THE PENGUIN
SPANISH DICTIONARY

COMPILED BY JAMES R. JUMP

SPANISH CONSULTANT: MANUEL CRIADO DE VAL

PENGUIN BOOKS

PENGUIN BOOKS

Published by the Penguin Group
Penguin Books Ltd, 27 Wrights Lane, London W8 5TZ, England
Penguin Books USA Inc., 375 Hudson Street, New York, New York 10014, USA
Penguin Books Australia Ltd, Ringwood, Victoria, Australia
Penguin Books Canada Ltd, 10 Alcorn Avenue, Toronto, Ontario, Canada M4V 3B2
Penguin Books (NZ) Ltd, 182–190 Wairau Road, Auckland 10, New Zealand

Penguin Books Ltd, Registered Offices: Harmondsworth, Middlesex, England

First published 1990
5 7 9 10 8 6 4

Printed in England by Clays Ltd, St Ives plc
Filmset in Linotron 202 Times

THE PENGUIN
SPANISH DICTIONARY

James R. Jump was born in 1916 in Wallasey, at that time in Cheshire but now a part of Merseyside. On leaving Wallasey Grammar School he worked as a newspaper reporter, first on Merseyside, then in Worthing, Sussex. As soon as he was twenty-one, he climbed over the Pyrenees to Spain, without a passport, to join the International Brigade in their fight against Franco, and was noted for bravery in dispatches from the battle of Ebro. He was invalided out of the Spanish Army in 1938 and after uneventful service in the Second World War decided to train as a teacher. He then spent thirteen years, until his retirement, as lecturer in Spanish at the Medway College of Technology, in Kent. After retiring he lived in Spain for five years, but was obliged to return to England because of ill-health. He wrote fourteen textbooks related to Spain, three of which have been translated into Swedish and German.

James R. Jump was married to a Spaniard and had two children, both of whom are bilingual. He died in 1990.

CONTENTS

NOTE ON THE DICTIONARY

In order to allow the fullest coverage of contemporary Spanish and English, and in order to make the dictionary as easy as possible to use, certain obsolete and archaic words have been omitted, as have some poetical usages and highly technical words.

Similarly, most of the following Spanish words have not been included:

(a) diminutive forms of nouns

(b) parts of verbs

(c) adverbs that are made by adding *mente* to the feminine form of the adjective.

From the Spanish–English section only, most of the following have also been omitted:

(a) words that are spelt the same, and have the same meaning, in Spanish and English

(b) feminine forms of nouns which end in **o**, **án**, **ín**, **ón** and **or**.

The author has assumed that English-speaking dictionary-users will have a basic knowledge of Spanish grammar. (If not, they are advised to read through the skeleton grammar on pp. xi–xxix.) In the English–Spanish section all irregular verbs are given a reference number, enabling the user to refer to one of the model irregular verbs listed on pp. xxii–xxix.

LIST OF ABBREVIATIONS

abbr	abbreviation	*ent*	entomology
adj	adjective	*equiv*	equivalent to
adv	adverb	*esp*	especially
aer	aeronautics	*euph*	euphemistic
agri	agriculture	*exclam*	exclamation
anat	anatomy	*expl*	expletive
arch	archeology	*fac*	facetious(ly)
archi	architecture	*fam*	familiar
Arg	Argentine	*fem*	feminine
art	article	*fig*	figurative(ly)
arts	in the arts	*freq*	frequently
astrol	astrology	*fut*	future
astron	astronomy	*gard*	gardening
aux	auxiliary	*geneal*	genealogy
bibl	biblical	*gener*	generally
bioch	biochemistry	*geog*	geography
biol	biology	*geol*	geology
Bol	Bolivia	*geom*	geometry
bot	botany	*gramm*	grammar
bui	building	*Gua*	Guatemala
Can	Canary Isles	*her*	heraldry
carp	carpentry	*hist*	history, historical
cer	ceramics		
chem	chemistry	*Hon*	Honduras
Chil	Chile	*hort*	horticulture
cin	cinéma	*imp*	imperative
Col	Colombia	*impers*	impersonal
comm	commerce	*incl*	including
conj	conjunction	*ind*	indicative
cont	contemptuous	*indef*	indefinite
		infin	infinitive
contr	contraction	*inter*	interrogative
Cub	Cuba	*interj*	interjection
cul	culinary	*invar*	invariable
def	definite	*iron*	ironical
dem	demonstrative	*joc*	jocular(ly)
		lang	language
dent	dentistry	*leg*	legal
dial	dialect	*lit*	literary
dim	diminutive	*log*	logic
Dom	Dominica	*masc*	masculine
eccles	ecclesiastical	*math*	mathematics
econ	economics	*mech*	mechanics
Ecu	Ecuador	*med*	medical
elect	electricity	*met*	metaphysics
emph	emphasis, emphatic	*metal*	metallurgy
		meteor	meteorology
eng	engineering	*Mex*	Mexico

mil	military		
min	mineralogy		
mot	motoring		
mus	music		
myth	mythology		
n	noun		
naut	nautical		
neg	negative		
neut	neuter		
Nic	Nicaragua		
numis	numismatics		
occ	occasionally		
opt	optics		
orni	ornithology		
o.s.	oneself		
Par	Paraguay		
part	participle		
past part	past participle		
pej	pejorative		
Per	Peru		
pers	person		
phil	philology		
philos	philosophy		
phon	phonetics		
phot	photography		
phys	physics		
physiol	physiology		
pl	plural		
poet	poetic(al)		
pol	politics		
pol/ec	political economy		
poss	possessive		
pref	prefix		
prep	preposition		
pres	present		
pres part	present participle		
print	printing		
pron	pronoun		
psych	psychology		
rad	radio		
refl	reflexive		
rhet	rhetoric(al)		
SA	Spanish America		
sci	science		

Sal	Salvador	*t*	transitive	*usu*	usually
sculp	sculpture	*tel*	telegraphy	*v*	verb
sing	singular	*text*	textiles	*v/aux*	auxiliary
sl	slang	*theat*	of the theatre		verb
s.o.	someone	*tr*	trade name	*vi*	intransitive
sp	sport		and/or		verb
Sp	Spanish		registered	*vt*	transitive
space	space		trademark		verb
	technology	*TV*	television	*Ven*	Venezuela
s.t.	something	*Uru*	Uruguay	*vet*	veterinary
superl	superlative	*US*	United	*vulg*	vulgar
sur	surveying		States	*zool*	zoology

PRONUNCIATION

Vowels

a   like a in happy, e.g. **las casas**
e   like e in merry, e.g. **el té**
i   like ee in queen, e.g. **mi primo**
o   like o in hot, e.g. **toro**
u   like oo in fool, e.g. **muro**

Consonants

b   at the beginning of a word or following **m**, like b in book, e.g. **banco**; otherwise like v in very, but the sound is made with the lips, e.g. **hablaba**
c   like c in cat, e.g. **cama**; but if it is followed by **e** or **i**, like th in think, e.g. **cinco**, **cebo**, except in Spanish America where it is like ss in kiss
ch   like ch in church, e.g. **muchacho**
d   like d in dog, e.g. **don**; but between vowels or at the end of a word, like th in those, e.g. **hada**
f   like f in farm, e.g. **Francisco**
g   like g in good, e.g. **goma**; but if followed by **e** or **i**, like ch in loch, e.g. **gitano**
h   always silent, e.g. **hombre**
j   like ch in loch, e.g. **ajo**

k   like k in kitten, e.g. **kilómetro**
l   like l in lion, e.g. **libro**
ll   like lli in million, e.g. **caballo**, except in Argentina, where it is like s in measure, and some regions, where it is like y in yes
m   like m in man, e.g. **como**
n   like n in now, e.g. **nada**
ñ   like ni in onion, e.g. **señor**
p   like p in paw, e.g. **pan**
q   like k in kitten. It is always followed by **ue** or **ui**, e.g. **querido**, **químico**
r   trilled more than in English, especially when following **l**, **n** or **s**, or at the beginning of a word, e.g. **ruedo**, **alrededor**, **enredo**
rr   strongly trilled, e.g. **perro**
s   like ss in kiss, e.g. **Sevilla**
t   like t in toffee, e.g. **todo**
v   like Spanish **b**, e.g. **viva**
x   like x in exert, e.g. **examen**, but if followed by a consonant, like s in sink, e.g. **experto**. In **México**, **mexicano** etc. (South American for **Méjico**, **mejicano** etc.) like Spanish **j**
y   like y in yes, e.g. **yeso**. When standing alone it has the same sound as Spanish **i**

MAIN POINTS OF SPANISH GRAMMAR

Punctuation

The principal features of Spanish punctuation that strike the English-speaking reader are:

1. Inverted question marks (¿...?) and exclamation marks are placed at the beginning of a question or exclamation – not always at the start of the sentence:

   ella no es rica pero ¿qué importa? (she isn't rich, but what does it matter?)

2. Dashes (– ...) are generally used in place of speech marks, and English speech marks or French *guillemets* at the beginning and end of a quotation within a speech:

   – Como dijo Hamlet, 'Ser o no ser'
   – contestó Juan ('As Hamlet said, "To be or not to be",' replied John)

3. Capital letters are not used for:
   1. nouns and adjectives of nationality
   2. days of the week, months of the year
   3. adjectives derived from proper nouns:

   los tiempos shakespearianos (Shakespeare's times)

4. titles:

   don Juan, el duque de Alba (Don Juan, the Duke of Alba)

Syllables, stress and accents

Syllables
The vowels **a**, **e** and **i** are strong vowels and each one makes one syllable:

cae (two syllables), **Bilbao** (three syllables).

The vowels **i** and **u** are weak vowels. One weak vowel alone makes a syllable:

rico (two syllables).

Two weak vowels together, or one weak and one strong together, make one syllable:

cuidado (three syllables), **fue** (one syllable, **auto** (two syllables).

Stress
Stress falls on the last syllable of a word, e.g. **comer**, unless the word ends in a vowel, **n** or **s**, in which case the stress falls on the next-to-last syllable, e.g. **andaba**, **comes**. All exceptions to this rule have an accent (´) on the vowel to be stressed: **lápiz, condición, magnífico**

Accents
The accent is also used to distinguish between two words spelt alike but with different meanings:

él (he) and **el** (the)
tú (you) and **tu** (your)

Nouns

Masculine and feminine

All Spanish nouns are masculine or feminine. As a general rule nouns that end in **-o** are masculine, while those that end in **-a** are feminine. In this dictionary *m* or *f* appears after any noun that does not follow the above rule; *mf* indicates that the word can be either masculine or feminine.

Plural

The rule for making nouns plural is: add **s** to a vowel; add **es** to a consonant:

reloj, relojes (watch, watches)

campo, campos (field, fields)

Nouns which end in **z** in the singular change the **z** to **c** in the plural:
lápiz, lápices (pencil, pencils)

Certain nouns which end in **s** and have an unstressed last syllable have the same form in the singular and plural:

crisis (crisis or crises)
paraguas (umbrella or umbrellas)

Most nouns that have an accented vowel in the last syllable drop the accent in the plural:

camión camiones, (lorry, lorries)

Articles

Definite

The Spanish for 'the' has four forms:

singular		*plural*	
masculine	*feminine*	*masculine*	*feminine*
el	**la**	**los**	**las**

el hombre (the man), **los hombres** (the men)

la mujer (the woman), **las mujeres** (the women)

The definite article is *omitted*:
1. before the number of a king, queen etc.:
   Felipe Segundo (Philip the Second)

2. before a noun in juxtaposition:
   Londres, capital de Inglaterra (London, the capital of England)

The definite article is *used*:
1. before an abstract noun:
   odiamos la hipocresía (we hate hypocrisy)

2. before a noun used in a general sense:
   me gusta el té (I like tea)

3. before Spanish titles (other than **don** and **doña**) except
   (a) in direct address:
   Sí, señor López, el señor Gómez está esperando (Yes, Mr Lopez, Mr Gomez is waiting)
   (b) when another title comes first:
   el dictador, General Franco (the dictator, General Franco)

4. before a geographical name accompanied by an adjective:
   la España prehistórica (prehistoric Spain)

5. before certain geographical names:
   El Perú (Peru) **La India** (India) **La Habana** (Havana)

6. before parts of the body, clothing and articles of personal adornment when, in English, the possessive adjective would be used:

movió la cabeza (he moved his head)

se pone los pendientes (she puts on her earrings)

me quité la corbata (I took off my tie)

The neuter article **lo** can be used with an adjective thus:

lo importante es tener éxito (the main thing is to be successful)

Indefinite

The Spanish for 'a' or 'an' has two forms:

masculine	*feminine*
un	una

The plural forms **unos** and **unas** are used to mean 'some':

un hombre (a man), **unos hombres** (some men)

una chica (a girl), **unas chicas** (some girls)

The indefinite article is *omitted*:

1. between **ser** (and a few other verbs) and a word indicating nationality, religion, politics, civil state, rank or profession, unless there is a qualifying adjective:

   ella es católica (she is a Catholic)

   ella no es una católica fanática (she is not a fanatical Catholic)

   Juan es médico (John is a doctor)

   fue nombrado presidente (he was nominated president)

2. before the object of **tener** used negatively:

   no tengo televisor (I haven't a television set)

   no tenemos hijos (we have no children)

3. before a noun in juxtaposition:

   Los Bravos, conjunto español (Los Bravos, a Spanish pop group)

The indefinite article is *used*:
before an abstract noun qualified by an adjective:

teníamos una sed incontrolable (we had an uncontrollable thirst)

Adjectives

Adjectives must agree in gender and number with the noun they accompany. Those which end in **-o** in the masculine singular have four forms; most others have only two forms.

masculine		feminine	
singular	*plural*	*singular*	*plural*
blanco	blancos	blanca	blancas
triste	tristes	triste	tristes
fácil	fáciles	fácil	fáciles

There are some exceptions:

1. Adjectives ending in **-án**, **-ón**, **-ín** and **-or** in the masculine singular add an **a** to form the feminine, dropping any accent they may have:

   hablador, habladora (talkative) **holgazán, holgazana** (lazy)

2. Adjectives of nationality ending in a consonant add **a** to form the feminine:

   francés, francesa (French) **alemán, alemana** (German)

3. Adjectives that end in **z** or **c** in the masculine singular change the last letter to **c** or **qu** respectively to form the plural:

   lápiz, lápices (pencil, pencils) **bic, biques** (biro, biros)

4. Colours that are the names of flowers, fruit etc. are invariable:

   un vestido rosa (a pink dress) (**la rosa** (the rose)

   un coche crema (a cream car)

Shortening of adjectives

1. The adjectives **alguno**, **ninguno**, **primero**, **tercero**, **bueno** and **malo** drop the final -o before a masculine singular noun:

   ningún amigo (no friend) **el primer capítulo** (the first chapter)

2. **Grande** drops the last syllable **-de** before any singular noun:

   La Gran Bretaña (Great Britain) **un gran militar** (a great soldier)

3. **Santo** drops the last syllable **-to** before the name of a male saint, unless that name begins with **Do-** or **To-**:

   San Pedro (St Peter) **Santo Tomás** (St Thomas)

4. **Ciento** drops the last syllable **-to** before a noun:

   cien soldados (a hundred soldiers) **ciento cincuenta soldados** (a hundred and fifty soldiers)

Possessive adjectives

singular		plural	
masculine	*feminine*	*masculine*	*feminine*
mi	mi	mis	mis
tu	tu	tus	tus
su	su	sus	sus
nuestro	nuestra	nuestros	nuestras
vuestro	vuestra	vuestros	vuestras
su	su	sus	sus

Like all adjectives, they agree in number and gender with the nouns that follow them:

nuestro padre, nuestras hijas

Because **su** and **sus** can mean 'his', 'her', 'its', 'your' and 'their', the words **de él, de ella, de usted, de ellos, de ellas** or **de ustedes** are often added if there is a possibility of misunderstanding:

su coche de ella (her car).

Spanish has no apostrophe to indicate possession. Instead the word **de** (meaning 'of', or 'belonging to') is used:

tengo la cartera de Paco (I have Paco's wallet)

Comparisons

Comparisons are made by placing the words

más ... que	(more ... than)
menos ... que	(less ... than)
tan ... como	(as ... as)

before and after the adjective:

Juan es más alto que su padre (John is taller than his father)

el té es menos fuerte que la cerveza (tea is weaker than beer)

el sargento luchó tan heroicamente como el general (the sergeant fought as heroically as the general)

To make the superlative form, **el**, **la**, **los** or **las** must precede the word **más** or **menos** and **de** follow the adjective:

el más inteligente de la familia (the most intelligent in the family)

la menos tímida de la clase (the least timid in the class)

There are four adjectives with irregular forms:

bueno	mejor
malo	peor
grande	mayor or más grande
pequeño	menor or más pequeño

There are four adverbs with irregular forms:

bien	mejor
mal	peor
mucho	más
poco	menos

The absolute superlative is often expressed by adding ísimo, -ísima, -ísimos or ísimas to an adjective. A spelling change is sometimes necessary to preserve the original sound:

contento, contentísimo (happy, very happy) **rica, riquísima** (rich, very rich)

Demonstratives

Adjectives

Spanish has three kinds of demonstratives:

este – to point to something near to the person speaking or writing, 'this'

ese – to point out something near to the person spoken or written to, 'that'

aquel – to point out something not near to either, 'that (over there)'

These are all adjectives and must agree in number and gender with the nouns they accompany.

	singular		plural	
	masculine	*feminine*	*masculine*	*feminine*
	este	esta	estos	estas
	ese	esa	esos	esas
	aquel	aquella	aquellos	aquellas

aquel libro es mío (that book is mine)

estas casas son blancas (these houses are white)

esa chica es francesa (that girl is French)

Pronouns

An accent on the stressed syllable of the above words turns them into pronouns:

éste (this one) **ésa** (that one) **aquéllos** (those ones) etc.

estas chicas son inglesas; aquéllas son rusas (these girls are English; those are Russian)

The neuter forms **esto**, **eso** and **aquello** are used when referring to anything that cannot be given a gender:

un hombre bien educado no hace eso (a well-mannered man does not do that (sort of thing))

Adverbs

Formation

Most descriptive adverbs which, in English, end in -ly, end in **-mente** in Spanish. To form an adverb **-mente** is attached to the feminine singular form of the adjective, thus:

cuidadoso (careful) **cuidadosamente** (carefully)

If the adjective bears an accent, this remains despite the addition of extra syllables:

rápido, rápidamente (rapid, rapidly)

Negative adverbs

In a negative sentence there must be a negative word before the verb. The most common of these is **no**.

no hablo japonés (I don't speak Japanese)

Others are **nada** (nothing), **nadie** (nobody), **nunca** and **jamás** (never), **nin-**guno, **ninguna, ningunos, ningunas** (not any) and **ni ... ni** (neither ... nor).

nunca van a la Costa Brava (they never go to the Costa Brava)

nadie viene a vistarnos (nobody comes to visit us)

If one of these negative words follows the verb, then **no** must be placed before the verb.

no iré jamás (I shall never go)

ellos no tienen ningún dinero (they haven't any money)

no encuentro ni sus gafas ni sus guantes (I can't find either his glasses or his gloves)

Pronouns

Personal pronouns

1. Subject pronouns

yo	I
tú	you (familiar)
él	he
ella	she
usted	you (formal)
nosotros (-as)	we
vosotros (-as)	you (familiar)
ellos (-as)	they
ustedes	you (formal)

Subject pronouns are normally omitted except:

(i) when it is necessary to avoid ambiguity:

Ella está triste; él está feliz (she is sad; he is happy)

(ii) to give emphasis:

usted lo hizo; yo no lo hice (you did it; I didn't do it)

2. Reflexive pronouns

me	myself
te	yourself (familiar)
se	himself, herself, itself, yourself (formal)
nos	ourselves
os	yourselves (familiar)
se	themselves, yourselves (formal)

Reflexive pronouns are placed immediately before most verbs.

me lavo antes de desayunar (I have a wash before breakfasting)

However, they are usually attached to the end of

(i) an infinitive

no voy a lavarme (I'm not going to have a wash)

(ii) a present participle (gerund)

ella esta peinándose (she is combing her hair)

no me voy a lavar and **ella se está peinando** are also correct.

Reflexive pronouns *must* be attached to a verb in the imperative form, unless it is negative:

lávese Vd. (wash yourself), but

no se lave Vd. (don't wash)

3. Direct object pronouns

me	me
te	you (familiar)
lo	it, him
le	him, you (formal)
la	her, you (formal)
nos	us
os	you (familiar)
los	them
les	them (people), you (formal)
las	them, you (formal)

4. Indirect object pronouns

These are the same as the direct object pronouns, with two exceptions:

le to him, to her, to it, to you (formal)

les to them, to you (formal)

The rules governing the position of reflexive pronouns apply also to direct and indirect pronouns.

When two pronouns come together indirect goes before direct:

te los enviamos (I am sending them to you)

¡dénmela! (give it to me!)

If **lo, la, le, los, las** or **les** (direct objects) appear together with **le** or **les** (indirect obects), then the latter are replaced by **se**:

se lo damos (we give it to them)

As **se** can mean to him, to her, to it, to you or to them, one may add, after the verb, **a él, a ella, a usted, a ellos, a ellas** or **a ustedes** to avoid confusion

se los regalaron a ella (they presented them to her)

5. Disjunctive pronouns
(pronouns following a preposition)
These are the same as the subject pronouns, with these exceptions:

mí	me
ti	you (familiar)
sí	himself, herself, itself, yourself, themselves, yourselves

van sin mí (they go without me)

Note the difference between

lo pone delante de sí (he puts it in front of himself) and

lo pone delante de él (he puts it in front of him (someone else))

The preposition **con** joins with **mí**, **ti** and **sí** to form the words

conmigo, contigo, consigo

¡Venga conmigo! (Come with me!)

María lleva el perro consigo (Mary takes the dog with her)

Formal and familiar 'you'

In Spanish there are two ways of addressing someone, the formal and the familiar. When speaking or writing to someone whom one does not know well, or to whom one wishes to show respect, the forms are **usted** (singular) and **ustedes** (plural). In writing, these words may be abbreviated to **Vd.** and **Vds.** As they are corruptions of the words **vuestra(s) merced(es)** (your honour(s)) they take the third person of the verb.

Tú is used when addressing a member of the family, an intimate friend, a child or an animal. **Vosotros** (masculine) and **vosotras** (feminine) are the plural forms of **tú**. But in South America the plural is **Vds.**

In practice it is advisable for the foreigner not to use the familiar form to a Spaniard unless invited to do so. Only the native Spaniard can tell when friendship has developed to such a point as to warrant the change from the formal to the familiar.

The personal 'a'

As word order in Spanish is more flexible than in English, the preposition **a** is placed before the direct object whenever:

(a) specific persons (or pets) are referred to:

no veo a mi amiga (I cannot see my friend)

Juanita quiere a su gatito (Jenny loves her little cat)

(b) there is a possibility of ambiguity:

la noche sigue al día (night follows day)

(c) the verb **tener** is used meaning 'to keep' or 'to hold':

tengo a mis hijos en la cama con la gripe (I have my children in bed with flu)

It is not used when **tener** simply means 'to possess':

Tengo dos hermanos y una hermana (I have two brothers and one sister)

Possessive pronouns

el mío	la mía	los míos	las mías (mine)
el tuyo	la tuya	los tuyos	las tuyas (yours)
el suyo	la suya	los suyos	las suyas (his, hers, its, yours)
el nuestro	la nuestra	los nuestros	las nuestras (ours)
el vuestro	la vuestra	los vuestros	las vuestras (yours)
el suyo	la suya	los suyos	las suyas (theirs, yours)

The article (**el, la, los, las**) is omitted after the verb **ser**:

Éste es mío; he perdido el tuyo (This is mine; I've lost yours)

These pronouns must be of the same gender and number as the nouns they represent.

> **Estos libros son míos. ¿Dónde ha dejado Vd. los suyos?** (These books are mine. Where have you left yours?)

As **suyo, suya, suyos, suyas** have so many meanings it is often advisable, for the sake of clarity, to use instead a phrase like:

> **el de Vd., las de él, la de ella,** etc.

The neuter article **lo** is used with the masculine singular pronoun when referring to something that cannot be given a gender.

> **toda nación defiende lo suyo** (every nation defends its own)

Relative pronouns

1. **Que** is used for persons or things, whether the subject or the direct object of the verb, in the relative clause:

> **la casa que vendió no valía más** (the house which he sold was not worth any more)

> **las chicas que vimos son españolas** (the girls whom we saw are Spanish)

> **la chica que vino anoche es mi prima** (the girl who came last night is my cousin)

2. If the object is preceded by a preposition, **quien** (plural **quienes**) is used for people:

> **la mujer con quien trabajo** (the woman with whom I work)

For things, use **que**:

> **el martillo con que pego el clavo** (the hammer with which I hit the nail)

3. **El cual, la cual, los cuales, las cuales, el que, la que, los que, las que** are used when the clause is separated from the noun to which it refers, or is governed by a compound preposition:

> **el fuego cerca del cual nos sentamos** (the fire near which we sit)

> **el padre de Cristina, el cual tiene un nuevo coche** (Christine's father, who has a new car)

4. **Cuyo, cuya, cuyos, cuyas** are the possessive relatives and mean 'whose' or 'of which'. They must 'agree' with the nouns that follow them.

> **el hombre cuya hija es violinista** (the man whose daughter is a violinist)

> **el mendigo cuyos zapatos están rotos** (the beggar whose shoes are worn out)

> **la casa cuyas ventanas necesitan una mano de pintura** (the house the windows of which need a coat of paint)

Verbs

Use of tenses and moods

The *present indicative* shows
1. what habitually happens or exists:

> **Londres está en Inglaterra** (London is in England)

2. what happens at any given time:

> **Juan llega a las doce** (John arrives at twelve)

The *present continuous* (present indicative of **estar** + present participle) shows what is happening at a given time:

> **María está bañándose** (Mary is having a bath)

The *imperfect* is used
1. to show what habitually happened or existed. (In English the past definite, the words 'used to' or 'would', are often used.)

> **yo le escribía todas las semanas** (I wrote to him every week)
> **el sol brillaba** (the sun was shining)

2. to express time in the past

> **eran las doce** (it was twelve o'clock)

The *imperfect continuous* shows what was happening at a given time:

ella estaba siguiéndome (she was following me)

The *past historic* shows completed events:

Colón descubrió América (Columbus discovered America)

The *perfect* (present indicative of **haber** + past participle) shows
1. what happened some time in the past:

he visto muchas películas de los hermanos Marx (I have seen many Marx Brothers' films)
2. completed actions in the very recent past (usually the same day):

esta mañana me he levantado a las ocho (this morning I got up at eight)

The *pluperfect* (imperfect tense of **haber** + past participle) shows what had happened:

ella había comido la pera (she had eaten the pear)

The *future* shows
1. what will be, or will happen:

el 5 de junio Cristina curaqlirá 17 años (on the 5th June Christine will be 17)
2. what will probably be, or happen:

ella tendrá 45 anos (she must be 45)

The *conditional* shows what would be, or would happen:

yo no lo comería (I would not eat it)

The *future perfect and conditional perfect* (future/conditional of **haber** + past participle) show what will have happened and what would have happened respectively:

habremos terminado el trabajo (we shall have finished the work)

yo no lo habría dicho (I would not have said it)

The *future continuous and conditional continuous* (future conditional of **estar** + present participle) show what will be happening/would be happening at a given time:

estaré comiendo a las ocho (I shall be dining at eight)

The *subjunctive* is used
1. In time clauses referring to the future

cuando nos vean nos saludarán (when they see us they will greet us)
2. After certain impersonal expressions involving doubt or uncertainty, such as **es posible que, es probable que, es necesario que, es dudoso que**:

es necesario que lo hagamos en seguida (it is necessary that we do it without delay)
3. After **tal vez** or any other expression meaning perhaps:

quizás ella tenga 21 años (maybe she is 21)
4. After verbs of emotion such as **estar contento de que, alegrarse de que, temer que**:

estoy contento de que puedas visitarnos (I am pleased that you can visit us)

If, however, only one person is involved, the infinitive is used:

Me alegro de verte (I'm happy to see you)
5. To express a prayer or fervent wish:

¡Viva la República! (Long live the Republic!)

!Ojalá que no llueva hoy! (I do hope it will not rain today)
6. In a dependent clause after a negative or indefinite antecedent:

no hay nadie que lo haga mejor que Vd. (there is no one who can do it better than you)

busco un alumno que sepa sumar
(I'm looking for a pupil who can add up – i.e. any pupil, providing he can add up)

Compare this with

Busco a un alumno que sabe sumar
(I'm looking for a pupil who can add up – i.e. I know this particular pupil exists)

7. After verbs of telling, commanding etc. when two or more persons are involved:

el oficial dice que liberen a los prisioneros (the officer tells them to free the prisoners)

8. After verbs of saying or believing used negatively, when two or more persons are involved:

no digo que lo hayas hecho querien- **do** (I don't say that you have done it on purpose)

9. (a) as the 'formal imperative':
vengan a vernos mañana (come and see us tomorrow)

(b) as the familiar imperative (negative only):
¡No lo hagas! (Don't do it!)

(c) meaning 'Let us' (first person plural imperative):
¡Cantemos! (Let us sing!)

Imperfect subjunctive in 'if' clauses
The imperfect subjunctive is used in 'if' clauses when some impossible or highly improbable circumstance is considered:

si los elefantes volasen ... (if elephants could fly ...)
si yo fuera rey ... (if I were king ...)

Verb tables

Regular verbs

The following verbs serve as models for all Spanish regular verbs (i.e. verbs which, in the English–Spanish section of this dictionary, are not followed by a number):

1. **–ar** verbs, e.g. **hablar** (to speak)

The following endings are added to the stem **habl-**:

Present:	–o, –as, –a, –amos, –áis, –an
Imperfect:	–aba, –abas, –aba, –ábamos, –abais, –aban
Past historic:	–é, –aste, –ó, –amos, –asteis, –aron
Future:	–aré, –arás, –ará, –aremos, –aréis, –arán
Conditional::	–aría, –arías, –aría, –aríamos, –aríais, –arían
Present subjunctive:	–e, –es, –e, –emos, –éis, –en
Imperfect subjunctive:	–ara, –aras, –ara, –áramos, –arais, –aran

or

–ase, –ases, –ase, –ásemos, –aseis, –asen

Imperative:	–a (tú), –ad (vosotros).

(For other persons, and for all negative forms, the present subjunctive is used.)

Present participle:	–ando
Past participle:	–ado

2. **–er** verbs, e.g. **comer** (to eat)

The following endings are added to the stem **com-**:

Present:	–o, –es, –e, –emos, –éis, –en
Imperfect:	–ía, –ías, –ía, –íamos, –íais, –ían
Past historic:	–í, –iste, –ió, –imos, –isteis, –ieron
Future:	–eré, –erás, –erá, –eremos, –eréis, –erán
Conditional:	–ería, –erías, –ería, –eríamos, –eríais, –erían
Present subjunctive:	–a, –as, –a, –amos, –áis, –an
Imperfect subjunctive:	–iera, –ieras, –iera, –iéramos, –ierais, –ieran

or

–iese, –ieses, –iese, –iésemos, –ieseis, –iesen

Imperative:	–e (tú), –ed (vosotros).

(For other persons and for all negative forms, the present subjunctive is used.)

Present participle:	–iendo
Past participle:	–ido

3. **–ir** verbs, e.g. **vivir** (to live)

The following endings are added to the stem **viv-**:

Present:	–o, –es, –e, –imos, –ís, –en
Imperfect:	–ía, –ías, –ía, –íamos, –íais, –ían
Past historic:	–í, –iste, –ió, –imos, –isteis, –ieron
Future:	–iré, –irás, –irá, –irémos, –iréis, –iran
Conditional:	–iría, –irías, –iría, –iríamos, –iríais, –irían
Present subjunctive:	–a, –as, –a, –amos, –áis, –an
Imperfect subjunctive:	–iera, –ieras, –iera, –iéramos, –ierais, –ieran

or

–iese, –ieses, –iese, –iésimos, –ieseis, –iesen

Imperative:	–e (tú), –id (vosotros).

(For other persons and for all negative forms, the present subjunctive is used.)

Present participle:	–iendo
Past participle:	–ido

Compound tenses

Compound tenses (e.g. perfect, pluperfect, present continuous etc.) are made by using:

haber (see irregular verb table p.xxvi) + past participle

or

estar (see irregular verb table p.xxv) + present participle

For example:

he comido
habíamos llegado
habré terminado
está comiendo
estabas durmiendo
estaré terminando

Irregular verbs

A number after a Spanish verb in the English–Spanish section means that the verb follows the pattern of the model verb bearing the same number in this list. Only the irregular forms are given below. If a tense or mood is not listed, it can be assumed that they follow the regular pattern.

1a. encontrar (to find, meet):

Present:	encuentro, encuentras, encuentra, encontramos, encontráis, encuentran
Present subjunctive:	encuentre, encuentres, encuentre, encontremos, encontréis, encuentren

1b. soler (to be in the habit of):

Present:	suelo, sueles, suele, solemos, soléis, suelen
Present subjunctive:	suela, suelas, suela, solamos, soláis, suelan

1c. dormir (to sleep):

Present:	duermo, duermes, duerme, dormimos, dormís, duermen
Past historic:	dormí, dormiste, durmío, dormimos, dormisteis, durmieron
Present subjunctive:	duerma, duermas, duerma, durmamos, durmáis, duerman
Imperfect subjunctive:	durmiera, durmieras, durmiera, durmiéramos, durmierais, durmieran

or

durmiese, durmieses, durmiese, durmiésemos, durmieseis, durmiesen

Imperative:	duerme (tú), dormid (vosotros)
Present participle:	durmiendo

2a. cerrar (to close):

Present:	cierro, cierras, cierra, cerramos, cerráis, cierran
Present subjunctive:	cierre, cierres, cierre, cerremos, cerréis, cierran

2b. perder (to lose):

Present:	pierdo, pierdes, pierde, perdemos, perdéis, pierden
Present subjunctive:	pierda, pierdas, pierda, perdamos, perdáis, pierdan

2c. herir (to wound):

Present:	hiero, hieres, hiere, herimos, herís, hieren
Present subjunctive:	hiera, hieras, hiera, heramos, heráis, hieran

3. pedir (to ask for):

Present:	pido, pides, pide, pedimos, pedís, piden
Past historic:	pedí, pediste, pidió, pedimos, pedisteis, pidieron
Present subjunctive:	pida, pidas, pida, pidamos, pidáis, pidan
Imperfect subjunctive:	pidiera, pidieras, pidiera, pidiéramos, pidierais, pidieran

or

pidiese, pidieses, pidiese, pidiésemos, pidieseis, pidiesen

4. **atacar** (to attack):

Past historic:	ataqué, atacaste, atacó, atacamos, atacasteis, atacaron
Present subjunctive:	ataque, ataques, ataque, ataquemos, ataquéis, ataquen

5. **pagar** (to pay (for)):

Past historic:	pagué, pagaste, pagó, pagamos, pagasteis, pagaron
Present subjunctive:	pague, pagues, pague, paguemos, paguéis, paguen

6. **averiguar** (to verify):

Past historic:	averigüé, averiguaste, averiguó, averiguamos, averiguasteis, averiguaron
Present subjunctive:	averigüe, averigües, averigüe, averigüemos, averigüéis, averigüen

7. **lanzar** (to launch):

Past historic:	lancé, lanzaste, lanzó, lanzamos, lanzasteis, lanzaron
Present subjunctive:	lance, lances, lance, lancemos, lancéis, lancen

8. **coger** (to catch):

Present:	cojo, coges, coge, cogemos, cogéis, cogen
Present subjunctive:	coja, cojas, coja, cojamos, cojáis, cojan

9. **fingir** (to pretend):

Present:	finjo, finges, finge, fingimos, fingís, fingen
Present subjunctive:	finja, finjas, finja, finjamos, finjáis, finjan

10. **delinquir** (to transgress):

Present:	delinco, delinques, delinque, delinquimos, delinquís, delinquen
Present subjunctive:	delinca, delincas, delinca, delincamos, delincáis, delincan

11. **distinguir** (to distinguish):

Present:	distingo, distingues, distingue, distingimos, distinguís, distinguen
Present subjunctive:	distinga, distingas, distinga, distingamos, distingáis, distingan

12. **vencer** (to conquer):

Present:	venzo, vences, vence, vencemos, vencéis, vencen
Present subjunctive:	venza, venzas, venza, venzamos, venzáis, venzan

13. **zurcir** (to darn):

Present:	zurzo, zurces, zurce, zurcimos, zurcís, zurcen
Present subjunctive:	zurza, zurzas, zurza, zurzamos, zurzáis, zurzan

14. **conocer** (to know):

Present:	conozco, conoces, conoce, conocemos, conocéis, conocen
Present subjunctive:	conozca, conozcas, conozca, conozcamos, conozcáis, conozcan

15. **reducir** (to reduce):

Present:	**reduzco, reduces, reduce, reducimos, reducís, reducen**
Past historic:	**reduje, redujiste, redujo, redujimos, redujisteis, redujeron**
Present subjunctive:	**reduzca, reduzcas, reduzca, reduzcamos, reduzcáis, reduzcan**
Imperfect subjunctive:	**redujera, redujera, redujera, redujéramos, redujerais, redujeran**

or

redujese, redujeses, redujese, redujésemos, redujeseis, redujesen

16. **huir** (to flee):

Present:	**huyo, huyes, huye, huimos, huis, huyen**
Imperfect:	**huía, huías, huía, huíamos, huíais, huían**
Past historic:	**huí, huiste, huyó, huimos, huisteis, huyeron**
Present subjunctive:	**huya, huyas, huya, huyamos, huyáis, huyan**
Imperfect subjunctive:	**huyera, huyeras, huyera, huyéramos, huyerais, huyeran**

or

huyese, huyeses, huyese, huyésemos, huyeseis, huyesen

Present participle:	**huyendo**

17. **leer** (to read):

Past historic:	**leí, leíste, leyó, leímos, leísteis, leyeron**
Imperfect subjunctive:	**leyera, leyeras, leyera, leyéramos, leyerais, leyeran**

or

leyese, leyeses, leyese, leyésemos, leyeseis, leyesen

Present participle:	**leyendo**
Past participle:	**leído**

18. **gruñir** (to growl):

Past historic:	**gruñí, gruñiste, gruñó, gruñimos, gruñisteis, gruñeron**
Imperfect subjunctive:	**gruñera, gruñeras, gruñera, gruñéramos, gruñerais, gruñeran**

or

gruñese, gruñeses, gruñese, gruñésemos, gruñeseis, gruñesen

Present participle:	**gruñendo**

19. Verbs that do not fall into any of the above groups

andar (to walk):

Past historic:	**anduve, anduviste, anduvo, anduvimos, anduvisteis, anduvieron**
Imperfect subjunctive:	**anduviera, anduvieras, anduviera, anduviéramos, anduvierais, anduvieran**

or

anduviese, anduvieses, anduviese, anduviésemos, anduvieseis, anduviesen

caber (to fit):

Past historic:	**cupe, cupiste, cupo, cupimos, cupisteis, cupieran**
Imperfect subjunctive:	**cupiera, cupieras, cupiera, cupiéramos, cupierais, cupieran**

or

cupiese, cupieses, cupiese, cupiésemos, cupieseis, cupiesen

caer (to fall):

Present:	**caigo, caes, cae, caemos, caéis, caen**
Past historic:	**caí, caíste, cayó, caímos, caísteis, cayeron**
Present subjunctive:	**caiga, caigas, caiga, caigamos, caigáis, caigan**
Imperfect subjunctive:	**cayera, cayeras, cayera, cayéramos, cayerais, cayeran**

or

cayese, cayeses, cayese, cayésemos, cayeseis, cayesen

Present participle:	**cayendo**
Past participle:	**caído**

dar (to give):

Present:	**doy, das, da, damos, dais, dan**
Past historic:	**di, diste, dio, dimos, disteis, dieron**
Present subjunctive:	**dé, des, dé, demos, deis, den**
Imperfect subjunctive:	**diera, dieras, diera, diéramos, dierais, dieran**

or

diese, dieses, diese, diésemos, dieseis, diesen

decir (to say):

Present:	**digo, dices, dice, decimos, decís, dicen**
Past historic:	**dije, dijiste, dijo, dijimos, dijisteis, dijeron**
Future:	**diré, dirás, dirá, diremos, diréis, dirán**
Conditional:	**diría, dirías, diría, diríamos, diríais, dirían**
Present subjunctive:	**diga, digas, diga, digamos, digáis, digan**
Imperfect subjunctive:	**dijera, dijeras, dijera, dijéramos, dijerais, dijeran**

or

dijese, dijeses, dijese, dijésemos, dijeseis, dijesen

Present participle:	**diciendo**
Past participle:	**dicho**
Imperative:	**di (tú), decid (vosotros)**

estar (to be):

Present:	**estoy, estás, está, estamos, estáis, están**
Past historic:	**estuve, estuviste, estuvo, estuvimos, estuvisteis, estuvieron**
Present subjunctive:	**esté, estés, esté, estemos, estéis, estén**
Imperfect subjunctive:	**estuviera, estuvieras, estuviera, estuviéramos, estuvierais, estuvieran**

or

estuviese, estuvieses, estuviese, estuviésemos, estuvieseis, estuviesen

haber (to have):

Present:	he, has, ha, hemos, habéis, han
Past historic:	hube, hubiste, hubo, hubimos, hubisteis, hubieron
Future:	habré, habrás, habrá, habremos, habréis, habrán
Conditional:	habría, habrías, habría, habríamos, habríais, habrían
Present subjunctive:	haya, hayas, haya, hayamos, hayáis, hayan
Imperfect subjunctive:	hubiera, hubieras, hubiera, hubiéramos, hubierais, hubieran

or

hubiese, hubieses, hubiese, hubiésemos, hubieseis, hubiesen

hacer (to do):

Present:	hago, haces, hace, hacemos, hacéis, hacen
Past historic:	hice, hiciste, hizo, hicimos, hicisteis, hicieron
Future:	haré, harás, hará, haremos, haréis, harán
Conditional:	haría, harías, haría, haríamos, haríais, harían
Present subjunctive:	haga, hagas, haga, hagamos, hagáis, hagan
Imperfect subjunctive:	hiciera, hicieras, hiciera, hiciéramos, hicierais, hicieran

or

hiciese, hicieses, hiciese, hiciésemos, hicieseis, hiciesen

Imperative:	haz (tú), haced (vosotros)
Past participle:	hecho

ir (to go):

Present:	voy, vas, va, vamos, vais, van
Imperfect:	iba, ibas, iba, íbamos, ibais, iban
Past historic:	fui, fuiste, fue, fuimos, fuisteis, fueron
Present subjunctive:	vaya, vayas, vaya, vayamos, vayáis, vayan
Imperfect subjunctive:	fuera, fueras, fuera, fuéramos, fuerais, fueran

or

fuese, fueses, fuese, fuésemos, fueseis, fuesen

Imperative:	ve (tú), id (vosotros)
Present participle:	yendo
Past participle:	ido

oír (to hear):

Present:	oigo, oyes, oye, oímos, oís, oyen
Past historic:	oí, oíste, oyó, oímos, oísteis, oyeron
Present subjunctive:	oiga, oigas, oiga, oigamos, oigáis, oigan
Imperfect subjunctive:	oyera, oyeras, oyera, oyéramos, oyerais, oyeran

or

oyese, oyeses, oyese, oyésemos, oyeseis, oyesen

Imperative:	oye (tú), oíd (vosotros)
Present participle:	oyendo
Past participle:	oído

poder (to be able):

Present:	puedo, puedes, puede, podemos, podéis, pueden
Past historic:	pude, pudiste, pudo, pudimos, pudisteis, pudieron
Future:	podré, podrás, podrá, podremos, podréis, podrán
Conditional:	podría, podrías, podría, podríamos, podríais, podrían
Present subjunctive:	pueda, puedas, pueda, podamos, podáis, puedan
Imperfect subjunctive:	pudiera, pudieras, pudiera, pudiéramos, pudierais, pudieran

or

	pudiese, pudieses, pudiese, pudiésemos, pudieseis, pudiesen
Present participle:	pudiendo
Past participle:	podido

poner (to put):

Present:	pongo, pones, pone, ponemos, ponéis, ponen
Past historic:	puse, pusiste, puso, pusimos, pusisteis, pusieron
Future:	pondré, pondrás, pondrá, pondremos, pondréis, pondrán
Conditional:	pondría, pondrías, pondría, pondríamos, pondríais, pondrían
Present subjunctive:	ponga, pongas, ponga, pongamos, pongáis, pongan
Imperfect subjunctive:	pusiera, pusieras, pusiera, pusiéramos, pusierais, pusieran

or

	pusiese, pusieses, pusiese, pusiésemos, pusieseis, pusiesen
Imperative:	pon (tú), poned (vosotros)
Present participle:	poniendo
Past participle:	puesto

querer (to want):

Present:	quiero, quieres, quiere, queremos, queréis, quieren
Past historic:	quise, quisiste, quiso, quisimos, quisisteis, quisieron
Future:	querré, querrás, querrá, querremos, querréis, querrán
Conditional:	querría, querrías, querría, querríamos, querríais,querrían
Present subjunctive:	quiera, quieras, quieras, queramos, queráis, quieran
Imperfect subjunctive:	quisiera, quisieras, quisiera, quisiéramos, quisierais, quisieran

or

	quisiese, quisieses, quisiese, quisiésemos, quisieseis, quisiesen

saber (to know):

Present:	sé, sabes, sabe, sabemos, sabéis, saben
Past historic:	supe, supiste, supo, supimos, supisteis, supieron
Future:	sabré, sabrás, sabrá, sabremos, sabréis, sabrán
Conditional:	sabría, sabrías, sabría, sabríamos, sabríais, sabrían
Present subjunctive:	sepa, sepas, sepa, sepamos, sepáis, sepan
Imperfect subjunctive:	supiera, supieras, supiera, supiéramos, supierais, supieran

or

supiese, supieses, supiese, supiésemos, supieseis, supiesen

salir (to leave):

Present:	salgo, sales, sale, salimos, salís, salen
Future:	saldré, saldrás, saldrá, saldremos, saldréis, saldrán
Conditional:	saldría, saldrías, saldría, saldríamos, saldríais, saldrían
Imperative:	sal (tú), salid (vosotros)

ser (to be):

Present:	soy, eres, es, somos, sois, son
Imperfect:	era, eras, era, éramos, erais, eran
Past historic:	fui, fuiste, fue, fuimos, fuisteis, fueron
Present subjunctive:	sea, seas, sea, seamos, seais, sean
Imperfect subjunctive:	fuera, fueras, fuera, fuéramos, fuerais, fueran

or

	fuese, fueses, fuese, fuésemos, fueseis, fuesen
Imperative:	sé (tú), sed (vosotros)

tener (to have):

Present:	tengo, tienes, tiene, tenemos, tenéis, tienen
Past historic:	tuve, tuviste, tuvo, tuvimos, tuvisteis, tuvieron
Future:	tendré, tendrás, tendrá, tendremos, tendréis, tendrán
Conditional:	tendría, tendrías, tendría, tendríamos, tendríais, tendrían
Imperfect subjunctive:	tuviera, tuvieras, tuviera, tuviéramos, tuvierais, tuvieran

or

	tuviese, tuvieses, tuviese, tuviésemos, tuvieseis, tuviesen
Imperative:	ten (tú), tened (vosotros)

traer (to fetch):

Present:	traigo, traes, trae, traemos, traéis, traen
Past historic:	traje, trajiste, trajo, trajimos, trajisteis, trajeron
Present subjunctive:	traiga, traigas, traiga, traigamos, traigáis, traigan
Imperfect subjunctive:	trajera, trajeras, trajera, trajéramos, trajerais, trajeran

or

	trajese, trajeses, trajese, trajésemos, trajeseis, trajesen
Present participle:	trayendo
Past participle:	traído

valer (to be worth):

Present:	valgo, vales, vale, valemos, valeis, valen
Future:	valdré, valdrás, valdrá, valdremos, valdréis, valdran
Conditional:	valdría, valdrías, valdría, valdríamos, valdríais, valdrían
Present subjunctive:	valga, valgas, valga, valgamos, valgáis, valgan

venir (to come):

Present:	vengo, vienes, viene, venimos, venís, vienen
Past historic:	vine, viniste, vino, vinimos, vinisteis, vinieron
Future:	vendré, vendrás, vendrá, vendremos, vendréis, vendrán
Conditional:	vendría, vendrías, vendría, vendríamos, vendríais, vendrían
Present subjunctive:	venga, vengas, venga, vengamos, vengáis, vengan
Imperfect subjunctive:	viniera, vinieras, viniera, viniéramos, vinierais, vinieran

or

	viniese, vinieses, viniese, viniésemos, vinieseis, viniesen
Imperfect subjunctive:	ven (tú), venid (vosotros)

ver (to see):

Present:	veo, ves, ve, vemos, veis, ven
Imperfect:	veía, veías, veía, veíamos, veíais, veían
Past historic:	vi, viste, vio, vimos, visteis, vieron
Present subjunctive:	vea, veas, vea, veamos, veáis, vean
Imperfect subjunctive:	viera, vieras, viera, viéramos, vierais, vieran

or

	viese, vieses, viese, viésemos, vieseis, viesen
Present participle:	viendo
Past participle:	visto

SPANISH–ENGLISH

A

¹ **a** *prep* at, ~ **la mesa** at the table; at a rate of, ~ **50 pesetas el kilo** at 50 pesetas a kilo; after, ~ **los pocos minutos** after a few minutes; by, ~ **puñadas** by the handful; from, **morir** ~ **veneno** to die from poison; in, **al aire libre** in the open air; on, ~ **la orilla del Ebro** on the bank of the Ebro; to, **iremos** ~ **Valencia** we shall go to Valencia; how to, **ella me enseñó** ~ **nadar** she taught me how to swim; up to, **con el agua al cuello** with water up to his neck; symbolizing the accusative case ~ is placed before personal, personalized and some other nouns and is then not translatable; **veo** ~ **María** I see Mary; ~ **ciegas** blindly; **¡**~ **comer!** come and eat!; ~ **conciencia** thoroughly; ~ **la francesa** in the French style; ~ **lo menos** at least; ~ **lo que usted dice** from what you say; ~ **mano/máquina** by hand/machine; ~ **los tres días** three days later; ~ **pie/caballo** on foot/horseback; ~ **veces** sometimes; **¡**~ **que no sabes …!** I bet you don't know …!

² **a** *f* (**aes** *pl*) letter a

ababol *m* poppy

ábaco abacus

abad *m* abbot

abadejo codfish; *ent* Spanish fly

abadesa abbess

abadía abbey

abajo below; **cuesta/escalera** ~ downhill/downstairs; **los de** ~ *fig* the underdogs

abalanzar to balance; ~**se** to rush, hurl o.s.; ~**se sobre** to pounce upon

abalaustrado with balustrade

abalizar to lay buoys; place cones on road

abanderado standard-bearer, colour sergeant

abanderar *naut* to register (a vessel)

abandonado abandoned; careless; lazy

abandonamiento abandonment; debauchery

abandonar to abandon, leave, desert; refrain, stop doing something; ~**se** to devote o.s.; give up personal hygiene, let o.s. go

abandono abandonment

abanicar to fan; ~**se** *sl* to scram

abanico fan; *fig* range of options *etc*; **en** ~ fan-shaped

abaniqueo fanning

abaratar to cheapen, lower the price; ~**se** to fall in price

abarca type of rustic leather slipper

abarcador monopolistic

abarcar to embrace; comprehend, include; corner, monopolize

abarquillar to curl up

abarrancadero rough road

abarrancamiento fall (into a hole); embarrassment

abarrancar to ditch; ~**se** to fall into a ditch; become embarrassed

abarrotar to strengthen with bars; *naut* stow

abarrote *m* food shop; article of food

abastecedor *n* supplier, purveyor

abastecer to supply

abastecimiento *n* supplying

abasto supply; ~**s** provisions, foodstuffs; food shop; **no dar** ~ to be unable to cope

abatatar to shame; intimidate

abatimiento depression, low spirits

abatir to bring down; humiliate; ~**se** to become disheartened

abayado berry-shaped

abazón *anat* cheek pouch

abdicación *f* abdication

abdicar to abdicate; ~ **en** to abdicate in favour of

abducción *f* abduction

abecé *m* a. b. c.; alphabet

abecedario alphabet; school primer

abedul *m bot* birch

abeja bee

abejar *m* beehive

1

abejarrón *m* bumble-bee

abejaruco *orni* bee-eater

abejón *m* drone

abejorro bumble-bee

abejuno *adj* pertaining to the bee

abellacarse to degrade o.s.

abellotado acorn-shaped

aberración *f* aberration

aberral *n* small crack; tiny opening; *adj* easily opened

abertura opening, fissure, gap

abertzale *n + adj* Basque separatist

abeto *bot* spruce; silver fir

abetunar to cover with pitch

abierto open, clear; unwalled, unfenced; candid, frank

abigarrar to paint with clashing colours; fleck

abigeato cattle-rustling

abigeo cattle-rustler

abisal abysmal *esp* pertaining to marine depths

abiselar to bevel

abisinio *n + adj* Abyssinian

abismal abysmal

abismar to sink; ~se to become engrossed in; think deeply

abismo abyss

abitaque *m archi* rafter; joist

abjuración *f* abjuration

abjurar to abjure

ablación *f med* ablation

ablactar to wean

ablandadizo easily persuaded

ablandamiento softening

ablandar to soften; mitigate; soothe; *mot* run in; *mil* soften up

ablande *m mot* running-in

ablativo ablative

ablución *f* ablution

abnegación *f* self-sacrifice, self-denial

abnegado self-sacrificing, self-denying

abnegarse to renounce

abobado silly, stupid

abobar to stupefy; ~se to grow stupid

abocado (of wine) mild; smooth

abocamiento meeting, parley

abocar to bring close; decant; ~se to meet by appointment

abocardar *carp* to countersink

abocetar to sketch, make a rough drawing of

abocinar to shape like a trumpet

abochornar to overheat; shame, make blush; *agri* wilt

abofetable deserving a slapping

abofeteador *n m* slapper; *adj* slapping

abofetear to slap

abogacía law (as a profession)

abogadear *iron* to play the lawyer

abogado lawyer, solicitor, barrister, attorney; ~ del diablo devil's advocate; ~ de secano quack lawyer; recibirse de ~ to be called to the bar

abogar to practise as a lawyer; plead

abolengo lineage

abolible abolishable

abolición *f* abolition; revocation; extinction

abolicionismo abolitionism

abolicionista *m + f* abolitionist

abolir to abolish; revoke, repeal

abolsado puckered; shaped like a pocket

abolladura dent

abollar to dent; ~se to get dented

abollonadura dent

abollonamiento *bot* budding

abollonar to dent

abominación *f* abomination; abhorrence

abominar to abominate; detest

abonado *n* subscriber; ticket-holder; *adj* trustworthy; *agri* manured

abonador *m* person who stands security; *agri* manurer

abonamiento bail, security

abonanzar *naut* to grow calm

abonar to bail; pay for; credit (an account); manure, fertilize; ~se to subscribe (to); buy a season ticket

abonaré *m* promissory note, I.O.U.

abono guarantee; subscription; season ticket; *agri* manure, fertilizer, compost

aboquillado filter-tipped

abordador *m naut* boarder

abordaje *m naut* boarding

abordar *vt naut* to board; approach (a person); tackle (a subject); *vi naut* to enter port

aborigen *adj* aboriginal; **aborígenes** *n mpl* aborigines

aborrascarse to become stormy

aborrecer to abhor, hate; *orni* desert the nest; ~se to hate each other

aborrecible abhorrent, hateful

aborrecimiento abhorrence, hate

abortar to miscarry, have an abortion;

space abort

abortista *m + f* abortionist

abortivo abortive

aborto miscarriage; ~ **provocado** abortion

abortón *m vet* abortion, miscarriage

abotagarse, abotargarse to become bloated

abotonador *m* button-hook

abotonar to button; ~se to button up (one's coat)

abovedar to arch, vault

aboyar to lay buoys

abozalar to muzzle

abra bay, cove; haven; creek

abrasador, abrasante *adj* burning

abrasamiento burning; excess of passion

abrasar to burn, scorch; feel passionately

abrasión *f* graze

abrasivo abrasive

abrazadera clasp, clamp

abrazar to embrace, hug; clasp, clamp; comprise; surround

abrazo hug, embrace

abrebotellas *m sing + pl* bottle-opener

abrecartas *m sing + pl* paper-knife

abrecoches *m sing + pl* doorman

ábrego south-west wind

abrelatas *m sing + pl* tin-opener

abrevadero watering place for farm animals; drinking trough

abrevar to water (cattle); irrigate; size (before painting/papering)

abreviación *f* abbreviation

abreviar to shorten, reduce, abridge

abreviatura abbreviation; **en** ~ in abbreviated form

¹ **abridor** nectarine

² **abridor** opener; stretcher; sleeper; wire for pierced ears; *agri* grafting-knife; ~ **de latas** tin-opener

abrigadero sheltered place; *naut* haven

abrigado *n* shelter; *adj* (of clothes) warm; sheltered

abrigar to shelter (from the elements); ~se to cover o.s.; warm; patronize

abril *m* April; ~es years (old); **los dieciséis** ~es sweet sixteen; **veinte** ~es twenty summers

abrileño *adj* April

abrillantador *m* polisher

abrillantar to polish; cut a diamond; *phot* to gloss

abrimiento *n* opening; cracking

abrir to open, unlock, unfasten; unseal; expand; separate; cut open; dig; ~ **brecha** to knock a hole; ~ **la mano** to be more generous; ~ **la procesión/ manifestación** to head the religious procession/demonstration; ~ **paso** to make way; ~ **un canal** to dig/cut a canal; ~se *sl* to scram, beat it; ~se una **vía de agua** *naut* to spring a leak

abrochador *m* button-hook

abrochadura fastening, lacing, buttoning

abrochar to fasten; button; do up; reprimand

abrogación *f* abrogation; repeal

abrogar to abrogate

abrojal *m* ground covered in thistles

abrojo thistle; prickle, thorn; *naut* underwater rocks

abroncar to annoy; vex; reprimand severely

abroquelarse to defend o.s.

abrumador overwhelming; crushing

abrumar to overwhelm, crush; ~se to worry; become misty

abrupto craggy; steep

abrutado brutish; bestial

absceso abscess

abscisión *med* incision

absentismo absenteeism

ábside *archi* apse

absintio *bot* absinthe; **licor de** ~ (drink) absinthe

absolución *f* absolution, pardon, acquittal

absolutismo absolutism, autocracy

absolutista *n m + f + adj* absolutist

absoluto *adj* absolute, unconditional; **dominio** ~ freehold; **en** ~ (in neg sentence) at all; *n* discharge from military service

absolvente absolving

absolver to absolve, acquit

absorbencia absorbancy, absorption

absorber to absorb; drink up; *comm* take over

absorción *f* absorption; *comm* take-over

absorto absorbed in thought

abstemio *n* teetotaller; *adj* abstemious; forbearing

abstención *f* abstention

abstencionismo *pol* abstentionism

abstencionista *n m + f + adj* abstentionist

abstenerse to abstain, refrain; ~ de hacer algo to abstain from doing something

absterger *med* to cleanse

abstersión *f med* cleansing

abstinencia abstinence; fasting

abstracción *f* abstraction

abstracto abstract; en ~ in the abstract

abstraer *vt* to abstract; *vi* to leave aside, do without; ~se to be mentally withdrawn/absent-minded

abstraído absent-minded, lost in thought

abstruso abstruse

absuelto absolved, acquitted

absurdidad *f* absurdity

absurdo *n* absurdity; ridiculousness; *adj* absurd, ridiculous

abubilla *orni* hoopoe

abuchear to boo; shout down

abucheo booing, catcalling

abuela grandmother; old woman; cuéntaselo a su ~ tell it to the marines

abuelo grandfather; old man; ancestor; mil *sl* conscript within six months of discharge

abulense *n m+f* native of Avila; *adj* of Avila

abulia pathological apathy

abúlico pathological apathetic; weak-willed

abultado bulky; big; ~ de facciones coarse-featured

abultar *vt* to enlarge; *vi* to be bulky; take up a lot of room

abundancia abundance; fruitfulness

abundante abundant

abundar to abound (de/en in/with); exaggerate

abundoso abundant

abuñolar, abuñuelar to shape like a fritter; turn over when frying

¡abur! good-bye!, au revoir!

aburar to burn

aburelar to give a reddish colour to

aburguesarse to become bourgeois/middle-class; adopt bourgeois attitudes

aburilar to engrave

aburrarse to become brutish

aburrido bored; boring

aburrimiento boredom, weariness, annoyance

aburrir to bore, weary, annoy; ~ a un muerto to bore to death; ~se to grow bored, get bored

abusador *n* person who takes unfair advantage

abusar to abuse; overdo; outstay one's welcome; ~ de to take unfair advantage of, impose upon

abusionero *n* fortune-teller, soothsayer; *adj* superstitious

abusivo abusive

abuso abuse, misuse; ~ de confianza breach of confidence

abyección *f* abjectness

abyecto abject

acá here, over here; ¿de cuándo ~? since when?; muy ~ right here; por ~ this way, hereabouts; ¡ven ~! come here/along!

acabable achievable; practicable

acabado *n* finish; *adj* finished; perfect; *fam* worn out; ruined

acabador *m* finisher

acabalar to complete, finish

acaballado like a horse

acaballerado gentlemanly

acaballonar *agri* to ridge

acabamiento end; completion

acabar to end, finish, complete; ~ con to destroy, put an end to, finish with; ~ de to have just; ~ por to end up + *gerund*; ~se to be finished, grow weak; ¡se acabó! it's all over!

acabildar to unite; form a group; ~se (contra) to gang up (on)

academia academy; school; learned society

académico *n* member of a royal society, academician; *adj* academic(al)

acaecedero eventual

acaecer to happen, occur

acaecimiento event, occurrence

acahual *m bot* sunflower

acaíta right here

acal *m* canoe

acalambrarse to get cramp

acalenturarse to become feverish

acalia *bot* marshmallow

acalorado heated; excited; angry

acaloramiento ardour; heat; excitement

acalorar to overheat; inflame; promote; ~se to grow warm; get excited

acallar *vt* to quiet

acamar (of rain, wind) to flatten, beat down

acampador *m* camper

acampamento *mil* encampment, camp

acampanado bell-shaped

acampar(se) to encamp

acanalado grooved, fluted, corrugated

acanalador *m carp* grooving-plane

acanalar to groove, flute, corrugate

acanelado cinnamon-coloured, cinnamon-flavoured

acantilado *n* cliff; *adj* steep, sheer

acanto *archi + bot* acanthus

acantonar *mil* to quarter, billet

acaparador *n m* monopolizer; *adj* monopolizing; hoarding

acaparamiento *n* monopoly; cornering; hoarding; *adj* monopolizing

acaparar to monopolize; corner; hoard

acaparrarse to close a deal

acaracolado *adj* spiral; winding

acarambanado covered with icicles

acaramelado sickly-sweet; overpolite; mealy-mouthed

acaramelar to cover with toffee; butter up; ~se to become excessively polite

acarar to face; confront

acardenalar to beat black and blue

acarear to face; brave

acariciador *n m* fondler; *adj* fondling

ácaro: ~ de queso cheesemite

acarreador *m* carrier; porter; bearer

acarreamiento cartage; transportation

acarrear to carry; transport

acarreo cartage

acartonarse to become shrivelled

acaso *n* chance; accident; *adv* maybe, perhaps; **por si** ~ in case

acastañado reddish-brown

acastillaje *m naut* superstructure

acatable deserving respect

acatamiento respect

acatar to respect, hold in high esteem

acatarrarse to catch cold

acaudalado opulent

acaudalador *m* hoarder

acaudalar to hoard; acquire a good reputation

acaule *bot* short-stemmed

acceder to accede; consent

accesibilidad *f* accessibility

accesible accessible; approachable

accesión *f* accession

accésit second prize

acceso access; *med* attack, bout; ~ **prohibido** no entry; **carretera de** ~ approach road

accesoria outbuilding

accesorio *adj* accessory

accidentado *n* casualty; *adj* troubled; eventful; (of terrain) undulating, broken

accidentarse to have an accident; become a casualty; be suddenly taken ill

accidente *m* accident; chance; *mus* accidental; *gramm* inflexion; *geog* feature

acción *f* action; feat; *leg* suit; gesture; battle; *comm* share

accionar *mech* to operate, function; gesticulate

accionista *m + f comm* shareholder

acebo holly(tree)

acecinar *cul* to salt and dry; ~se to grow old and wrinkled

acechadera vantage point

acechador *n m* look-out, observer, ambusher; *adj* spying, ambushing

acechar to lie in ambush; spy on; watch

acecho ambush, waylaying; **al** ~ in ambush

acedera *bot* sorrel

acedía acidity; heartburn; roughness of speech

acedo *adj* acid; unpleasant

acéfalo headless; without a leader

aceitar to oil; rub with oil

aceite *m* oil, *esp* olive oil; ~ **combustible** fuel oil; ~ **de colza** rape-seed oil; ~ **de quemar** lamp oil; ~ **pesado** diesel oil; **echar** ~ **al fuego** to add fuel to the flames

aceitera cruet; woman who sells oil

aceitería oil-shop

aceitero oil-seller; oil-can; ~s cruet

aceitillo light oil; *bot* snowberry

aceitoso oily

aceituna olive; ~ **rellena** stuffed olive; **llegar a las** ~s to arrive late

aceitunado, aceitunil olive-coloured

aceitunero olive harvester; olive dealer

aceitunillo satinwood

aceituno olive-tree; ~ **silvestre** satin-wood

aceleración *f* acceleration; haste; ~ **de gravedad** gravitational acceleration

acelerada burst of speed; revving

acelerado speedy

acelerador *m* accelerator

acelerante *adj* accelerating

acelerar to accelerate, hurry: ~**se** to make haste

acelerón *m see* **acelerada**

acelga spinach beet

acémila beast of burden; dolt

acemilero muleteer

acendrar *metal* to purify; free from blemish; refine

acento accent, stress; way of speaking; voice inflexion; ~ **ortográfico** written accent

acentuación *f* accentuation

acentuar to accentuate; emphasize

aceña water-mill

aceñero miller

acepción *f gramm* meaning, sense; *fig* ~ **de personas** favouritism

acepilladora *carp* planing machine

acepilladura wood-shaving

acepillar *carp* to plane; to brush (clothes)

aceptable acceptable

aceptación *f* acceptance; ~ **de personas** favouritism; **tener** ~ to be popular

aceptar to accept

acepto *n* acceptance; *adj* acceptable; agreeable

acequia irrigation ditch

acequiar to dig irrigation ditches

acequiero irrigation-ditch keeper

ácer *m bot* maple tree

acera pavement, *US* sidewalk

acerado made of steel, strong

acerar to edge with steel; harden; strengthen; pave; reinforce a wall with stone slabs; ~**se** to take courage

acerbidad *f* harshness; bitterness; asperity

acerbo harsh; bitter; cruel

acerca de about, concerning

acercamiento approximation; rapprochement

acercar to put near; bring up; ~**se** to come near; ~**se a** to approach

ácere *m bot* maple tree

acerico, acerillo pincushion

acero steel; ~ **dulce** soft steel; ~ **inoxidable** stainless steel

acérrimo very strong (of taste, flavour); very vigorous

acerrojar to lock; bolt

acertado correct; successful; well thought out; fit and proper

acertar to hit the mark; guess correctly; succeed; ~ **con** to find

acertijo riddle; guessing game

acervo heap; *leg* common property

acetábulo cruet

acetato acetate

acetileno acetylene

acético acetic

acetín *m bot* satinwood

acetona acetone

acetosa *bot* sorrel

acetre *m* small pail; *eccles* holy water basin

acezar to pant

acezoso panting; out of breath

aciago unlucky; unfortunate

aciano *bot* cornflower

acíbar *m bot* aloe-tree; bitterness

acibarar to make bitter

acicalado polishing, burnishing

acicalamiento polish, burnish

acicalar to polish, burnish

acicate *m* spur; incentive

acicatear to spur on

acicular needle-shaped

acidez *f* acidity

acidificar to acidify

ácido *n* acid; *adj* acid, sour, tart

acidular to acidulate; turn sour

acierto good shot/hit; correct guess; right move

ácimo: pan ~ unleavened bread

ación *f* stirrup-strap

acirate *m* landmark

aclamable laudable

aclamación *f* acclamation

aclamar to acclaim

aclamatorio acclamatory

aclaración *f* explanation

aclarador explanatory

aclarar to explain; clarify; make clear; rinse; thin down; ~ **la voz** to clear the throat; ~**se** *meteor* to clear up, brighten

aclaratorio explanatory

aclarecer to brighten, lighten, illuminate

aclimatación *f* acclimatization

aclimatar to acclimatize, *US* acclimate

acmé *m* top; highest point

acné *m med* acne

acobardar to daunt, intimidate; ~**se** to become terrified; lack courage; climb down

acochinado filthy

acochinar to corner and kill; corner a draughtsman; ~**se** to get filthy

acodadura nudging; bending the elbow; *hort* layering

acodar to bend the elbow; lean the elbow on; *hort* layer; ~**se** to rest on one's elbows

acodiciar to long for; covet

acodillar to bend the elbow/ankle; sag, give way under a load

acodo *hort* layer

acogedor sheltering; welcoming; cosy

acoger to welcome; receive with warmth; shelter; ~**se** to take shelter; ~**se bajo sagrado** to seek asylum/ sanctuary

acogeta *n* shelter; refuge; cover

acogida reception; welcome; hospitality; **buena/mala** ~ good/bad reception; **dar** ~ **a una letra** *comm* to honour a draft

acogimiento welcome

acogollar *hort* to force (by covering up)

acogotar to kill with a chop on the back of the neck

acohombrar *agri* + *hort* to earth up

acojinar to quilt; cushion

acojonado *sl vulg* shit-scared, yellow-bellied, lily-livered

acolada accolade

acolchar to quilt; pad

acólito acolyte

acollar *agri* + *hort* to earth up; *naut* to caulk

acollarar to harness; yoke; put on a leash; *fam* marry

acollonar *fam* to frighten; ~**se** to go into a (blue) funk

acomedirse to volunteer

acometedor *n m* attacker; *adj* aggressive

acometer to attack, assault; charge, go for; *mech* install; ~ **por la espalda** to attack from behind; ~**le a uno el sueño** to be overcome by sleep

acometida, acometimiento attack; *med* bout; *mech* connection, installation

acometividad *f* aggressiveness; fighting spirit

acomodable adaptable

acomodación *f* arrangement

acomodadizo obliging; accommodating

acomodado suitable; well-off; reasonable

acomodador *n* usher, attendant; *adj* accommodating, conciliating

acomodadora *cin* + *theat* usherette, attendant

acomodar *vt* to accommodate; settle; arrange; adapt; compound; *vi* to suit; ~**se** to put up with; adapt o.s. to; settle down

acomodaticio accommodating; conciliatory

acomodo employment; lodgings; situation; arrangement

acompañador *n* attendant; chaperon; *mus* accompanist; *adj* accompanying

acompañamiento retinue; *mus* accompaniment; *her* decoration round a coat-of-arms

acompañante companion; chaperon

acompañar to accompany, attend; join, unite; **le acompaño** *comm* I send you herewith; **le acompaño en sus sentimientos** please accept my deepest condolences; ~**se** *mus* to accompany o.s.

acompasado rhythmic; unhurried; measured by the compass

acompasar to measure with dividers; arrange in order

acomplejar *psych* to make s.o. develop a complex; ~**se** to develop a complex

aconchar *naut* to run aground

acondicionado: aire ~ air-conditioning

acondicionador *n* conditioner; ~ **de aire** air conditioner; *adj* conditioning

acondicionamiento conditioning

acondicionar to condition, prepare; repair; ~**se** to qualify (for a post)

acongojador afflicting

acongojar to afflict, sadden, grieve; ~**se** to be filled with anguish

acónito wolfsbane

aconsejable advisable

aconsejado: bien ~ well-advised; **mal** ~ ill-advised

aconsejador *n m* advisor; *adj* advising, advisory

aconsejar to advise, counsel; ~**se con la almohada** to sleep on it; ~**se mejor** to think better of it

aconsonantar to rhyme

aconstelado constellated

acontecer to happen, occur, take place; **lo acontecido** what has/had happened

acontecimiento event, occurrence

acopar to hollow

acopiamiento *comm* buying up, speculation

acopiar to gather; corner, speculate in

acopio gathering; cornering

acopladura coupling; junction

acoplamiento coupling, connection, joint; *space* docking; ~ **universal** universal joint

acoplar to couple, connect, join; adjust; yoke; *space* dock; *zool* mate; ~**se** to agree; make up; *fam* have sex

acoquinamiento daunting

acoquinar to frighten, daunt; intimidate; cow; ~**se** to get into a funk

acorazado *n* battleship, ironclad; ~ **de bolsillo** pocket battleship; *adj* armoured

acorazar to armour, armour-plate; ~**se contra** to shield o.s. against

acorazonado shaped like a heart

acordable tunable

acordar to decide; agree upon; remind; make flush; *mus* tune; be in agreement; ~ +*infin* to agree to +*infin*; ~**se con** to reach agreement with; ~**se de** to remember; **si mal no me acuerdo** if my memory serves me right

acorde *n m mus* chord; harmony; *adj* in agreement; *mus* in tune

acordelar to measure with a cord

acordemente by common consent

acordeón *m* accordion

acordeonista *m + f* accordionist

acordonar to make into the shape of a cord/rope; lace (shoes *etc*); cordon off; surround (with police/soldiers)

acornar, acornear to butt

acorneador *n m* animal that butts; *adj* butting

acorralamiento corralling

acorralar to round up, corral

acortamiento shortening

acortar to shorten, reduce, check; ~ **la marcha** to decelerate; ~**le a uno la palabra** to cut s.o. short; ~**se** to fall behind; become shy

acosador harassing

acosamiento pursuit, persecution

acosar to pursue; persecute, harass; vex; molest

acoso pursuit, harassment; corralling of bulls

acostado stretched out; lying down; in bed; *naut* on beam ends

acostamiento lying down; laying down; support; stipend

acostar to lay down, put to bed; *naut* bring alongside; ~**se** to lie down; go to bed; *naut* bring alongside; ~**se con las gallinas** to go to bed early

acostumbrado customary, usual

acostumbrar to be in the habit of; accustom; be used to, **ella acostumbra a trabajar** she is used to working; ~**se** to become accustomed to, get used to

acotación *f* boundary mark; *theat* stage directions; marginal note; *sur* elevation mark (on map)

acotada *bot* nursery

acotamiento limitation

¹ **acotar** to limit, put boundary marks on; annotate; *sur* to mark elevations

² **acotar** *bot* to prune

acotillo sledge-hammer

acracia *pol* opposition to authority

ácrata *pol* opposed to authority

¹ **acre** *adj* bitter; sour; acrimonious

² **acre** *n m* acre

acrecentamiento increase, growth

acrecentar(se), acrecer(se) to increase, grow; foster

acreditado reputable; held in high esteem

acreditar to assure, affirm; verify; give credence to; *comm* credit; guarantee; authorize; ~**se** to gain a reputation

acreditativo creditable

acreedor *n m* creditor; ~ **hipotecario** mortgagee; *adj* deserving, meritorious

acribador *n m* sifter; *adj* sifting

acribar to sift, sieve

acribillador *n m* tormentor; *adj* sievelike; tormenting

acribillar to pierce; riddle (with bullets); torment; *fam* pester, annoy; **estar acribillado de deudas** to be up to one's eyes in debt

acriminable incriminatory

acriminación *f* incrimination

acriminador *n m* accuser; *adj* accusing

acriminar to accuse

acrimonia acrimony; sourness; asperity

acrimonial, acrimonioso acrimonious

acriollarse to adopt local customs, go native

acrisolar to refine, purify; *metal* assay;

purge

acristianar to make Christian, baptize

acritud *f* acrimony

acrobacia *aer* stunt

acrobática acrobatics

acrobático acrobatic

acromatizar to achromatize

acróstico acrostic

acta record of proceedings; certificate of election; ~s records, minutes; file; ~s de los santos lives of the saints; **libro de** ~s minute-book

actitud *f* attitude, position

activar to activate, encourage, buck up

actividad *f* activity; **en** ~ in operation; **en plena** ~ in full swing

activista *m+f* activist

activo *n* assets; **en** ~ on active service; *adj* active, quick

acto act, action; public function; sexual intercourse; ~ **continuo,** ~ **seguido** immediately; **sala de** ~s assembly hall

actor *m* actor; *leg* claimant, plaintiff

actriz *f* actress; **primera** ~ leading lady

actuación *f* action; performance; behaviour; *leg* proceedings

actual present-day; topical

actualidad *f* present time; **en la** ~ at the present time; **ser de** ~ to be topical

actualizar to bring up-to-date; ~se to get up-to-date, *fam* get with it

actuante *m+f* performer; (at university) defender of a thesis

actuar to act; put into action; (at university) defend a thesis

actuario clerk of the court; actuary

acuafortista *m+f* etcher

acuarela water-colour painting

Acuario Aquarius

acuario aquarium

acuartelamiento *mil* billeting; quarters

acuartelar to billet, quarter; confine to barracks; ~se to take up quarters

acuático aquatic; **esquí** ~ water-skiing

acuatinta aquatint

acuatizaje *m aer* alighting on water

acuatizar *aer* to alight on water

acubarse to become intoxicated

acucia zeal, eagerness

acuciador, acuciante urgent

acuciamiento goading

acuciar to goad; harass

acucioso zealous, eager

acuclillarse to squat; crouch

acucharado shaped like a spoon

acuchillador *m* bully, thug

acuchillar to cut, stab, knife; hack; *carp* plane down; ~se to fight with knives/ swords

acudir to arrive at a place; attend (a function); answer a call; go to the rescue; keep (a date)

acueducto aqueduct

ácueo watery

acuerdo agreement, accord; *arts* harmony; **de** ~ all right, okay; **de** ~ **con** in accordance with; **de común** ~ unanimously

acuidad *f* acuity

acuitar to grieve, afflict

acular to force into a corner

acullá over on the other side

acumulación *f* accumulation; storing-up

acumulador *m* accumulator, storage battery

acumulante accumulating

acumular to accumulate; pile up; hoard

acumulativo accumulative

acunar to rock in a cradle

acuñación *f* coining, minting

acuñador *n m* minter, coiner; *adj* minting, coining

acuñar to coin, mint: *print* to quoin; ~ **una palabra** to coin a word

acuosidad *f* wateriness

acuoso watery

acupuntura acupuncture

acupunturista *m+f* acupuncturist

acurrucarse to huddle/curl up

acusación *f* accusation, indictment

acusado *n* accused, defendant; *adj* accused, marked

acusador *n m* accuser, prosecutor; *adj* accusing, prosecuting

acusar to accuse, charge, prosecute; acknowledge (receipt of); ~se de to confess to; **le acusaron de espía** they accused him of being a spy

acusativo accusative

acuse *m:* ~ **de recibo** acknowledgement of receipt

acusón *m,* **acusona** tale-bearer

acústica acoustics

acústico acoustic; **trompetilla acústica** ear-trumpet; **tubo** ~ speaking tube

acusticón *m* sound amplifier

acutángulo acute-angled

achacable imputable

achacar to impute

achacoso weak, ailing

achaflanar to chamfer

achantar *vi sl* to be quiet; *vt sl* to intimidate; ~**se** *fam* to climb down, sing small

achaparrarse *bot* to grow stunted

achaque *m* habitual illness; excuse; *fam* period, menstruation

achaquiento sickly, unhealthy

acharolar to paint with varnish; to japan

achatar to flatten

achicado timid; reserved

achicador *m naut* bailer, scoop

achicadura timidity; *naut* bailing

achicar to reduce, diminish; *fam* humble, belittle; *naut* bail; ~**se** to make o.s. small; climb down

achicoria chicory

achicharradero scorchingly hot place

achicharrador scorching, sizzling

achicharrar to scorch, roast; irritate; *sl* kill (with firearm), bump off

achilenarse to adopt Chilean habits

achinado like a Chinaman; of mixed (white and American-Indian) blood

achispado tipsy, merry

achispar to make s.o. tipsy; ~**se** to get tipsy

achocolatado chocolate-coloured

achubascarse to get showery/overcast

achuchador *n m* bully; *adj* bullying

achuchar to incite; push; jostle; **estar achuchado** to be broke

achulado *n* pimp; *adj* truculent, bullying

achularse to be kept by a woman

adagio proverb; *mus* adagio

adamada la-di-da woman

adamado effeminate

Adán Adam

adaptabilidad *f* adaptability

adaptación *f* adaptation

adaptador *n m* adapter; *adj* adapting

adaptar to adapt; make suitable; ~**se** to get used to

adarme *m* very tiny amount; **por** ~**s** sparingly

adecentar to clean up; tidy

adecuado adequate; suitable

adecuar to suit; make suitable

adefagia great hunger

adefesio nonsense; extravagant; exaggerated; ridiculous-looking

adehesar *agri* to convert to pasture

adelantado *n* governor-general; *adj* anticipated, developed; *bot* early; (of clocks) fast; **por** ~ in advance

adelantamiento progress, advancement, improvement, governor-generalship

adelantar to advance; promote; pay in advance; make progress; (of clocks) gain; ~**se** to take the lead; steal a march on

adelante *adv* ahead; forward, further off; **de hoy en** ~ henceforth; **hacia** ~ forwards; **más** ~ later on

adelanto advance, progress; *comm* advance payment

adelfa *bot* oleander; rose-bay

adelfilla *bot* willow-herb

adelgazador *adj* slimming

adelgazamiento *n* slimming

adelgazar *vt* to make slim; taper; *vi* to slim, lose weight; reduce; **régimen de** ~ slimming diet

adeliñar to make a bee-line for

adema *min* pit-prop

ademán *m* gesture

ademar *min* to prop

además moreover, besides; ~ **de** besides

adenoideo *adj* adenoid; **vegetación adenoidea** adenoids

adensarse to thicken

adentellar to bite; get one's teeth into

adentrarse to delve deeply into

adentro within, inside; **mar** ~ out at sea; **tierra** ~ inland; *interj* come in!

adentros *mpl* innermost being; *fam* innards

adepto *n* initiate; follower

aderezamiento adornment, embellishment; *cul* dressing

aderezar to adorn, embellish; *cul* dress; (of drinks) mix; (of wine, tea) blend

aderezarse to adorn, embellish; dress o.s.

aderezo dressing; finery; starch (for stiffening); furniture; ~ **de mesa** *cul* seasoning

adeudado in debt

adeudar to owe; *comm* debit; fall due; ~**se** to incur debts

adeudo indebtedness; custom-house duty; *comm* debit

adherencia alliance; adhesion; relationship; **tener** ~**s** to have connections

adherente *n m* adherent; follower; *adj*

adhesive, adherent

adherir to adhere, stick; ~**se** to stick fast

adhesión f adhesion, adherence

adhesividad f adhesiveness

adhesivo adhesive

adiamantado adamantine

adiamantar to adorn with diamonds

adición f addition, bill

adicional additional

adicionar to add to; extend

adicto n addict, devotee; adj addicted

adiestrable trainable

adiestrado broken in

adiestrador m trainer

adiestramiento training

adiestrar to train; ~**se** to practise

adietar to put on a diet

adinerarse to become rich

¡adiós! goodbye!, cheerio!

adiposidad f fatness

adiposo fat

aditamento addition; ~**s** accessories

aditivo n+adj additive

adivinable guessable

adivinación f guessing

adivinador n m soothsayer; adj divining

adivinaja puzzle, riddle

adivinamiento divination

adivinanza prediction; enigma; riddle, conundrum

adivinar to guess; divine; solve

adivinatorio divinatory

adivino soothsayer; fortune-teller; wizard; ent praying mantis

adjetivación f gramm agreement (of adjective/noun)

adjetivar gramm to make agree; use as an adjective

adjetivo n adjective; adj adjectival

adjudicación f award; adjudication; knocking down (at an auction); ~ **procesal** judicial award

adjudicador m adjudicator

adjudicar to adjudicate; award; ~ **el contrato** to award a contract; ~**se** to appropriate

adjudicatario successful bidder

adjudicativo adjudicative

adjuntar to add, join; enclose (in a letter)

adjunto n enclosure; partner; adj joined; enclosed; attached; associate; **professor** ~ lecturer

adjutor m assistant

administración f administration, management

administrador n m administrator, steward, bailiff; adj administrating; ~ **de correos** postmaster

administrar to administer, manage

administrativo administrative

admiración f admiration, wonder; gramm exclamation mark

admirador n m admirer, adj admiring

admirar to admire, wonder at; astonish; ~**se** to wonder, be astonished (at)

admirativo admiring, wondering

admisible admissible, allowable

admisión f admission, acceptance

admitir to admit, receive; concede; suffer

admonición f admonition, warning

adobado pickled pork

adobador n m dresser, preparer; adj pickling, preserving

adobamiento dressing; preserving; tanning

adobar to dress, prepare; pickle; cook; tan

adobasillas m sing+pl chair-mender

adobeño of adobe

adobería tannery

adobo repairing; pickle; sauce; ingredients for dressing leather

adocenado common; numerous

adocenamiento commonplaceness

adocenar to sell by dozens; ~**se** to become commonplace

adoctrinamiento indoctrination

adoctrinar to indoctrinate

adolecer to be afflicted with; suffer from; ~**se** to be sorry

adoleciente suffering, ailing

adolescencia adolescence

adolescente n m+f +adj adolescent; teenager

adolorido afflicted; grieved

adomiciliarse to set up house

adonde where; **¿adónde?** where?, whither?

adondequiera wherever; anywhere

adonis m handsome youth

adopción f adoption

adoptado adopted child

adoptador m, **adoptante** m adopter

adoptar to adopt, father; ~ **por hijo** to adopt as a son

adoptivo adopted
adoquier, adoquiera anywhere
adoquín *m* paving stone
adoquinar to pave
adoración *f* adoration, worship; **Adoración de los Reyes Magos** Epiphany, last day of Christmas
adorador *n m* adorer; *adj* adoring
adorar to adore, worship
adormecedor soporific
adormecer to make sleepy; lull asleep; ~**se** to fall asleep, grow benumbed
adormecido half-asleep
adormecimiento drowsiness, sleepiness
adormidera *bot* opium poppy
adormitarse to doze off
adornador *n m* decorator, adorner; *adj* adorning
adornar to adorn, decorate, embellish, garnish
adornista *m+f* decorator, painter
adorno adornment, decoration, finery
adosar to put back-to-back
adquir(i)ente *n m* acquirer; *adj* acquiring
adquirir to acquire, get; purchase
adquisición *f* acquisition; purchase
adquisidor *n m see* **adquir(i)ente**
adquisitividad *f* acquisitiveness
adquisitivo acquisitive; **poder** ~ purchasing power
adrede on purpose, deliberately
adrenalina adrenaline
adrián *m med* bunion; *orni* magpie's nest
Adriático Adriatic
adrizar *naut* to right
adrollar to swindle
adrollero dishonest trader
adscribir to assign; appoint
adscripción *f* nomination, appointment
aduana custom-house; *sl* hiding-place, refuge; **derecho de** ~ customs duty; **en la** ~ in bond
aduanar to pay duty on; put in bond
aduanero *n* customs officer; *adj* of the customs
aduar *m* Arab village; band of gipsies
aducción *f* adducing
aducir to adduce; cite
aduendado fairy-like; gnome-like; goblin-like
adueñarse to get control (**de** of)
adufe *m* tambourine

adula common pasture
adulación *f* adulation, flattery
adulador *n m* flatterer, fawner; *adj* flattering, fawning
adular to flatter, fawn
adulatorio flattering
adulón *n m* toady, creep; *adj* toadying, creeping
adulteración *f* adulteration; falsification
adulterador *n m* adulterer; *adj* adulterating; falsifying
adulterar to adulterate; corrupt; falsify; ~**se** to become corrupted/adulterated
adulterio adultery
adúltero *n* adulterer; *adj* adulterous; corrupted
adultez *f* adulthood
adulto adult, fully grown
adulzar to sweeten; to soften
adumbrar to shade
adunar to unite; ~**se** to become associated
adustez *f* grimness, gloom
adusto grim, gloomy
advenedizo *n* newcomer; *adj* newly arrived
advenidero forthcoming
advenimiento arrival; advent
adventista *n m+f+adj* Adventist
adverar to certify
adverbializar to employ as an adverb
adverbio adverb
adversario adversary, opponent
adversidad *f* adversity, calamity
adverso adverse
advertencia warning; advice
advertido forewarned; wide-awake
advertimiento warning
advertir to notice; warn; notify; advise; **es de** ~ it should be noticed; ~**se** to become aware
Adviento Advent
adyacencia adjacency; ~**s** neighbourhood
adyacente adjacent
aeración *f* aeration; ventilation
aerear to aerate
aéreo aerial; airy; overhead; fantastic; **combate** ~ dog-fight; **guerra aérea** air war(fare)
aeróbica aerobics
aerobús *m* airbus
aerodeslizador *m* hovercraft
aerodinámica aerodynamics

aerodinámico aerodynamic; streamlined
aeródromo aerodrome, airfield
aerofaro aerial beacon
aerofobia aerophobia
aeroforme streamlined
aerofoto aerophotograph
aerofotografía aerophotography; aero-photograph
aerofotografiar to photograph from the air
aerofumigación *f agri* crop-dusting
aerograma *m* aerogram
aerolínea air-line
aerolito meteorite
aeromapa *m* air-map
aeromodelismo model aircraft flying/building
aeromodelista *n m+f* model aircraft enthusiast; *adj* pertaining to model aircraft
aeromodelo model aircraft
aeronauta *m+f* aeronaut
aeronáutico aeronautic
aeronaval air-naval
aeronave *f* airliner; airship
aeropista air-strip
aeroplano aeroplane, airplane; ~ **nodriza** tanker plane, refuelling plane
aeropostal *adj* air-mail
aeroscala transit point; staging post
aeróstata *m+f* aerostat, balloonist
aerostática aerostatics
aerostático aerostatic
aeróstato air balloon
aerotransportar to airlift, transport by air
aerovía air corridor
afabilidad *f* affability
afable affable
afamar to make famous; ~**se** to become famous
afán *m* eagerness
afanador eager
afanar to toil, strive; *sl* rob; ~**se** to busy o.s.
afanoso eager
afantasmado ghost-like; *fam* vain
afasia *med* aphasia
afear to look ugly; deface; spoil; condemn
afeblecerse to grow feeble
afección *f* affection; fondness; *med* disease
afectable impressionable

afectación *f* affectation
afectar to affect, feign; influence
afectividad *f* affectibility
afectivo affective, emotional
afecto *n* affection, fondness; *adj* fond, well-affected
afectuosidad *f* fondness, affection
afectuoso fond, affectionate, loving
afeitada *n* shave
afeitadora electric shaver
afeitaduras *fpl* metal shavings
afeitar to shave; *bot* clip; trim a horse's mane/tail; cut the tips of fighting bull's horns; ~**se** to shave; make up
afeite *m* paint; make up; cosmetic
afelpado similar to plush
afeminación *f* effeminacy
afeminado effeminate
afeminarse to become effeminate
aferrado headstrong, obstinate
aferrador *n m* clamp; *adj* grasping
aferramiento obstinacy; grasping, seizing; *naut* mooring
aferrar to grasp, seize; *naut* moor, anchor; ~**se** to fasten to each other
Afganistán Afghanistan
afgano Afghan
afianzador *n m* guarantor; *adj* guaranteeing
afianzamiento security; guarantee, bail
afianzar to guarantee, vouch for, stand bail for; support; prop
afición *f* fondness, keenness, hobby; fans, supporters; **tener ~ a** to be fond of/keen on
aficionado *n* enthusiast; fan, supporter; amateur; addict; **ser ~ a** to be fond of/keen on
aficionar *vt* to get keen on; ~**se** to become fond of/keen on
afidávit *m* affidavit
afiebrado feverish
afijo *n gramm* affix
afilador *n m* knife-grinder; knife-sharpener; razor strop; *adj* sharpening
afiladura sharpening, whetting
afilalápices *m sing+pl* pencil-sharpener
afilamiento sharpening, whetting; slenderness (of fingers, face and nose)
afilar to sharpen; put an edge on; whet; taper; ~**se** to grow thin; taper away
afiliación *f* affiliation
afiliado *n* member; *adj* affiliated
afiligranado filigree, filigree-work,

decorated
afiligranar to filigree, decorate
afilón *m* whetstone, steel, strop, knife-sharpener
afinación *f* final touch; *metal* refining; *mus* tuning
afinado *n mus* tuning; *adj* in tune
afinador *n m* finisher; *mus* piano-tuner; tuning key; *adj* finishing, tuning
afinamiento refinement; good manners; completion
afinar to finish; polish; (bookbinding) trim; *metal* refine; *mus* tune; ~se to become cultured, wise, refined or polished
afincamiento settlement; settling-down
afincar to buy property/real estate; ~se to settle down
afinidad *f* affinity; relationship by marriage
afino *metal* refining
afirmación *f* statement, declaration, assertion
afirmado road-bed
afirmador *n m* asserter; *adj* asserting, declaring
afirmar to state, declare, assert; secure; ~se to steady o.s.; ~se en lo dicho to stick to one's guns
afirmativo affirmative
aflautado (of voice) high-pitched, squeaky
aflechado *bot* arrow-shaped
aflicción *f* affliction, sorrow, grief
aflictivo distressing, grievous; *leg* **pena aflictiva** corporal punishment
afligido distressing, grieving
afligimiento *see* aflicción
afligir to afflict, distress; ~se to grieve
aflojadura loosening, relaxation
aflojamiento slackening, abatement
aflojar to loosen, slacken, let up; *sl* pay, cough up, fork out; ~se to lose enthusiasm/courage
afloramiento *min* outcrop; sifting; gushing out
aflorar to sift, refine; ~se to gush forth
afluencia flow; rush, crowd; plenty; fluency, volubility
afluente *n m geog* tributary; *adj* inflowing; eloquent
afluir to flow in; flock in
afoliado *bot* leafless
afondarse *naut* to sink, founder

afonía loss of voice; *med* aphonia
afónico having lost one's voice
aforado privileged
aforador *m* appraiser; gauger
aforar to appraise; gauge; measure; hold, have room for; bestow privileges on
aforismo aphorism
aforo appraising; gauging; capacity
aforrar to line (clothes *etc*)
afortunado fortunate, lucky
afosarse *mil* to dig in
afrancesado frenchified; fond of the French
afrancesamiento frenchification
afrancesar to frenchify; ~se to imitate the French; copy things French
afrecho bran
afrenta affront; insult
afrentar to affront, insult
afrentoso insulting, outrageous
africanismo Africanism
africanista *m+f* Africanist
africano African
afro: peinado ~ afro hairstyle
afrodisíaco aphrodisiac
afrontamiento confrontation
afrontar to confront
afrutado (of wine) fruity
afta *med* thrush
afuera *adv* outside; in public; *interj* clear out!
afueras *fpl* outskirts, suburbs
afufar(se) *sl* to scarper; do a bunk
afuste *m* gun-carriage; gun emplacement
agabachar *pej* to frenchify; ~se to become frenchified
agachadiza *orni* snipe
agachar to lower; ~ las orejas to climb down; ~se to stoop, bend down, duck
agalgado like a greyhound
agallas *fpl* tonsils; fish-gills; courage; tener ~ to have guts
agamuzar to dress skins
ágape *m* banquet, love-feast
agareno Muslim
agarrada wrangle, row
agarraderas *fpl* influence, patronage
agarradero *m* handle
agarrado mean, miserly, stingy
agarrador *n m* handle; *adj* grasping, seizing
agarrafar to grapple; ~se to come to

grips

agarrar to hold, seize, grasp; *bot* take root; ~**se** (of illness) to take hold

agarre *m* grasp, hold

agarrochar to prick; goad

agarrotar to tie up; squeeze; garrotte; ~**se** become stiff; seize up

agasajado guest of honour

agasajador attentive

agasajar to regale, treat well, wine and dine

agasajo reception, welcome; lavish entertainment; party in s.o.'s honour

agasón *m* stable-boy

ágata agate

agateador *m orni* tree-creeper

agavanzo *bot* dog-rose

agavilladora *agri* mechanical harvester

agavillar to bind in sheaves; ~**se** to gang together

agazaparse to hide, lurk

agencia agency

agenciador *m* agent, promoter

agenciar to procure; bring about; ~**se** to manage; come by

agencioso diligent

agenda notebook, diary

agente *m* agent, promoter; policeman; ~ **de cambio y bolsa** stockbroker; ~ **fiscal** assistant attorney; ~ **inmobiliario** estate agent, *US* realtor; ~ **viajante** sales representative

agermanizar to copy things German

agigantado gigantic, enormous; exaggerated; **a pasos** ~**s** by leaps and bounds

agigantar to exaggerate

ágil agile, nimble

agilidad *f* agility

agilitar, agilizar to speed up; ~**se** to limber up

agio, agiotaje *m comm* speculation; usury

agiotador *m*, **agiotista** *m+f comm* speculator; usurer

agiotar to speculate; practise usury

agitable easily agitated

agitación *f* agitation; excitement

agitado agitated, stormy

agitador *m* agitator

agitanarse to adopt gipsy ways

agitar to agitate; excite; wave; ~**se** to become agitated/excited; to flutter; (of sea) to get rough

aglomeración *f* agglomeration; **horas de** ~ rush hours

aglomerado *n* agglomerate; briquette; chipboard

aglomerante *n m* binder

aglomerarse to pile up

aglutinación *f* agglutination

aglutinado agglutinate

aglutinante *n m* cementing agent

aglutinar to glue together; bind

aglutinativo agglutinative

agnación *f* blood-relationship

agnosticismo agnosticism

agnóstico agnostic

agobiado oppressed; overwhelmed; bowed down

agobiar to bow down; oppress; overwhelm; ~**se de/con** to become oppressed by

agobio oppression; burden

agolpamiento crowding; rush

agolpar to pile up; ~**se** to crowd, throng

agonía death-agony; agony, suffering

agonizante *m+f* dying person

agonizar *vt* to assist a dying person; *vi* to be on one's death bed; **estar agonizando** to be on the point of death

agorafobia agoraphobia

agorar to foretell, divine

agorería foretelling, divination

agorero *n* soothsayer, fortune-teller; *adj* ominous, ill-omened

agostadero summer pasture

agostar to wither up; spend August; ~**se** to fade away

agosto August; **hacer su** ~ to make hay while the sun shines

agotable exhaustible

agotado exhausted; (of books) out-of-print; *comm* sold out

agotador, agotante exhausting

agotamiento complete fatigue

agotar to exhaust, wear out; fritter away (money); drain off (a liquid); ~**se** to become exhausted; go out of print

agraciado favoured; good-looking; lucky

agraciar to favour; reward; pardon

agracillo *bot* barberry

agradable agreeable; enjoyable

agradar to please

agradecer to be thankful for

agradecimiento thankfulness

agrado pleasure, liking; **de mucho** ~ (of

people) agreeable

agrandamiento enlargement; aggrandizement

agrandar to enlarge; aggrandize

agrario agrarian

agravación *f* aggravation; worsening

agravador aggravating

agravamiento *n* worsening

agravante *f* aggravating circumstance

agravar to make worse; aggravate; put a tax on; ~**se** to become worse

agravatorio aggravating

agraviado *n* leg aggrieved party; *adj* injured, offended

agraviador *n m* offender; *adj* offending, wrongful

agraviante *adj* offending

agraviar to offend, wrong; ~**se** to take offence

agravio offence, insult; *leg* tort, injury; ~ **protervo** wanton injury; **deshacer** ~**s** to right wrongs

agravioso offensive, insulting

agraz *m* unripe grape; *cul* verjuice; displeasure

agrazar to embitter; taste sour

agrazón *m see* **agraz**; gooseberry bush

agredir to assault; attack

agregación *f* aggregation

agregado attaché; *bui* aggregate; *bui* concrete block

agregar to add, attach; collect

agremiación *f* unionization; union; guild

agremiado member of a guild

agremiar to form a guild/union

agresión *f* aggression; assault

agresividad *f* aggressiveness

agresivo aggressive

agresor *n m* aggressor; *adj* aggressive

agreste rustic, boorish

agrete sourish

agriar to make sour/bitter; embitter; exasperate; ~**se** to turn sour; become embittered/exasperated

agrícola *n* *m*+*f* agriculturalist; *adj* agricultural

agricultor *m* farmer, agriculturist

agricultura agriculture

agridulce sweet and sour; bitter-sweet

agridulzura bitter-sweetness

agrietamiento *n* cracking

agrietar(se) to crack, split

agrifolio *bot* holly

agrillarse *agri* to sprout

agrimensorio *adj* surveying

agrimensura land-surveying

agrimonia *bot* liverwort

agrio *n* sour fruit-juice; ~**s** citrus fruit; citrus fruit trees; citrus fruit juice; *adj* sour, tart, rough; *metal* unmalleable; (of colours) clashing

agrisado greyish

agrisarse to become greyish

agronomía, agronometría agronomics

agrónomo *n* agronomist; *adj* agronomic

agrumar to curdle, clot; ~**se** to become curdled/clotted

agrupación *f* crowd; grouping

agrupamiento *comm* association; cartel

agrupar to group; ~**se** to gather in crowds

agrura acidity; acerbity

agua water; rain; sea; *naut* leak; *bui* roof-slope; urine; ~ **abajo** downstream; ~ **arriba** upstream, against the current; ~ **corriente** running water; ~ **de Colonia** eau-de-Cologne; ~ **de seltz** soda-water; ~ **dulce** fresh water; ~ **fresca** cold water; ~ **gaseosa** mineral water; ~ **muerta** still water; ~ **mineral** spring-water; ~ **oxigenada** hydrogen peroxide; ~ **potable** drinking water; ¡~ **va!** look out!; ~ **verde** springtime rain; **cambiar el** ~ **al canario** to see a man about a dog; **echarse al** ~ to take the plunge; **hacer** ~ *naut* to leak; **tempestad en un vaso de** ~ storm in a teacup

aguacate *m* avocado

aguacero heavy shower, downpour

aguachar *m* puddle; *v* to flood

aguachirle *n f* watery food/wine; *adj* wishy-washy

aguada *bui* priming; *min* flood; *naut* fresh-water supplies; *arts* water-colour

aguadero drinking-trough

aguafiestas *m sing*+*pl fam* wet blanket

aguafuerte *f* etching

aguaje *m* sea-current; *naut* wake

aguajero blusterer, extrovert

agualluvia rainwater

aguamala jellyfish

aguamanil *m* water-jug; washstand

aguamanos *m sing*+*pl* wash-basin; water for washing the hands

aguamarina aquamarine

aguanieve *f* sleet

aguanieves *f sing + pl orni* pied wagtail

aguanoso watery

aguantable bearable, tolerable

aguantar *vt* to bear, put up with; endure; stand; *vi* to hold out, last out; stand one's ground; ~**se** to restrain o.s.; lump it

aguante *m* endurance, staying-power; patience

aguapié *m* cheap wine, plonk

aguar to water down; pour cold water on

aguardada wait, waiting

aguardar to wait (for)

aguardentería spirits-shop

aguardentero maker/seller of spirits

aguardentoso gruff voice

aguardiente *m* unmatured brandy; ~ **de caña** rum

aguarrás *f* oil of turpentine

aguasol *m bot* blight

aguatinta aquatint

aguaverde *f* green jellyfish

aguazal *m* marshy region

aguazarse to become marshy

agudeza sharpness; acuteness

agudizarse to become more acute/noticeable

agudo acute; sharp; subtle; *mus* high pitched; **ángulo** ~ acute angle

agüera irrigation ditch

agüero omen; **de mal** ~ ill-omened

aguerrir *mil* to season (troops); inure to war; ~**se** to become inured to war

aguijada lance; goad

aguijar to goad; incite

aguijón *m* prick; goad; thorn; *ent* sting

aguijonazo thrust with a goad

aguijoneador *adj* pricking

aguijonear to prick; goad

¹ **águila** *f* eagle; ~ **bicéfala** double-headed eagle; ~ **blanca** bald eagle; ~ **de mar** sea-eagle; ~ **pescadora** osprey; ~ **ratonera** buzzard; ~ **real** golden eagle

² **águila** *m* lynx; cunning fellow

aguileño aquiline; hook-nosed

aguilón *m* jib of crane; *bui* gable wall

aguilucho eaglet

aguinaldo Christmas box; Christmas bonus

aguja needle; (gramophone) stylus; (railway) points; (of watch) hand; *naut* compass needle; ~ **de gancho** crochet-hook; ~ **de hacer punto** knitting needle

agujazo prick with a needle

agujero hole; maker/seller of needles; *sl* refuge, safe house

agujeta shoe-lace; *orni* godwit; ~**s** cramp, pins-and-needles; **tener** ~**s** to have pins-and-needles, be all aches and pains

aguoso watery

¡agur! goodbye, au revoir

agusanado worm-eaten

agutí *m zool* agouti

aguzadero *n* whetstone; sharpener; *adj* sharpening

aguzanieves *f sing + pl* pied wagtail

aguzar to whet; sharpen; incite; goad on; ~ **las orejas** to prick up one's ears; ~ **los dientes** to whet one's appetite

ahebrado fibrous

ahechar to winnow

ahelear to gall; embitter

aherrojar to shackle; put in irons

aherrumbrar to make rusty; ~**se** to go rusty

aherrumbroso rusty

ahí there; **¡**~ **va!** look out!; **de** ~ **a poco** shortly afterwards; **por** ~ approximately in that direction

ahidalgado gentlemanly

ahijado godchild; protégé

ahijar *vt* to adopt; espouse (a cause); *vi agri* to bud, sprout

ahincar to urge; ~**se** to hurry

ahinco determination, insistence; tenacity

ahitar to gorge; stuff

ahito *n* indigestion, surfeit; *adj* gorged

ahogadero hangman's rope; throat-band; halter

ahogadizo unpalatable; heavier than water

ahogamiento drowning; suffocation; hardship

ahogar to choke, strangle; drown; quench; ~ **las penas** to drown one's sorrows; ~**se** to be suffocated/drowned; *naut* to founder

ahogo oppression; suffocation; distress; *med* tightness (of chest)

ahondar to deepen; go deeply into; ~**se** to become deeper

ahora now; a moment ago; right away; ~ **mismo** right now; **hasta** ~ until now; **desde** ~ from now on; **por** ~ for the present

ahorcado hanged person

ahorcadura, ahorcamiento *n* hanging

ahorcar to hang; ~**se** to hang o.s.

ahorita right now

ahorquillar to make fork-shaped; prop up (with fork-shaped timber *etc*)

ahorrador *n m* economizer; *adj* economizing

ahorramiento *n* saving

ahorrar to save, economize; spare; **no ~ esfuerzos para** to spare no efforts to; ~**se palabras** to save one's breath

ahorratividad *f* thrift

ahorrativo thrifty

ahorro saving, economy; ~**s** savings; **caja de** ~**s** savings bank

ahoyar to dig holes in

ahuchador *n m* miser; *adj* miserly

ahuchamiento hoarding, miserliness

ahuchar to hoard up

ahuecado hollow; pompous

ahuecamiento hollowing; pompousness

ahuecar to make hollow; fluff up; sound pompous

ahuesado bony

ahumado smoked, smoke-cured; **gafas ahumadas** dark glasses

ahumador *n m* smoker, curer; *adj* smoking, curing

ahumar *vt* to smoke; cure in smoke; fill with smoke; *vi* to emit smoke; ~**se** *fam* to get tipsy

ahuyentador frightening, scaring

ahuyentar to frighten away; drive out; ~**se** to run away

aijada goad

airado angry, furious; deprived

airamiento wrath, anger

airar to anger; ~**se** to grow angry

aire *m* air; wind; aspect, appearance; beauty; *mus* tune, melody; ~ **acondicionado** air-conditioning; ~ **colado** cold draught; **al** ~ **libre** in the open air; **estar en el** ~ to be in the balance; **tomar el** ~ to take a walk

airear to air, ventilate; ~**se** to take the air; cool down

airecillo gentle breeze

[1] **airón** *m* strong wind

[2] **airón** *m orni* crest; *orni* egret, grey heron

airoso light, graceful, elegant

aislación *f see* **aislamiento**

aislacionismo *pol* isolationist

aislacionista *n m+f+adj* isolationist

aislado isolated; insulated

aislador *n m* insulator; *adj* isolating; insulating

aislamiento isolation; insulation

aislar to isolate; insulate; ~**se** to isolate; become isolated

¡ajá! aha!

ajacintado like a hyacinth

ajada garlic sauce

ajado shopsoiled, faded

ajador *adj* fading, withering

ajamiento *n* fading, withering

ajamonarse to get fat

ajaquecarse to get a headache

[1] **ajar** *n* garlic field

[2] **ajar** to spoil, tarnish; cause to fade; ~**se** to wither, fade; get mussed

[3] **ajar** to chop, splinter

ajardinar to landscape

ajedrecista *m+f* chess-player

ajedrez *m* chess; chess set

ajedrezado *n* chequerwork; *adj* chequered

ajedrista related to chess

ajenabe *m*, **ajenabo** *bot* wild mustard

ajengibre *m bot* ginger

ajenjo *bot* wormwood; absinthe

ajeno another's; foreign; remote; strange; **en piso** ~ in another's flat; **por causas ajenas a nuestra voluntad** for reasons beyond our control

ajeo *orni* cry of the partridge; **perro de** ~ setter

ajetrear to harass; exhaust; ~**se** to wear o.s. out

ajetreo bustle

ají *m* chili; chili sauce; red/green pepper

ajiaceite *m* olive-oil-and-garlic sauce

ajicomino garlic-and-cumin-seed sauce

ajilimoje *m*, **ajilimójili** *m* pepper-and-garlic sauce

ajillo chopped garlic

ajimez *m arch* mullioned window

ajipuerro *bot* wild leek

ajo *bot* garlic; ~ **blanco** garlic soup; ~ **de chalote** shallot; ~ **moruno** chive; **diente de** ~ clove of garlic

ajolio garlic-and-olive-oil sauce

ajolote *m zool* axolotl

ajonjolí *m bot* sesame

ajoqueso *cul* cheese and garlic

ajorca bracelet; anklet

ajuanetado having bunions; having prominent cheekbones

ajuar *m* trousseau; bridal furniture/apparel; bottom drawer

ajudiado Jew-like

ajuiciado judicious

ajuiciamiento judiciousness, sagacity

ajuiciarse to come to one's senses

ajustabilidad *f* adjustability

ajustado exact; close-fitting; tight; **pantalón** ~ narrowed trousers; **salarios** ~**s** indexed wages

ajustador *n m print* pager; *mech* fitter; adjusting tool

ajustar *vt* to adjust, fit; regulate; engage; settle; fasten; fix; *print* page; (of clothes) be tight; ~**se** to come to terms, reach an agreement; ~**se a** to comply with

ajuste *m* (of clothes) fit, fitting, adjustment; settlement, compromise; engagement; *print* paging; making-up

ajusticiado executed convict

ajusticiar to put to death

al to the; at the; **al** + *infin* = on + *gerund*, ~ **salir** on leaving

ala *aer* + *orni* + *arch* + *sp* wing; row, file; *mil* flank; (of hat) brim; *anat* auricle; *aer* (of propeller) blade; (of fish) fin; (of table) leaf; ~ **en delta** *aer* delta wing; ~ **en flecha** *aer* swept-back wing

¡ala! *naut* pull!

Alá *m* Allah

alabador *n m* applauder, praiser; *adj* praising, complimentary

alabamiento praise

alabancero fawning

alabanza praise; glory; commendation; **cantar las** ~**s de alguien** to sing s.o.'s praises

alabar to praise, extol; ~**se** to boast

alabarda halberd

alabardero halberdier; *theat* hired applauder

alabastrado like alabaster

alabastro alabaster

álabe *m* blade of water-wheel; drooping branch

alabearse to become warped

alábega *bot* sweet basil

alabeo warping

alacena cupboard; *naut* locker

alacrán *m* scorpion

alacridad *f* alacrity, eagerness

alacha anchovy

alachero anchovy seller

Aladino Aladdin

alado *n* flutter of wings; *adj* winged; light

alajor *m* ground rent

alalía *med* aphonia

alamar *m* type of press-fastener; braid trimming

alambicado distilled, refined; ingenious; subtle

alambicar to distill, over-refine

alambique *m* still

alambrada *n* wire fence; wire netting; *mil* barbed-wire entanglement; *adj* wired

alambraje *m elect* wiring

alambrar to fence with wire; *elect* wire

alambre *m* wire; witty person; ~ **cargado** live wire; ~ **de púas** barbed wire; ~ **de tierra** earth wire; ~ **gemelo** *TV* twin lead

alambrera wire screen; wire cover (for food)

alambrista *m* + *f* high-wire performer, acrobat

alameda public walk; promenade; avenue; poplar grove

álamo *bot* poplar; ~ **de Italia** Lombardy poplar; ~ **temblón** aspen

alampar to crave; ~**se** to crave for

alancear to spear

alano wolf hound

alanzado spear-shaped

alarde *m mil* parade, review; display; ostentation; **hacer** ~ **de** to boast of

alardear to brag, boast, show off; ~ **de** to brag about

alardeo boastfulness, boasting

alardoso boastful, ostentatious

alares *mpl sl* trousers

alargar to lengthen, extend; prolong; *naut* pay out (rope *etc*); spin out (money); ~**se** to grow longer, lengthen, draw out

alarido yell

alarma alarm, alert; warning; **dar la** ~ to raise the alarm

alarmador *m* alarmist

alarmante alarming

alarmar to alarm, alert

alarmativo alarming

alármega *bot* wild rue

alarmista *n m* + *f* alarmist; *adj* alarming

alastrar *naut* to ballast; ~**se** to cower, lie flat (so as not to be seen)

alatinado Latinized; affected

alavense, alavés *n* + *adj* native of Alava

alazán *n m* chestnut-coloured horse; *adj* chestnut-coloured

alazo blow with a wing

alba dawn; *eccles* alb

albaca *see* albahaca

albacea *m* executor (of a will)

albahaca *bot* sweet basil

albanega hair-net; net for catching rabbits

albanés *n* + *adj* Albanian

albañal *m* sewer, drain, manure heap

albañil *m* bricklayer, mason; building worker

albañilería bricklaying, brickwork; masonry

albar white

albaracino leprous

albarán *m* placard listing objects available; *comm* invoice

albarca rustic shoe; sandal

albarda packsaddle

albardar to put a packsaddle on; *cul* lard

albaricoque *m* apricot

albaricoquero apricot-tree

albariza salt-water lagoon

albarizo *chem* whiting; dishcloth

albarrada dry-stone wall

albatros *m* albatross

albayaldar to paint with white lead

albayalde *m* white lead

albazano dark chestnut (colour)

albedrío free-will; *leg* precedent

albéitar *m* veterinary surgeon

albeitería veterinary surgery

albellón *m* sewer

alberca pond (*usu* artificial); swimming-pool

albérchigo apricot; clingstone peach; apricot-tree

alberchiguero apricot-tree; clingstone peach-tree

albergar to lodge, house; shelter; ~ **esperanzas** to cherish hopes

albergue *m* shelter, hostel, refuge; ~ **de la juventud** youth hostel; ~ **de turismo** tourist hotel

albericoque *m see* albaricoque

albinismo albinism

albo *lit* snowy, white

albohol *m bot* bindweed

albóndiga meatball; fishcake

albor *m* whiteness; dawn; beginning

alborada dawn, daybreak; *mus* aubade

alborear to dawn

albornoz *n* burnous; bathrobe

alborotado impetuous; in an excited state

alborotador *n m* rioter, disturber of the peace; *adj* riotous, agitating

alborotapueblos *m sing* + *pl* rabble-rouser

alborotar to stir up, rouse, agitate; cause a breach of the peace; ~**se** to riot, make a rumpus

alboroto riot, disturbance; hubbub, uproar

alborozar to fill with joy/merriment

alborozo joy, delight, mirth; rejoicing

albricias *fpl* reward for bringing good news; *interj* hurrah!, congratulations!

albufera large salt-water lagoon

álbum *m* album; ~ **de recortes** scrap-book

albuminoso albuminous

¹ **albur** *m* risk, chance

² **albur** *m* dace

alca *orni* razorbill

alcabala sales tax

alcabalero tax-collector

alcachofa artichoke; rose (on shower, watering-can *etc*)

alcachofal *m* artichoke bed/field

alcachofera artichoke plant

alcachofero artichoke grower/seller

alcahueta bawd, procuress; gossip-monger

alcahuete *m* pimp, procurer, go-between; gossip-monger

alcahuetear to pimp, procure; act as a front man

alcahuetería bawdry; pimping, procuring

alcaide *m* governor of a castle; gaoler

alcaidesa wife of a castle governor or gaoler

alcaldada abuse of authority

alcalde mayor; **tener el padre** ~ to have friends in high places

alcaldear to throw one's weight about

alcaldesa mayoress

alcaldía office of a mayor; town hall

álcali *m chem* alkali

alcalífero alkaline

alcalinidad *f* alkalinity

alcalino alkaline
alcaloide *m* alkaloid
alcana *bot* privet
alcance *m* reach, arm's length; extent; scope; range (of gun); capacity, ability; *mil* soldier's net pay after deductions; ~ **agresivo** *mil* striking range; **al ~ (de)** within reach (of); **al ~ del oído/la vista** within earshot/sight; **al ~ de la mano** within reach; **de corto/largo ~** short/long-range; **de cortos ~s** not very intelligent
alcancía money-box
alcandrón *m orni* shrike
alcanfor *m* camphor
alcanforar to camphorate
alcanforero camphor-tree
alcantarilla drain, culvert, sewer
alcantarillado drainage/sewage system
alcantarillero sewage worker
alcanzable attainable, within reach
alcanzar to attain, reach, overtake, catch up with, hit, understand; ~ **a** +*infin* to manage to; ~ **a/hasta** to reach as far as; ~ **el blanco** to hit the target/bullseye; ~**se** *impers v*: **no se me alcanza** I can't understand
alcaparra *bot* caper
alcaparro caper plant
alcaraván *m orni* stone curlew
alcaravea *bot* tare
alcarria barren plateau, moorland
alcatraz *m orni* gannet; *bot* arum
alcaudón *m see* **alcandrón**
alcazaba fort, citadel
alcázar *m* castle, fortress; *naut* quarter-deck
alce *m* moose, elk; harvesting of sugar-cane; *print* gathering together for binding
alción *m orni* kingfisher
alcista *n comm* bull; *adj* rising; *comm* bullish
alcoba bedroom; bedroom furniture; ~ **de huéspedes** guest room
alcohol *m* alcohol; ~ **desnaturalizado** methylated spirits; ~ **etílico** ethyl alcohol; ~ **para fricciones** surgical spirit; **lámpara de ~** spirit lamp
alcoholar *naut* to tar after caulking
alcohólico alcoholic
alcoholímetro, alcoholómetro breathalyser
alcoholismo alcoholism

alcoholizar to fortify (wine); ~**se** to become alcoholic
Alcorán *m* Koran
alcoranista *m* Koran scholar; student of the Koran
alcornoque *m* cork-oak, cork-tree
alcornoqueño *adj* pertaining to the cork-oak
alcorque *m* cork-soled clog; hollow (at foot of tree) to retain water
alcorza *cul* icing
alcorzar *cul* to ice; decorate
alcotán *m orni* hobby
alcotana pickaxe; mattock
alcurnia ancestry, lineage
alcuza oil-cruet; oil-can
aldaba door-knocker; *sl vulg* knocker, breast
aldabada knock, rap (with knocker)
aldabazo loud knock(ing)
aldabear to knock at the door
aldabeo knocking
aldabón *m* large knocker
aldabonazo *see* **aldabazo**
aldeaniego *adj* rustic
aldeano *n* villager, countryman; *adj* village, rustic
alderredor around; ~ **de** about
aldiza *bot* cornflower
aleación *f* alloy
¹ **alear** to alloy
² **alear** to flutter; move wings quickly; scramble (make unintelligible)
aleatorio fortuitous; **mensaje ~** scrambled message
aleccionar to teach
alechugado curled, pleated
aledaño *n* boundary, limit; *adj* confining, bordering
alegación *f* allegation; argument
alegar to allege; plead
alegato allegation; summing-up
alegórico allegoric
alegrador *adj* cheering, gladdening
alegrar to cheer up, delight; stir (fire); ~**se** to be glad; *fam* get tipsy
alegre happy, cheerful; sunny; tipsy
alegría joy, happiness; irresponsibility; *bot* sesame; *cul* small chilli
alegro *mus* allegro
alegrón *m* sudden happiness
alejamiento withdrawal; estrangement
Alejandría Alexandria
alejandrino Alexandrine

Alejandro Alexander

alejar to move away, drive away; ~**se** to go away, move further off

alelado bewildered; stupefied

alelamiento bewilderment; stupefaction

alelar to bewilder; stupefy; ~**se** to become bewildered

alelí *n bot* wallflower

aleluya hallelujah; *bot* wood-sorrel; ~**s** bad verse, doggerel

alemán *n + adj* German

Alemania Germany

alemánico Germanic

alentada deep breath

alentar *vt* to encourage, inspire; comfort; ~ **a** to encourage to; *vi* to breathe

alerce *m bot* larch-tree

alergia allergy

alérgico allergic

alero eaves; gable-end; splashboard; partridge snare

alerón *m aer* aileron; *sl* armpit

alerta *f* alert; watchword; *adv* on the alert

alertar to alert, put on guard

alerto vigilant, watchful

alerzal *m* larch-tree grove

aleta small wing; fin; leaf (of a hinge); blade (of a propeller); *mot* mudguard/wing

aletado *m* flap (of wings); *adj* winged; finned

aletargarse to become lethargic; *zool* hibernate

aletazo blow with a wing/fin

aletear to flutter; beat wings/fins

aleteo beating/flapping of wings/fins

aleve *m* traitor; *adj* treacherous

alevín, alevino *m* fry, young fish

alevinar to stock with fry

alevosía treason, treachery; **con premeditación y ~** with malice aforethought

alevoso treacherous

alfabético alphabetical

alfabetización *f* teaching how to read and write

alfabetizar to teach reading and writing; put into alphabetical order

alfabeto alphabet

alfalfa *bot* lucerne

alfalfal *m* lucerne field

alfanje *m* cutlass, scimitar; swordfish

alfaque *m naut* sandbar; shoal

alfarería pottery

alfarero potter

alfarje *m* lower stone of oil-mill

alfarma *bot* wild rue

alféizar *m* window-ledge, sill

alfeñicarse to become weak; be fussy

alfeñique *m* paste made of sugar and almond oil; delicate person

alferecía infantile epilepsy

alférez *m* second-lieutenant; standard bearer; ensign; ~ **de navío** lieutenant

alfil *m* (chess) bishop

alfiler *m* pin, brooch; ~**es** pin money

alfilerazo pin-prick; cutting remark

alfiletero pin and needle case

alfombra carpet, rug

alfombrar to carpet, fit a carpet

alfombrero maker/seller of carpets

alfombrilla small rug

alfombrista *m see* **alfombrero**

alforja saddlebag, knapsack

alforjero saddlebag maker/seller

Alfredo Alfred

alga *bot* seaweed, alga

algalia *med* catheter

algara cavalry raid; mounted foraging party; scouting expedition

algarabía Arabic; gibberish

algarada outcry; surprise attack; battering ram

algarroba *bot* locust-bean, carob-bean

algarrobal *m* carob grove

algarrobilla *bot* vetch

algarrobo carob-tree

algazara battlecry; din, uproar

álgebra algebra; *med* bone-setting

algebraico algebraic

algebrista *m + f* algebraist; bone-setter

algidez *f* hypothermia

álgido chilly; culminating

algo *adv* somewhat, rather; *pron* something; ¿~ **más?** anything else?

algodón *m* cotton; *bot* cotton plant; ~ **hidrófilo** cotton wool, *US* absorbent cotton; ~ **dulce** candyfloss; ~ **pólvora** gun-cotton; **criar entre algodones** to mollycoddle

algodonal *m* cotton plantation

algodonería cotton trade; cotton mill

algodonero *n* cotton dealer; *adj* pertaining to cotton

algodonoso cottony, woolly, covered with down

algoso full of seaweed
alguacil m constable; bailiff
alguaza hinge
alguien somebody, someone
algún some, any; not any; ~ **día** one fine day, some day
alguno some, any; not any; ~ **que otro** one or two; **alguna vez** occasionally
alhaja jewel, gem; fine fellow
alhajar to bejewel, adorn
alhelí m wallflower
alhóndiga public granary; wheat exchange; corporation store (of building materials, machinery etc)
alhorre m med skin eruption (of new-born babies)
alhucema f bot lavender
aliáceo garlic-like
aliado m ally; adj allied
aliaga bot gorse
aliancista n m+f pol member of Alianza Popular; adj of Alianza Popular
alianza alliance; wedding-ring
aliarse to become allies; form an alliance
alicaído crestfallen
alicantino n native of Alicante; adj of/ from Alicante
alicatado tiling
alicatar to tile; affix wall-tiles
alicates mpl pliers
Alicia Alice; ~ **en el país de las maravillas** Alice in Wonderland
aliciente m inducement, incentive
alicortar to clip the wings of
alicuota aliquot, proportional
alidada index of a quadrant; geometrical ruler
alienación f alienation; lunacy
alienado n lunatic; adj insane
alienar to alienate; leg transfer (property)
alienista m+f mental specialist
aliento breath, breathing; scent; courage; **cobrar** ~ to revive, take heart; **mal** ~ bad breath; **nuevo** ~ second wind; **sin** ~ breathless
alifafe m chronic complaint
aligación f phys mixture
aligar to unite, tie
aligeramiento lightening, hurrying, alleviation
aligerar(se) to lighten, hurry, alleviate
alijador m smuggler

[1] **alijar** m fallow land
[2] **alijar** to unload; smuggle; sandpaper
alimaña harmful animal; vermin
alimañero vermin exterminator; rat-catcher
alimentación f feeding, food; nourishment
alimentador nourishing, nutritious
alimentar to feed, nourish; sustain; nurture; cherish, foster; ~**se de/con** to feed on
alimentario nutritious
alimenticio pertaining to food; **productos** ~s food products, foodstuffs
alimento nourishment, nutriment; food; incentive; ~s foodstuffs; alimony, allowance
[1] **alindar** vt to mark; place boundary marks; vi to be contiguous; ~ **con** to border on
[2] **alindar** to adorn, embellish
alineación f alignment, lining-up; sp line-up; composition of a team
alinear to put in line; sp select a team
aliñar to adorn; cul to season
aliño ornament; cul seasoning
alioli garlic-and-olive-oil sauce
alionín m orni long-tailed tit
[1] **alisar** m alder-tree plantation
[2] **alisar** to smooth (down), flatten; carp plane; polish, burnish
alisios mpl trade winds
aliso alder-tree
alisón m bot alyssum
alistamiento enlistment, enrolment
alistar vt to recruit, enrol, enlist; ~**se** to enlist, enrol, join up
aliteración f alliteration
aliviadero overflow pipe; safety-valve
aliviador n m fence, receiver of stolen property; adj helping, labour-saving
aliviar to mitigate, soothe, lighten; assuage; sl steal, pinch, nick
alivio mitigation, relief, comfort; sl defence lawyer
aljaba quiver (for arrows)
aljafana wash-bowl
aljafifar see aljofifar
aljamía Spanish written in Arabic characters
aljibe m cistern
aljófar m imperfect pearl
aljofifa floor-mop

aljofifar to mop (up); clean

alma soul, mind, spirit, heart; substance, essence; strength, vigour; person; ghost, phantom; my love, my dearest; **no tener ~** to be heartless; **rendir el ~** to give up the ghost; **romperse el ~** to break one's heart

almacén *m* store, warehouse; department store; *SA* grocer's shop; **en ~** in store, in stock

almacenador *m* warehouseman

almacenaje *m* warehouse rent; storage, storage charges

almacenamiento warehousing, storage

almacenar to store; hoard

almacenista *m+f* warehouse owner; wholesaler; middleman

almádana, almádena, almádina large hammer for breaking stones

almadén *m* mine

almadía raft

almadiarse to become sea-sick

almadraba tunny fishery; tunny fishing; tunny net

almadreña clog

almagra *m* red ochre

almagrar to colour with red ochre; mark

almajara *hort* forcing-bed

almanaque *m* almanac, calendar

almanaquero almanac-seller

almanta space between rows of vines/olives; ridge between furrows; tree-nursery

almario *see* **armario**

almatriche *m* irrigation canal

almazara oil-mill

almazarero oil-miller

almazarrón *m see* **almagra**

almear *m* haystack; hayloft

almeja clam

almejar *m* clam-bed

almena battlement

almenaje *m* series of merlons; battlements

almenar to crown with merlons

¹ **almenara** beacon

² **almenara** overflow ditch

almendra almond; kernel; **~ de cacao** cocoa-bean; **~ garapiñada** sugared almond

almendrado *n* macaroon; *adj* almond-shaped

almendral *m* almond grove

almendrilla gravel

almendro almond-tree

almendruco unripe almond

almiar *m* haystack

almíbar *m* syrup

almibarar to sweeten; preserve in syrup

almidón *m* starch

almidonado starched; *fam* dapper

almidonar to starch

almiforero horse-thief

alminar *m* minaret

almiranta admiral's wife; flagship

almirantazgo admiralty

almirante *m* admiral

almirez *m* brass mortar

almizcle *m* musk

almizcleño *n* grape-hyacinth; *adj* musky

almizclera musk-rat

almizclero *n* musk-deer; *adj* musky

almofía wash-bowl

almohada pillow, bolster; pillow-case; **consultar con la ~** to sleep on it

almohadilla small pillow; sewing-cushion; *arch* roughstone wall

almohadón *m* large pillow

almohaza curry-comb

almohazar to groom with a curry-comb

almóndiga *see* **albóndiga**

almoneda public auction

almonedear to sell by auction

almorranas *fpl med* piles

almorzar to have lunch; have for lunch, **~ pescado** to have fish for lunch

almuédano muezzin

almuérdago mistletoe

almuerzo lunch(eon)

almunia kitchen garden

alnado stepchild

¡aló! hello

alocado crazy

alocución *f* allocution; harangue

alodial *leg* free, exempt

alodio *leg* freehold possession

aloja mead (drink)

alojado billeted soldier

alojamiento lodging, accommodation, billeting; *naut* steerage; **~s** *mil* quarters

alojar to lodge, let rooms, house, put up; *mil* billet; **~se** to lodge, take lodgings

alojería place where mead is made

alojero mead-seller

alón *m cul* wing of chicken

alondra *orni* lark; *sl* bricklayer, building

worker

alópata allopath

alopatía allopathy

alopático allopathic

aloque *n m* mixture of red and white wines; (of wines) pale red

alotar *naut* to reef, lash

alotropía *chem* allotropy

alotrópico *chem* allotropic

alotropo *chem* allotrope

alpaca *zool*+*text* alpaca; *metal* nickel silver

alpargata rubber-soled (*orig* hemp-soled) slipper, espadrille

alpargatería alpargata factory/shop

alpargatero alpargata maker/seller

Alpes *m pl* Alps

alpestre alpine

alpinismo mountaineering

alpinista *m*+*f* mountaineer

alpino alpine

alpiste *m* birdseed, canary-seed; *sl* wine

alquería farm-house

alquilador *m* renter, hirer; tenant

alquilamiento hiring, letting

alquilar to let, hire, rent; ~**se** to be for hire

alquiler *m* rent(al), hire, fee; act of hiring/letting; **de** ~ to let

alquimia alchemy

alquimila *bot* lady's mantle

alquimista *m* alchemist

alquitrán *m* tar, pitch; ~ **mineral/de hulla** coal-tar; ~ **vegetal** wood-tar

alquitranado *n naut* tarpaulin; **cabos** ~**s** *naut* tarred cordage; *adj* (of roads) tarred

alquitranar to tar, pitch

alrededor around; ~ **de** about

alrededores *mpl* outskirts, neighbourhood

Alsacia Alsace; ~-**Lorena** Alsace-Lorraine

alsaciano *n*+*adj* Alsatian

álsine *m bot* chickweed; ~ **rojo** *bot* scarlet pimpernel

alta *n* discharge (from hospital); release (from prison); *mil* record of enlistment; **dar de** ~ to declare fit for work/military service, discharge from hospital; **darse de** ~ to return to work/duty, discharge o.s. from hospital, join (an organization)

altabaque *m* work basket

altabaquillo *bot* dwarf bindweed

altanería arrogance, haughtiness; falconry

altanero arrogant, haughty; *orni* soaring

altar *m* altar; ~ **mayor** high altar; **llevar al** ~ *fam* to marry

altarero altar attendant; altar decorator

altarreina *bot* milfoil

altavoz *m* loudspeaker

altea *bot* marshmallow

alterabilidad *f* changeableness

alterable changeable; easily upset

alteración *f* alteration, change; disturbance, upset; irregularity (of breathing/pulse)

alterador, alterante altering, disturbing

alterar to alter, change; disturb, upset; corrupt; ~**se** to become disturbed/annoyed, be put out

altercado controversy, quarrel, row

altercador *n m* quarreller, arguer; *adj* quarrelling, arguing

altercar to quarrel, bicker

alternación *f* alternation

alternador *m elect* alternator

alternancia alternation

alternar to alternate; mix, mingle (at a social gathering)

alternativa *n* alternative, choice; *pol* option; (bull-fighting) ceremony of becoming a full matador; **tomar la** ~ to become an accepted matador

alternativo alternate, alternating; **cultivo** ~ rotation of crops

alterno alternate, alternating; every two days

alteza height; sublimity; (title) highness

altibajo uneven ground; ups and downs

altilocuencia grandiloquence

altilocuente grandiloquent, pompous

altillo hillock, attic, garret

altimetría *geom* altimetry

altimétrico *geom* altimetric

altímetro *n* altimeter; *adj* altimetric

altiplanicie *f*, **altiplano** high plateau; tableland

Altísimo the Most High

altisonante high-sounding

altitud *f* altitude, height

altivarse to put on airs

altivez *f* haughtiness, arrogance

altivo *f* haughty, arrogant, lofty

¹ **alto** *n* high place; pile; ~**s y bajos** ups and downs; *adj* high, tall; upper,

superior; strong; **alta mar** high seas; **altas horas** small hours; ~ **horno** blast furnace; **de ~ a bajo** from top to bottom; **de lo ~** from up above; **documento de alta seguridad** top-secret document; **en alta voz** in a loud voice; **estar en lo ~** to be at the top; ~**parlante** *see* **altavoz**

² **alto** *n mil* halt; **hacer ~** to halt; ¡~ **ahí!** stop there!

altozano height, hill

altramuz *m bot* lupin

altruismo altruism

altruista *n m + f* altruist; *adj* altruistic

altura height, elevation; altitude; summit, peak; *naut* latitude; ~ **de crucero** *aer* cruising altitude; **a estas ~s** at this stage; **estar a la ~ de** to be up to; **las ~s** heaven; **pesca/pesquero de ~** deep-sea fishing/fishing boat

alubia french bean, bean

alucinación *f* hallucination

alucinador *m* hallucinator

alucinar to dazzle, blind; ~**se** to deceive o.s.

alucinógeno hallucinogenic

alucón *m* barn-owl

alud *m* avalanche

aludir to allude, refer

aludo winged ant

alumbrado system of illumination

alumbrador illuminating

alumbramiento illumination; childbirth

alumbrante *n theat* lighting operator; *adj* illuminating

¹ **alumbrar** *vt* to light, illuminate; enlighten; *vi* to give light; give birth; ~**se** to get tipsy

² **alumbrar** to treat with alum

alumbre *m* alum

alumbrera alum-mine

alumbrico, alumbroso aluminous

aluminio aluminium, *US* aluminum

alumnado student body

alumno student, pupil

alunarse to go mad, be affected by the moon; *cul* become tainted, go off

alunizaje *m space* moon-landing

alunizar *space* to land on the moon

alusión *f* allusion, reference

alusivo allusive

alustrar to polish

aluvial alluvial

aluvión *m* alluvion; flood

álveo river-bed

alverja *see* **arveja**

alvino *med* alvine

alza *comm* rise; *mil* rear-sight (on gun); **jugar al ~** to speculate on rising prices

alzacuello parson's collar; dog-collar

alzada height (of a horse)

alzadamente for a cash settlement

alzado *n* cash settlement, lump sum; fraud; fraudulent bankrupt; *adj* raised; fixed, settled

alzamiento elevation, rise; (at auction) outbidding; **el Alzamiento** Franco's rebellion in 1936; fraudulent bankruptcy

alzapuertas *m sing + pl* dummy player; *theat* bit-part actor

alzar *vt* to raise, lift up, carry off; cut (at cards); *naut* heave; ~ **el precio** to put up the price; ~**velas** *naut* to set sail; ~**se** to rise; ~**se en rebelión** to rise in revolt

alzaválvulas *m sing + pl mot + mech* tappet

allá there, over there, yonder; ¡ ~ **ella/usted!** that's her/your business!; ~ **en Méjico** over there in Mexico; ~ **por los años cincuenta** way back in the fifties; ~ **veremos** we'll see; **el más ~** the afterlife; **más ~** further; **más ~ de** beyond, on the other side of; **por ~** thereabouts

allanador *m* leveller

allanamiento levelling; smoothing; consent; ~ **de morada** *leg* housebreaking

allanar to level, smooth; *fig* iron out; ~ **la casa** to break into the house; ~**se** to conform, abide by

allegado *n* relative, close friend; *adj* near, close, related; **pariente más ~** a next-of-kin

allegamiento collection, union; close friendship

allegar to collect, gather; add, unite; ~**se** to approach

allende beyond, on the other side

allí there, yonder; ~ **mismo** right there; **por ~** that way

ama landlady; mistress of the house; woman owner; ~ **de casa** housewife; ~ **de llaves** housekeeper; ~ **de leche** wet nurse; ~ **seca** children's nurse

amabilidad *f* kindness

amable kind

amaceno *bot* damson
amado beloved
amador *n m* lover; *adj* loving
amadrigar to welcome; ~**se** to burrow
amadrinar to yoke together; act as godmother
amaestramiento training, instruction
amaestrar to instruct, train; master, dominate; ~ **un caballo** to train a horse
amagar to threaten; feint; show signs of; ~**se** to hide
amago threat; threatening movement; *med* symptom
amainar *naut* to lower the sails; relax; moderate; **el viento ha amainado** the wind has slackened
amalgama *chem* amalgam
amalgamar to amalgamate; *metal* to alloy
amalgamación *f* amalgamation
amamantamiento suckling, nursing
amamantar to suckle, nurse, feed
amancebamiento concubinage
amancebarse to start living in concubinage/in sin
amanecer *m* dawn; **al** ~ at daybreak; *v* to dawn; arrive at daybreak; wake up
amanecida daybreak
amanerarse to adopt a mannerism
amansador *n m* tamer, appeaser; *adj* taming, appeasing, subduing
amansamiento *n* taming, soothing, appeasement
amansar to tame, subdue; pacify, appease; domesticate
amante *n m + f* lover; *adj* loving
amanuense *m* amanuensis
amañar to do cleverly; fake; ~**se** to be handy, be skilful; become expert; get on well (be popular)
amaño skill, cleverness; ~**s** tools; tricks
amapola *bot* poppy
amar to love
amáraco *bot* marjoram
amaraje *m aer* alighting on water
amaranto *bot* amaranth
amarar *aer* to alight/come down on water
amargado *n* embittered person; *adj* embittered
amargar to embitter; spoil (fun *etc*); ~**se** to become embittered
amargo bitter; painful; ~**s** bitters

amargón *m* dandelion
amargor *m* bitterness
amargoso bitterish
amarguera *bot* wild horse-radish
amargura bitterness
amaricado effeminate, queer, gay
amarilis *f sing + pl* amaryllis
amarillear to make yellow
amarillecer to turn yellow
amarillento yellowish
amarillez *f* yellowness; pallor
amarillo *n* yellow (colour); strike-breaker; scab; **sindicato** ~ company union; *adj* yellow
amarinar *cul* to salt; *naut* man (a vessel)
amarra *naut* cable, hawser; **cortar las** ~**s** to cut loose
amarradero hitching-post; *naut* mooring berth
amarradura *naut* moorage
amarraje *m* moorage dues
amarrar to tie, fasten; cheat at cards
amarre *m* fastening; mooring line
amartelamiento *fam* spooning, snogging, love-making
amartelar to make love-sick; ~**se de** to get a crush on; **están amartelados** they are crazy about each other
amartillar to hammer
amasadera kneading-trough
amasador *n m* kneader; mortar-mixer; *adj* kneading
amasadura *n* kneading
amasamiento kneading; *med* massage
amasar to knead, mix; *med* massage; ~ **dinero** to amass money
amasijo dough, mixture, medley, plot, mess, concoction
amatista amethyst
amazacotado stodgy, clumsy
amazona Amazon; mannish woman; horsewoman
ámbar *m* amber
Amberes Antwerp
ambición *f* ambition
ambicionar to aspire to
ambicioso *n* self-seeker; *adj* ambitious, greedy; *bot* climbing
ambidextro ambidextrous
ambientador *m* air-freshener
ambiental environmental
ambientar to set (the scene of); give atmosphere to; **película ambientada en Gales** film set in Wales

ambiente *n* atmosphere, environment; **allí no hay ~** there's nothing going on there; **tener ~** (of places) to be full of life

ambigüedad *f* ambiguity

ambiguo ambiguous

ámbito sphere, scope, field of action

ambivalencia ambivalence

ambivalente ambivalent

amblar to amble

ambligonio obtuse-angled

ambos both

ambulancia ambulance; **~ de correos** post-office on a train

ambulanciero ambulance driver; nurse

ambulante itinerant, wandering, nomadic, of no fixed abode

ambular to wander about

ambulativo itinerant, roving

ambulatorio ambulatory

ameba amoeba

amedrentador threatening, terrifying

amedrentar to intimidate; terrify

¹ **amén** besides; **~ de** in addition to

² **amén** amen, so be it

amenaza threat

amenazador threatening

amenazar to threaten; **~ de muerte** to threaten with death

amenidad *f* pleasantness

amenizar to make pleasant

ameno pleasant; **libro ~** book easy to read

amerar to soak with water; **~se** to become sodden

americana jacket

americanismo Americanism

americanista *m+f* student of things American

americanizar to Americanize; **~se** to become Americanized

americano *n+adj* American

amerindio *n+adj* American Indian

ameritar to prove one's worth

ametalado metallic

ametista amethyst

ametrallador *m* machine-gunner

ametralladora machine-gun

ametrallar to machine-gun, strafe

amezquindarse to become sad

amianto asbestos

amiba amoeba

amiboideo amoebic

amiento leather-thong; shoelace

amigable friendly

amigar to make friends; **~se** to become friends; live in sin

amígdalas *fpl* tonsils

amigdalitis *f* tonsillitis

amigdalotomía *med* tonsillectomy

amiga friend; mistress

amigo *n* friend, lover; **~ íntimo** bosom friend; **muy ~** great friend; *adj* friendly, fond; **ser ~ de** +*infin* to be fond of, be keen on +*gerund*

amigote *m* buddy, mate, pal

amiguete *m sl* friend (*esp* one with influence)

amiguismo *sl approx* old-boy network, patronage

amilanamiento fear, terror

amilanar to cow, frighten, terrify; **~se** to become cowed

amillonado *see* **millonario**

amimar to coax, wheedle

aminoácidos *mpl* amino acids

aminoración *f* lessening; diminution

aminorar to lessen; diminish

amistad *f* friendship; friend; concubinage; **hacer las ~es** to make up (after a quarrel); **romper las ~es** to fall out; **trabar ~** to become friends

amistar to reconcile; make friends; **~se** to become reconciled; become friends

amistoso friendly, cordial

amnésico amnesic

amnistía amnesty

amnistiar to declare amnesty; pardon

amo master; employer, boss; head of a family; proprietor; lord; **~ (de casa)** householder; **~s** master and mistress

amoblar to furnish

amodorrado drowsy, sleepy

amodorramiento drowsiness, sleepiness

amodorrante soporific

amodorrarse to get drowsy; fall asleep

amohecerse to grow rusty/mouldy

amohinar to irritate; **~se** to become irritated/vexed

amojamarse to shrivel up

amojonar to set up landmarks

amolador *n m* grinder; sharpener; *adj* grinding, sharpening; boring

amolar to grind, sharpen; bore

amoldar to brand (cattle); to adjust; **~se** to adapt oneself

amollar *naut* to pay out; ease off

amonarse to get drunk

amondongado *fam* flabby, fat
amonedado moneyed, rich
amonedar to mint, coin
amonestación *f* admonition, warning;
amonestaciones marriage banns; **correr las amonestaciones** to publish the
banns
amonestador *n m* admonisher; *adj*
admonishing, warning
amonestamiento admonition
amonestar to advise, warn, admonish;
publish (banns)
amoníaco ammonia
amonita *zool* ammonite
amontar to chase away (into the mountains); ~**se** to hide, take cover (in the
mountains)
amontonamiento heaping, amassing,
gathering, pile
amontonar to heap, pile; accumulate,
hoard, amass; crowd; ~**se** to pile up;
crowd together; (of snow) to bank up,
drift
amor *m* love, affection; loved one; *bot*
burdock; ~**es** gallantry, love affairs;
~**es mil** *bot* red valerian; ~ **mío** my
love, my dearest; ~ **propio** self-
esteem, pride
amoralidad *f* amorality
amoratado black-and-blue
amoratar to make black-and-blue; ~**se**
to turn black-and-blue
amorcillo flirtation; brief love-affair;
Cupid
amordazar to gag; muzzle
amorfo amorphous
amorío love-affair
amoriscado Moorish looking
amorosidad *f* amorousness
amoroso loving, affectionate
amorrar to lower one's head; *naut* pitch
(in heavy sea); ~**se** to sulk
amortajar to shroud (a corpse)
amortecer to deaden, muffle; ~**se** to die
away, faint
amortecimiento deadening, muffling;
swooning, fainting
amortiguación *f* dulling, deadening;
cushioning; absorbing
amortiguador *n m* softener; *mot* shock-
absorber, bumper, buffer; *adj* softening, absorbing, muffling
amortiguar to deaden, muffle, cushion,
absorb; (of colours) tone down; (of

fires) damp down
amortizable redeemable; payable
amortización *f* liquidation, paying off;
comm redemption; **fondo de** ~ *comm*
sinking fund
amortizar to pay off/back; recoup;
amortize; refund
amoscarse to get annoyed; become
suspicious
amostazar to annoy, irritate
amotinado *n* mutineer; *adj* mutinous
amotinar to incite to mutiny; ~**se** to
mutiny
amparar to protect, help, shelter, assist;
~**se** to enjoy protection; defend oneself; seek refuge; ~**se de** to seek the
protection of
amparo protection, shelter, help; *leg*
confiscation; asylum
amperio *elect* ampere
amperaje *m elect* amperage
amperímetro amperemetre
ampliación *f* enlargement, extension
ampliador *m* amplifier, enlarger
ampliar to enlarge, expand, broaden
ampliativo *adj* enlarging
amplificación *f* enlargement; amplification
amplificador *n m rad* amplifier; *adj*
amplifying; enlarging
amplificadora *phot* enlarger
amplio ample, extensive, roomy, broad,
wide; **amplia victoria** comfortable win
amplitud *f* greatness; fullness, roominess; amplitude
ampo snowflake
ampolla bubble; vial; *med* blister
ampollar to blister; hollow; ~**se** to
become blistered
ampolleta hour-glass
ampulosidad *f* pomposity, verbosity
ampuloso pompous, verbose
amputación *f* amputation
amputar to amputate
amueblar to furnish
amujerado effeminate
amujeramiento effeminacy
amuleto amulet
amuñecado doll-like; puppet-like
amura *naut* beam
amurallar to wall in
Ana Ann(e)
anabaptismo Anabaptism
anabaptista *m + f* Anabaptist

anacoreta anchorite, hermit
anacrónico anachronistic
anacronismo anachronism
ánade *m* + *f* duck
anadear to waddle
anadeja, anadino duckling
anadeo *n* waddle
anafe *m* portable stove
anagrama *m* anagram
anales *mpl* annals
analfabetismo illiteracy
analfabeto illiterate
analgésico analgesic
análisis *m sing* + *pl* analysis; *gramm* parsing
[1] **analista** *m* + *f* annalist
[2] **analista** *m* + *f* analyst
analítico analytical
analizar to analyse
analogía analogy
analógico analogical
análogo analogous
ananá(s) *f* pineapple
anaquel *m* shelf
anaquelería shelving
anaranjado *adj* orange(-coloured)
anarco *sl* anarchist
anarquía anarchy
anárquico anarchical
anarquismo anarchism
anarquista *n m* + *f* anarchist; *adj* anarchistical
anarquizar to spread anarchism
anata yearly income, annuity
anatema, anatematismo anathema
anatematizar to anathematize
anatomía anatomy
[1] **anatómico** anatomical
[2] **anatómico, anatomista** *m* + *f* anatomist
anatomizar to anatomize; dissect
anavajado knife-scarred
anca hindquarter; (horse's) croup; (frog's) leg; *fam* backside
ancianidad *f* old age
anciano *n* elderly person; *adj* elderly
ancillar ancillary
ancla anchor; ~ **de la esperanza** sheet-anchor; **echar** ~**s** to anchor; **estar al** ~ to be at anchor; **levar** ~**s** to weigh anchor; **uñas del** ~ arms of the anchor
ancladero anchorage
anclar to anchor
ancolia *bot* columbine

ancón *m* cove, inlet
áncora anchor
ancoraje *m* anchoring
ancorar to anchor, cast anchor
ancorca yellow ochre
ancorero anchor-maker
ancudo having a big backside
anchicorto wide and short
ancho *n* width; ~ **de vía** railway track gauge; *adj* wide; full, loose; loose-fitting; **ancha es Castilla** there is plenty of room for all opinions, it is a free country; **a sus** ~**s** at one's ease; **estar más** ~ **que largo** to be as happy as a sandboy
anchoa anchovy
anchura width, breadth; fullness; spaciousness
anchuroso wide, broad; ample; spacious
andadero *n* walker, runner; *adj* passable, fit for walking
andador *n m* good walker; messenger at court; *naut* good sailor; alley, garden path; *med* walking-frame; ~**es** child's reins; *adj* swift, good at walking/running
andadura gait
andahuertas *m sing* + *pl* *orni* garden-warbler
Andalucía Andalusia
andaluz *n m* + *adj* Andalusian
andaluzada anything typically Andalusian
andamiada, andamiaje *m* scaffolding
andamio scaffold, platform; *naut* gang-plank
andana row, line, file
andanada *naut* broadside; *fig* reprimand
andaniño child's walker, walking-frame
andante *n mus* andante; *adj* walking; **caballero** ~ knight-errant
andantesco pertaining to knight-errantry
andanzas *fpl* wanderings, adventures, doings
andar *n m* gait; walking; pace; **a un** ~ within walking distance; **el** ~ **del tiempo** the passing of time; *v* to walk, go on foot; go, come; (of a machine) function, work, run; ~ **a derechas** to work/function properly; ~ **a gatas** to go on all fours; ~ **de la ceca a la meca** to wander about aimlessly; ~ **en la danza** to be mixed up in the business/

matter; ~ **en palmas** to be successful/popular; ~ **listo** to go places; **andando el tiempo** in the course of time; **todo se andará** all in good time

andariego *n* good walker; *adj* wandering

andarín *n m* fast walker; *adj* walking

andarina *orni* swallow

andarríos *m sing+pl orni* pied wagtail

andén *m* (railway station) platform; pavement

andero litter/sedan-chair bearer

andinismo mountaineering

andinista *m+f* mountaineer

ándito sidewalk

andoba *sl* bloke, geezer, guy

andorga belly

andorrano *n+adj* Andorran

andorrear to gad about

andrajero rag-picker

andrajo rag, tatter

andrajoso ragged, tattered

Andrés Andrew

androide android

andrómina swindle, fraud

androsemo *bot* St John's wort

andurriales *mpl* by-ways

anea *bot* bulrush

aneblar to darken; ~**se** to become overcast

anécdota anecdote

anecdótico anecdotal

anecdotista *m+f* anecdotist

aneciarse to grow stupid

anegable liable to flooding

anegación *f* flooding

anegadizo easily flooded; subject to flooding

anegar to flood; drown; waterlog

anejo *n* annex; *eccles* church dependent on another

anélido annelid

anemia anaemia

anémico anaemic

anemómetro anemometer, wind-gauge

anémona, anémone *f bot* anemone; ~ **de mar** sea anemone

aneroide aneroid

anestesia anaesthesia

anestesiar to anaesthetize

anestético *n+adj* anaesthetic

anexar to annex

anexión *f* annexation

anexo *n* annexe; enclosure; *adj* annexed, joined

anfetamina amphetamine

anfibio *n* amphibian; *adj* amphibious

anfibología *rhet* amphibology; double meaning

anfiteatro amphitheatre

anfitrión *m* host

anfitriona hostess

ánfora amphora

angarillas *fpl* hand barrow

ángel *m* angel; angel-fish; ~ **custodio,** ~ **de la guarda** guardian angel; **tener** ~ to have charm

angelito little angel; *fam* baby; **con los** ~**s** in the land of Nod

angelote *m* large statue of an angel; chubby child

angina *med* angina, quinsy; ~ **de pecho** angina pectoris; ~**s** sore throat, tonsillitis

anglicanismo Anglicanism

anglicano Anglican

anglicismo anglicism

anglicón *sl pej* Englishman

anglo Angle

angloamericano Anglo-American

anglocatólico Anglo-Catholic

angloespañol Anglo-Spanish

anglófilo Anglophile

anglofobia Anglophobia

anglófobo Anglophobe

angloindio Anglo-Indian

anglomanía enthusiasm for England

anglómano Anglomaniac

angloparlante *n m+f* English-speaker; *adj* English-speaking

anglosajón *n m +adj* Anglo-Saxon

angoleño *n+adj* Angolan

angostar to narrow, contract

angosto narrow

angostura narrowness

angosturina angostura bitters

angra cove

anguila eel; ~ **de cabo** *naut* rope's end

anguilazo *naut* blow with a rope's end

anguilero eel-tank

anguiliforme eel-like

angula elver

angular angular; **piedra** ~ corner-stone

ángulo angle; corner; nook

anguloso angular

angustia anguish, anxiety; worry; distress; *sl* gaol

angustiar to produce anxiety/anguish; worry; ~**se** to suffer agonies of mind,

be deeply distressed
angustioso deeply distressing
anhelación f longing, yearning
anhelante see **anheloso**
anhelar to long for, yearn for, crave; gasp for breath
anhélito tightness of chest, breathing difficulty
anhelo yearning, longing
anheloso panting; yearning
anhídrido carbónico carbon dioxide
anidar orni to nest; shelter
aniego abnegation
anilina aniline
anilla curtain ring; ring-pull (on can of beer etc)
anillado ring-shaped
anillar to form into rings
anillo ring; circular band; sl fetters, irons; ~s bell-ringing at sunset; ~ verde green belt
ánima n soul; bore (of gun)
animación f animation, bustle, liveliness; **animaciones** floor-show, cabaret
animador n m animator; theat+TV entertainer, comedian, master of ceremonies; adj animating, encouraging
animadora hostess (in night-club etc)
animadversión f ill-will; antagonism
animal m animal, creature, brute; ~ doméstico pet
animalada stupid act or statement; large amount, hell of a lot
animalazo big animal/creature; hefty brute
animálculo animalcule
animalia animal kingdom
animalidad f animality
animalismo animalism
animalizarse to become an animal; sink to the level of an animal
animar to animate, enliven; entertain; inspire; ~se to cheer up, take heart
anímico of the mind
animismo animism
ánimo soul, spirit; mind; will; ¡~! cheer up!; **dar** ~ **a** to cheer up; **estado de** ~ state of mind; **presencia de** ~ presence of mind; **tener** ~ **de** to intend to
animosidad f animosity, ill-will; courage
animoso courageous, brave
aniñado child-like, childish
aniñarse grow childish
aniquilación f annihilation

aniquilador annihilating
aniquilamiento annihilation
aniquilar to annihilate; crush; ~se to decay, waste away; humble o.s.
anís m bot anise; aniseed; (drink) anís, anisette
anisar n aniseed field; v to flavour with anís
anisete m anisette
anivelar see **nivelar**
aniversario anniversary; annual requiem mass
anjeo burlap
ano anat anus
anoche last night
anochecedor nocturnal
anochecer n m dusk, nightfall; **al** ~ at dusk; v to grow dark; be at nightfall; **anocheció cansado** he was tired by dusk
anochecida nightfall
anodinar to give a pain-killing medicine to
anodinia painlessness
anodino anodyne; fam insipid, colourless, uninteresting
ánodo phys anode
anomalía anomaly
anómalo anomalous
anón m bot custard-apple tree
anona bot custard apple
anonadación f, **anonadamiento** annihilation, obliteration
anonadar to annihilate, obliterate, humiliate
anonimato: mantener el ~ to remain anonymous
anónimo n anonymous letter; anonymity; adj anonymous
anormal abnormal
anormalidad f abnormality
anorza bot white bryony
anotación f annotation, note
anotador n m annotator, commentator; adj annotating
anotar to note, jot down
anquilosar to fossilize, paralyse; ~se to become fossilized, paralysed
anquilosis f med+vet ankylosis, stiff joint
ánsar m goose, gander
ansarería goose-farm
ansarero goose-herd
ansarino n gosling; adj of geese

32

ansia anguish, longing; extreme hunger; ~s nausea

ansiar to long for

ansiedad f anxiety, longing

ansioso anxious, longing; extremely hungry

¹ **anta** zool elk

² **anta** obelisk

antagónico antagonistic

antagonismo antagonism

antagonista m+f antagonist

antaño, antañazo in days gone by

Antártica, Antártida Antarctica

antártico Antarctic

¹ **ante** n m suede, buckskin; arts buff-colour

² **ante** n m first course, starters

³ **ante** prep before; in the presence of; with regard to; ~ **el peligro** in the face of danger; ~ **todo** first of all

anteado buff-coloured

antealtar m chancel

anteanoche the night before last

anteanteanoche three nights ago

anteanteayer three days ago

antear to cover with suede

anteayer the day before yesterday

antebrazo anat forearm; vet shoulder

antecama bedside rug

antecámara antechamber

antecedencia antecedence; lineage

antecedente n m+adj antecedent; ~s **penales** criminal record; ~s **policiales** police record

anteceder to go before/in front of

antecesor n m predecessor; forefather; ~es ancestors; adj antecedent

antecoger to harvest too soon

antedatar to antedate

antedecir to foretell

antedía before the agreed day

antedicho aforesaid

antediluviano antediluvian

antehistórico prehistoric

anteislámico pre-Islamic

antelación f preference, priority (in time); **con** ~ in advance

antemano beforehand

antemeridiano in the morning

antena rad+TV aerial; ent antenna; ~s fpl sl ears

antenacido (of babies) premature

antenatal pre-natal

antenoche the night before last

antenupcial before marriage

anteojera spectacle-case; ~s blinkers

anteojero spectacle-maker/seller

anteojo spy-glass; ~ **de larga vista** telescope; ~ **de teatro** opera-glass; ~s spectacles; ~s **de camino** goggles

antepagar to pay in advance

antepecho breastwork, parapet; railing

antepenúltimo last but two

anteponer to prefer, place before; ~se to push forward, place o.s. first

anteportada fly leaf (bearing only the title)

antepuerta curtain in front of a door

antepuerto naut outer port

antera bot anther

anterior earlier

anterioridad: con ~ **a** prior to

antero worker in suede

antes before, formerly; earlier; first; better; ~ **ahora que luego** better now than later; ~ **de que** before; ~ **que** rather than; **cuanto** ~, **lo** ~ **posible** as soon as possible; **cuanto** ~ **mejor** the sooner the better; prep ~ **de** before

antesala anteroom; **hacer** ~ to dance attendance on; wait to be received

antetemplo eccles portico

antever to foresee

antevíspera two days before

antiácido antacid

antiaéreo anti-aircraft

antiafrodisíaco anti-aphrodisiac

antialcohólico anti-alcoholic

antiartístico unartistic

antiartrítico anti-arthritic

antiasmático anti-asthmatic

antibaby adj invar fam contraceptive

antibactérico antibacterial

anticanónico eccles unorthodox, anti-canonical

anticartel adj invar anti-monopoly

anticatarral med anti-catarrhal

anticatólico anti-catholic

anticiclón m anticyclone

anticientífico unscientific

anticipación f anticipation, foretaste; **con** ~ in advance

anticipado n unexpected thrust (in fencing); adj premature; agr early; comm in advance; **jubilación anticipada** early retirement

anticipador n m anticipator; adj

33

anticipating
anticipante anticipating
anticipar to anticipate; forestall; advance; ~se to be ahead of, jump the gun
anticipo *n* advance, advance payment; deposit (on making a purchase); foretaste
anticívico anti-civic
anticlericalismo anticlericalism
anticombustible non-inflammable
anticomunista *n* *m+f* *+adj* anti-communist
anticoncepcional contraceptive
anticonceptivo *adj* related to birth-control, contraceptive
anticongelante *m* antifreeze
anticonstitucional unconstitutional
anticristiano anti-Christian
Anticristo Antichrist
anticrítica counter-criticism
anticuado old-fashioned, out-of-date; obsolete
anticuar to outdate; ~se to become antiquated
anticuario antiquarian
anticuerpo antibody
antideportivo unsporting, unsportsman-like
antiderrapante, antideslizante *adj* non-skid, non-slip
antideslumbrante antidazzle, antiglare
antídoto antidote
antieconómico uneconomic, unprofitable
antiemético *med* anti-emetic
antiepiléptico *med* anti-epileptic
antiesclavista *n m+f +adj* anti-slave(ry)
antiespasmódico anti-spasmodic
antiestético unaesthetic; unsightly
antifaz *m* mask
antifebril *med* anti-febrile
antífona antiphon, anthem
antifonal, antifonario antiphonal
antifricción *f mech* anti-friction
antigás giving protection against poisonous gases; **careta ~** gas-mask
antígeno antigen
antigramatical ungrammatical
antigripal *adj* anti-flu
antigualla antique; out-dated article; ancient custom; old fogey, square
antiguarse to become out-of-date
antigüedad antiquity; olden times;

seniority
antiguo antique, ancient; old; senior; **a la antigua** in an old-fashioned way; **los ~s** the ancients
antiherrumbroso anti-rust
antihigiénico unhygienic
antihistérico *med* anti-hysteric
antihumano inhuman
antiinflacionista anti-inflationary
antilogía contradiction
antílope *m zool* antelope
antillano West Indian
antimilitarista *n m+f +adj* anti-militarist
antimonarquical anti-monarchical
antimonio antimony
antinacional anti-national
antinatural unnatural
antiobrero anti-labour
antipalúdico anti-malarial
antipapa antipope
antiparalítico *med* anti-paralytic
antiparras *fpl* spectacles
antipartido anti-party
antipatía antipathy, aversion; unpleasantness, unfriendliness
antipático disagreeable, unpleasant, nasty
antipatizar to feel antipathy/dislike
antipatriótico unpatriotic
anti-pestilencial *med* anti-plague
antípoda *adj geog* antipodal; *n* ~s antipodes
antipolítico anti-political
antiputrido *med* antiseptic
antiquismo archaism
antirrábico *med* anti-rabies
antirreglamentario against the rules
antirreligioso *n* anti-religious person; *adj* anti-religious
antirreumático *med* anti-rheumatic
antirrevolucionario anti-revolutionary
antirrino *bot* antirrhinum
antirrobo burglar-proof, anti-theft
antisemítico anti-Semitic
antisemitismo anti-Semitism
antiséptico antiseptic
antisifilítico anti-syphilitic
antisísmico earthquake-proof
antisonoro sound-proof
antiteísmo antitheism
antitérmico *phys* non-conducting
antítesis *f sing + pl* antithesis
antitóxico *med* antitoxic

34

antitoxina antitoxin
antituberculoso anti-tuberculosis
antivariólico *med* anti-smallpox
antivenenoso *n* antidote; *adj* antidotal
antivenéreo *med* anti-venereal
antiverminoso vermifugal
antófago flower-eating
antófilo flower-loving
antojadizo unpredictable
antojarse *v impers* to take a fancy to; **se me antoja** I fancy
antojera spectacle case; blinkers (for horse)
antojero spectacle-maker
antojo whim, caprice; birthmark; mole
antología anthology
Antonio Anthony
antónimo *gramm* antonym
antorcha torch; taper
antorchero torch-bearer
antracita anthracite
antracítico anthracitic
ántrax *m med* anthrax
antro cave; den; dangerous place
antropofagia cannibalism
antropófago cannibalistic
antropoide anthropoid
antropología anthropology
antropológico anthropological
antropólogo anthropologist
antropómetra *m+f* anthropometrist
antropometría anthropometry
antropomorfismo anthropomorphism
antropomorfista *m+f* anthropomorph- ist
antropomorfo anthropomorphous
antruejo carnival
antuviar to forestall; *fam* be the first to strike (a blow)
antuvión *m fam* unexpected blow; **de ~** unexpectedly
anual annual
anualidad *f* annuity; yearly pension
anuario year-book; annual report; di- rectory
anúbada call to arms
anubarrado cloudy
anublar to darken, dim; **~se** to become cloudy; *agri* become withered/mil- dewed
anublo mildew
anudar to knot; unite; resume; **~se** to become knotted; pine away
anuencia compliance

anuente complying
anuir to agree
anulación *f* nullification; cancellation
anulador *n m* repealer; *adj* repealing
[1] **anular** to annul, nullify, cancel; **~se** to take a back seat
[2] **anular** *n m* ring-finger; *adj* ring-shaped
ánulo circle, ring
Anunciación *f* Annunciation, Lady Day
anunciador *n m* announcer, advertiser; *adj* announcing, advertising
anunciante *see* **anunciador**
anunciar to announce, proclaim, adver- tise; foretell
anuncio announcement, advertisement, notice; sign, omen; *comm* advice; **~s por palabras**, **~s clasificados** classified advertisements, small-ads
anuo annual
anúteba *see* **anúbada**
anverso obverse
anzolero maker/seller of fish-hooks
anzuelo fish-hook; allurement
aña nanny
añadidura addition, extra; **por ~** furthermore, besides
añadir to add, increase
añafea: papel de ~ coarse paper
añagaza lure; bird-decoy
añal annual; **cordero ~** yearling lamb
añasco entanglement
añejar to make old; **~se** to grow old
añejo (of wine) old
añicos *mpl* bits, pieces, smithereens; **hacer ~ de** to smash to pieces
añil indigo; indigo dye
añilar to blue (washing); dye with indigo
añilería indigo plantation
añinos *mpl* lamb's wool; unshorn lamb- skin
año year; age; **~ económico** financial year; **~ secular** last year of the cen- tury; **al ~** yearly; **celebrar los ~s** to celebrate one's birthday; **entrado en ~s** getting on in years; **los ~s cin- cuenta/sesenta** the fifties/sixties; **per- der ~** to repeat a year's studies; **por ~** per annum
añojal fallow field
añojo yearling calf/lamb
añoranza nostalgia, longing, yearning
añorar to long for
añoso aged
añublo *agri* mildew, blight

añusgar to choke; be vexed

aojadura, aojamiento evil eye; witchcraft

aojo evil eye

aojusgar to choke while eating

aónides *fpl* the Muses

aoristo *gramm* aorist

aórtico aortic

aovar to lay eggs

aovillar to wind wool into balls

apabilar to trim the wick of a candle

apabullar to flatten, crush; confuse

apabullo flattening, crushing

apacentadero grazing land

apacentador *m* herdsman

apacentar to put out to graze; herd; ~se de/con to feed on

apacibilidad *f* pleasantness, gentleness, calmness

apacible pleasant, mild, calm

apaciguador *n m* pacifier, appeaser; *adj* pacifying, appeasing

apaciguamiento pacification, appeasement

apaciguar *vt* to pacify; calm; *vi naut* to abate; ~se to calm down

apache *n m* Apache; thug; *adj* Apache; thuggish

apadrinador *n m* patron, sponsor, backer; *adj* protecting, sponsoring

apadrinamiento sponsorship; backing

apadrinar to be second in a duel; be godfather; be best man (at a wedding); be patron to; back, sponsor

apagable extinguishable, quenchable

apagadizo difficult to keep alight, easily extinguished

apagado dull, lifeless; extinguished, out

apagador *n m* damper; extinguisher; *adj* extinguishing

apagaincendios *m sing+pl* fire-extinguisher

apagamiento dullness; lack of interest

apagar to extinguish, quench, put out; turn/switch off; *mech* deaden; *art* soften (colours); ~ la cal to slake lime; ~se to die out, go out

apagavelas *m sing+pl* snuffers

apagón *m* power-cut; black-out

apaisado oblong

apalabrar to agree orally to something

apalache Appalachian

apalancar to lever up; *fam* lump it; *sl* wait in hiding

apaleo heaping

apanalado honey-combed

apancora sea-urchin

apantallar to shield, hide

apantanar to flood; ~se to get bogged down

apañar to mend; arrange; patch; wrap; seize; **estar apañado** to have had it, be in a right mess; ~se to manage; ~se con to make do with; **apañárselas** to get fixed up; look after o.s.

apaño *m* repair

apañuscar to crumple; steal

apapagayado parrot-like

aparador *m* side-board, dresser; display-window

aparar to make ready; *carp* adze; dub; *agri* dress, weed; catch; ~se to prepare o.s.; get ready

aparasolado shaped like a parasol; *bot* umbelliferous

aparato apparatus, device, machine; system; set; pomp, ostentation; ~ **del partido** *pol* party machine; ~ **digestivo/respiratorio** digestive/respiratory system; ~ **de radio/televisión** radio/television set; ~ **vendedor** slot-machine, vending machine

aparatosidad *f* ostentation

aparatoso ostentatious, pompous

aparcadero parking place

aparcamiento parking; car-park, parking lot

aparcar to park

aparcero *agri* share-cropper

apareamiento matching, pairing, coupling, mating

aparearse to match, pair, couple; *zool* mate

aparecer(se) to appear, show up

aparecido ghost, phantom

aparejado ready, harnessed

aparejador *m* assistant architect; *bui* overseer; *naut* rigger

aparejar to get ready; harness; *naut* rig; size (before painting/papering); prime

aparejo preparation; harness, gear; priming, sizing (before papering/painting); *mech* tackle; *naut* rigging, tackle; *bui* bond; furniture; ~s apparatus; tools, instruments

aparentar to pretend, feign; look, seem; **él aparenta menos de cincuenta años**

he looks under fifty

aparente apparent, seeming; suited

aparición *f* apparition, appearance

apariencia appearance, looks; probability; **salvar las ~s** to keep up appearances

aparrado thick-set; vine-like

aparrar *hort* to espalier; **~se** to spread

aparroquiar to win clients/customers

apartación *f* distribution

apartadero lay-by; siding; free grazing at the side of a road

apartadijo share, portion; cubicle

apartadizo *n* cubicle, recess; *adj* stand-offish

apartado *n* alcove; special delivery mail; poste restante box; *metal* smelting, assaying; corralling (of bulls), dictionary entry; *adj* out of the way, off the beaten track; (of streets) back, side

apartador *m* separator; sorter; smelter

apartamento flat, apartment

apartamiento separation; remoteness; estrangement

apartar to separate, divide; put aside; pen; sort, shunt

aparte *n m* new paragraph; **punto y ~** full-stop and new paragraph; *adv* apart; aside; **dinero ~** money apart, apart from money

apartidar to side with

aparvar to heap up

apasionado *n* passionate admirer; devotee; *adj* passionate; devoted

apasionamiento passion

apasionante thrilling, exciting

apasionar to fill with enthusiasm; **~se de/por** to become very keen on

apatanado boorish

apatía apathy

apático apathetic

apatuscar to botch

apayasado clownish

apea hobble

apeadero halt (wayside station); horse-block

apeador *m* land-surveyor

apeamiento surveying

apear *vt* to help down; turn off (a bus etc); survey, chop down; take down; dismount; ford (rivers); overcome (obstacles); hobble (horse); *bui* prop up; **~se** to alight

apechugar to face with valour

apedazar to take to pieces; mend, repair

apedernalado flinty; insensitive

apedreado spotted, pock-marked

apedreamiento stoning to death

apedrear to stone

apedreo *see* **apedreamiento**

apegarse to grow fond of; attach o.s. to

apego fondness, inclination

apelación *f leg* appeal; *med* consultation; **no hay ~** it's a hopeless case

¹ **apelado** *leg* successful in appeal

² **apelado** (of horses) of the same colour

apelante *n leg* appellant

apelar to appeal, have recourse to; **~ a** to appeal to; **~ de** to appeal against

apelativo appellative

apelde *m* flight, escape

apelmazado heavy, stodgy, thick

apelmazadura, apelmazamiento heaviness, stodginess, thickness

apelmazar to cram together; make solid

apelotonar to make into balls; **~se** to crowd together

apellidar to name; call to arms; proclaim; **~se** be called

apellido surname, family name; epithet; mobilization order; call to arms; cry

apenachado crested, plumed

apenar to grieve

apenas hardly, scarcely; no sooner than

apencar *sl* to think; **~ con** *sl* to lump, put up with

apéndice *m* appendix

apendicitis *f* appendicitis

apeo survey; land mensuration; *archi* prop, stay

apeonar *orni* to run swiftly

apepsia *med* indigestion

aperador *m* wheelwright; *min* foreman

aperar to work as a wheelwright

apercibimiento preparation, foresight; advice; *leg* summons

apercibir to provide; warn; *leg* summon

apercollar to seize by the scruff of the neck; to steal

apergaminarse to become dried up

aperitivo *n* appetizer; *med* aperient; *adj* appetizing; *med* aperient

aperlado of pearly colour

aperreado wretched, miserable; **vida aperreada** a dog's life

aperrear to put the dogs on

37

apersonado: bien/mal ~ of good/bad appearance

apertura opening; reading (of a will)

aperturismo *pol* policy of opening-up, liberalization, glasnost

apesadumbrar to afflict

apestar *vt* to corrupt; vex, annoy; *vi* to stink

apestoso pestilent, foul-smelling

apétalo *bot* without petals

apetecer *vt* to fancy, hanker for; *vi* to be attractive

apetecible desirable

apetencia appetite; desire

apetitivo appetizing

apetito appetite, desire; **abrir el ~** to whet the appetite

apetitoso tasty, appetizing

apiadar to arouse pity; **~se de** to take pity on

apiario *n* apiary; *adj* bee-like

apicararse to go to the dogs; become a rascal

ápice *m* apex; crux; iota

ápices *mpl bot* anthers

apícola related to bee-keeping

apicultor *m* bee-keeper

apicultura bee-keeping

apilar to pile, heap up

apimplarse *sl* to get drunk

apimpollarse to germinate, bud

apiñadura, apiñamiento congestion, crowd, throng

apiñar to crowd, crush, press; **~se** to crowd

apio *m bot* celery; *sl* cissy, pansy

apiolar to seize; *sl* kill

apisonadora mechanical roller, steam roller

apisonamiento flattening, stamping down

apisonar to flatten, stamp down

aplacable appeasable

aplacamiento appeasement

aplacador *n m* appeaser; *adj* appeasing

aplacar to appease, calm down

aplacible pleasant

aplaciente pleasing

aplacimiento pleasure

aplanadera leveller, rollèr

aplanador *m* leveller; *mech* riveter; cylinder roller; *print* planishing mallet

aplanamiento levelling, flattening; dejection

aplanar to make level, flatten; make dejected

aplastante crushing

aplastar to crush, flatten

aplaudidor *m* applauder

aplaudir to applaud

aplauso applause

aplayar (of rivers) to overflow

aplazamiento postponement, adjournment

aplazar to postpone, adjourn

aplebeyar to debase

aplicable applicable

aplicación *f* application; diligence

aplicado studious, hard-working

aplicar to apply; impute; *leg* adjudge; **~se a** to get down seriously to

aplique *m elect* light-fitting

aplomado leaden; self-assured

aplomar *bui* to plumb; *archi* put vertically

apocado timid, spineless

Apocalipsis *m* Apocalypse

apocalíptico apocalyptic(al)

apocamiento timidity, spinelessness

apocar to humiliate; **~se** to be cowed, climb down

apocopar to shorten, apocopate

apócrifo apocryphal

apodar to nickname; make fun of

apoderar to empower, authorize; **~se de** to take hold of, seize

apodo nickname

apogeo *astron* apogee; climax, heyday

apolilladura moth-hole

apolillado moth-eaten; damaged by woodworm

apolillar to gnaw, eat, infest; **~se** to become moth-eaten

apologético apologetic

apología apology, apologia

apologista *m + f* apologist

apoltronarse to loaf

apomazar to smooth with pumice-stone

apoplejía apoplexy

apoplético apoplectic

aporcadura *agri* earthing up

aporreamiento clubbing, beating with a truncheon

aporrear to hit (*usu* with a truncheon)

aporreo beating

aporrillarse to swell in the joints

aportación *f* share, contribution

aportadero *naut* stopping-place; landing-place

aportar to bring, contribute; show up, turn up

aportillar to break down, knock a hole in; ~**se** to tumble down

aposentador *m* lodging-house keeper; innkeeper

aposentamiento lodging

aposentar to lodge; ~**se** to take lodgings

aposento room, lodging

aposesionar to give possession to; ~**se** to take possession

aposición *f gramm* apposition

apositivo *gramm* appositional

apósito *med* dressing

aposta deliberately

apostadero naval station; dockyard

apostador *m* better, punter

apostar to bet, wager; **apuesto a que ...** I bet ...

apóstata apostate

apostilla marginal note

apostillar to make marginal notes; ~**se** to break out in pimples

apóstol *m* apostle

apostolado the twelve apostles

apostólico apostolic

apóstrofe *m gramm* apostrophe

apostura poise

apote galore

apoteósico *adj* deifying, glorifying

apoteosis *f* apotheosis, deification

apoyabrazos *m sing + pl* armrest

apoyacabezas *m sing + pl* headrest

apoyadera, apoyador *n prop*, support

apoyar to lean, support; back up; rest (the head); ~**se** to rest on

apoyatura *mus* appoggiatura

apoyo prop, stay, support; **con** ~ **de** with backing from

apreciable valuable, esteemed, noticeable

apreciación *f* appreciation, appraisal; **error de** ~ error of judgement

apreciador *m* appraiser

apreciar to appreciate, appraise, estimate; ~ **en mucho** to think highly of

apreciativo appreciative

aprecio appreciation, esteem; valuation

aprehender to apprehend, seize; grasp; *phil* comprehend

aprehensión *f* seizure, capture; *phil* comprehension

apremiante urgent, pressing

apremiar to urge, press

apremio pressure

aprendedor *m* learner

aprender to learn; ~ **de memoria** to learn by heart

aprendiz *m* apprentice

aprendizaje *m* apprenticeship; **hacer un** ~ to serve an apprenticeship

aprensador *n m* presser; *adj* pressing

aprensión *f* apprehension, scruple; squeamishness; *med* hypochondria

aprensivo apprehensive; *med* hypochondriac

apresador *n m* privateer; plunderer; *adj* seizing, capturing

apresamiento capture, seizure

apresar to seize; arrest

aprestar to prepare, make ready; size (before papering); ~**se a** to get ready to

apresto preparation; *text* body

apresuración *f* haste

apresurado hasty

apresuramiento hastiness

apresurar to hurry, hasten

apretadero truss

apretado tight, compact; thick; cramped; difficult; dangerous; ~ **de dinero** short of money

apretador *n m* presser, rammer; waistcoat; hairnet; *adj* pressing, tightening

apretadura compression, constriction

apretar *vt* to press, tighten; squeeze; jam; pack tight; ~**le a uno la mano** to shake hands with s.o.; ~ **los dientes** to clench one's teeth; ~ **el cinturón** to tighten the belt; ~ **el paso** to go more quickly; *vi* to make itself felt; become severe

apretón *m* firm grasp; sharp pain; dash; ~ **de manos** hand-shake, hand-clasp

apretujar to squeeze, keep on squeezing

apretujón *m* hard squeeze

apretura crowd; want; need; fix, confined space

aprietatuercas *m sing + pl eng* wrench

aprieto fix, tight spot, difficulty, crush

aprisa quickly

aprisco sheepfold

aprisionar to imprison

aprobable approvable

aprobación *f* approval

aprobado (in exam) pass

aprobador, aprobante approving

aprobar to approve, (in exam) pass
aprobativo, aprobatorio approbatory
aprontar to prepare quickly
apropiador *n m* appropriator; *adj* appropriating
apropiar to appropriate, accommodate; ~**se** to appropriate to o.s.; ~**se (de) algo** to appropriate something
aprovechable serviceable, usable
aprovechado *n* opportunist; *adj* hard-working, selfish
aprovechamiento profit, benefit
aprovechar to profit by; be useful; ~**se de** to avail o.s. of; take advantage of, exploit
aprovisionador *m* provider, purveyor
aprovisionar to victual, supply
aproximación *f* approximation
aproximado approximate
aproximativo approaching, approximate
ápside *m astron* apogee; *archi* apse
aptitud *f* aptitude, fitness, capacity
apto apt, fit, suitable; ~ **para el frente** *mil* fit for frontline service; ~ **para todo** fit for anything
apuesta bet
apuesto smart, spruce
apuntación *f* annotation, memorandum; *mus* notation
apuntado pointed
apuntador *m theat* prompter
apuntalar to prop, shore up, support
apuntar *vt* to point, aim; point out, indicate; jot down; sketch; wager; fasten; sharpen; *theat* prompt; *vi* to begin to appear; hint; ~**se** to sign up; get tight; ~**se a** to join, become a member of; *mil* join up
apunte *m* annotation, memorandum, note, rough sketch; *theat* cue, prompt-book; rascal
apuntillar to finish off
apuñalado dagger-shaped
apuñalar to stab
apuración *f* refining, investigating; draining (to the dregs)
apurador *n m* refiner; candlestick; *adj* refining
apurar to purify; verify, investigate; consume, drain; hurry, push; ~**se** to become embarrassed; get into a flap/dither
apuro stringency, want; **estar en un** ~ to

be in a tight spot
aquejar to afflict
aquejoso afflicted
aquel *m*, **aquella** *adj* that
[1] **aquél** *m*, **aquélla** *pron* that one; the former
[2] **aquél** *m* charm
aquelarre *m* witches' sabbath
aquello *neut pron* that (which is referred to)
aquellos *mpl*, **aquellas** *fpl adj* those
aquéllos *mpl*, **aquéllas** *fpl pron* those ones
aquerenciarse to become attached to a place
aquí here; ~ **dentro** in here; ~ **fuera** out here; ~ **mismo** right here; **de** ~ **a seis meses** six months from now; **de** ~ **en adelante** from now on; **hasta** ~ so far; **he** ~ **lo** and behold; **por** ~ this way
aquiescencia acquiescence
aquietar to lull, pacify, set at rest
aquilatación assaying
aquilatar to assay
aquilea *bot* yarrow
aquilón *m* north wind
aquilonal northerly, wintry
Aquisgrán Aachen, Aix-la-Chapelle
aquistar to conquer
árabe *n* Arab; Arabic language; *adj* Arabian; ~ **saudí** Saudi Arabian
arabesco *n* arabesque; *adj* Arabian
arábiga: goma ~ gum arabic
arabismo Arabism
arabista *m+f* Arabist, Arabic scholar
arabizar to Arabize
arada ploughing, ploughed land
arado plough
arador *n m* ploughman; *adj* ploughing
aradura *n* ploughing
aragonés Aragonese
arameo Aramaic
aramio fallow land
arana trick
arancel *m* tariff; customs dues
arancelaria concerning customs dues
arándano cranberry
arandela *mech* ring, washer, rivet-plate
arandillo *orni* marsh warbler
aranero *n* trickster, cheat; *adj* deceitful
araña spider; *bot* crowfoot; *orni* bird net
arañada scratch
arañador *n m* scratcher; *adj* scratching
arañar to scratch, scrape; scrape

together
arañazo scratch
araño scratch, slight wound
arañuela *bot* love-in-a-mist
arañuelo red spider
arao *orni* guillemot
arapo rag, tatter
aráquida peanut
arar to plough
arbitración *f* arbitration
arbitrador *n m* judge, arbitrator, referee; *adj* arbitrating
arbitraje *m* arbitration
arbitrante arbitrating
arbitrar to arbitrate, adjuge; find ways and means
arbitrariedad *f* arbitrariness
arbitrario arbitrary; *leg* arbitral
arbitrio free-will; means, expedient; **propios y ∼s** ways and means
arbitrista *m + f* schemer, contriver
árbitro arbitrator, referee, umpire
árbol *m* tree; *naut* mast; *mech* axle, shaft; **∼ de levas** camshaft; **∼es** timber, *US* lumber; **no cae de los ∼es** it doesn't grow on trees
arbolado *n* woodland; *adj* wooded; *naut* masted; **mar ∼** high seas
arboladura *naut* masts and spars
arbolar to hoist, erect; *naut* mast; hoist a flag; **∼se** (of horses) to rear up
arbolario *bot* nursery
arboleda grove
arboledo woodland
arbolete *m* trap
arbolillo miserable little tree
arbolista *m + f* arboriculturist
arbóreo tree-shaped
arborizar to cultivate trees
arbotante *archi* vault; flying buttress
arbusto shrub
arca chest, coffer; safe; ark; lumberroom; **∼ cerrada** closed book, unknown quantity; **∼ de agua** watertower; **∼ de la alianza** Ark of the Covenant; **∼ de Noé** Noah's Ark; **∼s** treasury
arcabucear to shoot with an arquebus
arcabuco mountain covered with scrub
arcada retch(ing); *archi* arcade
arcaduz *m* conduit, pipe; bucket
arcaico archaic
arcaísmo archaism
arcaísta *m + f* archaist

arcaizar to archaize
arcángel *m* archangel
arcangelical, arcangélico archangelic
arcano secret, recondite, mysterious
arcar to arch
arce *bot* maple-tree
arcedianato archdeaconship
arcediano archdeacon
arcedo maple grove
arcén *m* border, brim, edge; (of road) hard shoulder; verge
arcilla clay
arcillar to clay
arcilloso clayey
arcipreste *m* archpriest
arco *geom* arc; *archi* arch, bridge; *mus* bow; *mil* bow; **∼ iris** rainbow
archibebe *m orni* greenshank
archicofradía privileged brotherhood
archidiácono archdeacon
archidiócesis *f* archdiocese
archiducado archdukedom, archduchy
archiducal archducal
archiduque *m* archduke
archiduquesa archduchess
archimillonario multimillionaire
archipámpano Great Panjandrum
archipiélago archipelago
archivador *m* filing cabinet; archivist
archivar to file; shelve (a matter)
archivero, archivista *m + f* archivist
archivo archive; file
arda squirrel
árdea *orni* stone-curlew
ardentía heat; phosphorescence (of the sea); heartburn
arder to burn, blaze, whine; (of compost) rot; be inflamed; **∼se** to burn up
ardeviejas *m sing + pl bot* gorse, furze
ardid *m* rusc, stratagem
ardido brave, bold, fearless
ardiente ardent, hot, fervent, fiery, feverish
ardilla squirrel; **andar como ∼** to fidget; **ser como una ∼** to be very quick
ardimiento conflagration, valour
ardiondo valiant
ardite *m* farthing; **no vale un ∼** it's not worth a farthing
ardor *m* ardour, heat, fervency; *med* fever; heartburn
ardoroso fiery, ardent
arduo arduous, difficult
área area

arefacción *f* drying

arelar to sift, sieve

arena sand; ~s *med* gravel; ~ **movediza** quicksand

arenáceo sandy

arenal *m* sandy ground

arenar to sand; cover with sand

arencar to salt and dry

arenería sand-pit

arenero sand-dealer

arenga harangue

arengador *n m* haranguer; *adj* haranguing

arenilla moulding sand; *med* calculus

arenisca sandstone

arenisco, arenoso sandy

arenque *m* herring; ~ **ahumado** kipper

arenquera herring-net; *fig* low woman

arenquero herring dealer

arete *m* ear-ring

arfada *naut* pitching (in rough sea)

arfar *naut* to pitch

argadijo reel, bobbin

argado trick; absurdity

argalia *med* catheter

argallera *carp* saw for cutting grooves

argamasar *vt* to mix (mortar); cement, plaster; *vi* to make mortar

árgana, árgano *mech* crane

argavieso whirlwind

argayar to fall (in landslide)

Argel Algiers

Argelia Algeria

argelino Algerian

argemone *f bot* horned poppy

argentado silvery

argentador *m* silversmith

argentar to silver; adorn with silver

argentario silversmith

argénteo silvery, silver-white

argentería embroidery in silver and gold

argentero silversmith

argentífero silver-bearing

argentino *n* Argentinian; *adj* silvery, Argentinian

argento silver; ~ **vivo** quicksilver

argo argon

argolla large ring; collar, hoop

árgoma *bot* gorse

argonauta *m* Argonaut

argot *m* slang

argüidor *n m* arguer; *adj* argumentative

argüir to argue

argumentación *f* argumentation

argumentador *n m* arguer; *adj* argumentative

argumentar to argue

argumentista *m* + *f* arguer

argumento argument; plot

arguyente *n m* + *f* arguer; *adj* arguing, opposing

aridecerse to become arid

aridez *f* dryness, aridity

árido arid, dry

arietar to ram

ariete *m* battering-ram, *sp sl* forward player, striker

arijo *agri* light, easily tilled

arillo ear-ring

ario Aryan

ariscarse to become sullen

arisco churlish, sullen, unsociable

aristocracia aristocracy

aristócrata *m* + *f* aristocrat

aristocrático aristocratic

aristón *m* barrel-organ

aritmética arithmetic

aritmético arithmetician

aritmómetro calculating machine

arlequín *m* harlequin

arlequinado parti-coloured

arlo *bot* barberry

arma arm, weapon; branch (of the services); ~ **blanca** bladed weapon; ~ **corta** pistol; ~ **de fuego** firearm; ~ **negra** fencing foil; ~s coat of arms; **las** ~s fighting forces; **maestro de** ~s fencing master; **pasar por las** ~s to put to the sword

armada navy, fleet; (hunting) party of beaters

armadía raft

armadijo snare

armado *eccles* (in procession) man dressed as a Roman soldier; **hormigón** ~ reinforced concrete

armador *m* outfitter; shipowner; privateer

armamento armament; *naut* equipment

armar to arm; man; put together, assemble, mount, rig up; reinforce (concrete); *naut* put in commission; ~ **caballero** to dub a knight; ~ **los remos** to man the oars; ~ **ruido** to make a din; ~ **una bronca/un escándalo** to start a row/shindy; ~se **un lío** to get into a muddle, *sl* have an erection

armario wardrobe, cupboard, *US*

closet; ~ **de luna** wardrobe with mirror

armatoste *m* unwieldy great object or machine; big useless person

armazón *m anat* skeleton; *f* framework; mounting

arménico Armenian

armería armoury; arsenal; gunsmith's shop; heraldry

armero armourer, gunsmith; rack for firearms

armífero warlike

armiñado trimmed/lined with ermine

armiño ermine

armisticio armistice

armón *m* gun-carriage

armonía harmony, concord

armónica harmonica

armónico harmonic, harmonious

armonio harmonium

armonioso +*fig* harmonious

armonista *m*+*f* harmonist

armonización *f* harmonization

armonizar to harmonize

arnaúte *n m*+*f*+*adj* Albanian

arnés *m* harness, armour; **arneses** trappings

¹ **aro** hoop; ring; **entrar por** ~ to settle down

² **aro** *bot* wild arum

aromaticidad *f* aromatic quality

aromático aromatic

aromatización *f* aromatization

aromatizador *n m* aromatizer; *adj* perfuming

aromatizante fragrant

aromatizar to perfume

arón *m bot* arum

arpa harp

arpado serrated

arpadura scratch

arpar to scratch, rend

arpegio *mus* arpeggio

arpella *orni* marsh harrier

arpía harpy, ugly old woman

arpillera sackcloth

arpista *m*+*f* harpist

arpón *m* harpoon

arponar, arponear to harpoon

arponero harpooner; harpoon maker

arqueada *mus* stroke with the bow; ~**s** retching; bandy

arqueaje *m*, **arqueamiento** *naut* gauging, tonnage measurement

¹ **arquear** *vt* to arch; ~ **las cejas** to raise the eyebrows; *vi* to retch

² **arquear** *naut* to gauge; check

¹ **arqueo** arching

² **arqueo** *naut* gauging; *naut* tonnage; checking

arqueología archaeology

arqueológico archaeological

arqueólogo archaeologist

arquería series of arches

¹ **arquero** archer; hooper

² **arquero** cashier, treasurer

arquetipo archetype

arquibanco bench with drawers

arquiepiscopal archiepiscopal

arquimesa escritoire

arquitecto architect

arquitectónico architectural

arquitectura architecture

arquitrabe architrave

arquivolta archivolt

arrabal *m* suburb, lower-class district; ~**es** outskirts

arrabalero suburbanite; ill-bred person

arrabio cast-iron

arracada pendant ear-ring

arracimarse to form bunches; cluster together

arraclán *m* alder-tree

arraigar to take root; ~**se** to settle down; become rooted

arraigo *bot* rooting; settling; landed property; **hombre de** ~ landowner, property owner; **fianza de** ~ guarantee by mortgage; **tener** ~ to own property

arraigue *m* settling down; taking root

arralar to become scarce

arranca plucking, picking

arrancaclavos *m sing*+*pl* claw (for nail pulling)

arrancada sudden departure; *naut*+*mot* sudden spurt of speed

arrancadero starting point

arrancador *n m* extirpator, destroyer; *adj* extirpating, destructive

arrancadura, arrancamiento extirpation, uprooting, destruction

arrancar *vt* to extirpate; uproot; force out; pull out; pull up; carry off; *mot* start (engine); ~ **de raíz** to tear out by the roots, eradicate; *vi* to get moving, start to move, rush forward; ~**se** to make a special effort

arranciarse to turn rancid

arranchar *naut* to coast; ~**se** to mess together

arranque *m* pulling up, wrench(ing); burst, sudden impulse, sudden start; *mot* starter; *fam* last drink

arrapar to snatch away, carry off

arrapiezo tatter, rag; ragamuffin

arras *fpl* security, earnest money; coins given by bridegroom to bride

arrasado satiny

arrasamiento levelling, razing to the ground

arrasar to level, raze to the ground, destroy; ~**se** *meteor* to clear up, turn fine; ~**se en lágrimas** (of eyes) to fill with tears

arrastradero *naut* careening place

arrastrado good-for-nothing, rascal; *adj* base, vile, wretched

arrastramiento *n* dragging, crawling

arrastrante *adj* dragging, crawling

arrastrar *vt* to drag, haul; attract; prompt; move; ~ **los pies** to shuffle; *vi* to creep, crawl; follow suit; ~**se** to humiliate o.s.; crawl

arrastre *m* dragging, haulage; **barco de** ~ trawler

arrastrero trawler; dredger

arrayán *m bot* myrtle

¡arre! gee up!

arrear to drive (horses *etc*); urge on; harness

arrebañaderas *fpl* grappling-irons (for dragging wells, ponds *etc*)

arrebañador *n m* gatherer; *adj* gathering, gleaning

arrebañadura *n* gathering; picking up; ~**s** scraps, left-overs

arrebatadizo excitable

arrebatado sudden, impetuous, violent

arrebatador captivating, enthralling

arrebatamiento rage, ecstasy, rapture

arrebatar to snatch; captivate, delight; ~**se** to become overcooked; *fig* get carried away

arrebatiña scrimmage, scramble

arrebato sudden attack, fit, rage, rapture

arrebatoso sudden, abrupt

arrebol *m* red sky; rouge

arrebolada red clouds

arrebolar to paint red; ~**se** to put on rouge

arrebolera rouge-box

arrebollarse to tumble

arrebozar, arrebozo *see* **rebozar, rebozo**

arreciar to grow stronger/worse, **el frío va a** ~ the cold is going to get worse

arrecife *m naut* reef

arrecirse to become frozen stiff

arrechucho fit of anger; *med* attack (of illness)

arredilar to pen (farm animals)

arredramiento terror, fear

arredrar to daunt; ~**se ante** to be daunted by

arreglado neat, tidy; reasonable

arreglar to arrange; *sp* 'fix' a game; repair; tidy; ~**se con alguien** to reach an understanding with s.o.; ~**se por las buenas** to settle things peacefully; ~**se solo** to manage by o.s.

arreglo arrangement, settlement, understanding; **con** ~ **a** in accordance with

arrejuntarse *sl* to live together as man and wife, live in sin

arrellanarse to loll, sprawl

arremangar to turn/tuck up; ~**se** to roll up one's sleeves/trousers

arrematar *see* **rematar**

arremediar *see* **remediar**

arremetedor *n m* assailant; *adj* aggressive

arremeter to attack, charge

arremetida attack, charge

arremolinarse to whirl about; eddy; throng together

arrendable rentable

arrendador *m* landlord; hirer, tenant; lessee

arrendamiento renting, letting, hiring

¹ **arrendar** to rent, let, hire

² **arrendar** to bridle, tie up (a horse)

³ **arrendar** to copy

arreo dress, ornament; ~**s** harness, trappings, accessories

arrendajo *orni* mocking-bird

arrepentida reformed woman; penitent

arrepentido penitent

arrepentimiento repentance; *leg* mitigating circumstance

arrepentirse to repent; regret

arrestado brave, audacious

arrestar *mil* to place under arrest; ~**se** to rush in

arresto *mil* arrest; daring, guts; **tener** ~**s**

to have guts

arria drove (of animals)

arriar *naut* to lower, strike, take in (sails, flags *etc*)

arriate *m gard* narrow flowerbed, path

arriba above, up, high up, upstairs, over; *naut* aloft; ¡~! get up!; **de** ~ from above; **calle** ~ up the street; **mirar de** ~ **abajo** to look up and down; **río** ~ upstream; ¡~ …! long live …!

arribada *naut* arrival; ~ **forzosa** emergency call; **de** ~ in distress

arribaje *m naut* arrival, landing

arribar *naut* to arrive; put into harbour

arribista *m+f* unscrupulous opportunist; go-getter; climber

arricete *m* sandbank

arriendo renting, letting, hiring

arriero drover, muleteer

arriesgado dangerous, risky

arriesgar to risk; ~**se** to take a risk

arrimar to bring, place near; *naut* stow; reject; ~ **el hombro** to put one's shoulder to the wheel; ~**se a** to lean against; join; seek the protection of; ~**se** (of bull fighting) allow the bull to come very close

arrimo *n* placing near; stick, crutch; help, support

arrinconar to corner; put into a corner; neglect; ~**se** to withdraw from the world

arriscado craggy

arriscar to risk; ~**se** to dare; be arrogant

arrisco risk

arrizar *naut* to reef, stow, lash

arroba arroba (approx 25lb.); **por** ~**s** in large quantities

arrobador entrancing

arrobamiento ecstasy

arrobar to entrance; fill with ecstasy

arrobinar to corrupt

arrobo ecstasy

arrocero *n* rice grower/merchant; *adj* of rice

arrocinarse to sink to the level of an animal; become stupid; fall head-over-heels in love

arrocito Venezuelan folk dance

arrodear *see* **rodear**

arrodillada (act of) kneeling

arrodilladura, arrodillamiento kneeling

arrodillar to force (s.o.) to kneel; ~**se** to

kneel down

arrogancia arrogance; fine bearing; valour; pride

arrogante arrogant; having a fine bearing; valiant

arrogar to claim; adopt

arrojadizo *adj* throwing, intended for throwing

arrojado intrepid, foolhardy

arrojar to throw, cast, fling; throw out, emit; *agri* shoot forth; *med* vomit

arrojo intrepidity, fearlessness

arrollador *n m* roller; *adj* rolling, sweeping

arrollamiento *elect* winding, coiling

arrollar to roll up; overwhelm

arromar to blunt

arropamiento *n* wrapping up

arropar to dress, wrap, clothe; *agri* earth up, cover the roots

arrope *m* grape syrup

arropea shackle, fetter

arrostrar to brave, face up to

arroyada gully, river valley

arroyar to make gullies in; ~**se** to form gullies

arroyo small river, stream, brook; gutter

arroz *m* rice; ~ **con leche** rice pudding; ~ **inflado** puffed rice

arrozal *m* rice-field, paddy-field

arrufianado roguish, scoundrelly

arruga crease, wrinkle

arrugación *f*, **arrugamiento** creasing, wrinkling

arrugar to crease, wrinkle, rumple; ~ **la frente** to frown; ~**se** *sl* to flee, do a bunk; become afraid

arruinador ruinous, destructive

arruinamiento ruin, destruction

arruinar to ruin, destroy; ~**se** to go to rack and ruin; to go bust/bankrupt

arrullador lulling, soothing

arrullar to bill and coo; sing to sleep; sing a lullaby to

arrullo billing and cooing; lullaby

arrumar *naut* to stow; ~**se** *naut* to become overcast

arrumazón *m naut* stowage; overcast horizon

arrumbar to put aside; put out of the way; *naut* steer the correct course; ~**se** *naut* to take bearings

arrurruz *m* arrowroot

arsenal *m* arsenal; dock-yard, shipyard

arsénico arsenic

arsolla *bot* lesser burdock

arta *bot* plantain

arte *m+f* art, skill; cunning, intrigue; ~ **manual** craft; **buen** ~ skill; **bellas** ~**s** fine arts; **mal** ~ clumsiness; ~**s y oficios** arts and crafts

artefacto contrivance; appliance

artejo knuckle; *ent* leg segment

arteria *anat* artery; main/trunk road

artería cunning, craftiness

arterioso arterial

artero crafty, cunning

artesa dug-out; baker's trough

artesanía craftwork, handicrafts

artesano craftsman, artisan

artesiano artesian

artesón *m archi* carved ceiling panel

artesonada ceiling of carved panels

artesonar *archi* to panel (ceilings)

artete *m* drag-net

artético arthritic

ártico arctic; **polo** ~ North Pole

articulación *f* articulation; joint

articulado articulate

articular to articulate; join

articulista *m+f* columnist; feature-article writer

artículo article; item; joint; ~ **de fondo** leader, editorial; ~ **de primera necesidad** essential

artífice *n* artificer

artificial artificial, man-made; **fuegos** ~**es** fireworks

artificio workmanship, craft; trick; guile; *mech* contrivance, device; **fuegos de** ~ fireworks

artificioso skilful; affected; false

artilugio useless device; trick

artillar to provide artillery; ~**se** to arm o.s.

artillería artillery, gunnery; *sp sl* (football) forward line

artillero gunner, artillery man; *sp sl* (football) forward with a powerful kick

artimaña snare; stratagem

artista *m+f* artist, craftsman; *theat+TV* performer

artístico artistic

artrítico arthritic

artritis *f* arthritis

artrón *m* arthrosis

Arturo Arthur

aruñar to scratch, scrape; scrape together

aruñazo scratch

arveja *bot* vetch

arza *naut* hoisting-tackle

arzobispado archbishopric

arzobispal archiepiscopal

arzobispo archbishop

arzón *m* saddle-tree

as *m* ace

asá: ni así ni ~ neither one way nor the other

asa handle

asado roast

asador *m* spit

asadura chitterlings, liver, lights, innards

asaetar to wound with arrows; annoy, vex

asainetado *theat* farcical

asalariado wage earner

asalariar to pay wages or a salary to

asalmonado salmon-like

asaltador *n m* assailant; *adj* assailing

asaltar to assault; surprise

asalto assault; (boxing, wrestling) round; **guardia de** ~ riot police

asamblea assembly, congress

asambleísta *m+f* member of an assembly

asar to roast, bake; *fam* pester; *sl* kill (with a firearm); ~**se de calor** to be scorching hot

asbestino of asbestos

asbesto asbestos

ascalonia *bot* shallot

ascendencia ancestry, lineage

ascendente ascendant

ascender *vt* to promote; *vi* to ascend, climb, go up, get promoted; ~ **a** *comm* to amount to

ascendiente *n m* ascendancy, influence; **tener** ~ **sobre** to have ascendancy over; *adj* ascendant

ascensión *f* ascension, ascent

ascensionista *n m+f* climber, balloonist; *adj* ascending, climbing

ascenso rise, promotion; climb

ascensor *m* lift, *US* elevator

asceta *m* ascetic

ascética ascetics

ascético ascetic

ascetismo ascetism

46

ascitis *f* dropsy

asco disgust, repugnance, loathing; **es un ~** it's quite disgusting; **me da ~** it makes me want to vomit

ascua ember, red-hot coal; **arrimar el ~ a la sardina** to look after yours truly; **estar sobre ~s** to be on tenterhooks; **hecho una ~** spick and span

aseado clean, neat

asear to clean, tidy up

aséchador *n m* waylayer; ensnaring

asechamiento, asechanza waylaying, snare

asechar to waylay

asediador *m* besieger

asediar to besiege, blockade

asedio siege, blockade

aseglararse to leave the priesthood

asegurable insurable

aseguración *f* insurance contract

asegurado policyholder, insured

asegurador *m* insurer, underwriter

aseguramiento insuring; *leg* security; safety

asegurar to secure; assure; preserve; *comm* to insure; **~se de** to make sure of; **~se de que** to make sure that

asemejar to make similar; **~se** to resemble

asenso assent, consent, credence

asentada *see* **sentada**

asentador *m* bricklayer; platelayer; razor-strop

asentamiento establishment; settlement

asentar *vt* to seat; place; lay down, settle, establish; note down; level, smooth; hone, sharpen; *vi* to be fitting, settle; **~se** to settle down

asentimiento assent, consent

asentir to assent, agree

asentista *m* contractor

aseo cleanliness; **cuarto de ~** washroom, toilet

asépalo *bot* without sepals

asepsia *med* asepsis

aséptico *med* aseptic

asequible attainable, reasonable

aserción *f* assertion

aserradero sawmill; saw-horse

aserrado serrated

aserrador *m* sawyer

aserradura sawing; **~s** sawdust

aserrar to saw, saw through; saw up

aserrín *m* sawdust

asertivo assertive

asertorio affirmatory

asesar to acquire prudence

asesinar to murder, assassinate

asesinato murder, assassination

asesino *n* murder, assassin; **~ de alquiler** hired killer

asesor adviser, consultant; **~ fiscal** tax-consultant

asesorar to advise; **~se** to have expert advice

asesoría adviser's/consultant's fee

asestadura aim; firing

asestar to aim; fire; try to injure; **~ un golpe** to strike a blow

aseveración *f* affirmation

aseverar to affirm

asfaltado asphalted surface

asfaltar to asphalt

asfáltico *adj* asphalt

asfalto asphalt

asfixia asphyxia

asfixiado *sl* broke, without a bean

asfixiador, asfixiante asphyxiating

asfixiar to asphyxiate, suffocate

así so, thus; this/that way; like this/that; **~ como** as well as; **~ pues** therefore; **~ que** therefore; **~ ~** so-so; **~ sea** so be it

asiático *n + adj* Asiatic

asidero handle; opportunity; pretext

asiduidad *f* assiduity

asiento seat; bottom (of a vessel *etc*); site; stability; *comm* entry; registry, roll; **de ~** prudent; **hacer ~** to establish o.s.; **no calentar el ~** to stay only a short while; **~s** backside, buttocks; **tomar ~** to sit down

asignable assignable

asignación *f* assignation; grant, subsidy, salary

asignar to assign, attribute

asignatura subject (academic discipline)

asilar to shelter

asilo asylum, sanctuary; harbourage; protection; old people's home

asilla small handle; slight pretext

asimetría asymmetry

asimétrico asymmetrical

asimilación *f* assimilation

asimilar to assimilate, absorb; grant (honours *etc*); **~se a** to resemble; be assimilated

asimilativo assimilative

asimismo in the same way

asincrónico asynchronous

asir *vt* to take hold of, seize, grasp; *vi agri* to strike, take root: ~**se de** to hang on to

Asiria Assyria

asirio *n* + *adj* Assyrian

asistencia attendance, presence, those present; ~**s** allowance, alimony

asistencial (of) welfare; **estado** ~ welfare state

asistenta daily (domestic) help, charwoman

asistente *n* *m* + *f* + *adj* assistant, one present; *mil* batman; *adj* attendant, attending

asistir *vt* to wait on; assist; *vi* to attend, be present

asma *med* asthma

asmático asthmatic

asna she-donkey; ~**s** *carp* rafters

asnada silly thing

asnal asinal

asnino asinine

asno ass; **bajarse del** ~ to admit an error

asocarronado sly, cunning

asociación *f* association, partnership

asociado *n* partner, associate; *adj* associate(d)

asociar to associate; ~**se** to form a partnership; ~**se a** to become a partner in

asolamiento desolation

asolanar to parch, dry up

asolapar to overlap

asolar to lay waste, devastate; burn

asoldadar, asoldar to hire, employ

asolear to expose to sunlight; ~**se** to sun o.s., become sunburnt

asomada brief appearance

asomar *vt* to show, stick out; *vi* to appear, stick out; ~**se por la ventana** to look out of the window

asombrador astonishing

asombramiento astonishment

asombrar to shade; astonish; ~**se de** to be surprised at

asombro astonishment

asombroso astonishing

asomo indication; sign; trace, hint; **ni por** ~ not by a long chalk

asonada mob, riot

asonancia assonance

asordar to deafen

asosegar *see* **sosegar**

aspa cross(-piece), arm (of windmill)

aspalato *bot* rosewood

aspaviento display of violent emotion

aspecto appearance, outlook

asperete *m* sour taste

aspereza asperity, roughness

asperger, aspergiar to sprinkle

asperjar to sprinkle, spray

áspero rough, harsh

aspersión *f* sprinkling

aspersor *m* water-sprinkler

áspid(e) *m* *zool* asp

aspillera *mil* loop-hole

aspiración *f* aspiration; intake

aspirador *m*, **aspiradora** vacuum cleaner

aspirante *n* *m* + *f* candidate, applicant; *adj* aspiring

aspirar to breathe in; aspirate; ~ **a** to aspire to

aspirina aspirin

asquear to revolt, disgust; feel nausea

asquerosidad *f* loathsome, disgusting or repulsive/filthy object

asqueroso disgusting, loathsome, revolting, filthy

asta shaft; flagstaff; handle; *zool* horn, antler; **a media** ~ at half-mast

ástaco crawfish, crayfish

astenia *med* debility

asterisco asterisk

asteroide *m* asteroid

astigmático astigmatic

astigmatismo *med* astigmatism

astil *m* handle (of axe, hammer *etc*); shaft (of arrow); beam (of balance)

astilla splinter

astillero shipyard

astilloso splintery

astracán *m* astrakhan

astrictivo astringent

astringencia astringency

astringente *n* *m* + *f* + *adj* astringent

astringir to contract, compress

astro heavenly body, star

astrolabio astrolabe

astrología astrology

astrológico astrological

astrólogo *n* astrologer; *adj* astrological

astronauta *m* + *f* astronaut

astronáutica astronautics

astronáutico astronautic(al)

astronave *f* spaceship

astronavegación *f* space travel

astronomía astronomy

astronómico astronomic(al); (of prices *etc*) exorbitant

astrónomo astronomer

astroso ill-fated; shabby, slovenly

astucia cunning, craftiness, astuteness

astucioso astute, shrewd

astur *m* native of Asturias, Asturian

asturiano *n* + *adj* Asturian

astuto astute, shrewd

asueto short holiday; day off work

asumir to assume

asunción *f* assumption

asunto matter; affair; business; ~s business; ~s exteriores foreign affairs

asustadizo easily scared; timid

asustar to frighten, scare

atabacado tobacco-coloured

atabal *m* kettle-drum

atabalear to drum

atabalero kettle-drummer

atacable attackable, vulnerable

atacado irresolute, undecided

atacador *m* ramrod; aggressor

atacadura, atacamiento *n* fastening, fitting

atacante attacking, irritating

atacar to fit tight to the body; button; attack, assault; irritate

ataderas *fpl* garters

atadero cord, rope; **no tener** ~ to be mad/uncontrollable

atadijo badly made parcel

atado *n* bundle, parcel; *adj* good-for-nothing; faint-hearted

atador *m*, **atadora** *agri* binder

atadura cord, fastening, union; **sin** ~s unrestricted

atafagar to choke; pester

atahorma *orni* osprey

atajadizo partition wall

atajador *m* interceptor; *mil* scout

atajamiento interruption

atajante intercepting

atajar *vt* to cut; cut short; intercept; partition off; *vi* to take a short cut; ~se to get embarrassed

atajo short cut; deletion; obstruction; interception

atalaya watch-tower, vantage point; *m* look-out/guard on watch-tower

atalayador *m* look-out; spy

atalayar to observe, watch; spy on

atalayero *mil* advance scout

atañer to be concerned

ataque *m* attack; *med* epileptic fit, onset of illness

ataquiza *agri* layering

ataquizar *agri* to layer

atar to tie, fasten; stop; ~ **cabos** to put two and two together; **loco de** ~ raving mad; ~se to become confused

atarazana arsenal, dockyard

atarazar to bite

atardecer *n m* evening; **al** ~ in the evening; *v* to grow late; find o.s. in the evening

atareado very busy

atarear to load with work; ~se to busy o.s.

atarjea drainpipe, sewer

atarquinar to bemire, smear with mud

atarugar to bung, plug

atascamiento bog; obstruction; blockage; traffic-jam

atascar to plug, bung up, obstruct, jam; ~se to get bogged down; stuff, gorge

atasco clogging, jamming; traffic-jam

ataúd *m* coffin, *US* casket

ataudado coffin-shaped

ataviar to deck, adorn, embellish

atávico atavistic

atavío dress, ornament, finery; gear

atavismo atavism

atediar to bore

ateísmo atheism

ateísta *m* + *f* atheist

atelar to harness

atemorizar to terrify

atemperación *f* tempering

atemperante soothing

atemperar to temper, soften; assuage; modify

Atenas Athens

atenazar to hold firmly

atención *f* attention; attentiveness; kindness; **atenciones** business affairs; **en** ~ **a** in view of; **prestar** ~ to pay attention

atendencia attention

atender to attend (to); be attentive (to); mind; heed; show kindness; *print* proof-read

atendible worthy of consideration

ateneo cultural club

atenerse to abide; ~ **a** to abide by

ateniense *n m* + *f* + *adj* Athenian

atentado *n* attempt on the life of s.o.; *adj*

49

prudent, tactful
atentar to attempt to commit a crime;
~**se** to restrain o.s.
atentatorio *leg* unlawful
atento *adj* attentive; polite, courteous;
~ **a** *adv* in view of, in consideration of
atenuación *f* attenuation
atenuante *adj* attenuating, lessening; *n*
~**s** *leg* extenuating circumstances
atenuar to attenuate, diminish; lessen
ateo *n* atheist; *adj* atheistic
aterciopelado velvety, like velvet
aterirse to become stiff with cold
aterrador terrifying
aterrajar *mech* to thread (a screw); tap
(with a die)
aterraje *m naut* landfall; *aer* landing
aterramiento ruin, destruction
aterrar *vt* to terrify; destroy, strike
down; *min* dump (waste); *vi* to land
aterrerar *min* to dump
aterrizaje *m aer* landing
aterrizar *aer* to land
aterrorizar to terrify, terrorize
atesorador *m* hoarder
atesorar to treasure, hoard
atestación *f* attestation
¹ **atestado** stubborn
² **atestado** certificate; ~**s** testimonials
atestadura, atestamiento cramming,
stuffing
¹ **atestar** to cram, pack
² **atestar** *leg* to attest, affirm
atestiguar to testify to
atezar to blacken; ~**se** to become
weathered/tanned
atiborrar to cram, stuff
aticismo elegant expression
ático attic
atiesar to stiffen
atigrado tiger-striped
atildado foppish, affected; neat
atildadura, atildamiento affectation
atildar to put a **tilde** on letter n; dress
affectedly
atinar to hit the mark
atiplar *mus* to raise the pitch of
atirantar to brace, make taut
atisbadero peep-hole
atisbador *adj* nosey, prying
atisbadura *n* prying, snooping
atisbar to pry, snoop
atisbo suggestion, hint, touch
atizadero fire-poker

atizador *m* inciting; fire-poker
atizar to prod, poke; incite, stir up
Atlántico *n* Atlantic (Ocean)
atlántico *adj* Atlantic
Atlas *m*: el ~ Atlas Mountains
atleta *m* athlete
atlético athletic
atletismo athletics
atmósfera atmosphere
atmosférico atmospherical
atoaje *m naut* towage
atoar *naut* to tow
atolón *m* atoll
atolondrado giddy, hare-brained, crazy;
bewildered
atolondramiento bewilderment; craziness
atolondrar to bewilder, fluster; ~**se** to
get flustered
atolladero mudhole; difficult situation
atollarse to get bogged down
atómico atomic
atomizar to atomize, spray
átomo atom
atónito thunderstruck, flabbergasted
átono *gramm* unaccented
atontamiento stupefaction
atontar to daze, stupefy, bewilder
¹ **atorar** to obstruct, choke; ~**se** to get
stuck
² **atorar** to cut firewood
atormentador *n m* tormentor; *adj* tormenting
atormentar to torment, torture; ~**se** to
suffer agony
atornillar to screw on/in/up
atosigamiento poisoning; harassment
¹ **atosigar** to poison
² **atosigar** to harass
atoxicar to poison
atóxico non-poisonous
atrabanco *n* hurry, hurrying
atracable *naut* easy to berth
atracadero *naut* landfall, landing-place,
berthing-place
atracador *m* armed bandit, robber
¹ **atracar** to hold up, rob; ~**se** to overeat
² **atracar** *naut* to berth, bring alongside
atracción *f* attraction; **parque de
atracciones** funfair, *US* carnival
atraco hold-up
atracón *m* gluttony, stuffing
atractivo *n* attraction, charm; *adj*
attractive, enchanting

atraer to attract, lure; charm

atragantarse to choke while eating; get something stuck in one's throat

atraíble attractable

atraicionar *see* **traicionar**

atraidorado treacherous; perfidious

atraillar to leash

atrancar to bar, block up; read hurriedly

atranco blockage, stoppage

atrapamoscas *m sing+pl bot* Venus flytrap

atrapar to catch, trap, ensnare, take in

atrás back, at the back, behind; in the rear; ¡~! get back!; **dejar** ~ to leave behind; **hacia** ~ backwards; **quedarse** ~ to get left behind

atrasado backward, behind the times; (of clocks) slow; in arrears

atrasar *vt* to slow down, put back, turn back, postpone; *vi* (of clocks) to be slow, lose; ~**se** to be late, take a long time; fall into arrears

atraso backwardness; delay; slowness (of clocks); ~**s** arrears

atravesado *fam* awkward; bloody-minded

atravesaño *see* **travesaño**

atravesar to cross, stretch across, go through; bet; *naut* lie to; ~**se** to interfere; cross the path of another

atrayente attractive

atreguarse to agree to a truce

atreverse to dare, venture

atrevido daring, audacious; insolent

atrevimiento daring, audacity, impudence

atribución *f* conferring; power; attribute

atribuible attributable

atribuir to attribute, ascribe; put down to

atribulación *f* tribulation, affliction

atribular to afflict, grieve

atributivo attributive

atributo attribute

atrición *f* attrition

atril *m* lectern

atrincheramiento entrenchment

atrincherar to entrench; defend with trenches

atrio porch, portico

atrocidad *f* atrocity; *fam* enormous amount

atrofia atrophy

atrofiar to atrophy; ~**se** to become atrophied

atrófico atrophic

atrojar *agri* to garner

atrompetado trumpet-shaped

atronador thundering

atronamiento thundering; deafening noise

atronar to deafen; make a din; stun; ~**se** to be affected by thunder

atropellado hasty, hurried

atropellador *n m* trampler, violator; *adj* trampling, violating

atropellamiento trampling, precipitation

atropellar to trample down; knock down; run over; abuse; misuse; violate; ~**se** to rush; act hastily

atropello upset; abuse; outrage; accident

atroz atrocious; tremendous, terrible

atruhanado scurrilous

atuendo pomp, show; get-up, dress

atufar to vex, annoy; irritate; stink, pong; ~**se** to be affected by heat/fumes; turn sour

atufo vexation, annoyance; fume

atún *m* tunny, tuna

atunara tunny fishing-ground

atunero tunny fisherman

aturdidor *adj* bewildering

aturdimiento bewilderment, fluster

aturdir to fluster, bewilder, confuse; ~**se** to become confused, dazed

aturrullar to confuse, perplex, bewilder

atusar to trim; smooth

auca goose

audacia audaciousness, boldness

audición *f* audition, hearing

audiencia audience; hearing; *leg* court; reception; **dar** ~ to hold audience

audífono hearing aid

audiofrecuencia audiofrequency

audiómetro audiometer

auditivo *n* telephone earpiece; *adj* auditive, auditory

auditor *m* judge, auditor; ~ **de guerra/de marina** military/naval legal adviser

auditoría office of auditor

auditorio *n* audience; auditorium; *comm* audit; *adj* auditory

auge *m* peak; *comm* boom

auguración *see* **augurio**
augurar to prophesy, foretell
augurio augury
augusto august, magnificent
aula classroom; lecture room
aulabús *m* school bus (belonging to a school)
aulaga *bot* gorse
aulagar *m* gorse-heath
aullador, aullante howling
aullar to howl
aumentable augmentable
aumentación *f* increase; *rhet* climax
aumentador augmenting
aumentar to increase, augment; magnify; grow
aumentativo augmentative
aumento increase, growth; rise, *US* raise; power of magnification; **en ~** on the increase
aun even, as yet; **~ así** even so; **~ cuando** even though
aún yet, still
aunar to unite, join; merge
aunque though, although
¡aúpa! up with you!, ups-a-daisy!; **de ~** super, fabulous, fantastic
aupar to help up; praise, encourage
aura *poet* gentle breeze, zephyr; favour, applause
áureo golden, gold
auréola, aureola glory; halo
aureolar to decorate with a halo; give a halo to
aurícula *anat* auricle; *bot* leaf-life
auricular *n* telephone ear-piece; *adj* auricular
aurífero, auriguero gold-bearing
aurora dawn, daybreak; **~ boreal** aurora borealis, northern lights
auscultación *f med* auscultation
auscultar *med* to auscultate; sound; listen (with stethoscope)
ausencia absence
ausentarse to be absent; depart
ausente absent, absent-minded
ausentismo absenteeism
auspicio auspice
austeridad *f* austerity
austero austere, severe
australiano Australian
austriaco Austrian
austro south wind
austrohúngaro Austro-Hungarian

autarcía, autarquía autarchy
auténtica original text; legal copy
autenticación *f* authentication
autenticar to authenticate
autenticidad *f* authenticity
auténtico *adj* authentic, genuine; *leg* attested
autillo *orni* barn-owl
autista autistic
¹ **auto** act; *leg* decree; sentence; warrant, writ; edict; **~s** *leg* pleadings; **~ sacramental** mystery play, allegorical religious play
² **auto** *fam* car
autoanálisis *m sing + pl* self-analysis
autobiografía autobiography
autobiográfico autobiographical
autobiógrafo autobiographer
autobomba autopump
autobombo self-praise; self-glorification; blowing one's own trumpet
autobote *m* motorboat
autobús *m* bus; **~ espacial** *fam* space shuttle; **~ de dos pisos** double-decker bus
autocamión *m* motor-lorry, motor-truck
autocar *m* motor-coach
autocarril *m* railcar
autocasa caravan, trailer
autoconciencia self-consciousness
autocopiar to duplicate
autocopista *m* duplicator; duplicating machine
autocracia autocracy
autócrata *m + f* autocrat
autocrático autocratic
autocrítica self-criticism
autóctono aboriginal
autodefensa self-defence
autodefinido self-styled
autodeterminación *f* self-determination
autodidacto *n* self-educated person; *adj* self-educated
autodidaxia facility for self-education
autodirigido self-guided
autodominio self-control
autódromo car-racing track
autoencendido self-ignition
auto-escuela driving school
autofecundación *f* self-fertilization
autofecundativo self-fertilizing
autogénesis *f sing + pl* autogeny
autógeno oxy-acetylene welded
autogobierno self-government

autografía facsimile reproduction
autografiar to autograph; duplicate
autográfico *adj* autographical; facsimile
autógrafo *n+adj* autograph
autohipnosis *f sing+pl* self-hypnotism
autoinducción *m elect* self-induction
autointoxicación *f path* autotoxaemia
automación *m* automation
autómata *m* automaton, robot; *fam* zombie
automático automatic
automatismo automatism
automatización *f* automation
automatizar to automate
automodelismo model car racing/making
automodelista *n m+f* model car enthusiast; *adj* pertaining to model cars
automotor *n m* autorail, railbus; *adj* self-propelling
automotriz *adj* self-propelling, self-moving
automóvil *n m* (motor-)car, *US* automobile; *adj* self-moving
automovilismo motoring
automovilista *n m+f* motorist, car-driver; *adj* driving
autonomía autonomy, home-rule; *aer+ orni* range
autonómico autonomous
autonomista *n m+f+adj* autonomist
autónomo autonomous, free
autopista motorway, *US* turnpike
autopropulsado self-propelled
autopropulsión *f* self-propulsion
autoprotección *f* self-defence, self-preservation
autoprotegerse to defend o.s.
autopsia autopsy, post-mortem
autor *m* author, writer; composer; *theat* manager; *leg* plaintiff; perpetrator of a crime
autorcillo third-rate author
autoridad *f* authority; reliable quotation; **sala de ~es** V.I.P. lounge
autoritarismo authoritarianism
autoritativo authoritative
autorizable authorizable
autorización *f* authorization
autorizado authoritative
autorizador *n m* authorizor; *adj* authorizing
autorizamiento *see* **autorización**
autorizar to authorize

autorretrato self-portrait
autorruta clearway, motor-road
autoservicio self-service shop, filling station *etc*; cash-and-carry
autostop *m* hitch-hiking; **hacer ~** to hitch-hike
autostopismo hitch-hiking
autostopista *m+f* hitch-hiker
autosugestión *f* autosuggestion
autosugestionarse to suggest to o.s.
autotécnica motor-engineering
autotipia *phot* autotype
autovía railcar
auxiliador *n m* helper, rescuer; *adj* helping, rescuing
¹ **auxiliar** *n+adj m* auxiliary
² **auxiliar** to help; attend s.o. who is dying
auxilio *m* aid, help; **~ en carretera** *mot* rescue service; **~ social** social work; **primeros ~s** first aid
aval *m* guarantee, surety; counter-signature
avalancha avalanche; flood
avalar to guarantee, endorse
avalentado arrogant, bragging
avalo slight movement, earthquake
avalorar to estimate, value, evaluate
avaluación *f* valuation, appraisement
avaluar to value, appraise, assess
avallar to fence in
avance *m* advance; *comm* statement, balance-sheet; advance payment; *cin+TV* trailer
avanecerse (of fruit) to become stale
avanzado *n* outpost, reconnoitring force; *adj* advanced, progressive, liberal
avanzar to advance; increase; come/go forward
avanzo *comm* tender, estimate; balance
avaricia avarice, greed
avaricioso *n* miser; *adj* avaricious, miserly
avaro *n* miser, tightwad; *adj* avaricious, greedy, miserly
avasallador *n m* enslaver; *adj* enslaving
avasallamiento enslavement, subjection
avasallar to enslave, subject
avatares *mpl* vicissitudes
ave *f* bird, fowl; **~ de corral** barnyard fowl; **~ de paso** bird of passage
avecinar to bring near; domicile; **~se** to approach, take up residence
avecindarse to take up residence; settle

down

avechucho miserable bird; *fam* strange fellow; ragamuffin

avejentar to age; **~se** to start to look old

avefría *orni* plover

avellana hazelnut, filbert

avellanador *n carp* countersink bit

[1] **avellanar** *m* hazel plantation

[2] **avellanar** *carp* to countersink

avellanero *bot* hazel-tree; dealer in hazel nuts

avellano *bot* hazel-tree

avemaría Ave Maria; rosary bead; **al ~** at nightfall; **en un ~** in a flash

avena *bot* oats; **sopa de ~** oatmeal gruel, porridge

avenal oatfield

avenar to drain

avenencia agreement

avenible adaptable

avenida avenue; flood

avenidor *n m* mediator, pacifier; *adj* mediating, pacifying

avenir to reconcile; **~se** to reach an agreement

aventajar to do better; surpass

aventamiento fanning, winnowing

aventar to fan, winnow; **~se** *fam* to swell (in the wind)

aventura adventure

aventurar to venture; **~se** to venture to

aventurero *n m* adventurer; *adj* adventurous

avergonzar to shame; **~se** to feel ashamed

avería breakdown; damage

averiar to damage; **~se** to break down

averiguación *f* investigation, inquiry

averiguador *n m* searcher, inquirer; *adj* investigating

averiguar to inquire into, verify

averío aviary; collection of birds

aversión *f* aversion

avestruz *m* ostrich

avetado veined; (of bacon) streaky

avetoro *orni* bittern

avezar to get used to

aviación *f* aviation; air force

aviador *m* aviator

[1] **aviar** to get ready to go; equip; *naut* caulk; **estar aviado** to be up the creek/ a gum-tree; **aviárselas** to get by

[2] **aviar** pertaining to birds

aviciar *agri* to encourage growth;

manure, feed

avícola pertaining to poultry-farming

avicultor *n m* poultry-farmer

avicultura poultry farming

avidez *f* greed, covetousness

ávido greedy, covetous

aviejarse to grow old

avieso twisted

avigorar to invigorate

avilantez *f* boldness, forwardness

avilés *n + adj* native of Avila

avillanar to debase

avinagrado vinegary, sour; peevish, bad-tempered

avinagrar to sour

Aviñón Avignon

[1] **avío** preparation; rations; equipment, tackle

[2] **avío** *sl* boy-friend, fiancé

avión *m aer* aeroplane; hop-scotch; *orni* martin; **~ a turbohélice** turbo-prop plane; **~ de reacción** jet-plane; **~ común** house-martin; **~ zapeador** sand-martin; **hacer el ~** *sl* to play a dirty trick; **por avion** by air mail

avioneta light aircraft; trainer plane

avisado level-headed; **mal ~** rash

avisador *n m* adviser, informer; *adj* advising, informing

avisar to inform; advise; warn

aviso notice, advice, warning, care; **estar sobre ~** to be on one's guard

avispa wasp

avispado smart, quick

avispar to stir up, spur on; **~se** to become alert

avispero wasp's nest

avispón *m* hornet

avistar to glimpse; **~se** to have an interview

avituallamiento victualling

avituallar to victual

avivador *m carp* rabbet-plane; *adj* enlivening

avivamiento *n* quickness, revival

avivar to quicken, enliven, brighten, inflame; revive, heighten (colours); **~ el fuego** to stoke the fire; *carp* rabbet

avizor *n m* spy; **~es** *sl* eyes; *adj* watchful

avizorador *n m* spy, watcher; *adj* watching

avizorar to spy on

avoceta *orni* avocet

avolcanado volcanic

avutarda buzzard

axila armpit
axioma *m* axiom
axiomático axiomatic
ay *m* sigh, moan; ¡~! alas!; ¡~ **de mí!** woe is me!
aya nanny, nurse-maid
ayear to bewail
ayer yesterday; formerly
ayuda help, aid; comfort; *med* enema; ~ **de cámara** valet; ~ **de parroquia** chapel-of-ease
ayudador *n m* assistant; *adj* helping
ayudanta female assistant
ayudante *n m* assistant; assistant lecturer; *mil* adjutant
ayudar to help, assist; ~ **a misa** to serve at Mass
ayunar to fast
ayuno fast, abstinence
ayuntamiento town council; town hall; corporation; municipal government
ayustar *naut* to splice
ayuste *m naut* splice
azabache *m* jet
azada *agri* spade
azadilla *gard* hoe
azadón *m* mattock
azafata lady-in-waiting; *aer* air hostess, stewardess; *TV* panel game hostess
azafrán *m cul* saffron; *bot* crocus
azafranado saffron-coloured
azafranal saffron/crocus plantation
azafranar to dye with saffron
azafranero saffron grower/dealer
azahar *m* flower of orange, lemon or citron; orange blossom
azar *m* chance, hazard; **al** ~ at random
azararse to get flustered
azaroso chequered; risky; dangerous
ázimo unleavened
ázoe *m chem* nitrogen
azófar *m* brass
¹ **azogue** *m* quicksilver
² **azogue** *m* market-place

azolar *carp* to adze
azor *m orni* goshawk
azorar to fluster
azotador *n m* whipper; *adj* whipping
azotaina *n* whipping, beating
azotamiento whipping
azotar to whip, beat; punish
azote *m* whip; spank; affliction
azotea flat roof; *sl* head
azozobrar to worry; fluster
azteca *n+adj* Aztec; Mexican
azúcar *m+f* sugar; ~ **glas de lustre** icing-sugar; ~ **de pilón** loaf-sugar; ~ **en terrón** lump-sugar; ~ **en polvo** granulated sugar; ~ **moreno** brown sugar; ~ **extrafino** caster sugar
azucarado sugary; *pej* smarmy; ~ **padre** sugar-daddy
azucarar to sugar, sweeten
azucarero *n* sugar-basin; *adj* pertaining to sugar
azucarillo candy-floss
azucena *bot* white lily
azud *m* dam; waterwheel
azuela adze
azuframiento sulphuration
azufrar to sulphurate
azufre *m* sulphur
azufroso sulphurous
azul blue; ~ **celeste** sky blue; ~ **de Prusia** Prussian blue; ~ **marino** navy blue; ~ **turquí** indigo
azulado bluish
azular to dye/colour blue
azulejar to tile
azulejería tile-works; tiling
azulejero tiler
¹ **azulejo** glazed tile
² **azulejo** *bot* cornflower; *orni* bee-eater
azulgrana blue-and-red; pertaining to Barcelona Football Club
azur *m* azure
azuzar to incite; egg on
azuzón *m* instigator

B

b *f* letter b

baba saliva; drivel; **caérsele a uno la** ~ to be delighted, be foolish

babaza slime

babear to slaver, dribble

babel *m* place of great confusion, bedlam

babeo *n* slavering, dribbling; drivelling

babero bib

babia: estar en ~ to be in a day-dream/in cloud-cuckoo-land

babieca *m*+*f* ignorant fellow; *adj* silly

babilónico Babylonian

bable *m* Asturian dialect

babor *m naut* port; **a** ~ **todo** hard a-port

babosa *zool* slug

baboso *adj* slavering, dribbling; drivelling; sloppy; slimy; *sl* lustful

babucha slipper

baca top of bus/coach; *mot* roof-rack

bacalada *sl* bribe; dried cod

bacalao codfish

bacanales *fpl* Bacchanalia

bacanal *adj* Bacchanalian

bacará *m* baccarat

bacelar *m* arbour *usu* with vines

bacía washbowl, shaving dish

bacilo bacillus

bacillar *m* newly planted vineyard

bacinero *eccles* man who passes round a collecting-box

bacineta *eccles* poor-box

bacinete *m* pelvis

bacteria bacterium

bacteriano, bactérico bacterial

bactericida bactericidal

bacteriología bacteriology

bacteriólogo bacteriologist

báculo support staff; *eccles* crozier

bache *m* pot-hole, rut; *fig* gulf

bachiller (degree) bachelor

bachillerato baccalaureate; bachelor degree

bachillería prattle

badajo idle chatter; bell clapper

badán *m anat* trunk

badana dressed sheepskin

badén *m* gully made by rainwater; rainwater conduit

badil *m*, **badila** fire-shovel

badomía nonsense

badulaque *m* untrustworthy person

bagaje *m mil* baggage; pack animal

bagajero *mil* pack-animal driver, muleteer

bagatela trifle

bagazo pulp; husk

bahía bay; harbour

bailable *mus* for dancing; **té** *m* ~ **thé dansant**

bailadero public dance-hall

bailador *m* dancer

bailaor *m* flamenco dancer

bailar to dance

bailarín *m* dancer

¹ **baile** *m* dance, ball; ~ **clásico** ballet; ~ **de disfraces/trajes** fancy-dress dance; ~ **de figuras** square-dance; ~ **de máscaras** masquerade; ~ **de San Vito** St Vitus's dance; ~ **serio** formal dance

² **baile** *m* sheriff, magistrate

bailotear to dance badly

baileteo bad dancing

baja *mil* casualty; *comm* fall in price; job vacancy; **dar de** ~ to drop from a list/membership of a club *etc*, discharge (from hospital)

bajada descent; slope; ~ **de aguas** downspout

bajamar *f* low tide

bajar *vi* to descend, come down, fall; lessen; ~ **de** to be less than; *vt* to lower, reduce; let down; humble; ~**se** to bend, crouch; grovel; alight, get out (of a vehicle); dismount

bajel *m naut* vessel

bajelero *naut* master; owner

bajero *adj* lower; **manta bajera** under-blanket

bajete *m pej* short fellow; *mus* counterpoint exercise

bajeza meanness, lowliness; contemptible act

bají *m sl* temper, humour

bajial *m* marsh

bajío sandbank, mudbank

bajista *m+f comm* bear; *mus* bassoon player

bajo *n* ground floor; sandbank, mud bank; turn-up (of trousers); *mus* bass; ~s hooves; *adj* low, short; shallow; humble; despicable; soft (of voice); subdued (of colours); common, vulgar; ~ **relieve** bas-relief; ~s **fondos** lowest districts; **por lo** ~ on the sly; *adv* underneath; *prep* under; ~ **cuerda/mano** in secret

bajón *m* bassoon; bassoon player; fall, drop

bajoncillo treble bassoon

bajonista *m+f* bassoon player

bala bullet; shot; ball; bale; ~ **de cadena** chain-shot; ~ **fría** spent bullet; ~ **perdida** stray bullet; ~ **rasa** cannon-ball; **como una** ~ like a shot

balada ballad

baladí trivial

balador *adj* bleating

baladrar to shout

baladrero shouter

baladro outcry

baladrón *m* braggart; bully

baladronear to brag; bully

balance *m* oscillation, swinging, rocking; hesitancy; *comm* balance; balance sheet; *aer* rolling; *SA* rocking-chair

balancear *vt* to balance, swing, rock; *vi* to swing, roll; hesitate

balanceo *n* rocking, swinging, swaying, wobbling

balancín *m* balance/oscillating beam; tightrope walker's pole

balandra *naut* sloop

balandrán *m* cassock

balandro fishing-boat

balanza scales, balance; tightrope walker's pole; judgement; ~ **de pagos/comercio** balance of payments/trade; **en** ~ at stake; **ponerle a uno en** ~ to make s.o. think again

balar to bleat

balata ballad

balate *m* border/parapet (of a trench)

balaustrada balustrade

balaustrado balustrade

balay *m* wicker basket

balazo shot, round; bullet wound

balbucear to stammer; babble

balbucencia *n* stammering

balbuceo babble

balcánico Balkan

balcón *m* balcony

baldadura, baldamiento physical handicap

baldaquín *m* canopy

baldar to cripple; obstruct; (at cards) trump

¹ **balde** *m* pail

² **balde** *m* trifle; **de** ~ free, gratis; without reward; **en** ~ in vain

baldear *naut* to swab the deck

baldíamente in vain

baldío *n* common land; *adj* uncultivated; common (of land); vain, lazy

baldón *m* insult

baldonar to insult

baldosa floor tile

baldosado tiled

baldosía small floor tile

balduque *m* red tape for tying documents

¹ **balear** to shoot

² **balear** *n* inhabitant of the Balearic Islands; Balearic language; *adj* Balearic; **islas Baleares** Balearic Islands

baleo round mat

balí *sl* five-peseta coin

balido *n* bleating

balín *m* pellet; **balines** buckshot

balística ballistics

balístico ballistic

baliza buoy

balneario *n* spa; *adj* medicinal, spa

balompié *m* football, soccer

balón *m* football; ball; balloon

baloncesto basketball

balonmano handball

balonvolea volleyball

balota ballot

balotaje *m* balloting

balotar to ballot

¹ **balsa** pond; *fig* ~ **de aceite** quiet

² **balsa** raft

balsadera, balsadero ferry crossing

balsámico balmy

balsamita *bot* tansy

bálsamo balsam, palm

balsar *m* marshy ground covered with undergrowth

balsear to ferry/navigate on a raft
balsero ferryman
balso balsa-wood
báltico Baltic
baluarte *m* bastion
balumbo bulky article
ballena whale; whalebone; train oil; *sl* very fat person
ballesta crossbow; spring (of a vehicle)
ballestada shot from a crossbow
ballestear to shoot with a crossbow
ballestería archery
ballestrinque *m* clove hitch
bambalina *theat* fly
bambarria fluke; lucky stroke at billiards
bambolear to sway, swing
bamboleo *n* swaying, swinging
bambolla *n* boast, humbug
bambú *m* bamboo
banana, banano banana
bananero *n* banana tree; banana boat; *adj* banana
banas *fpl Mex* banns (of marriage)
banasta large basket
banastero basket-maker
banasto large round basket
banca bench; *comm* banking, banks (in general)
bancada bench
bancario *n* bank employee; *adj* banking, financial
bancarrota bankruptcy; **hacer** ~ *comm* to fail; to go bankrupt
banco bench; form; pew; *mech* bed; *leg* dock; *carp* planing bench; school, shoal; *comm* bank (building); ~ **de ahorros** savings bank; ~ **de emisión** bank of issue; ~ **de hielo** iceberg; ~ **de nieve** snowdrift
banda sash, ribbon, band, strip; gang; *mus* band; *orni* covey, flock; border, edge; *naut* side (of ship); cushion (of billiard table); ~ **sonora** *cin* soundtrack
bandada *orni* covey, flock, flight
bandazo *naut* violent roll
bandeado striped
bandearse to shift for oneself; to move to and fro
bandeja tray; **ponérselo en** ~ **a ...** *fig* to hand it to ... on a plate
bandera flag, colour(s); infantry; ~ **de paz** flag of truce; ~ **de popa** ensign; ~

de proa jack; **a/con** ~ **desplegada** with flying colours, in broad daylight; **chica** ~ smashing girl; **de** ~ *sl* terrific, stupendous
bandereta small flag; ~**s** camp colours
bandería faction
banderilla (bullfighting) barbed dart
banderillear to stick **banderillas** in a bull's back
banderillero (bullfighting) **banderilla** man
banderín *m* stationmaster's flag; recruiting office; pennant
banderizar to band together
banderizo *adj* partisan
banderola streamer; pennant; signalling flag
bandidaje *m* banditry; gang of bandits
bandido bandit; outlaw; fugitive
¹ **bando** proclamation
² **bando** faction, group
bandola mandolin(e)
bandolera bandoleer; shoulder-belt; handbag with shoulder strap
bandolerismo banditry
bandolero highwayman, outlaw
bandullo *sl* belly
bandurria bandore, twelve-stringed guitar
banjo banjo
banquero *comm* (+ *gambling*) banker
banqueta footstool
banquete *m* banquet
banquetear to banquet
banquillo *leg* prisoner's seat; dock; gallows; bench
bañadera bathtub; *SA* open bus/motor-coach
bañadero bathing-place
bañado type of chamberpot
bañador *m* swimsuit
bañar to bathe, wash; coat; ~**se** to take/have a bath, to swim
bañera bathtub
bañero bath-house keeper/owner
bañil *m zool* water-hole
bañista *m+f* bather
baño bath, bathtub; bathing-place; bathroom; coating (of chocolate *etc*); ~ **(de) María** *cul* bain-marie; ~ **de vapor** vapour bath; ~ **revelador** *phot* developing bath
baptistería, bautistería baptistery
baquelita *tr* bakelite

58

baquetear to vex

baquiano n guide; adj expert

baraja pack (of cards), US deck

barajadura n shuffling

barajar to shuffle; entangle; cheat out of

baranda railing, banister; cushion (of billiard table)

barandada m balustrade

barandal m, **barandilla** railing, banister

barata n barter; bargain

barateador m barterer

baratear comm to undercut (prices)

baratería fraud

baratero cheapjack; haggler

baratijas fpl trinkets

baratillero peddler; second-hand dealer

baratillo second-hand shop; bargain counter

barato n reduction sale; gift from a successful gambler; adj cheap; **dar de ~** to concede for the sake of argument; **de ~** gratis

baratura cheapness

barba chin; beard; theat actor who plays old man's parts; **~s** head of a comet; bot root structure; orni vanes of a feather; **~ a ~** face to face; **~ cerrada** thick beard; **~ de ballena** whalebone; **en sus ~s** to his face; **por ~** per head; **tener pocas ~s** to be a novice

barbacana mil barbican; churchyard wall

barbacoa barbecue

barbacoar to barbecue, have a barbecue

baranda sl boss, guvnor

barbar to grow a beard; raise bees; hort +agri rot

barbárico barbarous, barbaric

barbaridad f barbarity, cruelty; impertinence; excess; wild statement; piece of nonsense; ¡qué ~! how dreadful!

barbarie f lack of culture; cruelty

barbarismo barbarism

barbarizarse to make exaggerated claims

bárbaro n barbarian; adj barbarous; rude; sl stupendous

barbechar to fallow; plough for seeding

barbecho fallow

barbechera fallowing season; ploughing

barbería barber's shop

barbero barber

barbiblanco n greybeard; adj grey-bearded, white-bearded

barbicano grey-bearded

barbiespeso thick-bearded

barbihecho freshly shaven

barbilampiño beardless

barbilindo dandy

barbilla chin; carp rabbet

barbinegro black-bearded

barbiponiente starting to grow a beard

barbirrubio blond-bearded

barbitúrico barbiturate

barbo barbel

barboquejo chin-strap

barbotar to mutter

barbudo adj long-bearded

barbulla loud prattling

barbullar to talk loudly and fast

barbullón m loud and fast talker

barca boat, barge; **~ de pasaje** ferry boat; **~ de pesca** fishing boat

Barça: el ~ fam Barcelona Football Club

barcada boatload

barcaje m ferriage

barcal m wooden vessel

barcarola barcarole

barcaza barge, lighter

barcelonés m inhabitant of Barcelona; adj of Barcelona

barcelonista m+f supporter of Barcelona Football Club

barcia chaff (of grain)

barcino (of cattle) brown/red and white

barco boat, barge, ship

barchilón m male nurse

barda thorny barrier

bardoma filth, mire

baré m sl five-peseta coin

bario barium

barítono baritone

barjuleta haversack; toolbag

barloar naut to grapple (before boarding)

barloventear naut to ply to windward

barlovento windward

Barna abbr Barcelona

barniz m varnish

barnizador n m varnisher; adj varnishing

barnizar to varnish

barógrafo barograph

barometría barometry

barométrico barometric

barómetro barometer
barometrógrafo barometrograph
barón *m* baron; *pol* party boss
baronesa baroness
baronía baronetcy
baroscopio baroscope
barquear to go in a boat
barquero boatman
barqueta punnet
barquilla wherry; basket (of a balloon)
barquillero wafer-seller
barquillo rolled wafer
barquín *m*, **barquinera** large bellows
barra beam, bar, rod; stripe; cart shaft; loaf; railing (in court-room); *theat* claque; *sp* group of fans; gang (*esp* of youths)
barrabasada mischievous act
barraca cottage, hut
barranco, **barranca** gorge, ravine; dry river bed
barrancoso rough
¹ **barrar** to smear
² **barrar** to bar, barricade
barrear to barricade; cancel, delete
barredera street-sweeping machine
barreduras *fpl* sweepings
barrena drill, gimlet; *aer* spin; ~ **de guía** centrebit; ~ **de gusano** wimble; *min* borer, drill
barrenado *n* boring, drilling; *adj* bored, drilled
barrenar to bore, drill; foil; transgress; ~ **una mina** to blast/explode a mine; ~ **un buque** to scuttle a ship
barrendero street sweeper
barrenero *min* blaster
barreno drilled hole; *fig* vanity; **dar** ~ *naut* to sink
barrer to sweep
barrera barrier, fence; tollgate; ~ **sónica** sound barrier; ~ **térmica** heat barrier
barrero potter
barretear to bar
barretina Catalonian cap (worn by men)
barriada *see* **barrio**
barrial *m* mire
barricada barricade
barrido *n* sweeping; *adj* swept
barriga belly; pregnancy
barrigón, **barrigudo** big-bellied
barriguera cinch
barril, **barrel** *m* water-cask

barrilero cooper
barrio district, quarter, precinct; ~ **chino** slum district; ~ **lata** shanty town; **el otro** ~ the next world, eternity
barrizal *m* mire; claypit
¹ **barro** mud, clay; earthenware
² **barro** pimple on the face
barroco baroque
¹ **barroso** muddy
² **barroso** pimply
barrote *m* thick iron bar; rung; ~**s** scantlings
barrullo: a ~ galore
barruntamiento *n* conjecturing
barruntar to conjecture
barrunto conjecture
bartola: a la ~ carelessly
bártulos *mpl* household property; means (of doing something)
baruca artfulness; trickery
barullo tumult; disorder, mess
barzón *m* stroll
barzonear to stroll about
basa base; pedestal; basis
basada stocks (for shipbuilding)
basalto basalt
basar to base, found; support; ~**se en** to base one's ideas on
basca nausea; squeamishness; swoon; *sl* gang, band
bascosidad *f* repulsiveness; filth
báscula platform scales; weighbridge
base *f* base; ~ **escala** *mil* staging post; **a** ~ **de** by
básico basic
basílica church
basilisco basilisk
basta coarse sewing
¡basta! enough!, that will do!
bastaje *m* carrier, porter
bastante enough; ~ **frío** fairly/pretty cold
bastar to be enough; ~**se** to be self-sufficient
bastarda *mech* bastard file
bastardear *vt* to bastardize; *vi* degenerate
bastardelo notebook; blotter
bastardo *n* bastard; *adj* degenerate
baste *f sl* finger
bastear (dressmaking) to baste
bastidor *m* frame; *arts* stretcher for canvas; *theat* wing; window-sash; **en-**

tre ~es *theat* behind the scenes
bastilla hem
bastimentar to victual
bastimento supply of victuals
bastión *m* bastion
¹ **basto** *n* pack-saddle; ace of clubs; ~s clubs
² **basto** *adj* coarse; rude
bastón *m* walking-stick; *mus* baton
bastonada, bastonazo blow with a stick
bastoncillo small stick; trimming lace; cotton-bud
bastonear to cane
bastonero walking-stick maker/seller
basura rubbish; refuse, garbage
basurero refuse/garbage collector; dustman; dunghill
bata dressing-gown; bath-robe; housecoat; doctor's white coat
batacazo bump (from a fall)
batalla battle; joust; inner struggle; fencing bout; ~ **campal** pitched battle
batallador *n m* fighter; *adj* fighting
batallar to fight; fence; struggle
batallón *m* battalion
batanero fuller
batata sweet potato
batatal *m* sweet-potato field
batayola *naut* rail
bate *m sp* bat
batear *sp* to bat
batel *m* small boat
batería *mil* battery; *mus* percussion instruments, drums; *cul* set of pans
batido *n cul* batter; milk shake; *adj* beaten; trodden; shot (of silk)
batidor *m cul* (+of game) beater
batidora food-mixer, whisk
batiente *m* door jamb; sill; *mus* piano damper; placc where waves break on the beach
batifondo row, tumult
batifulla, batihoja gold-beater
batir to beat, whisk; pound, hit; demolish; vanquish; reconnoitre, pound the beat; ~ **banderas** to salute with flags; ~ **el campo** to reconnoitre enemy terrain; ~ **las olas** to plough the waves; ~ **manos/palmas** to clap; ~ **moneda** to coin money; ~ **un record** to break a record; ~se to fight a duel; ~se **en retirada** to beat a retreat; **pista batida** *sp* hard court
batiscafo bathyscaphe

batisfera bathysphere
batista cambric
bato simpleton
batojar to knock fruit from a tree with a stick
batómetro bathymeter
baturrillo medley, potpourri
batuta *mus* baton; **llevar la** ~ to manage, direct, be the boss
baúl *m* trunk, chest
bauprés *m* bowsprit
bautismal baptismal
bautismo baptism
bautista *m* baptizer; **El Bautista** John the Baptist
bautisterio baptistery
bautizar to baptize, christen; add water to wine
bautizo baptism, christening
bauxita bauxite
bávaro *n+adj* Bavarian
Baviera Bavaria
baya berry
bayeta baize; duster
bayo *n* bay horse; *adj* bay
bayoneta bayonet
bayonetazo bayonet thrust
baza (cards) trick; opportunity; **no meter** ~ to mind one's own business
bazar *m* bazaar; fair
bazo *anat* spleen
bazofia offal; waste meat
bazuca bazooka
bazucar to mix liquids by shaking
bazuqueo *n* mixing (of liquids)
¹ **be** *f* letter b; ~ **por** ~ in minute detail
² **be** *m* baa, bleat
beata over-pious woman; prude; *sl* one-peseta coin
heatería excess of piety/prudery/bigotry
beaterio institution for pious old women
beatificación *f* beatification
beatificar to beatify
beatitud *f* beatitude
beato *n* over-pious person; *adj* happy; blessèd; devout; bigoted; over-pious
beatón *m* bigot, hypocrite
bebé *m* baby
bebedero *n* drinking place, trough; water-hole; *adj* drinkable
bebedizo *n* potion; poisonous drink; love-filter
bebedor *m* tippler, boozer
beber *n m* drinking; *v* to drink, swallow;

toast; ~ **a la salud de uno** to drink to s.o.'s health; ~ **como una cuba** to drink like a fish; ~ **de**, ~ **en** to drink from; ~ **los pensamientos de uno** to anticipate s.o.'s thoughts

bebible drinkable; pleasant to drink

bebida *n* drink, beverage; coffee/tea-break

bebido *adj* tipsy

beca scholarship; fellowship

becada *orni* woodcock

becario scholarship holder, fellow

becerra *bot* snapdragon

becerril bovine

becerro yearling calf; calfskin; church/town hall register; ~ **descarriado** dogie; *fam* stupid

becuadro *mus* natural

bedel *m* beadle

beduino *n+adj* Bedouin

befa jeer, taunt

befar to jeer, taunt

beibi *sl* girlfriend

béisbol *m* baseball

beisbolero *n* baseball player; *adj* baseball

beldad *f* beauty

belén *m* Christmas crib; *fig* confusion; **Belén** Bethlehem

beleño *bot* henbane

belfo *n zool* lip; *adj* having a thick lower lip

belga *n m+f+adj* Belgian

Bélgica Belgium

bélico warlike, bellicose

belicosidad *f* bellicosity

belicoso warlike, bellicose

beligerancia belligerency

bellacada den of rogues; knavish act

bellaco *n* rogue, villain; *adj* roguish, dishonest

bellaquear to swindle; (of horses) to buck

bellaquería roguishness; deceit

belleza beauty

bello beautiful; ~ **sexo** fair sex; **bellas artes** fine arts

bellota acorn

bellotear to feed on acorns

bellotera acorn season

bellotero oak-forest; acorn gatherer/seller

bembo thick-lipped

bemol *m mus* flat; **tener ~es** to be very difficult

bemolar *mus* to lower by one semitone

bencedrina benzedrine

bencina benzine

bendecidor *adj* blessing, blessed

bendecir to bless, consecrate

bendición *f* blessing, benediction; **bendiciones nupciales** wedding ceremony

bendito blessed, saintly; simple; foolish

bendícite *m* grace before meals

benedictino Benedictine

beneficencia charity; beneficence

beneficiado beneficiary; curate

beneficiador *m* benefactor; exploiter (of a mine *etc*)

beneficiar to benefit; exploit; cultivate; appoint to a sinecure; ~**se** to profit

beneficiario beneficiary

beneficio benefit; profit; *eccles* living; development, exploitation; *comm* profit, premium; ~ **bruto** gross profit; ~ **simple** sinecure

beneficioso beneficial; profitable

benéfico charitable; **obras benéficas** good works; **sociedad benéfica** charitable organization

Benemérita Civil Guard

benemérito meritorious, worthy; member of the Civil Guard

beneplácito approval, blessing, consent

benevolencia benevolence, kindness

benévolo benevolent, kind

bengala flare, luminous rocket

bengalí Bengali

benignidad *f* kindness

benigno kind, benign

benita Benedictine nun

benito Benedictine monk

benjamín *m* youngest son, baby of the family

benzol *m* benzol

beo *sl vulg* cunt

beodo *sl* drunk

berberecho *zool* cockle

berberí, berberisco, beréber Berber

berenjena eggplant, aubergine

bergante *m* impudent fellow; rogue

bergantín *m* brigantine

berilo beryl

berlinés *n* Berliner; *adj* of Berlin

bermejo bright red

bermejura ruddiness

bermellón *m* vermilion

bermudas *fpl* shorts
bernardina boast
berrear to cry like a calf; wail; howl
berrendo bi-coloured
berretín *m* caprice
berrido *n* bellowing
berrinche *m* temper; sulkiness; tantrum
berros *mpl* watercress
berrocal *m* craggy place
berza *n* cabbage; ~ **lombarda** savoy cabbage; ~s *adj sl* stupid, 'bananas'
besador *n* kisser; *adj* kissing
besamanos *m* hand-kissing (greeting)
besamel *m* white sauce, bechamel
besana *agri* first furrow
besar to kiss; touch
beso kiss; light collision
bestia beast; dunce; ill-mannered person; ~ **de carga** beast of burden
bestialidad *f* bestiality; *fig* stupidity
besucador fond of kissing
besucar to kiss frequently
besucón *m* inveterate kisser
besugo sea-bream; *fam* idiot
besuqueador *see* **besucador**
besuquear necking, snogging, excessive kissing
beta piece of string or cord
bético Andalusian
betún *m* bitumen, tar; shoe-blacking
bezo *med* proud flesh; thick lip
bezudo thick-lipped
biberón *m* feeding-bottle
Biblia Bible
bíblico biblical
bibliófilo book-lover
bibliografía bibliography
bibliográfico bibliographic
bibliómano bibliomaniac
biblioteca library
bibliotecario librarian
bicarbonato sódico bicarbonate of soda
bicéfalo two-headed
bici *f* bike
bicicleta bicycle
bicicletista *m + f* cyclist
bicoca trifle, bagatelle; fluke; bargain
bicolor, bicromático bi-coloured
bicúspide bicuspid
bichero boat-hook
bicho insect; grub, maggot, creepy-crawly; animal; **todo ~ viviente** every living creature
bidé *m* bidet

bidente *n sl* leg; *adj* two-pronged
biela connecting-rod
bielda pitchfork
¹ **bien** *m* good; benefit; righteousness; ~es possessions; ~es de fortuna worldly possessions; ~es dotales dowry; ~es forales leasehold estate; ~es inmuebles, ~es raíces real estate; **hombre de ~** upright man; **por ~ de** for the sake of
² **bien** *adv* well; all right; correct; happily; heartily, fully; quite; fairly; ~amado dearly beloved; ~andante prosperous; ~andanza prosperity; ~ (así) como just as; ~aventurado blessed, fortunate; *iron* simple; ~aventuranza bliss, well-being; beatitude; ~estar well-being; ~fortunado fortunate; ~hablado well-spoken; ~hadado lucky; ~ **hecho** well done; ~hechor do-gooder; ~intencionado well-meaning; ~mandado obedient; ~ **que** although; ~querer *n* esteem; *v* to think highly of, esteem; ~queriente *m* wellwisher; ~quisto esteemed, respected; ~venida *n* welcome; ~venido *adj* welcome, welcoming; ~vivir live in comfort; **ahora ~** now then; **de ~ en mejor** better and better; **hallar ~** to find satisfactory; **más ~** somewhat, rather; **no ~** just as; **o ~** or else; **por ~** willingly; **si ~** while, though; **y ~** now then; **¿y ~?** so what?; *interj* all right, O.K.
bienal biennial
bienio period of two years
bifásico *elect* two-phase
bife *m*, **biftek** *m* beef-steak; steak; ~ **de ternera** veal cutlet
bifurcación *f* bifurcation; branch railway line; fork(ing)
bifurcarse to fork; branch, divide into two
bigamia bigamy
bígamo *n* bigamist; *adj* bigamous
bigardear to live licentiously
bigardía jest
bigote *m* moustache
bigotudo having a large moustache
bigudí *m* hair-curler (pincer type)
bilbaíno *n* inhabitant of Bilbao; *adj* of/from Bilbao
bilingüe bilingual
bilingüismo bilingualism

bilioso bilious

bilis *f* bile

billa *n* (billiards) pocketing a ball 'in off' another

billar *m* billiards, pool

billarista *m*+*f* billiard player

billete *m* note, short letter; love letter; ticket; ~ **de banco** banknote; ~ **de ida y vuelta** return ticket; ~ **kilométrico** mileage ticket

billetera wallet

billón *m* billion (*Sp* million million, *SA* thousand million)

billonario billionaire

billonésimo billionth

bimensual bimonthly (twice a month)

bimestral bimonthly (every two months)

bimetálico, bimetalista bimetallic

bimotor twin-engined

binario binary

binóculo field-glasses, opera glasses

binomio binomial; ~ **de Newton** binomial theorem

binza thin membrane

biofísica biophysics

biografía biography

biográfico biographic

biógrafo biographer

biología biology

biológico biological

biólogo biologist

biombo folding screen

biopsia biopsy

bioquímica biochemistry

bioquímico *n* biochemist; *adj* biochemical

bióxido dioxide

bípedo *m* biped

biplano biplane

bipolar *elect* two-pole

birimbao jew's harp

birla bowling pin

birlador *m sl* thief

birlar *sl* to steal, pinch

birlocha paper kite

birlón *m* (bowling) jack pin

birmanés, birmano *n*+*adj* Burman

Birmania Burma

birreta biretta

birrete *m* cap

birria *fam* rubbish

bis twice; repeated

bisabuela great-grandmother

bisabuelo great-grandfather

bisagra hinge

bisanual *bot* biennial

bisbisar to mutter

bisbiseo muttering

bisbito *orni* meadow pipit

bisección *f* bisection

bisel *m* bevel; chamfer

biselar to bevel

bisiesto leap (year)

bisnieto *see* **biznieto**

bisonte *m* bison

bisoño *n* novice; *adj* inexperienced

bistec *m see* **bife**

bisturí *m surg* scalpel

bisulfato bisulphate

bisulfito bisulphite

bisulfuro bisulphide

bisutería trinkets; jeweller's (shop)

bitácora *naut* binnacle; **cuaderno de ~** *naut* log-book

bitoque *m* bung; plug

bitor *m orni* bittern

bituminizar to bituminize

bituminoso bituminous

bivalencia bivalency

bivalente bivalent

bivalvo bivalve

bizantino Byzantine

bizarrear to act courageously

bizarría bravery

bizarro brave, courageous

bizcar to squint

bizco cross-eyed

bizcocho sponge-cake

bizma poultice

biznieto great-grandson

bizquear to squint

blanca *sl* money; **sin ~** broke

blancanieves *f sing*+*pl sl* police patrol car; Snow White

blanco *n* white; target; goal; blank space; blank form; ~ **de España** blanco; ~ **de la uña** half-moon of the nail; ~ **de plomo** white lead; **dar en el ~** to hit the mark; **dejar en ~** to leave blank; **estar sin ~** to be broke; **quedarse en ~** to be disappointed; *adj* white

blancor *m* whiteness; fairness (of complexion)

blancote *n m* coward; *adj* cowardly

blancura whiteness

blancuzco whitish˜

blandeador *m* softener

blandear *vt* to soften; persuade, convince; *vi* to soften, weaken; ~**se** to change one's mind, give in

blandengue very kind; bland

blandir to brandish

blando soft; tender; bland; cowardly

blandón *m eccles* large candle

blandura *pol* soft line; softness

blanqueación *f* bleacher, whitener

blanqueadura *see* **blanqueo**

blanquear *vi* to whiten; *vt* to bleach, whiten; whitewash

blanquecimiento *n* blanching; *adj* whitish

blanqueo bleaching, whitening; whitewashing

blanquete *m* whitewash

blanquillo egg; supporter of Saragossa Football Club

blanquimiento bleaching solution

blanquizal *m* clay-pit

blasfemador, blasfemante *m* blasphemer

blasfemar to blaspheme

blasfematorio blasphemous

blasfemia blasphemy

blasfemo *n* blasphemer; *adj* blaspheming, blasphemous

blasón *m* armorial bearing; honour, glory

blasonador *m* boaster, braggart

blasonar to boast, brag; design a coat of arms

blasonería *n* boasting, bragging

bledo *bot* wild aramanth; **no me importa un ~** I don't care a fig

blenda *min* blende

blindado *n* armoured vehicle; ironclad; *adj* armoured

blindaje *m* armour; screening

blindar to armour(-plate)

bloc *m* note-pad, writing-pad

blocar (boxing) take the opponent's punches on the gloves

blondo blond, fair, flaxen

bloque *m* block

bloqueador *m* blockader

bloquear to blockade; to jam (phone lines *etc*); *comm* to treeze

bloqueo blockade

blusa blouse

boa *zool* boa-constrictor; boa (neckpiece)

boardilla *see* **buhardilla**

boato ostentation; pomp

bobada foolish behaviour

bobalicón *m* simpleton

bobear to talk/behave foolishly; fritter away

bobina bobbin; *elect* coil; ~ **de inducción** induction coil

bobo simpleton, fool, ninny; *orni* booby; **a lo ~** foolishly

boca mouth; entrance, opening; muzzle; bunghole; cutting edge (of tools); ~ **a ~** *m* kiss of life; ~ **abajo** prone, face down; ~ **arriba** supine, face up; ~**calle** *f* side street, turning; ~ **del estómago** pit of the stomach; ~ **del metro** underground/tube/subway entrance; ~ **de riego** fire hydrant; ~**manga** bottom of a sleeve; ~**mina** mine entrance, shaft; **a ~** by word of mouth; **a ~jarra** at point blank range; **a ~ llena** openly; **andar de ~ en ~** to be public knowledge; **como ~ de lobo** pitch dark; **no decir esta ~ es mía** to hold one's tongue

bocadillo sandwich; snack

bocado mouthful; small portion; **con el ~ en la boca** immediately after eating

bocal *m naut* narrows; *mus* mouthpiece

bocanada swig, slug; puff, drag (of smoke); ~ **de viento** gust of wind

bocata *see* **bocadillo**

bocaza large mouth; ~**s** *m sing+pl pej* bigmouth

boceto sketch, drawing

bocina trumpet; megaphone; fog-horn; *mot* horn; ear-trumpet

bocinar to blow a trumpet/bugle *etc*

bocinero trumpeter

bocio goitre

bocón big-mouthed

bocha bowl, ball; bag in ill-fitting garment

bochazo touch (of one bowl against another)

bochinche *m* disturbance of the peace

bochinchero rioter, disturber of the peace

bochorno sultry spell; scorching heat; blush; embarrassment

bochornoso sultry; embarrassing

boda wedding; ~ **de negros** noisy carousal; ~**s de Camacho** enormous banquet; ~**s de plata/oro** silver/golden wedding

bodega wine vault/cave/cellar; store-room; warehouse; grocer's shop; *naut* hold

bodegón *m* ale house; low-class restaurant; *arts* still life

bodegonear to go on a pub-crawl

bodegonero ale-house keeper

bodeguero butler; grocer

bodijo mésalliance; shotgun wedding

bodoque *m* pellet; dunce

bodoquera blow-pipe; pea-shooter

bodrio soup (from a charitable soup-kitchen); worthless work of art; badly cooked meal

bofe *m* lung; **echar los ~s** *sl* pant, gasp; slog away

bofetada, bofetón *m* slap (on the face)

bofia *m* policeman, copper; *f* cops, fuzz

[1] **boga** vogue

[2] **boga** *m+f* rower; *f* rowing stroke

bogador *m* rower, oarsman

bogar to row

bohardilla *see* **buhardilla**

bohemiano *n+adj* Bohemian (unconventional person)

bohemio *n+adj* Bohemian (of Bohemia); gypsy; bohemian (unconventional person)

boicot *m* boycott

boicoteador *m* boycotter

boicotear to boycott

boicoteo act of boycotting

boina beret

boj *m bot* box; boxwood

bojedal *m* plantation of box trees

bojiganga company of strolling players

bol *m* bowl (container)

bola ball, marble; game of bowls; **dar la ~** *sl* to obtain one's freedom; **dejar rodar la ~** to let things take their natural course; **salir en ~** to be released from prison

bolada (billiards) stroke

bolazo blow with a ball

bolchevique *n m + adj* Bolshevik

bolchevismo Bolshevism

bolchevista *m + f* Bolshevist

boleada shoe-polish

boleador *m* bootblack

bolear *vi* to play billiards; bowl; *vt* to cast, throw

boleo bowling; bowling green

bolera bowling/skittle alley

bolero bolero dancer

boleta draw ticket; money order; admission ticket; ballot; **~ de guardarropa** cloakroom ticket

boletería ticket office, booking office

boletero ticket agent

boletín *m* bulletin; price list; pay warrant

boleto draw ticket; football-pools coupon

boliche *m* (bowling) jack; cup-and-ball toy

bolichero owner of a small business

bólido shooting star; racing car

bolígrafo ball-point pen

bolívar *m* Venezuelan currency unit

boliviano *n+adj* Bolivian

[1] **bolo** ninepin; large pill; lacemaker's cushion; dunce; *sl* five-peseta coin

[2] **bolo** *sl* drunk

bolsa purse, pouch, bag; *anat* scrotum; *med* sac; *min* pocket; stock exchange; **~ de hielo** icepack; **~ de pastor** *bot* shepherd's purse; **~ de trabajo** job centre, employment office

bolsear to pucker, wrinkle

bolsera hair-net

bolsería handbag shop/factory

bolsero bag-maker/seller

bolsillo pocket; **rascarse el ~** to pay up, fork out; **tener a alguien en el ~** to have someone under one's thumb; **libro de ~** paperback

bolsín *m* minor stock exchange

bolsista *m+f* stockbroker

bolso handbag, bag

bolladura dent

bollar to emboss

bollera *sl* lesbian

bollería pastry cook's shop

bollero pastry cook

bollo breadroll; puff (in a dress); *metal* bruise; *med* swelling

bollón *m* button earring; *bot* bud; brass-headed nail

[1] **bomba** pump; fire engine; slide (of trombone); **~ alimenticia** feed pump; **~ al vacío** vacuum pump; **~ de estribo** stirrup pump; **~ marina** waterspout; **dar a la ~** to pump, work the pump

[2] **bomba** *n* bomb; shell; **~ de fragmentación** fragmentation bomb; **~ de hidrógeno** hydrogen bomb; **~ de mano** hand grenade; **~ de neutrones**

neutron bomb; ~ **de profundidad** depth charge; ~ **de tiempo** time bomb; ~ **fétida** stink bomb; *adj sl* extraordinary, stupendous

bombachos *mpl* loose trousers fastened at the ankle

bombarda *mus* bombardon

bombardear to bombard, bomb; ~ **en picado** to dive-bomb

bombardeo bombardment, bombing; ~ **de precisión** precision bombing; ~ **de saturación** saturation bombing; ~ **en picado** dive-bombing

bombardero bombardier; *aer* bomber, bombing-plane

bombástico bombastic

bombazo bomb explosion; bomb damage

bombear to pump; bombard

bombeo pumping

bombero fireman; pumper

bombilla *elect* light bulb

bombillo lamp chimney; small pump; *elect* light bulb

bombista *m+f* flatterer; newspaper writer of 'puffs'

bombo *n* bass drum; bass drum player; barge; **dar** ~ to praise effusively; write up; *adj* surprised, bewildered

bombón *m* filled chocolate; chocolate liqueur; choc-ice; *sl* attractive woman

bombona cylinder (*usu* for gas)

bombonera chocolate box

bonachón good-natured

bonaerense *adj* of or from Buenos Aires

bonancible calm; peaceful

bonanza prosperity; calm

bonazo good-natured

bondad *f* goodness; **tener la** ~ **de** please, kindly

bondadoso kind; big-hearted

bonetada raising the hat (in greeting)

bonete *m* bonnet; school cap

bonetería bonnet shop/factory

bonetero bonnet maker/seller

bonhomía bonhommie

boniato sweet potato; *sl* 1,000-peseta banknote

bonificación *f* bonus; discount

bonificar to credit; improve

¹ **bonito** striped tunny

² **bonito** pretty; nice; good

bono bond; certificate

boñiga cow dung, cowpat

boqueada *n* gasp; last breath

boquear to gasp; gape; utter; breathe one's last

boquera irrigation canal; opening; crack/sore at the corner of the mouth; *sl* prison officer

boquerón *m* kind of anchovy

boquiabierto open-mouthed, gaping

boquiancho wide-mouthed

boquiangosto narrow-mouthed

boquiconejuno hare-lipped

boquilla small mouth; *mus* mouthpiece; cigar/cigarette-holder; nozzle

boquirroto talkative

boquirrubio blabbing; simple-minded

boquiseco dry-mouthed

boquitorcido wry-mouthed

boquiverde given to risqué talk

borácico boracic

borbollar, borbollonear to gush out in bubbles

borborigmo rumbling of the bowels

borbotar to gush out; boil over

borbotón *m*: **hablar a borbotones** to talk impetuously

borceguí *m* laced boot

¹ **borda** gunwale; **fuera de** ~ outboard motor

² **borda** hut, cottage

bordada *n* going to and fro; **dar una** ~ *naut* to tack

bordado embroidery

bordador *m* embroiderer

bordadura embroidery

bordar to embroider

borde *m* border, edge, verge, ledge, brim, rim, side of a ship

bordo *naut* side of a ship; **a** ~ on board; **al** ~ alongside; **dar** ~s to tack; **de alto** ~ seagoing; *fig* important

bordón *m* pilgrim's staff; *mus* bass string; refrain; **bordones** outriggers

bordonear *vi* to test the ground with a stick; *vt* to beat

bordonería idle wandering

bordonero vagabond, tramp

bórico boric

borla tassel, tuft; tassel on (university) doctor's hood; **tomar la** ~ to take a doctorate

borneadizo pliant

bornear *vt* to bend, turn; *bui* hoist and put in place; *vi naut* to swing round at anchor; ~**se** to bulge

borneo *n* turning, twisting; swinging at anchor

borra flock

borracha leather wine-bottle

borrachear to get drunk frequently

borrachera, borrachería drunkenness; drinking bout, spree

borrachez *f* intoxication

borracho drunk

borrador *m* rough draft; eraser

borradura *n* erasing, striking out

borraj *m* borax

borraja *bot* borage

borrajear to scribble; doodle

borrajo hot embers

borrar *vt* erase, delete; obliterate; *vi* to grow dark

borrasca squall; storm; hazard

borrascoso squally, stormy

borrasquero *n* reveller; *adj* revelling

borrego lamb (up to one year old); simpleton

borrica female donkey; ignorant woman

borricada herd of donkeys; foolish speech or act

borrico donkey; *carp* saw-horse; ignorant man

borriqueño asinine

borriquero donkey owner/dealer

borro yearling lamb; dolt

borrón *m* blot, stain, blemish; rough draft

borronear to sketch, doodle, scribble

borroso blurred; faded; (of liquids) cloudy

boruca noise; uproar

boscaje *m* clump of trees; *arts* landscape

boscoso wooded

Bósforo Bosphorus

bosque *m* wood, forest; spinney

bosquejar to sketch, plan, outline; make a scale model of

bosquejo rough idea, sketch

bosquimano forest-dweller, bushman

bosta dung

bostezar to yawn

bostezo yawn

bota boot; leather wine-bottle; *naut* water-cask; ～ **de montar** riding-boot; **ponerse las ～s** to become rich, make a large profit; eat a lot

botado cheap

botador *m sp* pitcher; claw (for extracting nails); boat-hook

botalón *m* boom (of a crane)

botánica botany

botánico *n* botanist; *adj* botanical

botar *vt* to throw, pitch, cast; *naut* launch; squander; *vi* to bounce, rebound; ～**se** (of horses) to kick, caper

botaratada rash action

botarate *m* madcap, scatterbrain; spendthrift

¹ **bote** *m* thrust with a weapon; bound (of a horse); pitch-and-toss

² **bote** *m* can; jar

³ **bote** *m* boat; ～ **salvavidas** lifeboat

⁴ **bote** *m*: **de ～ en ～** chock-full

botella bottle; ～ **de Leiden** Leyden jar

botellería bottle factory

botellón *m* demijohn, large bottle

¹ **botero** maker of leather bottles

² **botero** boatman, ferryman

botica apothecary's shop; drugstore; medicines

boticario apothecary, chemist

botija earthenware jug

botijero maker/seller of water-jugs

botijo earthenware water-jar (with spout and handle)

¹ **botín** *m* baby's shoe; leggings; spat

² **botín** *m* booty, loot

botiquín *m* medicine chest/store, first-aid kit

botito man's gaiter

botivoleo *n* catching the ball on the rebound

boto wineskin

botón *m* button; *bot* bud; (fencing) tip of a foil; knob of door, window, radio *etc*; crankpin; dowel; **botones** bellboy, buttons

botonadura set of buttons

botonería button-shop

botonero maker/seller of buttons

botswanés Botswanian

bóveda vault; arch; cave; ～ **celeste** firmament; ～ **craneal** cranial cavity

bovedilla *bui* roof space

bovino bovine

boxeador *m* boxer

boxear to box

boxeo boxing

boya beacon; buoy; float

boyante buoyant; *naut* light, trim

boyar to float

boyera ox-stall

boyero oxherd

bozal *m* muzzle; harness bells; *adj* novice, greenhorn; stupid; untamed

bozo first downy growth of beard

braceaje *m* depth of water

bracear to swing the arms

braceo swinging of the arms

bracero labourer, hand; **de ~** arm-in-arm

bráctea *bot* bract

braga panties, knickers

bragazas *m sing+pl* henpecked husband

braguero *med* truss

bragueta fly (on trousers); **oír por la ~** to turn a deaf ear to

bramador *n m* roarer; *adj* roaring

bramar to roar, bellow; bluster

bramido (of animals and the elements) roar, howl

branquia *zool* gill

braña summer pasture

brasa red-hot coal; **estar en las ~s** to be on tenterhooks

brasero brazier; hearth

Brasil *m* Brazil

brasileño Brazilian

bravata bravado

braveador *m* bully

bravear to boast

bravera vent; chimney

braveza bravery; ferocity; (of elements) fury

bravío *n* fierceness (of a fighting bull); *adj* ferocious, untamed; unpolished

bravo brave; manly; angry; unpolished; (of terrain) rugged, rough; (of wine) excellent; *interj* bravo!

bravone *m* braggart

bravosidad *f* bravery

bravucón *m* boaster, braggart

bravura bravery

braza *sp* breaststroke; *naut* fathom

brazada armful

brazaje *m naut* depth

brazal *m* mourning-band (on sleeve)

brazalete *m* bracelet

brazo arm; *zool* foreleg; branch (of chandelier); *comm* wing/section of firm/factory; energy; **~ a ~** hand-to-hand; **~ de palanca** lever arm; **a ~** by hand; **con los ~s cruzados** with arms folded; **de ~s** arm-in-arm; **ser el ~ derecho de alguien** to be s.o.'s right-hand man; **~s** *fig* workers

brazuelo *zool* shoulder

brea pitch, tar

¹ **brear** to pitch, tar

² **brear** to vex; beat

brebaje *m* beverage, drink; grog

breca dace

brecha breach; **abrir ~** to make a breach; create an impression

brega fight, scrap; **andar a la ~** to toil; **dar ~** (of a task) to be laborious; **dar ~ a** to play a trick on

bren *m* bran

brenca *bot* maidenhair; sluice-post

breña, breñal *m* rough ground covered with brambles

breñoso craggy and brambled

bresca honeycomb

Bretaña Brittany; **Gran ~** Great Britain

bretón *m* Breton

breva early fig; good-quality cigar

breve *n f mus* breve; *adj* brief, short; **en ~** shortly

brevedad *f* brevity

brevete *m* memorandum

breviario breviary

brezal *m* heath, moorland

brezo heather

briba idleness

bribar to lead an idle life

bribón *m* vagrant; impostor; scoundrel

bribonada knavery; mischief

bribonear to loaf, loiter; lead a vagrant's life

bribonería life of a vagabond

bricho spangle

brida bridle; rein; curb; clamp

brigada brigade; gang of workmen; *mil approx* staff-sergeant

brigadista *m* member of the International Brigade

brígola battering-ram

brik *m* carton (*usu* for milk)

brillador, brillante brilliant, shining; glossy; excellent

brillar to shine, sparkle; **~ por su ausencia** to be conspicuous by his/her absence

brillo brightness, brilliance, lustre, magnificence; **en ~** *phot* glossy

brincador *n m* jumper; *adj* jumping

brincar *vi* to jump, leap; gambol; become excited; become angry; *vt* to omit; skip; throw a child up and down

brinco jump, leap; bounce; hop

brindar: ~ **por** to toast, drink s.o.'s health

brindis m toast

brío liveliness, vigour; courage

brioso lively, spirited, vigorous; courageous

brisa breeze

briscar to embroider with gold/silver thread

británica bot water dock

británico British

brizar to rock (a cradle)

brizna splinter, fragment; bot slip, sprig; shoot

briznoso full of fragments

brizo cradle

broca reel, bobbin; shoemaker's tack

brocado brocade

brocal m parapet (of a well)

brocha brush; loaded dice; **de** ~ **gorda** arts badly done

brochada brush stroke

brochadura hooks and eyes

broche m brooch; clasp; hasp; fastener

brocheta skewer

broma joke; practical joke; fun, merriment; **dar una** ~ to jest; **en** ~ in fun

bromar (of insects) to bore

bromear to joke; make fun

bromista m+f joker; adj full of fun

bromuro bromide

bronca wrangle, row

bronce m bronze; ~ **de cañón** gun metal; **edad** f **de** ~ Bronze Age

bronceado bronze-coloured; suntanned; **ligar** ~ sl to get a suntan

broncear to bronze

broncista m+f worker in bronze

bronco coarse, unpolished; harsh; peevish

bronconeumonía bronchopneumonia

broncoscopio bronchoscope

bronquedad f coarseness, roughness; peevishness

bronquial bronchial

bronquio bronchial tube

broquel m shield; protection; support

brota bud

brotadura n budding

brotar to bud; germinate; appear, issue

brote m outbreak; fragment, bit; bud

broza undergrowth; rubbish

brucero broom maker/seller

bruces: a/de ~ headlong

bruja witch; hag

brujear to practise witchcraft

brujería witchcraft, black magic

brujo wizard; sorcerer

brújula compass; magnetic needle

bruma mist, fog

brumal misty, foggy

brumazón m dense mist/fog

bruno dark, black

bruñido polish, lustre

bruñimiento polishing, burnishing

bruñir to polish, burnish

brusco rough; crude; curt

Bruselas Brussels

brusquedad f roughness; crudity; curtness

brutal brutal, brutish

brutalidad f brutality

brutalizar to brutalize

bruteza roughness; lack of polish

bruto n brute, beast; ignoramus; adj brutal, bestial; min crude; comm gross; unpolished

bruza horse-brush; scrubbing-brush

bruzar to brush

bu: hacer el ~ to scare, say 'Boo'

bucal oral

bucanero buccaneer

buceador m skin-diver; US scubadiver; deep-sea diver

bucear to skin-dive; US scubadive

bucéfalo Bucephalus; blockhead

buceo skin-diving; US scubadiving; deep-sea diving

bucero (of dogs) black-nosed

bucle m lock of hair; ringlet

¹ **buco** opening, gap

² **buco** zool buck

bucólico bucolic

buchada mouthful

buche m zool crop, maw, belly; (in clothing) pucker

buchete m cheek filled with air

buchón m orni pouter-pigeon

Buda m Buddha

budismo Buddhism

budista n m+f +adj Buddhist

buen good

buena sl right-hand side

buenamente easily, spontaneously

buenaventura good luck; fortune (told by a fortune-teller)

bueno adj good; nice; kind; suitable, fit;

pretty, fine; in good condition, admirable; desirable; easy; soft-hearted; **buena es ésa** that's a pretty kettle of fish; ~ **está lo** ~ enough is as good as a feast; ~**s días** good morning; **buenas noches** *adj* good night; **buenas tardes** good afternoon/evening; **de buenas a primeras** suddenly; *adv* well; all right; enough

buenparecer *m* good looks; **de** ~ good-looking

buey *m* ox, bullock; ~ **de caza** stalking ox; ~ **marino** sea-calf

bufalino *adj* buffalo

búfalo *n* buffalo

bufanda scarf, muffler

bufar to snort, puff

bufete *m* desk; lawyer's chambers; sideboard

bufido snort; bellow

bufo comic singer

¹**bufón** *n m* buffoon, clown; fool; *adj* comical

²**bufón** *m* street vendor

bufonada buffoonery

bufonearse to jest

bufonería buffoonery

bufonesco clownish

buga *m sl* motor-car

bugui *m* boogie-woogie

buhardilla, buharda garret; attic; skylight

buharro *orni* eagle owl

buhedera loophole

buhío hut, hovel

buho *orni* owl; unsociable person

buhonería pedlar's box

buhonero pedlar

buitre *m orni* vulture

buitrón *m* wickerwork fish trap; partridge net; snare

bujería knick-knack; bauble; toy

bujía candle; candlestick; candlepower; *mot* sparking-plug

bul *m vulg sl* arse

bula *eccles* bull

bulbo *bot* bulb

bulboso bulbous

buldocero bulldozer

bulevar *m* boulevard

búlgaro Bulgarian

bulo false rumour

bulto bulk; bulky article; bundle; pillowcase; *med* tumour, swelling; *mil*

sl recruit; **a** ~ wholesale; **de** ~ obvious; **escurrir/sacar el** ~ to sneak out/away

bululú *m* strolling player

bulla noise; bustle; fuss; mob; **armar una** ~ to create a din

bullaje *m* noisy crowd

bullanga tumult

bullanguero rioter; mobster

bullar to mark with a seal

bullebulle *m* busybody; tattler

bullicio bustle; noise; uproar; sedition

bullicioso merry; lively; (of the sea) rough

bullir to boil; bustle; hustle

bumerán *m* boomerang

buniato *see* **boniato**

bunker *m pol pej* most reactionary sector

bunkeriano *pol* extreme right-winger; diehard Francoite

buñolería bun shop

buñolero bun maker/seller

buñuelo bun; fritter; failure, flop

buque *m* ship; shipload; hull; ~ **de guerra** warship; ~ **de vapor** steamer; ~ **de vela** sailing ship; ~ **mercante** merchant ship

burbuja bubble

burbujeante bubbling

burbujear to bubble

burche *m* tower

burda *sl* door

burdel *m* brothel

burdo common, coarse

burel *m naut* marlinspike

bureta *chem* burette

burgalés *n* inhabitant of Burgos; *adj* of Burgos

burgués *m* bourgeois, middle-class person

burguesía bourgeoisie, middle-class

buriel *m* ropewalk

buril *m* engraving tool

burilar to engrave

burla scoff; sneer; hoax; jest; trick; ~ **pesada** practical joke in bad taste; ~**s aparte** joking aside; **de** ~**s** in fun; **hacer** ~**s de** to make fun of

burladero refuge in a bull ring

burlador *m* jester; scoffer; practical joker; seducer, casanova

burlar to mock, ridicule; scoff; evade; deceive; frustrate; ~**se de** to laugh at, make fun of

burlería fun; mocking; scoffing; deceit; yarn, fairy tale; banter; ridicule

burlesco burlesque

burlete *m* weather-strip; draught excluder

burlón *m* jester, scoffer

buró *m* bureau; desk

burocracia bureaucracy

burócrata *m+f* bureaucrat

burocrático bureaucratic

burra female donkey; ignorant woman; strong and hard-working woman; ~**s** *sl* bike

burrada drove of donkeys; stupid statement/act; blunder

burrear *sl* to cheat; steal

burro donkey; *carp* sawing-horse; windlass; obstinate person; *sl* thief, swindler

bursátil *adj* of the stock exchange; financial

busaca (billiards) pocket

busca search; pursuit; hunting party; terrier

buscada search; investigation

buscador *m* searcher; investigator; ~ **de**

oro gold prospector

buscaplé *m* hint; ~**s** squib, firecracker

buscapleitos *m sing+pl* trouble-maker

buscar to look for, search, seek; ~ **tres pies al gato** to pick a quarrel

buscavidas *m sing+pl* nosey-parker

buscón *m* searcher; filcher, pilferer

busilis *m* difficulty, snag; **dar en el** ~ to hit the target

buslar *sl* to gamble (especially at dice and cards)

búsqueda search; quest

busto bust; torso

butaca armchair; *theat+cin* stall

butano butane; natural gas

buten: de ~ *sl* excellent, first-class

butifarra Catalonian sausage; ill-fitting trousers; ham sandwich

butrino, butrón *m* fowling-net

buz *f* kiss (of respect)

buzo diver; diving-suit

buzón *m* letterbox, postbox; mill sluice; conduit, canal; *sl* large mouth

buzonear to deliver handbills *etc* from door to door

buzonera drain/gutter in courtyard

C

c *f* letter c

¡ca! *interj* come off it!

cabal *adj* exact, perfect; consummate; *adv* just so, exactly

cábala cabbala; intrigue

cabalar to complete

cabalgada cavalcade; raid

cabalgador *m* horseman

cabalgadura beast of burden; mount

cabalgante on horseback

cabalgar to ride; mount; go riding

cabalgata cavalcade; Christmas procession of men dressed as the Magi

cabalístico cabbalistic

caballa mackerel

caballar *adj* pertaining to horses, equine

caballerear to act the gentleman

caballeresco chivalrous

caballería horse-riding; cavalry; chivalry; horse

caballero knight, gentleman, horseman, sir, cavalier; ~ andante knight-errant; ~ cubierto grandee; de ~ a ~ as between gentlemen; espuela de ~ *bot* larkspur

caballerosidad *f* gentlemanliness

caballeroso gentlemanly

caballete *m carp* sawing-horse; trestle; bridge of the nose; easel; *orni* breastbone

caballista *m+f* horseman; highwayman

caballito pony; ~ del diablo dragonfly; ~ de mar sea-horse; ~s merry-go-round

caballo horse; (*Sp* playing-cards) queen; (chess) knight; *carp* trestle; crux (of argument); *sl* heroin; ~ blanco *theat* sponsor, backer; ~ de carrera race-horse; ~ del diablo dragonfly; ~ desbocado runaway horse; ~ de tiro draught horse; ~ de vapor horse-power

caballón *m agri* ridge

cabaña hut, cottage, cabin; *arts* landscape with dwelling

cabañal *m* village of huts; road used by flocks of sheep

cabe *f sp sl* header

cabeceador *naut* pitching (in rough sea)

cabecear to nod the head; *naut* pitch; *sp* head

cabeceo nodding; *naut* pitching

cabecera head (of bed, table *etc*); seat of honour; head board; end of bus/tram route; headline; provincial capital; bolster; médico de ~ family doctor

cabecilla rebel chief, leader

cabellera head of hair; *astron* tail of comet

cabello hair; ~ de angel sweetmeat of fruit cut into fine threads; asirse de un ~ to clutch at a straw

cabelludo hairy

caber to be able to be contained; go in, have enough room to fit in; *etc*); ella no cabe en sí she is quite beside herself with joy; no cabe duda there can be no doubt

cabestrillo *med* sling; llevar el brazo en ~ to have one's arm in a sling

cabestro halter; *sl* cuckold; leading ox

cabeza head; provincial capital; leader; *anat* end of a bone; ~ de chorlito scatterbrain; ~ de guerra warhead; ~ de perro *bot* celandine; ~ de turco scapegoat; ~ torcida hypocrite; a la ~ in front, ahead; de ~ head-first; ir de ~ to go to the dogs; por ~ per head; romperse la ~ to rack one's brains; ~ de familia *m* head of the family

cabezada shake (of the head), butt (with the head); nod; *naut* pitching; dar ~s to nod; echar una ~ to have forty winks

cabezal *m* small pillow; *med* compress

cabezazo butt; *sp* header

cabezo mountain summit

cabezón *n m* big head; fifty-peseta coin of Franco era; *adj* big-headed; pigheaded

cabezota *m+f* large-headed/pig-headed person

73

cabezudo *n* carnival figure with huge head; *adj* big-headed, stubborn
cabezuela *m + f* dolt, simpleton
cabida capacity
cabido landmark
cabildear to lobby, intrigue
cabildeo lobbying, scheming
cabildero lobbyist, schemer
cabildo meeting of chapter, municipal council
cabilla dowel; steel reinforcing rod
cabillo flower-stalk
cabina cabin; *cin* projection-room; ~ **telefónica** phone-box, *US* phone-booth
cabizbajo crestfallen; pensive
cable *m* cable, hawser
cablegrafiar to cable
cablegrama *m* cable
cablero cable-laying ship
cabo end, extremity; stub, stump; cape; *mil* corporal; ~ **suelto** loose end; **al fin y al** ~ in the end; **de** ~ **a rabo** from head to tail; **llevar a** ~ to carry out
cabotaje *m* coastal shipping
cabra goat; *mil* catapult
cabreado *sl* buggered
cabrearse to get into a foul temper; get mad
cabreo vile temper
cabrero goatherd
cabrestante *m* capstan
cabria *mech* hoist
cabrío *carp* joist, rafter
cabrío flock of goats; **macho** ~ he-goat; *adj* goatish
cabriola caper, leap
cabriolear to caper, cut capers
cabritilla kid(-skin)
cabrito kid, young goat; *sl* bugger
cabrón *m* he-goat; *fam* cuckold; *sl* bugger, bastard
cabronada rotten trick
cabronzuelo *sl* miserable little bugger
cabruno goatish
cabuya sisal-grass
caca *vulg* shit; filth; mess; botched job; thing of little value; ¡ ~! rubbish!
cacahuete *m* peanut
cacao cacao-tree; cocoa bean
cacaotal *m* cacao plantation
cacareador *adj* crowing; bragging
cacarear to crow; brag
cacatúa cockatoo

cacereño *n* native of Cáceres; *adj* of or from Cáceres
cacería hunt; hunting party, *arts* hunting-scene
cacerola saucepan
caceroleo *pol* organized pan-banging as a protest
cacica wife of tribal chief/party boss
cacique *m* chief; *pol* party boss; *fig* tyrant
caciquismo control by party bosses; jobbery
caciquista *m + f* supporter of **caciquismo**
caco *sl* petty thief
cacofonía din, cacophony
cacto cactus
cacumen *m* acumen, nous
cacha each of the two leaves of a knife handle; buttock
cachalote *m* cachalot, sperm whale
cachar to break; split; poke fun
cacharra *sl* pistol
cacharrería crockery store
cacharrero maker/seller of crockery
cacharro pot, pan; crock; *mot* old crock, jalopy; *sl* pistol; *sl* marihuana cigarette
cachaza slowness
cachazudo phlegmatic
cachear to frisk
cachemir *m*, **cachemira** cashmere
cacheo frisking
cachete *m* smack
cachetear to slap, smack
cachetina hand-to-hand fight
cachetudo chubby-faced
cachimba pipe
cachimbo pipe
cachiporra club, cudgel, truncheon
cachivache *m* worthless fellow; ~s pots and pans; goods and chattels; *fig* junk
cacho small piece
cachola *sl* head
cachondearse to get sexy; take the mickey
cachondeo sexiness; mickey-taking; mad behaviour
cachondez *f* sexual excitement
cachondo sexy, on heat, randy; sexually attractive; joking
cachorro puppy, cub
cachupín *m* Spaniard living in America
cada each; every; ~ **cual** everyone; ~ **vez más** more and more; ~ **vez que**

whenever; ¿~ **cuándo?** how often?

cadalso platform; scaffold; gallows

cadañal, cadañego yearly, annual

cadañero lasting a year

cadáver *m* corpse

cadavérico cadaverous

cadena chain; chain-gang; *fig* series; figure (in dancing); ~ **de montañas** mountain range; ~ **perpetua** life sentence

cadencia cadence, rhythm; *mus* cadenza

cadera *anat* hip

cadete *m* cadet

cadmio cadmium

cadoce *m* gudgeon

caducar to fall into disuse; become outdated; *comm*+*leg* expire; dote

caducidad *f* expiry; **fecha de ~** sell-by date

caduco senile, decrepit; *bot* deciduous; *comm*+*leg* expired, lapsed

caduquear *see* **caducar**

caduquez *f* senility

caedizo *bot* deciduous; on the point of falling

caer to fall, fall down or over, drop, tumble; droop, hang down; decrease, decline; fall due; realize, see the joke; ~ **bien** (of clothes) to fit well, suit; ~ **cerca** to be nearby; ~ **en cama** to fall ill; ~ **en gracia** to please; **dejar ~** to drop, let fall; **ella me cae bien** I like her; **no caigo** I don't get it, I don't see the point; **me ha caído el premio** I've won the prize

café *m* coffee; coffee-tree; café; ~ **con leche** white coffee; *sl* homosexual; ~ **cortado** coffee with very little milk; ~ **solo** black coffee

cafeína caffeine

cafetal *m* coffee plantation

cafetería café, coffee-bar

cafetera coffee-pot; *sl* jalopy, old crock

cafetero *n* coffee grower/maker/seller; café owner

cafeto *bot* coffee-tree

cafecultor *m* coffee-grower

cafecultura coffee-growing

cagada dung, shit; blunder

cagadero bog; shithouse

cagado *n* coward, miserable specimen; *adj* cowardly, shit-scared

cagalera diarrhoea, *sl* the shits; cowardice

cagancia *vulg sl* shit

cagar *vulg* to shit; mess up, soil, defile; ~**se** to shit o.s.

cagatintas *m sing*+*pl* pen-pusher

cagón *m* person suffering from diarrhoea; coward

caída fall; lapse; hang (of clothes *etc*); drop; fallen woman; ~ **del sol** sunset; downfall (of political extremist)

caídos *mpl* the fallen; **día de los ~** remembrance day

caimán *m* alligator

caja box, case; coffin; crate; chest; cash desk, till; *mil* stock (of rifle); drum; *bot* seed-case; ~ **alta/baja** *print* upper/lower case; ~ **de ahorros** savings bank; ~ **de caudales/fuerte** safe; ~ **de consulta** *leg* brief; ~ **de engranajes/velocidades/cambios** gearbox; ~ **de música** musical box; ~ **de reclutamiento** recruiting office; ~ **de resistencia** strike fund; ~ **registradora** cash register; ~ **tonta** *sl* telly, gogglebox; **en ~** in hand; **libro de ~** cash book

cajero cashier; box-maker; cashier; treasurer

cajetilla packet, *US* pack (of cigarettes)

cajista *m print* compositor

cajón *m* large box, chest; drawer; till; locker; trap (dog-track); ~ **de sastre** muddle, hotch-potch; **es de ~** it's obvious

cajonada *naut* locker

cajonería set of drawers; tallboy; chiffonier

cal *f* lime; ~ **apagada/muerta** slaked lime; ~ **viva** quicklime; **cerrar algo a ~ y canto** to shut something firmly

cala cove, creek; probe, test; dipstick; *naut* hold; first slice cut from a melon; *sl* peseta

calabacera *bot* pumpkin plant

calabacín *m* marrow, *US* squash; dolt

calabaza pumpkin; bumpkin; *sl* skeleton key; *sl* head

calabazar *m* pumpkin patch

calabazo gourd, calabash, pumpkin; *naut* old tub

calabobos *m sing*+*pl* drizzle

[1] **calabozo** dungeon; prison cell, goal

[2] **calabozo** *hort* pruning-hook

calada soaking, wetting-through; *sl* puff (of cigarette) caladero fishing-ground

calado *metal+carp+text* openwork; fretwork; lace cape; *mot* stalling

calador *m* perforator, borer; one who does openwork

calafate *m*, calafateador *naut* caulker

calafatear *naut* to caulk

calafateo, calafatería caulking

calafraga *bot* saxifrage

calamar *m* squid

calambre *m* spasm, twinge; cramp; electric shock

calamidad *f* calamity

calamitoso calamitous

calamoco icicle

calandria *orni* lark; *sl* peseta; town crier

calar to seep through, permeate; pierce, perforate; soak; *mech* wedge; see through; *sl* pick (pockets); ~ **bayonetas** to fix bayonets; ~ **un melon** to take a sample slice of a melon; ~**se** to get soaked (**hasta los huesos** to the skin)

calavera skull; *m* rake (person)

calaverada rakish behaviour

calca *sl* road; footsteps

calcañar *m* heel-bone

calcar to trample on; copy; *mot* give a parking ticket to; trace

calcáreo calcareous

calce *m* (iron) tyre; brake lining

calceta stocking; **hacer** ~ to knit

calcetería hosier's shop

calcetero hosier

calcetín *m* sock; *sl* french letter

calcificar to calcify

calcinar to calcine, burn, blacken

calcio calcium

calco tracing, (carbon) copy; *sl* shoe

calcografiar to engrave on copper

calcógrafo engraver; engraving machine

calcomanía transfer; infantile enthusiasm for transfers

calculación *f* calculation

calculador calculating

calculadora calculating machine; ~ **de bolsillo** pocket calculator

calcular to calculate; estimate; work out

calculatorio calculating

cálculo calculation; estimate; *med* gallstone

calda act of warming, heating; ~s hot springs

caldaico *n+adj* Chaldean

caldear to warm, heat

caldera boiler; big pot; shell (of kettledrum); ~ **de vapor** steam boiler

calderada cauldronful

calderero boilermaker, coppersmith, tinker

caldereta small cauldron; kettle, pot; kettleful; holy water basin; fish/lamb stew

calderilla small change; copper coins

caldero cauldron; copper pot

calderón *m mus* 'pause' sign

caldo broth, clear soup; consommé; **estar a** ~ *sl* to be broke; ~ **de cultivo** culture medium

caldoso thin, watery

calducho tasteless broth/stock

calé *n m* gipsy language; *adj* gipsy

caledonio Caledonian

calefacción *f* heating; ~ **central** central heating

calendario calendar

caléndula *bot* marigold

calentador *n m* heater; warming-pan; *fam* large watch; *adj* heating, warming

calentamiento heating, warming

calentar to heat, warm; ~**le a uno las orejas** to box s.o.'s ears; ~**se** to get warm, become heated, excited; *vet* be on heat

calentito nice and warm; sexy

calentón too warm/hot; very randy

calentura fever; *sl* sexual excitement

calenturoso feverish

calés *mpl sl* money, lolly

calesa chaise

calesero driver of a **calesa**

calibración *f* calibration

calibrador *m* calibre-gauge; callipers

calibrar to calibrate

calibre *m* calibre; **de mucho** ~ of excellent quality

calicó calico

caliche *m vulg sl* orgasm

calidad *f* quality; ~**es** conditions

calidez *f med* fever

cálido warm, hot

calidoscópico kaleidoscopic

calidoscopio kaleidoscope

calientacamas *m sing+pl* bed-warmer, warming-pan

calientapiernas *m sing+pl* leg-warmer

calientapies *m sing+pl* foot-warmer

calientaplatos *m sing+pl* plate-warmer

calientapollas *m sing+pl sl vulg* prick-tease

caliente warm, hot, heated

califa *m* caliph

califato *m* caliphate

calificable qualifiable

calificación *f* qualification; judgement; (in exam) grade

calificado qualified, skilled

calificador *m* censor; (in exam) moderator/examiner

calificar to qualify; grade, assess; authorize; ~se to prove one's ancestry

calificativo *n* epithet; *adj gramm* qualifying

californiano of California

caligrafía calligraphy, penmanship

caligrafiar to calligraph

caligráfico calligraphic

calígrafo calligrapher

calistenia callisthenics

cáliz *m* chalice; cup; *bot* calyx

calma calm; tranquillity, stillness, calmness; *fam* phlegm

calmante *n m +adj* sedative

calmar to calm down, pacify, soothe; calm; *naut* be becalmed; ~se to calm down, abate

calmo uncultivated; treeless; fallow

calmoso calm, tranquil; quiet

caló *m* gipsy slang

calofriarse to get chilled, catch a chill

calor *m* heat, warmth, ardour, feverishness; **entrar en** ~ to get warm; **hacer** ~ *meteor* to be warm; **tener** ~ to be hot

caloría calory

calórico caloric heat; ~ **radiante** radiant heat

calorífero *n* stove, heater; ~ **de aire** fan heater; *adj* heat-giving

calorífico calorific

calorífugo heat-resistant

calorímetro *phys* calorimeter

calumnia calumny, slander

calumniador *n m* calumniator, slanderer; *adj* calumniating, slanderous

calumniar to calumniate, slander

calumnioso calumnious, slanderous

caluroso warm, hot; enthusiastic

calva bald patch; (on lawn) bare patch; treeless place

calvario cross, ordeal; Calvary

calverizo (of the ground) having many bare patches

calvez *f*, **calvicie** *f* baldness

calvinismo Calvinism

calvinista *n m+f +adj* Calvinist

calvo *n* bald man; *adj* bald, hairless

calza wedge; ~s breeches

calzada causeway, roadway; **doble** ~ dual carriageway

calzado footwear

calzador *m* shoe-horn

calzar(se) to put on shoes/boots/spurs *etc*; **él calza un/el 42** he takes size 42 in shoes

calzón *m* safety-rope (used by painters, bricklayers *etc*); *SA* trousers, pants

calzones *mpl* trousers, breeches; **ponerse los** ~ to wear the trousers

calzonazos *m sing+pl* henpecked husband; stupid fellow

calzoncillos *m sing+pl* underpants

callado *n naut* lull in storm; *adj* silent, taciturn, reserved

callandito in a very low voice; secretly; slyly

callar to hush up; not to mention; keep quiet; ~ **la boca/el pico** to shut up; ~se to be quiet, remain silent; make no reply; stop talking; **¡cállese!** shut up!

calle *f* street; *sp* lane; *print* vertical space; ~ **arriba/abajo** up/down the street; **alborotar la** ~ to disturb the peace; **echar a/poner en la** ~ to chuck out, sack; **echarse a la** ~ to go out into the streets, riot

calleja alley

callejear to wander about the streets

callejeo strolling, wandering; loafing

callejero *n* street directory; *adj* gadabout; fond of gadding about; **manifestación callejera** street demonstration

callejón *m* narrow lane, alley; ~ **sin salida** blind alley, cul-de-sac

callicida corn-remover

callista *m+f* chiropodist

callo corn, callous; *sl* ugly woman; ~s tripe

callosidad *f* callosity

calloso corny, callous

cama bed, bedstead, lair, litter, bedding; *geol* stratum; ~ **sencilla** single bed; ~ **de agua** water-bed; ~ **de matrimonio** double bed; ~ **elástica** trampoline; **guardar** ~ to be confined to bed

camachuelo *orni* bullfinch

camada litter, brood; band of thieves

camafeo cameo

camaleón *m* chameleon; *fam* turncoat

camamila *bot* camomile

camándula hypocrisy, underhand dealing

camandular to pretend to be devout

camandulería hypocrisy, insincerity

cámara chamber, room, granary; *naut* cabin; *mot* inner-tube; *photo* camera; ~ **de comercio** chamber of commerce; ~ **de los comunes** House of Commons; ~ **fotográfica** camera; ~ **mortuaria** funeral parlour, chapel of rest; ~ **de los lores** House of Lords; ~s diarrhoea; **pintor de** ~ court painter; *m* cameraman

camarada *m+f* comrade, mate, chum, buddy

camaradería comradeship

camarera waitress; chambermaid; lady-in-waiting

camarero waiter, steward

camareta small bedroom; *naut* small cabin

camarilla *pol* clique; pressure group

camarín *m* small room; private office; *theat* dressing-room

camarista maid of honour to Spanish queen/princesses

camarón *m* large shrimp

camaronero shrimp and prawn seller

camarote *m naut* berth, cabin, stateroom

camarroya *bot* wild chicory

camastrón *n* artful person; *adj* artful, sly

cambalache *m* barter(ing), swap(ping)

cambalachear to barter, swap

cambalachero barterer

cambiable exchangeable

cambiada change of direction

cambiadizo changeable

cambiador *n m* barterer; money-changer; *adj* changing, bartering

cambiante *n m* banker, money-changer; ~s iridescence; *text* shot fabrics; *adj* changing, bartering

cambiar to change, alter; exchange; move; *meteor* veer; ~ **de idea** to change one's mind; ~ **de manos** to change hands; ~ **el agua al canario** to see a man about a dog

cambio change, alteration, small change, move, premium; *comm* quotation price, rate of exchange; barter; (railway) point, switch; **a** ~ **de** in exchange for; **en** ~ on the other hand; **letra de** ~ bill of exchange; **libre** ~ free trade

cambista *m+f* money-broker; **libre** ~ free-trader

Camboya Cambodia

camboyano *n+adj* Cambodian

cambrón *m bot* hawthorn; **cambrones** brambles

cambronal *m* thicket of brambles *etc*

cambur *m* banana; good employment

camedrio, camedris *m bot* germander, speedwell

camelador *n m* cajoler; *adj* cajoling

camelar to cajole, butter up, deceive; ~**se a alguien** *sl* to persuade s.o. by means of lies

camelia *bot* camellia

camelo blarney, gift of the gab; fake; false report

camella she-camel; *agr* ridge between furrows

camellear *sl* to traffic in drugs

camellero camel-driver

camello camel; *sl* drug pusher; *sl* stupid person

camellón *m agri* ridge; drinking trough

Camerón, Camerún Cameroons

cameronés, camerunés *n+adj* (native) of Cameroons

camilla stretcher, couch; table with heater underneath

camillero stretcher-bearer

caminada day's journey

caminador *m* good walker

caminante *m+f* wayfarer, passer-by, traveller

caminar to walk; travel, trek, hike; go, move along

caminata long walk/trek *etc*

caminero *adj* pertaining to roads; **peón** ~ road-mender

camino road, path, lane; way, route; ~ **de herradura** bridle-path; ~ **de Santiago** Milky Way; ~ **de sirga** towpath; ~ **hollado** beaten track; ~ **real** highway; ~ **vecinal** country road; **abrirse** ~ to make one's way; **estar fuera de** ~ to be up the creek/off the rails; **ir por buen** ~ to be on the right track; **ponerse en** ~ to set off;

quedarse a medio ~ to stop half-way; ~ **de Madrid** on the way to Madrid

camión *m* lorry, *US* truck

camionaje *m* haulage, truckage

camioneta motor-van, delivery van

camisa shirt, blouse, chemise; (of snake) cast-off skin; *bot* thin skin of onion, almond *etc*; *mech* casing, housing; gas-mantle; book-jacket; **en mangas de** ~ **de fuerza** straitjacket; **en mangas de** ~ in shirt-sleeves; **jugar hasta la** ~ to stake all

camisería shirt shop, men's outfitters

camisero shirt maker

camiseta vest, singlet; sports shirt, T-shirt

camisola blouse; labourer's shirt/smock; strip (of football team)

camisolín *m* shirt-front; tucker; dicky; modesty vest

camisón *m* nightshirt, nightdress, nightie

camomila *bot* camomile

camón *m* glass-enclosed balcony

camorra wrangle, quarrel; **armar** ~ to make trouble, pick a quarrel; **buscar** ~ to be itching for a fight

camorrista trouble-maker; quarrelsome person

camp outmoded, old-fashioned; affected, exaggerated

campa treeless

campal: batalla ~ pitched battle

campamento camp, encampment

campana bell; *phys* bell-jar; *gard* cloche; curfew; ~ **de buzo** diving-bell; ~ **de chimenea** chimney-hood; ~ **de rebato** alarm-bell; **a toque de** ~ at the sound of a bell; **doblar las** ~s to toll the knell; **echar las** ~s **a vuelo** to rejoice noisily; **tocar las** ~s to peal the bells

campanada stroke of a bell; sensational report

campanario bell-tower, steeple, belfry; **política de** ~ parish-pump politics

campanear to ring (bells); ~**se** to strut, swagger

campaneo bell-ringing; bragging

campanero bell-ringer, bell-founder; *orni* bellbird; *ent* praying mantis

campanil *m* belfry; *metal* bell-metal

campanilla small bell; doorbell; hand bell; small bubble; **persona de** ~s V.I.P.

campanillear to tinkle, reverberate

campanilleo tinkle, jingle

campanillero town crier

campano cow-bell

campanología campanology

campanólogo campanologist

campanudo bell-shaped

campaña level terrain; countryside; *mil* +*pol* campaign; ~ **naval** cruise

campar to camp, be encamped; excel; ~ **con su estrella** to be lucky

campeador *n m* warrior; *adj* very brave

campear to campaign; *mil* reconnoitre; be in the field; excel

campechano hail-fellow-well-met, frank

campeón *m* champion

campeonato championship; **de** ~ *sl* stupendous, fabulous

campero out-door; **fiesta campera** country festival

campesino *n* peasant, countryman; *adj* rustic, rural

campestre rural; (of flowers) wild; **merienda** ~ picnic

camping *m* camping; campsite; **hacer** ~ to camp, go camping

campiña landscape; flat tract of cultivated land

campista *m*+*f* camper

campo field, country(side); scope, range; *mil* camp; *arts* background; ~ **de honor** duelling-ground; ~ **raso** flat country; **a** ~ **travieso** cross-country; **hombre de** ~ country-lover; **levantar el** ~ to strike camp; ~ **de golf** golf course

camposanto graveyard, churchyard

camuesa *hort* pippin

camueso *hort* pippin-tree

camuflaje *m* camouflage

camuflar to camouflage

Camuñas: tío ~ bogeyman

¹ **can** *m* dog; trigger (of firearm)

² **can** *m* khan

cana white/grey hair; **tener** ~s to be old

Canadá *m* Canada

canadiense *n m*+*f* +*adj* Canadian; **tienda** ~ ridge tent

canal *m* canal, channel, waterway; *anat* duct; *m*+*f* narrow valley, water-pipe; conduit; gutter; slot; cleaned and gutted animal carcase; **Canal** *m* **de la Mancha** English Channel

canalado corrugated, fluted

canalete *m* paddle, small oar

canalización *f* canalization; *elect* wiring

canalizar to channel

canalón *m* gutter

canalla rabble, scum; *m* bounder, rotter

canallada rotten trick; caddish act

canana cartridge-belt

canapé *m* couch; savoury

Canarias *fpl* Canary Islands

canario *n orni* canary; Canary Islands folk dance; *adj* of/from the Canary Islands; **cambiar el agua al ~** to see a man about a dog

canasta basket, hamper

canastero basket maker/seller

canastilla layette; small basket

canasto basket; **¡~s!** crikey!

cancel *m* screen (partition), storm door; small porch (in church); draught-excluder

cancela front-door grating

cancelación *f* cancellation

cancelar to cancel, annul

cancelaría, cancelería chancellery

cancelario (university) chancellor

cáncer *m* cancer; **tener (un) ~** to have cancer

cancerar to render cancerous; consume; **~se** to get cancer

canceroso cancerous

canciller *m* chancellor

cancillerato chancellorship

cancillería chancellery

canción *f* song, rhyme; **~ de cuna** lullaby; **mudar de ~** to change one's tune

cancionero songbook; anthology of lyrics; *mus* book of tunes

cancioneta canzonet

cancionista *m+f* folksinger, songwriter

cancro canker; cancer

cancha cockfighting pit; sportsfield; tennis/pelota court; racecourse

canchal *m* rocky place

canchero expert

candado padlock

candar to lock

candeal (of flour) white and of finest quality

candela candle

candelabro candelabra

candelero candlestick; candle-maker/seller

candelilla *med* catheter; *bot* catkin

candencia white heat

candente white/red hot; **cuestión ~** burning question

candidato candidate

candidatura candidature; list of candidates

candidez *f* ingenuousness, simplicity

cándido guileless, simple

candil *m* oil-lamp; point (of cocked hat); **~ sin mecha** white elephant, useless object

candileja oil receptacle (for lamp); *bot* lucerne; **~s** *theat* footlights, limelight

candonga *sl* peseta

candor *m* candour; purity, simplicity; whiteness

candoroso ingenuous, simple-minded

canear to get white hair; *sl* hit, strike

caneca refuse bin

canela cinnamon; **~ fina** first-quality stuff

canelado cinnamon-coloured

canelo *n bot* cinnamon-tree; *adj* cinnamon-coloured

canelón *m* icicle; drainpipe; **canelones** *cul* cannelloni

canesú *m* yoke (of blouse/shirt)

caney *m* cabin

canforado camphorated

cangallo *sl* cart, car

cangilón *m* water-wheel bucket

cangrejal *m* crab ground

cangrejero one who catches and sells crabs and crayfish

cangrejo crab, crayfish; *naut* boom; *sl* 25 peseta coin; **~ de río** freshwater crayfish

cangri *m sl* church; *sl* prison

canguelo: tener ~ to be in a blue funk

canguro kangaroo; baby-sitter; *sl* Black Maria

caníbal *n m +adj* cannibal; savage

canibalismo cannibalism; savagery

canica marble; game of marbles

canicie *f* whiteness (of hair)

canícula, caniculares *mpl* dog-days; summer heat

canijo feeble, weak, sickly; *fam* small

canilla *anat* shinbone; tap, faucet, spigot; reel, bobbin; **irse de ~** to talk non-stop

canillado ribbed; striped

canillero faucet, spigot-hole (in barrel)

canino *n* dog excrement; *adj* canine; **diente** ~ canine tooth; **hambre canina** ravenous hunger

canje *m comm+mil+pol* exchange, swop; ~ **de prisioneros** exchange of prisoners

canjeable exchangeable

canjear to exchange, barter, swop

cano grey-haired, hoary

canoa canoe, (motor) boat; broad-brimmed hat

canódromo greyhound racing track; dog track

canoero canoeist

canon *m* canon, rule; standard, norm; licence-fee; *leg* land tax; *min* royalty

canonesa canoness

canónica conventual life

canónico canonical

canónigo canon, prebendary; **vida de** ~ easy life

canonizable worthy of canonization

canonización *f* canonization

canonizar to canonize; praise

canonjía canonry; *fam* sinecure

canoro harmonious

canoso grey-haired

cansable easily tired

cansado weary, tired, tiring, tiresome; **vista cansada** longsightedness

cansancio weariness, fatigue

cansar to tire, fatigue

cansino weary, tedious

canso tiresome

cantable *n* lyrics; simple melody; *adj* singable; *mus* sung slowly

cantábrico of Cantabria; **Mar Cantábrico** Bay of Biscay

cantada cantata

cantal *m* stony ground

cantalear *orni* to coo

cantaleta pun, jest; humbug; **dar** ~ **a** to poke fun at

cantalinoso pebbly

cantante *n m+f* singer; *adj* singing

cantaor *m* flamenco singer

cantar *n* song, tune, poem; ~ **de gesta** epic poem; **ése es otro** ~ that's another matter; *v* to sing, chant, praise; *sl* to denounce/confess to the police, spill the beans; ~ **de plano** to make a clean breast of it; ~ **misa** to say mass

cántara pitcher; milkchurn

cantarería shop where pitchers are sold

cantarera shelf (for jars *etc*)

cantarero potter

cantárida cantharis, Spanish fly

cantarín *adj* keen on singing

cántaro large pitcher; *vulg sl* knocker, breast; **a** ~**s** galore; **llover a** ~**s** to pour with rain

cantautor *m* singer who writes his own songs

cantazo blow with a stone

cante: ~ **flamenco** flamenco singing

cantear *vt* to stand on its narrow edge

cantera quarry; source; *sp+theat* nursery (for young players/actors)

cantería hewn stone

cantero stone-cutter; ~ **de pan** crust of bread

cántico canticle; hymn

cantidad *f* quantity, amount; **en** ~ in large amounts; **tener** ~ **de dinero** to have tons of money

cantiga troubadour poem

cantilena ballad; *fam* the same old story

cantimplora water-bottle; siphon; canteen

cantina canteen; station buffet

¹ **canto** singing; chant; song; canticle; ~ **llano** Gregorian chant, plainsong; **al** ~ **del gallo** at cockcrow

² **canto** end, edge; stone; back (of knife-blade); **de** ~ on edge

cantón *m* corner, cantonment

cantonear to hang about at street corners

cantonera *f* angle-iron, corner-bracket; streetwalker, prostitute

cantonero *n* loafer; *adj* loafing

cantor *n m* singer, song-bird; *sl* squealer, informer; *adj* singing

cantuariense of/from Canterbury

canturrear to hum, chant

canturrea humming, chanting

canutazo *sl* phone-call

canutillo thin tube; cane/straw tube; corduroy

canuto *n* tube; *sl* marihuana cigarette; *sl* telephone; *adj invar* stupendous, good-looking

caña *bot* cane, reed; walking-stick; stem; *anat* marrow; *naut* helm, tiller; small glass of beer; leg (of boot); *mus* reed; ~ **de pescar** fishing-rod; ~ **del pulmón** windpipe; ~ **dulce** sugar-cane

cañada glen, ravine; *cul* shin-bone

marrow

cañal *m* cane/reed plantation

cáñamo hemp; cloth made from hemp

cañamón *m* hempseed

cañar *see* **cañal**

cañareja *bot* fennel

cañaveral *m* cane-bed, reed-bed

cañaverero cane-retailer

cañazo blow with a cane

cañedo cane plantation, reed plantation

cañería pipe; pipeline

cañero conduit-maker; water-works manager

cañí *adj invar* gipsy

cañizar *m* cane-bed, reed-bed

cañizo hurdle

caño tube, pipe, conduit, gutter, spout; *mus* organ-pipes; *naut* channel at entrance to a port

cañón *m* cannon, gun; gun barrel; tube; canyon; quill pen; well (of staircase); ~ **de chimenea** chimney flue

cañonazo cannon-shot, cannon-fire

cañonear to shell, fire on

cañoneo bombardment, shelling

cañonero *m* gunboat; gunner; ~ **aéreo** helicopter gunship; *f mil* large tent; *naut* gun-port; **(lancha) cañonera** armed sloop; **diplomacia del** ~ gunboat diplomacy

caoba mahogany

caolín *m* kaolin

caos *m* chaos; shambles

caótico chaotic

capa cape, cloak, mantle; layer; coat(ing), covering; *bui* course, bed; outer leaf of cigar; **de** ~ **y espada** cloak-and-dagger; **ir de** ~ **caída** to be down-at-heel

capacidad *f* capacity, ability; means; *leg* qualification

capacitar to capacitate, equip, qualify

capacho hamper; shopping-bag; large basket

capador *m* gelder

capadura castration

capar to castrate, geld; *fam* curtail

caparazón *m zool* shell

capataz *m* foreman, overseer

capaz capacious, roomy; capable, fit, able

capazo hempen basket; carrycot

capciosidad *f* cunning, artfulness

capcioso cunning, artful; **pregunta cap-**

ciosa leading question

capea amateur bullfight with a calf (which is not killed)

capeador *m* amateur bullfighter

capear to fight a bull with the cape; *fam* dodge; fool; ~ **el temporal** to weather the storm

capelo cardinal's red hat

capellán *m* chaplain, padre; ~ **castrense** army chaplain; ~ **de navío** naval chaplain; ~ **mayor** chaplain-general

capellanía chaplaincy

capeo *see* **capea**

Caperucita Roja Little Red Riding Hood

caperuza pointed hood; ~ **de chimenea** chimney-cowl

capicúa palindrome, symmetrical number

capigorrista *m+f*, **capigorrón** *m* vagabond, sly fellow

capilar *n m + adj* capillary

capilla chapel; *bot* seed-case; *print* proof-sheet; ~ **ardiente** lying-in-state; **en** ~ awaiting execution; *fig* waiting to sit an examination

capillejo skein of sewing silk

capillita small chapel; niche; collection box; *m* church worker

capillo child's cap; christening cap; christening fee; hood (for hawk); net (for catching rabbits); *anat* prepuce; ~ **de hierro** helmet

capitación *f* capitation, poll-tax

capital *n f* capital city; main town *n m* capital (riches); *comm* capital stock; ~ **desembolsado** paid-up capital; ~ **social** share; *adj* capital, principal; great, essential; **enemigo** ~ chief enemy; **pecado** ~ deadly sin; **pena** ~ death penalty

capitalismo capitalism

capitalista *n m+f* capitalist; *adj* capitalist(ic)

capitalizable that can be capitalized

capitalización *f* capitalization

capitalizar to capitalize

capitán *m* captain, leader, commander (of a ship); ~ **de corbeta** lieutenant commander; ~ **de fragata** commander; ~ **de navío** captain; ~ **de puerto** harbour-master; ~**-general** de ejército field-marshal; ~**-general** commander-in-chief of a military

region
capitana flagship; captain's wife
capitanear to captain, command
capitanía captaincy; port dues; ~ **de puerto** harbour master's office
capitel *m archi* capital
capitulación *f* capitulation, surrender; **capitulaciones** marriage contract
capítulo chapter (of book); *eccles* chapter-house; ~ **de culpas** impeachment; ~**s matrimoniales** marriage articles; **llamar a** ~ to take to task
capó *m mot* bonnet
capoc *m*, **capoca** kapok
capón *n m* gelding; capon; faggot; thump/clout *usu* on the head; *adj* castrated, gelded
capona epaulette; shoulder-knot
caponera coop (for fattening poultry)
caporal ringleader, chief
capota bonnet, hood
capotar *mot* to turn over; *aer* nose-dive
capotazo (bullfighting) flourish with the cape
capote *m* cloak; (bullfighting) cape; poncho; *mil* greatcoat; thick mist; **echar un** ~ to help
capotear to fight (a bull) with a cape; to dodge
capoteo (bullfighting) capework
Capricornio Capricorn
capricho caprice, fancy, whim; *mus*+ *arts* caprice, capriccio
caprichoso capricious, flighty
cápsico *bot* capsicum
cápsula capsule
capsular *v* to cap (a bottle); *adj* capsular
captación *f* captation; capture; harnessing (of water); *rad* tuning, picking-up
captador *m* inveigler; *adj* captivating
captar to attract, catch, grasp, win over; *rad* pick up
captura *leg* seizure, catch, capture
capturar *leg* to apprehend, arrest, capture
capucha hood, cowl; *print* circumflex accent
capuchino Capuchin (monk); *bot* nasturtium
capuchón *m* lady's evening cloak with hood
capullo cocoon; *bot* bud; acorn-cup; *anat* prepuce; **en** ~ in embryo

caqui *m* khaki colour; **marcar el** ~ *sl* to do one's military service
¹ **cara** *n anat* face; look, appearance; cheek, impudence; *geom* plane; ~ **a** ~ face to face; ~ **de acelga** sallow face; ~ **de ajo** surly face; ~ **de aleluya** happy face; ~ **de cartón** wrinkled face; ~ **de hereje** ugly face; ~ **de juez** stern face; ~ **dura** cheek, nerve; ~ **de vinagre** sour face; ~ **o cruz** heads or tails; **a** ~ **descubierta** openly; **dar la** ~ to face the music; **echarle a uno en** ~ to tax s.o. with; **sacarle a uno la** ~ to defend s.o.; **tener** ~ **de** to have the appearance of; **tener buena/mala** ~ to look well/ill
² **cara** *adv* facing; ~ **alelante** forward; ~ **al sol** facing the sun; **de** ~ facing
carabela *naut* caravel
carabina carbine, rifle; *fam* chaperon; **es la** ~ **de Ambrosio** it's a dead loss, it's a waste of time
carabinazo carbine shot
carabinero carabineer; customs guard; large prawn
cárabo *orni* tawny owl
caracol *m zool* snail, winkle; **escalera de** ~ spiral staircase
caracolada *cul* dish of snails
caracolero snail-gatherer/seller
carácter *m* character, disposition, nature, temperament; *bio* characteristic; ~**es de imprenta** *print* types; **en su** ~ **de** in his capacity as
caracterismo characteristics
característica *n* character actress; characteristic, feature, attribute
característico *n* character actor; *adj* characteristic, typical
caracterizar to characterize; ~**se** to dress up/make up for the part
carado: bien ~ pleasant-faced; **mal** ~ evil-looking
caradura face, cheek, impudence; *m* cheeky fellow, thick-skinned rascal
carajillo black coffee with brandy or anis
carajo *vulg* prick, penis
¡caramba! I say!, Good Heavens!
carámbano icicle
carambola (in billiards) cannon; fluke; **por** ~ by a fluke
carambolear to cannon
carambolista *m* expert at scoring

cannons

caramelizar to make into caramel

caramelo sweet, toffee, *US* candy; ~s *sl* marihuana

caramillo small flute; deceit, trick

caramilloso peevish, touchy

carángano louse

carantoña ugly mask; ~s *pl* caresses, petting

caróta french bean

carapacho carapace

carátula mask

caratalero mask-maker

caravana caravan, *US* trailer; crowd, queue; *mot* tail-back

caravanera caravanserai

caravanero caravaneer

caravanista *m+f* caravaneer, caravanist

¡caray! Good Lord!, crikey!

carbol *m* phenol; carbolic acid

carbólico carbolic

carbón *m* coal, carbon; ~ **mineral**, ~ **de piedra** coal; ~ **vegetal** charcoal

carbonar to carbonize

carbonato *chem* carbonate

carboncillo *arts* charcoal pencil

carbonera wood ready for converting into charcoal; charcoal-bin; coal-bunker, coal-cellar; woman charcoal seller

carbonear to make into charcoal

carbonería coalyard, coal merchant's

carbonero *n* coalman, coal merchant; charcoal burner/seller; ~ **común** *orni* great-tit; ~ **garrapinos** *orni* coal-tit; *adj* pertaining to coal/charcoal

carbónico carbonic

carbonífero coal-bearing

carbonilla small coal; coal dust

carbonización *f* carbonization

carbonizar to carbonize, char

carbono *chem* carbon

carburador *m* carburettor

carburante *m* fuel

carburar to carburize; *mot* go/function well

carburo carbide

carca *m+f pol pej* diehard right-winger/Carlist; square

carcajada guffaw; peal of laughter; **reírse a** ~s to laugh heartily

carcajear to guffaw

carcamal *m* old fogey

caracamán *m naut* old tub

caracavón *m* gully formed by water

cárcel *f* prison, gaol; *carp* clamp

carcelaje *m* gaoler's fees

carcelario relating to prisons

carcelería imprisonment; bail; **guardar** ~ to be confined within bounds

carcelera gaoleress, wardress

carcelero *n* gaoler, warder; *adj* prison, gaol; **fiador** ~ one who stands bail for a prisoner; **fianza carcelera** bail, surety

carcoma wood-worm, death-watch beetle; worry

carcomer to gnaw, eat away, undermine

carcomido worm-eaten; rotten

carda *bot* cardthistle, teasel; *text* carding; reprimand; **dar una** ~ to reprimand severely; **gente de la** ~ ruffians

cardadería, cardería *text* carding factory

cardador *m text* carder

cardamina *bot* lady's smock, cuckoo-flower

cardar *text* to card, comb

¹ **cardenal** *m eccles* cardinal

² **cardenal** *m* weal, bruise

cardenalato *med* cardinalship

cardencha *bot* teasel; *text* card; comb

cardenillo verdigris

cárdeno *n bot* purple iris; *adj* mauve, bluish-purple

cardíaco *n* person suffering from heart-disease; *adj* cardiac

cardialgia *med* heart-burn

cardiografía *med* cardiography

cardiógrafo *med* cardiograph

cardiología *med* cardiology

cardiólogo cardiologist

cardo *bot* thistle; *sl* ugly woman; ~ **borriqueño** Scotch thistle; prickly customer

cardón *m bot* teasel; *text* carding

carear to bring face to face; *leg* confront witnesses and accused; compare; ~**se** to meet face to face

carecer to lack; ~ **de sentido** to make no sense

carena *naut* careening

carenadura *naut* careenage

carencia want, lack

carente lacking; ~ **de interés** lacking in interest

careo *leg* confrontation (of witnesses and accused); interrogation

carero (of things) dear, expensive; (of people) profiteering, charging high prices

carestía scarcity, famine; high cost of living

careta mask; fencer's/bee-keeper's mask; ~ **antigás** gas mask

carey *m* turtle, turtle shell

carga load, burden; cargo; loading; weight; *mil, min* charge; tax, duty; ~ **fija** *eng* dead load; ~ **real** land tax; ~ **útil** payload; **soltar la** ~ to throw off/give up a responsibility; **volver a la** ~ to harp on a topic

cargadero loading/unloading bay or platform

cargado loaded; *meteor* sultry; (of tea, coffee) strong; *elec* live; ~ **de espaldas** round-shouldered; **cargada** (of sheep) pregnant

cargador *m* shipper, loader; stevedore; carrier; porter

cargamento *naut* cargo, shipment

cargante annoying

cargar to load; make heavy; weigh down; impose, lay; annoy, get on the nerves of; *comm* debit, book, charge to an account; *mil* charge, assault; ~ **la mano** to go too far, overdo; ~ **los dados** to load the dice; ~**se** to incline towards; *comm* agree to the amount debited; *meteor* become duller/more sultry; get browned off; *sl* kill, bump off

cargareme *m* receipt, voucher

cargo load, burden; *comm* gross receipts; *leg* charge, accusation; post, position, office, duty, obligation; command; management; ~ **de conciencia** remorse; **hacerse** ~ **de algo** to take something on o.s.

cargoso heavy, annoying

carguero *n* cargo-boat; *adj* freight-carrying

cariacontecido down-in-the-mouth

cariacuchillado facially scarred

cariado (of teeth) decayed

carialegre smiling, cheerful

cariampollado chubby-faced

cariancho fat-faced

cariarse to become decayed

cariátide *f archi* caryatid

caribe *n m+f +adj* Carib, West Indian

caribeño *adj* Caribbean, West Indian

caribito fresh-water bream

caribobo stupid-looking

caribú *m zool* caribou

caricatura caricature, cartoon

caricaturista *m+f* caricaturist, cartoonist

caricaturizar to caricature

caricia caress, stroke

caricioso caressing

caricompuesto poker-faced

caricorto small-featured

caricuerdo grave-faced

carichato flat-faced

caridad *f* charity, alms

caridelantero brazen-faced

caries *fpl* caries, decay; *agri* blight

carifruncido frowning

carigordo fat-faced

cariharto round-faced

carilampiño beardless

carilargo long-faced

carilavado beaming

carilleno plump-faced

carillo on the dear side; rather expensive

carimohino glum-faced

carinegro swarthy

carininfo girlish-looking

cariño love, affection, fondness; dear, darling; **con** ~ lovingly

cariñoso loving, affectionate, fond; kind

caripálido pale-faced

carirredondo round-faced

carisma *m* charisma

carita sweet little face

caritativo charitable

cariz *m* aspect, appearance, look; **tener mal** ~ to look nasty

carlanca spiked collar; *sl* shirt collar

carleta *metal* file

carlinga *aer* cockpit

carlismo Carlism

Carlista *n+adj* Carlist

Carlitos Charlie

Carlos Charles

carmenador *m text* teaser, comber (man or machine); carding machine

carmenadura *text* teasing; carding

carmenar to unravel, disentangle; *text* tease, card; *fam* cheat, steal

carmesí *n m* cochineal powder; red silk material; *adj* carmine, crimson

carmín *n* carmine; rouge; cochineal colourant; *bot* wild red rose, rose of

Lancaster

carminativo *n + adj med* carminative

carminoso reddish

carnación *f arts + her* flesh colour

carnada bait; trap

carnadura muscularity, robustness

carnaje *m* carnage

carnal carnal, sensual, worldly; **primo ~** first cousin

carnalidad *f* carnality, sensuality

carnaval *m* carnival; the three days before Ash Wednesday

carnavalada carnival stunt

carnavalesco carnival-like

carnaza fleshy side (of skin); bait; fleshiness

carne *f cul* meat, flesh; pulp (of fruit); **~ de cañón** cannon-fodder; **~ de cerdo/cordero/vaca/ternera** pork, lamb, beef, veal; **~ de gallina** goose-flesh; **~ de horca ~** gallows-bird(s); **~ de membrillo** quince jelly; **~ de pelo** flesh of small edible quadrupeds (rabbits, hares *etc*); **~ de pluma** flesh of poultry; **~ salvajina** venison; **~ viva** raw flesh of a wound; **echar ~s** to put on weight; **ser sangre y ~** to be kith and kin; **ser ~ y hueso** to be flesh and blood; **ser uña y ~** to be thick as thieves

carné *m*, **carnet** *m* memorandum book; identity/membership card; **~ de conducir** driving-licence; **~ militar** pay-book

carnear to slaughter (animals)

carnerada flock of sheep

carneril *n m* sheep-walk; *adj* pertaining to sheep

carnero sheep, ram, mutton; **~ de simiente** breeding-ram

carneruno sheep-like

carnestolendas *f sing + pl* Shrovetide

carnet *m see* carné

carnicería butcher's shop; carnage, slaughter

carnicero *n* butcher; **~s** carnivora; *adj* carnivorous; bloodthirsty; fond of meat

cárnico pertaining to meat

carnívoro carnivorous

carniza left-over meat; cat's meat, dog's meat

carnosidad *f* fleshiness; *med* proud flesh

carnoso fleshy; (of fruit) pulpy

caro dear, expensive

caroba carob

carocha, carrocha *ent* eggs

carochar, carrochar *ent* to lay eggs

carona saddle-padding; *sl* shirt; **a ~ bare-backed**; **blando de ~** *adj* saddle-sore

caroquero *n* wheedler, flatterer; *adj* honey-tongued

carota *m + f* cheeky

carótida carotid artery

carótido carotid

carpa *zool* carp; tent

carpanta ravenous hunger

Cárpatos *mpl* Carpathians

carpe *m bot* hornbeam

carpedal *m bot* hornbeam plantation

carpelo *bot* carpel

carpeta file, folder, portfolio, letter-file

carpetazo: dar ~ a to shelve; put away and forget

carpintear to work as a carpenter

carpintería carpentry, woodwork, carpenter's shop/workshop

carpintero carpenter, joiner, woodworker; **~ de armar** carpenter who roofs houses; **~ de blanco** joiner; **~ de carretas** wheelwright; **~ de remos** oar-maker; **~ de ribera** shipwright; **pájaro ~** *orni* woodpecker

carpo *anat* carpus, wrist

carpófago fruit-eating

carpología carpology

carraca *orni* roller; *mus* rattle; old hulk/person

carrada cartload

carrasca holm-oak

carraspeante harsh

carraspear to clear one's throat

carraspeño hoarse, gruff

carraspeo hoarseness; clearing of the throat

carraspera frog-in-the-throat; sore throat

carraspique *m bot* candytuft

carrasposo chronically hoarse

carrera race, race-track, run; *astron* course, line; hair-parting; *archi* beam, girder; run (in stocking); professional or vocational training, course, profession; *naut* steamer route; **~s** races, horse-racing; **hacer la ~** to walk the streets, be a prostitute

carrerilla *mus* run, flourish

carrerista *m+f* punter, turf specialist, better; racing cyclist

carrero carter, carrier, vanman

carreta wagon, cart

carretada cart-load; **a ~s** by the cartload

carretaje *m* cartage, cartage fee

carretal *m* rough-hewn square stone

carrete *m* spool, bobbin; fishing-reel; *phot* roll; *elect+rad* induction coil; **dar ~ to** pay out (a line); **dar ~ a uno** to keep s.o. dangling/in suspense

carreteador *m* waggoner

carretear to cart; drive a cart

carretel *m* fishing-reel; *naut* log-reel

carreteo carting, cart transport; haulage

carretera road, highway; **~ de circunvalación** by-pass, *US* cut off; **~ nacional** trunk road

carretería carter's trade; cartwright's yard; wheelwright's shop

carretero: camino ~ cart-road; cart driver; **como un ~** like a trooper

carretilla small cart; hand cart; push-cart; wheelbarrow; railway wagon; baby-walker; squib; **de ~** by heart; **saber de ~** to know off pat

carretillada wheelbarrow load

carretillero s.o. who pushes a wheelbarrow/handcart

carretón *m* cart, go-cart, truck, dray; knife-grinder's cart; **~ de lámpara** *eccles* pulley for raising/lowering lamps

carretonada cartload, drayload

carretoncillo small go-cart; sledge, sleigh

carretonero drayman

carricero *orni* reed-warbler

carricoche *m* covered cart; *pej* decrepit cart/coach

carricuba water-cart

carril *m* cart-rut, narrow road, cartway; furrow; (railway) rail, track; lane (of road); vagabond's way of life

carrillar *m naut* hoisting-tackle

carrillada *cul* pig's cheek

carrillera chinstrap

¹ **carrillo** *anat* cheek; **masticar a dos ~s** to eat ravenously

² **carrillo** hoisting tackle; pulley

carrilludo round-cheeked

carriola truckle-bed

carrizo *bot* reed-grass

carro cart, carriage; *sl* car; cartload,

carriageful; supermarket trolley; *print* bed; carriage of press/typewriter; **~ de basura** dust-cart; **~ de combate** armoured fighting vehicle; **~ de riego** water-cart; **~ de volteo** tip cart; **Carro Mayor** Great Bear; **Carro Menor** Little Bear; **untar el ~** to bribe

carrocería *mot* bodywork; bodywork repair-shop

carrocero coachbuilder

carromatero carter

carromato covered wagon

carrón *m* hodful of bricks

carroña carrion

carroño putrid, rotten

carroñoso evil-smelling

carroza coach, carriage; decorated float (in procession); *naut* awning; *sl* old-fashioned person, square

carruaje *m* vehicle

carruajero driver

carrucha pulley

carrujado *n* (sewing) fluting; *adj* wrinkled, corrugated

carrusel *m* merry-go-round, roundabout

carta letter; playing card; chart; charter; menu; **~ de ajuste** TV test card; *comm* **~ de crédito** letter of credit; **~ blanca** carte blanche; **~ certificada** registered letter; **~ de examen** diploma; **~ de fletamento** charter-party; **~ de hidalguía** letters patent of nobility; **~ marítima** sea chart; **~ de pedido** order; **~ de presentación** letter of introduction; **~ de sanidad** bill of health; **~ de venta** bill of sale; **~ en lista** letter to be called for; **~ forera** royal grant of privileges; **~ viva** deliverer of an oral message; **a la ~** à la carte; **echar las ~s** to tell a fortune; **tomar ~s en** to take a hand in

cartabón *m* set square, triangle

cartafolio folio-sized sheet of paper

cartagenero *n* native of Cartagena; *adj* of/from Cartagena

cartaginense Carthaginian

Cartago Carthage

cartapacio writing-case, portfolio

cartear to play low-value cards; **~se** to correspond regularly

cartel *m* poster, mural display chart (in school); cartel; agreement; bill; sardine net; lampoon; **tener ~** to have a good reputation

cartelera bill-board, hoarding, entertainments guide

cartelero bill-poster; bill-sticker

cartelista *m + f* poster-artist

carteo correspondence; exchange of letters

cárter *m mech* housing; *mot* crankcase; **sumidor del** ~ sump, *US* oil-pan

cartera pocket-book; wallet, *US* billfold; document case, briefcase; satchel; pocket-flap; portfolio (office of cabinet minister); ~ **de pedidos** *comm* order-book

cartería post-office sorting room

carterista *m* pickpocket

cartero postman

cartílago cartilage

cartilla children's primer; ~ **de ahorros** savings book; ~ **de racionamiento** ration-book; **no saber la** ~ to have not a clue

cartita note

cartografía cartography

cartográfico cartographic

cartógrafo cartographer

cartología cartology

cartológico cartologic(al)

cartólogo cartologist

cartomancia fortune-telling by cards, cartomancy

cartomántico *n* fortune-teller, cardreader; *adj* related to cartomancy

cartón *m* pasteboard, cardboard; carton; *arts* cartoon (for tapestry *etc*); ~ **piedra** papier-mâché

cartonaje *m* cardboard packaging

cartonería cardboard factory

cartonero maker/seller of cardboard articles

cartuchera cartridge-box; cartridge-belt

cartucho cartridge; paper cornet; cylindrical packet containing coins, sweets *etc*; ~ **de fogueo** blank cartridge; **quemar el último** ~ to fire one's last shot

cartujo *n* Carthusian monk; hermit; *adj* Carthusian

cartulaje *m sl* pack (*US* deck) of cards

cartulina thin cardboard; cartridge paper

carvajal *m*, **carvallar** *m*, **carvalledo** oak grove

carvajo, carvallo *bot* oak

casa house, home; building; household; business house, firm; square (on chessboard); ~ **central/matriz** head office; ~ **consistorial** town hall; ~ **cuna** foundling home; ~ **de beneficencia** poor-house; ~ **de camas/citas/trato/mancebía** brothel; ~ **de corrección** reformatory; ~ **de empeños** pawn-shop; ~ **de fieras** menagerie; ~ **de huéspedes** boarding house; ~ **de juegos** gambling house; ~ **de labranza** farmhouse; ~ **de locos** madhouse; ~ **de vecindad** tenement; ~ **fuerte** influential family, stronghold; ~ **profesa** monastery; ~ **real** royal household; **echar la** ~ **por la ventana** to spend lavishly; **empezar la** ~ **por el tejado** to put the cart before the horse; **poner** ~ to set up house; **ser muy de** ~ to be fond of home life; **ya sabe donde tiene su** ~ make yourself at home; **a** ~ **home**

casaca dress-coat; **volver la** ~ to turn one's coat, change sides

casadero marriageable, of marrying age

casada married woman

casado *n* married man

casal *m* country house

casamata casemate

casamentero *n* match-maker; marriage-broker; *adj* match-making

casamiento marriage, matrimony

casar *vt* to marry, mate, unite in wedlock; (of colours *etc*) match; ~**se** to marry, get married; ~**se en segundas nupcias** to remarry; ~**se por poderes** to marry by proxy; ~**se por detrás de la iglesia** *sl* to live in sin; ~**se por el sindicato/de penalty** *sl* to marry, the bride being pregnant

casatienda shop and house combined

cascabel *m* sleigh-bell, jingle-bell; hawk-bell; **serpiente de** ~ rattle-snake; **tener un** ~ to be anxious

cascabelada jingle of small bells; crazy behaviour or act

cascabelero scatterbrained person; baby's rattle

cascada waterfall; cascade

cascajo gravel, rubble; *sl* wreck

cascamiento *n* cracking

cascanueces *m sing + pl* nut-cracker

cascapiedras *m sing + pl* stone-breaker

cascar to crack, break in pieces; crunch;

fam beat up; talk too much; ~**la** to kick the bucket; **estar cascado** to be a physical wreck

cáscara rind, husk, peel; *fam* homosexual

¡cáscaras! Good Heavens!

cascarón *m* thick rind; shell; ~ **de nuez** *naut* cockleshell; **salir del** ~ to come out of one's shell

cascarrabias *m sing + pl* irritable person

cascarudo thick-shelled

casco cranium; shard; crown (of hat); helmet; head-piece; cask; empty bottle; *naut* hull; *zool* hoof; ~ **de una casa** framework of a house; ~ **urbano** town centre; ~ **viejo** old quarter (of a town)

cascote *m* bit of rubble

caseína casein

cáseo curd

caseoso cheesy

casera (Basque Country) farmer's wife; landlady

caserío hamlet; (Basque Country) large farmhouse

casero *n* householder; landlord; caretaker; (Basque Country) farmer; *adj* home; **pan** ~ home-made bread; *sp* (of referees) favouring the home team

caseta shed, cabin; bathing-hut; *sp* changing-room

casete *m* cassette

casi almost, nearly; very nearly; ~ **nada** hardly anything

casilla railway guard's hut; gamekeeper's lodge; booth; locker; pigeon-hole, ruled column in account; ruled space on printed form; square on chequer board; **sacar a alguien de sus** ~**s** to drive s.o. crazy

casillero set of pigeon-holes/lockers; *sp sl* scoreboard

casillo *iron* trifling matter

casita little house, cottage; ~ **de campo** country cottage, weekend house

caso case, occurrence; event; ~ **fortuito** act of God; **a** ~ **hecho** on purpose; **caer en mal** ~ to get into a fix; **en** ~ **de que** in the event of; **en todo** ~ at all events; **estar en el** ~ to be in the picture; **hablar al** ~ to speak to the point; **hacer** ~ **de** to take notice of; **hacer** ~ **omiso de** to ignore; **el** ~ **es que** the fact remains that; **él es un** ~

he's a hopeless case, he's a bit of a lad; **en el mejor de los** ~**s** at best; **en el peor de los** ~**s** if the worst comes to the worst

casorio poor/hasty marriage

caspa dandruff

¡cáspita! Good gracious!

casposo covered with dandruff

casquetazo head-butt, header

casquete *m* helmet; skull-cap; wig; *mech* cap

casquijo *bui* ballast

casquillo tip, cap; ferrule, cartridge case

casquivano feather-brained; scatter-brained

casset *m sl* 1 kilo of marihuana

casta breed, lineage, caste; class; **toro de** ~ fighting bull; **cruzar** ~**s** to cross-breed

Castálidas *fpl* Muses

castaña chestnut; bore; pain in the neck; drunkenness; *sl* slap; ~ **de Brasil** Brazil nut; ~ **de Indias** horse-chestnut; **coger una** ~ to get tipsy; **dar la** ~ to bore to death

castañal *m*, **castañar** *m*, **castañeda**, **castañedo** chestnut grove

castañero dealer in chestnuts

castañeta castanet; snapping of the fingers

castañetazo sound of castanet; cracking of joints

castañete brownish

castañetear to rattle (castanets); chatter (teeth)

castañeteo clicking (fingers, castanets), chattering (teeth)

castaño *n* chestnut-tree; chestnut-wood; ~ **de Indias** horse-chestnut tree; *adj* chestnut-coloured

castañuelas *fpl* castanets; **estar como unas** ~**s** to be as happy as a sandboy

castañuelo *adj* chestnut-coloured

castellanismo expression peculiar to Castile

castellanizar to Castilianize

castellano *n + adj* Castilian; **a la castellana** in the Castilian fashion; **en** ~ in plain language

castellar *m bot* St John's wort

casticidad *f* purity (of language)

casticismo purism

casticista *m + f* purist

castidad *f* chastity

castigable punishable

castigación *f* castigation, punishment

castigador *n m* punisher; *adj* punishing

castigar to punish, chastise; overwork; break in (animals); be tough; be hard to get; *sport* penalize; afflict; ~ **la vista** to strain one's eyesight

castigo punishment, chastisement, correction, nuisance

Castilla Castile; **ancha es** ~ it takes all sorts to make a world

castillado castellated

castillejo small castle; scaffolding

castillo castle; ~ **de fuego** firework display; ~ **de naipes** house of cards, flimsy building; **hacer** ~**s en el aire** to build castles in the air

castizar to purify, refine

castizo of noble descent; pure-blooded; pure (of language), real; authentic; traditional

casto pure, chaste

castor *m zool* beaver

castoreño made of beaver-skin

castra pruning, pruning season

castración *f* castration, gelding

castrado eunuch

castrador *m* castrator, gelder

castrar to castrate, geld; *bot* prune

castrense of the army; **cura** ~ padre, chaplain

castro hopscotch

casual chance, accidental, casual

casualidad *f* chance, coincidence; **por** ~ by chance

casualismo casualism

casualista *m+f* casualist

casualmente *adv* by chance, by accident

casuario cassowary

casuca, casucha miserable house, hovel

casuista *n m+f* casuist; *adj* casuistic(al)

casuística casuistry

casuístico casuistic(al)

casulla *eccles* chasuble

casullero maker of chasubles and other vestments

cata trying, tasting; trial, sample; plummet; **dar** ~ to examine

catacaldos *m sing+pl* wine-taster

cataclismo cataclysm

catacumbas *fpl* catacombs

catador *m* taster, sampler; ~ **de vinos** wine-taster

catadura tasting

catafalco catafalque

catalán *n m+adj* Catalonian, Catalan

catalanista *m+f* Catalanist

catalejo telescope

catalepsia *med* catalepsy

cataléptico *med* cataleptic

Catalina Catherine, Kathleen; **rueda catalina** Catherine wheel

catalogable that can be catalogued

catalogación *f* cataloguing

catalogador *m*, **catalógrafo** cataloguer

catalogar to catalogue, list

catálogo catalogue, list

Catalunya, Cataluña Catalonia

catante tasting

cataplasma cataplasm, poultice; *m+f fam* pain-in-the-neck, bore

¡cataplum! bang!, crash!

catapulta catapult

catapún: del año ~ donkey's years old

catar to taste, try, sample; look at, examine, investigate

catarata waterfall; *med* cataract

catarral catarrhal

catarro catarrh; cold

catarroso *n* person subject to colds; *adj* having a cold

catarsis *f* catharsis

catártico cathartic

catástrofe *f* catastrophe

catastrófico catastrophic

catastrofismo doom-mongering

catastrofista *m+f* doom-monger

cataviento *naut* weathervane

catavinos *m sing+pl* wine-taster

cate *m fam* fail (exam mark)

catear to procure; *fam* flunk, fail (exam)

catecismo catechism

cátedra chair (of professor); professorship; *eccles* see; lecture room

catedral *f* cathedral

catedralicio pertaining to a cathedral

catedrático professor; *school* head of department

categoría category, class, rank; quality; **hombre de** ~ man of standing

categórico categoric(al); flat

catenaria catenary, chain; **reacción** ~ chain reaction

catequesis *f sing+pl* catechizing

catequismo catechism

catequista *m+f* catechist

catequización *f* catechizing

catequizante *n m+f* catechizer; *adj*

catechizing
catequizar to catechize
caterva crowd; load
catéter *m med* catheter
cateterizar to sound with a catheter
catódico cathodic
cátodo cathode
catolicismo Catholicism
católico *n* Catholic; *adj* Catholic; **no estar muy ~** to be not too good; (of food) be a bit off
catón *m* primer; children's reader; censor
catorce fourteen, fourteenth
catorceañero fourteen-year-old
catorceno fourteenth; aged fourteen
catorzavo fourteenth part
catre *m* cot, bed; **~ de mar** hammock; **~ de tijera** camp-bed
catrín *m* toff
caucáseo, caucásico Caucasian
Cáucaso *m* Caucasus
cauce *m* riverbed, mill-race; trench; course; **~s legales** official channels
caución *f* caution, security, pledge, bond
caucionar to take precautions against
caucho rubber
caudal *n m* fortune, wealth; stock; abundance; (river) flow, volume; **águila ~** red-tailed eagle; **caja de ~es** safe
caudaloso *adj* having much water; abundant; rich
caudillaje *m* leadership; tyranny
caudillismo dictatorship
caudillo leader, boss, chief; *mil* commander
causa cause; reason, motive; *leg* case, trial; **a ~ de** on account of, because of; **hacer ~ leg** to bring an action
causal *f* grounds on which action is taken; *adj gramm* causal, causative
causalidad *f* causality
causante *n m+f* causer; *adj* causative; causing; *fam* guilty
causar to cause; make
causativo causative
causón *m* high fever
causticidad *f* causticity; pungent satire
cáustico caustic, burning
cautela caution, care; artfulness; **absolver a ~** to give the benefit of the doubt

cautelar to prevent; **~se de** to guard against
cauteloso cautious, wary
cauterio cauterization
cauterizante cauterizing
cauterizar to cauterize
cautivador, cautivante captivating
cautivar to captivate, win over, charm, capture
cautiverio, cautividad *f* captivity
cautivo captive
cauto cautious
cava wine-cellar
cavacote *m* hillock
cavador *m* digger
cavadura digging
cavar to dig (out)
caverna cavern, cave
cavernidad *f* cavernousness
cavernoso cavernous
caviar *m* caviare
cavidad *f* cavity
cavilación *f* deep thought
cavilar to ponder (over)
cavilosidad *f* pondering
caviloso deep in thought
cayado shepherd's crook; bishop's crozier
cayo islet
cayuco fishing-boat
caz *m* mill-race
caza *n m* fighter-plane; *f* chase, hunt, hunting, game; **~ bombardero** fighter bomber; **~ furtiva** poaching; **~ mayor** big game; **~ menor** small game, fowling; **dar ~ a** to pursue; **ir de ~** to go hunting; **seguir la ~** to follow the scent
cazabe *m* cassava
cazaclavos *m sing+pl* nail-puller, claw
cazada ladleful
cazadero hunting-ground
cazador *n m* hunter, huntsman; **~ de dotes** fortune-hunter; **~ furtivo** poacher; *adj* hunting
cazadora huntress; hunting-jacket; jacket
cazar to chase, pursue, hunt; shoot, catch
cazasubmarinos *m sing+pl naut* submarine-chaser
cazatalentos *m sing+pl sp+theat* talent-scout
cazatorpederos *m sing+pl naut*

destroyer
cazcalear *fam* to fuss about
cazcorvo bow-legged
cazo ladle, scoop, saucepan; *fam* ugly woman
cazolada panful
cazoleja small saucepan
cazoleta small pan; boss (of shield); handguard (of sword); pipe-bowl
cazonete *m naut* toggle
cazuela earthen stew-pot; casserole; *theat* the gods
cazurro *n+adj* dour, surly; stupid
CC.OO (Comisiones Obreras) communist trade union
ce *f* letter c; ~ **por be** A to Z; **por** ~ **o por be** for one reason or another
cebada barley; ~ **perlada** pearl barley
cebadal *m* barley-field
cebadar to feed (animals)
cebadera nose-bag; barley-bin
cebadería barley-market
cebadero feeding-place; barley dealer; *arts* farmyard scene
cebadilla *bot* rye-grass
cebador *m* powder-horn
cebadura fattening (of farm animals)
cebar *vt* to fatten; feed; cram, stuff; prime (a firearm); bait (fish-hook); *vi* to penetrate; take hold of; ~**se en** to vent one's anger on
cebellina sable
cebo feed, fodder; fattening (of animals); bait; priming (of firearms)
cebolla onion; (flower) bulb; *sl* head; ~ **escalonia** shallot
cebollada onion stew
cebollana chive
cebollar *m* onion-patch
cebollero onion-seller
cebolleta spring-onion
cebollino onion-seedling, spring onion
cebolludo bulbous
cebón *m sl* fat; fattened pig
cebra zebra
cebrado striped like a zebra
cebú *m* zebu
ceca: de la ~ **a la meca** hither and thither
cecear to lisp; pronounce s as z
ceceo lisping; pronunciation of s as z
Cecilia Cecily
Cecilio Cecil
cecina cured meat
cecinar to dry and salt

cecografía braille
cecógrafo braille writer
cedacero sieve-maker, sieve-seller
cedente *m* conveyer; *adj* ceding, granting
ceder to yield, give up; transfer, convey; hand over; cede; ~ **a la razón** to give in to reason; ~ **el paso** to give way
cedizo putrid, rotten
cedro *bot* cedar
cédula slip of paper; bill; decree; warrant; share; government stock; ~ **de abono** order remitting a tax; ~ **personal identity documents; ~ **real** royal letters patent
cedulaje *m* fees paid for royal letters patent
cedulón *m* public notice; lampoon
cefalea migraine
céfalo mullet
céfiro zephyr
cegador blinding
cegajoso blear-eyed
cegar *vt* to blind; block up, close, wall up; cover over; ~ **un pozo** to stop up a well; *vi* to go blind
cegato short-sighted
ceguedad *f* blindness
ceja eyebrow; edging; brow (of hill); *mus* bridge; *carp* rabbet; **estar hasta las** ~**s de ...** to be up to one's eyes in ...; **fruncir las** ~**s** to frown; **quemarse las** ~**s** to burn the midnight oil
cejar to back away; give way; relax; take it easy
cejijunto, cejudo beetle-browed, frowning
cejilla *mus* bridge
cejo river mist
celada helmet; snare, ambush; artful trick; **caer en la** ~ to fall into the trap; **en** ~ secretly
celador *m* watchman; curator; vigilante
celaje *m* skylight; omen, harbinger; ~**s** *arts* cloud effects
celar to see to; watch, spy on (motivated by jealousy, fear *etc*); supervise, control, conceal
celda cell
celebérrimo extremely famous
celebración *f* celebration; acclaim
celebrador praising, applauding, celebrating
celebrante *m* celebrant

celebrar *vt* to celebrate; hold (a meeting *etc*); praise; be glad; **lo celebro** I'm very pleased (about it); **~se** to be held, take place; *vi* to say mass

célebre renowned, famous

celebridad *f* celebrity, fame, renown

celeridad *f* velocity, swiftness, speed

celeste celestial, heavenly; **azul ~** sky-blue

celestialidad *f* glory

celestina bawd, procuress

celibato celibacy

célibe *m+f* bachelor; spinster; celibate

celidonia *bot* celandine

¹ **celo: papel de ~** sellotape

² **celo** zeal, ardour, rut; heat; **~s** jealousy; **dar ~s a** to make jealous; **huelga de ~** work-to-rule; **tener ~s** to be jealous

celofán *m* cellophane

celosía lattice window

celoso zealous; jealous

celta *n m+f +adj* Celt, Celtic; *m* Celtic language

celtíbero, celtibérico Celtiberian

céltico Celtic

celtismo Celtism

celtista *m+f* Celtologist

célula *biol + pol* cell

celular: coche ~ Black Maria

celuloide *m* celluloid

celulósico *adj* cellulose; **cola celulósica** cellulose paste

celulosidad *f* cellulosity

celulosa cellulose, wood-pulp

celuloso *adj* cellulose

cellar *metal* forged

cementación *f* cementation

cementar to cement

cementerial relating to a cemetery

cementerio cemetery, graveyard

cemento cement

cementoso like cement

cena dinner, supper, evening meal

cenaaoscuras *m+f sing+pl* miser, recluse

cenáculo literary group

cenadero supper-room; summer-house

cenador *m* summer-house; arbour; open gallery round a patio

cenagal *m* bog, quagmire; predicament; mess

cenagoso muddy, marshy

cenar *vi* to have supper, dinner; *vt* have for supper

cenceño lean, thin, slender

cencerrada: dar la ~ to make fun of a woman on the first night of her second marriage; make noise

cencerrear (of cowbells *etc*) to jingle continually; kick up a racket

cencerreo jingling, din

cencerro cow-bell; **a ~s tapados** by stealth; **~ zumbón** bell worn by leading animal in herd; **estar como un ~** to be mad

cencido untilled, uncultivated

cenefa border, edge, hem; band; flounce; valance; *naut* awning

cenetista *m+f* member of **Confederación Nacional de Trabajo** (anarchist trade union)

cenicero ash-bin; ash-pan; ashtray

Cenicienta Cinderella

ceniciento ashen; ash-coloured

cenit, cénit *m* zenith

ceniza ash, ashes, cinders; **convertir en ~s** to reduce to ashes; **miércoles de ~** Ash Wednesday

cenizo *n bot* goosefoot; *sl* born loser; **ser un ~** to be a jinx/Jonah

cenizoso ashen

cenobio monastery

cenobita *m+f* monk; nun

cenotafio cenotaph

censal *m* annual ground-rent

censar to take a census

censo census; tax, ground rent; **~ electoral** electoral roll

censor *n m* censor; critic; auditor; **~ de cuentas** *comm* company auditor

censualista *m+f* lessor; copy-holder

censura censorship

censurador *n m* fault-finder, censor; *adj* censorious

censurante censorious

censurar to censor; censure; condemn; criticize

censurista *n m+f* critic, fault-finder; *adj* carping, critical

centaura *bot* centaury

centauro *myth* centaur

centavo *n* cent; *adj* hundredth

centella lightning, flash, spark; **como una ~** in a flash

centellador brilliant, gleaming, scintillating

centellante, centelleante gleaming, sparkling, flashing

centellar, centellear to gleam, flash, twinkle, sparkle

centelleo *n* gleam(ing), flash(ing), sparkle, twinkling

centena hundred

centenada hundred; a ~s by the hundred

centenal *m* rye-field

centenar *m* unit of one hundred; rye-field; a ~es by the hundred

centenario *n m* centenary; centenarian; *adj* centenary, centennial

centenero (of soil) suitable for rye

centeno rye

centesimal *adj* centesimal

centésimo *n* hundredth

centígrado centigrade

centigramo centigram

centilitro centilitre

centímetro centimetre

céntimo *n* hundredth part; *adj* hundredth; (coin) hundredth part of a peseta; cent; no tener un ~ not to have a penny

centinela *m*+*f* sentry, sentinel; *fig* lookout

centípedo *m* centipede; *adj* centipedal

centollo *zool* spider-crab

centón *m* patchwork quilt

centonar to pile, heap up

central *f* head office, headquarters; plant; ~ (telefónica) (telephone) exchange; ~ eléctrica power station; *adj* central, centric

centralismo centralism

centralista *m*+*f* centralist

centralita switchboard

centralización *f* centralization

centralizar to centralize

centrar to centre

céntrico central; en un lugar ~ near the town centre; punto ~ focal point

centrifugar to centrifuge

centrífugo centrifugal; bomba centrífuga centrifugal pump

centrípeto centripetal

centro centre, middle; centrepiece; town centre; ~ docente school; estar en su ~ to be in one's element

Centroamérica Central America

centroamericano *n m*+*f* +*adj* Central American

centrocampista *m sp* mid-field player

centuplicación *f* centuplication

centuplicador *adj* centuplicating

centuplicar to centuplicate; multiply a hundredfold; *fig* greatly increase

centuplo hundredfold

centurión *m* centurion

cenutrio *sl* fool

ceñido tight; tight-fitting; narrow-waisted; hard-up; curva ceñida tight/sharp bend

ceñidor *m* girdle, sash

ceñidura girding, contraction, restriction

ceñir to gird, circle; surround; hem in, reduce; contract; ~ espada to wear a sword; ~se to confine o.s., limit o.s.; cut down; ~se a lo justo to limit o.s. to bare essentials; ~se a to concentrate on; ~se a las circunstancias to adapt o.s. to circumstances

ceño frown, scowl; band, hoop, ring; arrugar/fruncir el ~ to frown

ceñudo frowning, grim, stern-looking

cepa vine-stock; stub (of tree-stem); stock; root; *archi* pier of arch; de buena ~ of good origin; de pura ~ authentic

cepellón *m* ball of earth round roots of a plant (for transplanting/repotting)

cepilladura *carp* planing; ~s shavings

cepillamiento *carp* planing

cepillar to brush; *carp* plane; *sl* flatter; *sl* cheat out of money; *sl* kill; *sp* deflect the ball; *vulg sl* lay, fuck; fail (exam)

cepillo almsbox, poorbox; *carp* plane; brush; ~ de dientes toothbrush; ~ para la ropa clothes brush

cepo *bot* branch, bough; stocks (for punishment); trap, snare; poorbox; clasp, clamp; ~ del ancla anchor-stock

ceporro old vine (pulled up for fuel); clod; stupid person; estar hecho un ~ to sleep like a log

cera wax, wax candles/tapers; no hay más ~ que la que arde that's all there is to it

ceráceo waxy

cerámica ceramics, pottery

cerámico ceramic

ceramista *m*+*f* potter, ceramist

cerapez *f* cobbler's wax

cerbatana *mil* blowpipe; pea-shooter; ear-trumpet; hablar por ~ to speak through a third person

cerca *n f* wall, fence; ~ viva hedge; *m*

tener buen/mal ~ to admit of/not to admit of close inspection; ~s *arts* objects in the foreground; *adv* nearby, near, close; ~ de *prep* near, close to; ~ de aquí near here; ~ de las dos about two o'clock; aquí ~ close by; de ~ at close quarters

cercado enclosure; fence; walled/fenced-in piece of land

cercador *n m* hedger; *adj* enclosing

cercadura enclosure; fence, wall, railing

cercamiento (act of) enclosing, surrounding

cercanía nearness; proximity; ~s vicinity, surroundings; outskirts; tren de ~s suburban train

cercano near; close

cercar to enclose, fence; hem in, encircle, surround; *mil* lay siege to

cercén all around, completely

cercenador *m*, cercenadora clipper, pruner

cercenadura clipping, retrenchment; ~s clippings

cercenar to clip, pare; cut off (extremities); abridge, reduce; curtail

cerceta *orni* teal; ~ carretona *orni* gargany

cerciorar to assure; ~se to check up, make certain

cerco *n* ring, hoop; rim, border, edge; halo; *mil* siege; frame (of door, picture *etc*); levantar el ~ to raise the siege; poner ~ a to lay siege to

cerchar to plant vine cuttings

cerda horsehair, bristle; *zool* sow; ~ de puerco hog's bristle; ~s snares

cerdada herd of swine; rotten trick

Cerdeña Sardinia

cerdito piglet, piggy, little pig

cerdo pig, hog; pork; ~ de matanza/de engorde fatted pig

cerdoso bristly

cerebelo cerebellum

cerebralidad *f* intellectual vigour

cerebrino cerebral

cerebro cerebrum; brain(s)

cereceda cherry-orchard

ceremonia ceremony, pomp, formality; *eccles* service; de ~ formal; de pura ~ as a pure formality; sin ~s informal, unceremoniously

ceremoniático ceremonious

ceremoniero fond of formality

ceremonioso ceremonious, formal

céreo waxy

cerería chandlery

cerero chandler

cerevisina brewer's yeast

cereza cherry

cerezal *m* cherry-orchard

cerezo cherry-tree; cherry-wood

cerífero wax-producing

cerificación *f* purifying of wax

cerificar to purify (wax)

cerilla wax taper, match; ear-wax

cerillero match seller, matchbox

cerneja fetlock

cerner to sift; scrutinize; ~se sobre to hover threateningly over; hang over

cernícalo *orni* kestrel; cloddish fellow; coger un ~ to get sozzled

cernido, cernidura sifting

cero zero; ser un ~ a la izquierda to be a mere cipher/a nobody

ceroma ointment

ceromático containing oil and wax

ceromiel *m* ointment of wax and honey

cerote *m* shoemaker's wax; *fam* panic, funk

cerotear to wax (thread)

cerquillo small circle, hoop; seam, welt

cerquita quite close; nice and handy

cerradero *n* lock, locker; purse-strings; *adj* locked, locking

cerradizo that can be locked or secured

cerrado *n* enclosure; *fam* blockhead; *adj* closed, shut; close, reserved, secretive; obtuse; (of accent) broad; *meteor* overcast, cloudy; (of beard) thick; a ojos ~s unquestioningly; a puerta cerrada secretly, in private; noche cerrada pitch-black night

cerrador *n m* fastener; locker; shutter; porter; doorkeeper; fastening; *adj* locking, shutting

cerradura locking up; lock; ~ de golpe/de muelle spring-lock; ~ embutida mortise-lock

cerraja lock; *bot* sow-thistle

cerrajear to work as a locksmith

cerrajería locksmith's trade/shop/workshop

cerrajero locksmith

cerrajón *m* steep, craggy cliff

cerramiento shutting/locking-up

cerrar to close, shut; lock, fasten; stop up, plug; turn off; clench; enclose, fence in; put an end to; engage (enemy); ~ **una carta** to seal a letter; ~ **un contrato** to conclude a contract; ~ **el paso** to bar the way; ~ **el pico** *sl* to shut up; ~ **la marcha** to bring up the rear; ~ **los oídos** to turn a deaf ear; **al** ~ **el día** at nightfall; ~**se** (of wounds) to heal up; ~ **con llave** to lock

cerrazón *f* gathering storm-clouds; mist; thick-headedness

correta *naut* bulwarks

cerril uneven, rough; unbroken, untamed; boorish; stupid

cerrilla die (for milling coins)

cerro *m* neck (of animal); backbone; hill; **en** ~ bareback

cerrojazo slamming (of a bolt)

cerrojo bolt, latch; *sp* purely defensive tactics; **tentar** ~**s** to try all ways and means

certamen *m* literary discussion; competition, contest

certería accuracy, good aim

certero accurate, on the mark; sure, certain

certeza certainty, certitude; **tener la** ~ **de que** to be certain that

certidumbre *f* certainty

certificable certifiable

certificación *f* certificate, certification; (of letter *etc*) registration

certificado *n* certificate; *adj* registered, certified

certificador *n m* certifier; *adj* certifying, registering

certificar to certify, guarantee; (of letters *etc*) register

certificativo certifying

certísimo absolutely true

certitud *f* certitude, certainty

cerumen *m* ear-wax

cerval, cervario pertaining to deer; **tener un miedo** ~ to be scared to death

cervantesco, cervantino in the style of Cervantes

cervantismo study of Cervantes

cervantista *m+f* student of Cervantes

cervantófilo admirer of Cervantes

cervatillo young fawn

cerveceo fermentation of beer

cervecería brewery, ale-house, bar

cervecero *n* brewer, ale-house keeper; *adj* pertaining to beer

cerveza beer, ale; ~ **de barril** draught beer

cervicabra gazelle

cérvidos *mpl* deer

cervillera helmet

cervino, cervuno cervine

cesación *f*, **cesamiento** cessation, pause

cesante *n m+f* suspended civil servant; *adj* suspended from office

cesantía suspension from civil service; pay received while suspended

cesar to cease, stop; be dismissed/suspended (from a post); ~ **de llover** to stop raining; **sin** ~ ceaselessly

César *m* Caesar; **o** ~ **o nada** all or nothing

cesario: operación cesárea Caesarian section

cese *m* cessation; dismissal, suspension; stoppage (of wages); end; ~ **de alarma** all-clear; ~ **de fuego** cease-fire

cesible *leg* transferable

cesión *f* cession, transfer; conveyance; ~ **de bienes** surrender of property

cesionario *leg* cessionary

cesionista *m+f* transferrer

césped *m* grass plot; turf; lawn, sward; ~ **inglés** lawn

cespitar to hesitate, vacillate

cesta basket, hamper, pannier; **llevar la** ~ to play gooseberry

cestada basketful

cestería basket-making; basket shop/factory

cestero basket-maker; basket-seller

cestico, cestillo, cestito small basket

cesto basket; ~ **de los papeles** waste-paper basket; **coger agua en** ~ to work in vain

cetáceo cetaceous

cetaria hatchery

cetrería falconry, hawking

cetrero falconer, hawker; verger

cetrino sallow

cetro sceptre; *eccles* rod; wand, perch, roost

ceutí *n+adj* (native) of Ceuta

C.I. (**coeficiente intelectual**) I.Q. (Intelligence Quotient)

Cía. (**Compañía**) Co. (Company)

ciaboga *naut* putting about

cianuro cyanide

ciar *naut* to back water; back-pedal; soft-pedal

ciática sciatica

ciático sciatic
cibernética cybernetics
cíbolo *zool* bison
cicatería niggardliness; meanness
cicatero *sl* pickpocket; stingy
cicatriz *f* scar
cicatrizante healing
cicatrizar to heal up
cicatrizativo healing
cicerón *m* eloquent orator
cicerone *m* guide
ciclamen *m*, **ciclamino** cyclamen
ciclamor *m* sycamore
ciclar to polish, burnish
cíclico cyclical
ciclismo cycling
ciclista *m* + *f* cyclist
ciclo *phys* cycle; season; course
ciclógrafo cyclograph
ciclometría cyclometry
ciclométrico cyclometric
ciclómetro cyclometer
ciclón *m* cyclone
ciclonal cyclonic
cíclope *m myth* + *zool* cyclops
ciclópeo cyclopean
ciclorama cyclorama
ciclostilar to cyclostyle
ciclostilo cyclostyle
cicuta *bot* hemlock
cicutado impregnated with hemlock juice
cicutina hemlock poison
cid *m* leader; **el Cid Campeador** Spain's national hero
cidra citron; type of water-melon
cidral *m* citron plantation
cidro citron plant
ciego *n* blind person; *adj* blind; (of pipes *etc*) blocked; **~ de ira** blind with rage; **a ciegas** blindly
cieguecico, cieguecito, cieguillo, cieguezuelo poor little blind creature
cielito little darling; Argentinian folk-dance
cielo sky, heaven; ceiling; darling; **~ benigno** mild climate; **~ de la boca** roof of the mouth; **bajado del ~** heaven-sent; **dormir a ~ raso** to sleep in the open; **poner el grito en el ~** to raise Cain; **ver el ~ abierto** to see a way out
ciempiés *m sing* + *pl* centipede
cien one hundred; *m sl* water-closet

ciénaga fen, marsh
ciencia science; knowledge, learning; **a ~ cierta** for certain
cienmilésimo hundred-thousandth
cienmilímetro hundreth part of a milli-metre
cieno mire, mud
científico *n* scholar, scientist; *adj* scientific
ciento hundred(th), one hundred; **por ~** per cent; **por ~s** by hundreds
cientopiés *see* **ciempiés**
cierne *m* flowering, blossoming; **en ~s** in its infancy
cierrapuertas *m sing* + *pl* automatic door-closing apparatus
cierre *m* closing, closure, shutting; lock-ing, lock; bolt, latch; clasp, fastener; **~ metálico** flexible roller-shutter (for shops); **~ patronal** lock-out
cierro closure
cierto certain, sure, true; **~ país** a certain country; **de ~** for certain; **lo ~** the truth; **por ~** certainly, (after a negative) by no means; **~s** some
cierva deer, hind
ciervo deer, stag; **~ volante** stag-beetle
cierzo cold north wind
cifra cipher; code; abbreviation; figure, number; **en palabras y en ~s** in words and figures; **en ~** in code
cifrador *m* person who writes in cipher
cifrar to cipher, write in code; abridge, summarize
cigala crayfish
cigarra cicada
cigarrera cigar-case; cigar-seller
cigarrería *SA* tobacconist's shop
cigarrillo cigarette; **~ de la risa** *sl* mari-huana cigarette
cigarro: **~ puro** cigar
cigoñino *orni* young stork
cigoñuela *orni* stilt
cigüeña *orni* stork; *mech* crank, winch
cigüeñal *m* crankshaft
cigüeñear to rattle with the beak
cigüeño male stork
cilantro *bot* coriander
cilicio hairshirt
cilindrada cylinder capacity
cilindrado rolling
cilindrar to roll
cilíndrico cylindrical
cilindrín *m sl* cigarette, fag

cilindro cylinder; drum; roller
cilindroide cylindroid
cilindroideo cylindrical
cima summit; top; **por ~** lightly, cursorily, superficially
cimar to clip the top (of hedge, shrub)
cimarrón *adj* wild, unruly; *naut* lazy
cimbalero cymbalist
címbalo cymbal
cimborio, cimborrio dome
cimbornales *mpl naut* scupper-holes
cimbra *archi* wooden frame used in building an arch
cimbrar, cimbrear to make vibrate; shake; bend; beat; **~se** to sway
cimbreante bending, swaying, flexible
cimentación *f* (laying of a) foundation
cimentar to lay the foundations of; found
cimiento foundation; basis; base, groundwork
cimitarra scimitar
cinabrio vermilion
cinc *m* zinc
cincel *m* chisel
cincelado *n* chiselling, engraving
cincelador *m* stone-cutter, engraver
cinceladura carving, chasing
cincelar to chisel, carve; engrave, chase
cincelería engraver's shop
cinco five, fifth; **saber cuántas son ~** to know what's what
cincoañal five-year-old (animal)
cincoañero five-year-old (child)
cincoenrama *bot* cinquefoil
cincomesino five-month-old
cincona *f bot* quinine
cincuenta fifty, fiftieth
cincuentañal *adj* fifty-year-old
cincuentavo, cincuenteno fiftieth
cincuentón *m* fifty-year-old man
cincha girth, cinch; saddle-strap; **ir rompiendo ~s** to go hell for leather
cinchar to girth, cinch up
cincho bellyband; belt, girdle; tyre
cine *m* cinema, films; **~ mudo** silent film; **~ sonoro** talking film; **~ en relieve** three-dimensional films; **ir al ~** to go to the movies/pictures
cineasta *m+f* cinema tycoon; film producer, film director; actor; actress
cinegética cynegetics
cinelandia filmland
cinemateca film library

cinemático cinematic
cinematografía cinematography
cinematografiar to film
cinematográfico cinematographic, film
cinematógrafo cinematograph; cinema
cinematurgo *cin* script-writer
cineraria: urna ~ cinerary urn
cinericio ashy
cineriforme ash-like
cingalés *n+adj* Singhalese
cíngaro gipsy
cinglar *naut* to scull
cíngulo (priest's) girdle
cínico *adj* cynical; barefaced, unprincipled; *n* cynic; brazen person; unprincipled person
cinismo cynicism; barefacedness; lack of principle; **¡que ~!** what a nerve!
cinocéfalo *zool* dog-faced baboon
cinquero zinc-worker
cinta ribbon, tape, band, strip; hempen net (for tunny-fishing); kerbstone; *archi* scroll; **~ aislante** insulating tape; **~ de freno** brake lining; **~ de teletipo** teletape; **~ de transporte** conveyor-belt; **~ magnetofónica** magnetic tape; **~ métrica** tape-measure
cintrado *archi* curved
cintura waist; girdle; waistline; throat (of chimney); *naut* rope knot; **meter en ~** to bring to heel
cinturilla waist ornament
cinturón *m* belt; sash; **~ de castidad** chastity-belt; **~ de seguridad** *aer* safety-belt; **~ salva-vidas** life-belt; **apretar el ~** *fig* tighten the belt
cipayo sepoy
cipote *vulg sl* penis
ciprés *m* cypress
cipresal *m* cypress grove
cipriota *n m+f+adj* Cypriot
circense of the circus
circo circus; amphitheatre
circuición *f* surrounding, encircling
circuir to surround, encircle
circuito circuit; track; **corto ~** short circuit; network; **~ impreso** printed circuit
circulación *f* circulation; traffic
circulador circulating
circulante circulating; **biblioteca ~** circulating library
circular *n f* circular letter; *adj* circular; *vt*

to circulate; circularize; *vi* to circulate, move, travel around; go from hand to hand; drive; (transport) run

circulatorio circulatory

círculo circle, ring

circuncidante circumcising

circuncidar to circumcise; clip; curtail

circuncisión *f* circumcision

circunciso circumcised; *fig* Jewish; Moslem

circundante surrounding, encircling

circundar to surround, encircle

circunferencia circumference

circunferencial circumferential, surrounding, circular

circunferente circumscribing

circunflejo circumflex

circunlocución *f* circumlocution

circunnavegación *f* circumnavigation

circunnavegante *m* circumnavigator

circunnavegar to circumnavigate

circunscribir to circumscribe, enclose, encircle

circunscripción *f* circumscription

circunspección *f* circumspection

circunspecto circumspect

circunstancia circumstance; ~ **agravante** aggravating circumstance; ~ **atenuante** extenuating circumstance; ~ **eximente** exonerating circumstance

circunstanciado circumstantial, detailed

circunstancial circumstantial

circunstante *adj* surrounding

circunstantes *mpl* bystanders

circunvalación *f* surrounding; **carretera de** ~ ring-road, by-pass

circunvalar to surround, encircle; by-pass

circunvecino neighbouring, adjacent

circunvención *f* circumvention

circunvenir to circumvent; over-reach

circunvolar to fly around

circunvolución *f* circumvolution

circunyacente surrounding, adjacent

cirial *m eccles* processional candlestick

cirigallo wastrel, idler

cirio wax taper, candle

cirolar *m see* **ciruelar**

cirolero *see* **ciruelo**

cirro *meteor* + *zool* cirrus

cirrosis hepática cirrhosis of the liver

ciruela plum; ~ **claudia** greengage; ~ **damascena** damson; ~ **de yema** yellow

plum; ~ **pasa** prune

ciruelar *m* plum-tree orchard

ciruelo plum-tree; *fam* fool

cirugía surgery; ~ **estética** cosmetic surgery; ~ **mayor/menor** major/minor surgery; ~ **nerviosa** neurosurgery; ~ **plástica** plastic surgery

cirujano surgeon

ciscar *vulg sl* to shit

cisco small coal; *fam* uproar; **armar un** ~ to kick up a shindy; **hacer** ~ to smash to smithereens; **estar hecho** ~ to be in a sorry state

cisión *f* incision

Cisjordania West Bank (Palestine)

cisma schism; *fig* disagreement

cismático schismatic

cismontaña situated on the side of a mountain

cisne *m orni* swan

cisterciense *m* + *f* Cistercian

cisterna cistern, water-tank

cita appointment, date; citation, quotation; meeting

citable quotable, citable

citación *f* citation, quotation

citador *n m* citer, quoter; *adj* citing, quoting

citar to make an appointment with; quote, cite; *leg* summon; (bull-fighting) incite the bull

cítara zither

citarista *m* + *f* zither-player

citatorio *n leg* summons; *adj* summoning

citrato citrate

cítrico *adj* citric

cítricos *mpl* citrus fruits

citrón *m* lemon

ciudad *f* city; town

ciudadanía citizenship

ciudadano *n* citizen, town-dweller; ~ **de a pie** man-in-the-street; *adj* of/from a town/city; civic

ciudadela citadel

civeta civet cat

civeto civet perfume

cívico civic, public-spirited; **espíritu** ~ public spirit

civil *n m* civilian; Civil Guard; salt herring; *adj* civil

civilidad *f* public-spiritedness, sociability

civilismo *see* **civismo**

civilista *m* + *f* student of civil law; anti-militarist

civilización f civilization

civilizador n m civilizer; adj civilizing

civilizar to civilize; ~se to become civilized

civismo public-spiritedness

cizalla shear; sheet-metal shears; paper cutters

cizallar to shear

cizaña bot darnel; discord

cizañador m one who sows discord

cizañero trouble-maker, trouble-making

cla m theat sl claque

clamador n m clamourer; adj crying-out

clamar to cry out for, clamour for; ~ al cielo to cry out to heaven

clamor m clamour, outcry; noise

clamorear to clamour; implore incessantly

clamoreo clamour(ing)

clamoroso clamorous; noisy

clamosidad f clamorousness

clan m clan; clique, faction; mob

clandestinidad f secrecy; pol underground

clandestino clandestine, secret; pol underground

clara sl shandy; white of egg

claraboya skylight

clarea mulled wine

clarear vt to brighten, give light to, make clear; rinse; vi to get light; clear up; dawn; ~se to show through; give o.s. away

clarecer to dawn, grow light

clarete m claret; rosé

claridad f clarity, brightness, clearness, light; ~ de vista clear-sightedness; ~es plain speech; con ~ clearly

clarificable that can be clarified

clarificación f clarification

clarificador n m clarifier; adj clarifying

clarificar to brighten, lighten, clarify

clarificativo clarifying

clarimente m arts colour-reviver; cosmetic oil

clarín m bugle/trumpet (player)

clarinete m clarinet; clarinettist

clarinetista m+f clarinettist

clarión m crayon, chalk

clarisa nun of the order of St Clare

clarividencia clear-sightedness

clarividente n m+f clear-sighted person; clairvoyant; adj clear-sighted

¹ claro n skylight; gap, space, interval; arts light; meteor clear period; space in a crowd; clearing, glade; ~ de luna moonlight; ~s loopholes; archi opening, window

² claro adj clear, bright, light; thin, sparse; weak; frank; **a las claras** plainly, clearly, adv of course; **poner en ~** to make clear; **sacar en ~** to get clear/straight

claror m brightness

claroscuro chiaroscuro, light and shade; monochrome

clarucho (of soup) watery, thinnish

clase f class, rank; kind; sort, species; family; form, class-room; lesson; **de cualquier ~** of any kind; ~ **alta** upper class; ~ **obrera** working-class; ~s **de tropa** mil other ranks; ~s **pasivas** pensioners; **tener mucha ~** to be very classy

clasicismo classicism

clasicista m+f classicist

clásico n classic; **armas clásicas** conventional arms; **los ~s** the classics; **lo ~** the same old story; adj classical, classic, traditional

clasificación f classification

clasificador n m filing-cabinet; classifier; adj classifying

clasificar to classify, class; sp to qualify

clasista class-conscious; snobbish

claudia greengage

claudicación f halting, submission, giving up, wavering; ~ **de las arterias** hardening of the arteries

claudicante adj halting, limping

claudicar to limp; waver, give in

claustrado cloistered

claustro cloister; university council; university staff; monastic state; ~ **materno** womb

claustrofobia claustrophobia

claustrofóbico claustrophobic

cláusula clause

clausura inner recess; closure; **monja de ~** enclosed nun

clausurar to terminate

clava cudgel; naut scupper

clavado studded with nails; dead right, spot on; spitting image; pinned

clavar to nail; overcharge; (of guns) spike; ~ **los ojos/la mirada en** to stare

at; ~ **el diente a** to sink one's teeth in;
~**se** to get; go in
clave m clavichord; key; f archi key-
stone; mus clef; code; **echar la ~** to
conclude; **en ~** in code
clavel m bot carnation; ~ **reventón**
double carnation
clavellina bot pink
clavelón m bot marigold
clavero nail-hole; keeper of the keys;
treasurer; bot clove tree
clavete m plectrum; tin-tack
clavetear to stud with nails; comm close
(a deal)
clavicordio clavichord
clavícula clavicle, collar-bone
clavija pin, peg, dowel; elect plug;
switch
clavijero hat-stand, clothes-rack
clavillo brad, tack, rivet
clavo nail; med corn (on toe); snag; surg
lint; bot + cul clove; naut rudder; min
rich vein; ~ **de herradura** hobnail; ~
romano picture-hook; ~**s** mot studs,
ramp; rumble-strip, sleeping policeman; **agarrarse a un ~ ardiendo** to
clutch at a straw; **como un ~** prompt,
on the dot; **dar en el ~** to hit the nail
on the head; **hacer ~** (of cement) to
set; **no dejar ~ ni estaca en pared** to
leave the place completely stripped;
no me importa un ~ I don't give a
damn
clemátide f bot clematis
clemencia clemency, mercy
clemente merciful
clementina clementine
clepsidra water-clock; hourglass
cleptomanía kleptomania
cleptomaníaco, cleptómano kleptomaniac
clerecía clergy, priesthood
clericalismo clericalism
clericato clergy, priesthood
clérigo clergyman, cleric; ~ **de corona**
tonsured priest; ~ **de misa y olla**
ignorant priest
clerizonte m fake priest; wretched priest
clero clergy
clerofobia hatred of clergy
clerófobo anti-clerical
cliente m+f customer, client, patron;
med patient
clientela clientele, customers, patrons;

med practice
clima m climate
climatérico climateric
climático climatic; changeable
climatología climatology
climatológico climatological
climatólogo climatologist
clínica clinic; private hospital
clínico clinical; **hospital ~** teaching
hospital
clip m paper-clip
clíper m naut clipper
clisado stereotyping; stereotypography
clisador stereotyper
clisar to stereotype
clisé m stereotype; cliché
clisos mpl sl eyes
clister m med clyster
clisterizar to administer clysters to
clo m cluck (of hen)
cloaca sewer, drain
clon m clown
clonación f biol cloning
clonar biol to clone
clono biol clone
cloque m boat-hook; gaff
cloquear vt to gaff; vi to cluck
cloqueo clucking
cloquera broodiness (in hens)
cloral chloral
clorato chlorate
clorhídrico hydrochloric
cloro chlorine
clorofila chlorophyll
clorofílico adj chlorophyll
clorofórmico adj chloroform
cloroformización f chloroforming
cloroformizar to chloroform
cloroformo chloroform
cloruro chloride; ~ **de cal** chloride of
lime; ~ **de sodio** sodium chloride
clubista m+f member of a club
clueco (of hens) broody
**C.N.T. (Confederación Nacional de
Trabajo)** anarchist trade union
coacción f compulsion, coercion
coacervación f heaping together
coacervar to heap together
coacreedor m joint creditor
coactivo compelling, coercive
coacusado n fellow-prisoner, co-
respondent; codefendant; adj jointly
accused
coacusar to accuse jointly

coadjutor coadjutor

coadjutoría coadjutorship; coadjutor's office

coadministrador *m* coadministrator, co-trustee

coadquiriente purchasing jointly

coadquiridor *m* joint purchaser

coadquisición *f* joint purchase

coadunación *f* close union

coadunar to join closely

coadyutor *m see* **coadjutor**

coadyuvador *m* fellow-helper

coadyuvante helping

coadyuvar to help

coagente *m* associate

coagulable easily coagulating

coagulación *f* coagulation, curdling

coagulador, coagulante coagulating, curdling

coagular(se) to coagulate, congeal, clot, curdle

coágulo clot, coagulum

coaguloso coagulated, coagulating

coalescencia coalescence

coalición *f* coalition

coalicionarse to form a coalition

coalicionista *m+f* coalitionist

coalla *orni* woodcock

coarrendador *m* joint lessor

coarrendamiento joint tenancy

coarrendar to rent jointly

coarrendatario joint-tenant

coartación *f* limitation, restriction

coartada alibi

coartador *n m* restrainer; *adj* restraining

coartar to restrain, limit, curtail

coartatorio limiting, restrictive

coasignatario joint-assignee

coasociación *f* co-partnership

coasociado co-partner

coasociarse to go into partnership

coautor joint author

coba flattery, adulation; soft-soap; **dar** ~ to creep; **dar** ~ **a** to butter up, soft-soap

cobalto cobalt

cobarde *n m+f* coward; *adj* cowardly

cobardear to behave in a cowardly way

cobardía cowardice, cowardliness

cobayo guinea-pig

cobertera lid, cover

cobertizo pent-roof, shed

cobertor *m* bedspread, blanket

cobertura coverage

cobija ridge-tile; *Mex* blanket, bed-clothes

cobijador protective, covering

cobijar to cover, protect; shelter, lodge

cobijo cover, protection, shelter, refuge

cobista *m+f* creep, flatterer

cobla sardana Catalonian band

Coblenza Coblenz

cobrable collectable, recoverable

cobrador *m* collector, receiver (of money); conductor (of bus *etc*); **perro** ~ retriever

cobranza collection, receiving, retrieving

cobrar to collect, receive, be paid, retrieve (game); gain, charge, pull in; ~ **ánimo** to take heart; ~ **carnes** to put on weight; ~ **fuerzas** to gather strength; ~ **un cheque** to cash a cheque; ¡**vas a** ~! you're going to cop it!; ~**se** to get one's money back

cobratorio collectable

cobre *m* copper; ~ **quemado** copper sulphate; ~**s** *mus* brass (instruments); **batirse el** ~ to fight tooth and nail

cobreño *adj* copper

cobrizo coppery; copper-coloured

cobro collecting, receiving (money *etc*); **poner en** ~ to keep in a safe place; **ponerse en** ~ to find a refuge; ~ **revertido** *tel* reversed charge

coca *bot* coca; *fam* head, blow on the head; *naut* knot (in rope); *sl* cocaine

cocador *n m* coaxer, wheedler, flatterer; *adj* coaxing, wheedling, flattering

cocaína cocaine

cocar to pull faces at; coax, flatter

cocción *f* boiling, cooking; *cer* baking, firing

coceador *n m* kicker; *adj* kicking

cocear to kick; ~ **contra el aguijón** to kick against the pricks

cocedizo easily cooked/boiled

cocedor *m* baking-oven

cocedura *n* boiling, cooking

cocer *vt* to boil, bake (bread, bricks *etc*); *vi* to boil, ferment, seethe

cocido *n* stew; *adj sl* drunk

cociente *m* quotient

cocimiento boiling, cooking

cocina cookery, cooking, cuisine; kitchen; cooker; *naut* galley; ~ **económica** kitchen range; ~ **eléctrica** electric cooker; **libro de** ~ recipe/

cookery book

cocinar to cook; *fam* meddle

cocinera cook

cocinero cook, chef

cocinilla small kitchen, portable stove

coco *bot* coco-palm; coconut; *fam* bogeyman; head, nut; ugly face; **hacer ~s (a)** to flirt (with); **lavado de ~, comida de ~** *fam* brain-washing; **más feo que un ~** as ugly as sin

cocodrilo *zool* crocodile

cocoliche *m SA* pidgin Spanish

cócora *m+f* bore, boring person

cochambre *m* filth; any filthy object

cochambrería heap of filth

cochambrero filthy

coche *m* coach, carriage, (motor) car, automobile; **~ cama** sleeping-car; **~ celular** Black Maria, patrol wagon; **~ de línea** long-distance bus/coach; **~ de plaza/de punto** hackney cab; **~ de San Fernando** Shanks's pony; **~ fúnebre** hearse; **~ patrulla** patrol car

cochecito pram, wheel-chair, baby-carriage

cocheras *fpl* bus/tram depot; coach-house; garage

cochero coachman

cochinada mean trick; filth

cochinear to behave in a filthy way

cochinería filthy act or speech

cochinero pig-sty

cochinilla cochineal (insect); wood-louse, pea-bug

cochinillo sucking-pig

cochina *n* sow

cochino *n* pig; *adj* filthy, rotten, vile

cochitril *m* pig-sty, filthy hovel

cocho boiled, baked

cochura baking, boiling; batch

cochurero boilerman, stoker

coda *mus* coda; *carp* wedge

codal *n m agri* vine-shoot; *archi* buttress; *carp* square; *adj* elbow-shaped

codazo nudge, dig with the elbow; **dar un ~** to nudge

codear to jostle, elbow; **~se (con)** to hobnob (with), rub shoulders (with)

codeína codeine

codelincuencia complicity

codelincuente accomplice

codemandante *m* co-plaintiff

codemandar to prosecute/sue jointly

codeo elbowing, nudging; hobnobbing

codera elbow-patch; baggy elbow

codetenido fellow-prisoner

codeudor *m* joint debtor

códice *m* codex

codicia greed, covetousness; **la ~ rompe el saco** grasp all, lose all

codiciable covetable, desirable

codiciador covetous

codiciante coveting

codiciar to covet

codicilo codicil

codicioso greedy, covetous, desirous; industrious

codificación *f* codification

codificador *n m* codifier; *adj* codifying

codificar to codify

código code (of laws); **~ civil** civil code; **~ de la circulación** highway code; **~ de señales** signal code; **~ territorial** *tel* exchange code

codillo bend, angle, elbow; shoulder (of meat), stirrup

codirector *m* joint director

codirectora joint directress

codo *anat* elbow; *mech* angle; shoulder (of quadruped); **~ a ~** shoulder to shoulder; **dar de ~** to nudge; **hablar por los ~s** to talk the hind legs off a donkey; **hasta los ~s** up to the eyes; **levantar el ~** to tipple, booze

codonante *m+f* co-donor

codorniz *f orni* quail

coeducación *f* coeducation

coeducar to coeducate

coeducativo coeducational

coeficiencia coefficiency

coeficiente *n m math* coefficient; **~ de seguridad** safety factor; **~ de trabajo** working stress; **~ intelectual** intelligence quotient; *adj* co-operating

coelector *m* joint-elector

coepíscopo co-bishop

coercer to coerce

coercitivo coercive

coesencial coessential

coetáneo *adj* contemporary; **~ de Goya** contemporary with Goya

coexistencia coexistence

coexistente coexistent

coexistir to coexist

cofa *naut* crow's nest

cofia head-dress, headgear; hairnet; cap

cofrade *m* confrère, brother; member of

a brotherhood/sisterhood

cofradía confraternity, brotherhood, sisterhood; guild

cofre *m* chest, trunk

cofrero chest-maker, chest-seller

cofundador *m* co-founder

cogajada *orni* crested lark

cogedera pole for gathering fruit

cogedero *n* handle; *adj* ready to be picked

cogedor *n m* dustpan; shovel; *adj* collecting

coger *vt* to catch, take, grab, grasp; seize; gather, pick; occupy; ~ **a puñados** to gather by the handful; ~ **desprevenido** to catch red-handed; ~ **las de Villadiego** to flee; ~ **toda la calle** to occupy the whole street; *vi* to fit in, have room; ~**se** to catch; ~ **la primera calle** take the first street

cogetrapos *m sing+pl* ragman, rag-and-bone man

cogida gathering, harvesting; (bullfighting) goring

cogido pleat, gather (in clothes)

cogitabundo pensive, musing

cogitación *f* meditation, reflection

cogitar to meditate, cogitate, reflect

cognación *f* cognation, relationship

cognado cognate, blood-relation

cognático *leg* cognate

cognominar to name; cognominate

cogollo heart (of cabbage, lettuce *etc*), shoot (of plant), tree-top; essence

cogorza *sl* drunken bout; state of drunkenness

cogotazo blow on the back of the neck

cogote *m* nape, back of the neck; crest (on helmet)

cogotera sun-bonnet (for beasts of burden)

cogotudo thick-necked; haughty

cogujada *orni* crested lark

cogulla monk's cowl

cohabitación *f* cohabitation

cohabitador *m* cohabiter

cohabitar to cohabit

cohechador *n m* briber, suborner; *adj* bribing

cohechar to bribe, suborn; plough immediately before sowing

cohecho bribery, graft; *agri* ploughing season

cohén *m+f* soothsayer; procurer, pimp

coheredar to inherit jointly

coheredera coheiress

coheredero co-heir

coherencia coherence; joint inheritance; *phys* cohesion

coherente coherent

cohesivo cohesive

cohete *m* rocket, sky-rocket

cohetería rocketry

cohibición *f* inhibition, embarrassment

cohibidor inhibiting

cohibir to inhibit, embarrass; make (s.o.) feel uncomfortable/ill at ease; restrain

cohobar to distil repeatedly

cohombrillo gherkin

cohombro cucumber

cohonestar to give a decent appearance to; whitewash

cohorte *m* cohort, crowd

coima gift, donation

coime *m*, **coimero** keeper of gaming-table

coincidencia coincidence

coincidente coincident, coinciding, coincidental

coincidir to coincide; agree; **coincidimos en la panadería** we were (by chance) in the baker's together

coinquilino joint tenant

cointeresado jointly interested

coipo *zool* coypu

coito coitus

cojear to limp, hobble; falter; wobble; ~ **del mismo pie** to have the same faults; **saber de qué pie cojea alguien** to know someone's weak spot

cojera lameness, limp

cojín *m* cushion; *naut* pillow

cojinete *m* small pillow, pad; *mech* bearing; ~ **de bolas** ball-bearing

cojo *n* lame person, cripple; *adj* lame, limping, unsteady, rickety (of furniture); **una frase coja** an incomplete sentence

cojón *m* testicle, ball; **tener cojones** *sl* to have guts

cojudo (of animals) not castrated

col *f* cabbage; **entre** ~ **y** ~ every now and then; ~ **lombarda** savoy cabbage; ~**es de Bruselas** Brussels sprouts

cola tail, (of dress) train; end (of roll of cloth), tail-end; hind part; queue; glue; *bot* cola; ~ **de caballo** (*bot*

+*hair-style*) pony-tail; ~ **de milano/de pato** *carp* dovetail; ~ **de pescado** fish-glue; ~ **de retal** painter's size; ~ **fuerte** adhesive gum; **a la** ~ in the end; **hacer** ~ to queue (up)

colaboración *f* collaboration

colaborador *m* collaborator

colaborar to collaborate

colación *f* collation; comparison; conferring (of degrees)

colacionar to collate, compare

colada wash, washing; soaking (of clothes) in bleach

coladera strainer, colander

coladero colander, strainer, drainer; filtering-bag

coladizo penetrating; runny; *fam* artful

colado: aire ~ cold draught; **hierro** ~ cast iron

colador *m* colander

coladora washerwoman, laundress

coladura straining; **coger una** ~ *sl* to drop a clanger

colapez *f* isinglass

colapso collapse

colar to sieve, strain; filter; bleach; *sl* pass (dud notes); **eso no cuela** that won't work; that is unbelievable; ~**se** to slip in, queue-jump

colateral collateral

colcha quilt, bedspread, counterpane

colchadura quilting

colchar to quilt

colchero quilt-maker

colchón *m* mattress; ~ **de plumas** feather-bed; ~ **neumático** air-cushion, air-bed

colchonería bedding

colchonero mattress-maker, mattress-vendor; *sp* supporter of Atlético de Madrid Football Club

coleada swish (of the tail)

coleador *m* cowboy who throws a bull by its tail

coleadura swishing (of tail)

colear to throw by the tail; wag, swish; wriggle; **vivo y coleando** alive and kicking

colección *f* collection

coleccionador *see* **coleccionista**

coleccionar to collect

coleccionista *m* + *f* collector

colecta *eccles* collect, collection

colectación *f* collecting (of taxes *etc*)

colectar to collect (taxes)

colectividad *f* collectivity, community

colectivismo collectivism

colectivista *m* + *f* collectivist

colectivo collective; *SA* bus

colector *m* collector, gatherer; water-pipe; *elect* commutator

colega *m* colleague

colegatario co-legatee, co-heir

colegiado collegiate; belonging to a professional body

colegial *n m* schoolboy; *adj* collegiate

colegiala schoolgirl, collegian

colegiarse to join a professional body

colegiata collegiate church

colegiatura fellowship, scholarship

colegio private school; academy; professional body; primary school

colegislador co-legislative

coleóptero *ent* coleopterous

¹ **cólera** *med* choler, bile; anger, fury; **montar en** ~ to fly into a rage

² **cólera** *m* cholera

colérico furious

coleta pigtail; postscript; **cortarse la** ~ to give up one's profession (*esp* bullfighting)

coletazo swish of the tail

coletear to flap, swish

coleteo flapping, swishing

coletilla short pigtail; postscript, rider; footnote; refrain

colgadero hanger, hook, peg

colgadizo *n m* penthouse; *adj* hanging

colgado hanging; **estar** ~ *sl* to be broke; *sl* be left in the lurch; *sl* (of drug addict) suffering withdrawal symptoms; under the influence of LSD; have failed an examination; **dejar** ~ to leave at a loose end; **quedarse** ~ to be left high and dry

colgadura hangings, drapery

colgajo hanging tatter

colgamiento *n* hanging

colgante *m archi* festoon; *mech* hanger; **puente** ~ suspension bridge; *adj* hanging

colgar to hang, suspend; *sl* fail (examination); string up; adorn; ~ **los hábitos** to give up holy orders

coliblanco white-tailed

colibrí *m* humming-bird

cólico colic, tummy-trouble

colicuar to dissolve, melt

coliflor *f* cauliflower
coligado associate
coligarse to confederate
coligrueso thick-tailed
colilla cigarette end
colimbo *orni* diver
colina hill
colinabo *bot* swede
colindante contiguous, adjoining
colindar to be contiguous, adjoin
coliquidador *m* joint liquidator
colirio *med* eye-drops
coliseo coliseum
colisión *f* collision, crash
colista *m* + *f sp* player/team at the foot of
  championship table; queuer
colitigante *m* + *f* joint-litigant
colmado grocer's shop; eating-house;
  adj plentiful
colmar to heap up; fill to the brim; fulfil;
  ~ **de mercedes** to heap favours on
colmena beehive; **como una** ~ well-
  stocked with provisions
colmenar *m* apiary
colmenero apiarist, bee-keeper; **oso** ~
  honey-bear
colmillada tusk wound
colmillo eye-tooth, canine-tooth, fang,
  tusk
colmilludo having prominent canine
  teeth
colmo top, limit; **es el** ~ it's the limit;
  llegar al ~ to reach the limit; **llenar**
  con ~ to fill to the brim; **para** ~ to
  crown all; **el** ~ **de** the height of
colocación *f* placing, arrangement; layout; employment, situation
colocado *sl* hooked on drugs; drunk
colocar to place; arrange; lay; situate; ~
  por orden to put in order; **estar**
  colocado de to be employed as; ~**se** to
  take up a position, place oneself
colofón *m* colophon; postscript; finishing touch
colofonia colophony
colofónico colophonic
colombiano *n* + *adj* Colombian
colombino of/about Columbus
colombófilo pigeon-fancier
Colón *m* Columbus
colonia colony, settlement; **agua de**
  Colonia eau-de-Cologne
colonial *adj* colonial, overseas; ~**es**
  groceries; **tienda de** ~**es** grocer's shop

colonización *f* colonization
colonizador *n m* colonizer; *adj* colonizing
colonizar to colonize
colono colonist, settler; tenant farmer
coloquio colloquy, dialogue, informal
  discussion
color *m* colour, hue, complexion,
  colouring; *sl* drug; ~ **muerto** pale
  colour; ~ **vivo** bright colour; **de** ~
  coloured; **mudar de** ~ to change
  colour; **ver de** ~ **de rosa** to see through
  rose-coloured spectacles
coloración *f* coloration
colorado red, ruddy, florid; **ponerse** ~ to
  blush
colorador *m arts* colourist
colorante *m* colouring
colorar, colorear to colour
colorido colouring
coloridor *m arts* colourist
colorín: ~ **colorado este cuento se ha**
  acabado and so our story ends
colorista *m* + *f arts* colourist
colosal colossal, huge
coloso Colossus, giant
columbino dove-like; innocent
columbrar to descry, glimpse; suspect
columna column, pillar; *naut* line of
  battleships; ~ **minguitoria** public
  urinal
columnar *m*, **columnata** colonnade
columpiar(se) to swing
columpio swing
colusión *f* collusion
colza *bot* rape; **aceite de** ~ rapeseed oil
collado hill
collalba *orni* wheatear
collar *m* necklace, charm collar
collarín *m* priest's collar; ring (of
  grenade fuse)
collera horse-collar; chain-gang
collón *m* coward, poltroon; *adj* cowardly
collonada, collonería cowardice
¹ **coma** comma; **punto y** ~ semicolon
² **coma** *m med* coma, stupor
comadre *f* midwife; procuress; gossip
  (old wife), neighbour
comadrear to gossip
comadreja weasel
comadreo gossiping
comadrería tittle-tattle
comadrero lazy and gossiping
comadrón *m* male midwife

comadrona midwife

comandancia command; commander's office

comandante *m* commander, commandant; major; ~ **en jefe** commander-in-chief

comandar to command jointly

comandita *f* silent partnership

comanditar *comm* to enter as a sleeping partner

comanditario: socio ~ *comm* sleeping partner, *US* silent partner

comando *mil* commando

comarca locality, district, region, area

comarcal regional, local

comarcano neighbouring, bordering on

comatoso comatose

comba skipping-rope; curve; warp; **saltar a la** ~ to skip (with a rope)

combadura curvature, warping

combar to curve, bend

combate *m* combat, fight; struggle; **fuera de** ~ out of action

combatidor *m* hard fighter

combatiente *n m* combatant, soldier; *orni* ruff; *adj* fighting

combatir to combat, fight, beat

combatividad *f* fighting spirit

combés *m naut* waist (of ship)

combi *f sl* petticoat

combinación *f* combination, permutation; (railway) connection; slip, petticoat

combinado cocktail

combinador combining

combinar to combine, join, unite, blend, *chem* compound

combinatorio combining, uniting

combo, comboso bent, warped

combustibilidad *f* combustibility

combustible *m* fuel, combustible

combustión *f* combustion, burning

combusto burnt, consumed

comedero *n* (animals') eating-place, eating-trough; *adj* eatable, edible

comedia play, drama, comedy; ~ **de capa y espada** cloak and dagger play; ~ **de costumbres** comedy of manners; ~ **de intriga** mystery play; **es una** ~ it's a farce; **hacer** ~ to put on an act

comedianta actress

comediante *m* actor

comediar to divide equally

comedido polite, discreet, moderate

comedimiento politeness, discretion

comediógrafo playwright, dramatist

comedirse to restrain o.s.

comedón *m* pimple, blackhead

comedor *m* dining-room; big eater

comendadora mother superior

comensal *m+f* retainer; fellow-diner

comentador *m* commentator

comentar to comment (on); gloss; gossip (about)

comentario commentary, comment; remark; ~s talk, gossip

comentarista *m+f* commentator

comento comment

comenzante *n m+f* beginner; *adj* beginning

comenzar to commence, start, begin

comer *n m* food; **ser de buen** ~ to have a good appetite; *vt* to eat (away); cause to fade; have for lunch; *vi* to eat, feed, dine, have lunch; ~ **a dos manos** to eat ravenously; ~ **con ganas** to eat heartily; ~ **de gorra** to eat at the expense of others; ~ **por cuatro** to eat like a horse; **dar de** ~ **a** to feed; **donde come uno comen dos** two can live as cheaply as one; **no tener qué** ~ to have nothing to eat; **quedarse sin** ~ to go hungry; ~**se** to eat up; ~**se las palabras** to mumble one's words; ~**se una letra** to miss out a letter; ~**se de celos** to be consumed with jealousy; ~**se una rosca** *sl* to pick up a girl

comerciable marketable

comercial commercial, trading, business; **ser** ~ to be a paying proposition

comercializar to commercialize

comerciante *n m* trader, dealer; *adj* trading

comerciar to trade; deal, have intercourse

comercio trade, commerce, traffic, business; shopping; shop; intercourse; card game; ~ **de cabotaje** coasting trade

comestible *adj* eatable, edible; *n* ~s food, victuals

cometa *f* kite; *m* comet

cometedor *n m* offender, criminal; *adj* offending

cometer to commit, charge, entrust, make; *comm* order; *gramm* to employ (figures of speech); ~ **una falta** to make a mistake

cometido commission, trust, duty; **esto no es mi ~** this is not my concern

cometología cometology

cometólogo cometologist

comezón *m* itch(ing); restlessness

comi *m sl* police station

comible eatable

comicalla *m+f* taciturn person; *adj* taciturn

comicial pertaining to elections

comicios *m sing+pl* assembly; election meeting; elections

cómico *n m* actor, player, comedian; **~ de la legua** strolling player; *adj* comic, ludicrous, comical; pertaining to the theatre

comida food, meal; dinner, lunch; **~ de coco** *sl* brain-washing; **reposar la ~** to rest after eating

comidilla gossip, topic of conversation; **~ de la ciudad** talk of the town

comienzo beginning, start; inception

comihuelga lazy, good-for-nothing

comilitón *m* fellow-soldier

comilón *n m* heavy eater; *adj* overeating

comilona heavy meal

comillas *fpl* inverted commas

comino *bot* cumin (plant and seed); **(no) me importa un ~** I don't care a damn

comiquear *theat* to put on amateur shows

comiquería amateur dramatic society

comisar to seize, confiscate

comisaría police station

comisariato commissariat

comisario commissary, commissar; (at horse-race) steward; **~ de policía** commissioner of police; **alto ~** high commissioner

comisión *f* commission; trust; committee; **~ mercantil** *comm* percentage

comisionado *n* commissioner, agent

comisionar to commission, empower

comisionista *m+f* commission-agent

comiso *leg* confiscation; confiscated goods; seizure

comisorio *leg* binding

comisquear to peck at

comistrajo hodge-podge

comisura joint; **~ de los labios** *anat* commissure

comité *m* committee

comitiva suite, retinue, procession

comix *m sing+pl* underground comic

como as, such as; since; like; if; that; about; **~ que**, **~ quiera que** since; **~ si** as if; **así ~** as soon as; **tanto ~** as much as; **tan ... como** as ... as

cómo *exclam+inter* how!; why!; how?; why?; what?; **¿~ no?** of course; **¡~!** it can't be so!

comodidad *f* comfort, convenience; **~es** creature comforts

comodín *m* joker (playing-card)

comodista *m+f* selfish person; comfort-loving person

cómoda chest of drawers; *US* dresser

cómodo comfortable, convenient

comodoro commodore

comorar to live together

compactibilidad *f* compactness

compacto compact, dense

compadecer to feel sorry for; **~se de** to pity; **~se con** to go well with

compadrar to become a godfather/godmother; become a sponsor

compadre *m* father/godfather (with respect to each other); mate; buddy

compadrería friendship, comradeship

compaginación *f print* paging

compaginador *m* combiner, collator

compaginar to arrange; *print* make up; reconcile; collate; **~se** to fit, agree

compañerismo comradeship

compañero companion, comrade, pal, buddy, mate; **~ de cuarto** roommate; **~ de viaje** +*pol* fellow-traveller

compañía company, companionship; fellowship; partnership; *theat* troupe; **~ anónima** stock company; **~ de la legua** company of strolling players; **en ~** together; **hacer ~ a** to keep company

compañón *m* testicle

comparación *f* comparison; **en ~ con** in/by comparison with

comparado comparative

comparar to compare, liken

comparativo comparative

comparecencia *leg* appearance (in court)

comparecer *leg* to appear (in court)

comparición *f leg* appearance

compariente kin, kindred

comparsa *theat* extra; puppet

compartimiento division; compartment; **~ estanco** watertight compartment

compartir to divide equally; share

compás m compass; pair of compasses; dividers; callipers; *mus* rhythm, beat; **~ de espera** cooling-off period; **a ~ de** in time with; **fuera de ~** out of time, off beat; **llevar el ~** to keep in time; **salirse del ~** to go off the rails

compasado measured, sensible

compasamiento measuring with compasses

compasar to measure; regulate; *mus* divide into bars

compasible compassionate; deserving compassion

compasillo *mus* quadruple time

compasión f compassion, pity

compasivo merciful, sympathetic, compassionate

compatibilidad f compatibility

compatriota m+f fellow-countryman, compatriot

compeler to compel

compendiar to summarize

compendio compendium; summary; **en ~** in brief

compendioso brief, condensed

compenetración f mutual understanding

compenetrarse to identify o.s.; understand each other

compensable that can be compensated

compensación f compensation; **banco de ~** clearing bank

compensador compensating

compensar to compensate; clear (a cheque); counter-balance

compensativo compensatory

competencia competition, competence; concern

competente competent, capable

competición f competition, contest

competidor n m competitor; *adj* competing, rival

competir to contest; compete

compilación f compilation

compilador n m compiler; *adj* compiling

compilar to compile

compinche m pal, crony, buddy

complacencia pleasure, satisfaction

complacer to please, humour, give satisfaction to; **me complace informarle que** I'm pleased to inform you that; **~se** to take pleasure in

complaciente obliging, helpful

complejidad f complexity

complejo n+adj complex, hang-up

complementar to complement

complementario complementary

complemento complement; *gramm* predicate

completar to complete

completas fpl eccles compline

completo n coffee, brandy and a cigar; *adj* complete; full up; full house; **por ~** fully, completely

complejidad f complexity

complexión f constitution; **de ~ recia** having a tough constitution

complicación f complication

complicador complicating

complicar to complicate, implicate, involve; **~se** to become complicated, involved

cómplice m+f accomplice, abettor

complicidad f complicity

complló m, **complot** m plot, conspiracy

componedor m repairer; *print* composing-stick; **amigable ~** *leg* arbitrator

componente n m +adj component

componer to compose; arrange; put together; repair; adorn; prepare; garnish; settle; **~se** to deck o.s.; consist of; **~las** to manage

componible repairable

comportamiento conduct

comportar to tolerate; **~se** to behave

comporte m behaviour, deportment

composición f composition, making-up, mending

compositor n m print compositor; *mus* composer; *adj* composing

compósitum m pharm mixture

compostura composition; accommodation; agreement; adjustment; mending; cleanliness; modesty

compota stewed fruit

compotera fruit-dish

compra purchase, buy; **~ a plazos** hire purchase, instalment plan; **hacer la ~** to do the shopping; **ir de ~s** to go shopping

comprable, compradero, compradizo purchasable

comprador n m buyer; *adj* buying, purchasing

comprar to buy, purchase; shop; **~ al contado** to buy cash down; **~ a plazos** to buy on hire purchase; **~ por kilos** to buy by the kilo

compraventa buying and selling; dealing; marketing

comprendedor comprehending, understanding

comprender to comprehend, understand; include; realize

comprensibilidad f comprehensibility

comprensible comprehensible; ~ **para todos** understandable to all

comprensión f comprehension

comprensividad f capacity for understanding

comprensivo understanding; comprising

compresa sanitary towel; *med* compress

compresibilidad f compressibility

compresible compressible

compresión f compression; pressure

compresivo compressive, condensing

compresor m compressor; ~ **de aire** air-compressor

comprimiente compressing, oppressing, containing

comprimible compressible

comprimido *med* tablet, pill

comprimidor compressive

comprimir to compress; restrain; ~**se** to control o.s.

comprobación f check, verification

comprobador n m checker, verifier; *adj* verifying, checking

comprobante n m check, proof, certificate, receipt; *adj* proving, attesting

comprobar to verify, check

comprofesor m fellow-teacher

comprometedor n m compromiser; *adj* compromising

comprometer to compromise; expose; jeopardize; endanger; bind; ~**se** to commit o.s.; compromise; ~**se a** to undertake to

comprometido risky, embarrassing; *pol* committed; engaged

comprometimiento undertaking, agreement, jeopardy

compromisario arbitrator, referee

compromiso obligation, agreement, embarrassment

compuerta hatch; half-door; sluice; floodgate

compuesto n compound; *adj* composed, neat and tidy

compulsa *leg* certified copy

compulsar to make an authentic copy/transcript

compulsivo compulsive, compulsory

compunción f contrition

compungirse to feel contrition, sorry

computación computation, calculation

computador *adj* computing, calculating; n computer

computadora computer

computar to compute, calculate

cómputo computation, calculation

comulgante m+f *eccles* communicant

comulgar vt to communicate; administer communion to; vi to communicate, receive communion; ~ **con ruedas de molino** to be very gullible

comulgatorio communion rail

común n m community; *adj* common, ordinary; **en** ~ in common; **por lo** ~ generally

comuna commune

comunal common, communal; **terreno** ~ common (land)

comunero n commoner; ~**s** villages with commonage; *adj* popular, common

comunes *mpl*: **los Comunes** the (House of) Commons

comunicabilidad f communicability

comunicable communicable

comunicación f communication, connection; **comunicaciones** post, telegraph

comunicado communiqué

comunicador n m communicator; *adj* communicating

comunicando: estar ~ *tel* to be engaged

comunicante m+f communicant; *adj* communicating

comunicar to communicate; ~**se** to be joined

comunicativo communicative, open

comunicatorio testimonial; **letras comunicatorias** testimonial letters

comunidad f community; **de** ~ in common, jointly

comunión f communion, fellowship

comunismo communism

comunista n m+f communist; *adj* communist(ic)

comunistizante n m+f *pol* fellow-traveller; *adj* with leanings towards communism

comunistizar to communize; ~**se** to become communist

comunitario communal; of the European Economic Community

con with; although, in spite of; in; towards; to; since; ~ **que** so that; ~ **comer menos** by eating less

conato endeavour, tendency, attempt

concavidad *f* concavity, hollow

cóncavo *n* concavity; *adj* concave, hollow

concebible conceivable

concebir to conceive; imagine; **no lo concibo** it's beyond my understanding

conceder to concede, grant

concejal *m*, **concejala** councillor

concejalía councillorship

concejo municipal council; **casa del ~** town hall

conceller *m* councillor (in Catalonia)

concentración *f* concentration

concentrado *n* concentrate

concentrador concentrating

concentrar(se) to concentrate; focus

concentricidad *f* concentricity

concéntrico concentric

concepción *f* conception; notion

concepcional conceptional; notional

conceptear to give smart answers

conceptibilidad *f* imaginativeness

conceptible imaginable

conceptismo ingenious style, euphemism

conceptista *m+f* ingenious stylist; punster; wit

conceptividad *f* conceivability

conceptivo conceptive

concepto concept, idea; flash of wit; pun

conceptuar to conceive, deem; judge; form an opinion

conceptuosidad *f* witticism, ingeniousness

conceptuoso witty, ingenious

concerniente concerning; **en lo ~ a** as for

concernir to concern, belong (to)

concertación *f* contest, dispute

concertador *n m* arranger; **maestro ~** choirmaster; *adj* arranging

concertante concerting; *mus* arranged for more than one voice

concertar *vt* to concert, arrange; *comm* close a deal; *mus* tune; (hunting) rouse the game; *vi* to agree, harmonize; ~**se** to be arranged, go hand-in-hand; agree

concertino leader of an orchestra

concertista *m+f* concert artist, soloist

concesión *f* concession; grant

concesionario *adj* concessionary; *n* concessionaire

conciencia conscience, consciousness, awareness; **a ~** conscientiously, thoroughly

concienciar to foster social/political awareness; ~**se** to get social/political awareness

concienzudo conscientious, thorough

concierto concert, contract, agreement, good order, arrangement; **de ~** in agreement

conciliable reconcilable

conciliábulo secret meeting

conciliación *f* conciliation; reconcilement; affinity

conciliador *n m* conciliator; *adj* conciliatory

conciliar to reconcile, harmonize, conciliate; ~ **el sueño** to go to sleep

conciliatorio conciliatory

concilio council

concisión *f* conciseness, brevity

conciso concise, brief

concitación *f* instigation, stirring-up

concitador inciting, provoking

concitar to stir up, incite

conciudadanía fellow-citizenship

conciudadano fellow-citizen

concluidor concluding

concluir *vt* to conclude, terminate; infer; *vi* to end; ~**se** to come to an end

conclusión *f* conclusion; *leg* winding-up

conclusivo conclusive, final

concluso concluded, closed; **dar por ~** *leg* to consider closed

concluyente conclusive

concofrade *m* member of the same brotherhood

concología conchology

concólogo conchologist

concomitancia concomitance

concomitante concomitant

concomitar to accompany

concordable agreeable

concordador *m* conciliator, moderator, peace-maker

concordancia concord, agreement; ~**s** concordance, index

concordante concordant

concordar to agree, conform; correspond; ~ **con** to conform to

concordato concordat

concordia concord, harmony; conformity; *leg* agreement

concretar to pinpoint, make specific/concrete

concreto concrete, specific, definite

concubina concubine

concubinato concubinage

concuñado brother-in-law, **concuñada** sister-in-law (used only of persons married to two brothers or sisters)

concupiscencia concupiscence, lust

concupiscente concupiscent, lustful

concurrencia concurrence; audience, crowd

concurrente concurrent, coinciding; attending

concurrido crowded, well-attended

concurrir to concur, coincide, converge, contribute; compete, go

concursante *m+f* competitor, participant; *comm* one who submits a tender

concursar *vt leg* to declare bankrupt; *vi* to compete, take part; *comm* to submit a tender

concurso contest, competition; attendance; help; *comm* invitation to submit tenders; ~ **de acreedores** meeting of creditors; **con el ~ de** with the help of; **fuera de ~** out of the running

concusión *f* concussion; *leg* extortion

concusionario extortioner

concha *f* shell, sea-shell; tortoisc-shell; *theat* prompter's box; **meterse en su ~** to go into one's shell

conchabar to join, unite; engage a servant; ~**se** gang up

conchado crustaceous; shelly; scaly

condado county; earldom

condal of an earl/count; **la Cuidad Condal** Barcelona

conde *m* earl, count; gipsy leader

condecente fit, proper

condecoración *f* decoration, medal

condecorar to decorate

condena *leg* sentence; term of imprisonment; punishment

condenable deserving condemnation

condenación *f* condemnation, damnation

condenado *n m* reprobate; *adj* damned, cursed, blasted, condemned

condenador *n m* condemner, censurer; *adj* condemning, censuring

condenar to condemn; damn; censure; convict; blame; ~**se** to be damned

condensabilidad *f* condensability

condensación *f* condensation

condensador *m* condenser; ~ **de fuerzas** accumulator; ~ **eléctrico** storage battery

condensante condensing

condesa countess

condescendencia willingness to comply; condescension

condescender to condescend; acquiesce; yield

condescendiente willing to comply, obliging

condestable *m* high constable; mastergunner

condestablía dignity of high constable

condición *f* condition, disposition; rank; nature; term; **a ~ de que** on condition that; **estar en condiciones de** to be in a position to; **hombre de ~** man of rank

condicional conditional; **libertad ~** *leg* parole, provisional liberty

condicionar to condition; determine

condimentador *adj* seasoning

condimentar to season

condimento seasoning

condiscípulo schoolfellow, classmate, fellow-student

condolencia condolence

condolerse to console; ~ **de** to be sorry for

condominio condominium; joint-ownership

condonación *f* condonation, pardoning

condonar to pardon, condone

cóndor *m orni* condor

conducción *f* conveyance, transportation; cartage; piping; conduction (of liquids); driving (of vehicles); **carné de ~** driving licence

conducente conducive

conducir to conduct, guide; convey; drive (a vehicle); **carné de ~** driving-licence; ~**se** to behave

conducta conduct, behaviour; handling; **mejorar de ~** to mend one's ways

conductibilidad *f* conductibility

conductividad *f* conductivity

conducto duct, conduit, channel; **por ~ de** through; **por ~s oficiales** through official channels

conductor *n m* leader, guide, driver;

phys conductor *m*; *adj* conducting, guiding

condueño co-owner

condumio *fam* food, grub, nosh

conectador *m* connector (contact-plug)

conectar *vt mech* to couple, connect; *vi* *rad+TV* to go over; **ahora vamos a ~ con Bilbao** we are now going over to Bilbao

conejal *m* rabbit warren

conejear to dodge; hide; cower

conejera rabbit burrow, warren

conejero *n* rabbit-breeder/vender; *adj* (of dogs) rabbit-hunting

conejillo little rabbit; **~ de Indias** guinea pig

conejito *f* bunny-girl

coneja doe rabbit; **ella es una ~** she breeds like a rabbit

conejo buck rabbit; **~ albar** white rabbit

conejuna rabbit fur

conejuno pertaining to rabbits

conexión *f* connection

conexionar to connect, contact

conexivo connective

conexo connected, *leg* united

confabulación *f* confabulation, plot

confabulador *m* schemer

confabularse to scheme, plot

confección *f* confection, making-up, tailoring

confeccionador *m* manufacturer (in the rag-trade)

confeccionar to make up, put together (clothes, prescriptions *etc*)

confederación *f* confederation

confederar to confederate; **~se** to combine

conferencia conference, speech; *tel* trunk call

conferenciante *m+f* lecturer

conferenciar to confer; talk, discuss

conferir to confer, bestow; award

confesa widow become a nun

confesado penitent

confesar to confess; **~se** to make/hear a confession

confesión *f* confession

confesional denominational, confessional

confeso lay brother; converted Jew

confesonario confessional(-box)

confesor *m* confessor

confeti *m* confetti

confiable trustworthy

confiado confident, trusting; gullible

confianza confidence; trust; familiarity; **en ~** in confidence; **persona de ~** trustworthy person; **tomarse ~s** to take liberties

confianzudo over-familiar

confiar *vt* to entrust; *vi* trust; **~se** to be trusting; confide

confidencia confidence, secret

confidencial confidential

confidente *n* *m+f* confidant(e); informer; *m* sofa for two people; *adj* faithful

configuración *f* configuration

configurar to configure; shape

confín *m* limit, boundary

confinamiento confining, confinement; banishment

confinante bordering

confinar *vt* to confine; banish; *vi* to border (**con** on)

confirmación *f* confirmation

confirmado *eccles* confirmee

confirmador *m eccles* confirmer

confirmar + *eccles* to confirm; **~se** to be confirmed

confiscación *f* confiscation

confiscar to confiscate

confitado hopeful

confitar to sweeten; preserve (in syrup)

confite *m* sweet(meat), confectionery

confitería confectioner's; sweetshop

confitera confectioner

confitero confectioner

confitura candied fruit, preserve

confiturería fruit preserving

confiturero fruit preserver

conflagración *f* conflagration

conflagrar to set on fire

conflátil fusible

conflictividad *f* controversial nature

conflictivo controversial

conflicto conflict, struggle

confluencia confluence (of people)

confluente *m* confluence (of rivers); *adj* confluent

confluir to converge, join

conformación *f* shape, structure

conformar to make conform; **~se** to resign o.s. (**con** to); conform

conforme *adj* in agreement; **estar ~** to be agreed/satisfied; *adv* as; **~ a** according to; **~ con** complying with

conformidad *f* conformity, approval, consent; **de/en ~ con** in accordance with

conformismo conformity

conformista *m+f* conformist

confort *m* comfort

confortable comfortable

confortación *f* comfort

confortador *n m* comforter, consoler; *adj* comforting

confortamiento consolation

confortante *m* comforting

confortar to comfort

confortativo comforting, consoling

confraternidad *f* confraternity, brotherhood

confraternizar to fraternize

confrontación *f* confrontation; **~ de las generaciones** generation gap

confrontante confronting

confrontar *vt* to confront; compare; *vi* to border (upon); **~se** to confront, face

confuciano, confucionista *m+f* Confucian

confundible indistinguishable

confundimiento confusion

confundir to confuse, mistake, mix up; throw into confusion, perplex; humiliate; **~se** to make a mistake, go wrong; mix

confusión *f* confusion, tumult; muddle

confusionismo deliberate clouding of issues

confuso confused, muddled, bewildered

congelación *f* freezing; **~ de salarios** wage-freeze

congelador *m* freezer

congelar(se) to freeze, deep-freeze; congeal

congenial akin, like

congenialidad *f* affinity

congeniar con to get on well with

congénito congenital

congestionar *med* to congest

congestivo *med* congestive

conglomeración *f* conglomeration

conglomerado conglomerate

conglomerar to conglomerate

congoja agony; grief; anguish

congoleño, congolés Congolese

congraciador ingratiating

congraciamiento ingratiation

congraciarse to ingratiate o.s.; **~se con alguien** to get into s.o.'s good books

congratular to congratulate, compliment; **~se** to be delighted

congratulatorio congratulatory

congregación *f* congregation, assembly

congregacionalismo Congregationalism

congregacionalista *n m+f+adj* Congregationalist

congregarse to congregate, assemble, gather

congresista *m+f* member of a congress

congreso congress

congrio conger-eel

congruencia congruence, congruity

congruente congruent, congruous

congruo apt, fit

cónico conical, cone-shaped

conífero *n* conifer; *adj* coniferous

conjetura conjecture, surmise

conjeturable conjecturable

conjeturador conjecturing

conjetural conjectural

conjeturar to conjecture

conjugación *f* conjugation

conjugar to conjugate, combine

conjunción *f* conjunction

conjunto whole, ensemble; set, team; pop-group; **en ~** as a whole; *adj* joint, united

conjurado conspirator

conjurador *m* conjuror; conspirator

conjuramentar to conjure; swear in

conjurante *n m* conjuror; conspirator; *adj* conjuring; conspiring

conjurar to bind by oath; entreat, implore; avert; conspire, plot; **~se** to conspire together

conjuro conjuration, exorcism; entreaty

conllevar to bear, suffer

conmemorable commemorable

conmemoración *f* commemoration

conmemorar to commemorate

conmemorativo, conmemoratorio commemorative

conmensurabilidad *f* commensurability

conmensurable commensurable

conmensuración *f* commensurability

conmensurativo commensurating

conmigo with me

conminación *f* threat

conminador threatening

conminar to threaten (**con** with); *leg* warn

conminativo threatening; warning

conmiseración *f* commiseration, pity

conmisto, conmixto mixed

conmoción *f* commotion; ~ **cerebral** concussion

conmovedor moving, touching

conmover to disturb, touch, affect, move (emotionally); ~**se** to be moved

conmutabilidad *f* commutability

conmutable commutable

conmutador *m elect* commutator; switch; *adj leg* commuting

conmutar *leg* to commute, exchange

connivencia connivance

connotación *f* connotation

connotar to connote

cono cone; **Cono Sur** *euph* South America

conocedor *m* connoisseur, expert

conocer to know; get to know; be acquainted with; meet; recognize; realize; ~**se** to know each other

conocible knowable

conocido *n* acquaintance; *adj* well-known

conocimiento knowledge, comprehension, understanding; acquaintance; ~ **de embarque** *comm* bill of lading; ~**s** knowledge, learning

conopeo canopy

conque so

conquibús *m fam* cash, wherewithal, lolly

conquiliología conchology

conquiliológico conchological

conquiliólogo conchologist

conquista conquest

conquistable conquerable

conquistador *n m* conqueror; *adj* conquering

conquistar to conquer; win

consabido well-known; timeworn; usual

consagrable consecratable

consagración *f* consecration, dedication

consagrado consecrated; dedicated; **una frase consagrada** a stock expression

consagrante consecrating

consagrar to consecrate, dedicate; ~**se** devote o.s. (**a** to)

consanguíneo consanguineous

consanguinidad *f* consanguinity

consciente conscious, aware

consectario co-religionist

consecuencia consequence; inference; **en** ~ therefore, as a result

consecuencial consequential

consecuente consequent; consistent

consecutivo consecutive

conseguir to get, obtain, achieve

consejera female adviser

consejero *n m* advisor, counsellor

consejo counsel, advice; consulting body; ~ **de guerra** court martial; ~ **de ministros** *pol* cabinet (meeting)

consenso consensus, assent; **un** ~ a bit of advice

consentido *n m* cuckold; *adj* spoiled (over-indulged); acquiescing

consentidor consenting, acquiescent

consentimiento consent

consentir *vt* to permit, tolerate; pamper, spoil; *vi* to consent, agree

conserje *m* caretaker, warden

conserjería wardenship; reception desk, porter's lodge

conserva preserve, jam, preserved food; convoy; **navegar en** ~ to sail in convoy

conservable preservable

conservación *f* preservation

conservador *n m* curator; *pol* conservative; *adj* preserving

conservaduría curatorship

conservadurismo *pol* conservatism

conservante preserving

conservar to preserve, conserve; keep; hold on to; ~**se** to wear well

conservativo conserving, preservative

conservatorio *n* conservatoire; *adj* conserving, preserving

conservería cannery

conservero *n* preparer of conserves; *adj* canning

consideración *f* consideration; respect; thought; **en** ~ **a** in consideration of; **de** ~ of importance

considerado considerate, thoughtful

considerando que *leg* whereas

considerante considering

considerar to consider, think over; deem

consiervo fellow-slave

consigna password, watchword; orders; left-luggage office, *US* check room

consignación *f* consignment, shipment

consignador *m comm* consignor

consignar to consign; record, put on record

consignatario *leg* trustee; *comm* consignee

consigo with oneself, with himself, with herself, with yourself, with themselves, with yourselves

consiguiente consequent, resulting; **por** ~ therefore

consiliario adviser

consistencia soundness, solidity, consistency

consistente firm, sound, solid; consistent; ~ **en** consisting of

consistir to consist (**en** in/of)

consistorial: casa ~ town hall

consistorio *eccles* consistory; town hall; town council

consocio partner, associate

consola console

consolación *f* consolation

consolador consoling, comforting

consolante comforting, soothing

consolar to console, comfort

consolativo, consolatorio consolatory

consólida *bot* comfrey; ~ **real** *bot* larkspur

consolidable that can be consolidated

consolidación *f* consolidation

consolidar to consolidate; fund (debts)

consonancia consonance, harmony, rhyme; **en** ~ **con** in keeping with

[1] **consonante** *m gramm* consonant

[2] **consonante** *n m* rhyme; *adj* consonant

consonar to harmonize, rhyme, agree

cónsono harmonious

consorcio partnership; consortium

consorte *m+f* consort, partner; ~**s** *pl leg* accomplices; associates

conspicuo conspicuous

conspiración *f* conspiracy

conspirador *n m* conspirator, plotter

conspirar to conspire, plot

constancia constancy; perseverance; certainty; proof

[1] **constante** *f math* constant

[2] **constante** *adj* constant, steady

Constantinopla Constantinople

constar to be on record; ~ **de** be composed of; be certain; **me consta que ...** I know for certain that ...; **hacer** ~ to make known, put on record; **que conste que ...** let it be known that ...

constelación *f* constellation; climate

consternación *f* consternation, panic

consternar to dismay; shock; ~**se** to be dismayed

constipación *f* cold (in the head)

constipado having a cold (in the head)

constipar to give a cold to; ~**se** to catch a cold

constitución *f* constitution

constitucional *n m* constitutionalist; *adj* constitutional

constitucionalidad *f* constitutionality

constitucionalismo constitutionalism

constituir to constitute, set up; represent; ~**se** to set o.s. up as

constituyente constituent; **las Cortes Constituyentes** Spanish parliament

constreñimiento constraint, compulsion

constreñir to constrain, compel; *med* constipate

constricción *f* constriction

constrictor constrictive

construcción *f* construction, building, structure; ~ **naval** shipbuilding; **obrero de la** ~ building worker

constructor *n m* builder, constructor; ~ **de buques** shipbuilder

construir to construct; build; *gramm* construe

construpador *m* rapist; corrupter

construpar to rape; corrupt

consubstancial consubstantial

consuegra fellow mother-in-law

consuegro fellow father-in-law

consuelo consolation; **sin** ~ disconsolately

consuetudinal customary; **derecho** ~ *leg* common-law

cónsul *m* consul

consulado consulate

consulta consultation; *med* surgery, practice; **hacerle a alguien una** ~ to consult s.o.; **horas de** ~ *med* consulting/surgery hours

consultación *f* consultation

consultante *m* consultant

consultar to consult, look up; discuss; ~ **con la almohada** to sleep on it; ~ **el bolsillo** to see how much money one has

consultivo consultative

consultor *n m* consultant, consulter, consultee, adviser; *adj* advising, consulting

consultorio information bureau; *med* surgery; readers' queries (section of periodical)

consumación *f* consummation; **hasta la**

~ **de los siglos** to the end of time

consumado *n sl* loot, booty; *adj* consummate, accomplished; **estafador** ~ consummate crook; **hecho** ~ fait accompli

consumador consummating

consumar to consume; carry out

consumero excise-officer

consumición *f* item consumed; minimum charge

consumido emaciated; worn out

consumidor *n m* consumer

consumir to consume, use up; grieve; ~**se** to waste away, wear out, fret

consumismo consumerism, mentality of the consumer society

consumista *n m+f* consumer; *adj* of the consumer society

consumo consumption

consunción *f* consumption, wasting away

consustancial consubstantial

consustancialidad *f* consubstantiality

contabilidad *f* accountancy, bookkeeping

contabilizar to reckon, tot up; enter in the accounts

contable *m+f* book-keeper, accountant

contactar to contact

contacto contact, touch; **ponerse en** ~ **con** to get in touch with

contadero *m* turnstile; *adj* countable

contado scarce, rare; **al** ~ cash down; **pago al** ~ cash payment; **tiene los días** ~**s** his days are numbered

contador *m* book-keeper, accountant, auditor, cashier; official receiver; counter, desk; meter (for water, gas *etc*); cash register

contaduría accountancy, counting-house; cashier's office; *theat* box office

contagiar to infect, transmit; contaminate; ~**se** to become infected

contagio contagion

contagiosidad *f* contagiousness

contagioso contagious, catching

container *m bui* skip

contaminación *f* contamination

contaminador contaminating

contaminar to contaminate

contante: dinero ~ **y sonante** ready money

contar to count, reckon; relate, tell; charge; ~ **con** rely on; **¡cuéntaselo a tu tía!** tell that to the marines!

contemperar to temper, moderate

contemplación *f* contemplation

contemplador contemplative

contemplar to contemplate, look at, humour

contemplativo contemplative, meditative

contemporaneidad *f* contemporaneousness

contemporáneo *n+adj* contemporary

contemporización *f*, **contemporizamiento** temporization

contemporizador *n m* temporizer; *adj* temporizing

contemporizar to temporize

contención *f* contention; restraining, holding; *leg* suit; **muro de** ~ containing/retaining wall

contencioso contentious

contendedor *m* contender

contender to contend, strive

contendiente *m+f* contending party, litigant

contendor *m* contender, antagonist

contenedor *n m* container, receptacle; *adj* containing

contener to contain, comprise, hold, embrace; ~**se** to restrain o.s., forbear

contenido contents

contenta welcome gift, present; certificate of good conduct; *comm* endorsement

contentadizo easily pleased

contentamiento contentment, joy

contentar to please; content, satisfy; *comm* endorse; ~**se** to be reconciled, be satisfied with

contentivo comprising, containing

contento *n* contentment; joy; *adj* content, happy

contera ferrule; end, completion

contérmino bordering

contertulio member of a group that meets for conversation

contestación *f* answer, reply; dispute, protest; ~ **a la demanda** *leg* answer to a complaint; **no tener** ~ to be unanswerable

contestador (automático) *tel* (automatic) answering machine

contestario *pol* protesting, bolshie

conteste *m+f* witness (whose evidence confirms that of other witnesses)

contexto context

contextuar to prove textually
contienda contest, dispute, struggle
contigo with you
contigüidad *f* proximity
contiguo contiguous, adjacent; ~ **al jardín** next to the garden
continencia continence
continente *m* continent, mainland; *adj* containing, continent
contingencia contingency
contingente *n m* quota, contingent; *adj* accidental
contingible that may happen
continuación *f* continuation, continuity; protraction; **a** ~ immediately afterwards
continuar to continue, go on, stay; ~ **cantando** to go on singing; ~ **en Valencia** to remain in Valencia
continuidad *f* continuity
continuo continual, continuous
contonearse to swagger
contoneo swaggering
contorcerse to contort, writhe
contorción *f* contortion, writhing
contornar to outline, to go around (a place)
contorneo turning, winding; outlining
contorno contour, outline; ~**s** environs; surroundings; **en** ~ round about
contorsión *f* contortion, twist
contorsionista *m + f* contortionist
contra *n m* opposite, opposite meaning; *mus* organ-pedal; *f* snag; *prep* against, contrary to, opposite; **en** ~ **de** in opposition to; **el pro y el** ~ the pros and cons; **llevar la** ~ **a** to oppose
contralmirante *m* rear-admiral
contraataque *m* counter-attack
contraaviso counter-advice
contrabajo *mus* double-bass; bass
contrabalancear to counterbalance, compensate; ~**se** to cancel each other out
contrabalanceo counterbalancing
contrabalanza *n* counterbalance
contrabandear to smuggle
contrabandista *m + f* smuggler; *adj* smuggling
contrabando contraband; smuggled goods; **pasar de** ~ to smuggle in
contrabasa pedestal
contrabatir *mil* to return the fire of
contracarril *m* safety-rail

contracción *f* contraction; *comm* slump
contracorriente *f* cross-current; **a** ~ against the current
contráctil contractile
contractabilidad *f* contractility
contracultural anti-establishment; underground, alternative
contrachapado plywood
contradancista *m + f* dancer of country dance/square dance
contradanza country dance, square dance
contradecir to contradict
contradenuncia *leg* counter-charge
contradicción *f* contradiction; **espíritu de** ~ contrariness
contradictor contradicting, conflicting
contradictorio contradictory
contraer to contract, limit; ~ **amistad** to strike up a friendship; ~ **una deuda** to incur a debt; ~ **una enfermedad** to get a disease; ~ **matrimonio** to marry
contrafuerte *m archi* buttress
contrafuga *mus* counterfugue
contragolpe *m pol* counter-coup; *sp* backstroke
contragolpear to strike back
contrahacer to counterfeit; *lit* pirate
contrahaz *f* wrong side (of a piece of cloth)
contrahecho deformed; fake
contrahilo: **a** ~ across/against the grain
contraluz *f* cross-light; **mirar a** ~ to hold up to the light
contramaestre *m naut* boatswain; foreman
contramandar to countermand
contraofensiva counter-offensive
contraoferta counter-offer
contraorden *f* countermand
contrapartida *comm* cross-entry (in book-keeping)
contrapelo: **a** ~ against the grain
contrapesar to counterpoise, counterbalance
contrapeso counterpoise, counterbalance; tight-rope walker's pole; plummet
contraponer to set against, contrast
contraproducente counter-productive, self-defeating
contrapuerta double door
contrapuntear *mus* to sing in counterpoint; be sarcastic

contrapuntístico *mus* contrapuntal
contrapunto *mus* counterpoint
contrariar to cross, thwart; vex
contrariedad *f* opposition; bother; set-back
contraria: llevar la ~ to argue against
contrario *n m* opponent; **al ~** on the contrary; **al ~ de María** unlike Mary; **de lo ~** otherwise; *adj* contrary, contradictory, opposed; opposite; **ser ~ a** to be opposed to
contrarreforma counter-reformation
contrarrestar to check; counteract; *sp* return (the ball)
contrarresto checking; *sp* player receiving (the service)
contrarrevolución *f* counter-revolution
contrarrevolucionario counter-revolutionary
contrasentido *m* contradiction; nonsense
contraseña countersign; *mil* password; *theat* pass-out ticket
contraste *m* contrast; assay(er)
contrata contract, deed
contratante *n m* party to a contract; *adj* contracting
contratar to contract; hire; engage
contratiempo mishap, setback; **a ~** *mus* syncopated
contratista *m + f* contractor
contrato contract, covenant, deed
contratorpedero (torpedo-boat) destroyer
contravención *f* contravention, violation
contraveneno antidote
contravenir to contravene
contraventana window-shutter
contribución *f* contribution; rates; municipal taxes
contribuidor *n m* contributor; *adj* contributing
contribuir to contribute, pay (as tax)
contribuyente ratepayer, taxpayer
contrincante *m* competitor, rival, fellow-candidate
contrito contrite
controlar to control, check
controversia controversy, dispute
contundente blunt, overwhelming, convincing; **argumento ~** crushing argument
contundir to contuse, bruise
conturbación *f* distress

convalecencia convalescence
convalecer to convalesce, be convalescent; recover (**de** from)
convaleciente convalescent
convalidar *leg* to ratify; authenticate
convecino neighbouring
convencedor convincing
convencer to convince, persuade
convencimiento conviction, certainty; **en el ~ de que** in the belief that; **tener el ~ de que** to be quite certain that
conveniencia suitability; profit; advantage
conveniente advantageous; suitable, fit, opportune
convenio convention; agreement
convenir to agree, be a good idea, suit; be desirable; **~ con** to agree with; **~ en** to agree about/on
convento convent, nunnery; monastery
convergencia convergence
convergente converging, convergent
converger, convergir to converge; agree
conversación *f* conversation; talk; topic; **él sacó la ~** he brought up the topic; **trabar ~** to start a conversation
conversador *m* good conversationalist
conversar to converse, talk; *mil* wheel (change direction)
conversión *f* conversion, transformation; *mil* wheel(ing)
convertibilidad *f* convertibility
convertidor *n m* converter
convertir to convert, transform; **~se** to be converted, become
convexidad *f* convexity
convexo convex
convicción *f* conviction
convicto *leg* convicted, found guilty
convidada invitation to have a drink
convidado guest
convidador *m* host; one who stands drinks
convidar to invite, treat; induce
convincente convincing
convite *m* feast, banquet; treat
convivencia living together; coexistence
conviviente *n m + f* cohabitant; *adj* living together
convivir to live together; coexist
convocación *f* convocation, summoning
convolvuláceo, convólvulo *bot* convolvulus, bindweed
convoy *m* convoy, train; cruet-stand;

retinue

convoyar to convoy, escort

convulsión *f* upheaval; *med* convulsion

convulsionar to cause upheaval in; *med* produce convulsions in

convulsivo convulsive

convulso convulsed

conyugal connubial; **vida** ~ married life

cónyuge *m* married partner

coña *fam* joking, facetiousness; joke (often in bad taste); **estar de** ~ to be in a joking mood

coñac *m* cognac, brandy

coñearse *fam* to joke; ~ **con** to take the mickey out of

coño *vulg* cunt; ¡~! bloody hell!

cooperación *f* cooperation

cooperador *n m* cooperator; *adj* co-operative

cooperante cooperating

cooperar to cooperate

cooperario cooperator

cooperativa cooperative society

cooperativo cooperative

coopositor *m* fellow candidate (in competitive examination)

coordinar to coordinate

copa cup, goblet, wine-glass; treetop; crown (of hat); ~**s** hearts (*Sp* playing-cards); **tomar una** ~ to have a drink

copar *pol* to sweep, win (all votes); (cards) win all tricks; *mil* cut off and capture; **estamos copados** we've had it, it's all up with us

Copenhague *m* Copenhagen

copera cabinet for glasses

copernicano Copernican

Copérnico Copernicus

copetudo tufted; uppish

copia copiousness, abundance; copy, duplicate, likeness

copiador *m* copyist, copier, transcriber; copying machine

copiar to copy, duplicate; ape, mimic

copilador *n m* compiler; *adj* compiling

copilar to compile

copiloto *aer* co-pilot

copioso copious, abundant

copista *m + f* copyist, transcriber

copla couplet, ballad

coplero folk singer, ballad singer

coplista *m + f* poetaster

coplones *mpl* bad verse

copo snowflake; ~**s de maíz** cornflakes

coproducción *f* joint production

copropietario joint-owner

cóptico Coptic

cópula copulation

copulación *f* copulation

copulador copulatory

copular to copulate

copulativo joining; *gramm* copulative

coque *m* coke

coquera coal-scuttle

coqueta flirt; dressing-table

coquetear to flirt

coqueteo flirting

coquetería flirtatiousness; coquetry

coqueto flirtatious; cute

coquetón *n m* one for the girls, lady-killer; *adj* sweet, cute, very flirtatious

coquetona terrible flirt

coquito gesture, grimace; *fam* Brazil nut

coraje *m* anger, spirit, guts; **me da** ~ it makes me see red

corajudo bad-tempered

coral *n m* coral; *adj* choral

Corán *m* Koran

corazón *m* heart, spirit; **de todo** ~ wholeheartedly; **hacer de tripas** ~ to pluck up courage; **llevar el** ~ **en la mano** to wear one's heart on one's sleeve; **tener el** ~ **bien puesto** to have lots of guts

corazonada hunch, presentiment

corbata necktie; cravat; ribbon; insignia; gin and Coca-Cola

corbatería necktie shop

corbatero maker/seller of neckties

corbeta *naut* corvette

Córcega Corsica

corcova hump, hunchback

corcovado hump-backed

corcovar to bend; make crooked

corchete *m* clasp; hook-and-eye; hook

corcho cork; beehive; (fishing) float; **tener cara de** ~ to be thick-skinned

corchoso corky

cordaje *m* cordage; *naut* rigging

cordel *m* cord, thin rope; **a** ~ in a straight line; **mozo de** ~ porter

cordelería rope trade; rope-walk; *naut* rigging

cordelero rope-maker

corderina lambskin

cordero lamb

cordial *n m* tonic; *adj* cordial, hearty

cordialidad *f* cordiality, heartiness
cordillera chain/range of mountains
cordita cordite
cordobés *n* native of Córdoba; *adj* Cordoban
cordón *m* cord, string; shoelace, *US* shoestring
cordoncillo milling (on coins)
cordura sanity, common-sense
Corea Korea; ~ **del Norte** North Korea; ~ **del Sur** South Korea
coreano *n+adj* Korean
corear to play/sing in a chorus; put a choral accompaniment to; chorus
coreografía choreography
coreográfico choreographic
coreógrafo choreographer
coriandro *bot* coriander
corista *m+f* chorus-singer, chorister
coriza *med* coryza
cormorán *m orni* cormorant; ~ **moñudo** *orni* shag
cornac *m* elephant keeper, mahout
cornada thrust with a bull's horn; gore
cornamenta *zool* horns, antlers
cornear to butt, gore
corneja *orni* crow
cornejo *bot* dogwood
cornero de pan crust of bread
corneta bugle
cornisa corniche, coastal promenade
Cornualles Cornwall
cornudo *n* cuckold; *adj* horned
coro choir; choir-loft; chorus; **a** ~ in chorus; **de** ~ by heart
corografía *see* **coreografía**
corográfico *see* **coreográfico**
corógrafo *see* **coreógrafo**
corolario corollary
corona crown, coronet; tonsure; halo; ~ **funeraria** wreath; *astron+bot* corona
coronación *f* coronation; *archi* coping (of walls)
coronado tonsured priest
coronamiento *naut* taffrail
coronar to crown; complete
coronario coronary
corondeles *mpl* watermark lines
coronel *m* colonel
coronilla *anat* crown; **andar de** ~ to be harassed; **estar hasta la** ~ to be browned off
corpiñera bodice-maker

corpiño bodice
corporación *f* corporation, guild; **en** ~ in a body
corporal corporal; **castigo** ~ corporal punishment; **daño** ~ bodily harm
corporativo corporative
corporificar to materialize
corpóreo corporeal
corpulencia corpulence
corpulento corpulent, heavily built
Corpus *m* Corpus Christi
corpúsculo corpuscle
corral *m* enclosure; farmyard; cattle-pen; **hacer** ~**es** to play truant
correa leather strap; lead; belt; watch-band; ~ **de transmisión** driving-belt; ~ **del ventilador** fan-belt; ~ **transportadora** conveyor-belt
correaje *m* leather straps; belting
correcalles *m sing+pl* gadabout
corrección *f* correction; correctness
correccional *m* reformatory, approved school; *adj* correctional
correccionalismo reformatory system
correccionario inmate of approved school
correcto correct, right; well-mannered, well-behaved
corrector *n m* corrector; proof-reader; *adj* correcting
corredera sliding panel; woodlouse; cockroach; lane; rail; guide, groove
corredero sliding
corredizo running, sliding; **nudo** ~ slip knot; **puerta corrediza** sliding door
corredor *m* runner; corridor, aisle; racing-driver; ~ **en pista** cyclist; *mil* scout, forager; *comm* broker; ~ **de cambios** stockbroker; ~ **de fincas** estate-agent, *US* realtor
correduría brokerage
corregibilidad *f* corrigibility
corregible corrigible
corregir to correct, amend; put right; adjust; temper
correinante reigning jointly
correlación *f* correlation
correlacionar to correlate
correlativo correlative
correligionario coreligionist
correntón *m* gadabout
correo courier, messenger; post, mail; *sl* small-time drug pusher; ~**s** post office; ~ **aéreo** air-mail; **echar al** ~ to

post, mail; **lista de** ~ poste restante
correoso leathery
¹ **correr** *vt* to overrun; pursue; race; push
home; draw (curtains); act as agent
for; undo (a knot); auction; **~la** to go
on a spree; ~ **los mares** to see the
world; ~ **monte** to hunt big game; ~
peligro to be in danger
² **correr** *vi* to run, hurry, flow, pass;
meteor blow; be worth; be common
talk/rumoured; ~ **con los gastos** to
bear the cost; **a todo** ~ flat out; **corre el
plazo** time is running out; **corre la voz**
it is said; **~se** to move over, slide out;
flow over; blush; (of paints) run
correspondencia correspondence, reciprocation; mail
corresponder to correspond; reciprocate; belong; **a quien corresponda** to
whom it may concern
correspondiente *n m+f* correspondent;
adj corresponding
corresponsal *m* (newspaper) correspondent
corresponsalía post of newspaper correspondent
correvedile, correveidile *m+f* tale-
bearer, gossipmonger
corrida sprint, run; *aer* taxiing; ~ **de
ratas** rat-race; ~ **de toros** bullfight; **de**
~ quickly
corrido *adj* running; cursive; unbroken;
worldly wise; **de** ~ by heart; **juerga corrida** constant fun
corriente *n f* current; trend; ~ **alterna**
alternating current; ~ **continua** direct
current; ~ **de aire** draught; **estar al** ~
(de) to be up-to-date (about); **poner al**
~ to put in the picture; *adj* running;
ordinary, normal, common
corrigendo reformatory inmate
corro ring/circle of (people); round enclosure; ring-a-ring-of-roses; round
dance/game; **hacer** ~ to form a circle
corroboración *f* corroboration
corroborador *n m* corroborator; *adj*
corroboratory
corroborar to corroborate, confirm
corroborativo corroborative
corroer to corrode; gnaw away
corromper to corrupt, spoil; bribe; rot;
~se to become corrupted; be spoilt
corrosión *f* corrosion
corrosivo corrosive; **ser** ~ to be an

undermining influence
corrupción *f* corruption, decay
corruptela corruption; *leg* abuse
corruptibilidad *f* corruptibility
corruptivo corruptive
corrupto corrupted, corrupt
corruptor *n m* corrupter, perverter; *adj*
corrupting
corsario corsair; privateer; pirate
corsé *m* corset
corsetería corset shop, corset factory
corsetero maker/seller of corsets
¹ **corso** privateering cruise
² **corso** Corsican
corta felling (of trees)
cortaalambres *m sing+pl* wire-cutters
cortacéspedes *m sing+pl* lawnmower
cortacigarros *m sing+pl* cigar-cutter
cortacircuitos *m sing+pl* *elect* cut-out;
circuit-breaker
cortado *n* coffee with a dash of milk;
ice-cream sandwich; *adj* cut; short; (of
milk) sour
cortador *n m* cutter (person); *adj* cutting
cortadora cutting machine, slicing
machine
cortadura cut
cortafuegos *m sing+pl* firebreak
cortante *n m* butcher; *adj* cutting; biting;
sharp
cortapapeles *m sing+pl* paper-knife
cortapicos *m sing+pl* earwig
cortapisa impediment, hindrance, restriction
cortaplumas *m sing+pl* pen-knife
cortapuros *m sing+pl* cigar-cutter
cortar to cut (out), shear, trim; interrupt; stop, switch off; curdle; ~ **de
raíz** to eradicate; ~ **el paso** to bar the
way; **~ le a alguien los vuelos** to clip
s.o.'s wings; ~ **un pase** *sp* to intercept
a pass; **~se** to become confused,
embarrassed; cut o.s.; **la leche se ha
cortado** the milk has curdled/gone
sour
cortauñas *m sing+pl* nail-clippers
cortavidrios *m sing+pl* glass-cutter (instrument)
cortaviento *aer* wind-shield; **~s** wind-
break
¹ **corte** *m* cut, cutting, trimming; length
(required for a garment); slit, slash;
hacer el ~ **de mangas** *equiv* to give the
two-fingered salute (reversed V-sign)

² **corte** *f* (royal) court; **la Corte** Madrid; **las Cortes** *Sp* parliament; **hacer la** ~ to court, woo

cortedad *f* smallness; shortness; stupidity; ~ **de medios** lack of funds

cortejador courting, wooing

cortejante *n m* beau, wooer; *adj* courting, wooing

cortejar to woo, court; escort

cortejo courting, wooing; cortège, procession

cortés courteous, polite, civil

cortesanía courtesy, politeness, civility

cortesano *n* courtier; *adj* courtly

cortesía courtesy, civility; *print* blank page between chapters; **hacer una** ~ to curtsy

corteza bark, peel, rind, crust, skin; boorishness

cortijada farm estate; farmhouse and its outbuildings

cortijero owner/manager of a farm estate

cortijo farm estate; **alborotar el** ~ to put a cat among the pigeons

cortina curtain; screen; covering; ~ **de fuego** artillery barrage; ~ **de humo** smoke screen; **a** ~ **corrida** in secret; **correr/descorrer la** ~ to draw/draw back the curtain

cortinal *m* plot, allotment

corto short, brief; shy; ~ **de luces** dull-witted, thick; ~ **de oído** hard of hearing; **a la corta o a la larga** sooner or later; **a** ~ **plazo** in the short term

cortocircuitar *elect* to short-circuit

cortocircuito *elect* short-circuit

cortometraje *m cin* short

coruñés *n* native of Corunna; *adj* of/from Corunna

corva back of knee; **hasta las** ~ knee-deep

corvadura curvature

corveta leap, bound

corvetear to leap, bound

corvina *zool* bass

corvo bent, crooked

corzo roe-deer

cosa thing, something, matter; *sl* marihuana; ~ **de oír/de ver** thing worth hearing/seeing; ~ **perdida** dead loss; ~**s de palacio** officialdom, bureaucracy; **es** ~ **de María** that's typical of Mary; **es** ~ **de media hora** it's a matter

of half an hour; **es** ~ **de nunca acabar** it's an endless business; **eso es** ~ **mía** that's my business; **no es** ~ **del otro jueves** it's nothing to write home about

cosaco Cossack

cosaquería savage raid

coscorrón *m* bump (on the head)

cosecha harvest, harvest-time; crop

cosechadora combine-harvester

cosechar to reap, harvest

cosechero grower

coser to sew, stitch; **es** ~ **y cantar** it's child's play, it's plain sailing

cosible that can be sewed

cosido sewing

cosmética cosmetics

cosmético cosmetic

cósmico cosmic

cosmografía cosmography

cosmográfico cosmographic

cosmógrafo cosmographer

cosmología cosmology

cosmológico cosmological

cosmólogo cosmologist

cosmonauta *m* cosmonaut, astronaut

cosmopolita *n m* + *f* + *adj* cosmopolitan

cosmopolitismo cosmopolitanism

coso main street; arena, bullring

cosquillas *fpl* tickling, ticklishness; **hacer** ~ **a uno** to tickle s.o.; **tener** ~ to be ticklish

cosquillear to tickle

cosquilleo tickling

cosquilloso ticklish, touchy

¹ **costa** cost; **a** ~ **de** at the expense of; **a poca** ~ with little effort; **a toda** ~ at all costs; ~**s** *leg* costs, expenses; **condenar en** ~**s** to sentence to pay costs; **vivir a** ~ **de alguien** to live off s.o.

² **costa** coast, shore; seaside; **aún hay moros en la** ~ the situation is still not clear; **dar a la** ~ *naut* to be blown towards the coast

costado side, flank; ~**s** lineage; **dolor de** ~ stitch (in the side); **por los cuatro** ~**s** to the backbone

costal: harina de otro ~ another kettle of fish

costanero coastal; **buque** ~ coastal vessel, coaster

costar to cost; **cueste lo que cueste** at all costs; **cuesta trabajo creerlo/conven-**

cerle it's hard to believe/convince him

costarricense, costarriqueño *n* + *adj* Costa Rican

coste *m* cost; ~ **de la vida** cost of living

¹ **costear** to pay for; defray the expenses of; **poder** ~ to afford; **vender una cosa para** ~**se otra** to sell one thing to pay for another

² **costear** *naut* to coast

costero *n bot* wood nearest to the bark; *adj* coastal

costilla *anat* rib; *cul* chop, cutlet; *fam* wife, better half; stave (of barrel); ~**s** shoulders, back; **medirle a alguien las** ~**s** to beat/cudgel s.o.

costo cost, price; charges, expenses; **a** ~ **y costas** at cost price

costoso dear, expensive, costly

costra crust, scab; filth, mess

costroso crusty, scabby; messy, filthy

costumbre *f* custom, habit; **novela de** ~**s** novel of manners; **usos y** ~**s** usage and custom; **las disculpas de** ~ the same old excuses; **de** ~ usually; **según** ~ according to custom; **depravar las** ~**s** to corrupt morals; **es** ~ it is customary; **tener la** ~ **de** + *infin* to be in the habit of + *gerund*

costumbrismo the writing of customs and novels of manners

costumbrista *m+f* author of novels of manners

costura needlework, sewing; seam, dressmaking; *naut* splicing; *carp* + *mech* joint; **sentar las** ~**s** to press the seams; **sin** ~**s** seamless; **alta** ~ high fashion

costurera seamstress, dressmaker

costurero work-box, work-basket; work-room

cota, cota de malla coat of mail

cotidiano daily, everyday

cotilla *m+f* gossip

cotillear to gossip

cotilleo gossip(ing)

cotizable quotable

cotización *f comm* quotation, price

cotizador *m* quoter, pricer, valuer

cotizar *comm* to quote, price; **estar muy cotizado** to be sought after; ~**se** to fetch; be quoted; be valued

coto reservation, preserve, boundary mark, limit; *zool* chub; ~ **de caza** game preserve; ~ **redondo** large

estate; **poner** ~ **a** to put a stop to

cotonada cotton goods

cotonía dimity

cotorra parakeet; chatterbox; talkative woman

cotorrear to chatter, gabble

cotorreo chattering, gossiping

cotorrera hen-parrot; chatterbox, talkative woman

cotorrería chattering (of women)

cotudo cottony, fluffy

cotutor *m* joint guardian

covachuela wretched little cave; poky little government office

covendedor *m* joint-vendor

coxcojilla, coxcojita hopscotch; **a** ~ hopping on one leg

coyuntura joint, articulation; *pol* juncture, situation

coz *f* kick; recoil (of firearm); flowing back (of liquids), butt (of pistol); **tratar a coces** to kick people around; **dar coces** to kick; **mandar a coces** to rule harshly

crac *m comm* failure, crash, bankruptcy; **hacer** ~ to go bankrupt; crack

cráneo skull, cranium; *fam* brain

crápula debauchery; *sl* libertine

crapuloso crapulous, debauched

craquear *chem* to crack

craqueo *n chem* cracking

crascitar to caw, croak

craso fat, greasy; crass

cráter *m* crater

creación *f* creation

creador *n m* creator; *adj* creative

crear to create, make, establish, found

crecepelos *m sing* + *pl* hair-restorer

crecer to grow, increase, become larger, rise; ~**se** to show guts; become too big for one's boots

creces *fpl* increase, rise, increment; **con** ~ abundantly

crecida swelling, rise, flood

crecido large, great; grown (up)

creciente *n f* swelling (of rivers *etc*); ~ **de la luna** crescent moon; ~ **del mar** flood tide; *adj* growing, increasing

crecimiento growth

credencial *adj* credential; *fpl* ~**es** credentials

credibilidad *f pol* credibility

crédito credit, credence; reputation; note, bill; **a** ~ on credit; **dar** ~ **a** to give credit/credence to

credo creed; **en un ~** in a trice/jiffy; **con el ~ en la boca** at death's door, in great danger

credulidad *f* credulity

crédulo credulous

creencia belief

creer to believe, think; **~ a ojos cerrados** to believe implicitly; **~se** to believe to be

creíble credible

creído vain, conceited

crema cream, liqueur; **~ de zapatos** shoe-polish; **~ de menta** crème de menthe

cremación *f* cremation

cremallera zipper, zip-fastener; *sl* mouth

crematística political economy

crematístico economic

crematólogo political economist

crematología political economy

crematológico relating to political economy

crematorio *n* crematorium; *adj* crematory

cremoso creamy

creosota creosote

creosotar to creosote

crepitación *f* crackling

crepitante *adj* crackling

crepitar to crackle

crepuscular *adj* of dusk/twilight

crepúsculo twilight, dusk

creso Croesus, wealthy man

crespina hair-net

crespo *n* curl; *adj* curly, frizzy, unmanageable; angry, haughty

cresta cock's comb; crest, tuft; **dar en la ~** to bring down a peg or two; **levantar la ~** to become arrogant

Creta Crete

cretense *n + adj* Cretan

cretinismo idiocy, cretinism

cretino cretin, idiot

cretona *text* cretonne

creyente *n m+f* believer; **los ~s** the faithful; *adj* believing

cría *zool* brood; rearing, breeding; litter; child; **~ de abejas** bee-keeping; **ama de ~** wet nurse

criada servant, maid

criadero *n bot* nursery; *zool* breeding-place; fish-hatchery

criado manservant

criador *n m* breeder, raiser

crianza nursing, lactation; manners; upbringing; breeding

criar to breed, rear, foster, nourish, grow, bring up; **~ carnes** to grow fat, put on weight; **~ molleja** to grow lazy; **~se** to grow up

criatura creature, infant, child; **eso es ~ de Pablo** that's Paul's doing

criba sieve, screen

cribadora sifter

cribador *n m* sifter; *adj* sieving, sifting

cribar to sieve, sift; screen

cric *m mot* jack

crica fissure, trench; *anat* vagina

crimen *m* crime, murder

criminal *n m* criminal, murderer; *adj* criminal, murderous; *fam* appalling, ghastly; **es ~** it's sheer murder

criminalidad *f* criminality; crime-rate

criminalista *m+f* criminal lawyer; criminologist

criminología criminology

criminólogo criminologist

criminosidad *f* criminality

criminoso criminal

crin *f zool* mane, horse-hair

crinado long-haired

crinolina crinoline

crío baby, infant, kid

criollo Creole; *SA* native

cripta crypt

criptograma *m* cryptogram

criptología cryptology

criquet *m* cricket

crisálida pupa, chrysalis

crisántemo chrysanthemum

crisma *sl* head, nut; **romperse la ~** to crack one's nut, bang one's head

crisol *m* crucible

crispación *f*, **crispamiento** twitch, twitching

crispante twitching, convulsive

crispar to convulse; twitch; **eso me crispa los nervios** that gets on my nerves

cristal *m* crystal, glass; pane of glass; **~ de aumento** magnifying glass; **doble ~** double glazing

cristalería glass-ware; glass-works

cristalero glassmaker, glass-dealer, glazier

cristalino *n anat* crystalline lens; *adj*

crystalline
cristalizable crystallizable
cristalización *f* crystallization
cristalizante crystallizing
cristalizar(se) to crystallize
cristalografía crystallography
cristalógrafo crystallographer
cristianar to baptize, christen
cristiandad *f* Christendom
cristianismo Christianity
cristianizar to christianize
cristiano Christian; **hablar en** ~ to use Castilian, use plain language
Cristina Christine
cristo crucifix; **Cristo** Christ
Cristóbal Christopher
criterio criterion, viewpoint; opinion
criticable open to criticism
criticador *n m* critic; *adj* critical, criticizing
crítica criticism, critique; review
criticar to criticize
crítico *n m* critic; *adj* critical
criticón *m* fault-finder
cro (caballero) gent (gentleman)
croar to croak
croata *n m + f + adj* Croatian
croché *m* crochet
cromática chromatics
cromático chromatic
cromo chrome, chromium; picture card; coloured picture; gaudy picture; **estar hecho un** ~ be gaudily attired
crónica chronicle, news report
crónico chronic
cronista *m + f* reporter, chronicler
cronología chronology, sequence
cronológico chronological
cronologista *m + f* chronologist
cronometrador *m* time-keeper
cronometraje *m* timing, timekeeping
cronometrar to time
cronometría chronometry
cronométrico chronometrical
cronómetro chronometer, stop-watch
croqueta croquette
croquis *m sing + pl* sketch, rough draft
cruce *m* crossing, cross-roads; ~ **giratorio** roundabout, *US* traffic-circle; **luz de** ~ dipped headlight
crucero *eccles* cross-bearer; *archi* transcept; *print* fold (in sheet of paper); *naut* cruise; **altitud/velocidad de** ~ cruising height/speed; **misil de** ~

cruise missile
crucífero *eccles* cross-bearer
crucificador *m* crucifier
crucificar to crucify
crucifijo crucifix
crucifixión *f* crucifixion
cruciforme cruciform
crudeza rawness, harshness; (of water) hardness; crudity
crudo raw, underdone; unripe; rough; (of linen) unbleached; (of water) hard; **cuero** ~ untanned leather
crueldad *f* cruelty
cruento bloody
crujidero creaky, rustling
crujido creak, crackle, rustle; **dar un** ~ to go bang
crujidor *m* glass-cutter (tool)
crujiente creaking, rustling, crackling; crunchy
crujir to creak, rustle, crackle; ~ **de dientes** to gnash/grind the teeth
crustáceo *n* crustacean
cruz *f* cross; reverse (of coin); *print* dagger; burden; *vet* withers; ~ **gamada** swastika; **cara o** ~ heads or tails; **en** ~ crosswise, with extended arms; **firmar con una** ~ to make one's mark, sign with a cross; ~ **y raya** that's that
cruzar *vt* to cross; go across; lay across; *naut* cruise; dub (knight); ~ **palabras** to quarrel; ~ **los brazos** to fold the arms; ~**se** to pass each other
cu *f* letter q
cuaderno exercise-book, notebook; ~ **de bitácora** *naut* log-book
cuadra stable
cuadrado *n* square; gusset; **de** ~ full-faced (view); *adj* square, stocky, broad; spot on
cuadragésimo fortieth
cuadrángulo *n* quadrangle; *adj* quadrangular
cuadrante *m* quadrant; quarter share of an inheritance; sun-dial; clock/watch face; *adj* squaring
cuadrar *vt* to square; form into a square; divide into squares; *vi* to fit, suit; tally; correspond; adjust; ~**se** *mil* to stand to attention; take a firm line; (horse-riding) stop short
cuadratura *astron + math* quadrature; squaring; ~ **del círculo** squaring of the

circle

cuadricenal every forty years

cuadrícula squared pattern

cuadriculado: papel ~ squared paper

cuadricular *adj* checkered, ruled in squares; *v* to rule in squares

cuadriforme square-shaped

cuadrilátero quadrilateral

cuadrilla team, gang, crew; troop, squad; armed patrol; group

cuadrillero leader of team/gang/crew; member of a patrol

cuadripartido quadripartite; divided into four

cuádriple, cuadriplicar *see* **cuádruple, cuadruplicar**

cuadro *n* square; *theat* scene, tableau; painting; square flower-bed; *print* platen; *mil* defensive square; staff (of a regiment); *elect* switchboard; *pol* cadre; *adj* square

cuadrúpedo *n* quadruped

cuádruple quadruple, fourfold

cuadruplicar to quadruplicate, quadruple

cuádruplo *n* quadruple

cuajada curd; ~ **de leche** junket

cuajado *n* minced meat with fruit and herbs; *adj* flabbergasted, curdled

cuajadura coagulation, curdling

cuajar *n m* rennet-bag; *vt* to curdle, coagulate; *vi* to take shape, come off; ~**se** to curd, curdle; coagulate; cake

cuajo rennet; curdling; coagulation; **arrancar de** ~ to tear by its roots

cuakerismo, cuákero *see* **cuaquerismo, cuáquero**

cual *adv* as, like; *rel pron* which; who; whom; **por lo** ~ for which reason; **cada** ~ each one; ~ **si** as if

cuál *inter pron* which?, what?, which one?

cualidad *f* quality

cualitativo qualitative

cualquier/a (*pl* **cualesquier/a**) *adj* any; *pron* anyone, anybody, whoever, whichever; **en** ~ **lugar** anywhere; **un** ~ a nobody

cuando (*interr* **cuándo**) *adv* when, if; *conj* whenever, though, although, since; even; ~ **más** at most; ~ **menos** at least; ~ **la guerra** during the war; ~ **no** otherwise, if not; ¿**de** ~ **acá?** since when?; **de** ~ **en** ~ from time to time;

¿**hasta** ~? till when?

cuantía amount, quantity, importance, degree; **de mayor** ~ serious; **de menor** ~ secondary, of little importance

cuantiar to value, estimate

cuantidad *f see* **cantidad**

cuantimás all the more

cuantioso copious, numerous, large

cuantitativo quantitative

cuanto *adj* as much as; all that; whatever; *adv* how much, how far, how long; the more; **en** ~ **a** respecting; **en** ~ as soon as

cuánto: ¡~ **dinero!** what a lot of money!; ¡~ **tiempo!** what a long time!; ¿~? how much?; ¿~**s?** how many?; ¿**a** ~**s estamos?** what is the date?

cuaquerismo Quakerism

cuáquero Quaker

cuarenta forty; **los años** ~ the forties

cuarentavo fortieth part

cuarentena period of forty days/forty months/forty years; quarantine

cuarentón *m* person in his forties

cuaresma Lent

cuaresmal Lenten

cuarta fourth part; (of cards) sequence of four; span (of hand)

cuartear to quarter; divide by four; make a fourth (at a game); ~**se** to split, crack

cuartel *m* quarter; district; lodging; barracks; clemency; *naut* hatch; ~ **general** headquarters; **dar** ~ to give quarter; **estar de** ~ to be on half-pay

cuartelada mutiny, coup

cuartelero *adj* pertaining to barracks; **lenguaje** ~ barrack-room language

cuartelillo police post

cuarteto *mus* quartet; *poet* quatrain

cuartilla sheet of paper

cuartillo *naut* dog-watch; half-litre

[1] **cuarto** *n* room, bedroom; ~ **de baño** bathroom; ~ **de aseo** wash-room

[2] **cuarto** *n* copper coin; **de tres al** ~ third-rate; **estar sin** ~ to be penniless; **tener** ~**s** to have money; *adj* fourth, quarter; ~ **creciente** first quarter (of moon); **en** ~ *print* quarto; 2 **y** ~ quarter past 2

cuarzo quartz

cuasi almost

cuatrero cattle-thief, rustler

cuatrimestre *n m* period of four months;

adj lasting four months

cuatrimotor *n m* four-engined plane

cuatrisílabo *n* quadrisyllable; *adj* quadrisyllabic

cuatro four; (date) fourth; **las** ~ four o'clock; **más de** ~ many

cuatrocientos four hundred

cuatrojos *m sing+pl sl* four-eyes; one who wears glasses

cuba cask, tub, vat; man with a big belly; **beber como una** ~ to drink like a fish; **estar como una** ~ to be sozzled

cubalibre *m* rum and Coca-Cola

cubano Cuban

cubata *see* **cubalibre**

cubertería cutlery

cubertura *Sp* grandee's right to wear a hat in the presence of the king

cubicar to calculate the cubic contents of; cube

cúbico cubic

cubierta cover, covering; envelope; wrapper; book-cover; *mot* tyre (casing); bonnet, engine cover; *naut* deck; ~ **alta** top deck; ~ **de aterrizaje** flight-deck; **entre** ~s between decks

cubierto cover, place; table service; fixed-price meal; table d'hôte; lean-to; *adj* covered; overcast; **ponerse a** ~ to take cover; ~s cutlery

cubil *m* animals lair; river-bed

cubilar *m* sheepfold, lair; *v* (of sheep) to take shelter

cubilla *ent* Spanish fly

cubismo cubism

cubista cubist

cubo pail, bucket; *math* cube; hub of wheel; ~ **mágico** Rubik's cube

cubrecama bed-cover, counterpane

cubremantel *m* fancy tablecloth

cubreplatos *m sing+pl* food cover; wire-net cover

cubrición *f* copulation (of animals)

cubriente copulating (of animals)

cubrir to cover, spread over; coat, face; shroud, cover up; (of animals) cover; ~ **los gastos** to meet the expenses; ~se to put one's hat on; *mil* cover off

cuca peanut; *sl* peseta; *sl* gambling woman; *sl* tart, slut; *vulg sl* prick

cucaña bargain, walk-over; piece of cake; (at fair) greasy pole with prize at top

cucar to wink

cucaracha cockroach

cucarachera cockroach trap; nest of cockroaches

cuclillas: en ~ squatting; **sentarse en** ~ to squat down

cuclillo *orni* cuckoo; cuckold

cucú *m* call of the cuckoo

cucurucho roll/cone of paper; (ice-cream) cornet

cuchara spoon, ladle; *bui* trowel

cucharada spoonful, ladleful; **meter su** ~ to stick one's oar in

cucharadita teaspoonful

cucharetear to stir

cucharilla, cucharita tea-/coffee-spoon

cucharón *m* ladle, scoop

cuchichear to whisper

cuchicheo whisper(ing)

cuchilla blade; kitchen-knife

cuchillada slash, gash; ~s quarrels; **andar a** ~s to be at daggers-drawn; **dar una** ~ to stab; play to the gallery

cuchillería cutlery, cutler's shop

cuchillero cutler

cuchillo knife; (sewing) gore; ~ **de monte** hunter's knife, sheath knife; ~ **mangonero** badly forged knife

cuchipanda bean-feast; blow-out

cuchitril *m* poky place, dump, pigsty

cucho pooch, doggie, pussy

cuchufleta quip

cuelga bunch (of fruit); string (of vegetables)

cuelgaplatos *m sing+pl* wire plate holder (for wall decoration)

cuelliangosto thin-necked

cuellicorto short-necked

cuellierguido stiff-necked; vain

cuelligrueso thick-necked

cuellilargo long-necked

cuello neck, throat; collar; **levantar** ~ to get on one's feet again

cuenca wooden bowl; *anat* eye-socket; *geog* river basin

cuenco earthenware bowl; hollow

cuenta account; count; bill, *US* check; bead; *sl* menstruation, period; ~ **corriente** current account; ~ **de la vieja** counting on one's fingers; ~ **pendiente** outstanding account; ~s **del Gran Capitán** exorbitant expenses; a ~ on account; **a esa** ~ at that rate; **ajustar** ~s to settle accounts; **caer en la** ~ to realize; **de** ~ important; **es** ~

mía that's my business; **llevar la ~** to keep a record; **no traer ~** to be not worthwhile; **pedir ~s** to demand an explanation; **por su (propia) ~** off one's own bat; **~ atrás** countdown

cuentacorrentista *m+f* current account holder

cuentagotas *m sing+pl med* dropper, drip-feed

cuentapasos *m sing+pl* pedometer

cuentecillo little story

cuentista *m+f* yarn-spinner, liar; short-story writer

cuento story, tale, yarn; lie; pretext; **tener ~** to make a fuss, exaggerate; **estar en el ~** to be in the picture; **no viene a ~** it's not the point

cuerda string, cord, rope, halter; spring; *anat* tendon; *mus* chord; cat-gut; mountain chain; **~ de presos** chain-gang; **~ falsa** *mus* out-of-tune string; **~ floja** tightrope; **dar ~ a un reloj** to wind up a watch; **dar una ~ falsa** to strike a wrong note; **(por) bajo ~** in an underhand way

cuerdero string-maker; string-seller

cuerdo sane; prudent

cuerna set of antlers/horns; hunting-horn

cuerno horn, antenna, feeler; hunting-horn; *naut* outrigger; **ponerle a alguien los ~s** to cuckold s.o.; **¡vete al ~!** go to hell!

cuero hide, leather, pelt; wine-skin; *sl* handbag; **~ cabelludo** scalp; **de ~** leathern

cuerpo body; *mil* corps; *print* size (of letters); staff (employees); corpse; **~ a ~** hand-to-hand; **~ muerto** *naut* mooring buoy; **~ volante** flying column, flying squad; **de ~ entero** *arts+phot* full-length; **de medio ~** *arts+phot* half-length; **de ~ presente** prepared for burial, in state

cuerva female crow

cuervo crow, raven; *sl* priest

cuesco stone (fruit); *vulg* noisy fart

cuesta slope, hill, incline; **~ abajo** downhill; **~ arriba** uphill; **a ~s** on one's back; **~ de enero** *comm* after-Christmas slump; **llevar a ~s** to carry on one's back

cuestación *f* charitable appeal

cuestión *f* question, matter, subject; **~**

candente burning question

cuestionable questionable

cuestionar to question, argue over

cuestionario questionnaire

cueto craggy hill

cueva cave; cellar; den

cuidado care, concern; **¡~!** look out!, mind!; **con ~** carefully; **de ~** dangerous; **no hay ~** not to worry, there's no fear of that

ciudadoso careful, painstaking

cuidante careful, vigilant

cuidar to take care of; look after; mind; *vi* **~ de** to look after; **~se** to take care of o.s.

cuita affliction, sorrow, worry

cuitado wretched, sorrowful

cuitamiento bashfulness, lack of spirit

culantrillo *bot* maidenhair fern

culata butt (of firearm); rear part; cylinder head; *zool* haunch; **salir el tiro por la ~** to misfire, backfire

culatazo recoil, kick (of gun)

culear *sl* to wiggle the bottom

culebra snake; **~ de cascabel** rattle-snake; **hacer ~** to wriggle

culebrear to wriggle, zigzag; twist and turn

culebreo wriggling, zigzagging; twisting

culera patch (on seat of trousers)

culero *n* nappy, *US* diaper; *vet* pip; *adj* lazy

culi *m* coolie

culinario culinary

culirroto having a hole in the seat of one's trousers

culito sweet little behind

culminación *f* culmination

culminante culminating

culminar to culminate

culo bottom, backside, behind, seat; arse; **~ de mal asiento** fidget; **~ de vaso** imitation precious stone

culón big-bottomed

culpa guilt; blame; fault; **echar la ~ a** to blame; **es ~ mía** it's my fault; **tener la ~ de** to be to blame for

culpabilidad *f* guilt

culpable *n m+f* culprit; offender; *adj* guilty

culpado *n* culprit; *adj* guilty

culpar to blame

cultivable cultivatable, arable

cultivador *m* cultivator

cultivadora cultivating machine
cultivar to cultivate; grow
cultivo cultivation, crop; *med* culture
culto *n m* cult, worship; *adj* cultured, cultivated, educated; **estilo ~** academic style
cultor *n m* worshipper; *adj* worshipping
cultura culture, civilization
cumbre *f* top, summit, peak; climax; highlight
cumpleaños *m sing + pl* birthday
cumplidero necessary
cumplido *n* compliment; formality; *adj* polite, formal; complete, full; **visita de ~** courtesy call
cumplidor *n m* executor (of a will); reliable, trustworthy
cumplimentador complimenting
cumplimentar to pay compliments to; congratulate
cumplimentero exaggeratedly courteous
cumplimiento courtesy; fulfilment; carrying out; completion; expiry; **al ~ del plazo** on the expiry of the stipulated period; **por ~** purely as a matter of form
cumplir *vt* to carry out, fulfil; **~ ... años** to reach the age of …; **~ una promesa** to keep a promise; *vi* to fall due; end; **~se** to come about, fall due
cumulativo cumulative
cúmulo pile; large number; *arch* cumulus
cuna cradle, cot, crib; rope bridge; **casa ~** foundling home; **de humilde/ilustre ~** of humble/noble birth
cunar to rock in a cradle
cundidor expanding, growing
cundir to grow, spread, expand; **~ mucho el dinero** to make one's money go a long way
cunear to rock, sway
cuneiforme cuneiform; wedge-shaped
cuneo rocking, swaying
cuneta ditch, open drain
cuña wedge, quoin; **meterse de ~** to elbow one's way in
cuñada sister-in-law
cuñado brother-in-law
cuñar to wedge
cuñete *m* keg, firkin
cuño *m* die, die-stamp; **de nuevo ~** freshly minted

cuota quota; subscription/membership fee
cuotidiano daily, everyday
eupé *m mot* coupé
cupido cupid
cuplé *m* ballad, cabaret song
cupletista *f* music-hall singer
cupo quota; contingent
cupón *m* coupon; dividend; ticket
cúprico of copper
cuproso copper-like
cúpula dome, cupola
¹ **cura** *m* priest; **~ de misa y olla** ignorant priest; **~ párroco** parish priest
² **cura** *f* cure, healing; **~ de aguas** water cure; **ella no tiene ~** she's quite hopeless; **tener ~** to be curable
curabilidad *f* curability
curación *f* cure, healing
curador *m* caretaker, overseer; *leg* guardian; administrator; curer, healer
curaduría guardianship
curalotodo cure-all
curandero quack; witch-doctor
curar to cure, heal, dress; cure, preserve; **~ al humo** to smoke; **~se** to be cured, recover
curativo curative
curato office of parish priest; care of souls
curdo *n + adj* Kurd, Kurdish
curia ecclesiastical court; bar; legal profession
curiosear to snoop, be nosey
curiosidad *f* curiosity
curioso *n* inquisitive person; *adj* curious, inquisitive; strange, odd, funny
currante *m sl* worker
currar, currelar *sl* to work
curre *m*, **currelo** *sl* work, labour
curro *sl* work, job
curruca *orni* whitethroat; **~ capirrotada** *orni* blackcap
cursado experienced
cursante *m + f* student, scholar; *adj* studious, assiduous; who follows a course
cursar to frequent; take (a training course); study; send (letters *etc*)
cursi pretentious, twee, in bad taste
cursilería pretentiousness
cursilón insufferably pretentious person
cursillo short course, intensive course
cursivo *n* cursive writing, italics; *adj*

cursive

curso course; route; educational session; academic year; **de ~ legal** legal tender

curtido *n* tanning; **~s** tanned leather; *adj* weather-beaten, tanned

curtidor *m* tanner, leather-dresser

curtiduría tannery

curtiente *m* tanning (material)

curtimbre *f*, **curtimiento** tanning (process)

curtir to tan (hide); sunburn; harden; **~se** to become sunburnt, tanned

curva curve, bend; **~ de nivel** contour-line; **tomar una ~** to negotiate a bend

curvatura curvature

curvilíneo curvilinear

curvo *adj* curved, bent, crooked

cusqui: hacerle la ~ a alguien to annoy s.o.; bugger s.o. up

cuscurro crust of bread

cuscuta *bot* dodder

cutáneo cutaneous

cúter *m naut* cutter

cutícula cuticle

cutis *m* skin, complexion

cutre *m* miser

cuyo whose, of whom, of which

cuzco mongrel

CH

ch *f* letter ch

cha tea

chabacanería lack of good taste; vulgarity

¹ chabacano awkward; in bad taste; vulgar

² chabacano type of apricot

chabola shanty, hut; poor dwelling

chacal *m* jackal

chácara leather shoulder-bag

chacarero farmer

chacarrachaca noisy argument, row

chacina spiced pork sausages

chaco snare

chacolí *m* light Basque wine

chacolotear to clatter

chacota noisy celebration; hacer ~ de to make fun of

chacotear to laugh loudly

chacoteo *see* chacota

chacotero waggish

chacra farm

chacuaco small foundry

chacha *fam* servant; lass

chachalaca *n* chatterbox; *adj* talkative

cháchara chit-chat, small talk

chacharear to prattle

chacharero prattler

chache: el ~ *sl* I, yours truly

chachi, chachipé *sl* fabulous, stupendous

chacho little boy

chadiano *n + adj* of Chad

chafadura *n* flattening; creasing; denting; destroying

chafaldita *fam* banter

chafalditero banterer

chafalote *m* rustic, countryman

chafalmejas *m sing + pl arts* dauber

chafallar to botch

chafallo botched job

chafallón *m* botcher

chafado speechless; crumpled

chafar to flatten; crease, crumple; *fam* spoil; beat in an argument; leave speechless

chafarote *m* sword

chafarrinada stain; *arts* daub, bad painting

chafarrinar stain; blot

chafarrinón stain; echar un ~ a to defame, sling mud at

chaflán *m* bevel

chaflanar to bevel; cant

chagra peasant

chai *f sl* girl, crumpet

chaira steel for knife-sharpening; cobbler's knife; *sl* pocket-knife

chal *m* shawl

chalado dotty, crazy, mad, head-over-heels in love

chalán *m* horse-trader; picador

chalana wherry

chalanear to buy/sell cleverly; break horses

chalanería sharp trading

chalanero cunning

chalate *m* nag, hack

chalé *m* chalet; one/two-storey detached house

chaleco waistcoat, vest; ~ salvavidas life jacket

chalote *m* shallot

chalupa *n* sloop; canoe; cornmeal pancake; *adj sl* foolish; in love

chalupero boatman

chama *sl* barter; trade

chamaco youngster

chamada *see* chamarasca

chamagoso greasy; dirty; vulgar

chamar *sl* to barter; trade

chamarasca, chámara brushwood; brushfire

chamarra sheepskin jacket; heavy woollen cardigan

chamarreta short jacket

chamarrillón *m* bad player at cards

chamarrón *m orni* long-tailed tit

chamba *fam* fluke, lucky break

chamberlán *m* chamberlain

chambón *n fam* botcher; novice; poor player; *adj* unskilled; awkward

132

chambonada *fam* blunder
chamiza kindling, firewood
chamizo half-burnt piece of wood; charred tree-trunk; premises used as a private bar/meeting-place during fiestas
chamorra closely cropped head
champán, champaña champagne
champiñón *m* mushroom
champú *m* shampoo
champurrar to mix cocktails
chamuchina mob
chamullar *sl* to speak incoherently
chamuscado tipsy; scorched; *fam* crossed
chamuscar to scorch
chamusquina *n* scorching, wrangling
chanada *fam* joke
chanar *sl* to comprehend
chancear to jest; ~se de make fun of
chancero jocose
chanciller *m* chancellor
chancla old shoe; slipper
chancleta slipper, mule; en ~ (of shoes) backless
chancletear to go in slippers
chancleteo clatter (of slippers)
chanclo clog; galosh
chancro *med* chancre
chancuco contraband tobacco
canchería butcher's shop
chanchi *see* chachi
chancho *n* pig; dirty person; ~ de monte *zool* agouti; *adj* filthy
chanchullero trickster; crook
chanchullo sharp practice; *fam* fiddle, dirty business
chanelar *sl* to understand
chanfaina offal stew
chanflón awkward
changa joke; witticism; portering
changar to break; spoil
changador *m* porter
chango joker; fussy person
changuear to jest
chantaje *m* blackmail
chantajista *m*+*f* blackmailer
chantar to erect; give a piece of one's mind
chantre *m* precentor
chantría precentorship
chanza joke; ~ pesada joke in bad taste
chanzoneta ballad
chanzonetero ballad-writer

chao chow
chapa veneer; *metal* sheet; plate; chaps; *fam* metal bottle-top; *sl* gong (medal); *sl* policeman's badge; copper, policeman; judgement; *sl* money, bean; ~s pitch and toss
chapado rosy-cheeked; ~ a la antigua old-fashioned; ~ en oro gold plated
chapaleo *n* splash, splatter
chapalear *see* chapotear
chapaletero noise of rain
chapar to plate, cover (with metal); *sl* shut
chaparrada rain-shower
chaparrear to pour with rain
chaparreras *fpl* (clothing) chaps
chaparro *adj* short
chaparrón *m* downpour
chapatal *m* mire
chapear *see* chapar
chapela beret
chapelo cap
chapera *bui* ramp
chapero *sl* male prostitute
chapín *m* clog
chapinería clog shop/factory
chapinero clog-maker
chapitel *m archi* capital of a column
chapodar to lop, cut
chapodo *n* lopping
chapón *m* ink blot
chapotear *vt* to sponge; *vi* paddle, dabble; (of water) lap
chapoteo splash
chapuceador *m* botcher; bungler
chapucear to botch; bungle
chapucería botched job
chapucero *m* blacksmith; bungling workman, 'cowboy'
chapul *m* dragonfly
chapurrar to jabber; speak a language badly
chapurreo *n* jabbering
chapuza botched job
chapuzar *vt* to duck; *vi* to dive; splash
chapuzón *m* dip
chaqueta jacket; *mech* casing; ~ de lana cardigan
chaquetear to change sides; change one's political allegiance
chaquetero turncoat
chaquetón *m* long jacket; overcoat
chaquira bead
chara American ostrich

charabán *m* charabanc

charada charade

charanga band of street musicians; brass band

charango small guitar

charanguero hawker, pedlar; bungler, botcher; small coastal ship

charca pool

charco puddle; small pond; **pasar el ~** to cross the ocean

charla chat

charlador *n m* chatterbox; *adj* talkative

charladuría indiscreet talk

charlante *m* chatterbox

charlao *sl* chat; **echar un ~** to have a chat

charlar to chat

charlatán *m* prattler; charlatan; quack; humbug

charlatanear to chat

charlotada mock and comic bullfight

charlotear *see* **charlar**

charloteo *see* **charla**

charnela, charneta hinge

charol *m* gloss; patent leather; **darse ~** to swank

charolar to polish

charolista *m+f* polisher

charpa *med+naut* sling

charque *m* dried food

charquear to dry food (in the sun)

charqueo cleaning the drains

charrada rustic speech/behaviour; country dance

[1] **charrán** *m orni* tern

[2] **charrán** *m* rascal

charrancito little tern

charranada rascally act

charranear to act like a rascal

charranería rascality

charrar *sl* to chat; reveal a secret

charrasca flick-knife

charrería *see* **charrada**

charretera epaulette

charro *n* ill-mannered person; cowboy; *adj* tawdry, flashy

chascar to click with the tongue; crunch

chascarillo funny anecdote

chasco trick; disappointment; **dar ~** to disappoint; **dar un ~ a** to play a trick on; **llevarse ~ con** to be disappointed in/with

chasis *m* chassis; *sl* skeleton

[1] **chasquear** to play a trick on; disappoint, let down

[2] **chasquear** to crack (a whip); creak

chasqui *m* emissary, messenger

chasquido creak

chata flat-bottomed boat; bedpan; **~ alijadora** *naut* lighter

chatarra scrap metal; *sl* loose change; *sl* jewellery; *sl* medals

chatarrero scrap metal dealer

chatear to go drinking with friends; go on a pub-crawl

chateo pub-crawl

chati *adj* (term of endearment) honey, dearest; love, ducky

chato *n* small glass of wine; *adj* pug-nosed

chauvinismo chauvinism

chauvinista *n m+f* chauvinist; *adj* chauvinistic

chava ragamuffin

chaval *m* lad

chavala lass

chaveta *n* wedge; forelock; *mech* pin; *adj* daft; **perder la ~** to lose one's reason; become angry

chavo: estar sin ~s *sl* to be without a bean

chaza: hacer ~s (of horses) to walk on hind feet

che *f* letter ch

checo *n+adj* Czech

checoslovaco *n+adj* Czechoslovak

Checoslovaquia Czechoslovakia

cheira *sl* flick-knife

cheli *m+f* Madrid drop-out; *m* Madrid drop-out slang

chelín *m* shilling

cheque *m* cheque

chequear to check

chequetrén *m* kind of mileage railway ticket

chequeo check-up; *med* thorough examination; *mot* periodic service

chica girl, girlfriend; maid

chicada childish act

chicana chicanery

chicanero cunning

chicano Mexican immigrant in USA

chicarrón *adj* big for one's age

chicle *m* chewing-gum; **~ blando/de globos** bubble-gum

chiclear to chew gum

chico boy, boyfriend; *fam* old chap; *sl cin* actor who portrays the leading

'goodie'; **ponerse como el ~ del esquilador** to have a whale of a time
chicolear to pay compliments to a
woman
chicoleo flattering remark
chicoria chicory
chicote *m+f* strong boy/girl; *naut* rope
end
chicotar to whip
chicha alcoholic maize drink; *fam* meat;
ni ~ ni limonada neither one thing nor
the other
chicharra cicada; kazoo; *sl* stub of a
marihuana cigarette
chicharrear (of cicadas) to chirp
chichear to hiss with displeasure
chicheo hiss, hissing
chichi *m sl* cunt
chichigua wet-nurse
chichinar to scorch
chichisbeador *m* wooer
chichisbeo wooing
chichón *m* bump (*usu* on the head)
chifla whistling, hissing
chifladera whistle
chiflado crazy; **~ por** crazy about, in
love with
chiflar to hiss, whistle
chiflarse por to lose one's head over
chiflato whistle
chiflido whistling sound
chifonía hurdy-gurdy
chileno Chilean
chilindrina trifle; trick; anecdote
chilindrinero trifler; joker
chillador *n m* screamer; *adj* screaming;
creaking
chillar to scream; (of colours) to clash
chillería rumpus; noisy gathering
chillido scream, shriek; child's bawling;
dar un ~ to utter a scream
chillón *n* screamer; *adj* screaming; (of
colours) loud
chimenea chimney; fireplace; funnel,
smokestack; kitchen range; *sl* head
chimento rumour
chimpancé *m* chimpanzee
¹ **china** small stone
² **china** maid, servant; girl
³ **china** *sl* enough marihuana to make one
cigarette
chinar *sl* to cut, slash
chinazo blow with a stone
chinchar to annoy

chincharrero fishing-boat
chinche *m* bedbug; drawing-pin, *US*
thumb tack
chincheta drawing-pin
chinchín *m* noisy advertising; noise of
street musicians
chinchorrería tale-bearing, impudence
chinchorrero malicious tale-bearer
chinchorro small rowing-boat; hammock
chindar *sl* to throw away
chinela slipper
chinero china cabinet
chinesco Chinese
chingar to annoy; *sl* spoil; *vulg sl* fuck;
~se to get drunk
chinito dearest, dearie
chino *n* Chinaman; servant; *adj* Chinese; **tinta china** Indian ink; **hablar ~**
to speak double Dutch
chinófilo Sinophile
chinorri *n m sl* little child; *n f sl* wench;
adj small
chinostra *sl* head
chipé, chipendi *n m* truth; *adj sl* stupendous, first-class
chipihusca *sl* prostitute
chipirón *m* small squid
Chipre Cyprus
chipriota *n m+f+adj* Cypriot
chiquero pigsty; bullpen
chiquillada childish act
chiquillería large number of children
chiquillo little child
chiquitear *see* chatear
chiquiteo *see* chateo
chiquito *n* small child; small glass of
wine; *adj* tiny; **hacerse ~** to be modest
chiri *m sl* marihuana cigarette
chiribitil *m* small room, 'den'
chirigota jest; **de ~** in fun
chirigotear to say things in fun
chirigotero jester
chirimbolos *mpl* odds and ends
chiringuito snackbar *usu* on the beach;
montarse un ~ to set o.s. up in business
chiripa fluke; stroke of good luck; **de ~**
by chance
chiripear to win by a fluke
chiripero lucky player
chirivía parsnip
chirla small clam
chirlador *m* loud prattler

135

chirlar to prattle noisily

chirle insipid

chirlo facial scar; knife wound

chirona *sl* prison

chirusa uneducated person

chirriado soaking wet

chirriador *adj* sizzling, hissing; (of hinge) creaking

chirriar to sizzle; hiss; creak; squeak

chirrido *n* *orni* chirping; *adj* sizzling, hissing, creaking

chirrión *m* two-wheeled cart; tumbril

chirrumen *m* common sense

¡chis! hush!

chisme *m* piece of gossip; *fam* gadget; *vulg sl* cunt, prick

chismear to gossip

chismografía gossip; tittle-tattle

chismoso *n* gossip-monger; *adj* gossipy

chispa *n* spark; twinkle; tiny quantity; drunken state; flash (of wit etc); ~s *sl* electrician, 'sparks'; **coger una** ~ to get tipsy; **echar** ~s to be very angry; **ser una** ~ to be lively; **tener** ~ to be witty/funny

chispazo spark; item of gossip; *sl* swig

chispeante sparkling, scintillating

chispear to sparkle, scintillate; drizzle

chisporrotear to spatter sparks

chisporroteo spattering; cracking

chisposo *adj* which emits sparks on burning

chisquete *m fam* swig of wine

chistar : **sin** ~ without saying a word

chiste *m* joke; ~ **inglés** a weak (unfunny) joke; ~ **verde** risqué joke; **dar en el** ~ to guess correctly

chistera top hat; basket in game of pelota; angler's basket

chistoso funny; witty

chistu *m* Basque flute

chistulari *m* Basque flute-player

chita : **a la** ~ **callando** on the quiet, by stealth

chiticalla *m+f* discreet person

chiticallando quietly; in secret; **a la** ~ noiselessly

chito : **irse a** ~s *fam* to go to the dogs; **¡**~**!** hush!

chiva *zool* female kid; **estar como una** ~ *sl* to be crazy, daft

chivar *vulg sl* to fuck; annoy; ~**se** to split, inform

chivata shepherd's staff; *sl* torch

chivato *zool* kid under one year old; *fam* talebearer, especially in prison; rascal; *sl* tallyman, overseer; *sl* intercom; *sl* peephole in cell door

chivatazo tale-bearing

chivero puma

chivo *zool* kid; ~ **expiatorio** scapegoat; **estar como un** ~ to be crazy

chivuto bearded

¡cho! whoa!

chocador disagreeable; repulsive

chocante disagreeable; surprising; strange

chocar *vi* to collide; clash; meet; fight; shock; *vt* provoke; surprise, displease; ~ **las manos** to shake hands

chocarrear to tell a coarse joke

chocarrería coarse joking; buffoonery

chocolate *m* chocolate; *sl* member of the Policía Nacional; *sl* marihuana

chocolatería shop where chocolate is sold

chocolatero chocolate seller

chocolatín *m* bar of chocolate

chocha, chochaperdiz *f orni* woodcock

chochada *sl* cunt

chochear to be senile; dote

chochera dotage; a senile person

chochete *m sl* girl, bird; crumpet

chocho *n* dotard; *adj* senile, doting

chófer *m* chauffeur, driver

chola, cholla *fam* skull; head

chollo *sl* bargain; sinecure

chonguear to jest

chopa seabream

chopal *m*, **chopera** grove of black poplars

chopo black poplar; *fam* rifle

choque *m* collision, clash; *mil* skirmish; *elect*+*med* shock; ~ **en cadena** *mot* multiple crash; **auto/coche de** ~ dodgem

choquezuela kneecap

chorar *sl* to pinch, nick; be on the fiddle

chorchi *m sl* soldier

chordón *m* raspberry

chori *m sl* petty thief

choricear *see* **chorar**

choricería sausage shop/stall

choricero sausage maker; *sl* petty thief

chorizar *see* **chorar**

chorizo *n* garlic sausage; tightrope walker's pole; *vulg sl* prick, penis; *sl* petty thief; fool; *adj* foolish

chorlito *orni* plover; ~ **negro** *orni* Kentish plover; **cabeza de** ~ scatterbrain

choro petty thief

chorrada foolishness; stupidity

chorreado (of cattle) striped

chorreadura (of rain *etc*) dripping

chorrear to drip, seep; be soaking wet; *sl* reprimand severely; make fun of

chorreo *n* dripping; *sl* severe reprimand

chorrera spout; mark made by water; (sewing) frill

chorretada spurt, jet

chorro jet, stream, flow; **a** ~**s** abundantly

chorroborro flood

chortal *m* lake fed by a spring

chorvo *sl* bloke, guy

chota *m sl* talebearer, nark; **estar como un** ~ to be crazy

chotacabras *m sing + pl orni* nightjar

chotear *fam* to banter; ~**se de** *sl* to make fun of

choteo *fam* banter

chotis *m* schottische

choto unweaned kid, calf

chova *orni* chough

chovinismo chauvinism

chovinista *m + f see* **chauvinista**

choza hut, shanty; hovel

chozpar to caper, gambol

chozpo caper, gambol

christmas *m* Christmas card

chubarba *bot* stonecrop

chubasco squally shower; adversity; ~ **de nieve** blizzard

chubascoso squally

chubasquero raincoat; *sl* french letter

chucha *sl* peseta

chuchear *vt* to fowl (with snares/nets); *vi* to whisper

chuchería trinket, titbit

chucho doggy, bow-wow

chueca joke; trick

chueco crooked; bent

chufa tigernut; *sl* peseta; *sl* slap, blow

chufar to mock

chufería place where tigernut drink is made

chufero tigernut seller

chufeta *fam* jest

chufleta *fam* taunt

chufletear to show contempt

chufletero *adj* sneering; taunting; contempt

chula woman (*usu* overdressed) from low districts of Madrid; flashy woman

chulada impolite behaviour; witty remark

chulapo, chulapón *m see* **chulo**

chulear to jest with; poke fun at; *sl* live off the earnings of a woman; boast, show off

chulería humorous speech or gestures; cheek

chuleta *cul* chop, cutlet; (golf) divot; *sl* written crib in an examination; *fam* slap

chulo *n* native of low districts of Madrid and who dresses with affectation; rascal; pimp; bullfighter's assistant; butcher's mate; *adj* rascally; picaresque; *adj invar sl* stupendous, fabulous

chumacera *naut* rowlock

chumbera, chumbo prickly pear

chuminada *sl* foolishness; stupid thing

chumino *sl* cunt

chunga *fam* jest; **de** ~ in fun

chungo *sl* bad; not genuine

chungón *m fam* jester

chunguearse to jest, chaff

chupa *sl* jacket, leather windcheater; **de** ~ *sl* smashing, stupendous

chupachú *m*, **chupachup** *m* lollipop

chupada sip; puff (of a cigarette); suck

chupadero *n* teething ring; *mech* suction tube; tippler; *adj* sucking, absorbing

chupado lean, emaciated; *sl* dead easy

chupaflor *m*, **chupamiel** *m*, **chupamirtos** *m sing + pl* humming-bird

chupano *sl* vagrant's temporary shelter

chupar to suck; sip; live as a scrounger; lick; *sl* drink; ~ **cámara** *cin* to hog the camera; ~**se los dedos** *fam* to enjoy eating, be overjoyed

chupatintas *m sing + pl* pen-pusher

chupete *m* baby's comforter, dummy; teething-ring

chupeteo sucking, suction

chupi *sl* magnificent; **pasarlo** ~ *sl* to have a swell time

chupito *sl* swig, mouthful (of liquid)

chupinazo *sp* powerful kick

chupón *m* sponger, parasite; *bot* sucker, side shoot; *mech* piston

chupóptero *fam* sponger, cadger

churdón *m* raspberry

churi *m sl* pocket-knife

churra yearling heifer; *sl* luck
churrascón *adj* scorching
churrero maker/seller of **churros**
churrigueresco *archi* overdecorated
churro light doughnut ring; *sl* fluke
churrellero gossip-monger
churrupear to sip
churruscarse to become scorched
churrusco over-toasted bread, crust
churumbel *m*, **churumbela** gipsy child
churumo juice
chus ni mus: no decir ni ~ not to say a
single word

chuscada pleasantry; joke
chusco droll
chusma rabble; crowd
chusquel *m sl* informer, nark
chut *m sp* shot at goal
chuta *sl* syringe
chutar *sp* to shoot; ~**se** *sl* to inject o.s.
with a drug; **va que chuta** *sl* it goes fine
chute *m sl* injection
chuzazo pike; any pointed object; **a** ~**s**
abundantly; **echar** ~**s** to boast; **llover**
a ~**s** to rain cats and dogs
chuzón crafty, artful

D

d *f* letter d
dable feasible, practicable
dabute *adj invar sl* excellent, super
dabuti *adv* excellently
dactilado shaped like a finger
dactilografía typewriting
dactilografiar to type
dactilográfico *adj* typing
dactiloscopia identification by finger-prints
dactiloscópico pertaining to fingerprints
dádiva gift, offering
dadivosidad *f* generosity
dadivoso generous
dado *n* die; **cargar los ~s** to load the dice; **como venga el ~** as things turn out; **corre el ~** we are in luck; *adj* given; **~ que** given that
dador *n m* donor, bearer; *comm* drawer (of bill of exchange); *adj* giving
daga dagger
daguerrotipado daguerreotype
daguerrotipar to daguerreotype
daguerrotipia daguerreotyping
daguerrotipo daguerreotype
dalia dahlia
daltoniano colour-blind
daltonismo colour-blindness
dama lady, mistress; concubine; (draughts) king; *cin+theat* leading lady; **~ de honor** bridesmaid, lady-in-waiting; **~ joven** *theat* juvenile lead; **~s** draughts, *US* checkers; **ser muy ~** to be very ladylike; **soplar la ~** (draughts) to huff the king
damajuana demijohn
damasco damask; damson (tree and fruit)
damasquinador *m* one who does damascene work
damasquinar to inlay, damascene
damasquino damascened
damería prudery
damero draught-board, *US* checker-board
damisela damsel

damnación *f* damnation
damnificador *n m* damager, injurer; *adj* damaging, injuring
damnificar to damage, injure
dandismo dandyism
danés *n m* Dane, Danish language; *adj* Danish
danone *m sl* police, patrol car
dante *m sl* queer, gay
dantesco Dantesque; nightmarish
Danubio Danube
danza dance, dancing; **~ de cintas** may-pole dance; **¿por dónde va la ~?** which way does the wind blow?
danzador *m* dancer
danzar to dance; *fam* butt in
danzarín *n m* fine dancer; *fam* meddler; *adj* given to dancing
dañable prejudicial
dañador harmful, destructive, injurious (persons)
dañar to harm, hurt, damage
dañino harmful, destructive, injurious (animals)
daño harm, hurt, damage, injury; **~s y perjuicios** *comm* damages; **en ~ de** to the detriment of; **hacer ~ a** to harm; **hacerse ~** to hurt o.s.
dañoso damaging, harmful, hurtful, injurious
dar *vt* to give; deal (cards); show; hit, strike; **~ a la luz** to publish; **~ a luz** to give birth; **~ de alta** to discharge; **~ de baja** to strike off a list, report absent; **~ diente con diente** to shiver; **~ el callo** *sl* to work hard; **~ fe** to certify; **~ guerra** to be a nuisance; **~ la cara por alguien** to stand up for someone; **~ la enhorabuena** to congratulate; **~ la razón a uno** to declare that someone is right; **~ que hacer** to cause trouble, make work; **~ razón de** to give an account of; **~ una carcajada** to let out a guffaw; **~ una vuelta** to go for a stroll; **no ~ golpe** not to do a stroke; *vi* to look out (**a** onto), overlook; (of

clocks) strike; ~ **con** to find; **dar en**+*infin* to take it into one's head to; ~ **de sí** to give, stretch; ~ **en beber** to take to drink; ~ **en ello** to hit on it; ~ **en vacío** to fall on deaf ears/stony ground

darse to give in, surrender; occur, happen; produce, yield; devote o.s. (**a** to); ~ **de baja** to resign, quit; ~ **por** to consider o.s.; ~ **por aludido** to take the hint; ~ **por vencido** to admit defeat; ~ **prisa** to make haste; ~ **un atracón** to have a blow-out (big meal)

dardo dart; *zool* dace; sarcastic remark

dares y tomares *mpl* give-and-take

dársena inner harbour, basin

darviniano Darwinian

darvinismo Darwinism

darvinista *m*+*f* Darwinist

data date; item (of statement/account); **de larga** ~ of long standing; **de mala** ~ in a bad temper

datar to date; *comm* credit; ~ **de** to date from

dátil *m bot* date; *sl* finger

datilera date-palm

dativo dative

dato datum, fact; detail; ~s data

¹ **de** of, from, out of, about, by, with, in, on; ~ **balde** gratis; ~ **día/noche** by day/night; ~ **golpe** suddenly; ~ **manera que** so that; ~ **María** Mary's; **hombre** ~ **bien** an honest man

² **de** *f* letter d

deambular to wander (about)

deán *m* dean

deanato, deanazco deanship

debajo *adv* below, under, underneath; ~ **de** *prep* under, underneath

debatible debatable

debatir to debate; ~**se** to struggle

debe *m comm* debit

deber *n m* duty, debt, school exercise; ~**es** homework, *comm* debit entries; **hacer sus** ~**es** to do one's exercises; **cumplir con el** ~ to do one's duty; to owe; **debo hacer eso** I must do that

debido due, proper; **como es** ~ as is correct

debiente *n m*+*f* debtor; *adj* owing

débil weak, feeble, slight

debilidad *f* weakness

debilitación *f* weakening

debilitar to weaken

débito debt

debutante *n m*+*f* beginner, debutante; *adj* beginning

debutar to begin; make a first appearance/debut

década decade

decadencia *n* decadent; *adj* decadence, decline

decadente *adj* decadent

decaer to decay, decline

decágono decagon

decagramo decagram

decaído low (in spirits or health)

decaimiento decline, decay, depression

decalaje *m* gap

decalitro decalitre

decálogo decalogue

decámetro decametre

decampar *mil* to decamp

decanato deanery

decano dean, doyen, grand old man

decantación *f* decantation

decantador *m* decanter

decantar to decant

decapitación *f* decapitation; beheading

decapitar to decapitate, behead

decasílabo decasyllable

decena half a score, ten; *mus* tenth; (about) ten

decenal decennial

decenar *m* ten; group/team of ten

decencia decency, modesty

decenio decade

decente decent, modest; respectable

decepción *f* disappointment, disillusionment

decepcionar to disappoint, disillusion

decible expressible

decidero that can be told

decidido resolute

decidir to decide, resolve; ~**se** to make up one's mind

decigramo decigram

decilitro decilitre

decímetro decimetre

décimo *n* tenth; tenth share of lottery ticket; *adj* tenth

decimoctavo eighteenth

decimocuarto fourteenth

decimonónico *adj* nineteenth-century, Victorian; old-fashioned

decimonono, decimonoveno nineteenth

decimoquinto fifteenth

decimoséptimo seventeenth

decimosexto sixteenth

decimotercero, decimotercio thirteenth

decir *n m* speech, way of speaking, saying; ~ **de las gentes** public opinion; **es un** ~ it's a figure of speech; *v* to say, tell; ~ **cuantos son cinco** to give a piece of one's mind; ~ **para sí/para su camisa** to say to o.s.; **dicho y hecho** no sooner said than done; **es** ~ that is to say; **por mejor** ~ more properly speaking; **querer** ~ to mean, signify; ~**se** to be called; be said; **se dice** it is said, they say

decisión *f* decision; resolution

decisivo decisive

declamación *f* declamation

declamador *n m* declaimer, reciter; *adj* declaiming, reciting

declamar to declaim, recite

declamatorio declamatory

declaración *f* declaration; proposal of marriage; *leg* deposition

declarado self-confessed

declarador declaring, stating

declarante *n m+f* witness, declarant; *adj* declaring, stating

declarar *vt* to declare, state; ~ **culpable** to find guilty; *vi* to make a statement; ~**se por/contra** to come out in favour/against

declarativo declarative

declaratorio declaratory

declinación *f gramm* declension; decline; deviation; *astron* declination

declinante declining, bending down

declinar to decline; refuse, reject

declinómetro declinometer

declive *m* declivity, slope, downhill; **en** ~ slanting, sloping

declividad *f* declivity

decoloración *f* discoloration

decomisar to confiscate, seize

decomiso confiscation, seizure

decoración *f* decoration; *theat* scenery; set

decorado decoration; *theat* scenery; setting; décor

decorar to decorate; recite

decorativo decorative

decoro decorum; respect, honour

decoroso decorous, decent

decrecer to diminish, decrease

decreciente diminishing, decreasing

decrecimiento, decremento decrease,

dimunition

decrépito decrepit, fallen into decay

decrepitud *f* decrepitude

decretar to decree; *leg* award a decree

decreto decree; act; **por real** ~ *sl* by force

decúbito recumbent

decuplar, decuplicar to multiply by ten

décuplo ten-fold

decuria group of ten (people)

decursas *fpl leg* arrears of rent

decurso lapse, passing of time

dechado sample, pattern, model; ~ **de virtudes** paragon of virtues

dedada small portion, sample, taste

dedal *m* thimble; thimbleful

dedalera *bot* foxglove

dédalo maze, labyrinth

dedeo *mus* fingering

dedicación *f* dedication, consecration

dedicante dedicating

dedicar to dedicate; ~**se** to dedicate o.s.; ~**se a** to devote o.s. to

dedicativo dedicative, dedicatory

dedicatoria dedication, inscription

dedignar to scorn, disdain

dedil *m* finger-stall

dedillo: saberse al ~ to have at one's fingertips

dedismo system of arbitrary appointment; jobs for the boys

dedo finger, toe, width of a finger; ~ **anular** ring-finger; ~ **gordo** big toe; ~ **meñique** little finger/toe; ~ **pulgar** thumb; **a** ~ (of an appointment) undemocratic(ally); **a dos** ~**s de** on the verge of; **chuparse los** ~**s** to lick one's lips; **derribar con un** ~ to knock down with a feather; **hacer** ~ *sl* hitch-hike

dedocracia *see* **dedismo**

dedocrático undemocratic(ally)

deducción *f* deduction, inference; *mus* diatonic scale

deduciente inferring, deducing

deducir to deduce, infer; *comm* deduct, discount; *math* derive

deductivo deductive

defalcar to lop off; embezzle

defecación *f* defecation

defecador defecating

defecar to defecate

defección *f* defection, desertion

defectible, defectivo defective, faulty

defecto defect, fault, flaw; **a** ~ *leg* by

default

defectuoso defective, faulty, deficient

defendedero defensible

defendedor *n m* defender; *adj* defending

defender to defend, protect; ~**se** to hold one's own; manage, get by

defenestración *f* defenestration

defenestrar to throw (a person) from a window

defensa defence; *sp* full-back; *zool* horns, antlers, tusks; *naut* fenders; ~ **escoba** *sp* sweeper

defensiva *n* defensive; **a la** ~ on the defensive

defensivo *n* protection; *adj* defensive

defensor *n m* defender, protector, defence lawyer; ~ **del pueblo** ombudsman; *adj* defending, protecting

defensorio plea, defence

deferencia deference

deferente deferential, deferring

deferir to defer, yield

deficiencia deficiency

deficiente defective, deficient

déficit *m* deficit

definible definable

definición *f* definition; **definiciones** military statutes

definido definite

definidor *n m* definer; *adj* defining

definir to define; put the finishing touches to; clarify

definitiva: en ~ in conclusion, to sum up

definitivo final

deflagración *f* deflagration, blaze

deflagrar to deflagrate, blaze up

deflector *m* deflector

deflexión *f* deflection

defoliación *f* defoliation

defoliante *m* defoliant

defoliar to defoliate

deformación *f* deformation; defacing; distortion

deformador deforming

deformar to deform, warp; *rad* to distort; ~**se** to become deformed/distorted

deformatorio deforming

deforme deformed; defaced, disfigured

deformidad *f* deformity

defraudación *f* fraud; tax-evasion

defraudador *n m* defrauder; *adj* defrauding

defraudar to defraud; cheat; dis-

appoint, let down

defuera on the outside

defunción *f* death, demise

degeneración *f* degeneration, degeneracy

degenerado *n* degenerate person; *adj* degenerate

deglución *f* swallowing

deglutir to swallow

degollación *f* throat-slitting

degolladero windpipe; scaffold; place of execution; **llevar al** ~ to lead to slaughter

degollado low-cut neck (in garment); beheaded

degollador *n* throat-cutter, executioner; *adj* throat-cutting

degolladura *see* **degollado**; cutting of the throat

degollante *n m+f* insufferable bore, pain in the neck; *adj* throat-cutting; unbearable

degollar to behead, cut the throat; mess up, ruin; interrupt a song

degollina slaughter, butchery

degradación *f* degradation, degrading

degradante degrading

degradar to degrade, debase; deprive (of honours, position); *arts* to shade down

degüello beheading, throat-cutting

degustación *f* tasting, sampling

dehesa pasture, cattle-range; farm

deidad *f* deity

deificación *f* deification

deificar to deify

deiforme god-like

deísmo deism

dejación *f* abandonment, relinquishment

dejada relinquishment

dejado indolent, lazy; ~ **de la mano de Dios** God-forsaken

dejadez *f* neglect; untidiness

dejamiento indolence, lassitude; neglect

dejar *vt* to leave; let; yield; ~ **caer** to let fall, drop; ~ **con la boca abierta** to astound; ~ **en cueros** to skin, leave with nothing; ~ **frío** to leave speechless; ~ **olvidado** to leave behind, forget; ~ **paso a** to make way for; ~ **plantado** to leave in the lurch; ~ **en paz** to leave alone; *vi* to leave off, give up, stop; ~ **de fumar/cantar** to stop smoking/singing; ~se to neglect o.s.; let o.s. go; ¡déjese de tonterías! stop talking nonsense!; ~se decir to let it slip out

deje m, **dejo** accent; after-taste

del contr of prep **de**+art **el** of the, from the, belonging to the

delación f delation, giving away; denunciation

delantal m apron, pinafore

delante adv before, ahead, in front; ~ de prep in front of, before; **ir** ~ to go ahead, lead; **pasar por** ~ **del hotel** to pass (walk by) the hotel

delantera fore, front; sp forward-line; lead, advantage; sl knockers, breasts; **coger la** ~ to get ahead

delantero n fore, front; sp forward; adj foremost, front

delatable that can be denounced

delatante denouncing

delator n m denouncer, informer; adj denouncing

delco mot distributor-head

deleble erasable

delectación f delight, pleasure

delegación f delegation; proxy; local branch

delegado delegate; local representative

delegante delegating

delegar to delegate

deleitable delightful, delectable

deleitamiento pleasure, delight

deleitante delighting

deleitar to please, delight; ~se (en/con) to take pleasure (in)

deleite m delight, pleasure

deleitoso delightful, pleasing

deletéreo deleterious

deletreador n m speller; adj spelling

deletrear to spell (out); interpret

deletreo spelling (out)

deleznable fragile, frail, perishable, crumbly

¹ **delfín** m zool dolphin

² **delfín** m dauphin

delfínidos mpl members of the dolphin family

delfino bot delphinium

delgadez f thinness, slenderness; ingenuity

delgado thin, lank, gaunt, slender; ingenious; (of soil) poor; **hilar demasiado** ~ to split hairs

delgaducho skinny

deliberación f deliberation

deliberado deliberate

deliberar to deliberate, consider

deliberativo deliberative

delicadez f, **delicadeza** delicacy; finesse; scrupulousness; tenderness; touchiness

delicado delicate; tender; dainty; scrupulous; touchy

delicia delight

delicioso delicious, delightful

delictivo unlawful

delimitación f delimitation

delimitar to delimit; mark off

delincuencia delinquency

delincuente n m+f delinquent, criminal; adj offending

delineación f delineation

delineador n m delineator; adj delineating

delineamiento delineation

delineante m+f draughtsman

delinear to delineate, outline

delinquir to commit an offence, transgress

delirante delirious, raving

delirar to be delirious, rave

delirio delirium; delusions

delito offence, crime; **Brigada de Delitos Monetarios** approx equiv Fraud Squad

deludir to delude, deceive

delusivo delusive, deceptive

delusorio delusory, fallacious, deceptive

demacración f emaciation

demacrar(se) to waste away, emaciate

demagógico demagogic

demagogo n m demagogue; adj demagogic

demanda demand, request, petition; alms-begging; search; enterprise; leg claim; **ley de la oferta y la** ~ law of supply and demand; **morir en la** ~ to die in the attempt; **poner** ~ leg to issue a writ, sue

demandado defendant, accused

demandador n m claimant, plaintiff; adj demanding

demandar to demand, request; claim; desire; leg sue

demarcación f demarcation

demarcador n m land surveyor; adj dividing, demarcating

demarcar to survey, mark the limits of

demás remaining, other; **los/las** ~ the others, the rest; **por lo** ~ apart from this, in addition

demasía excess; insolence, audacity; **en** ~ excessively

demasiado *adj+pron* too much; ~s too many; *adv* too, too much; ~ **frío** too cold; **él bebe** ~ he drinks too much

demasiarse to go too far

demasié *adv sl* too much; *sl* unbelievable

demencia insanity

dementar to drive insane; ~**se** to go insane

demente *n m+f* insane person, lunatic; *adj* insane

demérito demerit, fault

demeritorio undeserving

democracia democracy

demócrata *n m+f* democrat; *adj* democratic

democrático democratic

democratizar to democratize

democristiano Christian-Democrat

democristianismo Christian-Democracy

demografía demography

demográfico demographic

demógrafo demographer

demoledor *n m* demolisher; *adj* demolishing

demoler to demolish, pull down

demolición *f* demolition

demoníaco devilish, fiendish

demonio devil, demon, fiend; **de mil** ~**s** devilishly

demonología demonology

demora delay

demorar to delay, retard; linger; halt (during a journey); ~**se** to delay

demóstenes *m* eloquent speaker

demostrable that can be proved

demostración *f* demonstration; display, show

demostrador *n m* demonstrator; *adj* demonstrating

demostrar to demonstrate; prove, show

demostrativo demonstrative

demudar to change; ~**se** to turn pale

denegación *f* denial, refusal

denegar to refuse, turn down

denegatorio rejecting

denegrecer to blacken, darken; ~**se** to become black/dark

denegrido black(ened), dark(ened)

dengoso finicky, fussy

dengue *m* fussiness, finickiness (*usu* of women)

denigración *f* denigration, insult

denigrante insulting; degrading

denigrar to denigrate, insult

denigrativo denigrating, insulting

denodado valiant, resolute

denominación *f* denomination, name

denominador *n m* denominator; *adj* denominating

denominar to denominate, name

denominativo denominative

denostada insult, vilification

denostador *n m* vilifier; *adj* vilifying, insulting

denostar to revile, insult

denotar to denote; indicate

denotativo denoting

densidad *f* density; thickness

densificar to densify

densímetro *phys* densimeter

denso dense, thick

dentado dentated, serrated; cogged

dentadura (set of) teeth; denture; ~ **postiza** false teeth

dentar *vt* to cut teeth in, provide with cogs; *vi* to teethe

dentario *n bot* toothwort; *adj* dental

dentellada toothmark, bite; **a** ~**s** with the teeth

dentellado toothed, serrated

dentellar (of the teeth) to chatter

dentellear to nibble

dentera tingling pain in the teeth; **me da** ~ it puts my teeth on edge

dentición *f* dentition, teething

denticular denticulated

dentiforme dentiform

dentífrico dentifrice; **pasta dentífrica** toothpaste

dentina dentine

dentista *m+f* dentist

dentro *adv* inside, within; *prep* ~ **de** in, inside; ~ **de casa** at home; ~ **de poco** soon; **barrer para** ~ to look after number one; **dentro de dos días/una semana/un mes** in two days'/a week's/a month's time; **hacia** ~ inwards; **por** ~ inside

denudación *f* denudation

denudar to denude; lay bare

denuedo valour, intrepidity

denuesto affront, insult

144

denuncia denunciation, accusation, report (to the police); ~ **de un tratado** *pol* notification of unwillingness to ratify a treaty

denunciable which could be denounced; indictable

denunciación *f* denunciation, accusation

denunciador *n m* denouncer, accuser; *adj* denouncing

denunciante *m+f* accuser

denunciar to denounce, report (*esp* to the police); indicate; give notice of

denunciatorio denunciatory

denuncio *min* registration of a claim

denutrición *f* denutrition

deparar to supply, furnish; bring

departamental departmental

departamento department; (railway) compartment; administrative division

departidor *n m* talker; *adj* talking

departir to talk, converse

depauperización *f med* weakening

depauperar to impoverish; *med* debilitate, weaken

dependencia dependence, branch office; business; staff; ~**s** accessories; outbuildings

depender (de) to depend (on)

dependienta shop assistant, *US* salesclerk

dependiente *n m* shop assistant, *US* sales-clerk; *adj* dependent, subordinate

depilación *f* depilation, hair-removal

depilar to depilate, remove hair

depilatorio depilatory, hair-remover

deplorar to deplore, lament

deponente *n m+f* deponent; *leg* witness; *adj* deposing

deponer *vt* to put aside; declare; remove from office; lay down (arms); depose; *vi* to give evidence; to defecate

deportación *f* deportation

deportado deported person

deportar to deport

deporte *m* sport

deportismo sporting activity; addiction to sport

deportista *n m+f* sportsman, sportswoman; *adj* related to sport

deportividad *f* sportsmanship, sporting spirit, fair play

deportivo sporting; *fam* casual, cheery

deposición *f* deposition; removal from office; statement; evacuation (of the bowels)

depositador *n m* depositor; *adj* depositing, entrusting

depositar to deposit; place; entrust; ~**se** to settle (dregs *etc*)

depositaria depository; trust

depositario depository

depósito deposit; trust; *comm* warehouse, depot; tank; *mil* depot; *chem* precipitate, sediment; ~ **de cadáveres** mortuary; **en** ~ in trust

depravación *f* depravity

depravado depraved; degenerate

depravador *n m* depraver, corrupter; *adj* depraving, corrupting

depravar to deprave, corrupt; ~**se** to become depraved

deprecación *f* entreaty

deprecante entreating

deprecar to entreat

deprecativo entreating

depreciación *f* depreciation

depreciar to depreciate

depredación *f* depredation, plundering, pillaging

depredador *m* depredator

depredar to depredate, loot, plunder

depresión *f* depression; ~ **nerviosa** nervous breakdown

depresivo depressive, depressing

depresor *n m* oppressor; *adj* depressing

deprimir to depress, press down; humiliate; ~**se** to get depressed

depurable purifiable

depuración *f* purification

depurador *n m* purifier; *adj* purifying

depurar to purify

depurativo *n+adj med* depurative

depuratorio purifying

deputar *see* **diputar**

derby *m sp* local derby

derecha right-hand side; *pol* right; **a la** ~ on the right

derechera direct road

derechero *adj* honest, upright

derechismo *pol* right-wing doctrines/policies

derechista *n m+f pol* right-winger, conservative; *adj* right-wing

derecho *n* right, law; ~ **consuetudinario** common law; ~ **de visita** right of search; ~ **penal** criminal law; ~**s** dues, fees; ~**s aduaneros** customs dues; ~**s**

consulares consular fees; ~s **de almacenaje** storage charges; ~s **de entrada** import duties; ~s **de muelle** wharfage; ~s **reales** royal dues (on house purchase); **al** ~ the right way round; **de** ~ by right; **estudiar** ~ to study law; **según** ~ according to the law; *adj* right, straight, upright; **hecho y** ~ fully fledged; *adv* straight (on); **siga todo** ~ carry on right ahead

derechuelo simple sewing (as taught to children)

derechura rectitude; **en** ~ without delay

derelicción *f* dereliction

deriva *aer+naut* drift, drifting; **a la** ~ adrift

derivación *f* derivation; deduction; inference

derivado *n* by-product; derivative

derivar *vt* to derive; divert; turn aside; *vi* to be derived; go off course; drift

derivativo *n m+adj* derivative

dermatología dermatology

dermatológico dermatological

dermatólogo dermatologist

derogable repealable

derogación *f* repeal, abolition, revocation

derogador repealing, abolishing

derogar to revoke, repeal, annul; destroy

derogatorio *leg* repealing, annulling

derrabar to dock (the tail of an animal)

derramadero dumping place (*usu* for liquids); weir

derramado, derramador *adj* wasteful, prodigal

derramador *m* waster, spendthrift

derramamiento spilling, shedding, overflowing; ~ **de sangre** bloodshed

derramaplaceres, derramasolaces *m sing+pl* killjoy

derramar to spill, shed, scatter; spread; ~**se** to spill, overflow

derrame *m* spilling, loss, overflow; *naut* draught; *med* discharge, haemorrhage; ~ **cerebral** cerebral haemorrhage

derramo chamfer, bevel

derrapar to skid

derrape *m aer+naut* yawing; *mot* skidding

derredor: en ~, **al** ~ round about

derrelicto *naut* derelict

derrelinquir to abandon

derrenegar de to loathe

derrengar to cripple, sprain the hip of; màke crooked; ~**se** to tire o.s. out; **estar derrengado** to be worn out, be all aches and pains

derretido *n* concrete; *adj* soppy, sloppy; hopelessly in love; melted

derretimiento melting; soppiness, sloppiness; intense love

derretir(se) to melt; go soppy/sloppy; fall madly in love

derribar to demolish, overthrow; knock down; ~ **por tierra** to knock to the ground

derribo demolition, pulling down; ~s debris

derrocadero precipice

derrocamiento overthrow; throwing/pulling down

derrocar to throw down, overthrow

derrochador *n m* spendthrift, squanderer; *adj* wasteful, squandering

derrochar to squander, waste

derroche *m* squandering, waste, extravagance

derrochón *m* spendthrift

derrostrarse to injure one's face

derrota defeat; course, route

derrotar to defeat; bring low; ruin; *fam* get worn out; *sl* confess (to a crime)

derrotero *naut* course marked on chart; plan of action

derrotismo defeatism

derrotista *n m+f +adj* defeatist

derrubiar (of a river) to wash away the banks

derrubio erosion, washing away

derruir to demolish; **edificio derruido** ruined building

derrumbadero precipice; danger

derrumbamiento collapse

derrumbar to pull down; ~**se** to collapse, cave in

derrumbe *m* precipice; landslide; collapse

derviche *m* dervish

desabarrancar to pull out, disentangle

desabastecer to cut off supplies

desabastecimiento stopping of supplies

desabollar to remove dents from

desabonarse to cancel one's subscription

desabono cancellation (of subscription)

desabor *m* insipidity, tastelessness

desaborido tasteless, insipid

desabotonar to unbutton; *bot* bloom; ~se to undo one's buttons

desabrido insipid, tasteless; (of people) disagreeable; *meteor* unpleasant

desabrigar to uncover; deprive of shelter; ~se to remove one's outer clothes

desabrigo lack of covering/shelter/protection

desabrimiento insipidity; unpleasantness

desabrir to give a bad taste to; annoy; ~se to get annoyed

desabrochamiento unbuttoning; unfastening

desabrochar to unbutton; unfasten; to undo one's clothes; ~se to confide (a secret/one's feelings *etc*)

desacalorarse to cool off

desacatado disrespectful

desacatador *m* disrespectful person

desacatar to show contempt for; treat irreverently; disobey

desacatarrarse to get rid of a cold

desacato disrespect, irreverence; contempt of authority; *leg* contempt of court

desaceitar to remove the grease from

desacertar to be wrong, make a mistake

desacierto error, mistake

desacobardar to give courage to

desacomodado awkward, uncomfortable

desacomodar to make things awkward for; dismiss

desacomodo awkward circumstances; loss of employment

desacompañar to leave (s.o.'s company)

desaconsejable inadvisable

desaconsejado ill-advised

desaconsejar to dissuade

desacoplar to uncouple, disconnect

desacordar to cause disagreement; get out of tune; ~se to fall into disagreement

desacorde in disagreement, out of tune

desacorralar to release from a corral/farmyard

desacostumbrado unusual; unaccustomed

desacostumbrar to break the habit; ~se to lose the habit

desacotar to raise the ban on; reject, refuse to admit

desacreditar to discredit; ~se to become discredited

desacuerdo disagreement; forgetfulness; estrangement

desadeudarse to pay one's debts

desadormecerse to wake up

desadvertido inadvertent

desadvertimiento inadvertence

desadvertir to take no notice of

desafear to improve the appearance of

desafecto ill-will

desaferrar *naut* to weigh anchor

desafiadero duelling-ground

desafiador *n m* duellist, challenger; *adj* defying, defiant

desafiar to defy, challenge

desafición *f* disaffection

desafilar to blunt; ~se to become blunt

desafinado out of tune

desafinar to be out of tune; speak off the point; say s.t. indiscreet; ~se to get out of tune

desafío challenge; duel

desaforar to cancel privileges

desaforrar to remove the lining from

desafortunado unfortunate, unlucky

desafuero excess, outrage; *leg* infraction

desagarrar to let go, loosen the hold/grip

desagradable disagreeable, unpleasant

desagradar to displease

desagradecer to be ungrateful for

desagradecido *n* ungrateful person; *adj* ungrateful

desagradecimiento ingratitude

desagrado displeasure; **con** ~ reluctantly

desagraviar to make amends to; indemnify

desagravio amends, compensation

desaguar to drain; squander; (of rivers) flow into, reach

desagüe *m* outlet, drain

desaguisado *n* injury, wrong; *adj* unlawful, unjust

desahogado unencumbered, comfortably off; impudent; roomy; *naut* having sea-room

desahogar to ease; give vent to; ~se to find relief, give vent to one's feelings

desahuciar to evict; deprive of hope

desahucio eviction

desahumado smokeless; (of liquors) flat

desairado graceless; disregarded; **hacer un papel** ~ to cut a poor figure

desairar to slight, snub

desaire *n* slight, snub; **tragarse un** ~ to swallow an insult

desajustar to disarrange; ~**se** to get out of order

desajuste *m* disagreement; maladjustment; breach (of contract)

desalabanza disparagement

desalabar to disparage

desalabear *carp* to straighten; take the warp out of

desalarse to rush, dash

desalentador discouraging

desalentar to make breathless, discourage; ~**se** to get out of breath; become discouraged

desalfombrar to remove the carpets

desalforjarse to loosen one's clothing

desalhajar to strip (a room)

desaliento discouragement

desalineación *f* disalignment

desalinear to disalign

desaliñado slovenly, untidy

desaliñar to disarrange, ruffle

desaliño slovenliness; negligence; untidiness

desalivar to salivate

desalmado soulless, pitiless, inhuman

desalmamiento soullessness, pitilessness, inhumanity

desalmar to weaken; ~**se** to yearn

desalojamiento dislodging

desalojar to dislodge; clear out

desalquilado untenanted, vacant

desalquilar to vacate; ~**se** to become vacant

desalumbrado *see* **deslumbrador**

desalumbramiento *see* **deslumbramiento**

desamable unworthy of being loved

desamarrar *naut* to cast off

desamasado disunited

desambientado out of place, out of one's element

desamor *m* indifference, lack of affection, aversion

desamorado cold-hearted

desamoroso unloving

desamortización *f* disentailment

desamortizador disentailing

desamortizar to disentail

desamparar to forsake, leave helpless; *naut* dismast

desamparo abandonment, helplessness

desamueblado unfurnished

desamueblar to strip of furniture

desangramiento bleeding to death

desangrar(se) to bleed to death

desanidar *orni vi* to forsake the nest; *vt* to dislodge, expel

desanimado dull; dispirited; downhearted

desanimar to dishearten; discourage; ~**se** to get disheartened; get depressed

desánimo discouragement

desanudar to untie, unknot; disentangle

desapacibilidad *f* disagreeableness, unpleasantness, inclemency

desapacible disagreeable; unsettled

desaparecer to disappear, vanish

desaparecido: los ~**s** missing persons

desaparecimiento disappearing, vanishing

desaparición *f* disappearance

desaparejar to unharness

desapasionado lacking in passion; impartial

desapegar to detach, separate

desapego indifference; coldness

desapercibido unprepared; unnoticed; **pasar** ~ to be/go unnoticed

desapercibimiento unpreparedness

desapiadado pitiless, ruthless

desaplacible disagreeable

desaplicación *f* laziness; lack of application

desaplicado lazy, not given to study

desaplomar *see* **desplomar**

desapolillar to get rid of the moths in

desaposesionar to dispossess

desapreciar to scorn, despise

desaprender to forget (s.t. learnt)

desapretar to slacken, loosen

desaprisionar to release from prison

desaprobación *f* disapproval

desaprobar to disapprove

desapropiación *f*, **desapropiamiento** renunciation; dispossession (of property)

desapropiar to dispossess

desaprovechar to waste, misspend; fail to take advantage of; ~ **una ocasión** to miss a chance

desapuntar (sewing) to untack; unpick (stitches)

desarbolar *naut* to unmast

desarbolo *naut* unmasting

desarenar to remove the sand from

desarmador *m* trigger (of a firearm)

desarmadura, desarmamiento disarming, disarmament

desarmar to disarm; dismantle

desarme *m* disarmament

desarraigar to uproot, root out, extirpate

desarraigo uprooting, rooting out, extirpation

desarrancarse to give up membership (of an association *etc*); break off a relationship

desarrebozar to reveal

desarreglado disarranged; out of order; slovenly; untidy

desarreglar to disarrange, upset; ~se to get disarranged, get untidy

desarreglo disarrangement; disorder; slovenliness

desarrimar to separate

desarrollar to unroll, unfold; develop; ~se to develop, take place

desarrollo development; growth

desarropar to unwrap; undress

desarrugar to unwrinkle, take the creases out of

desarrumar *naut* (of cargo) to shift

desarticulación *f* disarticulation

desarticular to disarticulate; *mech* disconnect (a machine *etc*); upset/spoil (a plan *etc*)

desarzonar to unhorse, unseat; throw (a rider)

desasado without a handle; with a broken handle

desaseado dirty, slovenly

desasear to make dirty

desasentar to remove; displease; ~se to stand up

desaseo uncleanliness, slovenliness

desasir to release; ~se de malas costumbres to get rid of bad habits

desasociable unsociable

desasociar to separate

desasosegar to make uneasy

desasosiego uneasiness

desastrado wretched, unfortunate, shabby

desastre *m* disaster

desastroso disastrous

desatado crazy, frantic; undone

desatadura untying, loosening

desatancar to unblock, clear (an obstruction)

desatar to loose, unravel; undo (a knot); solve; ~se to lose all restraint; come untied; come undone

desatascar to free, unblock; get (s.o.) out of a difficult situation

desatención *f* lack of attention, disregard

desatender to disregard; neglect

desatento inattentive, heedless; discourteous

desatinar *vt* to drive crazy; *vi* to do/say crazy things; go off the rails

desatino utter nonsense, folly

desatontarse to face facts; come to one's senses

desatornillar to unscrew

desatraer to separate

desautorizar to take authority away from; ban; forbid

desaventajado disadvantageous

desavisado unaware

desayunar(se) to have breakfast; ~ de to receive the first news of

desayuno breakfast

desazón *m* insipidity, unease, restlessness; (of soil) unsuitability

desazonar to make insipid; worry; ~se to become uneasy

desbabar to dribble (saliva)

desbancar to win all the money from; ~ el casino to break the bank

desbandada *mil* rout; scattering; a la ~ in disorder

desbandarse to disband, flee in disorder

desbarajustar to throw into confusion

desbarajuste *m* disorder, shambles, chaos

desbaratado dissipated, broken, in a mess

desbaratador *m* destroyer, debaucher

desbaratamiento disorder, chaos

desbaratar to ruin, spoil; rout, throw into confusion; squander; ~se to go to pieces

desbarate *m*, **desbarato** disorder, routing; squandering

desbarbar(se) to shave

desbarrar to ramble, get off the point; act foolishly

desbastador *m* chisel; paring tool

desbastadura trimming, planing, hewing

desbastar to plane down, smooth down; trim; give a little education to

desbautizarse to become very angry

desbloquear *comm* to unfreeze; ~ **el tema de ...** to break the deadlock over ...

desbocar to break the rim of a vessel; ~**se** to run riot; use bad language; (horse) to bolt, run away

desbordamiento *n* overflowing

desbordante *adj* overflowing

desbordar to cause to overflow; ~**se** to overflow; run riot

desbragado *n* one of the dispossessed; *adj pej* unbreeched, sansculottes

desbravador *m* horse-breaker

desbravar to break in (horses); lose strength; (of liquors) go flat; ~**se** to moderate

desbridar to unbridle

desbullador *m* oyster-fork

desbullar to remove an oyster from its shell

descabalgadura dismounting (from a horse)

descabalgar to dismount

descabellado crazy, wild, absurd

descabellamiento absurdity

descabellar to dishevel, rumple (the hair); finish off (a bull) with a dagger in the back of the neck

descabello killing by stabbing in the back of the neck

descabezamiento beheading

descabezar to behead; lop the top off; ~**se** to rack one's brains

descabullirse to escape

descaecer to decline, languish

descaecimiento, descaimiento weakness, decay

descalabazarse to rack one's brains

descalabrar to wound in the head; ~**se** to hurt one's head

descalabro disaster, calamity; blow

descalandrajar to rip to shreds

descalificación *f* disqualification

descalificar to disqualify

descalzador *m* bootjack; crowbar

descalzar to take off the shoes/stockings; undermine; ~**se** to take off one's shoes; (of horses) lose a shoe

descalzo barefooted

descambiar to swap back

descaminar to lead astray; ~**se** to go off

the track, lose one's way

descamino smuggled goods

descamisado *n* one of the underprivileged, underdog; *adj* shirtless, destitute

descampado *n* wasteland; **en** ~ in open country; *adj* bare, open

descansadero resting-place

descansado quiet, tranquil; rested; **vida descansada** easy life

descansar to rest, pause; sleep; lie (buried); **en paz descanse** rest in peace

descansillo landing (of staircase)

descanso rest, pause; *theat* interval; **¡en su lugar** ~! *mil* stand at ease!

descantear to round off a sharp corner/edge

descañonar to pluck (poultry); fleece

descapotable *n m + adj mot* convertible

descapsulador *m* bottle-opener

descarado cheeky, saucy

descararse to be cheeky, be saucy

descarga discharge; unloading; volley; firing; ~ **de aduana** customs clearance

descargadero unloading bay

descargador *m* unloader; docker

descargar to discharge, unload, empty; bone (meat); inflict (blows); ~ **la conciencia** to ease one's conscience; ~ **la ira en** to vent one's anger on; ~**se** to clear o.s. (of an accusation); resign

descargo unloading, discharge, acquittal; *leg* plea; *comm* acquittance; **en su** ~ in his defence; **testigo de** ~ defence witness

descarnar to remove the flesh (from the bone); ~**se** to get thin

descaro impudence, sauciness, cheek(iness)

descarriar to lead astray, mislead; ~**se** to go astray

descarrilamiento derailment

descarrilar to derail; ~**se** to jump the track; go off the rails

descarrío going astray, losing one's way

descartar (in card games) to discard; dismiss (as untrue/unworkable); ~**se** to excuse o.s.

descarte *m* discarded cards; evasion

descasar to separate; *eccles* annul a marriage

descascar(ill)ar to peel, shell; ~**se** to peel, flake off

descastado cold, lacking affection

descatolizar to expel from the Catholic Church

descaudalado impoverished, penniless

descendencia descendants; offspring, issue

descendente descending, coming down

descender to descend, come down; (of temperature) fall

descendiente *m* descendant, offspring; *adj* descending

descendimiento descent, lowering

descenso descent, fall, decline; way down

descentrado off-centre

descentralización *f* decentralization

descentralizador decentralizing

descentralizar to decentralize

descentrar to knock off centre; unbalance; *fam* put off one's stroke

descercar to lift (a siege)

descerrajar to force open; shoot

descifrable decipherable

descifrador *m* decipherer

descifrar to decipher, decode

desclavador *m* nail-remover; claw-hammer

desclavar to remove nails from; take precious stones from a setting

descobijar to uncover; unfold

descoco cheek, impudence

descojonarse: ~ **de risa** *vulg* to piss o.s. with laughing

descolar *vet* to dock; cut the tail off

descolgar to unhang, take down; *tel* pick up; ~**se** to let o.s. down; appear suddenly

descolonización *f* decolonization

descolonizar to decolonize

descoloramiento discoloration, fading

descolorar, descolorir to fade, discolour

descolorido pale, pallid; faded

descollado lofty, haughty

descollante outstanding

descollar to stand out; tower over

descompás *m* excess; disproportion

descomponer to decompose, put out of order; break up; ~**se** to decompose, rot; show deep emotion; lose one's temper; *meteor* change for the worse

descomposición *f* decomposition, rotting; breaking down; discomposure; *med* looseness of bowels

descompostura untidiness; impudence; discomposition; breaking

descompresión *f* decompression

descompuesto broken; with diarrhoea; impudent, insolent; indisposed; immodest

descomulgado wicked, evil; excommunicated

descomulgar to excommunicate

descomunal monstrous, huge; extraordinary

desconceptuar to discredit, disqualify

desconcertado disorderly; disconcerted

desconcertador *m* disturber

desconcertadura disturbance

desconcertante disconcerting, bewildering

desconcertar to disconcert; upset; bewilder; confuse; *anat* dislocate; ~**se** to be disconcerted, put out; get confused

desconcierto disorder, chaos, bewilderment

desconchadura peeling (of plaster, glaze *etc*)

desconchar to strip (of plaster/glaze *etc*)

desconectar to disconnect, cut off; switch off; ~**se** to switch off; get disconnected

desconfiado distrustful, suspicious

desconfianza distrust, suspicion

desconfiar de to distrust, be suspicious of

desconformar to dissent; be of a different opinion; ~**se** to fall out

descongelación *f* defrosting, unfreezing

descongelar to defrost; defreeze

descongestión *f* decongestion

descongestionar to decongest

descongojar to console

desconocer not to know; be unaware of; not to recognize

desconocido *n* stranger; *adj* unknown, unfamiliar

desconocimiento ignorance, unawareness

desconsideración *f* inconsiderateness

desconsiderado thoughtless, rash; inconsiderate

desconsiderar to be inconsiderate

desconsolado grief-stricken, disconsolate

desconsolar to grieve; distress

desconsuelo grief, affliction; sorrow; *med* stomach debility

descontaminación *f* decontamination

descontaminar to decontaminate

descontar to discount, deduct; **dar por descontado** to take for granted

descontentamiento discontent, dissatisfaction

descontentar to discontent, dissatisfy

descontento *n* discontent, dissatisfaction; *adj* discontented, dissatisfied

descontinuación *f* discontinuation

descontinuar to discontinue

descontinuo discontinuous

desconvocar to call off (a strike)

descopar to lop off the top (*esp* trees)

descorazonado disheartened, dispirited

descorazonamiento down-heartedness, low spirits

descorchador *m* corkscrew

descorchar to uncork

descornar to dishorn; ~**se** to rack one's brains; *sl* bang one's head

descorrer *vt* to run back, open; draw (back); *vi* to trickle, drip

descorrimiento trickling, dripping

descortés discourteous, impolite

descortesía discourtesy, impoliteness

descortezar to peel; take off the crust/bark

descoser to unstitch, unpick the stitches; separate; *naut* unlash; **no ~ los labios** not to say a word; ~**se** to carry on prattling

descosido gossip; tear, open seam; **como un ~** wildly, without self-control

descostrar to pull the crust/scab off

descoyuntamiento *med* dislocation

descoyuntar *med* to dislocate

descrecer to diminish, decrease

descrecimiento *see* **decrecimiento**

descrédito discredit; loss of one's reputation/good name

descreer to disbelieve

descremar to skim, remove the cream; **leche descremada** skimmed milk

describir to describe

descripción *f* description

descriptible describable

descriptivo descriptive

descriptor *m* describer

descrismar to give s.o. a blow on the head; ~**se** to crack one's skull; become very angry

descristianar to clout the head of s.o.; get very angry

descristianizar to dechristianize

descrito described

descruzar to uncross

descuadernar to pull apart; unbind (books)

descuajar to unclot; pull up, uproot; dishearten

descuajaringarse to rest when fatigued; come apart; ~ **de risa** die of laughing

descuaje *m* unclotting

descuartizamiento carving up, cutting up of carcases

descuartizar to carve up

descubierta *cul* tart, pie without a top crust; *mil* reconnoitring, scouting; *naut* scanning of the horizon; **a la ~** in the open

descubierto *n comm* deficit; overdraft; **al ~** in the open, unconcealed; **en ~** overdrawn; **girar en ~** to make out a false cheque; *adj* obvious, manifest; exposed; uncovered; hatless, bareheaded

descubridero high place; look-out position

descubridor *n m* discoverer; *mil* scout; *adj* discovering, of discovery

descubrimiento discovery; disclosure, revelation

descubrir to uncover; discover; disclose, reveal; unveil; ~**se** to take off one's hat, bare one's head

descuello great height; loftiness

descuento discount

descuernacabras *m sing+pl* cold north wind

descuidado careless, negligent

descuidar *vt* to neglect, forget; *vi* to be careless; ¡**descuida!** don't worry!; ~**se** to be careless

descuidero pickpocket; sneak thief

descuido carelessness, negligence, oversight, slip; **al ~** casually, carelessly

descuitado without a care

desde *prep* since, after, from; ~ ... **hasta** from ... to; ~ **ahora** from now on; ~ **entonces** from then on; ~ **hace un mes/un año** for a month/year past; ~ **luego** of course, naturally; ~ **niño** from childhood; ~ **que** *conj* since

desdecir *vt* to belie, contradict; *vi* to be unworthy; ~**se** to take back one's words; go back on what one has said

desdén *m* disdain, contempt, scorn; **al ~** casually

desdentado toothless

desdentar to pull out the teeth of

desdeñable contemptible, despicable

desdeñador m scorner

desdeñar to disdain, scorn, treat with contempt; ignore; ~**se** to scorn to, not deign to

desdeñoso disdainful, contemptuous

desdibujarse to become blurred/faded

desdicha misfortune, adversity

desdichado n sorry wretch, poor devil; adj unlucky, unfortunate, wretched

desdinerar to impoverish (a country) by taking its money

desdoblamiento unfolding, splitting; ~ **de la personalidad** split personality

desdoblar to unfold, split

desdorar to remove the gilt; dishonour

desdoro dishonour, stain, blemish

desdramatizar to take the heat out of (a situation etc)

deseable desirable

deseado wished for, desired

deseador m wisher, desirer

desear to desire, wish for; want; **estar deseando** to be looking forward to

desecación f, **desecamiento** desiccation

desecante n m desiccator; adj drying

desecar to desiccate; dry up

desechar to reject, cast out; exclude; refuse

desecho rejected item; ~**s** scraps, refuse; scorn

deselectrización f elect discharge

deselectrizar elect to discharge

desellar remove the stamp from

desembalaje m unpacking

desembalar to unpack

desembanastar to lack discretion when talking; ~**se** (of an animal) to free

desembarazar to free, disencumber; ~**se** to get away from something unpleasant; get rid of something

desembarazo ease, disencumbrance

desembarcadero landing-stage; wharf

desembarcar vt to unload, unship; vi to disembark, go ashore; land; alight from a vehicle

desembarco disembarkation; unloading; landing (of stairs)

desembargar to remove the embargo on

desembargo lifting of an embargo/impediment

desembarque m disembarkation; unloading

desembarrancar naut to refloat

desembarrar to remove the mud from

desembaular to unpack a trunk; confide (usu troubles)

desembebecerse to come down to earth, return to reality

desembocadura estuary, mouth of a river; street-opening

desembocar to flow into; lead to

desembolsar to pay out, fork out, cough up

desembolso disbursement, payment; cost

desemborracharse to sober up

desembragar mot to declutch

desembrague m mot declutching

desembravecer to tame, calm

desembravecimiento taming, domesticating

desembrazar to throw with great force

desembridar to unbridle

desembrollar to unravel, disentangle

desembuchar to let the cat out of the bag, reveal a secret

desemejante unlike, dissimilar

desemejanza difference

desemejar to differ (**de** from)

desempacar to unpack; ~**se** calm down (after being angry)

desempachar to give relief from indigestion; ~**se** to gain relief from indigestion

desempacho ease, relief from indigestion

desempalagar to clear (a feeling of sickness)

desempalmar elect to disconnect a junction-box

desempañar to clean; de-mist; change a baby's nappy/diaper

desempapelar to strip (of wallpaper); unwrap

desempaque m unwrapping, unpacking

desempaquetar to unwrap, unpack

desempatar to play off a tie between; ~ **el voto a** to give a casting vote to

desempate m settlement of a tie; **partido de** ~ tie-breaker

desempedrar to roam the streets, pound the beat

desempeñar to redeem, take out of pawn; theat play a part; fill (a post); perform (duty); ~**se** to get clear

desempeño redeeming, performance, fulfilment

desempleo unemployment

desempolvadura dusting

desempolvar, desempolvorar to dust, remove dust from; *fig* revive

desenamorarse to fall out of love, stop being in love

desencadenar to unchain, unleash; trigger off; ~**se** to break out

desencajamiento disconnection; dislocation

desencajar to disconnect, put out of gear; disarticulate; ~**se** to become disjointed/haggard; come apart

desencaje *m* disconnection

desencajonar to take out of a box/crate

desencallar *naut* to refloat (a stranded vessel)

desencantamiento disenchantment

desencantar to disenchant, disillusion

desencanto disenchantment, disillusion

desencapotar *meteor* (of the sky) to clear

desencaprichar *vt* to talk out of; ~**se** to get over it, snap out of it

desencarcelar to release from prison

desencerrar to set free

desencogerse to lose one's inhibitions

desencogimiento naturalness

desencolerizarse to calm down

desencorvar to straighten, unbend

desenchufar to unplug, disconnect

desenfadado easy, nonchalant, uninhibited; disrespectful

desenfadar to appease; ~**se** to calm down

desenfado ease, nonchalance, absence of inhibitions; disrespect

desenfaldar (sewing) to lengthen a skirt, lower the hem of a skirt

desenfrenado unrestrained; frantic

desenfrenarse to give way to one's passions; run wild, throw caution to the wind

desenfreno unruliness, lack of restraint

desenfundar to unsheathe; draw (a firearm)

desenganchar to unhook, take down from a hook

desengañar to disabuse; open the eyes of; ~**se** to realize the truth

desengaño disappointment, disillusion

desengrasar to remove the grease from

desenguantarse to remove one's gloves

desenhebrar to unthread

desenjaular to uncage; *sl* release from prison

desenlace *m* dénouement; outcome; end

desenlazar to untie, loosen

desenmascarar to unmask; expose

desenredar to disentangle

desenredo disentangling; dénouement; unravelling

desenrollar to unroll; unwind

desenseñar to unlearn

desentenderse to wash one's hands (of); pretend not to know; repudiate

desenterramiento disinterment, exhumation

desenterrar to disinter, exhume, dig up

desentierramuertos *m sing+pl* one who insults the dead

desentonado out of tune, discordant

desentonar *vt* to hurt the pride of; *vi mus* to be out of tune; ~**se** to raise one's voice unnecessarily

desentono discord, false note

desentornillar to unscrew

desentorpecer(se) to liven up, smarten up

desentumecer, desentumir to restore life/feeling to

desenvainar to unsheath, uncover

desenvoltura easy manner, nonchalance, self-possession, forwardness

desenvolver to unfold; decipher; develop; enlarge upon; ~**se** to make do; get along, manage

desenvolvimiento unfolding, development

deseo desire, longing; wish; **a la medida de su** ~ in accordance with your wishes; **tener** ~**s de** to feel like

deseoso desirous, eager

desequilibrado *n* unbalanced person

desequilibrar to unbalance

desequilibrio unbalance

deserción *f* desertion; *leg* abandonment of a suit

desertar to desert, abandon

desértico *adj* deserted, uninhabited

desertor *m* deserter

deservicio disservice

deservir to serve badly; let down

desescamar to scale; remove the scales from

desescarchar to defrost (a refrigerator)

desescombrar to clear (of rubble)

desesperación *f* despair, desperation

desesperado *n* desperado; *adj* desperate, at one's wits' end; hopeless

desesperante exasperating

desesperanza despair; hopelessness

desesperanzar to deprive of hope

desesperar *vt* to make despair, exasperate; *vi* to despair, lose hope (**de** of); ~**se** to get exasperated; despair

desespero despair

desestima(ción) *f* lack of esteem

desestimador *n m* despiser; *adj* despising

desestimar to have no esteem for; reject

desfachatado shameless, brazen

desfachatez *f* impudence, effrontery

desfalcar to lop off; embezzle

desfalco embezzlement

desfasar *vt* to put out of phase/out of step/out of tune; **estar desfasado** not to be on the same wavelength; be badly adjusted

desfase *m* lack of coordination; gap; phase difference

desfavorable unfavorable

desfavorecer to disfavour

desfigurar to disfigure, deform, blur; ~ **las palabras de alguien** to twist s.o.'s words/meaning

desfiladero gorge, ravine

desfilar to march past, file by, parade

desfile *m* march past, parade, procession; *sp* walkover, easy win; ~ **de modelos** fashion show

desfloración *f* defloration

desfloramiento deflowering

desflorar to deflower, sully; skim over (a topic)

desfollonar *bot* to remove the leaves/shoots

desformar to disfigure, deform

desfondado without foundation

desgajar to tear off; ~**se** to break away

desgaje *m* breaking away

desgalichado out of line; gawky; clumsy

desgana, desgano lack of appetite; reluctance; **con** ~ reluctantly

desganarse to lose one's appetite, be off one's food

desgarbado gawky, ungainly

desgarbo gawkiness

desgargantarse to scream o.s. hoarse

desgaritar to get lost

desgarrado dissolute, shameless; torn

desgarrador heart-breaking

desgarrar to rend, tear

desgarro rent, tear; impudence; swagger

desgastar to wear away; use up

desgaste *m* wear and tear; erosion; **guerra de** ~ war of attrition

desgobernado ungovernable; disorderly

desgobernar to produce the fall of the government; misgovern; *med* dislocate; mismanage; ~**se** to get out of control

desgobierno misgovernment, mismanagement; maladministration; *med* dislocation

desgolletar to loosen clothing round the neck

desgracia misfortune, mishap; sorrow; bereavement; disgrace; accident; **por** ~ unfortunately

desgraciado *n* wretched creature, poor devil; *adj* unhappy, unlucky, graceless, disagreeable

desgraciar to spoil, mar; cripple; displease; deflower; ~**se** to get spoiled, broken

desgranar to take out the seeds from; shell (peas *etc*); ~**se** to come loose, wear away

desgrane *m cul* shelling

desgravación *f* allowance (against income-tax)

desgravar to reduce the tax on

desgreñar to dishevel

desguace *m naut* breaking up

deshabitado uninhabited, untenanted

deshabitar to leave; depopulate

deshabituarse to get out of a habit; get out of practice

deshacer to undo, break up; take apart; cancel; upset; ~ **agravios** to redress wrongs; **estar deshecho** to be fagged out; ~**se** to break up; come undone; ~**se de** to get rid of; ~**se en lágrimas** to dissolve into tears

deshambrido ravenous

desharrapado in tatters

desharrapamiento extreme poverty, destitution

deshebillar to unbuckle

deshebrar to unthread

deshecha *n* pretence; refrain; *adj* violent; **borrasca** ~ violent storm

deshechizar to remove a spell/curse

deshelar to thaw (out), defrost

desheredar to disinherit; ~se to degenerate

deshermanar to break up, unpair; lack brotherly/sisterly feelings

deshidratación *f* dehydration

deshidratar to dehydrate; ~se to become dehydrated

deshielo thaw

deshilada: a la ~ in single file

deshilvanar (sewing) to untack

deshilvanado (of thoughts/speech) incoherent

deshinchar to deflate, reduce the swelling of; ~se to go down (swelling)

deshipotecar to pay off the mortgage on

deshojar to defoliate

deshoje *m* defoliation; leaf-fall (in autumn)

deshollinador *m* chimney-sweep

deshollinar to sweep (chimneys)

deshonestidad *f* immodesty; lewdness, indecency

deshonesto immodest; lewd, indecent; dishonest

deshonor *m* dishonour

deshonra dishonour, disgrace; seduction

deshonrador *n m* seducer, dishonourer; *adj* dishonourable

deshonrar to dishonour, disgrace, defame, seduce

deshonrible shameful; contemptuous

deshonroso dishonourable, ignominious

deshora: a ~ inopportunely

deshorado untimely

deshuesadora fruit-stoning machine

deshuesar to stone (fruit); bone (meat)

deshumanizar to dehumanize

deshumano inhuman

deshumedecer to dry up

desiderable desirable

desiderata list of things to be bought (*esp* books)

desidia indolence

desidioso negligent; apathetic

desierto *n* desert, wilderness, wasteland; *adj* deserted, waste; **declarar** ~ to declare null and void

designación *f* designation

designar to designate, appoint

designio design, intention

desigual unequal, changeable, irregular, unfair; **pareja** ~ unsuited/ill-matched pair

desigualar to make unequal; ~se to excel

desigualdad *f* inequality, difference, unevenness, roughness; *math* sign of inequality

desilusión *f* disillusionment, disappointment

desilusionar to disillusion, disenchant; let down

desimanar *see* **desimantar**

desimantación *f* demagnetization

desimantar to demagnetize

desimpresionar to undeceive

desinclinar to disincline

desincrustar to remove the inlay from

desinencia *gramm* desinence, ending

desinfección *f* disinfection

desinfectante *m* disinfectant

desinfectar, desinficionar to disinfect

desinflar to deflate; ~se to be deflated

desinsectar to rid of insects; use insecticide

desintegración *f* disintegration

desintegrar to disintegrate

desinterés *m* disinterestedness, unselfishness

desinteresado disinterested, impartial; unselfish

desinteresarse to lose interest

desintoxicar to combat the poison, administer an antidote; ~se to sober up

desistir to desist; waive (a right); ~ de to give up, refrain from

desjarretar to hamstring

desjugar to extract the juice from

desjuntar to separate, sever

deslabonar to unlink, sever

desladrillar to unbrick

deslamar to clean mud from

deslastrar *naut* to remove ballast from

deslavado impudent; watery, insipid

deslavadura perfunctory rinsing

deslavar to wash superficially, rinse; remove the colour/taste/vigour from

deslavazado limp; disjointed

desleal disloyal

deslealtad *f* disloyalty

desleír to mix (in); ~se to dissolve

deslenguado brazen; foul-mouthed; outspoken

deslenguamiento foul-mouthedness

deslenguar to cut out the tongue of; ~se

to employ foul language

desliar to loosen, untie

desligadura untying

desligar to loosen, untie, unbind; *mus* play/sing staccato; ~**se** to break away from; come undone

deslindar to mark the boundaries; draw the line between

deslinde *m* demarcation

desliz *m* slip, slide; slip-up; blunder

deslizable liable to slip

deslizadero *n* slippery place; *mot* skid-pan; *adj* slippery

deslizadizo slippy, slippery

deslizador *m aer* glider; *naut* hovercraft

deslizamiento slip(ping), skid(ding)

deslizar to slip, slide; glide; ~**se** to slip, glide along; sneak in/out

deslomar to break the back of; ~**se** to fag o.s. out

deslucido tarnished, dull, shabby; **resultar** ~ to be a flop

deslucimiento tarnishing, dullness

deslucir to dull, tarnish

deslumbrador dazzling, glaring

deslumbramiento dazzle, glare; bewilderment

deslumbrante dazzling, glaring

deslumbrar to dazzle, daze; bewilder

deslustrar to dull, tarnish

deslustre *m* dulling, tarnishing; stain (on reputation)

deslustroso ugly

desmadrado *zool* motherless

desmadrar *zool* to take from its mother; ~**se** *sl* to behave unconventionally

desmadre *m* chaos, disorder

[1] **desmán** *m* excess, outrage

[2] **desmán** *m zool* muskrat

desmandar to countermand; revoke, repeal; ~**se** to run amuck; rebel against authority

desmangar to remove the handle from

desmantelado dismantled, dilapidated

desmantelamiento dilapidation; dismantling

desmantelar to dismantle; *naut* dismast

desmaña clumsiness, awkwardness

desmañado clumsy, awkward

desmarrido dejected, exhausted

desmayar to dismay; lose heart; ~**se** to faint

desmayo fainting-fit, swoon; dismay; *bot* weeping willow; **sin** ~ without

hesitation

desmedido disproportionate, excessive

desmedirse to go too far, forget o.s.

desmedrar to decline, weaken

desmedro weakening, frailty

desmejora(miento) deterioration

desmejorar to deteriorate, impair

desmelenar to dishevel, disarrange the hair

desmembración *f* dismemberment

desmembrar to dismember

desmemoriado *n* forgetful person; *adj* forgetful

desmemoriarse suffer from amnesia

desmenguar to lessen

desmentida, desmentido denial

desmentidor *n m* one who denies/contradicts; *adj* denying

desmentir to deny, contradict; ~**se** to take back one's words

desmenuzable crumbly, brittle, fragile

desmenuzador *adj* crumbling

desmenuzamiento *n* crumbling

desmenuzar to crumble; examine in great detail

desmerecedor unworthy

desmerecer *vt* to be unworthy of; *vi* to compare unfavourably with; deteriorate

desmerecimiento unworthiness

desmesura excess

desmesurado out of all proportion, excessive; rude, insolent

desmesurar to disorder, disarrange; ~**se** to go too far, forget o.s.

desmig(aj)ar to crumble (up)

desmilitarización *f* demilitarization

desmilitarizar to demilitarize

desmineralización *f* demineralization

desmirriado thin, wasted

desmitificación *f* debunking

desmitificador *m* debunker

desmitificar to debunk

desmochar to chop the top off

desmogar *zool* to renew horns/antlers

desmogue *m* renewal of horns/antlers

desmontar *vt* to clear of trees; uncock (a firearm); dismantle; *vi* to dismount (from bicycle, horse *etc*)

desmonte *m* felling, clearing; cleared terrain, waste ground

desmoralización *f* demoralization

desmoralizador *m* demoralizer

desmoralizar to demoralize

desmoronadizo crumbly

desmoronamiento crumbling

desmoronar *vt* to cause to crumble; ~**se** to crumble away

desmovilización *f* demobilization

desmovilizar to demobilize

desmugrar to clean, remove the grease/grime from

desmullir to squash flat

desnarigarse to bang one's nose

desnatado skimmed; **leche desnatada** skimmed milk

desnatar to skim; remove cream/scum from

desnaturalización *f* denaturalization

desnaturalizado unnatural; **alcohol ~** methylated spirits, *US* denatured alcohol

desnaturalizar to denaturalize, denature; change the nature of

desnevar (of snow) to melt

desnivel *m* unevenness; difference in standards; slope; **en ~** sloping

desnivelización *f* unevenness

desnivelar to make uneven; upset

desnucar to break/dislocate the neck of; give a rabbit punch to

desnuclearización *f* denuclearization

desnuclearizar to denuclearize

desnudador denuding

desnudamiento undressing

desnudar to undress, strip; *fam* fleece; *naut* unrig; ~ **la espada** to draw one's sword; ~**se** to undress, get undressed

desnudez *f* nakedness

desnudismo *theat* stripping; nudism

desnudista *theat* stripper; nudist

desnudo *n arts* nude; *adj* naked, nude, bare

desnutrición *f* malnutrition, undernourishment

desnutrirse to become undernourished

desobedecer to disobey

desobediencia disobedience

desobediente disobedient

desobligar to relieve from an obligation; offend

desobstrucción *f* clearing away of obstructions

desobstruir to clear

desocupación *f* leisure; unemployment

desocupado *n* idler, unemployed person; *adj* idle, unemployed

desocupar to vacate, leave empty; ~**se** to leave work

desodorante *m* deodorant

desoír to pay no attention to

desojarse to strain one's eyes

desolación *f* desolation

desolado desolate

desolar to lay waste; afflict, grieve

desoldar to unsolder, unweld

desollado impudent, brazen

desollador *m* flayer, extortioner; *orni* shrike

desolladura flaying, skinning; fleecing

desollar to flay, skin; fleece

desopinar to discredit

desorbitado excessive, disproportionate; (of eyes) bulging

desorbitar to exaggerate; ~**se** to leave orbit; bulge

desorden *m* disorder, untidiness, mess

desordenado untidy, slovenly

desordenamiento disorder

desordenar to disorder, make untidy; ~**se** to get muddled

desorejar to cut the ears off

desorganización *f* disorganization

desorganizador disorganizing

desorganizar to disorganize, throw into confusion

desorientación *f* disorientation, confusion; *aer* jet-lag

desorientar to disorientate, confuse; ~**se** to lose one's bearings, become confused

desorillar to trim; cut the edge from

desovar to spawn

desove *m* spawning

desovillar to unwind, unravel

desoxidación *f* derusting

desoxidante *n m* rust-remover; *adj* rust-removing, anti-rust

desoxidar, desoxigenar to derust

despabiladeras *f sing + pl!* snuffers

despabilado wide awake, alert, quick-witted

despabilador *m* snuffers

despabilar to snuff, trim the wick of; smarten up; ~**se** to wake up, snap out of it

despacio *adv* slowly, carefully; *interj* take it easy

despacioso sluggish

despacito *fam* nice and gently, slowly and carefully

despachar *vt* to dispatch; do quickly;

sell; clear (customs); ~ **con** to confer with; *vi* to do business; ~**se** to get finished

despacho dispatch, attending; clearance (customs); dismissal; private office; study, den; ~ **de billetes** ticket-office; ~ **de localidades** booking office; **secretaria de** ~ private secretary

despachurramiento squashing, flattening

despachurrar to squash, flatten; make a mess of

despajar to winnow

despampanar to prune (vines); *fam* stun; ~**se** *fam* to let off steam; tumble

desparejar to break up, split (a pair); **llevar los guantes/los zapatos desparejados** to wear odd gloves/shoes

desparpajar to prattle

desparpajo nonchalance, self-assurance

desparramar to spread, scatter; squander; *sl* pass (forged banknotes)

desparramo spreading, scattering

despatarrada the splits

despatarrado terrified

despatarrarse to do the splits; open one's legs wide

despavorirse to become terrified

despectivo derogatory, pejorative

despechar to annoy; drive to despair; *fam* wean; ~**se** to get angry

despecho spite, exasperation; **a** ~ unwillingly; **con** ~ angrily; **por** ~ in a fit of anger/spite

despechugar *cul* to cut the breast off (poultry); ~**se** to bare one's breasts, go topless

despedazamiento tearing/smashing to pieces

despedazar to tear/cut/smash to pieces; ~**se** to fall to pieces; ~**se de risa** to split one's sides laughing

despedida parting, leave-taking, farewell; dismissal; *mus* last stanza of popular song

despedir to emit, give off/out; dismiss, sack; see off, say goodbye to; ~**se** to leave, say goodbye; give one's notice; ~**se a la francesa** to take French leave

despedrar to remove stones (from land)

despegado detached; indifferent; lacking in feeling

despegar to unglue, unstick; **no** ~ **los**

labios not to say a word; ~**se** to come loose; grow cool/indifferent; *aer* take off

despego indifference; coldness

despegue *m aer* take-off

despeinar to ruffle the hair of; ~**se** to let down one's hair

despejado bright, clear-headed; *meteor* clear, cloudless

despejar to free, clear up; ~**se** to clear up, brighten up; (of fever) drop

despeje *m*, **despejo** freeing, clearing; brightness; clear-headedness

despelotado nude, undressed

despelotar to ruffle the hair of; ~**se** to put on weight; strip naked, undress; *sl* split one's sides laughing

despeluchar *text* to wear away the nap

despeluzar to rumple (hair); ~**se** (of hair) to stand on end

despellejar to skin, flay; tear to pieces; speak badly of s.o.

despenalización *f* legalization

despenalizar to legalize

despenar to console; put out of misery

dependedor *m* spendthrift

despender to squander

despensa larder, pantry; *naut* steward's room

despensería steward's office

despensero caterer, steward, dispenser

despeñadero *n m* precipice, cliff; *fig* danger; *adj* steep, sheer

despeñar to hurl down

despeño, despeñamiento hurling down; drop; *med* diarrhoea

despepitar to remove the pips from (fruit)

desperdiciador *m* squanderer

desperdiciar to waste, squander

desperdicio waste, refuse; ~**s** garbage, refuse

desperdigar to scatter

desperecerse to crave for

desperezarse to stretch one's limbs; rouse o.s.

desperfecto deterioration, wear and tear; damage; flaw

desperfilar *arts* to soften the lines of; *mil* camouflage; ~**se** to become shadowy; keep/show a low profile

despernada step (in dancing)

despernado weary and tired of walking

despertador *n m* alarm-clock; knockerup; *adj* awakening

despertamiento awakening

despertar to wake (up); awaken; whet; ~**se** to wake up

despiadado pitiless, ruthless

despicar to satisfy

despido dispatch; discharge; dismissal

despiece *m* break-down (analysis); cutting-up (of meat)

despierto awake; quick-witted; all there

despilchado badly dressed

despilfarrado ragged, tattered; wasteful

despilfarrador waster, spendthrift

despilfarrar to squander, waste

despilfarro waste, extravagance

despimpollar to prune (vines)

despinces *m sing+pl* tweezers

despintar to strip paint from; distort; ~**se** to fade

despiojar to delouse

despistado *n* absent-minded person; *adj* absent-minded; confused

despistar to give the slip to, throw off the scent; mislead; ~**se** to get lost; make a mistake; get the wrong idea

despiste *m* absent-mindedness; slip

desplacer *n m* displeasure; *v* to displease

desplantar to uproot

desplante *m* oblique posture (in fencing and dancing); act of defiance/arrogance

desplazamiento *naut* displacement; moving; movement

desplazar to displace; dislodge; move; transfer

desplegadura unfolding

desplegar to unfold, display; *mil* deploy; ~**se** to spread itself out; ~**se en abanico** to fan out

despliegue *m* unfolding, displaying; display; *mil* deployment

desplomar *vt* to put out of plumb; ~**se** to collapse, tumble; *aer* to pancake

desplome *m* tumbling down; *aer* pancaking

desplomo deviation from the vertical

desplumar to pluck; fleece

despoblación *f* depopulation

despoblado *n* open country, deserted place; **robo en** ~ highway robbery; *adj* uninhabited

despoblador depopulating

despoblar to depopulate; ~**se** to become deserted, lose its inhabitants

despojador *m* despoiler

despojar to despoil; fleece; ~**se de** to divest o.s. of; give up

despojo spoliation; plunder; ~**s** offal; mortal remains; second-hand building materials, left-overs

despolvar, despolvorear to dust

despopularizar to make unpopular

desposado *n* newly-wed; *adj* handcuffed

desposando person about to be married/betrothed

desposar *vt* to wed; ~**se** to be married

desposeer to dispossess

desposeído *n* underdog; *adj* deprived

desposorio betrothal, wedding

déspota *m* despot

despótico despotic

despotismo despotism

despotizar to tyrannize

despotricar to rant; complain

despreciable contemptible, despicable

despreciador despising, scorning

despreciar to scorn, despise; rebuff

despreciativo scornful, derogatory

desprecio scorn, contempt, rebuff

desprender to break away/off; give off/out; loosen; ~**se** to come loose; part with; be inferred

desprendido disinterested, selfless; loose; generous

desprendimiento detaching, coming loose, selflessness, indifference; *arts* descent from the Cross; ~ **de retina** *med* detached retina; ~ **de tierras** landslip

despreocupación *f* unconcern, nonchalance, casualness

despreocuparse to stop worrying o.s.; stop bothering

desprestigiar to damage the prestige of; discredit

desprestigio loss of prestige; discredit

desprevención *f* improvidence

desprevenido unprepared; **coger** ~ to catch unawares

desproporción *f* disproportion

desproporcionado disproportionate

desproporcionar to disproportion

despropositado absurd

despropósito absurdity, nonsense

desproveer to deprive of provisions

desprovisto de devoid of

después *adv* after, afterwards, later, then; ~ **de** *prep* after, next to; ~ **de**

que after; ~ **de todo** after all

despuntar *vt* to blunt, crop; *naut* round (a promontory); *vi* to bud, sprout

desquejar *bot* to slip

desqueje *m bot* slipping (for propagation)

desquerer to stop loving

desquiciado off balance; off one's rocker

desquiciamiento loss of balance; going off the rails

desquiciar to unhinge, disjoint; upset; ~**se** to lose control; go off the rails

desquitar to compensate for loss; ~**se** to get one's own back; get even

desquite *m* compensation; getting one's own back

desrabotar to dock; cut the tail off

desramar to strip off branches

desratización *f* rat-extermination

desratizar to clear of rats

desrazonable unreasonable

desreputación *f* disrepute

destacado outstanding, conspicuous; distinguished

destacamento *mil* detachment

destacar *mil* to detach, detail; emphasize; ~**se** to stand out

destajador *m* blacksmith's hammer

destajero, destajista *m+f* pieceworker

destajo piecework, task-work; **a** ~ on a piecework basis; eagerly; **hablar a** ~ to talk the hind legs off a donkey; **trabajar a** ~ to work hurriedly

destapada *n* pie without upper crust; tart; *adj* uncovered

destapar to uncover, unplug, take the lid off, open; ~**se** to get uncovered; lose one's bedclothes; undress

destape *m* taking the lid or covers off things; (*cin*+*theat*+magazines) nudism

destaponar to uncork

destartalado ramshackle; chaotic; rambling

destartalo lack of order

destechar to remove the roof from

destejar to untile; leave defenceless

destellar to sparkle, twinkle; flash

destello sparkle, twinkle; flash; ~ **de inteligencia** flash of intelligence

destemplado out of tune; intemperate, harsh; *meteor* unsettled

destemplanza *meteor* inclemency; intemperance; being out of sorts

destentar to lead out of temptation

desteñir to fade

desternillarse to break a tendon; ~ **de risa** to split one's sides laughing

desterradero wilderness, wilds; place of exile

desterrado exile

desterrar to exile; ~ **la tristeza** to put sorrow aside

desterronar *agri* to harrow

destetamiento weaning

destetar to wean

destete *m* weaning

destiempo: a ~ at the wrong time; at an inopportune time

destierro exile; place of exile

destilable distillable

destilación *f* distillation

destiladera still

destilador *n m* still; distiller; *adj* distilling

destilar to distil; filter; fall in drops

destilería distillery; ~ **de petróleo** oil-refinery

destinación *f* destination; *mil* posting

destinar to destine, send; *mil* post, station

destino destiny, fate; destination; job; post; use; **con** ~ **a** going to

destitución *f* removal from office, deprivation

destituir to remove from office, deprive

destocarse to bare one's head

destornillador *m* screwdriver

destornillar to unscrew

destoserse to clear the throat, feign a cough

destral *m* small axe

destrejar to act skilfully

destreza dexterity, skill

destripacuentos *m sing+pl* heckler, interrupter

destripador *m* ripper

destripamiento disembowelling

destripar to rip open; disembowel

destrizar to shatter; ~**se** to go to pieces; fly off the handle

destronamiento dethronement

destronar to dethrone

destroncar to chop down (a tree)

destrozador *m* destroyer

destrozar to smash to pieces; ruin; shatter

destrozo smashing to pieces; ~**s** damage

destrucción *f* destruction

destructibilidad *f* destructibility

destructividad *f* destructiveness

destructivo destructive

destructor *n m* destroyer; *adj* destructive

destruible destructible

destruir to destroy; ruin

desudar to wipe away perspiration from

desuncir to unyoke

desunión *f* disunion, discord; separation

desunir to disunite, separate

desusar to stop using

desuso disuse; **caer en ~** to fall into disuse

desvahar to remove dead parts (of a plant)

desvaído faded, pale, lank

desvainadura shelling (of peas *etc*)

desvainar to shell (peas *etc*)

desvalido helpless, unprotected, destitute

desvalijador *m* robber, filcher, rifler

desvalijamiento rifling, filching, robbing

desvalijar to rifle, filch, rob

desvalimiento helplessness, destitution

desvalorar *see* desvalorizar

desvalorización *f* devaluation

desvalorizar to reduce the value of; devalue

desván *m* attic, loft, garret

desvanecer to dispel, make vanish; **~se** to faint; disappear

desvanecimiento fainting, swooning; disappearance, vanishing; haughtiness

desvariar to be delirious; rave, rant

desvarío delirium; raving; whim

desvelar to keep awake; **~se** to be unable to sleep, stay awake; **~se por** to lean over backwards to

desvelo sleeplessness, anxiety

desvencijado tumble-down, dilapidated

desvencijar to make rickety

desvendar to unbandage; take the bandage off

desventaja disadvantage, drawback

desventajoso disadvantageous, unprofitable, detrimental

desventura mishap, misfortune

desventurado *n* unfortunate/wretched person; *adj* unfortunate, wretched

desvergonzado impudent, shameless

desvergonzarse to show one's true colours; throw modesty to the winds; behave in a shameless way

desvergüenza impudence, effrontery; shamelessness

desvestir(se) to undress, strip, disrobe

desviación *f* deviation; diversion; deflection

desviacionismo *pol* deviationism

desviacionista *n m+f +adj pol* deviationist

desviadero (railway) siding

desviar to divert, deflect, (railway) switch; **~se** to deviate, turn away, drift

desvío deviation; deflection, turning away; estrangement; (railway) siding

desvirtuar to weaken; detract from; impair

desvivirse ~ por to do anything for, go to any trouble to get

desyerbar to weed

deszocar to hurt, injure (the foot/hand)

deszumar to extract the juice from

detalle: al ~ retail

detallar to detail, particularize; retail; itemize

detalle *m* detail, particular; retail; detailed list; **al ~** retail; **vender al ~** to sell retail

detallista *n m+f* retailer; *adj* thoughtful, considerate, meticulous

detectar to detect

detención *f* detention, arrest, stop

detenedor *m* detainer, arrester, stopper

detener to detain, arrest, stop; **~se** to come to a halt, tarry

detenido thorough, painstaking, hesitant; *leg* arrested

detenimiento thoroughness, great care

detentar to hold; *leg* keep unlawfully

detergente *n m +adj* detergent

deterger *med* to cleanse

deteriorado shop-soiled, damaged

deteriorar to damage, spoil, impair; **~se** to deteriorate, go downhill; get damaged

deterioro deterioration, wear and tear

determinación *f* decision, determination; **tomar una ~** to take a decision

determinado determinate, definite; **a una hora determinada** at a given time; **en ~s casos** in certain cases

determinante *n m* determining factor; *adj* determining

determinar to determine, decide; ~se a to resolve to

determinativo determinative

determinismo *philos* determinism

determinista *n m+f+adj* determinist

detersión *f* cleansing

detestación *f* detestation

detestar to detest, loathe

detonación *f* detonation

detonador *m* detonator

detonar to detonate

detracción *f* detraction, slander

detractar to defame, slander

detractor *n m* slanderer; *adj* detracting, slandering

detraer to detract, take away; deface, slander

detrás behind, at the back/rear; ~ de behind, at the back of; **ir ~ de** to go after; **por ~** at the back; from behind

detrimento detriment, harm; **sin ~ de** without prejudice to

detrito detritus

deuda debt; ~ **consolidada** funded debt; ~**s activas** assets; ~**s pasivas** liabilities; **la ~ pública** national debt; **estar en ~ con** to be indebted to; **sin ~s** clear

deudo kinsman; ~**s** kith and kin

deudor *n m* debtor; *adj* indebted

devalar *naut* to drift off course

devanar to reel, wind; ~**se los sesos** to rack one's brains

devaneo delirium, craziness, foolish whim; passing love affair; flirtation

devastación *f* devastation

devastador devastating

devastar to devastate

devengar to collect, yield

devenir *v* to happen, become; *n* shape of things to come

deviación *f* deviation

devoción *f* devotion, devoutness, piety; **no es santo de mi ~** it/he/she is not my cup of tea

devocionario prayer-book

devolución *f* return, restitution, devolution

devolver to return, give back; *fam* vomit, spew up

devoniano, devónico *geol* Devonian

devorador ravenous; devouring

devorar to devour, wolf (down)

devoto devout, pious; fan

dextrosa dextrose

dezmable subject to payment of tithes

día *m* day, daytime, daylight; ~ **del juicio** doomsday; ~ **entre semana** weekday; ~ **festivo** holiday; ~ **laborable** working day; **al otro ~** (on) the next day; **buenos ~s** good day, good morning; **de ~** by day; **de hoy en ocho ~s** a week today; **el ~ 8** on the eighth; **el ~ menos esperado** when least expected; **en su ~** in due course; **entrado en ~s** elderly; **estar al ~** to be up to date, be with it; **hoy en ~** nowadays; **ser del ~** to be fresh, new-laid; **tener ~s** to have one's good/bad days; **un ~ sí y otro no** every other day; **vivir al ~** to live from hand to mouth

diabético diabetic

diabla, diablesa she-devil; **a la ~** carelessly

diablear to get up to mischief

diablo devil, fiend, demon

diablura prank, piece of mischief, lark

diabólico diabolic

diacatolicón *m* purgative made from senna, rhubarb and tamarind fruit

diaconato deaconship

diaconisa deaconess

diácono deacon

diadema diadem; tiara

diafanidad *f* transparency, diaphanousness

diafanizar to make diaphanous

diáfano transparent, diaphanous

diafragma *m* diaphragm

diafragmático diaphragmatic

diagnosticar to diagnose

diagnóstico *n* diagnosis; *adj* diagnostic

diagrama *m* diagram

dialéctica dialectics; *pol* debate

dialéctico dialectical

dialecto dialect

dialogar, dialogizar to dialogue, communicate

diálogo dialogue, debate, communication

dialoguista *m+f* dialogist

diamante *m* diamond; miner's lamp; ~ **en bruto** rough diamond

diamantífero diamond-bearing

diamantino adamantine

diamantista *m+f* diamond-cutter

diametral diametrical

diámetro diameter

diana bull's-eye; dart board; *mil* reveille; **hacer** ~ to score a bull's-eye

diapasón *m* diapason, tuning-fork; pitch-pipe

diapositiva colour-slide, transparency

diariamente every day, daily

diario *n* diary, daily newspaper; *comm* day-book, journal, daily expenses; ~ **de navegación** *naut* log-book; ~ *rad* + *TV* **hablado** news (bulletin)

diarismo journalism

diarista *n m* + *f* diarist, journalist

diarrea diarrhoea

diáspora *m* diaspora

diatómico *chem* diatomic

diatónico *mus* diatonic

diatriba diatribe

dibujante *m* + *f* designer, draughtsman, draughtswoman, cartoonist; sketcher

dibujar to draw, design; depict, sketch; ~**se** to stand out, be outlined; show

dibujo drawing, design, sketch, picture; ~ **del natural** drawing from life; ~ **lineal** technical drawing; ~**s animados** cartoon film(s)

dicacidad *f* mordacity; malevolence

dicción *f* diction

diccionario dictionary

diccionarista *m* + *f* lexicographer

díceres *m pl* murmurings

diciembre *m* December

dicotomía dichotomy

dicótomo dichotomous

dictado dictation; ~**s** dictates (of conscience *etc*); **escribir al** ~ to take down

dictador *m* dictator

dictadura dictatorship

dictáfono dictaphone

dictamen *m* judgement, decision; findings; opinion

dictaminar to express an opinion; consider; *leg* pass judgement

dictar to dictate

dictatorial, dictatorio dictatorial

dicterio vituperation; defamatory statement

dicha happiness, bliss; good luck; **por** ~ fortunately

dicharachero *n* joker, wag; *adj* witty, lively (in speech)

dicharacho crude expression, coarse word

dicho saying, adage; ~**s** marriage pledge; ~ **y hecho** no sooner said than done; **lo** ~ that's settled; **mejor** ~ properly speaking

dichoso happy, blissful, delighted; *fam* damned, blasted

didáctica didactics

didáctico didactic

didelfo *n zool* marsupials; *adj* pouched

diecinueve nineteen, nineteenth

diecinueveavo nineteenth

dieciochavo eighteenth

dieciséis sixteen, sixteenth

dieciseisavo sixteenth

diecisiete seventeen, seventeenth

diecisieteavo seventeenth

diedro *geom* dihedral

Diego James; **lindo Don** ~ conceited man

diente *m* tooth, fang; *mech* cog; prong (of fork); clove of garlic; ~ **de león** dandelion; **dar** ~ **con** ~ to chatter (with cold); **echar los** ~**s** to cut teeth; **hablar entre** ~**s** to mumble; **hincar el** ~ **en** to sink one's teeth in; **tener buen** ~ to have a good appetite

diéresis *f* diaeresis

diestra right-hand (side)

diestro *n* skilful fencer/bullfighter; bridle; **a** ~ **y a siniestro** blindly, wildly; *adj* right, skilful; dextrous; right-handed

dieta diet; stipend, honorarium; ~**s** daily expenses; **estar a** ~ to be on a diet

dietar to put on a diet

dietario record-book

dietética dietetics

dietético dietetic

dietista *m* + *f* dietician

diez ten, tenth; **a las** ~ at ten o'clock

diezmal *adj* tenth, decimal

diezmar to decimate; tithe

diezmero tithe-collector

diezmesino ten-month

diezmilésimo ten-thousandth

diezmilmillonésimo ten-thousand-millionth

diezmillonésimo ten-millionth

diezmo tithe

difamación *f* defamation, slander, libel

difamador defamatory, libellous

difamar to defame, libel

difamatorio defamatory, libellous

diferencia difference; **a** ~ **de, en** ~ **a** unlike; **hacer** ~**s** to discriminate; **partir**

la ~ to split the difference
diferenciación f differentiation
diferencial differential
diferenciar to differentiate; distinguish; ~**se** to be different, differ (**de** from)
diferendo difference, point of disagreement
diferente different
diferir vt to defer, postpone; vi to differ, be different
difícil difficult, hard, not likely; **es ~ que llegue hoy** he's unlikely to arrive today; **niño ~** problem child
dificultad f difficulty, hardness, obstacle; **tener ~ para comer** to have difficulty in eating
dificultador hindering, causing difficulty
dificultar to hinder, make difficult; consider difficult
dificultoso difficult, hard, laborious
difidación f declaration of war
difidencia distrust
difidente distrustful
difilo bot two-leaved
difluente adj wide-spreading
difluir to spread out, flow away
difteria med diphtheria
difumar to blur; ~**se** to fade away
difuminar to blur, make vague; arts shade
difumino blur, vagueness
difundir to diffuse, spread; publish, divulge
difunto n dead person; **día de los ~s** All Soul's Day; adj defunct, dead, late
difusible diffusible
difusión f diffusion, vagueness; rad + TV broadcasting
difusivo diffusive
difuso diffuse, vague, wordy
difusor diffusive; rad + TV broadcasting
digerible digestible
digerir to digest
digestibilidad f digestibility
digestión f digestion
digestivo digestive
digitación f fingering
digitado finger-shaped
digital n f bot foxglove, digitalis; adj digital; **impresión/huella ~** fingerprint
digitalismo see dedismo
dígito astron + math digit
dignación f condescension; deigning

dignarse to condescend, deign
dignatario dignitary
dignidad f dignity
dignificación f dignifying
dignificar to dignify
digno worthy, fitting; decent; ~ **de verse** worth seeing
digresión f digression
digresivo digressive
dije m charm, trinket; ~**s** bravado
dilaceración f ripping, laceration
dilacerar to lacerate
dilación f dilation, delay
dilapidación f squandering, waste
dilapidador adj squandering
dilapidar to squander
dilatación f dilation, expansion
dilatado extensive, numerous; dilated
dilatador adj dilating, expanding
dilatar to dilate, expand; prolong; spread abroad; ~**se** to linger; expand; dilate; ~**se en** to dwell on, go into great detail about
dilatoria delay; leg time allowed to pay, grace
dilatorio adj leg dilatory
dilección f predilection; affection
dilecto much loved
dilema m dilemma
díler m sl wholesale drug trafficker
diletante m + f dilettante; lover of the arts (esp mus)
diletantismo dilettantism
diligencia diligence; speed; stagecoach; ~**s** business
diligenciar to deal with, attend to
diligenciero agent
diligente diligent, quick
dilogía ambiguity, double meaning
dilucidación f elucidation
dilucidador elucidating
dilucidar to elucidate
dilución f dilution
diluir to dissolve; dilute, water down
dilusivo delusive
diluviano diluvian
diluviar to rain in torrents
diluvio flood, deluge; downpour
dimanación f origin, issuing
dimanar: ~ **de** to issue from, originate in
dimensión f dimension
dimes y diretes mpl bickering; **andar en** ~ to go in for bickering

diminución *f see* **disminución**

diminuir *see* **disminuir**

diminutivo diminutive

diminuto *adj* minute, tiny; defective, imperfect

dimisión *f* resignation (from office *etc*); **presentar la ~** to submit/tender one's resignation

dimisionario having submitted one's resignation

dimitir to resign

dimorfismo dimorphism

dimorfo dimorphic

din *m fam* cash; spondulicks; **el ~ y el don** money and quality

Dinamarca Denmark

dinamarqués *n m* Dane; Danish language; *adj* Danish

dinámica dynamics

dinámico dynamic

dinamismo dynamism

dinamista *n m+f* dynamist; *adj* dynamistic

dinamita dynamite

dinamitazo explosion, blast

dinamitero dynamiter

dínamo dynamo

dinamoeléctrico dynamo-electric

dinamómetro dynamometer

dinasta *m* dynast

dinastía dynasty

dinástico dynastic

dinastismo loyalty to a dynasty

dinerada, dineral *fam* fortune, packet, lot of money

dinerillo small amount of money *usu iron*; pretty penny

dinero money; **~ contante (y sonante)**, **~ en efectivo** spot cash, ready money; **~ suelto** petty cash, change; **estar mal de ~** to be hard up

dineroso moneyed

dinosaurio dinosaur

dintel *m* lintel

dintelar to fit lintels

diñar: ~la *sl* to snuff it, kick the bucket; **~se** to escape

diocesano *n m +adj* diocesan

diócesis *f sing+pl* diocese

dioptría *opt* diopter

dióptrico dioptric(al)

Dios *m* God; **armar un ~ es Cristo** to start a shindy; **¡bendito sea ~!** good heavens!; **como hay ~** as sure as two

and two make four; **como ~ manda** properly, correctly; **~ dirá** we shall see; **estar de ~** to be inevitable/fated; **no lo quiera ~** God forbid; **no servir ni a ~ ni al diablo** not to take sides, not to care either way; **¡por ~!** for heaven's sake!; **sabe ~** heaven alone knows; **tentar a ~** to tempt providence/fate; **¡válgame ~!** bless my soul!; **¡vaya con ~!** farewell!

dios *m* god, idol, image

diosa goddess

diostedé *m orni* toucan

diplomacia diplomacy

diplomado graduate

diplomar *vt* to award a diploma to, grant a degree to; **~se** to graduate, qualify

diplomática diplomacy

diplomático *n m* diplomatist, diplomat; *adj* diplomatic, tactful

diplopia *med* double vision

dipsomanía dipsomania

dipsómano dipsomaniac

díptero *ent* two-winged

díptico, díptica diptych

diptongar to diphthongize

diptongo diphthong

diputación *f* deputation; local government body; functions of an M.P.

diputado representative; member of the lower house of Spanish parliament, congressman

diputador *n m +adj* constituent

diputar to appoint as representative; delegate; deem, consider

dique *m* dyke, dam; barrier; *min* outcrop

diquelear *sl* to observe

dire *m+f cin sl* film director

dirección *f* direction, management; way; editorship; steering; postal address; **~ asistida** powered steering; **~ general** ministerial department; **~ única** one-way street

directiva *n* directive, instruction; board of directors/governors

directivo *n* director; *adj* directive, managing

directo direct, straight; **en ~** *rad+TV* live; **tren ~** through train; **velocidad directa** *mot* top (gear)

director *n m* director; manager; chief; editor; (prison) governor; **~ de escena** stage manager; **~ de orquesta** conductor; ~ **de pompas fúnebres** under-taker, *US* mortician; ~ **general** head of a ministerial department; director general; ~ **gerente** managing director

directorial pertaining to directories; managing

directorio *n* directory, directorate; *adj* directive, directorial

directriz *f geom* directrix; **líneas direc-trices** guidelines, norms

dirigente *n m+f* leader; *adj* leading, directing

dirigir to direct, manage; supervise; guide; write the address; *mus* con-duct; *naut* steer; aim (a gun); **~se a** to apply to, turn towards

dirigismo state control, centralized government

dirimente annulling

dirimible annullable

dirimir to annul, settle; solve (a prob-lem); dissolve

disanto holy day

discantar to descant

discante *m* descant; concert *esp* of stringed instruments

discarción *f tel* dialling

discar *tel* to dial

disceptación *f* discourse

disceptar to discourse

discernidor discerning

discernimiento discernment, insight, justice

discernir to discern, distinguish, dis-criminate, judge

disciplina discipline; lash, whip

disciplinado *bot* marbled; *bot* varie-gated; disciplined

disciplinal, disciplinante *adj* disciplinary

disciplinario disciplinary; **batallón ~** punishment squad/battalion

disciplinazo lash/whip stroke

discipulado discipleship, teaching; dis-ciples; pupils

discípulo disciple, pupil, student

disco disc; gramophone record; *sp* dis-cus; ~ **de señales** traffic-light(s); **soltar un ~** to repeat parrot-fashion

discoidal, discoide, discoideo disc-shaped

díscolo ungovernable

disconforme in disagreement

disconformidad *f* disconformity

discontinuidad *f* lack of continuity

discontinuo discontinuous, broken

disconveniencia *see* **inconveniencia**

disconveniente *see* **inconveniente**

discordancia discordance, disagreement

discordante discordant, dissonant

discordar to be discordant, disagree

discorde *adj* discordant; *mus* dissonant

discordia discord, disagreement

discoteca record library; discothèque

discotequero *adj* pertaining to disco-thèques

discreción *f* discretion, circumspection, wit; **a ~** at one's own discretion

discrecional discretional, optional; **pa-rada ~** request stop

discrepancia discrepancy

discrepar to differ, disagree

discretear to be discreet

discreto discreet, unobtrusive; witty; *fam* not bad

discrimen *m* risk

discriminación *f* discrimination

discriminar to discriminate

discriminatorio discriminatory

disculpa excuse, apology

disculpabilidad *f* excusability

disculpable excusable, pardonable

disculpar to excuse, forgive; **~se por** to apologize for

discurrir *vt* to think up, invent; devise; infer; *vi* to wander; (of time) pass; (of rivers) flow; think

discursante *m+f* speech-maker

discursar (sobre/acerca de) to discourse (about)

discursear *iron+pej* to speechify

discursista *m+f* person fond of speech-making

discursivo discursive

discurso discourse, speech; reasoning; course (of time); **partes del ~** *gramm* parts of speech

discusión *f* discussion; argument, dis-pute

discutible debatable; disputable; ques-tionable

discutidor *n m* arguer; *adj* arguing

discutir to discuss; dispute, argue (about); haggle (over)

disecable fit to be stuffed

disecación *f* stuffing, taxidermy

disecador *m* taxidermist

disecar to dissect, stuff (animals)

disección *f* dissection

disecea *med* high-frequency deafness

disector *m* dissector, anatomist

diseminación *f* dissemination, scattering

diseminador disseminating

diseminar to disseminate, scatter

disensión *f* dissension; disagreement

disenso dissent

disentería dysentery

disentérico dysenteric

disentimiento dissension

disentir to dissent, disagree; ~ **de** to disagree with

diseñador *m* designer

diseñar to design, draw, sketch

diseño design, drawing, outline, pattern

disertación *f* dissertation

disertador *adj* fond of discoursing

disertante *m+f* speaker

disertar (sobre/acerca de) to discourse (on)

diserto eloquent

disfavor disfavour; bad turn

disformar *see* **deformar**

disforme *see* **deforme**

disformidad *see* **deformidad**

disfraz *m* disguise, fancy-dress; **baile de disfraces** fancy-dress ball, *US* costume dance

disfrazar to disguise; cloak, cover up; ~**se** to disguise, masquerade (**de** as)

disfrutar to enjoy (o.s.)

disfrute *m* enjoyment, benefit

disfumar *see* **esfumar**

disgregación *f* disintegration

disgregar to disintegrate

disgregativo disintegrating

disgustar to displease, upset; annoy; **me disgusta** I don't like it; ~**se** to be annoyed, get/become angry

disgusto displeasure, upset; annoyance; nasty shock; row; **estar a** ~ not to feel at ease

disidencia dissidence, dissent

disidente *n m+f* dissenter, dissident; *adj* dissenting

disidir to dissent, disagree

disílabo disyllabic

disimetría dissymmetry

disimétrico unsymmetrical

disímil, disimilar dissimilar

disimilitud *f* unlikeness

disimulable concealable

disimulación *f* dissimulation

disimulado dissembling, undercover;

hidden; **hacerse el** ~ to pretend not to hear

disimulador *adj* dissembling

disimular to dissemble, feign, pretend; hide

disimulo pretence, covering-up; **actuar con** ~ to act in an underhand way

disipación *f* dissipation

disipador *n m* spendthrift; *adj* squandering

dislate *m* absurdity

dislexia dyslexia

disléxico dyslexic

dislocación *f*, **dislocadura** dislocation

dislocar to dislocate, disjoint

disminución *f* diminution; drop; decrease; reduction; **ir en** ~ to dwindle, shrink

disminuir to diminish, cut down, decrease, belittle; **sentirse disminuido** to feel small; ~**se** to diminish, dwindle, lessen

dismnesia *med* weak memory

disnea *med* difficulty in breathing

Disneylandia Disneyland

disociación *f* dissociation

disociar to dissociate

disolubilidad *f* dissolubility

disoluble dissoluble

disolución *f* dissolution, breaking-up; *chem* solution

disolutivo dissolvent

disoluto dissolute

disolvente *n m* dissolver; *adj* dissolvent

disolver to dissolve, break up

disón *m mus* discord

disonancia dissonance, discord

disonante dissonant

disonar to be dissonant/discordant

dísono dissonant

dispar dissimilar, different, unlike

disparadero trigger

disparador *m* trigger, release mechanism; ratchet-wheel

disparar to shoot, fire, discharge, release, let off; throw; ~**se** (of firearms) to go off, (of horses) bolt; *mot* race; *fam* lose control

disparatado crazy, preposterous

disparatador talking nonsense

disparatar to behave/talk crazily

disparate *m* crazy action or speech; rubbish; nonsense; ~ **de** hell of a lot of; ~ **escolar** school-boy howler

disparatorio speech/conversation/writing full of **disparates**
disparatoso given to talking nonsense
disparejo uneven
disparidad *f* disparity
disparo shot; shooting; firing; report; release
dispendio waste, excessive outlay
dispendioso costly, squandering
dispensa dispensation; exemption
dispensación *f* dispensation
dispensador *n m* dispenser; *adj* dispensing
dispensar to dispense, forgive; **dispense** I apologize, excuse me
dispensario clinic, surgery
dispepsia dyspepsia
dispéptico dyspeptic
dispersar to disperse, scatter
dispersión *f* dispersion, dispersal
disperso dispersed, scattered
displicencia superciliousness, indifference
displicente supercilious, indifferent; unpleasant
disponente disposing, arranging
disponedor *n m* arranger, disposer; *adj* arranging, disposing
disponer *vt* to dispose, arrange; *vi* ~ **de** to have at one's disposal; ~**se a** to get ready to
disponibilidad *f* availability; ~**es** resources
disponible available
disposición *f* disposition, layout, aptitude; disposal; willingness; **de** ~ *adj* stand-by; **tomar disposiciones** to take steps; **última** ~ last will and testament
dispositivo dispositive; device, mechanism
dispuesto ready, willing; arranged; **bien** ~ well-disposed; **estar** ~ **a** to be ready to; **mal** ~ ill-disposed
disputa dispute
disputable arguable, problematic
disputador disputing
disputar to dispute, argue over; haggle over; question; contend for
disquisición *f* disquisition
disruptivo disruptive
distancia distance; **a** ~ at a distance; **control/mando a** ~ remote control; **guardar la** ~ to keep one's distance
distanciamiento estrangement; spacing out

distanciar to place at a distance; estrange; separate; (horse-racing) disqualify; ~**se** to move away from; become estranged, separated; **están distanciados** they are estranged
distante distant, remote
distar to be distant/remote; ~ **de** to be (a certain distance) from
distender to distend
distensión *f* distension, relaxation; *pol* détente
distinción *f* distinctness; consideration, deference; **a** ~ **de** as distinct from, unlike
distinguible distinguishable
distinguido distinguished
distinguir to distinguish; tell; single out; make out; ~**se** to stand out; differ
distintivo *n m* distinctive mark; badge; *adj* distinctive
distinto distinct; different
distorsión *f* distortion, twisting
distorsionar to distort, twist
distracción *f* distraction, amusement; **por** ~ for amusement; through an oversight
distraer to distract; entertain, amuse; pilfer; ~**se** to amuse o.s.; relax; let one's attention wander
distraído entertaining; absent-minded; **hacerse el** ~ to pretend not to notice
distraimiento distraction; amusement
distribución *f* distribution; **tablero de distribuciones** switchboard
distribuidor *n m* distributor; ~ **automático** slot machine, vending machine; *adj* distributing
distribuir to distribute, deliver; apportion
distributivo distributive
distribuyente *n m+f* distributor; *adj* distributing
distrito district
disturbar to disturb, disrupt
disturbio disturbance, riot
disuadir to dissuade, deter, discourage
disuasión *f* dissuasion
disuasivo dissuasive, deterrent; **fuerza disuasiva nuclear** nuclear deterrent
disyunción *f* disjunction
disyuntiva dilemma, alternative
disyuntivo *adj* disjunctive
disyunto separated

disyuntor *m elect* circuit-breaker

dita security, bond, surety

diteísmo ditheism

diteísta *n m+f* ditheist; *adj* ditheistic

ditirámbico dithyrambic

ditirambo dithyramb

dítono *mus* ditone

diuca teacher's pet

diurético *med* diuretic

diurno diurnal

divagación *f* wandering, digression

divagador *n m* wanderer, digressor; *adj* digressing

divagar to wander, roam, digress

diván *m* divan

divergencia divergence

divergente divergent

divergir to diverge, dissent

diversidad *f* diversity, variety

diversificar to diversify

diversión *f* diversion, amusement

diverso diverse, different; ~s various

divertido amusing, funny, merry

divertimiento diversion, amusement

divertir to divert, amuse, entertain; ~se to amuse o.s.; have a good time

dividendo dividend

divididero divisible

dividir(se) to divide, split, share; separate, part

divieso *med* boil

divinatorio divinatory

divinidad *f* divinity, deity; *fam* delightful thing

divinización *f* divination

divinizar to deify; extol

divino divine; *fam* exquisite

divisa emblem, motto, slogan; foreign currency; *her* device

divisar to make out, descry, catch sight of

divisibilidad *f* divisibility

división *f* division

divisionario divisional, functional

divisivo divisive

divismo deification, hero-worship

diviso divided

divisor *n m math* divisor; *adj* dividing

divisoria *geog* divide; ~ **de aguas** watershed

divisorio *n print* copy-holder; *adj* dividing, divisionary

diva *poet* goddess; *mus* prima donna

divo *n mus* opera star; *adj poet* godlike

divorciar to divorce; ~**se** to get a divorce

divorcio divorce

divulgación divulgation, spreading, popularization

divulgador *n m* divulger, popularizer; *adj* divulging, spreading, popularizing

divulgar to divulge, spread, publish

diyambo metrical foot composed of two iambuses

dizque *m* rumour

do *m mus* do, C; ~ **de pecho** highest tenor note, top C

dobla: jugar a la ~ (betting) to keep on doubling one's stake

dobladillar (sewing) to hem

dobladillo hem; strong knitting yarn

doblado stocky, double-dealing; double(d)

dobladura fold, crease

doblaje *m cin* dubbing

doblamiento folding, creasing; doubling

doblar *vt* to double, fold, bend; *cin* dub; ~ **por** *cin+theat+TV* to understudy for (another actor/actress); ~ **una esquina** to go round (a corner); *vi* to toll a knell; ~**se** to bow, bend, give way, yield; double

doble *n m* double, fold, crease; toll of the death knell; large glass of beer; *cin+theat+TV* understudy; *adj* double, twin; *text* heavy; two-faced; ~ **calzada** dual carriageway

doblegable pliant, flexible

doblegadizo easily folded or bent

doblegar *vt* to bend, force to give way; ~**se** to bend, yield, give way

doblescudo *bot* shepherd's purse

doblete *n m* doublet; *adj* of medium thickness

¹ **doblez** *f* duplicity; **sin dobleces** frank, candid

² **doblez** *m* crease, fold, ply

doblón *m* doubloon; **escupir doblones** to flaunt one's wealth

doblonada *fam* lots of money

doce twelve, twelfth; **las** ~ twelve o'clock

doceavo twelfth

docena dozen; ~ **de fraile** baker's dozen

docencia teaching practice/experience

doceno twelfth

docente educational, teaching; **personal** ~ teaching staff

dócil docile

docilidad f docility

docto learned

doctora doctor's wife; blue-stocking; woman doctor

doctorado doctorate; **tener el ~ en** to be an expert on

doctoramiento conferring/taking of doctorate

doctorando n candidate for doctorate

doctorar to confer a doctorate on; **~se** to get one's doctorate

doctrina doctrine, learning; catechism

doctrinador n m instructor; adj instructing

doctrinal n m book of rules and precepts; adj doctrinal

doctrinario n + adj doctrinaire

doctrinar to indoctrinate

doctrino charity child

documentación f documentation; documents; identity papers

documental n m cin + TV documentary (film); adj documental, documentary

documentar to document; put in the picture; **~se** to obtain the necessary information, put o.s. in the picture

documento document

dodecaedro geom dodecahedron

dodecágono geom dodecagon

dogal m noose, slip-knot, halter; **con el ~ al cuello** in a fix, up to one's neck

dogmático n dogmatist; adj dogmatic

dogmatismo dogmatism

dogmatista m + f propounder of heretical dogmas

dogmatizador m, **dogmatizante** m dogmatizer, dogmatist

dogmatizar to dogmatize; teach heresy

dogo bulldog; doge

dolador m stone-cutter; timber-cutter

doladura stone chippings; shavings

dolar to shape and polish (wood/stone)

dólar m dollar

dolencia ailment, complaint; ache

doler to ache, hurt; **me duele la cabeza/el estómago** my head/stomach aches; **~se de** to feel sorry for; grieve

dolido aggrieved, complaining

doliente n mourner; adj aching, sick, suffering, sorrowing

dolménico pertaining to dolmens

dolo fraud, deceit

dolobre m stone-hammer

dolomía, dolomita min dolomite

dolor m pain, ache; sorrow; regret; **~ de muelas** toothache; **~ de oído** earache; **~ sordo** dull pain; **¡qué ~!** what a pity!

dolora short philosophical poem

dolorcillo twinge

dolorido aching, painful, sore

dolorosa sl bill, check

doloroso painful, distressing

doloso fraudulent, deceitful

doma breaking-in, taming, subduing

domable tamable; (of hair) manageable

domador m tamer; horse-breaker

domadura see doma

domar to tame; break in; subdue

dombo cupola

domeñable that can be subdued

domeñar to subdue, master

domesticable tamable

domesticar to tame, domesticate; **~se** to become civilized, tame

domesticidad f domesticity

doméstico n domestic servant; adj domestic

domestiquez f tameness

domiciliar to domicile, house; **estar domiciliado en** to live at; **~se** to take up residence

domiciliario n citizen, inhabitant; adj domiciliary; **arresto ~** house arrest

domicilio residence, domicile, home

dominación f domination; high ground; commanding position

dominador dominating; domineering

dominante domineering, dominant, commanding; **viento ~** prevailing wind

dominar to dominate, command, overlook; **domino dos idiomas** I have a knowledge of two languages; **~se** to control o.s.

dómine m Latin teacher; pedant

domingada Sunday fiesta

domingo Sunday; **~ de carnaval** Shrove Sunday; **~ de Ramos** Palm Sunday; **traje de ~** Sunday best, Sunday clothes

dominguero (of) Sunday; **conductor ~** pej Sunday driver

dominguillo tumbler toy, kelly

dominical (of) Sunday, dominical

dominicano Dominican; native of the Dominican Republic

dominico Dominican (nun or friar)

dominio dominion, control, mastery, domain; **perder el ~ de sí mismo** to lose one's self-control

dominó, dómino domino (robe); dominoes (game)

dompedro *bot* morning glory

¹ **don** *m* gentleman's title, used before the Christian name

² **don** *m* gift, talent; **~ de mando** aptitude for handling people; **~ de palabra** facility of speech; **tener ~ de gentes** to have a winning way with people

donación *f* donation, bequest

donada lay sister

donado lay brother

donador *n m* donor; *adj* donating

donaire *m* charm, wit

donairoso charming, witty

donante *m+f* donor; **~ de sangre** blood-donor

donar to donate

donativo donation

donatorio receiver of a donation

doncel mild; **pino ~** pine/deal without knots; **vino ~** mild-flavoured wine

doncella maid, damsel; lady's maid; chambermaid

doncellez *f* virginity, maidenhood

donde *adv* where; **~ no** otherwise; **~ las dan las toman** give and take; *pron* **¿dónde?** where?; **¿hacia ~?** whither?; **¿por ~?** which way?

dondequiera anywhere, wherever; **por ~** everywhere

dondiego dandy, fop

donillero card-sharper

donjuán dandy, lady-killer, casanova

donoso witty, charming

donostiarra *m+f* native of San Sebastian (Donosti)

doña title for ladies, used before Christian names

doñear to womanize

dopado *sl* drugged

doquier, doquiera *see* dondequiera

dorado *n* gilt, gilding; *adj* golden

dorador *m* gilder

doradura gilding

doral *m orni* fly-catcher

dorar to gild; *cul* brown; coat with sugar; **~ la píldora** to sugar the pill

dórico *archi* Doric

dormida night's sleep

dormidera *n bot* poppy; **~s** sleepiness

dormidero *n* resting-place for cattle; *adj* sleepy, soporiferous, narcotic

dormilón *n m* sleepy-head; *adj* sleepy-headed

dormilona garden poppy, pearl earring; sleepy-head

dormir *vt* to put to sleep; **~ la mona** to sleep it off; **~ la siesta** to take an after-dinner nap; *vi* to sleep, spend the night; **~ al sereno** to sleep under the stars; **~ a pierna suelta, ~ como un lirón** to sleep like a log; **~la** *sl* to sleep after a drunken bout; **~se** to go to sleep, fall asleep

dormitar to doze, snooze; have forty winks

dormitivo sleep-inducing

dormitorio dormitory, bedroom

dornajo trough

Dorotea Dorothy

dorsal *n m sp* number on player's back; *adj* dorsal

dorso back, reverse side; **véase al ~** please turn over

dos *n m* two, second, deuce; **~ de mayo** second of May; **de ~ en ~** two by two, in pairs, two abreast; **en un ~ por tres** in a flash; **las ~** two o'clock; **los/las ~** both of them; *adj* two; **vehículo de ~ ruedas** two-wheeled vehicle; **~ veces** twice

dosañal biennial

doscientos two hundred

dosel *m* canopy

dosificación *f* dosage

dosificar to dose, give medicine to

dosis *f sing+pl* dose

dotación *f* endowment, dowry; *naut* crew, ship's complement; staff, personnel

dotador *m* endower, donor

dotar to endow; give as dowry

dote *f* dowry; **~s** endowments, gifts; aptitudes

dozavado twelve-sided

dozavo twelfth part

draconiano Draconian

draga dredge; *naut* dredger

dragado dredging

dragaminas *m sing+pl* minesweeper

dragar to dredge; **~ minas** to sweep mines

dragón *m* dragon; *mil* dragoon; furnace, fire-box

dramático *n* dramatist, dramatic actor; *adj* dramatic

dramática dramatic art, dramatics

dramatismo drama, dramatic effect

dramatización *f* dramatization

dramatizar to dramatize

dramaturgia dramaturgy, dramatic art

dramaturgo dramatist

dramón *m* melodrama; blood-and-thunder play

drástico drastic

drenaje *m* drainage

drenar to drain

dríada, dríade *f* dryad, wood-nymph

driblar *sp* to dribble

dril *m text* drill, denim

driza halyard

droga drug, dope; deceit

drogadependencia drug-addiction, drug-dependence

drogadicto, drogota *m+f sl* drug-addict

droguería hardware shop, druggist's; drugstore; drysalter's

droguero, droguista *m+f* drysalter, druggist, hardware dealer

dromedario dromedary

druida *m* druid

druídico druidic(al)

druidismo druidism

druso Druse

dualidad *f* duality

dualismo dualism

dualista *n m* dualist; *adj* dualistic

dubio *leg* doubtful point

dubitable open to question

dubitación *f* doubt

dubitativo conjectural

ducado duchy; dukedom; ducat

ducentésimo two-hundredth

dúctil ductile

ductilidad *f* malleability

ductivo conducive

ductor *m* guide, leader; *med* probe

ducha shower

ducharse to have a shower

ducho skilled

duda doubt, misgiving; **poner en ~** to call in question; **sin ~** doubtless

dudable doubtful

dudar to doubt, hesitate

dudilla sneaking doubt

dudoso doubtful, dubious

duelista *m* duellist

duelo duel; sorrow, grief, bereavement, mourning; **~s** troubles

duende *m* (hob)goblin, gremlin, pixie, leprechaun; **tener ~** to have what it takes

duendecillo elf

duendo tame, gentle

dueña duenna, lady

dueño owner, proprietor, landlord, master; **~ de sí mismo** self-controlled; **hacerse ~ de** to make o.s. the master of

duermevela doze, snooze, fitful sleep

duerno trough; *print* double sheet of paper

dueto duo, duet

dúho bench, seat

dula common pasture

dulce *n* sweetmeat; **~ de membrillo** quince jelly; **~s** sweets, *US* candy; *adj* sweet, gentle; (of water) fresh

dulcecillo sweetish

dulcedumbre *f* sweetness

dulcémele *m mus* dulcimer

dulcera sweet jar

dulcería sweetshop

dulcero *n* confectioner; *adj* sweet-toothed

dulcificación *f* dulcification

dulcificante *adj* sweetening

dulcificar to sweeten; soften

dulcinea sweetheart, ideal woman

dulcísono sweet-toned

dulia cult of the saints

dulzaina *mus* flageolet

dulzainero flageolet-player

dulzaino *adj* cloying, oversweet

dulzor *m* sweetness

dulzura sweetness, mildness; **con ~** softly

duna dune

Dunquerque Dunkirk

dúo *mus* duo, duet

duodécimo twelfth

duodeno *m anat* duodenum; *adj* twelfth

dúplex *tel* duplex; **piso ~** split-level flat

duplicación *f* duplication

duplicado *n+adj* duplicate; **por ~** in duplicate

duplicar to duplicate

duplicador *n m* duplicator; *adj* duplicating

dúplice *adj* double

duplicidad *f* duplicity

duplo twice as much

duque *m* duke; **gran** ~ great duke

duquesa duchess

durabilidad *f* durability

duración *f* duration

duradero lasting, durable

duraluminio duraluminium

durante during, for; ~ **mucho tiempo** for a long time

durar to last; go on for; wear well

duraznero peach tree

durazno type of small peach

dureza hardness, firmness, toughness

durillo *n bot* dogwood; *adj* rather hard, toughish

durmiente dormer window; (railway) sleeper; *adj* sleeping

duro *n* five-peseta coin; *pol* hard-liner, hawk; *adj* hard, firm; stiff; harsh; **a duras penas** with difficulty; ~ **de corazón** hard-hearted; ~ **de mollera** thick-headed; ~ **de oído** hard of hearing; **ser** ~ **de pelar** to be a hard nut to crack

E

¹ e *f* letter e

² e and

ea: ¡~ pues! come on!

E.A. (Ejército de Aire) Air Force

easonense *n m+f* native of San Sebastian; *adj* of San Sebastian

ebanista *m* cabinet-maker

ebanistería cabinet-making

ébano ebony

ebonita ebonite

ebriedad *f* drunkenness

ebrio drunk

ebulición *f*, ebullición *f* boiling, bubbling over

eccehomo *fam* unfortunate wretch, poor devil

eclecticismo eclecticism

ecléctico eclectic

Eclesiástico Ecclesiasticus

eclesiástico *n* clergyman, parson; *adj* ecclesiastic(al)

eclipsar to eclipse; *fig* outshine, surpass

eclisa (railway) fish-plate

eclosión *f* blossoming; birth

eco echo; **hacer** ~ to echo, repeat word-for-word; **tener** ~ to catch on; *sl* that's it, correct

ecología ecology

ecológico ecological

ecologista *m+f*, ecólogo ecologist

economato discount store; company store; armed forces shop; trusteeship

economía economy; ~ **política** political economy, political economics

económico economic(al), saving

economista *m+f* economist

economizar to economize, save

ecónomo trustee

ectoplasma *m* ectoplasm

ecuable equitable; (of movement) uniform

ecuación *f* equation

ecuador *m* equator

ecuanimidad *f* equanimity

ecuánime calm, serene; impartial, fair

ecuatoguineano *n* inhabitant of Equatorial Guinea; *adj* of Equatorial Guinea

ecuatoriano Ecuadorian

ecuestre *adj* equestrian

ecuménico ecumenical

echacorvear to pimp, procure; swindle

echacorvería pimping, procuring; swindling

echacuervos *m sing+pl* pimp, procurer; swindler

echadero resting-place

echadillo, echadizo foundling

echado lazy, idle

echador *n m* thrower; *adj* throwing

echadura brood; brooding; hatching

echao pa'lante *sl* courageous

echaperros *m sing+pl* official who ejects dogs from church

echar to throw, cast, hurl; throw out, expel; dismiss; exude, give off; pour out; sprout; ~ **abajo** to knock down, pull down; ~ **a broma** to take as a joke; ~ **aceite al fuego** to add fuel to the flames; ~ **a correr** to run away; ~ **a la calle** to throw out, turn out of doors; ~ **a la lotería** to buy a lottery ticket; ~ **al correo** to post, mail; ~ **a llover** to begin to rain; ~ **al mundo** to give birth to; ~ **a perder** to spoil; ~ **a pique** *naut* to sink; ~ **bofes** to pant, gasp; ~ **bravatas** to boast; ~ **cara o cruz** to toss a coin; ~ **carnes** to get fat; ~ **cuentas** to reckon up, work it out; ~ **chispas** to become angry, show one's annoyance; ~ **de menos** to miss, regret the absence of; ~ **de ver** to notice, espy; ~ **el agua a** to baptize; ~ **el guante** to throw down the gauntlet, challenge; ~ **el hígado/los hígados por** to slave for; ~ **la culpa a** to put the blame on; ~ **las bendiciones a** to bless (*usu* on marriage); ~ **las cartas** to tell a fortune (from the cards); ~ **los dientes** to cut teeth; ~ **mano a** to take hold of; ~ **piropos** to pay compliments; ~ **por tierra** to knock down,

175

pull down; ~ **raíces** to take root; ~ **suertes** to draw lots; ~ **tierra a** to cover up, hide; ~ **una mano** to give/lend a hand; ~ **una partida** to have a game; ~ **una película** *cin* to project a film; ~ **un trago** to have a swig; ~ **vela** *naut* to put on sail; ~**se** to lie down; stretch out; ~**se a perder** to become spoilt; ~**se a reír** to burst out laughing; ~**se atrás** to draw back

echarpe *m* stole; scarf

eda lodger

edad *f* age

edén *m* Eden; paradise

edición *f* edition; publication; ~ **príncipe** first edition

edicto edict

edículo shrine; niche; small building

edificación *f* edification; construction

edificador *n m* builder; edifier; *adj* edifying; constructing

edificante edifying

edificar to edify, uplift; construct, build

edificativo edifying

edificio edifice, building

edil *m* councillor

Edimburgo Edinburgh

editar to publish

editor *n m* publisher; *adj* publishing

editorial *n m* editorial; *f* publishing house; *adj* publishing; editorial

editorialista *m+f* editorial-writer; leader-writer

Edipo Oedipus

edredón *m* eiderdown

Eduardo Edward

educación *f* education, training; breeding, manners; **falta de** ~ bad manners

educador *n m* educator; *adj* educating

educando pupil

educar to educate, train, teach; raise; bring up

educativo educational

educción *f* eduction

educir to educe

edulcoración *f* sweetening

edulcorante *m* sweetener

edulcorar to sweeten

EE.UU. (Estados Unidos) U.S. (United States)

efe *f* letter f

efectismo *arts* straining to achieve effect

efectista theatrical; artificial

efectividad *f* effectiveness; **con** ~ **desde** with effect from

efectivo *n m* cash; ~**s militares** military strength; **en** ~ in cash; *adj* effective; real; in operation, active

efecto effect, result; end, purpose; impression; ~**s** goods, personal property; **en** ~ in fact, actually; **llevar a** ~ to carry out; **surtir** ~ to come out as expected; give good results

efectuación *f* accomplishment

efectuar to effect, bring about, put into effect; carry out; ~**se** to take place

efémera *med* ephemeral (fever)

efémero *bot* stinking iris/lily

efervescencia *f* effervescence

efervescente effervescent

eficacia efficacy; efficiency; effectiveness

eficaz effective; active; efficient

eficiencia efficiency

eficiente efficient

efigie *f* effigy

efímero ephemeral, short-lived, brief

eflorescerse *chem* to effloresce

eflorescencia *chem* efflorescence

eflorescente *chem* efflorescent

efluvio emanation, exhalation; vapours

efusión *f* effusion

efusivo effusive

égida aegis

egipciano, egipcio Egyptian

Egipto Egypt

egiptología Egyptology

egiptólogo Egyptologist

égloga eclogue, idyll

egocéntrico egocentric, self-centred

egoísmo egoism, selfishness

egoísta *n m+f* egoist, selfish person; *adj* selfish

egolatra self-worshipping

egolatría self-worship

egotismo egotism

egregio egregious

egresar to leave; graduate

egreso egress

eje *m* axle; axis; ~ **auxiliar** countershaft; **partirle a uno por el** ~ to mess up s.o.'s plans

ejecución *f* execution, carrying out; performance; *leg* distraint, writ

ejecutable feasible, viable

ejecutante *n m* performer; *adj* executing

ejecutar to execute, carry out; perform; *leg* distrain

ejecutivo *n* executive; *adj* executive; prompt

ejecutor *n m* executor; ~ **de la justicia** executioner; *adj* executing

ejecutoriar *leg* to confirm (sentence)

ejecutorio *n leg* writ of execution; *adj* executory

ejemplar *n m* copy; specimen; *adj* exemplary, model

ejemplificar to exemplify

ejemplo example; model, pattern; **dar ~** to set an example

ejercer to practise (a profession); exert, exercise

ejercicio exercise; practice; *mil* drill; **el ~ hace maestro** practice makes perfect; **hacer ~** to take exercise

ejercitación *f* practice

ejercitar to practise, exercise; drill, train; **~se** to train oneself; practise

ejército army; **~s de tierra, mar y aire** armed forces

ejido common land

ejión *m archi* corbel

el *m def art* the; ~ **de** the one with, that one with; ~ **que** *rel pron* he who, the one that

él *pers pron* he; it; him (after a *prep*)

elaboración *f* manufacture, making; development

elaborado elaborate

elaborador *n m* maker; *adj* elaborating

elaborar to elaborate; make

elación *f* pomposity; magnanimity

elasticidad *f* elasticity

elástico *n m* elastic; elastic tape; wire spring; *adj* elastic; flexible

elche apostate

ele *f* letter l; **¡~!** *sl* hear-hear!; whacko!

eléboro hellebore

elección *f* election; choice

electivo elective

electo elect, chosen

elector *n m* elector, voter; *adj* electorial, electing

electorado electorate

electoralismo *n* electioneering

electoralista *n m+f* electioneer; *adj* electioneering

electorero *pol* election agent; canvasser

electricidad *f* electricity

electricista *m+f* electrician; electrical engineer

eléctrico electric, electrical

electrificación *f* electrification

electrificar to electrify; excite, thrill

electrizable electrifiable

electrizador *n m* electrifier; *adj* electrifying

electrizar to electrify

electroafeitadora electric shaver

electrocardiografía electrocardiography

electrocardiógrafo electrocardiograph

electrocutar to electrocute

electrodinámica electrodynamics

electrodinámico electrodynamic

electrodo electrode

electrodoméstico household electrical appliance

electroencefalografía electroencephalography

electroencefalógrafo electroencephalograph

electroencefalograma *m* electroencephalogram

electroimán *m* electro-magnet

electrólisis *f* electrolysis

electromagnético electromagnetic

electromagnetismo electromagnetism

electrometría electrometry

electromotor *m* electric motor

electromotriz *adj* electromotive

electrónica electronics

electrónico electronic

electroscopio electroscope

electrosoldador *m* electric welder

electrosoldadura electric welding

electrotecnia electrical engineering

electroterapeuta *m+f* electrotherapeutist

electroterapia electrotherapy

elefanta cow elephant

elefante *m* elephant; **patas de ~** exaggeratedly flared trousers

elefantiasis *f* elephantiasis

elefantina elephantine

elegancia elegance, grace, distinguished manner; smartness, stylishness

elegante elegant, graceful, polished; smart, stylish

elegía elegy

elegíaco elegiac, mournful

elegibilidad *f* eligibility

elegir to select, choose; elect

élego elegiac

elemental elementary, elemental, fundamental

elemento element; factor; *fam* bloke,

chap; ~s elements, fundamentals; ~s químicos chemical elements

elemí *m* gum resin

Elena Helen, Ellen

elenco index; *theat* cast

elepé *m* long-playing record

elevación *f* elevation; altitude; height; rise; rapture; raising

elevado elevated, lofty; grand; high

elevador *m* elevator, hoist

elevamiento elevation; rapture, ecstasy

elevar to elevate, raise, lift; ~se to ascend, climb; go up; soar

elfo elf

elidir *gramm* to elide

elijar to seethe; *cul* stew

eliminación *f* elimination, removal

eliminador *n m* eliminator; *adj* eliminating

eliminar to eliminate, remove; *sl* kill

elipse *f* ellipse

elipsis *f* ellipsis

elipticidad *f* ellipticity

elíptico elliptical

Elíseo Elysium

elisión *f* elision

elitario of the élite

elite *f* elite

elitismo elitism

elitista *adj* elitist

elocución *f* elocution

elocuencia eloquence

elocuente eloquent

elogioso *n m* eulogizer; *adj* eulogistic, praising

elogiar to praise

elogio praise

elongación *f* elongation

elucidación *f* elucidation, explanation

elucidar to elucidate, illustrate, explain

eludible avoidable

eludir to elude; avoid, dodge

ella *pers pron* she; her, (after a *prep*) it

elle *f* letter ll

ello *pron* it; ~ **es que** the fact is that

emaciación *f* emaciation

emanación *f* emanation, flow; odour; manifestation

emanar to emanate, spring, issue

emancipación *f* emancipation

emancipador *n m* emancipator; *adj* emancipating

emancipar to emancipate, set free; ~se to become free

emasculación *f* emasculation

embachar to pen (sheep) for shearing

embadurnador *m* dauber

embadurnar to daub

embaidor *adj* swindling, cheating

embair to swindle, cheat

embajada embassy; errand, mission

embajador *m* ambassador; ~ **cerca de ...** ambassador to ...

embajadora ambassadress; ambassador's wife

embalador *m* packer

embalaje *m* packing

embalar to pack; bale, crate; ¡no te embales! steady!, don't rush at it!; **papel de** ~ brown paper

embaldosar to pave with tiles

embalsadero swamp; stagnant pool

embalsamador *m* embalmer

embalsamamiento embalming

embalsamar to embalm; perfume

embalsar to dam

embalse *m* dam; reservoir

embalumar to burden; overload

embancar *naut* to run aground

embanderar to deck with flags

embarazada *n f* pregnant woman; *adj* pregnant; **quedar** ~ to become pregnant

embarazar to hinder, obstruct; make pregnant

embarazo impediment, obstacle; pregnancy; bashfulness; awkwardness

embarazoso embarrassing; cumbersome, unwieldy

embarcación *f* ship, boat; embarkation; ~ **de elijo** *naut* lighter; ~ **menor** small craft

embarbascarse to get muddled

embarbillar *carp* to rabbet

embarcadero wharf, pier

embarcador *m* shipper

embarcar to embark; send by boat, ship; ~se to embark, sail; engage (in)

embarco embarkation

embardar to thatch

embargar to impede; distrain; *leg* attach, seize, confiscate; lay an embargo on; **estar embargado de emoción** to be overcome with emotion

embargo embargo, restriction; distraint; confiscation; **sin** ~ nevertheless

embarnizadura varnishing
embarnizar to varnish
embarque *m* shipment
embarrador *m* plasterer; troublemaker
embarrancarse *naut* to run aground; get bogged down
embarrar to smear/daub with mud; roughcast with plaster
embarrullador *n* *m* muddler; *adj* muddling
embarrullar to muddle, mess up
embaucador *m* cheat, impostor, fraud
embaucamiento cheating
embaucar to fool, trick, swindle, deceive
embaular to pack in a trunk; *fam* stuff (with food); ~**se** to gorge
embausamiento astonishment
embazar to dye brown; be amazed
embebecer to enrapture
embebecido absorbed; amazed
embebecimiento absorption; rapture
embebedor *m* imbiber
embeber to imbibe, absorb; soak; shrink; (sewing) take in; ~**se** to be fascinated; be absorbed
embelecador *m* deceiver, impostor
embelecar to deceive
embeleco cheat; nuisance
embeleñar to charm; fascinate
embelesamiento charm, rapture; delight
embelesar to enrapture, delight, charm
embeleso delight, ecstasy
embellecer to embellish, beautify, adorn
embellecimiento embellishment, adornment
embestida (sudden) attack, onset; assault, charge
embestidor *n* *m* scrounger; *adj* charging, attacking
embestidura charge, onslaught
embestir to charge, attack
embetunar to blacken; cover with pitch
embijar to apply red-lead paint
emblandecer to soften
emblanquecer to whiten; bleach; become white; ~**se** to whiten, become white
emblanquecimiento bleaching, whitening
emblema *m* emblem
emblemático emblematic
embobamiento amazement, open-mouthed wonder, fascination

embobar to fool; amuse; fascinate; amaze; ~**se** to be amazed; be fascinated
embobinado reel (of a tape-recorder, computer)
embocadura mouth (of a river); entrance (through a narrow passage); *mus* mouthpiece
embochinchar to make a row
embodegar to store
embolada piston-stroke
embolado *theat* minor role; *fam* lie; *fam* trick; bull with protective wooden balls on its horns
embolar to polish
embolador *m* bootblack
embolia embolism, clot
embolismador detracting
embolismar to gossip about
embolismo embolism; *fam* lie, untruth
émbolo piston; plunger
embolsar to pocket; put into a purse; ~**se** to put into one's pocket
embolso pocketing (of money)
embonar to improve
emboñigar to daub with cow-dung
emboque *m* narrow passage
embornal *m* scupper-hole
emborrachador intoxicating
emborrachamiento drunkenness
emborrachar to intoxicate, make drunk; ~**se** to get drunk
emborronar to blot; scribble, doodle
emboscada ambush
emboscadura ambush(ing)
emboscar to ambush; ~**se** to lie in ambush; hide in a forest
embosquecer to become wooded
embotadura bluntness (of weapon), blunting
embotamiento dullness, bluntness; dulling, blunting
embotar to dull, blunt; enervate, weaken
embotellado *n* bottling; *adj* bottled
embotellador *m* bottler
embotelladora bottling works/machine
embotellamiento traffic-jam, bottling
embotellar to bottle; bottle up; ~**se** to become jammed
embovedar *archi* to vault, arch
embozar to muffle; cloak, conceal, disguise; muzzle; ~**se** to muffle oneself, wrap oneself up

embozo fold (in top part of sheet/ blanket); **quitarse el** ~ to put one's cards on the table

embracilado (of babies) in arms

embragar to throw in the clutch; *naut* sling

embrague *m mech* clutch; *naut* slinging; *fam* **patinar el** ~ to be a bit simple-minded

embreado *naut* tarring

embrear *naut* to tar

embriagar to make drunk, intoxicate; ~**se** to get drunk, get intoxicated

embriaguez *f* intoxication; drunkenness

embriología embryology

embriólogo embryologist

embrión *m* embryo

embrionario embryonic

embroca, embrocación *f* embrocation

embrollador *m* trouble-maker

embrollar to entangle; confuse, muddle, mess up

embrollo confusion, tangle; muddle, mess; lie, deception

embrollón *m* tale-bearer, mischief-maker

embrolloso tangled; confused

embromar to make fun of, kid, play jokes on

embrujar to bewitch, enchant

embrujo charm, enchantment; glamour

embrutecer to stupefy, make brutish; dull the mind, make insensible; ~**se** to become besotted, brutalized

embrutecimiento brutalization

embuchar to stuff

embudar to funnel in; trick

embudo funnel; trick; one-sided agreement

embuste *m* lie, fraud; ~**s** trinkets

embustear to lie; fraud, cheat

embustero *n* liar; *adj* deceitful, tricky

embutido sausage; inlaid work

embutir to insert, inlay; stuff; ~**se** to gorge

eme *f* letter *m*; *sl* shit

emendación *f* emendation, correction

emendador *m* corrector

emendar to amend; reform

emergencia emergency

emergente emergent; resulting

emerger to emerge, come out

emérito emeritus

emético emetic

emigración *f* emigration

emigrado émigré

emigrante *m* + *f* emigrant

emigrar to emigrate; migrate

Emilio Emil

Emilia Emily

eminencia eminence; height, summit, top; hill

eminente eminent; famous; high, lofty

emisario emissary

emisión *f* issue; radio broadcast; emission

emisor *n m* radio transmitter; *adj* transmitting; broadcasting, issuing

emisora broadcasting station

emitir to emit, give off; utter; send forth; issue; broadcast

emoción *f* emotion; feeling

emocional emotional

emocionante moving, touching; thrilling

emocionar to cause emotion, touch, move; ~**se** to be touched; be moved, be stirred

emolumento emolument, fee

emotivo emotional

empacador *m* packer

empacar to pack (up), wrap up; bale; ~**se** to be stubborn; get angry

empachado clogged; stuffed; suffering from indigestion; embarrassed; bashful

empachar to stuff, cram; cause indigestion; ~**se** to get upset; get clogged; be stuffed; suffer indigestion; get embarrassed

empacho indigestion; bashfulness; **no tener** ~ **en** to have no objection to; feel free to

empachoso embarrassing, bashful; (food) rich; annoying

empalagar to cloy; pall, become distasteful; disgust; annoy; sicken

empalagoso cloying; sickeningly sweet; boring, wearisome; smarmy

empalar to impale

empalizada stockade, palisade, fence

empalmar to splice; join; fit together; ~ **con** to join, make a junction with; (of trains) to connect; ~**se** *sl* to have an erection

empalme *m* junction; joint, connection; splice

empanadilla small pie, pasty

empanada pie; swindle, fraud; ~ **de**

carne/cerdo meat/pork pie

empanar to bake in a pie; coat in bread-crumbs; cover with bread/batter

empañar to blur; diminish; tarnish

empapada *n* drenching, soaking

empapado drenched, soaked

empapar to drench, soak, saturate; **~se** to get soaked/drenched

empapelado paper-hanging

empapelador *m* paper-hanger

empapelar to paper; wrap up in paper; *sl* charge, indict; *mot* give a parking ticket to; *mil* put on a charge

empaque *m* packing; looks, appearance, air; airs, importance

empaquetador *m* packer

empaquetadura *n* packing; *mot* gasket

empaquetar to pack; make a package; *mil sl* punish; **~se** to dress up, doll up

emparedado sandwich

emparedar to immure, wall up

emparejadura, emparejamiento matching

emparejar to even off, level up; pair off; match; catch up with; overtake

emparentado related by marriage

emparentarse become related by marriage

emparrado vine arbour

emparrillar *cul* to grill

empastar to paste; fill (a tooth); bind (books)

empaste *m* (tooth) filling; binding (of a book); *arts* impasto

empatar to tie (in a game), equalize; have an equal number of votes

empate *m* tie, draw, equal score; equal number of votes; **gol de ~** equalizing goal

empatía empathy

empavonar *metal* to blue

empecinado stubborn

empecinar to cover with pitch; **~se** to be stubborn

empedernido hardened; hardhearted; inveterate

empedernir to harden, toughen; **~se** to become hardened

empedrado *n* stone pavement; *adj* paved

empedrar to pave (with stones)

empegado tarpaulin

empegar to coat with pitch

empeine *m* instep

empelotarse to get undressed

empellón *m* push, shove; **a empellones** by pushing; **entrar a empellones** to push one's way in

empeñar to pawn; pledge; oblige, compel; engage (an enemy); **~se en** to persist in, insist on; apply oneself; go into debt; **~se por** to plead for

empeñero pawnbroker

empeño pledge, pawn; persistence, insistence; eagerness; perseverance; **casa de ~s** pawn shop; **tener ~ en** to be eager to

empeoramiento deterioration, worsening

empeorar to impair; make worse; become worse; **~se** to grow worse

empequeñecer to diminish; make smaller; belittle

emperador *m* emperor; *zool* swordfish

emperatriz *f* empress

emperezar to delay, put off

empernar to fasten with bolts

empero however, nevertheless

empezar to begin

empicotar to pillory

empiezo beginning

empinado steep; lofty; (of people) stuck-up, hoity-toity

empinadura elevation

empinar to raise, lift; incline, bend; **~se** to stand on tiptoes; rear up; rise high; *sl* have an erection; **~ el codo** to drink, 'raise the elbow'

empiojado lousy, full of lice

empírico empirical

empirismo empiricism

emplastar to plaster; poultice; paint the face

emplasto plaster, poultice; *fam* pain in the neck

[1] **emplazamiento** placing, positioning; site; location

[2] **emplazamiento** *leg* summons

[1] **emplazar** to place; site

[2] **emplazar** *leg* to summon

empleable employable

empleado employee

empleador *m* employer

emplear to employ; use; invest, spend; **~se en** to be employed in/on; **~se a fondo en** to give the full treatment to

empleo employment, occupation, job; employ; aim; investment

emplomar to cover/line *etc* with lead

emplumar to feather; decorate with feathers; tar and feather; *sl* arrest

empobrecer to impoverish; ~**se** to become poor, become impoverished

empobrecimiento impoverishment

empolvar to sprinkle powder; cover with dust; ~**se** to get dusty; powder one's face

empollador *m* incubator

empollar to hatch; *sl* swot; *sl* make pregnant; (of bees) breed

empollón *m* swot

emponzoñamiento *n* poisoning

emponzoñador *n m* poisoner; *adj* poisonous

emponzoñar to poison

emporio emporium

emporrarse to suffer the effects of marihuana smoking

empotrar to embed, grout; build in

emprendedor *n m* entrepreneur; *adj* enterprising

emprender to undertake; set out; ~**la con uno** to pick on s.o.

empreñar to impregnate; make pregnant

empresa enterprise, project, undertaking; device, symbol; company, management

empresarial managerial

empresario manager; impresario; promoter; entrepreneur

empréstito loan; ~ **público** government loan

empujar to push; shove; urge

empuje *m* push; shove; impulse

empujón *m* shove, push; **a empujones** by pushing, by shoving

empuñadura hilt

empuñar to grasp, grab, clutch; seize

empurar *mil sl* to punish

emulación *f* emulation

emulador *m* emulator; rival

emular to emulate

émulo rival, competitor

emulsificante *m* emulsifier

en in(to); (up)on; at; for; ~ **adelante** henceforth, in future; ~ **cantando** immediately after singing; ~ **casa** at home; ~ **vano** in vain; **se le conoce** ~ **su hablar** he is recognizable by his speech; ~ **tren/coche** by train, car; **pensar** ~ to think about

enaguas *fpl* waist-slip, petticoat

enajenación *f*, **enajenamiento** trance; absence of mind; transfer (of property); ~ **de los sentidos** loss of consciousness; ~ **mental** mental disorder

enajenar to estrange; drive mad; deprive (of one's senses); *leg* transfer property; dispossess; ~ **el afecto de** to alienate the affection of; ~**se** to be driven mad; become estranged

enaltecer to extol, exalt

enaltecimiento exaltation

enamarillecer to turn yellow

enamoradizo easily infatuated

enamorado *n m* sweetheart, lover; *adj* in love

enamorador *adj* wooing, courting

enamorar to make love to, woo, flirt with, court; ~**se** to fall in love

enano *n* dwarf; *adj* dwarfish; tiny, little

enarbolar to hoist (a flag); raise on high; ~**se** to rear, balk

enarcar to arch; hoop (barrels); ~ **las cejas** to arch one's eyebrows

enardecer to excite, fire with passion; anger; inflame; ~**se** to become excited; become passionate; get angry

enardecimiento passion; enthusiasm

encabezado (newspaper) headline; heading

encabezamiento heading; headline; list of taxpayers; registration (of taxpayers)

encabezar to give a heading to, give a title to; head; lead; (of wines) fortify

encabritarse to rear up, rise up (on the hind legs); *naut+aer* pitch; *sl* become angry

encadenación *f*, **encadenamiento** chaining, linking

encadenar to chain; link together; fetter

encajador *m* boxer who can take a lot of punishment

encajar to thrust in, fit into, insert; take; ~**se** to squeeze into; intrude, meddle; *sp* let in goals; **no** ~ not to add up, not to make sense

encaje *m* lace; adjustment; fitting together; socket, groove; inlaid work, inlay

encajero lace-maker

encajetillar to put in a packet

encajonar to pack in a box

encaladura *n* whitewashing, lime-washing

encalar to whitewash, lime-wash

encalomar *vulg sl* to fuck; ~**se** *sl* to go into hiding

encallar *naut* to run aground; get stuck; strand

encallecer to get corns; *fig* to get hard/callous

encamado bed-ridden

encamarse to be confined to bed

encaminar to direct, guide; ~**se** to go (towards); start out (on a road), take the road to

encandilar to dazzle

encanecer to grow white-haired; turn grey

encanijarse to get thin, become emaciated

encantado charmed, bewitched, enchanted; ~ **de conocerle** pleased to make your acquaintance

encantador *n m* charmer, enchanter; *adj* charming, enchanting

encantamiento enchantment

encantar to charm, enchant; delight

encante *m* open-air auction

encanto charm, enchantment; delight

encanutar to lay pipes

encañada *geog* gorge, ravine

encañado water-pipe

encañar *bot* to stake; channel (water)

encapotado cloaked; overcast, cloudy

encapotarse to become overcast, become cloudy; cover up, put on a cloak; frown

encapricharse to take a fancy (**con** to); get a crush (**con** on); acquire a whim/fancy

encarado: bien ~ well-favoured; **mal** ~ evil-looking

encaramar to raise; elevate; extol; ~**se** to climb; climb upon; perch on

encaramiento encounter; confrontation

encarar to face; ~**se con** to face; confront

encarcelación *f*, **encarcelamiento** imprisonment

encarcelar to imprison, gaol; *bui* embed (in cement); *carp* clamp

encarecer to make dear, raise the price of; exaggerate; extol; commend highly; enhance; ~**se** to go up in price

encarecidamente earnestly

encarecimiento price/cost increase

encargado *n* manager, person in charge; ~ **de negocios** chargé d'affaires; *adj* in charge

encargar to put in charge; entrust; commission; recommend, advise; order; ~**se de** to take charge of

encargo recommendation, advice; charge; order; commission; job; errand; assignment; **hecho de** ~ bespoke, made to order

encariñamiento affection, fondness, attachment

encariñar to arouse love; awake affection; ~**se (con)** to become fond (of); get attached to

encarnación *f* incarnation; *arts* flesh colour

encarnadino incarnadine

encarnado red; flesh-coloured; purple

encarnadura: buena ~ *med* flesh that heals quickly

encarnar to incarnate, embody; bait (a fish-hook); *arts* colour (a sculpture)

encarnecer to put on weight, grow fat

encarnizado bloody; hard-fought, fiercely contended; cruel, pitiless

encarnizamiento rage; cruelty

encarnizar to infuriate, enrage; ~**se** to get furious/enraged

encartar to outlaw, ban; *leg* summon

encasillar to pigeonhole; classify, sort out

encastar to improve by cross-breeding

encastillado haughty

encastillador *m* spiderman, scaffolder

encastillar to fortify with castles; ~**se** to stick to one's guns, nail one's colours to the mast

encastrar *eng* (of cog-wheels) to engage

encauchar to coat with rubber

encavarse (of animals) to go to earth

encebollado beef and onion stew

encefálico encephalic

encéfalo encephalon

encencerrado wearing a cow-bell

encendedor *n m* (cigarette-)lighter; *adj* incendiary

encender to light; switch on; ignite; ~ **la luz** to put on the light; ~**se** to light up; turn red

encendido *n mot* ignition; *adj* crimson; inflamed; ardent

encerado *n* blackboard; oilcloth; wax

coating; *adj* waxed; wax-coloured; **papel** ~ wax paper

encerar to wax; *bui* thicken (lime); *agri* (of grass) turn yellow

encerramiento enclosure; locking up; prison

encerrar to enclose; lock up; contain; ~**se** to shut oneself up; go into seclusion; lock oneself in

encespedar to turf, lay a lawn

encía *f anat* gum

encíclica *eccles* encyclical

enciclopedia encyclopaedia

enciclopédico encyclopaedic

enciclopedista *m+f* encyclopaedist

encierro confinement; retreat; prison; *pol* sit-in, occupation (as a protest)

encima above, over(head), on top; besides, in addition; ~ **de** on the top of; **estar siempre** ~ **de uno** to always watching s.o.; **mirar por** ~ **del hombro** to look askance; **poner las manos** ~ **a** to lay hands on; **por** ~ **de** over

encina evergreen oak, holm oak, ilex

encinal *m*, **encinar** *m* grove of evergreen oaks

encinta pregnant

encintado kerb

enclaustrar to cloister; shut up in a convent/monastery

enclavar to nail, fasten; hoodwink

enclenque *n m+f* sickly person, weakling; *adj* sickly, ailing

encobijar to shelter

encoger to shrink, shrivel; shorten, contract; ~**se** to shrink; shrivel; ~**se de hombros** to shrug one's shoulders

encogido shrunk, shrivelled; bent; bashful

encogimiento shrinking; timidity; ~ **de hombros** shrug, shrugging of shoulders

encolar to glue, gum

encolerizar to anger; ~**se** to get angry

encomendable commendable

encomendar to charge, advise; entrust; recommend, commend; ~**se** to entrust oneself to; send regards; pray (to), commend oneself to (God)

encomiador *n m* praiser; *adj* praising

encomiar to extol, praise

encomienda charge, commission; recommendation; parcel-post; package

encomio praise

encompadrar to become great friends

enconamiento inflammation; festering

enconar to inflame; irritate; ~**se** to become inflamed; get irritated

enconcharse to retire into one's shell

encono rancour, animosity, ill-will; festering; soreness

enconoso rancorous; resentful; inflaming

encontrado opposite; opposing; contrary; **estar** ~**s** to be at loggerheads

encontrar to encounter, meet; find; ~**se** to meet; coincide; be found, be situated; collide; conflict; ~**se con** to come across, meet, *US* meet up with

encontrón *m* bump, collision

encoñarse *sl vulg* to fall in love

encorchar to cork; (of bees) hive

encordar *mus* to string (an instrument)

encordelar to tie with string

encornadura set of horns/antlers

encornudar to cuckold

encorralar to corral, round up; enclose

encortinar to fit/hang curtains

encorvadura curvature; crookedness

encorvar to curve, bend; ~**se** to bend down, stoop

encostrar *bui* to roughcast; ~**se** to become crusty

encrespador *m* curling-tongs

encrespadura *n* curling

encrespamiento curling; (of hair) standing on end; (of the sea) roughness

encrespar to curl; ruffle; irritate; ~**se** to curl; get ruffled; become involved (in an affair); (of the sea) get rough

encrestado *orni* having a comb/crest; haughty

encrestarse *orni* to raise the crest/comb; become haughty

encrucijada crossroads, *US* street intersection; ambush

encuadernación *f* binding (of books)

encuadernador *m* bookbinder

encuadernar to bind (books)

encuadrar to enclose (in a frame); encompass; fit (into)

encubierta deceit; swindle

encubierto covered

encubridor *n m* concealer; procurer; pimp; *adj* hiding, concealing

encubrimiento hiding; *leg* sheltering (a criminal)

encubrir to cover; hide; hush up

encuentro encounter, meeting; find, finding; conflict; *sp* bout, match; collision; **salir al ~** to go out to meet

encuerado naked

encuerar to strip off s.o.'s clothes; skin; fleece; **~se** to strip, get undressed

encuesta search, inquiry, investigation; survey; **~ de opinión (pública)** (public) opinion poll

encumbrado elevated; exalted; high, lofty

encumbramiento elevation; exaltation; height; eminence

encumbrar to elevate; exalt, extol; **~se** to climb to the top, rise up, soar; become haughty

encurtidos *mpl* pickles

encurtir to pickle

enchapar veneer; *metal* cover with metal plates

enchilada pancake of chilli and maize

enchilado dish of seafood and chilli

enchilar to season with chilli

enchironar *sl* to put in clink/in the nick

enchufado person appointed to a post through influence

enchufar to plug in; obtain a post for a protégé; **~se** to obtain a post through influence

enchufe *m* socket; electric outlet; influence

enchufismo old-boy network, 'jobs for the boys'

ende: por ~ hence, therefore

endeble weak, frail; flimsy

endeblez *f* weakness, frailty; flimsiness

endécada *m* period of eleven years

endecha dirge

endechera paid mourner at a funeral

endechar to sing mournful songs; **~se** to grieve

endehesar to put out to graze

endémico endemic

endemoniado possessed (by the devil); devilish; mischievous

endemoniar to possess with a devil; infuriate

endentado serrated

endentar to indent; make notches in

enderezado suitable; straight

enderezador *n m* righter; **~ de agravios** redresser of wrongs; **~ de problemas** trouble-shooter

enderezar to straighten; correct; set upright; **~se** to go straight to; straighten up; sit up straight

endeudarse to get into debt

endevotado pious; devoted

endiablado devilish; possessed by the devil; ugly; wicked; mischievous

endiablar to possess with a devil; pervert; **~se** to become angry

endibia *bot* endive

endiosar to deify

endomingado dressed up in one's Sunday best

endorsar *see* endosar

endosante *m* endorser

endosar to endorse

endosatario endorsee

endose *m*, **endoso** endorsement

endulzura, endulzamiento *n* sweetening

endulzar to sweeten, soften; *arts* tone down

endurador *n m* miser; *adj* miserly

endurecer to harden; **~se** to get hardened; become cruel

endurecimiento hardening; hardheartedness

ene *f* letter n; *math* x (unknown quantity); **ser de ~** to be the logical consequence

enebro *bot* juniper

eneldo *bot* dill

enemigo *n* enemy; adversary; *adj* enemy; hostile; unfriendly; **ser ~ de una cosa** to dislike a thing

enemistad *f* enmity; hatred

enemistar to cause enmity between; **~se con** to become an enemy of, fall out with

energía energy; **~ nuclear** nuclear energy

enérgico energetic

enero January; **cuesta de ~** *comm* post-Christmas slump

enervación *f* enervation

enervador enervating

enervar to enervate, weaken

enésimo *math* nth

enfadadizo easily angered

enfadar to anger; annoy; **~se** to get angry

enfado anger; disgust; annoyance

enfadoso annoying

enfardar to bale, pack

énfasis *m* emphasis

enfático emphatic

enfebrecido feverish

enfermar to become ill; make ill; ~se to fall ill

enfermedad *f* sickness, illness, disease; ~ del sueño sleeping sickness

enfermería infirmary

enfermera nurse

enfermero male nurse

enfermizo sickly; unhealthy

enfermo *n* patient; *adj* sick, ill; feeble

enfermucho a bit off-colour

enfilar to line up; enfilade

enflaquecerse to become thin; weaken; lose weight

enflaquecimiento emaciation; loss of weight

enfocar to focus on; tackle; approach

enfoque *m* focusing; approach to a problem

enfrascar to bottle; ~se to get involved or absorbed

enfrenar to bridle; brake, put the brake on; check, curb

enfrentamiento confrontation; ~ de las generaciones generation gap

enfrentar to confront, put face to face; ~se con to confront, face; meet face to face

enfrente in front, opposite; ~ de in front of, opposite; la casa de ~ the house across the street

enfriamiento cooling; refrigeration; *med* chill, cold

enfriar to cool, chill; ~se to cool, cool off; get chilled; get a cold

enfrontar to confront

enfundar to sheathe

enfurecer to infuriate, enrage; ~se to rage; get furious; (sea) get rough

enfurecimiento fury, rage

engaitar to wheedle; trick

engalanar to adorn, decorate; ~se to dress up

enganchamiento hooking, coupling; *mil* enlistment

enganchado *sl* hooked (on drugs)

enganchar to hitch; hook; ensnare; ~se to engage, interlock; get hooked; enlist in the army

enganche *m* hooking; coupling; enlistment; *mil* draft (into the army); banderín *m* de ~ recruiting-office

engañabobos *m sing* + *pl* trap; trick

engañadizo easily tricked

engañador *n m* deceiver; *adj* deceitful, deceiving

engañapastores *m sing* + *pl orni* nightjar

engañar to deceive; mislead; ~se to deceive oneself; be mistaken, make a mistake; *sl* be maritally unfaithful; ~ la vista to be deceptive

engaño deceit, trick, fraud; mistake, misunderstanding

engañoso deceitful; tricky; misleading

engarrafar *fam* to snatch

engastar to mount, set (jewels)

engaste *m* setting (for a gem)

engatusador *n m* coaxer, wheedler; *adj* coaxing, wheedling

engatusar to coax, wheedle

engendrar to engender, beget, produce; cause

engendro foetus; *fig* bad piece of work

englobar to include

engolfarse to get deep (into); go deeply (into); become absorbed; become lost in thought

engomar to gum, glue; size

engorar to addle

engordar to fatten; ~se get fat, *fam* become rich

engorro tiresome business, bore

engorroso cumbersome; bothersome

engoznar to hinge

Engracia Grace

engranaje *m* gear, gears

engranar to gear; throw in gear, *US* mesh gears

engrandecer to aggrandize, enlarge; make greater; magnify; exalt

engrandecimiento aggrandizement

engrasación *f* oiling, greasing, lubrication

engrasador *m* oiler, greaser

engrasar to oil, lubricate, grease; stain with grease; manure, fertilize; dress (cloth); *sl* bribe

engrase *m* greasing, lubrication, oiling; *sl* bribe

engreído conceited, vain

engreimiento conceit, vanity

engreír to make vain/conceited; ~se to get conceited, puff o.s. up

engrillar to shackle

engringarse to adopt foreign ways

engrosar, engruesar to enlarge; thicken; fatten; *vi* to get fat

engrudo paste

enguirlandar to garland

engullir to gobble up, devour; gorge

engurrio blues, melancholy

enhebrar to thread (a needle); string (beads)

enhiesto straight, upright, erect

enhilar to thread; to put in line/in order

enhorabuena *n* congratulations; *adv* safely; well and good; all right; with much pleasure

enigmático enigmatic

enjabonadura soaping, lathering

enjabonar to soap; soft-soap, flatter; *fam* reprimand

enjaezar to harness

enjalbegadura whitewashing

enjalbegar to whitewash

enjambradera queen-bee; cell of a queen-bee

enjambre *m* swarm (of bees); crowd

enjarciadura *naut* rigging

enjarciar *naut* to rig

enjaular to cage; confine; gaol

enjertar *hort* to graft

enjerto *hort* grafting

enjuagar to rinse, rinse out

enjuague *m* mouthwash; rinse; rinsing

enjugar to dry; wipe; ~se to dry oneself

enjuiciar to indict; prosecute, bring suit against; try (a case); judge

enjuto dried; thin, skinny; **a pie** ~ without getting one's feet wet

enlabiar to coax, cajole

enlace *m* connection; link; tie, bond; marriage; *mil* runner

enladrillado brick floor; brickwork

enladrillador *m* bricklayer

enladrilladura brickwork

enladrillar to pave with bricks

enlatado canned; **música enlatada** canned music, muzak

enlatar to can, tin

enlazador *n m* uniter; binder; *adj* uniting; binding

enlazadura *n* uniting, binding, coupling

enlazar to connect; join, bind, tie; rope; link; ~se to join; marry; become related (through marriage)

enlodar to cover with mud; smear, sully, soil, dirty; ~se to get in the mud; get muddy

enloquecedor maddening

enloquecer to make crazy; drive mad; lose one's mind; ~se become mad

enloquecimiento madness

enlosado flagstone pavement

enlosar to pave (with flagstones)

enlucir *bui* plaster

enlustrecer to clean; polish

enlutarse to go into mourning

enmaderar *carp* to board/plank; lay floor-boards

enmadrarse to be tied to mother's apron-strings

enmagrecerse to lose weight, grow lean

enmalletado *naut* (of ropes) fouled

enmantar to cover with a blanket; ~se to grow sad

enmantecar to butter

enmarañar to entangle; snarl; confuse, mix up

enmarcar to frame

enmascarar to mask; ~se to put on a mask; masquerade

enmasillar *carp* to apply putty to

enmendación amendment

enmendar to amend, correct; rectify, compensate; *leg* revise (sentence); ~se to reform, mend one's ways

enmienda correction; amendment; reform; indemnity, compensation; **no tiene** ~ there's no hope; ~s fertilizer

enmohecer to rust; mould; ~se to rust, become rusty

enmohecido rusty; mouldy

enmohecimiento rustiness; mouldiness

enmudecer to silence; remain silent; lose one's voice; become dumb

ennegrecer to blacken; darken; ~se to become dark; get cloudy

ennegrecimiento darkening

ennoblecedor *adj* ennobling

ennoblecer to ennoble, dignify

ennoblecimiento ennoblement

enojadizo irritable, ill-tempered

enojado angry

enojar to make angry, anger; vex; annoy; ~se to get angry

enojo anger, annoyance

enojoso annoying, vexatious, tiresome

enorgullecer to fill with pride; ~se to swell with pride; be proud (**de** of)

enorgullecimiento pride

enorme enormous; huge; vast

enormidad *f* outrage; great number, large quantity; nonsense; enormity

..aizar to take root

enramada arbour, bower; (shady) grove

enrarecer to rarefy, thin; ~se to become rarefied; become scarce

enrarecimiento rarity, thinness (of the air)

enredadera n bot climber; adj climbing, twining; ~ **de campo** bindweed

enredador n m troublemaker; adj entangling

enredar to entangle, tangle up; snare; snarl; mess up, mix up; wind (on a spool); raise a rumpus; ~se to get tangled up, mixed up; get trapped; ~se con to have an affair with, get involved with (a woman); ~se en to become involved in

enredista m+f liar; talebearer

enredo tangle; confusion; intrigue; plot; ~s odds and ends

enredoso tangled up

enrejado trellis; grating; railing

enrejar to fence with railings

enrevesado turned around; intricate, complicated; unruly

Enrique Henry

enriquecedor wealth-producing

enriquecer to enrich; ~se to become rich

enriquecimiento enrichment

Enriqueta Henrietta

enrobustecer to strengthen; ~se to become stronger

enrocar (chess) to castle

enrojecer to redden; vi ~se to blush; become red

enrojecido red, reddened; fig blushing

enrollar to roll (up); coil; **nada me enrolló** sl nothing turned me on; ~se to become deeply involved

enromar to blunt

enronquecer to make hoarse; ~se to become hoarse

enroscar to twist; coil; ~se to coil; curl up

ensacar to put in a sack/bag

ensaimada custard tart made with flaky pastry

ensalada salad; medley

ensaladera salad-bowl

ensaladilla rusa Russian salad

ensalmador m bone-setter; quack

ensalmar to cure by magic; set bones

ensalmista m+f charlatan, quack

ensalmo charm; spell

ensamblador m joiner

ensambladura joinery

ensamblaje m joining

ensamblar to join, assemble

ensanchar to widen, enlarge; broaden; let out (a dress); ~se to expand; puff up

ensanche m widening, expansion; extension; urban expansion

ensangrentar to stain with blood; ~se to be covered with blood; get red (with anger)

ensartar to string; thread; link; skewer; rattle off (tales, stories)

ensayador m assayer; theat rehearser

ensayar to try, attempt; test; rehearse; ~se to practise; train oneself

ensaye m assay

ensayista m+f essayist

ensayo trail, attempt; rehearsal; test; experiment; essay

ensenada (small) bay, cove

enseñanza teaching; tuition; ~ **primaria/segundaria/superior** primary/secondary/higher education

enseñar to show; teach; instruct, train; point out

enseres mpl household goods; utensils; implements; equipment

ensillar to saddle

ensimismarse to become absorbed (in thought); become conceited

ensoberbecer to make proud; ~se to puff up with pride; become haughty; (sea) get rough, become choppy

ensoberbecimiento excessive pride

ensoñar to daydream

ensordecedor deafening

ensordecer to deafen; become deaf

ensordecimiento deafness

ensortijar to curl; ring the nose of (an animal); ~se to curl

ensuciamiento soiling, dirtying

ensuciar to dirty, soil; stain; ~se to get dirty; soil oneself

ensueño illusion, dream, day-dream; **de** ~ adj dream, ideal

entablación f flooring; boarding; eccles church register

entablado board/parquet floor; platform, stage

entabladura planking; flooring

entablar to board (up); plank; splint; ~

una conversación to start a conversation; ~ **un pleito** to bring a lawsuit

entable *m* position of chessmen on the board

entablillar to put in a splint

entalegar *sl* to put in gaol

entalingar *naut* to secure (a cable)

entalladura sculpture

entallar to carve; sculpture; (of clothing) fit

entapizar to upholster; cover with tapestry

entarimado parquet floor(ing)

entarimar to floor with parquet

ente *m* entity; being; *fam* fellow, bloke

entecado, enteco sickly, ailing; weak

entenada stepdaughter

entenado stepson

entender to understand; realize; ~ **de** to know about, be familiar with, be an expert in; ~ **en** to take care of, deal with; ~**se con** to have an understanding with, have dealings with; ~**se** to be understood, be meant, understand each other; ~**se en un asunto** to be in charge of a matter

entenderas *fpl* comprehension; **tener buenas** ~ to be a smart fellow

entendedor *m* one who understands

entendido understood; wise; prudent; agreed; well-informed; able, skilful

entendimiento understanding; intellect; mind

enterado informed; aware; **no darse por** ~ to pretend not to understand; not to take the hint; **ser** ~ **en** to be skilled in

enterar to inform, acquaint; report; ~**se** to know, learn, find out; understand; ~**se de** to find out about; hear of; **¡entérate!** pay attention!

entereza entirety; integrity; fortitude; serenity; presence of mind; firmness; perfection

entérico *med* enteric

enterezo whole

enternecedor touching, moving, pitiful

enternecer to soften, touch, stir, move; ~**se** to become tender; be touched, be moved

enternecimiento pity, compassion

entero *n math* integer, whole number; *adj* entire, whole; just, right; firm; **caballo** ~ stallion; **por** ~ fully, wholly

enterrador *m* grave-digger; *ent* sexton beetle

enterramiento burial

enterrar to bury; *fig* outlive; ~**se en vida** to avoid company

entibar *min* to shore up

entibo *min* pit-prop

entibiar to make lukewarm; ~**se** to become lukewarm

entidad *f* entity; unit, group, organization; ~ **comercial** business concern/enterprise; **de** ~ of value/importance

entierro burial; funeral; funeral procession

entintar to ink, dye; *arts* ink in

entoldado tent; group of tents; awning

entoldar to cover with an awning; ~**se** to swell with pride; *meteor* become overcast/cloudy

entomología entomology

entomológico entomological

entomólogo entomologist

entonación *f* intonation

entonado vain; haughty; in tune

entonador *m* organ-blower

entonar to sing in tune; be in tune; harmonize; strike up a tune; intone; (colours) harmonize, blend; ~**se** to put on airs; recover

entonatorio *eccles* book of sacred music

entonces then; at that time; **desde** ~ from then on; **hasta** ~ until then; **por aquel** ~ in those (far off) days; **pues** ~ well then

entono intoning, singing

entornar to half-open; tilt; leave ajar

entornillar to screw

entorno environment, surroundings

entorpecer to stupefy; benumb; delay, obstruct; thwart, frustrate

entorpecimiento numbness; dullness, sluggishness; delay; obstruction

entortar to make crooked; bend

entrada entrance, access; opening; gate; drive, avenue; attendance (at a function); *comm* entry; *comm* takings, cash receipts; *cul* starters, entrée; *theat+cin* admission charge; *theat +cin* ticket; *sp* challenge, tackle; ~ **de pavana** foolish remark; ~**s** income; ~**s de la frente** receding hair-line; **dar** ~ **a** to allow in; **de** ~ at the outset; **de primera** ~ in the first rush of enthusiasm; **derechos de** ~ import duty; **se**

prohibe la ~ no admission

entramado *carp* framework

entramar *carp* to make a framework for

entrampar to trap, ensnare; trick; burden with debts; ~**se** to get trapped, become entangled; run into debt

entrante entering; incoming; **el año** ~ next year

entraña entrail; innermost recess; heart; disposition, temper; ~**s** entrails, innards; **dar hasta las** ~**s** *fig* to shed one's lifeblood; **de buenas/malas** ~**s** good/evil-hearted; **echar las** ~**s** to vomit violently; **hijo de mis** ~**s** child of my heart; **no tener** ~**s** to be cruel, not to have a heart; **sacar las** ~**s** to remove everything, strip down

entrañable deep; intimate

entrañar to entail; imply

entrar *vt* to take in, bring in; get at; *vi* to get into; enter; come in(to); *naut* overtake; ~**le a uno en razón** to get s.o. to see reason; ~ **bien** to taste good, fit correctly; ~ **como Pedro por su casa** to walk in as if owning the place; ~ **en/a/por** to go in(to), enter; start; enter upon; ~ **en años** to be getting on in years; ~ **en la clase de los caballeros** to be counted as a gentleman; **aquel tipo no me entra** I can't abide that chap; **de estos entran pocos en docena** you don't find many as good as these; **en esto no entro ni salgo** this is no business of mine; **hasta bien entrada la noche** well into the night; **los zapatos no le entran** the shoes do not fit him; **tú entras ahora** now it's your turn; ~**se** to enter forcibly; slip in, sneak in

entre between; among; ~ **tanto** meanwhile; **dijo** ~ **sí** he said to himself

entreabrir to half-open, open halfway

entreacto interval, *US* intermission; intermezzo; small cigar

entrecano greyish; going grey

entrecejo space between the eyebrows; **fruncir el** ~ to wrinkle one's brow

entreclaro lightish

entrecoger to catch hold of; corner; defeat in argument

entrecoro chancel

entrecortado hesitating, (speech) faltering; breathless, choking; interrupted

entrecortar to cut halfway through; interrupt

entrecruzar to cross; interlace

entrecubiertas *naut* between decks

entrechocar to collide

entredicho prohibition, interdiction

entredoble of average thickness

entrega delivery; surrender; instalment (of a book); **novela por** ~**s** serial novel

entregador *n m* deliverer; *adj* delivering

entregar to deliver, hand over; give; ~**se** to surrender, submit, give up; devote oneself (to); abandon oneself (to); give in to; ~**la** to kick the bucket; **a** ~ to be called for

entreguismo appeasement

entrelazar to interlace; weave together

entrelistado striped; variegated

entremedias in between; **de** ~ among; between

entremés *m theat* one-act farce; **entremeses** *cul* hors-d'œuvres

entremesero hors-d'œuvres dish

entremesista *m + f* writer of **entremeses**

entremeter to insert; place between; ~**se** to meddle, intrude

entremetido *n* meddler; intruder; *adj* meddlesome

entremetimiento intrusion, meddling

entremezcladura intermixture

entremezclar to intermix, intermingle

entremorir to die away slowly

entrenador *m* trainer, coach

entrenamiento training; drill; coaching

entrenar to train, drill; coach; ~**se** to train, get o.s. fit

entreoír to half hear

entrepaño shelf; panel; *archi* space between pilasters

entrepierna *anat* inner part of thigh; gusset in crotch of trousers *etc*

entreponer to interpose

entrepuente *m naut* between-decks

entresacar to pick out, select; cull; *hort* thin (out); prune

entresuelo mezzanine

entresurco *agri* space between furrows

entretallar to carve in bas-relief; ~**se** to interlock

entretanto meanwhile

entretecho attic, loft

entretejer to interweave; intertwine

entretelar (sewing) to interline

entretenedor *n m* entertainer; *adj* entertaining

entretener to delay, detain; amuse, entertain; ~ **el tiempo** while away the time; ~**se** to amuse o.s., be detained/delayed; pass the time

entretenida kept woman

entretenido amusing, entertaining

entretenimiento entertainment; pastime; delay

entrever to glimpse, half-see, see vaguely; make out

entreverar to intermingle, intermix

entrevía (railway) gauge

entrevista interview; date, appointment

entrevistar to interview; ~**se con** to have an interview with

entristecer to sadden, make sad; ~**se** to become sad, become depressed

entristecimiento sadness

entrometer(se) *see* **entremeter(se)**

entrometido *see* **entremetido**

entrometimiento *see* **entremetimiento**

entronar to enthrone

entronerar (billiards) to pocket

entronización *f* enthronement

entronizar *see* **entronar**

entronque *m* relationship, family connection

entropía entropy

entruchado conspiracy, plot; dirty business

entruchar to ambush

entruchón *m* plotter, conspirator

entullecer to stop, check

entumecer to make numb; ~**se** to get numb; (sea) surge; swell

entumecimiento numbness, torpor

entumirse to get numb

entupir to choke; obstruct

enturbiar to make muddy; muddle; disturb; obscure; ~**se** to get muddy; get muddled

entusiasmar to excite, fill with enthusiasm; delight; ~**se** to become enthusiastic; get excited

entusiasmo enthusiasm; excitement

entusiasta *n m+f* enthusiast; *adj* enthusiastic

entusiástico enthusiastic

enumeración *f* enumeration, counting; listing

enumerar to enumerate, count; list

enunciación *f* statement; enunciation

enunciado terms of reference

enunciar to express, state, declare; enunciate

envainar to sheathe

envalentonar to encourage; ~**se** to become arrogant; get brave

envalijar to pack in a portmanteau/suitcase

envanecer to make vain; ~**se** to become vain

envanecimiento arrogance; conceit

envasar to pack, put in a container; bottle; can

envase *m* packaging, bottling, canning; jar, bottle, can

envejecer to age, make old; *vi* ~**se** to grow old; become out-of-date

envejecido aged; old(-looking)

envejecimiento process of ageing

envenenador *n m* poisoner; *adj* poisonous

envenenamiento poisoning

envenenar to poison; infect

enverdecer to turn green

envergadura spread (of a bird's wings); breadth (of sails); *aer* range; scope

envés *m* back, wrong side

envestidura investiture

envestir to invest

enviado envoy

enviar to send; ~ **a alguien por algo** to send s.o. for s.t.; ~ **a uno a paseo** to send s.o. packing, send s.o. about his business

enviciamiento corruption, depravity

enviciar to corrupt, deprave; spoil; ~**se con** to become addicted to

envidador *m* (cards) challenger, higher bidder

envidar (cards) to bid; bet

envidia envy

envidiable enviable, desirable

envidiar to envy

envidioso *n* envious person; *adj* envious, jealous

envilecer to debase, malign, degrade; ~**se** to degrade oneself; lower oneself

envilecedor degrading

envilecimiento degradation, debasement

envinagrar to add vinegar to

envinar to add wine to

envío remittance; shipment; act of sending; *lit* dedication

envite *m* (cards) bid, stake; offer

enviudar to be left a widow/widower

envoltorio bundle, package

envoltura wrapping, wrapper, cover; swaddling-clothes

envolvedor *n m* packer; *adj* wrapping, covering

envolvente *m* wrapping

envolver to involve, entangle; wrap (up); wind (wool *etc*); surround; *mil* outflank; ~**se** to become involved in, become entangled

envuelto (en) involved, entangled; wrapped up (in)

enyerbarse to become overgrown with grass; to get poisoned

enyesar to plaster; *med* put in a plaster cast

enzainarse to look askance; turn traitor

enzalamar to set dogs on; incite

enzamarrado sheepskin jacket

enzarzar to spread discord; ~**se** to get entangled in brambles *etc*; get involved in a complicated matter/argument; squabble

enzima *chem* enzyme

eñe *f* letter ñ

epactilla *eccles* devotional calendar

épica *n lit* epic

epicentro epicentre

épico *adj* epic

epicúreo epicure

epidemia *n* epidemic

epidémico *adj* epidemic

epidiascopio epidiascope

epifanía Epiphany, Twelfth Night

epiglotis *f* epiglottis

epigrama *m* epigram

epilepsia epilepsy

epiléptico epileptic

epilogar to sum up, recap

epílogo epilogue

episcopado bishopric; episcopate

episódico episodic

episodio episode

epístola epistle; letter

epitafio epitaph

epíteto epithet

epitimo *bot* lesser dodder

epitomar to epitomize

época epoch; time; age; hacer ~ to be of great importance

epopeya epic poem

epsomita Epsom salts

equidad *f* equity, justice, fairness

equidistancia equidistance

equidistante equidistant, equally distant; halfway, midway

equilátero equilateral

equilibrar to balance, poise

equilibrio equilibrium, balance; poise

equinoccio equinox

equipaje *m* baggage, luggage; equipment, outfit; crew

equipar to equip, fit out; man, provision (a ship)

equiparar to match, compare

equipo equipment, equipping; outfit; crew; team; gear; ~ **de música** music centre; ~ **de novia** trousseau

equipolente equivalent

equis *f* letter x; **estar hecho un** ~ to be legless (helplessly drunk)

equitación *f* horsemanship; horse-riding

equitativo fair, just

equivalencia equivalence

equivalente equivalent

equivaler (a) to be equivalent (to), be equal

equivocación *f* error, mistake

equivocar to mistake; ~**se** to be mistaken; make a mistake; ~**se de ...** to go to the wrong ...

equívoco *n* pun, play on words; misunderstanding; *adj* equivocal, ambiguous, vague

era era, age; threshing floor

erario public treasury

ere *f* letter r

erección *f* erection; establishment

eremita *m* hermit; recluse

eremítico isolated, solitary

erguir to erect, set upright; lift (the head); ~**se** to sit up, stand erect; become haughty

erguimiento erectness

erial *n m* uncultivated land; *adj* untilled; unploughed

erica *bot* heather

erigir to erect, build; found

eringe *f bot* sea-holly

erizado bristly, prickly; ~ **de** bristling with

erizar to set on end; bristle; ~**se** to bristle; (hair) stand on end

erizo hedgehog; thistle; irritable person; ~ **de mar** sea urchin

erizón *m* thistle

ermita hermitage

ermitaño hermit

erosión f erosion

erosionar to erode

erótico erotic

erotismo eroticism

erotizar to make erotic; give an erotic appearance to

erotomanía erotomania

erotómano erotomaniac

errabundo aimless; wandering

erradizo given to wandering

errado n (billiards) miscue; adj mistaken, erroneous

errante errant; roving, wandering

errar to err, make mistakes; miss (one's aim); take the wrong road, wander; ~ y porfiar to persist in making the same mistakes

errata misprint, printer's error; fe de ~s errata

errático erratic

erre f letter rr; ~ que ~ pig-headedly

erróneo erroneous, mistaken, wrong, incorrect

error m error, fault, mistake

ertzaina autonomous Basque police force; m member of that force

eructar to belch

eructo belch

erudición f erudition, learning

erudito n scholar; adj erudite, scholarly, learned; ~ a la violeta superficially learned

eruginoso rusty

erupción f eruption; outburst; rash

eruptivo eruptive

esa, ésa, esas, ésas fem form of ese, ése, esos, ésos

esbatimentar arts to shade

esbatimento arts shading

esbeltez f slenderness

esbelto slender

esbozar to sketch, outline; make a rough draft

esbozo sketch, outline; rough draft

escabechar to pickle; fam fail (an examination)

escabeche m pickle; pickled fish

escabel m stool, footstool

escabiosa bot scabious

escabioso med scabious

escabrosidad f roughness, unevenness; harshness; crudeness; coarse/im-

proper word

escabroso rough; rugged; scabrous, indecent, risqué

escabullamiento evasion

escabullirse to slip away; slip through; scurry

escacharrar to ruin, destroy

escafandra diving-suit; diving-helmet

escafandrismo skin-diving

escafandro wet-suit

escala ladder; scale; naut port of call; naut stay in port; stopover; ~ de cuerda/viento rope-ladder; hacer ~ en to stop over at, call at

escalada escalade; escalation

escalador n m climber; social climber; cat-burglar; adj climbing, scaling

escalafón m army register, army-list, roll

escalamera naut rowlock, US oarlock

escalamiento climbing, scaling

escálamo see escalamera

escalar to climb, scale; escalate; be a social climber

escaldada woman of ill-repute

escaldado cautious, wary; scalded

escaldadura scald

escaldar to scald; make red-hot; ~se to get scalded

escaleno geom scalene

escalera stairs, staircase; ladder; snakes and ladders; ~ mecánica escalator, moving staircase

escalerilla short ladder; run (at cards); steps

escaleta mot jack

escalfar cul to poach

escalmo see escalamera

escalofriante chilling; frightening

escalofriarse to get chilled, catch a chill

escalofrío chill; ~s feverish cold

escalón m step (of ladder etc)

escalonar to terrace; space out; ~se to rise in terraces

escalpar to scalp

escalpelo scalpel

escama (fish-)scale; suspicion

escamar to scale (fish); ~se to smell a rat

escamoso scaly; suspicious

escamoteador m conjuror; swindler

escamotear to snatch away, whisk out of sight; conceal by sleight of hand; skip

escampar to stop raining

escamujar hort to prune

escandalizar to scandalize, shock; ~se

to be shocked

escándalo scandal; bad example

escandaloso scandalous, shocking

Escandinavia Scandinavia

escandinavo Scandinavian

escandir *lit* to scan

escáner *m med* scanner

escansión *f lit* scansion

escaño seat (in parliament); bench

escañuelo footstool

escapada escape, flight; **en una** ~ in a moment, in a jiffy

escapar to escape, flee, avoid; ~**se** to run away, escape; slip out; slip away; **no se me escapa ninguno** I never miss one

escaparate *m* shop window; glass case/cabinet/cupboard

escaparatista *m+f* window-dresser

escapatoria escape; loophole; excuse; escapade, prank

escape *m* escape; vent, outlet; exhaust; **a** ~ rapidly, at full speed; hastily, in a hurry

escapismo escapism

escapo *bot* stem, stalk

escaque *m* square of chessboard

escaqueado checkered

escarabajo beetle

escaramucear to skirmish

escaramujo *bot* hip; dog-rose

escaramuza skirmish

escaramuzador *m* skirmisher

escaramuzar to skirmish

escarapela rosette; cockade

escarbar to scrape, scratch; dig out; pry into, research

escarbo scraping, scratching

escarcha frost

escarchado *n bot* ice-plant; *cul* frosting; *adj* frosted; **frutas escarchadas** glacé fruits

escarchar to frost, freeze; *cul* ice

escarda *hort* hoe

escardar to hoe, weed

escarificador *m agri* harrow

escarlata scarlet; scarlet fever; scarlet cloth

escarlatina scarlet fever

escarmentar to learn from experience; profit by an example; profit by one's misfortunes/punishment; ~ **en cabeza ajena** to profit by another's mistake or misfortune

escarmiento lesson, example, warning; punishment

escarnecer to jeer, insult, mock

escarnio jeer, scoffing remark

escarola endive

escarpa steep slope, bluff, cliff; scarp

escarpado steep; rugged

escarpia hook

escasear to be scarce; grow less, become scarce; stint

escasez *f* scarcity, lack, shortage; scantiness

escaso scarce, limited; scant; scanty; stingy

escatimar to stint, skimp; curtail; be mean

escatimoso stingy, cheeseparing; cunning

escatología eschatology

escatológico eschatological

escayola plaster; *med* plaster cast

escayolar to plaster; *med* put in a plaster cast

escena scene, scenery; *theat* stage

escenario *theat* stage; **poner en** ~ to stage, present

escénico scenic

escenificación *f* stage adaptation; staging, production

escepticismo scepticism; doubt, unbelief

escéptico sceptic

esclnco *zool* skink

escintilación *f* scintillation

escirro scirrhus

escisión *f* scission, split, division

esclarecedor enlightening

esclarecer to lighten, illuminate; elucidate; make clear, explain

esclarecimiento clarification, illumination, illustration; worth, nobility

esclava female slave; bracelet

esclavitud *f* slavery

esclavizar to enslave

esclavo slave; ~ **del tabaco** slave to tobacco

esclerosis *f* sclerosis

esclusa lock (of a canal); sluice, floodgate

escoba *bot* broom; besom

escobazo blow with a broom

escobera *bot* Spanish broom

escobero broom-maker

escobilla small broom

escocedura stinging pain

escocer to sting, smart

escocés *n m* Scot; Scotsman; *adj* Scottish, Scotch, Scots

Escocia Scotland

escocimiento stinging sensation

escofina *metal* file; *carp* rasp

escofinar *metal* to file; *carp* rasp

escogedor *n m* selector; *adj* choosing

escoger to select, choose

escogimiento selection, choice

escolar *n m* scholar; student; *adj* scholastic, academic

escolástico scholastic

escoliar to gloss

escolio *n* gloss

escolta escort; convoy

escoltar to escort; convoy

escollera jetty

escollo reef; danger; obstacle

escombrar to clean up; clear out

escombrera rubbish tip; slag heap

escombro debris, rubbish; ~s rubble

escondedero hiding-place

esconder to hide, conceal; ~se to hide, go into hiding

escondidas: a ~ on the sly, under cover; jugar a las ~ to play hide-and-seek

escondite *m* hiding-place; jugar al ~ to play hide-and-seek

escondrijo hiding-place

escopeta shotgun; ~ de cañones recortados sawn-off shotgun

escopetazo gunshot; gunshot wound

escopetear to fire at

escopeteo shooting; gun-fight

escopetero gunsmith; gunner

escopetón *m* fowling-piece

escoplo chisel

escorar to shore up

escoria slag; scum; volcanic ash

escorial *m* dump, dumping place, slag-heap

escorpión *m* scorpion

escotado with plunging neckline

escote *m* low neck; convite a ~ Dutch treat; pagar a ~ to go Dutch

escotilla hatchway

escotillón *m* hatch, hatchway; trap door

escozor *m* smarting sensation, sting

escriba *m* scribe

escribano lawyer's clerk; notary; *naut* purser; ~ cerillo *orni* yellow-hammer; ~ de agua *ent* water-skater

escribiente *m* clerk, *US* office clerk

escribir to write; spell; ~ a mano to write by hand; ~ a máquina to type; ~ largo y tendido to write at great length; ~se con to maintain correspondence with; ¿cómo se escribe? how is it spelt?

escrito *n* writing; manuscript; ~ de agravios *leg* writ; por ~ in writing, in black and white; *adj* written

escritor *m* writer, author

escritorcillo hack, third-rate writer

escritorio desk; study; office; objetos de ~ stationery

escritura writing, handwriting; document; *leg* deed(s); Sagrada Escritura Holy Scripture, Holy Writ

escrofuloso scrofulous

escroto scrotum

escrupulizar to have scruples/qualms/doubts

escrúpulo scruple, doubt; ~ de monja childish qualm/scruple

escrupulosidad *f* conscientiousness

escrupuloso scrupulous; particular, exact

escrutador *n m* scrutineer, examiner; inspector/returning-officer of an election; *adj* scrutinizing, examining; peering; penetrating

escrutar to scrutinize; count votes

escrutinio scrutiny; election returns

escuadra squadron; fleet; set-square, carpenter's square; angle-iron

escuadrar to square

escuadrón *m* squadron; ~ de la muerte *pol* death-squad

escualidez *f* squalor

escuálido squalid, filthy; thin, emaciated

escualor *m see* escualidez

escucha *m mil* scout; *rad* monitor

escuchador *n m* listener; *adj* listening

escuchar to listen; heed

escudar to shield

escudero squire

escudo shield; escutcheon, coat of arms

escudriñamiento scrutiny; prying

escudriñar to scrutinize; search; pry into

escuela school; ~ normal teacher-training college

escueto plain, unadorned, bare

esculpidor *m* engraver

esculpir to sculpt, carve

escultor *m* sculptor, carver

escultura sculpture

escultural sculptural

escullador *m* dipstick

escupidera cuspidor; spittoon; chamber-pot

escupir to spit; ~ **al cielo** to curse one's fate; ~ **doblones** to be well-heeled; **se prohibe** ~ spitting prohibited

escurreplatos *m sing + pl* plate rack

escurridizo slippery

escurrir to drip; drain; trickle; wring out (clothes); ~**se** to ooze out, trickle; slip out, sneak out

esdrújulo word with stress on the antepenultimate syllable

¹ **ese, esa** *dem adj* that; **esos, esas** those; **ése, ésa** *m + f dem pron* that one; **ésos, ésas** *m + f pl* those; the former

² **ese** *f* letter s; **hacer** ~**s** to reel, stagger

esencia essence; **por** ~ essentially

esencial essential

esfera sphere; (clock) dial

esférico spherical

esferoide *m* spheroid

esfinge *f* sphinx; *m* hawk-moth

esflorecer *chem* to effloresce

esforzado strong; valiant; courageous

esforzar to give strength; encourage; ~**se** to make an effort; strive, try hard

esfuerzo effort; spirit, courage; *eng + metal* stress

esfumar to shade, tone down; ~**se** to vanish, disappear

esgrima fencing

esgrimidor *m* fencer; fencing master

esgrimir to fence; brandish; wield

eslabón *m* link (of a chain); knife sharpener

eslabonador *m* chain-maker

eslabonar to link; join; connect

eslavo *n + adj* Slav

eslinga *naut* sling

eslogan *m* slogan

eslora *naut* length (of a ship)

eslovaco *n + adj* Slovak

esloveno *n + adj* Slovene

esmaltar to enamel; varnish

esmalte *m* enamel; ~ **para las uñas** nail-varnish

esmerado *adj* painstaking, careful, conscientious

esmeralda emerald

esmerar to polish, clean; ~**se** to take great pains, use great care

esmeril *m* emery

esmerilar to grind, sand

esmero care, precision

esmoquin *m* dinner-jacket, *US* tuxedo

esnob *n m + f* snob; *adj invar* snobbish

esnobismo snobbery

eso *dem pron* that, that thing/fact; ~ **es** that's it; ¡~! that's right!; **a** ~ **de** at about (referring to time); ~ **mismo** just so

esófago oesophagus

esotérico esoteric

espabiladeras *f pl* candle-snuffers

espaciador *m* space-bar (on typewriter)

espacial *adj* space; **vuelo** ~ space-flight

espaciar to space; spread; ~**se** to enlarge upon

espacio *n* space; delay; distance; period; ~ **exterior** outer space

espaciosidad *f* spaciousness

espacioso spacious; slow

espada sword; swordsman; matador; *sl* skeleton key; ~**s** swords (Spanish card suit = spades); ~ **negra** foil; **ceñir** ~ to be a professional soldier; **de capa y** ~ (of films, books *etc*) cloak-and-dagger; **entre la** ~ **y la pared** between two stools; **sacar la** ~ **por** to stand up for; **tirar de la** ~ to draw one's sword

espadachín *m* swashbuckler; bully

espadañar *orni* to spread the tail feathers

espadista *m sl* housebreaker/burglar who uses skeleton keys

espaguetis *mpl* spaghetti

espalda *anat* back; shoulders; *mil* rearguard; backstroke; ~**s** back, back part; ~**s de molinero** broad shoulders; **a** ~**s** behind the back of; **cargado de** ~**s** round-shouldered; **dar la** ~ **a** to turn one's back on; **de** ~**s** on one's back, with one's back turned; **hacer** ~**s a** to be a bodyguard to; **tumbar de** ~**s** to flabbergast

espaldar *m* back (of chair); trellis (for climbing plants)

espaldarazo pat on the back

espaldilla shoulder-blade; back of jacket/coat

espalduudo broad-shouldered

espantable frightful

espantada stampede; sudden scare; bolt

espantadizo scaring, *US* scary; shy, timid

espantajo, espantapájaros *m sing+pl* scarecrow

espantamoscas *m sing+pl* fly-trap

espantar to frighten, scare, scare away; ~**se** to be scared, be astonished

espanto fright, terror; astonishment

espantoso frightful, terrifying; astonishing

España Spain

español *n m* Spanish language; Spaniard; *adj* Spanish

españolada typically Spanish act/behaviour

españolismo love of things Spanish

españolista *m+f* person fond of things Spanish; supporter of Español Football Club

españolizar to make Spanish; ~**se** to adopt Spanish ways

esparadrapo sticking-plaster, *US* court-plaster

esparaván *m orni* sparrow-hawk

esparciata *m+f* Spartan

esparcido merry, joyful; scattered

esparcidor *n m* spreader; *adj* spreading

esparcimiento scattering; amusement, merriment; relaxation

esparcir to scatter, spread; ~**se** to relax, take recreation

esparrabar *sl* to burglarize, break in

esparrabo *sl* burglary, house-breaking

esparragador *m* asparagus-grower

esparragar to grow asparagus

espárrago asparagus

Esparta Sparta

espartano *n+adj* Spartan

espartero esparto seller; maker of esparto-work

espasmo spasm; horror

espástico spastic

espátula spatula; *arts* palette-knife; *orni* spoonbill

especería grocer's shop, spice shop

especia spice

especial special; **en** ~ in particular; specially

especialidad *f* speciality

especialista *m+f* specialist

especialización *f* specialization

especializar to specialize; ~**se (en)** to specialize (in)

especiar to add spice to

especie *f* species; kind, sort; pretext; idea

especiero grocer; spice rack

especificación *f* specification

especificar to specify; name

específico *n m med* specific; *adj* specific

espécimen *m* specimen, sample

especioso specious

espectacular spectacular

espectáculo spectacle, show; performance; **dar un** ~ to make a scene, cause a scandal

espectador *m* spectator; onlooker; ~**es** audience

espectral spectral

espectro spectre, ghost; spectrum

espectroscopio spectroscope

especulación *f* speculation

especulador *m* speculator

especular to speculate

especulativo speculative

espejado mirror-like

espejar to reflect

espejear to glitter

espejeo *see* espejismo

espejería mirror shop; glazier's

espejero mirror maker/seller; glazier

espejismo mirage; illusion

espejo mirror; ~ **de cuerpo entero** full-length mirror; **mirarse en ese** ~ to learn from that example

espeleología speleology

espeleólogo speleologist

espeluznante hair-raising, terrifying

espeluznar to ruffle the hair; be terrified

espera wait, stay; delay; be expecting; **compás de** ~ cooling-off period; **estar en** ~ **de** to be waiting for; **no tener** ~ to admit of no delay; **sala de** ~ waiting room

esperantista *n m+f +adj* Esperantist

esperanza hope, expectation; **tener (la)** ~ **(de)** to hope (for)

esperanzado hopeful

esperanzar to give hope to

esperar to hope; expect; wait, wait for; ~ **en alguien** to place confidence in someone

esperma sperm; ~ **de ballena** spermaceti

esperpento ugly thing; nonsense

espesamiento thickening; coagulation

espesar to thicken; ~**se** to thicken; become thick; *text* weave closely

espesativo *adj* thickening

espeso thick, dense; compact; slovenly; **aceite** ~ heavy oil

espesor *m* thickness; density

espesura density, thickness; thicket

espeta *m sl* police inspector

espetar *cul* to put on a spit; make listen; ~**se** to behave in a pompous way

espetera set of kitchen utensils; *sl* breasts, bust (*esp* if large)

espía *m+f* spy; ~ **doble** double agent

espiar to spy, spy on

espicanardo *bot* spikenard

espid *m sl* euphoria produced by drugs

espiga ear (of wheat); peg; spike; brad; fuse (of a bomb); clapper (of a bell); lace edging

espigado lanky

espigar *agri* to glean; ~**se** to go to seed; shoot up

espigón *m* sting of an insect; spike

espiguilla *bot* celandine; *text* herring-bone (pattern)

espina thorn; sharp splinter; fish bone; spine; fear, suspicion; **darle a uno mala** ~ to arouse s.o.'s suspicion; prick, goad

espinaca spinach-leaf; ~**s** spinach

espinar *m* thorn-brake; difficult business

espinazo spine, backbone

espinilla shin; blackhead

espino hawthorn; ~ **artificial** barbed wire

espinoso thorny; difficult, dangerous

espión *m* spy

espionaje *m* espionage, spying

espiración *f* breathing out

espiral spiral

espirar to exhale; emit, give off; die, expire

espirea *bot* spiraea

espiritismo *see* **espiritualismo**

espiritista *see* **espiritualista**

espíritu *m* spirit; soul; courage; vigour; essence; ghost, sprite; **Espíritu Santo** Holy Ghost

espiritual spiritual

espiritualismo spiritualism

espiritualista *m+f* spiritualist

espiritualizarse to grow very thin

espita spigot, tap, *US* faucet; *fam* drunkard; measure of length (21 cm)

esplendidez *f* splendour; generosity; magnificence

espléndido splendid, wonderful; generous

esplendor *m* splendour

esplendoroso resplendent, shining, radiant

espliego lavender

esplín *m* black humour; spleen

esplique *m* bird-snare

espolear to spur; incite

espolón *m* spur; buttress; breakwater; jetty; public walk, tree-lined avenue

espolvorear to powder, sprinkle with powder

esponja sponge; sponger; **pasar la** ~ to wipe the slate clean

esponjado fluffy; spongy; puffed up

esponjar to sponge; make spongy

esponjosidad *f* sponginess

esponjoso spongy

esponsales *mpl* betrothal

espontanearse to open one's heart

espontaneidad *f* spontaneity, ease, naturalness

espontáneo *n* person who breaks through a police cordon; spectator who interrupts a bullfight to show his bullfighting prowess; *adj* spontaneous

espora *bot* spore

esporádico sporadic; **huelga esporádica** stop-go strike

esposa wife; ~**s** handcuffs

esposar to handcuff

esposo husband; *eccles* bishop's ring

espuela spur; ~ **de caballero** *bot* lark-spur

espulgar to delouse; de-flea

espuma foam, froth; lather; head (on beer); scum; ~ **de jabón** soap suds

espumadera *cul* skimmer

espumajear to froth at the mouth

espumante frothing, foaming; (of wine) sparkling

espumar to froth, foam; *cul* skim off

espumarajo froth; **echar** ~**s** to froth at the mouth, be very angry

espumilla *text* voile

espumosidad *f* frothiness

espumoso foamy, frothy; (of wine) sparkling

espúreo spurious

esputar to spit

esputo spit, saliva, sputum

esqueje *m hort* cutting, slip

esquela note, letter; announcement; ~ **mortuoria/fúnebre** obituary notice

esquelético skeletal; bony; very thin

esqueleto skeleton; carcass; framework; outline

esquema *m* scheme, outline; sketch

esquemático schematic

esquematizar to provide an outline of

esquí *m* ski, ski-ing; ~ **acuático** water ski-ing

esquiador *m* skier

esquiar to ski

esquiciar to outline

esquicio outline, rough draft

esquife *m* skiff

esquila (small) bell; cow-bell; sheep-shearing

esquilador *m* sheep-shearer

esquilar to shear sheep; clip; crop

esquimal *n+adj* Eskimo

esquina corner, angle (outside)

esquinazo corner; **dar** ~ to avoid meeting someone; stand s.o. up; give the slip

esquinar *vt* to form a corner with; set at odds; *vi* to be on the corner; ~**se** to quarrel; have a chip on one's shoulder

esquinco *zool* skink

esquirol *m* strikebreaker, scab, blackleg

esquite *m* pop-corn

esquivar to avoid, dodge; shun; ~**se** to withdraw, shy away

esquivez *f* shyness, aloofness; disdain

esquivo reserved, shy; disdainful, aloof

esquizado mottled

esquizofrenia schizophrenia

esquizofrénico schizophrenic

estabilidad *f* stability

estabilización *f* stabilization

estabilizador *n m aer+naut* stabilizer; *adj* stabilizing

estabilizar to stabilize

estable stable, firm, steady

establecedor *m* founder

establecer to establish; found; decree, ordain; ~**se** to settle down; set up in business; establish oneself

establecimiento establishment; foundation; statute, law

establero groom, stable-boy

establo stable; cowshed, *US* barn

estaca stake, stick; picket (for a fence); peg

estacada stockade; picket fence; predicament; **dejarle a uno en la** ~ to leave s.o. holding the baby

estacar to stake; tie to a stake; stake off,

mark with stakes; ~**se** to remain rigid

estación *f* station; season; ~ **balnearia** spa

estacionar to station; place; *mot* park; ~**se** to remain stationary; park

estacionario stationary; motionless

estada sojourn, stay

estadía detention, stay; stay (of a vessel) in port; *arts* sitting

estadio stadium, sports complex

estadista *m* statesman

estadística statistics

estadístico *n* statistician; *adj* statistical

estado state, condition; station, rank; estate; ~ **civil** marital status; ~ **de ánimo** state of mind; ~ **llano** common people; ~ **mayor** army general staff; **en** ~ **(interesante)** pregnant; **hombre de** ~ statesman; **papel de** ~ government bonds

estadounidense from the United States, American

estafa swindle, fraud, trick; stirrup

estafador *m* swindler, crook

estafar to swindle, defraud, cheat

estafeta courier; diplomatic bag

estalactita stalactite

estalagmita stalagmite

estallar to explode, burst; creak, crackle; start, break out

estallido explosion, outburst; crash; creaking; crack (of a gun), report (of a gun)

estambre *m text* worsted; *bot* stamen

estampa image; print; stamp; picture; footprint; figure, appearance; **dar a la** ~ to send to press

estampación *f* printing

estampado print, printed fabric; printing

estampar to stamp; print

estampero seller of prints

estampida stampede

estampido crack, sharp sound; report (of a gun)

estampilla stamp, seal; **de** ~ **mil** (of rank) war substantive

estancación *f* stagnation

estancar to stem; staunch; stop the flow of; corner (a market); ~**se** to stagnate, become stagnant; become blocked up

estancia stay; hall, room; mansion; farm, cattle ranch

estanciero *n m* rancher, ranch-owner,

cattle raiser; *adj* pertaining to an **estancia**

estanco monopoly; government tobacconist's; cigar shop

estándar *n m* + *adj* standard; norm

estandardizar, estandarizar to standardize

estandarte *m* standard, flag, banner

estanque *m* pond, pool, reservoir; tank

estanquero keeper of an **estanco**

estanquillo tobacconist's; *Mex* cigar store

estante *m* shelf; bookshelf; prop, support

estantería shelving, shelves; book-case

estantío lifeless; stationary; dull

estañador *m* tinsmith

estañar to solder; tin

estañero seller of tin-ware

estaño tin; **papel de ~** silver-paper

estaquilla stake; peg

estar to be (indicating location or a temporary state/condition); **ella está contenta** she is happy; **Madrid está en España** Madrid is in Spain; **Juan no está** John is not in/at home; **él está fuera** he is out; **¿a cuántos estamos?** what is the date?; **estamos a ocho** it's the 8th; **el vino está a 50 pesetas el litro** wine is 50 pesetas a litre; **estamos con usted** we're with you/backing you; **mi hijo está con sarampión** my son has measles; **ella está de niñera** she works as a nanny; **~ por** to be inclined to; **~ para** to be in the mood for; **~ en** pay attention to; **~ sobre** to keep an eye on; **~ de prisa** be in a hurry; **~ le bien a uno** to suit one; **¡están verdes!** sour grapes!; **~ se** to keep, remain

estaribel *m sl* prison

estarcido stencilled drawing; tracing

estarcir to stencil; trace

estatal *adj* state

estática statics

estático static

estatua statue; **quedarse hecho una ~** to be petrified/thunderstruck

estatuar to adorn with statues

estatura stature, height

estatutario statutory

estay *m naut* stay

¹ **este, esta** *dem adj* this; **estos, estas** these, the latter

² **este** *m* east; east wind

éste, ésta *dem pron* this, this one, this thing, the latter; **éstos, éstas** these, these things, the latter

esteatita *min* soapstone

Esteban Stephen

estela *naut* wake; trail

estelar stellar

estelionato *leg* fraudulent conveyance

estenocardia *med* angina pectoris

estenografía stenography, shorthand

estenográfico stenographic

estenógrafo shorthand writer, *US* stenographer

estenordeste east-north-east

estentóreo stentorian, loud

estepa steppe; *bot* rock-rose

estera matting; mat

estercoladura *n agri* manuring, muck-spreading

estercolar *agri* to apply manure, fertilize with manure

estercolero manure heap/pile; manure collector

estercuelo *n* manuring

estéreo stereo; *sl* two kilograms of marihuana

estereofonía stereophony

estereofónico stereophonic

estereoscopio stereoscope

estereotipar to stereotype

estereotípico stereotypic

estereotipo stereotype

esterería shop where mats are sold

esterero mat-maker/seller

estéril sterile, barren

esterilidad *f* sterility

esterilizar to sterilize

esterilizador *n m* sterilizer; *adj* sterilizing

esterilla small mat

esterlina sterling; **libra ~** pound sterling

esternón *m* sternum, breastbone

estero estuary; fish-nursery; fishpond; swamp

esteroide anabolizante *m* anabolic steroid

estertor *m* snort; death-rattle

esteta *m* aesthete; *sl* homosexual

estética aesthetics

estético aesthetic

estetoscopio stethoscope

estevado bandy

estibador *m* stevedore, *US* longshoreman

estibar to stow; pack down, compress

estiércol *m* manure; fertilizer

estigio Stygian

estigma *m* stigma; birthmark; *eccles* stigmata

estigmatizador stigmatizing

estigmatizar to stigmatize; brand

estilar to use, be accustomed to using; ~**se** (clothes) to be in fashion; be used

estilete *m* stiletto; *surg* probe

estilista *m + f* stylist

estilizar to stylize

estilo *m* style; fashion; **algo por el** ~ something of the sort

estilográfico stylographic; **pluma estilográfica** fountain-pen

estima esteem; *naut* dead reckoning

estimabilidad *f* estimability, worth

estimación *f* esteem, regard; valuation

estimador esteeming; estimating

estimar to esteem, value, respect, regard highly; estimate, appraise; judge, think

estimativa judgement; appraisal

estimativo *adj* judging; appraising

estimulante *n m* stimulant; *adj* stimulant, stimulating

estimular to stimulate, excite

estímulo stimulation, incitement; stimulus

estío summer

estipendiar to pay a stipend to

estipendiario *n + adj* stipendiary

estipendio stipend, fee

estíptico styptic, astringent

estipulación *f* stipulation, specification, provision, proviso

estipulante stipulating

estipular to stipulate, specify

estirado stretched; extended; drawn out; conceited, stuck-up

estirador *m arts* drawing-frame

estirar to stretch, extend; pull; ~ **la pata** *fam* to die; ~**se** to stretch out, stretch oneself; give o.s. airs

estirón *m* pull, tug; stretch; **dar un** ~ to shoot up/grow quickly

estirpe *f* lineage, family; race

estival *adj* summer

esto *neuter pron* this; **en** ~ at this point; at that moment

estocada thrust, stab; stab wound

estofa stuff, cloth; quality; **gente de baja** ~ low-class people, rabble

estofado *n* stew, stewed meat; *adj* stewed

estofar to quilt; *arts* (of sculpture) size before gilding; *cul* stew

estoicismo stoicism

estoico stoic

estola stole; ~ **de visón** mink wrap

estólido stolid

estómago stomach; **tener mucho** ~ not to be squeamish

estonio Estonian

estopa burlap; oakum; *sl* tasteless food

estopear *naut* to caulk

estoque *m* rapier; matador's sword

estoqueador *m* matador

estoquear to stab

estoqueo stabbing

estorbar to hinder, obstruct, block; bother, disturb; get in the way of

estorbo hindrance, obstruction, bother, disturbance

estorboso hindering, in the way

estornino starling

estornudar to sneeze

estornudo sneeze

estovar *cul* to cook over a slow fire

estrabismo squint

estrabada road, way; **batir la** ~ *mil* to reconnoitre

estrafalario odd, eccentric; outrageous

estragado corrupted; spoiled; ruined; tired, worn out

estragamiento corruption, depravity; ruin

estragar to corrupt, contaminate; spoil; ruin

estrago havoc, ruin; destruction; **hacer** ~**s** to play havoc

estragón *m cul* tarragon

estrambosidad *f* squint(ing)

estrambótico odd, outrageous

estrangul *m mus* mouthpiece

estrangulación *f* strangulation

estrangulador *n m* strangler; *mot* throttle; choke; *adj* strangling

estrangular to strangle; choke, throttle

estraperlista *m + f* black marketeer

estraperlo black market

estratagema stratagem, scheme

estratega *m* strategist

estrategia strategy

estratégico *n m* strategist; *adj* strategic

estratificación *f* stratification

estratificar to stratify

estrato stratum, layer; *meteor* stratus

estratorreactor *m* supersonic jet plane

estratosfera stratosphere

estraza: papel de ~ brown paper

estrechamiento tightening

estrechar to tighten; make narrow; narrow down; embrace, hug; ~ **la mano** to shake hands; grasp s.o.'s hand; ~**se** to get narrow

estrechez *f* narrowness; tightness; austerity; dire straits; poverty; closeness

estrecho *n m* strait(s); narrow passage; *adj* narrow; tight; **de manga estrecha** narrow-minded; **una amistad muy estrecha** a close friendship

estrechura narrowness; narrow passage

estregadera scrubbing-brush

estregadura, estregamiento scrubbing, scouring

estregar to scrub, scour

estrella star; *fig* fate, destiny; ~ **de mar** starfish; ~ **de rabo** comet; ~ **fugaz** shooting-star, *US* falling-star; **barras y** ~**s** stars and stripes; **levantarse con las** ~**s** to get up very early in the morning

estrelladera egg-slice; spatula

estrellado starry, star-spangled; **huevos** ~**s** fried eggs, *US* eggs sunny side up

estrellamar *m* starfish

estrellar to shatter; dash to pieces; star; *cul* fry (eggs); ~**se** to shatter, break into pieces; crash; fail

estrellato *cin* + *theat* stardom

estremecedor frightful

estremecer to shake; ~**se** to shiver, shudder; vibrate

estremecimiento shiver, shudder; shuddering; vibration; shaking

estrena gift

estrenar to open/use/wear/perform for the first time; inaugurate; begin; ~**se** *theat* to present for the first time

estreno début, first appearance, first performance

estrenuo strong

estreñimiento constipation

estreñir to constipate; ~**se** to become constipated

estrepada *naut* long heave (on a rope)

estrépito racket, noise

estrepitoso noisy; boisterous

estriado fluted, grooved; streaked

estriar to groove; flute

estribación *f* spur (of a mountain); foothill

estribar to rest (upon); **eso estriba en que ...** the basis for it is that ...

estribera stirrup

estriberón *m* stepping-stone

estribillo refrain; chorus; favourite stock expression

estribo stirrup; footboard, running board; support; brace; spur (of a mountain); **perder los** ~**s** to lose one's balance; lose control of o.s.

estribor *m* starboard

estricnina strychnine

estricote: al ~ all over the place

estricto strict

estridencia stridency

estridente strident

estróbilo *bot* cone

estrofa strophe, stanza

estroncio strontium

estropajear to scrub, scour

etropajeo scrubbing, scouring

estropajo *m* pan-scrub; scourer; **tratar a uno como un** ~ to treat s.o. scornfully/like dirt

estropajoso indistinct; stingy; rough; fibrous

estropear to spoil, ruin, damage; cripple; ~**se** to get out of order; get damaged

estropeo rough use

estructura structure

estructurar to structure

estructural structural

estruendo *m* clatter; clamour, din, racket

estruendoso thunderous, uproarious, deafening

estrujamiento crushing, squeezing

estrujar to squeeze, press; crush

estrujón *m* squeeze, crush; smashing

estuario estuary

estucador *m* stucco-plasterer

estuco stucco; plaster

estuche *m* jewel box; instrument case, kit; casket; sheath; ~ **de montaje** *cin* splicing kit

estudiador studious

estudiantado the student body

estudiante *m* + *f* student

estudiantil *adj* student

estudiar to study

estudio study; research; studio; **dar ~s a** to pay for the education of; **tener ~s** to be well educated

estudiosidad *f* studiousness

estudioso *n m* learner; *adj* studious

estufa heater; stove; hothouse; steam room; **criar en ~** to mollycoddle

estulto stupid

estupa *m sl* member of Drug Squad (police)

estupefacción *f* stupefaction

estupefaciente narcotic

estupefacto stunned; speechless

estupendo stupendous, marvellous, wonderful

estupidez *f* stupidity

estúpido *n* stupid person; *adj* stupid

estupor *m* stupor; astonishment

estuprador *m* rapist

estuprar to rape

estupro rape

estuque *m* stucco

esturión *m* sturgeon

E.T. (Ejército de Tierra) army, land forces

E.T.A. Basque separatist movement

etapa stage, lap; epoch, period; **hacer ~ en** to break one's journey at; **quemar ~s** to do a non-stop journey

etarra *m+f* member of **E.T.A.**

éter *m* ether

etéreo ethereal; heavenly

eterizar to etherize

eternidad *f* eternity

eternizar to prolong; perpetuate, make eternal; **~se** to be endless; take ages

eterno eternal, everlasting; endless

ética ethics

ético ethical, moral

etileno ethylene

etilo ethyl

etimología etymology

etimológico etymological

etimólogo, etimologista *m+f* etymologist

etíope *m+f* Ethiopian (person)

Etiopía Ethiopia

¹ **etiqueta** etiquette; formality; **de ~** formal; **traje de ~** dinner jacket, *US* tuxedo

² **etiqueta** tag; label; ticket

etiquetero punctilious, fussy

étnico ethnic

etnografía ethnography

etnográfico ethnographic

etnógrafo ethnographer

etnología ethnology

etnológico ethnological

etnólogo ethnologist

etrusco *n+adj* Etruscan

eucalipto eucalyptus

eucaristía Eucharist

eucarístico Eucharistic

eufemismo euphemism

eufonía euphony

euforia euphoria, elation

eufórico euphoric, elated

eugenesia eugenics

eunuco eunuch

eurasio Eurasian

eurítmico eurhythmic

eurocracia Eurocracy

eurócrata *m+f* Eurocrat

eurocomunismo Eurocommunism

eurocomunista *n m+f +adj* Eurocommunist

euromisil *m* Euromissile

Europa Europe

europeizar to Europeanize

europeo European

Euskadi, Euzkadi Basque Country

euskera, euzkera Basque language

eutanasia euthanasia

Eva Eve

evacuación *f* evacuation; bowel movement

evacuante evacuating

evacuar to evacuate, empty; vacate

evadir to evade, elude; **~se** to slip away, escape

evagación *f* wandering (of the mind)

evaluación *f* evaluation

evaluar to evaluate, appraise

evalúo *comm* valuation

evangélico evangelical

evangelio gospel; **es el Evangelio** it's Gospel truth

evangelismo evangelism

evangelista *m+f* evangelist

evangelistero hot-gospeller

evangelizador *n m* evangelist; *adj* evangelizing

evangelizar to evangelize

evaporación *f* evaporation

evaporador evaporating

evaporar to evaporate; **~se** to evaporate; vanish, disappear

evaporizar to vaporize

evasión *f* evasion; dodge; escape; **de ~** escapist

evasiva evasive answer; evasion

evasivo evasive

evasor *m* evader, dodger

evento event; contingency

eventual *n m+f* temporary employee; *adj* fortuitous; temporary; possible; casual

evicción *f* eviction

evidencia evidence

evidenciar to prove, show, make evident

evidente evident

evitable avoidable

evitación *f* avoidance

evitar to avoid, shun

evocador evocative

evocar to evoke, call forth

evolución *f* evolution

evolucionar to evolve

evolucionismo evolutionism

evolucionista *m+f* evolutionist

evolutivo evolutionary

exabrupto outburst

exacción *f* extortion

exacerbación *f* exasperation

exacerbar to exasperate, irritate; aggravate, make worse

exactitud *f* accuracy, exactness; precision; punctuality

exacto exact, precise; punctual

exageración *f* exaggeration

excesivo excessive

exagerar to exaggerate

exagonal hexagonal

exágono hexagon

exaltación *f* exaltation; excitement; elation

exaltado elated; excited; hot-headed

exaltar to exalt, elevate, glorify; praise; **~se** to get excited, become upset; get carried away

examen *m* examination; inspection

examinador *m* examiner

examinando examination candidate

examinante examining

examinar to examine; inspect; observe; **~se** to sit an examination

exangüe lacking blood; anaemic; exhausted

exánime lifeless, motionless; weak, faint

exasperación *f* exasperation

exasperador, exasperante exasperating

exasperar to exasperate, irritate, vex

excarcelación *f* release from prison

excarcelar to release from prison

excavación *f* excavation

excavar to excavate, dig; dig out

excedente *n m* surplus; *adj* exceeding, extra

exceder to exceed, surpass; over-do; **~se** to go beyond the proper limit; misbehave

excelencia (title) excellency; excellence, superiority; **por ~** par excellence

excelente excellent; fine

excelso lofty, elevated; sublime; **El Excelso** the Most High

excentricidad *f* eccentricity

excéntrico eccentric; queer; odd

excepción *f* exception; **estado de ~** state of emergency

excepcional exceptional, unusual

excepto except, with the exception of

exceptuación *f* exclusion

exceptuar to except

excesivo excessive

exceso excess; crime; *comm* surplus; **~ de equipaje** excess baggage; **en ~** in excess, excessively

excitabilidad *f* excitability, nervousness

excitación *f* excitement

excitante exciting; stimulating

excitar to excite, stir; **~se** to get excited

excitativo stimulating

exclamación *f* exclamation

exclamar to exclaim

exclamativo exclamatory

exclamatorio exclamatory

exclaustración *f eccles* secularization (of nuns, monks *etc*)

exclaustrar to secularize (nuns, monks *etc*)

excluir to exclude; debar

exclusión *f* exclusion, debarment

exclusiva exclusive (report), scoop; sole right

exclusivo *adj* exclusive

excomulgación *f* excommunication

excomulgado excommunicated

excomulgador *m* excommunicator

excomulgar to excommunicate

excomunión *f* excommunication

excoriación *f* flaying

excoriar to flay; **~se** to graze o.s.

excrecencia, excrescencia excrescence

excreción *f* excretion

excremento excrement
excretar to excrete
exculpación f exoneration
exculpar to exonerate
excursión f excursion, trip, tour, picnic, outing
excursionista m+f tripper, picnicker
excusa excuse
excusado n lavatory, toilet, washroom; adj excused, exempt, superfluous; unnecessary; reserved, private
excusador m excuser
excusar to excuse; pardon; exempt (from); ~+infin to be excused from; ~se to apologize
exea mil scout
execración f execration
execrar to execrate
exención f exemption
exentar to exempt
exento exempt, freed; free, unobstructed
exequias fpl obsequies, funeral rites
exfoliación f defoliation
exfoliar to defoliate
exhalación f exhalation
exhalar to exhale; emit, give off; breathe forth; ~se to evaporate; run away
exhaustivo exhaustive
exhausto exhausted
exheredación f disinheritance
exheredar to disinherit
exhibición f exhibition; exposition
exhibicionismo exhibitionism; ~ **sexual** flashing
exhibicionista m+f exhibitionist; ~ **sexual** flasher
exhibir to exhibit; ~se to show off
exhortación f exhortation
exhortador m exhorter
exhortar to exhort, admonish
exhumación f exhumation
exhumar to exhume, disinter
exigencia exigency, demand
exigente adj demanding
exigir to demand
exiguo exiguous; small; scanty
exiliar to exile, banish; ~se to go into exile
exilio exile, banishment
eximente exempting; **circunstancias** ~s exonerating circumstances
eximio celebrated

existencia existence; ~s comm stocks, goods
existente existing; comm in stock
existimar to judge
existir to exist
éxito success; **tener** ~ to be successful
Éxodo Exodus
exoneración f exoneration
exonerar to exonerate
exorbitancia exorbitance
exorbitante exorbitant
exótico exotic
expandir to expand
expansión f expansion
expatriado expatriate
expatriarse to emigrate
expectación f expectation
expectante expectant
expectativa expectation; hope, prospect; **estar en** ~ **de algo** to be on the lookout for s.t.; be expecting s.t.
expectoración f expectoration
expectorante m med expectorant
expectorar to expectorate; cough up
expedición f expedition; dispatch, promptness
expedicionario n m member of an expedition; explorer; adj expeditionary
expedientado under enquiry
expediente m certificate; papers, documentation; expedient, means; promptness; leg action; proceedings; **cubrir el** ~ to keep up appearances; **formar** ~ **a** to start proceedings against
expedir to dispatch; issue; remit, send; pass (counterfeit notes)
expeditivo prompt
expeler to expel, eject
expendedor m dealer; agent; distributor of forged banknotes
expendeduría see **estanco**
expender to spend, lay out; deal in
expensas fpl expenses; **a** ~ **de** at the expense of
experiencia experience; experiment
experimentador m experimenter
experimentar to experiment, try, test; experience, feel
experimento experiment, trial
experto n m expert; adj expert, skilful
expiación f expiation, atonement
expiar to atone for; make amends for; purify

expiatorio expiatory

expiración *f* expiration

expirar to die; expire; come to an end

explanación *f* explanation; levelling (of land)

explanada esplanade, lawn

explanar to elucidate; level (land)

explayar to extend; ~**se** to become extended; relax; enlarge upon (a subject): ~**se con (un amigo)** to unbosom oneself (to a friend)

expletivo expletive

explicable explainable

explicación *f* explanation

explicaderas: tener buenas ~ to be good at explaining

explicador *m* demonstrator; explainer

explicar to explain; ~**se** to explain oneself; account for one's conduct; explain to oneself, understand; *sl* pay

explicativo explanatory, explaining

explícito explicit, express, clear, definite

exploración *f* exploration

explorador *n m* explorer; (boy) scout; *adj* exploring

explorar to explore

exploratorio exploratory

explosión *f* explosion, blast

explosivo explosive

explotable exploitable

explotación *f* exploitation; operation of a mine; development (of a business)

explotador *m* exploiter

explotar to exploit, operate, develop; utilize, use; profit by; explode

expoliación spoliation

expoliar to despoil

exponente *m* exponent; *comm* exhibitor (at trade fair *etc*)

exponer to expose, reveal; show, exhibit; display; explain; abandon (a child); ~**se a** to expose oneself to, run the risk of

exportación *f* exportation; export

exportador *m* exporter

exportar to export

exposición *f* exposition; exhibition; explanation; *phot* exposure

expósito *n + adj* foundling

expositor *m* exhibitor

exprés *m* express; express company

expresar to express; ~**se** to express o.s., speak

expresión *f* expression; utterance; **expresiones** regards

expresionismo expressionism

expresionista *n m + adj* expressionist

expresividad *f* expressiveness

expresivo expressive; affectionate

expreso *n m* express (train); *adj* expressed; express; clear, exact; fast; *adv* expressly, deliberately

exprimidera, exprimidero, exprimidor *m* squeezer; juice-extractor

exprimir to squeeze, extract (juice); wring out; express, utter

expropiación *f* expropriation

expropiar to expropriate

expuesto exposed; expressed; exhibited, displayed; risky, dangerous; **lo** ~ what has been said

expugnar *mil* to take by storm

expulsar to expel; eject; send down; *mil* cashier

expulsión *f* expulsion, expelling

expulsor *m* ejector

expurgación *f* expurgation; *pol* purge

expurgar to expurgate; *pol* purge

expurgatorio expurgatory

exquisitez *f* exquisiteness

exquisito exquisite

extasiar to delight; ~**se** to be in a state of ecstasy, be entranced

éxtasis *m* ecstasy

extático ecstatic

extemporáneo extemporaneous

extender to extend; spread out; unfold; draw up (a document); ~ **un cheque** to write out a cheque; ~**se** to extend, spread, become widespread

extendido widespread

extensible extendable

exterminador *m* exterminator

exterminar to exterminate

exterminio extermination; destruction

externado day-school

externo *n* day-pupil; *adj* external; outward

extinción *f* extinction, obliteration

extinguible extinguishable

extinguir to extinguish, put out; destroy; ~**se** to die (out), go out

extintivo extinctive

extinto extinct

extintor *m* extinguisher; ~ **de incendios** fire extinguisher

extirpación *f* extirpation

extirpador *n m* extirpator; *adj* extirpating

extirpar to root out, extirpate

extorno *comm* rebate

extorsión *f* extortion

extorsionar to extort, extract money, blackmail

extorsionista *m + f* extortioner; profiteer; racketeer

extra extra; **horas ~** overtime; **~ de** besides

extracción *f* extraction, lineage

extracto extract; abstract, summary; **~ de Saturno** white lead

extradición *f* extradition

extraer to extract

extrafino: azúcar ~ caster sugar

extralimitarse to overreach o.s.; go too far

extramuros *adv* outside

extranjerismo foreign/loan word

extranjerizar to adopt foreign ways

extranjero *n m* foreigner; *adj* foreign; **en el ~** abroad

extrañamiento wonder, surprise, amazement; banishment

extrañar to wonder at; miss; banish; **~se** to marvel; be astonished at

extrañeza strangeness; surprise, astonishment; oddity, odd thing

extraño *n m* stranger; *adj* strange; rare; odd

extraoficial unofficial

extraordinario extraordinary; **paga extraordinaria** bonus payment

extrarradio suburbs; outer parts

extrasensorio extrasensory

extraterrestre *m + f* creature from another galaxy/planet

extraterritorialidad *f* extraterritoriality

extravagancia extravagance; folly

extravagante extravagant, fantastic; odd

extraviar to lead astray; misplace; **~se** to lose one's way; get stranded; get lost; miss the way; be off course

extravío deviation, straying; error; misconduct; damage

extremado extreme

extremar to carry to an extreme; **~se** to take great pains; exert great effort

extremaunción *f* extreme unction

extremeño of Estremadura

extremidad *f* extremity; extreme degree; farthest part; **~es** extremities, hands and feet

extremismo extremism

extremista *n m + adj* extremist

extremo *n* extreme; end; **hacer ~s** to overdo it; *adj* extreme; farthest; **hasta el ~ de** to the point of

extremoso extreme; excessive

extrínseco extrinsic

extroversión *f* extroversion

extrovertido *n + adj* extrovert

exuberancia exuberance; **con ~** abundantly

exuberante exuberant

exudar to exude, ooze

exultación *f* exultation

exultar to exult, rejoice

exvoto votive offering

eyaculación *f* ejaculation

eyacular to ejaculate

eyectar to eject

eyector *m* ejector

F

f *f* letter f

f, fa *m mus* F, fa

f.a.b. (franco a bordo) f.o.b. (free on board)

fábrica factory, mill, plant, works; masonry; structure; building; fabric; manufacture; ~ **de cerveza** brewery; ~ **de conservas** canning factory; ~ **de gas** gas works; ~ **de (la) moneda** mint; ~ **de papel** paper mill; **marca de** ~ trademark

fabricación *f* manufacture; production; make; fabrication; ~ **en masa/en serie** mass production; **de** ~ **británica** British made; **de** ~ **casera** home-made; **de** ~ **nacional** home-produced; **estar en** ~ to be in production

fabricador *m,* **fabricante** *m* manufacturer, maker; factory owner

fabricar to manufacture, make; construct, build; fabricate; devise; ~ **en serie** to mass-produce

fabril *adj* manufacturing, factory

fabriquero manufacturer; factory owner; charcoal burner; churchwarden

fabuco *bot* beech-mast

fábula fable, story; plot (of play); rumour; falsehood; laughing-stock; **de** ~ fabulous

fabular to gossip, tell stories

fabulista *m+f* writer of fables

fabuloso fabulous; fictitious, imaginary; false; fantastic

f.a.c. (franco al costado) f.a.s. (free alongside)

faca jack-knife

facción *f* faction, party, band; feature, face; *mil* duty; ~ **de testamento** testamentary capacity; **estar de** ~ to be on (guard) duty

facciones *fpl* facial features

faccionario factional

faccioso *n* rebel; trouble-maker; *adj* partisan; rebellious, hostile

faceta facet

faceto cute, funny; affected

facial *adj* face, facial; **valor** ~ face value

fácil easy; probable; likely; glib; pliant; simple; wanton; ~ **de** easy to; **es** ~ **que** + *subj* it is likely that

facilidad *f* facility, ease; aptitude; fluency; **con** ~ easily; fluently; ~**es (de crédito)** credit facilities; ~**es de pago** easy terms

facilitar to facilitate; enable; let s.o. have, get s.t. for s.o., provide. supply, furnish; make s.t. seem easy; ~ **el ajuste** to expedite settlement; ~ **el dinero** to put up the money; ~ **el negocio** to expedite business

facilón *adj* very easy

facilona wanton; 'easy' woman

facineroso *n* criminal; *adj* villainous, wicked

facón *m* big knife; gaucho knife

faconazo stab

facoquero wart-hog

facsímil *m,* **facsímile** *m* facsimile

factibilidad *f* feasibility

factible feasible, practicable

facticio artificial; factitious

factor *m* factor; agent, commission agent; baggage master, freight agent; element; ~ **de seguridad** safety factor

factoraje *m comm* factoring, factorage

factoría trading post; agency; small factory; *comm* factoring

factótum *m* jack of all trades; busybody

factura invoice; bill; ~ **de gastos** expense account; ~ **de venta** bill of sale; ~ **por vencer** due bill; ~ **simulada** pro forma invoice; ~ **sin saldar** unpaid bill

facturación *f* invoicing; billing; booking (of goods); baggage registration/ checking

facturar to invoice, bill; register/check baggage

facultad *f* faculty; authority; power; ability; capacity; permission, authorization; option; ~ **de derecho,** ~ **de**

208

leyes Faculty of Law, law school; ~ **de Filosofía y Letras** Faculty of Arts; ~ **de ganar** earning power; ~ **de testar** testamentary capacity; ~ **de veto** power of veto; **tener** ~ **para** to be empowered to; **tener la** ~ **de** to have the power to

facultado authorized, empowered; qualified; commissioned

facultar to authorize, empower; commission

facultativo *n* doctor; surgeon; *adj* optional; permissive; medical; faculty; **dictamen** ~ medical opinion/report; **prescripción facultativa** doctor's prescription

facundia fluency, gift of expression, eloquence

facundo fluent, eloquent

[1] **facha** look, appearance; ~ **a** ~ face to face; **estar hecho una** ~ to look awful; **ponerse en** ~ *naut* to lie to; **ser** ~ to look a sight

[2] **facha** *n m+f +adj sl* fascist

fachada front, façade; frontage; title page; appearance, bearing; impudence, cheek; ~ **de almacén** shop front; **con** ~ **a** overlooking; **hacer** ~ **a/con** to face, look out on, overlook; **revocarse la** ~ *sl* to make up one's face

fachado: bien ~ good-looking; **mal** ~ ugly

fachear *naut* to lie to

fachenda *m fam* swank, conceited person, show-off; *f* ostentation; vanity; pretentiousness; airs and graces

fachendear *fam* to show off, swank; boast

fachendista, fachendón, fachendoso vain, ostentatious, pretentious

fachoso ridiculous, strange-looking

fada fairy; *bot* small pippin

faena task, job; shift; fatigue duty; work gang; (in bull fight) cape play; stunt; ~ **doméstica** housework; **estar de** ~ to be at work; **tener mucha** ~ to be very busy; **me hizo una mala** ~ he did me a bad turn

faetón *m* phaeton

fagot *m* bassoon; bassoonist

fagotista *m+f* bassoonist

faisán *m* pheasant

faisanero pheasant-breeder

faja band, sash; girdle, corset; bandage; strip; wave band; *archi* fascia; *TV* channel; (motorway) lane; parkway; ~ **de estacionamiento** parking lane; ~ **de pasar** overtaking/passing lane; ~ **postal** postal wrapper

fajador *m sp* attacking boxer

fajar to bind; wrap; bandage; whip; thrash; ~**se** to put on a belt; tighten one's belt; ~**se con** to come to blows with, lay into s.o.

fajardo vol-au-vent

fajín *m mil* sash

fajina toil; bundle; stook; *mil* lights-out, *US* taps

fajo sheaf, bundle; roll, wad (of notes, bills); ~**s** swaddling clothes

falacia fraud, deceit; fallacy; deceitfulness

falange *f* phalanx; **La Falange** the Falange (Spanish political party)

falangista *n m+f +adj* Falangist

falaris *f* coot

falaropo *orni* phalarope

falaz deceitful; fallacious; misleading

falbalá flounce

falca reaping-hook

falcado scythe-shaped

falcar to reap

falcón *m* falcon

falda skirt; lap; flap; fold; brim (of hat); slope, side, fold (of hill); ~ **escocesa** kilt; **a la** ~ **de la montaña** at the foot of the mountain

faldear to skirt (a hill)

faldero: hombre ~ ladies' man; **perro** ~ lapdog

faldicorto short-skirted

faldillas *pl* coat-tails

faldistorio *eccles* bishop's seat

faldón *m* coat tail; shirt tail; flap; gable; baby's garment

falencia mistake; misstatement; bankruptcy

falibilidad *f* fallibility

falible fallible

fálico phallic

falismo phallic cult

falocracia phallocracy, rule by males

falócrata *m* phallocrat; male chauvinist

falsada *orni* rapid swoop

falsario *n* crook; forger, counterfeiter; liar; *adj* lying

falsarregla bevel-rule

falseable falsifiable

falseador *m* crook; forger, falsifier

falseamiento falsification

falsear *vt* to falsify, forge; misrepresent; penetrate; *mus* hit the wrong note; falter; *vi* to weaken, give way; sag, slacken; be out of tune

falsedad *f* falsehood; falsity; false declaration; misrepresentation; ~ **consciente** deliberate lie

falseo bevelling

falsete *m* hung, spigot, plug; *mus* falsetto

falsía falsity; duplicity

falsificación *f* falsification; forgery; misrepresentation

falsificado falsified; counterfeit; **ser** ~ to be a forgery/fake

falsificador *m* forger; crook; ~ **de moneda** counterfeiter

falsificar to counterfeit, forge; fake; falsify

falsilla handwriting guide-lines

falso *adj* false; forged; counterfeit; fake; dishonest; sham; **coger en** ~ to catch s.o. out (in a lie); **dar un paso en** ~ to make a wrong move; **en** ~ falsely; mistakenly; without foundation; **joyas falsas** imitation jewellery; **jurar en** ~ to commit perjury

falta lack, want; failure; fault, flaw; deficiency; absence; mistake; misdemeanour; petty crime; **a** ~ **de** for lack of; **a** ~ **de personal** short-handed; **hacer** ~ to be lacking, needed; **me hace** ~ ... I need ...; **sin** ~ without fail; **te echo en** ~ I miss you

faltante lacking

faltar to lack; be lacking; be missing; be needed; offend; ~ **a** to be absent from, fail to keep (an appointment); ~ **a su palabra** to break one's word; **faltan diez minutos para las once** it's ten to eleven; **le falta dinero** he has no money; **¿le falta algo?** do you need anything?; is anything missing?; **¡No faltaba más!** The very idea!, That's the limit!

falto mean, base; stupid; short; defective; ~ **de juicio** insane; ~ **de peso** underweight; ~ **de recursos** short of funds

faltón unreliable; *sl* disrespectful; foul-mouthed

faltrero pickpocket

faltriquera pocket; hip-pocket; purse; **rasgar la** ~ to pay reluctantly

falúa *naut* tender, launch; gig

falla fault; defect, flaw, blemish; failure; *geol* fault; (in Valencia) fireworks, bonfire; ~ **de tiro** misfire

fallada trumping (cards)

fallar to fail; default; give way; miss; go wrong; pass sentence on; *leg* give a ruling; (cards) trump; ~ **un gol** to disallow a goal

fallecer to die, expire; die away

fallecido deceased; late

fallecimiento decease, death; expiration

fallido *n* bankrupt; ~ **no rehabilitado** undischarged bankrupt; *adj* unsuccessful; frustrated

fallo *n* decision; sentence, judgement; failure, breakdown; (cards) short suit; ~ **a muerte** death sentence; ~ **de freno** brake failure; ~ **de un tribunal** findings of a court; **estar** ~ (cards) to be unable to follow suit

fama fame, reputation; report; **es** ~ it is reported; **correr** ~ to be rumoured; **tener** ~ **de** to have the reputation of; **tiene mucha** ~ (he) is very famous

famélico famished, starved, ravenous

familia family; household; ~ **política** in-laws

familiar *n m* dependent; member of the family; relative; family servant; intimate friend; familiar spirit; *adj* informal; familiar; friendly; well-known; familial; domestic; **asuntos** ~**es** family affairs

familiaridad *f* familiarity; informality

familiarizar to familiarize; acquaint; ~**se** to acquaint oneself; become familiar with

famoso famous; excellent

fámula maidservant

famular *adj* of servants

famulato domestic service

fámulo man-servant

fanal *m* beacon; lighthouse; lantern; headlight; bell glass; glass lampshade; ~ **de aterrizaje** *aer* landing light; ~ **de tránsito/tráfico** traffic light

fanático *n* fanatic; enthusiast; sports fan; bigot; *adj* fanatical

fanatismo fanaticism; bigotry; enthusiasm

fanatizar to make fanatical

fanega *approx* bushel; ~ **de tierra** land measure *approx* 64,000 square yards but variable according to region

fanfa *m sl* braggart

fanfarria ostentation; bluster, bragging; fanfare

fanfarrón *m* braggart, boaster; bully; *adj* boastful, swaggering

fanfarronada boast, brag

fanfarronear to brag, boast; swagger

fanfarronería boasting; blustering

fanfarronesca swagger

fangal *m* bog

fango mud, mire; slush

fangoso muddy, miry; slushy; sticky

fantasear to fancy, imagine; fantasize; day-dream

fantaseador fanciful; dreaming

fantasía fancy, imagination; fantasy; whim; ~**s** string of pearls; **de** ~ fancy; **joyas de** ~ imitation jewellery

fantasioso *fam* conceited, vain

fantasma *m* phantom, ghost, shadow; *TV* ghosting; **gobierno** ~ shadow cabinet; *f* scarecrow; bogey-man

fantasmada *n sl* boasting

fantasmagoría phantasmagoria

fantasmagórico phantasmagoric; illusory

fantasmal ghostly, phantom

fantasmear to boast

fantástico fantastic; unbelievable; fancy; great, swell, weird

fantoche *m* puppet; nonentity

fañado (of animals) one-year-old

faquir *m* fakir

faradización *f elect* faradization

faradizar *elect* to faradize

faralá *m* frill

farallón *m* cliff; headland

farándula ballyhoo; bohemian life; strolling players; confidence trick

farandulear to show off; boast

farandulero strolling player; boaster

faraón *m* pharaoh

fardada *sl* ostentatious behaviour

fardado *sl* well-dressed

fardar *sl* to swank

fardel *m* knapsack; bundle; bag

fardo bundle; bale; pack; package; fat person; **pasar el** ~ to pass the buck

fardón *sl* elegantly dressed; swank

farellón *m* cliff, headland

farfallear to stutter; mumble

farfallón *n m,* **farfalloso** stutterer; *adj* stuttering

fárfara *bot* coltsfoot

farfolla nonsense; *bot* husk (of maize *etc*)

farfulla mumbling; nonsense talk

farfullador mumbling; gabbling; spluttering

farfullar to mumble; talk nonsense; splutter; blunder

farfullero mumbling; bungling

farináceo farinaceous, starchy

faringe *f* pharynx

farinigitis *f* pharyngitis

farisaico pharisaical; hypocritical; smug

farisaísmo, fariseísmo smugness; hypocrisy

fariseo pharisee; hypocrite

farmacéutico *n* pharmacist, druggist, chemist; *adj* pharmaceutical

farmacia pharmacy, chemist's, drug store; *sl* fly (on trousers); ~ **de guardia** all-night pharmacy; ~ **de turno** pharmacy open out of hours

farmacología pharmacology

farmacológico pharmacological

farmacólogo pharmacologist

farmacopea pharmacopoeia

faro lighthouse; beacon; headlight; floodlight; faro (game); ~ **de cruce** dipped headlight; ~ **de marcha atrás** reversing light; ~ **lateral** sidelight; ~ **piloto/trasero** rear light; ~**s** *sl* eyes

farol *m* lamp, lantern; lamp-post; bluff; ~ **de calle** street lamp; ~ **de tráfico** traffic light; ~ **de viento** hurricane lamp; **darse un** ~ to show off

farola street lamp; lamp-post; lighthouse

farolear to boast; show off; swank

faroleo *n* bluffing; boasting; blustering

farolero *n* lamplighter; boaster; *adj* vain, ostentatious

farolillo Chinese lantern; ~ **rojo** last person in a race/competition *etc*

farpado scalloped

farra revelry, noisy party; **ir de** ~ to go on the spree, paint the town red

fárrago hotch-potch; medley

farrear to go on the spree, carouse

farsa farce; sham, humbug, fraud; company of strolling players

farsante *n m+f* fraud, charlatan; actor

in a farce, comedian; *adj* fake

farseto quilted jacket

farsista *m* + *f* writer of farces

fas: por ~ o por nefas by hook or by crook; at any price

fascículo fascicule, part

fascinación *f* fascination, glamour

fascinador, fascinante fascinating, charming; glamorous

fascinar to fascinate, charm; bewitch, cast a spell on; allure

fascismo fascism

fascista *n* + *adj m* + *f* fascist

fascistoide *n m* + *f* + *adj* would-be fascist

fase *f* phase; aspect; **fuera de ~** out of phase

fastidiar to bother, bore, annoy; disappoint; cloy; spoil, harm; **~se** to get bored; get irritable; harm oneself; **¡fastídiate!** beat it!

fastidio boredom; disgust; annoyance; nuisance; nausea; distaste; **¡Que ~!** How annoying!

fastidioso annoying, tiresome; boring; squeamish; cloying

fastigio apex

fasto grandness, pomp

fastuoso lavish; ostentatious

fatal fatal; disastrous; deadly, mortal; unfortunate; evil; fateful; irrevocable; rotten; horrible; **fue ~** it was terrible

fatalidad *f* fatality; fate; misfortune

fatalismo fatalism

fatalista *n m* + *f* fatalist; *adj* fatalistic

fate, fati *sl* fat, short

fatídico fateful, ominous; prophetic

fatiga fatigue; weariness; hardship; **~ del metal** metal fatigue; **pasar ~s** to have a hard time

fatigador tiring; tiresome

fatigar to fatigue, weary; annoy; **~se** to grow tired

fatigoso fatiguing, tiring; annoying; difficult

fatuidad *f* fatuity; conceit

fatuo fatuous; conceited, pompous; foolish, stupid; **fuego ~** will-o'-the-wisp

fauces *fpl* jaws; gullet

fauno faun

fausto *n* pomp; *adj* fortunate

fautor *m* abettor, accomplice, accessory

favo *med* ringworm

favor *m* favour; good turn; **~es** patronage; **a ~ de** on behalf of, in favour of; to the order of; **a ~ de la noche** under cover of night; **de ~** gratis; **estar para hacer un ~** *sl* to be a smashing bit of crumpet; **haga el ~ de** +*infin* please ...; **por ~** please; excuse me

favorable favourable; advantageous

favorcillo small favour

favorecedor becoming, favouring, flattering

favorecer to favour; help; flatter; patronize (a shop); **ese color le favorece** that colour suits you

favoritismo favouritism

favorito *n* + *adj* favourite, pet

fayanca unsteady position; **de ~** carelessly

fayenco wickerwork basket

faz *f* face; appearance; aspect; (of coins) obverse

F.C. (ferrocarril) railway

Fco (Francisco) Francis

fe *f* faith; testimony; validity; testimonial; certificate; **~ de bautismo** baptismal certificate; **~ de casado** marriage certificate; **~ de erratas/errores** errata; **dar ~ a** to believe, credit; **dar ~ de** to attest, witness, certify; **de buena/mala ~** in good/bad faith; **en ~** consequently; **en ~ de ello/de lo cual** in witness whereof; **tener ~ en** to have faith in

fealdad *f* ugliness; immoral act; unseemliness

Febe Phoebe

feble feeble, weak; underweight

Febo Phoebus

febrera irrigation ditch

febrero February

febril feverish; hectic

fécula starch

feculencia dregs

feculento starchy; foul

fecundación *f* fertilization; **~ artificial** artificial insemination

fecundante *adj* fertilizing

fecundar to fertilize, fecundate

fecundidad *f* fertility, fecundity; fruitfulness; productiveness

fecundizar to fertilize

fecundo fertile, fruitful, fecund; prolific; productive

fecha date; **~ de cierre/de tope** closing

date; ~ **fijada/tope** deadline; **de ~ adelantada** post-dated; **de larga ~** outstanding, of long standing; **para estas** ~**s** by this time (with future reference); **por estas** ~**s** by this time (in the past); **sin ~** undated; **en ~ próxima** at an early date
fechador *m* date-stamp
fechar to date
fechoría misdeed, villainy
federación *f* federation
federalismo federalism
federalista *m*+*f* federalist
federalizar to federalize
federar to federate
federativo federative
Federico Frederick
féferes *mpl* tools; trinkets; goods and chattels
fehaciente authentic; attesting; evidencing
felacio fellatio
felandrio *bot* water-hemlock
feldespato feldspar
Felices Pascuas/Navidades Merry Easter/Christmas
feliciano *vulg sl* copulation, sexual intercourse
felicidad *f* happiness; luck; success; **¡felicidades!** congratulations!
felicitación *f* best wishes, congratulations; compliment
felicitar to congratulate; give one's best wishes; compliment
feligrés *m* church member, parishioner
feligresía church members, congregation; parish
felino feline, catlike
Felipa Philippa
Felipe Philip
Felisa Phyllis
feliz happy; lucky; **¡~ viaje!** pleasant journey!; **le(s) deseamos un ~ año nuevo** we wish you a Happy New Year
felón *n m* felon, criminal; *adj* criminal
felonía felony; treachery
felpa plush; tongue-lashing; hiding; *mil sl* reprimand; **toalla de ~** thick towel
felpada velvety; plush
felpilla chenille
felpudo *n* doormat; soft toy; *vulg sl* pubic hair; *adj* plushy
femenil feminine, womanly
femenino feminine; female

fementido treacherous, false, unfaithful
femineidad, feminidad *f* femininity
femíneo effeminate
feminismo feminism
feminista *m*+*f* feminist
fémur *m* femur
fenda fissure, crack
fenecer to terminate, conclude; die
fenecido deceased, dead
fenecimiento expiration; demise; death
fenicio *n*+*adj* Phoenician
fénico *adj* carbolic
fénix *m* phoenix
fenobárbito phenobarbital
fenobarbítono phenobarbitone
fenol *m* phenol
fenomenal phenomenal; tremendous, terrific
fenómeno *n* phenomenon; prodigy; freak; *adj fam* great, marvellous
feo *n* snub, slight; **dar ~ a** to insult; **hacer un ~ a** to slight s.o.; *adj* ugly; bad; nasty
feote very ugly; big and ugly
feracidad *f* fertility
feraz fertile, fruitful
féretro bier; coffin
feria fair; market; holiday; *leg* recess; vacation, day off; gratuity; *Mex* small change; ~ **de muestras** trade fair
feriado leave of absence; **día ~** holiday; **día medio ~** half holiday
ferial *m* fairground
feriante *m*+*f* pedlar, hawker; stallholder; exhibitor
feriar *Mex* to give small change for; buy at a fair
ferino wild, savage; **tos ferina** whooping cough
fermentación *f* fermentation
fermentar to ferment
fermento ferment; leavening
fernandina linen
Fernando Ferdinand
ferocidad *f* ferocity; cruelty
feroz ferocious, wild; cruel; ugly
férreo ferrous, iron; stern, inflexible; **vía férrea** railway, railroad
ferrería foundry; ironworks; hardware store
ferretería hardware store; hardware; ironmonger's
ferretero hardware dealer, ironmonger
férrico ferric

ferrocarril *m* railway, railroad; ~ **de cremallera** rack railway; ~ **de dos vías** double-track railway; ~ **de vía ancha/estrecha** broad-gauge/narrow-gauge railway; ~ **de vía única** single-track railway; ~ **funicular** cable railway; ~ **ramal** branch line; ~ **troncal** trunk line

ferrocarrilero *n* railway worker, railroader; *adj* railway, railroad

ferrohormigón *m* ferro-concrete

ferrón *m* iron-worker

ferroprusiato blue-print

ferroso ferrous; **metal no** ~ non-ferrous metal

ferrovía railway, railroad

ferrovial *adj* railway, railroad

ferroviario *n* railway worker, railroad employee; *adj* railway, railroad

ferruginoso containing iron

fértil fertile, productive

fertilidad *f* productivity, fertility

fertilización *f* fertilization; ~ **cruzada** cross-fertilization

fertilizador fertilizing

fertilizante *m* fertilizer

fertilizar to fertilize

férula ferule; birch; splint; rule; authority

férvido fervid; ardent; **fiebre férvida** burning fever

ferviente ardent, fervent

fervor *m* fervour; passion; zeal; (religious) devotion

fervorín *m* short sermon; short prayer

fervoroso fervent, ardent, zealous; pious, devout

festejante entertaining

festejar to celebrate; ~ **a alguien** to fête, entertain, give a party for s.o.; woo

festejo celebration, feast; festivity; wooing, courtship

festín *m* feast, banquet

festinación *f* haste

festinar to make haste, rush

festinado premature, precipitous

festividad *f* festivity; holiday; feast day; merrymaking; joviality; ~ **de beneficio** charity event

festivo festive, gay; witty; **día** ~ holiday

festón *m* festoon; garland, wreath; (sewing) edging, scallop

festonear to festoon; garland; (sewing) scallop

fetén *adj invar sl* smashing, fabulous

fetiche *m* fetish

fetichismo fetishism

fetichista *n m+f* fetishist; *adj* fetishist(ic)

fetidez *f* fetidness

fétido rank, fetid; foul-smelling

feto fetus, foetus; *sl* ugly person

feúcho ugly

feudalismo feudalism

feudo feud; fief; ~ **franco** freehold

FF.AA. (**Fuerzas Armadas**) armed forces

fiable trustworthy, responsible

fiado *n* credit; **al** ~ on credit, on trust; **dar** ~ to give credit; **en** ~ on bail; *adj* on credit

fiador *m* surety; guarantor, bondsman; sponsor; catch, fastener; safety catch; ~ **mancomunado** co-sponsor, fellow guarantor; **salir** ~ **por** to go bail for, stand security for

fiambre *n m* cold meat; buffet lunch/supper; stale news; old joke; *sl* corpse; ~**s** cold cuts, cold meats; *adj* (of food) cold; *fig* (of news *etc*) stale

fiambrera lunch basket; packed lunch; meat safe

fiambrería delicatessen store

fianza bail; bond, surety; guarantee; deposit; pledge; guarantor; **bajo** ~ on bail

fiar to give credit; sell on credit; guarantee, stand security for, go bail for; ~ **a** to entrust to; ~**se de** to trust, rely on; **ser de** ~ to be trustworthy

fiasco failure, fiasco

fiat *m* consent

fibra fibre; grain (of wood); *min* vein; energy, stamina; ~ **de vidrio** fibreglass; ~**s del corazón** heart-strings

fibroso fibrous

ficción *f* fiction; falsehood

ficcionario, ficticio, fictivo fictitious

ficha dossier, file; filing card; card index; (telephone) tally; token, check; chessman; domino; electric plug; ~ **antropométrica** personal record card; ~ **de índice** index card; ~ **perforada** punched card; ~ **policíaca** police file, dossier

fichado filed; indexed; known to the police

fichador *m*, **fichadora** filing clerk

fichar to index, file; play; sign on; clock in; ~ **por** *sp* to sign on for

fichero filing cabinet; card index; file, dossier

fidedigno trustworthy, reliable

fideero vermicelli-maker

fideicomisario *n* legatee; trustee; ~ **de quiebra** trustee in bankruptcy; *adj* trust; **banco** ~ trust company

fideicomiso trust; trusteeship; ~ **caritativo** charitable trust

fidelidad *f* faithfulness; fidelity; exactness, accuracy; loyalty; **alta** ~ high fidelity, hi-fi

fidelista *n* *m+f* supporter of Fidel Castro; *adj* pro-Castro

fideo noodle; ~**s** vermicelli; **sopa de** ~ noodle soup

fiduciario *n+adj* fiduciary

fiebre *f* fever; excitement; agitation; ~ **aftosa** foot and mouth disease; ~ **amarilla** yellow fever; ~ **del heno** hay fever; ~ **tifoidea** typhoid fever; **limpiarse de** ~ to recover from a fever; **tener** ~ to run a temperature, have a fever

fiel *n* public inspector, inspector of weights and measures; official receiver; needle of a balance/scale; **estar en el** ~ (of scales) to be accurate; **los** ~**es** the faithful, the congregation; *adj* faithful; true, accurate; honest

fieltro felt; felt hat; felt rug

fiera wild beast; fiend; **estar hecho una** ~ to be furious

fiereza ferocity; ugliness

fiero ferocious; ugly; **echar/hacer** ~**s** to utter threats

fierro iron

fiesta holiday; party; festivity; feast day, holy day; day off; ~ **de despedida** farewell party; ~ **de Navidad** Christmas holiday; ~ **de todos los santos** All Saints' Day; ~ **onomástica** saint's day (equivalent of birthday); ~**s** holidays, vacation; endearments; **aguar la** ~ to be a kill-joy; **estar de** ~ to be in a holiday/good mood; **hacer** ~ to take a day off; **hacer** ~ **s a** to make a fuss of s.o.; **por fin de** ~**s** to round it off, cap it all

fiestero *n* party-goer; reveller; *adj* festive, gay

fifí *m* playboy

figón *m* low eating-house

figura figure; face, countenance; character; drawing; diagram; form, shape; face card; figure of speech; marionette; *mus* note; ~ **de nieve** snowman; **hacer** ~ to cut a dash

figurable imaginable

figuración *f* figuration; rôle

figurado figurative

figurante *m* bit-part actor, walker-on; figurehead

figurar *vt* to figure; depict; represent; feign; *vi* to take part in, figure; ~ **como** to figure as; ~**se** to imagine, suppose; **¡figúrate!/¡figúrese!** just imagine!; **se me figura** ... I guess, I think ...; **ya me lo figuraba** I thought so

figurativo figurative

figurería grimace

figurero one who makes grimaces; statuette-maker

figurín *m* fashion plate; pattern book; dummy, model; design; dandy

figurina figurine, statuette

figurón *m* figurehead; pompous person

fijacarteles *m sing+pl* bill-poster

fijación *f* fixing; fixation; setting; ~ **de carteles** bill-posting; ~ **de daños y perjuicios** assessment of damages; ~ **de precios** price fixing

fijado *phot* fixing

fijador *n m* fastener; *phot* fixing-booth; hair fixative, hair spray; ~ **de carteles** bill-poster; *adj* fixing

fijamárgenes *m sing+pl* (typewriter) margin-stop

fijar to fix; affix; fasten, secure; set; determine, settle; establish; **¡fíjese!/ ¡fíjate!** just imagine!; ~ **carteles** to post bills; ~ **el pelo** to set hair; ~ **sellos** to stick on stamps; ~**se** to lodge, take up residence; ~**se en** to notice, pay attention to; stare at

fijativo fixative

fijeza firmness; fixity; **mirar con** ~ **a** to stare at

fijiano *n+adj* Fijian

fijo fixed, firm; agreed on; permanent; steady, secure; stationary; (colour) fast; **de** ~ certainly, without doubt

fil *m*: ~ **derecho** leap frog; **estar en un** ~ be equal; to be level

fila row; line; file; rank; dislike; ~ **de a uno** single file; ~ **de las manos** *sl* back row of cinema; ~ **india** Indian file; **de dos ~s** double-breasted; **en ~s** on active service; **romper ~s** *mil* to fall out, break ranks, dismiss

filacteria phylactery

Filadelfia Philadelphia

filadiz *m* ferret

filamento filament

filantropía philanthropy

filantrópico philanthropic

filántropo philanthropist

filar *sl* to watch; *sl* see through s.o. (discover his intentions)

filarmonía love of music

filarmónico *n* music-lover; *adj* philharmonic

filatelia philately, stamp collecting

filatélico, filatelista *n m+f* philatelist; *adj* philatelic

filatería talkativeness, verbosity

filatero *n* non-stop talker, chatterbox; *adj* talkative, garrulous

fileno delicate; effeminate

filera fishing-net

filete *m* fillet; steak; roasting-spit; thread (of screw); hem; ~ **de solomillo** filet mignon

filetear to fillet

filfa *fam* hoax; lie

fili *m sl* pocket; ~ **de la buena** *sl* inside breast-pocket; ~ **de la cula** *sl* hippocket

filiación *f* filiation; affiliation; relationship, descent; personal description; ~ **política** party affiliation, political leanings/ties

filial *n f comm* branch, subsidiary; **tomar la ~ a uno** to take down s.o.'s particulars; *adj* filial; affiliated

filibustear to filibuster

filibustero buccaneer; filibusterer

filigrana filigree; jewel; watermark

Filipinas: Islas ~ Philippine Islands

filipino *n+adj* Philippine; **punto ~** *fam* astute person

filisteísmo Philistinism

filisteo *n+adj* Philistine

film *m*, **filme** *m* film; ~ **sonoro** film with sound track

filmación *f* filming

filmar to film, shoot a film

fílmico *adj* film

filmina *phot* transparency; film strip; slide

filmoteca film library

filo blade; cutting edge; edge; ridge; dividing line; phylum; **dar ~ a** to sharpen; **de ~** resolutely; **de dos ~s** double edged; ~ **del viento** wind direction; **por ~** exactly

filocartista *m+f* postcard-collector

filocomunista *m+f* fellow-traveller, pro-Communist

filología philology

filológico philological

filologista *m+f*, **filólogo** philologist

filón *m* seam, layer, vein, load; *fig* gold mine

filosa *sl* face

filoso sharp-edged, sharp

filosofal: piedra ~ philosopher's stone

filosofar to philosophize

filosofía philosophy; ~ **política** political philosophy

filosófico philosophic(al)

filosofismo philosophism

filosofista *m+f* philosophist

filósofo philosopher

filoxera phylloxera; *fam* drunkenness

filtración *f* filtration; leak, seepage

filtrar to filter, strain; **~se** to filter through, percolate, seep through; be wasted, dissipated

filtro filter; philtre, love potion

filván *m* burr

fimo dung

fin *m* end, ending; terminus; aim, purpose; ~ **de la cita** unquote; ~ **de semana** weekend; **a ~ de** in order to; **a ~ de que** in order that; **a ~es de** about the end of; **a ese ~** with that end in view; **al ~** at last, finally; **al ~ y al cabo** in the end, after all; **en ~** well now; **en/por ~** finally; **poner ~ a** to put a stop to; **sin ~** endless(ly); **un sinfín de** no end of

finado late, deceased

final *n m* end, termination; *mus* finale; ~ **de escala** end of the scale; ~ **de la tarde** late afternoon; *f* terminal; (cup) final; *adj* final, last, ultimate

finalidad *f* object, purpose

finalista *m+f* finalist; *Cub fam* procrastinator

finalizar to finish, end, finalize, wind up; ~ **un contrato** to execute a contract

finamiento death

financiación *f* financing

financiador *m* financier

financiamiento financing; **agencia de ~** financing agency

financiar to finance

financiero, financista *n m+f* financier, banker; *adj* financial

finanzas finance, finances; financing; government funds

finar to die; **~se** to yearn

finca estate, real estate, landed property; house property; country house; ranch; **corredor de ~s** estate agent, *US* realtor

finchado stuck-up, conceited

fincharse to become vain

finés *m*, finesa Finn; *adj* Finnish

fineza fineness; courtesy, kindness; small gift; favour; (cards) finesse

fingido false; phoney, sham; pretended; deceitful; **con apariencias fingidas** under false pretences

fingidor *m* faker

fingimiento pretence; sham; faking

fingir to pretend; sham, feign; fake; **~se** to pretend to be; malinger

finiquitar to close (an account), settle up; finish, bring to an end

finiquito payment in full; settlement (of an account); discharge (of a debt); final receipt; **dar ~ a** to conclude

finir to end

finito finite

finlandés *n m* Finn; Finnish (language); *adj* Finnish

Finlandia Finland

fino fine; thin, slender, delicate; select; courteous; shrewd, subtle; cunning; **oro ~** refined gold; **ponerse ~** to be full of charm; **seda fina** sheer silk; **un hombre muy ~** a very courteous man

finta *sp* feint; **hacer ~(s)** to spar

finura fineness; daintiness; good manners; courtesy; charm; subtlety

fiordo fiord

firma signature; firm, business; trade name; partnership; **a la ~** for signature; **bajo/con mi ~** under my hand; **echar la ~** to sign one's name; **llevar la ~** to be empowered

firmal *m* bejewelled clasp

firmamento firmament, sky

firmante *m* signatory; **el abajo ~** the undersigned

firmar to sign; execute (a document)

¹ firme *n m* road surface, firm foundation; **de ~** firmly, steadily; **en ~** definitive, final; **estar en lo ~** to be in the right; **~s** material for road bed

² firme *adj* firm; solid, stable, sturdy; final, binding; **¡~s!** *mil* (stand to) attention!; *adv* firmly; **mantenerse ~** to stand fast

firmeza firmness; steadiness; soundness; binding clause; rigidity

¹ fiscal *n m* public prosecutor; district attorney; treasurer; auditor; controller

² fiscal *adj* fiscal, taxing; financial; **año ~** tax year, fiscal year

fiscalía office of public prosecutor

fiscalización *f* control, supervision; inspection; prosecution

fiscalizador *m* inspector; supervisor; controller; fault-finder

fiscalizar to inspect; oversee; audit; prosecute; pry into; criticize

fisco (public) treasury; exchequer

fisga harpoon; banter; mocking; **hacer ~ a uno** to tease s.o.

fisgador *m* harpooner; banterer

fisgar to harpoon; pry into; mock, tease

fisgón *n m* nosey-parker, snooper; mocker; *adj* prying, snooping

fisgonear to pry, snoop

fisgoneo snooping, prying

física physics; **~ del estado sólido** solid-state physics; **~ nuclear** nuclear physics

físico *n* physicist; physique; appearance; *adj* physical; vain; prudish

físil fissile

fisiocracia physiocracy

fisiócrata physiocrat

fisiología physiology

fisiológico physiological

fisiólogo physiologist

fisión *f* fission; **~ nuclear** nuclear fission

fisionable fissionable

fisionar to fission, split

fisioquímica physiochemistry

fisioterapia physiotherapy

fisioterapista *m+f* physiotherapist

fisípedo cloven-hoofed

fisonomía face, features; countenance; physiognomy

fístula *mus* reed; *bui* water-pipe; *med* fistule

fisura fissure; ~ **del paladar** cleft palate

flaccidez *f* weakness; flabbiness

fláccido flaccid; flabby

flaco *n* weak spot; weakness; foible; *adj* thin, lean, skinny; unstable; weak

flacucho scrawny

flacura thinness; weakness

flagelación *f* flagellation, whipping

flagelador *m* flagellator

flagelante *m+f* flagellant

flagelar to flay, whip, flagellate

flagelo scourge

flagrancia flagrancy

flagrante flagrant; **en** ~ red-handed, caught in the act, flagrante delicto

flai *m sl* marihuana cigarette

flama flame; firelight

flamante flaming; flashing, brilliant; brand-new

flameante flamboyant

flamear to flame; flutter, wave (flag)

¹ **flamenco** *n m* Flemish (language); Fleming; Andalusian gipsy; gipsy song or dance; *adj* Flemish; gipsy; flashy, gaudy; skinny; *sl* brave; *sl* provocative

² **flamenco** *orni* flamingo

flamenquilla *bot* marigold; small dish

flámeo *n* veil worn by a married woman; *adj* fluttering; flame-like

flamígero *arch* flamboyant

flámula streamer

flan *m* crème caramel; baked custard

flanco flank; side; **coger a uno por el** ~ to catch s.o. off his guard

Flandes *m* Flanders; **poner un pico en** ~ to set the Thames on fire

flanquear to flank; outflank

flanqueo flank attack

flaquear to weaken, flag, slacken; give way; become discouraged

flaqueza frailty, failing, weakness; leanness

flash *m phot* flash, flashlight; newsflash; *sl* exhilarating experience

flato flatulence, wind, gas; gloominess; hangover

flatoso flatulent; gloomy

flatulencia flatulence

flatulento, flatuoso flatulent, windy

flauta flute; *m+f* flautist; ~ **de Pan** pan-pipe; ~ **dulce** recorder; **pitos y** ~**s** six of one and half a dozen of the other

flautado *n mus* flute stop (on organ); *adj* flute-like

flauteado (of voice) flute-like

flautero flute-maker

flautín *m* piccolo

flavo golden-yellow

flébil mournful

flebitis *f* phlebitis

fleco fringe; tassel; flounce; ~**s** gossamer

flecha arrow; dart; member of Phalangist youth organization; **alas en** ~ *aer* swept-back wings

flechador *m* archer

flechaduras *fpl naut* ratlines

flechar to hit with an arrow; make a hit with s.o.; throw amorous glances at; ~ **un arco** to draw a bow

flechazo arrow wound; bowshot; amorous glance; love at first sight

flechería shower of arrows

flechero archer, bowman; quiver

flejar to put a steel band/hoop around

fleje *m* hoop; steel band

flema phlegm

flemático calm, phlegmatic

flemón *m* gumboil, swollen cheek

flemoso phlegmy

flemudo sluggish

flequillo fringe

Flesinga Flushing

fletador *n m* shipowner; charterer; *adj* charter

fletam(i)ento charter(ing); freight charter; charter party

fletante *m* (person) freighter; charterer; shipowner

fletar to freight; charter; hire; load; ~**se** to clear out, get out

flete *m* freight; cargo; charter; *sl* services of a prostitute; ~ **de vuelta** return freight paid; ~ **pagado** advance, prepaid freight; ~ **pagado a destino** freight collect; **echar un** ~ *sl* to fuck

fletero *n* freighter; freight carrier; *adj* charter

flexibilidad *f* flexibility; pliability

flexibilizar to make supple

flexible *n m elect* flex; soft hat; *adj* flexible, pliable; compliant

flexión *f* flexion; inflection; bend, bending

flipado *sl* drugged

flipante *sl* pleasant; attractive; charming

flipar *sl* to like very much; *sl* take drugs

flirt *m* flirtation; boy-friend; *f* girl-friend

flirteador *n m* flirt; *adj* flirtatious

flirtear to flirt

flirteo flirting; flirtation

flogisto phlogiston

floja: *sl* **me la trae** ~ I couldn't care less

flojear to weaken; slacken, ease up; flag; be lazy

flojedad *f* weakness; slackness; looseness; laziness

flojel *m* down; *text* nap; **pato de** ~ eider duck

flojera weakness; slackness

flojo *n* mop; *adj* loose, slack; weak, feeble; lazy; timid; **viento** ~ slight breeze

floqueado fringed

flor *f* flower, blossom, bloom; maidenhead, virginity; (of leather) grain; ~ **de andamio** *sl* ordinary tobacco; ~ **de la vida** prime of life; ~ **del campo** wild flower; ~ **de lis** fleur-de-lis; amaryllis; ~ **de muerto** marigold; ~ **de un día** flash-in-the-pan; ~ **y nata** the pick, flower, cream; **a** ~ **de** on a level; **a** ~ **de agua** afloat, at water-level; **a** ~ **de labios** on the tip of one's tongue; **a** ~ **de piel** skin-deep; **echar** ~**es a** to flirt with, pay compliments to; **en** ~ in flower, in bloom; **la** ~ **de la canela** the best of all

floración *f* flowering

floral floral; **arreglo** ~ flower arrangement; **juegos** ~**es** poetry contest; **ofrenda** ~ wreath, floral tribute

florar to flower, bloom

floreado flowery; flower-patterned; **pan** ~ first-quality loaf

florear *vt* to flower; bedeck with flowers; stack (cards); sift (flour); *mus* play with a flourish; choose the best; *vi* to flit, gad about; ~**se** to shine, excel

florecer to flower, bloom; flourish; thrive, prosper; ~**se** to become mouldy, get a bloom on

floreciente in flower, flowering; flourishing, prospering

florecimiento flowering, blossoming; flourishing

Florencia Florence

florentino Florentine

floreo *mus* flourish (on the guitar); idle chatter

florera flower girl

florero *n* vase, flower pot; *adj* flattering; given to flattery

florería florist's, flower shop

florescencia florescence

floresta wood, grove, glade; anthology

florete *m* (fencing) foil; cotton fabric

floretear to decorate with flowers

floretista *m+f* fencer, swordsman/swordswoman

floricultor *m* floriculturist, flower grower

floricultura flower growing

floridez *f* floweriness

florido flowery; florid; flowering; choice; **estar en** ~ to be in bloom; **Pascua Florida** Easter

florífero flower-bearing

florilegio anthology

florista *m+f* florist

floristería florist's, flower shop

flota fleet; ~ **mercante** merchant shipping

flotación *f* buoyancy; flotation; floating; **línea de** ~ waterline

flotador *n m* float; ballcock; *adj* floating

flotante floating; hanging loose; **barba** ~ flowing beard; **témpanos** ~**s** pack-ice

flotar to float; hang loose; ~ **al viento** to stream in the wind; ~ **a media asta** to fly at half mast; ~ **un empréstito** to float a loan

flote: **a** ~ afloat; **poner a/sacar a** ~ to refloat; **ponerse a** ~ to get out of a fix

flox *m* phlox

fluctuación *f* fluctuation; uncertainty

fluctuante fluctuating

fluctuar to fluctuate; waver, hesitate; float up and down

fluente flowing; fluent

fluidez *f* fluidity; fluency, easy flow

fluido *n* fluid; ~ **eléctrico** electric current; *adj* fluid, fluent; smooth; free-flowing

fluir to flow; run

flujo flow; flux; stream; rising tide; floodtide; menstruation; ~ **de risa** burst of laughter; ~ **de sangre** haemorrhage; ~ **de vientre** diarrhoea; ~ **y reflujo** ebb and flow

fluorescencia fluorescence

fluorescente fluorescent

fluorización *f* fluoridation

fluoroscopio fluoroscope

fluor *m* fluoride

fluvial *adj* freshwater; river; fluvial

flux *m sing+pl* (cards) flush; suit of clothes; **hacer** ~ to blow/spend all one's money; **tener** ~ to be in luck

fluxión *f med* congestion; flush; head cold

F.N.M.T. (Fábrica Nacional de Monedas y Timbres) *approx equiv* the Royal Mint

¡fo! phew!

fobia phobia

foca seal; *sl* fat and ugly person; ~ **de trompa** sea-elephant

focal focal; **distancia** ~ focal length

focino elephant-goad

foco focus; focal point; centre; core; headlight; electric light bulb; street lamp; *theat* spotlight; **fuera de** ~ out of focus

focha *orni* coot

fofo soft; spongy, porous; flabby; cheap; trashy

fogarada blaze

fogata bonfire; blaze, fire; camp fire

fogón *m* stove, kitchen range; firebox; *naut* galley; hearth, fireplace; bonfire

fogonazo flash; explosion

fogonero stoker; fireman

fogosidad *f* dash, verve; spirit, mettle; fieriness

fogoso fiery, high-spirited; ardent, lustful; (horse) frisky

foguear to become accustomed to gunfire

fogueo: cartucho de ~ blank cartridge

foja *orni* coot; *leg* folio

folgo footwarmer

foliación *f* foliation, numbering of pages

foliar to foliate, number the pages of

foliculario *pej* pamphleteer

folículo follicle

folklore *m* folklore; myth; *sl* rumpus, furore; jollification

folklórico *adj* folk; folkloric, folkloristic; traditional; quaint; picturesque

folklorismo trashy local products

folklorista *n m+f* student of folklore; *adj* folkloristic

folla medley; **con mala** ~ with bad intentions; **ni** ~ absolutely nothing

follada *cul* flaky pastry pie; *vulg sl* sexual intercourse

follaje *m* foliage; trashy ornament; floweriness of speech; verbosity; *vulg*

sl sexual intercourse

follapostes *m sing+pl tel+elect sl* repairer of overhead cables/wires

follar *vulg sl* to fuck; *sl* fail (in examination); *mil sl* punish; *vulg sl* fart silently

folletín *m*, **folletón** *m* newspaper serial; (newspaper) regular feature column; pamphlet; *fam* melodrama

folletinesco melodramatic

folletinista *m+f* newspaper columnist; writer of blood-and-thunder tales

folletista *m+f* pamphleteer

folleto pamphlet; folder, brochure; tract; booklet; railway time-table

follón *n m* fuss, complication; layabout; row, uproar; **tener un** ~ to be in a mess; have a row; *adj* indolent, lazy; arrogant; cowardly

follonero, follonista *m+f* trouble-maker

fomentación *f* fomentation; poultice

fomentador *m* promoter, developer; backer

fomentar to foment; foster; promote; instigate

fomento development, improvement; promotion; furtherance; fomentation, poultice

fonda inn, restaurant; railway station buffet

fondable suitable for anchoring

fondeadero anchorage, berth

fondear *vt* to plumb the depths; *vi* to drop anchor; ~**se** to save up, put money by

fondillos *mpl* seat of pants; buttocks, bottom

fondista *m+f* innkeeper; restaurant proprietor

fondo bottom; back, background; depth; fund, reserve; ~ **de amortización** sinking fund; ~ **de inversión** *approx* unit trust; ~ **del mar** sea-bed; ~ **falso** false bottom; ~**s** funds, finance; **a** ~ thoroughly; **andar mal de** ~**s** to be short of money; **artículo de** ~ editorial; **dar** ~ to drop anchor; **echar a** ~ to sink (a ship); **en el** ~ at bottom, in essence; **irse a** ~ to sink, go to the bottom; **tener buen** ~ to be good natured

fondón *adj* hefty; big-bottomed

fonema *m* phoneme

fonémico phonemic

fonética phonetics

fonético phonetic

fonetismo phoneticism

fonetista *m + f* phonetician

fónica phonics

fónico phonic

fonil *m* funnel

fonje spongy; flabby

fonocaptor *m* pick-up arm

fonografía phonography

fonográfico phonographic

fonógrafo phonograph, gramophone, record-player

fonograma *m* phonogram

fonología phonology

fonsado *mil* ditch

fontana fountain; spring

fontanal *m*, **fontanar** *m* spring (water)

fontanería plumbing; water supply

fontanero plumber

footing *n m* jogging

footingue.ro, footinguista *m + f* jogger

foque *m naut* jib

forajido *n* outlaw; fugitive; highwayman, bandit; *adj* fugitive

foral appertaining to privileges of an autonomous region

foráneo foreign, strange; alien

forastero *n* stranger; outsider; alien, foreigner; *adj* foreign, strange

forcej(e)ar to struggle, strive, resist, oppose

forcejeo struggle

forcejudo powerful, robust

fórceps *m sing + pl* forceps

forense: *n* **médico** ~ coroner; *adj* forensic; legal

forestal *adj* forest

fori *m sl* handkerchief

forja forge, foundry; blacksmith's, smithy; forging

forjado forged; wrought; **hierro** ~ wrought iron

forjador *m* forger, counterfeiter; blacksmith; gold beater; liar

forjadura forging

forjar to forge; shape; ~ **mentiras** to concoct lies; ~**se ilusiones** to build castles in the air

forma form, shape; way, means; manner, method; formula; form, blank; format; ~**s** social conventions; curves (of female figure); **dar** ~ **a** to put into final form; **de** ~ **que** so that, so; **de esta** ~ in this way; **de todas** ~**s**

anyway, at any rate; **en** ~ in order; **en debida** ~ in due form; **estar en** ~ to be in good form, be on form

formación *f* formation; shape; upbringing, training; education; ~ **profesional** vocational training

formador *adj* forming

formal formal; reliable; serious, sedate; regular, proper; businesslike

formaldehido formaldehyde

formalidad *f* form; formality; earnestness; seriousness, reliability; gravity, dignity; ~**es** formalities, red tape

formalista *n m + f* formalist; *adj m + f* over-formal; formalistic

formalización *f* formalization

formalizar to formalize; legalize, regularize; ~**se** to become serious; take offence

formar to form; shape, fashion; train; ~**se** to be trained; receive one's education; form up, get into formation; develop

formativo formative

formato format; size (of paper)

formicario, formícido stinging insect

fórmico formic

formidable formidable; tremendous; ¡~! that's fine!, swell!

formidoloso timid; fearful

formol *m* formaldehyde

formón *m* chisel

fórmula formula; prescription; solution; **por (pura)** ~ for form's sake, as a matter of form

formulación *f* formulation

formular to formulate; word; draw up; ~ **una queja** to lodge a complaint; ~ **una solicitud de** to make application for; ~ **una pregunta** to pose a question

formulario form, blank; order form; ~ **de inscripción** application form; ~ **de pedido** order blank

formulismo red-tape

formulista *n m + f + adj* formulistic

fornicación *f* fornication

fornicador *n m* fornicator; *adj* fornicating

fornicar to fornicate

fornicario *n* fornicator; *adj* fornicating

fornicio fornication

fornido strapping, hefty, robust

fornituras *fpl mil* leather shoulder-straps

foro forum; *leg* bar; the legal profession; court of justice; backstage

Foro: el ~ Madrid

forofo *sl* supporter, fan; buff

forrado lined; upholstered; bound; **~ de dinero** well-heeled

forraje *m* fodder; forage; foraging

forrajeador *m* forrager

forrajear to forage; gather

forrar to line, pad; lag; bind (a book); upholster; **~se** to save money, line one's pockets

forro lining; padding; lagging; book cover; upholstery; **~ de freno** brake lining; **ni por el ~** not by a long chalk

forsitia forsythia

fortalecedor fortifying

fortalecer to strengthen, fortify

fortalecimiento strengthening; encouragement

fortaleza fortress, stronghold; fortitude, courage; vigour

fortificable fortifiable

fortificación *f* fortification; fort

fortificante fortifying

fortificar to fortify; strengthen

fortín *m* fort, fortification

fortísimo fortissimo

fortuito fortuitous, accidental; chance

fortuna fortune; chance; luck; fate; success, good fortune; wealth; **correr ~** to ride the storm; **por ~** luckily; **probar ~** to try one's luck

forúnculo *med* boil

forzado *n* convict (sentenced to hard labour); *adj* forced; under pressure; hard; compulsory; **entrada forzada** forcible entry; **a marchas forzadas** at a rapid pace

forzador *m* ravisher

forzal *m* back of a comb

forzamiento *m* raping; forcing

forzar to force, compel; break open; enter by force; **por ~** take by storm; ravish, rape

forzoso compulsory; inevitable, unavoidable; necessary; **aterrizaje ~** forced landing

forzudo strong, tough

fosa pit; grave; cavity; *anat* fosse; **~ de los leones** lions' den; **~s nasales** nostrils

fosar to dig a ditch

fosca mist, haze

fosco dark; irritable; frowning, cross

fosfatina: estar hecho ~ *sl* to be weary

fosfato phosphate

fosforecer, foscorescer to glow, shine in the dark; be phosphorescent

fosforera matchbox

fosforero match-seller

fosforescencia phosphorescence

fosforescente phosphorescent

fósforo match; phosphorus; *astron* morning star; **~ de seguridad** safety match

fosforoso *adj* phosphorous

fósil *n m* fossil; *adj* fossil, fossilized

fosilización *f* fossilization

fosilizar to fossilize

foso hole, pit; ditch; trench; moat; *theat* pit; **~ de agua** water jump

fotero *sl* photographer

foto *f* photo; **~ fija** still

fotocélula photoelectric cell

fotocopia photocopy, print

fotocopiadora photocopier

fotocopiar to photocopy

fotoeléctrico photoelectric

fotogénico photogenic

fotograbado photogravure; photoengraving

fotograbar to photoengrave

fotografía photograph; photography; photographic studio; **~ instantánea** snapshot

fotografiar to photograph

fotográfico photographic

fotógrafo photographer; **~ de prensa** press photographer

fotograma *m cin* still

foto(gra)metría: ~ aérea aerial mapmaking

fotomatón *m* photograph-booth

fotómetro exposure meter, light meter, photometer

fotomontaje *m* photomontage

fotón *m* photon

fotostatar to photostat

fotostático photostatic

fotostato photostat

fototipia phototype

frac *m* (*pl* **fracs, fraques**) morning-coat; tails

fracasado *n* failure; *adj* failed; **intentona fracasada** abortive coup

fracasar to fail; be a failure; fall through; collapse; miscarry; *naut* break up

fracaso failure; stop; setback; slump; collapse

fracción f fraction; fragment; section; sub-paragraph; faction

fraccionamiento subdivision; dividing up; breaking up

fraccionar to divide up; subdivide; break up

fraccionario fractional

fractura fracture, break; ~ **complicada** compound fracture

fracturar to break, fracture; ~**se un brazo** to break one's arm

fraga raspberry

fragancia fragrance, perfume

fragante fragrant, sweet-smelling; **en ~** caught in the act, red-handed

fragaria strawberry

fragata frigate; *orni* frigate-bird; ~ **ligera** corvette

frágil fragile; frail; brittle

fragilidad f fragility; frailty; brittleness

fragmentación f fragmentation

fragmentar to fragment

fragmentario fragmentary

fragmento fragment

fragor m crash; din; uproar

fragoroso deafening

fragosidad f roughness; unevenness; denseness, thickness; rough path

fragoso rough, uneven; dense; deafening

fragua forge; smithy

fraguador n m schemer; adj scheming

fraguar vt to forge; devise, scheme; plot; vi to set (concrete etc); ~ **una mentira** to think up a lie; ~ **un complot** to hatch a plot

fraile m friar; monk; ~ **rezador** praying mantis

frailecillo puffin

fraileño monkish

frambuesa raspberry

frambueso raspberry cane

framea javelin

francachela spree; spread, feast; jamboree

[1] **francés** n m Frenchman; French (language); **mal ~** venereal disease; adj French

[2] **francés** vulg sl oral sex

francesilla buttercup

francesa n Frenchwoman; **a la ~** in a

French manner; **despedirse a la ~** to take French leave; **patatas a la ~** fried potatoes, chips, french-fries; **tortilla (a la) ~** plain omelette

francesada typically French behaviour

Francia France

Francisca Frances

franciscano n + adj Franciscan

Francisco Francis

francmasón m Freemason

francmasonería Freemasonry

Franco Frank

[1] **franco** n franc; Frank (nationality)

[2] **franco** adj frank, outspoken, open; free, gratis; exempt; generous; ~ **a bordo**, ~ **bordo** free on board; ~ **al costado vapor** free alongside; ~ **de derechos** duty-free; ~ **de porte(s)** prepaid; post free; post paid; carriage free

francófilo francophile

francófobo francophobe

francote frank, blunt, outspoken

francotirador m sharpshooter, sniper

franchute pej Froggy, Frenchy

franela flannel

frangente m mishap

frangir to shatter, smash to smithereens

frangollar to mess up, botch

frangollón adj botching

frángula bot alder

franja fringe; border; braid; strip; stripe; bank

franjar to trim

franqueado franked; pre-paid; **carta franqueada** stamped envelope; **carta franqueada de menos** 'postage due' letter

franqueadora franking machine

franquear to frank; pre-pay; exempt; free, liberate; open up, clear; pass through; despatch, send; expedite; ~ **el paso a** to permit the passage of; ~ **entrada** to grant access; ~ **una carta** to stamp, pre-pay a letter; ~**se con** to unbosom oneself to

franqueo postage; franking (letter); clearance; freeing

franqueza frankness, plain speaking; generosity; freedom; con ~ frankly

franquía clearing (of a vessel for sailing); sea room

franquicia exemption; privilege; franchise; enfranchisement; ~ **aduanera/arancelaria** exemption from customs' duty; ~ **diplomática** diplomatic privilege

franquismo Francoism

franquista n m+f supporter of General Franco, Francoite; adj pro-Franco

frasca dry leaves

frasco flask, bottle; jar; ~ **al vacío** vacuum flask

frase f sentence, phrase; expression; phrasing; ~ **hecha** stock phrase, cliché; proverb; ~**s duras** insulting remarks

frasear to phrase

fraseo mus phrasing

fraseología phraseology; wording; verbosity

fratás m bui plasterer's trowel

fratasar bui to smooth with a trowel

fraternal brotherly, fraternal

fraterna severe reprimand

fraternidad f brotherhood, fraternity

fraternización f fraternization

fraternizar to fraternize

fraterno fraternal, brotherly

fratricida m+f fratricide (person)

fratricidio fratricide (deed)

fraude m fraud; frame-up; faking; imposture

fraudulencia fraudulence; defrauding; deceit

fraudulento fraudulent

fray m (before a Christian name) friar, brother, Fra

frazada blanket

frazadero blanket-maker

frecuencia frequency; **alta** ~ high frequency; **baja** ~ low frequency; **con** ~ frequently, often

frecuentación f frequentation

frecuentador m frequenter

frecuentar to frequent, haunt

frecuentativo frequentative

frecuente frequent; common

fregadera, fregadero kitchen sink

¹ **fregado** n washing-up; scrubbing; mess; row; **dar un** ~ **a uno** to give s.o. a dressing-down; **hacer el** ~ to do the washing-up

² **fregado** adj annoying

fregador m dishcloth; sink

fregadora dishwashing-machine

fregajo swab; mop

fregar to wash up, wash dishes; mop; scrub; scour; annoy, tease, bother

fregasuelos m sing+pl floor mop

fregona, fregatriz kitchen-maid; wet mop

fregotear to scrub/wash up hurriedly

freiduría fried-fish shop

freír to fry; annoy; sl kill (with a firearm)

fréjol m see frijol

frenaje m braking

frenar to brake, put the brake on; bridle; check, restrain

frenazo see frenaje

frenesí m frenzy, madness

frenético frantic, frenzied, wild

frenillo naut ratline; **tener** ~ to lisp

freno brake; bit (horse); curb, check; fig stop; deterrent; ~ **de mano** handbrake; ~ **de pedal** footbrake; ~**s asistidos** powered brakes

frenología phrenology

frenológico phrenological

frenólogo phrenologist

frenópata m alienist

frenopatía alienism

frental of the forehead

¹ **frente** m front; front line, battlefield, firing line; face; ~ **a** in front of; compared with; ~ **a** ~ face to face; **a** ~ straight ahead, facing forward, abreast, resolutely; **en** ~ **de** in front of, against, opposite; **hacer** ~ **a** to face, confront

² **frente** f forehead, brow; face; **adornar la** ~ sl to be unfaithful to one's husband; **arrugar la** ~ to knit one's brow

fresa (usu wild) strawberry; bit, drill

fresadora metal milling machine

fresal m strawberry bed

fresar metal to mill

fresca fresh air; cool of the day; straight speaking; wisecrack; **tomar la** ~ to get a breath of fresh air

frescachón robust, glowing with health; cheeky; **mujer frescachona** buxom woman

frescal slightly salted

¹ **fresco** n cooling drink, refreshment; fresco; fresh air; coolness, freshness; cheeky person; **al** ~ out of doors, in the open air; **hace** ~ it is cool/fresh; **quedarse tan** ~ to remain unmoved; **tomar el** ~ to get some fresh air

² **fresco** adj fresh; cool; cheeky; new-laid; newly made

frescor m freshness; coolness, cool;

(painting) vivid colour

frescote *pej* buxom; blooming

frescura freshness; coolness; impudence, cheek; impudent remark; ¡qué ~! what a cheek!, what impudence!

fresera strawberry plant

fresero strawberry seller

fresnada ashgrove

fresnal of the ash tree

fresno ash (tree); ash (wood)

fresón *m* (cultivated) strawberry

fresquecillo, fresqueato, fresquito nice and cool

fresquera ice box; meat safe

fresquería ice-cream parlour, refreshment stall

fresquero fishmonger

fresquista *m+f* fresco painter

fresquito coolish; pleasantly cool

freudiano Freudian

freudismo Freudianism

frez *f* dung, animal droppings

freza spawn; spawning season; spawning; dung

frezar to spawn; *zool* defecate

friabilidad *f* friability

frialdad *f* coldness; coolness; indifference; *med* frigidity

fricación *f* friction, rubbing

fricar to rub

fricasé *m* fricassee

fricativo fricative

fricción *f* friction; rubbing; massage

friccionar to massage, rub

friega massage, rubbing; drubbing, beating; bother, fuss; nuisance

friegaplatos *m sing+pl* dishwasher

friera chilblain

frigidez *f* frigidity; coolness

frígido frigid; cool, cold

frigo *fam* fridge

frigorificación *f* refrigeration

¹ **frigorífico** *n* refrigerator; cold-storage plant; meat-packing plant; refrigerator ship

² **frigorífico** *adj* cold-storage, refrigerating

frijol *m* bean; kidney bean; french bean; ~ de media luna lima bean; ~ soya soya bean

fringílido *orni* member of the finch family

frío *n* cold; coldness, chill, fever; *adj* cold; cool; frigid; **bala fría** spent

bullet; **coger/tomar** ~ to catch cold; **hace** ~ it is cold; **tener** ~ to be cold

friolento, friolero sensitive to cold; shivery, chilly; cold-blooded

friolera trifle; trinket; snack; trifling matter

frisa frieze

frisado silk plush

frisar *vt* to rub; frizz; *vi* to agree; ~ con/ en to border on; **él frisa con los cuarenta** he's getting on for forty

Frisia Friesland

friso wainscot, baseboard; frieze; dado

frisol *m* kidney-bean

frisón *n m+adj* Friesian

frisuelo fritter

fritada fritter; fry-up

frito *n* doughnut; fried dish; ~s mixtos/ variados mixed grill; *adj* fried; *sl* in a mess, in a pickle; **estar** ~ *sl* to be asleep, be annoyed, be in a pickle; fed up; **traer** ~ to pester, annoy

fritura fritter

frivolidad *f* frivolity, frivolousness

frivolité *m* tatting

frívolo frivolous; trifling; **pretexto** ~ flimsy excuse

friz *f* beech flower

fronda frond, fern leaf; foliage

frondífero leaf-bearing

frondosidad *f* leafiness; luxuriance of growth

frondoso leafy, luxuriant

frontal *n m* altar frontal; *adj* frontal; of the forehead; **choque** ~ head-on collision

frontera frontier, border; boundary; façade

fronterizo *adj* frontier; boundary; facing; opposite

frontero facing, opposite

frontis *m sing+pl* façade, front

frontispicio frontispiece; title page

frontón *m* jai alai/pelota/handball court; pediment; gable; escarpment; **juego de** ~ handball

frontudo broad-browed

frotación *f*, **frotadura, frotamiento** rubbing; friction

frotador *m* rubber

frotar to rub; chafe; scour; ~ **una cerilla** to strike a match; **frotársela** *vulg sl* to masturbate; **quitar frotando** to rub off

frote *m* rub, rubbing; friction

frotis *m med* smear

fructífero fruitful; productive; interest-bearing

fructificación *f* fructification

fructificar to produce; bear fruit; yield (a crop, profit)

fructuoso fruitful; bearing fruit; productive; profitable

frugal frugal; thrifty

frugalidad *f* thrift; thriftiness; frugality

frugífero fruit-producing

fruición *f* enjoyment; delight; satisfaction

fruir to enjoy o.s.

frunce *m*, **fruncido, fruncimiento** pleat; puckering, gathering

fruncir to wrinkle (the brow); pucker; pleat, gather; ~ **el ceño/entrecejo** to frown, knit one's brows; ~ **la verdad** to twist the truth; ~ **los labios** to purse one's lips; ~**se** to frown

fruslería trifle; trinket; triviality

fruslero *n* rolling pin; *adj* trifling

frustración *f* frustration

frustráneo abortive, unsuccessful

frustrar to frustrate; thwart; foil; defraud; ~**se** to fail, be thwarted

frustrante *adj* frustrating

fruta fruit; *fig* consequence; ~ **del tiempo** fruit in season; ~ **de sartén** fritter, pancake; ~ **nueva** novelty

frutaje *m arts* painting of fruit/vegetables

frutal *n m* fruit tree; *adj* fruit-bearing, fruit

frutar to fruit, yield fruit

frutecer to begin to bear fruit

frutera fruit bowl

frutería fruit shop

frutero fruiterer; fruit dish, fruit bowl; *adj* fruit

fruticultura fruit-growing

frutilla rosary bead

fruto fruit; yield; result, consequence; ~ **del país** national products; ~**s** products, produce; proceeds; **sacar** ~ **de** to benefit from

fu: ¡~! faugh!; **ni** ~ **ni fa** neither one thing nor another; so-so

fúcar *m* wealthy man

fucilar to glisten

fucilazo sheet lightning

fuco bladder-wrack

fucsia *bot* fuchsia

¡**fucha**!, ¡**fuche**! phew!

fudre *sl* drunk

fuego fire, match, light; flame; beacon; hearth; ardour; skin rash; cold sore; ¡~! fire!; ~ **fatuo** will o' the wisp; ~**s artificiales** fireworks; **abrir** ~ to open fire; **echar** ~ to blow one's top; **echar** ~ **por los ojos** to look daggers; **hacer** ~ **sobre** to fire on; **pegar** ~ **a** to set fire to, set on fire; **prenderse** ~ to catch fire; **tocar a** ~ to ring the fire alarm

fuelle *m* bellows; cloud; wrinkle; tale-bearer; folding hood, folding top; ~ **de pie** foot pump

fuente *f* fountain; spring; source; serving-dish, plate, bowl; ~ **de agua** water supply; ~ **de gasolina** petrol/gasoline pump; ~ **de sodas** soda fountain; ~ **para beber** drinking fountain; ~**s solventes** reliable sources; ~ **termal** hot spring

fuer: a ~ **de** as, in the character of; by way of, by reason of

fuera *adv* outside, out; away; ¡~!, ¡~ **aquí**! get out!, go away!; ~ **de** out of, outside of; in addition to, besides; ~ **de eso** apart from that; ~ **de** +*infin* short of +*pres part*; ~ **de pagar** short of paying; ~ **de que** in addition to the fact that; **desde** ~ from the outside; **estar** ~ **de sí** to be beside o.s.; **por** ~ on the outside

fueraborda *m*, **fuerabordo** outboard motor

fuerino *Chil* outsider; drop-out; unprivileged person

fuero statute; code of laws; charter; privilege; jurisdiction, authority; **en su** ~ **íntimo** in his/her heart of hearts

fuerte *n m* fort, fortress; *mil* strong point; (person's) strong point; *mus* forte; *adj* strong; heavy; severe, intense; harsh; loud; *sl* incredible; ~ **en** well up in; *adv* loudly; strongly, excessively; hard

fuerza strength; force; power; intensity; effect; ~ **mayor** act of God, force majeure; ~ **motriz** motive power; ~ strength; (armed) forces; **a** ~ **de** by dint of; **a la** ~ forcibly; **por** ~ necessarily; **por (la)** ~ by force, forcibly; **por** ~ **mayor** under compulsion, by main force; by act of God; **ser** ~ to

be necessary
fuetazo lash, whipping
fuete *m* whip
fufar (of cats) to make a spitting noise
fuga flight; leak, escape; fugue; **darse a la** ~ to take to one's heels; **poner en** ~ to put to flight; **ponerse en** ~ run away
fugacidad *f* fleetingness
fugarse to flee, escape; ~**se con** to run away with
fugaz fleeting, passing; short-lived; elusive; **estrella** ~ shooting star
fugitivo *n+adj* fugitive
fuina *zool* marten
ful *f sl* shit; *adj sl* false
fulana tart, prostitute; ~ **de tal** Mrs So-and-So
fulano so-and-so; ~ **de tal** Mr So-and-So; ~, **sutano y mengano** Tom, Dick and Harry
fulastre *sl* false; of poor quality
fulcro fulcrum
fulero sham; poor-quality; untrue; blustering
fulgencia effulgence
fulgente brilliant, radiant
fulgor *m* radiance, brilliance; glow
fulguración *f* flash
fulgurante shining; shattering
fulgurar to gleam, shine, flash
fulguroso shining, flashing
fúlica *orni* coot
fuliginoso dark, murky
fulmar *m orni* fulmer
fulminación *f* fulmination
fulminante *n m* percussion cap; *adj* sudden; violent; fulminating; **éxito** ~ staggering success
fulminar to fulminate; utter threats; strike like lightning; explode
fulleresco *adj* swindling, cheating
fullería cheating; card-sharping
fullero *n* crook; cheat; card-sharper; *adj* shady, crooked; mischievous
fumable good for smoking
fumada whiff; draw (of cigarette); puff of smoke
fumadero smoke-room
fumado *sl* drugged
fumador *m* smoker; **no** ~ non-smoker
fumante *adj* smoking; fuming
fumar *vt* to smoke; *vi* to smoke, fume; ~**se algo** to squander s.t.; ~**se la clase**

to cut classes; **se prohibe** ~, ~ **prohibido** no smoking
fumarada puff; pipeful
fumarel *m orni* black tern
fumata *sl* gathering of marihuana smokers
fumeta *sl* marihuana smoker
fumigación *f* fumigation
fumigador *m* fumigator
fumigar to fumigate
fumista *m* stove-seller; chimney-sweep
fumistería stove repair-shop
fumosidad *f* smokiness
fumoso smoky
funambulismo tightrope walking
funámbulo, funambulista *m+f* tight-rope walker
función *f* function, duty; office, position; show, performance; **entrar en funciones** to take up a post; **alcalde en funciones** acting mayor, mayor designate; **gobierno en funciones** care-taker government
funcional functional
funcionamiento working, functioning; behaviour; **en** ~ working, in order
funcionar to work, function; behave; *vulg sl* fuck; **hacer** ~ to operate, work; **no funciona** out of order
funcionario official; civil servant; functionary; employee
funda case, cover; sheath, scabbard; covering, wrapping; holdall; *sl* French letter; ~ **de almohada** pillow-slip; ~ **de pistola** holster
fundación *f* foundation
fundado well-founded, justified
fundador *m* founder
fundamentalismo fundamentalism
fundamentalista *n m+f +adj* fundamentalist
fundamentar to lay the basis/foundations of
fundamento basis, foundation; grounds, reliability; groundwork; ~**s** fundamentals
fundar to found; establish; base; ~ **con dinero** to endow; ~**se en** to base one's opinion on
fundente *n m chem* flux; dissolvent; *adj* melting
fundible fusible
fundíbulo catapult
fundición *f* fusion; melting; smelting;

foundry, forge; *print* fount

fundido *fam* bankrupt

fundidor *m* foundryman

fundillos *mpl* seat of trousers; buttocks

fundir to fuse; melt (down); smelt; *sl* squander; ~**se** to blow a fuse; combine, merge; be ruined

fundo property in the country

fúnebre *adj* funeral; funereal; gloomy, lugubrious; **director de pompas** ~**s** undertaker, *US* mortician

funeral *m*, **funerales** *mpl* funeral (service)

funerala: a la ~ *mil* with reversed arms

funeraria undertaker's establishment, funeral parlour

funerario *n* funeral director, *US* mortician; *adj* funeral; funereal

funéreo funereal

funesto ill-fated, unfortunate; fatal, disastrous, baneful

fungicida *n m* fungicide; *adj* fungicidal

fungiforme fungiform

fungo fungus

fungosidad *f* fungus growth

fungoso fungous, spongy

funguelar *sl* to stink, pong

fuñicar to burgle

fuñique clumsy

furcia prostitute

furgón *m* van, truck; luggage van, freight car; guard's van, caboose

furgonero van man

furgoneta van, delivery truck; estate car, station wagon

furia fury, rage; speed

furibundo, **furioso** furious; violent, frantic

furor *m* fury, anger, rage; **hacer** ~ to be all the rage; **tener** ~ **por** to have a passion for

furriel *m mil* quartermaster

furtivismo poaching

furtivo *n* poacher; *adj* sly, furtive

fusa demi-semi-quaver

fusca *sl* pistol

fuselaje *m* fuselage

fusible *n m* fuse; **caja de** ~**s** fuse box; *adj* fusible

fusibilidad *f* fusibility

fusil *m* gun; rifle; ~ **de chispa** flintlock; ~ **de juguete** toy gun; ~ **de retrocarga** breech-loading rifle

fusilamiento shooting; execution (by firing-squad)

fusilar to shoot, execute; *sp* score a goal with great force

fusilazo gunshot, rifleshot; blow with a rifle

fusilería fusillade; rifle corps

fusilero rifleman, fusilier

fusión *f* fusion; melting; merger

fusionamiento merger, amalgamation

fusionar(se) to fuse, melt; merge

fusta horsewhip; rod; brushwood

fustán *m* fustian; (woman's) slip

fuste *m* wood, timber; **de** ~ wooden, timber; **hombre de** ~ man of substance

fustigador *adj* savage

fustigar to whip; scold, rebuke

futbito five-a-side football

fútbol *m* football, soccer; ~ **sala** five-a-side football

futbolero football enthusiast

futbolín *m* table-football

futbolista *m* footballer, soccer player

futbolístico *adj* football

futesa trifle

fútil futile, trifling

futilidad *f* futility, uselessness

futre *m* dandy

futura *fam* fiancée, future wife

futurible *pol* up-and-coming, promising

futurista, **futurística** futuristic

futuro future; *fam* fiancé, future husband; ~**s** *comm* futures; **en el/en lo** ~ in the future, hereafter

G

g *f* letter g; **(gramo)** gr (gramme)

gabacho *n* Frenchman, Froggy; Pyrenean; foreigner; yankee; *adj* French; frenchified; Pyrenean; **me salió gabacha** it turned out wrong for me

gabán *m* overcoat; jacket; cloak

gabardina raincoat; gabardine

gabarra barge, lighter; tender; ~ **de grúa** derrick barge; ~ **encajonada** covered lighter

gabarraje lighterage

gabarrero lighterman, bargee

gabela tax; duty; fee; ~ **de consumo** excise tax; ~ **por derechos patentarios** patent royalty

gabi *m sl* grub, nosh

gabinete *m* office; consulting room; study; studio; library (in a house); boudoir; sitting room; (government) cabinet; ~ **de archivo** filing cabinet; ~ **de lectura** reading room; ~ **de teléfono** telephone booth; ~ **de torturas** torture chamber; **estratega de** ~ armchair strategist

gablete *m* gable

gabón *m* powder magazine

gabonés *n m* +*adj* Gabonese

gacel *m*, **gacela** gazelle

gaceta gazette; newspaper; periodical; ~ **de los buques** shipping news; **Gaceta cameral** Congressional Record

gacetero newswriter, journalist; newspaper seller; gazetteer

gacetilla gossip column; short newspaper article; news in brief; newspaper miscellany; (person) gossip

gacetillero newspaper reporter; penny-a-liner, hack writer; gossip columnist; (person) gossip

gacetista *m*+*f* scandalmonger, gossip

gacha mush; mud; earthenware bowl, crock; ~s porridge; pap; ~s **de avena** oatmeal porridge; **a** ~s on all fours

gacheta spring lock, catch

gachí *f sl* attractive woman

gacho turned down; bent downwards; drooping, stooping; (of cattle) with horns turned downwards; **a gachas** stooping; on all fours; **con las orejas gachas** with lop/drooping ears; crestfallen; **sombrero** ~ slouched hat

gachó *m sl* bloke, fellow, guy

gachón attractive, charming, cute; (of a child) pampered, spoiled

gachupín *m Mex* Spaniard, Spanish settler

gaditano *n* native of Cadiz; *adj* of Cadiz

gaélico *n* Gael; Gaelic (language); *adj* Gaelic

gafar to destroy, tear down; bring bad luck to

gafas *fpl* spectacles; motorcyclist's goggles; grappling hooks; ~ **bifocales** bifocals; ~ **graduadas** prescription glasses; ~ **de sol/para sol** sunglasses; ~ **protectoras** protective goggles; ~ **submarinas** underwater goggles

gafe *m*+*f* jinx, bad luck; **ser** ~ to be always out of luck, be always making a mess of things

gafete *m* hook and eye; clasp

gafudo *sl* four-eyes, person who wears glasses

gaguear to stutter, stammer

gagueo stuttering, stammering

gaguera speech defect, stammer

gago stammerer

gaita flageolet; bagpipes; hand-organ, hurdy-gurdy; hard task; neck; good-for-nothing, lazy person; Galician; ~ **gallega** bagpipes; **estar de** ~ to be merry; **sacar la** ~ to stick one's neck out

gaitería brightly coloured clothing

gaitero *n* piper; *adj* gaudy, flashy; loud; too merry

gaje *m* fee; bonus; gage (challenge); ~ **del oficio** occupational hazard; customs of the trade; ~s perquisites, emoluments, salary

gajo cluster (of fruit); small bunch; slice, segment (of an orange); (broken)

229

branch (of a tree); spur (of a mountain)

gala elegance; ostentation, show; best suit; prize; tip; ~s regalia; ornaments; finery; ~s **de novia** bride's trousseau; **de** ~ **gala**, festive; **función de** ~ gala performance; **hacer** ~ **de** to boast of, make a show of; **ser la** ~ **de** to be the flower/pride of; **tener a** ~ to be proud to; **traje de** ~ dress suit; full dress uniform

galabardera *bot* dog rose; hip

galáctico galactic

galaico *adj* Galician

galafate *m* cunning thief, sneak-thief

galán *m theat* leading actor; handsome man; wooer; ladies' man; *adj* handsome, debonair

galancete *m* handsome young man; *theat* juvenile lead

galano tastefully dressed; elegant

galante gallant, attentive to the ladies; courteous, polite; (woman) wanton; **mujer** ~ courtesan

galanteador *m* lady's man; gallant; flatterer

galantear to court, woo; flirt with; make love to; flatter; compliment (a lady)

galanteo courtship, wooing; flirting; flirtation; flattery; gallantry

galantería compliment; flattery; gallantry; liberality; elegance; gracefulness; **decir una** ~ to pay a compliment

galantina galantine

galanura elegance, grace; beauty; charm

galápago turtle; terrapin; tortoise; pulley; ingot; mould; cheat; side saddle; *naut* batten

galardón *m* reward, recompense; prize

galardonador *m* rewarder

galardonar to reward, recompense; give a prize to

galaxia galaxy; galactite

galayo rocky outcrop

galbana idleness, sloth

galbanero, galbanoso idle, slothful

galeaza *naut* large galley (vessel)

galeno *naut* (of wind) gentle

gáleo dogfish; swordfish

galeón *m* galleon

galeote *m* galley slave

galera galley; large van; covered waggon; *print* galley; hospital ward;

woman's prison; shed, shanty; top hat, bowler hat

galerada galley proof; van load; waggon load

galerero *naut* master/captain of a galley

galería gallery; balcony; glass-covered porch; corridor; changing-room, cubicle; ~ **de tiro** shooting gallery; ~ **de viento** wind tunnel; ~ **policíaca** rogue's gallery; ~ **visitable** manhole; **hablar para la** ~ to play to the gallery

Gales *m* Wales; **el País de** ~ Wales; **la Nueva** ~ **del Sur** New South Wales; *text* **príncipe de** ~ check pattern

galés *n m* Welshman; Welsh (language); *adj* Welsh

galfarro wastrel

galga greyhound bitch; skid; mange; boulder

galgo *n* greyhound; ~ **ruso** borzoi; *adj* sweet-toothed; gluttonous

galgueño *adj* greyhound; to do with greyhounds

Galia *f* Gaul

Galiano: querer los palacios de ~ to be discontented with one's social position

galicano Gallic

galiciano *n* + *adj* Galician

galicismo Gallicism, French word/ expression; foreign word/expression generally accepted as Spanish

gálico *n* syphilis; *adj* Gallic, Gaulish

galicoso syphilitic

Galilea Galilee

galileo Galilean

galillo gullet

galimatías *mpl* gibberish

galio *cul* rennet

galiparla Frenchified Castilian

galo Gallic, Gaulish

galocha clog; galosh; overshoe

¹ **galón** *m* gallon

² **galón** *m* braid; *mil* stripe, chevron

galoneado trimmed with braid

galoneador *n m* trimmer

galop *m mus* gallop

galopada gallop; **pegar una** ~ to break into a gallop

galopante galloping

galopar, galopear to gallop; **echar a** ~ to break into a gallop

galope *m* gallop; **a** ~, **al** ~, **de** ~ at a gallop; **a** ~ **tendido** at full speed;

medio ~ canter

galopeado done hastily

galopillo scullion

galopín *m* young rascal

galpón *m* shed; toolshed; storehouse; garage

galvánico galvanic

galvanismo galvanism

galvanización *f* galvanizing; electroplating

galvanizar to galvanize; electroplate

galvanómetro galvanometer

gallardear to be elegant; carry o.s. well

gallardete *m* streamer; pennant

gallardetón *m* broad pennant

gallardía grace, elegance; deportment; gallantry, bravery

gallardo graceful, elegant; handsome; bold, brave; excellent

gallear *vt* (of cock) to tread, copulate; *vi* to excel, stand out; strut about; put on airs; shout threateningly

gallego *n+adj* Galician; *SA pej* Spaniard; *sl* coward; **viento ~** north-east wind

gallera cock pit

gallero breeder of fighting-cocks

galleta biscuit, cracker; slap, blow; telling-off; **~ de perro** dog biscuit; **colgarle la ~ a una persona** to sack s.o.; jilt

galletero biscuit-maker

gallina hen; timid person; coward; **~ ciega** blindman's buff; **~ clueca** broody hen; **~ de agua, ~ del río** coot; **~ de Guinea** guinea-fowl; **~ ponedora** laying hen; **~s** poultry; **~ sorda** woodcock; **carne de ~** goose-flesh, goose pimples

gallinaza poultry droppings

gallinazo turkey-buzzard

gallinería poultry market; poulterer's; flock of hens

gallinero henhouse; poultry yard; poultry dealer, poulterer; poultry basket; *theat* upper gallery, gods; bedlam

gallineta *orni* sandpiper

gallipuente *m* bridge without handrails

gallo cock, rooster; bully, domineering person, cock of the walk; boss; pilferer; frog in the throat; false note (in singing); *zool* dory; fishing float; **~ de pelea/de riña** game cock, fighting cock; **~ lira** *orni* grouse; **alzar el ~** to brag, boast; **llevar un ~** to serenade; **misa del ~** midnight mass (Christmas Eve); **no ser ~ para** to be no match for; **patas de ~** crow's feet; **peso ~** bantam weight; **vestirse de ~** to wear old clothes; **otro ~ nos cantará** it would have been different

gallofear to live on charity

gallofero wastrel; idler; vagabond

Gallup: sondeo ~ Gallup poll

gama doe; gamut; *mus* scale; *comm* range; gamma (Greek letter); **~ de frecuencias** frequency range

gamba prawn

gambado knock-kneed

gamberrada act of vandalism, hooliganism

gamberrismo hooliganism; vandalism

gamberro *n* lout, hooligan; vandal; *adj* loutish

gambiano Gambian

gambito gambit

gamella feeding trough; wash-tub

gamo buck, fallow deer

gamón *m bot* asphodel

gamuza chamois; chamois-leather; wash-leather; duster

gamuzado chamois-coloured

gana appetite, desire; inclination, will; **~ de comer** appetite; **darle a uno la ~ de, sentir/tener ~s de** to feel like, have a mind to; **de buena ~** willingly; **de mala ~** reluctantly, unwillingly; **no me da la ~** I don't want to, I don't feel like it

ganadería cattle, livestock; cattle-raising; cattle-dealing; breed, stock (of cattle); cattle ranch; stock farm

ganadero *n* cattleman; cattle-dealer; stock-farmer; cattle-breeder; *adj* cattle, pertaining to cattle

ganado *n* cattle, livestock; herd; **~ de cerda** swine; **~ de cría** breeding cattle; **~ en pie** cattle on the hoof; **~ lanar, ~ ovejuno** sheep; **~ mayor** cattle, horses, mules, asses; **~ menor** sheep, goats, pigs; **~ vacuno** cattle

ganador *n m* winner; *adj* winning, victorious; **apostar a ~ y colocado** to back (a horse) each way

ganancia profit, gain; **~ bruta, ~ en bruto** gross profit; **~ de capital** capital gains; **~ líquida** net profit; **~ por hora**

hourly earnings; ~s **previstas** anticipated profits; ~ **según los libros** book profit; ~s **y pérdidas** profit and loss

ganancial *adj* profit

gananciales *mpl* joint property (husband and wife)

ganancioso *n* winner, gainer; *adj* profitable, lucrative

ganapán *m* odd-job man; messenger; porter

ganar to win; gain; earn; get, obtain; ~ **dinero** to make money; ~ **el barlovento de** to get to the windward of; ~ **la costa** to make land/the shore; ~ **por la mano/de mano** to get the better of s.o.; beat s.o. to it; ~ **tiempo** to save time; ~ **vecindad** to establish legal residence; ~**se la vida** to earn one's daily bread; earn a living; **ir ganando** to lead

ganchada favour; **hacer una** ~ to do a favour

ganchillo hook; crochet hook; crochet work

gancho hook; shepherd's crook; crochet work; side saddle; bait, lure, attraction; sex appeal; ~ **de cabeza** hairpin; **echar un** ~ *sp* to deliver a hook; **tener** ~ to be attractive (of a woman), have a way with the men

ganchoso, ganchudo hooked, curved

gandaya life of idleness

gandujar to pleat; tuck; plait

gandul *m* loafer, idler, vagabond; *adj* lazy, loafing

gandulear to idle about, loaf

gandulería loafing; laziness, idleness

ganga bargain; cinch, easy job

ganglio ganglion; swelling

gangosidad *f* nasality, speech with a nasal twang

gangoso (of speech) nasal

gangrena gangrene

gangrenarse to become gangrenous

gangrenoso gangrenous

gangsterismo gangsterism

ganguear to talk through the nose; snuffle

gangueo talking through the nose; snuffling

ganguista *m+f* bargain hunter

Ganimedes *m* Ganymede

ganoso desirous; anxious; (of a horse) skittish, lively

gansa (hen) goose; **pasta** ~ *sl* lots of money, easy money

gansada stupid action/behaviour

gansear to say/do foolish things

ganso gander, goose; *fam* dunce; country bumpkin; slovenly or silly person; ~ **del norte** *orni* eider; ¡**no seas** ~! don't be stupid!

gante *n m* type of rough canvas; *adj* of Ghent

Gante Ghent

¹ **ganzúa** burglar; inquisitive person

² **ganzúa** hook; tool for picking locks; skeleton key; pass-key

gañán *m* farm hand, farm labourer; brawny man

gañanía farm labourers' quarters

gañido yelp, howl, squeal

gañir to yelp, howl; crow; croak; gasp, pant

garabatear *vt* to scribble; *vi* to doodle, scribble; beat about the bush; grapple

garabateo scribbling, doodling; beating about the bush

garabato hook, meat hook; hoe; grappling iron; (womanly) charm, sex appeal; scrawl; doodle; pothook; ~s scribbling; **hacer** ~s to scribble, scrawl

garabatoso covered with scribbles/doodles

garaje *m* garage; ~ **desatendido** unattended garage; ~ **de varios pisos** multi-storey car park; ~ **sin cerrar** all-night garage

garajista *m* garage attendant

garambaina ornament in bad taste, flashy ornament; ridiculously affected behaviour

garante *n m+f* surety; guarantor; referee (for a testimonial); *adj* responsible, acting as guarantor

garantía guarantee; warranty; surety; assurance; collateral, security; pledge, undertaking; bail, bond; covenant; ~ **crediticia** guarantee of credit; ~ **en efectivo** cash guarantee; ~ **hipotecaria** mortgage; ~ **subsidiaria** collateral

garantir *see* **garantizar**

garantizador *m* guarantor

garantizar to guarantee; vouch for; stand bail for

garañón m (stud) jackass; stallion, stud horse

garapiña sugar icing; pineapple drink

garapiñado glacé; sugar-coated

garapiñar to coat with sugar; candy; ice (a cake); clot (cream); freeze (ice-cream)

garapiñera ice-cream freezer

garapita net with a very fine mesh

garatusas: hacer ~ a uno to coax s.o.

garbancero seller of chick-peas

garbanzo chick pea; **cambiar el agua a los ~s** euph to see a man about a dog; **el ~ negro** the black sheep of the family

garbear to affect elegance, try to look glamorous

garbeo sl stroll

garbillar to sieve, sift; screen; riddle

garbillo sieve; sifter; screen

garbo elegance, grace; gracefulness; glamour; attractiveness; frankness; **andar con ~** to carry o.s. well

garbón m (male) partridge

garboso easy, graceful; attractive, glamorous; liberal, generous

garbullo confusion

garduño sneak-thief

garete: al ~ adrift; **estar al ~, ir al ~** to be adrift, be drifting

garfa claw

garfada clawing, scratching

garfio hook, gaff; grappling-iron; climbing-iron

gargajear to clear the throat

gargajeo clearing of the throat

gargajo phlegm

garganta throat; gullet; neck of bottle; singing voice; ravine, gorge; mountain pass, defile; **~ de pie** instep; **tener buena ~** to be a good singer

gargantear to warble, trill

garganteo warbling, trilling

gargantilla necklace

gárgara gargle; gargling; **hacer ~s** to gargle

gargarear to gargle

gargarismo gargling; gargle (solution); mouthwash

gargarizar to gargle

gárgola gargoyle

garguero windpipe; gullet; oesophagus

garita booth; sentry box; porter's lodge; watchman's hut; cabin; watch-tower;

~ de señales signal box

garitero gambler; gambling den

garito gambling den; (gambler's) winnings

garla chat, conversation

garlador m talker

garlito snare, trap; fish trap; **caer en el ~** to fall into a trap; **coger a uno en el ~** to catch s.o. red-handed, catch in the act

garnacha judge's gown

garra claw, talon; paw; clutch; strength; profit margin; appeal, attractiveness; **~s** rags and tatters; **caer en las ~s de** to fall into the clutches of; **echar la ~ a** to grab, snatch, arrest; **hacer ~s** to tear to shreds

garrafa carafe; decanter; big bottle

garrafal outrageous; monstrous

garrafón m demijohn, carboy

garrapata tick

garrapatear to scribble, scrawl; doodle

garrapato pothook; scribble, scrawl

garrar, garrear naut to drag the anchor

garrido elegant, pretty, good-looking

garroba bot locust bean, carob-bean

garrobal carob grove

garrocha goad; pole; picador's lance; vaulting-pole; **salto a la ~** pole jump(ing); **salto de ~** pole vault

garrón m orni spur; hook

garrotazo blow (with a club or stick)

garrote m cudgel, club, stick; tourniquet; brake; gallows; garrotte; **dar ~ a** to garrotte, execute by strangulation; **política del gran ~** big-stick policy

garrotear to beat, club

garrotero brakeman; loan-shark; bully; adj stingy

garrotillo croup

garrucha pulley

garrulador talkative

garrulería chatter; garrulity

garrulidad f garrulity, talkativeness

gárrulo garrulous; talkative; orni chirping; babbling (of brook)

garrulla smart-aleck

garúa drizzle; Scotch mist

garuar to drizzle

garza real heron

garzo blue-eyed; blue

garzón m boy, lad; waiter

gas m gas; vapour; fumes; gas-light;

petrol, *US* gasoline; ~**(es) asfixiante(s)** poison gas; ~ **de los pantanos** marsh gas, methane; ~ **de la risa** laughing gas; ~ **lacrimógeno** tear gas; **cámara de** ~ gas chamber

gasa gauze; crepe; chiffon; *fam* nappy, *US* diaper; ~ **hidrófila** cotton wool; **tira de** ~ mourning-band (on the hat)

gascón *m* Gascon

Gascuña Gascony

gaseosa soda water; aerated water, mineral water; ~ **de limón** fizzy lemonade

gaseoso gaseous; fizzy; aerated, gassy

gasfitero gas-fitter

gasificar to turn into gas

gasista *m* gas-man, gas-fitter

gasístico *adj* (of) gas

gasoducto gas pipeline

gas-oil *m* diesel oil

gasóleo diesel oil

gasolina petrol, *US* gasoline

gasolinera filling station, *US* gas station; motorboat

gastable expendable; dispensable

gastado exhausted, worn out; used up; spent; shopsoiled; hackneyed, outworn

gastador *n m* spendthrift; *mil* sapper, pioneer; *adj* lavish; extravagant, wasteful

gastar to spend; disburse; wear out; use up; wear; ~ **bigote** to sport a moustache; ~ **palabras** to waste one's breath; ~ **una broma** to play a joke; ~**se** to wear out, become exhausted, go to waste

gasto expense; spending, expenditure; outlay; wear, use; consumption; ~ **de agua** flow rate of water; ~ **de gas** gas consumption

gastos *mpl* expenses; cost, expenditure; ~ **acumulados** accrued expenses; ~ **bancarios** bank charges; ~ **de administración** overheads; ~ **de almacenaje** storage charges; ~ **de capital** capital charges; ~ **de cobranza** delivery charges; ~ **de correos** postage, postal charges; ~ **de explotación** operating expenses; ~ **de flete** freight charge; ~ **de locomoción** travelling expenses; ~ **de publicidad** advertising expenses; ~ **de representación** entertainment expenses; ~ **de viaje** travelling expenses; ~ **imprevistos** incidental expenses; ~ **menores** petty cash; ~ **ordinarios de operación** running expenses; ~ **varios** sundry expenses; **pagar los** ~ to pay the expenses, foot the bill

gastoso *adj* spendthrift

gástrico gastric

gastronomía gastronomy

gastronómico gastronomic

gastrónomo gourmet, gastronome

gata (she-)cat; mist, cloud (over a mountain); woman of Madrid; **andar/ ir a** ~**s** to walk on all fours, crawl, creep

gatada litter of kittens; artful dodge; scratching; typical feline behaviour

gatazo trick, swindle

gateado cat-like

gatear to clamber, climb; go on all fours; run after women

gatero cat-breeder/seller

gatillo trigger; dental forceps; kitten; sneak-thief; pickpocket; **de** ~ **alegre** trigger-happy

gatita, gatito pussy, kitten

gato cat, tomcat; *mech* jack; clamp; money-bag; petty thief, cat burglar; sly person; man from Madrid; gaucho dance or dancer; ~ **de algalia** civet cat; ~ **de Angora** Persian cat; ~ **montés** mountain cat, wild cat; ~ **romano** tabby cat; **comprar** ~ **por liebre** to buy a pig in a poke; **dar** ~ **por liebre** to cheat; **hay** ~ **encerrado** there's a catch in it somewhere, there's more in this than meets the eye

gatuno feline, cat-like

gatuperio deceit, fraud; intrigue; mixture, hotchpotch

gauchada typical gaucho exploit; good turn

gauchesco *adj* gaucho

gaucho gaucho, cowboy; *adj* crafty; rude

gaveta drawer (in a desk); till (in a shop); ~ **de dinero**, ~ **de pago** cash till

gavetero dresser; chest of drawers

gavia top-sail; *naut* crow's nest; ditch; seagull

gaviero *naut* look-out man

gavilán *m* sparrow-hawk; ingrowing toe-nail

gavilla wheatsheaf; bundle; gavel; gang, band (of thieves); **gente de** ~ rogues

gavión *m* great black-backed gull

gaviota gull; ~ **argéntea** herring-gull; ~ **cana** common gull; ~ **reidora** black-backed gull

gavota gavotte

gaya magpie; stripe

gayaba *bot* arbutus

gayo merry; showy; bright

gayola cage; prison, jail; *vulg sl* masturbation

gayumbos *mpl sl* underpants

gaza loop, noose

gazapa fib, lie

gazapera rabbit warren

gazapo cunning fellow; lie; slip (in speech or writing)

gazmoñería prudishness; hypocrisy

gazmoño *n* prude; hypocrite; *adj* prudish; hypocritical

gaznar *orni* to croak, caw, squawk

gaznate *m* windpipe, gullet; **remojar el** ~ to wet one's whistle

gazpacho cold vegetable soup

gazuza hunger

gazuzo hungry

ge *f* the letter *g*

géiser *m* geyser, hot spring

gel *m* **de baño** bubble-bath liquid

gelatina gelatine, jelly; ~ **explosiva** gelignite

gelignita gelignite

gema gem, precious stone; bud

gemela: apuesta ~ double (bet)

gemelo *n* twin; **buque** ~ sister ship; *adj* twin

gemelos *mpl* twins (*usu* identical); binoculars; opera glasses, cuff links; *astron* Gemini; ~ **de campaña,** ~ **de campo** field glasses; ~ **de teatro** opera glasses

gemido groan, moan, wail, cry

gemidor moaning, groaning, wailing

Géminis *m* Gemini

gemir to moan, groan, wail, howl; lament

genciana gentian

gendarme *m* policeman; gendarme

gendarmería police station

genealogía genealogy; pedigree; family tree

genealógico genealogical

genealogista *m+f* genealogist

generación *f* generation; lineage; (sexual) reproduction; issue, progeny

generador *n m* generator; *adj* generative, generating

¹ **general** *n m* general; ~ **de brigada** brigadier general; ~ **de división** major general; ~**es** *fpl* personal details, particulars, personal data

² **general** *adj* general; all-embracing; **en** ~, **por lo** ~ generally; **por regla** ~ as a rule

generala general alert; general's wife; *mil* call to arms

generalato generalship

generalidad *f* majority, most people, generality; greatest part; generalization, general statement

generalísimo generalissimo, supreme commander

generalizable that can be generalized

generalización *f* generalization; escalation

generalizador *adj* generalizing

generalizar to generalize; bring into general use; escalate; ~**se** to become general, become prevalent

generar to generate; ~ **fuerza** to generate power

generativo generative

genérico generic

género kind, sort, class; genus; gender; genre; material, stuff, cloth; ~ **chico** *Sp* short comic play, operetta; ~ **de punto** knitted goods, knitwear; ~ **humano** mankind, human race; ~ **principal** staple; *pl* goods, merchandise; commodities; ~ **averiados** damaged goods; ~ **de algodón** cotton goods; ~ **de consumo corriente** staple commodities

generosidad *f* generosity; courage

generoso generous; high-born; liberal; noble; **vino** ~ full-bodied wine, best wine, old wine

génesis *f* genesis; **Génesis** *m* (Book of) Genesis

genética genetics

genético genetic

genetista *m+f* geneticist

genial endowed with genius; brilliant, bright; genial, jovial; cheerful, pleasant

genialidad *f* genius, mark of genius; eccentricity; peculiarity (of temperament); characteristic manner

genialmente brilliantly; with a touch of genius; cheerfully

genio *m* nature, character, temper; disposition; genius; genie, spirit; **buen ~** good nature, good temper; **corto de ~** slow-witted, backward, timid; **de buen ~** good-tempered; **de mal ~** ill-tempered, bad-tempered; **mal ~** bad temper; **tener ~** to be temperamental

genista *bot* broom

genitor *adj* engendering

genitivo *n* genitive (case); *adj* generative, reproductive; genitive

genocida genocidal

genocidio genocide

Génova Genoa

genovés *n* + *adj* Genoese

Genoveva Genevieve

gente *f* people; nation, race; folk; crowd; relatives, family; **~ baja** rabble; **~ bien** upper class, smart set, top people; **~ de capa negra** city dwellers; **~ del rey** convicts; **~ de gavilla** crooks; **~ de mar** sea-dogs, seamen; **~ de medio pelo** lower middle class; **~ de pelo** wealthy people; **¡~ de paz!** friend (reply to 'Who goes there?'); **~ de seguida** armed robbers; **~ de trato** tradespeople; **~ forzada** convicts; **~ gorda** well-to-do people; **~ menuda** children; **~ parda** country folk; **~ perdida** vagabonds; **~ principal** gentry, worthies; **ser ~** to be someone of importance; **las ~s** the Gentiles

gentecilla riff-raff, rabble; people of no account

¹ **gentil** *n m* gentile, pagan

² **gentil** *adj* genteel, courteous; graceful, handsome; charming; remarkable; gentile

gentileza grace, elegance, charm; kindness; courtesy, politeness, graciousness; splendour, ostentation; gallantry

gentilhombre *m* gentleman; nobleman; **~ de cámara** gentleman-in-waiting

gentilicio national, of a nation, (of a) family; **nombre ~** family name

gentílico *adj* heathen, pagan

gentilidad *f* heathens, pagans

gentío crowd, throng, multitude

gentuza rabble, riff-raff

genuflexión *f* genuflection

genuinidad *f* genuineness

genuino genuine, true; pure; real; legitimate

G.E.O. (Grupo de Especiales Operaciones) *approx equiv* Serious Crime Squad

geo *m* member of G.E.O.

geocéntrico geocentric

geodesia geodesy

geodésico geodesic, geodetic

geofagía *f* land grabbing

geófago geophagus, earth-eating

geofísica geophysics

Geofredo Geoffrey

geografía geography

geográfico geographic(al)

geógrafo geographer

geología geology

geológico geological

geólogo geologist

geometría *f* geometry; **~ analítica** analytic geometry; **~ del espacio** solid geometry; **~ plana** plane geometry

geométrico geometric(al)

geomorfología geomorphology

geopolítica geopolitics

geopolítico geopolitical

geaniáceo *bot* geranaceous, of the geranium/pelargonium family

geranio geranium

Gerardo Gerald, Gerard

gerencia management; manager's office; (art of) management; administration; **~ de fabricación** production department; **~ de venta(s)** sales department

gerenciar to manage

gerente *m* manager, vice-president; **~ administrador** managing director; **~ de banco** bank manager; **~ de exportación** export manager; **~ de ventas** sales manager

geriatría geriatrics

geriátrico geriatric

germanía thieves' cant, slang

germánico, germano Germanic, German

germanizar to make German

germen *m* germ, seed, origin, source

germicida *n m* germicide; *adj* germicidal

germinación *f* germination

germinador *adj* germinating

germinar to germinate; sprout

gerontología gerontology

gerontólogo gerontologist

Gertrudis Gertrude

gerundense *n m+f* native of Gerona; *adj* of Gerona

gerundio gerund

gesta feat, deed; **cantar de** ~ heroic narrative poem, chanson de geste

gestación *f* gestation; hatching; **hallarse en** ~ to be hatching (a plot *etc*)

gestar to set up, create

gestear to make faces; grimace; gesticulate

gestero grimacing

gesticulación *f* gesticulation; grimace

gesticular to gesticulate; make faces

gestión *f* action, step, measure; démarche; effort; conduct of affairs; management, administration; ~ **procesal** court proceedings

gestionar to take steps to; negotiate (a deal); promote (an undertaking); ~ **el pago** to demand payment; ~ **el reembolso** to demand repayment; ~ **fianza** to ask for bail; ~ **fondos** to raise funds; ~ **un arreglo** to negotiate a settlement; ~ **un divorcio** to sue for divorce; ~ **un empréstito** to float a loan; ~ **una venta** to negotiate a sale

gestiones *fpl* negotiations, steps; business arrangements; **en** ~ under negotiation; **en** ~ **oficiales** on official business

gesto (facial) expression; face, countenance; appearance; grimace; gesture; **estar de buen/mal** ~ to be in a good/ bad temper; **hacer** ~s **a** to look displeased with, make faces at, make gestures/signs; **poner** ~ to show annoyance, anger; **poner mal** ~ to make a face; **tener mal** ~ to have an unpleasant expression

gestor *n m* manager; director; promoter; ~ **de negocios** agent, business representative; ~ **judicial** legal representative; *adj* managing; contriving; endeavouring

gestoría agency (for legal business)

gestudo *n* face-puller, grimacer; *adj* bad-tempered

Getsemaní Gethsemane

ghanés *n m +adj* Ghanaian

giba *f* hump (physical deformity); annoyance, nuisance

gibado hump-backed, hunch-backed

gibar to annoy, bother

gibón *m* gibbon

giboso hump-backed, hunch-backed

Gibraltar: el Peñón de ~ the Rock of Gibraltar

gibraltareño *n +adj* Gibraltarian

giganta giantess; sunflower

gigante *n m* giant; *adj* gigantic, giant

gigantesco gigantic

gigantez *f* gigantic size

gigantón *m* carnival giant

gili *sl* silly

gilipollas *m sing+pl vulg sl* silly prick, silly cunt

gilipollear *sl* to do stupid things

gilipollez *f sl* stupid action/behaviour

gimnasia gymnastics; physical training; ~ **respiratoria** deep-breathing exercises; ~ **sueca** Swedish drill; **confundir la** ~ **con la magnesia** *sl* to mistake chalk for cheese; **hacer** ~ to do gymnastics, go in for physical training

gimnasio gymnasium

gimnasta *n m+f* gymnast

gimnástica *n* gymnastics

gimnástico *adj* gymnastic

gimotear to whine, whimper; moan, grizzle

gimoteo whimper, whine, whining; grizzling, moan

Ginebra Geneva; Guinevere

ginebra gin; din, uproar, bedlam; gin rummy

ginebrés *n +adj* Genevan, Genevese

ginecología gynaecology

ginecológico gynaecological

ginecólogo gynaecologist

ginesta *f bot* broom

giñar *vulg* to shit

gira outing, excursion, trip, picnic; tour; **estar en** ~ *theat* to be on tour

girada draft

girado, girador *m* drawer (of cheque, draft), drawee

giralda weathercock

girar to revolve, rotate; whirl; gyrate, spin, turn; swivel; turn round; turn over (capital); manage (a business); issue, draw, send (cheques, drafts); *sl* stink, pong; ~ **contra/a cargo de** to draw on (an account); ~ **dinero** to draw cash; ~ **en descubierto** to overdraw (an account); ~ **una letra** to draw a bill/draft; ~ **un cheque** to draw a cheque

girasol *m* sunflower

giratorio revolving, rotary, swinging; swivel(ling); gyratory

giro rotation, turn, revolution, gyration; expression, turn of phrase; trade, line of business; bias, draft; ~ **a la vista** sight draft; ~ **a plazo** time draft; ~ **bancario** bank draft; ~ **en descubierto** overdraft; ~ **postal** money order; **tomar otro** ~ to take another course; change one's mind

girocompás *m* gyro-compass

giroscópico gyroscopic

giroscopio gyroscope

gis *m* chalk; crayon; slate pencil

gitana gipsy woman, gipsy girl; fortune-teller

gitanesco *adj* gipsy; full of tricks, sly

gitano *n* gipsy; *adj* gipsy; sly; wheedling; *sl* dirty; unbusinesslike

glaciación *f* glaciation

glacial very cold, freezing, icy; glacial

glaciar *m* glacier

gladiador *m* gladiator

gladiatorio gladiatorial

gladio, gladiolo, gladíolo gladiolus

glande *m* glans penis

glándula gland; ~ **cerrada** ductless gland; ~ **pituitaria** pituitary gland; ~ **prostática** prostate gland; ~ **tiroides** thyroid gland

glas: azúcar *m* ~ icing-sugar

glaseado glazed; glacé (of fruits *etc*); glossy; *cul* crystallized

glasear to glaze; make glossy, give a glossy finish to

glauco light green, sea-green

gleba clod of earth, lump of soil

glicerina glycerine

global in total, in all; overall; global

globo globe; orb; sphere; world; balloon; *sl* french letter; ~ **de barrera** barrage balloon; ~ **ocular** eye-ball; ~ **terráqueo** globe of the world; ~**s** *sl* breasts; **en** ~ as a whole, in bulk, in all

globoso, globular spherical, globular

glóbulo globule; corpuscle

gloria glory; heaven; delight; *eccles* gloria; *sl* marihuana; **estar en sus** ~**s**, **estar en la** ~ to be full of happiness, be in one's element; **hacer** ~ **de** to boast of, be proud of; **saber a** ~ to taste

divinely, be delicious

gloriarse: ~ **de** to boast of, pride oneself on; ~ **en** to rejoice in, glory in, delight in; boast of

glorieta bower; summerhouse; secluded nook (with a bench); square or circus where streets intersect; city park; *mot* roundabout

glorificación *f* glorification

glorificar to glorify, extol, praise, adore; ~**se de**, ~**se en** to glory in, take pride in; boast of

glorioso glorious; holy, blessed; proud, boastful, bragging; **la Gloriosa** the Blessed Virgin

glosa gloss, comment; explanatory note, annotation; audit; *mus* variation

glosador *m* auditor; commentator

glosar to gloss, explain (a text), comment upon; annotate; audit

glosario glossary

glose *m* audit

glosilla *print* minion (type)

glosopeda foot-and-mouth disease

glótico glottal

glotis *f* glottis

glotón *n m* glutton; *adj* gluttonous

glotonear to be greedy

glotonería gluttony

glucosa glucose

gluglú *m* gurgling; **hacer** ~ to gurgle; (turkey) gobble

gluglutear to gurgle; (turkey) gobble

glutinoso glutinous

gnómico gnomic

gnomo gnome

gnosticismo gnosticism

gnóstico *n* + *adj* gnostic

gobernable governable

gobernación *f* government; governing; administration; **Ministerio de la Gobernación** Ministry of the Interior

gobernador *n m* governor; *adj* governing, ruling

gobernadora governor's wife; female governor/ruler

gobernalle *m* rudder, helm

gobernante *n m+f* ruler, governor; boss; *adj* governing, ruling; ~**s** governing body; directors

gobernar to govern, rule; conduct (affairs), direct; manage, run; steer; ~**se** to control oneself; manage one's own affairs

gobi *f sl* police station, *US* precinct

gobierno government; management, control; administration; guidance, direction; governorship; district under a governor; steering; helm, rudder; ~ **de la casa** housekeeping, household management; ~ **en funciones** caretaker government; **para su** ~ for your guidance; **servir de** ~ to serve as a guide/rule; **mirar contra el** ~ *sl* to squint, look cross-eyed; **sin** ~ out of control, adrift

gobio gudgeon

goce *m* enjoyment; pleasure; possession

gocha *fam zool* sow

gocho hog, boar

godesco joyous

godo *n* Goth; Spaniard; *adj* Gothic; reactionary, conservative; **sangre de** ~**s** blue blood

Godofredo Godfrey

gofo stupid; coarse

gol *m* (football) goal; ~ **cantado** unsuccessful shot which looks a certain goal but misses the net; ~ **del cojo** goal scored by an injured (and therefore unmarked) player; ~ **fantasma** disputed goal

gola *m* throat, gullet; ruff, gorget; bib; *arch* ogee, cyma

goldre *m* quiver (for arrows)

golear to score a goal

goleada spate of goals

goleador *m* goal-scorer, striker

goleta schooner; sailing ship

golf *m* golf; golf course

golfa prostitute, shameless woman

golfán *m bot* water-lily

golfante *m* idler; rogue

golfear to loaf about

golfería loafing; scoundrels

golfillo urchin

golfín *m* member of a band of rogues

golfista *m+f* golfer

golfo gulf; bay; sea; vagabond, urchin; loafer, idler; rogue

Gólgota Golgotha

Goliat *m* Goliath

golilla ruff; lace collar

golillero collar-maker

golondrina *orni* swallow; swallow fish; ~ **de mar** tern

golondrinera *bot* celandine

golondrino *orni* male swallow; *mil sl* deserter

golosina tidbit, titbit; sweet, delicacy; yearning, fancy, desire, appetite; sweet tooth; greed

golosear to eat a lot of sweet things

goloso sweet-toothed, fond of sweets; greedy

golpazo blow, knock, swipe

golpe *m* blow, knock; hit, stroke; coup, shock; *sl* hold-up, mugging; collision; sledgehammer; ~ **bajo** low punch; ~ **de estado** coup d'état; ~ **de fortuna** stroke of luck; ~ **de gente** crowd; ~ **de gracia** coup de grâce, death blow; ~ **de mar** tidal wave; ~ **de teatro** coup de théâtre, dramatic turn of events; ~ **de tos** fit of coughing; ~ **de vista** glance; ~ **franco** free kick (football); ~ **frustrado** abortive coup; ~ **mortal** death blow; ~ **seco** sharp blow; **dar** ~ to astonish, be a sensation, make a hit; **dar** ~**s en** to thump; **de** ~ suddenly; **de un** ~ all at once, at one blow; **pestillo de** ~ spring catch, latch

golpeador *adj* beating

golpeadura battering, beating-up

golpear to strike, hit; knock, pound; beat; punch; ~ **la puerta** to knock at the door; **niños golpeados** battered children

golpecito tap, rap; **un** ~ **en la muñeca** a rap over the knuckles

golpetear to knock repeatedly; rattle, pummel; flap

golpeteo knocking, rapping; rattling; flapping; tapping; pounding

golpismo organizing of a coup d'état

golpista *m+f* rebel, one who takes part in a coup

gollería delicacy; treat; superfluity; **pedir** ~**s** to ask for too much

golletazo stab in a bull's neck (to finish it off)

gollete *m* throat; neck (of a bottle); **estar uno hasta el** ~ to be fed up to the teeth, have had enough

gollizo ravine, canyon

goma gum; rubber, elastic; eraser; elastic band; tyre, *US* tire; *sl* good-quality marihuana; *fam* rubber sheath, french letter; (police) truncheon; ~ **arábiga** gum arabic; ~ **de borrar** rubber, eraser; ~ **de masticar** chewing gum; ~ **espumosa** foam rubber; ~ **blanda**

bubble gum; ~s overshoes; rubbers; **estar de** ~ to have a hangover

gomero *n* gum tree; rubber tree; worker on a rubber plantation; rubber dealer; bottle of gum, glue-bottle; *adj* rubber

gomífero rubber-producing

gomigrafiar to rubber-stamp

gomígrafo rubber stamp

gomista *m* dealer in rubber

gomita elastic band, rubber band

gomosidad *f* stickiness, tackiness

gomoso *n* dandy, fop; *adj* sticky, gummy

góndola gondola; goods wagon, freight truck; ~ **de cable** cable car

gondolero gondolier

gonorrea gonorrhoea

gorda fat woman; thick tortilla; **ahora nos va a tocar la** ~ trouble's brewing, now we're in for it; **se armó la** ~ there was a great uproar, all hell broke loose

gordinflas *adj invar* tubby, fat; flabby

gordi(n)flón *n m* chubby person; *adj* chubby, fat, flabby

gordito plump, rather fat

gordo *n* fat person; *cul* fat, suet; grease; **los** ~s the wealthy, the rich; **ni** ~ absolutely nothing, not a bean; *adj* fat, plump, tubby; greasy, oily; big, large; thick; *text* coarse; **agua gorda** hard water; **dedo** ~ big toe, thumb; **hablar** ~ to talk big, boast; **hacer la vista gorda** to wink at, turn a blind eye to; **premio** ~ first prize in (Christmas) lottery; **me cae** ~ I can't stand him

gordura stoutness, fatness; *cul* fat; grease

gorgojo weevil; woodlouse; tiny person

gorgojoso full of weevils

gorgorito warble, trill; gurgle

gorgotear to gurgle

gorgoteo gurgle

gorguera muff; gorget

gorigori *m* wailing, dirge

gorila *m* gorilla; thug; *sl* bodyguard

gorja *anat* throat, gorge

gorjal *m* collar; *eccles* dog-collar

gorjeador *n m* warbler; *adj* warbling

gorjear to warble, chirp, twitter; ~**se** to babble, start to talk, crow (of a baby)

gorjeo warble, chirping; gurgling; babble, early attempts at speech, crowing (of a baby)

¹ **gorra** *m* parasite, sponger; **andar de** ~

to live at s.o. else's expense; **pegar la** ~, **vivir de** ~ to sponge, cadge

² **gorra** *f* cap; bonnet; academic cap; ~ **de paño** cloth cap; ~ **de visera** peaked cap

gorrear to live by scrounging

gorrero cap/bonnet-maker/seller

gorrinada dirty trick, underhand act

gorrinera pigsty; den

gorrino sucking pig, pig; *adj* piggish; *fam* dirty

gorrión *m* sparrow; ~ **molinero** tree-sparrow

gorrionería meeting place of people of ill-repute

gorro cap (for head), baby's bonnet; ~ **de dormir** nightcap; **poner el** ~ *sl* to be unfaithful to one's husband

gorrón *m* sponger, scrounger, parasite; pivot, gudgeon; pebble

gorronear to cadge, sponge; live off s.o.

¹ **gota** drop (of liquid); raindrop; ~ **a** ~ drop by drop; **caer a** ~**s** to drip, fall in drops; **no ver** ~ not to see a thing, see nothing; **sudar la** ~ **gorda** to sweat blood, work hard, work one's head off

² **gota** *med* gout; ~ **coral** epilepsy

goteado spotted, speckled

gotear to drip; trickle; dribble; leak; begin to rain; give/receive little by little

goteo dripping, drip; trickle; leak

gotera leak, hole (in the roof); gutter(ing); stain (left by water); valance; chronic illness; ~**s** outskirts, environs; **lleno de** ~**s** ailing, full of aches and pains

gotero dropper (for counting drops of medicine); drip

gótico *n m* Goth, Gothic (language); *adj* Gothic; noble, illustrious

gotita droplet; **una** ~ just a drop

gotoso gouty

goyesco characteristic of or similar to Goya's works

gozada *sl* great satisfaction

gozar to enjoy; have, possess; ~ **de** to enjoy s.t.; have the right to s.t.; ~ **en** +*infin* to take pleasure in +*gerund*; ~ **mucho** to have a good time; ~**se** to rejoice; enjoy oneself

gozne *m* hinge

gozo enjoyment, pleasure; gladness,

delight; **el ~ en un pozo** it's all up, it's ruined; **no caber de ~, no caber en sí de ~** to jump for joy, be beside o.s. with joy

gozoso joyful, glad, joyous; **~ de, ~ con** glad about

gozque *m*, **gozquejo** small/yapping dog

grabación *f* engraving; recording; transcription; **~ en cinta (magnetofónica)** tape recording; **hacer una ~** to make a recording

grabado engraving; print; woodcut; picture, illustration (in a book or newspaper); **~ al agua fuerte** etching; **~ al agua tinta** aquatint; **~ a puntos, ~ punteado** mezzotint; **~ en cobre** copper plate; **~ en hueco** die-sinking, punch-sinking; **~ rupestre** rock-carving

grabador *n m* engraver; die-sinker; *adj* recording

grabadora (de cinta) tape recorder

grabadura engraving

grabar to engrave; carve; imprint; record; **~ al agua fuerte** to etch; **~ en cinta, ~ sobre cinta (magnetofónica)** to (put on) tape, tape-record; **~ en disco** to record; **~ un disco** to cut/ make a record

gracejada crude joke; stupid action; buffoonery

gracejar to be witty

gracejo grace; wit; humour

gracia grace; charm; gracious action; favour; gift; pardon; commutation of sentence; remission of debt; boon; mercy; personal name; witty remark; wit; point (of joke); joke; talent; **caer de la ~ de uno** to lose s.o.'s favour; **caer en ~ a** to find favour with; **dar en la ~ de** to fall into the habit of; **de ~** gratis, free; **en ~ a** in consideration of; **hacer ~** to be funny, amusing; **hacer ~ a uno** to make s.o. laugh, strike s.o. as funny; **pedir una ~** to ask a favour; **por ~** gratuitously; **¡qué ~!** how funny!, what a cheek!, well, I like that!; **sin ~** not very funny; **tener ~** to be funny; **tiene ~ la cosa** that's funny, that's strange

gracias *fpl* thanks; **dar las ~** to give thanks, give a vote of thanks; **(muchas) ~** thanks (very much)

graciable affable, gracious

grácil subtle; delicate

graciosidad *f* grace, beauty; joke

gracioso *n* comic, funny man; *adj* funny, witty; gracious; charming; gratuitous, free; **a título ~** gratuitously; **lo ~** the funny thing

¹ **grada** step; tier, row (of seats); slipway; altar step

² **grada** prison; grille; *agri* harrow; **~ de mano** hoe

gradación *f* gradation; graded series; comparison; *mus* harmonic progression

gradar to harrow, hoe; level

gradeo *agri* levelling

gradería flight of steps; stands (in arena); rows (of seats); grading; **~ cubierta** grandstand

gradiente *m* gradient

grado step; (temperature+*geom*) degree; grade; rank; stage; **de buen ~** with pleasure, willingly; **de mal ~** unwillingly; **en sumo ~** highly, in the extreme

graduable adjustable

graduación *f* gradation, measurement; *mil* rank; grading; classification; alcoholic strength, proof; graduation; **~ del crédito** credit rating

graduado *n* graduate; *adj* graded; graduated; *geom* divided into degrees; *mil* brevet

gradual *n m eccles* responses between the epistle and the gospel; *adj* gradual

graduando student near to graduation

graduar to grade; classify; graduate; gauge, measure; calibrate; confer a degree on; **~se** to graduate, take a degree, *mil* receive a commission; **~se de** to obtain the degree of; **~se en** to take a degree in; **~ en honores** to take an honours degree

gráfica graph, chart; diagram; **~ de fiebre** *med* temperature chart

gráfico *n* chart, diagram; timetable; *adj* graphic; illustrated, pictorial; **~ de temperatura** temperature chart

grafioles *mpl* sweet S-shaped fritters

grafito graphite

grafología graphology

grafológico graphological

grafólogo graphologist

gragea dragee; sugar-coated pill

graja (hen) rook

grajear to caw

grajilla jackdaw

grajillo carrion crow

grajo rook

Gral (General) Gen. (General)

grama couch grass

gramática grammar; ~ **parda** shrewdness, native wit

gramático *n* grammarian; *adj* grammatical

gramatiquear to correct pedantically another's grammar

gramatiquería grammatical niceties; 'boring old grammar'

gramo gram(me)

gramófono gramophone, *US* phonograph; record-player

gran (contraction of **grande** before a *sing n*) big, great; ~ **premio** grand prix

grana cochineal; scarlet dye; scarlet cloth; ripening season, seedtime; small seed; **dar en** ~ to run to seed; **ponerse como la** ~ to turn red, turn scarlet

granada pomegranate; grenade; small mortar bomb; ~ **de mano** hand grenade

Granada Granada; Grenada

granadero grenadier; very tall man

granadilla passion fruit; passionflower

granadina drink made from pomegranate juice

granadino *n+adj* of Granada; of Grenada

granado *n* pomegranate tree; *adj* expert; mature; choice, select; ripe; **lo más** ~ the best, the pick

granar to ripen; run to seed

granate *m* garnet

granazón *f* seeding

Gran Bretaña Great Britain

¹ **grande** *m* grandee

² **grande** large; great; grand; tall; **a lo** ~ in high style; **en** ~ as a whole, on a grand scale; **estar en** ~ to be going strong; **pasarlo en** ~ to have a great time; **vivir en** ~ to live in style

³ **grande** *m sl* 1,000 pesetas

grandevo very old person, greybeard

grandeza grandeur; greatness; size; nobility

grandilocuencia grandiloquence

grandilocuente grandiloquent; boastful

grandillón *adj pej* over-large, too big

grandiosidad *f* grandeur; magnificence

grandioso grandiose, magnificent, grand

grandísono *lit* high-sounding

grandor *m* size

grandote huge

grandullón oversize; overgrown

graneado granulated

granear to sow (seed); grain (leather)

granel: a ~ in abundance; in bulk; in lots; **vino a** ~ wine by the barrel

granero barn, granary; grain-producing region; grain elevator

granítico *adj* granite

granito granite; granule; pimple

granívoro grain-eating

granizada hailstorm

granizado soft drink containing crushed ice; ~ **de café** iced coffee

granizar to hail

granizo hail

granja farm; farmhouse; country house; ~ **avícola** poultry farm

granjear to become rich through trading; win (friends, favour); obtain; ~**se** to win (for o.s.); ~**se la confianza de** to gain the confidence of

granjería farming; husbandry; gain, profit

granjero farmer

grano grain; seed; berry; pimple, boil; speck, particle; ~ **de café** coffee bean; ~ **de uva** one grape; ~**s** cereals, corn, grain; **de** ~ **fino** fine-grained; **de** ~ **gordo** coarse-grained; **ir al** ~ to come to the point; **tomarlo con un** ~ **de sal** to take it with a pinch of salt

granoso granular; granulated

granuja *m* rogue; urchin; *f* grape seed

granujada roguery

granujiento, granujoso pimply

granulación *f* granulation

granular *adj* granular; *vt* to granulate; ~**se** to break out in pimples

gránulo granule

granuloso granular

grapa clamp; staple; stick

grapadora stapler, stapling-machine

G.R.A.P.O. (Grupo Revolucionario Antifascista Primero de Octubre) left-wing terrorist organization

grapo *m+f* member of G.R.A.P.O.

grasa grease; fat; suet; filth; ~ **de ballena** blubber; ~ **para ejes** axle grease; ~ **vegetal** vegetable oil

grasiento, grasoso greasy, oily

graso n greasiness, oiliness; adj greasy, fatty

gratificación f gratification; bonus; expense allowance; perquisite; gratuity; fee; recompense

gratificador gratifying

gratificar to gratify; tip; reward; ~ **un deseo** to indulge a whim; **se gratificará** a reward will be given

gratitud f gratitude

grato pleasant, pleasing; gratifying; **me es ~ informarle** I am pleased to inform you

gratuito gratuitous; unjustified; free of charge

gratulatorio congratulatory

grava gravel

gravable taxable, dutiable

gravamen m burden; obligation; mortgage; tax assessment; ~ **del timbre** stamp tax; ~ **sucesorio** estate duty, inheritance tax

gravado aggrieved; leg encumbered; pledged; ~ **con hipoteca** mortgaged

gravar to burden, mortgage; encumber; tax; assess

grave grave, serious; heavy; mus bass; low; sedate; **acento ~** grave accent; **estar ~** to be seriously ill; **palabra ~** word accented on penultimate syllable

gravedad f gravity; importance; severity; dignity; **estar de ~** to be seriously ill

grávida pregnant; with young

gravidez f pregnancy

grávido loaded, full; abundant

gravitación f gravitation

gravitacional gravitational

gravitar to gravitate; ~ **sobre** to weigh down on; encumber

gravoso burdensome, oppressive; expensive; extortionate; **ser ~** to weigh on, be a burden to

graznar orni to croak, caw, squawk

graznido orni croak, caw, squawk

greca trellis; interlacing; border/frieze with geometrical pattern

Grecia Greece

grecolatino Greco-Roman

greda fuller's earth; clay

gredal m clay/fuller's earth pit

gredoso clayey

gregario gregarious; **instinto ~** herd instinct

gregarismo gregariousness

gregoriano Gregorian

Gregorio Gregory

greguizar to make Grecian/Greek

gremial adj guild; trade union

gremializar to unionize

gremio guild; trade union, labour union; occupational group; **ser del ~** sl to be a homosexual

greña mop of hair, matted hair; entanglement; **andar a la ~** to squabble, fight (esp pulling each other's hair)

greñudo matted; dishevelled

gresca squabble, quarrel; fight

grey m flock; congregation

Grial: el Santo ~ the Holy Grail

griego n+adj Greek

grieta cleft; crack; crevice; chink; chap (on skin)

grietado cracked; cleft

grifa sl marihuana

grifo tap, US faucet; spigot; griffin; **cerveza al ~** draught beer

grilo sl pocket

grilla ent female cricket

grillado sl crazy, round the bend

grillera sl Black Maria

grillete m fetter, shackle

grillo ent cricket; sl policeman; ~**s** fetters, shackles, sl handcuffs

grima disgust; horror; **me da ~** it gets on my nerves

gringo n foreigner (esp British/North American); Yankee; adj foreign

gripe f influenza, grippe

gris n m +adj grey

grisáceo greyish

grita outcry, uproar; **dar ~** to boo

gritador n m shouter; adj shouting

gritar to shout, cry; ~ **desafiante** to shout defiance; ~ **pidiendo auxilio** to shout for help

gritería, griterío shouting; outcry, clamour

grito shout, cry; **a ~ pelado** at the top of one's voice; **el último ~** the latest fashion; **estar en un ~** to complain about intense pain

gritón screaming, shouting; loudmouthed

grite (generalmente) generally

groenlandés *n m* Greenlander; *adj* Greenland

Groenlandia Greenland

grogui groggy

gromo yolk

grosella redcurrant; ~ **blanca/espinosa/silvestre** gooseberry; ~ **negra** blackcurrant

grosellero currant bush; gooseberry bush

grosería coarseness; rudeness; vulgarity; rude remark/action

grosero coarse; rude, uncouth; vulgar

grosor *m* thickness

grosura suet, fat

grotesco grotesque; absurd

grúa *mech* crane; derrick; hoist; *mot* car removal vehicle; ~ **de caballete** gantry; ~ **de pescante** jib crane; ~ **de pontón** floating crane

gruesa gross (12 dozen)

grueso *n* thickness; bulk; greater part; *adj* thick; stout; **en** ~ in bulk

gruir *orni* (of cranes) to call

grulla *orni* crane

grumete *m* cabin-boy

grumo clot; lump; ~ **de leche** curd; ~ **de uvas** bunch of grapes

grumoso clotted, lumpy

gruñido grunt; growl; snarl; (of doors *etc*) creak

gruñidor *n m* grumbler; *adj* grunting, growling, snarling

gruñir to grunt, growl; snarl; grumble; (of rusty hinge *etc*) creak

gruñón *n m* grouser, griper; *adj* grumpy, grumbling

grupa crupper; **volver** ~**s** to turn tail

grupada sudden squall/gust

grupera pillion; **ir en la** ~ to be a pillion passenger

grupo group; combine, group of companies; unit; cluster; *mech* plant; set; ~ **sanguíneo** blood group

gruta grotto, cavern

grutesco *see* **grotesco**

guacamayo macaw

guacamol *m* avocado salad

guacamote *m bot* yucca

guacia *bot* acacia

guachapear (of water) to splash against the legs

guáchara lie, untruth

guácharo sickly, ailing

guachinango joker; *joc* Mexican

guacho *n* orphan; chick; *adj* odd, unmatched

guadaña scythe

guadañada swath

guadañadora *agri* mowing machine

guadañar to scythe, mow

guadañero *agri* mower

guagua baby; bus; **de** ~ free, for nothing

guaje *m* smart-aleck

gualdo yellow, golden

Gualterio Walter

guampo log canoe

guanche *m+f* original inhabitant of the Canary Isles before the arrival of the Spaniards

guantada slap, blow with the open hand

guante *m* glove; **arrojar el** ~ to throw down the gauntlet, challenge; **echar el** ~ **a** to lay hands on, seize; **hacer** ~**s** *sp* to spar; **recoger el** ~ to take up the challenge

guantelete *m* gauntlet; face-flannel

guantera *mot* glove compartment

guantería glover's shop

guantero glover

guantón *m see* **guantada**

guapamente very well, excellently; beautifully

guapear to swagger; bluster; dress flashily

guapería swaggering; blustering

guapetón *n m* bully; *adj* good-looking; flashy

guapeza prettiness; flashiness; bravado

guapo *n* gallant; lover; swell; bully; *adj* good-looking; well dressed, smart; bold; *sl* interesting, good

guapote *adj* good-looking, handsome; good-natured

guaracha dance resembling the **zapateado**

guarache *m* leather sandal; tyre patch

guaraní *m* Paraguayan currency unit; Paraguayan Indian; Guaraní language

guarapo sugar-cane juice; drink made from fermented sugar-cane juice

guarapón *m* wide-brimmed hat

¹ **guarda** *m* guard; caretaker; custodian; watchman; ~ **de coto** gamekeeper; ~ **de dique** lockkeeper; ~ **jurado** security officer; ~ **nocturno** nightwatchman; **ángel de la** ~ guardian angel

² **guarda** *f* custody; safekeeping; flyleaf,

end paper; ward (of lock); guard, shield

guardabanderas *m sing+pl naut* seaman in charge of the binnacle

guardabarreras *m+f sing+pl* gatekeeper; level-crossing keeper

guardabarro(s) *m sing+pl* mudguard

guardabosque *m* forester, ranger; gamekeeper, gamewarden

guardabrisa *m* windscreen, *US* windshield

guardacabras *m sing+pl* goatherd

guardacenizas *m sing+pl* ashpan

guardacostas *m sing+pl* coastguard/revenue cutter

guardador *n m* guardian; *adj* watchful; protective; stingy

guardaequipajes *m* baggage master

guardaespaldas *m sing+pl* bodyguard

guardafango mudguard

guardafrenos *m sing+pl* brakeman

guardafuego(s) *m* fender (of fireplace)

guardagujas *m sing+pl* switchman, pointsman

guardalmacén *m* storekeeper; warehouseman

guardameta *m* goalkeeper

guardamuebles *m sing+pl* furniture repository

guardapapeles *m sing+pl* office file, filing cabinet

guardapelo locket

guardapolvo dust-cover, dustsheet; dust coat; overalls

guardar to hold, keep; watch over, protect; save, lay by; store; ~se to take care; ~se de to guard against, avoid; **¡guarda!** look out!

guardarrío *orni* kingfisher

guardarropa *m* cloakroom; wardrobe; *theat* property man; *m+f* cloakroom attendant

guardarropía *theat* wardrobe, property room; *theat* props

guardavía *m* (railway) linesman

guardavista *m* visor, sunshade

guardería: ~ **infantil,** ~ **para niños** crèche; nursery school

¹**guardia** *m* policeman; guardsman; guard; *naut* watch; ~ **civil** Civil Guard, *cul* salted herring; ~ **de la circulación/de la porra/de tráfico/urbano** traffic policeman; ~ **forestal** ranger, game-warden; ~ **jurado**

security guard; ~ **marina** midshipman; ~ **municipal** policeman

²**guardia** *f* guard (body of men); *mil* guard; *naut* watch; **Guardia Civil** Civil Guard; ~ **de asalto** riot police; ~ **de cuartillo** *naut* dog watch; ~ **de corps** bodyguard; ~ **de honor** guard of honour

³**guardia** *f* care; custody; defence, protection; (fencing) guard; *mil* guarding; **aflojar la** ~ to lower one's guard; **en** ~ on guard; **estar de** ~ to be on guard duty; keep watch; **estar en** ~ **contra** to be on guard against; **montar la** ~ to mount guard; **pelar** ~s *mil sl* to do guard duty; **relevar la** ~ to change guard

guardián *m* guardian; keeper; custodian; warden; policeman; watchman

guardilla garret

guardoso careful; stingy, mean

guarecer to shelter, protect; ~**se de** to take shelter from

guarida lair, den; hide-out

guarismo figure, digit; numeral

guarnecer to garnish; adorn; trim; equip, provide; garrison; ~ **una joya** to set a jewel; ~ **una pared** to plaster a wall

guarnecido *n* plaster

guarnición *f* adornment; trimming; setting, mounting (of jewel); guard (of sword); garrison

guarnicionar to garrison

guarnicionería harness-making

guarnicionero harness-maker

guarniciones *fpl* harness; fittings, fixtures; ~ **del alumbrado** light fittings

guarnigón *m orni* young quail

guaro small parrot

guarrada dirty trick, base act

guarrería filth; dirty trick

guarro pig

guasa jest; kidding; tastelessness; mockery; teasing; **de** ~ as a joke

guasearse to mock; fool around

guaso *n* gaucho; rustic; *adj* coarse, uncouth

guasón *n m* joker; *adj* humorous

guatemalteco *n+adj* Guatemalan

guateque *m* binge, party

guatusa *zool* agouti

guau *m* bark; **¡guau!** bow-wow!

guayaba guava (jelly); lie, untruth

guayabo guava tree

guayabera brightly coloured sports shirt

Guayana Guiana

guayanés *n* + *adj* Guianese

gubernamental *n m* government supporter, loyalist; *adj* governmental

gubernativo governmental

gubia *carp* gouge

guedeja lock of hair; long hair; lion's mane

güero blond

guerra war, warfare; ~ **atómica/nuclear** atomic/nuclear war; ~ **de nervios** war of nerves; ~ **fría** cold war; ~ **mundial** world war; **dar** ~ **a** to be a nuisance to; **de antes de la** ~ of good quality, well made; **en** ~ at war; **hacer la** ~ **a** to make war on

guerreador *n m* warrior; *adj* warlike; warring

guerrear to wage war

guerrera soldier's jacket

guerrero *n* soldier, warrior; *adj* warlike; martial; warring; *fam* troublesome

guerrilla guerrilla band; guerrilla warfare

guerrillear to wage guerrilla warfare

guerrillero guerrilla fighter

¹ **guía** *m* guide; courier

² **guía** *f* guide book; directory; handbook; timetable; *bot* leading shoot; signpost; guidepost; guidance; guiding principle, norm; ~ **de bicicleta** handlebars; ~ **de carga** ship's manifest; ~**s reins**; ~ **sonora** sound track; ~ **telefónica/de teléfonos** telephone directory

guiado holding a permit

guiar to guide; drive a car; lead; ~ **un pleito** to conduct a lawsuit

Guido Guy

guija pebble (*usu* small)

guijarral *m* shingle; pebbly beach; stony place

guijarreño pebbly; (of people) rugged

guijarro pebble; boulder; cobblestone

guijarroso pebbly; covered with boulders

guijo gravel; shingle

guijoso gravelly; pebbly

guil *m sl* five-peseta coin

guilla bumper harvest; **de** ~ in abundance

guillado crazy, round the bend

guillarse *sl* to leave hurriedly; go crazy

Guillermo William

guillote lazy, indolent

guillotina guillotine; **ventana de** ~ sash window

guillotinar to guillotine

¹ **guinchar** to goad

² **guinchar** to winch

guinche *m* winch; hoist; windlass

guincho goad

guinda cherry; **ponerse como una** ~ to blush scarlet

guindalera cherry orchard; **la quinta** ~ the back of beyond, far off the beaten track

guindaleta *naut* cable

guindaleza *naut* hawser

guindamaina *naut* greeting (signalled with flags)

guindar to hoist; hang up; *sl* steal, pinch; win a game

guinde *m sl* robbery

guindilla cayenne pepper, chilli; *joc* municipal policeman

guindillo capsicum, hot-pepper bush

guindola lifebuoy

guindón *m* thief

guineo *adj* (of) Guinea; **gallina guinea** guinea-fowl

guinga gingham

guiñada wink; blink; *naut* yaw

guiñador *adj* winking

guiñapo rug, rag-picker; ragged person; tatter; a nobody

guiñar to wink; blink; *naut* yaw

guiño wink; grimace; **hacer** ~**s** to wink; grimace

guión *m* hyphen, dash; outline, guide; handout; *cin* + *theat* + *TV* script, scenario; standard (flag), pennant; ~ **de codornices** *orni* corncrake

guionaje *m* conductor's/guide's duties and obligations

guipar *fam* to see

guipuzcoano *n* native of Guipúzcoa (province); form of the Basque language spoken in Guipúzcoa; *adj* of Guipúzcoa

guiri *m* + *f sl* foreigner, *esp* tourist

guirigai *m* jabber, unintelligible talk; confusion

guirlache *m* sweetmeat made of toasted almonds and caramel

guisa: a ~ **de** like, in the manner of; **de**

tal ~ in such a way
guisado *cul* stew
guisador *m* cook
guisante *m* pea; **~ de olor** sweet pea
guisar to cook, stew; prepare (a meal)
guiso stew; mess, disorder
guisote *m* slops; concoction; *cul* very bad stew
guita twine; *sl* money, dough
guitarra guitar; **chafar la ~ a uno** to steal a march on s.o.; queer s.o.'s pitch
guitarreo *pej* tiresome non-stop guitar-playing
guitarrero guitar-maker/seller; guitarist
guitarrista *m + f* guitarist
güitos *mpl vulg sl* testicles, balls
guitón *m* vagabond
guitonear to lead the life of a vagabond
guizgar to stimulate
gula gluttony, greed
gulosidad *f* gluttony
guloso gluttonous, greedy
gumía Moorish dagger
gurdo foolish
guri *m sl* soldier; policeman
guripa *m sl* municipal policeman; chap, bloke; stupid twit
gurrumina uxoriousness; trifle; cunning person
gurrumino *n* henpecked husband; uxorious husband; *adj* despicable; mean; uxorious; henpecked

gusa *sl* hunger
gusaniento worm-eaten; grub-infested
gusanillo small worm; maggot; *carp* auger, gimlet; *mech* small spring; *fam* bug; **~ de la conciencia** remorse
gusano worm, grub, maggot; caterpillar; **~ de luz** glow-worm; **~ de seda** silk-worm; **~ de tierra** earthworm; **criar ~s** to push up the daisies, be dead and buried
gusanoso worm-eaten; maggotty
gustable tastable
gustación *f* tasting; sampling
gustar *vt* to taste; try, test, sample; *vi* to please; like; **~ de** to like to; **me gustan las uvas** I like grapes
gustativo gustatory
gustazo great pleasure; fiendish delight
gustillo slight flavour
gusto taste; flavour; pleasure; liking; whim; **a ~** at will, to one's taste, at ease, *sl* drugged; comfortable; **con (mucho) ~** gladly; **de buen/mal ~** in good/bad taste; **dar ~ al dedo** *sl* to fire indiscriminately, be trigger-happy; **dar ~ a uno** to please s.o.; **mucho ~ (en conocerle)** pleased to meet you; **ser del ~ de** to be to the taste of; **tener ~ en** to be pleased to; **tomar ~ a** to take a liking to
gustoso tasty, savoury; enjoyable; **lo haré ~** I'll gladly do it
gutapercha gutta-percha

H

h *f* letter h

ha: diez años ~ ten years ago

haba *f* bean, broad bean, Lima bean; *sl* penis; ~ **de las Indias** sweet pea; **son** ~**s contadas** it's a cert/a sure thing

Habana: La ~ Havana

habanera *f* Cuban dance/song

habanero of/from Havana

habano *n m* Havana cigar; *adj* of Havana

habar *m* bean patch

¹ **haber** *m* credit; credit side (of a ledger); salary, wages; ~**es** *mpl* assets, property, cash

² **haber** to have; ~ **de** to have to; ~ **que** to be necessary; ~**se** to conduct oneself, behave oneself; **habérselas con** to have it out with s.o., cope with, deal with

habichuela *f* kidney bean; ~ **verde/ tierna** string bean; **ganar las** ~**s** to earn one's living

hábil skilful, clever, capable, able; **día** ~ workday, working day

habilidad *f* talent, aptitude; skill, ability; scheme, trick

habilidoso skilful; able

habilitación *f* qualification; financing; equipping

habilitado *n m* paymaster; *adj* qualified; made available

habilitar to enable; qualify; equip; fit out; provide capital for, finance

habitabilidad *f* habitability

habitable inhabitable, can be lived in

habitación *f* room, apartment; home, dwelling; habitation; habitat; bedroom

habitante *m* inhabitant; *sl* louse

habitar to inhabit; live in; dwell, reside

hábito habit, custom; **colgar/ahorcar el** ~ to abandon one's calling, cease to be a religious; **tener el** ~ **de, tener por** ~ to be in the habit of; **tomar el** ~ **to** become a monk/nun

habituado *n* habitué; *adj* accustomed,

habituated, inured

habitual habitual, usual, customary; regular

habituar to accustom, habituate; ~**se** to become accustomed to, inured to; get used to, accustom oneself to

habla speech, language; dialect; **al** ~ **de** within speaking distance of; **de** ~ **inglesa** English-speaking; **dejar sin** ~/ **quitar el** ~ to leave speechless; **ponerse en** ~ **con alguien** to get into verbal contact with s.o.; **¡al** ~! *tel* speaking!

hablado *adj* **bien** ~ well-spoken; **¡bien** ~! well said!, hear, hear!; **mal** ~ evil tongued

hablador *n m* chatterbox, gossip; *adj* talkative, gossiping

habladuría gossip, rumour; impertinent remark; sarcasm

hablante *n m+f* speaker; *adj* speaking

hablar to talk, speak; ~ **a gritos** to shout; ~ **alto** to talk loudly, in a loud voice; ~ **bajo** to speak quietly; ~ **claro** to speak plainly, speak out; ~ **con** to speak to; ~ **de** to speak about; ~ **entre dientes** to mumble, mutter; ~ **lo gordo** to talk big, boastfully; ~ **por** ~ to talk for the sake of talking; ~ **por los codos** to chatter, talk without stopping; **dar que** ~ to give people s.t. to talk about, set tongues wagging; **¡ni** ~! no way!; ~**se con** to be on speaking terms with; ~ **como un carretero** to swear like a trooper

hablilla rumour, (piece of) gossip

hablista *m+f* speaker

hacedero practicable, feasible

hacedor *m* maker; **el Supremo Hacedor** the Creator, Maker

hacendado *n* landlord, landowner; rancher, planter; cattleman, cattleowner; *adj* propertied, landed

hacendero, hacendoso industrious, diligent; thrifty

hacer to do; make; ~ +*infin* to cause to;

~ **alarde de** to boast of; ~ **agua** to leak; ~ **caso de** to take notice of, pay attention to, mind; ~ **daño** to hurt, harm; (of food) not to agree with; ~ **el papel de** to play the part of; ~ **frente a** to meet, oppose, face up to; ~ **la barba** to shave, flatter; ~ **la maleta** to pack; ~ **la vista gorda** to connive at; ~ **saber** to make known, notify, inform; ~ **uno su agosto** to make money, make hay while the sun shines; ~ **vela** to sail; put on sail; **hace frío/calor** it's hot/cold; **hace 3 años** 3 years ago

hacerse to become; turn into; ~ **a** to become accustomed to, get used to; ~ **con** to get hold of, acquire; ~ **el sueco** to pretend not to understand; ~ **el tonto** to play the fool; ~ **ilusiones** to fool oneself; ~ **(de) rogar** to want to be coaxed; ~ **un barro** to put one's foot in it; ~ **viejo** to grow old, kill time; **esto se me hace raro** that seems strange to me

haces *mpl* faeces

hacia towards, in the direction of; ~ **abajo** downwards; ~ **acá** this way; ~ **adelante** forwards; ~ **arriba** upwards; ~ **atrás** backwards; ~ **casa** homewards; ~ **dentro** inwards; ~ **fuera** outwards; ~ **las once** about eleven o'clock

hacienda estate; fortune; property; farm; cattle ranch; livestock; ~ **pública** public finances; **ministro de Hacienda** Finance Minister, Chancellor of the Exchequer

haciendas *fpl* household tasks

hacina sheaf (of grass), stock; pile, heap, stack

hacinar to stack sheaves; pack together; pile up; overcrowd

hacha axe, hatchet; torch, firebrand; ~ **de armas** battleaxe; **ser muy** ~ to be very skilful

hachazo blow/stroke with an axe or hatchet

hache *f* letter h; **por** ~ **o por be** for one reason or another

hachear to hew; top (with an axe)

hachemita *n m+f+adj* Hashemite

hachero woodcutter; *mil* sapper, pioneer; torch bearer

hachís, haxís *m* hashish

hada fairy; charming woman; ~ **ma-**

drina fairy godmother

hadar to put a spell on; enchant

hado fate, destiny; fortune

hagiografía hagiography

hagiográfico hagiographical

hagiógrafo hagiographer

Haití *m* Haiti

haitiano *n+adj* Haitian, from Haiti

¡hala!, ¡hale! pull!; hurry up!; come on!

halagador flattering; alluring; attractive

halagar to flatter; coax; attract, allure; please

halago flattery; caress; allurement; ~**s** blandishments, flattering words; coaxing

halagüeño flattering; pleasing, gratifying; attractive; promising

halar to haul, pull; tug

halcón *m* falcon

halconería falconry

halconero falconer

hálito breath; vapour

halo, halón *m* halo, nimbus

halterofilia weight-lifting

hallado found; **bien** ~ contented, at ease; **mal** ~ displeased

hallar to find; find out; discover; ~**se** to be present; find oneself; be, be situated; ~**se enfermo** to feel ill; ~**se bien con** to be contented with; **no** ~**se** to be uncomfortable

hallazgo find, thing found; discovery; reward (for finding); **cinco pesos de** ~ five pesos reward

hamaca hammock

hamacar to swing (in a hammock)

hamamelina, hamamelis *m* witch hazel

hambre *f* hunger; appetite; famine; *sl* sexual appetite; **morirse de** ~ to starve, die of hunger; **pasar** ~ to go hungry; **tener** ~ to be hungry, hunger; **tener** ~ **de** to hunger after, long for

hambrear to starve; be famished/hungry

hambriento hungry, starving; greedy; mean; *sl* sexually aroused

hambruna famine

Hamburgo Hamburg

hamburgués *n+adj* from/of Hamburg

hamburguesa hamburger

hamburguesería hamburger stall/shop

hamburguesero hamburger stallholder/shopkeeper

hampa underworld, criminals

hampón *m* thug

haragán n m idler, lazy person; adj idle, indolent, lazy

haraganear to idle, loaf about, be lazy

haraganería idleness, laziness

harapiento ragged, tattered

harapo m rag; tatter; **andar/estar hecho un ~** to be in rags and tatters

haraposo ragged, tattered

harén m harem

harina flour; meal; **~ de avena** oatmeal; **~ de huesos** bone meal; **~ de maíz** corn meal; **~ lacteada** malted milk; **~ leudante** self-raising flour; **es ~ de otro costal** that's quite another matter; **esparcidor de ~ recogedor de ceniza** penny wise pound foolish

harinero n flour merchant; adj flour

harinoso floury, farinacious

harmonía harmony

harnero sieve, sifter

harpa harp

harpía harpy

harpillera sackcloth; burlap

¡harre! hurry up!; gee up!

hartar to satiate; gorge, fill; overwhelm with; sicken, tire of; **~se de** to overeat, stuff o.s.; have too much of, tire of

hartazgo repletion; **darse un ~ de** to have one's fill of

¹ **harto (de)** satiated, sated, full of; sufficient of, enough of, more than enough of; **estar ~ de** to be fed up with

² **harto** adv enough; very; quite; too much, very much

hartura repletion, satiety; abundance

hasta prep till, until; up to, as far as; as much as; **~ ahora** up to now; **~ aquí** so far; **¿~ cuándo?** until when?; **~ la vista, ~ luego** goodbye, so long, see you later, I'll be seeing you; **~ mañana** see you tomorrow; **~ más no poder, ~ no más** to the utmost; conj even; **~ que** until

hastiar to cloy; surfeit; disgust; weary, bore; **~se de** to be weary of

hastío excess, surfeit; disgust, loathing; boredom, weariness

hatajo herd, flock; lot of, bunch of; gang, band; **un ~ de disparates** a lot of nonsense

hatillo bundle (of clothes); swag

hato flock, herd, livestock; sheepfold; shepherd's hut; cattle ranch; gang; crowd, bunch; kit, outfit, belongings; **liar el ~** to pack up one's traps; get ready to go

hawaiano Hawaiian

haxis, hachis m hashish

hay there is, there are; **~ que** +infin it is necessary to; **¿qué ~?** what's the matter?; how goes it? **no ~de que** you're welcome; don't mention it!

¹ **Haya: La ~** The Hague

² **haya** beech (tree); beech (wood)

hayuco m beechnut, beechmast

¹ **haz** m bundle (of sticks), bunch, faggot, sheaf; beam (of light); line, rank (of troops)

² **haz** f face; surface; surfacing; façade; **ser de dos haces** to be two-faced; **sobre la ~ de** on the surface of

hazaña deed, feat, exploit; achievement

hazañero fussy, prudish

hazañoso brave, heroic; courageous; gallant

hazmerreír m laughing-stock

HB (Herri Batasuna) pol Basque separatist party

he: **~ aquí** here is, here you have; **~ aquí que llegan** here they come; **~ allí** there is; **~lo aquí** here it is; **~los allá** there they are; **~me aquí** here I am

hebdomadario weekly newspaper

hebilla buckle, clasp

hebra thread; fibre; filament; (wood) grain; vein, lode; **de una ~** all at once, at one blow; **ni ~** nothing at all, absolutely nothing; **ser de/estar de buena ~** to be strong, robust; **pegar la ~** to talk too much; start a conversation

hebraico Hebrew, Hebraic

hebreo m+adj Hebrew; **jurar en ~** sl to display great anger

Hébridas: las ~ the Hebrides; **las Nuevas ~** the New Hebrides

hebroso fibrous, stringy

hecatombe f hecatomb; disaster; slaughter

heces fpl dregs; riff-raff, scum; faeces

hectárea hectare (10,000 square metres)

hectogramo hectogram

hectolitro hectolitre

hectómetro hectometre

Héctor m Hector

hechicera witch, enchantress

hechicería witchcraft, sorcery, magic; charm, fascination; enchantment

hechicero *n* wizard, sorcerer, magician; charmer; *adj* bewitching, charming, enchanting

hechizar to bewitch, charm, enchant; fascinate

hechizo *n* charm, spell, enchantment; fascination, glamour; *adj* feigned, false, artificial; home-made

¹ **hecho** *n* fact, deed, act; event; **de** ~ in fact, as a matter of fact; ~ **consumado** fait accompli; ~ **de armas** feat of arms

² **hecho** *adj* made, done, finished; full grown; ~ **de encargo/a medida** made to measure; ~ **y derecho** complete, perfectly done, finished; **a lo** ~ **pecho** what's done can't be undone, make the best of it; **bien** ~ well done; well shaped, well proportioned; **estar** ~ to be turned into, made to look like; **hombre** ~ a grown man; **mal** ~ badly done, wrong; badly shaped; **ropa hecha/traje** ~ ready-made clothing/suit; ¡**trato** ~! done!; it's a bargain!

Hechos de los Apóstoles Acts of the Apostles

hechura make; form, shape; cut, style; making up; workmanship; ~**s** cost of making; **no tener** ~ not to be practicable

heder to stink, reek

hediondez *f* stench, stink

hediondo stinking, evil-smelling; filthy, dirty; obscene

hedonismo hedonism

hedonista *n m+f* hedonist; *adj* hedonistic

hedor *m* stink, stench

hegeliano Hegelian

hegemonía hegemony

helada frost; ~ **blanca** hoar-frost

heladera refrigerator, ice-box; ice-cream freezer

heladería ice-cream parlour

heladero ice-cream seller

helado *n* ice-cream; ice, water-ice; *adj* frozen; icy, freezing; frosty; **quedarse** ~ to be frozen (with fear); **me quedé** ~ my blood ran cold

helador icy, freezing; **hace un frío** ~ it's freezing cold

helar *vt* to freeze, chill, ice; amaze; discourage; ~**se** to freeze up; be frozen; ~**se de frío** to freeze with cold

helecho fern; ~ **arbóreo** tree-fern

Helena Helen

heleno, helénico Hellenic

helenista *m+f* Hellenist

helero glacier

hélice *f aer* propeller; *naut* screw; spiral; helix; **Hélice** the Great Bear

helicóptero helicopter

helio helium

heliocéntrico heliocentric

heliógrafo heliograph

heliotropo heliotrope

helipuerto heliport

helitransportar to transport by helicopter

helvético *n+adj* Swiss

hembra *n* female; nut (of a screw); **macho y** ~ hook and eye, male and female; *adj* female

hembrilla eyelet

hemeroteca newspaper library

hemisferio hemisphere

hemisférico hemispherical

hemofilia haemophilia

hemofílico *n* haemophiliac; *adj* haemophilic

hemorragia haemorrhage

hemorroides *fpl* haemorrhoids, piles

henal *m* hayloft

henar *m* hayfield

henchidura filling, stuffing

henchir to fill, stuff; swell; ~**se de** to swell up, stuff oneself; ~**se de orgullo** to swell with pride

hender to crack; split, cleave

hendedura, hendidura crack, cleft, fissure, crevice, split, slot

henil *m* hayloft, barn

heno hay

heñir to knead (dough)

hepático hepatic, liverish

heptagonal, heptágono heptagonal

heptasílabo heptasyllabic

heráldica heraldry

heráldico heraldic

heraldo herald

herbáceo herbaceous

herbajar to graze, pasture; put out to graze

herbaje *m* grass, pasture; herbage

herbario *n* herbal (book); herbarium; collection of pressed plants; *adj* herbal

herbazal *m* field of grass

herbicida *n* weed-killer; *adj* herbicidal

herbívoro herbivorous

herboso grassy; full of weeds

herborizar to botanize

hercúleo Herculean

Hércules Hercules

heredable inheritable

heredad *f* estate; country property; farm; parcel of land

heredado inherited; landed

heredamiento estate, landed property

heredar to inherit; make heir to, bequeath, leave in a will; ~ **a** to inherit from

heredera heiress

heredero heir, inheritor; landed proprietor; ~ **forzoso** legal heir, heir apparent; ~ **presunto** heir presumptive; **príncipe** ~ crown prince

hereditario hereditary

hereje *m+f* heretic

herejía heresy; insulting remark; outrage

herencia *f* inheritance; heritage; heredity; estate

herida wound; injury; **renovar la** ~ to open an old wound; **tocar en la** ~ to touch on a raw spot; **hurgar en la** ~ to turn the knife in the wound

herido *m* wounded man; irrigation or drainage ditch; *adj* wounded, injured, hurt

herir to wound, injure; hurt; offend; strike

hermafrodita *n m* hermaphrodite; *adj* hermaphroditic

hermana sister; ~ **de leche** foster sister; ~ **lega** lay sister; ~ **política** sister-in-law; **media** ~ half-sister

hermanable fraternal; compatible

hermanar to match, mate, join; harmonize; make compatible; twin; **ciudades hermanadas** twinned towns

hermanastra step-sister

hermanastro step-brother

hermandad *f* brotherhood, fraternity; sisterhood; guild

hermano brother; ~ **de leche** foster brother; ~ **lego** lay brother; ~ **pequeño** *sl* penis; ~ **político** brother-in-law; ~**s** brothers, brother(s) and sister(s); ~**s siameses** Siamese twins; **medio** ~ half-brother; **primo** ~ first cousin

hermenéutico hermeneutic

hermético airtight; hermetic; silent, tight-lipped; impenetrable

hermetismo close secrecy

hermosear to beautify, adorn, embellish

hermoso beautiful; handsome, good-looking

hermosura beauty, loveliness; handsomeness, good looks; beauty, belle

hernia *med* rupture, hernia

herniado ruptured

Herodes *m* Herod

héroe *m* hero

heroico heroic

heroína heroine; heroin

heroinomanía heroin addiction

heroinómano heroin addict

heroísmo heroism

herpes *mpl+fpl* shingles, herpes

herrador *m* blacksmith, farrier

herradura horseshoe

herraje *m* ironwork; horseshoe and nails

herramienta iron tool; set of tools; implement; *sl* penis, tool

herrar to shoe (a horse); brand (cattle); ornament (with iron)

herrería blacksmith's shop, forge, smithy; ironworks

herrerillo *orni* blue tit

herrero blacksmith; ironworker

herrumbre *f* rust; irony taste

herventar to bring to the boil

hervidero bubbling (of liquid); spring; crowd, swarm; hotbed

hervido boiled; **agua hervida** boiling water

hervidor *m* boiler; kettle

hervir to boil; ~ **en** to swarm with, teem with; **hacer** ~ to boil (s.t.); to bubble, seethe

hervor *m* boiling; boiling point; **soltar el** ~ to bring to the boil

hervoroso fiery; impetuous

hesitación *f* hesitation

hesitar to hesitate

heterodino heterodyne

heterodoxo heterodox

heurístico heuristic

hexámetro hexameter

hiato hiatus

hibernación *f* hibernation

hibernar to hibernate

hibisco hibiscus

hibridación *f* hybridization

hibridar to hybridize

híbrido *n+adj* hybrid

hidalgo *n* gentleman; *adj* gentlemanly; courteous

hidalguez *f*, **hidalguía** nobility, gentlemanliness; courtesy, generosity

hideputa *m* son-of-a-bitch

hidratante moisturizing

hidratar to hydrate

hidratación *f* hydration

hidrato de carbono carbohydrate

hidráulica hydraulics; water-power

hidráulico hydraulic

hidroavión *m* seaplane

hidrocarburo hydrocarbon

hidrodinámica hydrodynamics

hidrodinámico hydrodynamic

hidroeléctrica hydroelectrics

hidroeléctrico hydroelectric

hidrófilo absorbent; **algodón ~** cotton-wool

hidrofobia rabies, hydrophobia

hidrófobo *n* hydrophobe; *adj* hydrophobic

hidrófono hydrophone

hidrófugo *adj* water-repellent

hidrógeno hydrogen

hidrografía hydrography

hidrográfico hydrographical

hidromiel *m* mead (wine)

hidrómetro water meter; hydrometer

hidropesía dropsy

hidrópico dropsical; very thirsty; insatiable

hidrostática hydrostatics

hiedra ivy

hiel *f* gall, bile; bitterness, rancour

hielo ice; frost; coldness, reserve; **~ flotante** pack ice; **romper el ~** *fig* to break the ice

hiena hyena

hierba grass; herb; weed; **mala ~** weed(s), black sheep; **~ callejera** stone crop; **~ caña** groundsel; **~ mate** Paraguayan tea, maté; **~ mora** nightshade

hierbabuena *bot* mint

hierro iron; tool, implement; weapon; **~ colado/fundido** pig iron, cast iron; **~ forjado** wrought iron; **llevar ~ a Vizcaya** to carry coals to Newcastle; **~s** fetters, chains; handcuffs; **machacar en ~ frío** to do something in vain, waste one's time

higa *f* (an obscene gesture made by placing the left thumb under the index finger); amulet or charm to ward off evil eye; **no dar dos ~s por** not to give a fig/a rap for

hígado liver; courage, valour

higiene *f* hygiene, cleanliness; sanitation; **~ pública** public health

higiénico hygienic, sanitary; **papel ~** toilet paper

higienista *m+f* hygienist

higo fig; *vulg sl* cunt; **~ chumbo**, **~ de tuna** prickly pear; **~ paso** dried fig; **no se me da un ~** I don't give a damn; **hecho un ~** wizened; **malos ~s** evil disposition; ill-will

higuera figtree; **~ (de) chumba/de tuna** prickly pear cactus; **~ india** banyan

hija daughter; **~ política** daughter-in-law

hijastra step-daughter

hijastro step-son

hijita little girl, small daughter; my dear

hijo son, child; junior; fruit, result; **~ adoptivo** adopted son; **~ de crianza** foster-son; **~ de familia** minor, unmarried son; **~ de leche** foster-son; **~ político** son-in-law; **cada uno es ~ de sus obras** a man must be judged by his deeds, not his birth; **~ de papá** lazy son of wealthy parents; **~ de puta**, **~ de cura**, **~ de la Gran Bretaña** *sl* son of a bitch; **~s** children, sons, sons and daughters

hila row, line, file; dressing, *med* lint; **a la ~** in single file

hilas, hilachas *fpl* rags and tatters

hilacha thread, shred of cloth; **~ de algodón** cotton waste; **mostrar uno su ~** to reveal one's worst qualities

hilachos *mpl* rags and tatters

hilachoso ragged, frayed

hilado *n* yarn, thread; spinning; *adj* spun

hilandera (woman) spinner

hilandería spinning, art of spinning; mill

hilandero spinner; spinning-room, mill

hilar to spin; **~ (muy) delgado** to split hairs; be very subtle

hilarante hilarious

hilaridad *f* hilarity

hilaza yarn, thread; **descubrir uno la ~** to show one's true nature

hilera file, line, row; **~ de perlas** string of pearls

hilguero goldfinch

hilo thread; grain, vein, seam; thin wire; filament; linen; ~ **de bramante** twine; ~ **de Escocia** lisle; ~ **de medianoche** dead on midnight; ~ **de mediodía** exactly at noon; **a** ~ uninterruptedly; **al** ~ along the weave; **al** ~ **del viento** all right, very well; **al** ~ **de medianoche** on the stroke of midnight; **de** ~ straight, uninterrupted; **de un** ~ continually, without stopping; **tener el alma en un** ~ to be in great suspense/anxiety; be frightened to death; **tomar el** ~ to pick up the thread of the conversation; **mover los** ~**s** to pull strings

hilván *m* tacking, basting; basting stitch; hem

hilvanar to tack, baste, sew together, string together; do hastily, plan s.t. hurriedly; hem

himen *m* hymen

himeneo marriage; hymen

himnario hymn book, hymnal

himno hymn; ~ **nacional** national anthem

hin *m* neigh, whinny

hincapié *m* stamping of the foot; **hacer** ~ to take a firm stand; **hacer** ~ **en** to stress, emphasize, insist upon

hincar to thrust in, drive, stick in; ~**la** *sl* to work; ~ **la rodilla** to bend the knee, go down on one knee; ~ **los dientes en** to sink one's teeth into, bite; ~**se (de rodillas)** to kneel down

hincha *m* football fan, supporter, follower; grudge, ill-will; pet aversion; **tener** ~ **a uno** to bear a grudge against s.o.; **tomar** ~ **a uno** to take a dislike to s.o.

hinchable inflatable

hinchada group of football fans

hinchado swollen; inflated, puffed up, bloated; vain, presumptuous

hinchar to swell; inflate, blow up; *sl* mess up, spoil; ~**se** to swell up, have one's fill, become swollen; swell with pride, become conceited, *sl* become rich

hinchazón *f* swelling, lump; conceit; bombast, bellyful

hindú *n m +adj* Hindu

hinduismo Hinduism

hiniesta *bot* gorse, broom, genista

hinojo *bot* fennel

hinojos *mpl*: **de** ~ kneeling; **caer de** ~ to fall on one's knees

hipar to hiccup; (of dogs) whimper, pant; ~ **por** to long for

hiperacidez *f* hyperacidity

hiperactivo hyperactive

hipérbaton *m gramm* hyperbaton

hipérbole *f* exaggeration; hyperbole

hiperbólicamente exaggeratedly

hipermercado hypermarket

hipersensibilidad *f* hypersensitivity

hipersensible hypersensitive

hipertensión *f* hypertension

hípico equine, pertaining to horses; equestrian; **concurso** ~ horse-riding competition, gymkhana

hípido hiccups

hipismo art, or knowledge of breeding, training or caring for horses; show-jumping

hipnosis *f* hypnosis

hipnótico hypnotic

hipnotismo hypnotism, hypnosis

hipnotizador *m* hypnotist

hipnotizar to hypnotize

hipo hiccup; longing; ill-will, grudge; **tener** ~ to have hiccups; **tener** ~ **contra uno** to have a grudge against s.o.; **tener** ~ **por** to long for

hipocondríaco *n + adj* hypochondriac

hipocresía hypocrisy

hipócrita *n m+f* hypocrite; *adj* hypocritical

hipodérmico hypodermic

hipódromo race course, race track; hippodrome

hipopótamo hippopotamus

hiposo hiccuping, having hiccups

hipoteca mortgage

hipotecar to mortgage

hipotecario mortgaging, mortgage

hipótesis *f sing + pl* hypothesis, theory

hipotético *adj* hypothetical

hiriente cutting, hurtful

hirsuto hirsute, hairy; bristly; gruff

hirviente boiling; seething

hisopo hyssop; holy-water sprinkler; paint brush

hispalense *n m + f + adj* Sevillian

hispánico Hispanic

hispanidad *f* Spanishness; **Día de la Hispanidad** 12 October, Columbus Day

hispanismo study or love of things Spanish

hispanista *m+f* Hispanist, student of Spanish culture

hispanizar to hispanize, make Spanish

hispano *n* Spaniard; *adj* Spanish, Hispanic

Hispanoamérica Spanish America, Latin America

hispanoamericano Spanish-American

hispanófilo *n+adj* hispanophile

hispanohablante, hispanoparlante Spanish-speaking

hispanomarroquí Spanish-Morrocan

histamina histamine

histerectomía hysterectomy

histérico *n* hysterical person; *adj* hysterical; **paroxismo ~** hysterics

histerismo hysteria

histología histology

histológico histological

histólogo histologist

historia history; story, tale, fable; historical painting; **~s** chatter, chit-chat; **dejarse de ~s** to stop beating about the bush, come to the point; **hacer ~ de** to give an account of, relate; **una mujer con ~** a woman with a past

historiado storied; over-decorated, ornate

historiador *m* historian

historial *m* case history, dossier, record; date; *adj* historic, historical

histórico historic, historical

historicidad *f* historicity, historicism

historieta short story, tale; **~ muda** comic strip

historiografía historiography

historiógrafo historiographer

histrión *m* actor; buffoon

histriónico histrionic

histrionismo acting; histrionics; actors

hito *n* landmark, milestone, boundary stone; guidepost; target; **dar en el ~** to hit the nail on the head, hit the mark; **mirar de ~ en ~** to look fixedly at, stare at; *adj* fixed

hno (hermano) brother; **~s (hermanos)** bros (brothers)

hocico snout, muzzle; **caer de ~s** to fall flat on one's face; **dar de ~s en/contra** to collide with, hit one's face against; **darse de ~s con** to fall flat on one's face; **estar con/de ~** to sulk, be sulky; **meter el ~ en todo** to stick one's nose into everything, meddle

hociquera muzzle

hogaño nowadays, at present; this year

hogar *m* fireplace, hearth; home

hogareño homeloving; homely, *US* homelike; of the home; of the family

hogaza large loaf

hoguera bonfire; *fig* blaze

hoja leaf; blade (of grass); petal; sheet of paper; pane, panel; (knife) blade; sheet of metal; **~ de afeitar** razor blade; **~ de aluminio** kitchen foil; **~ de lata** tin-plate; **~ de parra** fig leaf (in a painting, on a statue, to hide pubic parts); **~ de pedidos** *comm* order form; **~ de servicios** record of service (of an employee); **~ suelta** handbill, leaflet; **doblar la ~** to drop the subject; **le puso como ~ de perejil** he gave him a dressing-down; **volver la ~** to turn the page; change the subject; **de ~ perenne** evergreen

hojalata tin-plate

hojalatería tinware; tin shop

hojalatero tinsmith

hojaldrado made of puff pastry/flaky pastry

hojaldre *m+f* puff pastry, flaky pastry

hojarasca fallen leaves; abundant foliage; leaf mould; empty words; rubbish, trash

hojear *vt* to turn the pages of a book; thumb through a book; browse; *vi* to flutter (of leaves); flake

hojoso leafy

hojuela small leaf; leaflet; pancake; **~ de estaño** tin-foil

¡hola! hello!; ahoy there!

¹ Holanda Holland

² holanda holland linen

holandés *n m* Dutchman, Dutch language; **a la holandesa** in cloth binding, cloth-bound; *adj* Dutch

holgado comfortable; roomy, spacious; wide; loose; idle, at leisure; well-to-do

holganza leisure; idleness

holgar to rest, take one's ease; be idle; **~ con/de** to be glad about; **~se** to enjoy oneself, relax, have a good time

holgazán *n m* idler, loafer, lazy person, drone; *adj* lazy, idle

holgazanear to lounge about; idle; loiter

holgorio spree, frolic

holgura roominess, plenty of room; comfort, ease; rest; having a good time; **vivir con ~** to live in luxury, be well off

holocausto holocaust, slaughter; burnt offering, sacrifice

hollar to tread on, trample upon; humiliate

hollejo skin (of fruit *etc*); peel; husk

hollín *m* soot

holliniento sooty

hombrada manly deed; display of bravery

hombradía manliness; courage

hombre *m* man, husband; ¡**~**! good heavens!; ¡**~ al agua!, ¡~ a la mar!** man overboard!; **~ de armas** man-at-arms; **~ de a pie** man in the street; **~ de bien** honest man; **~ de bienes** man of property; **~ de buenas prendas** man of parts; **~ de campo** countryman; **~ de estado** statesman; **~ de letras** man of letters; **~ de mundo** man of the world; **~ de negocios** businessman; **~ de paja** man of straw; **~ hecho** fully grown man; **~-anuncio** sandwich-board man; **~ rana** frogman

hombrear to back, help; carry on the shoulders; **~ con** to vie with

hombrera epaulette; shoulder strap; shoulder pad

hombría manliness, courage; **~ de bien** honesty, uprightness, integrity

hombro shoulder; **arrimar/meter el ~** to lend a hand, help; **echar(se) al ~** to take the responsibility for; **encogerse de ~s** to shrug one's shoulders; **mirar por encima del ~** to ignore, shrug off; **salir a ~s** to be carried shoulder-high

hombruna mannish, masculine (said of a woman)

homenaje *m* homage; tribute; **rendir ~ a** to pay homage to, swear allegiance to

homeópata *m* + *f* homeopath

homeopatía homeopathy

homeopático homeopathic

Homero Homer

homicida *m* murderer, killer; *f* murderess; *adj* homicidal, murderous; **el arma ~** the murder weapon

homicidio murder, homicide

homilía homily

homínido hominid

homofonía homophony

homófono *n* homophone; *adj* homophonous, homophonic

homogeneidad *f* homogeneity

homogéneo homogeneous, of the same kind

homólogo homologous

homónimo *n* homonym; namesake; *adj* homonymous

homosexualidad *f* homosexuality

honda sling, slingshot

hondear *naut* to sound; unload; hit with a slingshot

hondo *n* depth, bottom; *adj* deep, profound; low; **de ~** in depth; **plato ~** soup plate

hondonada hollow; gully; ravine; dip, depression (in the ground); dale

hondura depth; **meterse en ~s** to get into trouble; get out of one's depth

hondureño *n* + *adj* Honduran

honestidad *f* honesty; modesty, decency; propriety, decorum; chastity, purity

honesto honest; modest, decent; pure, chaste, virtuous; (of prices) reasonable

hongo mushroom; fungus; bowler/derby hat

honor *m* honour, glory; dignity; reputation, good name; **de ~** honorary; **deuda de ~** debt of honour; **hacer ~ a** to honour; **palabra de ~** word of honour; **rendir ~es militares** to pay military honours to

honorable honourable, worthy

honorario *adj* honorary; **~s** honorarium, fee

honorífico honourable; honorary; honorific; **mención honorífica** honourable mention

honra honour; reputation, respect; **~s fúnebres** funeral rites; **tener algo a mucha ~** to regard s.t. as an honour, be proud of s.t.; **tener a mucha ~ +** *infin* to be proud of + *ger*

honradez *f* honesty, integrity; honour

honrado honest; honourable; honoured

honramiento honouring

honrar to honour, do honour to; **~se** to be honoured, consider it an honour

honrilla: por la negra ~ for the sake of appearances

honroso honourable; decorous, decent; honouring

hontanar *m geol+geog* place with springs

hora hour; time; ~s book of hours; las ~s canonical hours; **a buena** ~ punctually, on time, opportunely, in good time; **a estas** ~s at this time; **a última** ~ at the last moment; **dar** ~ to set the time; **dar la** ~ to chime, strike the hour; **de última** ~ latest, up-to-date; **es** ~ **de** it's time to; **la** ~ **de comer** dinnertime, meal-time; **la** ~ **punta** rush hour; **poner en** ~ to set the time; **¿qué** ~ **es?** what time is it?; **última** ~ *print* stop-press

horaciano Horatian

Horacio Horace, Horatius

horadación *f* perforation; piercing; boring, drilling

horadado perforated, pierced

horadar to perforate, pierce; drill; bore

horado *m* perforation, hole; cavern

horario *n* timetable, schedule; hour hand; watch; clock; hours; *adj* hourly

horca gallows; pitchfork, fork; forked prop; yoke; ~ **de ajos/cebollas** string of garlic/onions

horcadura fork of a tree; *anat* crotch, crutch

horcajadas: a ~ astride; **ponerse a** ~ to sit astride, straddle

horcajadillas: a ~ astride

horcajadura *anat* crotch, crutch

horcajo yoke; (of river) fork

horchata beverage made from tigernuts

horchatería, horchata stall

horchatero, horchata seller

horda horde

horizontal *n f sl* prostitute; *adj* horizontal

horizonte *m* horizon

horma mould, form; shoe tree; cobbler's last; dry wall; ~ **de sombrero** hat block; **encontrarse con/hallar la** ~ **de su zapato** to meet one's match, find what one has been looking for

hormaza dry-stone wall

hormiga ant; itching; itch; ~ **blanca** termite

hormigón *m* concrete; ~ **armado** reinforced concrete

hormigonera concrete-mixer

hormiguear to swarm (like ants); itch, tingle

hormigueo swarming; itching, tingling

hormiguero anthill; ant's nest; swarm, crowd; bonfire; **oso** ~ anteater

hormiguillo itching, tingling

hormiguita: ser una ~ to be industrious and thrifty

hormona hormone

hornada *cul+fig* batch

hornear to bake

hornero baker

hornilla kitchen grate; burner; nesting-hole in dovecot

hornillo portable stove; kitchen stove

horno furnace; oven; kiln; ~ **alfarero** pottery kiln; **alto** ~ blast furnace; ~ **de cal** limekiln; ~ **de cocina** kitchen stove; ~ **de cuba** blast furnace; ~ **de ladrillos** brick kiln; **fuente de** ~ oven-proof dish; **no está el** ~ **para bollos** this isn't the right time

horología horology

horólogo horologist

horóscopo horoscope; **hacer un** ~ to cast a horoscope

horqueta fork (of tree); forked stick

horquilla hairpin, kirby-grip; hatpin; pitchfork; forked pole; fork of tree; **viraje en** ~ hairpin bend

horrendo horrendous, horrible, frightful, hideous

horribilidad *f* horribleness, frightfulness

horrífico horrific, horrifying

horripilante horrifying, hair-raising

horripilar to horrify; cause revulsion

horror *m* horror; atrocity; **dar** ~ to horrify; **¡qué** ~**!** how terrible!; **me gusta un** ~ I like it very much

horrorizar to horrify; terrify; shock

horroroso horrible, horrid; hideous, frightful

hortaliza vegetable; ~s garden produce; vegetable garden

hortelano *n m* gardener, fruit farmer; *adj* garden

horterada act in bad taste

hortensia hydrangea

hortera *n m* Madrid shop assistant; person with bad taste; *f* wooden bowl; *adj* vulgar, in bad taste

hortícola horticultural

horticultor *m* horticulturalist

horticultura horticulture

hosco dark-coloured; dark brown; surly, sullen, bad-tempered; unsociable

hospedaje *m* lodging; board and lodging

hospedar to lodge; give board and lodging to; **~se** to put up at a hotel; lodge with; take a room/lodgings

hospedero inn-keeper

hospiciano inmate of an orphanage

hospicio workhouse, poorhouse; asylum; orphanage

hospital *m* hospital; **~ de campaña** field hospital; **~ de primera sangre** first-aid station

hospitalario hospitable; (of a) hospital

hospitalidad *f* hospitality

hospitalización *f* hospitalization

hospitalizar to hospitalize

hospitalmente hospitably

hosquedad *f* glumness; sullenness

hostería inn, tavern; hostel

hostia *eccles* consecrated wafer, Host (Holy Sacrament); offering, sacrificial victim; *sl* punch, thump; **de la ~** *sl* stupendous; **¡~!** *sl* damn it!

hostiar *sl* to punch, thump

hostigar to harass; tease, annoy; whip, lash; sicken, cloy; urge

hostil hostile

hostilidad *f* hostility; **romper las ~es** to begin hostilities

hotel *m* hotel; villa; detached suburban house; **~ del estado** *sl* gaol

hotelito semi-detached house; suburban villa

hotelero *n* hotel-keeper; *adj* hotel

hoy today; **~ (en) día** nowadays; **de ~ a mañana** any time now; **de ~ en adelante** from now on; **~ por ~** for the present, at present; **de ~ más** henceforth; **de ~ en 3 días** in 3 days' time

hoya pit, ditch; depression (in the ground); grave; seed-bed; river basin; dimple

hoyo hole, pit; dent; grave, tomb; *sl* death

hoyuelo dimple; little hole; (game) pitching pennies

hoz *f* sickle; ravine, defile; **de ~ en coz** recklessly

hozar (of pigs) to root

huarache *m* sandal

huaso *Chil* peasant, agricultural worker, cowboy

hucha chest; piggy-bank, money-box; nest egg; **tener una buena ~** to have a tidy sum put by

hueca *m* male homosexual

hueco *n* hole, gap, space, cavity; socket; **~ de la escalera** stairwell; **~ de la mano** hollow of the hand; **~ del ascensor** lift/elevator shaft; *adj* empty, hollow; vain, conceited, affected

huecograbado photogravure

¹ **huelga** strike; leisure; **~ de brazos caídos** sit-down strike; **~ de celo** work-to-rule; **~ de hambre** hunger strike; **~ de ritmo lento** go-slow strike; **~ de solidaridad** sympathy/secondary strike; **~ ilegal** unofficial strike; **~ legal** official strike; **~ salvaje** wildcat strike; **~ sentada** sit-down strike; **convocar una ~** to call a strike; **desconvocar una ~** to call off a strike; **declararse en ~, ir a la ~, ponerse en ~** to go on strike

² **huelga: ~ decir** needless to say

huelguista *m+f* striker

huelguístico *adj* striking

huella footprint, track; tread; rut; footstep; **~ dactilar/digital** fingerprint; **~ del sonido** sound track; **seguir las ~s de** to follow in the footsteps of; **dejar ~s** to leave one's mark

huerfanato orphanage

huérfano *n+adj* orphan; **~ de padre/madre** fatherless/motherless child

huero (of eggs) addled, rotten; empty; vain; **salir ~** to fail, flop, come to nothing

huerta vegetable garden; orchard; plantation; irrigated land

huertano *adj* garden

huerto kitchen garden; fruit patch; orchard

huesa grave, tomb

hueso bone; fruit stone, pit; dross; **a otro perro con ese ~** try it on s.o. else, tell it to the marines; **desenterrar los ~s de uno** to drag out the family skeleton/the skeleton in the cupboard; **estar en los ~s** to be all skin and bones; **la sin ~** the tongue; **soltar la sin ~** to talk too much; **mojarse hasta los ~s** to get wet through; **no dejar ~ sano a uno** to pick s.o. to pieces; **tener los ~s molidos** to be dog tired; be bruised; **un ~ duro de roer** a hard nut to crack

huesoso bony

huésped *m*, **huéspeda** *f* guest; lodger, boarder; host, hostess, landlord, landlady; **casa de** ~**es** boarding house

hueste *f* host, army; multitude; followers, partisans

huesudo bony, big-boned

hueva fish-roe; spawn

huevada *n sl* stupid action; *adv* **una** ~ *sl* greatly

huevera egg-cup; *sl* scrotum

huevería egg-merchant's stall/shop

huevero egg-merchant, egg-dealer

huevo egg; *sl* testicle; ~ **de Colón** task which looks difficult but proves to be easy; ~ **de Pascuas** Easter egg; ~ **duro** hard-boiled egg; ~ **en cáscara** soft-boiled egg; ~ **escalfado** poached egg; ~ **estrellado/frito** fried egg; ~ **mejido** drink made of egg, sugar and milk; ~ **pasado por agua**, ~ **tibio** soft-boiled egg; ~**s moles** egg-yolks beaten with sugar; ~**s pericos/revueltos** scrambled eggs; ¡~**s!** *vulg* balls!; **parecerse como un** ~ **a una castaña** to be as different as chalk and cheese; **tener** ~**s** *vulg* to be brave, have guts

huevón *adj sl* tranquil, easy-going

Hugo Hugh

hugonote *n m* + *adj* Huguenot

huida escape, flight; (of a horse) shying, bolting

huidero *n* lair; (of hunted animal) refuge; *adj* fleeing, escaping

huidizo fleeting; shy, elusive

huinche *m* winch

huir to flee, fly; run away, escape; ~ **de** to flee from; shun, avoid

hujier *m* usher

hule *m* rubber; rubber tree; oilcloth; oilskin; **habrá** ~ *sl* there's going to be a row/punch-up

hulla soft coal

hullera colliery

humada smoke-signal

humanar to humanize; ~**se** to become human; soften; ~**se a** to condescend to

humanidad *f* humanity, mankind; humaneness; human nature, human weakness; corpulence; ~**es** humanities

humanismo humanism; pragmatism

humanista *m* + *f* humanist; pragmatist

humanitario humanitarian; humane; kind, benevolent, charitable

humanitarismo humanitarianism

humanizar to humanize; ~**se** to become

human, take on human form; soften

humano *n* human being, mortal; *adj* human, mortal; humane, compassionate; **letras humanas** humanities; **linaje** ~ human race, mankind

humarada, humareda cloud of smoke

humazo dense smoke

humeada puff of smoke

humeante smoking, smoky; steaming

humear to smoke, give off smoke; fumigate; put on airs

humectador *m* humidifier

humectar to humidify

húmeda *sl* tongue

humedad *f* humidity, moisture, dampness

humedecer to wet, moisten, dampen; humidify; ~**se los labios** to lick/wet one's lips

húmedo wet, damp; moist, humid

humero chimney flue

húmero humerus

humildad *f* humility, humbleness; meekness

humilde humble, lowly; meek; submissive

humillación *f* humiliation, humbling; submission

humillador *adj* humbling, humiliating; mortifying; debasing

humillar to humiliate; humble, crush; ~**se** to humble oneself, lower oneself; bow low

humillo airs and graces; vanity, pride; conceit; ~**s** *vet* disease of young pigs

humo smoke; steam, vapour; fume; ~**s** airs, vanity, conceit; **darse** ~**s de grandeza** to put on airs; **irse todo en** ~ to go up in smoke

humor *m* humour; temper; mood, disposition; wit; **estar de buen** ~ to be in a good mood; **estar de mal** ~ to be in a bad mood; **no estar de** ~ **para** not to be in the mood for; **seguir el** ~ **a** to humour s.o.

humorada witticism; whim, caprice; *lit* epigrammatical composition

humorismo humour; humourousness

humorista *m* + *f* humourist

humorístico humorous

humoso smoky

hundible sinkable

hundimiento collapse; cave-in; sinking;

subsidence; foundering (of a ship); downfall, ruin

hundir to sink, submerge, plunge; destroy, ruin; ~**se** to sink, founder; collapse, cave in; subside; (of business) be ruined; fall off, diminish

húngaro *n* + *adj* Hungarian

Hungría *f* Hungary

huno Hun

hupe *m* touchwood, rotten wood, punk

huracán *m* hurricane

huraco hole (*esp* of ferret)

hurañez *f*, **huranía** diffidence; shyness; unsociability

huraño shy, diffident; unsociable, sullen; wild (of animals)

hurera burrow, hole, earth

hurgar to poke, stir; incite, rouse; ~**se la nariz** to pick one's nose; **peor es** ~ *approx equiv* to let sleeping dogs lie

hurgón *m* poker; stab

hurgonazo poke; jab; stab

hurgonear to poke the fire; stir up trouble

hurón *n m* ferret; snooper; *adj* shy; unsociable

huronear to ferret; ferret out; snoop

huronera ferret-hole

¡hurra! hurrah!

hurtadillas: a ~ slyly, on the sly, stealthily

hurtar to steal, rob; plagiarize; give short weight; give short change; encroach on (of the sea); ~ **el cuerpo** to dodge; shy away; duck; ~**se** to slip away; hide; withdraw

hurto theft, stealing, pilfering; stolen article; **a** ~ stealthily, on the sly; **coger con el** ~ **en las manos** to catch red-handed

húsar *m* hussar; **sombrero de** ~ busby; bearskin

husita *n m* + *f* + *adj* Hussite

husma snooping; **andar a la** ~ to snoop

husmeador *adj* snooping

husmear to scent, sniff, smell out; wind; pry into, snoop; (of meat) smell high

husmeo scenting, smelling, sniffing; prying, snooping; **estar al** ~ to watch for a good opportunity

huso *m* spindle; bobbin; ~ **horario** time zone

¡huy! ouch!

huyente: frente ~ receding brow; **ojeada** ~ shifty glance

I

i *f* (*pl* íes) letter i
ibérico *adj* Iberian
íbero *n* + *adj* Iberian
iberoamericano Iberoamerican; Spanish-American
íbice *m zool* ibex
ibicenco *n* inhabitant of Ibiza; *adj* from Ibiza
ibis *f orni* ibis
icono icon
iconoclasta *n m* + *f* + *adj* iconoclast
iconoclastía iconoclasm
iconografía iconography
iconógrafo iconographer
ictericia jaundice
ictiología ichthyology
ictiológico icthyological
ictiólogo ichthyologist
ida departure; outward journey; sally; ~s frequent visits; ~s y venidas comings and goings; ~ y vuelta there and back; billete de ~ y vuelta return ticket; en dos ~s y vueltas in a jiffy; partido de ~ *sp* first leg of a competition
idea idea; cambiar de ~ to change one's mind; no tener ni ~ not to have a clue; tener mala ~ to be ill-intentioned; tener ~s de bombero *sl* to have crazy ideas
idealidad *f* ideality
idealismo idealism
idealista *n m* + *f* idealist; *adj* idealistic
idealización *f* idealization
idealizar to idealize
idear to contrive; plan; think up
idéntico identical with
identidad *f* identity; documento de ~ identity papers
identificación *f* identification
identificar to identify
ideografía ideograph
ideográfico ideographical
ideología ideology
ideológico ideological
idílico idyllic

idilio idyll
idioma *m* language
idiomático idiomatic
idiosincrasia idiosyncrasy
idiosincrásico idiosyncratic
idiota *n m* + *f* idiot; *adj* idiotic, daft
idiotez *f* idiocy
idiotismo ignorance; *gramm* idiom, turn of speech
ido absent-minded; crazy; en tiempos ~s in days gone by
idólatra *n m* + *f* idolater; ardent lover; *adj* idolatrous
idolatrar to worship; idolize; adore
idolatría idolatry
idolátrico idolatrous
ídolo idol
idoneidad *f* fitness, aptness, capacity
idóneo fit; competent; suitable
iglesia church; ~ matriz metropolitan church; ~ mayor cathedral; ~ oriental Greek Orthodox Church; ~ ritualista high church; casarse por detrás de la ~ to live as man and wife without being married; casarse por la ~ to have a church wedding; llevar a una mujer a la ~ to get married
iglú *m* igloo
ignaro ignorant
ígneo igneous
ignición *f* ignition
ignícola fire-worshipping
ignífugo fireproof
ignito ignited, burning
ignominia ignominy
ignominioso ignominious
ignorancia ignorance; la ~ no quita pecado ignorance of the law is no excuse
ignorante *n m* + *f* ignoramus; *adj* ignorant; unaware
ignorar to not know
ignoto unknown
igual *n m* equal; *math* equal sign; ~es *sl* pair of Civil Guards; al ~ que the same as; en ~ de in lieu of; sin ~ un-

261

equalled, unrivalled; *adj* equal; level, even; unchangeable; ~ **a/que** equal to; **me es** ~ it's all the same to me; **no he visto cosa** ~ I've never seen such a thing

iguala agreement; stipulation; *med* agreed fee; *bui* level; **a la** ~ equally

igualación *f* equalization; levelling

igualado level; even

igualar to equalize; match, mate; level, smooth; *bui* size; *math* equate; *sp* be tied; trim; **~se a/con** to consider o.s. equal to

igualdad *f* equality; evenness; uniformity; ~ **de ánimo** equanimity; **en pie de** ~ on an equal footing; ~ **de opiniones** sameness of opinions

igualitario equitable

I.I. (índice de la inteligencia) I.Q. (Intelligence Quotient)

ikurriña, icuriña flag of **Euzkadi** (Basque Country)

ilegal illegal; (of strikes) unofficial

ilegalidad *f* illegality

ilegibilidad *f* illegibility

ilegible illegible

ilegitimar to make illegal

ilegitimidad *f* illegitimacy

ilegítimo illegitimate

ileso unhurt, unscathed

iletrado uncultured, ignorant

Ilíada Iliad

iliberal illiberal

iliberalidad *f* illiberality

ilícito illicit

ilicitud *f* unlawfulness

ilimitable illimitable, boundless

ilimitado unlimited

iliterato uncultured, ignorant

ilógico illogical

iludir to mock

iluminación *f* illumination

iluminador *n m* illuminator; *adj* illuminating

iluminar to illuminate; colour; enlighten

iluminaria light

iluminativo illustrating

ilusión *f* illusion; wishful thinking; **con** ~ hopefully; **esperar con** ~ to look forward to; **hacerse ilusiones sobre** to bank on; **tener ilusiones de** to entertain hopes of

ilusionar to build up somebody's hopes; **~se** to be thrilled

ilusionista *m+f* illusionist, conjurer; visionary

ilusivo false; apparent

iluso deceived

ilusorio illusive; *leg* null and void

ilustración *f* illustration; learning; enlightenment

ilustrado enlightened, cultured; illustrated

ilustrador *n m* illustrator; *adj* illustrative

ilustrar to illustrate; enlighten; elucidate; **~se** to become illustrious

ilustre illustrious, eminent

imagen *f* image

imaginación *f* imagination

imaginar to imagine; suspect; **~se** to picture in one's mind

imaginaria *mil* reserve guard; *mil* night guard in barracks dormitory

imaginario imaginary

imaginativa imagination; common sense

imaginativo imaginative; fanciful

imaginería fancy embroidery, pictorial embroidery; imagery

¹ **imán** *m* magnet; magnetism

² **imán** *m* imam

imanación *f* magnetism

imanar to magnetize

imantación *f* magnetizing

imantar to magnetize

imbatible unbeatable

imbécil *n + adj* imbecile

imbecilidad *f* imbecility

imberbe beardless

imbibición *f* imbibing

imbornal *m* drain; *naut* scupper, scupper-hole

imborrable indelible

imbuir (en) to imbue (with); persuade

imitación *f* imitation

imitado *adj* imitated

imitador *n m* imitator; *adj* imitative

imitámonos *m sing + pl* copycat

imitante imitating

imitar to imitate

imitativo imitative

impacción *f* impact

impaciencia impatience

impacientar to vex; exasperate, make s.o. impatient; **~se** to become impatient

impaciente (con/de) impatient (with)

impacto impact

impagable unpayable
impalpabilidad *f* impalpability
impar *math* odd; without equal, peerless
imparcial impartial
imparcialidad *f* impartiality
impartible indivisible
impartir to impart; share; concede
impasibilidad *f* impassiveness
impasible impassive
impavidez *f* composure
impávido dauntless; calm; *SA* cheeky
impecabilidad *f* impeccability
impecable impeccable
impedancia *elect* impedance; ~ **de entrada** input impedance
impedido disabled, crippled
impedidor *adj* impeding
impediente *adj* obstructing
impedimenta *mil* luggage, baggage
impedimento impediment; obstacle; snag
impedir to impede; bar (the way); prevent
impeditivo *adj* impeding, obstructing
impeler to impel; push; urge on
impender to spend (money)
impenetrabilidad *f* impenetrability
impenetrable impenetrable; incomprehensible; fathomless
impenitencia impenitence
impenitente impenitent
impensado unforeseen
impepinable *sl* unquestionable
imperante commanding; prevailing; *astrol* dominant
imperar to command; prevail
imperativo domineering; imperative
imperceptibilidad *f* imperceptibility
imperdible *n m* safety-pin; *adj* safe; impossible to lose
imperdonable unforgivable
imperecedero unperishable; undying; immortal
imperfección *f* imperfection
imperfecto *n gramm* imperfect; ~**s** damage; *adj* faulty, imperfect
imperforado imperforated
imperial *n m* upper seats on coach; top deck of bus; hood (of a vehicle); *adj* imperial
imperialismo imperialism
imperialista *n m+f +adj* imperialist
impericia inexpertness, lack of skill

imperio empire, command, sway
imperioso imperious; overbearing; necessary
imperito inexperienced; inexpert
impermeabilidad *f* impermeability
impermeabilizar to make water-proof
impermeable *n m* raincoat; *sl* french letter; *adj* impermeable; waterproof
impersonalidad *f* lack of personality
impertérrito intrepid
impertinencia impertinence; nonsense
impertinente *adj* not pertinent; impertinent; meddlesome; *n* ~**s** lorgnettes
imperturbabilidad *f* imperturbability
impétigo *med* impetigo
impetrar to obtain something asked for
ímpetu *m* impetus
impetuosidad *f* impetuosity
impetuoso impetuous
impiedad *f* impiety
impiedoso impious
impío *n* infidel, unbeliever; anti-religious person; *adj* impious, godless
implacabilidad *f* implacability
implantación *f* implantation
implantar to implant
implaticable unmentionable
implicación *f* involvement; contradiction
implicante contradictory; implicating
implicar to imply; to obstruct; implicate
implicatorio contradictory; implicatory
implícito implicit
imploración *f* entreaty
implorante imploring
implorar to implore
implume *orni* without feathers
impolítica discourtesy
impolítico indiscreet; unwise; discourteous
impoluto unpolluted
imponderabilidad *f* imponderability
imponedor *n m* imposer; *adj* imposing
imponente imposing; *fam* fabulous, stupendous
imponer to impose; advise; impute; inspire; *eccles* bless (by laying on of hands); ~**se** to assert o.s.; dominate; get one's own way
imponible dutiable; taxable
impopular unpopular
impopularidad *f* unpopularity
imporoso impermeable; non-porous

importación *f comm* imports; importation

importador *n m* importer; *adj* importing

importancia importance

importante important

importar *vi* to matter; *vt* to import; be worth

importe *m comm* cost, price

importunación *f* importunity

importunador *n m* importuner; *adj* importuning

importunar to importune

importunidad *f* importunity

importuno inopportune; annoying

imposibilidad *f* impossibility

imposibilitado disabled, crippled

imposibilitar to disable, cripple; render useless; make impossible

imposible impossible; ~ **de toda imposibilidad** quite out of the question; **hacer lo ~ para** to do all one can to

imposición *f* imposition; tax; ~ **de manos** *eccles* laying on of hands

imposta *archi* fascia; springer, impost

impostura imposture; deceit

impotable not fit for drinking

impotencia impotence

impotente impotent

impracticabilidad *f* impracticability

imprecación *f* imprecation

imprecar to imprecate

imprecatorio imprecatory

impreciso imprecise

impregnación *f* impregnation; saturation

impregnar to impregnate; saturate

impremeditado unpremeditated

imprenta printing; printing works; press

imprescindible indispensible, essential

impresentable unpresentable

impresión *f* impression; stamp(ing); print; edition; influence

impresionable impressionable

impresionante impressive

impresionar *vt* to impress, influence; *phot* expose; ~**se** to be moved

impresionismo *arts* impressionism

impresionista *n m + f arts* impressionist

impreso *n* printed form; pamphlet; printed matter; *adj* printed

impresor *m* printer

imprestable that cannot be lent

imprevisible unforeseeable

imprevisión *f* lack of foresight; thriftlessness

imprevisor improvident

imprevisto unforeseen; unexpected

imprimación *f* priming

imprimar to prime

imprimátur *m eccles* licence to print

imprimir to print; fix in one's mind

improbabilidad *f* improbability

improbar to disapprove

improbidad *f* dishonesty

ímprobo dishonest; arduous

improcedencia unrighteousness

improcedente against the law; unrighteous

improductivo unproductive

impronunciable unpronounceable

improperar to abuse

improperio insult, abuse

impropiedad *f* impropriety

impropio (a/de/en) inappropriate, unbecoming (for)

improporción *f* disproportion

improporcionado disproportionate

improrrogable that cannot be postponed

impróspero unprosperous

improvidencia improvidence

impróvido improvident

improvisación *f* improvisation

improvisador *m* improviser

improvisar to improvise

improviso unexpected

imprudencia imprudence, indiscretion; ~ **temeraria** criminal negligence

imprudente imprudent, unwise

impúber impuberate

impudente shameless, rude

impúdico immodest, unchaste

impudor *m* immodesty; shamelessness

impuesto *n* tax; duty; ~ **deducido a la fuente** tax deducted at source; ~ **sobre la renta** income tax; *adj* imposed; **estar ~ de** to be informed about

impugnación *f* opposition; refutation; *leg* challenge

impugnador *m* objector; refuter

impugnar to impugn; oppose; refute; challenge

impugnativo impugning

impulsar to impel; *mech* drive

impulsión *f* impulsion; impetus, drive

impulsividad *f* impulsiveness

impulsivo impulsive

impulso impulse, momentum; ~s del corazón promptings of the heart
impulsor *m* impeller
impune unpunished
impunidad *f* impunity
impureza impurity; obscenity; unchastity
impurificación *f* defilement
impurificar to defile; adulterate
impuro impure; adulterated; defiled
imputabilidad *f* imputability
imputación *f* imputation
imputador *n m* imputer; *adj* imputing
inabordable unapproachable
inacabable unending
inaccesibilidad *f* inaccessibility
inaccesible inaccessible
inacción *f* inaction
inacentuado unaccented
inaceptable unacceptable
inactividad *f* inactivity
inactivo inactive
inadaptable unadaptable
inadaptado maladjusted
inadecuado inadequate
inadmisible inadmissible
inadoptable unadoptable
inadvertencia oversight
inadvertido unnoticed; careless; pasar ~ to go unnoticed
inafectado unaffected
inagotable inexhaustible
inaguantable unbearable
inajenable inalienable
inalcanzable unattainable
inalterabilidad *f* unalterability
inalterable unalterable, imperturbable
inalterado unaltered, unperturbed
inameno unpleasant; dull
inamovible immovable
inamovilidad *f* immovability
inanalizable that cannot be analysed
inane useless, vain
inania, inanidad *f* inanity; uselessness
inanimación *f* inanimation
inanimado, inánime inanimate
inapagable unquenchable
inapetencia lack of appetite
inapetente having no appetite
inaplazable that cannot be deferred; pressing
inaplicable inapplicable
inaplicación *f* laziness
inaplicado lazy, careless

inapreciable invaluable
inapropiado inappropriate
inarmónico inharmonious
inarticulado inarticulate
inasequible unattainable
inastillable splinterproof
inatacable that cannot be attacked
inaudibilidad *f* inaudibility
inaudito unheard of; odd
inauguración *f* inauguration; (of monument *etc*) unveiling; (of building) ceremonial opening
inaugurar to inaugurate; unveil; declare open
inaveriguable unascertainable
inca *n + adj* Inca
incalificable indescribably bad, unspeakable
incandescencia incandescence
incandescente incandescent
incandescer to incandesce
incansable untiring
incantable unsingable
incapacidad *f* incapacity; incompetence
incapacitar to incapacitate; disable
incapaz incapable; incompetent
incasable unmarriageable
incasto unchaste
incautación *f leg* attachment, seizure (of property *etc*)
incautar *leg* to attach; ~se de *leg* to seize (property *etc*)
incauto gullible; unwary
incendiar to ignite; ~se to catch fire
incendiario *n* fire-raiser; *adj* incendiary
incendiarismo arson
incendio fire
incensar *eccles* to burn incense; *fig* flatter
incensario thurible, censer
incensurable unblamable
incentivar to provide an incentive/inducement to
incentivo incentive
incertidumbre *f* uncertainty
incesable, incesante unceasing
incesto incest
incestuoso incestuous
incidencia incident; *phys* incidence
incidente *n m* incident; ~s *comm* appurtenances; ~s de comercio lease and goodwill; *adj* incidental
incidir to cut into; ~ en to have an influence on, impinge on

incienso incense
incierto uncertain
incineración *f* incineration; cremation
incinerador *m* incinerator
incinerar to incinerate; cremate
incipiente incipient
incircunciso uncircumcised
incisión *f* incision, cut
incisivo *n* incisor tooth; *adj* incisive; keen; (of wit) biting
inciso cut; *gramm* subordinate clause
incitación *f* incitement
incitador *n* instigator; *adj* inciting
incitamiento incitement
incitante inciting
incitar to incite
incitativo *n* incitement; *adj* inciting
incivil uncivil
incivilidad *f* incivility
inclasificable unclassifiable
inclemencia inclemency; **a la ~** at the mercy of the elements
inclemente inclement
inclinación *f* inclination; tilt; slope; gradient; bow; nod; **~ de la brújula** *naut* tilt of the needle
inclinado, inclinador slanting, sloping
inclinar to incline; tilt; influence; **~se** to lean; sway; stoop; be inclined to
ínclito illustrious
incluido: todo ~ inclusive (hotel terms *etc*)
incluir to include; enclose
inclusa foundling home
inclusero foundling
inclusión *f* inclusion; friendship
inclusivo inclusive
incluso *adj* enclosed; included; *adv* + *prep* even
incluyente enclosing, including
incoagulabilidad *f* incoagulability
incobrable irretrievable, uncollectable
incógnita *math* unknown quantity; *fig* mystery
incógnito *n* unknown quantity; *adj* unknown; **de ~** clandestinely; **guardar el ~** to remain incognito
incoherencia incoherence
incoherente incoherent
incoloro colourless
incólume unharmed, unscathed
incolumidad *f* safety
incombinable uncombinable
incombustibilidad *f* incombustibility

incombusto unburnt
incomerciable unmarketable
incomestible, incomible uneatable
incomodar to disturb; inconvenience; **~se** to get vexed
incomodidad *f* inconvenience; vexation; discomfort
incómodo uncomfortable; inconvenient
incompartible indivisible
incompasivo pitiless; unsympathetic
incompatibilidad *f* incompatibility
incompensable unindemnifiable
incompetencia incompetence
incompetente incompetent
incompleto incomplete, unfinished
incomplexo incoherent; disjointed
incomponible irreparable
incomportable unsupportable
incomprensibilidad *f* incomprehensibility
incomprensible incomprehensible; unimaginable
incomprensión *f* misunderstanding
incomprimible uncompressible
incomunicabilidad *f* incommunicability
incomunicable incommunicable
incomunicación *f* isolation; lack of communication
incomunicado *n* prisoner; *adj* isolated; cut off
incomunicar to isolate; cut off; put into solitary confinement
inconcebible unconceivable
inconciliable irreconcilable
inconcluso unfinished
inconcluyente inconclusive
incondicional unconditional; **amigo ~** friend for life
inconducente non-conducive
inconexo unconnected
inconfesable shameful, unmentionable
inconfeso *n* accused who pleads innocence; *adj* unwilling to plead guilty
inconfundible unmistakable; characteristic
incongruencia incongruence
incongruo incongruous
inconmensurabilidad *f* incommensurability
inconmensurable immeasurable
inconmovible immovable; inexorable
inconmutable unchangeable
inconquistable unconquerable
inconsciente *n m* + *adj* unconscious; un-

aware
inconsecuencia inconsistency
inconsecuente inconsistent; inconsequential
inconservable unpreservable
inconsiderado ill-considered
inconsistencia inconsistency, flimsiness
inconsistente flimsy, unsubstantial
inconsolable unconsolable
inconstancia fickleness
inconstante unstable; changeable
inconstitucional unconstitutional
inconsútil seamless
incontaminado uncontaminated
incontenible unstoppable; uncontrollable
incontestable unquestionable, indisputable
incontinencia incontinence
incontinente incontinent
incontinenti right away, immediately
incontrastable irrefutable
incontrolable uncontrollable
incontrovertibilidad *f* incontrovertibility
inconveniencia inconvenience; impropriety; foolish deed or remark
inconveniente *n m* obstacle; snag; *adj* inconvenient; improper; undesirable; **no hay ningún ~** there is no objection
incordiar to annoy
incordio nuisance
incorporación *f* incorporation
incorporador incorporating
incorporal incorporeal
incorporar to incorporate; mix; **~se** to sit up; **~se a** to join, become a member of
incorpóreo incorporeal, formless
incorrección *f* inaccuracy; improper statement or deed
incorrecto incorrect
incorruptabilidad *f* incorruptability
incorrupto incorrupt; chaste
increado uncreated
incredibilidad, incredulidad *f* incredulity
incrédulo *n* unbeliever; *adj* incredulous
increíble incredible
incremento, incrementación *f* increment, increase
increpación *f* rebuke, upbraiding
increpador *n m* rebuker; *adj* rebuking, upbraiding

increpante *adj* rebuking
increpar to reprimand; rebuke
incriminación *f* incrimination
incriminar to incriminate
incruento without bloodshed
incrustación *f* incrustation; *arts* inlaying
incrustar to fix, mount; *arts* inlay
incubación *f* incubation
incubadora incubator
incubar to incubate
íncubo incubus; nightmare
incuestionable unquestionable
inculcación *f* inculcation; *print* locking
inculcar to inculcate; *print* lock up
inculpabilidad *f* guiltlessness
inculpable guiltless
inculpar to blame
inculto uncultivated; uncultured
incultura lack of culture/cultivation
incumbencia obligation; **no es de su ~** it's not his concern
incumbente incumbent
incumbir to be the responsibility of
incumplimiento failure to carry out; **~ de contrato** breach of contract
incumplir to fail to carry out
incuria negligence
incurioso negligent
incurrir to incur; commit (an offence)
incusar to accuse
indagación *f* verification; inquiry
indagar to verify; investigate
indagatoria statement (made to the police)
indagatorio *leg* investigatory
indebido improper; illegal
indecencia indecency; indecent act
indecente indecent
indecible unspeakable
indecisión *f* indecision, vacillation
indeciso undecided, hesitant
indecoro indecorum
indecoroso indecorous
indefenso defenceless
indefinido undefined; indefinite
indeleble indelible
indelicadeza indelicacy
indemne unhurt; undamaged
indemnización *f* compensation; redundancy pay, golden handshake
indemnizar to compensate
indemostrable that cannot be demonstrated
independencia independence

independiente independent
indescifrable undecipherable
indescriptible indescribable
indeseable undesirable
indestructibilidad *f* indestructibility
indeterminación *f* lack of determination
indeterminado undetermined; irresolute; *gramm* indefinite
indevoción *f* lack of piety
indevoto impious, irreligious
indianista *n m* + *f* + *adj* student/defender of American Indians
indiano settler who returns (rich) from America
Indias *fpl* Indies
indicación *f* indication
indicador *m* indicator
indicar to indicate
indicativo indicative
índice *m* index; forefinger; hand (of clock *etc*); gnomon; ~ **de crecimiento** growth rate; ~ **de materias** contents index
índico (East) Indian
indiferencia indifference
indiferente indifferent; *fam* immaterial
indígena *n m* + *adj* native
indigencia indigence
indigente indigent
indigerible indigestible
indigestarse to suffer indigestion
indigestión *f* indigestion
indigesto indigestible; disagreeable
indignación *f* indignation
indignado indignant
indignar to irritate; infuriate; ~**se** to get indignant
indignidad *f* indignity
indigno unworthy
indiligencia idleness
indio Indian; **hacer el** ~ *sl* to behave foolishly
indirecta hint; ~ **del padre Cobos** broad hint
indirecto indirect
indiscernible indistinct
indisciplina indiscipline
indisciplinado undisciplined, unruly
indiscreción *f* indiscretion
indiscreto indiscreet
indisculpable inexcusable
indiscutible indisputable
indisoluble indissoluble
indispensable indispensable

indisponer *vt* to make ill; ~ **a uno con** to set s.o. against; *vi* to become ill; ~**se con** to fall out with
indisposición *f* indisposition, illness
indispuesto indisposed; at variance
indistinto indistinct
individual *n m* individual; ~**es** singles match; *adj* individual
individualismo individualism
individualista *n m* + *f* + *adj* individualist
individualizar to individualize
individuo *n* individual; *pej* chap, fellow; *adj* individual
indivisibilidad *f* indivisibility
indivisión *f* entirety
indiviso undivided
indócil unruly
indocilidad *f* unruliness
indocto uncultured; uneducated
indochino Indo-Chinese
indoeuropeo Indo-European
índole inclination
indolencia indolence; insensitivity
indolente indolent; insensitive; painless
indoloro painless
indomable untamable; unmanageable
indomado untamed
indomesticable untamable
indoméstico untamed
indómito untamable
indonesio *n* + *adj* Indonesian
indostaní *n* + *adj* Hindustani
indotado without a dowry; unendowed
inducción *f* induction; **por** ~ inductively
inducimiento inducement
inducir to induce; instigate; persuade
indúctil not ductile
inductor *n m* inducer; *adj* inducting; *elect* inductive
indudable doubtless
indulgencia indulgence; leniency
indulgente indulgent; lenient
indultar *leg* to pardon; amnesty; exempt
indulto pardon; exemption
indumentaria clothing
industria industry; skill; **de** ~ deliberately
industrial *n m* manufacturer; factory; industrialist; *adj* industrial
industrializar to industrialize
industriar to train; ~**se** to find a way, manage
industrioso industrious
inedia undernourishment

inédito unpublished; unheard of
inefabilidad f ineffability
inefable ineffable
inefectivo ineffective
ineficacia inefficiency
ineficiente inefficatious
ineficaz inefficient
inelegante inelegant
ineludible inevitable
ineptitud f ineptitude
inepto inept
inequívoco unequivocal
inercia inertia
inerme lifeless; motionless; unarmed
inerrable infallible
inerrante astron fixed
inerte inert
inerudito unlearned
inescrutable inscrutable
inesperado unexpected
inestabilidad f instability
inestable unstable
inexactitud f inexactness
inexacto inexact
inexistente non-existent
inexperiencia inexperience
inexperto inexpert
inexplorado unexplored
inexpresivo unexpressive
inexpugnable unconquerable
inextinguible unextinguishable
infacundo not eloquent
infalibilidad f infallibility
infalible infallible
infamación f defamation, slander
infamador n m defamer, slanderer; adj
   slanderous
infamar to defame, slander
infamativo defamatory, slanderous
infame infamous; vile
infamia slander; infamy
infancia infancy; children
infando unmentionable
infanta Spanish royal princess
infante m Spanish royal prince; infant;
   eccles choirboy; mil infantryman
infantería infantry
infanticida m+f infanticide (person); sl
   man keen on young girls
infanticidio infanticide (crime)
infantil infantile, childish
infanzón m nobleman
infanzonía nobility
infarto swelling; obstruction; ~ car-

díaco cardiac arrest
infatigable untiring
infatuación f conceit
infatuar to make conceited
infausto unfortunate
infección f infection
infeccioso infectious
infectar to infect
infecto infected; vile
infecundidad f infertility; sterility
infecundo infertile, sterile
infelicidad unhappiness; ill-luck
infeliz n m+f unlucky person; person
   who has come down in the world; adj
   unhappy; unlucky; gullible
inferencia inference
inferioridad f inferiority
inferir to infer; inflict
infernáculo hop-scotch
infestación f infestation
infestar to infest; overrun, swamp
inficionar to defile; infect
infidelidad f infidelity; unbelief
infidencia faithlessness; treason; leg
   malfeasance
infidente unfaithful
infiel n m heathen; unfaithful person;
   unreliable person; adj heathen; unfaithful; unreliable
infiernillo portable stove
infierno hell
infiltración f infiltration
infiltrar infiltrate
ínfimo lowest; last; most inferior; vilest
infinidad f infinity
infinitésimo infinitesimal
infinitivo gramm infinitive
infinito n infinite; hasta lo ~ ad infinitum, adv immensely
inflación f inflation; vanity
inflacionismo inflationism
inflacionista n m+f +adj inflationist
inflado: arroz ~ puffed rice
inflagaitas m sing + pl sl fool
inflamable inflammable, US flammable
inflamación f blazing; med inflammation
inflamar to blaze; ~se to become angry;
   become inflamed
inflamatorio inflammatory
inflar to inflate; puff up; ~se to become
   vain
inflexibilidad f inflexibility
inflexión f inflexion, bending; tone
infligir to inflict

inflorescencia *bot* inflorescence
influencia influence; authority
influir to influence
influjo incoming tide; influence
influyente influential
información *f* information; *leg* brief
informador *n m* informer; media person; *adj* informing
informal informal; easy-going; unreliable; ill-mannered
informalidad *f* informality, unreliability
informar to inform; report; *leg* plead; ~**se** to find out
informática data processing
informativo informative
¹ **informe** *n* report; news item; instruction; *leg* plea
² **informe** *adj* formless; badly formed
informidad *f* shapelessness
infortunio misfortune
infracción *f* transgression; breaking of a law
infraccionar to break (a law)
infracto, infractor *m* law-breaker
infraempleado under-employed
infraempleo under-employment
infraestructura infrastructure
infrahumano subhuman
infrangible inviolable
infranqueable unsurmountable; impassable
infrarrojo infra-red
infrascrito *n + adj* undersigned
infrecuente infrequent
infringir to break (a pact, law *etc*)
infructuosidad *f* fruitlessness
infructuoso fruitless; useless
ínfulas *fpl* vanity, pride; *eccles* ribbon on a bishop's mitre; **tener** ~**s de ...** to have pretensions to ...
infundado false; groundless
infundir to infuse; instil
infusión *f* infusion; *eccles* baptism by sprinkling
ingeniar to invent; think up; engineer; ~**se** to manage, find a way
ingeniatura ingenuity; good management; *SA* engineering
ingeniería engineering
ingeniero engineer; ~ **agrónomo** agronomist, agricultural engineer; ~ **de caminos, canales y puertos** state-employed civil engineer; ~ **de marina** naval engineer; ~ **de minas** mining

engineer; ~ **de montes** forestry engineer; ~ **electricista** electrical engineer; ~ **hidráulico** hydraulic engineer; ~ **industrial** mechanical engineer; ~ **mecánico** production engineer
ingenio inventiveness; knack; wit; machine, appliance, apparatus; *SA* sugar-mill
ingeniosidad *f* genius, stroke of genius
ingenioso ingenious; witty
ingénito inborn
ingente huge, enormous
ingenuidad *f* ingenuity
ingenuo ingenuous, naïve
ingerencia interference; *agri* grafting
ingeridor *m agri* grafting-knife
ingeridura *n agri* grafting
ingerir to ingest; swallow; *agri* graft
Inglaterra England
ingle *f anat* groin
inglés *n* Englishman; *adj* English; (of jokes) unfunny; **a la inglesa** in the English fashion; **pan** ~ 'tin' loaf
inglesar to anglicize
inglesismo anglicism
ingobernable ungovernable
ingratitud *f* ingratitude
ingrato *n* ingrate; *adj* ungrateful; disagreeable
ingravidez *f* space absence of gravity; weightlessness
ingrávido weightless
ingrediente *m* ingredient
ingresar *vt* to deposit; *vi* to join
ingreso joining; entrance, admission; *comm* deposit; *comm* takings, receipts; **derecho/examen de** ~ entrance examination/fee
ingurgitación *f* swallowing
ingurgitar to swallow
ingustable unsavoury, nasty-tasting
inhábil unskilful; inept; tactless
inhabilidad *f* lack of skill; ineptness; tactlessness
inhabilitación *f* disqualification; incapacitation
inhabilitar to disqualify; debar (from holding public office)
inhabitable uninhabitable
inhabituado unaccustomed
inhalación *f* inhalation
inhalador *n m* inhaler; *adj* inhaling
inhalar to inhale

inhartable insatiable
inherente (a) inherent (in)
inhestar to erect
inhibición f inhibition
inhibir to inhibit; ~**se** to become inhibited; refrain
inhibitorio inhibitory
inhiesto erect, upright
inhonestidad f immodesty, indecency
inhonesto immodest, indecent
inhospitalario inhospitable
inhospitalidad f inhospitality
inhumación f burial
inhumanidad f inhumanity
inhumano inhuman, inhumane
inhumar to bury
iniciación f initiation
iniciador n m initiator; adj initiating
inicial n + adj initial
iniciar to initiate
iniciativa initiative
iniciativo initiatory
inicuo iniquitous
inimaginable unimaginable
ininteligible unintelligible
iniquidad f iniquity
injeridura n agri grafting
injerir to ingest; swallow; agri graft
injertar agri to graft
injerto agri graft, grafting
injuria abuse; slander, calumny
injuriador abusive, slanderous
injuriar to abuse, slander
injurioso abusive, slanderous
injusticia injustice
injustificable unjustifiable
injustificado unjustified
injusto unjust; unfair
inmaculado without blemish, faultless; **La Inmaculada** the Virgin Mary
inmadurez f immaturity; unripeness
inmaduro immature; unripe
inmaleable unmalleable
inmanejable unmanageable
inmarcesible unfading; that cannot wither
inmarchitable unfading
inmaterial immaterial
inmaturo immature
inmediaciones fpl immediate neighbourhood
inmediato adjoining, next-door; immediate; **de** ~ immediately; **historia inmediata** very recent history

inmedicable incurable
inmejorable unsurpassable
inmemorable immemorial
inmensidad f immensity
inmenso immense
inmensurable measureless
inmerecido, inmérito undeserved
inmeritorio undeserving
inmersión f immersion
inmigración f immigration
inmigrante n m + f immigrant
inmigrar to immigrate
inminencia imminence
inminente imminent
inmiscuir to mix; ~**se** to interfere; poke one's nose in
inmobiliaria estate agency; real estate office
inmobiliario property; **agente** ~ estate agent, US realtor
inmoble fixed, unmovable; unchanging
inmoderación f immoderation
inmoderado immoderate
inmodestia immodesty
inmodesto immodest
inmolación f sacrifice, immolation
inmolador sacrificing, immolating
inmolar to sacrifice, immolate
inmoral immoral
inmoralidad f immorality
inmorigerado inordinate
inmortalidad f immortality
inmortalizar to immortalize
inmotivado without reason
inmoto motionless
inmovible immovable
inmóvil fixed; motionless
inmovilidad f immobility
inmovilismo pol extreme reaction; die-hard resistance to change
inmueble leg real estate; ~**s** immovable property
inmundicia dirt; lewdness
inmundo dirty; lewd
inmune immune
inmunidad f immunity
inmunización f immunization
inmunizar to immunize
inmutabilidad immutability
inmutable unchangeable
innato inborn
innavegable unseaworthy
innatural unnatural

innecesario unnecessary
innegable undeniable
innoble ignoble
innocuo innocuous, harmless
innominado nameless
innovación *f* innovation
innovador *n m* innovator; *adj* innovatory
innovamiento innovation
innovar to innovate
innúmero innumerable
inobediencia disobedience
inobediente disobedient
inobservancia non-observance
inobservante unobservant
inocencia innocence; simplicity
inocentada simple act; innocent behaviour; silly joke; April fool joke
inocente innocent; naïve
inocentón *m* simpleton
inocuidad *f* innocuity
inoculación *f* inoculation
inoculador *n m* inoculator; *adj* inoculating
inocular to inoculate; ~**se** to get inoculated
inoculador inoculator
inocuo innocuous
inodoro *n* water-closet; *adj* odourless
inofensivo inoffensive
inolvidable unforgettable
inopia poverty; **estar en la** ~ to be in cloud-cuckoo land
inopinable indisputable
inopinado unexpected
inoportuno inopportune
inordenado lacking order
inorgánico inorganic
inoxidable stainless; non-rusting
inquebrantable unbreakable
inquietador disquieting
inquietante disturbing, worrying
inquietar to disturb, worry
inquieto uneasy; restless
inquietud *f* uneasiness; restlessness
inquilinato lease; **impuesto de** ~ municipal rates
inquilino tenant; *leg* lessee
inquina aversion; **tener** ~ **a** to bear a grudge against
inquinar to contaminate
inquiridor *n m* inquirer; *adj* inquiring
inquirir to investigate, check
inquisición *f* inquiry; inquest; inquisi-

tion
inquisidor *m* inquirer; inquisitor
inquisitivo inquisitive
inri *m* stigma; insult; **para más** ~ to make matters worse, add insult to injury
insabible unknowable
insaciabilidad *f* insatiability
insaciable insatiable
insalivación *f* insalivation
insalivar to insalivate
insalubre unhealthy
insalubridad *f* unhealthiness
insanable incurable
insania insanity
insano unhealthy; insane
insatisfecho unsatisfied
inscribir to engrave; enter on a list, enrol
inscripción *f* engraving; inscription; enrolment
insecable that cannot dry up; indivisible
insecticida *n m* + *adj* insecticide
insectívoro insectivorous
insecto insect, *US* bug
insectólogo entomologist; bug-hunter
inseguridad *f* insecurity; uncertainty
inseguro insecure; unsafe; uncertain
insembrado unsown
inseminación *f* insemination
inseminar to inseminate
insensatez *f* foolishness; stupidity
insensato nonsensical, senseless
insensibilidad *f* insensibility; insensitivity
insensibilizar to render insensitive/insensible
insensible insensitive; imperceptible
inseparabilidad *f* inseparability
insepulto unburied
inserción *f* insertion; *agri* engrafting
insertar to insert; introduce
inserto *n* insertion; *adj* inserting
inservible unserviceable; useless
insidia ambush, trap; insidious act
insidiar to plot against; ambush
insidioso insidious
insigne celebrated, eminent
insignia badge; standard; *naut* pennant; ~**s** insignia
insignificancia insignificance
insignificante insignificant
insinceridad *f* insincerity
insinuación *f* insinuation

insinuante suggestive
insinuar to insinuate; ~**se** to work one's way in; drop hints
insinuativo insinuating; slick, smooth
insipidez f insipidity
insípido insipid
insipiencia ignorance
insipiente ignorant
insistencia insistence
insistente insistent
insistir to insist
ínsito innate
insociabilidad f unsociability
insociable, insocial unsociable
insolación f sunstroke; heatstroke
insolar to expose to the sun; ~**se** to get sunstroke
insolencia insolence
insolentarse to behave insolently
insolente insolent
insólito unusual
insolubilidad f insolubility
insoluto unpaid
insolvencia insolvency
insolvente insolvent
insomne sleepless
insomnio insomnia
insondable fathomless; unfathomable
insonorización f sound-proofing
insonorizar to sound-proof
insonoro adj sound-proof; soundless
insoportable unbearable
insostenible indefensible
inspección f inspection; inspector's office
inspeccionar to inspect, oversee
inspector n m inspector, overseer; surveyor; superintendent; adj inspecting
inspiración f inspiration; med inhalation
inspirador n m inspirer; adj inspiring
inspirante inspiring
inspirar to inhale; inspire; ~**se en** to get inspiration from, be inspired by
inspirativo inspiring
instabilidad f instability
instalación f installation; fittings; eccles +mil induction; **instalaciones portuarias** port facilities
instalador m installer
instalar to install; ~**se** to settle in (house etc)
instancia demand; petition; application form; leg instance; **a** ~ **de** at the request of; **en ultima** ~ as a last resort

instantánea sl snapshot
instantáneo adj instantaneous; (of coffee) instant
instante n m instant; **a cada** ~ continuously; **al** ~ immediately; adj instant; urgent
instar to demand; press, urge
instauración f restoration
instaurar to restore
instaurativo restorative
instigación f instigation
instigar to instigate
instigador m instigator; adj instigating
instilar to pour drop by drop
instintivo instinctive
instinto instinct; **por** ~ instinctively
institución f institution; establishment
institucionalizarse to become institutionalized
instituir to found, establish; erect; appoint
instituto institute; state secondary school; corporation; rule
institutriz f governess
instituyente instituting
instrucción f instruction, education, learning; mil drill
instructivo instructive
instructor n m instructor; sp trainer; adj instructing
instruir to instruct, teach; leg institute (proceedings); mil drill
instrumentación f orchestration
instrumental n m med+surg set of instruments; adj instrumental
instrumentar to orchestrate
instrumentalista m+f instrumentalist
insuave rough
insubordinación f insubordination, rebellion
insubordinado insubordinate, rebellious
insubordinar to incite to rebellion; ~**se** to rebel
insubsanable unmendable
insubsistencia groundlessness
insubsistente groundless
insudar to toil
insuficiencia insufficiency
insuficiente insufficient
insufrible unbearable, intolerable
ínsula island; hamlet
insular n m islander; adj insular
insulina insulin

insulsez *f* insipidity
insulso insipid
insultada *SA* insult
insultador *n m* insulter; *adj* insulting
insultante insulting
insultar to insult; ~**se** to have a fit
insulto *n* insult
insumable incalculable
insume costly
insumergible unsinkable
insumisión *f* rebellion
insumiso rebellious
insurgente *m* insurgent, rebel
insurrección *f* insurrection; revolt
insurreccional insurrectional
insurreccionar to rebel, revolt
insurrecto rebel
insustancial insubstantial
insustituible irreplaceable
intáctil intangible
intacto intact; entire
intachable without blemish, perfect
integración *f* integration
integrante integral
integrar to integrate; make up; ~ **por** to
  consist of
integridad *f* integrity; wholeness; virginity
íntegro integral, complete; whole; (of
  people) upright
integumento disguise
intelectivo ability to understand
intelecto intellect
intelectualidad *f* intellectuality
inteligencia intelligence; **en ~ con** in
  league with; **en la ~ de que** on the
  understanding that
inteligente intelligent
inteligibilidad *f* intelligibility
inteligible intelligible
intemperancia intemperance
intemperante intemperate
intemperie *f* inclemency; **a la ~** exposed
  to the elements
intempestivo inopportune
intemporal timeless
intención *f* intention; ulterior motive;
  de/con ~ deliberately, on purpose; **de
  primera ~** on the first impulse; **segunda ~** hidden meaning; **tener mala
  ~** to be bloody-minded
intencionado deliberate; **frase intencionada** loaded remark
intencional intentional

intendencia administration
intendente *mil* quartermaster general
intensificar to intensify
intensión *f* intenseness
intensivo intensive; **curso ~** crash
  course
intenso intense
intentar to attempt, try; *leg* commence
  (a lawsuit)
intento attempt; **de ~** deliberately, on
  purpose
intentona coup d'état (*esp* if unsuccessful); rash attempt
intercadencia *med* intercadence
intercalación *f* interleaving; inserting
intercalar to interleave; insert
intercambiable interchangeable
intercambiar to exchange, interchange
intercambio exchange, interchange
interceder to intercede
intercepción *f* interception
interceptar to intercept
intercesión *f* intercession
intercesor *n m* one who intercedes; *adj*
  interceding
interciso split in halves; **día ~** half-
  holiday
intercomunicación *f* intercommunica-
  tion
intercomunicar to intercommunicate
interconectar to interconnect
interconexión *f* interconnection
intercostal *anat* between the ribs
interdecir to interdict
interdicción *f* interdiction, prohibition;
  ~ **civil** forfeiture of civil rights
interés *m* interest; **intereses** *comm* interest; **intereses creados** vested interests;
  tener ~ en to be keen on
interesable *adj* mercenary
interesado *n* interested party; egoist; *adj*
  interested
interesante interesting; (of prices)
  attractive; **estado ~** pregnancy
interesar interest; *comm* to produce
  interest; ~**se por** to be interested in
interestatal inter-state
interestelar interstellar
interfecto having suffered a violent
  death
interferencia interference; *rad* interference, (deliberate) jamming
interferir to interfere
interfoliar to interleave

interfono intercom
intergubernamental intergovernmental
ínterin *n* interim; *adv* meanwhile; *conj* while
interina domestic help, home help
interino substitute; **profesor** ~ supply teacher
interior *n m* + *adj* inside, interior; ~**es** entrails; innards; **asuntos** ~**es** *pol* home affairs
interjección *f* interjection
interlínea *print* space, lead
interlinear to write between the lines; *print* lead
interlocución *f* dialogue
intérlope interloping
interludio interlude
intermediar to mediate
intermediario *n* intermediary, middleman; *adj* intermediary
intermedio *n theat*+*TV* interval; *adj* half-way, intermediate
intermisión *f* intermission
intermitencia intermittence
intermitente *n m mot* indicator; *adj* intermittent; **luz** ~ *mot* winking light
internacional *n* member of the International Brigades; *adj* international
internacionalismo internationalism
internacionalista *n m*+*f* +*adj* internationalist
internacionalizar to internationalize
internado *n* boarding school; student body (of boarding-school); *adj* confined; interned
internar to intern; go inside; commit (to an institution); ~**se en** to penetrate into
interno *n* boarder; *adj* internal; boarding
inter nos in confidence, between you and me
interpelación *f* interpelation; appeal
interpelar to demand an explanation; ask the help of
interplanetario interplanetary
interpolación *f* interpolation
interpolar to interpolate, interrupt
interponer to interpose; ~**se** to get between
interprender *mil* to take/capture by surprise
interpresa *mil* surprise capture
interpretación *f* interpretation

interpretador *m* interpreter
interpretar to interpret; *theat*+*cin* act a role, play a part
intérprete *m*+*f* interpreter
interregno interregnum
interrogación *f* interrogation, questioning; question; *print* question-mark
interrogador *n m* interrogator, questioner; *adj* interrogating, questioning
interrogante *n m* question-mark; question; *adj* interrogating, questioning
interrogar to question, interrogate
interrogativo *adj* interrogative
interrogatorio interrogation, questioning
interrumpir to interrupt; obstruct, block
interrupción *f* interruption; stoppage, blockage
interruptor *n m* interruptor; *elect* switch; ~ **de dos direcciones** two-way switch; *adj* interrupting
intersecarse *geom* to intersect
intersección *f* intersection
intersticio interstice
interurbano inter-city; **conferencia interurbana** *tel* trunk call
intervalo interval; gap; **lúcido** ~ lucid interval (of a lunatic)
intervención *f* intervention; office of an intervenor; auditing of accounts
intervenir to intervene; audit; *tel* tap, bug
interventor *m* supervisor, inspector; auditor
interviú *m* interview
intestado intestate
intestino *n anat* intestine; *adj* internal; civil, domestic
intimación *f* intimation
intimar to intimate; become close friends
intimidación *f* intimidation
intimidad *f* intimacy; intimate/close friendship; privacy; **en la** ~ in private
intimidar to intimidate
íntimo *n* close friend; *adj* intimate
intitular to entitle, name
intocable untouchable
intolerabilidad *f* intolerability
intolerancia intolerance
intolerante intolerant
intoxicación *f* poisoning; food poison-

ing; **campaña de** ~ smear campaign
intoxicar to poison, to calumniate
intraducible untranslatable
intramuros inside a town/city
intranquilidad *f* worry, unease
intranquilizar to make uneasy; worry
intranquilo uneasy; worried
intransferible not transferable
intransigencia intransigence
intransigente intransigent
intransitable impassable
intransitivo intransitive
intrascendente not transcendental
intratable unamenable, unapproachable, unsociable
intravenoso intravenous
intrepidez *f* intrepidity, daring
intrépido intrepid, brave
intriga intrigue
intrigante *n m* intriguer; *adj* intriguing
intrigar to intrigue; scheme, plot
intrincado complicated, tangled
intrincar to ravel, tangle
intríngulis *m* essence, raison d'être; snag; **tiene su** ~ there's more to this than meets the eye
intrínseco intrinsic
introducción *f* introduction, prologue
introducir to introduce; insert; ~**se** to enter
introductorio, introductivo introductory
introito *eccles* introit; *theat* prologue
intromisión *f* intromission; meddling
introspección *f* introspection
introspectivo introspective
introversión *f* introversion
introverso introverted
introvertido introvert
intrusar to practise professionally without qualifications
intrusismo practising professionally without qualifications; gate-crashing
intruso *n* intruder; gate-crasher; *adj* intrusive
intuición *f* intuition
intuir to know by intuition, sense, feel
intuitivo intuitive
intuito glance, look; **por** ~ **de** in view of
intumescencia lump, swelling
inundación *f* flood, flooding; excess
inundante *adj* flooding
inundar to flood
inurbanidad *f* incivility
inurbano uncivil

inútil useless
inutilidad *f* uselessness; useless person, dead loss
inutilizar to render useless; disable
invadeable unfordable
invadir to invade
invalidación *f* invalidation
invalidar to invalidate
invalidez *f* invalidity
inválido *n* invalid; *adj* unfit; valueless; invalid; void
invariabilidad *f* invariability
invasión *f* invasion
invasor *n m* invader; *adj* invading
invectiva invective
invectivar to insult violently
invencibilidad *f* invincibility
invencible invincible
invención *f* invention
invencionero inventing, inventive
invendible unsaleable, unmarketable
inventar to invent
inventariar to take stock
inventario inventory
inventiva inventiveness
inventivo inventive
invento invention
inverecundo shameless
inverosímil improbable, unlikely
inverosimilitud *f* improbability, unlikelihood
invernáculo, invernadero hothouse, greenhouse
invernal wintry
invernar to winter
inversión *f* inversion; investment
inverso inverse; *sl* homosexual; **a/por la inversa** vice versa
invertebrado invertebrate; ~**s** invertebrata
invertido inverted; *comm* invested; *sl* homosexual
invertir to reverse, invert; spend (time); *comm* invest
investidura investiture
investigación *f* investigation
investigador *n m* researcher; investigator; *adj* investigating
investigar to investigate; do research on
investir to appoint; invest; install
inveterado inveterate; diehard
invicto invincible
invidencia blindness
invidente *n m + f* blind person; *adj* blind

invierno winter; *SA* rainy season
invigilar to invigilate, watch carefully
inviolabilidad *f* inviolability
inviolado inviolate
invincibilidad *f* invincibility
invisible invisible; hiding; **en un ~** in a jiffy
invitación *f* invitation
invitado guest
invitador *n m* inviter; *adj* inviting
invitar to invite; stand a round
invocación *f* invocation
invocar to invoke
invocador *n m* invoker; *adj* invoking
involucrar to mix; confuse
involuntario involuntary; unintentional
invulnerabilidad *f* invulnerability
inyección *f* injection
inyectable injectable
inyectado injected
inyectar to inject
ionización *f* ionization
ionizar to ionize
ir to go, walk; (of clothes) suit, fit; be convenient; match; **~ a** +*infin* to go and (do s.t.); **~ a caballo** to go on horseback; **~ a España** to go to Spain; **~ a gatas** to go on all fours; **~ a gran ir** to go at top speed; **~ a parar en ...** to end up in ...; **~ a pie andando** to go on foot; **~ de capa caída** to be crestfallen/down at heel; **~ en bicicleta/coche/tren** to go by bicycle/car/train; **~ por delante** to go ahead; **~ por partes** to take one thing at a time; **~se** to go away; fall to pieces; (of liquids) leak out; break wind
ira anger
iracundia anger; tendency to become angry
iracundo irascible, irate
iraní *n* +*adj* Iranian
iraquí *n* +*adj* Iraqi
iridio iridium
iridiscente iridescent
iris *m opt* iris; **~ de paz** mediator, peace-maker; **arco ~** rainbow
irisado rainbow-coloured
irisación *f phys* breaking down (of light)
irisar to iridesce
Irlanda Ireland; **~ del Norte** Northern Ireland
irlandés Irish, Irishman; *sl* Irish coffee; **norirlandés** Northern Irish

ironía irony
irónico ironic
irracional irrational
irracionalidad *f* irrationality
irradiación *f* radiation
irradiar to radiate
irreal unreal
irrealidad *f* unreality
irrealizable unrealizable
irrebatible indisputable
irreconciliable irreconcilable
irreconocible unrecognizable
irrecuperable irretrievable
irrecusable unimpeachable
irreemplazable irreplaceable
irreflexión *f* thoughtlessness
irreflexivo thoughtless
irreformable unreformable
irrefragable irrefutable
irrefrenable unstoppable, irrepressible
irregularidad *f* irregularity
irrelevante irrelevant
irreligión *f* irreligion
irreligiosidad *f* irreligiousness
irreligioso irreligious
irremisible unforgivable
irremunerado unremunerated, unpaid
irrenunciable unrenounceable
irreprensible irreproachable
irresoluble unsolvable
irresolución *f* irresolution, indecision
irrespirable unbreathable
irresponsable irresponsible
irresuelto wavering, vacillating
irrespetuoso disrespectful
irreverencia irreverence
irreverenciar to treat with disrespect
irreverente irreverent
irrevocabilidad *f* irrevocability
irrigación *f med* irrigation, enema
irrigar *med* to irrigate
irrisible laughable, derisory
irrisión *f* mockery, derision
irrisorio laughable, derisory
irritabilidad *f* irritability
irritación *f* irritation, anger
irritamente *leg* invalidly
irritamiento irritation, anger
irritante *n m* irritant; *adj* irritating
irritar to irritate; *leg* render null and void
irrito *leg* null and void
irrogar to damage
irrompible unbreakable

irrumpir to burst in, enter hurriedly
irrupción *f* irruption; raid
Isabel Elizabeth
isabelino Elizabethan
Isaías Isaiah
isatis *m* Arctic fox
Isidro Isidore
isidro yokel, bumpkin
isla island
islámico Islamic
islamismo Islamism, Mohammedanism
islamita *n m+f* Moslem; *adj* Islamic, Moslem
islamizar to Mohammedanize, Islamize
islandés *n* Icelander; *adj* Icelandic
Islandia Iceland
isleño *n* islander; *adj* island
isleo, isleta islet
islilla *anat* collar-bone
islote *m* isle (*usu* barren)
isoca caterpillar
isógono isogonic
isómero isomeric
isotermo isotherm
isótopo isotope

israelí Israeli
israelita *n m+f +adj* Israelite
ístmico isthmic
istmo isthmus
Italia Italy
italianini *m pej sl* Italian
italianizar to Italianize
italiano Italian
itálico Italic; **letra itálica** *print* italics
ítem likewise
iteración *f* repetition
iterar to repeat
itinerario itinerary
iza, izaje *m* hoisting; unfurling
izar to hoist (flag); unfurl (sail)
izquierda *n* left-hand side, left; *pol* left-wing
izquierdear to go astray, go awry
izquierdismo *pol* leftism
izquierdista *n m+f +adj pol* leftist, left-winger
izquierdizante *adj pol* leftish
izquierdo *n* left-handed person; *adj* left
izquierdoso *adj pol* leftish

J

j *f* letter j

¹ **ja** *sl* dame, bird

² **¡ja!** *interj* ha!; ¡~, ~, ~! ha, ha! ha! (laughter)

jabalí *m* wild boar

jabalina wild sow; javelin

jabardillo swarm (of insects); throng

jabato young wild boar

jabeque *m* facial scar caused by a knife

jabón *m* soap; cake of soap; ~ **de afeitar** shaving soap; ~ **de Castilla** Castile soap; ~ **de olor/de tocador** toilet soap; ~ **de sastre** french chalk; ~ **en polvo** soap powder, washing powder; **dar ~ a uno** to soft-soap s.o.

jabonada, jabonado soaping, lathering; clothes for the wash, washing

jabonadura soaping, lathering; ~s soap-suds; **dar una ~ a uno** to scold s.o.

jabonar to soap; scold, reprimand

jaboncillo tablet of soap

jabonera soap dish

jabonería soap factory; shop selling toilet requisites

jabonero soap maker

jabonete *m* cake of toilet soap

jabonoso soapy, lathery

jaca pony, cob

jacal *m* shack; Mexican hut

jácara merry song; merrymaking; merrymakers; bother, nuisance; lie

jácaro *n* swaggerer; *adj* swaggering

jacinto hyacinth

jacio *naut* dead calm

jaco nag

jacobino Jacobin

jactancia boasting; brag

jactancioso boastful, bragging

jactarse to boast, brag; ~**se de** to boast of

jaculatoria short prayer

jaculatorio *n* ejaculation; *adj* ejaculatory

jadeante panting, breathless

jadear to pant

jadeo pant; panting

jaez *m* harness; kind, sort; **jaeces** trappings

jagüey *m* pool

jai *f sl* girl, bird

jai alai *m* pelota (Basque game)

Jaime James

jalar to pull, haul; get out, scram; flirt with; *sl* nosh; *sl* snatch (a handbag); ~**se** to get drunk; fail an examination; go away

jalbegar to whitewash; *fig* make up (one's face)

jalbegue *m* whitewash; paint; make-up

jalea jelly; **hacerse una ~** to become sloppy

jalear to encourage (dancers *etc*) by clapping *etc*; make fun of; rouse/beat game

jaleo Andalusian dance; clapping, cheering; revelry; rumpus; brawl; **armar ~** to kick up a racket

jaletina gelatine; calf's foot jelly

jalón *m* surveyor's pole; landmark; swig (of liquor); drink; pull, tug; distance, stretch

jalonamiento staking, marking

jalonar to mark out, stake out

jalonear to pull, tug

jalonero surveyor's assistant; *sl* bag-snatcher

jalufa *sl* hunger

jamaica *m* Jamaica rum

jamaicano, jamaiquino *n + adj* Jamaican

jamancia *sl* hunger; grub, nosh

jamás never; ever; **nunca ~** nevermore; **por siempre ~** for evermore

jamba *archi* jamb

jambaje *m* frame (of door or window)

jame *m fam* woman's face

jamelgo nag, hack

jamón *m* ham; ~ **en dulce** cooked ham; ~ **serrano** home-cured ham; ~ **york** boiled ham; **raspar el ~** to play the guitar

jamona plump middle-aged woman;

279

fine figure of a woman

jándalo *n* + *adj fam* Andalusian

Japón: el ~ Japan

japonés *n m* + *adj* Japanese

jaque *m* check (chess); bully; ¡~ **de aquí!** beat it!; **dar** ~ **a** to put in check, check; **en** ~ in check; **tener a uno en** ~ to hold a threat over s.o., keep s.o. in check

jaque-mate *m* checkmate; **dar** ~ **a uno** to checkmate s.o.

jaquear to check (chess); ~ **al enemigo** to harass the enemy

jaqueca headache; migraine

jaquero fine-toothed comb

jara rock-rose; clump of reeds

jarabe *m* syrup; soothing words; tap dance; ~ **de palo** *sl* corporal punishment; ~ **de pico** empty words

jarana revelry; brawl; trick; joke; **ir de** ~ to go on a binge

jaranear to carouse, go on a binge

jaranero roisterer

jarcia *naut* rigging, shrouds; tackle

jardín *m* garden; field (baseball); ~ **de la infancia/infantil** kindergarten

jardinera window box, flower-pot stand; woman gardener; open tramcar

jardinería gardening

jardinero gardener; fielder (baseball)

jardinista *m* + *f* landscape gardener

jarocho uncouth

jarope *m* syrup; *fam* nasty medicine

jaroso covered with brambles

jarra jug, jar, pitcher; vase; beer mug; **de/en** ~**(s)** with arms akimbo

jarretera garter

jarro vase; ornamental urn

jarrón *m* jug, jar, pitcher; **echar un** ~ **de agua a** to pour cold water on

jaspe *m* jasper; ~**s** streaks, mottled marks

jaspear to mottle

jato calf

Jauja El Dorado; **vivir en** ~ to live a life of luxury and ease

jaula cage; gaol; lock-up garage

jauría pack (of hounds)

javanés *n* + *adj* Javanese

Javier Xavier

jazmín *m* jasmine

J.C. (Jesucristo) Jesus Christ

jebe *m* alum; elastic band; raw rubber;

sl arse

jefa woman boss

jefatura headship; leadership; position of chief; ~ **de policía** police headquarters

jefe *m* chief; leader; head, boss; ~ **de cocina** chef; ~ **de coro** choirmaster; ~ **de equipajes** baggage master; ~ **de estación** station-master; ~ **de gobierno** chief minister, prime minister; ~ **de estado** head of state; ~ **de redacción** editor-in-chief; ~ **de taller** foreman; ~ **de tren** (railway) guard, *US* conductor; **en** ~ chief, principal, head

Jehová *m* Jehovah; **Testigos de** ~ Jehovah's Witnesses

jején *m* gnat

jelatina gelatine

jengibre *m* ginger

jeque *m* sheik

jerarca *m* hierarch

jerarquía hierarchy

jerárquico hierarchical

Jeremías Jeremiah, whiner

jerez *m* sherry

jerezano native of Jerez de la Frontera

jerga coarse cloth; saddle pad; jargon; slang

jergón *m* straw mattress; shabby dress; clumsy fellow

jerigonza gibberish; jargon; slang; foolishness

jeringa syringe; nuisance; ~ **de engrase/grasa** *mech* grease-gun

jeringar to syringe; squirt; inject; vex, annoy; *fam* bugger up

jeringazo squirt; injection, jab

jeringuilla *med* syringe; *bot* mock-orange

jero *sl* face

jeroglífico *n* + *adj* hieroglyphic

Jerónimo Jerome

Jerusalén Jerusalem

Jesucristo Jesus Christ

jesuita *m* Jesuit; *sl* hypocrite; *fam* sly person

jesuítico Jesuit(ical); *sl* hypocritical

Jesús *m* Jesus; **en un decir** ~ in a twinkling of an eye; **morir sin decir** ~ to die suddenly

jeta thick lip(s); snout; face, mug; *sl* impudence, cheek; **poner** ~ to pout

jíbaro *n* peasant; *adj* rustic; uncivilized

jibia cuttlefish; *sl* cissy, pansy

jibión m cuttlefish bone

jícara chocolate cup; gourd, calabash (used as cup)

jifa offal

jifería slaughtering (of animals)

¡ji, ji! ha-ha!

jilguero goldfinch; bald-pate

jineta genet; horsewoman; **a la** ~ (riding) with short stirrups

jinete m horseman, rider; cavalryman

jineteada horse-breaking, bronco-busting; demonstration of horsemanship; rough-riding

jinetear vt to tame/break a horse; ride a bronco; vi to demonstrate horsemanship

jinglar to swing

jipijapa m Panama hat

jira tour, trip; excursion, picnic; strip of cloth

jirafa giraffe

jiroflé m bot clove tree

jirón m rag, tatter; shred, bit; pennant; facing (of a garment); **hacer jirones** to tear to pieces

jiste m yeast; head (on beer)

jitomate m tomato

jiu-jitzu m ju-jitzu

jocó monkey, ape

jocosidad f jocularity

jocoso jocular

jocoyote m+f youngest child, 'baby' of the family

jocundidad f jocundity

jocundo jocund

joder v vulg to fuck; mess up; **¡**~**!** interj fuck!; ~**se** to get messed up

jodido adj vulg fucking; vulg bloody; **estar** ~ to be ill/defeated/tired

jodienda vulg sl sexual intercourse

jofaina wash basin, wash bowl

jolgorio merriment

¡jolín!, ¡jolines! good heavens!

Jonás Jonah

jónico Ionic

jonrón m home run (baseball)

jorcar agri to winnow

Jordán m River Jordan; **ir al** ~ to be made young again

Jordania Jordan (country)

jordano Jordanian

jorfe m dry-stone wall

Jorge George

jorguina witch

jornada day's work; journey; day's journey; expedition; event; theat act; life-span; **a grandes/largas** ~s by forced marches; **ir por sus** ~s to go very carefully

jornal m day's wages; day's work; journal (book-keeping); **a** ~ (paid) by the day; ~ **mínimo** minimum wage

jornalero day labourer, journeyman

joroba hump, humpback; bother, nuisance; **¡**~**!** blimey!

jorobado n hunchback; adj hunchbacked

jorobar to annoy, bother; pester; sl mess up

joropo Venezuelan national dance

jorro dragnet

José Joseph

Josefina Josephine

jota letter j; iota; jot; Spanish dance/folksong; **no saber una** ~ not to know a thing; **sin faltar una** ~ with all i's dotted, without missing one detail

joven n m youth, young person; **de** ~ as a youth, as a young woman; adj young

jovialidad f joviality, gaiety, fun

jovial jolly, merry, jovial

joya jewel; gem; piece of jewellery; fam treasure; ~s jewels, jewellery; ~ **de familia** heirloom; ~s **de fantasía** costume jewellery

joyante glossy

joyel m small jewel

joyelero jewel case

joyería jeweller's shop; jewellery trade; jewellery

joyero jeweller; jewel case/casket

Juan John; ~ **español** the ordinary Spaniard; ~ **Lanas** dolt; ~ **Palomo** poor fellow; **San** ~ **Bautista** John the Baptist

Juana Joan, Jane, Jean; ~ **de Arco** Joan of Arc

juanete m bunion; high cheekbone; topgallant sail

juanetudo having bunions

jubilación f retirement; pension; annuity; ~ **anticipada** early retirement

jubilado n retired person; pensioner; adj retired, pensioned off

jubilar to pension off, retire; throw away; ~**se** to retire, be pensioned off; rejoice; play truant

jubileo jubilee; granting of indulgence

eccl; **por** ~ very rarely
júbilo jubilation, joy
jubiloso jubilant
jubón *m* jerkin; jacket; bodice; blouse
Judá Judah
judaico Judaic, Jewish
judaísmo Judaism
Judas Judas; traitor; **alma de** ~ evil person
judería Jewry; ghetto; tax on Jews
judía Jewess; kidney bean; **~s verdes/ tiernas** string beans, french beans
judiada unworthy act
judicatura judiciary; judicature, judge-ship
judiega olive of poor quality
judío *n* Jew; *adj* Jewish; ~ **de señal** converted Jew
Judit Judith
juego game; gambling; move, play; sport; works, mechanism; pack of cards; matching set; ~ **de alcoba** bed-room suite; ~ **de azar** game of chance; ~ **de bolas** ball bearings; ~ **de café** coffee set; ~ **de campanas** chimes; ~ **de comedor** dining-room suite; ~ **de la cuna** cat's cradle; ~ **de la pulga** tiddlywinks; ~ **del corro** ring-a-ring-a-roses; ~ **del salto** leap frog; ~ **de manos** conjuring; ~ **de palabras** pun; ~ **de prendas** forfeits; ~ **de suerte** game of chance; ~ **de té** tea-set; **hacer** ~ to match (a set); ~ **limpio** fair play; ~ **sucio** foul play; **hacer ~s malabares** to juggle; **no es cosa de** ~ it's no laugh-ing matter; **poner en** ~ to set in motion; co-ordinate; **por** ~ for fun
juerga spree, revelry; ~ **de borrachera** drinking bout; **ir(se) de** ~ to go on the spree
juerguista *m*+*f* reveller
jueves *m sing*+*pl* Thursday; **Jueves Santo** Maundy Thursday; **no es cosa del otro** ~ it's nothing to write home about
juez *m* judge; ~ **arbitrador/árbitro** arbi-trator, umpire; ~ **de instrucción** examining magistrate; ~ **de línea** *sp* linesman; ~ **de paz** justice of the peace; ~ **de primera instancia** judge of primary court, coroner; ~ **de salida** starter
jugada play, move, throw, stroke *etc*; trick, prank; **mala** ~ dirty trick

jugador *n m* player; gambler; ~ **de ma-nos** juggler/conjurer
jugar to play; gamble; wield (a wea-pon); toy; ~ **a la alza** *comm* to bull the market; ~ **a la baja** *comm* to bear the market; ~ **a la bolsa** to dabble in shares; ~ **al fútbol/tenis/escondite** to play football/tennis/hide-and-seek; ~ **en** to have a hand in; ~ **grueso** to play for high stakes; ~ **la a uno** *sl* to be-tray s.o. to the police; ~ **un papel** *theat*+*cin* to act a part; **~se** to risk, gamble; **~se el pellejo** to risk one's neck; **~se el todo por el todo** to stake all; **~se hasta la camisa** to put one's last penny; **jugársela a uno** to play a rotten trick on s.o.; **~se la vida** to risk one's life
jugarreta dirty trick
juglar *m* minstrel, jongleur
juglaresco *adj* minstrel
juglaría minstrelsy
jugo juice; gravy; substance, essence; sap; **sacar todo el** ~ **a** to get the most out of
jugosidad *f* juiciness
jugoso juicy; substantial, full of meat
juguete *m* toy, plaything; joke; ~ **có-mico** *theat* skit, sketch; **de/por** ~ for fun; **de** ~ *adj* toy; **soldado de** ~ toy soldier; **~-sorpresa** jack-in-the-box
juguetear to toy, trifle; romp, gambol; fool about with
jugueteo playing (with toys)
juguetería toyshop; toy-trade
juguetón playful, frisky
juicio judgement; sense; wisdom; sanity; *leg* trial, lawsuit; **el** ~ **final** the Last Judgement; **muela del** ~ wisdom tooth; **~ temeroso** hasty judgement; **a** ~ **de** in the opinion of; **estar en su sano** ~ to be in one's right mind; **estar fuera de su** ~ to be out of one's mind; **pedir un** ~ *leg* to sue; **perder el** ~ to go in-sane; **quitarle a uno el** ~ to drive s.o. mad
juicioso judicious; wise; sensible
jujana *sl* trickery, cheating
julay *m sl* fool; victim of a swindle
julepe *m* julep; scolding; fright; fuss
julepear to reprimand; scare; whip; tor-ment
Julián Julian
Julieta Juliet

Julio Julius

¹ **julio** July

² **julio** *elect* joule

jumear *sl* to stink, pong

jumenta she-ass

jumento ass, donkey

jumera drunken state

junar *sl* to see

juncada fritter

juncal *n m* reed-bed; *adj* reedy

juncia *bot* sedge

¹ **junco** rush, reed; ~ **de laguna** bulrush

² **junco** *naut* junk

juncoso reedy, full of rushes

jundunar *m sl* member of the Guardia
Civil

jungla jungle

junio June

junípero juniper

junquera *bot* rush

junquillo jonquil; reed; rattan; *archi*
round moulding

junta assembly; junta; board; council; meeting; junction; joint; seam;
washer; *mech* gasket

juntar to join, unite, put together;
collect, amass; half close a door/
window; assemble, congregate; ~**se**
to meet, assemble; ~**se a** to get close
to; copulate with; ~**se a/con** to
associate with

¹ **junto** *adj* joined, united, put together;
~**s** together; **las pagarás todas juntas**
you'll pay for this

² **junto** *adv* at the same time; near, hard
by, close at hand; together; ~ **a** next
to; ~ **con** together with; **en** ~ in all;
por ~ all together, in bulk; **todo** ~ all
at once, at the same time

juntura joint; juncture; coupling; seam

jura oath, pledge

jurado *n* jury; juror; *adj* sworn; **enemigo**
~ sworn enemy; **guardia** ~ security
guard

jurador *n m* swearer; *adj* swearing

juramentar to swear in; ~**se** to take an
oath

juramento oath; vow; swearword; ~
falso perjury; **prestar** ~ **a** to swear to

jurar to swear, vow; take an oath, be
sworn into (an office *etc*); curse,
swear; **jurársela a uno** to have it in for
s.o.

juratoria: fianza ~ release on parole

jurdos *mpl sl* money, lolly, bread

jurero false witness

jurguina witch

jurídico juridical; legal

jurisconsulto jurist; lawyer; legal expert

jurisdicción *f* jurisdiction

jurisdiccional jurisdictional

jurisperito legal expert; jurist

jurisprudencia jurisprudence

jurisprudente *m,* **jurista** *m+f* jurist

juro: de ~ certainly

justa joust, tournament; contest

justador *m* jouster

justamente justly; just, just at that
moment; tightly

justar to joust

justicia justice; **de** ~ fair, right; deservedly; **ir por** ~ to go to law, go to court;
la ~ the authorities; **tomar la** ~ **por su
mano** to take the law into one's own
hands

justiciable *leg* actionable

justiciero *n* stickler for justice; *adj*
strictly fair, just; stern

justificable justifiable

justificación *f* justification

justificado just; upright (of person);
justified

justificante *n* written excuse; proof; *adj*
justifying

justificar to justify; vindicate; clear of
blame

justillo undervest; jerkin

justipreciar to appraise

justipreciador *m* appraiser

justo *n* just person; *adj* just; correct;
pious; *adv* duly, rightly; exactly

juta goose

juvenil juvenile, youthful, young

juventud *f* youth; young people

juvia Brazil-nut tree

juzgado court of law; tribunal; court-
room

juzgamundos *m sing+pl* over-critical
person; fault-finder

juzgar to judge; consider; ~ **de** to pass
judgement on; **a** ~ **por** to judge by

K

k, ka f letter k
kaleidoscopio kaleidoscope
kantiano Kantian
kantismo Kantism
kárate m karate
karatista m+f exponent of karate
karting m go-cart; go-cart racing
Kenia Kenya
keniano Kenyan
kermese f charity fair
kerosene m, **kerosina, kerosín** m kerosene, paraffin, coal oil
keynsiano Keynesian
kg (kilogramo) kilogram(me)
kie m sl mate, pal
kifi f marihuana (esp from Morocco)
kilo n kilo, kilogram(me); sl one million pesetas; adv sl a great deal, very much
kilociclo kilocycle
kilogramo kilogram(me)
kilohercio kilohertz
kilolitro kilolitre
kilometraje m distance in kilometres; rate per kilometre

kilométrico kilometric; long-drawn-out; interminable; **billete** ~ runabout ticket
kilómetro kilometre; ~ **cero** centre of Madrid, Puerta del Sol
kilovatio kilowatt; ~ **hora** kilowatt-hour
kindergartenera nursery-school teacher
kiosko kiosk; newspaper stand/stall
kiosquero newsagent
kirieleisón kirie eleison; **cantar el** ~ to beg for mercy
km (kilómetro) kilometre
kph (kilómetros por hora) kilometres an hour
kv (kilovatio) kilowatt
kv-h (kilovatio-hora) kilowatt-hour
k.o. (knock-out) m knock-out (punch); **poner a uno** ~ to knock s.o. out
kodak f camera
koweití, kuweití n+adj Kuwaiti
krausismo Krausism, philosophy of Krause
krausista n m+f+adj Krausist
kremlinología kremlinology
kremlinólogo kremlinologist

L

l *f* letter l; (litro) litre

¹ **la** the; it; her; **dame ~ mano** give me your hand

² **la** *mus* lah

labelo *bot* labellum

laberíntico labyrinthine

laberinto labyrinth, maze; complicated matter

labia eloquence, gift of the gab

labiérnago *bot* laburnum

labihendido hare-lipped

labio lip; brim; **~ leporino** hare-lip

labor *f* work, task; design; needlework; embroidery; cultivation; **sus ~es** (occupation as given on completing a form) housewife

laborterapia occupational therapy

laborable *m* working day, weekday; *adj* workable; **día no ~** public holiday

laborar to till; work

laboratorio laboratory; **~ de idiomas** language laboratory

laboreo working; *min* exploitation

laboriosidad *f* industriousness

laborioso laborious

laborismo labourism

laborista *m + f* Labourite; **Partido Laborista** Labour Party

labra stone-carving; stone-cutting

labrada land ready for seeding

labrador *m* peasant farmer; farm labourer

labradora country woman, peasant

labrantío *n* farmland; *adj* arable, tillable

labranza farming, cultivation; farmland; **útiles de ~** agricultural implements

labrar to plough, till, cultivate; work, fashion; carve; build; embroider; bring about, cause; **~ el acta de una reunión** to write up the minutes of a meeting; **~ una acta** to draw up a memorandum

labriega countrywoman, peasant

labriego farmhand, peasant; small farmer

laburno *bot* laburnum

laca shellac; lacquer; **~ de/para uñas** nail varnish; **~s** lacquer ware

lacayo lackey, footman; *fig* hanger-on

lacear to drive (game); trap, snare; lasso; decorate with bows of ribbon

laceración *f* laceration; damage

lacerante lacerating

lacerar to lacerate, tear; damage

lacería poverty, hardship

lacerioso poor, needy

lacero expert with a lasso

lacio lank, straight; withered; limp

lacónico terse, laconic

laconismo terseness, brevity

lacra sore, scar; blot, blemish; defect; scum

¹ **lacrar** to leave a scar; cause injury to health; cause harm to, injure; **~se con** to suffer harm from

² **lacrar** to seal (with sealing wax)

lacre *n m* sealing wax; *adj* bright red

lacrimógeno tear-producing, tearful, sentimental; **gas ~** tear gas

lacrimoso tearful, lachrymose

lactación *f*, **lactancia** breast-feeding, lactation, nursing

lactante suckling; **mujer ~** nursing mother

lactar to breast-feed, suckle, nurse

lácteo milk, milky, lacteous; **Vía Láctea** Milky Way

láctico lactic

lactosa lactose

lacustre *adj* lake; marshy; **planta ~** marsh plant

ladeado tilted, inclined; leaning, lopsided; turned sideways

ladear *vt* to tip, tilt, incline to one side; avoid, get round; *aer* bank; skirt (a hill); *vi* to tilt, tip, lean; turn aside, turn off; **~se** to lean, incline; **~se a** to lean towards; **~se con** to be even with, be equal to

ladeo tipping, tilting; bending; leaning; inclination; *aer* banking, turning

285

ladera hillside; slope

ladero n railway siding; adj lateral, side

ladilla crab-louse; **pegarse como una ~** to cling like ivy

ladino n (Spanish speaking) Indian; half-breed; (Central American) white; **Ladino** Sephardic; adj cunning, sly

lado side; end; flank; **~ a ~** side by side; **~ débil** railway weak spot; **~ del debe** comm debit side; **¡a un ~!** make way!; **al ~** nearby; **al ~ de** beside; **dar a uno de ~** to neglect s.o.; **de ~** sideways; **dejar a un ~** to leave aside; **de otro ~** on the other hand; **echar a un ~** to cast aside; **hacer ~ a** to make room for; **hacerse a un ~** to move over, stand aside; **ir por otro ~** to go another way; **poner a un ~** to put aside; **por un ~ … por otro …** on the one hand … on the other …; **tener buenos ~s** to have plenty of backing, be well-supported

ladrar to bark

ladrería, ladrerío, ladrido barking; scandal

ladrillado brick floor

ladrillador m bricklayer

ladrillal m, **ladrillar** m brickyard

ladrillar v to brick, tile

ladrillera brickyard

ladrillo brick, tile; **~ de chocolate** block of chocolate; **~ de fuego, ~ refractario** firebrick

ladrón n m burglar, thief; **~ de bancos** bank robber; **~ de caminos** highway robber; **~ de corazones** lady-killer; **~ de ganados** cattle thief; **~ de tiendas** shoplifter; **¡al ~!** stop thief!; adj thieving

ladrona woman thief

ladronera theft; thieves' kitchen, den of thieves; piggy-bank

ladronicio larceny

ladronzuelo petty thief, small-time criminal

lagar m wine press; olive oil press

lagarta lizard; ent gipsy moth; sly woman; **¡~!** bitch!

lagartija small lizard

lagartijo lounge-lizard, idler

lagarto lizard; sly person; **¡~!** touch wood!; **~ de Indias** alligator

lago lake; **~ interior** inland lake

lagópodo ptarmigan

lágrima tear; drop; **beberse las ~s** to hold back one's tears; **deshacerse en ~s** to burst into tears; **llorar a ~ viva** to shed bitter tears

lagrimar to cry, weep

lagrimear to water (of eyes); be tearful; shed tears

lagrimoso tearful, lachrymose; **ojos ~s** watery eyes, eyes filled with tears

laguna pool; lagoon; loophole; gap, break; blank space; lacuna; hiatus; **~ de derecho, ~ de la ley** matter not covered by statute law

lagunajo puddle

lagunoso marshy

laicado laity

laical adj lay

laicismo laity; secularism, separation of church and state

laja flagstone, slab

Lalo Teddy

lama mud, slime; duckweed; lamé

lameculos m+f sing+pl vulg toady, bumsucker

lamedal m bog

lamedero salt lick (for cattle)

lamedura lick, licking

lamentable lamentable; regrettable; pitiful; **es ~ que** it is to be regretted that

lamentación f lamentation

lamentar to lament; mourn; regret; deplore; **~ que** to regret that; **~se (de/por)** to lament (over); complain (about)

lamento lament; moan, wail

lamentoso plaintive; lamentable; regrettable; pitiful

lamer to lick; lap; lap against; sl to creep, arselick

lametada lick, lap, lapping

lámina metal sheet, plate; illustration; engraving; stamp, die; **~ de fibra** fibreboard; **~s de acero** sheet steel

laminación f lamination

laminadero, laminador m rolling mill

laminar metal to laminate, roll

lámpara lamp, light; electric bulb; rad+TV valve, tube; grease-stain; **~ de alcohol** spirit lamp; **~ de arco** arc lamp; **~ de bolsillo** flashlight; **~ de lectura** reading light, desk light; **~ de pared** wall light; **~ de pie** standard lamp, floor lamp; **~ de señales** signalling light; ~ **de sobremesa** table lamp; ~ **de soldar** blow-lamp, blow-torch; ~ **de techo** ceiling light; ~ **inundante** floodlight; ~ **solar** sunray lamp

lamparero lamp-lighter; lamp-maker

lamparilla nightlight; small lamp; *bot* aspen

lamparón *m* large grease stain

lampiño clean-shaven, beardless; hairless

lampista *m* plumber, tinsmith; electrician; lamp-lighter; glazier

lana wool, fleece; ~ **de acero** steel wool; ~ **de algodón** cotton wool; ~ **de ceiba** kapok; ~ **en rama** uncombed wool; **de** ~ woollen

lanar *adj* wool; ~**es** sheep (in general); **ganado** ~ sheep

lance *m* throw, cast; catch (of fish); critical moment; incident, event; move, play, stroke; accident; quarrel; ~ **de honor** duel, affair of honour; **de** ~ secondhand; cheap; **tener pocos** ~**s** to lack interest, be dull

lancear to spear, pierce with a lance

lancero lancer

lanceta *surg* lancet; **abrir con** ~ to lance

lancetazo *surg* incision, lancing; cut

lancinante piercing

lancinar to pierce; lance

lancha launch; barge, lighter; longboat; ~ **motora** motor launch, motorboat; ~ **cañonera** gunboat; ~ **de auxilio** lifeboat; ~ **de carreras** speedboat; ~ **de desembarco** landing craft; ~ **neumática** rubber dinghy; ~ **de (la) policía** police launch; ~ **rápida** speedboat

lanchada barge-load

lanchaje *m* lighterage

lanchero boatman; lighterman

lanchón *m naut* lighter

landó landau

lanería wool shop; ~**(s)** woollens, woollen goods

lanero *n* wool merchant; *adj* wool, woollen

langosta lobster; *ent* locust

langostera lobster pot

langostín *m*, **langostino** crayfish

languidecer to languish, pine

languidez *f* languor, listlessness

lánguido languid, listless

lanilla nap; light-weight wool cloth

lanolina lanoline

lanoso, lanudo fleecy, woolly

lanza lance, spear, pike; nozzle; mercenary; **correr** ~**s** to joust; **cruzar** ~**s con** to cross swords with; **ser una** ~ to be smart

lanzabombas *m sing+pl* bomb release; mortar

lanzacohetes *m sing+pl* rocket launcher

lanzada lance-thrust; wound with lance

lanzadera *text* shuttle

lanzador *m* launcher; *sp* pitcher, thrower; promoter; *aer* ejector seat, pilot release gear; ~ **de cuchillos** knife thrower; ~ **de lodo** mud-slinger, slanderer

lanzaespumas *m sing+pl* foam fire extinguisher

lanzallamas *m sing+pl* flame-thrower

lanzamiento launching; throw, cast, firing, fling; promotion; airdrop, parachute jump; eviction, dispossession; ~ **de bandera** sp throw-in; ~ **de moneda** tossing (up) the coin; ~ **de pesos** putting the shot, putting the weight

lanzaminas *m sing+pl* minelayer

lanzamisiles *m sing+pl* missile launcher

lanzar to launch; throw, cast, fling; put forth, promote; *sp* pitch; vomit; evict, dispossess; ~**se** to throw oneself, hurl oneself; dart out; sprint; bale out; ~**se a** to embark upon

Lanzarote Lancelot

lanzatorpedos *m sing+pl* torpedo tube

laña *metal* clamp; rivet

lañar *metal* to clamp, rivet

laosiano Laosian

lapa limpet; hanger-on

lapicero pencil; **tacón de** ~ stiletto heel

lápida stone, stone tablet; ~ **mortuoria** tombstone

lapidación *f* stoning (to death)

lapidar to stone, stone to death, throw stones at; cut (precious stones)

lapidario lapidary; concise

lápiz *m* (lead) pencil; crayon; ~ **de cejas** eyebrow pencil; ~ **de plomo** graphite; ~ **estíptico** styptic pencil; ~ **labial/de labios** lipstick

lapizar to pencil

lapón *m*, **lapona** *f* Lapp, Laplander

Laponia Lapland

lapso lapse; ~ **de tiempo** passage of

time; ~ **para terminación** *leg* contract time

lapsus *m* slip, mistake; ~ **cálami** handwriting error

laqueado varnished, lacquered; **uñas laqueadas** painted nails

laquear to varnish, lacquer; shellac

lar *m* hearth; ~**es** hearth and home; family

lardear to baste, lard

lardo lard

lardoso fatty, greasy

larga long billiard cue; **a la** ~ in the long run; lengthwise; **dar** ~**s a** to postpone, put off; **saber** ~ to know one's way about

largamente at length; for a long time; **tratar** ~ to treat generously; **vivir** ~ to live in comfort, be well-off

largar to let go; release; slacken; set free; *sl* talk, tell; ~ **una vela** to unfurl a sail; ~ **un cable** to pay out a rope; ~**se** to clear off; sail away; start, begin; **¡lárgate!** beat it!

¹ **largo** *n* length; *mus* largo; ~**s** (stock exchange) bulls; **¿cuánto tiene de** ~**?** how long is it?; **tiene diez metros de** ~ it's ten metres long; **¡**~ **de aquí!** get out of here!

² **largo** *adj* long; lengthy; generous; cunning; tall; ~ **de lengua** talkative, indiscreet; ~ **de pelo** long-haired; ~ **de uñas** given to thieving; **a** ~ **plazo** long-term; **a lo** ~ lengthwise; at great length; far off; **a lo** ~ **de** along, alongside; throughout; **a lo más** ~ at most; **dejar pasar a uno de** ~ to give s.o. a wide berth; **estar de** ~ to wear a long dress; **hacerse a lo** ~ to make for the open sea; **pasar de** ~ to pass by (without stopping); miss; **ponerse de** ~ to dress in adult fashion, come out, make one's début; **vestir de** ~ to wear a long dress; **un kilo** ~ a good kilo (slightly over)

largor *m* length

larguero door jamb; beam, *sp* crossbar; bolster

largueza generosity, liberality; length; largeness

larguirucho lanky

largura length, extent

lárice *m bot* larch

laringe *f* larynx

laríngeo laryngeal

laringitis *f* laryngitis

laringoscopio laryngoscope

larva grub, maggot

lasca stone chip

lascar to slacken, pay out (a rope); chip (stone)

lascivia lasciviousness, lewdness

lascivo lascivious, lewd; wanton

lasitud *f* lassitude, tiredness; weakness

laso tired, exhausted; weak

lastar to pay up for s.o.; suffer for s.o. else

lástima pity; shame; complaint; compassion; **dar** ~ to arouse pity, be pitiful, be pathetic; **es** ~ **que** it's a pity that; **estar hecho una** ~ to be a sorry sight; **es una** ~ it's a shame; it's a pity; **¡qué** ~**!** what a pity!

lastimado *n* injured person; *leg* injured party; *adj* injured, hurt

lastimador hurtful; harmful, injurious

lastimadura sore, hurt; injury; bruise

lastimar to harm, injure; offend; feel pity for; arouse pity; ~**se** to hurt o.s.; ~**se de** to pity, feel sorry for; complain about

lastimero harmful, injurious; pitiful; sad, mournful

lastimoso pitiful

lasto receipt, voucher

lastra flagstone, slab

lastrar to ballast

lastre *m* ballast; dead weight; dead freight; trash; **ir en** ~ to sail in ballast

lata tin, can; tin plate; lath; bore, nuisance; drivel; **dar la** ~ to be a nuisance; pester; **en** ~ tinned, canned; **estar sin** ~**, estar en la** ~ to be broke; **es una** ~ it's a bore

latente latent; in abeyance

lateral *n m theat* wings, side of stage; *adj* lateral, side

látex *m* latex

latido heart beat; twinge, throb (of pain), palpitation

latifundia, latifundio large (landed) estate

latifundismo ownership of large estate

latifundista *m+f* owner of a large estate

latigazo lash, crack (of whip); tonguelashing, dressing-down

látigo whip; lash; crack (of whip)

latín *m* Latin; **saber (mucho)** ~ to be

(very) shrewd

latino *adj* Latin

Latinoamérica Latin America

latinoamericano *n + adj* Latin American

latir to beat, throb, palpitate; bark, yelp; **me late que …** I have a presentiment that …

latitud *f* latitude; area, extent; breadth

lato broad; extensive; wide

latón *m* brass

latonero brass merchant; brazier

latoso *n* bore; *adj* boring; annoying

latrocinante larcenous

latrocinio theft, larceny; thievishness

latvio, latviano *n + adj* Latvian

laúd *m* lute

laudable praiseworthy, laudable

láudano laudanum

laudar *leg* to make an award; give a decision on, decide

laudo *leg* decision, finding, award; ~ **arbitral** arbitrator's award/decision; **ir al** ~ to go to arbitration

laureado *n* laureate; *adj* distinguished, famous

laurear to honour, reward; crown with a laurel wreath

laurel *m* laurel; honour, reward; *cul* bay leaf; ~ **rosa** rosebay; **descansar/dormirse sobre sus** ~**es** to rest on one's laurels

lauréola *bot* daphne; laurel wreath

lauro laurel; honour, reward; glory

Lausana Lausanne

lava lava; *min* washing; **de** ~ **y pon** drip-dry

lavable washable

lavabo wash basin; washstand; washroom; lavatory, toilet

lavacoches *m sing+pl* car-wash; car-washer

lavadedos *m sing+pl* finger bowl

lavadero washroom; wash basin, laundry, wash-house; washing-place (in stream)

lavado wash; washing; laundering; laundry; ~ **a seco/en seco/químico** dry-cleaning; ~ **de cabeza** shampoo; ~ **de cerebro**/*sl* ~ **de coco** brain-washing

lavadora washing-machine; washer-woman, laundress

lavadura washing; dirty water

lavafrutas *m sing+pl* finger bowl, fruit bowl (to wash fruit)

lavamanos *m sing+pl* wash basin; lavatory

lavanda lavender

lavandera washerwoman, laundress; *orni* pied wagtail

lavandería laundry; ~ **automática** launderette

lavándula *bot* lavender

lavaojos *m sing+pl* eyebath, eye cup

lavaparabrisas *m sing+pl* windscreen/windshield washer

lavaplatos *m sing+pl* dishwasher

lavar to wash; launder; wash away, wipe away; ~ **a/en seco** to dry-clean; ~ **y marcar** shampoo and set

lavarropas *m sing+pl* (clothes) washing-machine

lavativa enema; nuisance

lavatorio washing; lotion; washstand; lavatory, washroom

lavavajillas *m sing+pl* dishwasher

lavazas *fpl* dirty water, dish water

laxante *n m+adj* laxative

laxidad *f*, **laxitud** *f* laxity, laxness

laxo lax, slack

laya spade; kind, sort; ~ **de puntas** garden fork

layar to dig (with a spade)

lazada bow, knot; bowknot; lassoing

lazar to lasso

lazarillo blind man's boy

lazarino *n* leper; *adj* leprous

Lázaro Lazarus; **lázaro** beggar

lazo bow, knot; bond, tie; snare, lasso; trap; hairpin bend; loop (in handwriting); link; shoelace; ~ **corredizo** slipknot; ~ **de amor** true love knot; **caer en el** ~ to fall into the trap; **tender un** ~ **a uno** to set a trap for s.o.

Ldo (Licenciado) licentiate, bachelor (degree)

le to him, to her, to it

leal *n m* loyalist; *adj* loyal, faithful; true; reliable; ~ **competencia** fair competition; **a mi** ~ **saber y entender** to the best of my knowledge and belief

lealtad *f* loyalty; trustworthiness; allegiance

leandra *sl* peseta

lebrel *m* greyhound

lección *f* lesson; class; warning; ~ **en práctica** object lesson; **dar** ~ to teach;

dar la ~ to recite the lesson

lectivo *adj* school; **año** ~ the school year

lector *m* reader; language-assistant; ~**mental** mind reader

lectura reading; ~ **de acusación** arraignment; ~ **del contador** meter reading; **libro de** ~ reader, reading book

lecturita *print* small pica

lechada whitewash; woodpulp; milking

lechar to whitewash; whitewash

leche *f* milk; semen; *fam* luck; ~ **condensada** condensed milk; ~ **desnatada** skim(med) milk; ~ **de manteca** buttermilk; ~ **en polvo** powdered milk, milk powder; ~ **pasterizada** pasteurized milk; **estar con/tener la ~ en los labios** to be a greenhorn, be inexperienced; **tener** ~ to be lucky; **mala** ~ bad blood, ill-feeling; **tener mala** ~ to be vindictive; ¡~! hell!

lechecillas *fpl* sweetbreads

lechera milkmaid, dairy maid; milk can; churn; (milch) cow; *sl* police patrol car; *sl* municipal policeman

lechería dairy

lecherita milk jug

lechero *n* milkman, dairyman; *adj* milk, dairy; lucky

lecho bed, couch; riverbed; layer, stratum; base; ~ **de plumas** featherbed; ~ **de roca** bedrock; ~ **mortuorio** deathbed

lechón *m* sucking pig, piglet; dirty person

lechona sow

lechoso milky

lechuga lettuce; frill; *sl* 1,000-peseta note

lechuguilla frill, flounce

lechuguino dandy

lechuza owl, barn owl

leer to read; ~ **en los labios** to lip-read; ~ **en voz alta** to read aloud

lega lay sister

legacía mandate; commission

legación *f* legation

legado bequest, legacy; endowment; legate; representative; ~ **a látere** Papal legate

legajo sheaf, bundle (of papers), file, dossier, docket; ~ **personal** personal file

legal lawful, legal; trustworthy; just; **huelga** ~ official strike

legalidad *f* legality, lawfulness; trust-

worthiness; ~ **técnica** legal technicality

legalista, legalístico legalistic

legalización *f* legalization; authentication; execution (of a document)

legalizar to legalize; authenticate; *leg* execute (a document)

legalmente legally; ~ **apto para testar** of sound mind; ~ **capacitado** eligible in law; ~ **responsable** liable in law

légamo silt; slime; mud; clay

legamoso slimy; muddy; clayey

legañoso bleary-eyed

legar to bequeath, leave to; send as a delegate/envoy; depute

legatario legatee; beneficiary

legendario legendary

legibilidad *f* legibility

legible, leíble legible

legión *f* legion

legionario legionnaire

legislación *f* legislation; ~ **derogativa** repeal legislation

legislador *n m* legislator; *adj* legislating, legislative

legislar to legislate, enact

legislativo legislative

legislatura legislative body; legislature, legislative assembly; ~ **extraordinaria** special session of the legislative assembly

legista *n m+f* lawyer; jurist; legal expert; *adj* law, forensic; **médico** ~ forensic lawyer, criminal pathologist

legitimación *f* legitimization

legitimar to legalize, legitimize; ~**se** prove one's claim to

legitimidad *f* lawfulness, legitimacy; authenticity; justice

legítimo lawful, legitimate; authentic; just; ~ **a defensa** *leg* self-defence; ~ **dueño** rightful owner

lego *n* layman, lay brother; *adj* lay, secular; uninformed, ignorant

legua league (approx. 5,500 metres); **a la ~, a ~ s** far away

legumbre *f* vegetable; legume

leguminoso leguminous

leíble legible, readable

leída reading

leído well-read

leísmo using **le** instead of **lo** and **la** as direct objects

290

lejanía distance, remoteness; distant place

lejano distant, remote; **Lejano Oriente** Far East; **pariente** ~ distant relative

lejía bleach; scolding

lejos _m_ distant view, glimpse; perspective; background; **tener buen** ~ to be good when seen from a distance; _prep_ ~ **de** far from; ~ **de la costa** off the coast; ~ **del local** away from the premises; _adv_ far, far away, far off; **a lo** ~ far off, in the distance; **de/desde** ~ from afar, from a distance

lelo stupid, foolish, slow-witted

lema motto, slogan; theme, watchword; caption; ~ **comercial** trade name, trade mark

lempira monetary unit of Honduras

lencería linen goods, dry-goods; lingerie; draper's shop, dry-goods store; linen cupboard, linen closet

lencero draper, dry-goods merchant

lendroso lousy

lengua tongue; language; clapper (of bell); ~ **de tierra** neck/spit of land; ~ **materna** mother tongue; ~ **viva** living language; **andar en** ~**s** to be talked about; **beber con la** ~ to lap up; **buscar la** ~ **a uno** to pick a quarrel with s.o.; **con la** ~ **fuera** panting; **hacerse** ~**s de** to rave about, extol; **írsele a uno la** ~ to let out a secret, blab; **morderse la** ~ to hold one's tongue; **no morderse la** ~ not to mince words; **tener mala** ~ to be evil tongued, be foul-mouthed; **tener mucha** ~ to have too much to say; **tirarle de la** ~ **a uno** to draw s.o. out, make s.o. talk

lenguado flounder, sole

lenguaje _m_ language, speech; diction; ~ **corriente** common parlance; ~ **literario** literary style

lenguaraz _n m + f_ linguist; _adj_ polyglot; foul-mouthed; loose-tongued

lengue _m sl_ handkerchief

lengüeta tongue (of shoe); needle, pointer (of instrument); barb (of arrow); tab; reed (of musical instrument); _anat_ epiglottis

lengüetada lick, lap

lengüetear to lick, stick one's tongue out; lap

lenidad _f_ leniency

lenificar to soften

leninismo Leninism

leninista _n m + f + adj_ Leninist

lenitivo _n_ balm; emollient; relief; _adj_ lenient

lenocinio pimping, procuring; **casa de** ~ brothel

lente _m + f_ lens; ~ **de aumento** magnifying glass; ~ **de contacto,** ~ **invisible** contact lens; ~**s** (eye)-glasses; ~**s de pinzas** pince-nez; ~**s oscuros** dark glasses

lenteja lentil; _sl_ dose of L.S.D.

lentejuela spangle, sequin

lenticular lentil-shaped

lentilla contact lens

lentitud _f_ slowness; sluggishness; **con** ~ slowly

lento slow, dull, sluggish

leña firewood; threshing; **echar** ~ **al fuego** to add fuel to the flames; **llevar** ~ **al monte** to carry coals to Newcastle

leñador _m_ woodcutter, woodman

leñazo punch, blow

leñera woodshed

leñero woodshed; timber merchant

leño wood, log, timber; blockhead

leñoso woody, ligneous

león _m_ lion; _fam_ footballer of **Athletic de Bilbao**

leona lioness

leonado tawny

leonera lion's den; lion's cage; lumber room; gambling den, joint

leonino leonine; one-sided, unfair

leontina watch chain

leopardo leopard; ~ **cazador** cheetah

leotardo leotard; tights

lepra leprosy

leprosería leper hospital

leproso _n_ leper; _adj_ leprous

lerdo dull; slow, slow-witted, clumsy, coarse

les for/to them/you; from them/you

lesa: ~ **majestad** lèse-majesty

lesbiana lesbian

lesbianismo lesbianism

lésbico, lesbio _adj_ lesbian

lescar _m_ Lascar

lesión _f_ wound, lesion; hurt; damage; ~ **corporal** bodily injury; ~ **de trabajo** occupational injury; ~ **mortal** fatal injury

lesionado _n_ injured person; _adj_ disabled;

injured

lesionar to wound, injure; damage; hurt; disable; ~**se** to get wounded, get hurt

lesivo injurious, harmful; prejudicial

lesna awl

leso injured; harmed; stupid

letal deadly, lethal

letanía litany

letárgico lethargic

letargo lethargy; stupor, drowsiness; slump (in shares)

letón *n m* + *adj* Lett, Lettish

Letonia Latvia

letra letter; handwriting; draft; lyric; *print* type; literal meaning; ~ **abierta** letter of credit; ~ **a la vista** sight draft; ~ **de cambio** bill of exchange; ~ **de imprenta** type; ~ **de mano** handwriting; ~ **de molde** block letter, printed letter; ~ **mayúscula** capital letter; ~ **menuda** fine print; ~ **minúscula** small letter; ~ **negrilla** bold face; ~ **redonda**, ~ **redondilla** roman; ~ **versal** capital letter; ~ **versalita** small capital letter; **al pie de la** ~ literally; **primeras** ~**s** primary education, ABC; **Facultad de** ~ Faculty of Arts

letrado *n* lawyer; **asesor** ~ counsellor, legal adviser; *adj* learned; pedantic

letrero sign, notice; inscription; caption; poster, placard; label

letrina latrine; sewer

letrista *m* + *f* song writer; calligrapher

leucemia leukaemia

leudar to leaven; ~**se** to rise (of bread, cakes)

leva draft, levy; lever, cam; weighing anchor, setting sail; **echar** ~ to draft, conscript; **echar** ~**s** to boast

levadura yeast, leaven; ~ **de cerveza** brewer's yeast; ~ **en polvo** baking powder

levantacoches *m sing* + *pl mot* jack, autojack

levantado elevated; high; sublime

levantador *m* lifter; ~ **de pesos** weight lifter

levantamiento lifting, raising; uprising, revolt; adjournment (of a meeting); ~ **del censo** taking of a census; ~ **de pesos** weight lifting; ~ **de planos**, ~ **de un plano** surveying

levantar to raise (up), lift (up), pick up;

stand up; raise, stir up; cheer up, uplift; build, construct; steal; recruit; ~ **el ancla** to weigh anchor; ~ **el campo** to break camp; ~ **fondos** to raise money; ~ **(la) casa** to move house; ~ **la mesa** to clear the table; ~ **la voz** to raise one's voice; ~ **planos** to make a survey, draw up plans; ~ **una sesión** to adjourn a meeting; ~**se** to get up (de from); raise o.s.; stand up; straighten o.s. up; rebel

levantaválvulas *m sing* + *pl mot* tappet

levante *m* east; east wind; **el Levante** the Levant, Near East; S.E. Mediterranean coast of Spain

levantino *n* Levantine; inhabitant of S.E. Mediterranean coast of Spain; *adj* Levantine

levar: ~ **el ancla**, ~ **anclas** to weigh anchor; ~**se** to set sail

leve slight; light; trivial, unimportant

levedad *f* levity; lightness; lack of importance

leviatán *m* leviathan

levita *f* frock coat; Levite

levitación *f* levitation

léxico *n* lexicon, dictionary; glossary, vocabulary list; *adj* lexical

lexicografía lexicography

lexicográfico lexicographical

lexicógrafo lexicographer

lexicología lexicology

lexicón *m* lexicon

ley *f* law; act, bill; rule; legal standard; norm; loyalty; ~ **del menor esfuerzo** line of least resistance; ~ **marcial** martial law; ~ **no escrita** unwritten law; **de** ~ genuine; **mala** ~ animosity, dislike; **plata de** ~ sterling silver; **tener** ~ **a, tomar** ~ **a** to be devoted to

leyenda legend; inscription

leyente *m* reader

lezna awl

liar to tie (up), bind; wrap up; confuse; ~ **un cigarillo** to roll a cigarette; ~**se con** to get involved with, have a liaison with, get tangled up in

libación *f* libation

libanés *n* + *adj* Lebanese

Líbano: el ~ Lebanon

libar to sip, taste; suck

libelar to start a lawsuit; sue for libel; file a complaint

libelo petition; complaint; libel, lam-

poon
libélula dragonfly
liberación *f* liberation; deliverance; release; settlement, quittance; redemption; exemption; ~ **de obligaciones** discharge of obligations
liberal liberal; generous
liberalidad *f* liberality; generosity
liberalismo liberalism
liberalizar to liberalize
liberar to free; deliver; release; ~ **acciones** to issue stock; ~ **a uno de** to exempt s.o. from; ~ **de responsibilidad** to free from liability
liberiano Liberian
libertad *f* liberty, freedom; licence; ~ **bajo fianza** on bail; ~ **bajo palabra** on parole; ~ **condicional**, ~ **vigilada** probation; ~ **de comercio** free trade; ~ **de cultos** freedom of worship; ~ **de enseñanza** academic freedom; ~ **de imprenta** freedom of the press; ~ **de los mares** freedom of the seas; ~ **de (la) palabra** free speech; ~ **de reunión** right of assembly; **tomarse la** ~ **de** to take the liberty of
libertado free, unrestrained; bold, daring; ~ **bajo/con fianza** released on bail
libertador *n m* liberator; deliverer; *adj* liberating
libertar to liberate, set free; save from, deliver from; ~ **bien** to succeed; ~ **mal** to fail
libertinaje *m* licentiousness; debauchery; profligacy; impicty
libertino *n* libertine, rake; free-thinker; *adj* loose-living; profligate; free-thinking
Libia Libya
libídine *f* libido; lust, lewdness
libidinoso libidinous, lustful, lewd
libio *n+adj* Libyan
libra pound; *sl* one hundred pesetas; ~ **esterlina** pound sterling
librado *m comm* drawer (of bill, cheque)
librador *m comm* drawer; deliverer
libramiento freeing, delivery; *comm* draft; bill of exchange
librante *m comm* drawer (of bill, cheque)
libranza bill of exchange, draft; ~ **de correos**, ~ **postal** money order
librar to free, release; exempt; relieve;

draw (cheques *etc*); **salir bien librado** to come out well; ~ **una batalla** to fight a battle; ~**se de** to free oneself from, get rid of
libre *n m sp* free kick; *adj* outspoken; free; immoral; ~ **de derechos** duty-free; ~ **de porte** postage prepaid; ~ **de vida** loose-living; **buffet** ~ running buffet
librea livery; **de** ~ liveried
librecambio free trade, free exchange
librecambista *n m+f* free-trader; *adj* free-trade
librepensador *n m* free-thinker; *adj* free-thinking
librepensamiento free thought
librería bookshop; bookcase; bookshelf; book-selling, book trade; library (in house); ~ **de ocasión**, ~ **de viejo** second-hand bookshop
libreril *adj* book
librero bookseller; bookbinder; bookshelf; bookcase; ~ **de viejo**, ~ **de libros usados** second-hand bookseller
libresco bookish
libreta notebook; ~ **de banco**, ~ **de depósitos** bank book, pass book
librete *m* booklet
libretista *m+f* librettist
libreto libretto
librillo hinge; book of cigarette papers
libro book; ~ **a la rústica** paperback; ~ **de actas** minute book; ~ **de apuntes** notebook; ~ **de bolsillo** paper-back; ~ **de caja** cash book; ~ **de cocina** cookery book, cookbook; ~ **de consulta** reference book; ~ **de cuentas** account book; ~ **de cuentos** story book; ~ **de cheques** cheque-book; ~ **de hojas cambiables** loose-leaf book; ~ **de lance** second-hand book; ~ **de mayor venta** bestseller; ~ **de memoria** memorandum book; ~ **de pedidos** order book; ~ **de reclamaciones** complaints book; ~ **de recuerdos** scrapbook; ~ **de teléfonos** telephone directory; ~ **de texto** textbook; ~ **de visitas** visitors' book; ~ **de vuelos** flight log-book; ~ **escolar** school record, school report; ~ **genealógico** stud-book; ~ **mayor** ledger; ~ **talonario** cheque-book; receipt book; counterfoil 'stub book'; **ahorcar/ arrimar los** ~**s** to give up studying,

leave the University; **hacer ∼ nuevo** to turn over a new leaf

librote *m* tome, dull book; big book

licencia licence, licentiousness; concession; permission; permit; leave of absence; *mil* furlough; **∼ absoluta** *mil* discharge; **∼ de armas** gun licence; **∼ de caza** game licence; **∼ de conducir, ∼ de conductor, ∼ de manejar** driving licence; **∼ de matrimonio** marriage licence; **∼ por enfermedad** sick leave; **∼ sin sueldo** unpaid leave; **dar su ∼** to give one's permission; **estar de ∼** to be on leave; **ir de ∼** to go on leave

licenciable licensable

licenciado *n* licentiate; lawyer; discharged soldier; graduate, Bachelor; *adj* pedantic; dismissed, discharged

licenciamiento discharge; disbandment

licenciar to license; permit; *mil* discharge; disband; confer a licentiate/degree on; **∼se** to take a degree; *mil* take a discharge, be discharged

licenciatura licentiate, degree; degree course

licencioso licentious

liceo high school; *Mex* elementary/primary school; lyceum

licitación *f* bid, bidding (auction)

licitador *m*, **licitante** *m* bidder; **∼ que vence en la subasta** successful bidder

licitar *vt* to bid for, bid on; buy or sell at auction; *vi* to bid

lícito lawful, legal; permitted; permissible; admissible, fair, just

licitud *f* legality; fairness, justness

licor *m* spirits, liquor; liqueur; liquid; **∼es puros** raw spirits

licorería distillery

licorista *m+f* distiller; seller of spirits

licoroso strong, alcoholic

licuación *f*, **licuefacción** *f* liquefaction

licuar to liquefy

licha *sl* street

lichtensteiniense *n m* Liechtensteiner; *adj* of Liechtenstein

lid *f* fight, combat; dispute; **en buena ∼** in a fair fight, fairly

líder *m* leader

liderar to lead, be in the lead

liderato leadership

lidia fight; bullfight; **toro de ∼** fighting bull

lidiador *m* fighter; bullfighter

lidiar to fight; fight in the bull ring; **∼ con/contra** to fight against

liebre *f* hare

Lieja Liège

lienza strip of cloth

lienzo linen, linen or cotton cloth; handkerchief; *arts* canvas; *archi* façade; *archi* curtain (wall)

liga garter, suspender; league; confederacy; mistletoe; birdlime; alloy; **∼ de goma** rubber band; **hacer∼s con** to get along with s.o.

ligación *f* union; bond

ligado *n* ligature; *adj+adv mus* legato

ligadura bond, tie; ligature

ligamento ligament

ligamiento bond, tie

ligar to bind, tie; put a ligature on; *mus* slur; glue; join; alloy; combine; draw matching cards; *fam* make friends with; *sl* chat up, pick up; **∼se** to bind o.s., be committed; band together, associate; **∼se con** to get involved in/with

ligazón *f* bond; union

ligereza lightness; swiftness; agility; frivolity; slightness; fickleness; tactlessness

ligero light; swift; agile; slight; superficial, fickle; **∼ de cascos** scatterbrained; **∼ de dedos** light-fingered; **∼ de lengua** loose-tongued; **∼ de pies** light-footed, swift; **∼ de ropa** scantily dressed; **a la ligera** quickly, superficially; rashly; **de ∼** thoughtlessly; **hacer algo a la ligera** to do something without fuss; **tomar algo a la ligera** to take something lightly; **obrar de ∼** to act recklessly

ligón *m sl* Don Juan, Casanova

lignito lignite

ligue *m sl* picking up; *sl* arrest

liguero *n* suspender-belt; *adj sp* league; **partido ∼** league game

ligustro privet

lija sandpaper; **∼ esmeril** emery paper

lijar *carp* to sand

Lila Lille

lila *n* lilac; *adj* lilac-coloured; *sl* simple person; *sl* victim of a robbery

lili: estar ∼ *mil sl* to be on leave

¹ **lima** lime; lime-tree

² **lima** *carp+metal* file; finish, polish; ∼

de/para las uñas nail-file

³ **lima** *sl* shirt

limar to file

limeño *n + adj* of Lima

limero lime-tree

limitación *f* limit, limitation; restriction, restraint; ~ **de velocidad** speed limit; **sin** ~ unlimited

limitado limited; slow-witted

limitar to limit, restrict; restrain, curtail, reduce; ~ **con** to border on, abut; be bounded by

límite *m* limit; border; boundary; ~ **de velocidad** speed limit; ~ **forestal** tree line

limítrofe contiguous; bordering

limo mud; slime; *sl* handbag

limón *m* lemon; lemon colour

limonada lemonade; ~ **natural** lemon squash

limonar *m* lemon grove

limonero lemon-tree

limosina limousine

limosna alms; **pedir** ~ to beg

limosnear to beg for alms

limosnero *n* almoner; beggar; poor box; *adj* charitable

limoso slimy, muddy

limpiabotas *m sing + pl* bootblack

limpiador *m* cleaner

limpiacristales *m sing + pl* windscreen/windshield wiper; window cleaner

limpiachimeneas *m sing + pl* chimney-sweep

limpiadura cleaning; ~s sweepings

limpianieves *m sing + pl* snowplough

limpiaparabrisas *m sing + pl* windscreen/windshield wiper

limpiapipas *m sing + pl* pipe-cleaner

limpiar to clean; cleanse; wipe; purge; shine shoes; *sl* steal; ~ **en seco** to dry clean; ~**se las narices** to wipe one's nose

límpido limpid

limpidez *f* limpidity

limpieza cleaning; cleansing; polishing; clearance; clean-up; cleanliness; integrity; honesty; fair play; ~ **de primavera,** ~ **general** spring cleaning; ~ **de sangre** racial purity; ~ **en seco** dry-cleaning; ~ **por vacío** vacuum-cleaning

limpio clean; neat; clear; pure; honest; ~ **de** free from; **copia en** ~ fair copy;

ganancia limpia net profit; **poner algo en** ~ to make sense of s.t.; **sangre limpia** pure blood; **jugar** ~ to play fairly

limusina limousine

linaje *m* lineage, family; line (of descent)

linajudo high-born, noble

linaza linseed; flax

lince *n m* lynx; wild cat; crafty person; **ser un** ~ to be crafty; *adj* crafty; shrewd; sharp-eyed

linchamiento lynching

linchar to lynch

lindante adjoining, contiguous; ~ **con** bordering on

lindar to adjoin; ~ **con** to border on, abut on, be bounded by

linde *m + f* boundary, limit

lindero *n* boundary, limit; edge; border; *adj* adjoining, contiguous; bordering

lindeza prettiness; loveliness; elegance; ~s pretty ways, *iron* insults

lindo pretty; lovely; elegant; fine, excellent

lindura prettiness; loveliness; elegance

línea *n* line; track; electric cable; outline; ~ **de alto el fuego** cease-fire line; ~ **de banda,** ~ **de centro,** ~ **de medio campo** *sp* half-way line; ~ **de gol,** ~ **de puerta** goal-line; ~ **de meta** finishing line; ~ **de montaje** assembly line; ~ **de partido** *pol* party line; ~ **de puntos** dotted line; ~ **de tiro** line of fire; ~ **lateral** *sp* side-line, touch; ~ **recta** straight line; **guardar la** ~ to keep one's figure

lineal linear, lineal; **aumento** ~ flat-rate increase, across-the-board increase; **dibujo** ~ line drawing

lineamentos *m + pl* lineaments

linear *v* to draw lines on; line; sketch, outline; **aumento** ~ flat-rate increase

linfa lymph

linfático lymphatic

lingotazo *sl* swig (of alcoholic drink)

lingote *m* ingot

lingüista *m + f* linguist

lingüística linguistics

lingüístico linguistic

linimento liniment

lino flax; linen; linseed

linóleo linoleum

linón *m text* lawn

linotipia linotype

linotipista *m* + *f* linotypist
linotipo linotype (plate)
linterna lantern; lamp; flashlight; spotlight; ~ **a pila, de pilas** electric torch
liño line (of trees or plants); ridge
lío pack; bundle; parcel; complication; tangle; muddle; row; love-affair, liaison; **armar un** ~ to kick up a fuss; **meterse en un** ~ to get into a fix; **tener un** ~ **con** to have an affair with
Liorna Leghorn
lique *m* kick; **dar el** ~ to sack
liquen *m* lichen
liquidable liquid, fluid (of assets)
liquidación *f* sale, closing-down sale; liquidation; winding-up (of a business); settlement (of an account); **entrar en** ~ to go into liquidation; **vender en** ~ to sell up, sell off
liquidador *m* receiver, liquidator
liquidar to liquidate; sell up; close down, close up (a business); settle (an account); pay off (a debt); sell off (stock); liquefy; *sl* to kill, bump off
liquidez *f* liquidity
líquido *n* net amount, balance; *adj* liquid, fluid; **ganancia líquida** net profit
¹ **lira** lyre
² **lira** lira (Italian currency unit)
lírica lyric poetry
lírico lyric; lyrical; **teatro** ~ music hall
lirismo lyricism; effusiveness
lirio iris; lily; ~ **de los valles** lily of the valley
lirón *m* dormouse; *fig* sleepy-head; **dormir como un** ~ to sleep like a log
lisamente smoothly, evenly; plainly
Lisboa Lisbon
lisboeta *n m* + *f* + *adj* of Lisbon
lisiado *n* cripple; wounded soldier; *adj* crippled, wounded
lisiar to cripple, injure; wound, maim
liso even; smooth; flat; plain; simple; impudent; ~ **y llano** pure and simple
lisonja flattery; fawning
lisonjear to flatter; fawn on; please
lisonjero *n* flatterer; *adj* flattering; pleasing, agreeable
lista list; roll (call); (school) register; schedule; strip (of cloth); stripe; slip (of paper); ~ **de bajas** casualty list; ~ **de correos** poste restante, general delivery; ~ **de espera** waiting list; ~

del triunfo popularity chart; ~ **de pagos** payroll; ~ **de platos** bill of fare; ~ **de precios** price list; ~ **de tandas** rota; ~ **de vinos** wine list; ~ **electoral** electoral roll; **pasar** ~ to call the roll
listar to list; enter in a list
listero time-keeper, time-clerk
listín *m* telephone directory
listo ready, prompt; alert; smart
listón *m* ribbon; tape; strip; lath
lisura smoothness; calmness; sincerity; insolence
lite *f* lawsuit; ~ **pendiente** suit pending
litera bunk; berth; litter; ~ **alta** upper berth; ~ **baja** lower berth
literario literary
literato *n* writer; *adj* literary
literatura literature
litigación *f* litigation; lawsuit
litigante *n m* + *f* + *adj* litigant
litigar to go to law; sue; argue, contend
litigio lawsuit; litigation; argument, plea
litigioso litigious; contentious
litio lithium
litis *f sing* + *pl* lawsuit; case (in law)
litisexpensas *fpl* legal costs
litografía lithograph; lithography
litografiar to lithograph
litoral *n m* waterfront; coast, shore; *adj* coastal
litro litre
liturgia liturgy
litúrgico liturgical
liviandad *f* frivolity; lewdness; fickleness; lightness
liviano frivolous; lewd; fickle; light (in weight)
lividez *f* lividness; pallor
lívido livid; pallid
liza lists; combat; **entrar en la** ~ to enter the lists; contest
¹ **lo** *m* him; it
² **lo** *neut* the; ~ **de siempre** the same old story; ~ **que** what, which; **a** ~ **que** according to what; **a** ~ **sumo** at (the) most; ~ **pesado que es** how tiring it is
loa praise; *theat* dramatic prologue
loable laudable, commendable
loar to praise
loba she-wolf
lobanillo wen, cyst
lobato, lobezno wolf-cub; cub scout
lobo wolf; half-breed; ~ **de mar** sea dog; ~ **marino** seal; ~ **solitario** lone wolf;

pillar un ~ *sl* to get drunk
lóbrego dark, dismal, gloomy
lobreguez *f* darkness, gloominess
lóbulo lobe
lobuno wolflike, wolfish
locación *f* lease; hiring, letting
local *n m* place, site; premises; *adj* local;
en el ~ on the spot; **equipo ~** *sp* home
team
localidad *f* locality; location; seat (on a
train, at a performance *etc*); ticket; **no
hay ~es** sold out; **sacar ~es** to get
seats, buy tickets
localización *f* location; placing
localizar to localize; locate, place, find
locatario leaseholder
loción *f* lotion; wash; **~ para después del
afeitado** after-shave
loco *n* madman; fool; *adj* mad, crazy,
huge; **~ de atar, ~ de remate, ~ rematado** raving lunatic; **un éxito ~**
stupendous success; **hacerse el ~** to
play dumb
locomoción *f* locomotion
locomotor *adj* locomotive
locomotora railway engine, locomotive;
~ de maniobras shunting engine,
shifting engine
locomotriz *adj* locomotive
locomóvil *n f* traction engine; *adj* movable
locuacidad *f* talkativeness, loquacity
locuaz talkative, loquacious
locución *f* idiomatic expression, locution
locura madness, insanity; folly
locutor *m*, **locutora** TV/radio announcer; compère
locutorio telephone box; locutory; **~
radiofónico** broadcasting studio
lodazal *m* muddy ground; quagmire
lodo mud, mire
lodoso muddy
logaritmo logarithm
logarítmico logarithmic
logia loggia; (masonic) lodge
lógica logic
lógico *n* logician; *adj* logical, reasonable
logística logistics
logístico logistic
logrado successful
lograr to get, obtain; achieve, attain; **~
+infin** to succeed in; *vi* to succeed;
~se to be successful
logrear to lend money for interest; be a

money-lender
logrero money-lender, usurer; profiteer; *adj* money-lending, profiteering
logro achievement, success; profit, gain;
usury; lucre; **dar a ~, prestar a ~** to
lend at a high rate of interest
Loira *m* Loire
loísmo use of the indirect object pronoun **lo** instead of **le**
loma low hill; slope; low ridge
Lombarda Lombardy
lombarda red cabbage
lombardo *n + adj* Lombard
lombriz *f* worm; **~ de tierra** earthworm;
~ solitaria tapeworm
lomo loin; back, spine; ridge (between
furrows); shoulder (of hill); railway
gradient; crease; **~s** ribs
lona canvas, sailcloth; burlap
loncha *see* **lonja**
lonchar to have lunch; have a snack
lonche *m* lunch; snack
lonchería snack bar, lunch counter
londinense *n* Londoner; *adj* of London
Londres *m* London
longanimidad *f* forbearance
longánimo forbearing, long-suffering;
magnanimous
longaniza long thin pork sausage
longevidad *f* longevity; life-span
longevo long-lived
longitud *f* length; longitude; **~ de onda**
wave-length
longitudinal lengthwise; longitudinal
lonja market, exchange; stock exchange; grocer's shop; thong; rasher
of bacon, slice of meat; strip
lonjista *m + f* grocer
lontananza background; **en ~** in the distance, on the horizon
loor *m* praise
loquear to act the fool; talk nonsense;
make merry
loquera mental hospital, mad-house;
padded cell
loquesco crazy; funny
lora female parrot
Lorenzo Lawrence
loro *n* parrot; *adj* dark brown
los *mpl* the; them, you; those; **~ que**
those who, those which
losa flagstone; stone slab; **~ sepulcral**
tombstone

losange *m* lozenge; diamond shape; *math* rhomb; (baseball) diamond

lote *m* lot; share, portion; lottery prize; plot of land

lotera, lotero seller of lottery tickets

lotería lottery; raffle; gamble

loto *bot* lotus

loza porcelain; crockery, earthenware; ~ **fina** china(ware); **hacer la** ~ to do the washing up

lozanear to grow profusely; be vigorous; be full of life

lozanía luxuriance

lozano lush; vigorous; lively; haughty; proud; robust

lubricación *f* lubrication

lubricador *n m* lubricant; *adj* lubricating, lubricant

lubricar to lubricate, grease, oil

lubricidad *f* lewdness, lubricity

lúbrico lewd; slippery

Lucas Luke, Lucas

lucera skylight

lucerna skylight; chandelier; loophole

lucérnula *bot* lucerne

lucero bright star; *astron* Venus; brilliance; ~ **del alba** morning star; ~ **de la tarde,** ~ **vespertino** evening star

lucidez *f* lucidity, clarity

lucido magnificent; sumptuous; elegant; successful; **quedarse** ~ *iron* to be a flop, make a mess of things

lúcido clear, lucid

luciente bright, shining; outstanding

luciérnaga firefly, glow-worm

Lucífero morning star

lucífugo that shuns light

lucimiento brilliance, lustre; dash, display; success; **quedar/salir con** ~ to come out with flying colours

lucio *n zool* pike; *adj* shiny

lucir *vt* to light up, illuminate; show off; show to advantage, display; *vi* to shine, sparkle; ~**se** to dress up; distinguish o.s.; *iron* make a mess of things, appear ridiculous, make o.s. a laughing stock

lucrar to get, obtain; ~**se** to make money, do well out of s.t.

lucrativo profitable, remunerative, lucrative

lucro profit, gain; lucre; ~**s y daños** profit and loss

luctuoso sad, mournful; gloomy

lucubración *f* lucubration

lucha fight; quarrel; struggle; ~ **de la cuerda** tug-of-war; ~ **de las clases** class-struggle; ~ **libre** all-in wrestling

luchador *m* fighter; wrestler

luchar to fight; quarrel; struggle; contend; wrestle

ludibrio derision, mockery

ludir to rub, rub together

luego next; then; therefore; soon; immediately; later; ~ **como,** ~ **que** as soon as; ~ **de** right after; **desde** ~ of course; **hasta** ~ goodbye, see you later

lúe *f* infection; ~ **canina** distemper; ~ **venérea** syphilis

lues *fpl* pestilence

lugano *orni* siskin

lugar *m* place, spot; room, space; seat; job, position; opportunity; village; ~ **común** commonplace, platitude; ~ **excusado** w.c.; ~ **religioso** burial ground; **dar** ~ to make room; **dar** ~ **a** to give cause for, give rise to; **en** ~ **de** instead of; **hacer** ~ **para** to make room for; make way for; **¿hay** ~? is there any room?; **no hay** ~ **para** there is no need for; **tener** ~ to take place

lugarejo hamlet

lugareño *n* villager; **los** ~**s** the locals; *adj* village

lugarteniente *m* deputy; substitute; lieutenant

luge *m* sled

lugre *m naut* lugger

lúgubre dismal, mournful, lugubrious

Luis Louis

Luisa Louise

lujo luxury; lavishness; abundance, profusion; ~ **de** abundance of, excess of; **de** ~ **de** luxe, luxury

lujoso luxurious, lavish; ostentatious

lujuria lust, lechery; lewdness

lujuriante luxuriant; lush; lustful

lujuriar to lust; be lustful

lujurioso lustful, lecherous

lulú: perro ~ lap-dog

lumbre *f* fire; light; brightness; fanlight; ~ **de agua** surface of the water; **echar** ~ *fam* to blow one's top; **ni por** ~ not for all the tea in China

lumbrera light; lamp; source of light; dormer window; skylight; vent, duct; luminary, leading light; ~ **de escape**

exhaust vent
luminar *m* luminary, leading light
luminaria lamp; luminary; ~s illuminations
luminiscencia luminescence
luminiscente luminescent
luminosidad *f* brightness; brilliance
luminoso bright, luminous; shining
luminotécnica lighting engineering
luminotécnico lighting engineer
luna moon; moonlight; mirror; plate glass; lens; whim, mood; ~ **creciente** waxing moon, crescent moon; ~ **de miel** honeymoon; ~ **llena** full moon; ~ **menguante** waning moon; ~ **nueva** new moon; **estar de buena** ~ to be in a good mood; **media** ~ half moon; **quedarse a la** ~ **de Valencia** to be disappointed; **vivir en la** ~ to be up in the clouds, out of touch with reality
lunar *n m* mole, beauty-spot; defect, blemish; ~ **postizo** artificial beauty spot; *adj* lunar
lunarejo having moles; *vet* spotted
lunario monthly calendar
lunático *n + adj* lunatic
lunchería snack bar
lunes *m* Monday; **hacer san** ~ to take Monday off work
luneta lens, eye-glass; stalls, orchestra seat; rear window; crescent-shape

lupa magnifying glass, lens
lupanar *m* brothel
lupia cyst; wen
lúpulo *bot* hop, hops
lusitano *n + adj* Portuguese, Lusitanian
lustrabotas *m sing + pl* bootblack
lustrador *m* polisher; bootblack
lustrar to polish, shine
lustre *m* polish, shine; gloss; lustre
lustro five-year period
lustroso bright, shining; glossy
luterano *n + adj* Lutheran
luto mourning; sorrow; ~ **riguroso** deep mourning; **estar de** ~, **llevar** ~ to be in mourning
luz *f* light; lighting; electricity; lamp, candle; daylight; window; span (of bridge); headroom; opening; ~ **de aparcamiento** *mot* sidelight; ~ **de cruce** *mot* dimmed/dipped headlight; ~ **destelladora/intermitente** flashing/winking light; ~ **lateral** *mot* sidelight; ~ **relámpago** *phot* flashlight; **a primera** ~ at first light, at daybreak; **dar a** ~ to give birth to, have a child; **entre dos luces** at twilight; tipsy, confused; **salir a** ~ to come to light, be published; **hombre de pocas luces** dim-witted man
Luzbel Lucifer

LL

ll *f* letter ll

llaga wound; sore, ulcer; grief; *bui* crack, seam; **poner el dedo en la ~** to put a finger on a sore spot; **renovar la ~** to open an old sore

llagar to wound; make sore; ulcerate

llama flame; passion; swamp; *zool* llama; **~ piloto** pilot light (on gas appliance); **saltar/salir de las ~s y caer en las brasas** to jump out of the frying pan into the fire

llamada call; signal, gesture; knock (at door), ring (of door bell); telephone call; reference mark; **~ a filas, ~ a quintas** call to military service; **~ de larga distancia, ~ interurbana** trunk call, long-distance call

llamado called, so-called

llamador *m* caller, messenger; push-button; door bell, (door) knocker

llamamiento call; vocation, calling; convening

llamar to call; send for; name; summons; knock, ring; **~ a la mili/a filas** to call up, draft; **~ a capítulo/a cuentas** to call to account; **~ la atención a/sobre** to call attention to; **~ por teléfono** to phone, ring up; **~se** to be called; *meteor + naut* to veer; **¿cómo se llama usted?** what's your name?

llamarada, llamarón *m* blaze, flare-up; outburst (of temper)

llamativo flashy, gaudy, loud; thirst-making

llamazar *m* swamp

llambria almost vertical rock-face

llamear to blaze, flame; flash

llana folio, page; plain; flat ground; *bui* trowel; **a la ~** straightforwardly; **dar de ~** to finish off with a trowel

llanada plain; flat ground

llanero plainsman, ranger, cowboy

llaneza plainness, simplicity; frankness, sincerity

llanito Gibraltarian

llano *n* plain; flat ground; landing; stair-head; iambus; *adj* flat, level; even, smooth; simple; straightforward; frank; sincere; **canto ~** plainsong; **de ~** openly, bluntly; **pueblo ~** common people; **palabra llana** word accented on the penultimate syllable

llanta tyre; rim (of wheel); **~ de goma** rubber tyre; **~ de oruga** caterpillar track; **~ de repuesto** spare tyre

llantén *m bot* plantain

llanto crying, weeping; lamentation; dirge; **dejar el ~** to stop crying; **en ~** weeping, in tears

llanura plain, prairie; flatness; evenness; smoothness

llapa occupational perk

llares *fpl* pothook(s)

llave *f* key; tap, *US* faucet; spigot, cock; switch; wrench; spanner; *mus* clef; (wrestling) lock; **~ de cambio** shift key; **~ de caño** pipe wrench; **~ de cierre, ~ de paso** stopcock; **~ de contacto** ignition key; **~ de flotador** ballcock; **~ inglesa** monkey wrench; **~ maestra** master key, skeleton key; **~ para tubos** pipe wrench; **bajo ~, debajo de ~** under lock and key; **echar la ~ a** to lock up

llavera housekeeper

llavero key-ring; gaoler, turnkey; locksmith

llavín *m* latchkey

lleco (of soil) virgin

llegada arrival, coming; **a la ~** on arrival

llegar *vt* to bring up, bring close, draw up; *vi* to arrive, come; amount to, be equal to; reach, attain; succeed; **~ a** to come to, succeed in; **~ a saber** to get to know; **~ a ser** to become; **~se** to draw near, approach, come close; **llegará el día en que** one fine day; **~ hasta** to go as far as; **me llega para vivir** I have enough to live on; **~ a +** *infin* to go so far as + *infin*; **~ a comprender** to come to understand; **~ a las manos** to come to blows; **~ a más**

300

to rise in the world; **él llegará lejos** he will go far, he will make a name for himself; **no le llega la camisa al cuerpo** he is petrified with fear

llena flood; overflow

llenado filling

llenador (of food) satisfying, filling

llenar to fill; fill in, fill up, fill out; fulfil; satisfy, meet (conditions); **a él le llenan los ojos** his eyes are bigger than his stomach; **~se** to fill up, stuff o.s.

¹ **lleno** n plenty, abundance; fullness; perfection; *theat* sell-out, full house; **de ~** fully, completely

² **lleno** adj full, filled, full up; **~ a rebosar**, **~ hasta el borde** brimful; **~ de goteras** full of aches and pains; **~ de polvo** covered in dust

llenura completeness, fullness

lleudar to leaven

lleva, llevada ride; carrying; **~ gratuita** free ride

llevadero tolerable, bearable; light, easy to carry

llevador m carrier

llevar to carry (away), transport; bear, produce; wear; lead; direct, manage; take (time); **~ a cabo** to carry out (to the finish); **~ adelante** to carry on, keep going; **~ calabazas** to be jilted; **~ el compás** to keep time; **~ la contraria** to contradict, take the opposite point of view; **~ la cuenta/los libros** comm to keep the accounts/the books; **~ la cuenta de** to keep track of; **~ la delantera** to lead the way; **~ a la práctica** to put into practice; **~se una caída** to take a fall; **él lleva viviendo aquí mucho tiempo** he has lived here a long time; **~ … años a** to be … years older than; **~se** to take away; **~se bien con** to get on well with; **~se un susto/chasco** to have a shock/disappointment

lloradero given to weeping

llorado late lamented; popular

llorar vt to weep over; cry about; mourn; vi to cry, weep; drip

lloriquear to snivel; whimper, whine

lloriqueo snivelling; whimpering, whining

lloro n weeping

llorón n m mute, hired mourner; crybaby; weepy person; **sauce ~** weeping willow; adj weeping, tearful, crying

llorona weeping woman; sl maudlin drunkenness

lloroso sad; tearful

llovedizo adj rainy; **agua llovediza** rainwater; **techo ~** leaking roof

llover to rain; come in abundance; **~ a cántaros** to rain cats and dogs; **llueva o no llueva** rain or shine

llovida shower, rain

llovido stowaway

llovizna drizzle

lloviznar to drizzle

lloviznoso drizzly; damp

lluvia rain; rainfall; fig flood; shower; **agua de ~** rainwater; **~ ácida** acid rain

lluvioso rainy; wet

M

m *f* letter m

maca bruise (in fruit), flaw, blemish; fraud

macabro macabre

macadamizar to macadamize

macadán *m* macadam

macagua South American snake

macana rubbish, piece of nonsense; wooden club

macanazo piece of utter nonsense; blow with a club

macanudo dandy, first-rate, fabulous

macareno *adj* pertaining to La Macarena; gaudily dressed

macarrón *m* piece of macaroni; **macarrones** *cul* macaroni; *naut* stanchions

macarrónico macaronic; ghastly, frightful; **latín** ~ very bad Latin

macarse to rot; (of fruit) be damaged by a fall/bruise

macazuchil *m* plant used to flavour chocolate

maceador *m* beater, hammerer

macear to beat, hammer, soften up; harp on

macedonia: ~ **de frutas** fruit salad; ~ **de verduras** mixed vegetables

macedónico *n* + *adj* Macedonian

macelo abattoir

maceración *f*, **maceramiento** softening up; mortification (of the flesh)

macerar to soften up; mortify

macerina saucer

macero mace-bearer

maceta small mace; mason's hammer; flower-pot, flower vase; *cul* haunch (of mutton)

macetero flower-pot stand

macicez *f* solidity

macilento pale, lean, wan

macillo hammer (of a piano)

macis *f cul* mace

maciza *sl* smashing bird, crumpet, *US* broad

macizar to fill up, make solid

macizo *n* flower-bed, clump; *bui* solid

wall; *adj* solid

maco *sl* prison, gaol

macolla *bot* clump

macona hamper

macrocefálico macrocephalous, large-headed

macrocosmo macrocosm

macuache *m* ignorant Mexican Indian

macuco *n* overgrown boy; *adj* sly

mácula stain, blemish

macular to stain; *print* mackle

maculatura *print* spoilt sheet

maculoso badly stained, spotted

macún *m* poncho

macutazo *mil sl* shit-house rumour

macuteno petty thief

macuto *mil* knapsack; alms-basket

machaca boring person

machacadera implement for pounding/crushing

machacadora crushing machine

machacador *adj* pounding, crushing

machacante *m sl* five-peseta coin

machacar *vt* to pound, crush; keep on contradicting; harp on a subject; grind

machacón *n m* bore, boring person; *adj* monotonous

machaconería monotonous insistence

machada stupidity; flock of he-goats

machamartillo: **a** ~ stoutly, steadfastly

machango coarse

machaqueo pounding, crushing

machar to pound

machear *zool* to beget more males than females

machetazo cut with a machete

machete *n* machete, cutlass

machetear to wound with a cutlass/machete

machetero sugar-cane cutter, one who clears ground/cuts a path through jungle with a machete; sabre-rattler

machi *m* + *f* quack, healer

machihembrado *carp* dovetailing

machihembrar *carp* to dovetail

machina crane; piledriver

302

machismo male chauvinism

machista *m* male chauvinist

macho male; mule; *eng* male piece; bolt (of a lock); *archi* buttress; hook (to catch in an eye); sledge-hammer; blockhead; ~ **cabrío** he-goat

machón *m archi* buttress

machorra barren female

machota mannish woman

machote *m* hammer; he-man

machucadura, machucamiento pounding, crushing

machucar *see* **machacar**

machucho level-headed; mature

machuelo clove of garlic; heart (of onion)

machuno mannish

madaleno *sl* secret policeman

madam *f sl* police (force)

madeja hank, skein; slovenly person; ~ **sin cuenda** hopeless muddle; **enredarse la** ~ to become involved; **(él) es una** ~ **de nervios** he is a bundle of nerves

¹ **madera** *sl* police (force)

² **madera** wood, timber; ¡**toca** ~! touch wood!; **saber a la** ~ to be a chip off the old block; **tener** ~ **de** to be made of the right stuff for

maderable (of trees) providing useful wood

maderaje, maderamen *m* timber-work

maderar to plank

maderería timber-yard, *US* lumber-yard

maderero *m* timber/lumber-merchant; carpenter

maderista *m* lumberman

¹ **madero** *sl* policeman

² **madero** beam; piece of wood; blockhead

madrastra stepmother; cruel mother

madraza over-affectionate mother

madre *m* mother; river-bed; ditch; main sewer; main piece; ~ **de leche** wetnurse; ~ **política** mother-in-law; **ésta es la** ~ **del cordero** this is the nub of the matter; **son ciento y la** ~ there's a whole mob of them; ¡~ **mía!** good heavens!

madrearse (of wine) to turn sour

madreperla mother-of-pearl

madrépora coral polyp; white coral

madrero attached to/dependent on one's mother

madreselva honeysuckle, woodbine

madridista *n m+f* fan of Real Madrid Football Club; *adj* of Real Madrid

madrigaleja short madrigal

madriguera warren, den

madrileño *n* native of Madrid; *adj* of Madrid

madrina godmother; patroness; **hada** ~ fairy godmother

madrona mother of spoilt children

madroñal grove of strawberry-trees

madroño strawberry-tree; tree strawberry; silk tassel

madrugada early morning; **de** ~ in the small hours

madrugador *n m* early-riser; *adj* early rising

madrugar to get up early; **a quien madruga Dios le ayuda** the early bird catches the worm

madrugón *n m* very early rising; one who habitually gets up very early; *adj* early rising

maduración *f* ripeness, maturity

madurante maturing, ripening

madurar to ripen, mature; ~**se** to ripen, grow ripe; *med* suppurate

madurez *f* maturity, ripeness, wisdom

madurillo almost ripe

maduro ripe; mature, middle-aged

maestra schoolmistress; master's wife; *bui* guideline; **abeja** ~ queen-bee

maestral *m* cell of the queen-bee; mistral, north-west wind

maestrante *m* member of a **maestranza**

maestranza fraternity of mounted knights or nobles; dockyard, arsenal

maestrazgo dignity of the grand-master (of a military order)

maestre *m* master of a military order; *naut* ship-master

maestrear *vt* to direct; trim, prune; *vi* to act domineeringly

maestrescuela cathedral canon

maestría mastery

maestro *n* master, primary teacher; maestro; *naut* mainmast; ~ **de armas** fencing master; ~ **de capilla** choirmaster; ~ **de cocina** chef; ~ **de escuela** schoolteacher; ~ **de obras** master-builder, building contractor; *adj* main, chief; **obra maestra** masterpiece; **perro** ~ trained dog

303

mafia mafia; criminal conspiracy

mafioso mafioso, member of a criminal conspiracy

maga enchantress

magante dull, torpid

magdalena madeleine, sponge-cake

magia *n* magic

mágica *n* sorceress

mágico *n* wizard; *adj* magic

magín *m* imagination, fancy

magisterio teaching; mastership; teaching profession; teachers; *chem* precipitate

magistrado magistrate, judge

magistral magisterial; pompous; pedantic

magistratura magistracy, judicature

magnanimidad *f* magnanimity

magnánimo magnanimous

magnesio magnesium; *phot* flash

magnesita meerschaum

magnético magnetic

magnetismo magnetism

magnetita lodestone

magnetización *f* magnetization

magnetizador magnetizing

magnetizar to magnetize

magnetoeléctrico electromagnetic

magnetófono, magnetofón *m* tape-recorder

magnificar to magnify, extol

magníficat *m* Magnificat; criticar el ~ to carp

magnificencia magnificence, splendour

magnífico magnificent

magnitud *f* magnitude, greatness

magno great (as epithet); Alejandro Magno Alexander the Great

mago magician, wizard; los Reyes Magos the Magi, the Three Wise Men

magosto fire (for roasting chestnuts)

magra rasher, slice of bacon

magrear *vulg sl* to grope (sexually)

magro *n* lean meat; *adj* lean

magrujo meagre

magrura leanness

magua joke; trick

magué *m sl* penis

maguey *m bot* aloe

maguillo crab-apple tree

magulladura bruise

magullamiento bruising

magullar to bruise

Maguncia Mainz

Mahoma Mohammed

mahometano Mohammedan

mahometanismo Mohammedanism

mahometista *m+f* Mohammedan

mahometizar *vt* to convert to Islam; *vi* to profess Islam

mahón *m* nankeen

mai *sl* marihuana cigarette

maicena cornflour; cornstarch

maído mewing

maitinante *m* one who attends matins

maitines *mpl* matins

maíz *m* maize, Indian corn

maizal *m* maize-field

maja beauty; attractive girl

majada sheep-fold; dung

majadal *m* pasture land of high quality

majadear *vi* (of sheep) to take shelter at night; *vt* to manure

majadería nonsense, stupidity

majaderillo bobbin (for lace-making)

majadero *n* pestle; bobbin; idiot; *adj* stupid

majador *adj* crushing, pounding

majadura *n* crushing, pounding

majagranzas *m sing+pl* stupid man

majal *m zool* school, shoal

majano landmark made of a pile of stones

majar to crush, pound; bore to death

majareta scatter-brained

majestad *f* majesty, royalty

majestuosidad *f* majesty

majestuoso majestic, stately, solemn

majeza flamboyant style/behaviour

majo *n* dandy; swaggering member of the lower classes; *adj* nonchalant; sportily dressed; blustering; *fam* handsome, smart, genial

majolar *m* white hawthorn grove

majuela fruit of white hawthorn; leather shoelace

majuelo *bot* white hawthorn

mal *n* badness, evil, injury, disease; ~ caduco epilepsy; ~ de muchos, consuelo de tontos *approx* companions in distress make sorrow the less; ~ de ojo evil eye; ~ francés syphilis; ~ menor lesser of two evils; *adj* bad, evil; *adv* bad(ly); ill; de ~ en peor from bad to worse; ~ hecho bad show; ¡menos ~! what a relief!; menos ~ que it's a good job that; sentar ~ (of food) to disagree with; tomar a ~ to take

offence at
malabar *adj:* **juegos ~es** juggling
malabarismo juggling
malabarista *m+f* juggler; confidence
trickster
Malaca Malay Peninsula
malacate *m* capstan, windlass
malaconsejado ill-advised
malacostumbrado having bad habits;
badly brought up
malacuenda sacking, oakum
málaga *m* Malaga wine
malagueña folksong of Malaga
malagueño *n* native of Malaga; *adj* of
Malaga
malandante unfortunate
malandanza misfortune, bad luck
malandar *m* wild boar
malandrín *n m* rascal; *adj* wicked
malaquita *min* malachite
Malasia Malaysia
malasio, malasiano *n+adj* Malaysian
malatía leprosy
malato leprous
malavenido at loggerheads
malaventura misfortune
malaventurado luckless
malaventuranza misfortune
malawiano *n* Malawi; *adj* of Malawi
malayo *n+adj* Malay, Malayan
malbaratador *adj* squandering
malbaratar to squander
malbaratillo junk-shop, cheap second-
hand shop
malcarado grim-faced
malcasado unfaithful (maritally)
malcasar to make s.o. marry; mismatch;
~**se** to marry an unsuitable person
malcaso treason
malcomer to eat badly
malcomido ill-fed, undernourished
malcontento *n* malcontent; *adj* discontented
malcriado ill-bred; spoilt; naughty
malcriar to spoil (a child)
maldad *f* evil; mischief
maldadoso, maldecido wicked
maldecidor *m* swearer; calumniator
maldecimiento calumny; back-biting
maldecir *vt* to curse; *vi* to speak ill (**de**
of)
maldiciente *n m+f* slanderer, backbiter;
adj evil-speaking, slanderous
maldición *f* curse

maldicho accursed
maldispuesto ill-disposed, reluctant
maldita *fam* tongue; **soltar la ~** to speak
one's mind
maldito accursed, damned; lowly; **el
Maldito** the Devil
maldivo Maldive; **Islas Maldivas** Maldive Islands
maleabilidad *f* malleability
maleable malleable
maleador *n m* corruptor, spoiler; *adj*
spoiling, corrupting
maleante *n m* evil-doer, crook; *adj*
corrupting, evil-doing
malear to spoil, damage; ~**se** to go
wrong, depart from the straight and
narrow
malecón *m* dyke, sea-wall; jetty
maledicencia slander, back-biting
maleducado *n* ill-mannered person;
boor; *adj* ill-mannered
maleficencia maleficence
maleficiar to hurt, injure; adulterate;
bewitch; corrupt
maleficio damage, injury; witchcraft,
spell
malejo poorish
maléolo ankle
malestar *m* malaise, uneasiness
maleta *f* suitcase; *mot* boot, *US* trunk;
hacer la ~ to pack (up); *fam m*
bungler, ham bullfighter
maletero railway porter; *mot* boot, *US*
trunk
maletilla *sl* aspiring bullfighter
maletín *m* small suitcase; medical bag
maletón *m* large suitcase
malevolencia malevolence
malévolo malevolent
maleza weeds, thicket
malformación *f* malformation
malgastador *n m* spendthrift; *adj* wasteful, extravagant
malgastar to misspend, squander
malgenioso angry
malhablado foul-mouthed
malhadado ill-fated
malhecho *n* misdeed; *adj* misshapen
malhechor *m* evil-doer
malherido gravely injured/wounded
malherir to injure/wound seriously
malhojo rubbish, garden refuse
malhumorado bad-tempered
malicia wickedness, malignance; sly-

ness, artfulness; innuendo

maliciar to suspect; ~**se** to have an inkling of

malicioso malicious; sly, mistrustful; risqué

malignar to malign; corrupt

malignidad *f* malignity

maligno malignant, wicked

malintencionado ill-meaning, ill-disposed

malito unwell, poorly

malmaridada *n* adultress; *adj* (of a wife) unfaithful

malmirado disliked; discourteous

malo *adj* bad, evil, mischievous, difficult, poor, wrong; **andar a malas** to be on bad terms; **de malas** in a nasty mood; **estar** ~ to be ill; **el** ~ the bad guy; **lo** ~ **es** … the trouble is …; **pie** ~ sore foot; **por malas o por buenas** by fair means or foul; **ser** ~ to be bad, naughty; **tener mala cara** to look off-colour

Malo: el ~ the Evil one; **por las malas** by force

malogrado unsuccessful, ill-fated; deceased

malograr to miss, lose; spoil; ~**se** to fail, come to naught, fall through, be a flop; come to grief; die young; break down

malogro failure; loss, waste; disappointment; early death

malón *m* Indian raid; unexpected attack

maloquear to raid

malparado in a bad state, damaged

malparar to damage, ill-treat

malparida woman who has miscarried

malparir to miscarry

malparto miscarriage

malpensado evil-minded

malquerencia ill-will, dislike

malquerer to dislike

malquistar to estrange, set at odds; ~**se** to fall out (**con** with)

malquisto disliked, unpopular

malrotador *n m* waster, spendthrift; *adj* squandering

malrotar to waste, squander

malsano unhealthy

malsín *m* talebearer, back-biter

malsinante *adj* back-biting

malsinar to speak ill of, run down

malsindad *f*, **malsinería** back-biting,

tale-bearing

malsonante ill-sounding; offensive to the ear

malsufrido impatient

malta malt

maltés *n* + *adj* Maltese

maltrabaja *m* + *f fam* idler

maltraer to treat badly

maltratamiento ill-treatment

maltrecho down-at-heel, in poor shape

malucho off-colour, groggy

malva *n bot* mallow; *adj* mauve

malvado evil

malvar to deprave

malvasía malmsey wine/grapes

malvavisco *bot* marshmallow

malvender to sell at a loss

malversación *f* embezzlement, misappropriation of funds

malversador *m* embezzler

malversar to embezzle, misappropriate

Malvinas: Islas ~ Falkland Islands

malvis *m orni* redwing

malvivir to live badly

malla mesh, meshed/netted fabric; mail (armour); tights; swimsuit

mallar *vt* to dress in a coat of mail; *vi* to make nets; be caught in a net

mallero net/mail-maker

mallete *m* gavel, mallet

mallo croquet; bowls; croquet mallet

Mallorca Majorca

mallorquín *n m* language/native of Majorca; *adj* Majorcan

mama breast; mamma

mamá mum(my), mamma

mamacallos *m sing* + *pl* simpleton

mamada *fam* suck, sucking

mamadera breast-pump; feeding-bottle; nipple

mamador *n m* sucker; *adj* sucking

mamaluco fool

mamancia foolishness

mamante, mamantón *adj* sucking

mamar to suck; *sl* booze; ~**se** to get drunk; learn without effort; **no** ~**se el dedo** to be no fool, get drunk; **dar de** ~ to suckle

mamario mammary

mamarrachada ridiculous object; botch, daub

mamarrachista *m* + *f* botcher, dauber

mamarracho ridiculous thing/person; laughing-stock; botch, daub

mambla small rounded hill

mameluco Mameluke; simpleton

mamellado nipple-shaped

mamífero n mammal; adj mamalian

mamila nipple (of man)

mamilar mammillary

mamola, mamona chuck under the chin

mamón n m bot shoot, sucker; adj fond of sucking

mamoso n panic grass; adj sucking

mamotreto memorandum book; weighty tome; bundle of documents; fam big book; monstrosity

mampara screen

mamparo naut bulkhead

mamporro blow, thump

mampostear bui to build with rubble

mampostería bui rubble-work

mampostero bui rubble-mason

mampresar to start to break in (horse)

mampuesta bui course (of bricks)

mampuesto bui rubble; rest (for fire-arm); parapet

mamujar to suck from time to time

mamullar to mutter; eat/chew having no teeth

mamut m mammoth

mana spring, source

maná manna

manada herd, pack, flock; team; a ~s in droves, galore

manadero n spring, source; herdsman, shepherd; adj springing, issuing

manante adj springing, issuing

manantial n m spring; fig source; adj flowing; agua ~ spring water

manar vt to pour out; vi to spring, flow, issue

manatí m, **manato** manatee, sea-cow

manaza large hand/paw; clumsy hand; ~s m sing + pl awkward/clumsy person

manca adj sl left, left-hand

mancamiento lack, want, deficiency; maiming

mancar vt to maim, disable; vi to be lacking

manceba concubine; lass; shop-assistant

mancebete m lad, youth

mancebía brothel

mancebo lad; shop-assistant; journey-man; bachelor

mancera plough-handle

mancilla spot, blemish; sin ~ immacu-late, pure

mancillar to stain, blemish, sully

mancipar to enslave

manco n one-armed/-handed person; sorry nag; adj one-handed/-armed; half finished

mancomún m concurrence; de ~ jointly, by consent

mancomunidad f fellowship, common-wealth

mancha spot, stain, blemish; sin ~ un-blemished; ~ solar sun-spot

manchadizo easily soiled

manchar to spot, speckle; stain; soil; discolour

manchego n native of La Mancha; adj of La Mancha

manda legacy, bequest

mandadera errand-girl

mandadero errand-boy, messenger

mandado command, order; message, errand

mandamás m big boss, top man, he-who-must-be-obeyed

mandamiento mandate, command; eccles commandment; leg writ

mandanga sluggishness

mandante commanding

mandar vt to command, order; lead; send; leave, bequeath; ~ a la mierda to tell to go to hell; ~ hacer algo to get/have something done; como Dios manda the right way, properly; vi to be in command; mi coche manda bien my car handles well; ~se to be able to get about (of invalids); be communi-cating (of rooms)

mandarina mandarin orange

mandatario leg attorney, agent

mandato mandate; injunction

mandíbula jaw; jaw-bone

mandibular pertaining to the jaw

mandil m apron (usu leather); coarse cloth

mandilar to rub (a horse) with a coarse cloth

mandilón m coward; long apron

mandioca tapioca

mando m command, mech drive; ~ a distancia remote control; ~s controls; alto ~ high command; cuadro de ~s instrument panel, dashboard; don de ~ talent for commanding; voz de ~ military order

mandoble blow with a double-handed sword; two-handed blow

mandón *n m* foreman, overseer, boss; *adj* domineering, bossy

mandrachero proprietor of gaming-house

mandracho gaming-house

mandrágora *bot* mandrake

mandria coward

mandril *m zool* mandrill; *eng* mandrel

mandrón *m* stone cannon-ball

manduca *sl* grub, nosh

manducación *f sl* eating, noshing

manducar *sl* to eat, nosh

manducatoria *see* manduca

manea fetters, shackles

manear to fetter, charm, shackle, hobble

manecilla small hand; vine tendril; watch/clock hand; *print* index

manejable manageable

manejar to manage; handle; *mot* drive

manejo handling, management; use; horsemanship; *mot* driving

maneota shackles, fetters, hobble

manera manner, way; **a ~ de** by way of; **a la ~ de** in the style of; **de mala ~** badly; **de ninguna ~** certainly not; **de todas ~s** anyway; **de ~ que** so that

manero (of hawks) tame

manflorita *m fam* cissy

manga sleeve; hose; whirlwind; *mil* line of troops; fishing net; *naut* beam; straining bag, poncho; **~ de agua** water spout; **¡a buenas horas ~s verdes!** it's about time!

mangana lariat, lasso

manganear to lasso

manganeo lassoing

manganilla trick, ploy; sleight of hand

mangante *m* scrounger, sponger; layabout; pilferer

mangar to scrounge, beg; pilfer

manglar *m* mangrove swamp

mangle *m bot* mangrove-tree

mango *bot* mango; handle

mangonada push

mangonear *vt* to handle, control, boss; *vi* to run the show, rule the roost

mangoneo running the show, ruling the roost

mangosta *zool* mongoose

mangueo *sl* scrounging, sponging; pinching

manguera hosepipe, wind-sail, water spout

manguero man who uses a hose

mangui *m sl* petty thief; untrustworthy person

manguitero leather-dresser; muff-maker

manguito muff; oversleeve; *mech* bush; collar, sleeve

maní *m* peanut

maní *f* (**manifestación**) demo (demonstration)

manía mania, craze, fad; **tener ~ a** to have a loathing for; **tener ~ de** to have a mania for; **tener ~ por** to be crazy about; **~ persecutoria** persecution complex

maníaco *n* maniac; *adj* maniacal

maniatar to handcuff, manacle

maniático *n* maniac, person with strange likes and dislikes; *adj* fussy, strange

manicomio lunatic asylum

manicorto tight-fisted

manicura manicure; manicurist

manida den, lair, haunt

manido *cul* (of game) high; trite, hackneyed

manifacero meddlesome; intriguing

manifactura form, shape

manifestación *f* manifestation, declaration; *pol* demonstration; *leg* writ

manifestador manifesting

manifestante *n m+f* demonstrator; *adj* manifesting

manifestar to manifest, show; state; *eccles* expose for adoration (the Blessed Sacrament); **~se** to demonstrate

manifiesto *n comm* manifest; *eccles* exposition; *adj* manifest, evident

manigua jungle

manigueta haft, handle

manija handle; shackles, handcuffs; brace, clamp

manijero manager

manilargo long-handed; sticky-fingered

manilense *m*, **manileño** native of Manila

manilla bracelet; handcuffs; hand (of watch)

maniobra handling, manoeuvre, shunting; *naut* rigging; tackle; **~s** *mil* manoeuvres

maniobrar to manoeuvre, shunt

maniobrero easy to handle/manoeuvre;

naut that responds well (to the rudder)

maniobrista *m naut* skilled manoeuvrer

maniota manacles, shackles

manipulación *f* manipulation

manipulador *n m* telegraph key; manipulator; *adj* manipulating

manipular to manipulate, handle

manípulo *eccles* maniple

maniqueísmo over-simplification

maniquí *m* mannequin, dummy, puppet

manir to hang (game, until it is high); *fam* handle frequently

manirroto extravagant, spendthrift

manirrotura extravagance, thriftlessness

manitas *m + f sing + pl* skilful person

manivacío empty-handed; idle

manivela *eng* crank; ~ **de arranque** *mot* starting handle

manjar *m* food, dish

manjúa sardine

mano *f* hand, forepaw, trotter; trunk (of an elephant); quire (of paper); coat (of paint), knock; ~ **de obra** labour; **a** ~ **to** hand; **a** ~ **derecha** on the (right side); **abrir la** ~ to hold out one's hand for money; **bajo** ~ underhandedly; **con las** ~**s en la masa** redhanded; **de buena** ~ on good authority; **dejado de la** ~ **de Dios** Godforsaken; **echar una** ~ to lend a hand; **hecho a** ~ hand-made; **llegar a las** ~**s** to come to blows; **tener** ~ **izquierda** to be tactful, have savoirfaire; **untar la** ~ to grease the palm of, bribe

manobrero cleaner of fountains and aqueducts

manojo handful; bunch (of keys *etc*); faggot, bundle (of twigs); **a** ~**s** abundantly

manolo low-class native of Madrid

manométrico manometric

manómetro manometer

manopla gauntlet; face-flannel; coachman's whip; knuckle-duster; mitten

manosear to handle, paw; rumple

manoseo handling; pawing; groping

manotada, manotazo slap, blow with the hand

manotear to slap, hit; wave the hands while talking; practise sleight-of-hand

manoteo hitting; waving about with the hands; sleight-of-hand

manquear to be/pretend to be onehanded

manquedad *f*, **manquera** lack of one hand/arm or both hands/arms; defect

mansalva: a ~ without danger

mansedumbre *f* mildness, gentleness; tameness

mansión *f* abode; mansion; **hacer** ~ to stop

¹ **manso** tame; meek, gentle; **mansa brisa** gentle breeze

² **manso** manor-house; manse

mansurrón too meek; gentle to a fault; very tame

¹ **manta** *m* good-for-nothing; bad workman

² **manta** blanket, travelling-rug; tossing in a blanket; **tirar de la** ~ to spill the beans, give the game away

mantaterilla coarse blanket

manteador *m* one who tosses s.o. in a blanket

mantear to toss in a blanket

manteca fat, lard, grease; *sl* lolly; ~ **de cacao** cocoa butter

mantecada type of shortcake

mantecado shortcake dough; vanilla ice-cream

mantecón *m* milksop

mantecoso greasy

manteísta *m* day-student in a seminary

mantel *m* table-cloth; *eccles* altar-cloth; **levantar los** ~**es** to clear the table

mantelería table-linen

manteleta mantelet, small scarf

mantelete *m eccles* bishop's mantle; *mil* bullet-proof screen

mantellina mantilla

mantenedor *m* president of tournament

mantenencia maintenance, support

mantener to maintain, support; hold; keep; ~**se** to live, keep o.s.; ~**se firme** to stand firm

mantenimiento maintenance; support; upkeep

manteo long cloak; tossing in a blanket; woollen skirt

mantequería dairy

mantequera churn

mantequero maker/seller of butter; butter-dish

mantequilla butter

mantero maker/seller of mantles

mantés *m* rogue, scoundrel

mantilla mantilla; saddlecloth; ~s swaddling-clothes; **estar en ~s** to be in its/one's infancy

mantillo *agri* humus; manure, compost

manto mantle, cloak; *min* stratum, layer, seam

mantón *m* large shawl; ~ **de Manila** large embroidered silk shawl

manuable manageable

manual *n m* manual, handbook; *eccles* ritual; *adj* hand

manubrio handle; crank

manucodiata *orni* bird of paradise

Manuel Emmanuel

Manuela Emma

manuella capstan bar

manufactura manufacture

manufacturar to manufacture

manufacturero *adj* manufacturing

manumisión *f* manumission, liberation

manumiso emancipated, free

manumisor *m* manumitter, liberator

manumitir to set free, emancipate

manuscribir to write by hand

manuscrito *n + adj* manuscript

manutención *f* maintenance, upkeep, support

manutener *leg* to maintain, support

manutisa *bot* sweet-william

manvacío empty-handed

manzana *bot* apple; knob; block (of houses *etc*); ~ **de Adán** Adam's apple; ~ **de la discordia** bone of contention

manzanal *m* apple orchard

manzanil *adj* of apples

manzanilla *bot* camomile; small knob; olive; pad (of animal's feet); type of pale sherry

manzano apple-tree

maña skill, cleverness, knack; bad habit; **darse ~** to manage

mañana *n m* tomorrow, future; *f* morning; ~ **por la ~** tomorrow morning; **de ~** in the morning; **de la noche a la ~** overnight; **muy de ~** early in the morning; **por la ~** in/during the morning

mañanear to rise with the lark

mañanero early-rising

mañanica, mañanita daybreak; bed-jacket

mañear to manage skilfully

mañería cunning

mañero clever, artful, handy

maño *fam* Aragonese

mañoco tapioca

mañoso skilful with one's hands; cunning

mañuela mean trick; cunning person

maoismo Maoism

maoista *n m + f + adj* Maoist

mapa *m* map

mapache *m* racoon

mapamundi *m* globe; map of the world

mapanare *f* poisonous snake

mapurite *m* *zool* skunk

maqueta scale model, maquette

maqueto (in Basque country) *pej* foreigner, 'Sassenach'

maquiavélico Machiavellian

maquiavelismo Machiavellism

maquiavelista *m + f* Machiavellian

Maquiavelo Machiavelli

maquillaje *m* make-up

maquillarse to make up

máquina machine, engine; *mil sl* machine-gun; *sl* motor-cycle; ~ **de afeitar** razor; ~ **de componer** *print* typesetter; ~ **de coser** sewing-machine; ~ **de escribir** typewriter; ~ **de vapor** steam engine; ~ **fotográfica** camera; ~ **tragaperras** slot-machine; **a toda ~** at full speed; **sala de ~s** *naut* engine-room

maquinación *f* machination

maquinador *m* contriver, schemer

maquinal mechanical; routine

maquinante planning, contriving

maquinar to machinate

maquinaria machinery; mechanics

maquinista *m + f* engine-driver; *naut* engineer

mar *m + f* sea, ocean; ~ **alta** rough sea; ~ **de fondo** swell; ~ **gruesa** heavy sea; ~ **llena, plena ~** high water; **alta ~** high seas; **baja ~** low tide; **hacerse a la ~** to put out to sea; **la ~ de** loads of, lots of

marabú *m* *orni* marabou

maracure *m* *bot* curare plant

maraña thicket, undergrowth; puzzle, fraud

marañón *m* *bot* cashew tree; cashew nut

marasmo *med* wasting away

maratoniano marathon runner

maravedí old Spanish gold coin

maravilla marvel, wonder; *bot* marigold; *bot* ivy-leaved morning glory; **a ~, a las mil ~s** very well; **de ~** marvellously; **por ~** by a fluke

maravillar to astonish; **~se** to be astonished

maravilloso marvellous

marbete *m* label, tag; sticker

marca mark; make, brand; standard; gauge; tag, label; brand; *sp* record; **~ de fábrica** trade-mark; **~ registrada** registered trade-mark; **de ~ mayor** outstanding, first-rate

marcación *f naut* bearing; taking a ship's bearing; *tel* dialling

marcador *n m* (sewing) sampler; marker; *sp* scorer, scoreboard; *adj* marking, branding

marcaje *m sp* marking; **sin ~** unmarked

marcapasos *m sing + pl med* pacemaker

marcar to mark; brand; show (the hour); *tel* dial; *sp* score; *naut* take a ship's bearing; **~ el compás** to beat time; **~ el paso** to mark time; **lavar y ~** to shampoo and set

marcear *meteor* to be rough/blustery; be March-like

marcescente withering

marcial martial, warlike

marcialidad *f* military bearing

marciano Martian

marco frame (picture, door, window *etc*); (currency unit) mark

márcola pruning-hook

marconigrama *m* marconigram, radio telegram

Marcos Mark

marcha march; progress; *mech* running; departure; *mot* gear; movement (of a watch); *naut* speed; **a largas ~s** quickly; **a toda ~** at full speed; **doblar las ~s** to go twice as fast; **en ~ atrás** in reverse; **poner en ~** to start off; **sobre la ~** on the way

marchamar to mark (goods at customs-house)

marchamo lead seal; customs-house mark

marchante *n m* dealer, shopkeeper; *adj* mercantile; commercial

marchapié *m* footboard; *naut* footrope

marchar to march, walk; go ahead; *mech* function, run; depart; *naut* make headway; **~se** to go away, depart

marchazo boaster, braggart

marchitable perishable

marchitamiento fading, withering

marchitar(se) to wither, fade

marchitez *f*, **marchidura** withering

marchito withered; faded

marea tide; gentle breeze; dew; drizzle; **~ creciente** flood tide; **~ menguante** ebb-tide; **~ muerta** neap tide; **~s vivas** spring tide; **contra viento y ~** against all opposition

mareado sick, seasick, travel-sick; dizzy

mareaje *m* seamanship; ship's course

mareante causing sea/travel-sickness; making dizzy; sea-faring

marear *vt* to sail (a ship); sell (goods); drive crazy; make dizzy; *vi* to navigate; **~se** to get sick/seasick; faint

marejada swell, surge

marejadilla slight swell

maremagnum *m* pandemonium

mareo sickness; air/sea/travel-sickness; dizziness; bother

marero *adj* (of wind) off the sea

Marfil: Costa de ~ Ivory Coast

marfil *m* ivory

marfileño *adj* (of) ivory; of the Ivory Coast

marfuz repudiated; deceitful, false

marga marl, loam; denim cloth

margar *agri* to dress with marl

margarina margarine

Margarita Margaret, Daisy

margarita pearl; *bot* marguerite, daisy; *zool* periwinkle; *min* margarite; **echar ~s a los cerdos** to throw pearls before swine; **~ de trigo** *bot* dog-daisy

margen *m* margin; edge, verge; fringe; marginal note; **~ de aproximación** margin of error; **~ de ganancia** profit-margin; **al ~ de** in addition to; on the fringe of; **estar al ~ de** to be out of it; *f* (river) bank, shore

marginación *f* underprivilege

marginado *n* underprivileged person, second-class citizen

marginal marginal; of secondary importance; **prensa ~** underground press

marginar to make notes in the margin; rule a margin/margins; leave out in the cold, leave on the fringe of society

marginoso with wide margins

margoso marly, loamy

311

marguera marl-pit
María Mary
maría *sl* housewife; *sl* marihuana; white wax taper; **baño ~** *cul* double boiler
mariano *eccles* Marian
marica *orni* magpie; thin asparagus; knave of diamonds; *m sl* queer, gay, homosexual
Maricastaña: en tiempos de ~ in olden times
maricón *m sl* queer, gay; *vulg* bugger
maricona *sl* man's handbag
maridable marriageable
maridaje *m* marriage, union
maridar to unite, join; marry; live as man and wife
marido husband
mariguana, marihuana, marijuana marihuana, cannabis
marimacho *m* mannish woman
marimandona bossy woman
marimanta hob-goblin
marimoña *bot* buttercup
marimorena *sl* shindy, punch-up
marina sea-coast; *arts* seascape; seamanship; navy, marine; **~ mercante** merchant navy
marinera sailor's blouse
marinero *n* seaman, mariner; *adj* marine; sailorlike; seaworthy; (of ships) easy to handle
marino *n* seaman, naval officer; *adj* nautical; sea
marión *m*, **marón** *n* sturgeon
marioneta puppet, marionette
maripérez *f* servant-girl
mariposa butterfly; **tuerca de ~** wing-nut; **válvula de ~** butterfly valve
mariposear to flutter about; be flighty
mariquita *ent* ladybird; *fam* pansy, queer, gay
marisabidilla know-all
mariscal marshal; **~ de campo** field-marshal
mariscar to gather shellfish
marisco shellfish; seafood
marisma swamp, morass
marisquera seafood shop/stall
marítimo maritime, marine
maritornes *f sing+pl* mannish maid-of-all-work
marjal *m* fen, marsh
marjoleta *bot* white hawthorn
marmita saucepan, stewpot

marmitón *m* scullion
mármol *m* marble; *print* imposing-stone/table
marmoleño marble-like
marmolería marble-work
marmolillo phlegmatic person; silly person
marmolista *m* marble-worker/dealer
marmoración *f* marbling; stucco
marmóreo made of marble
marmosete *m* vignette
marmota *zool* marmot; *sl* servant-girl
marmotear to jabber
maroma rope, cable, tightrope; acrobatics
maromero acrobat
marón *m* sturgeon
marqués *m* marquis
marquesa marquise
marquesina glass roof/canopy
marquesita *min* marquesite
marquetería marquetry
marquida, marquisa *vulg* prostitute
marquilla demy (paper size)
marra gap; stoneworker's hammer
márraga *text* grogram, ticking
marrajo *n m* shark; *sl* padlock; *adj* crafty, wily
marramao, marramáu *m* miaow
marranada filthiness; dirty/rotten trick; filthy thing
marranalla rabble
marrancho pig
marrana sow; filthy creature
marrano pig, swine; drum (of water wheel); *adj* filthy
marrar to miss, go astray
marras long ago; **de ~** well-known, well-remembered
marrasquino maraschino
marrazo mattock; machete
marro quoits; dodging; failure
marroco bread
marrón *n m* quoit; *sl* hundred-peseta note; **comerse un ~** to confess to a crime; *adj* brown
marroquí *n m+f* Moroccan; *m* Morocco leather; *adj* Moroccan
marroquinería Morocco leatherwork
Marruecos Morocco
marrullería *n* cunning; artful tricks; wheedling
marrullero *adj* crafty, cunning, wheedling

Marsella Marseilles

marsellés *n m* native of Marseilles; la Marsellesa the Marseillaise; *adj* of Marseilles

marsopa porpoise

Marta Martha

martagón *m bot* wild lily

Marte *m* Mars

martes *m sing+pl* Tuesday; ~ de carnestolendas/de carnaval Shrove Tuesday

martillador *adj* hammering

martillar to hammer; keep on at

martillazo hammer-stroke

martillejo smith's hammer

martilleo hammering, clattering

martillo *m* hammer; auction mart; hardware shop; hammer-headed shark; ~ pilón drop-hammer; de ~ *metal* wrought; rematear a ~ to dispose of by auction

martin pescador *m orni* kingfisher

martineta Argentinian partridge

martinete *m orni* night-heron; hammer; drop-hammer; piano hammer

martingala trick, cunning

Martinica Martinique

martinico goblin

mártir *m* martyr

martirio martyrdom

martirizador *n m* martyrizer, tormentor; *adj* martyrizing, tormenting

martirizar to martyr, torment

martirología martyrology

Maruja (familiar form of María) Molly

marxismo Marxism

marxista *n m+f +adj* Marxist

marzal *adj* (of) March

marzo March

¹ más *adv* more, most; ~ bien rather; a ~ de besides; a ~ tardar at the latest; cada vez ~ more and more; como el que ~ just like the best of them; de ~ too much; es ~ furthermore; gustar ~ to prefer; los ~ the majority; no ... ~ que only; ¿qué ~ da? what's the difference?; sin ~ ni ~ suddenly, without more ado; ya no ~ no longer

² más *m* plus; tener sus ~ y sus menos to have good and bad points

¹ mas *conj* but, yet; ~ que though; ~ si perhaps

² mas *n* farmhouse

masa mass; dough; mortar; en ~ en

masse

masada farmhouse

masadero farmer

masaje *m* massage

mascador *adj* chewing

mascadura *n* chewing

mascar to chew

máscara mask, masquerade; masquerader; baile de ~s fancy-dress ball

mascarada masquerade

mascarilla mask, half-mask; death mask

mascarón *m* large mask; ~ de proa *naut* figure-head

mascota mascot

mascujar *see* mascullar

masculinidad *f* masculinity

masculino masculine, male

mascullar to chew; mumble

masecoral *m*, masejicomar *m* sleight of hand

masera kneading-trough; cloth used for covering the dough

masería, masía farmhouse

masificación *f* mass-production

masificar to mass-produce

masilla putty

masita *mil* footwear and underclothing allowance

¹ masón *m* mash given to poultry

² masón *m* freemason

masónico masonic

masoquismo masochism

masoquista *n m+f* masochist; *adj* masochistic

masovero farmer

mastelerillo *naut* top-gallant mast

masticación *f* mastication

masticador *m* teething-ring; horse's bit

masticar to chew, masticate; ruminate

masticatorio masticatory

mastigador *m* horse's bit; upright post; trunk

mástil *m* mast; stem; shaft (of feather); neck (of stringed instrument)

mastín *m* mastiff; ~ lobero wolfhound

mástique *m* mastic

masto *hort* stock (into which the scion is grafted)

mastodonte *m* mastodon, mammoth

mastoides *adj* mastoid

mastuerzo *bot* peppercress; *fam* blockhead

masturbación *f* masturbation

masturbarse to masturbate

mata bush, shrub; brush, underbrush; *bot* mastic tree; head of hair; ~ **parda** dwarf oak; ~ **rubia** kermes oak; **saltar de la** ~ to come out of hiding

matacabras *m invar* north wind

matadero abattoir, slaughterhouse

matador *n m* killer, matador; *adj* killing

matadura *vet* harness sore

matafuego fire-extinguisher

matahombres *m sing+pl* Spanish fly

matajudío mullet

matalahuga, matala(h)uva *bot* anise; aniseed

mátalascallando *fam* hypocrite

matalobos *m sing+pl bot* wolfsbane

matalón, matalote *m* skinny old nag

matambre *m* large portion of meat

matamoros *m sing+pl* bully; braggart

matamoscas *m sing+pl* fly-swatter; fly-paper; fly spray

matanza killing, slaughter, massacre; pig-slaughtering; pig-slaughtering season; pork products

mataperrada mischievous prank

mataperros *m sing+pl* street urchin

matapiojos *m sing+pl* dragonfly

matapolvo light rain

matapulgas *m sing+pl* round-leafed mint

mataquintas *m sing+pl* cigarettes made with a cheap black tobacco

matar to kill, slay, slaughter, put to death; *carp* bevel; put out (fire/light); *arts* tone down; *sl* finish off (a marihuana cigarette); *fam* tire out; **matarlas callando** to be a wolf in sheep's clothing; **estar a** ~ to be at dagger's drawn; ~**se por** to go to any length to; ¡**que me maten!** I'll stake my life on it!

matarife *m* slaughterman, butcher

matarratas *m sing+pl* rat-poison; *fam* rot-gut

matasanos *m sing+pl* quack

matasellos *m sing+pl* postmark, cancellation stamp

matasiete *m* bully, braggart

mate *m* mate, checkmate; *bot* maté; gourd; ~ **ahogado** stalemate; **dar** ~ **a** to checkmate, make fun of

matear *bot* to shoot up, grow quickly

matemática(s) mathematics

matemático *n* mathematician; *adj* mathematical; automatic, unfailing

Mateo Matthew

materia matter, material, stuff; subject; ~ **colorante** dye-stuff; **en** ~ **de** with regard to; **entrar en** ~ to get to the point; ~ **prima** raw material

material *n m* material, stuff; equipment; ~ **fijo** permanent way; ~ **rodante** rolling stock; *adj* material, coarse

materialidad *f* materiality, outward appearance

materialismo materialism

materialista *n m+f* materialist; *adj* materialistic

materializar to materialize; ~**se** to become obsessed by material things

maternidad *f* maternity; motherhood; **casa de** ~ maternity hospital

materno maternal; **lengua materna** mother tongue

matero maté drinker

mates *fpl sl* mathematics

matidez *f* dullness

matigüelo, matihuelo kelly, tumbler (toy)

matildes *fpl sl* shares in the Compañía Telefónica, Madrid

matinal *adj* morning

matiné *m* matinée

matiz *m* tint, hue, nuance, mixing of colours; shade of meaning

matizado variegated; tinged

matizar to give a hue or shade of meaning to; blend the colours of

mato brake, coppice

matojo bush

matón *m* bully; *fam* bouncer, chucker-out

matorral *m* thicket, scrubland

matoso covered in scrub

matra woollen blanket

matraca rattle; pestering; **dar la** ~ **a** to make fun of

matraquear to rattle; make fun of

matraqueo rattle; jibing

matraquista *m+f* joker, teaser

matrería shrewdness

matrero *n* shrewd person; tramp; thug; *adj* shrewd; cunning, sly

matricida *n m+f* matricide (person); *adj* matricidal

matricidio matricide (deed)

matrícula register; matriculation; *mot* licence number; ~ **de mar** seaman's register

matriculado matriculated person
matricular to matriculate, enrol; ~se to register, enter (a competition)
matrimoniar *joc* to marry
matrimonio marriage, matrimony; *fam* married couple
matritense *adj* (of) Madrid
matriz *n f* womb; matrix, mould; *mech* female screw, nut; stub (of cheque-book); *adj* mother, head; **casa** ~ headquarters; **escritura** ~ original draft
matrona matron
matronaza respectable matron
matufia trick, fraud
Matusalén Methuselah
matute *m* smuggling
matutear to smuggle
matutero smuggler
matutinal, matutino *adj* morning
maula *f* trash, rubbish; remnant; deceit; *m+f* trickster, cheat; bad payer
maulería remnants stall/shop; trickery
maulero seller of remnants, trickster
maullador *adj* miaowing
maullar to miaow
maullido miaow
mauriciano Mauritian
Mauricio Maurice
mauritano Mauritanian
mausoleo mausoleum
maxilar maxillary
máxima maxim
máxime principally
máximo *n m* maximum; *adj* maximum, greatest
mayar to mew
mayestático majestic; **el nos** ~ the royal we/plural
mayo May; maypole; Mayday celebrations
mayólica majolica ware
mayonesa mayonnaise
mayor *n m m* major; **al por** ~ wholesale; *f* first proposition (of a syllogism); **los** ~**es** grown-ups, forefathers; *adj* greater, greatest; larger, largest; elder, eldest; main, principal; *eccles* high (altar, mass); *mus* major; **calle** ~ high street; **caza** ~ big game
mayoral coach driver; head herdsman; overseer
mayorazgo primogeniture; first-born son; heir to/owner of an entailed estate
mayordomear to manage (an estate)
mayordomía stewardship
mayordomo butler; steward
mayoría majority, coming of age
mayoridad *f* majority, full age, superiority
mayorista *m* wholesale trade; wholesaler
mayoritario *adj* majority
mayúscula capital letter
mayúsculo large, capital (of letters); tremendous
maza mace, war-club; bass drumstick; butt (of billiard cue); hub (of wheel); ~ **de gimnasia** Indian club; **la** ~ **y la mona** inseparable companions
mazacote *m* concrete; stodgy food; *fam* bore; monstrosity
mazacotudo stodgy, lumpy
mazada blow with a mace/club
mazagatos *m sing+pl* row, rumpus
mazagrán *m* cold coffee and rum
mazamorra boiled maize with honey; thick corn soup; *naut* mess made of broken biscuits
mazapán *m* marzipan
mazarí *m* thin flat brick; floor tile
mazmorra dungeon
maznar to knead; strike (hot iron)
mazo mallet; bell-clapper; bunch, bundle
mazonería masonry, brickwork
mazorca ear/cob of maize
mazorral rude, uncouth
mazote *m* mortar, cement
mazotear to strike with a club or mallet
mazurca mazurka
me me; to/for/from me; myself; to/for/from myself
meada urination; pissing; piss-stain; **la fiesta fue una** ~ the party was a laugh/scream
meadero *sl* urinal; piss-house
meados *mpl* urine, piss
meapilas *m sing+pl vulg* very devout person
mear to piss (on)
meauca *orni* shearwater
Meca Mecca
meca: andar de la ceca a la ~ to wander about aimlessly
¡mecachis! *interj* cor blimey!
mecánica mechanics; machinery; *mil sl*

fatigue duty; dirty trick

mecánico *n* mechanic, driver; *adj* mechanical; mean, servile

mecanismo mechanism

mecanizar to mechanize

mecano meccano; **un ~** a meccano set

mecanografía typewriting, typing

mecanografiar to typewrite, type

mecanográfico *adj* typewriting, typing

mecanógrafo typist

mecedor *n m* stirrer; *adj* rocking, swinging

mecedora *f* rocking-chair

mecedura *f* rocking

mecenas *m arts* patron; wealthy baker

mecha wick; fuse; match; roll of lint; larding bacon; lock (of hair); shoplifting; **aguantar ~** to stick it (out); **~s** (of hair) streaks; **a toda ~** at full speed

mechar to lard, stuff; shoplift

mechera *cul* larding-pin; shoplifter

mechero cigarette lighter, gas burner; shoplifter

mechoacán *m bot* bindwood

mechón *m* tuft, shock (of hair)

medalla medal

medallón *m* medallion; locket; large medal

médano, medaño sandbank, sand dune

media stocking; *math* mean; average; **~ diferencial** arithmetical mean; **~ proporcional** geometric mean

mediacaña picture-moulding; *carp* gouge; half-round file; curling-tongs

mediación *f* mediation

mediado *adj* half-full, half-view, halfway; **a ~s de** about the middle of

mediador *n m* mediator; *adj* mediating

mediana long billiard cue; *geom* median

medianería party wall/fence

medianero *n* mediator, go-between; *adj* middle; mediating

medianía, medianidad *f* mediocrity, moderate circumstances

mediano middling, medium; moderate, average; mediocre

medianoche *f* midnight; light savoury roll

mediante *adj* intervening; **Dios ~** God willing; *adv* by means of, through

mediar *vt* to half-fill; *vi* to be in the middle; be half-over; mediate; happen in the meantime

mediato *adj* mediatory, mediative

médica woman doctor; doctor's wife

medicación *f* medical treatment

medicamento medicine

medicar to give medicine to

medicastro quack doctor

medicina medicine; **~ casera** home remedies

medicinante medical student who practises before qualifying

medición *f* measurement, mensuration

médico *med* doctor, physician; **~ de cabecera** family doctor; **~ de plaza** bull-ring doctor; **~ forense** forensic expert; **~ partero** obstetrician

medicucho quack

medida measure(ment); step; moderation; **a ~ de** according to; **a ~ que** in proportion as; **en la ~ que** to the extent that; **hecho a ~** made to measure; **pesos y ~s** weights and measures; **tomarse las ~s** to have one's measurements taken

medidor *n m* measurer; *adj* measuring

¹ **mediero** stocking-manufacturer/-dealer; hosier

² **mediero** co-partner

medieval mediaeval, medieval

medio *n* half; middle, midst; medium; way; *pl* measures; **de ~ a ~** right in the middle; **por ~ de** by means of; **quitarse de en ~** to get out of the way; *adj* half (a); middle; average; medium; mid; **~ kilo** half a kilo; **un kilo y ~** one and a half kilos; **a ~ día** in the middle of the day; **distancia ~** average distance; **término ~** middle course; *adv* half, part(ly); **~ muerto** half-dead; **a ~ hacer** half done; **a medias** by halves

mediocridad *f* mediocrity

mediodía midday; south

medir to measure; *poet* scan; **~se** to behave with restraint

meditabundo pensive, thoughtful

meditación *f* meditation

meditar to meditate (on)

meditativo meditative

Mediterráneo Mediterranean

médium *n m* medium

medo *n + adj* Mede

medra thriving, prosperity, growth

medrar to thrive, prosper, grow

medre *m fam* rat-racc

medro progress; improvement

medroso fearful, timorous

médula *anat* marrow; **hasta la** ~ to the core

medular medullary

meduloso full of marrow

medusa jellyfish

mefítico pestilent, stinking, nauseating

megáfono megaphone

megalítico megalithic

megalito megalith

megalomanía megalomania

megalómano *n* megalomaniac

mégano dune; sandbank

mego gentle, mild

mejana islet (in a river)

mejicanismo Mexicanism

Méjico Mexico

mejido *cul* (egg) beaten with sugar and milk

mejilla *anat* cheek

mejillón *m zool* mussel

mejor *adj* better, best; ~ **postor** highest bidder; **a lo** ~ probably; **el** ~ **día** one fine day; **lo** ~ the best (thing); *adv* better, best; rather; ~ **dicho** rather, to be more exact; **tanto** ~ so much the better

mejora improvement, betterment; higher bid

mejorable improvable

mejoramiento improvement

mejorana *bot* sweet marjoram

mejorar to improve, better, ameliorate; raise (a bid), surpass; *leg* leave a special bequest to; **mejorando lo presente** present company excepted; ~**se** to improve, get better

mejunje *m* concoction

melada toast dipped in honey

melado *n* cane syrup; *adj* honey-coloured

meladura treacle

melampo *theat* prompter's candle

melancolía *bot n* melancholy, gloom

melancólico melancholic, gloomy

melancolizar to dispirit

melandro *zool* badger

melanesio *n + adj* Melanesian

melanita *min* melanite

melapia *bot* pippin

melar *adj* sweet; *v* to fill with honey; boil (sugar-cane juice) until clear

melaza molasses, treacle

melcocha honey-cake

melcochero maker of honey-cakes

melena (men's) long hair; (women's) loose hair; *zool* mane

melenudo long-haired

melero dealer in honey

melgacho dog-fish

melificado mellifluous

melificar to make honey (from)

melifluidad *f* mellifluousness

melifluo mellifluous

meliloto *n* sweet clover; *n + adj* fool(ish), simple(ton)

melindre honey fritter; over-nicety; fussiness

melindrear to act in a mincing way

melindroso mincing, over-nice, finicky

melocotón *m* peach

melocotonero peach-tree; peach seller

melodía melody

melódico melodic

melodioso melodious

melodramático melodramatic

meloja mead

melomanía melomania, fondness for music

melómano melomaniac, music-lover

melón *m* melon; *sl* head

melonar *m* melon-field

meloncillo mongoose

melonero melon-grower/seller

melosidad *f* sweetness; mildness

meloso honeyed, honey-tongued

mella nick, notch, dent; impression; **hacer** ~ **a** to leave a deep impression; cause trouble

mellar to nick, notch; dent; break a tooth from

mellizo twin (*usu* non-identical)

membrana membrane

membranáceo membranaceous

membranoso membraneous

membrete *m* letterhead, printed heading (on notepaper); memo

membrillar quince-tree orchard

membrillero quince-tree

membrillo quince; **carne de** ~ quince jelly

membrudo burly, robust

memela maize pancake

memez *f* foolish act/statement

memo *n* fool, idiot; *adj* foolish, idiotic

memorando *n* memorandum; *adj* memorable

memorándum *m* notebook; diplomatic

note
memorar to remember
memoria memory, recollection; memoir, record; dissertation; ~s a su hermana kind regards to your sister; borrarse de la ~ to fade from memory; de ~ by heart; ser flaco de ~ to have a poor memory
memorial *m* memorial, petition
memorialista *m* amanuensis
memorioso mindful
menaje *m* household furniture; school equipment
mención *f* mention
mencionar to mention, name
menchevique Menshevik
mendacidad *f* mendacity
mendaz mendacious
mendeliano Mendelian
mendicación *f* begging
mendicante *n m* mendicant; beggar; *adj* begging
mendicidad *f* mendicity, beggary
mendigante *m* beggar
mendigar to beg
mendigo beggar
mendiguez *f* beggary
mendoso mendacious
mendrugo crust of bread
meneador *adj* stirring, shaking
menear to shake, waggle; move; más vale no ~ to let sleeping dogs lie; ~se to get moving, get cracking; meneársela *vulg sl* to wank; ¡me la meneas! *vulg sl iron* big deal!
meneo shaking, wagging; shake, wag
menester *m* need, want; haber ~ to need; ser ~ to be necessary
menesteroso needy
menestra vegetable stew
menestral artisan, craftsman
menestralería craftsmanship
menestralía craftsmen, body/guild of craftsmen
menfita *min* onyx
mengano so-and-so; what's-his-name
mengua diminution; waning; decline; decrease; en ~ de to the detriment of
menguado *n* wretch; *adj* diminished, impaired; weak-spirited; wretched
menguante *n f* low water; decline; *adj* decreasing; waning
menguar to diminish, lessen; decline; fall off; wane

menhir *m* megalith; obelisk
menina maid-of-honour
menisco *phys* surface tension
menopausia menopause, change of life
menor *n m+f* minor; al por ~ retail; *adj* smaller, smallest; younger, youngest; ~ de edad under age
Menorca Minorca
menorquín *n m*, **menorquina** *f* native of Minorca; *adj* Minorcan
menos less, least; fewer, fewest; except (for); *math* minus; ~ mal que ... it's a good job that ...; a ~ que unless; de ~ less; echar de ~ to miss; las cuatro ~ cuarto a quarter to four; ni mucho ~ far from it; venir a ~ to come down in the world
menoscabar to lessen, detract from; *fig* whittle away; spoil
menoscabo lessening, impairing
menospreciable despicable
menospreciador *n m* despiser; *adj* despising
menospreciar to despise, undervalue, underestimate
menospreciativo despising
menosprecio contempt, scorn
mensaje *m* message
mensajería public conveyance; stage-coach; ~s shipping line; public transportation corporation
mensajero messenger
menstruación *f* menstruation
menstruar to menstruate
mensual monthly
mensualidad *f* month's pay/salary; monthly payment/instalment
ménsula bracket, elbow-rest; *archi* corbel
mensura measure
mensurabilidad *f* mensurability
mensurador, mensural *adj* measuring
mensurar to measure
menta *bot* mint, peppermint
mentalidad *f* mentality
mentalización *f* indoctrination
mentalizar to indoctrinate
mentar to name, mention
mente *f* mind
mentecatería foolishness, nonsense
mentecatez *f* stupidity
mentecato dim-wit, foolish person
mentir to lie; ~ con to disagree with; ~ más que siete to be an incurable liar

mentira lie; ~ **piadosa** white lie; **parecer** ~ to be hard to believe

mentirilla, mentirijilla white lie

mentiroso *n m* liar; *adj* lying

mentís *m* denial; **dar un ~ a** to give the lie to

mentol *m* menthol

menú *m* set menu; ~ **del día** today's special

menudear *vt* to give a detailed account of; repeat often; *vi* to happen often; become frequent; go into great detail

menudencia trifle, minute detail; ~s offal, giblets

menudeo repetition, recurrence; retail trade

menudero dealer in tripe, offal and giblets

menudillos *mpl* giblets

menudo *n* blood, stomach and feet of slaughtered livestock; ~s small change; *adj* small, tiny, petite; ¡**menuda sorpresa!** talk about a surprise!; **ganado ~** young livestock; **gente menuda** children, kids

meñique *n m* little finger/toe; *adj* little

meódromo *vulg joc* piss-house

meollo brains; essence, pith; marrow

meón *adj vulg* frequently pissing

meple *m bot* maple; ~ **moteado** bird's-eye maple

mequetrefe *m* conceited and ostentatious person

merar to mix (*usu* with water)

merca *fam* purchase

mercachifle *m* pedlar, street vendor; *pej* twopenny-halfpenny shopkeeper

mercadear to trade, traffic

mercader *m*, **mercadante** *m* merchant

mercadera tradesman's/shopkeeper's wife

mercadería merchandise

mercado market; ~ **nacional** home market

mercaduría merchandise

mercancía merchandise; article; **tren de ~s** goods train, *US* freight train

mercante *n m* merchant ship; *adj* merchant

mercantil mercantile

mercantilismo mercantilism

mercar to purchase

merced grace, favour, mercy; ~ **a** thanks to; **a ~ de** at the mercy of;

hacer la ~ de +*infin* to be so kind as +*infin*; **vuestra ~** your grace, your honour, sir

mercenario *n* + *adj* mercenary

mercería haberdasher's, draper's; *US* dry-goods store; haberdashery, drapery, dry goods

mercero draper, haberdasher

mercúrico mercuric

Mercurio Mercury

mercurio mercury, quicksilver

merdellón *adj* filthy, slovenly (*usu* of a servant)

merdoso filthy

merecedor deserving, worthy

merecer to deserve, merit; ~ **la pena** to be worth the trouble

merecido *n* just deserts; *adj* well-deserved

merecimiento merit

merendar *vt* to have for tea, picnic on; *vi* to have tea; have a snack, picnic

merendero place to have tea/a picnic; open-air café

merendona slap-up tea; beanfeast

merengue *n m* meringue; **los ~s** Real Madrid Football Club; *adj invar* of Real Madrid

meretricio meretricious

meretriz *f* prostitute

merey *f* cashew tree

merganzar *m orni* merganser

mergo *orni* diver

meridiana couch; nap, forty winks; meridian; **a la ~** at noon

meridiano *n* meridian; *adj* bright, meridian

meridional southern

merienda tea, afternoon snack; ~ **campestre** picnic

meritísimo most worthy

mérito merit, worth; **atribuirse el ~** to take the glory; **hacer ~ de** to mention, name-drop; **hacer ~s** to build up one's reputation

meritorio *n* employee who starts on a very low salary; *adj* meritorious

merla blackbird

Merlín: saber más que ~ to be very knowledgeable/wise

merlín *m* magician; *naut* marline

merlo dazed, stunned

merluza hake; *sl* **coger una ~** to get sozzled/pissed

merluzo *adj sl* foolish

merma decrease; leakage

mermar to decrease; leak; *fam* evaporate

mermelada jam; ~ **de naranja** marmalade

mero mere, simple

merodeador *n m* marauder; *adj* marauding

merodear to maraud; hang about

merodeo *n* marauding

merodista *m* marauder

mersa vulgar, uncouth person

mes *m* month; monthly wages; *med* menses; ~**es mayores** last months of pregnancy, last months before harvest; **al** ~ per month, monthly

mesa table, flat-topped desk; plateau; landing (of staircase); *print* case; board (meals); set, rubber (of cards); ~ **franca** open table; ~ **redonda** round table, table d'hôte; *naut* ~**s de guarnición** channels; **hacer** ~ **gallega** to make a clean sweep; **levantar la** ~ to clear the table; **media** ~ servants' table; **poner la** ~ to lay the table

mesada monthly pay

mesana mizzen-mast; mizzen-sail

mesar to pull the hair/beard

mescal, mezcal liquor made from the American agave

mescolanza medley, mixture; jumble

meseguería payment for guarding the harvest

meseguero harvest watchman

mesero worker paid by the month

meseta table-land; landing (of stairs)

mesiánico Messianic

mesianismo Messianism

Mesías *n* Messiah

mesilla small table; board; wager; ~ **de noche** bedside table

mesmedad *f* sameness

mesmerismo mesmerism

mesmo *see* mismo

mesnada armed retinue

mesnadería wages of an armed follower

mesnadero armed follower

mesón *m* inn

mesonaje *m* district where there are many inns

mesonero *n* innkeeper, host; *adj* serving at an inn

mesonista *m* waiter at an inn

mesta cattle-owners' guild

mestal *m* barren piece of land

mestizaje *m* cross-breeding

mestizar to cross(-breed)

mestizo *n + adj* half-breed, half-caste

mesura moderation, restraint; dignity

mesurar to moderate, restrain

meta goal; winning-post, finishing-line; aim

metabolismo metabolism

metafísica metaphysics

metafísico *n* metaphysician; *adj* metaphysical

metafonía metaphony

metáfora metaphor

metafórico metaphorical

metaforizar to employ metaphors; express by means of metaphors

metal *m* metal; timbre (of voice); *mus* brass; **el vil** ~ filthy lucre

metálica metallurgy

metálico *n* metal-worker; cash; *adj* metallic

metalizarse to become obsessed with money

metalurgia metallurgy

metalúrgico *n* metallurgist; *adj* metallurgical

metamórfico metamorphic

metamorfismo metamorphism

metamorfosear to metamorphose

metamorfosis *f sing + pl* metamorphosis

metano methane

metatarso *anat* metatarsus

metedor *m* smuggler

meteduría smuggling

metempsicosis *f* metempsychosis

metemuertos *m sing + pl theat* stagehand; nosey-parker

meteórico meteoric

meteorito meteorite

meteoro meteor

meteorología meteorology

meteorológico meteorological

meteorologista *m + f* meteorologist

meter to put, place, shove, introduce; *sp* score; stick in; cause, start; stake, bet; ~ **mentiras** to tell lies; ~ **ruido** to make a noise; **a todo** ~ as fast as possible; ~**se** to butt in, meddle; ~**se a** to set o.s. up as; ~**se con** to pick on; pick a quarrel with; ~**se en política** to get involved in politics

metesillas y sacamuertos *m sing + pl theat*

stagehand
meticón *m* busybody, nosey-parker
meticuloso meticulous
metido *n* punch below the ribs/below the belt; dressing-down; *adj* close, compressed; **estar ~ en** to be into; **estar muy ~ con** to be close with
metileno methylene
metílico, metilo methyl
metimiento interference
metódico methodical, formal
metodismo systematic method; *eccles* Methodism
metodista *m + f* Methodist
método method
metodología methodology
metoposcopia metoposcopy
metraje *cin* length; **corto ~** short film; **largo ~** feature film
metralla shrapnel; *sl* small change
metrallar to fire shrapnel
metralleta sub-machine gun
métrica prosody, poesy
métrico *adj* metrical, metric
metrificador *m* versifier
metrificar to put into verse
metro metre; underground (railway), tube, *US* subway
metrónomo metronome
metrópoli *f* metropolis; *eccles* archiepiscopal church
metropolitano *n* underground railway; metropolitan (archbishop); *adj* metropolitan
mexcal *see* **mescal**
meya spider-crab
mezcla mixture, blend; *text* tweed
mezclador *n m* mixer, blender; *adj* mixing, blending
mezcladora *cul* food-mixer
mezcladura, mezclamiento mixture, medley, mixing
mezclar to mix, mingle, blend; **~se** to mingle; intermarry
mezclilla *text* tweed
mezcolanza mixture; jumble
mezquindad *f* meanness, paltriness
mezquino mean, niggardly, paltry
mezquita mosque; *sl joc* toilet, lavatory
mezquital clump of mesquite bushes
¹ **mi** my
² **mi** *mus* mi
mí me, myself
miaja crumb; bit

miar to mew, miaow
miasmático miasmal, miasmatic
miau *m* mew, miaow
mica female monkey
Micaela Michèle
micción *f* micturition
micénico Mycenaean
mico *m* monkey, long-tailed ape; kid; brat; randy man; **volverse ~** to be at the end of one's tether
micología mycology
micra micron
micro *rad abbr* mike
microbio microbe; *sl* small child
microbiología microbiology
microbiológico microbiological
microbiólogo microbiologist
microbús *m* minibus
microcefalia microcephaly
microcéfalo microcephalic
microcosmo microcosm
microfilme *m* microfilm
micrófono microphone
micrografía micrography
microlentilla contact lens
micrómetro micrometer
micromilímetro micron
microordenador *m* home-computer
microorganismo micro-organism
microprocesador *m* silicon chip
microcomputador *m* minicomputer
microscópico microscopic(al)
microscopio microscope
microsurco microgroove, long-playing record
michino pussy-cat, kitty
micho puss
miedo fear, dread; **~ cerval** panic; **~ escénico** stage-fright; **dar ~ a** to scare, frighten; **de ~** terrific, fantastic; **tener ~** to be afraid
miedoso fearful; timorous
miel honey; **~ de caña** molasses; **luna de ~** honeymoon; **no hay ~ sin hiel** there's no rose without a thorn
mielgo twin; *bot* lucerne; *agri* winnowing fork
mielitis *f med* medullar inflammation
miembro member; limb
mienta *see* **menta**
mientes *fpl* mind, thought; **caer en ~** to come to mind; **poner ~ en** to think about; **traer a las ~** to call to mind
mientras while, whilst; **~ no** unless; **~**

que while; ~ **tanto** meanwhile

miércoles *m sing+pl* Wednesday; ~ **de ceniza** Ash Wednesday

mierda *vulg* shit, filth; mess-up, muck-up; *sl* marihuana; **¡vete a la ~!** go to hell!

mierdica little pip-squeak

mies *f* wheat, corn; harvest; **~es** grain fields

miga crumb (soft part of bread); marrow; essence; **~s** fried bread-crumbs; **tiene ~** there's something to it; **hacer buenas/malas ~s** to get on well/badly (**con** with); **hacer ~s** to smash

migaja scrap of bread

migajada, migajica, migajilla, migajuela tiny scrap of bread

migar to crumble; break into tiny pieces

migración *f* migration

migraña *med* migraine

migratorio migratory

Miguel Michael

miguelete *m* municipal policeman (in Basque Country)

Miguelito, Miguelín Mike, Mick, Mickey

mijar *m* millet-field

mijo millet

mil thousand, thousandth

miladi *f* milady

milagrero *adj* miracle-working

milagro miracle, wonder, marvel; **de ~** by a fluke, by the skin of one's teeth

milagroso miraculous, marvellous

milamores *f sing+pl bot* valerian

milano (negro) *orni* kite

mildeu *n* mildew

milenaria *n* millenarian

milenario *n* millennium; *adj* millennial; age-old

milenrama *bot* yarrow, milfoil

milésimo thousandth

¹**milhojas** *f sing+pl bot* milfoil, yarrow

²**milhojas** *m sing+pl* puff/flaky pastry

¹**mili** *f fam* military service, conscription; **tener mucha ~** to be very experienced

²**mili** *m+f* member of the military wing of ETA

miliamperio *elect* milliampere

milicia militia; military arts; military service

miliciano *n* militiaman; *adj* military

milico *sl pej* soldier

miligramo milligram

mililitro millilitre

milímetro millimetre

militante militant

militar *n* officer; soldier, army man; *adj* army, military; *v* to serve in the army; militate; **~ en** *pol* to be active in

militara wife/widow/daughter of a soldier

militarada military coup d'état

militarismo militarism

militarización *f* militarization

militarizar to militarize

militarón *m* old soldier, old campaigner

militarote *m* reactionary army officer, blimp

militroncho *sl* soldier

milo earthworm

miloca owl

milocha kite (plaything)

milonga family party; popular festival; song; folk-dance; *sl* lie, untruth

milor *m* milord; **~es** my lords

milpiés *m sing+pl* millipede

milla mile

millar thousand; **a ~es** by the thousand

millarada *approx* a thousand; **echar ~s** to pretend to be wealthy

millón *m* million

millonada large sum of money; **valer una ~** to be worth a fortune

millonario millionaire; having over a million inhabitants

millonésimo millionth

mimado pampered, spoilt

mimador *m* coaxer

mimar to pamper, spoil; pet, cuddle

mimbre *m bot* osier, willow; wicker

mimbrear(se) to sway, bend

mimbreño osier-like

mimbrera osier

mimbroso made of wickerwork

mimético mimetic

mimetismo mimetism, mimicry

mímica sign language; mimicry

mímico *adj* mimic

mimo mime; petting, caressing

mimoso pampered, spoilt; fussy, finicky

mina *min+mil* mine; lead (of a pencil); *fig* gold-mine; **beneficiar una ~** to work/exploit a mine; **volar la ~** to let the cat out of the bag

minador *n m* miner; *mil* sapper; mining engineer; *naut* minelayer; *adj* mining, minelaying

minal pertaining to a mine

minar to mine, burrow; sap, undermine

minarete *m* minaret

mineraje *m* mining; ~ **a tajo abierto** open-cast mining

mineral *n m* mineral, ore; spring, source; ~ **bruto** crude ore; **agua** ~ fresh spring water

mineralogía mineralogy

mineralógico mineralogical

mineralogista *m + f* mineralogist

minería mining, body of miners

minero *n* miner, mine operator; mine owner; *adj* mining

minga *vulg sl* penis, prick

mingitorio urinal

mingo red ball (in billiards); *vulg sl* penis, prick

miniatura miniature

miniaturista *m + f* miniature-painter

minifalda miniskirt

minifundio smallholding

minifundista *m + f* smallholder

mínima *mus* minim; tiny bit

minimizar to minimize, belittle

mínimo *n* minimum; *adj* minimal, least, smallest

minina *vulg sl* penis, prick

minino pussy-cat

minio red lead

ministerio ministry; **Ministerio de Hacienda** Treasury

ministrable *m* one in line for a ministerial appointment

ministrador, ministrante ministrant

ministrar *vi* to minister; *vt* to supply

ministril *m* minstrel

ministro minister; ~ **de Hacienda** *equiv* Chancellor of the Exchequer; ~ **sin cartera** minister without portfolio

minitaxi *m* minicab

minitaxista *m + f* minicab driver

minoración *f* minoration; reduction

minorar to lessen

minorativo *adj* lessening

minoría minority

minoritario *adj* (of) minority

minotauro Minotaur

minucia trifle, tiny point

minuciosidad *f* minuteness

minucioso minute, meticulous

minué *m* minuet

minusválido handicapped/disabled person; **los ~s** the handicapped/disabled

minuta first draft; bill for fees; menu

minutar to prepare a first draft of

minutero minute-hand (of clock/watch)

minuto minute

miñón *m* rural policeman

miñona *print* 7-point type

mío, mía, míos, mías my, mine; **ella es amiga mía** she is a friend of mine

miocardio *med* myocardium

miografía *med* myograph

miope *n m + f* short/near-sighted person; *adj* myopic, short-sighted

miopía short-sightedness

miosotis *f sing + pl bot* forget-me-not

miqueta chuck under the chin

mira gun-sight; levelling-rod; design; aim; *bui* rule; **a la ~** on the look-out; **con ~s a** with a view to

mirada look, glance, view, gaze; ~ **fija** stare; **echar una ~** to take a glance

miradero viewing-point

mirado thoughtful, considerate; discreet; **bien ~** all in all

mirador *m* balcony, viewing-point

miradura *n* looking

miraguano *bot* fan-palm

miramiento consideration, respect; **sin ~s** without ceremony

miranda elevated place; vantage-point

mirante *n m + f* onlooker; *adj* looking

mirar *vt* to look at/on; watch, observe; glance at; consider; ~ **con buenos ojos** to look upon favourably; ~ **de hito en hito** to look up and down; ~ **de reojo** to look askance at; **mirándolo bien** all things considered; *vi* to look, face; ~ **por** to look after, look out for; ~ **que** +*subj* to see to it that; **~se** to look at each other; **~se en él** to take an example/warning from him

mirasol *m bot* sunflower

miriagramo myriagram

mirialitro myrialitre

miriámetro myriametre

miriápodo, miriópodo *ent* centipede

mirífico marvellous, fabulous

mirilla peep-hole

miriñaque *m* crinoline; trinket, bauble

mirística nutmeg-tree

mirlarse to give o.s. an air of importance

mirlo *orni* blackbird; *sl* tongue; air of importance; ~ **blanco** rara avis

mirón *n m* looker-on; gawper, peeping-tom; *adj* gawping, gazing

mirra myrrh

mirrado perfumed with myrrh

mirto myrtle

misa mass; ~ **rezada/mayor** low/high mass; **ir a** ~ to go to church; ~ **del gallo** midnight mass; **ayudar a** ~ to serve mass; **eso va a** ~ it's the gospel truth; **¡que digan** ~**!** let them talk if they want to!

misacantano priest who celebrates mass for the first time

misal *m* missal

misantropía misanthropy

misantrópico misanthropic

misántropo misanthropist

misar *fam* to say/hear mass

misario acolyte, altar-server

miscelánea miscellany

misceláneo miscellaneous

miserable *n m* wretch; *adj* wretched, unhappy; mean, miserly, stingy; wicked, evil

miserear to be stingy

miseria misery, wretchedness; meanness, stinginess; pittance; poverty

misericordia mercy, pity; dagger; *eccles* misericord (on choir-stall seat); asylum, poor-house

misericordioso merciful

misero excessively church-going; sanctimonious

mísero wretched, unhappy; stingy, miserly

misil *m space* + *mil* missile; ~ **de crucero** cruise missile

misión *f* mission

misionar to reprimand; preach

misionario messenger, agent; *pol* member of a mission

misionero missionary

Misisipí *m* Mississippi

misiva missive, letter

misivo *adj* missive, sent

mismo *adj* same, self-same, very; **el** ~ **hombre** the same man; **él** ~ **lo hizo** he did it himself; **eso** ~ that very thing; **lo** ~ the same thing; *adv* right; **ahora** ~ right now; **aquí** ~ right here; **así** ~ likewise, also; **lo** ~ **que** just as (if), just like

misoginia misogyny

misógino *n m* misogynist; *adj* misogynous

mistar to mumble

míster *m fam* (football) trainer

misterio mystery

misterioso mysterious

mística study of the spiritual and contemplative life; mysticism

místico *n* mystic; *adj* mystical, dreamy

misticón hopelessly dreamy

mistificar to cheat, swindle; mystify

mitad *f* half, centre, middle; **a** ~ **de camino** half-way there; **a la** ~ half-way through; **por la** ~ down the middle

mítico mythical

mitigación *f* mitigation

mitigador, **mitigante** mitigating

mitigar to mitigate

mitin *m pol* meeting, rally; **dar un** ~ to kick up a rumpus

mito myth

mitología mythology

mitológico mythological

mitólogo, **mitologista** *m* + *f* mythologist

mitón *m* mitten

mitote *m* noisy party; uproar; fastidiousness

mitotero roistering; fastidious

mitra mitre

mitrado *n* bishop; archbishop; *adj* mitred

mixtifiori *m* pot-pourri; hotch-potch

mixto *n* compound; *adj* mixed, cross-bred; **tren** ~ combined passenger and goods train

mixtura mixture

mixturero mixing

miz(o) pussy; **¡**~ ~**!** puss, puss!

mnemónica, mnemotécnica mnemonics

mobiliario *n* furniture; *adj* movable, personal

moblaje *m* furniture

moblar to furnish

moca mocha

mocadero handkerchief

mocarro *pej* snot; **tener** ~**s** to have a snotty nose

mocasín *m* moccasin

mocear to sow wild oats

mocedad *f* youth

mocerío lads, boys

mocero lascivious, womanizing

mocetón *m* strapping youth

mocetona fine buxom lass

moción *f* motion

moco nasal mucous; *fam* snot; *metal* slag; wax drippings (from candle); *bot* love-lies-bleeding; **limpiarse los** ~s to blow one's nose; **no es ~ de pavo** it's not to be sneezed at; **tener** ~s to have a running nose

mocosidad *f* mucosity

mocoso *n* kid, brat; snotty-nosed child; *adj* dirty-nosed, snotty-nosed

mochales: estar ~ to be crazy

mocheta *archi* quoin, corner-stone

mochete *m orni* sparrow-hawk

mochil *m* farmer's boy

mochila rucksack, haversack

mochilero carrier

mocho *n* butt-end; *adj* shorn, lopped off, mutilated

mochuelo *orni* little owl; **cargar con el ~** to carry the can

moda fashion, mode, trend; **a la última ~** in the latest fashion, trendy; **estar de ~** to be fashionable; **pasado de ~** out of fashion

modales *mpl* manners

modalidad *f* kind, type; *sp* category

modelar to model, shape

modelo *f* fashion model; *m* pattern, model

moderación *f* moderation

moderado moderate

moderador *n m* moderator; *TV* chairman of informal discussion programme; *adj* moderating

moderante moderating

moderar to moderate, restrain

moderativo, moderatorio moderating

modernidad *f* modernity

modernismo modernism

modernista *n m+f* modernist; *adj* modernistic

modernizar to modernize; ~se to get up to date

moderno *n+adj* modern

modestia modesty

modesto modest

modicidad *f* moderateness

módico moderate

modificación *f* modification

modificador *n m* modifier; *adj* modifying

modificar to modify

modificativo modificative

modillón *m archi* bracket

modismo idiom

modista *m+f* dressmaker, courtier; ~ **de sombreros** milliner

modistería dressmaking; fashion shop, boutique

modistilla *fam* dressmaker, seamstress

modo way, manner; *gramm* mood; mode; ~ **de ser** disposition; **a ~ de** by way of; **a ~** correctly, properly; **al ~ de** in the manner of; **de este/ese ~** like this/that; **de otro ~** otherwise; **de todos ~s** in any case, anyhow; **malos ~s** brusqueness; ~ **de empleo** instructions for use

modorra lethargy, drowsiness

modorrar to make drowsy

modorrilla *mil* third night watch

modorro *adj* drowsy, lethargic, stupid

modoso well-behaved

modrego clumsy fellow

modulación *f* modulation

modulador *n m* modulator; *adj* modulating

modular to modulate

módulo *archi* module; *math* modulus; *mus* modulation; furniture unit; *numis* size of coins, medals *etc*

mofa scoffing; **hacer ~ de** to scoff at

mofador *n m* scoffer, jeerer; *adj* scoffing, jeering

mofadura *see* mofa

mofante *see* mofador

mofar to scoff, jeer; ~**se de** to scoff at

mofeta *min* fire-damp; *zool* skunk

mófler *m mot* silencer, muffler

moflete *m* chubby-cheek

mogol *n m* (**mogola** *f*)+*adj* Mogul, Mongol, Mongolian

Mogolia Mongolia

mogólico *adj* Mongolian

mogollón *m* sponger, scrounger; *sl* large quantity; **comer de ~** to sponge

mogote *m* hillock; corn-rick

mogrollo sponger; rustic

moharra spearhead

mohecer to become mildewed

mohín *m* grimace

mohina grudge

mohino *n* (cards) one playing solo against several; *adj* sullen; sad

moho mould, mildew

mohoso mouldy, mildewed

Moisés Moses

moisés *m* wicker cradle; carrycot

mojada, mojadura wetting, moistening

mojador *n m* soaker, wetter; *adj* soaking, wetting

mojama salted tuna

mojar to wet; dunk; *sl* celebrate (by drinking); **~se** to get wet

mojarrilla joker, punster

moje *m* broth

mojicón *m* punch (in the face); sponge-cake

mojiganga masquerade

mojigatería prudishness, narrow-mindedness

mojigato *n* prude; *adj* prudish

mojón *m* landmark; *vulg* turd

mojona placing of landmarks

mojonera landmark

mojonero gauger

moldadura moulding; **~ de inyecciones** injection moulding

moldar to mould, cast

molde *n* mould, matrix; **letra de ~** print; **pan de ~** sandwich loaf; **venir de ~** to be just right, just what the doctor ordered

moldeador *n m* cast-maker; *adj* moulding

moldear to mould, cast; make a moulding for

¹ **mole** *f* pile, heap

² **mole** *n m* meat fricassee with chilli sauce; *adj* soft

molécula molecule

moledor *n m* grinder, crusher; bore; *adj* grinding, crushing; boring

moledura grinding

molendero miller; chocolate-maker

moleña millstone

moler to mill, grind; *fam* bore; **~ a palos** to give a good hiding to

molestador *m* annoying person

molestar to disturb, annoy, irritate; **~se** to bother, put o.s. out

molestia annoyance, irritation, discomfort

molesto troublesome, annoying

molicie *f* softness

molienda milling, grinding

moliente: corriente y ~ common-or-garden

molificación *f* mollification

molificar to mollify

molificativo mollifying

molido: estar ~ to be fagged out

molimiento grinding

molinera miller's wife; mill-woman

molinero *n* miller; *adj* ready to be ground

molinete *m* windlass; turnstile; pinwheel; *naut* winch

molinillo hand-operated mill; coffee-grinder; (toy) windmill

molino mill, grinder; **~ de sangre** tread-mill; **comulgar con ruedas de ~** to swallow anything; **llevar agua al ~** to have one's eye on the main chance; **~ de viento/de agua** wind/watermill

molitivo mollient

molón *sl* attractive

molondro layabout

molotov: cóctel ~ Molotov cocktail

molusco mollusc

molla lean cut of meat; *fam* (of people) fat

mollar soft, tender; gullible

mollate *m* cheap table wine, plonk

mollear to grow soft and tender; give way easily

molleja gizzard, sweetbread

mollejón *m* millstone; fat slob

mollera *anat* crown; *fig* head, nut, brains; **duro de ~** thick-headed

molletudo chubby-faced

mollina, mollizna mist, drizzle

mollinar, mollizmar to drizzle

momentáneo momentary

momento moment; time; *mech* momentum; **al ~** at once; **de ~, por el ~** for the time being; **de un ~ a otro** any time now

momería mummery

momia mummy; *fam* very lean person

momificación *f* mummification

momificar to mummify, embalm

momio *n* bargain; cushy well-paid job; *adj* lean, meagre

momo buffoonery; bogeyman

mona female monkey; copy-cat; drunken bout; **coger una ~** to get sozzled; **dormir la ~** to sleep it off

monacal monastic, monkish

monacato monasticism

monacillo *see* **monaguillo**

monada monkey-trick; grimace; pretty little girl

monaguillo, monago acolyte, altar-server; choirboy

monarca *m* monarch

monarquía monarchy

monárquico monarchist, royalist

monarquismo monarchism

monarquista *n m+f +adj* monarchist.

royalist

monasterial monastic

monasterio monastery

monástico monastic

monda (act of) cleaning/peeling/pruning/ trimming; **es la** ~ it's really funny; it's the limit

mondadientes *m sing + pl* toothpick

mondador *n m* cleaner, pruner, peeler; *adj* cleaning, pruning, peeling

mondar to prune; peel; clean, clear; shell; shear; ~**se de risa** to split one's sides laughing

mondo bare, stripped clean; unadulterated

mondón *m* tree-trunk stripped of its bark

mondonga kitchen wench

mondongo entrails, innards; *vulg* turd

mondonguería tripe shop/stall

mondonguero tripe dealer

moneda coin; currency; ~ **común** commonplace; ~ **de vellón** debased currency; ~ **suelta** small change; **casa de** ~ mint; **pagar en la misma** ~ to repay in the same coin

monedar to coin

monedería mint

monedero purse; coiner; ~ **falso** counterfeiter

monegasco Monegasque

monería grimace; attractive ways (of little children); trifle, bauble

monesco monkeyish

monetario monetary

monfí *m* Moorish highwayman

mongólico *adj* Mongolian

monicaco scamp

monición *f* publication of banns

monigote *m* lay-brother; puppet; nobody; bad painting/sculpture

Monipodio: patio de ~ den of thieves

monis (*pl* **monises**) *m fam* money

monja nun

monje *m* monk

monjil nun-like, prudish

monjío nunship, taking of the veil

mono monkey, ape; scamp; overalls; *sl* drug withdrawal syndrome, cold turkey; assistant picador; *adj* pretty, attractive

monobsesivo having a one-track mind

monoceronte *m* unicorn

monociclo monocycle

monocilíndrico *adj* single-cylinder

monocordio monochord

monocromata *n* monochrome

monocromo *adj* monochrome

monóculo *n* monocle; *adj* one-eyed

monodía *mus* monody

monogamia monogamy

monógamo *n + adj* monogamous

monografía monograph

monográfico monographic

monograma monogram

monolítico monolithic

monolito monolith

monolitismo *pol* diehard patriotism

monologar to soliloquize

monólogo monologue, soliloquy

monomanía monomania

monopastos *m sing + pl* simple one-wheeled pulley

monopatín *n* skateboard

monopatinador *m* skateboarder

monopatinar to skateboard

monoplano *aer* monoplane

monopolio monopoly

monopolizar to monopolize

monosabio picador's assistant

monosilábico monosyllabic

monosílabo monosyllable

monoteísmo monotheism

monoteísta *n m + f* monotheist; *adj* monotheistic

monotipia monotype

monotipista *m* monotyper

monotonía monotony

monótono monotonous

monovalente: espejo ~ one-way mirror

monseñor *m* monseigneur

monserga same old rigmarole; gibberish

monstruo monster, freak

monstruosidad *f* monstrosity

monstruoso monstrous, hideous

monta amount, sum; *mil* bugle call to mount; mounting; stud farm; **de poca** ~ of small account

montacargas *m sing + pl* goods lift, hoist

montadero mounting-block

montado mounted; **artillería montada** horse artillery; **un hombre** ~ **a caballo** a man on a horse; *tech* set, built-in

montador *m* mounting block; *elect + mot* fitter

montadura trooper's accoutrements; setting (of gem)

montaje *m* setting up, installation,

assembly, montage; décor; ~ **publicitario** publicity stunt

montanero forester

montano mountainous

montantear to brag, boast

montaña mountain; highland

montañés *n* highlander; *adj* highland, mountain

montañoso mountainous

montar *vt* to mount, set (gem); cover (a mare); cock a gun; *vi* to ride; go on horseback; be important; ~ **en cólera** to fly into a rage; ~ **a pelo** to ride bareback; ~ **la guardia** to mount guard; ~ **una tienda/un negocio** to open a shop/start a business

montaraz *n m* forester; *adj* wild

monte *m* mountain, mount; woodland; (cards) pool, kitty; ~ **alto** forest; ~ **bajo** thicket, brush; ~ **de piedad** non-profit-making pawnshop; **no todo el** ~ **es orégano** life is not all a bed of roses

montecillo hillock

montepío widows' and orphans' fund

montera cloth cap; glass roof; *naut* skysail; bullfighter's cap; **ponerse ... por** ~ to cock a snook at

monterería cap-factory

monterero maker/seller of caps

montería hunting, hunt

montero hunter, huntsman

montés, montesino (of animals) wild

montgomery *m* duffle-coat

montículo mound

montón *m* heap, pile, stack; **un** ~ **de** a lot of

montonero guerrilla

montuoso hilly, wooded

montura mount, saddle; spectacles frame; mounting, setting (for gem)

monumento monument

monzón *m* monsoon

moño bun, topknot; crest; **estar hasta el** ~ to be fed up; **ponerse** ~**s** to put on airs

mopa mop

M.O.P.U. (Ministerio de Obras Públicas y Urbanismo) Ministry of Public Works and Town-Planning (*equiv* Ministry of Works)

moquear to snivel; (of the nose) run; be at the awkward age (between childhood and adulthood)

moquero handkerchief

moqueta moquette; fitted carpet

moquete *m* punch on the nose

moquetear to punch on the nose

moquillo *vet* distemper, pip

mora *bot* blackberry, mulberry

moraco *sl* Moroccan, Moor, Arab

morada abode, dwelling; stay, sojourn

morado purple

morador *m* dweller

¹ **moral** *f* morals, morale, morality

² **moral** *m* mulberry-tree

moraleja moral

moralidad *f* morality

moralista *m+f* moralist

moralizador *m* moralizer

moralizar to moralize

morar to dwell

moratoria *comm+leg* moratorium

morbidez *f* softness

mórbido soft; *med* morbid

morbilidad *f* sick rate

morbo disease; ~ **comicial** epilepsy; ~ **gálico** venereal disease; ~ **regio** jaundice

morbosidad *f* morbidity; *med* sickness rate

morboso morbid; sick

morciguillo *zool* bat

morcilla black pudding; *theat* stale joke; **meter** ~ *theat* to ad lib

morcillero maker of black puddings; *theat* gagger, ad libber

morcillo fleshy/muscular part of the arm

morcón *m* large black pudding

mordacidad *f* mordacity

mordaz mordant, biting

mordaza gag, muzzle; clamp; (railway) fishplate

mordedor biting

mordedura bite

morder to bite, nip, nibble; **no** ~**se la lengua** not to mince one's words; **está que muerde** he is hopping mad

mordicar to gnaw, nibble; sting

mordiente biting

mordisco bite, pinch

mordisquear to nibble (at), gnaw (at)

morena brown bread; *agri* new rick; brunette

morenazo dark and handsome

morenillo a little on the dark side

moreno *n* coloured/dark-complexioned person; *adj* brown, dark-complexioned, brunette

morera *bot* mulberry-tree

morería Moorish quarter

moretón *m* bruise

morfa *bot* citrus scab; *sl* morphine

morfema *m* morpheme

Morfeo Morpheus

morfina morphine

morfinómano morphine addict

morfología morphology

morfológico morphological

morganático morganatic

moribundo dying, moribund

moriche *m* palm-tree

moriego Moorish

morigeración *f* temperance, moderation

morigerado temperate, moderate

morigerar to restrain, moderate

morir to die; ~se to die away, be dying

morisco Moor converted to Christianity; animal that does not fatten

morisma Moorish faith; Moorish people

morisqueta Moorish trick; deception

mormón *m*, mormona Mormon

mormonismo Mormonism

moro *n m* Moor, Mohammedan; ~ de paz peace-loving person; ~s y cristianos rumpus; hay ~s en la costa there's trouble in the offing; *adj* Moorish

morocha vigorous

moroncha bald

morosidad *f* slowness

moroso *n* bad debt; person slow to pay debts; *adj* tardy, slow; defaulting (in payment)

morra *anat* crown

morrada punch in the face; butt with the head

morral *m* nose-bag, knapsack; *fam* clod, rustic

morrillo pebble

morriña nostalgia, melancholy, blues

¹ morro *zool* snout; *anat* thick lips; knob; pebble; headland; estar de ~s to be sulky

² morro purring

morrocotudo terrific

morrón *n m* crash; darse un ~ to come a cropper; *adj* red (of peppers)

morrudo big-snouted

morsa walrus

mortadela mortadella

mortaja shroud, winding-sheet; cigar-

ette paper

mortalidad *f* mortality

mortandad *f* slaughter; loss of life

mortecino dying, weak, feeble, dim

morterada *mil* discharge of shrapnel/grapeshot

mortero mortar

mortecino carrion

mortífero deadly, lethal

mortificación *f* mortification

mortificar to mortify

mortuorio *n* funeral; *adj* of the dead; casa mortuoria house of mourning

moruno Moorish

mosaico *n* mosaic; *adj* Mosaic, of Moses

mosaísmo Mosaic law

mosca fly; *fam* cash; ~ de burro horse-fly; es una ~ muerta he/she looks as though he/she is incapable of doing anything wrong; estar con la ~ detrás de la oreja to smell a rat; papar ~s to gape; por si las ~s just in case; ~s sparks; ~s volantes *med* black spots before one's eyes

moscarda gadfly, blowfly

moscardón *m* bumble-bee; drone; botfly; *fam* pest, bore; hornet; blue-bottle

moscareta *orni* flycatcher

moscatel *n m* +*adj* muscatel

mosco gnat, mosquito

moscón *n m* large fly, bluebottle; bore, pest; *adj* droning

moscona hussy

mosconear to pester

moscovita *n m*+*f* +*adj* Muscovite

Moscú *f* Moscow

mosén title given to clergymen in Aragon and Catalonia

mosqueado spotted; suspicious

mosqueador *m* fly-scarer; *fam* tail

mosquear to shoo off; ~se to get angry or suspicious

mosqueo fly-catching

mosquete *m* musket

mosquetero musketeer; *theat* spectator standing in the pit

mosquita small fly; ~ muerta hypocrite

mosquitero mosquito net; ~ común *orni* chiffchaff

mosquito gnat, mosquito

mostacero mustard pot

mostacho bushy moustache

mostachoso having a large moustache

mostaza mustard, mustard-seed; *mil* grape-shot

mostear (of wine) to put into old vats

mostela *agri* sheaf

mosto must; unfermented grape-juice

mostrable demonstrable

mostrador *n m* counter (of shop); bar (in café *etc*) clock-/watch-face; *adj* showing, pointing

mostrar to show

mostrenco stray(ed), homeless, ownerless; dense, stupid; **bienes ~s** unclaimed property

mota speck, mite, mote; bank of earth; *text* minor defect

mote *m* nickname

motear to speckle

motejador *m* mocker, scoffer

motejar to nickname

motete *m mus* motet

motilón *n m* lay-brother; *adj* with cropped hair

motín *m* mutiny

motivación *f* motivation

motivar to motivate, cause

motivo *n* cause, reason; motive; motif; **bajo ningún ~** in no circumstances; **con ~ de** because of

¹ **moto** *f* motorcycle

² **moto** guidepost, landmark

motobomba motor-pump

motocicleta motorcycle

motociclista *m+f* motorcyclist

motón *m naut* block, pulley

motonave *f* motor-ship

motor *n m* motor, engine; **~ de explosión** internal combustion engine; **~ de dos tiempos** two-stroke engine; **~ de reacción/a chorro** jet engine; *adj* motor

motora speedboat, motor-boat

motoricón *m sl* motorcycle policeman

motorismo motorcycling

motorista *m+f* motorcyclist; motorscooter rider; motorcycle policeman

motorizar to motorize

motril *m* boy shop-assistant

motriz *adj* motive, driving

movedizo movable, shifting; **arenas movedizas** quicksands

movedura movement; *med* miscarriage

mover *vt* to move, shift; persuade; excite, stir up; cause; *vi med* to miscarry; *agri* bud; **~se** to move, get a

move on; *naut* heave

movible movable; flighty, fickle

movida *sl* happening

moviente *adj* moving; motive

móvil *n m* motive; *adj* mobile, portable

movilidad *f* mobility

movilización *f* mobilization

movilizar to mobilize

movimiento move(ment), motion; life; *mus* tempo; *naut* heaving; **~ oratorio** oratorical gesture; **~ alternativo** reciprocating motion; **juguete de ~** mechanical toy, clockwork toy; *comm* **~ de mercancías** volume of business, turnover

moyana lie, falsehood; dog-biscuit

moza lass, girl; servant, waitress

mozalbete *m* lad, beardless youth

mozallón *m* strapping lad

mozambiqueño Mozambican

mozárabe *n m* Christian living in Moorish part of Spain; *adj* Mozarabic

mozo young man, youth; servant; waiter; **~ de estación** porter

mozuelo young lad

mtro (ministro) *pol* minister

¹ **mu** moo

² **mu** *sl* absolutely nothing, nix; **no decir ni ~** not to say a word

mucamo servant

mucilaginoso mucilaginous, slimy

mucílago slime

mucosidad *f* mucosity

mucoso mucous

muchacha girl; maid (servant)

muchachada childish prank; crowd of children

muchachear to fool about; play pranks

muchachería *see* **muchachada**

muchachez *f* puerility

muchachil youthful

muchacho boy, lad, young man

muchachote *m* hefty lad; tomboy

muchedumbre *f* crowd; a lot

mucho *adj* much, a lot of, loads of; *adv* much, a lot; hard; long; **~ más** a lot more; **como ~** at the outside, at best; **ni ~ menos** far from it; **trabajar ~** to work hard

muda change of clothes/bedlinen *etc*; *orni* moult(ing time)

mudable changeable

mudanza removal; mutation, change

mudar to change, move, remove,

moult; ~ **de color** to go pale; ~ **de parecer** to change one's mind/opinion;
~**se** to change, move house, change
one's clothes

mudéjar *m+f* Spanish Muslim living
under Christian rule; *adj* Mudejar

mudez *f* dumbness

mudo dumb, silent

mueblaje *m* furniture

mueblería furniture factory; furniture
shop

mueblista *m* furniture maker/seller

mueca grimace; **hacer** ~s to pull faces

muecín *m* muezzin

muela upper millstone; grindstone;
anat molar; flat-topped hill; ~ **del
juicio** wisdom tooth; **echar las** ~s
to cut one's teeth; **dolor de** ~s toothache

muellaje *m naut* port/harbour dues

muelle *n m* pier, jetty, quay, wharf, *US*
dock; railway goods platform; *adj*
soft, easy

muérdago *bot* mistletoe

muérgano useless thing/person

muermo *vet* glanders

muermoso *vet* glandered

muerte *f* death; **dar** ~ **a** to kill; **de mala**
~ of poor quality, grotty; **estar a la** ~
to be at death's door; **odiar a** ~ to hate
the guts of

muerto *n* dead man; *adj* dead; ~ **de frío**
frozen to death; ~ **de risa** helpless
with laughter; **estar** ~ **de curiosidad** to
be dying of curiosity/filled with curiosity; **hacerse el** ~ to feign dead, lie
doggo

muesca notch, nick

muestra sample, specimen; sign, sign-
board; model, pattern; *mil* roll-call; ~
de fuerza show of strength; **dar** ~s
de to show signs of; **feria de** ~s trade
fair

muestrario collection of samples;
sample-book

mufla muffle (of furnace); kiln

muga landmark

mugido bellow, lowing, mooing

mugir to bellow, low, moo

mugre *f* filth, grime

mugriento filthy, grimy

mugrón *m bot* shoot

muguete *m bot* lily-of-the-valley

mujer *f* woman, wife; ¡~! good gracious, woman!; ~ **de casa** housewife;
~ **de mala vida,** ~ **pública** prostitute;
~ **fatal** femme fatale

mujeriego *n* womanizer; *adj* keen on
women

mula she-mule

muladar *m* dung-heap

muladí *m* Spanish convert to Islam

mular *adj* of mules

mulatero *see* **mulero**

mulato mulatto

**MULC (Mando Único de Lucha Con-
traterrorista)** *Sp* special anti-terrorist
police force

mulero muleteer, mule-driver

muleta crutch, support; (bullfighting)
muleta

muletero *see* **mulero**

muletilla catch-phrase; slogan; cane

mulo mule

multa fine; **echar una** ~ to impose a fine

multar to fine

multicolor multicoloured

multicopiar to duplicate

multicopista *n m* duplicator; *adj* duplicating

multiforme having many forms/shapes

multimillonario multimillionaire

multinacional *n f* multinational (firm);
adj multinational

multiplicable multipliable

múltiple, múltiplo multiple

multiplicación *f* multiplication

multiplicador *m* multiplier

multiplicando *math* multiplicand

multiplicar(se) to multiply

multíplice *m see* **múltiple**

multitud *f* multitude

multitudinario multitudinous

mullido *n* soft filling; *adj* soft, sprung,
fluffed up

mullir to fluff up; loosen up; **mullírsela**
to chastise, mortify

mundanal *see* **mundano**

mundanalidad *f* worldly-mindedness

mundanear to be worldly-minded

mundanería worldliness, sophistication

mundano worldly-minded

mundial *adj* world; worldwide; **campeón**
~ world champion; **el Mundial** *fam*
World Cup

mundialmente all over the world, worldwide

mundificar to cleanse

mundificativo *adj* cleansing

mundillo world (in a limited sense); ~ **del espectáculo** world of show-business

mundo world; **el ~ es un pañuelo** it's a small world; **gran ~** high society, jet-set; **no es cosa del otro ~** it's nothing to write home about; **no ser de este ~** to be very unworldly; **tener ~** to be sophisticated; **todo el ~** everybody; **valer un ~** to be worth its/his *etc* weight in gold; **ver ~** to see the world

mundología savoir-faire

munición *f* munition, ammunition; **de ~** government issue; **municiones** provisions, supplies

municipal *n m* municipal policeman; *adj* municipal

municipalidad *f* municipality

munícipe *m* citizen, burgess

municipio township; town hall; municipality

munificencia munificence

muñeca *anat* wrist; doll; hopscotch; dressmaker's dummy

muñeco doll, puppet; ~ **de nieve** snow-man

muñequera watch-strap

muñequería over-dressing; (of men) effeminacy in attire

muñir to call, summon

muñón *m* stump (of limb); *mech* pivot; *mil* trunnion

muñonera *mech* socket; *mil* trunnion plate

murajes *mpl bot* pimpernel

muralla wall; *mil* rampart

murar to wall in/up/round

murciélago *zool* bat

murmujear *see* **murmurar**

murmullo murmur, whisper, rustle

murmuración *f* gossip-mongering, backbiting

murmurador *n m* murmurer, gossip-monger; *adj* murmuring, gossiping, gossipy

murmurar to murmur, whisper; rustle; ripple; gossip

murmurio *n* murmuring

muro wall; *mil* rampart

murria *n* melancholy, the blues; *adj* melancholy, blue

murtón *m bot* myrtleberry

murucuyá *bot* passion-flower

mus *m* card game of Basque origin

musa muse, inspiration

musaraña *zool* dormouse; shrew; **pensar en las ~s** to be in cloud-cuckooland

muscicapa *orni* fly-catcher

musco musk rat

músculo muscle, brawn

musculoso muscular, brawny

muselina muslin, cheesecloth

museo museum; art gallery

musgaño *see* **musaraña**

musgo *n* moss; *adj* dark brown

musgoso mossy

música *n* music; band; **dar ~ a un sordo** to waste one's time/breath

musicar *fam* to set to music

músico *n* musician; *adj* musical

musicógrafo musicographer

musicólogo musicologist

musicómano *n* music-lover; *adj* music-loving

musiú *m* foreigner (*esp* who speaks bad Spanish)

muslímico *n + adj* Muslim, Moslem

musmón *m* sheep-goat hybrid

mustela dogfish, rock-salmon

mustio faded, withered; gloomy

musulmán Muslim

muta pack of hounds

mutabilidad *f* mutability

mutación *f biol* mutation; *theat* change of scene

mutilación *f* mutilation

mutilado *n* crippled/physically handi-capped person; ~ **de guerra** crippled/maimed ex-serviceman; *adj* mutila-ted, maimed, crippled

mutilar to mutilate

mutis *m* refusal to talk; *theat* exit; **hacer ~** to keep quiet

mutismo voluntary silence

mutualidad *f* mutuality; mutual benefit society

mutualismo mutualism

mutuo mutual

¹ **muy** *f sl* tongue

² **muy** *adv* very

N

n *f* letter n
naba *agri* swede
nabab *m* nabob
nabal *m* turnip field
nabo turnip; bulb
nácar *m* mother-of-pearl
nacarado made of mother-of-pearl
nacarón *m* oyster shell
nacela *aer* nacelle
nacencia birth; tumour
nacer to be born; *bot* sprout; (of planets *etc*) appear; originate, issue; ~se to germinate; split near a seam
nacido *n* pimple; boil; *adj* born
naciente *n* east; *adj* very recent; rising
nacimiento birth; beginning; Christmas crib; (of moon *etc*) rising; lineage; (of river) source
nación *f* nation, country
nacional *n* native; *fam* member of the Policía Nacional; member of Franco's rebel army; *adj* national, domestic; de fabricación ~ home-produced, made in Spain
nacionalidad *f* nationality
nacionalismo nationalism
nacionalista *n m+f* nationallist; *adj* nationalist(ic)
nacionalización *f* nationalization; naturalization
nacionalizar to nationalize; naturalize
nacionalsindicalista *n m+f +adj* national syndicalist
nacionalsocialismo national socialism, nazism
nacionalsocialista *n m+f +adj* national socialist, nazi
nada nothing; nothingness; nonentity; not at all; de ~ (after thanks) don't mention it, it's a pleasure, you're welcome; ~ de eso not so; ~ de nuevo nothing new; ¡en ~! not at all!; ¡por ~ del mundo! no way!, in no circumstances!
nadaderas *fpl* water-wings
nadadero swimming place

nadador *n m* swimmer; *adj* swimming
nadar to swim; float; ~ en to abound in
nadería trifle, bagatelle
nadie nobody, no one; (after negation) anybody, anyone; Don Nadie nonentity
nado: a ~ afloat; cruzar a ~ to swim across
nafta naphtha; petrol
naftalina naphthaline
nagual *m* wizard, magician
naguas *fpl* petticoat
nailon *m* nylon
naipe *m* playing card; dar el ~ por otra cosa to be very skilful; dársele a uno el ~ to be lucky at cards
najarse *sl* to run away, escape
nalgas *fpl* buttocks, rump, backside
nalgatorio *fam* backside
nango stupid
nalgudo big-bottomed
nalguear to wiggle the backside
nana *fam* grandma; lullaby; nursemaid
¡nanai! *sl* no!; no fear!
nanear to waddle
nano *sl* little boy
nansa fish trap; fish-pond
nao *f naut* vessel; ~ capitana flagship
napea wood nymph
napelo *bot* wolfsbane
napoleónico Napoleonic
Nápoles Naples
napolitano Neapolitan
naquerar *sl* to speak
naranja *n* orange; ~ cajel/agria bitter orange; ~ sanguina blood orange; media ~ *fam* better half, spouse; *adj* orange-coloured; ¡ ~s de la China! rubbish!; nothing doing!
naranjada orangeade
naranjado orange-coloured
naranjal *m* orange grove
naranjero *n* orange grower; orange-tree; *sl* type of sub-machine gun; *adj* orange; orange-sized
naranjo orange-tree; dolt

narcisismo narcissism

narcisista *m+f* narcissist

¹ **narciso** *bot* narcissus; **∼ trompón** daffodil

² **narciso** fob, dandy

narcótico narcotic

narcotismo narcotism

narcotización *f* narcotization

narcotizador *n* narcotizer; *adj* narcotizing

narcotizar to narcotize

narcotraficante *m* drug trafficker

narcotráfico drug traffic

nardo *bot* spikenard

narigón *n m* large nose; *adj* big-nosed

narigudo long-nosed

narguile *m* hookah

nariz *f* nose; nostril; sense of smell; (of wine) bouquet; nozzle; *naut* cutwater; **¡narices!** balls!; **cerrar la puerta en las narices de alguien** to shut the door in s.o.'s face; **harto hasta las narices** fed up to the back teeth; **meter la ∼ por todas partes** to be a busybody; **tener (agarrado) por las narices** to lead by the nose

narizota large ugly nose

narizotas *m sing+pl* big-nosed person

narizudo big-nosed

narrable tellable

narración *f* narrative; narration

narrador *n m* narrator; *adj* narrating

narrar to narrate

narrativa narrative

narria sledge; fat woman

narval *n zool* narwhal

nasa fishnet; fish trap; angler's basket

nasalidad *f* nasality

nasalización *f* nasalization

nasalizar to nasalize

nasti *sl* no; quite impossible; not at all

nata cream; skin on coffee *etc*; best part; **∼s** sweetened whipped cream; **flor y ∼** flower, cream, the best of the best; **∼ batida** whipped cream

natación *f* swimming

natal natal; native; **día ∼** birthday

natalicio birthday

natalidad *f* birthrate

natarón *m* cottage cheese

natátil able to swim

natillas *fpl* custard

natividad *f* nativity, birth; Christmas

nativo native, indigenous; inborn; vernacular

nato inborn; born; **perdedor ∼** born loser

natura nature; *mus* major scale; sexual organs; **contra ∼** unnatural

naturaca *sl* naturally

natural *n* native; nature; *adj* natural; normal; plain, **es ∼** it stands to reason; **pintado del ∼** painted from life

naturaleza nature; **∼ muerta** *arts* still life; **carta de ∼** naturalization papers

naturalidad *f* naturalness; birthright

naturalismo naturalism; realism

naturalista *m+f* naturalist

naturalización *f* naturalization

naturalizar to naturalize; **∼se** to become accustomed, be naturalized

naturismo naturism; nudism

naturista *n m+f* naturist, nudist; *adj* naturist

naufragante sinking

naufragar to be shipwrecked; fall through

naufragio shipwreck; failure

náufrago shipwrecked person

náusea nausea; sick feeling; *fig* repulsion; **tener ∼s** to feel nausea

náuseo nauseousness

nauseabundo nauseous, loathsome, sickening

nauseante, nauseativo nauseating

nausear to feel nausea, feel sick

nauseoso *see* nauseabundo

nauta *m* sailor

náutica science of navigation

náutico nautical

nautilo *zool* nautilus

nava plain amid mountains

navaja razor; pocket-knife; *zool* razor clam; *zool* tusk of wild boar; **∼ de afeitar/de barba** razor; **∼ de resortes** flick-knife; **∼ de seguridad** safety razor

navajada knife thrust; razor slash

navajazo knife/razor wound

navajita penknife

navajo pool where cattle drink

Navarra Navarre

navarro Navarrese

¹ **nave** *f* ship, vessel; **∼ aérea** airship, zeppelin; **∼ de San Pedro** Roman Catholic Church; **∼ espacial** spaceship

² **nave** *archi* nave; large building

navecilla small ship; *eccles* censer
navegable navigable
navegación *f* navigation; sea voyage; shipping; ~ **costanera** coastal navigation; ~ **de bajura/altura** inshore/deep-sea navigation
navegacional navigational
navegador *n m* navigator; *adj* navigating
navegante *m* navigator
navegar *vi* to navigate; sail; steer a vessel; ~ **en conserva** to sail in convoy; *vt* to make (speed)
naveta small drawer; *eccles* censer
navicular boat-shaped
Navidad *f* Nativity, Christmas; **en ~es** at Christmas-time; **¡Felices ~es!** Merry Christmas!; **tener ... ~es** to be ... years old
navideño *adj* Christmas; **saludos ~s** Christmas greetings
naviero *n* shipowner; *adj* shipping
navío ship; ~ **de línea** battleship; ~ **de transporte** transport, cargo ship; ~ **de tres puentes** three-decker
náyade *f* naiad, water-nymph
nazareno *n* Nazarene; penitent in Holy Week procession; *fam* bucket-shop; bucket-shop owner; *adj* Nazarene
nazismo nazism
nazista *n m+f* nazi, nazist; *adj* nazi
nébeda *bot* catmint
nebladura *agri* damage caused by mist
neblina thin mist/fog
neblinoso misty
nebreda juniper grove
nebrina juniper berry
nebulón *m* hypocrite
nebulosidad *f* nebulousness
nebuloso nebulous, vague; misty, hazy
necear to talk nonsense
necedad *f* nonsense, foolishness
necesario *n* privy, toilet; *adj* necessary
neceser *m* toilet-case; sewing-case; workbox, workbasket; *mil* housewife
necesidad *f* necessity, emergency; need; evacuation of the bowel/bladder; **la ~ carece de ley** necessity knows no bounds; **hacer las ~es** *euph* to evacuate the bowel/bladder
necesitado needy
necesitar to need; compel; ~ **de** to be in need of; **se necesita camarero** waiter required
necio *n* fool; *adj* foolish, stupid

necro *sl* autopsy
necrocomio morgue, mortuary
necrófago carrion-eating
necrología necrology
necrológico necrological
necrópolis *m* burying-ground
necropsia autopsy, post-mortem examination
necroscópico pertaining to autopsy
nectarina nectarine
neerlandés *n* Dutchman; Dutch language; *adj* Dutch
nefando heinous
nefas: por fas o por ~ rightly or wrongly
nefasto ominous; sad; unlucky
nefritis *f* nephritis
negable deniable
negación *f* negation; denial; complete privation; *gramm* negative particle
negado inept; stupid
negador *m* disclaimer; denial
negalismo prohibitionism
negalista *m+f* total abstainer
negante denying, refusing
negar to deny, refuse; prohibit; disclaim; dissemble; ~ **el saludo a** to cut, refuse to greet, ignore; **~se a una visita** not to be at home to visitors; **~se a uno mismo** to exercise self-control
negativa negative; refusal
negativo *n m phot* negative; *adj phot, elect+math* negative
negligencia negligence; neglect
negligente *n* neglector; *adj* neglectful; negligent
negociabilidad *f* negotiability
negociación *f* negotiation
negociador *m* negotiator; *comm* agent
negociante *n m* businessman; dealer; *adj* engaged in trade; negotiating
negociar to negotiate; trade; deal
negocio business; transaction; affair; bargain; commerce; **~s** business matters; ~ **redondo** good business; **estar de ~s** to be on business; **viaje de ~s** business trip
negocioso active; diligent
negra negress; *mus* crochet; **~s** black chessmen
negrada crowd of negroes
negral blackish; very dark brown
negrear to turn black; look black
negrecer to blacken, become black

negrero *n* slave trader; slaver; *adj* slave trading

negreta *orni* coot

negrilla, negrita *print* bold face

negrizco *see* **negruzco**

negro *n* negro, black; ghost writer; ~ **de humo** lampblack; ~ **de la uña** tip of the finger-nail; *adj* black; gloomy; unfortunate; *sl* angry; **suerte negra** bad luck

negroide negroid

negror *m*, **negrura** blackness

negruzco blackish; very dark brown

neguijón *m* caries

neguilla *bot* love-in-a-mist; flat denial; age mark in horse's teeth

nema seal (of a letter)

nemerosa *bot* wood anemone

nemeroso sylvan

nen: de ~ *sl* not on your life, not for all the tea in China

nene *m*, **nena** *f fam* baby; darling

nenúfar *m* water-lily

neo *chem* neon; *sl* cancer

neocatolicismo Neo-Catholicism

neocatólico Neo-Catholic

neocelandés *n m* New Zealander; *adj* (of) New Zealand

neoescocés *n* + *adj* Nova Scotian

neófito neophyte, novice

neofobia neophobia, dislike of innovations

neoimpresionismo neo-impressionism

neoimpresionista neo-impressionist

neolítico neolithic

neologismo neologism

neomejicano New Mexican

neonazismo neo-nazism

neopreno: traje ~ wet-suit

neoyorquino *n* New Yorker; *adj* of New York

neozoico neozoic

nepalés *n m* Nepalese; Nepali (language); *adj* Nepalese

nepotismo nepotism

neptúneo Neptunian

Neptuno Neptune

nequáquam *adv sl* nothing doing, certainly not

nequicia perversity

nereida sea-nymph

Nerón Nero; cruel person

nerval, nerveo nerval; pertaining to the nerves

nervino *med* nerve-strengthening

nervio *anat* + *bot* nerve; *mus* string; (bookbinding) rib; *naut* stay; *fig* energy; **ataque de ~s** fit of hysterics; ~ **maestro** tendon; ~ **óptico** optic nerve

nerviosidad *f* nervousness; strength

nervioso nervous; energetic; *bot* having veins; **ponerse ~** to panic, get excited

nervosidad *f* nervousness; strength

nervoso nervous; strong; vigorous

nervudo strong-nerved; sinewy

nervura (bookbinder's) ribbing

nesciencia ignorance

nesciente ignorant

nesga (sewing) gore

néspera *bot* medlar

neto pure, unadulterated; clear; net; **en ~** net; **puro y ~** pure and simple

neumático *n* (pneumatic) tyre; *adj* pneumatic

neumococo pneumococcus

neumonía pneumonia

neumónico pulmonary

neurálgico neuralgic

neurastenia neurasthenia

neurasténico neurasthenic

neuro *sl* neurasthenia; neurasthenic

neurocirugía neurosurgery

neuroeje *m* neural

neurología neurology

neurólogo neurologist

neurona neurone, nerve cell

neurótico neurotic

neutoniano Newtonian

neutralidad *f* neutrality

neutralismo neutralism

neutralista *m* + *f* neutralist

neutralización *f* neutralization

neutralizar to neutralize

neutro neuter; neutral

nevada snowfall

nevado *n* snow-capped mountain; *adj* covered with snow

nevar to snow

nevasca snowstorm, blizzard

nevatilla *orni* pied wagtail

nevera icebox; refrigerator

nevereta *see* **nevatilla**

nevería ice-house

nevero ice seller

nevisca light snowfall

neviscar to snow lightly

nevoso snowy

nexo nexus, bond, link

ni neither, nor; ~ **con mucho** not by a long chalk; **¡~ hablar!** not on your life; ~ **que decir tiene** needless to say; ~ **siquiera** not even; ~ **tanto ~ tan calvo** moderation is best; ~ **un/una ...** not a single ...

niacina niacin

niara straw rick/stack

nicaragua *bot* garden balsam

nicaragüeño, nicaragüense Nicaraguan

nicena Nicene

nicobar *sl* to pinch, nick, filch

nicotina nicotine

nicotinismo nicotinism

nictálope *adj* night-blind

nictalopía *med* night-blindness

nicho niche

nidada clutch; brood; covey; nest of eggs

nidal *m* nest egg; basis; motive; *fam* hiding-place

nidificar to nest; build a nest

nido nest, eyrie; home; den; haunt

niebla mist, fog; *opt* film that dims the eyesight

nieta granddaughter

nieto grandson

nieve *f* snow; *sl* cocaine

nigeriano Nigerian

nigerino of Niger

nigola *naut* ratline

nigromancia necromancy

nigromante *m* necromantic

nihilismo nihilism

nihilista *n m+f +adj* nihilist

Nilo Nile

nilón *m* nylon

nimbo halo; nimbus

nimiedad *f* superfluity, triviality

nimio meticulous; insignificant

ninchi *sl* boy; friend, mate

ninfa nymph; girl; *ent* pupa

ninfea *bot* water-lily

ninfo *fam* effeminate man; pansy, cissy

ninfomanía nymphomania

ningún no, not one, not any; **de ~ modo** by no means

ninguno no, not one, not any; **de ninguna manera** by no means; **en ninguna parte** nowhere

niña little girl; baby girl; *opt* pupil; ~ **bonita** *sl* number fifteen

niñada childishness

niñear to behave childishly

niñera nursemaid; ~ **por horas** baby-sitter

niñería childish action; plaything; trifle

niñero fond of children

niñez *f* childhood

niño little boy; baby boy; child; ~ **bien** cissy; ~ **cebolla** *sl* child wearing many layers of clothing; ~ **de la piedra,** ~ **expósito** foundling; ~ **de la doctrina** charity child; ~ **de teta** babe in arms; ~ **probeta** test-tube baby; **de ~** as a child; **desde ~** from childhood

nipón *n m +adj* Nipponese, Japanese

níquel *m* nickel

niquelado nickel-plated

niqui, nikki *m* T-shirt

níspero *bot* medlar

nitidez *f* neatness, brightness

nitos *sl* nix, nothing

nitrato nitrate

nitrería saltpetre works

nítrico nitric

nitrito nitrite

nitro nitre, saltpetre

nitrogenado nitrogenous

nitrogenar to nitrogenize

nitrógeno nitrogen

nitroglicerina nitroglycerine

nitroso nitrous

nitruro nitride

nivel *m* level; plummet; watermark; ~ **de aire/burbuja** spirit level; ~ **de vida** standard of living; ~ **del suelo** ground level; ~ **longitudinal** *aer* fore-and-aft level; **a ~ level, curva de ~** contour line

nivelación *f* levelling; grading

nivelador *m* leveller; grader; ~ **de ruedas** *mot* wheel balancer

niveladora bulldozer

nivelar to level; grade; make even; ~ **el presupuesto** to balance the budget

níveo snowy

¹no no, not; ~ **bien** no sooner; ~ **obstante** notwithstanding; ~ **sea que** in case; ~ **... sino** not ... but; ~ **tal** no such thing; ~ **ya** not only; **a que ~** I bet you it isn't; **pues ~** not so; **ya ~** no longer

²no: ~ **partidista** non-party; ~ **sectario** non-sectarian

Nobel *n* Nobel Prize winner; **premio ~** Nobel Prize winner, Nobel Prize

nobelio nobelium

nobiliario pertaining to the nobility

nobilísimo most noble; honest

noble *n* nobleman; *adj* noble; honest

nobleza nobility; noblesse

nocedal *see* **nogueral**

nocente noxious; guilty

noción *f* notion; idea; element; **nociones** rudiments

nocional notional

nocivo noxious, harmful

noctambulismo sleepwalking

noctámbulo *n* sleepwalker; *fam* night-hawk; *adj* night-wandering

notffloro night-blooming

noctiluca glow-worm

noctívago *see* **noctámbulo**

nocturno *n* nocturne; *adj* nocturnal; **clase nocturna** evening class; **vida nocturna** night life

noche *f* night; evening; darkness; ignorance; night-time; **Nochebuena** Christmas Eve; **Nochevieja** New Year's Eve; **~ blanca, ~ toledana** sleepless night; **buenas ~s** good evening/night; **de ~** by night; **de la ~ a la mañana** overnight, suddenly; **esta ~** tonight; **muy de ~** late at night; **por la ~** at night; **quedarse a las buenas ~s** to be left in the dark, be disappointed

nocherniego night-wandering

nodo node

nodriza wet nurse

nódulo nodule

nogal *m*, **noguera** walnut-tree

noguerado walnut-coloured

nogueral *m* walnut-tree plantation

nolición *m* unwillingness

nómada *n m+f* nomad; *adj* nomadic

nomadismo nomadism

nombradía fame

nombramiento nomination; appointment; *mil* commission

nombrar to name; nominate; appoint; designate; **~ a dedo** to appoint undemocratically

nombre *m* name; title; reputation; renown; power of attorney; *gramm* noun; *mil* password; **~ apelativo** common noun; **~ de pila/de bautizo** Christian name; **~ postizo** alias; **~ y apellidos** full name; **de ~** by name; **no tener ~** to be unmentionable; **poner ~ a** to put a name to, set a price on; **por ~** by the name of

nomenclador *m*, **nomenclator** *m*, **nomenclatura** catalogue of names, technical vocabulary

nomeolvides *m sing+pl bot* forget-me-not

nómina list of names; payroll; money to be paid in wages

nominación *f* nomination; appointment

nominador *m* appointer

nominalismo nominalism

nominalista *n m+f* nominalist; *adj* nominalistic

nominar to nominate; name

nominativo personal; nominative; **~s** *fam* rudiments

nominilla voucher, pay warrant

nómino nominee

nomparell *print* nonpareil

non *n m* odd number; **¡~es!** *sl* not on your life!; **echar/dar ~es** to deny/refuse repeatedly; **pares y ~es** odds and evens; **quedar de ~es** to be left without a partner; *adj* odd, uneven

nonagenario *n+adj* nonagenarian

nonagésima nineteenth

nonato 'born' by Caesarean section

nono ninth

non plus ultra unsurpassable

nopal *m* prickly pear

noquear *sp* to knock out

noquero tanner

norabuena congratulations

noramala at a bad time

noray *m naut* bollard; mooring

nordestal north-eastern, north-easterly

nordeste *m* north-east

nórdico nordic

nordista *n m+f* supporter of the northern forces in U.S.A., Ireland, Vietnam *etc*; *adj* northerly

noria chain pump

norirlandés *n* inhabitant of Northern Ireland; *adj* Northern Irish

norma norm, pattern; standard

normalidad *f* normality

normalizar to normalize

Normandia Normandy

normando *n+adj* Norman

nornordeste *m* north-north-east

nornoroeste *m* north-north-west

noroeste *m* north-west

nortada northerly gale

norte *m* north; north wind; guide; *fig* aim; **~americano** North American

(*usu* from U.S.A.)

nortear to steer/stand to the northward

norteño *n* northerner; *adj* northern; northerly

nórtico northerly; northern

Noruega Norway

noruego Norwegian

nos us; to us; ourselves

nosotros we; us; ourselves

nostálgico nostalgic

nota note; mark; sign; grade in examination; annotation; renown; *comm* invoice, bill; price list; *sl* bloke; ~s notary's records, school report; **tener buenas ~s** to have a good report

notabilidad *f* notability

notabilísimo most notable

notable notable; remarkable; prominent; (school report comment) very good

notación *f* annotation; *math*+*mus* notation

notar to take note; remark; observe, notice, take notice of; annotate; criticize; reprehend; ~se to show; feel

notaría office/position of a notary

notariato title/practice of a notary

notario *n m* notary public; *adj* notarial

noticia news item; notice; piece of information; *comm* advice; ~ **remota** vague remembrance; ~s news; **atrasado de ~s** behind the times

noticiar to notify; inform

noticiario *rad*+*TV* news bulletin; *cin* newsreel

noticiero newscaster

notición *f* sensational news

notificación *f* notification

notificar to notify

notita brief note; memorandum

[1] **noto** well-known

[2] **noto** bastard

[3] **noto** south wind

notoriedad *f* notoriety

notorio notorious; well-known

novador *n* innovator; *adj* innovating

novatada joke played on apprentices, freshmen *etc*

novato novice, beginner

novecientos nine hundred

novedad *f* novelty; newness; latest news; surprise innovation; **no hay ~** there is no change; **sin ~** nothing new,

all quiet

novedoso new; novel, recent; innovating; fictional

novel new; inexperienced

novela novel; ~ **negra** crime novel; ~ **romántica** romantic novel; ~ **policíaca** detective story

novelar to write novels/stories

novelería collection of novels; fondness for novels

novelero *n* gossip-monger; tale-teller; *adj* fond of novels

novelesco novelistic, fictional

novelista *m*+*f* novelist

novelística novel-writing

noveno *adj* ninth; **novena**

noventa ninety; ninetieth

noventavo ninetieth

noventón *m* nonagenarian

novia bride; sweetheart; fiancée; *mil sl* rifle; **traje de ~** wedding dress

noviazgo betrothal, engagement

noviciado novitiate

novicio *n* novice, probationer; freshman; apprentice

noviembre *m* November

novilunio new moon

novilla heifer

novillada drove of young cattle; bullfight with young bulls

novillero pasture for young cattle; bullfight with young bulls; herdsman of young cattle

novillo young bull; **hacer ~s** to play truant/hookey

novio bridegroom; fiancé; boyfriend

novísimo newest; most recent; latest

nubada shower of rain; abundance, plenty

nubado cloudy; cloud-shaped

nube *f* cloud; multitude; *med* film on eye; shadow in precious stone; **estar entre ~s** to be in cloud-cuckoo land; ~ **de verano** passing cloud

nubecita little cloud; puff

nubífero cloud-producing

núbil nubile

nubilidad *f* nubility

nublado cloudy; overcast; *bot* blasted; mildewed

nubloso cloudy

nubosidad *f* cloudiness

nuca nape/scruff of the neck

nucleación *f* nucleation

nucleado nucleate

nuclearización *f* nuclearization

nuclearizar to nuclearize

núcleo nucleus; **fisión del ~** nuclear fission

nucleónica nucleonics

nudillo knuckle; *bui* plug; *carp* dowel

nudismo nudism

nudista *m+f* nudist

¹ **nudo** nude

² **nudo** knot; burl; tangle; *bot* joint; snag; tie, bond; *theat* crisis in drama; **~ en la garganta** lump in the throat

nudoso knotty; knotted

nuecero walnut vendor

nuégado nougat

nuera daughter-in-law

nuestro our; ours

nueva news, tidings

Nueva Escocia Nova Scotia

Nueva Zelanda New Zealand

nueve *n* nine; **a las ~** at nine o'clock; **el ~ de mayo** ninth of May; *adj* nine

nuevecito brand new; spanking new

nuevo new, modern; newly arrived; **nueva emisión** reissue; **~ flamante** brand-new; **de ~** anew, again; **¿qué hay de ~?** what's new?

nuez *f* walnut; Adam's apple; **~ de marañón** Brazil nut; **~ moscada** nutmeg

nueza *bot* bryony

nugatorio futile

nulidad *f leg* nullity; incompetency; insignificant person, a nobody; incompetent person

nulo null; of no account

numen *m* inspiration; genius

numeración *f* numeration, numbering

numerador *m* numerator, numberer

numerar to enumerate; number; calculate

numerario *n comm* cash; *adj* numerary

numérico numerical

número number; figure, numeral; (of shoes *etc*) size; (of periodicals) issue; *lit+mus* measure; rhythm; *mil* other rank, private; **~ de matrícula** *mot* registration number; **~ de serie** serial number; **~ impar** odd number; **~ par** even number; **~ sordo** *math* surd; **~ uno** number one, oneself; **hacer el ~** *sl* to behave scandalously/extravagantly; **sin ~** numberless; **tomar el ~ cambiado** to pull s.o.'s leg

numerosidad *f* numerosity

numeroso numerous

numismática numismatics

numismático *n* numismatist; *adj* numismatic

numulario *n* money-broker

nunca never; **~ más** never more; **~ jamás** *emph* never; **tierra de ~ jamás** never-never-land

nunciatura nunciature

nuncio nuncio; harbinger

nupcial nuptial

nupcialidad *f* marriage rate

nupcias *fpl* marriage

nutria otter; **~ marina** sea-otter

nutricio nutritious; *med* making up of prescriptions

nutrido: bien/mal ~ well/ill-nourished; **~ de** abounding with/in

nutrimiento food; nourishment; nutrition

nutrir to nourish, nurture; encourage, root for

nutritivo nourishing

Ñ

ñ *f* letter ñ
ñame *m* yam
ñam-ñam yum-yum
ñandú *m* American ostrich
ñaña sister, close friend
ñaño brother, close friend
ñapa bonus; **de** ~ as well, also
ñaque *m* collection of odds and ends;
rubbish
ñato snub-nosed
ñiquiñaque trash; despicable person
ñongo lazy; (of dice) loaded
ñoñería drivel; foolishness
ñoñez *f* senility, second childhood
ñoño senile
ñorda *sl* shit

O

¹ o *f* letter o

² o or; ~ sea in other words; o ... o either
... or

obcecación *f* blindness; obstinacy

obcecado blind; obstinate

obcecar to blind; ~se to go blind, get
into a disturbed state of mind

obduración *f* obduracy, obstinacy

obedecedor *n m* obeyer; *adj* obedient

obedecer to obey

obedecimiento, obediencia obedience

obediente obedient

obelisco obelisk; *print* dagger

obenques *mpl naut* shrouds

obertura *mus* overture

obesidad *f* obesity, fatness

obeso obese, fat

óbice *m* obstacle

obispado bishopric

obispal *adj* bishop

obispar to become a bishop

obispo bishop

óbito death, demise

obituario obituary

objeción *f* objection; ~ de conciencia
conscientious objection

objetar to object

objetivo *n* objective; aim; *phot* lens; *adj*
objective

objeto object; no tiene ~ there's no point
in it

objetor *n m+f* objector; ~ de conciencia conscientious objector; *adj* object-
ing

oblación *f* oblation

oblea wafer (for sealing letter); *eccles*
wafer

oblicuángulo oblique-angled

oblicuar to slant, cant

oblicuidad *f* slant, slope

oblicuo slanting, oblique

obligación *f* obligation, duty; obligaciones engagements; *comm* liabilities

obligacionista *m+f* bond-holder

obligado *n* public contractor; *mus*
obbligato; *adj* obligatory, obliged;
tight-fitting; es asunto ~ it's a must

obligante obliging

obligar to oblige, force; verse obligado a
to feel obliged to

obligatorio obligatory

obliteración *f* obliteration

obliterar to obliterate

oblongo oblong

obnubilación *f* blindness, bewilderment

óbolo obolus, coin of little value, farthing

obra work, piece of work, task; *theat*
play; *bui* fabric; building site; ~ de
about, approximately; a pie de ~ on
the spot; ~ de romanos mammoth
task; en ~ under repair; maestro de
~s clerk of works; mano de ~ labour,
work force; ¡manos a la ~! let's get
cracking; poner por ~ to put into
effect; por ~ de by virtue of

obrada day's work

obrador *n m* workshop; workman; *adv*
working

obraje *m* handicraft; manufacture

obrajero overseer, foreman

obrante *adj* working

obrar *vt* to work, carry out; *vi* to act,
behave; open one's bowels; obra en
nuestro poder su ... we are in receipt
of your ...

obrería workman's task; *eccles* repair
fund

obrerismo *pol* labour movement,
working-class movement

obrero *n* worker; *eccles* churchwarden;
adj working, labouring

obrizo (of gold) pure

obscenidad *f* obscenity

obsceno obscene

obscurantismo obscurantism; edad de ~
Dark Ages

obscurantista *n m+f+adj* obscurantist

obscuras: a ~ in the dark

obscurecer to grow dark

obscurecimiento, obscuridad *f* darkness,

shade
obscuro dark, shady, obscure, gloomy
obsequiar to entertain, treat; honour; present, give; offer
obsequias *fpl* funeral ceremony
obsequio attention, present; **ejemplar de ~** complimentary copy; **en ~ (de)** in honour (of)
obsequioso attentive
observación *f* observation, remark
observador *n m* observer; *adj* observing
observancia observance
observante observing
observar to observe, remark
observatorio observatory
obsesión *f* obsession
obsesionante obsessive, haunting
obsesionar to obsess, haunt
obsesivo obsessive
obseso obsessed
obsidiana *geol* obsidian
obsoleto obsolete
obstaculizar to obstruct
obstáculo obstacle; **carrera de ~s** obstacle race; (horse-racing) fence, jump
obstante: no ~ nevertheless
obstar to stand in the way; be an obstacle
obstétrico *n* obstetrician; *adj* obstetric
obstetricia obstetrics
obstinación *f* obstinacy
obstinado obstinate, stubborn
obstinarse en to persist in
obstrucción *f* obstruction
obstruccionismo obstructionism, bloody-mindedness
obstruccionista *n m+f +adj* obstructionist, bloody-minded (person)
obstruir to obstruct, block, clog; **~se** to get blocked up
obtención *f* obtaining
obtener to obtain, get
obturación *f* obturation, stopping up
obturador *m* stopper, plug; *med* obturator; *phot* shutter; *mot* choke, throttle
obturar to stop up, plug; *med* obturate; *mot* throttle
obtusángulo obtuse-angled
obtuso obtuse
obús *m mil* shell
obusera gunboat
obvención *f* perquisite
obviar *vt* to obviate; prevent; *vi* to stand

in the way
oca *orni* goose; *bot* oxalis
ocasión *f* occasion, chance, opportunity; **con ~ de** on the occasion of; **dar ~ a** to cause, give rise to; **de ~** second-hand
ocasionado provoking, insolent; dangerous
ocasionador causing, occasioning
ocasional *adj* occasional, chance; **mano de obra ~** casual labour
ocasionalmente by chance
ocasionar to cause, give rise to
ocaso sunset, twilight; decline
occidental western
occidente *m* west
occipucio *med* base of skull
occisión *f* slaughter; violent death
occiso slain
oceánico *adj* ocean; *naut* ocean-going
océano ocean
oceanografía oceanography
oceanográfico oceanographic(al)
oceanógrafo oceanographer
ocelote *m zool* ocelot
ociar to loiter, hang about, idle
ocio idleness; leisure
ocioso idle; lazy
ocluir *med* to occlude, close
ocre *m* ochre
octaedro octahedron
octágono octagon
octava *eccles* eight-day festival; *poet* eight-line composition; *mus* octave
octavar *m* to form octaves
octavilla leaflet; *print* octavo; *poet* eight-line stanza of octosyllabic lines; octet
octavín *m mus* piccolo
octavo *n m* eighth; *print* octavo; *adj* eighth
octogenario *n +adj* octogenarian
octógono *see* **octágono**
octosilábico octosyllabic
octosílabo octosyllable
octubre *m* October
óctuplo eight-fold, octuple
ocular *m* eye-piece, eye-glass; **testigo ~** eye-witness
oculista *n m+f +adj* oculist
ocultación *f* concealment
ocultador *n m* concealer; *adj* concealing
ocultar to conceal
ocultismo occultism
ocultista *m+f* occultist

oculto hidden; unknown

ocupación f occupation

ocupado occupied; (of toilets, phone-boxes etc) engaged

ocupador n m occupier; adj occupying

ocupante n m+f occupier, occupant; adj occupying

ocupar to occupy; employ; take up/hold (a post); ~se to concern o.s. (de with); look after, be in charge of

ocurrencia idea; witticism; remark

ocurrente witty

ocurrir to occur, happen; ~se a uno to come into one's head/mind; occur

ochavado eight-sided

ochavar to make eight-sided

ochavo piece of eight (coin)

ochenta eighty; los años ~ the eighties

ochentón n m +adj octogenarian, eighty-year-old

ocherón m octoroon

ocho eight; eighth; card with eight 'spots'; son las ~ it is eight o'clock

ochocientos eight hundred

oda ode

odalisca n odalisque; pantalón odalisca flared trousers

odiar to hate

odio hatred, hate; tener ~ a to hate

odiosidad f hatefulness

odioso hateful

odisea Odyssey

odontología odontology

odontólogo odontologist

odorante sweet-smelling, fragrant

odorífero, odorífico sweet-smelling, perfumed

odre m wineskin; joc drunkard

oesnoreste west-north-east

oesnoroeste m west-north-west

oeste m west; westerly, west wind; ~ cuarta al norte west by north; ~ cuarta al sur west by south

oessudoeste m west-south-west

ofendedor n m offender; adj offending

ofender to offend, insult; wrong; ~se to take umbrage

ofensa offence

ofensiva n mil offensive

ofensivo adj offensive

ofensor n m offender; adj offending

oferente n m+f offerer; adj offering

oferta offer; tender; bid; ley de (la) ~ y (la) demanda law of supply and demand

ofertorio offertory

office m scullery

offside: estar en ~ to be off-side/out of play

oficial n officer, official, senior apprentice; ~ mayor chief clerk; adj official

oficiala forewoman

oficialía clerkship

oficialidad f corps/body of officers

oficiar to officiate, minister, celebrate

oficina office; agency; horas de ~ business hours

oficinesco adj joc+pej office, pen-pushing

oficinista n+adj office-worker, clerk

oficio work, occupation, job; eccles service; role; official note; de ~ by trade, by profession; gajes del ~ occupational hazards; ¿qué ~ tiene usted? what is your job?

oficiosidad f officiousness

oficioso officious; unofficial; helpful, useful

ofidio zool ophidian

ofita min ophite

ofrecedor m offerer

ofrecer to offer; present; show; ~se to volunteer

ofreciente adj offering

ofrecimiento offer

ofrenda offering; ~ floral floral tribute

ofrendar to give as an offering

oftalmia med ophthalmia

oftálmico med ophthalmic

oftalmología ophthalmology

oftalmografía ophthalmography

oftalmoscopio ophthalmoscope

ofuscación f bewilderment, confusion; blindness

ofuscar to bewilder, confuse; blind

ogro ogre, bogeyman

ohmio elect ohm

óhmico elect ohmic

oíble audible

oída: de ~s by hearsay

oídio bot oidium

oído ear, hearing; aguzar los ~s to prick up one's ears; dolor de ~s ear-ache; pegarse al ~ mus to be catchy; tocar de ~ to play by ear

oidor m hearer, judge

oír to hear; listen; ~ decir que to hear that; ~ hablar de to hear of; ¡oiga!,

¡**oígame**! *tel* (on ringing up) hello

ojal *m* button-hole

¡**ojalá**! would to God!; I hope so; ~ **que** ... I do hope that ...

ojalar to make button-holes in

ojalatero armchair strategist, armchair general

ojaranzo *bot* hornbeam

ojeada glance

ojeador *m* beater (to disturb game)

ojear to glance at; raise (game)

ojeo raising (of game); shouting

ojera dark rings round eyes, bags beneath the eyes; eye-bath

ojeriza spite, ill-will; **le tengo ~** I've got it in for her

ojeroso having rings around the eyes

ojete *m* eyelet hole; *vulg sl* arsehole

ojeteador *m* stiletto

ojetear to make eyelet holes in

ojetera eyelet hole

ojialegre bright-eyed

ojienjuto dry-eyed

ojimoreno brown-eyed, dark-eyed

ojinegro black-eyed

ojiva ogive; (space travel) nose-cone; *mil* warhead

ojival ogival

ojo eye; hole; arch (of bridge); mesh (of net); ¡~! look out!; ~ **de buey** lamp cover (flush with ceiling); *naut* porthole; ~**s que no ven, corazón que no siente** what the eye does not see the heart does not grieve about; **a ~** roughly, by rule of thumb; **a ~s cerrados** without thought, *fig* blindfold; **abrir los ~s** to see things clearly/as they really are; **abrir los ~s a alguien** to undeceive s.o.; **clavar los ~s en** to fix one's gaze on, stare at; **comerse con los ~s** to devour with a look; **en un abrir y cerrar de ~s** in a flash; **hasta los ~s** *fig* up to the neck; **mal de ~** evil eye; **más valen cuatro ~s que dos** two heads are better than one; **no pegar los ~s** not to sleep a wink; **pagar el ~ de la cara** pay through the nose; **pasar los ~s por** to glance at, look over cursorily; **saltar a los ~s** to be clearly visible, appear suddenly; **tener ~** to be alert

ojuelo beady little eye

okey correct

ola wave, swell

olaje *m see* **oleaje**

ole *m* flamenco dance

¡**olé**! bravo!, well done!

oleáceo oleaginous, oily

oleada surge, waves, swell

oleaginosidad *f* oleaginousness, oiliness

oleaje *m* surge, waves

oleandro *bot* oleander

olear *eccles* to administer extreme unction

oleastro *bot* oleaster

oledero sweet-smelling, fragrant

óleo oil; *eccles* sacramental oil; ~**s** Holy Oil; **al ~** *arts* in oils; **cuadro/pintura al ~** oil painting

oleoducto oleoduct, oil pipe-line

oleografía oleograph

oleómetro oleometer

oleosidad *f* oiliness

oleoso oily

oler to smell, scent; suspect; nose into; ~ **a** to smell of

olfacción *f* smelling

olfatear to sniff, smell

olfato sense of smell; *fig* intuition

olfatorio olfactory

olíbano *bot* gum resin

oliente smelly, having a smell; **bien/mal ~** nice/evil-smelling

oliera *eccles* vessel for holy oil

oligarca *m* oligarch

oligarquía oligarchy

oligofrénico money-mad

Olimpiada Olympiad

olímpico Olympic; **juegos ~s** Olympic Games

Olimpo Olympus

olingo monkey

olio oil

oliscar to sniff; (of game) smell high

oliva olive (tree); olive branch

olivar grove of olive-trees

olivera, olivo olive-tree

olmeda clump of elm-trees, elm grove

olmo elm

O.L.P. (Organización para la Liberación de Palestina) P.L.O. (Palestine Liberation Organization)

ológrafo holograph

olor *m* smell, odour, scent; ~ **a ajo** smell of garlic; **sin ~** odourless

olorizar to perfume, scent

oloroso *n* sweet heavy sherry; *adj* fragrant, perfumed

olvidadizo forgetful; oblivious
olvidado forgotten; forgetful
olvidar to forget; leave behind
olvido oblivion; forgetfulness; oversight; **echar al/en ~** to put out of one's mind; **poner en ~** to forget
olla stewpot, whirlpool; **~ de grillos** pandemonium, deafening noise; madhouse; **~ podrida** stew, pot-pourri
ollería *m* pottery; crockery shop
ollero potter
ombligo navel, umbilical scar
ombría shady spot
ominar to augur, foretell
ominoso ominous
omisión *f* omission
omiso careless; **hacer caso ~ de** to omit, pass over, leave out
omitir to omit, miss out
ómnibus *m* (omni)bus; short stopping-train
omnímodo all-embracing
omnipotencia omnipotence, all-powerfulness
omnipotente omnipotent, all-powerful
omnipresencia omnipresence, every-whereness
omnipresente omnipresent, ubiquitous
omnisapiente omniscient, all-knowing
omnisciencia omniscience
omnisciente omniscient, all-knowing
omniscio omniscient
omnívoro omnivorous
omoplato, omóplato *anat* shoulder-blade
onagro wild ass; crossbow
onanismo onanism, masturbation
once eleven; eleventh; **a las ~** at eleven o'clock; **el ~ de febrero** (on) the eleventh of February
onceavo eleventh
oncejera snare
oncejo *orni* black martin
onceno eleventh
onda wave; flicker; *phys+rad* wave length; (sewing) scallop; **~ corta/larga/media** short/long/medium wave; **~ expansiva** *mil* shock wave (of bomb *etc*); **~ luminosa** light wave; **~ sonora** sound wave; **ella y yo estamos en la misma ~** she and I are on the same wavelength/understand one another perfectly; **estar en la ~** to be with it (modern in outlook)

ondeado (sewing) scalloping
ondeante wavy, undulating
ondear to wave, flutter, fluctuate; **~se** to sway, swing
ondeo waving
ondina water-sprite
ondisonante pounding
ondulación *f* undulation; roar (of a fast river)
ondulado undulating, rolling; corrugated
ondulante waving
ondular to wave, flutter; undulate
oneroso onerous
ónix *m min* onyx
onocrótalo *orni* gannet
onomástico *n* saint's day; *adj* onomastic; **fiesta onomástica** saint's day party
onomatopeya onomatopoeia
onomatopéyico onomatopoeic
ontogenia *bot* ontogenesis
ontogénico *bot* ontogenic
ontología ontology
ontológico ontological
ontologista *m+f* ontologist
onza ounce; **por ~s** sparingly, grudgingly
onzavo eleventh
oolito *geol* oolite
opacidad *f* opacity; opaqueness
opaco opaque; dark; dim
ópalo opal
opción *f* option, choice
OPEP (Organización de Países Exportadores de Petróleo) OPEC (Organization of Petroleum Exporting Countries)
ópera opera
operación *f* operation
operador *m* operator; *cin* cameraman; *surg* operating surgeon
operante operating, operative
operar to operate (on); **~se** to have an operation
operario workman; priest who visits sick/dying people
opereta operetta
operístico operatic
operoso wearisome
opiáceo opiate, soothing
opiado *see* **opiato**
opiata *n* opiate
opiato *adj* opiate, narcotic
opinable debatable, questionable

opinar to hold/express an opinion

opinión *f* opinion; **hacerse una** ∼ to form an opinion; **mudar de, cambiar de** ∼ to change one's opinion

opio opium

opíparo sumptious, lavish

oponer to oppose, resist; ∼**se a** to be opposed to, go against

oporto port wine

oportunidad *f* opportunity; *sp* opening

oportunismo opportunism

oportunista *n m+f +adj* opportunist

oportuno timely, appropriate

oposición *f* opposition, competitive examination; **hacer oposiciones (a)** to sit a competitive examination (for)

opositor *m* opponent; competitive examination candidate

opresión *f* oppression

opresivo oppressive

opresor *n m* oppressor; *adj* oppressive

oprimir to oppress; press (button/electric bell *etc*)

oprobiar to defame, calumniate

oprobio opprobrium

oprobioso opprobrious

optación *f rhet* optation

optar to opt, choose; ∼ **a** to aim at, be a candidate for; ∼ **por** to decide on

optativo optative

óptica optics; optician's stethoscope

óptico *n* optician; *adj* optical

optimismo optimism

optimista *n m+f* optimist; *adj* optimistic

óptimo best, most suitable/acceptable

optómetro optometer

opuesto opposed, contrary

opugnación *f* attack; refutation

opugnador attacking

opugnar to attack

opulencia opulence

opulento opulent

opúsculo short treatise

oquedad *f* hollow(ness), cavity

oquedal *m* grove of tall trees

oqueruela kink (in thread, wire *etc*)

ora now

oración *f eccles* prayer; *gramm* sentence; **partes de la** ∼ parts of speech; **oraciones** *eccles* angelus

oracional *m* prayer-book

orador *m* orator

orangután *m* orangutan

orante praying

orar to pray; make a speech

orate *m+f* lunatic; **casa de** ∼s lunatic asylum

oratoria oratory

oratorio *n m mus* orator; *adj* oratorical

orbe *m* orb, globe; world

órbita *astron* orbit; *anat* eye-socket

órdago: de ∼ first-class, super, fabulous

ordalías *fpl* trial by ordeal

¹ **orden** *f* order, command; ∼ **de batalla** battle-array; ∼ **del día** order(s) of the day

² **orden** *m* order, sequence; ∼ **del día** agenda; **llamar al** ∼ call to order; **por/en** ∼ in order; **sin** ∼ in a disorganized way

ordenación *f* disposición *f*, array; layout, arrangement

ordenada *geom* ordinate

ordenador *n m* ordainer; auditor; controller; computer; processor; *adj* ordering, arranging

ordenamiento edict, regulating; *eccles* ordaining

ordenancista *m+f* disciplinarian, martinet

ordenanza *m* messenger; *mil* orderly; (in prison) trusty

ordenar to arrange, sort out, put in order; *eccles* ordain

ordeñadero milk-pail

ordeñador *m* milker

ordeñar to milk; *agri* pick (olives); *fig* exploit

ordinariez *f* vulgarity, coarseness, rudeness

ordinario *n* ordinary; messenger; *adj* ordinary; coarse

ordinativo ordering, regulating

orea, oréada, oréade *f* wood-nymph

oreante cooling, refreshing

orear to cool, refresh, ventilate; ∼**se** to go out for a breath of fresh air

orégano marjoram

oreja (outer) ear; *fig* spy; *mech* lug; *naut* anchor-fluke; ∼ **de mercader** deaf ear; ∼ **de oro** *bot* primrose; **con las** ∼**s en punto** with ears pricked; **con las** ∼**s gachas** crestfallen

orejano (of livestock) unbranded

orejeado informed, forewarned

orejear (of dogs *etc*) to shake one's ears

orejera ear-muff, ear-cup

orejón *m* large ear; dried apple-ring,

dried peach
orejudo long-eared
oreo breeze, fresh air; airing
orfanato orphanage
orfandad f orphanhood; neglect; abandonment
orfebre m goldsmith
orfebrería gold-work
orfeón m choral society; choir
orfeonista m+f member of a choral society; chorister
organdí m organdie
organero organ-maker
orgánico organic
organillero organ-grinder, hurdy-gurdy man
organista m+f organist
órgano anat, mus (+ periodicals) organ
orgasmo orgasm
orgía orgy
orgiástico orgiastic
orgullo pride
orgulloso proud, haughty
orientación f bearings; aspect; orientation; tendency
orientador adj guiding
orientalismo orientalism
orientalista m+f orientalist
orientar to orientate, guide, direct; ~se to find one's bearings
oriente orient, east; east wind
orificar dent to give a gold filling to
orifice m goldsmith
oroficia goldsmith's craft
orificio orifice, hole
oriflama pennant, flag
origen m origin; extraction
originalidad f originality
originar to originate; ~se to originate
originario n native; adj original; native
orilla bank, shore, water's edge
orillar to trim (wallpaper); ~se mot to pull over to the side of the road
orillo selvedge
orín m rust
orina urine
orinal m chamber-pot
orinar to urinate
oriniento rustiness
orinque m naut buoy-rope
oriol m orni golden oriole
oriundo adj native
orla border, edging
orlador m borderer (one who makes borders)
orladura edge, border
orlar to border, edge; garnish
ormesí m satin
ornamentación f ornamentation
ornamentar to decorate, embellish
ornamento ornament; eccles vestments; archi moulding
ornar to ornament, decorate
ornato embellishment
ornitología ornithology
ornitológico ornithological
ornitólogo ornithologist
oro gold; ~ **batido** gold leaf; ~ **de ley** standard gold; ~ **en bruto** gold bullion; ~ **en polvo** gold dust; **de** ~ golden, of gold; **de** ~ **y azul** elegantly dressed; **hacer el** ~ **y el moro** to make one's fortune; **prometer** ~ to promise the earth; **la Edad del Oro** the golden age; **hacerse de** ~ to make a fortune
orografía orography
orográfico orographic
orógrafo orographer
orología orology
orondo fat; self-satisfied; puffed up
oropel m tinsel; cheap jewellery; flashy adornment
oropelero n tinsel maker; adj flashy, tawdry
oropéndola orni golden oriole
orozuz m licorice
orquesta orchestra; band
orquestación f orchestration
orquestar to orchestrate
orquídea orchid
orsay m: **estar en** ~ sp to be offside
ortega orni grouse
ortiga nettle
ortigarse to get stung by nettles
orto astron rising (of a star etc)
ortodoxia orthodoxy
ortodoxo orthodox, conventional
ortografía orthography, spelling
ortográfico orthographic
ortógrafo orthographer
ortopedia orthopaedics
ortopédico orthopaedic
ortopedista orthopaedist
ortóptero orthopterous
oruga caterpillar
orujo waste (from grapes/olives)
orvallar to drizzle
orvallo drizzle

orza preserving jar; *naut* luff
orzada *naut* luffing
orzaya nanny, nursemaid
orzaderas *naut* luff-boards
os you, ye; to you; yourselves
osa she-bear
osadía daring, bravery
osado brave, valiant
osar to dare
osario charnel-house
oscarizar *cin* to award an Oscar to
oscilación *f* oscillation
oscilador *n m phys* oscillator; *adj* oscillatory
oscilar to oscillate; fluctuate
oscilatorio oscillatory
oscitancia carelessness
oscular *joc* to kiss
ósculo *joc* kiss, kissing
oscuras: a ~ in the dark
oscurecer to grow dark
oscurecimiento, oscuridad *f* darkness, shade
oscuro dark, shady; obscure, gloomy
óseo osseous, bony
osera bear's lair/den
osero charnel-house
osezno bear-cub
osificación *f* ossification
osificar to ossify; ~se to become ossified
osífico ossific
osífraga *orni* osprey
oso bear; ~ **blanco** polar-bear; ~ **hormiguero** anteater; ~ **marino** fur-seal; ~ **de felpa, de trapo** teddy bear; **hacer el** ~ to act the goat
ososo bony
ostensión *f* show, manifestation
ostensivo showing, ostensive
ostentación *f* ostentation, show
ostentar to show (off); have, bear
ostentador *n m* boaster; *adj* boasting, boastful, ostentatious
ostento prodigy, wonder
ostentoso ostentatious
osteología osteology
osteológico osteological
osteólogo osteologist
osteomielitis *f* osteomyelitis
osteópata osteopath
osteopatía osteopathy
ostra oyster
ostracismo ostracism
ostral *m* oyster-bed

ostrero oysterman; oyster-bed
ostrícola, ostricultura oyster-farming
ostrífero oyster-producing
ostro south wind
ostrogodo Ostrogoth
ostugo chip, bit, piece
osudo bony
osuno bear-like
otalgia *med* ear-ache
otario silly, foolish
oteador watching (from above)
otear to watch (*usu* from a height); scan
otero hillock, knoll
oto *orni* tawny owl
otoba nutmeg-tree
otología otology
otólogo otologist
otomano Ottoman
otoñal *adj* autumnal; (of people) starting to age
otoño autumn, *US* fall
otorgador *n m* grantor; *adj* granting
otorgamiento *n* granting, awarding; *leg* drawing-up (of a will *etc*)
otorgante *m + f* grantor
otorgar to grant, award; agree to; execute (a will *etc*)
otorrinolaringología *med* study of the diseases of the ear, nose and throat
otorrinolaringólogo *med* ear, nose and throat specialist
otoscopio otoscope
otramente otherwise
otro *adj* (an)other; ~**s tantos** as many again; ~ **tanto** as much again; **al** ~ **día** the next day; **otra cosa** something else; **otra vez** again, once more; **por otra parte** on the other hand; *pron* another (one); ~**s** others
otrora in days of old
otrosí furthermore, moreover
ova seawrack; ~**s** roe
ovación *f* ovation
ovacionar to give an ovation to
ovalado, ovaloide oval, egg-shaped
ovar *orni* to lay
ovario ovary
oveja ewe; sheep; **cada** ~ **con su pareja** birds of a feather flock together
ovejero shepherd
ovejuno *adj* (of) sheep
overa *orni* ovary
overo egg-coloured; speckled; (of eyes) bulging

ovil *m* sheep-fold
ovillar to wind (string *etc*) into a ball;
~**se** to curl up into a ball
ovillo ball (of wool *etc*)
ovíparo oviparous
O.V.N.I. *m sing+pl* (**objeto volante no identificado**) U.F.O. (unidentified flying object)
ovniólogo student/believer in U.F.O.s
ovoide ovoid
ovoso full of roe
óvulo *anat* ovule
¡ox! shoo!
oxálico oxalic
oxalídeo *bot* oxalis

oxear to shoo away (*usu* birds)
oxiacanta *bot* hawthorn
oxidable liable to rust; *chem* oxidizable
oxidar to oxidize; *metal* rust; ~**se** to go rusty
oxigenable *chem* oxygenizable
oxigenar to oxygenate; ~**se** to get some fresh air
¡oxte! shoo!; keep off!; **sin decir oxte ni moxte** without so much as a by-your-leave
oyente *n m+f* listener; *adj* hearing
ozonizar to ozonize
ozono ozone

P

p *f* (letter) p; *abbr* (**página**) page

pabellón *m* pavilion; summer-house; bell-tent; national flag; outer ear

pabilo, pábilo candle-wick

Pablo Paul

pábulo food; encouragement

pacana pecan nut; pecan tree

pacedero *n* pasture, meadow, field; *adj* suitable for grazing

pacedura pasture

paceño inhabitant of La Paz, Bolivia

pacer to graze; eat away

paciencia patience

paciente *n* patient; ~ **externo** out-patient; *adj* patient

pacienzudo very patient

pacificación *f* pacification

pacificador *n m* peacemaker, appeaser; *adj* pacifying, appeasing

pacificar to pacify, calm; ~**se** to calm down

pacífico pacific, gentle

pacifismo pacifism

pacifista *n m + f + adj* pacifist

Paco Frank(ie)

paco sniper

pacotilla business venture; **de** ~ of poor quality

pacotillero pedlar, hawker

pactar to covenant, sign a pact

pacto pact, agreement; ~ **social** social contract

pachorra slowness; **gastar** ~ to be slow (at doing s.t.)

pachucho unwell, weak

padecer (de) to suffer (from); bear

padecimiento suffering

padrastro stepfather; obstacle, snag; hangnail

padrazo over-indulgent parent

padre *m* father, forebear; *vet* stallion, sire; *eccles* priest; *mil sl* conscript half-way through his military service; ~**s** parents; **Padre Nuestro** Lord's prayer; **darse o pegarse la vida** ~ to live like a king

padrear to breed; resemble one's father

padrenuestro Lord's prayer

padrino godfather; sponsor, patron; best man

padrón *m* electoral roll; census; commemorative plaque; indulgent father; stigma

paga pay, salary, wages; payment; **buena/mala** ~ prompt/slow payer

pagable payable

pagadero place/time of payment

pagado vain; ~ **de sí mismo** self-satisfied

pagador *n m* payer, paymaster, teller (in bank); *adj* paying

pagaduría paymaster's office

paganismo paganism, heathenism

pagano heathen; *fam joc* one who usually foots the bill

pagar to pay (for); repay; ~ **al contado** to pay cash down, pay on the nail; ~ **con la misma moneda** to pay like for like; ~ **el pato** to carry the can; ~ **en buena moneda** to give satisfaction; ~ **en especie** to pay in kind; ~ **un delito** to pay for a misdeed; ~ **una visita** to return a visit; ~**se de** to be conceited about

pagaré *m* promissory note; I.O.U.

página page, folio

paginación *f* pagination

paginar to page (a book)

pago payment; pay; wages; retribution; ~ **adelantado** payment in advance; ~ **contra reembolso** cash on delivery; ~ **inicial** down payment; ~ **total** full payment; **efectuar un** ~ to make a payment; **mediante el** ~ **de** on payment of

paica *m* boyfriend

painel *m carp* panel

pairar *naut* to lie to

país *m* country, land, nation; region; *arts* landscape; **del** ~ domestic, national; home-produced

paisaje *m* landscape

paisajista *m + f* landscape artist

paisana countrywoman; country dance

paisano countryman; fellow-countryman; civilian; **de** ~ in civvies

Países Bajos Low Countries, Netherlands

paja straw; trash, rubbish; **echar** ~**s** to draw lots; **hacerse una** ~ *vulg* to masturbate, wank; **hombre de** ~ man of straw, front man; **limpio de polvo y** ~ *comm* net; **no dormir en las** ~**s** to be alert

pajado straw-coloured

pajar straw-loft; rick (of straw)

pájara hen-bird; shrewd woman; paper kite; ~ **pinta** game of forfeits

pajarear to go bird-catching; loiter about

pajarera aviary

pajarería pet-shop; multitude of birds

pajarero *n* bird-catcher, bird-fancier; pet-shop keeper; *adj* merry; gaudy

pajarete *m* type of sherry

pájaro bird (*usu* small); *fam* sly fellow; *sl* delinquent, crook; ~ **bobo** *orni* booby; ~ **carpintero** woodpecker; ~ **de celda** gaol-bird; ~ **de cuenta** nasty customer; ~ **de sol** bird of paradise; ~ **gordo** big noise, V.I.P.; ~ **de mal agüero** bird of ill omen; ~ **mosca** humming-bird; ~ **polilla** kingfisher; **más vale** ~ **en mano que dos volando** a bird in the hand is worth two in the bush; ~ **reclamo** decoy; **tener** ~**s en la cabeza** to have bats in the belfry

pajarón *m* exceptionally clever fellow

pajarota hoax

pajarraco large bird; cunning fellow

pajarruco ugly bird

paje *m* page, valet; *naut* cabin-boy

pajear to feed well

pajera straw-loft/yard

pajizo, pajoso straw-coloured

Pakistán Pakistan

pala shovel, spade; scoop; leaf (of a hinge); bat, racket; blade (of oar/paddle/hoe *etc*); baker's peel; leaf (of cactus); dexterity; ~ **del timón** *naut* tiller; **a punta** ~ galore; **ser corta** ~ to know nothing

palabra word; password; speech; promise; floor (right to speak); ¡~! honest!, no kidding!; ~ **de caballero,** ~ **de honor** word of honour; ~ **de matrimonio** promise of marriage; ~**s mayores** insulting words; **dos** ~**s** a few words; **empeñar la** ~ to pledge one's word; **en buenas** ~**s** in plain speech; **en una** ~ to sum up; **libertad de** ~ freedom of speech; **llevar la** ~ to be the spokesman; **pedir la** ~ to ask for the floor; **tener la** ~ to have the floor

palabrada coarse/scurrilous language

palabrería wordiness, waffle

palabrero talkative

palabrista chatterbox

palabrimujer *m* man with an effeminate voice

palabrota coarse word/expression

palaciego *n* courtier; *adj* (of a) palace

palacio palace

palacra, palacrana gold nugget

palada shovelful, spadeful; *naut* stroke (of oars)

paladar *m* palate; roof of the mouth; taste; ~ **hendido** *med* cleft palate

paladear to relish, savour

paladeo (act of) relishing/savouring

paladial *gramm* palatal

paladino manifest, apparent

paladio palladium

palafito lake-dwelling

palafrén *m* palfrey

palafrenero groom, ostler; ~ **mayor** first equerry

palamenta *naut* set of oars

palanca lever, crowbar; thief's jemmy; ~ **del timón** *naut* rudder-bar, tiller

palancada blow with a crowbar

palancana, palangana wash-bowl

palanganero wash-stand

palangre *m* fishing-line with several hooks

palanguita para los dedos finger-bowl

palanquera fence made of logs

palanquero pile-driver

palanqueta small lever; dumbell; jemmy

palanquetazo *sl* robbery (using a jemmy)

palastro sheet metal

palatalización *f gramm* palatalization

palatino palatal, palatine

palatalizar *gramm* to palatalize

palazo blow with a spade/shovel

palco *theat* box, balcony

paleador *m* stoker

palenque *m* stockade, paling; *theat* passage from the stage to the pit

paleoceno Palaeocene

paleografía palaeography

paleográfico palaeographic
paleógrafo palaeographer
paleolítico palaeolithic
paleología palaeology
paleólogo palaeologist
paleontología palaeontology
paleontológico palaeontologic(al)
paleontólogo palaeontologist
palero shoveller; maker/seller of shovels/spades
Palestina Palestine
palestino Palestinian
palestra wrestling court/gymnasium; competition, contest
palestrita *m* wrestler; athlete
paleta small shovel; fire-shovel; *cul* skimmer; *bui+hort* trowel; *anat* shoulder-blade; *naut* propeller-blade; *arts* palette; ~ **de pescado** fish-knife; **de** ~ suddenly, without warning
paletada trowelful
paletazo thrust with a bull's horns
paletear *naut* to row without effect
paleteo flapping of the oars
paletilla shoulder-blade
paleto country bumpkin; rustic
palia *eccles* pall; altar-cloth
paliar to excuse, extenuate
paliativo *adj* palliative, extenuating, mitigating
palidecer to turn pale
palidez *f* paleness
pálido pale, ghastly; (of colours) light
paliducho palish, rather pale
palillero tooth-pick holder
palillo small stick; drumstick; toothpick; *bot* stem
palinodia public recantation
palio cloak; *eccles* pallium, canopy
palique *m* chitchat
palisandro *bot+carp* rosewood
paliza blow with a stick; beating, flogging
palizada palisade
palma *bot* palm(tree); palm leaf; *anat* palm; ~ **indiana** coconut palm; ~**s de tango** rhythmic clapping (as a protest); **andar en** ~**s** to be widely applauded; **ganarse/llevarse la** ~ to carry the day
palmáceo *bot* palmaceous
palmacristi *f bot* castor-oil plant
palmada pat; applause
palmar *n* palm-grove; *v sl* to die

palmario obvious
palmatoria candlestick
palmeado *bot* palmate; *zool* web-footed
palmear to clap the hands; applaud
palmera date-palm
palmeral *m* date-palm plantation
palmero pilgrim; *theat* flamenco artist who provides rhythmic clapping
palmípedo web-footed
palmito fan-palm
palmo span (measurement); ~ **a** ~ inch by inch
palmotear to applaud
palmoteo applause
palo stick; wood, timber; clout, thwack; handle; (cards) suit; *naut* mast; *Arg* one million pesos; mouthful, swig; *sl* criminal 'job', robbery; ~ **de mesana** *naut* mizzen-mast; ~ **de trinquete** foremast; ~ **dulce** licorice root; ~ **mayor** *naut* mainmast; **dar** ~**s de ciego** to hit out wildly; **moler a** ~**s** to thrash, beat
paloma pigeon, dove; timid person; honey, love (term of endearment); ~ **brava** rock-dove; ~ **buchona** pouter-pigeon; ~ **mensajera** carrier/homing-pigeon; ~ **silvestre** stock dove; ~ **torcaz,** ~ **zorita** wood-pigeon
palomar *m* dovecote, pigeon-house
palomariego tame, domestic (of pigeons)
palomear to shoot pigeons; breed pigeons
palomera bleak place
palomería pigeon-shooting
palomero pigeon breeder/fancier; pigeon seller
palomilla young pigeon; small butterfly; *ent* chrysalis; horse's backbone; white horse; wall-bracket; *mech* wing-nut; trestle; ~**s** *naut* white horses, white-caps
palomina type of black grape; pigeon-droppings
palomino young pigeon
palomitas de maíz pop-corn
palotada blow with a drumstick
palote *m* drumstick; down-stroke (in handwriting)
paloteado country-dance with sticks; noise
palotear to strike one stick against another; wrangle

paloteo fight with sticks
palpabilidad *f* palpability
palpación *f*, **palpadura** feeling, touching
palpar to feel, touch; consider self-evident; feel with one's hands; feel one's way in the dark
pálpebra *anat* eyelid
palpebral *adj* of the eyelids
palpitación *f* palpitation; quivering
palpitante *adj* palpitating; quivering
palpitar to palpitate; quiver
palpo *ent* + *zool* feeler
palquista *m* + *f sl* cat-burglar
palta *bot* avocado pear
palto *bot* avocado tree; jacket
palúdico malarial
paludismo malaria
paludoso marshy
palurdo *n* boor, rustic, country bumpkin; *adj* rustic, rude
palustre marshy
pallete *m naut* fender
pamela woman's wide-brimmed hat
pampa vast plain
pámpana vine leaf
pámpano young vine branch/tendril
pampanoso covered with tendrils
pampeano man from the pampa
pampear to travel over the pampa
pampero *see* **pampeano**
pamplacino *bot* cyclamen
pamplina *bot* chickweed; silly nonsense; trifle, bagatelle
pamplinada silly chatter
Pan: flauta de ~ Pan-pipe
pan *m* bread; loaf; crust (of a pie); wafer; food; **~ bazo** brown bread; **~ casero** home-made bread; **~ ácimo** unleavened bread; **~ de boda** wedding-cake; **~ de centeno** black bread; **~ de molde** sandwich loaf; **de oro** gold leaf; **~ de plata** silver leaf; **~ duro** stale bread; **~ inglés** 'tin' loaf; **~ integral** wholemeal bread; **~ rallado** breadcrumbs; **con su ~ se lo coma** it serves you/him *etc* right; **ganarse el ~** to earn one's living; **llamar al ~ ~ y al vino vino** to call a spade a spade; **venderse como ~ caliente** to sell like hot cakes
pana *text* plush; corduroy
panadera baker's wife
panadear to make bread
panadería bakery, baker's, bread-shop

panadero baker
panadizo *med* whitlow
panal *m* honeycomb; anything very sweet
Panamá Panama
panameño *n* + *adj* Panamanian
panamericano pan-American
pancarpia garland of flowers
pancarta placard
panceta dolt, fool; (rind of) bacon
pancilla *print* roman
pancista *m* + *f* one who sits on the fence, indecisive person
pancreático pancreatic
panchito *fam* peanut
pancho *n* paunch, belly; *adj sl* calm, self-controlled
panda: oso ~ *zool* panda; *archi* gallery of a cloister
pandear to bulge out
pandeo bulge
pandera tambourine
panderazo blow with a tambourine
panderetear to play the tambourine
pandereteo playing the tambourine; jollity, merriment
panderetero tambourine-player
pandero paper kite; tambourine
pandilla group, gang; *pol* faction
pandillero member of a gang/faction
pandillista *m* gang leader; *pol* leader of a faction
panecillo bread roll
panegírico *n* panegyric, eulogy; *adj* panegyrical
panegirista *m* + *f* eulogizer
panegirizar to eulogize
panel *m* panel; **~ de instrumentos** *mot* dashboard
panera granary; breadbasket
panero baker's basket
paneslavismo Pan-Slavism
paneslavista *n m* + *f* + *adj* Pan-Slavist
pánfilo easy-going person; gullible person
panfletista *m* + *f* lampooner
panfleto lampoon
pangermanismo Pan-Germanism
pangermanista *n m* + *f* Pan-German; *adj* Pan-Germanic
panhelénico Pan-Hellenic
panhelenismo Pan-Hellenism
panhelenista *m* + *f* Pan-Hellenist
paniaguado employee; protégé

pánico panic

panículo *bot* pellicle, membrane

panificación *f* bread-making

panificadora bakery

panificar to make bread

panislamismo Pan-Islamism

panislamista *n m+f + adj* Pan-Islamist

panizo maize, Indian corn

panocha, panoja corncob; *sl* cash, dough, lolly; *sl* red-haired girl

panojos *fpl sl* cash, dough, lolly

panoplia panoply

panorámico panoramic

panoso mealy

pantalón *m* (often used in plural) trousers; *fam* pants, panties; ~ bombacho wide trousers fastened at the ankle; **pantalones ajustados** narrowed trousers; **pantalones cortos** shorts; **pantalones odaliscas** flared trousers

pantalla lampshade; *TV+cin* screen

pantanal *m* marshy land, fen

pantano marsh, fen; dam; reservoir; snag

pantanoso marshy

panteísmo pantheism

panteísta *n m+f* pantheist; *adj* pantheistic

panteístico panthcistic

panteón *m* pantheon

pantera panther

pantográfico pantographic

pantógrafo pantograph

pantomima pantomime; mime; dumbshow

pantorrilla *anat* calf

pantufla slipper

panty, pantys *m* (pair of) tights

panza paunch, belly

panzada bellyful; push with the paunch

panzudo big-bellied

pañal *m* nappy, *US* diaper; ~es swaddling clothes; **estar en** ~es to be ignorant; be in its infancy

pañería drapery; draper's

pañero woollen-draper; clothier

paño cloth; woollen stuff; tapestry; drapery; dishcloth, teatowel; duster; *eccles* altar cloth; *naut* sailcloth, canvas; ~s **menores** underclothes

pañol *m naut* storeroom; ~ **de pólvora** powder magazine

pañolero handkerchief-maker

pañoleta headscarf, neckerchief

pañoso tattered

pañuelo handkerchief; kerchief, headscarf; ~ **de cuello** neckerchief

Papa Pope

papa potato

papá *m* dad(dy), papa; **Papá Noel** Father Christmas

papada double chin

papadilla flesh (under the chin)

papado papacy

papagayo parrot

papamoscas *m sing+pl orni* fly-catcher; simpleton

papanatas *m sing+pl* fool, simpleton

papar to swallow; *fam* eat

paparrucha fake; nonsense

papaya *bot* pawpaw

papear *sl* to eat, nosh

papel *m* paper; sheet of paper; document; treatise; tract; *cin+theat* part, role; ~ **atrapamoscas** fly-paper; ~ **cuadriculado** graph paper; ~ **de barbas** untrimmed paper; ~ **de calcar** carbon paper; ~ **de escribir** writing-paper; ~ **de envolver** wrapping paper; ~ **de Estado** government bond; ~ **de estaño** tinfoil, silver paper; ~ **de estraza** brown paper; ~ **de fumar** cigarette paper; ~ **de lija** sandpaper; ~ **de oficio** foolscap; ~ **de periódico** newsprint; ~ **de seda** tissue-paper; ~ **esmeril** emery-paper; ~ **higiénico** toilet-paper; ~ **pintado** wallpaper; ~ **reactivo** litmus paper; ~ **secante** blotting-paper; ~ **viejo** waste-paper; ~ **volante** leaflet, handbill; **hacer buen/mal** ~ to put on a good/poor show

papela *sl* identity card

papelear to glance through (a newspaper)

papeleo paper-work; red tape, bureaucracy

papelera waste-paper basket; litter basket/bin; paper mill

papelería stationer's; stationery; pile of papers

papelero stationer; paper-worker

papeleta card, ticket; slip; ballot-paper; *fig* problem; unpleasant job, drag; ~ **de préstamo** pawn ticket

papelucho scurrilous writing

paperas *fpl med* mumps

papilla pap, slops, soft food

papira *sl* letter
papiráceo papery
papiro papyrus; *sl* banknote
papismo Popery
papista *m + f* papist
papo double chin; *orni* gizzard
papú (*pl* papúes) Papuan
papudo having a double chin
paquebote *m* packet-steamer
paquete *m* packet, parcel; bundle (of papers); packet-steamer; package deal; *sl* one who is bad at his trade
paquetería shop selling prepacked goods
paquidermo *zool* pachyderm; *sl* thick-skinned person
Paquistán Pakistan
par *n m* pair, couple; team; brace; ~es o nones odds or evens; a ~es in twos; a la ~ jointly, at par; de ~ en ~ (of a door) wide open; estar al ~ de to be equal to; sin ~ peerless, without equal; *f anat + zool* placenta; *adj* equal, on a par, (of numbers) even
para for; in order to; to what end; to, towards; ~ con with, towards; ~ entre nosotros between you and me; ~ eso for that reason, therefore; ¿~ qué? what for?; ~ que in order that; dije ~ mi camisa I said to myself; estar ~ to be on the point of, be ready for
parabién *m* congratulation
parábola parable; *math* parabola
parabolero teller of parables
parabólico parabolic
parabrisas *mot* windscreen, *US* windshield
paracaídas *m sing + pl* parachute; *vulg sl* french letter
paracaidista *m + f* parachutist
parachoques *m sing + pl mot* bumper, *US* fender
parada (of buses, trams *etc*) stop; act of stopping; pause; *mil* halt; *mil* parade, review; dam; bank; ~ de autobuses bus-stop; ~ en seco dead stop
paradera sluice
paradero stopping place; (railway) halt; whereabouts; de ~ desconocido whereabouts unknown
paradigma *m* paradigm, example
¹ parado *n* unemployed person; *adj* unemployed; (of clock) stopped; (of factory) shut down

² parado slow; indolent; shy
paradoja paradox
paradojo, paradójico paradoxical
parador *m* state-run hotel (*usu* in an ancient building); road-house
parafernales, bienes parafernales *m pl* paraphernalia
parafina paraffin
parafraseador *m* paraphraser
parafrasear to paraphrase
paráfrasis *f* paraphrase
paragolpes *m sing + pl mot* bumper, *US* fender
paraguas *m sing + pl* umbrella
paraguayo *n* Paraguayan; kind of flat-shaped peach; *adj* Paraguayan
paragüero umbrella; umbrella stand/maker/repairer/seller
paraíso paradise; *theat* upper gallery; ~ fiscal tax haven; ave del ~ bird of paradise; ~ terrenal earthly paradise
paraje *m* place; condition
paralelar to parallel; compare
paralelas *f sing + pl* parallel bars
paralelepípedo parallelepiped
paralelo *n + adj* parallel
paralelogramo parallelogram
parálisis *f med* paralysis
paraliticarse to become paralysed
paralítico paralytic
paralización *f med* paralysation; *comm* stagnation
paralizado *med* paralysed; *comm* stagnant
paralogismo paralogism, false argument
paralogizar to paralogize, reason falsely
paramentar to adorn, embellish
paramento adornment, embellishment
paramera bleak place; moor
parámetro parameter
páramo high, exposed land
parancero bird-catcher
parangón *m* comparison
parangonar to compare
paraninfo best man (at a wedding); university auditorium, assembly hall
paranoico *n* paranoiac
parapetar(se) to hide behind a parapet
parapeto parapet
paraplejía *med* paraplegia
parapléjico *med* paraplegic
parar *vi* to stop, halt; *vt* to detain; arrest; ~ de nevar/llover to stop snowing/raining; sin ~ without stop-

ping, continuously; ~**se** to stop o.s.; halt, desist (**de** from); ~**se a …** to stop to …

pararrayos *m sing+pl* lightning conductor

parasemo *naut* figurehead

parasismo paroxysm, fit

parasiticida parasiticide

parasítico parasitical

parasitismo parasitism

parásito *n* parasite; ~**s atmosféricos** *rad* atmospherics, static; *adj* parasitic

parasitología parasitology

parasitólogo parasitologist

¹ **parca** fate; death

² **parca** windcheater

Parcas: las ~ the fates, Parcae

parcela plot of land

parcelar to divide into plots

parcial partial; partisan

parcialidad *f* partiality

parcidad *f* parsimony

parco scanty; parsimonious, frugal

parcómetro parking-meter

parche *m* patch (on clothing *etc*); *med* plaster; poultice; skin of a drum

parchista *m* sponger, scrounger

pardal *n m zool* leopard; *orni* sparrow; *bot* wolfsbane; *adj* rustic

pardear to appear/look greyish

¡**pardiez**! good heavens!

pardillo *n orni* linnet; peasant, yokel; *adj* brown, dark grey

pardusco greyish

pareado *lit* couplet

parear to match; mate

parecer *n m* opinion; appearance, look; *v* to seem, appear, turn up; resemble; **al** ~ to all appearances; **parece mentira** it's hard to believe; **según parece** by appearances; ~**se** to look alike, resemble one another/each other

parecido *n* resemblance; *adj* resembling; **bien/mal** ~ good/evil-looking

pareciente apparent; similar

pared *f* wall; *hort* box fence; ~ **maestra** main wall; ~ **medianera** party wall; **entre cuatro** ~**es** imprisoned, confined

paredaño separated by a wall

paredón *m* standing wall; place of execution by firing-squad

paregórico paregoric

pareja pair, couple; brace; team; part-

ner (at cards/dancing *etc*); pair of policemen/soldiers; ~**s mixtas** *sp* mixed doubles; **ir a** ~**s** to go together; **una** ~ *sl* two Civil Guards

parejo even; level; neck-and-neck; **por un** ~ on equal terms

parejura evenness; similarity

parentela kinsfolk

parentesco kinship

paréntesis *m sing+pl* parenthesis; **entre** ~ in brackets

pareo pairing, coupling

paria outcast, pariah

parición *f vet* parturition

parida *n* woman who has recently given birth; *adj* having recently given birth/ whelped

paridad *f* parity

parido: *sl* **bien** ~ good-looking

pariente *m+f* relation, kinsman; *f fam* wife, missus; old man

parihuela handcart; stretcher

parir to give birth; *fig* publish

París Paris

parisién, parisiense, parisino *n m+f +adj* Parisian

parka *tr* windcheater

parla talk

parlador *n m* chatterer; *adj* talkative

parladuría loquacity, garrulity

parlaembalde *m* chatterbox

Parlament *m* parliament of Catalonia

parlamentar to converse; *mil* parley

parlamentario *n* member of parliament; *mil* flag of truce; *adj* parliamentary

parlamento parliament

parlanchín *m* chatterer; *adj* chattery, talkative

parlante talking

parlar to speak fluently, chatter

parlatorio chat; parlour

parlería loquacity, talkativeness; *orni* chirping, cheeping; (of water) babbling

parlero loquacious, garrulous; chirping; babbling

parlón *n m* chatterer; *adj* talkative, garrulous

parlotear to prattle, chatter

parloteo prattle; small talk

parmesano Parmesan

Parnaso Parnassus

parné *m*, **parnés** *sl* dough, lolly, bread

¹ **paro:** ~ **carbonero** *orni* coal-tit

² **paro** unemployment; **en** ~ unemployed
parodia parody
paródico parodic, burlesque
parodista *m+f* parodist
parola idle talk
paronomasia pun
paronomástico *adj* punning
parótida *anat* parotid gland; *med* mumps
parotiditis *f med* mumps
paroxismal paroxysmal
paroxismo paroxysm
parpadear blink; flutter the eyelids
parpadeo blinking; winking; fluttering of the eyelids
párpado eyelid
parpar *orni* to quack
parque *m* park; paddock; parkland; *mot* parking zone; ~ **de atracciones** amusement park; ~ **de bomberos** fire-station; ~ **infantil** playground; playpen; ~ **zoológico** zoological gardens
parqueadero parking-place
parquear to park
parquedad *f* parsimony; moderation
parquímetro parking-meter
parra grapevine
párrafo paragraph
¹ **parral** *m* grape vine with long shoots; vine-bower
² **parral** *m* large earthenware jar (for honey) with two handles
parranda jollification, carousal; booze-up; **de** ~ on the spree
parrandero *n* reveller; *adj* fond of carousing
parricida parricide (person)
parricidio parricide (crime)
parrilla gridiron, grill; toaster; hotplate; **a la** ~ grilled
parro *orni* duck
párroco parish priest
parroquia parish; parish church; faithful of a parish; *comm* goodwill; clientèle
parroquiano *n* parishioner; *comm* customer, client; *adj* parochial
parsimonia parsimony; moderation; prudence
parsimonioso parsimonious; moderate; prudent
¹ **parte** *m* communiqué; ~ **meteorológico** weather report/forecast; **dar** ~ to inform; **en** ~ partly, in part

² **parte** *f* part; share; place; right/left side; *leg* party; *theat* role, character; ~ **de la oración** *gramm* part of speech; ~ **interesada** interested party; ~s genitals; ~s **pudendas/púdicas/vergonzosas** private parts; **de algún/mucho tiempo a esta** ~ for some time/a long time past; **de mi** ~ for my part, in my name, on my behalf; **en alguna** ~ somewhere; **en ninguna** ~ nowhere; **en/por todas** ~s everywhere; **ir a la** ~ to go shares; **la tercera/cuarta** ~ one third/a quarter; **por mi** ~ as far as I am concerned; **por otra** ~ on the other hand; **por** ~s bit by bit, by parts; **ser** ~ **en** to be a party to
partenogénesis *f* parthenogenesis
partenogénico parthenogenic
partera midwife
partería midwifery
partero accoucheur
parterre *m* small garden; flower-bed
partible divisible
partición *f* partition, distribution
particionero participant
participación *f* participation; portion; partnership; share (*esp* in a national lottery ticket)
participar *vt* to notify, communicate; *vi* to participate, take part (**en** in); ~ **de** to share in
partícipe *n m* participant; *adj* participating; sharing
participio *gramm* participle
partícula particle; ~s **de polvo** specks of dust
particular *n m* private individual; topic; **en** ~ particularly; *adj* special; private
particularidad *f* particularity; peculiarity; friendship; detail
particularizar to particularize; specify; ~se to be distinguished by
partida departure; death; item (in book-keeping); entry; record; parcel; lot; *mil* squad, platoon; gang, band, faction; *comm* shipment; *sp* game, match; ~ **de caza** hunting-party; ~ **de dobles/de simples** doubles/singles match; ~ **de nacimiento/matrimonio/defunción** birth/marriage/death certificate; ~ **doble** *comm* double entry
partidario *n* follower, supporter; partisan; *pol* party man; *adj* adherent;

partisan

partidismo partisanship; favouritism

partidista *m+f* supporter, partisan

partido *m* game, contest, match; team; *pol* party; *comm* profit; pact, agreement; district; **sacar ~ de** to profit by, take advantage of; **tomar ~** to take sides; *adj* divided; split

partidor *m* divider; *math* divisor; cleaver

partija division

partimento, partimiento *see* **partición**

partir *vt* to divide, split; break; *vi* to leave, depart; start (**de** from); **~ la diferencia** to split the difference; **~se** to break, split

partitivo *gramm* partitive

partitura *mus* score

parto childbirth, labour; **estar de ~** to be in labour

parva heap of grain; large quantity

parvedad *f*, **parvidad** *f* small quantity; smallness

parvo small; scanty

parvulez *f* smallness; simplicity

párvulo *n* small child, toddler; *adj* small; humble; **escuela de ~s** infant school

pasa raisin; **~ de Corinto** currant

pasacalle *m* parade (of circus artists *etc*); *mus* lively march

pasacintas *m sing+pl* bodkin

pasada pace; passage; **de ~** on the way, in passing; **mala ~** dirty trick

pasadero *n* stepping-stone; *adj* bearable, endurable

pasadizo passage; aisle; corridor; alley

pasado *n* past; turncoat; **~s** ancestors, forebears; *adj* past; *cul* stale; old-fashioned, square; **el mes/año ~** last month/year

pasador *m* pin, hat-pin; hair-slide; door-bolt; window fastener; sieve, colander; *naut* marlinspike

pasadura passage; transit; child's hysterical crying

pasaje *m* passage, voyage; fare; way; *geog* strait; *mus* change of voice; extract (from a book); **~ gratuito** free ticket, complimentary ticket

pasajero *n* passenger; *adj* passing, temporary, transitory

pasamanería passementerie

pasamanero passementerie-maker

pasamano banister, handrail; *naut* gang-

way

pasamontañas *m sing+pl* balaclava

pasante *m med* student assistant; *leg* articled clerk; **~ de pluma** barrister's clerk

pasapalo snack

pasapasa legerdemain; hocus-pocus

pasaporte *m* passport

pasar *vi* to pass; manage, get along; last; endure; die; *comm* be marketable/saleable; happen; **~ de** to exceed; **~ de largo** to pass without stopping, give a wide berth to; **~ por** to be taken for, call on, visit; **¿qué pasa?** what's up?, what's the matter?; *vt* to pass; go through/across; *comm* carry over/forward; pierce; smuggle; exceed; convey, transfer; suffer; swallow; omit; overlook; *cul* go stale, dry up; spend (time); *sl* give up (doing s.t.); **~ el rato** to kill time; **~ en claro** to omit, leave out; **~ (la) lista** to call the roll; **~lo bien** to have a good time; **~ plaza de** to set up as; **~ por las armas** to execute (as a punishment); **~se** *pol* to go over to another party; *cul* be stale; be overcooked; (of fire) burn out; permeate, go through; go too far

pasarela small bridge; *naut* bridge

pasatiempo pastime

pasavante *m* permit, licence; safe-conduct

pascua Passover; Easter; any church feast-day; **~ de (la) Navidad** feast of the Nativity, Christmas; **~ de (la) Resurrección** feast of the Resurrection, Easter; **dar las ~s** wish Merry Christmas; **de Pascuas a Ramos** from Easter to Palm Sunday, a long time; **estar como una ~** to be very jolly; **felices ~s** Merry Christmas; **~ florida** Easter

pascual *eccles* paschal

pase *m* pass, permit; **~ de pernoctar** *mil* overnight pass; *cin* screening, showing (of a film)

paseadero walk, avenue

paseador *n m* stroller; *adj* fond of walking

paseante *m+f* stroller, passer-by; **~ en corte** idler

pasear(se) to walk, stroll; ride; take a walk; **~ en coche/bicicleta** to ride in a car/on a bicycle

paseo walk, stroll; ride, drive; parade; avenue, boulevard; **dar un ~** to take a walk, go for a ride/drive; **mandar a ~** to send to blazes, dismiss abruptly; **¡vete a ~!** get lost!, drop dead!

pasero raisin seller/dealer

pasicorto taking short steps, short-striding

pasiego mountain-dweller of Santander province

pasilargo taking long steps, long-striding

pasillo corridor, aisle, passage

pasión *f* passion

pasional passionate; **crimen ~** crime of passion

pasionaria *bot* pasiflora, passion-flower

pasito short stride; **~ a ~** very gently, very softly

pasivo *n, usu* ~s *comm* liabilities; *adj* passive

pasma *sl* cops, police, fuzz

pasmar to stun; astound; chill; **~se** to wonder at; be astounded

pasmo wonder, prodigy; amazement; *med* lockjaw

pasmoso wonderful, prodigious

paso pace, step, stride; crossing; path; passage, alley; gait; occurrence; *theat* curtain-raiser; **~ a nivel** level-crossing; **~ de andadura** ambling pace; **~ inferior** underpass; **~ ligero** *mil* quick-step; **~ superior** flyover; **abrir ~** to make way; **a buen ~** at a good pace; **a cada ~** frequently; **a dos ~s** near to hand; **a ese ~** at that rate; **al ~** in passing; **a pocos ~s** at a short distance; **apretar el ~** to hurry, quicken one's step; **llevar el ~** to keep in step; **marcar el ~** to mark time; **ponerse al ~ de** to catch up with; **pro-hibido el ~** no entry, keep out

pasota *m+f* drop-out

pasotar to drop out

pasotismo drop-out (cult)

paspartú *m* passepartout

pasquín *m* lampoon; poster; leaflet

pasquinar to lampoon, ridicule

pasta paste; *cul* batter, dough; noodles, spaghetti *etc*; (bookbinder's) braid; wood-pulp; *sl* dough, lolly; **~ gansa** *sl* lots of money; **~ para sandwich** sandwich-spread; **gafas de ~** horn-rimmed spectacles

pastadero pasture, grazing

pastar to graze

pastel *m* cake; pie; *arts* pastel; *fam* mess

pastelería cake-shop, confectioner's; confectionery

pastelero pastry-cook, confectioner

pastelista *m+f arts* pastelist

pasterización *f* pasteurization

pasterizar to pasteurize

pastilla pastille; tablet; (of soap) cake

pastinaca *bot* parsnip; *zool* sting-ray

pasto pasture; grass for fodder; food; **~s comunes** common land; **a ~** abundantly

pastor *m* shepherd; *eccles* pastor

pastorear to pasture; tend; *eccles* feed (souls)

pastoría pastoral life

pastosidad *f* mellowness; softness

pastoso mellow; soft; doughy

pastura pasture; fodder

pasturaje *m* pasturage; money paid for pasturage

pata *zool* foot, paw; leg (of furniture/instruments *etc*); *fam* human leg/foot; **~ coja** hopscotch; **~s abajo** right side up; **~s arriba** upside down; **~s de gallo** wrinkles by the eyes; **a ~** *fam* on foot; **enseñar la ~** to reveal one's ignorance; **meter la ~** to put one's foot in it; **mala ~** bad luck

pataca Jerusalem artichoke

patache *m naut* tender

patacón *m* old silver coin; **sin un ~** without a bean

patada kick

patagón *m*, **patagónico** *n+adj* Patagonian

patalear to kick out; stamp one's feet hysterically/to show disapproval

pataleo kicking; tantrums

patán *n m* boor, rustic; *adj* boorish, churlish

patanada incivility; discourteous action

patanería incivility; churlishness

patata potato

patatal *m* potato field/patch

patatero *n* potato grower/dealer; *adj* fond of potatoes

patatús *m* fainting-fit

pateador (of horses) given to kicking

pateadura *n* kicking; stamping of feet; reprimand

patear to kick; stamp one's feet

patentar to patent

patente *n f* patent; warrant; *adj* patent, obvious, manifest; ~ de sanidad *naut* bill of health

patentizar to make manifest

páter *m mil sl* chaplain

paternalismo paternalism

paternalista *n m+f* paternalist; *adj* paternalistic

paternidad *f* paternity

paterno fatherly

paternoster *m* Lord's prayer

patético pathetic

patetismo pathos

patiabierto bow-legged

patibulario harrowing; sinister

patíbulo gibbet, scaffold, gallows

paticojo lame, limping

patihendido cloven-footed

patilargo long-legged

patilla sideburn; earpiece (of spectacles); pocket-flap

patín *m* skate; *aer+mot* skid; ~ de cola tail-spin; ~ de ruedas roller-skate

patinadero skating-rink

patinador *m* skater

patinar to skate; *aer+mot* skid; *mot* (of clutch) slip

patinazo skid, blunder; slip of the tongue

patinegro black-footed

patinete *m* child's scooter

patio small yard; *theat* pit; ~ de butacas stalls

patita small foot/leg/paw; poner de ~s en la calle to eject; throw out

patitieso stiff-legged; paralysed (with cold *etc*)

patito duckling

patituerto knock-kneed

patizambo bandy-legged

pato *orni* duck; ~ real *orni* mallard; ~ cuchara *orni* shoveller; pagar el ~ to be the scapegoat, be left holding the baby, carry the can

patochada blunder

patojo *adj* waddling

patología pathology

patológico pathological

patólogo pathologist

patoso clumsy-footed

patota group of noisy people

patraña fable; humbug

patria mother-country, fatherland; ~

chica native heath, place of birth

patriarca patriarch

patriarcal patriarchal

Patricio Patrick

patricio *n+adj* patrician

patrimonio *n* patrimony

patrio *adj* native; paternal

patriota *m+f* patriot

patriotería jingoism

patriotero jingoist

patriótico patriotic

patrocinador *n m* sponsor, backer; *adj* sponsoring

patrocinar to sponsor, back

patrocinio sponsorship, backing, patronage

patrón *m* patron, backer; host; protector; landlord; *eccles* patron saint; boss, employer; *naut* skipper; pattern, model; ~ de bote/lancha *naut* coxswain; ~ de oro gold standard

patronato, patronazgo patronage; protection; guardianship

patronímico *n+adj* patronymic

patrono patron, protector; employer, boss; lord of the manor

patrulla *n* patrol

patrullar to patrol

patudo having big feet/paws

paulatino slow, gradual

Paula Pauline

paulina offensive anonymous letter

paulonia *bot* paulownia

pauperismo abject poverty

paupérrimo very poor, poverty-stricken

pausa pause, delay; *mus* rest

pausado *adj* slow, calm; *adv* slowly

pausar to pause, hesitate; stop

pauta guide-lines (for handwriting); standard, pattern; dar la ~ to set a standard, establish a norm

pautada *mus* ruled staff

pava *orni* turkey-hen; coffee-pot; *sl* cigarette end; pelar la ~ to court

[1] pavero turkey breeder/dealer

[2] pavero wide-brimmed hat

pavés *m* large shield

pavesa ember; spark

pavía *bot* clingstone peach

pávido terrified

pavimentación *f* paving; pavement

pavimentar to pave

pavimento pavement

pavipollo turkey-chick

pavo *orni* turkey; *zool* peacock fish; ~ **real** *orni* peacock; *sl* five-peseta coin; *sl* ninny; **edad del** ~ awkward age; **subírsele el** ~ to blush

¹ **pavón** *m* peacock

² **pavón** *m metal* bluing

pavonada ostentation

pavonar *metal* to treat with bluing

pavonear to strut, show off

pavor *m* fright, terror

pavordear (of bees) to swarm

pavorido frightened; terrorized

pavoroso frightful, terrible

pavura fright, terror

payador *m* ballad-singer

payar to sing extemporaneously

payasada clownish behaviour; clownish action

payaso clown

payés *m* Catalonian peasant

payo non-gipsy

paz *f* peace; calm(ness), tranquillity; ¡~! hush!; **gente de** ~ friend (answer to challenge 'who goes there?')

P.C.E. (Partido Comunista de España) Spanish Communist Party

PD (posdata) PS (postscript)

pe *f* (letter) p; **de** ~ **a pa** thoroughly

peaje *m* toll; **autopista de** ~ toll motorway

peajero toll-collector

peal *m* foot (of stocking)

peana, peaña pedestal (of a statue); *eccles* step before the altar

peatón *m* pedestrian

peatonal for pedestrians; **zona** ~ pedestrian area

pebete *m* small child; joss-stick

pebetero air-purifier; perfumer; perfume censer

peca freckle

pecable sinful

pecado sin; excess; ~ **capital/mortal** deadly sin; ~ **contra la naturaleza** sodomy, masturbation; **de mis** ~**s** (following a *n*) of mine, my own

pecador *n m* sinner; *adj* sinning

pecaminoso sinful

pecante sinning; excessive

pecar to sin; offend; superabound; ~ **de** +*adj* to be too ...; **ella peca de tímida** she is too timid

pecarí *m zool* peccary

pecé *m*+*f* member of the Spanish Communist Party

peceño coloured like pitch; tasting of pitch

pecera fish-bowl; fish-tank

peciento coloured like pitch

pecina slime

pecinal slimy

pecio flotsam; wreckage

peciolo *bot* stem (of a leaf)

pecoso freckled

pectina pectin

pectoral *n m* breastplate; *eccles* pectoral cross; *adj* pectoral

pecuario *adj* cattle

peculado embezzlement

peculiaridad *f* peculiarity

peculio *leg* private property

pecunia *fam* money

pecuniario pecuniary

pechar *vt* to pay taxes; *vi* ~ **con** to bear, take on

pechblenda, pecblenda pitchblende

pechera shirt-front; chest-protector; *fam* bosom

pechería taxes

¹ **pechero** taxpayer

² **pechero** baby's bib

pechiblanco *orni*+*zool* white-breasted

pecho *anat* chest; breast, bosom; courage; slope, incline; **criar a los** ~**s** to instruct; **dar (el)** ~ to breast-feed, suckle; **de** ~ courageous; **entre** ~ **y espalda** in the stomach; **tener** ~ to endure patiently; **tomar a** ~ to take to heart

pechuga *cul* breast of fowl; *fam* bosom; slope

pedagogía pedagogy, teaching, education

pedagógico pedagogic, educational

pedagogo pedagogue, teacher

pedal *m* pedal; treadle

pedalear to pedal; ~ **en agua** to tread water

pedante *n m* pedant, prig; *adj* pedantic, priggish

pedantear to be pedantic, act pedantically

pedantería pedantry

pedantesco pedantic

pedantismo pedantry

pedazo piece; ~ **de animal** *cont* good-for-nothing; **a** ~**s** in pieces

pederasta *m* pederast

pederastia pederasty

pedernal *m* flint

pedernalino flinty, rock-hard

pedestre *adj* pedestrian; common, vulgar

pediatra *m+f* paediatrician

pediatría paediatrics

pediátrico paediatric

pedículo *bot* pedicle

pedicura chiropody

pediculo chiropodist

pedido demand; *comm* order

pedidor *m* petitioner

pedidura petitioning

pedigüeño persisting in begging

pediluvio footbath

pedimento petition; *leg* claim

pedir to ask for, request; beg, solicit; claim; inquire after; *comm* order; ~ cuentas to call to account; ~ la mano de to ask for the hand of (in marriage); a ~ de boca according to desire

pedo fart; estar ~ *sl* to be pissed

pedómetro pedometer

pedorrera flatulence, wind

pedorro *n* farter; *adj* given to farting

pedrada cast of a stone; blow with a stone

pedrea lapidation; fight with stones; hailstorm; small lottery prizes

pedregal *m* stony ground

pedregoso stony, rocky; *med* suffering from gravel

pedrejón *m* boulder

pedrera stone-quarry

pedrería precious stones

pedrero stone-mason

pedrisca shower of small thrown stones; hail shower

pedrisco hailstorm

Pedro Peter

pedrusco rough piece of stone

pedúnculo *bot* flower-stalk

peer to fart

pega joining, sticking together; appeal; snag, problem

pegadizo sticky; *med* (of illnesses) catching; *mus* (of tunes) catchy; (of people) leech

pegado patch

pegador *m* sticker; *min* blaster; ~ de carteles bill-poster

pegadura *n* sticking; appeal, catchiness, allure

pegajoso sticky; appealing, catchy; *fam* contagious

pegante glutinous, adhesive

pegar *vi* to take root; catch (fire); impress; make a hit; join; fit; match, suit; *vt* to glue, cement, stick; fasten; stitch, sew on; post (bills); infect with; hit, slap; no ~ los ojos not to get a wink of sleep; ~ un susto to give a fright; ~ un tiro to shoot; eso no pega that won't do, that doesn't make sense; ~se to stick, adhere, become addicted to; ~se un susto to get a fright

Pegaso Pegasus

pegata trick; swindle

pegatina sticker (*usu* non-political)

pegote *m* patch; *cul* thick stew; sponger, scrounger; sticker (*usu* political)

pegual *m* cinch

peguero maker/seller of pitch

pegujal *m*, pegujar *m* small-holding

pegujalero, pegujarero small-holder

pegunta pitch mark on sheep

peguntar to mark with pitch

peinado *n* hairdressing, hair-do; screening, investigation; *adj* effeminate in toilet/dress

peinador *m* hairdresser; dressing-gown

peinadura combing/dressing hair; ~s combings

peinar to comb; screen, investigate; touch lightly; ~ canas to be old, be ageing

peine *m* comb; *text* card; *anat* instep

peinería comb factory

peinero comb maker/seller

peineta ornamental high comb

peje *m* fish; crafty person; ~ palo stockfish; ~ sapo angler-fish

pejiguera nuisance, bother

pela *sl* peseta

peladilla sugared almond; pebble

pelado plucked; bald; bare; peeled, shelled; penniless, broke

pelador *m* plucker, peeler

peladura *n* plucking, peeling; peel

pelagatos *m sing+pl* ragamuffin; wastrel; nobody

pelagra *med* pellagra

pelagroso *med* suffering from pellagra

pelaje *m* pelt, skin (of an animal); apparel

pelambre *m*, pelambrera hair

pelar to remove hair; pluck; skin; peel; husk, shell; trick, rob; **eso es duro de ~** that's a hard nut to crack; **hace un frío que pela** it's bitterly cold; **~se** to lose one's hair; have one's hair cut; **pelárselas** to be in earnest; **él corre que se las pela** he runs like mad

pelargonio *bot* pelargonium

peldaño stair/step (of a staircase)

pelea fight; row; **~ de gallos** cock-fight

peleador *n m* fighter; *adj* quarrelsome person

peleante *adj* fighting

pelechar *zool+orni* to change the coat; grow new hair/feathers; slough; fledge

pelele *m* nincompoop, booby; stuffed figure, stuffed shirt; puppet; combs (garment)

¹ **peleón** *n m* quarrel, fight; *adj* fond of fighting

² **peleón: vino ~** cheap wine, plonk

peletería furrier's; shop where leather goods are sold; furs

peletero furrier; dealer in leather goods

peliagudo difficult, arduous

peliblanco white-haired

peliblando having soft, fine hair

pelicano grey-haired, hoary

pelícano *orni* pelican

pelicorto short-haired

película film, moving-picture; pellicle; **~ de dibujos animados** cartoon film; **~ protectora** protective coating

peliculero *n cin* scenario writer; film actor; one connected with the film industry; *adj* film, cinema, movie

peligrar to be in peril

peligro peril, danger; **correr ~** to run a risk

peligroso perilous, dangerous; risky

peligrosidad *f* danger, peril

pelilargo long-haired

pelillo short hair/fibre; slight bother; **echar ~s a la mar** to become reconciled; **no tener ~s en la lengua** not to be afraid to speak one's mind; **pararse en ~s** to split hairs, be over-scrupulous

pelilloso touchy

pelinegro black-haired

pelirrojo red-haired

pelirrubio fair-haired, blond

pelitieso straight-haired

pelitrique *m* trifle, bagatelle; fiddling

matter

pelma bore (person); indigestible food

pelmacería slowness

pelmazo sluggard; bore; flattened mass

pelo hair; fibre; filament; *bot+orni* down; *text* nap, pile; *carp* grain (of wood); *zool* coat; (watch-making) hair-spring; (billiards) kiss; *comm* raw silk; **~ arriba** against the grain; **~ de aire** breath of air; **~s y señales** finicky details; **a/al ~** along the grain; **de medio ~** low-class; **de ~ en pecho** brave; tough, strong; **montar a ~** to ride bareback; **escapar por un ~** to escape by the skin of one's teeth; **estar hasta los ~s** to have had quite enough, be fed up; **este asunto tiene ~s** there are snags to this; **hacerse el ~** to have a hair-do; **no tener ~s en la lengua** not to be afraid to speak one's mind; **ponérsele a uno los ~s de punta** to be scared stiff; **tomar el ~ a alguien** to tease, pull s.o.'s leg; **venir al ~** to come to the point; be just what the doctor ordered

pelón hairless; bald; penniless, destitute

pelona baldness; *med* alopecia

pelonería destitution, poverty

peloso hairy

¹ **pelota: en ~** stark naked

² **pelota** ball; *sp* fives; Basque national game, jai-alai; *sl* head; *vulg* testicle; *sl* yes-man, creep, boot-licker

pelotari *m* jai-alai player

pelotazo stroke/blow with a ball; *sl* glass of spirits

pelote *m sl* five-peseta coin

pelotear to play ball; quarrel; *comm* settle accounts

pelotera row, quarrel

pelotilla servility, adulation

pelotillero yes-man, creep

pelotón ball-maker

pelotón *m* large ball; *mil* platoon; crowd; posse

peltre *m* pewter

peltrero worker in pewter

peluca wig

peluche *m* felt; **muñeco de ~** soft toy

peludo hairy, shaggy

peluquería hairdresser's; barber's

peluquero hairdresser; barber

pelusa *bot* down; *text* nap, pile; fuzz; jealousy

pella pellet; round mass; cauliflower head; small portion of white food (meringue *etc*)

pellada *bui* trowelful of cement/mortar

pelleja skin, pelt, hide; *sl* life

pellejero leather-dresser

pellejo skin, pelt, hide; wineskin; **jugarse el ~** to risk one's life; **quitar el ~ a** to gossip about, speak ill of; **pagar con el ~** to pay the penalty with one's own life; **mudar el ~** to change one's habits/way of life, move house; **no quisiera estar en su ~** I shouldn't like to be in his shoes

pellico shepherd's jacket; garment made of skins/furs

pelliza pelisse; sheepskin coat/jacket

pellizcador pinching, tight

pellizcamiento pinching; pruning

pellizcar to pinch, nip; *orni* peck at

pellizco pinch, nip; tiny amount

pello fur jacket; *fam* bumpkin

¹ **pena** anguish, sorrow, mental pain; chagrin; hardship; penalty; **~ capital, ~ de muerte** capital punishment; **~ pecuniaria** fine; **~s eternas** hell fire; **a duras ~s** with great difficulty; **ahogar las ~s** to drown one's sorrows; **alma en ~** soul in purgatory; **¡qué ~!** what a shame!; **bajo/so ~ de** on pain of; **valer/merecer la ~** to be worth the trouble; **tener ~ de** to feel sorry for; **vivir sin ~ ni gloria** to lead a drab, humdrum life

² **pena** *orni* quill, feather

penable punishable

penachera tuft of feathers; crest, plume

penacho plume, crest, tuft; arrogance, haughtiness

penado *n* convict, prisoner; narrow-mouthed vessel; *adj* arduous; painful; sorrowful

penal *n m* prison (*esp* for those convicted of serious crimes); *adj* penal

penalidad *f* hardship; *leg* penalty

penalista *m+f* penologist; criminologist

penalizar to penalize

penalty *m sp* penalty; **casarse de ~** to have a shotgun wedding

penante arduous, difficult

penar *vi* to suffer; crave, long for; *vt* to punish, penalise; **~se** to mourn

penca *bot* fleshy leaf; whip, lash; **hacerse de ~s** to let o.s. be persuaded

pencazo whiplash

pencar *sl* to think

penco sorry nag, hack

pendejo *anat* pubic hair; *fam* good-for-nothing; coward

pendencia quarrel, row; affray; brawl

pendenciar to quarrel, row; brawl

pendenciero quarrelsome; given to brawling

pender to hang, dangle; depend (**de** on); be pending

pendiente *n m* ear-ring, pendant; *f* gradient, slope; **~s de la reina** *bot* fuchsia; *adj* hanging; sloping; pending; **cuenta ~** *comm* outstanding/unsettled account; **estar ~ de** to depend on

pendil *m* mantle; **tomar el ~** to depart

pendingue *m* french leave

¹ **péndola** pendulum

² **péndola** quill pen

pendolaje *m naut* plundering (of a captured ship); plunder from a captured ship

pendolero *adj* hanging

pendolista *m+f* penman

pendolón *m* large pendulum; *eng* king-post

pendón *m* banner, standard; pennant; *bot* shoot; *fam* tart, slut; despicable person

pendular swing

pendulazo swing (of a pendulum)

péndulo *n* pendulum; **~ sideral/sidéreo** *astron* chronometer, standard clock; *adj* pendulous; hanging

pene *m* penis

penedé *m+f* non-teaching member of a school staff

penetrabilidad *f* penetrability

penetrable penetrable; comprehensive

penetración *f* penetration; sagacity, wisdom

penetrador *n m* discerner; *adj* discerning, penetrating

penetral *m* innermost recess

penetrante penetrating; clear-sighted

penetrar *vt* to penetrate, pierce; permeate; break through; comprehend; *vi* **~ en** to enter/go in(to); penetrate

penicilina penicillin

península peninsula

peninsular living on a peninsula; peninsular; **España ~** mainland Spain

penique *m* penny

penisla peninsula

penitencia penitence; penance; **hacer ~** to take pot-luck; do penance

penitenciado *n* convict; *adj* punished, convicted

penitencial penitential

penitenciar to impose a penance on

penitenciaría *n* penitentiary

penitenciario *n* penitentiary

penitente *n m* + *f* + *adj* penitent

penol *m naut* yard-arm

penología penology

penológico penological

penólogo, penologista *m* + *f* penologist

penoso painful; arduous; unpleasant; shameful

pensado intentional, deliberate; thought-out; **bien ~** well-conceived, wise; **de ~** on purpose; **mal ~** ill-conceived, badly thought out; **tener ~** to have in mind, intend

pensador *n m* thinker; *adj* thinking

pensamiento thought, idea; epigram; suspicion; plan, project; *arts* first rough sketch; *bot* pansy; **en un ~** in a flash; **tener el ~ de** to intend

¹ **pensar** to think; intend to; **~ de** to think about, have an opinion about; **~ en** to think about, remember

² **pensar** to give fodder to

pensativo pensive, thoughtful

penseque *m* careless mistake

pensil *n m* hanging garden; *adj* hanging

pensión *f* pension; annuity; guest-house, boarding-house; price of board and lodging; scholarship; **~ vitalicia** life-pension; **media ~** halfboard

pensionado *n* pensioner; scholarship holder; boarding-school; **~ de señoritas** finishing school

pensionar to grant a pension to; impose a charge on

pensionario payer of a pension

pensionista *m* + *f* pensioner; boarder; **hogar del ~** *approx equiv* Darby-and-Joan club

pentaédrico pentahedral

pentaedro pentahedron

pentágono pentagon

pentagrama *m mus* manuscript paper; stave

pentámetro pentameter

pentasílabo (word) of five syllables

Pentateuco Pentateuch

pentatlo *sp* pentathlon

Pentecostés *m* Pentecost, Whitsun

penúltimo next-to-last, penultimate; *joc* last drink before going home

penuria penury, indigence, poverty

¹ **peña** rock, crag

² **peña** group of friends who meet regularly; youth club (*usu* of bull-fight supporters); **~ quinielista** pools syndicate

peñascal *m* craggy hill; rocky terrain

peñasco large rock

peñascoso rocky, boulder-strewn

peñón *m* large rock; rocky cliff; **el Peñón** Gibraltar

peón *m* labourer; footsoldier; draughtsman; pawn (chess); spinning-top; **~ de albañil** builder's labourer; bricklayer's mate

peonada one day's work

peonaje *m* gang of workmen

peonía *bot* peony

peonza spinning-top; fidgety person

peor worse, worst; **~ que** worse than; **~ que ~** worse and worse; **lo ~** the worst of it, the worst thing; **tanto ~** so much the worse

peoría deterioration

Pepa Josie

Pepe Joe, Joey

pepinar *m* cucumber plot/field

pepinazo *sp* short powerful shot at goal

pepinillo gherkin; pickled cucumber

pepino cucumber; **~ del diablo** bitter gherkin; **me importa un ~** I don't give a fig

¹ **pepita: ~ de oro** gold nugget

² **pepita** *bot* seed, pip

³ **pepita** *vet* pip, fowl distemper

pepito meat sandwich

¹ **pepitoso** full of seeds/pips

² **pepitoso** *vet* suffering from pip

pepón *m* water-melon

pepsina pepsin

péptico peptic

pequeñamente slightly, to a small degree

pequeñez *f* smallness; childhood, infancy; trifle; mean action; mean-spiritedness

pequeño *n* small child; *adj* small; young; mean-spirited; **de ~** as a child

pequeñuelo *n* very small child, toddler; *adj* very small; very young

Pequín Pekin

pequinés *m* pekinese (dog)

pera *n* pear; goatee beard; *sl* fence, receiver of stolen property; **chico ~** posh young man, young toff; **de uvas a ~s** once in a blue moon; **pedir ~s al olmo** to ask for the impossible, ask for the moon; **tomate ~** plum tomato

perada pear jam; perry (cider)

peral *m* pear-tree

peraleda pear-tree orchard

peralejo *bot* white poplar

peralte *m archi* rise (of an arch)

perca *zool* perch

percal *m* muslin; calico; *sl* money, lolly; **conocer el ~** to know one's stuff

percance perquisite; bad luck, misfortune; **~s del oficio** drawbacks of the job

percatarse to perceive; **~ de** to notice, become aware of

percebe *m* goose-barnacle; ignoramus

percebimiento warning; precaution

percepción *f* perception

perceptibilidad *f* perceptibility

perceptividad *f* perceptivity

perceptivo perceptive

perceptor *n m* perceiver; *adj* perceiving

percibir to perceive; receive, get; collect

percibo *n* receiving, collecting

percloruro perchloride

percolación *f* percolation, seepage

percolador *m* coffee-percolator

percudir to begrime; stain, tarnish

percusión *f* percussion

percutir to percuss, strike, beat

percusor *m* striker; (of firearm) percussion hammer

percha perch, pole; slat; *naut* spar; snare; clothes-rack; clothes-hanger; **de ~** off the peg, ready-made; **estar en ~** to be in the bag; **tener buena ~** to be well built

perchar *text* to card; raise the nap

perchonar to lay a snare (for game); prune vines

perchero clothes-rack

perchón *m* main vine shoot

perdedero cause of a loss; excuse for losing

perdedor *m* loser

perder to lose; fade; squander, ruin, miss (fail to catch); **~ cuidado** to have no fear; **~ de vista** to lose sight of; **~ el**
juicio/el seso to go mad; **~ el tiempo** to waste time; **~ los estribos** to fly off the handle; **~ la vista** to go blind; **echarse a ~** to go to the dogs, go to rack and ruin, go rotten; **~se** to get lost, go astray, miscarry; become flustered/bewildered; get damaged; go out of fashion; fall madly in love; **~se de vista** to go out of sight; **¡no te lo pierdas!** it's too good to be missed!

perdición *f* perdition; ruin; unbridled love

pérdida loss; damage; privation; waste; *comm* wastage, leakage, shortage; **~s y ganancias** profit and loss; **no tiene ~** you can't miss it, you can't lose your way; **vender con ~s** to sell at a loss

perdidizo lost deliberately; **hacer ~** to hide; **hacerse ~** to lose intentionally; **hacerse el ~** to sneak off, steal away

perdido *n* good-for-nothing, prodigal; *adj* lost; wasted; **~ de barro** covered in mud

perdidoso *adj* losing; easily lost

perdigar *cul* to broil; brown (meat); dispose

[1] **perdigón** *m* young partridge; decoy; **perdigones** lead shot, buckshot

[2] **perdigón** *m* wastrel, squanderer; reckless gambler

perdigonera shot-pouch

perdiguero retriever, gun-dog; game dealer

perdimiento loss

perdis *m* (of person) rake

perdiz *f* partridge; **~ blanca** ptarmigan

perdón *m* pardon; mercy; reprieve; cancellation (of debt); **¡~!** excuse me!; sorry!; **con ~** by your leave; **no tener ~** to be beyond forgiveness

perdonable pardonable, forgivable

perdonante forgiving

perdonar to forgive, pardon; excuse; remit (a debt)

perdonavidas *m sing + pl fam* bully

perdulario *n* rake; *adj* reckless

perdurable long-lasting; everlasting; enduring

perduración *f* long duration

perdurar to last a long time; endure

perecear to delay, put off, protract; waste time

perecedero *n* abject poverty; *adj* perishable

perecer to perish; come to an end; ~se to crave

pereciente *adj* perishing; craving

perecimiento *n* perishing; end; death

pereda pear orchard

peregrinación *f* pilgrimage

peregrinante travelling

peregrinar to go on a pilgrimage; travel; roam

peregrinidad *f* rareness; strangeness

peregrino *n* pilgrim; *adj* roaming, wandering; foreign; *orni* migratory; rare, strange

perejil *m bot* parsley; *fig* excessive adornment on a woman's dress

perendengue *m* ear-ring; trinket; cheap jewellery

Perengano so-and-so; what's-his-name?

perennal, perenne perennial; everlasting, perpetual

perennidad *f* continuity

perentoriedad *f* great urgency

perentorio peremptory; urgent

pereza laziness, idleness, sloth; slowness; **tener ~** to be lazy

perezoso lazy, idle, slothful; slow

perfección *f* perfection; **a la ~** perfectly

perfeccionador *n m* perfecter; *adj* perfecting

perfeccionar to make perfect; finish off; improve

perfeccionismo perfectionism

perfeccionista *m* + *f* perfectionist

perfectivo perfective

perfecto *n gramm* perfect tense; *adj* perfect, faultless; *fam* just right, O.K.

perficiente *adj* perfecting

perfidia perfidy, treachery

pérfido perfidious, treacherous

perfil *m* profile, outline; cross-section; **de ~** silhouetted, from the side; ~es finishing touches, etiquette

perfilado outlined; streamlined; well shaped

perfiladura outline

perfilar to outline, shape; polish; put the finishing touches to; ~se to stand sideways, stand up

perfoliado *bot* perfoliate

perforación *f* perforation, drilling, boring; ~ **petrolífera** oil-drilling

perforador *m* perforator, driller; drill; drilling-machine; *adj* drilling; boring

perforar to perforate; drill; puncture

perfumado perfumed, sweet-smelling

perfumador *adj* perfuming

perfumar to perfume

perfume *m* perfume; fragrance, aroma

performear to perfume

perfumería perfumery shop; perfume-making

perfumero perfumery shopkeeper

perfumista *m* + *f* perfumist

perfunctorio perfunctory

perfusión *f* sprinkling, bathing

pergaminero parchment-maker/seller

pergamino parchment; diploma; lineage, noble ancestry

pergeñar to outline; devise

pergeño look

pérgola pergola; roof-garden

peri *f* fairy

pericarpio *bot* pericarp

pericia expertise; know-how

pericial *adj* expert

Perico Pete; ~ **el de los palotes** any Tom, Dick or Harry

perico *orni* parakeet; periwig; (cards) queen of clubs; woman's curls; *fam* chamber-pot; ~ **entre ellas** man who prefers women's company

pericón *n m* large fan; *adj* multi-purpose

periferia periphery

periférico peripheric

perifollo *bot* chervil; frippery; ~s frills and flounces, excessive adornment

perifrasear to periphrase; employ circumlocutions

perífrasis *f* periphrasis

perifrástico periphrastic; circumlocutory

perigallo loose skin below the chin; hair-ribbon; tall thin man

perigeo *astron* perigee

perigonio *bot* perianth

perihelio *astron* perihelion

perilustre eminent, illustrious

perilla *bot* small pear; pear-shaped ornament; knob; goatee beard; earlobe; *elect* (pear-shaped) switch; **de ~** on purpose; at the right time; **venir de ~** to be just what the doctor ordered

perillán *m* knave, rogue

perímetro perimeter

perínclito highly illustrious

perindola small spinning-top

períoca synopsis

periodicidad *f* periodicity
periódico *n* newspaper; periodical; *adj* periodic(al)
periodismo journalism
periodista *m + f* journalist
periodístico journalistic
período period; *elect* cycle; age; *fam* menstruation; *mus* phrase
peripatético peripatetic
peripecia change of circumstances; incident
periplo journeyings, wanderings; seatrip, circumnavigation
peripuesto spruce; natty, dapper
periquete *m* jiffy, trice
periquillo sugar-plum
periquito *orni* parakeet, budgerigar; *sl* football fan
periscopio periscope
perista *m* fence, receiver of stolen goods
peritaje *m* technical college diploma
perito *n* expert, connoisseur; *adj* expert, skilful
peritoneo *med* peritoneum
perjudicante injurious, damaging
perjudicar to injure, damage, harm
perjudicial injurious, harmful, damaging
perjuicio detriment; harm, injury; damage
perjurador *m* perjurer
perjurar to commit perjury; speak profanely; ~se to perjure o.s.
perjurio perjury
perjuro *n* perjurer; *adj* perjured
perla pearl; *fig* gem, treasure; ~s fine teeth; **de ~s** perfectly; **venir de ~s** to be just what the doctor ordered
perlada pearled (of barley)
perlático paralysed, palsied
perlería collection of pearls
perlesía paralysis, palsy
perlino pearl-like; pearl-coloured
perlongar *naut* to coast, sail along the coast; *naut* cast a rope
permanecer to remain, stay; last, endure
permaneciente permanent, persisting
permanencia stay; duration; permanence
permanente *n f* perm, permanent wave; *adj* permanent
permanganato permanganate; ~ **de potasio** potassium permanganate

permeabilidad *f* permeability
permeabilizar to make permeable
permisible permissible
permisión *f* permission; permissiveness; permit, licence
permisivo permissive
permiso permit, licence; *mil* leave pass; **con ~** by your leave, excuse me; ~ **de pernoctar** *mil* overnight pass
permisor *m* permitter
permistión *f* mixture; concoction
permitiente *adj* permitting
permitidero permissible
permitidor permitting
permitir to permit, allow; enable; grant; ~se to take the liberty of, be allowed or permitted; **no se permite aparcar** parking is not allowed
permuta exchange; barter
permutable exchangeable
permutación *f* permutation, interchange
permutador *m* permuter
permutante permutant, exchanging
permutar to permutate; permute; interchange
pernada kick; *naut* leg (of a machine, appliance *etc*)
perneador strong-legged
pernear to kick; move the leg violently; fret
pernera leg (of a garment)
pernete *m naut* small peg; small bolt
perniabierto bandy-legged
pernicioso pernicious; injurious
pernil *m* hock (of an animal); ham; leg of pork; leg (of a garment)
pernio hinge of a door/window
pernituerto crooked-legged
perno bolt, pin; *mech* crank-pin
pernoctar to spend the night; stay out all night
¹ **pero** *bot* pear-tree
² **pero** *n* snag, difficulty; defect; **poner ~s** to raise objections, find fault; *conj* but, yet; **¡~ que muy bien!** very well indeed!
perogrullada truism; platitude
Perogrullo: verdad de ~ *see* **perogrullada**
perol *m* copper cooking vessel shaped like a half sphere
peroné *m anat* fibula
peroración *f* peroration
perorar to make a speech; urge

perorata harangue; rigmarole

peróxido peroxide; ~ **de hidrógeno** hydrogen peroxide

perpendicularidad *f* perpendicularity

perpendículo plummet; pendulum; *geom* altitude of a triangle

perpetración *f* perpetration

perpetrador *m* perpetrator

perpetrar to perpetrate

perpetuación *f* perpetuation

perpetuar to perpetuate; **~se** to drag on and on

perpetuidad *f* perpetuity

perpetuo perpetual, everlasting; **cadena perpetua** life imprisonment

perplejidad *f* perplexity

perplejo perplexed; unsure

perquirir to seek conscientiously

perra *vet* bitch; slut; tart; *fam* tantrum; ~ **chica** five-cent coin; ~ **gorda** ten-cent coin

perrada pack of dogs; mean act

perramente very badly

perrengue *m* morose person; bad-tempered person

perrera kennel; toil

perrería pack of dogs; gang of rogues; expression of anger; dirty trick

perrero dog-catcher; dog-fancier; master of hounds

perrezno whelp, puppy

perrillo little dog; ~ **faldero/de falda,** ~ **lulú** lap-dog

perrito little dog; ~ **caliente** *cul* hot dog

perro *n* dog; *sl* cop, policeman; ~ **alforjero** camp watch-dog; ~ **braco** setter; ~ **cobrador** retriever; ~ **chino** chihuahua; ~ **de aguas** poodle; ~ **de caza** gun-dog; ~ **de casta** thoroughbred dog; ~ **de lanas** lapdog, poodle; ~ **del hortelano** dog-in-the-manger; ~ **de muestra** show-dog; ~ **lebrel** whippet; ~ **mudo** *zool* racoon; ~ **pastor alemán** alsatian; ~ **viejo** old hand, one with great experience; ~ **zorrero** foxhound; **de ~s** lousy, very bad, **noche de ~s** dirty night

perroquete *m naut* topmast

perruno *adj* canine; dog-like

persa *n m + f + adj* Persian

persecución *f* persecution

persecutorio persecuting; **manía persecutoria** persecution complex

perseguidor *m* persecutor; pursuer

perseguimiento pursuing, pursuit

perseguir to persecute; pursue; importune

Perseo Perseus

perseverancia perseverance

perseverante persevering

perseverar to persevere

persiana venetian blind, *US* shade; *sl* gin and peppermint

persignarse to make the sign of the cross

pérsico *adj* Persian

persistencia persistence; obstinacy

persistente persistent; firm, obdurate; **reacción ~** sustained reaction

persistir to persist

persona person; personage; individual; **buena ~** decent person; **de ~ a ~** man-to-man; **en ~, por su ~** in person; **mala ~** nasty person; **muchas ~s** a lot of people; **tercera ~** mediator, third party; ~ **mayor** adult

personaje *m* personage; *theat* character

personal *n m* personnel, staff; people; *adj* personal, private

personalidad *f* personality; individuality; *leg* person

personalismo favouritism; nepotism; personality cult

personalizar to personalize

personarse to show up, appear in person; *leg* appear as an interested party

personería solicitorship

personero solicitor

personificación *f* personification

personificar to personify

perspectiva perspective; view, prospect; appearance; *fig* horizon

perspicacia, perspicacidad *f* perspicacity; acumen

perspicaz perspicacious

perspicuidad *f* perspicuity; clearness; transparency

perspicuo perspicuous; clear; transparent

persuadidor *m* persuader

persuadir to persuade; **~se** to be persuaded, let o.s. be convinced

persuasión *f* persuasion

persuasiva persuasiveness, persuasion

persuasivo persuasive; convincing

persuasor *m* persuader; persuasive person

persulfato persulphate

persulfuro persulphide

pertenecer to belong; concern; **pertenece al pasado** it's a thing of the past

pertenecido dependence

perteneciente belonging

pertenencia ownership; possession; **no es de mi ~** it's not my province

pértiga pole; pole-jumping; staff; staff of office

pertiguería vergership, verger's office

pertiguero verger

pertinacia pertinacity; stubbornness, doggedness

pertinaz pertinacious; obstinate

pertinencia relevancy; pertinence

pertinente pertinent; relevant; *leg* concerning

pertrechar to equip, supply

pertrechos *mpl* equipment; stores

perturbable easily perturbed

perturbación *f* perturbation; disorder

perturbador *n m* perturber; *adj* perturbing, upsetting

perturbar to perturb; disturb; unsettle

Perú Peru

peruano, peruviano *n + adj* Peruvian

perulero *see* perol

perversidad *f* perversity

perversión *f* perversion; depravation; corruption

perverso *n* pervert; *adj* perverse; depraved

pervertidor *m* perverter; *adj* perverting

pervertimiento perversion, perverting

pervertir to pervert

pervigilio sleeplessness

pervivencia survival

pervivir to survive

pervulgar to divulge

pesa weight; counter-weight; **~s y medidas** weights and measures; **según caigan las ~s** depending on how things turn out

pesacartas *m sing + pl* letter-scale

pesada weighing; quantity weighed at one time

pesadez *f* heaviness; slowness; sleepiness; obesity; dullness; **¡ que ~!** what a bore!

pesadilla nightmare

pesado *n* bore (person); *adj* heavy; sultry; stuffy (of atmosphere); obese; annoying; **broma pesada** practical joke, joke in bad taste

pesador *m* weigher

pesadumbre *f* grief, sorrow; heaviness

pesalicores *m sing + pl* hydrometer

pésame *m* condolence; **dar el ~** to offer one's condolences

pesante *adj* weighing

pesantez *f* heaviness; *phys* density

pesar *n* sorrow; regret; **a ~ de** in spite of; **a ~ nuestro** in spite of ourselves; *vi* to weigh, be weighty; be sorry; *vt* to weigh; think over, consider; **a ~** despite; **mal que le pese** though you may not like it; **pese a quien pese** whatever anyone thinks; **te pesará** you'll live to regret it

pesario *med* pessary

pesaroso sorrowful

pesca fishing; fishery; catch (of fish); **ir a la ~ de** to seek, look for; **ir de ~** to go fishing; **toda la ~** the whole caboodle

pescadería fishmonger's, fish-shop

pescadero fishmonger, *US* fish-dealer

pescadilla baby hake

pescado fish (not alive)

pescador *m* fisherman; angler

pescante *m* jib (of a crane); boom; *naut* davit; *theat* trap-door

pescar to fish; find and pick up; obtain, get; catch in the act

pescozón *m* grip round the neck; slap on the neck/head

pescuezo neck; throat; **cortar el ~** to cut the throat, decapitate; **retorcer el ~** to wring the neck

pesebre *m* crib; manger

pesebrera row of mangers; stable

peseta peseta; **cambiar la ~** *sl* to vomit, spew up

pesetero materialistic person; mercenary, stingy person

pésimamente very badly, atrociously

pesimismo pessimism

pesimista *n m + f* pessimist; *adj* pessimistic

pésimo very bad, atrocious

peso weight; heaviness; balance, scales; importance; burden; good sense; unit of currency in *Arg*, *Chi*, *Col*, *Cub* and *Mex*: **~ bruto** gross weight; **~ específico** *phys* specific gravity; **~ muerto** dead weight; **~ neto** net weight; **a ~ de oro** at an exorbitant price; **caerse de su ~** to be obvious; **de ~** of correct weight; **en ~** suspended; **llevar el ~ de**

to bear the burden of

pespuntador *m* (sewing) back-stitcher

pespuntar, pespuntear (sewing) to back-stitch

pespunte *m* back-stitch

pesquera fishery; fishing-grounds

pesquería fishing; fishery; fish business

pesquero *adj* fishing

pesquis *m* acumen; **tener mucho** ~ to be quick on the uptake

pesquisa investigation; inquiry; search

pesquisante investigating; inquiring; searching

pesquisar to investigate; inquire into

pesquisidor *m* inquirer; examiner; investigator

pestaña *anat* eyelash; *mech* flange; rim; *bot* hairs; sunshade

pestañear to blink; wink

pestañeo blinking; winking

pestañi *f sl* police (force), fuzz, cops

peste *f* plague, pestilence; bad smell; ~s angry words; ¡una ~ de ...! a plague on ...!; **echar** ~s to call every name under the sun

pestífero pestiferous, foul

pestilencia pestilence, plague; foulness; stench, stink

pestilencial, pestilencioso pestilential, foul

pestilente pestilent; foul; evil-smelling

pestillo door-bolt; latch; ~ **de golpe** automatic bolt, snap bolt; **correr el** ~ to slide the bolt

pestiño *cul* pancake, sweet fritter dipped in honey; *sl* bore, dull person

pesto beating

pestorejo scruff of the neck

pesuña half of cloven hoof; toe

petaca cigar-case; tobacco-pouch; leather case; leather-covered trunk

petalismo *pol* banishment

pétalo petal

petanca (game) petanque

petar to please, gratify; **no me peta** it doesn't appeal to me

petardear *mil* to blow up with petards; cheat; *mot* backfire

petardista *m* cheat

petardo petard; bomb; squib, firecracker; cheat, fraud; *mot* backfire; *sl* marihuana cigarette; bore, horror

petate *m* duffle-bag; *naut* kitbag; bedroll; sports bag; *naut* hammock;

sleeping-mat; *fam* cheat, swindler; **liar el** ~ to pack up and depart, kick the bucket

petenera Andalusian folk-song similar to the malagueña; **salir por** ~s to go off at a tangent

petera squabble; outburst of temper; obstinacy

peteretes *mpl* titbits, sweetmeats

petete *m* baby's bootee

petición *f* petition; claim; application; ~ **de mano** formal request for a woman's hand in marriage, proposal

peticionario petitioner

petigrís *m* squirrel-skin

petimetra stylish affected woman

petimetre *m* fob, dandy; mod

petirrojo *orni* robin

petitorio *n* repeated petition; *adj* petitionary

peto breastplate; (bullfighting) protective mattress for horses; **pantalones de** ~ dungarees

pétreo stony; of stone

petrificación *f* petrification

petrificante petrifying

petrificar to petrify

petrografía petrography

petróleo petroleum, mineral oil; ~ **combustible** fuel oil; ~ **crudo** crude oil

petrolero *n* seller of petroleum; incendiarist; *naut* oil-tanker; *adj* oil, petroleum

petrolífero oil-bearing

petrología petrology

petroquímico petrochemical

petroso stony, full of stones

petulancia petulance; arrogance

petulante petulant; arrogant

peyorativo pejorative, derogatory

¹ **pez** *f* tar, pitch; ~ **griega** resin

² **pez** *m* fish (alive); catch, haul; lazy student; ~ **de colores** goldfish; ~ **espada** swordfish; ~ **gordo** big noise, big shot; ~ **martillo** hammer-headed shark; ~ **sierra** sawfish; ~ **volador** flying-fish; **como** ~ **en el agua** in one's element; **picar el** ~ to be fooled, taken in

pezón *m* stem (of fruit); leaf/flower stem; *anat* nipple

pezonera *mech* linch-pin

pezpalo stockfish

pezpita *orni* wagtail

pezuña cloven-hoof; *sl* foot

piada chirping, tweeting

piador *n* chirper, tweeter; *adj* chirping, tweeting

piadoso pious, saintly, holy; **mentira piadosa** white lie

piafar (of horses) to paw the ground

piale *m* throw(ing) of a lasso

piamontés *n m +adj* Piedmontese

pian *m* *med* yaws

pian, piano softly, slowly

pianista *m+f* pianist; piano-maker

piano *adv* gently, softly

piano(forte) *m* piano; ~ **de cola** grand piano; ~ **de media cola** baby-grand piano; ~ **vertical** upright piano

piante *n sl* complainer, moaner, beefer; *adj* chirping, cheeping

piar to chirp, cheep; *fam* whine; *sl* complain

piara herd of mules, horses or pigs; mob

piastra piastre; *sl* peseta

piba *sl* girl, lass, bird

pibe *m + f* little child, tot, kid

pica pike, lance; goad, prod; *m sl* bus/ train ticket-inspector; **poner una ~ en Flandes** to obtain a triumph, set the Thames on fire

picacho summit, peak; crag

picada prick(ing), puncture; insect bite/ sting

picadero riding-school; *naut* stocks, boat-skid; stag's stamping-ground; bachelor flat

picadillo *cul* hash, minced meat; **hacer ~** *fig* to cut to pieces

picado *n cul* minced meat, hash; *aer* dive, diving; **bombardear en ~** to dive-bomb; *adj* (sewing) pinked; *med* pock-marked; vexed; (fruit) overripe

picador *m* mounted bullfighter armed with a goad; horse-breaker; (sewing) pinking-iron; file-cutter; chopping-block

picadura pricking; (sewing) pinking; puncture; sting, bite; slash; chopped tobacco; first signs of caries in teeth

picaflor *m* humming-bird

picajón, picajoso peevish; easily upset, touchy

pical *m* rural crossroads

picamaderos *m sing +pl* woodpecker

picana goad; *sl* electric-shock torture

picanear to goad; *sl* torture with electric

shock

picante *n m* piquancy; satire; ~**s** *sl* socks; *adj* piquant, highly seasoned, hot to the taste; stinging, pricking; satirical, biting

¹ picaño vagrant

² picaño patch (on a shoe)

picapedrero stone-cutter

picapica itching-powder; anything that causes itching

picapleitos *m sing+pl* litigious person; pettifogging lawyer

picaporte *m* bolt; latch; latchkey; door-knocker; door-knob

picaposte *m* woodpecker

picapuerco great spotted woodpecker

picar *vi* to be piqued; take offence; be moth-eaten; itch; start to decay/ decompose; *naut* (of sea) get choppy; *vt* to prick; pierce; *ent* sting, bite; *orni* peck; (of fish) bite, take the bait, nibble; *cul* mince, chop; take small bites of; incite; vex; *sl* kill; *sl* inject o.s. with a drug; *arts* stipple; ~ **la bomba** *naut* to work the pump; ~**se** to take offence; go bad; turn sour

picaraza *orni* magpie

picarazo rogue, knave

picardear to act the rogue; make trouble; lead into evil ways

picardía mischief, roguery, knavery; vileness; deliberate trick; wantonness; *sl* camiknickers; ~**s** offensive words

picaresca den of rogues

picaresco *n* life of knavery; *adj* picaresque; knavish, roguish; vile

pícaro *n* knave, rogue, scamp; ~ **de cocina** scullion; *adj* knavish, roguish; mischievous; crafty, sly; vile

picarón *m* great knave

picarona jade

picatoste *m* buttered toast; fried bread

¹ picaza magpie; ~ **marina** flamingo

² picaza mattock

¹ picazo (of horses) black and white

² picazo thrust with a pike; *orni* beak; young magpie; peck

picazón *f* itch, itching; fretfulness; disappointment

picea *bot* spruce

píceo tarry, pitchy

Picio: **más feo que ~** as ugly as sin

¹ pico sharp point; pick-axe; summit,

peak; *orni* beak, bill; *fam* mouth;
garrulity, talkativeness; small amount
extra; *sl* drug injection; ~ **de ancla**
naut bill of an anchor; ~ **de cigüeña**
geranium; ~ **de oro** honey-tongued
person, orator of great eloquence; ~s
odds and ends; **callar el** ~ to hold
one's tongue, shut up; **cuarenta y**
~ forty-odd; **hablar de** ~ to talk big
but do little; **hinchar el** ~ to kick the
bucket, snuff it; **las cuatro y** ~ just
after four o'clock; **perderse por el** ~
to talk too much; **salir por un** ~ to
cost a pretty penny; **sombrero de**
tres ~s three-cornered hat; **tener**
mucho ~ to have a lot to say, talk too
much

² **pico** *orni* woodpecker; ~ **verde**, ~ **real**
green woodpecker

picofeo *orni* toucan

picolete *m* bolt staple

picoleto *sl* member of the Civil Guard

picón *m* charcoal; *sl* louse

piconero charcoal-burner

picor *m* itching; piquancy, hot taste

picoso pitted by small pox; pock-marked

picota pillory; peak; spire; point; *sl*
nose; **poner en la** ~ to mock, hold up
to ridicule

picotazo *orni* peck; bite; mark of a bite/
peck

picote *m text* goat-hair cloth

picoteado pecked

picotear (of horses) to toss the head;
orni peck (at); ~**se** to chatter;
wrangle, squabble

picotería garrulity; gossiping

picotero garrulousness, chattering,
wrangling

pícrico picric

pictografía pictography

pictórico pictorial

picudo beaked, pointed; garrulous

picha *vulg* penis, prick

pichel *m* pewter tankard

pichelería tankard factory

pícher *m sp* pitcher

pichi *m* dungarees; pinafore

pichicos *m sing+pl* doggie, pooch

pichinga doll

pichón *m* young pigeon; clay pigeon;
fam darling, ducky; **tiro de** ~ clay-
pigeon shooting

pidientero beggar

pidón *adj* persistent in begging; always
asking for something

pie *m* foot; leg; stand, support; base,
pedestal; *bot* trunk, stem; *bot* slip,
cutting; bottom (of a page); (cards)
last player; *theat* cue; motive; foundation; rule; ~ **de amigo** *min* pit-prop; ~
de cabra crowbar; ~ **de imprenta**
printer's mark; ~ **de montar** left foot;
~ **derecho** *naut* stanchion; ~ **marino**
sea-legs; ~ **plano** flat foot; **a** ~ **on**
foot, walking; **a** ~ **de fábrica** ex-
works; **a** ~ **firme** resolutely; **a** ~s
juntillos emphatically; **al** ~ near to; **al**
~ **de la letra** literally; **caer de** ~ to land
on one's feet; **con buen o mal** ~ come
what may; **dar** ~ **a** to encourage; **de** ~
standing up; **de** ~**s a cabeza** from head
to foot; **en** ~ **de guerra** on a war
footing; **en** ~ **de igualdad** on an equal
footing; **entrar con buen** ~ to start off
on the right foot; **hacer** ~ to be able to
touch bottom (when in deep water);
hacer con los ~s to do/work in a ham-
fisted way; **ni** ~s **ni cabeza** neither
head nor tail; **perder** ~ to lose one's
foothold; **tomar** ~ **de** to use as an
excuse/justification

piedad *f* piety, saintliness; mercy; **por** ~
for pity's/Pete's sake

piedra stone; cobblestone; memorial
tablet; *med* gravel; flint; ~ **angular**
corner-stone; ~ **berroqueña** granite;
~ **bruta** rubble, hard core; ~ **caliza**
limestone; ~ **de amolar** grindstone,
whetstone; ~ **de molino** mill-stone; ~
de toque touchstone; ~ **falsa** imitation
precious stone; ~ **filosofal** philosopher's stone; ~ **fundamental** foundation stone; ~ **imán** lodestone; ~
lipis copper sulphate; ~ **millar** milestone; ~ **pómez** pumice-stone; ~
sepulcral gravestone, headstone; ~
viva solid rock; **no dejar** ~ **por mover**
to leave no stone unturned; **no dejar**
~ **sobre** ~ to raze to the ground; **tirar**
~s to go crazy

piel *f* skin, hide, pelt; leather; (of fruit
etc) peel; ~ **de gallina** goose-pimples,
goose-flesh; ~**es rojas** redskins; **ab-**
rigo de ~**es** fur coat; **ser de la** ~ **del**
diablo to be the very devil himself, be
of the devil's brood

piélago high seas; large number

¹ **pienso** fodder, animal feed; *sl* food, grub, nosh

² **pienso**: ¡ni por ~! not on your life!, not on your nelly!

piérides *fpl* Muses

pierna *anat* leg; downstroke (in handwriting); branch/leg of a pair of compasses/dividers; *mech* shank; ~ **de una sábana** width of a sheet; **a ~ suelta/tendida** at one's ease; **dormir a ~ suelta** to sleep like a log; **en ~s** bare-legged; **estirar la ~** *fam* to kick the bucket, snuff it; **estirar las ~s** to stretch one's legs, go for a stroll

piernitendido with legs outstretched

pieza piece, bit, fragment; *mech+mot* part, spare; *mus* piece, composition; *text* roll/bolt (of cloth); room (of a building); prey, quarry, game; coin; *theat* play; man (in chess, draughts *etc*); ~ **de artillería** piece of ordnance; ~ **de recibo** reception-room; ~ **de recambio**, ~ **de repuesto** spare part; ~ **por** ~ in great detail; **de una** ~ solid, in one piece; **hacer** ~**s** to break, smash; **quedarse de una** ~ to be flabbergasted; **un dos** ~**s** (clothes) two-piece suit

pifano *mus* fife; fife-player

pifia (billiards) miscue; error; whistling sound

pifiar (billiards) to miscue; breathe loudly, wheeze; make a blunder

pigmentación *f* pigmentation

pigmentario pigmentary

pigmento pigment

pigmeo pigmy

pignoración *f* pawn, pledge of security

pignorar to pawn, give as security

pigre lazy, slothful

pigricia laziness, slothfulness; carelessness; place in school for lazy pupils

pihuela leash; hindrance; ~**s** shackles, fetters

pijada *sl* stupidity

pijama *m* (*Sp*), *f* (*SA*) pair of pyjamas, *US* pajamas

pijo *sl* snob

pijota *zool* baby hake

pijote *m naut* swivel-gun

pijotero mean, niggardly; annoying

pila trough, basin; sink; *eccles* font, stoup; pile, heap; *eng+archi* pier; *elect* battery; **nombre de** ~ Christian name, *US* given name

pilada *bui* mixing; amount of cement mixed at one time; pile; *text* fulled cloth

pilar *m* basin of a fountain; *archi* column, pillar; pedestal, support; post; bedpost

pilastra *archi* pilaster

pilatero *text* fuller

Pilatos Pilate

pilcha man's suit

píldora pill, tablet; pellet; *fam* bad news; **dorar la** ~ to sugar the pill; **tragarse la** ~ to believe a tall story

pileo *eccles* cardinal's red hat

pileta swimming-pool; small basin; holy water stoup

pilífero *bot* hairy

pilón *m* basin of a fountain; drinking-trough; mortar (for pounding); loaf (of sugar); *bui* heap of cement; sliding weight of a balance; grapes ready for pressing; **martillo** ~ *bui* pile-driver

pilonero newsmonger

pilongo *adj* peeled and dried (chestnuts); sickly; weakly

¹ **pilotaje** *m naut* pilotage

² **pilotaje** *m eng* pilework

pilotar to pilot; drive racing cars; navigate

pilote *m eng* pile

pilotear *aer+naut* to pilot

pilotín *m naut* pilot's mate

piloto *aer+naut* pilot, navigator; first mate; pilot light/flame; ~ **de pruebas** test pilot; ~ **práctico** coast pilot; **casa/ piso** ~ show house/flat

piltra *sl* bed

piltraca, piltrafa lean and skinny flesh; *sl* wretch; ~**s** food scraps

pillador *m* pillager

pillaje *m* pillage

pillar to pillage, plunder, loot; catch (in the act); take hold of; run over; *sl* buy; ~**se los dedos** to catch/trap one's fingers

pillastre *m*, **pillastro, pillastrón** *m* rascal, knave

pimental *m agri* pepper field/plot

pimentero pepper-pot; *bot* pepper plant

pimentón *m* dried red pepper, paprika; ~ **picante** chilli powder

pimienta black pepper; ~ **malagueta** *bot*

myrtle

pimiento *bot* capsicum; *cul* red pepper; **~ morrón** sweet pepper; **~ de cometilla** hot pepper

pimpido dog-fish

pimpinela *bot* pimpernel

pimpollar *m bot* nursery

pimpollecer *bot* to bud, sprout

pimpollo *bot* bud, sprout; *bot* sucker; attractive child/youth; **~ de la flor** flower-bud; **~ lateral** side-shoot

pimpolludo *bot* full of buds, bearing many buds

pinabete *m bot* fir

pináceo *bot* pinaceous

pinacoteca picture-gallery

pináculo pinnacle

pinado *bot* pinnate

pinar *m* pine grove/wood

pinariego *adj* pine

pinastro wild pine

pinatar *m* pinetum; pine grove

pinaza *naut* pinnace

pincel *m arts* paint-brush; painter; painting

pincelada *arts* brush-stroke; touch; **dar la última ~ a** to put the finishing touch to

pincelar *arts* to paint; draw

pincelero *arts* brush-box; maker/seller of paint-brushes/pencils

pinchadiscos *m sing+pl* disc-jockey

pinchadura puncture; pricking

pinchar to puncture; prick; *fam* bug, tap (a phone); *med* inject; *fam* goad, tease; **no/ni pincha ni corta** to account for nothing, have no say in the matter

pinchauvas *m sing+pl* good-for-nothing

pinchazo *mot* puncture; *US* blow-out; *fam* phone-tapping/bugging

pinche *m* scullion, kitchen lad

pincho thorn, prickle; skewer; prod

pinchito savoury tit-bit

pindonga gadabout woman; gossiping woman

pindonguear to gad about

pineda pine grove/wood; braid for garters

pingajo rag

pingo rag; worthless garment; gadabout; **estar de ~** to gad about

pingoneo gadding about

pingorotudo posh

pingüe fat, greasy; plentiful, abundant

pingüedinoso fatty, greasy

pingüino penguin

pinguosidad *f* fatness

pinillo *bot* germander

pinitos *mpl* child's first steps; **hacer ~** to take one's first steps; have a try

pino *n bot* pine; **~ albar** Scotch pine; **~ alerce** larch; **~ rodeno/marítimo/bravo** red pine; *adj* steep, sheer

pinocha pine-needle

Pinocho Pinocchio

pinocho pine-cone

pinoso piny

pinreles *m pl sl* feet

pinsapo Spanish fir

¹ **pinta** pint (measure)

² **pinta** appearance, aspect; spot, mark; **tener ~ de ...** to look like ...

³ **pinta** good-for-nothing

pintacilgo *orni* goldfinch

pintada *orni* guinea-fowl; **~s** graffiti

pintado *adj* spotted, mottled; **el más ~** the best/cleverest; **venir ~** to be just right, fit correctly; **es ~ a su hermano** he is the spitting image of his brother

pintamonas *m sing+pl arts* dauber, bad painter

pintar to paint; stain; portray; draw; show signs of; **~se** to make up one's face; **~se solo para** to show an aptitude for, be better than anyone at; **no ~ nada** to be a nobody

pintarrajar, pintarrajear to daub, paint badly

pintarrajo *arts* daub, bad picture

pinto, pintojo mottled, speckled; spotted

pintor *m arts* painter; **~ a la aguada** water-colour painter; **~ de brocha gorda/de andamio** house-painter, bad artist

pintora *arts* woman painter; painter's wife

pintoresco picturesque

pintorreador *m* dauber, bad painter

pintorrear *arts* to daub, paint badly

pintura painting, picture; paint, pigment; **~ a la aguada** water-colour; **~ al fresco** fresco; **~ al óleo** oil painting; **~ al pastel** pastel picture; **~ figulina** painting on earthenware

pinturero affected, conceited

pinza (of lobsters *etc*) claw, nipper; clothes-peg; **~s** pincers, tweezers *med* forceps

pinzamiento twinge, stabbing pain

pinzón *m orni* chaffinch

piña pine-cone; pineapple; cluster

piñal *m* pineapple plantation

piñata children's party; **domingo de ~** first Sunday in Lent

[1] **piñón** *m orni* pinion

[2] **piñón** *m* pine-kernel; *bot* nut-pine

[3] **piñón** *m mech* pinion; **estar a partir un ~** to be as thick as thieves

piñonear click (of gun being cocked)

[1] **pío** pious, saintly; merciful

[2] **pío** (of horses) pied, piebald

[3] **pío** chirping; **~-~** (baby talk) dickey-bird; tweet-tweet; **¡~ ~ ~ ~ ~!** call made when feeding poultry; **no decir ni ~** not to say a word

piojento *see* **piojoso**

piojera *fam* nit-nurse

piojería lousiness; abject poverty

piojillo louse/vermin on birds

piojo louse; **~ pegadizo** crab-louse; **~ verde** *sl pej* member of the Civil Guard (traffic section)

piojoso lousy, lice-infested

pión *m*, **piona** chirping, tweeting

pionero pioneer

piorno *bot* broom

piorrea *med* pyorrhoea

pipa *bot* pip, seed *esp* of sunflower; pipe; *sl* pistol

pipar to smoke a pipe

pipería collection of casks/pipes

pipeta pipette

pipi *m mil sl* raw recruit, rookie

pipí *m* (baby talk) urine; **hacer ~** to pee

pipiar *orni* to chirp, cheep, peep

pipiolo novice, greenhorn

pipirijaina band of strolling players

pipiripao slap-up do, feast

pipo *orni* flycatcher

piporro *mus* bassoon

pipote *m* keg

pique *m* pique; **a ~** in peril; **echar a ~** *naut* to scuttle, sink; **estar a ~ de** to be on the point of; **irse a ~** to fail; *naut* founder

piqué *m* (sewing) piqué; cotton material

piquera entrance to a beehive; outlet; bung-hole

piquero pikeman

piqueta pickaxe; mattock; stone-mason's hammer

piquete *m* (sewing) small hole; stake; (strike) picket

piquetilla bricklayer's hammer

piquituerto *orni* crossbill

pira pyre

piragua canoe

piragüismo canoeing

piragüista *m + f* canoeist, canoer

pirámide *f* pyramid

piraña *zool* piranha, pirana

pirarse *sl* to depart, beat it, bugger off

pirata *n m* pirate, buccaneer; cruel person; **~ aéreo** hijacker; *adj* piratical; pirate

piratear to practise piracy

piratería piracy; robbery; **~ aérea** hijacking

pirático piratical

pirca dry-stone wall

pircar to enclose with a dry-stone wall

pirenaico Pyrenean

pírico *adj* (of) fireworks, pyrotechnic

piriforme pear-shaped

pirineo Pyrenean

Pirineos Pyrenees

pirita *min* pyrite

pirolatra *m + f* fire-worshipper

pirolatría fire-worship

piromancia pyromancy

piromanía pyromania

pirómano pyromaniac

pirómetro pyrometer

piropear to pay a spoken compliment/pass a cheeky remark (to a woman)

piropo spoken compliment/cheeky remark (to a woman); flattery; *min* type of garnet

piroscopio *phys* pyroscope

pirosis *f med* pyrosis, heart-burn

pirosfera *geog* pyrosphere

pirotecnia pyrotechnics

pirotécnico pyrotechnic

piroxilina gun-cotton

pirrarse: ~ por to long for, be mad over

pírrico Pyrrhic

pirueta pirouette, turn

piruetear *vi* to pirouette, turn

pirulí *m* cone-shaped lollipop

pisa treading (of grapes)

pisada footstep; footprint; stepping on s.o.'s foot; **seguir las ~s de** to dog s.o.'s footsteps

pisador *n m* treader (of grapes); (of horses) prancer; *adj* prancing

pisadura act of treading/stepping; foot-step

pisapapeles *m sing+pl* paperweight

pisar to tread on; step on; press (on); *orni* cover (copulate); ~ **fuerte** to act with determination

pisasfalto mixture of pitch and bitumen

pisauvas *m sing+pl* treader of grapes

pisaverde *m* fob, dandy, *US* dude

piscator *m meteor* almanac of meteorological forecasts

piscatorio piscatory

piscicultor *n* pisciculturist, fish-farmer; *adj* pisciculturistic

piscicultura pisciculture, fish-farming

pisciforme fish-shaped

piscina fish-pond; swimming-pool; *eccles* piscina

Piscis *astrol+astron* Pisces

piscívoro fish-eating

piscolabis *m sing+pl* snack, bite to eat

piso floor, storey; pavement; flat, apartment; ground level; tread; gait; ~ **bajo** ground floor; ~ **primero** first floor, *US* second floor

pisonear to ram

pisotear to trample; stamp on

pisoteo trampling, stamping

pisotón *m* stamp (on s.o.'s feet)

pispar *sl* to rob

pista trail, track; scent; clue; *sp* racecourse, track; ~ **de aterrizaje** landing-strip; ~ **de baile** dance-floor; ~ **de hielo** ice rink; ~ **de patinar** skating-rink; ~ **de tenis** tennis court; **estar sobre la** ~ to be on the track; **seguir la** ~ **(de)** to follow the trail (of)

pistacho pistachio nut

pistadero pestle

pistar to pound (with a pestle)

pisti *m sl* pistol

pistilo *bot* pistil

pisto *cul* vegetable stew; **darse** ~ to put on airs

pistola pistol

pistolera holster

pistolero gunman

pistoletazo pistol-shot; **dar un** ~ to fire a shot

pistolete *m* pocket pistol

pistón *m mech* piston; *mil* percussion-cap; primer

pita *bot* aloe; hiss/whistle (of disapproval); marble

pitaco *bot* aloe stem

pitada whistle-blast; whistling

pitagórico Pythagorean; **tabla pitagórica** multiplication table

pitancería distribution of alms/rations; distribution centre

pitancero distributor of alms/rations

pitanza pittance; alms; rations

pitaña bleariness

pitañoso bleary, blear-eyed

pitar to whistle, hiss; honk, hoot; **salir pitando** to leave in a hurry

pitarra bleariness

pitarroso blear-eyed

pitazo whistle-blast

pitezna spring (of a trap)

pitillera cigarette-case; woman cigarette-maker

pitillo cigarette, fag

pítima *fam* drunkenness

pitiminí *m* pussy-cat; **rosa de** ~ climbing rose

pitío whistling

pito whistle; fife; fife-player; *orni* woodpecker; *sl* prick; ~**s y flautas** six of one and half-a-dozen of the other; **no importar/no dársele un** ~ not to care a straw; **no vale un** ~ it's not worth a straw

pitoflero *mus* bad player

¹ **pitón** *m zool* python

² **pitón** *m zool* horn just starting to grow; tip of a bull's horn; lump; spout; *bot* shoot, sprig

pitonisa witch; fortune-teller

pitorra *orni* woodcock

pitorrearse de to mock, take the mickey out of

pitorreo mockery, mickey-taking

pitorro spout, nozzle

pituitaria *anat* pituitary gland

pituitario pituitary

pituso tiny, wee; cute

piular to tweet, chirp, cheep

pivote *m mech* king-pin; pivot

piyama *see* **pijama**

pizarra slate; blackboard

pizarral *m* slate quarry

pizarreño slate-coloured

pizarrero slate-quarryman, slate-cutter; roofer

pizarrín *m* slate pencil

pizarrón *m* blackboard

pizca speck, mite, bit; crumb; **ni** ~ not

one bit

pizcador m picker, harvester

pizcar to pick; glean

pizco pinch (small amount)

pizmiento pitch-coloured

pizpereta, pizpireta (of women) lively

pizpirigaña children's game

placa badge (policeman's, sheriff's *etc*); insignia (of order of knighthood); *mech+eng* plate; plaque; *med* spot, scab; ~ **de identidad** identity disc; ~ **de matrícula** *mot* number-plate; ~ **giratoria** (railway) turntable

placabilidad f placability

placarte m placard

placativo placatory

placear to publish, proclaim; retail

placel m *naut* sandbank

pláceme m congratulation

placentero merry, jolly; pleasant

[1] **placer** n m pleasure; **a** ~ at one's convenience; *vt* to please; humour; delight

[2] **placer** m *naut* sandbank; gold-bearing place; pearl fishing

placero n gadabout; market stall-holder; *adj* (pertaining to) market-place

placibilidad f agreeableness, placidity, serenity

placible agreeable, placid, serene

placidez f serenity, peacefulness

plácido placid, agreeable, serene

placiente pleasing

plafón m *archi* soffit

[1] **plaga** plague, pestilence; calamity; plenty, abundance, surfeit

[2] **plaga** *naut* cardinal point of the compass

plagar to infest, plague; ~**se de** to be overrun with

plagiar to plagiarize

plagiario n plagiarizer; *adj* plagiarizing

plagio plagiarism

plajo *sl* fag, cigarette

plan m plan; design, drawing, description; ~ **de estudios** curriculum; **a todo** ~ in grand style; **estar en** ~ to be ready; **no es** ~ that's no fun; **no hacer** ~ not to suit; **tener muchos** ~**es** to have lots of dates/engagements; **¡vaya** ~**!** what a lark!; **en** ~ **de broma** for a laugh

plana *bui* trowel; level terrain; side of a sheet of paper; ~ **mayor** *mil* general staff; **a toda** ~ (newspaper) full page; **(en) primera** ~ (on) the front page; **enmender la** ~ to find fault with, go one better

planada level ground, plain

plancton m plankton

plancha *metal* plate, sheet; flat-iron; paper-maker's mould; *naut* gangplank; howler, gaffe; ~ **de agua** *naut* punt, floating stage; ~ **de blindaje** *mil* armour-plate/-plating; ~ **eléctrica** electric iron; **hacer una** ~ to drop a clanger, put one's foot in it

planchada *naut* gun-apron

planchado ironing

planchador m ironer

planchar to iron, press

planchazo gaffe; howler, *US* boner; blunder

planchear *metal* to plate

planchuela fluting-iron

planeador m *aer* glider

planeamiento planning

[1] **planear** to plan

[2] **planear** *aer* to glide

planeo *aer* gliding

planeta m planet

planetario n planetarium; *adj* planetary

planetícola m+f inhabitant of another planet

planetoide m *astron* planetoid

planga *orni* gannet

planicie f plane (surface)

planificación f planning

planificar to plan; **economía planificada** planned economy

planimetría planimetry

planímetro planimeter

planisferio planisphere

plano n plan, map; survey; plane; level surface; flat part of a piece of wood; *aer* wing; *cin* shot; ~ **acotado** contour map; ~ **de deriva** *aer* tail-plane; ~ **geométrico** ground plan; ~ **inclinado** inclined plane; ~ **panorámico** pictorial map; **caer de** ~ to fall flat; **cantar de** ~ to make a full confession, make a clean breast of it; **de** ~ clearly, openly; **levantar un** ~ to make a survey; **primer** ~ foreground; close-up; *adj* plane, level, smooth, even, flat

planocóncavo plano-concave

planoconvexo plano-convex

planta *anat* sole; *bot* plant; plantation;

379

eng plan, horizontal projection; works, factory; building-site; ~ **baja** ground floor; **buena** ~ fine appearance; **echar** ~**s** to boast; **estar en** ~ to be up and doing

plantación *f* plantation; act of planting

plantado: dejar a uno ~ to fail to keep a date, leave in the lurch; **dejarlo todo** ~ to drop everything

plantador *m* planter

plantaina *bot* plantain

plantaje *m* collection of plants

plantar to plant; set up, fix vertically; post, place; strike, (a blow); establish, found; jilt, leave in the lurch; ~ **fuego a** to set fire to; ~ **un bofetón** to slap, hit; ~ **una pregunta** to pose a question; ~**se** to stand upright, reach; stop, halt

plantario *hort* nursery

plante *m* revolt

planteamiento planning; posing; statement; exposition; laying out; phrasing

plantear to execute, put into effect; plan; put into action; tackle; raise (for discussion); state; ~**se** to put/suggest to s.o.; think out; arise

plantel *m hort* nursery; training-ground

planteo, plantificación *f see* **planteamiento**

plantificar to put into execution; land (a blow); dump

plantilla *bot* young plant; inner sole (of footwear); *mech* templet, pattern; staff, employees; **de** ~ permanent, on the establishment/staff

plantío *n* plantation; planting; nursery (for trees); *adj agri* (of land) ready for planting

plantista *m+f* landscape-gardener; *m* bully

plantón *m bot* scion; *mil* sentry on guard as a punishment; watchman; doorkeeper; **dar un** ~ **a uno** to stand s.o. up; **estar de** ~ to cool one's heels; **llevar un** ~ to dance attendance

planudo *naut* flat-bottomed

plañidera hired mourner

plañidero mournful, weepy

plañido moan; weeping

plañir to lament, moan; whine

plaqué *m* gold/silver plating; plated ware

plaqueta *anat* platelet

plaquín *m* coat of arms

plasmador *n m* creator; maker; moulder; *adj* creative

plasmante *n m* moulder; *adj* moulding

plasmar to mould (with clay); capture

plasta anything soft (as clay, mud *etc*); anything flattened; paste; *fam* botch

plaste *m bui* size; filler

plastecer *bui* to smear with size; apply filler

plastecido *arts* sizing

plástica *arts* plastic arts

plasticidad *f* plasticity

plástico *n+adj* plastic; **de** ~ *sl* counterfeit, false; **pintura plástica** emulsion paint

plastificar to cover with plastic film; *sl* make a gramophone recording

plastilina *tr* plasticine

plastón *m* lump of any soft, wet substance, dollop

plata silver; silver coin; money; ~ **de ley** sterling silver; ~ **labrada** silverware; ~ **virgen** native silver; **como la** ~ clean and beautiful; **en** ~ in plain speech; **hablar en** ~ to speak bluntly, speak one's mind; **sin** ~ penniless, broke

plataforma platform; terrace; (railway) roadbed; *fig* springboard; ~ **continental** continental shelf; ~ **de lanzamiento** rocket-launching platform, launching pad

platal *m* riches, wealth

platanal *m*, **platanar** *m* banana-tree plantation

plátano banana (fruit and tree); *bot* plantain; ~ **falso** sycamore maple

platazo plateful; blow with a plate

platea *theat* pit; orchestra pit; **butaca de** ~ stall

plateado *n* silver-plating; *adj* silvered

platear to silverplate

platel *m* platter; tray

platense *m* native of La Plata (*Arg*)

plateresco *archi* plateresque

platería silversmith's trade/shop

platero silversmith; jeweller

plática sermon, homily; conversation, chat

platicar to chat, converse

platija *zool* flounder, plaice

platillo small plate; saucer; pan (of a balance); *mus* cymbal; alms-bowl; ~ **volante** flying-saucer

platinífero *min* platinum-bearing
platino platinum; ~s *mot* points
plato plate; dish; *cul* course; served food; pan (of a balance); ~ **de segunda mesa** makeshift, second fiddle; ~ **frutero** fruit-dish; ~ **hondo/sopero** soup-plate; ~ **llano** flat plate; **comer en el mismo** ~ to be close friends; **nada entre dos** ~s a lot of unnecessary fuss, much ado about nothing; **tener cara de nunca haber roto un** ~ to look as if butter wouldn't melt in his/her mouth; **no es** ~ **de mi gusto** it's not my cup of tea
platónico platonic
platudo monied, rich
plausibilidad *f* praiseworthiness
plausible praiseworthy, laudable; reasonable; acceptable
plausivo laudatory, plausive
playa shore, beach; coast; seaside, *US* ocean; seaside resort
playado having a beach
playazo big beach
playback: en ~ *TV* + *theat* mimed
playera beach-shoe; *mus* Andalusian folk-song
playero fisherman; *adj* of/for the beach; **ropa playera** beachwear
plaza square; market(-place); room, space; employment; ¡~, ~! make way!, make room!; ~ **de abastos** covered market; ~ **de armas** *mil* parade-ground, drill-ground; ~ **de toros** bullring; ~ **fuerte** stronghold; **hacer** ~ to make room; **sacar a** ~ to publish; **sentar** ~ *mil* to enlist
plazo term; date; day of payment; credit; **a corto/largo** ~ short/long range/term; **comprar a** ~s to buy on credit/on hire purchase; **en el** ~ **de una semana** in a week's time
pleamar *m* high tide
plebe *f* plebs, common people
plebeyez *f* plebeianism
plebeyo *n* + *adj* plebeian; ill-mannered
plebiscitar to hold a plebiscite
pleca *print* straight line, rule
plectro plectrum; *lit* inspiration
plegable, plegadizo folding, collapsible
plegadera paper-knife
plegado *n* folding; plaiting
plegador *n m* folder; plaiter; *adj* folding, collapsible

plegadora folding-machine
plegadura fold, crease; pleat
plegar to fold; plait; pleat; double; ~**se** to yield, submit; bend
plegaria prayer; angelus (bell)
pleguete *m bot* tendril
pleistoceno Pleistocene
pleitador *m* pleader, wrangler
pleitante *n m* litigant; *adj* litigating
pleitar to plead; litigate
pleitista *m* pettifogging lawyer
pleito *leg* suit, litigation; dispute, strife; ~ **de acreedores** bankruptcy proceedings; **poner** ~ **a** to sue; **ver un** ~ to try a case
plenamar *m* high tide
plenario complete, full, plenary
plenilunio full moon
plenipotencia full powers
plenipotenciario *n* + *adj* plenipotentiary
plenitud *f* plenitude, fullness; abundance
pleno *n* plenum; ~ **del ayuntamiento** full meeting of the corporation; *adj* full, complete; **en** ~ **campo** in open country; **en** ~ **día** in broad daylight; **en** ~ **invierno** in the depths of winter; **en** ~ **verano** at the height of summer
pleonasmo pleonasm
pleonástico pleonastic
plepa pain-in-the-neck (person)
plétora plethora, abundance
pletórico plethoric
pleuresía, pleuritis *f med* pleurisy
plexo *anat* plexus; network
Pléyades *fpl astron* Pleiades
plica matted hair; *leg* sealed will
pliego sheet (of paper); ~ **de cargos** *leg* charge sheet; ~ **de condiciones** *comm* tender, bid, specifications; ~ **de prensa** page proof; folded piece of writing-paper
pliegue *m* fold, crease; (sewing) gather, pleat
plieguecillo half-sheet of paper
plinto plinth
plioceno *geol* Pliocene
plomada lead pencil; plumb; plumb-line; *naut* sounding-lead; fishing net weight; cat-o'-nine-tails
plomar to affix a lead seal to
plomazo gun-shot wound
plombagina plumbago, graphite
plomería plumbing; lead roofing-sheet

plomero plumber

plomizo leaden, lead-coloured

plomo *n* lead; piece of lead; plumb-bob; bullet; fuse; ~ **derretido** molten lead; **andar con pies de** ~ to go very cautiously; *adj fam* full; boring; **a** ~ plumb, true; **caer a** ~ to fall flat

plomoso leaden; lead-coloured

pluma feather, plume; quill; pen; handwriting; *fig* writer; *lit* style; *sl* peseta; ~ **de agua** running water; ~ **fuente** fountain-pen; ~ **viva** eiderdown; **a vuela** ~ written spontaneously; **dejar correr la** ~ to scribble at length

plumado *adj* feathered, feathery

plumaje *m* plumage; crest, plume

plumajería plumage; feather-trade

plumajero feather-dealer

plumario *arts* painter of birds

plumazo feather pillow; feather mattress; stroke of the pen

plumbado bearing a leaden seal

plumbagina plumbago, graphite

plúmbeo *see* plomoso

plúmbico *chem* plumbic

plumeado *arts* hatching; darkening

plumear to write; *arts* hatch

plúmeo plumed, feathered

plumería pile of feathers

plumero plumage; feather-duster; **se te ve el** ~ I can see through you

plumífero *n sl* writer, author; journalist; *adj lit* feathered

plumilla nib

plumillista *m* pen-pusher

plumón *m* down, feather-bed

plumoso feathered

pluralidad *f* plurality; majority; **a** ~ **de votos** by a majority

pluralismo pluralism

pluralizar to pluralize

pluriempleado *n* moonlighter; *adj* having more than one paid job

pluriempleo moonlighting

plus *m* extra pay, bonus; ~ **ultra** beyond

pluscuamperfecto *gramm* pluperfect

plusmarquista *m+f sp* top scorer; record-breaker

plusvalía capital gains (tax); value added (tax)

plutocracia plutocracy

plutócrata *m+f* plutocrat

plutocrático plutocratic

Plutón *m astron* Pluto

plutónico *geol* plutonic

plutonio plutonium

plutonismo *geol* plutonism

pluvial rainy

pluvímetro, pluviómetro, pluviógrafo rain-gauge

pluvioso rainy

poa anual *bot* celandine

población *f* town, village; population

poblacho wretched/ugly village

poblachón *m* wretched/ugly town

poblado *n* town, settlement; *adj* inhabited

poblador *n m* settler; *adj* settling

poblar to populate; settle; colonize; stock; ~**se** *bot* to bud, burst into leaf; become peopled

pobo white poplar

pobre *n m+f* poor person, pauper; *adj* poor, needy; unfortunate; modest; unimportant, trifling; ~ **de solemnidad** really poor; **tan** ~ **como una rata** as poor as a church mouse

pobrería poor people, paupers; poverty

pobrero alms distributor

pobreta prostitute, harlot

probrete *n m* poor wretch; pauper; *adj* wretched, poor

pobretear to feign poverty

pobretería poor people, paupers; beggars

pobretón *n m* very poor person; *adj* very poor

pobreza poverty; lack, want

pobrismo pauperism; beggars; paupers

pocero well-digger; sewer-worker

pocilga pigsty; filthy place

pócima potion, concoction (*usu* of herbs)

poción *f* potion, drink (*usu* from a prescription)

poco *n* small quantity; short time; ~ **a** ~ little by little; ~ **antes** shortly before; **un** ~ **de** a little; ~**s** few; **unos** ~**s** a few, some; **a** ~ soon afterwards; **dentro de** ~ soon, in a little while; **por** ~ almost, nearly; **tener en** ~ to take a dim view of; *adj* little, not much; ~**s** few, not many; ~**s amigos** not many friends; **a los** ~**s días** a few days later; *adv* shortly, little; ~ **antes/después** shortly before/afterwards; ~ **dispuesto a** not very inclined to, not very keen on; ~ **más o menos** more or less

¹ **pocho** faded, discoloured; pale-faced, pallid, off-colour

² **pocho** large white kidney-bean

pocholo *sl* beautiful, honey, duckie

poda *agri+hort* pruning; pruning-season

podadera pruning-hook; hedging-bill

podador *m* pruner; hedger

podagra *med* gout

podar to prune; (of trees) lop

podazón *f* pruning-season

podenco hound *v, to be able to*

poder *n m* power, might, strength; possession; *leg* power of attorney; ~ **adquisitivo** purchasing power; ~ **judicial** judiciary; **a** ~ **de** by dint of; **en** ~ **de** in the hands of; **en el** ~ in power, in office; **plenos** ~**es** full powers; **por** ~**es** by proxy; *vi* can, be able to; may; **hasta más no** ~ to the limit; **no** ~ **con** not to be a match for; **no** ~ **más** to be worn out, weary; **no** ~ **menos de** cannot but, cannot help; ~**se** to be possible; **¿se puede?** may I?; **puede ser** maybe

poderhabiente *m* attorney

poderío might; wealth; jurisdiction

poderoso mighty, powerful; wealthy

podio podium

podólogo chiropodist

podómetro pedometer

podón *m* bill-hook, pruning-hook

podre *m+f med* pus; decayed matter

podrecer to decay, rot

podredumbre *f med* pus; corruption; grief

podredura putrefaction, corruption

podrimiento putrefaction

podrido putrid, rotten

podrir *see* pudrir

poema *m* poem

poemático poetic

poesía poetry; poem

poeta *m* poet

poetastro poetaster, bad poet

poético poetic

poetisa poetess

poetizar to write poetry

poíno gantry

polaco *n* Pole; Polish language; *adj* Polish

polainas leggings; gaiters

polaridad *f* polarity

polarización *f* polarization

polarizador *n m* polarizer; *adj* polarizing

polca polka

polcar to dance the polka

pólder *m* land reclaimed from the sea

polea pulley, tackle, block pulley; ~ **motriz** driving-pulley

poleadas *fpl* gruel, pap

poleame *m* set of pulleys

polémica polemics

polémico polemical

polemista *m+f* debater, controversialist

polemístico controversial

polemizar to engage in controversy

polen *m bot* pollen; **recuento de pólenes** pollen-count

polenta maize, gruel

poleo *bot* penny royal; *fam* stylish, posh; *meteor* strong cold wind

poli *f sl* cops, fuzz, police force

poliaccidentado accident-prone

poliandria *bot* polyandria

poliantea *bot* polyanthus

poliarquía polyarchy

poliárquico polyarchic(al)

pólice *m* thumb

policía *f* police (force); good breeding; *m* policeman; ~ **municipal** municipal/town police

policíaco *adj* of the police; *lit* detective; **novela policíaca** detective novel

policial *adj* (of the) police

policlínica *med* polyclinic

policopia multicopier

policopiar to multicopy

policromar to polychrome

policromático polychromatic

policromía polychromy

policromo polychromatic

policultura mixed farming

Polichinela Punch(inello); buffoon, clown

polidor *n sl* fence, receiver of stolen property

poliestérico *adj* polyester

poliéster *n* polyester

poliestireno polystyrene

polietileno *n* polythene, polyethylene

polietilénico *adj* polythene, polyethylene

polifacético many-sided, versatile

polifásica *elect* multiphase

polifonía *mus* polyphony

polifónico, polífono *mus* polyphonic

polígala *bot* milkwort
poligamia polygamy
polígamo *n* polygamist; *adj* polygamous
poligloto, polígloto polyglot
poligonal *n m sur* broken line; *adj* polygonal
polígono polygon; *mil* firing-range; industrial zone (of city)
polígrafo polygraph, lie-detector
polihédrico polyhedrical
polihedro polyhedron
polilla moth; clothes moth
polimería polymerism
polimerización *f* polymerization
polimerizar to polymerize
poli-mili *m* member of politico-military wing of E.T.A.
polimorfismo polymorphism
polimorfo polymorphous
polinesio *n+adj* Polynesian
polinización *f bot* pollination
polinizar to pollinate
poliomielitis *f* poliomyelitis
polipasto hoisting tackle
pólipo polyp; octopus; *med* polypus
polipodio fern
polisílabo *n* polysyllable; *adj* polysyllabic
polisón *m* bustle (on dress); pad
polistilo *archi* polystyle
politécnico polytechnic
politeísmo polytheism
politeísta *m+f* polytheist
política policy; politics; politeness; ~ **de mano dura** strong-arm policy; ~ **ficción** phoney politics; ~ **interior/exterior** home/foreign policy; **por** ~ for the sake of good manners, as a matter of policy
politicastro petty politician
político *n* politician; *adj* political; polite; well-mannered; **padre/hermano** ~ father/brother-in-law
politiquear to dabble in politics
politiquería corrupt politics
politiquero petty *usu* corrupt politician; political busy-body; wheeler-dealer
politizar to politicize
poliuretano polyurethane
polivalencia polyvalence
polivalente polyvalent
póliza *comm* policy; draft; payment; (tax) stamp; ~ **de seguro** insurance policy

polizón *m* stowaway; vagrant; hanger-on
polizonte *m sl* copper, policeman
polo *astron+geog* pole; support; lollipop; ice-lolly, water-ice; *sp* polo; ~ **de desarrollo** development zone
polonés *n* Pole; *adj* Polish
polonesa *mus* polonaise
Polonia Poland
poltrón *m* skiver; *adj* skiving, work-shy; lazy
poltrona easy chair
poltronería laziness, skiving
poltronizarse to become lazy/sluggish
polución *f* pollution; fog, smog; ~ **nocturna** wet dream
poluto polluted, dirtied
polvareda cloud of dust; rumpus
polvera powder-compact
polvillo fine dust
polvo dust; powder; pinch of snuff; ~s toilet powder; **oro en** ~ gold dust; ~ **de carbón** coal-dust; ~ **de lavar** washing-powder; ~ **de magnesio** *phot* flash-powder; ~s **de talco** talcum powder; ~s **de tocador** face-powder; **bota de** ~s powder-puff; **echar un** ~ *vulg sl* to have a fuck; **estar hecho** ~ to be weary, be fagged out; **hacer** ~ **a** to destroy completely; **leche en** ~ dried milk; **limpio de** ~ **y paja** *comm* net; **morder el** ~ to bite the dust; **sacudir el** ~ to beat, whip, flog
pólvora gunpowder; bad temper; liveliness; ~ **de algodón** gun-cutton; ~ **de caza** shotgun powder; ~ **fulminante** detonating powder; ~ **lenta** slow-burning powder; ~ **sorda** one who harms others in a quiet and dissimulating way; **gastar la** ~ **en salvas** to waste one's energy; **no ha inventado la** ~ he didn't set the Thames on fire; **ser una** ~ to be a live-wire
polvoramiento powdering
polvorear to sprinkle with powder
polvoriento dusty, covered with powder
polvorín *m* powder magazine; powder-flask; very fine powder
polvorista *m* gunpowder manufacturer; fireworks maker
polvorización *f* pulverization
polvorizar to pulverize
polvorosa *sl* road; **poner pies en** ~ to show a clean pair of heels

polvoroso dusty

polla pullet; attractive young woman; *sl* prick; ~ de agua *orni* waterhen

pollada *orni* flock, covey; cunning man; young blood; *mil* volley of mortar bombs

pollastra pullet

pollastro cockerel

pollazón *m* hatch, brood

pollear (of girls) to start trying to behave like a grown-up

pollera chicken-raiser/seller; hooped skirt; *astron* Pleiades

pollería poulterer's shop; young people

pollero poulterer; chicken-run

pollerón *m* riding-skirt

pollina young she-ass

pollino young jack-ass, donkey

pollita young chicken, chick; *fam* girl, bird

pollito *orni* nestling, chick; young bee; young boy

pollo chicken; young man; astute person

polluelo day-old chick

poma apple; smelling salts

pomada pomade, ointment, salve; hair-cream

pomar *m*, pomarada apple orchard

pomelo grapefruit

pómez: piedra ~ pumice stone

pomífero apple-bearing

pomo fruit containing pips; flagon; nosegay; pommel; knob, handle

pompa pomp, ostentation; pageant; bubble; ballooning (of clothes in the wind); spread (of a peacock's tail); *naut* pump; ~ **s fúnebres** undertaker's parlour, funeral ceremony; **director de ~s fúnebres** undertaker, *US* mortician

pompear to pump; make a show; ~se to strut

pompeyano *n+adj* Pompeian; of Pompeii

pompis *m sing+pl fam* bottom, backside

pomposidad *f* pomposity

pomposo pompous; splendid; inflated

pómulo cheekbone

ponchada bowlful of punch

ponche *m* punch (drink)

ponchera punch-bowl

¹ poncho soft, mild

² poncho *mil* cloak; poncho

ponderable praiseworthy

ponderación *f* consideration, exaggeration; circumspect; calm

ponderado: voto ~ card vote

ponderador *n m* ponderer; one who exaggerates; praiser; *adj* pondering; praising

ponderar to weigh up; consider; exaggerate; praise

ponderativo exaggerating; laudatory

ponderosidad *f* ponderousness; weightiness; circumspection

ponderoso ponderous; cautious; weighty; circumspect

ponedero *n* hen's nest; hen's nesting-box; nest egg; *adj* egg-laying

ponedor *n m* bidder; *adj* egg-laying

ponencia office/dignity of committee member; communication; report

ponente *m* arbiter, referee; committee chairman; *pol* proposer of a bill

ponentino *adj* western

poner to put, place, lay; arrange, set out; assume; put in charge; write, set down; bring forth; make, cause to become; ~ **al corriente** to inform; ~ **al día** to bring up-to-date; ~ **al sol** to expose to sunlight; ~ **aparte** to put on one side; ~ **a prueba** to test; ~ **casa** to start housekeeping, set up house; ~ **colorado** to make blush, shame; ~ **coto a** to stop; ~ **de manifiesto** to make public; ~ **de su parte** to do one's bit; ~ **de vuelta y media** to reprimand, tick off; ~ **en claro** to make clear; ~ **en duda** to call in question; ~ **en fuga** to put to flight; ~ **en la calle** to turn out of doors; ~ **en relieve** to describe in detail; ~ **en ridículo** to make ridiculous, hold up to ridicule; ~ **en venta** to put up for sale; ~ **en vida** to put to rights; ~ **en vigor** to enforce; ~ **fin a** to put a stop to, conclude; ~ **fuego a** to set fire to; ~ **la mesa** to lay the table; ~**le a uno** *tel* to put s.o. through; ~ **los puntos sobre las íes** to cross the t's and dot the i's; ~ **mal** to discredit, run down, denigrate; ~ **pies en polvorosa** to take to one's heels, flee; ~ **por escrito** to put down in black and white; ~ **(en) las nubes** to praise to the skies; ~ **reparos a** to raise objections to; **pongamos 50 pesetas** let's say 50 pesetas; ~**se** to apply o.s. to; put on (clothes); get, become;

astron set; arrive at; ~**se a** to begin to; ~**se a cubierto** to hide from danger; ~**se en jarras** to stand with one's arms akimbo; ~**se al corriente** to find out; ~**se colorado** to blush; ~**se de acuerdo** to reach an agreement; ~**se en camino,** ~**se en marcha** to set off; ~**se en pie** to stand up; ~**se en práctica** to get started, get cracking; ~**se a mal con uno** to get in s.o.'s bad books; **al ~se el sol** at sunset

poney *m* pony

[1] **pongo** *zool* orang-utan

[2] **pongo** dangerous ford

[3] **pongo** *SA* Indian servant

poniente *m* west; west wind

ponimiento act of putting (on)

ponleví *m* high-heeled shoe

pontaje *m* bridge toll

pontear to erect a bridge over

pontificado pontificate, papacy

pontificar to pontificate

pontífice *m* pontiff; **Sumo Pontífice** the Pope

pontificio pontifical

pontón *m* pontoon; prison-ship, hulk; *naut* lighter

pontonero *mil* pontoneer

ponzoña poison

ponzoñoso poisonous

popa *naut* poop, stern; **a/de ~** abaft; **de ~ a proa** entirely; **viento en ~** before the wind, *fig* swimmingly

popamiento cajoling, despising

popar to cajole, caress; despise

popelina *text* poplin

popero *adj* pop; **cultura popera** pop culture

popote *m* straw for broom-making

población *f* population

populachería clap-trap; cheap popularity; playing to the gallery; *pej* common herd, hoi polloi

populachero vulgar, common

populacho mob, rabble

popularidad *f* popularity

popularizar to popularize; ~**se** to become popular

populazo *see* **populacho**

populoso populous, crowded

poquedad *f* littleness, paucity; trifle; mite

poquillo *n* (a) little bit; *adj* very little

poquitín *m*: **un ~ de** a tiny bit of, wee bit of

poquito *n* tiny bit; *adj* very small; feeble (physically and mentally); **~ a poco** slowly; **a ~s** little by little; **~s** very few

por by; for; through; as; over, across; about, nearly; for the sake of; on behalf of; per; by way of, via; **~ ahí** thereabouts; **~ ahora** for now; **~ aquí** hereabouts; **~ (las) buenas o ~ (las) malas** like it or not; **~ carta de más** excessively; **~ carta de menos** insufficiently; **~ causa de** because of; **~ ce o ~ be** for one reason or another; **~ cien(to)** per cent; **~ cierto** indeed; **~ completo** completely; **~ cuanto** whereas; **~ decirlo así** so to speak; **¡~ Dios!** for heaven's sake!; **~ docena** by the dozen; **~ entre** among, through; **~ escrito** in writing; **~ eso** therefore; **~ este medio** by this means; **~ excelencia** par excellence; **~ favor** please; **~ fin** at last, in the end; **~ fuera** outside; **~ hacer** still to be done; **~ junto** together; **~ la mañana** in the morning; **~ la noche** at night; **~ la tarde** in the afternoon/evening; **~ más que** however much; **~ medio de** by means of; **~ mucho que** however much; **¿~ qué?** why?; **~ regla general** as a general rule; **~ si acaso, ~ si las moscas** (just) in case; **~ supuesto** of course; **~ turno** in turn; **~ turnos** by turns; **al ~ mayor** wholesale; **al ~ menor** retail; **de ~ sí** in itself; **estar ~** to be about to, be inclined to

porca earth between furrows

porcachón filthy

porcazo *zool* tapir

porcelana porcelain, china; enamel

porcentaje *m* percentage

porcino *n* young pig, piglet; bruise; *adj* piggish

porción *f* portion; *comm* share; allotment; **~ de gente** crowd of people

porcionero *n* participant; *adj* participating

porcionista *m+f* school boarder; *comm* shareholder

porcipelo *zool* bristle

porcuno porcine, piggish, swinish

porche *m* porch, portico

pordiosear to beg for alms

pordioseo, pordiosería begging for alms
pordiosero beggar
porfía obstinacy; stupidity; insistence; contradiction; **a** ~ in competition/rivalry
porfiado obstinate, stubborn
porfiar to persist; contradict; answer back
pórfido porphyry, jasper
porfirizar to pound to a powder
pormenor m detail
pormenorizar to itemize; give details of
pornografía pornography
pornográfico pornographic
pornógrafo pornographer
poro anat pore
porosidad f porosity
poroso porous
poroto type of bean; bean stew
porque because, for, as
porqué m reason why
porquera lair of a wild boar
porquería filth, grime; nastiness; dirty trick; trifle
porqueriza pigsty
porquerizo, porquero swineherd
porquerón m bumbailiff
porqueta woodlouse, peabug
porra truncheon, club; bore, pain in the neck; (in children's games) 'it'; **mandar a la** ~ to send packing; **vete a la** ~ go to the devil
porrada knock, blow (usu with a truncheon/hand); foolish remark
porrazo blow with a truncheon; injury caused by a fall
porrear to persist; annoy
porrería persistence; silliness
porreta green leaf of onion, leek or garlic; **en** ~ stark naked
porrilla small club
porrillo: a ~ galore
porrino young leek plant
porro n bot leek; sl marihuana cigarette, split; adj stupid
porrón n m narrow-spouted glass drinking vessel; orni pochard; adj heavy; slow; **a porrones** galore
porta naut gun-port
portaaguja needle-holder
portaaviones m sing+pl aircraft-carrier
portabandera socket for flagpole
portabombas m sing+pl aer bomb-rack
portabrocas m sing+pl mech drill-chuck

portacaja mil drum-strap
portacarabina mil scabbard for carbine
portacartas m sing+pl postman; mail-bag
portacoches m sing+pl car-transporter
portacontenedores m sing+pl container-ship
portada portal; frontispiece; print title-page
portadera chest
portadiscos m sing+pl gramophone turntable
portado: bien ~ well-dressed, well-mannered; **mal** ~ badly dressed, ill-mannered
portadocumentos m sing+pl briefcase
portador n m bearer; porter, carrier; biol carrier; tray; adj carrying, bearing
portaequipajes m sing+pl mot boot, US trunk
portaaeronaves m sing+pl aircraft-carrier
portaestandarte m mil colour-sergeant
portaféretro pall-bearer
portafolio briefcase
portafusil m rifle sling/strap
portaguión m standard-bearer (of dragoons)
portahelicópteros m sing+pl helicopter-carrier
portaherramientas m sing+pl tool-bag; mech chuck
portal porch; hall; city gate; Christmas crib
portalada portal
portalámparas m sing+pl elect lamp-holder; socket
portalápices m sing+pl, **portalapiceros** m sing+pl pencil-case
portalente m lens-holder
portalibros m sing+pl book-strap
portaligas m sing+pl suspender-belt
portalón m naut gangway; side-opening (of a ship)
portamanteo portmanteau, valise
portaminas m sing+pl propelling-pencil
portamisiles m sing+pl missile-carrier
portamonedas m sing+pl purse
portante quick pace (of a horse); **tomar el** ~ to go away, run off
portantillo easy pace, canter
portanuevas m sing+pl newsmonger
portañola naut port-hole; gun-port

portaobjeto microscope slide

portaparaguas *m sing+pl* umbrella rack/stand

portapliegos *m sing+pl* document case; large briefcase

portaplumas *m sing+pl* pen-holder

portar to carry; bear (arms); ~se to behave; ~se bien con to be kind to

portasenos *m sing+pl* bra

portátil portable

portavasos *m sing+pl* glass-rack

portavela candlestick

portaventanas, portaventanero *m sing +pl* carpenter specializing in windows and doors

portavoz *m* megaphone; spokesperson

portazgo toll

portazguero toll-collector

portazo slam(ming) of a door; **dar un ~** to slam a door

porte *m* bearing; capacity; *naut* tonnage; *comm* cost of carriage; freight; transport; postage; **~ franco** carriage paid

porteador *m* porter; carrier

portear to carry

portento portent, wonder

portentoso portentous, marvellous, wonderful

porteño *Sp* inhabitant of Puerto de Santa María, Cadiz; *SA* inhabitant of Buenos Aires

porteo cartage, postage

portería conciergerie; janitor's office; *sp* goal area; *naut* port-holes

portero janitor, concierge, door-keeper; *sp* goal-keeper; **~ de estrados** court usher

portezuela door (*usu* of a vehicle); flap; pocket-flap

pórtico portico, porch

portier *m* door-curtain

portilla opening; passage; *naut* port-hole

portillo gap, breach; gate; pass between hills; chip (in plate *etc*)

portón *bui* inner front-door

portorriqueño *n+adj* Puerto Rican

portuario docker, *US* longshoreman; *adj* port, harbour; dock

portugués *n m +adj* Portuguese

portuguesada *pej* typical Portuguese behaviour; exaggeration

portulano *naut* chart showing ports and harbours

porvenir *m* future

¡porvida! in the name of all that's holy!

pos: en ~ de in pursuit of

posa *eccles* halt (of a procession) to sing a response; *eccles* knell, bells rung for the dead; *fam* backside, bottom

posada inn; lodging-house; camp; bag/case containing knife, fork and spoon

posadera hostess, innkeeper's wife; ~s buttocks, backside

posadero host, innkeeper

posante resting; *naut* smooth sailing/passage

posar *vi* to lodge; sit down; rest; *orni* perch; *arts* pose; *vt* to lay down; ~se to alight; sit on; (of liquids) settle

posbélico *adj* post-war

poscafé *m* liqueur served with coffee

posdata post-script

poseedor *m* possessor, owner

poseer to possess, own

poseído conceited; **estar ~** to be convinced, be self-assured

posesión *f* possession; property; **posesiones** wealth, holdings; **dar ~ de** to give possession of; **tomar ~ de** to be sworn in; take possession of

posesivo possessive

poseso *n* person possessed by spirits; *adj* possessed by spirits

posesor *m* owner; holder

poseyente owning, holding

posfecha post-date, post-dating

posfechar to post-date

posfranquismo post-Franco era

posguerra *n+adj* post-war

posibilidad *f* possibility

posibilitar to make possible

posible possible; **en lo ~** in so far as is possible; **hacer lo ~** to do all that one can; **lo más pronto ~, lo antes ~** as soon as possible; **lo más ~** as much as possible

posición *f* position, standing, status; *leg* questions and answers of a cross-examination

positivismo positivism; matter-of-fact-ness

positivista *n m+f* positivist; realist; *adj* practical; matter-of-fact

positivo *n phot* positive; *adj* positive; real; matter-of-fact; **de ~** certainly

pósito co-operative society; public

granary

positura posture; disposition

posma *f* sluggishness; *m+f* sluggish person; pain-in-the-neck

posmeridiano *see* **postmeridiano**

poso sediment; repose

pospelo: a ~ against the grain; unwillingly

pospierna animal's flank

posponer to postpone, put off

posposición *f* postponement, putting-off

pospositivo postpositive

posta *m* courier; *f* pack-horses, relay; post-house; lead slug; memorial card; *cul* slice of meat/fish; **a** ~ on purpose; **por la** ~ rapidly

postal *n f* postcard; *adj* postal; **giro** ~ postal order

postdata post-script

postdiluviano post-diluvian; since the Flood

poste *m* post, stake; school punishment of being made to stand in a corner *etc*; blockhead; ~ **de amarre** *aer* mooring-mast; ~ **de meta** *sp* goalpost; **dar** ~ to keep s.o. waiting for a date/appointment; **llevar** ~ to wait for s.o. who fails to keep a date/appointment

postema *med* abscess; *fig* boring person

postemero *med* lancet

postergación *f* leaving behind; delaying; disregard of seniority

postergar to leave behind; delay; disregard seniority when considering s.o. for promotion

posteridad *f* posterity; posthumous fame; **con** ~ later

posterior *adj* posterior; rear, back; later

posterioridad *f* posteriority

posteta printed sheets stapled together

postfijo *gramm* suffix

postgraduado *n + adj* postgraduate

postguerra post-war era (*usu* after the Civil War of 1936–9)

postigo wicket; window-shutter

postila marginal note

postilación *f* marginal annotation

postilador *m* annotator

postilar to comment

postilla *med* scab; marginal note

postillón *m* postilion

postilloso scabby

postimpresionismo *arts* post-impressionism

postimpresionista *n m+f +adj arts* post-impressionist

postín *m* airs; snobbery; **darse** ~ to give o.s. airs; **de** ~ posh, snooty

postinero snob, vain person

postizo *n* false hair; hair-piece; type of castanet; *adj* false, artificial

postmeridiano postmeridian

postoperativo *med* post-operative

postor *m* bidder

postración *f* prostration; kneeling; *med* depression

postrado prostrate

postrador *m* choir footstool; prostrator, kneeler; *adj* prostrating, kneeling

postrar to prostrate; overthrow; debilitate; ~**se** to prostrate o.s., kneel down; be overcome

postre *n m* dessert; **a la** ~ at last; **llegar a los** ~**s** to arrive too late; *adj* last

postremo last

postrer(o), postrimero last, hindmost

postrimería last years of life; **en las** ~**s del imperio romano** in the last days of the Roman Empire

póstula, postulación *f* petition; postulation; nomination

postulado *n* postulate, nominee; *adj* postulated

postulador *m* postulator

postulante postulating

póstumo posthumous

postura posture; position; *agri* planting (of trees, plants *etc*); *comm* bid; wager; egg-laying

potabilizar to make potable/drinkable

potable drinkable, fit for drinking

potador *m* weights and measures inspector

potaje *m* vegetable stew, pottage; mixed drink; medley

potajería vegetable store

potala *naut* old tub, old ship; stone used as an anchor

potámide *f* river-nymph

potar to booze, tipple; inspect weights and measures

potasa potash

potásico potassic

potasio potassium

pote *m* jar; (flower)pot; **a** ~ galore

potencia power; dominion; possibility;

powerful nation; ~s del alma mental powers; ~ de freno *mot* brake horsepower; de ~ a ~ on equal terms; en ~ potentially
potencial potential
potencialidad *f* potentiality
potenciar to potentialize; increase, make possible; ~ la fuerza de los ríos to harness the power of the rivers
potenciómetro *elect* potentiometer
potentado potentate, magnate
potente powerful, mighty
poterna postern
potestad *f* power, dominion; jurisdiction; patria ~ parental authority
potestativo optional
potingue *m* medicinal concoction; physic
potista *m* boozer, tippler
potosí *m* unimaginable wealth; valer un ~ to be worth a king's ransom
potra filly; *med* hernia; tener ~ to have good luck
potrada herd of fillies/colts
potranca mare (under three years old)
potrear to tease
potrero herdsmen of young horses; pasture ground
potril *m* headstall
potrilla filly; *m* old man pretending to be young
potro foal, colt; nuisance; (vaulting) horse; instrument of torture; *med* obstetrical chair
potroso (of persons) ruptured; fortunate
poyal *m*, **poyo** stone seat
poza puddle; pool
pozal *m* pail; well-coping
pozanco pool beside a river
pozo well; deep hole in river bed; whirlpool; *min* pit, shaft; *naut* hold; ~ artesiano artesian well; ~ negro cesspit; ser un ~ de ... to be a mine of ...
pozol, pozole *m cul* stew of maize, onions, meat and chilli
práctica practice, custom; manner; routine; en la ~ in practice; poner en ~ to put into practice
practicaje *m naut* pilotage
practicanta practiser; practitioner
practicante *m* practiser; *approx* hospital intern/nurse; pharmacist's assistant; medical assistant

practicar to practise
práctico *n naut* harbour pilot; *adj* skilful, experienced, practical
pradal *m*, **pradeño, praderoso, pradera** meadow, meadowland
prado meadow; pasture-ground; lawn; ~ de deportes playing/sports field
pragmático *n* pragmatist; *adj* pragmatic(al)
pragmatismo pragmatism
pragmatista *n m+f* pragmatist; *adj* pragmatic(al)
prasma *min* dark green agate
pratense *adj* meadow
pratincola *orni* pratincole
pravedad *f* perversity, depravity
pravo perverse, depraved
pre *m mil* soldier's daily rate of pay
preámbulo preamble; digression; sin más ~s without more ado
preamplificador *m elect* preamplifier
preamplificar *elect* to preamplify
prebenda *eccles* benefice, prebend
prebendado *eccles* prebendary
prebendar *eccles* to confer a prebend on
prebostal provostal
prebostazgo provostship
preboste *m* provost
precalentamiento *sp* warming-up exercises
precalentar *sp* to warm up
precario precarious; a ~ by grace and favour
precaución *f* precaution, wariness
precaucionarse to be cautious
precautelar to take precautions against; fend off
precautorio preventive
precaver to try to prevent; obviate; ~se (contra) to be on one's guard (against); take precautions
precavido cautious; guarded; wary
precedencia precedence; primacy; priority
precedente *n m* precedent; *adj* preceding, foregoing
preceder to precede; be of higher rank than
preceptista *m+f* one who gives precepts
preceptivo preceptive
precepto precept; command; de ~ obligatory
preceptor *m* preceptor, teacher
preceptuar to give as a precept

preces *fpl* prayers asking help in time of need

preciado highly esteemed; prized; proud

preciador *m* valuer, appraiser

preciar to price, value, appraise; ~**se de** to boast (about); glory (in); pride o.s. (on)

precinta official seal; *naut* parcelling

precintar to seal; strap, bind; *naut* parcel the seams of

precinto sealing strap, sealed strap

precio price; premium; reward; value; ~ **al contado** cash price; ~ **corriente** market price; ~ **de apertura** *comm* opening price; ~ **de cierre** *comm* closing price; ~ **de costo** *comm* cost price; ~ **de entrega** delivery price; ~ **de oportunidad/ocasión** bargain price; ~ **de tarifa** list/catalogue price; ~ **de venta al público** retail price; ~ **rebajado** cut price; ~ **regular** standard price; **no tener** ~ to be priceless; **poner a** ~ **la cabeza de uno** to put a price on s.o.'s head

preciosidad *f* worth; rich/beautiful person; beautiful dream; beauty; marvel; ¡**qué** ~! how wonderful!

preciosismo affectation

precioso precious; beautiful; glorious; witty

precipicio precipice; chasm

precipitación *f* unwise haste; *chem* precipitation; ~ **radiactiva** radioactive fall-out

precipitadero steep cliff

precipitado *n chem* precipitate; *adj* hurried; abrupt

precipitante *n m chem* precipitant; *adj* precipitating

precipitar to rush, hasten; *chem* precipitate; hurl down; ~**se** to go headlong, hurry

precípite liable to fall

precipitoso hasty; rash, reckless

precipuo chief, main

precisar to fix, determine; compel; be urgent; be necessary

precisión *f* precision, accuracy; preciseness; compulsion, necessity; **bombardeo de** ~ precision bombing; **verse en la** ~ **de** to feel obliged to; **tengo** ~ **de marchar** I must go

preciso necessary; precise, exact; con-

cise; **tiempo** ~ just enough time

precitado aforementioned

precito reprobate

preclaro famous, celebrated

precocidad *f* precocity

precognición *f* precognition

precolombino pre-Columbian, before the discovery of America

preconcebir to preconceive

preconización *f* eulogy; preconception

preconizador *m* eulogizer, extoller; foreknower

preconizar to eulogize

preconocer to foreknow

precoz precocious

precursor *n m* forerunner; harbinger; *adj* preceding

predecesor *m* forerunner, predecessor

predecir to foretell, forecast; anticipate

predefinición predetermination

predefinir to predetermine

predestinación *f* predestination

predestinante *n m* predestinator; *adj* predestinating

predestinar to predestinate; foredoom

predeterminación *f* predetermination

predeterminar to predetermine

predial real; (of property) landed

prédica sermon (of a protestant minister)

predicable able to be preached; *log* predicable

predicación *f* preaching

predicadera pulpit; gift of preaching

predicado *log* + *gramm* predicate

predicador *n m* preacher; *adj* preaching

predicamento prestige, influence

predicante *n m* sectarian preacher; *adj* preaching

predicar to preach; make clear; *fam* reprimand; ~ **con el ejemplo** to practise what one preaches

predicho foretold

predigestión *f* predigestion

predilección *f* predilection, preference

predilecto favourite, preferred

predio real estate; landed property; inheritance

predisponer to predispose; prejudice

predisposición *f* predisposition; prejudice

predispuesto predisposed; inclined

predominación *f*, **predominancia** predomination, predominance

predominante predominant; prevailing

predominar to predominate; prevail; oversee; command

predominio predominance; superiority

preelegir to pre-elect

preeminencia pre-eminence

preeminente pre-eminent; superior

preescolar pre-school; **centro** ~ nursery school

preestablecer to pre-establish

preexcelso most illustrious

preexistencia pre-existence

preexistente pre-existent

preexistir to pre-exist

prefabricación f prefabrication

prefabricar to prefabricate

prefacio preface, prologue

prefecto prefect

prefectura prefecture

preferencia preference

preferente preferential

preferible preferable

preferir to prefer

prefiguración f prefiguration; foreshadowing

prefigurar to foreshadow; prefigure

prefijar to prefix

prefijo prefix; *tel* exchange code

prefinición f setting of a time limit

prefinir to set a time limit

prefulgente bright, dazzling

pregón m announcement by town-crier

pregonar to proclaim; *fam* gossip; make public

pregoneo crying of wares in the streets

pregonería office of town crier

pregonero n town crier; auctioneer; *adj* proclaiming, announcing; **no dar tres cuartos al** ~ to keep something hush-hush

preguerra pre-war (*usu* Civil War) era

pregunta question, query; **absolver las** ~s *leg* to answer under oath; **a la cuarta** ~ hard up, broke; **hacer una** ~ to ask a question

preguntador n m questioner; *adj* questioning

preguntar to ask, inquire; ~ **por** to ask after; ~**se** to wonder

preguntón inquisitive

pregustar to taste food before serving it

prehistoria prehistory

prehistórico prehistoric

preinserto previously inserted

prejudicial *leg* awaiting judicial decision

prejuicio, prejudicio prejudice

prejuzgar to prejudge; prejudice

prelacía prelacy

prelada abbess; mother superior

prelado prelate

prelatura prelacy

preliminar preliminary

prelucir to shine brilliantly

preludiar to prelude, herald

preludio introduction; *mus* prelude

prelusión f prologue

premamá *adj invar* maternity; **ropa** ~ maternity clothes

prematuro premature; unripe; *leg* impuberal, not nubile

premeditación f premeditation; *leg* malice aforethought

premeditadamente premeditatedly; *leg* with malice aforethought

premeditar to premeditate

premiador m rewarder

premiar to reward, award

premio prize, reward, award; **a** ~ at a premium; ~ **gordo** first prize in national Christmas lottery; ~ **Nobel** Nobel Prize, Nobel Prizewinner

premiosidad f slowness of speech

premioso tight; close-packed· troublesome; slow of speech; (of language) stilted; urgent

premisa n *log* premise; *leg* precedent; mark; *adj* premised

premonitorio *med* premonitory

premonición f premonition

premoriencia *leg* prior death

premorir to predecease

premura urgency; haste; pressure; tightness

prenatal antenatal

prenda garment; piece of jewellery; pledge, security; (in game) forfeit; ~ **de vestir** article of clothing; **en** ~ **de** as a pledge; **juego de** ~s (game) forfeits; **no soltar** ~ *sl* to keep one's mouth shut, stay mum; ~s **interiores** underwear

prendador n m pledger; pawner; *adj* pledging; pawning

prendar to pledge, pawn; charm, captivate; ~**se de** to become fond of

prendedero, prendedor m brooch; hook; nappy-pin; hair-ribbon

prender to catch, seize; pin, clasp; *zool*

mate; (of women) dress up; *hort+fig*
take root; ~ **fuego a** to set alight; ~**se**
fuego to catch fire; ~**se** to doll o.s. up
prendería second-hand clothes shop;
pawnbroker's
prendero second-hand clothes dealer;
pawnbroker
prendimiento seizure; arrest
prenoción *f philos* prenotion, first knowledge
prenombre *m* first name, Christian
name, *US* given name
prenotar to note in advance
prensa *print* printing-press; *mech* vice,
press; *phot* printing-frame; ~ **de lagar**
wine-press; ~ **de paños** clothes press;
~ **marginal** underground press; ~
periódica the press; ~ **sensacionalista** yellow press, gutter-press; **dar a
la** ~ to publish; **meter en** ~ to go to
press
prensado pressing; gloss
prensador *adj* pressing
prensadura pressure
prensar to press, squeeze
prensil prehensile
prensión *f* seizing, seizure; grasping
prensista *m+f* pressman, presswoman,
journalist, reporter; printing worker
prenunciar to predict, foretell
prenuncio prediction
preñado *n m* pregnancy; *adj* pregnant;
bulging
preñar to make pregnant; impregnate;
fill; ~**se** to get pregnant
preñez *f* pregnancy; gestation period;
confusion
preocupación *f* preoccupation, worry;
bias
preocupado preoccupied, worried
preocupar to preoccupy, worry; ~**se**
(de) to be worried (about)
preopinante *m* one who voices his
opinion first
preordinación *f eccles* pre-ordination
preordinar to pre-ordain
preparación *f* preparation; readiness; *sp*
training
preparado *n* preparation; *med* mixture;
adj prepared
preparador *m* preparer; (horse-racing)
trainer
preparamiento preparation; preparedness

preparar to prepare, get ready; *sp* train,
coach; ~**se** to get o.s. ready
preparativo *n* preparation; *adj* qualifying; preparatory
preparatorio preparatory; introductory
preponderancia preponderance
preponderante preponderant, prevailing; overwhelming
preponderar to preponderate, prevail;
overwhelm
preponer to put first; prefer
preposición *f gramm* preposition
preposicional *gramm* prepositional;
partícula ~ prefix
prepósito chairman; provost
prepositura office/dignity of a provost
prepositivo *gramm* prepositional
preposteración *f* inversion of order
preposterar to invert the order of
prepóstero in the wrong/inverse order
prepotencia prepotency
prepotente preponderant
prepucio *anat* prepuce, foreskin
prerrafaelismo Pre-Raphaelism
prerrafaelista *n m+f* +*adj* Pre-
Raphaelite
prerrogativa prerogative
presa capture, prey; (fishing) catch; *mil*
booty; dam; ditch; tusk; *orni* talon;
ave de ~ bird of prey; **hacer** ~ **en**
to seize on; **ser** ~ **de** to be the prey
of
presada reservoir
presado pale green
presagiar to foretell, presage
presagio omen
presagioso presaging, betokening
presago foreteller
presbicia *med* long-sightedness
présbita *n m+f* long-sighted person; *adj*
long-sighted
presbiterado priesthood
presbiteral priestly, sacerdotal
presbiterianismo Presbyterianism
presbiteriano Presbyterian
presbiterio presbytery; chancel
presbítero priest, presbyter
presciencia prescience, foreknowledge
presciente prescient
prescindible expendable; dispensable
prescindir to dispense with; do without
prescito damned
prescribir *vt* to prescribe; lay down; *vi*
lapse

prescripción *f* prescription
presea jewel
presencia presence; ~ **de ánimo** presence of mind; **en** ~ **de** in the presence of; **hacer acto de** ~ to turn up, put in an appearance
presencial: testigo ~ eyewitness
presenciar to witness; attend
presentación *f* presentation; display; lay-out; introduction; **a** ~ *comm* on sight
presentado *eccles* presentee
presentador *m* bearer; *TV+rad* presenter, announcer, compère
presentalla votive offering
presentáneo quick-acting
presentar to present; display, show; introduce (one person to another); nominate; make a present of; ~**se** to volunteer, offer o.s.; appear, turn up; ~**se como candidato** to stand, *US* run for election
presente *n m* gift; present time; **al/de** ~ at present; *adj* present, current; **cuerpo** ~ lying in state; **hacer** ~ to draw attention to, bring up; **mejorando lo** ~ present company excepted; **tener** ~ to bear in mind
presentemente now, at the present time
presentero *eccles* presenter (of a benefice)
presentimiento presentiment
presentir to have a presentiment of; foretell
presepio manger; stable
presero dam-keeper; dyke-keeper
preservación *f* preservation, conservation
preservador *n m* preserver; *adj* preserving
preservar to preserve, guard
preservativo *n* preservative, preventive; contraceptive; *adj* preserving
presidario see **presidiario**
presidencia presidency; chairmanship
presidenciable *adj* in the running for president; qualified to be president
presidencial presidential
presidencialismo presidentialism
presidenta president's wife; woman president/chairperson
presidente *m* president; chairman; *leg* presiding judge; ~ **en funciones** acting president

presidiable deserving imprisonment
presidiar *mil* to garrison
presidiario convict
presidio gaol, *US* jail, prison, *US* penitentiary; *mil* garrison, fortress
presidir to preside over; govern
presilla loop, noose; *naut* bight; (sewing) button-hole stitching; fastener
presión *f* pressure; ~ **arterial/sanguínea** blood-pressure; **grupo de** ~ *pol* lobby, pressure-group
presionar to pressurize; advocate; bring pressure to bear on
preso *n* prisoner; *adj* arrested; imprisoned
prest *m mil* daily rate of pay
prestación *f* loan, lending; service; ~ **personal** community service; ~ **por cese** redundancy pay
prestadizo that can be lent/borrowed
prestado borrowed, lent; **dar** ~ to lend; **de** ~ on a temporary basis; **tomar** ~ to borrow
prestador *m* lender
prestamera *eccles* benefice
prestamero *eccles* incumbent of a benefice
prestamista *m+f* pawnbroker; moneylender
préstamo loan; lending; borrowing; ~ **lingüístico** loan word; **dar a** ~ to lend; **recibir/tomar en** ~ to borrow
prestancia excellence of bearing
prestante excellent, fine
prestar *vi* to be useful; *vt* to lend, loan; ~ **juramento** take (an oath); ~ **atención** to pay attention; ~ **ayuda** to give help; ~**se** to offer o.s., be applicable; consent
prestatario *adj* borrowing
preste *m eccles* celebrant at high mass; **Preste Juan** Prester John
presteza quickness, promptitude; diligence
prestidigitación *f* prestidigitation; sleight of hand; conjuring
prestidigitador *m* conjurer; trickster
prestigiar to give prestige/distinction to; to perform sleights of hand
prestigio prestige; (of a conjurer) illusion; fascination
prestigioso prestigious; spell-binding
prestiño see **pestiño**
presto *adj* quick, prepared; *adv* quickly;

soon; **de** ~ promptly
presumible presumable, supposable
presumido _n_ vain/presumptuous person; _adj_ vain, conceited
presumir _vt_ to presume; suspect; _vi_ to give o.s. airs; ~ **de valiente** to consider o.s. valiant
presunción _f_ presumption
presuntivo presumptive
presunto presumed, alleged; ~ **asesino** alleged murderer; ~ **heredero** heir presumptive
presuntuoso presumptuous
presuponer to budget for, estimate for; presuppose
presuposición _f_ presupposition
presupuestario budgetary
presupuesto budget; estimate
presura oppression; grief; haste
presuroso hasty; urgent
pretencioso vain; pretentious
pretender to attempt; aim at/for; claim (as a right); woo
pretendienta claimant; job-seeker
pretendiente _m_ claimant; job-seeker; claimant; pretender; wooer
preterir to omit; pass over; leave out (an heir) from a will
pretérito _n_+_adj_ past
preternaturalizar to pervert
pretextar to offer as a pretext
pretexto pretext
pretil _m_ parapet; _mil_ breastwork (of a trench)
pretina _m_ girdle; belt
pretinazo blow with a belt; beating, belting
pretonero girdle/belt maker
pretorio praetorian
prevalecer to prevail; take root
prevaleciente, prevalente prevailing, prevalent
prevaler to prevail; ~**se** to avail o.s.
prevaricación _f_ betrayal, breach of trust
prevaricador _m_ corrupter, perverter; prevaricator
prevaricar to betray; fail to keep one's word
prevaricato _leg_ breach of faith
prevención _f_ prevention; foresight; preparation; prejudice; _mil_ guardroom; police station
prevenidamente beforehand
prevenido ready, prepared; fore-

warned; cautious
prevenir to prevent; prepare, make ready; foresee; surprise; ~**se** to get ready, be on one's guard; **más vale** ~ **que curar** prevention is better than cure
preventivo preventive, preservative
prever to foresee; anticipate
previo previous
previsión _f_ foresight; precaution; ~ **social** social security
previsor provident
prez _f_ glory; merit; honour
priesa haste, hurry
prieto tight, compressed; very dark; narrow-minded; mean
prima female cousin; _mil_ first quarter of the night's watch; _comm_ premium; _mus_ treble; ~ **de productividad** productivity bonus
primacía primateship; superiority
primada _n_ advantage taken of a simple-minded person
primado primeness; _eccles_ primate
primario principal; primary
primavera spring; _bot_ primrose
primaveral _adj_ spring, spring-like
primazgo cousinship
primearse to treat one another as cousins
primer (_contr_ of **primero**) first; ~ **galán** _theat_ male lead; ~ **grado** first degree; **Primer Ministro** Prime Minister; ~ **nombre** Christian name, _US_ given name, ~ **piloto** _naut_ first mate; ~ **piso** first floor, US second floor; ~ **plano** foreground; **en** ~ **lugar** in the first place
primeriza woman who has had one child
primerizo novice, beginner
primero _adj_ first, prime; foremost; main, principal; **primera cura** first aid; **primera dama** _cin_+_theat_ leading lady; **primera dama de la nación** first lady; **primera fila** front rank; **primera página** front page (of a newspaper); **primera piedra** foundation stone; ~**s auxilios** first aid; **a primera luz** at dawn; **a primera noche** soon after dark; **a primera vista** at first sight; **de primera** _comm_ of the finest quality; **de primera instancia** instantly; **primeras** (cards) first trick; _adv_ at first; **de primera** at the beginning

primevo primeval

primicerio *n* precentor; *adj* principal; first in line/queue

primicia first fruits; maiden effort

primichón *m* skein of soft silk

primilla *leg* pardoned for a first offence, conditionally discharged

primitivamente originally

primitivismo primitivism

primitivista *n m + f + adj* primitivist

primitivo primitive; original

primo *n* cousin; dupe; simpleton; ~ **carnal/hermano** first cousin; *adj* first; best, superior; prime; *adv* first(ly), in the first place; **hacer el** ~ to be taken for a ride

primogenio primogenial

primogénito first-born

primogenitura primogeniture

primor *m* beauty; excellence; care; dexterity; exquisiteness; **hacer ~es** to do wonders

primorear to perform with excellence

primorosamente painstakingly, neatly

primoroso exquisite; beautiful, graceful; dextrous; painstaking

prímula *bot* primula

primuláceo *bot* primulaceous

princesa princess

principada high-handed act

principado principality, princedom; primacy; pre-eminence

principal *n m comm* principal; stock; head of a firm *etc*; *mil* main guard; *theat* dress-circle, *US* balcony; *adj* principal, main; essential; renowned; most important; first; **piso** ~ first floor, *US* second floor; **lo** ~ the main thing

principalidad *f* principality; nobility

príncipe *m* prince; ruler; leader; **Príncipe de Asturias** Crown Prince of Spain; ~ **de sangre** prince of royal blood; **edición** ~ first edition

principesco princely, regal

principiador *m*, **principiante** *m* beginner, novice; apprentice

principiar to start, commence

principio principle; commencement; start; germ; motive; *cul* entrée, starters; *print* introductory matter (of a book); ~s rudiments; **a ~s del mes** at the beginning of the month; **al ~/a los ~s** at first; **dar** ~ **a** to start, begin; **en** ~ in principle; **en un** ~ at first

pringada toast soaked in gravy

pringado *sl* victim of a robbery

pringar to dip in/cover with grease; *fam* cover with dirt; spatter; slander; *sl* work hard; *sl* die, kick the bucket; *sl* catch venereal disease

pringón *n m* grease, stain; *adj* greasy; dirty; repugnant

pringoso greasy, sticky

pringote *m* hodge-podge

pringue *m* grease; fattiness

pringuera dripping-pan

prionodonte *m zool* giant armadillo

priora prioress

prioral *adj* of a prior/prioress

priorato priory; red wine from Tarragona

prioridad *f* priority

prioste *m* steward (of a religious community)

prisa haste, hurry; urgency; surprise attack; **a (toda)** ~ (very) quickly; **darse** ~ to make haste, hurry; **estar con/tener** ~ to be in a hurry

priscal *m* cattle-shelter

prisco peach

prisión *f* prison, gaol, *US* jail; imprisonment; **prisiones** chains, shackles, fetters; capture; *leg* custody; ~ **preventiva** protective custody; **reducir a** ~ to send to prison

prisionero captive; *mil* prisoner of war

prisma *m* prism

prismático *n:* ~s binoculars, field-glasses; *adj* prismatic

priste *m zool* sawfish

prístino pristine

privación *f* privation; lack; deprivation; ~ **del permiso de conducir** suspension of driving-licence

privada privy, w.c.; filth

privado *n* court favourite; *adj* secret, personal; *tel* ex-directory

privadero cesspit cleaner/emptier

privanza protection at court; private life

privar to deprive; ban, forbid; stun; *sl* booze, drink; ~se to deprive o.s.; **no se prive** go ahead, don't let me stop you; **no** ~ **de nada** to go short of nothing

privativo special, particular, exclusive

privatización *f* privatization, denationalization

privatizar to privatize, denationalize
prive *m sl* drink
privilegiadamente in a privileged way
privilegiado privileged, preferential
privilegiar to favour, privilege
privilegiativo enjoying a privilege
privilegio privilege; concession; exemption; franchise; copyright; ~ de fuero *eccles* privilege of being tried by a church court; ~ de introducción monopoly for the exploitation of an imported industrial method; ~ de invención patent; ~ odioso privilege that prejudices a third party; ~ personal non-hereditary privilege
pro *m+f* profit; advantage; ¡buena ~! much good may i. do you!; de ~ of note; en ~ de on behalf of; el ~ y el contra the pros and the cons; en ~ y en contra for and against
proa *naut* prow, bow; *aer* nose
proal *naut* forward
probabilidad *f* probability, likelihood; chance
probación *f* proof; probation period; test
probado tried, proved, tested
probador *m* taster, sampler; fitter; fitting-room
probar to try, endeavour; taste, sample; test; (of clothing) try on; suit, fit; ~ a cantarlo to try singing it; ~ fortuna to take one's chances; ~se to try on (clothes)
probatorio probationary; *leg* time allowed for producing evidence
probatura trial; experiment, test; fitting
probeta test-tube; pressure-gauge; *phot* developing tray; niño ~ test-tube baby
probidad *f* probity; honesty
problema *m* problem
problemática series of problems
problemático problematic(al)
problematizar to fill with problems
probo upright, honest
probóscide *f zool* proboscis
procacidad *f* lewdness, indecency; cheek
procaz lewd, indecent; foul; cheeky
procedencia origin; *naut* place of sailing
procedente *leg* fitting, proper; proceeding (de from)
proceder *n m* conduct, behaviour;

management; *v* to proceed, go on; come, arise; behave; take action; *leg* proceed against; concern; eso no procede that is not applicable
procedimiento procedure, method, manner, way
proceloso tempestuous
prócer *adj* noble, aristocratic; eminent
próceres *mpl* grandees of Spain
proceridad *f* nobility; eminence
procesado *n* defendant, accused; *adj* prosecuted, accused, indicted
procesamiento suing; indicting
procesar to sue; indict; prosecute, try
procesión *f* procession (*usu* religious)
procesional processional
proceso process, lapse of time; *leg* criminal case; trial; proceedings
procinto *mil* preparedness
proclama proclamation; marriage bann; publication of banns
proclamación *f* proclamation; acclamation; applause
proclamar to proclaim, promulgate; acclaim, cheer
proclive inclined to, prone to
proclividad *f* propensity
procomún *m*, procomunal *m* public welfare
procónsul *m* pro-consul
proconsulado pro-consulship
procreación *f* procreation, generation
procreador *n m* procreator, begetter; *adj* procreative
procreante procreating
procrear to procreate, beget; generate
procura power of attorney; careful management
procuración *f* care, careful management; *leg* power of attorney; *leg* chambers
procuraduría lawyer's chambers; proctorship
procurador *m leg* lawyer, solicitor, proctor; ~ de síndico attorney-general
procurar to try, endeavour; attempt to get; obtain; manage (on behalf of another); act as attorney; do one's best to
procurrente *m geog* peninsula
prodición *f* treachery, treason
prodigalidad *f* prodigality; abundance
prodigar to squander, lavish; ~se to

make an exhibition of o.s.; pay frequent visits

prodigio prodigy, wonder, marvel; miracle

prodigiosidad f prodigiousness

prodigioso prodigious, marvellous; miraculous

pródigo n spendthrift, wastrel; adj prodigal, wasteful

producción f production; crop; ~ **en serie** mass-production

producente producing; causing; generating

producidor n m producer; adj producing, productive

producir to produce; yield; ~**se** to explain o.s.; arise, occur, come about

productividad f productivity

productivo productive

producto product; production; ~s proceeds; ~s **de tocador** toilet articles; ~ **secundario** by-product ~s **de consumo** consumer goods

productor n m producer; adj productive

proejar naut to row against the wind/tide

proel m naut bow (oarsman); bows (of ship)

proemio preface, prologue

proeza prowess; feat, achievement

profanación f profanation, desecration

profanador n m profaner; violator; adj profaning, violating

profanar to profane, desecrate; defile; dishonour

profanidad f profanity, indecency

profano profane; unchaste; secular, lay; irreligious

profazar to speak evil of another

profecía prophecy; **Profecías** bibl Prophets

proferente adj uttering, expressing

proferir to utter, express

profesante professing

profesar vt to profess; practise (a profession); harbour (dislike etc); teach; vi join a religious order

profesión f profession; avowal; **de** ~ by profession

profesional n m professional; practitioner; adj vocational

profesionalismo professionalism

profesionalizar to professionalize

profeso eccles professed, having taken a

religious vow

profesor m teacher, instructor; professor; ~ **adjunto** lecturer; ~ **agregado** assistant professor; ~ **honorario** emeritus professor; ~ **particular** tutor, private teacher, coach

profesorado professorship; teaching staff; faculty; teaching profession

profesoral professorial, teaching

profeta m prophet

profético prophetic

profetisa prophetess

profetizador n m prophesier; adj prophesying

profetizar to prophesy

proficiente proficient

proficuo useful, advantageous

profiláctico n+adj prophylactic; n hygiene

profiláctico n med prophylactic; adj prophylactic, hygienic; preventive

profilaxia med preventive medicine

profilaxis f med prophylaxis

prófugo n+adj fugitive; mil deserter

profundar see **profundizar**

profundidad f profundity, depth; excellence; geom height, altitude

profundizar to deepen, investigate thoroughly; fathom; go into s.t. deeply

profundo n profundity; poet the deep; hell; poet sea; adj deep, profound; intense

profusión f profusion, lavishness, abundance

profuso profuse, lavish, abundant

progenie f lineage, descent

progenitura primogeniture

prognosis f meteor weather-forecast; prognosis

programa m programme; scheme; proclamation; pol platform; theat playbill; ~ **de urgencia** crash programme; ~ **doble** cin double feature

programación f TV+rad programme-planning; programming

programar to programme

progre n m+f +adj joc progressive

progresar progress, advance

progresión f progression

progresista n m+f +adj pol progressive, liberal

progresivo progressive; advancing

progreso progress; advancement

prohibición *f* prohibition
prohibicionismo *pol* prohibitionism
prohibicionista *m+f pol* prohibitionist
prohibido forbidden, prohibited; ~ **el paso** no entry, no admittance, no thoroughfare
prohibir to prohibit, forbid; **se prohibe fumar** no smoking
prohibitivo, prohibitorio prohibitory
prohijación *f* adoption
prohijador *m* adopter
prohijamiento adoption
prohijar to adopt
prohombre *m* great man; headman; master (of a guild)
proís *naut* hitching-post, mooring-berth, bollard; mooring rope/cable
prójima *sl* wife, better half; *sl* tart
prójimo fellow-creature, fellow-human; neighbour; individual; *sl* bloke
prolapso *med* prolapsus
prole *f* progeny, offspring
proletariado proletariat, working classes
proletario *n+adj* proletarian
proletariocracia rule by the proletariat
proliferación *f* proliferation
proliferante proliferating
prolífico prolific, fruitful
prolijidad *f* prolixity; nicety; tediousness
prolijo prolix; over-careful; fussy, troublesome
prologar to write a prologue for
prólogo prologue
prolongación *f* prolongation
prolongado *adj* oblong; prolonged
prolongador *adj* prolonging, extending
prolongar to prolong; *geom* produce; ~**se** to last longer
proloquio maxim
promanar to issue, stem
promediar to divide into two equal parts; halve; reach the middle (of a period of time); *comm* average; mediate
promedio average, mean
promesa promise, vow; good omen
prometedor *n m* promiser; *adj* promising
prometer to promise, betroth, be promising; ~**se** to expect, become betrothed; give/dedicate o.s. to God
prometido *n* promise, offer; fiancé; *adj*

betrothed; engaged; **lo ~ es deuda** a promise is a promise
prominencia prominence; protuberance; elevation
prominente prominent; protuberant, jutting out; elevated
promiscuar to be promiscuous; *eccles* to eat meat on a fast day
promiscuidad *f* promiscuity; ambiguity
promiscuo promiscuous; ambiguous
promisión *f* promise; **tierra de ~** promised land
promisorio promissory
promoción *f* promotion; group of officers/students commissioned/graduated at the same time; *comm* advertising, publicity; **campaña de ~** advertising campaign
promocional promotional; **montaje ~** advertising stunt
promocionar to promote, boost, hype
promontorio promontory, headland; height; anything bulky
promotor *n m* promoter; ~ **de la fe** *eccles* devil's advocate; ~ **fiscal** *leg* attorney; *adj* promotive
promovedor *n m* promoter; *adj* promoting
promover to promote; further
promulgación *f* promulgation
promulgador *n m* promulgator; *adj* promulgating
promulgar to promulgate; publish; proclaim
prono prone; inclined; disposed
pronombre *m gramm* pronoun
pronosticable foreseeable, prognosticable
pronosticación *f* prognostication, prediction; foresight
pronosticar to predict, forecast
pronosticador *n m* prognosticator, predictor; *adj* prognosticating
pronóstico prognostic, prediction; ~ **del tiempo** weather-forecast; ~ **reservado** *med* in a critical condition; ~**s deportivos** football pools
prontitud *f* promptness, swiftness; quick reply
pronto *n* sudden impulse/urge; fit of anger; *adj* prompt; rapid; ready; *adv* soon, quickly; **al ~** right away, at first; **de ~** suddenly; **lo más ~ posible** as soon as possible; **por de/por lo ~**

for the time being; **tan ~ como** as soon as

prontuario memorandum book; rule-book

pronunciable pronounceable

pronunciación *f* pronunciation

pronunciado *n* rebel, insurgent; *adj* pronounced, marked; steep

pronunciador *n m* pronouncer; *adj* pronouncing

pronunciamiento military insurrection/rising; *leg* pronouncement of a sentence

pronunciar to pronounce; deliver, make (a speech); *leg* give judgement; **~se** *mil* to rise in rebellion

propagación *f* propagation, spreading

propagador *n m* propagator; *adj* propagating

propaganda propaganda; dissemination; *comm* advertising

propagandismo propagandism

propagandista *n m+f +adj* propagandist

propagandístico *adj* publicity, advertising

propagante *adj* propagating; spreading

propagar to propagate, spread; disseminate; multiply

propagativo propagative, propagating

propalador *m* divulger, publisher

propalar to divulge, publish, spread abroad, make public

propano propane

propao *naut* bulkhead

propartida time immediately before a parting

propasar to transgress; **~se** overstep the limits; forget o.s.

propender to be inclined, tend

propensión inclination, tendency

propenso inclined, disposed

propiciación *f* propitiation, appeasement

propiciador *n m* propitiator, appeaser; *adj* propitiating, appeasing

propiciar to propitiate, appease

propiciatorio *adj* propitiatory; *n* prie-dieu

propicio propitious

propiedad *f* ownership, holding; property, lands, estate; propriety; possession; **~ intelectual/literaria** copyright; **~ mueble** goods and chattels; **~**

raíz real estate; **es ~ de ...** copyright by ...

propietaria proprietress, landlady

propietariamente *leg* with right of ownership

propietario *n* proprietor, owner; landlord; *adj* proprietary

propileno propylene

propileo *archi* propyleum, columned gallery

propina tip, gratuity; **de ~** into the bargain, as an extra

propinación *f* tipping; treat; invitation to have a drink

propinar to administer; treat; invite to have a drink

propincuidad *f* propinquity, proximity

propincuo contiguous, near

propio *n* messenger; publicly owned property; *adj* own; proper; suitable; typical; genuine; same; exact; **~ de** suited to, typical of; **de ~** specially; **es lo ~** it's the natural thing to do; **nombre ~** *gramm* proper noun

proponedor *m* proposer

proponente proposing

proponer to propose, suggest; nominate; **~se** to plan, intend

proporción *f* proportion; proposal, plan; tender, *US* bid; **en ~** proportionately; **a ~ que** as fast as

proporcionado proportioned; relevant

proporcional proportional

proporcionalidad *f* proportionality

proporcionar to proportion; adapt; provide; adjust; furnish, supply; **~se** to get, obtain

propósito purpose, intention; **a ~** apropos, by the way; on purpose; **a ~ de** in connection with; **de ~** on purpose, deliberately; **fuera de ~** irrelevant

propuesto *n* proposal; offer; nomination; *adj* proposed

propugnáculo fortress

propugnar to advocate; fight for

propulsa rejection, repulse

propulsar to propel, drive

propulsión *f* propulsion; **~ a chorro** jet-propulsion

propulsor *n m* propeller; *mech* driver; *adj* propellant, pushing

prorrata quota; **a ~** *comm* pro rata

prorratear to apportion

prorrateo pro rata division
prórroga, prorrogación f prorogation, extension; postponement; sp extra time
prorrogable capable of prorogation
prorrogar to prolong, extend; suspend; postpone
prorrumpir to burst out
prosa prose; fam verbiage
prosado in prose
prosador m prose writer
prosaico prosaic, dull
prosaísmo prosaism, dullness
prosapia lineage, ancestry
proscenio theat proscenium
proscribir to proscribe, forbid, prohibit
proscripción f proscription; banishment
proscriptor m proscriber
proscrito n proscribed person, exile; outlaw; adj proscribed
prosecución f prosecution; pursuit
proseguir to pursue, persecute; go on, continue
proselitismo proselytism
proselitista n m+f proselytizer; adj proselytizing, converted
prosélito proselyte, convert
prosificación f putting into prose
prosificar to put into prose
prosista m+f prose-writer
prosita short prose passage
prosodia prosody
prosódico prosodic
prosopopeya rhet personification; affected manner
prospección f min survey
prospecto prospectus
prosperar to thrive, make happy
prosperidad f prosperity
próspero prosperous
próstata med prostate
prostático prostatic
prosternarse to prostrate o.s.
prostésico prosthesist, artificial-limb maker
próstesis f prosthesis, artificial limb
prostético prosthetic
prostitución f prostitution
prostituido prostituted; corrupted
prostituir to prostitute; corrupt; ~se to prostitute o.s.; sell o.s.
prostituta prostitute
protagonismo cin+theat principal part/ role; leadership

protagonista m+f protagonist; hero; cin+theat star
prote f sl juvenile court
protección f protection; favour
proteccionismo protectionism
proteccionista n m+f+adj protectionist
protector m protector, defender; patron; mech safety guard; adj protecting
protectorado protectorate
protectriz f protectress
proteger to protect
protegido protégé, favourite
proteico, proteínico adj protein
proteína protein
protervia, protervidad f perversity
protervo perverse
prótesis f gramm prothesis; med prosthesis
protesta protest; ~ **denegada** objection over-ruled
protestación f protestation
protestante n m+f Protestant; adj Protestant, protesting
prostestantismo Protestantism
protestar to protest; affirm, state solemnly; complain; ~ **contra** to deny the validity of; ~ **de** to protest against
protestatario argumentative, bolshie
protestativo protesting
protoalbéitar m head veterinary surgeon
protocolar to formalize
protocolario ceremonial, formal
protocolizar to protocolize
protocolo protocol
protohistoria protohistory
protohistórico protohistoric
protomártir m protomartyr
protomédico physician to the king
protón m proton
protoplasma protoplasm
prototipo prototype
protráctil protractile
protuberancia protuberance
protuberante protuberant
provecto advanced (in years, experience etc)
provecho advantage; profit; ¡**buen ~**! may it profit you! (greeting before eating); **de ~** advantageous, profitable, useful; **hombre de ~** man of substance; **no hacer nada de ~** to do nothing useful; **ser de ~ para** (of food) to

401

be good for; **sacar** ~ **de** to gain advantage from

provechoso advantageous; beneficial; profitable

proveedor *m* purveyor

proveeduría purveyor's office/shop

proveer to provide, supply, provision; stock; dispose; transact; **~se (de)** to get one's supply (of)

proveído *leg* ruling, decision

proveimiento supplies

provena *bot* layer of vine

proveniente arising, resulting

provenir de to arise from, be due to

Provenza Provence

provenzal Provençal

proverbiador *m* collector of proverbs

proverbiar to employ proverbs

proverbio proverb, adage, saying

proverbista *m+f* one who employs clichés/proverbs

providencia foresight; means; judgement; providence

providencial providential

providenciar to take measures to decide; give judgement

providente, próvido provident; wise, prudent

provincia province

provincialismo provincialism

provinciano *n+adj* provincial

provisión *f* provision, supply; stock; decree; *comm* financial remittance; ~ **de alimento** catering

proviso: al ~ immediately

provisor *m* purveyor, supplier; *eccles* vicar-general

provisoria convent/college pantry

provisorio provisional, interim

provisto supplied, stocked; ~ **de** provided with

provocación *f* provocation, incitement

provocador *m* provocator, inciter

provocante provocative

provocar to provoke, incite; tempt; *fam* vomit

provocativo provocative, inciting; tempting

proxeneta *m+f* pimp, procurer/procuress of prostitutes

proxenetismo procuring; action of a pimp/procuress

proximidad *f* proximity

próximo next; neighbouring; **de** ~ soon;

no ~ nowhere near

proyección *f* projection; design; *cin* showing

proyectante projecting

proyectar to plan, design; *bot* shoot; *geom* project; *cin* show (a film); be thinking of; **~se** (of shadows, light *etc*) to fall

proyectil *m* projectile, missile; ~ **aire-tierra** air-to-ground missile; ~ **dirigido** guided missile

proyectista *m+f* designer, planner

proyecto *n* plan, project, scheme; draft; ~ **de ley** *pol* bill; ~ **de resolución** draft resolution; ~ **experimental** pilot project; *adj* projected; in perspective

proyector *n m* projector; searchlight; ~ **cinematográfico** film projector; *adj* projecting

proyectura projecture; *archi* projection

prudencia prudence, moderation

prudencial prudential, moderate

prudente prudent; wise

prueba proof; evidence; test; sample; sign; token tasting; acrobatic feat; card trick; (of clothing) fitting; *print+phot* proof; *sp* heat; ~ **de fuego** *fig* acid test; ~ **de indicios** circumstantial evidence; ~ **de inteligencia/aptitud** intelligence/aptitude test; **a ~** on trial; **a ~ de agua** waterproof; **a ~ de aire** airtight; **a ~ de balas/bombas/grasa** bullet-/bomb-/grease-proof; **poner a ~** to try, test

pruebista *m+f* acrobat

pruna prune

pruriginoso causing itching

prurito itching

Prusia Prussia

prusiano Prussian

prúsico prussic

pseudo pseud, pretentious person

pseudónimo nom-de-plume, pen-name

psicoanálisis *f* psychoanalysis

psicoanalista *m+f* psychoanalyst

psicoanalítico psychoanalytical

psicoanalizar to psychoanalyse

psicocirugía psycho-surgery

psicodélico psychedelic

psicogénesis *f* psychogenesis

psicología psychology; ~ **de masas** mass-psychology

psicológico psychological

psicólogo psychologist

psicometría psychometry
psicométrico psychometric
psicómetro psychometer
psiconeurosis *f* psychoneurosis
psiconeurótico psychoneurotic
psicópata psychopath
psicopatía psychopathy
psicosis *f* psychosis
psicosomático psychosomatic
psicoterapia psychotherapy
psicótico psychotic
psicosexual psychosexual
psique *f* psyche
psiquiatra *m+f* psychiatrist
psiquiatría psychiatry
psiquiátrico psychiatric
psíquico psychic(al)
psiquis *m* psyche; mind
P.S.O.E. (**Partido Socialista Obrero Español**) Spanish Socialist Workers' Party
P.S.U.C. (**Partido Socialista Unificado de Cataluña**) Unified Socialist Party of Catalonia (Communist Party of Catalonia)
psuquero member of **P.S.U.C.**
pta (**peseta**) peseta
Pte (**presidente**) Pres. (President)
pterodáctilo pterodactyl
ptomaína ptomaine
¡pu! bah!
púa prick; prong; tooth (of a comb); quill (of hedgehog); *hort* graft; *mus* plectrum; *sl* peseta; **alambre de ~s** barbed wire
puado set of prongs/teeth *etc*
pubertad *f*, **pubescencia** puberty
pubescente pubescent
pubescer to reach puberty
púbico, pubiano pubic
publicación *f* publication; proclamation; disclosure; *adj* publishing
publicador *m* publisher; proclaimer; discloser
publicano *bibl* publican
publicar to publish; proclaim; disclose
publicidad *f* publicity
publicista *m+f* publicist
publicitar to publicize
publicitario *adj* advertising
público *n* public; *adj* public; **en ~** publicly; **dar al ~** to publish
pucha *bot* bouquet
puchar *sl* to speak

púcher *m sl* (drug-)pusher
puchera cooking-pot
pucherito pouting (of a child about to cry); **hacer ~s** to pout
puchero saucepan, cooking-pot; stew, ragout; pouting of a child about to cry; **hacer ~s** to pout
pudelación *f*, **pudelaje** *m metal* puddling
pudelador *m metal* puddler
pudelar *metal* to puddle
pudendo *n* penis; *adj* shameful; obscene; **partes pudendas** private parts
pudibundez *f* prudishness
pudibundo shy, modest
pudicia modesty; chastity
púdico modest; chaste
pudiente powerful; rich, wealthy; **clase ~** ruling class, upper class
pudín *m* pudding
pudor *m* modesty; chastity
pudoroso shy, bashful; modest
pudrición *f* putrefaction
pudridero temporary burial place
pudrido putrid, rotten
pudrimiento *see* **pudrición**
pudrir to rot, decay, putrify; worry; gnaw at; **~se** to decay; *fig* die of grief
puebla village; *agri* sowing
pueblada mob, crowd; popular uprising; mass meeting of workers
pueblerino *n* villager, yokel; *adj* provincial, village
pueblo town, village; people, nation; common people
puente *m+f* bridge; *carp* transom, lintel; *naut* bridge; *naut* gun-deck; *mot* rear-axle; **~ aéreo** air-lift; **~ cerril** narrow bridge for cattle; **~ de barcas/pontones** pontoon bridge; **~ levadizo** drawbridge; **~ pivotante** swing-bridge; **hacer ~** to link up holidays, stay away from work between two public holidays
puerca *zool* sow; *fam* slut
puerco *n* hog, pig; low/dirty person; **~ de mar**, **~ marino** porpoise, dolphin; **~ espín** porcupine; **~ montés** wild boar; *adj* piggish, filthy
puericia childhood, infancy
puericultura child-care
pueril puerile, infantile, childish
puerilidad *f* puerility, childishness
puérpera woman who has recently given birth

puerperio afterbirth

puerro *bot* leek

puerta door, doorway; gate, gateway; ~ **corrediza/corredera** sliding-door; ~ **de dos hojas**, ~ **plegadiza** folding door; ~ **de emergencia** emergency exit; ~ **de vaivén** swing-door; ~ **franca** free entry; ~ **giratoria** revolving door; ~ **principal**, ~ **de la calle** front door, street door; ~ **trasera/excusada** back door; **a** ~**s** in abject poverty; **abrir la** ~ *fig* to provide a motive; **acompañar a alguien a la** ~ to see s.o. out/to the door; **cerrar la** ~ *fig* to make difficult; **coger a alguien entre** ~**s** to make s.o. stop sitting on the fence, force s.o. to make a decision; **coger la** ~ to depart; **detrás de la** ~ round the corner; **echar las** ~**s abajo** to bang loudly on the door; **enseñarle a alguien la** ~ to throw s.o. out of the house; **estar en** ~ **para** to be the next in line for; **fuera de** ~**s** outdoors; ~ **ventana** wooden window-shutter

puerto port, harbour, haven; pass (between mountains); shelter, refuge, asylum; ~ **de arribada/de escala** *naut* port of call; ~ **de mar** seaport; ~ **de marea** tidal harbour; ~ **de origen** home port; ~ **franco** free port; **derechos de** ~ harbour dues

puertorriqueño *n+adj* Puerto Rican

pues *adv* so, anyhow, anyway; *conj* for, as, since, because, well (introducing a statement); ~ **bien** well then; ~ **no** not so, not at all; ~ **que** since; *¿*~ **qué?** what about it?, what then?; ~ **sí** yes indeed, certainly; *¿*~ **y qué?** what else?

puesta *astron* set, setting; stake, bet; ~ **de sol** sunset; ~**-en-pie** pick-me-up

puesto place, space; booth, stall, exhibition stand; job, position; office, post; *mil* barracks; ~ **de avance** *mil* advance post, outpost; ~ **de control** check-point, control station; ~ **de escucha** *rad* monitoring-post, listening-post; ~ **de socorro** first-aid post; *adj* placed; set

¡puf! bah!

púgil *m* boxer, prizefighter

pugilato, pugilismo boxing, pugilism

pugilista *m* boxer, pugilist

pugna conflict, combat, row; **estar en** ~ **con** to be in conflict with

pugnacidad *f* pugnacity

pugnante *n m* opponent; *adj* fighting, struggling

pugnar to fight, struggle (**con** with); be opposed to; persist

pugnaz pugnacious, quarrelsome

puja out-bidding (at auction); higher bid

pujador higher bidder

pujante powerful, strong

pujanza power, strength

¹ **pujar** to outbid

² **pujar** to forge ahead; push through; falter; *fam* pout

pujo longing, desire

pulcritud *f* tidiness; neatness

pulcro tidy, neat; beautiful

pulga *ent* flea; silicon chip; **tener malas** ~**s**, **ser de malas** ~**s** to be ill-tempered; **tener** ~**s** to be restless

pulgada inch

pulgar *m* thumb

pulgarada inch

pulguero *sl* bed

pulgón *m* greenfly, aphid

pulgoso flea-ridden

pulguera flea-pit

pulguillas *m sing+pl* pugnacious man

pulicán *m* dentist's forceps

pulidero polisher, burnisher

pulidez *f* polish, cleanliness

pulido polished, clean

pulidor *n m see* **pulidero**; *adj* polishing, burnishing

pulimentar to polish, burnish

pulimento polish, gloss

pulir to polish, burnish; adorn, beautify; ~**se** to beautify o.s.; become polished

pulmón *m* lung; ~ **de acero** iron-lung

pulmonar pulmonary

pulmonaria *bot* lungwort

pulmonía pneumonia

pulmoníaco person suffering from pneumonia

pulpa *anat* flesh; pulp (of wood, fruit *etc*)

pulpejo any fleshy part of the body

pulpería general store; grocer's shop

pulpero grocer; octopus catcher

pulpeta slice of meat

púlpito pulpit

pulpo *zool* octopus

pulposo fleshy, pulpy

pulque *m* bar

pulquería tavern

pulsación *f* pulse, pulsation; rhythmic beating/tapping

pulsada pulse-beat

pulsador *n m* push-button; buzzer; *adj* pulsating

pulsante pulsating

pulsar to feel the pulse; finger gently; press (a button, knob *etc*); sound out; **~se** to pulsate, beat

pulsátil, pulsativo pulsating

pulsear to hand-wrestle

pulsera bracelet; *med* wrist bandage; lock of hair over the forehead; **reloj de ~** wrist-watch

pulsímetro *med* pulsimeter

pulso pulse, pulsation; wrist; care; **a ~ arts** freehand, by physical effort, the hard way; **tomar a ~** to test the weight by lifting; **tomar el ~ a** to feel the pulse of

pultáceo soft; *med* gangrened

pulular to germinate; bud; multiply rapidly; swarm

pulverización *f* pulverization, atomization

pulverizador *m* aerosol, spray, atomizer

pulverizar to pulverize, atomize, spray

pulverulento *see* **polvoriento**

pulla obscene expression; repartee; hint; taunt

pullista *m+f* one given to throwing out hints/quick repartee

¡pum! bang!

pumita pumice

puna bleak table-land

punción *f med* puncture

puncha prickle, thorn

punchar to puncture, prick

pundonor *m* point of honour; punctiliousness

pundonoroso punctilious; haughty

pungente pungent

pungir to prick; punch; sting

pungitivo pricking; punching; stinging

punible punishable

punición *f* punishment

púnico Punic, Carthaginian

punitivo punitive

punta point, sharp(ened) end; tip; top; *geog* headland, cape; cigar end; touch, tinge, trace; **~ de diamante** glass-cutter; **~ de París** wire nail; **~s** point-lace; **a ~ de lanza** meticulously; **de ~** at loggerheads; **de ~ a cabo** from end to end, from start to finish; **de ~ en blanco** all dolled up, dressed to kill; **horas ~** rush hours; **de ~s** on tip-toe; **sacar ~ a** to sharpen; **tener ~s de loco** to be a bit eccentric; **tener una ~ de artista/escritor** to be a very poor artist/writer; **tener … en la ~ de la lengua** to have … on the tip of the tongue; **tocar a alguien en la ~ de un cabello** to offend s.o.; **tener los nervios de ~** to be on edge

puntada (sewing) stitch; sharp dig; (bullfighting) gore; **echar ~s** to stitch

puntación *f see* **puntuación**

puntal prop, support; pillar; *cul* snack; *naut* depth of the hold

puntapié *m* kick; **echar a ~s** to kick out; **tratar a ~s** to treat like dirt

punteado *n* marking with dots; punctuation; *mus* plucking (of strings), pizzicato; *adj* dotted, speckled

puntear to stitch; *arts* stipple; *mus* play the guitar; *naut* tack; dot

puntera toe-cap; kick

puntería aim; good marksmanship; **tener buena/mala ~** to be a good/bad shot

¹ **puntero** pointer; mason's chisel

² **puntero** *n* good shot; *adj* first-rate

puntiagudo sharp; pointed

puntilla lace edging; tack, braid; *carp* nail; (bull-fighting) dagger; **de ~s** on tip-toe; **ponerse de ~s** to stick doggedly to one's opinion

puntillo *mus* dot, point

puntillón *m* kick

puntilloso punctilious

punto dot, point; place, spot; full-stop; nib; *med + sewing* stitch; (*of firearms*) sight; (*of nets*) mesh; knitting; hole in stockings; instant; **~ atrás** back-stitch; **~ cruzado** cross-stitch; **~ de admiración** exclamation mark; **~ de apoyo** fulcrum; **~ de cadeneta** chain-stitch; **~ decisivo** turning-point; **~ de comprobación** check-point; **~ de congelación/de hielo** freezing-point; **~ de ebullición** boiling-point; **~ de escala** *naut* stopover point; **~ de fuga** vanishing-point; **~ de fusión** melting-point; ~ **de inflamación** ignition-point; ~ **de interrogación** question-mark; ~ **de no regreso** point of no return; ~ **de partida** starting-point; ~ **de vista** point of view; ~ **en boca** silence, not a word; ~ **en cuestión** point at issue; ~ **menos** a little less; ~ **menos que imposible** barely possible; ~ **muerto** dead centre, deadlock; ~ **por** ~ point by point; ~**s cardinales** points of the compass; ~**s suspensivos** *print* dots, leaders; ~ **y coma** semi-colon; **a** ~ ready; **a** ~ **de** on the point of; **a** ~ **que** just when; **de** ~ knitted; **dos** ~**s** *gramm* colon; **en** ~ on the dot, sharp; **en** ~ **de** in regard to; **en** ~ **muerto** *mot* in neutral; **hasta cierto** ~ up to a point; **en su** ~ at its best; **ganar por** ~**s** *sp* to win on points; **poner** ~ **final a** to put a stop to, end; **poner los** ~**s sobre las íes** to cross one's t's and dot one's i's

puntoso sharply pointed; excessively punctilious

puntuación *f gramm* punctuation; marking; *sp* scoring

puntual punctual

puntualidad *f* punctuality

puntualizar to specify, detail

puntuoso punctilious

puntura puncture

punzada prick; stitch; twinge of pain/regret; compunction

punzador *m* pricking, stabbing

punzadura prick, puncture

punzante pricking, stinging; sharp

punzar to punch; perforate; prick; sting

punzó deep scarlet

punzón *m* punch; bodkin; awl; pick; *print* type mould; countersink

puñada fisticuff, punch

puñado handful, fistful; **a** ~**s** galore

puñal *m* dagger

puñalada stab-wound (with a dagger); ~ **encubierta** stab-in-the-back; **coser a** ~**s** to stab all over, stab over and over again

puñalero maker/seller of daggers

puñera double handful

puñeta annoying person/thing; **¡**~**s!** damn and blast it!

puñetazo fisticuff, punch

puñetero *sl* damned, blasted

puño fist; fistful; cuff, wristband; hilt; handle (of umbrella *etc*); **como un** ~ tight-fisted; **cerrar los** ~**s** to clench one's fists; **de su** ~ **y letra** in his/her own hand (writing); **hombre de** ~**s** strong man

pupa pimple; lip sore; *ent* pupa; (in baby-talk) pain

pupila *anat* pupil; *leg* ward

pupilaje *m* board and lodging; boarding-house; *leg* wardship

pupilero boarding-house keeper

pupilo boarder, inmate; *leg* ward

pupitre *m* school desk

pupo umbilical scar, belly-button

puré *m cul* purée

pureza purity, genuineness

purgación *f*, **purga** purgation, purge

purgante *n m* purgative; *adj* purging

purgar to purge, cleanse; atone for; refine; ~ **una condena** *leg* to serve a sentence; ~**se** to clear o.s. of guilt; take a laxative

purgativo purgative

purgatorio purgatory

puridad *f* purity; **en** ~ strictly speaking

purificación *f* purification

purificadero *adj* cleansing, purifying

purificador *n* purifier; *adj* purifying

purificante purifying

purificar to purify, cleanse; clarify; refine; ~**se** to be cleansed

purificatorio purifying

Purísima: la ~ the Virgin Mary

purismo purism

purista *m + f* purist

puritanismo Puritanism

puritano *n* Puritan; *adj* Puritanical

puro *n* cigar; *sl* punishment; *adj* pure; sterling; genuine; (of gold) solid, unalloyed; clean; mere, only; *adv* sheer; **de pura cepa** out-and-out; **de pura sangre** thoroughbred; **la pura verdad** the honest truth

púrpura purple; dignity of a king/cardinal; *med* purpura

purpurado cardinal

purpurar to colour purple; dress in purple

purpurear to have a purple tinge

purpurea *bot* burdock

purpúreo *adj* purple

purrela poor-quality wine, plonk

purulencia purulency

purulento purulent

pusca *sl* pistol
pusilánime faint-hearted
pusilanimidad *f* faint-heartedness
pústula *med* pimple
pustuloso pimply
puta whore, harlot, prostitute
putada *vulg sl* despicable act
putativo putative
puteado *vulg sl* buggered, fagged out
putear *vulg sl* to go whoring
puteo *vulg sl* whoring

putilla 'easy' girl
puto *vulg sl* male prostitute
putrefacción *f* putrefaction
putrefactivo putrefactive
putrefacto putrid, rotten
putridez *f* rottenness
puya goad; stick
puyazo prick
P.V.P. (precio de venta al público) retail price

Q

q *f* letter q

que *rel pron* who, which, that; *conj* that; **creo ~ va a llover** I think that it's going to rain

qué *inter pron* what, which; *demon pron* what, how; **¡~ bonito!** how lovely!; **¿~ chica?** what girl?; **¡~ chica!** what a girl!

quebrada ravine; gulch; bankruptcy

quebradero: ~ de cabeza worry

quebradizo brittle; fragile

quebrajar to split

quebrajoso brittle; full of cracks

quebrado *n math* fraction; *adj* broken; rough; bankrupt; *med* ruptured

quebradura breaking; fissure; *med* fracture, hernia

quebrantable brittle, easily broken

quebrantahuesos *m sing + pl orni* osprey

quebrantamiento breaking

quebrantaolas *m sing + pl* breakwater

quebrantar to break; crush, pound; tire, annoy; *leg* annul

quebranto breaking; crushing, pounding; tiring, annoying; *comm* loss, damages

quebrar *vt* to break, crush; interrupt; spoil; *vi comm* to go bankrupt; **~se** to get broken; rupture o.s.

queche *m naut* ketch

queda curfew bell; **toque de ~** curfew

quedar(se) to remain, stay, be left; **~se atrás** to be left behind; **~se bien** to acquit o.s. well; **~se con** *sl* to stare at; **~ en** to agree to; **~se ciego** to become blind; **~se fresco** not to mind in the least

quedo *adj* quiet; still, peaceful; *adv* softly; in a quiet voice; **~ a ~** little by little

quedón *m sl* joker, jester

quehacer *m* task, chore

queja complaint

quejarse to complain; protest

quejica *sl* moaner, beefer

quejido moan, complaint

quejoso ever-complaining; always moaning

quel *m sl* home

quema burning, combustion

quemado burnt; angry; **~ por el sol** suntanned

quemador *m* burner (on cooker)

quemadura burn; scar caused by burning

quemajoso *adj* smarting

quemar to burn; **~se** to get burnt; **~se las cejas** to burn the midnight oil

quemazón *m* combustion; burning sensation

quena *S.A.* native flute

querella complaint; *leg* accusation, charge

querellador *m*, **querellante** *m leg* complainant, plaintiff

querellarse to complain; *leg* take legal proceedings; contest a will

querencia fondness; (of animals) haunt, favourite spot

querer *n m* love; desire; *v* to want; love; be fond of; like; wish; **sin ~** unintentionally

querida *n* lover, paramour, mistress; *adj* darling

querido *n* lover, gallant; *adj* darling; (letter-writing) dear

queroseno kerosene

querubín *m* cherub

querúbico cherubic

quesear to make cheese

quesera cheese-dish; dairymaid

quesería cheese shop; cheese factory

quesero cheese maker/seller

queso cheese; *sl* foot

quevedos *mpl* horn-rimmed glasses

¡quiá! *interj* (expressing disbelief) come now!

quicio: fuera de ~ out of order; **sacar de ~** to unhinge; exasperate

quid *m* essence, gist, main point

quiebra break, crack; *comm* bankruptcy

quiebro dodge, feint; *mus* trill

408

quien who; he who; whom
¿quién? who?; whom?
quienquier, quienquiera, quienesquiera
whoever, whosoever, whomsoever
quietación f appeasement; calming
quietar to quieten; appease
quieto still, motionless; peaceful
quietud f stillness, peace
quijada jaw; Jew's harp
quijotada Quixotic deed
quijote m one who behaves like Don
Quixote
quijotesco quixotic
quijotismo quixotism
quilate m carat
quilo: sudar el ~ to work hard
quilla naut keel; orni breastbone
quillotrar to excite; make love to;
captivate; ~se to fall in love
quillotro excitement; love-making; very
dear friend
quimera chimera, illusion
quimérico chimeric, illusory
química chemistry
químico chemist
quimono kimono
quincalla comm hardware
quincallería hardware trade
quincallero hardware dealer
quince fifteen
quincena fortnight; por ~ fortnightly
quincenal fortnightly
quinceno fifteenth
quincuagenario fifty-odd-year-old
quincuagésimo fiftieth
quingentésimo five hundredth
quiniela football pool; pools coupon
quinielista m+f football pool competitor
quinientos five hundred
quinina quinine
quínola (cards) four of a kind
quinqué m oil-lamp
quinquefolio n bot cinquefoil; adj five-
leaved
quinquenal quinquennial

quinqui m sl tinker, didecai, pedlar
quinta country seat; mil call-up, draft;
mus fifth; ~ columna fifth column
quintacolumnista n m+f +adj fifth-
columnist
quintaescencia quintessence
quintal m measure approx 100 lb.; ~
métrico 100 kilogrammes
quintar mil to call up, draft
quinteto quintet
quintilla stanza of five lines
quintillizos mpl quintuplets
quinto n fifth; small bottle of beer; mil
conscript; national serviceman; adj
fifth
quintuplicación f quintuplication
quintuplicar to quintuplicate
quíntuplo quintuple
quinzavo n+adj fifteenth
quiosco kiosk
quiosquero kiosk owner; newsagent
quiquiriquí m cock-a-doodle-doo
quirófano operating theatre
quiromancia palmistry
quiromántico palmist
quiropedia chiropody
quiropedista m+f chiropodist
quirúrgico surgical
quisquilla bickering; shrimp
quisquilloso fastidious, fussy, particular
quiste m med cyst
quita leg discharge, release; de ~ y pon
detachable; non-iron
quitamanchas m sing+pl stain-remover
quitanieves m sing+pl snow-plough
quitapelillos m sing+pl flatterer, creep
quitapenas m sing+pl pocket-knife
quitapiedras m sing+pl cow-catcher
quitar to remove, take away, deprive of;
steal; math subtract; redeem (a
pledge); (fencing) parry; ~se to take
off; remove oneself
quitasol m sunshade, parasol
quite m obstacle; impediment
quito quit; clear; free
quizá, quizás maybe, perhaps

R

r f (letter) r

raba bait

rabada rump, hindquarter

rabadán m chief shepherd

rabadilla anat coccyx

rabanal m radish plot

rabanera shameless woman; radish seller

rabanero radish seller

rabanillo bot wild radish; (of wine) sour taste; med itch; bad temper

rabaniza bot radish seed

rábano radish; ~ **picante** horse-radish; **tomar el** ~ **por las hojas** to do things the wrong way round

rabazuz m licorice-juice

rabear to wag (the tail)

rabel m vulg arse

rabeo tail-wagging

rabera tail-end; chaff

rabero sl thief who operates on trains/buses; sl man who physically molests women and girls on trains/buses

rabí see rabino

rabia vet rabies; fury; **tener** ~ to be angry, bear a grudge; **tenerle a uno mucha** ~ to hate s.o.'s guts; **tomar** ~ **a** to take a dislike to

rabiar vet to suffer from rabies; rage; be furious; ~ **por** to long for

rabiazorras m sing+pl east wind

rabicán, rabicano white-tailed

rabicorto short-tailed

rabieta fit of temper; tantrum

rabihorcado n orni frigate-bird; adj fork-tailed

rabilargo long-tailed

rabinegro black-tailed

rabínico rabbinical

rabinismo rabbinism

rabinista m rabbinist

rabino rabbi

rabión m rapids

rabioso vet rabid; mad, in a rage; sl enormous; sl intense

rabisalsera impudent, cheeky, forward

rabiza tip of a fishing-rod; stick of a rocket (firework); end of a piece of rope

rabo tail; back, hind part; train (of garment); vulg sl penis; **aun hay que sudar el** ~ there's still a lot to be done; **de cabo a** ~ from end to end, from start to finish; **falta el** ~ **por desollar** the worst is yet to come; **mirar por el** ~ **del ojo** to look out of the corner of the eye

rabón vet docked, bobtailed

rabona soldier's wife; female camp-follower; **hacer** ~ to play truant

rabopelado opossum

rabosear to chafe, fret

raboso tattered, ragged

rabudo thick-tailed; long-tailed; bad-tempered

rábula pettifogger, petty lawyer; quack lawyer

raca sl motor-car

racanear sl to avoid work

rácano sl idle, lazy; stingy

racimado clustered

racimar to pick clusters/bunches of

racimo cluster, bunch

raciocinación f reasoning

raciocinar to reason, ponder

raciocinio reasoning

ración f portion; ration; supply; allowance; pittance; ~ **de hambre** starvation wages; **poner a** ~ to put on short commons

racional rational

racionalidad f rationality

racionalismo rationalism

racionalista m+f rationalist

racionamiento rationing

racionar to ration

racionero rations distributor; eccles prebendary

racionista m one who receives rations; theat odd-job man

racismo racism, racialism

racista n m+f+adj racist, racialist

410

racha gust of wind; stroke of luck; flaw; **mala** ~ bad spell, run of bad luck

racheado in gusts, in bursts

rachear to occur in gusts/bursts; *mil* fire in bursts

rada *naut* roadstead; bay

radiación *f* radiation

radiactividad *f* radioactivity

radiactivo radioactive

radiador *m* radiator

radial radial; radio; **locutor** ~ radio announcer

radiante radiant; ~ **de** beaming with

radiar to radiate; *rad+TV* broadcast; *med* treat with X-rays

radicación *f* radication, rooting, taking root

radical *n m math* radical, root; *gramm* root; *adj* radical, original

radicalismo radicalism

radicar to take root; have roots; lie; ~**se** to settle down; establish o.s.

radicoso radical

¹ **radio** *geom* radius; ~ **de acción** *aer* range; ~ **de gira** *mot* turning-circle

² **radio** radium

³ **radio** *f* (*m* in *SA*) radio, wireless; radio telegraphy; radio set; broadcasting; ~ **comando** walkie-talkie; ~ **macuto** *mil sl* grape-vine

radioactividad *f see* **radiactividad**

radioactivo *see* **radiactivo**

radioaficionado radio ham

radioamplificador *m rad* amplifier

radiobiología radiobiology

radiocarbono radio-carbon

radiocomunicación *f* radio communication system

radiodifundir to broadcast

radiodifusión *f* broadcasting

radiodifusora broadcasting-station

radioescucha radio listener, monitor

radioemisora radio station, broadcasting station

radiofaro radio beacon

radiofrecuencia radio-frequency

radiografía radiography; X-ray (photograph); *sl* pawing, groping

radiografiar to radiograph; *sl* paw, grope

radiográfico radiographic

radiograma *m* radio-telegram

radiogramola radiogram; ~ **tragaperras** juke-box

radioguía radio range-beacon

radiología radiology

radiológico radiological

radiólogo radiologist

radiómano radio fan

radiomensaje *m* radio message

radiometría radiometry

radiorevista radio magazine

radiorreceptor *m* radio receiver, receiving set

radioscopia radioscopy

radioso radiant; shining

radiotelefonía radiotelephony

radiotelefónico radiotelephonic

radiotelegrafía radiotelegraphy

radiotelegrafiar to radiotelegraph

radiotelegráfico radiotelegraphic

radiotelegrafista *m+f* radiotelegraphist

radiotelégrafo radiotelegraph

radiotelegrama *m* radio-telegram

radioscopio radioscope

radioterapia radio-therapy

radiotransmisor *m* radio transmitter

radioyente *m + f* listener

raedera scraper

raedor *n* scraper; *adj* scraping

raedura scraping

raer to scrape; rub off; wipe out, extirpate

raf *m sl* gin and Coca-Cola

rafa irrigation-ditch; *archi* buttress

Rafael Raphael

rafaelesco *n+adj* Raphaelite

ráfaga gust of wind; flash of light; *mil* burst of fire

rafia raffia

raglán *m* raglan

ragú *m* bait; hunger; suspicion

rahez base, despicable

raído frayed; bare; shabby

raigal *m* root

raigambre *f* root-structure; *fig* tradition

raigón *m bot* large root; root of a tooth

raíz *f* root, origin; **a** ~ **de** immediately after; **arrancar de** ~ to uproot; **bienes raíces** landed property, real estate; **cortar de** ~ to nip in the bud; **de** ~ completely; **echar raíces** to take root

raja split; (of food) slice; *vulg sl* cunt

rajá *m* rajah

rajable easily split

rajabroqueles *m sing+pl* bully

rajadizo easily split

rajado *sl* informal; *sl* untrustworthy; *sl* coward

rajadura cleft

rajar to split; (of food) slice; chatter; escape; *sl* wound with a knife

rajatabla: a ~ unswervingly, at any cost

raje *m* escape

ralea *pej* race, breed; quality; prey of predatory birds

raleza thinness

ralo thin

ralladera, rallador *m cul* grater

ralladura scratch, grating

rallar *cul* to grate; scratch

rallo grater; rasp

rama *bot* branch, bough; *print* chase; *sl* marihuana; **andarse por las ~s** to beat about the bush; **asirse a las ~s** to make silly excuses; **en ~** unprocessed, raw, crude; (of books) unbound

ramada arbour

ramaje *m* branches; foliage

ramal *m* branch; (railway) branch line; (of rope *etc*) strand

ramalazo lash; weal left by a lash; blow; sudden pain

rambla sandy ravine; tree-lined avenue

ramera prostitute, whore, harlot

ramería brothel, *US* cat-house

ramificarse to branch out

ramillete *m* posy, nosegay, small bouquet; *bot* cluster; **~ de Constantinopla** *bot* sweet william

ramilletero flower-vase; bouquet-maker

ramo branch, bough; bouquet; (of onions *etc*) string; *bot* cluster; *comm* department, line (of goods); **de Pascuas a Ramos** once in a blue moon; **domingo de Ramos** Palm Sunday; **ser del ~** *sl* to be gay/homosexual

ramoso having many branches

rampa ramp, slope; cramp

rampollo *hort* cutting for propagation

ramulla brushwood

rana frog; **~ arbórea** tree-frog; **~ de los prados** *bot* meadowsweet; **~ toro** bull-frog; **salir ~** to turn out to be a black sheep/wrong 'un

ranacuajo *see* **renacuajo**

rancajo splinter in the flesh

rancidez *f* rancidity, rancidness

rancio rancid; sour; stale

ranchear to build a hut; settle in a hut

ranchería settlement, camp; collection of huts

ranchero rancher; small farmer

¹ **rancho** farm; cattle-ranch; hut; camp; **~ de recreo** dude ranch

² **rancho** mess, messroom; food (*esp* in an institution); plain food; grub

¹ **randa** lace trimming

² **randa** *sl* pickpocket

randado lace-trimmed

randar *sl* to steal, rob

randera lace-maker

ranero vagabond, tramp, *US* hobo

rangífero *zool* reindeer

rango class; rank

ranúnculo *bot* buttercup

ranura groove, slot

rapa *bot* flower of the olive

rapacejo border; urchin

rapacidad *f* rapacity

rapapiés *m sing + pl* squib

rapapolvo sharp reprimand, ticking-off

rapar to shave; crop; steal; **~se** to shave one's head

¹ **rapaz** rapacious; predatory

² **rapaz** young boy

rapaza young girl

rapazada childish prank

rape: al ~ close-cropped

rapé *m* snuff

rapidez *f* rapidity; speed; velocity

rápido *n* express train; **~s** rapids; *adj* rapid, fast

rapiña robbery, plundering; **ave de ~** *orni* bird of prey

rapiñador *n m* plunderer, robber; *adj* plundering; robbing

rapiñar to plunder, pillage; rob

raposa vixen; astute person

raposear to behave astutely

raposera fox's lair

raposería foxiness, cunning

raposino foxy

raposo dog-fox

raposuno foxy

rapsodia rhapsody

rapsódico rhapsodic

raptar to kidnap (a woman); steal

rapto kidnapping (of a woman)

raptor *m* kidnapper (of a woman); thief

raquero *n naut* wrecker; *adj* piratical

raqueta *sp* racket; badminton; snow-shoe

raquetero maker/seller of rackets

raquis *m sing + pl bot* stalk; spinal

column

raquitis f, **raquitismo** med rickets

rara orni passerine

rarefacción f rarefaction

rarefacer to rarefy

rareza rarity; fad; curiosity; **por ~** rarely

raridad f rarity

rarificar to rarefy; make thin; **~se** to become thin, become rarefied

rarificativo rarefying

raro odd, strange; rare, scarce; precious

ras m level, even; **~ con ~** on the level; **a ~ de tierra** at ground level

rasa flat land

rasante f (railway) grade, gradient; adj levelling; **cambio de ~** brow of a hill

rasar to skim; touch lightly; level

rasca sl bout of drunkenness; sl hunger; sl cold

rascacielos m sing+pl skyscraper

rascadera curry-comb

rascador m scraper; rasp; bodkin

rascadura scraping, rasping

rascalino bot dodder

rascamiento scraping, scratching

rascamoño hatpin

rascar to scrape, scratch

rascazón m itching, tickling

rascón n m orni water-rail, marsh hen; adj acrid, sour

rasgadura rent, tear, rip

rasgar to rend, tear, rip; **de rompe y rasga** forthright, dauntless

rasgo stroke, flourish; flash (of wit etc); generous deed; characteristic; **~s** features; **a grandes ~s** in broad outline

rasgón m rip, rent, tear

rasgueado full of flourishes

rasguear to flourish; play flourishes on the guitar

rasgueo flourish; scroll-work

rasguñar to sketch, outline; scratch

rasguño sketch, outline; scratch

raso n satin; adj clear; plain; **a campo ~, al ~** in the open air; **cielo ~** clear sky; **hacer tabla rasa** to make a clean sweep; **soldado ~** private, trooper, ranker; **tiempo ~** fine weather

raspa carp wood-rasp; outer rind of nuts; sl servant-girl

raspadura erasure; rasping; abrasion; shavings

ráspano bot myrtle

raspante rasping, abrasive; (of wine) rough

raspar to erase; scrape, rasp; pare; steal; (of wine) sting

raspear to (of a pen) scratch

raspilla bot forget-me-not

rastra track, trail; sledge; agri harrow; string (of garlic/onions etc); **a la(s) ~(s), a ~s** dragging by force, unwillingly

rastrallar vi to crack (a whip etc); vt to lash

rastreador m tracker, scout, guide; naut mine-sweeper; trawler

rastrear to trace, track down; agri rake, harrow; drag (ponds etc); aer fly low, hedge-hop; comm sell (meat) wholesale

rastreo dragging (of ponds etc); searching; agri raking, harrowing; naut trawling

¹ **rastrero** adj crawling, grovelling, cringing; dragging; mean; aer low-flying

² **rastrero** slaughterhouse employee

rastrillador m raker

rastrillaje m raking

rastrillar to rake

rastrillo rake; portcullis; (cricket) wicket; **~ de pesebre** manger rack

rastro track, trail, scent; trace; agri rake, harrow; slaughterhouse

Rastro: el ~ flea-market in Madrid

rastrojera stubble-field

rastrojo stubble

rasura shaving

rasurado shave

rasuración f act of shaving

rasurar to shave

rata zool rat; pickpocket; sl miser, avaricious person; **~ de sacristía** sl very devout woman

rataplán m rub-a-dub (sound of a drum)

¹ **ratear** to apportion

² **ratear** to creep

³ **ratear** to steal, pinch; pick pockets

ratería pickpocketing; pinching

ratero pickpocket; petty thief

raticida rat poison

ratificación f ratification

ratificar to ratify

ratificatorio ratifying

ratigar to secure a load with a rope

ratina rateen

rato short period of time, little while; **a ~s** from time to time; **a ~s perdidos** in one's spare time; **al poco ~** shortly after; **lo tengo para ~** this is going to take me some time; **pasar el ~** to while away the time

ratón *m* mouse; **~ de archivo, ~ de biblioteca** book-worm; **~ de campo** fieldmouse, harvest-mouse

ratona female mouse; female rat

ratonera *n f* mouse-trap; mouse-hole; **caer en la ~** to fall into the trap; *orni* buzzard; *adj* good at catching mice

rauco raucous

raudal *m* torrent

raudo rapid, quick; impetuous

rauta road, way, route

¹ **raya** line; stripe; stroke, dash; frontier, boundary; score, mark; crease (in trousers); parting (of hair); *print* rule; firebreak; *sl* dose of cocaine or other drug in powder form; **~ de la meta** *sp* goal-line; **a ~** within bounds; **dar ciento y ~ a** to knock the living day-lights out of; **pasar de la ~** to go too far; **tener a ~** to hold at bay

² **raya** *zool* ray, skate

rayado lined, striped

rayadura ruling

rayano contiguous

rayar *vi* to excel; appear; verge on, border on; *vt* to draw lines on; scratch (furniture *etc*); stripe; underline; cross out

rayo ray, beam; spoke; thunderbolt; lightning-flash; **~s-X** X-rays; **~s infrarrojos** infra-red rays; **gustar/oler a ~s** to taste/smell awful

rayón *m* rayon

rayoso covered with lines/stripes

rayuela hop-scotch

rayuelo snipe

¹ **raza** race, lineage; **de ~, de pura ~** thoroughbred; **Día de la Raza** Columbus Day (12 October)

² **raza** crack, fissure

razón *f* reason, motive; reasonableness; fairness; explanation; *math* ratio; **~ de pie de banco** silly reason; **~ de ser** raison d'être; **~ social** trade mark; **a ~ de** at the rate of; **con ~ o sin ella** rightly or wrongly; **dar ~ de** to give an account of; **dar la ~ a** to agree with; **en ~ a** with regard to; **entrar en ~** to

listen to reason; **meter en ~** to convince; **no tener ~** to be wrong/mistaken; **perder la ~** to go mad; **por cuya ~** and therefore; **por ~ de** because of; **tener ~** to be right; **tomar ~ de** to record, make a record of/inventory of

razonable reasonable, fair

razonado reasoned out; itemized

razonador *n m* reasoner; *adj* reasoning

razonamiento reasoning

razonante reasoning

razonar to reason; itemize

rea accused woman

reabastecer to refuel

reabastecimiento (de combustible) re-fuelling

reabrir to reopen

reabsorber to reabsorb

reabsorción *f* reabsorption

reacción *f* reaction; **~ de la sangre** blood-test; **~ en cadena** chain reaction; **~ persistente** sustained reaction

reaccionar to react

reaccionario reactionary

reacio stubborn, reluctant

reacomodo readjustment

reacondicionamiento overhaul, re-conditioning

reacondicionar to overhaul, recondition

reactancia reactance

reactividad *f* reactivity

reactivo reactive

reactor *m* reactor; atomic pile; **~ re-productor** breeder reactor

readaptación *f* readjustment

readaptar to readapt

readmisión *f* readmission

reafirmación *f* reaffirmation

reafirmar to reaffirm

reagravación *f* reaggravation

reagravar to reaggravate

reagudo very acute

reajustar to readjust; *pol* shuffle (of cabinet)

reajuste *m* readjustment; *pol* shuffle (of cabinet)

¹ **real** real

² **real** *n* camp; fairground; obsolete *Sp* coin *equiv* 25 céntimos; **~ sitio** royal country house: **alzar los ~es** to break camp; **(a)sentar los ~es** to encamp; *adj* royal; royalist

realce *m* embossed work; splendour;

excellence
realdad *f* royal power
realegrarse to be very joyful
realengo *n* royal patrimony; *adj* royal
realeza royal dignity; royalty
realidad *f* reality, fact; truth; **en ~** as a matter of fact
realimentación *f elect* feedback
realineación *f* realignment
realinear to realign
[1] **realismo** realism
[2] **realismo** royalism
[1] **realista** *n m+f +adj* realist
[2] **realista** *n m+f +adj* royalist
realquilar to sublet
realizable realizable; *comm* marketable, saleable
realización *f* realization; fulfilment; *comm* sale
realizar to realize; fulfil; perform; *comm* sell off, market; convert into money
realzar to raise; emboss; brighten, enhance; **~se** to materialize
reanimación *f* reanimation; comfort
reanimar to reanimate; cheer, comfort
reanudación *f* renewal, resumption
reanudar to renew; resume
reaparecer to reappear
reaparición *f* reappearance
reapertura reopening
rearmar to rearm
rearme *m* rearmament
reasegurar to reinsure
reaseguro reinsurance
reasumir to reassume
reasunción *f* resumption
reata lariat, rope; **de ~** in single file, in Indian file
reatar to retie; tie tightly
reavivamiento revival
reavivar to revive
rebaja deduction; reduction; discount; **~s** sales; **precios de ~** bargain prices
rebajamiento lowering, reduction; humiliation
rebajar to lessen, reduce; underbid; *mil* discharge from service; *carp* plane down; *arts* tone down; **~se** to humble o.s.
rebajo *carp* rabbet; groove
rebalaje *m* eddy; current of water
rebalsa puddle, pool
rebanada slice

rebanador *m* slicing-machine
rebanar to slice
rebañadera drag-hook; grapnel
rebañar to gather, glean
rebañego easily led
rebaño flock, herd; *eccles* congregation
rebasar to exceed; overflow; *naut* sail past
rebate *m* contention
rebatible refutable
rebatido (sewing) overhand seam
rebatimiento refutation
rebatiña free-for-all; **andar a la ~** to grab and snatch
rebatir to drive back; refute; reject; beat repeatedly; *comm* deduct
rebato alarm; commotion; *mil* surprise attack; **tocar a ~** to sound the alarm
rebautizar to rebaptize
rebeca cardigan
rebeco *zool* chamois
rebelarse to rebel
rebelde *n m* rebel; *leg* defaulter; *adj* rebellious
rebeldía rebelliousness; stubbornness; truculence
rebelón (of horses) stubborn
rebencazo blow with a whip
rebenque *m* whip; *naut* ratline
rebién *fam* very well, jolly well
rebisabuela great-great-grandmother
rebisabuelo great-great-grandfather
rebisnieta great-great-granddaughter
rebisnieto great-great-grandson
reblandecer to soften
reblandecimiento softening; **~ cerebral** softening of the brain
rebocillo shawl
reborde *m* flange, border
rebosadura, rebosamiento overflow
rebosar to overflow; **~ de, ~ en** to teem with
rebotación *f* rebounding
rebotado *sl* ex-priest/monk; unfrocked priest
rebotadura rebound
rebotar to bounce; rebound; ricochet; clinch; vex, irritate; **~se** to change one's opinion; change colour; retract
rebote *m* rebound; ricochet; rebounding; irritation; **de ~** indirectly, on the rebound
rebozar to muffle up; *cul* dip in batter; **~se** to muffle o.s. up

rebozo muffler, shawl; muffling o.s. up; **de** ~ secretly; **sin** ~ openly

rebufo (of firearm) recoil, kick

rebujar to mix together; jumble

rebujina scuffle, mêlée

rebullicio tumult, clamour

rebullir to stir; start to move

rebusca remains; refuse; gleaning

rebuscado affected; unnatural

rebusco gleaning; search

rebuznador *adj* braying

rebuznar to bray

rebuzno bray, braying

recadero, recadista *m* messenger, errand-boy

recado message; errand; daily shopping; gift, present; ~ **de escribir** writing materials; **enviar** ~ to send word

recaer to fall back; relapse

recaída relapse; *leg* second offence

recalada *naut* landfall; soaking, drenching

recalar to soak, drench, saturate little by little; *naut* make landfall, sight land

recalcadura cramming, pressing, packing

recalcar to cram, pack, stuff; emphasize, stress; *naut* list, heel over

recalcitrante recalcitrant

recalcitrar to baulk

recalentamiento reheating

recalentar to reheat, warm up (food *etc*); excite sexually

recalmón *m naut* lull during a storm

recalvastro bald

recalzar *agri* to earth up; *archi* reinforce; *arts* colour

recalzo *agri* earthing up; *archi* reinforcement; rim of a cart-wheel

recamador *m* embroiderer

recamar to embroider with raised work

recámara bedroom, boudoir; *mil* gun-chamber

recambiar to exchange, re-exchange

recambio exchange, re-exchange; *mech* +*mot etc* spare part; refill

recañí *m sl* window

recamo raised embroidery

recantación *f* recantation, retraction

recantón *m* corner-stone

recapacitar to think over; refresh one's memory

recapitulación *f* recapitulation; summary

recapitular to recapitulate, recap; sum up

recargar to have an abundance of; surcharge; overload; *mil* re-load; recharge; *med* have a higher fever

recargo surcharge, extra tax, overload; *leg* fresh accusation; *leg* increase in sentence; *med* increase in temperature

recatado circumspect; shy, modest

recatar to conceal, secrete; ~**se** behave cautiously/modestly

recato circumspection; caution; shyness, modesty; coyness, virtue; **sin** ~ openly

recauchar *mot* to retread

recauchutaje *mot* retreading

recauchutado *mot* retread

recauchutar *mot* to retread

recaudación *f* collecting, collection (of taxes); tax-collector's office

recaudador *m* tax-collector

recaudamiento tax-collection; district (for tax purposes)

recaudar to gather, collect (rates, taxes *etc*); hold in custody

recaudo collection (of rates, taxes *etc*); precaution; *leg* bail, surety

recazo back (of a knife-blade); guard (of a sword)

recebar to gravel, cover with gravel

recebo gravel (for road repairs)

recelar to surprise; suspect; fear; (horses) excite sexually; ~**se** to have fears/suspicions; ~**se de** to fear, be afraid of

recelo fear, suspicion

recentadura leaven

recental *vet* suckling (of calves and lambs)

recentar to leaven, add yeast

recepción *f* reception; reception desk; acceptation; *leg* cross-examination

recepta *leg* record of fines

receptación *f leg* receipt of stolen property

receptáculo receptacle; refuge, shelter

receptar *leg* to receive stolen property; hide, shelter

receptividad *f* receptivity

receptivo receptive

recepto asylum, refuge

receptor *n m* receiver, fence; *adj* receiving

receptoría receiver's office; receivership
recercar to fence in
recesar to go into recess
recesión f recession
recésit m recess; vacation
receso recess; withdrawal; retirement
receta prescription; *cul* recipe; *comm* amount brought forward; memorandum
recetador m prescriber
recetar to prescribe
recetario *pharm* pharmacopoeia; list of prescriptions; *cul* recipe book
recetor m receiver; treasurer
recetoría treasury
recial m rapid (in a river)
recibí m *comm* receipt
recibidor m receiver, recipient
recibimiento reception; welcome; reception-room; drawing-room; hall
recibir to receive; accept; admit; welcome; suffer (an injury); ~se to graduate, be admitted to practise as
recibo reception; *comm* receipt; **acusar** ~ **de** to acknowledge the receipt of; **día de** ~ at-home day; **estar de** ~ to be at home (to visitors)
reciclaje m recycling
reciclar to recycle
recidiva *med* relapse
recidivar *med* to have a relapse
recién: ~ **casados** newly-weds; ~ **elegido** newly elected; ~ **llegado** just arrived; ~ **nacido** new-born
reciente new; recent
recinchar to gird
recinto place; enclosure; precinct
recio *adj* strong; coarse; loud; clumsy; uncouth; severe; *adv* strongly; coarsely; loudly; clumsily; severely; **hablar** ~ to talk loudly; **pisar** ~ to tread firmly
récipe m prescription; *fam* ticking-off
recipiente n m recipient; receptacle, container; *adj* receiving
recíproca *math* reciprocal; **a la recíproca** tit-for-tat
reciprocar(se) to match, reciprocate; repay (a favour)
reciprocidad f reciprocity
recíproco mutual, reciprocal
recircular *see* **reciclar**
recitación f recitation
recitado *mus* recitative; recitation

recital m poetry recital; *mus* concert, recital
recitar to recite
recitativo *mus* recitative
reclamación f reclamation; complaint; **libro de reclamaciones** complaints book
reclamante n m claimer; complainer; *adj* claiming; complaining
reclamar to claim; (hunting) decoy; *leg* subpoena; *orni* call; ~ **en juicio** to sue
reclamo decoy bird; decoy whistle; lure; *orni* courtship display; *orni* bird-call; claim; complaint; advertisement, publicity; catch-word
reclinación f reclining
reclinar to recline; ~se **(sobre)** to lean back (on)
reclinatorio couch; *eccles* priedieu, prayer-desk
recluir to shut in/up; lock up; keep in
reclusión f seclusion; retirement; prison, imprisonment; ~ **aislada** solitary confinement; ~ **perpetua** life imprisonment
recluso inmate; convict
reclusorio place of retirement/confinement
recluta f recruiting, recruitment; round-up (of cattle); m *mil* recruit, conscript
reclutador m *mil* recruiting-officer
reclutamiento recruiting, recruitment
reclutar to recruit; round up (cattle)
recobrable recoverable
recobrante *adj* recovering
recobrar to recover, regain; ~ **el tiempo perdido** to make up for lost time; ~se to recover, come to
recobro recovery; recuperation
recocer to reboil; reheat; cook too much; ~se to boil with rage
recocido n reheating, overcooking; *adj* overcooked
recocina pantry; back-kitchen
recochineo gloating
recochinearse *sl* to mock
recocho overdone, overcooked
recodarse to lean on one's elbows
recodo turn, angle; elbow-bend
recogedero catchment area
recogedor m gleaner, gatherer; dust-pan
recoger to retake; gather; glean, pick, collect; hoard; pick up; shorten; take in, shelter; ~ **velas** to climb down,

draw in one's horns; ~**se** to take shelter; withdraw; go home, retire

recogida withdrawal; retirement; harvesting

recogimiento house of correction, reformatory; concentration; devoutness; retirement

recolección *f* compilation; summary; crop, harvest; retirement

recolectar to gather, collect

recolector *m* tax-collector

recomendable commendable

recomendación recommendation, commendation; praise; ~ **del alma** prayers for the dead; **carta de** ~ letter of introduction

recomendar to (re)commend; ask; advise

recomendatorio (re)commendatory

recompensa recompense; **en** ~ in return

recompensable deserving reward

recompensación *f* compensation; reward

recompensar to compensate; reward

recomponer to recompose; mend, repair

reconciliación *f* reconciliation; *sl* baby-doll nightie

reconciliador *n m* reconciler; *adj* reconciling

reconciliar to reconcile; ~**se** to become reconciled; *eccles* return to the Faith

reconcomerse to scratch one's back

reconcomio scratching one's back; craving; fear

reconditez *f* reconditeness

recóndito recondite; concealed, hidden; abstruse

reconducir *leg* to renew a lease

reconocedor *n m* inspector, examiner; *adj* inspecting, examining

reconocer to recognize; examine; acknowledge; reconnoitre; ~**se** to confess one's guilt

reconocido acknowledged; accepted; grateful

reconocimiento recognition; acknowledgement; admission; inspection; reconnoitring; ~ **médico** medical check-up

reconquista reconquest

reconquistar to reconquer, recapture

reconstitución *f* reconstitution

reconstituir to reconstitute; *med* restore

reconstituyente *m med* tonic, restorative

reconstrucción *f* reconstruction

reconstruir to reconstruct

recontamiento narration

recontar to recount, relate, tell

recontento *n* deep satisfaction; *adj* very pleased, very satisfied

Recopa *sp* European Cup-Winners' Cup

recopilación summary, abridgement, compilation; digest

recopilador *m* abridger, summarizer, compiler

recopilar to abridge, summarize, compile

recordable memorable

recordación *f* recollection, memory

recordador *adj* reminding, remembering

recordante reminding

recordar to remind; *vt, vi* remember; ~ **algo a alguien** to remind s.o. to; ~**se** to remember

recordativo *n* reminder; *adj* reminiscent, mindful

recordatorio *n* reminder, souvenir

recordman *m sp* record-holder; champion

recorrer to cross, go over; haunt; run over; read through; go round; overhaul; cover; travel

recorrido course, trip, distance travelled; route, round; *mot* mileage

recortadura clipping, cutting

recortar to cut out; trim, clip; cut down to size

recorte *m* (press-)cutting, clipping; cutback, reduction; outline; ~**s** child's cut-out

recoser to sew again; mend

recostadero resting-place

recostado recumbent, leaning, reclining

recostar to lean; ~**se** to recline; lean back; tie back

recova dealing in poultry, eggs *etc*; place where poultry is sold

recoveco turning, twisting, bending; turn, bend; corner; trick; **sin** ~**s** straightforward; **tener muchos** ~**s** to be winding

recovero poultry dealer

recreación *f* recreation

recrear to amuse, delight; recreate

recreativo amusing, diverting, recreational

recrecer to increase, grow bigger; ~**se** to recover one's spirits

recrecimiento growth, increase

recreído intractable; *hort* having gone wild

recreo recreation; (in schools) break, playtime; **barco de** ~ pleasure boat; **casa de** ~ weekend house

recría repasturing

recriar to make a new pasture; redeem

recriminación *f* recrimination

recriminador *n m* recriminator; *adj* recriminating

recriminar to reproach, recriminate

recrudecer to recur; break out again; ~**se** to worsen

recrudescencia, recrudecimiento recrudescence

recrujir to squeak

recta straight line; ~ **final** *sp* final straight

rectángulo n rectangle; *adj* right-angled

rectificable rectifiable

rectificación *f* rectification

rectificador *n m* rectifier; *adj* rectifying

rectificar to rectify; ~**se** to correct o.s.

rectilíneo rectilinear

rectitud *f* rectitude, uprightness, correctness

¹ **recto** *n* right-angle; *adj* straight, erect; righteous, just; *adv* straight on (without deviation)

² **recto** *anat* rectum

rectorado rectorship

rectoría rectory; rectorship; curacy

recua drove of animals

recuarta extra (fourth) lute string

recubrir to cover (again); coat

recudimento, recudimiento authority to collect taxes, rates, rent *etc*

recudir to pay money to; rebound; revert

recuelo re-heated coffee, 'dishwater' coffee

recuento recount; inventory; ~ **de pólenes** pollen count

recuerdo recollection, memory; keepsake, souvenir; memorandum; ~**s** regards, greetings, compliments

recuero muleteer, mule-driver

recuesto slope, incline

reculada recoil; *naut* falling astern

recular to recoil; fall behind; go back; *naut* fall astern; *fig* back down

reculativo *adj* unfavourable

reculo (of poultry) tailless

reculones: a ~ *adv* moving backwards

recuperable recoverable

recuperación *f* recovery, recuperation; recovering

recuperador *n m* recuperator, recoverer; *adj* recovering

recuperar to recover; retrieve; (time) make up; ~**se** to recuperate; recover

recuperativo recuperative

recurrente *bot* recurrent; *leg* appellant

recurrir to appeal, resort (to), have recourse (to); revert

recurso recourse, resort; reversion; *leg* appeal; ~**s** resources; **de** ~**s** resourceful; **sin** ~ unavoidably

recusable refusable, exceptionable; *leg* challengeable

recusación *f* recusation

recusar to reject, recuse

rechazador *m* opponent

rechazamiento rejection; repulsion

rechazar to repel; reject

rechazo recoil, rebound, rejection; **de** ~ on the rebound

rechifla derisory hissing, hooting, booing

rechiflar to hiss, hoot, boo; ~**se** to mock, ridicule

rechinador, rechinante *adj* squeaking; creaking; grating

rechinamiento n squeaking; creaking; grating; gnashing

rechinar to squeak, creak, grate; gnash (the teeth); act reluctantly

rechistar to speak; **sin** ~ without opening one's mouth

rechoncho chubby, podgy

rechupete: de ~ *sl* super, fabulous, smashing, splendid

red *f* net; network; grating; grid; luggage-rack; snare; ~ **barredera** trawl-net; ~ **de espía** spy-ring; **caer en la** ~ to fall into the trap; **echar la** ~ to set the trap

redacción *f* editing, wording; editorial staff/office; essay

redactar to edit, word; write

redactor *m* editor; sub-editor, copy-editor; writer

redada casting of a net; netful, catch, haul; round-up (of suspects); raid

redaños guts, spunk, mettle

redar to net, catch in a net
redargución *f* retort; refutation
redargüir to retort; refute
redaya net
redecilla fine net; hair-net; *anat* reticulum
rededor *m* environs, surroundings; **al ~** round about
redención *f* redemption, ransom; recovery
redentor *n m* redeemer; *adj* redeeming
redero net-maker; one who nets birds
redescuento *comm* rediscount
redición *f* reiteration, repetition
redicho *adj* speaking with exaggerated preciseness
redifundir *rad* to broadcast
redifusión *f rad* broadcasting
redil *m* sheepfold
redimible redeemable
redimir to redeem, ransom, free
redingote *m* greatcoat
rédito revenue, yield, income, proceeds; interest
redituable, reditual profit-producing
redituar to yield, produce
redoblado *mil* double (step); stocky, heavy-built
redoblante drumming
redoblar to redouble, bend over; rivet; double; repeat; roll a drum; **~se** to grow louder and louder
redoble roll (of drums)
redoblegar to bend; redouble; clinch
redoblón *m* rivet, clinch nail
redoliente aching, painful
redolor dull pain/ache
redoma phial, flask
redomado dyed-in-the-wool; out-and-out
redonda neighbourhood; *naut* square-sail; pasture; *mus* semi-breve; **en cinco kilómetros a la ~** for five kilometres round about
redondeado almost circular/spherical
redondeamiento rounding
redondear to round off; make round; *comm* clear (debts *etc*)
redondel *m* circle; circular rug; bull-ring; *mech* flange; *mot* roundabout, *US* traffic circle
redondete roundish
redondez *f* roundness, rotundity; **toda la ~ de la tierra** the face of the earth

redondilla stanza of four octosyllabic lines rhyming abba; **letra ~** round-hand (writing)
redondo *n* locality, neighbourhood; pasture; *naut* square sail; hard cash; anything round; *sl* homosexual; *adj* round; *print* roman; flat, categorical; **~ de carne** *cul* joint; **en ~** all around; flatly, categorically; **en números ~s** in round figures
redondón *m* large sphere/circle
redopelo rubbing the wrong way; **a/al ~** against the grain
redor *m* round rug; **en ~** all around
reducción *f* reduction, decrease; cut, cutback; *mil* conquest; *comm* rebate, discount; **~ al absurdo** reductio ad absurdum
reducido small, miniature; compact; reduced
reducimiento reduction, reducement
reducir to reduce, cut down; subdue; convert; **~se** to cut one's costs; be reduced, diminish; **~se a** to come to, amount to
reducto redoubt
reductor *n m* reducer; *adj* reducing
redundancia redundancy
redundante redundant
redundar to redound; overflow; be redundant; **~ en** to result in
reduplicación *f* reduplication
reduplicar to reduplicate
reedificación *f* rebuilding
reedificador *m* rebuilder
reedificar to rebuild
reeditar to reprint, republish
reeducación *f* re-education
reeducar to re-educate
reelección *f* re-election
reelecto re-elected
reelegible re-eligible
reelegir to re-elect
reembalar to repack
reembarcar to reship
reembarco reshipment
reembargo *leg* re-attachment
reembolsable repayable, refundable
reembolsar to repay, refund; **~se** to get back money lent
reembolso refund, repayment; **contra ~** cash on delivery
reempacar to repack
reemplazable replaceable

reemplazar to replace, supersede
reemplazo replacement; *mil* annual call-up of conscripts; **de** ~ (officer) without a command
reencarcelamiento *leg* remand
reencarcelar *leg* to remand
reencarnación *f* reincarnation
reencarnarse to be reincarnated
reenganchamiento, reenganche *m mil* re-enlistment; re-enlistment bounty
reenganchar to re-enlist
reengendrado *n+adj* regenerate
reengendrador *m* regenerator
reengendrar to regenerate
reensayar to re-test; rehearse again
reensayo retrial; new test; fresh rehearsal
reenvasar to repack, refill
reenviar to forward, send on
reestreno *theat* revival; *cin* re-release
reestructuración *f* restructuring
reestructurar to restructure
reexaminación *f* re-examination
reexaminar to re-examine
reexpedición *f* forwarding
reexpedir to forward, send on
reexportación *f* re-export, re-exporting
reexportar to re-export
refacción *f* refection
refajo underskirt, slip
refección *f* refection; snack; repairing
refectorio refectory
referencia reference; testimonial
referéndum *m* referendum
referente referring, relating
referí *m sp* referee
referir to refer, report; tell; ~**se a** to refer to, allude to; be related to
refilón: de ~ slanting
refinación *f* refining, refinement
refinado refined, subtle; polished
refinador *m* refiner
refinadura refining
refinamiento refining; sophistication
refinar to refine; polish; make sophisticated
refinería refinery
refino *n comm* coffee, cocoa and sugar exchange; *adj* very refined
refirmar to confirm, ratify
refitolero *n* busybody, meddler; dandy, fop; *adj* officious
reflectante reflecting
reflector *n m* reflector; searchlight; *adj* reflecting

refleja observation, remark
reflejar to reflect, reveal; ~**se** to be reflected
reflejo *n* glare, reflex; ~**s** highlights; *adj* reflected; *gramm* reflexive; *physiol* reflex
reflexible reflectible
reflexión *f* reflection; **jornada de** ~ day preceding election day
reflexionar to think over; reflect
reflexivo reflective, reflexive; thoughtful
reflorecer to blossom anew
refluente flowing back; refluent
refluir to flow back; redound
refocilación *f* vulgar enjoyment; wallowing
refocilarse to enjoy o.s. coarsely; wallow
refocilo coarse pleasure
reforma reform, reformation; *bui* alteration, improvement; amendment
reformación *f* reformation
reformador *n* reformer; *adj* reforming
reformar to reform; alter; improve; reconstruct; amend; ~**se** to turn over a new leaf
reformatorio *m* reformatory; *adj* corrective
reformista *m+f* reformer, reformist
reforzada reinforcing tape
reforzar to reinforce, strengthen; cheer, support
refracción *f* refraction
refractar to refract
refractario refractory; unruly; fireproof
refracto refracted
refrán *m* proverb, adage, saying
refranero collection of proverbs
refranista *m+f* one who constantly uses proverbs
refregadura, refregamiento hard scrubbing
refregar to scrub; rub
refregón *m* scrubbing; abrasion
refreír to fry again; rehash; over-fry
refrenable stoppable
refrenamiento stopping, restraining, curbing
refrenar to stop; restrain, curb
refrendación *f* legalization; authorization; endorsement
refrendar to countersign; legalize; authorize; endorse

refrendario counter-signatory

refrendata counter-signature

refrendo legalization; authentication

refrescador, refrescante refreshing, cooling

refrescar to refresh, freshen, cool; turn chilly; ~**se** to get cool, cool off

refresco refreshment, refreshing drink; soft drink; **de** ~ once again

refriega affray, scuffle

refrigeración f refrigeration

refrigerador n m cooler, refrigerator, US ice-box; adj cooling

refrigerante n m cooling-chamber; space coolant; adj cooling

refrigerio coolness; comfort, consolation; light snack

refringir to refract

refrito n hash; adj over-fried

refuerzo reinforcement; welt (of footwear); aid

refugiado refugee, displaced person

refugiar to shelter; ~**se** to take shelter/refuge

refugio shelter, refuge; ~ **antiaéreo** air-raid shelter; ~ **de peatones,** ~ **contra el tráfico** traffic island

refulgencia refulgence, splendour, radiance

refulgente refulgent, radiant

refulgir to shine

refundición f recasting

refundir to recast

refunfuñador n m grumbler, moaner; adj grumbling, moaning

refunfuñadura grumbling, grousing, moaning

refunfuñar to grumble, grouse, moan

refunfuño grumble, grouse; snort (usu of disapproval)

refutación f refutation

refutador n m refuter; adj refuting

refutar to refute

regadera watering-can, sprinkler; irrigation trench; **estar como una** ~ sl to be crazy

regadero irrigation ditch

regadío irrigation; **tierra de** ~ irrigated land

regadizo irrigable

regador m irrigator

regadura irrigation, watering

regaifa Easter cake

regajal, regajo pool, streamlet

regala naut gunwale

regalado dainty, neat; comfortable

regalar to regale, present, give; treat; cajole, cheer

regalía regalia

regalismo regalism

regalista m+f regalist

regaliz m licorice

regalo gift, present; treat; pleasure; **con** ~ in luxury

regañadientes: a ~ protestingly

regañamiento grumbling

regañar to chide, scold, reprimand; grumble, quarrel

regañir to yelp

regaño scolding, reprimand; gesture of annoyance

regañón n m grumbler; adj grumbling

regar to water, irrigate; sprinkle; strew

regata regatta

regatear vi to haggle, bargain; sp dribble; race (in a regatta); vt to haggle over; give in dribs and drabs; avoid; ~**le a uno** to deny that s.o. has; **no** ~ **esfuerzos** to spare no efforts

regateo haggling; sp dribbling

regatería retail trade

regato brook, rivulet

¹ **regatón** m huckster, hawker

² **regatón** m ferrule

regatonear to sell retail

regatonería retail sale, retailing

regazar to tuck up

regazo anat lap

regencia regency

regeneración f regeneration

regenerador n m regenerator; breeder reactor; adj regenerating

regenerar to regenerate

regenerativo regenerative

regenta wife of a regent/magistrate; bossy woman

regente n m regent, director, magistrate, president of a tribunal; print foreman; adj ruling, governing

regentear to dominate, boss; manage; throw one's weight about

regicida m+f regicide (person)

regicidio regicide (crime)

regidor m alderman; governor; adj ruling, governing

regidora wife of an alderman/governor

regidoría, regiduría dignity of alderman

régimen m system, government, régime; *med* diet, régime; *gramm* government; **de ~** normal, ordinary

regimentación *f* regimentation

regimentar to regiment; form into a regiment

regimiento administration, government; *mil* regiment; *naut* pilot's sailing-book

regio royal, regal, kingly; *fam* splendid

región *f* region, area

regionalismo regionalism

regionalista *n m+f* regionalist, homeruler; *adj* regional, regionalistic

regir to rule; direct, manage; *gramm* govern; *naut* respond to the helm; **~se** to be in force, be operative; be guided

registrador *n m* registrar, recorder, controller; *adj* controlling

registrar to search, examine; register, record; mark; *min* prospect

registro search, examination, register, record, registry, registrar's office; manhole, inspection cover; census; regulator (of watch); *mus* organ-stop; **~ civil** registry (of births, marriages and deaths)

regitivo ruling, governing

regla rule, regulation; policy; (drawing) ruler, measure; *carp* straight edge; menstruation; **~ de cálculo** slide-rule; **~ de oro**, **~ de tres** *math* rule of three; **~ magnética** surveying compass; **echar la ~** to test by measuring; **en ~** in order, thoroughly; **por ~ general** as a general rule; **salirse de ~** to go too far

regladamente in an orderly fashion

reglamentación *f* establishment of rules and regulations

reglamentar to establish rules/regulations for

reglamentario *adj* obligatory; required

reglamento rules and regulations

reglar to rule lines; regulate; adjust

reglero ruler

regleta *print* lead, reglet

regletear *print* to lead

reglón *m* bui level

regnícola *m+f* writer on local matters

regocijado merry, festive, cheery

regocijador *n m* merrymaker, rejoicer; *adj* rejoicing

regocijar to make merry, cheer; **~se** to be merry, rejoice

regocijo merriment, rejoicing

regodeo pleasure, enjoyment

regodearse to take delight in

regoldar to belch, burp

regolfar to flow back; eddy

regordete chubby, plump

regostarse to delight

regraciar to show gratitude to

regresar to return, go/come back; *space* re-enter

regresión *f* regression

regresivo regressive

regreso return (journey); **de ~** back (again)

regruñir to growl, snarl

reguardarse to take good care of o.s.; look after number one

regüeldo belch, burp

reguera irrigation canal

regulación *f* regulation; adjustment

regulado according to rule

regulador *n m* regulator; *mech* governor; throttle; **~ de fuerza centrífuga** ball-governor

¹ **regular** regular; orderly; moderate, soso, middling; ordinary; **por lo ~** as a rule, usually

² **regular** to regulate; adjust; **~ la circulación**, **~ el tráfico** to control the traffic

regularidad *f* regularity; **con ~** regularly, steadily

regularización *f* regularization

regularizar to regularize, systematize

régulo petty chief

regurgitación *f* regurgitation

regurgitar to regurgitate

regusto after-taste

rehabilitación *f* rehabilitation

rehabilitar to rehabilitate

rehacer to do again; rebuild; mend; revive; **~se** to regain one's strength; *mil* rally, redeploy

rehacimiento renovation, recuperation, remaking, repairing, re-doing

rehecho sturdy, broad-shouldered

rehén *m* hostage

rehenchidura stuffing

rehenchimiento re-stuffing, refilling

rehenchir to re-stuff, refill

rehendija *see* **rendija**

rehilandera pinwheel

rehilar to twist too much; stagger, reel; whir

rehilete *m* shuttlecock; dart; small

arrow; cutting remark

rehilo shivering, trembling

rehogar to cook over a low flame; *cul* brown

rehuir to shun, shirk; retire; reject

rehurto feint, dodge

rehusar to refuse; decline

reidero laughable

reidor *adj* laughing; +*n* (of person)

reimportar to reimport

reimpresión *f* reprint

reimprimir to reprint

reina queen; queen bee; ~ **de la belleza** beauty queen; ~ **del carnaval** carnival queen; ~ **de los prados** meadowsweet; ~ **luisa** *bot* lemon verbena; ~ **mora** hopscotch; ~ **madre viuda** queen mother, dowager queen

reinado reign

reinante reigning, prevailing

reinar to reign, rule

reincidencia backsliding; *leg* repetition of an offence, recidivism

reincidente backsliding; *leg* recidivist

reincidir to backslide; relapse

reincorporación *f* reincorporation, rejoining

reincorporar to reincorporate; ~**se** to rejoin, be reunited to

reingresar to re-enter

reino kingdom, realm; **Reino de los Cielos** kingdom of heaven; **Reino Unido** United Kingdom

reinstalación *f* reinstallation; reinstatement

reinstalar to reinstall; reinstate

reintegrable *comm* reimbursable, repayable

reintegración *f* reintegration, repayment

reintegrar to reintegrate, repay; pay stamp duty on; ~**se** to get back; go back; ~**se de** to recover from

reintegro reintegration; repayment; stamp duty; refund prize (in state lottery)

reinversión *f* reinvestment

reír(se) to laugh; (of clothing) begin to go at the seams; ~ **a carcajadas** to laugh loudly, guffaw; ~ **el último** to have the last laugh; ~ **tontamente** to giggle; ~ **de** to laugh at

reiteración *f* reiteration

reiterar to reiterate

reiterativo reiterative, repetitive

reivindicable *leg* recoverable

reivindicación *f* *pol+comm* claim; *pol* admission of responsibility

reivindicar *pol+comm* to claim; *pol* claim responsibility for; *leg* regain possession of

reivindicatorio *adj* of a claim

reja grating, grille; railing; ploughshare; ploughing; coulter; **entre** ~**s** behind bars, in gaol

rejado grating, grille

rejal *m* pile of bricks on edge, each layer lying in opposite direction to the lower layer

rejería iron grating

rejero iron-grating maker

rejilla lattice(-work); lattice-window; grating, grille; grid; cane-work; luggage rack; foot-warmer

rejo spike; iron door-frame; *ent* sting; strength; *bot* caulicle

rejón *m* (bullfighting) short spear; dagger; spike

rejoneador *m* mounted bullfighter

rejonear to use a **rejón**; bullfight from horse-back

rejuvenecer to rejuvenate; ~**se** to be rejuvenated; be younger-looking

rejuvenecimiento rejuvenation

relación *f* relation(ship); report, account, description; story, tale, yarn; list; enumeration; ratio; *theat* speech; ~ **de compresión** *mot* compression ratio; **relaciones privilegiadas** *pol* special relationship; ~ **jurada** *leg* sworn statement; **hacer** ~ **a** to relate to; **tener relaciones con** to be acquainted with; be going out with

relacionado *n* acquaintance; *adj* related; concerning, regarding

relacionar to relate, connect; narrate; ~**se** to get acquainted

relajación *f* relaxation; looseness; *leg* reduction (of a sentence); release (from a promise/vow); rest; *med* rupture

relajado dissolute

relajador, relajante loosening, slackening, relaxing

relajar to relax; loosen; remit; mitigate; release from an obligation; corrupt; *med* rupture; **hablar relajado** to pronounce carelessly

relajo dissoluteness, degeneracy; bad

behaviour; absence of all decency; *sl* rest, repose

relamer to lick again and again; ~**se** to smack one's lips; ~**se de gusto** to lick one's lips with relish

relamido over-fastidious in attire; affected

relámpago lightning-flash; quick action

relampagueante lightning, flashing

relampaguear to flash with lightning

relampagueo lightning, flashing

relance *m* lucky event; chance; series of chances

relanzar to repulse, repel

relatador *m* narrator, teller

relatante narrating, reporting

relatar to narrate, tell

relatividad *f* relativity

relativo *n+adj* relative, comparative; **en lo** ~ relatively speaking

relato narrative, tale; report, account

relator *m* relater, narrator, teller; *leg* court-reporter

relatoría office of a court-reporter

relavar to rewash

relax *m* free time; relaxation

relé *m elect* relay

releer to re-read

relegación *f* relegation; banishment, exile

relegar to relegate; banish, exile; ~ **al olvido** to consign to oblivion

relej *m*, **releje** *m* wheel-rut; *archi* tapering (of a wall)

relejar *archi* to taper

relente chill (of the night); cheek, boldness

relentecer(se) to soften; become softened

relevación *f* relief, release; removal from office; remission, pardon; lifting-up

relevante outstanding

relevar to emboss, make stand out; relieve, free, release; *arts* stand out in relief

relevo relief, relay; change

relicario reliquary, locket

relieve *m* relief, raised work, embossment; **bajo** ~ bas-relief; **medio** ~ demi-relief; **poner de** ~ to highlight, stress

religar to tie again more tightly

religión *f* religion; **entrar en** ~ to enter the religious life

religionario religionist, Protestant

religiosidad *f* religiousness; **con** ~ without fail

religioso *n* one who has taken religious vows; *adj* religious, godly, scrupulous

relimpiar to clean again; polish

relimpio brightly clean

relinchador neighing, whinnying

relinchante *adj* neighing, whinnying

relinchar to neigh, whinny

relindo lovely, delightful

reliquia relic; ~**s** left-over(s)

reliquiario *see* **relicario**

reloco crazy, crackers, bananas, bonkers

reloj *m* watch, clock; ~ **de agua** waterclock; ~ **de arena** hour-glass, eggtimer; ~ **de bolsillo** pocket-watch; ~ **de péndulo** grandfather clock; ~ **de pulsera** wrist-watch; ~ **de repetición** repeater; ~ **de sol** sun-dial; ~ **despertador** alarm-clock; **como un** ~ like clockwork; **contra** ~ against the clock

relojera clock-case, watch-case; watchpocket

relojería watchmaker's shop; clockmaking; **bomba de** ~ time-bomb

relojero watchmaker, clockmaker

reluciente shining, glittering; sleek

relucir to shine, glitter

reluchar to struggle, strive

relumbrante resplendent

relumbrón *m* flash; **de** ~ flashy, tinselly

rellano landing (of staircase)

rellenar to refill, replenish; stuff; fill in

relleno *n* stuffing, forcemeat, filling; *mech* packing, gasket

remachado riveting, rivet-work

remachar to rivet; affirm; stress

remache *m* riveting

remador *m* rower, oarsman

remadura rowing

remallar to repair the meshes of

remamiento rowing

remanente *m* residue, remains; *adj* residual

remangar to roll up (sleeves); ~**se** to roll up one's sleeves, get ready (for work), show determination

remango rolling-up (of sleeves)

remansarse to become calm; stay awhile; stop flowing

remanso backwater; quiet spot

remante rowing

remar to row; paddle; toil

remarcar to mark again; emphasize

rematada whore

rematado sold (by auction); ruined; lost; ~ **a prisión** sentenced to prison

rematador *m* auctioneer

rematante *m* highest bidder

rematar to end, conclude; finish off; put the finishing touches to; (sewing) finish a seam; (knitting) cast off; *comm* sell by auction; ~ **de cabeza** (football) to head; **~se** to be destroyed, be ruined

remate *m* end, conclusion; finishing touch; *comm* auction, highest bid; ~ **de cabeza** (football) header; ~ **de cuentas** closing of an account; **de** ~ utterly; **loco de** ~ raving mad; **para** ~ as a finishing touch

remecer to rock to and fro; swing

remedable imitable

remedador *m* mimic, imitator

remedar to copy, imitate; mock

remediador *m* healer; comforter; helper

remediar to remedy, help; **no poder** ~ to be unable to help/prevent

remedio remedy, medicine; help; *leg* action; ~ **casero** household remedy; **no hay más** ~ **(que)** there's nothing that can be done (except); **no tener** ~ to be inevitable; **sin** ~ hopeless, unavoidable

remedión *m theat* makeshift performance

remedir to re-measure

remedo imitation, copy; mockery

remellado jagged, dented

remellar to remove the hair (from hides)

remellón jagged, dented

remembrar to remember

rememorar to remember, recall

rememorativo reminding; that brings to mind; commemorative

remendar to patch, repair; darn

remendón *n m* botcher; *adj* patching, mending, darning; **zapatero** ~ cobbler

remeneo rapid movement

rementir to lie like the devil

remera *orni* flight-feather

remero oarsman, rower

remesa shipment, consignment; delivery

remiendo patch; darning; repair; amendment; **a ~s** piece-meal; **echar un** ~ to sew on a patch; **echar un** ~ **a la vida** to have a bite to eat

remilgado fastidious, finicky; prudish

remilgo squeamishness, fastidiousness; prudery

remisible remissible

remisión *f* remission; sending back; forgiveness; indolence; relaxation; **sin** ~ without fail

remisivo remissive

remiso remiss, careless; reluctant

remitencia remittance

remitente *m* sender; consignee

remitir to remit, forward, send; forgive; waive; defer; slacken; rise; refer; submit; quote; **~se** to refer

remo oar; hard labour; *sp* rowing

remojadero steeping-vat

remojar to steep, soak; drench

remojo steeping, soaking; drenching; **dejar a/en** ~ to leave to soak

remolacha beetroot; ~ **azucarera** sugar-beet

remolar *m* oar-maker; master-carpenter

remolcador *n m naut* tug(-boat); *adj* towing

remolcar to tow; take in tow; haul

remolinar to whirl round; spin; **~se** to swirl, seethe

remolinear to spin; eddy; whirl about

remolino whirlwind; whirlpool; eddy; throng; commotion

remolón soft, lazy

remolonear to loiter, lounge; avoid work

remolque *m* towing, towage; trailer; **a** ~ in tow; **dar** ~ **a** to take in tow; **llevar a** ~ to have in tow

remondar to clean again thoroughly

remono very neat; very pretty

remonta *mil* remounting (cavalry)

remontar *vi* to elevate, rise; *vt mil* to supply remounts; repair (shoes), re-sole; **~se** *orni* to soar; date from

remonte *m* remounting; resoling; soaring

remorder to bite repeatedly; give cause for remorse; **~se** to express regret/ remorse; **me remuerde la conciencia** my conscience pricks me

remordimiento remorse

remoto remote; unlikely

remover to (re)move; transfer; dismiss, discharge; stir

removible removable

remozamiento rejuvenation

remozar to rejuvenate; ~**se** to look younger

rempujar to push; jostle

rempujo push; impulse

remuda change; change of clothes; ~ **de caballos** relay of horses

remudar to change; (re)move

remuneración f remuneration

remunerador n m remunerator; adj remunerating

remunerar to remunerate

remunerativo remunerative

remusgo cold fierce wind

renacentista adj Renaissance

renacer to be born again

renaciente renascent

renacimiento regeneration; Renaissance

renacuajo tadpole, US polliwog; despicable person; little runt

renano Rhenish

rencilla grudge; quarrel

rencilloso peevish, spiteful, quarrelsome

rencionar to set at odds, stir up trouble

renco lame (because of hip injury)

rencor m rancour, grudge

rencoroso rancorous, spiteful, bearing a grudge

rendaje m harness; set of bridles and reins

rendajo orni mocking-bird; mimic

rendición f surrender, submission; remission

rendido weary; obsequious; worn-out

rendija split, cleft, crack, chink

rendimiento yield; loyal allegiance; complete exhaustion; mech+met performance

rendir to subdue; surrender; render; comm yield, produce, bring in, remit; ~ **cuentas** to render an account; ~ **el alma** to give up the ghost; ~ **gracias** to give thanks; ~ **las armas** to throw down one's arms, surrender; ~ **marea** to stem the tide; ~**se** to become exhausted; yield, submit; give up

renegado renegade, apostate

renegador m swearer, blasphemer

renegar to deny, disown; hate; blaspheme

renegón m out-and-out blasphemer; moaner; adj blasphemous

renegrear to blacken

renegrido blackish; (of bruises) black and blue

Renfe f (Red Nacional de Ferrocarriles Españoles) Spain's national railway network; **estación de** ~ railway station

rengífero zool reindeer

renglón m written/printed line; **a** ~ **seguido** immediately after; **leer entre renglones** to read between the lines

renglonadura ruling (of lines on paper); ruled lines

rengo see **renco**

rengue m sl train

reniego blasphemy, curse; moaning

reniforme kidney-shaped

reno zool reindeer

renombrado renowned, celebrated, famous

renombre m renown; surname; nickname

renovable renewable; replaceable

renovación f renovation; replacement

renovador n m renovator; adj renovating

renovar to renovate, renew; replace

renquear to limp, hobble

renta profit, income; **declaración de la** ~ income-tax return/declaration; ~ **del trabajo** earned income; ~ **gravable** taxable income; **impuesto sobre la** ~ income tax; ~**s vitalicias** annuity

rentado adj living on investments

rentar to produce, yield; rent

rentero rural tenant; holder of a state monopoly

rentilla small income

rentista m+f financier, bondholder, person of independent means

rentístico financial

rento rent(al)

rentoso profitable

renuencia reluctance, unwillingness

renuente reluctant, unwilling

renuevo bot shoot, sprout

renuncia, renunciación f, **renunciamiento** resignation; waiving; renunciation

renunciante n m renouncer, resigner; adj renouncing; resigning

renunciar *vi* to resign; revoke (at cards); *vt* to renounce, give up; forgo; reject; relinquish

renunciatario one who profits from another's resignation

renuncio (cards) revoke; lie

renvalsar *carp* to rabbet

renvalso *carp* rabbet

reñido hard-fought; stubborn; at variance; on bad terms; incompatible

reñidor *m* quarreller

reñir to quarrel, fall out; reprimand; fight

reo *m* criminal, convict, culprit; *leg* accused, defendant; *adj* guilty, criminal

reojo: mirar de ~ to look out of the corner of the eye

reómetro *elect* rheometer

reorganización *f* rearrangement; reorganization

reorganizador *n* reorganizer; *adj* reorganizing

reorganizar to reorganize

reóstato *elect* rheostat

repajolero *sl* cursed, damned

repanchigarse, repantigarse to stretch o.s. while seated

repapilarse to stuff o.s., gorge

reparable reparable; objectionable; remarkable

reparación *f* reparation; repair; amends; atonement

reparado restored

reparador *m* repairer; fault-finder; fortifying, refreshing; **sueño ~** beauty-sleep

[1] **reparar** to repair, restore; consider; make up for; atone for; put the final touch to

[2] **reparar** to stop, stay over; parry, defend; **~se** to forbear, refrain

reparativo reparative

[1] **reparo** repair(ing); reparation; advice, warning; difficulty; reserve

[2] **reparo** defence; defect

reparón *n m* fault-finder, carper; *adj* fault-finding, carping

repartible distributable

repartidero to be distributed

repartidor *n m* distributor; dealer (at cards); tax-inspector; tax-assessor; *adj* distributing

repartimiento distribution, division; sharing; assessment

repartir to distribute; apportion; divide; assess

reparto distribution; division; assessment; *theat* dramatis personae; *cin* + *TV* credits

repasadera *carp* smoothing-plane, finishing-plane

repasar to pass again; re-examine; revise, scan; mend (clothing)

repaso revision, re-examination; final check; clothes repairing; reprimand

repatear *sl* to annoy, displease

repatriación *f* repatriation

repatriar to repatriate

repechar to go uphill

repecho steep slope

repelente *adj* repellent

repeler to repel

repelo anything that goes against the grain; aversion; dispute

repelón *m* pulling out the hair/loose thread in cloth; **a repelones** by degrees; **de ~** in a hurry

repeloso touchy

repensar to re-think, think over

repente *m* sudden movement; impulse; **de ~** suddenly

repentino sudden

repentista *m+f* improviser; impetuous person

repentizar to improvise; act hastily

repentón *m* sudden impulse

repeor much worse

repercudida rebound

repercudir to rebound

repercusión *f* repercussion

repercusivo repercussive

repercutir to reverberate; rebound; have repercussions

repertorio repertoire

repetición *f* repetition; repeater (watch); *theat* encore; *arts* replica

repetidor repeating

repetir to repeat; say again; echo; do again; *arts* make a replica of; **~se** to repeat o.s.

repetitivo repetitive

repicar *cul* to chop, mince; (of bells) ring, jingle; **~se** to boast

repintar to repaint

repipi: niño ~ bonny child

repique *m cul* chopping, mincing; (of bells) peal; dispute

repiquete *m* joyful ringing/jingling of bells; opportunity

repiquetear to ring, jingle; have a row

repiqueteo ringing, jingling; dispute, row

repisa mantelpiece; shelf

repitente repeating

repizcar to pinch

repizco pinch

replantear to lay out on the ground (a plan of a building); restate (a problem)

repleción *f* repletion

replegable folding

replegar to fold more than once; ~se *mil* retreat, fall back, re-deploy

repleto completely full; packed

réplica reply; repartee

replicador *m* replier

replicante *n m* replier; *adj* replying

replicar to answer back

repliegue *m* fold(ing), crease

repoblación *f* repopulation; ~ **forestal** reafforestation

repoblar to repopulate; restock; reafforest

repollo cabbage; head (of a plant)

reponer to put back; reinstate; reply; *cin+TV* re-release, show again; ~se *med* to recover, get better

reportación *f* moderation, forbearance

reportado moderate, forbearing

reportaje *m* report; reportage

reportamiento forbearance, restraint

reportar to check; bring, carry; ~se to refrain; control o.s.; calm down

reporte *m* report; information, news

repórter *m*, **reportero** reporter

reporterismo reporting

reposado calm, tranquil

reposar to rest, lie down; stand on; ~se (of liquids) to settle

reposición *f* reinstatement; *med* recovery; *theat* revival; *cin* re-release; *TV* repeat showing

repositorio repository

reposo rest, repose; tranquillity

repostar to stock up, take in supplies

reposte *m* pantry, larder

repostería pantry, larder; confectionery; cake-shop, pastry-cook's

repostero pastry-cook

repregunta *leg* cross-examination

repreguntar *leg* to cross-examine

reprender to reprehend, chide, reprimand

reprendiente reprimanding, chiding

reprensible reprehensible

reprensión *f* reprehension, reprimand, reproof

reprensor *m* reprehender, reprover

represa dam; damming; checking, holding back; *naut* recapture

represalia reprisal; retaliation

represaliado victim of reprisals

represaliar to take reprisals (against), victimize

represar to dam (up); check; *naut* recapture; *fig* repress

representación *f* representation; description; *theat* performance; production; image, figure; petition; *leg* right of succession; **en ~ de** as a representative of

representante *n m* representative, agent; *theat+cin* actor, performer; *adj* representing

representar to represent; state, express; signify, mean; *theat+cin* perform; **ella representa menos que sus años** she looks younger than her age

representativo representative

represión *f* repression; curbing

represivo repressive

reprimenda reprimand, telling off

reprimir to repress, check

reprivatación *f* reprivatization

reprivatizar to reprivatize

reprobable blameworthy, reprehensible

reprobación *f* reprobation

reprobado *adj* failed in an examination; reprobate

reprobador *n m* condemner, reprover; *adj* reproving

reprobar to condemn, reprove; fail

réprobo *n* reprobate; damned person

reprochar to reproach

reproche *m* reproach; reproof

reproducción *f* reproduction; *arts* print, facsimile copy

reproducir to reproduce; reoccur

reproductible reproducible

reproductividad *f* reproductiveness

reproductivo reproductive

reproductor *n m* reproducer, breeding animal; *adj* reproductive, reproducing

repropiarse (of horses) to shy

repropio (of horses) skittish

reprueba *print* new proof
reptar to crawl, creep, slither
reptil *m* reptile
república republic
republicanismo republicanism
republicano *n+adj* republican
repúblico prominent citizen; patriot, statesman
repudiación *f* repudiation
repudiar to repudiate
repudio repudiation
repudrir to rot; ~**se** to rot away
repuesto *n* stock, store, supply; sideboard; pantry; spare part; **de** ~ spare, extra; *adj* secluded; recovered; replaced
repugnancia repugnance, loathing, disgust; aversion
repugnante repugnant, loathsome, disgusting
repugnar to cause repugnance/loathing; disgust, nauseate; reject; ~**se** contradict
repujado repoussé; embossed *esp* on metal/leather
repujar to emboss; do repoussé work on
repulgado affected
repulgar to border, put an edging on; (sewing) hem
repulgo hem, fringe, border; ~**s** ridiculous scruples
repulido all dolled up; dressed up to the nines
repulir to dress showily/affectedly; repolish
repulsa check, reproof; rejection, refusal
repulsar to check, reprove; reject, refuse
repulsión *f* repulsion, loathing; rejection
repulsivo repulsive
repullo leap, bound; jerk, start (with shock/surprise)
repunta point, headland; disagreement, dispute; turning point
repuntar to begin to appear, come into sight; collect, round up; ~**se** to be on the point of going sour
repunte *m naut* turn (of the tide); rounding-up
reputación *f* reputation
reputante *m* appraiser
reputar to repute; estimate
requebrar to court, woo; flatter; break

into even smaller pieces
requemar to parch; *cul* be hot to the taste, overcook; *bot* dry up, wither; ~**se** to be passionately in love
requerimiento summons; requisition, demand
requesón *m* cottage cheese
requeté *m* military unit of the Carlist Party; member of the **requeté**
requiebro flattery; compliment (to a woman)
réquiem *m eccles* requiem mass; *mus* requiem
requilorios *mpl* beating-about-the-bush
requintador *m* outbidder
requintar to outbid; *mus* raise/lower the pitch by five tones; exceed
requinto rise of one-fifth in bidding; *mus* treble clarinet (player); small guitar
requisa tour of inspection; *mil* requisition, confiscation
requisar to inspect; requisition
requisición *f* requisition
requisito requisite, requirement
res *f* head of cattle, sheep *etc*; ~ **brava** fighting-bull
resaber to know perfectly well
resabiarse to contract bad habits
resabido *adj* pretending to be knowledgeable; pedantic
resabio bad habit; unpleasant taste
resaca *naut* surf; undertow; *fam* hangover; *comm* redraft
resacar *naut* to underrun, haul; *comm* redraw, redraft
resalado charming; dear, darling; very amusing
resalir to jut out
resaltar to bounce, rebound; be self-evident; stand out; **hacer** ~ to emphasize
resalte *m*, **resalto** prominence, protuberance
resaludar to return a greeting
resalutación *f* return of a greeting
resarcimiento compensation
resarcir to compensate; repair; ~**se de** to make up for
resbaladero *n* slippery place; *adj* slippery, elusive
resbaladizo slippery, elusive
resbalador *n m* backslider; *adj* sliding
resbaladura slide, sliding; skid
resbalante sliding, slipping

resbalar to slip, slide; slip up; skid; go astray; **me resbala** I couldn't care less

resbalo steep slope

resbalón *n* slip(-up)

resbaloso slippery

rescaldar to scald

rescaño remains; fragments, scraps

rescatador *m* ransomer; redeemer; rescuer

rescatar to ransom; redeem; barter; rescue

rescate *m* ransom money; barter; rescue, recovery

rescindir to rescind

rescisión *f* rescission, cancellation

rescisorio *adj* rescinding

rescoldera *med* heart-burn

rescoldo embers, hot ashes; scruple, qualm

rescontrar to set off, offset

resecar to dry up

reseco *n* dryness (of mouth); drying-up (of plants); *adj* dried-up, parched

resello surcharge

resentido resentful; bitter

resentimiento resentment; bitterness

resentirse to resent

reseña description, critical review; *mil* march-past, inspection

reseñar to describe, sketch; review

reserva reserve, reservation; reticence, caution, prudence; (of wine) vintage; **a ~ de** intending to; **de ~** in reserve, (of wine) vintage; **en ~** confidentially; **guardar ~** to act discreetly; **sin ~** openly

reservación *f* reservation, booking; **~ anticipada** advance booking

reservado *n* private room (in a restaurant *etc*); *eccles* consecrated bread kept in the ciborium; *adj* reserved, secret; private; (of information) classified, restricted

reservar to reserve, retain; keep secret; postpone; **~se** to bide one's time; be careful

reservista *m mil* reservist

resfriado *med* cold; *agri* irrigation of land before ploughing

resfriador *n m* fridge; *adj* cooling, refrigerating

resfriante cooling

resfriar to cool, chill; start to feel cold; **~se** to catch cold

resfrío *med* cold, chill

resguardar to preserve; **~se** to take refuge/shelter/precautions

resguardo preservation; safety; *comm* security; counterfoil, stub (of cheque); voucher

residencia residence, dwelling; **~ sanitaria** social security hospital; **~ de ancianos** old people's home

residencial residential

residenciar to call (an official) to account; impeach

residente *n m* resident; *adj* residing

residir to reside

residuo residue, remainder, remnant; *math* difference

resigna resignation

resignación *f* resignation, submission; conformity

resignante *n m* resigner; *adj* resigning

resignar to resign

resina resin, rosin

resinar to draw resin from

resinero, resinoso resinous

resinífero resin-bearing

resistencia resistance, endurance; strength; *elect* resistor, hot-plate (on cooker); **oponer ~** to offer resistance; **~ al avance** *aer* drag

resistente resistant; strong, tough

resistero hottest part of the day; place where the sun's heat is most concentrated

resistibilidad *f* resistibility

resistidor *m* resister

resistir(se) to resist, endure

resma ream

resobrina grand-niece

resobrino grand-nephew

resol *m* glare of the sun

resolana sunny place, sun-trap

resolano sunny

resolución *f* resolution; courage; *math* solution; *leg* lapse, nullification

resoluto resolute, daring; brief

resolutorio resolute

resolvente resolving, resolvent

resolver to resolve; sum up; *math* solve; *leg* annul; **~se** to determine, make up one's mind to; be solved

resollar to breathe loudly; snort

resonación *f* resounding, re-echoing

resonancia resonance; **hacer ~** to attract attention; **tener ~** to cause a stir

resonante resonant, resounding

resonar to resound, echo; clatter

resoplar to breathe noisily; snort

resoplido noisy breathing, puffing and panting; snorting

resorte *m* means, resources; elasticity; *mech* spring; **tener ~s** to have pull/influence

respaldar *n* back (of a chair); *v* to endorse, back up; answer for, guarantee; **~se** to lean back; *vet* dislocate the backbone

respaldo back; backing, endorsement; back (of a chair)

respectar to regard, concern; **por lo que respecta a** as regards

respectivo respective

respecto respect; relation, proportion; **~ a/de** with regard to; **a este ~** concerning this; **al ~** relative to

résped *m ent* sting; snake's tongue; biting remark

respetabilidad *f* respectability; deserving respect

respetable *n sl theat* (+ bullfighting) audience; *adj* respectable, considerable; deserving respect

respetar to respect; revere

respetivo respectful

respeto respect, observance; **de ~** very special; **campar por sus ~s** to do as one pleases; **faltar al ~** to show disrespect; **por ~ a** with respect to

respetoso, respetuoso respectful

réspice *m* retort, sharp reproof

respigador *m* gleaner

respigar to glean

respingado turned-up; (of the nose) snub

respingar to grunt, snort; answer back; resist

respingo jump

respingón *n m* grumbler, grunter; *adj* grumbling, grunting; **nariz respingona** snub nose

respingoso skittish; gruff, sour

respirable breathable

respiración *f* breathing; ventilation; **faltar la ~** to choke

respiradero air-hole, vent; breathing-tube, snorkel; skylight; *fam* breather, respite

respirador *n m* respirator; snorkel; *adj* respiratory, breathing

respirante *adj* breathing

respirar to breathe; take a breather/rest; get back one's breath

respiratorio respiratory

respiro breathing, breather, respite, relief; *comm* extension of time for payment

resplandecencia resplendency, splendour; lustre

resplandecer to glitter, shine; stand out

resplandeciente glittering, shiny, bright

resplandina sharp reproof

resplandor *m* brilliance, radiance, gleam(ing); glow, blaze

respondedor *m* answerer

responder to answer, reply; re-echo; yield, produce; do what is required; vouch; **~ a** to answer, match; **~ de/por** to answer for

respondiente *n m* answerer; *adj* answering

respondón *adj* pert, saucy, truculent, cheeky

responsabilidad *f* responsibility, accountability

responsabilizarse to accept responsibility for

responsable responsible, accountable

responsar, responsear to pray for the dead; scold

responso *eccles* responsory for the dead; scolding

respuesta reply, answer; echoed sound; **~ aguda/picante** repartee

resquebradura crack, split, crevice

resquebradizo easily cracked

resquebrajar, resquebrar to crack

resquemar to burn (the mouth); smart; **~se** to get parched

resquemo pungency; burning passion; smell/taste of burnt food

resquemor *m* smarting, resentment

resquicio chink, cleft, crack

resta *math* subtraction; remainder, difference

restablecer to re-establish; restore; **~se** *med* to recover, recuperate

restablecimiento re-establishment; restoration; *med* recovery

restallar to crack (as a whip); crackle

restante *n m* remainder; *adj* remaining

restañadero estuary

restañar to stop, stem (bleeding *etc*); **~se** to stagnate

restañasangre *f min* bloodstone

¹ **restaño** staunching, stemming; stagnation

² **restaño** cloth of gold/silver

restar *vt* to deduct, subtract; return/hit back (a ball *etc*); *vi* to be left; **solo me resta...** I have only ... left

restauración *f* restoration; repairing; *med* recovery

restaurador *n m* restorer, repairer; *adj* restoring, repairing

restaurante *n m* restaurant, restorer; *adj* restoring

restaurar to restore; retrieve; renew

restaurativo + *adj* restorative

restitución *f* restitution

restituible restorable

restituidor *m* restorer; *adj* restorative

restituir to restore; give back refund; ~**se** to go back to the place of departure

restitutivo, restitutorio restitutive

resto remainder, rest, residue; *sp* return (of a ball); ~**s** remains, left-overs; **echar el** ~ to stake one's all

restorán *m see* **restaurante**

restregadura, restregamiento scrubbing, rubbing

restregar to scrub, rub; ~**se** to rub/ scratch o.s. (against s.t.)

restregón *m* scrubbing, rubbing

restribar to lean heavily

restricción *f* restriction; cut, reduction

restrictivo restrictive

restricto restricted, limited

restringente, restriñente restringent, restricting

restriñidor *n m* restringent; *adj* restringent; *med* constipating

restriñimiento contraction, constriction; *med* constipation

restriñir to contract, constrict; constipate

resucitación *f* resuscitation, resurrection

resucitador *adj* reviving, resuscitating

resucitar to resuscitate; resurrect; revive; modernize

resudación *f* slight perspiration; oozing

resudar to perspire slightly; ooze

resudor *m* slight perspiration

resuelto resolute, determined; solved

resuello breath, breathing; **meter el** ~ **a** to put the wind up; **sin** ~ out of breath, panting

resulta result, resolution; ~ **secundaria** after-effect; **de** ~**s de** as a result of

resultado result, outcome, upshot; end product; consequence

resultando *leg* (in legal documents) whereas

resultante *n f mech* resultant (force *etc*); *adj* resulting, consequent

resultar to result; follow; turn out, work out; be a good thing; *fam* work (well/ badly); **resulta extraño que ...** it seems odd that ...; **resultó que** (introducing an anecdote) it so happened that ...

resultón *m sl* pleasant person, good fellow

resumen *m* résumé, summary, précis; recapitulation; *leg* brief; **en** ~ to sum up, cut a long story short

resumido abridged, summarized; **en resumidas cuentas** in short

resumir to abridge, abstract; ~**se** to be abridged

resunción *f* résumé, summary

resurgente resurgent, reappearing

resurgimiento reappearance, revival

resurgir to reappear; spring up again

resurrección *f* resurrection, revival, resuscitation

resurtida rebound, repercussion

retablo altar-piece

retacería remnants for making a patchwork quilt

retacar (billiards) to hit the ball twice

retaco short fellow

retador *n m* challenger; *adj* challenging

retaguardia rearguard; *sl* arse; **picar la** ~ to harass an enemy in retreat; **a** ~ in the rear, behind the lines

retahíla string, line, series

retajar to cut round; circumcise

retal *m* clipping, remnant, off-cut

retama *bot* broom; ~ **macho** *bot* Spanish broom; ~ **negra** *bot* furze; **tan seco como la** ~ as dry as dust

retamal *m*, **retamar** *m* land covered with broom

retambufa *sl* arse

retar to challenge, dare

retardación *f* delay

retardado (mentally) retarded

retardar to delay, slow down

retardatriz retardative

retardo delay; *mus* sustaining (of a chord)

retasa, retasación *f* price-reduction; re-assessment

retasar to reduce the price of; re-assess

retazar to tear to pieces

retazo fragment, portion, remnant

retejar to re-tile

retejer *text* to weave closely

retejo re-tiling

retemblar to tremble, shake, quiver

retemblor trembling, shaking

retén *m* stock, store, supply; *mil* reserves; *mech* ratchet

retención *f* keeping back, retention

retener to retain; withhold; catch; arrest, detain

retenida guy-rope

retenimiento *see* **retención**

retentiva memory

retentivo retentive

reticencia innuendo, double meaning; hint, suggestion

reticente hinting, insinuating

retín *m* tinkling, jingling, clink

retina retina; **desprendimiento de ~** detached retina

retinoscopio *med* retinoscope

retinte *m* jingling sound

retintín *m* jingling, tinkling, clinking

retinto reddish brown

retiñir to jingle, tinkle, clink, ring; (of rain) pitter-patter

retirada withdrawal; *mil* retreat; place of refuge; privy; *sl* withdrawal method of birth control; menopause

retiradamente in secret

retirado retired; remote; isolated

retirar to withdraw; reserve; take away; **~se** to retire; move back; *mil* retreat

retiro retirement; secluded place; retirement pay/pension

reto challenge, threat

retobado grumbling; false

retobarse to distrust; become surly

retocador *m* retoucher

retocar to touch up, put the finishing touch to

retoñar *bot* to reappear, sprout

retoño *bot* sprout; sucker; kid

retoque *m* finishing touch

retorcedura twisting, writhing

retorcer to twist; contort; wring; distort; misconstrue; **~se** to writhe, squirm

retorcimiento twisting, contorsion, distortion, writhing, squirming

retórica rhetoric; **~s** quibbling

retórico *n* rhetorician; *adj* rhetorical

retornamiento return

retornante returning

retornar *vi* to return, recede; *vt* to give/send back; twist

retorno return; going home; repayment; barter; exchange

retorta *chem* retort

retortero rotation; **andar al ~** to hang about; **traer al ~** to deceive by false pretences

retortijar to twist

retortijón *m* twist(ing), cramp

retozador frisky, lively

retozar *v* to frisk, caper, gambol

retozo *n* frisk, caper, gambol

retozón frolicsome, frisky

retracción *f* retraction

retractación *f* retraction, recantation

retractar to retract, recant

retracto *leg* right of redemption

retráctil retractile

retraer to bring back; dissuade; *leg* redeem; **~se** to shelter, take refuge; live quietly

retraído incommunicative, phlegmatic

retraimiento seclusion; refuge; sanctum; incommunicativeness

retransmisión *f* *rad* + *TV* relay

retransmitir *rad* + *TV* to relay

retrasado backward, mentally retarded; (of clocks) slow; late, behind

retrasar *vi* to go back, decline; *vt* to defer, put off; (of clocks) set back, put back; **~se** to be backward; be late; (of clocks) be slow

retraso backwardness, delay; (of trains *etc*) **llegar con ~** to arrive late

retratar to portray; draw/paint/photograph a portrait; depict; *sl* (of women) display underclothing when sitting down/crossing their legs; **~se** to have one's portrait painted/drawn/photographed; be depicted

retratista *m* + *f* portrait painter; photographer

retrato portrait, picture; description

retrechar (of a horse) to go backwards

retreta retreat, tattoo; *mil* evening parade

retrete *m* sanctum, private room; toilet, loo

retribución *f* fee, reward

retribuir to reward, pay, remunerate
retributivo remunerative
retro *sl* old-fashioned person, square
retroacción *f* retroaction
retroactividad *f* retroactivity
retroactivo retroactive
retrocarga: de ~ breech-loading
retroceder to go backwards; *mot* reverse
retrocesión *f* backwards movement; retrocession
retroceso going back; backwards movement; receding; *med* getting worse; (of firearm) recoil
retrocohete *m space* retrorocket
retrogradación *f* retrogression
retrogradar *astron* to retrograde; recede
retrógrado retrograde, retrogressive; *pol* reactionary
retrogresión *f* retrogression
retronar to thunder
retropropulsión *f* jet-propulsion
retroproyección *f cin* back-projection
retroproyector *m cin* back-projector
retrospección *f* retrospection
retrospectivo *n cin*+*lit* flash-back; *adj* retrospective
retrotracción *f leg* antedating
retrotraer *leg* to pretend that s.t. happened at an earlier date than it actually did
retrovender to sell back; cancel a sale
retrovisor *mot* rear-view mirror
retumbante pompous, bombastic; resonant
retumbar to re-echo; reverberate; sound loudly; resound
retumbo echo; reverberation; loud noise
retundir *bui* to point
reuma *m med* rheumatism; *f med* gathering
reumático rheumatic
reumatismo rheumatism
reunión *f* meeting, assembly; get-together; party
reunir to unite, accumulate; assemble; fulfil; **~se** to join, get together; hold a meeting
reuntar to reanoint
reválida admission to a higher faculty; university entrance examination
revalidar to be admitted to a higher faculty; ratify

revalorar to revalue, reappraise
revalorización *f*, **revaluación** *f* revaluation
revancha revenge; *sp* return match; (boxing) return fight
revejecer to grow old before one's time
revelación *f* revelation
revelado *phot* developing
revelador *n m phot* developer; *adj* revealing
revelamiento revelation; *phot* developing
revelante revealing, disclosing
revelar to reveal, disclose; *phot* develop
revenar *bot* to sprout
revendedor *m* retailer; ticket-tout
revender to retail; tout tickets
reventa re-sale; touting of tickets
reventar to burst; smash, wreck; **~ de risa** to burst out laughing; **~se** to burst, explode; (of waves) break, splash; burst forth; *bot* sprout, blossom
reventón *n m* explosion; *mot* puncture, US blow-out; uphill work; *adj* bursting
rever to review, revise; *leg* re-try
reverberación *f* reverberation
reverberar to reverberate
reverbero reverberation; reflection; street-lamp
reverdecer to become green again
reverencia bow; reverence
reverenciable worthy of reverence
reverencial reverential
reverenciar to revere
reverendísimo most reverend
reverendo reverend
reverente showing reverence; respectful
reversibilidad *f* reversibility
reversión *f* reversion
reverso reverse; near side, back
revertir to revert; **(a) cobro revertido** *tel* (with) reversed charge
revés *m* reverse, back, opposite side, wrong side; *sp* back-hand stroke; blow with the back of the hand; **al ~** the wrong way, in the wrong direction; **de ~** from left to right; **del ~** inside out; back to front; **punto del ~** (knitting) purl stitch
revesa *naut* backwater
revesado complicated, difficult; obscure; untamable

revesar to vomit

revestimiento *bui* covering, coating; facing; finish

revestir to cover; dress; *bui* coat, face; ~se to be arrogant

revezar to replace, substitute

revirado *bot* twisted

revisar to revise, re-examine; ~ las cuentas to audit the accounts

revisión *f* revision; inspection

revisor *m* reviser, censor; *comm* auditor; (on train) guard, ticket inspector

revisoría office/work of a revisor

revista revision, review; re-examination; *leg* new trial; *mil* parade, muster; magazine, journal; revue; pasar ~ to review

revistar to review, inspect

revistero *lit* reviewer

revitalizar to revitalize

revivificación *f* revivification

revivificar to revivify

revivir to revive, resuscitate; live again

revocabilidad *f* revocability

revocación *f* revocation

revocador *n m* revoker; *bui* plasterer; *bui* painter; *adj* revoking

revocar to revoke, repeal, cancel, countermand; *bui* plaster, paint

revocatorio revocatory

revoco *n* revoking, cancellation

revolar *orni* to hover about, fly around

revolcadero *zool* animal's wallowing-place

revolcadura wallowing

revolcar to trample on; ~se to wallow

revolotear to flutter about

revoloteo fluttering

revoltijo, revoltillo mess, jumble; ~ de huevos scrambled eggs

revoltoso mischievous; seditious, mutinous; intricate, full of twists and turns

revolución *f* revolution

revolucionar to rebel, rise up against authority

revolucionario revolutionary

revolucionarse to rebel, revolt

revolvedor *n m* agitator; *adj* rebellious, seditious

revolver to turn around; turn over; stir, mix, agitate; wrap; revolve; ponder

revólver *m* revolver

revolvimiento disturbance, commotion; revolution

revoque *m* plastering; white-washing

revotarse to change one's voting habits; support a different party

revuelco wallowing

revuelo *orni* bird's second flight; *aer* gyration while flying; disturbance; de ~ by the way

revuelta second turn, revolution, revolt; dissension, change

revuelto *cul* (of eggs) scrambled; topsy-turvy; boisterous; mischievous; unsettled

revuelvepiedras *m sing+pl orni* turnstone

revulsivo, revulsorio revulsive

rey *m* king, chief; *ent* queen bee; ~ de armas king at arms; Reyes Magos Magi, wise men from the East; ni ~ ni roque not a living soul; no temer ni ~ ni roque to fear no man; a ~ muerto ~ puesto the king is dead, long live the king

reyerta squabble, quarrel

reyezuelo petty king; *orni* goldcrest

rezado *eccles* divine service; prayer

rezador *m* one who prays a lot

rezaga rearguard

rezagado, rezagante laggard, straggler

rezagar to outstrip, leave behind; ~se to lag behind

rezago remains, left-overs, remainder; weak animal removed from herd/flock

rezar to pray; ~ misa say mass; la frase reza así the phrase reads like this

rezno *ent* tick; *bot* castor-oil plant

rezo prayer, devotions

rezongador *m* grumbler, beefer

rezongar to mutter; grumble; growl

rezongo muttering; grumbling; growling

rezumadero cesspool, septic tank

rezumarse to ooze, percolate, filter through

ría estuary; tidal waters of a river

riada flood

riba sloping bank

ribaldería knavery, rascality

ribaldo *n* rogue, rascal, knave; *adj* knavish, roguish

ribazo *see* riba

ribera water's edge, shore, beach

ribereño *n+adj* riparian

ribero river bank

ribes *f sing+pl* currant-bush

ribete *m* (sewing) binding, reinforcement; border

ribeteado (of the eyes) red; irritated

ribetear (sewing) to bind, reinforce

riboflavina *chem* riboflavine

rica: estar ~ (of a woman) *sl* to have a fine figure

ricacho very rich and vulgar

ricadueña, ricahembra wife of a grandee

ricino *bot* castor-oil plant; **aceite de ~** castor oil

rico *n* rich man; **los ~s** the rich (people); *adj* rich, wealthy; (of food) delicious, tasty, savoury; (of children) cute

ricohombre *m* grandee of Spain

ricura wealth; lovely little girl/boy

ridiculez *f* ridiculous action or thing; ridicule; oddity

ridiculizar to ridicule, mock, make fun of

¹ **ridículo** *n* ridicule; *adj* ridiculous; odd, outlandish; absurd; **poner en ~** to expose to ridicule; **ponerse en ~** to make o.s. appear ridiculous

² **ridículo** reticule

riego irrigation, watering; water for irrigation

riel *m* ingot; rail

rielar to glisten, shine

rienda rein; moderation; **~s** reins, ribbons; **a ~ suelta** without restraint, with a free hand; **tener las ~s** to be in control; **tirar de las ~s** to restrain, hold back, check

riente smiling, laughing

riesgo risk, danger, peril; **seguro a todo ~** comprehensive insurance

riesgoso daring

rifa raffle, draw, lottery

rifador *m* raffler

rifar to raffle; quarrel; *naut* (of a sail) split

rifirrafe *m* quarrel, row

riflero rifleman

rigidez *f* rigidity, stiffness; **~ cadavérica** rigor mortis

rígido rigid, stiff

rigodón *m* quadrille

rigor rigour, sternness, severity; **de ~** indispensable; **en ~** in fact

rigorismo austerity

rigorista *n m+f* very strict person; *adj* very strict

rigoroso rigorous, strict, severe, austere

rigurosidad *f* severity, sternness

riguroso *see* **rigoroso**

rija dispute, row, quarrel

rijador *m* quarreller

rijo lust

rijoso quarrelsome, cantankerous; lustful, lascivious

rilado *vulg sl* shit-scared

rilar to tremble, shake

¹ **rima** heap, mound, pile

² **rima** rhyme; **~s** lyrics; **~ imperfecta** assonance

rimado versified, in verse

rimador *m* versifier, rhymer

rimar to rhyme; write verses

rimbombancia resonance; ranting; ostentation

rimbombante ostentatious; bombastic; high-falutin

rimbombar to resound, re-echo

rímel *tr m* mascara

rimero heap, mound; rhymer

rincón *m* (inside) corner; angle; cosy place; remote place; hiding-place

rinconada corner

ringla, ringle *f*, **ringlera** line, file, row; swath

ringorrango exaggerated flourish in handwriting; superfluous decoration

rinoceronte *m* rhinoceros

rinología *med* rhinology

rinoplastia *surg* rhinoplasty

rinoscopia *med* rhinoscopy

riña quarrel, dispute, row, wrangle; scuffle

riñón *m* kidney; *fig* centre of a country; **~ artificial** kidney machine; **costar un ~** to be very expensive; **tener cubierto el ~** to be well-heeled, be loaded, be wealthy

riñonada *cul* kidney dish; *anat* layer of fat about the kidney; loin

río river; **a ~ revuelto** in confusion; **cuando el ~ suena agua lleva** there's no smoke without fire

riojalibre *m sl* wine and Coca-Cola

riojano *n+adj* Riojan, of the Rioja region

rioplatense *n+adj* Argentinian/Uruguayan from the River Plate region

riostra *n* stay, brace

riostrar to stay, brace

ripia roofing-shingle

ripio debris, refuse; *lit* padding, verbiage; **no perder** ~ not to miss an opportunity

riqueza wealth, riches; abundance; ~**s naturales** natural resources

risa laugh, laughter; ironic smile, sneer; **descoyuntarse/destornillarse de** ~ to split one's sides with laughing; **es de** ~ it's a laughing matter

risada belly laugh

riscal *m* craggy place

risco cliff, crag

riscoso craggy, rocky

risibilidad *f* risibility

risible laughable, ludicrous, derisory

risita titter, giggle; false laughter

risotada outburst of laughter

ristra string (of onions, garlic *etc*); file, line, row; **en** ~ on a string

ristrel *m archi* wooden moulding

risueño smiling

rítmico rhythmic

ritmo rhythm; rate; ~ **moderno** pop music

rito rite

ritual *m* ritual; *eccles* prayer-book

ritualidad *f,* **ritualismo** ritualism; high church movement in the Anglican Church

ritualista *n m + f* ritualist; *adj* ritualistic

rivalidad *f* rivalry

rivalizar to rival, vie with, compete against

rivera creek, stream

riza green stubble

rizado *n* fluting, crimping; *adj* curly

rizador *n m* crimping-iron; curling-iron; *adj* crimping, curling

rizar to crimp; curl; flute; corrugate; (of water) ripple; ~**se** to curl

rizo *n* curl, ringlet; *aer* loop; **rizar el** ~ *aer* to loop the loop; **tomar** ~**s** to reef (sails); *adj* naturally curly

rizoma *bot* rhizome

rizón *m naut* anchor with three flukes

rizoso naturally curly

ro-ro-ro crooning sound to lull a baby to sleep

roano *vet* roan

róbalo *zool* sea bass

¹ **robar** to rob, steal; abduct; draw (a card from the pool); ~ **a** to steal from; **me robó la cartera** he robbed me of my wallet, he stole my wallet

² **robar** to chamfer; round off (anything pointed)

robezo *zool* chamois

robín *m* rust, oxidized metal

robinia *bot* false acacia

robladura riveting

roblar to rivet

roble *m bot* oak

robledal *m,* **robledo** oak wood/forest

roblizo *adj* strong, sturdy; hard

roblón *m* rivet

roblonar *see* **roblar**

robo robbery, theft; number of playing-cards taken from the pool

roboración *f* corroboration, confirmation

roborante corroborating, confirming

roborar to corroborate, confirm

roborativo corroborative, confirmatory

robótica robotics

robustecedor strengthening, body-building

robustecer to strengthen

robustez *f* robustness, strength

robusto robust

roca rock

rocalla fallen rocks/stones; stone chippings

rocalloso rocky, stony

roce *m* rubbing, stroking; intercourse, physical contact; friction

rociada sprinkling; *naut* spray; dewfall; severe reprimand

rociadera watering-can

rociado dewy

rociador *m* sprinkler, spray

rociadura, rociamiento *see* **rociada**

rociar to fall as dew; sprinkle, spray, scatter

rocín *m* nag, hack; ignorant person

rocinante *m* skinny horse

rocío dew; spray; sprinkling

rococó *archi* rococo

rocoso rocky

rochela racket, noise

rocho roc

rockero *see* **roquero**

roda *sl* motor-car

rodaballo *zool* turbot; astute man

rodada rut, wheel-track

rodadero, rodadizo easily rolled

rodado *n* vehicle; *adj* wheeled; rounded; fluent; **canto** ~ pebble; **venir** ~ to come to the surface

rodador *n m* roller; *adj* rolling

rodadura rolling, rut; *mot* tyre-tread

rodaja disc; wheel; slice

rodaje *m* set of wheels; *mot* running-in period; **en ~** running in; *cin* filming, shooting

rodal *m* spot, place

rodante *n m sl* motor-car; *adj* rollable; **material ~** rolling-stock

rodapelo *n* going against the grain; affray

rodapié *m bui* skirting; foot-rail

rodar to roll, roll down; run on wheels; wander about; *cin* shoot, film; **~ de suelo** *aer* to taxi; **~ por** to serve; **dejar ~** to let things follow their natural course

rodeabrazo *adv* swinging of the arm to throw/bowl

rodear to surround; (of cattle) round up; *mil* invest, besiege; beat about the bush

rodela buckler, round shield

rodeo turn; roundabout route; detour; round-up; rodeo; corral; beating about the bush, evasion; trickery

rodeón *m* complete turn

rodera cart-track

rodete *m* horizontal water-wheel; ring round which hair is wrapped to form a bun; cloth ring placed on the head when carrying a heavy weight

rodezno horizontal water-wheel

rodilla *anat* knee; ward (of a lock); **a media ~** kneeling on one knee; **de ~s** on one's knees; **doblar la ~** to kneel down, humble o.s.

rodillada, rodillazo blow/push with the knee

rodillera knee-patch; knee-protector; bagginess of trousers at the knees

rodillo roller; road-roller; *print* ink-roller; *cul* rolling-pin; *mech* drum

rodo: a ~ galore, in abundance

rododafne *f bot* daphne

rododendro *bot* rhododendron

rodrigar *agri+hort* to prop up plants *esp* vines

Rodríguez *m sl* husband who remains working (and enjoying himself) while his family are on holiday

rodrigón *m agri+hort* cane/stake to support a plant

roedor *n m* rodent; *adj* gnawing; corroding

roedura act of gnawing; signs of gnawing

roer to gnaw, eat away

roete *m* tonic wine made from pomegranate juice

rogación *f* request, petition; **rogaciones** *eccles* rogation

rogador *n m* supplicant; *adj* supplicating

rogante requesting, praying

rogar to request, entreat; crave

rogativa *adj eccles* rogation

rogativo supplicatory

rojal reddish

rojeante reddening

rojear to redden; blush

rojete *m* rouge

rojez *f* redness

rojizo reddish

rojo *n* red, *fam* communist; *adj* red; (of hair) auburn; (of eggs) brown; **~ alumbrado** bright red; **al ~** red hot

rojura *see* **rojez**

rol *m* list, roll; catalogue

rolar *naut* to veer; go round in circles

roldana pulley-wheel; caster

¹ **rolla** horse's collar

² **rolla** nursemaid

rollar *see* **arrollar**

rollizo chubby; stocky, sturdy

¹ **rollo** anything round/cylindrical/spherical; roller; *cin* reel; *cul* rolling-pin

² **rollo** annoyance, nuisance; *sl* anything difficult/complicated; bore

³ **rollo** world of drugs; drug sub-culture; **estar en el ~** to be with it

Roma Rome

romadizarse to catch cold

romadizo head-cold; hay fever

romaico modern Greek (language)

romana steelyard, balance; **venir a la ~** to be of correct weight

romanador *m* weighmaster

romanar to weigh with a steelyard

romance *n m* Spanish language; romance; historic ballad; verse in octosyllabic metre; **en ~** in plain speech

romancear to translate into Spanish; paraphrase

romancero ballad-singer; collection of ballads

romancista *m+f* novelist

romanear to weigh with a steelyard

romanero weighmaster

romanesco novelistic
romanía: de ~ crestfallen
románico *archi* romanesque, *approx equiv* Norman; **lenguas románicas** Romance languages
romanización *f* Romanization
romanizar to Romanize
romano *n+adj* Roman; **ir de ~ mil sl** to go in uniform; **saludo ~** nazi/fascist salute
romanticismo romanticism
romántico romantic
romanzar *see* **romancear**
rombal, rómbico rhombic
rombo rhombus
romboidal rhomboidal
romboide *m* rhomboid
romeral *m* place where rosemary grows
romería pilgrimage; picnic near a holy shrine
¹ romero pilgrim; one who goes to a **romería**
² romero *bot* rosemary
romo blunt, unsharpened, dull
rompecabezas *m sing+pl* puzzle, *esp* jigsaw puzzle
rompedero fragile, easily broken; perishable
rompedor *n m* breaker; *adj* breaking
rompedura breakage
rompeesquinas *m sing+pl* lounger, loafer
rompegalas *m sing+pl* untidy person
rompehielos *m sing+pl naut* ice-breaker
rompehuelgas *m sing+pl* strikebreaker, scab
rompenueces *m sing+pl* nut-cracker
rompeolas *m sing+pl* breakwater
rompepoyos *m sing+pl* idle person
romper to break, smash; crush; *med* fracture; *agri* break up (land) *bot* sprout, bud; interrupt; **~ el alba/la aurora** to dawn; **~se el alma** to break one's heart; **~se la cabeza** to rack one's brains
rompesquinas *m sing+pl* street-corner loafer
rompible breakable
rompido newly broken land
rompiente *n m* shoal, reef; *adj* breaking
rompimiento break, breakage; fracture; rupture, infringement, violation; *agri* breaking up of virgin land
ron *m* rum

roncador *n m* snorer; *adj* snoring
roncar to snore; *zool* cry/call at rutting time
ronce *m* wheedle, wheedling
roncear to wheedle; *naut* sail slowly
roncería slowness, sluggishness; *naut* sluggish sailing
roncero slow, sluggish; wheedling; grumbling
Roncesvalles: ser un ~ to be a memorable battle/disaster
ronco hoarse; gruff
roncón *m mus* drone (of bagpipe)
¹ roncha weal; bump; lump (of insect-bite *etc*)
² roncha thin slice
ronda rounds (of night patrol); policeman's beat; round of drinks; serenade
rondador *m* roundsman; patrolman; night wanderer
rondalla funny story; group of serenaders
rondar to go the rounds; pound the beat; walk the streets at night; haunt
rondó *mus* rondo
rondón: de ~ daringly; unexpectedly
ronquear to be hoarse; suffer from pharyngitis
ronquedad *f*, ronquera, ronquez *f* hoarseness
ronquido snore
ronronear to purr; *aer* whirr (of a propeller)
ronroneo *n* purring
ronzal *m* halter
ronzar to crunch
roña *vet* scab; crust of dirt on s.o.; rust; stinginess, meanness
roñería, roñosería stinginess, meanness
roñoso scabby; filthy; rusty; stingy
ropa clothes, clothing, apparel; wardrobe; **~ blanca** linen; **~ hecha** ready-made clothes; **~ interior** underwear; **~ vieja** old clothes, cast-off clothes; **a quemar ~** suddenly, pointblank
ropaje *m* clothes; *eccles* vestments
ropavejería old-clothes shop
ropavejero old-clothes dealer
ropería clothing-trade, rag-trade; clothing shop; wardrobe; cloakroom; **~ de viejo** old-clothes shop
ropero clothier; wardrobe-keeper; cloakroom; wardrobe

ropita baby's clothes

roque *m* (chess) rook, castle

roqueda rocky place

roqueño hard, flinty

¹ **roquero** *adj* built on rocks

² **roquero** *n* rocker (of the rocker fashion/cult)

roqueta turret (of a castle)

rorro babe-in-arms

rosa *bot* rose; rosette; **novela ~** romantic novel; (colour) pink; **ver todo color de ~** to see everything through rose-coloured spectacles

rosáceo *bot* rosaceous

rosada frost

rosadelfa *bot* azalea

rosado pink; rose-coloured

rosal *m* rose-bush, rose-tree; **~ de pitiminí** climbing rose; **~ silvestre** dog-rose, wild rose

rosaleda rose-arbour; rose-garden

rosariero rosary-seller

rosario *eccles* rosary; *fig* string

rosarse to blush

rosbif *m* roast beef; roast meat; **~ de ternera** roast veal

rosca screw and nut; screw thread; spiral; ring-shaped cake/bread/biscuit; **hacer la ~** to flatter; **no comerse una ~** *sl* to fail to pick up a girl

roscado *mech* having a thread

roscar to cut a thread on; **máquina de ~** screw-threading machine

rosco *sl* nil, no marks (in an examination)

roscón large ring-shaped loaf; *sl* nil (in an examination)

rosear to turn pink

róseo rosy

roseta rose (of shower, watering-can *etc*); rosette

rosetón *m* large rosette; *archi* rose window

¹ **rosmarino** *bot* rosemary

² **rosmarino** light red

rosmaro walrus; manati

¹ **roso** threadbare; bald

² **roso** red, rosy

rosqueado twisted

rosquilla ring-shaped cake; **venderse como ~s** to sell like hot cakes

rosquillero seller of **rosquillas**

rostro face, countenance; *orni* bill, beak; rostrum; **~ a ~** face to face; **~**

pálido paleface; **hacer ~ a** to face up to; **tener ~** to be cheeky

rota *mil* defeat

rotación *f* rotation; **~ de cultivo** crop-rotation

rotamente barefacedly

rotante rotating

¹ **rotar** to rotate; roam

² **rotar** to belch

rotario Rotarian; Rotary

rotarismo Rotarianism

rotativo *n print* rotary press; newspaper; *adj* rotary

roten *m bot* rattan

roto *n* tear (in a garment); *adj* broken, torn, chipped, ragged, tattered; battered

rotograbado rotogravure

rótula *anat* knee-cap; lozenge

rotulador *n m* labeller; felt-tipped pen; *adj* labelling

rotulata label, mark

rótulo label, mark, poster, placard; shop-sign

rotundidad *f* rotundity, roundness

rotundo round, sonorous

rotura fracture, break

roturación *f agri* breaking-up (of virgin land)

roturador *m agri* Rotavator

roturar *agri* to break up land; Rotavate

roya *bot* mildew; tobacco

rozadura rubbing, abrasion, friction; chafed spot

rozamiento rubbing; disagreement; *mech* friction

rozar *agri* to clear virgin land, grub; scrape, pare; chafe, rub, graze; be bordering on; **~se con** to be on intimate terms with, associate with

¹ **roznar** to bray

² **roznar** to crunch

¹ **roznido** bray (of a donkey)

² **roznido** crunching noise

rúa village street, highroad

ruandés Ruandan

ruano roan

ruar *sl* to roam the streets

rúbeo ruby-coloured; reddish, rosy

rubescencia rosiness, reddishness

rubescente rosy

¹ **rubia** *bot* madder; *zool* red gournard

² **rubia** *n+adj* blonde; *fam* one-peseta coin; *mot* estate car with wooden

bodywork

rubial reddish (*esp* of soil)

rubiales *m+f sing+pl* person with a fair complexion

rubicundez *f* ruddiness, reddishness

rubicundo ruddy, reddish, rosy-cheeked

rubificar to redden, make red

rubio *n* blond, fair man/boy; *adj* blond, fair; (of tobacco) Virginia-type

rublo rouble

rubor *m* blush; shyness, timidity, bashfulness

ruborizarse to blush

ruboroso shy, bashful, timid

rúbrica flourish added to a signature; *eccles* rubric; **de ~** according to custom

rubricante signing; affirming

rubricar to sign with a flourish; sign and seal; *fig* round off

rucio *n* donkey; *adj* (of animals) silver-grey

rucho ass

ruda *bot* rue

rudeza rudeness; coarseness; vulgarity

rudimental, rudimentario rudimentary

rudimento rudiment; vestige

rudo rude, coarse; vulgar; unpolished; severe; stupid

rúe *f sl* street

rueca *text* distaff

rueda wheel, roller, caster; group/circle of people; slice, round; rack (torture); **~ catalina** Catherine-wheel; **~ de andar** treadmill; **~ de prensa** press conference; **~ de recambio, de repuesto** *mot* spare wheel; **hacer la ~ a** to cajole

ruedo turn, rotation; circumference; round rug/mat; bottom of a skirt; bullring

ruego request, petition

rufián *m* ruffian; pimp

rufianada villainy

rufianear to play the villain; act the pimp

rufianería villany; pimping

rufianesco *n* gang of ruffians/villains; *adj* ruffianish, villainish

rufianismo rowdyism, hooliganism

rufo red; blond

rugido roar; bellow; rumble of the intestines

rugiente roaring, bellowing

rugir to roar, bellow; *sl* stink, pong; **~se** *impers* to be whispered about, be said; **se ruge que ...** it is said that ...

rugosidad *f* wrinkled state

rugoso wrinkled; corrugated

ruibarbo *bot* rhubarb

ruido noise, sound; report; stir; **hacer/meter ~** to make a noise, attract attention; **mucho ~ y pocas nueces** empty vessels make most noise

ruidoso noisy, loud

ruin *n* mean/vile/stingy man; *adj* mean; base, despicable; *pej* little, puny; malicious; stingy, avaricious; (of animals) vicious

ruina ruin; downfall; destruction; *sl* long prison sentence; **~s** ruins, debris

ruinar to ruin, destroy

ruindad *f* baseness; base/vile action

ruinoso ruinous, worthless

ruiseñor *m orni* nightingale

rular to roll, revolve

ruleta roulette

¹ **rulo** ball; road-roller

² **rulo** *print* ink-roller

Rumania Romania

rumano *n+adj* Romanian; *sl* gipsy, Romany language

rumbático ostentatious

rumbo course, direction, trend; *fam* ostentation, vanity; *naut* scuttle; **(con) ~ a** bound for, heading for; **poner ~ a** to head for

rumboso generous; pompous

rumiante *n m +adj* ruminant

rumiar to ruminate; ponder

rumor *m* rumour; murmuring; sound of voices

rumorearse *v impers* to be rumoured, be said

rumoroso giving rise to rumours

runa rune

rúnico, runo runic

runrún *m* rumour; buzz

runrunearse (of a rumour) to spread

rupestre inscribed/painted on rocks; **arte ~** cave art

rupia rupee; *sl* peseta

rupicabra *zool* chamois

ruptura rupture; breaking, break; **~ del núcleo** nuclear fission

Rusia Russia

rusificar to make Russian; spread

Russian ideas *etc*

ruso Russian; **montaña rusa** switchback, big dipper

rusticación *f* rustication

rustical rustic, wild

rusticidad *f* rusticity; simplicity; clumsiness

rústica: en ~ paperbacked

rusticano *bot* wild; reverted

rústico *n* peasant, countryman, rustic; *adj* rustic, rural; coarse; clumsy; ill-mannered

ruta route

rutilante sparkling, twinkling

rutilar to sparkle, twinkle

rutina routine; rut; **salir de la ~** to get out of a rut; **una cuestión de mera ~** a pure formality

rutinario *adj* routine

S

s *f* (letter) s; *abbr* (**su, sus**) his, her, its, your, their; *abbr* (**siglo**) century

S.A. (Su Alteza) His/Her/Your Highness

sábado Saturday; ~ **de gloria** Easter Saturday; ~ **inglés** half-holiday, Saturday afternoon off

sábalo *zool* shad

sabalera fishing-net; fire-grate

sabana savanna

sábana bed sheet; *eccles* altar cloth; *sl* 1,000-peseta note; **pegársele las** ~s to oversleep, rise late

sabandija grub, creepy-crawly

sabanear to scour the plain

sabanero *n* plainsman; *adj* (of the) savanna

sabanilla small sheet; piece of linen; *eccles* altar cloth; table napkin; head scarf

sabañón *m* chilblain; **comer como un** ~ to devour, eat like a horse

sabatario Sabbatarian

sabatino *n eccles* Saturday mass; *adj* Saturday

sabatizar to keep the Sabbath

sabedor *n m* knowledgeable person; *adj* knowing; ~ **de** aware of, knowing about

sabelotodo *m+f* know-all

¹ **saber** *vt* to know; know how to, be able to; ~ **cuántos son cinco** to know how many beans make five; ~ **donde aprieta el zapato** to know which side one's bread is buttered; **a** ~ to wit; **que yo sepa** as far as I know; **sabérselas todas** to have an answer for everything; **un no sé que** a certain something

² **saber:** ~ **a** a taste of/like

sabidillo know-all

sabido learned

sabiduría knowledge, learning

sabiendas: a ~ knowingly

sabiente *adj* knowing

sabihondez *f* conceited claim to be knowledgeable

sabihondo know-all

sabina *bot* savin

¹ **sabino** sabine

² **sabino** roan (horse)

sabio *n* scholar, sage; *adj* wise

sablazo sabre-thrust; *fam* sponging, scrounging; **dar un** ~ to touch for a loan

¹ **sable** *m* sabre; **régimen de los** ~s military rule

² **sable** *her* black, sable

sablista *m+f* sponger, scrounger

sablón *m* coarse sand

sabor *m* flavour; zest; **a** ~ to one's taste; ~ **local** local colour; ~ **a naranja** orange flavour

saboreamiento relish(ing)

saborear *vi* to relish, enjoy; *vt* to flavour, give zest to; ~**se en** to take joy in

sabotaje *m* sabotage

saboteador *m* saboteur

sabotear to sabotage

Saboya Savoy

saboyano *n+adj* Savoyard

sabroso savoury, delicious

sabucal *m bot* alder

sabuco *bot* alder

sabueso bloodhound; *fig* detective

sábulo coarse sand

¹ **saca** extraction, drawing out; **estar de** ~ to be marriageable

² **saca** large sack; ~ **de correos** mail-bag

sacabrocas *m sing+pl* tack claw, pincers

sacabuche *m mus* sackbut; *naut* hand-pump; fool, ninny

sacaclavos *m sing+pl* nail-extractor

sacacorchos *m sing+pl* corkscrew

sacada territory separated from a province

sacadineros *m sing+pl* catchpenny

sacador *m* drawer, extractor

sacamanchas *m sing+pl* stain-remover

sacamiento drawing out, taking out

sacamuelas *m sing+pl fam pej* dentist; quack

sacapasta f profitable venture, money-spinner

sacaperras m sing+pl slot-machine

sacar to extract, take out; pick (out); protrude; get, purchase; phot take; (tennis) serve; (of emotions) excite; draw (lots); sp kick off; ~ **a bailar** to ask for a dance; ~ **a la luz** to bring out, publish; ~ **de paseo** to take for a walk; ~ **de pila** to act as godfather/godmother; ~ **de quicio** to make one lose patience; ~ **el ascua/la brasa con la mano del gato** to have another do one's dirty work; ~ **el jugo** to work s.o. hard; ~ **en claro/limpio** to get straight; ~ **la cara** to stand up for; ~ **la cuenta** to figure out; ~ **a uno de sus casillas** to drive one crazy; ~ **ventaja de** to profit by; **yo saco** I kick off/start (in a game)

sacarina saccharin

sacasillas m sing+pl theat stage hand

sacatachuelos m sing+pl see sacabrocas

sacate m hay, grass

sacerdocio priesthood, ministry

sacerdotal priestly

sacerdote m priest, minister

sacerdotisa priestess

saciable satiable

saciar to satiate

saciedad f satiety

sacio satiated

saco sack(ful), bag(ful); jacket; sp hitting the ball on the rebound; mil pillage; naut cove, inlet; sl 1,000-peseta banknote; sl prison; ~ **de noche** valise; **caer en ~ roto** to fall on deaf ears; **entrar a ~, poner en ~** to pillage, loot; **no echar en ~ roto** not to ignore, not to overlook

sacral adj taboo, ritualistic

sacramentado eccles having received the last sacraments

sacramental n f brotherhood devoted to the sacrament of the altar; adj sacramental

sacramentar eccles to administer the last sacraments; consecrate; ~**se** to be transubstantiated

sacramente in a sacred way

sacramento sacrament; **incapaz de ~s** a complete idiot

sacratísimo most sacred

sacrificable expendable

sacrificadero place of sacrifice

sacrificador n m sacrificer; adj sacrificing

sacrificante sacrificial

sacrificar to sacrifice; slaughter (animals); ~**se** to sacrifice o.s.

sacrilegio sacrilege

sacrílego sacrilegious

sacristán m sacristan, sexton; hoop skirt

sacristana sacristan's wife; nun in charge of a sacristy

sacristanía office of sacristan/sexton

sacristía sacristy, vestry

¹ **sacro** sacred

² **sacro** anat sacrum

sacrosanto sacrosanct

sacudida shake, jerk

sacudido intractable, determined

sacudidor n m shaker; adj shaking

sacudidura shaking, cleaning

sacudimiento shake, jerk, jolt

sacudir to shake, jerk; beat, spank; throw off; shake off; naut (of sails) flap; ~**se** to shake off, reject

sachadura weeding, hoeing

sachar to weed, hoe

sacho hoe, weeding-tool

sádico n sadist; adj sadistic

sadismo sadism

sadista m+f sadist

sadístico sadistic(al)

saduceo n+adj Sadducee

saeta arrow, dart; hand (of clock/watch); bot bud of vine; eccles spontaneous verse sung as Holy Week procession passes

saetada arrow-wound

saetear to shoot with arrows

saetera loophole; small window

saetero n archer, bowman; adj arrow

safo sl handbag

¹ **saga** saga, legend

² **saga** witch

sagacidad f sagacity

sagaz sagacious; keen-scented

sagita geom sagitta, segment

sagital arrow-shaped

sagitaria bot sagittaria

Sagitario astrol+astron Sagittarius

sago loose coat

sagrado n refuge; adj sacred, consecrated; **enterrar en ~** to give a Christian burial to; **sagrada escritura** Holy Writ

sagrario sanctuary; tabernacle; *eccles* ciborium

sagú *m* sago

saguntino *adj* of Sagunto

sahariano, saharaui Saharan, of the Sahara

sahornarse to chafe

sahorno chafing

sahumador *m* fumigator; perfuming pot; clothes-drier

sahumadura fumigation; perfuming

sahumar to fumigate; perfume; (of food) smoke

sahumerio fumigation; perfuming; aromatic smoke

saín *m* dirt/grease on clothes

sainar to fatten (animals)

sainete *m theat* one-act farce; zest, relish

sainetear to act in one-act farces

sainetero writer of one-act farces

sainetesco comical, burlesque

saja, sajadura cut, incision

sajar to slice open

sajón *n+adj* Saxon; **genitivo** ~ use of the possessive apostrophe

Sajonia Saxony

sal *f* salt; *fig* wit; charming ways; ~ **de la higuera** Epsom salts; **~es de fruta** health salts; ~ **gema** rock salt; ~ **marina** sea salt; ~ **piedra** rock salt; **echar en** ~ to preserve in salt

sala drawing-room, parlour, lounge; hall; large room; hospital ward; *leg* courtroom; ~ **de autoridades** (at airport) V.I.P. lounge; ~ **de batalla** P.O. sorting office; ~ **de espectáculos** theatre, cinema; ~ **de espera** waiting room; ~ **de máquinas** *naut* engineroom; **guardar** ~ to observe rules of protocol

salabardo scoop-net

salabre *m* landing-net

salacidad *f* salaciousness, lechery

salacot *m* pith helmet

saladar *m* salt-marsh

saladería meat-salting factory

saladero salting-tub

salado *n* saline land; *adj* salty, brackish, briny; funny; witty; winsome; likeable

¹ **salador** *m* salter, curer

² **salador** *m* salting-place

saladura salting, curing; salted food

salamandra salamander; ~ **acuática** newt

salamanqués *m* native of Salamanca

salamanquesa salamander

salame unhappy

salangana *orni* oriental swift whose nest is used to make soup

salar to salt; preserve in brine

salarial *adj* (of) wage(s)

salariar to pay a wage/salary to

salario salary, wages, pay; ~**s congelados** frozen wages

salaz salacious, lecherous

salazón *f* salting; salted meat/fish

salbanda *min* selvedge

salce *m bot* willow; ~ **llorón** weeping willow

salceda, salcedo willow grove

salcereta dice-box

salcochar to boil in salt water

salcocho food boiled in salt water

salchicha sausage

salchichería sausage-shop

salchichero sausage-maker, sausage-seller

salchichón *m* salami

saldado *comm* paid, settled

saldar *comm* to settle, liquidate; hold a sale of; sell at reduced prices

saldista *m* liquidation broker; dealer in remnants and discontinued lines

saldo *comm* balance; settlement; remnants; sale (at reduced prices); ~ **acreedor/deudor** credit/debit balance

saledizo *n* projection, ledge; *archi* corbel; *adj* salient, jutting out

salera salt-mine

salero salt-cellar; salt-store; wit; charm

saleroso witty; charming, amusing

salgar to feed salt to cattle

salguera, salguero *bot* osier

salicílico *chem* salicylic

salicina *chem* salicin

sálico Salic

salicor *m bot* saltwort

salida departure, start; exit; result; projection; *comm* saleability; *comm* outlay; *naut* headway; *mil* sally, sortie; epithet, witty remark; opening; *mech* outlet; ~ **de emergencia** emergency exit; **calle sin** ~ cul-de-sac; **tener** ~ *comm* to sell well

salidizo *n archi* overhang, projection, corbel; *adj* jutting out

salido projecting; *vet* in season

saliente *n f* projection, lug; *adj* project-

ing; retiring
salífero salt-bearing
salificar to turn into salt
salín *m* salt-store
salina salt-pan; salt-mine
salinero salter; salt-dealer
salinidad *f* saltiness
salino saline
salinómetro salinometer
[1] **salir** to go/come out; depart, leave; *naut*
sail; get out (of a vehicle); come forth,
show up; *astron* rise; *sp* begin; *theat*
enter, come on stage; result; do
(well/badly); be elected; end up;
grow; ~ **adelante** to be successful; ~
al padre to turn out just like one's
father; ~ **con** to come out with; ~ **de**
to part with; leave; ~ **de sus casillas** to
lose one's temper; ~ **ganando/
perdiendo** to end up a winner/loser; ~
mal to do badly; **salga lo que saliere**
come what may
[2] **salir: ~se** to leak; boil over; overflow;
go off; fly off; **~se con la suya** to get
one's own way; **~se de madre** to lose
one's self-control
salitral *m* saltpetre bed, saltpetre works;
adj nitrous
salitrar to impregnate with saltpetre
salitre *m* saltpetre
salitrero *n* saltpetre worker; *adj* saltpetre
salitroso nitrous
saliva saliva, spittle; **tragar** ~ to suffer
in silence; **gastar** ~ **en balde** to waste
one's words
salivación *f* salivation, spitting
salivadera spittoon
salivar to salivate, spit
salivazo spit
salivoso excessive spitting
salmantino native of Salamanca
salmear to sing psalms
salmista *m* psalmist, psalm-singer
salmo psalm
salmodia psalter; psalmody
salmodiar to sing psalms
salmón *m* salmon
salmonado salmon-like; **trucha salmo-
nada** salmon trout
salmonera salmon-net
salmonete red mullet
salmorejo game sauce
salmuera brine

salobral *n m* salty land; *adj* salty, briny
salobre, salobreño brackish
salobridad *f* brackishness, saltiness
saloma *naut* shanty
salomar to sing shanties
Salomón Solomon
salón *m* drawing-room; assembly-room;
large hall
saloncillo small drawing-room; waiting-
room; rest-room
salpicadero dashboard
salpicado spattered, blotchy
salpicadura splash(ing)
salpicar to splash; sprinkle
salpicón *m* splashing; ~ **de mariscos**
sea-food cocktail
salpimentar to season with salt and
pepper
salpimienta mixture of salt and pepper
salpresar to preserve with salt
salpullido *med* rash
salpullir *med* to break out in a rash
salsa sauce, dressing, gravy; ~ **de San
Bernardo** hunger; ~ **mahonesa**
mayonnaise
salsedumbre *f* saltiness
salsera gravy-boat
salsero *n bot* Spanish thyme; *adj* nosey-
parker, busy-body
salsifí *m bot* salsify
saltabancos *see* **saltimbanco**
saltabardales *m sing+pl* wild youth
saltabarrancos *m sing+pl* gadabout
saltacaballo *archi* crossette; **a** ~ *archi*
overlapping
saltación *f* leaping, hopping; dancing
saltacharquillos *m sing+pl* jaunty fellow
saltadero leaping-place; fountain
saltadizo snapping, breaking
saltador *n m* jumper, hopper, leaper;
skipping; *adj* jumping, hopping
saltamontes *m sing+pl* grasshopper
saltante *adj* jumping, leaping; salient
saltaojos *m sing+pl bot* peony
saltaparedes *see* **saltabardales**
saltar *vi* to jump, leap, spring, bound,
hop, skip; spurt; shoot up; fly apart;
snap; burst; come off, come loose;
stand out; *vt* to jump over; (of
animals) cover (the female); ~ **a la
vista** to be obvious; ~ **de alegría** to
jump for joy; ~ **a tierra** to disembark;
hacer ~ **el edificio** to blow up the
building; **~se a la torera** to disregard;

saltársele las lágrimas to burst into tears

saltarén *m* grasshopper; *mus* tune on the guitar

saltarín *adj* hopping; jumping; skipping; dancing

saltarina dancer; dancing-mistress

saltarregla slide-rule; bevel square

saltaterandate *m* embroidery

saltatrás *m sing + pl* throwback

saltatriz *f* ballet-dancer

saltatumbas *cont m sing + pl* priest who makes a living from funerals

salteador *m* highwayman

salteadora woman footpad; woman living with highwaymen

salteamiento highway robbery; *cul* frying

saltear to hold up, waylay, ambush; do things by fits and starts; *cul* sauté

salteo highway robbery

salterio psalter

saltero highlander

saltígrado *zool* leaping, jumping

saltimbanco, saltimbanqui *m* mountebank; quack; acrobat

salto jump; leap; spring; hop; skip; omission; gap; ~ **atrás** *cin* flashback; ~ **de agua** waterfall; ~ **del ángel** swallow-dive; ~ **de cama** dressing-gown; ~ **de trucha** tumbling; ~ **de viento** sudden change of wind; ~ **mortal** somersault; **a** ~**s** by hops, by fits and starts; **dar un** ~ to take a jump; **de un** ~ at one jump; **en un** ~ in the twinkling of an eye; **por** ~**s** irregularly; **vivir a** ~ **de mata** to live from hand to mouth

saltón *n m* grasshopper; *adj* given to hopping/leaping; (of eyes) protruding

salubre healthy, salubrious

salubridad *f* healthfulness, wholesomeness

salud *f* health; welfare; ¡~! cheers!; ¡a su ~! your health!; **beber a la** ~ **de** to drink the health of; **bien/mal de** ~ in good/poor health; **gastar** ~, **gozar de buena** ~ to enjoy good health

saludable salutary, healthy, wholesome

saludador *m* greeter, saluter; quack

saludar to greet, salute; give regards to; *naut* dip the flag; **le/les saluda atentamente** yours faithfully

saludo salute; greeting; bow

salutación *f* salutation; greeting; bow; salute; *eccles* Ave Maria

salutífero healthy, salubrious

¹ **salva** salver, tray

² **salva** round of applause; *mil* salvo

³ **salva** ordeal; oath; vow; assurance

salvación *f* salvation, redemption

salvadera sand-box (for sprinkling on writing)

salvado bran

salvador *n m* saviour, redeemer, deliverer; *adj* redeeming; delivering, rescuing

salvadoreño *n* Salvadorean; *adj* of Salvador

salvaguardar to safeguard

salvaguardia *f* safeguard; security; protection; *m* guard; watchman

salvajada (act of) savagery; atrocity

salvaje *n m* savage, barbarian; *adj* savage; *bot + zool* wild

salvajería, salvajez *f*, **salvajismo** savagery, brutish behaviour

salvamano without taking any risk; in a cowardly fashion

salvamanteles *m sing + pl* table-mat

salvamento, salvamiento salvage, salvaging; rescuing, life-saving; place of safety; **bote de** ~ lifeboat

salvante except

salvar to save, rescue; overcome, surmount; avoid (danger); make allowances for; make an exception of; ~**se** to escape; survive; *eccles* save one's soul; ~ **la reputación** to save face, preserve one's image; ~ **las apariencias** to keep up appearances; ¡**sálvese quien pueda!** every man for himself!

salvavidas *m sing + pl* life-preserver; lifebelt; **chaleco** ~ life-jacket; lifeguard; **bote** ~ lifeboat

¡**salve!** hail!

salvedad *f* reservation, exception

salvia *bot* salvia; sage

salvilla salver, tray

salvo *adj* saved, safe; **a** ~ safe; **dejar a** ~ to leave out, leave on one side; **en** ~ at liberty; *adv* save, except; ~ **que** only if, unless; **ponerse a** ~ to reach safety

salvoconducto safe conduct, pass

salvohonor *m fam* behind, backside

salladura weeding

sallar to weed

sallete *m* weeding-tool
sámago dry rot
samaritano Samaritan
samaruguera fishnet (stretched across a river)
sambenitar to denounce publicly
sambenito garment worn by penitents; disgrace; public dishonour
samblaje *m* joinery, carpentry
samoano *n + adj* Samoan
samoyedo Samoyed
sampaguita *bot* tropical jasmine
sampán *m* sampan
San (Santo) Saint
sanable curable, healable
sanador *m* healer
sanalotodo cure-all, panacea
sanar to heal, cure; ~**se** to recover
sanativo curative
sanatorio sanatorium
sanción *f* sanction; penalty
sancionar to sanction; penalize
sanco stew; porridge; thick mud
sancochar to parboil; cook badly
sancocho meat and vegetable stew; half-cooked meat
sanctasanctórum *m* holy of holies
sanchopancesco like Sancho Panza; worldly, materialistic
sandalia sandal
sandalino *adj* (of) sandalwood
sándalo sandalwood
sandez *f* silly/stupid deed/statement
sandía watermelon
sandiar *m* watermelon field
sandio stupid, silly
sandunga *fam* elegance, style; charm
sandunguero *fam* elegant, stylish; charming; amusing
sandwichera sandwich-maker/toaster
saneado clear, unencumbered; drained; sound
saneamiento *leg* surety, guarantee; bail; drainage; land improvement; sanitation; ~**s** bathroom/toilet fittings
sanear to give security/bail; indemnify; drain; improve (land); put right
sanedrín *m* Sanhedrin
sanforizar *tr* to sanforize
sanfrancia quarrel
sangradera *med* lancet; basin for blood-letting; sluice, drain
sangrador *m* outlet, opening; *med* blood-letter

sangrar to bleed; drain; ~**se** to be bled
sangraza contaminated blood
sangre *f* blood; race; kindred; ~ **azul** blue blood; ~ **fría** aplomb, composure; **a** ~ **caliente** impulsively, in the heat of the moment; **a** ~ **fría** in cold blood; **a** ~ **y fuego** with fire and sword; **la** ~ **tira** blood is thicker than water; **no llegó la** ~ **al río** they didn't come to blows; **subirse la** ~ **a la cabeza** to become excited; **tener mala** ~ to be bloody-minded
sangría bleeding, blood-letting; drainage; drain, outlet; tap; inner angle of the elbow; *print* indentation; drink made of iced red wine, orange juice, oranges and lemons
sangriento bloody, blood-stained; savage
sangüesa *bot* raspberry
sangüeso *bot* raspberry cane/bush
sanguijuela *zool* leech
sanguinaria *bot* knot-grass; *min* blood-stone
sanguinario sanguinary, blood-thirsty
sanguíneo *adj* sanguine, red; **grupo** ~ blood group
sanguinolencia blood condition
sanguinolento bloody, blood-stained, dripping blood
sanguinoso *adj* (of) blood; bloody
sanguiñuelo *bot* dogberry, wild cornel
sanguis *m eccles* consecrated wine
sanguisorba *bot* great burnet
sanguja *see* sanguijuela
sanidad *f* health; public health department; ~ **marina** quarantine officials; **carta de** ~ bill of health
sanitario *n* health official; *mil* stretcher-bearer; *adj* healthy, hygienic, sanitary
sanjuanada St John's Day festival
sanjuanero *agri* ripe by St John's Day
San Lorenzo St Lawrence (river)
sanmarinense *n* native of San Marino
San Martín pig-slaughtering time, 11 November; **a cada puerco le llega su** ~ everyone meets his Waterloo
sanmiguelada Michaelmas-tide
sanmigueleño *agri* ripe by Michaelmas
sano sound; healthy; fit; wholesome; ~ **y salvo** safe and sound; **cortar por lo** ~ to cut one's losses
sánscrito Sanskrit
Sansón Samson

sansón *m* very strong man

santa saint

santabárbara *naut* powder-magazine

Santa Elena St Helena

santamente correctly; **ha hecho** ~ he's done what is right

santanderino *n* native of Santander; *adj* (of) Santander

Santelmo *naut* St Elmo's fire

santero *n* seller of holy images; guardian of a sanctuary; *sl* criminal who plans a crime but does not take part; *adj* over-zealous in devotion to the saints

Santiago St James

¡Santiago! war-cry of Spaniards fighting the Moors

santiagueño *agri* ripe by St James' Day

santiagués *n* native of Santiago de Compostela; *adj* (of) Santiago de Compostela

santiamén *m* instant, flash; **en un** ~ in a jiffy

santidad *f* saintliness, holiness; **Su Santidad** His/Your Holiness

santificación *f* sanctification; ~ **de las fiestas** keeping/observing holy days

santificador *n m* sanctifier; *adj* sanctifying

santificante sanctifying

santificar to sanctify, consecrate, hallow; keep holy days; ~**se** to justify, clear from guilt, declare o.s. innocent

santiguada sign of the cross

santiguador *m* one who heals by making the sign of the cross

santiguamiento crossing o.s.

santiguar to bless; heal by blessing; make the sign of the cross; *fam* hit, beat; ~**se** to cross o.s.

santimonia sanctity, holiness; *bot* corn marigold; chrysanthemum

santísimo most holy; **hacer la santísima a** to play a dirty trick on

santito *iron* regular little saint

santo *n* saint; saint's day; image of a saint; book illustration; *mil* watchword; ~ **titular,** ~ **patrón** patron saint; **comerse los** ~**s** to be excessively devout; **dar el** ~ **y seña** to give the password; **desnudar a un** ~ **para vestir a otro** to rob Peter to pay Paul; **no es** ~ **de mi devoción** it's not my cup of tea; **quedarse para vestir** ~**s** to remain an old maid; **Todos los Santos** All Saint's

Day; *adj* saintly; holy, sacred; *fam* simple-minded; ~ **varón** simple man; **su santa voluntad** his/her own sweet will; **todo el** ~ **día** the whole blessed day; **una santa bofetada** a good slap

santol *m* sandalwood tree

santón *m* holy man; hypocrite

santónico *bot* wormwood

santoral *m* book of (lives) of the saints; church choir-book

santuario sanctuary

santucho hypocrite

santurrón *n m* sanctimonious person; *adj* sanctimonious

santurronería sanctimoniousness, sanctimony

saña anger; savage cruelty

sañero *sl* wallet; *sl* pickpocket

sañoso, sañudo savage, cruel

sao *bot* laburnum

sapajú *m* capuchin monkey

sapidez *f* sapidity

sápido sapid, tasty

sapiencia knowledge

sapiente wise

sapina *bot* glasswort

sapino fir-tree

sapo toad

saponáceo soapy

saponaria *bot* soapwort

saponificación *f* saponification

saponificar to saponify

saporífero saporific, imparting flavour

saque *m* (football) kick-off; (hockey) bully-off; (tennis) serve, service; ~ **de banda** throw-in; ~ **de esquina** corner-kick; **tener buen** ~ to be a good drinker or eater

saqueador *n m* looter, pillager; *adj* plundering, looting

saqueamiento looting, pillaging, plundering

saquear to loot, pillage, plunder

saqueo *see* **saqueamiento**

saquera sacking-needle

saquería sack-making, collection of sacks

saquero sack-maker

saquete *m* cartridge-bag

saragüete *m* informal party, get-together

sarampión *m* measles

sarao soirée

sarape *m* Mexican blanket worn by

men; shawl

sarapico *orni* curlew

sarasa *m* cissy, pansy

sarcasmo sarcasm

sarcástico sarcastic

sarcia burden, load

sarcocola resin gum

sarcófago sarcophagus, tomb

sardana national dance of Catalonia

sardesco sardonic; crude; small (of donkeys)

sardina sardine; **como ~s en lata** packed like sardines

sardinero *n* seller of sardines; *adj* sardine, sardine-like

sardineta small sardine; *naut* lanyard; **~s** *mil* chevrons

¹ **sardo** *n*+*adj* Sardinian

² **sardo** (of cattle) red, white and black

sardonia *bot* crowfoot

sardónica *min* sardonyx

sardónico sardonic

¹ **sarga** *text* serge, twill; *arts* fabric painted in oil/distemper

² **sarga** *bot* osier

sargado serge-like

sargal *m* clump of osiers

sargazo gulf-weed

sargenta sergeant's wife; well-built woman; *fam* tyrant

sargentería sergeant's drill

sargentía office of sergeant

sargento sergeant; **~ mayor** sergeant-major

sargentona heavily built woman; *fam* old battle-axe; tyrant

sarilla *bot* marjoram

sarmentar to glean pruned vine shoots (for fuel)

sarmentera place where pruned vine-shoots are stored (for fuel)

sarmentoso dried-up; wrinkled

sarmiento pruned vine-shoot

sarna *med* itch, scabies; *vet* mange; **más viejo que la ~** as old as the hills

sarnazo malignant/chronic itch

sarnoso itchy; scabby; mangy

sarpullido rash; flea-bite

sarpullirse to have a rash; be flea-bitten

sarraceno *n* Saracen, Moor; *adj* Saracen, Moorish

sarracina scuffle, fight; massacre

sarria rope net; fruit basket

sarrillo *bot* arum; death-rattle

sarro crusted deposit on vessels; tartar/plaque on teeth

sarroso crusty; covered with tartar

sarta string, line, file; series

sartén *f* frying-pan; **tener la ~ por el mango** to be in control

sartenada frying-panful

sartenazo blow with a frying-pan

sarteneja small frying-pan

sartorio sartorial

sastra tailoress; tailor's wife

sastre *m* tailor; **~ remendón** repairer; **traje ~** tailored suit

sastrería tailor's shop; tailoring

Satán, Satanás Satan

satánico satanic

satelitario *adj* satellite

satélite *m* satellite; *fig* follower, supporter; **estado ~** satellite/puppet state

satelizar to put into orbit

satén, satín *m* satin

satinado (of paint) with silk finish

satinador *m* calender; polishing tool; *phot* burnisher

satinar *v* to calender; *phot* burnish

satinete *m* *text* satinette

sátira satire; innuendo

satírico *n* satirist; *adj* satirical, sarcastic

satirio *zool* water-vole

satirizante satirizing

satirizar to satirize

sátiro satyr

satisfacción *f* satisfaction; complacency; **a ~** fully; **tomar ~** to vindicate o.s.

satisfacer to satisfy; make amends; settle; repay; indemnify; explain, convince; **~ una letra** *comm* to honour a draft; **~se** to be avenged/satisfied

satisfaciente satisfying

satisfactorio satisfactory, satisfying

satisfecho satisfied; self-satisfied, smug

sativo sown, cultivated

sátrapa *m* satrap; cunning fellow

satrapía satrapy

saturación *f* saturation

saturar to saturate; satiate

saturnales *fpl* Saturnalia

saturnino saturnine; gloomy, morose

saturnismo *med* lead poisoning

Saturno *astrol*+*astron* Saturn

saturno lead

sauce *m* *bot* willow; **~ llorón** weeping-willow

sauceda, saucedal *m*, **saucera** willow

plantation
saucillo *bot* knot-grass
saúco *bot* elder
saurio *zool* saurian
sausería palace larder
sausier *m* head of a palace larder
sauz *m bot* willow
sauzal *m* willow plantation
savia *bot* sap; *fig* strength, vigour
sáxeo stony
saxífraga, saxifragia *bot* saxifrage
saxo *fam* saxophone player
saxófon *m*, **saxófono** saxophone
sayal *m* sackcloth; coarse material; skirt
sayalero sackcloth-weaver
sayalete *m approx* flannelette
sayo smock; frock; tunic; loose garment; **cortar un ~ a** to talk behind the back of; **decir para su ~** to say under one's breath; **hacer de su capa un ~** to do just as one pleases
sayón *m* executioner; fierce-looking person
sazón *f* ripeness, maturity; season, occasion; taste; seasoning; **a la ~** at that time; **en ~** ripe, in season, opportune
sazonado seasoned; mellow, ripe; witty; pertinent
sazonador *m* seasoner
sazonar *vi* to ripen, mature; *vt* to season
scaléxtrix *m tr fam* complex of underpasses and flyovers; spaghetti junction
schotis *m mus* schottische
se himself, herself, itself, oneself, yourself, themselves, yourselves; (to) each other, (to) one another; (used to give emphasis) **~ lo bebió** he drank it up; (used to replace the passive voice) **aquí ~ habla inglés** English is spoken here; **~ dice que** it is said that; **no ~ sabe** no one knows
sebáceo sebaceous, greasy, tallowy
sebe *f* wattle fence
sebillo tallow; toilet soap
sebo tallow, suet; candle-grease; fat, grease
seboso tallowy, greasy; unctuous
seca drought; *naut* dry sandbank
secacristales *m sing + pl* squeegee
secadal *m* barren ground
secadero *n* drying-shed; fruit-drier; *adj* suitable for drying
secadillo almond meringue
secador *n m* drier; hair-drier; *adj* drying

secadora *n* drier; **~ centrífuga** spin-drier
secamiento drying, desiccation
secano unirrigated land; dry region or land; *naut* dry sandbank; **cultivo de ~** dry farming
secansa (cards) sequence, run
secante *n* blotting-paper; (football) player who marks his opponent well; annoying person, hanger-on; *adj* drying, blotting; **papel ~** blotting-paper
secar to dry, wipe dry; desiccate; (football) mark well; **~se** to dry up; become very thirsty; wipe away
secaral *m* drought
secatón *adj* very curt, brusque
secatura insipidity; dullness
sección *f* section; cross-section; department, division; cutting
seccionado in sections
seccionar to section
seccionario sectional
secesión *f* secession
secesionista *n m + f + adj* secessionist
seceso excrement, stool
seco *n* drought; dry season; *naut* dry sandbank; **~s** *naut* rocks, sandbanks; *adj* dry, dried up; lean, thin; plain, unadorned; curt, abrupt; rude; cold; (of pain) dull; *bui* without mortar; **a secas** just, merely; **a secas y sin llover** out of the blue; **dejar ~** *fam* to bump off, shoot; **golpe ~** quick blow; **parar en ~** to stop dead
secreción *f med* secretion
secreta private examination/graduation; *eccles* secret; secret investigation; privy, closet; secret police
secretar *med + physiol* to secrete
secretaría secretary; secretary's wife
secretaría secretariat; secretary's office; secretaryship; government department
secretariado secretariat
secretario secretary
secretear to talk confidentially; whisper
secreteo confidential whispering
secreter *m* bureau, writing-desk
secretista *m* dealer in secrets; naturalist
secreto *n* secret; secrecy; caution; concealment; secret drawer; **~ a voces** open secret; **en ~** in private/confidence; *adj* secret, confidential
secretorio *med* secretory
secta sect

sectario sectarian

sectarismo sectarianism

secuaz *m+f* henchman, supporter, follower

secuela sequel, upshot, result

secuencia sequence; *gramm* word-order

secuestrable *leg* sequestrable; likely/ liable to be hijacked/kidnapped

secuestración *f leg* sequestration; hijacking; kidnapping

secuestrador *m leg* sequestrator; hijacker; kidnapper; ~ **aéreo** aeroplane hijacker

secuestrar *leg* to sequester; hijack; kidnap

secuestro *leg* sequestration; hijacking; kidnapping; ~ **aéreo** aeroplane hijacking

sécula seculórum for ever and ever, world without end

secular secular; age-old; time-honoured

secularidad *f* secularity

secularista *m+f* secularist

secularización *f* secularization

secularizar to secularize

secundar to second, back, support

secundario *n* second-hand (of watch); *adj* secondary; (of schools) secondary, high; subordinate; subsidiary

secundinas *fpl* after-birth

secundípara mother for the second time

secura dryness, drought

sed *f* thirst; dryness, drought; eagerness; longing; ~ **de** thirst for; **apagar la** ~ to quench the thirst; **tener** ~ to be thirsty

seda silk; *zool* bristles of wild boar; **como la** ~ smooth as silk

sedal *m* angling line; *surg* seton

sedalina *text* silk and cotton mixture

sedante *m* sedative; *adj* sedative; soothing

sedar to allay; soothe; sedate

sedativo sedative

sede *f eccles* see; ~ **social** *comm* headquarters/head office

sedear to clean/polish gems

sedentario sedentary

sedente seated

sedeña flaxen tow

sedeño silky, silk-like; made of hair

sedera jeweller's polishing-brush

sedería silks, silk; silk shop

sedero *n* silk-weaver, silk-dealer; *adj*

silk, silken

sedición *f* sedition; mutiny

sedicioso *n* rebel; trouble-maker; *adj* seditious, mutinous

sediento thirsty; ~ **de** thirsty for, longing for

sedimentación *f* sedimentation

sedimentar to deposit; ~**se** to settle

sedimentario sedimentary

sedimento sediment; dregs; grounds

sedoso silky, silk-like

seducción *f* seduction; fascination

seducir to seduce; allure, entice; lead astray; fascinate, attract; **le sedujo la idea** the idea tempted her

seductivo seductive; enticing, captivating

seductor *n m* seducer; deceiver; enchanting person; *adj* seductive; tempting; fascinating

sefardí, sefardita *m* Sephardi, Sephardic Jew; language of the Sephardim; *adj* Sephardic

segable ready for reaping

segada harvest

segadera sickle, reaping-hook

segadero *see* segable

segador *m* harvester (person); reaper; mower

segadora harvester (machine+woman); ~ **de césped** lawn-mower; ~ **trilladora** combine harvester

segar to reap, mow; cut off; mow down

segazón *f* reaping; reaping season

seglar *n m* layman; *f* laywoman; *adj* lay, secular

segmentación *f* segmentation

segmentar to segment

segmento segment

segoviano native of Segovia

segregación *f* segregation; ~ **celular** solitary confinement

segregacionista *n m+f* +*adj* segregationist

segregar to segregate; *med* secrete

segregativo segregative; *med* secretory

seguida continuation, succession; **de** ~ in succession, at once; **en** ~ right away, immediately

seguidamente immediately afterwards, right after that

seguidero guide-lines (for handwriting)

seguidilla four/seven-line poem; popular song and dance of Andalusia

seguido continued; successive; straight, direct; **acto** ~ at once; **todo** ~ straight on, straight ahead

seguidor *m* follower, henchman

seguimiento pursuit; chase, hunt; continuation

seguir to follow; continue; keep on; take; **suma y sigue** *comm* balance carried forward; **~se** to follow (logically), be deduced

según *adv* it all depends; it depends; depending on; ~ **y como/conforme** it all depends on how; *conj* according as; depending on; ~ **que** it all depends on whether; *prep* according to

segunda double turn of a key in the lock; double meaning; second class

segundar *vt* to repeat; second; *vi* to be/come in second

segundario secondary

segundero *n* second-hand (of watch); *adj* second (crop the same year)

segundilla call-bell (in a convent)

segundillo second helping of food; *mus* accidental

segundo *n* second (of time); second in command; *naut* mate; **sin** ~ without equal; *adj* second; ~ **fontanero** plumber's mate; ~ **galán** *m theat* actor with a walk-on role; **de segunda mano** second-hand

segundogénito second-born

segundogenitura *leg* rights of a second son

segundón *m* younger son

segur *f* axe; sickle

segurador *m* surety, bondsman

seguramente very likely, very probably; indeed

segurar *see* **asegurar**

seguridad *f* security; surety; certainty; assurance, bond, guarantee; **caja de** ~ safety deposit-box; **con (toda)** ~ with (absolute) security/certainty

seguro *n* insurance, assurance; safety; safety-catch; *mech* pawl, ratchet; (of lock) tumbler; ~ **contra accidentes** accident insurance; ~ **contra incendios** fire insurance; ~ **contra terceros** third-party insurance; ~ **de desempleo** unemployment insurance; ~ **a todo riesgo** comprehensive insurance; ~ **de viaje** travel insurance; **a buen** ~ undoubtedly; **en** ~ in safety;

irse del ~ to throw discretion to the winds; **sobre** ~ without risk; *adj* secure, safe; sure, certain; constant; dependable

segurón *m* large axe

seis six; sixth (of the month); six-spotted domino/card; **(a) las** ~ (at) six o'clock

seisavado hexagonal

seisavo *n* one sixth, sixth part; hexagon; *adj* sixth

seiscientos six hundred; six hundredth; *m sing + pl* **Seat** ~ mini car

seise *m* one of six choirboys who sing and dance in some cathedrals

seiseno sixth

seisillo *mus* sextolet

seísmico seismic

seistiros *m sing + pl* six-shooter

seísmo earth tremor

selección *f* choice; *sp* team (*usu* national)

seleccionador *n m* selector; *sp* manager; *adj* selecting

seleccionamiento *n* selecting, choosing

seleccionar to select, choose, pick

selectas *fpl lit* analects, gleanings

selectivo selective

selecto select; excellent; selected

selenita *m + f* inhabitant of the moon; selenite

self *f elect* self-induction coil

selva forest (*esp* tropical), jungle; **Selva Negra** Black Forest

selvático wild, (of the) forest, jungle

selvatiquez *f* wildness; uncouthness

selvicultura forestry, silviculture

selvoso sylvan, wooded

sellador *m* sealer

selladura sealing

sellar to seal; stamp; close; ~ **los labios** to seal the lips, keep mum

sello seal; stamp; stamp office; signet; *pharm* sachet, wafer capsule; ~ **de aduana** docket; ~ **postal/de correos** postage stamp

semafórico semaphoric

semáforo semaphore; traffic-light

semana week; **Semana Santa** Holy Week; **entre** ~ on weekdays; **estar de** ~ to be on duty for the week

semanal weekly

semanario *n* weekly (periodical); *adj* weekly

semanería work done in a week

semanero n weekly worker; adj engaged by the week

semántica semantics

semántico semantic

semasiología see **semántica**

semblante n look, appearance; countenance; **mudar de** ~ to change colour, take on a different appearance

semblanza biographical note

sembrada sown/cultivated land

sembradera sowing-machine; seeding machine; seed drill

sembradío arable; ready for sowing

sembrado cultivated field; sown land

sembrador m sower

sembradora sowing-machine

sembradura sowing, seeding

sembrar to sow, seed, disseminate

semeja resemblance, likeness; mark

semejable, semejado resembling, like

semejante n m fellow-creature; likeness, resemblance; adj alike, similar, such (as)

semejanza similarity; **a** ~ **de** like, in the likeness of

semejar to resemble

semen m semen; seed

semencera sowing

semencontra m pharm vermifuge

semental n m breeding animal; stallion, stud-horse; adj seminal

sementera sowing, seeding; seed-bed; cultivated land; seed-time; beginning; fig hotbed

sementero seed-bag; seed-bed

sementino adj (related to) seed/seed-time

semestral adj half-yearly

semestralmente adv half-yearly

semestre m semester, half-year

semiárido semi-arid

semiautomático semi-automatic

semicabrón satyr

semicalificado semi-skilled

semicapro see **semicabrón**

semicilindro half-cylinder

semicírculo semicircle

semicivilizado half-civilized

semiconsciente semi-conscious

semicopado syncopated

semicorchea semiquaver

semidiáfono semi-diaphanous

semidiámetro radius

semidifunto half-dead

semidiós m demigod

semidiosa demigoddess

semidormido half-asleep

semieje m mot half axle-tree

semiesfera hemisphere

semiesférico hemispherical

semifinalista m+f semifinalist

semifluido semi-liquid

semiforme half-formed

semihombre m half-man

semilunio half-moon

semilla seed

semillero seed-bed; nursery

semilloso seedy

seminación f semination

seminario eccles seminary; seminar; hort seed-bed, seed-box

seminarista m theological student, seminarist

seminífero seed-bearing

semínima mus crochet

seminuevo euph second-hand

semiologías, semiótica semiology, semiotics

semiplena leg (of evidence) inconclusive

semiplenamente leg half-proved

semiprecioso semi-precious

semirecto geom of forty-five degrees

semirrubio half-blond, almost blond

semisalvaje half-wild

semita m+f Semite

semítico Semitic

semitono semitone

semitransparente almost transparent

semivivo half-alive

semivocal f semivowel

sémola semolina

sempiterno everlasting, eternal; bot evergreen

sen f bot senna

Sena m Seine

sena: ~s double sixes (on dominoes/dice)

senado senate; senate house

senador m senator

senaduría senatorship

senario senary

senatorio senatorial

sencillez f simplicity; candour

sencillo simple; unmixed; uncomplicated; candid; text plain

senda footpath, path, trail

senderar, senderear vi to adopt unusual methods; vt to cut a path through

sendero path, footpath, by-way

sendos, sendas one each, one for each; each

senectud *f* old age, senility

senegalés *n m* + *adj* Senegalese

senil senile

seno breast, bosom; womb; *med* sinus; innermost recess; *math* sine; *archi* spandrel; *naut* bulge of a sail

senojil *m* garter

sensación *f* sensation, feeling

sensacional sensational

sensacionalismo sensationalism

sensacionalista *n m* + *f* + *adj* sensationalist

sensatez *f* sense, good sense

sensato sensible, level-headed

sensibilidad *f* sensitivity

sensibilizar to sensitize, make sensitive

sensible sensitive; perceptible; keen; grievous; *phot* sensitized; tender

sensiblería over-sentimentality

sensiblero gushy, maudlin

sensitiva *bot* sensitive plant, mimosa

sensitivo sensitive, of the senses

sensorio *n anat* sensorium; *adj* sensorial, sensory

sensualidad *f* sensuality

sensualismo sensualism

sensualista sensualistic

sentada sitting, session; sit-in; sit-down protest; **de una ~** at one go/sitting

sentaderas *fpl* behind, backside

sentadero place where one can sit

sentadillas: a ~ side-saddle

sentado sitting, seated; steady

sentamiento *archi* settling

sentar *vt* to seat; set up, establish; *vi* fit; suit; agree with; **~ la cabeza** to settle down; **~ plaza** to join up; **dar por sentado** to take for granted; **los tengo sentados en la boca del estomago** I can't abide them, I can't stomach them; **~se** to sit (down); settle (down); subside, sink

sentencia sentence; judgement, verdict; penalty; *comm* award; dogma; **pronunciar la ~** to pass judgement

sentenciador *m* one who passes judgement

sentenciar to sentence; pass judgement on; condemn; decide; lay down the law

sentención *f* harsh sentence

sentencioso sententious

senticar *m* thicket

sentido sense, perception, feeling; understanding; meaning; direction; **~ común** common sense; **con los cinco ~s** with all one's heart and soul; **en el ~ de que** to the effect that; **costar un ~** to cost the earth; **no tener ~** not to make sense; **perder el ~** to lose consciousness; **sin ~** meaningless

sentimental sentimental, emotional

sentimentalismo sentimentalism, emotionalism

sentimentalista *m* + *f* sentimentalist

sentimiento sentiment, feeling, sorrow, grief; **le acompaño en el ~** please accept my condolence

sentina cess-pit; *naut* bilge; *fig* place of iniquity

sentir *n* feeling; opinion; judgement; **para nuestro ~ de hoy** by today's standards; *v* to feel, judge; foresee; perceive; suffer; feel sorry, regret; grieve, mourn; **sin ~** unnoticed; **~se** to be moved/affected

senyera flag of Catalonia/Valencia

seña sign, mark; signal, nod; *mil* password; **por ~s** by signs; **por más ~s** to be more precise; **santo y ~** password; **~s** address

señal *f* sign, mark; trace; signal; landmark; book-mark; *comm* deposit; traffic-sign; dialling tone; **~ acústica** *mot* horn; **código de ~es** signals code; **en ~ de** as a token of; **ni ~ de** not a sign of

señalado eminent, distinguished, notable; **ocasiones señaladas** special occasions

señalamiento appointed day; marking with signs

señalar to mark, stamp; indicate, make known; fix; make signs; **~ con el dedo** to point a finger at; **~se** to distinguish o.s.

señalización *f* signposting

señalizar to signpost

señera ancient banner

señero solitary

señolear to catch birds with a decoy

señor *n* sir; lord; master; Mr; gentleman; **el Señor** Our Lord; **muy ~ mío** dear sir; **muy ~es míos** dear sirs; **todo**

un ~ a perfect gentleman; *adj* noble, grand; fine, super

señora lady; mistress; Mrs; madam; gentlewoman; **~ de compañía** lady's companion, chaperon; **~ de García** Mrs García; **~ mayor** matron, middle-aged woman; **ella es muy ~** she's every inch a lady; **Nuestra Señora** Our Lady (Virgin Mary)

señorada lordly gesture

señoreador *m* domineering person

señoreante domineering

señorear to dominate, master; tower over; lord it over; be senior (in rank) to; **~se** to put on airs

señoría lordship, ladyship, seigniory

señorial manorial; lordly; feudal; elegant

señoril lordly

señorío lordship; aristocracy, upper class; grand manner, self-control

señorita young lady, Miss; mistress of the house; shop assistant (married or not)

señorito young gentleman; *pej* young toff; *sl* playboy; *fam* master of the house

señuelo lure; decoy

seo cathedral church

sépalo *bot* sepal

separable separable, detachable

separación *f* separation, parting, dismissal; *pol* secession

separado: por ~ separately

separador *m* separator

separar to separate; disconnect; divide; remove; put aside; dismiss; **~se** to part company; come off, come loose; resign, leave, withdraw; separate; part with

separata *print* pull-out section/supplement; off-print

separatismo separatism, secessionism

separatista *m* + *f* separatist, secessionist

sepelio funeral, burial

sepia *zool* cuttlefish

sepsis *f med* blood-poisoning

septena group of seven

septenario *n* period of seven days

septenio period of seven years

Septentrión *m astron* Great Bear

septentrional northern

septeto *mus* septet

septicémico *med* septicemic

séptico septic

septiembre *m* September

séptima run of seven cards; *mus* seventh

séptimo *n* + *adj* seventh

septisílabo of seven syllables

septuagenario septuagenarian

septuagésimo *n* + *adj* seventieth

septuplicar to septuple

séptuplo sevenfold

sepulcro sepulchre, tomb, grave

sepultador *m* grave-digger

sepultar to bury; hide

sepulto buried

sepultura burial, interment, sepulchre, tomb, grave

sepulturero grave-digger

sequedad *f* dryness, sterility; lack of irrigation; gruffness, surliness

sequedal *m*, **sequeral** *m* dry, barren soil

sequero arid and unirrigated land

sequeroso moistureless

sequete *m* dry crust; stale bread; blow, thump; harshness; shock; *fam* curt reply

sequía drought, dryness

sequillo rusk

sequío unirrigated farm land

séquito retinue, suite; followers

sequizo dryish

ser *n m* being, existence; essence; *v* to be, become, belong (to); **~ con** to agree with (another's opinion); **~ de** to be made of; **~ de ver** to be worth seeing; **~ para poco** not be of much use; **~ para todo** to be fit for everything; **de no ~ por** were it not for; **érase que se era, érase una vez** once upon a time; **eso es** that's it; **o sea** that is to say; **no sea que** unless; **si yo fuera usted** if I were you

sera large pannier

seráfico seraphic

serafín *m* seraph

serafina fine baize

serena serenade; evening dew

serenar *vi* to become calm; *vt* to calm (down); **~se** to sober up; calm down

serenata serenade

serení *m naut* jolly-boat; yawl

serenidad *f* serenity, calmness, tranquillity

[1] **sereno** serene, calm, tranquil; *fam* sober

[2] **sereno** member of municipal night police force; night-watchman; **al ~** in

the night air
sergas *fpl* exploits, feats
seriado stereotyped; mass-produced
seriar to mass-produce
sérico silken
sericultura silk culture
serie *f* series, set; **de** ~ mass-produced;
   fabricar en ~ to mass-produce; **fuera**
   de ~ out of the ordinary; **restos de** ~
   remainders
seriedad *f* seriousness; reliability
serio serious, earnest; solemn; reliable;
   en ~ seriously; **una cosa seria** no small
   matter
sermón *m* sermon
sermonario collection of sermons
sermonear to preach (to), lecture
sermoneo preaching, lecturing
serna cultivated field
seroja withered leaf; brushwood
serón *m* pannier, hamper
serpa *bot* layer, runner; sucker
serpear to wriggle, wind
serpentario *orni* secretary bird
serpentear to wriggle, squirm; wind
serpentín *m* coil
serpentina paper streamer
serpentino *adj* serpentine, snake-like;
   winding; sinuous; venomous
serpentón *m mus* serpent
serpiente *f* serpent, snake; ~ **de cascabel**
   rattle-snake
serpigo *med* ring-worm
serpol *m* wild thyme
serpollar *v bot* to sprout, shoot
serpollo *n bot* sprout, shoot
serradizo ready to be sawn
serrado serrated
serrador *m* sawyer
serraduras *fpl* sawdust
serrallo seraglio, harem; brothel
serranía mountain ridge; mountainous
   land
serrano highlander; mountaineer
serrato serrated, denticulated
serrátula *bot* saw-wort
serrín *m* sawdust
serrino *med* (of pulse) irregular
serrucho handsaw; ~ **braguero** sawpit
servato *bot* hog-fennel
serventesio four-line verse rhyming
   a b a b
servible useful, serviceable
servicial serviceable; accommodating;

obsequious; helpful
servicio service, duty; servants; tea/
   coffee/dinner set; toilet; service
   charge; ~ **de escuchas** *rad* monitoring
   service; ~ **de té** teaset; ~ **de recambios**
   spares service; **de** ~ on duty; **hacer un**
   flaco ~ to do scant service
servidero useful, fit for service
servido pleased; **ser** ~ to please, deign
servidor *m* servant, waiter; wooer; ~ **de**
   usted at your service
servidumbre *f* servitude, serfdom; staff
   of servants; obligation; *leg* right; ~ **de**
   la vía (railway) right of way; ~ **de paso**
   right of way, right of access
servil servile, base; humble
servilismo servility, abjectness
servilleta serviette, table-napkin; **doblar**
   la ~ *euph* to die; kick the bucket
servilletero serviette-ring
servio Serbian
servir *vi* to serve, wait at table; do (for);
   be of use; *vt* to serve; help; wait on;
   tend; ~ **para** to serve as, serve for;
   ¿para qué sirve? what's the good of
   it?; **estar servido** to have had it; **para**
   ~ **a usted** at your service; ~**se** to help
   o.s., serve o.s., deign to; **sírvase usted**
   entrar please come in
servitud *f* servitude
servocroata *n m+f* Serbo-Croat
servodirección *f mot* power steering
servomecanismo servomechanism
sesada *cul* fried brains
sésamo sesame
sesear to pronounce c (before e or i) as
   an s
sesenta sixty; sixtieth
sesentavo *n+adj* sixtieth
sesentón *n m* sixty-year-old; *adj* sixty
   years old
seseo pronunciation of c (before e or i)
   as an s
sesera brain-pan
sesga (sewing) gore
sesgadamente on the bias, askew
sesgado oblique, bevelled
sesgadura obliquity, bevel
sesgar to slope; bevel; cut on the bias
sesgo *n* slope; bevel; bias; obliqueness;
   adj sloping; biased; aslant; bevelled;
   severe
sesil *bot* sessile
sesión *f* session, sitting; consultation;

levantar la ~ to adjourn the meeting
sesionar to meet, hold a meeting
[1] **seso** stone to keep a pot steady
[2] **seso** brain(s); intelligence; **devanarse los ~s** to rack one's brains; **levantarse la tapa de los ~s** to blow one's brains out; **no tener ~s** to be lacking in common-sense; **perder el ~** to go mad; **sin ~(s)** scatter-brained
sesquidoble two and a half times
sesquimodio bucket and a half
sestear to take a nap, have forty winks; take a rest/a siesta
sesudo brainy, wise; discreet
seta mushroom; bristle
setecientos seven hundred
setena group of seven; **pagar con las ~s** to suffer excessive punishment
setenta seventy; seventieth
setentavo seventieth
setentón *m* septuagenarian
setiembre *m* September
sétimo *n + adj* seventh
seto fence, paling; enclosure; **~ vivo** hedge
seudo pseudo, false
seudo-artístico arty-arty
seudónimo *n* pseudonym, nom-de-plume; fictitious name
severidad *f* severity, harshness; strictness; austerity
severo severe, harsh; strict; austere
sevicia fierceness
sevillanas *fpl* Sevillan song and dance
sevillano *n + adj* Sevillan
sevillista *n m + f* supporter of Seville Football Club
sexagenario sexagenarian
sexagésimo sixtieth
sexímbolo sex symbol
sexmo administrative district
sexmero mayor of a small town
sexo sex; sexual organs; **~ débil** weaker sex; **bello ~** fair sex; **cambiar de ~ to** change sex; **cambio de ~** sex-change
sexta *m mus* sixth; sequence of six cards
sextante *m naut* sextant
sexteto *mus* sextet
sextilla *lit* six-line verse
sexto sixth
sextuplicación *f* multiplication by six, sextuplication
sextuplicar to sextuple, multiply by six
sextuplo six-fold

sexuado sexed
sexualidad *f* sexuality
sexy *n* sex appeal; *adj* sexy
seycheliano *n + adj* (native) of the Seychelles
shakespeariano Shakespearian
[1] **si** *m mus* B, si
[2] **si** if, whether; **~ bien** although; **por ~ acaso** just in case; **~ ... ~** whether ... or
[1] **sí** himself, herself, itself, oneself, yourself, yourselves, themselves; **de ~** spontaneously; **de por ~** in itself; **fuera de ~** beside o.s. (with emotion); **volver en ~** to come to, recover consciousness
[2] **sí** *n* assent, consent, yes; **dar el ~** to say yes; **por ~ o por no** in any case, at all events; **porque ~** just for the hell of it; **un ~ es no es** just a little; **un día ~ y otro no** every other day; *adv* (used for emphasis): **yo ~ la quiero** I really do love her
siamés *n m + adj* Siamese
sibarita *n m + f + adj* Sybarite
sibarítico Sybaritic
sibaritismo Sybaritism
sibil *m* cave, cellar
sibila sibyl
sibilante sibilant, hissing
sicalipsis *f* erotica, sexiness
sicalíptico erotic, sexy, suggestive
sicario hired assassin
sicativo *chem* drying agent
sicigia *astron* conjunction of sun and moon
Sicilia Sicily
siciliano Sicilian
siclo shekel
sicoanálisis psychoanalysis
sicofanta, sicofante *m* informer, slanderer; sycophant, toady
sicología *see* **psicología**
sicomoro *bot* sycamore
sicosis psychosis
SIDA (síndrome de inmunodeficiencia adquirida) AIDS (acquired immune deficiency syndrome)
sideral, sidéreo sidereal
siderurgia iron and steel industry, siderurgy
siderúrgico siderurgical
sidra cider
sidrería cider-shop

siega reaping, mowing; harvest

siembra sowing, seeding; seed-time; sown field

siempre always; ~ **que** provided that; **para** ~, **por** ~ forever; **por** ~ **jamás** for ever and ever; **lo de** ~ the usual

siempreviva *n bot* everlasting flower; ~ **mayor** houseleek; ~ **menor** stonecrop

sien *f anat* temple

sierpe *f* snake, serpent; *bot* sucker

sierpecilla small snake; winding skyrocket

sierra saw; mountain range; *zool* sawfish; ~ **abrazadera** lumberman's saw; ~ **caladora** coping-saw; ~ **de agua** sawmill; ~ **de arco** bow-saw; ~ **de cinta** band-saw; ~ **de ingletes** tenonsaw; ~ **de mano** hand-saw; ~ **de marquetería** fret-saw; ~ **de trozar** crosscut-saw

siervo servant; serf; slave

sieso *anat* rectum

siesta nap, siesta; hottest part of the day; **echar la** ~ to have a siesta

siete seven, seventh; V-shaped tear in cloth; seventh of the month; **(a) las** ~ (at) seven o'clock; **los** ~ **grandes** the big seven (Spain's seven largest banks)

sieteañal septennial

sieteenrama *bot* tormentil

sietemesino *n* seven-month baby; *fam* little runt; *adj* premature, born seven months after conception

sieteñal *see* **sieteañal**

sífilis *f* syphilis

sifilítico syphilitic

sifón *m* syphon; soda-water

sifosis *f* crooked back

sigilación *f* impression; seal; mark

sigilar to seal; conceal, keep secret

sigilo seal, concealment; discretion; ~ **profesional** professional secrecy; ~ **sacramental** secrecy of the confessional

sigilosidad *f* quality of silence

sigiloso silent; discreet

sigla initials used as an abbreviation

siglo century, age; ~ **de oro** Golden Age; ~s **medios** Middle Ages; **hace** ~s **que** ... it's ages since ...; **por los** ~s **de los** ~s for ever and ever

signáculo signet, seal

signar to mark with a signet; ~**se** to cross o.s.

signatario *n* signatory; *adj* signing

signatura sign, mark; signature

significación *f*, **significado** meaning, significance

significante significant, meaningful

significar to signify, mean; indicate

significativo significant, meaning

signo mark, sign; symbol; nod; flourish (in a signature); *eccles* benediction; *mus* character; ~ **de exclamación,** ~ **de admiración** exclamation mark; ~ **de interrogación** question-mark; ~ **externo** status symbol; ~ **más** *math* plus sign; ~ **menos** *math* minus sign

siguemepollo ribbon adornment hanging down the back

siguiente next, following

sil *m* yellow ochre

sílaba syllable

silabario phonetic reader (book); primer

silabear to syllabize

silabeo syllabication

silábico syllabic

silba *theat* whistle/whistling (showing disapproval); whiz (of a bullet)

silbador *m* whistler, hisser, booer; *adj* whistling, hissing, booing

silbar to whistle, hiss; *fig* hoot, boo; catcall; ring

silbato whistle; crack from which liquid/air hisses

silbido whistle; hiss; hoot, boo; whiz; ~ **de oídos** ringing in the ears

silbo whistle, hiss; whiz

silboso *adj* whistling, hissing; whizzing

silenciador *m mot* silencer, *US* muffler; (on firearm) silencer

silencio silence; quiet(ness); stillness; secrecy; *mus* rest; **guardar** ~ to keep quiet; **pasar en** ~ to omit, not mention

silencioso silent; still; quiet

silepsis *f* syllepsis

silero *agri* silo

silesiano Silesian

sílfide *f*, **silfo** sylph

silicato silicate

sílice *min* silica, silex

silicio *n* silicon

silogismo syllogism

silogístico syllogistic(al)

silogizar to syllogize; reason

silueta silhouette; (of a person) figure
siluro *zool* catfish; *mil* torpedo
silva verse; anthology; miscellany
silvático rustic, sylvan
silvestre wild; uncultivated; rustic
silvicultor *m* forester
silvicultura forestry
silvoso sylvan, wooded
silla chair; *eccles* see; ~ **de la reina** chair made by two persons holding hands; ~ **de manos** sedan chair; ~ **de montar** saddle; ~ **de posta** post-chaise; ~ **de ruedas** wheel-chair; ~ **de tijera** folding-chair; ~ **giratoria** revolving chair; ~ **plegadiza** folding chair, camping chair; ~ **poltrona** easy chair; ~ **volante** gig; **de** ~ **a** ~ tête-à-tête, heart to heart
sillar *m archi* ashlar stone; back (of a horse)
[1] **sillería** chair factory; set of chairs
[2] **sillería** *eccles* ashlar masonry
silleta small chair; bedpan
silletero chair-maker; sedan-chair carrier
sillín *m* harness saddle; mule chair; cycle saddle
sillón *m* armchair; side-saddle
sima abyss, chasm
simado deep
simbiosis *f* symbiosis
simbiótico symbiotic
simbólico symbolic(al)
simbolismo symbolism
simbolización *f* symbolization
simbolizar to symbolize, typify
símbolo symbol; ~ **de la fe** creed, articles of religion; ~ **fálico** phallic symbol
simetría symmetry
simétrico symmetric(al)
simia female ape
símico simian
simiente *f* seed, grain; sperm; **quedar para** ~ to go to seed
simiesco ape-like
símil *n m* similarity; simile; comparison; *adj* similar, like, alike
similitud *f* similarity
similitudinario similar
similor *m* poor-quality brass; **de** ~ sham, fake
simio ape, simian
simón *m* hack, cab; cabby

simonía simony
simoníaco simoniacal
simpatía friendliness; fellow-feeling; *med* sympathy; **tener** ~ **por** to like, be fond of
simpaticectomía *med* sympathectomy
simpático friendly, congenial, pleasant; **me cae** ~ I like him/her
simpatizador *adj* sympathizing
simpatizante *n m+f* supporter; sympathizer; *adj* favouring, supporting
simpatizar to have a liking (**con** for); hit it off (**con** with), sympathize
simple *n m+f* simpleton; *adj* simple, mere; single; foolish; plain; insipid
simpleza foolishness; foolish act; rusticity; ~s nonsense
simplicidad *f* simplicity
simplificación *f* simplification
simplificar to simplify
simplista *n m+f* simplist; herbalist; *adj* simplistic; oversimplifying
simposio symposium
simulación *f* simulation, pretence
simulacro simulacrum, idol; mockery, sham; *mil* sham battle
simulador *n* dissembler; *adj* dissembling
simular to simulate, feign; fake, sham
simultaneidad *f* simultaneity
simultáneo simultaneous
simún *m* sandstorm; sirocco
sin without, besides, not counting; ~ **comentarios** no comment; ~ **comerlo ni beberlo** undeservedly; ~ **decir oxte ni moxte** without more ado; ~ **embargo** however, nevertheless; ~ **pies ni cabeza** without rhyme or reason; ~ **satisfacer** unsatisfied; ~ **terminar** unfinished; ~ **ton ni son** without rhyme or reason
sinagoga synagogue
sinalefa *gramm* synalepha
sinapismo sinapism, mustard plaster; bore
sincerador *m* exculpator, excuser
sincerar to exculpate; vindicate; ~**se** to open one's heart (**con** to), speak frankly (**con** with)
sinceridad *f* sincerity
sincero sincere
síncopa *gramm* syncope; syncopation
sincopar to syncopate; abridge; ~**se** *med* (of the heart) to miss a beat
síncope *f* fainting-fit; syncope

461

sincopizar to produce a fainting fit in; produce a syncope; ~**se** to faint, have a fit, miss a beat

sincrónico synchronous, synchronic

sincronismo synchronism

sincronizar to synchronize

sindéresis *f* good judgement, discretion

sindicado syndicate

sindical *adj* syndical; trade union

sindicalismo syndicalism; trade-union-ism

sindicalista *n m+f +adj* syndicalist; trade-unionist

sindicalizar to syndicalize; organize into a trade union

sindicar to accuse; syndicate; ~**se** to band into a trade union; join a union

sindicato trade union; syndicate; ~ **vertical** company union; **casarse por el** ~ to marry, the bride being pregnant

síndico receiver; syndic

sindiós *n m+f* unbeliever, atheist; *adj* godless

síndrome *m* syndrome; ~ **de abstinencia** withdrawal syndrome

sinecura sinecure

sinéresis *f sing+pl gramm* syneresis

sinfín *m* no end, endless amount/number

sínfito *bot* comfrey

sinfonía symphony

sinfónico symphonic

sinfonista *m+f* symphonist

singa *naut* sculling (over the stern)

Singapur Singapore

singladura *naut* day's run; voyage

singlar *naut* to sail

singlón *m naut* futtock

singularidad *f* singularity; oddity

singularización *f* singularization; singling out

singularizar to singularize; single out; ~**se** to make a name for o.s.; be the odd man out

singulto hiccough; sob

sínico Chinese

siniestra left-hand; left-hand side

siniestrado victim (of flood, fire *etc*)

siniestro *n* perverseness; wreck; disaster; accident; *comm* damage, loss; *adj* sinister; left-hand; ill-omened

sinnúmero endless succession; **un ~ de** no end of

[1] **sino** but, except, only; **no solo ... ~**
también not only ... but also

[2] **sino** fate, destiny

sinodal synodal; *astron* synodic

sínodo synod

sinófilo sinophile

sinojaponés Sino-Japanese

sinología Sinology

sinologista *m+f* Sinologist

sinónimo *n* synonym; *adj* synonymous

sinopsis *f* synopsis

sinóptico synoptic

sinrazón *f* unreason; wrong, injustice

sinsabor *m* displeasure; anxiety; trouble

sinsonte *m orni* mocking-bird

sinsostenismo 'no-bra' craze, 'burn-the-bra' movement

sinsostenista 'burn-the-bra' advocate; extreme feminist

sinsubstancia *m+f* fat-head

sintáctico syntactic(al)

sintaxis *f sing + pl gramm* syntax

síntesis *f sing+pl* synthesis

sintético synthetic

sintetizar to synthesize

síntoma *m* symptom

sintomático symptomatic(al)

sintonía tuning, tune; theme song

sintonización *f* tuning

sintonizador *n m rad* tuner; *adj* tuning

sintonizar *rad* to tune; ~ **con** to tune in to

sinuosidad *f* sinuosity; deviousness

sinuoso sinuous; winding; devious

sinvergüencería shamelessness; caddish behaviour

sinvergüenza scoundrel, rascal; cad, rotter; cheeky person

Sión Zion

sionismo Zionism

sionista *n m+f +adj* Zionist

siquiatría psychiatry

síquico psychic(al)

siquier, siquiera (al)though; scarcely, hardly; even; ~ **un poco** a little bit; **ni** ~ not even

sirena mermaid; siren, foghorn

sirga tow rope; **a la** ~ tracking from the shore; **caballo de** ~ canal-barge horse

sirgadura towing

sirgar to tow, track

sirgo twisted material made of silk

sirguero goldfinch

Siria Syria

siriano, sirio Syrian

sirte *f naut* hidden shoal/sandbank

sirvienta servant-girl, maid

sirviente *m* serving-man, manservant

¹ **sisa** gilder's size

² **sisa** petty theft; (sewing) dart; excise; armhole

sisador *m* petty thief, pilferer

¹ **sisar** to pilfer; (sewing) take in; put a tax on

² **sisar** to size

sisear to hiss

siseo hiss, hissing

sisero excise-man

sísmico seismic

sismógrafo seismograph

sismograma *m* seismogram

sismología seismology

sismológico seismological

sismómetro seismometer

sisón *n m* pilferer; *orni* little bustard; *adj* pilfering

sistema *m* system, method; **el** ~ the establishment; ~ **de guía** *space* guidance system; ~ **de guía a la base de origen** homing system; ~ **nervioso** nervous system

sistemático systematic

sistematización *f* systemization

sistematizar to systematize

sistematología systematology

sitacosis *f* psittacosis, parrot-fever

sitiador *n m* besieger; *adj* besieging, investing

sitial *m* seat of honour; president's chair

sitiar to besiege, invest; hem in, surround

sitibundo thirsty

sitio place, spot, site, location; room, space; siege; country seat; royal residence; **cambiar de** ~ to change places; **dejar** ~ **a** to make/leave room for; **en cualquier** ~ anywhere; **poner** ~ **a** to lay siege to; **quedarse en el** ~ to die on the spot

sito located, situated

situación *f* situation, position, location; condition, state; ~ **activa** active service/position/office; ~ **pasiva** position of a retired person; **en** ~ **de** in a position to

situar to place, put, situate; locate; *comm* remit; ~**se** to get/take a position; settle down in a place

sixtino Sistine

skay *m* imitation leather

slip *m* briefs; knickers; underpants; swimming-trunks

smoking *m* dinner-jacket, *US* tuxedo

snifada *sl* inhalation of a narcotic drug

¹ **so** under, below; ~ **capa de** under pretext of; ~ **pena de** under sentence of, on pain of

² **¡so!** whoa!, stop!

soasar to half-roast; cook lightly

soba pawing, petting; beating, beating up; kneading

sobaco *anat* armpit; *bot* axil

sobadero tannery

sobado *n* beating, flogging; *adj* hackneyed; (of bread) close-textured; shabby, worn

sobadura, sobajadura kneading; rubbing

sobajanero *fam* errand-boy

sobajar to squeeze; rub hard

sobao kind of sponge-cake

sobaquera arm-hole (in garment)

sobar to knead; finger, paw; *fam* pet, neck, snog

sobarbada sudden check; reprimand, scolding

sobarbo *mech* cam, pawl

sobarcar to carry under the arm; pull clothes up to the arm-holes

soberanear to domineer, lord it

soberanía sovereignty

soberano *n* sovereign; *adj* sovereign; supreme

soberbia *n* (excessive) pride, arrogance

soberbio haughty, overproud, vain; superb, magnificent; high-spirited

sobina wooden peg

sobón *m* one fond of necking/petting

sobordo *naut* checking of a ship's manifest

sobornación *f see* **soborno**

sobornado badly shaped loaf of bread

sobornador *n* briber, suborner

sobornal *m* overload

sobornar to bribe, suborn; incite

soborno bribe; bribery; incitement

sobra excess, surplus; remains; ~**s** leftovers; **de** ~ more than enough; **estar de** ~ to be superfluous, be not wanted; **saber de** ~ to know only too well

sobradar to add a loft to

sobradillo loft, penthouse

sobrado *n* attic, loft; *adj* more than enough, to spare; exaggerated; ostentatious

sobrancero *adj* unemployed

sobrante *n m* surplus, excess; *adj* remaining, left over, surplus

sobrar to be surplus, be left-over, be more than enough; **le sobra dinero** he has too much money; **le sobra razón** he has every right, right is on his side

sobrasada type of sausage

sobrasar *cul* to add fuel

sobre *n m* envelope; sachet; *prep* (up)on, above, over, concerning; in addition to; ~ **poco más o menos** more or less; ~ **que** on top of the fact that; **estar** ~ **sí** to be out of control, be on the look-out; **ir** ~ to go in pursuit of; **2 grados** ~ **cero** 2 degrees above freezing; ~ **todo** above all; ~ **las 3** about 3 o'clock

sobreabundancia superabundance

sobreabundante superabundant

sobreactuación *f* overacting

sobreactuar to overact

sobreaguar to float

sobreagudo *mus* highest treble

sobrealiento gasping, difficulty in breathing

sobrealimentación *f* overfeeding

sobrealimentar to overfeed

sobrealzar to extol, over-praise

sobreañal over a year old

sobreasada *see* **sobrasada**

sobreasar to re-roast

sobrebarato dirt cheap

sobreboya *naut* marking-buoy

sobrecaja outer casing

sobrecalentar to overheat

sobrecalza leggings

sobrecama bedspread, coverlet

sobrecarga overload; surcharge; extra trouble

sobrecargar to overload; surcharge; overcharge

sobrecargo *naut*+*aer* purser

sobrecarta envelope

sobreceja forehead

sobrecejo, sobreceño frown

sobrecercar (sewing) to welt

sobrecerco (sewing) welt

sobrecogedor startling

sobrecoger to overawe; take by surprise;

catch red-handed; ~**se** to become afraid; be startled

sobrecogimiento fear, apprehension

sobrecomida dessert

sobrecopa lip of a cup

sobrecoser (sewing) to whip

sobrecrecer to grow on top; outgrow

sobrecreciente growing on top; outgrowing

sobrecostura (sewing) whip-stitch

sobrecubierta book jacket; *naut* upper deck

sobredicho above-mentioned, aforesaid

sobredorar to plate with gold; gloss over

sobreedificar to build over/on top of

sobreexcitación *f* over-excitement

sobreexcitar to over-excite

sobrefalda overskirt

sobrefaz *f* surface; outside

sobrefino superfine

sobreguarda second/reserve guard

sobrehaz *f see* **sobrefaz**

sobreherido slightly wounded

sobrehilar (sewing) to overcast

sobrehueso *vet* splint; *fig* burden

sobrehumano superhuman

sobrehusa fried fish stew

sobreimpresión *phot* overprint, double exposure

sobreimpuesto super-tax, surtax

sobrellave *m* keeper of the keys at a royal residence

sobrellenar to overfill; overflow

sobrelleno overfull

sobrellevar to ease another's burden; endure; suffer in silence

sobremanera exceedingly

sobremesa tablecloth; dessert; after-dinner conversation; **de** ~ after dinner

sobrenadar to float; remain on the surface

sobrenatural supernatural

sobrenombre *m* nickname

sobrentender to understand; ~**se** to go without saying, be taken for granted

sobrepaga extra pay; increased pay; bonus

sobrepaño outer cloth; wrapper

sobreparto confinement after giving birth

sobrepasar to exceed

sobrepeine *n m* hair-trimming; *adv* slightly, briefly

sobrepelliz *f* surplice

sobrepeso excess weight

sobreponer to place above/over/upon; superimpose; ~**se** to overcome; pull o.s. together

sobreposición *f* superposition

sobreprecio extra charge, surcharge

sobreproducción *f* over-production

sobreproducir to over-produce

sobrepuerta *archi* cornice; door-curtain; pelmet

¹ **sobrepuesto** *n* honeycomb (made outside the hive)

² **sobrepuesto** superposed

sobrepuja outbidding

sobrepujante excelling, surpassing

sobrepujanza great strength

sobrepujar to excel, surpass

sobreropa overalls; overcoat

sobresaliente *n m* 'distinction' mark (in examination); substitute, understudy; *adj* outstanding, excellent; projecting

sobresalir to stand out, protrude; excel; be prominent

sobresaltar *vi* to stand out; *vt* to startle; ~**se** to be startled

sobresalto start, scare, fright; **de** ~ suddenly, unexpectedly

sobresanar to heal superficially, heal over

sobresano superficially healed, healed over

sobrescribir to superscribe; address (a letter *etc*)

sobrescrito address (of a letter *etc*)

sobreseer *leg vi* to desist; *vt* to stay

sobreseimiento suspension; *leg* stay (of proceedings)

sobresembrar to sow again

sobresolar to re-pave; resole (footwear)

sobrestante *m* foreman; overseer, supervisor

sobresueldo additional pay, extra pay

sobresuelo overlaid floor

sobretarde *f* dusk, twilight

sobretodo *n* overcoat, *US* topcoat

sobreveedor *m* chief supervisor

sobrevenida supervention; unexpected arrival

sobrevenir to arrive unexpectedly; happen suddenly

sobreverterse to overflow, run over

sobrevestir to put on over other clothes

sobrevidriera window-grille; storm window

sobrevienta sudden gust of wind; *fig* surprise attack

sobreviento gust of wind; *naut* **estar a** ~ to have the wind of

sobrevista beaver (of a helmet)

sobreviviente *n m+f* survivor; *adj* surviving

sobrevivir to survive; ~ **a** to outlive

sobrexcedente exceeding, surpassing

sobrexceder to surpass, exceed

sobrexcitación *f* over-excitement

sobrexcitar to over-excite

sobriedad *f* sobriety, moderation

sobrina niece

sobrino nephew

socaire *m naut* lee; **al** ~ **de** under the shelter of; **estar al** ~ *fam* to shirk work

socairero *naut* shirker; skulker

socaliña cunning ruse

socalzar *archi* to underpin

socapa pretext; **a** ~ on the sly

socarra singe(ing); cunning

socarrar to singe, scorch

socarrén *m* gable-end; eave

socarrena space between rafters

socarrón ironic, wryly funny; sly

socava, **socavación** *f* undermining; digging round trees

sociabilidad *f* sociability

social social; **razón** ~ trade name; **sede** ~ head office (of a company)

socialdemócrata *m+f* social democrat

socialismo socialism

socialista *n m+f* socialist; *adj* social-ist(ic)

socialistizante *n m+f +adj* (one) having socialist leanings

socialización *f* socialization, nationalization

socializar to socialize, nationalize; live in a commune

sociedad *f* society, company; ~ **anónima** limited company; ~ **benéfica** charitable organization; welfare state; ~ **colectiva** joint-stock company; ~ **en comandita** partnership; **entrar en** ~ to come out (in society)

socio partner, member; chap, guy; ~ **capitalista** financial partner; ~ **comanditario** sleeping partner, *US* silent partner; ~ **industrial** working partner; **hacerse** ~ **de** to join, become a member of

socioeconómico socio-economic

sociología sociology

sociológico sociological

sociólogo sociologist

socolor *m* pretext, pretence

socollada *naut* pitching (in rough weather)

socorredor *n m* helper; *adj* helping

socorrer to help, succour; give alms to

socorrido helpful; handy, useful

socorrista *m+f* first-aider

socorro help, succour, aid, assistance; alms; *comm* part payment of an account; **puesto de** ~ first-aid post

socrático Socratic

socucho den, dive; poky place

sochantre *m eccles* choirmaster

sódico sodic; **carbonato** ~ sodium carbonate

sodio sodium

sodomía sodomy

sodomita *n m+f +adj* sodomite

sodomítico sodomitical

soez filthy, obscene

sofá *m* couch, sofa, *US* davenport

sofaldar to tuck up, lift up

sofaldo tucking up

sofión *m* snort (of disapproval); dressing down

sofisma sophism

sofista *m+f* sophist

sofistería sophistry

sofisticación *f* sophistication; falsification; adulteration

sofisticar to sophisticate; falsify; adulterate

sofístico sophistical

sofito *arch* soffit

soflamar to make blush; deceive; ~**se** to get scorched; be taken in (deceived)

soflamero trickster

sofocación *f* suffocation; choking; embarrassing situation

sofocante suffocating, choking

sofocar to suffocate, choke, smother; extinguish, quench; make blush; ~**se** to suffocate, choke; blush, become embarrassed, get all het up, get hot and bothered

sofoco suffocation; annoyance; upset, vexation; shame

sofocón *m* annoyance

sofrenada severe reprimand

sofrenar to check sharply

sofrenazo *see* **sofrenada**

sofrito *n cul* anything lightly fried; *adj* lightly fried

¹ **soga** rope, halter, cord; *bui* face (of brick); **con la** ~ **al cuello** *fig* with water up to one's neck; **dar** ~ **a** to take the mickey out of; **echar la** ~ **tras el caldero** to throw the whole thing up; **hacer** ~ to lag behind; **mentar la** ~ **en casa del ahorcado** to be tactless

² **soga** cunning person

soguear to measure with a cord

soguería rope-walk; rope-making

soguero rope-maker/dealer

soja soya

sojuzgador *n m* conqueror, subduer; *adj* conquering, subduing

sojuzgamiento subjugation

sojuzgar to conquer, subdue, subjugate

¹ **sol** *m* sun(light); day; silver coin; *fam* darling; **a** ~ **puesto** at sunset; **al salir el** ~ at daybreak, at sunrise; **arrimarse al** ~ **que más calienta** know on which side one's bread is buttered; **de** ~ **a** ~ from dawn to sunset; **hace (mucho)** ~ it is (very) sunny; **limpio como un** ~ clean as a whistle; **tomar el** ~, **tomar baños de** ~ to sunbathe

² **sol** *m mus* sol, G

solada dregs, lees, sediment

solado pavement; tiled floor; paving

solador *m* paver; tiler

soladura paving, flooring; paving/flooring materials

solampiar to eat alone and in a hurry

solana sunny place; sun-trap; hottest part of the day

solanera sunstroke; hot sunshine; hot and sunny place

solano hot east wind; *bot* nightshade

solapa lapel; book-jacket; **de** ~ sneakily; **junta de** ~ lap joint

solapado artful, cunning

solapadura overlap

solapar to put lapels on; overlap; conceal

solape *m*, **solapo** lapel, pretence; **a** ~ sneakily

¹ **solar** *m* building plot, *US* lot; ancestral home; lineage

² **solar** *adj* solar, (of the) sun

³ **solar** *v* to pave, floor; sole (footwear)

solariego manorial; **casa solariega** ancestral home

solas: a ~ alone

solaz *m* solace, relaxation; **a ~** pleasantly

solazar to solace

solazo scorching sun

solazoso affording solace

soldada wages; pay

soldadesca *n* soldiery, indisciplined troops

soldadesco *adj* soldier

soldado soldier; **~ raso** private, ranker

soldador *m* solderer, welder; soldering-iron

soldadote *m fam* thick-headed soldier; blimp

soldadura soldering, solder; welding; correction; **~ autógena** welding

soldán *m* sultan

soldar to solder; weld; mend

soleá song and dance of Andalusia

solear to sun; put in the sun

solecismo solecism

soledad *f* solitude, loneliness; lonely place; *mus* Andalusian song and dance

solejar *m* place exposed to the sun

solemne solemn; sober-looking

solemnidad *f* solemnity; ceremony; impressiveness; **~es** formalities; **pobre de ~** poor as a church mouse

solemnización *f* solemnization

solemnizador *n m* solemnizer; *adj* solemnizing

solemnizar to solemnize, celebrate

solenoide *m elect* solenoid

soler to be in the habit of; **solía vivir en Madrid** he used to live in Madrid; **suele venir los martes** he usually comes on Tuesdays

solera *archi* crossbeam; rib; lintel; stone slab; **vino de ~** vintage wine

solercia shrewdness

solería flooring, paving; leather for soles

solero lower mill-stone

solerte shrewd

solevación *f*, **solevamiento** *see* **sublevación**

solevantado worried

solevantar, solevar *see* **sublevar**

solfa *mus* sol-fa; musical annotation; music harmony; spanking; **tomar a ~** to see the ridiculous side of

solfear *mus* to sol-fa; *fam* spank

solfeo *mus* sol-fa; *fam* spanking

solferino reddish-purple

solfista *m+f* sol-fa-ist, singer

solicitación *f* request

solicitado in demand, sought after

solicitador *n m* agent; *adj* soliciting

solicitante *n m+f* applicant; *adj* soliciting

solicitar to request, apply for

solícito solicitous; keen to please

solicitud *f* solicitude; application; request

solidar to make firm, consolidate

solidaridad *f* solidarity, sympathy

solidario *leg* jointly liable; **hacerse ~ de/con** to express one's sympathy for/with

solidarizar *leg* to make jointly liable; **~se** to express sympathy (**con** for)

solidez *f* solidity; firmness; soundness

solidificación *f* solidification

solidificar(se) to solidify

sólido solid; strong; sound; (colour) fast

soliloquiar to soliloquize

soliloquio soliloquy, monologue

solista *m+f* soloist

solitaria *med* tapeworm

solitario *n* hermit, recluse; (game) patience, solitaire; *adj* solitary, lone(ly)

sólito usual, customary

solitud *f* solitude, loneliness; lonely place

soliviantado worried

soliviantar to stir up, incite

soliviar to raise up, prop up

solo alone, by o.s., lone; **a solas** alone

sólo only, solely; just

solomillo *cul* sirloin

solsticial solstitial

solsticio solstice

soltadizo easily untied

soltador *adj* loosening

soltar to untie, unfasten; slacken; release; let go, let out; *naut* cast off; *fam* utter; *fam* give (a kick/slap *etc*); tell; *sl* cough up (pay); **~ una carcajada** to burst out laughing; **~se** to become loose, come undone; begin to get fluent

soltería bachelorhood, spinsterhood

soltera spinster, unmarried woman

soltero *n* bachelor, unmarried man; *adj* unmarried, single

solterón *m* confirmed bachelor

solterona old maid

soltura looseness; ease; fluency; confidence

solubilidad *f* solubility

solución *f* solution; loosening, untying; **no tiene** ~ it's a waste of time, it's a dead loss; **sin** ~ **de continuidad** without interruption

solucionar to solve, sort out

solvencia solvency; trustworthiness

solventar to settle (debts); solve

sollamar to scorch, singe

sollastre *m* scullion, kitchen boy; rogue

sollastría scullery

sollo sturgeon

sollozar to sob

sollozo sob

somalí *adj* Somali

Somalia Somalia

somatén *m* volunteer defence force; alarm call

somatología somatology

somatológico somatological

sombra shade, shadow; rough likeness; *astron* umbra; **hacer** ~ **a** to shade; **ni por** ~ not by any stretch of the imagination; **poner a la** ~ to put away; **tener buena** ~ to be likeable; be lucky; **tener mala** ~ to be dull, be tactless; be unlucky

sombraje *m* hut roofed with branches

sombrajo shed, hut, shack; *fam* shadow cast by one person on another

sombrar to overshadow

sombreado *arts* shading

sombrerera milliner; hatter's wife; hat-box

sombrerería milliner's shop; hat-factory

sombrerero hatter

sombrerete *m* bonnet, cap

sombrero hat; ~ **apuntado** cocked hat; ~ **de copa** top-hat; ~ **de jipijapa** panama hat; ~ **de paja** straw hat; ~ **de tres picos** three-cornered hat; ~ **flexible** felt hat, trilby; ~ **hongo** bowler, *US* derby; ~ **jarano** Mexican straw hat

sombría shady place

sombrilla parasol, sunshade

sombrío *n* shady place; *adj* gloomy, sombre, murky; taciturn; *arts* shaded

sombroso shady

somero slight, superficial

someter to submit, subject; subdue; ~**se** to yield; acquiesce

sometimiento submission, acquiescence

somier *m* bedspring

somnambulismo *see* sonambulismo

somnámbulo *see* sonámbulo

somnífero *n* sleeping draught, sleeping pill; *adj* somniferous; soporific

somnílocuo *adj* talking while asleep

somnolencia sleepiness, drowsiness

somnoliento somnolent

somo summit

somorgujador *orni* diver

somorgujar *vi* to dive; *vt* to duck

somorgujo *orni* grebe; **a lo** ~ under water

son *m* sound; tune; rumour; **¿a qué** ~? why on earth?; **bailar al** ~ **que le tocan** to dance to any tune (change according to circumstances); **en** ~ **de …** in a … way; **sin ton ni** ~ without rhyme or reason

sonable sonorous; loud

sonada tune

sonadera blowing the nose

sonadero handkerchief

sonado much talked of, famous; crazy

sonador *n m* handkerchief; *adj* noise-producing

sonaja jingle, timbrel

sonajero baby's rattle

sonambulismo somnambulism, sleep-walking

sonámbulo *n* somnambulist, sleep-walker; *adj* sleep-walking

sonante sounding; **dinero contante** y ~ ready cash

sonar to sound; ring; chime; tinkle; have a familiar sound; **como suena** it's as true as I'm standing here; **suena a mentira** it sounds like a lie; ~**se** to blow one's nose

sonda *n med* catheter; probe; *naut* heaving the lead

sondable that can be sounded

sondaleza *naut* lead-line

sondar, sondear to sound; probe; conduct an opinion poll

sondeo opinion poll; investigation; *min* drilling; sounding

sonetear to write sonnets

sonetista *m* + *f* writer of sonnets

soneto sonnet

sónico sonic; **estampido** ~ sonic boom

sonido sound, noise

sonochada *mil* evening watch

sonochar *mil* to keep watch during the early evening

sonoridad *f* sonority

sonoro sonorous, loud; *phon* voiced; **banda sonora** sound-track

sonreír to smile

sonrisa smile

sonrisueño smiling

sonrojar, sonrojear to cause to blush; ~**se** to blush

sonrojo blush; word which makes s.o. blush; shame

sonrosado pink

sonrosar, sonrosear to dye red; ~**se** to blush, flush

sonroseo blush, flush

sonsaca wheedling; enticing; drawing out

sonsacador *m* wheedler, coaxer; enticer; petty thief

sonsacamiento wheedling; extortion

sonsacar to wheedle, coax; pilfer

sonsaque *m* wheedling; enticement; petty theft

sonsonete *m* sing-song tone; rhythmical tapping; scornful tone

soñador *n m* dreamer; *adj* dreaming, dreamy

soñar to dream; ~ **con** to dream about; ~ **despierto** to daydream; ni ~**lo** not on your life

soñera, soñolencia sleepiness, drowsiness

soñollento sleepy, drowsy; lazy, sluggish

sopa soup; ~ **de gato** thin soup; **a la ~ boba** sponging; **hecho una ~** wet through

sopaipa honey fritter

sopalancar to raise with a lever

sopanda brace; lintel joist

sopapear to slap; call names

sopapo chuck under the chin

sopar, sopear to dunk; trample; maltreat

sopera soup tureen

sopero *n* soup plate; *adj* (of) soup; fond of soup

sopesar to weigh up

sopetear to dunk; maltreat

sopeteo dunking, dipping

[1] **sopetón**: de ~ suddenly

[2] **sopetón** *m* toasted bread in oil; slap

sopicaldo watery soup

sopista *m+f* one who lives on charity

sopita light soup; lovely soup

sopitipando *fam* faint, swoon

¡sopla! bless my soul!

sopladero blow-hole

soplado *n min* deep fissure; *adj* overnice, stuck up; drunk

soplador *m* blower, blowing-fan; *adj* blowing

sopladura blow-hole

soplamocos *m sing+pl* slap

soplar to blow (on), fan; blow up; blow out; *fam* filch, pinch; (draughts) huff; whisper; prompt; drink up; *sl* inform (the police); ~**se** to eat up; booze up; give the game away

soplete *m* blowpipe; blow-lamp

soplido puff, blast; *sl* information (given to the police)

soplo puff, breath; gust; blowing; *fam* jiffy; *sl* tip-off; **ir con el ~** to blow the gaff, spill the beans

soplón *m sl* informer, squealer, grass

soponcio fainting

sopor *m* drowsiness, lethargy

soporífero soporiferous

soporífico soporific; sleeping-draught, sleeping-pill

soportal *m* arcade, portico

soportable tolerable, endurable, bearable

soporte *m* support; bracket; stand

sopuntar to underline with dots

sor *f eccles* sister

sorbedor sucking, absorbing

sorber to sip, suck; absorb; soak up; swallow up

sorbete *m* sherbet; water-ice

sorbetón *m* large draught; gulp

sorbible that can be sipped

sorbo sip; swallow; gulp, swig

sordera, sordez *f* deafness

sordidez *f* sordidness, squalor; stinginess

sórdido sordid, squalid; stingy

sordina *mus* mute; damper (on piano); **a la ~** on the quiet

sordino *mus* small fiddle

sordo *n* deaf person; *adj* deaf, mute; noiseless; muffled; (of pain) dull; irrational; ~ **como una tapia** deaf as a post; **a la sorda, a sordas** noiselessly; **hacerse el ~** to feign deafness

sordomudez *f* deaf-mutism

sordomudo *n* deaf-mute; *adj* deaf and

dumb

soriano *n* native of Soria; *adj* from Soria

sorna sarcasm, irony; malice; sluggishness

soroche *m* mountain sickness; shortage of breath at high altitudes

sorprendente surprising

sorprender to surprise, astonish; come upon; overhear; catch red-handed

sorpresa surprise; **de ~** by surprise

sorrostrada insolence, brusqueness; **dar ~ to** taunt, mock; insult

sorteable that can be raffled; avoidable; *mil* eligible to be conscripted

sorteador *m* one who draws lots; one who gets around; skilled bullfighter

sorteamiento raffling, drawing lots; casting lots

sortear to draw/cast lots; dodge, get round; (bullfighting) dodge, avoid

sorteo raffle; drawing/casting of lots; dodging

sortero fortune-teller

sortiaria fortune-telling by cards

sortija ring; hair-curl; **~ de sello** signet ring

sortilegio sorcery; charm, spell

sortílega sorceress

sortílego sorcerer

sosa soda; kelp

sosaina *m+f* dull person; one lacking in personality

sosal *m*, **sosar** *m* soda-bearing land

sosegado quiet, peaceful, calm

sosegador *n m* appeaser, peacemaker; *adj* calming, quieting

sosegar *vi* to rest; *vt* to calm, quiet; **~se** to become quiet, calm down

sosería dullness; tranquillity

sosero soda-yielding

sosia *m* double

sosiego rest after toil; nightcap

soslayar to place sideways; dodge

soslayo oblique, slanting; **al/de ~** obliquely, slantingly; askance

soso insipid, tasteless; dull, dreary

sospecha suspicion

sospechable suspicious, suspect

sospechar *vi* to be suspicious; *vt* to suspect; imagine; **~ de** to suspect, distrust

sospechoso *n* suspect; *adj* suspicious

sospesar to weigh up

sosquín *m* treacherous blow; back-

hander

sostén *m* support, maintenance; *naut* stability (of a ship); bra

sostenedor *n m* supporter, upholder; *adj* supporting

sostener to support, hold up; sustain; uphold

sostenido supported; kept up; upheld; *mus* sharp

sostenimiento sustenance; maintenance, upkeep; support; **muro de ~** retaining wall

sota knave/jack (cards); hussy; jade; **es ~ caballo y rey** there's only Hobson's choice

sotacola crupper

sotana cassock; *fam* flogging, beating

sotanear to beat, flog; reprimand

sótano cellar, basement

sotaventarse *naut* to fall to leeward

sotavento *naut* lee(ward); **a ~** under the lee

sotayuda assistant steward

sotechado shed, hut

soterramiento burial

soterraño underground, subterranean

soterrar to bury; conceal

sotillo copse

soto *n* copse; *prefix* under, beneath, below

sotreta nag, sorry horse

sotrozo *mech* axle-pin, linch-pin

soviético *adj* Soviet

sovietizar to sovietize

Sr (Señor) Mr

Sra (Señora) Mrs

Srta (Señorita) Miss

standing *m* high class; top quality

statu quo *m* status quo

striptisismo strip-tease

su, sus his, her, its, your, their, one's

suasorio suasive

suave smooth; soft; mild, gentle

suavidad *f* smoothness; softness; mildness; gentleness

suavizador *n m* razor-strop; softener; *adj* softening; mollifying

suavizar to smooth; soften; mollify

subacuático undersea, underwater

subafluente *m* tributary (of a river)

subalternar to subdue, subject

subalterno *n+adj* subaltern; subordinate

subarrendador *m* sub-letter; sub-lessee;

sub-tenant

subarrendamiento sub-letting, sub-leasing

subarrendar to sub-let; sub-lease

subarrendatario sub-lessor; sub-lessee; sub-tenant

subarriendo sub-renting; sub-lease

subasta, subastación *f* auction sale; tender; **sacar a pública ~** to sell by auction

subastador *m* auctioneer

subastar to auction (off), sell by auction

subcampeón *m sp* runner-up

subclase *f biol* sub-class

subcolector *m* assistant collector

subcomendador *m* deputy-commander

subcomisión *f* sub-commission, sub-committee

subconsciente *n m + adj* subconscious

subcontratar to sub-contract

subcontratista *m* sub-contractor

subcontrato sub-contract

subcutáneo subcutaneous

subdesarrollado underdeveloped

subdesarrollo underdevelopment

subdiácono sub-deacon

subdirector *m* assistant manager

súbdito *n + adj* subject, citizen

subdividir to subdivide

subdivisión *f* subdivision

subejecutor *m* deputy executor; sub-agent

subdominante *f mus* subdominant

subentender to understand what is merely implied

subestimar to underestimate

subgénero *biol + zool* sub-genus

subgobernador *m* deputy-governor

subida *n* ascent, climbing; accession; rise

subidero *n* ladder; up-gradient; uphill road; *adj* climbing, raising

subido raised up; high; fine, superior; (of colours) vivid; risqué

subidor *m* lift, *US* elevator

subiente rising, ascending

subilla awl

subimiento rising; climbing

subinquilino sub-tenant

subinspector *m* assistant inspector

subir *vi* to rise; climb; mount; grow; increase; *vt* to raise, lift up; bring up; take up; go up; **~se** to climb; get on; **~se a la cabeza** (of drinks) to go to one's head

subitáneo sudden

súbito sudden, suddenly

subjefe *m* second-in-command

subjetividad *f* subjectivity

subjetivismo subjectivism

subjetivo subjective

subjuntivo subjunctive

sublevación *f*, **sublevamiento** rising, rebellion, insurrection

sublevado rebel

sublevar to incite to revolt; **~se** to rise in revolt, rebel

sublimación *f* sublimation

sublimado sublimate

sublimidad *f* sublimity

submarino *n + adj* submarine; *pol* mole, fifth-columnist

submúltiplo *math* sub-multiple

suboficial non-commissioned officer

subordinación *f* subordination

subordinado *n + adj* subordinate

subordinar *v* to subordinate

subprefecto sub-prefect, deputy prefect

subproducto by-product

subrayar to underline; emphasize

subrepción *f* underhand proceeding

subrepticio surreptitious

subrogación *f* subrogation; substitution

subrogar to subrogate; substitute

subsanable excusable; remediable

subsanar to excuse; amend; compensate for

subscribir(se) to subscribe (**a** to)

subscripción *f* subscription, *US* dues

subscriptor *m* subscriber

subsecretario under-secretary; assistant secretary

subsecuente subsequent

subsidiario subsidiary

subsidio subsidy; **~ de paro** unemployment benefit; **~ familiar** family allowance

subsiguiente subsequent, succeeding

subsistencia subsistence; livelihood

subsistente subsisting

subsistir to subsist

subsolano east wind

subsónico subsonic

substancia substance; essence

substantivo *n + adj* substantive

substituto substitute

subsuelo subsoil

subtender to subtend

subteniente *m* second lieutenant, sub-lieutenant

subterfugio subterfuge

subterráneo *n* underground passage; *adj* underground, subterranean

subtítulo sub-title, sub-heading

suburbano *n* underground railway, tube; *adj* suburban

suburbial *adj* slum

subversión *f* subversion

subversivo subversive

subvertir to subvert

subyacente underlying

subyugación *f* subjugation, subjection

subyugador subjugating, subjecting; captivating

subyugar to subjugate; subject; captivate

succión *f* suction

succionar to suck in

sucedáneo substitute

suceder to succeed, follow on; happen

sucedido happening, event

sucediente following, succeeding

sucesión *f* succession; estate; offspring

sucesivamente: y así ~ and so on

sucesivo succession; **en lo** ~ in the future

suceso event, happening

sucesor *m* successor

suciedad *f* dirt, filth; nastiness

sucintarse to be brief, be expressed succinctly

sucinto succinct

sucio dirty, filthy; nasty; unfair

suco sap, juice

sucoso juicy

sucrosa sucrose

súcula windlass, winch

suculencia succulence, juiciness

suculento succulent, juicy

sucumbir to yield; die; *leg* lose (a suit)

sucursal *m comm* branch; *adj* subsidiary

sud *m* south; south wind

sudación *f* sweating

sudadero handkerchief; *sp* sweat-band

sudado sweaty

sudador *m* one who perspires freely

Sudáfrica South Africa

sudafricano South African

Sudamérica South America

sudamericano South American

sudanés Sudanese

sudar to perspire, sweat; ooze; ~ **la gota gorda** to sweat one's guts out

sudario shroud, winding-sheet

sudatorio *see* **sudorífico**

sudeste *n m* +*adj* south-east

sudoeste *n m* +*adj* south-west

sudor *m* sweat, perspiration

sudorífico *n* + *adj* causing perspiration

sudoroso sweaty

sudsudeste *n m* + *adj* south-south-east

sudsudoeste *n m* + *adj* south-south-west

sudueste *see* **sudoeste**

Suecia Sweden

sueco *n* Swede; **hacerse el** ~ to pretend not to hear; *adj* Swedish

suegra mother-in-law

suegro father-in-law

suela sole (of shoe); tip (of billiard cue)

suelda *bot* comfrey

sueldo salary; soldier's pay; ~ **básico** basic wage; ~ **mínimo** minimum wage; **a** ~ wage-earning

suelo ground; soil, land; earth, terra firma; storey; plot of land; underside; *vet* hoof; ~ **natal** native land; **dar consigo en el** ~ to fall down; **medir el** ~ to lie down flat; fall flat; **por el** ~, **por los** ~s quite out of favour; **venirse al** ~ to topple

suelta *n* loosening; freeing; fetters

suelto *n* small change; short newspaper paragraph; *adj* loose; free; fluent; odd; single (copy); ~ **de lengua** outspoken; **dormir a pierna suelta** to sleep like a top

sueño sleep, sleepiness; dream; experience of very brief duration; ~ **eterno** death; ~ **pesado** deep sleep; ~ **reparador** beauty-sleep; **echar un** ~, **descabezar un** ~ to take a nap; **en/entre** ~s in the land of dreams; **ni por** ~ by no means; **tener** ~ to be sleepy

suero whey; scum; *med* serum; ~ **de la verdad** truth drug

sueroso serous, watery

suerte *f* chance, luck; good luck; condition; destiny; fate; sort, kind; manners; *theat* trick, feat; **caerle a uno en** ~ to fall to one's lot; **de** ~ **que** in such a way that; **echar a** ~s to draw lots; **entrar en** ~ to take part in a raffle; **por** ~ by chance; **tener** ~ to be lucky

sueste *m see* **sudeste**

suéter *m* sweater

suficiencia sufficiency, ability; **a** ~

sufficiently
suficiente sufficient; fit
sufijo suffix
sufragáneo n eccles suffragan
sufragar to favour; aid; defray; pay
sufragio suffrage; favour
sufragismo suffragism
sufragista m suffragist; f suffragette
sufrible, sufridero bearable, endurable
sufrido enduring; long-suffering; (of colours) subdued; hard-wearing; that do not show the dirt; **mal ~** impatient
sufridor n m sufferer; adj suffering
sufrimiento suffering
sufrir to suffer; bear up; undergo (an operation); receive (an injury); tolerate; put up with; do (penance)
sugerencia suggestion
sugerente suggestive
sugerir to suggest; insinuate
sugestión f suggestion, insinuation
sugestionar to influence; hypnotize
sugestivo suggestive; fascinating
suicida m+f suicide (person); adj suicidal
suicidarse to commit suicide
suicidio suicide (deed)
Suiza Switzerland
suizo n sugared/Swiss bun; adj Swiss; **ventilador ~** electric fan
sujeción f subjection; control; coercion; **con ~ a** in accordance with
sujetador n m fastener, clip; bra; adj fastening
sujetalibros m sing+pl book-end
sujetapapeles m sing+pl paper-clip
sujetar to subject; fasten; hold tight; **~se a** to adhere to, stick to
sujeto n subject, individual; adj subject; held tight; fixed
sulfato sulphate
sulfhidrato hydrosulphate
sulfito sulphite
sulfurar to make angry; irritate; **~se** to become furious
sulfúrico sulphuric
sulfuroso sulphorous
sultán m sultan
sultanato, sultanía sultanate
suma sum, total; summary; **~ de la vuelta** balance brought forward; **~ y sigue** comm balance carried forward; fam and so on and so forth; **en ~** in short, to sum up

sumadora: máquina ~ adding-machine
sumar to add (up); amount to; recapitulate; **máquina de ~** adding-machine
sumario n summary; leg indictment; adj summary
sumarísimo expeditious; **consejo ~ mil** drum-head court martial; **juicio ~** summary judgement/trial
sumergible n m submarine; adj submersible, sinkable
sumergimiento submerging, sinking
sumergir to immerse, plunge under; **~se** to submerge; dive, plunge
sumersión f submersion, immersion
sumidad f apex, peak
sumidero drain; sewer; gully; sump, US oilpan
sumido sunken
sumillería chamberlain's office
suministración f supply, provision
suministrador m supplier, purveyor
suministrar to supply, purvey
suministro supply, provision
sumir to sink; **~ en la tristeza** to depress
sumisión f submission
sumiso meek, submissive, humble, obedient
sumo high; supreme; great; extreme; **Sumo Pontífice** Pope; **~ sacerdote** high priest; **a lo ~** at most; **de ~** fully; **en ~ grado** to a great extent
sunción f eccles partaking of the eucharist
sunsún m orni humming-bird
suntuario sumptuary
suntuosidad f sumptuousness, magnificence
suntuoso sumptuous
supeditación f subordination, subjection
supeditar to subordinate, subject, oppress
superabundante superabundant
superante surpassing, exceeding
superar to surpass, better; excel; overcome, surmount; **~se** to set one's sights higher and higher; aim (ever) higher
superávit m surplus
supercarretera expressway
superchería fraud, trick
superchero n trickster, cheat; adj fraudulent
supercrítico hypercritical

superdominante *mus* submediant
supereminencia supereminence
supereminente supereminent
superentender to superintend, oversee, supervise
superestructura superstructure
superficialidad *f* superficiality, shallowness
superficie *f* surface; area; ~ **de rodadura** *mot* tread (of a tyre)
superficionario lease-holder
superfino superfine
superfluidad *f* superfluity
superfluo superfluous, unnecessary
superfortaleza *aer* superfortress
superfosfato superphosphate
superheterodino *rad* superheterodyne
superhombre *m* superman
superhumano superhuman
superintendencia superintendence
superintendente *m+f* superintendent
superior *n m* superior; *adj* superior; higher, upper; better, first-class; **cirugía** ~ major surgery; **piso** ~ upper storey, top deck (of a bus)
superiora mother-superior
superioridad *f* superiority
superlativo *n* superlative; *adj* superlative; **en grado** ~ in the highest degree
supermercado supermarket
superno supreme, highest
supernumerario supernumerary
superpetrolero *naut* supertanker
superponer to superpose; superimpose
superposición *f* superposing
superpotencia *elect+pol* super-power
superproducción *f* super-production; over-production
supersensible hypersensitive
supersónico supersonic
superstancial superstantial; **pan** ~ *eccles* Host
superstición *f* superstition
supersticioso superstitious
supérstite surviving
supervención *f* supervention
superveniente supervening
supervenir to supervene
supervisar to supervise
supervisión *f* supervision
supervisor *n m* supervisor; *adj* supervising
supervivencia survival; ~ **del más apto**

survival of the fittest
superviviente *n m+f* survivor; *adj* surviving
superyacente overhanging
supino supine; **ignorancia supina** crass ignorance
suplantación *f* supplanting
suplantador *n m* supplanter; *adj* supplanting
suplantar to supplant; forge, alter fraudulently; impersonate
suplementar to supplement
suplementario supplementary
suplemento supplement; supply
suplente *n m+f* substitute, replacement, locum; *adj* standing-in, substituting
supletorio supplementary; additional
súplica entreaty; **a** ~ by request
suplicación *f* entreaty; petition; *leg* appeal; **a** ~ on petition, by request
suplicar to beg, entreat; *leg* appeal against
suplicio execution; place of execution; torture; grief
suplir to supply, provide; substitute
suponedor *n m* supposer; *adj* supposing
suponer *vt* to suppose, assume; mean; entail; involve; attribute; *vi* to have authority, carry weight
suportación *f* endurance
suposición *f* supposition; exalted position
supositivo suppositive
supositorio *med* suppository
supradicho aforesaid; above-mentioned
suprarrenal *med* supra-renal
supremacía supremacy
supremo supreme; final
supresión *f* suppression; elimination; abolition; *math* cancelling-out
supresivo suppressive
supresor *n m* suppressor; *adj* suppressing
suprior *m eccles* subprior
supriora *eccles* subprioress
supuesto *n* supposition, hypothesis; *adj* supposing; assumed; ~ **que** granted that; **esto** ~ that being understood; **por** ~ of course, obviously
supuración *f* suppuration
supurante suppurating
supurar *med* to suppurate
supurativo, supuratorio suppurating
suquero member of PSUC (communist

party of Catalonia)

sur *n m* south, south wind; *adj* southern, south

surafricano South African

suramericano South American

surcado furrowed

surcador *m* ploughman

surcar to plough, furrow; cut through

surco rut, wrinkle; *agri* furrow

surcoreano South Korean

surculado *bot* single-stemmed

súrculo *bot* stem without branches

sureño *n* southerner; *adj* south, southern, southerly

surfismo surf-riding; ~ **a vela** sailboarding

surfista *m+f* surf-rider; ~ **a vela** one who practises sail-boarding

surgente *adj* salient

surgidero *naut* anchorage

surgidor *adj* anchoring

surgir to issue; appear; *bot* sprout; *naut* anchor

surrealismo surrealism

surrealista *n m+f* surrealist; *adj* surrealist(ic)

surtida *mil* sortie, sally; *naut* slipway

surtidero conduit; ~ **de agua** reservoir

surtido *n* assortment; **de** ~ in common use; *adj* assorted

surtidor *m* purveyor, supplier; jet, spout; ~ **de gasolina** petrol-pump

surtimiento supply, stock

surtir *vt* to supply, furnish, stock; *vi* spout; ~**se** to provide o.s. with

surto at rest; *naut* anchored

sus *see* **su**

susceptibilidad *f* susceptibility

susceptivo susceptible

suscitación *f* excitement, stirring up

suscitar to excite, stir up

suscribir(se) to subscribe (**a** to)

suscripción *f* subscription, *US* dues

suscriptor *m* subscriber

susidio worry, anxiety

susodicho aforesaid

suspender to suspend, hang up; discontinue; (in examination) fail; adjourn; ~ **la paga** to stop payment; ~**se** (of horses) to rear up

suspensión *f* suspension; discontinuance; ~ **de armas/de fuego** cease-fire

suspensivo: puntos ~**s** row of dots

suspenso *n* eager anticipation; (in examination) fail mark; *adj* hanging; perplexed, bewildered; **en** ~ in abeyance

suspicacia distrust

suspicaz distrustful, suspicious

suspirado longed-for, looked forward to

suspirar to sigh; ~ **por** to crave for

suspiro sigh; *mus* brief pause; **exhalar el último** ~ to die, give up the ghost

suspirón *m* 'sigher'

sustancia substance, essence

sustenido *mus* sharp

sustentable defensible

sustentación *f* sustenance

sustentáculo support, prop

sustentador *n* sustainer; *adj* sustaining

sustentamiento sustenance

sustentante *n m+f* supporter, defender; *adj* sustaining

sustentar to sustain, support, nourish

sustento sustenance, support, maintenance; *fig* food

sustitución *f* substitution

sustituidor *n m* one that substitutes; *adj* substituting

sustituir to substitute, replace, stand in for

sustituto substitute

sustituyente substituting

susto shock, fright, scare

sustracción *f* stealing; *math* subtraction

sustraer to remove, take away, steal; ~**se a** to evade, dodge

susurración *f* whispering

susurrador *n m* whisperer; *adj* whispering

susurrante whispering

susurrar to whisper; rustle; murmur, hum

susurro whisper, rustle, murmur, humming

susurrón *n m* moaner, malcontent; *adj* whispering, murmuring

sute *Col+Ven* ailing

sutil subtle; keen; slender; delicate

sutileza subtlety; fineness; slenderness; hair-splitting; ~ **de manos** light-fingeredness *esp* pickpocket's skill; *zool* animal instinct

sutilizar to make thin/slender; refine; polish

sutorio *adj* shoemaking

sutura seam; suture

suturar to seam; suture

suversión *f* subversion
suversivo subversive
suvertir to subvert
suyo(s), suya(s) his, hers, its, theirs, yours; **los suyos** his/her/their folk;

salirse con la suya to get one's own way; **una de las suyas** one of his/her/their tricks

svástica swastika

T

t f (letter) t

¡ta! (*usu* repeated) bah!

taba ankle bone; ~s (game) fivestones, jackstones

tabacal m tobacco plantation/field

tabacalero n tobacco grower/dealer; *adj* tobacco

tabaco tobacco; *fam* cigarettes; ~ **de vena** cigarette tobacco; ~ **en polvo** snuff; ~ **holandilla** Dutch tobacco; ~ **negro** dark tobacco; ~ **rubio** Virginia-type tobacco

tabacoso nicotine-stained; *bot* suffering from blight

tabalada heavy fall; slap

tabalear *vi* to drum with the fingers; *vt* to swing/rock to and fro

tabaleo drumming with the fingers; swinging/rocking to and fro

tabanque m treadle (of potter's wheel)

tabaola hubbub

tabaquería tobacconist's shop

tabaquero tobacconist

tabaquismo addiction to smoking

tabaquista m+f smoking addict

tabardete m, **tabardillo** sunstroke; typhus; crazy person

tabardo tabard

tabarra boring person; nuisance

tabasco banana

tabellar *text* to fold (cloth); *text* mark with a trade mark

taberna tavern, wine-shop

tabernáculo tabernacle

tabernario vulgar, low

tabernera barmaid; tavern-keeper's wife

tabernero tavern-keeper, innkeeper

tabes f sing + pl med consumption

tabica panel

tabicar to partition off

tabicón m thick wall/partition

tabique m partition wall; inside wall

tabla plank; board; slab; bench; list; (sewing) box pleat; strip (of land); *math* table; ~ **de surf** surfboard; ~s *theat* boards; **a raja** ~ by the book, according to the rules; **hacer** ~ **rasa** to make a clean sweep; **hacer** ~s to draw, finish up equal; **salvarse en una** ~ to save o.s. by the skin of one's teeth; **tener** ~s to know the ropes

tablacho sluice-gate

tablado n scaffold; platform, stage; tableau; decorated float; *theat* boards; **sacar al** ~ to publish, make known

tablaje m pile of planks; gaming-house

tablajería betting, gambling; butcher's shop

tablajero butcher; tax-collector; scaffold-maker; *theat* carpenter; *joc* hospital surgeon

tablar m set of garden plots

tablazón m flooring; planking; *naut* decks; boards; timber

tablear *hort* to divide into beds; *carp* saw into boards; (sewing) make box-pleats

tableo sawing into boards; division (of land) into plots; *sur* levelling; (sewing) box-pleating

tablero board; panel; gaming table/house; shop counter; wood ready for sawing; tailor's cutting-table; draughts/chess board; notice board; ~ **contador** abacus; ~ **de cocina** dresser; ~ **de distribución** *elect* switchboard; ~ **de instrumentos** control panel; *mot* dashboard

tableta tablet; writing-pad; clapper; (chocolate) bar; **estar en** ~s to be in suspense

tabletear to rattle

tableteo rattling; clatter; tapping

tablilla tablet; slab; notice-board; *med* splint; ~ **de mesón** inn-sign; **por** ~ indirectly

tabloide m tabloid (newspaper)

tablón m plank; ~ **de anuncios** notice-board; **llevar un** ~ to be drunk

tabloncillo floor-board; bullring seats furthest from the arena

tabloza *arts* palette

tabú *m* taboo

tabuco hovel, shack

taburete *m* stool; ~*s theat* pit benches

taca cupboard (*usu* in kitchen)

tacada (billiards) stroke; *naut* wedge

tacañear to be mean/stingy

tacañería stinginess, meanness

tacaño *n* stingy/mean person, miser; *adj* stingy, tight-fisted

tacar *vi* to have one's turn (at billiards); *vt* to mark

tacatá *m* child's walking-frame

tacazo (billiards) stroke

tácito taciturn; understood

taco plug; stopper; piece of wood; log (for burning); billiard cue; writing pad; swear-word, coarse expression; muddle; snack; **armarse un** ~ to get in a muddle

tacógrafo *mot* tachograph

tacón *m* heel (of shoe); ~ **de cuña** wedge heel; ~ **de lapicero** stiletto heel

taconazo heel click; stamp with a heel

taconear to drum with the heels (in flamenco dancing)

taconeo heel-stamping/tapping

táctica tactics

táctico *n* tactician; *adj* tactical

táctil tactile

tacto touch; tact

tacha blemish, flaw; **poner** ~ **a** to find fault with

tachar to call; cross out; *leg* challenge (a witness); ~ **a alguien de …** accuse s.o. of …

tachero tinsmith

tacho pail; boiler; pot; **irse al** ~ to go to rack and ruin

tachón *m* erasure; (sewing) trimming; gilt-headed tack

tachonar to adorn with spangles; (sewing) trim; decorate with gilt-headed tacks

tachonería decorative work with gilt-headed tacks

tachoso faulty

tachuela tack, hobnail

tafetán *m* taffeta; **tafetanes** flags, bunting

tafilete *m* Moroccan leather

tagalo *n* + *adj* Tagalog

tagarote *m* pen-pusher; penniless aristocrat

taguán *m* flying squirrel

Tahití Tahiti

tahona bakery, baker's shop; flour mill

tahonero baker; miller

tahur *n m* + *f* card-sharper; gambler; *adj* addicted to gambling

tahurería gambling; cheating at cards

taifa faction

Tailandia Thailand

tailandés *m* + *f* Thai

taimado sly, astute; stubborn

taita daddy

taitano Tahitian

tajada cut, slice; hoarseness; *fam* drunkenness; **coger una** ~ to get drunk; **sacar** ~ to get something out of it

tajadera chopping-knife; *carp* gouge

tajadero chopping-block

tajadilla *cul* dish of lights

tajado steep, sheer; *her* divided diagonally

tajador *m* cutter; cutting edge

tajadura cutting, chopping

tajamar *m naut* cutwater

tajante cutting; categorical

tajaplumas *m sing* + *pl* penknife

tajar to cut, chop; cut off

tajea drain, gutter; watercourse

Tajo Tagus

tajo cut(ting), slash, slice; ravine; chopping-block; **vamos al** ~ let's show willing, let's get cracking

tajón *m* chopping-block

tal *adj* such, such a; like; **un** ~ **García** a fellow named García; *adv* so, thus; **¿qué** ~? how are things?; *pron* someone; ~ **para cual** two of a kind; *conj* **con** ~ **que** on condition that

tala tree-felling; destruction; tipcat (game)

talabartería saddlery

talabartero saddler, harness-maker

talador *adj* tree-felling

taladradora drill, drilling machine

taladrador *adj* drilling

taladrar to drill, perforate

taladro *n* drill, auger; drill-hole; drilling bit

talán *m* ding-dong

talante *m* mood; **de buen/mal** ~ in a good/bad mood, with good/bad grace

talar to fell (trees); lay waste

talco talcum; **polvos de** ~ talcum powder

478

talcualillo fair to middling, so-so

talega bag; money-bag; nappy; hairnet

talego bag; clumsy person; *sl* money, dough

talento talent, cleverness

talentoso talented, clever

talentudo a little too clever

talio thallium

talismán *m* talisman

talmente literally

talón *m anat* heel; cheque; voucher, coupon; **apretar los talones** to hurry up; **pisar los talones de** to be hard on the heels of

talonada kick with the heel; back-kick

talonario cheque-book; counterfoil book

talonear to walk rapidly

talquina ruse, artful trick

talud *m* embankment

talla carving; height, stature; size (of shoes, clothes *etc*); ransom; **no dar la ~** not to be up to standard

tallador *m* carver, engraver; die-sinker; croupier

talladura engraving

tallar *n m* trees ready for felling; *adj* ready for felling; *vi* to deal (cards); chat; woo; *vt* to carve, engrave, cut (diamonds *etc*)

talle *m* figure; fit; waist

tallecer to sprout

taller *m* workshop; studio; **~ de reparaciones** repair-shop; **~ de teatro** theatre workshop

tallista *m* engraver; wood-carver

tallo *bot* stalk, stem

talludo having a long stalk; overgrown

tamal *m* meat pasty made with cornflour

tamango shoe worn by gauchos

tamañito undersized; very small

tamaño *n* size; **de ~ natural** life-size; *adj* so big, very big

támara palm-tree; bunch of dates

tamarindo tamarind (tree and fruit)

tamarisco, tamariz *m* tamarisk

tamba loin-cloth

tambalco *n* staggering, reeling

tambaleante *adj* staggering, reeling, wobbling

tambalearse to stagger, reel; wobble

tambaleo *n* staggering, reeling, wobbling

también also, too, as well

tambo hostelry; dairy farm; cowshed

tambor *m* drum; drummer; roaster (for coffee, chestnuts *etc*); *anat* eardrum; **~ mayor** drum-major

tambora bass drum

tamborete *m* timbrel

tamboril *m* small drum played with one stick

tamborilada, tamborilazo fall onto the backside

tamborilear *vi* to drum, tap; *vt* to praise, laud

tamborileo *n* drumming

tamborón *m* large bass drum

Támesis *m* Thames

tamiz *m* sieve, riddle; **pasar por ~** to sift, sieve

tamizar to sieve, sift

tamo fluff, fuzz; dust

tampoco neither, not either

tamujo *bot* buckthorn

tan so, as; **~ siquiera** even if only; **~ sólo** only just; **¡qué chica ~ guapa!** what a beautiful girl!!; **tan ... como** as/so ... as

tanaceto *bot* tansy

tanate *m* bundle

tanda turn, shift; task, job; game (of billiards); batch

tándem *m* tandem

tanganillas: en ~ shakily

tangencia tangency

tangente *f* tangent

Tánger Tangier

tangerina tangerine

tangerino *n* native of Tangier; *adj* of Tangier

tanguearse *pol pej* to change parties

tánico tannic

tanino tannin

tanque *m* tank; *sl* handbag

tantarantán *m* rub-a-dub-dub; drum-beat; slap

tanteador *m+f* scorekeeper, marker; *m* scoreboard

tantear to try; test; sound out; *arts* sketch; make a rough estimate of; keep score; **~se** to ponder carefully

tanteo trial; test; sounding out; rough estimate; *sp* score

tanto *n* amount; *sp* point, goal, run; scorer; *comm* rate; **~ alzado** lump sum; **~ por ciento** percentage; **apuntarse un ~** to score a point/goal *etc*; **entre ~** meanwhile; **otro ~** as much again; ¡y ~!, ¡y ~ que sí! you're telling me!, not half!; **estar al** ~ to be up to date/in the picture; *adj* as/so much; ~s as/so many; *adv* as/so much; ~ **como** as much as; ~ **Juan como María** both John and Mary; **un** ~ a little, not much

tanzano Tanzanian

tañedor *m mus* player

tañente *n mus* playing

tañer *mus* to play (an instrument); ring (a bell)

tañido tune, melody; rhythm; ringing

tañimiento *mus* playing (an instrument)

taoísmo Taoism

taoísta *m+f* Taoist

tapa cover, lid, cap; heel (of shoe); *mot* cylinder head; book cover; flap (of pocket); titbit (eaten in bars)

tapaboca slap across the mouth

tapacubos *m sing+pl* hub-cap

tapaculo *bot* dog-rose; rosehip

tapada veiled woman

tapadera cover, lid

tapadero stopper, plug

tapadillo hiding (of a woman's face); **de** ~ secretly

tapadizo shed

tapado *n* woman's overcoat; hidden treasure; *zool* (of an animal's skin) unspotted

tapador *n m* cover, lid; stopper, plug; *adj* covering

tapadura *n* covering

tapadujo: de ~ secretly; as an alibi

tapagujeros *m sing+pl* botcher, unskilled bricklayer

tapamiento *n* covering

tápana *bot+cul* caper

tapapiés *m sing+pl* very long coat

tapar to cover (up); plug (up); cap; cork; wrap up; ~**se** to wrap o.s. up

taparrabo bathing trunks; loin cloth

tapera abandoned house; ruins of a village

taperujarse to cover one's face with clothing/bedclothes

tapetado dark brown

tapete *m* rug; tablecloth; ~ **verde** gambling table; **estar sobre el** ~ to be under discussion

tapia enclosing wall; boundary wall *usu* of mud bricks; **sordo como una** ~ deaf as a doorpost

tapiador *m* builder of **tapias**

tapiar to wall (up/in); block up

tapicería tapestry-making; tapestries; upholstery

tapicero tapestry maker; upholsterer

tapido closely woven

tapiz *m* tapestry

tapizar to cover with tapestry; upholster

tapón *m* stopper, plug; cork; bung; *mot* traffic jam/hold-up; *med* tampon; *fam* short stocky chap; **estado** ~ *pol* buffer state

taponamiento *mot* traffic jam/hold-up; *med* tamponage

taponar to tampon, plug up

taponazo pop (of a cork)

taponería corkshop/factory; corks

taponero *n* corkseller/maker; *adj* (of) cork

tapujarse to wrap o.s. up

tapujo jiggery-pokery, funny business; **sin** ~s honestly, no kidding

taque *m* knock at a door; noise of a door being locked

taquera billiard cue rack

taquigrafía shorthand

taquigrafiar to write in shorthand

taquígrafo shorthand writer

taquilla box office; ticket office; booking office; till; receipts

taquillero *n* booking/ticket office attendant; *adj* box office; **éxito** ~ box-office success

taquimeca (taquimecanógrafa) shorthand-typist

tara *comm* tare; tally; defect; **menos la** ~ making allowances for exaggeration

tarabilla latch, bolt; fastener; *fam* chatterbox; featherbrained person; **soltar la** ~ to start chattering

taracea inlaid work; marquetry; mother-of-pearl inlaid work

taracear to inlay

tarado imperfect, defective; maimed

taraje *m bot* tamarisk

tarambana *m+f* madcap

tarando reindeer

tarángana poor-quality black-pudding

tarantela *mus* tarantella

tarantín *m* rubbish; shop

tarántula tarantula

tarará *f* toot, sound of a trumpet

tararear to hum (a melody)

tararira loud laughter

tarasca virago; shrew

tarascada bite; shrewish behaviour; snappy answer

tarascar to bite

tarascón *m* bite, mouthful

taray *m bot* tamarisk

tarazana *naut* building yard

tarazar to bite; harass

tardador *m* one who delays, procrastinator

tardanza delay

tardar to take a long time; delay; **a más ~** at the latest; **¿cuánto tarda?** how long does it take?

tarde *n f* afternoon, evening; **buenas ~s** good afternoon/evening; *adv* late, too late; **~ o temprano** sooner or later; **de ~ en ~** infrequently; **hacerse ~** to get late; **más vale ~ que nunca** better late than never

tardecer *v impers* to grow late

tardecica evening, twilight

tardígrado *zool* slow-moving

tardío, tardo late; slow

tardón *m* slowcoach

tarea task, job; piece of work; homework

tarifa price-list, tariff

tarima movable platform/dais

tarja tally, check; **beber sobre ~** to get drunk on credit

tarjador *m* tally-keeper

tarjeta card; **~ de visita** visiting-card; **~ postal** postcard

tarjetero, tarjetera card-case

tarjetón *m* show-card

tarquín *m* slime

tarraconense of Tarragona

tarro jar, bottle; *sl* shoe

tarso *anat* tarsus; *orni* shank

tarta cake; **~ helada** ice-cream cake

tártago misfortune; practical joke

tartajear to stutter, stammer

tartajoso stuttering, stammering

tartalear to stagger, reel

tartaleta *cul* tart

tartamudear to stutter, stammer; falter

tartamudeo *n* stuttering, stammering

tartamudo *n* stutterer; *adj* stuttering

tartán *m* tartan

tartana two-wheeled cart/carriage; *naut* single-sailed vessel

tartanero driver/captain of a **tartana**

tártaro tartar; cream of tartar; plaque (on teeth)

tartera baking-tin

tártrico tartaric

tartufo hypocrite

tarugo *n* wooden stopper/plug/bung; *adj fam* stupid

¡tas – tas! smack-smack! (warning given to a child)

tasa rate, valuation, measure; **sin ~** without limit

tasación *f* valuation

tasador *m* valuer

tasajo hung beef; slice of meat

tasar to value, price; keep within limits

tasca eating-house; den, dive

tascador *m* bodkin

tascar: ~ el freno to champ at the bit

tasquera wrangle, row

tastana hard crust (on soil)

tastaz *m* polishing powder

tasugo *zool* badger

tata nurse (baby language)

tatarabuela great-great-grandmother

tatarabuelo great-great-grandfather

tataradeudo distant relation; ancestor

tataranieta great-great-granddaughter

tataranieto great-great-grandson

tato lisping and stammering (*esp* pronouncing s as t)

tatuaje tattoo, tattooing

tatuar to tattoo

taurino *adj* bullfighting

Tauro *astrol* Taurus

taurómaco expert on bullfighting

tauromaquia art of fighting bulls

tautología tautology

tautológico tautological

taxativo definite; limited

taxidermia taxidermy

taxidermista *m + f* taxidermist

taxímetro taxi

taxista *m + f* taxi-driver

taz a taz on an even basis

taza cup(ful); basin (of fountain/toilet)

tazón *m* large cup; bowl

TBO comic (periodical)

te you, to you, for you; yourself; thee; to/for yourself; **~ lo he terminado** I have finished it for you; **¡cepíllate los dientes!** clean your teeth!

té *m* tea

tea brand, torch; *naut* anchor hawser

teatral theatrical

teatralidad *f* exaggerated theatrical/dramatic quality

teatrero theatregoer, theatre buff

teatro theatre; drama; plays

tebeo comic (periodical)

¹ **teca** teak

² **teca** *eccles* reliquary

tecla key (of typewriter/calculator/piano *etc*); **dar en la ~** to put one's finger on the spot, hit the mark

teclado keyboard (of typewriter/piano *etc*)

teclear to test; touch on, tackle; strum, play a few notes; tap with the fingers

tecnicismo technicality; technical expression

técnica technique

técnico *n* technician; *adj* technical

tecnócrata technocrat

tecnología technology

tecnológico technological

tectónica techtonics

tectónico techtonic

techado roof; ceiling; **bajo ~** indoors

techador *m* roofer, thatcher

techar to roof, put a roof on

techo roof, ceiling

techumbre *f* roofing

tedero candlestick

tedeum *m eccles* Te Deum

tedex (técnico en desactivación de artefactos explosivos) *m* bomb-disposal expert

tediar to hate

tedio boredom; annoyance

tedioso tedious

teguillo thin board/lath

tegumento covering

teína caffeine

teinada cattle-shed

teísmo theism

teísta *m+f* theist

¹ **teja** roof tile; **a toca ~** cash down; **de ~s abajo** here below, in this life; **de ~s arriba** up above, in heaven; **sombrero de ~** shovel hat

² **teja** *bot* linden-tree

tejadillo roof (of a vehicle); shed; trick

tejado tiled roof

tejano Texan; **~s** jeans

tejar *m* tile-works; *v* to cover with tiles

tejaroz *m* eaves

tejazo blow with a tile

tejedera, tejedora weaver

tejedor *n m* weaver; schemer; water-flea; *adj* weaving

tejedura weaving; texture

tejeduría weaving; weaving-mill

tejemaneje *m* jiggery-pokery

tejer to weave; scheme (up), plot

tejera, tejería tile factory/works

tejero tile-maker

tejido weave, texture; textile; material, fabric; *anat* tissue

tejo quoit; disc; *bot* yew; *mech* bush; hopscotch

tejoleta brickbat, piece of tile

tejón *m zool* badger

tejuelo book label; quoit; *mech* bush, socket

tela fabric, material; film, membrane; *sl* money, lolly; **~ de araña** cobweb; **~ de juicio** legal proceedings; **~ encerada** buckram; **~ metálica** wire-netting; **aquí hay mucha ~** there's more in this than meets the eye; **en ~** cloth-bound; *sl* **soltar/aflojar la ~** to cough up the dough

telar *m text* loom; *theat* gridiron; (bookbinding) stitching-machine

telaraña cobweb; **mirar las ~s** to be in a brown study

tele *f fam* telly

telecomunicación *f* telecommunication

telediario *TV* news bulletin

teleférico cable-railway

telefilm(e) *m* television film

telefio *bot* stonecrop

telefonazo telephone call

telefonear *v* to telephone

telefonema *m* telephone message

telefonía telephony; **~ sin hilos** wireless telephony

telefónica: cabina ~ telephone kiosk; phone booth

telefónico telephonic

telefonista *m+f* telephonist

teléfono telephone

telefoto telephoto

telefotografía telephotography

telefotografiar to telephotograph

telegrafía telegraphy; **~ sin hilos** wireless telegraphy

telegrafiar to telegraph

telegráfico telegraphic

telegrafista *m+f* telegraph operator

telégrafo telegraph; **~ marino** nautical signals; **~ óptico** semaphore

telegrama *m* telegram

telele *m* fit; **les dará un ~** they'll go round the bend/have a fit

telemando remote control

telemetría telemetry

telemétrico telemetric

telémetro range-finder

telendo lively, full of beans

telépata *m+f* telepathist

telepatía telepathy

telepático telepathic

telera corral, cattle-pen; *mech* jaw (of a clamp *etc*)

telescópico telescopic

telescopio telescope

telesilla ski-lift, chair-lift

telespectador *m TV* viewer

telestudio television studio

teleta blotting paper

teletipia teletype machine, ticker-tape machine

teletipo teletype; teleprinter

teletón *m* strong silk material

televidente *m+f TV* viewer

televisar to televise

televisión *f* television

televisivo *adj* (of) television

televisor *m* television set

televisual *adj* (of) television

telilla flimsy cloth

telina clam

telón *m theat* curtain; **~ de acero** *pol* iron curtain; **~ de fondo** *theat* back-curtain, background; **~ de seguridad** *theat* safety curtain

telonio customs house; inland revenue office

telúrico *adj* telluric, back-to-earth

telurio tellurium

telliz *m* horse-cloth

telliza bedspread, coverlet

¹ **tema** *m* theme, topic; **~ celeste** astronomical map; **~s de actualidad** current affairs

² **tema** *f* mania, obsession; **cada loco con su ~** we all have our pet ideas

temario agenda; set of topics (to study)

temático thematic

tembladal *m* quagmire

tembladera tankard; quagmire

tembladero quagmire

temblador *n m* trembler; *adj* trembling, shaking; shivering

temblante *adj* trembling, quivering

temblar to tremble, quiver; shiver

tembleque *m* trembling/shivering fit

temblequear to tremble; shiver; shake

temblón tremulous, shaking; **álamo ~** *bot* aspen

temblor *m* trembling; **~ de tierra** earth-tremor

tembloroso, tembloso tremulous; shivering; trembling

temedero dread, fearful

temedor *adj* dreading, fearing

temer *vt* to fear, be afraid (of); *vi* **+ ~se** to be afraid

temerario rash, foolhardy

temeridad *f* temerity, rashness

temerón *adj* blustering, hectoring

temeroso fearful; **~ de Dios** God-fearing

temible fearful

temor *m* fear, dread; **~ a/de** fear of

temoso obstinate

témpano *mus* kettledrum; drum-skin; flitch (of bacon); **~ de hielo** ice-flow; **~s flotantes** pack-ice

temperación *f* tempering

temperamento temperament; weather

temperancia temperance, moderation

temperar *v* to temper, calm

temperatura temperature

temperie *f* weather, elements

tempero seasonableness

tempestad *f* tempest; storm

tempestear to storm, rage

tempestividad *f* timeliness

tempestivo timely, seasonable

tempestuoso tempestuous

¹ **templa** *anat* temple

² **templa** *arts* tempera; size, distemper

templadera sluice-gate

templado temperate, warm; lukewarm; brave; level-headed; slightly drunk; frugal

templador *n m+f* tuner; *m* tuning-key; *adj* tempering, tuning

templadura tempering, tuning

templanza temperance; *arts* blend

templar *vi* to ease up; *vt* to temper, moderate; tune; *naut* trim (sails); (falconry) train; *arts* blend; **~se** to use moderation; *meteor* become warmer

templario Knight Templar

temple temperature; *metal* temper; mood; tuning; determination; distemper; order of the Knights Templar; **al ~** distempered; *arts* in tempera

templete *m* small temple; pavilion; ~ **de música** bandstand

templo temple, church

témpora Ember Week

temporada season; period of time, while; **estar de** ~ to be on one's holidays

temporal *n m* storm, rainy weather; temporal zone; *adj* temporary; temporal

temporalidad *f* temporality

temporalizar to make temporary; secularize

temporario, temporáneo temporary, passing

temporejar *naut* to lie to

temporero *n* seasonal worker; *adj* seasonal

temporizador *m* temporizer

temporizar to temporize; waste one's time

tempranal (of fruit trees) early (-fruiting)

tempranero early-rising; *bot* early

tempranilla early grape

temprano *n agri* early crops; *adj+adv* early

tena cattleshed

tenacear to be stubborn

tenacero maker of tongs/pincers

tenacidad *f* tenacity

tenacillas *fpl* pincers; small tongs; sugar-tongs; curling irons

tenada *see* **tena**

tenallas *fpl* pair of tongs/pincers

tenaz tenacious

tenaza pincer; (of lobster *etc*) claw, nipper; *med* forceps; ~**s** pincers, tongs

tenazada gripping/biting hard

tenazón: a/de ~ blindly; unexpectedly

tenca *zool* tench

tención *f* holding

tendajo miserable little shop

tendal *m* clothes-line; awning

tendalero drying-place

tendedero clothes-line

tendedor *m* stretcher; spreader

tendedura stretching; spreading out; hanging out (of washing)

tendel *m* plumb-line

tendencia tendency, inclination

tendencioso tendentious, prejudiced; having an ulterior motive

tendente tending

ténder *m* (railway) tender

tender *vi* to tend; *vt* to spread out; stretch out; hang out (washing); lay; throw; *bui* coat with plaster; ~**se** to lie down; stretch out

tenderete *m* stall, stand; articles for sale scattered on the ground

tendero shopkeeper; tent-maker

tendido *n* laying down; spreading; hanging (washing); batch; coat (of plaster); slope (of roof); seats (in bullring); *adj* full tilt

tendón *m* tendon

tenebrario *eccles* candelabra of fifteen candles used in Holy Week

tenebrosidad *f* darkness, gloom

tenebroso dark, gloomy

tenedero *naut* anchorage

tenedor *m* fork; holder, keeper; ~ **de libros** book-keeper; ~ **de póliza** policy-holder

teneduría: ~ de libros book-keeping

tenencia holding, possession; tenancy; tenure; ~ **ilícita de armas** unlawful possession of arms

tener to have, possess; keep; hold; be of the opinion; have with one; *cin* play opposite; ~ **hambre/sed/sueño/miedo** to be hungry/thirsty/tired/afraid; ~ ... **años** to be ... years old; **ahí lo tiene** there you have it, there you are; ~ **que** to have to; **no** ~ **que ver con** to have nothing to do with; **¿qué tiene usted?** what's the matter with you?, what's wrong with you?; **no tiene nada de particular** there's nothing special about it; **ya tienen** they already have some; ~**se** *fig* hold on; to stop, halt; ~**se de pie** to stand, remain standing; **tenérselas con** to have it out with; ~**se tieso, tenérselas tiesas** to stand firm, be resolute

tenería tannery

tenguerengue shaky, wobbly

tenia *med* tape-worm

tenida meeting (of masonic lodge)

teniéntazgo lieutenantship; office of deputy

teniente *n m* lieutenant; deputy; **primer** ~ **de alcalde** first deputy mayor; *adj* holding, owning; unripe; stingy

tenífugo *adj med* anti-worm

tenis *m* tennis

tenista *m+f* tennis player

tenor *m* purpose, drift; *mus* tenor; **a ~ de** in agreement with; on the lines of; **a este ~** at this rate

tenorio *fam* lady-killer, Casanova

tensión *f* tension; tautness; stress; pressure; voltage; blood-pressure; **tener la ~ alta** to have high blood-pressure

tenso tense; taut

tentación *f* temptation

tentaculado having tentacles

tentáculo tentacle

tentadero round-up (where young fighting bulls are tried out)

tentador *n m* tempter; *adj* tempting

tentadora temptress

tentalear to feel (with the fingers)

tentar to tempt; feel; try

tentativa trial, test

tentativo *adj* tentative

tentemozo (self-righting) doll, kelly; prop, support

tentempié *m* snack, bite

tentenelaire *m* half-caste

tentetieso *see* **tentemozo**

tentón *m* rough treatment/handling

tenue tenuous; subdued; faint; slight, unimportant

tenuidad *f* tenuousness; faintness; slightness; mere bagatelle

tenuta *leg* rights of a temporary tenant

tenutario temporary tenant

teñible that can be dyed

teñidura dyeing

teñir to dye, tinge

teocracia theocracy

teocrático theocratic(al)

teodolito theodolite

teologal theological

teología theology; **no meterse en ~s** not to meddle in complicated matters

teológico theological

teologizar to theologize

teólogo *n* theologian; *adj* theological

teomanía delusion under which the sufferer thinks he/she is divine

teorema *m* theorem

teoría theory

teórico theoretical; hypothetical

teorizar to theorize

teoso resinous

teosofía theosophy

teósofo theosophist

tepe *m* turf; sod

terapeuta *m+f* therapist

terapéutica therapeutics

terapéutico therapeutic

terapia therapy

tercena tobacco warehouse

tercenista *m* wholesale tobacco merchant

tercer *see* **tercero**

tercera *n* (cards) piquet; *mus* third string of an instrument; bawd; *adj* third; **~ edad** old age

tercero *adj* third; *nm* mediator; pimp

tercerón *m* mulatto

terceto tercet; trio; triplet

tercia third part; run of three cards; storehouse

terciado *n* cutlass; ribbon; *adj* slanting, cross-wise; **azúcar ~** brown sugar; **pan ~** ground rent paid in grain

terciana, tercianario *med* tertian fever

terciar to place slanting/diagonally; divide by three; bear arms; arbitrate; participate; **~se** to crop up; **si se tercia** if the occasion presents itself

terciario tertiary

tercio one third; *mil* infantry regiment; **~s** strong limbs; **hacer buen ~** to come in useful; **irse al ~ mil** to join the Foreign Legion

terciopelado velvety

terciopelero velvet weaver

terciopelo velvet

terco obstinate

terebinto *bot* terebinth

terebrante (of pain) stabbing

teresa, teresiana Carmelite nun

tergiversación *f* distortion (of facts)

tergiversar to distort, misrepresent

terliz *m text* ticking, sackcloth; sailcloth

termal thermal

termas *fpl* hot springs/baths

termes *m sing+pl* termite

térmico thermal; **ropa térmica** thermal clothing

terminación *f* ending, conclusion, termination

terminacho vulgar expression

terminador *adj* ending, terminating

terminante categorical, flat

terminar(se) to end, finish, conclude

terminativo terminative

término end, finish, conclusion; limit; term; district; *med* crisis; *mus* pitch, tone; ~ **medio** average; **en primer** ~ in the foreground, in the first place; **en último** ~ as a last resort, in the background; **llevar a** ~ to carry on to the end; **poner** ~ **a** to put an end to, conclude

terminología terminology

terminológico terminological

terminote *m joc* big word

termita termite

termitero termite nest, anthill

termo Thermos flask

termodinámica thermodynamics

termométrico thermometric

termómetro thermometer

termoplástico thermoplastic

termoscopio thermoscope

termostático thermostatic

termostato thermostat

terna triad; three names submitted for election of a candidate; (dice) pair of threes; set of dice

ternario *n eccles* three days of devotion; *adj* ternary

terne *n m* bully, roughneck; *adj* obstinate; bullying; tough

ternejal *m* bullying

ternejón *n m* very emotional person; *adj* easily moved

ternera calf; **carne de** ~ veal

ternero male calf

ternerón *see* **ternejón**

terneza tenderness; softness; endearment; **decir** ~**s** to whisper sweet nothings

ternilla cartilage, gristle

ternilloso cartilaginous, gristly

terno set of three; three-piece suit; *eccles* celebrant's vestments; oath; **echar** ~**s** to curse

ternura tenderness; affection; tender word

terquear to display obstinacy

terquedad *f*, **terquería**, **terqueza** obstinacy, pig-headedness, bloody-mindedness

terracota terracotta

terrada bitumen

terrado *bui* terrace; flat roof

terraje *m* ground-rent

terrajero lessee of farmland

terral *n m* land breeze; *adj* (from the) land

Terranova Newfoundland

terraplén *m* mound; earthworks; (railway) embankment

terraplenar to terrace, raise up, bank; fill in

terráqueo *n* earthling, terrestrial; *adj* terraqueous, (of the) earth

terrateniente *m* landowner, landlord

terraza terrace; *hort* border; ~ **del café** pavement in front of a café

terrazgo ground-rent; arable land

terrazo landscape

terrecer to terrify

terremoto earthquake

terrenal earthly, worldly; terrestrial

terrenidad *f* earthliness, worldliness

terreno *n* land, ground; plot of land; **ceder** ~ to give way; **ganar/perder** ~ to gain/lose ground; **medir el** ~ to see how the land lies; **sobre el** ~ on the spot

térreo earthy, of earth

terrera steep uncultivable ground; *orni* skylark

terrero *n* mound/bank of earth; *bui* terrace, flat roof; dump; *adj* of earth, lowly; *orni* low-flying

terrestre *n m* earthling; *adj* terrestrial

terribilidad *f* awfulness

terrícola *m+f* earthling, inhabitant of the earth

terrífico terrifying, frightful

terrígeno earth-born

terrino *see* **térreo**

territorialidad *f* territoriality

territorio territory; ground

terrizo *see* **térreo**

terromontero hillock

terrón *m* clod of earth; lump (of sugar)

terrorífico horrific

terrorismo terrorism

terrorista *n m+f +adj* terrorist

terrosidad *f* earthiness

terroso earthy

terruño plot of land; one's own place of origin

tersar to smooth; polish

tersidad *f* smoothness

terso smooth; *lit* (of style) polished

tersura smoothness; *lit* (of style) polish

tertulia *n* group (for conversation); social gathering; *theat* gallery; card-room; **hacer** ~ to sit and chat

tertulio *n* member of a **tertulia**; *adj* of a conversation group

teruelo ballot box

terzón *m* three-year-old bull

terzuelo third part; *orni* male falcon

tesar *naut* to haul taut

tesauro thesaurus

tesela mosaic piece

teselado tessellated

Teseo Theseus

tésera countersign

tesina short thesis; extended essay

tesis *f sing + pl* thesis

teso taut, pulled tight

tesón *m* tenacity, doggedness; inflexibility

tesonería obstinacy, doggedness, pigheadedness

tesorería treasury, exchequer

tesorero treasurer; *eccles* priest in charge of church treasure/relics

tesoro treasure; treasury, exchequer

tespíades *fpl* las ~ the Muses

testa head; forehead; front; *fam* common sense; ~ **coronada** crowned head

testación *f* erasure, crossing-out

testada obstinacy, stubbornness; blow with the head

testado *leg* testate

testador *m* testator

testadora testatrix

testadura erasure, crossing-out

testaférrea *n*, **testaferro** man of straw; dummy; front-man

testamentaria executrix

testamentaría execution of a will

testamentario *n* executor; *adj* testamentary

testamento *leg* will, testament

testar to make a will

testarada butt with the head; obstinacy

testarazo butt with the head

testarrón pig-headed

testarronería, testarudez *f* pig-headedness, bloody-mindedness

testarudo pig-headed, stubborn, bloody-minded

teste *m* testicle

testera front part; animal's forehead; wall

testero front part; back plate (of fireplace); large log; wall

testículo testicle

testificación *f* attestation, affirmation

testificante attesting, witnessing

testificar to attest, certify, testify

testificata affidavit

testificativo attesting, solemnly declaring

testigo witness; ~ **de cargo** prosecution witness; ~ **de descargo** defence witness; ~ **presencial/ocular/de vista** eyewitness

testimonial *adj* attesting, giving evidence

testimoniales *fpl* reference, certificate of good character

testimoniar to testify to

testimoniero calumniating

testimonio evidence; affidavit; **falso** ~ false evidence

testuz *m anat* nape; forehead

tesura *f* stiffness

teta teat; breast; hillock; ~ **de vaca** cone-shaped meringue; **dar la** ~ **a** to breast-feed; **niño de** ~ babe in arms

tetánico *med* tetanic

tétano(s) lockjaw, tetanus

tetar to suckle, breast-feed

tetera teapot; kettle; nipple, teat

tetero feeding-bottle

tetigonia cicada

tetilla male's nipple; rubber teat (on feeding bottle)

tetón *m* stub (of pruned branch)

tetona big-breasted, having large teats, busty

tetraedro tetrahedron

tetrágono tetragon

tetragrama *mus* stave

tetramotor *m* four-engined plane

tetrarca *m* tetrarch

tétrico gloomy, grim

tetuda *see* **tetona**

teucrio *bot* germander

teucro *n + adj* Trojan

teúrgia black magic

teutón *n m + adj* Teuton

teutónico *n* Teutonic language; *adj* Teutonic

teuvé *f fam* Spanish television service

teuvecracia *joc* television control, director of T.V.E.

T.V.E. (Televisión Española) Spanish television

textil *n m + adj* textile

texto text; **libro de** ~ textbook

textorio *adj* textile

textual textual, the actual words used

textualmente textually; **dijo** ~ ... he said, quote, ...

textura texture

tez *f* skin, complexion

tezado jet-black

ti you, thee; yourself

tía aunt; old woman; *fam* tart, bit of stuff; ~ **buena** smashing bit of homework; **cuéntaselo a tu** ~ tell that to the marines; **no hay tu** ~ you might as well give up hope

tianguis *m* market

tiara triple crown (worn by the Pope); tiara

tiberio hubbub, uproar

tibetano Tibetan

tibia *anat* tibia, shin-bone; *mus* flute

tibieza lukewarmness

tibio lukewarm; careless; **poner** ~ **a alguien** to call s.o. every name under the sun; **ponerse** ~ **de comida** to gorge o.s.

tibor *m cer* large jar

tiburón *m* shark

tictac *m* tick-tock

tiemblo *bot* aspen

tiempo time; age; season; weather; *gramm* tense; *mus* tempo; ~**s idos** days gone by; **a** ~ **in** time; **acomodarse al** ~ to move with the times; **a su** ~ all in good time, in due course; **a su debido** ~ at the proper time; **con el** ~ in the course of time; **¿cuánto** ~? how long?; **de** ~ **en** ~ from time to time; **del** ~ **de Maricastaña/del rey Wamba** as old as the hills; **demasiado** ~ too long; **el** ~ **dirá** time will tell; **en** ~ **hábil** at/within the appointed time; **en aquellos** ~**s** in the good old days; **en los** ~**s de Maricastaña/del rey Wamba** in olden times; **hacer** ~ to mark time; **hacer buen/mal** ~ to be fine/bad weather; **haga buen o mal** ~ come rain or shine; **tomarse** ~ to take one's time

tienda shop; tent; *naut* awning; ~ **de autoservicio** self-service shop; ~ **de campaña** tent; ~ **de campaña canadiense** ridge tent; ~ **de ultramarinos** grocer's shop; **ir de** ~**s** to go shopping; **poner** ~ to open a shop

tienta testing (of fighting bulls); sounding rod; probe; **andar a** ~**s** to feel one's way

tientaguja sounding rod

tientaparedes *m+f sing+pl* groper

tiento feel, touch, tact; blow, cuff; pole (of tightrope walker); caution; *zool* tentacle; *mus* opening flourish, tuning up; **a** ~ by touch; **con** ~ very carefully; **dar un** ~ to have a bash/go at; **perder el** ~ to lose one's touch

tierno soft, tender; gentle; sweet-natured; **de edad tierna** of tender years

tierra earth; land; soil; country; region; ~ **campa** land without trees; ~ **de pan llevar** grain country; **echar por** ~ to demolish; **echar** ~ **a** to hush up; **en toda** ~ **de garbanzos** everywhere; **faltarle a uno la** ~ to stumble and fall; ~ **firme** mainland; **poner** ~ **por medio** to get away, clear off; **tomar** ~ to land; **torno de** ~ landing, landfall; **ver** ~ to sight land; **ver** ~**s** to see the world

tieso rigid, stiff; haughty; **quedarse** ~ to get frozen stiff; **tenerse** ~ to stick to one's guns

tiesto pot; flowerpot

tiesura rigidity, stiffness

tífico *adj* having typhus

¹ **tifo** see **tifus**

² **tifo** glutted, satiated

tifoidea *n* typhoid fever

tifoideo *adj* typhoid

tifón *m* typhoon

tifus *m* typhus; ~ **asiático** cholera; ~ **de América** yellow fever; ~ **de oriente** bubonic plague

tigra female jaguar

tigre *m* tiger; jaguar; cruel person

tigresa tigress

tija shaft (of a key)

tijera scissors, shears; *carp* saw-horse; draining trench; sheep-shearer; ~**s** boom (across a river); **de** ~ folding; **silla de** ~ deckchair

tijereta small scissors; *ent* earwig; *bot* vine tendril

tijeretada *n* snip/cut with scissors

tijeretear *v* to cut with scissors

tijereteo noise made by scissors; cutting

tila *bot* linden-tree, lime-tree; linden flower; linden tea

tildar to put a **tilde** over; cancel, erase; find fault with; call, name, brand

tilde *f* sign over letter n; dash; fault

tildón *m* long dash

tiliche *n* knick-knack

tilichero pedlar

tilín *m* ting-a-ling; ring; chime; **en un ~** in a flash; **no me hace ~** I'm not struck on it

tilingo stupid, foolish

tilma blanket used as a cloak by Mexican peasants

tilo *see* **tila**

tilla gangway; deck planking

tillado wooden floor

tillar *v* to floor, plank

timador *m* swindler

tímalo *zool* grayling

timar to cheat, swindle; **~se** (of sweethearts) to wink at each other

timba gambling-house

timbal *m* kettledrum

timbaleo beat of the kettledrum

timbalero kettledrummer

timbrador *m* rubber stamp; stamping machine

timbrar to stamp

timbre *m* stamp; revenue stamp; push-bell; *fam* belly button; **~ metálico** metallic sound

timidez *f* timidity, shyness

tímido timid, shy

¹ **timo** *zool* grayling

² **timo** swindle; **dar un ~ a** to cheat, swindle

timocracia timocracy

timón *m* helm, rudder; *aer* joystick; rocket-stick; **~ de profundidad** *aer* elevator

timonear to steer

timonel *m* helmsman

timonera wheelhouse; *zool* tail feather

timonero *see* **timonel**

tímpano *anat* eardrum; *mus* kettledrum

tina large earthen jar

tinaco wooden tub

tinaja *see* **tina**

tinajería jar-shop

tinajero maker/seller of jars

tinción *f* dyeing

tinelo servants' dining-room

tinerfeño *adj* of Tenerife

tinge *m* *orni* black owl

tingible *adj* that can be dyed

tinglado shed; temporary stage; set-up; complicated matter; machination

tiniebla(s) darkness; **estar en ~** to be in the dark/in complete ignorance

tino knack, skilful touch; good aim; moderation; **a ~** gropingly; **a buen ~** at a guess; **con ~** well, successfully; **perder el ~** to lose one's touch; **sin ~** wildly

tinta *n* ink; dye; **~ china** Indian ink; **~ simpática** invisible ink; **de buena ~** on good authority; **recargar las ~s** to overdo it

tintar to dye, tinge

tinte *m* dye, dyeing; tint; hue, shade; dry cleaner's

tinterillo lawyer with scant knowledge

tintero inkwell; *print* ink table; **dejar en el ~** to leave unsaid

tintilla sweet red wine *esp* of Rota (Cadiz)

tintillo light-coloured wine

tintín *m* clang, clink

tintineo clinking, clanging; tinkle

tintirintín *m* shrill sound

tinto *n* red wine; *adj* deep-coloured; red; dyed; **vino ~** red wine

tintorería dyer's, dry-cleaner's

tintorera female shark

tintorero dyer; dry-cleaner

tintura dyeing; make-up; tincture; stain

tinturar to dye, tinge, stain; imbue

tiña *med* scalp ringworm; *fam* poverty

tiñería *fam* poverty; stinginess

tiñoso scabby, mangy; *fam* stingy

tiñuela *bot* dodder

tío uncle; *fam* bloke, geezer, chap

tiovivo merry-go-round

tipiadora *fam* typist

típico typical

tiple *m* treble/soprano voice; treble guitar; *f* soprano singer

tiplisonante treble, shrill

tipo type, figure; *comm* rate; *fam* bloke, fellow, guy

tipográfico typographical

tipógrafo typographer

tipometría typometry

tipómetro type-gauge

típula *ent* daddy-long-legs

tíquet *m* ticket

tiquismiquis *mpl* hairsplitting

tira strip; thong; shred; strap

tirabala pop-gun

tirabotas *m sing + pl* boot-hook

tirabraguero *med* truss

tirabuzón *m* corkscrew; curl, ringlet

tiracantos *m sing+pl* despicable person; a nobody

tiracol *m* sword-belt

tirada throw; distance; space; lapse of time; series; *print* edition, run-off; *mus* tirade; ~ **aparte** extra printing, reprint, off-print; **de una** ~ at one go

tiradera strap; trace (harness); long arrow

tiradero (hunting, shooting) +*phot* hide

tirado *n* drawing, pulling; printing; *adj* flowing; *naut* long and low (hull); (of prices) give-away; walk-over; trash

tirador *m* drawer; thrower; marksman; handle, knob; bell-pull

tirafondo *carp* screw

tiralíneas *m sing+pl* drawing-pen

tiramiento *n* stretching, drawing

tiramira long distance; long mountain ridge; long line of people, traffic *etc*

tirana ancient Spanish folksong

tiranía tyranny

tiranicida *m+f* tyrannicide (person)

tiranicidio tyrannicide (deed)

tiránico tyrannical

tiranización *f* tyrannizing

tiranizar to tyrannize

tirano *n* tyrant; *adj* tyrannical

tirante *n m* trace (harness); *mech* brace, tie-rod; ~**s** pair of braces, *US* suspenders; *adj* tight

tirantez *f* tenseness; tension; strained relations

tiranuelo petty tyrant

tirar *vi* to attract (interest *etc*); draw (of a furnace); aim at; have a tinge/hint of; pull; ~ **a la derecha/izquierda** to turn/veer to the right/left; ~ **de** to pull; ~ **de espada** to draw one's sword; **ir tirando** to get by, manage; **tira y afloja** give and take; ~**se** to rush, hurl o.s.; jump; *vt* to throw, cast; throw away; cast off; fire (a shot); give (a kick); draw; stretch; knock over, upset; draw (a line); print; squander

tirela *text* striped material

tiricia *fam* jaundice

tirilla edging; neckband

tirios y troyanos opposing factions

tiritaña flimsy material; trifle

tirita sticking plaster dressing

tiritar to shiver; shake

tiritón *m* shivering, chill

tiritona affected shivering

Tiro Tyre

tiro throw, cast; shot; discharge; aim; firing; sound of firing; *mil* piece of ordnance; target practice; firing-range; trace (harness); flight (of stairs); petty theft; length of a piece of cloth; prank; ~**s** sword belts; **a** ~ within range; **a** ~ **de piedra (de)** a stone's throw (from); **a** ~ **hecho** on purpose; **al** ~ immediately; ~ **al blanco** target-practice; **errar el** ~ to miss the target; **ni a** ~**s** not for all the tea in China; **salir el** ~ **por la culata** to backfire; **de** ~**s largos** dressed to kill; **pegar un** ~ to fire a shot

tirocinio apprenticeship; period of probation

tiroides *m sing+pl* thyroid gland

¹ **tirolés** *n m sing+pl +adj* Tyrolean

² **tirolés** *m sing+pl* pedlar

tirón *m* pull, tug; novice; *sl* bag-snatcher; **de un** ~ in one go, at a stretch; **ni a tirones** hopeless, impossible

tirona fishing-net

tiroriros *mpl fam* wind instruments

tirotear to shoot at; ~**se** to exchange shots

tiroteo shooting; gun-fight; exchange of shots

tirria dislike; **tener** ~ **a** to bear a grudge against

tirso wand, staff

tirulato astonished, speechless

tisana infusion

tísico *med* consumptive

tisis *f sing+pl med* consumption

tisú *m* tissue

titánico titanic

titanio titanium

titear to mock

títere *m* puppet, marionette; ~**s** puppet show; **no dejar** ~ **con cabeza** to cause complete destruction, wreak havoc

titeretada underhand trick

tití *m* small monkey

titilación *f* titillation; quivering; twinkling

titilador, titilante titillating; quivering; twinkling

titilar *vi* to quiver; twinkle; *vt* to titillate

titímalo *bot* spurge

titirimundi *m* peepshow

titiritaina din

490

titiritar to shiver
titiritero puppeteer
titubeante vacillating, hesitating
titubear to stutter; vacillate, hesitate
titubeo vacillation, wavering, hesitation
titulado *n* titled person; professionally qualified person; *adj* qualified; entitled
titular *n m* holder, incumbent; headline; *f* capital letter; *vi* to obtain a title/qualification; *vt* to title; call, entitle
titulillo petty title; *print* page heading; **andar en** ~s to split hairs
título title; titled person; university degree; qualification; certificate, bond; **a** ~ **de** by way of, as; **a** ~ **individual/particular** on one's own account, in a private capacity; ~ **de propiedad** title-deed
tiza chalk
tizar to draw, design
tizna lampblack
tiznadura *n* smudging
tiznajo stain, smudge
tiznar to blacken, smudge
tizne *m* soot, smut, lampblack
tiznón *m* smut, smudge
tizo half-burnt charcoal
tizón *m* brand; half-burnt wood; *hort* blight, mildew; **negro como el** ~ black as pitch
tizonada, tizonazo *fam* hell-fire
tizonear to poke (a fire)
tizonero poker
toa hawser, rope
toalla towel
toallera towel-rack
toar to tow
toballeta napkin
tobillera *sp* ankle support
tobillo ankle
tobogán *m* toboggan; slide, chute; helter-skelter
toca coif; head-dress; bonnet
tocable playable
tocadiscos *m sing+pl* record-player, gramophone, *US* phonograph; ~ **tragaperras** juke-box
tocado *n* head-dress; *adj* daft, crazy
tocador *m* dressing-table, dressing-room; toilet case; *mus* player, performer; **artículos de** ~ toilet articles
tocadura coiffure, headgear
tocamiento *n* touching

tocante *adj* touching; ~ **a** concerning
tocar *vi* to be one's turn; be related to; do one's hair; touch, (billiards) kiss; appertain to; ~ **de cerca** to affect closely; ~ **en lo vivo** to wound to the quick; ~ **a la puerta** to knock at the door; **me tocó el coñac** I won the brandy; **por lo que** ~ **a** as regards; **toca marcharnos** it's time for us to go; *vt* to touch; (of clocks) strike; touch upon; *mus* play; inspire; ~ **a muerto** to sound the knell; ~ **diana** to beat/sound the reveille; ~ **fondo** *naut* to strike ground; ~**se** to cover one's head
tocasalva rack for glasses
tocata *fam* beating; *mus* toccata
tocateja: a ~ cash down, cash on the nail
tocayo namesake
tocino speck; streaky bacon; fat; fast skipping
toco *sl* share of stolen goods
tocología obstetrics
tocólogo obstetrician
tocón *n m* stump (of tree/limb); *adj* overfond of touching
tocotoco *orni* pelican
tochedad *f* coarseness; rusticity
tocho *n* metal bloom; (Scout's) woggle; *adj* coarse, uncouth
tochura *see* **tochedad**
todabuena *bot* St John's-wort
todavía still, yet; ~ **no** not yet
todito *fam* every little bit (of)
todo *n* whole, all, everything; ~s everybody, everyone; **ante** ~ first of all; **con** ~ for all that; **de** ~ a bit of everything; **del** ~ altogether; **jugarse el** ~ **por el** ~ to stake all; **sobre** ~ above all; **vieja y** ~ despite her age; *adj* all, entire; each, every; **a** ~ **color** *TV* in full colour; **a** ~ **correr** flat out; ~ **confort** all mod. cons.; *adv* all, completely; *pron* all, everything; **es** ~ **uno** it's one and the same thing; ~ **incluído** inclusive charges, no extras
todopoderoso all-powerful, almighty
tofo *med* tumour
toga toga; academic gown; judge's robe
togado robed
togolés *n+adj* Togolese
toisón de oro *m* Golden Fleece
tojal *m bot* patch of gorse
tojo *bot* gorse

tola shrub, bush

tolanos *mpl* short hair on the neck

toldadura awning

toldar to cover with an awning

toldería Indian camp/village

toldo awning; blinds, *US* shades; pomp; Indian tent

tole *m* hubbub, outcry; expression of disapproval

toledano *n+adj* Toledan; **noche tole-dana** sleepless night

tolerancia tolerance; toleration

tolerante tolerant

tolerantismo toleration; religious freedom

tolerar to tolerate; bear

tolete *m naut* thole(-pin)

tolmo tor

tolondro *n* bump; scatterbrain; *adj* scatterbrained

tolondrón *n m* bump; **a tolondrones** by fits and starts; *adj* scatterbrained

tolteca *n m+f+adj* Toltec

tolvanera cloud of dust

tolla bog, fen

tollo *photo* (and hunting) hide; bog, fen

tollón *m* gorge, ravine

toma taking; dose; capture; *elect* current collector, tap; *rad* terminal; ~ **de tierra** *aer+naut* landing

tomacorriente *m elect* socket, plug

tomada capture

tomadero handle; drain opening, outlet

tomador *n m* taker, receiver; retriever (dog); *naut* gasket; *comm* drawee; *adj* taking; (of dogs) retrieving; boozing

tomadura taking; ~ **de pelo** teasing, leg-pulling

tomaína ptomaine

tomajón *fam* sticky-fingered, light-fingered

tomar to take; have (drink *etc*); take hold of; take up; get, gather; **¡toma!** well, well!; **¡tómalo con calma!** take it easy!; ~ **algo a mal** to take s.t. badly; ~ **el fresco** to take the air; ~ **el pelo** to tease; ~ **el sol** to sunbathe; ~ **estado** to marry, take holy orders; ~ **fuerzas** to gain strength; ~ **la delantera a** to overtake; ~ **las de Villadiego** to clear out; ~ **lenguas** to make inquiries; ~ **puerto** to make port; ~ **represalias a** to victimize; ~ **tierra** *aer* to land; ~ **un cariz feo** to begin to look nasty/

serious; ~**se** to get rusty

Tomás Thomas

tomatada tomato fry

tomatal *m* tomato field

tomatazo blow with a tomato

tomate *m usu* beef tomato; ~ **canario** small tomato; *fam* hole (in heel of sock *etc*); **aquí hay mucho** ~ there's a lot to be done here

tomatera tomato plant

tomatero *n* tomato grower/seller; tomato boat; *adj* of tomato(es); fond of tomatoes

tomavistas *m sing+pl* cine-camera

tómbola charity raffle

tómbolo long sandbank joining two pieces of land

tomillar *m* thyme bed/field

tomillo *bot* thyme

tomo volume, tome; **de** ~ **y lomo** dyed-in-the-wool

tomón *n m* thief; *adj* sticky-fingered

ton: sin ~ **ni son** without rhyme or reason

tonada tune; accent

tonadilla musical interlude; light tune

tonadillero composer of light music

tonalidad *f* tone; *tel* ringing tone (of phone); shade

tonado *archi* round moulding

tonel *m* barrel; cask

tonelada ton

tonelaje *m naut* tonnage; *comm* tonnage dues

tonelería cooper's shop/workshop; cooper's trade; barrels, casks; *naut* water-casks

tonelero cooper

tonelete *m* keg; short skirt

tonga layer, stratum

tongano *n+adj* Tongan

tongo *sp* cheat; **¡hay** ~! it's a fix!

tónica *mus* keynote; tonic water

tónico *n+adj* tonic; accented (syllable)

tonificador, tonificante *adj* tonic, strengthening, fortifying

tonificar *med* to fortify, tone up

tonillo monotonous tone; accent

tonina *zool* dolphin

tono tone; tune; *med* strength; *mus* pitch, key; **a ese** ~ at that rate; **bajar el** ~ to lower one's voice; **dar el** ~ to set the standard; **darse** ~ to give o.s. airs; **de buen/mal** ~ in good/bad taste; **ir a**

~ **con** to be in tune with; **fuera de** ~ out of place, unsuitable; **ponerse a** ~ *mil* to get in step/in line; **salida de** ~ tasteless, in bad taste; **subido de** ~ bright

tonsila *med* tonsil

tonsilitis *f med* tonsillitis

tonsura tonsure; sheep-shearing; fleecing

tonsurar to shear, cut (hair or wool); fleece; give the tonsure to

tontada foolishness, nonsense

tontaina *m+f* dolt

tontear to fool about; flirt

tontería *see* **tontada**

tontico little twit

tontiloco harebrained

tontillo bustle; hoop-skirt

tontina tontine

tontivano foolishly proud

tonto *n* fool, ninny; ~ **de capirote** dunce; **hacer el** ~ to play the fool; **hacerse el** ~ to pretend not to understand; **volver a uno** ~ to drive s.o. crazy

tontuna foolishness

toña tipcat (game); large loaf; *fam* intoxication

¡top! *naut* hold!, stop!

topa butt (of an animal)

topacio topaz

topador *m* animal given to butting; gambler

topar to butt; come up against; meet, find

tope *m* top, end; stop, stopper; obstacle; quarrel; bump; (railway) buffer; *naut* mast-head; ~ **salarial** wages ceiling; **a/al** ~ full up; **a todo** ~ at the very most; **estar hasta el** ~ to be packed full

topera mole-hole

topero *sl* burglar/housebreaker who uses a jemmy

topetada butt, bump

topetar to butt; knock against

topetazo, topetón *m* butt; bump, collision

topetudo given to butting

tópico *n* cliché; *adj* local

topinada *fam* awkwardness

topinera mole-hole; mole-hill

topista *m see* **topero**

topo *zool+pol* mole; clumsy person; half-blind person

topográfico topographical

topógrafo topographer, surveyor

toponímico *adj* toponymic

topónimo toponym

toque *m* touch; sounding, ringing (of bells), beat (of drums); trial, test; hint; ~ **a muerto/de difuntos/de ánimas** knell; ~ **de corneta** bugle call; ~ **de diana** reveille; ~ **de queda** curfew; **a** ~ **de campana** at the double; **ahí está el** ~ there's the rub; **dar un** ~ **a** to drop a hint to, sound out

toqueado clapping, stamping

toquetear to finger, paw, mess about

toqueteo fingering, pawing, messing about

toquero veil-maker; head-dress maker

toquilla shawl

tora figure of a bull in fireworks display

toral *m* copper bar; *adj* main, principal, chief

tórax *m* thorax, chest

torbellino whirlwind

torca *geol* funnel

torcal *m* cavernous region

torcaz (of pigeons) wild; **paloma** ~ ring-dove

torcecuello *orni* wryneck

torcedero twisting

torcedor *n m* twister; cause of grief; ~ **de tabaco** cigar-maker; *adj* twisting

torcedura twisting; sprain

torcer to twist; turn; bend; sprain; ~ **el gesto** to pull a face; **estar torcido con** to be on bad terms with; ~**se** to get twisted/sprained; go awry; **si no se tuerce** so long as nothing happens to prevent it

torcida wick

torcido *n* twisted silk; *adj* twisted; tortuous; oblique; crooked; bent

torcijón *m* twist; sprain; bend; warping; circumlocution; bellyache

torculado shaped like a screw

tórculo *print* small press

tordella *orni* missel-thrush

tordillo grizzled, greyish

tordo *n orni* thrush; ~ **loco** solitary thrush; *adj* speckled, dappled

torear to fight (bulls); *fam* lead a merry dance; fluster

toreo bullfighting

torero *n* bullfighter; *adj* bullfighting

torera short, tight jacket; **saltarse a la** ~ to disregard (the rules *etc*)

torete *m* rumour; absorbing topic; difficult problem; young bull

toril *m* bull-pen

torillo little bull; *carp* dowel

torio thorium

toriondez *f* rutting (of cattle)

torloroto rustic flute

tormenta storm, thunderstorm

tormentar to suffer torment

tormentario *n* gunnery, artillery

tormento torment, torture; **dar ~ a** to put to torture

tormentoso stormy

tormo tor; turf, sod

torna restitution; return; **volver las ~s a** to turn the tables on; **se cambiaron las ~s** the tables are turned

tornaboda day after a wedding; first day of honeymoon

tornada return (journey)

tornadizo *n* turncoat; *adj* changeable

tornadura recompense

tornamiento turn, change

tornapunta *naut* stay, brace

tornar to return; give back; turn, change; go/come back; **~ en sí** to come to, come round; **~se** to become, turn

tornasol *m* sunflower; litmus; iridescence

tornasolado changing colour, iridescent

tornátil *adj* changeable, fickle; *carp+ mech* turned (on a lathe)

tornatrás *m+f sing+pl* throw-back

tornavía turntable

tornaviaje *m* return trip

tornavirón *m* slap, box

torneador *m* turner; tilter (at a tournament)

torneadura lathe shavings

tornear to shape by turning; turn, go round; tilt (at tournaments); meditate

torneo tournament; turning

tornero turner

tornillero *fam mil* deserter

tornillo screw; clamp; **~ de banco** vice; **apretar los ~s** to put the screws on; **hacer ~ mil** to desert; **le falta un ~** he has a screw loose

torniquete *m* tourniquet; turnstile; turnpike

torno wheel; axle-tree; winch, windlass; spinning wheel; spindle; serving hatch; **~ de alfarero** potter's wheel; **en ~ a** round about; **volver al ~** to go back to the grind

toro bull; *astron+astrol* Taurus; **~ bravo** fighting bull; **~ corrido** old hand; **~s** bullfighting, bullfight; **~s y cañas** quarrel; **dejar en los cuernos del ~** to leave in the lurch; **ver los ~ desde la barrera** to sit on the fence

toronja grapefruit

toroso robust, strong

torozón *m* gripes; *vet* enteritis

torpe clumsy; dull-witted; lewd

torpedear to torpedo; wreck

torpedeo torpedoing

torpedero torpedo-boat

torpedo torpedo; streamlined car; **~ de fondo, ~ durmiente** naval mine

torpeza clumsiness, stupidity

torrar *cul* to toast

torre *f* tower, turret; belfry; steeple; (chess) rook, castle; **~ de control** *aer* control tower; **~ de costa** watch-tower, Martello tower; **~ de luces** *naut* lighthouse; **~ de viento** castle in the air

torrear to fortify with towers

torrefacción *f* torrefaction, toasting

torrefacto (of coffee beans) toasted with added sugar

torrejón *m* badly built/shaped turret

torrencial torrential; overwhelming

torrentada strong current

torrente *m* torrent, rush; avalanche; abundance

torrero tower-guard; **~ de faro** light-house-keeper

torreznero lazy person

torrezno fritter of streaky bacon

tórrido torrid, parched

torrija sweet fritter of bread dipped in milk

torsión *f* torsion, twist

torta cake; pancake; pie; *print* font, forme; *fam* slap, smack; **~s y pan pintado** trifles, child's play; **hacer un pan con unas ~s** to make a mess of things; **ser una ~** to be very stolid; **no veo ni ~** I can't see a thing

tortada meat/chicken pie

tortedad *f* twistedness

tortel *m* flat bun

tortera pie-dish; baking-pan

torticero unjust

tortícolis *f* stiff neck

tortijón *m see* **torcijón**

tortilla omelette; pancake; ~ **española** potato omelette; ~ **(a la) francesa** plain omelette; **cuando se vuelva la** ~ when the boot is on the other foot; **hacerse** ~ to get flattened

tortillera *vulg sl* lesbian

tortita waffle; pancake

tórtola turtle-dove

tortolilla little love-bird

tortuga tortoise, turtle; **a paso de** ~ at a snail's pace

tortuosidad *f* tortuosity

torturar to torture

torva whirl of snow/rain

torvo sullen; sinister

torzal *m* silk twist; silk cord

torzonado contracted, twisted

torzuelo *orni* male falcon

tos *f* cough; ~ **ferina** whooping-cough

tosco rough, coarse; clumsy; uneducated

tosegoso *adj* coughing

toser *vi* to cough; *vt* to needle, aggravate; **no hay quien le tosa** no one can touch him; no one is his equal

tosidura coughing

tosigar to poison

tósigo pain; poison

tosigoso poisonous; coughing

tosquedad *f* coarseness; clumsiness

tostada piece of toast; *fam* bore

tostador *m* toaster

tostadura toasting

tostar to toast; tan, brown; ~**se al sol** to sunbathe

tostón *m* buttered toast; sucking-pig; *fam* bore, drag

total *n* sum total; *adj* total; *adv* to sum up; so; after all

totalidad *f* totality, whole; **la** ~ **de los jugadores** all the players

totalitario totalitarian

totalitarismo totalitarianism

totalizar to amount to

totemismo totem-worship

totilimundi *m* raree-show; peep-show

totuma cup made from a calabash

totumo calabash tree

toxicar to poison

tóxico *n* poison; *adj* poisonous

toxicología toxicology

toxicológico toxicological

toxicomanía drug-addiction

toxicómano *n* drug addict; *adj* drug-addicted

toxina toxin

tozal *m* summit

tozar to butt with the head

tozo *n* log, stump; block of wood; piece of bark; *adj* stocky, squat; dwarf

tozolada blow on the neck

tozudez *f* stubbornness, pig-headedness

tozudo stubborn, pig-headed

traba binding; bond; fetter; hobble; hindrance; wedge; **poner** ~s to hinder; **sin** ~s unrestrained(ly)

trabacuenta error (in accounts); dispute

trabadero pastern

trabado thickened; robust; (of horses) having white forefeet

trabadura bond, union

trabajado elaborate, carefully done

trabajador *n m* worker; *adj* hard-working

trabajante *adj* working, toiling

trabajar to work; *agri* till; work at/on/out; bother; deal in; ~ **a destajo** to do piece-work; ~ **a ritmo lento** to go slow

trabajillo little job

trabajo work, labour; job, task; trouble; hardship; ~ **a destajo** piece-work; ~s **forzados** hard labour; **cuesta** ~ it's hard work; **dar** ~ to make work; give work; **pasar** ~s to experience difficulties

trabajoso toilsome, laborious

trabalenguas *m sing + pl* tongue-twister

trabamiento joining, uniting

trabar to join, fasten, bind; shackle; fetter; begin, strike up; thicken; *carp* set (a saw); ~ **amistad** to make friends; ~ **batalla** to join battle; ~ **conversación** to begin a conversation; **trabársele a uno la lengua** to get tongue-tied

trabilla strap; (knitting) dropped stitch

trabón *m* fetter, hobble

trabuca fire-cracker

trabucación *f* mix-up

trabucaire arrogant; daring

trabucante muddling

trabucar to confuse, mix up; turn upside down; ~**se** to get mixed up

trabucazo shot with a blunderbuss; sudden surprise

trabuco blunderbuss; ~ **naranjero** punt-gun

trabuquete *m* catapult

traca series of fire-crackers/rockets set to go off in succession

trácala gang; swindle

tracalada mob

tracamundana hubbub, bustle; barter

tracción *f* drive, traction; ~ **delantera** front-wheel drive; ~ **trasera** rear-mounted engine, rear-wheel drive

tracería *archi* tracery

tracista *m+f* designer; schemer

tracoma trachoma

tracto period of time; distance

tractor *m* tractor; traction engine; ~ **oruga** caterpillar tractor

tractorista *m+f* tractor driver

tradición *f* tradition

tradicional traditional

tradicionalismo traditionalism

tradicionalista *n m+f* traditionalist

traducción *f* translation

traducible translatable

traducir to translate; convert; ~**se en** to result in

traductor *m* translator

traedizo portable

traedor *m* porter, conveyer

traer to bring; fetch; carry; bring about; result in; wear; ~ **a colación** to bring up; ~ **a cuento** to mention; ~ **algo entre manos** to be up to no good; ~ **a mal** ~, ~ **de cabeza** to treat roughly; ~ **entre ojos** to be suspicious of; ~ **loco** to drive mad; ~ **y llevar** to bandy about; **por la cuenta que le trae** in his own interests; ~**se entre manos** to be occupied with

traeres *mpl* ornaments, finery

trafagante dealing, trafficking

trafagar to deal, traffic; wander; hustle; do tiring work

tráfago dealing, trafficking; trade; bustle; things happening

trafagón *n m* hustler; *adj* industrious

traficación *f* traffic, commerce

traficante *n m* trafficker, trader; *adj* trafficking, trading

traficar to traffic, trade; deal; roam

tráfico traffic, trade, commerce

trafulla cheating, swindling

tragacanto tragacanth

tragacete *m* dart, javelin

tragaderas *fpl* gullet; **tener buenas** ~ to be very gullible; to eat a lot

tragadero gullet; pit; vortex; *naut* trough (of the sea)

tragador *m* glutton

tragahombres *m sing+pl* bully

tragaldabas *m sing+pl* glutton

tragaleguas *m sing+pl* good walker; fast walker

tragaluz *f* skylight

tragantada big swig

tragante *adj* swallowing

tragantón gluttonous

tragantona spread, feast

tragar to swallow; put up with; believe; ~ **quina** to grin and bear it; ~**se un insulto** to pocket one's pride

tragasantos *m sing+pl cont* Bible-basher

tragavirotes *m sing+pl fam* stuffed shirt, pompous person

tragazón *f* gluttony

tragedia tragedy

trágico *n* tragedian; writer of tragedies; *adj* tragic

tragicomedia tragi-comedy

tragicómico tragi-comical

trago gulp; swallow, swig; **a** ~**s** little by little; **echar un** ~ to have a drink; **pasar malos** ~**s** to have a rough time of it; **de un** ~ at one gulp

tragón *n m* glutton, gannet; *adj* greedy, gluttonous

tragonear to gorge, stuff o.s.

tragontina *bot* arum lily

traición *f* treason, treachery; **a** ~ treacherously; **alta** ~ high treason

traicionar to betray

traicionero treacherous; deceptive

traído thread-bare

traidor *n m* traitor; *adj* treacherous; disloyal

trafilla lash, whip; leash; machine for levelling roads

traillar to level

traína seine net; sardine net

traite *m text* raising the nap

traje *m* suit; lounge suit, *US* business suit; costume; ~ **charro** ostentatious riding habit; ~ **de etiqueta** evening dress; ~ **de luces** bullfighter's costume; ~ **neopreno** wet-suit; **baile de** ~**s** fancy-dress dance

trajear to clothe

trajín *m* hustle, bustle; carriage

trajinante *m* carrier

trajinar *vi* to bustle; potter about;

traipse about; *vt* to cart, carry

trajinería carrying, carting; toing and froing

trajinero carrier

tralla whip-lash; cord

trallazo crack (of whip); lash

trama texture; plot, conspiracy; *bot* blossoming

tramador *n m* plotter, schemer; *text* weaver; *adj* weaving; plotting

tramar to weave; plot, conspire; (of olive-trees) bloom

tramilla twine

tramitación *f* procedure; formalities

tramitar to arrange; put through

trámite *m* arrangement, formality

tramo strip of land; flight (of stairs); section (of road); span (of bridge)

tramontana north wind; pride; **perder la ~** to lose control of o.s.

tramontano tramontane; north side

tramontar *vi* to go over the mountains; *vt* to help to escape

tramoya intrigue; *theat* stage machinery

tramoyista *m theat* stage hand, stage carpenter; scene shifter; schemer, plotter

trampa trap, snare; trap door; (of trousers) fly; bad debt; cheat; **caer en la ~** to fall into the trap; **coger en la ~** to trap; **hacer ~s** to cheat

trampal *m* bog, quagmire

trampantojo trick; optical illusion

trampeador *m* borrower; swindler

trampear *vi* to live by borrowing; scrape by; *vt* to deceive

trampería trickery, chicanery

trampilla peep-hole; door of kitchen stove; trapdoor

trampista *m* cheat; card-sharper

trampolín *m* spring-board; person used by another for ulterior motives

tramposo *n* cheat, swindler; *adj* cheating, swindling

tranca club, cudgel; thick stick; crossbar; drunkenness; **a ~s y barrancas** through thick and thin; **llevar/coger una ~** to get drunk

trancada long stride; clout; **en dos ~s in** a jiffy

trancahilo knot used by surgeons

trancar *vi* to stride along; *vt* to bolt (a door)

trancazo clout; bout of flu

trance *m* trance; critical situation; *leg* seizure; **a todo ~** at all costs, come what may

tranco threshold; long stride; **a ~s in a** hurry; **en dos ~s in** a jiffy

tranchete *m* cobbler's knife

tranquera palisade, fence; gate

tranquero *bui* angular stone (of jamb/lintel)

tranquilar *comm* to balance (accounts); check off

tranquilidad *f* tranquillity, peace; ease of mind

tranquilizante *n m* tranquillizer; *adj* tranquillizing

tranquilizar to tranquillize, calm; **~se** to calm down, take it easy

tranquilo tranquil, calm, peaceful; with one's mind at rest; ¡**~!** calm down, take it easy

tranquilla bar, pin; lug; trap

tranquillo knack

transacción *f* transaction; arrangement

transalpino transalpine

transandino trans-Andean

transar to compromise

transatlántico *n* transatlantic liner; *adj* transatlantic

transbordador *m* ferry; **~ espacial** space shuttle; *adj* transhipping, transferring

transbordar to transfer, tranship

transbordo transfer; transhipment; **hacer ~** to transfer, change

transcendencia *see* **trascendencia**

transcendental *see* **trascendental**

transcendentalismo *see* **trascendentalismo**

transcendente *see* **trascendente**

transcender *see* **trascender**

transcribir to transcribe

transcripción *f* transcription

transcurrir to pass; take place, happen

transcurso passing; lapse; course

transeúnte *n m* passer-by; *adj* transient

transferencia transfer, transference

transferidor *m* transferrer

transferir to transfer

transfigurable transformable

transfigurar to transfigure; **~se** to be transfigured

transfijo transfixed

transfixión *f* transfixion

transflor *m* enamel painting

transflorar *vi* to show through; *vt* to

paint on metal; trace against the light

transflorear to paint on metal

transformación *f* transformation

transformador *m* transformer

transformar to transform; ~**se** to be transformed, change

transformativo transformative

transformista *n m+f theat* quick-change artist; *adj* transformistic

transfretano *adj* situated across a stretch of water

transfretar *vi* to spread, extend; *vt* to cross (the sea)

tránsfuga *m*, **tránsfugo** deserter, fugitive; turncoat

transfundir to transfuse; spread

transfusión *f* transfusion; ~ **de sangre** blood transfusion

transgredir to transgress

transgresión *f* transgression

transgresor *m* transgressor

transición *f* transition

transido overwhelmed, stricken

transigencia tolerance, compromise

transigente broadminded, tolerant, accommodating

transigir to compromise (**en** on); ~ **con** to countenance

transitable practicable; passable

transitar to pass, go, travel (through/ along)

transitivo *gramm* transitive; *leg* transferable

tránsito traffic; transit; transition; death; ~ **rodado** wheeled traffic; **de** ~ passing through; **hacer** ~ to make a stop

transitorio transitory

translación *see* **traslación**

translimitación *f* trespass; intervention

translimitar to go beyond the bounds (of reason, decency *etc*)

translucidez *f* translucence

translúcido, transluciente translucent

transmarino transmarine

transmigración *f* transmigration

transmigrar to transmigrate

transmisibilidad *f* transmissibility

transmisible transmissible

transmisión *f* transmission; **transmisiones** *mil* signals (unit)

transmisor *n m* transmitter; *adj* transmitting

transmitir to transmit, broadcast

transmudación *f* transmutation, change

transmudar to transfer; change

transmutable convertible

transmutación *f* transmutation

transmutar to transmute

transmutativo transmitting

transparencia transparency

transparentarse to show through

transparente *n m* altar window; window shade; *adj* transparent

transpirable perspirable

transpiración *f* perspiration

transpirar to transpire; perspire

transpirenaico trans-Pyrenean

transponedor *n m* transplanter; transposer; *adj* transposing

transponer to transpose; transplant; turn; ~**se** to go down; go to sleep; disappear

transportación *f* transportation, conveyance

transportador *n m* transporter, carrier; *adj* transporting, conveying

transportamiento transportation, carriage; ecstasy

transportar to transport, convey; *mus* transpose; ~**se** to get carried away

transporte *m* transport; conveyance; shipment

transportista *m* transport worker

transposición *f* transposition

transterminar to transfer

transubstanciación *f* transubstantiation

transubstancial transubstantial

transubstanciar to transubstantiate

transvasar to decant

transverberación *f* transfixion

transversal, transverso transverse

tranvía *m* tram, *US* streetcar; trolley

tranviario *n m+f* tramway worker; *adj* of trams

tranza *leg* seizure

tranzadera knot of plaited ribbons

tranzar to cut; plait

Trapa: la ~ Trappist order

trapa tramp(ing) of feet; hubbub, uproar

trapacear to swindle, cheat, defraud

trapacería cheat, swindle; fraud

trapacero *n* cheat, swindler; *adj* cheating, swindling

trapacista *m+f* cheat, deceiver

trapajo rag

trapajoso ragged, tattered; **lengua tra-**

pajosa indistinct speech

trápala stamping of feet; noise of a galloping horse; confusion; deceit; *m+f* prattler

trapalear to chatter; lie; cheat; rattle along; make a clatter with the feet

trapalón *n m* liar; cheat; *adj* lying; cheating

trapatiesta row, argument

trapaza trick; fraud

trapazar to cheat, trick

trape *m* buckram

trapecio trapeze; *geom* trapezium

trapense *m* Trappist

trapería rags; old clothes shop; rag-shop

trapero *n* rag-and-bone dealer; rag picker; *adj* **puñalada trapera** underhand trick; stab in the back

trapezoide *m* trapezoid

trapiche *m* olive-press; sugar-refinery; *min* ore-crusher

trapichear to scheme, be on the fiddle; retail

trapicheo fiddling, plotting, shady dealing

trapichero shady character

trapiento tattered

trapillo *fam* nest-egg; squalid love affair; **de ~** casually dressed

trapío *naut* sails; glamour; covetousness; (bullfighting) fighting spirit (of bull)

trapisonda scheming; *fam* shindig, uproar; *naut* white-caps, breakers

trapisondear to scheme, cause a riot

trapisondista *m+f* schemer; troublemaker

trapito small rag; **~s** clothes; **en ~s de cristianar** in one's Sunday best

trapo rag; duster; *naut* sails, canvas; bullfighter's **muleta**; **a todo ~** full tilt, with all sails set; **manos de ~** butterfingers; **poner como un ~** to give a dressing-down; **soltar el ~** to burst into tears/laughter

traque *m* fuse, touch-paper (of firework); noise of exploding fireworks; **a ~ barraque** at any time

tráquea trachea, windpipe

traquear *see* **traquetear**

traqueo *see* **traqueteo**

traqueotomía *med* tracheotomy

traquetear *vi* to rattle, crackle; *vt* to shake up, jolt; move about

traqueteo rattling; crackling; jolting

traquido crack (of a firearm); creak (of wood)

tras *prep* after; behind; beyond; furthermore; **~ de** after, in addition to; *n fam* backside

trasalcoba alcove (off a bedroom)

trasalpino *see* **transalpino**

trasaltar *m* reredos, altar-screen

trasanteanoche three nights ago

trasanteayer, trasantier three days ago

trasañejo *vet* three years old

trasatlántico *see* **transatlántico**

trasbordar *see* **transbordar**

trasca leather thong

trascabo (wrestling) leg-hold; trip

trascantón *m* corner stone of curb; **dar ~** to escape, give the slip

trascendencia transcendency, importance

trascendental transcendental, exceedingly important; far-reaching

trascendentalismo transcendentalism

trascendente transcendent

trascender to transcend, leak out, extend; have important consequences

trascendido acute, far-reaching

trascocina back-kitchen, scullery

trascolar to percolate, strain

trasconejarse to get lost/mislaid

trascordarse to forget

trascoro space behind the choir-stalls

trascorral *m* backyard

trascribir *see* **transcribir**

trascripción *see* **transcripción**

trascuarto small room off a larger one

trasdobladura trebling

trasdoblar to treble

trasdós *m archi* extrados

trasechador *m* waylayer

trasechar to waylay

trasegar *vi* to booze; *vt* to decant; transfer; turn on end

traseñalar to mark again, countermark

trasera back (of house/cupboard/door *etc*)

trasero *n* behind, backside, buttocks; **~s** forebears, ancestors; *adj* back, rear, hind

trasferencia *see* **transferencia**

trasferir *see* **transferir**

trasfigurar *see* **transfigurar**

trasformación *see* **transformación**

trasformador *see* **transformador**

trasformar see **transformar**

trasfregar to rub, scour

trasfuga see **transfuga**

trasfundir see **transfundir**

trasfusión see **transfusión**

trasgo (hob)globin, gnome, sprite; *fig* disobedient child

trasgredir see **transgredir**

trasgresor see **transgresor**

trasguear to behave as a hobgoblin; make mischief

trashoguero *n* back of a grate; large log; *adj* stop-at-home

trashojar to flip through the pages (of a book *etc*)

trashumancia changing pasture in the spring and autumn

trashumante (of flocks) nomadic

trashumar to move from winter to summer pasture (and back)

trasiego disorder, chaos, upset; decanting; moving to and fro

trasijado lank, lean, meagre

traslación *f*, **trasladación** *f* moving, transfer; postponement; translation; transcription

trasladador *m* mover, transferrer, translator

trasladar to (re)move, transfer; translate; adjourn, postpone; transcribe, copy

traslado removal, moving, transfer; transcript, copy; *leg* notification

traslapar to overlap, superpose

traslaticio figurative, metaphorical

traslativo transferring

traslato see **traslaticio**

trasloar to give fulsome praise to, adulate

traslucidez see **translucidez**

trasluciente see **translucido**

traslucirse to shine/show through; leak out; be revealed

traslumbramiento dazzlement

traslumbrar to dazzle; ~se to be dazzled; disappear, go quick as a flash

trasluz *m* reflected/diffused light; **al** ~ against the light

trasmallo trammel-net; handle of hammer/mallet

trasmano (cards) second player; **a** ~ out of the way, in the wilds

trasmañanar to postpone, delay; leave until tomorrow

trasmatar *fam* to wish (a person) dead

trasmigración see **transmigración**

trasminar to percolate, undermine

trasmisible see **transmisible**

trasmisión see **transmisión**

trasmontar to pass beyond, climb over

trasmosto poor-quality wine, plonk

trasmudar see **transmudar**

trasmutación see **transmutación**

trasnochada sleeplessness; sleepless night; last night; *mil* night raid, night attack

trasnochado out-of-date, old-fashioned, démodé; pale-faced, wan

trasnochador *m* one who stays up late/stays up all night

trasnochar to stay out late; sleep away from home

trasnoche *m*, **trasnocho** staying out late

trasnombrar to make a mistake in s.o.'s name

trasoír to misunderstand; mishear

trasojado having deep-set eyes

trasoñar to get all wrong, imagine incorrectly

traspalar to shovel away; hoe; weed

traspaleo shovelling; hoeing; weeding

traspapelar to mislay; ~se to get mislaid

trasparencia see **transparencia**

trasparente see **transparente**

traspasador *m* trespasser; transgressor

traspasar to transfer; cross over; pierce; transgress

traspaso transfer; crossing; piercing; transgressing; payment for fittings; key-money

traspatio backyard

traspeinar to touch up (hair with a comb)

traspellar to shut, close

traspié *m* stumble, trip, slip; (wrestling) leg-hold; **dar** ~**s**, **dar un** ~ to slip, slip up

traspillar to shut, close; ~se to grow thin

traspintar to play a card after showing another; ~se to turn out the opposite of what one anticipated

traspirar see **transpirar**

trasplantar to transplant, re-pot; ~se to migrate

trasplante *m* transplantation, repotting; migration; *med* transplant

trasponer see **transponer**

traspontín *m mot* folding seat; under-mattress; *fam* bottom, backside

trasportación *see* **transportación**

trasporte *see* **transporte**

¹ **traspuesta** transport; corner, turning; disappearance; concealment; hiding-place; flight, escape

² **traspuesta** backyard, backgarden; back-door; outbuilding at the back of a house

traspunte *m theat* prompter

trasquero leather-cutter

trasquiladero place where sheep are sheared

trasquilador *m* sheep-shearer

trasquiladura shearing, clipping; bad haircut

trasquilar to shear (sheep); cut the hair unevenly; *fig* curtail; diminish; rob through a trick

trasquilimocho *fam* close-cropped

trasquilón *m* clipping, cutting, shearing; money lost through a trick; **a trasquilones** irregularly, unevenly

trastabillar to stagger, reel

trastada *fam* underhand trick; bad turn; prank

trastazo *fam* hard blow

traste *m* wine-glass used for sampling; *mus* fret; **dar al ~ con** to scotch, wreck, ruin, put paid to

trasteado *mus* set of frets (on a guitar)

trasteador *n m* rummager; *adj* moving things around

trastear *vt mus* to fret a guitar; *mus* play the guitar; (bullfighting) incite by waving the **muleta**; manipulate; *vi* rummage about; talk excitedly

trastejador *m* roof-tiler

trastejar to roof; repair

trastejo roofing, tiling; fuss

trasteo (bullfighting) playing the bull; skilful and tactful handling (of things/people)

trastería heap of junk; mean trick; mob

trastero *n* lumber, junk; lumber-room; *adj* (of) lumber, (of) furniture not being used

trastesado stiff, rigid

trastienda room at the rear of a shop; *fig* astuteness

trasto piece of lumber/junk; unused piece of furniture/tackle; piece of furniture; tool, implement; *theat* set-piece; smart customer; **tirarse los ~s a la cabeza** to have a set-to; **~s viejos** junk

trastocar to upset; change around; **~se** to lose one's reason

trastornable easily upset

trastornador *adj* upsetting

trastornadura, trastornamiento *n* up-setting

trastornar to upset, make topsy-turvy; put into a crazed/dazed state

trastorno upheaval, upset, mess-up; dis-order; inconvenience

trastrabarse to get tied up/tongue-tied

trastrabillar to reel, stagger; hesitate; stammer; trip up

trastrás *m* last but one, next to last

trastrocamiento switching round

trastrocar to switch round

trastrueco, trastrueque *m* switching round

trastulo toy, pastime

trastumbar to drop, let fall; roll (a ball *etc*)

trasudar to sweat slightly

trasudor *m* slight sweat

trasuntar to abridge; copy

trasunto abridgement; copy, transcript; likeness

trasver to see through; glimpse

trasversal *see* **transversal**

trasverter to overflow

trasvolar to fly across

trata slave-trade; **~ de blancas** white-slave traffic

tratable approachable

tratado treaty; treatise

tratador *m* mediator

tratamiento treatment; title

tratante *m* dealer, trader

tratar *vi* to deal (with), be about; try (to); *vt* to treat; deal with; discuss; **~ de tú/de usted** to be familiar/formal with; **~se** to deal, behave; **no me trato con** I'm not friends with; **¿ de qué se trata?** what's it all about?

trato treatment; manner; address; title; deal; agreement; **¡~ hecho!** it's a deal!; **~ de gentes** gift of getting on well with people; **cerrar un ~** to close/clinch a deal; **malos/buenos ~s** bad/good treatment; **tener buen ~** to be pleasant/well-mannered

traumático traumatic

traumatismo traumatism

traumatizar to subject to a traumatic experience

traumatología traumatology

traumatólogo traumatologist

través *m* slant; *mil* traverse; *archi* cross-beam; **a ~ de** across, through; **de ~** cross-wise; **mirar de ~** to look askance

travesaño cross-beam, transom, cross-bar; bolster (long pillow)

travesar to cross, go across/through

travesear to joke, jest; caper, romp; be mischievous; be quick at repartee

travesero *n* bolster (long pillow); *adj* transverse, cross

travesía cross-road; crossing; crosswise position; *naut* side wind; *naut* pay/wages for one voyage; wasteland

travesío *n* cross-road; *adj* traversing; oblique

travesti *m sl* transvestite; *theat fam* female impersonator

travestido *n m* transvestite; *adj* disguised

travesura piece of naughtiness; mischievous prank

traviesa distance across; (railway) sleeper; *archi+bui* rafter; transverse wall; *min* cross-gallery

travieso *adj* cross; mischievous

trayecto stretch; fare-stage; route

trayectoria trajectory; path

trayente *adj* bringing, carrying

traza design; scheme, plan; means; mark; trace; **darse ~s** to find a way; **por las ~s** by the looks of him/her *etc*; **tener ~s de** to look like, show signs of

trazado plan; outline; layout

trazador *m* planner, designer

trazar to plan; design, draw; outline; map out; trace

trazo line; outline; **al ~** drawn in outline

trazumarse to ooze

trébedes *m+f sing+pl* tripod; trivet

trebejo plaything; chess piece; **~s** tools

trébol *m* clover; shamrock, trefoil; (cards) club

trece *n* thirteen; **seguir en sus ~** to refuse to budge; *adj* thirteenth

trecemesino of thirteen months

trecenario (period of) thirteen days

treceno thirteenth

trecentista *adj* fourteenth-century

trecésimo thirtieth

trecientos three hundred

trechear to pass round (from hand to hand); take from one place to another

trechel *m* spring wheat

trecho stretch, distance; **buen ~** long way; **de ~ en ~** here and there, now and again; **del dicho al hecho hay gran ~** there's many a slip twixt the cup and the lip

tredécimo thirteenth

trefe thin; not genuine

tregua truce, cease-fire; respite

treinta *n* thirty; *adj* thirtieth

treintanario (period of) thirty days

treintañal containing thirty years

treintavo thirtieth

treintena group of thirty; thirtieth part

treinteno *n* about thirty; *adj* thirtieth

treja (billiards) cushion shot

tremebundo dreadful, fearful

tremedal *m* marsh, fen, quagmire

tremendismo *lit* shockingly realistic style

tremendo tremendous, fearful, terrific, terrible

tremente *adj* trembling

trementina turpentine

tremés, tremesino *adj* three-month-old

tremó *m*, **tremol** *m* frame of wall-mirror

tremolante *adj* fluttering, waving

tremolar to flutter, wave; hoist, unfurl (a flag *etc*)

tremolina rustling (of wind *etc*); *fam* hubbub

trémolo tremolo

tremor *m* tremor, trembling

tremulante, tremulento, trémulo tremulous, quivering

tren *m* train; gear, outfit; ostentation; *sp* speed; **~ ascendente** up train; **a todo ~** regardless of the cost; **~ correo** mail train; **~ de aterrizaje** *aer* undercarriage; **~ de mercancías** goods train; **~ de montaje** assembly line; **~ de recreo** excursion train; **~ de vida** pace of life; **~ descendente** down train; **ella está como un ~** she's a honey; **jefe de ~** guard, *US* brakesman

trena sash, scarf; *sl* clink, nick, stir; *sl* girl, bird

trenado *n* mesh; *adj* reticulated

trenca trench coat; tap-root (of vine)

trencia, trencilla, trencita plait, braid

trencillar to decorate with braid

502

treno dirge

trenza plait; braided hair; tress(es)

trenzadera tape

trenzado braided hair; prance (of a horse)

trenzar *vi* to caper; prance; *vt* to plait, braid

trepa climbing; boring, drilling; trimming (of clothes); *fam* flogging; *fam* cunning trick; somersault

¹ **trepado** (of animals) robust, healthy

² **trepado** trimming/edging of clothes; drilling, boring

trepador *n m* climbing place; *adj bot* climbing, creeping ·

trepadora *bot* climber, creeper

trepajuncos *m sing+pl orni* reed-warbler

trépano *med* trepan

trepante artful; climbing

trepar *vi* to climb (up); *vt* to bore, drill; (sewing) put a wavy edging on

trepatroncos *m sing+pl orni fam* blue-tit

trepe *m fam* telling-off

trepidación *f* throbbing, vibration

trepidar to throb, vibrate

tres *adj* three, third; *n m* three; third; (cards) trey; **(a) las ~ (at)** three o'clock

tresañal, tresañejo *adj* three-year-old

trescientos *mpl* three hundred

tresdoblar to triple, treble; fold three times

tresdoble *m* threefold

tresillo three-piece suite; ring with three stones; *mus* triplet

tresnal *m agri* stook

trestanto *n* triple amount; *adv* three times as much

treta trick; (fencing) feint

trezavo thirteenth

tría sorting out

triaca antidote

triangulado, triangular triangular

triángulo *n* triangle

triar to sort out; (of bees) swarm in and out

tribu *f* tribe

tribuente attributing

tribulación *f* tribulation, adversity

tribuna tribune; platform; grandstand; political life

tribunal *m* tribunal; *leg* court; board (of examiners/adjudicators); **~ tutelar de**

menores juvenile court; **~ supremo** supreme court

tribuno *pol* orator

tributación *f* tribute, contribution; taxation (system)

tributante *m* taxpayer

tributar to pay (taxes *etc*)

tributario tributary; (of) tax

tributo tribute, tax

tricenal *adj* thirty-year

tricentésimo three hundredth

tricésimo thirtieth

triciclo tricycle

tricípite three-headed

tricolor three-coloured

tricorne three-horned

tricornio three-cornered hat

tricot *m* knitwear

tricotar to knit

tricotomía trichotomy

tricotosa knitting-machine

tridente *m* trident

trienal triennial

trienio triennium, period of three years

trifásico *elect* three-phase

trífido *bot* trifid

trifinio place where three boundaries/frontiers meet

trifolio *bot* trifolium, clover, trefoil

triforme triform

trifurcado trifurcate

trigal *m* wheatfield, cornfield

trigémino triplet

trigésimo thirtieth

trigo wheat; **~ candeal** summer wheat; **~ chamorro** winter wheat; **~s** cornfields, crops

trígono *astron* trigon; *geom* triangle

trigonometría trigonometry

trigonométrico trigonometrical

trigueño wheat-coloured; of light brown complexion; (hair) light brown

triguero *n* grain-merchant; corn-sieve; *adj* wheaten, wheat-growing

trilátero trilateral, three-sided

trilero three-card trickster, thimble-rigger

trilingüe trilingual; speaking three languages; written in three languages

trilito dolmen made of three stones

trilogía trilogy

trilla threshing; threshing time; toothed harrow

trilladera toothed harrow

trillado threshed; stale, hackneyed; **camino ~** beaten track

trillador *m* thresher

trilladora threshing machine; **~ segadora** combine harvester

trilladura threshing

trillar to thresh, tread out, beat; repeat

trillo threshing harrow; threshing machine; path

trillón *m* trillion, *US* quintillion

trimestral trimensual; quarterly

trimestre *m* term, quarter; period of three months; quarterly payment

trimotor *m aer* three-engined plane

trinado trill, warble

trinar to trill, warble, twitter; get angry

trincar *vi naut* to lie to; *fam* booze; *vt* to break; leap; tie; lash; *fam* pinch, snaffle; *vulg sl* fuck

trincadura *naut* two-masted barge

trincafía *naut* marline

trincar *vi naut* to lie to; *fam* booze; *vt* to break; leap; tie, lash; *fam* pinch, snaffle; *vulg sl* fuck

trinchador *m*, **trinchadora** *n* carver; *adj* carving

trinchante *n m* carver; carving-knife; butcher's knife; stone-mason's hammer; *adj* carving

trinchar to carve

trinche *m* table fork; sideboard

trinchera trench; ditch; trench coat; **abrir ~s** *mil* to begin a siege

trinchero trencher; sideboard

trinchete *m* paring-knife, fruit-knife

trineo sled, sledge, toboggan

Trinidad *f* Trinity

trinitaria *bot* heartsease

trinitario Trinitarian

trino *n astron* trine; *mus* trill; *adj* trinal

trinomio trinomial

trinquete *m naut* foresail, foremast; *mech* pawl, catch; *sp* squash; **a cada ~** at every step

trinquis *m sl* drink, booze

trióxido trioxide

tripa belly; gut, intestine; sausage skin; **~s** *fam* innards; **echar ~** to grow fat; **hacer de ~s corazón** to pluck up courage, take heart; **me revuelve las ~s** it turns my stomach

tripada bellyful

tripartir to divide by three

tripartito tripartite

tripería tripe-shop

tripero belly-band; tripe-seller

tripi *m sl* L.S.D. (drug)

tripicallero tripe-seller

tripita *fam* belly-button

triplano *aer* triplane

tríplica *leg* rejoinder

triplicación *f* triplication

triplicar to triple, treble; *leg* rejoin

tríplice *adj* triple, treble

tripón *fam* pot-bellied

tríptico triptych

triptongo triphthong

tripudiar to dance

tripudio dance

tripudo pot-bellied

tripulación *f aer + naut* crew

tripulante *m aer + naut* crew-member

tripular *aer + naut* to man, crew; fit out

trique *m* crack, sharp noise; **a cada ~** every moment

triquete: a cada ~ at every step

triquinosis *f med* trichinosis

triquitraque *m* clatter(ing); firecracker

tris *m* ting, clink (noise of breaking glass); **~ tras** monotonous repetition; **en un ~** within an ace

trisar *orni* (of swallows) to chatter, chirrup

trisca noise of stamping on cinders *etc*; merriment

triscador *n m* set of saws; *adj* noisy, lively

triscar to mix, mingle; *carp* set the teeth of a saw; stamp the feet; romp about

trisecar to cut into three parts

trisemanal three times a week

trisílabo trisyllabic

trismo *med* lockjaw

triste sad, miserable; gloomy; depressed; of sorry appearance

tristeza sadness, misery; gloom; depression; sorry state

tristón saddish, dull, dreary

tristura *see* **tristeza**

tritíceo wheaten

tritón *m* newt

tritono *mus* minor third

trituración *f* trituration; shredding; grinding; crushing

triturador *n m* crusher; shredder; *adj* crushing

trituradora crushing-machine; shredding machine

triturar to triturate, crush; shred, tear to pieces

triunfador *n m* winner, victor; *adj* triumphing

triunfal triumphal

triunfalismo policy of exaggerating achievements and successes and of minimizing failures and defeats; a we've-never-had-it so-good attitude

triunfalista *n* one who goes in for **triunfalismo**; *adj* triumphalist

triunfante triumphant, victorious

triunfar to triumph, win

triunfo triumph; spoils of war; trump card

triunvirato triumvirate

trivial trite, commonplace

trivialidad *f* triviality, triteness

triza mite, scrap, bit; *naut* rope, cord; **hacer ~s** to smash to bits

trocable changeable

trocado *n* change (money); *adj* changed, permuted

trocador *m* exchanger, barterer

trocaico trochaic

trocamiento change, exchange, barter

trocante *adj* changing; exchanging; altering

trocar to change; exchange, barter; switch

trocear to cut into pieces

troceo cutting up

trocla pulley

trocha narrow path, trail

trochemoche pell-mell

trofeo trophy; *mil* insignia

troglodita *m+f* troglodyte, cave-dweller

troje *f* granary

trojero granary-keeper

trojezado minced, chopped

trola lie, fib

trole *m*, **trolebús** *m* trolleybus

trolero liar, fibber

tromba waterspout

trombón *m* trombone; trombonist

trombosis *f sing+pl med* thrombosis

¹ **trompa** *f* horn; *zool* trunk, proboscis; humming-top; *archi* projecting arch; **~ de Eustaquio** Eustachian tube; **~ de Falopio** Fallopian tube; **estar ~** to be canned/sozzled

² **trompa** *m+f* horn player

trompada, trompazo bump, collision; wallop

trompar, trompear to spin a top

trompero *n* maker/seller of spinning-tops; *adj* deceitful

¹ **trompeta** trumpet; bugle

² **trompeta** *m+f* trumpeter; bugler; *fam* noodle, twit

trompetada silly remark

trompetazo trumpet blast; *fam* clout, wallop

trompetear to sound the trumpet; blow the bugle

trompeteo sounding the trumpet; blowing the bugle

trompetería trumpets; bugles

trompetero trumpeter; bugler

trompetilla small trumpet; ear-trumpet; *ent* proboscis

trompicar to trip up; *fam* promote out of turn

trompicón *m* stumble, stumbling; **a trompicones** by fits and starts

trompo spinning-top; chessman; **ponerse como un ~** to stuff o.s.

trompón *m* large top; collision; bump; *bot* daffodil; **de ~** in an unruly way

tronada thunderstorm

tronado worn-out; broke, penniless

tronador thundering, thunderous

tronar to thunder; *fam* go bust; **~ con** to break with

tronco trunk; log; stem; two-horse team; *fam* fathead; *sl* mate, buddy; **él está hecho un ~** he is fast asleep

tronchar to split, break off; cut down; **~se** to split; fall down; **~se de risa** to split one's sides laughing

tronchazo long stalk

troncho *n* stalk, stem; *adj* crooked

tronchudo having a long stalk

tronera dormer; skylight; opening; embrasure; (billiards) pocket-hole; squib; *naut* porthole

tronerar to make embrasures in

tronero rake, mad-cap

tronga *vulg sl* mistress, kept woman

trónica *fam* gossip

tronido thunderclap; bankruptcy

tronitoso thundering, resounding

trono throne; *eccles* shrine

tronzador *m* two-handed saw; crosscut saw; mechanical saw

tronzar to shatter; crosscut; wear out; (sewing) pleat

tropa troop(s), soldiers; crowd; drove

of cattle; **de** ~ in the army

tropel *m* rush, stampede; **en** ~ in a throng

tropelía outrage

tropero cattle-drover; cowboy; cattle-dealer

tropezadero stumbling place

tropezador *n m* stumbler; *adj* stumbling

tropezadura *n* stumbling

tropezar to stumble, trip; ~ **con** to bump into, come up against; ~**se con** to light upon, come across

tropezón *n m* tripping, stumbling; solid piece of food in soup *etc*; obstacle, difficulty; **a tropezones** by fits and starts; *adj* stumbling often

trópico *n* tropic; *adj* tropical

tropiezo trip, stumble; hitch, snag; solid morsel in soup

tropo *rhet* trope

troquel *m* die (for coins *etc*)

troquelar to mint, coin

troqueo trochee

trotaconventos *f sing+pl fam* procuress, bawd

trotador *adj* trotting

trotamundos *m+f sing+pl* globe-trotter

trotar to trot, hustle

trote *m* trot; hustle, bustle; **al** ~ at a trot; **para todo** ~ all-purpose; **viejo para estos** ~**s** not up to it any more

trotón *n m* trotter, horse; *adj* trotting

trotona chaperon; *fam* street-walker, prostitute

trotonería continual trotting

trova verse, song

trovador *m* minstrel, troubador

trovar *vi* to write verse; *vt* to parody; misconstrue

trovista *m* minstrel

trovo love-poem

Troya Troy; **aquí fue** ~ that's how it all began; **va a arder** ~ there'll be hell to pay

troyano Trojan

troza log; portion

trozar to cut into logs

trozo bit, piece, chunk

trucar to employ trickery; (snooker) pocket a ball

truco trick; knack; **coger el** ~ to get the knack

truculento truculent

trucha trout; portable shop/stall

truchero *n* trout fisherman; trout seller; *adj* trout

truchimán *m* artful creature; unscrupulous person

truchuelo thin dried cod

trueco exchange; **a/en** ~ in exchange

trueno thunderclap; *fig* bombshell; young tearaway/hoodlum

trueque *m* exchange, barter; **a/en** ~ in exchange

trufa lie; *bot* truffle

trufador *n m* liar, fibber; *adj* lying, untruthful

trufar *vi* to lie, fib; *vt* to stuff with truffles

truhán *m* rascal; knave; jester

truhanada knavish trick; rascally behaviour

truhanear to cheat, swindle; play the fool

truhanería rascality; clownishness

truhanesco knavish; clownish

trujamán *m* dragoman; interpreter; expert trader

trujamanear to act as interpreter; barter; trade; act as broker

trujamanía brokerage

trulla trowel; bustle, hurly-burly; crowd

truncado truncated

truncamiento truncation, maiming

truncar to truncate; cut (speech *etc*); leave unfinished

trunco truncated, cut down; mutilated

trusas *fpl* breeches

tsetsé *f* tsetse fly

tu(s) your, thy, thine

tú you, thou; **tratar de** ~ to be on first-name terms (with)

tuba tuba; snorkel; **falda tuba** tight skirt

tuberculina *med* tuberculine

tuberculización *f* tuberculosis

tubérculo tubercle, tuber

tuberculoso *n* tubercular person; *adj* tubercular

tubería tubing, piping; drains; factory where pipes *etc* are made

tuberosidad *f* tuberosity; protuberance

tuberosa spikenard

tuberoso tuberous

tubo tube, pipe, duct; *sl* telephone; ~ **acústico** speaking-tube; ~ **de ensayo** test-tube; ~ **lanzallamas** flame-thrower; ~ **lanzatorpedos** torpedo-tube; ~ **respiradero** snorkel

tubuloso tube-shaped

tucán *m* toucan

tuco armless, one-armed; glow-worm

tudesco *n* German; *adj* Germanic, Teutonic

tueco stub, stump; wormhole in wood

tuerca nut, female screw

tuerce *m* sprain, twisting; bad luck

tuero dry wood, brushwood; fuel

tuerto *n* one-eyed man; injury, wrong; ~s birth pangs; *adj* one-eyed; **a tuertas o a derechas** rightly or wrongly

tueste *m* toast, toasting

tuétano bone marrow; *bot* pith; *fig* essence, core; **hasta los** ~s to the very marrow

tufarada stink, pong

tufillo slightly unpleasant smell; stuffiness

tufo vapour, fume; bad smell, stink, *sl* pong; ~s airs, conceit

tugar *m* game similar to hide-the-thimble

tugurio hovel; shepherd's hut; den, dive; ~s slums

tuición *f leg* guardianship, protection

tuitivo *leg* protective

tul *m* tulle

tulipa small tulip; (tulip-shaped) lampshade

tulipán *m* tulip

tullidez *f*, **tullimiento** crippled state; paralysis

tullir to cripple, maim; paralyse; illtreat

tumba tomb, grave; coach roof; driver's seat (on state coach); somersault

tumbacuartillos *m sing + pl* sot, boozer

tumbado *archi* vaulted

tumbaga copper-gold alloy

tumbar *vi* to tumble, fall down; *naut* heel over; *vt* to knock down, lay out; ~se to lie down; put one's feet up

tumbo tumble, fall; rise and fall; deedbook; ~ **de dado** imminent danger; **dar** ~s to stagger

tumbón *m* trunk with rounded lid; couch; lazybones; *adj* lazy; idle

tumbona easy chair; lazybones

tumefacción *f* swelling

túmido, tumefacto swollen; pompous; *archi* domed

tumor *m* tumour

túmulo tomb, sepulchre; monument; catafalque; funeral pile

tumulto tumult, uproar, riot

tumultuante spreading sedition

tumultuar to mob, raise a tumult; ~se to rise up in arms

tumultuario, tumultuoso tumultuous

tuna *n mus* strolling group of student musicians; loafing; **correr la** ~ to loaf around; *adj* crooked, rascally

tunanta shrewd rascally woman

tunantada knavish trick

tunante *n m* loafer; rogue, rascal; *adj* loafing; crooked, rascally

tunantear to loaf; act in a rascally way

tunantería rascality; vagrancy

tunar to loiter about, loaf; lead a loose life

tunda beating, flogging

tundear to give a beating to

tundición *f* shearing of cloth

tundidor *m* cloth-shearer

tundidora cloth-shearing machine

tundidura shearing

tundir to shear (cloth); beat, flog

tunear to act the knave

tunecino *n + adj* Tunisian

túnel *m* tunnel; ~ **aerodinámico** windtunnel

Túnez Tunis

tungsteno tungsten

túnica tunic, gown; *bot* tunicle

Tunicia Tunisia

túnico tunic, gown

tuno student minstrel

tuntún: al buen ~ thoughtlessly; without knowledge

tupa tight packing

tupamaro Uruguayan urban guerrilla

tupé *m* toupee

tupido dense; close-woven; dull, stupid

tupinambo Jerusalem artichoke

tupir to pack tightly, make compact; ~se to stuff o.s.

turba mob, rabble; peat

turbación *f* confusion; embarrassment

turbador *n m* trouble-maker; *adj* flustering; troubling; disturbing

turbal *m* peat-bog

turbamulta mob, rabble

turbante *m* turban

turbar(se) to alarm, disturb, upset; confuse; embarrass

turbera peat-bog

turbidez *f* turbidity
túrbido turbid
turbiedad *f*, **turbieza** turbidity, muddiness; obscurity
turbina turbine
turbia muddiness
turbio *adj* turbid, troubled; cloudy; muddy; dubious; obscure; *n m pl* ~s dregs
turbión *m* squall; whirlwind
turbohélice *adj aer* turbo-prop
turbonada storm and whirlwind
turbulencia turbulence; turbidity
turbulento turbulent; turbid
turca: coger una ~ to get sozzled
turco *n* Turk, Turkish language; *adj* Turkish
túrdiga leather strip
turgencia swelling
turgente turgent, swollen, prominent; *lit* (of style) pompous
turibular *eccles* to cense with a thurible
turibulario *eccles* thurifer, censer-bearer
turífero incense-bearing
turismo tourism; touring; private car; saloon car, *US* sedan
turista *m + f* tourist
turístico *adj* tourist
turma testicle; ~ **de tierra** truffle
turnarse to take turns
turnio cross-eyed
turno turn, shift; go; ~ **de día/de noche** day/night shift; **el/la del** ~ the person on duty
turolense *adj* of Teruel
turquesa *n* turquoise
turquesada *adj* turquoise
turquí, turquino deep blue
Turquía Turkey
turrar to roast, toast
turrón *m* Christmas sweetmeat of almonds, honey and sugar; **comer del** ~ to hold a sinecure
turronería shop that sells **turrón**
turronero maker/seller of **turrón**
turulato dumbfounded
turumbón *m* bump on the head
tus: sin decir ~ **ni mus** without daring to say boo to a goose
tusílago *bot* coltsfoot
[1] **¡tuso!** (to dogs) get away!
[2] **tuso** pitted by smallpox
[1] **tusón** *m* fleece of a sheep
[2] **tusón** *m* colt under two years old
tusona filly under two years old; *fam* whore, strumpet
tute *m* card game
tutear to be on first-name terms with
tutela tutelage, guardianship
tutelar tutelary
tuteo being on first-name terms with
tutiplén: a ~ galore, in abundance
tutor *m* guardian, protector; prop, cane (for supporting plants)
tutoría guardianship, tutelage
tuyo, tuya, tuyos, tuyas yours, thine; **los tuyos** your folks

U

¹ **u** *f* letter u; **en U** U-shaped
² **u** or
U (usted) *pl* **UU (ustedes)** you
ubérrimo very fruitful
ubicación *f* location
ubicar to locate; **~se** to be located
ubicuidad *f*, **ubiquidad** *f* ubiquity
ubicuo ubiquitous
ubre *f* udder
ucase *m* ukase
U.C.D. (Unión de Centro Democrático) *pol* Centre Democratic Union
ucedismo policies of U.C.D.
ucedista *n m+f* member/supporter of U.C.D.; *adj* of U.C.D.
Ucrania Ukraine
ucranio *n+adj* Ukrainian
Ud (usted) *pl* **Uds (ustedes)** you
udómetro rain-gauge
uesnoreste, uesnorueste *see* **oesnoreste, oesnoroeste**
ueste *see* **oeste**
¡uf! phew! (denoting tiredness, heat or annoyance)
ufanarse to boast; display conceit
ufanía conceit, vanity
ufano conceited, vain
ufo: a ~ *adv* on the scrounge, on the cadge
ufología ufology
ufólogo ufologist
ugandés Ugandan
ugetista *n m+f* member of U.G.T.; *adj* of U.G.T.
U.G.T. (Unión General de Trabajadores) General Workers' Union
ujier *m* usher, janitor
úlcera ulcer
ulceración *f* ulceration
ulcerar(se) to ulcerate
uliginoso swampy
ulterior further; subsequent
ulteriormente in time to come; later
ultimar to end; put the finishing touches to
ultimidad *f* final stage

último last, latest, final; farthest, utmost; best; **~ suplicio** death penalty; **a la última** in the latest fashion; **a última hora** at the eleventh hour, at the last minute; **a ~s de ...** at the end of ... (month, year *etc*); **estar a lo ~** to be well-informed; **por ~** finally; **en ~ caso** in the final resort, when the crunch comes
¹ **ultra** *m+f* right-wing extremist; *adj* extreme right-wing
² **ultra** besides, beyond
ultracongelar to deep freeze
ultrajador *n m* outrageous/insulting person; *adj* outrageous
ultrajar to outrage; insult
ultraje *m* outrage; insult
ultrajoso outrageous; insulting
ultramar *m* place abroad; foreign country
ultramarino *n* (colour) ultramarine; *adj* ultramarine; overseas
ultramarinos *mpl* groceries; **tienda de ~** grocer's shop
ultramoderno ultramodern
ultramundo: el ~ the next world
ultranza: a ~ at all costs
ultraterreno unearthly
ultrasónico ultrasonic
ultratumba beyond the grave
ultravioleta ultraviolet
úlula owl
ululante howling, screeching
ulular to hoot, screech
umbelífero *bot* umbelliferous
umbráculo *hort* shady place; screen to give shade
umbral *m* threshold; commencement; *archi* lintel
umbría shady place
umbrío, umbroso shady; giving shade
un (uno) a; one; **~ año sí y otro no** every other year
unánime unanimous
unanimidad *f* unanimity; **por ~** unanimously

509

unción f unction, anointing; **extrema ~** *eccles* extreme unction

uncir to yoke

undécimo eleventh

undécuplo eleven times as much/as many

undoso wavy, undulating

undulación undulation, wave motion

undulante undulating

undular to undulate; wriggle

undulatorio undulatory

U.N.E.D. (Universidad Nacional de Educación a Distancia) *approx equiv* Open University

ungido anointed one (king *etc*)

ungir to anoint

ungimiento anointing

ungüento ointment

ungulado *zool* ungulate

único only, sole; unique

unicolor *adj* monochrome

unicornio unicorn; **~ de mar** narwhal

unidad f unity; unit; **~ de vigilancia intensiva** *med* intensive care unit

unido united; unified

unificación f uniformity; standardization

uniformar to standardize; wear uniform

uniforme *n m* uniform, regimentals; *sp* strip; **~ de campaña** battledress; *adj* uniform; standardized

uniformidad f uniformity

unigénito only-begotten

unión f union; agreement, harmony; mixture of ingredients; marriage; *mech+carp* joint; *comm* merger; railway junction

unionismo unionism

unionista *m+f* unionist

unípede one-footed

unipersonal *adj* for one person; one-man

unir to unite; join, couple; connect; mix; harmonize; **~se** to join; mix; adhere; concur; *comm* merge, consolidate

unisex *adj invar*: **moda ~** unisex fashion

unísono *n* unison; **al ~** in unison; *adj* sounding alike

unitario *n+adj* unitarian

unitarismo unitarism

universalidad f universality

universalismo universalism

universalista *m+f* universalist

universalizar to universalize

universidad f university

universitario *n* university student; *adj* university

universo *n* universe

¹ **uno, una** *adj* one; **~ que otro/otra** a few; **~ sí y otro no** every other one; **~s** some; approximately; **~s cuantos/cuantas** a few

² **uno** *pron* one; someone; **~ a otro** each other, mutually; **~s** some people; **~s a otros/otras** one another; **~ y otro/otra** both; **cada ~** each one; **de ~** one's

³ **uno, una** (number) one; **~ por ~** one by one, one after another; **a una** unanimously; **de una** at once; **de ~ en ~** in single file; **todo es ~** it's all the same, there's no difference; **una vez y no más** never more; **el ~ de mayo** the first of May

untador *m* greaser, oiler; painter

untadura *n* greasing, oiling; painting; coating

untar to anoint; smear, daub; grease; paint; coat; bribe; **~ las manos** to bribe; **~se** to be bribed

unto grease, animal fat; ointment; **~ amarillo** cash bribe; **~ de cerdo** lard

untuosidad f greasiness

untuoso greasy

uña fingernail, toe-nail; claw, talon; sting; *bot* thorn; *mech* claw; *mus* plectrum; *naut* anchor fluke; **~ de caballo** *bot* coltsfoot; **a ~ de caballo** at a gallop; **afilar las ~s** to sharpen one's wits; **hincar las ~s** to overcharge, sting; **ser ~ y carne** to be hand in glove; **tener ~s** to be a hard job/a difficult task

uñada scratch

uñero ingrowing toenail

uñizo long-nailed, long-clawed

¡**upa!** ups-a-daisy

uperizada : leche ~ U.H.T. milk

upupa *orni* hoopoe

uralita uralite

uranio uranium

Urano Uranus

urbanizable: terreno ~ land allocated for housing development

urbanidad f civility; good manners

urbanismo *m+f* town-planning

urbanista *m+f* town-planner

urbanística science of town-planning

urbanístico related to town-planning
urbanizar to urbanize; build on
[1] **urbano** urban
[2] **urbano** polite, well-mannered
urbe *f* big city
urdimbre *f text* warp
urdir *text* to warp; plot, scheme
urgencia urgency; obligation; **cura de** ~ first aid; **salida de** ~ emergency exit
urgente urgent
urgir to need, require; be urgent
úrico uric
urinación *f* urination
urinario *n* urinal; *adj* urinary
urna urn, casket; ballot box
urogallo *orni* type of woodcock
urología urology
urólogo urologist
uroscopia *med* urine examination/test
urraca *orni* magpie
Ursa: ~ **Mayor** Great Bear; ~ **Menor** Little Bear
urso corpulent man
usado worn out; second-hand; used; accustomed
usanza usage, custom; *comm* usance
usar *vt* to use, wear, enjoy the use of; *vi* to be accustomed to; ~**se** to be in fashion; be used to
usgo loathing
usía your lordship; milord
usina *elect* power station; factory
uso use, usage; custom, habit, practice; wear, wear and tear; *comm+leg* usance; ~ **de razón** understanding; **al** ~ according to custom; **en buen** ~ in good condition
U.S.O. (**Unión Sindical Obrera**) Workers' Trade Union
usted you; ~**es** you *pl*, ye; **de usted/**

ustedes your, yours
ustible inflammable
ustión *f* burning, consummation by fire
ustorio *adj* burning
usuario user
usufructo *n* right to use; *leg* usufruct
usura usury
usurar, usurear to practise usury; profiteer
usurero usurer; money-lender; pawnbroker; profiteer
usurpación *f* usurpation
usurpador *m* usurper
usurpar to usurp
utensilio utensil; tool
uterino uterine
útero *anat* uterus; womb
útil *adj* useful; profitable, effective; *n mpl* ~**es** tools, equipment, utensils
utilería *theat* props, properties
utilero *theat* property manager
utilidad *f* utility, usefulness; profit
utilitario *n* small economical car, runabout; *adj* utilitarian
utilizable available
utilización *f* utilization; **base de** ~ **conjunta** *mil* joint base
utilizar to utilize, use
Utopía Utopia
utópico Utopian
uva grape; *med* wart on eyelid; ~ **de Corinto** currant; ~ **de raposa** *bot* nightshade; ~ **espina** gooseberry; ~ **lupina** *bot* wolfsbane; ~ **pasa** raisin; **hecho una** ~ paralytic drunk; **estar de mala** ~ *fam* to be bloody-minded
uve *f* letter v; ~ **doble** letter W
uxoricida *m* wife-murderer
uxoricidio wife-murder

V

v f letter v; **en V** V-shaped
V (usted) you; **VV (ustedes)** you, ye
vaca cow; ~ **de San Antón** ladybird; ~
lechera milch cow
vacacional *adj* holiday
vacaciones *fpl* vacation, holidays; ~ **de
Semana Santa** Easter holidays
vacada drove of cows
vacancia vacancy
vacante *nf* vacancy; *adj* vacant, unoccupied
vacar to take a holiday; ~ **de** to lack; (of
jobs) remain vacant; not to work
vaciadero drain, sump
vaciado *arts* cast in a mould; emptying
vaciador *m* casting; moulding; emptying
vaciar *vt* to empty; cast, mould;
excavate, hollow; *vi* to discharge; flow
into; fall; ~**se** to become empty;
over-flow
vaciedad *f* piece of nonsense
vacilación *f* hesitation, vacillation;
staggering
vacilante *adj* hesitating, vacillating;
staggering
vacilar to hesitate, waver
vacío *n* void; emptiness; hiatus, blank;
opening; (for casting) hollowness;
vacancy; ~ **de poder** power vacuum;
de ~ empty; **envasado al** ~ vacuum-
packed; *adj* void, empty, vacant;
stupid; fruitless; hollow; defective;
presumptuous
vaco (of jobs) vacant
vacuidad *f* vacuity, emptiness
[1] **vacuna** *vet* cowpox
[2] **vacuna, vacunación** *f med* vaccination;
vaccine
vacunador *m* vaccinator
vacuno bovine; **ganado** ~ cattle
vadeable fordable
vadear to ford, wade through; ~**se** to
behave
vademécum *m* school portfolio
vadera ford
vado ford; *mot* right-of-way; **al** ~ **o al**

puente one way or the other; **no hallar**
~ to be at a loss what to do
vadoso shallow
vagabundear to rove, loiter
vagabundo *n* vagrant, rover, vagabond;
adj vagrant, roving
vagamundear, vagamundo *see* **vagabundear, vagabundo**
vagancia vagrancy, roving; laziness
vagar *n* leisure; idleness; *v* to loiter;
rove, wander
vagaroso *adj* errant; roving, vagrant
vagido cry of newborn baby
vagneriano Wagnerian
[1] **vago** *n* vagabond, vagrant; wanderer;
tramp; idle loafer; *adj* lazy, roving,
wandering; vague; vacillating; lax;
arts indistinct
[2] **vago** piece of wasteland
vagón *m* truck, waggon; railway coach/
car; ~ **cama** sleeping-car; ~ **cuadra**
cattle truck; ~ **de carga/de mercancías**
goods wagon, freight truck; ~ **de cola**
caboose, guard's van; ~ **de plataforma** flatcar; ~ **negro/de prisión**
Black Maria; ~ **tanque** tank wagon
vagonada waggon-load; car-load; van-
load
vagoneta open delivery cart
vaguada watercourse in a valley
vagueación *f* restlessness; unsteadiness;
flight of fancy
vagueante *adj* wandering
vaguear to rove, loiter, wander, tramp,
idle
vaguedad *f* vagueness
vaguido *n* dizziness; *adj* dizzy
vahaje *m* gentle breeze
vahar to exhale
vaharada breath, breathing
vahear to give off (vapour, fumes *etc*)
vahído dizziness, vertigo
vaho vapour
vaina scabbard, sheath; *bot* pod, husk
vainilla vanilla
vaivén *m* fluctuation; giddiness; risk;

512

mech swing, oscillation, see-saw movement; *naut* line, rope

vajilla tableware; dinner/tea-set; ~ **de plata** silverware

¹ **vale** agreed; O.K.

² **vale** bet (at cards); *comm* bond, I.O.U., promissory note; sales slip

³ **vale** farewell; valediction

valedero binding, valid

valencia *chem* valency

valenciano *n* + *adj* Valencian

valentía valour, bravery; feat; boast; *arts* mastery in copying nature; **pisar de** ~ to strut

valentón *n m* bully; *adj* blustering, arrogant; bullying

valentona, valentonada brag, boast

valer *n* value, merit; *vt* to protect, patronize; cost, amount to; be valued at; be equal to; ~ **la pena** to be worth the trouble; ~ **lo que pesa** to be worth its weight in gold; **ni cosa que lo valga** nor anything like it; **valga lo que valiere** whatever may happen; *vi* to be of value; possess merit, be worthy; prevail; have power/authority; be valid/binding; be equivalent to; be good/useful; ~ **por** to be equal to; **hacer** ~ to turn to account; **más vale tarde que nunca** better late than never; **no poder** ~**se** to be helpless; **no vale para nada** it is of no use; it's a waste of time; **¡válgame Dios!** good heavens!, ~**se** to keep o.s., look after o.s.; ~**se de** to make use of

valeriana *bot* valerian

valerosidad *f* valour

valeroso brave; strong; active

valía value; credit; favour; influence; faction; **a las** ~**s** at the highest price

validar to validate

valido *n* + *adj* favourite

válido *adj* favoured, esteemed

valiente *n* brave person; bully; *adj* valiant; strong; efficacious; valid; eminent; **¡**~ **amigo!** *iron* what a friend!

valija valise; kit-bag; mail bag

valimiento value; use; favour; favoritism

valioso valuable; highly thought of; wealthy

valisoletano *see* **vallisoletano**

valor *m* value, price; amount; equiva-

lence; validity, meaning; *fam* impudence, cheek; ~ **adquisitivo** purchasing power; ~**es** *comm* bonds, securities; stocks; ~**es fiduciarios** *comm* notes

valorar, valorear to value, appraise, price; *chem* discover the strength of

valoría price; worth, value

valorizar *see* **valuar**

valquiria Valkyrie

vals *m* waltz

valsador *m* waltzer

valsar to waltz

valuable rateable, appraisable

valuación *f* valuation, appraisement

valuador *m* valuer, appraiser

valuar to value, appraise; price

valva *zool* + *bot* valve

valvasor *m* nobleman

válvula valve; ~ **de campana** two-stroke valve; ~ **de corredera** slide valve; ~ **de estrangulación** throttle; ~ **de expansión** cut-off valve

valla fence, paling, railing; stockade; barrier, barricade; *sp* hurdle; **100 metros** ~**s** 100-metres hurdles; **saltar la** ~ to take the lead in a difficult matter

vallado obstacle; stone wall; fence

vallar to fence; enclose; hedge

valle *m* valley, vale, dale, glen; ~ **de lágrimas** vale of tears

vallisoletano *n* + *adj* (inhabitant) of Valladolid

vampiro vampire

vanadio vanadium

vanagloria vainglory, conceit

vanagloriarse to be vainglorious; boast

vanaglorioso vainglorious

vandálico Vandalic

vandalismo vandalism

vándalo vandal

vanear to talk nonsense

vanguardia vanguard

vanguardismo vanguardism

vanguardista *n m* + *f* + *adj* vanguardist; avant-garde

vanidad *f* vanity; shallowness; foppishness; **hacer** ~**es** to boast

vanidoso vain, conceited; foppish

vanilocuencia verbosity, loquaciousness

vanilocuo verbose, loquacious

vaniloquio verbosity; empty talk

vanistorio affected person; exaggerated vanity

vano empty, sterile; conceited; **en ~** in vain

vánova bedspread, quilt

vanse *theat* (stage direction) exeunt

vapor *m* steam; mist; faintness; vapour; *naut* steamer; **~es** attack of hysteria; **al ~** rapidly, *cul* steamed; **a todo ~** at top speed, under full steam

vaporable volatile

vaporación *f* vaporization

vaporar, vaporear to vaporize

vaporización *f* vaporization

vaporizador *m* vaporizer

vaporizar, vaporizarse to vaporize

vaporoso ethereal; cloudy

vapular to whip, flog

vapuleo whipping, flogging

vaquería herd of cattle; work done by cowboys; dairy

vaquerizo herdsman, cowherd

vaquero cowboy, cowhand; **~s** jeans

vara twig, thin stick, wand; staff, pole; staff of office; unit of length (*approx* 0.8 metre); cartshaft; **~ buscadora** divining-rod; **~ de cortina** curtain rod; **~ de medir** measuring stick; **~ de pescar** fishing-rod

varada *naut* running aground, beaching

varano monitor lizard

varar *naut* to be stranded/beached

varazo blow with a pole/staff

vareador *m* harvester who knocks fruit down with a pole

vareaje *m* knocking down the fruit with a pole

vareta lime twig for catching birds

varga steepest part of a slope

várgano fence rail

variabilidad *f* variability

variación *f* variation, change

variante *n f* difference; discrepancy; *m* **~s** mixed pickles; *adj* varying, deviating; changeable

variar to vary, change; shift; diversify; **para ~** for a change

varicela chicken-pox

varicoso varicose

varilla small rod; spindle; wand; rib (of umbrella); whalebone stiffener; **~ mágica** conjurer's/magic wand; **~s** *cul* wire whisk

varillaje *m* ribs of a fan/umbrella

vario varied; changeable; undecided; variegated; **~s** various, several

varita : ~ mágica magic wand

varón *m* human male; respectable man; **buen ~** wise man; **hijo ~** male child; **santo ~** good fellow but not very clever

varona mannish woman

varonil virile, manly

varraquear to grunt; (of a child) bawl, yell

vasallaje *m* vassalage

vasallo *n + adj* vassal, subject

vasar kitchen shelf

vasco, vascongado *n + adj* Basque

Vasconia Basque Country

vascuence *n m* Basque language; *adj fig* gibberish

vase *theat* (stage direction) exit

vaselina *tr* vaseline

vasera shelf for glasses

vasillo cell of honeycomb

vaso drinking glass; tumbler; vessel; glassful; **~ de engrase** *mot* greasebox; **~ de noche** chamber-pot; **culo de ~** imitation precious stone

vástago *bot* stem; sucker, side-shoot; scion

vastedad *f* vastness

vasto vast

vataje *m* *elect* wattage

Vaticano Vatican

vaticinador *m* prophet; diviner

vaticinar to divine, predict

vaticinio prediction, foretelling

vatihora *elect* watt-hour

vatio *elect* watt

vatímetro *elect* wattmeter

¡vaya! *iron* come on!, indeed!

ve *f* letter v

veces see **vez**

vecinal neighbouring; adjacent

vecindad *f* neighbourhood; vicinity; **hacer mala ~** to be a troublesome neighbour

vecindario population of district/neighbourhood/block of flats

vecino *n* neighbour; tenant; citizen; *adj* neighbouring, nearby, next-door

veda prohibition; close season

vedado enclosure; park

vedamiento prohibition

vedar to forbid; prohibit

vedagambre *bot* hellebore

vedeja *zool* mane

vedija tangled hair/wool; matted hair

veedor *m* peeping-tom; voyeur; supervisor, inspector; spy
vega fertile plain, flatland
vegetación *f* vegetation
vegetal *n m* +*adj* vegetable, plant
vegetalista *n* +*f* *see* vegetariano
vegetar to vegetate
vegetarianismo vegetarianism
vegetariano vegetarian
vegetativo vegetative; **por proceso** ~ by
natural wastage
¹ veguero meadowy
² veguero cigar; tobacco grower
vehemencia vehemence
vehemente vehement
vehículo vehicle; ~ **K** unmarked police
car
veintavo twentieth
veinte twenty, twentieth
veintena score, collection of twenty
veintenal lasting twenty years
veintésimo twentieth part
veinticinco twenty-five
veinticuatro twenty-four
veintidós twenty-two
veintinueve twenty-nine
veintiocho twenty-eight
veintiséis twenty-six
veintitrés twenty-three
veintiún, veintiuno twenty-one
veintuplo twenty-fold
vejación *f* vexation
vejar to vex
vejatorio vexatious, annoying
vejecito little old man
vejestorio *pej* old person
vejete *m* silly old man
vejez *f* old age
vejiga *anat* bladder; blister; *arts* tube for
paint; ~ **de la bilis/hiel** gall-bladder; ~
para tabaco tobacco pouch
vejigatorio blistering
¹ vela *n* candle; vigil, wake; watchfulness;
watchman; pilgrimage; **en** ~ vigi-
lantly, without sleeping
² vela *naut* sail; sailing-ship; awning;
windmill arm; ~ **mayor** mainsail;
acortar la ~ to shorten sail; **alzar** ~**s**
to prepare to sail; **a toda** ~ with all
sails set; in full swing; **a** ~ **y remo** with
all heart and soul; **barco de a** ~ sailing
ship; **hacer fuerza de** ~ to crowd sail;
hacerse a la ~ to set sail; **recoger** ~**s** to
contain o.s.; **tender las** ~**s** to seize an

opportunity
velación *f* watch, vigil, wake; **velaciones**
time when the church permits marriages
velada soirée
¹ velador *m* watchman; caretaker
² velador *m* pedestal table; tall candlestick
velaje *m* *naut* set of sails; canvas
¹ velar to watch; stay awake; keep vigil,
guard; work at night; invigilate
² velar to cover with a veil; hide
veleidad *f* fickleness
veleidoso fickle
velero sailmaker; sailing-boat/ship;
candle seller
veleta weathercock; pennant; (fishing)
float; fickle person
velicar *med* to lance, open
velo *n* veil; disguise; curtain; confusion;
perplexity; ~ **del paladar** soft palate;
correr un ~ **sobre** to drop (a topic);
descorrer el ~ to reveal; **tomar el** ~ to
become a nun
velocidad *f* speed, velocity; ~ **de ascen-**
sión *aer* rate of climb; ~ **de liberación**
aer + *space* escape velocity; *mot* gear;
caja de ~**es** gearbox; **confundir el**
tocino con la ~ to confuse chalk with
cheese
velocímetro speedometer
velocipedismo *sp* cycling
velocipedista *m* +*f* cyclist
velocípedo velocipede, bicycle
velódromo cycle racing track
velomotor *m* autocycle, moped
veloz quick, rapid; fleeting
vellido downy; hairy
vellón *m* fleece
vellorita *bot* cowslip
vellosidad *f* downiness, hairiness
velloso downy, hairy
velludillo velveteen
velludo *n* velvet; plush; *adj* downy,
hairy, shaggy, woolly
vena vein, blood-vessel; *bot* fibre; *min*
seam; underground stream; stripe in
marble, wood *etc*; inspiration; ~ **coro-**
naria cardiac vein; **dar en la** ~ to hit
on the best means; **estar de** ~ **para** to
be in the mood for; **estar en** ~ to be inspired
venablo javelin; dart
venadero *n* place frequented by deer;

adj deer; deer-hunting
venado deer, venison
¹ **venal** venous
² **venal** venal, mercenary
venalidad *f* venality
vencejo *orni* swift; martin
vencedor *n m* victor, conqueror; *adj* victorious, triumphant
vencer to conquer, defeat; *comm* to expire, fall due; (of emotions) to control, subdue; (of roads *etc*) to turn
vencible conquerable
vencido conquered, beaten; *comm* due, overdue; **él cobra por meses ~s** he is paid at the end of the month; **ir/estar de ~** to be on the wane, be past its best
vencimiento victory, conquest; *comm* expiry, maturity
venda bandage; blindfold; **tener una ~ en los ojos** to refuse to accept the truth
vendaje *m* bandaging; tip, gratuity
vendar to bandage; blindfold; deceive
vendaval *m* strong (*usu* south) wind
vendedor *n m* salesman, seller; **aparato ~** slot/vending machine
vendehumos *m sing + pl* one who trades on having influential acquaintances
vender to sell; **~ al contado** to sell for cash; **~ al por mayor/menor** to sell wholesale/retail; **~ a plazos** to sell on credit/easy terms; **~ como pan caliente** to sell like hot cakes; **sin ~ una escoba** nothing done yet; **~se** to sell out; accept a bribe; be for sale
vendible marketable; saleable
vendimia grape harvest; vintage; large profit
vendimiar to harvest grapes; make excessive profits
veneciano Venetian
veneno poison
venenosidad *f* poisonousness
venenoso poisonous
¹ **venera: empeñar la ~** to spare no expense
² **venera** scallop-shell
venerabilidad *f* venerability
veneración *f* veneration
venerando venerable
venerar to venerate; revere; worship
venéreo *n* venereal disease; *adj* sensual; *med* venereal
venero spring; origin; *adj* vengeful
venezolano Venezuelan

vengable deserving revenge
vengador *m* avenger
venganza revenge, vengeance
vengar to avenge; **~se de** to take revenge on
vengativo revengeful; vindictive
venia permission; forgiveness
venida arrival; **idas y ~s** comings and goings
venidero *n* posterity; *adj* future, coming
venir to come, arrive; result; fit, suit; grow; **~ a** to attain; **~ a buscar** to come and get; **~ a menos** to come down in the world; **~ a ser** to become, amount to; **~ en** to decide; **¿a qué viene éso?** what has that got to do with it?; **¿a qué viene usted?** how does this concern you?; **en lo por ~** in the future/hereafter; **... que viene** next ...; **venga lo que viniere** come what may; **~se** to ferment; have an ejaculation; come back; **~se abajo** to collapse, fall; **~se al suelo** to collapse, fall
venosidad *f med* venosity
venoso venous; veined
venta sale, selling; roadside inn; inhospitable place; shop, store; **~ al por mayor** wholesale sale; **~ al por menor** retail sale, retailing; **~ pública** auction sale; **de ~, en ~** for sale
ventada gust of wind
ventaja advantage; gain, profit; **llevar ~ a** to be ahead of, have the better of
ventajoso advantageous; profitable
ventalla *bot* pod
ventalle *m* fan
ventana window; window frame; window shutter; **~ de la nariz** nostril; **echar la casa por la ~** to spare no expense
ventanear to be continually looking out of the window
ventaneo window-gazing
ventanero window-maker; peeping tom
ventanilla window (of vehicle, ticket office *etc*); small window
venteo bung, bunghole
ventero innkeeper
ventilación *f* ventilation; discussion
ventilador *m* ventilator; **~ suizo** electric fan
ventilar to ventilate; air; discuss
ventisca blizzard
ventiscar to snow (with a strong wind)

ventiscoso full of snowdrifts; having frequent snowstorms
ventisquear *see* **ventiscar**
ventisquero snowstorm; snowdrift; glacier; snow-capped mountain
ventolera gust of wind; *fam* **darle la ~** have a crazy idea
ventolina *naut* light breeze
ventor *m* foxhound
ventosa vent; suction cup; *zool* sucker
ventosear to fart, break wind
ventosidad *f* flatulence
ventoso windy, stormy; flatulent; inflated
ventregada brood; litter; multitude
ventrera bellyband; cummerbund, sash
ventrículo ventricle
ventrílocuo ventriloquist
ventriloquia ventriloquism
ventroso, ventrudo big-bellied
ventura luck, fortune; chance, hazard; venture; risk; **a la buena ~** at hazard; **buena ~** fortune (told by a fortune-teller); **por ~** by chance; **probar ~** to try one's luck
venturado, venturoso lucky, fortunate
venturanza happiness
venturero *n* fortune-hunter; adventurer; *adj* lucky, adventurous
venturo *adj* future
venusiano Venusian
venustidad *f* beauty
venusto beautiful
[1] **ver** *n* sense of sight, seeing; looks; **a mi ~** in my opinion, the way I see it; **de buen ~** of good appearance; **de mal ~** of bad appearance
[2] **ver** *v* to see, look at; examine; **~ es creer** seeing is believing; **~ las estrellas** to see stars, feel pain; **~ mundo** to see the world; **~ visiones** to build castles in the air; **a ~** in order to see; **¡a ~!** let's have a look!; **a ~ si …** let's see whether…; **allá veremos** we shall see, time will tell; **estar por ~** it remains to be seen; **no poder ~ a** to detest, abhor; **no tener nada que ~ con …** to have nothing to do with …
[3] **ver:** **~se** to be seen; be conspicuous; be (situated); be obvious; have an interview; **~ con** to have a talk with; **ya se ve** it's obvious
veracidad *f* veracity, truthfulness
veranada summer season (livestock)

veranadero summer pasture
veranar, veranear to spend the summer
veraneante *m* summer resident, holiday-maker
veraneo summer holidays; **lugar de ~** holiday resort
veraniego *adj* summer
veranillo: **~ de San Martín** Indian summer
verano summer; (Central America) dry season
veras *fpl* reality; truth; **de ~** really, truly
veraz truthful |
verbena *bot* vervain; festival/open-air dance on eve of a saint's day
verbenear to be plentiful
verberar to lash, whip, beat
verbigracia for example
verbo verb; **echar ~s** to curse; **el Verbo** the Word; **en un ~** at once
verborrea, verbosidad *f* verbosity, wordiness
verboso verbose, wordy
verdad *f* truth; **¿~?** isn't that so?; **~ de Perogrullo** truism; **a decir ~** in reality, as a matter of fact; **bien es ~ que …** it is quite true that …; **decir cuatro ~es** to speak one's mind; **de ~** honestly; **¿no es ~?** isn't it?, don't you?, will she? *etc*
verdadero true, real; truthful
verde *n* green; verdure; **darse un ~** to amuse o.s. for a while; *adj* green, verdant; (of fruit) unripe; immature; inexperienced, young; risqué; **~ botella** bottle green; **~ limón** bright green; **chiste** *m* **~** dirty joke; **viejo ~** dirty old man
verdear, verdecer to turn green, look green
verdecillo *orni* greenfinch
verdegal *m* green field
verdemar sea-green
verdesmeralda emerald-green
verdete *m* verdigris
verdín *m* pond scum; mildew; verdigris
verdinegro dark green; green and black
verdino bright green
verdiseco half dry
verdor *m* verdure, greenness; *fig* youth
verdoso greenish
verdugo public executioner; leather whip
verdugón *m* weal

517

verdulería greengrocer's shop
verdulero greengrocer
verdura *cul* greens, vegetables; garden produce; *arts* foliage
verecundo bashful
vereda footpath, track; **entrar por la ~** to see reason
veredero messenger; runner
veredicto verdict; **~ abierto** open verdict
verga *naut* yard; *anat* penis
vergel *f* flower garden
vergelero gardener
vergonzante shamefaced; shameful
vergonzoso *n zool* armadillo; *adj* shameful, disgraceful; shamefaced; shy
verguear to hit with a stick
vergüenza shame; bashfulness, modesty; disgrace; public punishment; **tener ~** to be ashamed/shy; **~s** *anat* private parts
vericueto wilderness
verídico truthful
verificable verifiable
verificación *f* verification
verificar to verify; prove, test; carry out; **~se** to be verified, prove true; carry out; occur, take place
verificativo corroboratory
verisímil likely; credible
verisimilitud *f* likelihood
verja grating; iron fence
vermes *mpl med* intestinal worms
verminoso verminous
vermívoro worm-eating
vermut *m* vermouth
vernáculo vernacular
verónica *bot* veronica, speedwell; (bullfighting) pass with the cape
verraquear to grunt; (of children) cry
verraquera crying spell
verriondez *f zool* ruttish season; *bot* time when plants wither
verriondo *zool* ruttish; *bot* withered
verruga wart
verrugo miser
verrugoso warty
versal *m + f + adj print* capital letter
versar to go around; **~ sobre** to treat of; **~se** to become versed
versátil versatile; changeable
versatilidad *f* versatility; changeability
versería poems
versiculario *eccles* singer of versicles

versículo verse (*esp* in Bible)
versificación *f* versification
versificador *m* versifier
versificante *adj* versifying
versificar to versify
versión *f* translation; version
versista *m + f* versifier
verso line of poetry; verse (of the Bible); **~ blanco** blank verse; **~s** poems
vertebrado *n + adj* vertebrate
vertedero rubbish dump
vertedor *m* drain; emptier
verter to pour, cast; empty; dump, tip; translate, construe; divulge, publish; **~se** to flow
vertibilidad *f* convertibility
vertible changeable; movable
vertical vertical; **sindicato ~** company union
vértice *m* vertex; apex
verticillo *bot* whorl
vertiente *n f* watershed; slope; *adj* flowing; emptying
vertiginoso giddy
vértigo vertigo; dizziness; frenzy; fit of madness
vesánico mentally disturbed
vesícula *anat + bot* vesicle; *med* blister; **~ biliar** gall bladder; **~ elemental** *biol* cell
vespertina evening lecture at university
vespertino *adj* evening
vestíbulo vestibule; hall; lobby
vestido dress, clothing, costume; ornament; **~ de corte** court dress; **~ de etiqueta** evening dress; **~s usados** second-hand clothes
vestidura garment; *eccles* vestments
vestigio vestige, trace; sign; postmark; ruins, remains; *chem* traces
vestimenta clothes; *eccles* ceremonial robes, vestments
vestir *vt* to dress, clothe; adorn; palliate; put on, wear; cover; *bui* roughcast; *vi* to dress in a particular way; **~ bien/mal** to dress well/badly; **~ de uniforme** to wear uniform; **~se** to get dressed; dress up; **~ de** to dress up as
vestuario clothes, wardrobe, dress; *mil* equipment, outfit; *eccles* vestry; *theat* green room; *sp* dressing-room
veta *min* vein, seam; (of wood) grain; stripe; **descubrir la ~** to show one's

hand

vetado, veteado striped; **jamón ~** streaky bacon

vetar to veto

vetear to grain; variegate

veterano *n* veteran; *mil* ex-serviceman; *adj* veteran; experienced

veterinaria *n* veterinary medicine

veterinario *n* veterinary surgeon; *adj* veterinary

vetisesgado striped diagonally

vetustez *f* antiquity; old age

vez time, occasion; turn; **a la ~** at the same time; **a la ~ que** while; **alguna ~** sometime, ever; **alguna que otra ~** occasionally; **a su ~** in one's turn; **a veces** occasionally; **cada ~ que ...** every time that ...; **de una ~** at a stroke, at once; **de ~ en cuando** from time to time; **dos veces** twice; **érase una ~** once upon a time; **muchas veces** often; **otra ~** again; **pocas/varias veces** seldom/often; **tal vez** maybe; **todas las veces que** whenever; **una que otra ~** occasionally; **una ~** once

veza *bot* vetch

vezar to accustom

vía road; way, route; (railway) track, line; gauge; **~ aérea** air-lane; **~ ancha/estrecha** wide/narrow gauge; **~ de agua** *naut* leak; **~ férrea** railway; **Vía Láctea** Milky Way; **~ muerta** (railway) siding; **~ pública** public thoroughfare; **en ~ de** in the process of; **en ~ recta** straight ahead; **por ~ de** by way of

viabilidad *f* viability

viaducto viaduct

viajante *m* commercial traveller, *US* drummer

viajar to travel; work as a commercial traveller

viajata trip, excursion

viaje *m* journey, voyage; trip, excursion; passage; drug bout; errand; water main/supply; **~ de ida y vuelta** return journey; **~ de novios** honeymoon; **~ espacial** space trip/journey; **¡buen ~!** bon voyage!; **estar de ~** to be away from home (travelling)

viajero passenger, traveller, excursionist; **¡~s al tren!** all aboard!

vial *adj* pertaining to road

vialidad *f* road engineering; road system

viandante *m* traveller, passenger; tramp

viandas *fpl* food, victuals

viático travelling expenses; preparations for a journey

víbora viper

vibración *f* vibration

vibrador *m* vibrator; *adj* vibrating

vibrante vibrating, shaking

vibrar to vibrate

vibrátil capable of vibrating

viburno *bot* viburnum

vicaría, vicariato vicarage, vicarship

vicario *n* vicar; **~ de coro** choirmaster; **~ general** vicar-general; *adj* vicarious

vicealmirantazgo vice-admiralty

vicealmirante *m* vice-admiral

vicecanciller *m* vice-chancellor

vicecónsul *m* vice-consul

viceconsulado vice-consularship; vice-consulate

vicegerencia assistant manager's office

vicegerente *m* assistant manager

vicegobernador *m* vice-governor

vicenal every twenty years; of twenty years' duration

vicepresidencia vice-presidency

vicepresidente *m*, **vicepresidenta** vice-president

vicerrector assistant director; vice-rector

vicerregente vice-regent

vicesecretaría assistant-secretaryship

vicesecretario assistant secretary

vicésimo twentieth

vicetesorero vice-treasurer

vicetiple mezzosoprano

viceversa *n* illogical statement; non sequitur; *adv* vice versa

vicia *bot* tare

viciar to mar, spoil; counterfeit; adulterate; make void; deprave, pervert, corrupt; **~se** to abandon o.s.; acquire a bad habit, lead a life of vice

vicio vice, bad habit; defect, blemish; fraud; exaggerated desire; excessive appetite; *bot* excessive growth; **de ~** by habit; **tener el ~ de** to be in the habit of

vicioso vicious; given to vice; faulty; licentious, (of children) spoilt; *bot* overgrown

vicisitud *f* vicissitude

víctima victim

victimizar to victimize

¡vítor! hurrah!

victorear to cheer; give an enthusiastic welcome to

victoria victory, triumph; **cantar la** ~ to celebrate a victory; **cantar** ~ to boast of a victory

victorial *adj* victory

victoriano Victorian

victorioso victorious

vid *f bot* grapevine

vida life, living; sustenance; lifetime; condition; activity; *leg* period of ten years; ~ **ancha** good living; ~ **mía, mi** ~ my darling; **buena** ~ high living; **buscarse la** ~ to earn an honest livelihood; **dar mala** ~ to ill-treat, abuse; **darse buena** ~ to live comfortably; **de mala** ~ disreputable; **de por** ~ for life; **en** ~ while alive; **en la** ~ never; **ganarse la** ~ to earn one's living; **hacer** ~ to live together

vidente *n* prophet; person with eyesight; *adj* seeing

vidita my darling

vidriado glazed ware

vidriar to glaze

vidriera stained-glass window; glass partition; show case, display cabinet

vidriería glassworks; glazier's shop

vidriero glazier

vidrio glass; anything made of glass; anything brittle; ~ **coloreado/de color** stained glass; **pagar los** ~**s rotos** to be punished undeservedly, carry the can

vidriosidad *f* glassiness

vidrioso glassy; brittle; (of snow) slippery; peevish

viejarrón *m* old codger

viejecito little old man

viejo *n* old man; *adj* old; stale; worn-out; old-fashioned; ~ **verde** dirty old man

vienés Viennese

vientecillo light wind

viento wind; petty pride; (of dogs) scent; *naut* course; ~ **calmoso** light variable wind; ~ **contrario** foul wind; ~ **de bolina** scant wind; ~ **de la hélice** *aer* slipstream; ~ **de tierra** land breeze; **ir** ~ **en popa** get along very well; ~ **escaso** slack wind; ~ **fresco** fresh breeze; ~**s alisios** trade winds; **con** ~ **contrario** against the wind; **contra** ~ **y marea** against all odds

vientre *m* abdomen, belly; stomach;

womb; bowels; pregnancy; *naut* widest part of a hull

viernes *m sing* + *pl* Friday; **Viernes Santo** Good Friday

vietnamita *n m* + *f* + *adj* Vietnamese

viga beam, girder; rafter; ~ **armada** trussed beam; ~ **de aire** joist; ~ **de alma llena** plate girder; ~ **maestra** chief supporting beam

vigencia state of being in force; operative; 'life' of an organization; **en** ~ in force; **tener** ~ to be operative

vigente in force

vigésimo twentieth

vigía *f* watchtower; *naut* shoal, rock; *m* lookout, watchman

vigilancia vigilance

vigilante *n m* watchman; guard, vigilante; ~ **jurado** security guard; *adj* vigilant, watchful; careful

vigilar to watch over; look out for; invigilate

vigilativo *adj* causing sleeplessness

vigilia sleeplessness; watchfulness; study at night; *eccles* vigil, fast, eve (of feast day); **comer de** ~ to abstain from eating meat

vigor *m* vigour; **en** ~ operative, in force

vigorar *see* **vigorizar**

vigorizador, vigorizante *adj* invigorating

vigorizar to invigorate

vigoroso vigorous

viguería *bui* timberwork

vigués *n* inhabitant of Vigo; *adj* of/from Vigo

vil vile, base

vilano thistledown

vileza vileness, baseness; bad conduct

vilipendiador *adj* reviling; despising

vilipendiar to revile; condemn

vilipendio *n* revulsion; contempt

vilipendioso contemptible

vilo: en ~ in suspense, in the air

vilordo lazy

vilorto type of reed; snare

viltrotear to wander, loaf

villa town, city; villa

Villadiego: tomar las de ~ to take french leave, beat it

villanada despicable act

villancico Christmas carol

villanciquero carol singer

villanería lowness of birth

villanesco rustic; boorish

villanía lowness of birth; vile deed

villano *n* villain; contemptible person; rustic; *adj* rustic; boorish; base, villainous

villar *m* hamlet

vimbre *m bot* willow

vinagre *m* vinegar; sourness; **cara de ~** disagreeable person

vinagrera cruet; heartburn

vinagrero vinegar merchant

vinagreta *cul* vinegar sauce

vinagroso vinegary; sourish; grouchy

vinariego vineyard owner

vinario pertaining to wine

vinatería wine trade

vinatero *n* wine merchant; *adj see* **vinario**

vinazo strong wine

vincapervinca *bot* periwinkle

vinculación *f leg* entail

vincular to found upon; perpetuate

vínculo tie, bond; *leg* entail

vindicación *f* vindication

vindicador *m* vindicator

vindicar to vindicate, avenge; assert (one's rights); *leg* reclaim, repossess

vindicativo vindictive, revengeful

vindicta vengeance, revenge; **~ pública** public punishment

vinícola *m n* vineyard owner; *adj* wine, vinicultural

vinícolo *adj* wine

vinicultor *m* viniculturist

vinicultura viniculture, wine-making

vinil *n* vinyl

vinílico of vinyl, vinylic

vinillo weak wine

vino wine; **~ clarete/rosado** rosé; **~ cubierto** darkened wine; **~ de cuerpo** full-bodied wine; **~ de Jerez** sherry; **~ de Oporto** port; **~ espumoso** sparkling wine; **~ flojo** weak wine; **~ generoso** strong old wine; **~ peleón** cheap wine, plonk; **~ seco** dry wine; **~ tinto** red wine; **tomarse el ~** to get drunk; **tener mal ~** to be quarrelsome when drunk

vinolencia excessive wine-drinking

vinolento fond of wine

vinoso vinous

viña vineyard

viñadero vineyard keeper

viñador *m* viniculturist

viñedo *see* **viña**

viñero *see* **viñadero**

viñeta vignette

violáceo violet-coloured

violación *f* violation; rape

violador *m* violator; rapist

¹ **violar** to violate, rape; desecrate

² **violar** *m* bed of violets

violencia violence; **parto sin ~** *med* natural childbirth

violentar to do violence to; break into; **~se** to force o.s. to do something unpleasant

violento violent; irascible; strained; absurd; embarrassing; difficult

violero viola player

violeta violet

violín *m* violin; violin player

violinista *m+f* violin player

violón *m mus* double-bass; double-bass player; **tocar el ~** to talk through one's hat

violoncelista *m+f* cellist

violoncelo violoncello, cello

vipéreo, viperino venomous

vira welt (of shoe)

virada *naut* tack, tacking

viraje *m* change of direction

virar *naut* to tack

virazón *m* sea breeze

virgen *n f +adj* virgin; (of video-tapes *etc*) blank; unused

Virgilio Virgil

virginia Virginia tobacco

virginidad *f* virginity

virgo virginity

vírgula small rod; short line; cholera bacillus

viril virile, manly

virilidad *f* virility

viripotente nubile

virolento pock-marked

virología virology

virólogo virologist

viroso poisonous

virote *m* dart; arrow; April fool's trick

virotillo *mech* bolt; stay rod

virotismo conceit

virreina viceroy's wife

virreinato viceroyship

virrey *m* viceroy

virtud *f* virtue; power; vigour; courage; **en ~ de** by virtue of

virtuoso *n mus* virtuoso; *adj* virtuous, chaste

viruela smallpox; **~s bastardas/locas**

chicken-pox
virulencia virulence; acrimony
virulento virulent; acrimonious
viruta wood-shaving
visado *n* visa; *adj* countersigned, visaed
visaje *m* grimace
visar to visa, countersign; O.K.
visceral *adj* visceral; **reacción ~** gut reaction
visco birdlime
viscosidad *f* viscosity
viscoso viscous
visera peak (of cap); peaked cap; eyeshade
visibilidad *f* visibility
visigodo Visigoth
visigótico Visigothic
visillo window curtain; net curtain
visión *f* sight, vision; phantom; **ver visiones** to be deluded
visionario *n + adj* visionary
visir *m* vizier
visita visit; visitor, caller; visitation; inspection; **~ de cumplido/cumplimiento** courtesy visit; **~ de médico** doctor's visit, *iron* hurried call; **~ de sanidad** health inspection; **~ domiciliaria** social worker's visit; **hacer una ~** to pay a visit; **pagar una ~** to return a call; **tener ~** to have company
visitación *f* visitation
visitador *m* visitor, caller; searcher, inspector; **~ de registro** *naut* customs inspector
visitante *n m* visitor; *adj* visiting
visitar to visit; call on; inspect, examine; *leg* make a judicial search; (of ghosts) appear; **~se** to visit one another
visiteo frequent visiting
vislumbre *f* glimpse
vislumbrar to glimpse
viso outlook; lustre, sheen; slip (worn under a transparent frock); **de ~** prominent; **de dos ~s** with a double design; *text* sideways view (to see the sheen); **tener ~s de** to have the appearance of, look like
visón *m* mink
visor *m phot* viewfinder
visorio *n* expert inspection; *adj* optic, visual
víspera eve, day before; forerunner; **en ~s de** on the eve of
¹ **vista** sight, seeing, vision; appearance;

meeting; knowledge, perception; connection; comparison; opinion; trial; **~ cansada** long-sightedness; **~ corta** short-sightedness; **a ~ de** in the presence of; **a la ~** in sight, *comm* at sight; **a simple ~** at a first glance; **a primera ~** at first sight; **dar una ~** to give a quick glance; **de ~** by sight; **echar una ~ a** to watch; **en ~ de** in view of; **estar a la ~** to be obvious; **hacer la ~ gorda** to wink at; **hasta la ~** au revoir; **perder de ~** to lose sight of; **saltar a la ~** to be obvious; **tener ~** to be showy; **tener a la ~** to have before one's eyes
² **vista** *m* customs officer
³ **vista** meeting, conference; interview; **~s** presents given to each other by bride and groom
vistamiento *n* sighting
vistaria *bot* wisteria
vistazo glance; **dar/echar un ~ a** to glance at
vistillas *fpl* place with a good view
visto *n leg* clause beginning with 'whereas'; *adj* obvious, evident; *leg* whereas; **~ bueno** approval; **~ que** considering that; **bien ~** proper; **mal ~** improper; **no ~ nunca** unheard of; **por lo ~** apparently
vistoso beautiful; loud; showy
visual *n f* line of sight; *adj* visual
vitalicio *n m* life-insurance policy; *adj* for life
vitalicista *m+f* holder of life-insurance policy
vitalidad *f* vitality
vitalizar to vitalize
vitamina vitamin
vitela vellum
viticultor *m* grape-grower
viticultura grape-growing
vito lively dance; jig
vitorear to cheer
vitral stained-glass window
vítreo glassy
vitrina showcase, display cabinet
vitriólico vitriolic
vitriolo vitriol
vituallas *fpl* victuals, provisions
vituallar *mil* to victual
vítulo marino *zool* seal
vituperación *f* vituperation
vituperante vituperative

vituperar to vituperate

viuda widow, dowager; ~ **del jardín** *bot* scabious

viudedad *f* widow's pension; widowhood

viudez *f* widowhood; *fam* widow's pension

viudo widower

viva *n* cheer, shout of acclamation; *interj* long live!

vivac *mil* bivouac

vivacidad *f* liveliness, vivaciousness

vivaque *m mil* bivouac

vivaquear to bivouac

vivar *m* burrow; vivarium

vivaracho sprightly

vivaz lively, vigorous; *bot* evergreen, perennial

víveres *mpl* provisions; *mil* stores

vivero hatchery; *bot* nursery

viverista *m* nurseryman

viveza liveliness, sprightliness; vehemence; acuteness; quickness; witticism; splendour

vividero habitable

vívido vivid

vividor *n m* sponger; *adj* thrifty

vivienda dwelling, residence; housing

viviente living

vivificación *f* vivification

vivificador *m* vivifier

vivificante life-giving

vivificar to vivify; animate

vivificativo life-giving

vivíparo viviparous

vivir *n m* life; way of life; **mal** ~ riotous living; *v* to live, dwell; be alone; endure, last; ¡**viva** …! long live …!; ~ **de** to live on; ¿**quién vive?** *mil* who goes there?

vivisección *f* vivisection

vivo *n* edging, border; (sewing) piping; *vet* mange, itch; *adj* (a)live, living; (of colours) intense; acute; ingenious; bright; lively; diligent; lasting; (of wounds) open; **a lo** ~ to the life, realistic; **en** ~ living, *TV* live; **en carne viva** (of wound) open; **tocar en lo** ~ to cut to the quick

vizcaíno *n* inhabitant of Vizcaya; Basque; *adj* Vizcayan

vizcondado viscountcy

vizconde *m* viscount

vizcondesa viscountess

vocablo word; term

vocabulario vocabulary

vocabulista *m + f* lexicographer

vocación *f* vocation

vocal *f gramm + print* vowel; *m* voter in a meeting; *adj* vocal, oral

vocalización *f mus* vocalization

vocalizar to vocalize, articulate

voceador *m* town crier; vociferator

vocear *vi* to vociferate, shout; *vt* to proclaim, publish

vocejón *m* harsh voice

vocería shouting

vocero spokesman (for another)

vociferador *n m* shouter, boaster; *adj* shouting, boasting

vociferante vociferating

vociferar to vociferate, shout; boast about

vocinglería clamour, outcry

vocinglero *n* loud talker; *adj* vociferous; prattling

¹ **volada** short flight

² **volada** bad turn

voladero *n* abyss; precipice; *adj* flying

voladizo *n archi* corbel; *adj* jutting out

volador *n m* rocket (firework); flyingfish; *f mech* flywheel; *adj* flying; moving quickly; hovering in the air

voladura blast(ing), explosion

volandas: en ~ off the ground, in the air

volandero *orni* ready to fly; fluttering; fleeting

volando at top speed

volante *n m mot* steering-wheel; *mech* flywheel; (sewing) flounce; note, memorandum; lackey; *sp* shuttlecock

volantón *adj orni* capable of flying

volapié *m* bullfighting feat

volar *vi* to fly, flutter; hover; go quickly, vanish; act fast; make rapid progress; explode, burst; spread quickly; **echar a** ~ to disseminate; *vt* to blow up, explode; disseminate, publish; **echarse a** ~ to fly away

volatería *sp* fowling; falconry; flock of birds; **de** ~ in passing

volátil volatile; flying; fickle, changeable

volatilidad *f chem* volatility

volatilizar *chem* to volatilize, evaporate

volatín *m* acrobatic feat

volatinero aerialist, acrobat

volavérunt it's gone; the bird has flown

volcán *m* volcano

volcánico volcanic

volcanología vulcanology

volcanólogo vulcanologist

volcar to overturn; capsize; ~se to spare no expense; change one's mind

volea *sp* volley

voleador *m sp* batsman, batter

volear *sp* to volley; (baseball) bat; *mil* fire a volley

voleo *sp* volley; (dancing) high kick; **de un ~** at one go, in a flash

volframio tungsten

volición *f* volition

volitar to flutter

volquearse to tumble, flounder

volquete *m* tip-cart

voltaje *m* voltage

voltariedad *f* inconstancy, fickleness

voltario fickle, inconstant

volteador *m* tumbler, acrobat

voltear *vt* to overturn, turn round; alter the order of; *archi* vault; *vi* to turn over, roll over; revolve; tumble (acrobatics); ~se to turn over

voltejear to whirl; *naut* tack

voltereta somersault; turning up a card to make trumps

volteo whirl, turn, revolution; overturning; tumbling

voltímetro voltmeter

voltio volt

voltizo twisted; versatile; fickle

volubilidad *f* volubility

voluble voluble; easily moved; *bot* climbing

volumen *m* volume, size; corpulence; volume (book)

voluminoso voluminous, bulky

voluntad *f* will(-power); kindness; desire; disposition; **de buena ~** willingly; **de mala ~** unwillingly

voluntariedad *f* wilfulness

voluntario *n + adj* volunteer

voluntarioso wilful; self-willed

voluptuosidad *f* voluptuousness

voluptuoso voluptuous

voluta *archi* volute; ~s **de humo** smoke rings

volver *vt* to turn; turn up/over/upside down/inside out; return; give/pay/send back; vomit; reflect; give change (in a shop); ~ **la cara** to turn/look round; ~ **loco** to drive crazy; *vi* to return, come/go back; come again; change direction; ~ **a hablar** to speak again; ~ **atrás** to come/go back; ~ **en sí** to come round, recover consciousness; ~ **por** to stand up for; ~ **por sí** to stand up for o.s.; ~ **sobre sí** to make up one's losses, turn over a new leaf; ~ **sobre sus pasos** to retrace one's steps; ~se to turn, become; turn sour; turn around; change one's opinions; ~se **atrás** to retreat; **cuando se vuelva la tortilla** when the tables are turned; ~se **loco** to go crazy

volvible that can be turned over

vómico *n + adj* emetic

vomipurgante *n m +adj* emetic and purgative

vomitar to vomit; reveal

vomitivo emetic

vómito vomit; ~ **negro** yellow fever

voracidad *f* voracity

vorágine *f* vortex, whirlpool

voraginoso full of whirlpools

voraz voracious

vórtice *m* vortex, whirlpool; whirlwind; eye of a hurricane

vos, vosotros you

votación *f* voting, balloting

votador *n m* voter; *adj* voting

votante *m* voter (in a meeting)

votar to vote (on); express an opinion; ~ **una partida** to make an appropriation

votivo votive

voz *f* voice; word; authority to speak (at a meeting); opinion; *mus* singer; *mil* command; shout, cry; ~ **activa** right to vote, *gramm* active voice; ~ **argenta** clear voice; ~ **de mando** *mil* word of command; ~ **pasiva** right to be elected, *gramm* passive voice; ~ **pastosa** mellow voice; **a media ~** in an undertone; **dar voces** to scream, shout; **en ~ alta** aloud; **en ~ baja** in an undertone, in a whisper; **pedir a voces** to clamour for; **secreto a voces** open secret

voznar *orni* to cackle

vudu *m* voodoo

vuelco *m* tumble, fall; upset; **me dio un ~ el corazón** I had a presentiment

vuelo flight, flying; distance flown; *orni* wing; fullness, bagginess (of clothes);

elevation; loftiness (of thoughts); ~ **espacial** space flight; ~ **libre** hang gliding; ~ **planeado** gliding; ~ **tripulado** manned flight; ~ **sin tripulación** unmanned flight; **al** ~ *agri* scattered at random; **alzar el** ~ to take off; **coger algo al** ~ to understand immediately; **de alto** ~ of very great importance

vuelta turn, revolution (of a wheel *etc*); curve; recompense; recapitulation; *naut* hitch; short walk, stroll; change (in state or condition); return; sleeve, cuff; *cer* potter's wheel; witticism; round; turn-up; ~**s de coral** coral necklace; **a la** ~ round the corner, on returning, p.t.o., *comm* carried forward; **a** ~ **de correo** by return post; **andar en** ~s to employ trickery; **estar de vuelta** to have returned/be back; **no hay que darle** ~s there are no two ways about it, that's all there is to it; **partido de** ~ *sp* second leg; return game; **poner de** ~ **y media** to give a dressing-down

vuelto change (money returned after payment)

vuestro your, yours

vulcanita vulcanite

vulcanizar to vulcanize; *mot* repair a puncture

vulcanizador *n m* vulcanizar; *adj* vulcanizing

vulgacho rabble, mob

vulgaridad *f* vulgarity

vulgarismo vulgarism

vulgarizar to vulgarize

Vulgata Vulgate

vulgo common people

vulnerabilidad *f* vulnerability

vulneración *f* breaking (of a law *etc*); damage to s.o.'s reputation

vulnerar to injure; break (a law); damage s.o.'s reputation

vulnerario *adj* healing, curative

vulpécula, vulpeja vixen

vulpino foxy, crafty

vultuoso redfaced (with anger *etc*)

W

w *f* letter w

wagón *m* railway carriage, railroad car; wagon; van

warrant *m* receipt for goods deposited in customs warehouse

wat *m* watt

wáter *m* w.c., lavatory, toilet

waterpolista *m*+*f* water-polo player

wélter *m* welterweight

X

x *f* the letter x
xenófilo admirer of foreigners
xenofobia xenophobia
xenófobo *n* xenophobe; *adj* xenophobic
xerocopia xerox (copy)
xerocopiar to xerox
xilofonista *m+f* xylophonist

xilófono xylophone
xilografía xylography; wood engraving, xylograph
xilográfico xylographic
xtano (cristiano) Christian
Xto (Cristo) Christ

527

Y

¹ y *f* letter y

² y *conj* and; **~/o** and/or; **¿~ bien?** well
then ...?; **~ eso que** even though; **¿~
que ...?** is it true that ...?; **¿~ qué?** so
what?

¹ ya *adv* already; now, right away, at
once; presently, soon; eventually; **~
dicho** aforesaid; yet; **~ es tarde** it's too
late now; **~ no** no longer; **~ pasan de
las once** it's after eleven o'clock; **~
pronto** any minute now; **~ se acabó**
it's all over, it's finished; **~ verá Vd**
you'll soon see

² ¡ya! *interj* of course!; quite!; at last!;
¡~!, ¡~! all right!, O.K.!; yes, yes! **¡~
lo creo!** of course!, I should say so!; **~
se ve** that's obvious; **pues ~** naturally,
of course; **~ que** since, seeing that, inasmuch as, now that; **no ~ ... sino** not
only ... but also; **si ~** if only; **~ ves** you
see

³ ya *conj* whether, or

yac *m naut* (flag) jack; yak

yacaré *m* alligator, cayman

yacer to rest; lie (buried); be situated; **~
con** to sleep with (a woman); **aquí yace
...** here lies ...

yaciente lying down, recumbent

yacija bed; couch; grave; **ser de mala ~**
to be restless, sleep badly

yacimiento *min* bed, layer, deposit; **~ de
petróleo, ~ petrolífero** oilfield

yacio rubber-tree

yámbico iambic

yambo iambus

yanacón *m* Andean Indian

yanqui *n m + f + adj* Yankee

yapa tip, bonus, something extra; **de ~**
for good measure

yarda (measure) yard; yardstick

yardaje *m* yardage

yate *m* yacht

yaya granny; scratch, wound

yayo grandad

ye *f* letter y

yedra ivy

yegua mare; cigar(rette) butt; slattern;
~ de tripa breeding mare

yeguada, yegüería herd of horses; stud

yeísmo pronunciation of ll as y

yeli *m* jelly

yelmo helmet

yema shoot, bud; egg yolk; candied
yolk; best part, cream; **~ del dedo**
finger tip; **~ mejida** egg nog; **dar en la
~** to hit the nail on the head; **en la ~
del invierno** in the dead of winter

yentes: ~ y vinientes *mpl* habitués,
frequenters; passers-by

yerba grass; herb; *sl* marihuana; **~ mate**
Paraguay tea, maté

yerbabuena mint, peppermint

yerbajo weed

yerbazal *m* place full of weeds

yermar to lay waste

yermo *n* desert, wilderness; *adj*
deserted, uninhabited; (ground) unsown; (woman) barren, not pregnant;
tierra yerma wasteland

yerno son-in-law

yernocracia nepotism

yero (plant) tare; lentil

yerro error, mistake; fault; **~ de cuenta**
miscalculation; **~ de imprenta** typo-
graphical/printer's error

yerto stiff, rigid; motionless; terrified; **~
de frío** stiff with cold

yesca tinder; touchwood, kindling;
echar una ~ to strike a light (with a
flint)

yesería plastering; plasterwork; plasterer's shop

yesero plasterer

yeso plaster; blackboard chalk; gypsum;
plaster cast; **~ blanco** whitewash; **~
mate, ~ de París** plaster of Paris

yesoso *adj* of plaster; like plaster/chalk

yeta evil eye; bad luck

ye-ye *adj invar* with it, trendy; **cantante
~** pop singer

yip *m* jeep

yo I; **~ mismo** I myself; **soy ~** it's me/I;

528

el ~ the ego
yodo iodine
yodoformo iodoform
yogui *m* yogi
yogur *m* yoghurt; *sl* police patrol car
yogurtera yoghurt-maker (appliance)
yoi *m*, **yoin** marihuana cigarette, joint
yol *m*, **yola** *naut* yawl
yonqui *sl* junkie
yóquey *m* jockey
yuca cassava; yucca
yucateco (inhabitant) of Yucatán
yudo judo
yugar to work
yugo yoke; burden; **sacudir el** ~ to
　throw off the yoke
Yugo(e)slavia Yugoslavia

yugo(e)slavo Yugoslav
yuguero ploughman
yugular *m* jugular vein
yumbo (Ecuadorian) Indian
yungas *fpl* (Andean) jungle valleys
yungla jungle
yunque *m* anvil; drudge; **estar al** ~ to be
　long-suffering; **hacer de** ~, **servir de** ~
　to accept hardships
yunta yoke of oxen; team of horses; ~**s**
　cufflinks; pair, couple
yuntero ploughman
yute *m* jute
yuxtaposición *f* juxtaposition
yuxtapuesto juxtaposed
yuyo weed

Z

z f letter z

¡za! shoo!

zabarcero middleman (dealing in fruit)

zabordar to run aground, strand

zabucar to mix

zabullir vt to duck; give a ducking to; throw, hurl; ~se to dive

zacapela, zacapella rumpus, row

zacate m grass, hay; thatch

zacatín m street/square where an open-air market is held

zacear to shoo away (animals)

zafada lightening (of a ship)

zafado brazen, impudent; alert, wide-awake; daft; out of joint

zafar to set free, loosen, untie; dislocate, put out of joint; adorn, bedeck; ~ un buque to lighten (a ship); ~se to run away, make oneself scarce; ~se de (un compromiso) to get out of (an engagement); avoid, dodge

zafarrancho naut clearing the decks; havoc; scuffle; ~ de combate clearing the decks for action

zafiedad f coarseness, crudeness

zafio crude, coarse, uncouth, rude

zafir, zafiro sapphire

zafo unhurt; intact; naut free, clear

zafra sugar crop; sugar harvest; sugar-making season; olive-oil vat

zaga rear; rearguard; sp sl defence; a ~, a la ~, en ~ behind, in the rear; ir a la ~ to lag behind; no irle a la ~ a uno not to be inferior to s.o.; no quedarse en ~ not to be left behind

zagal m shepherd boy; office boy; stripling

zagala shepherdess; lass, maiden

zagalejo petticoat, short shirt; shepherd boy; lad

zagual m naut paddle

zaguán m (entrance) hall, foyer, vestibule

zaguero n laggard; sp back, backstop, defender; adj back, rear; lagging behind

zahareño disdainful

zaherir to reproach, reprove, censure; hurt s.o.'s feelings, offend s.o.

zahones mpl hunting breeches; chaps

zahora noisy feast

zahorí m seer, soothsayer; diviner; clairvoyant; keen observer

zahorra naut ballast

zahúrda pigsty, pigpen; hovel

zaino treacherous, false; (horse) vicious; (horse) chestnut-coloured; **mirar de ~/a lo ~** to look sideways; give a shifty look

zairense n m+f+adj Zairean

zalagarda row; snare; ambush

zalama, zalamería flattery

zalamero n flatterer; adj flattering, fawning

zalea (undressed) sheepskin, pelt

zalema salaam, deep bow

zamacuco stupid person, dolt

zamacueca Chilean dance

zamarra sheepskin jacket; sheepskin

zambaigo half-breed (Indian and Negro)

zambiano Zambian

zambo bandy-legged; half-breed (Indian and Negro); monkey

zambomba peasant drum (used at Christmas); ¡~! phew!, wow!

zambombazo noise made with a **zambomba**; loud explosion; blow with a truncheon

zambombo rough; ignorant man

zambra merrymaking; uproar; gipsy dance

zambullida dive, plunge; (fencing) thrust; ducking

zambullidura n diving; plunging; ducking

zambullir to plunge in water, duck; throw (in water); hurl; ~se to dive, plunge; go into hiding

zampa archi pile

zampar to throw; gobble up; ~se to gatecrash; ~se en to dash into

zampoña *mus* pipes of Pan

zanahoria carrot

zanca shank, long leg; leg of a fowl/frog

zancada long stride; **en dos ~s** in a jiffy

zancadilla booby trap; trip; tripping up; **echarle la ~ a uno** to trip s.o. up

zancajear to go to and fro, go from one place to another

zancajo heel-bone, heel; **no llegarle a los ~s a uno** not to be the equal of s.o.

zancajoso down-at-heel; slovenly

zanco stilt; **andar en ~s** to walk on stilts; rise above one's station

zancón lanky, long-legged; (of dress) very short

zancudo *orni* wader; mosquito; *adj* long-shanked, long-legged

zanfonía barrel-organ, hurdy-gurdy

zangamanga deceit, trick

zanganada insult, impertinence, rude remark

zangandungo lazy awkward person

zanganear to loaf, live in idleness, make impertinent remarks

zángano drone; idler, loafer; scrounger

zangarrear to strum a guitar

zangolotear to shake, rattle; fidget; **~se** to waddle, sway from side to side; (of windows) rattle, slam

zangoloteo rattle, rattling; fuss, bother; fidgeting

zangón *m fam* tall uncouth boy

zanguanga malingering; **hacer la ~** to malinger, swing the lead

zanguango *n* shirker, loafer, malingerer; fool; *adj* lazy, indolent, malingering

zanja ditch, trench, gully; irrigation ditch; **abrir las ~s** to lay the foundations

zanjar to dig a ditch, excavate a trench; settle a dispute; overcome difficulties; **~ un delito** to compound a felony

zanjón *m* ditch; ravine

zanquear to waddle

zanquilargo long-legged

zanquillas *m sing+pl* man with thin, short legs

zanquituerto bandy-legged

zapa spade; trench; sharkskin; shagreen

zapador *m mil* sapper; **labor de ~** undermining; subversion

zapallo pumpkin, gourd; stroke of luck

zapapico mattock, pickaxe

zapar to mine; excavate; undermine

zapata half-boot; lintel; **~ de freno** brake shoe; **~ de la quilla** *naut* false keel

zapatazo blow with a shoe; bump, thud; stamping (of horses)

zapateado tap-dance

zapateador *n* tap-dancer

zapatear to tap (with feet), stamp; tap dance; stamp on the ground

zapateo tap-dance; tapping (with feet), stamping

zapatería shoe shop; shoemaker's; shoe factory; cobbler's

zapatero shoemaker; (games) player who does not score; **~ remendón, ~ de viejo** cobbler

zapatilla slipper; pump; gasket; washer; button (on fencing foil); cloven hoof

zapato shoe; **~s de goma/hule** galoshes, rubbers, overshoes; **~s de tacón alto** high-heeled shoes

zapatobús *m joc sl* shanks' pony

[1] **zape** *m sl* homosexual

[2] **¡zape!** shoo!, scat!; gee!

zaque *m* wineskin; drunkard

zaquizamí *m* garret; hovel

zar *m* czar

zarabanda saraband; public dance; thrashing; row

zaragata quarrel; fight

zaragatero hooligan

zaragatería hooliganism

zaragozano *n+adj* of Zaragoza

zaranda sieve, screen, sifter, colander

zarandar, zarandear to winnow; sieve, screen, sift; jiggle; shake; **~se** to wear o.s. out, toil; abuse, maltreat; strut, swagger; waddle, sway the hips

zarapito curlew

zaraza printed cotton, chintz; **~s** ground glass used as pesticide

zarceño brambly

zarcero real *orni* sedge-warbler

zarcillo earring; tendril; earmark; trowel

zarco blue-eyed; light blue

zarigüeya opossum

zarina czarina

zarpa paw, claw; weighing anchor; **echar la ~ a** to seize, grab

zarpada, zarpazo blow with a paw/claw; clawing; grabbing zarpar to weigh anchor

zarrapastroso down-at-heel; seedy

zarza bramble, blackberry bush

zarzal *m* bramble patch

zarzamora blackberry

zarzaparrilla sarsaparilla

zarzarrosa dog rose

zarzo hurdle; wattle fence; ring

zarzoso brambly

zarzuela *Sp* musical comedy; ~ **del género chico** one-act musical comedy; ~ **grande** three-act musical comedy

¡zas! bang!, smack!

zascandil *m* busybody; intriguer; frivolous person

zascandilear to meddle; intrigue; behave frivolously

zeda letter z

zedilla cedilla

zenit *m* zenith, peak

zeta letter z; *sl* police car

Zetlandia: Islas de ~ Shetland Islands

zigzaguear to zigzag

zigzagueo zigzagging

Zimbabue Zimbabwe

zipizape *m* rumpus, row; **estar de** ~ to be squabbling

ziszás *m* zigzag

¡zis, zas! wham!; swish!

zoca, zócalo public square, plaza; base of a pedestal; baseboard; skirting-board

zocato left-handed; (of fruit) over-ripe

zoclo clog, wooden shoe, sabot

zoco *n* left-handed person; *adj* left-handed; one-armed

zodíaco, zodiaco zodiac

zoilo carping critic

zombi: estar ~ *sl* to be crazy

zona zone, district; belt; *med* shingles; ~ **a batir** *mil* target area; *meteor* ~ **de depresión** airpocket; ~ **de seguridad** safety zone; ~ **peatonal** pedestrian precinct; ~ **portuaria** waterfront; ~ **verde** green belt, conservation area

zoncería inanity, foolishness; boredom

zonzo *n* fool, bore; *adj* stupid; tasteless

zoófito zoophyte

zoología zoological

zoólogo zoologist

zopenco *n* blockhead, dunce; *adj* stupid, dull

zopilote *m* turkey buzzard

zopisa pitch; pine-resin

zopo *n* cripple; *adj* crippled; deformed; gauche

zoquete *m* block, chunk of wood, chuck; blockhead, fool; ugly person; ~ **de pan** crust of (stale) bread; *adj* doltish

zoquetillo shuttlecock

zorra vixen; foxy person; drunkenness, 'skinful'; prostitute; hand truck; ~ **de levante** portable elevator; **pillar una** ~ to get drunk/'soused'

zorrera fox-hole; anxiety; drowsiness

zorrería cunning, craftiness

zorrillo skunk

¹ zorro *n* fox; foxy person; ~ **argentado/ plateado** silver fox; ~ **hediondo** skunk; ~ **negro** racoon; **estar hecho un** ~ to be drowsy; **hacerse el** ~ to pretend stupidity, play dumb; play deaf

² zorro *adj* foxy, crafty; slow, lazy

zorzal *m orni* thrush; ~ **alirrojo** redwing; ~ **real** fieldfare

zozobra sinking; capsizing; anxiety

zozobrar to sink, founder, capsize; be in danger; worry, fret; vacillate

zueco clog, sabot

zulú *n m+f adj* Zulu

zullenco, zullón *m* wind (in bowels), flatulence

zumaque *m* sumac tree; ~ **venenoso** poison ivy

zumba cowbell, sheep-bell; raillery, banter; beating

zumbador *m* buzzer; humming-bird

zumbar to buzz, hum; mock, scoff at, make fun of; throw out; beat; *sl* steal; ~**se** to clear out, beat it; ~**le a uno los oídos** to have a buzzing/ringing in one's ears; ~**se de uno** to make fun of s.o.

zumbido buzzing, humming, ringing (in one's ears); blow, whack, smack; ~ **de ocupación**, ~ **de ocupado** *tel* 'number engaged' sound, busy signal

zumbón *n* jester, wag; *adj* playful, funny; sarcastic

zumiento juicy, succulent

zumo juice; profit

zumoso juicy

zunchar to put a band/hoop around

zuncho hoop (on barrel), band; ferrule

zupia dregs, lees; poor-quality drink; refuse, trash

zurcido darn; invisible mending

zurcidor *m* darner, mender; invisible mender

zurcidura *n* darning

zurcir to darn; patch; make up lies

zurdazo left hook; blow with the left hand

zurdo *n* left-handed person; *adj* left-handed; **mano zurda** left hand; **a zurdas** clumsily, with the left hand

zurear *orni* to coo

zureo *n orni* cooing

zuri: darse el ~ *sl* to escape

zuro corn-cob

zurra dressing (skins); tanning, currying; thrashing

zurrador *m* tanner, skin dresser

zurrapa dregs

zurrar to dress skins/leather, tan; thrash, flog

zurriagar to whip, horsewhip

zurriago *n* whip

zurriar to hum, buzz

zurrido blow, smack

zurrón *m* (shepherd's) pouch, leather bag; shoulder bag

zutano so-and-so, such a one (in the combination **fulano, megano** y ~)

zuzón *m bot* groundsel

ENGLISH–SPANISH

A

¹ **a** (letter) a (aes) *f*; A *mus* la *m*; **from ~ to z** de pe a pa; **AA gun** cañón (-ones) *m* antiaéreo; **A-bomb** *n* bomba atómica, *v* emplear armas nucleares (contra)

² **a, an** un *m*, una; **fifty pence ~ pound** 50 peniques la libra; **is there ~ bank here?** ¿hay algún banco aquí?; **he earns two thousand pesetas ~ day** él gana dos mil pesetas por día/al día; **~ fine thing** ¡bonita cosa!; **what ~ man!** ¡qué hombre!; **~ certain Mr So-and-So** cierto Señor Tal

A1 de primera (calidad)

aback *naut* en facha; **taken ~** desconcertado

abandon *n* abandono; *v* abandonar; (renounce) renunciar; **the crew ~ ship** la tripulación abandona el navío; **~ o.s. to** entregarse⁵ a

abandoned (left) abandonado; (depraved) vicioso; **~ child** niño desamparado

abandonment abandono

abase: ~ o.s. humillarse

abasement humillación *f*

abashed avergonzado

abate (lessen) disminuir¹⁶; (stop) hacer¹⁹ cesar; **the storm ~d** la tempestad se calmó

abatement (lessening) disminución *f*; (stopping) cesación *f*

abattoir matadero

abbess abadesa

abbey abadía; **~ church** iglesia abacial

abbot abad *m*

abbreviate abreviar

abbreviation (short form) abreviatura; (summary) resumen *m*

ABC abecé *m*; **it's as easy as ~** es el abecé; **the ~ of** los rudimentos de

abdicate abdicar⁴; **~ in favour of** renunciar en favor de

abdication (of throne) abdicación *f*; (of rights) renuncia

abdomen abdomen (-ómenes) *m*

abdominal abdominal

abduct raptar; secuestrar

abduction rapto; secuestro

abductor abductor *m*

aberrance aberración *f*

aberrant aberrante

aberration aberración (-ones) *f*; *astron* desvío aparente; *med* locura parcial

abet instigar⁵; **to aid and ~** ser cómplice de

abetter instigador *m* (-ora *f*)

abeyance: in ~ en suspenso; (without a claimant) vacante; **that law is in ~** aquella ley está en desuso; **the matter is in ~** el asunto está en suspenso

abhor aborrecer¹⁴

abhorrence aborrecimiento; **hold in ~** detestar

abhorrent repugnante; **it is ~ to me** me es repugnante

abide *vi* (remain) permanecer¹⁴; *vt* (endure) soportar; **~ by** atenerse¹⁹ a; **I can't ~ strong cheese** no aguanto el queso fuerte; **I ~ by what I say** cumplo con mi palabra; **I shall ~ by your wishes** obraré de acuerdo con sus deseos

abiding permanente

ability capacidad *f*; (cleverness) habilidad *f*; **he did it to the best of his ~** él lo hizo lo mejor que pudo; **man of great ~** hombre *m* de talento

abject despreciable; **~ apologies** disculpa rastrera

abjectly sumisamente

abjure (doctrine *etc*) abjurar; (rights) renunciar

ablative ablativo; **~ absolute** ablativo absoluto

ablaze (on fire) en llamas; **be ~ with anger** echar chispas; **the city was ~ with lights** la ciudad estaba brillante de luces

able capaz (-ces); (manually) mañoso; **~ to work** capaz de trabajar; **~ man** hombre mañoso; **be ~ to** poder (ue)^{1b} +*infin*; **~-bodied** robusto; **~ seaman**

537

marino de primera

ablution(s) ablución (-ones) *f*

ably hábilmente; con maña

abnegate renunciar

abnegation renuncia

abnormal anormal

abnormality anormalidad *f*

aboard a bordo; **go ~ (ship)** embarcarse[4] (en un barco); **all ~!** ¡viajeros al tren!, *SA* ¡vámonos!

abode domicilio; **of no fixed ~** sin domicilio

abolish abolir

abolition abolición *f*

abolitionist abolicionista *m+f*

abominable detestable; (taste) pésimo

abominate detestar

abomination asco

aboriginal *n +adj* indígena *m+f*

aborigine aborigen (-ígenes)

abort abortar; *space* terminar el vuelo (espacial)

abortion aborto provocado

abortionist abortista *m+f*

abortive abortivo

abortiveness abortamiento

abound abundar (**with/in** en)

abounding abundante (**with/in** en)

about *adv* alrededor; (here and there) por ahí; alrededor de; **~ turn!** ¡media vuelta!; *prep* (approximately) a eso de; **they arrived at ~ six** llegaron a eso de las seis; **it's ~ time** ya es hora; (concerning) sobre, de; **he said it ~ me** lo dijo de mí; **a book ~ Goya** un libro sobre Goya; **she is ~ ten** ella tiene unos diez años; **~ to** a punto de +*infin*; **have ~ one** tener[19] encima; **~-face** *n*: **do an ~-face** pasar al partido opuesto, dar[4] media vuelta

above encima; **~ all** sobre todo; (over) sobre; **lamp ~ the door** lámpara sobre la puerta; (more than) más de; **I'll not pay ~ 100 pesetas** no pagaré más de 100 pesetas; **one ~ the other** uno encima de otro; **he is ~ lying** él es incapaz de mentir; **he is (socially) ~ me** él es mi superior; **go ~ (exceed)** pasar; **~-board** *adj* franco; **~-mentioned** susodicho; **~-named** arriba citado

abrasion raspadura; *med* abrasión (-ones) *f*

abrasive *n+adj* abrasivo

abreast de … en …; **they marched four ~** marcharon de cuatro en cuatro; **~ of** *fig* al corriente de; **he keeps ~ of the news** está al corriente de las noticias; **come ~ of** alcanzar[7]

abridge abreviar; *lit* compendiar; **~d edition** edición reducida

abridgement resumen *m*; *lit* compendio

abroad en el extranjero; **go ~** ir[19] al extranjero; **the story is spread ~ that** corre la voz de que; **back from ~** de vuelta del extranjero; **live ~** vivir en el extranjero; **scatter ~** esparcir[13] por todas partes

abrogate abrogar[5]

abrogation abrogación *f*

abrupt (steep) abrupto; (sudden) repentino; (rude) brusco

abruptness (of slope) precipitación *f*; (of manner) brusquedad *f*

abscess absceso; **turn into an ~** formarse un absceso

abscond fugarse[5] (**from** de)

absence ausencia (**from** de); **~ of mind** distracción *f*; **in the ~ of** a falta de; **leave of ~** permiso

absent *adj* ausente (**from** de); **~ without leave** ausente sin permiso; **~-minded** despistado; **he kissed her ~-mindedly** él la besó de una forma indiferente; **~-mindedness** distracción *f*; *v* **~ o.s. (from)** ausentarse (de)

absentee ausente *m+f*; **~ landlord** absentista *m*

absenteeism absentismo

absinth(e) ajenjo

absolute absoluto; **~ ceiling** *aer* techo absoluto; **~ monarch** monarca *m* absolutista; **~ pitch** *mus* afinación perfecta; **it's the ~ truth** es la pura verdad; **the ~ limit of cunning** el no va más de la astucia

absolutely (yes) categóricamente; (completely) completamente, absolutamente

absolution absolución *f*; **public ~** absolución general

absolutism absolutismo

absolutist *n+adj* absolutista *m+f*

absolve absolver (ue)[1b] (*past part* absuelto) (**from** de); *eccles* perdonar; **~ from a promise** redimir de una promesa

absorb absorber (*past part* absorto); *fig*

asimilar; ~ **a shock** amortiguar[6] un choque; ~**ed in** (engrossed in) absorto en, (enthusiastic about) embebido en
absorbent absorbente
absorbing (interesting) cautivador
absorption absorción *f*; (mental) preocupación *f*
abstain abstenerse (ie)[19] (**from** de); ~ **from meat** abstenerse de comer carne
abstainer (teetotaller) abstemio total
abstemious abstemio
abstemiousness sobriedad *f*
abstention abstención *f*
abstinence abstinencia; **day of** ~ día *m* de ayuno; **total** ~ abstinencia total
abstinent abstemio
abstract *n* resumen (-úmenes) *m*; **in the** ~ en abstracto; *adj* abstracto; ~ **painter** pintor *m* abstracto; ~ **painting** pintura abstracta; *v* (extract) extraer[19] de; (summarize) resumir
abstraction abstracción *f*; **fit of** ~ momento de abstracción
abstractionism *arts* abstraccionismo
abstractionist *arts n*+*adj* abstraccionista *m*+*f*
abstruse abstruso
abstruseness oscuridad *f*
absurd absurdo; **it's** ~ es ridículo; **theatre of the** ~ teatro del absurdo
absurdity disparate *m*; **height of** ~ colmo de lo absurdo
abundance abundancia; **in** ~ en abundancia
abundant abundante; **be** ~ (**with**) abundar (en)
abundantly abundantemente; ~ **clear** absolutamente claro
abuse *n* (ill-treatment) maltrato; (insult) insultos *mpl*; (misuse) abuso; *v* (illtreat) maltratar; (insult) insultar; (misuse) abusar de
abusive *adj* abusivo
abusiveness vituperación *f*
abut lindar (**on/against** con)
abutment contigüidad *f*
abutting lindante (**on** con)
abysmal abismal; ~ **ignorance** ignorancia profunda
abyss abismo
Abyssinia Abisinia
Abyssinian *n*+*adj* abisinio
a.c. (**alternating current**) c.a. (corriente alterna)

acacia acacia
academic *n*+*adj* académico; (theoretical) teórico; (scholarly) erudito; ~ **year** año escolar
academician académico
academy academia; ~ **of fine arts** academia de bellas artes; ~ **of music** conservatorio; **military** ~ escuela militar
acanthus *archi*+*bot* acanto
accede (agree) acceder (**to** a); ~ **to an office** tomar posesión de un puesto; ~ **to a treaty** firmar un tratado; ~ **to the throne** subir al trono
accelerate acelerar
acceleration aceleración *f*
accelerator acelerador *m*; ~ **pedal** pedal *m* del acelerador
accelerometer *space* acelerómetro
accent *n* acento; **acute/grave** ~ acento agudo/grave; *v* acentuar
accentuate acentuar; *fig* agudizar[7]
accentuation acentuación *f*
accept (receive) recibir; (admit) admitir
acceptability aceptabilidad *f*
acceptable aceptable; ~ **gift** regalo adecuado
acceptance (receipt) aceptación (-ones) *f*; (approval) acogida; ~ **of a proposal** aprobación (-ones) *f* de una proposición; **without** ~ sin recepción
access acceso; (of emotion) arrebato; *med* ataque *m*; ~ **road** camino de acceso; **easy/difficult of** ~ fácil/difícil de acceso; **gain** ~ **to** acceder a
accessible accesible (**to** a)
accession (growth) acrecentamiento; *leg* accesión (-ones) *f*; ~(**s**) (**to library**) nueva adquisición (-ones) de libros; ~ **of funds** adquisición *f* de fondos; ~ **to the throne** advenimiento al trono
accessory *n* (extra piece of equipment) accesorio; (accomplice) cómplice *m*+*f*; **be an** ~ **to a crime** ser cómplice de un delito; ~ **after the fact** encubridor *m* (-ora *f*); ~ **before the fact** instigador *m* (-ora *f*); *adj* accesorio
accidence *gramm* accidente *m*
accident accidente *m*; (chance) azar *m*; *mot* atropello; ~ **insurance** seguro contra accidentes; **meet with an** ~ sufrir un accidente; (quite) **by** ~ por casualidad; **road** ~ accidente *m* de carretera; ~**-prone** propenso a tener

accidentes; *fam* accidentado

accidental *n mus* accidente *m*; *adj* accidental; ~ **death** muerte *f* accidental

accidentally por casualidad; (unintentionally) sin querer

acclaim aclamar; **he was ~ed king** fue proclamado rey

acclamation aclamación (-ones) *f*; **carried by ~** aprobado con aplausos

acclimatization aclimatación *f*

acclimatize aclimatar; **become ~d** aclimatarse

accolade acolada

accommodate (lodge) alojar; (adjust) ajustar; (oblige) complacer[14]; ~ **o.s. to** amoldarse a

accommodating *adj* complaciente

accommodation acomodación *f*; (agreement) arreglo; ~ **address** dirección (-ones) *f* de conveniencia; ~ **bill** *comm* letra de favor; **living ~** alojamiento; **sleeping ~** habitación (-ones) *f*

accompaniment acompañamiento; **musical ~** acompañamiento musical

accompanist acompañante *m+f*

accompany acompañar; **he accompanies the singer on the piano** él acompaña al cantante en el piano; **be accompanied by** estar[19] acompañado por

accomplice cómplice *m+f*; **be an ~ to a crime** ser cómplice de un delito/crimen

accomplish llevar a cabo; ~ **one's ambition** llevar a cabo su ambición; ~ **one's object** dar[19] en el blanco; **~ed** (talented) competente, (completed) cumplido

accomplishment realización *f*; **difficult of ~** difícil de realizar; **~s** talentos *mpl*

accord *n* acuerdo; **of one's own ~** espontáneamente; **with one ~** de común acuerdo; *v* ~ **with** estar[19] de acuerdo con

accordance acuerdo; **in ~ with** de acuerdo con

according: ~ **to** según; ~ **to age** según la edad; ~ **to him** según lo que dice; ~ **to plan** según el plan; ~ **to whether** según que

accordingly en consecuencia; **to act ~** actuar en conformidad

accordion acordeón (-ones) *m*

accordionist acordeonista *m+f*

accost abordar

account *n comm* cuenta; (story) relación (-ones) *f*; ~ **book** libro de cuentas; ~ **rendered** girado a cuenta; **~s sheet** hoja de cuentas; **~s department** departamento de teneduría; **current ~** cuenta corriente; **credit/debit an ~** abonar/cargar[5] en cuenta; **do the ~s** hacer[19] las cuentas; **give a grim ~ of** cargar[5] la tinta sobre; **of great/no ~** de gran/ninguna importancia; **make up an ~** *comm* hacer[19] una cuenta; **on ~ a** cuenta; **on ~ of** por motivo de; **on no ~** de ninguna manera; **profit and loss ~** cuenta de pérdidas y ganancias; **settle an ~** liquidar una cuenta; **take into ~** tener[19] en cuenta; **he turned the matter to good ~** él sacó buen provecho del asunto; *v* ~ **for** explicar[4]; (be responsible for) responder de; **how can one ~ for that?** ¿cómo se explica éso?; **are all ~ed for?** ¿están contados todos?

accountability responsabilidad *f*

accountable responsable (**for** de); **he is not ~ for his actions** él no es responsable de sus acciones

accountancy contabilidad *f*

accountant contable *m*; **chartered ~** contador colegiado

accounting contabilidad *f*; ~ **department** departamento de teneduría; **there's no ~ for tastes** hay gustos que merecen palos; **~-machine** contabilizadora

accoutrements pertrechos *fpl*; equipo

accredit (authorize) autorizar[7]; (vouch for) acreditar; **~ed to** acreditado a; **~ed** (to be of a certain grade) certificado; **~ed opinions** opiniones *fpl* acreditadas

accretion aumento

accrue derivar[5] (**to/from** a/de); **~d dividend/interest** dividendo/interés devengado

accumulate acumular(se)

accumulation acumulación (-ones) *f*

accumulator acumulador *m*; ~ **bet** apuesta múltiple

accuracy (correctness) corrección *f*; (punctuality) precisión *f*

accurate exacto; *math* correcto; (of aim) certero; **take ~ aim** apuntar con certeza; **this watch is ~** este reloj

es puntual
accursed *adj* maldito; *eccles* excomulgado
accusation denuncia; **make an ~** poner[19] una denuncia
accusative acusativo
accuse acusar, denunciar; **I ~d him of being Frenchified** le taché de ser afrancesado; **~d** *n* acusado
accuser acusador *m* (-ora *f*)
accustom acostumbrar a; **~ o.s. to** acostumbrarse a, *fam* hacerse[19] a; **~ed** acostumbrado, (habitual) habitual
ace *n* (card + person) as *m*; **within an ~ of** a dos dedos de; *adj* sobresaliente
acetate acetato
acetylene *n* acetileno; **~ cutting** corte *m* oxiacetilénico; **~ equipment** equipo de soldadura autógena; **~ lamp** lámpara oxiacetilénica; **~ welding** soldadura autógena
ache *n* dolor *m*; **I have toothache/a headache** tengo dolor de muelas/de cabeza; **I'm all ~s and pains** me duele todo el cuerpo; *v* doler (ue)[1b]; **my head ~s** me duele la cabeza; **it makes my heart ~** me rompe el alma
achieve (accomplish) llevar a cabo; (attain) conseguir (i)[3]; **he will never ~ anything** él nunca hará nada
achievement (feat) hazaña; (end) realización (-ones) *f*
Achilles Aquiles; **~ tendon** tendón *m* de Aquiles; **~ heel** punto débil; talón *m* de Aquiles
aching *n* dolencia; *adj* doliente; **I have an ~ tooth** tengo una muela que me duele
achromatic acromático
acid *n*+*adj* ácido; **~ test** prueba definitiva; **~ rain** lluvia ácida
acidify acidificar[4]
acidity acidez *f*
ack-ack fuego antiaéreo
acknowledge (recognize) reconocer[14]; (admit) admitir; **~ receipt of** acusar recibo de; **~ with thanks** dar[19] las gracias por
acknowledgement (recognition) reconocimiento; (admission) admisión *f*; (of letter *etc*) acuse *m* de recibo; **~s** (author's) agradecimiento
acme cima; **~ of perfection** colmo de la

perfección
acne acné *m*
acolyte acólito; *fam* monaguillo
acorn bellota; **~ cup** cúpula de bellota
acoustic *adj* acústico
acoustics *n* acústica; **this hall has good ~** este salón tiene buena acústica
acquaint informar; **~ o.s. with** enterarse de; **be ~ed with** conocer[14]; **he is ~ed with the facts** está enterado de los hechos
acquaintance (person) conocido; (friendship) relaciones amistosas; **make someone's ~** conocer[14] a uno; **I'm glad to make your ~** tengo mucho gusto en conocerle; **he improves on ~** él mejora al conocerle; **his ~ with the subject** su conocimiento del asunto; **I have a long ~ with ...** tengo relaciones amistosas con ... desde hace mucho tiempo; **she has a wide circle of ~s** ella tiene un círculo amplio de conocidos; **~ship** familiaridad *f*; **wide ~ship with** familiaridad profunda con
acquiesce (agree) consentir (ie)[2c] (en); (submit to) someterse a
acquiescence (agreement) consentimiento; (submission to) sumisión *f* a
acquiescent: ~ to *adj* conforme con
acquire (receive) adquirir (ie)[2c]; (by one's efforts) ganar; **~ a habit** coger[8] un vicio; **~ a taste for** tomar gusto por; **~d** *adj* adquirido; **~d characteristic** rasgo característico; **~d taste** gusto contraído
acquirement adquisición *f*; **~s** conocimientos *mpl*; **man of great ~s** hombre *m* de grandes talentos
acquirer adquiridor *m* (-ora *f*)
acquisition adquisición (-ones) *f*
acquisitive adquisitivo
acquit (declare blameless) absolver (ue)[1b]; (set free) poner[19] en libertad; **~ o.s. well/badly** portarse bien/mal
acquittal (of a duty) descargo; *leg* absolución *f*
acre acre *m* (0,4 hectáreas)
acreage número de acres
acrid acre; (smell) pungente
Acrilan *tr* Leacril *m*
acrimonious áspero
acrimony aspereza
acrobat acróbata *m*+*f*

acrobatic *adj* acrobático; ~ **feat** hazaña acrobática; ~**s** *n* acrobacia

across *adv* a través; (crossword clues) horizontales; **the distance** ~ la distancia de un lado a otro; *prep* (over) a través de; (on the other side of) al otro lado de; (from one side to another) de un lado a(l) otro; ~ **the river** de un lado al otro del río

acrostic *n+adj* acróstico

acrylic: ~ **fibre** fibra acrílica

act *n* acción (-ones) *f*; *leg* ley *f* (de parlamento); *theat* acto; (variety turn) actuación (-ones) *f*; **(by an)** ~ **of God** (por) fuerza mayor; **put on an** ~ *fig* disimular; *v* actuar; (behave) hacer[19]; ~ **honestly/openly** comportarse bien; ~ **the fool** hacer[19] el tonto; ~ **a part** desempeñar un papel; **the brakes failed to** ~ los frenos no funcionaron; ~ **as** (substitute) hacer[19] de; ~ **on impulse** obrar impulsivamente

acting *n* desempeño; actuación *f*; *adj* interino

action acción (-ones) *f*; *leg* proceso; (movement of hand *etc*) gesto; *theat* argumento; ~ **committee** comité *m* de acción; **bring an** ~ **against** entablar un pleito contra; **killed in** ~ muerto en batalla; **take** ~ tomar medidas

actionable procesable

activate activar; *phys* ionizar

activator activador *m*

active activo; **he is on** ~ **service** está en activo; (vigorous) vigoroso

activism activismo

activist *n+adj* activista *m+f*

activity actividad *f*; (social) vida social

actor actor *m*; **film** ~ actor de cine; ~-**producer** intérprete-director *m*

actress actriz (-ces) *f*

actual (real) efectivo; (of the moment) actual; (true) verdadero; **this is the** ~ **pen that García Lorca used** ésta es la misma pluma que usaba García Lorca

actuality realidad *f*; (present time) actualidad *f*

actually (despite appearances) a decir verdad; (really) en efecto

actuary actuario; ~ **tables** tablas *fpl* de mortalidad

actuate actuar; ~**d by jealousy** movido por los celos

acumen perspicacia

acupuncture acupuntura

acute agudo; *med* crítico; (of perception) finísimo; (situation) grave; ~ **accent** acento agudo; ~-**angled** acutángulo

A.D. (Anno Domini) A.C. (Año de Cristo)

ad anuncio; ~-**man** agente *m* de publicidad

adage refrán (-anes) *m*

Adam Adán; ~'**s apple** nuez (-ces) *f*

adamant firme; **be** ~ ser[19] firme

adapt adaptar (**to** a); (edit) refundir; ~ **o.s. to** amoldarse a; ~**ed** adaptado; **well** ~**ed to** bien adaptado a; **play** ~**ed from the French** comedia adaptada del francés

adaptability adaptabilidad *f*

adaptable adaptable (**to** a)

adaptation adaptación (-ones) *f*; ~ **of ... to** adaptación de ... a

adapter, adaptor (editor) refundidor *m* (-ora *f*); *elect* adaptador *m*; *phot* objetivo

add añadir (**to** a); ~ **together** sumar; ~ **up to** equivaler[19] a; **to** ~ **insult to injury** por más injuria/inri

addendum adición (-ones) *f*

adder víbora

addict *med* adicto; (enthusiast) fanático; **drug** ~ toxicómano; ~**ed to** *fig* aficionado a; **become** ~**ed to** entregarse[5] a; enviciarse con

addiction afición (-ones) *f*; **drug** ~ toxicomanía

adding adición *f*; ~-**machine** máquina de sumar, sumadora

addition adición (-ones) *f*; *math* suma; **do an** ~ sumar; **in** ~ **to** además de

additional adicional; ~ **payment** pago suplementario

additionally además

additive *n* aditivo

addled podrido; **addle-headed** chiflado

address *n* (residence) dirección (-ones) *f*; (formal letter) memorial; (speech) discurso; **name and** ~ señas *fpl*; **of no** ~ sin domicilio; **home** ~ dirección *f* de casa; **what is your** ~? ¿dónde vive usted?; **deliver an** ~ dar[19] una conferencia; **form of** ~ tratamiento; *v* (a letter) poner[19] las señas; (speech) dirigir[9] la palabra; ~ (send) **a letter to**

s.o. enviar una carta a uno; **this letter is badly ~ed** esta carta tiene las señas equivocadas; ~ **a meeting** dar[19] una conferencia; ~ **s.o. as ...** tratar a uno de ...; ~ **a petition** presentar un memorial; ~**-book** libro de señas

addressee destinatario

addressograph *tr* máquina de imprimir direcciones

adduce aducir[15]

adenoids vegetaciones adenoideas

adept *n* experto; *adj* hábil; **be ~ at** ser[19] hábil para

adequacy adecuación *f*

adequate adecuado; **he has ~ resources** tiene recursos adecuados; ~ **to** adecuado para

adhere pegarse[5] (**to** a); (remain loyal to) permanecer[14] fiel a

adherence apego (**to** a); lealtad (**to** a)

adherent *n* + *adj* (supporter) partidario; (glue) adhesivo

adhesion adhesión *f*

adhesive pegajoso; ~ **plaster** tirita; ~ **tape** cinta adhesiva

ad hoc: ~ **committee** comité *m* ad hoc

adieu adiós *m*

ad infinitum ad infinitum

adjacent adyacente (**to** a); ~ **buildings** edificios *mpl* vecinos

adjectival adjetival

adjective adjetivo

adjoin lindar con

adjoining *adj* contiguo; ~ **house** casa vecina; ~ **room** habitación (-ones) inmediata

adjourn aplazar[7]; ~ **the meeting until** levantar la sesión hasta; ~ **to the next room** trasladarse a la habitación inmediata

adjournment aplazamiento

adjudge adjudicar[4]; (pass sentence) pronunciar la sentencia

adjudicate adjudicar[4]; ~ **a claim** dar[19] fallo sobre una reclamación

adjudication adjudicación *f*

adjudicator adjudicador *m* (-ora *f*); (in competition) juez (-ces) *m*

adjunct *n* + *adj* adjunto

adjust (adapt o.s.) acostumbrarse (**to** a); (alter slightly) ajustar; (regulate, settle) arreglar

adjustable adaptable; ~ **head-rest** cabecera regulable; ~ **pipe wrench** llave

corrediza; ~ **screw** tornillo de ajuste; ~ **seat** *mot* butaca abatible; ~ **shelves** estantes *mpl* graduables; ~ **spanner** llave inglesa

adjustment arreglo; *mech* ajuste *m*; **social** ~ adaptación (-ones) *f* social

adjutant ayudante *m*; ~**-general** ayudante general *m*

ad lib *n* improvisación (-ones) *f*; *adv* a elección; *v* improvisar

administer administrar; ~ **justice** dispensar la justicia; ~ **the last sacrament** dar[19] la extremaunción; ~ **medicine** dar[19] medicina; ~ **an oath** tomar juramento; ~ **relief** distribuir[16] ayuda (material)

administration administración (-ones) *f*; (of a country) gobierno; (of a drug) administración; (of law) aplicación *f*; (of state) intendencia

administrative administrativo

administrator administrador *m*

administratrix administradora

admirable admirable

admiral almirante *m*; **red ~ ent** vanesa atalanta

admiralty (office, dignity) almirantazgo; (government department) ministerio de marina

admiration admiración *f*; **she is the ~ of all** ella es admirada por todos; **struck with ~** atónito de admiración

admire admirar; ~ **o.s. in the mirror** contemplarse en el espejo

admirer admirador *m* (-ora *f*); (wooer) pretendiente *m*

admissibility admisibilidad *f*

admissible admisible

admission entrada; **no ~** se prohíbe la entrada; **what is the ~ fee?** ¿cuánto cuesta la entrada?; ~ **free** entrada libre; ~ **of guilt** confesión *f* de culpabilidad

admit admitir; (grant) reconocer[14]; (let in) dejar entrar; **please ~ the bearer** se ruega dejar pasar al portador; **I'll ~ of no excuse** no aceptaré ninguna disculpa; **be admitted to** (hospital *etc*) internarse en, (society) ingresar en

admittance entrada

admittedly de acuerdo que

admixture mezcla

admonish (reprimand) reprender; (warn) amonestar

admonition (reprimand) reprensión (-ones) *f*; (warning) amonestación (-ones) *f*

admonitory exhortatorio

ado ruido; **much ~** mucho ruido; **without further ~** sin más ni más

adolescence adolescencia

adolescent adolescente *m+f*

Adolph(us) Adolfo

adopt adoptar; **~ a fashion** seguir[8] una moda; **~ed country** país adoptado; **~ed daughter** hija adoptiva

adoption adopción (-ones) *f*

adoptive adoptivo

adorable adorable

adoration adoración *f*

adore adorar

adorn adornar (**with** con/de); **~ o.s. with** adornarse con/de

adornment adorno

adrenalin adrenalina

Adriatic Adriático; **~ Sea** mar Adriático

adrift a la deriva; *fig* abandonado; **go ~** ir[19] a la deriva

adroit diestro

adulation adulación *f*

adult *n+adj* adulto; *fam* pornográfico; **for ~s (only)** (reservado) para mayores; **~ suffrage** derechos *mpl* de votar los mayores

adulterate adulterar

adulteration adulteración *f*

adulterer adúltero

adulteress adúltera

adulterous adúltero; **~ union** enlace adúltero

adultery adulterio

advance *n* (money) adelanto; (forward move) avance *m*; **~ booking office** despacho de entradas para teatros y conciertos; **~ guard** avanzada; **in ~** de antemano; **pay in ~** pagar[5] por adelantado; **make an ~** (payment) conceder un adelanto; **make the first ~s** dar[19] los primeros pasos; *v* adelantar; *mil* avanzar[7]

advanced (for one's age) precoz (-ces); (not elementary) difícil

advancement progreso

advantage (+ tennis) ventaja; **~ rule** *sp* ley *f* de la ventaja; **have the ~ over s.o.** llevar la ventaja a uno; **take ~ of** (avail o.s. of) aprovecharse de, (abuse s.o.)

abusar de; **show to ~** lucir[15]

advantageous ventajoso

advantageousness provecho

advent advenimiento; **Advent** *eccles* Adviento

adventitious adventicio

adventure *n* aventura; **~ story** cuento de aventuras; *v* arriesgar[5]

adventurer aventurero

adventurous, adventuresome aventurado

adverb adverbio

adverbial adverbial

adversary adversario

adverse (opposite) contrario; (unfavourable) desfavorable; **~ balance** balance *m* desfavorable; **~ wind** viento contrario

adversity adversidad *f*

advert *n* (advertisement) anuncio; *v* **~ to** referirse (ie)[2c] a

advertise (inform) anunciar; (promote sales) hacer[19] propaganda; **~ for** (in newspaper) poner[19] un anuncio pidiendo

advertisement aviso comercial; (in newspapers) anuncio; (placard) cartel *m*; **classified ~s** anuncios *mpl* por palabras; **~ columns** anuncios *mpl*

advertiser anunciante *m*

advertising publicidad *f*; **~ agency** empresa publicitaria; **~ manager** director *m* de publicidad; **~ medium** medio de publicidad; **~ rates** tarifas *fpl* para anuncios; *adj* publicitario

advice (counsel) consejo; (information) noticia, aviso; **act on s.o.'s ~** seguir (i)[3+11] los consejos de alguien; **he will not listen to ~** no quiere que se le aconseje; **piece of good ~** buen consejo; **take legal ~** asesorarse

advisability conveniencia

advisable aconsejable; **as is ~** como convenga; **it may be ~ to ...** quizás sea prudente ...

advise (counsel) aconsejar; (inform) informar, avisar; **~ against** aconsejar que no *+subj*; **~ to** aconsejar que *+subj*; **be (well) ~d to** ser[19] prudente que *+subj*; **you would be well ~d to speak to him** sería prudente que le hable usted; **I shall keep you ~d** le tendré al corriente; **ill-~d** imprudente; **well-~d** prudente

advisedly deliberadamente

adviser consejero; *mil* asesor *m*; **legal** ~ abogado; **spiritual** ~ confesor *m*

advisory consultivo; ~ **service** servicio consultivo

advocacy (profession) abogacía; ~ **of a cause** defensa de una causa

advocate *n* (lawyer) abogado; ~ **of a cause** partidario de una causa; *v* propugnar; *leg* abogar[5] por

Aegean (Sea) (mar) Egeo

aegis escudo; **under the** ~ **of** bajo el patrocinio de

aerated: ~ **water** agua de sifón

aerator aereador *m*

aerial *n rad* antena; *adj* aéreo; ~ **mine** mina aérea; ~ **photography** fotografía aérea; ~ **railway** teleférico; ~ **torpedo** torpedo aéreo

aerobatics acrobacia aérea

aerodrome aeródromo

aerodynamic aerodinámico; ~ **lift** *phys* fuerza ascensional; ~**s** aerodinámica

aero-engine aeromotor *m*

aerogramme aerograma *m*

aeronaut aeronauta *m+f*

aeronautical aeronáutico

aeronautics aeronáutica

aero-photographic(al) aerofotográfico

aero-photograph(y) aerofotografía

aeroplane avión (-ones) *m*

aerosol disparador atómico, aerosol *m*

aerospace *n* aeroespacio; *adj* aeroespacial

Aeschylus Esquilo

Aesop Esopo

aesthete esteta *m+f*

aesthetic(al) estético

aesthetics estética

afar (from afar) desde lejos

affability afabilidad *f*

affable afable

affair asunto; (happening) acontecimiento; **the Dreyfus** ~ el caso Dreyfus; ~ **of honour** lance *m* de honor; **love** ~ amorío; **it's no** ~ **of mine** no tiene nada que ver conmigo; **that's your** ~ allá usted/tú

affect (act on) afectar; (feign) fingir[9]; (influence) influir[16] en; (move) conmover (ue)[1b]

affectation afectación (-ones) *f*

affected *adj* afectado; (artificial) amanerado; *fam* cursi; *med* atacado;

(impaired) alterado

affectedly con afectación

affecting (concerning) tocante a

affection cariño

affectionate cariñoso

affectionately cariñosamente; **yours** ~ de Vd. afmo.

affianced prometido

affidavit declaración jurada

affiliate afiliar

affiliation afiliación (-ones) *f;* ~ **order** orden *f* de pagar manutención para un hijo ilegítimo

affinity afinidad *f*

affirm afirmar

affirmation afirmación (-ones) *f*; *leg* declaración (-ones) *f*

affirmative *n* afirmativa; **the answer is in the** ~ la respuesta es sí; **reply in the** ~ dar[19] una respuesta afirmativa, *fam* contestar que sí; *adj* afirmativo

affirmatively: he answered ~ contestó que sí

affix fijar

afflict afligir[9]

afflicting penoso

affliction aflicción (-ones) *f*

affluence (abundance) afluencia; (wealth) opulencia

affluent *adj* opulento

afford tener[19] medios para; (provide) proveer[16]; ~ margen; **I cannot** ~ **it** está fuera de mis medios, no tengo bastante dinero; **it** ~**ed us the opportunity** nos proporcionó la oportunidad (**to de**); **I can't** ~ **to have you living here** (it is not convenient) no me conviene tenerle viviendo aquí; **I can't** ~ **not to work** no puedo permitirme el lujo de no trabajar

afforestation repoblación *f* forestal

affranchise manumitir

affray riña

affright espantar

affront *n* afrenta; *v* afrentar

Afghan *n+adj* afgano

Afghanistan Afganistán *m*

afield lejos

afire ardiendo

aflame en llamas

afloat a flote; **keep/stay** ~ mantener(se) a flote

afoot en movimiento

aforementioned, aforenamed, aforesaid
susodicho

aforethought premeditado; **with malice**
~ con premeditación *f*

afraid asustado; ~ **of** temeroso de; **be** ~
tener[19] miedo, *fam* tener[19] canguelo;
I'm ~ **that** (sorry that) (me) temo que

afresh de nuevo

Africa África

African *n*+*adj* africano

Afrikaner africano de raza holandesa,
afrikander *m*

Afro-Asian *n*+*adj* afroasiático

aft *naut* a popa

after *adv* (place) detrás; (time) después;
the day ~ al día siguiente; *prep* (place)
detrás de; (time) después de; **one** ~
another uno tras otro; ~ **Goya** (in the
style of Goya) a la manera de Goya; ~
all después de todo; ~ **this/that**
(henceforth) en adelante; ~ **you!** (you
go first) ¡usted primero!; ~ **a while** al
poco tiempo; **it's ten** ~ **five** son las
cinco y diez; **be** ~ **s.o.** (trying to attract) andar[19] detrás de alguien; **go** ~
(look for) ir[19] por; **look** ~ cuidar de;
soon ~ a poco de; ~**birth** secundinas *fpl*; ~**-care** *n* asistencia pos-
operatoria; ~**-dinner** *adj* de sobremesa; ~**-effect** efecto secundario; ~**-
glow** resplandor *m* (crepuscular); ~**-
hour(s)** a deshora; ~**-life** vida futura;
~**math** consecuencias *fpl*; ~**noon**
tarde *f*; ~**noon mass** *fam* misa de las
sinvergüenzas; ~**noon tea** té *m* de las
cuatro; ~**-sales service** servicio post-
ventas; ~**-shave lotion** loción (-ones) *f*
para después del afeitado; ~**taste**
resabio, *fig* disgusto; ~**thought** reflexión (-ones) tardía; ~**wards** después;
~**s** (dessert) postre *m*

again otra vez; **do something** ~ volver
(ue)[1b] (*past part* vuelto) a +*infin*; **he
interrupted** ~ él volvió a interrumpir;
~ **and** ~ repetidas veces; **half as much**
~ cincuenta por ciento más; **never** ~
nunca más; **now and** ~ de vez en
cuando; **once** ~ una vez más; **same** ~!
¡otro(s) tanto(s)!

against *adv* en contra; **votes for and** ~
votos a favor y en contra; *prep*
(opposed to) contra, en contra de;
(close to) junto a; **be** ~ (opposed to)
oponerse[19] a; **the ladder was** ~ **the**

wall la escalerilla estaba contra la
pared; ~ **any eventuality** para
cualquier eventualidad; ~ **the light** al
trasluz; ~ **the grain** a contrapelo; **go** ~
the grain *fig* ir[19] a contrapelo de la voluntad; ~ **the rules** antirreglamentario

agate ágata

age *n* (number of years) edad *f*; (of
baby) tiempo; (period) época; **what is
his** ~? ¿cuántos años tiene?, (of baby)
¿qué tiempo tiene?; **at the** ~ **of ten** a la
edad de diez años; **of** ~ mayor de
edad; **not of** ~, **under** ~ menor de
edad; **the people of my** ~**-bracket/**
~**-group** la gente de mi edad; ~**-old**
antiguo; **I haven't seen her for** ~**s**
hace mucho que no la veo; **old** ~
vejez *f*, *euph* tercera edad; *v* enveje-
cerse[14]

aged *see also* **age**; (old) anciano

ageism discriminación *f* contra los viejos

ageless sempiterno; (of people) siempre
joven

agency acción (-ones) *f*; *comm* agencia;
through the ~ **of** por mediación de

agenda orden *f* del día

agent agente *m*; *comm* representante *m*;
ticket ~ taquillero

agglomerate aglomerar

agglomeration aglomeración (-ones) *f*

aggrandize engrandecer[14]

aggrandizement engrandecimiento

aggravate (make worse) agravar;
(annoy) molestar

aggravation agravamiento; (annoyance) molestia; *leg* circunstancia
agravante

aggregate total; **in the** ~ en total

aggress atacar[4]; *sp* jugar (ue) agresiva-
mente

aggression agresión *f*; *psych* agresividad *f*

aggressive agresivo

aggressor agresor *m* (-ora *f*); ~ **nation**
país *m* agresor

aggrieve afligir[9]

aghast horrorizado; *fam* con la boca
abierta

agile ágil

agility agilidad *f*

agitate agitar; ~ **for** hacer una campaña
en favor de; ~**d** perturbado; **be** ~**d**
agitarse

agitation (mental state) perturbación *f*;

pol agitación *f*

agitator *mech*+*pol* agitador *m*; (in washing machine) hélice *f*

aglow encendido

Agnes Inés

agnostic *n*+*adj* agnóstico

agnosticism agnosticismo

ago hace; **how long ~?** ¿cuánto tiempo hace?; **two months ~** hace dos meses; **long ~** hace mucho; **a short time ~** hace poco; **some time ~** hace tiempo

agog excitado; (inquisitive) curioso; **be all ~** excitarse, estar[19] lleno de curiosidad

agonizing agonizante

agony agonía; **~-column** pequeños anuncios personales

agoraphobia agorafobia

agoraphobic agorafóbico

agrarian agrario

agree (get on well) entenderse (ie)[2b] bien; (concur) estar[19] de acuerdo; **~d!** ¡de acuerdo!, *fam* ¡vale!; (to come to an agreement) llegar[5] a un acuerdo **~ about** estar[19] de acuerdo sobre; **~ to** convenir (ie)[2c] en; **~ to differ** no llegar a un acuerdo

~ with (person) estar[19] de acuerdo con; (of food) sentar (ie)[2a] bien, **strong coffee doesn't ~ with me** el café fuerte no me sienta bien; **I don't ~ with divorce** no admito el divorcio

agreeable agradable; (in conformity with) conforme con; **~ personality** carácter simpático; **be ~ to** estar[19] de acuerdo con +*infin*

agreement acuerdo; (arrangement) arreglo *m*; (compact) convenio; (conformity) conformidad *f*; *gramm* concordancia; (harmony) concordia; (treaty) pacto; **be in ~ with ... (about/over)** estar[19] de acuerdo con ... (en); **by mutual ~** por acuerdo mutuo; **come to/reach an ~** llegar[5] a un acuerdo; **wages ~** convenio sobre salarios

agrément *pol* cargo de agregado

agricultural agrícola; **~ show** feria agrícola

agriculture agricultura

agriculturist agricultor *m*

aground *naut* encallado; *fig* empantanado; **run ~** encallar[18]

ague escalofrío

ahead adelante; *naut* por la proa; **be ~** (with work) ir[19] adelantando, (in front) ir[19] adelante; **full steam ~!** ¡avante a toda máquina!; **get ~ of** adelantarse a; **go ~** seguir (i)[3+11] hacia delante, (carry on) seguir (i)[3+11]; **go straight ~** seguir (i)[3+11] todo recto; **look ~** mirar al frente, *fig* pensar (ie)[2a] en el futuro

ahoy **ship ~!** ¡ah del bote!

aid *n* ayuda, auxilio; **approach ~** *aer* aparato (de precisión) para aproximación; **deaf ~** audífono; **financial ~** subvención *f*; **first ~** primeros auxilios *mpl*; **come to the ~ of** acudir a la defensa de; **in ~ of the poor** en pro de los pobres; **what's all this in ~ of?** *fam* ¿de qué viene todo esto?; *v* ayudar; **~ed** (financially) subvencionado

aide-de-camp edecán *m*

A.I.D.S. (Acquired Immune Deficiency Syndrome) S.I.D.A. (Síndrome *m* de inmunodeficiencia adquirida)

ail estar[19] enfermo; **what ~s you?** ¿qué le pasa?

aileron *aer* alerón (-ones) *m*

ailing enclenque

ailment indisposición (-ones) *f*

aim *n* puntería; (ambition) fin *m*; (purpose) objeto; **miss one's ~** errar el blanco; **take ~** apuntar; *v* apuntar; **~ at** (aspire to) aspirar a; **~ higher** *fig* picar[4] más alto

aimless (lacking ambition) vago; (pointless) sin objeto

aimlessly sin objeto fijo

air aire *m*; (appearance) aspecto; **~s and graces** remilgos *mpl*; **give o.s. ~s and graces** entonarse, *fam* darse postín; **by ~** por avión; **get a breath of fresh ~** ventilarse; **in mid-~** entre cielo y tierra; **in the ~** (overhead) (por) arriba; **in the open ~** al aire libre; **be on the ~** *rad* radiodifundirse, *SA* peridonearse; **go off the ~** terminar el programa del día; **take the ~** tomar el aire; **~borne** aerotransportado; **become ~borne** despegar[5]; **we are now ~borne** ya estamos en el aire; **~-brake** freno de aire comprimido; **~ bus** autobús aéreo; **~-compression chamber** cámara de compresión del aire; **~-condition** climatizar[7]; **~-conditioned** con aire acondicionado;

~**-conditioner** acondicionador *m* de aire; ~**-conditioning** acondicionamiento del aire; ~**-cooled** refrigerado por aire; ~**-corridor** aeroruta; ~**-craft** avión (-ones) *m*; ~**craft-carrier** portaviones *m sing*; ~**craftman** soldado del ejército del aire; ~**-crew** tripulación *f* de avión; ~**-cushion** cojín (-ines) *m* de aire; ~**-drill** taladro neumático; ~**-drome** aeródromo; ~**-drop** *n* lanzamiento, *v* lanzar[7]; ~**-duct** conducto de aire; ~**field** campo de aviación; ~**-filter** filtro de aire; ~**force** fuerzas *fpl* aéreas; ~**-freight** aerotransporte *m*; ~**-freighter** carguero; ~**-freshener** ambientador *m*; ~**-gun** escopeta de aire comprimido; ~**-hole** respiradero; ~**-hostess** azafata; ~**intake** entrada de aire; ~**-lane** aeroruta; ~**-letter** carta por correo aéreo; ~**-lift** *n* puente *m* aéreo, *v* abastecer[14] por vía aérea; ~**line** línea aérea; ~**liner** avión *m* de pasajeros; ~**lock** burbuja de aire; ~**mail** correo aéreo; ~**mail edition** edición (-ones) *f* aérea; **by** ~**mail** por avión; ~**mail envelope/stamp** sobre/sello aéreo; ~**man** aviador *m*; ~**-mattress** colchón (-ones) *m* de aire; ~**-minded** aficionado a la aviación; ~**mindedness** afición *f* a la aeronáutica; ~**-mine** mina aérea; ~**-passage** canal *m* de aereación; ~**-pistol** pistola de aire comprimido; ~**-pocket** bache *m* aéreo; ~**-pollution** contaminación atmosférica; ~**port** aeropuerto; ~**power** potencia aérea; ~**pump** bomba de aire comprimido; ~**-raid** ataque *m* aéreo; ~**-raid drill** simulacro de ataque aéreo; ~**-raid precautions** defensa antiaérea; ~**-raid shelter** refugio antiaéreo; ~**-raid warning** alarma aérea; ~**-rifle** escopeta de aire; ~**-route** aeroruta; ~**-screw** hélice *f* (de avión); ~**-sea rescue service** servicio aéreo de rescate; ~**ship** dirigible *m*; ~**-sick** mareado (en el avión); ~**-sickness** mareo (en el avión); ~**-sock** veleta de manga; ~**space** espacio aéreo; ~**speed** velocidad *f* con respecto al aire; ~**-stewardess** azafata; ~ **supremacy** supremacia en el aire; ~**strip** pista de aterrizaje; ~ **surveying** tipografía aérea; ~**-**

terminal terminal *m* del aeropuerto; ~**tight** hermético; ~**-to-ground missile** proyectil *m* aire–tierra; ~**-to-sea missile** proyectil *m* aire–mar; ~**umbrella** protección *f* aérea; ~**way** ruta aérea; ~**ways** línea(s) aérea(s); ~**woman** aviadora; ~**worthy** apto para volar; *v* ventilar
airily a la ligera
airing ventilación *f*; ~**-cupboard** ropero
airplane avión (-ones) *m*
airy airoso; ~**-fairy** *adj* ilusorio
aisle pasillo
aitch-bone (rump bone) sacro
ajar entreabierto
Ajax Ayax
akimbo en jarras; **place the arms** ~ ponerse[19] en jarras
akin (of same family) consanguíneo (**to** a); (similar to) parecido a
alabaster *n* alabastro; *adj* de alabastro
à la carte a la carta
alacrity alacridad *f*
Aladdin Aladino
alarm *n* alarma; ~**-bell** timbre *m* de alarma; ~**-cord** cordón *m* de alarma; ~**-clock** despertador *m*; **set the** ~**clock** poner[19] el despertador; ~**-signal** rebato; *v* alarmar; **be/become** ~**ed** alarmarse
alarming alarmante
alarmist *n* + *adj* alarmista *m* + *f*
alarum rebato
alas! ¡ay (de mí)!
alb alba
Albania Albania
Albanian *n* + *adj* albanés *m* (-esa *f*)
albatross albatros *m*
albeit aunque
Albert Alberto
albino albino
album álbum *m*
albumen albúmina
alchemist alquimista *m* + *f*
alchemy alquimia
alcohol alcohol *m*
alcoholic *n* + *adj* alcohólico
alcoholism alcoholismo
alcove (room) gabinete *m*, *SA* recámara; (niche) nicho
alder aliso
alderman regidor *m*
ale cerveza (inglesa); ~**house** cervecería
alert *n* alarma; **be on the** ~ estar[19] sobre

aviso; *adj* alerta; **be ~** ser[19] vivo; **~ child** niño listo; *v* poner[19] sobre aviso

alertness (liveliness) viveza; (of guard) vigilancia

Alexander Alejandro

Alexandra Alejandra

Alexandria Alejandría

alfalfa alfalfa, lucerne

Alfred Alfredo

algae alga(s)

algebra álgebra

algebraic algebraico

Algeria Argelia

Algerian *n* + *adj* argelino

alias *n* seudónimo; *adv* por otro nombre; alias

alibi coartada; **cast-iron ~** coartada férrea

Alice Alicia; '**~ in Wonderland**' 'Alicia en el país de las maravillas'

alien *n* extranjero; *adj* extraño; (foreign) extranjero; **~ to his character** contrario a su carácter

alienate (person) apartar; (property) enajenar

alienation (of person) alejamiento; (of property) enajenación *f*

alienist *med* alienista *m* + *f*

alight *adj* (on fire) encendido; (lit up) iluminado; *v* (settle) posarse; (from vehicle) bajar; **~ (on the sea)** *aer* amarar

align alinear; **~ o.s. with** ponerse al lado de

alignment alineación (-ones) *f*

alike *adj* parecido; **you are all ~** ustedes son todos parecidos; **they are very much ~** son muy parecidos; *adv* igualmente

alimentary alimentario

alimony pensión alimenticia

alive vivo; **the fireman brought her out ~** el bombero la sacó viva; **he is still ~** aún vive; **keep ~** mantener[19] vivo; **stay ~** mantenerse[19] vivo; **~ and kicking** vivito y coleando; **~ to** sensible a; **~ with fleas** lleno de pulgas

alkali álcali *m*

alkaline alcalino

all *adj* todo; **~ day (long)** todo el día; **~ hands on deck** ¡todo el mundo arriba!; **~ modern conveniences** todo confort; **~ rights reserved** todos los derechos reservados; **~-weather** para todo

tiempo; **All Fools' Day** día *m* de los Inocentes; **All Saints'/Souls' Day** día *m* de Todos los Santos/de los Difuntos; **~-metal** todo metálico; **~-purpose** polivalente; **~-wool** de lana pura; *adv* completamente; **~ agog** lleno de curiosidad; **~ alone** a solas; **~ along** (**~ the time**) siempre, (**~ the way**) a lo largo de; **~ at once** de repente, (in unison) todos juntos; **~ but** (almost) por poco, **I ~ but fell** por poco caí; **he is ~ ears** él es todo oídos; **~ in** (weary) rendido, **I'm ~ in!** ¡ya no puedo más!; **~ out** (rapidly) a toda velocidad; **~ over** (done) terminado, **it's ~ over** se acabó; **~ right** (safe) sano y salvo, (in agreement) vale, (exclamation) ¡bueno!, (trustworthy) de confianza; **I'm ~ right now** ya pasó; **that's ~ right with/by me** me conviene; **~-round sportsman** deportista *m* acabado; **~ the better/worse** tanto mejor/peor; **~ the same** sin embargo; **~ there** *fig* despierto; **~ too** excesivamente; **~ up with** despachado; **he will come soon if he comes at ~** vendrá pronto si es que viene; **I don't like it at ~** no me gusta nada; **not at ~** (don't mention it) de nada; **he is not at ~ friendly to me** conmigo no es nada simpático; **~-in insurance** seguro a todo riesgo; **~-in wrestling** lucha libre; **~ over** (completely) completamente, (everywhere) por todas partes; **on ~ fours** a gatas; *pron* todo(s), toda(s), (everyone) todo el mundo; **~ the best!** ¡que le vaya bien!; **~ but** todo(s)/toda(s) menos; **~ in order** todo en regla; **~ there is** todo lo que hay; **~ who / ~ that** cuantos todos que; **in ~** en total; **that's ~** eso es todo; **when ~'s said and done** al fin de cuentas; **~-clear** cese *m* de alarma, *fig* señal *f* de seguir adelante; **~-out** acérrimo; **~-star show** espectáculo de muchas estrellas

Allah Alá *m*

allay (fear) calmar; (hunger *etc*) aliviar

allegation alegato

allege alegar[5]

allegiance lealtad *f*; (to a superior) obediencia; **oath of ~** (to a flag) juramento de lealtad, (to a king) juramento de fidelidad; **swear ~ to** rendir (i)[3] homenaje a

allegorical alegórico

allegory alegoría

allergic alérgico

allergy alergia

alleviate aliviar

alleviation alivio

alley callejuela; (tennis) espacio lateral; **blind ~** callejón *m* sin salida; **bowling ~** bolera, *SA* boliche *m*

alliance alianza; **enter into an ~** contraer[19] una alianza

allied aliado; (related) relacionado

alligator caimán *m*, *SA* lagarto; **~ pear** avocado, aguacate *m*

alliterate usar aliteración

alliteration aliteración (-ones) *f*

allocate (allot) asignar; (distribute) distribuir[16]

allocation distribución (-ones) *f*; (portion allocated) cuota, ración (-ones) *f*

allot (assign) asignar; (distribute) distribuir[16]

allotment (commission) asignación (-ones) *f*; (share) parte *f*; (land) parcela, huerta

allow (permit) dejar, permitir; (grant) conceder; **he ~s me a ten per cent discount** me concede un descuento del diez por ciento; **she ~ed herself to be cheated** ella se dejó engañar; **~ for** (take into account) tener[19] en cuenta, (put aside) dejar para; **you must ~ for some money for expenses** usted tiene que dejar algún dinero para gastos; **~ to** dejar +*infin*; **he won't be ~ed to leave** no le dejarán salir

allowable permisible

allowance (money) pensión (-ones) *f*, pago; (price reduction) rebaja; (concession) concesión (-ones) *f*; (against income tax) desgravación (-ones) *f*; **make an ~ for** tener[19] en cuenta; **monthly ~** mensualidad *f*; **he has a petrol ~** él recibe una asignación para gasolina

alloy *n* aleación (-ones) *f*; *v* alear

allude aludir (**to a**)

allure *v* atraer[19]

allure(ment) atractivo

alluring atractivo

allusion alusión (-ones) *f̄*; **make an ~ to** hacer[19] alusión a

allusive alusivo

alluvial aluvial

alluvium aluvión (-ones) *f*

ally *n* aliado; *v* **~ o.s. to/with** aliarse a/con

almanac almanaque *m*

almighty todopoderoso; **there was an ~ explosion** hubo una explosión tremenda; **Almighty (God)** (Dios) Todopoderoso

almond almendra; (tree) almendro; **~ essence/oil** aceite *m* de almendras; **~ paste** mazapán *m*; **~-shaped** de forma de almendra

almoner limosnero; *med* trabajador *m* (-ora *f*) medicosocial (agregado a un hospital)

almost casi

alms limosna; **~ box** limosnero; **~-giving** acto de dar limosna; **~house** hospicio

aloe áloe *m*

aloft arriba

alone *adj* solo; **leave ~** (not touch) no tocar[4]; **leave me ~!** (don't bother me) ¡déjeme en paz!; **let ~** (besides) sin mencionar; *adv* solamente

along *adv* **come ~!** ¡venga conmigo!; **all ~** desde el principio; **~ with** junto con; *prep* por, **they walked ~ the street** pasearon por la calle; **~side** a lo largo, *naut* al costado; **come ~side** atracarse al costado; **another bus will be ~ soon** otro autobús vendrá pronto

aloof reservado

aloud en voz alta

alphabet alfabeto

alphabetical: ~ order orden alfabético

alpine *n hort* planta alpina; *adj* alpestre

Alps Alpes *mpl*

already ya

Alsace Alsacia

Alsatian Alsaciano

alsatian perro pastor (perros pastor)

also también

altar altar *m*; **~-piece** retablo; **~-rail** comulgatorio

alter cambiar; *bui* reformar; (clothes) arreglar; (*US* castrate) capar

alterable alterable

alteration cambio; *bui* reforma; (clothes) arreglo

altercate altercar[4]

altercation altercado

alterer alterador *m* (-ora*f*)
alternate *adj* alterno; **on ~ days** un día sí y otro no; *v* alternar
alternately alternativamente
alternating alternante; ~ **current** corriente alterna
alternative *n* alternativa; *adj* alternativo
although aunque
altimeter altímetro
altitude altura
alto contralto
altogether *n*: **in the ~** completamente desnudo; *adv* (assembled) en conjunto; (completely) completamente
altruism altruismo
altruist altruista *m+f*
altruistic altruista
alum alumbre *m*
aluminium (*US* **aluminum**) aluminio
alumna graduada
alumnus graduado
always siempre
alyssum alisón *m*
a.m. (morning) de la mañana, **at seven ~** a las siete de la mañana; (very early) de la madrugada, **at two ~** a las dos de la madrugada
amalgamate amalgamar(se)
amalgamation amalgamación *f*
amass amontonar
amateur aficionado; ~ **theatricals** teatro de aficionados
amateurish *pej* chapucero
amatory amatorio
amaze asombrar
amazement asombro
amazing asombroso
Amazon (río) Amazonas *m*
ambassador embajador *m*
ambassadorial propio de un embajador
ambassadress embajadora
amber ámbar *m*; ~ **light** *mot* luz amarilla
ambidextrous ambidextro
ambiguity ambigüedad *f*
ambiguous ambiguo
ambit ámbito
ambition ambición (-ones) *f*
ambitious ambicioso
ambivalence ambivalencia
ambivalent ambivalente; *fam* homosexual
amble deambular
Ambrose Ambrosio

ambrosia ambrosía
ambulance ambulancia; ~ **driver** ambulanciero, conductor *m* de ambulancia; ~ **orderly** enfermero de ambulancia
ambulatory ambulatorio
ambush *n* emboscada; **lay an ~** tender (ie)[2a] una emboscada; **lie in ~** estar[19] emboscado; *v* emboscar[4]
Amelia Amalia
ameliorate mejorar(se)
amelioration mejora
amen *n*+*interj* amén *m*
amenable bien dispuesto (**to** a); **become ~ to reason** entrar en razón
amend enmendar (ie)[1a]
amendment enmienda
amends compensación *f*; **make ~ (for)** compensar (por)
amenity amenidad *f*
America América *f*; (U.S.A.) Estados Unidos *mpl*
American americano; (of the U.S.A.) norteamericano, *pej* yanqui *m*, *SA* gringo
Americanism americanismo
Americanize americanizar[7]
amethyst amatista
amiability amabilidad *f*
amiable simpático
amicable amistoso
amid en medio de; ~**ships** en medio del navío
amidst en medio de
amiss mal; **take ~** llevar a mal; **what is ~?** ¿qué pasa?
amity amistad *f*
ammeter amperímetro
ammonia amoníaco
ammunition munición (-ones) *f*; ~ **dump** depósito de municiones
amnesia amnesia
amnesty *n* amnistía; *v* amnistiar
amoeba amiba
among, amongst entre; **from ~** de entre
amoral amoral
amorous amoroso
amorphous amorfo
amount (quantity) cantidad *f*; (sum) suma; (money) importe *m*; **net ~** importe neto; **gross ~** importe bruto; **to the ~ of** hasta un total de; *v* ~ **to** (money) ascender a, (total) llegar[5] a; **it ~s to the same thing** da lo mismo; **it doesn't ~ to much** no sube a mucho,

fig no significa mucho; **what does it ~ to?** ¿a cuánto asciende?, *fig* ¿a qué viene eso?; **it didn't ~ to anything** no tuvo importancia

ampere amperio

ampersand el signo & (y)

amphetamine anfetamina *m*

amphibian anfibio

amphibious anfibio

amphitheatre anfiteatro

ample amplio; **he has ~ means** él tiene recursos adecuados

amplification ampliación *f*; *rad* amplificación *f*; *opt* aumento

amplifier amplificador *m*

amplify *elect* amplificar⁴; (increase) aumentar

amplitude amplitud *f*

amputate amputar

amputation amputación (-ones) *f*

Amsterdam Amsterdám

amuck: run ~ atacar⁴ a ciegas; volverse loco

amulet amuleto

amuse divertir (ie)²ᶜ; entretener; **~ o.s.** divertirse (ie)²ᶜ

amusement diversión (-ones) *f*; **~ park** parque *m* de atracciones; **~ machine** tragaperras *m sing+pl*

amusing divertido; (witty) salado

anachronism anacronismo

anachronistic anacrónico

anaemia anemia

anaemic anémico

anaesthesia anestesia

anaesthetic anestésico

anaesthetist anestesista *m+f*

anaesthetize anestesiar

anagram anagrama *m*

anal anal

analgesic analgésico

analogical, analogous análogo

analogue término análogo

analogy analogía

analyse analizar⁷

analysis análisis *m+f*; *US* (p)sicoanálisis *m+f*

analyst analista *m+f m*; *US* (p)sicoanalista *m+f*

analytical analítico

anarchic anárquico

anarchism anarquismo

anarchist *n+adj* anarquista *m+f*

anarchy anarquía

anathema anatema *m+f*

anatomical anatómico

anatomist anatomista *m+f*

anatomy anatomía

ancestor antepasado; *+fig* ascendiente

ancestral hereditario; **~ home** casa solariega

ancestry estirpe *f*; *fig* ascendencia; **of noble ~** de noble estirpe

anchor *n* ancla; **cast ~** echar el ancla; **ride at ~** estar¹⁹ anclado; **~ chain/fluke** cabo/uña de ancla; *v* anclar; **~ed** anclado

anchorage (place) ancladero; (process) anclaje *m*

anchovy anchoa

ancient antiguo

ancillary auxiliar

and y; (before i or hi) e; **~/or** y/o; **~ so** conque, **~ so forth** etcétera; **~ yet** sin embargo

Andalusia Andalucía

Andalusian *n+adj* andaluz *m* (-uza *f*)

Andean andino

Andes Andes *mpl*

Andorra Andorra

Andorran *n+adj* andorrano

Andrew Andrés

anecdotal anecdótico

anecdote anécdota

anemone anémona

aneroid aneroide

anew de nuevo

angel ángel *m*; *fig* pedazo de pan; **~-cake** bizcocho en molde; **~-face** cara de cielo

angelic angélico

anger *n* cólera; *v* enfadar

angina angina; **~ pectoris** angina de pecho

angle *n* ángulo; (point of view) punto de vista; **at an ~** inclinado; *v* **~ for** pescar⁴

angler pescador *m*

Anglican anglicano

anglicism anglicismo

anglicize adaptar al inglés

angling pesca (con caña)

anglophile anglófilo

anglophobe anglófobo

anglophobia anglofobia

Anglo-Saxon *n+adj* anglosajón *m* (-ona *f*)

Angolan *n+adj* angolés *m* (-esa *f*),

angoleño

angry enfadado; *SA* bravo; *med* inflamado; ~ **sea** mar agitado; ~ **words** contienda (de palabras); **get** ~ **with** enfadarse con; **make** ~ enfadar

angst angustia

anguish angustia

angular angular

aniline: ~ **dye** tinte *m* de anilina

animadversion animadversión *f*

animal animal *m*; ~ **spirits** vivacidad *f*

animalcule animálculo

animalism animalismo

animate (encourage) animar; (enliven) despabilar; ~**d** vivo; ~**d cartoons** dibujos animados

animation animación *f*

animosity animosidad *f*

anise (+ liquor) anís *m*

aniseed (grano de) anís

ankle tobillo; ~ **bone** hueso del tobillo; ~**-deep** hasta los tobillos

anklet (decorative ring) brazalete *m* para el tobillo; (sock) calcetín (-ines) *m* corto

annalist analista *m*+*f*

annals anales *mpl*

Anne Ana

anneal recocer (ue)[1b]

annex, annexe *n* anexo; *v* anexar; (document) adjuntar

annexation anexión (-ones) *f*

annihilate aniquilar

annihilation aniquilación *f*

anniversary aniversario

Anno Domini Año de Cristo

annotate anotar

annotation anotación (-ones) *f*

announce anunciar

announcement declaración (-ones) *f*; *comm* anuncio; **engagement/wedding** ~ participación (-ones) *f* de enlace/boda; **official** ~ comunicado

announcer *rad* locutor *m* (-ora *f*)

annoy molestar; *fam* fastidiar; (tease) tomar el pelo; (bore) aburrir

annoyance molestia; fastidio; (boredom) aburrimiento

annoying molesto; *vulg* jodón (-ona *f*)

annual *n bot* planta anual; (year-book) anuario; *adj* anual

annuity anualidad *f*; **life** ~ renta vitalicia

annul anular

annulment anulación (-ones) *f*

Annunciation Anunciación *f*

anode ánodo

anodyne anodino

anoint untar

anointment untamiento; *eccles* ungimiento

anomalous anómalo

anomaly anomalía

anon *adj* anónimo; *adv* en seguida

anonymity anónimo; **preserve one's** ~ conservar el anonimato

anonymous anónimo; ~ **letter** carta anónima

another otro; **the children love one** ~ los niños se quieren (unos a otros)

answer *n* (reply) contestación (-ones) *f*; (refutation) refutación (-ones) *f*; *leg* contestación (-ones) *f* a una demanda; (to puzzle +*math*) solución (-ones) *f*; *v* contestar; (to a description) corresponder; ~ **the door** abrir (*past part* abierto) la puerta; ~ **a letter** contestar a una carta; ~ **the telephone** contestar el teléfono; ~ **by return post** contestar a vuelta de correo; ~ **a purpose** servir (i)[3] a propósito

~ **back** descararse; replicar; *fam* contestar

~ **for** responder de

~ **to (the name of)** llamarse

answerable responsable (**to** a)

answering-machine contestador automático

ant hormiga; ~**-hill** hormiguero; ~**-eater** oso hormiguero

antagonism antagonismo

antagonist antagonista *m*

antagonistic antagónico

antagonize contrariar

Antarctic *n*+*adj* antártico; ~ **Circle** círculo polar antártico

antecedence precedencia

antecedent *n*+*adj* antecedente *m*

antechamber antecámara

antedate antedatar

antediluvian antediluviano

antelope antílope *m*

ante-natal antenatal

antenna *ent*+*rad* antena

anterior anterior

anteroom antesala

anthem himno; **national** ~ himno nacional

anthologist antólogo
anthology antología
Anthony Antonio
anthracite antracita
anthrax *vet* lobado; *med* ántrax *m*
anthropoid *n+adj* antropoide *m*
anthropological antropológico
anthropologist antropólogo
anthropology antropología
anti-aircraft antiaéreo; ~ **fire** fuego
   antiaéreo; ~ **gun** cañón (-ones) *m*
   antiaéreo
antibiotic antibiótico
antibody anticuerpo *m*
antic cabriola, gracia
anti-Catholic anticatólico
anticipate anticipar(se); esperar; **she ~d
   our wishes** ella se anticipó a nuestros
   deseos
anticipation anticipación *f*
anticipatory anticipante
anticlerical anticlerical
anticlimax anticlimax *m*
anti-clockwise en sentido contrario a las
   agujas del reloj
antics travesuras *fpl*
anticyclone anticiclón (-ones) *m*
anti-dazzle antideslumbrante
antidote antídoto
anti-fascism antifascismo
anti-fascist *n* antifascista *m+f*
anti-Franco antifranquista
anti-freeze anticongelante
anti-Jewish antijudío
anti-knock *n+adj mot* antidetonante
Antilles Antillas *fpl*
antimony antimonio
antipathetic antipático
antipathy antipatía
anti-personnel antipersonal
anti-Phalangist *n+adj* antifalangista
   m+f
antiphon antífona
antipodes antípodas *fpl*
antiquarian anticuario
antiquary anticuario
antiquated anticuado
antique *n* antigüedad *f*; ~ **dealer** vendedor *m* (-ora *f*) de antigüedades; ~
   dealer's tienda de antigüedades; *adj*
   antiguo
antiquity (age) antigüedad *f*
anti-racialism antirracismo
antirrhinum antirrino

anti-rust: ~ **paint** pintura antioxidante
anti-Semite antisemita *m+f*
anti-Semitic antisemítico
anti-Semitism antisemitismo
antiseptic antiséptico
anti-social antisocial
anti-Soviet antisoviético
anti-submarine: ~ **defence** defensa contra submarinos
anti-tank antitanque; ~ **gun** cañón
   (-ones) *m* antitanque
anti-tetanus: ~ **injection** inyección
   (-ones) *f* antitetánica
anti-theft: ~ **device** aparato antirrobo
antithesis antítesis *f*
antithetic antitético
antitoxin *med* antitoxina
antler asta, cuerno; ~s cornamenta
antonym antónimo
Antwerp Amberes
anus ano
anvil yunque *m*
anxiety ansiedad *f*; (desire) afán (**to** de)
anxious ansioso (**about** de); (desirous)
   deseoso (**to** de)
any *adj* (some) algún (-una *f*); (whatever) cual(es)quier; ninguno; **I
   haven't** ~ **idea** no tengo ninguna idea;
   can you give me ~ **bread?** ¿puede
   usted darme algo de pan?; ~ **place**
   dondequiera; en cualquier sitio;
   have you ~ **potatoes?** ¿tiene usted
   patatas?; ~ **way at all** de cualquier
   modo; **I haven't** ~ **friends** no tengo
   amigos; **in** ~ **case** de todos modos, en
   todo caso; ~**body** alguien, cualquier
   (a); ~**body knows that** todo el mundo
   lo sabe; ~**how**, ~**way** (at all events)
   de todas maneras, (in any manner) de
   cualquier manera; ~**thing** algo; nada;
   she didn't ask me ~**thing** ella no me
   preguntó nada; ~**thing but** todo
   menos; ~**thing else?** ¿algo más?;
   ~**where** en cualquier parte; *pron*
   cual(es)quiera; ~ **of us** cualquiera de
   nosotros
aorta aorta
apace con presteza
apart aparte; (in pieces) en pedazos; ~
   from aparte de; **come** ~ deshacerse[19];
   keep ~ mantener[19] separado; **set** ~
   poner[19] a un lado; **take** ~ desmontar
apartheid apartamiento, separación *f*

racial

apartment piso; *SA* apartamento; *Chil* departamento; ~ **hotel** hotel *m* de familias; ~ **house** casa de pisos, *SA* casa de departamentos; **furnished** ~ piso amueblado

apathetic apático

apathy apatía

ape *n* mono; *v* imitar

aperient *n+adj* laxante *m*

apéritif aperitivo

aperture abertura

apex ápice *m*

aphasia afasia

aphis áfido

aphorism aforismo

aphoristic aforístico

aphrodisiac *n+adj* afrodisíaco

apiary abejar *m*

apiece cada uno

aping imitación *f*

apish simiesco

aplomb aplomo

apocalypse apocalipsis *m*

apocalyptic apocalíptico

Apocrypha libros *mpl* apócrifos

apocryphal apócrifo

apocynthion *space* apocintio

apogee apogeo

Apollo Apolo

apologetic apologético; ~**s** apologética

apologist apologista *m+f*

apologize disculparse (**to ... for** con ... por)

apology disculpa

apolune *space* apolunío

apoplectic apoplético

apoplexy apoplejía

apostasy apostasía

apostate *n* apóstata *m+f*; *adj* falso

apostatize apostatar

apostle apóstol *m*; **Apostles' Creed** Símbolo de la Fe

apostolate apostolado

apostolic apostólico

apostrophe apóstrofe *m*

apothecary boticario; ~**'s** (shop) botica

apotheosis apoteosis *f*

appal espantar

appalling espantoso

apparatus aparato

apparel *n* ropa; *v* vestir (i)[3]

apparent (evident) evidente; (obvious) claro; (seemingly) aparente; **heir-~**

heredero forzoso

apparently al parecer

apparition aparición (-ones) *f*

appeal *n* petición (-ones) *f*; (charm) atracción (-ones) *f*, *fam* gancho; *leg* apelación (-ones) *f*; *pol* llamamiento; ~**-court** tribunal *m* de apelación; *v* pedir (i)[3]; (charm) atraer[19]; ~ **against** suplicar[4] contra, *leg* apelar contra; **when we need money we** ~ **to our friends** cuando necesitamos dinero recurrimos a nuestros amigos

appealing atractivo

appear (arrive) presentarse; (be published) salir[19]; (reveal o.s.) aparecer[14]; (seem) parecer[14]; **it** ~**s that she is ill** parece que ella está enferma; **we do not** ~ **to have received your letter** no vemos haber recibido su carta; *theat* salir[19] a escena; ~ **on T.V.** salir[19] en la T.V.; **he** ~**ed in 'Blood Wedding'** él actuó en 'Bodas de Sangre'; **fantastic monsters** ~ **in my dreams** monstruos fantásticos aparecen en mis sueños; ~ **in court** comparecer[14]; ~ **for** *leg* representar

appearance (look) aspecto; *theat* intervención *f*; *fam* pinta, **that man has the** ~ **of a drunkard** aquél hombre tiene pinta de borracho; (coming in view) aparición *f*; **girl of splendid** ~ chica de buena presencia; **first** ~ (of actor, clothing *etc*) estreno; **the last** ~ **of the comet** la última aparición del cometa; **put in an** ~ dejarse ver; **personal** ~ **is compulsory** la comparecencia personal es obligatoria; **judge by** ~**s** fiarse de las apariencias; **keep up** ~**s** salvar las apariencias; **to all** ~**s** según parece

appease apaciguar[6]

appeasement apaciguamiento; *pol* entreguismo

appellant apelante *m*

appellation título

append añadir

appendage accesorio; *bot+zool* cola

appendectomy apendectomía

appendicitis apendicitis *f*

appendix *lit+med* apéndice *m*

appertain relacionarse (**to** con); (belong) pertenecer

appetite apetito; *fig* anhelo

appetizer aperitivo

appetizing apetitoso

applaud aplaudir; (praise) alabar
applause aplauso; **he received a lot of** ~ recibió muchos aplausos
apple manzana; (tree) manzano; ~ **of the eye** niña de los ojos; **upset the ~-cart** zafar por completo; ~ **juice** zumo de manzana; ~**jack** licor *m* hecho de sidra; ~ **pie** pastel *m* de manzanas; **in ~-pie order** en perfecto orden; ~ **sauce** compota de manzanas
appliance aparato
applicable aplicable (**to** a)
applicant solicitante *m*
application aplicación (-ones) *f*; *med* compresa; (request) petición (-ones) *f*; ~ **form** solicitud *f*
applied aplicado; ~ **sociology** sociología aplicada
apply aplicar[4]; (hold good) ser[19] aplicable; ~ **the brakes** frenar; ~ **o.s. to** dedicarse[4] a; **the paint can be** ~ **with brush, roller or spray** la pintura puede aplicarse a brocha, a rodillo o a pistola; **to whom must I** ~? ¿a quién debo dirigirme?; ~ **to me if you need help** recurra usted a mí si necesita ayuda; **the orders** ~ **to everyone** las órdenes comprenden a todos; **that doesn't** ~ **to me** eso no me es pertinente; ~ **for** solicitar
appoint (a time) señalar (una hora); (person, committee *etc*) nombrar; **at the ~ed time** a la hora señalada; **be ~ed as** ser[19] nombrado
appointment (engagement) cita; (employment) empleo; (nomination) nombramiento; **hold an** ~ retener[19] un puesto; **keep an** ~ acudir a una cita; **make an** ~ **with ... for** citarse con ... para; **the hairdresser gave me an** ~ la peluquera me dio hora
apportion repartir
apportionment repartimiento
apposite apropiado
appositeness propiedad *f*
apposition yuxtaposición *f*; *gramm* aposición *f*
appraisal valorización (-ones) *f*
appraise estimar
appraiser tasador *m*
appreciable apreciable
appreciate *vt* apreciar; (be grateful for) agradecer[14]; (recognize) reconocer[14]; *vi* aumentar en valor; (of shares) subir

appreciation aprecio; (gratitude) agradecimiento; (recognition) reconocimiento; aumento en valor; **deep** ~ **of music** profundo aprecio por la música
appreciative apreciativo; **be** ~ **of** apreciar
apprehend (arrest) prender; (understand) comprender
apprehension (arrest) detención (-ones) *f*; (fear) aprensión (-ones) *f*
apprehensive aprensivo; **be** ~ **about** estar inquieto por
apprentice *n* aprendiz *m* (-iza *f*); ~**ship** aprendizaje *m*; *v* (take on as ~) tomar de aprendiz; **my father** ~**d me to a carpenter** mi padre me puso de aprendiz con un carpintero; **be** ~**d (to)** ir[19] de aprendiz (con)
apprize valuar
approach acercamiento; *mil* aproche *m*; ~ **light** *aer* luz (-ces) *f* de acercamiento; ~ **road** carretera de acceso; **you must find the right** ~ *fig* usted tiene que buscar el mejor camino; ~**es** cercanías *fpl*; **make** ~**es** dar[19] los primeros pasos; *v* (go near) acercarse[4] a; (turn to) dirigirse a; ~ **s.o. about** preguntarle a uno acerca de; **he is very easy to** ~ él es muy abordable; **she is** ~**ing forty** ella ronda los cuarenta
approachable abordable
approbation aprobación *f*
approbatory aprobatorio
appropriate *adj* (corresponding) correspondiente; (suitable for) apropiado para; *v* (take) apropiarse de; (allot money) asignar
appropriation apropiación (-ones) *f*
approval aprobación *f*; **on** ~ a prueba
approve (of) aprobar (ue)[1a]; (authorize) autorizar[7]; ~**d school** reformatorio
approvingly con aprobación
approximate *adj* aproximado; *v* ~ **to** aproximar(se) a
approximation aproximación *f*
appurtenance pertenencia
apricot albaricoque *m*; *Mex* chabacano; ~ **tree** albaricoquero
April abril *m*; ~ **showers** chubascos de abril; ~ **Fools' Day** día *m* de los Inocentes/*fam* tontos
apron delantal *m*; *aer* plataforma de

aviones; ~ **strings** cintas *fpl* del delantal; **he is tied to her ~ strings** él está cosido a sus faldas; ~ **stage** escenario salido hacia el auditorio

a propos a propósito

apse ábside *m*

apt (quick to learn) competente; (suitable) apto; (to the point) acertado; **be ~ to** (capable of) ser[19] capaz (-ces) de, (inclined to) estar[19] dispuesto a, (liable to) ser[19] propenso a

aptitude, aptness aptitud *f*; ~ **test** prueba de aptitud

aqualung botella de oxígeno

aquamarine *n min* aguamarina *f*; (colour) aguamarina *m*; *adj invar* aguamarina

aquarium acuario

Aquarius Acuario

aquatic acuático; ~s deportes acuáticos

aquatint acuatinta

aqueduct acueducto

aquiline aguileño

Arab *n* árabe *m+f*; (horse) caballo árabe; *adj* árabe

arabesque arábigo

Arabia Arabia *f*

Arabian *n+adj* árabe; '~ **Nights**' 'Mil y una noches'; ~ **Sea** mar *m* de Omán

Arabic *n* (language) árabe; *adj* arábigo

arable cultivable

Aragon Aragón

Aragonese aragonés (-esa *f*)

Aramaic *n+adj* arameo

arbiter árbitro

arbitrariness arbitrariedad *f*

arbitrary arbitrario

arbitrate arbitrar

arbitration arbitraje *m*; ~ **board** cámara arbitral; **go to ~** recurrir a una cámara arbitral

arbitrator árbitro

arboriculture arboricultura

arbour glorieta

arc *n* arco; ~ **lamp** luz (-ces) *f* de arco; ~ **lights** reflectores *mpl* de arco; **Joan of Arc** Juana de Arco

arcade cubierta con tiendas a cada lado

arcane arcano

[1] **arch** *n* arco; *anat* planta; **the trees made an ~ over the road** los árboles formaron bóveda sobre la carretera; **fallen ~es** pies planos; **triumphal ~** arco de triunfo; ~**way** pasaje abo-

vedado; *v* arquear; ~ **the eyebrows** arquear las cejas; **the cat ~ed its back** el gato se arqueó; ~**ed bridge** puente *m* arqueado

[2] **arch** *adj* (coy) coquetón (-ones); (leading) grande; **he is an ~-thief** él es un grandísimo ladrón; ~-**enemy** enemigo principal, (Satan) el demonio

archaeological arqueológico

archaeologist arqueólogo

archaeology arqueología

archaic arcaico

archaism arcaísmo

archangel arcángel *m*

archbishop arzobispo

archbishopric arzobispado

archdeacon arcediano

archduchess archiduquesa

archduke archiduque

archer (cross-bowman) ballestero; (long-bowman) arquero

archery ballestería; tiro de arco

archetypal arquetípico

archetype arquetipo

archiepiscopal arzobispal

Archimedes Arquímedes

archipelago archipiélago

architect arquitecto

architectural arquitectónico

architecture arquitectura

architrave arquitrabe *m*

archives archivo *sing*

archivist archivero

archness sutileza de ingenio

Arctic *n+adj* ártico; ~ **Circle** círculo polar ártico; ~ **Ocean** océano Ártico

ardent ardiente; *fig* apasionado

ardour ardor *m*

arduous (laborious) arduo; (steep) empinado

arduousness arduidad *f*

area (court) patio; (extent) extensión (-ones) *f*; *geom* área; (region) zona; (surface) superficie *f*

arena redondel *m*; (of bull-ring) ruedo; (of circus) pista

Argentina, Argentine (La) Argentina

Argentinian argentino

argon argón *m*

Argonauts Argonautas *mpl*

arguable discutible

argue discutir; (dispute) disputar; (infer) inferir; (maintain) sostener[19]; (prove) probar(se)[1a] con argumentos;

(reason) razonar; ~ **against** hablar en contra de; ~ **that** sostener²ᵇ que

argument discusión (-ones) *f*; (dispute) disputa; (reasoning) razonamiento; (theme) argumento; **fierce** ~ forcejeo; ~ **against/in favour** argumento en contra/a favor

argumentation argumentación *f*, argumentos *mpl*

argumentative argumentativo

aria aria

arid árido

aridity, aridness aridez *f*

aright bien; **set** ~ arreglar

arise (come into being) elevarse; (get up) levantarse; (rebel) sublevarse; (return to life) resucitar; *fig* surgir⁹; ~ **from** originarse de

aristocracy aristocracia

aristocrat aristócrata *m+f*

aristocratic aristocrático

Aristophanes Aristófanes

Aristotle Aristóteles

arithmetic *n* aritmética; ~ **lesson** lección (-ones) *f* de aritmética

arithmetical aritmético

arithmetician aritmético

ark arca; **Noah's** ~ arca de Noé

arm *n* anat+*mil* brazo; *eng* palanca; ~ **of a chair** brazo de un sillón; ~ **in** ~ cogidos del brazo; **babe in** ~**s** niño de pecho; **at** ~**'s length** a una brazada, (at bay) a distancia; **bear/lay down/take up** ~**s** llevar/rendir (i)³/empuñar las armas; **rise up in** ~**s** alzarse⁷ en armas; **present** ~**s!** ¡presenten armas!; **shoulder** ~**s!**¡armas al hombro!; **to** ~**s!** ¡a las armas!; **under** ~**s** sobre las armas; **with folded** ~**s** con los brazos cruzados; **within** ~**'s reach** al alcance; ~**band,** ~**let** brazalete *m*; ~**-chair** sillón (-ones) *m*; ~**-chair general** general *m* de sillón; ~**-hole** sobaquera; ~**pit** sobaco; ~**-rest** apoyabrazos *m sing+pl*; **side-**~**s** armas *fpl* de cinta; **small** ~**s** armas *fpl* portátiles; *v* armar; ~**ed forces** fuerzas *fpl* armadas; ~**ed robbery** robo a mano armada; **open-**~**ed** con los brazos abiertos

armada (flota) armada

armadillo armadillo

armament armamento

armature (dynamo) inducido; (magnet) armadura

Armenia Armenia

Armenian armenio

armful brazada

armistice armisticio

armorial: ~ **bearings** blasón (-ones) *m* (heráldico)

armour *n* (body-armour) armadura; (armour-plate) blindaje *m*; ~**-piercing** taladrante; *v* armar; **proteger¹⁴** con blindaje; ~**ed/**~**-plated car** coche blindado; ~**ed division** división (-ones) *f* acorazada

armourer armero

armoury armería

army ejército; *fig* multitud *f*; ~ **corps** cuerpo de ejército; ~ **doctor** médico militar; ~ **list** presupuesto para el ejército; ~ **of occupation** ejército de ocupación; **join the** ~ alistarse; **standing** ~ ejército permanente

aroma aroma *m*

aromatic *n+adj* aromático

around *adv* (near by) cerca; (on all sides) alrededor; **all** ~ por todos lados; **he's somewhere** ~ él está por aquí; **turn** ~ dar¹⁹ la vuelta; *prep* (approximately) cerca de; (on all sides of) alrededor de; ~ **the corner** a la vuelta de la esquina; ~ **here** por aquí; **go** ~ **the world** dar la vuelta al mundo

arouse (waken) despertar (ie)²ᵃ; (emotions) mover (ue)¹ᵇ; (interest) estimular; ~ **o.s.** (pull o.s. together) despabilarse; ~ **suspicions** despertar (ie)²ᵃ sospechas

arpeggio arpegio

arraign denunciar

arrange arreglar; *mus* adaptar; ~ **alphabetically** poner¹⁹ en orden alfabético; ~ **to** hacer¹⁹ arreglos para; ~ **with** arreglarse con; ~ **a date** fijar una fecha

arrangement (agreement) acuerdo; (order + act of arranging) arreglo; (layout) disposición (-ones) *f*; *mus* adaptación (-ones) *f*; (plan) proyecto; **make** ~**s for** hacer¹⁹ los preparativos para

arrant consumado

array *n* formación *f*; (large number) muchedumbre *f*; *v* formar

arrears atrasos *mpl*; **in** ~ atrasado

arrest detención *f*; **be under** ~ estar¹⁹

558

detenido; **be under house ~** estar[19] bajo arresto domiciliario; **warrant of ~** orden *f* de detención; *v* (take into custody) detener (ie)[2b]; (stop) contrarrestar; *sl* pringar

arresting llamativo

arrival llegada; *naut* arribada; **new ~** recién llegado; **on ~** al llegar; **safe ~** feliz llegada; **train ~s and departures indicator** indicador *m* de trenes y andenes

arrive llegar[5]; *naut* arribar; (happen) suceder; **~ at a decision** llegar[5] a una decisión

arrogance arrogancia

arrogant arrogante

arrogate arrogarse[5]

arrow flecha; **~head** punta de flecha; **~-shaped** asaeteado

arrowroot arrurruz *m*

arse culo

arsenal arsenal *m*

arsenic arsénico

arson incendio provocado

art arte *m+f*; **driving is an ~** la conducción es un arte; (skill) habilidad *f*; **~ gallery** galería de pintura; **~ school** instituto de bellas artes; **~s and crafts** artes y oficios; **fine ~s** bellas artes; **work of ~** obra de arte; **Arts** (university course) Filosofía y Letras

artefact artefacto

arterial: ~ road ruta nacional

arteriosclerosis arteriosclerosis *f*

artery arteria

artesian: ~ well pozo artesiano

artful astuto

arthritic artrítico

arthritis artritis *f*

Arthur Arturo

artichoke alcachofa; **Jerusalem ~** cotufa

article *n* (object) objeto; *leg* cláusula; (in periodical) artículo; *gramm* artículo; **~ of clothing** prenda de vestir; **~ of furniture** pieza; **~s of war** código militar; **sign ~s** (of apprenticeship) comprometerse por contrato; **~writer** articulista *m+f*; *v* **be ~d to** estar[19] escriturado en

articulate *adj* articulado; *v* articular; **~d lorry** camión articulado

articulation articulación *f*

artifice artificio

artificer artífice *m*

artificial artificial; (insincere) afectado; (imitation) falso; **~ flower** flor *f* artificial; **~ insemination** fecundación *f* artificial; **~ leg** pierna artificial; **~ respiration** respiración *f* artificial; **~ teeth** dientes postizos

artificiality artificialidad *f*; (of people) afectación *f*

artillery artillería; **field/heavy ~** artillería de campaña/pesada; **~man** artillero

artisan artesano

artist artista *m+f*; (painter) pintor *m* (-ora *f*)

artistic artístico

artistry talento artístico

arty que presume de artístico sin serlo

arum *bot* aro

Aryan *n+adj* ario

as (because, how) como; (when) mientras (que); **~ a child** de niño; **~ I was there I saw it all** estando yo allí lo vi todo; **~ ... ~** tan ... como, **he is ~ tall ~ his father** él es tan alto como su padre; **it's ~ good ~ lost** puede darse por perdido; **~ ... ~ possible** lo más ... posible; **~ soon ~ possible** lo antes posible; **~ big again** dos veces más grande; **~ far ~** hasta; **~ far ~ it concerns me** por lo que a mí me toca; **~ far ~ I know** que yo sepa; **~ for/to** en cuanto a; **~ if (~ though)** como si +*subj*; **~ if to** como para; **~ is** *comm* tal cual; **~ it is** así como así; **~ it were** por decirlo así; **~ long** tan largo; **~ many ~** tantos como; **~ much ~** tanto como; **~ many ~ two hundred arrived** hasta doscientos llegaron; **~ of** fechado; **~ often ~** siempre que; **~ per** *comm* según; **~ a rule** por regla general; **~ sure ~ can be** sin duda alguna; **~ the case may be** según el caso; **~ they well know** como bien saben; **~ though** como si +*subj*; **~ usual** como de costumbre; **~ well** también; **~ well ~ can be expected** tan bien como se puede esperar; **~ yet** aún; **~ you please** como (usted) quiera; **~ much ~ you need** cuanto usted necesite; **reject ~ useless** rechazar[7] por inútil; **tall ~ I am, I cannot ...** alto y todo, no puedo ...

asbestos amiamto; ~ **roof(ing)** cubierta de fibrocemento

ascend ascender; ~ **a street/river** ir[19] calle/río arriba; ~ **to the throne** subir al trono

ascendancy ascendiente *m*

Ascension Ascensión *f*; ~ **Day** fiesta de la Ascensión

ascent ascenso

ascertain averiguar[6]

ascertainable averiguable

ascertainment averiguación *f*

ascetic *n* asceta *m*; *adj* ascético

ascetism ascetismo

ascribable atribuible

ascribe atribuir[16]

aseptic aséptico

asexual asexual

[1] **ash** ceniza; ~**es** (+ mortal remains) cenizas *fpl*; **Ash Wednesday** Miércoles *m* de Ceniza; ~**-can** cubo de la basura; ~**-coloured** ceniciento; ~**tray** cenicero

[2] **ash** *bot* fresno

ashamed avergonzado; **be** ~ tener[19] vergüenza; **be** ~ **to** darse[19] vergüenza +*infin*; **aren't you** ~ **of yourself?** ¿no le da vergüenza?

ashen, ashy ceniciento

ashore a tierra; en tierra; **go** ~ desembarcar[4]

Asia Asia; ~ **Minor** Asia Menor

Asiatic, Asian *n*+*adj* asiático

aside *n theat* aparte *f*; *adv* a un lado; **put** ~ dejar a un lado; **all joking** ~ bromas *fpl* aparte; **set** ~ apartar, *leg* anular; **stand** ~ apartarse

asinine asnal

ask (inquire) preguntar; (request) pedir (i)[3]; ~ **a favour** pedir (i)[3] un favor; ~ **permission** pedir (i)[3] permiso; ~ **a question** hacer[19] una pregunta

~ **after** preguntar por

~ **for** pedir (i)[3]; ~ **for information about** pedir (i)[3] información sobre; ~ **for the impossible** pedir (i)[3] lo imposible; **he** ~**ed a thousand pesetas for the book** él pidió mil pesetas por el libro

~ **in** invitar a entrar

~ **out** invitar a salir

askance de soslayo; **look** ~ mirar de reojo

askew ladeado

asking *n* súplica; **it's yours for the** ~

puede usted tenerlo con sólo pedirlo; **third time of** ~ tercera amonestación; ~**-price** primer precio

aslant de soslayo

asleep dormido; **fall** ~ quedarse dormido; **he is fast** ~ él está (dormido) como un tronco; **my foot is** ~ tengo el pie dormido

asp víbora

asparagus espárragos *mpl*; ~ **bed** arriate *m* de espárragos; ~ **tips/stalks** puntas *fpl*/tallos *mpl* de espárragos

aspect aspecto; **financial** ~ **of the matter** aspecto monetario de la cuestión; **southern** ~ vistas *fpl* al sur

aspen tiemblo

asperity aspereza

aspersion *eccles* aspersión *f*; ~**s** calumnias *fpl*; **cast** ~**s on** decir calumnias de

asphalt asfalto; ~ **roof(ing)** cubierta de tela asfaltada

asphyxiate asfixiar

asphyxiating asfixiante

aspic gelatina de carne

aspidistra aspidistra

aspirant aspirante *m*+*f*

aspirate *n* letra aspirada; *adj* aspirado; *v* aspirar

aspiration aspiración (-ones) *f*

aspire aspirar (**to** a)

aspirin aspirina

aspiring: ~ **boxer** aspirante *m* a boxeador

ass burro; *fig* ganso; *US vulg* culo

assail asaltar

assailable asaltable

assailant asaltador *m* (-ora *f*)

assassin asesino

assassinate asesinar

assassination asesinato

assault *n* asalto; **criminal** ~ atraco; ~ **and battery** falta de palabra y obra; ~ **force** fuerzas de asalto; **indecent** ~ atentado contra el pudor; **take by** ~ tomar por las armas; *v* asaltar; (criminal) atracar

assay *n* ensaye *m*; *metal* ensaye *m*; (weights and measures) contraste *m*; ~ **balance** balanza de precisión; ~**-marked gold** oro de ley; *v* ensayar; contrastar

assemblage montaje *m*

assemble (meet) reunirse; (collect)

reunir; (put together) montar

assembly (meeting) reunión (-ones) *f*; (putting together) montaje *m*; ~ **line** tren *m* de montaje; ~ **room** sala de sesiones; ~ **shop** taller *m* de montaje; **national** ~ asamblea nacional

assent *n* consentimiento; *v* ~ **to** consentir (ie)[2c] en

assert afirmar; ~ **o.s.** imponerse; ~ **one's dignity** sostener su dignidad; ~ **one's rights** hacer[19] valer sus derechos

assertion aserción (-ones) *f*; afirmación (-ones) *f*

assess gravar; valorar; ~ **at** tasar en; ~ **damages** *leg* fijar los daños

assessable gravable

assessment gravamen (-ámenes) *m*; evaluación (-ones) *f*

assessor tasador *m*; asesor *m*

asset posesión (-ones) *f*; *comm* partida del activo; *fam* ventaja; ~**s** *comm* bienes *mpl*; **personal** ~**s** bienes muebles; **real** ~**s** bienes raíces

assiduous asiduo

assiduousness asiduidad *f*

assign (allot) asignar; (ascribe) señalar; (designate) designar; (fix) indicar[4]; *leg* (convey) traspasar

assignation cita

assignment (allotment) asignación (-ones) *f*; (appointment) cita; (attribution) señalamiento; *comm* cesión (-ones) *f*; (homework) deber *m*; (task) misión (-ones) *f*; *leg* traspaso; **deed of** ~ escritura de traspaso

assimilate asimilar

assimilation asimilación *f*

assist (help) ayudar; (be present) asistir (**at** a); ~ **in** tomar parte en

assistance ayuda; **public** ~ auxilio (público)

assistant *n* ayudante *m+f*; (in shop) dependiente *m+f*; *adj* ayudante; ~ **director** subdirector; ~ **master** profesor auxiliar; ~ **secretary** subsecretario

assizes sesión *f* de tribunal judicial

associate *n* socio; *adj* asociado; ~ **professor** profesor adjunto; *vt* ~ ... **with** asociar ... con; relacionar; **I always** ~ **poison with the Borgias** siempre asocio veneno a los Borja; *vi* ~ **with** frecuentar la compañía de; **be** ~**d**

with estar[19] asociado con, (be connected with) estar[19] mezclado con

association asociación (-ones) *f*; *comm* sociedad *f*; ~ **football** fútbol *m*; ~ **of ideas** carga semántica

assorted surtidos

assortment surtido

assuage mitigar[5], aliviar

assume asumir; ~ **responsibilities** asumir las responsabilidades; (pretend to possess) imaginarse; (suppose) creer[17], suponer

assuming: ~ **that** dado que

assumption suposición (-ones) *f*; ~ **of power** toma de poder; *eccles* **Assumption** (fiesta de la) Asunción

assurance seguridad *f*; *comm* seguro; **he gave me an** ~ me prometió

assure asegurar

assuredly seguramente

asterisk asterisco

astern en popa; **go** ~ ir[19] hacia atrás

asteroid asteroide *m*

asthma asma

astigmatism astigmatismo

astonish sorprender

astonishing sorprendente; *fam* de aúpa

astonishment asombro

astound pasmar

astrakhan astracán *m*

astral astral

astray extraviado; **go** ~ extraviarse; *fig* ir[19] por el mal camino; **lead** ~ llevar por el mal camino

astride a horcajadas; (riding) montar a horcajadas; **stand** ~ estar[19] de pie con las piernas abiertas

astringent *n+adj* astringente *m*; ~ **lotion** loción *f* astringente

astrologer astrólogo

astrological astrológico

astrology astrología

astronaut astronauta *m+f*

astronautic astronáutico; ~**s** astronáutica

astronomer astrónomo

astronomic, astronomical astronómico

astronomy astronomía

astro-physicist astrofísico

astro-physics astrofísica

Asturian asturiano

astute astuto

astuteness astucia

asunder (in pieces) a pedazos; (in two

pieces) en dos

asylum (refuge) asilo; (mental institution) manicomio; **political** ~ asilo político

asymmetric asimétrico

asymmetry asimetría

at (place) a, en; ~ **Alicante** en Alicante; ~ **Ann's** en casa de Ana; ~ **the baker's/hairdresser's** en la panadería/peluquería; ~ **arm's length** a una brazada; ~ **a distance (of)** a una distancia (de); ~ **the door** a la puerta; ~ **the end of the street** al final de la calle; ~ **home** en casa; **they went to her** ~**-home** ellos fueron a su día de recibo; ~ **large** en libertad; ~ **sea** en el mar, *fig* perplejo; ~ **the seaside** a orillas del mar; ~ **the side of** al lado de; ~ **table** a la mesa

(time) a, de, en, por; ~ **(about) two o'clock** a eso de las dos; ~ **the age of** a la edad de; ~ **the beginning/end of May** a primeros/fines de mayo; ~ **Christmas** en/por Navidades; ~ **daybreak** al amanecer; ~ **the earliest/latest** lo más pronto/tarde; ~ **first** al principio; ~ **intervals** a intervalos; ~ **infrequent intervals** de tarde en tarde; ~ **last** al fin; ~ **least** al menos, por lo menos; ~ **length** por fin; ~ **midday** al mediodía; ~ **midnight** a la medianoche; ~ **night** de noche; ~ **nightfall** al anochecer; ~ **once** en seguida; ~ **present** actualmente; ~ **the right moment** al momento oportuno; ~ **that** en eso; ~ **that time** en aquel momento, (in that epoch) en aquella época; ~ **the same time** al mismo tiempo, (on the other hand) por otra parte; ~ **times** a veces; ~ **the very moment** en el mismísimo momento; **two** ~ **a time** dos a la vez

(rate) a; ~ **sixty kilometres an hour** a sesenta kilómetros la hora; ~ **forty pesetas a dozen/metre** a cuarenta pesetas la docena / el metro; ~ **a rate of** *comm* a razón de, (speed) a una velocidad de; ~ **any rate** en todo caso; ~ **this rate** de esta manera

(condition, degree, manner) a, en, de; **I don't like it** ~ **all** no me gusta nada; ~ **all events** de todas maneras; **if** ~ **all possible I'll do it** si es posible lo haré; **not** ~ **all** de ninguna manera; ~ **bay**

acorralado; ~ **best** a lo más; ~ **ease** como en casa; ~ **the end of one's tether** sin recursos; **be** ~ **fault** tener[19] la culpa; ~ **first hand** de buena tinta; ~ **first sight** a primera vista; ~ **hand** a mano; ~ **heart** en el fondo; ~ **its best** a punto; ~ **least** por lo menos; ~ **leisure** desocupado; ~ **length** extensamente; **be** ~ **liberty to** tener[19] permiso para; **be** ~ **a loose end** estar[19] sin nada que hacer; ~ **a loss** *comm* perdiendo, *fig* perplejo; **be** ~ **a loss for words** no saber[19] qué decir; ~ **the mercy of** a la merced de; ~ **most** a lo sumo; ~ **odds** riñendo; ~ **one stroke** de un solo golpe; **be** ~ **one with** estar[19] de acuerdo con; ~ **peace/war** en paz/guerra; ~ **a pinch** en un apuro; ~ **play/rest/work** jugando/descansando/trabajando; ~ **the sight of** a la vista de; ~ **sixes and sevens** por los cerros de Úbeda; ~ **stake** en juego; ~ **a standstill** parado; ~ **that** en eso; ~ **will** a voluntad; **he's** ~ **his wit's end** él no sabe qué hacer; ~ **worst** en el peor de los casos; **be good** ~ **drawing** tener[19] facilidad para dibujar; **be bad** ~ no tener[19] facilidad para; ~ **your service!** ¡mande usted!

atavism atavismo

atheism ateísmo

atheist ateo

atheistic(al) ateo

Athenian *n + adj* ateneo

Athens Atenas *f*

athlete atleta *m + f*; ~'s **foot** pie *m* de atleta

athletic atlético

athletics atletismo; **European Athletics Championships** Campeonatos Europeos de Atletismo

Atlantic Atlántico; ~ **Charter** Carta del Atlántico

Atlantis Atlántida

atlas atlas *m*

atmosphere atmósfera

atmospheric atmosférico

atmospherics perturbaciones atmosféricas

atoll atolón (-ones) *m*

atom átomo; ~-**bomb** bomba atómica

atomic atómico; ~ **pile** pila atómica

atomize pulverizar[7]

atomizer pulverizador *m*

atonal atonal
atone: ~ **for** expiar
atonement expiación (-ones) *f*
atrocious atroz (-ces)
atrocity atrocidad *f*
atrophy *n* atrofia; *v* atrofiar(se)
attaboy!, attagirl! ¡bravo!
attach (stick) pegar⁵; *fig* atribuir¹⁶; *leg* embargar⁵; (fasten) sujetar; ~ **great importance to** dar¹⁹ gran importancia a; ~ **o.s. to** pegarse⁵ a; **shirt with collar** ~**ed** camisa con cuello unido; **be** ~**ed to** (fond of) estar¹⁹ apegado a, *sp* ser¹⁹ aficionado a; **he is** ~**ed to the regiment** él está agregado al regimiento
attachable separable
attaché agregado; **military** ~ agregado militar; ~ **case** maletín (-ines) *m*
attachment apego; (affection) cariño; *leg* embargo; *mech* accesorio; *fig* enlace *m*; **form an** ~ enlazarse⁷
attack *n* ataque *m*; (of wild animal) embestida; **make an** ~ **on** hacer¹⁹ un ataque contra; ~ **of fever** acceso de fiebre; **heart** ~ ataque de corazón; *v* atacar⁴; acometer
attackable atacable
attacker atacador *m* (-ora *f*)
attain alcanzar⁷; ~ **to** llegar⁵ a
attainable al alcance
attainment logro; ~**s** conocimientos *mpl*
attar esencia de rosas
attempt *n* tentativa; (effort) esfuerzo; (~ to kill) atentado (**on** contra); **make an** ~ hacer¹⁹ una tentativa; **he made an** ~ **to reach them** hizo un esfuerzo por alcanzarlos; **at the first** ~ a la primera tentativa; *v* (try) intentar; ~ **on the life of** atento contra la vida de; ~ **the impossible** intentar lo imposible; ~ **to (do something)** intentar (+*infin*) (algo); ~**ed murder** asesinato frustrado
attend (be present at) asistir a; (go regularly) soler (ue)¹ᵇ ir; **they** ~ **church** suelen ir a la iglesia; **the doctor** ~**ed the patient** el médico atendió al paciente; ~ **to** (pay attention to) escuchar, (care for) cuidar de; ~ **to your work!** ¡ocúpese de su trabajo!; ~ **to that lady!** ¡atienda a aquella señora!
attendance (crowd) concurrencia; (pre-

sence) asistencia; *leg* comparecencia ante el tribunal; **be in** ~ **on** servir (i)³ a; **dance** ~ **on** servir (i)³ obsequiosamente, *fam* hacer¹⁹ antesala
attendant *n* encargado; criado, criada; *cin*+*theat* acomodador *m* (-ora *f*); (museum *etc*) guarda *m*; *adj* ~ **on** acompañante de
attention atención *f*; ~! (take care) ¡cuidado!, *mil* ¡firmes!; ~ **please!** ¡atención por favor!; **be at/stand to** ~ *mil* estar¹⁹ cuadrado; **call to** ~ hacer¹⁹ presente; **get/attract s.o.'s** ~ llamar la atención de alguien; **pay** ~ **to** hacer¹⁹ caso de, (woo) hacer¹⁹ la corte a; **we shall give this matter prompt** ~ atenderemos a este asunto lo más pronto posible
attentive atento (**to** a)
attenuate atenuar
attenuating atenuante
attenuation atenuación (-ones) *f*
attest atestiguar⁶; *leg* dar¹⁹ fe; **where can I get my signature** ~**ed?** ¿dónde pueden legalizar mi firma?
attestation atestación (-ones) *f*
attic desván (-anes) *m*
attire *n* atavío; *v* ataviar
attitude (viewpoint) actitud *f*; (+space) posición *f*
attorney abogado; **power of** ~ poder *m*; ~ **at law** procurador *m* judicial; ~ **general** (England) fiscal *m* de la corona, *US* fiscal *m* del estado
attract atraer¹⁹; ~ **attention** llamar la atención
attraction atracción (-ones) *f*; (personal) atractivo; **main** ~ *theat etc* número principal; **big** ~ **of the show** atracción *f* mayor del espectáculo
attractive atractivo; **that girl is** ~ *fam* aquella chica está como un tren; ~ **secretary** una secretaria bombón
attributable atribuible
attribute *n* atributo; *v* atribuir¹⁶
attribution atribución (-ones) *f*
attrition roce *m*; **war of** ~ guerra de desgaste
attune afinar
atypical atípico
aubergine berenjena
auburn castaño rojizo
auction *n* subasta; ~ **bridge** bridge-remate *m*; ~ **room** sala de subastas;

sale by ~ venta en subasta; *v* vender en subasta (pública)

auctioneer subastador *m*

audacious (daring) osado; (cheeky) descarado

audacity (daring) osadía; (check) descaro

audibility audibilidad *f*

audible audible

audience (public) público; (interview) audiencia

audio-visual audiovisual

audit *n* revisión (-ones) *f* de cuentas; *v* revisar; ~**ed and found correct** revisado y conforme

auditing revisión *f* (de cuentas); ~ **department** sección *f* de intervención de cuentas

audition *n* audición (-ones) *f*; *v* dar[19] audición

auditor revisor *m*, interventor *m* (de cuentas); *Cub, Mex* auditor *m*

auditorium salón (-ones) *m* de actos; *theat* anfiteatro

auditory auditivo

auger taladro

aught algo

augment aumentar(se)

augmentation aumento

augur *n* agüero; *v* agorar; **it ~s ill/well** es de mal/buen agüero

august augusto

August agosto

Augusta Augustina

Augustine Agustín *m*

Augustus Augusto

auk alca

aunt tía; ~ **and uncle** tíos *mpl*

au pair (girl) au pair *f*

aura aura

aural auricular

aureola aureola

auricle aurícula

aurora borealis aurora boreal

auspices protección *f*; **under the ~ of** bajo el auspicio de

auspicious propicio

austere austero

austerity austeridad *f*

Australia Australia

Australian *n* + *adj* australiano

Austria Austria

Austrian *n* + *adj* austriaco

authentic auténtico

authenticate autenticar[4]

authentication autenticación *f*

authenticity autenticidad *f*

author autor *m*; ~**'s royalties** derechos de autor

authoress autora

authoritarian autoritario

authoritarianism autoritarismo

authoritative autoritario

authoritativeness calidad *f* de autoritario

authorities autoridades *fpl*

authority autoridad *f*; **I have it on good ~** lo tengo de buena fuente, *fam* lo sé de buena tinta; **on the ~ of** por parte de

authorization autorización (-ones) *f*; **by ~ of** por autorización de

authorize autorizar[7]; ~**d signature** firma autorizada; ~**d to act**, ~**d for use** habilitado

authorship paternidad literaria

autobiographical autobiográfico

autobiography autobiografía

autocade desfile *m* de coches

auto-change: ~ **record player** tocadiscos automático

autocracy autocracia

autocrat autócrata *m* + *f*

autocratic autocrático

autocycle ciclomotor *m*

autograph *n* + *adj* autógrafo; ~ **hunting** petición *f* de autógrafos

automate automatizar[7]

automatic *n* (pistol) (pistola) automática; (rifle) fusil automático; *adj* automático; ~ **gear change** cambio automático; ~ **landing** *aer* aterrizaje *m* por instrumentos; ~ **loading** (camera) de introducción automática; ~ **pilot** *aer* piloto automático; ~ **transmission** *mot* transmisión automática

automation automatización *f*

automaton autómata *m* + *f*

automobile automóvil *m*

autonomous autónomo

autonomy autonomía

autopsy autopsia

auto-suggestion autosugestión *f*

autumn otoño

autumnal otoñal

auxiliary auxiliar

avail *n* ventaja; **of no ~** inútil, *fam* en balde; *v* servir (i)[3] para; ~ **o.s. of**

aprovecharse de

availability disponibilidad *f*

available (obtainable) disponible; ~ **assets** *comm* activo disponible; (valid) válido

avalanche alud *m*; *fig* torrente

avant-garde *n* vanguardia; *adj* vanguardista *m*+*f*

avarice avaricia

avaricious avaro

Ave Maria avemaría

avenge vengarse[5] de

avenger vengador *m* (-ora *f*)

avenging vengador

avenue avenida; **explore every ~** investigar[5] todas las posibilidades

aver afirmar

average *n* promedio; *naut* avería; **on the ~** por término medio; **rough ~** término medio aproximado; *adj* medio; ~ **temperature** temperatura media; **at an ~ speed of** a una velocidad media de; *v* (calculate) tomar el promedio; **he ~s twelve thousand pesetas a month** saca un promedio de doce mil pesetas por mes

averse adverso (**to** a); **be ~ to** ser contrario a

aversion aversión (-ones) *f*; **my pet ~** lo que más odio

avert (prevent) prevenir[19]; (turn away) apartar; ~ **one's eyes** quitar la vista

aviary pajarera

aviation aviación *f*; ~ **spirit** *aer* gasolina de aviación

aviator aviador *m* (-ora *f*)

avid ávido

avidity avidez *f*

Avignon Aviñón

avocado aguacate *m*

avocation distracción (-ones) *f*

avocet avoceta

avoid (someone) huir[16] de; (something) evitar; **he drove ~ing the pot-holes** condujo salvando los baches; **you are ~ing the issue** usted se sale por la tangente

avoidable evitable

avoidance evitación *f*

avow declarar

avowal declaración (-ones) *f*

avuncular de un tío

await esperar; ~**ing signature** *comm* a la firma

awake *adj* (not asleep) +*fig* despierto; (aroused) despabilado; **be ~** estar[19] despierto/despabilado; **be ~ to** darse[19] cuenta de; **half ~** medio despierto; **wide ~** bien despierto

awake(n) *v* (from sleep) despertar(se) (ie)[2a]; (rouse) despabilar(se); ~ **suspicion** suscitar sospechas

awakening *n* despertar *m*

award *n* premio; *v* (prize) adjudicar[4]; (honour) conferir (ie)[2c]

aware enterado; **to be ~ of** estar[19] enterado de; **not that I'm ~ of** no, que yo sepa; **you are ~ that** *comm* le(s) consta a usted(es) que

awash a flor de agua

away fuera; ~ **back in 1500** allá por 1500; ~ **from home** fuera de casa; **Real Madrid are playing ~ (from home)** el Real Madrid juega fuera; ~ **game** partido fuera (de casa), *fam* salida; ~ **with you!** ¡lárguese!; **far ~** (a lo) lejos; **far and ~** con mucho; **they are six miles ~** están a seis millas de aquí; **fire ~!** ¡fuego!; **a few days ~ from work** unos días alejado del trabajo

awe temor *m*; ~**-inspiring** imponente; ~**-struck** aterrado

awesome imponente

awful espantoso; (very bad) pésimo; ~ **weather** tiempo terrible; **I feel ~** me siento fatal; **he looks ~ today** él tiene un aspecto muy malo hoy; **an ~ lot of** una barbaridad de; **how ~!** ¡qué barbaridad!

awfully (very) muy; **I love you ~** te quiero horrores

awhile un rato

awkward (clumsy) desmañado; (difficult) incómodo; ~ **job** trabajo incómodo; ~ **question** pregunta delicada; ~ **customer/fellow** un tipo de poco fiar; (embarrassed) tímido; **he is very ~ with girls** es muy tímido con las chicas; (embarrassing) violento; **it was very ~ for me** me fue muy violento; ~ **situation** situación *f* desagradable

awkwardness (clumsiness) torpeza; (difficulty) incomodidad *f*; (embarrassment) timidez *f*, lo violento

awl lezna

awning toldo

awry torcido

axe *n* hacha; *v* (chop) hachear; *fig* (sack) despedir (i)[3]; (reduce) reducir[15] drásticamente

axiom axioma *m*

axiomatic(al) axiomático

axis eje *m*

axle eje *m*; ~-**tree** eje *m* de carretón

azalea azalea

Azores Azores *mpl*

Aztec *n* + *adj* azteca *m* + *f*

azure *n* + *adj* azul (celeste) *m*

B

b (letter) be *f*; **B** *mus* si *m*

B.A. (Bachelor of Arts) Br. en A. (Bachiller en Artes); *Sp equiv* Licenciado en Filosofía y Letras

baa *n* be *m*; *v* balar

babble balbucear; **the brook** ~s el arroyo susurra

babbler hablador *m* (-ora *f*); charlatán *m* (-ana *f*)

babbling *n* (garrulousness) garrulería; (of stream) susurro; *adj* hablador; (of stream) que susurra

babe niño; ~ **in arms** niño de pecho

baboon babuino

baby *n* bebé *m*; (animal) cría; (term of endearment) rica; ~ **bed** *US* cuna; ~ **boy** nene *m*; ~**-buggy**, ~**-carriage** coche(cito) de niño; ~ **girl** nena; ~ **grand** piano de media cola; ~**-linen** canastilla; ~**-sit** hacer[19] de niñera (por horas); ~**-sitter** niñera por horas, *fam* canguro; ~**-stroller** silla de paseo; ~**-talk** media lengua

babyhood niñez *f*

babyish infantil

Babylon Babilonia

Babylonian *n* + *adj* babilónico

baccarat bacará *m*

Bacchanalia bacanales *fpl*

Bacchus Baco

bachelor soltero; **old** ~ solterón (-ones) *m*; ~ **flat** piso de soltero; ~ **girl** soltera; ~**hood** soltería

Bachelor Bachiller *m*; ~ **of Arts** Bachiller en Artes, *Sp equiv* Licenciado en Filosofía y Letras; ~ **of Law** Bachiller en Leyes, *Sp equiv* Licenciado en Derecho

bacillus bacilo

back *n* (human) espalda; (animal) lomo; (of chair) respaldo; (of clothing) parte trasera; (of knife) canto; (spine of book) lomo; *sp* defensa *m*; (of throat) fauces *mpl*; (reverse side) dorso; **on the** ~ al dorso; ~ **of beyond** el quinto pino; **at**

the ~, **in** ~ (**of**) detrás (de); **at the** ~ **of one's mind** en lo recóndito del pensamiento; **behind one's** ~ + *fig* a espaldas de uno; **I should like to see the** ~ **of her** quisiera librarme de ella; **on one's** ~ (lying) boca arriba, (carrying) a cuestas; **put your** ~ **into it** hágalo con más esfuerzo; **turn one's** ~ **on** volver (ue)[1b] (*past part* vuelto) la espalda a; **with one's** ~ **to the wall** con la espalda a la pared; ~**bite** murmurar; ~**biter** murmurador *m* (-ora *f*); ~**biting** calumnia; ~**breaking** agobiante; ~**less dress** vestido sin espalda; ~**-slapping** espaldarazos *mpl*, *fig* bombo mutuo; ~**-to-**~ de espaldas; ~**-to-front** al revés

adj trasero; ~**bencher** diputado sin ningún cargo especial; ~**bone** espinazo, *fig* firmeza; **he is the** ~**bone of the family** él es el pilar de la familia; **to the** ~**bone** hasta los tuétanos; ~**-cloth** telón (-ones) *m* de fondo; ~ **door** puerta trasera; **enter by the** ~ **door** *fig* entrar por la puerta falsa; ~**drop** *theat* foro; ~**ground** fondo, *fig* (environment) ambiente *m*, (social) medio; **I prefer to remain in the** ~**ground** prefiero estar en segundo término; ~**ground music** música ambiental; ~**hand** *n sp* revés (-eses) *m*, *adj* de revés; ~**handed** de revés, *fig* irónico; ~**hander** (slap) golpe *m* de revés, (remark) observación irónica; ~**lash** reacción *f*; ~**log** atrasos *mpl*; ~**number** (publication) número atrasado, *fig* cero (a la izquierda); ~ **pay** sueldo atrasado; ~ **pocket** bolsillo posterior; ~**-projection** *cin* retroproyección *f*; ~ **room** pieza trasera, (of shop) trastienda; ~**-room boy** sin renombre *m*; ~ **row** *cin etc* última fila; ~ **seat** asiento de atrás; **take a** ~ **seat** *fig* ceder el puesto; ~**side** trasero, *fam* culo; ~**-stage** entre bastidores; ~**-stairs**

567

escalera de atrás, *fig* vías indirectas; ~**stitch** *n* pespunte *m*, *v* pespuntar; ~**stroke** (swimming) braza de espalda; ~ **tooth** muela; ~**track** retirarse; ~**water** *n* remanso, *v naut* remansar; ~ **yard** patio interior

adv (in reverse) (hacia) atrás; (returned) de vuelta; **ah, you're ~!** ¡ah, está usted de vuelta!; ~ **and forth** de una parte a otra; **some years ~** hace unos años; ~**chat** réplica; ~**date** poner[19] fecha atrasada; ~**fire** *n* falsa explosión, *mot* petardeo, *v mot* petardear, *fig* salir[19] el tiro por la culata; ~**pedal** contrapedalear, *fig* retirarse; ~**somersault** *n* voltereta hacia atrás, *v* dar[19] una voltereta hacia atrás; ~**slide** reincidir; ~**slider** reincidente *m+f*; ~**sliding** reincidencia; ~**spacer** (typewriter) tecla de retroceso

v (go ~) retroceder; *mot* dar[19] marcha atrás (a); (bet on) apostar (ue)[1a] por; apoyar

~ **down** ceder; *fam* rajarse

~ **out** volverse (ue)[1b] (*past part* vuelto) atrás

~ **off** retroceder de

~ **up** apoyar; *fam* sacar la cara a

interj ¡atrás!

backer (gambler) apostador *m*; (supporter) partidario; *theat* caballo blanco, mecenas *m*

backgammon chaquete *m*; ~**board** tablas *fpl* reales

backing *n* (support) apoyo; (pop-music) batería; ~**sheet** hoja posterior

backward torpe; **he is not ~ in coming forward** él no es de los que se echan atrás; ~**looking** *fig* retrógrado; ~**s** atrás; al revés

backwardness torpeza

bacon bacon *m*; **eggs and ~** huevos *mpl* con jamón; **save one's ~** salvar el pellejo; ~**slicer** cortafiambres *m sing+pl*

bacteria bacterias *fpl*

bacterial bactérico

bacteriological bacteriológico; ~ **warfare** guerra bacteriológica

bacteriologist bacteriólogo

bacteriology bacteriología

bad malo; (decayed) podrido; (harmful) dañoso; (ill) enfermo; ~ **blood** *fig*

mala sangre; ~ **breath** mal aliento; ~ **cold** resfriado fuerte; ~ **debt** deuda morosa; (in) ~ **faith** (de) mala fe; ~ **form** mala educación; **with a ~ grace** de mala gana; ~ **joke** chiste *m* inglés; ~ **language** palabrotas *fpl*; **use ~ language** soltar (ue)[1a] tacos; ~ **lot** mal sujeto; ~ **luck** mala suerte; ~ **news** mala(s) noticia(s); ~ **money** moneda falsa; ~ **visibility** mala visibilidad; **be in ~ with** (out of favour with) estar[19] a mal con; **from ~ to worse** de mal en peor; **I feel ~ about it** lo siento mucho; **go ~** (food) pasarse; **go to the ~** caer[19] en el mal; **in ~ taste** cursi; **a piece of ~ taste** cursilada; **joke in ~ taste** broma de mal gusto; **it will be ~ for you** le hará daño a usted; **not too ~** regular; **that's not a ~ idea** eso no está mal; **too ~!** ¡qué lástima!; ~**lands** tierras *fpl* yermas; ~**mannered** mal educado; **be ~tempered** tener[19] mal genio

badge insignia; (policeman's) placa

badger *n* tejón (-ones) *m*; *v* molestar

badly mal, de mala manera; **he is ~ in need of** él se pierde por; **I am ~ off** ando muy mal de dinero; ~ **made** mal hecho; ~ **wanted** muy necesario

badminton (juego del) volante *m*

badness (evil) maldad *f*; (pus) podredumbre *f*

baffle frustrar; ~**plate** *mot* deflector *m*

baffling desconcertador (-ora *f*)

bag saco; (handbag) bolso, *sl* tanque *m*; (man's) *sl* maricona; (shopping-bag) capacho; (grip) bolso de viaje; (paper) bolsa de papel; (game) caza; **in the ~** *fig* en el bolsillo; **I let the cat out of the ~** se me escapó el secreto; **the whole ~ of tricks** todo; **he's a ~ of bones** él está en los huesos; ~**s** (under eyes) ojeras, (trousers) pantalón *m*; **there's ~s of room** hay sitio de sobra; ~**snatcher** ratero; *v* (capture) coger[8]; (hunt) cazar[7]

bagatelle bagatela

baggage equipaje *m*; *SA* bagaje *m*; (hussy) fulana; ~**room** consigna

baggy: ~ trousers pantalón (-ones) *m* dados de sí

bagpipe gaita

bagpiper gaitero

Bahamas Islas Bahamas

bail *n* fianza; **on ~** bajo fianza; **go/stand ~ for** salir[19] fiador por; *v* **~ out** *naut* achicar[4]

bailiff alguacil *m*

bait *n* cebo; **swallow/take the ~** *fig* tragar[5] el anzuelo; *v* cebar; *fig* acosar

baize bayeta; **green ~** tapete *m* verde

bake *cer+cul* cocer (ue)[1b] (en el horno); **~d** asado; **~d fish** pescado al horno; **half-~d** a medio cocer, *fig* inexperto

bakehouse, bakery panadería

bakelite *tr* baquelita

baker panadero; **~'s (shop)** panadería

baking hornada; *cer* cocción *f*; **she likes ~ a** ella le gusta hacer[19] tortas; **~-powder** levadura; **~-tin** molde *m*

balalaika balalaika

balance *n* (scales) balanza; (equilibrium) equilibrio; (surplus) saldo; *comm* balance *m*; (in picture) harmonía de dibujo; **~ due** saldo debido; **~ in hand** saldo disponible; **~ in your favour** saldo a su favor; **~ of payments** balanza de pagos; **~ of power** equilibrio político; **~ of trade** balance *m* comercial; **~ outstanding** saldo pendiente; **have a favourable ~** *comm* tener[19] un saldo favorable; **in the ~** *fig* en balanza; **lose one's ~** perder (ie)[2b] el equilibrio; **show a ~** arrojar un saldo; **~-sheet** balance *m*; **~-wheel** balancín (-ines) *m* (de reloj); *vt* balancear; *vi* equilibrarse; **~ a budget** comparar un presupuesto; **~ the account(s)** saldar cuentas; **~ the ledger** saldar el mayor; **~ up** igualar; **~d diet** régimen equilibrado; **he is a well-~d man** él es un hombre bien equilibrado

balcony balcón (-ones) *m*; *theat* galería, *fam* paraíso

bald calvo; *fig* directo

balderdash disparate *m*

balding que se va quedando calvo

baldness calvicie *f*

bale *n* fardo; *v* enfardar; **~ out** *aer* lanzarse[7] (en paracaídas)

Balearic Islands Islas Baleares

baleful funesto

baler (for baling straw) embaladora

balk *n* (obstacle) estorbo; (timber) viga; (billiards) cabaña; *v* frustrar

Balkan balcánico

Balkans Balcanes *mpl*

[1] **ball** (tennis *etc*) pelota; (football) balón (-ones) *m*; (sphere) esfera; **~-and-socket joint** articulación esférica; **~ game** juego de pelota; **~ of the foot** región *f* tenar; **~ of wool** ovillo de lana; **keep the ~ rolling** *fig* mantener[19] en marcha (la conversación); **play ~** jugar a la pelota, *fig* ponerse[19] de acuerdo; **cannon-~** bala de cañón; **~-bearing** bola de acero; **~-bearings** cojinete *m* de bolas; **~-cock** válvula de flotador; **~-park** campo de deportes; **~-(point) pen** bolígrafo, *fam* bic (-ques) *m*; **eye-~** globo del ojo; **~s** *+interj vulg* cojones *mpl*; **make a ~-up of** *vulg* joder

[2] **ball** (dance) baile *m*; **~ dress** vestido de baile; **fancy-dress ~** baile *m* de disfraces; **~-room** salón (-ones) *m* de baile; **~-room dance/dancing** baile *m* de sociedad

ballad romance *m*; **~-singer** cupletista *m+f*

ballast *n* *bui* balasto; *naut* lastre *m*; **in ~** lastrado; *v* lastrar

ballerina bailarina

ballet ballet *m*; **~-dancer** bailarín *m* (-ina *f*)

ballistic: ~ missile proyectil balístico; **~s** balística

balloon globo; **~ barrage** barrera anti-aérea de globos cautivos; **~-tyre** neumático de baja presión

ballot *n* votación (-ones) *f*; **~-box** urna (electoral); **~-paper** papeleta para votar; *v* **~ (for)** votar (por)

ballyhoo propaganda sensacionalista

balm bálsamo

balmy balsámico

baloney necedad *f*

balsam bálsamo

Baltic Sea mar Báltico

balustrade balaustrada

bamboo bambú *m*

bamboozle engañar

bamboozler engañador *m* (-ora *f*)

ban *n* prohibición (-ones) *f*; *v* prohibir; **he was banned from playing** le prohibieron que jugase

banal trivial

banality trivialidad *f*

banana plátano; *SA* banana; **~ boat** bananero; **~ tree** banano; **~s** (crazy) chiflado

¹band (thin strip) faja; *archi* listón (-ones) *m*; *rad* banda; (on cigar) anillo; **Band-Aid** *tr* tirita; **~-box** sombrerera de cartón; **~-saw** sierra sin fin

²band *n* (gang) pand(ill)a; *mus* banda (de música); *US* ~ **of sheep** rebaño de ovejas; **join the ~-wagon** ir¹⁹ al sol que más calienta; **~master** director *m* de banda; **~sman** músico de banda; **~stand** glorieta de música; *v* ~ **together** agruparse

bandage *n* vendaje *m*; *v* vendar

bandanna pañuelo

bandit bandido; **one-armed** ~ máquina tragaperras *f sing+pl*

banditry gangsterismo

bandy(-legged) patizambo

bane perdición *f*

baneful pernicioso

bang *n* (noise) estrépito; (blow) golpe *m*; **with a** ~ con un golpe violento; *v* (hit) golpear, *fam* pegar⁵; (sound) disparar; ~ **the door** dar¹⁹ un portazo; ~ **the head** golpearse la cabeza; *interj* ¡pan!

bangle pulsera

banish desterrar (ie)²ᵃ

banishment destierro

banister pasamano

banjo banjo

¹bank *n* (institution+building) banco; (gaming) banca (de juego); ~ **account** cuenta de banco; ~ **book** libreta de banco; ~ **clerk** empleado de banco; ~ **counter-clerk** empleado de ventanilla; ~ **holiday** (día *m* de) fiesta nacional; ~ **manager** director *m* de banco; **~note** billete *m*, *sl* papiro; ~ **rate** tipo bancario; ~ **statement** estado de la cuenta; **run on the** ~ gran demanda al banco; **savings** ~ caja de ahorros; *v* depositar, ingresar en el banco

²bank (of river) ribera; *aer* inclinación *f* al virar; (mound of earth) terraplén (-enes) *m*; *naut* bajo; (of flowers) banco; (row of lights) batería; ~ **of snow** montón (-ones) *m* de nieve; **fog-~** banco de niebla; *v aer* inclinar al virar; ~ **on** contar (ue)¹ᵃ con; ~ **up** (fire) cubrir

bankable admisible en un banco

banker banquero; (football pool) fijo; **~'s order** letra de cambio; **be** ~ (in game) tener¹⁹ la banca

banking *n* banca; *adj* bancario; **~-house** casa de banco

bankrupt *n+adj* quebrado; **go** ~ quebrar (ie)²ᵃ

bankruptcy quiebra

banner bandera; ~ **headline** grandes titulares *mpl*

banns amonestaciones *fpl*; **publish the** ~ decir¹⁹ las amonestaciones

banquet *n* banquete *m*; *v* banquetear

banqueting *n* banqueteo *m*

banshee espíritu *m* cuya presencia presagia la muerte

bantam gallinilla; ~ **weight** *sp* peso gallo

banter burlarse de

banterer burlón *m* (-ona *f*)

bap panecillo escocés

baptism (sacrament) bautismo; (action) bautizo

baptismal: ~ **certificate** fe *f* de bautismo

Baptist anabaptista *m+f*; **St John the** ~ San Juan Bautista

baptistry bautisterio

baptize bautizar⁷

bar *n* barra; (barrier) barrera; (public house) bar *m*; (counter) mostrador *m*; *leg* foro; *mus* compás *m*; *naut* barra; (obstacle) traba; (of soap *etc*) pastilla; **be at the** ~ *leg* ser¹⁹ abogado recibido; **be called to the** ~ recibirse de abogado; ~ **line** *mus* raya; **~maid** moza de bar; **~man,** ~**-tender** mozo de taberna, *SA* barman *m* (bármanes); *v* atrancar, poner barrotes a; (fasten) cerrar (ie)²ᵃ con barras; (exclude) excluir¹⁶; (hinder) impedir (i); *prep* (except) excepto

barb púa; **~ed** armado con púas; **~ed remark** observación (-ones) *f* mordaz; **~ed wire** alambre *m* de púas

Barbados Barbados

Barbara Bárbara

barbarian *n+adj* bárbaro

barbaric, barbarous bárbaro

barbarism (speech) barbarismo

barbarity barbaridad *f*; **an act of** ~ una crueldad

Barbary Berbería

barbecue *n* barbacoa; *adj* asado en la barbacoa; *v* asar en barbacoa

barbel barbo

barber peluquero; **~'s shop** peluquería

barbiturate barbitúrico

Barcelona Barcelona; **inhabitant of** ~

barcelonés *m* (-esa *f*)

bard poeta *m*

bardic de los bardos

bare (naked) desnudo; (hairless) pelado; (uncovered) descubierto; (unadorned) seco; (just enough) escueto; (truth) pura; **the ~ details** los detalles escuetos; **lay ~** (reveal) revelar; **~-back(ed)** a pelo; **~-faced** descarado; **~-faced lie** mentira gorda; **~-footed** descalzo; **~-handed** (unarmed) a brazo partido; **~-headed** descubierto; **~legged** en pernetas; *v* desnudar; descubrir (*past part* descubierto)

barely apenas

barette pasador *m*

bargain *n* (cheap purchase) ganga, *fam* bicoca; (agreement) convenio; **make/strike a ~** cerrar (ie)²ᵃ un convenio; **~ basement** sección *f* de rebajas; **~ counter** oportunidades *fpl*; **~ prices** precios *mpl* de oportunidad; **give into the ~** dar¹⁹ además; *v* hacer¹⁹ convenio; (haggle) regatear; **~ with ... for** negociar con ... para

bargaining (negotiation) convenio; (haggling) regateo

barge *n* (admiral's) falúa; (with sails) gabarra; (with engine/sails) barcaza; (towed) lancha remolque; *v* **~ into** tropezar⁷ con; (deliberately) dar¹⁹ empujones

bargee barquero

baritone barítono

barium bario; **~-meal** comida de bario

bark *n* (of dog) ladrido; (of tree) corteza; **his ~ is worse than his bite** perro ladrador poco mordedor; *v* (of dog) ladrar (at a); **strip ~ from** descortezar⁷; **~ one's shin** despellejarse la espinilla; **~ up the wrong tree** descaminarse

barley cebada; **pearl ~** cebada perlada; **~corn** grano de cebada; **~-sugar** alfeñique *m*; **~-water** hordiate *m*

barm levadura

barmy lerdo

barn pajar *m*; *US* cochera; **~dance** baile *m* rural; **~-owl** lechuza; **~yard** corral *m*

barnacle percebe *m*

barometer barómetro

baron barón (-ones) *m*; **~ of beef** solomillo

baroness baronesa

baronet baronet *m*

baronetcy rango de baronet

baronial relativo a la baronía o al barón

barony baronía

baroque barroco

barrack *v* abuchear; interrumpir a voces

barracks cuartel *m*

barrage presa; *mil* cortina de fuego

barrel barril *m*; (of rifle *etc*) cañón (-ones) *m*; **~-maker** tonelero; **~-organ** organillo

barrelled embarrillado; **double-~** de dos cañones

barren *agr*+*fig* árido; *biol* estéril

barrenness *agr*+*fig* aridez *f*; *biol* esterilidad *f*

barricade *n* barricada; *v* cerrar (ie)²ᵃ con barricadas

barrier barrera; **ticket ~** barrera (del revisor)

barring excepto

barrister abogado recibido

barrow carretilla; **~-boy** vendedor *m* que lleva sus mercancías en una carretilla; (mound) túmulo

barter *n* trueque *m*; *v* traficar⁴

Bartholomew Bartolomé

basalt basalto

base *n*+*mil* base *f*; (cosmetic) crema base; **~ball** béisbol *m*; **~ball player** beisbolista *m*; **~board** rodapié *m*; **~ camp** (mountaineering) refugio de partida; **~ line** *sp* línea de saque; **~ metal** metal *m* común; *adj* vil; *v* basar; **be ~d on** estar¹⁹ basado en

baseless sin fundamento

basement sótano

baseness vileza

bash *n* golpe *m* aplastante; *v* golpear; **he kept on ~ing away** él siguió golpeándole

bashful vergonzoso

bashfulness vergüenza

basic básico; **~ industry** industria básica; **~ wage** salario-base *m*

Basil Basilio

basil *bot* albahaca

basilica basílica

basilisk basilisco

basin *cul* fuente *f*; (for holy water) pila; (of river) cuenca; **hand-~** palangana

basis base *f*; **on a competitive ~** sobre una base competitiva

bask calentarse (ie)²ᵃ; ~ **in the sun** tomar el sol

basket cesta, cesto; ~**ball** baloncesto, basquetbol *m*; ~**ball player** basquetbolista *m+f*; ~**ful** cestada; ~**-maker** cestero; ~**-making/work** cestería

Basle Basilea *f*

Basque *n+adj* vasco; (language) vascuence *m*, euzkera; ~ **Provinces** Provincias Vascongadas, Euzkadi *m*

bas-relief bajo relieve

bass *n* (fish) perca; *adj mus* bajo; ~ **clef** clave *f* de fa; ~ **control knob** *rad etc* regulador *m* de notas graves

basset perro zarcero

bassoon bajón (-ones) *m*

bastard bastardo; (term of abuse) *vulg* hijo de puta

baste *cul* rociar⁵; (sewing) hilvanar

bastion bastión (-ones) *m*

¹ **bat** *n* (aircraft signaller's) disco de señal; *sp* palo; **off his own** ~ por su cuenta y riesgo; *v* golpear con un palo; **he didn't** ~ **an eyelid** él ni parpadeó

² **bat** *n* murciélago; **blind as a** ~ ciego como un topo; **be/have** ~**s in the belfry** tener¹⁹ pajaritos en la cabeza

batch lote *m*; *cul* hornada

bath *n* baño; (vessel) bañera; **have a** ~ tomar un baño; ~**s** piscina; ~**-chair** silla de ruedas; ~**-robe** bata de baño; ~**room** cuarto de baño; ~**-salts** sales *fpl* de baño; ~**-towel** toalla de baño; ~**tub** bañera; ~**water** agua del baño; *v* bañar(se)

bathe *n* baño; *vi* bañarse; *vt* bañar; (wound) lavar

bather bañista *m+f*

bathing baño; ~**-beauty** bañista bella; ~**-cap** gorro de baño; ~**-costume** bañador *m*; ~**-hut** caseta; ~ **resort** balneario; ~**-trunks** taparrabo

bathos paso *m* de lo sublime a lo ridículo

bathysphere batisfera

batman *mil* ordenanza *m*

baton *mil* bastón (-ones) *m* de mando; *mus* batuta; (policeman's) porra; *sp* testigo; ~**-charge** ataque *m* con porras

bats (crazy) chiflado; mochales

batsman jugador *m* que golpea la pelota en el cricket o béisbol; bateador *m*

battalion batallón (-ones) *m*

batten *n* listón (-ones) *m* de madera; *v* ~ **down the hatches** cerrar (ie)²ᵃ las escotillas

batter *n* (baseball *etc*) bateador *m*; (beating) golpeo; **in** ~ *cul* rebozado; *v* golpear; ~ **down** derribar; ~**ed** (worn out) muy estropeado; ~**ed wives** esposas golpeadas

battering golpeo; ~**-ram** ariete *m*

battery *mil* batería; *elect* pila; *leg* agresión *f*; ~ **hen** gallina de batería; ~ **water** agua de acumulador

battle *n* batalla; combate *m*; (struggle) lucha; ~ **for life** lucha por la vida; ~ **of words** riña; **do** ~ librar batalla; **fight a** ~ dar¹⁹ batalla; **in** ~ **array** en orden de batalla; **pitched** ~ batalla campal; **that is half the** ~ lo más difícil está hecho; ~**-axe** hacha de combate, *fig* arpía; ~**-cruiser** crucero de batalla; ~**-cry** grito de guerra; ~**-dress** *mil* uniforme cotidiano; ~**field** campo de batalla; ~**-royal** riña promiscua; ~ **ship** acorazado; *v* batallar, *fig* luchar

battlements muralla almenada

bauble chuchería

baulk *see* **balk**

Bavaria Baviera

Bavarian bávaro

bawd alcahueta

bawdy obsceno, escandaloso; ~**-house** burdel *m*

bawl chillar; (weep) llorar

bawling chillidos; (weeping) lloro

¹ **bay** *n geog* bahía; (small) cala; (section of factory) división (-ones) *f*; ~ **window** mirador *m*; **Bay of Biscay** mar Cantábrico

² **bay** *n bot* laurel *m*; *adj* (colour) bayo

³ **bay** *v* aullar; **at** ~ acorralado; **keep at** ~ mantener¹⁹ a raya

baying aullido

bayonet *n* bayoneta; *v* (kill) matar/ (wound) herir (ie)²ᶜ de un bayonetazo

Bayonne Bayona

bazaar bazar *m*

bazooka bazuca

B.C. (Before Christ) a de J.C. (antes de Jesucristo)

be (when sudden change is impossible or unlikely) ser¹⁹; **I am English** soy inglés; **she is a communist** ella es comunista; **we are soldiers** somos soldados; **they are Catholics** son católicos; **it is one o'clock** es la una; **it is half past two** son las dos y media; **it will ~ about seven o'clock** (it probably is about seven o'clock) serán las siete; **snow is cold** la nieve es fría; **we are from London** somos de Londres; **I am not myself today** hoy no soy yo; **it is I** soy yo; **it is she** es ella; **it cannot ~** no puede ser; **~ that as it may** sea como fuere; **it is likely (that)** es probable (que); **it is possible (that)** es posible (que); **they are young** son jóvenes; **America was discovered by Columbus** América fue descubierta por Colón; **so ~ it** así sea

(in a temporary state or in a place) estar[19], encontrarse (ue)[1a], hallarse, verse[19]; **the door is open** la puerta está abierta; **my coffee is cold** mi café está frío; **I'm all right** estoy bien; **she is all for going now** ella está por ir ahora; **they are ill** están enfermos; **how are you?** ¿cómo está usted?; **we were playing** estábamos jugando; **I was about to leave** yo estaba para salir; **she was on the point of speaking** ella estaba a punto de hablar; **I was obliged to follow them** me vi obligado a seguirles; **the church is on a hill** la iglesia está/se encuentra/se halla en una colina

(in certain idiomatic expressions) tener[19]; **she is six** ella tiene seis años; **I am hungry** tengo hambre; **you are right** usted tiene razón; **they are keen to ...** ellos tienen ganas de +*infin*; **she was afraid** ella tenía miedo; **~ careful** tener[19] cuidado; **~ careful!** ¡(tenga) cuidado!; (to describe the weather) hacer[19]; **the weather is bad** hace mal tiempo; **it is fine today** hace sol hoy; **it is cold** hace frío; **it is sunny** hace sol; **there is, there are** hay; **there will ~** habrá; **there would ~** habría; **there was, there were** había; **there cannot ~** no puede haber; **we shall ~ going to Spain next year** vamos/iremos a España el año que viene; **it's a long time since I ...** hace mucho tiempo que yo ...; **it is nothing to me** no me hace nada; **~ off with you!** ¡lárguese!; **~ quick** darse[19] prisa; **~ quiet** callarse; **~ sorry** sentirlo (ie)[2c]; sentir +*infin*/ que +*subj*; **she is looking for them** anda buscándolos; **how much is it?**

¿cuánto vale?; **Spanish is spoken in Mexico** en Méjico se habla español; **her husband to ~** su futuro marido; **what is that to me?** ¿qué me importa?; **~-all and end-all** el no va más allá; **~-in** reunión (-ones) *f* de hippyes

beach *n* playa; *adj* playero; **~-comber** vago de las playas; **~-head** *mil* cabeza de playa; **~-robe** albornoz (-ces) *m*; **~-umbrella** parasol *m*; **~-wear** ropa playera; *v* (accidentally) encallar en la playa; (deliberately) arrastrar a la playa

beacon *naut* faro *m*; **~-fire** fuego de alarma

bead cuenta; (sweat, blood *etc*) gota; **draw a ~ on** (aim at) apuntar a; **string of ~s** collar *m* de cuentas; **tell one's ~s** rezar[7] el rosario

beading listón (-ones) *m*

beady como abalorio

beagle (dog) especie *f* de perro de caza; (person) alguacil *m*

beak pico

beaker vaso; *chem* cubeta de precipitación

beam *n* viga; *naut* manga; *rad* (+of light) rayo; **on the ~** *naut* al lado; **be on one's ~ ends** *naut* estar[19] a punto de volcar, *fig* estar[19] a la cuarta pregunta; *v* destellar; *rad* radiar; (smile) sonreír (i)[3] genialmente

beaming sonriente

bean alubia; **full of ~s** *fig* lleno de energía; **without a ~** a la cuarta pregunta; **~-feast** bodas *fpl* de Camacho; **~-pole** rodrigón (-ones) *m*; **~-stalk** tallo de judía; **broad ~** haba; **French/ kidney ~** alubia, *SA* (+Andalusia) frijol *m*; **runner-~** judía; **soya ~** fruto de la soja

[1] **bear** *n* oso; *comm* bajista; **~-cub** osezno; **~-skin** piel *f* de oso, (headgear) gorro de piel; **she-~** osa

[2] **bear** *vt* (carry) llevar; (endure) aguantar; (give birth to) dar[19] a luz a; **~ arms** llevar armas; **~ the blame** tener[19] la culpa; **~ the brunt of** aguantar lo más fuerte de; **~ fruit** *fig* dar[19] fruto; **~ a grudge (against)** guardar rencor (a); **~ interest** producir[15] interés; **~ in mind** tener[19] en cuenta; **~ a resemblance (to)** tener[19] semejanza (con); **~ witness** atestiguar[6]; **this letter**

does not ~ a date esta carta no está
fechada; *vi* dirigirse[9] a; **~ to the left/
right** tirar a la izquierda/derecha
~ down on caer[19] sobre
~ out confirmar
~ up *vt* sostener[19]; *vi* (cheer up) cobrar
ánimo; **~ up!** ¡ánimo!
~ with aguantar
bearable soportable
beard *n* barba; **have a ~** llevar barba; *v*
arrancar[4] las barbas; **~ed** barbudo
beardless imberbe
bearer (of a document) portador *m*; (of
a litter) andero
bearing *n* (conduct) conducta; (deportment) porte *m*; (direction) dirección
(-ones) *f*; (endurance) aguante *m*;
mech cojinete *m*; **have no ~ on** no
tener[19] relación con, *fam* no tener[19]
nada que ver con; **find/get one's ~s**
orientarse; **lose one's ~s** des-
orientarse
beast +*fig* bestia; **~ of burden** bestia de
carga
beastliness bestialidad *f*
beastly bestial; *fig* detestable
beat *n mus* compás *m*; (of drum) redoble *m*; (of heart) pulsación (-ones) *f*;
(policeman's) ronda; **~ music** música
rítmica; *adj* fatigado; **I'm dead ~**
estoy completamente rendido; **~
generation** la generación de disidencia
social; *v* golpear; *cul* batir; (carpet)
sacudir; (drum) tocar[4]; *sp* (dribble
past) regatear; (defeat) vencer[12];
(pulsate) palpitar; **~ about the bush**
andarse[19] por las ramas; **~ black and
blue** moler (ue)[1b] a palos; **~ hollow**
vencer[12] por mucho; **~ a record** batir
un récord; **~ a retreat** (on drum)
tocar[4] la retirada, (withdraw) emprender la retirada; **he ~ me to it** él
llegó antes que yo; **~ time** marcar[4] el
compás; **this ~s the band!** ¡esto ya
pasa de la raya!; **~ it!** ¡lárguese!
~ back rechazar
~ down (price) regatear
~ up apalear
beaten (defeated) vencido; *cul*+*metal*
batido; **off the ~ track** en el quinto
pino
beater batidor *m* (-ora *f*)
beatific beatífico
beatification beatificación *f*

beatify beatificar[4]
beating(-up) apaleamiento
beatitude beatitud *f*; **the Beatitudes** las
Bienaventuranzas
beatnik joven *m*+*f* disidente
Beatrice Beatriz
beau galán (-anes) *m*
beautician maquilladora
beautiful hermoso; (people only)
guapo, *fam* (*esp* of children) mono
beautify embellecer[14]
beauty (person) preciosidad *f*; (quality)
hermosura, belleza; **~ contest** concurso de belleza; **~ parlour** salón
m de la belleza; **~ queen** reina de belleza; **~ sleep** sueño reparador; **~ spot**
anat lunar *m*, (place) lugar bonito
beaver castor *m*
becalmed encalmado
because porque; **~ of** a causa de
beck (gesture) ademán *m*
beckon hacer[19] señas
become volverse (ue)[1b] (*past part*
vuelto); (sad *etc*) ponerse[19]; (change
into) convertirse (i)[3] en; (to get to be)
llegar[5] a ser; (suit) caer[19] bien; **what
will ~ of her?** ¿qué será de ella?; **what
has ~ of them?** ¿qué les ha pasado?
becoming *adj* correcto; (clothing) que
cae bien
bed *n* cama, *pej* catre *m*; *bui*+*eng*
cimiento; (*hort* macizo; (of river) cauce
m; *sp* (of dartboard) sección *f*; **get into
~** meterse en la cama; **go to ~**
acostarse (ue)[1a], *fam* ir(se) a la cama;
put to ~ acostar (ue)[1a]; **~bug** chinche
m; **~-chamber**, **~room** dormitorio;
~fellow compañero de cama, *fig*
asociado; **~-jacket** mañanita; **~-linen**
ropa de cama; **~-pan** chata; **~-post**
pata de la cama; **~-ridden** encamado;
~-rock *min* lecho de roca, *fig* último
extremo; **~-settee** sofá-cama *m*; **~side**
lado de cama; **~side book** libro de
cabecera; **~side table** mesilla de noche; **~-sitter** estudio; **~sore** encama-
miento; **~spread** colcha; **~stead**
armazón *m* de la cama; **~time** hora de
acostarse; *v* **~ out** *hort* trasplantar
bedaub ensuciar
bedazzle deslumbrar
bedding ropa de cama
bedevil endemoniar
bedlam manicomio

Bedouin *n+adj* beduino
bedraggle ensuciar (la ropa)
bee abeja; **have a ~ in one's bonnet**
tener[19] manía (**about** sobre); **~-eater**
orni abejaruco; **~hive** colmena; **~-**
keeper colmenero; **~-keeping** apicultura; **make a ~-line for** ir[19] en línea
recta a; **~swax** cera de abejas
beech haya
beef *n* carne de vaca; **~-steak** filete *m*,
SA bife *m*; **~ tea** caldo de carne
beefy robusto
Beelzebub Belcebú
beer cerveza; **glass of ~** caña; **bottled ~**
cerveza de botella; **draught ~** cerveza
de barril; **~-house** cervecería; **~-mat**
fieltro (de cerveza)
beery (fond of beer) cervecero;
(smelling of beer) que huele a cerveza; (tasting of beer) que sabe a cerveza
beet(root) remolacha; **~ sugar** azúcar *m*
de remolacha
beetle escarabajo; **~-browed** cejijunto,
(sullen) ceñudo
befall suceder a
befitting conveniente
befog envolver (ue)[1b] en niebla; *fig*
atolondrar
before *adv* (place) delante; (time) antes;
(+*infin*) antes de; *prep* (in front of)
delante de; (facing) ante; antes de; **he**
appeared ~ the judge él compareció
ante el juez; **~ one's time** antes de
tiempo; **~ the wind** (con el) viento en
popa; **~hand** de antemano; **~-**
mentioned susodicho; *conj* antes (de)
que
befriend ofrecer[14] amistad a
befuddle aturdir
beg (request) pedir (i)[3]; rogar (ue)[1a+5];
(ask for money) mendigar[5]; **~ the**
question desviar la cuestión; **I ~ to**
differ! ¡permítame disentir!
beget engendrar
beggar mendigo
beggarly pobre
begging mendicidad *f*; **go ~** dedicarse[4] a
la mendicidad, *fig* no tener[19] demanda
begin empezar (ie)[2a+7]; ponerse[19] a
+*infin*; **they ~ to sing** se ponen a
cantar; (in game) salir[19]; **it's Mary's**
turn to ~ a María le toca salir; (originate) iniciar; **to ~ with** en primer

lugar
beginner principiante *m+f*; **~'s luck**
suerte *f* del principiante
beginning comienzo; **at the ~ of March** a
primeros de marzo
begonia begonia
begrudge envidiar, escatimar; **he ~s**
spending money no le gusta gastar
dinero
beguile seducir[15]
behalf provecho; **on ~ of** en nombre de;
on ~ of the homeless en pro de los desamparados; **he did it on my ~** lo hizo
por mí
behave comportarse
behaviour conducta; **be on one's best ~**
portarse lo mejor que uno pueda
behavioural relativo a la conducta
behaviourism teoría que la conducta depende exclusivamente de reacciones y
estímulos
behead descabezar[7]
beheading descabezamiento
behind trasero; *fam* culo; *adv* atrás;
detrás; **stay (a long way) ~** quedarse
(a mucha distancia) atrás; *prep* detrás
de; **~ s.o.'s back** a espaldas de uno;
with one's hands ~ one's back con las
manos detrás; **he has a lot of experi-**
ence ~ him él tiene mucha experiencia
a sus espaldas; **~ time** con atraso,
(trains *etc*) con retraso; **~ the times**
atrasado de noticias, (of fashion)
fuera de moda; **~hand** atrasado
behold *v* contemplar; *interj* ¡he aquí ...!
beholden agradecido
behove convenir[19]
beige beige *invar*
being ser *m*; **human ~** ser humano;
come into ~ llegar[5] a ser; **for the time**
~ por el momento
bejewelled enjoyado
belabour apalear
belated retrasado; atrasado
belch *n* eructo; *v* eructar; **smoke ~ed**
from the volcano el humo salió con
fuerza del volcán
beleaguer sitiar
belfry campanario
Belgian *n+adj* belga *m+f*
Belgium Bélgica
Belgrade Belgrado
belie desmentir (i)[3]
belief (faith) fe *f*; (opinion) opinión

(-ones) *f*; **past all** ~ increíble; **to the best of my** ~ según mi leal saber y entender, *fam* que yo sepa

believable creíble

believe creer[17] (**in** en); **I don't** ~ **a word of it!** ¡qué va!; **he is** ~**d to have died in Africa** se cree que murió en África; **you'll never** ~ **it,** but parece mentira, pero; **make** ~ *adj* de mentirijillas, *v* fingir[9]; **I don't** ~ **in smoking** soy antitabaquista

believer creyente *m+f*

Belisha beacon señal *f* de un paso de peatones

belittle empequeñecer[14]

bell *n* (large) campana; (small) campanilla; (door) timbre *m*; (jingle-bell) cascabel *m*; (boxing) gong *m*; **ring a** ~ tocar[4] una campana/un timbre *etc*, *fig* (call to mind) sonarle (ue)[1a] a uno; **saved by the** ~ *sp+fig* salvado por la campana; ~-**bottoms** pantalón *m* acampanado; ~-**boy,** ~-**hop** botones *m sing+pl*; ~-**push** perilla del timbre; ~**ringer** campanero; ~**ringing** campanología; ~-**rope** cuerda de campana; ~-**shaped** campaniforme; ~-**tent** tienda (de campaña) redonda; *v* acampanar

belladonna belladona

belles-lettres bellas letras

bellicose belicoso

belligerence beligerancia

belligerent *n+adj* beligerante *m*

bellow *n* bramido; *v* bramar

bellows fuelle *m*

belly barriga; (of violin *etc*) caja; ~ **of pork** panceta; ~-**ache** *n* dolor *m* de vientre, *v* refunfuñar; ~-**button** *fam* tripita, *joc*·timbre *m*; ~-**dance** danza del vientre; ~-**flop** (diving) plancha

bellyful panzada

belong pertenecer[14]; **I** ~ **to Glasgow** soy de Glasgow

belongings posesiones *fpl*

beloved querido

below *adv* abajo; de abajo; *prep* debajo de; ~ **the belt** *fig* antideportivo; ~ **par** con pérdida; ~ **zero** bajo cero

Belshazzar Baltasar

belt *n* cinturón (-ones) *m*; *eng* correa de transmisión; *geog* zona; *sl* (blow) golpe; **below the** ~ *fig* antideportivo; **tighten one's** ~ apretarse el cinturón;

v (strike) golpear; ~ **up!** ¡cállate!

bemoan deplorar

bemuse confundir

bench (seat) banco; (of stone) poyo; *carp* banco; *leg* tribunal *m*

bend *n* curve; (of river, street *etc*) recodo; (of pipe) codillo; *naut* nudo; **be round the** ~ *fig* estar[19] chiflado; ~**s** *med* enfermedad *f* de los buzos; *v* doblar; (of roads *etc*) torcer (ue)[1b]; (relent) doblegar[5]; ~ **the knee** doblar la rodilla; ~ **the oars** *fig* hacer[19] fuerza; ~ **down** doblarse; ~ **over** inclinarse (sobre); ~ **over backwards to** *fig* hacer[19] el máximo de concesiones para +*infin*/para que +*subj*

bender: to go on a ~ ir[19] de parranda

beneath debajo de; *adv* debajo; ~ **contempt** indigno de atención; ~ **his station** indigno de su rango

Benedict Benedicto

Benedictine benedictino

benediction bendición *f*; **Benediction** Exposición *f* del Santísimo

benefaction beneficio

benefactor protector *m* (-ora *f*)

benefice beneficio

beneficence beneficencia

beneficent bienhechor (-ora *f*)

beneficial benéfico

beneficiary beneficiario

benefit *n* beneficio; *sp* partida/*theat* función (-ones) *f* benéfica; (insurance) lucro; **for the** ~ **of** a beneficio de; *v* ~ **(from)** sacar[4] beneficio (de)

Benelux Benelux

benevolence benevolencia

benevolent benévolo; ~ **fund** fondos benéficos *pl*; ~ **society** sociedad benéfica

Bengal Bengala

Bengali *n+adj* bengalí *m+f*

benighted ignorante

benign benigno

Benny Benito

bent *n* inclinación *f* (**for** a); *adj* torcido, *fig* deshonesto; (homosexual) mariquita; **be** ~ **on** estar[19] resuelto a +*infin*

benzedrine *tr* bencedrina

benzine bencina

bequeath legar[5]

bequest legado

berate regañar

Berber *n*+*adj* bereber *m* (-cra *f*)
bereaved *n*+*adj* afligido
bereavement aflicción (-ones) *f*
beret boina, chapela
Berlin Berlín *m*
Bermuda Islas *fpl* Bermudas
Bernard Bernardo
Berne Berna
berry baya
berserk frenético
berth *n* (anchorage) anclaje *m*; (bed)
litera; (cabin) camarote *m*; *sl* (job)
empleo; **give a wide ~ to** evitar a
alguien; *vt* atracar⁴; *vi* llegar⁵ a puerto
Bertha Berta
Bertram Beltrán
beryl berilo
beryllium berilio
beseech suplicar⁴
beseeching suplicante
beset obstruir¹⁶; **~ with difficulties** lleno
de dificultades
besetting: ~ sin vicio habitual
beside al lado de; **she is quite ~ herself**
ella está fuera de sí; **be ~ o.s. with joy**
estar¹⁹ loco de alegría; **that is ~ the
point** eso no viene al caso; **~s** *adv*
además; *prep* además de
besiege *fig* asediar
besmear, besmirch ensuciar
besom (broom) escoba de palma; (hag)
tarasca
bespatter salpicar⁴
bespeak encargar⁵
bespectacled con gafas
bespoke hecho a la medida; **~ tailor** sastre *m* que confecciona a medida
besprinkle salpicar⁴
best mejor; **she is the ~ in the class** ella es
la mejor de la clase; **~ of all** lo mejor
de todo; **~ part of** (most of) la mayor
parte de; **as ~ one can** lo mejor que
pueda uno; **at ~** a lo más; **act for the ~**
actuar con las mejores intenciones; **be
at one's ~** esmerarse; **do one's ~**
esmerarse; **I had ~ do it** más vale que
yo lo haga; **get the ~ of** vencer¹²; **in the
~ way (possible)** de la mejor manera;
it is ~ that lo mejor es que +*subj*; **I
think it ~ that** creo que será mejor que
+*subj*; **like s.o./s.t. ~** preferir (ie)²ᶜ;
make the ~ of sacar⁴ el mejor partido
de; **make the ~ of a bad job** salir¹⁹ lo
mejor posible de un mal negocio; **the**

~ of it is that lo mejor es que; **to the ~
of my knowledge** a mi leal saber y
entender; **one's ~ Sunday clothes** sus
mejores galas; **you know ~** usted sabe
mejor; **~ man** padrino (de boda);
~seller libro de más venta; **~-selling
record** disco más vendido; **second- ~**
mejor después del primero
bestial bestial
bestiality bestialidad *f*; (sexual) zoofilia
bestir excitar; **~ o.s.** despabilarse
bestow conferir
bestride cruzar⁷ de un tranco
bet *n* apuesta; **lay a ~** poner¹⁹ una
apuesta; *v* apostar (ue)¹ᵃ, *fam* ir¹⁹;
how much do you ~? ¿cuánto va/
apuesta usted?; **will you ~ on it?** ¿(te)
apuestas algo?; **I ~ a hundred to one**
apuesto ciento contra uno; **you ~!** *fam*
¡digo!, ya lo creo
bête noire coco
Bethlehem Belén *m*
betoken indicar⁴
betray (commit treason) traicionar;
(show) revelar
betrayal traición (-ones) *f*
betrayer traidor *m* (-ora *f*)
betrothal noviazgo
betrothed *n* novio, novia; *n*+*adj* prometido
¹ **better** *adj* mejor; (socially) superior; **our
~s** nuestros superiores; **the ~ part of**
la mejor parte de; **~ half** esposo,
esposa; *adv* mejor; **~ and ~** cada vez
mejor; **~ late than never** más vale
tarde que nunca; **~ off** más acomodado; **all the ~** tanto mejor; **be ~
than** valer¹⁹ más que; **a pin would be ~
than a nail** un alfiler sería más
indicado que un clavo; **for ~ or for
worse** en la suerte o en la adversidad;
get ~ (after illness) reponer(se)¹⁹; **it's
~ so** más vale así; **it's ~ that** más vale
que +*subj*; **know ~** estar¹⁹ mejor
enterado; **he knows it ~ than I** él lo
sabe mejor que yo; **you know ~ than
to do a thing like that** usted sabe que
no se debe hacer semejante cosa;
know someone ~ conocer a uno más a
fondo; **I know her ~ than you (do)** la
conozco mejor que usted; **no ~ and no
worse** ni mejor ni peor; **so much the ~**
tanto mejor; **think ~ of** mudar de
opinión sobre; **you'd ~ do it** más vale

que usted lo haga; **whatever I do, he always tries to go one** ~ no importa lo que yo haga, él siempre intenta hacer más; v ~ **o.s.** adelantar, mejorar

² **better** (gambler) apostador m (-ora f)

betterment mejoramiento

betting apostar m; ~**-shop** timba

between entre; ~ **now and then** de aquí a entonces; ~ **the devil and the deep blue sea** entre la espada y la pared; ~ **you and me** entre usted y yo

bevelled biselado

beverage brebaje m

bevy grupo (de mujeres)

bewail lamentar

beware tener[19] cuidado (**of** de); ~ **of …!** ¡cuidado con …!; ~ **of pickpockets!** ¡ojo rateros!

bewilder aturdir

bewilderment aturdimiento

bewitch hechizar[7]

bewitching hechicero

beyond n vida futura; adv más allá; prep más allá de; ~ **the bounds of possibility** completamente imposible; ~ **compare** incomparable; ~ **control** ajeno a la voluntad; **owing to difficulties** ~ **our control** debido a dificultades ajenas a nuestra voluntad; ~ **dispute** incontestable; ~ **doubt** fuera de duda; ~ **expression** indecible; ~ **measure** desmesuradamente; ~ **reach** fuera de alcance; ~ **reproach** sin tacha; **from** ~ **the grave** de ultratumba; **back of** ~ en el quinto pino; ~ **the pale** al margen de la sociedad; **it's** ~ **me** no lo comprendo; **it's** ~ **my understanding** es cosa que no entiendo

Biafra Biafra

Biafran n + adj biafreño

biannual semianual, semestral

bias n bies m; (prejudice) prejuicio; ~ **against/in favour (of)** inclinación f contra/a favor (de); **cloth cut on the** ~ tela cortada al bies

bias(s)ed tendencioso

bib babero

Bible Biblia; ~ **paper** papel m de Biblia; ~ **thumper** predicador fanático

biblical bíblico

bibliographer bibliógrafo

bibliography bibliografía

bibliophile bibliófilo

bibulous bebedor (-ora f)

bicarbonate: ~ **of soda** bicarbonato sódico; fam bicarbonato

bicentenary bicentenario

bicentennial (lasting two hundred years) que dura doscientos años; (every two hundred years) que ocurre cada doscientos años

biceps bíceps m sing

bicker altercar[4]

bickerer camorrista m + f

bickering guerra de palabras

bicoloured de dos colores, bicolor

bicycle n bicicleta; v ir[19] en bicicleta

bicyclist ciclista m + f

bid n (auction) oferta; (cards) subasta; (attempt) tentativa; **higher** ~ puja; **make a** ~ **for** hacer[19] una oferta por; v (auction) ofrecer[14]; (cards) declarar; ~ **against s.o. else** hacer[19] una oferta contra otra persona; ~ **for** hacer[19] una oferta por; ~ **farewell** despedirse (i)[3]; ~ **higher** pujar; ~ **s.o. welcome** darle[19] a uno la bienvenida

bidder postor m; **highest** ~ mejor postor

bidding (auction) postura; (cards) subasta m; (request) invitación f

bide: ~ **one's time** esperar el momento oportuno

bidet bidé m

biennial n planta bienal; adj bienal

bier féretro

biff n tunda; v tundir

bifocal bifocal; ~ **glasses** gafas fpl graduadas

bifurcate bifurcarse[4]

bifurcation bifurcación (-ones) f

big grande; (elder, grown-up) mayor; **this coat is too** ~ **for me** este abrigo me está demasiado grande; ~ **business** alto negocio; ~ **businessman** negociante m en gran escala; ~ **dipper** montaña rusa, US astron osa mayor; ~ **end** mot cabeza (de la biela); ~ **game** animales mpl de caza mayor; ~**-game hunting** caza mayor; ~**-headed** fig engreído; ~**-hearted** bondadoso; ~**-mouth** bocazas m + f sing; ~ **noise/shot** personaje m, fam pez (-ces) gordo; ~ **prize** (in lottery) gordo; ~ **toe** dedo gordo del pie; ~ **top** recinto de circo; **in a** ~ **way** en gran escala; **talk** ~ fanfarronear, fam echárselas

bigamist bígamo

bigamous bígamo
bigamy bigamia
bight *naut* seno (de un cabo)
bigness grandeza
bigot fanático; (religious) beato
bigoted fanático, beato
bigotry fanatismo
bike *sl* bici *f*
bikini bikini *m*
bilateral bilateral
bilberry arándano
bile bilis *f*; *fig* displicencia
bilge *naut* pantoque *m*; **talk ~** decir[19] idioteces
bilingual bilingüe
bilious +*fig* bilioso; ~ **attack** bilis *f*; **have a ~ attack** arrojar bilis
¹ **bill** *n orni* pico; ~**-hook** honcejo; *v* ~ **and coo** acariciarse
² **bill** *n* cuenta, nota; (invoice) factura; (of parliament) proyecto de ley; (poster) cartel *m*; (*US* banknote) billete *m*; ~ **of credit** carta de crédito; ~ **of exchange** letra de cambio; ~ **of fare** minuta; ~ **of health** certificado/patente *m* de sanidad; ~ **of lading** conocimiento de embarque; ~ **of sale** escritura de venta; **fill the ~** satisfacer los requisitos; **make out the ~** preparar la cuenta/factura; **pass a ~** *pol* aprobar (ue)[1a] una ley; **stick no ~s!** ¡prohibido fijar carteles!; ~**-board** cartelera; ~**-broker** agente *m* de cambio; ~**fold** cartera; ~**-head** modelo de factura; ~**-poster** cartelero; *v* anunciar por carteles
billed: ~ **programme** programa *m* anunciado
billet *n* acantonamiento; *v* acantonar
billet-doux cartita de amor
billetee alojado
billiard: ~**-ball** bola de billar; ~**-cue** taco de billar; ~**-player** billardista *m*+*f*; ~**-table** mesa de billar; ~**s billar** *m*; **play ~s** jugar (ue)[1a] al billar
billion (U.K.) billón (-ones) *m*; **a ~ ...** un billón de ...; (U.S.A.) mil millones
billow *n* oleada; *v* hinchar(se)
billowy ondulado
billy-goat macho cabrío
bimonthly (every two months) cada dos meses; (twice a month) dos veces al mes
bin arca; (large) arcón (-ones) *m*;

bread~ panera; **dust~** cubo de la basura
binary binario
bind *n* **it's a bit of a ~** es una leche; *v* (tie) atar[5]; (of books) encuadernar; *med* vendar; ~ **over** amonestar a uno que no repita el delito; ~**weed** correhuela
binder (person) encuadernador *m* (-ora *f*); *agri* agavilladora; (for magazines *etc*) faja
binding (of books) encuadernación *f*; (sewing) cinta; **hard-cover ~** pastas *fpl*; ~ **on** obligatorio para
binge *fam* juerga; **go on a ~** correr la gran juerga
binnacle bitácora
binoculars gemelos *mpl*
biochemist, biochemical bioquímico
biochemistry bioquímica
biodegradable biodegradable
biographer biógrafo
biographical biográfico
biography biografía
biological biológico
biologist biólogo
biology biología
biorhythms bioritmos *mpl*
bipartisan compuesto de dos partidos (políticos)
bipartisanship composición *f* de dos partidos (políticos)
bipartite bipartido
biped bípedo
biplane biplano
birch *n* (rod) vara de abedul; (tree) abedul *m*; ~**-bark** corteza de abedul; *v* azotar
¹ **bird** *n* ave *f*; (small) pájaro; ~ **call** reclamo; ~ **of paradise** ave *f* del paraíso; ~ **of passage** ave *f* de paso; ~ **of prey** ave *f* de rapiña; **kill two ~s with one stone** de un camino dos mandados; **a ~ in the hand is worth two in the bush** más vale pájaro en mano que ciento volando; ~**s of a feather flock together** Dios los cría y ellos se juntan; ~**-bath** pila para pájaros; ~**-cage** jaula; ~**-fancier** pajarero; ~**lime** liga; ~**seed** alpiste *m*; ~**-watcher** ornitólogo; ~**-watching** ornitología
² **bird** *sl* (girl) musaraña, jai *f*; *vulg* tía
birdie *sp* birdie *m*
biretta birrete *m*

biro *tr* bolígrafo; *fam* bic (biques) *m*

birth nacimiento; *fig* origen *f*; (ancestry) linaje *m*; **give ~** parir; **give ~ to** dar[19] a luz a; **~ certificate** partida de nacimiento; **~ control** control *m* de la natalidad; **~-mark** marca de nacimiento; **~place** lugar *m* de nacimiento; **~-rate** natalidad *f*; **~right** derechos *mpl* de nacimiento

birthday cumpleaños *m sing+pl*; **happy ~!** ¡feliz cumpleaños!; **~-cake** tarta de cumpleaños; **~ present** regalo de cumpleaños

Biscay Vizcaya; **Bay of ~** mar Cantábrico

biscuit *cul* galleta; *cer* bizcocho; **~-coloured** beige *invar*

bisect dividir en dos partes

bisexual bisexual

bishop *eccles* obispo; (chess) alfil *m*

bishopric obispado

bismuth bismuto

bison bisonte *m*

bit *n* (small piece) pedacito; (small amount) poquito; *eng* taladro; (harness) bocado; **~ by ~** a poquitos; **he's a ~ of a Don Juan** él es un tanto Don Juan; **not a ~** ni pizca; **not a ~ of it!** ¡qué va!; **do one's ~** ayudar en lo que pueda; **take the ~ between the teeth** tomar control, (rebel) rebelarse; **my puppy is four months and a ~** mi perrito tiene cuatro meses y pico; **smash to ~s** hacer[19] añicos; *adv* algo, un poco; **wait a ~!** ¡espere un poco!; **a ~ drunk** algo/un poco borracho

bitch *n* perra; (shrew) mujer *f* de mal genio; (prostitute) ramera; **son of a ~** hijo de puta; *v* quejar

bitchiness mal genio

bitchy malicioso

bite *n* mordisco; (of insect) picadura; (morsel) bocado; **I have a ~!** (fishing) ¡ya pica!; **have a ~ to eat** comer algo; *v* morder (ue)[1b]; (of insects, fish *+fig*) picar[4]; **what's biting you?** ¿qué le pica?; **~ one's nails** morderse (ue)[1b] las uñas; **~ the dust** morder (ue)[1b] la tierra

biting mordiente; (sarcastic) mordaz; (of wind) penetrante, *fam* que pela

bitter amargo; **to the ~ end** hasta vencer[12] o morir; **~ almond** almendra amarga

bitterly amargamente; **the weather is ~ cold** hace un frío que pela; **I'm ~ cold** tengo mucho frío

bittern *orni* avetoro

bitterness amargura

bittersweet *n bot* dulcamara; *adj* (flavour) agridulce

bitumen betún *m*

bituminous bituminoso

bivalence, **bivalency** bivalencia

bivalve *n* molusco bivalvular; *adj* bivalvular

bivouac *n* vivaque *m*; *v* vivaquear

biweekly (every two weeks) quincenal; (twice a week) dos veces por semana

bizarre grotesco

B.L. (Bachelor of Law) Licenciado en Derecho

B/L (bill of lading) carta de embarque

blab chismorrear

blabber *n* chismoso; *v* chismorrear

black *n* negro, negra; (mourning) luto; **work like a ~** trabajar como un negro; **in ~ and white** por escrito; *adj* negro; (proscribed by strikers) proscrito; (bought on black market) de estraperlo; **~ and blue** amoratado; **~ as pitch** negro como el tizón; **~ art** nigromancia; **~ball** *v* dar[19] bola negra; **~ beetle** cucaracha; **~berry** (zarza-) mora; **~berry bush** zarza; **~bird** mirlo; **~board** pizarra; **I'm in her ~ books** estoy en su lista negra; **with a ~ border** con orla de luto; **~-coated worker** oficinista *m*; **~ coffee** café solo; **~currant** grosella negra; **~ day** día funesto; **Black Death** peste *f* (del siglo XIV); **~-eyed** ojinegro; **~ flag** bandera de pirata; **Black Forest** Selva Negra; **~guard** *n* tunante *m*, *v* abusar; **~head** espinilla; **~ jack** (club) cachiporra, (flag) bandera de pirata; **~leg** (strike-breaker) esquirol *m*; **~list** *n* lista negra, *v* poner[19] en lista negra; **~-listed** en la lista negra; **~ look** mirada asesina, (appearance) aspecto funesto; **~mail** *n* chantaje *m*, *v* hacer[19] un chantaje; **~mailer** chantajista *m+f*; **Black Maria** coche *m/SA* carro celular; **~ mark** estigma; **~ market** estraperlo, (of money) bolsa negra; **~marketeer** estraperlista *m+f*; **~marketing** estraperlismo; **Black Moslems** musulmanes negros; **~-out** *n* apagón *m*, *theat* mutación *f* al oscuro, *fig* (of news) censura, *v* apagar[5] las luces; ~ **pepper** pimienta negra; ~ **pudding** morcilla; **Black Sea** mar Negro; ~ **sheep** oveja negra; ~**smith** herrero; ~**smith's** herrería; ~ **spot** (trouble centre) sitio gafe, *mot* lugar peligroso; ~**thorn** endrino; ~ **tidings** malas noticias *fpl*; *v* ~ **s.o.'s eyes** hincharle a uno los ojos

blacken ennegrecer[14]; *fig* denigrar

blacking betún *m*

blackish negruzco

blackness negrura

bladder vejiga

blade (of grass) brizna; (of knife) hoja; (of propeller) paleta

blamable culpable

blame *n* (guilt) culpa; (censure) censura; *v* (find fault with) censurar; (put the ~ on) echar la culpa a; **who is to ~?** ¿quién tiene la culpa?

blameless sin culpa *invar*

blanch blanquear; *cul* pelar

Blanche Blanca

blancmange manjar blanco

blanco blanco de España

bland blando, (soft) suave

blandish lisonjear

blandishment halago

blank en blanco; ~ **cartridge** cartucho de fogueo; ~ **cheque** cheque *m* en blanco; ~ **form** blanco; ~ **verse** verso suelto; **draw a ~** no tener[19] suerte; **leave a ~** dejar un espacio; **at point-~ range** a quemarropa

blanket *n* manta; ~ **of snow** capa de nieve; **he's a wet ~** él es un aguafiestas; *v* cubrir (*past part* cubierto); *rad* paralizar[7] por medio de interferencia

blankly estúpidamente

blankness espacio

blare *n* sonido como de trompeta; *v* sonar (ue)[1a] a modo de trompeta

blarney labia; **he's full of ~** él tiene mucha labia

blasé hastiado

blaspheme blasfemar

blasphemer blasfemo

blaspheming *n* blasfemia; *adj* blasfemo

blasphemous blasfemo

blasphemy blasfemia

blast *n* (of wind) ráfaga; (of fire)

bocanada; (explosion) onda de expansión; *mus* toque repentino; **in full ~** en plena marcha; ~**-furnace** alto horno; ~**-off** lanzamiento; *v* volar (ue)[1a]; ~ **rocks** barrenar[4] rocas; (swear) maldecir[19]; ~**ed** maldito; *interj* ~ **it!** ¡maldito sea!; ~ **off** lanzar[7]

blasting voladura; ~**-charge** carga explosiva

blatant vocinglero; evidente

blatantly descaradamente

blaze *n* (conflagration) incendio; (bonfire) fogata; (of flames) llamarada; (of light) resplandor *m*; ~**s!** ¡maldito sea!; **go to ~s!** ¡váyase a freír espárragos!; *v* (burst into flames) encenderse (ie)[2b] en llamas; (burn fiercely) arder con llamas; (of lights) resplandecer[15]

blazer chaqueta de sport

blazing llameando; (with lights) resplandeciendo; *fig* furioso

bleach *n* lejía; *vt* emblanquecer[14]; (in sun) blanquear al sol; (of clothing) colar (ue)[1a]; ~ **the hair** teñirse (i)[3] de rubio el pelo; *vi* desteñirse (i)[3]

bleaching *n* blanqueo; *adj* ~ **powder** cloruro de cal

bleak (exposed) desolado; (cold) frío; *fig* triste; ~ **region** páramo

blear(y) legañoso; ~**-eyed** legañoso

bleat *n* balido; *v* balar

bleating balido

bleed sangrar; ~ **to death** morir (ue)[1c] (*past part* muerto) desangrado; ~ **white** desangrar, *fig* arrancar[4] hasta el último céntimo; **his nose is ~ing** él está echando sangre por la nariz

bleep *n* señal electrónica, plic *m*; *v* llamar por señal electrónica

bleeper busca electrónica

bleeping plic-plic *m*

blemish *n* defecto; *fig* deshonra; *v* dañar; manchar

blench recular; (bleach) blanquear

blend *n* mezcla; (of colours) matiz (-ces) *m*; *v* mezclar(se); (of colours) matizar(se)[7]

bless bendecir[19]; (make happy) hacer[19] feliz; ~ **my soul!** ¡válgame Dios!; ~ **you!** (after a sneeze) ¡Jesús!

blessed *n* bienaventurados *mpl*; *adj* bendito; *iron* maldito; **the whole ~**

day todo el santo/maldito día; **not a ~ fish did I catch** ni un solo pez pesqué

blessing bendición (-ones) *f*; **~ in disguise** beneficio disfrazado; **what a ~ that…!** ¡menos mal que…!

blight *agri* añublo; *fig* mala suerte; *v agri* agostar; *fig* marchitar; **the cold wind has ~ed the leaves** el viento frío ha marchitado las hojas

blighter *sl* bribón *m*

blimey! ¡vaya!

blimp dirigible pequeño

blind *n* (window shade) cortinilla; **venetian ~** persiana; **the ~** los ciegos; *adj* ciego, *fig* ignorante; **go ~** quedarse ciego; **~ in one eye** tuerto; **as ~ as a bat** tan ciego como un topo; **~-alley** callejón (-ones) *m* sin salida; **~ corner** rincón (-ones) *m* sin visibilidad; **~ date** concertada con uno que no se conoce; **~ flying** vuelo sin visibilidad; **~fold** *v* vendar los ojos, *adv* con los ojos vendados; **~ landing** aterrizaje *m* a ciegas; **~-man's-buff** gallina ciega; **~ side** lado difícil; **~ spot** punto ciego; **turn a ~ eye** hacer[19] la vista gorda

blindage blindaje *m*

blinding cegador (-ora *f*)

blindly a ciegas

blindness ceguera

blink *n* parpadeo; *v* parpadear

blinker (harness) anteojera

bliss deleite *m*

blissful dichoso

blissfully felizmente

blister ampolla; **~ed** ampollado; **~ed paintwork** pintura ahuecada

blithe feliz (-ces)

blitz *n* guerra relámpago; *v* atacar[4] repentinamente; (lay waste) devastar

blizzard chubasco de nieve

bloated hinchado

bloater arenque ahumado

blob gota; *sp* cero

bloc bloque *m*

block *n* (piece) trozo; (of wood) zoquete *m*; (office) edificio de oficinas; (of building) manzana; (of flats) casa de vecindad, bloque *m* de pisos; *mot* bloque *m* de cilindros; (traffic jam) atasco; (obstacle) obstrucción (-ones) *f*; *print* plancha grabada; **~ letter** letra de imprenta; **~ booking** *cin+theat*

reserva en bloque; **~ road** *mil* barricada, (police) barrera; **~ and tackle** aparejo de poleas; **~head** zoquete *m*, animal *m*; *v* obstruir[16], bloquear; **~ s.o.'s way** cerrarle (ie)[2a] el paso a uno

blockade *n* bloqueo; **~-runner** violador *m* de bloqueo; *v* bloquear; **~d area** zona bloqueada

bloke *fam* tío

blonde *n* rubia; **dumb ~** rubia estúpida; *adj* rubia

blood *n* sangre *f*; **of noble ~** de noble linaje/parentesco; **~ is thicker than water** la sangre tira; **in cold ~** a sangre fría; **draw ~** derramar sangre; **it makes my ~ boil** me bulle la sangre; **what I saw made my ~ run cold** lo que vi me dejó helado; **~-bank** banco/depósito de sangre; **~-bath** carnicería; **~-brother** primo carnal; **~-clot** coágulo; **~-count** hemograma; **~-curdling** horripilante; **~-donor** donante *m+f* de sangre; **~-feud** venganza a muerte **~-group** grupo sanguíneo; **~-heat** temperatura del cuerpo; **~hound** sabueso; **~-letting** sangramiento; **~-lust** sed *f* de sangre; **~-money** precio pagado por un asesinato; **~-orange** naranja sanguínea; **~-plasma** plasma sanguíneo; **~-poisoning** septicemia; **~-pressure** tensión *f* arterial; **~-red** color *m* de sangre; **~-relationship** consanguinidad *f*; **~ serum** suero sanguíneo; **~-shed** matanza; **~-shot** ensangrentado; **~-stain** mancha de sangre; **~-stained** manchado de sangre; **~-stream** caudal sanguíneo; **~-sucker** sanguijuela, *fig* usurero; **~-test** análisis *m* de sangre; **~-thirsty** sanguinario; **~ transfusion** transfusión (-ones) *f* de sangre; **~-vessel** vaso sanguíneo

bloodily de modo sanguinario

bloodless sin sangre

bloody sangriento; **don't be such a ~ fool!** ¡no seas idiota!; **what a ~ life!** *vulg* ¡puta vida!; **~ mary** jugo de tomate con vodka; **~-minded** tozudo; **~-mindedness** tozudez *f*

bloom *n* florecimiento; (flower) flor *f*; (on fruit) vello; *fig* lozanía; **~ of youth** lozanía de la juventud; *v* florecer[14]

bloomer metedura de pata
bloomers pololos
blooming en flor; *fig* lozano; **all ~ night** toda la santa noche
blossom *n* flor *f*; *v* florecer[14]; **~ out** desarrollarse; (flower) abrirse
blot *n* borrón (-ones) *m*; *fig* mancha; *v* emborronar; manchar; **~ out** borrar
blotch *n* mancha; (on skin) erupción (-ones) *f*; *v* marcar[4] con manchas
blotchy manchado; (of skin) marcado de erupciones
blotter papel *m* secante
blotting: **~-pad** secafirmas *m sing*; **~-paper** papel *m* secante
blotto *sl* piripi
blouse blusa; **battle-dress** ~ guerrera
[1] **blow** *n* golpe *m*; (with fist) puñetazo; (with club) porrazo; (with whip) latigazo; *fig* (disappointment) desilusión (-ones) *f*; (shock) susto; **come to ~s** llegar[19] a las manos; **strike a ~ for freedom** dar[19] un golpe por la libertad
[2] **blow** *n* soplo; **~-hole** respiradero; **~-lamp** lámpara de soldar/soplete; **~-pipe** *mech* soplete *m*; *v* (wind) soplar; *mus* tocar[4]; (puff) resoplar; *sl* (squander) derrochar; **~, man!** *sl* ¡lárguese, hombre!; **~ hot and cold** vacilar entre el sí y el no; **~ the nose** sonarse (ue)[1a] la nariz; **~ a whistle** pitar; **~ one's own trumpet** alabarse; **I'll be ~ed!** ¡no me lo diga!; **~ it** (die) *sl* diñarla
~ away arrebatar
~ in entrar de sopetón
~ off steam dejar salir vapor
~ on enfriar soplando
~ open abrirse (*past part* abierto) con el viento
~-out *n* *mot* pinchazo
~ out *v* (light) apagar[5] de un soplido
~ over pasarse, olvidarse
~-up *n* *phot* ampliación (-ones) *f*
~ up *v* (explode) volar (ue)[1a]; (inflate) inflar; *phot* ampliar; **~ up in anger** enfadarse
blower soplador *m* (-ora *f*)
blowfly moscarda
blowing soplido, soplo
blown (of flowers) marchito; (of fuse) fundido; **the fuse has ~** se ha fundido el plomo

blowy ventoso
blowzy desaliñado; (of face) coloradote
blubber *n* (whale's) grasa (de ballena); *sl* (weeping) llanto; *v* (weep) lloriquear
bludgeon *n* (cachi)porra; *v* aporrear; **they ~ed him into …** le obligaron a porrazos a +*infin*
blue *n* (colour) azul *m*; (washing) añil *m*; *fig* (sea) mar *m*; **out of the ~** cuando menos se esperaba; **~s** *mus* blues *mpl*; (melancholy) morriña; *adj* azul; (sad) triste; **true ~** leal; **~ baby** niño que nace con cianosis; **Bluebeard** Barba Azul; **~-bell** campanilla; **~-berry** arándano; **~-bird** azulejo norteamericano; **~-black** azul oscuro; **~ blood** sangre *f* azul; **~-blooded** de sangre azul; **~-book** *pol* libro de informes oficiales; **~-bottle** moscarda; **~-eyed** ojiazul, *fig* predilecto; **be in a ~ funk** tener[19] mucho miedo, *fam* estar[19] muerto de miedo; **~-jacket** marino (de un buque de guerra); **~ joke** chiste verde; **once in a ~ moon** de Pascuas a Ramos; **~-nose** puritano fanático; **~ pencil** (censor's) lápiz (-ces) *m* rojo del censor; **~-pencil** *v* tachar; (censor) censurar; **Picasso's ~ period** período azul de Picasso; **Blue Peter** *naut* bandera de salida; **~print** cianotipo, *fig* programa *m*; **~ ribbon** primer premio; **~-stocking** marisabidilla; **~tit** herrerillo; *v* azular(se); *metal* pavonar; (washing) añilar
blueness azul *m*
bluff *n* farol *m*; *geog* escarpado; *geol* risco; **call s.o.'s ~** cogerle[8] la palabra a uno; *adj* franco; *v* engañar; **he's ~ing** él está faroleando
bluffer farolero
bluish azulado
blunder *n* desatino; *fam* plancha; *v* desatinar; *fam* meter la pata
blunderbuss trabuco
blunt *adj* (not sharp) romo; desafilado; (brusque) brusco; *v* embotar
bluntness embotadura; (brusqueness) brusquedad *f*
blur *n* trazo borroso; *v* hacer[19] borroso
blurb advertencia en la solapa de un libro
blurred borroso; **the photo is ~** la foto ha salido borrosa

blurt out *vt* soltar (ue)[1a] bruscamente; *vi* hablar inconsideradamente

blush *n* rubor *m*; *v* ruborizarse[7]

blushing *n* rubor *m*; *adj* ruborizado; *fig* modesto

bluster *n* (of waves, wind) tumulto; *fig* jactancia; *v* fanfarronear

blusterer fanfarrón *m* (-ona *f*)

blustering, blustery tumultuoso

B.O. tufo

boa *zool* boa

boar verraco; **wild** ~ jabalí *m*, *SA* pecarí *m*

[1] **board** *n* (plank) tabla; (chess, draughts *etc*) tablero; (for notices) tablero; (card) cartón *m*; (table) mesa; (food) comida; ~**s** *theat* escenario; **above** ~ franco; ~ **and lodging, bed and** ~ pensión completa; ~**-walk** paseo entablado; (at hotel *etc*) estar[19] de pupilo; (at school) ser[19] interno; *vt* (feed) hospedar; *bui* entablar; ~ **up** (window *etc*) cerrar (ie)[2a] con tablas

[2] **board** *n* (group of officials) junta; *comm* directiva; ~ **of directors** junta directiva; ~ **meeting** reunión (-ones) *f* de la directiva; ~ **of examiners** tribunal *m* de examen; **Board of Trade** Ministerio de Comercio; ~ **of trustees** consejo de administración; ~**-room** sala de juntas/sesiones

[3] **board** *n naut* bordo; **on** ~ a bordo; **free on** ~ franco a bordo; *v* (try to capture ship) abordar; (go on ~) embarcarse[4] en; (vehicle) subir a

boarder *naut* abordador *m*; (guest) huésped *m*; (scholar) interno

boarding: ~ **house** pensión (-ones) *f*; ~ **school** escuela de internos; ~**-out** comer *m* fuera todos los días

boast *n* jactancia; *v* jactarse (**about** de); **it's nothing to** ~ **about** no es cosa del otro jueves

boaster fanfarrón *m* (-ona *f*)

boastful jactancioso

boasting *n* jactancia; *adj* jactancioso

boat *n* (small) bote *m*, barca; (large) lancha; (ship) barco; **be in the same** ~ estar[19] en iguales circunstancias; **burn one's** ~**s** quemar las naves; ~**-builder** constructor *m* de barcas; ~**-building** construcción *f* de barcas; ~**-deck** cubierta de botes; ~**-hook** bichero; ~**-house** cobertizo para botes; ~**-load**

barcada; ~**man** barquero; ~**-race** regata; ~**swain** contramaestre *m*; ~**swain's mate** segundo contramaestre; ~**-train** tren *m* que enlaza con un barco; **gravy/sauce** ~ salsera

boater (straw hat) sombrero de paja

boating canotaje *m*; **go** ~ ir[19] (de paseo) en bote

bob *n* (of clock pendulum) lenteja; (of fishing-line) corcho; (of hair) pelo cortado a lo garsón; (of horse) cola cortada; (of plumb-line) plomo; (jerky movement) sacudida; *sl* (shilling) chelín (-ines) *m*; ~**cat** gato montés; ~**-sled,** ~**-sleigh** trineo articulado; ~**-tail** cola corta, (horse) caballo rabón; **rag, tag and** ~**tail** canalla; *vt* (of hair) cortar corto/a lo garsón; *vi* menearse; ~ **up and down** subir y bajar rápidamente

bobbed: ~ **hair** pelo cortado a lo garsón

bobbin bobina

[1] **bobby** *sl* polizonte *m*

[2] **bobby:** ~**-pin** sujetador *m* de pelo; ~**-socks** tobilleras *fpl*; ~**-soxer** tobillera

Boche *pej* teutón *m* (-ona *f*)

bock cerveza rubia

bode presagiar; ~ **ill/well** ser[19] un mal/ buen agüero

bodice corpiño

bodiless sin cuerpo

bodily *adj* corporal; *adv* en persona

bodkin (needle) aguja roma; (for punching holes) punzón (-ones) *m*

body *anat* cuerpo; (dead) cadáver *m*; (of tree) tronco; (of statue) torso; (individual) persona; (group) grupo; (officially constituted group) gremio; *mil* formación *f*; (of letter) texto; (intensity) densidad *f*; (of wine) fuerza; **wine of good** ~ vino fuerte; ~ **odour** tufo; ~ **politic** estado político; **in a** ~ en masa; **heavenly** ~ cuerpo celestial; **learned** ~ docta corporación (-ones) *f*; **main** ~ mayor parte *f* de; **this dress has a silk** ~ este vestido tiene el cuerpo de seda; ~**-builder** (food *etc*) comida fortificante; ~**-building** *n* desarrollo físico, *adj* fortificante; ~**guard** (individual) guardaespaldas *m sing*, (force) guardia personal; ~**-snatcher** ladrón (-ones) *m* de cadáveres; ~**work** carrocería

Boer bóer *m*; ~ **War** guerra del

Transvaal

boffin científico

bog *n* pantano; (of peat) turbera; (toilet) letrina; *v vulg* cagar[5]; **get bogged down** hundirse

bogey(man) coco

boggle recular; **the mind** ~s es absolutamente increíble

boggy pantanoso

bogie (wheels) bogie *m*

bogus falso

Bohemia Bohemia

Bohemian bohemio

[1] **boil** *n* hervor *m*; **it's on the** ~ está hirviendo; **bring to the** ~ calentar (ie)[2a] hasta (el punto de) hervir; *v* hervir (i)[3]; ~ **down** reducir por cocción, *fig* reducir(se)[15] a su más simple forma; ~ **over** hervir (i)[3] hasta rebosar; ~ **with rage** estar[19] fuera de sí; **his behaviour made me/my blood** ~ su comportamiento me hizo enfurecerme; ~**ed** cocido, hervido; ~**ed egg** huevo pasado por agua; **hard-**~**ed egg** huevo duro; ~**ed potatoes** patatas cocidas

[2] **boil** *med* divieso

boiler *cul* (stewpot) marmita; (fowl) gallina demasiado vieja para asar; *mech* caldera; ~**-house/room** sala de calderas; ~**-maker** calderero; ~**-making** fabricación *f* de calderas; ~**suit** mono

boiling ebullición *f*; ~**-hot** hirviendo; ~**-point** punto de ebullición

boisterous bullicioso; (noisy) ruidoso; (children) revoltoso

boisterousness bulla, ruido

bold atrevido; **be so** ~ **as to** atreverse a +*infin*; **in** ~ **relief** en relieve; ~**-faced** descarado; ~**(-faced) type** *print* letra negrita

boldness atrevimiento

bole tronco

bolero (dance) bolero; (clothing) chaquetilla

Bolivia Bolivia

Bolivian *n*+*adj* boliviano

bollard *naut* bolardo; (on traffic island) poste *m*

boll-weevil gorgojo del algodón

Bologna Bolonia

boloney tonterías *fpl*

Bolshevik, Bolshevist *n*+*adj* bolchevique *m*+*f*

Bolshevism bolchevismo

Bolshevize hacer[19] bolchevique

bolshie *n*+*adj* (bolshevik) bolchevique *m*+*f*; (rebel) rebelde *m*+*f*

bolster *n* almohadón (-ones) *m*; *v* ~ **up** sostener[19]; (of spirits) animar

[1] **bolt** *n* (of door, rifle) cerrojo; *carp*+*mech* perno; (arrow) saeta; (of paper *etc*) rollo; (lightning) rayo; ~ **from the blue** suceso inesperado; ~ **upright** erguido; **nut and** ~ tuerca y perno; **shoot one's** ~ hacer[19] un último esfuerzo; *v* (door) echar el cerrojo; *carp*+*mech* empernar

[2] **bolt** *n* (escape) fuga repentina; **he went out with a** ~ él salió de repente; *v* (escape) salir[19] de repente; ~ **food** tragar[5] la comida sin mascarla; ~**-hole** escondite *m*

bomb *n* bomba; **drop a** ~ +*fig* hacer[19] estallar una bomba; **it cost me a** ~ *sl* me costó un ojo de la cara; **it went like a** ~ tuvo gran éxito, *US* fracasó; *v* ~**ed** fracasó; ~ **crater** embudo de bomba; ~**-disposal** desactivación *f* de bombas; ~**-proof** a prueba de bombas; ~**-rack** portabombas *m sing*+*pl*; ~**shell** bomba, *fig* gran sorpresa; ~**-shelter** refugio antiaéreo; ~**-sight** mira de bombardeo; ~**-site** solar *m* arrasado (por una bomba); *v* bombardear

bombard bombardear; ~ **with neutrons** activar con neutrones

bombardier bombardero

bombardment, bombing bombardeo

bombast ampulosidad *f*

bombastic ampuloso; *SA* bombástico

bomber (aeroplane) avión (-ones) *m* de bombardeo; (person) bombardero

bombing *n* bombardeo; *adj* de bombardeo

bona fide de buena fe

bonanza *min* bonanza; *fig* operación (-ones) lucrativa

bonbon confite *m*

bond *n*+*fig* lazo; *comm* bono; (surety) título; (bail) fianza; **in** ~ en depósito bajo fianza; ~ **holder** obligacionista *m*+*f*; ~ **issue** emisión (-ones) *f* de bonos; ~**s** (fetters *etc*) cadenas *fpl*; ~**sman** fiador *m*; *v* (join together) unir(se); *comm* poner[19] en depósito afianzado; ~**ed goods** mercancías *fpl*

cn depósito; ~ed **warehouse** almacén
(-enes) *m* de depósito
bondage cautiverio
bone *n* (human, animal) hueso; (fish)
espina; ~ **china** porcelana de fosfato
de cal; ~ **of contention** manzana de la
discordia; **be all skin and** ~ estar[19] en
los huesos; **dry as a** ~ seco como la
retama; **chilled to the** ~ helado hasta
los tuétanos; **cut costs to the** ~
reducir[15] los gastos al mínimo; **he
made no** ~**s about it** él no vaciló en
decirlo; **I have a** ~ **to pick with you**
tengo que arreglar cuentas con usted;
~**-dry** seco como la retama; ~**head**
imbécil *m*; ~**headed** lerdo; ~**-idle**
perezosísimo; ~**meal** harina de huesos; ~**-shaker** bicicleta antigua, *mot*
cacharro; *v* quitar el hueso/las espinas
a; ~**d** sin huesos, (fish) sin espinas
boneless deshuesado; (fish) sin espinas
boner (howler) disparate *m*
bonfire hoguera
bonhomie jovialidad *f*
Boniface Bonifacio
bonito atún *m*
bonkers chiflado
bon mot dicho agudo
bonnet gorro/gorra de mujer; *mot* capot
m
bonny bonito; *fam* mono
bonus prima
bony huesudo; (fish) con espinas; *med*
huesudo
boo *n* abucheo; **she never says** ~ ella
nunca dice ni pío; *v* abuchear; *interj*
¡fuera!
boob *n* (person) bobo; (gaffe) plancha;
vulg sl teta; *v* cometer una plancha
booby (person) bobo; ~**-prize** premio
para el peor jugador; ~**-trap** engañabobos *m sing*; *mil* trampa explosiva
book *n* libro; (volume) tomo; (of
tickets, cheques *etc*) talonario; (words
of opera) letra; *sp* lista de apuestas; **be
in s.o.'s bad/good** ~**s** estar[19] mal/bien
con alguien; **bring s.o. to** ~ pedir (i)[3]
cuentas a alguien; **it suits my** ~ me
conviene; **take a leaf out of s.o.'s** ~
imitar a alguien; ~**binder** encuadernador *m*; ~**binding** encuadernación *f*; ~**case** librería; ~ **club** círculo
de lectores; ~**-end** sujetalibros *m
sing+pl*; ~ **of instructions** folleto ex-

plicativo; ~ **jacket** camisa; ~**keeper**
tenedor *m* de libros; ~**keeping**
teneduría de libros; ~**-learning**
teoría; ~**-lover** bibliófilo; ~**maker** corredor *m* de apuestas; ~**mark**
marcador *m* de libro; ~**-plate** ex libris
m sing+pl; ~ **of reference** libro de
consulta; ~**-rest** atril *m*; ~ **review**
reseña; ~ **rights** propiedad literaria;
~**seller** librero; ~**stall** puesto de periódicos y libros; ~**shop,** ~**store** librería; ~**-token** cupón regalo (de libros); ~**worm** polilla, *fig* ratón
(-ones) *m* de biblioteca; *v* (buy a
ticket) sacar[4] un billete; *cin+theat* sacar[4] una entrada; (reserve a room)
reservar una habitación; (engage an
entertainer) contratar a un artista;
(request a trunk-call) pedir (i)[3] una
conferencia; **the police** ~**ed him** la
policía le puso una multa; ~ **in** (hotel)
inscribirse (*past part* inscrito); ~ **out**
(hotel) marcharse; ~**ed up** (full) completo, (busy) ocupado; **I'm completely**
~**ed up** tengo todas las horas dadas
bookable reservable
bookie corredor *m* de apuestas
booking (entering in book) registro; (of
seats) reserva; (of actor) contrato; ~-
clerk taquillero; ~**-office** taquilla
bookish libresco
booklet folleto
[1] **boom** (barrier) cadena de puerto; *naut*
(spar) botavara; (arm for microphone
etc) barra supletoria, jirafa
[2] **boom** *n* (noise) estampido; trueno; *v*
retumbar
[3] **boom** *n comm* auge *m*; ~ **town** pueblo
en bonanza; *v* estar[19] en auge
boomerang *n* bumerán *m*; *v fig* rebotar
boon *n* bendición *f*; *adj* íntimo
boor rústico; *fig* gamberro
boorish grosero
boost *n* empujón (-ones) *m* hacia arriba;
(of prices) alza
booster *elect* elevador *m* de tensión; *med*
inyección (-ones) *f* secundaria; *space*
cohete *m* de refuerzo
[1] **boot** *n* bota; (woman's) botín (-ines) *m*;
(child's woollen) patuco; **die with
one's** ~**s on** morir (ue)[1c] (*past part*
muerto) al pie del cañón; **I'm glad I'm
not in your** ~**s** me alegro de no estar[19]
en su pellejo; **the** ~ **is on the other foot**

es lo contrario de lo que usted supone; **get the ~ in** dar[19] patadas; **give s.o. the ~** despedir (i)[3] a uno; **to ~** de añadidura; **~black, ~s** limpiabotas *m sing+pl*; **~lace** cordón (-ones) *m* de zapato; **~leg** de contrabando; **~legger** contrabandista *m+f*; **~legging** contrabando; **~licker** *sl* pelota *m*, *vulg* lameculos *m sing+pl*; *v* dar[19] una patada; **~ out** despedir (i)[3]

²**boot** *mot* portaequipajes *m sing+pl*

bootee botita; (woolly) patuco

booth (stall) puesto; (for voting) casilla; (telephone) cabina

bootless descalzo

booty botín *m*

booze *n* bebida alcohólica; **go on the ~** ir[19] de chateo; *v* coger[8] una tajada; **~-up** *n* borrachera; **~d up** achispado; **get ~d up** achisparse

boozer (person) bebedor *m* (-ora *f*); (place) tasca

boozy achispado

boracic bórico

borax borax *m*

Bordeaux Burdeos; (wine) vino de Burdeos

border *n* borde *m*; (dressmaking) orla; (frontier) frontera, *fam* raya; (of garden) arriate *m*; (of wallpaper) orilla; **~land** tierras fronterizas; **~line** límite *m*; **~line case** caso dudoso; *adj* fronterizo; *v* confinar; (dressmaking) orlar; **~ on/upon** lindar con

borderer habitante fronterizo

bore *n* (hole) barreno; *eng* diámetro interior; (wave) ola causada por la marea; *fig* (person) pelma; **what a ~!** ¡qué lata!, ¡qué pesadez!; *v* (drill) taladrar; *eng+min* sondear; (tire) aburrir, *fam* dar[19] el tostón; **be ~d with** estar[19] aburrido de; **~d stiff** aburrido como una ostra

boredom aburrimiento

boring aburrido; **be ~** ser[19] aburrido/ *fam* pesado

born nacido; **to be ~** nacer[14]; **be ~ again** renacer[14]; **~ to be** destinado a ser; **he is a ~ teacher** es un maestro por naturaleza; **~ leader** jefe nato *m*; **~ loser** perdedor nato, *sl* ceniza

boron boro

borough municipio incorporado; **~ council** ayuntamiento

borrow pedir (i)[3] prestado; *fam* sablear

borrower que pide prestado; *fam* sablista *m*; **~'s ticket** (library) papeleta de empeño

borstal reformatorio para delincuentes jóvenes

bosom pecho; *fig* corazón *m*; (dressmaking) pechera; **~ friend** amigo íntimo

Bosphorus Bósforo

boss *n* jefe *m*; *fam* patrón (-ones) *m*; *pol* barón *m*; *v* dominar

bossy mandón (-ona *f*)

bosun (boatswain) contramaestre *m*

botanical botánico; **~ gardens** jardín (-ines) *m* botánico

botanist botánico

botany botánica

botch *v* chapucear; **I don't want you to make a ~ of it** no quiero que hagas una chapuza

both ambos (-as *f*), los/las dos; **~ my uncle and my aunt speak Polish** tanto mi tío como mi tía hablan polaco

bother *n* molestia; **what a ~!** ¡qué lata!; *v* molestar; *fam* chinchar; **don't ~ about me** no se moleste por mí

botheration molestia

bothersome molesto

bottle *n* botella; **five pesetas on the ~** cinco pesetas por el casco; **have a lot of ~** *sl* tener[19] mucha fuerza; **~-green** verde botella *invar*; **~-neck** cuello de botella, *fig* embotellamiento; **~-opener** descapsulador *m*, abrebotellas *msing*; **~-party** guateque *m* al que cada invitado lleva una botella; **~-top** cierre *m* de botella; **hot-water ~** bolsa de agua caliente; *v* (+ **~ up**) embotellar

bottom *n* fondo; (of lake *etc*) lecho; (of page) pie *m*; (posterior) pompis *m*, *sl* culo; **~ up(wards)** boca abajo; **at ~** en realidad; **be at the ~ of** ser[19] causa de, (be to blame for) tener[19] la culpa de; **from the ~ of one's heart** de todo corazón; **get to the ~ of** descubrir (*past part* descubierto); **go to the ~** *naut* irse[19] a pique: **touch ~** tocar[4] fondo; **rock-~** lo más profundo; *adj* inferior; (in class) último; **~ dollar** último dólar; **~ drawer** cajón (-ones) *m* de abajo, *fig* ajuar *m*; **in ~ gear** en primera; **~most** más hondo; *v* **~ out**

587

acabar paulatinamente

bottomless sin fondo

boudoir tocador *m*

bough rama

bouillon caldo

boulder canto

boulevard bulevar *m*

Boulogne Boloña

bounce *n* rebote *m*; **he is full of** ~ él lanza muchas bravatas; *vi* rebotar; *vt* hacer[19] botar

bouncer el que echa a los alborotadores de una función

bouncing *fig* frescachón (-ona *f*); ~ **baby** niño fuerte

bouncy seguro de sí mismo

[1] **bound** *n* salto; *v* saltar

[2] **bound** *n* límite *m*; **beyond the ~s of possibility** completamente imposible; **fix the ~s** fijar los límites; **in ~s** a raya; **out of ~s** fuera de los límites; **keep within ~s** +*fig* no traspasar los límites; **within the ~s of possibility** dentro de lo factible; *v* limitar; señalar los límites

[3] **bound** *adj* (of books) encuadernado; (indentured) puesto en aprendizaje; (tied) atado, *fig* obligado; **she is ~ to win** seguramente ella ganará; ~ **up with** relacionado con

[4] **bound:** ~ **for** con rumbo a

boundary límite *m*; ~**-line** ámbito; ~**-mark** mojón (-ones) *m*

bounder sinvergüenza *m*+*f*

boundless ilimitado

bounteous, bountiful generoso

bounty generosidad *f*; ~**-money** *mil* enganche *m*; (reward) premio de enganche; **royal** ~ merced *f*

bouquet (of flowers) ramillete *m*; (of wine) nariz (-ces) *f*

Bourbon Borbón (-ones) *m*; **House of** ~ casa de Borbón; (whiskey) whiskey americano

bourgeois *n*+*adj* burgués *m* (-esa *f*); *print* tipo de 9 puntos

bourgeoisie burguesía

bourse bolsa

bout turno; *med* ataque *m*; (boxing *etc*) encuentro; **main** ~ encuentro de fondo; **return** ~ revancha

boutique boutique *f*

bovine bovino; *fig* lerdo

[1] **bow** (bend) reverencia; **make one's** ~

presentarse; *v* hacer[19] una reverencia; ~ **to** *fig* someterse a

[2] **bow** *naut* proa; (oarsman) remo en la proa; ~**sprit** bauprés (-eses) *m*

[3] **bow** (knot) lazo; (weapon + violin) arco; **have two strings to one's** ~ tener[19] dos medios para conseguir algo; **tie a** ~ hacer[19] un lazo; ~**-legged** patiabierto; ~**man** arquero; ~**-saw** *carp* sierra de arco; ~**string** cuerda de arco; ~**-tie** pajarita; ~**-window** mirador *m*; *v mus* arquear

bowdlerize expurgar[5] y mutilar

bowels entrañas *fpl*

bower glorieta

bowie-knife cuchillo de monte

[1] **bowl** cuenco; (for washing) palangana; (small) tazón *m*; (cavity) hueco; (of pipe) hornillo; (of spoon) paleta; ~**ful** cuenco lleno, palangana llena

[2] **bowl** *n* bolo; **play ~s** jugar (ue)[1a] a los bolos; *v* (bowls) bolear; (cricket) lanzar[7] la pelota; ~ **along** rodar (ue)[1a]; ~ **over** derribar

bowler jugador *m* de bolos; (cricketer) lanzador *m* de la pelota; ~**-hat** bombín (-ines) *m*

bowline bolina

bowling: ~ **alley/green** bolera

bow-wow (sound) guau-guau *m*; (dog) perrito; *fam* chuchi *m*+*f*

[1] **box** *n* caja; (large) cajón *m*; (chest) cofre *m*; (for animals) establo; (for jewellery) estuche *m*; (for matches) caja; (*sl* television) tele *f*; *theat* palco; ~ **camera** cámara rígida; ~**-car** furgón (-ones) *m*; ~**-kite** cometa celular; (**Post Office**) ~ **number** apartado (de correos); ~**-office** taquilla; **the ~-office is sold out** la taquilla está agotada; ~**-office success** triunfo taquillero; ~**-pleat** pliegue *m* de tabla; ~**-spanner** llave *f* tubular; *v* encajonar

[2] **box** *n* (blow) golpe *m*; *v* (fight) boxear; (hit) abofetear

[3] **box** *bot* boj *m*

boxer (pugilist) boxeador *m*; (dog) bóxer *m*

boxing boxeo; *Mex* box *m*; ~**-glove** guante *m* de boxeo; ~**-boot** borceguí (-íes) *m* (de boxeo); (several bouts) velada de boxeo; ~**-ring** ring *m*, *fam* cuadrilatero

Boxing Day día *m* de los aguinaldos

boy chico, muchacho; (baby) niño; ~-**friend** amigo, (affianced) novio, *sl* avío; ~**hood** mocedad *f*; ~-**scout** explorador *m*

boycott *n* boicot *m*; *v* boicotear

boycotti.g boicoteo

boyish de muchacho; infantil

boysenberry especie *f* de frambuesa

bra sostén (-enes) *m*

brace *n* (pair) par; *bui* tirante *m*; *carp* berbiquí *m*; *mech* refuerzo; ~**s** (clothing) tirantes *mpl*; ~ **and bit** berbiquí y taladro; *v* reforzar (ue)[1a+7]; ~ **o.s.** vigorizarse[7]

bracelet pulsera

bracing vigorizante

bracken helecho

bracket *n* soporte *m* (en la pared); (lamp) brazo de lámpara; *print* corchete *m*; *v* poner[19] entre corchetes, *fig* poner[19] en una misma clase

brackish salobre

bract bráctea

brad puntilla

bradawl lezna

brag *n* fanfarronada; *v* fanfarronear

braggart fanfarrón *m* (-ona *f*)

braid *n* (hair) trenza; *mil* galón *m*; *v* trenzar[7]

braille escritura para ciegos, braille *m*

brain *n* cerebro; ~**s** sesos *mpl*; **he was the ~s behind the plot** él fue el cerebro del complot; **rack one's ~s** estrujarse el cerebro; ~-**child** invento; ~-**drain** fuga de cerebros; ~-**fever** fiebre *f* cerebral; ~-**storm** ataque violento de locura; ~(**s**) **trust** grupo de intelectuales; ~**wash** lavar el cerebro; ~**washing** lavado de cerebro; ~-**wave** idea luminosa; ~-**work** trabajo intelectual; *v* romper (*past part* roto) la crisma a

brainless tonto

brainy inteligente, listo; ~ **person** cerebral *m*

braise estofar

■ **brake** *bot* soto

2 **brake** *n* freno; **apply the ~(s)** echar el freno; ~-**block** zapata de freno; ~-**drum** tambor *m* de freno; ~-**fluid** líquido de frenos; ~ **horse-power** potencia de freno; ~-**lever** palanca de freno; ~-**lining** forro de freno; ~**man** guardafrenos *m sing+pl*; ~ **parachute**

aer paracaídas *m sing+pl* de freno; ~ **shoe** zapata de freno; **hand/foot** ~ freno de mano/pie; *v* frenar

braking *n* frenazo; ~ **distance** distancia de freno

bramble zarza

bran salvado; ~-**tub** *approx* tómbola

branch *n* rama; (sphere) ramo; *comm* sucursal *f*; (of armed forces) arma; (of family) rama; (of river) afluente *m*; ~-**line** ramal *m*; *v* bifurcar[4]; ~ **out** ramificarse[4], *fig* extenderse (ie)[2b]

brand *n* marca; (animals) hierro; (torch) tea; ~-**new** flamante; *v* (animals) herrar (ie)[2a]; ~**ed goods** mercancías *fpl* de marca

brandish blandir

brandy coñac *m*

brash atrevido

brass *metal* latón *m*; (memorial) placa; *mus* cobre *m*; *mil* alto mando; *sl* (money) pasta; **get down to ~ tacks** ir[19] al grano; ~ **band** banda de música

brassière sostén (-enes) *m*

brassy de latón; (of sounds) metálico; *fig* (cheeky) descarado

brat mocoso

bravado bravata

brave *adj* valiente; *v* desafiar

bravery valor *m*

bravo! ¡bravo!

brawl *n* alboroto; *v* alborotar

brawler alborotador *m* (-ora *f*)

brawling alborotos *mpl*

brawn fuerza; *cul* carne *f* en gelatina

brawniness fortaleza

brawny forzudo

bray rebuznar

braying rebuzno

braze soldar

brazen (hecho) de latón; **she is ~** ella tiene mucha cara

brazier brasero

Brazil Brasil *m*; ~ **nut** castaña del Brasil, *fam* coquito

Brazilian *n+adj* brasileño

breach *n* brecha; (of contract) ruptura; (of good faith) abuso de confianza; ~ **of promise** falta de palabra (de casamiento); ~ **of the peace** perturbación *f* del orden público; **cause a ~ of the peace** alterar el orden público; ~ **of contract** incumplimiento de contrato

bread pan *m*; *sl* (money) parné *m*; ~

and butter pan *m* con mantequilla; **earn one's ~ and butter** ganarse el pan; **be on ~ and water** estar a pan y agua; **break ~ with** sentarse (ie)[2a] a la mesa con; **know which side one's ~ is buttered** saber[19] a que carta quedarse; **brown/white ~** pan bazo/blanco; **fresh ~** pan tierno; **stale ~** pan duro; **wholemeal ~** pan *m* integral; **~-basket** cestilla del pan, *fig* estómago; **~-bin** panera; **in ~-crumbs** empanado; **~-crumb** miga; **in ~-crumbs** empanado; **~-knife** cuchillo del pan; **to be on the ~-line** vivir de limosna; **~-winner** el que mantiene a la familia

breadth anchura

break *n* ruptura; (billiards) partida; (day's holiday) asueto; (interval) descanso; (interruption) interrupción (-ones) *f*; *meteor* cambio (de tiempo); (at school) recreo; **~ of day** alba; **give s.o. a ~** abrirle (*past part* abierto) a uno la puerta; **even ~** oportunidad justa; **lucky ~** suerte *f*; **without a ~** sin parar; **~neck** rapidísimo; **~water** rompeolas *m sing+pl*; *vt* romper (*past part* roto); (shatter) quebrantar; (solve a cipher) descifrar; (tame) domar; **~ the bank** quebrar (ie)[2a] la banca, (cards) hacer[19] saltar la banca; **~ a blood-vessel** *fig* montar en cólera; **~ camp** levantar el campo; **~ a fall** cortar una caída; **~ the flag** izar[7] la bandera; **~ gaol** escaparse de la cárcel; **~ a habit** desacostumbrarse; **she is ~ing my heart** ella me está partiendo el alma; **~ into pieces** hacer[19] añicos; **~ a journey** interrumpir un viaje; **~ the law** cometer un delito; **~ loose** separarse, (escape) escaparse; **~ the news** dar[19] las noticias; **~ new ground** principiar una nueva empresa; **~ one's back** *fig* echar los hígados; **~ one's neck** desnucarse[4]; **~ one's word, ~ a promise** faltar a la palabra; **~ a record** batir un récord; **~ the rule(s)** salir(se)[19] de la regla; **~ the silence** romper (*past part* roto) el silencio; **~ the spell** romper (*past part* roto) el encanto; **~ surface** salir[19] a flote; **~ wind** (belch) eructar, *euph* sacar[4] un provecho; *vi* romperse (*past part* roto); (shatter) quebrantarse; (film) cortar; (flag) desplegarse (ie)[2a]; (waves) reventarse (ie)[2a]; (weather)

cambiar; **his voice will ~ soon** pronto cambiará su voz

~ asunder partir

~ away *n* escapada; *adj* (of trade union *etc*) independiente

~ away from desprenderse de

~down *n* (negotiations *etc*) ruptura; *mot etc* avería; *med* crisis *f*; (of marriage) desavenencia conyugal; **~down gang** equipo de auxilio en las carreteras; **~down truck** furgoneta de auxilio

~ down *vt* derribar; *math* descomponer[19]; *vi mot etc* tener[19] una avería; (burst into tears) deshacerse[19] en lágrimas; **the prisoner broke down and confessed** el prisionero no pudo resistir más y confesó

~ even salir[19] sin ganar ni perder

~ in forzar (ue)[1a+7]; *leg* escalar; (tame) domar; **~ in upon** sorprender

~ into forzar (ue)[1a+7]; **~ into laughter** soltarse (ue)[1a] en risa; **~ into a run** echar a correr

~ off arrancar[4]; (engagement) romper (*past part* roto) un noviazgo; (negotiations) dejar sin concluir; (speech) interrumpir(se)

~ open abrir (*past part* abierto) a la fuerza

~-out *n* fuga

~ out *v* (war) estallar; (of prison) escaparse; **~ out in spots** cubrirse (*past part* cubierto) de granos

~through *n mil* brecha; *sci etc* avance *m* sensacional

~ through *v* hacer[19] una brecha

~ up (school) cerrar(se) (ie)[2a]; *naut* desmenuzarse[7]; (meeting) levantarse; **~ up in disorder** acabar como el rosario de la aurora; **they decided to ~ up the estate** decidieron parcelar la finca

~ with romper con

breakable quebradizo

breakage fractura

breaker ola rompiente; *rad* radioaficionado

breakfast *n* desayuno; *v* desayunar

breaking ruptura; **~ point** punto de romperse; **~ load** *eng* carga de fractura; **~ and entering** allanamiento de morada; **~-in** *US* en rodaje; **~-up** (of gang) desarticulación *f*

bream brema; **sea-~** besugo

breast *n* pecho; *vulg* teta; (of poultry)

pechuga; **make a clean ~ of it** confesar francamente; **~-bone** esternón (-ones) *m*; **~ cancer** cáncer *m* de la mama; **~-fed** amamantado; **~-feed** dar el pecho, *fam* tetar; **~-pocket** bolsillo de pecho; **~-stroke** braza de pecho; **do the ~-stroke** nadar a braza; *v* arrostrar resueltamente

breath respiración (-ones) *f*; (of air) soplo; **be short of ~** estar[19] sin aliento; **get a ~ of fresh air** ventilarse; **hold one's ~** contener[19] la respiración; **in the same ~** al mismo tiempo; **out of ~** sin aliento; **save one's ~** ahorrarse las palabras; **take a ~** respirar; **take a deep ~** respirar hondo; **under one's ~** en voz baja; **waste one's ~** hablar en balde; **with bated ~** pasmado; **~-taking** conmovedor

breathable respirable

breathalyser alcoholímetro

breathe respirar; **~ one's last** dar[19] el último suspiro; **don't ~ a word** no revele usted nada; **she didn't ~ a word all morning** ella no dijo ni palabra en toda la mañana; **~ in** aspirar; **~ out** exhalar

breather *n* descanso; **take a ~** descansar

breathing respiración *f*; (alive) vivo; **he's still ~** aún vive; **~-apparatus** aparato de oxígeno; **~-pipe** tubo respiradero; **~-space** descanso

breathless sin aliento; **~ness** desaliento

bred: born and ~ nacido y criado; **pure-~ dog** perro de pura raza; **well-~ young man** joven bien educado

breech recámara

breeches calzones *mpl*; **wear the ~** *fig* llevar los pantalones; **~-buoy** pantalón *m* de salvamento

breed *n* raza; **of a different ~** *fig* de madera distinta; *v* criar

breeder (of cattle *etc*) criador *m*; **~-reactor** *phys* reactor *m* reproductor

breeding (of animals) cría; (good manners) educación *f*; **~-ground** criadero; **~ mare** yegua de tripa

breeze *n* brisa; *poet* céfiro; **~-way** pasillo cubierto; *v* **~ in** entrar sin preocupación

breezy airoso; (jolly) vivo; **it is ~** hace brisa

Bremen Brema

Bren gun ametralladora ligera

brethren hermanos *mpl*

Breton bretón (-ones) *m*

breve *mus* breve *f*

breviary breviario

brevity brevedad *f*

brew *n* mezcla; *vt* (beer) fabricar;[4] (tea) hacer[19] (una infusión de); *vi* hacerse; **a storm is ~ing** una tempestad amenaza; **~ over an idea** cocer[1a] una idea

brewer cervecero

brewery fábrica de cerveza

brewing fabricación *f* de cerveza

briar, brier zarza; (for pipe-making) brezo

bribe *n* soborno; *fam* unto amarillo; *v* sobornar; *fam* untar las manos (de); **be ~d** dejarse sobornar

briber sobornador *m* (-ora *f*)

bribery soborno

bric-à-brac baratijas *fpl*

brick *n* ladrillo; (toy) taquito; *fig* buen chico; **drop a ~** meter la pata; **~bat** pedazo de ladrillo; **~-kiln** horno; **~-layer** albañil *m*; **~-red** de color (de) ladrillo; **~work** enladrillado, (craft) albañilería; **~works** fábrica de ladrillos; *v* **~ up** enladrillar

bridal nupcial; **~ bed** tálamo; **~ cake** tarta de la boda; **~-suite** suite *f* nupcial

bride novia; **~groom** novio; **~smaid** madrina de boda

bridge *eng, mus, naut etc* puente *m*; (of nose) caballete *m*; (game) bridge *m*; **~-player** jugador *m* (-ora *f*) de bridge; **~-head** cabeza de puente; *v* tender (ie)[2b] un puente sobre; **~ a gap** *fig* llenar un vacío

Bridget Brígida

bridging loan crédito de puente

bridle *n* brida; **~-path** camino de herradura; *v* erguirse[11]

brief *n* escrito; **hold no ~ for** no defender (ie)[2b]; **~s** (men's) braslip *m*, (woman's) braga; **~-case** portapapeles *m sing+pl*; *adj* breve; *v* **leg** dar[19] un informe a; *mil* dar[19] instrucciones a

briefing instrucciones *fpl* (preliminares)

brier *see* **briar**

brig bergantín (-ines) *m*

brigade brigada

brigadier brigadier *m*; **~-general** general *m* de brigada

brigand bandido

bright (clever) listo; (shiny) reluciente; **look on the ~ side** ser[19] optimista; ~ **colour** color vivo; ~ **day** día claro; ~ **idea** idea luminosa; ~ **lights** luces *fpl* brillantes, *US mot* faros *mpl*; ~ **sky** cielo claro; **cloudy with ~ periods** nubosidad *f* con claros; **~-eyed** ojialegre

brighten *vt* pulir; *fam* sacar[4] brillo a; *vi* ~ **(up)** +*fig* animar; alegrar; **the sky is ~ing** el cielo está despejándose

brightness brillantez *f*; *TV* luminosidad *f*

brilliance brillantez *f*; (of intellect) talento

brilliant brillante; (clever) talentoso

brilliantine brillantina

brim borde *m*; (hat) ala

brimful rebosante

brimming: ~ **over** lleno hasta el borde

brimstone azufre *m*; **fire and ~** fuego y azufre *m*

brindled manchado

brine salmuera

bring traer[19]; ~ **o.s. to** resolverse (ue)[1b] a +*infin*; ~ **pressure to bear on** ejercer[12] presión en

~ **about** efectuar

~ **back** traer[19] de vuelta

~ **down** bajar; (with great force) abatir; (hunting) matar; ~ **down the house** promover (ue)[1b] grandes aplausos; ~ **down a plane** aterrizar[7] un avión, (shoot down) derribar un avión; ~ **down a peg or two** humillar

~ **forth** producir[15]

~ **forward** *comm* pasar a nueva cuenta

~ **home to** demostrar (ue)[1a] a

~ **in** (milk *etc*) entrar; (a meal) servir (i)[3]; ~ **in a bill** presentar un proyecto de ley; ~ **in a good price** venderse a buen precio; ~ **in money** producir[15] dinero; ~ **in a verdict** dar[19] el veredicto

~ **into play** poner[19] en juego

~ **off** llevar a cabo

~ **on** (an illness) causar; ~ **on oneself** buscar[4] con la actitud; **he brought it on himself** lo buscó con su actitud

~ **out** (a book) sacar[4] a luz; (a new model) estrenar; ~ **out a point** presentar un argumento; ~ **out a play** poner[19] en escena una obra; ~ **out a young lady** presentar a una señorita

~ **round** *med* resucitar; (persuade) convencer[12]

~ **to** sacar[4] de un desmayo; *naut* ponerse[19] a la capa; ~ **to book** pedir[3] cuentas; ~ **to a head** provocar[4]; ~ **to light** descubrir (*past part* descubierto); ~ **to a standstill** parar; ~ **to task** censurar

~ **together** reunir

~ **up** (upstairs) (hacer[19]) subir; (educate) educar[4]; (vomit) devolver (ue)[1b] (*past part* devuelto); ~ **up for discussion** traer[19] a discusión; ~ **up the rear** cubrir (*past part* cubierto) la retaguardia; ~ **up to date** poner[19] al corriente

bringing-up educación *f*

brink borde *m*; **on the ~ of** a punto de; **~manship** política arriesgada

briny *n fig* (sea) mar *m*+*f*; *adj* salobre

briquet(te) briqueta

brisk vigoroso

brisket pecho (de un animal)

briskness energía

bristle *n* cerda; *v* erizar(se)[7]; ~ **with difficulties** estar[19] (rodeado) de dificultades

bristly cerdoso

Britain: Great ~ Gran Bretaña

British *n* (people) pueblo británico; *adj* británico; ~ **Commonwealth** Mancomunidad Británica

Briton británico; **ancient ~** britano

Brittany Bretaña

brittle quebrantable

broach (subject) mencionar por primera vez; abordar; (a barrel) espitar

broad *n sl* jaia *f*; *adj* (wide) ancho; (roomy) amplio; (vast) extenso; ~ **hint** indicación clara; **it's as ~ as it is long** es igual en todos los sentidos; **in ~ daylight** en pleno día; **~-brimmed** de ala ancha; **~cast** *n* emisión (-ones) *f*, *v* transmitir, (spread) esparcir[13], *agri* sembrar a voleo; **~caster** locutor *m* (-ora *f*); **~casting** radiodifusión *f*; **~casting studio** estudio de emisión; **~casting station** emisora; **~cloth** popelina; **~-gauge** de vía ancha; **~-minded** tolerante; **~-shouldered** ancho de espaldas; **~side** *mil*+*naut* andanada

broaden ensanchar(se); *fig* ampliar(se)

broadly: ~ **speaking** hablando de una manera general

brocade brocado

broccoli brécol *m*

brochure folleto

brogue (shoe) zapato grueso con adornos; (speech) acento irlandés

broil *n* riña; *v cul* asar

broiler *cul* pollo tomatero

broke *fam* sin perra

broken roto; (shattered) quebrado; (tamed) domado; ~ **accent** acento extranjero; ~ **chord** acorde roto; ~ **sleep** sueño interrumpido; ~-**down** decrépito; ~-**hearted** angustiado

broker corredor *m*; **stock**~ corredor *m* de cambios

brokerage corretaje *m*

bromide bromuro

bronchial bronquial

bronchitis bronquitis *f*

bronco potro cerril; ~-**buster** domador *m* de potros cerriles

brontosaurus brontosaurio

Bronx cheer *see* **raspberry**

bronze *n* bronce *m*; *v* broncear; ~**d** (sunburnt) bronceado por el sol; **Bronze Age** edad *f* del bronce

brooch alfiler *m*

brood *n* nidada; *v* empollar; ~ **over** rumiar con melancolía, amargura *etc*

broody clueca; *fig* melancólico; **become** ~ enclocar[4]

brook *n* arroyo; *v* (put up with) aguantar

[1] **broom** escoba; ~**stick** palo de escoba

[2] **broom** *bot* retama

broth caldo

brothel burdel *m*; *euph* casa de niñas

brother hermano; *eccles* fraile *m*; ~(**s**) **and sister(s)** hermanos; ~**hood** (relationship) fraternidad *f*, (organization) cofradía; ~-**in-law** cuñado

brotherly fraternal

brow frente *f*; (of hill) cima; ~**beat** intimidar; ~**beating** intimidación *f*

brown *n*+*adj* (hair, eyes) marrón (-ones); castaño; (swarthy) moreno; **be in a** ~ **study** estar[19] en babia; ~ **bread** pan bazo; ~ **paper** papel *m* de estraza; ~ **sugar** azúcar moreno; ~-**eyed** ojimoreno; *v cul* tostar (ue)[1a]; ~**ed** (sunburnt) bronceado por el sol; ~**ed off** (fed up) fastidiado, *vulg* cabreado; **be** ~**ed off with** estar[19] harto de

brownie duende *m*

brownish que tira a castaño/moreno

browse (graze) pacer[14]; ~ **through a**

book hojear un libro; ~ **about,** ~ **around** curiosear

Bruges Brujas

bruise *n* contusión (-ones) *f*; cardenal *m*; (on fruit) maca; *v* magullar; (fruit) golpear

bruiser boxeador *m*

brunette *n*+*adj* morena

brunt lo más fuerte; **bear the** ~ pagar[5] el pato; **bear the** ~ **of** aguantar lo más recio de

brush *n* cepillo; (broom) escoba; *elect* escobilla; (large paint-brush) brocha; (small paint-brush) pincel *m*; (of fox) hopo; (undergrowth) matorral *m*; *fig* (fight) escaramuza; **have a** ~ **with** desavenir(se)[19] con; ~**wood** broza; *v* cepillar; (with the hand) frotar; ~ **clean** limpiar con cepillo; ~ **the teeth/ hair** cepillar los dientes/el pelo

~ **aside** echar a un lado

~ **back/forward: he had his hair** ~**ed back/forward** él tenía el pelo echado para atrás/delante

~ **by/past** pasar muy cerca

~ **up** (revise) repasar

brusque brusco

Brussels Bruselas; ~ **sprout** col *f* de Bruselas

brutal brutal

brutality brutalidad *f*

brutalize embrutecer[14]; (*US* ill-treat) agredir

brutalizing embrutecedor

brute bruto; ~ **force** fuerza bruta

brutish abrutado

Brutus Bruto

bubble *n* burbuja; *fig* ilusión *f*; ~ **and squeak** sobras *fpl* fritas de patatas y legumbres; **blow** ~**s** hacer[19] burbujas; ~-**bath** baño de espuma; ~ **bath liquid** gel *m* de baño; ~-**car** coche-cabina *m*, *fam* huevo; ~-**gum** chicle *m* blando de globos

bubbly *n* (champagne) champán *m*; cava *m*; *adj* espumoso

bubonic bubónico; ~ **plague** peste bubónica

buccaneer corsario

Bucephalus Bucéfalo

Bucharest Bucarest *m*

buck *n zool* gamo; (male) macho; (redskin) indio varón; (dandy) petimetre *m*; (dollar) dólar *m*; **pass the** ~ dejar a otro la responsabilidad; ~-**shot** perdigón *m* grande; ~**skin** piel *f* de ante; ~-**tooth** diente *m* saliente; ~**wheat** alforfón *m*; *v* (jump wildly) corcovear; ~ **up!** ¡ánimo!

bucket cubo; (of canvas or wood) balde *m*; **a drop in the** ~ una nonada; **kick the** ~ *fam* estirar la pata, *sl* diñarla); ~-**shop** nazareno

bucketful cubo; **by the** ~ a punta pala

buckle *n* (fastener) hebilla; (bend) comba; *v* (fasten) hebillar; (bend) combar(se); ~ **down to** dedicarse⁴ con empeño a; ~**d** combado, (twisted) torcido

buckram bucarán *m*

bucolic bucólico

¹ **bud** *n* botón (-ones) *m*; (*esp* of rose) capullo; *v* abotonar

² **bud** camarada *m+f*

Buddha Buda *m*

Buddhism budismo

Buddhist *n+adj* budista *m+f*

budding en capullo; *fig* futuro

buddy camarada *m+f*; *sl* tronco

budge mover(se) (ue)¹ᵇ

budgerigar periquito

budget *n* presupuesto; *v* ~ **(for)** hacer¹⁹ el presupuesto (para)

buff (color *m* de) ante *m*; (enthusiast) aficionado

buffalo búfalo

buffer (railway) tope *m*; ~ **state** país tapón *m*

¹ **buffet** (furniture) alacena; (meal) comida de fiambres; (railway restaurant) cantina; ~-**lunch** buffet *m*; ~-**car** vagón (-ones) *m* donde se sirven comidas

² **buffet** (blow) *n* bofetada; *v* abofetear

buffeting zurra

buffoon bufón (-ones) *m*; **act the** ~ hacer¹⁹ bufonadas

¹ **bug** *n* bicho; ~**bear** pelma; **bed**~ chinche *m*

² **bug** *n* micrófono escondido; *v* escuchar por medio de un micrófono escondido; (annoy) molestar

bugaboo coco

bugger *n* sodomía *m*; *vulg* cabrón *m*; *v* cometer sodomía; *sl* (exhaust) cabrear; ~ **off!** ¡vete a hacer puñetas!; ~**ed** (exhausted) *vulg* jodido

buggery sodomía

bugle corneta; ~-**call** toque *m* de corneta

bugler corneta *m*

build *n* (construction) construcción *f*; (of person) figura; *v* construir¹⁶; ~ **up** *bui* edificar, *mil* concentrar, *mech* montar; ~ **up a firm** ampliar un negocio; ~ **up illusions** forjar(se) ilusiones

builder (master-~) constructor *m*; (building worker) obrero de la construcción, *fam* albañil *m*

building (product) edificio; (action) construcción *f*; ~ **society** *approx* sociedad *f* de inversión inmobiliaria; ~ **trade** ramo de la construcción

built construido; ~-**in cupboard** armario empotrado; ~-**up area** zona edificada

bulb *bot* bulbo; *elect* bombilla; (of thermometer *etc*) ampolleta; **flash-**~ *phot* flash *m*

bulbous bulboso

Bulgaria Bulgaria

Bulgarian *n+adj* búlgaro

bulge *n* comba; *v* combarse

bulging saliente; ~ **eyes** *fam* ojos saltones

bulk bulto; **in** ~ a granel, en grueso; ~**head** mamparo

bulky abultado

¹ **bull** *n* toro; (male elephant, whale *etc*) macho; *mil* (~**shit**) disciplina excesiva; **he's talking a load of** ~ él está diciendo idioteces; ~-**dog** dogo; ~-**dozer** niveladora; ~'**s-eye** blanco; ~-**fight** corrida (de toros); ~**fighter** torero; ~**fighting** tauromaquia; **I like** ~**fighting** (taking part) me gusta torear, (watching) me gustan los toros; ~**finch** camachuelo; ~**frog** rana mugidora; ~**headed** terco; ~-**necked** cuellicorto; ~-**ring** plaza de toros; ~-**terrier** bull-terrier *m*

² **bull** *eccles* bula

bullet bala; ~-**proof** a prueba de balas

bulletin boletín (-ines) *m*

bullion *comm* metálico

bullock buey *m*

¹ **bully** *n* matón *m*; *v* intimidar

² **bully** (corned beef) carne *f* (de vaca) en lata

bulrush junco

bulwark baluarte *m*

bum *n* *anat* trasero, *fam* culo; *fig* (loafer) vago; (scrounger) sablista *m*; (tramp) trotamundos *m* *sing+pl*; *vt* (scrounge) sablear; *vi* vivir a expensas de otro; (tramp) llevar una vida errante

bumble-bee abejorro

bumf (toilet paper) papel higiénico; *fig* papeleo

bump *n* golpe *m*; (swelling) hinchazón (-ones) *m*; (in road) bache *m*; *v* pegar⁵; ~ **into** dar¹⁹ con; (meet) encontrarse (ue)¹ᵃ con; ~ **off** cargarse⁵ a

bumper *n* *mot* parachoques *m* *sing+pl*; *adj* (excellent) abundante

bumpkin palurdo

bumptious presumido

bumpy (road) lleno de baches

bun *cul* bollo; (hair) moño

bunch *n* manada; ~ **of flowers** ramo de flores; ~ **of grapes** racimo de uvas; ~ **of keys** manojo de llaves; *v* agrupar(se)

bundle bulto; (large) fardo

bung *n* tapón (-ones) *m*; *v* taponar⁵; ~ **it in here** métalo por aquí; ~**hole** agujero de bitoque

bungalow chalé *m*

bungle chapucear

bungler chapucero

bungling *n* chapucería; *adj* chapucero

bunion juanete *m*

bunk *n* (bed) litera; (nonsense) patrañas *fpl*; *v* (run away) escaparse

bunker (for coal) carbonera; (golf) hoyo de arena; *mil* búnker *m*

bunkum tonterías *fpl*

bunny conejito; ~**-girl** conejita

Bunsen burner mechero de Bunsen

bunting (decorations) banderas *fpl*; *orni* escribano; **corn-**~ triguero

buoy *n* boya; *v* boyar

buoyancy flotabilidad *f*; *fig* confianza

buoyant boyante; optimista; ~ **economy** economía boyante

burble *n* burbujeo; *v* burbujear

burden carga; **beast of** ~ bestia de carga; ~**some** pesado

bureau (desk) escritorio; (chest of drawers) cómoda; (dressing-table) tocador *m*; (office) despacho; (organization) agencia; **weather-**~ oficina meteorológica

bureaucracy burocracia

bureaucrat burócrata *m+f*

bureaucratic burocrático

burg ciudad *f*

burgess ciudadana

burgher ciudadano

burglar ladrón (-ones) *m*; ~**-alarm** alarma contra robo; ~**-proof** a prueba de ladrones; **cat-**~ gato

burglarize *see* **burgle**

burglary robo con allanamiento de morada

burgle *v* robar (de una casa habitada) con allanamiento de morada

burgomaster alcalde *m*

Burgundy Borgoña

burial entierro; ~ **service** oficio de difuntos; ~**-ground** camposanto, cementerio

burlesque *n* parodia; *adj* burlesco; *v* parodiar; ~ **show** espectáculo de bailes y cantos

burly fornido

Burma Birmania

Burmese birmano

burn *n* quemadura; *vi* arder; *vt* quemar; ~ **one's boats** quemar las naves; ~ **one's fingers** quemarse los dedos, *fig* cogerse⁸ los dedos; ~ **the midnight oil** quemarse las cejas; ~ **to a cinder** carbonizar⁷; **he is** ~**ing with rage** él está ardiendo de rabia

~ **down** quemar(se) de arriba abajo

~ **out** *n* *space* extinción *f*

~**-up** *n* vuelta rápida en coche/motocicleta

~ **up** *v* quemar(se) por completo

burner quemador *m*; (of gas cooker *etc*) mechero

burning *n* quemado; **there's a smell of** ~ hay olor a quemado; *adj* (very hot) abrasador

burnish bruñir

burnt quemado; ~ **out** (bulb) fundido; **be** ~ **to death** morir (ue)¹ᶜ (*past part* muerto) en un incendio; ~ **sienna** siena tostada

burp *n* eructo; *v* eructar

burrow *n* madriguera; *v* amadrigar⁵

bursar tesorero

bursary beca

burst *n* reventón (-ones) *m*; (of bomb) estallido; *mil* (~ **of gunfire**) ráfaga de tiros; ~ **of energy/enthusiasm** explosión (-ones) *f* de energía/entusiasmo; *adj* reventado; (tyre) pinchado; ~ **pipe** tubería rota; *v* reventar (ie)[2a]; ~ **into blossom** brotar; **he ~ into the room** él irrumpió en la habitación; ~ **into tears** deshacerse[19] en lágrimas; ~ **open** forzar (ue)[1a]; ~ **out crying** romper a llorar; ~ **out laughing** soltar (ue)[1a] una carcajada; ~ **with envy/pride** reventar (ie)[2a] de envidia/orgullo

bursting: ~ **into bud** eclosión *f* de la primavera

bury enterrar (ie)[2a]; *fam* dar[19] tierra a; (hide) esconder; ~ **the hatchet** hacer[19] las paces; ~ **one's head in the sand** esconder la cabeza debajo de la manta

bus autobús (-uses) *m*; (long-distance) coche *m* de línea; ~ **conductor** cobrador *m* (de autobús); ~ **depot** cochera; ~ **driver** conductor *m* de autobús; ~ **route** línea de autobuses; ~ **station** estación (-ones) *f* de autobuses; ~ **stop** parada de autobuses; **by** ~ **en** autobús; **my old** ~ mi coche; *v* ir[19] en autobús

busby gorro de húsar

bush (plant) arbusto; (scrubland) terreno cubierto de malezas; **beat about the** ~ andarse[19] por las ramas; ~-**telegraph** *mil sl* radio macuto; **the** ~-**telegraph says that** corre la voz que

bushel medida de áridos (*UK* 36,35 litros, *US* 35 litros)

bushy peludo; ~ **eyebrows** cejas *fpl* pobladas

busily diligentemente

business *n* negocio; (firm) empresa; (matter) asunto; (obligation) obligación *f*; (profession) oficio; ~ **is** ~ el negocio es el negocio; **she means** ~ ella habla en serio; **mind your own** ~ métase en sus asuntos; **it's not my** ~ no es cuenta mía; **they sent me about my** ~ me mandaron a paseo; **set up** ~ establecer[14] un negocio; **let's settle this** ~ arreglemos este asunto; **he is in the family** ~ él trabaja en el negocio de familia; ~-**like** práctico; ~-**man** negociante *m*, hombre *m* de negocios; *adj* comercial; ~ **efficiency** eficiencia comercial; ~ **management** gestión *f* comercial; ~ **manager** gerente *m+f*; ~-**suit** *US* traje *m* de calle

busker actor *m*/músico callejero

bust *n art* busto; *anat* (bosom) pecho; *v* (break) reventar (ie)[2a]; **I'm** ~ (penniless) estoy barrido; ~-**up** riña

bustle *v* apresurarse

bustling animado

busy *n* ocupado; (thronged) concurrido; ~ **life** vida activa; ~ **bee** *fig* hormiguita; ~-**body** entrometido; *v* ~ **o.s. (about/with)** ocuparse (con)

business actividad *f*

but pero; (after a negative) sino, **he is not German,** ~ **Austrian** él no es alemán sino austriaco; **she is** ~ **a child** ella no es más que una niña; **had I** ~ **known** si yo hubiera sabido; ~ **for** si no fuera por; ~ **that ...** a no ser que ...; **I cannot** ~ **laugh** no puedo (por) menos de reír; **last** ~ **one** penúltimo; **none** ~ **the brave** sólamente los valientes; **not only ...** ~ **also ...** no sólamente ... sino también ...

butane butano

butcher carnicero; *fig* hombre sanguinario; ~'s **shop** carnicería; *v* matar; *fig* dar[19] muerte cruel

butchery matanza

butler mayordomo

butt *n* cabo; (cigarette end) colilla, *SA* chicote *m*; (person) hazmerreír *m*; (target) blanco; *v* embestir (i)[3]; ~ **in** meter baza

butter *n* mantequilla; ~-**cup** botón (-ones) *m* de oro; ~-**dish** mantequillera; ~-**fingered** desmañado; ~-**fly** mariposa; ~-**fly stroke** braza de mariposa; ~-**fly nut** tuerca de orejas; ~-**knife** cuchillo para la mantequilla; ~-**milk** suero de la leche; ~-**scotch** dulce *m* de mantequilla y azúcar; *v* poner[19] mantequilla en; ~-**ed toast** tostada con mantequilla; ~ **up** hacer la pelota a

buttock *fam* trasero; nalga

button botón (-ones) *m*; (of a bell) timbre *m*; *mech* botón (-ones) *m* de control; ~-**hole** ojal *m*, (flower) flor *f* (para llevar en el ojal), *v fig* importunar; ~-**wood** plátano falso; ~ **up** abotonar

buttress *n archi* contrafuerte *m*; *fig* apoyo; *v* apoyar

buxom rollizo

buy comprar; ~ **on credit** comprar al fiado; ~ **on HP** comprar a plazos

~ **off** librarse de ... con dinero

~ **out** comprar la parte de
~ **up** acaparar
buyable comprable
buyer comprador *m* (-ora *f*)
buzz *n* zumbido; *v* zumbar
buzzard águila ratonera
buzzer (bell) timbre *m*
buzzing *n* zumbido; *adj* zumbador
by *prep* por; **written** ~ **Iriarte** escrito por Iriarte; **six metres** ~ **ten metres** seis metros por diez; ~ **winning the battle he became famous** con ganar la batalla se hizo célebre; ~ **working you will become rich** trabajando usted se hará rico; **do it** ~ **tomorrow** hágalo para mañana; **I'll be there** ~ **seven** estaré allí antes de las siete; **he will reach Madrid** ~ **Sunday** él llegará a Madrid el domingo; **I haven't it** ~ **me** no lo tengo conmigo; **one must play** ~ **the rules** se debe jugar⁵ según las reglas; ~ **air** por avión; ~ **all means** por todos los medios, (certainly) naturalmente; ~ **and** ~ pronto, luego; ~ **and large** de manera general; ~ **birth** de nacimiento; ~ **cable** por cable; ~ **chance** por casualidad; ~ **day** de día; ~ **degrees** poco a poco; ~ **dint of** a fuerza de; ~ **the dozen** por docenas; ~ **experience** por experiencia; ~ **far** con mucho; ~ **force** por la fuerza; ~ **God!** ¡Por Dios!; ~ **good luck** afortunadamente; ~ **heart** de memoria, *fam*

de carretilla; ~ **itself** (on its own) de por sí; ~ **land** por tierra; ~ **letter** por carta; ~ **the light of** a la luz de; ~ **means of** por medio de; ~ **mistake** erróneamente, sin querer; ~ **moonlight** a la luz de la luna; ~ **name** de nombre; ~ **night** de noche; ~ **no means** de ninguna manera; ~ **now** ya; ~ **oneself** (alone) a solas; ~ **order of** por mandato de; ~ **profession** de profesión; ~ **radio** por radio; ~ **rail** por ferrocarril; ~ **road** por carretera; ~ **stealth** a hurtadillas; ~ **then** para entonces; ~ **turns** por turnos; ~ **water**, ~ **sea** por mar, por vía marítima; ~ **way of** por vía de; ~ **the way** a propósito; ~ **wire** por telegrama
adv junto, cerca, al lado; **close** ~ muy cerca, juntito; **~stander** espectador *m*
pref secundario; **~-election** *n* elección (-ones) *f* parcial; **~-law** estatuto/reglamento local; **~-pass** *n* desvío, *v* evitar; **~-play** acción (-ones) secundaria; **~-product** producto secundario; **~-road** carretera secundaria
bye-bye adiós
bygone pasado; **let ~s be ~s** lo pasado, pasado
byword dicho
Byzantine bizantino
Byzantium Bizancio

C

c (letter) ce *f*; **C** *mus* do
cab (taxi) taxi *m*; (horse-drawn) coche *m* de punto; (of locomotive) cabina del maquinista; (of lorry, truck) cabina; ~-**driver,** ~-**man** taxista *m*, cochero; ~-**rank,** ~-**stand** parada de taxis/coches
cabal cábala
cabaret cabaret *m*; ~ **show** espectáculo de cabaret
cabbage col *f*; ~ **butterfly** mariposa blanca
cabbalistic(al) cabalístico
cabby taxista *m*, cochero
cabin (hut) cabaña; *naut* camarote *m*; (of lorry, plane) cabina; ~-**boy** paje *m* de escoba, mozo de camarote; ~-**cruiser** crucero de placer; ~-**trunk** baúl *m*
cabinet (private room) gabinete *m*; (furniture) vitrina; *rad+TV* caja; *pol* consejo de ministros; ~ **minister** ministro; ~ **reshuffle** reajuste *m* ministerial; ~-**maker** ebanista *m*
cable *n elect+naut+tel* cable *m*; ~ **address** dirección cablegráfica; ~**gram** cablegrama *m*; ~-**railway** funicular *m*; ~-**stitch** punto en cruz; *v* cablegrafiar
caboodle: the whole ~ toda la pesca
caboose cocina en la cubierta de un buque; *US* vagón (-ones) *m* de cola en un tren de carga, furgón
cabriolet cabriolé *m*
cacao cacao
cache *n* escondite *m*; *v* esconder
cachet sello; *fig* marca distintiva
cackle *n* cacareo; (laughter) carcajada; (chatter) cháchara; *v* cacarear; reírse (i)[3] a carcajadas; chacharear
cackler cacareador *m*; (chatterer) chacharero
cackling cacareo; (chattering) cháchara
cacophonous cacofónico
cacophony cacofonía
cactus cacto
cad sinvergüenza *m+f*

cadaver cadáver *m*
cadaverous cadavérico
caddie *n* muchacho que lleva los palos en el juego de golf; ~-**bag** carcaj *m* (para los palos); *v* servir (i)[3] de caddie
caddish mal educado
caddy (golf) *see* **caddie;** *cul* cajita para té
cadence, cadency cadencia
cadenza cadencia
cadet cadete *m*
cadge *vt* pedir (i)[3]; *vi* vivir de gorra
cadger gorrón *m* (-ona *f*)
Cadiz Cádiz *m*
cadmium cadmio
cadre *pol+mil* cuadro
Caesar César *m*
caesarean: ~ **operation** operación cesárea
café café *m*; *SA* restaurante *m*; ~ **au lait** café con leche; ~ **noir** café solo
cafeteria cafetería
caffeine cafeína
cage *n* jaula; *v* enjaular
cagey cauteloso
cahoot compañía; **be in** ~s asociarse
Caiaphas Caifás *m*
Cain Caín *m*; **to raise** ~ armar camorra
cairn montón (-ones) *m* de piedras sobre una tumba; ~ **terrier** perro ratonero de patas cortas
Cairo El Cairo
caisson arcón (-ones) *m*; *mil* furgón (-ones) *m* de municiones
cajole halagar[5]; ~ **s.o. into** conseguir (i)[3+11] por medio de halagos que +*subj*
cajoler lisonjero
cajolery zalamería
cake *n* (large) tarta; (small) pastel *m*; (of soap) pastilla; **share the national** ~ repartir la tortilla nacional; **that takes the** ~ eso gana el premio; ~-**tin** molde *m*; *v* (harden) endurecerse[14]; **his shoes are** ~**d with mud** sus zapatos están cubiertos de lodo

598

calabash calabaza
calamine calamina
calamitous calamitoso
calamity calamidad *f*
calcification calcificación *f*
calcify calcificar(se)[4]
calcium calcio; ~ **carbonate** carbonato de calcio
calculable calculable
calculate *v* calcular; ~ **on** contar (ue)[1a] con; **be ~d to ser**[19] a propósito para
calculating de calcular; *fig* astuto; ~-**machine** (máquina) calculadora
calculation cálculo
calculator (person) calculador *n* (-ora *f*); (machine) calculadora
calculus cálculo
Calcutta Calcuta
Caledonian caledonio
calendar calendario; ~ **month** mes *m* del año; ~ **year** año civil
calf (animal) ternero; *anat* pantorrilla; (binding) piel *f*; **kill the fatted** ~ celebrar una fiesta de bienvenida; ~-**love** amor *m* juvenil; **in** ~**skin** en becerro
calibrate calibrar
calibration graduación (-ones) *f*
calibre calibre *m*; **large/small** ~ grueso/pequeño calibre
calico percal *m*
California California
Californian californiano
caliph califa *m*
calk *see* **caulk**
call *n* llamada; *mil* toque *m*; (telephone) llamada (telefónica); (visit) visita; *naut* escala; (vocation) vocación (-ones) *f*; *orni* reclamo; *theat* llamamiento; **in the** ~ **of duty** en el cumplimiento del deber; **on** ~ disponible; (doctor *etc*) localizado; **pay a** ~ hacer[19] una visita, *naut* hacer[19] escala; **within** ~ al alcance de la voz; ~-**box** cabina telefónica; ~-**boy** (hotel) botones *m sing+pl*, *theat* traspunte *m*; ~-**collect** cobro revertido; ~-**girl** chica de plan; *v* llamar; (loudly) gritar; (wake) despertar (ie)[2a]; (cards) marcar[4]; (name) llamar; **be** ~**ed** llamarse; **I'm** ~**ed John but my friends** ~ **me Johnny** me llamo Juan pero mis amigos me llaman Juanito; ~ **a bluff** coger[8] la palabra a;

~ **attention to** llamar la atención sobre; ~ **(in) the police** llamar la ayuda de la policía; ~ **it a day** parar (el trabajo); ~ **it quits** hacer las paces; ~ **a meeting** convocar[4] una reunión; ~ **a strike** convocar[4] una huelga; ~ **names** insultar, *fam* poner[19] verde; ~ **the roll/register** pasar lista; ~ **a spade a spade** llamar[19] al pan pan y al vino vino
~ **after** poner[19] el mismo nombre que; **be** ~**ed after** llevar el mismo nombre que
~ **again** llamar de nuevo; (come back) volver (ue)[1b] (*past part* vuelto)
~ **at** visitar; *naut* hacer[19] escala en
~ **away** llamar; **she was** ~**ed away to Madrid** la llamaron de Madrid
~ **back** mandar volver
~ **by** *US* visitar
~ **(s.o.) down(stairs)** hacer[19] bajar (a alguien)
~ **for** ir[19]/venir[19] por; ~ **for me at eight o'clock** venga usted a buscarme a las ocho; (require) necesitar
~ **forth** hacer[19] salir
~ **in** hacer[19] entrar; *comm* retirar
~ **off** suspender
~ **on** (visit) visitar; (invite) pedir (i)[3] a +*subj*
~ **out** hacer[19] salir; (shout) gritar
~ **to (someone)** llamar a (uno); ~ **to account** llamar a cuentas; ~ **to arms** (call up) llamar al servicio (militar), *fam* llamar a la mili; (sound the alarm) tocar[4] la alarma; ~ **to the bar** recibir de abogado; ~ **to mind** recordar (ue)[1a]; ~ **to order** llamar al orden; ~ **to witness** tomar por testigo
~ **together** convocar[4]; reunir
~-**up** *n* llamamiento (al servicio militar)
~ **up** *v* llamar al servicio (militar); (summon) recordar (ue)[1a]; (on telephone) llamar por teléfono
caller visita *m+f*; (in bingo hall) locutor *m* (-ora *f*)
calligraphy caligrafía
calling vocación (-ones) *f*; ~-**card** tarjeta de visita
callipers calibrador *m*
callous insensible
callousness insensibilidad *f*
callus callo
calm *n* calma; *adj* tranquilo; *v* calmar; ~

down tranquilizarse[7]; (weather) calmarse

calmness tranquilidad *f*

calorie caloría

calorific calorífico

calumniate calumniar

calumnious calumnioso

calumny calumnia

Calvary Calvario

calve parir

Calvin Calvino

Calvinism calvinismo

Calvinist calvinista *m+f*

calypso calipso

cam *mech* leva; **~-shaft** eje *m* de levas

camaraderie camaradería

camber comba

Cambodia Camboya

Cambodian *n+adj* camboyano

cambric batista

camel camello; **~('s) hair** *adj* de pelo de camello

camellia camelia

cameo camafeo

camera máquina (fotográfica); *TV* cámara; **in ~** *leg* a puerta cerrada; **~-man** operador cinematográfico, cámara

Cameroons Camerún *m sing*

Camille Camila

camomile camomila; **~ tea** manzanilla

camouflage *n* camuflaje *m*; *v* camuflar

[1] **camp** *n* campamento; **(holiday ~)** colonia; **(~-site)** camping *m*; **~-bed** camilla de tijera; **~-fire** hoguera de campaña; **~-follower** acompañante *m* civil, (woman) mujer *f* de la tropa; **~-site** (terreno de) camping *m*; **~-stool** catrecillo; *v* acampar, hacer[19] camping

[2] **camp** *sl* camp *invar*; **~ around** fanfarronear

campaign *n* *mil+pol* campaña; *v* *pol* hacer[19] campaña

campaigner *mil* veterano; *pol* propagandista *m+f*

campanologist campanólogo

campanology campanología

camper campista *m+f*; (at a holiday camp) colono; (*US* caravan) coche *m* vivienda (coches vivienda)

camphor alcanfor *m*

camphorated alcanforado

camping camping *m*; **Camping Gaz** *tr*

butagás *m*

campus recinto de universidad/escuela

[1] **can** *n* lata; *fam* (gaol) jaula; **~-opener** abrelatas *m sing*; *v* enlatar

[2] **can (be able to)** poder[19]

Canada el Canadá

Canadian *n+adj* canadiense *m+f*

canal canal *m*; (irrigation) acequia

canalize canalizar[7]

canary canario; **~-breeder** canaricultor *m* (-ora *f*); **~-seed** alpiste *m*

Canary Islands Islas *fpl* Canarias

cancan cancán *m*

cancel (debt, booking) cancelar; *math* suprimir; (stamps) poner[19] matasellos

cancellation cancelación (-ones) *f*; *math* supresión *f* (de factores comunes); (stamps) obliteración *f*, franqueo

cancer cáncer *m*; **Tropic of Cancer** Trópico de Cáncer

cancerous canceroso

candelabra candelabro

candid cándido

candidate candidato; (in competitive examination) opositor *m* (-ora *f*)

candidature, candidacy candidatura

candied: **~ peel** cáscara de naranja almibarada

candle vela; (large) cirio; **it's not worth the ~** no vale la pena; **~-grease** sebo; **~-light** luz *f* de una vela; **~-power** bujía; **~-stick** palmatoria; **~-wick** pabilo

candour candor *m*

candy caramelos *mpl*; *SA* bombón (-ones) *m*; **~-box** bombonera, confitera; **~-floss** algodón azucarado; **~-store** confitería

cane *n* caña; (stick) bastón (-ones) *m*; (material) mimbre *m*; **~-bottomed chair** silla con asiento de mimbre; **~-sugar** azúcar *m* de caña; *v* bastonear

canine canino; **~ tooth** colmillo

caning apaleamiento

canister bote *m*

canker *med* úlcera maligna; *bot* cancro

cannabis cáñamo

canned en conserva; **~ goods** conservas *fpl*; **~ music** música enlatada grabada; (drunk) achispado; **get ~** coger[8] una trompa

cannelloni canelones *mpl*

cannery fábrica de conservas

cannibal caníbal *m+f*

cannibalism canibalismo

cannibalization empleo de piezas de un avión/coche averiado para reparar otro

cannibalize aprovechar piezas de un avión/coche averiado para reparar otro

canning *adj* conservero; ~ **factory** fábrica conservera

cannon cañón (-ones) *m*; (billiards) *n* carambola; ~-**ball** bala de cañón; ~-**fodder** carne *f* de cañón; *v* (billiards) hacer[19] carambola

cannonade *n* cañoneo; *v* cañonear

canny sagaz (-ces), astuto

canoe *n* piragua; *v* pasear en piragua

canoeist piragüista *m*+*f*

canon *eccles* canónigo; (rule + *mus*) canon *m*; ~ **law** derecho canónico

canonical canónico; ~s vestiduras

canonize canonizar[7]

canonry canonjía

canoodle besuquearse

canopy dosel *m*; *SA* (over door) marquesina; (awning) toldo, palio; ~ **of heaven** bóveda celeste

cant hipocresía; (slang) jerga; (slope) inclinación (-ones) *f*

cantankerous avinagrado

cantata cantata

canteen (dining-room) cantina; (water-vessel) cantimplora; ~ **of cutlery** juego de cubiertos

canter *n* medio galope; *v* ir[19] a medio galope

Canterbury Cantorbery *m*

canticle cántico

cantilever *n* viga voladiza; *adj* voladizo; ~ **bridge** puente *m* de contrapeso

canto canto

canton *n* cantón (-ones) *m*

cantonment acantonamiento

cantor *eccles* chantre *m*; (Jewish) cantor *m*

Canute Canuto

canvas lona; *arts* lienzo; *naut* vela; **under** ~ *mil* en tienda, *naut* con las velas izadas

canvass *n* solicitación *f* de votos/pedidos; *v* solicitar votos; buscar[4] pedidos

canvasser solicitador *m* (-ora *f*) de votos; *comm* agente *m* de pedidos

canvassing *see* **canvass**; ~ **trip** viaje *m* en

busca de pedidos/votos

canyon cañón (-ones) *m*

cap (dress) gorro, gorra; (peaked ~) visera; (of fountain pen *etc*) capuchón (-ones) *m*; (of bottle) cápsula, *fam* chapa; (percussion) fulminante *m*; ~ **and bells** gorro de campanillas; ~ **and gown** toga y bonete; **put on one's thinking** ~ reflexionar; **that** ~s **everything** eso es el colmo

capability capacidad *f*

capable capaz (-ces)

capacious extenso

capacity (ability) aptitud *f*; (contents) capacidad *f*; (status) calidad *f*; ~ **load** carga máxima; **in the** ~ **of** en calidad de; **in a private** ~ a título particular

cape *geog* cabo; (dress) capa

Cape Horn Cabo de Hornos

Cape of Good Hope Cabo de Buena Esperanza

Cape Town ciudad del Cabo

Cape Wrath el Cabo de las Tormentas

caper *n* (leap) cabriola; (prank) travesura; *v* (leap) cabriolar; (perform pranks) hacer[19] travesuras

capillary *n* vaso capilar; *adj* capilar

capital *archi* capitel *m*; *econ* capital *m*; (city) capital *f*; ~ ! ¡estupendo!; **make** ~ **out of** sacar[4] beneficio de; ~ **equipment** equipo-capital; ~ **expenditure** inversión *f* de capital; ~ **gains** ganancias *fpl* de capital; ~ **gains tax** plusvalía; ~ **goods** bienes *mpl* de capital; ~ **letter** mayúscula; ~ **levy** impuesto sobre la propiedad; **love with a** ~ **L** amor *m* con mayúscula; ~ **punishment** pena de muerte; ~ **reserves** reservas *fpl* de capital; ~ **ship** acorazado; ~ **turnover** giro/movimiento de capital; **working** ~ capital activo

capitalism capitalismo

capitalist *n* +*adj* capitalista *m*+*f*

capitalization capitalización *f*

capitalize capitalizar[7]; ~ **on** aprovecharse de

capitulate capitular

capitulation capitulación *f*

capon capón (-ones) *m*

capped: be ~ *sp* (play for one's country) vestir (i)[3] la camiseta nacional

caprice capricho

capricious caprichoso
Capricorn: Tropic of ~ Trópico de Capricornio
capsize zozobrar
capstan cabrestante *m*
capsule cápsula; *space* cofia
captain *n* capitán (-anes) *m*; ~ **of industry** gran industrial *m*; *v* capitanear
captaincy capitanía
caption título; *cin* subtítulo
captious capcioso
captivate encantar, cautivar
captivating encantador
captive *n*+*adj* cautivo *f*
captivity cautividad *f*
captor apresador *m* (-ora *f*)
capture *n* (of a person) captura; (of a town) toma; (thing captured) botín *m*; (person captured) presa; *v* apresar, tomar; ~ **attention** captar la atención
capuchin (monje) capuchino, (monja) capuchina
car coche *m*; *SA* carro; *SA* (of elevator) caja; ~-**ferry** transbordador *m* de vehículos; ~**load** coche lleno (**of** de); ~-**park** aparcamiento; ~-**port** cobertizo (para automóviles); ~-**rental** alquiler *m* de coches; ~-**wash** lavacoches *m sing*+*pl*; ~-**worker** obrero de la industria automovilística
carabineer carabinero
carafe garrafa
caramel caramelo; ~ **chocolate** bombón (-ones) *m* de caramelo; ~ **custard** flan *m*
carat quilate *m*; **nine**-~ **gold** oro de nueve quilates
caravan (convoy of vehicles *etc*) caravana; (trailer) coche-vivienda *m*
caravanette pequeño coche-vivienda, roulotte *f*
caraway alcaravea; ~-**seed** carvi *m*
carbide carburo
carbine carabina
carbohydrate hidrato de carbono
carbolic fénico; ~ **acid** ácido fénico
carbon carbono; ~-**14 test(ing)** prueba del carbono 14; (in car engine) carbonilla; ~-**copy** copia en papel carbón; ~-**paper** papel *m* carbón; ~ **dioxide** dióxido de carbono; ~ **monoxide** monóxido de carbono; ~ **steel** acero ordinario
carboniferous carbonífero

carbonization carbonización *f*
carbuncle *med* carbunco; *geol* carbúnculo
carburettor carburador *m*
carcass (animal) res muerta; (for food) canal *m*; (bird) caparazón (-ones) *m*
carcerogenous carcerógeno
card (cardboard) cartón *m*; (thin) cartulina; (playing) carta, naipe *m*; (index) ficha; (postcard) postal *f*; **it's on the** ~**s that** es probable que +*subj*; **I'm going to put my** ~**s on the table** voy a poner mis cartas en el tapete; **play** ~**s** jugar (ue)[1a] a los naipes; ~**board** cartón *m*; ~-**case** tarjetero; ~-**catalogue**, ~-**index** fichero; ~-**game** juego de naipes; ~-**party** tertulia de cartas; ~-**sharper** tahur *m*; ~-**table** mesa de juego; ~-**trick** juego de manos empleando naipes; ~ **vote** voto ponderado; **visiting**-~ tarjeta de visita
cardiac cardíaco
cardigan chaqueta de punto; *fam* rebeca
[1] **cardinal** *adj* cardinal; ~ **number** número cardinal; ~ **point** punto cardinal
[2] **cardinal** *eccles* cardenal *m*
cardiograph cardiógrafo
cardiology cardiología
care *n* (anxiety) ansiedad *f*; (attention) esmero; (carefulness) cuidado; ~ **of** (address c/o) suplicado en casa de; (**in the**) ~ **of** al cuidado de; **he is under my** ~ él está a mi cargo; **take** ~! ¡cuidado!; **take** ~ **of** cuidar de, encargarse[5] de; **take** ~ **of o.s.** cuidarse; **take** ~ **not to** guardarse de, tener cuidado de no ...+*inf*; **without a** ~ sin cuidado; *v* (be concerned) importar; **I don't** ~ no me importa; **I don't** ~ **to** ... no tengo ganas de ... +*infin*; **I couldn't** ~ **less** igual me da; ~-**free** libre de cuidados; ~-**taker** conserje *m*; ~**taker government** gobierno en funciones; ~-**worn** agobiado
career *n* carrera; *adj* (professional) de carrera; *v* correr a toda velocidad
careful cuidadoso; (**be**) ~! ¡cuidado!
careless descuidado; **be** ~ descuidar
carelessness descuido
caress *n* caricia; *v* acariciar
caressing cariños *mpl*
cargo carga(mento); ~ **boat** barco de

carga; ~ **rates** *comm* tipos de flete; ~ **ship** carguero

Caribbean Caribe; ~ **Sea** mar *m* Caribe

caricature *n* caricatura; *v* caricaturizar[7]

caricaturist caricaturista *m+f*

caries caries *f sing+pl*

carillon carillón (-ones) *m*

Carlist *n* carlista *m+f*; *adj* carlista

Carmelite carmelita *m+f*; ~ **Order** Orden *f* del Carmen

carmine carmín *m*

carnage matanza

carnal carnal

carnation clavel *m*; *adj* (colour) encarnado

carnival *n* carnaval *m*; *US* feria; *adj* carnavalesco

carnivorous carnívoro

carol *n* villancico; *v* cantar alegremente; (of birds) gorjear

Caroline Carolina

carousal juerga

carouse hacer[19] una juerga

carp *n* carpa; *v* criticar[4]

Carpathian Mountains montes Cárpatos *mpl*

carpenter carpintero

carpentry, carpenter's shop carpintería

carpet *n* alfombra; **be on the ~** *fig* estar[19] sobre el tapete; ~**-bag** bolsa de viaje; ~**-slipper** zapatilla, pantufla; ~**-sweeper** limpialfombras *m sing+pl*; *v* alfombrar

carpeting alfombrado

carping caviloso

carriage coche *m*; (ceremonial) carroza; (railway) vagón (-ones) *m*; (pram) cochecito (de niño); *aer* tren *m* de aterrizaje; (transport) (trans)porte *m*; (bearing) presencia; (typewriter) carro; ~ **free** *comm* franco de porte; ~ **paid** porte pagado; ~**way** firme *m*

carrier (transporter) transportador *m*; (person) transportista *m+f*; (pannier) alforja; (on bicycle) portaequipajes *m sing+pl*; *med* portador *m*; *aer* portaviones *m sing+pl*; ~**-bag** bolsa; ~**-pigeon** paloma mensajera

carrion carroña; ~ **crow** corneja

carrot zanahoria

carroty (hair) pelirrojo

carry llevar; transportar; (have in stock) tener[19] surtido de; *math* llevar(sc); ~ **conviction** ser[19] convincente; ~ **the**

day llevarse la palma; ~ **insurance** *comm* estar[19] asegurado; ~ **a motion** aceptar una propuesta; ~ **a stock** mantener[19] existencias; ~ **weight** ser[19] de peso; **his name carries weight** su nombre pesa; ~ **with it** (results) llevar consigo; **he carried the meeting** conquistó a la junta; ~**-cot** moisés *m sing*

~ **away** llevarse; *fig* encantar; **be carried away** *fig* perder (ie)[2b] los estribos

~ **forward** *comm* pasar a otra hoja; **carried forward** suma y sigue

~ **off** llevarse

~ **on** (continue) seguir (i)[3+11]; **she's likely to ~ on for some time** ella tiene cuerda para rato; (behave badly) hacer[19] travesuras; ~ **on a business** llevar un negocio; ~ **on a conversation** charlar; ~ **on negotiations** negociar; ~ **on with** continuar con; **he is carrying on with her** él tiene relaciones con ella

~ **out** (a plan) llevar a cabo

~ **with one** llevar con uno; **I never ~ it with me** nunca no llevo conmigo; **the consumption of drugs carries with it grave problems** el consumo de drogas acarrea problemas graves

carryings-on conducta frívola

cart *n* (four-wheeled) carro; (two-wheeled) carreta; (trolley) carretilla; ~**-horse** caballo de tiro; ~**load** carretada; ~**-track** rodada; ~**-wheel** rueda de carro, (gymnastics) voltereta de lado; *v* acarrear; ~**wright** carretero

cartage porte *m*

carte blanche carta blanca

cartel cartel *m*

carter carretero

Carthage Cartago

Carthaginian cartaginés (-esa *f*)

Carthusian cartujo; ~ **Order** Cartuja

cartilage cartílago

cartographer cartógrafo

cartography cartógrafo

carton (caja de) cartón *m*; ~ **of milk** brik *m* de leche

cartoon caricatura; *cin* película de dibujos animados; (comic strip) historieta muda

cartoonist caricaturista *m+f*

cartridge cartucho; ~**-belt** *Sp* cartuchera, *SA* canana; ~**-case** cápsula de cartucho; ~**-paper** papel *m* de dibujar

carve (wood) tallar; (stone) esculpir; (engrave) grabar; (meat) trinchar

carving escultura; talla; (ceiling) artesonado *m*; ~**-fork** tenedor *m* de trinchar; ~**-knife** cuchillo de trinchar

caryatid cariátide *f*

Casanova Don Juan *m*

cascade cascada

case *m* (box) caja; (small box) estuche *m*; (container) funda; (suitcase) maleta; ~**load** número total de pacientes/clientes; **pillow-~** funda de almohada; (sheath) vaina; (circumstance) caso; *leg* pleito; *gramm+med* caso; ~ **in point** caso en cuestión; **in** ~ por si acaso; **in any** ~ en todo caso; **in that** ~ entonces; **in the** ~ **of** en cuanto a; **such being the** ~ siendo así; *v* (study the scene of a planned robbery *etc*) reconocer el terreno

casement (window) ventana batiente; (part of window) marco (de ventana)

cash *n* (money) metálico; (means of payment) al contado; ~ **advance** anticipo; ~ **balance** saldo en efectivo; ~**book** libro de caja; ~**-box** caja; ~ **carrier** (in shop) conductora mecánica de dinero; ~ **in hand** efectivo en caja; ~ **on delivery** entrega contra reembolso; ~ **payment** pago al contado; ~ **purchase** compra al contado; ~**-register** caja registradora; ~ **sale** venta al contado; ~ **value** valor efectivo; **in** ~ en metálico; **pay** ~ **(down)** pagar[5] al contado; **petty-~** gastos menores de caja; **ready** ~ dinero contante; *v* hacer[19] efectivo; **I must** ~ **a cheque** tengo que cobrar/cambiar un cheque; **will you** ~ **this cheque?** ¿quiere usted cambiarme este cheque?; ~ **in on** sacar[4] provecho de

cashew(-nut) anacardo

cashier *n* cajero, cajera; ~**'s desk** caja; *v* *mil* degradar

Cashmere Cachemira

cashmere cachemir *m*

casing cubierta; *mech* camisa

casino casino

cask barril *m*; (wine) pipa

casket (for valuables) estuche *m*; (*US* coffin) ataúd *m*

Caspian Sea mar Caspio

Cassandra Casandra

casserole (dish) cacerola; (food) cazuela

cassette cassette *f*; ~ **tape-recorder** magnetófono de cassette

cassock sotana

cast *n* (throw) lanzamiento; (fishing) echada; (mould) molde *m*; *theat* reparto; (of the eye) ligero estrabismo; *adj* fundido; ~ **iron** *n* hierro fundido, *adj* de hierro fundido; **a ~-iron alibi** una coartada férrea; *v* (throw) lanzar[7]; (fishing) echar el anzuelo; *theat* repartir los papeles; *metal* fundir; (light) difundir; ~ **anchor** dar[19] fondo; ~ **a glance at** echar una ojeada a; ~ **lots for** echar suertes para; ~ **a skin** mudar la piel; ~ **a vote for** dar[19] un voto por; ~ **pearls before swine** echar margaritas a los puercos

~ **about for** buscar[4]

~ **aside** desechar

~**-down** *adj* abatido

~ **down** *v* abatir; bajar

~**-off:** ~**-off clothes** ropa desechada

~ **off** *v* (throw away) tirar; (knitting) dejar; *naut* desamarrar

~ **on** (knitting) echar

~ **out: be** ~ **out** ser[19] despedido, *fam* puesto de patitas en la calle

~ **up** (vomit) vomitar

castanets castañuelas *fpl*

castaway náufrago

caste casta; **lose** ~ desprestigiarse

caster: ~ **sugar** azúcar fina

castigate castigar[5]

Castile Castilla

Castilian castellano

casting *metal* (operation) fundición *f*; (result) pieza fundida; ~ **vote** voto de calidad

castle *n* castillo; ~**s in Spain** castillos en el aire; (chess) roque *m*; *v* enrocar[4]

castor (furniture) ruedecita; ~ **oil** aceite *m* de ricino; ~ **sugar** azúcar fina

castrate castrar

castration castración *f*

casual casual; (off-hand) despreocupado; ~ **payment** pago accidental; ~ **ward** asilo de pobres; ~ **wear** ropa informal; ~ **work** trabajo eventual

casually distraídamente; casualmente ~ **dressed** vestido de sport; **he answered quite** ~ él contestó sin darle importancia

casuals (shoes) zapatos cómodos; (garments) ropa cómoda

casualty (occurrence) accidente *m*; (victim) víctima; *mil* baja; ~-**list** lista de bajas

casuistry casuística

cat gato; *fig* mujer maliciosa; (jazz player) jacista *m*+*f*; (cat-o'-nine-tails) azote *m* de nueve colas; ~'s **eyes** pequeños reflectores al margen de una carretera; ~'s **whiskers** *rad* detector *m*; **let the** ~ **out of the bag** revelar un secreto; **it's raining** ~s **and dogs** está lloviendo a cántaros; ~-**burglar** gato; ~**call** grito; ~**fish** siluro; ~**gut** cuerda de tripa, *surg* catgut *m*; ~-**nap** sueñecito; ~'s-**paw** testaferro; ~**walk** pasarela

cataclysm cataclismo

catacombs catacumbas *fpl*

Catalan, Catalonian *n*+*adj* catalán (-anes) *m* (-ana *f*)

catalogue *n* catálogo; *v* catalogar[5]

Catalonia Cataluña, Catalunya

catalyst catalizador *m*

catamaran catamarán (-anes) *m*

catapult *n* catapulta; (toy) tiragomas *m* *sing*+*pl*; *v* catapultar

cataract catarata

catarrh catarro

catastrophe catástrofe *f*

catastrophic catastrófico

catch *n* (of a door) pestillo; (fishing) pesca; *mech* enganche *m*; (trick) trampa; *sp* cogida de la pelota en vuelo, (for marriage) buen partido; ~ **question** pega; ~ **crop** siembra intermedia; *v* coger[8], *Arg* tomar; (take hold of) agarrar; (trap) atrapar; (fish) pescar[4]; (understand) comprender; (disease *etc*) contagiarse de, *fam* coger[8]; (for marriage) pescar[4]; ~ **a chill** resfriarse; ~ **cold** (in the head) constiparse, (*usu* on chest) coger[8] un catarro; ~ **fire** encenderse (ic)[2b]; ~ **a glimpse of/sight of** alcanzar[7] a ver; ~ **s.o.** sorprender a alguien +*pres part*; **they caught the girl leaving without permission** sorprendieron a la muchacha saliendo sin permiso; ~ **s.o.'s eye** atraer[19] la atención de alguien; **you'll** ~ **it** *fam* ¡vas a cobrar!; ~ **the train** coger[8] el tren; **I've been caught like that before** ese truco (me) lo sé de memoria; ~**penny** baratija; ~**word**

lema, *theat* pie *m*

~ **on** (fashion) ponerse[19] de moda; (understand) caer[19] (en la cuenta)

~ **out** (deceive) engañar

~ **up with** alcanzar[7]; ~ **up with one's work** ponerse al día

catcher cogedor *m* (-ora *f*); (baseball) receptor *m*

catching *med* contagioso; *fam* pegadizo; (attractive) cautivador

catchment: ~ **area** zona de captación

catchy *mus* (easily remembered) pegadizo; (easy to sing) tarareable; (of question) capcioso

catechism catecismo

categorical categórico

categorize clasificar[4]

category categoría

catenary catenaria

cater proveer[17]; ~ **to s.o.'s tastes** complacer[14] a uno en sus gustos

caterer proveedor *m* (-ora *f*)

catering abastecimiento de alimento

caterpillar oruga; ~ **tractor** tractor *m* oruga (tractores oruga)

caterwaul maullar

caterwauling maullido

catharsis catarsis *f*

cathartic catártico

cathedral catedral *f*

Catherine Catalina; ~-**wheel** rueda de fuegos artificiales

catheter *med* sonda

cathode cátodo; ~ **ray** rayo catódico

catholic *adj*, **Catholic** *n*+*adj* católico

Catholicism catolicismo

catkin amento

Cato Catón

cattiness malicia

cattle ganado (vacuno); ~-**man,** ~-**dealer** ganadero; ~-**grid** reja en la carretera para no dejar pasar animales; ~-**raising** ganadería; ~-**ranch** ganadería; ~-**show** feria de ganado; ~-**thief** cuatrero; ~-**truck** vagón (-ones) *m* de ganado

catty malicioso y chismoso

Caucasian caucásico; (*US* white-skinned) blanco

Caucasus Cáucaso

caucus junta (de un partido)

caul redecilla; *anat* membrana

cauldron caldera

cauliflower coliflor *f*; ~-**ears** orejas abo-

lladas
caulk calafatear
causal causal
causality causalidad *f*
causative causativo
cause *n* causa; *v* causar; hacer[19]; ~ **havoc** hacer[19] estragos
causeway calzada; (at sea) arrecife *m*
caustic cáustico; ~ **soda** sosa cáustica
cauterize cauterizar[7]
caution *n* (care) cautela, cuidado; (warning) advertencia; *v* avisar
cautionary preventivo
cautious cauto, cauteloso
cavalcade cabalgata
cavalier *n* galán (-anes) *m*; *adj* altivo
cavalry caballería; ~**man** soldado de caballería
cave *n* cueva; ~**-man** troglodita *m+f*; ~**-in** *n* derrumbe *m*; *v* ~ **in** hundirse
caveat escrito en que se ruega el aplazamiento de un proceso
cavern caverna
cavernous cavernoso
caviare caviar *m*
cavil cavilar
cavity cavidad *f*; (in tooth) picadura; **there is a** ~ **in my tooth** tengo un diente picado/una muela picada
cavort corvetear; *fig* cabriolar
caw graznar
cayenne: ~ **pepper** cayena
cayman caimán (-anes) *m*
cease dejar de +*infin*; ~**-fire** *n* alto del fuego, *v* suspender el fuego; ~ **fire!** ¡alto el fuego!
ceaseless incesante
cedar cedro
cede ceder
cedilla cedilla
ceiling techo; *fig* límite *m*; *aer* techo; ~ **price** precio máximo
celebrant celebrante *m*
celebrate *v* celebrar; *fam* ir[19] de parranda; ~ **High Mass** cantar misa; ~ **Low Mass** decir[19] misa
celebrated célebre
celebration celebración (-ones) *f*; *fam* juerga
celebrity (quality) celebridad *f*; (person) persona célebre
celerity celeridad *f*
celery apio
celestial celeste; ~ **guidance/mechanics**

space navegación/mecánica celeste
celibacy celibato
celibate célibe, soltero
cell (prison) celda; *biol+pol* célula; *elect* elemento de una pila
cellar sótano; (for wine) bodega
cellarage almacenaje *m* en una bodega
cellist violoncelista *m+f*
cello violoncelo
cellophane celofán *m*
cellular celular; ~ **vest/sock** camiseta/calcetín (-ines) *m* transpirable
celluloid celuloide *m*
cellulose *n* celulosa; *adj* celular
Celt celta *m+f*; ~**iberian** *n+adj* celtíbero, celtibérico
Celtic céltico; (language) celta *m*
cement *n* cemento; ~**-mixer** hormigonera; *v* revestir (i)[3] con cemento; (stick) pegar[5]; *fig* cimentar; ~ **a friendship** consolidar una amistad
cemetery cementerio
cenotaph cenotafio
censer incensario
censor *n* censor *m*; *v* censurar; **this letter has been** ~**ed** esta carta ha sido cortada por la censura
censorious severo
censorship censura
censurable censurable
censure *n* censura; *v* censurar
census censo; **to take the** ~ levantar el censo
cent céntimo; *SA* centavo
centaur centauro
centenarian centenario
centenary centenario
centennial *n+adj* centenario
centigrade centígrado
centigramme centigramo
centilitre centilitro
centimetre centímetro
centipede ciempiés *m sing+pl*
central central; ~ **heating** calefacción *f* central; ~ **reservation** faja mediana; **Central America** Centroamérica; **Central American** *n+adj* centroamericano
centrality posición *f* central
centralization centralización *f*
centralize centralizar[7]
centre *n* centro; ~ **parting** (hair) raya en medio; ~ **of gravity** centro de gravedad; **she likes to be the** ~ **of at-**

traction a ella le gusta figurar; ~-
forward *sp* delantero centro; ~-half
sp medio centro; ~-line (rugby) línea
de centro; ~piece centro de mesa; ~-
punch punzón (-ones) *m* de marcar;
adj central; *v* colocar[4] en el centro; *sp*
centrar; ~ on, around girar en torno a

centrifugal centrífugo; ~ force fuerza
centrífuga

centripetal centrípeto

century siglo

ceramics cerámica

Cerberus Cerbero

cereal *n* + *adj* cereal *m*

cerebral cerebral

ceremonial *n* + *adj* ceremonial *m*

ceremonious ceremonioso; *SA* etiquetero

ceremony ceremonia; (polite behaviour) formalidad *f*; **don't stand on** ~!
¡no gaste cumplimientos!, *SA* ¡no sea
etiquetero!

cerise color *m* de cereza

certain cierto; **for** ~ por cierto; **our
victory is** ~ nuestra victoria está
segura; **you may be** ~ **that** usted
puede estar seguro de que; **to a** ~ **degree** hasta cierto punto; **they will meet
at a** ~ **time** se encontrarán a una hora
determinada; **a** ~ **Mr Smith** un tal Sr
Smith; **his aim is** ~ su puntería es
certera; **it is** ~ **that** es cierto que
+ *indic*; **make** ~ asegurar

certainly por cierto; **she** ~ **is pretty!**
¡cuidado que es bonita!; *interj* con
mucho gusto; ~ **not!** ¡de ninguna manera!

certainty certeza; **with** ~ a ciencia cierta

certificate certificado; (of birth *etc*)
partida; *leg* título

certificated certificado

certified (mad) excluido; ~ **public accountant** *US* contable diplomado

certify certificar[4]

certitude certidumbre *f*

cervical cervical

cervix cerviz (-ces) *f*

cessation cese *m*; ~ **of hostilities** suspensión *f* de hostilidades

cession cesión *f*

cesspool pozo negro (de letrina)

Cévennes Cevenes *mpl*

Ceylon Ceilán *m*

Ceylonese *n* + *adj* ceilanés *m* (-esa *f*)

C.F.I. (Cost, Freight and Insurance) csf
(coste, seguro y flete)

chafe rozar[7]; *fig* irritar

chaff *n* arista; (banter) burla; *v* burlarse
de

chaffinch pinzón (-ones) *m*

chafing rozadura

chagrin mortificación *f*

chain *n* cadena; ~ **of mountains** cordillera; ~ **of office** cadena; ~ **of super-
markets** cadena de supermercados;
~-armour/mail cota de malla; ~-drive
transmisión *f* por cadena; ~-gang
cuerda de presos; ~-letter carta de
cadena; ~-reaction reacción (-ones) *f*
en cadena, *fig* reacción progresiva;
~-smoke fumar un pitillo tras otro;
~-smoker fumador *m* (-ora *f*) de un
pitillo tras otro; ~-stitch punto de cadeneta; ~-store tienda de una cadena;
v encadenar

chair *n* silla; (academic) cátedra; (at
meeting) sillón *m* del presidente;
(chairman) presidente; ~-cover funda
de sillón; ~-lift telesilla; *v* (take the
~) presidir; **he** ~**ed the meeting** él presidió la reunión

chairman presidente *m*; *TV* (of discussion programme) moderador *m*

chairmanship presidencia; **under the** ~
of bajo la presidencia de

chairwoman presidenta

chaise-longue tumbona

Chaldea Caldea

chalet chalet *m*; chalé *m*

chalice cáliz (-ces) *m*

chalk (rock) roca cretácea; (blackboard) tiza; (tailor's) jaboncillo; **be
unable to tell** ~ **from cheese** confundir
el tocino con la velocidad; ~-pit cantera de yeso; *v* marcar[4]/escribir (*past
part* escrito) con tiza; ~ **up** *sp* marcar[4]
(un tanto)

chalky cretáceo

challenge *n* desafío; *mil* quién vive *m*; *v*
desafiar; *mil* dar[19] el quién vive

chamber cámara; *mech* depósito; (of
firearm) cámara; ~s despacho de
abogado/juez; ~ **of commerce** cámara
de comercio; ~ **of horrors** galería de
terror (en el Museo de Cera); **Chamber of Deputies** cámara de diputados,
Sp Cortes *fpl*; ~-maid camarera; ~-
music música de cámara; ~-pot

orinal *m*

chamberlain chamberlán (-anes) *m*

chameleon camaleón (-ones) *m*

chamois gamuza; ∼**-leather** piel *f* de gamuza

champ *v* mordisquear

champagne champán (-anes) *m*; cava *m*

champion *n* campeón (-ones) *m* (-ona *f*); *v* abogar[5] por

championship campeonato

chance *n* azar *m*; (prospect) oportunidad *f*; **by** ∼ por casualidad, *fam* de chiripa; **take a** ∼ aventurarse; **there is no** ∼ no hay posibilidad; **wait for a** ∼ esperar la oportunidad; *adj* casual; ∼ **bargain** compra de ocasión; ∼ **meeting** encuentro imprevisto; *vt* arriesgar; *vi* suceder; **I** ∼**d to see her** la vi por casualidad; ∼ **upon** tropezar (ie)[2a+7]con

chancel (entre)coro; ∼**-arch** arco del altar

chancellery cancillería

chancellor canciller *m*; (university) rector *m*; **Chancellor of the Exchequer** Ministro de Hacienda

chancery cancillería; **in** ∼ en litigio

chancy incierto

chandelier candelabro, *fam* araña

chandler proveedor *m* de granos; **ships'** ∼ chiplichandle *m*

change *n* cambio *m*; (of clothes) muda; (money) (dinero) suelto; (money returned after payment) vuelta; (alteration) alteración (-ones) *f*; (something new) novedad *f*; (transformation) transformación *f*; **for the better** mejoría; ∼ **for the worse** empeoramiento; ∼ **of heart** cambio de opinión; ∼ **of life** retirada; ∼ **of scene** *theat* mutación *f*; ∼ **of voice** muda de voz; **for a** ∼ para variar; **keep the** ∼! ¡quédese con la vuelta!; *v* cambiar; (alter) alterar; ∼ **the bed-linen** hacer[19] el aseo de la cama; ∼ **clothes** (completely) mudarse la ropa, (outer garments) cambiarse; ∼ **colour** cambiar de color; ∼ **gear** *mot* cambiar la marcha; ∼ **hands, owners** cambiar de dueño; ∼ **money** cambiar dinero; ∼ **one's mind** cambiar de opinión; ∼ **one's tune** cambiar de actitud; ∼ **places** cambiar de sitio; ∼ **position** cambiar de postura; ∼ **round the**

furniture cambiar de sitio los muebles; ∼ **sides** *pol fam* chaquetear; ∼ **the subject** desviar la conversación; ∼ **trains** cambiar de tren; ∼**-over** cambio completo; ∼**-purse** *US* monedero

changeability mutabilidad *f*

changeable variable; (person) veleidoso

changeless inmutable

changeling niño cambiado por otro

changing *n* cambio; ∼ **of the guard** relevo de la guardia; *adj* cambiante

channel *n* canal *m*; (of river) lecho; *rad*+*TV* cadena; **I prefer** ∼ **1** prefiero la primera cadena; (way of communication) vía; *v* canalizar[7]

chant *n* (song) canción (-ones) *f*; *eccles* canto llano; *v* cantar

chantry capilla

chaos caos *m sing*

chaotic caótico

chap pollastre *m*; *pej* tío, tipo

chapel capilla; (nonconformist) iglesia no conformista; ∼ **of ease** ayuda de parroquia

chaperon *n* señora de compañía; *fam* carabina; *v* acompañar

chaplain capellán (-anes) *m*; *mil* capellán castrense

chaplaincy capellanía

chapped agrietado

chaps (clothing) chaparreras *fpl*

[1] **chapter** capítulo; ∼ **and verse** con pelos y señales

[2] **chapter** *eccles* cabildo; ∼ **house** sala capitular

[1] **char** *m* (cleaner) fregatriz (-ices) *f*, *euph* asistenta; *v* hacer[19] las faenas domésticas

[2] **char** (burn) carbonizar[7]

[3] **char** *sl* (tea) té *m*

charabanc charabán (-anes) *m*

character *n* (disposition) carácter *m*; (person) personaje *m*; (odd person) tipo raro; (reference) testimonio (de conducta); (sign) letra; *theat* papel *m*; (in novel) personaje *m*; *adj* ∼**-actor** actor de carácter

characteristic *n* característica; *adj* característico

characterization caracterización (-ones) *f*

characterize caracterizar[7]

characterless sin carácter

charade charada

charcoal (fuel) carbón *m* de leña; *arts* carboncillo; **~-burner** (person) carbonero, (instrument) horno para hacer carbón de leña; **~-sketch** dibujo al carbón

charge *n* (responsibility) carga, cargo; (accusation) acusación (-ones) *f*; *elect* (+ explosive) carga; (fee) derechos *mpl*; (instruction) recomendación *f*; (price) precio; *mil* ataque *m*; *sp* acometida; (of wild animal) embestida; **~ account** cuenta abierta; *sl* empaquelar; **delivery ~(s)** gastos *mpl* de remisión; **free of ~** gratis; **be in ~ of** ser[19] encargado de/ responsable por; **is there any ~?** ¿hay que pagar algo?; **lay a ~** (accuse) acusar, (place explosives) poner[19] una carga; **in ~ of** a cargo de; **take ~ of** hacerse[19] cargo de; *v* (put in) cargar[5]; (accuse) acusar, *sl* empapelar; **they ~d him with stealing** le acusaron de robar; (ask a price) pedir (i)[3]; *fam* soplar, **they ~d me 100 pesetas** me soplaron 100 pesetas; (command) dar[19] órdenes; (urge) exhortar; *mil* atacar[4]; (of wild animal) embestir (i)[3]; **~ it (up) to my account** póngalo a mi cuenta; **they ~ too much in that shop** piden demasiado en aquella tienda; **~-hand** jefe *m* (de un grupo de obreros); **~-sheet** hoja de acusaciones

chargeable to a cargo de

chargé d'affaires encargado de negocios

charger (horse) caballo de guerra; corcel *m*; *elect* cargador *m*

chariness cautela

chariot carro (de dos ruedas)

charioteer auriga *m*

charitable caritativo; **~ deeds** obras caritativas; **~ society** asociación (-ones) *f* benéfica

charities obras *fpl* de caridad

charity (virtue) caridad *f*; (organization) asociación (-ones) *f* benéfica; (alms) limosna; **~ begins at home** la caridad empieza por uno mismo; **~ performance** función (-ones) *f* benéfica; **~-box** cepillo de los pobres

charlatan charlatán (-anes) *m*; *med* curandero

charlatanism charlatanismo

Charlemagne Carlomagno

Charles Carlos

Charlie Carlitos; (fool) idiota *m+f*; **~**

Chaplin Charlot

Charlotte Carlota

charlotte *cul* carlota

charm *n* (attraction) encanto; (spell) hechizo; (talisman) dije *m*; *v* encantar

charmer encantador *m* (-ora *f*); *fam* castigador *m* (-ora *f*)

charming encantador (-ora *f*); **very ~!** *iron* ¡muy galante!

charnel-house osario

chart *n* mapa *m*; *naut* carta de navegación; **~s** *mus* lista de popularidad; **in the ~s** clasificado; **it continues to move up the ~s** sigue escalando puestos en la lista; *v* trazar[7] el mapa; *comm* incluir[11] en el cuadro; **~ a course** trazar[7] una ruta

charter *n* carta constitucional/fuero; **~ of U.N.O.** carta de la O.N.U.; **~-flight** vuelo chárter; **~-party** *comm* contrato de fletamiento; **~-planes** aviones *mpl* chárter; *v naut* (+ bus) fletar; (train, plane) alquilar; **~ed accountant** contable diplomado

charterhouse cartuja

chartreuse licor *m* preparado por los cartujos

charwoman fregatriz (-ces) *f*

chary cauteloso

Charybdis Caribdis *f*

chase *n* (hunt) caza; (pursuit) persecución *f*; *v* perseguir (i)[3]; **~ away** ahuyentar

chased: ~ work piezas encajadas

chaser perseguidor *m*; (drink) (vaso de) cerveza después de una copita de whisky

chasing: ~ tool encajador *m*

chasm precipicio

chassis chasis *m sing+pl*

chaste honesto; (style) casto

chasten, chastise castigar[4]

chastening *n* corrección *f*; *adj* correccional

chastisement castigo

chastity castidad *f*; **~-belt** cinturón (-ones) *m* de castidad

chasuble casulla

chat *n* charla; *v* charlar; **~ up** (someone of opposite sex) ligar

chattels bienes muebles *mpl*

chatter *n* cotorreo; *fam* cháchara; *v* cotorrear; *fam* chacharear; (teeth) castañetear; (birds) chirriar; **~-box**

cotorrón *m* (-ona *f*), *fam* chacharón *m* (-ona *f*)

chattering *n* cotorreo; *adj* locuaz (-ces)

chatty familiar; *fam* charlatán (-ana *f*)

chauffeur chófer *m*

chauvinism chauvinismo

chauvinist chauvinista *m*+*f*

chauvinistic patriotero; antifeminista

cheap (inexpensive) barato; (bad) malo; (avaricious) tacaño; **feel ~** sentirse (i)[3] inferior; **hold ~** tener[19] en poco; **make o.s. ~** rebajarse; **~skate** tacaño; **~ trip** viaje *m* a precio reducido; **~jack** buhonero, *Arg fam* tudoavinte *m*; **dirt-~** baratísimo

cheapen abaratar; **~ o.s.** despreciarse

cheapness baratura; (flashiness) cursilería

cheat *n* (person) estafador *m* (-ora *f*); (action) engaño; *v* engañar; *sp* enfullar; **~ out of** privar por engaño de; **he ~ed me out of my inheritance** él me privó por engaño de mi herencia; (financial) estafar de

cheating engaño

[1] **check** *n* (chess) jaque *m*; **in ~** en jaque; **~mate** mate, *v* dar[19] mate a

[2] **check** *n* (bill) cuenta; (receipt) talón (-ones) *m*; (cheque) cheque *m*; (obstacle) obstáculo; (restraint) freno; (inspection) inspección (-ones) *f*; **~-point** punto de inspección/control; **~-room** guardarropa; *adj* (pattern) de cuadros; *v* (stop) contrarrestar; (verify) verificar[4] y marcar[4]

~ in inscribirse (*past part* inscrito)

~ off dar[19] visto bueno a

~-out *n* (exit) salida; (from self-service store) caja

~ out *v* pagar[5] la cuenta e irse[19]

~-up revisión *f*; *med* reconocimiento, *fam* chequeo

~ up *v* verificar[4]

checker inspector *m* (-ora *f*); (piece) dama; **play ~s** jugar (ue)[1a+5] a las damas

cheek *n anat* mejilla; (impertinence) descaro; **~ by jowl** cara a cara; **with one's tongue in one's ~** fingidamente; **~-bone** pómulo; *v* descararse

cheeky descarado

cheep piar

cheeping pío-pío *m*

cheer *n* (happiness) regocijo; (applause)

viva *m*; **~leader** líder *m* de hinchas; *v* (comfort) consolar; (applaud) aplaudir; **~ on** (a team) animar; **~ up** *vt* (re)animar, *vi* alegrarse; **~ up!** ¡ánimo!

cheerful alegre

cheerily alegremente

cheeriness alegría

cheering *n* ovaciones *mpl*; *adj* animador (-ora *f*)

cheerio! (farewell) ¡adiós y hasta la vista!

cheerless triste

cheers (applause) vivas *fpl*; (thanks) gracias; (toast) salud; **three ~ for ...!** ¡viva ...!

cheery alegre

cheese queso; **~-cloth** estopilla; **~-mite** ácaro de queso; **~-monger** quesero, quesera; **~-straw** canapé *m* de queso

cheesy caseoso

cheetah leopardo cazador

chef jefe *m* de cocina

chemical *n* substancia química; *adj* químico; **~ warfare** guerra química

chemin de fer juego parecido al bacará

chemise camisa de mujer

chemist químico; (pharmacist) farmacéutico; **~'s (shop)** farmacia

chemistry química

chenille felpilla

cheque cheque *m*; **bearer ~** cheque al portador; **blank ~** cheque en blanco; **~-book** talonario de cheques

chequered de cuadros; **~ career** vida accidentada

chequers (juego de) damas

cherish (love) querer[19]; (protect) abrigar[5]; **~ ill-will** guardar rencor; **~ a hope** abrigar[5] una esperanza

cheroot puro de Sumatra

cherry *n* cereza; **~-tree** cerezo; *adj* (hecho) de cereza; **~-brandy** aguardiente *m* de cerezas; **~-red** rojo cereza; **~-stone** hueso de cereza

cherub querubín *m*

chess ajedrez *m*; **~-board** tablero (de ajedrez); **~-man** pieza de ajedrez; **~-player** ajedrecista *m*+*f*; **~-set** ajedrez *m*; **~ tournament** torneo de ajedrez

chest (box) cajón (-ones) *m*; *anat* pecho; **~ of drawers** cómoda; **~ cold** catarro bronquial; **she has a ~ complaint** ella tiene algo pulmonar; **get it off one's ~**

desahogarse[5]

chesterfield tipo de sofá

chestnut n castaña; ~-**tree** castaño; (wood) madera de castaño; adj (colour) castaño

chevron sardineta

chew mas(ti)car[4]; (animals) rumiar; ~ **the cud**, ~ **over** +fig rumiar

chewing-gum chicle m

chiaroscuro claroscuro

chic elegante; 'chic'

chicanery tramposería

chick polluelo; (term of endearment) chica; **day-old** ~ pollito (de un día); ~**pea** garbanzo; ~**weed** álsine m

chickadee orni pavo americano; (endearment) cariño mío

chicken n pollo; ~ **broth** caldo de gallina; ~-**farm** granja avícola; ~-**feed** comida para gallinas; ~-**hearted** cobarde, fam gallina, vulg cagado; ~-**pox** viruelas fpl locas; v ~ **out** rajarse

chicory achicoria

chide reprender

chief n jefe m; (of tribe) cacique m; ~ **of state** jefe m de estado; adj principal; ~ **clerk** oficial m mayor; ~ **engineer** ingeniero jefe, naut jefe m de máquinas; ~ **justice** presidente m del tribunal supremo; ~ **mourner** (persona) que preside un entierro; ~ **of police** jefe m de policía; ~ **of staff** mil jefe m de estado mayor; ... **in** ~ ... en jefe

chieftain cacique m

chiffchaff orni mosquitero

chiffon gasa

chilblain sabañón (-ones) m

child niño, niña; (son) hijo; (daughter) hija; **with** ~ embarazada; ~ **care** puericultura; ~ **guidance** pediatría; ~ **guidance clinic** centro de pediatría; ~ **labour** trabajo de menores; ~**'s play** cosa fácil; ~ **welfare** protección f de la infancia; ~**bearing** maternidad f; **she is past** ~**bearing** ella ha pasado la edad de dar a luz; ~**birth** parto; ~**like** infantil

childhood niñez f; **since** ~ desde niño/niña

childish infantil; ~ **behaviour** niñada; ~ **thing** (done or spoken) niñería

childishness puerilidad f

childless sin hijos

Chile Chile m

Chilean chileno

chill n resfriado; **catch a** ~ resfriarse; **take the** ~ **off** entibiar; adj frío; v enfriar

chilli pimentón picante m, SA ají m; ~ **sauce** salsa de guindilla

chilliness frialdad f

chilly frío; ~ **reception** acogida fría

chime n repique m (de campanas); **clock-**~**s** juego de campanas; v repicar[4]; **the clock** ~**d three** el reloj dio las tres

chimera quimera

chiming: ~ **clock** reloj m de carillón

chimney (fireplace) chimenea; (outside) tubo (de chimenea); ~-**breast** campana de chimenea; ~-**corner** rincón m al lado de la chimenea; ~-**piece** manto de chimenea; ~-**pot** tubo de chimenea; ~-**stack** fuste m de chimenea; ~-**sweep(er)** deshollinador m

chimpanzee chimpancé m

chin barb(ill)a; ~-**strap** barboquejo; **keep one's** ~ **up** no desanimarse; **put a violin to one's** ~ encarar un violín

China China; ~**man** chino; ~**town** barrio chino

china porcelana; ~ **clay** kaolín m; ~ **cupboard,** ~ **cabinet** vitrina

chinchilla zool chinchilla; (fur) piel f de chinchilla

Chinese n (language) +adj chino

chink n (crack) grieta; resquicio; (sound) tintineo; v tintinear

chintz quimón m

chip (of wood) astilla; (of glass) pedacito; (of china) desconchado; cul patata frita, SA papa frita; elect microprocesador m, sl pulga; (fragment) saltadura; (money token) ficha; **he's a** ~ **off the old block** él es hijo de su padre; **he has a** ~ **on his shoulder** él es un resentido; ~-**board** madera aglomerada; v astillar(se), desconchar(se); ~ **in** (pay one's share) contribuir[16] su cuota, (interrupt) meterse en una conversación

chipmunk especie f de ardilla

chipolata salchicha delgada

chipped desconchado

chiropodist pedicuro

chiropody pedicura

chirp n chirrido; v chirriar

chisel n carp escoplo; (metal and stone)

cincel *m*; (cold steel) cortafríos *m* *sing+pl*; *v carp* escoplear; (metal and stone) cincelar; *fig* (cheat) estafar; (scrounge) comer/beber a expensas de otro

chiseler (scrounger) gorrón *m* (-ona *f*)

chit nota; ~ **of a girl** muchachita; ~**-chat** chismorrerías

chivalrous (knightly) caballeresco; (gentlemanly) caballeroso

chivalry (knighthood) caballería; (gallantry) caballerosidad *f*

chive cebollino

chivvy acosar

chlorate clorato

chloride cloruro

chlorinate tratar con cloro

chlorination cloración *f*

chlorine cloro

chloroform *n* cloroformo; *v* cloroformizar[7]

chlorophyll clorofila

chock cuña; ~**-a-block** (full) apretado, *fig* harto; ~**-full** de bote en bote

chocolate chocolate *m*; **filled** ~ bombón (-ones) *m*; ~**-cake** tarta de chocolate; ~**-drop** lengua de gato; ~ **ice-cream** helado de chocolate; ~**-covered** bañado en chocolate

choice *n* (preference) preferencia; (selection) selección *f*; **have no** ~ **in the matter** no tener[19] ni voz ni voto; **make/take a** ~ seleccionar; *adj* escogido

choir coro; (large) orfeón (-ones) *m*; ~**boy** niño de coro; ~**-loft** coro; ~**master** maestro de capilla; ~**-stalls** sillería

choke *n eng* cierre *m*; *mot* mariposa (del aire); *vt* estrangular; (clog) estancar[4]; *vi* (become clogged) estancarse[4]; (splutter while eating) atragantarse

choky *sl* jaula

cholera cólera *m*

choleric colérico

choose escoger[8]; ~ **between** optar entre; ~ **to** optar por +*infin*

choosy especial

chop *n* (meat) chuleta; (blow) golpe *m* cortante; ~**s** labios *mpl*; ~**-house** restaurante barato; ~**sticks** palillos (para comer); *v* cortar; ~ **finely** repicar[4]; ~ **and change** cambiar de parecer; ~ **down a tree** derribar un

árbol (con hacha); ~ **off** tronchar; ~ **up** desmenuzar[7]

chopped: ~ **herbs** *cul* hierbas finas

chopper (axe) hacha; (butcher's) cuchilla; **meat-**~ picadora de carne; *aer* helicóptero; *vulg* (penis) pito

choppiness agitación *f* (de mar)

chopping: ~**-block** tajo; ~**-board** tajador *m*

choppy (of sea) picado; (of wind) variable

chop-suey plato chino de carne con arroz, cebollas *etc*

choral *adj* coral; ~ **society** sociedad *f* coral

chorale coral *m*

chord *geom* cuerda; *mus* acorde *m*; **that strikes a** ~ eso me suena

chore quehacer *m*

choreographer coreógrafo

choreography coreografía

chorister corista *m+f*

chortle reír (i)[3] entre dientes

chorus *mus+theat* coro; *poet* estribillo; ~**-girl** corista; ~**-singer** corista *m+f*

chosen people pueblo escogido

chough chova

chow *sl* comida; perro chino

chowder sopa de almejas

chrism crisma

Christ Cristo; ~**-child** Niño Jesús; **Jesus** ~ Jesucristo; ~**-like** parecido a Cristo

christen bautizar[7]

Christendom cristiandad *f*

christening bautizo

Christian cristiano; ~ **Democrat** *n+adj* cristianodemócrata *m+f*; ~ **name** nombre *m* de pila; **give s.o. a** ~ **burial** enterrarle a uno en sagrado

Christianity cristianismo

Christianize cristianizar[7]

Christine Cristina

Christmas *n* (pascua de) Navidad *f*; ~**box** aguinaldo; ~**-card** christmas *m*, felicitación *f* de pascuas; ~ **carol** villancico; ~ **crib** belén *m*, SA nacimiento; ~ **Day** día *m* de Navidad; ~ **draw** *Sp* sorteo del Niño; ~ **Eve** Nochebuena; ~ **greens** *US* ramos *mpl* de acebo *etc* con los cuales se decoran las casas en Navidad; ~ **pudding** pudín *m* de Navidad; ~**time,** ~**tide** pascuas, Navidad; ~**-tree** árbol *m* de Navidad; *adj* navideño

Christopher Cristóbal
chromatic cromático
chrome n cromo; v cromar; ~-**yellow** amarillo de cromo
chromium cromo; ~-**plated** cromado
chromosome cromosoma m
chronic crónico; ~ **disease** enfermedad crónica, fam fatal m
chronicle n crónica; v narrar; (make a record) anotar
chronicler cronista m+f
chronological cronológico
chronology cronología
chronometer cronómetro
chrysalis crisálida
chrysanthemum crisantemo
chub cacho
chubby gordinflón (-ona f)
chuck n eng portabroca f; v (throw) tirar; ~ **under the chin** hacer[19] la mamola; ~ **up a job** dejar un empleo
chucker-out expulsador m
chuckle n risita ahogada; v reír (i)[3] entre dientes
chuckling risueño
chuffed contento
chug n resoplido (de una locomotora); v resoplar
chum n compinche m; **be** ~**s with** ser[19] compinche de; v ~ **up with** entablar amistad con
chummy muy amigable
chump tonto; ~ **chop** chuleta de lomo
chunk trozo grande
chunky (plump) rechoncho; (containing lumps) con pedazos/tropiezos
church (building + institution) iglesia; **go to** ~ ir[19] a la iglesia/a misa; **member** (of the ~) feligrés m (-esa f); **Church of England** iglesia anglicana; ~ **calendar** santoral m; ~-**goer** fiel m; ~ **music** música sagrada; ~ **service** oficio; ~**warden** capiller m; ~**yard** cementerio
churching misa de alumbramiento
churlish palurdo; (niggardly) mezquino
churn n mantequera; v agitar; (make butter) batir manteca
chute salto de agua; (for coal) tolva; (in swimming-pool) tobogán (-anes) m
chutney salsa picante
cicada cigarra
cicatrice cicatriz (-ces) f

Cicely Cecilia
Cicero Cicerón
cicerone cicerone m
C. I. D. (Criminal Investigation Department) approx B. I. C. (Brigada de Investigación Criminal)
cider sidra; ~-**press** prensa para estrujar manzanas
c.i.f. (cost, insurance and freight) c.f.s. (costo, flete y seguro)
cigar puro; ~-**band** anillo de cigarro; ~-**box** cigarrera; ~-**case** petaca; ~-**cutter** cortapuros m sing+pl; ~-**holder** boquilla; ~-**store** estanco
cigarette cigarrillo, fam tabaco; **have you any** ~**s?** ¿tiene usted tabaco?; ~-**case** pitillera; ~-**end** colilla; ~-**holder** boquilla; ~-**lighter** encendedor m; ~-**paper** papel m de fumar
cinch (strap) cincha; (certainty) breva
cinder ceniza; **burn to a** ~ quedar carbonizado; ~-**track** pista de ceniza
Cinderella la Cenicienta
cine: ~-**camera** tomavistas m sing+pl; ~-**film** película; ~-**projector** proyector m de cine
cinema cine m; ~ **newsreel** tr No-Do (Noticias Documentales); ~-**organ** órgano de cine; ~-**projector** proyector m de cine
Cinemascope, Cinerama: Cinemascope m, Cinerama
cinematic cinemático
cinematograph cinematógrafo
cinematography cinematografía
cinnamon canela
cipher cifra; (zero) cero; v cifrar
circa cerca de
circle n geom círculo; (social) círculo social; theat anfiteatro; v rodear
circlet anillo pequeño
circling circulante
circuit circuito; ~-**breaker** cortacircuitos m sing+pl
circuitous tortuoso
circular n (carta) circular f; adj circular; ~ **movement** movimiento giratorio; ~-**saw** sierra circular
circularity circularidad f
circularize enviar circulares a
circulate circular; ('mix' at a party) alternar
circulating: ~ **library** biblioteca circulante

circulation circulación *f*; (of a periodical) tirada; **in ~** (money) corriente
circumcise circuncidar
circumcision circuncisión (-ones) *f*
circumference circunferencia
circumflex circunflejo
circumlocution circunlocución (-ones) *f*
circumnavigate circunnavegar[5]
circumnavigation circunnavegación (-ones) *f*
circumscribe circunscribir (*past part* circunscrito)
circumscription circunscripción (-ones) *f*
circumspect circunspecto
circumspection circunspección *f*
circumstance circunstancia; **in (under) the ~s** en las circunstancias; **in (under) no ~s** de ninguna manera; **in easy ~s** acomodado; **in his ~s** con sus medios
circumstantial circunstanciado; ~ **evidence** evidencia circunstancial
circumstantiality minuciosidad *f*
circumstantiate corroborar
circumvent (outwit) burlar; (avoid) evitar; (entrap) embaucar[4]
circumvention estratagema
circus *n* circo; (urban open space) plaz(olet)a; *adj* circense; ~**-ring** pista
cirrhosis (of the liver) cirrosis *f* hepática
cirrus (cloud) cirro
cislunar *space* cislunar
cissy sarasa *m*
Cistercian *n+adj* cisterciense
cistern cisterna
citadel ciudadela
citation cita; (for bravery) mención (-ones) *f*; *leg* citación (-ones) *f*
cite (quote) citar; (for bravery) mencionar; *leg* citar (a juicio); (refer to) referirse (ie)[2c] a
citizen ciudadano
citizenry ciudadanos *mpl*
citizenship ciudadanía; ~ **papers** carta de ciudadanía; **British ~** nacionalidad británica
citrate citrato
citric cítrico; ~ **acid** ácido cítrico
citron (fruit) cidra; (tree) cidro; (candied peel) cidrada
citrus: ~ **fruit(s)** agrios *mpl*
city *n* ciudad *f*; *adj* urbano; ~ **council**

ayuntamiento; ~ **editor** redactor *m* financiero, *US* redactor encargado de noticias locales; ~ **hall** casa consistorial, ayuntamiento; ~**-state** ciudad-estado *f*
civic cívico
civics cívica
civil civil; (polite) cortés; ~ **defence** defensa civil; ~ **disobedience** resistencia pasiva; ~ **engineer** ingeniero civil; ~ **liberty** libertad *f* civil; ~ **rights** derechos *mpl* civiles; ~ **servant** funcionario (del estado); ~ **service** administración pública; ~ **war** guerra civil; **Civil Guard** (force) Guardia Civil; (person) (guardia *m*) civil, *sl* verde
civilian paisano; ~ **dress** traje *m* de paisano
civility cortesía
civilization civilización *f*
civilize civilizar[7]
civvies: in ~ (vestido) de paisano
clad vestido
claim *n* reclamación (-ones) *f*; *leg* demanda; (right) derecho; ~**-check** comprobante *m*; *v* reclamar; ~ **damages** reclamar por daños; ~ **to pretender** (ie)[2b] +*infin*
claimable reclamable
claimant reclamante *m*; (to a title *etc*) pretendiente *m*
clairvoyance clarividencia
clairvoyant clarividente *m+f*
clam almeja; **shut up like a ~** callarse como un muerto
clamber trepar; (on all fours) gatear; ~ **up** subir gateando/trepando
clammy pegajoso
clamorous clamoroso
clamour *n* (demand) clamor *m*; (noise) vocería; *v* clamar; vociferar
clamp *n eng* grapa; *agri* ensilado; *v* agrapar; *agri* ensilar; ~ **down (on)** ponerse[19] severo (con)
clan clan *m*; ~**sman** miembro de un clan
clandestine clandestino
clang *n* sonido metálico; *v* sonar (ue)[1a] metálicamente
clanger: drop a ~ cometer una plancha
clanging (of bells) campaneo
clank *n* sonido metálico; *vt* hacer[19] sonar fuerte; *vi* sonar fuerte
clannish exclusivista
clap *n* (with hands) palmada; (blow)

golpe *m*; (venereal disease) gonorrea;
~ **of thunder** trueno; *v* (applaud)
aplaudir; (strike) golpear; ~ **eyes on**
echar la vista encima; ~ **one's hands**
dar[19] palmadas

clapboard chilla

clapped: ~ **out** (people) rendido,
(things) gastado

clapper (of bell) badajo; (person) pal-
moteador *m* (-ora *f*); **he ran like the** ~**s**
él corrió como una liebre, *fam* perdió
el culo

clapping aplausos *mpl*

claptrap charlatanería

claque claque *f*

Clare Clara

claret clarete *m*

clarification clarificación *f*

clarify clarificar[4]

clarinet clarinete *m*

clarion clarín *m*

clarity claridad *f*

clash (collision) choque *m*; (disagreement) conflicto; (noise) estruendo; *v*
~ **with** chocar[4] con; **that tie** ~**es with
my shirt** esa corbata desentona con mi
camisa; ~**ing colour** color *m* chillón

clasp *n* (fastening) cierre *m*; (hug) abrazo; (of hands) apretón (-ones) *m*;
~-**knife** navaja; *v* (embrace) abrazar[7];
(fasten) abrochar; ~ **hands** apretar
(ie)[2a] las manos

class *n* clase *f*; (quality) buena calidad;
that woman has ~ esa mujer tiene
elegancia; **every social** ~ **in the city**
todo estamento social de la ciudad;
first/second ~ de primera/segunda
clase; ~-**conscious** consciente de clases; ~-**distinction** clasismo; ~-**list**
lista, (exam results) lista de resultados
de examen; ~-**mate** condiscípulo;
~**room** (sala de) clase; ~-**struggle** lucha de clases; *v* clasificar[4]

classic *n* obra clásica; *adj* clásico

classical clásico; ~ **music** música clásica;
~ **scholar** humanista *m+f*

classicism clasicismo

classicist clasicista *m+f*

classification clasificación *f*

classifiable clasificable

classified clasificado; (secret) secreto; ~
advertisements anuncios *mpl* por
palabras

classify clasificar[4]

classless sin clases

classy elegante

clatter estrépito; (of hoofs) trápala; *v*
resonar (ue)[1a] ruidosamente

Claude, Claudius Claudio

clause cláusula; *leg* artículo; *gramm*
oración (-ones) *f* dependiente

claustrophobia claustrofobia

clavichord clavicordio

clavicle clavícula

claw *n orni+zool* garra; (crab) pinza;
eng etc gancho; *v* arañar; ~-**hammer**
martillo de orejas

clay *n* arcilla; *adj* de arcilla; ~-**pigeon
shooting** tiro de pichón (de barro); ~
pipe pipa de tierra; ~-**pit** barrera

clean *adj* limpio; *fig* honesto; *sp* deportivo; (having no criminal record)
limpio, *sl* legal; ~ **bill of health**
patente limpia de sanidad; ~ **joke**
chiste *m* de color de rosa; ~ **linen**
muda limpia; ~ **sweep** limpieza total;
~ **water** agua pura; **make a** ~ **breast of**
it confesar de plano; **show a** ~ **pair of**
heels tomar las de Villadiego; ~-**living**
decente; ~-**shaven** afeitado; *v* limpiar; (fish + poultry) destripar; ~
house poner[19] la casa en orden; ~
one's nails arreglarse las uñas; ~ **one's**
teeth limpiarse los dientes; ~ **shoes**
limpiar los zapatos; ~ **out** vaciar; *fig*
limpiarle a uno; **be** ~**ed out** quedar
limpio; ~-**up** *n* limpieza general; ~ **up**
vt limpiar completamente, (gambling)
hacer[19] mesa limpia; *vi* limpiarse; *adv*
completamente; **I** ~ **forgot it** lo olvidé
completamente; **come** ~ confesarlo
todo

cleaning limpieza; ~ **fluid** quitamanchas
m sing; ~ **woman** asistenta, *pej* fregona

cleanliness limpieza

cleanse limpiar

cleansing-cream crema limpiadora

clear (neat) limpio; (cloudless) despejado; (distinct) claro; (innocent) absuelto; (obvious) claro; (transparent)
transparente; (resolved) claro; (unimpeded) libre; ~ **of** (free from) libre de;
~ **soup** consomé *m*; ~ **water** agua
cristalina; **in the** ~ libre de sospecha;
he has a ~ **head** tiene la cabeza des-
pejada; **three** ~ **days** tres días com-
pletos; *adv* por completo, completa-

mente; **he got ~ away** se escapó por
completo; **get ~ (of)** escaparse (de);
make o.s. ~ explicarse⁴; **~-cut** bien
definido; **~-eyed** de ojos brillantes;
~-headed inteligente; **~-sighted** perspicaz; **~ way** autoruta; *v* (of guilt) absolver (ue)¹ᵇ; *meteor* despejarse; **~
(up) a debt** arreglar una deuda; **~ the
decks for action** despejar las cubiertas
para el combate; **~ the table** levantar
la mesa; **~ the throat** carraspear; **he
~ed the wall with one leap** de un salto
pasó por encima de la muralla
~ away (tidy) recoger⁸
~ out (empty) vaciar; (take out) sacar⁴;
(go away) largarse⁵
~ up (a problem) aclarar; (tidy) recoger⁸; (clarify) clarificar⁴; *meteor* despejarse el tiempo
clearance (customs) despacho de aduana; **~ sale** liquidación *f*; **six-centimetre
~** espacio libre de seis centí-
metros
clearing (in wood) claro; **~-house** banco
de liquidación
clearly claramente; **I can see it all ~** lo
veo todo claro
clearness claridad *f*
cleavage hendidura; *anat* raya (del pecho)
cleave hender²ᵇ; **~ to** pegarse⁵ a
cleaver cuchilla de carnicero
clef clave *f*
cleft grieta; **~ palate** fisura del paladar
clematis clemátide *f*
clemency clemencia; *meteor* benignidad *f*
Clement Clemente
clench agarrar; **~ the fist** cerrar (ie)²ᵃ el
puño; **~ the teeth** apretar (ie)²ᵃ los
dientes
clerestory claraboya
clergy clero
clergyman, cleric clérigo; (protestant)
pastor *m*
clerical (of clergy) clerical; (of a clerk)
de oficina; **~ collar** cuello de clérigo;
~ error error *m* de pluma; **~ work**
trabajo de oficina
clericalism clericalismo
clerk (in office) escribiente *m*; *leg* escribano; (*US* shop assistant) dependiente *m+f*; (bank) empleado
clever listo; inteligente; *fam* hacha *m+f*;

(with the hands) mañoso; **he has such
~ hands** él tiene manos de oro
cleverness listeza; (with the hands)
maña
cliché tópico *m*; *print* clisé *m*
click *n* golpe seco; (of a gun) piñoneo;
(of heels) taconeo; (of the tongue)
chasquido; *v* hacer¹⁹ tictac; *fam* (be
successful) tener¹⁹ éxito; **~ the heels**
hacer¹⁹ sonar los tacones; **~ the
tongue** chasquear la lengua
client cliente *m+f*
clientele clientela
cliff precipicio; risco; (by the sea)
acantilado; **~-hanger** episodio emocionante; **the election was a ~-hanger**
la elección fue llena de suspenso
climacteric climatérico
climate clima *m*
climatic climático
climatology climatología
climax punto culminante
climb *n* escalada; *v* escalar; **~ down**
bajar, *fig* rebajarse; **~ up** subir
climbable escalable
climber escalador *m* (-ora *f*); *bot*
enredadera; **social ~** arrivista *m+f*
climbing-irons trepadores *mpl*
clinch *n* agarro; *sp* clincha; **in a ~**
(boxing) cuerpo a cuerpo; *v* agarrar;
fig confirmar; **~ the deal** cerrar (ie)²ᵃ
el trato
cling agarrarse (to a); (hang on to)
colgarse (ue)¹ᵃ (de); *fig* (to a habit)
persistir en; (continue to trust) confiar
en
clinging (close-fitting) ceñido; (of a person) pegajoso
clinic clínica
clinical clínico; **~ chart** gráfica de un
enfermo; **~ thermometer** termómetro
clínico
clink *n* (sound) tintín *m*; *sl* (gaol) jaula;
vt hacer tintinear; **~ glasses** chocar
copas; *vi* tintinear
clinker escoria de hulla
clip *n* pinza; (for papers) sujetapapeles
m sing+pl; (cut with scissors) tijeretada; *cin* secuencia; *fam* (blow)
puñetazo; **~-joint** casa de fulanas; **at a
fast ~** a gran velocidad; *v* (with
scissors) cortar; (tickets) picar⁴;
(sheep) esquilar; *fam* (strike) aporrear; **~ s.o.'s wings** cortarle a uno el

vuelo

clipper *naut+aer* clíper *m*

clippers (hairdressing) maquinilla para cortar el pelo; (pruning) tijeras *fpl* podadoras; (shearing) tijeras *fpl* de trasquilar; *metal* cizalla

clipping (action) corte *m*; (newspaper cutting) recorte *m*

clique pandilla

cliquish exclusivista

cloak *n* capa; *fig* disimulo; *adj* ~ **and dagger/sword** de capa y espada; *v* encapotar; *fig* disimular

cloakroom ropería; (lavatory) servicio

clobber (hit) apalear; *sl* (give work to) cargar[5]

clock reloj *m*; (on sock) cuadrado; ~-**face**, ~-**dial** esfera de reloj; ~-**maker** relojero; ~-**tower** torre *f* del reloj; *v* medir (i)[3] el tiempo; *sp* cronometrar; ~ **off** fichar la salida del trabajo; ~ **on** fichar la entrada al trabajo

clockwise en el sentido de las agujas del reloj

clockwork *n* maquinaria de reloj; **like** ~ como un reloj; *adj* con movimiento de cuerda; **everything was going like** ~ todo iba sobre ruedas

clod (earth) terrón (-ones) *m*; (blockhead) zoquete *m*

cloddish rústico

clodhopper papanatas *m sing+pl*; (footwear) zapatón (-ones) *m*

clog *n* chanclo; ~-**dance** zapateado; *v* obstruir[16]; ~ **up** estancar

cloister(s) *n* claustro; *v* enclaustrar

¹ **close** *n* recinto; *adj* (intimate) íntimo; (miserly) avaro, *fam* roñoso; (nearby) cercano; (almost equal) casi igual; (accurate) fiel, ~ **copy** copia fiel; (of texture) compacto; (sultry) bochornoso, **it's** ~ **today** hace bochorno hoy; (uncommunicative) callado; ~ **call** escape *m* por un pelo; **have a** ~ **shave** afeitarse a ras, *fig* escaparse por un pelo; ~ **examination** registro minucioso; ~ **season** veda; **at** ~ **quarters** (fight) cuerpo a cuerpo; (at ~ range) a quemarropa; *adv* cerca; ~ **by** cerca; ~ **on** cerca de, **there were** ~ **on forty people in the garden** había cerca de cuarenta personas en el jardín; **she is** ~ **on thirty** ella ronda los treinta; ~ **to** cerca de; ~ **to the wind** de

bolina; ~-**cropped** rapado; ~-**fisted** manicorto; ~-**fitting** ceñido; ~-**up** *phot* de cerca, *cin* primer plano; **people** ~ **to the Pope** personas allegadas al Papa

² **close** *n* fin *m*, terminación *f*; (closure) clausura; (of day) caída; *v* cerrar (ie)[2a]; (put lid or cover on) tapar; (end) terminar; (a meeting) clausurar; *comm* (an account) liquidar; ~ **a deal** cerrar (ie)[2a] un trato; ~ **the door against** *fig* cerrar (ie)[2a] el paso hacia; ~ **ranks (against)** estrechar filas (contra); ~**d chapter** asunto concluido; ~**d circuit television** circuito cerrado de televisión; ~**d shop** (place) taller agremiado, (principle) agremiación obligatoria

~ **down** cerrar (ie)[2a]

~ **in** acercarse[4]; **night is closing in** la noche está cerrando; ~ **in on** rodear

~ **with** (enemy) venir[19] a las manos con

closed cerrado; ~ **prison** cárcel *f* de régimen cerrado

closely de cerca

closeness intimidad *f*; (air) falta de ventilación

closet (room) gabinete *m*; (lavatory) servicio; (cupboard) armario

closing: ~ **prices** precios *mpl* de liquidación; ~ **time** hora de cerrar

closure *n* clausura

clot *n* coágulo; *fig* idiota *m+f*; *v* cuajarse; **clotted cream** crema cuajada

cloth (material) tela; (rag) trapo; ~-**binding** encuadernación *f* en tela; ~-**table** ~ mantel *m*

clothe vestir (i)[3]; ~ **with authority** investir (i)[3] de autoridad

clothes ropa; ~-**basket** cesto de la ropa; ~-**brush** cepillo de la ropa; ~-**hanger** percha; ~-**horse** secarropa de travesaños; ~-**line** tendedero; ~-**peg**/*US* ~-**pin** pinza; ~-**wringer** máquina de exprimir

clothier (seller of cloth) pañero; (seller of clothes) ropero; ~'**s** pañería, ropería

clothing ropa

cloud *n* nube *f*; ~ **bank** mar *m* de nubes; ~ **of dust** nube *f* de polvo; ~ **of smoke** humareda; **be in** ~-**cuckoo-land** estar[19] en el limbo; **under a** ~ desacreditado; ~-**burst** chaparrón (-ones) *m*; ~**-capped** coronado de nubes; *v* ~ **over** anublarse

clouded (a)nublado

cloudless despejado

cloudy (weather) nublado; (liquid) turbio

clout *n* (smack) bofetada; **of little** ~ de poca influencia/poder; *v* abofetear

clove clavo; ~ **of garlic** diente *m* de ajo

cloven hendido; ~**-hoofed** patihendido, *fig* diabólico

clover trébol *m*; **in** ~ en abundancia; **be in** ~ vivir rodeado de lujo

clown *n* payaso; *fig* hazmerreír *m*; *v* hacer[19] payasadas

clowning payasadas *fpl*

clownish bufonesco

cloy empalagar[5]

[1] **club** *n* (stick) porra; (golf) palo; (society) club *m*; **in the** ~ (pregnant) embarazada, *sl* cepillada, *Arg* de compras; ~**-car** coche bar *m*; ~**-foot** pie *m* de zopo; ~**-footed** de pie de zopo; ~**house** casino; ~**land** barrio de clubs; ~**man**, ~**woman** clubista *m+f*; *v* aporrear; ~ **together (for)** (unite) reunirse (para); (contribute) contribuir[16] (a), pagar[5] entre todos

[2] **club** (cards) *Eng* trébol *m*; *Sp* basto

clubbed en forma de maza

cluck *n* cloqueo; *v* cloquear

clue pista; **I haven't a** ~ no tengo idea, (in answer to a question) en absoluto

clueless (baffled) desorientado; (foolish) tonto

clump (trees, bushes) boscaje *m*; (sound of footsteps) pisada recia

clumsy torpe; **be** ~ **with one's hands** ser[19] un manazas; ~ **fellow** patoso; ~ **clot!** ¡pedazo de bruto!

cluster *n* grupo; (grapes *etc*) racimo; ~ **round** agruparse alrededor (de); ~**ed columns** *archi* columnas agrupadas

clutch *n* (eggs) nidada; *mot* embrague *m*; **put in/US throw in the** ~ embragar[5]; **let out the** ~ desembragar[5]; **fall into the** ~**es of** caer[19] en las garras de; *v* agarrar(se); ~ **at** intentar agarrar

clutter: ~ **up** alborotar

Co. (Company) Cía (Compañía); (county) condado

C.O. (Commanding Officer) comandante *m* en jefe

c/o (care of) al cuidado de

[1] **coach** (horse-drawn) coche *m*; (ceremonial) carroza; (railway) vagón (-ones) *m*; *mot* autocar *m*; ~**-builder** carrocero; ~**-building** carrocería; ~**man** cochero; ~**work** carrocería

[2] **coach** *n* (tutor) preceptor *m*; *sp* entrenador *m*; *v* (for exam) dar[19] clase particular; *sp* entrenar

coaching clases *fpl* particulares; *sp* entrenamiento

coagulate cuajar

coagulation cuajamiento

coal *n* carbón *m*; **carry** ~**s to Newcastle** llevar hierro a Vizcaya; **haul over the** ~**s** reprender severamente; ~**-bin**, ~**-bunker** carbonera; ~**-black** negro como el tizón; ~**-burning cooking stove** cocina económica; ~**-cellar** carbonera: ~**-dust** polvo de carbón; ~**-face** tajo; ~**-field**, ~**-measure** *geol* yacimiento de carbón; ~**-fire** fuego de carbón; ~**-gas** gas *m* (de hulla); ~**-house** carbonera; ~**man/-merchant** carbonero; ~**-mine** mina de carbón; ~**-miner** minero; ~**-scuttle** cubo de carbón; ~**-seam** filón (-ones) *m* de carbón; ~**-shovel** pala de carbón; ~**-tar** alquitrán *m* (de hulla); ~ **tit** *orni* carbonero garrapinos; ~**-wharf** muelle carbonero; ~**-yard** parque *m* de carbón; *v* proveerse[17] de carbón

coalesce fundirse

coalescence fusión *f*

coaling toma de carbón; ~**-station** puerto de toma de carbón

coalition coalición *f*; ~ **government** gobierno de coalición

coarse (rough) tosco; (thick) grueso; (vulgar) grosero, *fam* feo; ~ **cloth** tela burda; ~ **joke** chiste *m* verde; ~ **words** palabras groseras; ~**-grained** de fibra gruesa

coarsen curtirse; (of people) embrutecer[14]

coast *n* costa; **the** ~ **is clear** no hay moros en la costa; ~**guard** guardacostas *m* *sing+pl*; ~**guard cutter** escampavía (de guardacostas); ~**guard service** servicio costero; ~**line** costa; ~**ward(s)** hacia la costa; *v* navegar[5] a lo largo de la costa; *mot* seguir (i)[3+11] rodando libremente

coastal de la costa; costero; ~ **defence**

defensa de la costa; ~ **fishing** pesca costera; ~ **trade** cabotaje *m*

coaster barco de cabotaje; (table-mat) salvamanteles *m sing*

coasting cabotaje *m*

coat (garment) abrigo; (animal's) pelo; (paint) mano *f*; **cut one's ~ according to one's cloth** amoldarse a las circunstancias; ~**-hanger** percha; ~**-of-arms** (escudo de) armas; ~**-of-mail** cota (de malla); ~**-pocket** bolsillo del abrigo; ~**-tail** faldón *m*; *v* ~ **with** cubrir de, bañar en; ~**ed with chocolate** bañado en chocolate; ~**ed with mud** cubierto de barro

coating (paint) capa; (plaster) enlucido

coax engatusar; ~ **s.o. into** persuadirle a uno a que +*subj*

coaxer engatusador *m* (-ora *f*)

coaxing *n* engatusamiento; *adj* lleno de engatusamiento

cob (corn) mazorca de maíz; (horse) jaca; *orni* cisne macho; **corn on the ~** maíz *m* en la mazorca, *SA* tusa de maíz

cobalt cobalto; ~ **blue** azul cobalto

¹ **cobble** (stone) guijarro

² **cobble** remendar (ie)²ᵃ zapatos

cobbler zapatero; ~**s!** *vulg* ¡huevos!

cobelligerent cobeligerante *m*

cobnut avellana

cobra cobra

cobweb telaraña

Coca-Cola *tr* Coca-Cola *m*

cocaine cocaína

cock *orni* gallo; (tap) grifo; (penis) *vulg* pito; ~ **of the walk** gallito del lugar; **it's a lot of ~** es completamente falso; ~**-a-doodle-do** quiquiriquí *m*; ~**-a-hoop** jubiloso; ~ **and bull story** patraña; ~**-crow** canto del gallo; ~**-eyed** bizco, *fam* (crazy) loco, (drunk) achispado; ~**-fight(ing)** riña de gallos; ~**-sure** seguro de sí mismo; *v* montar (un arma de fuego); ~**ed hat** sombrero de tres picos

cockade cucarda

cockalorum hombrecito engreído

cockatoo cacatúa

cockle berberecho; ~**-shell** concha de berberecho

cocker: ~ **spaniel** perro cocker

cockerel gallito

cockiness engreimiento

cockney *n* + *adj* londinense *m* + *f*

cockpit cabina de piloto

cockroach cucaracha

cocktail coctel *m*; ~ **bar** mueble-bar *m*; ~**-frock** vestido de cóctel; ~**-party** cóctel *m*; ~**-shaker** coctelera

cocoa cacao; ~**-bean** almendra de cacao

coconut coco; ~ **palm** cocotero; ~ **plantation** cocotal *m*

cod bacalao; ~**-liver oil** aceite *m* de hígado de bacalao; ~**-fishery** pesca de bacalao; ~ **war** disputa sobre los derechos de pescar en aguas territoriales

C.O.D. (cash on delivery) entrega contra reembolso

coddle mimar

code *n leg* código; (cipher) clave *f*, cifra; **in ~** en clave; **put in ~** cifrar; ~ **message** carta en clave; ~ **of honour** código de honor; ~**-word** consigna; *v* cifrar

codeine codeína

codicil codicilo

codification, coding codificación *f*

codify codificar⁴

co-ed alumno (de un instituto mixto); ~ **school** (primary) escuela mixta, (secondary) instituto mixto

co-editor coredactor *m*

coeducation coeducación *f*

coeducational coeducacional, mixto

coefficient coeficiente *m*

coerce obligar⁵

coercion coerción *f*

coexist coexistir

coexistence coexistencia; **peaceful ~** coexistencia pacífica

coextensive coextensivo

coffee (black) café solo; **white ~** café con leche; ~ **with very little milk** café cortado; **iced ~** café granizado; ~**-bar** cafetería; ~**-bean** grano de café; ~**-break** descanso (para tomar café); ~**-coloured** de color café; ~**-grinder** molinillo (de café); ~**-grounds** posos *mpl* del café; ~**-house** café *m*; ~**-mill** molinillo de café; ~ **plantation** cafetal *m*; ~**-pot** cafetera; ~**-room** salón (-ones) *m* de café; ~**-set** servicio de café; ~**-spoon** cucharita de café; ~**-stall** quiosco (de café); ~**-strainer** colador *m* de café; ~**-table** mesa de café

coffer cofre *m*; ~**s** (wealth) tesoro; fondos *mpl*

coffin ataúd *m*; *fam* caja
cog diente *m* de rueda; **~-wheel** rueda dentada
cogency fuerza lógica
cogent convincente
cogitate meditar
cogitation meditación *f*
cognac coñac *m*
cognate análogo
cognition cognición *f*
cognizance conocimiento; *leg* competencia
cohabit cohabitar, convivir (**with** con)
cohabitation cohabitación *f*
cohere adherirse (ie)²ᶜ a
coherence coherencia
coherent coherente
cohesion cohesión *f*
cohesive cohesivo
cohort cohorte *f*
coiffure peinado
coil *n* (rope) rollo; *elect* carrete *m*; *v* enrollar; (a cable) *naut* adujar; **~ up** (snake) enroscarse
coin moneda; *fam* dinero; (cash) metálico; *v* (mint) acuñar; **~ a phrase** inventar una frase; **~ money** *fig* enriquecerse¹⁴ rápidamente, (make false coins) falsificar⁴ monedas
coinage sistema monetario
coincide coincidir
coincidence casualidad *f*
coincidental coincidente
coiner falsificador *m* (-ora *f*)
coition, coitus coito; **coitus interruptus** coitus interruptus *m*
coke (fuel) cok *m*; (drink) Coca-Cola *m*; cocaína
Col. (colonel) cnel. (coronel *m*)
colander colador *m*
cold *n* (lack of heat) frío; *med* catarro; **catch (a) ~** constiparse; **have a ~** (in the head) estar¹⁹ constipado, (on the chest) tener¹⁹ catarro; **I have a bit of a ~** estoy un poco resfriado; **leave out in the ~** dejar a la luna de Valencia; *adj* frío; (indifferent) reservado; *fig* (not near the thing sought) lejos; **be ~** (person) tener¹⁹ frío, (thing) estar¹⁹ frío, (weather) hacer¹⁹ frío; **become ~** enfriarse; **~ comfort** triste gracia; **blow hot and ~** vacilar; **get ~ feet** volverse (ue)¹ᵇ (*past part* vuelto) tímido; **leave one ~** dejar a uno

indiferente; **throw ~ water on** *fig* desanimar; **turn down ~** rechazar⁷ sin consideración; **in ~ blood** a sangre fría; **~-blooded** inhumano, *zool* de sangre fría; **~ cream** crema limpiadora; **~ dish** plato frío; **~ frame** invernáculo pequeño; **~ front** *meteor* frente frío; **~-hearted** insensible; **~ meat** fiambres *mpl*; **give the ~ shoulder to** tratar con frialdad; **~ snap/spell** período de frío agudo; **~-sore** herpe *m* labial; **~ steel** armas *fpl* blancas; **~ storage** frigorífico; **~ sweat** sudor frío, escalofrío; **~ war** guerra fría; **~-wave** permanente *f*
coldness frialdad *f*
coleslaw ensalada de col picada
colic cólico
collaborate colaborar
collaboration colaboración *f*
collaborator colaborador *m* (-ora *f*)
collage cuadro hecho de pedazos de tela, papel *etc*
collapse *n* (buildings *etc*) derrumbamiento; *med* colapso; *comm* fracaso; *v* (building) derrumbarse; *med* desmayarse; *comm* fracasar
collapsible plegadizo; **~ steering-column** dirección telescópica
collar cuello; (dog) collar *m*; (horse) collera; **~-band** cuello de camisa; **~-bone** clavícula; **~-stud, ~-button** botón (-ones) *m* del cuello; **~ stay, ~ stiffener** ballena; *v* coger⁸ (por el cuello)
collate colacionar
collateral colateral *n*+*adj m*
collation colación (-ones) *f*
collator colacionador *m* (-ora *f*)
colleague colega *m*+*f*
collect *vt* (pick up) recoger⁸; (gather together) juntar; (make a collection of) hacer¹⁹ colección de; **~ a debt** cobrar una deuda; **~ dust** atraer¹⁹ el polvo; **~ taxes** recaudar contribuciones; **~ one's thoughts** poner¹⁹ las ideas en orden; *vi* juntarse, reunirse; **~ed works** obras *fpl* completas
collection colección (-ones) *f*; (taxes *etc*) recaudación (-ones) *f*; (for charity) colecta; (compilation) recopilación (-ones) *f*; **~ agency** agencia de cobros
collective colectivo; **~ agreement** convenio colectivo; **~ bargaining** trato co-

lectivo; ~ **farm** granja colectiva; ~
security seguridad colectiva

collectivism colectivismo

collectivization colectivización *f*

collector (hobby) coleccionista *m*+*f*;
(compiler) compilador *m* (-ora *f*);
elect colector *m*; ~ **of customs** (at a
port) administrador *m* de aduanas; ~
of taxes recaudador *m* de contribuciones; **debt** ~ cobrador *m* de
deudas; **ticket** ~ revisor *m*

college *n* escuela superior; *adj* estudiantil; ~ **yell** grito que sirve para distinguir los estudiantes de cada college

collide chocar[4] (**with** con); *fig* estar[19] en
conflicto (**with** con)

collie perro pastor

collier (man) minero; (ship) (barco)
carbonero

colliery mina (de carbón); ~ **disaster**
catástrofe *f* en una mina

collision choque *m*; *fam* trompazo; **in** ~
en colisión; **on a** ~ **course** en trayectoria de choque

colloid *n*+*adj* coloide *m*

colloquial familiar

colloquialism expresión *f* familiar

colloquially en lenguaje coloquial

colloquy coloquio

collotype (fotografía de) colotipia

collude coludirse

collusion colusión *f*; **be in** ~ **with** estar[19]
en inteligencia con

collusive colusorio

Cologne Colonia; **Eau-de-**~ agua de
Colonia

Colombia Colombia

Colombian *n*+*adj* colombiano

colon *anat* colon *m*; *gramm* dos puntos

colonel coronel *m*

colonial *n* colono; *adj* colonial; ~ **secretary** ministro de colonias

colonialism colonialismo

colonist (colonizer) colonizador *m* (-ora
f); (inhabitant of a colony) colono

colonization colonización (-ones) *f*

colonize colonizar[7]

colonizing *n* colonización *f*; *adj* colonizador (-ora *f*)

colonnade columnata

colony colonia

colophon colofón (-ones) *m*

colophony colofonia

Colorado: ~ **beetle** escarabajo de la
patata

coloratura floreos *mpl* en el canto; ~ **soprano** soprano *f* aficionada a floreos
en el canto

colorific colorativo

colossal colosal

colossus coloso

colour *n* +*fig* color *m*; ~s *mil* bandera,
naut pabellón (-ones) *m*; **be off** ~
estar[19] indispuesto; **call to the** ~s
llamar al servicio militar; **change** ~
cambiar de color; **get one's** ~s ser[19]
seleccionado (para un equipo); **give/
lend** ~ **to** hacer[19] verosímil; **he lays
the** ~s **on too thick** él recarga las tin-
tas; **in (full)** ~ a (todo) color; **show
one's** ~s dejar ver su verdadero
carácter; **show me the** ~ **of your
money!** ¡afloje la pasta!; **under** ~ **of** a
pretexto de; **with flying** ~s triunfante;
~-**bar** barrera de color; ~-**blind**
daltónico; ~-**blindness** daltonismo; ~
chart cuadro de color; ~ **film** película
en color; ~ **filter** *phot* filtro de colores;
~ **photography** fotografía en color; ~
plate (in book) grabado a color; ~
prejudice racismo; ~ **problem** problema *m* racial; ~ **sensitiveness** *phot*
sensibilidad cromática; ~-**sergeant**
sargento abanderado; ~ **slide** diapositiva; ~ **television** televisión *f* en
color; ~s (paints) pinturas *fpl*; *vt*+*fig*
colorear, *phot* colorir; *vi* (blush)
ruborizarse; ~**ed** *n* gente *f* de color,
(in South Africa) mestizos *mpl*; *adj*
coloreado; (of people) de color; *fig*
(distorted) falseado

colourable colorable

colourful lleno de color; *fig* vívido

colouring (act) coloración *f*; (complexion) color *m*; (pigment) colorante
m; (distortion) falsificación (-ones) *f*

colourist colorista *m*+*f*

colourless sin color; *fig* (dull) soso

colt potro; *fig* mozuelo; ~**sfoot** uña de
caballo

columbine aguileña; **Columbine** *theat*
Colombina

Columbus Colón; ~ **Day** (12 October)
Día *m* de la Hispanidad/de la Raza

column columna; (regular newspaper
feature) crónica

columnist periodista *m*+*f*

coma coma *m*; *astron* cabellera

comatose comatoso

comb *n* peine *m*; (for a horse) almohaza; (cock's) cresta; (honeycomb) panal *m*; (wool) carda; (of wave) cresta; *v* peinar; (horse) almohazar[7]; (wool) cardar; ~ **one's hair** peinarse; ~ **out** cardar

combat *n* combate *m*; ~ **troops** tropas *fpl* de combate; ~**-duty** servicio de frente; ~**-fatigue** neurosis *f* de guerra; *v* combatir

combatant *n* + *adj* combatiente *m*

combative peleador (-ora *f*)

comber *mech* cardador *m* (-ora *f*); (wave) ola encrestada

combinable combinable

combination combinación (-ones) *f*; ~**s** camisa pantalón *f*; ~**-lock** cerradura de combinación

combine *n comm* asociación (-ones) *f*; (monopoly) monopolio; ~**-harvester** cosechadora; *v* combinar(se); ~**d operations** maniobras conjuntas

combings peinaduras *fpl*

combustibility combustibilidad *f*

combustible *n* + *adj* combustible *m*

combustion combustión *f*

come (approach) venir[19]; (arrive) llegar[5]; **here they** ~ ya vienen; ~ **here!** ¡ven(ga) aquí!; **I'm coming** ya voy; ~ **and …** venir[19] a + *infin*; ~ **and go** ir[19] y venir[19]; ~**-~!** ¡ánimo!; ~ **clean** confesarlo todo; ~ **a cropper** caer[19] (un trompazo), *fig* fracasar; ~ **hard on** venir[19] mal a; ~ **home** regresar a casa; ~ **loose** aflojarse; ~ **across with it!** llegar[5] a las manos de uno; ~ **quietly!** ¡venga sin resistir!; ~ **true** realizarse[7]; ~ **undone** desatarse, (of buttons) desabrocharse, *fig* fracasar; ~ **what may** venga lo que venga; **how** ~? ¿cómo (es) eso?; **for years to** ~ por años; (have an orgasm) venirse

~ **about** (happen) acaecer[14]; **it came about that** acaeció que; **I've** ~ **about the cooker** vengo para ver la cocina

~ **across** (cross over) atravesar; (find, meet) dar[19] con; ~ **across with it!** *fam* ¡entrégamelo!; **his words did not** ~ **across** (were not convincing) sus palabras no convencieron

~ **after** (follow) seguir (i)[3+11]; (seek) buscar[4]

~ **again** venir[19] otra vez; *fam* (repeat) repetir (i)[3]

~ **along!** ¡venga!; (hurry!) ¡dese prisa!; ~ **along with** acompañar

~ **at** (attack) atacar[4]; (reach) alcanzar[7]

~**-at-able** *adj* accesible

~ **away** marcharse; ~ **away from there** ¡quítese de allí!

~**-back** *n* (counter-attack) contrataque *m*; (rehabilitation) rehabilitación *f*; (retort) respuesta aguda; **stage a** ~**-back** rehabilitarse

~ **back** *v* volver (ue)[1b] (*past part* vuelto); (retort) replicar[4]

~ **before** llegar[5] antes; **he will** ~ **before the judge** él comparecerá ante el juez

~ **between** interponerse[19] entre; **p** ~**s between o and q** la p viene entre la o y la q

~ **by** (achieve) conseguir (i)[3+11]; (acquire) obtener[19]; (pass) pasar por; *v* (visit) visitar

~**-down** *n* revés *m* de fortuna; **what a** ~**-down!** ¡qué chasco!

~ **down** *v* (descend) bajar; (collapse) derrumbar; (fall) caer[19]; (of prices) rebajarse; *aer* aterrizar[7], (on water) amarar, (on the moon) alunizar[7]; ~ **down in the world** venir[19] a menos; ~ **down to** (of a problem) reducirse[15] a; **it has** ~ **down to me** (by inheritance) lo tengo de mis antepasados; **she came down on me like a ton of bricks** ella me regañó terriblemente; **it has** ~ **down from Roman times** ha llegado desde los tiempos romanos; ~ **down with** *med* enfermarse de

~ **for** venir[19] por

~ **forth** salir[19]; (of flowers) brotar

~ **from** venir[19] de

~**-hither** *adj* seductor (-ora *f*)

~ **in** entrar (en); (race/contest) llegar[5]; ~ **in!** ¡pase!; ~ **in for** (abuse) ser[19] objeto de abuso; ~ **in handy** ser[19] útil

~ **into** (enter) entrar (en); (inherit) heredar; ~ **into bloom** florecer[14]; ~ **into demand** sobrevenir[19] la demanda; ~ **into fashion** ponerse[19] de moda; ~ **into one's own** tomar posesión de lo suyo; ~ **into sight/view** aparecer[14]; ~ **into the world** nacer[14]

~ **of** (be caused by) resultar de; **that's what comes of …** eso es lo que trae el + *infin*; ~ **of age** llegar a la mayoría de edad

~ **off** (become detached) soltarse (ue)[1a]; (get down from) bajar de; (of a stain) quitarse; (happen) celebrarse; (succeed) tener[19] éxito; ~ **off it!** ¡déjate de tonterías!; ~ **off badly/well** salir[19] mal/bien; ~ **off best/worst** salir[19] ganando/perdiendo

~ **on** (advance) avanzar[7]; (develop) desarrollarse; (grow) crecer[14]; (improve) mejorar; (prosper) prosperar; ~ **on!** (let's go) ¡vamos!, (hurry!) ¡dese prisa!, (have courage!) ¡ánimo!; ~ **on stage** salir[19] a escena

~ **out** salir[19] (of de); (of a book) publicarse[4]; (of buds) brotar; (of a girl in society) ponerse[19] de largo; (of a new model) estrenarse; (of news) revelarse; (of a stain) quitarse; ~ **out on strike** declararse en huelga; ~ **out with** (declare) soltar (ue)[1a], (disclose) revelar

~ **over** (cross) pasar al otro lado; ~ **over all queer** venir[19] mareos; **what's ~ over him?** ¿qué le pasa?

~ **round** (visit) venir[19] a ver; (recover consciousness) volver (ue)[1b] (*past part* vuelto) en sí; (accept another's point of view) asentir (ie)[2c]

~ **through** pasar por; (tribulations) salir[19] de

~ **to** (reach) llegar[5] a; (amount to) sumar a; *med* (revive) volver (ue)[1b] (*past part* vuelto) en sí; ~ **to an agreement** llegar[5] a un acuerdo; ~ **to anchor** llegar[5] al fondeadero; ~ **to a bad end** acabar mal; ~ **to blows** venirse[19] a las manos; ~ **to an end** acabarse, (die) morir (ue)[1c] (*past part* muerto); ~ **to grief** fracasar; ~ **to grips with** afrontar; ~ **to hand** llegar[5] a manos de uno; ~ **to a head** *med* madurar, *fig* definirse; ~ **to life** nacer[14]; ~ **to life again** resucitar; ~ **to light** descubrirse (*past part* descubierto); ~ **to mind** venir[19] a la memoria; ~ **to one's knowledge** enterarse de, **it came to my knowledge that** me enteré de que; ~ **to nothing** frustrarse; ~ **to one** venirle[19] a uno a una idea, **the idea came to me** me vino la idea; ~ **to one's senses** volver (ue)[1b] (*past part* vuelto) sobre sí; ~ **to pass** acaecer[14]; ~ **to the point** venir[19] al caso; ~ **to the rescue** acudir

(a uno); ~ **to rest** pararse; ~ **to the same thing** venir[19] a ser lo mismo; ~ **to stay** ser[19] permanente, venir a quedarse; ~ **to terms** aceptar; **I was just coming to that** precisamente a eso iba yo

~ **together** juntarse

~ **under** estar[19] bajo la jurisdicción de; (be included in) figurar entre

~ **up** subir; (of sun *etc*) salir[19]; (of plants) brotar; (of problems) surgir[9]; (in conversation) mencionarse; *leg* comparecer[14]; ~ **up against a problem** tropezar[7] con un problema; **she came up to me in the park** ella se acercó a mí en el parque; ~ **up to** (be as good as) ser[19] tan bueno como, (be as high as) llegar[5] a, (equal) igualar; ~ **up to expectations** ser[19] tan ... como; **it came up to my expectations** era tan bueno como yo imaginaba; ~ **up with an idea** proponer[19] una idea

~ **upon** (discover) descubrir (*past part* descubierto); (find, meet) encontrarse (ue)[1a] con; ~ **upon evil days** venir[19] a menos

~ **within** ser[19] incluido en

comedian cómico (*- a f*)

comedy comedia; ~ **act** (in circus *etc*) número cómico

comeliness hermosura

comely hermoso

comer el/la que viene; **all ~s** todos los que vengan; **first-~** primer llegado

comestibles comestibles *mpl*

comet cometa *m*

comeuppance: get one's ~ llevarse lo merecido

comfort *n* comodidad *f*; (consolation) consuelo; (encouragement) ánimo; (ease from pain) alivio; (help) ayuda; **live in ~** vivir con comodidad; **she is a great ~ to me** ella me ayuda mucho; **~-loving** comodón (-ona *f*); *v* (console) consolar; (encourage) animar; (ease from pain) aliviar; (help) ayudar

comfortable cómodo; (of income) suficiente; **make o.s. ~** ponerse[19] cómodo; **child of a ~ family** hijo de una familia acomodada; ~ **living** vida holgada; ~ **win** *sp* victoria amplia

comforter (person) consolador *m* (-ora *f*); (baby's) chupete *m*; (scarf) bufanda de lana; (eiderdown) edredón

(-ones) *m*
comforting consolador (-ora *f*)
comfortless desolado; (inconsolable) inconsolable
comfy confortable
comic *n* (person) cómico; (publication) tebeo; *adj* cómico; ~ **opera** opera cómica; ~ **strip** historieta muda
comical cómico
Cominform oficina de información comunista
coming *n* llegada; ~ **of our Lord** advenimiento de Nuestro Señor; ~-**back** *n* vuelta; *adj* (approaching) que se acerca; (of month, year) próximo; (promising) de porvenir; ~ **of age** mayoría de edad *f*; ~**s and goings** entradas *fpl* y salidas *fpl*; ~-**out** (of a girl) puesta de largo; (of a new model) estreno; ~-**out party** fiesta de largo
Comintern internacional *f* comunista
comity cortesía
comma coma; **in (inverted)** ~**s** entre comillas
command *n* orden (órdenes) *f*; (control of one's feelings) dominio; *mil* mando; **he was given** ~ **of the army** le dieron la comandancia del ejército; ~ **post/module** puesto/módulo de mando; **at one's** ~ a la disposición de uno; **be in** ~ estar[19] al mando; **by royal** ~ por real orden; **have a** ~ **of** (a language) dominar; **under the** ~ **of** bajo el mando de; *v* mandar; (control of feelings) dominar; (have at one's ~) disponer[19] de; *mil* comandar; ~ **a good price** venderse por un buen precio; **she** ~**s sympathy** ella merece compasión; **they** ~**ed silence** ellos impusieron silencio
commandant comandante *m*
commandeer +*mil* requisar; *fam* apoderarse de
commander *mil* comandante *m*; *naut* capitán (-anes) *m* de fragata; ~-**in-chief** comandante *m* en jefe, (General Franco) generalísimo
commanding comandante; *fig* imponente; ~ **appearance** apariencia señorial; ~ **officer** comandante *m*; ~ **personality** personalidad *f* dominante
commandment mandamiento
commando comando
commemorate conmemorar

commemoration conmemoración (-ones) *f*; **in** ~ **of** en conmemoración de
commemorative conmemorativo
commence empezar (ie)[2a+7]; ~ (doing something) empezar a +*infin*
commencement principio
commend (to) encomendar (ie)[2a] (a)
commendable loable
commendation alabanza
commendatory laudatorio
commensurable conmensurable
commensurate proporcionado; ~ **with** conforme a
comment *n* comentario (**on** sobre); (in conversation) dicho; **'no** ~**'** 'sin comentarios'; *v* ~ **on** comentar; ~ **that** observar que
commentary comentario
commentate hacer[19] un comentario
commentator comentarista *m*+*f*; *rad*+ *TV* locutor *m* (-ora *f*)
commerce comercio; **chamber of** ~ cámara de comercio
commercial *n* *rad*+*TV* anuncio publicitario; *adj* comercial; ~ **bank** banco comercial; ~ **break** *rad*+*TV* espacio publicitario; ~ **traveller** viajante *m* (de comercio), *SA* viajero; **a record with** ~ **possibilities** un disco de corte comercial
commercialism comercialismo
commercialize comercializar[7]
commiserate compadecerse (**with** de)
commissariat comisaría
commissar(y) comisario
commission (of a crime) perpetración (-ones) *f*; *mil* nombramiento; (order) encargo; (body of people) comisión (-ones) *f*; (money) porcentaje *m*; **out of** ~ fuera de servicio, (not working) que no funciona; *v* encargar[5]; *mil* nombrar; *naut* poner[19] en servicio activo; ~**ed officer** oficial *m*
commissionaire portero
commissioner (for oaths) notario público
commit (crime) cometer; ~ **suicide** suicidarse, *fam* matarse; ~ **to memory** aprender de memoria; ~ **to prison** encarcelar; ~ **to writing** poner[19] por escrito
commitment (obligation) compromiso; *leg* auto de prisión; (crime) ejecución *f*

committal *leg* encarcelamiento
committee comité *m*; **go into ~** constituirse[16] en comité
commode (chest of drawers) cómoda; **night-~** bacín (-ines) *m*
commodious espacioso
commodity mercancía; artículo
commodore comodoro
common *n* pastos comunes *mpl*; *adj* común; (ordinary) corriente; (vulgar) vulgar; **~ gull** gaviota cana; **~ people** (commoners) estado llano; **~ sense** sentido común; **Common Market** Mercado Común; **~ to** común a; **in ~** en común; **in ~ with** de acuerdo con
Commons: House of ~ Cámara de los Comunes
commonness ordinariez *f*
commonplace *n* lugar *m* común; (expression) perogrullada; *adj* ordinario
commonwealth nación (-ones) *f*; **British Commonwealth** Mancomunidad *f* británica
commotion tumulto
communal comunal
commune comuna
communicable comunicable
communicant comulgante *m+f*
communicate comunicar[4] (**with** con); (of buildings) mandarse (**with** con)
communication comunicación (-ones) *f*; **be in ~ with** estar[19] en contacto con; **~ satellite** satélite *m* de comunicaciones; **~-trench** trinchera de acceso; **~s** sistema *m* de comunicaciones; *adj* comunicativo; **~ cord** cordón *m* de alarma
communicative comunicativo
communicator comunicante *m+f*
communion comunión *f*; **take ~** comulgar[5]
communiqué comunicado; *mil* parte *m* (de guerra)
communism comunismo
communist *n+adj* comunista *m+f*
communistic comunista
community comunidad *f*; (local) vecindad *f*; **the ~** la nación; **~ centre** centro social; *US* **~ chest** fondo municipal de contribuciones para gastos de caridad; **~ singing** canto al unísono; **~ spirit** civismo
commutable conmutable

commutation-ticket billete *m* de abono
commutator conmutador *m*
commute ir[19] al trabajo (en coche, tren *etc*); *leg* reducir; **the death sentence was ~d to one of imprisonment** la pena de muerte fue conmutada por la de prisión
commuter viajero abonado; *elect* conmutador *m*
compact *n* (agreement) convenio; (for face-powder) polvera; *adj* compacto
compacted apretado
compactness densidad *f*
companion (friend) compañero, camarada *m+f*; (one who accompanies) acompañante *m+f*; (chivalry) caballero (de una orden); **~s in distress make sorrow the less** *approx equiv* mal de muchos consuelo de tontos; **~-way** *naut* escalerilla
companionable sociable
companionship compañerismo
company *comm+mil+theat* compañía; *naut* tripulación (-ones) *f*; **she has this evening** ella tiene visita esta tarde; **keep ~ with** asociarse con, *fam* cortejar; **part ~** separarse; **~ commander** jefe *m* de compañía; **~ union** sindicato de empresa; **limited liability ~** sociedad *f* de responsabilidad limitada
comparable comparable (**with/to** con)
comparative comparativo
compare *vt* comparar (**with** con); **~ notes** comparar datos/impresiones; *vi* poderse[19] comparar (**with** con); **he is not to be ~d with my brother** él no puede compararse con mi hermano; **~ well with** no perder (ie)[2b] por comparación con; **beyond ~** sin igual
comparison comparación (-ones) *f*; **beyond ~** sin comparación; **in ~ with** comparado con; **~s are odious** toda comparación es odiosa
compartment departamento
compass (range) límites *mpl*; (magnetic) brújula; *mus* extensión *f* (de la voz/de un instrumento); **~ needle** aguja de brújula; **box the ~** cuartear la aguja
compasses compás *m sing*
compassing cercano
compassion compasión *f*
compassionate compasivo; **~ leave** permiso especial; **on ~ grounds** por compasión

compatibility compatibilidad *f*
compatible compatible
compatriot compatriota *m+f*
compel compeler (**to** a); **I feel compelled to tell you** me veo obligado a decírselo
compelling irresistible; ~ **desire to** deseo irresistible de +*infin*
compendious compendioso
compendium compendio
compensate compensar (**with** con); ~ **for** indemnizar[7] por
compensation compensación (-ones) *f*
compensatory compensador (-ora *f*)
compère *n* presentador *m*; *v* presentar a los artistas
compete competir (i)[3] (**for** para, **with** con); ~ **in a race** participar en una carrera
competence competencia; *leg* capacidad *f*
competent +*leg* competente
competing: ~ **line** *comm* renglón *m* competidor
competition concurso; competición (-ones) *f*; *comm* competencia; (exam) oposición (-ones) *f*; **in** ~ **with** en competencia con
competitive competidor (-ora *f*); ~ **examination** oposición (-ones) *f*; ~ **post** puesto de oposición; ~ **price** precio competitivo; ~ **spirit** espíritu *m* de competición
competitor competidor *m* (-ora *f*); (in competitive examination) opositor *m* (-ora *f*); (in contest) participante *m+f*; (in race) corredor *m* (-ora *f*)
compilation compilación (-ones) *f*
compile compilar
complacency satisfacción (-ones) *f* de sí mismo
complacent satisfecho de sí mismo (**about** de)
complacently con satisfacción
complain quejarse (**about** de); *leg* demandar (**about** de); **she ~ed to the manager** ella se quejó al gerente
complainant demandante *m+f*
complaining quejoso
complaint queja; *leg* demanda; *med* enfermedad *f*; **lodge/make a** ~ hacer[19] una queja, *leg* presentar[19] una demanda
complaisance complacencia
complaisant complaciente

complement, *n* *gramm*+*math* complemento; *naut* personal *m*; *v* complementar
complementary, complemental complementario
complete *adj* (entire) entero; (finished) acabado; *fam* (utter) de remate; *v* (finish) llevar a cabo; (make whole) completar; ~ **a form** (re)llenar un impreso; **I've ~d twenty years with this firm** he cumplido veinte años con esta compañía
completion cumplimiento; (finish) terminación (-ones) *f*
complex *n* *comm*+*psych* complejo; *fam* manía; **inferiority/superiority** ~ complejo de inferioridad/superioridad; *adj* complicado
complexion cutis *m*; *fig* carácter (-acteres) *m*; **that puts a different** ~ **on it** eso cambia el asunto por completo
complexity complejidad *f*
compliance sumisión *f* (**with** a); **in** ~ **with** de acuerdo con
compliant sumiso
complicate complicar[4]
complication complicación (-ones) *f*
complicity complicidad *f* (**in** en)
compliment *n* cumplido; (spoken ~ **to a** woman) piropo; ~**s** (greetings) saludos *mpl*; **give my** ~**s to** saludos a; ~**s of the season** felices navidades; *v* (congratulate) felicitar (**on** por); (praise) lisonjear, decir[19] un piropo
complimentary lisonjero; ~ **copy/ticket** ejemplar *m*/billete *m* de obsequio
compline completas *f pl*
comply conformarse (**with** con); (give way) ceder; (law) acatar
component *n*+*adj* componente *m*
comport: ~ **o.s.** comportarse
compose *mus*+*print* componer[19]; ~ **o.s.** tranquilizarse[7]; ~**d** tranquilo; (**be**) ~**d of** (estar[19]) compuesto de
composer compositor *m* (-ora *f*)
composing *mus*+*print* composición *f*; ~**-frame** *phot* bastidor *m* para la ampliación; ~**-stick** *print* componedor *m*
composite *n*+*adj* compuesto; ~ **number** número compuesto
composition composición (-ones) *f*; (essay) ensayo; (at school) redacción; *print* tipo; (sketch) diseño

compositor cajista $m+f$
compost abono compuesto; ~ **heap** montón (-ones) m de abono compuesto
composure tranquilidad f
compote compota
compound n compuesto; (enclosed space) empalizada; *adj* compuesto; ~ **fraction** quebrado compuesto; ~ **fracture** fractura complicada; ~ **interest** interés compuesto; ~ **number** número denominado; ~ **word** vocablo compuesto; v componer[19]; ~ **a felony** agravar un delito; ~ **with** capitular con
comprehend comprender; (contain) encerrar (ie)[2a]
comprehensible comprensible
comprehension comprensión f; **beyond** ~ incomprensible
comprehensive comprensivo; ~ **insurance** seguro contra todo riesgo
comprehensiveness extensión f
compress n compresa; v comprimir; ~ed **air** aire comprimido
compressibility compresibilidad f
compression compresión f; ~ **chamber** *mot* cámara de compresión; ~ **ratio** *mot* índice de compresión
compressor compresor m
comprise comprender
compromise n arreglo; **come to/make a** ~ llegar[5] a un arreglo; *vt* arreglar; (jeopardize) arriesgar[5]; *vi* transigir[9]; ~ **o.s.** comprometerse
compromising comprometedor (-ora f)
comptometer (máquina) calculadora
comptroller interventor m
compulsion compulsión f
compulsive compulsivo
compulsory obligatorio; ~ **figures** (skating) figuras *fpl* fundamentales; ~ **powers** *pol* poderes *mpl* absolutos; ~ **purchase** expropiación forzosa
compunction escrúpulo f; **without** ~ sin escrúpulo
computable calculable
computation cálculo
compute calcular
computer (operator) calculista $m+f$; (machine) computadora, ordenador m; ~ **science** informática
computerize calcular por medio de una computadora

comrade camarada $m+f$; ~ **in arms** compañero de armas
comradeship camaradería
[1] **con: pros and** ~s el pro y el contra
[2] **con** (learn by heart) aprender de memoria
[3] **con** *naut* gobernar (ie)[2a] un buque
[4] **con** n: ~-**man** timador m; v timar; **he conned me into ...** por engaño me hizo +*infin*
concatenate concatenar
concatenation concatenación f
concave cóncavo
concavity concavidad f
conceal (from) esconder (de); *leg* encubrir (*past part* encubierto); ~ed escondido; ~ed **assets** activo oculto; ~ed **lighting** iluminación indirecta; ~ed **turning** (on road) viraje oculto
concealment encubrimiento; (of feelings) disimulo m; (place of concealment) escondite m
concede conceder
conceit presunción f
conceited presumido; ~ **style** estilo conceptuoso
conceitedness presunción (-ones) f
conceivable concebible
conceivably posiblemente
conceive *med* concebir (i)[3]; (imagine) imaginar; (understand) comprender; ~ **a plan** idear un plan
concentrate n concentrado; v concentrar(se); ~ **on** concentrar la atención en, (dedicate oneself to) dedicarse[4] a; ~d **fire** *mil* fuego concentrado
concentration concentración (-ones) f; ~-**camp** campo de concentración
concentric concéntrico
concept concepto
conception concepción f
conceptual conceptual
conceptualize conceptualizar[7]
concern n (importance) interés m; (firm) empresa; (affair) asunto; (anxiety) preocupación (-ones) f; **it is no** ~ **of mine** a mí no me importa; v importar; **to whom it may** ~ a quien corresponda; ~ed **in** (involved) interesado en; ~ed **(about)** (worried) preocupado (por)
concerning tocante a
concert concierto; **in** ~ de acuerdo; *mus* **a coro**; ~-**pitch** tono normalmente

empleado en conciertos
concerted proyectado mutuamente
concertina concertina
concerto concierto
concession concesión f
concessionaire concesionario
conch concha
concierge portero
conciliate conciliar
conciliation conciliación f
conciliatory conciliatorio
concise conciso
conciseness brevedad f
conclave cónclave m
conclude concluir[16]
concluding concluyente
conclusion (end) fin m; (result) conclusión (-ones) f; in ~ por conclusión; to a ~ hasta el fin
conclusive conclusivo; (decisive) decisivo
concoct confeccionar; fig tramar
concoction (fabrication) invención (-ones) f; (mixture) mezcla; (bad food) comistrajo; (drink) brebaje m
concomitant concomitante m
concord concordia; gramm+mus concordancia
concordance concordancia; (index) concordancias fpl
concordat concordato
concourse concurso; US gran salón m de estación
concrete n hormigón m; SA concreto; ~-block bloque m de hormigón; reinforced ~ hormigón armado; ~-mixer hormigonera; adj bui de hormigón; (concept) concreto; v cubrir (past part cubierto) con hormigón
concubine concubina
concupiscence concupiscencia
concupiscent concupiscente
concur estar[19] de acuerdo (with con)
concurrence concurrencia
concurrent concurrente
concuss conmocionar
concussion concusión f; ~ of the brain conmoción f cerebral
condemn (deplore) censurar; (declare unfit) prohibir el uso de; (sentence) condenar; ~ed cell celda de los condenados a muerte; ~ed person condenado

condemnation condenación (-ones) f; (reproof) censura
condensation condensación (-ones) f; (abridgement) compendio
condense condensar; (abridge) abreviar; ~d milk leche condensada
condenser condensador m
condescend condescender (ie)[2b]
condescendence, condescension condescendencia
condescending condescendiente
condign condigno
condiment condimento
condition (stipulation) condición (-ones) f; (state) condición f; on ~ that a condición de que +subj; v (a)condicionar; ~ed reflex reflejo condicionado
conditional condicional; ~ upon a condición de que +subj
conditions condiciones fpl; ('strings') cortapisa sing
condole dar[19] el pésame (with a)
condolence(s) pésame m
condominium condominio
condonation condonación f
condone condonar
conduce conducir[15]
conducive conducente (to a)
conduct n conducta; v (lead) conducir[15]; (affairs) dirigir; (orchestra) dirigir[9], fam llevar la batuta; elect+phys ser[19] conductor de; ~ o.s. comportarse
conduction conducción f
conductivity conductividad f
conductor mus director m; (bus) cobrador m (-ora f); elect conductor m; lightning ~ pararrayos m sing+pl
conductress cobradora
conduit conducto
cone cono; mot pino; ice-cream ~ helado en cucurucho; ~-shaped cónico
coney conejo
confab(ulation) plática; have a confab platicar[4]
confectionary see confectionery
confectioner pastelero; (seller of sweets) confitero, Can dulcero; ~'s (cake-shop) pastelería, (sweet-shop) confitería
confectionery dulces mpl; (place)

confitería, *Can* dulcería
confederacy, confederation confederación *f*
confederate confederado; (criminal) cómplice *m* + *f*
confer *vt* conferir (ie)²ᶜ; *vi* ~ **with** consultar (con)
conference (assembly) congreso; (business) conferencia; reunión (-ones) *f*; ~**-table** tapete *m* verde
conferring consultación *f*
confess (admit) confesar (ie)²ᵃ; *sl* cantar; (to something) admitir; ~ **one's sins** (to a priest) confesar(se) (ie)²ᵃ
confession confesión (-ones) *f*; *eccles* (act of faith) credo
confessional *n* + *adj* confesionario
confessor (priest) confesor *m*; (penitent) confesante *m* + *f*
confetti carnavalinas *fpl*
confidant(e) confidente *m* + *f*; *fam* compinche *m* + *f*
confide fiarse (**in** de)
confidence confianza; **I have ~ in you** me fío de usted; ~ **trick** estafa; ~ **trickster** estafador *m* (-ora *f*); **full of ~** lleno de confianza; **in (the strictest) ~** con (la mayor) reserva; **self-~** presunción *f*
confident seguro; **she is ~ that** ella está segura de que
confidential confidencial; ~ **agent** confidente *m* + *f*
confidentially en confianza
confiding confiado
confine (enclose) limitar; (shut up) encerrar (ie)²ᵃ; **be ~d** *med* estar¹⁹ de parto, (imprisoned) estar¹⁹ encerrado; **be ~d to bed** guardar cama
confinement (detention) prisión (-ones) *f*; (birth) parto
confines *n* límites *mpl*
confirm (corroborate) confirmar; (ratify) ratificar⁴; *eccles* confirmar; ~**ed bachelor** solterón empedernido; ~**ed drunkard** borracho inveterado, *fam* borracho perdido
confirmation confirmación (-ones) *f*; (ratification) ratificación (-ones) *f*
confirmatory confirmativo
confiscable confiscable
confiscate confiscar⁴
confiscation confiscación (-ones) *f*
confiscator confiscador *m*

conflagration conflagración (-ones) *f*
conflict *n* conflicto; *v* ~ **with** estar¹⁹ en conflicto con; (contradict) contradecir¹⁹
conflicting contradictorio
confluence confluencia
conform conformar (**with, to** con)
conformable conforme
conformist conformista *m* + *f*
conformity conformidad *f*; **in ~ with** con arreglo a
confound confundir; ~ **it!** ¡maldito sea!; ~**ed** maldito
confraternity cofradía
confrère compañero
confront (face) enfrentar; ~ (**with**) confrontar (con); **be ~ed with** encararse con
confrontation confrontación (-ones) *f*; *mil* enfrentamiento
confuse confundir; ~ **the issue** complicar las cosas; **she ~s onions with leeks** ella confunde cebollas con puerros; ~**d** confuso
confusion confusión *f*
confutation refutación *f*
confute refutar
conga conga
congeal coagular(se)
congenial agradable
congenital congénito
conger: ~ **eel** congrio
congest apiñar; *med* congestionar
congested obstruido; *med* congestionado; **a ~ area** una región superpoblada
congestion *med* congestión *f*; **traffic ~** atasco
conglomerate aglomerar(se)
conglomeration conglomeración (-ones) *f*
Congo Congo
Congolese *n* + *adj* congoleño
congratulate felicitar; **I ~ you on having won** le felicito por haber ganado
congratulations felicitaciones *fpl*
congratulatory congratulatorio
congregate congregar(se)⁵
congregation *eccles* congregación (-ones) *f*
congregational, congregationalist congregacionalista *m* + *f*
congregationalism congregacionalismo
congress congreso; ~**man** miembro de

un congreso; *SA* congresista *m* + *f*
congressional congresional; ~ **district**
distrito electoral
congruence congruencia
congruent, congruous congruente
congruity congruencia
conic, conical cónico
conifer conífero
coniferous conífero
conjectural conjetural
conjecture *n* conjetura; *v* conjeturar
conjugal conyugal; ~ **bond** lazo conyugal
conjugate conjugar⁵
conjugation conjugación (-ones) *f*
conjunction conjunción (-ones) *f*
conjunctivitis conjuntivitis *f sing* + *pl*
conjure *vt* pedir (i)³ con instancia; ~ **up**
hacer¹⁹ aparecer; *vi* escamotear
conjurer prestidigitador *m*
conjuring prestidigitación *f*; ~ **trick** escamoteo
conker castaña; ~**s** juego infantil con
castañas
connect conectar (**with/to** con/a); (associate) asociar (**with** con); (relate)
relacionar (**with** con); (telephone)
poner¹⁹ en comunicación (**with** con);
(trains) empalmar (**with** con); **be well**
~**ed** ser¹⁹ de buena familia
connecting de unión; ~ **link** nexo; ~-**rod**
biela
connection (link) conexión (-ones) *f*;
(relationship) parentesco; (trains)
empalme *m*; ~**s** (circle of acquaintances) amistades *fpl*; **in** ~ **with** con
relación a; **in this** ~ con respecto a
esto
conning: ~ **tower** torreta
connivance connivencia
connive consentir (ie)²ᶜ (**with** con)
conniver cómplice *m* + *f*
connoisseur conocedor *m* (-ora *f*); perito; (of wine) catador *m*
connotation connotación (-ones) *f*
connote connotar
connubial conyugal
conquer *vt* (land) conquistar; (enemy)
vencer¹²; *vi* triunfar
conquering conquistador (-ora *f*)
conqueror conquistador *m*
conquest conquista
consanguineous consanguíneo
consanguinity consanguinidad *f*

conscience conciencia; **my** ~ **is clear**
tengo la conciencia tranquila; **my** ~
does not trouble me no tengo remordi-
mientos de conciencia; **guilty** ~ conciencia sucia; ~-**stricken** remordido
por la conciencia
conscientious concienzudo; ~ **objection**
objeción *f* de conciencia; ~ **objector**
objetor *m* de conciencia
conscious consciente; **be** ~ (fully awake)
tener¹⁹ conocimiento; **be** ~ **of** ser¹⁹
consciente de; ~ **mind** consciente *f*
consciously con conocimiento
consciousness conocimiento; **lose/re-**
cover ~ perder (ie)²ᵇ/recobrar el
conocimiento
conscript *n* quinto; *v* reclutar
conscription reclutamiento
consecrate consagrar; ~**d** consagrado
consecration consagración (-ones) *f*
consecutive consecutivo
consensus consenso; ~ **of opinion** opinión *f* general
consent *n* consentimiento; **by common**
~ de común acuerdo; **silence gives**
~ quien calla otorga; *v* consentir (**to**
en)
consequence consecuencia; **as a** ~ **of**
como consecuencia de; **in** ~ en consecuencia; **be of no** ~ no ser¹⁹ de ninguna importancia; **take the** ~**s** aceptar
las consecuencias
consequent consiguiente (**on** de)
consequential consiguiente; (important)
importante
consequently por lo tanto
conservancy, conservation conservación *f*
conservatism conservadurismo
conservative *n* + *adj pol* conservador *m*
(-ora *f*); (cautious) cauteloso
conservatoire conservatorio de música
conservatory *bot* invernadero; *mus*
conservatorio
conserve *n* conserva; *v* conservar
consider (believe + meditate on) considerar; (take into account) tomar en
cuenta
considerable considerable
considerate considerado
consideration consideración (-ones) *f*;
(money) remuneración (-ones) *f*; **in** ~
of en consideración a; **take into** ~
tomar en cuenta; **without (due)** ~ sin

(debida) reflexión

considering visto que; ~ **that** en vista de que

consign consignar

consignee destinatario

consigner consignador *m*

consignment consignación (-ones) *f*

consist consistir (**of** en)

consistency consistencia; (logical) consecuencia

consistent consistente (**with** con); (logic) consecuente (**with** con)

consistently firmemente

consistory consistorio

consolable consolable

consolation consuelo; ~ **prize** premio de consolación

console *n* consola; *v* consolar (ue)[1a]

consolidate consolidar

consolidation consolidación *f*

consoling consolador (-ora *f*)

consols títulos *mpl* de la deuda consolidada

consommé caldo

consonance consonancia

consonant consonante *f*

consort *n* consorte; *v* ~ **with** asociarse a

consortium consorcio

conspectus (summary) sumario; (survey) ojeada

conspicuous conspicuo; **be** ~ **by one's absence** brillar por su ausencia

conspiracy conspiración *f*

conspirator conspirador *m* (-ora *f*)

conspire conspirar

constable (agente *m* de) policía *m*; guardia *m*

constabulary policía; guardia

Constance Constanza

constancy constancia

constant *n* + *adj* constante *m*

Constantine Constantino

Constantinople Constantinopla

constellation constelación (-ones) *f*

consternation consternación *f*

constipated estreñido

constipation estreñimiento

constituency *pol* distrito electoral

constituent *n* elector *m*; *adj* constitutivo; ~ **assembly** asamblea constituyente

constitute (form) constituir[16]; (appoint) establecer[14]; (person) nombrar

constitution (nature) composición *f*; (of a person) constitución *f*; *pol* constitu-

ción *f*

constitutional constitucional; ~ **law** (jurisprudence) derecho político, (body of rules) ley orgánica

constrain constreñir (i)[3+18]

constraint apremio

constrict (squeeze) apretar; (shrink) encoger[8]

constriction constricción (-ones) *f*

constrictive constrictivo

constrictor *zool* boa *m* constrictor

construct construir[16]

construction construcción (-ones) *f*; **under** ~ en construcción; (structure) estructura; (interpretation) interpretación (-ones) *f*; *gramm* construcción *f*

constructive constructivo

construe (analyse) interpretar; (translate) traducir[15]

consul cónsul *m*; ~ **general** cónsul general

consular consular

consulate consulado

consult consultar

consultant consultor *m*

consultation consultación (-ones) *f*; *med* consulta

consultative consultivo

consulting: ~ **hours** horas *fpl* de consulta; ~ **room** consultorio

consumable consumible

consume consumir(se)

consumer *n* + *adj* consumidor *m* (-ora *f*); ~ **goods** bienes *mpl* de consumo; ~ **nation** nación (-ones) *f* consumidora; ~ **society** sociedad *f* de consumo

consumerism consumerismo

consummate *v* consumar; *adj* absoluto

consumption consumo; *med* tisis *f*

consumptive *n* + *adj* tísico

contact *n* contacto; ~ **adhesive** adhesivo de contacto; ~ **breaker** *elect* interruptor automático; ~ **lens** lentilla/lente *m* + *f* de contacto; ~ **man** representante *m* (de una empresa); ~ **print** *photo* prueba de contacto; ~ **rail** carril *m* conductor; ~s relaciones *fpl*; *v* poner(se)[19] en contacto con; *comm* establecer[14] relaciones comerciales con

contagion contagio

contagious contagioso; *fam* pegadizo

contain contener[19]; ~ **o.s.** contenerse[19]

container envase *m*; (large) contenedor

m; ~ **-ship** portacontenedores *m*
sing + *pl*

contaminate contaminar

contamination contaminación *f*

contemplate (look) contemplar; (intend) tener[19] la intención de + *infin*

contemplation contemplación *f*

contemplative contemplativo

contemporary *n* contemporáneo; *adj* contemporáneo; (fashion) moderno, *fam* yeyé *invar*

contempt desprecio; ~ **of court** contumacia; **hold in** ~ despreciar

contemptible despreciable

contemptuous despectivo; ~ **of** desdeñoso con

contend (maintain) sostener[19]; ~ **with ... over** contender (ie)[2b] con ... sobre

contender: number 1 ~ aspirante *m* + *f* número uno

[1] **content** *n* (pleasure) contento; **to one's heart's** ~ a gusto; **be** ~ **with** quedar contento de

[2] **content** (capacity) cabida; (what is contained) contenido; ~**s unknown** se ignora el contenido; ~**s table** tabla de materias

contented *adj* contento

contention disputa

contentious porfiado

contentment contento

contest (argument) disputa; (fight) contienda; *sp etc* concurso; **a fifteen-round** ~ un combate de quince asaltos; *v* disputar; *sp etc* tomar parte en un concurso; (election) ser[19] candidato en

contestant (in argument) disputante *m* + *f*; (in fight) contendiente *m* + *f*; (in sport) concursante *m* + *f*

context contexto

contiguity contigüidad *f*

contiguous contiguo

continence continencia

continent *n* continente *m*; **on the** ~ en la Europa continental; *adj* continente

continental continental

contingency eventualidad *f*

contingent *n* contingente *m*; *adj* contingente; ~ **upon** (de)pendiente de

continual continuo

continuance, continuation continuación *f*

continue continuar; ~ **speaking** seguir (i)[3+11] hablando; **please** ~ siga (usted) por favor; **to be** ~**d** continuará; ~**d from page eight** seguido de la página ocho

continuing continuo

continuity continuidad *f*; *cin* escenario

continuous continuo

continuum *math* continuo

contort retorcer(se) (ue)[1b+12]

contortion retorcimiento

contortionist contorsionista *m* + *f*

contour contorno; *geog* curva de nivel; **I like her** ~**s** me gustan sus curvas

contra contra

contraband *n* contrabando; **take/bring in** ~ colar (ue)[1a] matute; *adj* de contrabando

contrabandist contrabandista *m* + *f*

contraception anticoncepción *f*

contraceptive *n* + *adj* anticonceptivo; ~ **pill** píldora anticonceptiva

contract *n* contrato; **break a** ~ rescindir un contrato; **by** ~ por contrato; ~ **bridge** bridge contrato; **marriage-**~ esponsales *mpl*; *vt* (acquire) contraer[19]; ~ **a debt** contraer[19] una deuda; ~ **a disease** contraer[19]/*fam* coger[8] una enfermedad; *vi* contraer(se)[19]

~ **for** contratar

~ **out** salir[19] de un contrato

~ **to** comprometerse por contrato a

contracting: ~ **party** contratante *m*

contraction contracción (-ones) *f*

contractor contratista *m* + *f*

contractual contractual

contradict contradecir[19]

contradiction contradicción (-ones) *f*

contradictory contradictorio

contralto contralto *f*, (voice) *m*

contraption aparato; *sl* cacharro

contrariness terquedad *f*

contrary *n* contrario; **on the** ~ al contrario; **to the** ~ en contra; *adj* contrario; ~ **to** en contra de

contrast *n* + *TV* contraste *m*; **in** ~ por contraste; **in** ~ **to** en contraposición a; *v* ~ **with** contrastar con

contravene contravenir[19]

contravention contravención (-ones) *f*

contribute contribuir[16] (**to** a/para); ~ **to a periodical** colaborar en un periódico

contribution contribución (-ones) *f*; (in

periodical) artículo

contributor (money) contribuidor *m* (-ora *f*); (in periodical) colaborador *m* (-ora *f*)

contributory contribuidor (**to** a)

contrite contrito

contrition contrición *f*

contrivance invención (-ones) *f*; (device) artificio, *fam* aparato

contrive inventar; ~ **to** ingeniarse para

control *n* control *m*; ~ **of the seas** dominio de los mares; **be in** ~ tener[19] el mando; **have under** ~ tener[19] bajo control; **get under** ~ conseguir (i)[3+11], dominar; **remote** ~ mando a distancia; ~**-panel** tablero de instrumentos; ~**-tower** *aer* torre *f* de control; ~**s** mando(s); **at the** ~**s** en control; *v* controlar, dominar; ~ **the market** abarcar[4]; ~ **prices** regular precios; ~ **the traffic** regular la circulación; ~ **o.s.** controlarse

controller interventor *m*

controlling predominante; ~ **interest** interés *m* predominante

controversial polémico

controversy polémica

contumely contumelia

contusion contusión (-ones) *f*

conundrum adivinanza

conurbation aglomeración *f* de unidades urbanas

convalesce convalecer[14]

convalescence convalecencia

convalescent convaleciente; ~ **home** casa de reposo

convection convección *f*; ~ **heater** calentador *m* por convección

convene: ~ **a meeting** convocar[4] una reunión

convenience conveniencia; **at your earliest** ~ tan pronto como le sea posible; **marriage of** ~ matrimonio de conveniencia; (lavatory) servicio

convenient conveniente; **a** ~ **place** un sitio conveniente; **a** ~ **time** una hora oportuna

convent convento (de monjas); ~ **school** escuela de monjas

convention (meeting) asamblea; (agreement) convenio; (custom) convención (-ones) *f*

conventional convencional; ~ **weapons**

armas *fpl* clásicas

conventionality precedente *m* convencional

conventionalize hacer[19] convencional

converge convergir[9] (**upon** en)

convergence convergencia

conversant versado (**with** en); **become** ~ **with** familiarizarse[7] con

conversation conversación (-ones) *f*; (interview) entrevista; **hold** ~**s** (political *etc*) entrevistarse

conversational de conversación

converse *n* contraria; *adj* contrario; *v* ~ (**with**) conversar (con)

conversely al contrario

conversion conversión (-ones) *f*; (into cash) realización (-ones) *f*; (rugby) transformación (-ones) *f*; ~ **table** tabla de conversión

convert *n* convertido; (*esp* of pagans) converso; *v* ~ (**into**) convertir (i)[3] (en); (rugby) transformar; ~ **into cash** realizar[7]; ~ **to one's own use** apropiarse para uso propio; ~**ed try** *sp* gol *m* de transformación

converter (steel) convertidor *m*; *elect* transformador *m*

convertible *n mot* descapotable *m*; *adj* convertible; *mot* descapotable

convex convexo

convey (transport) transportar; (communicate) comunicar[4]; *leg* traspasar

conveyance (act of transporting) porte *m*; (vehicle) vehículo; *leg* traspaso; (document) escritura de traspaso

conveyancing *leg* traspasos *mpl*

conveyor portador *m*; ~ **belt** transportador *m*

convict *n* preso; *v* sentenciar

conviction *leg* sentencia; (belief) convicción (-ones) *f*

convince convencer[12]; **be finally** ~**d that** llegar[5] al conocimiento de que

convincing convincente

convivial alegre

conviviality buen humor *m*

convocation convocación (-ones) *f*

convoke convocar[4]

convolvulus convólvulo, enredadera

convoy *n* convoy *m*; *v* convoyar

convulse convulsionar; ~ **with laughter** torcerse (ue)[1b+12] de risa; **be** ~**d with**

pain retorcerse (ue)[1b+12] de dolor
convulsion convulsión (-ones) *f*; **fit of ~s** ataque *m* de convulsiones
convulsive convulsivo
cony *see* **coney**
coo *v* (of dove) arrullar
cooing *n* (of dove) arrullo
cook *n* cocinero, cocinera; **too many ~s spoil the broth** barco que mandan muchos pilotos pronto va a pique; **~-book** libro de cocina; **~-house** cocina; *v* cocer (ue)[12]; **~ breakfast/ lunch** preparar el desayuno/la comida; **~ the books** falsificar[4] las cuentas; **~ up** tramar; **what's cooking?** ¿qué pasa?
cooker cocina (de gas/eléctrica/de carbón)
cookery (arte *m* de) cocina; **~-book** libro de cocina
cookie (biscuit) galleta
cooking *n* (arte *m* de) cocina; *adj* de cocina; **~-range** cocina económica; **~-salt** sal gorda; **~-utensils** batería de cocina
cool *n* fresco, frescura; (self-control) autocontrol *m*; **keep one's ~** (not be involved) no estar[19] comprometido (en un asunto), (keep calm) guardar la calma; **lose one's ~** perder (ie)[2b] la calma; *adj* fresco; (cheeky) fresco; ('pop' *sl*) yeyé *invar*; (indifferent) indiferente; **~ as a cucumber** fresco como una lechuga; **he asked a ~ million** pidió un buen millón; **~-headed** sereno; *v* refrescar[4]; **~ one's heels** hacer[19] antesala
cooler refrigerador *m*; *sl* (gaol) jaula
coolie culi *m*
cooling refrescante; **~ system** sistema *m* de refrigeración; **~-off period** compás *m* de espera
coolish fresquito
coolness fresco, frescura; (of character) serenidad *f*
coon *zool* mapache *m*; *pej* negro
coop *n* gallinero; *v* **~ up** enjaular
co-op cooperativa
cooper tonelero
co-operate cooperar
co-operation cooperación *f*
co-operative *n* (sociedad) cooperativa; *adj* cooperativo
co-operator cooperador *m*

co-opt nombrar a uno miembro de un comité por votación extraordinaria
co-ordinate coordinar
co-ordination coordinación *f*
coot *orni* focha común
cop *n* (policeman) madero *m*; **~s** bofia; *v* coger; *fam* pescar[4]
co-partner consocio
cope *n* *eccles* capa pluvial; *v* **~ (with)** poder[19] (con)
Copenhagen Copenhague *m*
Copernicus Copérnico
co-pilot segundo piloto, copiloto
coping-stone albardilla; (well) pozal *m*
copious copioso
copper *n* *metal* cobre *m*; (boiler) caldera; (policeman) *fam* polizonte *m*, *Arg* cana; **in ~** (coins) en calderilla; **~-coloured** cobrizo; *adj* de cobre; **~-bottomed** de fondo de cobre; **~-plate** *n* (writing) letra inglesa, **~-smith** calderero; *v* encobrar
coppers (coins) calderilla; *sl* (police) bofia, madera
coppice bosquecillo
copra copra
co-production *cin* coproducción (-ones) *f*
copse bosquecillo *m*
Copt, Coptic copto
copulate copular
copulation coito
copy *n* copia; (example) ejemplar *m*; *print* original *m*; **~-book** cuaderno; **~-cat** copión *m* (-ona *f*); **~-writer** escritor *m* publicitario; *v* copiar
copying *adj* de copiar; **~-ink** tinta de copiar; **~-(-ink)-pencil** lápiz (-ces) *m* tinta; **~-machine** multicopista
copyist copista *m* + *f*
copyright derecho de autor; **~ by** es propiedad de; **~ laws** leyes *fpl* de la propiedad intelectual
coquetry coquetería
coquette coqueta
coquettish coquetón (-ona *f*)
coracle barquilla de cuero
coral *n* coral *m*; *adj* de coral; **~-reef** arrecife *m* de coral
cor anglais oboe *m* tenor
cord cuerda; (in pyjamas) trenzón (-ones) *m*; **~-tyre** *mot* neumático de cordones; **~s** pantalón de pana
cordial *n* cordial *m*; *adj* cordial

cordiality cordialidad *f*

cordite cordita

cordon *n hort+mil* cordón (-ones) *m*; *v* ~ **off** acordonar

Cordova Córdoba

Cordovan *n+adj* cordobés (-esa *f*)

corduroy pana; ~s pantalón (-ones) *m* de pana

core parte *f* central; *phys* núcleo; *elect* alma (de cable); ~ **of an apple** corazón *m* de una manzana; **I'm frozen to the** ~ estoy helado hasta los tuétanos; *v* quitar el corazón/el centro

co-respondent codemandado

Corinth Corinto

Corinthian *n+adj* corintio

cork *n* (material) corcho; ~ **tree** alcornoque *m*; ~**screw** sacacorchos *m sing+pl*; *v* tapar con corcho; ~**ed** (of wine) que sabe a corcho

corkage derechos *mpl* de descorche

corm bulbo

cormorant cormorán (-anes) *m*

¹ **corn** (grain) mies *f*; (wheat) trigo; (maize) maíz *m*; ~**field** campo de trigo, *US* campo de maíz; ~**flakes** copos *mpl* de maíz, *SA* hojuelas *fpl* de maíz; ~**flour**, ~**starch** harina de maíz; ~ **on the cob** maíz en la mazorca, *SA* tusa de maíz

² **corn** (on foot) callo; ~**-pad**, ~**-cure** callicida *m*; ~**-plaster** emplasto para los callos; ~**-remover** quitacallos *m sing+pl*

cornea cornea

corned: ~ **beef** carne *f* en lata

Cornelius Cornelio

corner *n* ángulo; (interior) rincón (-ones) *m*; (exterior) esquina; (remote place) rincón *m*; *sp* saque *m* de esquina; *fig* (predicament) apuro; **drive into a** ~ poner[19] entre la espada y la pared; **out of the** ~ **of one's eye** por el rabillo del ojo; **take a** ~ *sp* sacar[4] un córner; **turn a** ~ doblar una esquina; *adj* angular; (interior) rinconero; (exterior) esquinal; ~ **cupboard** armario rinconero; ~**-flag** *sp* banderín (-ines) *m*; ~ **house** casa de la esquina; ~**-kick** saque *m* de esquina; ~ **seat** asiento en la esquina; ~ **shop,** ~ **store** tienda de la esquina; ~**stone** piedra angular; *v* (trap) acorralar; (house) hacer esquina; *comm*

monopolizar[7]; (draughts) acochinar; (turn a corner) doblar una esquina; **this car** ~**s well** este coche toma bien las curvas

cornet corneta; **ice-cream** ~ helado en cucurucho; ~**-player** corneta *m+f*

cornice cornisa

Cornish de Cornualles

corn pone pan *m* de maíz

Cornwall Cornualles *m*

corny calloso; *fig* muy sentimental; (in poor taste) cursi; ~ **joke** chiste *m* inglés

corollary corolario

corona *astron* corona

coronary coronario; ~ **thrombosis** trombosis coronaria

coronation coronación (-ones) *f*

coroner médico forense; ~**'s inquest** pesquisa dirigida por el médico forense

coronet corona (de un título nobiliario)

corp. (**corporal**) cabo; (**corporation**) sociedad anónima

corporal *n* cabo; *adj* corpóreo

corporate social; ~ **name** razón *f* social

corporation corporación (-ones) *f*; (city administration) ayuntamiento; (firm) compañía

corporeal corpóreo

corps cuerpo

corpse cadáver *m*

corpulence corpulencia

corpulent corpulento; *fam* tripudo

Corpus Christi Corpus Cristi *m*

corpuscle corpúsculo; *anat* glóbulo

corpuscular corpuscular

corral *n* corral *m*; *v* acorralar

correct *adj* correcto; (behaviour) formal; **be** ~ (right) tener[19] razón; *v* corregir (i)[3+9]; (admonish) censurar

correction corrección (-ones) *f*; (punishment) castigo; (admonishment) censura; (in newspaper) (nota de) rectificación (-ones) *f*; ~**s** *print* fe *f* de erratas

corrective correctivo

correctness exactitud *f*

corrector corrector *m*

correlate correlacionar

correlation correlación *f*

correlative correlativo

correspond corresponder (**to, with** a); ~ **with** (write) cartearse con

correspondence correspondencia; *comm* correo; ~ **school** escuela por correspondencia

correspondent *n* (press) corresponsal *m*; (letter writer) el (la) que escribe cartas; *adj* correspondiente

corresponding correspondiente

corridor pasillo; ~**-train** tren corrido

corrigible corregible

corroborate corroborar

corroboration corroboración *f*

corroborative corroborante

corrode +*fig* (cor)roer(se)

corrosion corrosión *f*

corrosive corrosivo

corrugated ondulado; ~ **cardboard** cartón acanalado; ~ **iron** chapa ondulada

corrupt *adj* corrompido; *v* corromper; (with money) sobornar

corruptible corruptible

corruption, corruptness corrupción *f*; (bribery) soborno

corsage (bodice) corpiño; (flowers) ramillete *m*

corsair corsario

corset corsé *m*

Corsica Córcega

Corsican *n*+*adj* corso

cortège procesión (-ones) *f* funeraria; (people) cortejo

cortex corteza

cortisone cortisona

Corunna La Coruña

corvette corbeta

cosiness comodidad *f*

cosmetic cosmético; ~ **surgery** cirugía estética

cosmetics cosméticos *mpl*

cosmic cósmico

cosmographer cosmógrafo

cosmography cosmografía

cosmonaut cosmonauta *m*+*f*

cosmopolitan *n*+*adj* cosmopolita *m*+*f*

cosmos cosmos *m*

Cossack *n*+*adj* cosaco

cosset mimar

cost *n* precio; ~ **accounting** contabilidad *f* de costos; ~**, insurance and freight** costo, seguro y flete; ~ **price** precio de coste; ~ **of living** coste *m* de vida; at ~ *comm* ál coste; **at any** ~, **at all** ~s a toda costa; **at low** ~ a precio bajo; **count the** ~ estudiar los riesgos antes de obrar; *v* costar (ue)[1a]; **how much does it** ~? ¿cuánto cuesta?; **it** ~ **me a pretty penny** buen dinero me costó; ~ **what it may** cueste lo que cueste; *comm* (calculate the cost) sacar[4] el coste

co-star *n* coprotagonista *m*+*f*; *v* coprotagonizar[7]

Costa Rican *n*+*adj* costarriqueño

coster(monger) vendedor *m* ambulante de frutas *etc*

costing cálculo de costes

costly caro

costs *leg* costas *fpl*

costume traje *m*; (fancy dress) disfraz (-ces) *m*; ~ **jewellery** bisutería; ~ **play** obra de época; **tailored** ~ traje *m* sastre

costumier sastre *m* de teatro

cosy cómodo y agradable

cot (cradle) cuna; (small bed) camita de niño; (bunk) catre *m*

coterie tertulia

cottage casita de campo; ~ **cheese** requesón *m*; ~ **industry** industria casera

cotton *n* algodón *m*; ~**-bud** bastoncillo; ~ **candy** algodón azucarado; ~ **exchange** lonja del algodón; ~ **mill** algodonería; ~**-plant** algodonero; ~ **plantation** algodonal *m*; ~**tail** conejo norteamericano; ~ **waste** desperdicios *mpl* de algodón; ~**-wood** álamo; ~**-wool** algodón (hidrófilo); *adj* de algodón; *v* ~ **on(to)** entender (ie)[2b]

cottony algodonoso

couch *n* canapé *m*; sofá *m*; ~**-grass** hierba rastrera; *v* expresar

couchette litera

cough *n* tos *f*; ~**-drop** pastilla para la tos; ~**-mixture, ~-syrup** jarabe *m* para la tos; *v* toser; ~ **up** (pay) producir[15] dinero, *sl* sacar[4] la pasta; ~ **it up!** (say it) ¡suéltelo!

could (was able) *past hist* pude, pudiste *etc*; *imperf* podía, podías *etc*; (would be able) *condit* podría, podrías *etc*; ~ **have** *pluperf subj* hubiera podido, hubieras podido *etc*

council consejo; (municipal body) ayuntamiento; *eccles* concilio; ~**-house** vivienda protegida, *fam* casa social

councillor concejal *m*

counsel *n* (advice) consejo; (lawyer) abogado; ~ **for the defence** defensor *m*; ~ **for the prosecution** fiscal *m*; **keep one's own** ~ guardar silencio; **take** ~ **with** consultar; *v* aconsejar

counsellor consejero

count (calculation) cuenta; **lose** ~ perder la cuenta; (boxing) cuenta; **out for the** ~ fuera de combate; *leg* cargo; (title) conde *m*; *v* contar (ue)[1a]; *pol* (of votes) *n* escrutinio, *v* escrutar; **I don't** ~ (I have no authority) no pinto nada; **that doesn't** ~ eso no vale; ~ **on one's fingers** contar con los dedos; **don't** ~ **your chickens before they are hatched** no vendas la piel del oso antes de haberlo muerto

~**-down** *n* cuenta atrás

~ **down** *v* contar (ue)[1a] (a cero)

~ **for** valer[19]

~ **on** (rely on) contar (ue)[1a] con; **I shall** ~ **on you** contaré con usted

~ **out** no contar (ue)[1a]; ~ **me out** (don't ~ on me) no cuente conmigo; (boxing) declarar vencido

~ **up** contar (ue)[1a]

countable contable

countenance *n* aspecto; **be out of** ~ estar[19] desconcertado; *v* aprobar (ue)[1a]

counter *n* (shop) mostrador *m*; (game) ficha; **Geiger-**~ contador *m* Geiger; *v* oponerse[19]; *prep+adv* en contra; *adj* ~ **to** opuesto a

counteract contrariar; contrarrestar

counter-attack *n* contraataque *m*; *v* contraatacar[4]

counter-attraction atracción *f* rival

counter-balance *n* contrapeso; *v* contrapesar

counterblast respuesta vigorosa

counter-charge recriminación (-ones) *f*

counter-check *n* segunda comprobación *f*; *v* comprobar por segunda vez

counter-claim *n* reconvención (-ones) *f*; *v* reconvenir[19]

counter-clockwise en sentido contrario a las agujas del reloj

counter-espionage contraespionaje *m*

counterfeit *n* falsificación (-ones) *f*; *adj* falsificado; (of money) falso, ~ **note** billete falso; *v* falsificar[4]

counterfeiter falsificador *m* (de moneda)

counterfoil talón (-ones) *m*

counter-intelligence contrainteligencia

countermand revocar[4]

counter-move jugada defensiva

counter-offensive contraofensiva

counter-order contraorden (-órdenes) *f*

counterpane colcha

counterpart copia; (person) homólogo

counter-plot contramaniobra

counterpoint contrapunto

counterpoise *n* contrapeso; *v* contrapesar

counter-proposal contrapropuesta

counter-punch puntuar; *fam* contar (ue)[1a]

Counter-Reformation contrarreforma

countersign *n* contraseña; *v* refrendar

countersink avellanar

countersunk avellanado

counter-tenor contralto

countess condesa

counting: *pol* (of votes) escrutinio; ~**-house** despacho de contabilidad

countless incontable

countrified rústico

country *n* (nation) país *m*; ~ **of origin** país *m* de origen; (not town) campo; **in the** ~ en el campo; **in open** ~ en pleno campo; (region) región (-ones) *f*; **go to the** ~ *pol* celebrar elecciones generales; **live off the** ~ vivir del país; *adj* de campo; ~ **bumpkin** pardillo; ~ **club** club *m* campestre; ~ **dance** baile *m* regional; ~ **estate** finca; ~ **house** casa de campo; ~**man** campesino; ~**side** campo; ~**wide** nacional; ~**woman** campesina

county *n* condado; *fig* aristocracia; *adj* aristocrático; ~ **town** cabeza de condado/provincia

coup golpe *m*; ~ **d'état** golpe *m* de estado; ~ **de grâce** (with firearm) tiro de gracia, (blow) golpe *m* de gracia

coupé *mot* cupé *m*

couple *n* (things) par *m*; (persons, *esp* man and woman) pareja; ~ **of hours** par *m* de horas; *v* acoplar

couplet pareado

coupling acoplamiento

coupon cupón (-ones) *m*; (counterfoil) talón (-ones) *m*; (voucher) vale *m*; **football pools** ~ boleto (de las quinielas)

courage valor *m*; ~! ¡ánimo!; **pluck up**
~ hacer[19] de tripas corazón

courageous valiente

courier mensajero; (diplomatic) correo
diplomático; (tourist) guía *m+f*

course (academic) curso; *cul* plato;
(procedure) proceder *m*; (water) corriente *f*; (golf) campo de golf;
(track) pista; (horse-racing) hipódromo; (ship's) rumbo; *bui* hilada; **in
due** ~ a su debido tiempo; **in the** ~ **of**
durante; **in the** ~ **of time** andando el
tiempo; **let life take its** ~ dejarse llevar
por la vida; **of** ~ desde luego; **of** ~
not claro que no; **take a** ~ **with** seguir
(i)[3] un curso con; **crash** ~ cursillo; *v* ~
along correr

coursing cacería de liebres con galgos

court *n* (royal) corte *f*; (yard) patio; *leg*
tribunal *m*; ~ **of appeal** tribunal de
apelación; ~ **of final appeal** tribunal
supremo; ~ **of first instance** tribunal
de primera instancia; **tennis** ~ pista de
tenis; **out of** ~ fuera de banda; ~ **card**
figura; ~ **dress** traje *m* de corte; ~-
house palacio de justicia, ~ **jester**
bufón (-ones) *m*; ~ **martial** *n* consejo
de guerra; (try by) ~ **martial** someter
a consejo de guerra; ~ **order** apremio;
~**room** sala de tribunal; *v* (woo)
cortejar; ~ **disaster** arriesgarse[5]

courteous cortés *m+f*

courtesan prostituta; cortesana

courtesy cortesía; ~ **call** visita de cumplido; ~ **title** título honorífico; ~ **costs
nothing** lo cortés no quita lo valiente

courtier cortesano

courting cortejo; ~ **couple** pareja de
novios

courtly galante

courtship galanteo; (of lovers) noviazgo

cousin primo, prima

cove cala

coven reunión (-ones) *f* de brujas

covenant *n* convenio; *vt* concertar

covenanter contratante *m*; (Scots) presbiteriano escocés

cover *n* (lid of pan *etc*) tapadera; (lid of
chest *etc*) tapa; (envelope) sobre *m*;
first-day ~ sobre *m* del primer día de
emisión; (furniture) funda; (at table)
cubierto; (of book) cubierta; (of
magazine) portada; (insurance) (extensión *f* del) seguro; (layer) capa;

(pretence) pretexto; (refuge) abrigo;
(animal's lair) guarida; *mil* refugio;
give ~ *mil* dar[19] fuego de protección;
take ~ buscar[4] abrigo; **under** ~
(sheltered) bajo techo, *comm* (in an
envelope) bajo sobre; **under separate**
~ (en sobre) aparte; **outer** ~ (tyre)
cubierta; ~-**charge** precio del
cubierto; ~-**girl** muchacha de una
portada; **dust-**~ *mech* cubierta contra
el polvo, (book) camisa, (furniture)
funda guardapolvo; *v* cubrir (*past part*
cubierto); (book, furniture *etc*) forrar; (distance) recorrer; (boxing) cubrirse (*past part* cubierto); (journalism) cubrir; informar sobre; (include) abarcar[4]; (recoup) recobrar;
(with firearm) apuntar a; *comm*
asegurar; ~**ed by insurance** con póliza
de seguro; ~ **the cost** cubrir (*past part*
cubierto) el costo

~ **in** (hole) llenar

~ **off** *mil* cubrirse (*past part* cubierto)

~ **over** cubrir (*past part* cubierto) completamente

~ **up** (against cold) abrigar(se)[5]; (hide)
ocultar; (boxing) cubrirse (*past part*
cubierto)

coverage (newspaper +*rad*) cobertura

covering *n* (refuge) abrigo; (furniture)
funda; (wrapping) envoltura; *adj* cubriente; ~ **fire** fuego de protección; ~
letter carta adjunta

coverlet colcha

covert refugio; (hunting) guarida

covertly en secreto

covet codiciar

covetous codicioso

covetousness codicia

cow *n* vaca; ~-**bell** cencerro; ~**boy**
vaquero, *Arg* gaucho, *Ven* llanero,
(bad workman) chapucero; **play** (at)
~**boys and Indians** jugar (ue)[1a] a
policías y ladrones; ~-**catcher** quitapiedras *m sing+pl*; ~-**dung**, ~-**pat**
boñiga; ~-**elephant** hembra del
elefante; ~-**hand, ~-herd** vaquero;
~-**heel** pata de vaca; ~-**pox** vacuna;
~**shed** establo; *v* amilanar; **be** ~**ed**
amilanarse

coward cobarde *m+f*; *fam* gallina *m+f*;
vulg cagado

cowardice cobardía; *vulg* cagalera

cowardly cobarde; *vulg* cagado

cower agacharse

cowl (clothing) capucha; *bui* sombrerete *m* de chimenea

cowling cubierta (de la cabina)

co-worker colega *m*

cowslip vellorita

coxswain timonel *m*

coy tímido

coyly recatadamente

coyness timidez *f*

coyote coyote *m*

coypu coipo

crab cangrejo; ~-louse ladilla; **catch a ~** *fig* dar un falso golpe con el remo; ~-apple manzana silvestre; ~-apple tree manzano silvestre

crabbed, crabby avinagrado

crack *n* (sound) chasquido; ~! ¡pam!; (fissure) grieta; (joke) chiste *m*; (slit) rendija; **at the ~ of dawn** al romper el alba; *adj* de primera (categoría); ~-brained chiflado; ~-pot *n* tarambana *m*; ~ **shot** tiro certero; *vt* (split) agrietar; *chem* craquear; (a code) descifrar; ~ **a bottle** despachar una botella; ~ **a joke** contar (ue)[1a] un chiste; ~ **jokes** gastar bromas; ~ **a problem** solucionar/resolver (ue)[1b] un problema; ~ **nuts** cascar[4] nueces; ~ **a safe** forzar[7+1b] una caja de caudales; ~ed agrietado, (voice) ronco, (crazy) chiflado; *vi* agrietarse; (window) rajarse

~ **down on** castigar[5] severamente

~ **open** forzar[7+1a]

~-up *n aer* aterrizaje violento; *comm* fracaso; *med* colapso

~ **up** *v aer* estrellarse; *comm* fracasar; *med* perder (ie)[2b] la salud

cracker (firework) petardo; (biscuit) cracke(r) *m*; ~s chiflado

[1] cracking excelente

[2] cracking *n chem* craqueo

crackle crujir; *rad* chirriar

crackling (noise) crujido; (pork) chicharrón *m*

Cracow Cracovia

cradle *n* cuna; *bui* plataforma colgante; ~-song canción (-ones) de cuna; *v* acunar

[1] craft (occupation) oficio; (skill) destreza; (slyness) astucia

[2] craft *naut* embarcación (-ones) *f*

craftsman artesano

crafty astuto

crag peña

craggy escarpado

cram llenar; (study) preparar intensivamente para exámenes, *fam* empollar; (with food) hartarse; ~-full completamente lleno

crammer empollón (-ones) *m*

cramp *n med* calambre *m*; *carp* cárcel *f*; *eng* pinza de unión; **get ~** tener[19] un calambre; ~-iron grapa; *v* sujetar, grapar; ~ **s.o.'s style** cortarle las alas a uno

crampon crampón (-ones) *m*

cranberry arándano

crane *n mech* grúa; *orni* grulla; *v* estirar el cuello

cranial craneal

cranium cráneo

crank *n* (eccentric person) chiflado; *mech etc* manivela; ~-case cárter *m*; ~-handle manivela; ~-shaft cigüeñal *m*

crankily de mal humor

cranky chiflado

cranny hendidura

crap (excreta) mierda; (rubbish) tontería; (game) juego de los dados; **shoot ~** jugar (ue)[1a] a los dados; *v fam* cagar[5], *vulg* giñar

crape crespón *m*

crash *n* (noise) estallido; (collision) choque *m*; *comm* quiebra; *adj* (quick) rápido; (urgent) de urgencia; ~ **course** curso intensivo, cursillo; ~ **programme** programa *m* de urgencia; ~-dive *n* sumersión (-ones) *f* instantánea, *v* sumergirse[9] rápidamente; ~-helmet casco protector; ~-land aterrizar[7] forzadamente; ~-landing aterrizaje forzoso; *v* (fall down) derrumbarse estrepitosamente; *mot* chocar(se)[4]; *aer* estrellar(se); *comm* quebrar (ie)[2a]; ~ **into** chocar(se)[4] con, estrellarse contra; **gate~** entrar de gorra

crass craso

crate *n* embalaje *m* (de tablas); *v* ~ (up) embalar

crater cráter *m*

cravat corbata

crave anhelar; ~ **for** suspirar por

craven cobarde

craving anhelo (for de); gana(s) (for de); (during pregnancy) antojo

crawfish cangrejo de río

crawl *n* arrastramiento; (swimming) crawl *m*; *v* arrastrarse; (on all-fours) ir[19] a gatas; (swimming) hacer[19] crawl; (abase oneself) humillarse; (flatter) hacer[19] coba; ~ **along** ir[19] a paso de tortuga

crawler (abject flatterer) cobista *m+f*

crawling *adj* (abject) pelotillero

crayfish cangrejo de río

crayon pastel *m*; pintura de cera

craze (madness) manía; (fashion) moda; **mini-skirts were all the ~ in 1968** las minifaldas estaban de moda en 1968

crazed enloquecido

crazy (demented) loco, chiflado; (ridiculous) desatinado; **be ~ about** estar[19] chiflado por; **go ~** volverse loco

[1] **creak, creaking** *n* crujido

[2] **creak** *v* crujir

cream *n* (+ cosmetic) crema; *fig* flor y nata *f*, **the ~ of our youth** la flor y nata de nuestros jóvenes; ~ **bun** bollo con crema; ~ **cake** tarta de nata; ~ **cheese** queso de nata; ~ **jug** jarrita de crema; ~ **of tartar** crémor tártaro; *adj* color crema; **the houses are ~** (~-**coloured**) las casas son color crema; *v* (remove the ~) desnatar; ~ **the butter** batir la mantequilla

creamery mantequería

creamy que tiene nata/crema

crease *n* arruga; ~-**resisting** inarrugable; **there's no ~ in my trousers** mi pantalón no tiene raya; *v* arrugar(se)[5]; (fold) doblar

create crear, **God ~d the heavens and the earth** Dios creó los cielos y la tierra; (appoint) nombrar; (bring about) ocasionar; (produce) producir[15]; (make a fuss) armar un lío

creation creación *f*

creative creador (-ora *f*); *arts* imaginativo

creativity inventiva; creatividad *f*

creator creador *m*; **the Creator** el Creador

creature criatura

crèche guardería infantil; *fam* belén *m*

credence creencia; **give ~ to** dar[19] crédito a

credentials credenciales *fpl*

credibility credibilidad *f*; **the President's**

~-**gap is widening** la credibilidad (del pueblo) en el presidente está disminuyendo

credible creíble

credit *n* (trust) confianza; (honour) honor *m*; (reputation) reputación *f*; *comm* crédito; ~**s** *cin+TV* reparto; **buy on ~** comprar a plazos; **give ~** reconocer[14] el mérito, *comm* dar[19] crédito; **give s.o. ~ for** reconocer a uno el mérito de; **take ~ for** atribuirse[16] el mérito; ~ **balance** saldo acreedor; ~-**card** tarjeta de crédito; ~ **entry** asiento de crédito; *v* (believe) creer; (grant credit) conceder crédito; (enter on credit side) pasar al haber

creditable loable

creditor acreedor *m* (-ora *f*); ~ **nation** nación (-ones) acreedora

credulity credulidad *f*

credulous crédulo

creed credo; (religion) creencia

creek (inlet) cala; (river) río; **up the ~** (mistaken) desacertado, (crazy) chiflado

creep *n fam* cobista *m+f*, *vulg* lameculos *m sing+pl*; **it gives me the ~s** me da hormigueo; *v* (crawl) arrastrarse; (adulate) dar[19] coba, *sl* lamer

~ **in(to)** +*fig* deslizarse; **some errors have crept into the work** algunos errores se han deslizado en la obra

~ **out** escurrirse

~ **up** subir gradualmente; ~ **up on** acercarse[4] insensiblemente a

creeper *bot* trepadora; (person) el que se arrastra; *fam* cobista *m+f*

creeping *bot* trepador (-ora *f*); (abject) pelotillero

creepy horripilante; ~-**crawly** bichito

cremate quemar

cremation cremación (-ones) *f*

crematorium crematorio

crème: ~ **caramel** flan *m*; ~ **de menthe** crema de menta

creole *n+adj* criollo

creosote *n* creosota; *v* creosotar

crêpe crespón *m*; ~ **de chine** crespón *m* de seda, ~ **paper** papel rizado; ~ **rubber** goma de crespón

crepuscular crepuscular

crescendo crescendo

crescent creciente *f*

cress berros *mpl*

crest *orni* cresta; (of a hill) cima; (of a wave) cresta; *her* timbre *m*; (coat of arms) escudo; **~-fallen** alicaído

Cretan *n+adj* cretense *m+f*

Crete Creta

cretin cretino

cretonne cretona

crevasse grieta profunda (en un glaciar)

crevice grieta

crew *naut+aer* tripulación (-ones) *f*; **~-cut** pelo cortado al ras; **~-member** tripulante *m*

crib *n* (Christmas ~) belén (-enes) *m*; (cot) cuna; (store) granero; (aid) chuleta; *v* llevar chuletas

cribbage cierto juego de naipes

crick: ~ **in the neck** tortícolis *f sing+pl*

cricket (insect) grillo; *sp* cricket *m*; *fig* deportismo; **that's not** ~ eso es anti-deportivo; ~ **bat** palo de cricket; ~ **player, cricketer** jugador *m* de cricket; ~ **pitch** campo de cricket

crier pregonero

crikey! *fam* ¡joroba!

crime (serious) crimen (-ímenes) *m*; (minor offence) delito; (general) criminalidad *f*; *mil* falta de disciplina; ~ **novel** novela negra; ~ **passionel** crimen pasional; ~ **wave** ola de crímenes

Crimea Crimea

criminal *n* (serious offender) criminal *m*; (minor offender) delincuente *m+f*; (accused) reo; *adj* criminal; **with** ~ **intent** con intención delictiva; ~ **act** maniobra criminal; ~ **lawyer** abogado criminalista; **Criminal Investigation Department** *approx equiv* Brigada de Investigación Criminal

criminologist criminologista *m+f*

criminology criminología

crimp rizar[7]

crimson carmesí

cringe (through fear) encogerse[8]; temblar ante un peligro; (fawn) adular

cringing rastrero

crinkle *n* arruga; *v* (shrink up) arrugarse[5]; (rustle) crujir

crinkly arrugado; (hair) rizado

crinoline crinolina

cripple *n* mutilado; (with leg injury) cojo; (with arm injury) manco; *v* mutilar; (arm) dejar manco; (leg)

dejar cojo; **~d** lisiado; **~d ship** barco estropeado

crisis crisis *f sing+pl*

crisp *n* patata frita; *adj* crespo; (of food) crujiente; (of lettuce) fresca; (of punches) seco; ~ **style** *lit* estilo directo

crispness encrespadura

crispy crespo

criss-cross cruzado; (intertwined) entrelazado; ~ **stitch** zurcido

criterion criterio

critic crítico; *cin+theat* crítico (de cine/de teatro); *mus* comentarista *m+f* musical

critical (causing anxiety) peligroso; *med* crítico; (discriminating) crítico; ~ **temperature** *chem* temperatura crítica

critically: ~ **ill** gravemente enfermo

criticism crítica; (of a book, film *etc*) reseña

criticize criticar[4]

critique crítica

croak (of frog) croar; (of raven) graznar; (die) morir (ue)[1c] (*past part* muerto), *sl* diñarla; ~! ¡roac!

croaker graznador *m* (-ora *f*); *fig* (complainer) refunfuñador *m* (-ora *f*)

croaking (of frog) croar *m*

Croat, Croatian *n+adj* croata *m+f*

Croatia Croacia

crochet *v* hacer[19] ganchillo; **~-work** ganchillo

crock (*naut + mot*) cacharro

crockery vajilla; *fam* cacharros *mpl*

crocodile cocodrilo; (of schoolchildren) fila doble de alumnos de paseo; ~ **tears** lágrimas *fpl* de cocodrilo

crocus azafrán (-anes) *m*

croft pegujal *m*

crofter pegujalero

croissant cuerno

cromlech cromlech *m*

crone vieja; bruja

crony compinche *m*

crook (shepherd's) cayado; (criminal) estafador *m*; *sl* pájaro

crooked (bent) encorvado; (awry) ladeado; (twisted) doblado; (criminal) criminal, delincuente

crookedly torcidamente; *fig* pícaramente

crookedness encorvadura; *fig* perversidad *f*

croon canturrear

crooner canturreador *m* (-ora *f*)

crooning canturreo

crop *n agri* cosecha; *orni*+*zool* buche *m*;
~**-dusting** aerofumigación (-ones) *f*;
~**-eared** desorejado; *v* (harvest)
segar[5]; (eat grass) pacer[14]; (cut short)
rapar; **this apple-tree is going to** ~ **well
this year** este manzano va a dar mucho
este año; ~ **out** *min* aflorar; ~ **up**
(happen) producirse[15], (appear) aparecer[14]; **something has cropped up** ha
surgido un imprevisto

cropped: ~ **hair** pelo rapado

cropper caída (de cabeza), **he came a** ~
cayó de cabeza; *fig* fracasar

croquet croquet *m*; ~ **mallet** martillo de
croquet

croquette croqueta

crosier báculo (del obispo)

cross *n* cruz (-ces) *f*; *fig* aflicción *f*;
(hybrid) híbrido; (blow) cruzado;
left/right ~ *sp* cruzado de izquierda/
derecha; **a** ~ **marks the spot** una equis
indica el lugar; ~**-bar** tranca, *sp*
travesaño (de la portería); ~**-bearer**
eccles crucero; ~ **bill** *orni* piquituerto;
~**bones** fémures cruzados; ~**bow** ballesta; ~**-bred** mestizo; ~**-breed** *n* híbrido, *v* cruzar[7] (plantas o animales);
~**-breeding** cruzamiento de razas; ~**-
Channel** a través del Canal de la Mancha; ~**-country** *adj* a campo traviesa;
~**-country race** cross *m*; ~**-current** corriente contraria; ~**-cut file** lima de
picadura cruzada; ~**-cut saw** sierra de
trozar; ~**-examination** interrogatorio;
~**-examine** interrogar[5]; ~**-eyed** bizco;
~**-fire** *mil* fuego cruzado; ~**-grained**
veteado; ~**-legged** con las piernas
cruzadas; ~**-patch** gruñón *m* (-ona *f*);
~**-piece** pieza transversal, *carp*
crucero; **we are at** ~**-purposes** vamos
por vías opuestas; ~**-question** repreguntar; ~**-reference** contrarrefe-
rencia; ~**-road** cruce *m* (de caminos),
fig momento decisivo; ~**-section**
corte *m* transversal; ~**-section of the
population** grupo representativo
de la población; ~**-stitch** *n* punto de
cruz, *v* hacer[19] punto de cruz; ~**-talk**
diálogo humorístico (que suele consistir en preguntas y respuestas); ~**-tie**
traviesa; ~**ways** cruce *m*; ~**wind**
viento contrario; ~**wise** en (forma de)

cruz; ~**word puzzle** crucigrama *m*; *adj*
enojado; *v* (go over) cruzar[7]; (animals
of different breeds) cruzar[7]; (mark
with a cross) marcar[4] con una equis;
our letters ~**ed** nuestras cartas se
cruzaron; ~ **a cheque** cruzar[7] un
cheque; ~**ed cheque** cheque cruzado;
~ **o.s.** santiguarse[6]; ~ **one's heart**
jurar; ~ **one's mind** ocurrírsele; ~
one's palm untarle a uno las manos; ~
one's path encontrarse(ue)[a] con uno;
~ **one's t's and dot one's i's** poner[19] los
puntos sobre las íes; ~ **swords with**
medir (i)[3] las armas con

~ **out, off** borrarme; **you may** ~ **me off
your list of friends** usted puede borrarme de la lista de sus amistades

~ **over** pasar de un lado a otro

~ **with** estar[19] enfadado con

crossing cruce *m*; (voyage) travesía; ~**-
sweeper** barrendero; **level-**~ paso a
nivel; **level-**~ **watchman** guardabarrera *m*; **pedestrian-**~ paso de peatones; **zebra-**~ paso de cebra

crossness mal humor *m*

crotch entrepiernas *m sing*+*pl*

crotchet *mus* negra

crotchety (bad-tempered) malhumorado; (having odd ideas) chiflado

crouch acurrucarse[4]

croup garrotillo

croupier crupier *m*

croûton corteza de pan frito

crow *n orni* corneja; (call of cockerel)
canto (del gallo); **as the** ~ **flies** a vuelo
de pájaro; ~**'s-feet** patas *fpl* de gallo;
~**'s-nest** cofa de vigía; *v* cantar; *fig*
cantar victoria

crowbar palanca

crowd *n* gentío; (at a sporting event)
multitud *f*; **I don't go about with this** ~
no voy con este grupo; **it will pass in a**
~ no es nada bueno pero servirá;
come and help to make a ~ venga
usted para hacer cuadrilla; **two's
company, three's a** ~ hay sitio para
dos pero no para tres; *v* amonto-
nar(se); ~ **sail** *naut* hacer[19] fuerza de
vela

~ **in** entrar en tumulto

~ **out** salir[19] en tumulto; **they** ~**ed me
out** no dejaron sitio para mí

~ **together** agruparse

crowded lleno; **the room was** ~ la

habitación estaba de bote en bote; ~
city ciudad superpoblada
crown *n* corona; (of head) coronilla; (of
hat) copa; (of tooth) corona; ~ **colony**
colonia de la Corona; ~ **jewels** joyas
fpl de la Corona; ~ **land(s)** patrimonio
real; ~ **prince** príncipe heredero; ~
princess princesa heredera; *v* coronar;
fig (reward) premiar; **that** ~**s all** eso
pasa la raya
crowning *n* coronación (-ones) *f*; *adj*
más importante
crozier *see* **crosier**
crucial decisivo
crucible crisol *m*
crucifix crucifijo; *fam* cristo
crucifixion crucifixión (-ones) *f*
cruciform cruciforme
crucify crucificar[4]; *fig* atormentar
crude (uncouth) tosco; (raw) sin cocer;
~ **oil** petróleo bruto
crudity crudeza
cruel cruel
cruelty crueldad *f*
cruet vinagrera; ~ **stand** vinagreras
cruise *n* crucero; ~ **missile** misil *m* de
crucero; *v* cruzar[7]; *mot* ir[19] lentamente
cruiser crucero
cruising *adj* de crucero; ~ **height/speed**
altura/velocidad *f* de crucero; **at** ~
speed en crucero
crumb *n* miga; ~**s!** ¡Jesús!; ~-**brush**
cepillo de mesa; *v* migar[5]
crumble desmenuzar(se)[7]
crumbly desmenuzable
crummy (dirty) sucio; (poor quality) de
mala muerte
crumpet especie *f* de bollo; *sl* las
mujeres; **bit of** ~ *sl* jai *f*
crumple arrugar[5]
crunch *n* quebrantamiento; (testing-
time) momento decisivo; **then the** ~
came entonces se armó la gorda; *v*
(break) cascar[4]; (eat noisily) mascar[4];
vi crujir
crupper (horse) grupa
crusade *n* cruzada; *v* llevar una campaña
(contra algún abuso)
crusader cruzado
crush *n* (act of crushing) estrujamiento;
(crowd) aglomeración (-ones) *f* de
gente; **there was a dreadful** ~ **in the
cinema** hubo un gentío formidable en

el cine; (infatuation) infatuación
(-ones) *f*; ~-**barrier** valla; *v* aplastar;
(put down) suprimir
crushing *adj* aplastante
crust costra; (of bread) corteza; (stale
piece of bread) mendrugo; (of pie)
pasta; **earth's** ~ corteza terrestre
crustacean crustáceo
crusted encostrado (**with** de)
crusty costroso; (person) brusco
crutch muleta
crux lo esencial
cry *n* (shout) grito; (spell of weeping)
lloro; (call) llamada; (bird's call)
canto; **a far** ~ **from** un camino largo
de; **in full** ~ acosando de cerca; **have a
good** ~ desahogarse[5] llorando; **within**
~ al alcance del oído; ~-**baby** llorón
m (-ona *f*); **war** ~ grito de guerra; *v*
(shout) gritar; (weep) llorar; ~ **one's
eyes out** llorar amargamente
~ **down** desacreditar; (shout down) hacer[19] callar a fuerza de gritos;
~ **for** pedir (i)[3] llorando; ~ **for mercy**
pedir (i)[3] gracia
~ **off** renunciar; *fam* rajarse
~ **out** gritar; ~ **out against** gritar en contra de
crying *n* llanto; *adj* llorón (-ona *f*);
(notorious) escandaloso
crypt cripta
cryptic enigmático
cryptogram criptograma *m*
cryptographer criptógrafo
crystal cristal *m*; (watch glass) cristal *m*
de reloj; ~ **ball** bola de cristal (del
adivino); ~-**clear** claro como el agua;
~-**gazer** adivinador *m* (-ora *f*); ~-
gazing adivinación *f* (por medio de
una bola de cristal); ~-**set** *rad*
receptor *m* de galena
crystalline cristalino
crystallize cristalizar(se)[7]; ~**d fruit** fruta
glaseada/escarchada
crystallography cristalografía
C.S. gas gas lacrimógeno
cub *zool* cachorro; *fig* (lad) rapaz (-ces)
m; ~-**reporter** aprendiz (-ces) *m* de
periodista; **Cub Scout/Wolf Cub** lobato
Cuba Cuba
Cuban cubano
cubby-hole cuarto muy pequeño; *mot*
guantera

cube n cubo; (of sugar) terrón (-ones) m; ~ **root** raíz (-ces) f cúbica; **Rubik's** ~ cubo mágico; v cubicar[4]; elevar al cubo; **ten ~d (10³)** diez al cubo

cubic cúbico; ~ **measure** medida de capacidad

cubicle cubículo

cubism cubismo

cubist cubista m+f

cubit codo

cuckold n cornudo; v poner[19] los cuernos a

cuckoo (bird) cuclillo; (call) cucú m; (crazy) chiflado; ~-**clock** reloj m de cuclillo

cucumber pepino; **cool as a** ~ fresco como una lechuga

cud rumia; **chew the** ~ rumiar, fig meditar

cuddle n abrazo; v abrazar[7]; ~ **up to** arrimarse a

cudgel n porra; **take up ~s on behalf of** ir[19] a la defensa de; v aporrear; ~ **one's brains** devanarse los sesos

cue n (billiards) taco; theat apunte m; **take one's** ~ **from** seguir (i)[3+11] el ejemplo de; v theat apuntar

cuff n (blow) bofetada; (on sleeve) puño; (trouser turn-up) dobladillo; ~-**links** gemelos mpl; v abofetear

cuisine cocina

cul-de-sac calle f sin salida

culinary culinario

cull entresacar[4]

cullender see **colander**

culminate (in) culminar (en)

culmination culminación (-ones) f; fig colmo

culotte (garment) falda-pantalón m (pl faldas-pantalón)

culpability culpabilidad f

culpable culpable

culprit culpable

cult culto

cultivate +fig cultivar; ~ **s.o.** buscar amistad con alguien; ~**d** fig culto

·cultivation cultivo

cultivator cultivador m (-ora f); (machine) cultivadora

cultural cultural

culture n cultura; (of bacteria) cultivo; ~ **medium** medio de cultivo; v (bacteria) cultivar; ~**d** culto

culvert alcantarilla

cumber estorbar

cumbersome molesto

cumulative acumulativo

cumulus cúmulo

cuneiform cuneiforme

cunning n astucia; (skill) habilidad f; adj astuto

cunt vulg coño; euph chisme m

cup n taza; eccles cáliz (-ces) m; sp copa; **be in one's ~s** estar[19] bebido; ~-**bearer** copero; ~-**final** final f de la copa; ~-**shaped** en forma de taza; ~-**tie** partido eliminatorio (de la copa)

cupboard armario; ~ **love** amor m interesado

cupful taza

Cupid Cupido

cupidity codicia

cupola cúpula

cupreous cobrizo

cupro-nickel cuproníquel m

cur perro de mala raza; fig canalla m+f

curability curabilidad f

curable curable

curaçao curasao

curacy vicaría

curate vicario

curative curativo

curator conservador m; (of museum etc) director m; leg (in Scotland) curador m

curb n (of bridle) barbada; (kerb) bordillo; (stone) encintado, Arg cordón m de la acera; fig restricción (-ones) f; v refrenar; fig refrenar

curd cuajada; ~**s and whey** requesón m y suero; ~ **cheese** queso fresco

curdle cuajar(se); fam pasarse; ~ **the blood** horripilar

cure n cura; eccles cura; (remedy) remedio; **take a** ~ tomar una cura; ~-**all** panacea; v med curar; (by smoking) ahumar; (with salt) salar; fig (remedy) remediar

curer (for smoking) ahumador m (-ora f); (with salt) salador m (-ora f)

curfew (toque m de) queda

curia curia

curing med curación (-ones) f; (with salt) saladura; (with smoke) ahumadura

curio, curiosity curiosidad f

curious curioso

[1] **curl** sp jugar (ue)[1a] al curling

[2] **curl** *n* rizo; (lock of hair) bucle *m*; (ringlet) tirabuzón (-ones) *m*; (of smoke) espiral *m* de humo; **in ~s** rizado; *v* rizar(se)[7]; ~ **one's lips** hacer[19] una mueca de desdén; ~ **up** arrollarse, (of a person) acurrucarse[4]; ~ **up with laughter** torcerse (ue)[1b] de risa

curler rizadora

curlew *orni* zarapito, *fam* chorlito

curliness ensortijamiento

[1] **curling** *sp* (juego de) curling *m*

[2] **curling**: ~**-paper** papel *m* para rizar el pelo; ~**-tongs**, ~**-irons** rizador *m*, tenacillas *fpl*

curly rizado

curmudgeon erizo

currant (dried) pasa de corinto; (fresh) grosella; ~**-bush** grosellero

currency dinero en circulación; *fig* uso corriente

current *n+fig* corriente *f*; *elect* corriente *f*, *fam* luz *f*; *adj* corriente; ~ **account** cuenta corriente; ~**-account holder** cuentacorrentista *m+f*; ~ **affairs** temas *fpl* de actualidad; ~ **events** actualidades *fpl*; ~ **number** (of a periodical) último número

curriculum programa *m* de estudios

[1] **curry** *n* curry *m*; ~**-powder** especias en polvo para preparar el curry; *v* preparar con curry

[2] **curry** (a horse) almohazar[7]; (leather) curtir; ~**-comb** almohaza; ~ **favour** buscar favores, *fam* chupar del bote

curse *n* maldición (-ones) *f*; (oath) palabrota; (ruin) perdición *f*; **put a ~ on** echar una maldición; *vt* maldecir[19]; ~ **it!** ¡maldito sea!; *vi* blasfemar; ~ **and swear** soltar (ue)[1a] palabrotas; ~**d** maldito, (hateful) odioso; **be ~d with** tener[19] que aguantar

cursing maldiciones *fpl*; (blasphemy) blasfemias *fpl*

cursive cursivo; ~ **handwriting** letra inglesa

cursory superficial; ~ **glance** mirada rápida

curt brusco

curtail abreviar; (deprive) privar de

curtailment reducción (-ones) *f*; (deprivation) privación *f*

curtain *n* cortina; (lace) visillo; (heavy) cortinón (-ones) *m*; *theat* telón (-ones)

m; **draw the ~** correr la cortina; **drop/ raise the ~** *theat* bajar/subir el telón; **it's ~s for him** ya no tiene futuro; ~ **of fire** cortina de fuego; ~**-call** llamada al escenario (para recibir aplausos); ~**-lecture** reprimenda conyugal; ~**-raiser** pieza preliminar; ~**-ring** anilla (de la cortina); ~**-rod** barra de la cortina; *v* ~ **off** separar con cortina(s)

curtness brusquedad *f*

curtsy *n* reverencia; *v* hacer[19] una reverencia

curvaceous (of a woman) curvilínea

curvature curvatura; ~ **of the spine** desviación *f* de la espina

curve *n* curva; *mech* codo; *mot* (of road) viraje *m*; *v* encorvar(se); **the road ~s to the left** la carretera tuerce a la izquierda; ~**d** curvo

cushion *n* cojín (-ines) *m*; (billiards) baranda; *v* proteger[8] con cojines; *mech* acojinar; *fig* amortiguar

cushy (easy) fácil; (pleasant) agradable; ~ **number** empleo bien pagado y de poco trabajo; *fam* chollo

cuspidor escupidera

cuss *see* curse; ~**ed** terco

cussedness terquedad *f*

custard natillas *fpl*

custodian custodio

custody custodia; (of child) tenencia; **in ~** en la carcel; **in safe ~** en un lugar seguro; **take into ~** arrestar

custom (habit) costumbre *f*; (clientele) parroquia; (usage) uso; ~**-made** hecho a (la) medida

customary acostumbrado; **as is ~** según es norma

customer cliente *m+f*; *sl* tío; **ugly ~** tipo antipático

customs aduana; ~ **authorities** autoridades *fpl* aduaneras; ~**-duty** derechos *mpl* de aduana; ~**-house** aduana; ~**-officer** aduanero; ~**-post** puesto aduanero; **go through the ~** pasar por la aduana

cut *n* corte; (blow) golpe *m* cortante; (of cards) corte *m*; (of clothing) hechura; *comm* (lowering) reducción (-ones) *f*; *cul* (of meat) tajada; (deletion) corte *m*; (of electric power) apagón (-ones) *m*; (insult) desaire *m*; (knife-blow) cuchillada; *med* herida; *surg* incisión (-ones) *f*; (share) parte *f*; **he is a ~ above** él no se rebajaría a +*n*/*infin*; **~-price, ~-rate** a precio rebajad(ísim)o; **~-purse** carterista *m*+*f*; **~-throat** asesino; *adj* cortado, *mech* labrado; **~-and-dried** hecho; **~-and-dried ideas** ideas *fpl* cerradas; **~-glass** cristal tallado; **he has well-~ features** él tiene facciones regulares; *v* (+ cards) cortar; *comm* (losses) abandonar; (divide) partir; (stone) tallar; (wheat) segar (ie)[2a+5]; *fig* negarse (ie)[2a+5] a saludar; **~ and run** poner[19] los pies en polvorosa; **~ capers** cabriolear; **~ class** no asistir a la clase; **~ o.s.** cortarse; **I've ~ my hand** me he cortado la mano; **I'm going to have my hair ~** voy a cortarme el pelo; **~ costs** reducir los gastos; **~ prices** rebajar los precios; **~ to the quick** herir (ie)[2c] en lo más vivo; **it ~s both ways** es un arma de dos filos; **it ~s no ice** no cuenta; **the road was ~ by the floods** el camino estaba cortado por las inundaciones; **baby has ~ a tooth** al niño le ha salido un diente

~ across cortar al través; (go across) atravesar; *fig* ir[19] en contra de

~ away *n* chaque *m*

~-back *n* reducción (-ones) *f*

~ back *v* acortar; (expenses) reducir

~ down derribar (cortando); **~ down to size** reducir[15], *fig* rebajar

~ in interrumpir; (at dance) cortar; *elect* conectar

~ off cortar; *surg* amputar; (isolate) aislar; **~ off with a shilling** desheredar; **~ off in one's prime** segado en flor; (isolated) incomunicado

~ open abrir (*past part* abierto) cortando

~-out *n* diseño para recortar; *elect* cortacircuitos *mpl*; *mech* válvula de escape

~ out *v* recortar; (of stone) tallar; *fig* suprimir; **~ out a hole** hacer[19] un agujero; **be ~ out for** tener[19] un talento especial para; **have one's work ~ out to** tener[19] trabajo de sobra para poder +*infin*; **one of the engines ~ out** uno de los motores falló; **~ it out!** ¡déjese de eso!; **~ out smoking** dejar de fumar

~ short abreviar; (interrupt) interrumpir

~ up +*cul* picar[4]; **~ up rough** ponerse[19] furioso; **be ~ up (about)** acongojarse (por)

cute mono

cuteness monería

cuticle cutícula

cutlass chafarote *m*

cutler cuchillero

cutlery cuchillería

cutlet chuleta

cutter (person) cortador *m* (-ora *f*); *mech* cortadora; *naut* cúter *m*

cutting *n* +*cin* corte *m*; *hort* esqueje *m*; (from periodical) recorte *m*; (railway) desmonte *m*; (cloth) retal *m*; *adj* cortante, *fig* mordaz (-ces); **~ edge** filo

cuttlefish jibia

cyanide cianuro; **potassium ~** cianuro de potasio

cybernetics cibernética

cyclamate ciclamato

cyclamen ciclamino

cycle *n* ciclo; (bicycle) bicicleta; *v* ir[19] en bicicleta

cyclic(al) cíclico

cycling ciclismo

cyclist ciclista *m*+*f*

cyclone ciclón (-ones) *m*

cyclopaedia enciclopedia

Cyclops Cíclope *m*

cyclostyle *n* ciclostilio; *v* ciclostilar

cyclotron ciclotrón *m*

cygnet pollo de cisne

cylinder cilindro; *mech* tambor *m*; (of gas) bombona; **~-block** bloque *m* de cilindros; **~-capacity** *mot* cilindrada; **~-sleeve** camisa

cylindrical cilíndrico

cymbal címbalo; platillo

cymbalist cimbalero

cynic cínico

cynical cínico

cynicism cinismo

cypress ciprés *m*; **~-grove** cipresal *m*

Cypriot *n*+*adj* chipriota *m*+*f*

Cyprus Chipre

Cyril Cirilo

cyst quiste *m*

cystic quístico

cystitis cistitis *f*

czar *see* tsar

czarina *see* tsarina

Czech *n*+*adj* checo

Czechoslovak(ian) checoslovaco

Czechoslovakia Checoslovaquia

D

d (letter) de *f*; D *mus* re *m*

¹ **dab** (light blow) golpecito; (small quantity) untadura; *v* frotar suavemente; ~ **one's eyes** secarse⁴ los ojos; ~ **on** untar

² **dab** (fish) lenguado

³ **dab** (fingerprint) huella, *sl* fusella digital

dabble mojar; (in water) jugar (ue)¹ᵃ; (with the feet) chapotear; ~ **in** *fig* ser¹⁹ aficionado a; ~ **in politics** meterse en la política; ~ **in shares** jugar(ue)¹ᵃ a la bolsa

dabbler aficionado; **be a** ~ **in** ser¹⁹ aficionado a

dace (fish) albur *m*

dachshund perro tejonero

dad, daddy papá *m*; *SA* tata *m*

dadaism dadaísmo

dadaist *n+adj* dadaísta *m+f*

daddy-long-legs segador *m*

dado *archi* dado

daffodil narciso

daft bobo

dagger puñal *m*; **be at** ~**s drawn** estar¹⁹ a matar; **look** ~**s at** mirar con odio; ~-**blow** puñalada

dahlia dalia

Dáil parlamento de la República Irlandesa

daily *n* (newspaper) diario; *adj* diario; **our** ~ **bread** el pan nuestro de cada día; ~ **dozen** ejercicio diario; ~ **help** interina; *adv* diariamente

daintiness delicadeza

dainty *n* golosina; *adj* (appetizing) sabroso; (fastidious) delicado

dairy lechería; ~ **butter** mantequilla de granja; ~ **cattle** vacas *fpl* lecheras; ~ **farming** industria lechera; ~**maid** lechera; ~**man** lechero; ~ **products** productos lácteos

dais estrado

daisy margarita; ~-**chain** cadenita de margaritas

dale valle *m*

dalliance coqueteo

dally (waste time) tardar; (flirt) coquetear

Dalmatian dálmata

dalmatian (dog) perro dálmata

¹ **dam** *n* presa; ~ (**up**) *v* embalsar

² **dam** (animal) madre *f*

damage *n* daño(s); ~**s** indemnización (-ones) *f*; **collect** ~**s** recaudar una indemnización; **sue for** ~**s** demandar por daños y perjuicios; *v* estropear; ~**d goods** mercancías estropeadas

damaging perjudicial

Damascus Damasco

damask damasco

dame dama; *fam* tía

damn *n* maldición (-ones) *f*; **it's not worth a** ~ no vale un comino; **I don't care/give a** ~ no me importa un bledo; *adj* maldito; *v* condenar (a la pena eterna); (curse) maldecir¹⁹; **he** ~**ed my plans** él arruinó mis proyectos; *interj* ¡caramba!; ~ **it (all)!** ¡maldito sea!; ~ **you!** ¡al diablo con usted!

damnable infame

damnably horriblemente

damnation condenación *f*; **eternal** ~ eterna condenación

damned maldito; **the king be** ~! ¡llévese el rey al diablo!; **the** ~ los condenados (a la pena eterna)

damning condenatorio

damp *n* humedad *f*; *adj* húmedo; ~ **course** aislante hidrófugo; ~-**proof** impermeable

dampen (make damp) humedecer¹⁴; (cover the fire) cubrir (*past part* cubierto) el fuego

dampening humedecimiento

damper apagador *m*; regulador *m* de tiro (de la chimenea)

dampish algo húmedo

dampness humedad *f*

damsel doncella

damson (fruit) (ciruela) damascena; ~-**coloured** de color damasco

dance *n* baile *m*; danza; (function) baile

m; ~-**band** orquesta de baile; ~-**floor** pista de baile; ~-**hall** salón (-ones) *m* de baile; ~-**music** música de baile; *v* bailar, danzar[7]; **shall we** ~? ¿bailamos?; ~ **attendance on** servir[3] constantemente, *fam* no dejar ni a sol ni a sombra; ~ **for joy** saltar de alegría; ~ **with rage** saltar de rabia

danceable bailable

dancer bailador *m* (-ora *f*); (professional) bailarín *m* (-ina *f*)

dancing *n* baile *m; adj* de baile; ~-**lesson** clase *f* de baile; ~-**partner** compañero/compañera de baile; ~-**saloon** salón (-ones) *m* de baile; ~-**shoe** escarpín (-ines) *m*

dandelion amargón (-ones) *m*, diente *m* de león

dander: get s.o.'s ~ **up** enojar a uno

dandle mecer[14]

dandruff caspa

dandy *n* alfeñique *m; adj* estupendo; **fine and** ~ de primera

Dane, Danish danés *m* (-esa *f*)

danger peligro; (hidden) escollo; ~ **ahead!** ¡peligro en frente!; ~-**money** prima de riesgos; ~ **signal** señal *f* de peligro; ~ **zone** zona de peligro; ~, **road up!** ¡atención, obras!; **in** ~ en peligro; **be in** ~ **of** estar[19] en peligro de, *fam* estar[19] en un tris de; **out of** ~ fuera de peligro; **on the** ~ **list** estar[19] de cuidado; **run into** ~ encontrar (ue)[1a] peligro; **there is no** ~ no hay miedo; **there's no** ~ **of** *fig* no hay posibilidad de +*infin*/de que +*subj*

dangerous peligroso; *med* grave

dangerously peligrosamente; (seriously) gravemente

dangle *vt* colgar (ue)[1a+5]; *vi* columpiarse; **the child sat with his legs dangling** el niño estaba sentado balanceando las piernas

Danish *n+adj* danés *m* (-esa *f*)

dank húmedo

dankness humedad *f*

Danube Danubio

Daphne Dafne

dapper apuesto

dapple-grey rucio moteado

Dardanelles Dardanelos *mpl*

dare atreverse (**to** a); ~ **s.o. to** desafiarle a uno a +*infin*; **don't (you)** ~ **to** cuidado con +*infin*; ~ **say** figurarse; ~-

devil atrevido

daring atrevido; *fam* de pelo en pecho

dark *n* oscuridad *f*; (dusk) tinieblas *fpl*; **after** ~ después del anochecer; **in the** ~ a oscuras; **be (kept) in the** ~ *fig* ignorar; *adj* oscuro; (of complexion) moreno; **get/grow** ~ anochecer; **keep it** ~! ¡ocúltelo usted!; **Dark Ages** edad *f* del obscurantismo; ~ **colour** color oscuro; ~-**eyed** de ojos negros; ~ **horse** caballo no favorito, *fig* candidato desconocido; ~-**room** cámara oscura; ~ **screen** *TV* pantalla negra; ~-**skinned** moreno

darken oscurecer[14]; **don't** ~ **my door!** ¡no venga aquí más!

darkish morenillo

darkness oscuridad *f*

darling *n* querido, *fam* sol *m*; (favourite) predilecto; **what a** ~ **dress!** ¡qué vestido tan bonito!

[1] **darn** *v* (repair) zurcir[13]

[2] **darn** (damn) maldición (-ones) *f*; **I don't give a** ~ no me importa un bledo; **he doesn't know a** ~-**(ed) thing** él no sabe ni jota; ~ **(it)!** ¡caramba!

darning *n* zurcido; *adj* de zurcir; ~-**mushroom** seta de zurcir; ~-**needle** aguja de zurcir

dart *n* dardo; (dressmaking) sisa; **make a sudden** ~ hacer[19] un avance repentino; ~**s** juego de dardos; *v* lanzar(se)[7]; ~-**board** diana; ~ **out/away** marcharse rápidamente

Darwinian *n+adj* darwiniano

dash *n* (small quantity) poco; **with a** ~ **of water** con un poco de agua; *print* raya; (race) carrera; **hundred-metre** ~ cien metros lisos; (hurry) avance rápido; (energy) brío; (show) ostentación *f*; **cut a** ~ hacer[19] gran papel; **make a** ~ **for** correr hacia; **he made a** ~ **for the bus** él salió corriendo para coger el autobús; **with a** ~ **of the pen** con un rasgo de la pluma; ~-**board** *mot* tablero de instrumentos; *v* (disappoint) frustrar; **my plans were** ~**ed** mis proyectos fueron frustrados; (hurry) precipitarse; (throw) arrojar/tirar con violencia

~ **against** estrellarse contra; (of waves) romperse (*past part* roto) contra

~ **along** ir[19] rápidamente

~ **away** marcharse de prisa

~ **down** *vi* bajar aprisa; *vt* volcar[1a]

~ **off** (depart) marcharse rápidamente; (write quickly) escribir (*past part* escrito) de prisa; (do quickly) hacer[19] de prisa

~ **out** lanzarse[7] a la calle

~ **through** atravesar rápidamente; (finish quickly) terminar de prisa

~ **to pieces** hacer[19] añicos

~ **up** llegar[5] a prisa

dashing (hurried) precipitado; (person) garboso; ~ **young man** joven gallardo

dastardly cobarde

data datos *mpl*; ~**-processing** informática

datable que se puede fechar

[1] **date** *n* fecha; (appointment) cita; **what is the ~?** ¿a cuántos estamos?; ~ **of issue** fecha de expedición; **to ~** (up to now) hasta la fecha; **break a ~ with** dar[19] esquinazo a; **have a ~ with** tener[19] cita con; **make a ~ with** citarse con; **fix the ~** señalar la fecha; **out of ~** anticuado, (*esp* of fashion) pasado de moda, (of persons) atrasado de noticias; **be up to ~** estar[19] al corriente; **bring up to ~** renovar, (of persons) poner[19] al corriente; ~**-line** línea de fecha; ~**-stamp** fechador *m*, (postmark) matasellos *m sing+pl* con fecha; *v* poner[19] fecha; (appointment) salir[19] con; ~ **from** remontarse de

[2] **date** (fruit) dátil *m*; ~**-palm** (palma) datilera

dateless sin fecha

dative dativo; **in the ~** en dativo

datum dato; ~**-line** plano de referencia

daub *n* (smear) mancha; (bad painting) pintarrajo; *v* untar; ~**ed with mud** manchado de barro

dauber pintor *m* de brocha gorda

daughter hija; ~**-in-law** nuera

daughterly como (una) hija

daunt acobardar

dauntless intrépido

dauphin delfín (-ines) *m*

davenport escritorio decorado; *US* sofá *m*

davit pescante *m*

Davy: ~ **Jones' locker** fondo del océano; ~ **lamp** lámpara de seguridad (para minas)

dawdle andar[19] despacio

dawdler gandul *m* (-ula *f*)

dawdling lento

dawn *n* amanecer *m*; **at ~** al amanecer; ~ **of civilization** comienzo de la civilización; *v* amanecer[14]; **it has ~ed on me that** se me ocurre que

dawning *n* alborada

day día *m*; **the ~ after** (on the following day) al otro día; ~ **after the battle** día *m* después de la batalla; ~ **after ~,** ~ **in ~ out** día tras día; **the ~ after tomorrow** pasado mañana; **the ~ before** el día *m* anterior; **(on) the ~ before** el día anterior; **the ~ before my birthday** la víspera de mi cumpleaños; **the ~ before yesterday** anteayer; ~ **by ~** día a día; ~**-to-~ matters** asuntos corrientes; **all ~ long, all the livelong ~** todo el día; **by ~** de día; **by the ~** al día; **before ~** antes del amanecer; **call it a ~** dar[19] por terminada la jornada; **give the time of ~** dar[19] los buenos días; **good ~!** ¡buenos días!; **it's all in a ~'s work** son gajes del oficio; **my ~ begins at seven** mi jornada empieza a las siete; **name the ~** poner[19] fecha (de la boda); **the next ~** el día siguiente; **(on) the next ~** al otro día; **one fine ~** el día menos pensado; **one of these ~s** un día de estos; **this ~ and age** hoy día; **this ~ week** de hoy en ocho días; **this has made my ~** ya está completa mi felicidad; **to this very ~** hasta hoy mismo; **twice a ~** dos veces al día; **win the ~** salir[19] victorioso; **the ~ is ours** la victoria es nuestra; **St George's ~** fiesta de San Jorge; ~ **of grace** *comm* plazo de respiro; ~ **of judgement** día del juicio; ~ **off** día *m* de descanso, (servant's) día *m* de salida; ~ **out** día *m* de excursión; ~**-boarder** medio pensionista; ~**-book** libro diario; ~**-boy** alumno externo; ~**break** amanecer; **at ~break** al amanecer; ~**-cream** (cosmetics) crema de día; ~**-dream** *n* ensueño, *v* soñar despierto, *fam* estar[19] en Babia; ~**-dreamer** soñador *m* (-ora *f*); ~**-dreaming** sueños *mpl*; ~**-girl** alumna externa; ~**-labour** jornal *m*; ~**-labourer** jornalero; ~**-light** luz *f* del día, (as opposed to artificial light) luz *f* natural; ~**-light-saving time** hora de verano; **before ~light** antes del amanecer; **hours of ~light** horas *fpl* de sol; **it's ~light robbery!**

¡es un robo!; **I'm beginning to see ~light** empiezo a comprender; **~-nursery** guardería de niños; **~ school** escuela/colegio de externos; **~ shift** turno de día; **~'s holiday** día *m* libre; **~'s work** jornada; **~ ticket** billete *m* de excursión; **~time** día *m*; **in the ~time** de día

days (time) tiempos *mpl*; (years) años; **my ~ in the army** mis años en el ejército; (life) vida; **my ~ as a soldier** mi vida de soldado; **in the ~ of Napoleon** en los tiempos de Napoleón; **in olden ~** en la antigüedad, *fam* en los tiempos de Maricastaña; **in our ~** en nuestros tiempos; **in my younger ~** en mi juventud; (in) **these ~** hoy día; (in) **those ~** en aquellos tiempos; **those were the ~!** ¡qué tiempos aquéllos!

daze *n* deslumbramiento; **be in a ~** estar[19] trastornado; *v* trastornar

dazzle deslumbrar

dazzling deslumbrador (-ora *f*)

d.c. (**direct current**) c.c. (corriente continua)

D.D. (**Doctor of Divinity**) Doctor en Teología

D-Day día *m* D

deacon diácono

deaconess diaconisa

dead *n* muertos *mpl*; **speak ill of the ~** hablar mal de los muertos, *fam* desenterrar (ie)[2a] los muertos; **in the ~ of night** en las altas horas de la noche; **in the ~ of winter** en pleno invierno

adj (not alive) muerto; (withered) marchito; (numb) entumecido; (complete) completo; *elect* sin corriente; (switched off) interrumpido; **~-ball** *sp* pelota fuera de juego; **~-ball line** (rugby) línea de balón muerto; **~ body** cadáver *m*; **~ calm** calma profunda, *naut* calma chicha; **~ centre** *mech* punto muerto; **~ certainty** certeza completa; **~-end** callejón (-ones) *m* sin salida; **~ ground** *mil* terreno libre al alcance de fuego; **~ heat** empate *m*; **~ hours** horas *fpl* muertas; **~ key** (typewriter) clave muerta; **~ language** lengua muerta; **~ letter** carta devuelta, *leg* letra muerta, *fig* papel mojado; **~-letter office** sección *f* de cartas devueltas; **~line** fecha tope; **~lock** punto muerto; **the talks**

reached **~lock** las conversaciones llegaron a punto muerto; **~ loss** pérdida total; **he is a ~ loss** él no vale para nada; **~ march** marcha fúnebre; **~-pan** cara sin expresión; **~ reckoning** estima; **~ set on** empeñado en; **~ shot** tirador certero; **~ silence** silencio absoluto; **~ slow** al paso de tortuga; **~ sound** ruido sordo; **~ stop** parada en seco; **come to a ~ stop** pararse en seco; **~ to the world** insensible; **~ weight** peso muerto, *fig* estorbo; **~ wood** *fig* cosa inútil; **be ~** haber[19] muerto, estar[19] muerto; **be a ~ man** *fig* tener[19] la muerte segura; **drop (down) ~** caer[19] muerto; **the fire is ~** el fuego está apagado; **in ~ earnest** en serio; **I'm in ~ earnest** estoy hablando en serio; **in a ~ faint** desmayado como muerto; **Dead Sea** mar Muerto

adv (exactly) exactamente; (completely) del todo; (deeply) profundamente; **~ beat** rendido, *fam* hecho polvo, *vulg* jodido; **~ broke** sin cinco; **~ certain** segurísimo; **~ drunk** borracho perdido; **~ easy** facilísimo, *sl* chupado; **~ level** absolutamente llano; **~ sure** absolutamente seguro; **~ tired** muerto de cansancio; **be ~ against** estar[19] completamente opuesto a; **stop ~** parar(se) en seco

deaden amortiguar[6]

deadening amortiguador (-ora *f*)

deadliness carácter *m* mortal

deadly mortífero; *med* mortal; **~ enemy** enemigo mortal; **~ nightshade** belladona; **~ sin** pecado mortal; **seven ~ sins** siete pecados capitales

deadness (lack of spirit) desanimación *f*; (numbness) entumecimiento; (of flowers *etc*) marchitez *f*

deaf sordo; **he was ~ to my entreaties** él se hizo el sordo a mis súplicas; **become ~** ensordecer[14]; **fall on ~ ears** caer[19] en saco roto; **as ~ as a doorpost** tan sordo como una tapia; **~-aid** audífono; **~ and dumb, ~ mute** sordomudo; **~-and-dumb alphabet** alfabeto manual

deafen ensordecer[14]

deafening ensordecedor (-ora *f*)

deafness sordera

[1] **deal** *n* (transaction) negocio; (agreement) convenio; **do/make a ~** llegar[5] a

un convenio; **it's a ~!** ¡trato hecho!;
(at cards) reparto; **whose ~ is it?** ¿a
quién le toca dar?; **good/great ~** mucho; (satisfactory settlement) buen
negocio; **bad ~** mal negocio; **~ between two parties** convenio entre dos
interesados; **raw ~** mal trato; **square
~** buen trato; *v* (at cards) dar[19],
repartir; **~ a blow** dar[19] un golpe, *fig*
destruir de un golpe; **I always ~ at
that shop** siempre hago las compras en
aquella tienda; **this book ~s with life
in Egypt** este libro trata de la vida en
Egipto
~ in comerciar en
~ out repartir
~ with (do business with) negociar con
² **deal** (wood) pino
dealer comerciante *m*; (cards) el que da
las cartas, *SA* tallador *m*
dealings relaciones *fpl*; *comm* transacciones *fpl*
dean decano; *eccles* deán *m*
deanery decanato; *eccles* deanato
dear *n* querido, querida; *adj* (beloved)
querido; (charming) encantador
(-ora *f*); (expensive) caro; **~ Sir/
Madam** Muy señor mío/señora mía;
Sirs Muy señores míos/nuestros; **~
me!, oh ~!** ¡Dios mío!
dearest queridísimo
dearly (with affection) cariñosamente;
~-bought pagado caro; **love ~** querer
mucho
dearness (of price) precio alto
dearth escasez *f* (of de)
death muerte *f*; *leg* óbito; **be at ~'s door**
estar[19] a la muerte; **be worked to ~**
estar[19] muerto de tanto trabajar; **put
to ~** ajusticiar; **to the ~** hasta la
muerte; **~-bed** lecho de muerte; **~-
benefit fund** fondo de defunción; **~-
blow** golpe *m* mortal; **~ certificate**
partida de defunción; **~ duties** derechos *mpl* de herencia; **~ knell** toque *m*
de difuntos; **~-like** sepulcral; **~-mask**
mascarilla; **~ penalty** pena de muerte;
~ rate mortalidad *f*; **~ rattle** estertor
m; **~ ray** rayo mortífero; **~-roll** lista
de las víctimas; **~'s head** calavera; **~-
trap** lugar peligroso; **~ warrant**
sentencia de muerte; **~ watch** vela(torio); **~-watch beetle** reloj *m* de la
muerte; **~ wound** herida mortal

deathless inmortal
deathly de la muerte
deb debutante *f*
débâcle desbordamiento
debag quitarle a uno los pantalones
debar excluir[16]; **~ s.o. from** privar a
alguien de
debark desembarcar[4]; (remove the
bark) quitar la corteza
debarkation desembarco
debase degradar; (coinage) falsificar[4]
debasement degradación *f*; (of coinage)
falsificación (-ones) *f*
debatable discutible
debate *n* debate *m*; *v* debatir
debater polemista *m+f*
debauch corromper
debauch(ery) libertinaje *m*
debenture obligación (-ones) *f*; **~-
holder** obligacionista *m+f*
debilitate debilitar
debility debilidad *f*
debit debe *m*; débito; **~ balance** saldo
deudor; **~ and credit** debe y haber *m*;
~s and credits gastos e ingresos; **~
entry** asiento de débito; **on the ~ side**
en la columna de gastos; *v* cargar[5] (en
una cuenta)
debonair gallardo
deboost *space* desaceleración *f*
Deborah Débora
debouch desembocar[4]
debris escombros *mpl*
debt deuda; **~ collector** cobrador *m* de
deudas; **~ of honour** deuda de honor;
run into ~ contraer deudas; *fam* entramparse
debtor deudor *m*; *comm* cargo
debunk desmitificar
debunker desmitificador *m* (-ora *f*)
debunking desmitificación *f*
début debut *m*; *theat* estreno; **make
one's ~** debutar
débutante debutante *f*
decade década
decadence decadencia
decadent decadente
decagram(me) decagramo
decalitre decalitro
decalogue decálogo
decametre decámetro
decamp escaparse; *fam* tomar las de Villadiego; *sl* zafarse
decant decantar

decanter garrafa
decapitate decapitar
decapitation decapitación (-ones) *f*
decarbonize descarbonizar[7]
decasualization finalización *f* de trabajos eventuales
decathlon decatlón *m*
decay *n* (rot) pudrimiento; (teeth) caries *f sing*; (withering) marchitez *f*; (decline) caída; *v* (rot) pudrirse; (of teeth) carearse; (decline) decaer[19]
decease defunción *f*; ~**d** *n* + *adj* difunto
deceit(fulness) engaño
deceitful engañoso
deceitfully engañosamente
deceivable fácil de engañar
deceive engañar; (disappoint) desilusionar
deceiver impostor *m* (-ora *f*)
deceiving engañador (-ora *f*)
decelerate disminuir[16] la velocidad
deceleration deceleración *f*
December diciembre *m*
decency decencia; (chastity) pudor *m*; (honour) honradez *f*; **the decencies** buenos modales *mpl*
decent decente; (chaste) honesto; (fairly good) módico; (honourable) honrado; (likeable) simpático; **make/earn a ~ living** ganar lo suficiente (para vivir)
decentralization descentralización *f*
decentralize descentralizar[7]
deception decepción (-ones) *f*; (mistake) desengaño
deceptive engañoso
deceptiveness decepción *f*
decibel decibelio
decide decidir; *leg* determinar; ~ **to do something** resolver (ue)[1b] hacer algo
decidedly categóricamente
deciding decisivo
deciduous caedizo
decigramme decigramo
decilitre decilitro
decimal *n* fracción (-ones) *f* decimal; *adj* decimal; ~ **coinage** sistema *m* decimal de moneda; ~ **point** coma (de decimales); ~ **system** sistema *m* decimal; **correct to one/two/three ~ place(s)** correcto en décimas/centésimas/milésimas; **recurring ~** fracción decimal periódica
decimalize reducir[15] al sistema decimal

decimate diezmar
decimetre decímetro
decipher descifrar
decipherable descifrable
decision decisión (-ones) *f*; *leg* sentencia; (agreement) acuerdo; (firmness) resolución (-ones) *f*; **reach/come to a ~** llegar[5] a un acuerdo
decisive decisivo
[1] **deck** *n naut* cubierta; **go (up) on ~** subir a cubierta; **on ~** sobre cubierta; **all hands on ~!** ¡todo el mundo arriba!; ~ **of cards** baraja, *SA* naipe *m*; ~**-chair** tumbona; ~**-hand** marinero (de cubierta); ~**-house** camareta sobre cubierta; ~**-load** carga de cubierta; ~**-tennis** tenis *m* de cubierta
[2] **deck** *v* engalanar; ~ **o.s.** engalanarse
declaim declamar
declaimer declamador *m* (-ora *f*)
declamation declamación (-ones) *f*
declamatory declamatorio
declarable declarable
declaration declaración (-ones) *f*
declare declarar; ~ **o.s. against** declararse contra
declension *gramm* declinación (-ones) *f*
declination declinación (-ones) *f*
decline *n* decadencia; (in prices) baja; (in demand) disminución *f*; (in trade) depresión *f*; *med* debilitación *f*; **the patient is in a ~** el enfermo va perdiendo sus fuerzas; *v* (fall off) decaer[19]; (refuse) rehusar; *med* debilitarse; *gramm* declinar; ~ **to (do s.t.)** negarse (ie)[2a+5] a (+ *infin*); ~ **an invitation to** rechazar[7] una invitación a + *infin*; **his health has ~d** su salud ha empeorado
declivity pendiente *m*
declutch desembragar[5]
decoct hacer[19] un cocimiento
decoction decocción *f*
decode descifrar
decoder descifrador *m*
decoding desciframiento
decoke descarburar
de-colonize descolonizar[7]
de-colonization descolonización *f*
décolleté escotado
decompose descomponer[19]
decomposition descomposición *f*
decompress descomprimir
decompression descompresión *f*; ~

chamber cámara de descompresión
decompressor descompresor *m*
decontaminate descontaminar
decontamination descontaminación *f*; ~
squad equipo de descontaminación
decontrol *n* terminación *f* de control; *v*
terminar el control de
décor decorado; *theat* escenografía
decorate decorar; (a person) adornar;
(confer a medal *etc*) condecorar
decoration decoración (-ones) *f*; (personal) adorno; (medals *etc*) condecoración (-ones) *f*
decorative decorativo
decorator decorador *m* (-ora *f*); **painter
and** ~ pintor *m* y empapelador *m*;
interior ~ decorador *m* de interiores
decorous decoroso
decorum decoro
decoy *n* señuelo; ~ **bird** pájaro de reclamo; *v* atraer[19] con señuelo; *fam* entruchar
decrease *n* disminución (-ones) *f*; ~ **in
the death rate** descenso de la mortalidad; *v* disminuir[16]
decreasing decreciente
decreasingly cada vez menos
decree *n* decreto; ~ **nisi** divorcio provisional; *v* decretar
decrepit decrépito
decrepitude decrepitud *f*
decry desacreditar
dedicate dedicar[4]; ~ **o.s. to** dedicarse[4] a
dedication dedicación (-ones) *f*; (of a
book) dedicatoria
dedicatory dedicatorio
deduce deducir[15]
deducible deducible
deduct restar; (make a deduction from a
price) descontar (ue)[1a]
deductible deductible
deduction (conclusion) deducción
(-ones) *f*; (money) descuento
deed hecho; (outstanding) hazaña; *leg*
escritura; ~ **of gift** escritura de donación; ~ **of conveyance** escritura de
traspaso; ~-**poll** escritura legal
dee-jay *rad* comentarista *m*+*f de discos*;
fam pinchadiscos *m sing*+*pl*
deem considerar
deep *adj* profundo; **it is two metres** ~
tiene dos metros de profundidad; **the
crowd waited ten** ~ la muchedumbre
esperaba diez en fondo; (intense)

fuerte; (bass) profundo; (astute) astuto; ~ **in debt** cargado de deudas; ~
in thought ensimismado; ~-**dyed**
redomado; ~-**felt** hondamente sentido; ~-**fried** frito en mucho aceite;
~ **mourning** luto riguroso; ~ **sea** alta
mar; ~-**sea diving** submarinismo; ~-
sea fishing pesca de altura; ~-**rooted**,
~-**seated** arraigado; ~-**set eyes** ojos
hundidos; **be in** ~ **water** *fig* estar[19] con
el agua hasta el cuello; **go in at the** ~
end arrojarse sin miedo en un asunto;
go off the ~ **end** enfurecerse[14]
deepen *vt* profundizar[7]; (increase) aumentar; ~ **a colour** intensificar[4] el
tono de un color; *vi* hacerse más pro-
fundo/más hondo; *fig* intensificarse[4];
the sound ~ed el ruido se hizo más
grave
deep-freeze *n* congelador; **in** ~ congelado; *v* congelar
deepness profundidad *f*; (astuteness)
astucia
deer ciervo; ~-**stalker** (person) cazador
m de acecho, (hat) sombrero de cazador
de-escalate desescalar
de-escalation desescalada
deface desfigurar; (damage) estropear
defacement desfiguración *f*
de facto de hecho
defalcate desfalcar[4]
defalcation desfalco
defamation calumnia; ~ **of character**
difamación *f*
defamatory calumnioso
defame calumniar
default *n* omisión (-ones) *f*; **by** ~ *leg* en
rebeldía; **in** ~ moroso; **in** ~ **of** a falta
de; *v* faltar; ~ **in payment** faltar en el
pago
defaulter delincuente *m* + *f*
defeat *n* derrota; *v* derrotar; ~ **one's
own ends** defraudar sus propias intenciones
defeatism derrotismo
defeatist *n*+*adj* derrotista *m*+*f*
defecate defecar[4]
defecation defecación *f*
defect *n* defecto; *v* desertar; ~ **to the
enemy** desertar al enemigo
defection defección *f*; deserción (-ones)
f
defective defectuoso

defectiveness deficiencia

defence +*leg* defensa; (justification) justificación *f*; ~s *mil* defensas, (fortifications) fortificaciones *fpl*; ~ **in depth** defensa en fondo; ~ **lawyer** abogado defensor, *sl* alivio; **in ~ of** en defensa de; **Minister of Defence** Ministro de Defensa; ~**man** (baseball) defensa *m*

defenceless indefenso

defencelessness indefensión *f*

defend defender (ie)[2b]; *fig* vindicar[4]; ~ **one's good name** vindicarse[4]; ~ **one's title** (boxing *etc*) jugarse (ue)[1a+5] el título

defendant acusado

defender defensor *m* (-ora *f*); *sp* (fullback) defensa *m*

Defense: ~ **Department** *US* ministerio de defensa

defensible defendible; (justifiable) justificable

defensive *n* defensiva; *adj* defensivo; **be on the ~** estar[19] a la defensa

defer (put off) aplazar[7]; ~ **to** deferir (ie)[2c] a

deference deferencia; **in ~ to** teniendo respeto a

deferential respetuoso

deferment aplazamiento

deferred: ~ **payment** pago a plazos; **by ~ payments** a plazos

defiance desafío; **in ~ of** en contra de

defiant desafiador (-ora *f*)

deficiency deficiencia (**in** en); ~ **disease** enfermedad *f* por carencia

deficient deficiente (**en** in)

deficit déficit *m*

defier desafiador *m* (-ora *f*)

defile *n* desfiladero; *v* (pollute) ensuciar; *mil* desfilar

defilement contaminación *f*

defiler corruptor *m*

definable definible

define definir; *leg* determinar

definite definido; ~ **article** *gramm* artículo definido

definition definición (-ones) *f*; (meaning) acepción (-ones) *f*; *opt* precisión *f*

definitive definitivo

deflate desinflar; (money) reducir[15] (el valor de); (enthusiasm) desilusionarse

deflation desinflación *f*; *econ* reducción *f*

deflect desviar(se)

deflection desvío

deflector desviador *m*

defloration desfloración *f*

deflower desflorar; *fig* violar

defoliate deshojar

defoliation defoliación *f*

deforest desmontar; *SA* desboscar[4]

deforestation desmonte *m*

deform deformar

deformation deformación (-ones) *f*

deformed deforme

deformity deformidad *f*

defraud defraudar

defray sufragar[5]; costear

defrayment subvención (-ones) *f* (de gastos)

defreeze, defrost descongelar; (windscreen) desescarchar

defrock degradar

deft diestro

deftness destreza

defunct difunto

defuse desactivar

defy desafiar; (face) arrostrar; (contravene) contravenir[19]

degauss neutralizar[7] las minas magnéticas

degeneracy, degeneration degeneración *f*

degenerate *n*+*adj* degenerado; *v* degenerar

degradation degradación *f*

degrade degradar

degrading degradante

degree grado; (academic) título; **by ~s** poco a poco; **in the highest ~** en sumo grado; **to a (certain) ~** hasta cierto punto; **take a ~** graduarse

degression decrecimiento

dehumanize deshumanizar[7]

dehumidifier secadora

dehydrate deshidratar

dehydration deshidratación *f*

de-ice descongelar

de-icer descongelador *m*

deification deificación *f*

deify deificar[4]

deign dignarse (**to** a)

deism deísmo

deist deísta *m*+*f*

deity deidad *f*

dejected descorazonado

dejection melancolía

de jure legalmente

dekko mirada; **let's have a ~** a ver

delay *n* tardanza, retraso; **without further** ~ sin más tardar; *v* (put off) diferir; (be late) tardar; (obstruct) impedir (i)³; **my wife ~ed me** mi esposa me entretuvo; **~ed-action** (de) acción retardada

delectable deleitable

delegacy delegación *f*

delegate *n* delegado; *v* delegar⁵

delegation delegación (-ones) *f*

delete borrar

deletion supresión (-ones) *f*

delft loza fina

deliberate *adj* (intentional) premeditado; (slow) pausado; **his foolishness is** ~ su necedad es buscada; *v* deliberar

deliberately (intentionally) con premeditación, *fam* queriendo; (slowly) pausadamente

deliberation (consideration) reflexión *f*; (discussion) discusión (-ones) *f*; (slowness) lentitud *f*

deliberative: ~ **body** cuerpo deliberativo

delicacy (choiceness) delicadeza; (food) manjar *m* (exquisito)

delicate delicado; (sickly) enfermizo; (difficult) difícil; (of taste) exquisito

delicatessen ultramarinos *mpl*

delicious delicioso; *fam* rico

delight *n* delicia; *v* encantar; ~ **in** deleitarse en

delighted encantado; ~ **(to know you!)** ¡encantado!; **be** ~ **to** tener¹⁹ mucho gusto en +*infin*; **be** ~ **with** estar¹⁹ encantado con

delightful encantador (-ora *f*)

Delilah Dalila

delimit delimitar

delineate delinear

delinquency delincuencia; **juvenile** ~ delincuencia juvenil

delinquent *n+adj* delincuente *m+f*; **juvenile** ~ delincuente juvenil

delirious delirante

delirium delirio; ~ **tremens** delirium *m* tremens

deliver (free) liberar; (hand over) entregar⁵, repartir; (bring) traer¹⁹; ~ **a baby** asistir a un parto; **be ~ed of a child** dar¹⁹ a luz; ~ **a judgement** *leg*

pronunciar; ~ **the mail** repartir el correo; ~ **the goods** (do what is expected) hacer¹⁹ lo prometido; ~ **a speech** pronunciar un discurso; **we shall** ~ **it** lo llevaremos a su casa; ~ **up** entregar; **~ed free** *comm* porte pagado

deliverance liberación *f*

deliverer salvador *m*

delivery entrega; (birth) alumbramiento; (post) reparto; (of speech) pronunciación *f*; (of singing) claridad *f*; **on** ~ **of** a la entrega de; **~-man** recadero *m*; **~-note** nota de entrega; **~-room** *med* sala de alumbramiento; **~-van** furgoneta de reparto

delouse despiojar

delphinium espuela de caballero

delta (letter) delta *f*; (of river) delta *m*; ~ **wing** ala en delta; **~-winged plane** avión *m* con alas en delta

delude engañar; ~ **o.s.** engañarse

deluge *n* diluvio; *fig* inundación (-ones) *f*; *v* diluviar; *fig* inundar

delusion engaño; **be under the** ~ **that** equivocarse⁴ creyendo que

de luxe de lujo

delve (dig) cavar; ~ **into** (investigate) investigar⁵

demagogic demagógico

demagogue demagogo

demagogy demagogia

demand *n* petición (-ones) *f*; *comm, pol, leg* demanda; *econ* consumo; ~ **note** pagaré a la vista *m*; **be in** ~ scr¹⁹ popular, *comm* tener¹⁹ demanda; **on** ~ al solicitarse; *v* pedir (i)³; (claim) reclamar

demanding exigente

demarcate demarcar⁴

demarcation demarcación (-ones) *f*; ~ **line** línea de demarcación; ~ **dispute** disputa laboral acerca de la distribución de trabajo

demean: ~ **o.s.** rebajarse **(to a)**

demeanour conducta

demented demente

demerit demérito

demesne tierra solariega

demigod semidiós *m*

demigoddess semidiosa

demijohn damajuana

demilitarization desmilitarización *f*

demilitarize desmilitarizar⁷

demimonde mujeres *fpl* de la vida
demise fallecimiento
demisemiquaver fusa
demo (demonstration) mani *f* (manifestación)
demobilization desmovilización *f*
demobilize desmovilizar[7]; ~**d** (having completed military service) licenciado, (at end of general mobilization) desmovilizado
democracy democracia
democrat demócrata *m+f*
democratic democrático
democratize democratizar[7]
demolish demoler (ue)[1b]
demolition demolición *f*
demon demonio
demoniac(al) demoníaco
demonology demonología
demonstrable demostrable
demonstrate (show) demostrar (ue)[1a]; *pol* manifestarse
demonstration demostración (-ones) *f*; *pol* manifestación (-ones) *f*
demonstrative demostrativo
demonstrator demostrador *m* (-ora *f*); *pol* manifestante *m+f*
demoralization desmoralización *f*
demoralize desmoralizar[7]
demoralizing desmoralizador (-ora)
demote rebajar en grado; *mil* degradar
demotion descenso de grado; *mil* degradación *f*
demur *n* (hesitation) vacilación *f*; (objection) inconveniente *m*; *v* (hesitate) vacilar; (raise objections) poner[19] inconvenientes, *fam* sacar[4] peros
demure modesto
demureness gravedad *f*
den (lair) madriguera; (of thieves) guarida; (study) gabinete *m*; (in zoo) recinto
denationalization desnacionalización *f*
denationalize desnacionalizar[7]
denaturalize desnaturalizar[7]
denatured: ~ **alcohol** alcohol desnaturalizado
deniable negable
denial negación (-ones) *f*; **self-~** abnegación *f*
denier (of nylons) denier *m*, *fam* cabo
denigrate denigrar, *fam* poner[19] a uno como un trapo
denim tela fuerte de algodón; ~ **trou-**

sers, ~**s** pantalón (-ones) *m* vaquero
denizen habitante *m*
Denmark Dinamarca
denominate denominar
denomination clase *f*; *eccles* secta
denominational sectario
denominator denominador *m*
denotation denotación *f*
denote (mean) denotar; (designate) designar
denouement desenlace *m*
denounce denunciar; *fam* soplar
denouncement denuncia; *fam* soplo
denouncer denunciante *m+f*; *fam* soplador *m* (-ora *f*)
dense denso; ~ **fog** niebla espesa; ~ **wood** bosque tupido; **he is very** ~ él es muy torpe
densely densamente; ~ **populated country** país (-íses) *m* con gran densidad de población
denseness densidad *f*; (of the mind) estupidez *f*
density densidad *f*
dent *n* abolladura; *v* abollar(se); ~**ed** abollado
dental dental; ~ **mechanic** mecánico dentista; ~ **surgeon** odontólogo
dentifrice dentífrico
dentist dentista *m+f*; ~**'s** (surgery) consulta del dentista
dentistry odontología
denture dentadura; **he wears** ~**s** él lleva dentadura postiza
denturist mecánico dentista
denude despojar (**of** de)
denunciation denuncia
deny (contest) negar (ie)[5]; (refuse) denegar (ie)[2a+5] a; (give up) renunciar; ~ **o.s.** negarse[2a+5]
deodorant *n+adj* desodorante *m*
deodorize desodorizar[7]
depart irse[19]; (turn aside) desviarse; (die) morir[1c] (*past part* muerto); **the train** ~**s at two** el tren sale a las dos
departed (dead) difuntos *mpl*; (person who has left) ido
department departamento; (of a store) departamento; *pol* ministerio; ~(**al**) **store** almacén (-enes) *m*; **Department of the Navy** ministerio de Marina; **Department of the Interior** ministerio de la Gobernación
departmental departamental

departure salida; ~ **platform** andén (-enes) *m* de salida

depend depender (**on** de); **it** ~s **on you** depende de usted; **it** ~s **on whether** depende de si; **it** (**all**) ~s depende; **you can** ~ **on me** usted puede contar conmigo

dependable seguro; (of a person) digno de confianza

dependant dependiente *m+f*

dependence dependencia

dependency dependencia

dependent *adj* dependiente *m+f*; ~ **upon** (waiting for) pendiente de; (owing livelihood to) dependiente de

depict representar

depilate depilar

depilatory depilatorio

deplete agotar

depletion agotamiento

deplorable deplorable

deplore deplorar

deploy desplegar[5+2a]

deployment despliegue *m*

depopulate despoblar (ue)[1a]

depopulation despoblación *f*

deport deportar

deportation deportación (-ones) *f*

deportee deportado

deportment conducta

depose destronar; *leg* declarar; **the** ~**d mayor** el cesado alcalde

deposit *n* (money) depósito; ~ **account** cuenta de ahorros; (sediment) poso; *chem* precipitado; *geol* yacimiento; **put down a** ~ *comm* hacer un depósito; *v* (place) colocar[4]; (money) ingresar; (sand) sedimentar; *chem* precipitar

deposition deposición (-ones); *leg* testimonio

depositor depositador *m* (-ora *f*)

depository almacén (-enes) *m*

depot (store) almacén (-enes) *m*; *mil* depósito; *mil* (vehicle store) parque *m*; (for trams, buses etc) cochera; (*US* railway station) estación (-ones) *f*

depravation depravación *f*

deprave depravar

depravity perversión (-ones) *f*

deprecate desaprobar (ue)[1a]

deprecatingly con desaprobación *f*

deprecatory deprecativo

depreciate depreciar(se); *mot etc* perder

(ie)[2b] el valor; (have poor opinion of) menospreciar

depreciation   *comm*   depreciación (-ones) *f*; *fig* desprecio

depredation depredación (-ones) *f*

depress (dispirit) entristecer[14]; *comm* bajar; (press down) deprimir

depressed triste

depressing (pressing down) deprimente; (sad) triste; ~ **weather** tiempo muy triste

depressingly con tristeza/melancolía

depression (hollow) hoyo; (sadness) desaliento; *comm+med+meteor* depresión *f*; *comm* (prices) baja

depressive depresivo

deprivation privación *f*

deprive privar (**of** de); *eccles* destituir[16] (**of** de); ~ **o.s.** privarse (**of** de)

depth profundidad *f*; **be ... metres in** ~ tener[19] ... metros de profundidad; (thickness) espesor *m*; (of feelings) intensidad *f*; (wisdom) sagacidad *f*; **in the** ~ **of winter** en pleno invierno; **study in** ~ estudio detallado; **be out of one's** ~ cubrirle (*past part* cubierto) a uno el agua, *fig* estar[19] en honduras; **be in the** ~ **of despair** estar[19] en el abismo de desesperación; ~s profundidades *fpl*, lo más hondo; ~-**charge** carga de profundidad

deputation diputación (-ones) *f*

depute diputar, delegar

deputize: ~ **for** sustituir[16] a

deputy (representative) representante; *pol* diputado; (*US* policeman) policía *m*; ~-**governor** vicegobernador *m*; ~-**head** subjefe *m*

derail descarrilar

derailment descarrilamiento

derange (disturb) desordenar; (mentally) trastornar (el juicio)

deranged trastornado (el juicio)

derangement (disorder) desorden (-órdenes) *m*; (mental) trastorno

de-rate desgravar

de-rating *n* desgravación *f*

Derby carrera del Derby

derby (*US* hat) sombrero hongo; **local** ~ *sp* derby *m*

derelict *n naut* derrelicto; *adj* abandonado

dereliction desamparo; abandono; ~ **of duty** descuido del deber

deride burlarse de
derision irrisión *f*
derisive irrisorio
derisory irrisorio; *fam* guasón (-ona *f*); **a ~ amount** una cantidad irrisoria
derivation derivación (-ones) *f*; (origin) proveniencia
derivative derivativo
derive derivar; **~ from** proceder de; **~ pleasure (from)** sacar[4] gusto de; **~ profit (from)** sacar[4] provecho (de)
dermatitis dermatitis *f*
dermatologist dermatólogo
dermatology dermatología
derogate detractar (**from** de)
derogation detracción *f*
derogatory despectivo
derrick (crane) grúa; (oil-~) torre *f* (de perforación)
dervish derviche *m+f*
descant *n+adj mus* discante *m*; *v mus* discantar; **~ on** disertar sobre
descend descender (ie)[2b]; bajar; **the sun ~s in the west** el sol se pone en el oeste; **~ from** descender (ie)[2b] de; **when I die this crown will ~ to you** cuando muera esta corona pasará a ti; **~ upon** caer[19] sobre, (turn up unexpectedly) llegar[5] inesperadamente, (invade) invadir
descendant descendiente *m+f*
descending descend(i)ente; **~ arpeggio** arpegio descendente; **~ series** serie *f* descendente
descent descenso; (slope) declive *m*; (family) estirpe *f*; **of noble ~** de noble linaje; (invasion) invasión *f*; **Descent from the Cross** Descendimiento de la Cruz
describable descriptible
describe describir (*past part* descrito); (draw) dibujar
description descripción (-ones) *f*; (type) clase *f*
descriptive descriptivo
descry divisar
desecrate profanar
desecration profanación *f*
desegregate desegregar[5]
desegregation desegregación *f*
desert *n* desierto; (merit) mérito; **~s** lo merecido; **get one's ~s** recibir su merecido; *adj* desierto; *v* abandonar; *mil* desertar (ie)[2a]

deserted (left) abandonado; (uninhabited) despoblado
deserter desertor *m*
desertion *leg* abandono; *mil* deserción (-ones) *f*
deserve merecer[14]
deservedly merecidamente
deserving merecedor (-ora *f*); **be ~ of** merecer(se)[14]
desiccate desecar[4]; **~d coconut** coco rallado
desiccation desecación *f*
design *n* (project) proyecto; (intention) intención (-ones) *f*; (pattern) dibujo; **he is studying ~** él estudia el arte de dibujo; **have ~s on** codiciar; *v* (plan) proyectar; (draw) diseñar, dibujar
designate *adj* nombrado; **bishop ~** obispo designado; *v* (point out) designar; (appoint) nombrar
designation designación *f*
designer dibujante *m*
designing *n* arte *m* de dibujo; *adj* intrigante
desirability conveniencia
desirable deseable; (convenient) conveniente
desire *n* deseo; gana(s); (will) voluntad *f*; **I have a (great) ~ to** tengo (muchas) ganas de *+infin*; *v* desear; (command) mandar; (request) rogar (ue)[1a]
desirous deseoso (**of** de)
desist desistir; **~ from** dejar de *+infin*
desk (school) pupitre *m*; (office) escritorio; (with pigeon-holes) casillero; **~-clerk** recepcionista *m+f*; **~-sergeant** (police) sargento de servicio
desolate *adj* (forlorn) desolado; (uninhabited) desierto; *v* desolar
desolation desolación *f*
despair *n* desesperación *f*; **be in ~** estar[19] desesperado; *v* desesperar(se); **~ of** desesperar(se) de *+n/infin*
despairing desesperado
despatch *see* dispatch
desperado bandido
desperate desesperado; **~ criminal** malhechor violento
desperately desesperadamente; (furiously) furiosamente
desperation desesperación *f*; (fury) furia
despicable despreciable
despicably bajamente
despise despreciar

despite a pesar de
despoil despojar
despoliation despojo
despondency desaliento
despondent desalentado
despondently con desaliento
despot déspota *m*
despotic despótico
despotism despotismo
dessert postre *m*; **~-spoon** cuchara sopera; **~-spoonful** cucharada grande
de-Stalinize desestalinizar[7]
destination destino
destine destinar
destiny destino
destitute desamparado; **~ of** privado de
destitution indigencia; destitución
destroy destruir[16]; (put an end to) acabar con; (kill) matar; **be ~ed** ser[19]/estar[19] destruido
destroyer (person + *naut*) destructor *m*
destructible destructible
destruction destrucción *f*
destructive destructivo; **the elephant is a ~ animal** el elefante es un animal destructor; **~ criticism** censura no constructiva
desultory pasajero, esporádico
detach separar(se); (unstick) despegar[5]; *mil* destacar[4]; (stand out) destacar(se)[4]; *mech* desmontar
detachable separable; *mech* desmontable; (of clothing) de quita y pon; **~ collar** cuello postizo
detached separado; (impartial) imparcial; **~ house** casa independiente
detachment (objectivity) objetividad *f*; *mil* destacamento
detail *n* detalle *m*; *mil* destacamento; **in ~** en detalle, detalladamente, *fam* ce por be; **go into ~s** explicar[4] detalladamente, entrar en (los) detalles; *v* detallar, particularizar[7]; *mil* destacar[4]
detailed detallado; **~ specification** especificaciones detalladas; **make ~ calculations** hacer[19] cálculos detallados
detain detener[19]; (delay) atrasar
detainee detenido
detect descubrir (*past part* descubierto); **you will be ~ed by the police** usted será descubierto por la policía; (notice) percibir; *elect* detectar
detectable perceptible
detection descubrimiento

detective *n* detective *m*; *adj* de detectives; **~ novel** novela policíaca
detector (person) descubridor *m* (-ora *f*); *rad* rectificador *m*; *elect* detector *m*; *naut* detector *m* (de torpedos)
detente distensión *f*
detention (arrest) detención *f*; (confinement) encierro
deter desanimar; (dissuade) disuadir; (prevent) impedir (i)[3]; **~ from** disuadir de
detergent detergente *m*
deteriorate empeorar(se)
deterioration empeoramiento *f*
determination determinación *f*
determine (resolve) decidir; (insist) empeñarse en; (fix) señalar; determinar; **~ the results** determinar los resultados
determined (resolved) resuelto; (of prices *etc*) fijo; **it is ~ by** depende de; **be ~ to** empeñarse en
determining: **~ factor** determinante *n*
determinism determinismo
deterrent *n* fuerza disuasiva; **act as a ~** servir (i)[3] como un freno; **nuclear ~** fuerza disuasiva nuclear; *adj* disuasivo
detest detestar
detestable detestable
detestation aborrecimiento
dethrone destronar
dethronement destronamiento
detonate *vi* estallar; *vt* hacer[19] estallar
detonating detonante; **~ powder/gas** pólvora/gas *m* detonante
detonation detonación (-ones) *f*
detonator detonador *m*; (railway signal) señal *f* detonante
detour *n* desvío, desviación *f*; **make a ~** hacer[19] un desvío; *v* desviar
detract quitar mérito (from a)
detraction detracción *f*
detractor detractor *m*
detriment perjuicio; **to the ~ of** con menoscabo de
detrimental (to) perjudicial (a/para)
detritus *med + geol* desperdicios *mpl*
deuce (cards) dos *m*; (tennis) deuce *m*, cuarenta iguales; **what the ~!** ¡diablos!; **there's going to be the ~ of a row** va a arder Troya
deuced maldito
Deuteronomy Deuteronomio
devalu(at)e desvalorizar[7]

devaluation desvalorización (-ones) *f*
devastate devastar
devastation devastación *f*
develop desarrollar(se); *phot* revelar
developer *phot* revelador *m*
developing (of countries) en vía de desarrollo; ~ **tank** *phot* tanque *m* revelador
development desarrollo; *phot* revelación *f*; (event) acontecimiento; (exploitation) explotación *f*
deviance desviación *f*; **sexual** ~ desviación sexual
deviate desviar(se)
deviation desviación (-ones) *f*
deviationism desviacionismo
deviationist desviacionista *m+f*
device (invention) invención (-ones) *f*; (contrivance) aparato, mecanismo; (motto) divisa; (scheme) plan *m*; (trick) estratagema *m*
devil *n* diablo; **little** ~ diablillo; **the Devil** Satanás; ~'**s advocate** abogado del diablo; ~ **worship** adoración *f* de espíritus malos; **go to the** ~! ¡vete a freír churros/espárragos!, *vulg* ¡vete a la mierda!; **play the (very)** ~ **with** arruinar por completo; **poor** ~ pobre diablo; **the** ~ **take it!** ¡lléveselo el diablo!; **what the** ~! ¡qué diablos!; **what the** ~ **do you want?** ¿qué diablos quiere usted?; ~-**may-care** audaz (-ces); *v cul* poner[19] mucho picante
devilish endiablado
devilishly endiabladamente
devilled *cul* picante
devilment, devilry diablura; (wickedness) maldad *f*
devious tortuoso
deviousness extravío
devise idear
deviser autor *m* (-ora *f*)
devitalize desvitalizar
devoid desprovisto (**of** de)
devolution devolución *f*; *pol* autonomía
devolve corresponder (**on** a)
devote dedicar[4]; ~ **o.s. to** dedicarse[4] a
devoted (enthusiastic) fervoroso; (loyal) leal
devotedly con devoción
devotee aficionado; (religious) devoto; (admirer) admirador *m* (-ora *f*)
devotion (religious) devoción *f*; (to task *etc*) dedicación *f*; (keenness) celo;

(loyalty) lealtad *f*; ~**s** rezo(s)
devotional devoto
devour devorar; *fig* destruir[16]
devouring devorador (-ora *f*)
devout devoto
devoutness devoción *f*
dew rocío; ~**drop** gota de rocío
dewlap papada
dewy rociado
dexterity destreza
dextrous diestro
diabetes diabetes *f*
diabetic *n+adj* diabético
diabolic(al) diabólico
diadem diadema
diaeresis diéresis *f*
diagnose diagnosticar[4]
diagnosis diagnóstico
diagnostic *n+adj* diagnóstico
diagonal *n+adj* diagonal *f*
diagonally diagonalmente
diagram esquema *m*
diagrammatic esquemático
dial *n* cuadrante *m*; (of clock) esfera; (of phone) disco; (of machine) indicador *m*; *v* (telephone) marcar[4] (el número); (call by phone) llamar (por teléfono); ~ **the police** llamar (por teléfono) a la policía
dialect dialecto
dialectal dialectal
dialectic dialéctico; ~**s** dialéctica
dialling: ~ **tone** señal *f* de llamada
dialogue diálogo
diameter diámetro; **three cm in** ~ tres centímetros de diámetro
diametric(al) diametral
diamond diamante *m*; (cards) diamante *m*, (*Sp* cards) oro; ~ **cutter** cortavidrios *m sing*; ~-**shaped** en forma de diamante; ~ (**wedding**) **anniversary** bodas *fpl* de diamante
Diana Diana
diaper paño higiénico; pañal *m*
diaphanous diáfano
diaphragm diafragma *m*; *elect+mech* membrana; ~ **pump** bomba de membrana
diapositive diapositiva
diarist diarista *m+f*
diarrhoea diarrea
diary (libro) diario; (pocket) agenda
diatonic diatónico
diatribe diatriba

dice *n* dados *mpl;* *v* jugar (ue)[1a] a los dados; *cul* cortar en cubos pequeños
dicey (doubtful) dudoso; (risky) arriesgado
dichotomy dicotomía
dick detective *m*; **clever ~** sabihondo; *vulg sl* (penis) pito
dicky pechera postiza; (seat) trasera; **~-bird** piopío
Dictaphone *tr* dictáfono
dictate (command) mandar; (give dictation) dictar; **I don't like being ~d to** no me gusta que me manden
dictation dictado
dictator dictador *m*
dictatorial dictatorial
dictatorship dictadura
diction dicción *f*
dictionary diccionario
dictum (order) dictamen (-ámenes) *m*; (saying) dicho; *leg* fallo
didactic didáctico
diddle engañar; (financially) estafar; **~ out of** quitar por engaño
[1] **die** (*pl* dice) *n* dado; **the ~ is cast** la suerte está echada; *eng etc* troquel *m*; **~ sinker** grabador *m* en hueco
[2] **die** *v* morir (ue)[1c] (*past part* muerto); fallecer[14]; (finish) cesar; (wither) marchitarse; **~ early/young** morir (ue)[1c] joven; **~ laughing** morirse (ue)[1c] de risa; **~ like flies** morir (ue)[1c] (*past part* muerto) como chinches; **~ a natural death** morir (ue)[1c] por causas naturales; *fam* morir (ue)[1c] en la cama; **I'm dying to go** me muero por ir; **I'm dying with curiosity** estoy muerto de curiosidad; **never say ~!** ¡mientras hay vida hay esperanza!
~ away desaparecer[14] poco a poco; (light) palidecer[14]; (noise) dejar de oírse; (go from sight) desaparecer[14]
~ down extinguirse[11] poco a poco; (conversation) acabarse; (wind) amainar; (sound) dejar de oírse
~ off ir[19] muriendo
~ out (be forgotten) olvidarse; (go out of fashion) pasarse de moda; (become extinct) dejar de existir
diehard *n+adj* tradicionalista *m+f*
Dieppe Diepa
diesel *adj* diesel *invar*; **~-electric** dieseleléctrico; **~ engine** motor *m* diesel; **~ fuel** gas-oil *m*; **~ train** tren *m* diesel

diet *n* dieta; régimen (regímenes) *m* (dietético); (assembly) dieta; **be on a ~** estar[19] a dieta; *vt* poner[19] a dieta; *vi* estar[19] a dieta
dietary, dietetic dietético
dietetics dietética
dietician dietista *m+f*
differ (disagree) no estar[19] de acuerdo; **~ from** (be different from) diferir (ie)[2c] de
difference +math diferencia; (disagreement) desacuerdo; (argument) disputa; **it makes no ~ (to me)** (me) es igual
different (not the same) distinto; (diverse) diverso; **he is of quite a ~ breed** él es de madera distinta
differential *n* mot diferencial *m*; *adj* diferencial; **~ calculus** cálculo diferencial
differentiate diferenciar(se)
differentiation diferenciación *f*
differing diferente
difficult difícil
difficulty dificultad *f*; **be in ~** estar[19] en dificultades; (perplexed) estar[19] confuso; **get into ~** meterse en dificultades; **make difficulties** (raise objections) *fam* sacar[4] peros
diffidence modestia
diffident modesto
diffract difractar
diffraction difracción *f*
diffuse difundir; *chem* mezclarse
diffused difuso; **~ lighting** iluminación difusa
diffusion difusión *f*; *chem* mezcla
dig *n arch* excavación (-ones) *f*; (poke) empujón (-ones) *m*; (with the elbow) codazo; **~s** (lodgings) alojamiento; *v arch* excavar; **~ the soil** cultivar la tierra; (poke) dar[19] un empujón, (with the elbow) dar[19] un codazo; (rummage) escarbar; (understand, appreciate) apreciar; **~ that crazy music!** ¡escucha esa música fantástica!; **I don't ~ Chopin** no me gusta Chopin; **~ a mine** zapar
~ in *mil* abrir (*past part* abierto) trincheras; *fam* (eat heartily) comer vorazmente
~ (deeply) into one's pocket *fig* rascarse[4] el bolsillo

~ **out** excavar; ~ **one's way out** escaparse cavando

~ **up** desenterrar (ie)2a; ~ **up potatoes** sacar4 patatas; (find) hallar; (seek information) averiguar6

digest n resumen (-úmenes) m; leg digesto; v (food) digerir (ie)2c; (knowledge) asimilar; **easy to** ~ fácil de digerir

digestibility digestibilidad f

digestible digerible

digestion digestión f; (of ideas) asimilación f

digestive digestivo; ~ **juices** jugos biliarios; ~ **system** aparato digestivo

digger cavador m (-ora f); (machine) excavadora; fam australiano

digging acción f de cavar; ~s minas fpl; arch excavaciones fpl

digit math cifra; anat dedo

digital digital; ~ **computer** computadora digital

digitalis digital f

dignified majestuoso

dignify dignificar4

dignitary dignatario

dignity dignidad f; (rank) cargo; (pride) altivez f; (stateliness) majestad f; **stand on one's** ~ darse19 importancia

digress divagar5

digression divagación (-ones) f

dike n (wall) dique m; (ditch) canal m; (irrigation) acequia; v represar

diktat mandato

dilapidated arruinado; (shabby) raído

dilapidation ruina f

dilate dilatar(se) (**upon** sobre)

dilation dilatación f

dilatoriness (slowness) lentitud f; (delaying) tardanza

dilatory (causing delay) dilatorio; (slow) lento

dilemma dilema m; **be in a** ~ estar19 en un aprieto

dilettante diletante m+f

diligence diligencia; (care) cuidado; (vehicle) diligencia

diligent diligente; (careful) concienzudo

dilly-dally perder (ie)2b el tiempo; fam pasearse el alma por el cuerpo

dilute adj diluido; v diluir16

dilution dilución (-ones) f

diluvial diluvial

dim adj (dark) oscuro; (indistinct) confuso; (stupid) lerdo; ~ **light in the distance** luz (-ces) f tenue a lo lejos; **my sight is** ~ tengo la vista turbia; **it's a** ~ **look-out** el prospecto es malo; **I take a** ~ **view of that** no me gusta eso; **in the** ~ **and distant past** fam en los tiempos de Maricastaña; v oscurecer14; (of lights) reducir15 la intensidad de una luz; **time** ~s **my memory** el tiempo borra mi memoria

dime moneda estadounidense de diez céntimos; ~-**novel** novelucha; ~-**store** tienda donde se venden artículos de poco valor

dimension dimensión (-ones) f; ~s (measurements) medidas fpl

dimensional dimensional

diminish disminuir16; ~**ed seventh** mus séptima disminuida

diminishing menguante

diminution disminución f

diminutive n+adj diminutivo

dimly indistintamente, vagamente

dimmer elect regulador m de luces

dimness oscuridad f; (of light) tenuidad f

dimple hoyuelo

dimpled con hoyuelos

dimwit lerdo

din estrépito; fam barullo; **the traffic made a great** ~ el tráfico armó mucho barullo; ~ **it into** metérselo en la cabeza

dine (in evening) cenar; (at midday) comer; ~ **s.o.** convidar a cenar/comer a uno; ~ **out** comer/cenar fuera

diner (person) comensal m; (on train) coche m comedor

ding-ding tintín m

ding-dong talán talán m

dinghy bote m

dinginess suciedad f; (of a person) desaseo

dingle valle estrecho y arbolado

dingy sucio; (dress) deslustrado; (person) desaseado

dining: ~-**car** coche m comedor; ~-**room,** ~-**hall** comedor m, (in institution) refectorio; ~-**table** mesa (de comedor)

dinky pequeñ(it)o

dinner (in evening) cena; (at midday) comida; ~'**s ready** la cena/la comida está servida; **have** ~ comer, cenar;

over the ~ **table** de sobremesa; ~ **hour** la hora libre (para comer); ~**-jacket** smoking *m*; ~**-party** cena; ~**-service** vajilla; ~**-time** hora de comer; ~-**waggon** carrito

dinosaur dinosaurio

dint: by ~ **of** a fuerza de

diocesan diocesano

diocese diócesis *f sing+pl*

diode diodo

dioxide dióxido

dip *n* (bathe) baño; **take a** ~ tomar un baño; (immersion) zambullida; *geol* pendiente *f*; ~ **in the ground** declive *m* en el terreno; ~**stick** varilla (de aceite); *v* bañar; ~ **into a book** hojear un libro; ~ **the flag** bajar la bandera; ~ **the headlights** bajar los faros; **the road** ~**s** la carretera se inclina hacia abajo; **she** ~**s the biscuit in the milk** ella moja la galleta en la leche

diphtheria difteria

diphthong diptongo

diphthongize diptongar[5]

diploma (title) diploma *m*; (document) título

diplomacy diplomacia; **gunboat** ~ diplomacia de la cañonera

diplomat, diplomatist diplomático

diplomatic diplomático; ~ **corps** cuerpo diplomático

dipper (ladle) cazo; *orni* mirlo acuático; **big** ~ montaña rusa; **Big Dipper** *astron* Osa Mayor; **Little Dipper** Osa Menor

dipsomania dipsomanía

dipsomaniac dipsómano

dire horrendo

direct *adj* directo; (not crooked) recto; (straightforward) inequívoco; ~ **action** acción directa; ~ **current** corriente continua; ~ **object** acusativo; ~ **opposite** todo lo contrario; ~ **ratio** razón directa; ~ **speech** oración directa; ~ **taxation** contribución directa; ~ **train** tren directo; **score a** ~ **hit** dar[19] en el blanco; *v* (show the way) dirigir[9]; (command) ordenar; **he was** ~**ed to wait** le ordenaron que esperase/esperara; ~ **a firm/film** dirigir[9] una empresa/una película

direction dirección (-ones) *f*; **in the** ~ **of** con rumbo a; (command) dirección (-ones) *f*; (on letter) señas *fpl*; ~

finder radiogoniómetro; **sense of** ~ orientación *f*; ~**s** (instructions) instrucciones *fpl*; ~**s for use** instrucciones para el uso; **in all** ~**s** por todas partes

directional director (-ora *f*); *rad* direccional

directly directamente; (right away) en seguida; (absolutely) precisamente

directness franqueza

director director *m* (-ora *f*); **managing** ~ (director) gerente *m*; **board of** ~**s** consejo de administración; ~**s** (of football club) directiva

directorate junta directiva

directorship *n* directorio

directory guía; **business** ~ guía comercial; **telephone** ~ guía telefónica

dirge lamento

dirigible *n+adj* dirigible *m*

dirk puñal *m*

dirt suciedad *f*; (mud) lodo; (soil) tierra; (dust) polvo; (excrement) excremento, *fam* mierda; (dishonesty) inmundicia; ~ **cheap** baratísimo; ~-**road** carretera blanca; ~**-track** (racing) (carreras *fpl* en) pista de ceniza

dirtiness suciedad *f*; (meanness) bajeza

dirty *adj* sucio; **his hands are** ~ él tiene las manos sucias; **get** ~ ensuciarse; (muddy) enlodado; (indecent) indecente, *fam* verde; ~ **joke** chiste *m* verde; ~ **look** mirada desagradable; **give someone a** ~ **look** mirar a uno despectivamente; ~ **night** (bad weather) noche *f* de perros; ~ **old man** viejo verde; ~ **trick** mala pasada; ~ **weather** tiempo de perros; *v* ensuciar

disability incapacidad *f*; (injury) inhabilitación *f*

disable incapacitar; *leg* imposibilitar

disabled incapacitado; inválido; *naut* fuera de servicio; ~ **soldier** mutilado (de guerra); **the** ~ los inválidos, los mutilados

disablement invalidez *f*; *leg* impedimento

disabuse desengañar (**of** de)

disaccustom desacostumbrar

disadvantage desventaja; **be under the** ~ **of** estar en la desventaja de + *inf*; **have s.o. at a** ~ tener[19] a uno en situación desventajosa

disadvantageous desventajoso
disaffect hacer[19] desleal
disaffected desafecto
disaffection desafección *f*
disagree (a person) no estar[19] de
    acuerdo (**with** con); (an argument)
    discrepar (**with** de); **I ~ with what you
    say** no estoy de acuerdo con lo que
    usted dice; (food) sentarle (ie)[2a] mal
    (a uno), **sardines ~ with me** las sar-
    dinas me sientan mal
disagreeable (things) desagradable;
    (people) antipático
disagreement desacuerdo; (quarrel) al-
    tercado
disallow rechazar[7]; (goal) *sp* anular
disappear desaparecer[14]
disappearance desaparición (-ones) *f*
disappoint desilusionar; (annoy) con-
    trariar
disappointed desilusionado; **be ~** sen-
    tir(ie)[2c] desilusión
disappointedly con desilusión
disappointing decepcionante
disappointment desilusión (-ones) *f*;
    fam chasco; **have a ~** sufrir una des-
    ilusión, *fam* llevarse un chasco
disapprobation, disapproval desaproba-
    ción *f*
disapprove (of) desaprobar (ue)[1a]
disapproving de desaprobación
disapprovingly con desaprobación
disarm desarmar(se); *fig* apaciguar[6]
disarmament desarme *m*; **nuclear ~**
    desarme nuclear
disarming (innocent) ingenuo
disarrange desarreglar; (of plans) tras-
    tornar; **the room is ~d** la habitación
    está sin recoger
disarray *n* desorden (-órdenes) *f*; *v* des-
    ordenar
disassemble desmontar
disassociate (o.s.) disociar(se) (**from** de)
disaster desastre *m*
disastrous desastroso
disavow repudiar
disavowal, disavowment repudiación *f*
disband *vi* desbandarse; *vt mil* licenciar
disbar *leg* excluir[16] del foro
disbarment exclusión *f* del foro
disbelief incredulidad *f*
disbelieve no creer[17]
disbeliever incrédulo
disburden descargar[5]; **~ o.s.** *fig* quitarse

un peso de encima
disburse desembolsar
disbursement desembolso
disc disco; **~ brakes** frenos de disco; **~-
    jockey** *rad* comentarista *m+f* de dis-
    cos, *fam* pinchadiscos *m sing+pl*
discard *n* (cards) descarte *m*; *v* dese-
    char; (cards) descartar(se)
discern percibir
discernible perceptible
discerning perspicaz (-ces)
discernment discernimiento
discharge *n* (cargo) descarga; (debt)
    pago; (duty) ejecución *f*, cumpli-
    miento; (exoneration) exoneración *f*;
    (weapon) disparo, *fam* tiro; *elect* des-
    carga; (from employment) despido;
    (from hospital) el alta, **John received
    his ~** le dieron de alta a Juan; *mil*
    licencia; *med* (from intestine) flujo,
    (of blood) derrame *m*, (of pus) su-
    puración *f*; *v* descargar[5]; (arrow) lan-
    zar[7]; (cargo+*elect*) descargar[5]; (fire-
    arm) disparar, *fam* tirar; (from court)
    exonerar; (from detention) liberar;
    (from hospital) dar[19] de alta a; (from
    work) despedir (i)[3]; *mil* licenciar;
    (pay) pagar[5]; (perform) ejecutar; **the
    wound is discharging** la herida está
    supurando
disciple discípulo
disciplinarian ordenancista *m+f*
disciplinary disciplinario
discipline disciplina; (punishment) cas-
    tigo; *v* disciplinar; (punish) castigar[5]
disclaim rechazar[7]; *leg* renunciar
disclaimer renuncia
disclose revelar
disclosure revelación (-ones) *f*
disco discoteca
discoloration descoloramiento
discolour desteñir(se) (i)[3]; **~ed** desco-
    lorido, desteñido
discomfit desconcertar (ie)[2a]
discomfiture confusión *f*
discomfort incomodidad *f*
discompose descomponer[19], perturbar
discomposure inquietud *f*
disconcert desconcertar (ie)[2a]
disconcerting desconcertante
disconnect separar; *mech* desconectar;
    elect desenchufar; (rolling stock) des-
    acoplar
disconnected   incoherente;   des-

conectado

disconnection desunión *f*; *elect* desconexión (-ones) *f*; *mech* desacoplamiento

disconsolate desconsolado

disconsolateness desconsuelo

discontent *n* descontento; *v* desagradar

discontented descontento

discontentment descontento

discontinuance descontinuación *f*

discontinue discontinuar; (payments, negotiations) suspender

discontinuity discontinuidad *f*

discontinuous descontinuo

discord (disagreement) discordia; *fig* cizaña; *mus* disonancia

discordant discordante; *mus* disonante

discotheque discoteca

discount *n* descuento; ~ **for cash** descuento por venta al contado; ~ **of twenty per cent** descuento de un veinte por ciento; **at a** ~ con descuento; **give a** ~ hacer[19] un descuento; ~ **coupon** cupón (-ones) *m* de rebaja; ~ **price** precio con descuento; ~ **store** economato; ~ **rate** tipo de descuento; *v* descontar (ue)[1a]; (attach little importance to) dar[19] poca importancia a

discountenance desaprobar (ue)[1a]

discourage (dishearten) desanimar; (dissuade) disuadir (**from** de + *infin*)

discouragement desánimo; disuasión *f*

discouraging desalentador (-ora *f*)

discourse *n* discurso; (treatise) disertación (-ones) *f*; *v* disertar

discourteous descortés *m*+*f*; (very ~) grosero

discourtesy descortesía

discover descubrir (*past part* descubierto); (realize) darse[19] cuenta de

discoverer descubridor *m* (-ora *f*)

discovery descubrimiento

discredit *n* descrédito; *v* desacreditar

discreditable deshonroso

discreet discreto

discrepancy discrepancia

discrete discreto

discretion discreción *f*; **at your (own)** ~ a su discreción; **age of** ~ edad *f* de discreción

discriminate distinguir[11]; ~ **between** distinguir[11] entre; ~ **against/in favour of** hacer[19] una distinción en contra de/en

favor de

discriminating discriminatorio

discrimination (discernment) discernimiento; (prejudice) discriminación *f*

discursive discursivo

discus disco; ~-**thrower** lanzador *m* (-ora *f*) de disco; **throwing the** ~ lanzamiento de disco

discuss discutir; (deal with) tratar de

discussion discusión (-ones) *f*

disdain *n* desdén *m*; *v* desdeñar

disdainful desdeñoso

disease enfermedad *f*; *fig* mal *m*

diseased enfermo; *fig* depravado

disembark desembarcar(se)[4]

disembarkation desembarque *m*

disembodied incorpóreo

disembody separar del cuerpo

disembowel destripar

disenchant desencantar

disenchantment desencanto

disengage (free) liberar; (of gears) desembragar[5]; *mil* romper (*past part* roto) el contacto (con); (uncouple) desenganchar; ~**d** (loose) suelto; (free) libre

disentangle desenredar

disentanglement desenredo

disestablish *eccles* separar del estado

disestablishment separación *f* del estado

disfavour *n* desaprobación *f*; **be in** ~ estar[19] en desgracia; **fall into** ~ caer[19] en desgracia; *v* desaprobar (ue)[1a]

disfigure desfigurar; (mar) estropear

disfigurement, disfiguration desfiguración (-ones) *f*

disfranchise privar de los derechos políticos

disfranchisement privación (-ones) *f* de los derechos políticos

disgorge vomitar; devolver (ue)[1b] (*past part* devuelto)

disgrace *n* ignominia; (scandal) escándalo; **in** ~ fuera de favor; en desgracia; (of child) castigado; *v* deshonrar; **you** ~ **me** (let me down) usted me avergüenza

disgraceful deshonroso; (scandalous) escandaloso

disgruntled descontento; (moody) veleidoso

disguise *n* disfraz (-ces) *m*; **in** ~ disfrazado; **wear a** ~ llevar un disfraz; *v* disfrazar[7]; ~**d (as)** disfrazado (de)

disgust *n* repugnancia; *v* repugnar

disgusting repugnante

dish (vessel + food) plato; *chem* cápsula (de evaporar); ~es platos *mpl*, vajilla *f sing*; ~-**cloth** trapo de fregar; ~-**cover** cubreplatos *m sing*; ~-**rack** escurreplatos *m sing*; ~-**towel** paño de cocina; ~-**washing machine** lavavajillas *m sing+pl*; ~-**water** agua de fregar la vajilla; *v* ~ **up** servir (i)[3]

disharmony discordia

dishearten descorazonar

disheartening descorazonador (-ora *f*)

dishevelled desaseado; (of hair) despeinado

dishful plato

dishonest fraudulento

dishonesty fraude *m*

dishonour *n* deshonra; *v* deshonrar; ~ **a debt** no pagar[5] una deuda

dishonourable deshonroso

disillusion *n* desilusión *f*; *v* desilusionar

disillusionment desilusión *f*

disinclination mala gana

disinclined: be ~ **to** estar[19] poco dispuesto a

disinfect desinfectar

disinfectant *n m+adj* desinfectante

disinfection desinfección *f*

disinfest desinfestar

disingenuous disimulado

disinherit desheredar

disintegrate desintegrar(se)

disintegration desintegración *f*

disinterested desinteresado

disjointed dislocado

disk *see* **disc**

dislike *n* aversión (-ones) *f* (of/for a); **take a** ~ **to** coger[8] antipatía a; *v* no gustarle a uno; **I** ~ **that man** aquel hombre no me gusta; ~**d** malquisto

dislocate dislocar[4]

dislocation dislocación *f*

dislodge desalojar

disloyal desleal

disloyalty deslealtad *f*

dismal triste; ~ **failure** fracaso total

dismantle *mil+naut* desmantelar; (house) desamueblar

dismasted desarbolado

dismay *n* consternación *f*; **fill with** ~ desanimar; **to my (great)** ~ para mi (gran) consternación; *v* consternar

dismember desmembrar

dismiss despedir (i)[3]; (from an official position) destituir[16]; *leg* absolver (ue)[1b]; *mil* dar[19] la orden de romper filas; ~! ¡rompan filas!; (parliament) disolver (ue)[1b]; (cricket) despachar; ~ **from one's mind** apartar de su pensamiento

dismissal (from job) despido; (from office) destitución *f*; (parliament) disolución *f*

dismount (from horse) desmontar; (from vehicle) apearse; (take to pieces) desarmar

disobedience desobediencia

disobedient desobediente

disobey desobedecer[14]

disobliging poco complaciente

disobligingly descortésmente

disorder *n* desorden (-órdenes) *m*; *med* indisposición (-ones) *f*; (mental) enajenación (-ones) *f* mental; **in** ~ en desorden; *v* desarreglar; (mind) trastornar; ~**ed** en desorden; *med* enfermo; (of mind) trastornado

disorderly desordenado; ~ **conduct** conducta escandalosa

disorganization desorganización *f*

disorganize desorganizar[7]

disorientate desorientar

disorientation desorientación *f*

disown repudiar

disparage (belittle) desacreditar; (scorn) despreciar

disparagement detracción *f*

disparaging menospreciativo

disparate disparejo

disparity disparidad *f*

dispassionate imparcial

dispatch *n* (message) mensaje *m*; *mil* parte *f* (de guerra); *v* (send) enviar; (finish) despachar; (kill) matar

dispel disipar

dispensable dispensable

dispensary dispensario

dispensation exención (-ones) *f*; dispensa

dispense dispensar; *leg* (of justice) administrar; ~ **with** prescindir de

dispenser dispensador *m*; *pharm* farmacéutico, farmacéutica

dispersal dispersión *f*

disperse *vi* dispersarse; *vt* dispersar

dispersion dispersión *f*

dispirited desanimado

dispiritedness desánimo
displace desalojar, desplazar⁷; ~**d persons** personas *fpl* desplazadas
displacement desalojamiento; *naut* desplazamiento
display *n* exhibición (-ones) *f*; *mil* maniobras *fpl* (militares); (ostentation) ostentación *f*; ~ **cabinet** vitrina; *v* exhibir; (show off) ostentar; ~ **ignorance** demostrar la ignorancia
displease desagradar
displeasing desagradable
displeasure desagrado
disport: ~ **o.s.** divertirse (ie)²ᶜ
disposable disponible; (of empty container) sin vuelta
disposal disposición *f*; (of garbage) recolección *f*; (sale) venta; **at your** ~ a su disposición
dispose disponer¹⁹; ~ **of** (finish) terminar; (get rid of) deshacerse¹⁹ de; (give) regalar; (kill) matar; (sell) vender; (transfer) ceder, (transfer houses *etc*) traspasar; (prove wrong) refutar
disposed: ~ **to** dispuesto a
disposition (arrangement) disposición *f*; (temperament) carácter *m*
dispossess desposeer¹⁷ (**of** de); *leg* desahuiciar (**of** de)
dispossession desposeimiento; *leg* desahuicio
disproportion desproporción *f*
disproportionate desproporcionado
disprovable refutable
disprove refutar
disputable disputable
disputant disputador *m* (-ora *f*)
disputation disputa
disputatious disputante
dispute *n* disputa; **it's beyond** ~ es indiscutible; *vi* (argue) discutir; *vt* (refute) refutar; poner en duda
disqualification incapacidad *f*; *sp* descalificación (-ones) *f*
disqualify incapacitar; *sp* descalificar⁴
disquiet inquietud *f*
disquieting perturbador (-ora *f*)
disquisition disquisición *f*
disregard *n* desatención *f*; (scorn) desdén *m*; *v* desatender (ie)²ᵇ; (scorn) desdeñar
disrepair mal estado
disreputable de mala fama
disrepute mala fama; **come into** ~ caer¹⁹ en desgracia
disrespect falta de respeto
disrespectful irreverente
disrobe desnudar(se)
disrupt interrumpir
disruption interrupción (-ones) *f*
dissatisfaction descontento
dissatisfy descontentar
dissect disecar⁴; *fig* analizar⁷
dissection disección (-ones) *f*; *fig* análisis *m*
dissemble disimular
disseminate diseminar
dissemination diseminación *f*
dissension disensión *f*
dissent *n* disentimiento; *v* no estar¹⁹ conforme (**from** de); disentir
dissenter disidente *m* + *f*
dissentient disidente
dissertation disertación (-ones) *f*
disservice deservicio
dissidence disidencia
dissident *n* + *adj* disidente *m* + *f*
dissimilar desigual
dissimilarity disparidad *f*
dissimulate disimular
dissimulation disimulo
dissipate disipar; (waste) desperdiciar
dissipated disipado; (of person) disoluto
dissipation disipación *f*; (waste) derroche *m*; (dissoluteness) disolución *f*
dissociate: ~ **o.s. from** disociarse de
dissociation disociación *f*
dissoluble disoluble
dissolute disoluto
dissoluteness disolución *f*
dissolution disolución *f*
dissolve disolver (ue)¹ᵇ; (parliament) prorrogar⁵; (marriage) anular; ~ **into tears** deshacerse¹⁹ en lágrimas
dissonance disonancia
dissonant disonante
dissuade disuadir (**from** de)
dissuasion disuasión *f*
distance distancia; **at a** ~ a alguna distancia; **from a** ~ desde lejos; **go the** ~ (boxing) ir¹⁹ a la distancia; **what is the** ~ **from ... to ...?** ¿qué distancia hay desde ... a ...?; **keep at a** ~ mantener¹⁹ lejos; **keep one's** ~ mantenerse¹⁹ a distancia
distant lejano; (unfriendly) frío; **he is a** ~ **relative of mine** él es un lejano pariente mío

distaste aversión (-ones) *f*

distasteful desagradable

distemper *n vet* moquillo; (paint) (pintura al) temple; *v* pintar al temple

distend distender

distended dilatado; (swollen) hinchado

distension dilatación (-ones) *f*; *med* distensión (-ones) *f*

distil destilar

distillation destilación *f*

distiller destilador *m*

distillery destilería

distinct (clear) claro; (different) distinto; (precise) preciso; **as ~ from** a diferencia de

distinction (difference) distinción (-ones) *f*; (honour) honor *m*; **man of great ~** hombre muy distinguido

distinctive distintivo

distinctness claridad *f*

distingué distinguido

distinguish distinguir[16]; (honour) honrar; **~ between** diferenciar entre; **~ o.s.** distinguirse[16]

distinguishable distinguible

distinguishing distintivo; **has it any ~ features?** ¿tiene algo que lo distinga?

distort torcer (ue)[1b]; (of sound) distorsionar

distortion (physical) deformación (-ones) *f*; (of meaning) tergiversación (-ones) *f*

distract distraer[19]; (madden) enloquecer[14]

distraction (amusement) distracción *f*; (confusion) confusión *f*; (madness) locura; **you drive me to ~** me pones loco

distraught desesperado

distress *n* aflicción *f*; *leg* embargo; **ship in ~** barco en peligro; **the ship put in in ~** el barco entró de arribada forzosa; **~ signal** señal *f* de socorro; *v* afligir[9]; *leg* embargar[5]

distressing, distressful angustioso

distribute distribuir[16]

distribution distribución (-ones) *f*

distributive distributivo

distributor distribuidor *m* (-ora *f*)

district distrito; (of country) región (-ones) *f*; (of town) barrio

distrust *n* desconfianza; *v* desconfiar de

distrustful desconfiado

disturb (bother) molestar; (disarrange)

desordenar; (interrupt) interrumpir; (worry) inquietar; **~ the peace** perturbar el orden público; **~ed** (anxious) inquieto, (disarranged) desordenado, (in the mind) trastornado

disturbance alboroto; **cause a public ~** causar un alboroto público; (of mind) trastorno

disturbing inquietante

disunion desunión *f*

disunite desunir(se)

disunity desunión *f*

disuse *n* desuso; **fall into ~** caer en desuso; *v* dejar de usar

ditch *n* zanja; (for irrigation) acequia; *mil* foso; (roadside) cuneta; **to the last ~** hasta el último cartucho; **~-water** agua de zanja; *v* (leave behind) deshacerse[19] de, *sl* zafarse de, **we're trying to ~ her** estamos intentando deshacernos de ella/*sl* zafarnos de ella

dither *n* temblor *m*; **she's all of a ~** ella está muy agitada/nerviosa; *v* temblar; (hesitate before choosing) vacilar

dithyramb, dithyrambic ditirambo

ditto idem

ditty cancioncilla

diurnal de día

diurnally diariamente

divan cama turca

¹ dive *n* zambullida; *aer* picado; **~-bomb** bombardear en picado; **~-bombing** bombardeo en picado; *v* tirarse (de cabeza); zambullirse; *aer* picar[4]; (of a submarine) sumergirse[9]; (swim under water) bucear

² dive (low tavern) tasca

diver zambullidor *m* (-ora *f*); (deep-sea ~) buzo; *orni* somorgujo; (underwater swimmer) buceador *m* (-ora *f*)

diverge divergir[9]

divergence divergencia

divergent divergente

divers varios

diverse variado

diversification diversificación *f*

diversify variar

diversion (pleasure +*mil*) diversión (-ones) *f*; (change of route) desviación (-ones) *f*

diversity diversidad *f*

divert (amuse) divertir (ie)[2c]; (traffic) desviar; **~ s.o.'s attention** distraer[19]; **my attention was ~ed and I fell** me descuidé y caí

diverting divertido

divertissement *theat* pieza ligera; *mus* divertimiento

divest desnudar(se); *fig* ~ **of** despojar de

divide *vt* dividir; ~ **the sheep from the goats** apartar el grano de la paja; ~**d highway** carretera de doble calzada; ~**d skirt** falda pantalón *f*; *vi* dividirse

dividend dividendo

dividers *geom* compás *m* de división

divination adivinación (-ones) *f*

divine *n* teólogo; *adj* divino; *v* (guess) adivinar; (forecast) pronosticar[4]

diviner adivino; (water-~) zahorí *m*

diving zambullida; (underwater activity) buceo; *aer* picado; ~**-bell** campana de buzo; ~**-board** trampolín (-ines) *m* (de saltar al agua), *SA* palanca; ~**-suit** escafandra

divining-rod vara de adivinación/de zahorí

divinity divinidad *f*

divisible divisible

division *math*+*mil* división *f*; (distribution) reparto; (partition between rooms) tabique *m*; (department of firm) ramo; (voting) votación (-ones) *f*; **without a** ~ sin votar; ~ **of labour** división del trabajo

divisional divisional; ~ **H.Q.** cuartel *m* general de división

divisive divisivo

divorce *n* divorcio; *v* divorciarse (de); **to** ~ **o.s. from** *fig* apartarse de; ~**d from reality** apartado de la realidad

divorcee divorciado

divulge divulgar[5]

dizzily vertiginosamente

dizziness mareo

dizzy vertiginoso; (crazy) chiflado; **feel** ~ sentirse (ie)[2c] mareado

do *n* (party, celebration) fiesta, juerga; **fair** ~**s!** ¡sea imparcial!; *v* hacer[19]; (acquit o.s.) salir[19]; (carry out) ejecutar; (cause) causar; (cheat) engañar; (clean) limpiar; (finish) dejar de, **I have done smoking** he dejado de fumar; (study) estudiar, **he is doing law** él está estudiando derecho; (suit) valer[19], **you'll** ~ usted vale; (travel) ir[19] a, **this car does a hundred miles an hour** este coche hace cien millas por hora; (visit, *esp* as tourist) visitar;

(walk) caminar, **yesterday I did twenty miles** ayer caminé veinte millas; ~ **bad(ly)** hacer[19] mal; ~ **the cooking/darning** cocinar[14]/zurcir[15]; ~ **a day's work** trabajar, **he's never done a day's work in his life** no ha dado golpe en toda su vida; ~ **a favour** hacer[19] un favor; ~ **good** hacer[19] bien, **it did me a world of good** me hizo la mar de bien; ~ **a good turn** hacer[19] un favor; ~ **harm** hacer[19] daño; ~ **justice** ejecutar justicia; ~ **one's best/utmost** hacer[19] lo posible; ~ **one's duty** cumplir con su deber; ~ **one's hair** peinarse; ~ **right** obrar bien; ~ **a sum/an exercise** hacer[19] una suma/un ejercicio; ~ **time** (in prison) cumplir una condena; **he did a year in gaol** estuvo un año en la cárcel; **don't!** ¡no haga eso!; ~ **you speak Chinese?** ¿habla usted chino?; **I** ~ **not like garlic** no me gusta el ajo; **he had nothing to** ~ **all day** él pasó el día en blanco; ~ **tell me your name** le ruego me diga cómo se llama; ~ **to death** matar; **I** ~ **want to visit your sister** yo sí quisiera visitar a su hermana; **may I open it? please** ~ ¿puedo abrirlo? ábralo; **how** ~ **you** ~? ¿cómo está usted?, *fam* ¿qué tal?; **I can't** ~ **on the money he gives me** no me llega el dinero que me da; **have nothing to** ~ no tener[19] nada que hacer; **make** ~ (manage) aguantar; **never did I see such a thing!** ¡en mi vida he visto semejante cosa!; **so** ~ **I** yo también; **that will** ~ (that's enough) eso basta, *fam* déjate de eso; **these things are just not done** estas cosas no se hacen; **that will never** ~ eso no se hace; **what are you going to** ~? ¿qué piensa usted hacer?; **what to** ~? ¿qué hay que hacer?; **well done!** ¡bravo!

~ **again** volver[1b] (*past part* vuelto) a hacer

~ **away with** (abolish) suprimir; (eliminate) eliminar; (get rid of) quitar; (kill) *fam* cargarse[5] a

~ **by** tratar; **he did the right thing by her** él la trató bien

~ **for** (ruin) arruinar; (kill) matar, *fam* cargarse[5] a; (look after) cuidar de; **he is** ~**ing all right for himself** él sabe cuidarse; **what wouldn't I** ~ **for a glass** of water! ¡lo que no haría yo por un vaso de agua!; **it does for my needs** basta para mí; **what do you ~ for a living?** ¿a qué se dedica usted?; **~ what one can for** hacer todo lo posible por, **I ~ what I can for my clients** me debo a mis clientes

~ in (kill) cargarse[5] a

~ out (clean thoroughly) limpiar bien; **~ out of** (cheat of) engañar a

~ over redecorar; (assault) golpear

~ up (button) abrochar; (repair) reparar; (tie) atar; (wrap) envolver (*past part* envuelto); **I'm all done up** (weary) estoy rendido

~ well (prosper) prosperar; **the patient is doing well** el enfermo está mejorando; **they ~ you well at this restaurant** se come bien en este restaurante; **~ well to** convenirle (ie)[19] a uno (+ *infin*)

~ with (concern) tener[19] que ver con, **I have nothing to ~ with this matter** no tengo nada que ver con este asunto; **this novel has to ~ with life in Canada** esta novela trata de la vida en el Canadá; (need) necesitar; **I could ~ with that** me convendría tener eso; **~ without** pasar sin

docile dócil

docility docilidad *f*

dock *naut* dársena; *leg* banquillo; *bot* bardana; **~ area** dársenas *fpl*; **~yard** arsenal *m*; *v naut* atracar[4]; (deduct money) descontar (ue)[1a]; (remove the tail) descolar; **~ with** *space* acoplar con

docker obrero portuario, estibador *m*

docket minuta

docking *space* (operación *f* de) acoplamiento

doctor *n med* médico, doctora; (holder of doctorate) doctor *m* (-ora *f*); **he is a ~ of** es doctor en; **become a ~ of** doctorarse en; *v med* curar; *vet* (castrate) capar

doctorate doctorado

doctrinaire doctrinario

doctrinal doctrinal

doctrine doctrina

document documento

documentary *n* (película) documental; *adj* documental

documentation documentación *f*

dodder chochear; *bot* cuscuta

dodderer chocho, (-a *f*)

doddering chocho

dodge *n* (avoiding action) regate *m*; (trick) truco; *v* (avoid a blow) evadir, esquivar; (avoid a difficulty) eludir; **~ the issue** evadir el tema

dodgem(-car) automóvil *m* de choque

dodger sablista; (*US* deadbeat) sinvergüenza

doe (deer) gama; (rabbit) coneja

doer autor *m* (-ora *f*); persona activa

doeskin piel *f* de gama

doff quitarse (el sombrero)

dog *n* perro; **~-biscuit** canil *m*; **~-collar** collar *m* de perro, *eccles* alzacuello; **~-eared** con las puntas de las hojas dobladas; **~-end** *fam* colilla, *SA* chicote *m*; **~-fight** lucha de perros, *aer* combate aéreo; **~fish** lija; **~-house** perrera, **I'm in the ~-house** estoy en desgracia; **~ in the manger** perro del hortelano; **~-kennel** perrera; **~-Latin** latinajo; **~-licence** licencia de perros; **~-racing** carreras *fpl* de galgos; **~-rose** escaramujo; **~-show** exposición canina; **~-tag** disco de identidad; **~-tired** cansadísimo; **~-track** canódromo; **~-watch** guardia de cuartillo; **~wood** cornejo; **~sbody** lacayo; **~'s life** vida miserable; **~'s meat** comida de perros; **every ~ has its day** a cada cerdo le llega su San Martín; **go to the ~s** estar[19] arruinado; *v* **~ s.o.'s steps** seguir (i)[3+11] los pasos de uno

dogged tenaz (-ces)

doggerel coplas *fpl* de ciego

doggy perrito

dogie becerro descarriado

dogma dogma *m*

dogmatic dogmático

dogmatism dogmatismo

dogmatize dogmatizar[7]

do-gooder bienhechor *m* (-ora *f*)

doily panito/papel *m* de adorno

doing acción *f*; **it's his ~** es obra suya; **nothing ~** no hay nada (que hacer); **there's something ~** algo pasa; **be up and ~** darse[19] prisa, *fam* menearse; **~s** hechos *mpl*

doldrums calmas *fpl* ecuatoriales

dole *n* limosna; (unemployment benefit) subsidio de paro; **be on the ~** vivir de limosna/subsidio de paro; *v* **~ out** distribuir[16]

doleful triste

doll n muñeca; ~'s **house** casa de muñecas; v (dress up) engalanar(se); **she's all ~ed up** fam ella está de punta en blanco

dollar dólar m; ~ **deficit** déficit m de dólares; ~ **diplomacy** diplomacia del dólar; ~ **gap** escasez f de dólares

dollop masa informe

dolly muñequita

dolmen dolmen (dólmenes) m

dolphin delfín (-ines) m, Mex tonina

dolt papanatas m sing

doltish lerdo

domain +fig dominio

dome cúpula; ~d **roof** techo con bóveda; ~-car vagón (-ones) m de observación

domestic n criada; adj (home-loving) casero; (national) nacional; ~ **animal** animal doméstico; ~ **appliance** aparato de uso doméstico; ~ **flight** aer vuelo interno

domesticate domesticar[4]; **become ~d** (of people) hacerse[19] casero

domesticity domesticidad f

domicile domicilio

domiciled domiciliado (**in** en)

dominance ascendiente; predominio

dominant n+adj dominante f

dominate dominar

domination dominación f

domineer tiranizar[7]; ~ **over** mandar en

domineering mandón (-ona f); ~ **woman** fam marimandona, comozacha

Dominican n+adj dominicano

Dominican Republic República Dominicana

dominie maestro de escuela

dominion dominio

domino dominó m; ~es (game) (juego del) dominó

[1] **don** n (Spanish title) don m; (at university) profesor universitario; **Don Juanish** donjuanesco

[2] **don** v ponerse[19]

donate donar

donation donativo

done hecho; cul cocido/asado en su punto; **it's finished and ~ with** se acabó; **what's ~ is ~** lo pasado pasó; ~! (agreed!) ¡de acuerdo!; ~ **for/in** (beaten) vencido, (ruined) arruinado,

(worn out) agotado; ~ **out of** defraudado de; ~ **up** renovado

donkey burro; ~-**engine** máquina auxiliar

donnish erudito; pedante

donor +med donante m+f

doodle n garabato; v hacer[19] garabatos

doom (ruin) ruina; (death) muerte f; (fate) destino; (sentence) sentencia; ~ed condenado a morir, fig estar[19] predestinado a la ruina; **Doomsday** día m del juicio final; ~-**monger** jeremías m, catastrofista m+f

door puerta; (of block of flats) puerta principal; **out of ~s** al aire libre; **show s.o. the ~** echar a alguien; **throw open one's ~s** dar[19] hospitalidad f; ~-**bell** timbre; **ring the ~-bell** tocar[4] el timbre; ~-**chain** cadena para la puerta; ~-**frame** marco de la puerta; ~-**keeper**, ~-**man** portero; ~-**knob** pomo; ~-**knocker** aldaba; ~-**mat** esterilla; ~-**plate** placa; ~-**step** umbral m; ~-**stop** tope m de puerta; ~-**way** portal m

dope n (drugs) drogas, narcóticos mpl; (information) información f; (foolish person) bobo; mot+aer (fuel) combustible m de alta calidad; aer barniz (-ces) m para aviones; ~-**fiend** toxicómano; ~-**pedlar** vendedor m (-ora f) de narcóticos, sl camello; v narcotizar[7]; **be ~d** estar[19] narcotizado

doping sp doping m

doric dórico

dormant durmiente

dormer: ~ **window** buhard(ill)a

dormitory (room + hall of residence) dormitorio; ~ **town** pueblo residencial

dormouse lirón (-ones) m

dosage dosis f; dosificación f

dose n dosis f sing+pl; ~ **of flu** ataque m de gripe; v dosificar[4]; ~ **o.s.** curarse

doss-house tugurio

dossier documentación (-ones) f

dot n punto; mus puntillo; ~s gramm puntos mpl suspensivos; ~s **and dashes** puntos y rayas; **on the ~** en punto; v ~ **an i** poner[19] el punto sobre la i

dotage chochera; **be in one's ~** estar[19] chocheando

dotard viejo chocho

dote estar[19] loco (**on** por)

doting (affectionate) mimador (-ora *f*); (senile) chocho

dotted salpicado (with de); ~ **line** línea de puntos, (for signature) línea para la firma

dottle posos *mpl* de tabaco

dotty chiflado

double *n theat* (+ dominoes) doble *m*, *Chil* chancho; (type of bet) apuesta doble; **at/on the** ~ **mil** a paso ligero, *fig* rápidamente; *adj* doble; **a house** ~ **the size** una casa el doble de grande; ~**agent** espía *m+f* doble; ~-**barrelled** de dos cañones; ~-**bass** contrabajo; ~ **bed** cama de matrimonio; ~ **brandy** coñac *m* doble; ~-**breasted** cruzado; ~ **chin** papada; ~ **cream** doble nata; ~-**cross** traicionar; ~-**date** cita de dos parejas; ~-**dealer** traidor *m* (-ora *f*); ~-**dealing** doblez *f*; ~-**decker** (bus) (autobús (-uses) *m*) de dos pisos; ~ **doors** puerta doble; ~-**Dutch** chino; ~-**edged** de dos filos; ~ **entry** *comm* partida doble; ~ **exposure** *phot* doble revelación *f*; ~ **feature** *cin* programa *m* doble; ~ **glazing** cristal *m* doble; ~-**headed** bicéfalo; ~-**jointed** de articulaciones dobles; **with a** ~ **meaning** con doble sentido; ¡**te apuesto doble o nada!**; ~-**park** *mot* estacionar en doble fila; ~-**parking** estacionamiento en doble fila; ~-**play** (recording tape) de doble duración; ~ **pneumonia** pulmonía doble; ~-**quick** a paso ligero; ~ **room** habitación (-ones) *f* para dos personas, (with ~ bed) habitación *f* con cama de matrimonio; ~ **rose** rosa doble; ~ **somersault** salto mortal; **in** ~-**spacing** con separación doble; ~-**stop** *mus* tocar[4] dos tonos (en un instrumento); ~-**talk** habla ambigua; ~-**think** habilidad *f* de sostener dos ideas opuestas; ~-**time** (pay) paga doble; ~-**track** *n* vía doble, *adj* de doble vía; *v* (fold) doblar; (make twice as great) duplicar[4]; *naut* doblar; **mil** ir[19] a paso ligero; ~ **the bid** doblar la oferta; ~ **one's efforts** redoblar sus esfuerzos; ~ **one's capital** doblar su capital; ~ **back** (return) volver (ue)[1b] (*past part* vuelto) sobre sus pasos; ~ **up** (bend in agony or laughter) retorcerse (ue)[1b];

(hurry) apresurarse; *adv* (en) doble; **I paid** ~ pagué doble

doubling doblamiento

doubly doblemente

doubt *n* duda; **beyond all** ~ fuera de duda; **if in** ~ en caso de duda; **no** ~ indudablemente; **there's no** ~ (**about it**) (de eso) no cabe duda; *v* dudar de; **I** ~ **that** dudo que +*subj*

doubter escéptico

doubtful dudoso; (ambiguous) ambiguo; (perplexed) perplejo; **it's** ~ **that** es dudoso que +*subj*; **I'm** ~ **about** estoy dudoso de, dudo de; ~ **character** persona de poco fiar

doubtless sin duda

douche (shower) ducha; (enema) lavativa; *med* jeringa; *v* duchar(se); irrigar

dough masa; *sl* (money) pasta; ~**nut** buñuelo, *fam* frito

doughy pastoso

dour hosco

dourly severamente

Douro Duero

douse mojar

dove +*pol* paloma; ~**cot** palomar *m*

Dover Dóver *m*

dovetail *n* ensambladura a cola de milano; *v* empalmar a cola de milano; *fig* encajar

dowager viuda; ~ **duchess** duquesa viuda

dowdiness desaliño

dowdy desaliñado; ~ **hat** sombrero pasado de moda

dowel *n* tarugo; *v* sujetar con tarugos

¹**down** *n* (feather) plumón *m*; (hair) vello; (on fruit) pelusilla; (on youth's chin) bozo; (from plant) vilano

²**down** *n*: **he has a** ~ **on me** me trata severamente sin justa causa; *adj* pendiente; (of crossword puzzle clues) vertical; (fallen) caído; (of trains) procedente de la capital; (sad) triste; ~ **and out** *sp* fuera de combate, *fig* completamente arruinado, (penniless) sin cinco; ~ **at heel** descuidado; ~ **in the mouth** cariacontecido; ~ **to the last detail** hasta en el menor detalle; ~ **payment** depósito, (first instalment) primer plazo; *adv* (hacia) abajo; (on the ground) por tierra; (stretched out) tendido, **he threw himself** ~ **on the sand** se tumbó tendido en la arena;

mil ~! ¡a tierra!; ~-**river** río abajo; ~ **to** hasta; ~ **with ...!** ¡abajo ...!; **John is** ~ **with flu** Juan tiene la gripe; **boil** ~ reducir[15] hirviendo, *fig* reducirse[15]; **come/go** ~ (+ prices, temperature) bajar; **this legend has come** ~ **to us through the centuries** esta leyenda ha perdurado a través de los siglos; **the sun goes** ~ se pone el sol; **our profits have gone** ~ nuestras ganancias han disminuido; **the wind has gone** ~ el viento ha cesado; **let's get** ~ **to work** vamos a trabajar en serio; ~ **tools** declararse en huelga; ~**cast** cabizbajo; ~**fall** caída, *fig* ruina; ~**grade**, ~**hill** cuesta abajo; ~**hearted** descorazonado; **become** ~**hearted** perder (ie)[2b] ánimo; ~-**link** *space* enlace *m* de superficie; ~ **payment** entrada; ~**pour** chaparrón (-ones) *m*; ~**right** *adj* categórico, *adv* absolutamente; ~**stairs** planta baja; ~**stairs room** habitación (-ones) *f* en la planta baja; **she ran** ~**stairs** ella corrió escaleras abajo; ~**stream** río abajo; ~**town** centro comercial de la ciudad; **go** ~**town** ir[19] al centro; ~ **trend** tendencia a empeorar; ~**trodden** pisoteado, *fig* oprimido; ~**ward(s)** hacia abajo; *v* vencer[12]

³ **down:** ~**land**, ~**s** región *f* de terreno ondulado

downy velloso

dowry dote *f*

doyen decano

doze *n* sueño ligero; *v* dormitar; ~ **off** adormecerse[14], *fam* quedarse frito

dozen docena; **a** ~ **oranges** una docena de naranjas

doziness somnolencia

dozy adormecido

drab *n* (prostitute) ramera; *adj* (colour) gris amarillento; (monotonous) monótono

draft *n* (outline) bosquejo *m*; **rough** ~ borrador *m*; *mil* destacamento, *US* conscripción *f* militar; *comm* letra de cambio; *v* (draw up) redactar; (outline) bosquejar; *mil* (detach) destacar[4]; (recruit) reclutar

draftee quinto

drafting *mil* reclutamiento; (of a bill *etc*) redacción (-ones) *f*

draftsman delineante *m*

drag *n* (obstacle) estorbo; (bore) aburrimiento; **what a** ~! ¡que aburrimiento!; *fam* (puff of cigarette) chupada; **take a** ~ dar[19] una chupada; *theat* ropa de mujer (llevada por un hombre); **in** ~ disfrazado de mujer; ~-**net** red barredera; ~-**rope** *naut* sonda; *v* (pull) arrastrar; (go slowly, *esp* time) pasar lentamente; (make slow progress) avanzar[7] penosamente; *fam* (puff) chupar; ~ **the river** dragar[5] el río

dragging (of rivers *etc*) rastreo

draggle ensuciar arrastrando

dragon dragón (-ones) *m*; ~-**fly** libélula, *fam* caballito del diablo

dragoon *n* dragón (-ones) *m*; *v* imponer una disciplina muy severa; ~ **into** obligar[5] a la fuerza a +*infin*/a que +*subj*

drain *n* (gutter, sewer) alcantarilla; (of sink) desaguadero; *mech* (tubería de) desagüe *m*; *agri* (ditch) acequia; ~-**plug** tapón (-ones) *m* de desagüe; *v* (land) desaguar; (put in drain-pipes) encañar; (lakes) secar; (remove water from food, clothes *etc*) escurrir; (empty by drinking) vaciar; (exhaust) agotar; **that land is well** ~**ed** ese terreno tiene buen drenaje; **it's a great** ~ **on our resources** está consumiendo nuestros recursos; **it's money down the** ~ *fig* es dinero tirado por la ventana; ~ **the sump** *mot* vaciar la culata; ~ **away/off** vaciar

drainage desagüe *m*

drain(ing-)board escurridero

drake pato (macho)

dram (weight) dracma; (small drink) trago

drama drama *m*

dramatic dramático; ~ **art** dramática; **the** ~ **quality of the work** el dramatismo de la obra; **amateur** ~**s** piezas representadas por aficionados

dramatis personae personajes *mpl*

dramatist dramaturgo

dramatization adaptación *f*; dramatización *f*

dramatize dramatizar[7]

drape: *n* ~**s** *US* cortinas *fpl*; *v* colgar[5]

draper pañero; ~**'s shop** pañería

drapery colgaduras *fpl*

drastic drástico

drat maldecir[19]; ~ **that boy!** ¡maldito sea aquel niño!

draught *n* (air-current) corriente *f* (de aire), *SA* chiflón (-ones) *m*; (of a chimney) tiro; (drink) trago; *naut* calada, **that boat has a ~ of ...** aquel barco tiene ... de calada; *adj* suelto; **do you sell ~ wine?** ¿vende usted vino suelto?; ~ **beer** cerveza de barril; ~-**excluder** burlete *m*; ~ **horse** caballo de tiro

draughtiness corrientes *fpl*

draughts (game) (juego de) damas *fpl*; **let's play ~** vamos a jugar a las damas; ~ **board** tablero de damas; ~**man** peón (-ones) *m*

draughtsman (designer) delineante *m*

draughty expuesto a corrientes de aire

[1] **draw** *n* (attraction) atracción (-ones) *f*; (lottery) sorteo; (raffle) rifa; *sp* empate; **box-office ~** fuerza taquillera; ~**bridge** puente levantizo; ~-**ticket** boleto de lotería; *v* (pull) tirar (de); (extract) sacar[4]; ~ **a gun/a cork** sacar[4] una pistola/un corcho; (take liquid from barrel) sacar[4]; (disembowel) destripar; (stretch) estirar; (attract) atraer[19]; **this film will ~ the crowds** esta película atraerá a la gente; *sp* empatar; ~ **blood** hacerle[19] a uno sangrar; ~ **breath** respirar; ~ **a cheque** girar un cheque; ~ **to a close** irse[19] acabando; ~ **comfort (from)** tomar consuelo (de); ~ **comparisons** hacer[19] una comparación; ~ **a conclusion** sacar[4] una conclusión; ~ **courage** sacar[4] fuerzas; ~ **the curtains** correr las cortinas; ~ **inspiration (from)** inspirarse (en); ~ **level with** alcanzar[7]; ~ **lots (for)** echar suertes (para); ~ **money** cobrar; ~ **a number** (in lottery) sortear; ~ **a sword** desenvainar una espada; **the fire ~s well** el fuego tira bien

~ **along** arrastrar

~ **alongside** acostarse (ue)[1a]

~ **aside** *vi* apartarse; *vt* llevar a un lado; (curtains) descorrer

~ **away** (leave behind) ir[19] alejándose; (remove) quitar

~**back** *n* desventaja

~ **back** *v* retirarse

~ **forth** hacer[19] salir; (develop) desarro-

llar; (provoke) provocar[4]

~ **in** (of days) acortarse[6]; **the cat ~s in its claws** el gato retrae sus garras

~ **into** retirarse dentro de

~ **off** (liquid) sacar[4]

~ **out** *vt* (of days) alargar[5]; (of elastic) estirar; (make s.o. talk) sacarle[4] a uno; *vi* hacerse largo

~ **together** reunir(se)

~ **up** (raise) levantar; (bring near) acercar[4]; (halt) parar(se); (prepare a document) redactar; (prepare a plan) proyectar

~ **upon** recurrir a

[2] **draw** (sketch) dibujar; ~ **the line (at)** no pasar más allá (de)

drawer (of pictures) dibujante *m*; (of water) tirador *m* (-ora *f*); *comm* girador *m*; (furniture) cajón (-ones) *m*; ~**s** (men's garment) calzoncillos *mpl*, (women's garment) braga(s)

drawing (sketch) dibujo; (plan) esquema; (of lots) sorteo; (of money) cobranza; ~-**board** tablero de dibujo; ~ **paper** papel *m* de dibujo; ~-**pen** tiralíneas *m sing*; ~-**pin** chincheta; ~-**room** salón (-ones) *m*

drawl *n* habla *f* lenta; *v* arrastrar las palabras

drawn (tired) ojerosa; (with pain) desencajado; *sp* empatado; ~ **game** empate *m*; ~ **sword** espada desnuda

dray carro

dread *n* temor *m*; **be in ~ (of)** estar[19] con miedo (de); **have a ~ of** tener[19] miedo de; *adj* temible; *v* tener[19] miedo de

dreadful (frightening) terrible; **it's ~ the way she talks to her parents** es de miedo como ella habla a sus padres; **something ~ has happened** ha ocurrido una desgracia; **something ~ is going to happen** va a ocurrir algo gordo; (very bad) tremendo, **I've had a ~ day** he pasado un día horrible; **I feel ~ making you wait** me sabe mal hacerle esperar

dream *n* sueño; **in a ~** despistado; **sweet ~s!** ¡duerme bien!; *adj* de ensueño; **your ~ house** su casa de ensueño; ~**land** tierra de la fantasía; ~**like** como un sueño; ~ **world** mundo de las ilusiones; *v* soñar (ue)[1a] (**of** con); **I wouldn't ~ of it!** ¡ni pensar!

dreamer soñador *m* (-ora *f*)

dreamily como en sueño

dreamless sin sueños

dreamy soñador (-ora *f*)

dreariness tristeza

dreary triste

dredge dragar[5]; (sprinkle) espolvorear

dredger draga; (for sugar) azucarera; (for flour) harinero

dredging dragado; (sprinkling) salpicadura

dregs heces *fpl*; (people) gentuza

drench mojar; ~ed como un trapo; **I got** ~**ed** me puse como un trapo

Dresden Dresde *m*

dress *n* (clothing) ropa; (frock) vestido; *adj* de etiqueta, ~ **suit** traje *m* de etiqueta; (with tail-coat) traje *m* de frac; ~ **uniform** uniforme *m* de gala; ~ **circle** anfiteatro; ~ **clothes** traje *m* de etiqueta; ~ **coat** frac *m*; ~-**designer** diseñador *m* (-ora *f*) de modelos; ~-**designing** arte *m* de modista; ~-**maker** modista *m*+*f*; ~-**making** costura; ~-**rehearsal** ensayo general; ~-**shirt** camisa de etiqueta; *v* vestir (i)[3]; ~ **o.s.** vestirse (i)[3]; *naut* empavesar; ~ **a wound** vendar una herida; ~ **in one's best clothes** vestirse[3] sus mejores galas; ~ed (**chicken**) (pollo) limpio; **all** ~**ed up** de punta en blanco, (disguised) disfrazado

dressage obediencia hípica

dresser (furniture) aparador *m*; (kitchen) armario de cocina; (maid) doncella; (valet) ayuda de cámera; *theat* mamá *f*

dressing vestir(se)[3] *m*; (of textiles) apresto; (of skins) adobo; (sauce) salsa; (seasoning) condimentación *f*; (*US* stuffing) relleno; *med* vendas *fpl*; ~-**case** neceser *m*; ~-**down** regaño, *fam* rapapolvo; **give s.o. a** ~-**down for** ... regañarle a uno por ...; ~-**gown** bata, (of towelling) albornoz (-ces) *m*; ~-**room** *theat* camarín (-ines) *m*, *sp* vestuario; ~-**station** puesto de socorro; ~-**table** tocador *m*

dressy vistoso

dribble gotear; (baby) babear; *sp* driblar

driblet gotita; **in** ~**s** a (cuenta) gotas

dribs: in ~ **and drabs** poco a poco

dried seco, (of fruit) paso; ~ **peach** orejón *m*; ~ **up** (withered) marchito

drier secadora

drift *n* (current) corriente *f*; (conversation) giro; (snow) ventisquero; ~ **to the towns** emigración *f* interior; *v naut* ir[19] a la deriva; (go with the crowd) dejarse arrastrar; (snow) amontonarse; *vt* llevar, encaminar; ~ **into** deslizarse[7] en, *fig* (war *etc*) entrar sin querer

drifter pesquero

drifting a la deriva; ~ **sand** arena movediza

driftwood madera de deriva

drill *mech* taladro; *min* sonda; (dentist's) torno (dental); (physical training) educación *f*/instrucción *f* física; *mil* instrucción *f* militar; *agri* (máquina) sembradora; (seed-~) hilera; (cloth) dril *m*; ~-**ground** (school) patio (de recreo), *mil* patio (de un cuartel); ~-**sergeant** sargento instructor; *vt mech* taladrar; ~ **a tooth** perforar un diente; *mil* enseñar la instrucción; *vi* hacer[19] la instrucción (militar/física)

drink *n* bebida; **have a** ~ tomar una cop(it)a, *fam* echar un trago; **may I have a** ~ **of water?** ¿quiere usted darme un poco de agua?; ~**s on the house!** ¡la casa paga!; *v* beber, tomar; *fam* soplar; **he** ~**s all his wages** él gasta todo su sueldo en beber

~ **in** *fig* absorber

~ **to** brindar por

~ **up** beberse; ~ **it all up!** ¡bébetelo!

drinkable potable

drinker bebedor *m* (-ora *f*)

drinking *n* beber *m*; *adj* (of a person) que bebe, *pej* aficionado a la bebida; (of things) para beber; ~-**bout** ataque *m* de embriaguez; ~-**fountain** fuente *f* de agua potable; ~-**song** canción (-ones) *f* de taberna; ~-**trough** abrevadero; ~-**water** agua potable

drip *n* gota; *sl* persona de poco carácter; ~-**dry shirt** camisa de lava y pon; *v* gotear; ~-**feed** *med* alimentación (-ones) *f* parenteral, *fam* gotagota *m*

dripping *n* goteo; (fat) pringue *m*; *adj* que gotea; (soaked) mojado hasta los huesos

drive *n* (roadway) avenida; (path) paseo de coches; (distance) trayecto; **a day's** ~ un trayecto de un día; (journey)

viaje *m* en coche; (campaign) campaña, **sales** ~ campaña de venta;
(energy) energía; (golf) golpe *m*;
mech acción *f*; *mil* ataque *m*, (advance) avance *m*; **go for a** ~ dar un
paseo (en coche); **take for a** ~ llevar
en coche; **~way** paso de coches; *v*
(vehicle) conducir[15]; (animals) llevar;
(game birds) batir; *mil* atacar[4], avanzar[7]; *sp* golpear; *mech* hacer[19] funcionar, mover (ue)[1b]; (oblige) compeler; ~ **a bargain** hacer[19] un negocio;
~ **a hard bargain** regatear mucho;
~ **slowly!** ¡marcha moderada!; ~
mad/round the bend volver (ue)[1b]
(*past part* vuelto) loco; **what are you
driving at?** ¿qué quiere Vd. decir?

~ **away** *vt* repeler; (frighten) espantar;
vi marcharse (en coche); (after parking) desparcar[4]

~ **back** *sp* devolver (ue)[1b] (*past part*
devuelto); (return) volver (ue)[1b] (*past
part* vuelto) (en coche)

~ **home** regresar (en coche); ~ **home
the point/argument** remachar el clavo

~-in *adj*: **~-in bank** banco cuyos clientes no necesitan salir de sus coches;
~-in cinema cine *m* al aire libre para
automovilistas

~ **in** *v* entrar en coche; (nail) clavar;
(stake) hincar[4]; (animals) hacer[19] entrar

~ **into a rage** provocar[4] al enfado

~ **off** (after parking) desparcar[4]

~ **on** seguir[3+11] conduciendo

~ **out** expulsar

~ **to despair** desesperar

drivel *n* disparates *mpl*; *v* decir[19] disparates; (in senility) chochear

driver +*mot* conductor *m* (-ora *f*); (of
locomotive) maquinista; (of cart) carretero; (of carriage) cochero; (of
cattle) ganadero; (golf) dríver *m*

driving *n* conducción *f*; **he is the ~ force
behind** él es el cerebro de; *adj* de
conducir; *mech* motor (-ora *f*); ~ **rain**
lluvia violenta; **~-instructor** instructor *m* de conducir; **~-licence**
carnet *m* de conducir; **~-mirror** re-
trovisor *m*; **~- school** autoescuela; **~-
seat** asiento del conductor; **~-test**
examen (-ámenes) *m* de conducción;
~-wheel volante *m*

drizzle *n* llovizna; *v* lloviznar

droll gracioso
drollery chuscada
dromedary dromedario
drone *n* abejón (-ones) *m*, *fig* zángano;
(sound) zumbido; *v* zumbar; ~ **on and
on** seguir (i)[3] hablando monótona-
mente
droning zumbador (-ora *f*)
drool: ~ **over** deleitarse en
droop inclinarse; (wither) marchitarse;
(pine) desanimarse
drooping caído; (sad) decaído; ~ **ears**
orejas *fpl* gachas; ~ **moustache** bigote
m llorón
drop *n* (liquid) gota; (fall) caída; ~ **of
thirty metres** caída de treinta metros;
(slope) pendiente *f*; (in prices) baja;
(by parachute) lanzamiento; (sweet)
pastilla; **at the ~ of a hat** con cualquier
pretexto; **by ~s** a gotas; **get the ~ on
s.o.** disparar el primero; **~-curtain**
theat telón (-ones) *m* de boca; **~-kick**
sp boterpronto; **~-leaf table** mesa
plegable; *v* dejar caer; (lower) bajar;
(leave) dejar (de); (descend) descender; ~ **anchor** fondear; ~ **a brick**
fig cometer una plancha, meter la
pata; ~ **a clanger** *sl* pegar una coladora; ~ **a hint** echar una indirecta; ~
a line escribir (*past part* escrito); ~
the subject dejar el tema; ~ **a letter
in the post** echar una carta; **let the
matter** ~ dejar el asunto; **the temperature has dropped** la temperatura
ha bajado; **the wind has dropped** el
viento ha amainado; **will you please ~
me at …?** ¿le importaría dejarme
en …?
~ **asleep** dormirse (ue)[1c]
~ **astern/behind** quedar atrás
~ **in** (call on) ir[19] a ver; **they often ~ in
on his uncle** ellos visitan a menudo a su
tío; ~ **in at** caer[19] por, **I sometimes ~
in at the little café** a veces caigo por el
cafetín
~ **off** (fall asleep) dormirse (ue)[1c]; (decrease) disminuir; **can I ~ you off anywhere?** ¿quiere usted que le deje en
algún sitio?
~-out *n* (from university *etc*) rebotado;
fig disidente *m*+*f* social, *sl* pasota
~ **out** *v* rebotar, disidir
droplet gotita
dropper *med* cuentagotas *m sing*+*pl*

droppings excrementos *mpl*; *fam* cagadas *fpl*

dropsical hidrópico

dropsy hidropesía

dross escoria; (rubbish) basura

drought sequía

drove (sheep) rebaño; (people) muchedumbre *f*; **in ~s** a montones

drover ganadero, vaquero

drown *vt* ahogar[5]; (flood) inundar; *fig* (shouts *etc*) ahogar[5]; **~ one's sorrows** ahogar[5] las penas; *vi* ahogarse[5]

drowse adormecerse[14]

drowsiness somnolencia

drowsy (sleepy) medio dormido; (sleep-inducing) soporífero; **become/grow ~** adormecerse[14]; **make ~** adormecer[14]

drub apalear

drubbing paliza; *fig* derrota decisiva

drudge *n* ganapán (-anes) *m*; *v* fatigarse[5]

drudgery trabajo duro y monótono

drug *n* droga; (narcotic) estupefaciente; medicina *m*; **~-addict** toxicómano, drogadicto; **~-addiction** toxicomanía; **~-pedlar** vendedor *m* (-ora *f*) de drogas, *sl* camello; **~-squad** brigada especial de estupefacientes; **~-store** farmacia; **~-taking** consumo de estupefacientes; **~-traffic** tráfico de drogas; **it's a ~ on the market** es invendible; *v* drogar, administrar drogas; (mix with ~s) poner[19] drogas en

druggist farmacéutico; **~'s** farmacia

druid druida *m*

drum *n* *mus* tambor *m*; (container) bidón (-ones) *m*; (of ear) tímpano; **~-beat** toque *m* de tambor; **~-major** tambor *m* mayor; **~-majorette** directora de una banda (de muchachas) en un desfile; **~-stick** *mus* palillo (de tambor), *cul* pata de ave; **~s** (in band) batería (de jazz); **with ~s beating** con tambor; *v* (with fingers) teclear; (with heels) taconear; **~ into** machacar[4]; **~ up sales** fomentar ventas

drummer tamborilero; *mus* (in group) batería; (*US* commercial traveller) viajante *m*

drunk borracho; **be ~** estar[19] borracho, *fam* estar[19] trompa; **get ~** emborracharse, *fam* coger[8] una tajada; **make ~** emborrachar; **~ as a lord** borracho como una cuba

drunkard borracho

drunken borracho; **~ (way of) life** vida crapulosa; **~ driving** conducción *f* cuando borracho

drunkenness borrachera

dry *adj* seco, árido; (thirsty) sediento; **I am ~** tengo sed; (wine) seco, **~ sherry** jerez seco, **~ vermouth** vermú blanco; (squeezed) exprimido; (boring) aburrido; **~-clean** lavar en seco; **~-cleaner's** tintorería; **~-cleaning** lavado en seco; **~-dock** dique *m* de carena; **~-eyed** sin llorar; **~-fly fishing** pesca con mosca artificial; **~ goods** lencería; **~-goods store** lencería; **~ land** tierra firme; **on ~ land** en seco; **~ measure** medida para áridos; **~ rot** carcoma; **~ season** estación *f* de sequía; **~ shampoo** champú *m* en polvo; *v* secar(se)[4]; (wipe) enjugar[5]; **~ up** secarse[5]; (of dishes) secar[5] la vajilla; (of speech) dejar de hablar

dual doble; **~ carriageway** doble calzada; **~ control** (de) mandos *mpl* gemelos; **~ personality** doble personalidad; **~-purpose** que sirve a dos fines

dub (grant knighthood) armar caballero; (give nickname) apodar; *cin* doblar

dubbin adobo impermeable

dubbing *cin* doblaje *m*

dubious dudoso

dubiousness incertidumbre *f*

duchess duquesa

duck *n* pato; (darling) vida mía; *sp* (nil) cero; (cloth) dril *m*; (movement) agachada; **~weed** lenteja de agua; *v* (jerk) agacharse; (in water) chapuzarse[7]; **~ the head** bajar la cabeza

ducking chapuzón (-ones) *m*

duckling patito

duct canal *m*

ductile dúctil

dud falso; **~ shell** obús (-uses) *m* que no explota

dude petimetre *m*; **~ ranch** rancho para turistas

due *n* merecido; impuesto; **~s** (taxes) impuestos, (subscription) cuota; *adj* debido; *comm* pagadero; (fitting) propio; (expected) esperado; **in ~ course** a su tiempo debido; **~ to** debido a; *adv*: **~ west** derecho hacia

oeste
duel *n* duelo; *v* batirse en duelo
duelling (batirse *m* en) duelo
duenna dueña
duet dúo
duettist duetista *m+f*
duffel-coat brenca, *fam* montgómery *m*
duffer estúpido
dug-out refugio subterráneo; (canoe) piragua
duke duque *m*
dukedom ducado
dulcimer dulcémele *m*
dull *adj* (stupid) lerdo; (blunt) romo; (boring) aburrido; (dreary) triste; *meteor* nublado; ~ **weather** tiempo nublado; (not polished) mate; *comm* inactivo; ~ **colour** color agapado; ~ **girl** chica sosa; ~ **light** luz sombría; ~ **pain/sound** dolor/ruido sordo; **he is ~ of hearing** él es duro de oído; *v* (weaken) debilitar; (pain) aliviar; (blunt) embotar; (remove shine) hacer[19] mate
dullness (stupidity) estupidez *f*; (bluntness) embotamiento; (boredom) aburrimiento; (sadness) tristeza; (of hearing) dureza; (of people) sosera *f*; (of style) prosaísmo
dully (not brightly) sin brillo; (stupidly) sin comprender; (sadly) tristemente
duly debidamente
dumb mudo; **become ~** quedarse mudo; **strike ~** dejar sin hablar/mudo; *fig* (stupid) lerdo; **~-bell** pesa de gimnasia; **~-waiter** montaplatos *m sing+pl*
dumbfounded aturdido
dumbness mudez *f*; (stupidity) estupidez *f*
dum-dum bala explosiva
dummy *n* (baby's) chupete *m*; (tailor's) maniquí *m*; (at cards) muerto; **be ~** (at cards) ser[19] el muerto; *adj* fingido
dump vertedero; (for stores) depósito; **ammunition ~** depósito de municiones; **this town is a ~** este pueblo es un lugar aburrido; **be (down) in the ~s** estar[19] con murria; **~-truck** camión (-ones) *m* de volquete; *v* verter (ie)[2b]; **~ goods** inundar el mercado
dumper (truck) dúmper *m*
dumping inundación (-ones) *f* del mercado
dumpling bola de masa cocida

dumpy gordito
¹ **dun** *adj* pardo
² **dun** *v* exigir[9] pago
dunce tonto; **~'s cap** orejas *fpl* de burro
dune duna; **~-buggy** coche *m* que se usa en la playa
dung estiércol *m*; (of sheep, goats *etc*) cagarruta; (of poultry) gallinaza; **~hill** muladar *m*
dungarees mono *m sing*
dungeon calabozo
Dunkirk Dunquerque *m*
duo dúo
duodenal: ~ **ulcer** úlcera duodenal
dupe *n* víctima; (fool) tonto; *v* engañar; **be ~d** hacer[19] el primo
duplex: ~ **house** apartamento de dos pisos
duplicate *n* copia; **in ~** por duplicado; *v* duplicar[4]; **~d** a multicopista
duplicating machine, duplicator multicopista
duplication duplicación *f*
duplicity duplicidad *f*
durability durabilidad *f*
durable duradero
duration duración *f*; **for the ~ of** hasta que termine
duress coacción *f*; **under ~** bajo coacción
during durante/cuando, ~ **the Republic** durante/cuando la República
dusk anochecer *m*; **at ~** al anochecer
dusky (dim) oscuro; (swarthy) moreno
dust *n* polvo; **fine ~** polvillo; **~-bin** cubo de la basura; **~-bowl** terreno estéril a causa de la erosión; **~-cart** camión (-ones) *m* de (recoger) la basura; **~-cover** funda; **~-man** basurero; **~pan** recogedor *m* (de basura); **sweep the ~** barrer el polvo; *v* (powder) espolvorear; (remove ~) quitar el polvo de
duster bayeta; (of feathers) plumero
dusting limpieza; **she is going to do the ~** ella va a quitar el polvo; **~-powder** polvos *mpl* de talco
dusty polvoriento; **it is very ~** tiene mucho polvo; **get ~** llenarse de polvo
Dutch holandés (-esa *f*); ~ **cheese** queso de bola; ~ **courage** coraje falso, (drink) ginebra; **double-~** chino; **~man** holandés, **... or I'm a ~man!** ¡... o mi culo es torero!; **~woman** holandesa; **go ~** pagar[5] cada uno su

consumición, ir[19] a escote
dutiful obediente
duty obligación (-ones) *f*; (moral obligation) deber *m*; (payment) derechos *mpl* de aduana; **off** ~ libre de servicio, *mil* franco de servicio; **do one's** ~ cumplir con su deber; **on** ~ de servicio; **pay** ~ **on** pagar[5] derechos de aduana por; ~**chemist's** farmacia de turno; ~**-free** libre de impuestos; ~**-sergeant** (police) sargento de servicio
D.V. (Deo volente) S.D.Q. (si Dios quiere)
dwarf *n* enano; (in circus) liliputense *m*+*f*; *adj* enano; ~ **rose** rosal *m* enano; *v* achicar[4]
dwell habitar; ~ **on** (think about) meditar sobre, (speak at length about) hablar largamente de, (insist on) insistir en, (pause over) detenerse[19] en
dwelling domicilio

dwindle disminuir[16]; ~ **to** reducirse[15] a
dwindling disminución *f*
dye *n* tinte *m*; ~**-stuff** materia colorante; ~**-works** tintorería; *v* teñir (i)[3]; ~**d-in-the-wool** fanático
dyeing tinte *m*
dyer tintorero; ~**'s** tintorería
dying moribundo; **his** ~ **wish** su último deseo; **be** ~ estar[19] agonizando; **be** ~ **for** morirse[1c] (*past part* muerto) por
dyke *see* **dike**
dynamic dinámico
dynamics dinámica
dynamite *n* dinamita; *v* volar (ue)[1a] con dinamita
dynamo dínamo *f*
dynastic dinástico
dynasty dinastía
dysentery disentería
dyspepsia dispepsia
dyspeptic *n*+*adj* dispéptico

E

e (letter) e *f*; E *mus* mi *m*

each *adj* cada *invar*; **they gave presents to ~ other** se hicieron regalos uno(s) a otro(s); **they love ~ other** se quieren; **they visit ~ other** se visitan mutuamente; *pron* cada uno/una; **~ of them** cada uno de ellos

eager ansioso; deseoso (**to** de); **~ efforts** esfuerzos *mpl* ambiciosos

eagerly con ansia

eagerness ansiedad *f*; (zeal) fervor *m*

eagle águila; (golf) eagle *m*; **~-eyed** con ojos de lince; **~-owl** buho, *Peru* carancho

eaglet aguilucho

ear (external) oreja; (internal) oído; (ability to hear) oído; *bot* espiga; **I'm all ~s** soy todo oídos; **by ~** de oído; **have a good ~ for** tener[19] buen oído para; **turn a deaf ~** hacerse[19] el sordo; **~-ache** dolor *m* de oído(s); **~-drum** tímpano (del oído); **~-flap** orejera; **~mark** separar para un fin especial; **~-phone**, **~-piece** auricular *m*; **~-plug** tapón *m*; **personal ~-plug** *rad* audífono personal; **~ring** pendiente *m*; **within ~shot** al alcance del oído; **~-splitting** ensordecedor (-ora *f*); **~-syringe** jeringa de oídos; **~-trumpet** trompetilla

earful: **did you get an ~ of that?** ¿oyó usted eso?

earl conde *m*

earldom condado

earlier más temprano; *hist* más antiguo; (first) primero; **not ~ than five** a las cinco lo más pronto

earliest el más temprano; *hist* el más antiguo; (first) primero

earliness lo temprano; *hist* antigüedad *f*

early *adj* temprano; (primitive) primitivo; (of an artist's work) primero; *hort* tempranal; (approaching) próximo; **~ date** fecha próxima; **~ age** (of child) tierna edad; **~-bird**, **~-riser** madrugador *m* (-ora *f*); **~**

diagnosis diagnóstico precoz; **~ retirement** jubileo anticipado; **~ hours of the morning** altas horas de la noche; **~ train** tren *m* de la madrugada; **in my ~ years** en los años de mi niñez; *adv* temprano; (in the month) a primeros de; (in the day) temprano; **~ in the morning** muy de mañana; **as ~ as possible** lo más temprano posible; **be ~** llegar[5] antes de tiempo; **five minutes ~** con cinco minutos de anticipación; **get up ~** madrugar[5]; **the ~ bird catches the worm** a quien madruga Dios le ayuda; **~-rising** *adj* madrugador (-ora *f*); **~-warning system** sistema *m* de aviso inmediato

earn ganar; **~ one's living** ganarse la vida; **~ good money** *fam* ganar buenas perras

earnest serio; **be in ~** estar[19] en serio; **~ money** arras *fpl*; **~ prayers** oraciones *fpl* fervorosas

earnestly en serio

earnestness seriedad *f*

earnings (wage) jornal *m*; (salary) salario; *comm* ingresos *mpl*

earth *n* tierra; (fox's lair) madriguera; **on ~** sobre la tierra; **~-bound** terrestre; **~-man** terrestre *m*; **~-nut** cacahuete *m*; **~quake** terremoto; **~-satellite** satélite *m* terrestre; **~-ward(s)** hacia la tierra; **~-wire**, **~-cable** cable *m* de toma de tierra; **~works** terraplén (-enes) *m*; **~worm** lombriz (-ces) *m*; *v elect* conectar con la tierra; **~ up** *agri* acollar

earthen de barro; **~ware** alfarería; *adj* de barro

earthiness terrosidad *f*

earthling terrestre *m+f*

earthly terrenal; (worldly) mundano; **there's not an ~ chance** no hay la más mínima posibilidad

earthy terroso; *fig* grosero

earwig tijereta

ease (tranquillity) tranquilidad *f*; (comfort) bienestar *m*; (freedom from embarrassment) naturalidad *f*; (freedom from pain) alivio; **at** ~! *mil* ¡en su lugar descansen!; **be at** ~ estar[19] a/en sus anchas; **life of** ~ vida desahogada; **with** ~ con facilidad; *v* (loosen) aflojar; (remove difficulty) hacer[19] más fácil; (lessen pain) aliviar; ~ **off,** ~ **up** apaciguarse[6]

easel caballete *m*

easement descarga

easily fácilmente; *sp* (by clear lead) de lejos

easiness sencillez *f*; (of manner) naturalidad *f*

easing (of repressive laws *etc*) suavización *f*

east *n* este *m*; **the East** el Oriente; *adj* oriental; **East Germany** Alemania Oriental; **East Indies** Indias Orientales; **Far East** Lejano Oriente; **Middle East** Oriente Medio; **Near East** Cercano Oriente; ~**-bound** hacia el este; ~**-north-**~ estenordeste *m*; ~**south-**~ estesudeste *m*; ~ **wind** viento del este, *Sp* levante *m*

Easter Pascua de Resurrección; ~ **egg** huevo de Pascua; ~ **Monday** lunes *m* de Pascua; ~ **Sunday** domingo de Pascua; ~ **Saturday** (before Easter) sábado de gloria, (after Easter) sábado santo; ~**tide** tiempo de Pascua

easterly (towards the east) hacia el este; (from the east) del este

eastern oriental

easterner (person) oriental *m*; (wind) viento del levante

easternmost lo más al este/más oriental

eastwards hacia oriente

easy (not difficult) fácil; (unconcerned) despreocupado; (of ~ virtue) *fam* facilona; ~ **to get on with** simpático; ~ **to manage** de fácil manejo; ~ **come** ~ **go** los dineros del sacristán cantando vienen y cantando se van; **I'm** ~ (I don't care either way) me es igual; **be in** ~ **street** vivir espléndidamente; **I don't feel** ~ **here** no estoy a gusto aquí; **now I feel** ~ **about the matter** ahora estoy tranquilo sobre el asunto; **it's dead** ~ *sl* está chupado; **of** ~ **virtue** de moralidad relajada; **take it** ~! ¡tómelo con calma!; **take the** ~ **way**

out tirar por la calle de en medio; ~ **chair** sillón (-ones) *m*; ~**-going** bonachón (-ona *f*), *Arg* manfichista *m*+*f*; **be** ~**-going** tener[19] mucha pachorra; ~ **money** dinero ganado sin esfuerzos, *comm* dinero en abundancia, *sl* pasta gansa

eat comer; (corrode) corroer; ~ **breakfast** desayunar(se); ~ **dinner** (midday) almorzar (ue)[1a], comer; (evening) cenar; ~ **lunch** almorzar (ue)[1a]; comer; ~ **like a horse** comer como una fiera; ~ **a snack** tomar un tentempié; ~ **supper** cenar; ~ **humble pie** rebajarse; ~ **one's heart out** sufrir un disgusto en silencio; **the journalist had to** ~ **his words** el periodista tuvo que tragarse sus palabras; **... I'll** ~ **my hat** *vulg* ... me la corto

~ **into** (of acids *etc*) corroer; (capital) gastar

~ **out** comer fuera

~ **up** comerse; ~ **it all up at once!** ¡cómetelo en seguida!

eatable comestible; ~**s** comestibles *mpl*

eater el *m* (la *f*) que come; **he's a good** ~ tiene buen apetito

eating comer *m*; ~ **and drinking** el comer y beber; ~**-house** fonda

eau de cologne (agua de) Colonia

eaves alero *m sing*; ~**drop** escuchar a la puerta; ~**dropper** el que escucha escondido

ebb *n* (tide) menguante *f*; *fig* declinación *f*; ~**-tide** marea menguante; *v* (tide) menguar[6]; *fig* declinar; ~ **and flow** fluir[16] y refluir[16]

ebony ébano

ebullience exuberancia

ebullient exuberante

ebullition (boiling) hervor *m*; *fig* efervescencia

eccentric *n* chiflado; *adj geom*+*mech* excéntrico; (strange) raro, *fam* extrafalario

eccentricity chifladura; excentricidad *f*

Ecclesiastes Eclesiastés *m*

ecclesiastic(al) *n*+*adj* eclesiástico

echelon escalón (-ones) *m*

echo *n* eco; **produce an** ~ producir[15] un eco; ~**-sounder** sonda acústica; *v* reverberar; **he** ~**ed my words** repitió mis palabras

echoic ecoico

echoing *n* eco; *adj* retumbante
éclair bollo de crema
éclat esplendor *m*
eclectic *n*+*adj* ecléctico
eclecticism eclecticismo
eclipse *n* eclipse *m*; be in ∼ estar¹⁹ en eclipse; *v*+*fig* eclipsar
ecliptic *n* eclíptica; *adj* eclíptico
ecological ecológico
ecologist ecologista *m*+*f*
ecology ecología
economic(al) económico; economic blockade bloqueo económico; ∼ prices precios *mpl* asequibles
economics economía (política)
economist economista *m*+*f*
economize *vt* economizar⁷; *vi* hacer¹⁹ economías
economy economía; (frugality) frugalidad *f*
ecosystem ecosistema *m*
ecstasy éxtasis *m*; be in ∼ estar¹⁹ en éxtasis
ecstatic extático
ectoplasm ectoplasma *m*
Ecuador Ecuador *m*
Ecuadorian *n*+*adj* ecuatoriano
ecumenical ecuménico
ecumenism ecumenismo
eczema eczema
eddy *n* remolino; *v* remolinar(se)
edelweiss edelweiss *f*
Eden Edén *m*; Garden of ∼ Jardín *m* del Edén
edge *n* borde *m*; (end) extremidad *f*; (of coin) canto; (of river *etc*) orilla; (sharpened part) filo; my teeth are on ∼ tengo dentera; on the ∼ of the table al borde de la mesa; put an ∼ on (sharpen) afilar; I have the ∼ on him tengo una ventaja sobre él; she is on ∼ (agitated) ella está nerviosa; *fam* tiene los nervios de punta; ∼-tool herramienta cortante; *v* poner¹⁹ un borde a; (sewing) ribetear; (sharpen) afilar; ∼d (bordered) bordeado, (sewing) ribeteado, (sharpened) afilado; black-∼d orlado de luto; double-∼d +*fig* de dos filos
∼ away escurrir(se)
∼ forward avanzar⁷ con dificultad
∼ into deslizarse⁷ en
∼ one's way through abrirse (*past part* abierto) paso por

edgeways de lado; I can't get a word in ∼ no puedo meter baza
edging orla; (wallpaper) orilla
edgy irritable
edibility calidad *f* de comestible
edible comestible
edict edicto
edification edificación *f*
edificatory constructivo
edifice edificio
edify edificar⁴
edifying edificante
Edinburgh Edimburgo
edit (prepare an edition) editar; (prepare for press) redactar; (correct) corregir⁹; (be in charge of a newspaper) ser¹⁹ director de; this newspaper is ∼ed by este periódico está bajo la dirección de; text ∼ed by edición de
editing (preparation of an edition) trabajo editorial; (preparation for press) redacción *f*; (correction) corrección *f*
edition edición *f*; *print* tirada
editor (text) editor *m* (-ora *f*); (newspaper) redactor *m* (-ora *f*); ∼-in-chief director *m* (-ora *f*); *cin* jefe *m* de corte
editorial *n* artículo de fondo/del editor; *adj* editorial; ∼ office/staff redacción *f*
editorship dirección *f*
Edmund Edmundo
educability educabilidad *f*
educable educable
educate instruir¹⁶; (also give moral training) educar⁴
education (manners) educación *f*; (public) enseñanza; (training) instrucción *f*
educational pedagógico, *SA* educacional; (in morality and manners) educativo
educative educativo
educator, educationalist pedagogo
Edward Eduardo
Edwardian perteneciente a la época de Eduardo VII
E.E.C. (European Economic Community) C.E.E. (Comunidad Económica Europea)
eel anguila
eerie misterioso
efface borrar; ∼ o.s. retirarse

effacement borradura

effect *n* efecto; (result) resultado; (meaning) significado; **~s** (belongings) bienes *mpl*; **the aspirins are taking ~** las aspirinas están haciendo efecto; **come/go into ~** entrar en vigor; **it has no ~ on us** no nos hace ningún efecto; **she does it for ~** ella lo hace para producir efecto; *v* efectuar; **~ a payment** realizar[7] un pago

effective en vigor; **the orders became ~** las órdenes entraron en vigor; (efficient) eficaz (-ces)

effectiveness eficacia

effectual eficaz (-ces)

effeminacy afeminación *f*

effeminate afeminado; **~ man** afeminado, *fam* marica *m*

effervesce hervir (i)[3]

effervescent efervescente

effete estéril

effeteness decadencia

efficacious, efficient eficaz (-ces); (capable) competente

efficacy, efficiency eficacia; *mech* rendimiento

effigy efigie *f*; **burn in ~** quemar en efigie

efflorescence *bot* florescencia; *chem* eflorescencia

effluent efluente *m*

effort esfuerzo; (attempt) intento; **my first literary ~** mi primer intento literario; **~ prize** premio de aplicación; **make an ~** hacer[19] un esfuerzo; **make an ~ to** esforzarse[1a+7] por

effortless(ly) sin esfuerzo

effrontery descaro

effusion efusión (-ones) *f*

effusive efusivo

e.g. (exempli gratia) p.ej. (por ejemplo)

egalitarian igualitario

egalitarianism igualitarismo

egg *n* huevo; **~-cup** huevera; **~-custard** flan *m*; **~-flip** huevo batido con ron; **~-head** cerebral *m*; **~-plant** berenjena; **~-rack** (in refrigerator) departamento de los huevos; **~-shaped** aovado; **~-shell** cáscara de huevo; **~-slicer** cortahuevos *m*; **~-spoon** cuchar(it)a para huevos; **~-timer** reloj *m* de arena (para cocer huevos); **~-whisk** batidor *m* de huevos; *v* **~ on** incitar

eglantine eglantina

ego yo *m*; **go on an ~ trip** jactarse

egocentric egocéntrico

egoism, egotism egoísmo

ego(t)ist egoísta *m+f*

ego(t)istic egoísta

egregious notorio

egress salida

egret *orni* airón (-ones) *m*

Egypt Egipto

Egyptian egipcio

Egyptologist egiptólogo

Egyptology egiptología

eh? ¿qué?

eider (duck) pato de flojel; **~down** edredón (-ones) *m*

eight *n+adj* ocho *m*; (boat) ocho de carrera; **have one over the ~** tener[19] una copa de más; **~-day clock** reloj *m* con cuerda para ocho días; **~-hour day** jornada de ocho horas

eighteen *n+adj* dieciocho *m*; **she is ~** ella tiene dieciocho años; **~ months ago** hace un año y medio; **eighteen-fifty** mil ochocientos cincuenta

eighteenth decimoctavo; **~ of July** dieciocho/diez y ocho de julio; (of monarchs) dieciocho; (fraction) decimoctava parte

eighth *n* octavo; *fam* octava parte; **~ of May** el ocho de mayo; **Henry the ~** Enrique octavo; *adj* octavo

eightieth octogésimo

eighty *n+adj* ochenta *m*; **be in one's eighties** tener[19] sus ochenta años

Eire Eire *m*

either *adj* cada *invar*; **on ~ side of the road** a cada lado/a ambos lados de la carretera; **in ~ case** en ambos casos; *adv* tampoco; **I don't swim ~** no sé nadar tampoco; **not/nor Mary ~** ni María tampoco; *pron* cualquiera (de los dos); **pick ~** escoja usted cualquiera; **John is taller than ~** Juan es más alto que los dos; **~ ..., or o ... o;** **I don't like ~ of them** no me gusta ni uno ni otro

ejaculate exclamar; *med* eyacular

ejaculation exclamación (-ones) *f*; *med* eyaculación (-ones) *f*

ejaculatory eyaculatorio

eject expulsar; (emit) emitir

ejection expulsión (-ones) *f*; (emission) emisión (-ones) *f* ejector eyector *m*

eke: ~ out escatimar; ~ out a livelihood
ganarse la vida a duras penas

elaborate *adj* complicado; (detailed)
detallado; *v* ~(upon) elaborar

elaboration elaboración *f*

elapse transcurrir

elastic *n+adj* elástico; ~ band goma
elástica; ~ bandage venda elástica

elasticity elasticidad *f*

Elastoplast *tr* esparadrapo; ~ dressing
tirita

elate alegrar

elation alegría

elbow *n* codo; ~-grease jugo de muñeca;
~-room libertad *f* de movimiento; *v*
codear; ~ one's way abrirse (*past part*
abierto) paso a (fuerza de) codazos

[1] elder *n* persona mayor; *eccles* dignatario; *adj* mayor *m+f*; ~ statesman
viejo político

[2] elder *bot* saúco; ~berry baya del saúco

elderly de edad; an ~ lady una señora de
edad

eldest el/la mayor; (firstborn) primogénito

Eleanor Leonor

elect *n* electos *mpl*; *adj* electo; mayor ~
alcalde electo; *v* elegir (i)[3]; be ~ed
salir[19] electo·

election elección (-ones) *f*; ~ meeting
mitin *m* electoral

electioneer hacer[19] propaganda electoral; (canvass) pedir (i)[3] votos

electioneering campaña electoral

elective electivo

elector elector *m* (-ora *f*); (prince)
elector *m*

electoral electoral; ~ register lista de
electores, censo

electorate electorado

electric eléctrico; ~ blanket manta eléctrica; ~ chair silla eléctrica; ~ cord
US cable eléctrico; ~ current corriente (eléctrica); ~ light luz (-ces)
eléctrica; ~ motor motor *m* eléctrico;
~ shaver máquina de afeitar; ~ shock
sacudida eléctrica; ~ wire conductor
eléctrico

electrical eléctrico; ~ engineer ingeniero electricista; ~ engineering ingeniería eléctrica

electrically por electricidad

electrician electricista *m+f*

electricity electricidad *f*; *fam* luz *f*; this
appliance uses a lot of ~ este aparato
usa mucha luz

electrification electrificación *f*

electrify electrificar[4]

electrocardiogram electrocardiograma
m

electrocardiograph electrocardiografía

electrocute electrocutar

electrocution electrocución *f*

electrode electrodo

electro-dynamics electrodinámica

electrolysis electrólisis *f*

electrolyte electrólito

electromagnet electroimán (-anes) *m*

electromagnetism electromagnetismo

electromotive: ~ force fuerza electromotriz

electromotor motor eléctrico

electron electrón (-ones) *m*; ~ microscope microscopio electrónico

electronic electrónico

electroplate platear, galvanizar[7]

electroplating galvanoplastia

elegance elegancia

elegant elegante

elegantly con elegancia

elegiac elegíaco

elegy elegía

element elemento; (factor) factor *m*;
(component) componente *m*; *eccles*
pan *m*; *chem* cuerpo simple; ~s
(weather) elementos; naturaleza; be
in one's ~ (in one's natural·
environment) estar[19] en su propia
salsa, (in a happy state) estar[19] a sus
anchas

elemental elemental

elementary elemental; (education) de
primera enseñanza

elephant elefan·e *m*, elefanta *f*; ~-
keeper, ~-trainer naire *m*

elephantiasis elefancia

elevate (raise) elevar; (honour) enaltecer[14]; (promote) ascender; (improve
the mind) educar[4]; *eccles* ~ the Host
alzar[7] la hostia

elevated (raised) elevado; (exalted)
exaltado; ~ railway ferrocarril aéreo

elevation elevación (-ones) *f*; (height)
altitud *f*; *archi* alzado (de un edificio);
~ to the House of Lords ascenso a la
Cámara de los Lores

elevator (lift) ascensor *m*; *agri* elevador

m; *eng* transportador *m*

eleven *n+adj* once *m*; *sp* (team) equipo

elevenses bocadillo de las once

eleventh undécimo; (of monarchs) once; ~ **of March** el once de marzo; (fraction) undécima parte; **at the ~ hour** a última hora

elf duende *m*

elfin, elfish de duende

elicit sacar[4]

elide elidir

eligibility elegibilidad *f*

eligible elegible; ~ **bachelor** buen partido

Elijah Elías

eliminate eliminar

eliminating: ~ **heat/test** (carrera/prueba) eliminatoria

elimination eliminación (-ones) *f*; **by a process of** ~ por exclusión

eliminatory eliminador (-ora *f*)

Elisha Eliseo

elision elisión *f*

élite la flor y nata

elitism elitismo

elixir elixir *m*

Elizabeth Isabel

Elizabethan isabelino

elk alce *m*

ellipse elipse *m*

elliptic(al) elíptico

elm olmo; ~**-grove** olmeda

elocution declamación *f*; ~ **class** clase *f* de declamación

elocutionist declamador *m* (-ora *f*)

elongate alargar(se)[5]

elongation alargamiento

elope fugarse[5] (with con)

elopement fuga

eloquence elocuencia

eloquent elocuente

else más; **anyone/anything** ~ alguien/algo más; **everyone** ~ todos los demás; **nobody/nothing** ~ nadie/nada más; **or** ~ si no; **somewhere/nowhere** ~ en otra/en ninguna otra parte; **I can do nothing** ~ no puedo (hacer) más; **there's nothing** ~ **to do** no hay más remedio; **what** ~? ¿qué más?; ~**where** en otra parte

elucidate elucidar

elucidation elucidación *f*

elude eludir

elusive fugaz (-ces); (hard to under-

stand) difícil de comprender

elusiveness fugacidad *f*

Elysian elíseo; ~ **fields** campos *mpl* elíseos

Elysium Elíseo

emaciate demacrar; **become** ~**d** demacrarse

emaciation demacración *f*

emanate emanar (**from** de)

emanation emanación (-ones) *f*

emancipate emancipar

emancipation emancipación *f*

emancipator emancipador *m* (-ora *f*)

emancipatory emancipador (-ora *f*)

emasculate emascular; *euph* mutilar

embalm embalsamar

embalmer embalsamador *m* (-ora *f*)

embalming *n* embalsamamiento

embankment declive *m*; (dike) dique *m*; (quay) muelle *m*

embargo embargo; **put an** ~ **on** embargar[6]; **remove an** ~ sacar[4] de embargo

embark embarcarse[4]; *fig* empezar (ie)[2a] con; ~ **on a career** emprender una carrera

embarkation (of people) embarcación *f*; (of goods) embarque *m*

embarrass (hinder) impedir (i)[3]; (financially) apurar; (confuse) desconcertar (ie)[2a]; (make ill at ease) poner[19] en un aprieto; (shame) avergonzar[7]

embarrassed (confused) confuso; (ill at ease) apurado; (ashamed) avergonzado

embarrassing desconcertante; **it is** ~ **for me** me es violento

embarrassment apuro; (shame) vergüenza; (confusion) turbación *f*; **financial** ~ apuro financiero

embassy embajada

embed empotrar

embellish adornar

embellishment adorno

ember ascua; **Ember-days** témporas *fpl*

embezzle desfalcar[4]

embezzlement desfalco

embezzler desfalcador *m* (-ora *f*)

embitter amargar[5]; **have an** ~**ed look** *fam* tener[19] cara de mala uva

embitterment amargura

emblazon blasonar

emblazonry blasón *m*

emblem divisa

emblematic emblemático
embodiment personificación f
embody personificar[4]; (include) incluir[16]
embolden animar
embolism embolismo; *med* embolia
emboss estampar en relieve; ~**ed** en relieve
embrace n abrazo; v abrazar[7]; (include) abarcar[4]; (accept) aceptar
embrocation embrocación (-ones) f
embroider bordar
embroiderer bordador m (-ora f)
embroidery bordado; ~ **frame** bastidor m; ~ **silk** hilo de bordar
embroil enredar (**in** en)
embryo n embrión (-ones) m; *adj* embrionario
embryology embriología
embryonic embrionario
emend enmendar (ie)[2a]
emendation enmienda
emerald n esmeralda; *adj* de color de esmeralda; ~ **green** verde esmeralda
emerge emerger[8]; (of ideas) aparecer[14]
emergence emergencia
emergency n (caso de) necesidad f; **break glass in** ~ rómpase el cristal en caso de emergencia; ~ **dressing** cura individual; ~ **exit** salida de urgencia; ~ **hospital** casa de socorro; ~ **kit** botiquín (-ines) m de urgencia; ~ **landing** aterrizaje forzoso; ~ **landing field** campo de emergencia; ~ **measure** medida de urgencia; ~ **ward** sala de urgencia
emergent emergente
emeritus emérito
emery esmeril m; ~-**paper** papel m de esmeril
emetic n + *adj* emético
emigrant n + *adj* emigrante m + f
emigrate emigrar
emigration emigración (-ones) f
émigré emigrante m + f
Emily Emilia
eminence (hill) elevación f; (title) eminencia
eminent eminente
emir emir m
emissary emisario
emission emisión (-ones) f
emit emitir; (gas) exhalar
Emmanuel Manuel

emolument emolumento
emotion emoción (-ones) f; **display of** ~ aspaviento
emotional emotivo; emocional
emotionalism sentimentalismo
emotive emotivo
empathy empatía
emperor emperador m; ~**ship** dignidad f imperial
emphasis énfasis m
emphasize dar[19] énfasis a
emphatic enfático
emphatically con énfasis
empire imperio; ~-**building** *fig* ensanchamiento por un empleado de su esfera de influencia
empiric(al) empírico
empiricism empirismo
emplacement emplazamiento
employ n empleo; v emplear; (give employment to) dar[19] trabajo a
employable empleable
employee empleado
employer patrón m (-ona f)
employment empleo; (post) puesto; (situation) colocación (-ones) f; ~ **exchange** bolsa del trabajo
emporium emporio; (store) almacén (-enes) m
empower autorizar[7] (**to** a)
empress emperatriz (-ces) f
emptiness vaciedad f
empty n (container) embalaje m vacío; (bottle) botella vacía, *fam* muerto; *adj* vacío; (hungry) hambriento; (unoccupied) desocupado; (vain) frívolo; ~ **phrase** frase hueca; ~ **vessels make most noise** mucho ruido y pocas nueces; ~-**handed** con las manos vacías; ~-**headed** casquivano; v vaciar; (unload) descargar[5]
emu emú m
emulate emular
emulation emulación f
emulative emulador (-ora f)
emulsify emulsionar
emulsion emulsión (-ones) f
enable habilitar (**to** para); **they** ~ **him to live here** le permiten vivir aquí
enact *leg* promulgar[5]; (a play) representar; (a part) desempeñar
enactment promulgación (-ones) f
enamel n esmalte m; ~-**remover** quitaesmaltes m *sing*; v esmaltar

enamour enamorar; **be ~ed of** (a person) estar[19] enamorado de, (a thing) ser[19] aficionado a

en bloc en bloque

encamp acampar

encampment campamento

encase encajar

enchain encadenar

enchant encantar

enchanter encantador (-ora *f*)

enchanting encantador (-ora *f*)

enchantment encanto

enchantress bruja; *fig* mujer seductora

encircle cercar[4]

encirclement cerco

enclave enclave *m*

enclose cercar[4]; (with letter) acompañar; encerrar; **she ~d him in her arms** ella le abarcó con sus brazos; **~d** *adj* (with letter) adjunto

enclosure (wall) tapia; (area) recinto; (with letter) contenido

encompass rodear; **~ the globe** dar[19] la vuelta al mundo

encore *n* repetición (-ones) *f*; *v* hacer[19] repetir; **be ~d** ser[19] aplaudido hasta repetir; **~!** *interj* ¡bis!

encounter *n* encuentro; *v* encontrarse (ue)[1a] con

encourage animar; (approve) aprobar (ue)[1a]; (foster) fomentar

encouragement ánimos *mpl*; (approval) aprobación *f*; (fostering) fomento; **Society for the Encouragement of** sociedad para el fomento de

encouraging alentador, estimulante; (favourable) favorable

encouragingly con aprobación

encroach pasar los límites (**upon** de); (of the sea) hurtar; **~ upon someone's kindness** abusar de la bondad de uno

encroaching usurpador (-ora *f*)

encroachment invasión (-ones) *f*; *fig* usurpación *f*

encrust incrustar

encumber estorbar; (load) cargar[5]

encumbrance (burden) carga; **~ on** estorbo para, (estate) gravamen (-ámenes) *m* sobre

encyclical encíclica

encyclopaedia enciclopedia

encyclopaedic enciclopédico

end *n* (conclusion) fin *m*, final *m;* (death) muerte *f*; (extremity) ex-

tremidad *f*; (of moustache) guía; (of rope) cabo; (piece) fragmento; (of anything pointed) punta; (of a word) terminación (-ones) *f*; *theat+sp* (denouement) desenlace *m*; (of a street) final *m*; **he took the ball to the Leeds United ~** llevó el balón al lado de Leeds United; **~ of work** (for the day) salida; (purpose) fin *m*; (result) resultado; **at the ~ of November** a fines de noviembre; **that would be the ~!** ¡sería el colmo!; **the ~ justifies the means** el fin justifica los medios; **~-on** de punta; **~-game** última táctica; **~ product** producto; **~ to ~** cabeza contra cabeza; **be at an ~** haberse[19] acabado, **the war is at an ~** la guerra se ha acabado; **at the ~** (finally) por fin; **be at the ~ of one's tether** estar[19] sin recursos; **at a loose ~** desocupado; **come to an ~** terminarse; **come to a bad ~** terminar mal; **from ~ to ~** de cabo a cabo; **gain one's ~s** alcanzar[7] su objetivo; **in the ~** al fin (y al cabo); **keep up one's ~** defenderse bien; **make an ~ of** acabar con; **make ~s meet** pasar con lo que se tiene; **I can't make ~s meet** no me salen las cuentas; **it's at the ~ of your nose!** ¡está delante de sus ojos!; **no ~ of** (plenty of) la mar de, *fig* una infinidad de; **on ~** de pie, (of hair) erizado; **for hours on ~** durante una infinidad de horas; **two days on ~** dos días seguidos; **put an ~ to** poner[19] fin a; **to no ~** en vano; **to the ~ that** a fin de que +*subj*; **world without ~** por los siglos de los siglos; *vt* terminar; *vi* acabar(se); **this will ~ his career** esto hundirá su carrera; **~ up** ir[19] a parar; **where would we ~ up?** ¿dónde iríamos a parar?

endanger poner[19] en peligro

endear hacer[19] querer

endearing que inspira cariño

endearment cariño; (spoken) palabra de cariño

endeavour (attempt) intento; (effort) esfuerzo; *v* (attempt) intentar; (make an effort) esforzarse (ue)[1a] (**to** por)

endemic endémico

ending (conclusion) fin *m*; final *m*; (death) muerte *f*; (of a word) terminación (-ones) *f*; (denouement) desenlace *m*; (cessation) cesación (-ones)

f; ~ **of a dynasty** ocaso de una dinastía
endive escarola
endless interminable
endlessly sin fin
endorse (support) apoyar; (guarantee) garantizar[7]; ~ **a cheque** endosar un cheque; ~ **a driving licence** escribir los detalles de una sanción en el carnet de conducir
endorsement (support) apoyo; (guarantee) garantía; (on cheque) endoso; (on driving licence) nota de inhabilitación
endow dotar (**with** de)
endowment dotación (-ones) *f;* ~ **fund** fondos *mpl* de dotación; ~ **insurance/policy** póliza dotal
endurable soportable
endurance resistencia; **beyond** ~ inaguantable; ~ **test** prueba de resistencia
endure (put up with) aguantar; (last) (per)durar
enduring durable
endways, endwise longitudinalmente
E.N.E. (east-north-east) *n+adj* E.N.E. (estenordeste) *m*
enema enema
enemy *n+adj* enemigo; **how's the ~?** *fig* ¿qué hora es?
energetic enérgico
energize dar[19] energía a
energy *n* energía; *mech* fuerza; *adj* energético; ~ **crisis** crisis energética
enervate enervar
enervating enervante
enervation enervación *f*
enfeeble debilitar
enfilade *n* fuego de enfilada; *v* enfilar
enfold envolver (ue)[1b] (*past part* envuelto); (in one's arms) abrazar[7]
enforce (compel obedience) hacer[19] cumplir; *leg* poner[19] en vigor; (get by force) conseguir (i)[3+11] por fuerza; (urge) insistir en
enforcement ejecución *f* (de una ley)
enfranchise *fig* emancipar
enfranchisement *fig* emancipación *f*
engage (reserve) reservar; (employ) emplear; (promise) contratar; (in conversation) entretener[19]; (start fighting) trabar contacto con; *mech* (of wheels) endentar con; ~ **gears** meter las velocidades; ~ **the clutch**

embragar[5]
engaged (busy) ocupado; (having an appointment) comprometido; (betrothed) prometido; **they are** ~ son novios; **an** ~ **couple** una pareja de novios; **be** ~ **to** ser[19] novio a/de; **become** ~ prometerse; (telephone) comunicando *invar;* (washroom *etc*) ocupado; **be** ~ **in** dedicarse[4] a
engagement (obligation) compromiso; (date) cita; **I have an** ~ **at eight o'clock** tengo una cita a las ocho; (battle) batalla; (betrothal) palabra de casamiento; ~**-ring** anillo de compromiso
engaging atractivo
engagingly de un modo atractivo
engender engendrar
engine motor *m;* (railway) locomotora; ~**-driver** maquinista *m;* ~**-failure,** ~**-trouble** avería de motor; ~ **man** maquinista *m;* ~**-room** sala de máquinas; ~**-shed** depósito de locomotoras
engineer *n* ingeniero; (mechanic) mecánico; *naut* maquinista *m;* **chief** ~ jefe *m* de máquinas; **second-**~ segundo maquinista; *mil* (sapper) zapador *m;* (*US* locomotive driver) maquinista *m;* *v* dirigir[9] como ingeniero; (arrange) arreglar; ~ **a plot** maquinar un complot
engineering ingeniería
England Inglaterra
English *n* los ingleses *mpl;* *adj* inglés (-esa *f);* **she speaks** ~ ella habla inglés; **I don't understand** ~ no comprendo el inglés; ~ **Channel** Canal *m* de la Mancha; **in the** ~ **style** a la inglesa; ~**man** inglés (-eses); ~**woman** inglesa
engrain inculcar[4]
engrave grabar
engraver (person) grabador *m;* (tool) cincel *m*
engraving (picture) grabado; *arts* arte *m* de grabar
engross absorber (*past part* absorto) (**in** en)
engrossing absorbente
engulf hundir; (surround) rodear
enhance realzar[7]
enhancement realce *m*
enigma enigma *m*
enigmatic enigmático
enjoin ordenar; *leg* prohibir; ~ **upon** recomendar (ie)[2a] a

enjoy (possess) poseer[17]; (take pleasure in) disfrutar de, gozar[7] de; **he ~s working** le gusta trabajar; **~ a meal** comer a gusto; **~ good health** gozar[7] de buena salud; **~ o.s.** pasarlo bien; **he ~ed himself** lo pasó bien

enjoyable agradable

enjoyably de una manera agradable

enjoyment (possession) posesión *f*; (pleasure) placer *m*; (satisfaction) satisfacción *f*

enkindle encender (ie)[2b]

enlarge ensanchar; *phot* ampliar; **~ upon** tratar detalladamente

enlargement ensanche *m*; *phot* ampliación (-ones) *f*

enlarger ampliadora

enlighten iluminar; **can you ~ me about …?** ¿puede Vd ayudarme en el asunto de …?

enlightened culto

enlightening (revealing) revelador (-ora *f*); (instructive) instructivo

enlightenment cultura

enlist *vt* reclutar; **~ the support of** buscar el apoyo de; *vi* **~ in** alistarse en; *fam* engancharse

enlistment alistamiento; *fam* enganche *m*

enliven animar

en masse en masa

enmesh enredar

enmity enemistad *f*

ennoble ennoblecer[14]

ennoblement ennoblecimiento

ennui aburrimiento

enormity enormidad *f*

enormous enorme

enormously enormemente; *fam* horrores, **I liked it ~** me gustó horrores

enough *n* (lo) bastante; **~ and to spare** de sobra; **~ is ~** basta y sobra; **~ is as good as a feast** lo poco agrada, lo mucho enfada; **be ~** bastar; **as if that were not ~** por si fuera poco; **curiously ~ he was born in China** por raro que parezca nació en China; *adj+adv* bastante; *interj* ¡basta!

en passant al vuelo

enquire, enquiry *see* **inquire, inquiry**

enrage enfurecer[14]

enraged enfurecido

enrapture entusiasmar; (charm) encantar

enrich enriquecer[14]; *agri* fertilizar[7]

enrichment enriquecimiento; *agri* abono

enrol alistar(se); (for school or university) matricular(se)

enrolment alistamiento; matriculación *f*

en route con rumbo (**for** a)

ensconce acomodar; **~ o.s.** acomodarse

ensemble *mus* conjunto; (clothing) traje *m* (de mujer) compuesto de dos piezas

enshrine poner[19] en sagrario

enshroud cubrir (*past part* cubierto)

ensign (flag) bandera; (officer) alférez (-ces) *m*; (*US* navy) subteniente *m*

enslave esclavizar[7]

enslavement esclavitud *f*

ensnare coger[8] en un lazo; *fig* enredar

ensue conseguir (i)[3+11]

ensuing (next) que viene; (resulting) resultante

ensure asegurar

entail *n leg* vinculación *f*; *v* traer[19] consigo; *leg* vincular

entangle enredar

entanglement enredo; *mil* alambrada; (love affair) intriga amorosa

entente pacto; **~ cordiale** convenio cordial

enter entrar en; **~!** ¡pase(n)!; (join) hacerse[19] miembro de; (enrol) alistarse; (at university) matricularse; **~ the church** (take holy orders) hacerse[19] cura; (make a note of) apuntar; *comm* (make an entry) asentar (ie)[2a]; *theat* salir[19] (a escena); **~ in alphabetical order** disponer[19] en orden alfabético; **it didn't ~ my mind/thoughts** no se me occurió; **~ for a race** inscribir(se) (*past part* inscrito) en una carrera

~ into (a matter) entrar en (materia); **~ into an agreement** celebrar un convenio; (sign) firmar un convenio; **~ into conversation with** entablar una conversación con; **~ into details** entrar en detalles; **~ into negotiations** iniciar negociaciones; **~ into the spirit of** encajar en el ambiente de

~ up poner[19] en la lista; (diary) poner[19] al día

~ upon emprender

enteric entérico; **~ fever** fiebre tifoidea

enteritis enteritis *f*

enterprise (undertaking) empresa; (initiative) iniciativa

enterprising (forceful) aventurero; (of initiative) de mucha iniciativa

entertain *vt* (amuse) entretener[19]; (offer hospitality) hospedar; (consider) considerar; (hold) mantener[19], **I cannot ~ the idea** no puedo mantener la idea; **~ doubts as to** concebir (i)[3] dudas sobre; *vi* dar[19] fiestas; **they ~ a lot** ellos reciben mucho en casa

entertainer (host) anfitrión (-ones) *m*; (in public) artista *m+f*; (singer) vocalista *m+f*

entertaining *n* hospitalidad *f*; *adj* entretenido

entertainment entretenimiento; (spectacle) espectáculo; (hospitality) hospitalidad *f*; **~-tax** impuesto sobre espectáculos

enthrall (enslave) esclavizar[7]; *fig* dominar

enthralled (enslaved) esclavizado; *fig* encantado

enthralling absorbente

enthrone entronizar[7]

enthronement entronización (-ones) *f*

enthuse entusiasmarse (**about/over** por)

enthusiasm entusiasmo

enthusiast entusiasta *m+f*

enthusiastic entusiástico; **be ~ about** entusiasmarse por

enthusiastically con entusiasmo

entice: ~ away seducir[15]

enticement seducción (-ones) *f*

enticing seductor (-ora *f*)

entire (total) entero; (undivided) íntegro

entirety totalidad *f*

entitle titular; (give the right) autorizar[7]; **his position ~s him to respect** él merece que le respeten por su posición

entity entidad *f*

entomb sepultar

entomological entomológico

entomologist entomólogo

entomology entomología

entourage séquito

entr'acte entreacto

entrails entrañas *fpl*

entrain subir al tren

entrainment subida al tren

entrammel enredar

[1] **entrance** *n* (act of entering) entrada; (way in) entrada; (door) puerta; (porch) portal *m*; *theat* salida (a escena); (beginning) principio; (to society/a profession) ingreso; (right to enter) entrada; (of tunnel or cave) boca; **~ examination** examen (-ámenes) *m* de ingreso; **~ fee** cuota de entrada, (to school *etc*) derechos *mpl* de matrícula; **is there an ~ fee?** ¿hay que pagar por entrar?; **~ forbidden!** ¡se prohibe la entrada!; **~ hall** vestíbulo

[2] **entrance** *v* encantar

entrancing encantador (-ora *f*)

entrant *sp* competidor *m* (-ora *f*)

entreat rogar (ue)[1a+5]

entreaty ruego

entreating suplicante

entreatingly de modo suplicante

entrée *cul* entremeses *mpl*; (to society) entrada

entrench atrincherar

entrenching: ~ tool atrincheradora

entrenchment atrincheramiento

entrepreneur empresario

entresol entresuelo

entrust: ~ s.o. (with something) confiarle a uno (algo)

entry (entrance) entrada; **no ~** prohibido el paso; (passage) pasadizo; (note in book) anotación (-ones) *f*; *sp* apuntación (-ones) *f*; (competitor) competidor *m* (-ora *f*); **there was one ~** había un competidor; (football pools) boleto, **I do a six-line ~** hago un boleto de seis; *comm* partida; **~ corridor** *space* corredor *m* de entrada

entryism infiltración *f*

entwine entrelazar[7]

enumerate enumerar

enumeration enumeración *f*

enunciate enunciar

enunciation enunciación *f*

envelop envolver (ue)[1b] (*past part* envuelto)

envelope sobre *m*; (of airship) cubierta exterior

envelopment envolvimiento

enviable envidiable

envious envidioso

enviously con envidia

environment (medio) ambiente *m*; **out of one's ~** desambientado

environmental ambiental

environs vecindad *f*
envisage prever[19]; imaginarse
envoy enviado
envy *n* envidia; *v* envidiar; **I ~ him** le tengo envidia
enzyme enzima
epaulette charretera
ephemeral efímero; *fig* pasajero
Ephesus Éfeso
Ephesian *n* + *adj* efesio
epic *n* epopeya; *adj* épico; **~ poem** poema épico; **~ poetry** épica
epicure, epicurean epicúreo
epidemic *n* epidemia; *adj* epidémico
epidermis epidermis *f*
epiglottis epiglotis *f*
epigram epigrama *m*
epigrammatic epigramático
epigraph epígrafe *m*
epilepsy epilepsia
epileptic *n* + *adj* epiléptico; **~ fit** ataque epiléptico
epilogue epílogo
Epiphany día *m* de los Reyes (Magos)
episcopacy episcopado
episcopal, episcopalian episcopal
episcopate episcopado
episode (occurrence) incidente; *lit* episodio
episodic episódico
epistle epístola
epistolary epistolar
epitaph epitafio
epithet epíteto
epitome epítome *m*
epitomize resumir; *fig* ser la personificación de
epoch época; **~-making** trascendental
Epsom: ~ salts sal *f* de la Higuera
equability ecuanimidad *f*
equable ecuánime
equably con ecuanimidad
equal *n* igual *m* + *f*; **among ~s** entre personas iguales; *adj* igual; **all men have ~ rights** todos los hombres tienen los mismos derechos; **without ~** sin igual; **that makes the scores ~** eso iguala el tanteo; **he is not ~ to the work** él no sirve para el trabajo; **on an ~ footing** en pie de igualdad; *v* igualar; **your ignorance ~s your obstinacy** tu ignorancia corre pareja con tu tozudez; **~s sign** *math* igual *m*
equality igualdad *f*

equalization igualación (-ones) *f*
equalize igualar; *sp* lograr el empate
equally igualmente
equalizing igualador (-ora *f*)
equanimity ecuanimidad *f*
equate igualar (**with** a)
equation ecuación (-ones) *f*
equator ecuador *m*
equatorial ecuatorial
equerry caballerizo real
equestrian *n* jinete *m*; *adj* ecuestre; **~ statue** estatua ecuestre
equidistant equidistante
equilateral equilátero
equilibrium equilibrio; **be in a state of ~** equilibrarse
equine hípico
equinoctial equinoccial
equinox equinoccio
equip equipar
equipment equipo
equipoise equilibrio
equitable equitativo
equitably con justicia
equity equidad *f*; **~ security** *comm* acción (-ones) *f* ordinaria
equivalent *n* + *adj* equivalente; **be ~ to** equivaler[19] a
equivocal equívoco
equivocate usar palabras equívocas
equivocation equívoco
equivocator equivoquista *m* + *f*
era época
eradiate (ir)radiar
eradiation radiación *f*
eradicate erradicar[4]
eradication erradicación *f*
erasable borrable
erase borrar
eraser goma (de borrar)
Erasmus Erasmo
erasure borradura
ere *prep* antes de; *conj* antes de (que)
erect *adj* erguido; (standing) de pie; *v* (build) construir[16]; (set up) levantar; **~ a tent** montar una tienda (de campaña)
erection + *anat* erección (-ones) *f*; (building) construcción (-ones) *f*; **have an ~** *sl* tener la verga en ristre
erector constructor *m*
ergonomics ergonomía
Eric Erico
ermine *zool* armiño; (fur) piel *f* de

armiño
Ernest Ernesto
erode (acid *etc*) corroer[17]; *geol* desgastar
Eros Eros *m*
erosion erosión *f*
erosive desgastador (-ora *f*); erosivo
erotic erótico
eroticism erotismo
err pecar[4]; ~ **on the side of** pecar[4] por exceso de
errand recado; **do an ~ for** hacer[19] un recado por parte de; ~**-boy** recadero
errant errante; **knight-~** caballero andante
errantry vida errante (de un caballero)
errata erratas *fpl*; (list) fe *f* de erratas
erratic irregular; (of behaviour) excéntrico; (of work) desigual
erring extraviado
erroneous erróneo
error (mistake) error *m*; (sin) pecado; ~ **of judgement** entendimiento errado; **do something in ~** hacer[19] algo por equivocación
ersatz sucedáneo; ~ **coffee** café *m* de malta
Erse gaélico
erstwhile de otro tiempo
erudite erudito
erupt estar[19] en erupción; (begin to ~) entrar en erupción
eruption erupción (-ones) *f*
eruptive eruptivo
erysipelas erisipela
Esau Esaú
escalade *n* escalada; *v* escalar
escalate escalar
escalation escalada
escalator escalera rodante/mecánica
escallop *see* **scallop**
escalope venera; (badge of pilgrim to Santiago de Compostela) concha
escapade escapada
escape *n* escapada; (leak) escape *m*; (of gas) fuga; **have a narrow ~** salvarse por un pelo; ~**-hatch** escotilla de urgencia; ~**-velocity** *space* velocidad *f* de escape; ~**-wheel** *mech* rueda de áncora; *v* escapar; (avoid) evitar; (leak) escaparse (**from** de); ~ **notice** pasar inadvertido; ~ **with one's life** salvar(se) la vida; **a cry ~d me** no pude contener un grito; **her name ~s me** se me olvida su nombre

escaped (from detention) suelto; ~ **lunatic** loco suelto
escapee evadido
escapement *mech* áncora
escaping fugitivo
escapism evasión *f* (de la realidad)
escapist de evasión; ~ **literature** literatura de evasión
escapologist especialista *m+f* en desatarse
escarpment escarpa
eschew evitar
escort *n* (person) acompañante *m*; *mil* escolta; ~ **vessel** buque *m* de escolta; *v* acompañar; *mil* escoltar
escritoire escritorio
escutcheon escudo
E.S.E. (east-south-east) *n+adj* E.S.E. (estesudeste) *m*
Eskimo *n+adj* esquimal *m+f*
esoteric esotérico
espalier espaldera
esparto esparto
especial especial
Esperantist esperantista *m+f*
Esperanto esperanto
espionage espionaje *m*
esplanade paseo; *mil* explanada
espousal desposorio; ~ **of a cause** adhesión *f* a una causa
espouse desposar(se) (con), casarse con; ~ **a cause** abrazar[7] una causa
espresso exprés *invar*; ~ **bar** bar *m* exprés; ~ **coffee** café *m* exprés; ~**-coffee machine** máquina exprés
esprit de corps compañerismo; *mil* moral *f*
espy divisar
esquire escudero; (landowner) hacendado; (title, used only before Christian name) don
essay *n* (attempt) tentativa; *lit* ensayo; *v* intentar
essayist ensayista *m+f*
essence esencia
essential *n* artículo de primera necesidad; ~**s** rudimentos *mpl*; *adj* esencial
establish (set up) establecer[14]; (erect) erigir[9]; (prove) probar (ue)[1a]; **he can't ~ his identity** no puede demostrar su identidad; *hort+agri* arraigarse[5]; ~**ed church** iglesia oficial
establishment establecimiento; (autho-

rities) autoridades *fpl*; (of institution) fundación *f*; (staff) (plantilla de) personal *f*

estate (land) finca; (inheritance) patrimonio; *leg* bienes *mpl*; (personal possessions) fortuna personal; **~-agent** corredor *m* de fincas; **~-car** *fam* rubia

esteem *n* estima *f*; *v* estimar

Esther Ester, Esther

esthete estete *m+f*

esthetic estético

estimable estimable

estimably de modo estimable

estimate estimación *f*; *comm* presupuesto; **~s free** presupuestos gratuitos; **make an ~** hacer[19] un presupuesto; *v* estimar; (value) valorar; (submit an ~) hacer[19] un presupuesto

estimation opinión (-ones) *f*; (esteem) estima

estrange enajenar; **~d couple** matrimonio separado; **become ~d** malquistarse

estrangement enajenación (-ones) *f*

estuary estuario

etc etc (etcétera)

etch grabar al agua fuerte

etcher grabador *m* al agua fuerte

etching (art form) grabado (al agua fuerte); (picture) aguafuerte *f*

eternal eterno; **~ triangle** triángulo amoroso

eternity eternidad *f*

ether éter *m*

ethereal etéreo

etherize eterizar[7]

ethic ético

ethical ético

ethics ética

Ethiopia Etiopía

Ethiopian etíope *m+f*

ethnic étnico

ethnographer etnógrafo

ethnographic etnográfico

ethnography etnografía

ethnological etnológico

ethnologist etnólogo

ethnology etnología

ethos lo característico de una cultura

ethyl etilo

etiolate descolorar(se)

etiquette etiqueta

Etna Etna *m*

Eton: **~ collar** cuello de colegial; **~ crop** pelo a lo garsón

Etruscan *n+adj* etrusco

etymological etimológico

etymologist etimólogo

etymology etimología

eucalyptus eucalipto

eucharist eucaristía

eucharistic eucarístico

Euclid Euclides

Euclidean euclidiano

Eugen(e) Eugenio

eugenic eugenésico

eugenics eugenesia

eulogize elogiar

eulogy elogio

eunuch eunuco

euphemism eufemismo

euphemistic eufemístico

euphonic eufónico

euphonium eufonio

euphony eufonía

euphoria euforia

Eurasian *n+adj* eurasiático

eureka! ¡eureka!

eurhythmic eurítmico

eurhythmics euritmía

Eurocracy administración *f* del Mercado Común Europeo

Eurocrat funcionario del Mercado Común Europeo

Euromissile euromisil *m*

Europe Europą

European *n+adj* europeo; **(in) ~ fashion** a la europea

Europeanize europeizar[7]

Eustace Eustaquio

euthanasia eutanasia

evacuate evacuar

evacuation evacuación (-ones) *f*

evacuee evacuado

evade evadir; **~ taxes** eludir impuestos

evaluate evaluar

evaluation evaluación (-ones) *f*

evanescent fugaz (-ces); evanescente

evangelic(al) evangélico

evangelism evangelismo

evangelist evangelista *m+f*

evangelize evangelizar[7]

evaporate evaporar(se); **~d milk** leche evaporada

evaporation evaporación *f*

evasion evasión (-ones) *f*; (escape) fuga

evasive evasivo; **take ~ action** tomar

medidas evasivas

evasiveness carácter *m* evasivo

Eve Eva

eve víspera; *eccles* vigilia; **on the ~ of** la víspera de

even *adj* (level) llano; (smooth) liso; (uniform) uniforme; (calm) tranquilo; **~ number** (not odd) (número) par *m*, (approximate) número redondo; **of ~ date** de la misma fecha; **on an ~ keel** en iguales calados, *fig* estable; **get ~ with** desquitarse con; **break ~** cubrir (*past part* cubierto) los gastos; **~-handed** imparcial; **~-tempered** de genio tranquilo; *v* (make even) igualar; *adv* aun hasta; incluso; **~ the old people helped** ayudaron hasta los viejos; (in negative phrase) ni siquiera, **he can't ~ walk** ni siquiera puede andar; **not ~ wild horses would make me go in** ni a la de tres entraría; **~ as** así como; **~ if** aun cuando; **~ now** todavía; **~ so** suponiendo que sea así, aun así; **~ though** aunque, **I shall do it ~ though it kills me** lo haré aunque me mate

evening tarde *f*; (nightfall) anochecer *m*; (after dark) noche *f*; **good ~!** ¡buenas tardes/noches!; **in the ~** por la tarde/noche, al anochecer; **on Monday ~** el lunes por la tarde; **~ class** clase nocturna; **~-dress** (gown) vestido de noche, (suit) traje *m* de etiqueta; **~ paper** periódico de la tarde; **~ star** estrella vespertina; (Venus) lucero de la tarde

evenness igualdad *f*; (smoothness) lisura; (of temper) serenidad *f*

evensong vísperas *fpl*

event acontecimiento *m*; *sp* competición (-ones) *f*; (race) carrera; **at all ~s** de todas maneras; **in the ~ of** en caso de; **in the ~ that** en caso de que +*subj*; **in such an ~** en tal caso

eventful memorable

eventual final, eventual

eventuality eventualidad *f*

eventually al fin

ever (always) siempre; (at any time) alguna vez; (after negative) nunca, **I don't visit him ~** no le visito nunca; **~ after** desde entonces; **~ and anon** de vez en cuando; **~ since** desde entonces; **~ so (many)** la mar de; **she is ~ so nice** ella es la mar de simpática; **for ~ para siempre**; **for ~ and ~** por siempre jamás; **for ~ more** eternamente; **hardly ~** casi nunca; **well, did you ~!** ¡hábrase visto!

evergreen *n* planta de hoja perenne; *adj* de hoja perenne; **~ oak** encina

everlasting eterno; (of something disagreeable) interminable; **~ flower** (flor) siempreviva

every todo, todos los *mpl*, todas las *fpl*; **~ one** cada uno; **~ soldier knows** todo soldado sabe; **~ day** todos los días; **~ four days** cada cuatro días; **~ other day** un día sí y otro no; **~ bit as good as** de ningún modo inferior a; **~ man for himself** sálvese quien pueda; **~ mother's son** cada hijo de vecino; **~ now and then** de vez en cuando

everybody, everyone todo el mundo

everyday diario, cotidiano; (ordinary) córriente

everything todo; **~ possible** todo lo posible; **~'s all right** (no harm done) nada se pierde

everywhere en todas partes; (wherever) por dondequiera que +*subj*, **~ I go** por dondequiera que yo vaya

evict desalojar

eviction evicción (-ones) *f*

evidence prueba; *leg* testimonio; **give ~** dar[19] testimonio; **in ~** (in sight) a la vista

evident evidente; **be ~** ser[19] patente

evil *n* maldad *f*; mal *m*; **speak ~ of** s.o. hablar mal de uno; *adj* malo; **~-doer** malhechor *m* (-ora *f*); **~-eye** mal *m* de ojo; **~-minded** mal pensado, *SA* maldoso; **~-smelling** maloliente; **~-spoken person** mala lengua; **~ spirit** demonio

evilness maldad *f*

evince evidenciar

evocation evocación *f*

evocative evocador (-ora *f*)

evoke evocar[4]

evolution evolución *f*; *mil* + *naut* maniobra

evolutionary evolutivo

evolve evolucionar

ewe oveja; **~-lamb** cordera

ewer aguamanil *m*

exacerbate exacerbar

exacerbation exacerbación *f*

exact *adj* exacto; (of person) metódico; ~ **amount** cantidad correcta; ~ **opposite of** polo opuesto de; *v* exigir[9]

exacting exigente; ~ **work** trabajo arduo

exaction exacción (-ones) *f*

exactness, exactitude exactitud *f*

exaggerate exagerar

exaggeration exageración (-ones) *f*

exalt exaltar; (praise) ensalzar[7]

exaltation exaltación *f*; (ecstasy) éxtasis *m*

exalted eminente

examinable averiguable

examination (investigation) investigación (-ones) *f*; (customs) inspección (-ones) *f*; *leg* interrogatorio; *med* reconocimiento (médico), *fam* chequeo; (test) examen (-ámenes) *m*; **take an** ~ examinarse; **oral/written** ~ examen oral/escrito; ~**-paper** papel *m* de examen; **passport** ~ control *m* de pasaportes

examine (inspect) inspeccionar; *leg* interrogar[5]; *med* reconocer[14]; (test) examinar; ~ **in great detail** escrutar

examinee examinando, (-a *f*)

examiner examinador *m* (-ora *f*); ~**s** tribunal *m*

examining que examina; *leg* ~ **magistrate** interrogante *m*; ~ **board** tribunal *m* de examen

example ejemplo; (warning) escarmiento; **for** ~ por ejemplo; **make an** ~ **of s.o.** castigarle[5] a uno para que sirva de ejemplo; **set an** ~ dar[19] un ejemplo

exasperate exasperar

exasperating exasperante

exasperation exasperación *f*

excavate excavar; (hollow out) vaciar

excavation excavación (-ones) *f*; *arch* vaciado

excavator (person) excavador *m*; *mech* excavadora

exceed (be greater than) exceder; (go beyond) traspasar; **he** ~**ed the speed limit** él sobrepasó la velocidad permitida

exceeding excesivo

exceedingly sumamente

excel sobresalir[19]

excellence, excellency excelencia; **Your Excellency** Su Excelencia

excellent excelente; (of school work) sobresaliente

except *v* exceptuar; *prep* salvo, excepto; ~ **for**, ~**ing** con excepción de

exception excepción (-ones) *f*; (protest) protesta; **make an** ~ **of** hacer[19] una excepción de; **with the** ~ **of** con excepción de; **take** ~ **to** protestar contra

exceptionable recusable

exceptional excepcional

excerpt *n* extracto; *v* extraer[19]

excess exceso; *fam* empache *m* (of de); **in** ~ **(of)** en exceso (de); **to** ~ demasiado, *fam* más de la cuenta; ~ **material** material *m* sobrante; ~ **fare** suplemento; ~ **luggage** exceso de equipaje; ~ **postage** sobrecarga; ~ **profits tax** impuesto sobre beneficios extraordinarios

excessive excesivo

excessively exageradamente

exchange *n* (inter)cambio: (of money) cambio; (building) bolsa; (telephone-~) central (telefónica), (private telephone ~) centralita; ~ **of prisoners** canje *m* de prisioneros; ~ **of ideas** intercambio de ideas; ~ **of credentials** canje *m* de credenciales; **bill of** ~ letra de cambio; **in** ~ **for** a cambio de; **rate of** ~ cambio monetario; **when I bought this car they took the old one in part** ~ cuando compré este coche me hicieron una deducción por cambio; *adj* cambiable; ~ **control** control *m* de divisas; *v* (inter)cambiar; ~ **blows** darse[19] golpes; *mil* (+diplomacy) canjear; (replace) reemplazar[7]; ~ **for** cambiar por

exchangeable cambiable

exchequer (funds) fondos *mpl*; (public finance) Hacienda Pública

excise *n* impuesto sobre el consumo; ~ **duty** derecho de aduanas; *v* cortar

exciseman recaudador *m* de impuestos

excision excisión (-ones) *f*

excitability excitabilidad *f*

excitable excitable

excitant excitante *m*

excite emocionar; (provoke) provocar[4]; ~ **interest** despertar (ie)[2a] interés; **she is** ~**d about her sister's wedding** ella

está ilusionada con la boda de su hermana; **become** ~**d** emocionarse, (angry) enfadarse, (upset) agitarse
excitedly con emoción
excitement emoción (-ones) *f*; ~ **in the streets** animación *f* en las calles
exciting emocionante
excitingly de modo emocionante
exclaim exclamar
exclamation exclamación (-ones) *f*; ~-**mark** punto de admiración
exclamatory exclamatorio
exclude excluir[16]
exclusion exclusión (-ones) *f*
exclusive exclusivo; ~ **club** club *m* exclusivista; ~ **of** sin contar; ~ **rights** exclusiva, **he has** ~ **rights to my invention** él tiene la exclusiva de mi invento
exclusively exclusivamente; **something** ~ **English** una cosa privativa de los ingleses
exclusiveness carácter exclusivo
excommunicate excomulgar[5]
excommunication excomunión (-ones) *f*
excrement excremento
excrescence excrecencia
excreta excrementos *mpl*
excrete excretar; *fam* hacer[19] del vientre
excretion excreción *f*
excretory excretorio
excruciating agudísimo
exculpate exculpar
exculpation exculpación (-ones) *f*
excursion excursión (-ones) *f*; ~-**boat,** ~-**steamer** vapor *m* de excursiones; ~-**ticket** billete *m* de excursión; ~-**train** tren *m* de recreo, *fam* tren *m* botijo
excursionist excursionista *m+f*
excursus exposición (-ones) detallada de un punto especial de una obra literaria
excusable disculpable
excuse *n* disculpa; (pretext) pretexto; **make** ~**s** sacar[4] disculpas/pretextos; **give an** ~ pretextar; *v* disculpar; (pardon) perdonar; (defend) defender (ie)[2b]; ~ **me** perdone(n) usted(es), (*US* what did you say?) ¿qué dice usted?
ex-directory privado
execrable execrable
execration execración *f*

executant ejecutante *m+f*
execute (carry out) realizar[7]; (kill) ajusticiar; *mus* ejecutar; *leg* otorgar[5], legalizar (un documento); ~ **a will** cumplir un testamento
execution (realization) realización (-ones) *f*; (killing) ejecución (-ones) *f* de la pena de muerte; *mus* ejecución (-ones) *f*; *leg* legalización *f*; ~ **of a will** cumplimiento de un testamento
executioner verdugo
executive *n* director *m*; *adj* administrativo, ejecutivo; ~ **assistant** ayudante *m* de dirección; *adj* ~ **committee** comisión (-ones) directiva; ~ **power** poder ejecutivo
executor ejecutor testamentario
executrix ejecutora testamentaria
exegesis exégesis *f*
exemplary ejemplar
exemplification ejemplificación (-ones) *f*
exemplify ejemplificar[4]
exempt *adj* exento; ~ **from taxes** exento de impuestos; *v* librar (**from** de)
exemption exención (-ones) *f* (**from** de)
exercise *n* ejercicio; *mil* maniobra; (*US* ceremonies) ceremonias *fpl*; ~-**book** cuaderno; *v* (**take** ~) hacer[19] ejercicio; (wield) ejercer[12]; ~ **a dog** llevar de paseo a un perro; ~ **a horse** entrenar un caballo
exert emplear; **he** ~**ed his influence** él empleó su influencia; ~ **pressure** hacer[19] presión; ~ **o.s.** esforzarse (ue)[1a+7] (**to** por); **don't** ~ **yourself** *iron* no te hernies
exertion esfuerzo; (exercise) ejercicio; ~**s** buenos oficios
exes (expenses) gastos *mpl*
exeunt vanse; ~ **soldiers** soldados vanse
ex-factory franco en fábrica
ex-gratia sin obligación
exhalation (from lungs) espiración (-ones) *f*; (of gases *etc*) exhalación (-ones) *f*
exhale exhalar
exhaust *n* escape *m*; ~-**fumes** gases *mpl* de escape; ~-**pipe** tubo de escape; ~-**valve** válvula de escape; *v* (tire) cansar; (empty) vaciar; (end) agotar; (debilitate) debilitar; ~ **a topic** tratar detalladamente un tópico
exhaustible agotable

exhausting agobiante
exhaustion (tiredness) cansancio; (finish) agotamiento
exhaustive minucioso
exhibit *n* objeto expuesto; *leg* prueba; *v* (a film) presentar; (a notice) mostrar; (paintings *etc*) exponer; (reveal) revelar
exhibition exposición (-ones) *f*; (performance) función (-ones) *f*; (scholarship) beca; (display) manifestación (-ones) *f*; **make an ~ of o.s.** ponerse[19] en ridículo; **~-grounds** ferial *m*; **~-hall** palacio de exposiciones; **boat/book ~** salón (-ones) *m* náutico/del libro
exhibitionism exhibicionismo
exhibitionist *n*+*adj* exhibicionista *m*+*f*
exhibitor expositor *m* (-ora *f*)
exhilarate alborozar[7]
exhilarating vigorizador (-ora *f*); estimulante
exhilaration alborozo
exhort exhortar
exhortation exhortación (-ones) *f*
exhumation exhumación (-ones) *f*
exhume exhumar
exigency exigencia
exigent exigente
exiguous exiguo
exile *n* destierro; (person) desterrado; *v* desterrar (ie)[2a]; **be ~d, be in ~** estar[19] desterrado
exist existir
existence existencia; **be in ~** existir
existent existente
existential existencial
existentialism existencialismo
existentialist *n*+*adj* existencialista *m*+*f*
exit *n* salida; *theat* mutis *m*; *v* va(n)se, **~ Don Carlos** Don Carlos vase
exodus éxodo
ex-officio de oficio
exonerate exonerar
exonerating exonerante
exoneration exoneración (-ones) *f*
exorable exorable
exorbitance exorbitancia
exorbitant exorbitante
exorcism exorcismo
exorcist exorcista *m*+*f*
exorcize conjurar, exorcizar[7]
exoteric exotérico

exotic exótico; **~ plant** planta de estufa
expand (make bigger) extender (ie)[2b]; (become bigger) ensancharse, **the city has ~ed** la ciudad se ha ensanchado; (develop) desarrollar; (enlarge temporarily) dilatar(se), **he ~ed his chest** dilató el pecho; (swell up) hincharse; (unfold) desplegar (ie)[2a+5], **the bird ~ed its wings** el pájaro desplegó las alas; **metals ~ with heat** los metales se dilatan con el calor; **the market is ~ing** el mercado expansiona; *fig* (become talkative) dilatarse (**on** sobre), volverse expansivo
expanding: ~ file (for documents) clasificador *m* auxiliar; **~ suitcase** maleta expansible
expanse extensión (-ones) *f*
expansion dilatación *f*; (development) desarrollo
expansionism expansionismo
expansionist: ~ policy política expansionista
expansive expansivo; (talkative) comunicativo
expansiveness expansibilidad *f*; (talkativeness) afabilidad *f*
expatiate extenderse (ie)[2b] (**on** en)
expatiation digresión *f*
expatriate *n* expatriado; *v* expatriar(se)
expatriation expatriación *f*
expect *vt* esperar; **I ~ to see him** espero verle; (wait for) esperar; (demand) exigir[9]; (rely on) contar (ue)[1a] con, **in August you can ~ fine weather** en agosto se puede contar con buen tiempo; (rely on … to) contar (ue)[1a] con … para, **I ~ you to finish the work** cuento con usted para terminar el trabajo; **when least ~ed** el día menos esperado; *vi* creer[17]; **I ~ he will arrive soon** creo que llegará pronto
expectance, expectancy expectación *f*
expectant: ~ mother mujer embarazada
expectantly con esperanza(s)
expectation esperanza; *leg* esperanza de heredar; **~ of life** índice *m* vital
expectorate escupir, expectorar
expectoration expectoración *f*
expediency conveniencia; **for the sake of ~** para evitar inconveniencias
expedient *n* expediente *m*; *adj* conve-

niente; **be** ~ convenir[19]

expedite (send) despachar; (make easy) facilitar; (speed) acelerar

expedition expedición (-ones) *f*; **go on an** ~ salir[19] de expedición; (speed) celeridad *f*

expeditionary: ~ **force** fuerza(s) expedicionaria(s)

expeditious expedito

expel (spit out) expeler; (from school *etc*) expulsar

expend (money) gastar; (time) perder (ie)[2b]

expendable gastable; (people) prescindible; *mil* sacrificable

expenditure gasto(s); (of time) pérdida

expense gasto; *comm* coste *m*; **at great** ~ con mucho gasto; **go to great** ~ **to** gastar mucho dinero para + *infin*; **they laughed at my** ~ rieron a mi costa; ~ **account** cuenta de gastos; ~ **chit/ voucher** comprobante *m* de gastos; ~**s** gastos pagados; ~**s incurred** gastos originados; **salary plus** ~**s** salario con gastos pagados

expensive caro; (inclined to overcharge) carero

expensively costosamente

expensiveness lo costoso

experience *n* experiencia; **by** ~ por experiencia; **gain** ~ lograr experiencia; *v* experimentar; ~ **difficulty** tener[19] dificultad

experiment experimento; *v* experimentar

experimental experimental

experimenter experimentador *m* (-ora *f*)

expert *n* experto; *adj* experto (**at/in** en); ~ **testimony** peritaje *m*; ~ **witness** testigo pericial

expertise, expertness maestría

expiate expiar

expiation expiación *f*

expiatory expiatorio

expiration (termination) terminación *f*; *comm* vencimiento; (exhaling) espiración *f*; (death) muerte *f*

expire (come to an end) vencer[12]; (die) fallecer[14]; **this ticket** ~**s today** este billete caduca hoy

expiry expiración *f*; *comm* vencimiento; ~ **date** plazo, (sell-by date) fecha de caducidad

explain (describe) explicar[4]; (clarify) aclarar; (justify) justificar[4], **let me** ~ **my actions** permítame justificar mis acciones; ~ **a plan** exponer[19] un plan; ~ **away** justificar[4] con facilidad; ~ **o.s.** explicarse[4]

explainable explicable

explanation explicación (-ones) *f*; (solution) aclaración (-ones) *f*; (justification) justificación (-ones) *f*

explanatory explicativo

expletive *n* voz (-ces) expletiva; (oath) palabrota; *adj* expletivo

explicable explicable

explicate explicar[4]

explication explicación (-ones) *f*

explicit explícito

explode *vt* volar (ue)[1a]; (show to be false) refutar; *vi* estallar; ~ **with anger** reventar de ira

exploit *n* hazaña; *v* explotar

exploitation explotación *f*

exploration exploración (-ones) *f*

exploratory preparatorio; *med etc* exploratorio

explore explorar; ~ **every avenue** revolver (ue)[1b] (*past part* revuelto) Roma con Santiago; ~ **the possibilities of** examinar las posibilidades de

explorer explorador *m* (-ora *f*)

explosion explosión (-ones) *f*

explosive *n*+*adj* explosivo; ~ **charge** carga explosiva; ~ **power** fuerza explosiva; ~ **situation** situación (-ones) peligrosa

exponent exponente *m*+*f*; *math* exponente *m*

export *n* (article) (artículo de) exportación *f*; (process) exportación *f*; ~ **bonus** subvención (-ones) *f* de exportación; ~ **duty** derechos *mpl* de exportación; ~ **firm/house** casa exportadora; ~ **model** modelo de exportación; ~ **trade** comercio de exportación; *v* exportar

exporter exportador *m*

exporting *n* exportación *f*; *adj* exportador (-ora *f*)

expose exponer[19] (a la luz); (unmask) desenmascarar; ~ **o.s. to** exponerse[19] a; ~**d** (unprotected) desabrigado, *mil* desguarnecido; ~**d nerve** nervio descubierto

exposé (explanation) explicación (-ones) *f*; (disclosure) revelación (-ones) *f*

exposition exposición (-ones) *f*; (unmasking) desenmascaramiento

expositor expositor *m*

expository expositivo

expostulate altercar⁴ (with con)

expostulation altercado

exposure +*phot* exposición (-ones) *f*; (of a plot) descubrimiento; **die from ~** morir de frío; **~-meter** exposímetro; **~-time** tiempo de exposición; **~-timer** cronometrador *m* de exposición

expound explicar⁴

ex-president ex-presidente *m*

express *n* expreso; *adj* (stated) explícito; (rapid) rápido; **~ train** expreso; **~man** empleado de una compañía de porteo; **~ letter** carta urgente; *v* expresar

expressible expresable

expression expresión (-ones) *f*; **accept this as an ~ of my gratitude** acepte esto como muestra de mi agradecimiento; *mus* matiz *f*; **give ~** matizar⁷

expressionism expresionismo

expressionist *n*+*adj* expresionista *m*+*f*

expressive expresivo

expressway autorruta

expropriate expropiar

expropriation expropiación (-ones) *f*

expulsion expulsión (-ones) *f*

expunge borrar

expurgate expurgar⁵

expurgation expurgación *f*

exquisite exquisito; **an ~ girl** *fam* una chica de rechupete

ex-serviceman excombatiente *m*

extant existente

extemporaneous, extemporary improvisado

extempore *adj* improvisado; *adv* de improviso

extemporize improvisar

extend extender (ie)²ᵇ; (lengthen) alargar(se)⁵; (offer) proferir (ie)²ᶜ; (time) prolongar⁵; **~ a building** ensanchar un edificio; **~ a hand** tender (ie)²ᵇ una mano; **~ thanks** dar¹⁹ las gracias; **~ a welcome to** dar¹⁹ la bienvenida a; **~ a visa** prolongar un visado; **~ed-play**

record disco de duración extendida

extendible: ~ seat asiento extensible

extensible extensible

extension extensión (-ones) *f*; *bui* anexo; (increase) aumento; (length) alargamiento; (space) ampliación (-ones) *f*; *comm* prórroga; (telephone) supletorio; **~ ladder** escalerilla extensible, (fireman's) escala extensible; **~ line** *tel* línea derivada; **~ loudspeaker** altavoz (-ces) *m* exterior

extensive extenso; (comprehensive) comprensivo

extent extensión *f*; **to a certain ~** hasta cierto punto; **to the full ~** hasta su extensión; **to a great ~** en gran parte; **to such an ~** hasta tal punto; **to what ~?** ¿hasta qué punto?

extenuate atenuar

extenuating: ~ circumstances circunstancias *fpl* atenuantes

extenuation atenuación *f*

exterior *n* exterior *m*; *adj* exterior; **~ decorator** decorador *m* de exteriores

exterminate extirpar

extermination extirpación *f*

exterminator exterminador *m* (-ora *f*)

external *adj* externo; **for ~ use only** para uso externo; **~ trade** comercio con el extranjero; **~s** *n* apariencias *fpl*

extinct extinto; (quenched) apagado; **~ volcano** volcán apagado

extinction extinción *f*

extinguish extinguir¹¹

extinguisher extintor *m* (de incendios)

extirpate extirpar

extirpation extirpación (-ones) *f*; *surg* excisión *f*

extol alabar

extort extorsionar

extortion extorsión *f*

extortionary que implica extorsión

extortionate exorbitante; *comm* gravoso

extortioner desollador *m*

extra *n* (additional charge) suplemento, recargo; (accessory) accesorio; (newspaper) edición (-ones) extraordinaria; *theat*+*cin* extra *m*+*f*; **~s** *theat*+*cin* comparsería, (additional charges/expenses) gastos *mpl* extraordinarios; **are there any ~s?** ¿hay algo que no está comprendido en esto?; **earn a little ~ on the side** sacar[4] de sobresueldo; *adj* de más, extra, adicional; **I have an ~ rubber I can lend you** tengo una goma más que puedo prestarle; **~ time** *sp* prórroga; **Barcelona won after ~ time** el Barcelona ganó después de una prórroga

extract *n* trozo; *med* extracto; *v* sacar[4]; *lit* extractar; *sci* extraer[19]

extraction *n*+*fig* extracción *f*; **of French ~** de extracción francesa

extractor extractor *m*; **~-fan** extractor *m* de aire

extraditable sujeto a la extradición

extradite conceder la extradición

extradition extradición *f*

extra-judicial extra-judicial

extra-marital fuera de matrimonio

extra-mural fuera (del recinto) de la escuela/universidad; **~ course** curso para estudiantes libres

extraneous extraño; (irrelevant) ajeno

extraordinary extraordinario

extrapolate extrapolar

extrasensory extrasensorial

extra-special excepcional

extraterritorial extraterritorial

extraterritoriality extraterritorialidad *f*

extravagance extravagancia; (strangeness) rareza; (waste) derroche *m*; **life of ~** vida de lujo

extravagant (eccentric) extravagante, *fam* estrafalario; (wasteful) despilfarrado; **~ living** vida muy lujosa; **~ price** precio excesivo

extravaganza extravagancia

Extremaduran *n*+*adj* extremeño

extreme *n* extremo; **carry to ~s** llevar a extremos; **from one ~ to another** de un extremo a otro; **go to ~s** tomar medidas extremas; **in the ~** en sumo grado; *adj* extremo; **Extreme Unction** Extremaunción *f*

extremely sumamente; *fam* muy

extremism extremismo

extremist *n*+*adj* extremista *m*+*f*

extremity extremidad *f*; extremities *anat* extremidades *fpl*, (measures) medidas extremas; **be driven to extremities** verse[19] obligado a pasar de lo razonable

extricate extraer[19] (**from** de); (of a per-

son) librar (**from** de); **~ o.s. from** librarse de

extrication liberación *f*

extrinsic extrínseco

extroversion extraversión *f*

extrovert(ed) extravertido

extrude sacar[4]

exuberance exuberancia

exuberant exuberante

exude exudar

exult exultar (**in/at** por)

exultant exultante

exultation exultación (-ones) *f*

ex-works franco en fábrica

eye *n* ojo; (of needle) ojo; (dressmaking) corchete *m*; **an ~ for an ~ and a tooth for a tooth** ojo por ojo y diente por diente; **be all ~s** ser[19] todo ojos; **be up to one's ~s in** tener[19] hasta encima de las cejas; **black ~** ojo amoratado; **have an ~ for** tener[19] buen ojo para; **have one's ~s on, keep an ~ on** vigilar; **in the ~s of the King a** los ojos del rey; **it's all my ~!** ¡es puro cuento!; **make ~s at** hacer[19] ojitos a; **see ~ to ~ with** estar[19] de acuerdo con; **see with half an ~** ver[19] con los ojos cerrados; **she has bad ~s** ella sufre de los ojos; **shut one's ~s to** (pretend not to see) hacer[19] la vista gorda a; **there's more in this than meets the ~** hay gato escondido; **there's something in my ~** se me ha metido algo en el ojo; **with an ~ to** pensando en; **~-ball** globo del ojo; **~-bath** lavaojos *m sing*+*pl*; **~brow** ceja; **~brow pencil** lápiz (-ces) *m* de cejas; **~-catching** vistoso; **~-hole** órbita del ojo; **~lash** pestaña; **~lid** párpado; **~-lotion** loción (-ones) *f* de ojos; **~-ointment** pomada *f* para los ojos; **~-opener** revelación (-ones) *f*; **~-patch** parche *m* de ojo; **~piece** ocular *m*; **~-shade** visera (parasol); **~shadow** sombra de ojos; **~shot** alcance *m* de la vista; **~sight** vista; **have bad ~sight** estar[19] mal de la vista; **~sore** monstruosidad *f*; **~-strain** vista cansada; **~-tooth** colmillo; **~wash** mentira; **~-witness** testigo presencial; **~s front!** ¡vista!; **~s left/right!** ¡vista a la izquierda/a la derecha!; *v* (stare at) mirar (detenidamente); (glance at) ojear

eyeful ojeada
eyelet ojete *m*
eyrie aguilera

Ezekiel Ezequiel
Ezra Esdras

F

f (letter) efe *f*; **F** *mus* fa *m*
fable (legend) fábula; (lie) mentira
fabled legendario; (famous) célebre
fabric *archi* fábrica; (cloth) tela
fabricate fabricar[4]; (invent) inventar
fabrication fabricación *f*; (lie) mentira
fabulous fabuloso
façade fachada
face *n* (of persons) cara; (of clock) esfera, *SA* carátula; (effrontery) desfachatez *f*; (grimace) mueca; **make/ pull a ~** hacer[19] muecas; (look) aspecto; (of a coin) anverso; (prestige) reputación *f*; (surface) superficie *f*; **~ of the earth/moon** faz *f* de la tierra/luna; **~ down(wards)** boca abajo; **~ to ~** cara a cara; **~ up(wards)** boca arriba; **in the ~ of** ante, (despite) a pesar de; **he shut the door in my ~** él cerró la puerta en mis narices; **keep a straight ~** contener[19] la risa; **lose ~** perder (ie)[2b] prestigio; **on the ~ of it** a primera vista; **save ~** salvar las apariencias; **show one's ~** dejarse ver; **throw in one's ~** *fig* echar en cara; **to my ~** en mi cara; **with a long ~** cariacontecido; **~-card** figura; **~-cloth** (for washing) manopla; **~-cream** crema para la cara; **(go in for) ~-lift(ing)** (hacerse[19]) cirugía plástica de la cara, **~-pack** lodos *mpl*; **~-powder** polvos *mpl*; **~ value** significado literal, *comm* valor *m* nominal; **~-worker** (miner) picador *m*
v mirar hacia; (cover) revestir (i)[3] con; **~ with concrete** revestir (i)[3] con hormigón; **~ the enemy** enfrentarse con el enemigo; **~ facts** aceptar los hechos; **~ the music** pagar[5] el pato; **~ a problem** afrontar un problema; **~ the wall** ponerse[19] de cara a la pared; **the house ~s the park** la casa da al parque
~ about dar[19] media vuelta; *SA* voltearse
~ on to dar[19] a
~ up to dar[19] cara a; hacer frente a; **~**

up to it reconocerlo[14]; **~ up to the idea of death** enfrentarse con la idea de la muerte
faced revestido (**with** de); (sewing) forrado, **~ with silk** forrado de seda
facet faceta
facetious chistoso
facetiousness festividad *f*
facial *n* masaje *m* facial; *adj* facial; **~ expression** expresión *f* de la cara
facile fácil
facilitate facilitar
facilities medios *mpl*; instalaciones
facility facilidad *f*
facing *n* revestimiento; **~s** (sewing) vueltas *fpl*; *prep* frente
facsimile *n* + *adj* facsímil *m*
fact hecho; **~ or fiction** lo verdadero o lo imaginario; **~s** hechos *mpl*; *sci* datos *mpl*; **~s and figures** hechos y cifras; **~s of life** verdades *fpl* de la vida; **~-finding** de indagación; **the ~ is that** (la pura verdad) es que; **as a matter of ~,** **in (point of) ~** en realidad; **know for a ~** saber[19] a ciencia cierta
faction (quarrelling) disensión *f*; (group) facción *f*
factitious facticio
factor factor *m*; (person) agente *m*
factorize descomponer[19] en factores
factory fábrica; (small) taller *m*, *SA* usina, *Mex* factoría; **~-hand** operario; **~-made** hecho en fábrica; **~-tested** inspeccionado en fábrica
factotum factotum *m*
factual verdadero
faculty (aptitude) facultad *f*; (teaching staff) profesorado
fad (craze) manía; (whim) capricho
faddist, faddy caprichoso
fade (lose colour) discolorarse; (diminish) disminuir[16]; (of flowers) marchitarse; *rad* perder (ie)[2b] intensidad
~ away desvanecerse[14]
~ in/up *cin* + *TV* fundir
~ out desaparecer[14] gradualmente

702

fading desvanecimiento

faeces heces *fpl*

fag (cigarette) pitillo; ~**-end** colilla; (task) trabajo antipático

fagged(-out) rendido

faggot (of wood) gavilla; (meat ball) albóndiga

Fahrenheit: ~ **thermometer** termómetro de Fahrenheit

faience fa(y)enza

fail (be unsuccessful) no tener[19] éxito; **an examination** ser[19] suspendido en un examen; (become weak) decaer[19]; **my strength is** ~**ing** se me acaban las fuerzas; (betray trust) decepcionar; (disappoint) faltar; (of supplies) acabarse; **he** ~**ed three candidates** suspendió a tres candidatos; **the brakes** ~**ed** los frenos no funcionaron; **the electricity** ~**ed** la electricidad se cortó; **words** ~ **me** no encuentro palabras (para expresarme); **without** ~ sin falta; ~ **to** (in an attempt) no lograr; **I** ~ **to understand** no comprendo; **don't** ~ **to write** no deje(n) de escribir; **he** ~**ed to keep his word** faltó a su palabra; **she** ~**ed to arrive** ella no llegó; ~**-safe** interruptor *m* automático

failing *n* defecto; *adj* decaído; *prep* en la ausencia de

failure (non-success) fracaso; (in examination) suspenso; *comm* quiebra; *mech* avería; (of an organ) debilitamiento; (omission) omisión *f*; ~ **to honour an obligation** incumplimiento de una obligación; **be a** ~ malograrse; **be a born** ~ ser un fracasado nato

faint *n* desmayo; *adj* (not clear) indistinto; (weak) débil; (dizzy) desmayado; **feel** ~ estar[19] mareado; ~ **colour** color pálido; **there is a** ~ **resemblance** hay una ligera semejanza; ~**-hearted** cobarde, *fam* gallina *invar*, *vulg* cagado; ~ **recollection of** vago recuerdo de; *v* desmayarse

faintest: I haven't the ~ **idea** no tengo la menor idea

fainting-fit desmayo

faintness (weakness) debilidad *f*; (indistinctness) vaguedad *f*

[1] **fair** *n* parque *m* de atracciones; (market) mercado; (exhibition) feria, exposición *f*; ~**-ground** real *m*

[2] **fair** *adj* (beautiful) hermoso; (blond) rubio; (fresh) claro; *meteor* (calm) sereno, (cloudless) despejado; ~ **sex** sexo bello; (good) bueno; (not too bad) regular; (just) justo; ~ **and square** honrado a carta cabal; **it's not** ~! ¡no hay derecho!; **it's only** ~ **to say that** hay que decir que; ~ **chance of** buenas posibilidades de; **by** ~ **means** por medios rectos; **by** ~ **means or foul** de una manera o de otra; **if it's a** ~ **question, why …?** si no le importa decirme, ¿por qué …?; **be in a** ~ **way to** estar[19] en buen camino de; ~ **copy** copia en limpio; **make a** ~ **copy** poner[19] en limpio; ~ **dealing** negocio honrado; ~ **enough!** ¡de acuerdo!; ~ **game** caza legal, *fig* objeto legítimo; ~**-minded** imparcial; ~**-mindedness** imparcialidad *f*; ~ **play** juego limpio; ~ **price** precio asequible; ~**-sized** (quite large) bien grande, (large enough) de un tamaño adecuado; *adv* (honourably) honradamente; (politely) cortésmente; justo; **act** ~ obrar con imparcialidad; **play** ~ jugar (ue)[1a] limpio; **she hit him** ~ **on the face** ella le pegó en plena cara

fairing *space* carenaje *m*

fairly (justly) con imparcialidad; (slightly) ligeramente; (adequately) bastante; ~ **good** regular

fairness (beauty) hermosura; (of complexion) blancura; (of hair) rubio; (justice) justicia

fairway paso libre; (golf) paso; *naut* canal *m* navegable

fairy hada; (homosexual) mariquita *m*; ~**-cycle** bicicleta para niño; ~**-godmother** hada madrina; ~**-lamps, -lights** lucécitas *fpl* en el árbol de Navidad; ~**land** tierra de las hadas; ~**-like** como una hada; ~**-ring** círculo mágico; ~**-tale** *n* cuento de hadas, *adj* de ensueño

fait accompli hecho consumado

faith fe *f*; (religion) religión *f*; (trust) confianza; ~**-healing** curación *f* por fe; **break** ~ **with** faltar a la palabra dada a; **in good** ~ de buena fe; **keep** ~ **with** cumplir su palabra dada a; **have** ~ **in** fiarse de; **have no** ~ **in** no tener[19] confianza en

faithful fiel; **the** ~ los fieles; ~ **account** informe *m* veraz

faithfully con fidelidad; (accurately) con exactitud; **yours ~ le(s) saluda atentamente**
faithfulness fidelidad *f*
faithless infiel
faithlessness infidelidad
fake *n* imitación *f*; (person) impostor *m* (-ora *f*); *adj* (imitation) falso; (dishonest) fraudulento; (tampered with) falsificado; *v* (counterfeit) falsificar[4]; (simulate) fingir[9]
fakir faquir *m*
falcon halcón *m*
falconer halconero
falconry halconería
Falkland Islands Islas Malvinas
fall *n* caída; (in temperature) baj(ad)a; (in ground) declive *m*; (of rocks, earth) desprendimiento; (of tide) reflujo; (of water) catarata; (*US* autumn) otoño; (downfall) ruina; *comm* (of shares) baja, (in prices) reducción *f*, (in value) depreciación *f*; **the Fall (of Man)** la Caída (del hombre); **~ of snow** nevada; **there was a heavy ~ of snow** nevó mucho; **~ of the city** *mil* toma de la ciudad; *adj* (autumnal) otoñal; *v* caer[19]; (of temperature, prices) bajar; *mil* rendirse (i)[3]; *theat* (of curtain) bajar; *leg* (be inherited) pasar; (collapse) derrumbarse; (decrease) disminuir[16]; (die) caer[19] muerto; (happen) suceder; (sin) caer[19]; (of spirits) ponerse[19] triste; (of wind) amainar; **their faces fell** pusieron una cara de desengaño
~ again recaer[19]
~ among caer[19] entre
~ apart despedazarse[7]
~ asleep dormirse[1c]
~ away (depart) dejar; (grow weak) enflaquecer[14]; (disintegrate) desmoronarse
~ back (lag behind) quedarse atrás; (retreat) retroceder;
~ back on recurrir a, *mil* replegarse[5] hacia
~ behind quedarse atrás; **he fell behind with his payments** se retrasó en los pagos
~ between two stools fracasar por no saber a qué carta quedarse
~ down caerse[19]; (of a building) de-rrumbarse
~ downstairs rodar[1a] las escaleras abajo
~ due vencer[12]
~ flat caer[19] de bruces; *fig* tener[19] mal éxito
~ for enamorarse de, *fam* chiflarse por, *sl* hacer[19] tilín por; (be fooled by) ser[19] engañado por; **you fell for that** usted picó
~ foul of chocar[4] con
~ ill caer[19] enfermo
~ in caer[19] en; (collapse) hundirse, *mil* alinearse; *leg* caducar[4]; **~ in line** formar cola, (conform) seguir (i)[3] la corriente; **~ in love with** enamorarse de; **~ in with** (meet) encontrarse (ue)[1a] con, (agree) estar[19] de acuerdo con
~ into (be divided into) dividirse en; **they fell into the hands of the enemy** cayeron en manos del enemigo; **this letter has fallen into my hands** esta carta ha llegado a mis manos; **~ into a habit** adquirir (ie)[2c] la costumbre
~ off caer de; (lessen) disminuir[16]; (worsen) empeorar; **in autumn the leaves ~ off the trees** en otoño las hojas se desprenden/se separan de los árboles
~ on caer de; **~ on one's back** caer[19] de espaldas; **~ on one's feet** caer[19] de pie, *fig* salir[19] del vado; **~ on one's hands** caer[19] sobre las manos; **my birthday ~s on a Monday** mi cumpleaños cae en lunes; **~ on bad times** venir[19] a menos
~ out *n* caída radiactiva; **~out shelter** refugio contra caída radiactiva
~ out *v mil* salir[19] de las filas; (be dismissed) romper filas; **~ out!** ¡rompan filas!; **~ out of the window** caer[19] por la ventana; **~ out with** perder (ie)[2b] las amistades con
~ over volcar[4], caer[19]; (trip) tropezar[7] con
~ overboard caer[19] al agua
~ short ser[19] insuficiente; **~ short of expectations** no llegar[5] a lo esperado
~ through caer[19] por; (fail) fracasar
~ to (begin) ponerse[19] a +*infin*; (be incumbent upon) tocar[4] a; **~ to pieces** caer[19] en pedazos
~ under caer[19] (de)bajo; (incur) merecer[14]

704

~ **upon** (attack) atacar[4]

fallacious erróneo˜

fallacy error *m*; engaño

fallen *n* (killed in action) caídos *mpl*; *adj* caído; ~ **angel** ángel caído; ~ **arches** pies *mpl* planos

fallibility falibilidad *f*

fallible falible

falling caída; ~ **off** (lessening) disminución *f*, (worsening) deterioro *f*; ~ **star** estrella fugaz

Fallopian tubes trompas *fpl* de Falopio

fallow *n* barbecho; *adj* en barbecho; ~ **deer** gamo *m*

false falso; (of a person) desleal; (sham) fingido; **be/play** ~ traicionar; **bear** ~ **witness** dar[19] testimonio falso; ~ **alarm** falsa alarma; ~ **beard/nose** barba/nariz postiza; ~ **bottom** doble fondo; ~**-bottomed** de doble fondo; ~ **imprisonment** detención *f* ilegal; ~ **pretences** estafa; **with** ~ **pretences** con engaño; ~ **pride** falso orgullo; ~ **step** paso en falso; ~ **teeth** dientes *mpl* postizos; ~**-hearted** pérfido

falsehood mentira

falseness falsedad *f*

falsetto *n+adj* falsete *m*

falsification falsificación *f*

falsify falsificar[4]

falsity falsedad *f*

falter (hesitate) vacilar; (in speech) balbucear

faltering vacilante; (of speech) balbuceante

falteringly con dificultad, vacilantemente; (of speech) con voz temblorosa

fame fama

familiar familiar; (everyday) corriente; (cheeky) fresco; **his face is** ~ **to me** su cara me es conocida; **be** ~ **with** (know about) estar[19] enterado de, (know thoroughly) ser[19] versado en; **be/get too** ~ tomar demasiadas confianzas

familiarity familiaridad *f*

familiarize: ~ **o.s. with** (get to know) familiarizarse[7] con; (accustom o.s. to) acostumbrarse a

family *n* familia; *adj* familiar; ~ **celebration** fiesta familiar; **in the** ~ **way** (pregnant) embarazada, *sl* cepillada, *Arg* de compras; **put s.o. in the** ~ **way** embarazar[7]; ~ **allowance** subsidio

familiar; ~ **business** negocio de familia; ~ **doctor** médico de cabecera; ~ **gathering** reunión *f* familiar; ~ **income** entradas *fpl* familiares; ~ **life** vida de familia; ~ **man** padre de familia; ~ **name** apellido; ~ **planning** planificación *f* familiar; ~ **seat** casa solariega; ~**-size** (of containers) de tamaño familiar; ~ **ties** lazos familiares; ~ **tree** árbol genealógico

famine hambre *f*; (shortage of goods) carestía

famished hambriento; **be** ~ tener[19] mucha hambre, *fam* morirse (ue)[1a] (*past part* muerto) de hambre

famous famoso (**for** por)

fan *n* +*archi* abanico; (ventilator) ventilador *m*; (supporter) aficionado; (admirer) hincha; ~**-belt** correa de transmisión del ventilador; ~**light** ventana de abanico; ~**-mail** cartas escritas por admiradores; *v* abanicar(se)[4]; *mech* ventilar; *fig* atizar[7]; ~ **out** salir[19] en todas direcciones; ~ **the embers** avivar el rescoldo

fanatic *n*+*adj* fanático

fanaticism fanatismo

fancied (favourite) favorito; (imaginary) imaginario

fancier aficionado; (breeder) criador *m* (-ora *f*)

fanciful fantástico

fancy *n* (imagination) fantasía; (whim) capricho; (liking) cariño; *adj* de capricho/fantasía; (of clothing) de adorno; ~**-dress ball** baile *m* de disfraces; ~**-free** sin novio/novia; ~ **goods** artículos de fantasía; ~ **ideas** ideas *fpl* extrafalarias; ~ **price** precio exorbitante; ~ **work** labor artística, (embroidery) bordado; *v* (suppose) imaginar(se); (like) encapricharse de; ~ **that!** ¡fíje(n)se!; ~ **meeting you!** ¡qué casualidad encontrarle a usted!; **she fancies you** a ella le gusta usted

fandango fandango

fanfare toque *m* de trompetas

fang colmillo; *mech* diente *m*

fanny *sl* (arse) culo; *vulg* (cunt) coño

fantasia, fantasy fantasía

fantasize fantasear

fantastic fantástico

far *adj* lejano; ~**-off** remoto; **Far East**

Lejano Oriente; *adv* lejos; **how ~ are we going?** ¿hasta dónde vamos?; **how ~ is it from here to Soria?** ¿cuánta distancia hay de aquí a Soria?; **~ and near/wide** por todas partes; **from ~ and near** de todas partes; **~ and away** con mucho; **~ apart** muy separado; **~ away** remoto, *fig* abstraído; **by ~ the best** con mucho el/la mejor; **~ better** mucho mejor; **~ beyond** mucho más allá; **~ easier** *etc* mucho más fácil *etc*; **~ enough** bastante lejos; **~ from** lejos de; **~ from doing his duty** en vez de hacer su deber; **she is ~ from well** ella no está nada bien; **~ into the night** hasta las altas horas de la noche; **~ more** mucho más; **~ off** a lo lejos; **~ be it from me to** no permita Dios que yo +*subj*; **as ~ as** (up to, until) hasta; **he can't walk as ~ as you** él no puede andar tan lejos como usted; **as ~ as I am aware** que yo sepa; **be not ~ wrong** no estar[19] muy lejos de la verdad; **carry s.t. too ~** no saber[19] cuando terminar; **it's a ~ cry from … to …** dista mucho desde … hasta …; **he will go ~** él prosperará; **~-fetched** traído por los pelos; **~-flung** extenso; **~-reaching** de gran alcance; **~-seeing, ~-sighted** previsor (-ora *f*); **~-sightedness** previsión *f*

farce tontería; *theat* farsa

farcical ridículo

fare *n* (payment) precio (del billete); (passenger) pasajero; (food) comida; **~-stage** parada donde cambia el precio del billete; **how much is the ~ to?** ¿cuánto cuesta el billete a?; *v* pasarlo; **~ well/ill** pasarlo bien/mal

farewell *n* despedida; *interj* adiós

farinaceous farináceo

farm *n* granja; *SA* estancia, rancho; **~ girl** labradora; **~-hand, ~-labourer** peón *m*; **~-house, ~-stead** cortijo; **~ produce** productos *mpl* agrícolas; **~-school** escuela-granja; **~-yard** corral *m*; *v* cultivar (la tierra); (be a farmer) ser[19] agricultor

farmer agricultor *m*, granjero; *SA* estanciero

farming *n* agricultura; *adj* agrícola; **~ land** labrantío

farrier herrador *m*

farrow *n* lechigada de cerdos; *v* parir

fart pedo

farther *adj* más lejano; *adv* más lejos; **~ on** más adelante; **be ~ away** estar[19] más lejos

farthest *adj* más lejano; *adv* más lejos

farthing cuarto de penique

fascinate fascinar; (charm) encantar

fascinating fascinante; fascinador (-ora *f*)

fascination fascinación *f*; (charm) encanto

Fascism fascismo

Fascist *n*+*adj* fascista *m*+*f*, *sl* facha *m*+*f*

fashion *n* (dress) moda; (way) manera; (custom) costumbre *f*; **~ magazine** revista de modas; **~-designer** modista; **~-model** maniquí *f*; **~-parade** desfile *m* de maniquíes; **~-plate** figurín (-ines) *m* de modas; **after a ~** en cierto modo, (not very well) no muy bien; **be in ~** estar[19] de moda; (of colours *etc*) privar, **this year blue is in ~** este año priva el azul; **be out of ~** estar[19] pasado de moda; **come into ~** ponerse de moda; **go out of ~** pasarse de moda; **set the ~** imponer[19] la moda; *v* formar; (design clothes) diseñar

fashionable de moda

fashionably de moda, a la moda

[1] **fast** *n* ayuno; **~-day** día de ayuno; **break a ~** romper (*past part* roto) el ayuno; *v* ayunar; **she is fasting** ella está ayunando

[2] **fast** *adj* (quick) rápido; (secure) seguro; (fixed) fijo; (tight) firme; (non-fading) sólido; (dissipated) disoluto; **~ friend** amigo leal; **~ train** (tren) rápido; **my watch is (two minutes) ~** mi reloj está adelantado (dos minutos); **pull a ~ one on** jugar (ue)[1a] una mala pasada a; **she is a ~ woman** ella es muy coqueta; **~-wind** (on tape-recorder) rebobinado rápido; *adv* rapidamente; **hold ~** mantenerse[19] firme; **make ~** *naut* amarrar; **make it ~!** (do it quickly!) ¡pronto!; **she is ~ asleep** ella está profundamente dormida

fasten *vt* (fix) fijar; (of clothing) abrochar; (stick) pegar[5]; (tie) atar; *naut* amarrar; **~ the door** cerrar (ie)[2a] la puerta; **~ up** (of clothing) abrochar; (nail) clavar; *vi* fijarse; pegarse[5]; **~ the**

blame on echar la culpa a; ~ **on** agarrarse de/a; *fig* fijarse en

fastener (bolt) pestillo; (lock) cerrojo; (buckle) hebilla; (on dress) cierre *m*; (for papers) sujetapapeles *m*

fastening (action) sujeción *f*; (joining together) unión *f*; (of clothing) brochadura; (on a handbag) cierre *m*

fastidious (fussy) melindroso, *fam* especial; (critical) crítico

fastidiousness melindres *mpl*; sentido crítico

fasting ayuno

fastness (stronghold) fortaleza; (dissipation) libertinaje *m*

fat *n* (stoutness) gordura; (lard) lardo; *cul* manteca; (of meat) grasa; ~ **of the land** lo mejor de la tierra; **the ~ is in the fire** va a arder Troya; *adj* (stout) gordo, grueso; (greasy) grasiento; (of meat) que tiene mucha grasa; ~ **profit** ganancia excesiva, *fam* pingüe; **get ~** engordar, *fam* echar carnes; **a ~ lot you know!** ¡muy poco sabe usted!; ~**head** estúpido

fatal fatal; (mortal) mortal

fatalism fatalismo

fatalist *n*+*adj* fatalista *m*+*f*

fatalistic fatalista *adj*

fatality fatalidad *f*; (person) muerto

fate destino, suerte; **as ~ would have it** como si fuese predestinado

fated (pre)destinado

fateful decisivo; (ominous) ominoso

Fates Parcas *fpl*

father *n* +*eccles* padre *m*; ~ **and mother** padres *mpl*; **God the Father** Dios Padre; **he's been (like) a ~ to me** él se ha portado como si fuera mi padre; **like ~ like son** de tal palo tal astilla; **Father Christmas** Papá *m* Noel; ~**confessor** director *m* espiritual; ~**figure** representación paterna; ~**in-law** suegro; ~**land** (madre) patria; ~**s** (ancestors) antepasados *mpl*; *v* prohijar; *fig* patrocinar; **she ~ed the child on ...** ella atribuyó su hijo a ...; ~**s of the Church** padres *mpl* de la Iglesia

fatherhood paternidad *f*

fatherless sin padre

fatherliness amor *m* paternal

fatherly paternal

fathom *n* braza; *v naut* sondear; *fig* desentrañar

fathomless insondable; *fig* incomprensible

fatigue *n* cansancio, fatiga; *eng* pérdida de resistencia; *mil* faena; ~**-party** destacamento de trabajo; *v* cansar; **be ~d** estar[19] cansado

fatness gordura

fatten *v*/*i* ponerse[19] gordo/grueso; ~ **up** *v*/*t* engordar; (animals) cebar

fatty *n* (nickname) gordinflas *m sing*; *adj* grasiento; ~ **degeneration** degeneración grasosa; ~ **tissue** tejido adiposo

fatuity fatuidad *f*

fatuous fatuo

faucet (tap) grifo; *SA* bitoque *m*

fault *n* (blame) culpa; (defect) defecto; (error) falta; *elect* avería; *geol* falla; *sp* falta; (in cloth) canilla; **be at ~** (to blame) ser[19] culpable, (mistaken) estar[19] equivocado; **find a ~ in** encontrar (ue)[1a] un defecto en; **find ~ with** culpar; **it's his ~** él tiene la culpa; **to a ~** excesivamente; ~**-finder** criticón (-ona *f*), *fam* sacafaltas *m*+*f sing*; ~**finding** manía de criticar; *vi sp* cometer una falta; *vt* tachar

faultiness imperfección *f*

faultless intachable

faulty defectuoso; (of reasoning) ilógico

faun fauno

fauna fauna

Faust Fausto

faux pas error *m*; **commit a ~** tirarse una plancha, *fam* meter la pata

favour *n* (kindness) favor *m*; (badge) colores *mpl*; (letter, order) grata; (support) amparo; (token) prenda; ~**s** (of women) favores *mpl*; **do a ~** hacer[19] un favor; **be in ~** tener[19] aceptación; **be in ~ of** (in agreement) estar[19] por, (support) ser[19] partidario de; **be in ~ with** tener[19] el apoyo de; **fall out of ~** caer[19] en desgracia; **find ~ with** caer[19] en gracia a; **I'm in your ~** estoy a su favor; *v* (be in favour of) favorecer[14]; (support) ser[19] partidario de; (take after in looks) parecerse[14] a; **that colour ~s you** ese color le favorece

favourable favorable

favoured favorecido; **well-~** bien parecido; **ill-~** mal encarado

favouring favoritismo

707

favourite *n* favorito; **the king's** ~ el privado del rey; **the queen's** ~ (lover) el amante de la reina; *adj* predilecto

favouritism favoritismo

fawn *n* cervato; *adj* color *m* de cervato; *v* ~ **on** adular; (of an animal) acariciar

fawning adulador

fear *n* miedo; *fam* canguelo; **for** ~ **of** por miedo de; **for** ~ **that** por miedo de que +*subj*; **from** ~ de miedo; **go in** ~ **of one's life** temer por su vida; **no** ~! ¡ni hablar!; **there's no** ~ **of/that** no hay peligro de/de que +*subj*; ~**less** intrépido; *v* tener[19] miedo de; (be sorry) sentir (ie)[2c]

fearful (of people) temeroso (**of** de); (of things) espantoso

fearlessly sin miedo

fearlessness intrepidez *f*

fearsome temible

feasibility posibilidad *f*

feasible factible

feast *n* (meal) banquete *m*; *eccles* fiesta; ~**-day** día *m* de fiesta; *v* festejar; ~ **one's eyes on** recrear la vista (mirando); ~ **on** regalarse con

feat hazaña; (in circus) ejercicio (más difícil)

feather *n* pluma; (from tail) pena; ~**-bed** colchón *m* de plumas; ~**-brained** casquivano; ~**-duster** plumero; ~**-weight** peso pluma; ~ **in one's cap** triunfo personal; **in fine** ~ de buen humor; ~**s** plumaje *m*; *v* emplumar; ~**ed** emplumado; ~ **one's nest** hacer[19] su agosto, *fam* ponerse[19] las botas

feathery ligero como una pluma

feature *n* característica; *cin* atracción *f* principal; *geog* accidente *m*; ~ **article** (in newspaper) artículo; ~ **film** largo metraje; ~**-writer** articulista *m*+*f*; **the main** ~ lo más sobresaliente; ~**s** (facial) facciones *fpl*; *v* destacar; *cin* presentar

featuring presentando

featureless sin rasgos distintivos

febrile febril

February febrero

feckless incapaz

fecund fecundo

fecundity fecundidad *f*

fed: ~ **up** harto; **be** ~ **up (with)** estar[19] harto (de), *SA* estar[19] hasta el copete (de)

federal *n* federalista *m*+*f*; *adj* federal; ~ **government** gobierno federal; ~ **state** (part) estado confederado, (whole) estado federal

federalize federar

federate *adj* confederado; *v* confederar

federation (con)federación *f*

fee honorario; (for admission) precio de entrada; (for membership) cuota; (tip) propina; ~**s** (school *etc*) coste (de la enseñanza)

feeble débil; (feckless) irreflexivo; (light) tenue; ~**-minded** (mentally defective) anormal, deficiente mental; (weak-willed) vacilante

feebleness debilidad *f*; (mental) anormalidad *f*

feed *n* alimento; (meal) comida; (for animals) pienso; *mech* (tubo de) alimentación *f*; ~**-back** *rad* realimentación *f*; ~**-pipe** alimentación *f*; *vt* dar[19] de comer; (animals) cebar; *mech* alimentar; *fig* nutrir; *vi* comer; (graze) pastar; ~ **on** alimentarse de, *fig* nutrirse de

feeder (child's bib) babero; (eater) comedor *m* (-ora *f*); (invalid cup) pistero; *mech* alimentador *m*

feeding *n* alimentación *f*; *adj* alimenticio; ~**-bottle** biberón *m*; ~**-trough** pesebre *m*

feel *n* tacto; **you can tell by the** ~ se conoce por el tacto; **it has a nice** ~ es suave al tacto; **I don't like the** ~ **of this shirt** no me gusta la sensación de esta camisa; **get the** ~ **of** *fig* coger[8] el tino a; *vt* sentir (ie)[2c]; (touch) palpar; (believe) creer[17] (**that** que); *vi* sentirse (ie)[2c]; **how do you** ~? ¿cómo se siente usted?; **I** ~ **fine** me siento perfectamente; **I** ~ **wonderful** me siento divinamente; ~ **certain that** estar[19] seguro de que; ~ **cold/hot** tener[19] frío/calor; ~ **the cold/the heat** sentir (ie)[2c] el frío/el calor; ~ **equal to** sentirse en plan de; ~ **hungry/thirsty** tener[19] hambre/sed; ~ **like** (resemble) parecer, (want to) tener[19] ganas de +*infin*; **I** ~ **like eating** tengo ganas de comer; ~ **like nothing on earth** encontrarse (ue)[1a] muy mal; ~ **the loss of** sentir la pérdida de; ~ **the need to** sentir (ie)[2c] la necesidad de; ~ **one's way** ir[19] a tientas; ~ **the pulse** tomar el pulso; ~ **strongly about** tener[19] opiniones muy decididas sobre; ~ **well/sad** sentirse (ie)[2c] bien/triste; **it ~s cold in here** se siente frío aquí; **she doesn't ~ quite herself** ella no está muy bien de salud; **your hand ~s cold** tu mano está fría; **the measures are making themselves felt** las medidas dejan sentir sus efectos

~ **for** compadecerse[14] de

~ **out** (seek) averiguar[6]

~ **up to** sentirse (ie)[2c] con ánimo(s) para

feeler antena; *fig* tentativa; **to put out ~s** *fig* hacer[19] una tentativa

feeling (sentiment) emoción *f*; (sensation) sensación *f*; (sympathy) compasión *f*; (touch) tacto; sensibilidad; ~s sentimientos *mpl*; **I hurt his ~s** le ofendí; **I've no ~ in my hand** mi mano no tiene sensibilidad

feelingly expresivamente

feet *see* **foot; have one's ~ firmly on the ground** *fig* pisar el suelo

feign fingir[9]; ~ **madness/sleep** fingirse[9] loco/dormido; ~**ed** fingido

feint *n* disimulación *f*; (boxing) desplante *m*; (fencing) finta; *mil* ataque simulado; *v* hacer[19] una finta/un desplante

felicitate felicitar

felicitation felicitación *f*

felicitous (happy) feliz (-ces); (opportune) oportuno

felicity felicidad *f*

feline *n*+*adj* felino

fell (hilly region) altura; (moor) páramo; *adj* cruel; *v* derribar

fellah fela *m*

felling tala; ~-**axe** hacha de tala

fellow hombre; *fam* tipo; *pej* andoba; **get a move on, old ~!** ¡corre, hombre!; (colleague) colega *m*; (equal) igual *m*+*f*; (at university) becario (posgraduado); (of a society) socio; (one of a pair) pareja; ~ **citizen** conciudadano; ~ **countryman** compatriota *m*+*f*; ~ **creature** prójimo; ~-**feeling** interés *m* común; ~ **member** (of a society) consocio; (of staff) colega *m*; ~ **passenger** compañero de viaje; ~ **prisoner** compañero de prisión; ~ **student** condiscípulo; ~ **traveller** compañero de viaje, *pol* filocomunista *m*+*f*; ~ **worker** compañero de trabajo, (co-

llaborator) colaborador *m* (-ora *f*)

fellowship (feeling) camaradería; (body) confraternidad *f*; (at university) colegiatura; (university grant) beca

felon reo

felonious delincuente; **with ~ intent** con intención delictiva

felony delito (de mayor cuantía)

felt fieltro; (for roofing) tela asfáltica

female *n* hembra; *adj* femenino; ~ **screw** *mech* tornillo hembra

feminine *n* femenino; *adj* femenino; *pej* (of men) afeminado; ~ **fashions** modas para señoras; **in the ~ (gender)** en el género femenino

femininity feminidad *f*

feminism feminismo

feminist feminista

femoral femoral

femur fémur *m*

fen pantano

[1] **fence** valla; (of stakes) empalizada; (horse-racing) obstáculo; **sit on the ~** estar[19] indeciso; *v* vallar; ~ **in** cerrar (ie)[2a] con valla; ~ **off** separar con valla

[2] **fence** *sp* esgrimir; *fig* defenderse (ie)[2b] con respuestas evasivas

[3] **fence** (receiver) comprador *m* de cosas robadas; *fam* perista *m*

fencer esgrimidor *m* (-ora *f*)

[1] **fencing** *n* materiales *mpl* para vallar; ~-**post** poste *m* de valla

[2] **fencing** *sp* esgrima; ~ **foil** florete *m*; ~ **master** maestro de esgrima

fend: ~ for o.s. valerse por sí mismo; (earn one's living) ganarse la vida; ~ **off** parar

fender (round a fire) guardafuegos *m sing*+*pl*; *naut* defensa; *mot* parachoques *m sing*+*pl*; (on locomotive) quitapiedras *m sing*+*pl*, *Arg* miriñaque *m*, *Chil* trompa

Fenian feniano

fennel hinojo

Ferdinand Fernando

ferment *n* fermento; (of beer) fermentación *f*; *pol* agitación *f*; *v* +*fig* (hacer[19]) fermentar

fermentation fermentación *f*

fern helecho

ferocious feroz (-ces)

ferocity ferocidad *f*

ferret *n* hurón *m*; *v* cazar[7] con hurones;

~ **about** buscar[4] revolviendo todo; ~ **out** indagar[5]; he ~ed **out the secret** el logró descubrir el secreto

ferreting caza con hurón/hurones

ferriage *comm* barcaje *m*

ferris-wheel noria

ferro-concrete hormigón armado *m*

ferrous ferroso

ferrule regatón (-ones) *m*

ferry *n* transbordador *m*; ~**-boat** barca de pasaje; ~**-man** barquero; *vt* transportar … de una a otra orilla; *vi* pasar un río en barca

fertile fértil

fertility fertilidad *f*

fertilization fertilización *f*

fertilize *agri+biol* fertilizar[7]

fertilizer fertilizante *m*

fervency fervor *m*

fervent, fervid fervoroso

fervour fervor *m*

festal festivo

fester supurar

festival *n* festival *m*; *eccles* fiesta; *adj* de fiesta

festive festivo; **the ~ season** Navidades *fpl*

festivity festividad *f*

festoon *n* guirnalda de papel; *v* festonear

fetch traer[19]; (go and bring) ir[19] por; **this car will ~ £1000** este coche se venderá por mil libras; ~ **down** bajar; ~ **in** (hacer[19]) entrar

fetching atractivo

fête fiesta; *v* festejar

fetid fétido

fetish fetiche *m*

fetishism fetichismo

fetlock cerneja

fetter grillete *m*; **in ~s** en cadenas; *v* encadenar; *fig* estorbar

fettle: in fine ~ en buenas condiciones

feud enemistad heredada; *leg* feudo

feudal feudal; ~ **lord** señor *m* feudal

feudalism feudalismo

fever fiebre *f*; (excitement) agitación *f*; **be in a ~** tener[19] fiebre, *fig* estar[19] muy impaciente/agitado; ~ **hospital** hospital *m* de aislamiento

feverish febril; **become ~** empezar (ie)[2a+7] a tener fiebre

feverishly sin paciencia

feverishness calentura; (impatience) impaciencia

few *n*: **the ~** los menos; **fashions for the ~** modas para los menos/la minoría; *adj* (not many) pocos (-as); (some) (alg)unos; **he has ~ friends** él tiene pocos amigos; **he has a ~ friends** tiene (alg)unos amigos; ~ **and far between** poquísimos; **every ~ minutes** cada cuatro minutos; **not a ~** no pocos; **quite a ~, a good ~** bastantes

fewer menos; **she has ~ than six** ella tiene menos de seis; **she has ~ friends than I** ella tiene menos amigos que yo; **the ~ the better** cuantos menos mejor

fewness escasez *f*

fey destinado a morir; (weak) débil

fez fez *m*

fiacre simón (-ones) *m*

fiancé novio

fiancée novia

fiasco fracaso

fiat fiat *m*

fib *n* mentirilla; *SA* papa; *v* decir[19] mentirillas; *SA* echar papas

fibber mentirosillo; *SA* paparruchero

fibre fibra; *fig* carácter *m*; ~**glass** fibravidrio

fibrin fibrina

fibrositis reumatismo muscular

fibrous fibroso

fibula peroné *m*

fickle veleidoso; ~ **person** mariposón *m* (-ona *f*); **be ~** mariposear

fickleness veleidad *f*

fiction ficción *f*; *lit* literatura novelesca; **I read only ~** leo sólo novelas

fictional novelesco

fictitious ficticio

fiddle *n* violín (-ines) *m*; (trick) trampa; ~**-de-dee!, ~ sticks!** ¡qué disparate!; **be as fit as a ~** andar[19] como un reloj; **play second ~** tocar[4] el segundo violín, *fig* ser[19] plato de segunda mesa; *v* tocar[4] el violín; (cheat) engañar (con una trampa); (fidget) moverse (ue)[1b] nerviosamente; ~ **around** (waste time) perder (ie)[2b] el tiempo; ~ **(about) with** manosear

fiddler violinista *m+f*; (cheat) tramposo

fiddling *n* (cheating) engaños; *adj* trivial

fidelity fidelidad *f*

fidget *n* persona inquieta; ~s movimientos *mpl* nerviosos; **have the ~s** tener[19] hormiguillo; *v* moverse (ue)[1b] nerviosamente; (with the hands) manosear

fidgety nervioso

fief feudo

field *n* campo; (cultivated) sembrado; (meadow) prado; (hunting) caza; *sp* campo de deportes; (competitors) competidores *mpl* en una carrera, (horses in a race) campo; *mil* campo (de batalla); (campaign) campaña; (speciality) esfera (de actividades); ~ **of fire** campo de tiro; ~ **of vision** campo visual; **in the** ~ *mil* en campaña; **take the** ~ *mil* entrar en campaña, *sp* presentarse; ~ **ambulance/artillery/kitchen/telephone** ambulancia/artillería/cocina/teléfono de campaña; ~**-day** día *m* de maniobras, *fig* día *m* triunfal; ~**-dressing** botiquín *m* de urgencia; ~ **events** saltos *mpl* y lanzamientos *mpl*; ~**fare** *orni* zorzal *m* real; ~**-glasses** prismáticos; ~**-hospital** hospital *m* de sangre; ~**-marshal** capitán *m* general (del ejército); ~**mouse** ratón *m* campesino; ~**-officer** (teniente) coronel *m*; ~**-work** labores *mpl* del campo; *v* recoger[8] y devolver (ue)[1b] (*past part* devuelto) la pelota

fielder, fieldsman *sp* el que recoge la pelota

fiend demonio; (person) malvado; **he is a ~ for** es fanático de +*infin*

fiendish diabólico; (of a person) malvado

fierce feroz; (of heat) intenso

fierceness ferocidad *f*; (of heat) intensidad *f*

fieriness ardor *m*; (bad temper) irritabilidad; (vehemence) vehemencia; (of horses) fogosidad *f*

fiery (burning) ardiente; (hot) caliente; (of horses) fogoso; (of speech) apasionado

fiesta fiesta

fife pito, pífano

fifteen *n*+*adj* quince *m*

fifteenth décimoquinto; (of months + monarchs) quince; **Fifteenth Brigade** Quince Brigada

fifth *n* quinto; *fam* quinta parte; **Henry the Fifth** Enrique quinto; *adj* quinto; ~ **column** quinta columna; ~ **columnist** quintacolumnista *m*+*f*

fifthly en quinto lugar

fiftieth cincuentavo

fifty *n*+*adj* cincuenta *m*; ~-~ mitad y mitad; **the fifties** los años cincuenta

fig higo; (tree) higuera; **I don't care a ~** no me importa un higo; **it's not worth a ~** no vale un ardite; ~**-leaf** hoja de higuera, (on statue) hoja de parra

fight *n* pelea; *SA* riña; (conflict) conflicto; (quarrel) riña; (struggle) lucha; *sp* combate *m*; **have a ~** tener[19] una pelea; **he still has ~ left in him** le queda fuerza para luchar; **in fair ~** en buena lid; **pick a ~ with** meterse con; **he put up a (good)** ~ resistió (bien); **show** ~ enseñar los dientes; *v* pelear (con); (quarrel with) reñir (i)[3] con; (struggle against) luchar (con); ~ **a battle** librar una batalla; ~ **a tendency** combatir una tendencia; ~ **one's way** abrirse (*past part* abierto) paso a la fuerza

~ **against** luchar contra; ~ **against heavy odds** luchar con gran desventaja

~ **for** luchar por

~ **off** rechazar[7]

~ **on** seguir (i)[3+11] luchando

~ **out** *fig* disputar; ~ **it out** decidir a golpes, *fig* decidir a argumentos

~ **to a finish** decidir por la fuerza

fighter luchador *m* (-ora *f*); *mil* combatiente *m*; (boxer) boxeador *m*; *aer* (avión *m* de) caza *m*; ~**-bomber** cazabombardero *m*; ~**-escort** escolta de caza; ~**-pilot** piloto de caza

fighting *n* lucha; (boxing) boxeo; *adj* combatiente *m*; (aggressive) belicoso; ~**-cock** gallo de pelea; ~**-man** guerrero

figment invención (-ones) *f*

figurative figurativo

figuratively en sentido figurado

figure (shape) forma; (of human body) talle, (*esp* woman's) silueta, *fam* tipo; (*geom*, dance, skating) figura, (illustration) lámina; (number) cifra; (price) precio; (statue) estatua; (on fabric) dibujo; ~ **three** la cifra tres; ~**-of-eight** curva de ocho; ~ **of speech** figura de dicción; **cut a** ~ hacer[19] buen papel; **cut a fine** ~ *iron* hacer[19] el ridículo; **fine** ~ **of a woman** real hembra; **have a good** ~ tener[19] buena figura; **she worries about her** ~ se preocupa por su línea; **he's good at** ~s él es fuerte en matemáticas; ~**-head** +*naut* figurón *m*; ~**-skating** patinaje artístico; *v* figurar; (imagine) imaginarse; (think) opinar; **it** ~**s** (makes sense) tiene sentido; ~ **on** (count on) contar (ue)[1a] con, (plan) esperar; ~ **out** (calculate) calcular, (understand) comprender

figures (of cloth) estampado

figurine figurilla

filament filamento

filbert avellana

filch sisar; *sl* birlar

[1] **file** *n* (for bills *etc*) archivador *m*; (for documents) carpeta; (records) archivo; *comm*+*leg* expediente *m*; ~s archivos *mpl*, (for record cards) fichero; ~**-card** ficha; **on** ~ archivado; *v* (put away documents) archivar; (classify) clasificar[4]; ~ **a petition** presentar una demanda; ~ **a suit** entablar un pleito

[2] **file** *carp*+*mech n* lima; *v* limar

[3] **file** (row) *n* fila; **line up in single** ~ ponerse[19] en fila; *v* marchar en fila; ~ **in/out** entrar/salir[19] en fila; ~ **past** desfilar; ~**-past** desfile *m*

filial filial

filiation filiación *f*

filibuster *n* (action) obstruccionismo; (person) filibustero; *v* usar maniobras obstruccionistas

filibustering filibusterismo

filigree *n* filigrana

[1] **filing** clasificación *f*; (of a petition) presentación *f*; ~ **cabinet** archivador *m*; ~ **card** ficha; ~ **clerk** archivador *m*

[2] **filing** (action) limar *m*; ~s limaduras *fpl*

fill *n* hartazgo; **I've eaten my** ~ me he hartado; **I've had my** ~ **of** +*fig* estoy harto de; ~ **of tobacco** pipa de tabaco; *v* llenar; *cul* rellenar; (tooth) empastar, (with gold) orificar[4]; (inflate) inflar; (occupy) ocupar; ~ **a prescription** hacer una receta; ~ **(in) a form** rellenar una hoja; ~ **a hole** (re)llenar

~ **in** llenar; ~ **in the details** añadir los detalles; ~ **in time** esperar que pase el tiempo; ~ **in for** hacer[19] por

~ **out** (grow fat) ponerse[19] gordo; ~ **out a request** despachar un pedido

~ **up** (re)llenar

~ **with** llenar(se) de

filler lo que sirve para llenar; (of fountain pen) cargador *m*

fillet *n cul*+*archi* filete *m*; *v* (cut in pieces) cortar en filetes; (of fish) quitar la raspa y destripar

filling *n* +*cul* relleno; (in tooth) empaste *m*, (gold ~) orificación *f*, *Arg* emplumadura; *adj* que llena; ~**-station** *mot* gasolinera, *SA* estación de gasolina

fillip estímulo

filly potra(nca)

film *n* (coating) capa; (on liquid) tela; (over eye) nube *f*; *cin*+*phot* película; **go into** ~s colocarse[4] en el cine; ~ **actor** actor *m* de cine; ~ **actress** actriz (-ces) *f* de cine; ~ **club** cineclub *m*; ~ **distributor** distribuidor *m* de películas; ~ **library** cinemateca; ~ **producer** cineasta *m*+*f*; ~ **slide** diapositiva; ~ **society** cineclub *m*; ~**-star** (female) estrella de cine, (male) astro de cine; ~**-strip** tira de película; ~ **studio** estudio de cine; ~**-test** prueba (de un aspirante a las películas); *v* (make a ~) filmar; (show a ~) proyectar una película; ~ **(over)** nublarse

filming rodaje *m*

filmy diáfano; ~**-eyed** con los ojos nublados

filter *n* filtro; ~**-paper** papel *m* (de) filtro; ~**-tank** depósito de filtrador; ~**-tip** filtro; ~**-tipped** con filtro; *v* filtrar(se); (of news) divulgarse[5]; ~ **through** infiltrarse en

filth(iness) porquería; *fam* roña; (corruption) corrupción *f*; (obscenity) obscenidad *f*

filthy mugriento; (obscene) obsceno, *fig* asqueroso; ~ **joke** chiste *m* verde

fin aleta

final *n* (cup-~) final *f* (de la copa); ~s (examination) examen (-ámenes) *m* final; *adj* final; ~ **edition** (of newspaper) última edición

finale final *m*

finalist finalista *m*+*f*

finality finalidad *f*

finalization finalización *f*

finalize finalizar[7]

finally por fin

finance *n* finanzas *fpl*; (government department) Hacienda Pública; ~s

712

fam medios *mpl*; ~ **officer** administrador *m* de finanzas; *v* financiar

financial financiero

financier financiero

financing financiación *f*

finch pinzón (-ones) *m*

find *n* hallazgo; *v* hallar; *leg* decidir; **a husband has to ~ money for his family** un marido tiene que proveer[17] por su familia; ~ **difficulty in** encontrar dificultad en; ~ **o.s.** encontrarse (ue)[1a]; ~ **one's way** encontrar (ue)[1a] el camino; ~ **pleasure in** gustarle a uno; ~ **time for** hallar tiempo para; **all found** todo incluido; **I found it (im)possible to go** me fue (im)posible ir; **I hope to ~ you at home** espero encontrarle en casa; ~ **for** *leg* decidir a favor de; ~ **out** (investigate) averiguar[6], (discover) descubrir (*past part* descubierto), (discover the truth about) darse cuenta de, **they found me out** se dieron cuenta de cómo era yo, me descubrieron; ~ **out about** informarse sobre

finder el/la que halla; *phot* visor *m*

finding(s) *leg* sentencia

[1] **fine** *n* multa; **the tribunal imposed on him a ~ of 10,000 pesetas** el tribunal le puso una multa de 10.000 pesetas; *v* multar

[2] **fine** *adj* (delicate) fino; (beautiful) hermoso; (excellent) excelente; (pointed) agudo; (refined) refinado; (subtle) sutil; (thin) fino; (tiny) menudo; ~ **arts** bellas artes; ~ **figure of a man** hombre *m* de un aspecto espléndido; ~ **print** letra pequeña; ~ **weather** tiempo agradable; ~ **young man** buen mozo; ~ **young woman** real moza; **become** ~ *meteor* mejorar; **have a ~ time** pasarlo bien; **that's ~!** ¡estupendo!; **you're a ~ fellow!** *iron* ¡buena pieza es usted!; *adv* muy bien; **I feel ~** *fam* estoy de primera; **cut it ~** llegar justo a tiempo; ~**-drawn,** ~**-spun** muy tenue; ~**-grained** compacto

fineness fineza; (beauty) hermosura; (delicacy) finura; (excellence) excelencia; (thinness) delgadez *f*

finery (mejores) galas *fpl*

finesse sutileza

finger *n* dedo, ~**s** *sl* dátiles; **first ~** dedo índice; **little ~** dedo meñique; **middle**

~ dedo del corazón; **ring-~** dedo anular; **burn one's ~s** *fig* cogerse[8] los dedos; **have a ~ in the pie** meter su cucharada; **put one's ~ on** señalar; **it slipped through my ~s** se me escapó de entre los dedos; **she twists me round her little ~** ella hace conmigo lo que le da la gana; ~**-board** (of piano) teclado, (of stringed instrument) diapasón *m*; ~**-bowl** lavafrutas *m sing*; ~**-nail** uña; ~**-print** huella dactilar; ~**-print expert** perito en dactiloscopia; **take s.o.'s ~prints** tomarle a uno las huellas dactilares; ~**-stall** dedil *m*; ~**-tip** punta del dedo, **have at one's ~-tips** saber[19] al dedillo; *v* tocar[4] con los dedos; (piano) teclar; (violin) pulsar

fingering toqueteo; (instructions on music) digitación *f*; (piano) tecleo; (violin) pulseo

finicky especial; **be ~** andar en tiquismiquis; ~ **work** trabajo intrincado

finish *n* fin *m*; *sp* (of race) llegada, (end of game) final *m*; **be in at the ~** estar[19] presente al final/a la llegada; (final appearance) acabado, **this car has a good ~** este coche tiene un buen acabado; **dull/gloss(y) ~** acabado mate/brillante; **put a ~ on** dar[19] la última mano a; **wood with a rough ~** madera al natural; *v* terminar; (exhaust) agotar; (leave off) dejar de +*infin*; (put an end to) poner[19] fin a; (reach the end) llegar al fin; ~**ed** completo; (polished) puli(menta)do; ~ **off** (conclude) terminar, (destroy) destruir[16], (kill) matar, *fam* acabar con, *sl* cargarse[5] a; ~ **up** acabar, (eat) comerse, (drink) beberse; ~ **up at** ir[19] a parar a; ~ **up with** terminar con

finisher acabador *m* (-ora *f*)

finishing concluyente *m*; ~**-post** meta; ~**-school** colegio de educación social (para señoritas); ~ **touch** remate *m*; **put the ~ touches to** dar[19] la última mano a

finite finito

fink *n* soplón *m*; esquirol *m*; *v* soplar

Finland Finlandia

Finn finlandés *m* (-esa *f*)

Finnish *n* + *adj* finlandés (-esa *f*)

fiord fiordo

fir abeto; **Scotch** ~ pino; ~**-cone** piña (de abeto)

fire *n* fuego; (conflagration) incendio; *fig* ardor *m*; **be on** ~ estar[19] ardiendo, *fig* estar[19] lleno de pasión; **between two** ~**s** entre dos aguas; **by** ~ **and sword** a sangre y fuego; **(be) under enemy** ~ (estar[19]) bajo el fuego del enemigo; ~**-alarm** alarma de incendios; ~**arm** arma (de fuego); ~**-box** caja de fuego; ~**brand** (person) incendiario, *fig* agitador, (torch) tea; ~**break** cortafuegos *m sing+pl*; ~**brick** ladrillo refractario; ~**-brigade** (cuerpo de) bomberos *mpl*; ~**-bug** incendiario; ~**-chief** jefe *m* de bomberos; ~**-cracker** triquitraque *m*; ~**-damp** grisú *m*; ~**-dog** morillo; ~**-drill** ejercicio para caso de incendio; ~**-eater** tragafuegos *m*, *fig* matamoros *m sing*; ~**-engine** coche *m* de bomberos; ~**-escape** escalera de incendios; ~**-extinguisher** extintor *m* (de incendios); ~**-fighter** bombero; ~**fly** luciérnaga; ~**guard** guardafuego; ~**hose** manguera de incendios; ~**hydrant,** ~**-plug** boca de incendios; ~**-insurance** seguro contra incendios; ~**-irons** badil *m* y tenazas; ~**-lighter** encendedor *m*; ~**man** bombero, (*naut* + railway) fogonero; ~**place** chimenea; ~**-policy** póliza contra incendios; ~**-power** potencia de fuego; ~**proof** a prueba de fuego; ~**-raiser** incendiario; ~**-raising** incendio premeditado; ~**ship** brulote *m*; ~**side** hogar *m*; ~**-station** (*US* ~**-hall**) parque de bomberos; ~**-warden,** ~**-watcher** vigilante *m* de incendios; ~**-watching** vigilancia de incendios; ~**wood** leña; ~**works** fuegos *mpl* artificiales; *v* (set ~ to) encender (ie)[2b]; *cer* cocer[14]; (gun) disparar; *mot* dar[19] explosiones; *fig* (dismiss) despedir (i)[3]; (excite) excitar; ~**!** ¡fuego!; ~ **away** (begin) empezar (ie)[2a+7]

firing (of arms) disparo; *cer* cocción *f*; (dismissal) despedida; **within** ~ **range** a tiro; ~**-kiln** horno; ~**-line** línea de fuego; ~**-party** (ceremonial) piquete *m* de salvas; (for executions) pelotón de ejecuciones; ~**-pin** aguja de percusión; ~**-squad** pelotón *m* de ejecuciónes

[1] **firm** *n* empresa

[2] **firm** *adj* firme; (of persons) inflexible; ~ **order** pedido en firme

firmament firmamento

firmly con firmeza

firmness firmeza; (of purpose) resolución *f*

first *n* (of month) (día *m*) primero; (academic degree) grado de primera clase; ~ **to do something** primero en hacer algo; **from the** ~ desde el principio; **from the very** ~ desde el primer momento; *adj* primero; ~**-aid** primeros auxilios; ~**-aid box** botiquín *m* de urgencia; ~**-aid station** puesto de socorro; ~ **base** *sp* primera base; ~**-born** primogénito; ~**-class** de primera clase, *fam* de aúpa; ~**-cousin** primo/prima carnal; ~**-day cover** sobre *m* de primer día; ~ **edition** edición *f* príncipe; *f* ~ **finger** dedo índice; ~ **floor** piso principal, *US* planta baja; ~**-footer** el primero que cruza el umbral el 1º de enero; ~**-fruits** frutos primerizos; ~**-hand** de primera mano; ~**-hand account** informe *m* de fuentes originales; ~ **lieutenant** teniente *m*; ~ **mate** piloto; ~ **name** nombre *m* de pila; ~ **night** *theat* estreno, (wedding-night) noche *f* de bodas; ~ **offender** delincuente *m+f* por primera vez, *Arg* ojo; ~**-rate** de primera categoría; **have** ~ **refusal** tener[19] derecho de ser el primero a quien se ofrezca algo; **at** ~ **sight** a primera vista; **love at** ~ **sight** flechazo; ~ **thing** (early) a primera hora, (most important) lo primero; **he doesn't know the** ~ **thing about** él no sabe nada de; ~**-year pupil** alumno/alumna de primer grado; *adv* primero; (for the ~ time) por primera vez; **at** ~ al principio; ~ **and foremost,** ~ **of all** ante todo

firstly en primer lugar

fiscal fiscal; ~ **year** año fiscal

fish *n* (live) pez *m*; (for eating) pescado; **be neither** ~ **nor fowl** no ser[19] ni carne ni pescado; **have other** ~ **to fry** tener[19] otras cosas más importantes que hacer; **like a** ~ **out of water** como reo en capilla; **he's an odd** ~ él es un tipo raro; ~**-bone** espina de pescado; ~**bowl** pecera; ~**-cake** croqueta de pescado; ~**-fingers** palitos de pescado; ~-**glue** cola de pescado; ~-**hook** anzuelo; ~-**knife/fork** pala/tenedor *m* de pescado; ~-**market** (wholesale) lonja de pescado, (retail) pescadería; ~**monger** pescadero; ~**monger's** pescadería; ~-**net** red *f*; ~-**paste** pasta de pescado; ~**plate** carp cubrejunta *m*, (railway) eclisa; ~-**pond** vivero; ~-**server**, ~-**slice** pala para pescado; ~ **stew** sopa de pescado; ~-**tank** acuario; ~**wife** pescadera; *v* pescar[4], *fig* buscar[4]; ~ **in troubled waters** *prov* a río revuelto ganancia de pescadores; ~ **for** tratar de pescar; ~ **for compliments** andar[19] a la pesca de requiebros; ~ **out** sacar[4]

fisherman pescador *m*
fishery pesquería; industria pesquera
fishily de manera sospechosa
fishiness (smell) olor *m* a pescado; (taste) sabor *m* a pescado
fishing *n* pesca; *adj* de pescar; **go** ~ ir de pesca; ~-**boat** barca de pesca; ~-**grounds** pesquera; ~-**line** sedal *m*; ~-**net** red *f*; ~-**reel** carrete *m*; ~-**rod** caña de pescar; ~-**tackle** aparejo de pesca; ~ **village** pueblo de pescadores
fishy de pescado; *fig* sospechoso; **it tastes** ~ sabe a pescado; **it smells** ~ huele a pescado, *fig* huele a camelo; ~ **tale** cuento extravagante
fission fisión *f*
fissionable, fissile fisionable
fissure grieta; *SA* rajadura
fist puño; ~-**fight** pelea con los puños
fistful puñado
fisticuffs puñetazos *mpl*
fit *n* +*med* ataque; (of emotional excitement) acceso; (cut of clothing) corte *m*; (size) ajuste *m*; **by** ~**s and starts** a saltos; *adj* (suitable) apto; (healthy) sano; (in training) en forma; (capable) capaz (-ces); (just) justo; ~ **and proper** justo y conveniente; ~ **for a king** digno de un rey; ~ **for service** *mil* apto para el frente; **the horse is not** ~ **for work** el caballo no está en condiciones para trabajar; **I'm** ~ **for anything** estoy listo para todo; **I am not** ~ **to travel** no estoy para viajar; ~ **to eat** comestible; **this is not** ~ **to eat/drink** esto no se puede comer/beber; **think** ~ juzgar[5] conveniente; *v* ajustar; (place in position) colocar[4];

(try on) probar (ue)[1a]; **this suit** ~**s you** este traje le viene bien; ~ **the description** cuadrar con la descripción; ~ **the facts** estar[19] de acuerdo con los hechos; **a key to** ~ **this lock** una llave (que sirve) para este cerrojo
~ **in(to)** *vt* encajar; *vi* caber[19], *fig* adaptarse
~ **in with** encajarse en; (get on well with) llevarse bien con
~ **out (with)** equipar (con); *naut* armar
~ **together** encajar
~ **up** (assemble) montar
fitful (capricious) caprichoso; (spasmodic) espasmódico
fitfully a ratos
fitment equipo; mueble
fitness (suitability) aptitud *f*; (health) vigor *m*
fitter *mech* mecánico ajustador; (tailoring) cortador *m* (-ora *f*); (dressmaking) probador *m* (-ora *f*)
fitting *n* encaje *m*; *mech* pieza de armadura, (of clothes) prueba; (size) medida; ~-**out** equipo; ~-**up** *mech* montaje *m*, (of a house) muebles *mpl*; ~-**room** probador *m*; ~**s** instalaciones *fpl*, (accessories) accesorios *mpl*; *adj* propio
five *n*+*adj* cinco *m*; ~-**peseta coin** duro, *sl* bali *m*; ~ **hundred** quinientos; ~-**thousand-peseta note** *sl* fantasma; ~-**year plan** *m* quinquenal; ~-**a-side soccer** futbito ~-**finger exercise** *mus* ejercicio de cinco dedos
fiver billete *m* de cinco libras
fives juego de pelota; ~-**court** frontón *m*
fix *n* (dilemma) apuro; (of drugs) inyección *f*, *sl* chute *m*; *sp* tongo; **be in a (tight)** ~ estar[19] en un apuro, *fam* tener[19] la negra; **get (o.s.) into a** ~ meterse en un lío; **give o.s. a** ~ (drug) *sl* chutarse; *v* (fasten) fijar; (agree) quedar en; (establish) establecer[14]; (of drugs) pegarse[5] un chute; *photo*+*chem* fijar; (repair) arreglar; (revenge o.s.) pagar[5] en la misma moneda, **I'll** ~ **him once and for all** voy a arreglarle las cuentas de una vez; *sp* hacer[19] tongo; **it's been** ~**ed** hay tongo; ~ **a bayonet** calar una bayoneta; ~ **the blame on** echar[5] la culpa a; ~ **a drink** preparar una bebida; ~ **one's eyes on** clavar los ojos

en; ~ **one's hopes on** poner[19] las esperanzas en; ~ **the price** determinar el precio; ~ **up** (arrange) organizar[7], (decide on) decidir, (repair) arreglar; ~ **up with** (provide) proveer[17]

fixation fijación f

fixative fijador m

fixed fijo; ~ **assets** activo fijo; ~ **bayonet** bayoneta calada; ~ **idea** obsesión (-ones) f; ~ **income** renta fija; ~ **star** estrella fija

fixer fijador m

fixing (of a date) fijación f; ~**-bath** phot baño fijador

fixity fijeza

fixture (action) instalación f; (thing) cosa fija; sp partido; fig (person) ostra; ~s (in a shop) habilitaciones fpl, elect guarniciones fpl de alumbrado; ~**-card** calendario deportivo

fizz n siseo; v sisear

fizzle sisear débilmente; (of fire) chisporrotear; ~ **out** no dar[19] resultado

fizzy efervescente; ~ **drink** gaseosa

flabbergast pasmar

flabbiness flaccidez f; (of character) debilidad f

flabby blanducho

flaccid fláccido

[1] **flag** n bandera; (small) banderín m; ~ **of truce** bandera de parlamento; **show the** ~ fig hacer ostensible su presencia; ~**-bearer** portaestandarte m; ~**-day** (for charity) día m de la banderita, US día m de la Bandera (14 de junio); ~**-pole** asta de bandera; ~**-officer** jefe m de escuadra; ~**ship** capitana; ~**staff** asta de bandera; ~**-stop** US apeadero; ~**wagger** patriotero; ~**wagging** patriotería; v hacer[19] señal(es) con bandera; **he flagged me down** me hizo señal de parada; **the linesman flagged** el juez de línea marcó con la bandera

[2] **flag** bot (yellow) lirio amarillo; (purple) lirio cárdeno

[3] **flag** n (stone) losa; v (pave with stones) enlosar

[4] **flag** (decline) decaer[19]; (weaken) debilitarse; (of conversation) languidecer[14]; (of enthusiasm) enfriarse

flagellate flagelar

flagellation flagelación f

[1] **flagging** n (flagstones) pavimentación f

[2] **flagging** adj lánguido

flagon frasco

flagrant flagrante

flail n mayal m; v azotar

flair aptitud f (for para + n/infin)

flak fuego antiaéreo

flake n escama; (of snow) copo (dc nieve); vt separar en escamas; vi desprenderse en escamas

flaky escamoso; ~ **pastry** hojaldre m

flamboyance extravagancia

flamboyant extravagante

flame n llama; fig (person) amor; **in** ~s en llamas; ~**-thrower** lanzallamas m sing; v llamear; ~ **up** inflamarse, fig (blush) ruborizarse[7]

flamenco flamenco

flaming llameante; (of emotions) apasionado; ~ **red** rojo encendido; **be in a** ~ **temper** estar[19] rabioso

flamingo flamenco

flammable inflamable

flan pastel m de fruta

Flanders Flandes

flange reborde m

flank (animal's) ijada; (human's) costado; (of hill) lado; mil flanco; v flanquear; **be** ~**ed by** tener[19] a su lado; ~**ing movement** movimiento de flanqueo

flannel franela; (face-cloth) toallita dc cara; ~s pantalones mpl de franela; adj de franela

flannelette franela de algodón

flap n (of envelope, book jacket) solapa; (of pocket) cartera; (of shoe) oreja; (of table) hoja (plegadiza); (of sail, flag) zapatazo; (of wings) aletazo; (sound of wings flapping) aleteo; fig (panic) pánico; vt agitar; vi batir, fig consternarse

flapjack torta de sartén

flare n llamarada; (signal) cohete m dc señales; (dressmaking) vuelo; ~**-path** trayecto iluminado (para el aterrizaje nocturno); ~**-up** n llamarada, (of anger) arranque m, (of rioting) estallido; v llamear; ~**d** (of a skirt) con vuelo; ~ **up** encenderse (ie)[2b], (in anger) encolerizarse[7]

flash n (of light) destello; (of lightning) relámpago; (of a firearm) fogonazo; (moment) instante; **in a** ~ en un santiamén, (of emotions) acceso; ~ **in**

716

the pan éxito pasajero; ~ **of wit** rasgo de ingenio; **like a** ~ como un relámpago; ~**-back** *cin*+*TV* escena retrospectiva; ~**-bulb** *pnot* flash; ~**-gun**, ~**-lamp** *phot* aparato de luz relámpago, flash; ~**light** *phot* flash de magnesio, (torch) linterna (eléctrica); ~ **photography** fotografía relámpago; ~**-point** punto de inflamación; *adj see* **flashy**; *v* destellar; (of lightning) relampaguear; (display with pride) ostentar; (indecently) exponerse sexualmente; ~ **a light at** dirigir[9] un rayo de luz hacia; **an idea** ~**ed into his mind** una idea iluminó su mente

flasher exhibicionista *m* sexual

flashily llamativamente

flashing *n* centelleo; (of lightning) relampagueo; exhibicionismo sexual; *adj* centellador (-ora *f*); (of lightning) relampagueante; ~ **light** luz *f* intermitente; **she looked at me with** ~ **eyes** ella me miró con ojos de fuego

flashy llamativo; (of persons) achulado; (of colours) chillón

flask frasco; *chem* redoma; (vacuum) *tr* termos *m sing*+*pl*

flat *n* (dwelling) piso, *SA* apartamento; *mot* pinchazo, *SA* llanta volada; *mus* bemol *m*, A ~ A bemol; *naut* banco; (terrain) llanura; *theat* bastidor *m*; ~ **of the hand** palma; ~ **of the sword** plano de la espada; *adj* (level) llano; (horizontal) plano; ~**-bottomed** (of boats) de fondo plano; (smooth) liso; **100 metres** ~ **(race)** 100 metros lisos; (lying) tumbado; (spread out) tendido; *fig* (downright) categórico, ~ **denial** negativa categórica; (dull) aburrido; (of liquid) insípido; *mot* (of battery) descargado, (of tyres) desinflado; (nett) neto; *mus* desafinado; **he has** ~ **feet** él tiene los pies planos; ~**-car** vagón *m* de plataforma; ~**fish** lenguado; ~**-foot** *sl* (policeman) polizonte *m*; ~**-footed** de pies planos; ~**- iron** plancha; ~**-nosed** chato; ~ **rate** tarifa fija; (of salaries) ~**rate increase** aumento lineal; *adv* (*see* **flatly**) **be** ~ **broke** estar[19] barrido; **go** ~ **out** ir[19] a toda velocidad; **fall** ~ caer[19] de bruces; **the joke fell** ~ el chiste no tuvo éxito; **lie** ~ **on the ground** tumbarse en

el suelo; **turn down** ~ rechazar[7] de plano

flatlet pisito

flatly de plano; (categorically) categóricamente; (plainly) netamente; **refuse** ~ negarse[8] en rotundo

flatness planicie *f*; (evenness) igualdad *f*; (insipidness) insipidez *f*

flatten (make level) allanar; (crush) aplastar; (destroy) derribar; *fig* (defeat in argument) desconcertar; ~ **out** allanar

flatter adular; *fam* pasar la mano; ~ **o.s.** felicitarse; **that photo** ~**s you** esa foto le favorece a usted

flatterer adulador *m* (-ora *f*)

flattering favorecedor; halagüeño; ~ **compliment** chicoleo

flattery adulación *f*; **it's not** ~ **but a fact** no es una galantería sino un hecho

flatulence flatulencia

flatulent flatulento

flaunt *vt* ostentar; *vi* pavonearse

flaunting ostentoso

flautist flautista *m*+*f*

flavour *n* sabor *m*; **in vanilla and many other** ~**s** en vainilla y otros muchos gustos; *v* sazonar

flavouring condimento; *fig* dejo

flavourless soso

flaw defecto; (in a precious stone) pelo; (crack) grieta; *geol* falla

flawless perfecto; (character) irreprochable

flax, flaxen de lino; (of hair) muy rubio

flay desollar (ue)[1a]; *fig* flagelar

flea pulga; ~**-bag** saco de montaña; ~**-bite** picadura de pulga, *fig* bagatela; ~**-bitten** *fig* dilapidado; ~**-pit** cine barato

fleck *n* punto; mota; *v* puntear; ~ **with** salpicar[4] de; ~**ed** moteado

fledged plumado; **fully** ~ completamente plumado, *fig* hecho y derecho

fledgling volantón (-ones) *m*

flee huir[17] (**from** de); *fam* chaquetear (**from** de)

fleece *n* vellón (-ones) *m*; *v* esquilar; *fig* desplumar

fleecy lanudo; (of cloud) aborregado; ~ **lining** forro de lana

[1] **fleet** *n* flota; (armed) armada; ~ **of cars** parque *m* de coches

[2] **fleet** ligero; ~**-footed** veloz (-ces)

fleeting fugaz (-ces)

Fleming, Flemish flamenco

flesh carne *f*; (of fruit) pulpa; *fig* (mankind) la humanidad; **in the ~** en persona; **sins of the ~** pecados *mpl* carnales; **~-coloured** encarnado; **~-eating** carnívoro; **~-pot** marmita, *fig* lujo; **~-wound** herida superficial

fleshly carnal

fleshy gordo; (of fruit) pulposo

fleur-de-lis flor *f* de lis

flex *n* cordón (-ones) *m* (de la luz); *v* doblar

flexibility flexibilidad *f*

flexible flexible

flick golpecito; (of the finger) capirotazo; (of whip) chasquido; **~-knife** navaja de muelles; *v* (fingers) dar[19] un capirotazo; (with whip) chasquear; **~ away** quitar con un golpecito

flicker (of light) luz mortecina; (of flame) llama vacilante; (of eyes) parpadeo; **without a ~ of** sin la menor señal de; *v* (of light) brillar con luz mortecina; (of a flame) flamear; *fig* fluctuar

flickering centelleo; (of eyes) parpadeo

flics cine *m*

flies *theat* bambalina

flight vuelo; (trajectory) trayectoria; (escape) fuga; **~ of aeroplanes** escuadrilla de aviones; **~ of birds** bandada de pájaros; **~ of fancy** sueño; **~ of stairs** tramo de escalera; **two ~s up** dos pisos más arriba; **put to ~** ahuyentar; **take ~** alzar[7] el vuelo; **take to ~** ponerse[19] en fuga; **~-deck** cubierta de despegue y aterrizaje

flightiness veleidad *f*

flighty veleidoso; frívolo

flimsiness fragilidad *f*; (of argument) futilidad *f*

flimsy débil; (fragile) quebradizo; (of paper, cloth) fino; **~ excuse** excusa floja

flinch acobardarse (**from** ante); **without ~ing** sin vacilar

fling (dance) baile *m* escocés; (of dice *etc*) echada; **go on a ~** hacer[19] la juerga; *v* arrojar

~ away desechar

~ back devolver (ue)[1b] de un tiro

~ down tirar al suelo; **~ o.s. down** tumbarse

~ o.s. headlong lanzarse[7]

~ open abrir de repente

~ out echar a la fuerza; poner de patitas en la calle

flint (stone) pedernal *m*; (for making fire) piedra de encendedor

flinty de pedernal; *fig* empedernido

flip *see* **flick**; **~ a coin** echar a cara o cruz; **~-side** lado B

flippancy (frivolity) frivolidad *f*; (pertness) impertinencia

flippant (frivolous) frívolo; (pert) impertinente

flipper aleta; (for swimming) pie *m* de pato

flirt *n* (person) coqueta *f*, coquetón *m*, *fam* castigador *m* (-ora *f*); (action) flirteo; *v* coquetear, flirtear (**with** con); *fig* **~ with an idea** acariciar una idea con poca seriedad; **~ with death** jugar (ue)[1a] con la muerte

flirtation coqueteo

flirtatious (of woman) coqueta; (of men) galanteador

flit revolotear; **~ by** pasar rápidamente

flitter *see* **flutter**

flivver coche barato; *fam* cacharro

float *n* (on fishing net) flotador *m*; (on fishing line) veleta; (on sea-plane) flotador *m*; (for learning to swim) nadadera; *naut* (raft) balsa; (decorated vehicle) carroza; **~s** *theat* candilejas; *vi* flotar, *naut* boyar; (while bathing) flotar, hacer[19] la plancha; *vt* hacer[19] flotar; *naut* **~ a ship** poner[19] a flote un barco, (grounded ship) desencallar; **~ a company** lanzar[7] una compañía; **~ a loan** poner[19] en circulación un empréstito

floatation flotación *f*

floating *n* flotación *f*; *adj* flotante; **~ dock** dique *m* flotante; **~ population** población *f* flotante; **~ voter** votante *m*+*f* indeciso (-a)

flock *n* (of animals) rebaño; (of birds) bandada; (wool) borra; *eccles* grey *f*; *v* congregarse[5]; **~ to** reunirse en gran número en; **come ~ing** venir[19] en masa

floe témpano de hielo

flog azotar; (sell) vender, *sl* (steal) birlar

flogging azotamiento

flood *n* inundación *f*; *bibl* Diluvio; *fig* torrente *m*; **~ of tears** chorro de lágrimas; ~-**gate** compuerta; ~**light** *n* foco, *v* iluminar con focos; ~**lighting** iluminación *f* con focos; ~-**tide** pleamar *f*; *v* (of river) desbordar(se); ~ **with** +*fig* inundar de

flooding inundación (-ones) *f*

floor *n* (ground) suelo; (of the sea) fondo; (storey) piso; **ground** ~ planta baja; **ask for/have the** ~ pedir (i)³/ tener¹⁹ la palabra; **take the** ~ salir¹⁹ a bailar; ~-**cloth** bayeta; ~-**lamp** lámpara de pie; ~-**plan** planta; ~-**polish** cera para el suelo; ~-**polisher** lustrador *m* (de piso); ~-**show** espectáculo de cabaret; ~**walker** guardalmacén *m*; *v* (knock down) derribar; *fig* dejar sin réplica

flooring tablado; suelo

flop (splash) chapoteo; (failure) fracaso; ~**house** posada de mala muerte; *v* caerse¹⁹ flojamente; (fail) fracasar

floppy colgante; flojo

flora flora

floral floral; ~ **tribute** ofrenda floral

Florence Florencia

Florentine florentino

florescence florescencia

florescent en flor

florid (complexion) encarnado; *lit* figurado

florist florista; ~s floristería

floss seda floja

flotation flotación *f*

flotilla flotilla

flotsam pecios *mpl*

flounce *n* volante *m*; *v* ~ **out** salir¹⁹ airado

flounder *n* (fish) platija; *v* revolcarse⁴; (fall into error) cometer errores

flour harina; ~-**bin** tina; ~-**merchant** harinero; ~-**mill** molino (harinero)

flourish (movement) gesto; (fencing + *rhet*) floreo; (of the hand) ademán *m*; (in writing) rasgo; (under signature) rúbrica; *mus* (fanfare) toque *m* de clarín; (guitar-playing) floreo; *v* (prosper) florecer¹⁴; (wave) agitar en el aire; (weapon) blandir; (cudgel) menear

flourishing (prosperous) próspero; (healthy) como un reloj; *bot* floreciente

floury harinoso

flout burlarse de

flow *n* corriente *f*; (of tide) flujo; *comm* (output) producción *f* total; ~ **of words** torrente *m* de palabras; ~-**chart** *comm* gráfica de movimiento; *v* fluir¹⁶; (of blood) derramarse; *fam* correr; (of tide) subir

~ **away** escaparse

~ **back** refluir¹⁶

~ **down** fluir¹⁶ hacia abajo; **the tears** ~**ed down her cheeks** las lágrimas le corrieron por las mejillas

~ **from** (di)manar de; *fig* proceder de

~ **in** entrar en abundancia

~ **into** desembocar⁴ en

~ **over** rebosar

~ **through** fluir¹⁶ por

~ **together** confluir¹⁶

flower *n* flor *f*; **no** ~**s by request** no (llevar) flores por deseo del finado; ~-**bed** cuadro (de jardín); ~-**garden** jardín *m*; ~-**girl** florista; ~-**market** mercado de flores; ~-**people** (members of cult) niños floridos; ~-**pot** tiesto; ~-**shop** floristería; ~-**show** exposición *f* de flores; ~-**stand** jardinera; ~-**vase** florero; *v* florecer¹⁴; ~**ed** con (dibujos de) flores

flowering *n* florecimiento; *adj* floreciente; ~ **season** época de floración; ~ **shrub** arbusto de flores

flowery florido

flowing *n see* **flow**; *adj* fluente; (of tide) creciente; (of style) fluido; (waving) ondeante

flu gripe *f*, *fam* trancazo

fluctuate fluctuar

fluctuation fluctuación (-ones) *f*

flue cañón *m* de chimenea; (of boiler) tubo (de caldera)

fluency fluidez *f*; **his** ~ **in French** su dominio del francés

fluent fluido; **be** ~ **at Spanish** dominar el español

fluently con facilidad

fluff pelus(ill)a

fluffy cubierto de pelusa; (of hair) encrespado; (feathered) plumoso; (woolly) lanoso

fluid *n* + *adj* fluido

fluidity fluidez *f*

fluke (fish) platija; (of anchor) uña; (chance) chiripa; **by a** ~ por chiripa

flume (channel) acequia; *geog* cañada; (chute) canal *m*

flummox confundir

flunk: ~ **an exam** ser[19] suspendido en un examen

flunkey lacayo

fluorescence fluorescencia

fluorescent fluorescente

fluoridation: ~ **of water** fluorización *f* del agua

fluoride fluor(uro)

flurry *n* conmoción *f*; (of snow, wind) ráfaga; *v* poner[19] nervioso

flush *n* (blush) rubor *m*; (cards) flux *m*; *adj* (level) nivelado; ~ **with** a ras de; (generous) liberal; (rich) adinerado; **be** ~ tener[19] dinero, *sl* tener[19] pasta; *v* (turn red) ruborizarse[7]; (of birds) levantar el vuelo; (wash out) limpiar con un chorro de agua; (w.c.) tirar de la cadena; ~ **out** enjuagar[5]

fluster *n* aturdimiento; *v* atolondrar; **be** ~**ed** estar[19] atolondrado

flute flauta; ~**player** flautista *m*+*f*

fluted acanalado

fluting *archi* acanaladura; (sewing) rizado

flutter *n* (of wings) aleteo; (of heart) palpitación *f*; (of flags) ondeo; (excitement) excitación *f*; (confusion) alboroto; (speculation) especulación *f*; (bet) apuesta; **have a** ~ poner[19] una apuesta; *v* (tremble) temblar; (of birds) aletear; (of heart) palpitar; (of flags) ondear

fluvial fluvial

flux flujo

fly *n* (insect) mosca; (for fishing) mosca artificial; (of tent) toldo; (of trousers) bragueta; *theat* bambalina; (vehicle) calesín (-ines) *m*; ~**blown** contaminado (por las moscas); ~**catcher** *orni* papamoscas *m sing*; ~**fishing** pesca con mosca artificial; ~**leaf** (hoja de) guarda; ~**over** paso superior; ~**paper** papel *m* cazamoscas; ~**past** desfile *m* de aviones; ~**sheet** papel volante; ~**swatter** matamoscas *m sing*; ~**way** ruta migratoria de aves; ~**weight** *sp* peso mosca; ~ **weight champion** campeón *m* de peso mosca; ~**wheel** volante *m*; *adj* (artful) avispado; *vi* volar (ue)[1a]; (go by plane) ir[19] en avión; (hurry) precipitarse; darse prisa; **I must** ~ tengo que correr; (flee) huir[16]; *vt* hacer[19]

volar; (transport by air) transportar por avión; ~ **a flag** enarbolar una bandera; **what flag is that ship** ~**ing?** ¿qué bandera lleva aquel barco?; ~ **a kite** hacer[19] volar una cometa; ~ **a plane** volar (ue)[1a] un avión; ~**by-night** *n* trasnochador *m* (-ora *f*); **let** ~ **at** atacar[4]

~ **away** emprender el vuelo

~ **in** volar (ue)[1a] adentro; *aer* llegar[5] (en avión)

~ **into** volar (ue)[1a] dentro de; ~ **into a rage/temper** montarse en cólera, *fam* ahumarse a uno el pescado

~ **low** volar (ue)[1a] a poca altura

~ **off** emprender el vuelo; (of buttons) saltar; ~ **off at a tangent** salir(se)[19] por la tangente; ~ **off the handle** encolerizarse

~ **open** (of doors *etc*) abrirse (*past part* abierto) de repente

~ **out at** atacar[4] violentamente

~ **over** sobrevolar (ue)[1a]

flyer aviador *m*; (airwoman) aviadora; (train) tren rápido

flying *n* vuelo; *adj* volante; (of aviation) de aviación; (fast) rápido; **with** ~ **colours** con mucho éxito; ~ **accident** accidente de avión; ~**boat** hidroavión *m*; ~ **column** *mil* cuerpo volante; ~**field** campo de aviación; ~**fish** pez *m* volador; ~ **jib** *naut* petifoque *m*; ~**kit** equipo de volar; ~**machine** avión (-ones) *m*; ~ **saucer** platillo volante; ~**squad** equipo volante; ~ **start** salida lanzada; **get off to a** ~ **start** empezar (ie)[2a+7] muy felizmente; ~**test** examen (-ámenes) *m* de pilotaje

foal *n* potro; *v* parir (la yegua)

foam *n* espuma; ~**extinguisher** extintor *m* de espuma; ~**rubber** goma espuma; *v* espumar; ~ **with rage/at the mouth** echar espuma por la boca

foaming espumoso

f.o.b. (**free on board**) f.a.b. (franco a bordo)

fob *n* faltriquera del reloj; *v* ~ **off** dejar (un propósito) con excusas; ~ **off with** hacer[19] aceptar por engaño

focal focal; ~ **distance/length** distancia focal; ~ **point** punto focal

focus *n* foco; **in** ~ enfocado; **out of** ~ desenfocado; *v* enfocar[4]; ~ **attention**

on concentrar(se) en

focusing *n* enfoque; *adj* de enfoque; ~-
eyepiece ocular *m* de enfoque; ~-**lens**
objetivo del visor

fodder forraje *m*

foe enemigo

foetal fetal

foetus feto

fog *n* niebla; *phot* velo; *fig* confusión *f*;
~-**bank** masa (densa) de niebla; ~-
bound inmovilizado por la niebla; ~-
horn sirena de niebla; ~-**signal** señal *f*
de niebla; *v phot* velar(se); ~ **an issue**
oscurecer[14] un asunto

fogey viejo de ideas anticuadas; *fam*
viejo chocho

foggy nebuloso; **it is** ~ **today** hay niebla
hoy; *phot* velado; *fig* confuso

foible flaqueza *m*

foil *n* (fencing) florete *m*; ('silver paper')
papel *m* de estaño; (contrast) con-
traste; **serve as a** ~ **for** servir (i)[3] de
contraste a; **he is a good** ~ **for his
wife's repartee** él hace resaltar las
agudezas de su esposa; **kitchen-**~
aluminio de cocina; *v* frustrar

foist on lograr con engaño que uno
acepte

fold *n*+*geol* pliegue *m*; (wrinkle)
arruga; (for sheep) redil *m*; *eccles* congregación *f*; *suff* veces *fpl*, **three**~ tres
veces; *v* doblar; ~ **one's arms** cruzarse[7] los brazos; ~ **up** *vt* doblar, (*esp*
paper) plegar (ie)[2a+5]; *vi* doblarse; *fig*
fracasar; **the firm** ~**ed up** la firma que-
bró

folder (for documents) carpeta; (prospectus) folleto

folding *n* doblamiento; (book-binding)
pliego; *adj* plegadizo; ~ **chair** silla de
tijera; ~ **screen** biombo

foliage follaje *m*

folio *n* (page) folio; (book) libro en
folio; *adj* en folio; ~ **edition** edición *f*
en folio

folk (people) gente *f*; (nation) nación
(-ones) *f*; **my** ~(**s**) mi familia; **hello** ~**s!**
¡hola amigos!; *adj* popular; ~-**dance**
danza popular/típica; ~-**lore** folklore
m; ~-**music** música popular; ~-**song**
canción popular/típica; ~-**tale** cuento
tradicional

folkloric folklórico

folklorist folklorista

follicle folículo

follow seguir (i)[3+11]; (obey) ejecutar;
(understand) entender (ie)[2b]; (watch)
observar; (be a consequence of) ser[19]
el resultado de; **from the evidence it**
~**s that** según el testimonio es
evidente que; ~ **the advice of** seguir
(i)[3+11] los consejos de; ~ **in another's
footsteps** seguir (i)[3+11] los pasos de
otro; ~ **a profession/trade** ejercer[12]
una profesión/un oficio; ~ **the news**
estar[19] al corriente; ~ **suit** jugar (ue)[1a]
el mismo palo, *fig* hacer[19] lo mismo;
have s.o. ~**ed** hacer[19] seguir a uno (by
por); **it's as** ~**s** es como sigue; ~ **on
from** ser[19] la consecuencia lógica de;
~ **through** continuar con una acción
hasta su conclusión; ~-**my-leader**
juego de seguir al primero; ~ **up**
proseguir (i)[3+11]; ~-**up** seguimiento

follower partidario; (pursuer) perseguidor; ~**s** séquito *m sing*, seguidores
mpl

following *n* séquito; (what follows) lo
siguiente; *adj* siguiente; ~ **wind** *naut*
viento en popa, *sp* viento a favor

folly locura

foment fomentar

fomentation +*med* fomento

fond cariñoso; ~ **mother** madre *f*
(demasiado) indulgente; **be** ~ **of** (a
person) estar[19] encariñado de, (a
thing) gustarle a uno, **I'm** ~ **of wine**
me gusta el vino, (an activity) ser[19]
aficionado a; **become/grow** ~ **of**
(people) tomar cariño a, (things)
aficionarse a

fondle (stroke) acariciar; (play with)
jugar (ue)[1a] con

fondness cariño; (for things) afición *f*
(for a)

font pila bautismal; *print* fundición *f*

food comida; alimento; (of animals)
pasto; **I gave him** ~ le di de comer;
it gave me ~ **for thought** me dio en
qué pensar; ~-**mixer** batidora; ~-
poisoning botulismo; ~-**safe** fresquera; ~-**stuffs** comestibles *mpl*; ~-
supplies abastecimiento de víveres;
~-**value** valor nutritivo/alimenticio

fool *n* tonto; (jester) bromista *m*+*f*;
(court jester) bufón (-ones) *m*;
(laughing-stock) hazmerreír *m*; **I'm
no** ~ no soy ningún niño; ~**'s errand**

misión f inútil; ~'s **paradise** felicidad ilusoria; **make a ~ of** ponerle[19] a uno en ridículo; **make a ~ of o.s.** ponerse[19] en ridículo; ~**hardiness** temeridad f; ~**hardy** temerario; ~**proof** a toda prueba; v engañar; ~ **about, play the ~ hacer**[19] payasadas; ~ **around with** juguetear con; ~ **away the time** malgastar el tiempo

foolery tontería

fooling n payasada; fam chunga; **no ~** hablando en serio; **I was only ~** estaba bromeando

foolish tonto; (empty-headed) insensato; (ridiculous) ridículo; (unwise) imprudente; ~ **act/thing** tontería; **for ~ reasons** por razones mpl idiotas

foolishness necedad f; (imprudence) imprudencia

foolscap papel m de folio (43 cm x 34 cm)

foot (human) pie m, sl pata; (of animal or object) pata; (measurement) pie m; **at the ~ of** al pie de; **my ~!** ¡mi tía!; **on ~** a pie; **be on one's feet** estar[19] de pie; **put one's ~ down** adoptar una actitud firme (**about** sobre); **put one's ~ in it** meter la pata; **set ~ on** pisar; **set on ~** (initiate) promover (ue)[1b]; **under~** debajo de los pies; **flat-~ed** de pies planos; ~-**and-mouth disease** glosopeda; ~**board** estribo; ~-**brake** freno de pie; ~**bridge** puente m para peatones; ~-**fall** paso; ~**hills** colinas fpl al pie de una montaña; ~**hold** pie firme m; ~**lights** candilejas fpl, fig el teatro; ~-**loose** libre; ~**man** lacayo; ~**note** anotación f (al pie de la página); ~**path** senda; ~**plate** (railway) plataforma de la cabina; ~**platemen** maquinistas mpl y fogoneros; ~**print** huella, pisada; ~-**pump** fuelle m de pie; ~-**rest** apoyapié m; ~-**rule** regla de un pie; ~**sore** con los pies doloridos; ~**step** paso; **follow in the ~steps of** seguir (i)[3+11] los pasos de; ~-**soldier** soldado de infantería; ~**stool** escabel m; ~-**sure** de pies seguros; ~-**switch** elec pedal m interruptor; ~**wear** calzado; ~**work** sp manejo de los pies; ~-**worn** (path) trillado, (person) despeado; v ~ **it** ir[19] andando; ~ **the bill** pagar[5] la cuenta, fam pagar[5] el pato

football n (game) fútbol m; (ball) balón m (de fútbol); adj futbolístico; ~ **game/match** partido de fútbol; ~ **pools** quinielas fpl, SA pronósticos deportivos; ~ **team** equipo de fútbol; ~**(ing) world** mundo futbolístico; **play ~** jugar (ue)[1a] al fútbol

footballer futbolista m

footing bui faja del cimiento; (climbing) pie m; **gain a ~** lograr establecerse; **lose one's ~** perder (ie)[2b] pie; **on an equal ~** en pie de igualdad (**with** con); **the firm is on a sound ~** la compañía tiene una base firme; **on a war ~** en pie de guerra

footling trivial

fop petimetre m

foppery afectación f

foppish afectado

for prep (duration) por (espacio de), **he sat ~ a few minutes** se quedó sentado por (espacio de) unos minutos; (in exchange ~) por, **I gave ten pesetas ~ the book** di diez pesetas por el libro; (in favour of) a favor de, **I'm (all) ~ (doing) that** estoy a favor de (hacer[19]) eso; (instead of) por, **I did it ~ her** lo hice por ella; (on account of) por, **he went to Switzerland ~ his health** él fue a Suiza por su salud; (on behalf of, for the sake of) por, **die ~ one's country** morir (ue)[2c] (past part muerto) por la patria; (purpose) para, **it is not ~ drinking** no es para beber; **it's time ~ a rest** es hora de descansar; (reason) por, **I went to the chemist's ~ aspirins** fui a la farmacia por aspirinas; (until) hasta, **leave it ~ tomorrow** déjelo hasta mañana; ~ **all that** a pesar de eso; ~ **ever (and ever)** para siempre; ~ **example** por ejemplo; ~ **fear that** por miedo de que +subj; ~ **hire** para alquilar; ~ **keeps, ~ good** para siempre; ~ **love** por amor, fig (for nothing) desinteresadamente; ~ **money** por dinero; ~ **now/the present** por ahora; ~ **my part** por mí; ~ **one's age** para la edad que tiene uno; ~ **the sake of** (a person, an ideal) por amor de; ~ **shame!** ¡qué vergüenza!; ~ **short** para abreviar; ~ **what reason?** ¿para qué?; ~ **a while** por un rato; ~ **the reason that** por la razón de que; **bends ~ five kilometres** curvas en cinco kilómetros; **he hasn't been here ~ two days** hace dos días que no está aquí; **I shall be away** ~ **a month** estaré fuera un mes; **if it were not** ~ **him/that** si no fuera por él/eso; **I'm in business** ~ **myself** tengo negocios por mi propia cuenta; **I won't be back** ~ **a week** no volveré antes de una semana; **it is easy** ~ **us to** nos es fácil +*infin*; **it's** ~ **you to decide** le toca a usted decidir; **jump** ~ **joy** saltar de alegría; **not** ~ **all the tea in China** ni por el forro; **now you're** ~ **it!** ¡ahora le va a tocar la gorda!; **play** ~ **a team** jugar (ue)[1a+5] en un equipo; **he's tall** ~ **his age** él es alto para su edad; ~ **or against** en pro o en contra; **the train** ~ **Salamanca** el tren de Salamanca; *conj* ya que, pues

forage forraje *m*; ~**-cap** gorra de cuartel; *v* forrajear; *fig* buscar[4]

foraging forraje *m*; **go** ~/**on a** ~ **expedition** ir[19] a buscar forraje

forasmuch: ~ **as** por cuanto; ya que

foray incursión *f*

forbear *v* (be patient) ser[19] paciente; ~ **to** abstenerse[19] de; ~ **with** ser[19] indulgente con

forbearance indulgencia

forbearing indulgente

forbears *see* **forebears**

forbid prohibir (**to** que +*subj*); *leg* vedar; **God** ~! ¡Dios no lo quiera!

forbidden prohibido; *leg* vedado; **smoking** ~ prohibido fumar; ~ **fruit** fruto prohibido

forbidding formidable; (unpleasant) repugnante

force *n* fuerza; *mil* cuerpo; (police) policía; ~**s** *mil* fuerzas (armadas); ~ **of gravity** fuerza de gravedad; **in** ~ en gran número; **by** ~ a la fuerza; **by** ~ **of** a fuerza de; **be in** ~ (prices) regir (i)[3], *leg* estar[19] en vigor; ~ **of habit** fuerza de la costumbre; *v* forzar (ue)[1a+7]; (compel) obligar[5]; (impose) imponer[19]; *agri*+*hort* forzar (ue)[1a+7]; ~ **a door** forzar[1a+7] una puerta; ~ **one's way** abrirse (*past part* abierto) paso a la fuerza; ~ **o.s. to** hacer[19] un esfuerzo por +*infin*; ~ **the pace** forzar (ue)[1a+7] el paso; ~ **a smile** esforzarse (ue)[1a+7] por sonreír; **I am** ~**d to tell you** me veo obligado a decirle; ~**-feed** alimentar a la fuerza; ~**-feeding** alimentación forzada

~ **back** hacer[19] retroceder

~ **down** obligar[5] a bajar; (swallow) (hacer[19]) tragar[5] a la fuerza; *aer* obligar[5] a aterrizar

~ **in** introducir[15] por fuerza; (person) obligar[5] a entrar en

~ **into** meter a la fuerza

~ **open** forzar (ue)[1a+7]; (by breaking the lock) descerrajar

~ **out** echar a la fuerza

~ **upon s.o.** forzar (ue)[1a+7] a uno a aceptar

forced forzado; (artificial) afectado; ~ **flowers** flores tempranas; ~ **labour** trabajos forzados *mpl*; ~ **landing** aterrizaje forzoso; ~ **march** marcha forzada; ~ **smile** sonrisa artificial

forceful vigoroso; (of character) dominante

forcemeat relleno

forceps *surg* pinzas *fpl*; (dentist's) tenazas *fpl* de extracción; (obstetrics) forceps *mpl*

forcible fuerte; (of character) enérgico; *lit* enérgico; ~ **entry** allanamiento de morada; ~ **feeding** alimentación forzada

forcibly a la fuerza

forcing: ~**-frame** semillero; ~**-house** invernadero

ford *n* vado; *v* vadear

fordable vadeable

fore *n* proa; **bring to the** ~ hacer[19] destacar en primer plano; *adj* delantero; *naut* de proa; ~ **and aft** de popa a proa; ~ **and aft sails** velas *fpl* al tercio; ~**arm** antebrazo; ~**castle** castillo de proa; ~**court** patio exterior; ~**finger** dedo índice; ~**foot** pata delantera, *SA* mano; ~**knowledge** presciencia; ~**land** promontorio; ~**leg** pata delantera; ~**mast** (palo del) trinquete *m*; ~**-part** parte delantera; ~**sail** trinquete *m*; ~**-sight** (of gun) punto; ~**stroke** *sp* golpe derecho

forebears *n* antepasados *mpl*

forebode presagiar

foreboding presentimiento; *fam* corazonada

forecast *n* pronóstico; *comm* previsión *f*; (football pools) acierto; *v* pronosticar[4]; (of football pools) acertar (ie)[2a]

forecaster pronosticador *m* (-ora *f*); (of football pools) acertante *m*+*f*; *meteor* meteorologista *m+f*

foreclose excluir[16]; ~ **on a mortgage** ejecutar una hipoteca

foreclosure ejecución (-ones) *f* de una hipoteca

forefathers antepasados *mpl*

forefront vanguardia

foregather *see* **forgather**

forego preceder

foregoing *n* lo que antecede; *adj* precedente

foregone decidido de antemano; ~ **conclusion** conclusión (-ones) *f* prevista

foreground: in the ~ en el primer plano

forehand directo

forehanded (looking ahead) previsor *m*; (timely) temprano

forehead frente *f*

foreign extranjero; (strange) ajeno; **it is** ~ **to his nature** es ajeno a su índole; ~ **affairs** asuntos exteriores; ~ **body** *med* cuerpo ajeno; ~-**born** nacido en el extranjero; ~ **exchange** divisas *fpl*; ~-**made** de fabricación extranjera; **Foreign Office** Ministerio de Relaciones Exteriores; ~ **trade** comercio exterior

foreigner extranjero

forelock mechón *m*; **take time by the** ~ tomar la ocasión por los cabellos

foreman capataz (-ces) *m*; (in printing works) regente *m*; *SA* caporal *m*; ~ **of the jury** presidente *m* del jurado

foremost (in position) delantero; (in quality) principal

forename nombre *m* (de pila); ~**d** susodicho

forenoon mañana

forensic forense; ~ **medicine** medicina forense

forerunner precursor *m* (-ora *f*); *mil* explorador *m*

foresee prever[19]

foreseeable previsible

foreshadow prefigurar

foreshore desplaya *m*

foreshorten escorzar[7]

foresight previsión *f*

foreskin prepucio

forest *n* bosque *m*; *adj* del bosque

forestall prevenir[19]

forester ingeniero forestal; (keeper) guardabosques *m sing+pl*

forestry silvicultura

foretaste goce anticipado

foretell pronosticar[4]

forethought providencia; premeditación *f*

forever para siempre

forewarn avisar

foreword prólogo

forfeit *n* prenda; ~**s** juego de prendas; *v* perder (ie)[2b]; *leg* perder (ie)[2b] el derecho a

forfeiture pérdida

forgather reunirse

forge *n* (fire) fragua; (blacksmith's) herrería; *metal* fundición (-ones) *f*; *v metal* forjar; (counterfeit) falsificar[4]; ~ **ahead** avanzar[7] constantemente

forger falsificador *m* (-ora *f*)

forgery falsificación (-ones) *f*

forget olvidar; **I forgot to do it** olvidé hacerlo; (leave behind) dejar olvidado; ~ **it!** *fam* ¡no se preocupe!; ~ **o.s.** propasarse; ~ **about** olvidarse de; ~-**me-not** nomeolvides *m sing*

forgetful olvidadizo

forgetfulness olvido

forgivable perdonable

forgive perdonar

forgiveness perdón *m*; **ask** ~ pedir (i)[3] perdón

forgiving clemente

forgo renunciar a

fork *n* tenedor *m*; *agri* horca; (road junction) bifurcación (-ones) *f*; (in tree) horcadura; ~-**lift truck** carretilla elevadora; *v agri* cultivar con horca; (of roads) bifurcarse[4]; ~ **left** doblar a la izquierda; ~ **out** producir el dinero, *sl* sacar la pasta

forked en forma de horca; ~ **lightning** relámpago en zigzag

forkful tenedor lleno

forlorn abandonado; (appearance) infeliz (-ces); ~ **hope** empresa desesperada

form *n* forma; **in the** ~ **of** en forma de; (bench) banco; (class) clase *f*; (condition) estado; (formality) formalidad *f*; (of person, ghost) figura; (stationery) hoja; (style) estilo; **be in great** ~ (physically) estar[19] en (gran) forma, (witty) estar[19] en vena; **for** ~'s **sake** por pura fórmula; **it is bad** ~ es de mal gusto; **it is not good** ~ no es de buena educación; **matter of** ~ pura formalidad; **in due** ~ en debida forma; *v* formar; (make up) constituir[16]; ~ **an alliance with** aliarse con; ~ **fours** *mil* formar a cuatro; ~ **a habit** adquirir (ir)[2c] la costumbre; ~ **an opinion** formular una opinión; ~ **public opinion** moldear la opinión pública; ~ **a queue** hacer[19] cola; ~ **up** *mil* alinearse

formal formal; (ceremonious) ceremonioso; (of dress) de etiqueta; ~ **agreement** contrato formal; ~ **dress** vestido de etiqueta; ~ **speech** discurso solemne; ~ **visit** visita de cumplido

formalism formalismo

formality formalidad *f*; **without formalities** sin ceremonia

formalize formalizar[7]

format formato

formation formación *f*; (order) arreglo; ~ **dancing/flying** bailar/volar en formación

formative formativo

forme *print* forma

former *n* aquél(los), aquélla(s); *adj* anterior; *fam* que fue; *suff* ex-, ~ **mayor** ex-alcalde *m*; **in** ~ **times** antiguamente

formerly antes; (in days gone by) antiguamente

formic: ~ **acid** ácido fórmico

formica formica

formidable formidable

formless informe

formula fórmula

formulate formular

fornicate fornicar[4]

fornication fornicación *f*

fornicator fornicador *m*

forsake abandonar

forswear (renounce) renunciar; *leg* (swear falsely) perjurar(se)

fort fortín *m*

forte *n* fuerte *m*; *adj mus* forte

forth (forward) (a)delante; (out) (a)fuera; **from this day** ~ de hoy en adelante; **and so** ~ y así en lo sucesivo; **come/go** ~ salir[19]; **walk back and** ~ pasear arriba y abajo

forthcoming próximo; (obliging) cooperativo

forthright (blunt) directo; (honest) recto

forthwith en el acto

fortieth cuadragésimo; *fam* cuarenta; (fraction) cuadragésima parte

fortification fortificación *f*

fortified fortificado; (of wine) encabezado

fortify fortificar[4]; ~ **o.s.** fortalecerse[14]

fortitude fortaleza

fortnight quince días *mpl*

fortnightly *adj* quincenal; *adv* cada quince días

fortress fortaleza

fortuitous fortuito

fortuity casualidad

fortunate afortunado

fortune (chance) fortuna; (wealth) fortuna; *fam* dineral *m*; **make a** ~ enriquecerse[14], *fam* hacer[19] los oros y los moros; ~-**hunter** aventurero; ~-**teller** adivino; ~-**telling** adivinanza

forty *n+adj* cuarenta *m*; **have** ~ **winks** echar una siesta

forum (place) foro; (body) tribunal *m*

forward *n sp* delantero, ~-**line** (línea) delantera; **centre-**~ delantero centro; *adj* (of position) delantero; (advanced) adelantado; (pert) descarado; ~ **delivery** pronta entrega; ~ **gears** velocidades *fpl* de avance; ~-**looking** progresivo; ~ **pass** *sp* pase adelantado; ~ **position** *mil* avanzadilla; *adv* (hacia) adelante; *naut* hacia la proa; ~**s** hacia adelante; ~ **march!** de frente ¡marcha!; **come** ~ adelantarse; **go** ~ avanzar[7]; **from that day** ~ desde aquel día en adelante; **look** ~ **to** esperar con ilusión; **the scheme is going** ~ el proyecto está en marcha; *v* (send on) reenviar; *comm* expedir (i)[3]; (promote) promover (ue)[1b]; **please** ~! ¡haga seguir!; (mail) remítase al destinatario

forwarding *comm* envío, expedición *f*; ~ **agency** agencia de embarques; ~ **agent** agente *m* expedidor; ~ **documents** documentos *mpl* de envío

forwardness precocidad *f*; *fam* descaro

fossil fósil *m*; (person) anticuado

fossilized fosilizado

foster criar; (encourage) fomentar; ~-**brother** hermano de leche; ~-**child** hijo/hija de leche; ~-**home** hogar *m* de adopción; ~-**mother** madre adoptiva; ~-**parents** padres *mpl* adoptivos

foul *n sp* falta, *SA* chapuza; *adj* asqueroso; (of air) fétido; (coarse) indecente; (despicable) despreciable; (unsporting) antideportivo; ~ **language** lenguaje obsceno; ~**-mouthed** mal hablado; ~ **play** juego antideportivo; ~**-smelling** maloliente; ~ **weather** tiempo muy malo; ~ **wind** viento contrario; **fall** ~ **of** ponerse[19] a malas con; *vt* (make dirty) ensuciar; *sp* cometer una falta contra, *naut* chocar[4]; *vi sp* violar las reglas; *naut* enredarse (en); ~**ed** enredado

foulness asquerosidad *f*; (coarseness) indecencia

found *metal* fundir; (set up) fundar; **be** ~**ed on** fundarse en; ~**ed on fact** bien fundado

foundation (creation) fundación (-ones) *f*; (endowment) dotación (-ones) *f*; (basis) base *f*; ~**s** *bui* cimientos *mpl*; **without** ~ sin justificación; **that accusation is without** ~ esa acusación es injusta; ~ **garment** corsé *m*; ~ **school** escuela dotada; ~**-stone** +*fig* primera piedra

[1] **founder** *n* fundador *m*; *metal* fundidor *m*

[2] **founder** *v* (sink) irse[19] a pique; *fig* fracasar

founding fundación *f*; *metal* fundición *f*

foundling niño expósito; ~ **hospital** casa de expósitos, inclusa

foundress fundadora

foundry fundición *f*

fount fuente *f*; *print* fundición (-ones) *f*

fountain fuente *f*; (spring) manantial *m*; (jet) chorro; ~**-head** fuente *f* (origen); ~**-pen** (pluma) estilográfica, *Arg* lapicera fuente

four *n*+*adj* cuatro *m*; ~**-course** *cul* de cuatro platos; ~**-engined plane** cuatrimotor *m*; ~**-eight time** *mus* tiempo de cuatro por ocho; ~**-figure number** número de cuatro cifras; ~ **figures** mil (libras esterlinas) o más; **it will reach** ~ **figures** llegará a mil; ~**fold** cuatro veces; ~**-footed** cuadrúpedo; ~**-time** *mus* compasillo; ~**-leaf clover** trébol *m* de cuatro hojas; ~**-legged** de cuatro patas; ~**-letter word** palabra grosera; ~**-part song** canción *f* a cuatro voces; ~**-poster** cama imperial; ~**-seater** cuatriplaza *m*; ~**some** (group of ~) grupo de cuatro, *sp* juego de cuatro personas; ~**-speed gearbox**

mot cambio de cuatro velocidades; ~**-square** (firm) firme, (of a person) sincero; ~**-stroke** *mot* de cuatro tiempos; ~**-wheel drive** *mot* tracción *f* de cuatro ruedas

fourteen *n*+*adj* catorce *m*

fourteenth décimocuarto; (of dates and monarchs) catorce

fourth *n* cuarto; *fam* cuarta parte; (of dates+monarchs) cuatro; (fraction) cuarta parte; *mus* cuarta justa; *adj* cuarto

fourthly en cuarto lugar

fowl *n* (bird) ave *f*; (poultry) ave *f* de corral; (chicken) pollo; ~**-pest** peste *f* aviar; *v* cazar[7] aves

fowling caza (de aves)

fox *n*+*fig* zorro; (vixen) raposa; ~**glove** dedalera; ~**-hole** raposera; ~**hound** perro raposero; ~**-hunt(ing)** cacería de zorros; ~**-terrier** fox-terrier *m*; ~**-trot** fox *m*; *v* (mystify) mistificar[4]

foxiness zorrería

foxy zorrero

foyer vestíbulo; *US* pasillo

fracas gresca

fraction *math* fracción (-ones) *f*; (small part) parte pequeña

fractional fraccionario

fractious peleón

fracture *n* rotura; *med* fractura; *v* romper(se) (*past part* roto); fracturar(se)

frag matar con una bomba de fragmentación

fragile frágil

fragility fragilidad *f*

fragment *n* fragmento; **break into** ~**s** *vt* fragmentar; *vi* fragmentarse, *fam* romperse (*past part* roto) en pedazos

fragmentary fragmentario

fragmentation fragmentación *f*; ~ **bomb** bomba de fragmentación

fragrance fragancia

fragrant fragante

frail frágil; (weak) débil

frailty fragilidad *f*; (weakness) debilidad *f*

frame *n* (structure) armazón *m*; *anat* talle *m*; (of bicycle) cuadro; *eng* armadura; (for embroidery) bastidor *m*; (of picture) marco; (of spectacles) armadura; ~**-of-mind** disposición *f*; ~**-up** estratagema *m* para incriminar a uno; ~**work** armazón *m*, (of government *etc*) constitución *f*; *v* (picture) enmarcar[4]; (formulate) formular; (incriminate) incriminar por estratagema; ~ **a law/contract** redactar una ley/un contrato; ~ **up a charge** forjar una acusación

franc franco

France Francia

Frances Francisca

franchise derechos *mpl* políticos

Francis Francisco

Franciscan *n + adj* franciscano

Francoism franquismo

Francoite franquista *m + f*

Frank (nationality) franco; (name) Paco

frank *n* sello de franqueo; *adj* franco; *v* franquear

frankfurter salchicha de Francfort

Frankie Paquito

frankincense incienso

franking franqueo

frankness franqueza; **with complete ~** con el corazón en la mano

frantic frenético; (despairing) desesperado; (worried) desquiciado

fraternal fraternal

fraternity (con)fraternidad *f*; *eccles* hermandad *f*; (trade association) gremio; *US* club *m* estudiantil

fraternization fraternización *f*

fraternize fraternizar[7]

fratricidal fratricida

fratricide (act) fratricidio; (person) fratricida *m + f*

fraud (action) fraude, *SA* chapuza; (financial swindle) estafa; (person) impostor *m* (-ora *f*)

fraudulence fraude *m*

fraudulent fraudulento

fraught: ~ **with** cargado de; ~ **situation** situación peligrosa

[1] **fray** *n* lucha

[2] **fray** (of cloth) *vt* deshilachar, *fam* desgastar; *vi* deshilacharse; ~**ed nerves** nervios *mpl* de punta

frazzle triza; **beat to a ~** cascar[4]

freak *n* (of nature) monstruo; (phenomenon) fenómeno; (of imagination) capricho; ~ **conditions** condiciones anormales; *v* ~ **out** volverse (ue)[1b] (*past part* vuelto) loco

freakish (capricious) caprichoso;

(grotesque) monstruoso; (unusual) anormal

freckle *n* peca; ~**d** pecoso

Frederica Federica

Frederick Federico

free *adj* libre; en libertad; (bold) atrevido; (disengaged) libre; (of persons) desocupado; (gratuitous) gratuito, *fam* sin pagar; ~ **church** iglesia no oficial; ~ **ticket** *theat* billete *m* de favor; (liberal) liberal; (loose) suelto; (self-governing) autónomo; ~ **and easy** familiar, (of persons) poco ceremonioso; ~ **of charge** gratuito; ~ **on board** franco a bordo; **be ~ from** (exempt) estar[19] exento de, (immune) ser[19] inmune contra; **be ~ to** poder[19] libremente +*infin*; **be ~ with money** ser[19] generoso, *fam* ser[19] manirroto; **give a ~ hand to** dar[19] rienda suelta a; ~ **translation** traducción *f* libre; **make ~ with** usar como si fuera suyo; **of one's own ~ will** por su propia voluntad; ~ **enterprise** libre empresa; ~-**fight**, ~-**for-all** lucha general, *fam* sarracina; ~ **flight** (de) vuelo libre; ~-**hand** a pulso; ~-**hand drawing** dibujo a mano; ~-**handed** generoso; ~-**hold** dominio absoluto; ~**hold deeds** escrituras *fpl* de dominio absoluto; ~**holder** poseedor *m* (-ora *f*) de fuero franco; ~ **kick** (saque) libre *m*; ~-**lance** independiente; ~-**lance journalist** periodista *m + f* independiente; ~ **love** amor *m* libre; ~**man** hijo de honor; ~ **market** mercado libre; **Freemason** (franc)masón *m*; **Freemasonry** (franc)masonería, *fig* compañerismo; ~ **port** *comm* puerto franco; ~-**range eggs** huevos *mpl* camperos; ~ **speech** libertad *f* de palabra; ~-**spoken** franco; ~-**style** *sp* (de estilo) libre; ~-**thinker** librepensador *m* (-ora *f*); ~-**thinking** librepensamiento; ~ **time** tiempo libre; ~ **trade** libre cambio; ~**trader** librecambista *m + f*; ~ **verse** verso libre; ~**way** autorruta; ~**wheel** *n* rueda libre, *v* ir[19] a rueda libre; ~ **will** libre albedrío; *v* libertar, liberar

freebie regalo

freedom libertad *f*; (autonomy) autonomía; (exemption) exención *f*; (immunity) inmunidad *f*; ~ **from hunger/want** inmunidad *f* contra el hambre/la carestía; (looseness) soltura; **give the ~ of the city to** nombrarle hijo predilecto de la ciudad; **receive the ~ of the city** recibir ciudadanía de honor; ~ **of speech/the press** libertad *f* de palabra/prensa; ~ **of thought/worship** libertad *f* de pensamiento/cultos; ~**-fighter** luchador *m* (-ora *f*) por la libertad

freeing liberación *f*; emancipación *f*

freely (frankly) francamente; (generously) generosamente

freeze *n* congelación *f*, ~**-up** *meteor* helada, (of water pipes) congelación *f*; ~**-dried** leofilizado; **wage-~** congelación *f* de salarios; *v* helar (ie)[2a]; *v* congelar; ~ **to death** morir (ue)[1c] (*past part* muerto) de frío; **my hands are freezing** se me hielan las manos; ~ **wages** congelar los salarios

freezer congeladora

freezing *n* congelación *f*; *adj* frigorífico; glacial; congelante; ~**-mixture** sal frigorífica; ~**-point** punto de congelación; ~ **weather** tiempo glacial

freight (load) carga; (payment) porte *m*, flete; *adj* de mercancías; ~ **car** vagón *m* de mercancías; ~ **plane** (avión) carguero; ~ **train** tren *m* de mercancías

freightage carga •

freighter fletador *m*; (ship) buque *m* de carga

French *n* (people) los franceses *mpl*; (language) francés *m*; *adj* francés; ~ **bean** judía verde; **french chalk** talco; ~ **fries** (potatoes) patatas fritas, *SA* papas fritas; ~ **horn** trompa (de pistones/de cilindros); **french letter** goma *vulg*, camisa de amor; **french polish** barniz *m* para los muebles; ~ **poodle** perro de lanas; **french window** puerta ventana; **take** ~ **leave** despedirse (i)[3] a la francesa

Frenchie gabacho

Frenchified afrancesado

Frenchman francés (-eses) *m*

Frenchwoman francesa

frenzied frenético

frenzy frenesí *m*; delirio

frequency frecuencia

frequent *adj* frecuente; *v* frecuentar

frequenter frecuentador *m*

frequently a menudo

fresco fresco

fresh fresco; (new) nuevo; (newly arrived) recién llegado; (not tinned) fresco; (impertinent) fresco, descarado; ~ **air** aire fresco/puro; **have/ take a breath of** ~ **air** ventilarse un poco; ~**water** agua dulce, *SA* bisoño; ~**water fish** pez *m* de río; ~ **wind** viento fresco

freshen (of wind) levantarse

freshly nuevamente; (recently) recientemente; ~ **painted** recién pintado

freshman estudiante *m* de primer año

freshness frescura; (newness) novedad *f*

[1] **fret** (worry) inquietarse

[2] **fret** *carp* adornar con calados; ~**saw** sierra de calados; ~**work** calado

fretful inquieto

Freudian freudiano

friable friable

friar fraile *m*; (title) Fray

friary convento de frailes

fricassee fricasé *m*

fricative fricativo

friction fricción; (ideological) choque *m* de ideas

Friday viernes *m*; **Good** ~ Viernes Santo

fridge frigorífico

fried frito

friend amigo, amiga; ~ **of mine/his** amigo mío/suyo; ~**(s)!** (to a sentry) ¡gente de paz!; **be** ~**s with** ser[19] amigo de; **make** ~**s with** establecer[14] amistad con; (with s.o. of opposite sex) *fam* ligarse[5] con; (Quaker) cuáquero

friendless sin amigos

friendly amistoso, simpático; ~ **country** país amigo; ~ **game** partido amistoso; ~ **place** lugar *m* acogedor; ~ **smile** sonrisa acogedora

friendship amistad *f*

frieze *text* frisa; *archi* friso

frigate fragata

fright (shock) susto; **you gave me a** ~ usted me dio un susto; (person) espantajo; *fam* pinta *m*+*f*; **look a** ~ estar[19] hecho una pinta

frighten (shock) asustar; (terrify) atemorizar[7]; ~ **away/off** espantar; **be** ~**ed** asustarse, espantarse; **be** ~**ed out of one's wits** estar[19] muerto de miedo

frightful de miedo; *fam* tremendo

frightfulness horror *m*

frigid frígido

frigidaire frigorífico

frigidity frigidez *f*

frill volante; **~s** (superfluous adornments) ringorrangos *mpl*; (on a woman) perifollos *mpl*; *fig* afectación *f*

frilly (clothes) con volantes; (speech) afectado

fringe (tasselled border) fleco; (edge) orla; (hair) flequillo; **on the ~ of** al margen de; **~ benefits** beneficios complementarios; *v* **~ with** orlar de

frippery perifollos *mpl*

frisbee disco-juguete

frisk saltar; (search) cachear, *SA* esculcar[4]

frisking cacheo

frisky juguetón

fritter *n* fritura; *v* **~ away** disipar; (money) malgastar, *fam* triturar

frivolity frivolidad *f*

frivolous frívolo; (trivial) trivial

frizz rizo

frizzle *cul* freír (i)[3] (*past part* frito) chisporroteando; (noise) sisear

frizzy rizado

frock vestido; **~-coat** levita

frog rana; **have a ~ in the throat** padecer[14] carraspera; **~-man** hombre-rana *m*; **~-march** llevar a un preso empleando la fuerza

Frog(gy) (Frenchman) gabacho

frolic *n* (game) juego; (mischief) travesura; *v* (play) juguetear; (get into mischief) hacer travesuras

frolicsome (playful) juguetón; (mischievous) travieso

from (place) de, desde, **~ above/below** desde arriba/abajo; (number) de, **she counted ~ one to twenty** ella contó de uno a veinte; (cause) de, por, **he died ~ hunger/lack of food** él murió de hambre/por falta de comida; (time) desde, de, **~ Tuesday to Friday** desde martes hasta viernes; **~ time immemorial** desde los tiempos más remotos; (price) desde, **ties ~ fifty pesetas** corbatas desde cincuenta pesetas en adelante; **~ day to day** de día en día; **~ life/nature** del natural; **~ memory** de memoria; **~ this day forward** (des)de hoy en adelante; **~ head to foot** de pies a cabeza; **~ time to time** de

vez en cuando; **~ what I see** por lo que veo; **~ what you say** según lo que usted dice; **judging ~ appearances** a juzgar por las apariencias; **tell her this ~ me** dígale a ella de mi parte

~ afar (des)de lejos

~ among de entre

~ henceforth desde ahora en adelante

~ on high desde lo alto

frond fronda

front *n* parte delantera; *meteor+ mil+pol* frente *m*; *theat* auditorio; (façade) fachada; (of shirt) pechera; *fig* apariencia falsa; *adj* delantero; (first) primero; **go in ~** (lead the way) tomar la delantera; **in ~ of** delante de; (facing) frente a; **in the ~ of the book** al principio del libro; **the number on the ~ of his cap** el número en la parte delantera de su gorro; **she likes to take the ~ seat** *fig* a ella le gusta figurar; **~ door** puerta principal/de la calle; **~ elevation** elevación frontal; **~-end loader** avión que se carga por delante; **~ line** *mil* primera línea (de fuego); **~-mounted engine** motor delantero; **~ page** primera página/plana; **~-page news** noticias *fpl* muy importantes; **~ porch** soportal *m*; **~ room** habitación *f* que da a la calle; **~ row** primera fila, (*cin+theat+bullring*) delantera; **~ seat** asiento delantero; **~ tooth** diente incisivo; **~ view** vista de frente; **~-wheel drive** tracción delantera; *v* **~ on to** dar[19] a

frontage frontal *m* de carretera; **fifty-metre ~** frontal *m* de cincuenta metros

frontal frontal; *mil* de frente

frontier *n* frontera; *fam* raya; *fig* límite; *adj* fronterizo

frontispiece portada

frost escarcha; **~-bite** congelación *f*; **~-bitten** congelado; **~-bound** parado por el hielo

frosted escarchado; **~ glass** vidrio esmerilado

frosting *cul* alcorza

frosty escarchado; *fig* glacial

froth *n* espuma; *fig* frivolidad *f*; *v* echar espuma; **~ at the mouth** echar espumajos por la boca

frothy espumoso; *fig* frívolo

frown *n* ceño; **with a ~** frunciendo el

ceño; *v* fruncir[13] el ceño; ~ **at** mirar
con ceño; ~ **on** desaprobar (ue)[1a]
frowzy desaseado
frozen helado, congelado; *geog* glacial;
~ **over** cubierto de hielo; **I am** ~ estoy
helado (de frío); ~ **assets** valores
congelados; ~ **foods** alimentos congelados; ~ **wages** salarios congelados
fructify fructificar[4]
frugal frugal; (thrifty) ahorrador (-ora
f)
frugality frugalidad *f*
fruit *n* fruta; *fig* fruto; ~**-bearing** frutal;
~ **cake** plumcake *m*; ~ **dish** frutero;
~**-juice** jugo de fruta; ~**-knife** cuchillo
de postre; ~ **pie** empanadilla de fruta;
~ **salad** macedonia de frutas; ~ **stall**
puesto de frutas; ~ **store** frutería; ~**-
tree** árbol *m* frutal; *v*+*fig* dar[19] fruto;
dried ~ frutos secos
fruiterer frutero; ~**'s** (shop) frutería
fruitful (fertile) fructífero; (profitable)
provechoso; (productive) productivo
fruitiness (smell) olor *m* a fruta; (taste)
sabor *m* a fruta
fruition fruición *f*; **come to** ~ realizarse[7]
fruitless infructuoso; **he avoided** ~ **arguments** él evitaba discusiones inútiles
fruity de fruta; (taste) con sabor a fruta;
(voice) melodioso; (obscene) verde
frump espantajo
frumpish fuera de moda
frustrate frustrar
frustration frustración *f*
fry *n cul* fritada; (fish) pececillos *mpl*;
small ~ gente menuda; *v* freír (i)[3]
frying freír *m*; ~**-pan** sartén (-enes) *f*;
out of the ~**-pan into the fire** de mal en
peor
fuchsia fuscia; *fam* pendientes *mpl* de la
reina
fuck *n vulg sl* polvo; *v*+*interj* joder; ~
off! ¡vete a la mierda!; ~**ing** *adj* jodido
fuddled emborrachado
fuddy-duddy viejo de ideas antiguas
fudge caramelo de azúcar y leche
fuel *n* combustible *m*; *esp aer*+*mot*
carburante *m*; *fig* pábulo; ~ **cell** *space*
célula de combustible; ~ **filter** filtro de
gas-oil/de gasolina; ~**-oil** gas-oil *m*;
~**-pipe** tubería de alimentación; ~**-
pressure gauge** manómetro de combustible; ~**-pump** *mot* bomba de
gasolina; ~ **tank** tanque *m* (de

gasolina *etc*); *v* aprovisionar(se) de
combustible
fuelling abastecimiento (de combustible)
fug atmósfera cargada
fugitive *n* fugitivo; *adj* fugaz; *fig* de
interés pasajero; (of persons) fugitivo
fugue fuga
fulcrum fulcro
fulfil llevar a cabo; **this machine** ~**s a
dual purpose** esta máquina realiza dos
trabajos; (obey) obedecer[14]; (satisfy)
llenar
fulfilment cumplimiento; (achievement)
logro; (obedience) ejecución *f*
full lleno; (of vehicle *etc*) completo; (abundant) abundante; (complete) ínte-
gro; (detailed) detallado; (thinking
of) pensando en, **he is** ~ **of his
own problems** él está pensando en sus
propios problemas; (satisfied) harto;
fig pleno, **life** ~ **of sorrow** vida llena de
dolor; **at** ~ **blast** a toda velocidad;
with ~ **board** con pensión completa;
in ~ **colour** a todo color; **in** ~ **dress**
(formal attire) vestido de etiqueta; ~
dress uniform uniforme *m* de gala; ~
dress-rehearsal ensayo general; ~ **employment** pleno empleo; **at** ~ **gallop** a
galope tendido; ~**-grown** desarrollado; ~ **house** (at cards) máxima,
cin+*theat* cine/teatro completo; ~**-
length** (portrait) de cuerpo entero;
~**-length film** (película de) largo metraje *m*; ~ **moon** luna llena; ~ **name**
nombre *m* y apellidos; ~ **price** precio
íntegro; **with** ~ **sail** a toda vela; ~**-
scale** de tamaño natural; ~ **skirt** falda
de vuelo; **at** ~ **speed** a toda velocidad;
~ **speed ahead!** ¡avante a toda
máquina!; **at** ~ **steam** a todo vapor; ~
stop punto; **come to a** ~ **stop** *fig*
pararse en seco; **in** ~ **swing** en plena
actividad; **at** ~ **throttle** a todo gas; **at**
~ **tilt** a todo correr; ~**-time** jornada
completa; **in** ~ por completo; **in** ~
view enteramente visible; **to the** ~
completamente; **he won by a** ~ **minute**
él ganó por un minuto largo; **on a** ~
stomach en plena digestión
fuller batanero; ~**'s earth** tierra de
batán
fullness plenitud *f*; (of dress) amplitud *f*;
(corpulence) gordura; **in the** ~ **of time**

a su debido tiempo

fully completamente, enteramente; ~ **fashioned** de costura francesa; ~ **fledged** *fig* hecho y derecho

fulminate *n* fulminato; *v* fulminar; ~ **against** tronar (ue)[1a] contra

fulsome servil; (exaggerated) exagerado

fumble (grope) ir[19] a tientas; (bungle) chapucear; ~ **for** buscar[4] a tientas; ~ **with** manejar torpemente; ~ **the ball** dejar caer la pelota

fumbling inhábil

fume *v* echar humo/gas; (with rage) encolerizarse[7]

fumes humo; gas *m*

fumigate fumigar[5]

fumigation fumigación *f*

fuming encolerizado

fun (joy) alegría; (amusement) diversión *f*; (jocularity) broma; **in** ~ en broma; **be** (**great**) ~ ser[19] (muy) divertido; **have** ~ divertirse (ie)[2b], *fam* darse[19] la fiesta; ~**fair** parque *m* de atracciones; **make** ~ **of, poke** ~ **at** burlarse de

function *n* (purpose) función *f*; (ceremony) ceremonia; (task) cargo; *v* funcionar

functional funcional

functionary *n* funcionario; *adj* funcional

functioning funcionamiento

fund *n* fondo (**for/in aid of** para); ~s (resources) fondos *mpl*; **be in** ~s tener fondos

fundamental *n* principio; **get down to** ~s ir[19] al grano; *adj* fundamental

fundamentalism fundamentalismo

fundamentalist fundamentalista *m+f*

funeral *n* (church ceremony) funeral *mpl*; (at cemetery) entierro; **go to the** ~ **of** asistir a los funerales de; *adj* fúnebre; ~ **director** director *m* de pompas fúnebres; ~**-house,** ~**-parlour** funeraria; ~**-march** marcha *f* fúnebre; ~ **procession** cortejo fúnebre; ~**-pyre** pira funeraria; ~ **service** misa de réquiem/de difuntos

funereal fúnebre

fungicide fungicida *m*

fungous fungoso

fungus hongo

funicular (**railway**) (ferrocarril) funicular *m*

funk *n* (fear) miedo; *fam* canguelo; **in a**

~ aterrado, *vulg* cagado (de miedo)

funky *sl* fabuloso

funnel *n* (utensil) embudo; *naut* chimenea; *v* canalizar[7]

funnily (*see* **funny**) de una manera cómica/rara; ~ **enough** aunque parezca increíble

funny cómico; (odd) raro; **it struck me as** ~ **that** (comical) me hizo gracia que, (odd) me pareció raro que +*subj*; (mysterious) misterioso; **I had a** ~ **feeling** experimenté una sensación rara; ~**-bone** hueso de la alegría

fur *n* (of animal) piel *f*; (deposit in pipes *etc*) sarro; (on tongue) saburra; *adj* de piel; ~**-coat** abrigo de pieles; ~**-collar** cuello de piel; ~ **trade** peletería; ~**-trader** peletero; *v* (of pipes *etc*) formarse sarro

furbish pulir

furious furioso; **at a** ~ **pace** a toda velocidad

furl (flag) plegar (ie)[2a+5]; (sail) aferrar

furlong estadio

furlough *n* permiso; **on** ~ de permiso; *v* dar[19] permiso a

furnace horno

furnish amueblar; (provide) proveer[17] de; ~ **information** facilitar información; ~ **proof** ofrecer[14] una prueba; ~ **with** equipar con; ~**ed** amueblado; ~**ed with** provisto de

furnisher vendedor *m* de muebles; ~**'s** (shop) tienda de muebles

furnishing provisión *f*; ~**s** mobiliario; (accessories) accesorios *mpl*

furniture muebles *mpl*; **piece of** ~ mueble *m*; ~ **dealer/maker** mueblista *m*; ~**-polish** crema para muebles; ~**-van** camión (-ones) *m* de mudanzas

furore furor *m*

furred (of tongue) cubierta de saburra, *fam* sucia; (of kettle *etc*) cubierto de sarro

furrier peletero; ~**'s** peletería

furrow *n* *agri* surco; (on brow) arruga; *v* *agri* surcar[4]; ~ **one's brow** fruncir[13] el entrecejo

furry peludo

further *adj* (distance) más lejano; (additional) adicional; **on the** ~ **side** al otro lado; ~ **degree** (university) grado superior a la licenciatura/al doctorado; ~ **education** educación *f* después de la segunda enseñanza; **till ~ orders** hasta nueva orden; *adv* (distance) más lejos; (in addition) además, ~ **on** más allá; *v* (promote) adelantar, fomentar; (aid, support) apoyar

furtherance promoción *f*; (aid) apoyo

furthermore además

furthermost más lejano

furthest *adj* más lejano; *adv* (lo) más lejos; **at the ~** a lo sumo

furtive furtivo

furtively a hurtadillas

fury furia; **like a ~** como una furia

furze tojo

fuse *n* (explosive) mecha; *elec* fusible *m*, *fam* plomo; **the ~ has blown** se ha fundido el plomo; **~-box** caja de fusibles; **~-wire** fusible; *v* fundirse

fuselage fuselaje *m*

fusible fundible

fusilier fusilero

fusillade descarga cerrada; *fig* torrente *m*

fusion fusión *f*; *metal+fig* fundición *f*

fuss (noise, bustle) jaleo; (exaggerated display) aspaviento; (formalities) ceremonia; (scandal) escándalo; (trouble) lío; **kick up a ~** dar[19] cuatro voces; **make a ~** armar un lío/escándalo; **make a ~ of** ser[19] muy atento a, (child) hacer[19] carantoñas; **don't make a ~!** (don't trouble yourself) ¡nada de etiqueta!; **don't make such a ~** no es para tanto; **~-pot** persona muy exigente; *vi* agitarse; *vt* poner[19] nervioso; ~ **around/about** andar de acá para allá

fussy (particular) exigente, *fam* especial; (nervous) inquieto, nervioso; **be ~** (selective) **about** ser exigente con; **she was never ~ about what people gave her** ella nunca fue escrupulosa en lo que la gente le daba

fustian fustán *m*

fusty mohoso; *fig* (of ideas) pasado de moda

futile inútil

futility inutilidad *f*

futon colchón delgado

future *n* porvenir *m*; *fam* el día de mañana; **in ~** de aquí en adelante; **in the near ~** en fecha próxima; **what the ~ has in store (for us)** lo que (nos) reserva el porvenir; *adj* futuro, venidero; **for ~ reference** para información futura; **~ tense** tiempo futuro

futureless sin porvenir

futuristic futurista

futurity lo futuro

fuzz pelusa; (policeman) *sl* bofia *m*

fuzzy (covered with fuzz) velloso; (of hair) muy encrespado; (indistinct) indistinto

G

g (letter) ge *f*; **G** *mus* sol *m*
gab parloteo; **gift of the ~** mucha labia
gabardine gabardina
gabble *n* (chatter) cotorreo; (quick talking) algarabía; *v* (chatter) cotorrear; (talk quickly) hablar atropelladamente; (pronounce badly) pronunciar mal
gabbler cotorrón *m* (-ona *f*)
gabion gavión (-ones) *m*
gable *archi* faldón (-ones) *m*; **~-end** alero
Gabon el Gabón
Gabonese gabonés *m* (-esa *f*)
¹ gad lingote *m*
² gad: ~ about pendonear
gadabout *n* persona callejera; *adj* callejero
gadder callejero
gadding callejeo, vagabundeo
gadfly tábano
gadget artefacto, chisme *m*
gadgetry chismería
gadwall *orni* ánade friso
Gael gaélico
Gaelic gaélico
¹ gaff (fish-spear) garfio; *naut* (boat-hook) bichero
² gaff: blow the ~ chivarse, *sl* soplar
gaffe plancha
gaffer (boss) patrón *m*, (foreman) capataz (-ces); (old man) vejete *m*
gaffle espolón *m*
gag *n* mordaza; *theat* morcilla; *v* amordazar[7]; *theat* meter morcilla
gage prenda
gaggle *orni* bandada; *v* graznar
gaiety alegría
¹ gain *n* (financial) ganancia; (advantage) provecho; (increase) aumento; *v* ganar; aprovechar; aumentar; (of clocks) adelantar; **~ on** ir[19] alcanzando; **~the day** vencer[14]
² gain (mortise) *n* mortaja; *v* hacer[19] una mortaja
gainer ganador *m* (-ora *f*)

gainful provechoso, ganancioso; (paid) remunerado
gainfulness provecho, ganancia
gainsay contradecir[19]
gainsaying contradicción *f*; **there's no ~** no puede negarse
gait modo de andar
gaiter polaina
gala *n* fiesta; *adj* de fiesta
galactic galáctico
galantine *cul* galantina
galaxy galaxia; **war of the galaxies** guerra de las galaxias
galbanum *bot* gálbano
gale (*usu* from north or west) galerna; (*usu* from south or south-west) vendaval *m*
Galilean galileo
galipot galipot(e) *m*
gall *n anat* bilis *f*; hiel *f*; (on animals) rozadura; *fig* amargura; **~-bladder** vejiga (de la hiel); **~stone** cálculo hepático; *v* irritar
gallant *n* galán (-anes) *m*; *adj* (chivalrous) caballeresco; (amorous) galante; (brave) valiente
gallantry galantería; (bravery) valor *m*
galleon galeón (-ones) *m*
gallery galería; *theat* paraíso; (audience) galería; (of paintings) museo; **play to the ~** actuar para la galería
galley (ship) galera (de esclavos); (rowing-boat) falúa (de capitán); (kitchen) cocina; *print* galera; **~-proof** galerada; **~-slave** galeote *m*
Gallic galo
gallicism galicismo
galling irritante
gallivant callejear; *fam* pindonguear
gallivanting callejero; **go ~** ir[19] de pindongueo
gallon galón (-ones) *m* (UK 4,54 litros; USA 3,78 litros)
gallop *n* (fast pace) galope *m*; (fast horse-ride) galopada; **go at full ~** ir[19] a rienda suelta; *vi* galopar; *vt*

733

hacer[19] galopar
~ **away** marcharse a galope
~ **past** desfilar a galope
~ **through** cruzar[7] a galope; *fig* hacer[19] muy de prisa
galloping +*med* galopante
gallows horca; ~-**bird** carne *f* de horca
Gallup: ~ **poll** sondeo Gallup
galore en abundancia
galoshes chanclos *mpl*
galvanize galvanizar[7]; *fig* (shock) escandalizar[7]
galvanometer galvanómetro
gambit (chess) gámbito; *fig* táctica
gamble *n* jugada; *fig* riesgo; **it's a** ~ es un gran riesgo; *v* jugar (ue)[1a]; apostar; *fig* arriesgar[5]; ~ **on the Stock Exchange** jugar en la bolsa; ~ **away** perder (ie)[2b] en el juego; ~ **everything** jugar el todo por el todo
Gambian gambiano
gambler jugador *m* (-ora *f*); (impulsive) tahur *m*
gambling *n* juego; (impulsive) tahurería; *adj* de juego; ~-**den** garito de tahurería
gamboge gutagamba
gambol *n* brinco; *v* brincar[4]
[1] **game** *n* juego; (match) partido; **what's his** ~? ¿qué está haciendo él?; ~**s** deportes *mpl*, (athletics) juegos *mpl* atléticos; ~**s master/mistress** profesor *m*/profesora de deportes/gimnasia; ~ **of chance** juego de azar; *fig* **the** ~ **is up** ya se acabó; **make** ~ **of** burlarse de; **play a** ~ jugar[1a] un partido; **play the** ~ *fig* jugar [1a+5] limpio; **he plays a good/bad** ~ él juega bien/mal; (hunting) caza; ~-**bag** morral *m* ; ~-**bird** ave *f* de caza; ~ **cock** gallo de pelea; ~ -**keeper** guardamonte *m*; ~-**laws** ley *f* de caza y pesca; ~-**licence** licencia de caza; ~-**reserve** coto de caza; ~**smanship** arte *m* de desmoralizar al oponente para ganar un juego; *adj* (brave) valiente; (hunting) de caza; **I'm** ~ **for** estoy dispuesto a; **she is** ~ **for anything** ella se atreve a todo; **he put up a** ~ **fight** se defendió con brío; ~, **set and match** tanto, set y partido; *v* jugar (ue)[1a+5] (por dinero)
[2] **game** (crippled) *see* **gammy**
gamely con valor
gameness valentía

gamester jugador *m*
gamete gameto
gaming *n* juego; *adj* de juego; ~-**den,** ~-**table** garito/mesa de juego
gamma gama; ~-**radiation** irradiación *f* de rayos gama; ~-**ray** rayo gama (rayos gama)
gammon jamón (ahumado)
gammy inútil; **he has a** ~ **hand** le falta el uso de una mano
gamut gama
gander ganso (macho)
gang *n* pandilla; (of workmen) cuadrilla; ~ **member** pandillero; ~-**plank** pasarela, *naut* plancha; ~-**warfare** guerra entre pandillas; *v* ~ **up** organizarse[7] en cuadrilla; ~ **up on** conspirar contra; ~ **up with** conchabarse con
ganger capataz (-ces) *m* de una cuadrilla
gangling delgaducho
ganglion ganglio
gangrene gangrena
gangrenous gangrenoso
gangster gángster *m*
gangsterism gangsterismo
gangway pasarela; (passage between seats) pasillo; *naut* (door in ship's side) portalón *m*; (from ship to quay) escala; ~! ¡abran paso!
gannet alcatraz (-ces) *m* común; *fig* comilón *m* (-ona *f*)
gantry caballete *m*; (railway) puente *m* transversal de señales; ~-**crane** puente grúa *m*
gaol *n* cárcel *f*; (for worst criminals) presidio; *v* encarcelar; ~-**bird** (prisoner) pájaro de celda, (ex-prisoner) expresidiario; ~-**break** fuga de una cárcel; ~-**sentence** condena
gaoler carcelero
gap abertura; (breach) brecha; *geog* (fissure) quebrada; (crack) hendidura; (empty space) vacío; (hole) boquete *m*; (in mountain range) paso; (space between two things) espacio; (in the wall) portillo; ~-**toothed** de dientes separados
gape (stare in amazement) quedar embobado (*at* de); (look stupidly around) mirar boquiabierto; (yawn) bostezar[7]
gaping boquiabierto; (yawning) que bosteza; ~ **wound** herida abierta
garage *n* garaje *m*; (for buses) cochera;

~ **proprietor** garajista *m*; *v* poner[19] en garaje

garb *n* vestido; *v* vestir(se) (i)[3]

garbage basura; ~-**can** cubo de basura; ~-**collection** recolección *f* de basura; ~-**collector** basurero

garbled (of speech) incomprensible; (of a text) falseado (por selección)

garden *n* jardín (-ines) *m*; (for vegetables) huerto; *fig* (fertile region) huerta; **Garden of Edén** jardín del Edén; ~-**city** ciudad *f* jardín; ~-**party** fiesta de jardín; ~-**suburb** barrio jardín; ~-**warbler** *orni* andahuertas *m sing+pl*; *v* trabajar en el jardín/huerto

gardener jardinero; (vegetable-~) hortelano

gardenia gardenia

gardening jardinería

gargantuan gigantesco

gargle *n* (action) gárgaras *fpl*; (liquid) gargarismo; *v* hacer[19] gárgaras; *SA* gargarear

gargoyle gárgola

garish chillón (-ona)

garishness cursilería

garland *n* guirnalda; *archi* festón *m*; *v* enguirnaldar

garlic ajo; *cul* **with** ~ al ajillo

garment prenda (de vestir); ~s ropa *f sing*

garner almacenar

garnet granate *m*

garnish (decorate) (ad)ornar; *cul* aderezar[7]; ~**ed with** aderezado con

garnishing, garniture adorno

garret desván (-anes) *m*

garrison *n* guarnición *f*; ~ **town** plaza de armas; *v* guarnecer[14]

garrotte *n* garrote *m*; *v* ajusticiar a garrote

garrulity garrulidad *f*

garrulous gárrulo

garter liga; **Order of the Garter** Orden *m* de la Jarretera; ~-**belt** liguero *m sing+pl*

gas *n* gas *m*; *mil* gas *m* asfixiante; *min* grisú *m*; (petrol) gasolina; (talk) parloteo; **I'm out of** ~ no me queda gasolina; **step on the** ~ acelerar (la marcha); ~-**attack** ataque *m* con gases asfixiantes; ~-**bag** charlatán *m* (-ana *f*); ~-**burner** mechero de gas; ~-**canister** *mil* granada de gas; ~-

chamber cámara de gas; ~-**cooker** cocina de gas; ~-**engine** motor de gas; ~-**fire** estufa de gas; ~-**fitter** gasista *m*; ~-**gauge** medidor *m* de gasolina; ~-**holder** gasómetro; ~-**jet** mechero de gas, (flame) llama de gas; ~-**light** luz *f* de gas; ~-**lighter** encendedor *m* de gas; ~-**main** cañería principal de gas; ~-**mantle** camiseta incandescente; ~-**mask** careta antigás; ~-**meter** contador *m* de gas; ~-**oil** gas-oil *m*; ~-**pipe** tubería de gas; ~-**pipeline** gasoducto; ~-**proof** a prueba de gas(es); ~-**ring** hornillo de gas; ~-**station** gasolinera; ~-**stove** cocina de gas; **portable** ~-**stove** hornillo *m* de gas; ~-**turbine** turbina de gas; ~-**works** fábrica de gas; *v* asfixiar con gas; *mil* atacar[4] con gas; (talk) parl(ote)ar

Gascon *n+adj* gascón *m* (-ona) *f*

Gascony Gascuña

gaseous gaseoso

gash *n* herida abierta; *v* acuchillar

gasify gasificar[4]

gasket *mech* junta (de culata); *naut* tomador *m*

gasoline gasolina

gasometer gasómetro

gasp *n* boqueada; **at the last** ~ al último extremo; *v* boquear; ~ **for breath** jadear; ~ **for** *fig* anhelar; ~ **out** decir[19] con voz entrecortada

gassing asfixia *m* con gas

gassy gaseoso

gastric gástrico; ~ **fever** dispepsia aguda; ~ **ulcer** úlcera de estómago

gastritis gastritis *f*

gastronome gastrónomo

gastronomic gastronómico

gastronomy gastronomía

gat arma de fuego; revolver

gate *n* puerta; (small) portón; (of iron) verja; (at level crossing) barrera; (of lock) compuerta; **a good** ~ **is expected for today's match** se espera mucho público para el partido de hoy; ~-**crash** colarse (ue)[1a] en; ~-**crasher** intruso; ~-**keeper** guardabarrera *m*; ~-**legged table** mesa de alas abatibles; ~-**money** ingresos de entrada; ~-**post** soporte *m* de la puerta; ~-**way** (puerta de) entrada; *v* hacer[19] volver a cierta hora, no dejar salir (a un estudiante)

gather *vt* reunir; (collect) acumular; ~ **flowers** (re)coger[8] flores; (dressmaking) fruncir[13]; **dress ~ed at the waist** vestido fruncido a la cintura; (infer) deducir[15]; ~ **from** inferir(se) (ie)[2c] de; **I ~ from Mary** según lo que me dice María; ~ **dust** llenarse de polvo; ~ **speed** cobrar velocidad; ~ **strength** cobrar fuerzas; ~ **in** (crop) (re)coger[8]; ~ **up the threads** *fig* recoger[8] los hilos; *vi* (~ **together**) juntarse; *med* supurar

gathering *n* (of crops) recolección *f*; (of taxes) recaudación *f*; (of people) reunión *f*; *med* absceso; **social ~** fiesta; (on dress) fruncimiento, pliegues *mpl*

gauche torpe

gaucherie torpeza

gaudily ostentosamente

gaudiness ostentación *f*

gaudy llamativo

gauge *n* (measurement) calibre *m*; (instrument) calibrador *m*; (dial) indicador *m*; (of railway track) entrevía, *SA* trocha; **narrow-~/broad-~ railway** ferrocarril *m* de vía estrecha/ancha; *v* calibrar; *fig* estimar

Gaul *n* Galia; (person) galo

gaunt flaco; (of building) lúgubre

gauntlet guante *m*; **throw down the ~** arrojar el guante; **take up the ~** recoger[8] el guante; **run the ~** correr por entre dos filas de personas hostiles

gauze gasa

gauzy diáfano

gavel martillo

gavotte gavota

gawky desgarbado

gay *n* invertido, homosexual; *adj* (happy) alegre; (lively) animado; (of colours) brillante; **lead a ~ life** llevar una vida de placeres; **make ~** alegrar; **the ~ twenties** los felices años veinte

gaze *n* mirada fija; **direct one's ~ on** dirigir[9] una mirada hacia; *v* ~ **at** mirar con fijeza; ~ **upon** contemplar

gazebo mirador *m*

gazelle gacela

gazette *n* gaceta; *v* nombrar en la gaceta oficial

gazetteer diccionario geográfico

G-clef clave *m* de sol

[1] **gear** *n* (attire) atavío(s); (equipment) equipo; *naut* aparejo; (tools) herramientas *fpl*; *mech* engranaje *m*; *mot* marcha; **~s** velocidades *fpl*; **be in ~** estar[19] engranado; **put in ~** engranar; **(in) bottom/low/first ~** (en) primera velocidad; **(in) neutral ~** (en) punto muerto; **(in) reverse ~** (en) marcha atrás; **(in) second ~** (en) segunda velocidad; **(in) top ~** (en) tercera/cuarta velocidad; **out of ~** desengranado, *fig* desquiciado; **put out of ~** desengranar, *fig* desquiciar; **~-box**, **~-case** caja de velocidades; **~-lever**, **~-shift** palanca de cambios; **~-ratio** relación *f* de multiplicación; ~ **twist grip** (motor-cycle) puño giratorio de cambios; **~-wheel** rueda dentada; *v* (equip) aparejar; *mech* engranar; **be ~ed to** engranar con; ~ **down** desmultiplicar[4]; ~ **up** multiplicar[4]

[2] **gear** *adj* fabuloso

gee (whiz)! ¡caray!

gee-gee caballito

gee-up! ¡arre!

geezer tío

Geiger: ~ **counter** contador *m* Geiger

geisha geisha

gelatine gelatina

gelatinous gelatinoso

geld castrar

gelding caballo castrado

gelignite gelatina explosiva

gem piedra preciosa; *fig* preciosidad *f*

Gemini Géminis *mpl*

gender género

gene gen *m*

genealogical genealógico

genealogy genealogía

general *n* general; **~-in-chief** generalísimo; **become ~** generalizarse[7]; **in ~**, **as a ~ rule** por lo general; *adj* general; ~ **election** elecciones *fpl* generales; **~-knowledge test** examen (-ámenes) de cultura general; ~ **meeting** mitin *m* general; ~ **opinion** opinión *f* general; **General Post Office** Oficina Central de Correos; ~ **practitioner** médico de cabecera; ~ **public** público; ~ **staff** estado mayor; ~ **strike** huelga general

generalissimo generalísimo

generality generalidad *f*

generalization generalización *f*

generalize generalizar[7]

generally por lo general; ~ **speaking** en rasgos generales

generalship generalato; (strategy) estrategia

generate engendrar; *mech* generar

generating: ~ **station** central generadora

generation *mech* generación *f*; ~ **gap** conflicto de las generaciones

generator generador *m*; *US* dínamo

generic genérico

generosity generosidad *f*

generous (abundant) abundante; (liberal) generoso

genesis génesis *m*

genetic *adj* genético; ~**s** *n* genética

Geneva Ginebra

genial afable

geniality afabilidad *f*

genie genio

genitals órganos genitales

genitive (case) genitivo; **in the** ~ en genitivo

genius (person) genio; (quality) talento; **have a** ~ **for** tener[19] talento para

Genoa Génova

genocide genocidio

Genoese *n* + *adj* genovés *m* (-esa *f*)

genre género

genteel gentil; *iron* afectado

gentian genciana

gentile *n* + *adj* gentil *m*

gentility gentileza; *iron* cursilería

gentle de buena familia; (benign) benigno; (loving) cariñoso; (slow) lento; (soft) suave; ~ **animal** animal dócil; ~**folk** gente *f* de bien; ~ **knock at the door** golpe leve a la puerta

gentleman caballero; señor *m*; (at court) gentilhombre *m*; ~**-in-waiting** gentilhombre de cámara; ~**'s agreement** acuerdo verbal; **he is a perfect** ~ él es todo un caballero; **I am no** ~ no soy caballero

gentlemanly caballeroso

gentlemanliness caballerosidad *f*

gentleness suavidad *f*; (kindness) bondad *f*

gentlewoman dama (de servicio)

gently suavemente; (slowly) despacio

gentry alta burguesía

genuflect doblar la rodilla

genuflexion genuflexión *f*

genuine auténtico; (of people) sincero

genuineness autenticidad *f*; (of people) sinceridad *f*

genus género

geographer geógrafo

geographic(al) geográfico

geography geografía

geological geológico

geologist geólogo

geology geología

geometric(al) geométrico

geometrician geómetra *m*

geometry geometría

geophysicist geofísico

geophysics geofísica

geopolitics geopolítica

George Jorge

geranium geranio

gerfalcon gerifalte *m*

geriatric geriátrico; ~**s** geriatría

germ (bacterium) bacteria; (microbe) microbio; (beginning) germen (gérmenes) *m*; ~**-carrier** portador *m* (-ora *f*) de microbios; ~**-proof** a prueba de bacteria; ~**-war(fare)** guerra bacteriológica

German *n* alemán *m* (-ana *f*), *pej* teutón *m* (-ona *f*); (language) alemán *m*; *adj* alemán (-ana *f*), *pej* teutónico; ~ **measles** rubéola

germane afín (**to** a)

Germanic germánico

Germany Alemania

germicide germicida

germinate *vi* germinar; *vt* hacer[19] germinar

germination germinación *f*

gerontologist gerontologista *m* + *f*

gerontology gerontología

gerrymander dividir injustamente en distritos electorales

Gertrude Gertrudis

gerund gerundio

Gestapo Gestapo *f*

gestation gestación (-ones) *f*

gesticulate gesticular

gesticulation gesticulación (-ones) *f*

gesture *n* gesto; (of face) mueca; (of hands) ademán *m*; ~ **of good will** gesto de buena voluntad, *fig* indicación *f*; **mere** ~ pura formalidad; *v* decir[19] por gestos

get (obtain) obtener[19]; (receive) recibir; (bring) traer[19]; (collect *usu* money)

cobrar; (arrest) arrestar; *med* coger[8];
(win) ganar; (take) tomar; (seize)
agarrar, *SA* recibir; ~ **him!** (to a dog)
¡a él!; (make contact with) localizar[7], **I
couldn't ~ him at the office** no pude
localizarle en la oficina; (arrive) llegar[5]; (be) ser[19], ~ **killed** ser matado;
(become) volverse (ue)[1b] (*past part*
vuelto), **he improved only to ~ worse
again** él se restableció para volver a
enfermar; (succeed in) conseguir
(i)[3+11], **we shall ~ you elected** con-
seguiremos que le elijan; (persuade)
persuadir; (cause) hacer[19]; (understand) comprender; (kill) matar; (let
o.s. be) dejarse +*infin*, **don't ~
caught** no te dejes coger; ~ **better**
mejorar; ~ **the better of** vencer; **sleep
got the better of me** el sueño me
venció; (hit) dar[19] en, **he got the
bullseye** él dio en el blanco; ~ **busy/
cracking** moverse (ue)[1b]; ~ **going** *vi*
ponerse[19] en marcha, *vt* organizar[7]; ~
hold of coger[8], (comprehend) comprender; ~ **it (in the neck)** cobrar; ~ **it
bad** sufrir mucho; ~ **knotted!** ¡váyase
a freír espárragos!; ~ **o.s. up as** disfrazarse[7] de; ~ **rid of** deshacerse[19] de,
(throw away) tirar; ~ **s.o.** (revenge
o.s.) cargarse[5] a uno, **I'll ~ him** me lo
cargaré; ~ **something done** hacer[19]
hacer algo; **I'm going to ~ a garage
built** voy a hacer construir un garaje;
~ **a start over** coger[8] la delantera a; ~
talking (to) entrar en conversación
(con); ~ **that inside you** (eat that)
écheselo entre pecho y espalda; ~
well again restablecerse[14]; ~ **a woman
with child** poner[19]　encinta a una
mujer

~ **about/around** moverse (ue)[1b]; (travel) viajar; (after illness) levantarse
y salir; (of rumours) correr

~ **above** subir a un nivel más alto

~ **across** cruzar[7]; (convince) hacer[19]
entender; *theat* tener[19] éxito

~ **ahead** (take the lead) adelantarse;
(progress) hacer[19] progresos; (progress in one's career) situarse; ~
ahead of adelantarse a

~ **along** (leave) marcharse; (continue)
seguir (i)[3+11]; (manage) ir[19] tirando;
how are you getting along? ¿cómo le
va?; **he can ~ along all right in Spanish**

él se defiende bien en castellano; ~
along well/badly with llevarse bien/
mal con; ~ **along without** pasarse sin;
~ **along with you!** ¡no diga(s) tonterías!

~ **at** (reach) alcanzar[7]; (refer to) aludir
a; (attack) reñir[4]; (find out) descubrir
(*past part* descubierto); **what are you
getting at?** ¿qué quiere usted decir con
eso?

~ **away** (depart) marcharse (**from** de);
(escape) escaparse (**from** de); ~ **away
with** (take) llevarse; ~ **away with it** (~
one's own way) salirse[19] con la suya; ~
away with you! ¡no diga(s)
tonterías!

~ **back** (retreat) volver (ue)[16] (*past part*
vuelto); (step back) ir[19] hacia atrás;
(recover) recobrar; **I got it back** me lo
devolvio/devolvieron

~ **behind** ponerse[19] detrás (de); ~ **thee
behind me Satan** vete Satanás; (delay)
quedarse atrás

~ **by** (pass) pasar; (avoid) eludir;
(manage) arreglárselas

~ **clear** *vt* hacer[19] entender bien; *vi*
entender (ie)[2b] bien

~ **down** bajar; ~ **down!** (throw o.s. to
the ground) ¡cuerpo a tierra!; (swallow) tragar[5]; (write) escribir (*past part*
escrito); ~ **down to business** ir[19] al
grano; ~ **down to work** ponerse a
trabajar; **it got me down** (depressed
me) me desanimó, (annoyed me) me
irritó

~ **in** entrar (en); *pol* ser[19] elegido; (go
home) volver (ue)[1b] (*past part* vuelto)
a casa; ~ **in first** (race) llegar[5] el primero, (in speech) hablar el primero; **I
couldn't ~ a word in (edgeways)** yo no
podía meter baza; ~ **in with** hacerse[19]
amigo de; **they got it all in the report**
incluyeron todo en el informe

~ **into** entrar (en); (vehicle) subir a;
(clothes) ponerse[19]; (trouble) meterse
en; ~ **into bed** acostarse (ue)[1a]; ~ **into
debt** endeudarse; ~ **into the habit of**
acostumbrarse a

~ **nowhere** no resultar en nada

~ **off** (vehicle *etc*) bajar de; (depart)
marcharse; (on a journey) ponerse[19]
en camino; salir; *aer* despegar[5];
(punishment) librarse de; **my lawyer
got me off** mi abogado me defendió

con éxito, *fam* mi abogado me sacó del apuro; **I told him where he gets off** le dije cuántos son cinco; **~ off!** ¡suelta(me)!, ¡fuera!; **~ off my back!** ¡no me moleste tanto!; **~ off with** enamorar, *fam* ligar, conquistar

~ on ponerse[19] encima de; (vehicle) subir(se) a; (horse) montar en; (progress) progresar; **~ on (in years)** envejecer[14]; **he's getting on to fifty** él ronda los cincuenta; **~ on in the world** progresar; **~ on one's nerves** ponerle[19] a uno los nervios de punta; **~ on with the work** hacer[19] el trabajo; **~ on well with** llevarse bien con; **it's getting on for nine** falta poco para las nueve; **she's always getting on to me** ella siempre me critica

~ out (take out) sacar[4]; (publish) publicar[4]; (news) hacerse[19] público; **~ out of** salir[19] de, (vehicle) bajar de, (escape from) escaparse de; **~ out of bed** levantarse de la cama; **~ out of a habit** perder[2b] la costumbre; **~ out of hand** llegar[5] a ser incontrolable; **~ out of one's depth** perder[2b] pie; **~ out of s.o.** sacarle[4] a uno, **they got the secret out of Mary** le sacaron el secreto a María; **~ out of the way** apartarse; **~ out (of here)!** ¡fuera (de aquí)!

~ over pasar por encima de; (illness *etc*) reponerse[19] de; (convince) hacer[19] entender; **~ over a difficulty** vencer[14] un obstáculo; **~ over a surprise** recobrarse de un susto; **let's get it over quickly** vamos a terminarlo pronto

~ past lograr pasar

~ round (avoid) esquivar; (persuade) convencer[12]; (become known) divulgarse[5]

~ there (be successful) tener[19] éxito

~ through pasar por; (reach a destination) llegar, **the convoy will ~ through** el convoy llegará; (spend money) gastar; (spend time) pasar; (pass an examination) aprobar (ue)[1a]; (on telephone) lograr comunicar; (message) *vi* llegar; *vt* hacer[19] llegar; **I shan't be able to ~ through my work** no podré terminar mi trabajo; **the minister got the bill through parliament** el ministro hizo aprobar el proyecto de ley

~ to (reach) llegar[5] a; (manage to) conseguir (i)[3+11]

~-together tertulia

~ together *vt* reunir; *vi* reunirse

~ under ponerse[19] debajo (de); **~ under way** (vehicle) ponerse[19] en marcha; **they got production under way** encarrilaron la producción

~-up (clothes) atavío; (appearance) aspecto

~ up (climb) subir; (from bed) *vt* levantar, *vi* levantarse; (stand up) ponerse[19] de pie; (arrange) organizar[7]; **~ up a subject** preparar un tema; **the wind got up** el viento empezó a soplar; **I wonder what she is getting up to now** me pregunto lo que ella estará haciendo ahora

get-at-able asequible

getaway *n* escapada

gew-gaw chuchería

geyser geiser *m*; (water-heater) calentador *m* de agua; *sl* (person) tío

G-force *space* fuerza G

Ghana Ghana

Ghanaian *n+adj* ghanés *m* (-esa *f*)

ghastliness horror *m*; (paleness) palidez *f* mortal; (nasty appearance) aspecto miserable

ghastly horrible; (pale) pálido; (unpleasant) muy desagradable

gherkin pepinillo

ghetto judería; gueto

ghost fantasma *m*; (spirit) espíritu *m*; **(have) not the ~ of a chance of** no tener[19] ni la menor posibilidad de +*infin*; **lay a ~** conjurar un fantasma; **~-story** cuento de fantasmas; **~-write** escribir (*past part* escrito) para otra persona; **~-writer** negro; **Holy Ghost** Espíritu Santo

ghostliness lo misterioso

ghostly espectral

ghoul (vampire) demonio necrófago; *fig* persona de gustos macabros

ghoulish excesivamente cruel

GI soldado norteamericano

giant *n* gigante *m*; *adj* gigantesco

giantess giganta

gibber farfullar

gibberish galimatías *m sing*; *fam* griego; *joc* dialecto del castellano hablado en Gibraltar

gibbet horca

gibbon gibón *m*

gibe *n* mofa; *v* ~ **at** mofarse de

gibing mofador (-ora *f*)

gibingly con sorna

giblets menudillos *mpl*

Gibraltar Gibraltar *m*; **Rock of** ~ Peñón *m* de Gibraltar; **Plain of** ~ campo de Gibraltar

Gibraltarian *n* + *adj* gibraltareño

giddily vertiginosamente

giddiness vértigo

giddy mareado; (frivolous) casquivano; **make** ~ marear; **feel** ~ tener[19] mareos; ~ **height** altura vertiginosa

gift regalo; (act of giving) donación (-ones) *f*; (offering) ofrenda; *sl* (bargain) ganga; (personal quality) don *m*, **have a** ~ **for** tener[19] un don para; **I don't want it even as a** ~ no lo quiero ni regalado; **don't look a** ~ **horse in the mouth** a caballo regalado se le mira el diente; ~ **of the gab** labia; ~-**voucher** cupón *m* de regalo

gifted talentoso

gig (carriage) birlocho; *naut* lancha; *mus sl* cita para tocar

gigantic gigantesco

giggle *n* risa tonta; *v* reírse (i)[3] por nada; (nervously) reírse (i)[3] nerviosamente

gigolo gigoló; *sl* ligón *m*

Gilbert Gilberto

gild *v* bañar en oro; *fig* pintar color de rosa; ~ **the pill** dorar la píldora

gilder dorador *m*

gilding doradura

¹ **gill** (of fish) branquia; (of mushroom) laminilla

² **gill** (liquid measure) medida de líquido (aproximadamente 1/8 litro)

gillyflower minutisa

gilt dorado; ~-**edged** (of book) con los cantos dorados; ~-**edged securities** valores *mpl* del estado

gimballed: ~ **motor** *space* motor *m* cardán

gimbals balancines *mpl* de la brújula

gimcrack *n* chuchería; *adj* mal hecho

gimlet barrena de mano; *US* ginebra con jugo de lima agria

gimmick artilugio; **sales**-~ truco publicitario

gimmickry empleo excesivo de artilugios

gimmicky tramposo

¹ **gin** (drink) ginebra; ~-**sling** ginebra con

vermut

² **gin** (trap) trampa

ginger *n* jengibre *m*; *fig* (liveliness) brío; **Ginger** (nickname) Zanahoria; ~-**ale**, ~-**beer** cerveza de jengibre; ~**bread** pastel *m* de jengibre; ~-**group** grupo de activistas; ~ **hair** pelo rojo; ~-**haired** pelirrojo; ~-**snap** galletita de jengibre; ~-**wine** vino de jengibre; *v* ~ **up** animar

gingerly cautelosamente

gingham guinga

gipsy gitano; ~ **girl** gitanilla; ~ **lad** gitanillo

giraffe jirafa

gird ceñir; ~ **o.s. for** prepararse para

girder viga

girdle *n* (belt) cinturón *m*; (corset) faja; *v* fajar; (go round) cercar

girl (child) niña, muchacha, *fam* chavala; (young woman) chica, moza; (servant) muchacha; ~-**friend** amiga, (fiancée) novia; **Girl-Guide**, *US* **Girl-Scout** exploradora, guía scout

girlhood (childhood) niñez *f*; (youth) juventud *f*

girlish de niña; (infantile) pueril

giro giro

girth (harness) cincha; (circumference) circunferencia

gist substancia; lo esencial

give *n* (elasticity) elasticidad *f*; (flexibility) flexibilidad *f*; ~ **and take** concesiones mutuas; *v* dar[19]; (as present) regalar; (donate) donar; (grant) conceder; (hand over) entregar[5]; (impart) comunicar[4]; (produce) producir[15]; *med* contagiar; ~ **an injection** poner[19] una inyección; **I don't want to** ~ **you my cold** no quiero contagiarle mi catarro; (cause) causar, ~ **pain** causar dolor; (collapse) hundirse, **the floor began to** ~ **under his weight** el suelo empezó a hundirse bajo su peso; (slacken) aflojarse, **in time the cords will** ~ con el tiempo las cuerdas se aflojarán; (stretch) dar[19] de sí; *theat* representar; ~ **chase to** dar[19] caza a; ~ **evidence** prestar declaración; ~ **ground** ceder terreno; ~ **a hand** echar una mano; ~ **it to s.o.** *fig* regañar a alguien; ~ **judgement** fallar; ~ **a lead** dar[19] ejemplo; ~ **lessons** dar[19] clase; ~ **the lie to** desmentir (ie)[2c]; **can you** ~

me a lift to ¿quiere usted llevarme a?;
~ **a piece of one's mind** decir[19] cuántos
son cinco; **I shall** ~ him plenty of rope
fig le daré largas; **I'd** ~ **my right hand
to** yo daría mi mano derecha por; ~
rise to producir[15]; ~ **a sigh/a laugh**
echar un suspiro/una carcajada; ~ **the
slip** evadir(se); ~ **trouble** causar
molestia; ~ **a wide berth** pasar de
largo

~-**away** *n* revelación indiscreta; **at** ~-
away prices a precios regalados

~ **away** *v* regalar; (get rid of) deshacerse[19] de; (reveal) revelar; (sell
cheaply) vender a un precio bajo; (betray) traicionar; ~ **away the bride**
ser[19] padrino de la novia

~ **back** devolver (ue)[1b] (*past part* devuelto)

~ **forth** publicar[4]; (smell) emitir

~ **in** (hand in) entregar[5]; (surrender)
rendirse (i)[3]; ~-**in to** (agree with) asen-
tir(ie)[2c] en; ~ **in to your little sister!**
¡haz lo que quiere tu hermanita!

~ **off** despedir (i)[3]

~ **out** *vt* (allege) afirmar; (allocate)
asignar; (distribute) repartir; (publish) publicar[4]; (reveal) revelar; *vi* (be
exhausted) acabarse, **my strength is
giving out** se me acaban las fuerzas

~ **over** (transfer) traspasar; (stop) dejar
de +*infin*

~ **up** (hand over) entregar[5]; (abandon)
abandonar; (cede) ceder; (sacrifice)
sacrificar[4]; (stop) dejar de +*infin*;
(surrender) rendirse(i)[3]; (lose hope)
perder (ie)[2b] la esperanza; (not to expect) no creer; **they had given me up**
creían que ya no iba a venir; ~ **up
as lost** dar[19] por perdido; ~ **up an
attempt to** renunciar a +*infin*; ~ **up
the priesthood** secularizarse[1], *fam*
botar/colgar la sotana

~ **way** ceder; (make room) ceder el
paso; (not hold tight) aflojarse; **his
legs gave way (beneath him)** le fla-
quearon las piernas

given dado; ~ **that** dado que; **be** ~ **to**
ser[19] aficionado a, (in the habit of)
soler (ue)[1b] +*infin*; **by a** ~ **time** en un
momento dado; ~ **name** nombre *m* de
pila

giver d(on)ador *m* (-ora *f*)

giving generoso

gizzard molleja; **it sticks in my** ~ *fig* no
puedo tragarlo

glacé helado; (sugared) escarchado

glacial glacial

glaciation helamiento

glacier glaciar *m*

glacis glacis *m*

glad (content) satisfecho; (happy) alegre; **be** ~ **of** alegrarse de +*infin*; **be** ~
that alegrarse de que +*subj*; **be** ~ **to**
(pleased to) tener[19] mucho gusto en
+*infin*; **be** ~ **of** (need) agradecer[14]; ~
to meet you! ¡encantado!

gladden alegrar

glade claro (en un bosque)

gladiator gladiador *m*

gladiatorial gladiatorio

gladiolus gladiolo

gladly (willingly) con mucho gusto;
(with enjoyment) de buena gana

gladness alegría

glamorize romantizar[7]

glamorous encantador (-ora *f*);
(sophisticated) sofisticado

glamour encanto; (sex-appeal) atractivo
sexual; ~-**girl** chica atractiva

glance *n* ojeada; (blow) golpe *m* de
soslayo; **sidelong** ~ mirada de reojo; *v*
(hit) golpear de soslayo; (look) echar
una mirada; ~ **off** rebotar de soslayo;
~ **over** (revise) repasar; ~ **through (a
book)** hojear (un libro)

gland glándula

glandular glandular; ~ **fever** fiebre *f*
glandular

glare *n* (of light) deslumbramiento;
(angry look) mirada feroz; *v* (dazzle)
deslumbrar; ~ **at** mirar enfurecido a

glaring (dazzling) deslumbrador (-ora
f); (of colours) chillón; (angry-
looking) de mirada feroz; *fig* (obvious) que salta a la vista

glass *n* cristal *m*; (tumbler) vaso, **it is
sold by the** ~ se vende al vaso; (for
beer) caña; (for wine) copa; (for
liqueur) copita; (mirror) espejo;
(barometer) barómetro; (telescope)
catalejo; ~**es** gafas; ~-**blower** soplador *m* de vidrio; ~-**blowing** soplado *m* de vidrio; ~-**cloth** paño de
cocina; ~-**cutter** (diamond) diamante
m de vidriero, (wheel-type) cortavidrios de disco; ~-**works** cristalería;
adj de cristal; ~ **door** puerta de

cristales; ~ **eye** ojo de cristal; ~**house** *hort* invernadero, *mil* cárcel *f* militar; ~**-paper** papel *m* de lija; ~ **roof** montera; ~**ware** cristalería

glassful (tumbler) vaso (lleno) (**of** de); (wineglass) copa (llena) (**of** de)

glassiness vidriosidad *f*

glassy cristalino; ~**-eyed** con ojos vidriosos

glaucous de color verdemar; *bot* glauco

glaze *n cer* vidriado; *v* vidriar; (fix window-panes) poner[19] cristales a; ~**d tile** azulejo

glazier vidriero

glazing vidriado

gleam *n* destello; (of metal) brillo; *fig* rayo, ~ **of hope** rayo de esperanza; ~ **in her eyes** chispa en sus ojos; *v* destellar; (reflect) reflejar; (of metal) brillar

gleaming reluciente

glean espigar[5]; *fig* recoger[8]

gleaner espigador *m* (-ora *f*)

gleanings moraga; *fig* fragmentos recogidos

glee alegría; *mus* canción *f* para voces solas; ~**-club** orfeón (-ones) *m*

gleeful alegre

gleefully con alegría

glen cañada

glib locuaz (-ces); *fam* de mucha labia; ~ **excuse** disculpa fácil

glibness facilidad *f*; *fam* labia

glide *n* deslizamiento; *aer* planeo; *mus* ligadura; *v* deslizarse[7]; *aer* planear; ~ **away** escurrirse

glider planeador *m*; ~**-pilot** piloto de planeador

gliding vuelo sin motor

glimmer *n* luz *f* débil; *fig* rayo; ~ **of hope** rayo de esperanza; *v* brillar débilmente

glimpse *n* vistazo; **catch a** ~ dar[19] un vistazo; *v* vislumbrar

glint *n* destello; (in the eye) chispa; *v* destellar; (reflect) reflejar

glisten brillar; **all that** ~**s is not gold** no es oro todo lo que reluce

glitter *n* centelleo; *v* centellear

glittering resplandeciente; ~ **uniform** uniforme *m* deslumbrante

gloaming crepúsculo

gloat deleitarse (**over** en)

global esférico; (of the whole world)

mundial

globe globo; *geog* globo terráqueo; ~ **artichoke** alcachofa; ~**-trotter** trotamundos *m sing + pl*

globule glóbulo

gloom (darkness) oscuridad *f*; (depression) melancolía

gloomy (dark) oscuro; (depressed) melancólico; ~ **face** cara sombría

glorification glorificación *f*

glorify glorificar[4]

glorious glorioso; ~ **weather** tiempo espléndido

glory *n* gloria; *v* ~ **in** (rejoice) gloriarse en, (boast) gloriarse de; ~ **be to ...!** ¡alabado sea ...!

gloss *n* (shine) brillo; (note) glosa; **put a** ~ **on** sacar[4] brillo a; ~**-paint** pintura esmalte; *v* (shine) lustrar; (make a note) glosar; ~ **over** disculpar

glossary glosario

glossy lustroso; ~ **magazine** revista de lujo; ~ **paper** papel *m* con brillo

glottal glótico

glottis glotis *f*

glove guante *m*; ~ **compartment** *mot* guantera; ~ **shop** guantería

glover guantero

glow *n* incandescencia; (redness) rojez *f*; (in the sky) arrebol *m*; (heat) calor *m*; ~ **of health** (appearance) aspecto de salud, (feeling) sensación *f* de bienestar; ~ **of pleasure** sensación *f* de placer; ~**-worm** luciérnaga; *v* brillar; estar[19] al rojo; ~ **with** (pride *etc*) enardecerse[14] de

glower mirar con ceño

glowing ardiente; *fig* (enthusiastic) entusiasta *m + f*

glucose glucosa

glue *n* cola; *v* pegar[5] con cola; **my eyes were** ~**d on her** yo tenía los ojos fijos en ella

gluey pegajoso

glueyness pegajosidad *f*

glum malhumorado

glut *n* superabundancia; **be a** ~ **on the market** abarrotar el mercado

glutinous glutinoso

glutton glotón *m*; *fam* comilón *m* (-ona *f*); **I'm a** ~ **for** soy insaciable de

gluttony glotonería

glycerine glicerina

G-man agente secreto federal (de los

Estados Unidos)

G.M.T. (Greenwich Mean Time) hora solar

gnarled nudoso; (weather-beaten) curtido

gnash: ~ **one's teeth** rechinar los dientes

gnat mosquito; *SA* jején (-enes) *m*

gnaw roer

gnawing roedor (-ora *f*)

gneiss gneis *m*

gnome gnomo

gnomon gnomon *m*

gnu ñu *m*

go *n* (energy) energía; (attempt) intento; (turn) turno; **at one** ~ de un tirón; **be full of** ~ estar[19] lleno de energía; **be on the** ~ estar[19] activo; **it's all the** ~ **now** está muy de moda ahora; **have a** ~ **(at)** (take a turn) tener[19] un turno (a), (make an attempt) tratar (de) +*infin*, (try one's luck) probar (ue)[1a] suerte (a); **it's a** ~! ¡trato hecho!; **it's my** ~ me toca a mí; **(it's) no** ~ es perder tiempo; **make a (good)** ~ **of** tener[19] éxito en; ~**-ahead** *n* permiso, *adj* progresista; ~**-between** intermediario, (pimp) alcahuete *m*; ~**-cart** go-cart *m*; ~**-getter** buscavidas *m sing*

v ir[19]; (depart) irse[19]; (disappear) desaparecer[14]; (die) ir(se)[19], **he's** ~**ing fast** va de prisa; (of time) pasar; (become) hacerse[19]; (work) funcionar, *fam* andar[19]; (belong) (deber) colocarse[4], **the screw doesn't** ~ **there** el tornillo no se coloca/debe colocarse allí; (fit) caber[19], **the books won't** ~ **in the box** los libros no caben en la caja; (sell) venderse, **this car will** ~ **for £1,000** este coche se venderá por mil libras; (read) rezar[7], **the first paragraph** ~**es like this** el primer párrafo reza así; (sound) sonar (ue)[1a], **the bell will** ~ **at seven** el timbre sonará a las siete; (break) romperse (*past part* roto); ~ **and ...** ir(se)[19] a +*infin*; ~ **and listen!** ¡vaya a escuchar!; ~ **it** ir[19] a toda velocidad; ~ **it alone** obrar a solas; ~ **one better** quedar por encima; **as far as it** ~**es** dentro de sus límites; **here** ~**es!** ¡vamos a ver!; **how** ~**es it?** ¿qué tal?, ¿qué hay?; **who** ~**es there?** ¿quién va?

~ **aboard** ir[19] a bordo

~ **about** (wander) dar[19] vueltas; *naut* virar de bordo; ~ **about one's business** meterse en lo que le importa

~ **abroad** ir[19] al extranjero

~ **across** atravesar, *fam* pasar

~ **after** (follow) seguir (i)[3+11]; (pursue) perseguir (i)[3+11]

~ **against** ir[19] contra; ~ **against the grain** repugnarle a uno

~ **ahead** adelantarse; (lead) ir[19] a la cabeza; ~ **ahead with** proseguir (i)[3+11] con

~ **all out** hacer[19] todo lo posible(**to** para); (quickly) ir[19] a toda velocidad

~ **along with** (accompany) acompañar a; (agree) estar de acuerdo con

~ **amiss** ir[19] mal a uno

~ **ashore** desembarcarse[4]

~ **astray** extraviarse

~ **at** atacar[4]

~ **away (from)** irse[19] (de); (further off) alejarse (de)

~ **back** (return) regresar; (withdraw) retirarse; ~ **back on one's word** faltar a su palabra

~ **backwards** andar lo andado; *mot* ir[19] en marcha atrás; ~ **backwards and forwards** ir[19] para atrás y para adelante

~ **before** (precede) preceder; (lead) ir[19] a la cabeza (de)

~ **behind** ir[19] detrás de; ~ **behind s.o.'s back** obrar a espaldas de uno

~ **beyond** ir[19] más allá de; (exceed) exceder

~ **by** (pass) pasar (por); (be ruled by) atenerse[19] a; ~ **by appearances** juzgar[5] por las apariencias; **to** ~ **by what he says** a juzgar por lo que dice; ~ **by air** ir[19] por/en avión; ~ **by bus/ car/train** ir[19] en autobús/coche/tren; ~ **by default** condenarse en rebeldía; ~ **by the name of** llamarse

~ **down** bajar; (sun) ponerse[19]; *naut* hundirse; *comm* fracasar; (leave university) salir[19] de la universidad; ~ **down in history** pasar a la historia; ~ **down on one's knees** *fig* implorar; ~ **down with** *med* caer[19] enfermo con

~ **easy** (slowly) ir[19] despacio; ~ **easy on/with!** ¡cuidado con!

~ **far** ir[19] lejos; *fig* hacer[19] grandes progresos

~ **for** (seek) ir[19] por; (attack) atacar[4]; ~

for a ride by dar[19] una vuelta en ; ~ **for a walk** dar[19] un paseo; ~ **for in a big way** entusiasmarse mucho por; **it all went for nothing** todo fue una pérdida de tiempo; **that ~es for me too** yo también

~ **forth** salir[19]

~ **forward** adelantar

~ **hard with s.o.** irle[19] mal a uno

~ **in** entrar; (of the sun) desaparecer[14]; ~ **in and out** entrar y salir[19]; ~ **in for** (try) intentar, (compete) concurrir, (be keen on) dedicarse a

~ **into** entrar en; (investigate) investigar[5]; ~ **into films** colocarse[4] en el cine; ~ **into hysterics** ponerse[19] histérico; ~ **into mourning** vestirse (i)[3] de luto

~ **off** marcharse; (be fired) dispararse, **the pistol went off** la pistola se disparó; (explode) estallar; (ring) sonar (ue)[1a], **the alarm-clock went off at six** el despertador sonó a las seis; (go sour) cortarse; (go bad) pasarse; ~ **off at a tangent** tirar por la tangente; ~ **off one's food** perder[2b] el apetito; ~ **off one's head** perder (ie)[2b] el juicio; ~ **off the rails** descarrilarse, *fig* (go mad) volverse (ue)[1b] (*past part* vuelto) loco; ~ **off to sleep** dormirse (ue)[1c]; ~ **off well/badly** salir[19] bien/mal

~ **on** seguir (i)[3+11]; *theat* salir[19] en escena, (last) durar; (happen) pasar, **what's going on?** ¿qué pasa?; **how are you going on?** ¿qué tal?; **this hat won't ~ on me** no puedo ponerme este sombrero; ~ **on to** pasar luego a +*infin*; **he went on to thank the mayor** pasó luego a dar las gracias al alcalde; (complain) quejar(se), *fam* echar pestes; ~ **on at** (nag) reñir[3] a; **don't ~ on like that!** ¡no se ponga así!; ~ **on!** ¡vaya!, ¡anda!; ~ **on with** continuar con

~ **out** salir; (of light, fire) apagarse[5]; (of fashion) pasar de moda; ~ **out to** (do s.t.) salir[19] a (+*infin*); **they ~ out to work** salen a trabajar

~ **over** pasar por encima de; (repeat) revisar[19]; (betray) pasar al otro lado; **the general went over the conquered territory** el general recorrió el terreno conquistado; (revise) repasar

~ **round** dar[19] la vuelta (a); (visit) visitar; (be enough for all) haber[19] para todos; ~ **round a corner** doblar una esquina; **when the hat went round** cuando pasó el gorro

~-**slow** *n* huelga de ritmo lento

~ **slow** *v* trabajar a ritmo lento

~ **through** pasar por; (check) examinar; (experience) experimentar; (spend) gastar; (squander) malgastar; (suffer) sufrir; **this book went through many editions** este libro se reimprimió con gran frecuencia; ~ **through with** llevar a cabo

~ **to** (visit) ir[19] a ver; (fall to) tocarle[4] a uno

~ **together** (of colours) (h)armonizar[7]

~ **under** pasar por debajo de; (sink) hundirse; (fail in business) fracasar; **he goes under the name of Vincent** se llama Vicente

~ **up** subir; (explode) estallar; (go to the capital/university) ir[19] a; ~ **up in one's opinion** mejorar en la estimación de uno

~ **upstairs** subir la escalera

~ **well/badly** ir[19] bien/mal (**with** con)

~ **with** (of clothes *etc*) ir[19] bien con; **it ~es with everything** pega con todo

~ **without** pasarse sin; ~ **without saying** sobreentenderse (ie)[2b]; **it goes without saying** *fam* ni que decir tiene

~ **wrong** (fail) salir[19] mal; *mech* dejar de funcionar

goad *n* aguijón *m*; *v* aguij(one)ar; incitar; ~ **into** provocar[4] a; ~ **into fury** irritar hasta la furia

goal *sp* gol, tanto; (~posts) portería, *SA* arco; *fig* meta; **be in/keep** ~ ser[19] portero; **score a** ~ meter un gol, *sl* golear; ~ **aggregate** goleada; ~ **area**, ~-**line** área/línea de meta; ~**keeper** portero, *SA* arquero; ~-**kick** saque *m* de puerta; ~**less draw** empate *m* a cero; ~-**post** poste *m* de la portería; ~-**scorer** goleador *m*

goat cabra; **he gets my** ~ él me da mala espina; **she**~ cabra; **he**-~ macho cabrío; ~**herd** cabrero; ~**skin** piel *f* de cabra

goatee perilla

gob (saliva) salivazo; (mouth) morro

gobbet pedacito

gobble *n* (noise) gluglú *m*; *v* gluglutear; (eat) engullir[18]

gobbledegook jerga burocrática

gobbler pavo

goblet copa

goblin duende *m*

god dios *m*; ~s *theat* paraíso; **God keep you!** ¡vaya con Dios!; **God knows!** ¡Dios sabe!; **God knows what will happen** sabe Dios lo que sucederá; **God forbid!** ¡(que) no lo quiera Dios!; **God willing** si Dios quiere; **for God's sake!** ¡por (el amor de) Dios!; ~**child** ahijado (-a); ~**-daughter** ahijada; ~**father** padrino; **God-fearing** piadoso; ~**-forsaken** dejado de la mano de Dios, (isolated) solitario; ~**head** divinidad *f*; ~**like** divino; ~**mother** madrino; ~**parents** padrinos *mpl*; ~**son** ahijado; **God-speed!** ¡buen viaje!

goddess diosa

godless descreído

godlessness impiedad *f*

godliness piedad *f*

godly piadoso

godsend buena suerte

goggle *n* mirada fija; ~s gafas *fpl*, *SA* antiparras *fpl*; ~**-box** *TV pej* caja tonta; ~**-eyed** con ojos saltones; *v* mirar fijamente

going (outward journey) ida; (departure) salida; (road conditions) estado del camino, *sp* estado del terreno, (racing) estado de la pista; **the ~ was easy** *mot* el conducir era fácil; **while the ~ is good** mientras hay condiciones favorables; ~**-over** (beating) paliza, apaleamiento, (revision) repaso; ~**s-on** (behaviour) conducta, (happenings) sucesos *mpl*; *adj* que va; (functioning) funcionando; (for sale) en venta; ~ **concern** negocio en marcha

goitre bocio; *SA* buche *m*

gold *n* oro; (colour) color *m* oro; ~**-bearing** *geol* aurífero; ~ **bullion** oro en barras; ~**-dust** oro en polvo; ~**-fever** fiebre *f* del oro; ~**-field** yacimiento de oro; ~**-lace** encaje *m* de oro; ~**-leaf** oro batido; ~**-mine** mina de oro, *fig* potosí *m*; ~**-plated** dorado; ~**-rimmed** con armadura de oro; ~**-rush** fiebre del oro; ~**-smith** orfebre *m*; ~ **standard** patrón oro; *adj* de oro; ~**crest** reyezuelo sencillo; ~**finch** jilguero; ~**fish** pez *m* de colores

Gold Coast Costa de Oro

golden (made of gold) de oro; (covered with gold) dorado; **become ~** dorarse; ~ **age** edad *f* de oro; ~ **eagle** águila real; **Golden Fleece** Vellocino de Oro; ~**-haired** de cabellos de oro; ~ **jubilee** quincuagésimo aniversario; ~ **mean** justo medio; ~ **oriole** *orni* oropéndola; ~ **plover** avefría; ~ **rule** regla; ~ **spaniel** cocker dorado; ~ **wedding** bodas *fpl* de oro

Goldilocks Trenzas de Oro

golf golf *m*; ~**-club** (stick) palo de golf, (society) club *m* de golf; ~**-course/links** campo de golf

golfer jugador *m* (-ora *f*) de golf

Golgotha Gólgota

golliwog muñeco negro de trapo

gonad gónada

gondola góndola

gondolier gondolero

gone *past part* of **go**; **it's all ~** ya no hay más; **it's ~ six (o'clock)** son las seis pasadas; **she's ~ on him** ella está chiflada por él

goner (person) dado por muerto

gong tantán *m*; (boxing) gong *m*; (medal) *sl* chapa

gonk muñequita cómica o fantástica

gonorrhoea gonorrea

goo cola; *fig* exceso de sentimentalismo

good *n* (advantage) bien; **do ~** hacer[19] bien; **the ~** (abstract) lo bueno, (people) los buenos *mpl*; **for the ~ of** para el bien de; **for ~ (and all)** para siempre; **to the ~** de sobra; **what's the ~ of?** ¿para qué sirve?; **the tablets did me ~** las pastillas me hicieron bien; **it's no ~ doing that** no vale la pena hacer[19] eso; **they are up to no ~** ellos están tramando algo malo; **make ~** (make up) resarcirse[13] de; ~**s** bienes *mpl*, *comm* géneros *mpl*; ~**s-van** furgón (-ones) *m*; ~**s station/train** estación (-ones) *f*/tren *m* de mercancías; *adj* bueno; **be ~** ser[19] bueno; ~ **afternoon/evening** buenas tardes; **Good Book** Santa Biblia; ~ **day/morning** buenos días; ~ **night** buenas noches; ~ **luck!** ¡buena suerte!; ~ **Friday** Viernes Santo; **it is very ~ of you** usted es muy amable; **carrots are ~ for children** las zanahorias son buenas para los niños; **do a ~ turn** hacer[19] un favor; **have a ~ time** pasarlo bien; **it's a ~ thing you came**

menos mal que usted llegó; **on ~ authority** de fuente fidedigna; **~ leg** (the other being injured) pierna válida; **it is a ~ time to** es el momento oportuno para; **be ~ at** ser[19] perito en; **be ~ for** (useful for) servir (i)[3] para; **they are no ~** no sirven para nada; **he's ~ for 1,000 pesetas** él podría contribuir 1.000 pesetas; **have a ~ mind to** tener[19] ganas de; **in ~ time** a tiempo; **(all) in ~ time!** ¡no sea(s) impaciente!; **~ bit/deal of** mucho/bien de; **~ half** (algo) más de la mitad; **~ many** muchos (-as); **~ way** (distance) buen trecho; **~ while** buen rato; **~-humoured/tempered** de buen humor; **~-looking** guapo; **~-natured** bondadoso; **~-for-nothing** sinvergüenza *m+f*

goodbye adiós *m*

goodish bastante; **for a ~ bit** durante bastante tiempo

goodly considerable; (good-looking) de buena apariencia

goodness bondad *f*; (nourishment) sustancia *f*; **~!** ¡Dios mío!; **for ~' sake** ¡por el amor de Dios!

goodwill buena voluntad; *comm* clientela; **~ visit** visita de buena voluntad

goody (sweet) caramelo; **~-~** *n+adj* beato; **play (at) goodies and baddies** jugar (ue)[1a] a policías y ladrones

gooey pegajoso; *fig* excesivamente sentimental

goofy embobado

goolies *vulg* huevos *mpl*; *sl* cojones *mpl*

goon payaso

goose ganso; **~-flesh, ~-pimples** carne *f* de gallina; **~-step** paso de ganso

gooseberry grosella blanca

gopher ardilla terrestre

gore *n* sangre (derramada); (sewing) nesga; *v* cornear; (sewing) nesgar[5]

gorge *n* (throat) garganta; (food) atracón *m*; *geog* cañón *m*; **it made my ~ rise** me dio (un) asco; *v* **~ upon** engullirse

gorgeous magnífico

gorgeousness magnificencia

Gorgon Gorgona

Gorgonzola queso de Gorgonzola

gorilla gorila *m*

gormandize glotonear

gormless lerdo

gorse aulaga

gory ensangrentado

goshawk azor *m*

gosling ansarino

gospel evangelio; **~ according to St John** evangelio según San Juan; **~ truth** (verdadero como) el evangelio

gospeller evangelista *m+f*

gossamer (hilos *mpl* de) telaraña; *fig* gasa finísima

gossip *n* (conversation) cotorreo; (person) chismoso; (scandal) chismorreo; **piece of ~** chisme *m*; **~-column** gacetilla, ecos de sociedad; *v* (chat) cotorrear; (talk scandal) chismorrear

gossipy chismoso

got *see* get

Goth godo

Gothic gótico, de estilo gótico; **(in) ~ characters** (en) letra gótica

gouge *n* gubia; *v* escoplar (con gubia); **~ out** (empty) vaciar; (remove) sacar[4], **~ out s.o.'s eyes** sacarle[4] los ojos a alguien

goulash sopa picante húngara

gourd calabaza

gourmand glotón *m* (-ona *f*)

gourmet gastrónomo

gout gota

gouty gotoso

govern gobernar (ie)[2a]; (regulate) regular; *fig+gramm* regir (i)[3]

governable gobernable

governess institutriz (-ces) *f*

governing administrativo; **~ body** junta directiva; **~ principle** principio rector

government gobierno; **~ bonds** papel *m* del estado; **~ grant** subvención *f* del estado

governmental gubernativo

governor gobernador *m* (-ora *f*); (of a prison) director *m*; (father) padre *m*; *SA fam* viejo; (boss) jefe *m*; *eng* regulador *m*; **~-general** gobernador *m* general

gown (woman's) vestido; *eccles* sotana; (academic) toga

grab *n* agarro; (theft) robo; *mech* gancho arrancador; **make a ~ at** intentar agarrar; **~-bag** tómbola; **~-bucket** pala de doble concha; *v* agarrar; *fig* tomar

Grace (name) Engracia, Gracia

grace *n* gracia; (gracefulness) elegancia;

(good manners) educación *f*; *theol*
gracia; (prayer before eating) bendición *f*; **with a bad/good** ~ de mala/
buena gana; **Your Grace** Vuestra
Ilustrísima, *eccles* Su Reverendísima;
be in s.o.'s good ~**s** gozar⁷ del
favor de alguien; **by** ~ **and favour a**
precario; **get into s.o.'s good** ~**s** congraciarse con alguien; ~-**note** *mus*
nota de adorno; *v* adornar, embe-
llecer¹⁴; ~ **with one's presence** honrar
graceful gracioso
gracefulness gracia
graceless sin gracia
gracious bondadoso; ~ (**me**)! ¡caray!;
¡Dios mío!
graciousness bondad *f*
gradation graduación *f*; *mus* gradación *f*
grade categoría; (quality) calidad *f*;
(slope) pendiente *f*, *SA* gradiente *m*;
(marks) nota(s); (*US* class) clase *f*;
best/top ~ de primera calidad; **make
the** ~ lograr tener éxito; ~-**crossing**
paso a nivel; ~-**school** *US* escuela de
primera enseñanza; *v* clasificar⁴; **be**
~**d** (according to scale) estar¹⁹ graduado
gradient pendiente *f*
grading graduación *f*
gradual gradual
graduate *n* graduado; **he is a** ~ **of
Salamanca** se graduó en Salamanca;
US ~ **nurse** enfermera diplomada; ~-
studies estudios *mpl* de licenciatura;
do ~ **studies** cursar asignaturas superiores; *v* graduar(se), licenciarse
graduation graduación *f*; *US* ~ **exercises**
ceremonia de graduación
graffiti pintadas *fpl*
graft *n hort* injerto; *surg* transplante *m*;
(corruption) chanchullo, *SA* mor-
dida; **hard** ~ trabajo muy duro; *v hort*
injertar; *surg* trasplantar
grafting injerto; ~-**knife** navaja de in-
jertador
Grail: the Holy ~ el Santo Grial
grain *n* (cereals) cereales *mpl*; (seed)
grano; (tiny piece) +*fig* pizca; (of
leather) flor *f*; (of marble *etc*) veta; (of
wood) hebra; (**go**) **against the** ~ **carp**
(ir¹⁹) contra la hebra, *fig* (ir¹⁹) a contra
pelo; **with the** ~ **carp** a hebra; *v* vetear
grammalogue gramálogo *m*
grammar gramática; (book) (libro de)

gramática; ~-**school** instituto (de segunda enseñanza)
grammarian gramático
grammatical gramático
gram(me) gramo
gramophone gramófono, tocadiscos *m
sing*+*pl*, *SA* fonógrafo; ~ **pick-up**
pick-up *m*; ~-**record** disco (de gramófono)
grampus orca
granary granero
¹ **grand** *n* mil dólares; *adj* (large) grande;
(main) principal; (imposing) impo-
nente; (haughty) altivo; *sl* fabuloso;
~**child** nieto *m*, nieta *f*; ~**children**
nietos *mpl*; ~**dad** abuelito, *SA* papá *m*
grande; ~ **duchess** gran duquesa; ~
duke gran duque *m*; ~**father** abuelo;
~**father clock** reloj de pesas; **Grand
Jury** Gran Jurado; ~**ma** abueli(ta),
SA mamá grande; ~**mother** abuela; ~
opera ópera; ~**pa(pa)** abuelito;
~**parents** abuelos *mpl*; ~ **piano** piano
de cola; ~**stand** tribuna (cubierta); ~
style *lit* estilo elevado; ~ **total** importe
m total
² **grand:** ~ **prix** gran premio
grandee grande *m* (de España o de Portugal)
grandeur grandeza
grandiloquence grandilocuencia
grandiloquent grandilocuente
grandiose grandioso; (pretentious) hinchado
grandly grandiosamente
grange casa de campo
granite *n* granito; *adj* de granito
granny abuel(it)a, nana; *SA* mamá
grande; (old woman) viejecita; (knot)
nudo al revés
grant *n* donación *f*; (subsidy) subvención *f*; (for study) beca(-salario);
(transfer) traspaso; ~-**aided** subvencionado; *v* (concede) conceder;
(agree to) acceder a; (bestow) donar;
(transfer) traspasar; ~**ed that** dado
que; **take for** ~**ed** dar¹⁹ por supuesto
granular granular
granulate granular(se); ~**d sugar** azúcar
m+*f* en grano
granule gránulo
grape (grano de) uva; **a lot of** ~**s** mu-
cha(s) uva(s); ~-**juice** mosto; ~-**shot**
metralla; ~-**vine** vid *f*, (climber) pa-

rra, *fig* vía clandestina de información/rumor, *mil sl* radio macuto

grapefruit toronja; ~ **juice** zumo de toronja

graph *n* diagrama gráfico; **~-paper** papel cuadriculado; *v* ~ **(out)** representar gráficamente

graphic gráfico

graphite grafito

graphologist grafólogo

graphology grafología

grapnel *naut* garabato; *aer* áncora

grapple *n mech* garfio; *naut* garabato; (wrestling) presa; *v* (seize) aferrar; ~ **with** luchar a brazo partido con, *naut* aferrar con, *fig* esforzarse[7] con … para resolver; **he had been grappling with some very difficult problems** él ha estado resolviendo unos problemas muy difíciles

grappling (struggling) lucha a brazo partido; *naut* aferramiento; **~-iron** garabato

grasp *n* (hold) agarro, *fam* puño; (handclasp) apretón (-ones) *m*; (understanding) conocimiento, **have a good** ~ **of** tener[19] un buen conocimiento de; **have within one's** ~ tener[19] al alcance; **it's within his** ~ está a su alcance; *v* agarrar, empuñar; (understand) comprender; **I can't** ~ **it** no lo comprendo, *fam* no me cabe en la cabeza

grasping tacaño

grass *n* (plant) hierba; *sl* marihuana; (pasture) pasto; (lawn) césped *m*, *SA* grama; *sl* (police informer) soplón *m* (-ona *f*); ~ **court** campo de tenis de hierba; **~hopper** saltamontes *m sing*; **~land** pradera; **~roots** *n* origen (-ígenes) *m* popular, raíz; *adj* popular; **~roots movement** movimiento popular; ~ **runway** *aer* pista de hierba; **~-seed** semilla de césped; ~ **skirt** falda de rafia; **~-snake** culebra de collar; ~ **widow** mujer *f* cuyo marido está ausente; *v* cubrir (*past part* cubierto) con hierba; *sl* (inform) soplar

grassy herboso; herbáceo; *SA* pastoso

grate *n* parilla del hogar *m*; *v* raspar; *cul* rallar; (irritate) irritar; **it ~s on my nerves** me ataca los nervios; ~ **on the ear** herir (ie)[2c] el oído

grateful agradecido; **be** ~ agradecer[14]

gratefulness agradecimiento

grater rallador *m*

gratification satisfacción *f*

gratified complacido; **be** ~ complacerse[14]

gratify satisfacer (*conj like* hacer[19]); complacer[14]

gratifying satisfactorio; **be** ~ serle[19] grato a uno +*infin*; **it is very** ~ **to have your reply** me/nos es muy grato tener su contestación

gratin *cul* gratín; **cauliflower au** ~ coliflor *f* al gratín

grating *n* (iron cover) reja; (noise) rechinamiento; *adj* rechinante (-ora *f*); (annoying) molesto al oído

gratis *adj* gratuito; *adv* gratis, *fam* de balde

gratitude gratitud *f*

gratuitous gratuito; (uncalled-for) sin fundamento; ~ **statement** afirmación arbitraria

gratuity gratificación *f*; (tip) propina

gravamen querella más grave (de una acusación)

[1] **grave** *n* sepultura; **~-digger** sepulturero; **~stone** lápida sepulcral; **~yard** cementerio; *adj* (serious) grave; (solemn) solemne

[2] **grave:** ~ **accent** acento grave

gravel grava; *med* mal *m* de piedra; ~ **path** senda de arenilla

gravelly arenisco

graven: ~ **image** ídolo

graver (tool) buril *m*

graving-dock dique *m* de carena

gravitate gravitar

gravitation gravitación *f*

gravitational: ~ **pull** fuerza de gravedad *f*

gravity +*phys* gravedad *f*; **~-feed** *mech* alimentación *f* por gravitación

gravy salsa; **with** ~ en salsa; **~-boat** salsera

gray *see* **grey**

grayling tímalo

graze *n* rozadura; *f*; (mere touch) roce *m*; *vt* (scratch) raspar; (merely touch) rozar[9]; *agri* pastar, *SA* pastear; *vi agri* +*vt* pacer[14]

grazier ganadero

grazing apacentamiento; **~-land** pasto

grease *n* grasa; (of candle) sebo; (dirt)

mugre *f*; ~**-box** caja de engrase; ~**-gun** engrasador *m* de presión; ~**-paint** maquillaje *m*; ~**-proof** a prueba de grasa; ~**-proof paper** papel apergaminado; ~**-spot** lamparón (-ones) *m*; *v* engrasar; ~ **the palm of** untar la mano a

greaser engrasador *m*; *sl* joven (jóvenes) motorista *m*; *US* mejicano

greasiness graseza

greasing engrasado; *mot* engrase *m*

greasy grasiento; ~ **surface** *mot* piso resbaladizo

great grande; **that's ~!** ¡estupendo!; **that's a ~ idea** eso es una buena idea; ~ **deal of** mucho; ~ **man/writer** gran hombre/escritor; ~ **many** muchos; ~ **powers** grandes potencias *fpl*; ~ **while** largo rato; ... **the Great** (of monarchs) ... el/la Grande; **Great Bear** *astron* Osa Mayor; **Great Britain** la Gran Bretaña, ~**-aunt** tía abuela; ~**-coat** sobretodo; ~ **dane** perro gran danés; ~**-grandchild** biznieto *m*, (-a *f*); ~**-granddaughter** biznieta; ~**-grandfather** bisabuelo; ~**-grandmother** bisabuela; ~**-grandparents** bisabuelos *mpl*; ~**-grandson** biznieto; ~**-hearted** magnánimo; ~**-tit** carbonero común

greatly grandemente

greatness grandeza

grebe *orni* somorujo

Greco-Roman grecorromano; ~ **wrestling** lucha grecorromana

Greece Grecia

greed (avarice) avaricia; (gluttony) glotonería; (selfishness) egoísmo; *fig* (longing) anhelo

greedy (avaricious) avaricioso; (gluttonous) glotón; (selfish) egoísta; *fig* anhelante

Greek *n*+*adj* (+language) griego; **that's ~ to me** no entiendo ni pío de aquéllo; ~**-Cypriot** griegochipriota

green *n* (colour) verde *m*; (golf) green *m*; *adj* verde; (credulous) crédulo, *fam* bobo; (inexpert) inexperto; (unripe) crudo; ~ **fingers/thumb** habilidad *f* para la jardinería; **turn** ~ verdear; ~ **light** señal *f* verde, *fig* permiso; ~ **vegetables**, ~**s** verdura(s); ~**back** *US* billete *m* de banco; ~**finch** verderón *m*; ~**fly** pulgón (-ones) *m*; ~**gage** ciruela verde, claudia; ~**grocer**

verdulero, verdulera; ~**grocer's** verdulería; ~**horn** novicio; ~**house** invernadero; ~ **room** *theat* camerino; ~**sand** *geol* arenisca verde; ~**wood** selva frondosa; **bottle-~** verde botella; **sea-~** verdemar

greenery verde *m*

greenish verdoso

Greenland Groenlandia

Greenlander groenlandés *m* (-esa *f*)

greenness (*see* green) verdor *m*; credulidad *f*; inexperiencia

greet saludar; (receive) acoger[8]; (welcome) dar[19] la bienvenida a; ~ **the sight/ears** presentarse a la vista/al oído

greeting saludo; (reception) acogida; ~**s!** ¡salud!; ~**s to** (in letter) recuerdos a; ~**s telegram** telegrama de felicitación

gregarious gregario

gregariousness sociabilidad *f*

Gregory Gregorio

gremlin duendecillo

Grenada Granada

grenade granada

grenadier granadero

grey *n* (color *m*) gris *m*; (horse) caballo rucio; *adj* gris; (of animals) pardo; (of horses) rucio; (of weather) triste; **be ~ at the temples** tener[19] las siencs grises; **my hair is turning ~** mi pelo se vuelve canoso; ~**-haired** de pelo gris; ~ **hairs** canas *fpl*; ~ **matter** seso(s); ~**hound** galgo; ~**hound-racing** carreras *fpl* de galgos; ~**hound-(racing-)-track** canódromo

greyish grisáceo; ~ **hair** pelo entrecano

greyness lo gris

grid (network) red *f*; *rad* malla; (draincover) alcantarilla; (old car/bicycle) armatoste *m*; ~**iron** parrilla

griddle (over fire) plancha; (for cakes) tartera

grief pena, aflicción *f*; **come to ~** fracasar; ~**-stricken** desconsolado

grievance agravio

grieve afligirse[9]; ~ **for** llorar; ~ **over** afligirse[9] por

grievous doloroso; **commit ~ bodily harm** herir (ie)[2c] gravemente

griff: give the ~ (on) revelar los detalles (de)

grill *n* parrilla; ~**-room** parrilla; *v cul* asar a la parrilla; (question) interrogar⁵ (severamente)

grille (screen) verja; (on window) reja; (over counter) rejilla; *mot* parrilla

grilling interrogación (severa)

grim (ferocious) horrendo; (severe) severo; *fam* (dull) muy aburrido; ~ **facts** hechos *mpl* inexorables; **give a ~ account of** cargar⁵ la tinta sobre

grimace *n* mueca; *v* hacer¹⁹ muecas/una mueca

grime, griminess mugre *f*

grimness (ferociousness) horror *m*; (severity) severidad *f*

grimy mugriento

grin *n* sonrisa abierta; (mocking) sonrisa burlona; (grimace) mueca; *v* sonreírse (i)³ (enseñando los dientes); ~ **and bear it** ponerle¹⁹ buena cara

grind *n* trabajo aburrido; **daily ~** rutina diaria; **it's a ~** es un calvario; *v* moler (ue)¹ᵇ; (sharpen) afilar; ~ **(down)** (oppress) oprimir; ~ **out** producir¹⁵ laboriosamente; ~ **one's teeth with rage** rechinar los dientes de rabia; **~stone** afiladero; **have one's nose to the ~stone** batir el yunque; **have a ~** (have sex) *vulg sl* follar

grinder (person) afilador *m*; (machine) molin(ill)o

grinding *n* pulverización *f*; (of teeth) rechinamiento

grip *n* (action) agarro; (handle) agarradero; (bag) maletín (-ines) *m*; (handclasp) apretón (-ones) *m*; (pressure) compresión; **come to ~s with** luchar con; **get a ~ on** agarrar; **get a ~ on o.s.** contenerse¹⁹; **in the ~ of** poseído de, (in the clutches of) en las garras de; **in the ~ of winter** en pleno invierno; **lose one's ~** perder (ie)²ᵇ control (de sí mismo); *v* agarrar; (squeeze) apretar; (of tyres) agarrarse; **the film gripped me** la película me emocionó

gripe *v* (complain) quejarse

griping quejas *fpl*

gripping emocionante

grisly horripilante

grist molienda; **all is ~ to the mill** todo es bueno para el convento

gristle ternilla

gristly ternilloso

grit arenilla; (in the eye) polvo; (spirit) determinación *f*; *geol* arenisca; *v* ~ **one's teeth** rechinar los dientes, *fig*

(suffer in silence) aguantar

gritty arenoso

grizzle gimotear; ~ **about** quejarse de

grizzled grisáceo

grizzling (of children) lloriqueo

grizzly(-bear) oso pardo

groan *n* gemido; (complaint) queja; *v* gemir; (complain) quejarse

grocer tendero de comestibles; *Cub* bodeguero; *Mex* abarrotero; ~**'s shop** tienda de ultramarinos, *Cub* bodega, *Chil+Arg* almacén *m*, *Mex* tienda de abarrotes

groceries ultramarinos *mpl*; *SA* abarrotes *mpl*; (*US* shopping) compras *fpl*

grog grog *m*

groggy (unsteady) inestable; (dazed) aturdido; (half drunk) medio borracho; (weak) débil; (boxing) grogui

groin *anat* ingle *f*; *archi* arista de crucería

groom *n* mozo de cuadra; (bride~) novio; *v* (horse) almohazar⁷; (for a post) preparar; ~ **o.s.** peinarse; **he is always well ~ed** él siempre va muy bien puesto

groove *n* acanaladura; (slot) ranura; (in gramophone record) surco; *v* acanalar; ~ **along** divertirse (ie)²ᶜ; **let's ~ along together** vamos a salir juntos

grooviness yeyeísmo

groovy de moda; **have a ~ time** divertirse (ie)²ᶜ mucho

grope andar a tientas; ~ **for** buscar⁴ a tientas, *fig* avanzar⁷ lentamente hacia

gropingly a tientas

gross *n* gruesa; **by the ~** (al) por mayor; **in ~** en conjunto; *adj* (large) enorme; *comm* total; (bad-mannered) grosero; ~ **amount** importe *m* total; ~ **earnings/profit** beneficios *mpl* brutos; ~ **error** error craso; ~ **income** renta total; ~ **lie** mentira gorda; ~ **tonnage** tonelaje bruto; ~ **weight** peso bruto

grotesque grotesco

grotesqueness lo grotesco

grotto gruta

grotty malo; *sl* chucho

grouch *n* mal humor *m*; (person) refunfuñón (-ona *f*); **have a ~ against** guardar rencor a; *v* refunfuñar

grouchy refunfuñador (-ora *f*)

¹ **ground** *n* suelo; (earth) tierra; (land) terreno; *naut* fondo; *sp* campo; **football**

~ campo de fútbol; *fig* (basis) motivo; ~s (estate) finca, (gardens) jardines *mpl*, (sediment) poso; ~(s) for motivos *mpl* de; from the ~ up de abajo arriba; he covered a lot of ~ él hizo un gran recorrido; it fits/suits you down to the ~ le está como un guante; on the ~ sobre el suelo; on the ~(s) of por motivo de; on the ~(s) that por +*infin*, porque +*indic*; stand one's ~ no ceder terreno; what ~s have you for saying that? ¿qué razones tiene usted para decir eso?; ~-plan proyección *f* horizontal; ~-rent canon (cánones) *m*; ~sheet tela impermeable; ~ swell mar *m* de fondo; ~-wire cable *m* de tierra; ~work base *f*; ~-to-air missile proyectil *mpl* tierra-aire; *adj* terrestre; ~-crew, ~-staff personal *m* de tierra; ~floor planta baja; ~-nut cacahuete *m*; *v* poner[19] en tierra; *naut* encallar; *aer* aterrizar[7]; the plane was ~ed el avión no pudo despegar; well ~ed in bien versado en

² ground (in powder) en polvo; ~-beef carne *f* de buey picada

grounding instrucción básica
groundless infundado
groundsel hierba cana
groundsman jardinero

group *n* grupo; *mus* conjunto; ~-captain jefe de escuadrilla; *adj* colectivo; ~ therapy terapéutica colectiva; *vt* ~ (together) agrupar; *vi* agruparse
grouping agrupación (-ones) *f*
¹ **grouse** *orni* ortega; (American) guaco
² **grouse** (complaint) queja; (cause for complaint) motivo de queja; *v* quejarse (about de)
grouser gruñón *m* (-ona *f*)
grout lechada; ~ed sujet(ad)o con lechada
grove arboleda; *SA* alameda
grovel (crawl) arrastrarse; (abase o.s.) humillarse
groveller persona servil; *fam* cobista *m+f*
grovelling *n* servilismo; *adj* servil; *fam* cobista
grow crecer[14]; (cultivate) cultivar; (develop) desarrollarse; (increase) aumentar; (become) hacerse; ~ angry enfadarse; ~ better mejorar; ~ bigger

agrandarse; ~ cold enfriarse, *meteor* empezar[2a+7] a hacer[19] frío; ~ dark anochecer[14]; ~ fat engordar; ~ late hacerse[19] tarde; ~ less disminuir[16]; ~ longer alargarse[5]; ~ old envejecer[14]; ~ pale ponerse[19] pálido; ~ shorter acortarse; ~ smaller achicarse; ~ tired cansarse; ~ warm calentarse, *meteor* empezar[2a+7] a hacer[19] calor
~ on one gustarle a uno cada vez más; that melody ~s on me aquella melodía me gusta cada vez más; (become habitual) arraigar[5] en uno
~ out of (originate) resultar de; the branches ~ out of the trunk las ramas salen del tronco; (abandon the habit) perder (ie)[2b] la costumbre de; we all ~ out of childish games al crecer todos abandonamos los placeres infantiles; (become too big for) hacérsele pequeña a uno la ropa
~ to llegar a +*infin*; I grew to love her llegué a quererla
~ up crecer[14]; (become grown-up) llegar[5] a ser mayor; (of customs) imponerse[19]

grower cultivador *m*
growing *n* crecimiento; *agri+hort* cultivo *f*; *adj* creciente; ~ business negocio en crecimiento
growl *n* gruñido; *v* gruñir[18]
growler gruñón *m* (-ona *f*)
grown crecido; ~ man hombre maduro; be fully ~ estar[19] completamente desarrollado; ~ over with cubierto de; ~-up *n* persona mayor; ~-ups mayores *mpl*; for ~-ups only exclusivamente para mayores; ~-up *adj* adulto
growth crecimiento; (development) desarrollo; (increase) aumento; (progress) progreso; (vegetation) vegetación *f*; *med* tumor *m*; four days' ~ on the chin barba de cuatro días
groyne malecón (-ones) *m*
¹ **grub** *n* gusano; *v* ~ about escarbar; ~ out/up (clear weeds *etc*) desherbar (ie)[2a], *SA* desmalezar[7]
² **grub** (food) comida; *sl* rancho; ~ up! ¡a comer!
grubbiness suciedad *f*
grubby mugriento
grudge *n* inquina; (motivo de) rencor *m*; have/bear a ~ against guardar rencor a; *v* dar[19] de mala gana

grudging *adj* de mala voluntad
grudgingly de mala gana
gruel gachas *fpl*
gruelling riguroso
gruesome macabro
gruff (of manner) brusco; (of voice) ronco
gruffly (of manner) bruscamente; (of voice) con la voz ronca
gruffness (of manner) brusquedad *f*; (of voice) ronquera
grumble *n* queja; (noise) ruido sordo; *v* murmurar; ~ **about** quejarse de
grumbler refunfuñador *m* (-ora *f*)
grumbling gruñón *m*
grumblingly refunfuñando
grumpiness mal humor *m*
grumpy malhumorado
grunt *n* gruñido; *v* gruñir[18]
Gruyère queso gruyere
G-string *mus* primera cuerda; (attire) taparrabos *m sing+pl*
guano guano
guarantee *n* garantía; *leg* fianza; caución *f*; **give a** ~ dar[19] garantía; *v* garantizar[7]
guarantor fiador *m* (-ora *f*)
guaranty caución *f*, fianza
guard *n* (in general) guarda *m*; (body of soldiers *etc*) guardia *f*; (soldier *etc* on duty) guardia *m*; (escort) escolta; (on train) jefe *m* de tren; (sentry) centinela *m*; (safeguard) salvaguardia; (boxing *etc*) defensa; (of a sword) guarnición *f*; *mech* (protective device) rejilla protectora; ~**'s van** (on train) furgón (-ones) *m*; **be off one's** ~ estar[19] desprevenido; **be on one's** ~ estar[19] prevenido; **be on** ~ estar[19] de guardia; **keep** ~ estar[19] de guardia; **keep a close** ~ **on** guardar una estrecha vigilancia; **let down one's** ~ descuidar la guardia; ~**-duty** guardia; ~**-house**, ~**-room** cuerpo de guardia, (detention cell) prisión (-ones) *f* militar; ~**-rail** barrera de protección, *bui* pasamano, *mech* rail *m* de defensa; *v* guardar; (protect) proteger[8]; (watch) vigilar; ~ **against** guardarse de +*n*/*infin*
guarded (cautious) cauteloso
guardian guardián (-anes) *m*; *leg* tutor *m*; ~ **angel** ángel *m* de la guarda
guardianship tutela
guardsman guardia *m*

Guatemala Guatemala
Guatemalan *n*+*adj* guatemalteco
gudgeon (fish) gobio; *mech* gorrón (-ones) *m*; ~**-pin** perno de émbolo
guer(r)illa guerrilla; (person) guerrillero; ~ **warfare** guerrilla
guess *n* suposición (-ones) *f*; **at a** ~ a primera vista; **that's a good** ~ es una buena suposición; ~**-work** conjetura(s); *v* adivinar; (suppose) suponer[19]; **this will keep you guessing** esto le hará pensar; ~ **at** estimar aproximadamente; ~ **right** acertar (ie)[2a]; ~ **wrong** no acertar (ie)[2a]
guest (at hotel) huésped *m* (-a *f*); (at meal) convidado; ~ **of honour** agasajado; ~**-house** casa de huéspedes; ~**-night** tarde *f* para visitas; ~**-room** cuarto de invitados
guesstimate adivinación aproximada/presupuesto aproximado
guff patraña
guffaw *n* carcajada; *v* reírse (i)[3] a carcajadas
Guiana Guayana
Guianese *n*+*adj* guianés *m* (-esa *f*)
guidance (act of guiding) dirección *f*; (advice) consejo; ~ **system** *space* sistema *m* de navegación
guide *n* (book) guía; (clue) indicación *f*; (inspiration) norte *m*; (person) guía *m*+*f*; *mech* guía; ~**-dog** perro-guía *m*; ~**-line sheet** (for writing) falsilla; ~**-rails** railes-guía *mpl*; ~**-rope** cuerda de arrastre; *v* guiar; (govern) gobernar (ie)[2a]; ~**d** (by remote control) teledirigido; **be** ~**d by** dejarse llevar por
guiding: ~ **line** pauta
guild gremio; *eccles* cofradía; ~**hall** (casa del) ayuntamiento; ~ **member** gremial *m*
guilder florín (-ines) *m* holandés
guile astucia
guileful astuto
guileless ingenuo
guillemot *orni* alca
guillotine *n* guillotina; *v* guillotinar
guilt culpa(bilidad) *f*; (sin) pecado; ~ **complex** complejo de culpa(bilidad); **admit** ~ confesarse culpable
guiltily como si fuera culpable
guiltiness culpabilidad *f*
guiltless inocente

guilty culpable; **have a ~ conscience** sentir (ie)[2c] remordimiento(s) de conciencia; ~ **party/person** culpable m+f; **find** ~ declarar culpable; **plead** ~ confesarse culpable; **plead not** ~ declararse inocente

Guinea Guinea

guinea guinea; ~**-fowl** gallina pintada; ~**-pig** conej(ill)o de Indias

guise pretexto; **under the** ~ **of** con el pretexto de; **in this** ~ de esta manera

guitar n guitarra; sl jamón m; adj de guitarra

guitarist guitarrista m+f

gulch barranco

gulf n golfo; (abyss) abismo; fig vorágine f; **Gulf Stream** corriente f del Golfo (de Méjico)

gull n orni gaviota; v (cheat) engañar

gullet garganta

gullibility credulidad f

gullible crédulo

gully barranco; (gutter) canal m

gulp n (of food) bocado; (of liquid) trago; ~ **of air** bocanada de aire; v engullir[18]; (under emotional stress) tragarse[5] la saliva

[1] **gum** anat encía; ~**boil** flemón (-ones) m; ~**-shield** (boxing) protector m dental

[2] **gum** (adhesive) cola; (chewing-~) chiclé m; ~**-arabic** goma arábiga; ~**-drop** pastilla; ~**-tree** eucalipto; **be up a ~-tree** estar[19] en un apuro; v pegar[5] con cola; ~ **up** atascar[4]

gumption sentido común

gun n arma de fuego; (cannon) cañón (-ones) m; (pistol) pistola; (rifle) fusil m; (shotgun) escopeta; **fire a 21-~ salute** disparar un saludo de 21 cañonazos; **stick to one's ~s** quedarse en lo suyo; ~ **barrel** cañón (-ones) m de fusil; ~**-boat** cañonero; ~**-carriage** cureña; ~**-cotton** algodón de pólvora; ~**-fight** tiroteo; ~**fire** cañoneo; ~**-flash** llamarada (de cañón/de fusil); ~**-licence** permiso de (llevar) armas; ~**man** bandido armado, pistolero; ~**-metal** bronce m de cañón; ~**powder** pólvora; ~**-room** armería; ~**-runner** contrabandista m de armas; ~**-running** contrabando de armas; ~**shot** (of cannon) tiro de cañón, (of shot~) escopetazo, (of rifle) tiro de fusil; **within** ~**shot** a tiro de fusil;

~**shot wound** herida de escopetazo; ~**-sight** punto; ~**smith** escopetero, mil armero; ~**smith's** armería; ~**-turret** torreta; ~ **wound** balazo; v cazar[7] con escopeta/fusil; ~ **down** matar a tiros

gunner artillero

gunnery artillería

gunwale borda

guppy pececillo oriundo de Venezuela

gurgle n (of baby) gorjeo; (of liquid) borboteo, fam gluglú m; v (of baby) gorjear; (of liquids) borbotear, fam hacer[19] gluglú

guru gurú m

gush n (jet) chorro; (of emotions) efusión f; (of words) torrente m; v chorrear; (of a person) ser[19] demasiado efusivo; ~ **out** saltar a chorros; ~ **over** hablar efusivamente de

gusher (oil) reventón (-ones) m

gushing efusivo

gusset escudete m

gust (of wind) ráfaga; fig acceso

gusto entusiasmo; placer m

gusty borrascoso

gut n intestino; mus cuerda de tripa; ~ **reaction** reacción f visceral; v (of fish etc) destripar; (by fire) quemar completamente

guts (bowels) tripas fpl; **I have ~-ache** tengo dolor de tripa; (courage) valor m; **have the ~ to** tener[19] agallas para, vulg tener[19] huevos para +infin

gutta-percha gutapercha f

gutter n bui canal m; (in street) cuneta, arroyo; ~ **press** prensa sensacionalista; ~**snipe** golfillo; v (of candle) correrse

guttering tubería externa

guttural n sonido gutural; adj gutural

[1] **guy** n (rope) naut retenida; (of tent) viento

[2] **guy** n (ridiculously dressed person) espantapájaros m sing; (fellow) tío; v burlarse de (imitando); **they ~ed their teacher** se burlaron del profesor imitándole

guzzle (eat) engullir[18]; (drink) beber con exceso; (swallow) tragar[5]

guzzler (greedy eater) comilón m (-ona f); (drinker) borracho

gym gimnasio; ~**-shoes** zapatillas de tenis

gymkhana competencia de habilidad *f*
  ecuestre
gymnasium gimnasio
gymnast gimnasta *m+f*
gymnastic gimnástico
gymnastics gimnasia
gynaecological ginecológico
gynaecologist ginecólogo
gynaecology ginecología

gypsum yeso
gypsy *see* **gipsy**
gyrate girar
gyration giro
gyratory giratorio
gyro-compass girocompás *m*
gyro-pilot piloto giroscópico
gyroscope giroscopio

H

h (letter) hache *f*; **drop one's ~'s** comerse las haches

ha! (expression of surprise) ¡ah!; (laugh) ja

haberdasher mercero; *SA* camisero; **~'s** mercería; *SA* camisería

haberdashery mercería, *SA* camisería

habilitate habilitar

habilitation habilitación *f*

habit costumbre *f*; (*esp* dress) hábito; **acquire the ~** adquirir (ie)[2c] la costumbre; **be in the ~ of** soler (ue)[1b] +*infin*; **break o.s. of a ~** perder (ie)[2b] la costumbre; **have the bad ~ of** tener[19] la mala costumbre de +*infin*; **have bad ~s** estar[19] malacostumbrado; **man of good ~s** hombre *m* de buen carácter; **~-forming** enviciador (-ora *f*), (of drugs) adictivo; **riding-~** traje *m* de montar

habitability habitabilidad *f*

habitable habitable

habitat habitación *f*

habitation habitación *f*; **be unfit for human ~** no reunir las condiciones (mínimas) de habitabilidad

habitual habitual; **~ thief** ladrón avezado

habituate habituar (**to a**)

habitué tertuliano

hack *n* (axe-blow) hachazo; *mech* piqueta; (horse) rocín *m*; (writer) estorzuelo; **~ on the shin** puntapié *m* en la espinilla; **~ work** trabajo de rutina; *adj* mercenario; (hackneyed) gastado; *v* (cut) cortar; (with knife) acuchillar; (with axe) dar[19] hachazos a; **~ the shin** dar[19] un puntapié en la espinilla; **~ down** (a tree) talar; **~ to pieces** cortar en pedazos

hacker operador *m* ilegal de computadora

hacking: **~ cough** tos seca

hackle (neck feathers/fur) plumas *fpl*/ piel *f* del pescuezo; **it made my ~s rise** me enfureció

hackney-carriage coche *m* de alquiler

hackneyed gastado

hacksaw sierra para metales

had *see* have

haddock pescadilla

Hades infierno

haemoglobin hemoglobina

haemophilia hemofilia

haemorrhage hemorragia

haemorrhoids hemorroides *fpl*; *fam* almorranas *fpl*

haft puño; mango

hag (old woman) viejota; (witch) bruja

haggard (gaunt) demacrado; (tired) ojeroso

haggardness aspecto ojeroso

haggis morcilla escocesa hecha de avena e hígado de oveja

haggish de bruja

haggle regatear

haggler regatero

haggling *n* regateo; *adj* regateador

Hague: The **~** La Haya

[1] hail *n meteor* granizo; *fig* (shower) pedrisco; **~ of bullets** granizada de balas; **~-stone** piedra de granizo, (large) pedrisco; **~-storm** granizada; *v* granizar[7]; *fig* (throw) lanzar[7]

[2] hail *n* (acclamation) aclamación *f*; (call) llamada; (greeting) saludo; **~!** ¡salud!; (shout) grito; **within ~(ing distance)** al habla; *v* (acclaim) aclamar; (call) llamar; (greet) saludar; (shout) gritar; **~-fellow-well-met** amigo de todos; **Hail Mary** Avemaría *f*

[3] hail: **~ from** proceder de

hair *n* (single strand) pelo; (on head) pelo, *sl* lana, **he has fair ~** él tiene pelo rubio; (on body) vello; (on plants) filamento; (of cloth) pelus(ill)a; (of violin bow) mecha; **long ~** (*esp* on a man) melena; **keep your ~ on!** ¡no te pongas así!; **let down one's ~** *fig* echar una cana al aire; **put one's ~ up** recogerse el pelo; **it makes my ~ stand**

755

on end me pone los pelos de punta; **tear one's** ~ mesarse los cabellos; **not turn a** ~ no mudarse; **wash one's** ~ lavarse la cabeza; ~**-bow**, ~**-ribbon** lazo/cinta del pelo; **by a** ~**'s breadth** por un pelo; ~**-cream** fijapelo; ~**-curler** (roller) rulo; (pincer) bigudí *m*; ~**-cut** *n* corte *m* de pelo; **have a** ~**-cut** cortarse el pelo; **I want a** ~**-cut** quiero que me corte el pelo; ~**-do** peinado; ~**dresser** peluquero; ~**dresser's** peluquería; ~**-dressing** peinado; ~**-drier** secador *m* para el pelo; ~**-line** línea delgadísima; ~**-net** red(ecilla) para el pelo; ~**-oil** aceite *m* del pelo; ~**pin** horquilla, *SA* ganch(it)o (para el pelo); ~**pin bend** viraje *m* de horquilla; ~**-raising** espeluznante; ~**-remover** depilatorio; ~**-restorer** vigorizador *m* de cabello; ~**-shirt** cilicio; ~**-slide** pasador *m*; ~**-splitting** *n* sofistería, *adj* rebuscón; ~**spray** laca para el pelo; ~**-spring** pelo *m* de reloj; ~**-style** peinado; ~**-styler** moldeador *m* de pelo; ~**-styling** moldeado de pelo; ~**-tonic** tónico capilar; ~**-trigger** pelo de una pistola

hairiness pelaje *f*; (of body) vellosidad *f*

hairless sin pelo; (bald-headed) calvo; (of body) sin vello

hairlessness (baldness) calvicie *f*

hairy peludo; (of body) velludo; ~**-chested** de pelo en pecho

Haiti Haití *m*

Haitian *n*+*adj* haitiano

hake merluza

halcyon: ~ **days** días *mpl* felices

hale robusto; ~ **and hearty** sano y fuerte

half *n* mitad *f*; ~ **my money** la mitad de mi dinero; ~ **and** ~ mitad y mitad; **in** ~ por la mitad; *sp* tiempo, **after ten minutes of the first** ~ después de diez minutos del primer tiempo; *adj* medio, semi-; **one hour and a** ~ una hora y media; ~ **(a) dozen** media docena (de); ~ **a litre of milk** medio litro de leche; ~ **as big** la mitad de grande; ~ **as long again** otra mitad de largo; ~ **a loaf is better than no bread** cuando no hay pan buenas son tortas; *adv* medio, a medias; **I was** ~ **asleep** yo estaba medio dormido; **my battery**

is ~ **flat** tengo la batería a medias; **his appearance was** ~ **apostolic and** ~ **revolutionary** tenía el aspecto entre apostólico y revolucionario; ~**-believe** creer[13] a medias; ~ **close** (the eyes) entornar; ~ **dressed** a medio vestir; **not** ~ (completely) completamente, **not** ~! ¡toma no!; ~ **naked** medio desnudo; ~**-back** *sp* medio; ~**-back line** (línea) media; ~**-baked** incompleto, poco maduro; ~**-breed/caste** mestizo; ~**-brother** medio hermano; ~ **calf** encuadernación *f* de la mitad en piel; **at** ~ **cock** en seguro; **set at** ~ **cock** poner el seguro; ~**-cooked** a medio cocer; ~ **dead (with)** medio muerto (de); ~**-finished** a medio acabar; ~**-hearted** indiferente; ~**-hitch** cote *m*; ~**-holiday** medio día festivo, (on Saturday) *fam* sábado inglés; ~**-hour** media hora; ~**-hourly** cada media hora; ~**-length** (portrait) retrato de medio cuerpo; ~**-made** a medio hacer; **at** ~ **mast** a media asta; ~**-measure** medida a medias; ~ **moon** media luna; ~**-mourning** medio luto; ~**-nelson** agarro de un adversario pasando un brazo por el axilar y al mismo tiempo sujetándole por la nuca; ~**-note** *mus* nota blanca; ~**-open** entreabierto; ~**-past** y media, ~**-past three** las tres y media; **(on)** ~ **pay (a)** medio sueldo; ~**penny** medio penique; ~**-pint** (*see* **pint**) media pinta; ~ **price** a mitad de precio; ~**-sister** hermanastra; ~**-starved** medio muerto de hambre; ~**-timbered** de paredes entramadas; ~**-time** *sp* descanso; ~**-title** portadilla; ~**-tone** fotograbado; ~**-truth** media verdad *f*; ~**-volley** medio voleo; ~**way** a medio camino; ~**-witted** bobo; ~ **year** semestre *m*

halibut hipogloso

halitosis halitosis *f*

hall (auditorium) salón *m*, auditorio; (country mansion) casa de campo; (entrance) vestíbulo, hall *m*; (passage) pasillo; (~ of residence) residencia; ~**mark** (marca de) contraste *m*, *fig* sello; ~**-marked** contrastado; ~ **porter** conserje *m*; ~**-stand** perchero; ~ **table** taquillón *m*; ~**way** (entrance) vestíbulo, (passage) pasillo

hallelujah aleluya

hallo! ¡hola!; (answering phone) ¡diga/dígame!; (calling by phone) ¡oiga/óigame!

halloo n llamada; v llamar; (hunting) azuzar[7]; ~! ¡sus!

hallow santificar[4]

Hallowe'en víspera del día de los Difuntos

hallucination alucinación (-ones) f

hallucinatory alucinante

hallucinogen n+adj alucinógeno

halo halo; fig aureola

[1] **halt** n alto; (railway) apeadero; (bus, tram) parada; **bring to a ~** parar; **call a ~** mil mandar hacer alto; **call a ~ to** mandar parar; **come to a ~** pararse; (of flow on production line) interrumpirse, **there has been a ~ in the production of** se ha interrumpido la producción de; vt parar; vi (stop) pararse; (hesitate) vacilar; (stammer) tartamudear; (walk with a limp) cojear; mil hacer[19] alto; **~! who goes there?** ¡alto!, ¿quién vive?

[2] **halt: the ~ and the blind** los cojos y los ciegos

halter n cabestro; (noose) dogal m; ~ **neck-line** escote ancho y profundo; v (en)cabestrar

halting (of speech) tartamudo; (of walk) cojo

halve partir por la mitad; **by ~s** a medias; **in ~s** en dos mitades; **go ~s** ir[19] a medias

halyard driza

ham n jamón m; anat pernil m; (bad actor) racionista m de teatro; rad radioaficionado; **~-fisted, ~-handed** desmañado; **~-roll, ~-sandwich** bocadillo de jamón; v theat actuar mal

Hamburg Hamburgo

hamburger hamburguesa; ~ **meat** carne picada; **~-seller** hamburguesero; **~-stall** hamburguesería

hamlet aldehuela

hammer martillo; (mason's) piqueta; (of firearm) percusor m; (of piano) macillo; ~ **and sickle** la hoz y el martillo; ~ **and tongs** como perros y gatos; **come under the ~** subastarse; **throw the ~** sp lanzar[7] el martillo; **~-blow** martillazo; **~-head** cabeza de martillo; **~-throwing** sp lanzamiento del

martillo; v (a)martillar; ~ **away at** dar[19] martillazos a, fig insistir en; ~ **into** clavar, fig inculcar[4]

hammering martilleo; (knocking on door) repiqueteo; **receive a ~** (boxing) recibir leña

hammock hamaca; SA chinchorro; naut coy m

hamper n cesto; v estorbar

hamster hámster m

hamstring n tendón m de la corva; v desjarretar; fig incapacitar

hand n mano f; (of animal) pata; (applause) aplauso; **big ~** gran ovación f; (at cards) mano f; (influence) mano f, **he had a ~ in that** él tomó parte en eso; (of clock) manecilla, **hour/-minute ~** manecilla pequeña/grande; (of dial) aguja; (farm worker) peón (-ones) m; (factory worker) operario; (sailor) tripulante m; (signature) firma; (writing) letra; (measure) palmo; (side) mano f, **on the one/other ~** por un lado/otro lado; **be ~ in glove** ser[19] uña y carne; ~ **in ~** cogidos de la mano; **go ~ in ~** ir[19] juntos; ~ **over fist** rápidamente; ~ **over ~** mano sobre mano; **~s off!** ¡fuera las manos!; **keep your ~s off it!** ¡no lo toque!; **~s up!** ¡manos arriba!; **all ~s** todo el personal; **all ~s on deck!** ¡todo el mundo arriba!; **the ship sank with all ~s** el buque se hundió con toda su tripulación; ~ **to ~** de mano en mano, (of fighting) a brazo partido; **ask for the ~ of** (in marriage) pedir (i)[3] la mano de; **at ~** a mano; **at first ~** de primera mano; **at the ~s of** a manos de; **by ~** a mano; **shake by the ~** estrechar la mano a; **be a good ~ at** tener[19] buena mano para; **be an old ~** ser[19] perro viejo/perra vieja; **change ~s** cambiar de mano, (change owners) cambiar de dueño; **get one's ~ in** (acquire the knack) hacerse[19] la mano; **have no ~ in** no tener[19] arte ni parte en; **have a free ~** tener[19] carta blanca; **have one's ~s full** estar[19] ocupado; **have the upper ~** tener[19] la sartén por el mango; **hold one's ~** detenerse[19]; **hold ~s** cogerse[8] las manos, (when in love) hacer[19] manitas; **in ~** (money) contante; **in our ~s** comm en nuestro poder; **be in**

757

good ~s estar¹⁹ en buenas manos; **I've
put it in the ~s of my lawyer** lo he
puesto en (las) manos de mi abogado;
put in ~ empezar (ie)²ᵃ⁺⁷; **show one's
~** poner¹⁹ las cartas boca arriba; **stock
in ~** mercancias en almacén; **take in ~**
hacerse¹⁹ cargo de; **keep one's ~ (in/
at)** conservar la práctica (en/de); **lay
~s on** echar mano a; **lend a ~** echar
una mano; **live from ~ to mouth** vivir
al día; **on ~** (handy) a mano, (available) en existencia; **go on one's ~s and
knees** andar a gatas, *fig* suplicar; **I
have my father on my ~s** tengo que
ocuparme de mi padre; **on the right/
left~ (side)** a la derecha/izquierda; **out
of ~** (immediately) en seguida,
(unruly) incontrolable; **set one's ~ to**
meter mano a; **shake ~s** estrechar²ᵃ la
mano; **take s.t. off one's ~s** quitar de
encima; **to ~** a mano; **come to ~**
venir¹⁹ a mano, **your letter has not yet
come to ~** su carta todavía no ha
venido a mano; **turn one's ~ to**
dedicarse⁴ a; **with his ~s behind his
back** con las manos a la espalda
adj de mano, manual; ~**bag** bolsa, *sl*
tanque *m*, (man's) maricona, *US* monedero, *SA* cartera; (valise) maletín
m, *SA* valija; ~**ball** balonmano; ~-
basin palangana; ~-**bell** campanilla;
~**bill** hoja volante; ~**book** manual,
(guide) guía; ~-**brake** freno de mano;
~**cart** carretilla de mano; ~-**control**
control *m* manual; ~**cuff** *v* poner las
esposas; ~**cuffs** esposas *fpl*; ~-**drill**
taladro de mano; ~-**grenade** granada
(de mano); ~**hold** sitio donde agarrarse; ~-**lever** palanca de mano; ~-
loom telar *m* de mano; ~-**luggage**
equipaje *m* de mano; ~-**made** hecho a
mano; ~-**made paper** papel *m* de tina;
~**maiden** sirvienta; ~-**me-downs** traje
m de segunda mano; ~-**operated** (de
operación) manual; ~-**out** nota de
prensa, (alms) limosna; ~-**picked**
escogido a mano; ~-**propelled** de
propulsión a mano; ~-**pump** bomba
de mano; ~-**rail** pasamano; ~-**saw** sierra de mano; ~-**shake** apretón (-ones)
m de manos; ~-**spring** voltereta sobre
las manos; ~-**stand** farol *m*; ~**work**
trabajo (hecho) a mano, (sewing)
labor *m* de aguja; ~**writing** letra; **in**

one's own ~writing de su puño y letra;
~-**written** escrito a mano; *adv* a mano
v entregar⁵; *fam* pasar; **will you ~ me the
salt?** ¿quiere pasarme la sal?; **one must
~ it to John that he ...** hay que
reconocer que Juan es ...; **for rudeness
~ it to him** a imprudencia él gana
~ **back** devolver (ue)¹ᵇ (*past part* devuelto)
~ **down** bajar; (of traditions) transmitir;
(as inheritance) pasar (de padres a
hijos); (of clothes) pasar a un
hermano/hermana menor
~ **in** entregar⁵; ~ **in one's resignation**
dimitir
~ **off** (rugby) rechazar⁷ con la mano
~-**out** (money) ayuda financiera; (press
report) nota de prensa
~ **out** distribuir¹⁶; (pay) pagar⁵
~ **over** entregar⁵; ~ **over power to** traspasar los poderes a
~ **round** pasar de mano en mano; (offer)
ofrecer¹⁴ (a todos)
~ **up** subir
handful puñado
handicap *n* obstáculo; *sp* handicap *m*; *v*
estorbar; *sp* conceder un handicap;
handicapped *med* inválido; **be handi-
capped** estar¹⁹ en situación de inferioridad
handicraft obra hecha a mano; (skill)
destreza manual; ~s artesanía
handicraftsman artesano
handily diestramente
handiwork labor hecha a mano
handkerchief pañuelo
handle *n* mango; (lever) palanca; *mech*
manivela; (of cup/basket) asa; (of
cart) tirador *m*; (of door/drawer)
pomo; (of hammer/axe) asta; (of
sword) puño; (of window) manubrio;
~-**bar(s)** manillar *m*, *SA* manubrio; *v*
manosear; (control) manejar, **this car
~s easily** este coche se maneja con
facilidad; (cope with) tratar; (deal in)
comerciar en; ~ **the ball** (football)
hacer¹⁹ mano; ~ **a situation** dominar
la situación; ~ **with care** tratar con
cuidado; ~ **with kid gloves** tratar con
muchos miramientos; **he's able to ~
the problem** él es capaz de resolver el
problema
handless sin mano
handling manoseo; (control) manejo;

(manipulation) manipulación *f*; (of a person) trato; (of a situation) dominio
handsome guapo, hermoso; (generous) generoso; ~ **offer** buena oferta; ~ **sum** suma considerable
handsomely: he paid ~ **for it** él pagó mucho dinero por ello
handy (near to hand) a mano; (easy) fácil de manejar; (skilled) diestro; (useful) útil; **it will come in** ~ vendrá bien; ~**man** factótum *m*
hang *n* (of clothes) caída; **get the** ~ **of** coger[8] el tino de; **now I get the** ~ **of it** ya lo entiendo; **I don't care a** ~ no me importa un ardite; *vt* colgar[1a+5]; (wallpaper) pegar[5]; (execute) ahorcar[4]; *vi* (of garments) caer[19], **your skirt** ~**s well** su falda cae bien; ~ **o.s.** ahorcarse[4]; ~ **fire** estar[19] en suspenso; ~ **the head** inclinar la cabeza; ~ **in the balance** estar[19] en un hilo; ~ **it all!** ¡por Dios!; **I'll be** ~**ed if I will!** ¡que me cuelguen si lo hago!; ~**dog** avergonzado
~ **about/around** rondar, frecuentar
~ **back** no querer (ie)[2b] adelantarse; (hesitate) vacilar
~ **down** colgar[1a+5]
~ **on** (resist) resistir; (stay) quedarse; (wait) esperar; ~ **on to** (hold) agarrarse a, (retain) guardar
~ **out** (washing) tender (ie)[2b]; (lean out) asomarse (**of** por); (live) vivir
~**over** *n* resaca, *SA* goma, *Mex* crudo
~ **over** *v* cernerse sobre; (threaten) amenazar[5]
~ **together** mantenerse[19] unidos; (of an argument) ser[19] consistente
~**up** complejo; (prejudice) prejuicio
~ **up** colgar (ue)[1a+5]; (washing) tender (ie)[2b]; ~ **up on s.o.** (telephone) colgarle a uno (el teléfono), **she hung up on me** ella me colgó
~ **upon s.o.'s words** beber la palabras de uno
hangar hangar *m*
hanger colgadero; (coat-~) percha; ~-**on** parásito, *fam* pegote *m*
hanging *n* (execution) ahorcadura; (of pictures *etc*) colgamiento; ~**s** colgaduras *fpl*; *adj* colgante
hank madeja
hanker: ~ **after** añorar
hankering añoranza (**after** por)

hanky pañuelo; ~-**panky** truco
Hannah Ana
Hannibal Aníbal
hansom cabriolé *m*
haphazard *adj* casual
haphazardly al azar
hapless desventurado
happen suceder, pasar; **I** ~**ed to see her** la vi por casualidad; **I don't** ~ **to have a pencil** el caso es que no tengo lápiz; **it so** ~**s that** resulta que; **it won't** ~ **again** no volverá a ocurrir; **whatever** ~**s** suceda lo que suceda; **it** ~**ed one day that** sucedió un día que; **what's** ~**ed to you?** ¿qué le ha pasado?
happening suceso, acontecimiento; *sl* movida
happily felizmente; (luckily) afortunadamente
happiness felicidad *f*
happy fcliz (-ces); *fam* entre dos luces; **be** ~ **about** estar[19] contento de; **be** ~ **to** tener[19] mucho gusto en +*infin*; ~-**go-lucky** despreocupado; ~ **medium** justo medio; **Happy Christmas!** ¡Felices Navidades!; **Happy New Year!** ¡Feliz Año Nuevo!
Hapsburg Habsburgo
hara-kiri harakiri *m*
harangue *n* arenga; *v* arengar[5]
harass acosar; *mil* hostigar
harassment acosamiento; *mil* hostigamiento
harbinger *n* precursor *m*; *v* anunciar
harbour *n* puerto; ~-**dues** derechos *mpl* portuarios; ~-**bar** barra del puerto; ~-**master** capitán (-anes) *m* de puerto; *v* (give shelter to) abrigar[5]; ~ **a criminal** amparar a un criminal; ~ **a doubt** mantener[19] una duda
hard *adj* duro; (difficult) difícil; (stern) severo; *meteor* áspero; ~ **winter** invierno riguroso/severo; ~ **to deal with** intratable; **be** ~ **on** (a person) ser[19] duro con, (clothes) gastar; **go** ~ endurecerse[14]; **have a** ~ **time** pasar apuros, *fam* pasar las de Caín; **we've been through** ~ **times** hemos pasado estrecheces; **it's** ~ **to believe** parece mentira; **it's rather** ~ **to do** cuesta un poco hacerlo; ~ **to please** difícil de contentar; **take a** ~ **look at** mirar fijamente, *fig* investigar[5] detenidamente; ~ **and fast rule** regla inflexible;

~-back libro de tapa dura; ~ blow golpe *m* fuerte; ~board tabla de fibras prensadas; (in) ~ cash (en) metálico; ~ core *bui* firme *m* del suelo, *fig* parte *f* principal; ~ court (tennis) pista de tierra (dura); (in) ~ covers (of books) (en) pastas *fpl*; ~ currency moneda fuerte; ~ drinker bebedor *m* empedernido; ~ drinking el beber demasiado; ~ facts hechos *mpl* innegables; ~ knot nudo apretado; ~ labour trabajo forzado; ~ landing *aer* aterrizaje duro; ~-liner *pol* duro; ~ luck! ¡mala suerte!, *fam* ¡mala pata!; ~ liquor licor espirituoso; ~ news noticias *fpl* de gran importancia; ~ of hearing duro de oído; ~ sell publicidad agresiva; ~ usage/wear mal trato; ~ware ferretería, *mil* material *m* de guerra pesado; ~ware store ferretería; ~ water agua gorda; ~ words palabras *fpl* imperiosas; ~ work trabajo duro; ~ worker trabajador asiduo, trabajadora asidua *adv* (diligently) diligentemente; (with difficulty) con dificultad *f*; (with physical effort) duro; *naut* todo; go ~ with irle[19] mal a uno; I was ~ put to encontré difícil +*infin*; I work ~ for my money gano a pulso mi dinero; ~-baked +*fig* duro; ~-boiled (of eggs + people) duro; ~-earned ganado a pulso; ~-faced descarado; ~-fought reñido; ~-handed despótico; ~-headed astuto; ~-hearted duro de corazón; ~-heartedness insensibilidad *f*; ~-hitting vigoroso; ~-pressed acosado, (financially) apurado; ~-pushed apurado; ~-wearing durable; ~-won ganado con el sudor de la frente; ~-working muy trabajador (-ora *f*)

harden endurecer(se)[14]; *comm* (of shares) entonarse; *metal* templar(se); become ~ed to acostumbrarse a

hardening endurecimiento; *metal* temple *m*; ~ of the arteries arteriosclerosis *f*

hardihood temeridad *f*

hardiness robustez *f*; (daring) audacia

hardly duramente; (with difficulty) difícilmente; (sternly) severamente; (scarcely) apenas; there are ~ any ... casi no hay ...; ~ ever casi nunca

hardness dureza; (of character) severidad *f*; (inhumanity) inhumanidad *f*; (stiffness) tiesura; (of hearing) dureza (de oído); (of water) gordura

hardship penas *fpl*; (privation) privación *f*; (suffering) sufrimiento

hardy robusto; (daring) audaz (-ces); *hort* resistente, ~ annual planta anual resistente

hare *n* liebre *f*; ~bell campanilla azul; ~-brained casquivano; ~-lip labio leporino; ~-lipped labihendido; ~s and hounds (game) caza de papelitos; *v* ~ after correr detrás de

harem harén (-enes) *m*

haricot (fresh) judía; (dried) alubia

hark escuchar; ~! ¡oiga(n)!; ~ back to (something) volver (ue)[1b] (*past part* vuelto) a, (recall) recordar (ue)[1a]

harlequin arlequín (-ines) *m*

harlequinade arlequinada

harlot ramera

harm daño; (danger) peligro; (misfortune) desgracia; there's no ~ (in) no hay ningún mal (en); out of ~'s way fuera de peligro; keep (o.s.) out of ~'s way evitar el peligro; I hope no ~ will come to you espero que no le ocurra ninguna desgracia; *v* dañar, hacer[19] daño; all his life he never ~ed a soul en su vida ha hecho daño a nadie

harmful dañoso; (of insects *etc*) dañino; (dangerous) peligroso; be ~ (of food) hacer[19] mal

harmless inocuo; (of people) inocente

harmonic *n* armónica; *adj* armónico

harmonica armónica

harmonious armonioso

harmonium armonio

harmonize armonizar[7] (with con)

harmony armonía; be in ~ with *fig* estar[19] de acuerdo con

harness *n* arreos *mpl*; *mil* arnés *m*; die in ~ morir (ue)[1c] (*past part* muerto) con las botas puestas; get back in ~ volver[1b] (*past part* vuelto) a la rutina; ~-maker talabartero; *v* enjaezar[7]; *fig* utilizar[7]

harp *n* arpa; *v* ~ on *fam* machacar[4]

harpist arpista *m*+*f*

harpoon *n* arpón (-ones) *m*; ~ gun cañón (-ones) arponero; *v* arponear

harpooner arponero

harpsichord clavicordio

harpy arpía

harridan bruja

harrier (person) corredor *m* a través del campo; (dog) perro lebrel; *orni* aguilucho

harrow *n* grada; *v agri* graduar; *fig* horrorizar[7]

harrowing *n agri* gradeo; *adj* horripilante

harry acosar

harsh áspero; (of behaviour) severo; (of colours) chillón

harshness aspereza; (of behaviour) severidad *f*; (of colour) discordancia

hart ciervo europeo

harum-scarum *n* tarambana *m+f*; *adj* alocado

harvest *n* cosecha; (of grain) siega; (of grapes) vendimia; ~ **festival** fiesta de la cosecha; ~**-home** fiesta de segadores; ~ **moon** luna de la cosecha; ~ **time** tiempo de la cosecha; *v +fig* cosechar

harvester (person) segador *m* (-ora *f*); (machine) cosechadora

has-been cosa/persona ya pasada de moda

hash *n* (*see* **hashish**); *cul* picadillo; *fig* estropicio; **make a** ~ **of** estropear; *v* picar[4]; *fig* estropear

hashish hachís *m*; *fam* grifa; *sl* mierda

hasp aldaba (de candado)

hassle *n* (argument) discusión (-ones) *f*; (confusion) atolondramiento; *v* (argue) discutir; (confuse) atolondrar

hassock cojín (-ines) *m*

haste prisa; **in** ~ de prisa; **make** ~ darse[19] prisa; **more** ~ **less speed** vísteme despacio que voy de prisa

hasten *vt* acelerar; ~ **one's steps** apretar el paso; *vi* darse[19] prisa; ~ **to** apresurarse a +*infin*

hastily de prisa, sin reflexión

hastiness precipitación *f*

hasty (hurried) apresurado, *fam* a bocajarra; (impatient) impaciente; (impulsive) impulsivo; (quick-tempered) de genio vivo; ~ **job** trabajo hecho a la ligera

hat sombrero; **take off one's** ~ quitarse el sombrero; **take off one's** ~ **to** hacer[19] reverencia a; ~**s off!** ¡descúbra(n)se!; ~**s off to** ¡todo honor a!; **at the drop of a** ~ en un santiamén; ...

I'll eat my ~ que me ahorquen si …; **keep it under your** ~ de esto no diga usted nada; **pass round the** ~ pasar el cepillo; **talk through one's** ~ decir[19] disparates; ~**-band** cinta (del sombrero); ~**-box** sombrerera; ~**-pin** horquilla de sombrero; ~**-shop** sombrerería; ~**-stand/rack** perchera; **do the** ~**-trick** ganar tres veces seguidas, (football) meter tres goles en un partido

[1] **hatch** (trap-door) puerta caediza; (in ceiling) lumbrera del desván; (half-door) compuerta; (serving-~) ventanilla de servicio; *naut* (~way) escotilla; ~**-back** *mot* coche *m* con puerta trasera; ~**-cover** cubierta de escotilla

[2] **hatch** *n orni* (of chickens) pollada; (of wild birds) nidada; *vi* salir[19] del cascarón; *vt* empollar; ~ **a plot** tramar un complot

hatchery criadero

hatchet hacha; **bury the** ~ hacer[19] las paces; ~**-faced** de/con rostro afilado

hatching (shading) sombreado; *orni* incubación *f*

hate *n* odio; *v* odiar; ~ **the sight of** no poder[19] ver; **I** ~ **to bother you but** siento mucho molestarle pero; **I** ~ **to see you do that** no me gusta verle hacer eso; **he** ~**s all work** le repugna todo trabajo

hateful odioso

hatless sin sombrero; *fam* descubierto

hatred *see* **hate**

hatter sombrerero; ~**'s** (shop) sombrerería; **mad as a** ~ loco como una cabra

haughtiness altanería

haughty altanero

haul *n* (pull) tirón *m*; (catch of fish) redada; *fam* (booty) botín *m*; **it's a long** ~ **to** hay buen trecho a; *v* (pull) tirar (de); ~ **at the ropes** arriar: ~ **down the flag** arriar la bandera; ~ **in** *naut* cazar[7]; ~ **over the coals** regañar

haulage transporte *m*; ~ **costs** gastos *mpl* de transporte; ~ **contractor** contratista *m* de transportes

haunch *anat* cadera, anca; (of meat) pierna

haunt *n* lugar *m* de reunión; (lair) guarida; *v* (of ghosts) aparecer en, +*fig* recorrer, **a spectre is** ~**ing Europe** un fantasma recorre Europa;

(frequent) rondar por; **the memory ~s me** el recuerdo me obsesiona; **~ed house** casa embrujada

hauteur altivez *f*

Havana La Habana; (cigar) puro de La Habana

have *n* **the ~s and the ~-nots** los ricos y los pobres, (of nations) los países desarrollados y los subdesarrollados; *v* (possess) tener[19]; (take) tomar, **please ~ one** tome uno por favor; (eat/drink) tomar, **what will you ~?** ¿qué tomará usted?; (smoke) fumar, **he had a cigarette** él fumó/*fam* él echó un cigarrillo; (spend) pasar, **they will ~ a day in Seville** pasarán un día en Sevilla; (walk, ride *etc*) dar[19], **they ~ a long walk** dan un paseo largo; (suffer) padecer[14]; (allow) tolerar, **I can't ~ that** no puedo tolerar eso; (swindle) engañar, **you've been had** le han engañado; (maintain) insistir en que; (as auxiliary *v*) haber[19], **I ~ seen it** lo he visto; **~ a bath(e)** tomar un baño; **~ a child** dar[19] a luz a un niño; **~ a dance** bailar; **~ a dream** tener[19] un sueño; **~ done with** acabar con; **I ~ had a (wonderful) idea** he tenido una idea (luminosa); **~ just** acabar de +*infin*, **I ~ just arrived** acabo de llegar; **I'm going to ~ it repaired** voy a hacerlo reparar; **~ on good authority** tener[19] de buena tinta; **~ one's eye on** (keep watch on) vigilar, (want) desear; **~ one's own way** hacer[19] lo que uno quiera; **~ one's revenge** vengarse[5] (on de); **~ one's say** dar[19] su opinión; **I ~ it!** ¡ya está!; **as Sancho Panza has it** según Sancho Panza; **I had all my money stolen** me robaron todo el dinero; **I ~ you** (I've caught you) le tengo cogido; **I had rather** yo preferiría; **I will not ~ it** (I don't want it) no lo quiero, (I'll not permit it) no lo permitiré; **let him ~ it** (hit him) dele una paliza, (give him a telling-off) dígale cuatro verdades; **you had better** más vale que +*subj*; **she had better do it** más vale que lo haga ella; **you've had it/your chips** se acabó para usted

~ about one (friends) estar[19] rodeado de; (money) tener[19] encima

~ back (regain possession) tener[19] otra vez; **when shall I ~ it back?** ¿cuándo

me lo devolverán?

~ it away (with) *see* **~ it off (with)**

~ it in for s.o. quererle (ie)[2b] mal a uno

~ it off (with) tener[19] relaciones sexuales (con); *sl* tirarse a, *vulg* joder

~ it out with resolverlo (ue)[2b] con

~ on (wear) llevar puesto; (tease) tomar el pelo; **I ~ something on tonight** (I am engaged) tengo una cita esta tarde

~ out: I'm going to ~ a tooth out voy a sacarme una muela

~ to (must) tener[19] que; **I shall ~ to do it myself** tendré que hacerlo yo mismo; **~ (s.t.) to do with** estar[19] relacionado con

~ up (in court) llevar ante los tribunales

haven *naut* puerto; (refuge) refugio

haversack mochila

havoc estrago; **play ~ (among)** hacer[19] estragos (entre/en)

[1] **haw** *hort* baya de espino

[2] **haw: hum and ~** vacilar al hablar

Hawaiian hawaiano

hawk *n orni*+*pol* halcón *m*; **~-eyed** de ojos de lince; *v* cazar[7] con halcones; (sell) vender por las calles; (shout wares) pregonar

hawker buhonero

hawser cable *m*

hawthorn espino

hay heno; **hit the ~** ir[19] a dormir; **make ~ while the sun shines** hacer[19] su agosto; **~-cock** montón (-ones) *m* de heno; **~-fever** fiebre *f* del heno; **~-field** henar *m*; **~-fork** horca; **~-loft** henil *m*; **~-making** henaje *m*; **~-rick, ~-stack** almiar *m*; **~-seed** rústico; **~-wire** (mad) loco, (in disorder) en desorden

hazard *n* azar *m*; (danger) peligro; *v* arriesgar[5]; **~ a remark** aventurar una observación

hazardous peligroso

haze *n* neblina; *fig* confusión *f*; *v* burlarse de

hazel avellano; (colour) de color de avellana; **~-nut** avellana

hazy nebuloso; *fig* confuso

hazzle discutir

H-bomb bomba H

H.C.F. (highest common factor) M.C.D. (máximo común divisor)

H.E. (His Excellency) S.E. (Su Excelencia); **(His Eminence)** Su Eminencia; **(high explosive)** explosivo violento

he él; ~ **who** quien; **a** ~ **or a she?** ¿varón o hembra?; ~**-goat** macho cabrío; ~**man** machote *m*, *fam* hombre *m* de pelo en pecho

head *n anat* cabeza; *sl* cocorota; (hair) cabellera; *lit* testa, **crowned** ~**s of Europe** testas coronadas de Europa; (talent) cabeza, **he has a good** ~ **for business** él tiene buena cabeza para los negocios; (chief) jefe *m*; (of a school) director *m* (-ora *f*); (of state) jefe *m* de Estado; (top part) parte *f* superior; (of a list) cabecera, **Real Madrid is at the** ~ **of the table** el Real Madrid está a la cabecera de la clasificación; (of a page) cabeza; (person) persona, **per** ~ por persona, *fam* por barba; (of cattle) res *f*, **fifty** ~ cincuenta reses; (of an arrow *etc*) punta; (of coin) cara, ~**s or tails** cara o cruz; (of flower) cabezuela; (of pins *etc*) cabeza; (of bed, table *etc*) cabecera; (of a bridge) cabeza; (froth) espuma; (of river) cabecera; (of water in plumbing) altura de caída; ~ **first** de cabeza; **be off one's** ~ estar[19] fuera de sí; **be it on your** ~ a su responsabilidad, *fam* allá usted/tú; **be above one's** ~ (too difficult) estar[19] fuera del alcance; **bring to a** ~ provocar[4]; **come to a** ~ (reach crisis point) llegar[5] a un punto decisivo, (of a boil) abrirse; **from** ~ **to foot** de pies a cabeza; **get it into your** ~ **that** métaselo en la cabeza que; **I shall give him his** ~ le daré rienda suelta; **go to one's** ~ (success, drink) subírsele a uno a la cabeza; **go over s.o.'s** ~ saltar por encima de uno; **keep one's** ~ mantener[19] calma; **lose one's** ~ *fig* perder (ie)[2b] los estribos; **make neither** ~ **nor tail of it** no encontrarle (ue)[1a] ni pies ni cabeza; **out of one's own** ~ de su cosecha; ~**-over-heels** patas arriba, (completely) completamente; ~**-over-heels in love with** locamente enamorado de, *fam* chiflado por; **let's put our** ~**s together** vamos a cambiar ideas (para resolverlo); **she took it into her** ~ **to** se le ocurrió a ella +*infin*; **turn one's** ~ (with praise) envanecer(se)[14]; ~

down cabizbajo; **with** ~**(s) held high** con la frente alta; ~**ache** dolor *m* de cabeza, *fig* problema *m*; ~**board** cabecera; ~ **cook** primer cocinero; ~**-dress** tocado; **Red Indian** ~**-dress** tocado de jefe indio; ~**-gear** (hat) sombrero, (cap) gorro; ~ **guard** (boxing) chichonera; ~**-hunter** cazador *m* de cabezas; ~**-hunting** caza de cabezas; ~**lamp**, ~**light** *mot* faro; ~**land** promontorio; ~**line** (of chapter) epígrafe *m*, (of newspaper) titular *m*, **in bold** ~**lines** a grandes titulares; ~**long** de cabeza; ~ **man** jefe *m*; ~**master** director *m*; ~**mistress** directora; ~ **office** oficina central; ~**-on** de frente; ~**-on collision** choque *m* de frente, frontal; ~**phone** auricular *m*; ~**-phones** audífonos gemelos; ~**piece** (helmet) casco, (brains) cabeza, *rad* auricular *m*; ~**quarters** cuartel *m* general, (of firm) oficina central; ~**rest** apoyacabezas *m sing*; ~**-room** altura; ~**ship** dirección *f*; ~**sman** verdugo; ~**stone** lápida sepulcral, *archi* piedra angular; ~**strong** terco; ~ **waiter** maestresala; ~**way** progreso; **make** ~**way** progresar; ~**wind** viento en proa; ~**-work** trabajo mental

adj (in the lead) primero, delantero; (principal) principal; (central) central

v (be first) estar[19] a la cabeza de; **he** ~**ed the cortège** él presidió el cortejo fúnebre; (football) cabecear; *aer* conducir[15]; ~ **off** desviar, *fig* distraer[19]; ~ **for/towards** dirigirse[9] hacia, ~**ing for** con rumbo a

header (head-first dive) salto de cabeza; (football) cabezazo

headiness (of person) terquedad *f*; (of wine) fuerza

heading título; (on stationery) membrete *m*; (summary at the beginning of a chapter) epígrafe *m*

heady fuerte

heal *vt* curar; *vi* curarse; ~ **(up)** (of a cut) cicatrizarse[7]

healer curador *m* (-ora *f*); (unqualified) curandero

healing *n* cura(ción) *f*; (of cut) cicatrización *f*; *adj* curativo; (of cut) cicatrizante

health salud *f*; **how is your** ~? ¿cómo

está usted de salud?; (public ~) sanidad *f*; **be in bad/good** ~ estar[19] mal/bien de salud; **drink (to) the** ~ **of** beber a la salud de; **good** ~! ¡(a su) salud!; **bill of** ~ patente de sanidad; ~-**certificate** certificado de salud; ~-**giving** saludable; ~ **inspector/officer** inspector *m* de sanidad; ~ **insurance/service** seguro de enfermedad; ~ **resort** balneario

healthy (of a person) sano; (of a place *etc*) saludable; **be** ~ (person) tener[19] buena salud; (place *etc*) ser[19] saludable

heap *n* montón (-ones) *m*; **in a** ~ amontonado; **in** ~**s** a montones; **we have** ~**s of time** nos sobra tiempo; *v* amontonar; ~**ed (with)** repleto (de); ~ **together** juntar; ~ **up** apilar, *fig* acumular; ~ **favours on** colmar de favores

hear oír[19]; (listen) escuchar; **I** ~ **that** ... oigo decir que ...; ~ **a case** *leg* ver[19] un pleito; ~, ~! ¡bravo!

~ **about** oír hablar de

~ **from** tener[19] noticias de; **I hope to** ~ **from you** espero tener noticias suyas

~ **of** (learn about) enterarse de; (permit) permitir; **I won't** ~ **of it** no quiero ni oírlo; **he was never** ~**d of again** no se volvió a saber de él

hearer oyente *m*+*f*

hearing (sense) oído; (examination) audiencia; *leg* vista; *mus* audición *f*; **be out of** ~ estar[19] fuera del alcance del oído; **be within** ~ estar[19] al alcance del oído; ~-**aid** audífono

hearken: ~ **to** escuchar, (take notice of) hacer[19] caso de

hearsay rumor *m*; ~ **evidence** testimonio indirecto; **by** ~ de oídas

hearse coche *m* fúnebre

heart corazón (-ones) *m*; (of cabbage *etc*) cogollo; *fig* (centre) centro; **in the** ~ **of Africa** en medio de África; **in the** ~ **of the country** en pleno campo; ~ **and soul** con todo el alma; ~ **of stone** corazón de piedra; ~-**to**-~ **talk** discusión franca; **after my own** ~ a mi gusto, **girls after my own** ~ chicas de las que me gustan; **at** ~ en el fondo; **be sick at** ~ tener[19] la muerte en el alma; **you will break my** ~ me romperá el alma; **by** ~ de memoria, *fam* de carre-

tilla; **do one's** ~ **good** alegrarle a uno el corazón; **eat one's** ~ **out for** penar por; **from the** ~ de todo corazón; **have a** ~! ¡tenga compasión!; **have no** ~ *fig* no tener[19] entrañas; **have the** ~ **to** tener[19] valor para; **have one's** ~ **in one's mouth** tener[19] el alma en un hilo; **in good** ~ lleno de confianza, (of soil) en buen estado; **in my** ~ **of** ~**s** en lo más recóndito de mi corazón; **lose** ~ desanimarse; **lose one's** ~ **to** enamorarse de; **set one's** ~ **on** poner[19] el corazón en; **take** ~ cobrar ánimo, *fam* hacer[19] de tripas corazón; **take to** ~ tomar a pecho; **to one's** ~'**s content** sin restricción; **wear one's** ~ **on one's sleeve** llevar el corazón en la mano; **with all my** ~ con toda mi alma; **I am French at** ~ soy francés de corazón; ~-**ache** (anguish) angustia; ~-**attack** ataque *m* cardíaco; ~-**beat** latido de corazón; ~**break** congoja; ~**breaking** angustioso; ~**broken** afligido; ~**burn** acedía; ~-**burning** descontento; ~ **complaint** afección cardíaca; ~ **disease** enfermedad *f* del corazón; ~-**failure** colapso cardíaco; ~-**felt** sincero; **accept my** ~-**felt sympathy** le acompaño en sus sentimientos; ~-**rending** desgarrador (-ora *f*); ~-**searching** examen *m* de conciencia; ~-**sease** *bot* trinitaria; ~-**shaped** acorazonado; ~-**sore** desconsolado; ~-**strings** fibras *fpl* del corazón; ~-**throb** latido del corazón, (film star *etc*) ídolo; **she is my** ~-**throb** ella es la que me chifla; *v* (of cabbages *etc*) formar cogollo; ~**ed** de corazón; **hard**-~**ed** duro de corazón

hearten alentar (ie)[2a]

heartening animador (-ora)

hearth hogar *m*; ~-**rug** alfombra para poner delante del fuego; ~-**stone** solera del hogar

heartily cordialmente; **eat** ~ comer con buen apetito; **be** ~ **sick of** estar[19] harto de; **laugh** ~ reír[3] a carcajadas

heartiness cordialidad *f*

heartless inhumano

heartlessness inhumanidad *f*

hearty (friendly) cordial; (healthy) robusto; ~ **meal** comilona; **he is a** ~ **eater** él tiene buen diente; ~ **welcome** cordial recibimiento

heat n calor m; **in the ~ of the day** a pleno sol; (of animals) celo, **on ~** en celo; fig ardor m, **in the ~ of the moment** en el ardor del momento; (of an argument) acaloramiento; sp eliminatoria; **dead ~** empate m; **~-barrier** muro del calor; **~ haze** neblina estival; **~-proof** termoresistente; **~-rash** calentura; **~-resistant** resistente al calor; **~-shield** space blindaje m del calor; **~ stroke** insolación f; **~-wave** ola de calor; v calentar (ie)[2a]; **~ed** (excited) excitado; **~ed swimming-pool** piscina aclimatizada

heater calentador m

heath (place) brezal m; bot brezo; **native ~** patria chica

heathen n+adj pagano

heathenish pagano

heather brezo; **~-mixture** tela verdosa jaspeada

heating calefacción f; **central ~** calefacción f central

heave n (pull) tirón m; (push) empujón (-ones) m; **one more ~** un esfuerzo más; (retch) náusea; v (move up and down) subir y bajar; (pull) tirar (**at** de); (throw) arrojar; **~ coal** cargar[5] carbón; **~ a sigh** dar[19] un suspiro; **~ the lead** naut echar el escandallo; **~ overboard** echar al agua; **~ to** naut fachear; **~ to!** ¡a la capa!

heaven cielo; **~ forbid!** ¡no lo quiera Dios!; **~-sent** providencial; **thank ~!** ¡gracias a Dios!; **~s** firmamento; **~!** ¡madre mía!, ¡Dios mío!

heavenly +fig celestial; astron celeste; **~ body** astro

heavenwards hacia el cielo

heaver cargador m

heavily pesadamente; (sadly) tristemente; **it rained ~** llovió mucho; **she fell ~** ella cayó de plomo

heaviness peso; fig letargía; (of crops) abundancia; **~ of heart** tristeza

heavy pesado; **be ~** pesar mucho; **how ~ is it?** ¿cuánto pesa?; (serious) grave; **there was ~ buying on the Stock Exchange** hubo mucha compra en la Bolsa; **~ artillery** artillería pesada; **~ drinker** beberrón m (-ona f); **~-eyed** con ojeras; **~ fire** mil fuego intenso; **~-handed** severo; **~-hearted** triste; **~ industry** industria pesada;

~-laden recargado; **~ loss** comm pérdida considerable; **~ losses** mil pérdidas cuantiosas; **~ meal** comida pesada; **~ rain** lluvia fuerte; **~ sea** mar grueso/gruesa; **~ shower** chaparrón m; **~ sky** cielo encapotado; **~ sleep** sueño profundo; **be a ~ sleeper** dormir (ue)[1c] bien; **~ soil** tierra mala; **~ traffic** circulación densa; **~ water** agua pesada; **~ weather** mal tiempo; **make ~ weather** progresar con gran dificultad; **~weight** (boxeador m) de peso pesado; **~ work** trabajo duro

Hebraic hebraico

Hebrew n+adj hebreo

heckle interrumpir

heckler objetante m+f

hectare hectárea

hectic agitado

hectogramme hectogramo

hectograph hectógrafo

hectolitre hectolitro

hector intimidar

hectoring intimidante

hedge n seto (vivo); **~hog** erizo; **~-hop** v volar (ue)[1a] a ras de tierra; **~-hopping** vuelo a ras de tierra; **~row** seto (vivo); **~-sparrow** acentor m común; vt cercar[4] con seto; **~ a bet** hacer[19] apuestas compensatorias; vi (hesitate) vacilar, (reply evasively) contestar con evasivas

~ about rodear (**with** de)

~ in (enclose) encerrar (ie)[2a]; (restrict) poner[19] obstáculos a

~ off separar (por un seto)

hedonism hedonismo

hedonist(ic) hedonista m+f

heed n atención f; **pay ~ to** prestar atención a; **take ~ (of)** hacer[19] caso de; v hacer[19] caso (de)

heedful atento (**of** a)

heedless desatento

heedlessness desatención f

heedlessly sin hacer caso

hee-haw rebuzno

heel n anat talón (-ones) m; (of shoe) tacón (-ones) m; (of sock) talón (-ones) m; (person) sinvergüenza m+f; **be at one's ~s** pisarle los talones a uno; **come to ~** seguir[11] a su amo, fig dejar de sublevarse; **cool one's ~s** hacer[19] antesala; **down-at-~** mal vestido; **take to one's ~s** echar a correr;

~-**clicking** taconazo; ~-**tapping** taconeo; v (repair footwear) poner[19] una tapa a; (football) talonar; ~ed (having money) adinerado, (carrying a firearm) llevando arma de fuego; **high-~ed, low-~ed** de tacón alto/bajo; ~ **over** naut zozobrar

heft levantar

hefty fuerte; fam de chapa

hegemony hegemonía

heifer novilla

heigh! ¡oye!; ~-**ho!** ¡ay!

height altura; **what is the ~ of that mountain?** ¿qué altura tiene aquella montaña?; (high ground) cerro; fig colmo, ~ **of folly** colmo de la locura; (of fame) apogeo; (of fever) crisis f; **be at the ~ of fashion** estar[19] muy de moda

heighten elevar; fig (enhance) intensificar[4]

heinous atroz (-ces)

heir heredero; **be ~ to** heredar; ~-**apparent**, ~-**at-law** heredero forzoso; ~-**loom** reliquia de familia; ~-**presumptive** presunto heredero

heiress heredera

Helen Elena

helical helicoidal

helicopter helicóptero; ~-**carrier** porta-helicópteros m sing+pl; ~ **gun-ship** cañonero aéreo

heliocentric heliocéntrico

heliograph helió grafo

heliogravure, heliotype heliograbado

heliotrope heliotropo

heliport helipuerto

helium helio

hell infierno; ~! ¡demonio!; ~ **for leather** a toda prisa; **she gave me** ~ **ella me las hizo pasar moradas; go to** ~! ¡vete al diablo!; **just for the ~ of it** por diversión; **like** ~! ¡ni hablar!; **make a ~ of a row** hacer[19] un ruido imponente; **what the** ~ **are you doing here?** ¿qué demonios haces aquí?; ~-**fire** fuego del infierno

Hellene heleno

Hellenic helénico

hellish infernal; fam horrible

hello! see **hallo!**

helm timón (-ones) m; ~**sman** timonel m; **be at the ~** gobernar

helmet mil casco, sl cacerola; (knight's) yelmo; (miner's) casco de plástico; (motor-cyclist's) casco protector

help n ayuda; **by/with the ~ of** con la ayuda de; ~! ¡socorro!; **call for ~** pedir (i)[3] socorro; **can I be of (any) ~?** ¿puedo servirle (en algo)?; **come to the ~ of** acudir a la ayuda de; **there's no ~ for it** eso no tiene remedio; **daily ~** (servant) asistenta; ~**mate** compañero, compañera; v (assist) ayudar; (rescue) socorrer; (serve) servir (i)[3], **may I ~ you to more potatoes?** ¿puedo servirle a usted más patatas?; ~ **o.s.** (at table) servirse (i)[3], ~ **yourself** sírvase usted; **I can't ~ it** no puedo remediarlo; **I can't ~ +ger** no puedo menos de +infin; **couldn't be ~ed** no había más remedio; **I shan't go if I can ~ it** no iré si puedo evitarlo; **these tablets will ~ the pain** estas pastillas mitigarán el dolor

~ **down from/out of** (vehicle) ayudarle a uno a salir/a bajar

~ **off with** (clothes) ayudarle a uno a quitarse

~ **on** (a vehicle) ayudarle a uno a subir a; **I ~ed her on with her coat** le ayudé a ponerse el abrigo

helper ayudante m

helpful útil; (of a person) atento

helping n porción (-ones) f; **take another ~** servirse (i)[3] otra vez; adj ayudante; **give a ~ hand** echar una mano

helpless n: **the ~** los desamparados; adj (needing help) desamparado; (incompetent) inútil; (powerless) imposibilitado

helplessness (need of help) desamparo; (powerlessness) impotencia; (incompetence) incompetencia

helter-skelter n tobogán m; adv a trochemoche

[1] **hem** n dobladillo; ~-**line** bajo (de un vestido); ~-**stitch** calado; v dobladillar; ~ **in** encerrar (ie)[2a]; **my car was hemmed in** mi coche estaba tapado

[2] **hem** n (coughing sound) ejem m; v vacilar

he-man machote m

hemisphere hemisferio

hemlock cicuta

hemp cáñamo; ~**en** cañameño

hen gallina; ~-**coop**, ~-**house** gallinero; ~ **ostrich** hembra del avestruz; ~-

party reunión *f* de señoras

hence (from now on) de aquí; (therefore) por lo tanto; ~**forth** de aquí en adelante

henchman secuaz (-ces) *m*

henna alheña

henpeck dominar (al marido); ~**ed** dominado por su mujer; ~**ed husband** *fam* calzonazos *m sing*

Henrietta Enriqueta

Henry Enrique

hepatic hepático

heptagon heptágono

her *poss adj* su(s); *pron* (direct object) la, **I saw** ~ la vi; (indirect object) le, **I gave** ~ **the prize** le di (a ella) el premio; (after *prep*) ella, **they came with** ~ vinieron con ella; **she put it behind** ~ (~self) lo puso detrás de sí

herald *n* heraldo; *fig* precursor *m*; *v* anunciar; *fig* ser[19] precursor de

heraldic heráldico

heraldry heráldica

herb hierba; **pot-** ~**s** hortalizas *fpl*

herbaceous herbáceo; ~ **border** arriate herbáceo

herbal herbario

herbalist herbolario

herbarium herbario

herbivorous herbívoro

Herculean hercúleo

Hercules Hércules

herd *n* manada; (pigs) piara; (people) muchedumbre *f*, **common** ~ vulgo; ~ **instinct** instinto gregario; ~**sman** vaquero, (shepherd) pastor *m*; *vt* reunir en manada; *vi* ~ **together** ir[19] juntos

here aquí; (after *v* of movement) acá, **come** ~! ¡ven(ga) acá!; ~! (in answer to one's name) ¡presente!; ~ **and now** ahora mismo; ~ **and there** acá y allá; ~, **there and everywhere** por todas partes; ~ **below** aquí abajo; ~ **goes!** ¡ahí va!; ~ **lies the body of** aquí yacen los restos de; ~'**s to!** ¡a la salud de!; ~ **we are** ya estamos; ~ **you are** (this is what you want) aquí lo tiene usted; ~'**s your sister** aquí está su hermana; **that's neither** ~ **nor there** eso no viene al caso; ~**about(s)** por aquí cerca; ~**after** *n* vida futura, *adv* de aquí en adelante; ~**by** por la presente; ~**in** aquí dentro; ~**tofore** hasta ahora; ~**upon** en esto; ~**with** adjunto

hereditary hereditario

heredity herencia

heresy herejía

heretic hereje *m+f*

heretical herético

heritage herencia

hermaphrodite hermafrodita *m+f*

hermetic hermético

hermetically: ~ **sealed** cerrado herméticamente

hermit ermitaño

hermitage ermita

hernia hernia

hero héroe *m*; ~-**worship** culto a los héroes

Herod Herodes

heroic heroico; ~ **verse** poesía épica; ~**s** *n* heroica; **mock** ~**s** heroicocómica

heroin heroína; ~ **addict** heroinómano; ~ **addiction** heroinomanía

heroine heroína

heroism heroísmo

heron garza real

herpes herpes *mpl+fpl*

herring arenque *m*; ~-**boat** barca *m* para la pesca de arenques; ~**bone pattern** dibujo de espiga; ~**bone stitch** punto de escapulario, *fam* pata de gallo; ~ **gull** gaviota argéntea; **red** ~ arenque ahumado, *fig* artimaña para distraer la atención

hers (el) suyo, (la) suya, (los) suyos, (las) suyas; **that pen is** ~ esa pluma es suya/de ella; **a friend of** ~ un amigo suyo/de ella

herself *refl pron* se; *emph* misma, **she did it** ~ ella misma lo hizo;(after *prep*) sí misma, **she was speaking for** ~ ella hablaba por sí misma; **she is not** ~ **today** ella no es la misma hoy

hesitance, hesitancy vacilación *f*; (in speaking a foreign language) chapurreo

hesitant vacilante

hesitate vacilar; (over a word) titubear; **don't** ~ **to** no vacile en +*infin*

hesitation vacilación *f*; (in speech) titubeo

hessian tejido hecho de cáñamo y yute

heterodox heterodoxo

heterodoxy heterodoxia

heterodyne heterodina

heterogeneity heterogeneidad *f*

heterogeneous heterogéneo

heterosexual heterosexual

het-up apasionado; **get (all) ~ (about/over)** acalorarse (por)

heuristic heurístico

hew (chop) hachear; (cut) cortar; **~ down** talar; **~ out** excavar

hewer (person) talador *m*; (pitcher) cántaro

hexachlorophene hexaclorofeno

hexagon hexágono

hexagonal hexagonal

hexameter hexámetro

hey! *see* **hi (there)!**

heyday apogeo

H.H. (His/Her Highness) S.A. (Su Alteza); (His Holiness) S.S. (Su Santidad)

hi (there)! (greeting) ¡hola!; (call to attract attention) ¡oiga!, *fam* ¡oye!

hiatus vacío; *gramm+poet* hiato

hibernate invernar (ie)[2a]

hibernation hibernación *f*; **go into ~** invernar

hibiscus hibisco

hiccup, hiccough *n* hipo; *vi* tener[19] hipo; *vt* decir[19] hipando

hick rústico

hickory nogal americano; (walking-stick) bastón *m* (de nogal)

hidden escondido; (secret) secreto; **~ reserves** reserva oculta

¹ **hide** *n* (skin) piel *f*; (tanned) cuero; **he has a thick ~** él tiene la cara muy dura; **tan the ~ of** *fig* azotar; **~-bound** estrecho, tradicionalista

² **hide** *n* (for hunting, photography *etc*) paranza; **play ~-and-seek** jugar (ue)[1a] al escondite; **~-out** escondite *m*; *vt* esconder (from de); (one's feelings) disimular; *vi* esconderse; **~ behind** esconderse detrás de, *fig* escudarse tras, **he hid behind his secretary and would not see me** se escudaba tras su secretaria y no me recibió

hideous espantoso

hiding (thrashing) paliza; **in ~** escondido; **~-place** escondite *m*

hierarchic(al) jerárquico

hierarchy jerarquía

hieroglyphic *n+adj* jeroglífico

hi-fi (de) alta fidelidad

higgledy-piggledy revuelto; *fam* patas arriba

high *n* cifra record; (euphoric state produced by drugs) *sl* viaje *m*; *adj* alto, **it is fifty metres ~** tiene cincuenta metros de altura; **how ~ is that mountain?** ¿qué altura tiene aquella montaña?; (of temperature, proportion *etc*) elevado; (of quality) superior; (of wind) fuerte; (of meat) pasado; *mus* agudo; (drugged) estupefacto; (drunk) borracho; **~ and dry** varado, *fig* en seco; **leave s.o. ~ and dry** dejarle a uno plantado; **look ~ and low** buscar[4] por todas partes; **~ and mighty** *iron* orgulloso; **~ blood-pressure** hipertensión *f*, *fam* tensión *f*; **~ cards** cartas altas; **she has ~ cheekbones** ella tiene los pómulos salientes; **hold in ~ esteem** tener[19] en gran estima; **hold one's head ~** ir[19] con la cabeza alta; **get on one's ~ horse** darse[19] importancia; **have a ~ opinion of** tener[19] en mucho; **~ rate of interest** interés crecido; **it's ~ time that** ya es hora de +*infin*/de que +*subj*; **on ~** en alto; **we knew her when she was so ~** la conocimos cuando era niña; **~ altar** altar *m* mayor; **~-altitude flight** vuelo a altitudes mayores; **~-ball** whisky *m*/cognac *m* con sifón; **~binder** gangster *m*; **~-born** noble; **~-bred** de raza (pura); **~brow** intelectual; **~ chair** silla alta; **High Church** iglesia ritualista (en la secta anglicana); **~-class** de primera categoría, (of people) elegante; **~ colour** color *m* fuerte; **~ command** alto mando; **High Commissioner** alto comisario; **~ court** tribunal supremo; **~ day** día festivo; **~ diving** saltos *mpl* acuáticos/de trampolín; **~ explosive** explosivo violento; **~-falutin(g)** rimbombante; **~-fidelity** (de) alta fidelidad; **~-flier** persona muy ambiciosa; **~-frequency** de alta frecuencia; **~-frequency broadcasting** radiodifusión *f* de alta frecuencia; **~ gear** (toma) directa; **put (a car) into ~ gear** poner[19] los cambios (de un coche) en directa; **~-grade** de alta calidad; **~-handed** arbitrario; **~-hat** *adj* engreído, *v* tratar con desprecio; **~-heeled shoe** zapato de tacón alto; **~ jinks** juerga; **~ jump** salto de altura; **~land(s)** tierra(s) alta(s); **~lander** montañés *m* (-esa *f*); **~-level** de alto nivel; **~ life** vida de gran mundo; **~light** *n* mo-

culminante, *v* (emphasize) subrayar;
High Mass misa mayor; **~-minded**
magnánimo; **~-mindedness** magnanimidad *f*; **~-necked** con cuello alto; ~
noon pleno mediodía; **~-octane fuel**
combustible *m* de alta potencia; **~-**
pitched (roof) (tejado) empinado; **~-**
pitched voice voz *f* aguda; **~-powered**
de alta potencia, *mot* de muchos caballos; ~ **precision** suma precisión; **~-**
pressure a/de alta presión, *fig*
enérgico; **~-priced** de precio alto; ~
priest sumo sacerdote; **~-principled**
concienzudo; **~-riser**, **~-rise block**
rascacielos *m* *sing+pl* de
apartamentos; ~ **school** instituto; ~
seas alta mar; **~-speed** de alta
velocidad; **at ~ speed** a toda
velocidad; **~-spirited** alegre; **~ spirits**
alegría; ~ **spot** punto saledizo; **~-**
stepping (of horse) pisador (-ora *f*),
fam (gay life) vida alegre; ~ **street** calle *f* mayor; ~ **summer** pleno verano;
~-tail escaparse; **~-tension** de alta
tensión; ~ **tide** marea alta; ~ **treason**
alta traición; ~ **up** muy alto; **~-up** *n*
persona importante; **~-voltage** de alto
voltaje; ~ **water** marea alta; **~-water**
mark límite de la marea, *fig* colmo;
~way (old) camino real, (modern) carretera nacional; **~way code** código
de la circulación; **~way robbery**
atraco; **~wayman** atracador *m*
higher más alto, más elevado *etc* (*see*
high); ~ **education** enseñanza superior; **on a ~ plane** en un nivel más alto;
~ **up** más arriba
highest el más alto, la más alta *etc*; ~
common factor máximo común divisor; **I gave him the ~ references** le di
informes inmejorables; **glory to God**
in the ~ gloria a Dios en las alturas
highly altamente, sumamente, (before
adj) muy; **think very ~ of s.o.** tener[19]
en mucho a alguien; **~-seasoned** picante; **~-strung** nervioso
highness alteza; **your ~** su alteza
hijack secuestrar
hijacker secuestrador *m*; pirata *m* del
aire; *SA* aeropirata *m*
hijacking secuestro de camiones/de
aviones; *SA* aeropiratería
[1] **hike** *n* caminata; *v* dar[19] una caminata
[2] **hike** (rise in cost) alza; *v* ~ **up** subir(se)

hiker caminante *m+f*
hilarious divertidísimo
hilarity hilaridad *f*
hill colina; (slope) cuesta; **as old as the**
~s tan viejo como caracuca; **~-billy**
serrano; **~-climbing** escalada; **~side**
falda de montaña; **~top** cumbre *f* de
una colina; **down~** cuesta abajo; **up-**
~ cuesta arriba
hilliness montuosidad *f*
hillock altozano
hilly montañoso
hilt empuñadura; **up to the ~** *fig* hasta
las cachas
him *pron* (direct object) le, *esp SA* lo, **I**
saw ~ le/lo vi; (indirect object) le, **I**
gave ~ the book le di el libro; (after
prep) él, **they came with ~** vinieron
con él; **he put it in front of ~** (~self) lo
puso delante de sí
himself *refl pron* se; *emph adj* mismo, **he**
did it ~ él mismo lo hizo; (after *prep*)
sí mismo; **he is not ~ today** él no es el
mismo hoy
[1] **hind** (deer) cierva
[2] **hind:** ~ **leg** pata trasera; **~most** último;
~quarters cuarto trasero; **~sight** percepción tardía
[1] **hinder** *adj* trasero
[2] **hinder** *v* estorbar (**from** de +*infin*)
hindrance estorbo
Hindu *n+adj* hindú *m+f*
Hindustani *n+adj* indostanés *m* (-esa *f*);
(language) indostaní
hinge *n* bisagra; *fam* librillo; **off its ~s**
desquiciado; *v* bisagrar; ~ **upon** *fig*
depender (ie)[2b] de
hint *n* indirecta; (advice) consejo; **take**
the ~ captar la alusión; **drop a ~**
lanzar[7] una indirecta; **he had a slight ~**
of a moustache tenía un amago de
bigote; **with a ~ of blue** tirando a azul;
v echar indirectas; ~ **at** insinuar
hinterland región *f* interior
[1] **hip** *anat* cadera; **65 centimetres round**
the ~s 65 centímetros de caderas; **~-**
bath baño de asiento; **~-bone** cía; **~-**
flask frasco para licor; **~-pocket** bolsillo de atrás, bolsillo de cadera
[2] **hip** *bot* escaramujo
[3] **hip:** ~, ~, **hurray!** ¡viva!
hippodrome hipódromo
hippopotamus hipopótamo
hippy hippy (-yes) *m+f*

hire *n* alquiler *m*; (wages) jornal *m*; **for ~** de alquiler; **~ purchase** compra a plazos; **~-purchase agreement** contrato de compra a plazos; **~-purchase instalment** plazo; **~-purchase sale** venta a plazos; *v* alquilar; (employ) emplear; **~ a vessel** fletar un buque; **~d assassin** asesino profesional; **~ out** alquilar

hireling mercenario

hirer alquilador *m* (-ora *f*)

hirsute hirsuto

his *poss adj* su(s); *poss pron* (el) suyo, (la) suya, (los) suyos, (las) suyas; **those dogs are ~** esos perros son suyos/de él; **he washed ~ hands** él se lavó las manos; **friend of ~** amigo suyo

Hispanic hispánico

Hispanicism españolismo

Hispanophile hispanófilo

hiss *n* silbido; *v* silbar; **~ one's s's** sisear

hissing silbido; (of one's s's) seseo

historian historiador *m* (-ora *f*)

historic(al) histórico

history historia; **~-book** libro de historia; **natural ~** ciencias *fpl* naturales; **medical ~** historia médica

histrionic histriónico

histrionics histrionismo

hit *n* (blow) golpe *m*; (shooting) tiro certero; (success) éxito; **be a ~** tener[19] éxito; **score a direct ~** dar[19] en el blanco; **~-and-miss** a la (buena) ventura; **~-and-run** atropello y fuga; **~-and-run driver** conductor *m* de atropello y fuga; **make a ~ with** caer[19] en gracia a; **make a ~ in society** destacar[4] en sociedad; *v* (strike) pegar[5]; (shooting) hacer[19] blanco en; **he was ~ in the head by a bullet** fue alcanzado por una bala en la cabeza; **~ the mark/target** dar[19] en el blanco; **~ the jackpot** ganar el (premio) gordo; **~ the nail on the head** dar[19] en el clavo; **the town was ~ by floods** la ciudad sufrió inundaciones; **~ the trail** ponerse[19] en camino

~ (o.s.) against golpearse contra

~ back defenderse (ie)[2b]

~ off (mimic) imitar; **~ it off with** simpatizar[7] con

~ out (at) atacar[4]; *fig* denunciar; *sp* golpear (la pelota) fuera

~ upon dar[19] con

hitch *n* (knot) cote *m*; (obstacle) dificultad *f*; (pull) tirón (-ones) *m*; **without a ~** sin contratiempo; **I asked for a ~ from Madrid to Bilbao** pedí a un automovilista que me llevara desde Madrid a Bilbao; *v* (knot) amarrar; **~ the horse to the cart** enganchar el caballo al carro; **~ up one's trousers** subirse el pantalón; **~-hike** hacer[19] (el) autostop; **~-hiker** autostopista *m*+*f*; **~-hiking** autostop *m*

hither hacia acá; **~ and thither** para atrás y para delante; **~to** hasta ahora

Hitlerian hitleriano; **~ moustache** bigote hitleriano

Hitlerism hitlerismo

Hitlerite *n*+*adj* hitlerista *m*+*f*

hitter golpeador *m* (-ora *f*)

hive colmena; **~ of activity** centro de actividad; *v* (of bees) enjambrar; **~ off** (go away) marcharse; (take away) quitar

hives *med* urticaria

H.M. (His/Her Majesty) S.M. (Su Majestad)

hoard *n* acumulación *f*; (of wealth) tesoro; *v* acumular; (food) acaparar; (wealth) atesorar

hoarder acumulador *m* (-ora *f*); (of food) acaparador *m* (-ora *f*); (of wealth) atesorador *m* (-ora *f*)

hoarding acumulación; (of food) acaparamiento; (of wealth) atesoramiento; *bui* valla de construcción; (for posters) valla publicitaria

hoar-frost escarcha

hoarse ronco; **she is a little ~** ella tiene la voz tomada

hoarseness ronquera

hoary vetusto; (of hair) canoso

hoax *n* engaño; *v* engañar

hoaxer burlador *m* (-ora *f*)

hob repisa interior de la chimenea

hobble *n* (gait) cojera; (on horse's legs) maniota; *vi* (limp) cojear; *vt* (a horse) manear

hobby pasatiempo; **~-horse** caballito (de niños), (fixed idea) caballo de batalla

hobgoblin duende *m*

hobnail clavo de botas; **~ed boots** botas *fpl* claveteadas

hob-nob codearse (**with** con)

hobo vagabundo

Hobson's choice: you have ~ usted no puede escoger

hock n (wine) vino del Rin; *anat* corvejón m; **in** ~ (pawned) empeñado, (in gaol) encarcelado; ~**-shop** casa de empeños; v empeñar

hockey hockey m; ~**-stick** palo de hockey; **ice-**~ hockey m sobre hielo; **roller-skate** ~ hockey m sobre patines

hocus-pocus birlibirloque m

hod capacho (de albañil)

hoe n azada; v azadar

hog n +*fig* cerdo, puerco; (glutton) glotón (-ones) m; **go the whole** ~ llegar[8] hasta el final; ~**shead** pipa; ~**skin** piel f de cerdo; ~**-wash** bazofia; v acaparar; ~ **the camera** *cin*+*TV* chupar cámara

hoggish puerco

hoist n montacarga, *SA* elevador m; v alzar[7]; *naut* izar[7]; ~ **the flag** izar la bandera

hoity-toity presuntuoso

hokum exceso de sentimentalismo

hold n (grip) agarre m; (place to grip) asidero; (wrestling) presa; *naut* bodega; (influence) dominio; **get** ~ **of** (seize) agarrar, (obtain) adquirir; **let go one's** ~ soltar (ue)[1a]; **have a** ~ **on/over** tener[19] poder sobre; v tener[19]; **he held the knife between his teeth** él tenía el cuchillo entre los dientes; (contain) caber[19], **this case will not** ~ **all the clothes** en esta maleta no cabe toda la ropa; (keep) guardar; (a meeting) celebrar; (a party) ofrecer[14], **she held a cocktail party** ella ofreció un cóctel; *mus* sostener[19]; (not break) resistir; (of weather) seguir[11] bueno; (be of an opinion) sostener[19]; ~ **one's breath** contener[19] la respiración; ~ **a conversation (with)** tener[19] una conversación (con); ~ **the fort/one's ground** mantenerse[19] firme; ~ **hands** cogerse[8] de la mano, (when in love) hacer[19] manitas; ~ **hard!** ¡quieto!; ~ **in check** refrenar; ~ **in high esteem** tener[19] en gran estima; ~ **the key to** tener[19] la clave de; ~ **the line** *mil* no retirarse, (telephone) no colgar (ue)[1a]; ~ **office** ocupar el cargo, (of government) estar[19] en poder; ~ **o.s. well** tener[19] buena postura; ~ **o.s. in readiness**

mantenerse[19] preparado; ~ **responsible (for)** juzgar[1a+5] responsable (de); ~ **the stage** dominar la escena; ~ **one's tongue** callarse; ~ **your tongue!** ¡cállese!; **he can** ~ **his drink** él resiste bien su bebida; ~ **true/water** ser[19] válido; **what the future** ~**s in store for us** lo que nos reserva el porvenir; ~**all** bolsa

~ **against** (reproach) echar en cara

~ **back** *vi* refrenarse; *vt* refrenar; **she held back her tears** ella contuvo sus lágrimas

~ **down** tener[19] sujeto; (employment) mantenerse[19] en

~ **forth (about)** arengar[5] (sobre)

~ **good** aplicarse[4]

~ **off** (of rain) no llegar[5]; (resist) mantener[19] a distancia

~ **on to** (grip) agarrarse de; (retain) retener[19]

~ **open** mantener[19] abierto

~ **out** (offer) ofrecer[14]; (resist) resistir; ~ **out against** resistir +*direct object*; ~ **out one's hand** tender (ie)[2b] la mano; ~ **out for a better offer** esperar una oferta mejor; ~ **out hopes of** ofrecer[14] la esperanza de; ~ **out hopes that** ofrecer[14] la esperanza de que +*subj*

~ **over** (postpone) aplazar[7]; ~ **over one's head** (threaten) amenazar[7] con

~ **tight (to)** agarrarse bien (de)

~ **to:** ~ **to a belief** seguir (i)[3+11] fiel a; ~ **to a promise** exigir[9] lo prometido

~ **together** (of people) mantenerse[19] juntos; (of things) pegarse[5]; ir unidos

~**-up** n (delay) paro; (robbery) atraco; (of traffic) embotellamiento

~ **up** v (lift) levantar; (support) sostener[19]; (delay) detener[19]; **the plane was held up by snow** el avión llegó con retraso a causa de la nieve; (stop) parar; (rob) atracar[4]; (display) mostrar (ue)[1a]; ~ **up as an example** poner[19] como modelo; ~ **up to the light** mirar a/contra la luz; ~ **up to ridicule** poner[19] en ridículo

~ **with** estar[19] de acuerdo con

holder poseedor m (-ora f); *comm* tenedor m (-ora f); portador m; (clip) sujetador m; (handle) mango

holding: ~ **company** holding m; ~**s** valores *mpl*

hole n agujero; (cavity) cavidad f; *min*

(for explosive) barreno; (in clothing) roto; (in ground) hueco; (in road) bache *m*; (lair) guarida; (golf) hoyo; *fig* (difficult situation) apuro; **what a dreadful ~!** ¡qué sitio tan terrible!; **pick ~s in** encontrar[1a] defectos en; **~-and-corner** furtivo; *v* (golf) meter en el hoyo

holiday (día *m* de) fiesta; **take a ~** tomar unas vacaciones; **on ~** de vacaciones; **go on ~** ir[19] de vacaciones; **be on ~** estar[19] de vacaciones; **~s** vacaciones *fpl*, *SA* fiestas *fpl*; **~s with pay** vacaciones pagadas; **~ camp** campamento de vacaciones; **~-maker** veraneante *m+f*; **~ season** temporada (de vacaciones)

holiness (+title) santidad *f*

Holland Holanda

holland (cloth) holanda

holler llamar a gritos

hollow *n* hueco; *geog* barranco; (groove) ranura; (of the back) curvadura; *adj* hueco; *fig* falso, **~ words** palabras falsas; **~ sound** ruido sordo; **~-eyed** con los ojos hundidos; *v* **~ out** ahuecar; *adv* completamente; **beat ~** ganar con facilidad

hollowness cavidad *f*; *fig* falsedad *f*

holly acebo

hollyhock malva real

Hollywood *adj* hollywoodense

holm-oak encina

holocaust holocausto

holograph hológrafo

holster pistolera

holy santo; **most ~** santísimo; **make ~** santificar[4]; **Holy of Holies** sanctasanctórum *m*; **Holy Bible** Santa Biblia; **~ Communion** Sagrada Comunión; **Holy Father** Santo Padre; **Holy Ghost/Spirit** Espíritu Santo; **Holy Land** Tierra Santa; **~ orders** órdenes *m* sacerdotales; **Holy Sacrament** Santísimo (Sacramento); **Holy See** Santa Sede; **~-day** día *m* de fiesta; **Holy Thursday** Jueves Santo; **~ water** agua bendita; **~-water stoup** acetre *m*; **Holy Week** Semana Santa; **Holy Writ** Sagrada Escritura

homage homenaje *m*; **pay ~ to** rendir (i)[3] homenaje a

homburg sombrero de pelo de liebre

home *n* casa; (district) patria chica;

(reformatory) reformatorio; (refuge) refugio; *sp* meta; **~ for the aged/poor** asilo de ancianos/pobres, *fam* misericordia; **at ~** en casa; **she held an at ~** ella tuvo un día de recibo; **I felt at ~ with them** yo estaba a gusto con ellos; **make yourself at ~!** ¡está usted en su casa!; *adj* de casa, doméstico; **~ address** dirección *f* del domicilio; **~ appliances** aparatos *mpl* para el hogar, *elect* aparatos electrodomésticos; **~-coming** regreso (al hogar); **~ cooking** cocina casera; **~-brewed, ~-cured** casero; **~ economics** economía doméstica; **~ front** frente doméstico; **on their ~ ground** *sp* en su campo; **~-grown** del país, (from garden) de cosecha propia; **~land** tierra natal; **~ life** vida de familia; **~-loving** hogareño; **~-made** casero; **~-made bread** pan *m* de fabricación casera; **~ market** mercado nacional; **Home Office** Ministerio del Interior/de la Gobernación; **~-plate** (baseball) base *f* de bateador; **~ port** puerto de origen; **~-produced** de producción nacional, *agri* del país; **~-rule** autonomía; **~-run** (baseball) golpe *m* que habilita al bateador a una vuelta completa; **Home Secretary** Ministro del Interior/de la Gobernación; **~sick** nostálgico; **be ~sick** tener[19] nostalgia, *fam* tener[19] morriña; **be ~sick for** añorar; **~sickness** nostalgia, *fam* morriña; **~spun** casero; **~stead** hacienda; **~ stretch** último trecho de una carrera; **~ team** *sp* equipo local; **~ town** ciudad *f* natal; **a few ~ truths** cuatro verdades *fpl*; **~work** trabajo para hacer en casa, (school prep) deberes *mpl*; **~-worker** obrero a domicilio; *adv* a/en casa, (to one's country) a la patria; **be ~ soon** estar[19] de vuelta en seguida; **come ~** volver (ue)[1b] (*past part* vuelto) a casa; **get ~** llegar[5] a casa, *fig* (of a blow) dar[19] en el blanco, (in a race) llegar[5] a la meta; **bring ~ to s.o.** hacerle[19] a uno comprender; **it came ~ to me** me llegó al alma; **the arrow went ~** la flecha dio en el blanco; *v mil* buscar[4] al blanco; (of pigeons) volver (ue)[1b] (*past part* vuelto) al palomar

homeless *n* destituidos *mpl*; *adj* sin casa

homelessness destitución *f*

homeliness sencillez *f*; (*US* ugliness) fealdad *f*

homely sencillo; (*US* ugly) feo

Homer Homero

Homeric homérico

homeward hacia casa; ~-**bound** de regreso

homey casero

homicidal homicida *m+pl*

homicide homicidio

homily homilía

homing: ~ **device** instrumento autodirigido buscador del blanco; ~ **instinct** instinto de volver a casa; ~-**pigeon** paloma mensajera

homoeopathic homeopático

homoeopathy homeopatía

homogeneous homogéneo

homogenize homogeneizar[7]

homologous homólogo

homonym homónimo

homophone palabra homófona

homosexual *n+adj* homosexual

homosexuality homosexualidad *f*

homunculus homúnculo; *fam* enano

Honduran hondureño

Honduras Honduras *f*

hone *n* piedra de afilar; *v* afilar

honest honrado; (chaste) honesto; ~ **as the day is long** honradote; ~-**to-goodness** honradísimo

honestly de veras

honesty honradez *f*

honey miel *f*; (term of endearment) cielo; **it's a ~ of a cooker** es una cocina de ensueño; ~-**bee** abeja doméstica; ~-**coloured** color de miel; ~**comb** panal *m*; ~**combed** apanalado; ~**moon** (time) luna de miel, (journey) viaje *m* de novios; ~**suckle** madreselva verdadera; ~**ed,** ~-**tongued** meloso

honk *n* (of geese) graznido; (of motorhorn) bocinazo; *v* graznar; bocinar

honky-tonk club *m* de mala fama

honorarium honorario

honorary honorario; ~ **degree** título honoris causa; ~ **member** socio de honor; ~ **rank** mando honorífico

honour *n* honra; (distinction) honor *m*; ~**s** (cards) naipes *mpl* de más valor; **I have the ~ to inform you** me es grato informarle; **in ~ of** en honor de; **on my**

~ **a fe mía**; **on my (word of)** ~ palabra (de honor); **point of** ~ amor propio; **Your Honour** vuestra merced, *leg* Su Señoría; **with** ~**s** calificado de sobresaliente; **pass with** ~ calificarse[4] de sobresaliente; **do the** ~**s** hacer[19] los honores; ~**s list** cuadro de honour; *v* honrar; ~ **a cheque** aceptar un cheque; ~ **an obligation** hacer[19] honor a un compromiso

honourable honorable; ~ **mention** mención de honor; **Right Honourable** Ilustrísimo

hooch licor *m*

hood capucha; (graduate's) capirote *m*; *mot* capota, (bonnet) capó *m*; *US sl* gamberro; *v* cubrir (*past part* cubierto); ~**ed** encapuchado, (of eyes) tapado

hoodlum gamberro

hoodoo aojo; **put the** ~ **on** aojar

hoodwink engañar

hooey tonterías *fpl*

hoof *n* casco; *v* ~ **it** ir[19] a pie; ~**ed** (having hoofs) ungulado

hoo-ha jaleo

hook *n* (+ *boxing*) gancho; (clothes hanger) colgadero; (dress fastener) corchete *m*; ~**s and eyes** corchetes y corchetas *mpl*; (fishing) anzuelo; ~ **and line** caña y anzuelo; ~, **line and sinker** todo; **by** ~ **or by crook** por fas o por nefas; ~-**up** *rad+TV* emisoras acopladas; *v* enganchar; (fishing +*fig*) pescar[4]; ~ **up** enganchar; (clothing) abrochar; ~**ed** ganchudo; **be** ~**ed on** (addicted to) ser[19] adicto a; ~**ed beak** pico corvo; ~**ed nose** nariz aguileña; ~**worm** anquilostoma, (disease) anquilostomiasis *f*

hooker (rugby) talonador *m*; (prostitute) ramera

hookey: play ~ hacer[19] novillos

hooligan gamberro

hooliganism gamberrismo

hoop *n* aro; ~-**la** juego de los aros; ~-**skirt** miriñaque *m*; *v* enarcar[4]

hooper tonelero

hoopoe abubilla

hoosgow *sl* jaula

hoot *n* (shout) grito; (of horn) bocinazo; (of owl) ululato; (of siren) toque *m* de sirena; ~ **of laughter** carcajada; **I don't give a** ~ no me importa un bledo; *v* (cry) gritar; (of horn, siren) tocar[4]; (of owl) ulular; ~ **at** (with derision) silbar; ~ **with laughter** echar una carcajada

hooter *mot* bocina; (siren) sirena; *sl* (nose) jeta

Hoover *tr n* aspiradora; *v* pasar la aspiradora

hop *n* salt(it)o; *aer* vuelo; (dance) baile *m*; *agri* lúpulo; ~**, skip and jump** triple salto; ~**-garden** huerto de lúpulo; ~**-picker** recolector *m* (-ora *f*) de lúpulo; ~**-pole** estaca para la cultivación de lúpulo; ~**scotch** infernáculo, *fam* tejo; ~**-o-my-thumb** Pulgarcito; *v* saltar; (on one leg) saltar a la pata coja; ~ **on** subir; ~ **off** bajar; ~ **it!** ¡lárguese!

hope *n* esperanza; **give up** ~ perder (ie)[2b] la esperanza; **beyond** ~ sin esperanza; *v* esperar; **I** ~ **so/not** espero que sí/que no; ~ **against** ~ esperar desesperadamente; ~ **for the best** tener[19] esperanzas

hopeful esperanzado; **be** ~ tener[19] esperanza, (optimistic) ser[19] optimista *m+f*; **be** ~ **that** esperar que +*subj*; ~ **signs** indicios que dan esperanza

hopefully con esperanza

hopeless desesperado; *med* (incurable) desahuciado; **a** ~ **case** un caso irremediable

hopelessly sin esperanza

hopelessness desesperación *f*

hopper tolva; *ent* langosta joven

hopping: ~ **mad** enfurecido

Horace Horacio

horde horda

horizon horizonte *m*; **on the** ~ en el horizonte

horizontal horizontal; ~ **bar** barra fija

hormone hormona

horn *n* cuerno; (of bull or stag) asta; (hunting-~) trompa de caza; (of insect) antena; (of snail) tentáculo; *mot* bocina; *mus* trompa; (pair of) ~**s** cornamenta *f sing*; ~ **of plenty** cuerno de la abundancia; **on the** ~**s of a dilemma** entre la espada y la pared; ~**beam** carpe *m*; ~**bill** *orni* cálao; ~**pipe** baile *m* (de marineros); ~**rimmed glasses** gafas de concha; ~**shaped** corniforme; ~**-thrust** cornada; *v* ~ **in** (intrude) entrometerse;

~**ed** cornudo

hornet avispón (-ones) *m*; **stir up a** ~**'s nest** armar una gorda

hornless sin cuernos

hornswoggle engañar

horny córneo; ~**-handed** de manos callosas; (sexy) cachondo

horology relojería

horoscope horóscopo; **cast a** ~ sacar[4] un horóscopo

horrendous horripilante

horrible horrible

horrid horroroso

horrific horroroso

horrify horrorizar[7]

horror horror *m*; **have a** ~ **of** tener[19] horror a; ~**s** espasmo de horror; ~ **film** película de miedo; ~**-struck** horrorizado

hors de combat fuera de combate

hors d'œuvre entremeses *mpl*; ~ **dish** entremesero

horse *n* (+ gymnastic) caballo; **ride a** ~ montar a caballo; *mil* caballería, **regiment of** ~ regimiento de caballería; (stand) caballete; **dark** ~ caballo desconocido; **eat like a** ~ comer como una vaca; **get on one's high** ~ darse[19] importancia; **hold your** ~**s!** ¡para!; **that's a** ~ **of a different colour** esa es harina de otro costal; **white** ~ (breaker) cachón (-ones) *m*; ~**artillery** artillería montada; **on** ~**back** (montado) a caballo; ~**-blanket** sudadero; ~**-box** vagón *m* para caballos; ~**-breeding** cría caballar; ~ **butcher** vendedor *m* de carne de caballo; ~**chestnut** (tree) castaño de la India, (fruit) castaña de la India; ~**-collar** collera; ~**-dealer** chalán (-anes) *m*; ~**doctor** veterinario; ~**-drawn** tirado de caballo; ~**-faced** de cara de caballo; ~**-fly** tábano, ~ **guards** guardia montada; ~**-hair** pelo de caballo, (cloth) tela de crin; ~**-laugh** carcajada; ~**man** jinete *m*; ~**manship** equitación *f*; ~**meat** carne *f* de caballo; ~**-play** (clowning) payasadas, (friendly fight) pelea amistosa; ~**-power** caballo (de fuerza); **ten h.p.** de diez caballos; ~**race** carrera de caballos; ~**-radish** rábano picante; ~**-sense** sentido común; ~**shit** *US sl* tonterías *fpl*; **don't give me that** ~**shit!** ¡no me digas tonterías!; ~**shoe** herradura; ~**-show** concurso hípico; ~**-tail** cola de caballo, *bot* belcho; ~**-thief** cuatrero; ~**-trough** abrevadero; ~**-whip** *n* látigo, *v* pegar[5] con látigo; ~**woman** amazona; *v* ~ **about** hacer[19] payasadas

horsy *n* caballito; *adj* aficionado a caballos

horticultural hortícola; ~ **show** exposición *f* de flores

horticulturalist horticultor *m* (-ora *f*)

horticulture horticultura

hosanna hosana *m*

hose *n* (socks) calcetines *mpl*; (stockings) medias *f*; (~-pipe) mang(uer)a; ~**-coupling** cople *m* de manguera; *v* (wash with ~) lavar con manga; (water plants) regar (ie)[2a] con manga

hosier calcetero

hosiery géneros de punto

hospice hospicio

hospitable hospitalario

hospital (health service) residencia, (private) clínica, (for the poor) hospital *m*; ~**-ship**, ~**-train** buque *m*/tren *m* hospital

hospitality hospitalidad *f*

hospitalize hospitalizar[7]

hospitalization hospitalización *f*

host huésped *f*; (at a meal) anfitrión (-ones) *m*; (at an inn) hospedero; *bot*+*zool* huésped *f*; (crowd) multitud *f*; *eccles* hostia; *mil* hueste *f*; **Lord of Hosts** Señor *m* de los ejércitos

hostage rehén (enes) *m*

hostel hostal *m*, posada; (students') residencia (de estudiantes); (youth ~) albergue *m* de la juventud

hostelry hostal *m*, posada

hostess huéspeda; (at an inn) patrona; *aer* azafata; *TV* (of panel game) azafata

hostile (to) hostil (a)

hostility hostilidad *f*; **hostilities** actos *mpl* de agresión; **start hostilities** romper (*past part* roto) las hostilidades

hot *adj* caliente; **her hands are** ~ ella tiene las manos calientes; (of climate) cálido; (of day) caluroso; (taste) picante; (radioactive) radiactivo; (dangerous) peligroso; **be** ~ (of people) tener[19] calor, (of things) estar[19] caliente, (of weather) hacer[19] calor; **get** ~ calentarse (ie)[2a]; **make** ~

calentar (ie)[2a]; **make it** ~ **for s.o.** fastidiarle a uno; **she is** ~ **stuff** ella es de rechupete; **he is** ~ **stuff at** él es experto en; (near the thing sought) muy cerca, **you are getting very** ~ te estás quemando; **in** ~ **pursuit,** ~ **on the scent** siguiendo la pista muy de cerca; ~ **and cold running water** agua corriente caliente y fría; **be in** ~ **water** estar[19] en un lío; ~ **air** *fig* palabrería; ~**-air balloon** globo de aire caliente; ~**bed** *hort* almajara, *fig* foco; ~**-blooded** apasionado; **sell like** ~ **cakes** venderse como pan nuevo; ~**-dog** perrito caliente; ~**-foot** aprisa; ~**-head(ed)** temerario; ~**house** invernadero; ~**house plant** planta de estufa; ~ **line** *pol* teléfono rojo; ~ **money** dinero robado; ~ **news** últimas noticias *fpl*; ~**-plate** placa calentadora, *fam* plancha; ~**-pot** estofado de carne y patatas; ~**-rod** bólido; ~ **scent** rasco fresco; ~ **seat** silla eléctrica; **be in the** ~ **seat** estar[19] en una situación difícil; ~ **spring** termas *fpl*; ~**-tempered** de genio vivo; ~ **tip** *sp* soplo seguro; ~**-water bottle** bolsa de agua caliente; ~**-water heater** calentador *m* de agua; ~**-water tank** depósito de agua caliente; *v* ~ **up** *mot* superalimentar, **hotted up** superalimentado; (reheat) recalentar; ~ **it up** *mus* tocar[4] con más viveza

hotchpotch *cul* olla podrida; *fig* mezcolanza

hotel hotel *m*; ~ **chain** cadena hotelera; ~**-keeper** hotelero

hotelier hotelero

hotly con vehemencia

Hottentot *n*+*adj* hotentote *m* (-ta *f*)

hound *n* sabueso; *pej* canalla *m*; *v* perseguir[3+11]

hour hora; *fig* momento; **half an** ~ media hora; **quarter of an** ~ cuarto de hora; **thirty miles an** ~ treinta millas por hora; **at the eleventh** ~ al último momento; **by the** ~ por horas; **keep late** ~**s** acostarse (ue)[1a] tarde; **strike the** ~ dar[19] la hora; ~ **of death** hora suprema; **after** ~**s** después de las horas de trabajo; **in the early** ~**s** en la madrugada; ~**-glass** reloj *m* de arena; ~**-hand** horario

hourly (de) cada hora; (by the ~) por

horas

¹ **house** *n* casa; ~ **and home** hogar *m*;(in school) división administrativa de una escuela; (building in zoo) departamento; *cin*+*theat* público; **bring down the** ~ provocar⁴ grandes aplausos; *comm* casa comercial; (lineage) familia; *pol* cámara, **House of Commons/Lords** Cámara de los Comunes/Lores; ~ **of cards** castillo de naipes; ~ **of ill fame** burdel *m*; **it's on the** ~ la casa paga; **keep** ~ llevar la casa; **keep open** ~ tener¹⁹ la mesa puesta; ~**-agent** corredor *m* de casas; **(under)** ~**-arrest** (bajo) arresto domiciliario; ~**boat** casa flotante; ~**bound** atado a la casa; ~**breaker** demoledor de casas, (thief) ladrón *m* de casas, (with skeleton key) *sl* espadista *m*, (with jemmy) *sl* topista *m*; ~**breaking** robo de una casa; ~**coat** bata; ~**-detective** detective *m* de la casa; ~**-dog** perro guardián; ~**-fly** mosca (doméstica); ~**-furnisher** mueblista *m*+*f*; ~**-furnishings** artículos domésticos; ~**hold** casa; ~**hold appliances** aparatos domésticos; ~**hold cavalry/troops** caballería/guardia real; **be a** ~**hold word** andar en lenguas; ~**holder** amo/ama de casa; ~**keeper** ama de llaves; ~**keeping** (management) gobierno de la casa, (money) dinero para la casa, (tasks) quehaceres *mpl* de la casa; ~**maid** criada; ~**maid's knee** rodilla de fregona; ~**-martin** *orni* avión *m* común; ~**master** maestro responsable por el bienestar de los alumnos en su 'house'; ~**-painter** pintor *m* de brocha gorda; ~**-party** convite *m* de varios días; ~**-physician,** ~**-surgeon** médico/cirujano residente; ~**-proud** orgulloso de su casa; ~**-room** alojamiento; **give** ~**-room to** tener¹⁹ en casa; ~**-to-**~ **search** registro casa por casa; ~**sparrow** gorrión *m*; ~**-top** tejado; ~**-trained** limpio; ~**-warming** fiesta de inauguración de una casa; ~**wife** ama de casa, (sewing kit) estuche de costura; ~**wifery** economía doméstica; ~**work** trabajo(s) de casa

² **house** *v* alojar; *mech* encajar; *naut* estibar; **be** ~**ed** alojarse; **this flat will not** ~ **them** no cabrán en este piso

houseful casa llena

housey-housey bingo

housing viviendas *fpl*; (storage) almacenaje *m*; *mech* cubierta de la caja; ~ **estate** colonia de viviendas; ~ **policy** programa *m* de viviendas; ~ **shortage** escasez *f* de viviendas

hove: ~ **to** al pairo

hovel casucha

hover cernerse; ~ **between life and death** estar¹⁹ con el credo en la boca; ~ **near** rondar; ~**craft** aerodeslizador *m*

how como; ~ **are you?** ¿cómo está usted?; ~ **are things?** ¿qué hay?; ~ **goes it?** ¿qué tal?; ~ **is it that?** ¿cómo es que?; ~ **about it?** ¿qué le parece?; ~ **about eating?** ¿qué tal si comiéramos?; ~ **come?** ¿cómo?; ~ **come that ...?** ¿cómo resulta que ...?; ~**d'ye-do** *n* lío, (formal greeting) tanto gusto; **this is** ~ **...** así es como ...; ~ **far is it to?** ¿cuánta distancia hay a?; ~ **long is it?** (distance) ¿cuánto mide?, (time) ¿cuánto dura?; ~ **long it is!** ¡qué largo es!; **we know** ~ **long it is** sabemos lo largo que es; ~ **long will it last?** ¿cuánto tiempo durará?; ~ **many** cuántos (~**as**); ~ **much?** ¿cuánto?; ~ **much are the plums?** ¿qué precio tienen las ciruelas?; ~ **often?** ¿con qué frecuencia?; ~ **old is she?** ¿cuántos años tiene ella?; ~'**s that?** (*US* pardon?) ¿qué dice usted?; ~ **to do it** cómo hacerlo; ~ **I'd like to ...!** ¡cuánto me gustaría ...!; ~ **shall I tell her?** ¿cómo decirle?; ~ **to use this appliance** modo de uso de este aparato; **see** ~ **little she cares!** ¡mire lo poco que le importa!

howdy? ¿qué tal?

however (notwithstanding) sin embargo; ~ **much it is** por mucho que sea; ~ **late it may be** por muy tarde que sea; ~ **much it may cost** por mucho que cueste

howitzer obús *m*

howl *n* (animal's) aullido; (human's) grito, ~ **of pain** grito de dolor; *rad* silbido; *v* aullar; ~ **with laughter** reírse (i)³ a carcajadas; ~ **with pain** gritar de dolor; ~ **down** abuchear

howler plancha

howling *n* aullido; (weeping) lamento; *adj* aullador (-ora *f*); ~ **mob** muchedumbre clamorosa; **it was a ~ success** tuvo un éxito formidable; **~ wind** viento rugiente

hoy! ¡hola!

H.R.H. (**Her/His Royal Highness**) S.A.R. (Su Alteza Real)

hub cubo; *fig* centro; **~cap** tapacubos *m sing*

hubbub barullo

hubby marido

Hubert Huberto

huckleberry variedad *f* de arándano

huckster buhonero

huddle (group) grupo; (heap) montón *m*; **go into a ~** consultar en secreto; *vt* amontonar; *vi* amontonarse

hue (colour) matiz (-ces) *m*; **~ and cry** griterío

huff *n* mal humor *m*; **in a ~** enfadado; *v* (draughts) soplar

huffily petulantemente

huffy malhumorado

hug *n* abrazo; *v* abrazar[7]; **~ the coast** no apartarse de la costa

huge enorme

hugeness inmensidad *f*

hugger-mugger confusión *f*

Hugh Hugo

Huguenot *n+adj* hugonote *m* (-ta *f*)

huh? ¿eh?

hulk casco; **great ~ of a man** armatoste *m*

hulking grande y pesado

hull *n naut* casco; (shell) vaina; *v naut* +*mil* dar[19] en el casco; (remove the shell) mondar; **~ed** *naut* averiado en el casco, (shelled) sin cáscara

hullabaloo alboroto

hullo! *see* hallo!

hum *n* (of insect/motor) zumbido; (of crowd) murmullo; (of person) tarareo; *sl* (smell) hedor *m*; *v* (of insect/motor) zumbar; (of person) tararear; *sl* (smell) heder (ie)[2b]; **~ and haw** vacilar; **make things ~** avivarlo

human *n+adj* humano; **~ being** ser humano; **~ touch** don *m* de gentes; **~kind** humanidad *f*

humane humanitario; **~ killer** *vet* martillo inglés de matanza

humanism humanismo

humanist *n+adj* humanista *m+f*

humanitarian *n+adj* humanitario

humanity humanidad *f*; **the humanities** las humanidades

humanize humanizar[7]

humble *adj* humilde; (timid) sumiso; **eat ~ pie** humillarse; **~ folk** gente de garbanzo; **in my ~ opinion** a mi ver; **your ~ servant** su servidor; **the most ~ position in the firm** el último puesto en la empresa; *vt* humillar; **~o.s.** humillarse, *fam* rebajarse

humbug hipocresía; **religious ~** tartufería; (fraud) embuste *m*; (nonsense) paparrucha; (person) charlatán *m* (-ana *f*); (sweet) caramelo de menta

humdinger algo sobresaliente

humdrum monótono

humerus húmero

humid húmedo

humidify humedecer[14]

humidity humedad *f*

humiliate humillar

humiliating humillante

humiliation humillación *f*

humility humildad *f*

humming *n* zumbido; (of a tune) tarareo; *adj* zumbidor (-ora *f*); **~-bird** pájaro mosca; **~-top** trompa

hummock montecillo

humoresque capricho musical

humorist humorista *m+f*

humorous humorístico; (of a person) chistoso

humour *n* humor *m*; (temperament) disposición *f*; (whim) capricho; **be in a bad/good ~** estar[19] de mal/buen humor; **be in the ~ to** estar[19] de humor para +*infin*; **sense of ~** sentido del humor; *v* complacer[14]; (spoil) mimar

humourless sin sentido del humor

hump *n* joroba; (hillock) montecillo; **~-back(ed)** jorobado; *v* llevar al hombro

humph! ¡qué va!

Humpty-Dumpty (rotund person) retaco

humpy (uneven) desnivelado

humus humus *m*

Hun huno; *pej* (German) teutón *m* (-ona *f*)

hunch *n* (idea) corazonada, *SA* pálpito; *v* **~ up** encorvar(se); **~ one's shoulders** encogerse[8] de hombros; **~-back(ed)** jorobado

hundred ciento; **a ~ men** cien hombres; **one ~ and ten men** ciento diez hombres; ~s **of men** centenares *mpl* de hombres; **by** ~s/**by the** ~ a centenares; ~**fold** cien veces; ~ **peseta note** *sl* marrón *m*; ~ **pesetas** *sl* libra; ~ **thousandth** cienmilésimo; ~**weight** *approx* quintal *m* (50 kilos)

hundredth (ordinal) ciento, **the** ~ **man** el hombre número cien; (fraction) centésimo

hung: ~ **up (on)** obsesionado (con); ~ **council** consejo en el que ningún partido tiene mayoría

Hungarian *n+adj* húngaro; (language) húngaro

Hungary Hungría

hunger *n* hambre *f*; *fig* (desire) anhelo **(for** de); ~**-strike** huelga de hambre; ~ **is the best sauce** (proverb) a pan duro diente agudo; *v* ~ **for** anhelar

hungry hambriento; **be (very)** ~ tener[19] (mucha) hambre; **feel** ~ sentir (ie)[2c] hambre; **go** ~ pasar hambre; *fig* **be** ~ **for affection** tener[19] sed de cariño; **be** ~ **as a horse** tener[19] hambre de lobo

hunk pedazo grueso

hunky satisfactorio

hunt *n* caza; (of a person) persecución *f*; (search) busca, **on the** ~ **for** a la busca de; *v* cazar[7]; (a person) perseguir[3+11]; (search) buscar[4]

hunter cazador *m* (-ora *f*); (horse) caballo de caza

hunting caza; (of a person) persecución *f*; **go** ~ ir[19] de caza; ~**-box**, ~**-lodge** pabellón (-ones) *m* de caza; ~**-crop** látigo mocho; ~**-dog** perro de caza; ~**-ground** cazadero; ~**-horn** corneta de monte; ~ **season** tiempo de caza; **autograph-**~ petición *f* de autógrafos

huntress cazadora

huntsman cazador *m*

hurdle *n* valla; ~**-race** carrera de vallas; **hundred metres** ~s cien metros vallas; (obstacle) obstáculo; *v* saltar vallas

hurdler corredor *m* (-ora *f*) en una carrera de vallas

hurdy-gurdy organillo

hurl lanzar[7]; ~ **o.s.** lanzarse[7]; ~ **o.s. against/at** arrojarse contra/a; ~ **abuse** proferir insultos

hurly-burly tumulto

hurrah! ¡viva!; ~ **for Bilbao Athletic!** ¡viva el Athletic de Bilbao!

hurricane huracán (-anes) *m*; ~**-lamp** lámpara sorda

hurry *n* prisa; **be in a (great)** ~ tener[19] (mucha) prisa; **there's no** ~ no hay prisa; **I shan't speak to him again in a** ~ no pienso hablarle nunca más; *vt* apresurar; *vi* apresurarse; **hurried** hecho de prisa

~ **away** marcharse de prisa

~ **back** volver (ue)[1b] (*past part* vuelto) en seguida

~ **over** pasar rápidamente por; (do quickly) hacer[19] con prisa; (finish quickly) terminar a prisa

~ **up** darse[19] prisa; *fam* correr

hurt *n* daño; (injury) herida; *v* hacer[19] daño; **it didn't** ~ **(me)** no me hizo daño; (injure) herir (ie)[2c], **five people were** ~ **in the accident** cinco personas resultaron heridas en el accidente; ~ **o.s.** hacerse[19] daño; **my leg** ~s me duele la pierna; *fig* ofender; ~ **deeply** herir (ie)[2c] en el alma; ~ **s.o.'s pride** herir el amor propio de uno

hurtful dañoso; ~ **comment** comentario dañino

hurtle lanzar(se)[7]

husband *n* marido, esposo; *v* economizar[7]

husbandry agricultura; **animal** ~ zootécnica; cría de ganado

hush *n* silencio; ~-~ secreto; ~**-money** precio del silencio (de una persona); *v* acallar; ~ **up** echar tierra a; ~ **s.o. up** hacer[19] callar a uno; ~! ¡chitón!

hushaby! ¡duerme!

husk cáscara

huskiness ronquera

husky *n* perro de esquimal; *adj* ronco; (tough) fornido

hussar húsar *m*

hussy sinvergonzona; *fam* suripanta

hustings elecciones *fpl*

hustle *n* actividad *f*; ~ **and bustle** ajetreo; *vt* empujar; *vi* darse[19] prisa, *fam* menearse

hustler trafagón *m* (-ona *f*); (prostitute) ramera

hut cabaña; *SA* bohío; *mil* barraca

hutch conejera; (*US* dresser) armario

hutment campamento de barracas

hyacinth jacinto

hybrid *n+adj* híbrido

hybridize cruzar[7]

hydra hidra

hydrangea hortensia
hydrant boca de riego; **fire-~** boca de incendio
hydrate hidratar
hydraulic hidráulico; **~s** hidráulica; **~ brake** freno hidráulico
hydraulically: **~ operated** de energía hidráulica
hydrocarbon hidrocarburo
hydrochloric clorhídrico; **~ acid** ácido clorhídrico
hydrochloride clorhidrato
hydrodynamics hidrodinámica
hydroelectric hidroeléctrico
hydrofoil hidroala
hydrogen hidrógeno; **~-bomb** bomba de hidrógeno; **~ peroxide** agua oxigenada
hydrogenation hidrogenación *f*
hydrology hidrología
hydrolysis hidrólisis *f*
hydrophobia hidrofobia
hydrophobic hidrofóbico
hydroplane hidroplano; *aer* hidroavión *m*
hydrostat hidrostato
hydrostatic hidrostático
hydrotherapy hidroterapia
hydroxide hidróxido
hyena hiena
hygiene higiene *f*
hygienic higiénico
hymen himeneo; *anat* himen *m*
hymn himno; **~-book** himnario
hyperbola hipérbola
hyperbole hipérbole *f*
hypercritical hipercrítico

hyperrealism *arts* hiperrealismo
hyperrealist *n+adj* hiperrealista *m+f*
hypersensitive quisquilloso
hypersonic supersónico
hypertension hipertensión sanguínea
hypertrophy hipertrofia
hyphen guión (-ones) *m*
hyphenate escribir (*past part* escrito) con guión; **~d word** voz compuesta
hypnosis hipnosis *f*
hypnotic hipnótico
hypnotism hipnotismo
hypnotist hipnotizador *m*
hypnotize hipnotizar[7]
hypo *phot* hiposulfito sódico
hypochondria hipocondría
hypochondriac *n+adj* hipocondríaco
hypocrisy hipocresía
hypocrite hipócrita
hypocritical hipócrita *m+f*; *fam* mojigato
hypodermic hipodérmico; **~ needle/ syringe** aguja/jeringa hipodérmica
hypotenuse hipotenusa
hypothesis hipótesis *f*
hypothesize *vt* concluir[16] por hipótesis; *vi* hacer[19] hipótesis
hypothetic(al) hipotético; *fam* imaginario
hyssop hisopo
hysterectomy histerectomía
hysteria histerismo, histeria
hysteric(al) histérico
hysterics paroxismo histérico; **go into ~** ponerse[19] histérico; **~ of laughing/ tears** paroxismo de risa/lágrimas

I

i (letter) i (íes) f

I n el yo; *pron* yo (often omitted in speech and writing), **I dine at eight** ceno a las ocho; **it is** ~ soy yo

iambic yámbico

iambus yambo

Iberia Iberia

Iberian íbero; ~ **Peninsula** Península Ibérica

ibex íbice m

ibis ibis f

Ibizan ibicenco

ice n hielo; **break the** ~ +*fig* romper (*past part* roto) el hielo; **skate on thin** ~ tomar riesgos; ~ **age** período glacial; ~**-axe** picolet m; ~**berg** iceberg m; *fig* témpano; ~**-bound** (port) bloqueado por el hielo, (road) cubierto de hielo, (ship) preso entre los hielos; ~**-box** nevera; *SA* refrigerador m; ~**breaker** rompehielos m *sing*; ~**-cap** casquete m glacial; ~**-cold** *see* icy; ~**-cream** (cornet/sandwich) (cucurucho/corte m de) helado; ~**-cream parlour** heladería; ~**-cube** cubo de hielo; ~**-field** campo de hielo; ~**-floe** témpano; ~**-hockey** hockey m sobre hielo; ~**-lolly** polo; ~**-man** vendedor m de hielo; ~**-pack** *geog* masa de hielo flotante, *med* bolsa de hielo; ~**-rink** pista de hielo; ~**-skate** n patín (-ines) m de cuchilla, v patinar sobre hielo; ~**-skating** patinaje m sobre hielo; v (freeze) helar (ie)[2a] (up/over por encima); *cul* garapiñar; ~**d cake** pastel garapiñado; ~**d coffee** café granizado, *fam* (white coffee) blanco y negro; ~**d drink** bebida helada; ~**d water** agua con hielo

Iceland Islandia

Icelander islandés m (-esa f)

Icelandic islandés (-esa f)

icicle carámbano

iciness +*fig* frialdad f

icing *aer* hielo; (on road) formación f de hielo; *cul* glaseado

icon icono

iconoclasm iconoclasia

iconoclast iconoclasta m+f

iconography iconografía

icy (covered with ice) cubierto de hielo; (frozen) congelado; +*fig* glacial; **my hands are** ~(**-cold**) tengo las manos helad(ísim)as

idea idea; (intention) intención (-ones) f; **bright/great** ~ idea luminosa; **form an** ~ **of** hacerse[19] una idea de; **I have an** ~ **that he is a doctor** me parece que él es médico; **I haven't the slightest** ~ no tengo la menor idea; **I had no** ~ **that you were Spanish** yo no sabía que usted es español; **my** ~ **is to** mi intención es; **that's the** ~**!** ¡eso es!; **the very** ~**!** ¡ni hablar!; **what an** ~**!** (how strange!) ¡vaya una ocurrencia!; **what's the** ~**?** (what are you up to?) ¿qué hace usted?

ideal n+*adj* ideal m

idealism idealismo

idealist idealista m+f

idealistic idealista m+f

idealization idealización f

idealize idealizar[7]

idem ídem

identical idéntico (**with** a)

identicalness identidad f

identifiable identificable

identification identificación f; ~**-mark** señal f de identificación; ~**-parade** rueda de presos

identify identificar[4]; ~ **o.s.** identificarse[4]

Identikit: ~ **picture** foto(grafía)-robot f

identity identidad f; **lose one's sense of** ~ perder (ie)[2b] el sentido de identidad; **mistaken** ~ identificación errónea; ~**-card** cédula personal, *fam* carnet m de identidad; ~**-disc** *mil* placa de identidad

ideogram, ideograph ideograma m

ideological ideológico

ideology ideología

780

idiocy idiotez (-ces) *f*
idiom (expression) modismo; (language) idioma *m*
idiomatic idiomático
idiosyncrasy idiosincrasia
idiosyncratic idiosincrático
idiot idiota *m+f*; *fam* tonto
idiotic idiota
idle *adj* ocioso; (lazy) perezoso; (not working) parado; (of no use) vano; (unemployed) sin trabajo; *comm* (of capital) inactivo; **stand ~** estar[19] parado; **~ fancies** ilusiones *fpl*; **~ fellow** holgazán *m*; **~ hours** ratos perdidos; **~ question** pregunta inútil; **~ talk** charla frívola; **indulge in ~ talk** hablar a tontas y a locas; *v mot* marchar en vacío; **~ away** gastar ociosamente; **~ away the time** pasar el rato
idleness, idling ociosidad *f*; (laziness) pereza; (uselessness) inutilidad *f*
idler holgazán *m* (-ana *f*); *fam* gandul *m* (-ula *f*)
idol ídolo
idolater idólatra *m*
idolatress idólatra *f*
idolatrous idólatra *m+f*
idolatry idolatría
idolize idolatrar
idyll idilio
idyllic idílico
i.e. (id est) es decir
if *n* hipótesis *f*; **~s and buts** peros *mpl*; *conj* si; (whenever) en caso de que +*subj*; **~ I were you** yo que usted; **~ necessary** si fuese necesario; **~ not** si no; **~ only …!** ¡ojalá que +*subj*¡; **~ only to prove that** aunque sólo sea para demostrar que; **~ so** si es así; **as ~** (though) como si +*subj*; **as ~ to** como para; **even ~** aunque +*subj*
igloo iglú *m*
igneous ígneo
ignite *vt* encender (ie)[2b]; *vi* encenderse (ie)[2b]
ignition ignición *f*; *mot* encendido; **~ key** llave de contacto; **~-switch** contacto, *SA* switch *m* (de ignición)
ignoble innoble
ignominious ignominioso
ignominy ignominia
ignoramus ignorante *m+f*
ignorance ignorancia
ignorant ignorante; (bad-mannered)

inculto, *fam* burro; **~ of** ignorante de; **be ~ of** ignorar
ignore no hacer[19] caso de; (pretend not to see) hacer la vista gorda; (refuse to listen) desoír[19]; **~ an order** desobedecer[14] una orden
iguana iguana
ilex encina
ilk clase *f*; **of that ~** de la misma especie
ill *n* desgracia; *adj* (bad) malo; (sick) enfermo; **be ~** estar[19] enfermo; **become ~** ponerse[19] enfermo; **fall ~** caer[19] enfermo; **~ fame** mala fama; **do ~** hacer[19] mal; **do s.o. an ~ turn** hacer[19] a uno una mala faena; *adv* mal; **he took it ~** él lo tomó a mal; **I can ~ afford it** está fuera de mi alcance; **I can ~ afford to offend him** no me conviene ofenderle; **it ~ becomes him** no le va bien; **~ at ease** incómodo; **~-advised** malaconsejado; **~-advisedly** imprudentemente; **~-assorted** mal juntado; **~-bred** maleducado; **~-breeding** mala educación; **~-clad** mal vestido; **~-conceived** mal ideado; **~-considered** imprudente; **~-deserved** no merecido; **~-disposed** (towards) malintencionado (hacia); **be ~-disposed to** no estar[19] dispuesto a +*infin*; **~-famed** de mala fama; **~-fated** aciago; **~-favoured** feo; **~-feeling** hostilidad *f*; **~-founded** infundado; **~-gotten** maladquirido; **~ health** mala salud; **~ humour** mal humor *m*; **~-humoured** malhumorado; **~-informed** malinformado; **~-intentioned** de malas intenciones; **~-judged** imprudente; (by) **~-luck** (por) mala suerte; **~-mannered** maleducado; **~-matched** mal aparejado; **~-natured** malicioso; **~-omened** de mal agüero; **~-pleased** descontento; **~-qualified** inapto; **~-spent** malgastado; **~-spoken** de mala lengua; **~-starred** malhadado; **~-suited** impropio; **~-tempered** de mal genio; **~-timed** inoportuno; **~-treat** maltratar; **~-treatment** maltrato; **~-use** *n* maltrato, *v* maltratar; **~will** mala voluntad; **I bear her no ~will** no le guardo rencor
illegal ilegal
illegality ilegalidad *f*
illegibility ilegibilidad *f*
illegible ilegible

illegitimacy ilegitimidad *f*
illegitimate ilegítimo
illiberal iliberal
illiberality intolerancia *f*
illicit ilícito
illimitable ilimitable
illiteracy analfabetismo
illiterate analfabeto
illness enfermedad *f*
illogical ilógico
illogicality falta de lógica
illuminate iluminar; *fig* aclarar; ~d
  manuscript manuscrito iluminado;
  ~d sign letrero luminoso
illuminating revelador
illumination iluminación (-ones) *f*; ~s
  (city lights) luces *fpl* de la ciudad
illumine iluminar
illusion ilusión (-ones) *f*; be under the ~
  that creer erróneamente; have no ~s
  about no tener[19] ilusiones sobre; optical ~ ilusión óptica
illusionist ilusionista *m+f*
illusive, illusory ilusorio
illustrate ilustrar; (demonstrate) demostrar (ue)[1a]; (provide examples)
  ejemplificar[4]; ~d magazine revista ilu-
  strada
illustration ilustración *f*; (clarification)
  aclaración *f*; (picture) grabado, lámina
illustrative ilustrativo
illustrator ilustrador *m* (-ora *f*)
illustrious ilustre
I.L.O, (International Labour Office)
  O.I.T. (Oficina Internacional del Trabajo)
image *n* imagen (-ágenes) *f*; he is the (living) ~ of his father él es el vivo retrato
  de su padre; (metaphor) metáfora; *v*
  representar
imagery imágenes poéticas
imaginable imaginable
imaginary imaginario
imagination imaginación *f*; his ~ runs
  away with him él se deja llevar por la
  imaginación
imaginative imaginativo
imagine imaginar(se); ~ things fanta-
  siar; just ~! ¡imagínese!; I can just ~
  it me lo figuro; I ~ so creo que sí
imbalance desequilibrio *m*
imbecile *n+adj* imbécil *m+f*; (fool,
  foolish) tonto

imbecility imbecilidad *f*
imbibe (em)beber; *fig* embeberse de/en
imbroglio embrollo
imbue imbuir[16]; ~d with imbuido de
imitable imitable
imitate imitar
imitation *n* imitación (-ones) *f*; *adj* de
  imitación; (of jewellery) falso; ~
  leather skay *m tr*
imitative imitativo
imitator imitador *m* (-ora *f*)
immaculate inmaculado; Immaculate
  Conception Purísima Concepción
immanent inmanente
immaterial inmaterial; (unimportant)
  sin importancia: it's ~ to me no tiene
  importancia para mí
immature inmaduro; *fam* verde
immaturity inmadurez *f*
immeasureable inmensurable; (enormous) inmenso
immediacy proximidad *f*
immediate (of place) cercano; (of time)
  próximo; (urgent) urgente; take ~
  action tomar acción inmediata; ~
  needs necesidades urgentes; ~ relatives parientes *mpl* allegados
immediately en seguida; ~ he saw me he
  … en cuanto me vió …
immemorial inmemorial
immense inmenso
immensely enormemente; *fam* horrores, I love him ~ le quiero horrores
immensity inmensidad *f*
immerse sumergir[9]; ~ o.s. sumergirse[9]
  (in en), *fig* enfrascarse[4] (in en)
immersion *n* inmersión *f*; ~-heater
  calentador *m* de inmersión
immigrant *n+adj* inmigrante *m+f*
immigrate inmigrar
immigration inmigración *f*
imminence inminencia
imminent inminente
immobile inmóvil
immobility inmovilidad *f*
immobilize inmovilizar[7]
immoderate inmoderado
immodest inmodesto
immodesty inmodestia *f*
immolate inmolar
immolation inmolación *f*
immoral inmoral
immorality inmoralidad *f*
immortal inmortal

immortality inmortalidad *f*
immortalize inmortalizar[7]
immovable inmóvil
immune inmune (**from/to** contra); (taxes) exento (**from** de)
immunity inmunidad *f*
immunization inmunización *f* (**against** contra)
immunize inmunizar[7]
immunology inmunología
immure emparedar
immutability inmutabilidad *f*
immutable inmutable
imp +*fig* diablillo
impact impacto
impair (injure) perjudicar[4]; (weaken) debilitar
impairment perjuicio
impale empalar
impalpable impalpable
impart comunicar[4]; ~ **courage** dar[19] ánimo
impartial imparcial
impartiality imparcialidad *f*
impassable intransitable
impasse punto muerto
impassibility impasibilidad *f*
impassible impasible
impassioned apasionado
impassive impasible
impassivity impasibilidad *f*
impatience impaciencia
impatient impaciente (**at/with** con/de/por); (intolerant) intolerante (**of** con/para); **be** ~ ser[19] impaciente; **become** ~ impacientarse (**of/with** ante/con)
impeach acusar (de alta traición); ~ **s.o.'s honour** poner[19] en tela de juicio el honor de alguien
impeachable censurable
impeachment procesamiento (de alta traición)
impeccability impecabilidad *f*
impeccable impecable
impecunious indigente
impedance *elect* impedancia
impede estorbar
impediment impedimento; *leg* estorbo (**to** para); (in speech) defecto del habla
impedimenta equipaje *m*; *mil* impedimenta
impel impeler
impend pender

impending inminente
impenetrability impenetrabilidad *f*
impenetrable impenetrable (**by/to** a)
impenitence impenitencia
impenitent incorregible
imperative imperativo; ~ **mood** modo imperativo; (necessary) indispensable
imperceptible imperceptible
imperceptive incapaz (-ces) de percibir
imperfect +*gramm* imperfecto
imperfection imperfección (-ones) *f*
imperial imperial
imperialism imperialismo
imperialist *n*+*adj* imperialista *m*+*f*
imperialistic imperialista
imperil poner[19] en peligro
imperious imperioso
imperishable imperecedero
impermeable impermeable
impermissible inadmisible
impersonal +*gramm* impersonal
impersonality impersonalidad *f*
impersonate hacerse[19] pasar por; *theat* imitar
impersonation personificación *f*; *theat* imitación *f*
impersonator representador *m* (-ora *f*); *theat* imitador *m* (-ora *f*)
impertinence impertinencia
impertinent impertinente
imperturbability imperturbabilidad *f*
imperturbable imperturbable
impervious impermeable (**to** a); *fig* insensible (**to** a)
impetigo impétigo
impetuosity impetuosidad *f*
impetuous impetuoso
impetus ímpetu *m*
impiety impiedad *f*
impinge chocar[4] (**on** con); (infringe) violar
impingement choque *m*
impious impío
impish travieso
implacability implacabilidad *f*
implacable implacable
implant implantar; (in the mind) infundir
implausible inverosímil
implement *n* utensilio; ~**s** (of war) elementos de guerra; *v* poner[19] en vigor
implementation ejecución *f*
implicate implicar[4] (**in** en)

implication implicación f
implicit implícito; ~ **faith** fé absoluta
implicitly a pie juntillas; **he believed his friend** ~ él creyó a pie juntillas a su amigo
implore implorar
imploring suplicante
imply (give to understand) dar[19] a entender; **this implies that** esto significa que; (mean) querer (ie)[2b] decir; **with all that it implies** con todo lo que ello encierra
impolite descortés m+f
impoliteness descortesía
impolitic impolítico
imponderable imponderable; ~s elementos imponderables
import n importación f; (meaning) significado; ~ **duty** derechos mpl de importación; ~**-licence** licencia de importación; v importar; (mean) significar[4]
importance importancia; **it is of no** ~ (**at all**) no importa (nada)
important importante; (of people) de categoría, fam gordo; **be** ~ tener[19] importancia; **it is** ~ **that** es importante que +subj
importation importación (-ones) f
importer n+adj importador m (-ora f)
importunate importuno
importune importunar
importuning n pedidura; adj pedigüeño
importunity importunidad f
impose imponer[19]; ~ (**up)on** abusar de (la amistad de), (deceive) engañar
imposing imponente
imposition imposición f; (unreasonable demand) abuso; (at school) ejercicio de castigo
impossibility imposibilidad f
impossible n lo imposible; adj imposible; (insufferable) insoportable; **it's** ~ **for me to** me es imposible +infin, es imposible que yo +subj; **make** ~ imposibilitar; **that's** ~ eso es imposible
impostor impostor m (-ora f)
imposture impostura
impotence impotencia
impotent impotente
impound (animals) encerrar; (goods) confiscar[4]; leg depositar
impoverish empobrecer[14]

impoverishment empobrecimiento
impracticability impracticabilidad f
impracticable impracticable
impractical impráctico
impracticality lo que no es práctico
imprecate imprecar[4]
imprecation imprecación (-ones) f
impregnable inexpugnable
impregnate impregnar; biol fecundar; **become** ~**d** impregnarse
impregnation impregnación f; biol fecundación f
impresario empresario
impress n huella; v (mark by pressing) imprimir; (convince) convencer[12]; fig (make a lasting impression) impresionar; fig (make a good impression on) hacer[19] un buen tanto con; ~ **on the memory** grabar en la memoria
impression impresión f; huella; (notion) idea; **be under the** ~ **that** tener[19] la idea de que; **make an** ~ **upon** impresionar; **it gives the wrong** ~ parece otra cosa
impressionable impresionable
impressionism impresionismo
impressionist n+adj impresionista m+f
impressive impresionante
imprimatur imprimátur m
imprint n impresión f; print pie m de impresión, fig huella; v imprimir; (on the mind) grabar
imprison encarcelar
imprisonment encarcelamiento
improbability improbabilidad f
improbable improbable
impromptu adj improvisado; adv de improviso
improper impropio; (of behaviour) indecoroso
impropriety impropiedad f
improvable mejorable
improve vt mejorar; (beautify) embellecer[14]; (increase) aumentar; (reform) reformar; (strengthen) fortificar[4]; vi mejorar(se); (become beautiful) embellecerse[14]; (increase) aumentar; **he** ~**s on acquaintance** él gana mucho cuando se le conoce; ~ **on an idea** mejorar una idea; ~ **one's knowledge of** perfeccionar; ~ **land** abonar[4] la tierra
improvement mejora; agri abono; (in appearance) embellecimiento; (in-

crease) aumento; *med* mejoría; (reform) reforma; **an ~ on last week** mejor que la semana pasada; **there is room for ~** se puede mejorar todavía

improver trabajador *m* recién calificado
improvidence imprevisión *f*
improvident imprevisto
improving educativo
improvisation improvisación *f*
improvise improvisar
imprudence imprudencia
imprudent imprudente
impudence descaro
impudent descarado
impugn impugnar
impulse impulso; *elect* impulso *f* eléctrico; **on ~** de repente
impulsive impulsivo
impulsiveness irreflexión *f*
impunity impunidad *f*; **with ~** impunemente
impure adulterado; (of morals) deshonesto; (language) incorrecto
impurity impureza
imputation imputación *f*
impute imputar

[1] **in** *prep* en; **~ Madrid** en Madrid; **~ Spanish** en español; **~ 1971** en (el año) 1971; (during) durante; (inside) dentro de, **~ a cave/week's time** dentro de una cueva/una semana; **~ the rain** bajo la lluvia; (after a *superl*) de, **the most intelligent ~ the family** el más inteligente de la familia; **~ all** en suma; **~ being existente**; **~ saying this** al decir esto; **~ threes** de tres en tres; **be ~ the army/business** ser[19] militar/comerciante; **be ~ on** estar[19] en el secreto; **be (well) ~ with** ser[19] (muy) íntimo de; **one ~ five** uno de cada cinco; **she has it ~ her to** ella es capaz de +*infin*; **there's nothing ~ it** (it's not true) no es verdad, (they are equal) van muy iguales; **there's nothing ~ it for me** no me beneficia; **~-law** *see* law; *adv* (inside) (a)dentro; (at home) en casa; **is Mary ~?** ¿está María?; (in fashion) de moda; **the Liberals are ~** los liberales están en el poder; **you're ~ for it!** ¡vas a pagarlo!; **~s and outs** recovecos *mpl*

[2] **in** *sl*: **the ~ group/sport** el grupo/deporte *m* in; **~ joke** chiste comprendido solamente por los miembros de un

círculo
inability incapacidad *f*
inaccessibility inaccesibilidad *f*
inaccessible inaccesible
inaccuracy inexactitud *f*
inaccurate inexacto
inaction inacción *f*
inactivate hacer[19] inactivo
inactive inactivo
inactivity inactividad *f*
inadequacy insuficiencia
inadequate insuficiente
inadmissibility inadmisibilidad *f*
inadmissible inadmisible
inadvertence inadvertencia
inadvertent inadvertido
inadvertently sin querer
inadvisability inconveniencia
inadvisable desaconsejable
inalienable inalienable
inane necio
inanimate inanimado
inanity sandez (-ces) *f*
inapplicability inaplicabilidad *f*
inapplicable inaplicable
inapposite inoportuno
inappreciable inapreciable
inapproachable inaccesible
inappropriate impropio
inappropriately fuera del caso
inapt inadecuado
inaptitude ineptitud *f*
inarticulate inarticulado; (of people) incapaz (-ces) de expresarse
inartistic antiartístico
inasmuch: ~ as ya que
inattention desatención *f*
inattentive desatento
inaudibility inaudibilidad *f*
inaudible inaudible
inaugural inaugural
inaugurate inaugurar
inauguration inauguración (-ones) *f*
inauspicious poco propicio
inborn innato
inbred (innate) innato; (resulting from inbreeding) engendrado por endogamia; **~ family** familia endogámica
inbreeding endogamia
Inc. (Incorporated) S.A. (Sociedad Anónima)
Inca *n*+*adj* inca *m*+*f*
incalculable incalculable
incandescence incandescencia

incandescent incandescente
incantation conjuro
incapability incapacidad *f*
incapable incapaz (-ces); **drunk and ~** incapacitado por borrachera
incapacitate incapacitar
incapacitation inhabilitación *f*
incapacity incapacidad *f*
incarcerate encarcelar
incarceration encarcelamiento
incarnate *adj* encarnado; *v* encarnar
incarnation encarnación *f*
incautious incauto
incendiarism incendiarismo premeditado
incendiary incendiario; *fig* subversivo; **~-bomb** bomba incendiaria
incense *n* incienso; **~d** (angry) exasperado; **~-burner** incensario; *v* exasperar
incentive incentivo
inception incepción *f*
incessant incesante
incest incesto
incestuous incestuoso
inch *n* pulgada (2,54 cm); **~ by ~** palmo a palmo; **every ~ a man** todo un hombre; **be within an ~ of** estar[19] a punto de +*infin*; *v* **~ forward** adelantarse palmo a palmo
inchoate incoado
incidence incidencia; **high ~ of** gran incidencia de
incident (episode) episodio; (event) acontecimiento, **~s on the border** acontecimientos en la frontera
incidental *n* (accessory) cosa accesoria; **~s** (unexpected costs) imprevistos *mpl*; *adj* incidental; **~ music** *cin* música de fondo
incidentally (by chance) por casualidad; (by the way) a propósito
incinerate incinerar
incineration incineración *f*
incinerator incinerador *m*
incipience principio
incipient incipiente
incise cortar
incision incisión (-ones) *f*
incisive incisivo; (of speech) mordaz (-ces)
incisor diente incisivo
incite incitar
incitement incitación *f*

inciter incitador *m* (-ora *f*)
incivility descortesía
inclemency inclemencia; (of weather) intemperie *f*
inclement inclemente; (of weather) destemplado
inclination (slope) inclinación *f*; (bow) reverencia; *geom* inclinación *f*; (liking) afición *f* (**for** a); (tendency) propensión *f*
incline inclinar (**to** a); inclinarse (**to** a); (tend) tener propensión (**to** a); **be ~d to** (in the habit of) ser[19] propenso a; **I am/feel ~d to** me inclino a +*infin*; **I do it because I feel ~d to** lo hago porque me da la gana
include incluir[16]; (comprise) comprender; (enclose with a letter) adjuntar; **everything ~d** todo comprendido
including incluso; **not ~** no comprendido
inclusion inclusión *f*
inclusive *adj* inclusivo; **~ terms** todo incluido; *adv* inclusive; **Tuesday to Friday ~** de martes a viernes inclusive
incognito *adj* incógnito; *adv* de incógnito
incoherence incoherencia
incoherent incoherente; **what he says is quite ~** lo que él dice no tiene ni pies ni cabeza
incombustible incombustible
income ingreso(s) *m*; (unearned) renta de inversiones; **~ and expenditure** entrada y salida; **~-tax (return)** (declaración *f* del) impuesto sobre la renta; **~s policy** política salarial
incoming entrante; **~ tide** marea ascendente
incommensurable, incommensurate inconmensurable
incommode incomodar
incommodious inconveniente
incommunicable incomunicable
incommunicado incomunicado
incomparable incomparable
incompatibility incompatibilidad *f*
incompatible incompatible (**with** con)
incompetence incompetencia; *leg* incapacidad *f*
incompetent incompetente; *leg* incapaz (-ces)
incomplete incompleto
incompleteness estado incompleto

incomprehensibility incomprensibilidad *f*, uninteligible
incomprehensible incomprensible
incomprehension incomprensión *f*
incomprehensive incomprensivo
inconceivability inconcebibilidad *f*
inconceivable inconcebible
inconclusive inconclusivo; (unconvincing) poco convincente
inconclusiveness indeterminación *f*
incongruity incongruencia
incongruous incongruo
inconsequential inconsecuente
inconsiderable insignificante
inconsiderate desconsiderado
inconsideration desconsideración *f*
inconsistency inconsistencia
inconsistent inconsecuente (**with** a)
inconsolable inconsolable
inconspicuous que no llama la atención; *fam* desapercibido
inconstancy veleidad *f*
inconstant inconstante; (fickle) veleidoso
incontestable incontestable
incontinence +*med* incontinencia
incontinent +*med* incontinente
incontrollable ingobernable
incontrovertible incontrovertible
inconvenience *n* incomodidad *f*; *v* incomodar; *comm* perjudicar⁴
inconvenient incómodo; (inopportune) inoportuno; **at an ~ time** a deshora; **I find it ~** no me conviene
inconvertible inconvertible
incorporate incorporar(se) (**into/with** a/con/en)
incorporation constitución en sociedad anónima; incorporación *f*
incorporeal incorpóreo
incorrect incorrecto
incorrectness incorrección *f*
incorrigibility incorregibilidad *f*
incorrigible incorregible
incorruptible incorruptible
increase *n* aumento; **be on the ~** estar¹⁹ en crecimiento; *vt* aumentar(se)
increasing creciente
increasingly cada vez más
incredibility incredibilidad *f*
incredible increíble
incredulity incredulidad *f*
incredulous incrédulo
increment incremento; **unearned ~**

plusvalía *f*
incriminate incriminar
incriminating incriminador (-ora *f*)
incrimination incriminación *f*
incrust incrustar
incrustation incrustación (-ones) *f*
incubate empollar
incubation incubación *f*
incubator empollador *m*
incubus +*med* íncubo
inculcate inculcar⁴
incumbency *eccles* duración *f* de un beneficio eclesiástico
incumbent *n eccles* beneficiado; *adj* obligatorio; **be ~ upon** incumbir a
incur incurrir en; **~ a debt** contraer¹⁹ una deuda
incurability incurabilidad *f*
incurable incurable; (of a habit) irremediable
incurious poco curioso
incursion incursión *f*; *mil* correría; *fig* penetración *f*
indebted (in debt) adeudado; (under an obligation) reconocido; **be ~ to** (owing money) estar¹⁹ en deuda con, (under an obligation) estar¹⁹ agradecida
indebtedness (debt) deuda; (obligation) obligación *f*
indecency indecencia
indecent indecente; **~ assault** atentado contra el pudor; **~ exposure** exhibicionismo sexual
indecipherable indescifrable
indecision indecisión *f*
indecisive indeciso
indecorous indecoroso
indeed (really) verdaderamente; **I do ~ visit them** yo sí les visito; **~?** ¿de veras?; **~ not!** ¡claro que no!; **yes, ~!** ¡por cierto!
indefatigable infatigable
indefensible indefendible; (of an argument) insostenible
indefinable indefinible
indefinite indefinido
indefinitely por tiempo indefinido
indelible indeleble; **~ pencil** lápiz imborrable *m*
indelicacy grosería
indelicate grosero
indemnify indemnificar⁴
indemnity indemnización (-ones) *f*

indent *n* +*mil* (order for goods) requisición *f*; (notch) mella; *print* sangrado; *v* +*mil* requisar; (cut notches) mellar; *print* sangrar

indentation *see* **indent** *n*

indenture *n* contrato (de aprendizaje); *v* contratar (como aprendiz); ~**d labour force** mano de obra contratada a largo plazo

independence independencia; *pol* autonomía; (complete ~) *pol* separación *f*

independent independiente; *pol* autónomo; **be** ~ (financially) vivir de sus rentas; ~ **of** libre de; **of** ~ **means** acomodado; ~ **suspension** *mot* suspensión *f* independiente

indescribable indescriptible

indestructibility indestructibilidad *f*

indestructible indestructible

indeterminable indeterminable

indeterminate indeterminado

index *n* índice *m*; *eccles* índice expurgatorio; *math* exponente *m*; ~**-cabinet** estantería de ficheros; ~**-card** ficha; ~**-finger** (dedo) índice; *v* (prepare an ~) poner[19] índice (a); (enter in the ~) poner[19] en el índice

India la India; ~**-paper** papel *m* biblia; ~**-rubber** goma de borrar

Indian *n*+*adj* (from India/America) indio; ~ **corn** maíz *m*; ~ **file** fila india; ~ **head-dress** tocado de jefe indio; ~ **ink** tinta china; ~ **Ocean** Océano Índico; ~ **summer** veranillo de San Martín

indicate indicar[4]; (show) mostrar (ue)[1a]

indication indicación *f*

indicative indicativo; **be** ~ **of** indicar[4]

indicator indicador *m*; *mot* luz *f* intermitente (de dirección), *fam* piloto

indict acusar (ante el juez) (**on a charge of** de)

indictable procesable; ~ **offence** delito

indictment denuncia; *leg* procesamiento

indifference indiferencia; (coolness) frialdad *f*

indifferent indiferente; (cool) frío; (not very good) de calidad *f* regular

indifferently con indiferencia; (impartially) imparcialmente; (coolly) fríamente

indigence indigencia

indigenous indígena

indigent indigente

indigestible indigerible

indigestion indigestión *f*; *fam* empacho

indignant indignado

indignantly con indignación

indignation indignación *f*

indignity indignidad *f*

indigo *n*+*adj* añil; ~ **blue** azul (de) añil

indirect indirecto; ~ **free kick** *sp* (tiro) indirecto

indiscernible imperceptible

indiscipline indisciplina

indiscreet indiscreto

indiscretion indiscreción (-ones) *f*

indiscriminate sin discriminación

indiscriminately sin distinción

indiscrimination falta de discriminación

indispensable indispensable

indispose indisponer[19]

indisposed *med* indispuesto; (unwilling) mal dispuesto (**to** para)

indisposition +*med* indisposición *f* (**to** para)

indisputable incontestable

indissoluble indisoluble

indistinct indistinto

indistinctness indistinción *f*; confusión *f*

indistinguishable indistinguible

individual *n* individuo; *pej* sujeto; *adj* individual; ~ **taste** gusto original

individualism individualismo

individualist *n*+*adj* individualista *m*+*f*

individuality individualidad *f*

individualize individualizar[7]

indivisibility indivisibilidad *f*

indivisible indivisible

Indo: ~**-China** Indochina; ~**-European** indoeuropeo

indoctrinate adoctrinar (**with** en); *fam* lavar el cerebro

indoctrination adoctrinamiento; *fam* lavado del cerebro

indolence indolencia

indolent +*med* indolente

indomitable indómito

Indonesia Indonesia

Indonesian *n*+*adj* indonesio

indoor *adj* interior; ~ **aerial** antena interior; ~ **clothing** ropa de (estar por) casa; ~ **football** futbito; ~ **games** juegos *fpl* de salón; ~ **plant** planta de salón; ~ **swimming-pool** piscina cubierta; ~ **track** *sp* pista cubierta

indoors en casa; **go** ~ entrar; **stay** ~ quedarse en casa indubitable indubitable

induce +*elect* inducir[15] a; **I'll ~ her to sleep** la persuadiré a que duerma; **~d current** corriente inducida

inducement incentivo

induct +*eccles* instalar

induction +*elect* inducción *f*; *eccles* instalación *f*; **~-coil** carrete *m* de inducción

inductive inductivo

indulge *vt* dar[19] rienda suelta a; (pamper) mimar; *vi* **~ in** darse[19] el gusto de

indulgence +*eccles* indulgencia; (pleasure) exceso

indulgent indulgente

industrial industrial; **~ tribunal** tribunal *m* industrial; **~ securities** valores industriales; **Industrial Revolution** revolución *f* industrial

industrialism industrialismo

industrialist industrial *m*

industrialize industrializar[7]

industrious diligente

industry industria; **heavy/light ~** industria pesada/ligera; (diligence) laboriosidad

inebriate *n*+*adj* borracho; *v* emborrachar

inebriation embriaguez *f*

inedible incomible

inedited inédito

ineducable ineducable

ineffable inefable

ineffective, ineffectual, inefficient ineficaz (-ces)

ineffectiveness, ineffectuality, inefficiency ineficacia

inefficacious ineficaz (-ces)

inefficacy ineficacia

inelegance inelegancia

inelegant inelegante

ineligibility inelegibilidad *f*

ineligible inelegible

inept inepto

ineptitude ineptitud *f*

inequality desigualdad *f*

inequitable injusto

inequity injusticia

ineradicable imborrable

inert inerte

inertia inercia

inertial de inercia; **~ guidance** *space* navegación *f* por inercia

inescapable ineludible

inessential *n* cosa no esencial; *adj* no esencial

inestimable inestimable

inevitability inevitabilidad *f*

inevitable inevitable

inexact inexacto

inexactness inexactitud *f*

inexcusable imperdonable

inexhaustibility lo inagotable

inexhaustible inagotable

inexorability inexorabilidad *f*

inexorable inexorable

inexpediency inoportunidad *f*

inexpedient inoportuno

inexpensive económico

inexperience falta de experiencia

inexperienced, inexpert inexperto; **be ~** *fam* ser[19] rana

inexplicable inexplicable

inexpressible indecible

inexpressive inexpresivo

inextinguishable inapagable

inextricable inextricable

infallibility infalibilidad *f*

infallible infalible

infamous infame

infamy infamia

infancy infancia; *leg* minoría de edad; **from ~** desde niño; **in my ~** durante mi niñez

infant *n* criatura; *fam* nene *m*, nena *f*; *leg* menor *m*+*f*; **~ school** escuela de párvulos; *adj* infantil

infanta infanta

infante infante *m*

infanticide (crime) infanticidio; (person) infanticida *m*+*f*

infantile infantil; **~ paralysis** parálisis *f* infantil

infantry infantería; **~man** soldado de infantería

infatuate apasionar; **be ~d with** apasionarse por/de, *fam* chiflarse por/de

infatuation apasionamiento; *fam* chifladura

infect infectar; **~ s.o. with** contagiar a alguien con

infection infección (-ones) *f*

infectious +*fig* infeccioso; *fam* pegajoso

infelicitous infeliz (-ces)

infelicity infelicidad *f*

infer inferir (ie)[2c]

inferable deducible

inference inferencia

inferior *n+adj* inferior *m+f*; (in rank) subordinado

inferiority inferioridad *f*; ~ **complex** complejo de inferioridad

infernal infernal; ~ **machine** máquina infernal

inferno infierno

infertile estéril

infertility esterilidad *f*

infest infestar; **be** ~**ed with** estar[19] plagado de

infestation infestación *f*

infidel *n+adj* infiel *m+f*

infidelity infidelidad *f* (**to** con)

infield *sp* diamante *m*

infighting (boxing +*fig*) lucha cuerpo a cuerpo *m*

infiltrate infiltrar(se) (en)

infiltration infiltración (-ones) *f*

infinite infinito

infinitesimal +*math* infinitesimal; ~ **part** parte infinitésima

infinitive infinitivo

infinity infinidad *f*

infirm achacoso; (weak) débil; ~ **of purpose** irresoluto

infirmary enfermería

infirmity achaque *m*; (weakness) debilidad *f*; ~ **of purpose** flaqueza

inflame inflamar(se)

inflammability inflamabilidad *f*

inflammable inflamable; (*US* not burnable) ininflamable

inflammation inflamación *f*

inflammatory inflamatorio; (subversive) subversivo

inflate inflar; +*fig* hincharse; ~**d prices** precios *mpl* inflacionarios

inflation inflación *f*

inflationary inflacionista *m+f*

inflator bomba de aire; *SA* inflador *m*

inflect *gramm* declinar; (of the voice) modular

inflexibility inflexibilidad *f*

inflexible inflexible

inflexion *gramm* flexión *f*; (of voice) modulación *f*

inflict infligir (**on** a); ~ **damage** causar daño; ~ **o.s. on s.o.** imponer su presencia a alguien

infliction imposición *f*

inflow flujo; *fig* entrada

influence *n* influencia; **have** ~ **on** tener[19] influencia sobre; **have** ~ **with** tener[19] influencia con; *v* influenciar

influential influyente; ~ **people** gente *f* influyente

influenza gripe *f*; *fam* trancazo

influx afluencia

inform informar (**about** sobre/de); **be (well)** ~**ed about** estar[19] al corriente de; **well-**~**ed source** fuente *f* bien informada; **keep s.o.** ~**ed** tener[19] a alguien al corriente (**about** de); ~ **against** denunciar

informal sin ceremonia; (unofficial) extraoficial; ~ **visit** visita de confianza; ~ **dress** ropa de sport

informality falta de ceremonia

informally sin ceremonia; **be** ~ **dressed** estar[19] (vestido) de sport

informant informante *m+f*

information información *f*; *leg* delación, denuncia *f*; **piece of** ~ información *f*; **for** ~ **only** a título puramente informativo; **give** ~ **to** dar[19] información a; **I want** ~ **on** deseo informarme sobre; ~ **bureau** oficina de información

informative informativo

informer delator *m* (-ora *f*); *sl* soplón *m* (-ona *f*)

infra: ~ **dig** poco digno; ~-**red** infrarrojo; ~-**red telescope** *astron* telescopio de infrarrojos; ~**structure** infraestructura

infraction infracción *f*

infrequency infrecuencia

infrequent infrecuente

infringe violar (**upon** a)

infringement violación *f*

infuriate enfurecer[14]; *fam* poner[19] negro

infuriating irritante

infuse *vi* infundir (**into** a/en); *vt* hacer[19] una infusión

infusion infusión *f*

ingenious ingenioso; *fam* mañoso

ingenuity ingeniosidad *f*; *fam* maña

ingenuous ingenuo

ingenuousness ingenuidad *f*

ingest ingerir

ingestion ingestión *f*

ingle-nook rincón *m* de la chimenea

inglorious ignominioso

ingoing entrante; ~**s and outgoings** entradas *fpl* y salidas *fpl*

ingot lingote *m*; ~ **steel** acero en lingotes

ingrained arraigado

ingratiate: ~ **o.s. with** congraciarse con

ingratiating insinuante
ingratitude ingratitud *f*
ingredient ingrediente *m*
ingrowing que crece hacia dentro; ~ **toe nail** uñero
inhabit habitar
inhabitable habitable
inhabitant habitante *m*
inhabitation habitación (-ones) *f*
inhalation inspiración *f*; *med* inhalación *f*
inhale inspirar; *med* inhalar
inhalent inhalación *f*
inhaler inhalador *m*
inharmonious discordante
inhere ser[19] inherente
inherent inherente
inherit heredar (**from** de)
inheritance herencia
inheritor heredero
inhibit inhibir; *eccles* prohibir (**from** de)
inhibition inhibición (-ones) *f*
inhibitory inhibitorio
inhospitable inhospitalario
inhospitability inhospitalidad *f*
inhuman(e) inhumano
inhumanity inhumanidad *f*
inimical enemigo (**to** de)
inimitable inimitable
iniquitous inicuo
iniquity iniquidad *f*
initial *n+adj* inicial *f*; *v* firmar con las iniciales
initiate *n+adj* iniciado; *v* iniciar (**into** en)
initiation iniciación *f*; ~ **fee** cuota de ingreso
initiative iniciativa; **on his own** ~ por su propia iniciativa; **take the** ~ tomar la iniciativa
initiator iniciador *m* (-ora *f*)
initiatory iniciador
inject inyectar (**into** en); *fig* introducir[15]
injection inyección (-ones) *f*; (space) inserción *f*; ~ **moulding** moldeado por inyección
injudicious indiscreto
injunction mandato; entredicho
injure *n* (hurt) dañar; *med* lesionar; (permanently) lisiar; (offend) injuriar; ~ **o.s.** hacerse[19] daño
injurious dañoso, injurioso
injury (to body) daño; *med* lesión *f*; (offence) agravio

injustice injusticia; **do s.o. an** ~ hacer una injusticia a alguien
ink tinta; **write in** ~ escribir (*past part* escrito) con tinta; ~ **eraser/rubber** goma para tinta; ~**-fish** calamar *m*; ~**-pad** almohadilla de entintar; ~**-stand** escribanía; ~**-well** tintero; *v* entintar; ~ **in** pasar en tinta
inkling sospecha
inky (black as ink) (negro) como la tinta; (stained with ink) manchado (de tinta)
inlaid: ~ **floor** entarimado; ~ **work** taracea
inland *adj* (del) interior; ~ **town** ciudad *f* del interior; ~ **navigation** navegación *f* fluvial; ~ **revenue** impuestos *mpl* interiores, (department) delegación *f* de contribuciones; ~ **waterways** ríos *mpl* y canales *mpl*; *adv* tierra adentro; **go** ~ internarse (en un país)
in-laws familia política
inlay *n* taracea; *v* taracear
inlet *geog* cal(et)a; *mech* admisión *f*, ~ **valve** válvula de admisión
inmate residente *m+f*; (of a hospital) enfermo; (of an institution) internado; (of a mental hospital) internado; (of a prison) preso
inmost (más) interior; *fig* más íntimo
inn posada, fonda; (poor) venta; **Inns of Court** colegio de abogados (en Londres); ~**keeper** posadero, fondista *m+f*, ventero
innate innato
innately instintivamente
inner interior; *fig* secreto; ~**most** (más) interior, *fig* más íntimo; ~**-tube** cámara (de aire)
innings *sp* turno; *fig* oportunidad *f*
innocence inocencia
innocent *n+adj* inocente (**of** de)
innocuous inocuo
innovate innovar
innovation innovación (-ones) *f*
innovator innovador *m* (-ora *f*)
innuendo indirecta
innumerable innumerable; *fam* un sinfín de
inobservance inobservancia
inoculate inocular; **I have been** ~**d against** me han inoculado contra
inoculation inoculación (-ones) *f*
inoffensive inofensivo

inoffensiveness inocuidad *f*
inoperable inoperable
inoperative inoperante
inopportune inoportuno; **at an ~ moment** a deshora
inordinate desmesurado
inorganic inorgánico
in-patient paciente *m+f* interno
input *elect+mech* entrada; (money) cantidad recibida
inquest pesquisa; **have an ~ on** investigar[5] la muerte de; *fig* investigar
inquietude inquietud *f*
inquire: ~ about pedir (i)[3] informes sobre; **~ after** preguntar por; **~ into** investigar[5]
inquirer (investigator) investigador *m* (-ora *f*); (questioner) interrogante *m+f*
inquiring curioso; (investigating) investigador (-ora *f*)
inquiry (investigation) investigación *f* (**into** de); (question) pregunta; *leg* pesquisa; **make inquiries about** pedir (i)[3] informes sobre; **~-desk** mesa de información
inquisition inquisición *f*; **Holy Inquisition** Santo Oficio
inquisitive curioso; (given to asking questions) preguntón
inquisitiveness curiosidad *f*; manía de preguntar
inquisitor inquisidor *m*
inquisitorial inquisitorial
inroad incursión *f*; *fig* invasión *f*; **make ~s upon** invadir
inrush afluencia
insalubrious insalubre
insane loco; (senseless) insensato; **become ~** volverse (ue)[1b] (*past part* vuelto) loco; **~ asylum** manicomio
insanitary antihigiénico
insanity locura
insatiable insaciable
inscribe inscribir (*past part* inscrito); **~ a book** dedicar[4] un libro
inscription inscripción *f*; (in a book) dedicatoria
inscrutability inescrutabilidad *f*
inscrutable inescrutable
insect insecto; **~-powder** polvos *mpl* insecticidas
insecticide insecticida
insectivorous insectívoro

insecure inseguro
insecurity inseguridad *f*
insemination inseminación *f*; **artificial ~** fecundación artificial
insensate insensato; (without feelings) insensible
insensibility insensibilidad *f*
insensible insensible (**to** a)
insensitive insensible (**to** a)
inseparability inseparabilidad *f*
inseparable inseparable
insert *n* hoja insertada; *v* insertar; **~ an advert** insertar un anuncio, *fam* poner[19] un anuncio
insertion inserción *f*; (sewing) entredós *m*
inset *n* inserción *f*; (in book) grabados *mpl*/mapas *mpl* en el centro; *adj* (sewing) cortado
inshore *adj* cercano a la orilla; **~ fishing** pesca de bajura; *adv* cerca de la orilla; (towards the shore) hacia la orilla
inside *n* interior *m*; (working parts) *fam* entrañas *fpl*, *sl* tripas *fpl*; **~ out** al revés; **know ~ out** conocer[14] a fondo; **on the ~** por dentro; **on the ~ of the pavement** parte interior de la acera; *adj* interior; **this must have been an ~ job** esto lo ha hecho alguien desde dentro; **~ forward** *sp* interior *m*; **~ information** información confidencial; **~-left/-right** *sp* interior izquierdo/derecho; **~ measurement** (of sleeve or leg) tiro; *adv* (a)dentro; **go/come ~** entrar; *prep* dentro de; **I knew ~ me that he was lying** ya sabía yo que él estaba mintiendo
insider socio; persona enterada
insidious insidioso
insidiousness insidia
insight penetración *f*; **get an ~ into** formarse una idea de
insignia insignias *fpl*
insignificance insignificancia
insignificant insignificante
insincere poco sincero
insincerity falta de sinceridad
insinuate insinuar; **~ o.s. into** insinuarse en
insinuating insinuante
insinuation indirecta
insipid soso
insipidity sosería
insist insistir; **~ on** insistir en +*infin*

insistence insistencia
insistent insistente
insobriety embriaguez *f*
insofar: ~ as en cuanto a
insole plantilla
insolence insolencia
insolent insolente
insolubility insolubilidad *f*
insoluble insoluble; *math* indescifrable
insolvency insolvencia; ~ **proceedings** concurso de acreedores
insolvent insolvente
insomnia insomnio
insomuch: ~ as ya que; ~ that hasta tal punto que
inspect (formally) registrar; (informally) inspeccionar; *mil* pasar revista a
inspection (formal) registro; (informal) inspección *f*; *mil* revista; ~-**pit** foso de reconocimiento
inspector inspector *m* (-ora *f*); (public official) interventor *m*; (police) policía superior al sargento; **ticket** ~ revisor *m*
inspectorate inspectoría
inspiration inspiración *f*; **find** ~ **(in)** inspirarse (en)
inspire inspire **(to a)**
inspiring inspirador *m* (-ora *f*)
inst. (**instant**) del corriente
instability inestabilidad *f*
instable inestable
install instalar; **be** ~**ed in** tomar posesión de
installation instalación (-ones) *f*
instalment *comm* plazo; (part of story) entrega; *rad*+*TV* episodio; ~ **plan** plan *m* de venta a plazos; **pay by** ~**s** pagar[5] a plazos
instance *n* ejemplo; *leg* (urgent request) instancia; **for** ~ por ejemplo; **in the first** ~ en primer lugar; *v* citar como ejemplo
instant *n* instante *m*; (present month) corriente *m*; **on the 12th** ~ el 12 del corriente; **in an** ~ en seguida; **let me know the** ~ **he comes** avíseme en cuanto llegue; **this** ~ ahora mismo; *adj* inmediato; ~ **coffee** café instantáneo
instantaneous instantáneo; ~ **exposure** *phot* instantánea
instantly en el acto

instate instalar
instead en cambio; ~ **of** en lugar de
instep empeine *m*
instigate instigar[5]
instigation instigación *f*; **at the** ~ **of** a instigación de
instigator instigador *m* (-ora *f*)
instil inculcar[4]
instillation inculcación *f*
instinct instinto
instinctive instintivo
institute *n* instituto
institution institución *f*; (home for orphans *etc*) asilo; (act of setting up) establecimiento; *fam* (person) persona muy conocida, (thing) cosa muy conocida
institutional institucional; *US* que da prestigio
institutionalize (admit to institution) meter en una institución; **he has become** ~**d and can no longer look after himself** él ha vivido tanto tiempo en un asilo que ya no sabe cuidarse
instruct (teach) instruir[16] (**about/in** de/en); (command) mandar (**to a**)
instruction (education) instrucción *f*; (command) orden (órdenes) *f*; ~**s** (information) instrucciones *fpl*; (orders) órdenes *fpl*; ~**s for use** modo de empleo; **on the** ~**s of** por orden de
instructional instructivo
instructive instructivo
instructor instructor *m*; *US* profesor *m* auxiliar
instructress instructora
instrument +*med, mus* instrumento; ~-**panel** tablero de mandos
instrumental instrumental; ~ **music** música instrumental; **be** ~ **in** contribuir[16] (materialmente) a
instrumentalist instrumentalista *m*+*f*
instrumentality agencia
instrumentation instrumentación *f*
insubordinate insubordinado
insubordination insubordinación *f*
insubstantial insubstancial
insubstantiality insubstancialidad *f*
insufferable inaguantable
insufficiency insuficiencia
insufficient insuficiente
insular insular; *fig* estrecho de miras
insularity insularidad *f*; *fig* estrechez *f* de miras

793

insulate aislar

insulating aislador (-ora *f*); ~ **tape** cinta aislante

insulation aislamiento

insulator aislante *m*

insulin insulina

insult *n* insulto; *v* insultar; *fam* pringar⁵

insulting insultante

insuperable insuperable

insupportable insoportable

insuppressible que no se puede suprimir

insurable asegurable

insurance seguro; ~ **agent** agente *m* de seguros; ~ **broker** corredor *m* de seguros; ~ **company** compañía de seguros; ~ **policy** póliza de seguros; ~ **premium** prima de seguro

insure asegurar(se) (**against** contra); **be** ~**d for** estar¹⁹ asegurado en; **whom do you** ~ **with?** ¿qué seguro lleva usted?

insurer asegurador *m* (-ora *f*)

insurgency insurrección *f*

insurgent *n+adj* insurrecto

insurmountable insuperable

insurrection insurrección *f*

insurrectionary insurreccional

insurrectionist *n+adj* insurreccionista *m+f*

insusceptibility insensibilidad *f*

insusceptible no susceptible

intact intacto

intaglio talla

intake admisión *f*; *mech* entrada; (of a mine) ventilador *m*; (quantity) cantidad admitida; (students, recruits *etc*) número admitido

intangibility intangibilidad *f*

intangible intangible; ~ **assets** *comm* activo inmaterial

integer (número) entero

integral *n math* integral *f*; *adj* entero; *math* integral; ~ **calculus** cálculo integral; ~ **parts** partes *fpl* integrantes

integrate integrar

integration integración *f*

integrity integridad *f*

integument integumento

intellect intelecto

intellectual *n+adj* intelectual; *SA* doctor (-ora)

intelligence inteligencia; (information) información *f*; (news) noticias *fpl*; ~ **quotient** cociente *m* intelectual; ~ **service** servicio de espionaje; ~ **test**

test *m* de inteligencia

intelligent inteligente

intelligentsia intelectuales *mpl*; *SA* doctores *mpl*

intelligibility inteligibilidad *f*

intelligible inteligible

intemperance intemperancia

intemperate inmoderado; *meteor* destemplado; ~ **weather** intemperie *f*

intend pensar (ie)²ᵃ; (wish) querer¹⁹, **that is not what she** ~**ed** eso no es lo que ella quería; ~**ed for** destinar a; **is this** ~**ed for me?** ¿es para mí?; ~ **to** pensar (ie)²ᵃ +*infin*; **I** ~**ed you to** yo quería que usted +*subj*

intended *n* novio, novia

intense intenso; (of a person) apasionado

intenseness intensidad *f*; (of a person) apasionamiento

intensification intensificación *f*

intensifier intensificador *m*

intensify intensificar⁴

intensity intensidad *f*; (of feelings) profundidad *f*

intensive intensivo; ~ **course** cursillo

intent *n* intento; **with felonious** ~ con intención delictiva; **with** ~ **to** con intención de +*infin*; **to all** ~**s and purposes** en realidad; *adj* ~ **on** absorto en; (resolved to) resuelto a

intention intención *f*

intentional intencional

intentionally a propósito; *fam* queriendo

inter enterrar (ie)¹ᵇ

interact obrar recíprocamente

interaction interacción *f*

inter-allied interaliado

interbreed cruzar⁷

interbreeding hibridación *f*

intercede interceder; **Israel asked France to** ~ **with Algeria for the return of the plane** Israel ha pedido a Francia que interceda con Argelia para la devolución del avión

intercept interceptar; *geom+sp* cortar

interception intercepción *f*

interceptor (plane) interceptor *m*

intercession intercesión *f*

interchange *n* intercambio; (*US* road junction) enlace *m*; *v* (inter)cambiar(se)

interchangeable intercambiable

intercom interfono
intercommunicate intercomunicarse[4]
intercommunion intercomunión *f*
interconnect interconectar
intercontinental intercontinental; ~ **ballistic missile** cohete *m* intercontinental
intercourse *comm* intercambio comercial; (social) trato; **have sexual ~** tener[19] trato sexual
interdenominational interconfesional
interdependence interdependencia
interdependent interdependiente
interdict entredicho[19]
interdiction interdicción *f*
interest *n* interés *m*; (shareholding) participación *f*; (dividend) interés *m*; ~**-free** sin interés; ~ **of eight per cent** interés del ocho por ciento; **pay with** ~ pagar[5] con creces; **in one's own** ~ en provecho propio; **in the** ~**s of** en interés de; **it's of no** ~ **to me** me tiene sin cuidado; **look after one's (own)** ~**s** ocuparse de sus (propios) intereses; *v* interesar; ~**ed party** interesado; **be** ~**ed in** interesarse en/por
interesting interesante
interface superficie entremetida
interfere intervenir[19]; *fam* meterse (**with** con); *phys+rad* interferir; ~ **in** meterse en; ~ **with** meterse en, *fam* manosear; (obstruct) impedir (i)[3], **he** ~**d with the progress of the work** él impidió el progreso del trabajo
interference intervención *f*; (hindrance) impedimento; *phys+rad* interferencia
interfering entrometido; *fam* mangoneador (-ora *f*)
inter-governmental intergubernamental
interim *n* ínterin *m*; **in the** ~ entretanto; *adj* interino
interior *n* interior *m*; ~ **decoration** decoración *f* de interiores; ~ **decorator** decorador *m* de interiores
interject interponer[19]
interjection interjección *f*
interlace entrelazar(se)[7]
interlard interpolar; ~ **with** salpicar[4] de
interleave interfoliar
interline interlinear; (sewing) entretelar
interlining (of clothing) entretela
interlock encajar(se); *mech* endentar; enganchar

interlocking: ~ **device** sistema *m* de cierre; ~ **stitch** punto indesmallable
interlocutor interlocutor *m* (-ora *f*)
interlope entremeterse sin permiso
interloper intruso
interlude *mus* interludio; *theat* intermedio; **it was a sad** ~ **in his life** fue un período triste de su vida
intermarriage (of relations) matrimonio entre parientes; (racial) matrimonio entre personas de distintas razas
intermarry (of relations) casarse (entre personas emparentadas); (of races) casarse (entre distintas razas)
intermediary *n+adj* intermediario
intermediate intermedio; ~ **stop** escala
interment entierro
intermezzo *mus* intermezzo; *theat* intermedio
interminable interminable
intermingle entremezclar(se); (at a party) alternar
intermission intervalo; *theat* entreacto
intermittent intermitente
intermittently a intervalos
intermix *see* **intermingle**
intern *n* interno *m* de hospital; *v* internar
internal interno; ~ **injuries** lesiones *fpl* internas; ~**-combustion engine** motor *m* de combustión interna; ~ **problems** *pol* problemas *m* domésticos
international *n sp* (game) partido internacional; (player) jugador *m* internacional; **Third International** Tercera Internacional *f*; *adj* internacional; ~ **law** derecho internacional; **International Brigades** Brigadas Internacionales *fpl*
internationalism internacionalismo
internationalize internacionalizar[7]
internecine de aniquilación mutua
internee internado
internment internamiento; ~ **camp** campo de internamiento
interpellation interpelación *f*
interphone interfono
interplanetary interplanetario
interplay interacción *f*
interpolate interpolar
interpolation interpolación *f*
interpose interponer(se)[19]
interpret interpretar; (explain) explicar[4]; (translate) traducir[15]

interpretable interpretable

interpretation interpretación f; (explanation) explicación f; (translation) traducción f

interpreter intérprete m+f

interracial interracial

interregnum interregno

interrelation relación recíproca

interrogate interrogar⁵

interrogation interrogación f; ~ **mark** (punto de) interrogación f

interrogative interrogativo

interrogator interrogador m (-ora f)

interrogatory n interrogatorio; adj interrogativo

interrupt interrumpir

interrupter +elect interruptor m

interruption interrupción (-ones) f

intersect vt cruzar; math cortar; vi intersecarse⁴; cruzarse

intersection intersección f; (cross-roads) cruce m

intersperse esparcir¹³ (**with** de)

inter-state interestatal

interstellar interestelar

interstice intersticio

intertwine entrelazar(se)⁷

interval +mus intervalo; sp descanso; theat entreacto; **at** ~**s** (time) a intervalos, (distance) de trecho en trecho; **at** ~**s of five metres** cada cinco metros

intervene intervenir¹⁹; (mediate) mediar

intervening interventor (-ora f)

intervention intervención f; (mediation) mediación f

interventionist intervencionista m+f

interview n entrevista; (press +TV) interviú m; **have an** ~ **with** entrevistarse con; ~-**room** (in police station) sala de interrogatorios; v entrevistar; (press +TV) interviuar

interviewer entrevistador m (-ora f)

interweave +fig entretejer

interweaving entretejimiento

intestacy falta de testamento

intestate intestado

intestinal intestinal

intestine intestino; **large/small** ~ intestino grueso/delgado

intimacy intimidad f; (sexual) relación sexual íntima

intimate n amigo de confianza; adj íntimo; (profound) profundo; **become**

~ **with** intimar con; v intimar

intimation indicación f

intimidate intimidar

intimidation intimidación f

intimidatory amenazador (-ora f)

into en; ~ **the park** al parque; **he fell** ~ **the water** él cayó al agua; **put it** ~ **the drawer** métalo dentro del cajón; ~ **Spanish** al castellano

intolerable intolerable

intolerance intolerancia

intolerant intolerante

intonation entonación f

intone entonar; eccles salmodiar

intoxicant bebida alcohólica

intoxicate emborrachar; med intoxicar

intoxication borrachera f; med intoxicación f

intractability intratabilidad f

intractable intratable; (of a problem) insoluble

intransigence intransigencia

intransigent intransigente

intransitive n+adj intransitivo

intravenous intravenoso

intravenously por vía intravenosa

intrench see entrench

intrepid intrépido

intrepidity intrepidez f

intricacy intrincación f

intricate intrincado

intrigue n intriga; fam trapicheo; **petty** ~ tiquismiquis mpl; v intrigar⁵

intriguer intrigante m+f

intrinsic intrínseco

introduce (a person) presentar; **may I** ~? permítame presentarle a; (insert) introducir¹⁵ (**into** en); ~ **a bill** pol presentar un proyecto de ley; ~ **a book** prologar⁵

introduction introducción f; lit prólogo; (of a person) presentación f, **letter of** ~ carta de recomendación

introductory introductorio

introspection introspección f

introspective introspectivo

introversion introversión f

introvert introverso; ~**ed** introvertido

intrude vt introducir¹⁶ por fuerza; vi meterse (**upon** con)

intruder intruso

intrusion intrusión f

intrusive intrusivo

intuition intuición f

intuitive intuitivo

inundate inundar

inundation inundación (-ones) *f*

inure acostumbrar (**to** a)

invade +*fig* invadir

invader invasor *m* (-ora *f*)

[1] **invalid** *n* inválido; enfermo; ~-**carriage** cochecito de inválido; ~-**chair** silla *m* para inválidos; *v* ~ **out** *mil* dar[19] la baja por invalidez

[2] **invalid** *adj* inválido

invalidate invalidar

invalidation invalidación *f*

invalidity invalidez *f*

invaluable inestimable

invariability invariabilidad *f*

invariable *n* invariante *m*; *adj* invariable

invariably sin excepción; *fam* (usually) generalmente

invasion +*fig* invasión *f* (**of** de)

invective invectiva

inveigh usar invectivas (**against** contra)

inveigle: ~ **into** engatusar para que +*subj*

inveiglement engatusamiento

invent inventar

invention invención (-ones) *f*

inventive inventivo

inventiveness inventiva

inventor inventor *m* (-ora *f*)

inventory *n* inventario; *v* hacer[19] un inventario

inverse inverso; **in** ~ **ratio** (**to**) en razón inversa (a)

inversion inversión (-ones) *f*

invert volver (ue)[1b] (*past part* vuelto) al revés; ~**ed** (gay) homosexual; **in** ~**ed commas** entre comillas *fpl*

invertebrate invertebrado

invest *comm* invertir (i)[3]; *mil* sitiar; ~ **with** (a decoration) investir (i)[3] de/con

investigate investigar[5]

investigation investigación *f*

investigator investigador *m* (-ora *f*)

investiture investidura

investment inversión *f*; ~**s** inversiones, fondos *mpl* invertidos; ~ **securities** valores *mpl* de inversión; ~ **trust** sociedad *f* inversionista

investor inversionista *m*+*f*

inveterate inveterado; *fam* incurable

invidious odioso; (unjust) injusto

invigilate vigilar (durante un examen)

invigilator vigilante *m*+*f* (durante un examen)

invigorate vigorizar[7]

invigorating vigorizador (-ora *f*)

invigoration tonificación *f*

invincibility invencibilidad *f*

invincible invencible

inviolability inviolabilidad *f*

inviolable inviolable

inviolate inviolado

invisibility invisibilidad *f*

invisible invisible; ~ **exports** exportaciones *fpl* invisibles; ~ **ink** tinta simpática; ~ **mending** (sewing) zurcido invisible

invitation invitación (-ones) *f*

invite *n* invitación *f*; *v* invitar; (to food or drink) convidar; ~ **criticism** exponerse[19] a la crítica; (ask for) pedir; **they** ~**d me to speak** me invitaron a hablar; ~ **to dance** sacar[4] a bailar

inviting (attractive) atrayente; (of food) apetitoso

invocation invocación *f*

invoice *n* factura; ~ **form** modelo de factura; *v* facturar

invoicing facturación *f*

invoke invocar[4]

involuntary involuntario

involve (complicate) envolver[1b] (*past part* envuelto); (entangle) enredar; (entail) traer[19] consigo; (implicate) comprometer; **be** ~**d in** verse[19] envuelto en

involvement envolvimiento; (entanglement) enredo; (unwilling association) compromiso; (love affair) amorío

invulnerability invulnerabilidad *f*

invulnerable invulnerable

inward *adj* interior; *adv* ~(**s**) hacia dentro

inwardly (to o.s.) para sí

iodine yodo

iodize yodar

ion ion *m*

ionize ionizar[7]

ionosphere ionosfera

iota (letter) iota; *fig* pizca

I.O.U. pagaré *m*

ipecacuanha ipecacuana

I.Q. (intelligence quotient) c.i. (cociente *m* de inteligencia)

Iran Irán *m*

Iranian *n*+*adj* iranés *m* (-esa *f*), iraní (-íes)

Iraq Irak *m*
Iraqi *n*+*adj* iraquí (-íes) *m*+*f*
irascibility irascibilidad *f*
irascible irascible
irate colérico
Ireland Irlanda
iridescence iridiscencia
iridescent iridiscente
iris *hort* lirio; *opt* iris *m*
Irish irlandés (-esa *f*); ~ **Free State** Estado Libre de Irlanda; ~**man** irlandés; ~ **Sea** mar *m*+*f* de Irlanda
irk fastidiar
irksome fastidioso
iron *n* hierro; (for ironing) plancha; (golf club) (palo de) hierro; ~**s** (manacles *etc*) hierros, (leg support) hierro (para corregir una deformidad); **in** ~**s** (in chains) encadenado; **put in** ~**s** encadenar; ~ **and steel industry** industria siderúrgica; **strike while the** ~ **is hot** a hierro caliente batir de repente; ~ **age** edad *f* de hierro; ~**clad** *n* acorazado, *adj* blindado; **Iron Curtain** telón *m* de acero; ~ **foundry** fundición *f* de hierro; ~**lung** pulmón (-ones) *m* de acero; ~**-master** fabricante *m* de hierro; ~**monger** ferretero; ~**mongery**, ~**monger's shop** ferretería; ~ **ore** mineral *m* de hierro; ~ **pyrites** pirita; ~ **ration** reserva de víveres; ~ **tonic** reconstituyente ferruginoso; ~**ware** artículos de ferretería; ~ **will** voluntad *f* de hierro; ~**work** herraje *m*; ~**works** herrería; *adj* férreo, de hierro; *v* planchar; ~ **out** +*fig* allanar
ironic irónico
ironing planchado; **she has finished the** ~ ella ha terminado de planchar; ~**board** tabla de planchar
irony ironía
irradiance luminosidad *f*
irradiant luminoso
irradiate irradiar; *fig* derramar
irradiation irradiación *f*
irrational irracional
irrationality irracionalidad *f*
irreclaimable irrecuperable
irrecognizable irreconocible
irreconcilable irreconciliable
irrecoverable irrecuperable
irredeemable irredimible
irreducible irreduc(t)ible

irrefutable irrefutable
irrefutability calidad *f* de irrefutable
irregular irregular; *mil* *n*+*adj* guerrillero; (of procedure) antirreglamentario
irregularity irregularidad *f*
irrelevant fuera de propósito
irreligious irreligioso
irremediable irremediable
irremissible irremisible
irremovable inamovible
irreparable irreparable
irreplaceable insustituible
irrepressible irreprimible
irreproachable irreprochable
irresistible irresistible
irresolute indeciso
irresolvable irresoluble
irrespective of aparte de
irresponsibility irresponsabilidad *f*
irresponsible irresponsable
irretrievable irrecuperable
irreverence irreverencia
irreverent irreverente
irreversible irreversible; (decision) irrevocable
irrevocability irrevocabilidad *f*
irrevocable irrevocable
irrigate regar (ie)[2a]; *med* irrigar[5]
irrigation riego; *med* irrigación *f*
irritability irritabilidad *f*
irritable irritable
irritant irritante
irritate +*med* irritar
irritating irritante
irritation irritación *f*
irruption irrupción *f*
Isaiah Isaías
Islam Islam *m*
Islamic islámico
island *n* isla; (traffic) refugio para peatones; *adj* isleño
islander isleño
islet islote *m*
isolate aislar
isolation aislamiento; *chem* separación *f*; ~ **hospital** hospital preventorio
isolationism aislacionismo
isolationist *n*+*adj* aislacionista *m*+*f*
isosceles isósceles *m sing*+*pl*; ~ **triangle** triángulo isósceles
isotherm línea isoterma
isotope isótopo
Israel Israel *m*

Israeli *n+adj* israelí (-íes) *m+f*

Israelite *n+adj* israelita *m+f*

issue *n* (*esp* of coins, stamps and bonds) emisión *f*; (copy of periodical) número; *med* flujo; (exit) salida; (matter) cuestión *f*; (outcome) resultado; (offspring) sucesión *f*, *fam* prole *f*; **at** ~ en disputa; **avoid/evade the** ~ esquivar la pregunta; **face the** ~ afrontar la situación; **force the** ~ forzar (ue)[1a] una decisión; **join** ~ **with** llevar la contraria a; **without** ~ sin sucesión; *vt* publicar[4]; *comm* poner[19] en circulación; (a command) expedir (i)[3]; (a decree) promulgar[5]; *vi* salir[19]; ~ **forth** echar; ~ **from** brotar de

isthmus istmo

it *pron* (subject) él *m*, ella *f* (often not translated); ~ **is cold** hace frío; (direct object) lo, la; (indirect object) le; (after prep) él *m*, ella *f*, ello *neuter*; **that's** ~! ¡eso es!

Italian *n+adj* italiano; *pej* macaroni *m+f*

italic itálico; ~s letra bastardilla; **in** ~s en bastardilla

italicize poner[19] en (letra) bastardilla

Italy Italia

itch *n* picor *m*; *med* sarna; *v* picar; **be itching to** suspirar por +*infin*

itchy picante; *med* sarnoso

item ítem *m*; (on programme) número; **every single** ~ cada detalle

itemize especificar[4]

itinerant ambulante

itinerary *n+adj* itinerario

its *adj* su(s); *pron* (el) suyo, (los) suyos, (la) suya, (las) suyas

itself mismo; **the book** ~ el libro mismo; *reflex pron* se; **in** ~ en sí; **of** ~ de sí

ivory *n* marfil *m*; **ivories** *fam* (billiard balls) bolas *fpl*, (piano keys) teclas *fpl*; *adj* marfileño; ~ **tower** torre *f* de marfil

ivy hiedra

J

j (letter) jota

jab *n* (prick) pinchazo; (poke) hurgonazo; (with elbow) codazo; *fam* (injection) inyección *f*; (boxing) golpe dado sin extender el brazo; *v* (*see n*) pinchar; hurgonear; dar[19] un codazo; golpear

jabber *n* jerigonza; *v* parlotear

Jack Juanito

jack *n* *mot* gato; (cards) sota; (bowls) boliche *m*; *mil* bandera de proa; ~**ass** burro; ~**boots** botas altas/militares; ~**-in-the-box** caja sorpresa; ~**-of-all-trades** hombre *m* de muchos oficios; ~**-of-all-work** factótum *m*; ~**pot** (cards) bote *m*, (in lottery, pools *etc*) (premio) gordo; **hit the ~pot** dar[19] en el blanco; *v* ~ **up** alzar[7] con gato; ~ **up the price** subir el precio; ~ **it in** darse[19] por vencido

jackal chacal *m*

jackdaw grajilla

jacket chaqueta; *SA* saco; (of a book) sobrecubierta; *mech* camisa; **potatoes in their ~s** patatas *fpl* enteras

Jacobean de la epoca de Jacobo I, jacobino

Jacobin *n*+*adj* jacobino

jade *n* (horse) rocín (-ines) *m*; *min* jade *m*; (woman) picarona; *v* (exhaust) cansar; (surfeit) saciar

jaffa naranja de Israel

jag *n* (protrusion) diente *m*; (tear) siete *m*; *v* rasgar[5]

jagged dentado

jaguar jaguar *m*

jail *see* **gaol**

jailer *see* **gaoler**

jalopy *sl* cacharro

jam mermelada; (of people) agolpamiento; (of vehicles) atasco; *fig* apuro; **I'm in a** ~ estoy en un lío; ~**jar** tarro *m* (para confitura); ~**-session** reunión *f* informal de músicos de jazz; *vt* (block up) interferir; *rad* enredar; (ram) apretar; (wedge) trabar; *vi*

(become blocked) estancarse[4]; (of traffic) atascarse[4]; ~ **into** apiñar en; ~ **one's finger in the door** cogerse[8] el dedo en la puerta; ~ **on the brakes** frenar con violencia; ~ **one's hat on** encasquetarse el sombrero; **the wheels are jammed** las ruedas están bloqueadas; **jammed with people** atestado de gente

Jamaica Jamaica

Jamaican *n*+*adj* jamaicano

jamb jamba

jamboree rallye *m* de niños exploradores; *fig* (celebration) reunión *f* convivial

James Jaime, Santiago

jamming *rad* interferencia; ~ **on of brakes** frenazo

Jane Juana

jangle *n* (metallic sound) cencerreo; *v* cencerrear

janitor portero; (at university) bedel *m*

January enero

Japan el Japón *m*

Japanese *n*+*adj* japonés *m* (-esa *f*); (language) japonés *m*

japanned lacado

japonica camelia japonesa

¹ **jar** (container) tarro; (with handles) jarra

² **jar** *n* (jolt) choque *m*; (noise) ruido fuerte; (shock) sorpresa desagradable; **it gave me a nasty** ~ me hizo una impresión muy desagradable; **door on the** ~ puerta entreabierta; *v* (jolt) sacudir; (of sounds) desentonar; (of colours) chocar; **it** ~**s on my nerves** me ataca los nervios

jargon jerigonza; (technical) jerga; (gibberish) guirigay *m*

jarring discordante

jasmine jazmín *m*

jasper jaspe *m*

jaundice ictericia; ~**d** ictérico; *fig* amargado

jaunt *n* excursión *f*; **go on a** ~ hacer[19]

una excursión
jauntily con garbo
jauntiness garbo
jaunty garboso
Javanese n+adj javanés m (-esa f)
javelin jabalina; ~-**throwing** sp lanzamiento de jabalina
jaw n mandíbula; mech mordaza; **in its** ~**s** en su boca; ~**s of death** garras fpl de la muerte; ~-**bone** mandíbula; v charlar
jay orni arrendajo; ~-**walk** cruzar[7] la calle sin consideración para los demás; ~-**walker** peatón m imprudente (que no sigue por la acera)
jazz n jazz m; ~ **musician** jacista m+f; ~-**band** orquesta de jazz; adj jacístico; v ~ **up** sincopar; (dance) bailar el jazz
jazzy alegre
jealous celoso; **be (very)** ~ **(of)** tener[19] (muchos) celos (de); **make s.o.** ~ dar[19] celos a uno
jealousy celos mpl
jeans (pantalones) tejanos, vaqueros
jeep jeep m
jeer n mofa; (shout) grito sarcástico; v ~ **at** mofarse de, burlarse
jeerer burlón m (-ona f)
jeering n burlas fpl; adj burlón
Jehovah's Witnesses Testigos mpl de Jehová
jejune aburrido
jell solidificarse[4]
jellied en gelatina
jello jalea
jelly n gelatina; (sweet) jalea; ~-**baby** approx equiv osito de goma; ~-**fish** medusa, fam aguamala; ~-**roll** brazo (de) gitano; v convertirse (ie)[2c] en jalea
jemmy palanqueta
jennet jaca española
jeopardize arriesgar[5]
jeopardy peligro; **put in** ~ poner[19] en peligro
Jeremiah Jeremías
jerk n tirón (-ones) m; **by** ~**s** a tirones; US sl haragán (-anes) m; **physical** ~**s** ejercicios mpl físicos; v (pull) dar[19] un tirón; (shake) sacudir; **she** ~**ed it out of my hand** ella me lo arrancó de la mano; **she** ~**ed herself free** ella se libró de una sacudida
jerkin justillo

jerry: ~-**builder** tapagujeros m sing+pl; ~-**built** de pacotilla
jersey (garment) jersey (-eyes) m
Jerusalem Jerusalén m; ~ **artichoke** aguaturma
jest n broma; (esp spoken) chiste m; **in** ~ en broma; v bromear
jester (at court) bufón (-ones) m; (joker) bromista m+f
jesting n bromas fpl; adj burlón
jestingly en broma
Jesuit n+adj Jesuita m+f
Jesus Jesús
[1] **jet** min azabache m; ~-**black** azabachado
[2] **jet** n (burner) mechero; (pipe) surtidor m; (stream) chorro; ~-**engine** reactor m; ~-**plane** avión m a reacción; ~-**propelled** a reacción, fig (speedy) rapidísimo; ~-**propulsion** propulsión f por reacción; ~-**set** flor y nata social
jetsam echazón m
jettison echar al mar; fig desechar
jetty embarcadero
Jew judío; ~'**s harp** birimbao
jewel joya, alhaja; (of watch) rubí (-íes) m; ~-**case** joyero
jewelled (of watch) de rubíes
jeweller joyero; ~'**s (shop)** joyería
jewellery joyas fpl, alhajas fpl; ~-**store** joyería
Jewess judía
Jewish judío
Jewry pueblo judío
jib n naut foque m, mech aguilón m; ~-**boom** botalón de foque; v (of a horse) plantarse; ~ **at** negarse (ie)[2a] a
jiffy instante m; **in a** ~ en un santiamén
jig n (dance) jiga; mech plantilla de grúa; ~-**saw** sierra de vaivén; ~-**saw puzzle** rompecabezas m sing+pl; v (dance) bailar la jiga; mech fabricar[4] piezas idénticas; fig ~ **about** moverse (ue)[1b] a saltitos
jigger naut cangreja de mesana; mech+rad jigger m
jiggery-pokery chalaneo
jilt dar[19] calabazas a
Jim Crow segregación f de color
jingle n (rhyme) rima infantil; (sound) retintín m; ~-**bell** cascabel m; ~-**jangle!** ¡tilín-tilín!; v cascabelear
jingling cascabeleo
jingo patriotero; **by** ~! ¡caramba!

jingoism patriotería

jingoist(ic) patriotero

jinks: high ~ jolgorio

jinx gafe *m*; (evil influence) mala suerte

jitney moneda estadounidense de cinco céntimos

jitter: you give me the ~s usted me pone nervioso; **~-bug** (aficionado a) bailar el jazz; *v* temblar (ie)²ᵃ

jittery nervioso

jive bailar el jazz

j-nib plumilla de punto grueso

job (employment) empleo; (work) trabajo; (duty) obligación *f*; (task) tarea; *sl* curro; (*esp* in the house) quehacer *m*; *fam* (affair) asunto; (robbery) robo; **bad ~** *fig* mala situación; **be on the ~** estar¹⁹ trabajando, *fam* (be alert) estar¹⁹ al pie; **be out of a ~** estar¹⁹ sin trabajo; **have more than one regular ~** hacer¹⁹ el pluriempleo; **I had a ~ to control myself** me costó controlarme; **it's a good ~ (that)** menos mal (que); **just the ~** perfecto; **lose one's ~** perder (ie)²ᵇ el empleo; **take on the ~ of** estar¹⁹ comprometido a +*infin*; **you've made a good ~ of it** lo ha hecho usted muy bien; **~-lot** colección miscelánea, *comm* lote suelto de mercancías

jobber (odd-~) trabajador *m* a destajo; *comm* corredor *m* de bolsa

jobbery chanchullos *mpl*; **piece of ~** chanchullo

jobbing ocasional; **~ gardener** jardinero por horas

jockey *n* jockey *m*; *v* **~ for (a) position** maniobrar para obtener una ventaja

jocose, jocular jocoso

jocularity jocosidad *f*

jocund jocundo

jodhpurs pantalón (-ones) *m* de montar

jog *n* empujoncito; (with elbow) codazo; **~-trot** trote corto; *v* empujar ligeramente; (with elbow) dar¹⁹ con el codo; (go jogging) hacer¹⁹ el footing; **~ along** andar a trote corto, *fig* ir¹⁹ tirando; **~ s.o.'s memory** (hacer¹⁹) recordar (ue)¹ᵃ

jogger footinguista *m+f*

jogging footinguismo

joggle *n* sacudida; *v* sacudir suavemente

John Juan; **~ the Baptist** Juan Bautista

john retrete *m*, servicio

join *n* juntura; (sewing) costura; *v* unir; (link up) acoplar; *mech* ensamblar; (become a member of) hacerse¹⁹ socio de; (meet) ir¹⁹/venir¹⁹ a buscar, **I'll ~ you later** iré a buscarle más tarde; (of roads) juntarse; *fig* (have a drink with) acompañar, **will you ~ me?** ¿me acompaña (en una bebida)?; **~ at table** sentarse (ie)¹ᵇ en la mesa con; **~ battle** librar batalla; **~ a firm** ingresar en una empresa; **~ forces** unirse; **~ hands** darse¹⁹ la mano; **~ issue with** disputar con; **~ one's regiment/ship** incorporarse a su regimiento/barco

~ in tomar parte en; **~ in a group** ir¹⁹ con un grupo; **~ in the chorus** ponerse¹⁹ a cantar en coro

~ together juntar(se)

~ up *mil* alistarse; *sl* engancharse

joiner carpintero

joinery carpintería

joint *n* juntura; *anat* articulación *f*; *elect* empalme *m*; (hinge) bisagra; (meat) cuarto; *mech* ensambladura; *sl* fonducho; *sl* cigarillo de marihuana; **out of ~** descoyuntado, *fig* fuera de compás; **put out of ~** descoyuntar, *anat* dislocar; *adj* mutuo; unido; **~ account** cuenta compartida; **~ base** *mil* base *m* de utilización conjunta; **~ committee** comisión mixta; **~ communiqué** comunicado conjunto; **~ liability** responsabilidad solidaria; **~ owner** copropietario; **~ ownership** copropiedad *f*; **~ responsibility** responsabilidad solidaria; **~-stock** capital *m* social; **~-stock company** sociedad anónima; *v* juntar; **~ed** articulado; **~ed fishing-rod** caña de pescar montable

jointly en común; **~ and severally** todos y cada uno por sí; **~ owned** de varios

joist viga

joke *n* broma; (*esp* spoken) chiste *m*; (laughing-matter) cosa de reír; (laughing-stock) hazmerreír *m*; **for a ~** de chunga; **play a ~ (on)** gastar una broma a; **take a ~** aguantar una broma; **tell a ~** contar (ue)¹ᵃ un chiste; *v* bromear, *sl* chunguear

joker bromista *m+f*; (card) comodín (-ines) *m*

joking *n* chistes *mpl*; **~ aside** hablando en serio; *adj* chistoso

jokingly de chunga

jollification, jollity regocijo

jolly *adj* alegre; (amusing) divertido; (slightly drunk) achispado; *adv* muy; ~ **good fellow** hombre estupendo; ~ **good show!** ¡bravo!; **you** ~ **well must** usted no tiene más remedio; *v* ~ **along** hacer[19] correr

jolt *n* sacudida; *fig* (shock) choque *m*; *v* sacudir; (of a vehicle) traquetear

jolting traqueteo

jolty (of a vehicle) que traquetea; (uneven) desnivelado

Jonah Jonás, *fig* cenizo

jonquil junquillo

Jordan (country) Jordania; (river) Jordán *m*

Jordanian *n+adj* jordano

Joseph José

josh *n* engaño; *v* engañar

Joshua Josué

joss-stick pebete *m*

jostle *n* empujón (-ones) *m*; *v* dar[19] empujones

jostling empujones *mpl*

jot *n* jota; **not one** ~ ni pizca; **she doesn't care a** ~ **(about)** a ella le importa un bledo; *v* ~ **down** apuntar

jotting apunte *m*

journal (diary) (libro) diario; (newspaper) diario; (review) revista; *mech* gorrón *m*; ~**-bearing (box)** cojinete *m*

journalese jerga periodística

journalism periodismo

journalist periodista *m+f*

journalistic periodístico

journey *n* viaje *m*; **go on a** ~ hacer[19] un viaje; ~**-man** oficial *m*; *v* viajar

joust *n* justa; *v* justar

jousting justas *fpl*

Jove Júpiter *m*; **by** ~ ¡caramba!

jovial jovial

joviality jovialidad *f*

jowl (cheek) carrillo; (of animals) papada; (jaw) quijada

joy alegría; **filled with** ~ lleno de alegría; **a** ~ **to the eye** un gozo para la retina; **it gives me great** ~ **(to)** me da gran placer (+*infin*); **it's a** ~ **to** a gusto +*infin*; **wish s.o.** ~ desearle a alguien suerte; ~**-ride** excursión en coche/avión robado; ~**-stick** *aer* palanca de mando

joyful alegre

joyless triste

joyous alegre

J.P. (Justice of the Peace) *approx* juez *m* de paz

jr, jun. (junior) hijo

jubilant jubiloso

jubilate regocijarse

jubilation regocijo

jubilee jubileo; **golden/silver** ~ bodas de oro/de plata

Judaic judaico

Judaism judaísmo

Judas Judas

Judea Judea

judge *n+leg* juez *m*; (connoisseur) conocedor *m* (-ora *f*); *sp* árbitro; **be a good** ~ **of** ser[19] buen juez de; **be no** ~ **of** no entender (ie)[2b] de; **Judge Advocate** auditor *m* de guerra; *v* juzgar[5]; *sp* arbitrar; ~ **for o.s.** formar su propia opinión; **judging from/by** a juzgar por

judgement juicio; (of court) sentencia; (opinion) opinión *m*; **pass** ~ juzgar[5]; **sit in** ~ **on** ser[19] juez de; **my** ~ **is good** mis elementos de juicio son buenos; **to the best of my** ~ según mi leal saber y entender; ~ **day** día *m* del juicio; ~**-seat** tribunal *m*; **Last Judgement** juicio final

judicature judicatura

judicial judicial; ~ **inquiry** investigación *f* judicial; ~ **murder** asesinato legal; ~ **proceedings** diligencias judiciales; ~ **separation** separación *f* legal

judicious sensato

judo judo

jug *n* jarro; *sl* (gaol) jaula; *v* (imprison) encarcelar

jugful jarro lleno

jugged: ~ **hare** liebre *f* en estofado

juggernaut monstruo destructivo; *mot* camión (-ones) *m* enorme

juggins inocentón *m* (-ona *f*)

juggle *n* juego de manos; *vi* hacer[19] juegos de manos; *vt* escamotear; ~ **with** arreglar de otra manera, *fig* falsificar[4]

juggler malabarista *m+f*

juggling malabarismo

Jugoslavia Yugoeslavia

Jugoslav *n+adj* yugoeslavo

jugular yugular; ~ **vein** vena yugular

juice jugo, zumo; *fam elect* luz *f*; *sl mot* gasolina; **in its** ~ *cul* en su jugo

juicy jugoso, *fam* sabroso

ju-jitsu jiu-jitsu *m*

jujube pastilla

juke-box tocadiscos *m sing+pl* traga-perras

julep julepe *m*

julienne (soup) sopa juliana

July julio

jumble *n* (disordered state) revoltijo; (objects) artículos usados; **be in a ~** estar[19] todo revuelto; **~ sale** venta de artículos usados; *v* (confuse) confundir; (mix) mezclar; **~d** confuso, mezclado

jump *n* salto; (surprise) sobresalto; **~ in pay** aumento de salario; **~ in temperature** subida rápida de temperatura; **with one ~** de un salto; **go and take a running ~!** ¡vete a hacer gárgaras!; **~-jet** *aer* reactor *m* de despegue vertical; *v* saltar; (in draughts) comer; (with surprise) dar[19] un salto/*fam* un respingo; **~ a horse** hacer[19] saltar a un caballo; **~ ship** desertar (ie)[2a] del buque; **~ the gun** madrugar[5]; **~ the queue** colarse; **~ the rails** descarrilarse; **~ed-up** recién subido

~ at lanzarse[7] sobre; *fig* aprovecharse a aceptar

~ down bajar de un salto

~ on (get quickly on) saltar a; (reprimand) regañar

~ out of bed saltar de la cama

~ over saltar por encima de; *fig* (omit) pasar por alto de

~ to: **~ to a conclusion** sacar[4] precipitadamente una conclusión; **~ to conclusions** juzgar[5] al tuntún; **~ to it!** ¡date prisa!

~ with joy saltar de alegría

jumper saltador *m* (-ora *f*); (garment) jersey (-eyes) *m*, *US* vestido de mujer; (sailor's) blusa

jumpiness nerviosidad *f*

jumping *n* saltos *mpl*; *adj* saltador (-ora *f*); **~-bean** frijol *m* saltador; **~-board** trampolín *m*; **~-jack** títere *m*; **~-off place** *mil* base avanzada, *sp* trampolín *m*; **~-pit** foso de caída; **~-pole** pértiga; **~-rope** comba

jumpy asustadizo

junction unión *f*; (of pipes, railway lines *etc*) empalme *m*; (of rivers) confluencia; (of roads) bifurcación *f*; **~-box** *elect* caja de empalmes, (railway)

estación *f* de empalme

juncture coyuntura; **critical ~** trance *m*

June junio; **junebug** abejorro

jungle jungla; *fig* maraña; **~-cat** gato salvaje; **~-fever** fiebre palúdica

junior *n* joven (jóvenes) *m+f*; **he is my ~ by two years** él tiene dos años menos que yo; **John Smith ~** John Smith hijo; *adj* **~ (to)** más joven (que); **~ college** (*US* technical college) instituto técnico; **~ partner** socio menor; **~ school** escuela elemental

juniper enebro

junk trastos viejos *mpl*; (cheap goods) baratijas *fpl*; (refuse) basura; (scrap metal) chatarra; *naut* junco; (nonsense) disparates *mpl*; **~-dealer** chatarrero; **~-room** cuarto trastero; **~-shop** chatarrería; **~-yard** depósito *m* de chatarra

junket dulce *m* de leche cuajada

junketing festividades *fpl*

junky toxicómano

junta junta

Jupiter Júpiter

juridical jurídico

jurisdiction jurisdicción *f*; **within my ~** dentro de mi jurisdicción

jurisprudence jurisprudencia

jurist jurista *m+f*

juror (miembro de un) jurado

jury jurado; **be/serve on the ~** formar parte del jurado; **~-box** tribuna del jurado; **~-man** jurado

just *adj* (exact) exacto; (fair) justo; (of a decision) justificado; (well-deserved) merecido; *adv* (exactly) exactamente; (only ~) muy justamente; **~ about** poco más o menos; **~ a moment!** ¡un momento, por favor!; **~ arrived/married** recién llegado(s)/casado(s); **~ as** (like) tal como, **~ as I said** como dije; **he did ~ as he was told** hacía exactamente lo que le decían; **~ as I was leaving** en el momento que yo salía; **~ as you wish** como quiera; **~ beyond** un poco más allá (de); **~ by** muy cerca (de); **~ call me John** llámeme Juan a secas; **~ for the asking** nada más que por no más; **~ imagine!** ¡imagínese!; **~ in case** por si acaso, *fam* por si las moscas; **~ like** (the same as) de la misma manera que; **~ now** ahora mismo; **~ so** ni más ni menos, (perfect) perfecto; ~ **the job** exactamente lo que hacía falta, *interj* ¡bravo!; ~ **the person** la persona indicada; **(not)** ~ **yet** todavía (no); I **only** ~ **missed being shot** por poco me fusilan; it's ~ **the same to me** me es igual; it's ~ **wonderful!** ¡es absolutamente maravilloso!; **I was** ~ **going out** yo estaba a punto de salir; **to have** ~ acabar de +*infin*; **I have/had** ~ **done it** yo acabo/acababa de hacerlo

justice justicia; (person) juez *m*; (magistrate) juez municipal; **do o.s.** ~ quedar bien

justifiable justificable

justifiably con justicia

justification justificación *f*

justify justificar[4]; (excuse) disculpar

justly con justicia

jut: ~ **out** sobresalir[19]

jute yute *m*

Jutland Jutlandia

juvenile *n* joven (jóvenes) *m+f*; *adj* juvenil; (childish) infantil; ~ **court** tribunal *m* tutelar de menores; ~ **delinquency** delincuencia juvenil; ~ **delinquent** delincuente *m+f* juvenil; ~ **lead** *theat+cin* galán *m* joven

juxtapose yuxtaponer[19]

juxtaposition yuxtaposición *f*

K

k (letter) ka *f*
kaffir *n*+*adj* cafre *m*+*f*
kaiser káiser *m*
kale col rizada
kaleidoscope calidoscopio; *fig* escena animada y variada
kaleidoscopic calidoscópico; *fig* abigarrado
kamikase, kamikazi kamikase *m*
kangaroo canguro; ~ court tribunal *m* no oficial
kaolin caolín *m*
kapok miraguano
karate kárate *m;* ~ fighter karatista *m*+*f*
kayak kayac *m*
keel *n* quilla; lay down a ~ poner[19] la quilla; on an even ~ de igual calado, *fig* estable; *v* ~ over (fall) caer[19] patas arriba, *naut* dar[19] de quilla; (faint) desmayarse
keelage *comm* derechos *mpl* de puerto
keen agudo; (sharp-edged) afilado; (enthusiastic) entusiasta; ~ appetite muy buen apetito; ~ intelligence/mind inteligencia/mente aguda; ~ prices precios *mpl* muy reducidos; ~ satire sátira mordaz; ~ sportsman muy aficionado a los deportes; ~ to help ansioso de ayudar; ~ wind viento fuerte; be ~ on ser[19] aficionado a; be ~ about tener[19] entusiasmo por; I'm not ~ on him no es santo de mi devoción; I'm not ~ on beer no me gusta la cerveza; have a very ~ ear tener[19] el oído muy agudo; ~-edged afilado; ~-sighted de buena vista
keenness agudeza, entusiasmo
keep *n* (tower) torre *f* de homenaje; (maintenance) subsistencia; earn one's ~ ganarse la vida; for ~s para siempre (jamás); ~-net (fishing) red *f* vivero; ~sake recuerdo; *vt* (possess, have in stock) tener[19], he ~s rabbits él tiene/cría conejos; (provide accommodation) alojar; (retain) quedarse

con; (celebrate) celebrar; (manage) ser[19] director de; ~ an appointment acudir a una cita; ~ the books/a record *comm* llevar los libros/ un registro; ~ a diary llevar un diario; ~ in (a good state of) repair conservar en buen estado; ~ informed mantener[19] informado; ~ late hours acostarse (ue)[1a] tarde; ~ the law observar la ley; ~ one's word cumplir una promesa; ~ order mantener[19] el orden; ~ the peace mantener[19] la paz; ~ quiet callarse; ~ a secret guardar un secreto; ~ s.o. waiting hacer[19] esperar a alguien; I shan't ~ you long no le entretendré mucho tiempo; she kept her honour ella defendío su honor; the speaker could not ~ their attention el orador no podía retener[19] su atención; we'll ~ this room for you le reservaremos esta habitación; when she stays indoors I ~ her company cuando ella se queda en casa yo la acompaño; *vi* (continue) seguir (i)[3+11]; (of food) guardarse; (remain) quedarse
~ at it (~ trying) seguir[3+11] intentando
~ awake *vt* no dejar dormir; *vi* no poder dormir
~ away *vt* no dejar acercarse; *vi* no acercarse
~ back (a crowd) no dejar avanzar; (feelings, tears) contener[19]; (secrets, evidence) ocultar
~ down no dejar subir; (of prices) mantener[19] bajo
~ from: ~ s.o. from +*ger* no dejar +*infin* a una persona; ~ from s.o. ocultar a una persona
~ in no dejar salir; (fire) mantener[19] encendido; ~ in with mantener[19] amistad con; they will ~ him in gaol le detendrán en la carcel
~ off tener[19] a raya; ~ off the grass prohibido pisar la hierba; ~ off! (don't touch) ¡no toque!; ~ off a subject evitar un tema

806

~ **on** seguir (i)$^{3+11}$; **she kept on talking** ella siguió hablando; **don't ~ on about it!** ¡no le des tantas vueltas!

~ **out** no dejar entrar; ~ **out of trouble** no meterse en líos

~ **to** limitarse a; ~ **to the path** seguir (i)$^{3+11}$ la senda; ~ **to one's bed** guardar cama; **she kept it to herself** lo guardo para sí sola

~ **under** subyugar^5; ~ **under control** controlar

~ **up** (in good condition) conservar en buen estado; ~ **up appearances** guardar las formas; ~ **up prices** sostener^{19} los precios; ~ **up one's spirits** no desanimarse; **he always ~s me up late** siempre me hace trasnochar; ~ **one's end up** mantenerse^{19} firme; ~ **up with** mantenerse^{19} al ritmo de

keeper guarda $m+f$; (game-~) guardabosques m $sing+pl$; (of museum) director m (-ora f); (of park/zoo) guardián; (of prison) carcelero; **am I my brother's ~?** ¿soy yo guardián de mi hermano?; ~ **of records** archivero; ~ **of the keys** llavero

keeping (celebration) celebración f; (observance) observación f; (custody) custodia; (maintenance) mantenimiento; **in safe ~** en buenas manos; **in ~ with** de acuerdo con; **out of ~ with** en desacuerdo con; ~ **back** retención f

keg barril m

ken (alcance m de la) vista; (understanding) conocimiento; v $dial$ conocer^{14}, saber^{19}

kennel n perrera; (of hounds) jauría; v encerrar (ie)^{2a} en perrera

Kenyan keniano

kepi quepis m $sing+pl$

kept: ~ **woman** manceba

kerb(stone) encintado; Arg cordón m de la acera

kerchief pañuelo de cabeza

kernel (of fruit) pepita, (nut) almendra; (of wheat) grano; fig meollo

kerosene petróleo; (US paraffin) parafina; SA keroseno m; lámpara de petróleo

kestrel $orni$ cernícalo (vulgar)

ketch queche m

ketchup salsa de tomate

kettle hervidor m; Arg pava; **here's a** pretty ~ **of fish!** ¡vaya una olla de grillos!; ~-**drum** timbal m

key n llave f; $mech$ chaveta; mus tonalidad f; (on piano, typewriter) tecla; tel manipulador m; (solution) clave f; **in** ~ mus a tono; **in the ~ of G** en clave de sol; **off** ~ mus desafinado; ~**board** teclado; ~**hole** ojo de la cerradura; ~**hole saw** sierra de punta; ~-**money** traspaso; ~-**note** nota tónica, fig idea fundamental; ~-**ring** llavero; ~ **signature** mus clave; ~-**stone** clave f (de arco), fig piedra angular; adj principal; ~ **industry** industria clave; ~ **man** hombre m indispensable; ~ **position** posición estratégica; ~ **word** palabra clave; v $mech$ achavetar; mus afinar; ~**ed up** excitado

Keynesian keynsiano

K.G. (Knight of the Garter) Caballero de la Orden de la Jarretera

khaki n caqui m; adj de (color) caqui

khan kan m

kibbutz granja colectiva

kick n patada; (usually of an animal) coz (-ces) f; (of a firearm) culatazo; ~ **on the shin** patada en la espinilla; **get a ~ out of** hallar placer en; **for ~s** para divertirse; **this beer has a ~** esta cerveza tiene mucha fuerza, SA esta cerveza tumba; **free ~** sp libre m; **drop-**~ puntapié m de botepronto; **place-**~ puntapié colocado; ~-**starter** pedal m de arranque m; v dar^{19} una patada; (usually of an animal) dar^{19} coces; (of a child in a temper) patalear; (of a rifle) recular; sp (football) chutar; ~ **s.o. on the shin** poner^{19} zancadillas; ~ **a goal** marcar^4 un gol; ~ **one's heels** esperar con impaciencia; ~ **the bucket** sl diñarla, SA palmar; ~ **it** sl dejar de tomar drogas

~ **about** dar^{19} patadas a

~ **against** fig protestar contra; ~ **against the pricks** dar^{19} coces contra el aguijón

~ **away** quitar con el pie

~ **downstairs** echar escaleras abajo

~-**off** n (football) saque m inicial, fig comienzo

~ **off** (football) sacar^4; fig comenzar (ie)$^{2a+7}$

~ **out** echar a la calle

~ **over the traces** rebelarse

~ **up**: ~ **up a row** (make a noise) armar un escándalo, *SA* armar un bochinche; (show anger) armar camorra; ~ **up the dust** levantar una polvareda; *fig* armar follón

kicker (horse) caballo coceador; *sp* chutador *m*

kicking pataleo; (of animals) acoceamiento

kid *n* (goat) cabrito; (child) chaval *m* (-ala *f*); (leather) cabritilla; ~ **gloves** guantes *mpl* de cabritilla, *fig* trato muy suave; *adj* (más) joven; **my ~ brother** mi hermano menor; *v* engañar; *SA* chotear; **are you kidding?** ¿está usted bromeando?; **I was only kidding** lo decía en broma; **no kidding!** ¡nada de bromas!

kiddy nene *m*, nena

kidnap secuestrar

kidnapper secuestrador *m* (-ora *f*)

kidnapping secuestro

kidney riñón (-ones) *m*; *cul* riñones *mpl*; ~**-bean** judía, *SA* frijol *m;* ~ **failure** insuficiencia renal

kill *n* (act of killing +*fig*) golpe *m* final; (prey) presa; (total number of animals killed) piezas *fpl*; **be in at the** ~ presenciar el golpe final; **close in for the** ~ rodearle para darle muerte/*fig* para el golpe final; *v* matar, *sl* cargarse a; (of feelings) amortiguar[6]; (of pain) aliviar; (of taste) quitar; (greatly amuse) hacer[19] morir de risa; ~ **a bill** *pol* ahogar[5] un proyecto de ley; ~**ed in committee** suprimido por el comité; ~ **off** exterminar; ~ **time** matar el tiempo; ~ **two birds with one stone** matar dos pájaros de un tiro; ~ **with kindness** colmar de favores; ~**ed muerto; ~ed in action** muerto en batalla; ~**-joy** aguafiestas *m+f sing+pl*, *sl* plasta *m+f*

killer *n* asesino; *adj* matador (-ora *f*); ~ **disease** enfermedad *f* fatal; ~**-whale** orca

killing *n* matanza; asesinato; *fam* **make a** ~ tener[19] un gran éxito financiero; *adj* destructivo; asesino; *fig* (funny) cómico; (tiring) abrumador (-ora *f*)

kiln horno

kilocycle kilociclo

kilo(gramme) kilo(gramo)

kilometre kilómetro

kilometric kilométrico

kilowatt kilovatio; ~**-hours** kilovatios hora *mpl*

kilt falda escocesa

kimono quimono

kin parientes *mpl*; *fig* especie *f*; **next of** ~ pariente(s) más próximo(s); ~**ship** parentesco, *fig* afinidad *f*; ~**sman** pariente *m*; ~**swoman** parienta

[1] **kind** *n* especie *f*; (breed) raza; (~ **of person**) tipo; ~ **of** (somewhat) algo; **all** ~**s of** toda clase de; **in** ~ en especie; **nothing of the** ~ nada de eso; **two of a** ~ dos iguales; **a job of that** ~ tal trabajo

[2] **kind** bondadoso, amable; **be** ~ **to** ser[19] bueno con; **my** ~ **regards to** (spoken) muchos recuerdos a, (written) saludos afectuosos a; **would you be** ~ **enough to** tenga la bondad de +*infin*; ~**-hearted** de buen corazón; ~**-heartedness** bondad *f*

kindergarten jardín (-ines) *m* de (la) infancia

kindle *vt* encender (ie)[2b]; *vi* encenderse (ie)[2b]

kindliness benignidad *f*

kindling (act) encendimiento; (wood) leña menuda, SA charamuscas *fpl*

kindly *adj* amable; *adv* amablemente; **will you** ~ haga el favor de + *infin*; **take** ~ **to** aceptar de buen grado; **not take** ~ **to** no poder (ue)[1b] aguantar; ~ **disposed** bien dispuesto (**towards** hacia)

kindness amabilidad *f*; (favour) favor *m*; **do a** ~ **to** hacer[19] un favor a; **show** ~ **to** mostrarse (ue)[1a] cariñoso con

kindred *n* parentela; *adj* afín (-ines); ~ **soul** persona con ideas afines

kinetic cinético

king *n* (+ cards, chess) rey *m*; (draughts) dama; ~**cup** *bot* botón (-ones) *m* de oro; ~**fisher** martín *m* pescador; ~**pin** perno real, *fig* persona principal, *fam* gallo; ~**post** pendolón *m*; ~**ship** realeza, (reign) reinado; ~**-size** (large) de tamaño extra, (long) (super)largo

kingdom reino; ~ **of heaven** reino de los cielos

kingly real

kink *n* pliegue *m*; *fig* chifladura; *v* plegar[2a+5]

kinky (of hair) rizado, *SA* grifo; *fam* (attractive) hechizo; (eccentric) raro; (perverted) pervertido

kinsfolk familia

kiosk quiosco

kip *n* sueño; *v* ~ **down** echarse

kipper *n* arenque ahumado; *v* ahumar

kirbigrip horquilla para el pelo

kismet destino

kiss *n* beso; (long drawn-out) besazo; (short) besín (-ines) *m*; *fig* (mere touch) roce *m*; (of billiard-balls) pelo; ~ **of life** boca-a-boca *m*; **give the ~ of life** hacer[19] el boca-a-boca; **throw a** ~ echar un beso; ~**-curl** bucle *m*; ~**-proof** (of lipstick) indeleble; *v* besar; (repeatedly) besuquear; ~ **each other** besarse; ~ **one's hand to** echar un beso a; ~ **away** (pain, tears) quitar con un beso

kit *n* equipaje *m*; *mil* equipo; (tools) caja de herramientas; **cleaning-**~ avíos *mpl* para la limpieza; **first-aid** ~ botiquín (-ines) *m* de urgencia; **repair** ~ cajita de reparación; ~**-bag** bolsa para excursiones, *mil* saco; *v* ~ **(out)** equipar

kitchen cocina; ~**-cabinet** armario de la cocina; ~**-garden** huerta; ~**-maid** pincha; ~ **range** cocina económica; ~**-sink** fregadero; ~ **utensils** batería *f sing* de cocina

kitchenette cocina pequeña

kite cometa; *SA* volantín *m*; (plane) avión *m*; *orni* milano real; **fly a** ~ hacer[19] volar una cometa; ~**-balloon** globo cometa; ~**-flying** remonte *m* de la cometa

kith: ~ **and kin** parientes *mpl* y amigos *mpl*

kitten *n* gatito; *v* (of a cat) parir

kittenish coquetón

kittiwake risa

kitty (kitten) gatito; (in games) fondo *m*; **start off the** ~ abrir (*past part* abierto) el fondo

kiwi kiwi *m*

klaxon klaxon *m*

Kleenex *tr* Kleenex *m*

kleptomania cleptomanía

kleptomaniac cleptómano

knack tino; **learn the** ~ **of** coger[8] el tino de +*infin*

knacker matarife *m* de caballos;

(house/ship breaker) contratista *m* de derribos; ~**s** *vulg* cojones *mpl*; ~**'s (yard)** matadero; ~**ed** *vulg* cabreado

knapsack mochila

knave pícaro; (cards) sota

knavery picardía

knavish pícaro

knead (massage) dar[19] masaje; (mix dough) amasar; ~ **into shape** formar

kneading-trough amasadera

knee *n* rodilla; (of animals) codillo; (of trousers) rodillera; **bring s.o. to his ~s** humillar; (**fall**) **on one's ~s** (caerse[19]) de rodillas; **go down on one's bended ~s** suplicar[4] de rodillas; **gone at the ~s** con las rodilleras desgastadas; ~**-bend** (gymnastics) flexión *f* de piernas; ~**-breeches** calzón (-ones) *m sing* corto; ~**-cap** rótula; ~**-deep** (metido) hasta las rodillas; ~**-high** (que llega) hasta la rodilla; ~**-jerk reflex** reflejo rotuliano; ~**-joint** *anat* articulación *f* de la rodilla, *mech* articulación *f* angular; ~**-pad** rodillera; *v* dar[19] un rodillazo; (football) dar[19] con la rodilla

kneel (**down**) arrodillarse

kneeler el que se arrodilla

kneeling arrodillado

knell toque *m* de difuntos; *fig* mal agüero

knickerbockers calzón (-ones) *m sing* corto

knickers braga(s); (*US* plus-fours) pantalón (-ones) *m* bombacho; *interj* ¡mierda!

knick-knack baratija

knife *n* cuchillo; (carving-~) trinchante *m*; (pocket-~) navaja; **have one's** ~ **into** tener[19] enemigo a; ~**-box** portacubiertos *m sing*; ~**-edge** filo de cuchillo, (of balance) eje *m* de apoyo; ~**-grinder** amolador *m*; ~**-sharpener** afilón (-ones) *m*; ~**-thrust** cuchillada; *v* acuchillar

knight caballero; (chess) caballo; ~**-errant** caballero andante; ~**-errantry** caballería andante; **Knight Templar** templario; *v* armar caballero

knighthood título de caballero; (collectively) caballería

knightly caballeresco

knit *vi* hacer[19] punto; (of bones) unirse; *vt* tricotar; ~ **one's brows** fruncir el ceño; ~ **together** enlazar(se)[7]; ~**wear**

géneros *mpl* de punto
knitted de punto
knitting trabajo de punto; ~**-machine** tricotosa; ~**-needle** aguja de punto
knob protuberancia; (on door) pomo; (on drawer) tirador *m*; (on radio *etc*) botón *m*; (on walking-stick + decoration on furniture) puño; ~ **of butter** nuez (-ces) *f* de mantequilla
knobb(l)y nudoso
knock *n* golpe *m*; (at the door) llamada; *mot* martilleo; *fig sp* (*esp* cricket) turno; ~**-for-**~ (agreement) acuerdo recíproco; ~**-kneed** patizambo; *v* golpear; *mot* martillear; (on door) llamar; (criticize) hablar mal de

~ **about** (damage) golpear; (ill-treat) maltratar; (wander) vagabundear
~**-about:** ~**-about comedy** farsa bulliciosa
~ **against** chocar[4] contra; (with the head) dar[19] con la cabeza contra
~ **at** (door) llamar a
~ **back** *sl* (drink) soplar
~ **down** derribar; (building) demoler (ue)[1b]; (at an auction) rematar (**to** a); ~ **down the price** rebajar el precio; *mot* atropellar; ~**-down prices** precios rebajadísimos
~ **in** (of nails) clavar
~ **off** quitar de un golpe; (cause to fall) hacer[19] caer; ~ **off work** dejar de trabajar, (leave the place of work) dejar el lugar del trabajo; **he will** ~ **off five per cent** él descontará (el) cinco por ciento; ~ **off s.o.'s head** *fig* descalabrar a uno
~**-out** *n* fuera de combate *m*; **by a** ~**-out** por fuera de combate
~ **out** *v* (stun) atontar; (boxing) poner[19] fuera de combate, *fam* noquear; ~ **out of s.o.'s hands** arrancar[4] de la mano (de un golpe)
~ **over** derribar; *mot* atropellar
~ **up** (waken) despertar (ie)[2a]; (score) marcar[4]; ~ **up against** chocar[4] contra
knocker aldaba; ~**s** *vulg* tetas
knocking golpeo; (on door) aldabeo; *mot* martilleo
knoll otero
knot *n* +*bot*+*naut*+*fig* nudo; (bow) lazo; (of hair) moño; (group) corrillo; ~**-hole** agujero de un nudo; **Gordian** ~ nudo gordiano; *vt* atar; *vi* hacer[19]

nudos
knotted nudoso; **get** ~! ¡lárgate!
knotty nudoso; *fig* difícil
knout knut *m*
know *n*: **be in the** ~ estar[19] en el secreto; *v* (be acquainted with) conocer[14]; (be aware of) saber[19]; ~ **how to** saber[19] +*infin*; (recognize) reconocer[14]; (understand) comprender; ~ **for certain** saber[19] a ciencia cierta; ~ **only too well** saber[19] de sobra; ~ **o.s.** conocerse[14] a sí mismo; ~ **one's place** *fig* saber[19] con quien se habla; ~ **one's way around** *fig* tener[19] mucho mundo; ~ **the ropes** saber[19] el juego; ~ **what's what** saber[19] cuántas son cinco; **as far as I** ~ que yo sepa; **do you** ~ **the story about?** ¿ha oído usted el cuento de?; **get to** ~ **s.o.** llegar[5] a conocer a uno; **get to** ~ **s.t.** enterarse de algo; **how can I** ~? ¿cómo lo voy a saber yo?; **who** ~**s?** ¿quién sabe?; **worth knowing** digno de saberse; **known to the police** conocido por la policía; **make known** publicar[4]; **it is (well) known that** es (bien) sabido que; ~**-all** sabelotodo *m*+*f*; ~**-how** conocimiento

~ **about** estar[19] enterado de; **not to** ~ **about** estar[19] a oscuras sobre
~ **best** ser[19] el mejor juez; **mother and father** ~ **best** los padres siempre tienen razón
~ **better: you should** ~ **better than to** ya sabe usted que no debe +*infin*; **you should** ~ **better** (you ought to be ashamed) usted sabe como debe portarse
~ **by heart** saber[19] de memoria
~ **by sight** conocer[14] de vista
~ **of** conocer[14]; **do you** ~ **of a good doctor here?** ¿conoce usted un buen médico aquí?; (have news of) tener[19] noticias de; **not that I** ~ **of** no que lo sepa yo
knowable conocible
knowing *n*: **there's no** ~ no hay modo de saberlo; *adj* **with a** ~ **look** con un aire como de quien sabe
knowingly queriendo; a sabiendas
knowledge saber *m*; (aquaintance) conocimiento; (learning) erudición *f*; (skill) pericia; **be common** ~ ser[19] notorio; **have a thorough** ~ **of** conocer[14]

a fondo; **not to my** ~ que yo sepa, no; **to the best of my** ~ según mi leal saber y entender; **without my** ~ sin saberlo yo

knowledgeable sabedor (-ora *f*); *fam* sabihondo

knuckle *n* nudillo; (of meat) jarrete *m*; ~-**bone** nudillo, hueso del metacarpo; ~-**duster** puño de hierro; ~-**joint** *anat* articulación *f* de los dedos, *mech* unión *f* de gozne; *v* ~ **down to work** ponerse[19] a trabajar con ahinco; ~ **under** someterse

koala bear koala *m*

Koran Alcorán, Corán *m*

Korea Corea

Korean *n* + *adj* coreano

kosher autorizado por la ley judía; *fam* (of good quality) bueno; (true) verdadero

kowtow humillarse (**to** ante)

kraal corral *m*

Kremlin Kremlin *m*

Kt (knight) Cro(caballero)

kudos prestigio

Kurd *n*, **Kurdish** *adj* curdo

Kuwaiti kuweití *m* + *f*

kybosh: put the ~ **on** zafar por completo

kyrie eleison kirieleisón *m*

L

l (letter) ele *f*; (left) izqda (izquierda); (litre) litro

la(h) *mus* la

lab laboratorio

label *n* etiqueta; (on reserved seat) etiqueta de reserva; (on luggage) etiqueta (con la dirección); (gummed) etiqueta engomada; (manufacturer's) marbete *m*, etiqueta; (on exhibit) letrero; *sl* (nickname) apodo; *v* etiquetar; *fig* calificar[4] (as de)

labelling acto de etiquetar; *fig* (group description) clasificación *f*; ~ **machine** máquina de etiquetar

labial labial

laboratory laboratorio; ~ **assistant** ayudante *m+f* de laboratorio

laborious laborioso

labour *n* trabajo; **hard** ~ trabajos forzados; (job of work) faena; ~ **of Hercules** *fig* faena ardua; (labouring class) clase obrera; (manual workers) los obreros *mpl*; (as opposed to capital) mano *f* de obra; ~ **costs** gastos *mpl* de la mano de obra; *pol* los laboristas, **Labour will win the election** los laboristas ganarán la elección; (pains of childbirth) dolores *mpl* del parto; **be in** ~ estar[19] de parto; ~ **camp** campamento de trabajo; **Labour Day** primero de mayo; ~ **dispute** conflicto laboral; ~ **exchange** bolsa de trabajo; ~ **laws** legislación *f* de trabajo; ~ **leader** jefe *m* de sindicato obrero; ~ **market** mercado del trabajo; **Labour Party** Partido Laborista; ~**-saving** que ahorra trabajo; ~**-stoppage** paro (de trabajo); ~ **turnover** movimiento de obreros; ~**-union** sindicato obrero; *adj* laboral; ~ **ward** sala de partos; *vt* elaborar; *vi* trabajar; ~ **in vain** trabajar en balde; (move with difficulty) moverse (ue)[1b] penosamente; (struggle) luchar; ~**ed** (of breathing) fatigoso, (of style) forzado

~ **at** trabajar en

~ **to** esforzarse (ue)[1a] en +*infin*

~ **under** sufrir; ~ **under a delusion** estar[19] equivocado; ~ **under the delusion that** equivocarse[4] creyendo que

labourer obrero; (day-~) jornalero; (farm-~) labrador *m*; (unskilled) bracero

labouring *n* trabajo; *adj* trabajador (-ora *f*)

Labrador Labrador *m*

labrador perro de Labrador

laburnum lluvia de oro

labyrinth laberinto

labyrinthine laberíntico

lace *n* (fabric) encaje *m*; (trimming) puntilla; (decorative braid) galón (-ones) *m*; (for shoe) cordón (-ones) *m*; (liquor) licor *m* (*esp* en una taza de café); ~ **cuff** puño de adorno; ~ **curtain** visillo; ~ **frills** volantes *mpl* de puntilla; ~**-maker** encajero; ~ **pillow** almohadilla para hacer encajes; *v* (fasten with cords) atar con cordones; (pass a cord through holes) entrelazar[7]; (pour spirits) echar (un poco de) licor a; ~ **into** *fam* azotar

lacerate lacerar

laceration laceración *f*

lachrymal lacrimal

lachrymose lacrimoso

lack falta; (need) necesidad *f*; **for** ~ **of** por falta de; *v* carecer[14] de; (need) necesitar; **I** ~ **money** me hace falta dinero; **he** ~**s the will to do it** le falta la voluntad para hacerlo

lackadaisical distraído

lackey +*fig* lacayo; *Chil* librea

lacking *adj* faltante; (feeble-minded) lerdo; **be** ~ (in need of) faltar; *prep* no teniendo

lacklustre deslustrado

laconic lacónico

lacquer laca; ~ **remover** quitaesmaltes *m sing+pl*; ~ **work** labor *f* en laca

lacrosse juego de pelota (del Canadá)

lactic lácteo

lactose lactoso

lacuna laguna

lad muchacho; *fam* chaval *m*; (apprentice) pipiolo; **he's a bit of a ~** él es poco formal

ladder *n* escalera de mano; +*naut* escala; *fig* escalón (-ones) *m*; (in stocking) carrera; **climb the ~** *fig* progresar en su carrera; **~-proof** indesmallable; *v* **~ one's stockings** hacerse una carrera en las medias

ladies see **lady**

lading cargamento; **bill of ~** conocimiento de embarque; **clean bill of ~** conocimiento limpio

ladle *n* cucharón (-ones) *m*; *v* servir (i)[3] con cucharón; **~ out** vaciar con cucharón

lady señora; (noble) dama; *euph* (female animal) hembra; **~ of the house** señora de la casa; **~-in-waiting** dama de honor; **he's fond of the ladies** él es Perico entre ellas; **Our Lady** *eccles* Nuestra Señora; **young ~** señorita, (fiancée) novia; **~ assistant** (in shop) dependienta *f*; **~-bird, ~-bug** mariquita; **~ bountiful** bienhechora; **Lady Chapel** capilla de la Virgen; **Lady Day** día de la Anunciación, *fam* día de la Virgen; **~ doctor** +*med* doctora; **~-finger** *bot* vulneraria; **~-friend** amiga; **~'s-help** interina; **~-killer** tenorio; **~like** bien educada, (of a man) afeminado; **~ love** querida; **~ship** señoría; **your ~ship** su señoría; **'ladies'** (lavatory) señoras; **ladies and gentlemen!** ¡señoras y señores!; **ladies' hairdresser's** peluquería para señoras; **lady's smock** *bot* mastuerzo

lag *n* (delay) retraso; (hardened convict) presidiario; *v* (go slowly) ir[19] despacio; (insulate) revestir (i)[3]; **~ a boiler** calorifugar[5] una caldera

lager cerveza tipo Pilsen

laggard holgazán *m* (-ana *f*)

lagging revestimiento

lagoon laguna

lah-di-dah postinero

laicize laicizar[7]

laid: ~ paper papel *m* vergé; **new-~** (of eggs) recién puestos; **be ~ up** tener[19] que guardar cama; **she is ~ up with flu**

ella tiene que guardar cama a causa de la gripe; **my car is ~ up** mi coche está fuera de circulación

lair cubil *m*

laird hacendado escocés

laissez-faire laissez faire *m*

laity legos *mpl*

lake lago; (colour) laca; **~ dwelling** vivienda lacustre; **~land** región *f* de lagos

lam azotar

lama lama *m*

lamb *n* +*fig* corder(it)o; (meat) carne *f* de cordero; **~ chop** chuleta de cordero; **~skin** piel *f* de cordero; **~swool** añinos *mpl*; *v* parir

lambaste dar[19] una paliza a; *fig* criticar[4] severamente

lambing: ~ season la temporada de parir las ovejas

lame *n* los mutilados; *adj* cojo; *Arg* rengo; **~ excuse** disculpa poco convincente; **~ duck** persona *f* incapacitada, *comm* persona/firma insolvente; **~ ship** buque averiado; *v* lisiar; (*esp* of leg) dejar cojo

lamé lamé *m*

lamely con cojera; *fig* imperfectamente

lameness cojera; *fig* defecto

lament *n* lamento; *poet* elegía; *v* lamentarse de; **~ for** llorar; **the late-~ed mayor** el difunto alcalde

lamentable lamentable; (wretched) miserable

lamentation lamentación (-ones) *f*

laminate *n* laminado; *v* laminar; **~d glass** vidrio inastillable

lamp lámpara; (oil) lámpara de aceite; (in street) farol *m*; *mot* faro; (*naut* + railway) farol *m*; **~black** negro de humo; **~-bracket** brazo de lámpara; **~-light** luz *f* de (la) lámpara; **~-lighter** farolero; **~-post** poste *m* de farol; **~-shade** pantalla; **~-stand** pie *m* de lámpara

lampoon *n* pasquín (-ines) *m*; *v* pasquinar

lamprey lamprea

lance *n* lanza; **~-corporal** cabo interino; **~-sergeant** sargento interino; *v* alancear; *med* abrir (*past part* abierto) con lanceta

lancer lancero; **~s** (dance) lanceros *mpl*

lancet lanceta; **~ arch** ojiva aguda; **~**

window ventana ojival

land tierra; (soil) suelo; (piece of ~) terreno; parcela; (nation) país *m*; ~ of promise tierra prometida; see how the ~ lies mirar la configuración del terreno, *fig* considerar todas las circunstancias; make ~ *naut* hacer[19] escala; ~-agent corredor *m* de fincas; ~-based de tierra; ~-breeze terral *m*; ~fall recalada, make a ~ fall hacer[19] escala; ~-girl labradora voluntaria (en tiempo de guerra); ~-grant concesión gubernamental de terreno; ~-hunger sed *f* de tierra; ~lady patrona, (owner) propietaria; ~line cable telegráfico sobre la tierra; ~-locked cercado de tierra; ~lord patrón *m* (-ona *f*), (owner) proprietario, (lessor) arrendador *m*; ~-lubber hombre *m* de tierra; ~mark jalón (-ones) *m*, *fig* punto culminante; be a ~mark marcar[4] época; ~mine mina terrestre; ~owner terrateniente *m+f*; ~-power *mil* fuerzas *fpl* terrestres; ~-register registro de la propiedad; ~-rover *mot* landrover *m*; ~slide corrimiento de tierras; ~-surveyor agrimensor *m*; ~-tax contribución *f* territorial; *vi* (fall to the ground) caer[19] al suelo; (of a bird) posarse; ~ on one's feet/head caer[19] de pies/de cabeza; *aer* aterrizar; ~ on the moon alunizar[7]; ~ on water amarar; *vt aer* aterrizar[7]; *naut* desembarcar[4]; (catch a fish) echar en tierra; *fig* obtener[19], the firm has ~ed a big contract la empresa ha obtenido un contrato grande; ~ a blow dar[19] un golpe; ~ (up) in gaol ir[19] a parar a la cárcel

landau landó *m*

landed: ~ gentry los hacendados *mpl*; ~ property bienes *mpl* raíces

landing (on stairs) rellano; *naut* (of cargo) desembarque *m*, (of people) desembarco; *aer* aterrizaje *m*; (on sea) amaraje *m*; ~ on the moon alunizaje *m*; make a soft ~ space posarse; ~-craft lancha de desembarco; ~-deck cubierta de aterrizaje; ~-gear tren *m* de aterrizaje; ~-ground campo de aterrizaje; ~-net salabardo *m*; ~-place (on voyage) escala; ~-run recorrido de aterrizaje; ~-stage desembarcadero; ~-strip pista de aterrizaje

landscape paisaje *m*; ~-gardener artista *m+f* en jardines; ~-painter paisajista *m+f*

landward hacia tierra

lane (road) camino vecinal, (in town) callejuela; (cart-track) senda; *aer+naut* zona (de tránsito); (athletics) calle *f*; *mot* carril *m*, six-~ motorway autopista de seis carriles; you are in the wrong ~ usted se ha confundido de línea

language idioma *m*; (choice of words) lenguaje *m*; ~ laboratory laboratorio de idiomas; bad ~ palabrotas *fpl*; he uses bad ~ él es mal hablado; strong ~ palabras *fpl* mayores; modern/dead ~ lengua viva/muerta

languid lánguido

languish languidecer[14]

languishing lánguido

languor languidez *f*

languorous lánguido

lank (of hair) lacio; (long and thin) alto y flaco

lankiness flaqueza

lanky larguirucho

lanolin lanolina

lantern +*archi* linterna; (*naut* + of lighthouse) farol *m*; ~ lecture conferencia con proyecciones; ~-slide diapositiva

lanyard acollador *m*; (of gun) cuerda y gancho de disparo

Laotian *n+adj* laosiano

¹ lap *n anat* regazo; *fig* seno; ~dog perro faldero; in the ~ of the gods en las manos de los dioses

² lap *n sp* vuelta; *mech* traslapo; *theat* (of stage) etapa; *v sp* aventajar en una vuelta entera; *mech* ~ (over) traslapar(se) a

³ lap *n* (act/sound of lapping) lametada; (of waves) chapaleteo; *v* lamer; (of waves) chapalear; ~ up beber con la lengua, *fig* (believe) tragar[5]

lapel solapa

lapidary lapidario

lapis lazuli lapislázuli *m*

Lapland Laponia

Laplander, Lapp lapón *m* (-ona *f*)

lapping (licking) lamedura; (of waves) chapoteo; (of a stream) murmullo

lapse *n* lapso; (of time) intervalo; (decline) recaída; (mistake) equivocación (-ones) *f*; *leg* caducidad *f*; **after a ~ of two weeks** después de dos semanas; **with the ~ of time** en el transcurso de los años; *v* (of time) transcurrir; (err) caer[19] en el error; *leg* (+ expire) caducar[4]; **she is a ~d catholic** ella es ex-católica; **~ into** recaer[19] en

lapwing avefría

larboard *n* babor; *adj* de babor

larceny latrocinio; **petty ~** latrocinio de menor cuantía

larch alerce *m*

lard *n* manteca (de cerdo); *v cul* mechar; *fig* adornar (**with** con)

larder despensa

large grande; **as ~ as life** de tamaño natural; (in person) en persona; **at ~** en libertad; **in ~ type** en letras grandes; **on the ~ size** algo grande; **~-handed** de manos grandes, *fig* generoso; **~-hearted** bondadoso; **~ intestine** intestino grueso; **~-scale** en gran escala; **~-sized** de tamaño grande

largely en gran parte

largeness gran tamaño; (of a person) gran talle *m*; (generosity) magnanimidad *f*

largesse limosna; (generosity) liberalidad *f*

largo *mus* largo

lariat lazo

lark *n orni* alondra; (joke) broma; (fun) juerga; **rise with the ~** levantarse con las gallinas; *v* **~ about** (get into mischief) hacer[19] travesuras; (go on the spree) andar de parranda

larking *n* travesuras *fpl*

larkspur espuela de caballero

larva larva

larval larval

laryngeal laríngeo

laryngitis laringitis *f*

larynx laringe *f*

lascivious lascivo

lasciviousness lascivia

laser laser *m*; **~ beam** rayo laser (*pl* rayos laser)

lash (whip) látigo; (thong) tralla; (blow) latigazo; (eye~) pestaña; *v* (hit) azotar; (of waves) romper (*past part* roto) (**against** contra); (of rain, hail, wind) azotar; (provoke) provocar[4] (**into** hasta); (fasten) atar; *naut* trincar[4]; **~ the tail** agitar la cola; **~ out**

dar[19] coces, (verbally) fustigar[5]

lashings (fastenings) ataduras *fpl*; (blows) latigazos *mpl*; (of rain, hail, wind) azotes *mpl*; **there were ~ of food** había una cantidad enorme de comida

lass(ie) chica; *fam* chavala; *Arg* piba

lassitude lasitud *f*

lasso *n* lazo; *v* lazar[7]

last *n* último, última; (end) fin *m*; (cobbler's) horma; **at ~** por fin; **at long ~** al fin y al cabo; **~ but not least** el último pero no el peor; **be the ~ to** ser[19] el último en +*infin*; **see the ~ of** no volver (ue)[1b] (*past part* vuelto) a ver; **breathe one's ~** exhalar el último suspiro; *adj* último; (next to ~) penúltimo; **his latest novel is not as long as his ~ one** su última novela no es tan larga como la anterior; (final) final; (previous) anterior, **~ generation** generación *f* anterior; *euph* (often used by superstitious Spaniards) penúltimo, **let's have a ~ drink!** ¡vamos a tomar la penúltima!; **to the ~ ditch** hasta el último cartucho; **~ Friday** el viernes pasado; **~ hope** último recurso; **Last Judgement** juicio final; **be on one's ~ legs** no poder[19] más; **at the ~ moment** a la orilla; **~ night** anoche; **~ post** (collection) última recolecta de cartas, (delivery) último reparto de cartas, (bugle-call) toque *m* de retreta; **~ (dying) request** última voluntad; **this is the ~ straw** esto es el colmo; **Last Supper** última cena; **~ thing at night** a última hora; **if it's the ~ thing I do** por encima de todo; **for the ~ time** por última vez; **~ week** la semana pasada; **~ word** palabra final, (in fashion) última moda, (supreme) cosa inmejorable; *v* durar; **his shoes never ~ long** sus zapatos nunca duran mucho; (continue) continuar, **the meeting ~ed until dawn** la reunión continuó hasta la madrugada; **~ a very long time** perdurar; **~ out** resistir, **that competitor will not ~ out to the end of the race** aquel competidor no resistirá hasta el fin de la carrera; *adv* finalmente, por última vez; **I ~ saw him in Segovia** le vi por última vez en Segovia; **how have you been since I ~ saw you?** ¿cómo le va desde la última vez que le vi?

lasting duradero; (of colours) sólido

lastingness permanencia

lastly en conclusión

latch picaporte *m*; **on the ~** cerrado con picaporte; **off the ~** entreabierto; **~ key** llave *f* de la puerta, (Yale type) llavín *m*

late *adj* tardío; (deceased) difunto; **~ arrival** recién llegado; **~ in the morning** a última hora de la mañana; **~ in years** de edad avanzada; **~ of** recién salido de; **keep ~ hours** acostarse (ue)[1a] tarde; **~ tackle** *sp* entrada retardada; **~-tenth-century poetry** poesía de fines del siglo diez; **my ~ husband** mi difunto (marido) (que en paz descanse); **~-comer** el que llega tarde; *adv* tarde; **be ~** llegar[5] tarde; **it is ~** es tarde; **I was ~ in** + *pres part* tardé en +*infin*; **the train arrived ten minutes ~** el tren llegó con diez minutos de retraso; **~ at night** a altas horas de la noche; **it's getting ~** se hace tarde; **of ~** últimamente; **better ~ than never** más vale tarde que nunca

lately últimamente; *fam* hace poco

latency estado latente

lateness retraso; **~ of the hour** lo avanzado de la hora

latent latente

later (on) más tarde; (afterwards) después; **~ and ~** cada vez más tarde; **sooner or ~** tarde o temprano

lateral lateral

latest (*see* late) último, más reciente

latex látex *m*

lath listón (-ones) *m*

lathe torno

lather *n* espuma (de jabón); *vi* hacer[19] espuma; *vt* enjabonar; *sl* (thrash) zurrar

latifundia latifundios *mpl*

Latin *n* latín *m*; *adj* latino; **print** medieval; **~ America** Hispanoamérica; **~ American** hispanoamericano; **~ races** razas *fpl* de origen latino

Latinism latinismo

Latinist *n+adj* latinista *m+f*

latinize latinizar[7]

latitude latitud *f*; *fig* libertad

latitudinal latitudinal

latrine letrina

latter *pron* éste *m*, ésta; *adj* (most recent) más reciente; (of two) segundo; **at the ~ end of** May a fines de mayo; **~ half** segunda mitad; **~-day** de nuestros días; **Latter-day Saints** mormones *mpl*

latterly últimamente

lattice *n* enrejado; **~ bridge** puente *m* de celosía; **~ girder** viga de celosía; **~-work** celosía; *v* enrejar

Latvia Letonia

Latvian *n+adj* letón *m* (-ona *f*)

laud *n* alabanza; *eccles* laudes *fpl*; *v* alabar

laudability laudabilidad *f*

laudable loable

laudanum láudano

laudatory laudatorio

laugh *n* risa; (loud) risotada; **have the ~ of** quedar por encima de; **have the last ~** ser[19] el último en reírse; *v* reír(se); **be ~ed at** servir (i)[3] de irrisión; **he who ~s last ~s loudest** ríe mejor quien ríe el último

~ at reírse de

~ down ridiculizar[7]

~ in s.o.'s face reírse de uno en las barbas

~ off tomar a risa; **~ one's head off, die ~ing** morirse de risa, *fam* mearse de risa

~ on the other side of one's mouth arrepentirse

~ out reír(se) a carcajadas; **his plan was ~ed out** acabaron con su plan por el ridículo

~ up one's sleeve reírse por lo bajo

laughable risible

laughing *n* risa; *adj* risueño; **it's no ~ matter** no es ningún chiste; **~-gas** gas *m* hilarante; **~-stock** hazmerreír *m*

laughter risa

launch *n* (act of launching) botadura; (boat) lancha; **motor ~** lancha motora; **steam~** bote *m* de vapor; *v naut* botar; *space* lanzar[7]; (throw, initiate, publicize) lanzar[7]; *comm* emitir; **~ forth** lanzarse[7]; **~ out** lanzarse[7]; **~ out into** emprender

launching *naut* botadura; *space* lanzamiento; **~-pad** plataforma de lanzamiento; **automatic ~** *space* autolanzamiento; **~-tube** lanzatorpedos *m sing*

launder *vt* lavar (y planchar); *vi* resistir el lavado; (money) blanquear

launderette lavandería automática
laundress lavandera
laundry (establishment) lavandería; (clothes for washing) ropa sucia; (washed clothes) ropa lavada; ~-**bag** bolsa del lavado; ~-**list** lista del lavado; ~-**man** lavandero; ~-**tub** cuba de colada
laureate n poeta laureado; adj laureado
laurel laurel m; **rest on one's** ~**s** dormirse[1c] sobre sus laureles; ~-**wreath** corona de laurel
Lausanne Lausana
lava lava
lavatory servicio; (washroom) lavabo; **public** ~ servicios públicos; ~ **bowl/pan** taza del retrete; ~ **seat** asiento del retrete
lavender lavanda; ~-**water** agua de lavanda
lavish adj pródigo (**in** en, **of** de); v prodigar[5] (**on** sobre)
lavishly con profusión
lavishness prodigalidad f
law ley f; sp regla; sl (police) bofia; sl (policeman) polizonte m; (study) derecho; **civil/constitutional/criminal/international** ~ derecho civil/político/penal/internacional; **maritime** ~ código marítimo; **mercantile** ~ código de comercio; ~ **and order** orden público; **according to the** ~ según la ley; **go to** ~ recurrir a los tribunales; **he's a** ~ **unto himself** él no tiene ni rey ni roque; **have the** ~ **on s.o.** llevar a uno a los tribunales; **lay down the** ~ hablar autoritariamente, (chide) hablar severamente; **take the** ~ **into one's own hands** tomarse la justicia por su mano; **in** ~ según la ley; **in-**~ político, **my sister-in-**~ mi hermana política; ~ **of diminishing returns** ley f de rendimiento decreciente; ~ **of nature** ley f natural; ~ **of supply and demand** ley f de oferta y demanda; ~-**abiding** observante de la ley; ~-**breaker** infractor m de la ley; ~ **court** tribunal, (room) sala de audiencia; ~-**giver**, ~-**maker** legislador m; ~ **school** escuela de derecho; ~ **student** estudiante m+f de derecho; ~-**suit** pleito
lawful legal
lawfulness legalidad f
lawless (of a person) desordenado; (of a country) sin leyes
lawlessness rebeldía
[1] **lawn** césped m; ~-**mower** cortacéspedes m sing; ~ **tennis** tenis m sobre hierba
[2] **lawn** (cloth) linón m
Lawrence Lorenzo
lawyer abogado; ~'s **office** bufete m
lax laxo
laxative laxante m
laxity laxitud f
[1] **lay** laico; ~ **brother** hermano lego; ~ **figure** maniquí m (-íes); ~-**man** lego; **I am a** ~-**man when it comes to architecture** soy lego en arquitectura; ~ **sister** hermana lega; ~ **studies** estudios mpl profanos
[2] **lay** (poem) romance m; (song) canción f
[3] **lay** poner[19]; (flatten) aplastar, **the rain will** ~ **the wheat** la lluvia aplastará el trigo; (spread out) extender (ie)[2b]; vulg tirarse a; ~ **bare** revelar; ~ **a bet** apostar (ue)[1a]; ~ **the blame** echar la culpa (**on** a); ~ **a cable** tender (ie)[2b] un cable; ~ **charges against** acusar a; ~ **claim to** reclamar; ~ **claim to the throne** pretender (ie)[2b] al trono; ~ **the dust** asentar el polvo; ~ **an egg** poner[19] un huevo; ~ **eyes on** ver[19]; ~ **a fire** preparar un fuego; ~ **the foundations** echar los cimientos (**for/of** de); ~ **the foundation stone** colocar[4] la primera piedra; ~ **a ghost** conjurar un fantasma; ~ **hands on** (find) encontrar (ue)[1a], (hit) pegar[5]; ~ **hold of** agarrar(se) a; ~ **a place for** poner[19] un cubierto para; ~ **to rest** enterrar (ie)[2a]; ~ **siege to** sitiar, fig importunar; ~ **stress on** subrayar; ~ **the table** poner[19] la mesa; ~ **waste (to)** asolar (ue)[1a]
~ **about** n holgazán m
~ **about** v (hit out) dar[19] palos de ciego
~ **aside** arrinconar
~-**by** n mot parking m
~ **by** v poner[19] a un lado; (store) ahorrar
~ **down** dejar; (assert) afirmar; ~ **down a job** dimitir; ~ **down one's arms** deponer[19] las armas; ~ **down money** (as wager) apostar (ue)[1a] dinero, (as instalment) depositar dinero; ~ **down one's life** sacrificar la vida (**for** por); ~ **down a principle** formular un principio

~ **in** proveerse de[17]

~ **low** derribar

~**-off** *n* despido (de un empleado)

~ **off** *v* (sack) despedir (i)[3]; (cease) dejar de +*infin*

~ **on** (services) instalar; (food) ofrecer[14]; (paint) dar[19]; ~ **it on** exagerar

~**out** *n* plan *m*; (of furniture *etc*) disposición *f*; *print* montaje *m*; ~**out design** proyecto de diseño

~ **out** *v* (prepare for burial) amortajar; (spend) desembolsar; (display) desplegar (ie)[2a]; ~ **a garden** trazar un jardín

~ **to** *naut* capear

~ **up a ship** desarmar un barco

layer *n* capa; *geol* estrato; (hen) ponedora; *hort* acodo; ~ **cake** tarta; *v hort* acodar

layering *hort* propagación *f* por acodo

layette canastilla

laying (placing) colocación *f*; (spreading) tendido; (of eggs) puesta; ~**-on of hands** imposición *f* de manos; ~**-out** (of corpse) amortajamiento, (of money) empleo

laze: ~ **about** gandulear

laziness pereza

lazy perezoso; *fam* tumbón; ~**-bones** gandul *m* (-ula *f*)

l.c. (lower case) min. (minúsculas); (letter of credit) carta de crédito

L.C.M. (least common multiple) **M.C.M.** (mínimo múltiple común)

[1] **lead** *n* plomo; (in pencil) mina; *naut* + *bui* sonda; *print* regleta; **swing the** ~ fingirse[19] trabajador; ~**-line** *naut* sondaleza; ~**-pencil** lápiz (-ces) *m*; ~ **poisoning** saturnismo; *v* (cover with ~) emplomar; *print* regletear; ~**ed lights** cristales emplomados

[2] **lead** *n* (dog's) correa, **on a** ~ sujeto con correa; *elect* conexión *f*; (first place) +*sp* delantera, **be in/take the** ~ llevar la delantera; **play the** ~ hacer el papel principal; (at cards) salida, **it's my** ~ salgo; (hint) indicación *f*, **give me a** ~ deme una indicación; (influence) influencia; (initiative) iniciativa; **have a two-stroke** ~ **over** (golf) aventajar en dos golpes a; **have a good** ~ (clue) tener[19] una buena pista; *v* (guide) conducir[15]; *mil* (command) mandar; (go ahead of) encabezar[7]; (come first)

encabezar[7]; ~ **the cortege** presidir el cortejo fúnebre; ~ **nowhere** no ir[19] a ningún sitio, *fig* no conducir[15] a nada; ~ **the way** llevar la delantera; ~ **a good life** llevar buena vida; ~ **astray** desviar, *fig* seducir[15]

~**-in** *adj elect* de entrada

~ **off** empezar (ie)[2a+7]; *sp* abrir (*past part* abierto) el juego; (take away) llevar

~ **on** *fig* incitar

~ **out** (remove) llevar afuera; **this room** ~**s** (**out**) **into the kitchen** esta habitación lleva a la cocina

~ **to** conducir[15] a; **it could** ~ **to mistakes** podría prestarse a indiscreciones

~ **up to** conducir[15] a; **what is all this leading up to?** ¿qué significa todo esto?

leaden de plomo; (of colour, sky) plomizo; *fig* triste

leader líder *m*; **who is your** ~? ¿quién es su líder?; ~ **of men** capitán (-anes) *m* de hombres; (of gang of workmen) cuadrillero; (of gang of ruffians) cabecilla *m*; (fishing line) hijuela; (draught horse) caballo de varas; *mil* caudillo; *pol* gobernante *m*+*f*; *mus* (of dance-band) director *m*; (of orchestra) primer violinista *m*+*f*; (on recording-tape) cabecera; (article) artículo editorial; (signed article) artículo de fondo; ~**-writer** editorialista *m*+*f*; **follow-my-**~ (game) seguir *m* la fila; **loss-**~ *comm* reclamo; ~**ship** liderato, *mil* mando

[1] **leading** *bui* emplomadura

[2] **leading** *n* (guidance) dirección *f*; *adj* principal; **he is a** ~ **surgeon** él es un cirujano eminente; ~ **article** artículo editorial; ~ **card** primer naipe *m*; ~ **counsel** abogado principal; ~**-edge** *aer* borde *m* de ataque; ~ **lady** primera actriz (-ces) *f*; ~ **man** primer galán (-anes) *m*; ~ **question** pregunta capciosa

leaf *n* (*bot* + of paper, table *etc*) hoja; (of bridge) ala elevable; ~ **tobacco** tabaco de hojas; **shake like a** ~ temblar (ie)[2a] como una hoja; **turn over the leaves of a book** hojear un libro; **turn over a new** ~ hacer[19] libro nuevo; **take a** ~ **from s.o.'s book** seguir (i)[3+11] el ejemplo de alguien; ~**-bud** yema;

~-**mould** hojarasca; *v* ~ **through** hojear

leafless sin hojas; (having lost its leaves) deshojado

leaflet folleto; *bot* hojita

leafy frondoso

league *pol*+*sp* liga; (measure) legua; **League of Nations** Liga de las Naciones; ~ **championship** campeonato de liga; **be in** ~ **with** aliarse con, *fam* estar[19] conchabado con; *v* *pol* ligar(se)[5]

leak *n* (through roof) gotera; (from pipe) escape *m*, **gas** ~ fuga de gas; *elect* cortacircuito por falta de aislamiento; (hole) agujero, **there's a** ~ **in this bucket** este cubo tiene un agujero; *pol* filtración *f*; *naut* (vía de) agua, **spring a** ~ abrirse (*past part* abierto) una vía de agua; **have a** ~ *fam* hacer[19] pis; *vi* (of a container) calar, **this tank** ~**s** este tanque cala; *naut* hacer[19] agua; (drip) gotear; (escape from a container) perderse (ie)[2a]; **water is leaking from my radiator** estoy perdiendo agua de mi radiador; ~ **out** (of information) divulgarse[5]; ~ **through** filtrar por; *vt* (of information) divulgar[5] subrepticiamente; *pol* dejar filtrar

leakage (of gas *etc*) escape *m*; (of information) divulgación subrepticia

leaky (roof) con goteras; (container) agujereado; *naut* que hace agua

¹ **lean** *n* (of meat) lo magro; *adj* (thin) flaco; (of meat) magro; ~ **year** año de carestía

² **lean** inclinar(se)

~ **against** recostar(se) (ue)[1a] contra

~ **back** recostarse (ue)[1a]

~ **forwards/backwards** inclinarse para adelante/para atrás

~ **on** apoyarse en

~ **out of** asomarse a

~ **over** inclinarse sobre; **he** ~**ed over the wall** él se apoyó sobre la muralla; **I** ~**ed over backwards to help him** hice todo lo que pude para ayudarle

~-**to** *n* colgadizo

~ **towards** inclinarse hacia

~ **upon** +*fig* apoyarse sobre

leaning +*fig* inclinación *f* (**towards** hacia)

leanness flacura; (of meat) magrez *f*

leap *n* salto; **by** ~**s and bounds** a pasos agigantados; **with one** ~ de un salto; ~ **in the dark** salto en el vacío; **play** ~-**frog** jugar (ue)[1a] a la mula; ~-**year** año bisiesto; *v* saltar (**over** a)

learn aprender (**to** a); (get to know) enterarse (**about** de); ~ **by heart** aprender de memoria; ~ **from experience** aprender por experiencia; ~ **about** enterarse de

learned sabio; ~ **body** docta corporación; ~ **profession** profesión *f* liberal

learner principiante *m*+*f*; ~-**driver** uno/una que está aprendiendo a conducir

learning (act of ~) aprender *m*; (wisdom) erudición *f*

lease *n* arrendamiento; **on** ~ en arriendo; **get a new** ~ **of life** recobrar su vigor; ~**hold** *n* bienes *mpl* raíces, *adj* arrendado; ~**holder** arrendatario; *v* (grant a ~) dar[19] en arriendo; (obtain a ~) tomar en arriendo; (*US* hire) alquilar

leash *n* trailla; *v* atraillar

least *n* lo menos; *adj* el menor, la menor *etc*; **at** ~ por lo menos; **at the very** ~ lo mínimo; **not in the** ~ de ninguna manera; **to say the** ~ por no decir más; ~ **of all** ni mucho menos

leather *n* cuero; *fam* pellejo; (binding) piel *f*; (~ sole) suela; (wash-~) gamuza; ~-**trade** comercio en cuero; ~-**jacket** *ent* típula; ~-**neck** soldado de marina estadounidense; *adj* de cuero

leathery correoso; (like leather) como el cuero; (of skin) curtido

leatherette cuero artificial

leave *n* permiso; *esp mil* licencia; (leave-taking) despedida; **by your** ~ con permiso de usted; **on** ~ con permiso, *esp mil* con licencia; **take one's** ~ despedirse (i)[3] (**of** de); **take French** ~ despedirse (i)[3] a la francesa; *v* (go away) marcharse; (depart, of trains, buses *etc*) salir[19] (de); (from employment) darse[19] de baja (de); (abandon) abandonar; (say goodbye) despedirse (i)[3] (**to** de); (as surety) empeñar; (in a will) legar[5]; ~ **in the dark** dejar a oscuras; ~ **in the lurch** dejar colgado; ~ **it at that** dejarlo así; ~ **it to me** yo me encargaré de eso; **I left word at the desk** dejé recado en la recepción; **it** ~**s**

much to be desired deja mucho que desear; ~ **the priesthood** secularizarse[7]; **two from four** ~s **two** cuatro menos dos son dos

~ **alone** dejar en paz; (refrain from touching) no tocar[4]

~ **behind** (forget to bring) dejar olvidado; (travel faster than) distanciarse de

~ **off** dejar de +*infin*; (of clothing) dejar de llevar; (of habit) renunciar

~ **out** omitir

leaven *n* levadura; *vi* fermentar; *vt* echar levadura a

leaving salida; ~s sobras *fpl*

Lebanese *n*+*adj* libanés *m* (-esa *f*)

Lebanon Líbano

lecher lascivo

lecherous lascivo

lechery lascivia

lectern atril *m*

lectionary leccionario

lector lector *m*

lecture *n* (talk) conferencia; (academic) clase *f*; (scolding) sermoneo; **give a** ~ dar[19] una conferencia (**on** sobre); ~-**room** sala de conferencias; (at university) clase; ~**ship** cátedra; *v* dar[19] una conferencia; (scold) sermonear

lecturer (speaker) conferenciante *m*+*f*; *SA* conferencista *m*+*f*; (academic) profesor *m* (-ora *f*) de universidad; **assistant** ~ profesor *m* (-ora *f*) auxiliar

ledge borde *m*; (shelf) anaquel *m*; (of window) antepecho

ledger libro mayor

lee *n* sotavento; *adj* de/a sotavento, sotaventado; ~ **shore** costa de sotavento; ~**way** deriva; **make** ~**way** derivar; **make up** ~**way** salir[19] del atraso

leech sanguijuela

leek puerro

leer *n* mirada con una sonrisa maligna; *v* mirar con una sonrisa maligna

lees heces *mpl*

leeward *adj* sotaventado; **to** ~ a sotavento

[1] **left** *see* **leave**; **be** ~ **over** sobrar; **be** ~ **behind** quedarse atrás; **they** ~ **me standing** me dejaron plantado; ~-**luggage office** consigna; ~-**overs** sobras *fpl*

[2] **left** *n pol* izquierdas *fpl*; *adj* izquierdo;

on/to the ~ a la izquierda; ~ **and right** (on both sides) a diestro y a siniestro, (in all directions) a derecha e izquierda; ~, **right and centre** a derecha e izquierda; ~ **back** *sp* defensa *m* izquierdo; ~ **half** *sp* medio izquierdo; ~ **turn!** ¡izquierda!; ~ **wheel!** ¡cabeza variación a la izquierda!; ~ **hand** mano izquierda; ~-**hand drive** conducción *f* a la izquierda; ~-**hand screw** tornillo zurdo; ~-**hand thread** de rosca a izquierdas; ~-**handed** zurdo; ~-**handed compliment** cumplido ambiguo; ~-**hander** (jugador) zurdo; ~-**wing** *adj pol* izquierdista, *pol* ala izquierda; ~-**winger** *pol* izquierdista *m*+*f*, *sp* extremo izquierdo

leftism izquierdismo

leftist *n*+*adj* izquierdista *m*+*f*

leftward hacia la izquierda

leg *n* (human) pierna; (of animal/furniture) pata; (support) pie *m*; (of meat/trousers) pernil *m*; (of stocking) caña; *sp* (lap, game) etapa; (cricket) la parte de un campo de cricket detrás del bateador; **pull s.o.'s** ~ tomar el pelo a uno; **be on one's last** ~s estar[19] en las últimas; ~-**hold** (wrestling) presa de pierna; ~**less** (drunk) borracho; ~-**pulling** tomadura de pelo; ~-**up** (help in climbing) pie *m*; ~ -**warmers** calientapiernas *m sing*; *v* ~ **it** ir[19] a pie

legacy legado; (inherited) herencia

legal legal; ~ **action** medidas *fpl* judiciales; **take** ~ **action** proceder judicialmente; ~ **adviser** abogado; ~ **aid** asistencia jurídica; ~ **costs** litisexpensas *fpl*; ~ **holiday** fiesta oficial; ~ **proceedings** proceso; **take** ~ **proceedings** (**against**) redactar mandamientos judiciales (contra); ~ **status** estado civil; ~ **studies** estudios *mpl* jurídicos; ~ **tender** moneda de curso legal

legality legalidad *f*

legalize legalizar[7]

legally legalmente; ~-**minded** legalista

legate legado

legatee legatario

legation legación *f*

legend leyenda; (on coin) inscripción *f*

legendary legendario

legerdemain juego de manos

legged de … piernas/patas (*see* **leg**);

three-~ table mesa de tres patas
leggings polainas *fpl*
leggy patilargo
legibility legibilidad *f*
legible legible
legion legión (-ones) *f*
legionnaire, legionary legionario
legislate legislar
legislation legislación *f*
legislative legislativo
legislator legislador *m*
legislature legislatura
legitimacy legitimidad *f*
legitimate legítimo
legitimize legitimar
leguminous leguminoso
leisure tiempo libre; ~ **moments** ratos perdidos; **be at ~** estar[19] desocupado; **I shall do it at my ~** lo haré cuando tenga tiempo
leisured desocupado; ~ **classes** clases acomodadas
leisurely *adj* pausado; *adv* despacio
leitmotif leitmotiv *m*
lemming leming *m*
lemon *n* limón (-ones) *m*; ~ **cheese/curd** conserva de limón; ~ **grove** limonar *m*; ~ **sole** especie de platija; ~ **squash** zumo de limón; ~**-squeezer** exprimidor *m*; ~ **tree** limonero; *adj* (~-coloured) de color limón; (~-flavoured) de limón
lemonade limonada; (fizzy) gaseosa (de limón)
lemur lémur *m*
lend prestar; ~ **an ear to** prestar atención a; ~ **a hand** echar una mano; **it doesn't ~ itself to** no se presta a; ~**-lease** préstamo y arriendo
lender prestador *m*; (of money) prestamista *m+f*
lending prestación *f*; ~**-library** biblioteca de préstamo
length largo; **two metres in ~** dos metros de largo; (piece) trozo, ~ **of cane** trozo de caña; (of cloth) corte *m*; (of track/road) tramo; (of wallpaper) hoja; (duration) duración *f*; *naut* eslora; (of swimming-pool) largo; **at ~** largamente; **at (great) ~** detenidamente; **by a ~** (racing) por un cuerpo; **go to any ~s** no pararse en barras; **go to the ~ of** llegar[5] al extremo de; **he will not go to such ~s** él

no llegará a tal extremo; **keep at arm's ~** guardar las distancias; **full-~** (portrait) de cuerpo entero, (film) de largo metraje; ~**ways** a lo largo
lengthen alargar[5]; (of days) crecer[14]
lengthening alargamiento; (of days) crecimiento
lengthily largamente
lengthiness largueza; (of speech) verborrea
lengthy largo; (of speech) verboso
lenience lenidad *f*
lenient indulgente
Leningrad Leningrado
lens lente *m+f*; *phot* objetivo; (of the eye) cristalino; ~ **cap/shutter** tapa/obturador *m* de objetivo; ~**man** fotógrafo
Lent Cuaresma
Lenten cuaresmal
lentil lenteja; ~ **soup** sopa de lentejas
Leonard Leonardo
leonine leonino
leopard leopardo
Leopold Leopoldo
leper leproso; ~ **colony** leprosería
lepidoptera lepidópteros *mpl*
leprechaun duende *m* irlandés
leprosy lepra
leprous leproso
lesbian lesbiana, *vulg* tortillera
lèse-majesté lesa majestad
lesion lesión (-ones) *f*
less *adj* menor; *adv* menos; ~ **than** menos que, **he eats ~ than I** él come menos que yo; (before a number) menos de, ~ **than six** menos de seis; ~ **and ~** cada vez menos; **no ~ (than)** nada menos (que); **no ~ a person than** no otro que; **grow ~** disminuir[16]
lessee arrendatario; (house) inquilino
lessen *vt* disminuir[16]; *vi* disminuirse[16]
lessening disminución *f*
lesser menor; ~ **celandine** celidonia menor; ~ **of two evils** mal *m* menor
lesson lección *f*; (Bible-reading) capítulo; (class) clase *f*; (experience that serves to warn) escarmiento; **learn one's ~** escarmentar (ie)[2a]; **give a ~** dar[19] clase, *fig* dar[19] una lección a
lessor arrendador *m*
lest para que no +*subj*
[1] **let** (rent) alquilar, **house to ~** casa para alquilar; (allow) dejar; ~**'s ... vamos a**

+*infin*; ~'s **dance** vamos a bailar; ~'s **get moving!** ¡en marcha!; ~ **alone/be** dejar en paz, (apart from) por no hablar de; ~ **well alone** dejar las cosas como están, *prov* peor es meneallo; ~ **the chance slip** perder (ie)[2b] la ocasión; ~ **the cat out of the bag** tirar de la manta; ~ **it pass** (take no notice) dejar pasar; ~ **them go!** ¡que se vayan!; ~ **fall** dejar caer; ~ **s.o. know** hacer[19] saber; ~ **fly (at)** disparar (a), *fig* (verbally) soltar (ue)[1a] insultos (a); ~ **go (of)** soltar (ue)[1a]; ~ **it be a lesson to you** que le sirva de escarmiento; ~ **o.s. be seen/heard** dejarse ver/oír; ~ **o.s. go** desahogarse, (in appearance) dejar de cuidarse

~**-down** n chasco, desilusión (-ones) f
~ **down** v bajar; (~ air out of) desinflar; *fig* (disappoint) desilusionar; ~ **down one's hair** +*fig* despeinarse

~ **in** dejar entrar; (visitor) hacer[19] pasar
~ **into** dejar entrar en; ~ **into a secret** divulgar[5] un secreto
~ **off** (gun) disparar; (free) dejar libre; (forgive) perdonar; ~ **off lightly** castigar[5] sin severidad
~ **on** admitir
~ **out** dejar salir; (see to the door) acompañar a la puerta; (free) libertar; (dressmaking) alargar[5]; ~ **the fire out** dejar apagarse el fuego; ~ **out of one's sight** soltar (ue)[1a] de la mano
~ **through** dejar pasar (por)
~**-up** n cesación f, disminución f
~ **up** v moderarse; (work less) trabajar menos

[2] **let: without** ~ **or hindrance** sin estorbo ni obstáculo

lethal (*esp* of poison) letal; ~ **weapon** arma mortífera
lethargic letárgico
lethargy letargo
letter n (of alphabet) letra; (communication) carta; *comm* escrito; **by** ~ por escrito; **to the** ~ al pie de la letra; ~ **of credit** carta de crédito; ~ **of introduction** carta de presentación; ~ **of the law** la ley estrictamente interpretada; ~**s patent** título de privilegio; ~**s** (academic) (bellas) letras *fpl*; **man of** ~**s** literato; ~**-balance** pesacartas m *sing*; ~**-bomb** carta explosiva; ~**-box** buzón m; ~**-card**

carta-tarjeta; ~**-file** carpeta; ~**-head** membrete m; ~**-opener** abrecartas m *sing*; ~**-press** impreso; ~**-rack** casillero del correo; ~**-writer** escritor de cartas; v rotular
lettering rótulo; ~**-brush** pincel m para rótulos
letting arrendamiento
lettuce lechuga
leukaemia leucemia
Levant Levante m
Levantine levantino
levee dique m; (at court) recepción f
level n (state + instrument) nivel m; *min* galería horizontal; **on a** ~ **with** +*fig* al nivel de; **be on the** ~ ser[19] sincero; **find one's** ~ situarse; ~**-crossing** paso a nivel; ~**-headed** (stable) estable; *adj* (flat) llano; *sp* igual; **dead** ~ completamente llano; ~ **with a nivel con**; *adv* a nivel; v nivelar; (be frank) ser[19] franco; (flatten) allanar; **the village was levelled to the ground** la aldea fue arrasada; **he levelled his rifle at me** me apuntó con el fusil

~ **down** rebajar al mismo nivel; igualar
~ **off** nivelarse; *aer* enderezarse[7]; (of prices) estabilizarse[14]
~ **up** levantar al mismo nivel
lever n palanca; v apalancar[4]
leverage apalancamiento, *fig* influencia
leveret lebrato
leviathan leviatán (-anes) m
levitate vt levantar por levitación; vi levantarse por levitación
levitation levitación f
levity levedad f
levy n impuesto; *mil* reclutamiento; v exigir; *mil* reclutar
lewd lascivo
lewdness lascivia
lewis hijo de francmasón
lexicographer lexicógrafo
lexicography lexicografía
lexicon léxico
liabilities obligación f; *comm* pasivo; deudas
liability (responsibility) responsabilidad f; (risk) riesgo, *fam* desventaja; (insurance) suma asegurada; (tendency) propensión f
liable (responsible) responsable (**for** de); (risking) expuesto (**to** a); (likely) propenso (**to** a)

liaise enlazar[7]

liaison coordinación *f;·phon* enlace *m*; (relationship) relaciones *fpl*; (love-affair) amorío; ~ **officer** oficial *m* de coordinación

liar mentiroso

libation libación (-ones) *f*

libel *n* libelo (**on/against** contra); *v* difamar

libellous difamatorio

liberal *n* liberal *m+f; adj* tolerante; *pol* liberal; (abundant) generoso

liberalism liberalismo

liberality *pol* liberalidad f; (abundance) generosidad *f*

liberalize liberalizar[7]

liberate liberar; (energy) descargar[5]; (gas *etc*) dejar escapar

liberation liberación *f*, (of energy) descargo; (of gases *etc*) escape *m*; **National Liberation Front** Frente *m* de Liberación Nacional

liberator libertador *m* (-ora *f*)

Liberia Liberia

Liberian liberiano

libertinage libertinaje *m*

libertine libertino

liberty libertad *f*; **be at** ~ estar[19] en libertad; **be at** ~ **to** tener[19] derecho a +*infin*; **set at** ~ poner[19] en libertad; **take liberties with** tomar(se) libertades con; **may I take the** ~ **of saying** ...? ¿me permite usted decir ...?; **civil liberties** derechos *mpl* civiles; ~ **horse** caballo de circo

libidinous libidinoso

libido líbido

librarian bibliotecario

library biblioteca; (private) librería

librettist libretista *m+f; fam* letrista

libretto libreto

licence (permission) permiso; (*esp* document) licencia; (concession) concesión *f; mot* (driving-~) carnet *m* de conducir; (freedom) licencia; ~**-plate** matrícula

license autorizar[7]; *mot* matricular; ~**d house** taberna o tienda en donde se permite la venta de bebidas alcohólicas

licensee concesionario

licentiate licenciado

licentious licencioso; *fam* crapuloso

lichen liquen (líquenes) *m*

lichgate puerta de cementerio

lick *n* lamedura; ~**spittle** pelotillero, *fam* lameculos *m sing*; *v* lamer; *sl* (hit) cascar[4]; ~ **one's lips** pasar la lengua por los labios, relamerse, (in anticipation of food) chuparse los dedos; ~ **into shape** adiestrar; ~ **s.o.'s boots** adular servilmente a alguien, *vulg* lamer el culo a alguien; *sl* dar[19] coba

licking lamedura; *sl* (beating) zurra

licorice regaliz *m*

lid (of container) tapa(dera); *anat* párpado; *sl* (hat) techo; **that's put the** ~ **on it** eso es el colmo

lido piscina pública al aire libre

[1] **lie** *n* (untruth) mentira; *fam* filfa; *Arg* macana; **big** ~ mentira gorda; **white** ~ mentirilla piadosa; **it's a** ~! ¡cuento!; **tell a** ~ mentir (ie)[2c]; **give the** ~ **to** desmentir (ie)[2c]; ~**-detector** detector *m* de mentiras; *v* mentir (ie)[2c]; ~ **one's way out of** escaparse con mentiras

[2] **lie** *n* disposición *f*; ~ **of the land** configuración *f* del terreno, *fig* estado de las cosas; (golf) posición *f* de la pelota; *v* (be recumbent) estar[19] echado; (be situated) estar[19] situado; (be buried) yacer[14]; **here's...** aquí descansa...; ~ **fallow** estar[19] en barbecho; ~ **at the heart of/root of** estar[19] en el fondo de; ~ **heavy on** pesar mucho sobre; ~ **low** esconderse; ~ **idle** estar[19] parado

~ **about** (scattered) estar[19] esparcido; *fam* (of a person) gandulear

~ **alongside** *naut* atracar[4]

~ **at anchor** estar[19] anclado

~ **back** recostarse (ue)[1a]

~ **down** acostarse (ue)[1a]; ~ **down!** (to a dog) ¡échate!; **take it lying down** soportarlo sin protestar

~ **in** levantarse tarde; ~ **in state** estar[19] en capilla; ~ **in wait for** acechar; **it** ~**s in your power** depende de usted

~ **over** (wait) aplazarse[7]; *comm* caducar[4]

~ **to** *naut* estar[19] al pairo

~ **up** descansar

~ **with** dormir (ue)[1c] con; **it** ~**s with you** la responsabilidad recae sobre usted

lief: I would ~ preferiría +*infin*

liege feudatario; ~**man** vasallo; ~ **lord** señor *m* feudal

Liège Lieja

lien derecho de retención

lieutenant *mil* teniente *m*; (naval) teniente de fragata; **~-colonel** teniente *m* coronel; **~-commander** teniente *m* de corbeta; **~-general** teniente *m* general; **sub-~**, **second-~** alférez *m*, (naval) alférez de navío

life vida; (liveliness) animación *f*; (period of usefulness) vigencia; **~ to come** vida después de la muerte; **come to ~** empezar (ie)[2a+7] a vivir; **depart this ~** partir de esta vida; **risk one's ~, take one's ~ into one's hands** jugarse (uc)[1a] la vida; **lay down one's ~ (for)** entregar[5] la vida (por); **take one's ~** suicidarse; **(matter of) ~ and death** (cuestión *f* de) vida o muerte; **for ~** por toda la vida; **for the ~ of me** aunque me maten; **for dear ~** para salvar la vida; **she is the ~ and soul of the party** ella es el alma de la fiesta; **see ~** ver[19] mundo; **this is the ~!** ¡esto es jauja!; **not on your ~!** ¡ni pensar!; **from ~** *arts* del natural; **~ annuity/pension** renta/pensión vitalicia; **~-belt** cinturón (-ones) *m* salvavidas; **~-blood** sangre *f*, *fig* nervio; **~boat** lancha de socorro; **~-buoy** boya salvavidas; **~ expectancy** índice *m* de vida; **~-giving** que da vida; **~-guard** socorrista *m+f*; **~ insurance** seguro de vida; **~ insurance company** compañía de seguro(s) de vida; **~ interest** usufructo vitalicio (**in en**); **~-jacket** chaleco salvavidas; **~-like** (hecho al) natural; **~-line** cuerda salvavidas, (diver's) cuerda de señales, (palmistry) línea de la vida; **~-long** de toda la vida; **~-preserver** cachiporra; **~-raft** balsa salvavidas; **~-saving** *n* salvamento, *adj* salvavidas; **~-sentence** cadena perpetua; **you deserve a ~ sentence** usted merece cadena perpetua; **~-size** de tamaño natural; **~time** transcurso de la vida; **for a ~-time** para toda la vida; **~ work** trabajo de la vida

lifeless sin vida; *fig* desanimado

lifelessness falta de vida; *fig* desanimación *f*

lift (elevator for people) ascensor *m*; (elevator for goods) montacargas *m sing+pl*; *aer+phys* fuerza ascensional; *mech* altura de elevación; (stimulus) estímulo; (help) ayuda; (in car) viaje *m* en coche ajeno, **can I give you a ~ anywhere?** ¿puedo dejarle en alguna parte?; **~-boy**, **~-girl** ascensorista *m+f*; **~-shaft** hueco del ascensor, *v* (raise) levantar; (pick up) coger[8]; *aer* transportar en avión; (remove) suprimir; **they ~ed the restrictions** suprimieron las restricciones; *sl* (steal) chorar; **~ one's hat** quitarse el sombrero; **I wouldn't ~ a finger to** no haría ningún esfuerzo por +*infin*; **the fog will ~ soon** pronto se disipará la niebla

~ down bajar

~-off *n space* despegue *m*

~ off/up *v* (raise) levantar; **she tried to ~ up the child** ella intentó levantar en brazos al niño

lifting levantamiento

ligament ligamento

ligature *mus+surg* ligadura

¹ **light** *n* luz *f*; (lamp) lámpara; *mot* faro; (window) ventana; (for cigarette) fuego, **give me a ~** deme fuego/*sl* candela, **~s** *theat* luces *fpl*; **upper ~s** *theat* diabla; **against the ~** al trasluz; **at first ~** al rayar el día; **in the ~ of** *fig* a la luz de; **put a ~ to** encender (ie)[2b]; **according to his ~s** según Dios le da a entender; **bring to ~** sacar[4] a luz; **come to ~** descubrirse (*past part* descubierto); **shed/cast ~ on** aclarar; **see the ~** caer[19] en la cuenta, *eccles* convertirse (i)[3]; **~-buoy** boya luminosa; **~-bulb** bombilla; **~-fitting** guarnición (-ones) *f* del alumbrado; **~-house** faro; **~-house keeper** torrero; **~-meter** fotómetro; **~-ship** buque *m* faro; **~-switch** interruptor *m* (de la luz); **~-wave** onda luminosa; **~-year** año de luz; *vt* **~ (up)** encender (ie)[2b]; (illuminate) iluminar; *vi* **~ (up)** encender(se) (ie)[2b]; **her face lit up** su cara se iluminó

² **light** (colour) *adj* claro (of hair, beer, tobacco, wood) rubio; (of complexion) blanco

³ **light** (not heavy) ligero; (slight) leve; *naut* en lastre; **travel ~** viajar con poco equipaje, (truck) ir[19] vacío; **~ aircraft** avioneta; **~ alloy** metal ligero; **~ opera** opereta, *Sp* zarzuela; **make ~ of** no dar[19] importancia a; **~ reading** lectura de entretenimiento; **~-fingered** largo de uñas; **~-footed**

ligero de pies; **~-headed** (dizzy) mareado, (frivolous) casquivano; **~-hearted** alegre; **~weight** ligero, (boxing) de peso ligero; *v* ~ **upon** dar[19] con, (of bird) posarse en

[1] **lighten** iluminar(se); (lightning) relampaguear

[2] **lighten** (in weight) aligerar; (emotions) alegrar(se)

lighter (cigarette-~) encendedor *m*; *naut* gabarra; **~man** gabarrero

lighting *+theat* luminotecnia; (of a scene) iluminación *f*; ~ **arrangements** disposición *f* de iluminación; **~-up time** hora de encender los faros

[1] **lightness** claridad *f*; (luminosity) luminosidad *f*

[2] **lightness** (lack of weight) ligereza; (slightness) levedad *f*

lightning relámpago; **at** ~ **speed** como una flecha; **~-bug** luciérnaga; **~-conductor** pararrayos *m sing*; **~-flash** relampagueo; **~-strike** huelga relámpago

lights (offal) bofes *mpl*

ligneous leñoso

lignite lignito

[1] **like** *n* (similar) semejante *m+f*; **and the** ~ y otro(s) por el estilo; **I've never seen the** ~ **of it** nunca' he visto cosa igual; **the ~s of him** otros como él; *adj* (similar) parecido (a); (characteristic of) típico de; (equivalent) equivalente; **a car** ~ **mine** un coche como el mío; **teeth** ~ **pearls** dientes *mpl* como perlas; **it's not** ~ **Mary to do that** no es propio de María hacer eso; **that's just** ~ **her** así es ella; **so it's** ~ **that, is it?** así andamos, ¿eh?; ~ **father** ~ **son** de tal palo tal astilla; **in** ~ **cases** en casos parecidos; **in** ~ **manner** de la misma manera; **be** ~ (resemble) parecerse[14] a; **it looks** ~ **rain** parece que va a llover; **there's nothing** ~ **a good meal** no hay nada como una buena comida; **what does it look** ~? ¿cómo es?; **I feel** ~ tengo ganas de *+infin*; **~-minded** teniendo los mismos gustos e ideas; *adv* como; (in the same way as) lo mismo que; (just ~) así como

[2] **like** *n*: **~s and dislikes** gustos *mpl* y aversiones *fpl*; (fads) caprichos *mpl*; *v* gustarle a uno, **I** ~ **oranges** me gustan las naranjas; (be an enthusiast for) ser[19] aficionado a, **he ~s fishing** él es aficionado a la pesca; (be fond of a person) querer[19], **I** ~ **her very much** la quiero mucho; (wish) querer[19], **I'll give you what you** ~ le daré a usted lo que quiera; **I** ~ **the look of this** esto tiene buen aspecto; **I should** ~ **to ...** quisiera *+infin*; **if you** ~ si le parece; **how do you** ~ **my kitchen?** ¿qué le parece mi cocina[2]

likeable simpático; (in appearance) atractivo

likelihood probabilidad *f*

likely probable; **be** ~ **to** ser[19] probable que *+subj*; **you are** ~ **to see her tomorrow** es probable que la vea usted mañana; **that's a** ~ **story!** ¡vaya cuento (más improbable)!

liken comparar (**to** con)

likeness (similarity) semejanza; (portrait) retrato

likewise de la misma manera

liking (*see* [2]**like**) gusto (**for** de); afición *f* (**for** por); **to one's** ~ al gusto de uno; **have a** ~ **for** ser[19] aficionado a; **take a** ~ **to** (people) tomar cariño a, (things) aficionarse a

lilac lila; (colour) (de) color lila

Lilliputian liliputiense *m+f*

lilt (melody) canción (-ones) *f* con ritmo marcado; (accent) acento

lily lirio; **Madonna** ~ azucena; ~ **of the valley** muguete *m*; **~-livered** gallina, *vulg* cagado; **~-white** blanco como la nieve

Lima: ~ **bean** haba

limb *anat* miembro; (of tree) rama; **be out on a** ~ estar[19] en un atolladero

limber *adj* flexible; *v* ~ **up** hacer ejercicios de precalentamiento

[1] **limbo** limbo; **be in** ~ estar[19] en el limbo

[2] **limbo: ~-dancer** bailador acrobático de las Antillas

[1] **lime** *n chem* cal *f*; (for catching birds) liga; **~-kiln** calera; **~-light** luz *f* de calcio, *theat* luz *f* del proyector, *fig* primer plano; **she likes to be in the ~-light** le gusta a ella figurar; **~-stone** caliza; *v agri* abonar con cal; (to catch birds) untar con liga

[2] **lime** (citrus tree) limero; (fruit) lima; **~-juice** zumo de lima

[3] **lime** (linden tree) tilo

limerick especie *f* de quintilla humorística

Limey inglés *m* (-esa *f*)

limit *n* +*fig* límite *m*; (restriction) restricción *f*; **you are the ~!** ¡usted es el colmo!; **this is the ~!** ¡no faltaba más!; **know no ~s** ser[19] infinito; **to the ~** hasta no más; *v* limitar; (restrict) restringir[9]; **to a ~ed extent** hasta cierto punto; **he is a very ~ed person** él es una persona con muchas limitaciones; **~ed liability** responsabilidad limitada; **~ed company** sociedad anónima

limitation limitación (-ones) *f*; **know one's ~s** reconocer[14] sus faltas

limousine limusina

limp *n* cojera; **have a ~** cojear; *adj* (not stiff) flojo; (of person) débil; (of hair) lacio; (of binding) de tapa blanda; *v* cojear; *Arg* renguear; **~ down/up** bajar/subir cojeando

limpet lapa

limpid cristalino

limping *n* cojera; *adj* cojo

limpness (not stiff) flojedad *f*; (of person) debilidad *f*; (of hair) laciedad *f*

linchpin pezonera

linctus jarabe *m*

linden tilo

[1] **line** +*tel* línea; **cross the ~** (Equator) pasar la línea, (railway) cruzar[7] la vía; (string) cuerda; (fishing) sedal *m*; (wrinkle) arruga; *print* renglón (-ones) *m*; (railway, tram *etc*) vía; (route) línea, **air~** línea aérea; (row of houses *etc*) hilera; (row of soldiers) fila; (queue) cola, **form a ~** hacer[19] cola; *comm* (of business) ramo, (of goods) género; *sp* (touch-~) banda, (finishing-~) línea de llegada, (serving-~) línea de saque, (starting-~) línea de salida; *poet* verso; (short letter) cuatro líneas, *fam* unas letras; (boundary) raya; (profession) oficio; (speciality) especialidad *f*; (lineage) linaje *m*, **in a direct ~** (of descent) en línea recta; **~ of life** línea de la vida; **all along the ~** por todas partes; **along/on the ~s of** conforme a; **draw the ~** (at) no pasar más allá (de); **fall into ~** (with) conformarse (con); **toe the ~** obedecer[14] órdenes; **follow/obey the party ~** seguir[3+10] la línea del partido;

front ~ *mil* frente *m*; **get a ~ on s.o.** descubrir (*past part* descubierto) un secreto sobre alguien; **hard ~s!** ¡mala suerte!; **hold the ~!** *tel* ¡no cuelgue usted!; **in a straight ~** en línea recta; **in ~ with** (in agreement with) de acuerdo con; **on the ~s of** conforme a; **on the right ~s** por buen camino; **read between the ~s** leer[17] entre líneas; **ship of the ~** barco de línea; **shoot a ~** fanfarronear; **soldier of the ~** soldado de línea; **he took an aggressive ~** él adoptó una actitud agresiva; **~-drawing** dibujo de líneas; **~-shooter** fanfarrón *m* (-ona *f*); **~sman** (railway) reparador *m* de la vía, *sp* juez *m* de línea, *SA* abanderado; *v* **~ up** formar fila, (queue) hacer[19] cola; **~-up** alineación *f*; **~ the streets** congregarse[5] a lo largo de las calles; **~d** (wrinkled) arrugado, (of paper) rayado

[2] **line** (clothing) forrar; *mech* revestir (i)[3]; (brakes) guarnecer[14]

lineage linaje *m*

lineal lineal

lineament facción *f* (del rostro)

linear lineal; *bot*+*zool* linear; **~ equation** ecuación (-ones) *f* de primer grado; **~ measure** medida de longitud

linen lino; (piece of ~) lienzo; (sheets, underclothing *etc*) ropa blanca; **soiled ~** ropa sucia; **~-cupboard** armario para la ropa

liner transatlántico

[1] **ling** *bot* brezo

[2] **ling** (fish) especie *f* de abadejo

linger (delay departure) tardar en marcharse; (continue to live) tardar en morir; (be slow to disappear) persistir; **~ over** hacer[19] despacio; **~ over a meal** comer/cenar *etc* despacio

lingerie ropa interior de mujer

lingering prolongado; (of illness, smell *etc*) persistente

lingo lengua; (specialized language) jerga

lingua franca lengua franca

linguist lingüista *m*+*f*

linguistic lingüístico; **~s** lingüística

liniment linimento

lining (of clothes) forro; (of brakes) guarnición *f*; *mech* revestimiento

link *n* (of chain) eslabón (-ones) *m*; *fig*

enlace *m*; (*esp* with the past) vínculo; (of beads) sarta; *mech* varilla; *rad* enlace *m*; (**golf**) ~s campo de golf; *v* ~ (**up**) eslabonar(se); ~**-up space** *n* empalme *m*; ~ **up** *v* space empalmar; ~ **arms** cogerse[14] del brazo

linkage (of chain) eslabonamiento; *fig* enlace *m*; *mech* varillaje *m*

linnet pardillo común

linoleum linóleo

Linotype linotipia; (strip of type) linotipo; ~ **operator** linotipista *m*

linseed linaza; ~ **cake** bagazo; ~**-oil** aceite *m* de linaza

lint hilas *fpl*

lintel dintel *m*

lion león *m*; ~'s **den** leonera; ~**-hearted** valiente; ~**-tamer** domador *m* (-ora *f*) de leones; ~'s **share** mayor parte *f*

lioness leona

lionize tratar como una celebridad

lip labio; (of jug) pico; (of cup) borde *m*; *fig* insolencia; ~**-read** interpretar el movimiento de los labios; ~**-reading** labiolectura; ~**-service** jarabe *m* de pico; ~**stick** lápiz *m* labial

liquefaction licuefacción *f*

liquefy licuar(se); (of butter, metals *etc*) derretirse (i)[3]

liqueur licor *m*; ~ **glass** copita

liquid *n* líquido; ~ **air** aire *m* líquido; ~ **assets** valores *mpl* realizables; ~ **measure** medida para líquidos; *adj* líquido

liquidate *comm+mil+pol* liquidar

liquidation *comm+mil+pol* liquidación *f*; **go into** ~ liquidarse

liquor bebida alcohólica; ~**-store** tienda de vinos y licores

liquorice regaliz *m*

Lisbon Lisboa

lisle hilo de Escocia

lisp *n* ceceo; (childish way of talking) balbuceo; *v* cecear; balbucear

lissom ágil

list *n* lista; *esp comm* catálogo; (register) lista; *naut* escora; (tournament) liza; ~**-price** precio de catálogo; *v* (make a list) catalogar[5]; (put on a list) poner[19] en una lista; *naut* escorar; **enter the** ~**s** entrar en liza; ~**ed** *comm* cotizado; ~**ed securities** valores *mpl* cotizables

listen (to) escuchar; (obey) atender (ie)[2b] (a); ~ **for** escuchar; ~ **in (to the**

radio) escuchar (la radio); ~ **to reason** atender a razones

listener oyente *m+f*; *rad* radioyente *m+f*

listening-post escucha

listless apático

listlessness apatía

litany letanía

literacy capacidad *f* de leer y escribir; ~ **campaign** campaña de alfabetización

literal literal

literally: take ~ tomar al pie de la letra

literary literario

literate, literate person literato

literati literatos *mpl*

literature literatura; (pamphlets) impresos *mpl*; *comm+pol* propaganda

lithe ágil

lithograph *n* litografía; *v* litografiar

lithographer litógrafo

lithographic litográfico

lithography litografía

Lithuania Lituania

Lithuanian *n+adj* lituano

litigant *n+adj* litigante *m+f*

litigate litigar[5]

litigation litigio

litigious litigioso

litmus (paper) (papel *m* de) tornasol *m*

litre litro

litter (rubbish) basura; (carrier) litera; (animal's bedding) lecho/paja; (brood) camada; ~**-bug**, ~**-lout** uno que tira basura en lugares públicos; ~**-basket**, ~**-bin** papelera; cubo de la basura; *v* (leave in an untidy state) dejar en desorden; (throw away rubbish) tirar basura; (provide bedding) dar[19] paja; (give birth) parir; ~**ed with** sucio de, **the room was** ~**ed with paper** la habitación estaba sucia de papeles

little *n* poco; **very** ~ poquito; ~ **by** ~ poco a poco; **the** ~ **I know** lo poco que sé; ~ **he knows!** ¡maldito lo que él sabe!; **make** ~ **of** sacar[4] poco provecho de; **think** ~ **of** tener[19] mal concepto de; **not a** ~ no poco; *adj* pequeño; (mean) mezquino; **for a** ~ **while** por un rat(it)o; **I'll go a** ~ **way with you** le acompañaré un poco; **he has no** ~ **influence** él no tiene poca influencia; **I adore her** ~ **ways** adoro sus cositas; **Little Bear** *astron* Osa

Menor; ~ **finger** dedo meñique; ~ **one** (child) chiquillo; ~ **owl** mochuelo; ~ **people** (fairies) hadas *fpl*; **Little Red Riding Hood** Caperucita Roja; *adv* poco; **he is a ~ worse today** él está un poco peor hoy; **I was not a ~ drunk** yo estaba muy borracho

littleness pequeñez *f*; (meanness) mezquindad *f*

littoral litoral *m*

liturgic(al) litúrgico

liturgy liturgia

live *adj* vivo; *elect* con corriente, ~ **rail** raíl con corriente; **this is a ~ issue** ésto es un asunto de actualidad; ~ **bait** pez vivo; ~ **bomb** bomba sin explotar; ~ **coal** ascua; ~ **programme** *rad+TV* programa *m* en directo; ~ **weight** peso en vivo; ~ **wire** alambre *m* con corriente, cargado, (person) polvorilla; ~**stock** ganado; *v* vivir; **how long have you ~d there?** ¿cuánto tiempo lleva usted viviendo allí?; ~ **and learn** vivir para ver; ~ **and let** vivir y dejar vivir; **long ~ …!** ¡viva …!; ~ **well** darse[19] buena vida; ~ **one's life** pasar (toda) la vida; **I ~d the part** me identifiqué con mi papel; ~**long** todo, **the ~long day** todo el santo día

~ **again** volver (ue)[1b] (*past part* vuelto) a vivir

~ **at** vivir en; **they ~ at number ten** ellos viven en el número diez

~ **beyond:** ~ **beyond one's income** gastar más de lo que uno gana

~ **by** vivir de; ~ **by one's wits** vivir del cuento

~ **down** lograr borrar

~ **for** vivir por; **she ~s only for her children** ella vive solamente por sus hijos

~ **in** habitar; (as an inmate) estar[19] interno; ~ **in sin** (with) vivir amancebado (con)

~ **off** vivir de

~ **on** vivir de; **have enough to ~ on** tener[19] de qué vivir; (continue living) seguir (i)[3+11] viviendo

~ **out:** ~ **out one's life** pasar el resto de la vida

~ **to** vivir para; ~ **to see** (the day when) vivir bastante para ver; ~ **to tell the tale** vivir para contarlo

~ **together** convivir

~ **up:** ~ **up to expectations** cumplir con

lo prometido; ~ **up to one's income** vivir al día; ~ **up to one's position** vivir en conformidad con su posición; ~ **it up** *sl* pulir en verde

~ **within:** ~ **within one's means** vivir con arreglo a los ingresos

livelihood sustento; **make a ~** ganarse la vida

liveliness viveza

lively (of people) vivo; (*esp* of streets *etc*) animado; (fast) rápido, ~ **pace** paso rápido; (of colours) brillante

[1] **liver** *anat* hígado; ~ **complaint** mal *m* de hígado

[1] **liver** (person) vividor *m* (-ora *f*); **fast ~** calavera

livery librea; ~ **company** gremio de la ciudad de Londres; ~**man** criado de librea; ~ **stables** cochería de alquiler

livid lívido; **be ~** estar[19] negro

living *n* vida; **earn one's ~** ganarse la vida/*fam* el cocido; *eccles* beneficio (eclesiástico); **the ~** los vivientes; ~**conditions** condiciones *fpl* de vida; ~**quarters** alojamiento *f*; ~**room** cuarto de estar, *US* sala: ~**space** espacio vital; ~ **wage** sueldo mínimo; *adj* vivo; **he is still ~** él vive aún; ~ **image of** vivo retrato de; **in ~ memory** que se recuerda; ~ **soul** ser *m* viviente, *fam* bicho viviente

lizard lagarto; (small) lagartija

llama llama

LL.D (Doctor of Laws) Doctor en Derecho

load *n* carga; ~ **of manure** carretada de estiércol; *elect* corriente suministrada en un tiempo dado; *mech* resistencia; ~**s of** *fam* gran cantidad *f* de; **you're talking a ~ of rubbish** estás hablando sandeces; ~**capacity** capacidad *f* de carga; ~**line** línea de flotación; ~**shedding** distribución equitativa de corriente; *vt* cargar[5]; (burden) agobiar (with con/de); ~ **favours on s.o.** colmar a alguien de favores; ~**ed dice** dados cargados; ~**ed question** pregunta intencionada; *vi* ~ **up** tomar carga

loader cargador *m*

loading operación *f* de carga; ~**-bay,** ~**-ramp** rampa de carga; ~**-wharf** muelle *m* de carga; ~**-yard** (railway) cargadero

loadstone imán *m*

loaf *n* pan *m*; (small) panecillo; (long) barr(it)a de pan; ~ **sugar** azúcar *m* en pilón; *v* gandulear

loafer gandul *m* (-ula *f*)

loam *n* marga; *v* poner[19] marga

loan *n* préstamo; *comm* empréstito; **government** ~ empréstito gubernamental; **be on** ~ **to** estar[19] en préstamo a; **have on** ~ tener[19] prestado; **I'll ask for the** ~ **of his car** pediré prestado su coche; ~**-word** extranjerismo; *v* prestar

loath poco dispuesto (to a); **nothing** ~ de buena gana

loathe detestar; **she** ~**s me** me odia

loathing asco

loathingly con asco

loathsome asqueroso

lob *n sp* voleo alto; ~**scouse** cocido de carne y patatas; ~**worm** lombriz *m* para pescar; *v sp* volear en alto

lobate lobulado

lobby *n* (passage) pasillo; (anteroom) antesala; *pol* grupo de presión; *v pol* ejercer presión; cabildear

lobbying presión *f*, cabildeo

lobbyist cabildero

lobe +*anat* lóbulo; *fam anat* perilla; ~**d** lobulado

lobelia lobelia

lobotomy lobotomía

lobster langosta; ~**-pot** trampa de mimbre para coger langostas

lobule lóbulo

local *n* (pub) tasca; **the** ~**s** (people) el vecindario; *adj* local; (of anaesthetic) externo; **I'm a** ~ **man** soy de aquí; ~ **authorities** ayuntamientos *mpl*; ~ **call** (telephone) llamada urbana; ~ **colour** color *m* local; ~ **government** administración *f* local; ~ **option** derecho de un distrito a establecer sus propios estatutos; ~ **produce** productos *mpl* de la región; ~ **tax** contribución *f*; ~ **train** tren *m* suburbano

locale local *m*

locality localidad *f*

localization localización *f*

localize localizar[7]

locate (put) colocar[4]; (find) hallar; **be** ~**d** hallarse

location situación *f*; *cin* exteriores, **on** ~ en rodaje fuera del estudio

locative locativo

[1] **lock** *n* cerradura; (of firearm) cerrojo; *mech* (stoppage) bloqueo; *mot* ángulo de giro; (of canal) esclusa; (wrestling) presa; **under** ~ **and key** bajo llave; ~, **stock and barrel** por completo; ~**-gate** compuerta (de esclusa); ~**-jaw** tétano; ~**-keeper** esclusero; ~**-nut** contratuerca; ~**smith** cerrajero; ~**smith's** cerrajería; ~**-stitch** punto de cadeneta; *v* cerrar (ie)[2a] con llave; *mech* bloquear

~ **in** encerrar (ie)[2a]

~**-out** *n* cierre *m* patronal

~ **out** *v* dejar en la calle; (industry) cerrar (ie)[2a] una fábrica (los dueños)

~ **together** enlazar[7]

~**-up** *n* cárcel *f*, *sl* jaula; ~**-up garage** garaje *m* particular

~ **up** *v* encerrar (ie)[2a] con llave; (at night) cerrar (ie)[2a] las puertas y ventanas; (imprison) encarcelar, *sl* enjaular

[2] **lock** (of hair) mechón *m*; (ringlet) bucle *m*; ~**s** cabellos *mpl*

lockable con cierre

locker armario; (small) cajón (-ones) *m* con cerradura; *naut* cajonada

locket guardapelo

locking cierre *m*; ~ **device/mechanism** trinquete *m*

locomotion locomoción *f*

locomotive *n* locomotora; *adj* locomotor

locomotor: ~ **ataxy** ataxia locomotriz

locum interino, *med* médico suplente

locus lugar *m*

locust *ent* langosta; (bean) algarroba; ~ **tree** algarrobo

locution locución *f*

lode filón *m*; ~**star** norte *m*; ~**stone** imán *m*

lodge *n* (porter's) portería; (hunting) pabellón (-ones) *m*; (masonic) logia; *vt* alojar; *vi* alojarse; (remain stuck) quedar cogido; ~ **a complaint** presentar una queja

lodger huésped *m* (-eda *f*)

lodging(s) alojamiento; ~**-house** casa de huéspedes

loft desván *m*; (for hay *etc*) pajar *m*; *eccles* galería

loftiness (height) altura; *fig* dignidad *f*; (haughtiness) altanería

lofty alto; *fig* eminente; (haughty)

altanero

log leño; *naut* diario de navegación; *aer* libro de vuelo; **sleep like a** ~ dormir (ue)[1c] como un lirón; ~ **boom/jam** apiñadura de troncos; ~**-cabin** caney *m*; ~**-line** corredera; *v* apuntar en el diario de navegación/en el libro de vuelo

loganberry especie *f* de zarzamora

logarithm logaritmo

logarithmic logarítmico

logger maderero

loggerheads: be at ~ estar[19] (siempre) disputando (**with** con)

loggia galería

logging corte *m* y transporte *m* de troncos

logic lógica

logical lógico

logician lógico

logistic logístico; ~**s** logística

loin ijada; ~**-cloth** taparrabo

loiter vagar[5]

loiterer vago

loll recostarse(ue)[1a] (**against** en); ~ **out** (of tongue) colgar (ue)[1a+5] hacia fuera; ~ **about** repantigarse[5]

lolly, lollipop (sweet) *tr sl* chuchapú; (ice-cream) polo; *sl* (money) pasta

Lombardy Lombardía; ~ **poplar** chopo lombardo

London *n* Londres *m*; *adj* londinense

Londoner londinense *m*+*f*

lone solitario; ~ **wolf** (persona) solitaria

loneliness soledad *f*

lonely sol(itari)o

lonesome solo y triste

[1] **long** *n* mucho tiempo; (**not**) **for** ~ (no) mucho tiempo; **before** ~ dentro de poco; **the** ~ **and short of it is that** en su esencia; *adj* largo; **it is three metres** ~ tiene tres metros de largo; (of grass) alto; **as** ~ **as** tan largo como; **be a** ~ **way off** estar[19] lejos; **in the** ~ **run** a la larga; **of** ~ **standing** desde hace mucho tiempo; **a** ~ **time** (**ago**) hace mucho tiempo; ~ **barrow** *arch* dolmen (dólmenes) *m*; ~**boat** falúa; ~**bow** arco; ~**-distance** bus coche *m* de línea; ~**-distance call** (telephone) conferencia; ~**-distance race** carrera de fondo; ~ **division** división *f* en que se escriben los productos parciales; ~**-eared** de orejas largas; ~**-faced** carilarga; ~**-haired** dc/con cl pclo largo; ~**-hand** escritura normal; ~**-headed** *fig* astuto; ~ **johns** calzoncillos *mpl* largos; ~ **jump** salto dc longitud; ~**-life milk** leche *f* larga vida; ~**-lived** longevo; ~**-lost** perdido hace mucho tiempo; ~ **odds** pocas probabilidades *fpl*; **it is** ~ **odds that** hay pocas probabilidades dc quc +*subj*; ~**-playing record** disco dc larga duración; ~**-range** dc largo alcancc; **at** ~ **range** a larga distancia; ~**shoreman** estibador *m*; ~ **sight** presbicia; ~**-sighted** présbita, *fig* previsor; ~**-sleeve(d)** (dc) manga larga; ~**-standing** viejo; ~ **stride** zancada; ~**-suffering** sufrido; ~**-tailed** dc cola larga; ~**-term** a largo plazo; ~ **trousers** pantalón (-oncs) *m* (largo(s)); ~ **vacation** vacacioncs *fpl* (*esp* universitarias) dc verano; ~**-wave** *rad* dc onda larga; ~**ways** a lo largo; ~**-winded** gárrulo; *adv* mucho tiempo; **will you be here** ~? ¿cstará ustcd aquí mucho ticmpo?; **as** ~ **as** micntras quc +*subj*; ~ **ago** hacc mucho (ticmpo); **not** ~ **ago** hacc poco; **as** ~ **ago as 1800** ya cn 1800; ~ **before** mucho antcs; ~ **since** desde hacc mucho ticmpo; **not** ~ **since** desde hacc poco; **how** ~ **is it since …?** ¿cuánto ticmpo hacc quc no …?; **be** ~ **in** tardar cn +*infin*; **so** ~! ¡hasta lucgo!; ~**-forgotten** olvidado hacc mucho ticmpo

[2] **long:** ~ **for** anhclar; ~**ed-for** anhclado

longevity longevidad *f*

longing anhclo

longish bastante largo

longitude longitud *f*

longitudinal longitudinal

loo servicio

loofah esponja vcgetal

look *n* mirada; **take a** ~ **at** lanzar[7] una mirada a; (glance) vistazo, **take a** (**quick**) ~ (**at**) echar un vistazo (a); (appearance) aspecto; **good** ~**s** bucn parecer *m*; **I like the** ~ **of them** mc hacen buena imprcsión; *v* mirar; (seem) parcccr[14], **she** ~**s tired** clla parece cansada; ~ **like** tcncr[19] pinta de, **they** ~ **like ruffians** ticncn pinta de gamberros; **it** ~**s like rain** parccc quc va a llover; **it** ~**s as though he's not coming** parece quc no vicnc; **it just**

doesn't ~ right to me no queda bien a mi parecer; **you ~ lovely today** estás preciosa hoy; **it ~s well on you** le sienta bien a usted; **~ alive** parecer[14] vivo, *fig* darse[19] prisa; **~ before you leap** *prov* antes que te cases, mira lo que haces; **~ daggers** echar chispas; **~ daggers at** mirar echando chispas; **~ here!** ¡oye!; **~ hopeful** prometer bien; **~ sharp** darse[19] prisa; **~-see** mirada rápida

~ about mirar alrededor; **~ about one** mirar a su alrededor, *fig* considerar las cosas; **~ about for** ir[19] buscando

~ after cuidar de; **~ after number one** arrimar el ascua a su sardina

~ at mirar; (consider) considerar

~ away apartar la vista (**from** de)

~ back mirar hacia atrás; (in time) pensar (ie)[2a] en lo pasado; **after moving to Canada he never looked back** después de trasladarse al Canadá jamás se volvió atrás

~ down mirar hacia abajo; **~ down on** despreciar; **the mountains ~ down on the plain** las montañas dominan la llanura

~ for buscar; **~ for what isn't there** buscarle[4] cinco pies al gato; (hope for) esperar; **~ed for** esperado

~ forward to esperar (con ilusión)

~-in *n*: **not get a ~-in** no poder[19] intervenir, *fam* no poder[19] meter baza

~ in *v* mirar dentro de; (visit) visitar; *TV* ver[19] la televisión; **~ s.o. in the face** mirar a alguien cara a cara

~ into mirar adentro; (investigate) investigar[5]

~ on (as spectator) estar[19] de mirón; (consider) considerar; **~ on the dark side** ser[19] pesimista *m+f*

~ onto dar[19] a

~-out *n* (watch) vigilancia; (person) centinela, *sl* ojo; (place) puesto de observación; *fig* (prospect) perspectiva; **it's a poor ~-out ...** lástima si no ...; **keep a careful ~-out** estar[19] ojo avisor; **that's his/their ~-out** allá él/ellos; **~ out** *v* (watch) vigilar; (seek) buscar[4]; **~ out!** ¡cuidado!; **~ out for** (hope) esperar, (be careful with) tener[19] cuidado con; **~ out (of)** (window) mirar por; **~ out over** dar a, **the windows ~ out over the park** las

ventanas dan al parque

~ over mirar por encima de; (revise) repasar; (take a quick look at) ojear

~ round mirar hacia atrás; (inspect) inspeccionar

~ through mirar por; (revise) repasar; (search among) rebuscar[4] entre; **~ through s.o.'s pockets** registrarle a uno los bolsillos, cachearle a uno

~ to esperar de; (take care of) cuidar; (trust) tener[19] puestas las esperanzas en

~ up levantar los ojos; (call for) ir[19] a buscar; (visit) visitar; **things are looking up** las cosas van mejorando; **~ s.o. up and down** mirar a alguien de arriba abajo; **~ up to** admirar

~ upon: I ~ upon him as my son le considero como un hijo mío

~ upwards mirar hacia arriba

looker-on espectador *m* (-ora *f*)

looking: clean ~ de aspecto limpio; **~-glass** espejo

[1] **loom** (machine) telar *m*

[2] **loom** *v* (up) asomar; **~ large** abultar, *fig* ser[19] de importancia

loony loco; **~-bin** manicomio

loop *n* lazo; (sewing) presilla; (curve) curva; *elect* circuito cerrado; **~ aerial** antena de cuadro; **~-hole** *mil* aspillera, *fig* escapatoria; **~-line** (railway) vía de circunvalación, *elect* circuito en bucle; *vi* formar curvas; *vt* hacer[19] lazos con; (fasten) abrochar con presilla; **~ the ~** rizar[7] el rizo

loose *adj* (free) suelto; (not tight) flojo; (~-fitting) holgado; *elect* desconectado; *mech* loco, desmontable; *fig* (not precise) inexacto; **~ thinking** pensamiento ilógico; (dissolute) disoluto; **at a ~ end** desocupado; **~ morals** moral relajada; **on the (fast and) ~** de parranda; **~-box** (for horse) establo; **~-leaf** de hojas sueltas; **~-reined** a rienda suelta; *v see* **loosen**

loosen (free) soltar (ue)[1a]; (slacken) aflojar; (relax) relajar; (untie) desatar; **~ one's grip** relajar la presión; **~ the tongue** empezar (ie)[2a+7] a hablar; **~ up** (muscles) desentumecer[14]

looseness (freedom) soltura; (slackness) flojedad *f*; (relaxation) relajamiento *f*; (dissolution) disolución *f*; *med* diarrea

loot *n* botín *m*; *sl* (money) pasta; *v* saquear

looter saqueador *m*

looting saqueo

lop (tree) mochar; ~ **off** cortar; ~**-eared** de orejas caídas; ~**-sided** desproporcionado, (off balance) desequilibrado

lope correr a paso largo

lopping desmoche *m*

loquacious locuaz (-ces)

loquaciousness locuacidad *f*

lord *n* señor *m*; (British title) lord (*pl* lores); **the Lord** el Señor; **my** ~ su señoría; ~ **mayor** alcalde *m*; **Lord Chief Justice** presidente *m* del (Tribunal) Supremo; **Lord's Prayer** padrenuestro; **House of Lords** cámara de los lores; ~**ship** (title) señoría, (rule) señorío; *v* ~ **it** (over) señorear

lordliness munificencia; (haughtiness) arrogancia

lordly señorial; (haughty) altivo

lore saber *m* popular

lorgnette impertinentes *mpl*

lorgnon quevedos *mpl*

lorry camión *m*; **tip-up** ~ volquete *m*; ~ **driver** camionero *m*; ~**-load** camión lleno

lose perder (ie)[2b]; (of clock) atrasar; **a wrong answer will** ~ **you the prize** una contestación incorrecta le hará perder el premio; ~ **control of o.s.** perder (ie)[2b] el dominio de sí mismo; ~ **count** perder (ie)[2b] la cuenta; ~ **face** desprestigiarse; ~ **one's grip** *fig* perder (ie)[2b] pie; ~ **ground** perder (ie)[2b] terreno; ~ **hope** perder (ie)[2b] la esperanza; ~ **one's head** perder (ie)[2b] los estribos; ~ **heart** desanimarse; ~ **height** bajar; ~ **one's life** fallecer[14]; ~ **an opportunity (to)** perder (ie)[2b] la ocasión (de); ~ **patience** perder (ie)[2b] la paciencia; ~ **sight of** perder (ie)[2b] de vista; ~ **strength** perder (ie)[2b] fuerzas; ~ **one's temper** enfadarse; ~ **the thread** (of an argument) perder (ie)[2b] el hilo; ~ **time** perder (ie)[2b] el tiempo; ~ **one's voice** perder (ie)[2b] la voz; ~ **one's way/o.s.** perderse

loser perdedor *m* (-ora *f*); **born** ~ perdedor *m* nato, *sl* cenizo

losing perdedor; *sp* ~ **team** equipo vencido; **fight a** ~ **battle** luchar sin esperanza de ganar

loss pérdida; **at a** ~ *comm* perdiendo, *fig* perplejo; **I was at a** ~ **for words** no sabía qué decir; **be at a** ~ **for** no encontrar (ue)[1a]; **sell at a** ~ vender perdiendo; ~ **of face** desprestigio; **be at a** ~ estar[19] desesperado; **be at a** ~ **to understand** no poder (ue)[1b] comprender; ~**-leader** *comm* reclamo

lost perdido; **be** ~ **in thought** estar[19] ensimismado, *fam* estar[19] en babia; ~ **to view** perdido de vista; **that joke was** ~ **on him** ese chiste no le aprovechó; ~ **property (office)** (oficina de) objetos *mpl* perdidos; ~ **sheep** oveja descarriada

lot (share) porción *f*; **that's your** ~ *fam* se acabó para usted; *comm* lote *m*; (building-plot) solar *m*; (fate) suerte, **throw in one's** ~ **with** unirse a la suerte de; **draw** ~**s** echar suertes; **a** ~ **of,** ~**s of** mucho, mucha, muchos, muchas, *fam* un montón de; **the** ~ todo; **he's a bad** ~ *fam* él es un tipo malo

lotion loción *f*

lottery lotería; ~**ticket** billete *m* de lotería

lotto: lotería

lotus loto

loud (of noise) fuerte, alto; (of colours) chillón; (in bad taste) cursi; **in a** ~ **voice** en voz alta; ~**-hailer** megáfono; ~ **laughter** carcajada; ~**-mouthed** deslenguado; ~ **pedal** (on piano) pedal *m* fuerte; ~**speaker** altavoz *m*

loudness (noisiness) ruido; (force) fuerza; (of colours) mal gusto

Louis Luis; ~ **Seize chair** silla de estilo de Luis XVI

lounge *n* salón *m*; ~**-suit** traje *m* de calle; *v* ponerse[19] a sus anchas; ~ **about** tirarse a la bartola

lounger azotacalles *m sing*

lour *see* [2]**lower**

louse piojo

lousy +*fig* piojoso

lout gamberro

loutish grosero

loutishness grosería

louvre celosía para la ventilación

lovable amable

love *n* amor *m*; (enthusiasm) afición *f*;
(darling) querido; (tennis) cero; ~ **at
first sight** flechazo; **be in** ~ **with** estar[19]
enamorado de; **fall in** ~ **(with)**
enamorarse de, *fam* chiflarse por;
make ~ **(to)** hacer[19] el amor (a), (woo)
cortejar; **she's a** ~ ella es una preciosidad; **for** ~ por amor; **for the** ~ **of**
por el amor de; **not for** ~ **or money** ni
por el forro; ~**-affair** intriga amorosa;
~**bird** periquito; ~**-child** niño ilegí-
timo/natural; ~**-in** reunión *f* de jóvenes para practicar el amor libre; ~**-
letter** cart(it)a de amor; ~**-lies-
bleeding** *bot* amaranta; ~**-life** vida
sexual; ~**-lorn** enamoradísimo; ~**-
making** trato sexual, (courtship)
galanteo; ~**-match** matrimonio por
amor; ~**-play** juego erótico; ~**-potion**
filtro; ~**-seat** asiento para dos personas hecho en forma de S; ~**-sick**
enfermo de amor; ~**-story**, ~**-song**
cuento/canción *f* de amor; *v* (person)
amar, querer (ie)[2b], **I** ~ **you** te quiero;
(enthuse over) ser[19] aficionado a; **he
~s bullfights** él es aficionado a los
toros; (like) gustar; **I** ~ **oranges** me
encantan las naranjas; **I'd** ~ **to do it**
me gustaría mucho hacerlo

loveliness (beauty) hermosura; (de-
lightfulness) encanto

lovely (beautiful) hermoso; (delightful)
encantador (-ora *f*), *fam* bonito, ~
film película bonita

lover amante *m+f*; (sweetheart) novio,
novia; ~ **of music** aficionado a la
música

loving cariñoso; ~ **kindness** benevolencia

low *n meteor* área de baja presión; *mot*
(bottom gear) primera marcha; (~
point) punto más bajo, **production
reached a new** ~ la producción llegó a
un nuevo punto bajo; *adj* bajo; (of
supplies) escaso; (of character) vil; (of
rank) humilde, (rude) grosero; **be** ~
(in spirits) sentirse (ie)[2c] abatido, (in
health) débil; **she has a** ~ **opinion of
me** ella tiene una mala opinión de mí;
in a ~ **voice** en voz baja; **run** ~
escasear; **be laid** ~ (buried) ser[19] ente-
rrado, (knocked down) ser[19] derri-
bado; ~ **blood-pressure** tensión baja;
~**-born** de humilde cuna; ~ **bow** reve-

rencia profunda; ~**-bred** malcriado;
~**brow** *adj* de poca cultura; ~ **comedy**
farsa; **Low Countries** los Países Bajos;
~**-down** *fam* información *f*; **give the
~-down (on)** revelar los detalles (de);
~ **dress** vestido escotado; ~ **fire** fuego
bajo; ~ **flying** vuelo a baja altitud; ~
frequency baja frecuencia; ~**-grade** de
calidad inferior; ~**-heel(ed shoe)** (zapato de) tacón bajo; ~ **joke** chiste *m*
verde; **he spoke in a** ~ **key** habló con
moderación; ~**land(s)** tierra(s) ba-
ja(s); ~**-level attack** ataque desde
poca altura; ~**-lying** bajo; **Low Mass**
misa rezada; ~ **neck** escote *m*; **very
~-necked** con mucho escote; ~ **note**
mus nota grave; ~**-pitched** *mus* grave;
~**-pressure tyre** neumático de baja
presión; ~ **price** precio módico; ~
relief bajo relieve; ~**-slung engine**
motor *m* bajo el piso; ~**-spirited** abatido; ~ **spirits** abatimiento; ~**-
temperature** a baja temperatura; ~**-
trick** mala pasada; ~ **water** bajamar
m, (of river) estiaje *m*; ~**-water mark**
línea de nivel mínimo; *v* mugir[9]

[1] **lower** *adj* (*see* low) más bajo *etc*; ~**-case
print** letras *fpl* minúsculas; ~ **class** (de
la) clase baja; ~ **middle class** clase
media baja; ~ **deck** cubierta inferior;
~ **jaw** mandíbula inferior; ~ **topsail**
gavia baja; ~**-grade work** trabajos *mpl*
inferiores; *v* bajar; (flag) abatir; (sails)
arriar; ~ **one's guard** (boxing) aflojar
la guardia; ~ **one's head** agachar la
cabeza; ~ **one's voice** hablar más bajo

[2] **lower** fruncir[15] el ceño; ~ **at** mirar con
ceño

[1] **lowering** *n* (decline) descenso

[2] **lowering** amenazador (-ora *f*); (of sky)
encapotado

lowest el/los más bajo(s), la/las más
baja(s); **the** ~ **of the low** el más bajo de
todos

lowing mugido

lowliness humildad *f*

lowly humilde

loyal leal

loyalist gubernamental; *esp Sp* republicano

loyalty lealtad *f*

lozenge (shape) losange *m*; (tablet)
pastilla

L.P. (long-play) L.D. (larga duración)

L.S.D. (drug) L.S.D. *m*

L-shaped en (forma de) L

Ltd (Limited) Ltda (Limitada)

lubber *m* marinero de agua dulce

lubricant *n+adj* lubricante *m*

lubricate lubricar⁴; *esp mot* engrasar

lubricating-oil aceite *m* lubricante

lubrication lubricación *f*; engrase *m*

lubricator lubricante *m*

lubricious incierto, lúbrico

Lucerne Lucerna

lucerne *bot* alfalfa

lucid lúcido; **in his ~ moments** en sus momentos de claridad mental

lucidity lucidez *f*; (mental) claridad *f* mental

luck suerte *f*; (chance) casualidad *f*; **be in ~** tener¹⁹ suerte; **be out of ~** tener¹⁹ mala suerte; **be down on one's ~** estar¹⁹ de malas; **bring good/bad ~** traer¹⁹ buena/mala suerte; **as ~ would have it** por suerte; **try one's ~** probar (ue)¹ᵃ fortuna; **with any ~** a lo mejor; **no such ~!** ¡ojalá!; **hard ~!** *fam* ¡mala suerte!; **what rotten ~!** *fam* ¡qué perra suerte!

luckily por fortuna

luckless desdichado

lucky afortunado; (bringing luck) que trae buena suerte; **be ~** tener¹⁹ suerte; **seven is my ~ number** siete es mi número de la suerte; **you ~ devil!** *fam* ¡chusquero de provecho!; **~ break/shot** chiripa; **~ dip** tómbola

lucrative lucrativo

lucre lucro; **filthy ~** el vil metal

lucubration lucubración *f*

Lucy Lucía

ludicrous ridículo

ludicrousness ridiculez *f*

ludo parchís *m*

luff orzar⁷

lug *n* (pull) tirón *m*; (ear) oreja; *mech* (projection) orejeta; **~-sail** vela de tercio; **~-worm** lombriz *f* de cebo; *v* tirar de; **~ about** llevar consigo

luggage equipaje *m*; **~-boot** *mot* maletero; **~-label** marbete *m* (con la dirección); **~-rack** (on train) rejilla, *mot* portaequipajes *m sing+pl*; **~ van** furgón *m* de equipajes

lugger lugre *m*

lugubrious lúgubre

Luke Lucas

lukewarm tibio; *fig* frío

lull *n* pausa; *v* (soothe) calmar; (a child) arrullar

lullaby nana

lulu *sl* chica bandera

lumbago lumbago

lumbar lumbar; **~ region** región *f* lumbar

lumber *n* (rubbish) trastos *mpl* viejos; **~ room** cuarto de trastos; (timber) madera de sierra; **~-jack**, **~-man** leñador *m*; **~-jacket** cazadora, *SA* campera; **~-yard** depósito de maderas; *v* **~ about** andar¹⁹ pesadamente; **be ~ed with** *fam* tener¹⁹ que cuidar de

lumbering corte *m* y transporte *m* de troncos

luminary lumbrera

luminous luminoso; **~ paint** pintura luminosa

lump *m* masa; (piece) pedazo; (of sugar) terrón *m*; (swelling) hinchazón (-ones) *m*; totalidad; **~ in the throat** nudo en la garganta; **~ sugar** terrones *mpl* de azúcar; **~ sum** precio global/total; (buy) **by the ~** (comprar) a bulto; **he's on the ~** él trabaja por su propia cuenta; *v* **~ together** amontonar; **~ it** aguantarlo

lumpish como masa; (of people) torpe

lumpy aterronado; con bultos

lunacy locura

lunar lunar; **~ landing** alunizaje *m*; **~ month/year** mes *m*/año lunar; **~ module** módulo lunar

lunatic *n+adj* loco; **~ asylum** manicomio; **~ fringe** minoría de elementos extremistas

lunch *n* (midday meal) almuerzo, comida; (snack) bocado; **~-basket** fiambrera; **~-box**, **~-pail** caja para la merienda; **~-counter** barra de cafetería; **~-time** hora de almorzar/comer; *v* almorzar (ue)¹ᵃ⁺⁷, comer; (eat a snack) merendar (ie)²ᵃ

lung pulmón (-ones) *m*; **~ cancer** cáncer *m* de pulmón

lunge *n* acometida; (fencing) estocada; *v* acometer (at contra); (fencing) dar¹⁹ una estocada (at contra)

lupin altramuz (-ces) *m*

lurch *n* sacudida; **the ship gave a sudden ~** el buque guiñó de repente; **leave in the ~** dejar colgado; *v* (walk) andar¹⁹

tambaleando; *naut* guiñar
lure *n* señuelo; *fig* aliciente *m*; *v* atraer[19]
con señuelo; *fig* tentar (ie)[2a]; ~ **away**
atraer[19]
lurid sensacional; (horrifying) espeluznante; ~ **sky** cielo rojizo
lurk (hide) esconderse; (move furtively) moverse (ue)[1b] furtivamente
lurking (in ambush) escondido; **I have a**
~ **fear** tengo un miedo oculto
luscious delicioso
lush fresco y lozano
lust *n* lascivia; ~ **for power** anhelo de
poder; *v* lujuriar; ~ **after** codiciar
lustful lascivo
lustiness vigor *m*
lustre lustre *m*
lusty vigoroso
lute laúd *m*
Luther Lutero
Lutheran luterano
Luxembourg Luxemburgo
luxuriance lozanía

luxuriant lozano
luxuriate crecer[14] con exuberancia
luxurious lujoso
luxury *n* lujo; **luxuries** artículos de lujo;
adj de lujo
lychgate puerta de cementerio
lye lejía
lying (reclining) acostado; (untruthful)
mentiroso; ~-**in** *med* parto, ~-**in hospital** (casa de) maternidad *f*; ~-**to** *naut*
al pairo
lymph linfa
lymphatic linfático
lynch linchar; ~ **law** ley de Lynch
lynching linchamiento
lynx lince *m*; ~-**eyed** con ojos de lince
lyre lira; ~-**bird** pájaro lira
lyric *n* poesía lírica; (words of song) letra de una canción; ~-**writer** letrista
m+f; *adj* lírico
lyrical lírico; *fam* elocuente
lyricism lirismo

M

m (letter) eme *f*; (metre, minute) m
(metro, minuto)
M.A. (Master of Arts) M. en A. (Maestro en Artes)
ma mamá
ma'am señora
macabre macabro
macadam macadán *m*
macadamize macadamizar[7]
macaroni macarrones *mpl*; ~ cheese
macarrones *mpl* con queso
macaroon *approx* almendrada
macaw guacamayo
mace (spice) macia; (staff of office)
maza; (tear-gas) gas lacrimógeno; ~-
bearer macero
Macedonia Macedonia *m*
macerate macerar
machete machete *m*
Machiavelli Maquiavelo
machiavellian maquiavélico
machination maquinación *f*
machinator maquinador *m* (-ora *f*)
machine *n* máquina; *pol* organización *f*
(de un partido); *fam* (bicycle) bici *f*;
~ fitter montador *m*; ~-gun ametralladora; ~-gunner ametrallador *m*;
~-made hecho a máquina; ~-shop taller *m* de maquinaria; ~-tool máquina
herramienta; ~ translation traducción *f* a máquina; *v* elaborar a
máquina; (dressmaking) coser a
máquina
machinery maquinaria; (mechanism)
mecanismo, *fam* tripas *fpl*; *pol*
sistema; *theat* tramoya
machinist operario de máquina,
maquinista *m+f*
machismo machismo
macho macho
mackerel caballa; ~ sky cielo aborregado
mackintosh impermeable *m*
macrobiotic macrobiótico
macrocosm macrocosmo(s)
mad loco; (angry) furioso; she's a little

~ ella está majareta; get ~ encolerizarse[7]; go ~ enloquecer[14], (of dog)
ponerse[19] rabioso; you drive me ~
usted me vuelve loco; like ~ como un
loco; ~cap locuelo; ~ dog perro
rabioso; ~house +*fig* manicomio;
~man loco; ~woman loca
madam señora
made hecho; ~ to measure hecho a la
medida; you've got it ~ su futuro está
asegurado; ~-up artificial, (with cosmetics) maquillado
madness locura
Madonna Virgen *f*; ~ lily azucena
madrigal madrigal *m*
maelstrom remolino
maestro maestro
mafia mafia
mafioso mafioso
magazine (periodical) revista; (of firearm) depósito; (explosives store) polvorín *m*; (explosives store on ship)
santabárbara
magenta *n* magenta; *adj* de color
magenta
maggot gusano
maggoty agusanado
Magi (Reyes *mpl*) Magos *mpl*
magic *n* magia; *fig* encanto; as if by ~
como por encanto; *adj* mágico; ~
lantern linterna mágica; ~ wand varita mágica
magical mágico
magician mágico; *theat* ilusionista *m+f*
magisterial magistral
magistracy magisterio
magistrate juez *m* municipal
Magna Carta Carta Magna
magnanimity magnanimidad *f*
magnanimous magnánimo
magnate magnate *m*
magnesia magnesia
magnesium magnesio
magnet imán *m*
magnetic magnético; ~ bearing rumbo
magnético; ~ field/pole campo/polo

magnético; ~ **needle** brújula; ~ **tape** cinta magnetofónica; ~s ciencia del magnetismo

magnetism magnetismo

magnetize magnetizar[7], imantar; *fig* atraer[19]

magneto magneto

magnetophone magnetófono

Magnificat Magníficat *m*

magnification *opt* aumento; *fig* exageración *f*

magnificent magnífico

magnifico magnífico

magnify aumentar; (praise) magnificar[4]

magnifying de aumento; ~ **instrument** instrumento de aumento; ~ **glass** lupa

magniloquence grandilocuencia

magnitude magnitud *f*

magnolia magnolia

magnum botella de dos litros

magpie urraca

Magyar *n + adj* magiar *m + f*

maharajah maharajá *m*

mahogany caoba; (colour) de color caoba

Mahomet Mahoma *m*

Mahometan *n + adj* mahometano

maid (young girl) doncella; (servant) criada; (mu)chacha, *SA* mucama; **old ~** solterona; ~**-of-all-work** criada para todo; ~**-of-honour** dama de honor; ~**servant** criada

maiden *n* doncella; *adj* (de) soltera; ~ **aunt** tía soltera; ~ **name** apellido de soltera; ~ **speech/voyage** primer discurso/viaje; ~**hair** *bot* culantrillo; ~**head** himen *m*; ~**hood** doncellez *f*

maidenly *adj* recatada

[1] **mail** (armour) malla; **coat of ~** cota de malla; ~**ed** de malla; ~**ed fist** puño de hierro

[2] **mail** (postal service) *n* correo; **by return ~** a vuelta de correo; ~**-bag** valija; ~**-boat** vapor *m* correo; ~**-box** buzón (-ones) *m*; ~**man** cartero; ~**-order** pedido postal; ~**-order firm** casa de ventas por correo; ~**-train** (tren *m*) correo; ~**-van**, ~**-truck** coche *m* correo; *v* echar al correo

maim mutilar; ~**ed** mutilado

main *n* (gas, water) conducto; *elect* red *f*; **connected to the ~(s)** conectado a la red/al conducto; ~**s switch** interruptor *m* de red; ~**s voltage** tensión *f*

de la red; **in the ~** por lo general; *adj* principal; ~ **thing** lo más importante; **by ~ force** por fuerza mayor; ~ **clause** *gramm* oración *f* principal; ~ **dish** (of meal) plato fuerte; ~ **feature** (in newspapers *etc*) plato fuerte; ~**land** continente *m*; ~**land Spain** España peninsular; ~ **line** (railway) línea principal; ~**mast** palo mayor; ~ **office** oficina central; ~ **road** carretera nacional; ~**sail** vela mayor *m*; ~**spring** muelle *m* mayor; ~**stay** estay *m* mayor, *fig* sostén (-enes) *m* principal; ~**stream** tradicionalista; ~ **street** calle *f* mayor

maintain mantener[19]; (affirm) sostener[19]; *mech* mantener

maintenance manutención *f*; (cost of upkeep) (gastos *mpl* de) conservación *f*; (affirmation) sustento; *mech* mantenimiento; ~ **allowance** pensión *f* para la manutención; ~ **shop** taller *m* de mantenimiento

maisonette casa pequeña; (flat) piso completo en sí mismo

maize maíz *m*; ~ **cob** mazorca

majestic majestuoso

majesty majestad *f*; **your ~** su majestad

majolica mayólica

major *n* mayor *m + f* de edad; (*US* university) especialidad *f*; *mil* comandante *m*; ~**-general** general *m* de división; *adj* importante; (main) principal; (elder) mayor; ~ **disaster** desastre *m* en gran escala; ~ **key/scale** *mus* tono/escala mayor; ~ **operation** *surg* operación *f* superior; ~ **road** carretera de prioridad; *v* (*US* university) graduarse

Majorca Mallorca

Majorcan *n + adj* mallorquín *m* (-ina *f*)

major-domo mayordomo

majorette batonista

majority mayoría; *mil* comandancia; **be in the ~** tener[19] una mayoría; **reach one's ~** llegar[5] a la mayoría de edad

make *n* (form) hechura; (of clothes) confección *f*; (brand) marca; **of German ~** de marca alemana; (product) producto; **he is on the ~** él lleva el agua a su molino; **our own ~** de fabricación propia; ~**-believe** *n* pretexto, *v* fingir[9]; **land of ~-believe** reino de los sueños; ~**-weight** contrapeso

v gen hacer[19]; **I'll ~ you eat it** le haré comerlo; (manufacture) fabricar[4]; (build) construir[16]; (create) crear; (arrange) arreglar; (prepare) preparar, **she is making breakfast** ella está preparando el desayuno; (reach) llegar[5] a, **that ship will not ~ port** aquel barco no llegará al puerto; (earn) ganar, **he ~s a million pesetas a year** él gana un millón de pesetas al año; (appoint) constituir[16], **they made him king** le constituyeron rey; (compel) obligar[5] a, **they will ~ me stay** me obligarán a quedar; (equal) ser[19], **two and two ~ four** dos y dos son cuatro; (agree on) convenir[19] en, **they will ~ a pact** ellos convendrán en un pacto; (become) ponerse[19], **she ~s herself ridiculous** ella se pone en ridículo; **~ o.s. known** darse[19] a conocer (**to** a); **~ as if** hacer[19] como si; **~ the best of** aprovecharse de; **~ do with** contentarse con; **~ good** (compensate) indemnizar[7], (repair) reparar, (be successful) tener éxito; **~ good one's promise** cumplir la palabra; **~ one of** ser[19] uno de; **~ or break** hacer[19] la fortuna o ser[19] la ruina de; **~ it** (be successful) tener[19] éxito; **what time do you ~ it?** ¿qué hora tiene usted?; **~shift** *n* arreglo provisional, *adj* improvisado

~ after seguir (i)[3+11]

~ away with (take) llevarse; (abolish) abolir; **~ away with o.s.** suicidarse

~ for dirigirse[9] a; (attack) atacar[4]; (help to achieve) contribuir[16] a

~ into convertir (ie)[2c] en

~ of (interpret) sacar[4] de

~ off largarse[5]; **~ off with** llevarse

~ out (see) distinguir[16]; (decipher) descifrar; (understand) entender, comprender; (declare) declarar; (prepare) preparar; (give an impression) dar[19] a entender; (pretend) fingir[16]; **~ out a bill** hacer[19] una cuenta; **~ out a cheque** extender (ie)[2b] un cheque; **how did you ~ out?** ¿cómo te fue?

~ over to traspasar

~ to hacer[19] ademán de +*infin*

~ towards dirigirse[9] a

~-up *n* pintura; *theat* maquillaje *m*; **~-up artist** maquillador *m* (-ora *f*); (formation) composición *f*; (charac-

ter) modo de ser

~ up *v* hacer[19]; fabricar[4]; (invent) inventar; (of clothes) confeccionar; *print* compaginar; (constitute) formar; (with cosmetics) pintarse; *theat* maquillar(se); **~ up the fire** echar carbón al fuego; **~ up a prescription** preparar una receta; **~ up one's mind** decidirse (**to** a/por); **~ up one's mind about** formar una opinión sobre; **~ up for** compensar; **~ up for lost time** recobrar el tiempo perdido; **~ up to** congraciarse con, (flirt with) galantear; **~ it up with** arreglárselas con

maker fabricante *m*; (of clothes) confeccionador *m* (-ora *f*); **our Maker** Dios *m*

making fabricación *f*; (of clothes) confección *f*; **in the ~** en vía de formación; **be the ~ of** ser[19] la causa del éxito de; **~s** elementos necesarios; **have the ~s of** tener[19] madera de

malachite malaquita

maladjusted inadaptado; (sexually) invertido

maladjustment inadaptación *f*; (sexual) inversión *f*

maladministration mala administración

maladroit torpe

malady enfermedad *f*

malaise malestar *m*

malapropism expresión impropiamente aplicada que resulta grotesca

malaria paludismo

malarial palúdico

Malay *n+adj* malayo

Malaysia Malasia

Malaysian malasio

malcontent *n+adj* descontento

male *n* varón *m*; (animal) macho; *adj* masculino; (animal) macho; **~ child** hijo varón; **~ issue** sucesión masculina; **~ nurse** enfermero; **~ prostitute** *sl* chapero; **~ prostitution** *sl* chaperismo; **~ screw** *mech* tornillo macho

malediction maldición *f*

malefactor malhechor *m*

malevolence malevolencia

malevolent malévolo

malformation deformidad *f*

malformed mal formado

malice malicia; **~ aforethought** intención delictuosa; **bear ~ (for)** guardar rencor (por)

malicious malicioso
malign *adj* maligno; *v* calumniar
malignant + *med* maligno; pernicioso
malignity malignidad *f*
malinger fingirse[9] enfermo
malingerer calandria *m+f*
mall alameda
mallard pato real
malleable +*fig* maleable; ~ **iron** hierro forjado
mallet mazo
mallow malva
malmsey malvasía
malnutrition desnutrición *f*
malodorous maloliente
malpractice abuso de autoridad/posición
malt *n* malta; *v* maltear; ~**ed milk** harina lacteada y malteada
maltese *n*+*adj* maltés *m* (-esa *f*); ~ **cross** cruz (-ces) *f* de Malta
Malthusian maltusiano
maltreat maltratar
maltreatment maltrato
maltster preparador *m* de malta
mamma mamá
mammal mamífero
mammalian mamífero
mammary mamario
mammon espíritu *m* de la codicia
mammoth *n* mamut *m*; *adj* mastodóntico, *fam* enorme
mammy mamaíta
man *n* hombre *m*; (human race) el género humano; *mil* soldado; *naut* marinero; (servant) criado; (worker) obrero; (chess *etc*) pieza; **a ~ must do what is necessary** uno tiene que hacer lo necesario; **every ~, woman and child** todo el mundo, *fam* todo bicho viviente; **to a ~** todos; **no ~** nadie; ~ **about town** hombre de mundo; ~ **alive!** ¡hombre!; ~ **and boy** desde pequeño; ~ **and wife** marido y mujer; **Man Friday** criado leal; ~ **in the moon** mujer *f* de la luna; ~ **in the street** hombre de/a pie; ~ **of God** clérigo; ~ **of letters** hombre *m* de letras; ~ **of means** hombre adinerado; ~ **of straw** testaferro, hombre de paja; ~ **of the world** hombre de mundo; ~ **overboard!** ¡hombre al agua!; **see a ~ about a dog** cambiar el agua a los garbanzos ~**-at-arms** hombre *m* de armas; ~**-day** día-

hombre *m*; ~**-eater** caníbal *m+f*, (animal) fiera que come carne humana; ~**-eating** antropófago, (animal) que come carne humana; ~**handle** maltratar, *mech* manipular a brazo; ~**-hater** mujer *f* que odia a todo hombre; ~**-hole** registro; ~**-hole cover** tapa del registro; ~**hood** virilidad *f*; ~**-hour** hora-hombre *f*; ~**-hunt** persecución *f* de un criminal; ~**kind** raza humana; ~**-made** artificial; ~**-made fibres** fibras *fpl* artificiales; ~**-of-all-work** hombre *m* para todo; ~**-of-war** buque *m* de guerra; ~**-power** mano de obra, *mil* fuerzas *fpl* (militares); ~**-servant** criado; ~**sized** bastante grande para un hombre; de hombres; ~**slaughter** homicidio sin premeditación; ~**-trap** cepo; *v naut* tripular, *mil* guarnecer; ~ **the pumps** armar las bombas
manacle *n* manilla; ~**s** esposas *fpl*; *v* poner[19] esposas a
manage *vt* (handle) manejar; (animal, person) controlar, **the rider ~s his horse very well** el jinete controla muy bien su caballo; (do) hacer[19], **I can ~ it** puedo hacerlo; (cope with) poder[19] con, **she can't ~ all the work** ella no puede con todos los quehaceres; (eat) comer, **can you ~ another meatball?** ¿puede usted comer otra albóndiga?; (direct) administrar; *comm* dirigir[9]; *vi* (cope) arreglárselas, **she could never ~ when they had guests** ella nunca podía arreglárselas cuando tenían invitados; (get along) ir[19] tirando, **I haven't much money but I ~** no tengo mucho dinero pero voy tirando; (in speaking a foreign language) defenderse (ie)[2b], **he ~s well in Italian** él se defiende bien en italiano; ~ **to** lograr +*infin*; ~ **without** pasarse sin
manageable manejable; (of animals, people) controlable; (of hair) domable
management (use) manejo; (administration) administración *f*; *comm* (act of managing) gerencia; (group of executives) dirección *f*; *theat* empresa; **he is studying ~** él estudia administración comercial; ~ **consultant** consultante *m* de administración
manager gerente *m*; *fam* jefe *m*; *theat*

empresario; **she is a good** ~ ella es buena administradora

manageress directora, jefa

managerial directivo

managing: ~ **board** dirección *f*; ~ **director** director *m* gerente

mandarin (language) mandarín *m*; (fruit) mandarina

mandatary mandatario

mandate mandato; ~**d territory** territorio *m* bajo mandato

mandatory obligatorio

mandolin(e) mandolina

mandrake mandrágora

mandril mandril *m*

mane crin *f*; (of person) melena; ~**d** con crines/melena

manful valiente

manganate manganato

manganese manganeso

mange *vet* sarna

manger pesebre *m*

manginess estado sarnoso

mangle *n* exprimidor *m* de la ropa; *v* pasar por el exprimidor; (mutilate) mutilar; (damage) estropear

mangling mutilación *f*

mango mango

mangold remolacha forrajera

mangrove mangle *m*

mangy sarnoso

manhattan cóctel *m* de whisky y vermut

manhood (masculinity) machismo; (valor) valentía

mania manía; *fam* chifladura; **have a** ~ **for** tener[19] manía de +*inf*, estar[19] chiflado por +*n*

maniac maniático

maniacal, manic maníaco

manicure *n* manicura; ~**-set,** ~**-case** estuche *m* de manicura; *v* hacer[19] la manicura

manicurist manicura

manifest *n naut* manifiesto; *adj* manifiesto; **make** ~ poner[19] de manifiesto; *v* hacer[19] patente

manifestation manifestación (-ones) *f*

manifesto manifiesto

manifold *n mot* tubo múltiple; *adj* múltiple; ~ **paper** papel *m* para hacer copias

manikin enano; (tailor's dummy) maniquí *m*

Manilla Manila; ~ **shawl** mantón *m* de

Manila

manilla (hemp) abacá

manipulate manipular

manipulation manipulación *f*

manipulator manipulador *m* (-ora *f*)

manliness virilidad *f*; *fam* machismo

manly varonil, de hombres; **he is very** ~ él es muy macho

manna maná *m*

manned tripulado; *space* pilotado

mannequin maniquí *m*; ~ **parade** desfile *m* de maniquíes

manner manera; (style) estilo; (sort) clase; **after the** ~ **of** según el estilo de; **all** ~ **of** toda clase de; **in a** ~ **of** speaking por decirlo así; **in this** ~ de este modo; **to the** ~ **born** avezado desde la cuna; **have bad/good** ~**s** tener[19] malos/buenos modales; **she has no** ~**s** ella no tiene educación; **it was a piece of bad** ~**s** fue mala educación

mannered amanerado; **well-**~ bien educado

mannerism idiosincrasia; *theat* latiguillo

mannerist artista amanerado

mannerly cortés *invar*

mannish masculino; (of a woman) hombruna

manoeuvrability maniobrabilidad *f*

manoeuvrable maniobrable

manoeuvre *n* maniobra; *vt* (manipulate) manipular; *vi* hacer[19] maniobras

manoeuvring maniobras *fpl*; (plotting) intrigas *fpl*

manometer manómetro

manor (land) finca; (rights) feudo; *sl* distrito; **lord of the** ~ señor *m* feudal, *fam* cacique *m*; ~**-house** casa solariega

manse rectoría

mansion palacio, casa grande; (block of flats) casa de vecinos

mantelpiece repisa (de chimenea)

mantilla mantilla

mantis mantis *m*

mantle *n* + *fig* manto; (gas-~) manguito incandescente; *v* cubrir (*past part* cubierto)

manual *n* (handbook) manual *m*; (keyboard) teclado de órgano; *adj* manual; ~ **labour** trabajo manual, (workers) mano *f* de obra

manufacture *n* fabricación *f*; (product) manufactura; *v* fabricar[4]

manufacturer fabricante *m*

manufacturing *n* fabricación *f*; *adj* manufacturero; ~ **town** ciudad *f* industrial

manure *n* estiércol *m*; *v* estercolar

manuscript manuscrito

many *n* gran número; **a good** ~ un buen número de; **for the** ~ para muchos; *adj* muchos, muchas; **how** ~? ¿cuántos?; ~ **a man** muchos hombres; ~ **people** mucha gente; ~ **a time** muchas veces; **as** ~ **as** tantos como; **she has as** ~ **as I** ella tiene tantos como yo; **he has as** ~ **as 500 books** él tiene hasta 500 libros; **too** ~ demasiados; **two too** ~ dos de más; ~**-coloured** multicolor; ~**-headed** de muchas cabezas; ~**-sided** multilátero, (person) polifacético

Maoism maoismo

Maoist *n* + *adj* maoista *m* + *f*

Maori *n* + *adj* maorí *m* + *f*

map *n* mapa *m*; (chart) carta; **off the** ~ remoto; ~ **of the world** mapamundi *m*; ~**-maker** cartógrafo; ~**-making** cartografía; ~**-read** interpretar un mapa; ~**-reading** interpretación *f* de los mapas; *v* trazar[7] un mapa; *fig* ~ **(out)** proyectar

maple arce *m*; (wood) madera de arce; ~**-syrup** jarabe *m* de arce

mapping cartografía; ~**-pen** pluma para trazar mapas

maquette maqueta

maquis maquis *m*

mar (spoil) estropear; (disfigure) desfigurar; *fig* (take away enjoyment) aguar[6]

maraschino marasquino

marathon(-race) (carrera de) maratón *m*

maraud merodear

marauder merodeador *m*

marble *n* mármol *m*; (toy) canica; **play** ~**s** jugar[1a+5] a las canicas; *adj* marmóreo; *v* jaspear

marcasite marcasita

March marzo; **mad as a** ~ **hare** loco como una cabra

march *n* marcha; (step) paso; *fig* (progress) marcha; **steal a** ~ **on** tomar la delantera a; **strike up a** ~ batir la marcha; *vi* marchar; *vt* hacer[19] marchar

~ **back** *vt* volver (ue)[1b] (*pàst part*

vuelto) a pie; *vt* hacer[19] volver a pie

~ **in** entrar a pie

~ **off** marcharse

~ **on** seguir (i)[3+11] adelante

~ **on to** subir a

~**-past** *n* desfile *m*

~ **past** *v* desfilar ante

marching de marcha; ~ **order** orden *m* de marcha; **get one's** ~ **orders** ser[19] despedido; ~ **song** canción (-ones) *f* de marcha

marchioness marquesa

mardi gras martes *m* de carnaval

mare yegua; ~**'s nest** hallazgo ilusorio

Margaret Margarita

margarine margarina

margin +*print* margen (márgenes) *m*; (profit) ganancia; **in the** ~ al margen; ~ **of error** margen *m* de error; ~**-release** (typewriter) tecla de margen

marginal marginal; ~ **note** nota al margen *f*

marginalia notas al margen *fpl*

marguerite margarita

Maria María; **Black** ~ coche *m* celular, *SA* carro celular, *sl* lechera

marie biscuit galleta maría

marigold caléndula

marihuana marihuana; *sl* grifa; ~ **smoker** grifota *m* + *f*

marinade escabeche *m*

marinate escabechar

marine *n* soldado de marina; ~**s** (force) infantería de marina; **tell that to the** ~**s!** ¡a otro perro con ese hueso!; *adj* marítimo; ~ **insurance** seguro marítimo; ~ **law** derecho marítimo

mariner marinero; ~**'s compass** brújula

marionette marioneta

marital matrimonial; ~ **status** estado civil

maritime marítimo; ~ **law** derecho marítimo; ~ **code** código marítimo

marjoram mejorana

Mark Marcos; **Gospel according to St** ~ evangelio de San Marcos

mark *n* señal *f*; (stain) mancha; (trade-~) marca; (for schoolwork) nota; *sp* raya; (target) blanco, **hit the** ~ dar[19] en el blanco; (coin) marco; **make one's** ~ firmar con una cruz, *fig* distinguirse[11]; **up to the** ~ satisfactorio; **wide of the** ~ alejado de la verdad; ~**sman** tirador *m*; ~**smanship**

puntería; *v* señalar; **the page you wanted is** ~**ed** la página que usted buscaba está señalada; (stain) manchar; (price) poner[19] precio (a); (correct) corregir (i)[3+9]; (award a ~) dar[19] nota a; (characterize) caracterizar[7]; (observe) observar; ~ **a player** *sp* marcar[4]/*fam* doblar a un jugador; ~ **time** marcar[4] el paso, *fig* hacer[19] tiempo; ~**ed** marcado, señalado; (stained) manchado; **she speaks with a** ~**ed accent** ella habla con marcado acento; ~**ed man/woman** futura víctima

~**-down** *n* rebaja

~ **down** *v* rebajar; (make a note of) apuntar

~ **off** señalar

~ **out** trazar[7]; (indicate) indicar[4]; (select) escoger[8]

~ **up** *comm* aumentar el precio de; *sp* (score) apuntar

marker (billiards) marcador *m*; (football *etc*) tanteador *m*; (in book) registro

market *n* mercado; *fam* plaza; (stock ~) bolsa; **Common Market** Mercado Común; **buyer's** ~ mercado de precios bajos; **be in the** ~ **for** estar[19] dispuesto a comprar; **on the** ~ a venta; **put on the** ~ intentar vender; **play the** ~ jugar (ue)[1a+5] la bolsa; **black** ~ estraperlo, *SA* bolsa negra; **ready** ~ fácil salida; ~**-day** día *m* de mercado; ~**-garden** huerto; ~**-gardener** hortelano; ~**-place** plaza del mercado, (usually covered) plaza de abastos; ~**-price** precio corriente; ~ **research** análisis *m* del mercado; ~ **researcher** investigador *m* de mercados; ~**-stall** tabanco; ~ **survey** examen (-ámenes) *m* del mercado; *v* (sell) vender en un mercado; **they are going to** ~ **this product** van a explotar este producto

marketability posición *f* (de un producto) frente a los compradores

marketable vendible

marketeer *pol* partidario del Mercado Común

marketing intercambio comercial; (sales methods) método de venta, *SA* mercadotecnia; ~ **list** lista de compras

marking señal *f*; (on animal) pinta; (of

exercises) corrección *f;* **I have a lot of** ~ **to do** tengo mucho que corregir; ~**-ink** tinta de marcar

marl marga

marline merlín *m*; ~**spike** pasador *m*

marly margoso

marmalade mermelada de naranja

marmoset tití *m*

marmot marmota

[1] **maroon** *n* petardo; *adj* marrón

[2] **maroon** abandonar en una isla desierta

marquee gran tienda de campaña

marquetry marquetería

marquis marqués *m*

marquise marquesa

marriage matrimonio; (wedding) boda, *fig* alianza de oro, *fig* unión *f*; **by** ~ político, **he is my uncle by** ~ él es mi tío político; **related by** ~ emparentado; ~ **without sex** matrimonio blanco; ~ **allowance** subsidio matrimonial; ~ **certificate** partida de matrimonio; ~ **licence** licencia de matrimonio; ~ **portion** dote *m*; ~ **rate** nupcialidad *f*; ~ **register** acta matrimonial; ~ **vows** votos *mpl* del matrimonio

marriageable casadero

married casado; ~ **couple** matrimonio; **get** ~ **(to)** casarse (con); ~ **life** vida matrimonial

marrow (vegetable) calabacín (-ines) *m*; (in bone) tuétano, ~ **bone** hueso con tuétano; ~**fat** especie *f* de guisante

marry *vi* casarse con; *vt* (give/join in marriage) casar, *fig* unir(se); ~ **again** casarse en segundas nupcias; ~ **for money** casarse por dinero, *fam* dar[19] el braguetazo; ~ **into** emparentar(se) con; ~ **off (to)** casar (con)

Mars Marte *m*

Marseillaise marsellesa

Marseilles Marsella

marsh pantano; ~ **fever** paludismo; ~ **gas** gas *m* de los pantanos; ~ **harrier** aguilucho lagunero; ~**mallow** *bot* malvavisco, (sweet) caramelo de merengue blando; ~**-marigold** calta

marshal *n* mariscal *m*; (*US* police chief) jefe *m* de policía; *v* ordenar; (procession) formar; (arguments) reunir

marshalling ordenación *f*; (of procession) formación *f*; (of arguments) reunión *f*; ~**-yard** plaza de clasificación

marshy pantanoso

marsupial *n+adj* marsupial *m*

mart emporio; (auction-room) martillo

Marte *m* Mars

marten marta

Martha Marta

martial marcial; ~ **law** ley *f* marcial; **under** ~ **law** en estado de sitio; ~ **spirit** marcialidad *f*

Martian *n+adj* marciano

Martin Martín

martin vencejo

martinet ordenancista *m+f*

Martinique Martinica

martyr *n* mártir *m+f*; *v* martirizar[7]

martyrdom martirio

martyrize martirizar[7]

marvel *n* maravilla; *v* maravillarse (at de)

marvellous maravilloso

Marxism marxismo

Marxist *n+adj* marxista *m+f*

Mary María

marzipan mazapán *m*

mascara rimel *m*

mascot mascota

masculine +*gramm* masculino; (*esp* of a woman) hombruno

masculinity masculinidad *f*; (virility) machismo

mash *n* amasijo; (animal feed) mezcla (de granos); (brewing) malta remojada; *v* triturar, mezclar; ~**ed potatoes** puré *m* de patatas/*SA* papas

mashie mashie *f*

mask *n* máscara; *mil* (gas-mask) careta; *surg* mascarilla; *v* enmascarar; (hide) ocultar; ~**ed ball** baile *m* de máscaras

masochism masoquismo

masochist masoquista *m+f*

mason albañil *m*; cantero; (freemason) (franc)masón (-ones) *m*

masonic masónico; ~ **lodge** logia de (franc)masones

masonry albañilería; (freemasonry) (franc)masonería

masque fiesta dramática

masquerade *n* mascarada; *fig* farsa; *v* disfrazarse[7] (**as** de); *fig* hacer[19] el papel (as de)

[1] **mass** *eccles* misa; **hear/say** ~ oír[19]/celebrar misa; **High Mass** misa mayor/cantada; **Low Mass** misa rezada; **black** ~ misa negra; ~**-book** libro de misa

[2] **mass** *n* +*phys* masa; (shape) bulto; (heap) montón (-ones) *m*; (of people) muchedumbre *f*; **the** ~**es** las masas; **the (great)** ~ la mayoría de; **in the** ~ en conjunto; **in** ~ **formation** en columna cerrada; ~ **media** medios *mpl* de comunicación de masa; ~ **meeting** mitin *m* popular; ~ **murder** matanza en masa; ~**-produce** producir[15] en serie; ~**-production** producción *f* en serie; ~ **psychology** psicología de masas; ~ **unemployment** desempleo en masa; *v* juntarse

massacre *n* matanza; *v* masacrar

massage *n* masaje *m*; *v* dar[19] masaje a

masseur, masseuse masajista *m+f*

massif macizo montañoso

massive (large) abultado; (solid) macizo

massiveness (largeness) gran bulto; (solidity) macicez *f*

[1] **mast** *n* *naut* mástil *m*; *rad+TV* torre *f*; ~**head** tope *m*; *v* *naut* arbolar

[2] **mast** (beech) hayuco; (oak) bellota

master *n* (of house) señor *m*, amo; (young) señorito; (form of address) señor(ito); (owner) dueño; (expert) perito (**of** en); (graduate) licenciado, **Master of Arts** Maestro en Artes; (junior-school teacher) maestro; (secondary-school teacher) profesor *m*; (of university college) director *m*; *naut* capitán (-anes) *m*; (of small vessel) patrón (-ones) *m*; (of military order) maestre *m*; **the Master** (Christ) el Señor; **be** ~ **of the situation** ser[19] dueño de la situación; **be one's own** ~ ser[19] dueño de su persona, (be self-employed) trabajar por su propia cuenta; **old** ~ *arts* antiguo pintor, (painting) cuadro de un antiguo pintor famoso; ~ **of ceremonies** maestro de ceremonias; ~ **of the hounds** cazador *m* mayor; ~**-builder** contratista *m* de construcciones; ~ **clock** reloj *m* principal; ~ **copy** copia matriz; ~**-gunner** condestable *m*; ~**-hand** mano *f* maestra; ~ **key** llave maestra; ~**-mariner** capitán *m* de un buque mercantil; ~**-mind** *n* cerebro, *v* ser[19] el instigador de; ~**piece** obra maestra; ~**-stroke** golpe maestro; ~ **switch** interruptor maestro; ~**-touch** mano de genio; *v* (tame) domar; (subdue)

vencer[12]; (become expert in) llegar[5] a
ser maestro en, (language) dominar

masterful imperioso

masterly maestro

mastery (authority) autoridad *f*; (victory) dominio; (skill) maestría

mastic mastique *m*; *med* almáciga

masticate masticar[4]

mastication masticación *f*

masticatory masticatorio

mastiff mastín (-ines) *m*

mastodon mastodonte *m*

mastoid apófisis *f* mastoides

masturbate masturbarse

masturbation masturbación *f*

masturbatory masturbatorio

[1] **mat** *n* estera; (door-~) felpudo; (table-~) salvamanteles *m sing*, (of lace) tapetito; *v* (become matted) entretejerse; (of hair) enredarse

[2] **mat** (not glossy) mate

matador matador *m*

[1] **match** *n* cerilla, fósforo, cerillo; (fuse) mecha; ~**box** caja de cerillas; ~**-seller** fosforero; ~**wood** madera para fósforos, *fig* astillas *fpl*

[2] **match** *n* igual; *sp* partido, **football ~** partido de fútbol; (marriage) alianza; **be a ~ for** poder[19] con; **be more than a ~ for** ser[19] más fuerte que; **be a good ~** (in marriage) ser[19] buen partido, (of colours) hacer[19] juego con; **meet one's ~** hallar la horma de su zapato; ~**-maker** casamentero; *v* igualar; (of a pair) emparejar; (of colours) hacer[19] juego con; ~ **s.o. against** enfrentar a uno contra; **I want to ~ this cup** busco una taza igual a esta

matching a juego (con); **gloves ~ her coat** guantes *mpl* a juego con su abrigo; (of colours) a tono (con)

matchless incomparable

[1] **mate** *n* (marriage partner) cónyuge *m+f*; *zool* (male) macho, (female) hembra; (assistant) ayudante *m*; (unskilled assistant) peón (-ones) *m*, **bricklayer's ~** peón de albañil; *naut* piloto; (one of a pair) pareja; (friend) compañero; *v* (marry) casar(se) con; *zool* aparear(se)

[2] **mate** (chess) mate *m*

maté mate *m*

materfamilias madre *f* de familia

material *n* material *m*; (cloth) tela; *adj*

material; (essential) esencial

materialism materialismo

materialist *n+adj* materialista *m+f*

materialistic materialista

materialization materialización *f*

materialize materializarse[7]

materially materialmente

maternal materno; (of feelings *etc*) maternal, ~ **instinct** instinto maternal

maternity maternidad *f*; ~ **benefit** subsidio de natalidad; ~ **gown** baby *m*; ~ **clothes** ropa premamá; ~ **hospital** (casa de) maternidad *f*

matey amigable

mathematical matemático; ~ **instruments** instrumentos de dibujo

mathematician matemático

mathematics, math(s) matemática(s); **applied/pure ~** matemáticas prácticas/teóricas

matinée función *f* de la tarde; ~**-coat** chaquetita de punto

mating apareamiento; ~ **season** época de celo

matins maitines *mpl*

matriarch matriarca

matriarchal matriarcal

matriarchy matriarcado

matricide (criminal) matricida *m+f*; (crime) matricidio

matriculate matricular(se) (**from** de)

matriculation matriculación *f*

matrimonial matrimonial; ~ **agency** agencia matrimonial

matrimony vida conyugal

matrix matriz (-ces) *f*

matron matrona; *med* enfermera jefa; (of school) ama de llaves; ~ **of honour** madrina

matronly de matrona; (dignified) serio

matted enredado; (of undergrowth) enzarzado

matter *n* materia; (content) contenido; *comm* asunto *m*, **we are considering the ~** estamos considerando el asunto; *med* pus *m*; **a ~ of** (about) unos (-as), **we visited a ~ of fifty houses** visitamos unas cincuenta casas; **it's a ~ of importance** es cuestión de importancia; ~ **in hand** asunto de que se trata; ~ **of course** cosa natural; **as a ~ of course** por rutina; **in the ~ of** en cuanto a; ~ **of fact** (truth) hecho positivo; **as a ~ of**

fact en realidad; **~-of-fact** *adj* prosaico; **~ of form** pura formalidad; **~ of opinion** cuestión de opinión; **no ~ no** importa; **no ~ how** de cualquier modo que +*subj*; **no ~ who** quienquiera que +*subj*; **to make ~s worse** para colmo de las desdichas; **for that ~** en cuanto a eso; **what's the ~?** ¿qué pasa?; **what's the ~ with?** (what's the harm in?) ¿qué inconveniente hay en +*infin*?; *v* importar; **what does it ~?** ¿qué importa?; **it doesn't ~ to me** no me importa

Matthew Mateo

matting estera

mattock azadón (-ones) *m*

mattress colchón (-ones) *m*; **spring ~** colchón (-ones) *m* de muelles

maturation maduración *f*

mature *adj* maduro; *comm* vencido; *v* madurar; *comm* vencer[12]

maturity madurez *f*; *comm* vencimiento

matutinal matutino

maudlin llorón

maul magullar; *fig* sobar

maunder chochear

Maundy: ~ Thursday Jueves Santo; **~ money** limosna real

Maurice Mauricio

mauser (rifle) máuser *m*

mausoleum mausoleo

mauve (de) color *m* malva

maverick res *f* sin marcar; *pol* disidente *m*

maw estómago; (of bird) molleja; *fig* abismo

mawkish sensiblero

mawkishness sensiblería

maxillary *n*+*adj* maxilar *m*

maxim máxima

maximal máximo

Maximilian Maximiliano

maximize exagerar

maximum *n*+*adj* máximo

May mayo; **~ Day** (fiesta del) primero de mayo; **~ Queen** maya; **maybug** abejorro; **mayflower** flor *f* del cuclillo; **mayfly** cachipolla; **maypole** mayo

may poder[19]; **~ I go?** ¿puedo irme?; (to express possibility) es posible que +*subj*; **he ~ not come** es posible que no venga; (to express a wish) *subj used* **~ you be very happy!** ¡(que) sean muy felices!; **~ I come in?** ¿se puede

pasar?; **~ I visit your daughter?** ¿me da usted permiso para hacerle una visita a su hija?; **if I ~** si me lo permite usted; **you ~ not remember me** usted quizás no se acordará de mí

Maya(n) *n*+*adj* maya *m*+*f*

maybe tal vez, quizá(s)

mayhem mutilación *f* criminal; *fam* gamberrismo

mayonnaise mahonesa

mayor alcalde *m*

mayoral de alcalde

mayoralty alcaldía

mayoress alcaldesa

maze laberinto

mazurka mazurca

mazy laberíntico

M.C. (master of ceremonies) maestro de ceremonias

me *pron* me; **they hate ~** me odian; (after all *preps* except con) mí, **they went without ~** fueron sin mí; (emphatic) mí, **don't ask ~!** ¡no me pregunte a mí!; **dear ~!** ¡ay de mí!; **with ~** conmigo

[1] **mead** aguamiel *m*

[2] **mead** *m poet* (meadow) prado

meadow prado; **~-pipit** *orni* bisbito común; **~-sweet** *bot* reina de los prados

meagre (lean) flaco; (scanty) escaso

meagreness escasez *f*

meal comida; (flour) harina; **have a ~** comer; **have a good ~** comer bien; **~-time** hora de comer

mealie harina de maíz

mealy harinoso; (pale) pálido; **~-mouthed** mojigato

[1] **mean** *n* (midpoint) medio; (average) (pro-)medio; *math* media; **~s** medios *mpl*, (money) recursos *mpl*; **live on one's ~s** vivir de sus rentas; **she lives beyond her ~s** ella gasta más de lo que gana; **man of ~s** hombre acomodado; **~s to an end** medio para conseguir un fin; **by ~s of** por medio de; **by all ~s!** (certainly) ¡por supuesto!, (with pleasure) con mucho gusto; **by any ~s** de cualquier modo; **not by any ~s** de ninguna manera; **by fair ~s or foul** por las buenas o por las malas; **by this ~s** de esta manera; **~s test** investigación *f* de rentas

[2] **mean** *adj* (miserly) tacaño, *fam* roñoso; (despicable) vil; (humble) humilde;

(of poor quality) malo; (*US* bad-tempered) malo; ~ **trick** jugada mezquina

[3] **mean** *v* querer[19] decir; **what do you ~ by that?** ¿qué quiere usted decir con eso?; (signify) significar[4], **what does that word ~?** ¿qué significa esa palabra?; ~ **business** (be determined) estar[19] resuelto, (talk seriously) hablar en serio; **I really ~ it** lo digo en serio; **she ~s well** ella tiene buenas intenciones; ~ **to** pensar (ie)[2a] +*infin*; **I didn't ~ to do it** lo hice sin querer; **be meant for** ser[19] destinado para; **this picture is meant to be Prince Charles** este retrato se supone que es el príncipe Carlos

meander *n* serpenteo; *v* serpentear; (in talk) divagar[5]

meandering serpenteo; (of talk) divagaciones *fpl*

meaning significado *f*, sentido; (intention) intención *f*; (of a word) acepción *f*; **what is its ~?** ¿qué significa?; **that joke has a double ~** ese chiste tiene doble sentido

meaningful significativo; **give a ~ look** echar una mirada significativa

meaningless sin sentido

meanness (miserliness) tacañería, *fam* roña; (humility) humildad *f*; (poor quality) mezquindad *f*

meanwhile, meantime mientras tanto

measles sarampión *m*

measly mezquino

measurable mensurable

measure *n* medida; ~, **made to** ~ hecho a medida, (for measuring) regla; **tape-** ~ metro; *mus* compás *m*; *pol* proyecto de ley; **beyond** ~ interminable; **for good** ~ por añadidura, *fam* de propina; **in a great** ~ en gran manera; **in some** ~ hasta cierto punto; **take ~s to** tomar medidas para +*infin*; *v* medir (i)[3]; (for height) tallar; (take measurements) tomar las medidas (de); ~ **off/out** medir (i)[3]; ~ **up to** ser[19] igual a; ~**d** mesurado, acompasado, (of words) deliberado; **with ~d steps** a pasos contados

measureless inmensurable

measurement medida; **take ~s** (for clothes) tomar las medidas; (act of measuring) medición *f*

meat carne *f*; *fig* sustancia; **cold ~s** fiambres *fpl*; ~ **pie** empanada de carne; ~**-ball** albóndiga; ~**-extract** extracto de carne; ~**-grinder** picadera; ~**-safe** fresquera

meaty carnoso; *fig* sustancioso

Mecca la Meca

Meccano *tr* Mecano; ~ **set** un Mecano

mechanic mecánico

mechanical mecánico; ~ **engineering** ingeniería mecánica; ~ **saw** motosierra

mechanics mecánica

mechanism mecanismo; *fam* tripas *fpl*

mechanize mecanizar[7]; *mil* motorizar[7], ~**d column** columna motorizada

mechanization mecanización *f*

medal medalla; *sl* chapa

medallion medallón (-ones) *m*

medallist medallista *m+f*

meddle (entro)meterse (**with/in** con)

meddler entremetido; *fam* metementodo *m+f*

meddlesome entremetido; **be ~** meterse en todo

meddling entremetimiento

mediaeval *etc see* **medieval**

media medios *mpl* de comunicación; ~ **person** informador *m* (-ora *f*)

medial medio

median *n+adj* mediano; ~ **strip** faja mediana

mediate mediar (**between** entre); ~ **in the war** mediar en la guerra

mediation mediación *f*

mediator mediador (-ora *f*)

mediatory de mediador

medic médico

medical *n* reconocimiento (médico); (~ **student**) estudiante *m+f* de medicina; *adj* médico, de medicina; ~ **certificate** certificado médico; ~ **examination** reconocimiento (médico); *fam* cheques; ~ **officer** *mil* médico militar; ~ **officer** (**of health**) jefe *m* de sanidad municipal; ~ **practitioner** médico, doctora; ~ **school** escuela de medicina; ~ **service** servicio de sanidad; **army ~ corps** cuerpo de sanidad militar

medicate medicar[4]

medication medicación *f*

medicinal medicinal

medicine medicina; **take one's ~** pagar[5] las consecuencias; ~**-chest** botiquín

(-ines) *m*; ~**-man** hechicero *m*

medico (doctor) médico; (student); *fam* cheques; estudiante *m*+*f* de medicina

medieval medieval

medievalism medievalismo

medievalist medievalista *m*+*f*

mediocre mediocre

mediocrity mediocridad *f*; (person) medianía *f*

meditate meditar

meditation meditación *f*

meditative contemplativo

Mediterranean *n* (mar) Mediterráneo; *adj* mediterráneo

medium *n* medio; (person) médium *m*; ~ **cut** (tobacco) picadura entrefina; ~ **wave** *rad* onda media; **happy** ~ justo medio; **through the** ~ **of** por medio de; ~**-sized** de tamaño regular

medlar (fruit) níspola; (tree) níspero

medley mezcla; *mus* popurrí *m*; ~ **relay** *sp* relevo combinado

medulla médula

medullary medular

Medusa Medusa; (jellyfish) aguamala

meek manso; ~ **and mild** mansurrón

meekness mansedumbre *f*

¹ meet *n sp* concurso; (hunting) reunión *f* para una cacería; *vt* encontrar(se) (ue)¹ᵃ; (come across) tropezar⁷ con; (make acquaintance) conocer¹⁴, **I met her yesterday** la conocí ayer; (keep appointment) ver¹⁹; **he's going to** ~ **his fiancée** él va a ver a su novia; (welcome) esperar, **I shall** ~ **you at the station** le esperaré en la estación; (connect with) empalmar con, **this bus** ~**s your train** este autobús empalma con su tren; (answer) responder a, **she always** ~**s my arguments with laughter** ella siempre responde a mis argumentos con risa; (pay) pagar⁵, **I shall** ~ **the bill** pagaré la cuenta; (suffer) tener¹⁹ que aguantar; (fight) batirse con, *sp* enfrentarse con; ~ (boxing) pelear con; *vi* (*see vt*) encontrarse (ue)¹ᵃ; conocerse¹⁴; verse¹⁹; batirse; enfrentarse; empalmarse; (of rivers) confluir¹⁶; **till we** ~ **again** hasta la vista; ~ **a charge** refutar una acusación; ~ **a cheque** dar¹⁹ crédito a un cheque; ~ **the eye** saltar a la vista; ~ **half-way** hacer¹⁹ concesiones a; ~ **an obligation** cumplir una obligación; ~

one's requirements/wishes satisfacer¹⁹ (*conj* like **hacer**¹⁹) los requisitos/ deseos de uno; ~ **with an accident** tener¹⁹ un accidente; ~ **(up) with** tropezar⁷ con; **there's more in this than** ~**s the eye** hay gato encerrado

² meet *adj* conveniente

meeting encuentro; (assembly) reunión (-ones) *f*, **call a** ~ convocar⁴ una reunión; (public ~) mitin *m*; (session) sesión *f*; (by appointment) cita; (interview) entrevista (**between** entre); (of rivers) confluencia; *sp* encuentro; ~**-house** *eccles* capilla protestante; ~**-place** lugar *m* de reunión/ de cita

megacycle megaciclo

megalomania megalomanía

megalomaniac megalómano

megaphone megáfono

megaton megatón *m*

melamine melamina

melancholic melancólico

melancholy melancolía

mêlée pelea confusa

mellifluous melífluo

mellow *adj* maduro; *fig* suave; (drunk) alegre; ~ **wine** vino añejo, *fam* vino entre dos luces; *v* madurar; *fig* suavizarse⁷

mellowness madurez *f*

melodic melódico

melodious melodioso

melodrama melodrama

melodramatic melodramático

melody melodía

melon melón (-ones) *m*; **water-**~ sandía; ~**-shaped** amelonado

melt (of metal) fundir(se); (of snow) derretir(se) (i)³; (dissolve) disolver(se) (ue)¹ᵇ; *fig* ablandar(se), **it** ~**s my heart** me ablanda el corazón; ~ **into tears** deshacerse¹⁹ en lágrimas; ~ **away** disolver(se) (ue)¹ᵇ, (disappear) desaparecer¹⁴, *fam* (depart) escurrirse; ~ **down** fundir, derretir (i)³

melting *n* fusión *f*; derretimiento; *adj* fundente; ~**-point** punto de fusión; ~**-pot** +*fig* crisol *m*

member (limb) miembro; (of association) socio; (of committee) vocal *m*; (of parliament) diputado; (one of a group) componente *m*+*f*, miembro, **he is a** ~ **of a pop group** es componente de un conjunto musical

membership calidad *f* de socio; (number of members) número de socios; ~ **fee** cuota (de socio)

membrane membrana

memento recuerdo

memoir biografía; ~**s** autobiografía; (published reminiscences) memorias *fpl*

memorable memorable

memo(randum) apunte *m*; *pol* memorándum *m*; ~**-pad** libro de notas

memorial *n* monumento; (petition) memorial *m*; *adj* conmemorativo; ~ **tablet** lápida mural con inscripción; ~ **stone** lápida conmemorativa, (on tomb) lápida sepulcral

memorialize presentar un memorial

memorize aprender de memoria

memory memoria; (thing recalled) recuerdo; **from ~ de** memoria; **in ~ of a** la memoria de; **if my ~ serves me right** si la memoria no me falla; **what a ~ you have!** ¡qué cabeza la suya!

men *see* **man**; ~ **at work** (road sign) obras *fpl*; ~**folk** hombres *mpl*; ~**'s room** (sign) caballeros; ~**swear** artículos *mpl* para caballero

menace *n* amenaza; *v* amenazar[7]

menacing amenazador (-ora)

menacingly con amenazas

ménage familia

menagerie colección *f* de fieras

mend *n* reparación *f*; (patch) remiendo; (darn) zurcido; (of broken bone) soldadura; *v* arreglar; (darn) zurcir[13]; (patch) remendar (ie)[2a]; (scw) recoser; (get better) curarse; (broken bone) soldarse; ~ **one's ways** enmendarse (ie)[2a]

mendacious mendaz (-ces)

mendacity mendacidad *f*

mender reparador *m* (-ora *f*); (by darning) zurcidor *m* (-ora *f*); (by patching) remendón *m* (-ona *f*)

mendicant *n+adj* mendigo; ~ **order** *eccles* orden *m* de frailes mendicantes

mendicity mendicidad *f*

mending reparación *f*; (by darning) zurcidura; ~**-wool** lana de zurcir

menial *n* criado; *adj* servil; (low) bajo

meningitis meningitis *f*

meniscus *phot* menisco

menopause menopausia; *fam* retirada

menstrual menstrual; ~ **cycle** ciclo menstrual

menstruate menstruar

menstruation menstruación *f*; *fam* regla

mensuration mensura

mental mental; (intellectual) intelectual; ~ **arithmetic** aritmética mental; ~ **case** paciente *m+f* con desarreglo mental, *fam* loco; ~ **defective** subnormal *m+f*; ~ **deficiency** deficiencia mental; ~ **home/hospital** manicomio; ~ **illness** desarreglo mental; ~ **reservation** reserva mental; ~ **work** trabajo intelectual

mentality mentalidad *f*

mentally mentalmente; ~ **deficient** subnormal; ~ **ill** alienado

menthol mentol *m*; ~ **cigarette** cigarrillo (a)mentolado

mentholate (a)mentolar

mention *n* mención *f*; (passing) alusión *f*; *mil* (in dispatches) nombramiento; *v* mencionar; (in passing) aludir, *mil* citar; **don't ~ it!** (in reply to thanks) ¡de nada!; **do not (dare to) ~ that!** ¡ni hablar de eso!; **not to ~** y no digamos

mentor mentor *m*

menu carta; (set meal) menú *m*

Mephistopheles Mefistófeles

Mephistophelian mefistofélico

mercantile mercantil; ~ **law** derecho mercantil; ~ **marine** marina mercante

mercenary *n+adj* mercenario

mercer mercero

mercerize mercerizar[7]

merchandise *n* mercancías *fpl*; **staple ~** mercancías *fpl* de consumo corriente; *v* comercializar[7]

merchandiser comerciante *m*

merchandising ciencia de la comercialización

merchant *n* comerciante *m*; *fig* tío; *adj* mercantil, *naut* mercante; ~**man** buque *m* mercante; ~ **seaman** marinero mercante; ~ **service/navy** marina mercante; ~ **ship** buque *m* mercante

merchantable comerciable

merciful compasivo; **be ~** tener[19] compasión

merciless implacable

mercurial mercurial; *fig* veleidoso

mercury mercurio

mercy compasión *f*; **beg (for) ~** pedir (i)[3] clemencia; **be at the ~ of** estar[19] a la

merced de; **at the ~ of the elements** a la
intemperie; **it's a ~ that** es un milagro
que; **~-killing** eutanasia; **~-seat** trono
de Dios

[1] **mere** n lago

[2] **mere** adj mero; **a ~ man** un simple hombre; **~ words** nada más que palabras

merely nada más que

merest (más) mínimo; **~ nonsense** tontería

meretricious llamativo

merganser mergánsar m

merge unir(se); comm fusionar(se)
(**with** con); **~ into** perderse (ie)[2b] en

merger comm fusión f

meridian n+adj meridiano

meridional meridional

meringue merengue m

merit n mérito; **~s of the case** circunstancias fpl del caso; v merecer[14]

meritorious meritorio

merlin esmerejón (-ones) m

mermaid sirena

merman tritón (-ones) m

merriment alegría

merry alegre; (drunk) achispado; **become ~** alegrarse, (drunk) achisparse;
make ~ divertirse (ie)[2c]; **~ Christmas**
felices navidades fpl; **~-go-round** tiovivo m; **~-making** festividades fpl

mesalliance matrimonio contraído con
una persona inferior

mescalin mescalina

mesentery mesenterio

mesh n malla (de red); **~es** +fig red f;
mech engranaje m; v mech engranar
(**with** con); fig enredar

mesmerism mesmerismo

mesmerize hipnotizar[7]

[1] **mess** n (piece of bad work) birria, **who
made this ~?** ¿quién hizo esta birria?;
(dirtiness) suciedad f; (untidiness)
desorden m; (muddle) confusión f;
(predicament) lío, **get into a ~** hacerse[19] un lío; **make a ~ of** ensuciar,
desordenar, (spoil) echar a perder;
my hair is in a ~ tengo greñas; v **~
about** entretenerse[19] en tonterías,
(work without enthusiasm) trabajar
con desgana, (idle) vaguear; **~ about
with** manosear; **don't ~ about!**
¡déjese de tonterías!; **~ up** desordenar, ensuciar, fam chafar, **they
have ~ed up my holidays** han chafado

mis vacaciones; **what ~ed me up was**
lo que me fastidió fue

[2] **mess** n (food) ración (-ones) f (de comida); mil+naut rancho; (dining-
room) comedor m, **officers' ~** comedor de oficiales; **~-jacket** mil+naut
chaqueta que se lleva para comer; **~-
kit** batería de cocina; **~mate** compañero de rancho; **~-tin** plato de
campaña; v comer el rancho

message mensaje m; (call, errand) recado, **leave a ~** dejar un recado

messenger mensajero; **~-boy** botones m
sing+pl

Messiah Mesías m

Messianic mesiánico

Messrs sres (señores) mpl

messy sucio; desordenado; fig confuso

metabolic metabólico

metabolism metabolismo

metacarpal: ~ bone hueso del metacarpo

metal n metal; (road) grava; fig ánimo;
~s (railway) railes mpl; **~ polish** lustre m para metales; **~-shears** tijera
para chapa; **~ work** metalistería; **~
worker** metalista m+f; adj metálico; v
(road) macadamizar[7]

metallic metálico

metallurgic(al) metalúrgico

metallurgist metalúrgico

metallurgy metalurgia

metamorphic metamórfico

metamorphose metamorfosear

metamorphosis metamorfosis f

metaphor metáfora

metaphorical metafórico

metaphysical metafísico

metaphysics metafísica

mete: ~ out dar[19]

meteor meteoro

meteoric meteórico

meteorite meteorito

meteorologist meteorólogo

meteorology meteorología

meter: electricity/gas ~ contador m de la
electricidad/del gas; **read the ~**, US
refer to the ~ leer[17] el contador; v
medir (i)[3] con contador

methane metano

methedrine metedrina

methinks me parece

method método; (systematic arrangement) orden (órdenes) m

methodical metódico

Methodism metodismo

Methodist *n+adj* metodista *m+f*

methodology metodología

meths alcohol desnaturalizado

methyl metilo; ~ **alcohol** alcohol metílico

methylated: ~ **spirits** alcohol desnaturalizado

meticulous meticuloso

metre +*poet* metro; **three** ~**s long** tres metros de largo

metric(al) métrico; ~ **system** sistema métrico

metro (underground railway) metro

metronome metrónomo

metropolis metrópoli *f*

metropolitan *n+adj eccles* metropolitano

mettle ánimo; **be on one's** ~ estar¹⁹ dispuesto a hacer grandes esfuerzos; **put s.o. on his** ~ picar⁴ el amor propio de uno

¹ **mew** *orni* gaviota

² **mew** (of cat) *n* maullido; *v* maullar

mewing maullido

mews caballeriza

Mexican mejicano; *SA* mexicano

Mexico Méjico; *SA* México

mezzanine entresuelo

mezzo soprano mezzo soprano *f*

mezzotint mezzotinto

mi *mus* mi *m*

miaow *n* miau *m*; *v* maullar

miasma miasma

miasmal miasmático

mica mica

Michael Miguel

Michaelmas fiesta de San Miguel

¹ **mickey** (mouse) ratón (-ones) *m*

² **mickey:** **take the** ~ **out of** pitorrearse de; ~**-taking** pitorreo

microbe microbio

microbial microbiano

microbiologist microbiólogo

microbiology microbiología

microcosm microcosmo(s)

microfilm microfilm *m*

microgroove microsurco

micrometer micrómetro

micron micrón *m*

microphone micrófono

micro-photography microfotografía

microscope microscopio

microscopic microscópico

microwave: ~ **receiver/oven** receptor/horno *m* de microondas

micturate orinar

micturition acción *f* de orinar

mid: in ~**-air** en pleno vuelo; **in** ~**-ocean** en plena mar; **in** ~**-September** a mediados de setiembre; **from** ~**-May to** ~**-June** desde mediados de mayo hasta mediados de junio; ~**-morning** media mañana; **my** ~**-morning coffee** mi café de media mañana; **in** ~**-stream** en medio del río, *fig* a media carrera

midday *n* mediodía *m*; *adj* de mediodía; **at twelve o'clock** ~ a las doce del mediodía

middle *n* medio; (waist) cintura; **in the** ~ **of** en medio de, (month, year) a mediados de; **in the** ~ **of nowhere** donde Cristo dio las tres voces; **I'm in the** ~ **of working** estoy (ocupado) trabajando; ~**-aged** de edad madura; **Middle Ages** Edad Media; ~**brow** de gustos medios; **Middle East** Medio Oriente; ~ **class** (de la) clase media; ~ **distance** segundo término; ~ **ear** oído medio; **Middle English** inglés *m* de la edad del oscurantismo; ~ **finger** dedo del corazón/medio; ~**man** intermediario; ~ **management** mando medio; ~**most** más céntrico; ~**-of-the-road** *adj fig* neutral; ~**-sized** de tamaño mediano; ~**weight** (boxing) *n* peso medio; de peso medio

middling mediano; (of quality) mediocre; **fair to** ~ regular

midfield: ~ **player** centrocampista *m*

midge jején (-enes) *m*

midget *n+adj* enano

midinette dependienta parisiense

midland del interior (de un país); **Midlands** región *f* central de Inglaterra

midnight medianoche *f*; **at** ~ a medianoche; **burn the** ~ **oil** quemarse las cejas; **Midnight Mass** misa del gallo; ~ **sun** sol *m* de medianoche

midriff diafragma *m*

midship *n* medio del buque; ~**s** en medio del buque; ~**man** guardiamarina *m*

midst medio; **in the** ~ **of** en medio de, (surrounded by) rodeado de; **in your** ~ entre ustedes

midsummer pleno verano; ~**'s day**

fiesta de San Juan; 'A Midsummer Night's Dream' 'Sueño de una noche de verano'

midway *adj+adv* a mitad del camino; ~ **between** equidistante de

midweek (de) entre semana

midwife partera

midwifery partería

midwinter pleno invierno

mien semblante *m*

[1] **might** *n* poder(ío) *m*; **with ~ and main** con todas sus fuerzas

[2] **might: it ~ be that** puede ser que +*subj*; **it ~ be true or it ~ not** podría o no podría ser verdad; **you ~ well do that** bien podría usted hacer eso; **the accident ~ have been avoided** el accidente podía haberse evitado

mighty *adj* poderoso; *adv fam* enormemente

mignonette reseda

migraine migraña; **have a ~** sufrir de migraña

migrant *orni+fig* ave *f* de paso; *adj* migratorio

migrate emigrar

migration migración *f*

migratory migratorio

Mike Miguelito

mike (microphone) *fam* micro

mild suave; (of people) pacato; (of drinks) ligero; *med* benigno; *meteor* templado; ~ **steel** acero dúctil

mildew mildiu *m*

mildly: to put it ~ para no decir más

mile milla; **nautical ~** milla marina; **~stone** piedra miliaria; **this is a ~stone in our history** es un hito en nuestra historia

mileage recorrido en millas; *approx* kilometraje *m*

milfoil *bot* milenrama

milieu ambiente *m*

militancy belicosidad *f*; *pol* activismo

militant *n* persona belicosa; *pol* activista *m+f*; *adj* militante; *pol* activista

militarism militarismo

militarist militarista *m+f*

militaristic militarista

militarization militarización *f*

militarize militarizar[7]

military *n* los militares; *adj* militar; ~ **academy** colegio militar; ~ **equipment** equipo de guerra; ~ **law** código mili-

tar; ~ **police** policía militar; ~ **policeman** policía *m* militar; ~ **service** servicio militar, *fam* mili *f*; ~ **target** objetivo militar; ~ **transport plane** carguero militar

militate: ~ **against** oponerse a

militia milicia; **~man** miliciano

milk *n* leche *f*; **condensed ~** leche condensada; **powdered ~** leche en polvo; ~ **chocolate** chocolate *m* con leche; ~ **of magnesia** leche *f* de magnesia; ~ **of human kindness** compasión *f*; **~-and-water** *fig* débil; **~-bar** cafetería; **~-can** lechera; **~-float** carro de lechero; **~-jug** jarra de leche; **~maid** lechera; **~man** lechero; **~ products** productos lácteos; **~-shake** batido de leche; **~sop** marica; **~-tooth** diente *m* de leche; *vt* ordeñar; *fig* chupar; *vi* dar[19] leche

milkiness lactescencia

milking ordeño; ~ **machine** ordeñador *m*; **~-stool** taburete *m*

milky lechoso; **Milky Way** vía láctea

mill *n* molino; (factory) fábrica, **paper ~** fábrica de papel; (spinning) hilandería; (weaving) fábrica de tejidos; (for coffee) molinillo; *US* milésimo de un dolar estadounidense; **go through the ~** aprender por experiencia; **~-board** cartón *m* prensado; **~-dam** esclusa de molino; **~-hand** obrero; **~-owner** dueño de una fábrica; **~-pond** cubo; **~-race** caz (-ces) *m*; **~stone** piedra de molino, *fig* montón (-ones) *m*; **a wife like that is a ~stone** una mujer como ella es una rémora; **~-wheel** rueda de molino; *vt* moler (ue)[1a]; *mech* fresar; (coin) acordonar; (cloth) abatanar; **~ed edge** cordoncillo; *vi* ~ **about/ around** arremolinarse

millenary *n+adj* milenario

millennial milenario

millennium milenio

millepede milpiés *m sing+pl*

miller molinero

millet mijo

milliard mil millones *mpl*

milligramme miligramo

millilitre mililitro

millimetre milímetro

milliner sombrerero; **~'s (shop)** sombrerería

millinery (occupation) (ocupación de)

sombrerería; ~ **department** sección *f*
de sombreros

milling *n* molienda; (on coin) cordoncillo; *adj* desordenado; ~ **crowd** muchedumbre desordenada

million millón *m*; **two ~ men** dos millones de hombres; ~ **pesetas** *sl* kilo

millionaire millonario

millionth millonésimo

milometer cuentakilómetros *m sing+pl*

milt lechecillas *fpl*

mime *n* pantomima; (mimicry) mímica;
v hacer[19] en pantomima; (mimic)
imitar

mimeograph *n* multicopista; *v* reproducir[15] a multicopista

mimic *n* imitador *m* (-ora *f*); *adj* mímico;
v imitar

mimicry mímica

mimosa mimosa

minaret minarete *m*

minatory amenazador (-ora *f*)

mince *n* carne picada; ~**meat** conserva
de frutas secas y especias; ~**-pie** pastel
m relleno de conserva de fruta; *vt*
picar[4]; ~ **matters** medir (i)[3] las palabras; **not to ~ one's words** no tener[19]
pelos en la lengua; *vi* andar con pasos
pequeños

mincer picadora, máquina de picar
carne

mincing *n* acción *f* de picar; *adj* afectado; ~ **machine** picadora, máquina
de picar carne

mind *n* mente *f*; (intellect) inteligencia;
(inclination) inclinación *f*; (spirit)
espíritu *m*; (opinion) parecer *m*; ~
reader adivinador *m* (-ora *f*) del
pensamiento ajeno; ~ **reading** adivinación *f* del pensamiento ajeno; ~**'s
eye** imaginación *f*; **presence of ~** presencia de ánimo; **be of one ~** estar[19]
unánimes; **be in one's right ~** estar[19]
en su sano juicio; **bear in ~** tener[19] en
cuenta; **make up one's ~ (to)** decidirse
(a); **change one's ~** cambiar de opinión; **be out of one's ~** estar[19]
fuera de sí; **go out of one's ~ (go mad)**
perder (ie)[2b] el juicio, (forget)
olvidársele a uno, *fam* escapársele a
uno; **it slipped my ~** se me olvidó; **give
one's ~ to** entregarse[5] al estudio de; **I
gave him a piece of my ~** le dije cuatro
verdades; **have on one's ~** pensar

(ie)[2a] en; **you haven't got your ~ on
what you are doing** no está usted en lo
que hace; **have something on one's ~**
estar[19] preocupado; **I have a good/half
a ~ to** tengo ganas de +*infin*; **have in
~** pensar (ie)[2a] en; **she knows her own
~** ella sabe lo que quiere; **set one's ~
on** estar[19] resuelto a; **speak one's ~**
decir[19] su parecer; hablar sin rodeos;
out of sight, out of ~ ojos que no ven,
corazón que no siente; **it takes my ~
off things** me distrae de las cosas; *v*
(care about) importarle a uno; **I don't
~ at all** no me importa nada; (pay
attention to) hacer[19] caso de; (take
care of) cuidar (de); ~ **the baby** cuidar
al niño; (be careful) tener cuidado;
cuidarse; ~ **out!** ¡cuidado!; ~ **the
door!** ¡cuidado con la puerta!; ~ **you
don't** tenga cuidado de no +*infin*/que
no +*subj*; ~ **your own business**
métase en sus asuntos; ~ **you, he is no
fool** conste que él no es tonto; **do you
~ the window open?** ¿le molesta la
ventana abierta?; **do not ~ him** no se
preocupe de él; **never ~** no se preocupe, (take no notice) no haga caso;
would you ~ giving me a light?
¿quiere darme fuego?

minder guardaespaldas *m sing*, *sl* gorila

mindful atento (**of** a)

mindless sin inteligencia *f*

[1] **mine** *poss pron* (el) mío, (la) mía *etc*

[2] **mine** *n* +*mil*+*fig* mina; ~**-detector** detector *m* de minas; ~**field** campo de
minas; ~**-layer** buque *m* minador; ~**-
sweeper** dragaminas *m sing+pl*; **land
~** mina terrestre; **magnetic ~** mina
magnética; *v* excavar; (work a ~) explotar una mina; *mil* sembrar (ie)[2a]
minas

miner minero

mineral *n*+*adj* mineral *m*; ~**-oil** petróleo; ~ **water** (spring ~) agua
mineral, (fizzy drink) gaseosa

mineralogist mineralogista *m*+*f*

mineralogy mineralogía

minestrone sopa minestrone

mingle mezclar(se) (**with/in** con); (of
people) asociarse (**with/in** con)

mingy *fam* roñoso, tacaño

mini *mot* minicoche *m*; ~**bus** microbús
m; ~**cab** minitaxi; ~**cab driver** minitaxista *m*; ~**dress** minitraje *m*; ~**skirt**

minifalda; **a very ~ ~skirt** una minifalda muy mini

miniature *n* miniatura; *adj* en miniatura,
~ **trains** trenes *mpl* en miniatura; ~
edition edición *f* diamante; ~ **football**
futbolín *m*; ~ **rifle range** (at fair) barraca de tiro al blanco, *fam* tiro

minim blanca

minimal mínimo

minimize reducir[15] al mínimo; *fig* menospreciar

minimum *n* + *adj* mínimo

mining *n* minería; ~ **engineer** ingeniero
de minas; *adj* minero; ~ **industry**
industria minera

minion lacayo

minister *n* ministro; *eccles* pastor *m*; *v*
(ad/su)ministrar; ~ **to** atender (ie)[2b] a

ministerial ministerial

ministrant ministrador *m*; *eccles* oficiante *m*

ministration ayuda; *eccles* ministerio

ministry ministerio

mink visón *m*

minnow alevino

minor *n* menor *m* + *f* de edad; *adj* menor
de edad; (secondary) secundaria; *mus*
menor, **in the ~ key** en tono menor; ~
detail detalle *m* sin importancia; ~
planet pequeño planeta *m*

Minorca Menorca

Minorcan *n* + *adj* menorquín *m* (-ina *f*)

minority minoría; (of age) minoría de
edad *f*; ~ **government** gobierno minoritario; ~ **programme** *rad* + *TV* programa *m* de minorías

minster catedral *f*; iglesia monesterial

minstrel juglar *m*; (black-faced) cómico
disfrazado de negro

¹ **mint** *n bot* hierbabuena; (peppermint)
menta; (sweet) pastilla/caramelo de
menta; *adj* de menta

² **mint** *n* casa de moneda; ~ **of money**
potosí *m*; *adj* (of stamps, coins) sin
usar; *v* acuñar; *fig* inventar

mintage acuñación *f*

minuet minué *m*

minus *n* (sign) menos *m*; *adj* negativo;
prep sin

¹ **minute** *adj* menudo

² **minute** *n* minuto; *fig* momento, **just a ~**
un moment(it)o; (note) minuta; ~**s**
actas *fpl*; **at the last ~** al último
momento; **be up to the ~** estar[19] al co-

rriente; ~-**book** libro de actas; ~-
hand minutero; *v* minutar

minutely detalladamente

minuteness minuciosidad *f*

minutiae detallitos *mpl*

minx chica descarada

miracle milagro; **perform a ~** hacer[19] un
milagro; ~ **play** auto sacramental; ~-
worker milagrero

miraculous milagroso

mirage espejismo

mire fango, lodo

mirror *n* + *fig* espejo; *mot* retrovisor *m*;
look (at o.s.) in the ~ mirarse al
espejo; ~-**writing** escritura al revés; *v*
reflejar

mirth alegría

mirthful alegre

mirthless triste

miry fangoso

misadventure desgracia

misalliance casamiento desigual

misanthrope, misanthropist misántropo

misanthropic misantrópico

misanthropy misantropía

misapplication mal uso

misapply hacer[19] mal uso de

misapprehend entender (ie)[2b] mal

misapprehension equivocación *f*; **be
under a ~** estar[19] equivocado

misappropriate malversar

misbegotten bastardo

misbehave portarse mal; **don't ~!** (to a
child) ¡no seas malo!

misbehaviour mal comportamiento

misbelief error *m*

miscalculate calcular mal

miscalculation cálculo equivocado

miscall nombrar impropiamente

miscarriage aborto; **have a ~** abortarse;
~ **of justice** error *m* judicial

miscarry *med* abortar, (of plans) fracasar

miscast dar[19] (a un actor) un papel
inadecuado

miscegenation entrecruzamiento de
razas

miscellaneous misceláneo

miscellany miscelánea

mischance mala suerte *f*

mischief (behaviour) picardía; (wilfulness) travesura; (harm) daño; (child)
diablillo; **get into ~** hacer[19] diablu-
ras; ~-**maker** malicioso; (gossip)

chismoso

mischievous (roguish) pícaro; (harmful) dañino; (wilful) travieso; ~ **look** mirada maliciosa, (roguish) pícara

mischievousness *see* **mischief**

misconceive entender (ie)[2b] mal

misconception equivocación (-ones) *f*

misconduct *n* mala conducta; (adultery) adulterio; *vt* dirigir[9] mal; *vi* ~ **o.s.** portarse mal

misconstruction mala interpretación

misconstrue interpretar mal

miscount *n* cuenta errónea; *v* contar (ue)[1a] mal

miscreant *n* bribón *m* (-ona *f*); *adj* vil

miscue *n* pifia; *v* pifiar

misdeal dar[19] mal

misdeed mal hecho

misdemeanour mala conducta; *leg* delito de menor cuantía

misdirect dirigir[9] mal

misdirection instrucción errónea

mise-en-scène puesta en escena

miser avaro

miserable miserable; (pitiful) lastimoso; (poor quality) despreciable; **she's feeling** ~ **today** ella se encuentra fatal hoy

miserere *eccles* miserere *m*; *archi* misericordia (de un asiento en el coro)

misericord misericordia

miserly avar(ient)o

misery miseria

misfile archivar mal

misfire *n* falla de tiro; *mot* falla de encendido; *v* fallar de tiro/de encendido

misfit persona inadaptada

misfortune desgracia

misgiving recelo

misgotten mal adquirido

misgovern gobernar (ie)[2a] mal

misgovernment mala administración

misguide aconsejar mal

misguidedly mal aconsejado

mishandle maltratar

mishap contratiempo

mishit *n* golpe desacertado; *v* golpear mal

misinform informar mal

misinformation informaciones *fpl* falsas

misinterpret interpretar mal

misinterpretation mala interpretación

misjudge juzgar[5] mal

misjudgement juicio errado

mislay extraviar

mislead despistar; (deceive) engañar

misleading engañoso

mismanage administrar mal; (of child) criar mal

mismanagement mala administración; (of children) mala crianza

misnamed mal llamado

misnomer nombre inapropiado

misogamist misógamo

misogamy misogamia

misogynist misógino

misogyny misoginia

misplace colocar[4] mal; (in the wrong place) poner[19] fuera de su lugar; ~**d affection** cariño malogrado

misplacement colocación *f* fuera de lugar

misprint *n* errata; *v* imprimir mal

mispronounce pronunciar mal

mispronunciation pronunciación incorrecta

misquotation cita equivocada

misquote citar mal

misread leer[17] mal; (misinterpret) entender (ie)[2b] mal

misrepresent falsificar[4]

misrepresentation falsificación *f*

misrule *n* desgobierno; *v* gobernar (ie)[2a] mal

[1] **miss** señorita; *fam* niña precoz

[2] **miss** *n* tiro errado; (failure) fracaso; (mistake) desacierto; **near** ~ tiro errado por poco; *v* (not hit) no dar[19] en; fallar; **the arrow just** ~**ed him** por poco la flecha le toca; (not catch) perder (ie)[2b], **she** ~**ed the train** ella perdió el tren; ~ **the boat** *fig* perder (ie)[2b] el tren; (not find) no encontrar (ue)[1a]; (overlook) pasar por alto, **the policeman** ~**ed the clue** el guardia pasó por alto el indicio; (not understand) no entender (ie)[2b], **I** ~**ed the meaning** no entendí el significado; ~ **the point** no comprender el verdadero sentido; (be absent from) faltar a, **I could not** ~ **the wedding** no podía faltar a la boda; (regret absence of) echar en falta; ~ **a class** ausentarse de la lección; ~ **one's footing** perder (ie)[2b] pie; **I** ~**ed your final words** se me escapó lo que usted dijo al final; **I** ~**ed that programme** perdí aquel programa; ~ **out** pasar por alto

missal misal *m*

misshapen deforme

missile proyectil *m*; ~**-carrier** portamisiles *m sing+pl*; ~**-launcher** lanzamisiles *m sing+pl*; ~ **launching** lanzamiento de proyectiles; **guided** ~ proyectil teledirigido

missing extraviado; (absent) ausente; *mil* desaparecido; **report a** ~ **person** dar[19] parte de la desaparición de alguien; ~ **link** eslabón perdido

mission misión (-ones) *f*; ~ **completed** misión cumplida

missionary *n+adj* misionero

missis: the ~ la mujer

Mississippi Misisipi *m*

missive misiva

Missouri Misuri *m*

misspell deletrear mal

misspelling error *m* de ortografía

misspend malgastar

misstate relatar mal

misstatement relación falsa

mist *n* niebla; (at sea) bruma; (slight) calina; **Scotch** ~ llovizna; *v* ~ **over** (a)nublar(se)

mistakable confundible

mistake *n* equivocación *f*; (in exercise) falta; **by** ~ por equivocación; **make a** ~ equivocarse, (in exercise) cometer una falta; **and no** ~! ¡toma no!; *v* (err) equivocarse[4]; (misunderstand) entender (ie)[2b] mal; **they** ~ **me for my brother** me toman por mi hermano

mistaken equivocado; **be** ~ equivocarse[4]; **if I am not** ~ si no me equivoco; ~ **identity** identidad equivocada

mister señor *m*

mistily a través de la niebla

mistime hacer[19] a destiempo

mistiness *see* mist

mistle-thrush zorzal *m*

mistletoe muérdago

mistral mistral *m*

mistranslate traducir[15] mal

mistranslation traducción inexacta

mistress (Mrs) señora; (lover) querida; (teacher) profesora; ~ **of the house** señora de la casa

mistrust *n* desconfianza; *v* desconfiar de

mistrustful desconfiado; **be** ~ **of** recelar de

misty nebuloso; *fig* vaporoso; **it is** ~ hay niebla; ~ **eyes** ojos *mpl* llenos de lágrimas

misunderstand entender (ie)[2b] mal

misunderstanding equivocación *f*; (disagreement) desavenencia

misuse *n* abuso; (of money) malversación *f*; (ill-treatment) mal trato; *v* abusar de; (of money) malversar; (ill-treat) maltratar

mite (contribution) óbolo; *ent* ácaro; *fam* (child) criatura

mitigable mitigable

mitigate mitigar[5]

mitigation mitigación *f*

mitre *n eccles* mitra; *mech* inglete *m*, ~ **joint** ensambladura de inglete; *v eccles* mitrar; *mech* ingletear

mitt (glove) mitón; (hand) mano *f*

mitten mitón *m*

mix *vt +cul* mezclar; (concrete, plaster etc) amasar; (drinks) preparar; **if you** ~ **your drinks you will get drunk** si usted mezcla las bebidas se emborrachará; (salad) aderezar[7]; *vi* mezclarse; (of people) asociarse (**with** con), (socially) alternar (**with** con); ~ **in/ with high society** frecuentar la alta sociedad; ~**ed** mezclado, (assorted) variado, *sp* mixto, ~ **doubles** parejas mixtas; ~**ed company** compañía de dos sexos; ~**ed marriage** matrimonio mixto (entre dos razas/religiones); ~**ed number** *math* número mixto; **have** ~**ed feelings (about)** estar[19] indeciso (sobre); ~**-up** *n* confusión *f*; ~**ed up** (in disorder) en desorden, (person) confuso; ~**ed up with** implicado en; **get** ~**ed up in/with** mezclarse en

mixer *+rad* mezclador *m*; (person) persona sociable; **concrete-**~ hormigonera; **food-**~ batidora

mixing acción *f* de mezclar; ~**-stage** *cin* tablero de mezcla

mixture mezcla; *med* medicina; (of cloth) mezclilla

mizzen: ~**-mast** palo de mesana; ~**-sail** mesana

mizzle *sl* (depart) zafarse; (drizzle) llovíznar

mnemonic mnemotécnico

moan *n* gemido; (complaint) queja; *v* gemir (i)[3]; (complain) quejarse (**about** de)

moaning gemidos *mpl*; (grumbling)

quejas *fpl*

moat foso; ~ed fosado

mob *n* (crowd) muchedumbre *f*; (rabble) populacho; (gang) pandilla; ~-law ley *f* de Lynch; *v* atacar⁴ en masa; **the youngsters ~ their idols** los jóvenes festejan tumultuosamente a sus ídolos

mob-cap cofia

mobile móvil; *mil* motorizado, ~ **column** columna motorizada; **socially** ~ adaptable; ~ **canteen** cantina ambulante; ~ **home** coche *m* vivienda, *fam* rulote *f*

mobility movilidad *f*

mobilization movilización *f*

mobilize movilizar⁷

mobster gángster *m*

moccasin mocasín (-ines) *m*

mocha (café) moca

mock *n* burla; **make ~ of** poner¹⁹ en ridículo; *adj* fingido; (burlesque) burlesco; ~-**heroic** heroicoburlesco; ~ **modesty** modestia fingida; ~-**orange** *bot* jeringuilla; ~ **turtle soup** sopa a imitación de tortuga; *v* burlarse de; (mimic) imitar; ~-**up** *n* maqueta en escala natural

mocker guasón *m* (-ona *f*)

mockery burla; **make a ~ of** mofarse de

mocking *n* burlas *fpl*; *adj* burlón; ~-**bird** sinsonte *m*

mod *n* petimetre *m*

modal modal

mode (method) manera; (fashion) moda; **à la ~** de moda

model *n* +*fig* modelo; *archi* maqueta; (artist's, fashion) modelo *m*+*f*; *adj* modelo *m only*; ~ **house** casa modelo; (miniature) en miniatura, ~ **railway** ferrocarril *m* en miniatura; ~ **aeroplane** aeromodelo; ~ **aeroplane flying** aeromodelismo; ~ **car racing** automodelismo; **she is a ~ student** ella es una alumna modelo; *vt* modelar (**on** sobre); (plan) planear (**after** según); *vi* hacer¹⁹ de modelo

modeller modelador *m* (-ora *f*)

modelling *n* modelado; *adj* de modelar; ~ **clay** arcilla de modelar

moderate *n pol* moderado; *adj* +*pol* moderado; (of prices) módico; *v* moderar; (of wind) amainar

moderation moderación *f*; **in ~** con moderación

moderator moderador *m*; (arbitrator) árbitro; *eccles* presidente *m* de la asamblea de la iglesia escocesa

modern *n*+*adj* moderno; **he is one of the ~s** él es uno de los modernos; **fashions for the ~ miss** modas para chicas modernas; ~ **languages** lenguas modernas

modernism modernismo

modernist *n*+*adj* modernista *m*+*f*

modernistic modernista *m*+*f*

modernity modernidad *f*

modernize modernizar⁷

modest modesto; (chaste) púdico; (moderate) moderado

modesty modestia; (chastity) pudor *m*

modicum porción pequeña

modifiable modificable

modification modificación *f*; **make ~s to** hacer¹⁹ modificaciones a

modify modificar⁴

modifying modificante

modish en boga

modiste modista *m*+*f*

modulate modular

modulation modulación *f*; **frequency ~** modulación *f* de frecuencia

modulator modulador *m*

module módulo

Mogul mogol; **the Great ~** el Gran Mogol; (tycoon) magnate *m*

mohair moer *m*, mohair *m*

Mohammedan *n*+*adj* mahometano

Mohican *n*+*adj* mohicano

moiety parte *f*

moiré muaré

moist húmedo

moisten humedecer(se)¹⁴

moistening-sponge esponjilla humedecedora

moisture humedad *f*

moisturize hidratar

moisturizing: ~ **cream** crema hidratante

molar *n* muela; *adj* molar

molasses melaza

mold, molding, moldy *etc see* **mould** *etc*

mole (on skin) lunar *m*; (pier) muelle *m*; *zool* topo; *pol* (infiltrator) quintacolumnista *m*+*f*, *sl* submarino; ~-**hill** topera; **make a mountain out of a ~-hill** hacer¹⁹ de una pulga un elefante; ~-**skin** piel *f* de topo

molecular molecular

molecule molécula
molest importunar
molestation importunidad *f*
moll *sl* ramera
mollification apaciguamiento
mollify apaciguar[6]
mollusc molusco
mollycoddle mimar
Molotov: ~ **cocktail** cóctel *m* molotov
molten fundido; ~ **glass** vidrio fundido; ~ **lava** lava líquida
molybdenum molibdeno
moment momento; (importance) importancia; **at any** ~ de un momento a otro; **at/for the** ~ de momento; **at the present** ~ (nowadays) actualmente; **at this** ~ en este momento; **eat it this** ~! ¡cómelo en seguida!; **in a** ~ en un momento; **just a** ~, **please** un momentito, por favor; **your big** ~ **has come** ha llegado su oportunidad
momentarily (in a moment) en un momento; (for a moment) por un momento
momentary momentáneo
momentous trascendental
momentum +*fig* ímpetu *m*
Monegasque monegasco
monarch monarca *m*
monarchic(al) monárquico
monarchist *n*+*adj* monarquista *m*+*f*
monarchy monarquía; **absolute/constitutional** ~ monarquía absolutista/constitucional
monastery monasterio
monastic(al) monástico
monasticism vida monástica
Monday lunes *m*; **on** ~ el lunes; **on** ~**s** los lunes
monetary monetario
money dinero; *esp SA* plata; *sl* pasta; (coins) monedas *fpl*; **paper** ~ papel *m* moneda; **ready** ~ dinero contante; **make** ~ ganar dinero; **make a lot of** ~ hacer[19] los oros y los moros; **keep in** ~ proveer[17] de dinero; **get one's** ~**'s worth out of** sacar[4] el valor de; **throw good** ~ **after bad** echar la soga tras el caldero; ~ **for jam/old rope** ganga; **play cards for** ~ jugar (ue)[1a] el dinero a los naipes; ~ **talks** *prov* poderoso caballero es Don Dinero; ~**-bags** talega, (person) ricachón (-ones) *m* (-ona *f*); ~**-box** hucha; ~**-changer**

cambista *m*; ~**-grubber** avaro; ~**-lender** prestamista *m*; ~**-making** hacer *m* dinero, *adj* lucrativo; ~ **market** mercado monetario; ~**-order** *n* giro postal; ~**-saving** que ahorra dinero; ~**-spinner** producto rentable, *fam* sacapasta *m*
moneyed adinerado
Mongol(ian) *n*+*adj* mongol *m* (-ola *f*)
mongoose mangosta
mongrel *n* perro callejero; *adj* mestizo
monitor *n* (school) monitor *m*; *rad* radiorreceptor *m* de contrastación; *rad* (person) escucha *m*+*f*; *v* vigilar; *rad* radiocaptar
monk monje *m*
monkey *n* mono; *fig* diablillo; *mech* maza; **make a** ~ **out of** tomar por primo; ~ **business/tricks** trucos *mpl*; ~**-nut** cacahuete *m*; ~**-puzzle** araucaria, *Chil* pehuén *m*; ~**-wrench** llave inglesa; *v* ~ **about** hacer[19] payasadas; ~ **about with** meterse con
monkish de monje
monochrome monocromo
monocle monóculo
monocular monocular
monody monodia
monogamist monógamo
monogamy monogamia
monogram monograma *m*
monograph monografía
monolith monolito
monolithic monolítico
monologue monólogo
monomania monomanía
monomaniac monomaníaco
monoplane monoplano
monopolist monopolista *m*+*f*
monopolization monopolización *f*
monopolize monopolizar[7]
monopoly monopolio; **have a** ~ **on** tener[19] un monopolio de
monorail monocarril *m*; ~ **train** tren *m* monocarril
monosyllabic monosílabo
monosyllable monosílaba
monotheism monoteísmo
monotheist monoteísta
monotone monotonía *m*+*f*
monotonous monótono
monotony monotonía
Monotype *tr* monotipia; ~ **operator** monotipista *m*

monoxide monóxido
monseigneur monseñor *m*
monsoon monzón (-ones) *m*
monster *n* monstruo; *adj* (large) enorme
monstrance custodia
monstrosity monstruosidad *f*
monstrous monstruoso
montage montaje *m*
month mes *m*; **8,000 pesetas a ~** 8,000 pesetas mensuales; **two ~s ago** hace dos meses; **in a ~ of Sundays** en mucho tiempo; **a ~'s notice** aviso de despedida dentro de un mes
monthlies menstruación *f*, *fam* regla
monthly *n* revista mensual; *adj* mensual; **~ payment** mensualidad *f*; *adv* mensualmente
monument monumento; **~ to s.o.** monumento conmemorándole a uno
monumental monumental
moo *n* mugido; *v* mugir[9]
mooch: ~ about vagar[5]
[1] **mood** humor *m*; **be in a good/bad ~** estar[19] de buen/mal humor; **be in the ~ for** estar[19] de humor para
[2] **mood** *gramm* modo
moodiness mal humor *m*; (sulkiness) murria; (indulging in varying moods) carácter caprichoso
moody de mal humor; (sulky) moroso; (changeable) caprichoso
moon *n* luna; *poet* (month) mes *m*; **once in a blue ~** de Pascuas a Ramos; **next blue ~** (never) cuando San Juan baje el dedo; **~ probe** *space* sonda lunar; **~beam** rayo de luna; **~-faced** carirredondo; **~-landing** alunizaje *m*; **~-launch** lanzamiento de un cohete hacia la luna; **~light** *n* luz *f* de la luna; **in the ~light** a la luz de la luna; **~light flit** mudanza a la chita callando; **~light** *v* tener[19] empleo adicional; **~lighter** persona que tiene pluriempleo; **~-lighting** pluriempleo; **~lit** (night) de luna, (room) iluminado por la luna; **~rise** salida de la luna; **~scape** paisaje *m* lunar; **~shine** licor destilado ilegalmente; **~-shiner** fabricante *m* de licor ilegal; **~shot** lanzamiento de un cohete a la luna; **~stone** adularia; **~-struck** chiflado; *v* **~ about** vagar[5]; estar en la luna
moonless sin luna
moony (absent-minded) distraído;

(crazy) chiflado
Moor *n* moro
[1] **moor** *n* (heath) brezal *m*; **~hen** polla de agua; **~land** brezal *m*, páramo
[2] **moor** *v* *naut* amarrar
mooring: ~-place amarradero; **~s** amarras *fpl*
Moorish moro; *archi + lit etc* árabe
moose alce norteamericano
moot *adj* discutible; *v* proponer[19] para la discusión
mop *n* (for floor) fregona; (for dishes) estropajo; (untidy hair) greña; *v* fregar (ie)[2a]; **he mopped his brow** él se enjugó la frente; **~ up** secar[4], *mil* limpiar de enemigos
mope *n* melancolía; *v* entregarse[5] a la melancolía
moped ciclomotor *m*
moping, mopish melancólico
mopping-up fregado; **~ operation** *mil* operación *f* de limpieza
moquette moqueta
moraine morena
moral *n* moraleja; **~s** moralidad *f*; *adj* moral; **~ certainty** evidencia moral; **~ victory** victoria moral
morale moral *f*
moralist moralista *m + f*
morality moralidad *f*
moralize moralizar[7]
morass + *fig* cenagal *m*
moratorium moratoria
morbid (of feelings) malsano; (gruesome) horripilante; (pathological) morboso; **~ curiosity** curiosidad *f* malsana
morbidity (feelings) lo malsano; (pathological) morbosidad *f*
mordant mordaz (-ces)
more más; **~ than** más que, (followed by a number) más de, tengo más de cinco caballos (followed by verb) más de lo que, **he has ~ than you think** él tiene más de lo que usted cree; **~ and ~** cada vez más; **no ~, not any ~** no más, (no longer) ya no; **~ or less** (poco) más o menos; **once ~** una vez más; **the ~ the merrier** cuanto más, mejor; **all the ~** tanto más; **the ~ he shouts the ~ she weeps** cuanto más grita él, más llora ella
morello cherry guinda
moreover además

morganatic morganático
morgue depósito de cadáveres
moribund moribundo
Mormon *n* mormón *m* (-ona *f*); *adj* mormónico
morning *n* mañana; (before dawn) madrugada; **good ~!** ¡buenos días!; **in the ~** por la mañana; **at seven o'clock in the ~** a las siete de la mañana; *adj* matinal; **~ coat** chaqué *m*; **~ paper** diario de la mañana; **~ sickness** náuseas *fpl* (que se tienen por la mañana); **~ star** lucero del alba
Moroccan *n+adj* marroquí
Morocco Marruecos; **~ leather** marroquí *m*
moron imbécil *m+f*
moronic de imbécil
morose malhumorado
morphine morfina
morphology morfología
morris: **~ dance** mojiganga
morrow (future time) mañana; (day after) día *m* siguiente; **on the ~** el día de mañana, el día siguiente
Morse (code) (alfabeto) Morse *m*
morsel bocado
mortal *n+adj* mortal *m+f*
mortality mortalidad *f*
mortar *mil* mortero; **~-board** birrete *m*
mortgage *n* hipoteca; *v* hipotecar[4]
mortgagee acreedor *m* (-ora *f*)
mortgagor deudor hipotecario
mortician empresario de pompas fúnebres
mortification humillación *f*; **~ of the flesh** mortificación *f* de la carne
mortify humillarse; *med* gangrenarse; **~ the flesh** mortificar[4] la carne; **be mortified** avergonzarse[1a+7]
mortise *n* muesca; *v* hacer[19] muescas
mortuary *n* depósito de cadáveres; *adj* mortuario
mosaic mosaico
Moscow Moscú
Moslem musulmán *m* (-ana *f*)
mosque mezquita
mosquito mosquito; **~-net** mosquitero
moss musgo; *geog* pantano
mossy musgoso
most *n* la mayor parte; **at ~** a lo más; **make the ~ of** sacar[4] el mejor partido de, (exaggerate) exagerar; *adj* más, muy; **~ children** la mayoría de los

niños; **for the ~ part** generalmente; *adv* más; (*US* almost) casi; **~ of all** sobre todo; **a ~ exciting film** una película sumamente emocionante
mostly principalmente
motel motel *m*
motet motete *m*
moth mariposa nocturna; (clothes-~) polilla; **~-ball** bola de naftalina; **~-eaten** apolillado, *fig* anticuado; **~ hole** agujero hecho por la polilla; **~-proof** a prueba de polillas
mother *n* madre *f*; **Mother Church** (Christian Church) Santa Madre Iglesia; (chief church of country) iglesia metropolitana; **~ country** (madre) patria; **~ love** amor *m* maternal; **~-ship** buque *m* nodriza; **~ superior** superiora; **~-tongue** lengua materna; **every ~'s son** todo bicho viviente; **Mother's Day** día *m* de la Madre; **~-in-law** suegra; **~-of-pearl** *n* nácar *m*, *adj* nacarado; *v* servir (i)[3] de madre; (give birth to) dar[19] a luz
motherhood maternidad *f*
Mothering Sunday cuarto domingo de cuaresma
motherless huérfano de madre
motherliness cariño maternal
motherly maternal
mothy apolillado
motif *arts+mus* tema; (sewing) adorno
motion *n* movimiento; (gesture) señal *f*, (with the hand) ademán *m*; (parliamentary) moción *f*; *med* movimiento del vientre; **in ~** en marcha, *mech* en operación; **~-picture** *n* película, *adj* motor *m+f* cinematográfico; *vt* indicar[4] (con la mano); **~ to s.o. to do s.t.** indicar[4] a uno que +*subj*; *vi* hacer[19] señas
motionless inmóvil
motivate motivar
motivation motivación *f*
motive *n* motivo; *adj* motor *m+f*, motriz (-ces) *f*; **~ power** fuerza motriz
motiveless sin motivo
motley *n* botarga; *adj* abigarrado
motor *n* motor *m*; **~-bike**, **~-cycle** motocicleta; **~-boat** motora; **~-bus** autobús *m*; **~ car** coche *m*, *SA* carro; **~-coach** autocar *m*; **~-cyclist** motorista *m+f*; **~-home** coche *m* vivienda; **~-launch** lancha motora; **~-lorry**, **~-truck** ca-

mión (-oncs) *m*; ~**man** conductor *m*
de tranvía/tren eléctrico; ~**-scooter**
vespa; ~**-spirit** gasolina; ~**way** autopista; *v* viajar en coche

motorcade caravana de coches

motoring *n* automovilismo; *adj* automovilista

motorist automovilista *m+f*

motorization motorización *f*

motorized: ~ **troops** tropas motorizadas

mottle jaspear

motto lema; *her* divisa

¹ **mould** (fungus) moho

² **mould** *n* molde *m*; (cast) pieza
moldeada; *fig* carácter *m*; *v* moldear;
fig amoldar

¹ **moulder** (away) convertirse (ie)²ᶜ en
polvo

² **moulder** moldeador *m* (-ora *f*)

mouldiness moho

moulding amoldamiento, moldeado;
bui moldura

mouldy mohoso; *fig* sin valor

moult *n* muda; *v* mudar la pluma/piel

mound *n* montón (-ones) *m*; *archi* túmulo; *v* amontonar

mount *n* montaña; (horse) montura; *vt*
montar; (climb) subir (on to en/a);
(put on a horse) montar a caballo;
(provide with horses) proveer¹⁷ de
caballos; (jewel) engastar; ~ **guard**
montar la guardia; *vi* subir a caballo;
~ **up** aumentar

mountain *n* montaña; (pile) montón
(-ones) *m*; ~ **ash** serbal *m*; ~ **chain**
cordillera; ~**-dew** whisky *m* de contrabando; ~**-lion** puma *m*; ~**-range**
sierra; ~**side** falda de una montaña;
adj montañés (-esa)

mountaineer (mountain dweller) montañés *m* (-esa *f*); (climber) montañero

mountaineering, mountain climbing
montañismo

mountainous montañoso

mountebank saltimbanqui *m*

mounting *n* montadura; *mech* montaje
m; (of jewel) montura *m*; *adj* ~ **costs**
gastos *mpl* crecientes

mountie agente *m* de la policía
canadiense

mourn *vt* llorar la muerte de; (wear
~ing) llevar luto por; *vi* lamentarse,
estar¹⁹ de luto

mourner doliente *m+f*

mournful triste

mournfulness tristeza

mourning *n* (grief) duelo; (clothing)
luto; **be in/wear** ~ estar¹⁹ de luto; **be
in/wear** ~ **for** llevar luto por; **deep** ~
luto rigoroso; **half-**~ medio luto; *adj*
de luto

mouse *n* ratón (-ones) *m*; ~**-hole** ratonera; ~**-trap** ratonera; *v* cazar⁷ ratones

mouser gato cazador de ratones

mousse postre de huevos y crema batidos

moustache bigote *m*; **he has a** ~ él lleva
bigote; **grow a** ~ dejarse bigote;
drooping ~ bigote *m* llorón

mousy como un ratón; (colour) pardusco; (shy) tímido

mouth *n* *anat*+*fig* boca; *fam* hocico; (of
river) desembocadura; **down in the** ~
alicaído; **keep one's** ~ **shut** (refrain
from talking) callarse, (keep a secret)
guardar un secreto; **make one's** ~
water hacerse¹⁹ agua la boca; **not to
open one's** ~ no decir¹⁹ esta boca es
mía; **by word of** ~ de palabra; ~**-
organ** (h)armónica; ~**piece** *mus* (+ of
pipe *etc*) boquilla, (of phone) micrófono, (spokesman) portavoz (-ces)
m; ~**-ulcer** boquera; ~**-wash**, ~**-rinse**
enjuague *m*; ~**-watering** apetitoso; *v*
pronunciar con afectación; hablar con
movimientos de la boca exagerados

mouthful bocado

movability movilidad *f*

movable *n*: ~**s** bienes *mpl* muebles; *adj*
movible

move *n* (movement) movimiento;
(manoeuvre) maniobra; (in game)
jugada; (to new house) mudanza; **on
the** ~ en movimiento; **she's always on
the** ~ ella está siempre en movimiento; **get a
~ on** darse¹⁹ prisa, *fam* menearse; **get
a ~ on!** ¡despabílate!; **make a** ~ dar¹⁹
un paso; **make the first** ~ dar¹⁹ el
primer paso; **it's time we made a** ~
(it's time we set off) ya es hora de
ponernos en camino; **have first** ~ (in
game) salir¹⁹; **it's your** ~ le toca a
usted; **is it my** ~? ¿a mí me toca?;
whose ~ **is it?** ¿a quién le toca?

vt mover (ue)¹ᵇ; (from one place to
another) trasladar; (disturb) remover
(ue)¹ᵇ; (shake) menear; (purpose)

proponer[19]; (of emotions) conmover (ue)[1b]; ~ **house** mudar de casa; ~ **s.o. to** +*infin* mover (ue)[1b] a una persona a +*infin*

~ **aside**, ~ **away** apartar

~ **on** hacer[19] circular

~ **up** subir

vi moverse (ue)[1b]; (set off) ponerse[19] en marcha; (to another place) trasladarse; (go to a new house) mudar de casa; (of bowels) exonerarse

~ **about** ir[19] y venir[19]

~ **along** circular; ~ **along, please!** (in bus *etc*) ¡más adentro por favor!

~ **aside** retirarse

~ **away** apartarse

~ **forward** avanzar[7]

~ **in** instalarse (en)

~ **on** avanzar[4]; (keep moving) circular

~ **out** salir[19]; mudarse de casa

~ **over** (to the side of the road) *mot* orillarse

~ **round** (spin) dar[19] vueltas; (move in circles) rodar

~ **up** subir; (make room) moverse (ue)[1b]

movement movimiento; *mech* mecanismo; (of bowels) defecación *f*; *comm* actividad *f*; *mus* tiempo; (of traffic) circulación *f*

mover instigador *m* (-ora *f*); (proposer) autor *m* (-ora *f*); **prime** ~ *mech* máquina motriz; *fig* promotor *m* (-ora *f*)

movie película; ~-**goer** aficionado al cine; ~-**house**, ~-**theatre** cine *m*; ~-**land** cinelandia; ~-**star** (female) estrella de cine, (male) astro de cine

[1] **moving:** *US* ~-**company** agencia de mudanzas

[2] **moving** *adj* movedizo; (of emotions) conmovedor; ~-**picture** película; ~ **spirit** alma

mow down segar (ie)[2a+5]

mower (person) segador *m*; (machine) segadora; **lawn-**~ cortacéspedes *m sing+pl*

mowing *n* siega; (harvest) cosecha; ~-**machine** segadora (mecánica)

Mozambican mozambiqueño

Mozarab(ic) mozárabe *m+f*

much mucho; ~ **wealth** mucha riqueza; (before *past part*) muy; ~ **admired** muy admirado; (by far) con mucho; ~ **ado about nothing** mucho ruido, pocas nueces; ~ **of a muchness** lo mismo poco más o menos; ~ **the same** casi lo mismo; **as** ~, **so** ~ tanto; **as** ~ **as** tanto como, **I have as** ~ **money as you** tengo tanto dinero como usted; **as** ~ **again**, **as** ~ **more** otro tanto más; **how** ~? ¿cuánto?; **however** ~ por mucho que +*subj*; **make** ~ **of** dar[19] mucha importancia a, (person) agasajar; ~ **as he would wish** por mucho que él quisiera; **not** ~ **of a ... ...** de poca cuantía; **not so** ~ **as** ni siquiera; **think** ~ **of** estimar en mucho; **not think** ~ **of** tener[19] en poco; **I thought as** ~ ya me lo figuraba; **too** ~ demasiado; **very** ~ muchísimo; **thank you very** ~ muchísimas gracias

muck *n* (dirt) suciedad *f*; (manure) estiércol *m*; *lit* (worthless work) porquería; ~-**rake** escarbar en vidas ajenas; ~-**raker** revelador *m* de escándalos

~ **about** perder (ie)[2b] el tiempo; ~ **about with** manosear

~ **around** ocuparse en fruslerías

~-**up** *n* (mess) desorden; (failure) fracaso

~ **up** *v* (damage) estropear; (dirty) ensuciar; (make untidy) desordenar

mucky sucio

mucous mucoso; ~ **membrane** mucosa

mucus moco

mud barro; +*fig* fango; **throw/sling** ~ **at** calumniar; ~-**bath** lodos *mpl*; ~-**flats** marisma; ~-**guard** guardabarros *m sing+pl*; ~-**lark** golfillo; ~-**pack** mascarilla de belleza; **stick in the** ~ atascarse; **stick-in-the-**~ retrógrado

muddle *n* (confusion) confusión *f*; (disarray) desorden *m*; (bewilderment) aturdimiento; **get into a** ~ embrollarse; **get s.o. into a** ~ embrollarle a uno; **make a** ~ armar un lío; ~-**headed** atontado; *vt* embrollar; (person) aturdir; ~ **up** confundir; *vi* obrar sin ton ni son; ~ **through** tener[19] éxito sin saber cómo

muddy *adj* fangoso; (of liquids) turbio; *v* manchar de barro; (of liquids) enturbiar

[1] **muff** manguito

[2] **muff** *n* (fool) tonto; *v* perder (ie)[2b] la ocasión; (fail to catch a ball) dejar escapar la pelota

muffin especie *f* de panecillo que se come tostado

muffle *n* mufla; *v* (wrap up) embozar(se)[7]; (~ the noise of) amortiguar[6] el ruido de; (of drums) enfundar

muffler (scarf) bufanda; *mus* sordina; (*US* silencer) silenciador *m*

mufti traje *m* de paisano; **in** ~ vestido de paisano

[1] **mug** tazón *m*; **beer-**~ jarra

[2] **mug** *n* (face) *sl* hocico; (fool) primo; **~-shot** fotografía de identidad; *v* ~ **up** (swot) empollar

[3] **mug** *v* (attack and rob) atracar[4]

mugger atracador *m*

mugging atracos *mpl*

mugwump *US* republicano independiente

muggy bochornoso

mulatto mulato

mulberry *n* mora; (tree) moral *m*; *adj* (colour) morado

mulch cubrir (*past part* cubierto) con estiércol, paja *etc*

mulching acción *f* de cubrir con estiércol *etc*

mulct *n* multa; *v* multar; ~ **of** quitar

mule *zool* mula; (slipper) babucha; (obstinate person) testarudo

muleteer mule(te)ro

mulish terco

mull calentar (ie)[2a] con especias; ~ **over** meditar sobre

mullet (red) salmonete *m*; (grey) mújol *m*

mulligatawny sopa muy condimentada

mullion parteluz (-ces) *f*; **~ed** dividido con parteluz

multicoloured multicolor

multifarious vario

multiform multiforme

multilateral (many-sided) multilátero; *pol* multilateral

multimillionaire multimillonario

multiple *n* múltiple *m*; **in** ~ *elect* en paralelo; *adj* múltiple; ~ **crash** *mot* choque *m* en cadena; ~ **store** almacén *m* (de una cadena)

multiplexing *space* multiplaje *m*

multiplication multiplicación *f*; ~ **table** tablas *fpl* de multiplicar; ~ **sign** signo de multiplicación

multiplicity multiplicidad *f*

multiplier multiplicador *m*

multiply *vt* multiplicar[4] (by por); *vi* multiplicarse[4]

multi-purpose para varios usos

multi-storey de varios pisos; ~ **block** (of flats) rascacielos *m sing+pl*; ~ **car park** garaje *m* de varios pisos

multitude multitud *f*

multitudinous muy numeroso

[1] **mum** *n* mamá

[2] **mum** *n* ~'**s the word!** ¡chitón!; **keep** ~ callarse; *adj* callado

mumble *n* refunfuño *f*; *v* musitar entre dientes

mumbo-jumbo mojiganga

mummer histrión *m*

mummification momificación *f*

mummify momificar[4]

[1] **mummy** (mother) mamaíta

[2] **mummy** (corpse) momia

mumps paperas *fpl*

munch mascar[4]

mundane mundano

municipal municipal; ~ **council** ayuntamiento; ~ **utilities** servicios *mpl* municipales

municipality municipio

munificence munificencia

munificent munífico

munition: ~ **works** fábrica de municiones; **~s** municiones *fpl*; **~s dump** depósito de municiones

mural *n* cuadro mural; *adj* mural

murder *n* asesinato; *leg* homicidio; ~ **trial** proceso de un homicida; ~ **weapon** arma (con la cual se cometió el asesinato); *v* asesinar; (play) degollar; (song) cantar mal; (language) estropear

murderer asesino; *leg* homicida *m*

murderess asesina

murderous sanguinario

murk oscuridad *f*

murky oscuro; +*fig* tenebroso

murmur *n* murmullo; *v* ~ (**against**) +*fig* murmurar (contra)

murmuring murmuración *f*

murrain morriña

muscatel *n*+*adj* (grape, wine) moscatel *m*

muscle *n* músculo; *fig* fuerza muscular; **~-bound** con los músculos agarrotados; *v* ~ **in** (on) entrar por fuerza (en)

Muscovite *n*+*adj* moscovita *m*+*f*

862

muscular muscular; ~ **man** hombre musculoso

Muse musa

muse meditar (**upon** en)

museum museo

mush *cul* gachas de harina de maíz; *rad* interferencia; *fam* sentimentalismo exagerado; (person) *sl* tío; (face) *sl* morro

mushroom *n* champiñón (-ones) *m*; *adj* de champiñones; *fig* rápido; ~ **cloud** hongo atómico; ~ **growth** crecimiento rapidísimo; *v* (appear) aparecer[14] de la noche a la mañana; (grow) crecer[14] rápidamente

mushy pulposo; *fig* excesivamente sentimental

music música; (score) partitura; **set to** ~ poner[19] musica a, *fam* musicar[4]; **face the** ~ pagar[5] el pato; ~-**box** caja de música; ~ **publisher** editor *m* de obras musicales; ~-**hall** teatro de variedades; ~-**master** profesor *m* de música; ~ **school** conservatorio; ~ **shop** tienda de música; ~-**stand** atril *m*; ~-**stool** taburete *m* de piano

musical *theat* obra musical; **be** ~ (have talent) tener[19] talento para la música, (enjoy music) ser[19] aficionado a la música; ~ **box** caja de música; ~ **chairs** juego de la silla; ~ **comedy** opereta, *Sp* zarzuela; ~ **instrument** instrumento musical

musicality armonía

musician músico; **street** ~ músico ambulante; ~-**ship** calidad *f* de músico

musicology musicología

musk almizcle *m*; ~-**deer** almizclero; ~-**melon** melón *m*; ~-**ox** buey almizclero; ~-**rat** (rata) almizclera; ~-**rose** (rosa) almizcleña

muskeg turbera

musket mosquete *m*

musketeer mosquetero

musketry mosquetes *mpl*; (troops) fusilería; (fire) tiro(s) de fusilería

musky almizclado

muslin muselina

musquash almizclera

muss *n* *US* desarreglo; *v* desarreglar, desordenar

mussel mejillón *m*

Mussulman *n* + *adj* musulmán (-ana *f*)

[1] **must** *n* necesidad *f*; *v* (have to) tener[19]

que, **I** ~ **finish this work** tengo que terminar este trabajo; (ought to) deber, **she** ~ **return the book** ella debe devolver el libro; ~ **be** (probably is/are) deber de ser/estar, **you** ~ **be cold** usted debe de tener frío; **it** ~ **be six o'clock** serán las seis; **it** ~ **have been four o'clock** serían las cuatro; **she** ~ **be at least forty** ella tendrá por lo menos cuarenta años; ~ **have** haber[19] tenido que; **you** ~ **have seen her** usted ha tenido que verla

[2] **must** (mould) moho

[3] **must** (wine) mosto

mustang potro mesteño

mustache *see* **moustache**

mustard mostaza; ~-**gas** gas *m* mostaza; ~-**plaster** sinapismo; ~-**pot** mostacera

muster *n* + *mil* (gathering) asamblea; (review) revista; (~-roll) lista; *naut* rol *m*; **pass** ~ pasar revista; *v* convocar[4] una asamblea; *mil* juntar para pasar revista; ~ **up** juntar, ~ **up courage** hacer[19] de tripas corazón

mustiness moho

musty (mouldy) mohoso

mutability mutabilidad *f*

mutable mutable

mutant mutante *m*

mutate mutar

mutation mutación (-ones) *f*

mute *n* mudo; *mus* sordina; **deaf**-~ sordomudo; *adj* mudo; ~ **swan** cisne mudo; *v* poner[19] sordina a

mutilate mutilar

mutilation mutilación *f*

mutineer amotinado

mutinous rebelde

mutiny *n* motín (-ines) *m*; *v* amotinarse

mutism mutismo

mutt bobo

mutter *n* murmullo; *v* (speak softly) murmurar; (grumble) refunfuñar

muttering murmullo; (grumbling) refunfuño

mutteringly en voz baja

mutton carne *f* de carnero; **leg of** ~ pierna de carnero; ~-**chop** chuleta de carnero; ~-**head** tonto

mutual mutuo; ~ **aid** ayuda mutua; (by) ~ **consent** (de) común acuerdo; ~ **benefit association** mutualidad *f*; ~ **funds** cooperativa de inversión; ~ **in-**

surance seguros mutuos
mutuality mutualidad *f*
muzzle *n anat* hocico; (leather guard) bozal *m*; (gag) mordaza; (of firearm) boca; **~-loading** que se carga por la boca; *v* abozalar; (gag) amordazar[7]; *fig* imponer[19] silencio en
muzzy confuso
my mi (mis *pl*); **~ ~!** ¡hombre!
mycosis micosis *f*
myelitis mielitis *f*
myope miope *m*+*f*
myopia miopía
myopic miope
myosotis miosota
myriad *n* miríada; *adj* sin cuento; innumerable
myrmidon esbirro
myrrh mirra
myrtle mirto

myself *refl pron* me; **I look after ~** me cuido; (emphatic) yo mismo (-a), **I did it ~** lo hice yo mismo; (after *prep*, except con) mí, **written by ~** escrito por mí (mismo)
mysterious misterioso
mystery misterio; **~ play** auto sacramental
mystic *n*+*adj* místico
mystical místico
mysticism misticismo
mystification mistificación *f*
mystify mistificar[4]
mystique mística
myth mito
mythical mítico
mythological mitológico
mythologist mitólogo
mythology mitología
myxomatosis mixomatosis *f*

N

n (letter) +*math* (unknown number) ene *f*; n^th enésimo; N (North) N (norte)

nab atrapar; *fam* pescar⁴

nabob nabab *m*

nacre nácar *m*

nadir nadir m

naff: ~ off! ¡vete a la mierda!

¹ nag *n* jaca; *pej* rocín *m*

² nag *v* regañar; his conscience ~s him le remuerde la conciencia

nagger renegón *m* (-ona *f*)

nail *n anat* uña; *mech* clavo; bite one's ~s morderse (ue)¹ᵇ las uñas; hit the ~ on the head dar¹⁹ en el clavo; pay on the ~ pagar⁵ a toca teja; ~-brush/file cepillo/lima para las uñas; ~-polish, ~-varnish esmalte *m* (para uñas); ~-varnish remover quitaesmalte *m*; ~-scissors tijeras *fpl* para las uñas; *v* clavar; *fig* (show the falsity of) demostrar (ue)¹ᵃ la falsedad de

~ down sujetar con clavos; (person) comprometer (to a)

~ to clavar en

~ together fijar con clavos

~ up cerrar (ie)²ᵃ con clavos

naïve ingenuo

naïveté, naïvety ingenuidad *f*

naked desnudo; (of birds) implume; stark ~ en cueros (vivos), *fam* en pelota; to the ~ eye a simple vista; with a ~ sword con la espada desenvainada; ~ light llama descubierta; ~ truth pura verdad

nakedness desnudez *f*

namby-pamby *n* + *adj* ñoño

name nombre *m*; Christian ~ nombre (de pila); (surname) apellido; (nickname) apodo; (of book) título; what is your ~? ¿cómo se llama usted?; my ~ is me llamo; have a good ~ tener¹⁹ buena reputación; make one's ~ (become famous) hacer¹⁹ su numerito; by ~ de nombre; by the ~ of bajo el nombre de; in ~ only nada más que de nombre; in his ~ de parte de él; in the ~ of God/religion por Dios/la fe; ~ of the game lo esencial (de una acción); call s.o. ~s poner¹⁹ motes a, (insult) insultar; ~-calling palabras abusivas; ~-day santo; ~-dropping: alusiones *fpl* frecuentes de personajes célebres para impresionar a los demás; ~-plate letrero, (on manufactured article) placa de fábrica, (private) letrero profesional; ~sake tocayo; *v* nombrar; (christen) bautizar⁷; (give surname) apellidar; (mention) mencionar; (fix) fijar, he ~d the price él fijó el precio

nameless anónimo; (inexpressible) indecible; ~ wickedness maldad *f* nefasta

namely es decir

naming nombramiento; (of child, ship) bautizo

nancy-boy mariquita *m*

nanny niñera; ~-goat cabra

¹ nap (short sleep) sueño ligero; (in afternoon) siesta, take a ~ echar la siesta; catch s.o. napping coger⁸ a uno desprevenido

² nap (on cloth) lanilla; (on plants) pelusilla

³ nap (cards) napolitana; go ~ jugarse (ue)¹ᵃ el todo; (racing) pronóstico seguro

napalm napalm *m*; ~ bomb bomba napalm (bombas napalm)

nape nuca

naphtha nafta

naphthalene naftalina

napkin (baby's) pañal *m*; (table-~) servilleta; ~-ring servilletero

Naples Nápoles *m*

Napoleon Napoleón

Napoleonic napoleónico

nappy pañal *m*

narcissism narcisismo

narcissus narciso

narcosis narcosis *f*

narcotic narcótico
narcotize narcotizar[7]
nark *n sl* (informer) soplón *m* (-ona *f*); *v* (inform) soplar; (annoy) fastidiar, **get ~ed** enfadarse; **~ it!** (stop it!) ¡quieto!
narrate narrar
narration narración *f*
narrative *n* narrativa; *adj* narrativo
narrator narrador *m* (-ora *f*)
narrow: **~s** *n* estrecho; *adj+fig* estrecho; (constricted) reducido; (mean) avaro; **~-boat** barca de canal; **~ circumstances** escasez *f* de medios; **~ escape** escapada por los pelos; **have a ~ escape** escapar por los pelos; **~-gauge** *n* vía estrecha, *adj* de vía estrecha; **~-minded** intolerante; **~-mindedness** intolerancia; *v* estrechar(se), **the road ~s** el camino se estrecha; **the man's eyes ~ed** se le entornaron los ojos al hombre; **~ down to** reducirse[15] a
narrowing estrechamiento
narrowly estrechamente; **he ~ missed drowning** por poco él se ahoga
narrowness estrechez *f*; (of ideas) intolerancia
nasal *n* nasal *f*; *adj* nasal; (of voice) gangoso
nasalize nasalizar[7]
nasally nasalmente; **speak ~** hablar por la nariz
nascent naciente
nastiness (dirtiness) suciedad *f*; (ugliness) fealdad *f*; (repulsiveness) repugnancia; (spite) malicia; (obscenity) indecencia
nasturtium capuchina
nasty (dirty) sucio; (ugly) feo; (repulsive) repugnante; (spiteful) malicioso; (obscene) indecente; (difficult) difícil; (dangerous) peligroso; **be in a ~ mess** *fig* tener[19] el agua al cuello; **turn ~** ponerse[19] desagradable; **video ~** vídeo repugnante u obsceno
nat. (national) nac. (nacional)
natal natal
natch obviamente
Nathaniel Nataniel
nation nación *f*; (people) pueblo; **~hood** calidad *f* de ser nación; **~wide** por toda la nación
national *n+adj* nacional *m+f*; **~ anthem** himno nacional; **(Spanish) ~ costume**

traje típico (español); **~ dance** baile *m* típico; **~ debt** deuda pública; **~ government** gobierno de unión nacional; **~ hero** héroe *m* nacional; **~ holiday** fiesta nacional **~ insurance**; seguro social; **~ monument** monumento nacional; **~ park** parque *m* nacional; **~ service** servicio militar, *fam* mili *f*; **National Socialist** *n+adj* nacional-socialista *m+f*
nationalism nacionalismo
nationalist *n+adj* nacionalista *m+f*
nationality nacionalidad *f*
nationalization nacionalización *f*
nationalize nacionalizar[7]
nationally desde el punto de vista de la nación; (nationwide) por toda la nación
native *n* natural; **I am a ~ of Logroño** soy (natural) de Logroño; (indigenous) indígena *m+f*; *adj* (indigenous) indígena; (innate) innato; *geol* nativo; **go ~** vivir como los indígenas; **~ land** patria; **~ language** idioma *m* natal
Nativity Navidad *f*; (painting) nacimiento (de Cristo); **~ play** auto del nacimiento
N.A.T.O. (North Atlantic Treaty Organization) O.T.A.N. (Organización del Tratado del Atlántico Norte)
natter (chatter) charlar; (grumble) quejarse
natty elegante; *fam* chulo; *sl* chuli
natural *n+adj +mus* natural; (artless) (persona) sencilla; **in a ~ state** en estado natural; **~ child** hijo ilegítimo; **~ colour** color crudo; **~ gas** gas *m* natural; **~ history** historia natural; **~ resources** riqueza natural; **~ science** ciencias *fpl* naturales; **~ selection** selección *f* natural; **by ~ wastage** por proceso vegetativo
naturalism naturalismo
naturalist naturalista *m+f*
naturalistic naturalista
naturalization naturalización *f*; **~ papers** carta de naturaleza; **take out ~ papers** tomar carta de naturalización
naturalize naturalizar[7]; **become ~d** naturalizarse[7]
naturally (by nature) naturalmente; (of course) desde luego
naturalness naturalidad *f*
nature *n* naturaleza; (essence) esencia;

(type) género; **he is violent by** ~ él es violento de por sí; ~ **cure** naturismo; **from** ~ del natural; **in the** ~ **of** algo como; **good** ~ bondad *f*; ~**-lover** naturalista *m+f*; ~ **reserve** parque *m* nacional; ~**-study** estudio de la naturaleza; ~**-worship** culto de la naturaleza

natured: good-, evil-~ de buen/mal carácter

naturism nudismo

naturist nudista *m+f*

naught nada; (figure) cero; **all for** ~ todo en balde; **bring to** ~ frustrar; **come to** ~ malograrse; **set at** ~ despreciar

naughtiness travesura(s) *f*

naughty travieso; (of story) verde; **be** ~ (of child) ser[19] malo

nausea náusea; *fig* asco

nauseate dar[19] náuseas; *fig* dar[19] asco

nauseating, nauseous nauseabundo; *fig* asqueroso

nautical náutico; ~ **mile** milla marina

naval naval; ~ **architect** arquitecto naval; ~ **attaché** agregado de marina; ~ **base** base *f* naval; ~ **dockyard** arsenal *m*; ~ **engagement** batalla naval; ~ **estimates** presupuesto de la Marina; ~ **forces** fuerzas *fpl* navales; ~ **officer** oficial *m* de marina; ~ **power** fuerzas *fpl* navales, (nation) poder marítimo; ~ **reservist** marinero de reserva; ~ **warfare** guerra naval

Navarre Navarra

Navarrese navarro

nave nave *f*

navel ombligo; *fam* timbre *m*; ~ **orange** naranja de ombligo

navicert certificado de navegación

navigability practicabilidad *f* de navegar

navigable navegable

navigate navegar[5]

navigation navegación *f*; (science of ~) náutica; ~ **light** luz *f* de navegación; **aerial** ~ navegación aérea

navigational de navegación

navigator navegante *m*; *aer* piloto

navvy peón (-ones) *m*

navy marina (de guerra); **Navy Department** Ministerio de Marina; **merchant** ~ marina mercante; ~**-blue** azul marino *invar*

Nazarene *n+adj* nazareno

Nazareth Nazaret *m*

Nazi *n+adj* nazi *m+f*

Nazism nazismo

N.B. (nota bene) N.B. (nótese bien)

N.E. (north-east) N.E. (noreste *m*)

Neanderthal neandertal

neap: ~ **tide** marea muerta

Neapolitan *n+adj* napolitano

near *adj* cercano; (of time) inminente, **their defeat is** ~ su derrota es inminente; (of friends) íntimo; (of guess) próximo; (mean) tacaño; **Near East** Cercano Oriente; ~ **future** futuro próximo; ~ **miss** tiro que anda cerca; ~ **relative** pariente cercano (-a); ~**side** *mot* lado izquierdo, *US+Sp* lado derecho; ~**-sighted** miope, *fam* corto de vista; ~**-sightedness** miopía; ~ **thing** escape *m* por un pelo, **that was a** ~ **thing** nos escapamos/me escapé *etc* por un pelo; ~ **translation** traducción aproximada; *adv* cerca; ~ **to** cerca de; ~ **at hand** a mano; **bring** ~ acercar[4] (**to** a); **come/go/draw** ~ acercarse[4] (**to** a); *prep* cerca de; ~**-by** *adj* cercano

nearly casi; **not** ~ ni con mucho; **I** ~ **missed the bus** por poco pierdo el autobús

nearness proximidad *f*; (intimacy) intimidad *f*

neat (tidy) pulcro, arreglado; (clean) limpio; (attractive) atractivo; (of writing) legible; (deft) diestro; (cleverly said) bien dicho; (without water) solo; (*Scots*) pequeño; ~ **and tidy** arregladito; **make a** ~ **job of** hacerlo[19] bien

neatness (tidiness) pulcritud *f*, arreglo; (cleanliness) limpieza; (attractiveness) esbeltez *f*; (of writing) legibilidad *f*; (deftness) destreza

neb (*Scots*) pico; (of cap) visera

nebula nebulosa

nebular, nebulous nebuloso

necessary *n* requisito indispensable; *adj* necesario; **be** ~ hacer[19] falta; **in modern society money is** ~ en la sociedad moderna hace falta dinero

necessitate necesitar

necessitous necesitado

necessity necesidad *f*; **of** ~ de necesidad; **in case of** ~ en caso de urgencia

neck *n* cuello; (animal's) pescuezo; (of

bottle) gollete *m*; (of violin) mastil *m*;
(of dress) escote *m*; **low ~ed**
escotado; **high ~ed** sin escote; **~ and
~ parejo**; **~ or nothing** a toda costa;
get it in the ~ cargársela[5], *fam* cobrar;
~-band cabezón (-ones) *m*; **~-guard**
(on helmet *etc*) cubrenuca *m*; **~-line**
escote *m*; **(with a) plunging ~-line**
(con) mucho escote; **~lace**, **~let** collar *m*; **pearl ~lace** collar de perlas;
~tie corbata; *v* besuquear

neckerchief pañuelo; *Mex* mascada
necking besuqueo
necrology necrología
necromancer nigromante *m*
necromancy nigromancia
nectar néctar *m*
nectarine nectarina
née nacida; **Carmen García, ~ López**
Carmen López de García
need *n* necesidad **(for** de); **(urgent ~)**
urgencia; (poverty) pobreza; (lack)
falta **(of** de); **have ~ of** necesitar; **if ~
be** si fuese necesario; **in case of ~** en
caso de necesidad/urgencia; **in ~ of** a
falta de; **if ~s must** si hace falta; *vt*
hacer[19] falta; **do we ~ it?** ¿nos hace
falta?; **she doesn't ~** me no le hago
falta (a ella); **that dog ~s watching** hay
que vigilar aquel perro; **be ~ed** ser[19]
necesario; **an exit permit is ~ed** se
requiere un permiso de salida; *vi* (be
needy) ser[19] necesitado; **~ to** (have
to) tener[19] que +*infin*; **I ~ to see him**
tengo que verle
needful necesario
needle *n* aguja; **~-case** alfiletero; **~-
woman** costurera; **she is a good ~-
woman** ella cose muy bien; **~work** labor *m* de aguja, (embroidery) bordado; *v* pinchar; *fam* (annoy) meterse
(con frasecitas bien colocadas)
needless superfluo; **~ to say** claro está,
fam ni que decir tiene
needy necesitado
ne'er-do-well perdulario; **he is a ~** es un
gandul
nefarious nefario
negate negar[5]
negation negación *f*
negative *n* (denial) negativa; (answer)
contestación negativa; *phot* negativo;
adj negativo; *elect* electricidad negativa; *v* (reject) rechazar[7]; (veto) po-

ner[19] el veto a
neglect *n* descuido; (self-neglect) dejadez *f*; (state of neglect) abandono;
(non-observance) inobservancia; **fall
into ~** caer[19] en desuso; *v* descuidar,
(person) desatender (ie)[2a]; (omit
carelessly) perder (ie)[2a]; **~ to** dejar de
+*infin*
neglectful negligente
négligé salto de cama; ropa interior
negligence negligencia
negligent negligente
negligible insignificante
negotiability negociabilidad *f*
negotiable negociable; (of road) transitable
negotiate negociar; (obstacle) pasar por;
(difficulty) vencer[12]; **~ a bend** *mot*
tomar una curva; **~ from strength**
negociar desde una posición de fuerza
negotiation negociación; (of an obstacle) salto; (of a bend) toma; **enter into
~s with** entrar en tratos con
negotiator negociador *m* (-ora *f*)
negress negra
negro negro
negroid negroide
Negus negus *m*
negus (drink) vino y agua caliente
neigh *n* relincho; *v* relinchar
neighbour vecino; *bibl* prójimo (-a); **~s**
(people next door) gente *f* de al lado;
~hood vecindad *f*, (local community)
vecindario; **in the ~hood of** cerca de,
(approximately) alrededor de; *v*
estar[19] cercano a
neighbouring vecino; (next door) de al
lado
neighbourliness buena vecindad
neighbourly amistoso; **be ~** ser[19] de
buena vecindad
neither ninguno (**of them** de los dos); **~
answer is correct** ninguna contestación es correcta; **~ ... nor** ni ... ni, **I
like ~ cheese nor fish** no me gusta ni el
queso ni el pescado; **~ will I tell you** yo
tampoco se lo diré; **~ do I** ni yo tampoco
Nemesis Némesis *f*
neo-colonialism neocolonialismo
neolithic neolítico
neologism neologismo
neon neón *m*; **~-lamp**, **~-tube** lámpara/
tubo de neón; **~-sign** anuncio

luminoso de neón
neophyte neófito
nephew sobrino
nephritis nefritis *f*
nepotism nepotismo; *joc sl* yernocracia
Neptune Neptuno
nerd (fool) lerdo
nereid nereida
Nero Nerón
nerve *n anat+bot* nervio; (bravery) valor *m*; (daring) atrevimiento; *fig* (cheek) descaro; **get on s.o.'s ~s** crisparle a alguien los nervios; **have one's ~s on edge** tener[19] los nervios de punta; **lose one's ~** perder (ie)[2b] la cabeza; **strain every ~** hacer[19] un gran esfuerzo; **suffer from ~s** sufrir de los nervios; **what a ~!** ¡qué frescura!; **~-cell** célula nerviosa; **~-centre** centro nervioso, *fig* corazón *m*; **~-gas** gas *m* neurotóxico; **~-racking** horripilante; **~-racking time** mal rato de nervios; *v* animar; **~ o.s.** animarse
nerveless sin sistema nervioso; (weak) débil
nerviness nerviosidad *f*
nervous nervioso; (timid) tímido; **~ breakdown** depresión *f* nerviosa; **~ exhaustion** agotamiento nervioso; **~ strain** tensión nerviosa; **~ system** sistema nervioso
nervousness nerviosidad *f*; (timidity) timidez *f*
nervy nervioso
nest *n* nido; (animal's) madriguera; (brood) nidada *m*; (of drawers, tables) juego; *fam* (home) hogar *m*; **~ of thieves** guarida de ladrones; **feather one's ~** barrer para adentro; **~-egg** nidal *m*, *fam* dinerillos *mpl*; *v* anidar; (search for nests) buscar[4] nidos
nesting período de anidar; **~-box** ponedero
nestle arrimarse (**up to** a); **~ down** anidarse
nestling pajarito (en el nido)
[1] **net** *n* red *f*; (mesh) malla; (fabric) tul *m*; **~-ball** balonred *m*; **~work** red *f*, *rad+TV* cadena; **hair-~** redecilla; *v* coger[8] con red
[2] **net** *adj* neto; **~ amount/price** importe/precio neto; **~ earnings** ganancias *fpl* netas; **~ loss** pérdida neta; **~ proceeds** réditos netos; **~ weight** peso neto; *v*

obtener[19] un beneficio neto
nether más bajo; **~ regions** infierno
Netherlands Países Bajos
netting red *f*; **wire-~** malla de alambre
nettle hortiga; **~-rash** urticaria; *v* irritar
neural neural
neuralgia neuralgia
neuralgic neurálgico
neurasthenia neurastenia
neurasthenic neurasténico
neuritis neuritis *f*
neurologist neurólogo *m+f*
neurology neurología
neuron neurona
neurosis neurosis *f*
neurotic neurótico
neuter neutro
neutral *n mot* punto muerto; (person) neutral *m+f*; *adj* neutral; *bot+ chem+elect+zoo* neutro; **~ corner** (boxing) ángulo neutral
neutrality neutralidad *f*
neutralization neutralización *f*
neutralize neutralizar[7]
neutron neutrón (-ones) *m*
never nunca, jamás; **she ~ talks to herself** ella nunca habla sola; (in no circumstances) de ningún modo; (not even) ni (siquiera), **he ~ said a word** él no dijo ni (siquiera una) palabra; **were he ~ so humble** por más humilde que fuese él; **~ again** nunca (ja)más; **~ fear** no se preocupe, **~ a glance** ni una mirada; **~ mind** (don't worry) no se preocupe, (it doesn't matter) no importa; **~ a one** (not a single one) ni siquiera uno/una; **he was ~ a one to** él nunca+*imperf*; **better late than ~** más vale tarde que nunca; **~-ending** eterno; **~-failing** que nunca falla; **~more** nunca (ja)más; **~theless** sin embargo; **~-to-be-forgotten** inolvidable; **~-~ land** tierra de nunca jamás
new nuevo; (fresh) fresco; **~ milk** leche fresca; (another) otro, **a ~ job** otro trabajo; (inexperienced) inexperto; **~ to** recién venido a; **~ bread** pan tierno; **as good as ~** como nuevo; **what's ~?** ¿qué hay de nuevo)?; **~-born** recién nacido; **~comer** recién llegado; **~fangled** recién inventado; **~-found** recién hallado; **New Guinea** Nueva Guinea; **~-laid eggs** huevos *mpl* frescos; **~ moon** luna nueva,

(time) novilunio; **New Orleans** Nueva Orlcans; ~ **paragraph** aparte; ~ **potato** patatita; ~ **rich** *n* nuevos ricos *mpl*, *adj* nuevo rico; **New South Wales** Nueva Gales del Sur; **New Testament** Nuevo Testamento; **New World** Nuevo Mundo; **New Year('s Day)** (día del) Año Nuevo; **Happy New Year** Feliz Año Nuevo; **New Year's Eve** Nochevieja; **New Year resolution** propósito del Año Nuevo; **New York** Nueva York; **New Yorker** neoyorquino; **New Zealand** Nueva Zelandia/Zelanda; **New Zealander** neozelandés *m* (-esa *f*)

Newfoundland Terranova; (dog) perro de Terranova

newish bastante nuevo

newly (afresh) nuevamente; (recently) recién, ~-**wed** recién casado

newness novedad *f*; (of a person) inexperiencia

news noticias *fpl*; **piece of** ~ noticia; **what's the** ~? ¿qué hay de nuevo?; **be (very much) in the** ~ estar[19] de (excepcional) actualidad; **it was** ~ **to me** me cogió de nuevas; **he has a nose for** ~ él es buen gacetillero; **no** ~ **is good** ~ *prov* malas noticias corren a prisa; ~ **agency** agencia de información; ~**agent**, ~-**dealer** vendedor *m* (-ora *f*) de periódicos; ~**agent's** tienda de periódicos; ~**boy** (chiquillo) vendedor *m* de periódicos; ~-**bulletin** noticiario, *TV* telediario; ~**caster** cronista *m*+*f* de radio/televisión; ~ **conference** rueda de prensa; ~ **coverage** reportaje *m* de noticias; ~-**editor** redactor *m* (-ora *f*) de noticias; ~ **flash** noticia de última hora; ~ **headlines/highlights** noticias *fpl* más destacadas; ~ **item** noticia; ~**letter** boletín (-ines) *m* informativo; ~**paper** periódico, (daily) diario, (weekly) semanario *m*; ~**paper advertising** publicidad *f* de la prensa; ~**paper cutting** recorte *m* de periódico; ~**paperman** periodista *m*; ~**paper rack** revistero; ~**print** papelprensa *m*; ~**reader** *rad*+*TV* locutor *m* (-ora *f*); ~**reel** *cin* noticiario, *Sp tr* No-do; ~**reel camera** cámara de reportero; ~-**reporter** reportero; ~-**room** sala de redacción; ~-**stand** quiosco de periódicos; ~-**theatre** cine

m de actualidades; ~-**vendor** vendedor *m* (-ora *f*) de periódicos; ~**worthy** que merece publicarse

newsy lleno de noticias

newt tritón (-ones) *m*

Newtonian neutoniano

next *adj* (in order) siguiente, ~ **please!** ¡que pase el/la siguiente!; (in future) próximo, ~ **Saturday** el sábado próximo; (in position) vecino, ~ **house** casa vecina; ~ **street** calle *f* de al lado; ~ **but one/two** el primero/segundo después de éste ~ **day** día siguiente; ~ **door** casa de al lado; ~ **door but one** a dos casas (de aquí); ~-**door neighbours** vecinos *mpl* de al lado; ~ **door to** al lado de, *fig* que raya en; ~ **of kin** pariente más cercano; ~ **time** la próxima vez; **on the** ~ **page** a la vuelta; ~ **week/month** semana/mes *m* que viene; *adv* después; ~ **best** segundo; ~ **best thing** lo mejor después de es(t)o; **what** ~? ¿qué más?; ~ **to** (comparison) después de, (place) al lado de; ~ **to impossible** casi imposible; ~ **to nothing** casi nada; **in** ~ **to no time** acto continuo; **wear** ~ **to the skin** llevar sobre la piel

nib plumilla; (of fountain pen) plumín (-ines) *m*

nibble *n* mordisco; *v* mordiscar[4]; (of mice *etc*) roer; (of fish) picar[4]; (of horses) rozar[1]; ~ (**at**) *fig* considerar

niblick niblick *m*

Nicaragua Nicaragua

Nicaraguan *n*+*adj* nicaragüense *m*+*f*

nice (attractive) bonito; (dainty) fino; (kind) simpático; (pleasant) amable; ~ **and** muy, *suff* -ito; ~ **and cool** fresquito; ~ **and warm** calentito; **the weather's** ~ **and warm** hace un calor agradable; ~ **distinction** distinción delicada; ~-**looking** guapo, *fam* mono; ~ **people** (friendly) gente *f sing* simpática, (well-bred) gente buena; **not** ~ (not good manners) feo; **have a** ~ **time** pasarlo bien

nicely (attractively) muy bien; (pleasantly) amablemente; (in a friendly way) con simpatía; ~-**spoken** redicho

niceness (attractiveness) lo bonito; (daintiness) lo fino; (pleasantness) amabilidad; (friendliness) simpatía

nicety exactitud *f*; **niceties** detalles *mpl*;

to a ~ con la mayor precisión
niche nicho; *fig* posición *f* conveniente;
find a ~ for o.s. situarse
Nicholas Nicolás
Nick: Old ~ Patillas *m*
[1] **nick** *n* (cut) muesca; *sl* (gaol) chirona, **in
the** ~ en chirona; *sl* (police-station)
comisaría; **in the** ~ **of time** de perilla; *v*
(cut) hacer[19] muescas (en); *sl* (steal)
afanar, mangar; *sl* (arrest) pescar[4]
[2] **nick: in good** ~en buena condición
nickel níquel *m*; *US* moneda de cinco
centavos; ~**-plated,** ~**-plating** niquelado
nickname *n* apodo; *v* apodar
nicotine nicotina
niece sobrina
niggardliness tacañería
niggardly tacaño
nigger negro; **work like a** ~ trabajar
como un negro; ~ **in the woodpile** gato
encerrado; ~**-heaven** *theat* paraíso
niggle sacar[4] faltas pequeñas
niggling (annoying) irritante; (insignificant) minucioso
night noche *f*; **good** ~! ¡buenas noches!;
at/by ~, **in the** ~ (~**-time**) de noche;
last ~ anoche; ~ **before last** anteanoche; **make a** ~ **of it** estar[19] de juerga
toda la noche; **stay out all** ~ trasnochar; **the** ~ **is young** la noche es joven;
~**bird** ave *f* nocturna, (person) trasnochador *m* (-ora *f*); ~**-blindness**
nictalopia; ~**-bomber** bombardero
nocturno; ~**cap** gorro, *fig* última
bebida antes de acostarse; ~**-clothes**
ropa de dormir; ~**-club** cabaret *m*;
~**-commode** sillico bacín; ~**-cream**
(cosmetic) crema de noche; ~**dress**
camisón (-ones) *m*; ~**fall** anochecer
m; ~**-fighter** *aer* caza *m* nocturno; ~**-
flying** *aer* vuelo nocturno; ~**gown**
camisón (-ones) *m*; ~**jar** *orni* chotacabras *m* *sing+pl*; ~**-life** ambiente
nocturno; ~**light** mariposa; ~ **mail**
(last post) último correo, (train) tren
correo de noche; ~**mare** pesadilla;
~**marish** traumático; ~**-owl** *fig*
trasnochador *m* (-ora *f*); ~**-porter**
portero de noche; ~**-school** escuela
nocturna; ~**shade** dulcamara; **deadly**
~**shade** belladona; ~ **shift** turno de
noche; ~**shirt** camisón (-ones) *m*; ~**-
stick** porra; ~ **tariff** tarifa nocturna;

~**-time** horas *fpl* de la noche; ~
walker ramera; ~**watchman** vigilante
m de noche, *Sp* (policeman) sereno
nightingale ruiseñor *m*
nightly (at night) por las noches; (every
night) todas las noches
nihilism nihilismo
nihilist *n+adj* nihilista *m+f*
nil cero; *sp* **three** ~ tres a cero
Nile Nilo
nimble ligero; ~**-fingered** ligero de
dedos; ~**-witted** alerto
nimbus nimbo
nincompoop bobo
nine *n+adj* nueve *m*; ~ **hundred** novecientos (-as); **in** ~**-eight time** *mus* en
nueve *m* por ocho; **be dressed up to
the** ~**s** estar[19] hecho un brazo de mar,
fam estar[19] todo pimpante; **number**
~**s** (laxative medicine) purga; ~**fold**
nueve veces; ~**pins** juego de bolas
nineteen *n+adj* diecinueve *m*; **talk** ~ **to
the dozen** hablar por los codos
nineteenth decimonono; *fam* diecinueve, ~ **century** siglo diecinueve;
fig ~ **(hole)** bar *m* de un club de golf
ninetieth nonagésimo; *fam* noventa
ninety *n+adj* noventa *m*; **Paris in the
nineties** París en los años noventa;
he's in his nineties él tiene más de
noventa años
ninny bobo
ninth *n* noveno; *fam* novena parte; (of
month) nueve; (of monarch) noveno;
(of Pope) nono; *adj* noveno
ninthly en noveno lugar
nip *n* (bite) mordisco; (pinch) pellizco;
Nip *sl* (*esp US*) japonés *m* (-esa *f*);
there's a ~ **in the air today** hace frío
hoy; ~ **of whisky** copita de whisky; ~
and tuck empate *m*; *v* (bite)
mordiscar[4]; (pinch) pellizcar[4]; (of
wind) picar[4]; *vi* (hurry) correr; (cold)
cortar; ~ **in** colarse (ue)[1a]; ~ **in the
bud** cortar en flor; ~ **out/off** pirarse
nipper (of crab) pinza; (boy) chavalín
(-ines) *m*; ~**s** *elect* tenazas *fpl*
nipple *anat* pezón *m*, *US* teta; (of male)
tetilla; (on feeding bottle) tetilla; *eng*
(for greasing) engrasador *m*
nippy (of person) activo; (of car, boat)
manejable; **the wind is** ~ el viento
pica
nirvana nirvana

Nissen: ~ hut casucha de hierro acanalado

nit liendre *f*; *fig* (~wit) atontolinado;
~-nurse *fam* piojera; ~-picking pedante

nitrate nitrato

nitric nítrico; ~ acid ácido nítrico

nitrite nitrito

nitrogen nitrógeno

nitrogenous nitrogenado

nitro-glycerin nitroglicerina

nitrous nitroso; ~ oxide óxido nitroso

nitty-gritty realidades *fpl* (de un asunto)

nitwit bobo

nix *sl* nada

N.N.E.   (north-north-east)   *n+adj*
N.N.E. (nornordeste) *m*

N.N.W.   (north-north-west)   *n+adj*
N.N.O. (nornoroeste) *m*

no *n* no *m*; *adj* ninguno(s); ninguna(s);
she has ~ friends ella no tiene ningún
amigo/ningunos amigos; I have ~
money no tengo dinero; '~ comment'
'sin comentarios'; ~ dice! ¡claro que
no!; ~ doubt sin duda; ~ entry prohibida la entrada; ~ flowers by request
se ruega no mandar flores; it's ~ good
no vale; it's ~ good running no vale la
pena correr; ~ kidding? ¿de veras?;
~ kidding! ¡déjate de bromas!; ~
longer ya no, I ~ longer see her ya no
la veo; ~ more no más (than de); ~
parking prohibido aparcar; ~ passing/
overtaking prohibido adelantarse; ~
place en ningún sitio; ~ sooner than
tan pronto como; ~ sooner said than
done dicho y hecho; ~ thoroughfare
prohibido el paso; ~ tipping se ruega
no dar propinas; whether or ~ sea o
no sea; with ~ (without) sin, he came
with ~ books vino sin libros; ~body *n*
don nadie *m*; I'm just a ~body here no
pinto nada aquí; ~body else nadie
más; vote of ~ confidence voto de desconfianza; ~-go area zona controlada
por rebeldes; ~-good *n* inútil *m+f*;
~how de ninguna manera; ~-man's
land tierra de nadie; ~ one *see* ~body;
~way(s) de ningún modo

no. (number) núm. (número); nos.
núms. (números)

Noah Noé; ~'s Ark arca de Noé

nob (head) crisma; (toff) pez (-ces)
gordo

nobble (horse) narcotizar[7]; (bribe
jockey) sobornar

nobbling (of horse) narcotización *f*; (of
jockey) soborno, *sl* tongo; (of jury)
soborno

Nobel (prize + prizewinner) nobel *m*

nobility nobleza; (of behaviour) hidalguía

noble *n+adj* noble; (in rank) aristocrático; (of building) magnífico; of ~
descent linajudo; ~ (unsuccessful)
gesture quijotada; ~man aristócrata
m, noble, hidalgo; ~-minded magnánimo; ~woman aristócrata

nobleness nobleza

nocturnal nocturno

nocturne *mus* nocturno

nod *n* (movement) cabezada; (sign)
señal *f* con la cabeza, I signalled to him
with a ~ le hice una señal con la
cabeza; a ~ is as good as a wink a buen
entendedor pocas palabras; *v* (in
assent) asentir (ie)[2c] con la cabeza, he
nodded to me me saludó con la cabeza;
(doze) dar[19] cabezadas; (of trees)
mecerse[14]; give s.o. the ~ echar a uno
una indirecta; on the ~ con solamente
consentimiento formal

nodal nodal

nodding: ~ acquaintance conocimiento
de vista

node *med+phys* nodo; *bot* nudo

nodular nodular

nodule nódulo

noggin vaso pequeño; (measure) medida de licor (1,42 decilitros; (*US*
mountain pass) desfiladero

noise *n* ruido; make a ~ hacer[19] ruido;
he's a big ~ él es un pez gordo; *v*
about/abroad publicar[4]

noiseless(ly) sin ruido

noisome malsano

noisy ruidoso

nomad nómada *m+f*

nomadic nómada

nom-de-plume nombre artístico

nomenclature nomenclatura

nominal nominal; ~ value valor *m*
nominal/simbólico

nominate nombrar; *pol* proponer[19]
como candidato

nomination nombramiento; (as candidate) propuesta

nominative *n+adj* nominativo

nominee candidato nombrado/propuesto

non: ~ **sequitur** conclusión falsa; ~-**acceptance** rechazo; ~-**aggression** no agresión *f*; **treaty of** ~-**aggression** pacto de no agresión; ~-**alcoholic** no alcohólico; ~-**allergic** an(ti)alérgico; ~-**appearance**/-**attendance** ausencia; ~-**breakable** irrompible; ~-**combatant** *n+adj* no combatiente *m*; ~-**commissioned officer** suboficial; ~-**committal** evasivo; ~-**compliance** desobediencia (**with** de); ~-**conformist** *n+adj* disidente *m+f*, *eccles* no conformista *m+f*; ~-**conformity** no conformismo; ~-**cooperation** falta de cooperación; ~-**delivery** falta de entrega; ~-**denominational** no sectario; ~-**descript** inclasificable; ~-**drinker** abstemio; ~-**effective** ineficaz (-ces); ~-**entity** nulidad *f*; ~-**essential** no esencial; ~-**execution** incumplimiento; ~-**existence** no existencia; ~-**existent** inexistente; ~-**ferrous** no ferroso; ~-**fiction** no novelesco; ~-**flam** ininflamable; ~-**flam film** película de seguridad; ~-**freezing** no congelante; ~-**fulfilment** incumplimiento; ~-**inflammable** ininflamable; ~-**intervention** no intervención *f*; ~-**iron** (of clothing) de no planchar; ~-**laddering** indesmallable; ~-**marketable** no vendible; ~-**member** no miembro; ~-**observance** inobservancia *f*; ~-**pareil** (cosa/persona) sin par, *print* nonpareil *m*; ~-**party** *pol* independiente; ~-**payment** falta de pago; ~-**perishable** no perecedero; ~-**plus** dejar perplejo; ~-**plussed** perplejo; ~-**plus-ultra** *print* nonplusultra; ~-**practising** sin ejercici;o ~-**professional** aficionado; ~-**profit-making** sin fines lucrativos; ~-**proliferation** (**treaty**) (pacto de) no proliferación *f*; ~-**recurring** que no se repite; ~-**renewable** no prorrogable; ~-**resident** *n+adj* no residente *m+f*; ~-**returnable** sin devolución *f*; ~-**returnable bottle** botella sin vuelta; ~-**scheduled** no programado; ~-**scientific** anticientífico; ~-**sectarian** *n+adj* no sectario; ~-**shrink** inencogible; ~-**skid** (**tread**) (relieve *m*) antideslizante; ~-**smoker** (person) no fumador *m*, (railway compartment) departamento de no fumadores; ~-**starter** cualquier cosa que no tendrá éxito; ~-**stop** directo, *aer+mot* sin escalas; **they went** ~-**stop to Paris** ellos fueron a París sin parar; ~-**stop work** trabajo continuo; ~-**technical** no técnico; ~-**transferable** intransferible; ~-**union** no sindicado; ~-**unionist** *n+adj* antisindicalista *m+f*; ~-**violence** no violencia; ~-**violent** no violento; ~-**voter** abstencionista *m+f*; ~-**white** *n+adj* no blanco

nonagenarian *n+adj* noventón *m* (-ona *f*)

nonchalance indiferencia

nonchalant indiferente

none (person) nadie; (+thing) ninguno; ~ **but** solamente; ~ **of us** ninguno de nosotros; ~ **too good** no muy bueno; **be** ~ **the worse/better (for)** no hallarse peor/mejor (por)

nonentity (thing) cosa que no existe; (person) nulidad *f*, *fam* don nadie

nonetheless sin embargo

nonsense tontería; ~! ¡tonterías!; **talk** ~ hablar sin ton ni son

nonsensical ridículo

noodle fideo; ~ **soup** sopa de fideos; (fool) mentecato

nook escondrijo

noon *n* mediodía *m*; **at** (**high**) ~ al mediodía; ~**day**, ~**tide** mediodía *m*; *adj* de mediodía

noose *n* lazo; (with slip-knot) lazo corredizo; (hangman's) soga *m*; *v* coger[8] con lazo

nor: neither ... ~ *see* **neither**; ~ **I** ni yo tampoco; ~ **was this all he said** y esto no fue todo lo que él dijo

Nordic *n+adj* nórdico

norm norma

normal *n* lo normal; **everything is back to** ~ todo se ha normalizado; *adj* normal; **why don't you wear** ~ **clothes?** ¿por qué no lleva usted ropa corriente?; **become** ~ normalizarse[7]

normality normalidad *f*

normalization normalización *f*

normalize normalizar[7]

Norman *n+adj* normando

Normandy Normandía

Norse escandinavo; ~**man** (antiguo) escandinavo

north n norte m; adj del norte; ~ **wind** viento del norte; ~ **of the port** al norte del puerto; **North America** Norteamérica; **North American** norteamericano; **North Pole** polo norte; **North Sea** mar m del Norte; **North Korea/Vietnam** Corea/Vietnam del Norte; **North Korean/Vietnamese** n+adj norcoreano, norvietnamita m+f; **North Star** estrella polar; ~ **by east/west** norte cuarta noreste/ noroeste; ~-**east** n+adj noreste m; ~-**easterly/eastern** (towards the north-east) hacia el noreste, (from the north-east) del noreste; ~-**west** n+adj noroeste m

northerly (towards the north) hacia el norte; (from the north) del norte

northern del norte; **Northern Cross** crucero; ~ **hemisphere** hemisferio norte; ~ **Ireland** Irlanda del Norte; **Northern Irishman/Irishwoman** irlandés/irlandesa del Norte, fam norirlandés/norirlandesa; ~ **lights** aurora boreal; ~ **provinces** fpl (provincias) norteñas; ~**most** más norte

northerner habitante m+f del norte

northwards hacia el norte

Norway Noruega

Norwegian n+adj noruego

nose n nariz f; sl jeta; (animal's) hocico; (of aeroplane) morro; (of ship) proa; (sense of smell) olfato; **bleed at the ~** echar sangre por la nariz; **blow one's ~** sonar(se) (ue)[1a] las narices; **follow one's ~** ir[19] todo seguido; **have a ~ for** tener[19] buen olfato para; **keep one's ~ to the grindstone** batir el cobre; **lead s.o. by the ~** tener[19] a alguien agarrado por las narices; **look down one's ~ (at)** mirar por encima del hombro; **pay through the ~** pagar[5] un ojo de la cara (for por); **pick one's ~** hurgarse[5] las narices; **poke one's ~ in** fig meter el hocico en; **speak through the ~** hablar con voz gangosa; **turn up one's ~ (at)** desdeñar; **under the very ~ of** en las mismas barbas de; ~-**bag** morral m; ~-**bleed** hemorragia nasal; ~-**cap** (of rocket) caperuza; ~-**cone** mil + space ojiva; ~-**dive** n aer picado (vertical), (fall) caída de morros, v aer descender en picado; ~**gay** ramillete m; ~-**ring**

(of bull) narigón (-ones) m; v ~ **about** curiosear; ~ **out** descubrir (past part descubierto); ~ **one's way** avanzar[7] con cautela

nosey curioso; **Nosey Parker** fisgón m (-ona f)

nosh n sl rancho: v sl zampar, Arg morfar

nostalgia nostalgia

nostalgic nostálgico

nostril (ventanilla de la) nariz (-ces) f

nostrum medicina de expectación

not no; ~ **I** yo no; ~ +past part sin +infin, ~ **thinking that** sin pensar que; ~ **at all** de ningún modo, (don't mention it) ¡de nada!; **he is ~ at all handsome** él no es nada guapo; ~ **in the least** de ninguna manera; ~ **even**, ~ **so much as** ni siquiera; ~ **guilty** no culpable; ~ **one** ni uno; ~ **that** no es que +subj, ~ **that she will sing** no es que ella vaya a cantar; ~ **until** no antes de; ~ **without** no sin; ~ **a word** ni pío; **I didn't dare to say a word** no me atreví a decir ni pío; ~ **yet** todavía no; **I believe ~** creo que no; **did he do it or ~?** ¿lo hizo o no?; **why ~?** ¿por qué no?

notability notabilidad f; (person) persona de importancia

notable n+adj notable m+f (for por)

notarial notarial

notarize autorizar[7] ante notario

notary notario; ~'**s office** notaría

notation notación f

notch n muesca; (in cog-wheel) rebaja; v cortar muescas en

note n apunte m; +mus nota; (pitch) tono; (money) billete m, **500 peseta ~** billete de 500 pesetas, sl papiro de 500; (letter) recado, fam cuatro líneas fpl; **of ~** notable; **make a ~ of** apuntar; **take ~ of** poner[19] atención a; **take ~s** tomar notas; **diplomatic ~** nota diplomática; ~ **of hand** pagaré m; ~**book** cuaderno; ~-**pad** bloc m; ~-**paper** papel m de escribir; ~**worthy** digno de notarse; v (notice) observar; (~ down) apuntar; ~**d for** notable por

nothing n nada; **I have ~ in my hand** no tengo nada en la mano; math cero; **mere ~** nadería; **sweet ~s** expresiones fpl de ternura; **for ~** (free) gratis, (for no reward) de balde, (in vain) en

balde; **come to** ~ fracasar; **make** ~ **of** no entender (ie)[2b], (fail to take advantage of) no aprovechar; **think** ~ **of** (despise) tener[19] en poco, (take no notice of) no hacer[19] caso de; ~ **but** no más que; ~ **else** nada más; **there's** ~ **for it but to** no hay más remedio que +*infin*; **be** ~ **of the kind** no ser[19] nada de eso; **have** ~ **to do** no tener[19] nada que hacer; **I had** ~ **to do all day** pasé el día en blanco; **it has** ~ **to do with me** no es cuenta mía; **it is** ~ **to me** no me importa nada, *fam* no me hace ni fu ni fa; **look like** ~ **on earth** tener[19] aspecto de espantajo; **next to** ~ casi nada; ~ **(much) to speak of** poca cosa; ~ **new** nada nuevo; **that is** ~ **to what I shall do** eso no es nada en comparación con lo que haré yo; *adv* de ninguna manera; ~ **daunted** sin amedrarse; ~ **less** no menos; **be** ~ **like** no parecerse[8] en nada a; ~ **short of** nada menos que +*infin*/de +*num*
nothingness inexistencia; nada
notice *n* (announcement) anuncio; (warning) aviso; (attention) atención *f*; (poster) letrero; (critical review) reseña; ~ **to quit** desahucio; **at short** ~ a corto plazo; **until further** ~ hasta nuevo aviso; **attract** ~ llamar la atención; **be beneath one's** ~ no merecer[8] la atención; **bring to the** ~ **of** dar[19] noticia de; **escape** ~ pasar desapercibido; **give a month's** ~ avisar con un mes de anticipación, (of dismissal) despedir (i)[3] con un mes de plazo, (of leaving) dar[19] la dimisión con un mes de plazo; **give** ~ **of** hacer[19] saber; **give** ~ **that** avisar que; **take** ~ **of** hacer[19] caso de; **take no** ~ **of** hacer[19] el sueco; ~**-board** tablero de avisos/anuncios; *v* observar; notar; (pay attention to) hacer[19] caso de
noticeable evidente
notifiable de declaración obligatoria
notification notificación *f*
notify notificar[4]
notion noción *f*; idea; ~**s** (novelties) novedades *fpl*
notional nocional
notoriety notoriedad *f*; *fam* mala fama
notorious notorio; *fam* de mala fama
notwithstanding *adv* no obstante; *prep* a pesar de

nougat *approx* turrón *m*
nought nada; *math* cero; **come to** ~ malograrse; ~**s and crosses** juego de tres en línea
noun nombre *m*, substantivo
nourish nutrir; *fig* fomentar
nourishing nutritivo
nourishment nutrición *f*; alimento
nous sentido común
nouveau riche *n* nuevos ricos *mpl*; *adj* nuevo rico
Nova Scotia Nueva Escocia
novel *n* novela; *adj* original
novelette novela corta; (trashy) novelucha
novelist novelista *m+f*
novella novela/narrativa corta
novelty novedad *f*; (newly-marketed item) novedad
November noviembre *m*; **typical** ~ **weather** tiempo típico de noviembre
novena novena
novice +*eccles* novicio
novitiate noviciado
novocaine novocaína
now *n* actualidad *f*; *adv* ahora; (nowadays) hoy día: ~ **and again/then** de vez en cuando; ~ **that** ya que; **from** ~ **on** de aquí en adelante; **here and** ~ actualmente; **just** ~, **right** ~ ahora mismo; ~ **then** bueno; **two days from** ~ hoy en dos días; **until** ~ hasta el presente; ~! *interj* ¡vamos!
nowadays hoy día
nowhere en ninguna parte; ~ **else** en ninguna otra parte; ~ **near** ni con mucho; nada cerca
nowise de ningún modo
noxious nocivo
nozzle boquilla; (of spray) pulverizador *m*
nuance matiz (-ces) *m*
nub protuberancia; *fig* lo más importante
nubile núbil
nuclear nuclear; ~ **energy/reactor** energía/reactor *m* nuclear; ~ **test** ensayo nuclear; ~ **test ban treaty** pacto para la prohibición de pruebas nucleares; ~ **war(fare)** guerra nuclear
nuclearization nuclearización *f*
nuclearize nuclearizar[7]
nucleus núcleo
nude *n+adj* desnudo; **in the** ~ en

cueros, *fam* en pelota
nudge *n* codazo; *v* dar[19] un codazo a
nudism (des)nudismo
nudist *n+adj* (des)nudista *m+f*; ~ **camp** colonia de (des)nudistas
nudity (des)nudez *f*
nugatory insignificante
nugget pepita; **gold** ~ pepita de oro
nuisance (annoyance) molestia, *fam* lata; (person) pelma(zo); **become a** ~ (of a person) ponerse[19] pelma; **commit a (public)** ~ portarse indecorosamente; **make a** ~ **of o.s.** dar[19] la lata; **what a** ~**!** ¡qué lata!; **what a** ~ **you are!** ¡qué pelma eres!
nuke *n* misil *m* nuclear; *v* destruir[16] con armas nucleares
null inválido; ~ **and void** sin validez
nullify invalidar
nullity nulidad *f*; ~ **decree** anulación *f* del matrimonio
numb *adj* entumecido; (with cold) sin sentido, **my fingers are** ~ se me han dormido los dedos (de la mano); *v* entumecer[14]
number *n* +*gramm*+*mus* número; (crowd) muchedumbre *f*; (of periodical) ejemplar, **back** ~ ejemplar atrasado; *math* (sign) cifra; (science) teoría de los números; *sp* (on a player's back) número dorsal; **a** ~ **of** unos cuantos; **in great** ~ en gran número; **one of our/their** ~ uno de entre nosotros/ellos; ~**-one seed** *sp* número uno, **the two** ~**-one seeds** los dos número uno; **look after** ~ **one** cuidar de sí mismo, *fam* arrimar el ascua a la sardina; **even** ~ (número) par *m*; **odd** ~ (número) impar *m*; ~**s game** lotería; ~**-board** (racing) indicador *m*; ~**-plate** *mot* (placa de) matrícula; *vi* (amount to) ascender (ie)[2b] a; **I am** ~**ed among his friends** figuro entre sus amigos; **her days are** ~**ed** ella tiene los días contados; *vt* (count) contar; (pages of a book) numerar; ~ **off** numerar(se)
numberless sin número
numbness entumecimiento
numeral *n see* **number**; *adj* numeral
numerate contar (ue)[1a]
numeration numeración *f*
numerator numerador *m*
numerical numérico

numerous numeroso; **I have** ~ **friends in Seville** tengo muchos amigos en Sevilla
numismatic numismático
numismatics numismática
numismatist numismático
numskull zote *m*, tonto
nun monja; **become a** ~ meterse a monja
nunciature nunciatura
nuncio nuncio (apostólico)
nunnery convento de monjas
nuptial nupcial; ~ **mass** misa de velaciones
nuptials nupcias *fpl*
nurse *n* (of sick) enfermera; **male** ~ enfermero; (children's) niñera, *fam* chacha; **wet** ~ nodriza; ~**maid** niñera, *fam* chacha; *vt* (the sick) cuidar de; (feed) criar; *fam* dar[19] el pecho a; (in arms) mecer[14]; (caress) acariciar; *fig* fomentar; ~ **a cold** intentar curar un resfriado; *vi* ser[19] enfermera
nursery *n* cuarto de los niños; *agri* semillero; *bot* vivero; *sp+theat* cantera; ~**man** encargado de un semillero/vivero; ~ **rhyme** canción (-ones) *f* infantil; ~ **school** guardería infantil; ~ **slope** pista (de esquí) para principiantes; *adj* de niños
nursing (of sick) profesión *f* de enfermera; (suckling) lactancia; ~**-home** clínica; ~ **mother** madre lactante; ~ **sister** (nun) hermana enfermera
nurture *n* nutrición *f*; (upbringing) crianza; *v* nutrir; (bring up) criar
nut (fruit) nuez (-ces) *f*; *mech* tuerca; *sl* (head) chola; *sl* (toff) currutaco; *sl* (~case) tonto; **be** ~**s (about)** estar[19] chiflado (por); **you drive me** ~**s** me vuelves loco; **hard** ~ **to crack** *fig* hueso duro de roer; ~**case** chiflado; **(pair of)** ~**-crackers** cascanueces *m* *sing+pl*; ~**hatch** trepador *m* azul; ~**shell** cáscara de nuez; **in a** ~**shell** en una palabra
nutmeg nuez moscada; ~**-grater** rallador *m* de nueces
nutrient nutritivo
nutriment (alimento) nutritivo
nutrition nutrición *f*
nutritional de valor nutritivo
nutritious, nutritive nutritivo
nutter chiflado
nutty (of taste) que sabe a nueces;

(crazy) chiflado (**about** por)

nuzzle hocicar[4]; ~ **up to** arrimarse cómodamente a

N.W. (north-west) N.O. (noroeste *m*)

nylon nilón *m*; ~s (stockings) medias *fpl*

de nilón

nymph ninfa; ~-**like** como una ninfa

nymphet chica sexualmente atractiva

nymphomania ninfomanía

nymphomaniac ninfómana

O

O (telephone and serial numbers) cero; **1300** trece-cero-cero; **130220** trece-cero-dos-veinte

o (letter) o *f*

oaf zoquete *m*

oafish lerdo

oafishness tontería

oak *n* (tree) roble *m*; (wood) madera de roble; **~-apple** agalla (de roble); **~ forest** robledal *m*; **~-wood** robledo; *adj* ~(en) de roble

oakum estopa (de calafatear)

O.A.P. (old age pensioner) jubilado por vejez

oar remo; (person) remero; **pull on the ~s** tirar de los remos; **rest on one's ~s** descansar; **(un)ship the ~s** (des)armar los remos; **put one's ~ in** *fig* meter baza; **~ed** de remos; **~lock** horquilla; **~sman** remero; **~smanship** arte *m* de remar; **~-stroke** palada

O.A.S. (Organization of American States) O.E.A. (Organización de Estados Americanos)

oasis oasis *m*

oast horno para secar lúpulo; **~-house** fábrica de lúpulo

oatcake torta de avena

oath juramento; (blasphemy) blasfemia; (swearword) palabrota, **let out a string of ~s** soltar (ue)[1a] palabrotas; **on ~** bajo juramento; **put s.o. on ~** hacer[19] prestar juramento a alguien; **swear on ~** jurar; **administer an ~ to** tomar juramento (**to a**); **break an ~** violar un juramento; **~ of allegiance** juramento de lealtad; *mil* jura de bandera; **swear an ~ of allegiance** jurar lealtad

oatmeal harina de avena

oats avena; **crushed/rolled ~** copos *mpl* de avena; **sow one's wild ~** andarse a la flor del berro

obbligato obligado

obduracy obstinación *f*

obdurate obstinado

obedience obediencia (**to a**); **blind ~** obediencia ciega

obedient obediente; **your ~ servant** su seguro servidor

obeisance reverencia; **pay ~ to** tributar homenaje a

obelisk obelisco

obese obeso

obesity, obeseness obesidad *f*

obey obedecer[14]; (instructions) cumplir; (natural law) seguir (i)[3+11], **~ the law of gravity** seguir la ley de gravedad; **~ the speed limit** respetar la velocidad máxima

obfuscate ofuscar[4]

obfuscation ofuscamiento

obit exequias *fpl*

obituary *n* necrología; **~ column** sección *f* necrológica; **~ notice** esquela de defunción

¹ **object** *n* objeto, cosa; *gramm* complemento; *pej* individuo; (purpose) propósito; (ambition) ambición *f*; **cost/distance no ~** no importa precio/distancia; **~ lesson** lección práctica; **~-finder, ~-lens** objetivo

² **object** *vt* objetar; *vi* poner[19] reparos a **+***infin*; **if they do not ~** si ellos no tienen inconveniente

objection objeción *f*; **raise an ~** hacer constar una protesta; **raise ~s to** poner[19] reparos a; **have no ~** no tener[19] inconveniente; **(if) there is no ~** (si) no hay ningún inconveniente; **~ overruled** protesta denegada

objectionable (annoying) molesto; (unpleasant) desagradable; (offensive) ofensivo

objective objetivo; (destination) destinación *f*; (purpose) propósito; *adj* objetivo; *gramm* acusativo, **~ case** caso acusativo

objectivity objetividad *f*

objector objetante *m+f*

objet d'art pequeño artículo de valor artístico

oblation oblación *f*; (gift) oblata

obligate obligar[5]

obligation obligación *f*; **of** ~ *eccles* de precepto; **be under an** ~ **(to)** deber un favor (a); **place under an** ~ obligar a hacer algo; **without** ~ sin compromiso

obligatory obligatorio

oblige (compel) obligar[5]; (do a service to) hacer[19] un favor (**with** de), **he** ~**d me with a loan** me hizo el favor de un préstamo; **much** ~**d** muy agradecido (**for** por); **much** ~**d!** ¡se agradece!; **I'm very much** ~**d to you** le quedo muy agradecido; **I should be** ~**d if** agradecería si +*subj*

obliging atento

obligingness cortesía

oblique oblicuo; (indirect) indirecto; ~ **angle** ángulo oblicuo

obliquely al sesgo; (indirectly) indirectamente

obliterate (rub out, cross out) borrar; (destroy) destruir[16]; **be** ~**d** borrarse, quedar destruido

obliteration (rubbing out, crossing out) borradura; (destruction) destrucción *f*

oblivion olvido; **sink into** ~ caer[19] en el olvido

oblivious olvidado (**of** de)

oblong *n* +*adj* oblongo

obloquy deshonra

obnoxiousness odiosidad *f*

oboe oboe *m*

oboist oboísta *m*+*f*

obscene obsceno; *fam* (of jokes) verde

obscenity obscenidad *f*

obscurantism oscurantismo

obscurantist *n*+*adj* oscurantista *m*+*f*

obscure *adj* +*fig* oscuro; *v* ocultar; **become** ~**d** oscurecerse[14]

obscurity oscuridad *f*

obsequies exequias *fpl*

obsequious obsequioso

obsequiousness obsequiosidad *f*

observable observable

observance observancia; *eccles* rito

observant observador (-ora *f*)

observation (seeing) observación *f*; (remark) comentario; **be under** ~ estar[19] vigilado; **escape** ~ pasar inadvertido; ~ **car** (railway) vagón-mirador *m*; ~ **post** puesto de observación; ~ **ward** sala de vigilancia

observatory observatorio

observe observar; (comment) decir[19];

(obey) cumplir con; *eccles* (keep) guardar, ~ **a fast** guardar un día de ayuno; ~ **silence** guardar silencio; ~ **two minutes silence** guardar dos minutos de silencio

observer observador *m* (-ora *f*)

obsess obsesionar (**with** con)

obsession obsesión *f*; **have an** ~ **about** tener[19] una obsesión por; *fam* manía (**about** por)

obsessive obsesivo

obsidian obsidiana

obsolescence caída en desuso

obsolescent que cae en desuso

obsolete anticuado; *biol* atrofiado

obstacle obstáculo; **put** ~**s in the way of** hacer[19] difícil, (raise objections) sacar[4] peros; ~~**race** carrera de obstáculos

obstetric(al) obstétrico

obstetrician tocólogo

obstetrics obstetricia

obstinacy obstinación *f*

obstinate obstinado; *fam* terco; **be** ~ **about** obstinarse en

obstreperous turbulento

obstruct obstruir[16]; (hinder) dificultar; (prevent an action) estorbar; (stop the flow) estancar[4]; **become** ~**ed** obstruirse[16]; estancarse[4]

obstruction obstrucción *f*; **cause an** ~ (in street) cerrar (ie)[2a] el paso

obstructionism obstruccionismo

obstructionist *n*+*adj* obstruccionista *m*+*f*

obstructive obstructivo

obstructor obstructor *m*

obtain *vt* obtener[19]; sacar; ~ **by false pretences** conseguir (i)[3]+[11] por engaño; ~ **by threats** arrancar[4] por medio de amenazas; *vi* (hold good) prevalecer[14]

obtainable asequible; **be** ~ (of goods) estar[19] en venta; **be easily** ~ ser[19] fácil de obtener

obtrude *vt* imponer[19] (**on** a); *vi* entremeterse

obtrusion, obtrusiveness imposición *f*, entremetimiento

obtuse obtuso; ~ **angle** obtusángulo; (stupid) torpe

obverse *n* anverso; *adj* del anverso

obviate obviar

obvious evidente; **it's** ~ **that** claro está

que, *fam* se ve que

obviously claro; ~ **he is a gipsy** claro que él es gitano; (affirmative comment) claro que sí; ~ **not** claro que no; **the door was ~ locked on the inside** la puerta estaba a todas luces cerrada por dentro

occasion *n* ocasión *f*; (happening) acontecimiento, **it was a great ~** fue un gran acontecimiento; (opportunity) oportunidad *f*; **on the ~ of her birthday** por motivo de su cumpleaños; **as ~ demands** en caso necesario; **on ~** de vez en cuando; **on one ~** una vez; **have ~ to** haber[19] de +*infin*; **rise to the ~** estar[19] a la altura de las circunstancias; **this is the ~ for** éste es el momento para; *v* ocasionar

occasional poco frecuente; **he has an ~ glass of beer** él toma una que otra caña de cerveza; ~ **table** mesilla

occasionally de vez en cuando

occident occidente *m*

occidental occidental

occipital occipital

occiput occipucio

occlusion oclusión *f*

occlusive oclusivo

occult *n* lo oculto; *adj* oculto

occultism ocultismo

occultist ocultista *m*+*f*

occupancy ocupación *f*; (tenancy) tenencia

occupant ocupante *m*; (tenant) inquilino

occupation *mil* ocupación *f*; (action) toma de posesión; (tenancy) inquilinato; *pol* (as protest) encierro; (job) oficio, **what is your ~?** ¿qué oficio tiene usted?; **reading is his main ~** lo que más hace es leer

occupational de oficio; ~ **disease** enfermedad *f* profesional; ~ **hazard** gaje *m* del oficio; ~ **therapist** terapeuta *m*+*f* laboral; ~ **therapy** terapia laboral

occupied ocupado; (of dwelling) alquilado; (of toilet) ocupado; **he is ~** (engaged) él está ocupado, (very busy) él está atareado; **be ~ in/with** entretenerse[19] con; ocuparse en

occupier inquilino; ocupante *m*+*f*

occupy +*mil* ocupar; (live in) habitar; (of time) emplear

occur (happen) suceder; (be found) encontrarse (ue)[1a], **diamonds ~ in Africa** se encuentran diamantes en África; ~ **to** (come to mind) ocurrirse a, **it ~s to me that** se me ocurre que +*infin*

occurrence acontecimiento; (existence) existencia; **it is a frequent ~** sucede a menudo

ocean océano; *fig* ~**s of** la mar de; ~ **lane** ruta de alta mar; ~**-going** de alta mar; **go to the ~** (*US* go to the seaside) ir[19] a la playa

Oceania Oceanía

oceanic oceánico

oceanography oceanografía

ocelot ocelote *m*

ochre ocre *m*

o'clock: it is one ~ es la una; **it is two ~** son las dos; **at four ~** a las cuatro; **what ~ is it?** ¿qué hora es?

octagon octágono

octagonal octagonal

octahedron octaedro

octane octano; ~ **numbering/rating** octanaje *m*; **high-~ petrol** gasolina de alto octanaje, *fam* gasolina super

octave octava

octavo (libro) en octavo

octet octeto

October octubre *m*

octogenarian ochentón *m* (-ona *f*)

octopus pulpo

octosyllabic octosilábico

ocular ocular

oculist oculista *m*+*f*

odd (strange) extraño, raro, **how ~!** ¡qué raro!; (of numbers) impar, ~ **or even** pares o impares; (of stamps, volumes) suelto; (of gloves, shoes) desparejado, *fam* sin pareja; (not the same) desiguales; **at ~ moments** en momentos de ocio; **at ~ times** de vez en cuando; **in some ~ corner** en algún que otro rincón; **fifty-~** cincuenta y pico; ~**-job man** chapucero; ~ **lot** colección variada; **be ~ man out** (be different) diferenciarse de los demás, (be excluded) estar[19] excluido, (be left over) estar[19] de más

oddity (person) persona rara; (thing) objeto curioso; (quality) rareza

oddly singularmente; ~ **enough** aunque parece increíble

oddment artículo suelto; **sale of ~s** venta de retales

oddness rareza

odds (betting) puntos *mpl* de ventaja, **give ~** dar[19] ventaja; **the ~ are that** lo más probable es que; **fight against the ~** luchar contra fuerzas superiores; **what's the ~?** ¿qué importa?; **~ and ends** (remains) sobras *fpl*, (trifles) chucherías *fpl*; **be at ~ with** estar[19] reñido con; **it makes no ~** lo mismo da; **what's the ~?** ¿qué importa?; **set at ~** enemistar

ode oda

odious odioso

odium odio

odontologist odontólogo

odontology odontología

odoriferous odorífero

odorous (pleasant) oloroso; (nasty) hediondo

odour olor *m*; **~ of sanctity** olor *m* de santidad; **be in bad/good ~** tener mala/buena fama; **be in bad ~ with** llevarse mal con

odourless inodoro

Odysseus Ulises

odyssey odisea

Oedipus: ~ complex complejo de Edipo

oesophagus esófago

oestrogen estrógeno

of de; **~ the** (before *m sing*) del, (before *f sing*) de la, (before *mpl*) de los, (before *fpl*) de las; **it was very kind ~ you to** ha sido muy amable en +*infin*; **a friend ~ ours** un amigo nuestro; **a friend of my sister's** un amigo de mi hermana; **they robbed him ~ his wealth** a él le robaron su riqueza; **love ~ (one's) country** amor *m* a la patria; **a quarter ~ five** *US* las cinco menos cuarto; **dream ~** soñar (ue)[1a] con; **smell ~** oler[19] a; **taste ~** saber a; **think ~** pensar (ie)[2a] en

off *adj elect* (light) apagado, (supply) desconectado; (of gas, water) cortado; *mech* parado; (of brake) desapretado; (of food) pasado; (removed from menu) quitado; (cancelled) cancelado; **~ season** temporada baja; *adv* (away) a (distancia), **two metres ~ a** (una distancia de) dos metros; **far ~** muy lejos; **~ sick** en el seguro; **he's been ~ sick for six days** hace seis días

que está en el seguro; **day ~** día libre; **my birthday is three days ~** faltan tres días para mi cumpleaños; **be/go ~** marcharse, irse[19]; **they're ~** (in race) ¡ya van!; **~ with you!** ¡lárguese!; **be ~** (the menu) no quedar; **he has his shoes ~** él está descalzo; **~ and on** de vez en cuando; **hands ~!** ¡fuera las manos!; **how are you ~ for …?** ¿qué le queda de …?; **be badly ~** andar mal de dinero; **be well ~** estar[19] acomodado; **five per cent ~** descuento del cinco por ciento; **there's nothing ~** (no reduction) no hay descuento; *prep* (not on) de, **it fell ~ the table** (se) cayó de la mesa; (near) cerca de, **~ the coast** cerca de la costa; **five kilometres ~ the coast** a cinco kilómetros de la costa; **she has a button ~ her blouse** a su blusa le falta un botón; **a street ~ the main road** una calle que sale de la calle principal; **~ the beaten track** donde Cristo dio las tres voces; **be ~ duty** estar[19] libre; **~-beat** (syncopated) tiempo débil, (unusual) raro; **~-chance** posibilidad remota; **on the ~-chance of** con poca esperanza de +*infin*; **~ colour** pachucho; **~-day** día malo; **this is one of my ~-days** hoy no estoy para nada; **~-duty** *adj* libre de servicio; **~-hand** *adj* casual, (curt) brusco, (extempore) improvisado, *adv* sin cumplidos ni ceremonia, (extempore) sin preparación; **~-the-peg garment** prenda confeccionada; **~ one's head** loco; **~-licence** *approx* bodega; **~ the map** en el quinto pino; **~-peak traffic** circulación *f* fuera de las horas de aglomeración; **~-peak heater** calentador que se recarga durante las horas de poco consumo; **~-print** tirada aparte (de un artículo); **~-putting** desconcertante; **~ the record** extraoficial(mente); **~-set** *n* compensación *f*, *geog* estribación *f*, *print* offset *m*, *v* compensar; **~-shoot** *bot* vástago, (of family *etc*) ramal *m*; **~-shore** *adj* costanero, *adv* (a corta distancia) de la costa; **~-shore wind** viento de la costa; **~-side** *mot* de la derecha, *Sp, SA, US* de la izquierda, *sp* orsay *m*, **to be ~** estar en orsay; **~-spring** hijo(s); **~-stage** en los mutis; **~-white** blanco sucio; *interj* ¡fuera de aquí!

offal (food) asadura; (waste) desperdicios *mpl*

offence ofensa; *leg* delito; **technical ~** cuasidelito; **commit an ~ against** ofender contra; **give ~ to** ofender; **take ~** ofenderse; **no ~ (meant)** sin intención de ofenderle

offend *v/i* pecar⁴ (**against** contra); *v/t* ofender; **be ~ed** tomar a mal

offender delincuente *m+f*; **first ~** delincuente sin antecedentes penales; **old ~** delincuente reincidente

offensive *n* ofensiva; **take the ~** tomar la ofensiva; *adj* ofensivo; (aggressive) agresivo

offer oferta; (of help) promesa; **on ~** en oferta; *v* ofrecer¹⁴; (opportunities *etc*) brindar; (apology, congratulations *etc*) dar¹⁹; **~ one's seat to** ceder el asiento a; **~ resistance to** oponer¹⁹ resistencia; **~ to** ofrecerse¹⁴ a; **~ up** ofrecer¹⁴

offering ofrecimiento; *eccles* ofrenda

offertory ofertorio; **~-box** cep(ill)o

office (place of work) oficina; (room) despacho; (agency) agencia; (*US* doctor's) consulta; (lawyer's) bufete *m*; (of newspaper) redacción *f*; (state department) ministerio; (function) oficio; (post) cargo; *eccles* oficio; **through the good ~s of** por favor especial de; **be in ~** *pol* estar¹⁹ en el poder; **party in ~** partido en el poder; **~ block** bloque *m* de oficinas; **~-boy** mozo de oficina; **~ hours** horas *fpl* de oficina/consulta; **~-seeker** aspirante *m+f*; **~-work** trabajo de oficina; **~-worker** oficinista *m+f*; **~s** (lavatory *etc*) servicios *mpl*

officer *n* +*mil* oficial *m*; (policeman) (agente *m* de) policía *m*; **~ of the watch** oficial *m* de guardia; **~s** (of society) (miembros de la) junta directiva; *v* proveer¹⁷ de oficiales; **be well ~ed** tener¹⁹ buenos oficiales

official *n* oficial *m*; *adj* oficial; **go through the ~ channels** hacer¹⁹ los trámites; **~ receiver** comisario (de quiebras); **Official Secrets Act** ley *f* de secretos oficiales

officialdom burocracia

officialese jerga empleada en documentos oficiales

officialism burocracia

officiant oficiante *m*

officiate oficiar (**as de**)

officious oficioso

offing: in the ~ (in sight) visible; **there's a general election in the ~** es probable que haya una elección general, *fam* una elección general danza en el aire

oft: ~-told, ~-repeated contado/repetido a menudo

often a menudo, muchas veces; **how ~?** (how many times?) ¿cuántas veces?, (how frequently) ¿con qué frecuencia?; **not ~** pocas veces, con poca frecuencia; **as ~ as not** no pocas veces; **it is not ~ that** no ocurre con frecuencia que

ogive ojiva

ogle echar miradas amorosas a; *fam* guiñar el ojo a

ogling miradas *fpl* amorosas; *fam* guiño

ogre ogro

ogress ogresa

oh! ¡ay!, ¡oh!

ohm ohmio

oil *n* aceite *m*; (petroleum) petróleo, **strike ~** encontrar (ue)¹ᵃ petróleo, *fig* enriquecerse¹⁴; (*eccles*+painting) óleo, **~ painting** cuadro al óleo; **burn the midnight ~** quemarse las cejas; **pour ~ on troubled waters** mojar la pólvora; **~-bearing** petrolífero; **~-box** engrasador *m*; **~-burner** quemador *m* de petróleo; **~-burning** de combustión de aceite; **~-cake** bagazo; **~-can** aceitera; **~-cloth** hule *m*; **~-colour** pintura al óleo; **~-drilling** perforación petrolífera; **~-drum** bidón *m* de aceite; **~-field** campo petrolífero; **~-filter** separador *m* de aceite; **~-fired** de combustión de fuel-oil; **~-gauge** manómetro de aceite; **~-lamp** velón (-ones) *m*; **~-pan** cárter *m*; **~ pipeline** oleoducto; **~-refinery** destilería de petróleo, (olive oil) refinería de aceite; **~-rig** plataforma petrolífera; **~-ring** anillo de lubricación; **~skin** tela encerada, *naut* chubasquero; **~-stone** piedra afiladera; **~-stove** *cul* cocina de petróleo, (for heating) estufa de petróleo; **~-sump** depósito de aceite; **~-tanker** *naut* petrolero, (lorry) camión petrolero; **~-well** pozo de petróleo; *v* lubricar⁴; *esp mot+mech* engrasar; ~ **s.o.'s palm** untarle la mano a uno; **well ~ed** (drunk) achispado

oiliness oleosidad *f*

oiling engrasado

oily aceitoso; (of person) zalamero

ointment ungüento

O.K., okay *n* visto bueno; **give s.o. the ~ to** darle a uno la autorización para +*infin*; **is it ~ for me to go?** ¿puedo marcharme?; **it's ~ for you but** está bien para usted, pero; *adj* satisfactorio; *v* aprobar (ue)¹ᵃ; *interj* vale

okra quimbombó *m*

old *n* (people) los viejos; **the ~ and the new** lo viejo y lo nuevo/moderno; *adj* viejo; (former) antiguo; (of wine) añejo; (worn out) gastado; **how ~ is she?** ¿cuántos años tiene?, (of a baby) ¿cuánto tiempo tiene?; **she is two years ~** ella tiene dos años; **grow ~** envejecer¹⁴, *fam* ir¹⁹ para viejo/vieja; **good ~ Peter** el bueno de Pedro; **of ~** antiguamente; ~ **age** vejez *f*, *euph* tercera edad; **die of ~ age** morir²ᶜ (*past part* muerto) de viejo; **~-age pension** subsidio de vejez; **~-age pensioner** jubilado; ~ **boy** antiguo alumno, *fam* chico; **Old Boys' Day** día *m* de reunión de ex-alumnos; ~ **clothes** ropa usada; ~ **clothes dealer** ropavejero; ~ **crock** *mot* coche *m* de época; **~-established** establecido desde hace muchos años; **~-fashioned** anticuado; ~ **folk** viejos *mpl*, (parents) padres *mpl*; ~ **guard** vieja guardia; **Old Glory** bandera de los Estados Unidos; ~ **hand** experto, *fam* perro viejo, **he's an ~ hand at** él es perro viejo en +*infin*; **~-looking** de aspecto viejo; ~ **maid** solterona, **remain an ~ maid** quedarse para vestir santos; ~ **man** anciano, *fam* amigo mío, (boss) jefe *m*, (father) *fam* viejo *m*, (husband) marido; ~ **master** (painter) pintor *m* célebre, (painting) lienzo de un pintor célebre; ~ **moon** luna vieja; ~ **salt** lobo de mar; ~ **school/style** a la antigua; ~ **soldier** ex soldado, *fig* hombre astuto; **Old Testament** Antiguo Testamento; **~-time** de tiempos pasados; **~-timer** anciano; ~ **wives' tale** patraña; ~ **woman** vieja, (mother) parienta,

(wife) mujer *f*; **Old World** Viejo Mundo; **~-world** de los tiempos pasados

olden: in ~ times en tiempos pasados

older más viejo; **he is two years ~ than I** él me lleva dos años

oldish bastante viejo

oldness edad *f*

oleaginous oleaginoso

oleander adelfa

olfactory olfatorio

oligarchy oligarquía

olive *n* aceituna; (tree) olivo; ~ **branch** rama de olivo, *fig* emblema de la paz; **~-green** verde aceitunado; **~-grove** olivar *m*; ~ **oil** aceite *m* de oliva; **~-press** lagar *m*; *adj* aceitunado; **~-skinned** con tez aceitunada

olympiad olimpiada

Olympian olímpico

Olympic Games Juegos *mpl* Olímpicos

ombudsman Defensor *m* del Pueblo

omelette tortilla; **cheese/potato ~** tortilla de queso/de patata; **plain ~** tortilla francesa

omen agüero

ominous ominoso

omissible que se puede omitir

omission omisión *f*; **sins of ~** pecados *mpl* de omisión

omit omitir; **I omitted to say that** dejé de decir que

omnibus *n* autobús (-uses) *m*; *adj* completo; ~ **volume** volumen (-úmenes) *m* de obras completas

omnipotence omnipotencia

omnipotent omnipotente

omnipresence omnipresencia

omnipresent omnipresente

omniscience omnisciencia

omniscient omnisciente

omnivorous omnívoro

on *prep* en; ~ **the floor** en el suelo; (on top of) encima de, sobre, ~ **the shelf** encima del/sobre el estante; (concerning) sobre, **a speech ~ the Vietnam war** una conferencia sobre la guerra de Vietnam; (by) en, **London is ~ the Thames** Londres está en el Támesis; (belonging to) de, **he is ~ the committee** él es del comité; (towards) hacia, **the troops marched ~ Paris** las tropas marcharon hacia París; ~ **the second of May** el dos de mayo; ~

Sunday el domingo; **I'll see you ~ Sunday** le veré el domingo; **~ Sundays, she goes to Mass ~ Sundays** ella va a misa los domingos; ~ **my birthday** el día de mi cumpleaños; ~ **entering they stopped speaking** al entrar dejaron de hablar; ~ **and after a** partir de; **this is ~ me** yo pago; **this is ~ the house** la casa paga; **have (money) ~ one** tener[19] dinero encima, **I have no money ~ me** no tengo dinero encima; ~ **my appointment** a mi nombramiento; **be ~ bad/good terms (with)** llevarse mal/bien (con); **get ~ a train/bus** subir a un tren/autobús; **turn one's back ~** volver (ue)[1b] (+*past part* vuelto) la espalda a; ~ **business/duty/holiday** de negocios/ servicio/vacaciones; **the biggest ~ earth** el/la más grande del mundo; **are you ~ the phone?** ¿tiene usted teléfono?; ~ **the left/right** a la izquierda/derecha; ~ **the next page** en la página siguiente; *adv* puesto, **she had her gloves ~** ella tenía puestos los guantes; (of brake) apretado; *elect* (connected) conectado, (switched on) puesto, (light) encendido, *fam* dado; (of gas, water) abierto; *mech* puesto (en marcha); ~ **and ~** sin cesar; ~ **and off** de vez en cuando; ~**-and-off switch** interruptor *m*; **and so ~** y así sucesivamente; **farther ~** más allá; **have s.o. ~** (tease) tomar el pelo a alguien; **that's not ~!** ¡éso no se hace!; **be ~** (have started) haber empezado, **the battle is ~** la batalla ya ha empezado; **what's ~?** *theat* ¿qué representan?; **there's a new play ~ at the Teatro Miramar** se ha estrenado una nueva comedia en el teatro Miramar; **what film is ~ at the Kursaal?** ¿qué película están proyectando/*fam* echando en el Kursaal?; *interj* ¡adelante!

once *n* una vez; **just this ~** solamente esta vez; *adv* (on one occasion) una vez; (formerly) en otro tiempo: **~ a day** una vez al día; **at ~** (immediately) en seguida, (in one go) de una vez, (simultaneously) simultáneamente, (suddenly) de repente; ~ **(and) for all** ya de una vez; ~ **in a while** de tarde en tarde; ~ **more** otra vez; **more than ~** más de una vez; **not ~** ni siquiera una vez; ~ **too often** una vez demasiado; ~ **upon a time** (ages ago) en tiempos de Maricastaña, (starting a story) érase una vez; **give the ~-over** hacer[19] una inspección rápida; *conj* una vez que; ~ **he had left** una vez que se marchó/ hubo marchado

oncoming *n* proximidad *f*; *adj* próximo

one uno, una; (before *m sing n*) un, ~ **man** un hombre; (sole) único, **my ~ hope** es mi única esperanza es; ~ **García** un tal García; ~ **and the same** idéntico; ~ **by ~** uno por uno; ~ **day** algún día; ~ **of these days** algún día de estos; ~ **more** uno más; ~ **or two** (a few) unos pocos; **it's all ~ to me** me es igual; **be ~ up (on)** llevar ventaja por un punto (a); ~**-armed** manco; ~**-armed bandit** máquina tragaperras; ~**-crop economy** monocultivo; ~**-eyed** tuerto, (strange) raro; ~**-horse** *adj* de poca importancia; ~**-man** monohombre; ~**-man crane** grúa monohombre; ~**-man office** oficina unipersonal; ~ **o'clock** la una; ~**-off** insólito; ~**-piece** de una pieza; ~**-sided** parcial; ~**-string fiddle** violín *m* de una sola cuerda; ~**-time** antiguo; ~**-track** de una sola vía; **he has a ~-track mind** el sólo piensa en una cosa; **Tyson gave Bruno a ~-two** Tyson dio a Bruno un uno-dos; ~**-way street** calle *f* de dirección única; ~**-way ticket** billete de ida; ~**-way traffic** dirección obligatoria; *pron* uno; (*reflex* form of *v* often used) **here ~ can eat well** aquí se come bien; (sometimes not translated) **the white ~** el blanco; ~ **must eat to live** hay que comer para vivir; ~ **and all** todos; ~ **another** uno(s) a otro(s); **he is ~ of those** él es marica; **this ~, that ~** *see* this, that; **little ~s** los chiquillos

oneness unidad *f*

onerous oneroso

oneself *reflex pron* se; (after *prep*) sí (mismo); (emphatic) uno mismo; **be ~** ser[19] natural

ongoing continuo

onion cebolla; ~ **seed** cebollino; ~**-seller** cebollero; **string of ~s** ristra de cebollas

onlooker espectador *m* (-ora *f*)

only *adj* único, solo; ~ **child** hijo único; *adv* sólo; **not** ~ **but also** no sólo sino también; **I would be** ~ **too happy to me** daría mucho placer +*infin*; **he has** ~ **three** él no tiene más de tres; **I** ~ **wanted to greet her** yo quería saludarla nada más; **if** ~ ...! ¡ojalá que ...! +*subj*; ~ **just** apenas, (a short time ago) hace un momento; *conj* ~ **(that)** solo que, pero

onomatopoeia onomatopeya

onrush arremetida; (attack) ataque *m*; (of water *etc*) torrente *m*

onset +*med* comienzo

onslaught embestida

onto *adj*; **he got** ~ **the train** el subió al tren

ontological ontológico

ontology ontología

onus responsabilidad *f*; ~ **of proof** obligación *f* de probar

onward *adj* progresivo; *adv* (hacia) delante; ~**(s)!** ¡adelante!

onyx ónice *m*

oodles: ~ **of** la mar de

oological oológico

oologist oólogo

oology oología

oops-a-daisy! ¡aúpa!

ooze *n* cieno; *vi* rezumarse; *vt* exudar, *fam* sudar; ~ **away** escaparse poco a poco; **he** ~**s hypocrisy** él derrocha hipocresía

opacity opacidad *f*

opal ópalo

opalescent opalescente

opaque opaco

open *n*: **in the** ~ al aire libre; **bring out into the** ~ hacer[19] público; *adj* abierto; ~ **door** puerta abierta; (frank) franco, ~ **look** mirada franca; (public) público; (uncovered) descubierto; (unfenced) descercado; (unfolded) desplegado; *comm* libre, ~ **market** mercado libre; **leave** ~ (unresolved) dejar sin resolver; **(in the)** ~ **air** (al) aire libre; ~**-air theatre** teatro al aire libre; **welcome with** ~ **arms** dar[19] la bienvenida a; ~**-cast mine** mina a cielo abierto; ~ **cheque** cheque abierto; **in** ~ **country** en pleno campo; ~**-eared** escuchando atentamente; ~**-eyed** alerta; ~ **goal** *sp* puerta libre; ~**-handed** generoso, *fam* manilarga; ~**-hearted** sincero; ~**-heart surgery** cirugía a corazón abierto; ~ **hearth** *metal* horno de revertero; **keep** ~ **house** tener[19] la casa abierta para todos; ~ **letter** carta abierta; ~ **mind** mente receptiva; ~**-minded** imparcial; ~**-mouthed** boquiabierto; ~ **prison** prisión *f* sin rejas; ~ **question** cuestión *f* pendiente; ~ **sea** alta mar; ~ **season** (hunting) tiempo de caza, (fishing) tiempo de pesca; ~ **secret** secreto a voces; ~ **shop** (trade union) taller *m* franco; ~ **to persuasion** dispuesto a dejarse convencer; ~ **to suggestions** dispuesto a recibir sugerencias; ~ **university** universidad *f* a distancia; ~ **verdict** veredicto del juez en el que admite la inhabilidad de determinar la causa de muerte; ~ **work** enrejado, (embroidery) calado; *vi* abrirse (*past part* abierto); *theat* estrenarse, **the play** ~**s tonight** la obra de teatro se estrena esta noche; (of buds) brotar; *vt* abrir (*past part* abierto); (of clothing) desabrochar; (of parcels) abrir (*past part* abierto); (inaugurate) inaugurar; **she died without** ~**ing her lips** ella murió sin despegar[5] los labios; ~ **fire on** hacer[19] fuego sobre; ~ **the discussion** empezar (ie)[2a+7] la discusión; ~ **the scoring** marcar[4] el primer tanto

~ **into** comunicar[4] con; (of street) desembocar[4] en

~ **on(to)** dar[19] a

~ **out** (unfold) desplegar[5]; (spread) extender(se) (ie)[2b]

~ **up** abrir (*past part* abierto); (explore) explorar; (speak freely) franquearse; (start shooting) romper (*past part* roto) el fuego

opener abridor *m*; (for tins) abrelatas *m* *sing*+*pl*; (opening goal) primer tanto

opening apertura; *theat* estreno; (of buds), brotación *f*; (inauguration) inauguración *f*; (hole in wall) brecha; (in forest) claro; (employment) vacante *f*; (opportunity) oportunidad *f*; ~ **move** primera jugada; ~ **night** estreno; ~ **number** primera canción; ~ **price** precio de apertura; ~ **session** sesión *f* inaugural

openness (spaciousness) espaciosidad *f*; (candour) candor *m*

opera ópera; ~ **singer** cantante *m+f* de ópera; ~**-glasses** gemelos *mpl* de teatro; ~**-hat** clac *m*; ~**-house** teatro de la ópera

operable operable

operate *vi* funcionar; *vt* hacer[19] funcionar; *mech* manejar; *surg* operar (on a); ~**d by electricity** accionado por electricidad

operatic operístico

operating operante; ~ **expenses** gastos *mpl* de explotación; ~**-table** mesa de operaciones; ~**-theatre** quirófano

operation +*mil* operación (-ones) *f*; (functioning) funcionamiento; (*mech* + handling) manejo; *surg* intervención *f* (quirúrgica); *leg* vigencia; *min* explotación *f*; **be in** ~ *mech* estar[19] en funcionamiento; *leg* estar[19] en vigor; **put into** ~ poner[19] en funcionamiento; (law) poner en vigor

operational *mil* en condiciones de servicio; *mech* capaz (-ces) de funcionar

operative *n* operario; *adj* operativo; **this law will become** ~ **in May** esta ley entrará en vigor en mayo

operator *cin+surg* operador *m* (-ora *f*); *mech* maquinista *m+f*; (telephone) telefonista *m+f*; (on Stock Exchange) corredor *m* de bolsa

operetta opereta; *Sp* zarzuela

ophthalmia oftalmía

ophthalmic oftálmico

ophthalmologist oftalmólogo

opiate *n+adj* opiato

opine opinar

opinion opinión *f*; (judgement) dictamen (-ámenes) *m*; **I am of the** ~ **that** opino que; **in my** ~ a mi parecer; **have a high** ~ **of** tener[19] en mucho; **have a high** ~ **of o.s.** pagarse[5] de sí mismo; ~ **poll** sondeo de opinión

opinionated porfiado

opium opio; ~ **den** fumadero de opio; ~ **poppy** adormidera

opossum zarigüeya

opponent adversario; *pref* anti (often used): ~ **of Franco** antifranquista *m+f*

opportune oportuno

opportunism oportunismo

opportunist *n+adj* oportunista *m+f*

opportunity oportunidad *f*

oppose oponerse[19] a; (fight against) combatir

opposed: be ~ **to** oponerse[19] a

opposing: ~ **forces** fuerzas enemigas

opposite *n* lo contrario; **the exact** ~ **of** el polo opuesto de; *adj* opuesto; (facing) de enfrente; ~ **number** persona que ocupa un puesto correspondiente, (friend) compañero; ~ **sex** sexo contrario; *adv* enfrente; *prep* ~ **to** enfrente de

opposition oposición *f*

oppress oprimir

oppression opresión *f*

oppressive opresivo; ~ **weather** tiempo bochornoso

oppressor opresor *m* (-ora *f*)

opprobrious oprobioso

opprobrium oprobio

opt optar (**for** por); ~ **out** decidir no participar

optic óptico

optical óptico; ~ **illusion** ilusión óptica: ~ **navigation** *space* navegación óptica

optician óptico

optics óptica

optimism optimismo

optimist optimista *m+f*

optimistic optimista; **I'm** ~ (**about**) soy optimista (sobre)

optimum óptimo

option opción *f* (**on** a); ~ **to purchase** opción de comprar

optional discrecional; ~ **equipment** equipo optativo

optometrist oculista *m+f*

opulence opulencia

opulent opulento

opus obra; *mus* opus *m*

or o; (before o- and ho-) u, **seven** ~ **eight** siete u ocho; **either...** ~ o...o; ~ **else** si no; **five minutes** ~ **so** unos cinco minutos

oracle oráculo; **work the** ~ obrar entre bastidores

oracular fatídico

oral *n* examen (-ámenes) *m* oral; *adj* oral

orange naranja; (colour) de color naranja; ~ **blossom** azahar *m*; ~**-grove** naranjal *m*; ~**-grower** naranjero; ~**-juice** zumo de naranja; **Orangeman, Orangewoman** *pol* orangista *m+f*; ~ **marmalade** mermelada de naranja; ~**-peel** cáscara de naranja; ~**-stick**

limpiauñas *m sing*; ~ **tree** naranjo

orangeade naranjada; (fizzy) gaseosa de naranja

orangery naranjal *m*

orang-outang orangután *m*

orate perorar

oration discurso

orator orador *m* (-ora *f*)

oratorical oratorio

oratorio oratorio

oratory oratoria; *eccles* oratorio

orb orbe *m*

orbit *n* órbita; **in** ~ en órbita; **go/put into** ~ entrar/colocar[4] en órbita; *v* orbitar

orbital orbital

orchard huerto; (of apples) pomar *m*

orchestra orquesta; ~ **stall/seat** butaca de platea

orchestral orquestal

orchestrate orquestar

orchestration orquestación (-ones) *f*

orchid orquídea

ordain ordenar; **be ~ed as** ordenarse de

ordeal prueba (rigurosa); **go through an** ~ *fam* pasar las de Caín

order *n* (arrangement) orden (órdenes) *m*, **in battle** ~ en orden de batalla; (command) orden (órdenes) *f*; *comm* (for goods) pedido, ~ **book** libro de pedidos; (class) categoría; (tidiness) arreglo; (peace) orden *m*, **public** ~ orden público; (decoration) orden *m*; (to view a house) permiso; (for money) giro; *eccles* orden *f*, **take** ~**s** ordenarse; **in** ~ (tidy) ordenado, *leg* en regla, *mech* en funcionamiento; **the engine is in good running** ~ el motor funciona bien; **in** ~ **that** para que +*subj*; **in** ~ **to** para +*infin*; **of the** ~ **of** del orden de; **on the** ~**s of** por orden de; **out of** ~ *mech* que no funciona, (on notice) no funciona, (in meeting) fuera de orden; **his stomach is out of** ~ él no está bien del estómago; **made to** ~ hecho por encargo especial, (of clothes) hecho a la medida; **until further** ~**s** hasta nueva orden; **be on** ~ estar[19] pedido; **call to** ~ llamar al orden; **give** ~**s** mandar; **keep** ~ mantener[19] el orden; ~! ¡silencio!; **put in** ~ arreglar; **that's a tall** ~! ¡eso es pedir mucho!; **to the** ~ **of** a la orden de; ~ **form** impreso de pedido; ~ **of the day** orden *f* del día, *fig* moda; ~

paper orden *f* del día

v (give ~s) mandar; (arrange) ordenar; (tidy) arreglar[5]; (bespeak) encargar[5]; ~ **a suit** mandar hacer[19] un traje

~ **about** dar[19] muchas órdenes

~ **back** hacer[19] volver

~ **down** decir[19] a uno que baje

~ **off** mandar marcharse

~ **out** mandar salir

~ **up** hacer[19] subir

ordered: well-~ **mind** mente lógica

orderliness ordenanza

orderly *n mil* ordenanza *m*; *med* enfermero; *adj* (in good order) ordenado; (law-abiding) formal; (tidy) arreglado; (systematic) metódico; (well-disciplined) bien disciplinado; ~ **officer** oficial del día

ordinal *n* + *adj* ordinal *m*

ordinance ordenanza

ordinand ordenando

ordinarily por lo general

ordinariness ordinariez *f*

ordinary *n eccles* ordinario de la misa; **out of the** ~ fuera de lo común; *adj* común, (of wine) corriente; ~ **seaman** simple marinero; ~ **wear and tear** desgaste *m* normal por el uso

ordination ordenación *f*

ordnance artillería; (supplies) material *m* de guerra; **Ordnance Survey** agrimensura; **Ordnance Survey map** *approx* mapa *m* del estado mayor

ordure suciedad *f*; *fam* mierda

ore mineral; **iron** ~ mineral de hierro; ~ **deposit** yacimiento mineral

oregano orégano

organ (all meanings) órgano; ~**-blower** entonador *m*; ~**-grinder** organillero; ~**-loft** tribuna del órgano; ~**-pipe** cañón de órgano; ~**-stop** registro de órgano

organdie organdí *m*

organic orgánico; ~ **food** comestibles *mpl* producidos sin abono artificial; **an** ~ **whole** una entidad orgánica

organism organismo

organist organista *m* + *f*

organization organización (-ones) *f*; ~ **chart** *comm* organigrama *m*

organizational organizacional

organize organizar[7]

organizer organizador *m* (-ora *f*)

organizing *adj* organizador

orgasm orgasmo; **to have/reach an ~** orgasmar; *vulg sl* venirse[19]
orgiastic orgiástico
orgy orgía
oriel mirador *m*
orient oriente *m*
oriental *n+adj* oriental *m+f*
orientalist orientalista *m+f*
orientate orientar
orientation orientación *f*
orifice orificio
origami papiroflexia
origin origen (-ígenes) *m*; (extraction) procedencia
original *n+adj* original *m*; ~ **sin** pecado original
originality originalidad *f*
originate *vt* originar, causar; *vi* originarse; ~ **from/in** traer[19] su origen de; **this style ~d with Picasso** este estilo es de Picasso; ~ **a fashion** empezar[2a+7] una moda
origination principio
originator originador *m* (-ora *f*)
oriole oropéndola
Orion Orión *m*
Orkneys Orcadas *fpl*
orlon *equiv* tergal *m*
ormolu bronce dorado
ornament *n* adorno; *fig* ornamento; (trinket) chuchería; *v* adornar
ornamental decorativo
ornamentation adornos *mpl*
ornate ornado; (of language) florido
ornithological ornitológico
ornithologist ornitólogo
ornithology ornitología
orotund orotundo
orphan *n+adj* huérfano; *v* dejar huérfano a; ~**ed** huérfano
orphanage orfanato
Orpheus Orfeo
orthodox ortodoxo; ~ **church** iglesia ortodoxa
orthodoxy ortodoxia
orthographic ortográfico
orthography ortografía
orthopaedic ortopédico; ~**s** ortopedia
O.S. *see* **outsize**
oscillate oscilar; (of mind) vacilar
oscillating oscilante; ~ **circuit** circuito de corriente alterna
oscillation oscilación *f*
osculate besar

osier (material) mimbre *f*; *bot* mimbrera
osmosis ósmosis *f*, osmosis *f*
osmotic osmótico
osprey quebrantahuesos *m sing+pl*
ossify osificar(se)[4]
ossuary osario
Ostend Ostende *m*
ostensible aparente
ostentation ostentación *f*; *fam* ínfulas *fpl*
ostentatious ostentoso; *fam* rimbombante
osteopath osteópata *m*
osteopathy osteopatía
ostler mozo de cuadra
ostracism ostracismo
ostracize excluir[16] de la sociedad
ostrich avestruz (-ces) *m*
other otro; **this one and three ~s** éste y otros tres; **I heard them talking on the ~ side of my door** les oí hablando a través de mi puerta; **the ~ day** el otro día; **some ~ day** otro día; **every ~ day** un día sí y otro no; **this man and the ~** este hombre y el otro; **someone or ~** alguien; **the ~s** los demás, **I don't care what ~ people think** no me importa lo que piensan los demás; ~ **than** otra cosa que; ~ **side of the picture** *fig* otra cara de la moneda; **look the ~ way** mirar hacia otra parte; **no ~** ningún otro; ~ **world** mundo sobrenatural; ~**-worldliness** espiritualidad *f*; ~**-worldly** espiritual
otherwise (differently) de otra manera; (if not) si no; (in other respects) por lo demás
otiose ocioso
otter nutria
ottoman diván (-anes) *m*; **Ottoman** *n* otomana; *adj* otomano
ouch! ¡huy!
ought (to) deber; **I ~ to say it** debería decirlo; **I ~ to have said it** debería haberlo dicho; **he ~ to have done it** (he probably has …) él debe (de) haberlo hecho; **you ~ to have seen** era (cosa) de ver; **you ~ to have told me** usted debería habérmelo dicho; **you ~ to eat more** le convendría a Vd. comer más
ounce onza (=28.35 gramos); *fig* pizca
our nuestro(s), nuestra(s); ~**s** el nuestro, la nuestra *etc*; **a friend of ~s** un amigo nuestro; **Our Father** Padre

Nuestro; **say the Our Father** rezar[7] el padrenuestro

ourselves nosotros mismos; *reflex pron* nos; (after *prep*) nosotros

oust desposeer[17]

out fuera; **have a day ~** pasar el día fuera; **be ~** (not at home) no estar[19], **daddy is ~** no está papá; (of a fire) estar[19] apagado; (of buds) haber[19] brotado; (of clock) estar[19] mal; (of publication) haberse[19] publicado; (of secret) haber[19] salido a luz; (of tide) estar[19] baja; *sp* estar[19] fuera del juego; (on strike) estar[19] en huelga; **be ~ to** tener[19] intención de +*infin*; **come ~** (of girls in society) ponerse[19] de largo, (of sun) salir[19]; *in combination with v* **run/jump ~** salir[19] corriendo/saltando; **say ~ loud** decir[19] en voz alta; **just ~** (book *etc*) recién salido, *cin* recién estrenado; **~-and-~** completo; **~ and about** andando fuera; **~ of** (~side) fuera de, (lacking) sin, **I'm ~ of money** estoy sin dinero; **we are ~ of size forty** ya no tenemos la talla cuarenta; **I am ~ of sugar** se me ha acabado el azúcar; **~ of the ordinary** discordante; **~ of print** agotado; **~ of spite/pride** por despecho/orgullo; **~ of time** *mus* fuera del compás; **~ of tune** desafinado; **read ~ of a book** leer[17] en un libro; **a scene ~ of the play** una escena de la obra de teatro; **a verse ~ of the Bible** un verso de la Biblia; **four ~ of five** de cada cinco, cuatro; **~ of work** sin trabajo; **I threw him ~** (of the house) le puse en la calle; **~ of my way!** ¡aparte!; **~ with it!** ¡habla sin rodeos!; **~ with the dictator!** ¡fuera con el dictador!; **~ you go!** ¡fuera de aquí!; **~-of-date** pasado de moda; **~-of-doors** al aire libre; **~-of-the-way** inaccesible; **~-general** ganar por mejor táctica

outbalance contrapesar; *fig* compensar

outbid sobrepujar; (at cards) sobrepasar

outbidder sobrepujador *m* (-ora *f*)

outboard: **~ motor** motor *m* fueraborda

outbreak principio; (of crime) serie *f*; *med* brote *m*; (of war) comienzo

outbuilding dependencia; (shed) cobertizo

outburst explosión *f*; **~ of laughter** carcajada

outcast paria *m*+*f*

outclass ser[19] muy superior a

outcome resultado

outcrop afloramiento

outcry protesta ruidosa

outdated anticuado

outdistance dejar atrás

outdo exceder; **~ o.s.** excederse; **be outdone** quedarse atrás

outdoor al aire libre; **~ relief** ayuda a domicilio; **~s** fuera de casa, (in the open) al aire libre

outer exterior; **~ space** espacio extraterrestre/exterior

outermost más exterior

outface mirar fijo; (defy) desafiar

outfall desembocadura

outfield *sp* jardín *m*

outfielder *sp* jardinero

outfit equipo; (clothes) ropa; *mil* cuerpo

outfitter camisero; **~'s** camisería

outflank flanquear

outgoing *n*: **~s** gastos; *adj* saliente; (of tide) descendiente

outgrow hacerse[19] demasiado grande para; (of clothes) ya no caber[19] en; **I've outgrown my shoes** se me quedan pequeños los zapatos

outhouse dependencia

outing excursión *f*; **go on an ~** ir[19] de excursión

outlandish estrafalario

outlast durar más que

outlaw *n* proscrito; *v* proscribir (*past part* proscrito)

outlawry proscripción *f*

outlay desembolso

outlet +*fig* salida; *elect* toma; (to sea) desembocadura

outline *n* contorno; (preliminary plan) anteproyecto; **in ~** a grandes rasgos; *v* bosquejar; (plan) prefigurar; **~d against** destacado contra

outlive sobrevivir; **~ its usefulness** durar más que el tiempo en que puede servir

outlook +*fig* perspectiva; (viewpoint) punto de vista

outlying remoto; **~ districts** afueras *fpl*

outmanoeuvre vencer[14] por mejor táctica

outmoded pasado de moda

outnumber ser[19] más que

outpace dejar atrás

out-patient enfermo externo (de un

hospital); ~s' **department** consulta de los enfermos externos, ambulatorio

outplay jugar (ue)[1a] mejor que

outpoint (boxing) ganar por puntos

outpost puesto avanzado

outpouring +*fig* efusión *f*

output producción *f*; *elect* potencia de salida; *mech* rendimiento

outrage *n* ultraje *m*; *fig* abuso; *v* ultrajar

outrageous atroz (-ces); *fam* monstruoso; (ridiculous) ridículo; **dress in an ~ way** estar[19] matador

outrange tener[19] mayor alcance que

outré cursi

outride cabalgar[5] más a prisa que

outrider (on horseback) escolta *m* a caballo; (on motorcycle) motorista *m* de escolta

outrigger (bote *m* con) portarremos *m sing* exterior

outright *adj* absoluto; *adv* de una vez

outrival sobrepujar

outrun correr más que; (exceed) exceder

outset comienzo

outshine brillar más; (eclipse) eclipsar

outside *n* exterior *m*; (appearances) apariencia; ~ **left/right** *n* extremo izquierdo/derecho; **at the ~** (at most) a lo sumo; **on the ~ of** fuera de; *adj* exterior; ~ **shutter** contraventana; *adv* fuera; (out of doors) al aire libre; **come ~!** (for a fight) ¡salgamos al campo!; *prep* fuera de

outsider forastero; *fam* persona maleducada

outsize de tamaño extra

outskirts afueras *fpl*; **on the ~ of** en las afueras de

outsmart engañar; ser más listo que

outspoken franco; **she is very ~** ella no tiene pelos en la lengua

outspread extendido

outstanding (excellent) destacado; *fam* fuera de serie; (awaiting attention) pendiente; (unpaid) sin pagar

outstare: ~ **s.o.** hacer[19] bajar la vista mirando a uno

outstay (one's welcome) quedarse más tiempo de (lo conveniente)

outstretch extender (ie)[2b]

outstrip distanciar

outvote recibir más votos que; **be ~d by** recibir menos votos que

outward exterior; ~ **journey** viaje *m* de ida; **to (all) ~ appearances** aparentemente; ~-**bound** de salida; *adv* ~s hacia fuera

outwear (last) durar más que; (wear out) gastar

outweigh pesar más que; *fig* valer[19] más que

outwit ser[19] más listo que; ~ **the police** despistar a la policía

outwork *n* trabajar más que

outworker empleado que trabaja en su propia casa

outworn gastado; *fig* anticuado

oval *n* óvalo; *adj* ovalado

ovary ovario

ovation ovación *f*; **give an ~ to** recibir con aplausos; **give a standing ~ to s.o.** ponerse[19] de pie y recibir con aplausos

oven horno; ~**ware** cacharros *mpl* para el horno

over *n* (cricket) serie *f* de seis saques; *adj* terminado; **it's all ~** todo se acabó; **now that it's all ~** después de que todo pasó; *adv* (above) por encima; (across) de un lado a otro; (on the other side) al otro lado; **all ~** (everywhere) por todas partes; (all) ~ **again** otra vez; ~ **and ~** (again) una y otra vez; **I looked him ~** le miré de pies a cabeza; ~ **to you!** *adj rad* ¡cambio!; ~ **and out!** ¡corto!; *prep* (above, upon) sobre; (with *v* of movement) por encima de, **it went ~ his head** pasó por encima de su cabeza; (across) a través de, **jump ~ the stream** saltar el arroyo; (during) durante, ~ **the last few days** durante los últimos pocos días; (more than) más de; (on the other side of) al otro lado de, ~ **the wall** al otro lado del muro; ~ **and above** además de; ~ **here** acá; ~ **there** allá; ~ **the way** en frente; **he's ~ me at work** él es mi superior en el trabajo; **he's just ~ twenty** él tiene veintipocos años; **all ~ Scotland** por toda Escocia; **the child is all ~ mud** el niño está cubierto de lodo; ~ **my dead body!** ¡por encima de mi cadáver!; (as prefix) demasiado, ~-**anxious** demasiado ansioso

overabundance superabundancia

overabundant superabundante

overact exagerar (un papel)

overall *n* (clothing) bata; ~s mono; *adj* global, **the ~ influence** la influencia global; ~ **length** largo total

overarm por lo alto

overawe intimidar

overbalance perder (ie)²ᵇ el equilibrio

overbearing dominante

overblown marchitado

overboard al agua; **throw ~** echar al agua, *fig* abandonar; **man ~!** ¡hombre al agua!

overboot zapato de goma, chanclo

overburden sobrecargar⁵

overcast *adj* nublado; *v* (sewing) sobrehilar

overcharge *n* suplemento; *v* cobrar demasiado

overclothes ropa exterior

overcloud nublar

overcoat abrigo

overcome *adj* (by emotion) turbado; (by sleep) rendido; *v* (conquer), vencer¹²; (difficulties) superar

overcompensate compensar demasiado (**for** por)

overconfidence demasiada confianza

overconfident demasiado confiado

overconsumption superconsumo

overcrowd apiñar

overcrowding superpoblación *f*

overdeveloped superdesarrollado; *phot* revelado demasiado

overdo exagerar; *cul* recocer¹ᵃ⁺¹⁴; **don't ~ it!** ¡no trabaje demasiado!, *fam iron* ¡no te hernies!

overdone hecho más de lo necesario; *cul* demasiado hecho

overdose dosis excesiva

overdraft giro en descubierto; **ask for an ~** pedir³ un crédito

overdraw girar en descubierto; **I'm ~n** estoy al descubierto

overdress vestirse (i)³ con exceso

overdrive *mot* superdirecta

overdue (train) atrasado; *comm* sobrevencido

overeat comer con exceso

overemployment superempleo

overestimate tener¹⁹ un concepto exagerado de

overexertion esfuerzo excesivo

overexpose *phot* sobreexponer¹⁹

overexposure exceso de exposición

overflight: ~ **zone** zona sobrevolada

overflow *n* desbordamiento; (pipe) cañería de desagüe, *fig* exceso; *v* +*fig* desbordar(se) (**with** de)

overfly sobrevolar (ue)¹ᵃ

overgarment prenda exterior

overgrown cubierto de herbaje; (of child) grande para su edad

overhand *sp* tirado de volea alta; (sewing) sobrehilado

overhang *n* saliente; *v* sobresalir¹⁹

overhaul *n* reparación *f*; *v* (repair) revisar y reparar; (overtake) alcanzar⁷

overhead *adj* aéreo; ~ **expenses** (~s) gastos *mpl* generales; ~ **railway** ferrocarril elevado; *adv* por encima de la cabeza

overhear oír por casualidad

overheat recalentar (ie)²ᵃ; **become ~ed** recalentarse (ie)²ᵃ; (of people) enfadarse

overheating recalentamiento

overindulge mimar demasiado

overindulgence exceso (**in** de)

overjoyed lleno de alegría

overkill más que las bombas nucleares necesarias para destruir al enemigo

overladen sobrecargado

overland por tierra

overlap montarse sobre; *fig* coincidir en parte

overlapping *n* solapa; *adj* montado sobre

overlay *n* cubierta; *v* cubrir (*past part* cubierto) (**with** de)

overleaf a la vuelta

overload *n* sobrecarga; *v* sobrecargar⁵

overlook dar¹⁹ a; **the house ~s the park** la casa da al parque; (not notice) no fijarse en; (take no notice) pasar por alto; (wink at) hacer¹⁹ la vista gorda a; (forgive) perdonar

overlord señor *m*

overly demasiado

overmuch demasiado

overnight de la noche a la mañana, **it made him famous ~** le hizo célebre de la noche a la mañana; **stay ~** pasar la noche; ~ **bag** saco de noche; ~ **journey** viaje de noche; ~ **pass** *mil* pase *m* de pernoctar

overpaid que gana demasiado

overpass (road) paso superior; *joc sl* scalectrix *m*

overpitch lanzar⁷ con demasiada fuerza

overplay *sp* golpear la pelota con demasiada fuerza; *theat* hacer[19] un papel con exageración

overpopulated superpoblado

overpopulation superpoblación *f*

overpower vencer[12]; (senses) embargar[5]

overpowering abrumador (-ora *f*)

overpraise alabar demasiado

overprice recargar[5] el precio

overprint *n* sello rehabilitado; *v* sobreimprimir; (postage stamp) rehabilitar

overproduction superproducción *f*

overproof de concentración alcohólica superior a su debido porcentaje

overprotect proteger[16] demasiado

overrate exagerar el valor de; ~d de un valor exagerado

overreach: ~ **o.s.** excederse

override anular

overriding decisivo

overrule anular; *leg* denegar (ie)[2a+5]

overrun invadir; (of vermin) infestar; (of time) exceder

overseas *adj* de ultramar; *adv* en ultramar

oversee supervisar (ie)[2b]

overseer superintendente *m+f*; (foreman) capataz (-ces) *m*

oversew sobrehilar

oversexed hipersexuado

overshadow sombrear; (eclipse) eclipsar

overshoe chanclo

overshoot: ~ **the mark** pasar de la raya; ~ **the runway** sobrepasar la pista

oversight *n* inadvertencia; (supervision) vigilancia

overskirt sobrefalda

overslaugh bajo de arena en una ría

oversleep dormir (ue)[1c] demasiado; **I overslept** durmiendo se me pasó la hora, *fam* se me pegaron las sábanas

overspend gastar demasiado

overspill desparramamiento de población; ~ **town** ciudad *f* de habitantes trasladados de otra mayor

overstate exagerar

overstatement exageración *f*

overstay quedar(se) demasiado tiempo

overstep exceder; ~ **the mark** propasarse

overstock tener[19] surtido excesivo de

overstrain *n* tensión excesiva; *v* fatigar[5] demasiado

overstrung nervioso; (of piano) cruzado

oversubscribe contribuir[16] más de lo pedido

overt manifiesto

overtake alcanzar[7] (y adelantarse a)

overtax oprimir con tributos; (with work) sobrecargar[5]; ~ **o.s.** fatigarse[5] demasiado

overthrow *n* derrocamiento; *v* +*fig* derrocar[4]

overtime horas *fpl* extra; **work** ~ trabajar horas extra

overtone *mus* armónico; *fig* sugestión *f*

overtop descollar entre

overture propuesta formal; *mus* obertura; *pol* proposición *f*

overturn volcar (ue)[1a+4]; *naut* zozobrar

overweening presuntuoso

overweight excesivamente pesado; **be** ~ pesar demasiado

overwhelm abrumar; ~ **with kindness** colmar de favores

overwhelming abrumador (-ora *f*)

overwind (clock *etc*) saltar la cuerda a

overwork *n* trabajo excesivo; *vi* trabajar demasiado; *vt* hacer[19] trabajar demasiado

overwrought sobreexcitado

oviform oviforme

ovum huevo

owe *vt* deber; *vi* tener[19] deudas

owing debido (to a); **he died** ~ **a lot of money** él murió debiendo mucho dinero

owl lechuza; **little** ~ mochuelo común; **long-eared** ~ buho chico

owlet lechuza pequeña

owlish parecido a un buho

own *adj* propio; **my** ~ **car** mi propio coche; **get one's** ~ **back (on)** vengarse[5] (de); **get one's** ~ **way** salirse[19] con la suya; **our** ~ **make** de la casa; *pron* lo mío/suyo/nuestro *etc*; **come into one's** ~ entrar en posesión de lo suyo; **hold one's** ~ mantenerse[19] firme; **on one's** ~ (alone) solo; **on one's** ~ (account) por su propia cuenta; *v* poseer; (acknowledge) reconocer[14]; ~ **up (to)** confesar (ie)[2a]

owner dueño; ~-**driver** automovilista *m/f* con su propio coche; ~-**occupier** propietario ocupador

ownerless sin dueño

ownership posesión *f*

ox buey *m*; ~ **blood** (colour) color *m* de sangre de toro; ~ **bow** collera de yugo; ~-**bow bend** curva en U

oxalic oxálico

Oxford: ~ **accent** acento oxfordiano

oxide óxido

oxidize oxidar(se)

oxidizer +*space* oxidante *m*

oxlip prímula

Oxonian oxoniano

oxyacetylene: ~ **burner** soplete *m* de acetileno

oxygen oxígeno; ~-**mask** máscara de oxígeno; ~ **starvation** falta de oxígeno; ~-**tent** tienda de oxígeno

oxygenize oxigenar

oyez! ¡oíd!

oyster ostra; ~-**bed** criadero de ostras; ~-**catcher** *orni* ostrero

ozone ozono

P

p (letter) pe *f*; (penny) penique *m*; (page) pág (página); **mind one's ~'s and q's** tener[19] cuidado de no meter la pata

pa papá *m*

pabulum pábulo

pace (step) paso; (of horse) andadura; (speed) velocidad *f*, **go the ~** (go quickly) +*fig* mantener[19] velocidad; **go at a snail's ~** ir[19] a paso de tortuga; **go at a good ~** ir[19] a buen paso; **keep ~ with** ir[19] al mismo paso que; **put through one's ~s** demostrar (ue)[1a] las cualidades de uno; **set the ~** establecer[14] el paso; **~-maker** el que marca el paso, *fig* el que da el ejemplo, *med* marcapasos *m sing+pl*; *v* ~ **(up and down)** pasearse (de un lado a otro); ~ **(out)** medir (i)[3] a pasos (a); **did he ~ out the length of the garden?** ¿midió él a pasos la longitud del jardín?; ~ **s.o. in a race** marcar[4] el paso para uno en una carrera

pachyderm paquidermo

pacific pacífico; **Pacific Ocean** Océano Pacífico

pacification pacificación *f*

pacifier chupete *m*

pacifism pacifismo

pacifist *n+adj* pacifista *m+f*

pacify pacificar[4]

pack *n* (load) bulto; (rucksack) mochila; (of cards) baraja; (of cigarettes) paquete, cajetilla; (of hounds) jauría; (of wolves) manada; (rugby) delanteros *mpl*; (of rogues) pandilla; ~ **of lies** montón *m* de mentiras; ~ **animal** bestia de carga; **~-horse** caballo de carga; **~-ice** témpanos flotantes; **~-saddle** enjalma; **~-thread** bramante *m*; *v* (suitcase) hacer[19] la maleta; (in trunk) embaular; (in box) encajar; (cram) apretar; (fill with supporters) llenar de partidarios; *mech* empaquetar; (crowd) atestar, **streets ~ed with tourists** calles atestadas de turistas; **the glasses were ~ed in tissue paper** los vasos estaban envueltos en papel de seda; **~ed like sardines** como sardinas en lata; **the bus was ~ed** el autobús estaba lleno de bote en bote; **send packing** despedir (i) con cajas destempladas, *fam* mandar a freír espárragos

~ **in:** ~ **it in** (stop it) dejarlo

~ **off** (a person) despachar

~ **up** (finish) terminar; (tidy) recoger[8] todo; (make parcel) empaquetar; **my car has ~ed up** se ha roto mi coche; ~ **it up** (stop it) dejarlo

package paquete *m*; ~ **deal** *comm+pol* paquete *m*

packaging envase *m*

packer embalador *m* (-ora *f*)

packet paquete *m*; (of cigarettes *etc*) paquete; **~-boat** paquebote *m*

packing embalaje *m*; (inner protective material) relleno; (lagging) guarnición *f*; **do one's ~** hacer[19] las maletas; **~-case** cajón (-ones) *m* de embalaje

pact pacto; **sign a ~ (with)** pactar (con)

pad *n* almohadilla; (ink-pad) almohadilla (para entintar); (for polishing) muñeca; (on wound) cabezal *m*; (shin protector) espinillera; (of paw) pulpejo; (of paper) bloque *m*; (blotting-paper) secante; (launching platform) plataforma; *vt* rellenar; acolchar; ~ **out** (in writing) meter mucha paja; *vi* (walk about) caminar sin ruido

padded acojinado; acolchado; ~ **cell** celda acolchada

padding relleno; (in writing) paja

paddle *n* (oar) canalete *m*; (on paddle-wheel) paleta; (wading) baño a media pierna; **~-box** tambor *m* (de rueda); **~-steamer** vapor *m* de ruedas; **~-wheel** rueda de paletas; *v* remar con canalete; (wade) bañarse a media pierna

paddler remero; bañador *m* (-ora *f*) a

media pierna

paddling baño a media pierna; ~-**pool** estanque *m* de juegos

paddock prado; (racing) corral *m*

paddy: ~ **field** arrozal *m*; (fit of temper) rabieta

padlock *n* candado; *v* cerrar (ie)[2a] con candado

padre capellán *m* militar; *fam* cura *m*

paediatrician pediatra *m+f*

paediatrics pediatría

pagan *n+adj* pagano

paganism paganismo

[1] **page** *n* (boy) paje *m*; *v* buscar[4] llamando

[2] **page** *n* (in book) página; **on** ~ **ten** en la página diez; (of newspaper) plana, **on the front** ~ en primera plana; ~-**proofs** pruebas *fpl* de imprenta; *v* paginar

pageant representación *f* teatral de un episodio histórico; (festival) fiesta

pageantry pompa

pagination paginación *f*

paging (of book) paginación *f*

pagoda pagoda

paid: **put** ~ **to** acabar con; ~-**up share** acción liberada

pail cubo; ~**ful of water** cubo de agua

pain *n* dolor *m*; **I have a** ~ **in my arm** me duele el brazo; **be in** ~ estar[19] con dolor; **labour** ~**s** dolores *mpl* del parto; **he took great** ~**s to** él se esforzó en/por; **on** ~ **of** so pena de; **get for one's** ~**s** lograr después de tanto trabajo; ~**staking** concienzudo; ~**ed look** expresión *f* de disgusto; **he's a** ~-**in-the-neck** él es un pelmazo; ~-**killer** *med* analgésico; *v* doler (ue)[1b]; *fig* dar[19] lástima

painful doloroso; (task) penoso

painless sin dolor/pena

paint *n* pintura; (for preserving metal) pavón (-ones) *m*; (rouge) colorete *m*; (make-up) maquillaje *m*; ~-**box** caja de pinturas; ~-**brush** (small) pincel *m*, (large) brocha; ~-**roller** rodillo de pintura; ~-**spray** pistola de pintar; *v* pintar; **she** ~**ed it green** ella lo pintó de verde; ~ **o.s.** (with make-up) pintarse; ~ **a black picture of** cargar[5] tinta sobre; ~ **the town red** ir[19] de parranda

painted pintado

[1] **painter** pintor *m*

[2] **painter** *naut* amarra

painting (act) pintura; (colouring) coloración *f*; (picture) cuadro

paintress pintora

pair *n* par *m*; (of people) pareja; ~ **of pyjamas** pijama; ~ **of scales** balanza; ~ **of scissors** unas tijeras; *v* emparejar(se) ~ **off** (animals) aparearse

pajamas *see* **pyjamas**

Pakistan Pakistán *m*

Pakistani pakistaní (-íes *pl*) *m+f*

pal *n* amigo, *sl* tronco *v* ~ **up** (with) hacerse[19] amigo (de)

palace *n* palacio

palaeography paleografía

palaeolithic paleolítico

palaeontologist paleontólogo

palaeontology paleontología

palatable sabroso

palatal *n+adj* palatal *m*

palate *anat* (+ taste) paladar *m*

palatial palaciego; (sumptuous) suntuoso

palaver conferencia; *fam* lío

[1] **pale** pálido; (of colours) claro; **turn** ~ palidecer[14], (of colours) descolorarse

[2] **pale: beyond the** ~ (que merece ser) excluido de la buena sociedad

paleness palidez *f*; (of colours) claridad *f*

Palestine Palestina

Palestinian *n+adj* palestino

palette paleta; ~ **knife** espátula

palfrey palafrén (-enes) *m*

palindrome palabra palíndroma

paling (stake) estaca; (fence) estacada

palisade estacada

[1] **pall** paño mortuorio; (of smoke) capa; *eccles* palio; ~-**bearer** doliente *m+f*

[2] **pall** dejar de gustar (**on a**)

pallet, palliasse jergón (-ones) *m*

palliate paliar

palliative *n+adj* paliativo; **take** ~ **measures** tomar medidas paliativas

pallid pálido

pallor palidez *f*

pally amistoso

[1] **palm** (tree) palmera; ~ **grove** palmar *m*; ~-**oil** aceite *m* de palma; **Palm Sunday** Domingo de Ramos

[2] **palm** *n* (of hand) palma; **grease s.o.'s** ~ untar la mano a alguien; *v* (card) escamotar; ~ **off on** encajar a

palmist quiromántico

palmistry quiromancia

palpability palpabilidad *f*

palpable +*fig* palpable
palpitate palpitar
palpitation palpitación (-ones) *f*; **get ~s** sufrir de palpitaciones
palsy perlesía
paltriness (insignificance) insignificancia; (contemptibility) mezquindad *f*; (poverty) pobreza
paltry (insignificant) insignificante; (contemptible) mezquino; (poor) pobre
pampas pampas *fpl*
pamper mimar
pamphlet folleto; *comm*+*pol* folleto de propaganda
pamphleteer folletista *m*+*f*
pan *n* cazuela; (frying-pan) sartén (-enes) *f*; (of balance) platillo; *min* gamella; **~cake** *n* tortita; **~cake-landing** aterrizaje *m* de vientre; *v* (for gold) separar en la gamella; *cin*+*TV* panoramicar⁴, **~ right** girar a la derecha; **~ out** (turn out) resultar, (succeed) tener¹⁹ exito
panacea panacea
panache penacho
Panama Panamá *m*; **~ hat** (sombrero de) jipijapa *m*; **~ Canal** canal *m* de Panamá
Panamanian *n*+*adj* panameño
panchromatic pancromático
pancreas páncreas *m*
panda panda *m*+*f*
pandemonium pandemonio
pander *n* (pimp) alcahuete *m*; *v* (act as pimp) alcahuetear; **~ to** procurar complacer
pane cristal *m*; **~ of glass** cristal *m* de vidriera
panegyric *n*+*adj* panegírico
panel *n* (wall) panel *m*; (ceiling) artesón (-ones) *m*; (door) entrepaño; *arts* tabla; (sewing) paño; (of instruments) tablero de instrumentos; (jury) tribunal *m*; **~-doctor** médico de seguros; **~-game** *TV* programa *m* concurso; *v* (see *n*) revestir con entrepaños/paneles, artesonar
panelling (wall) paneles *mpl*; (ceiling) artesonado; (door) entrepaños *mpl*
pang (pain) punzada (de dolor); (anguish) angustia; **~s of childbirth** dolores *mpl* de parto; **have ~s of conscience** tener¹⁹ remordimiento

panic *m* pánico; **cause ~** provocar⁴ pánico; **~-stricken** lleno de terror; *v* dejarse dominar por el pánico
panicky asustadizo
pannier alforja
panoply panoplia
panorama panorama
panoramic panorámico
pansy *bot* pensamiento; (effeminate man) sarasa *m*
pant *n* jadeo; *v* jadear; **~ for** suspirar por
pantechnicon camión *m* de mudanzas
pantheism panteísmo
pantheistic panteísta
pantheon panteón *m*
panther pantera
panties braga(s)
panting *n* jadeo; *adj* jadeante
pantomime pantomima; (Christmas show) obra musical de Navidad
pantry despensa
pants (underclothing) calzoncillos *mpl*; (trousers) pantalones *mpl*; (women's underclothing) braga(s)
pap (food) papilla
papa papá *m*
papacy papado
papal papal
paper *n* papel *m*; (newspaper) periódico; (article) artículo; (essay) trabajo; (exam) papel escrito; (wallpaper) papel pintado; (lecture) comunicación *f*, **give a ~** (on) dar¹⁹ una conferencia (sobre); **the police asked for his ~s** la policía le pidió su documentación *f*; **only on ~** nominalmente; **take the ~ off** (a toffee) pelar; **sheet of ~** cuartilla; **~ back** libro de bolsillo; **~ bag** bolsa de papel; **~-bound** en rústica; **~-boy** repartidor *m* de periódicos; **~-chase** rallye-papel *m*; **~-clip** sujetapapeles *m sing*+*pl*; **~ cone** cucurucho; **~-fastener** (wire staple) grapa; **~-hanger** empapelador *m*; **~-knife** abrecartas *m sing*; **~-maker** fabricante *m* de papel; **~-mill** fábrica de papel; **~ money** papel *m* moneda; **~-weight** pisapapeles *m sing*+*pl*; **~ work** papeleo; *v* empapelar
papier-mâché cartón *m* piedra
papist *n*+*adj* papista *m*+*f*
paprika pimentón *m*

Papuan papú (úes) *m+f*

papyrus papiro; (document) documento en papiro

par paridad *f*; **above** ~ a premio; **below** ~ a descuento; **be on a** ~ **with** ser[19] igual que

para soldado paracaidista; ~**s** tropas paracaidistas

parable parábola

parabola parábola

parabolic parabólico

parachute *n* paracaídas *m sing*; ~ **troops** paracaidistas *mpl*; *v* lanzar(se)[7] en paracaídas

parachutist paracaidista *m+f*

parade *n* (road) paseo; (procession) desfile *m*; (military review) revista; (ostentation) alarde *f*; ~**-ground** plaza de armas; *v* (*see n*) pasear; desfilar; pasar revista; alardear; *pol* hacer[19] una manifestación; ~ **up and down** pasearse

paradise paraíso

paradox paradoja

paradoxical paradójico

paraffin petróleo; ~ **lamp** lámpara de petróleo; ~ **wax** parafina

paragon modelo; **she is a** ~ **of** ella es un modelo de; *print* tipo de veinte puntos

paragraph párrafo; **new** ~ (punto y) aparte

Paraguay Paraguay *m*; **she lives in** ~ ella vive en el Paraguay

Paraguayan *adj n+adj* paraguayo

parakeet periquito

parallel *n* paralelo; *adj* paralelo (**to** a); (comparable) igual; *elect* en paralelo; ~ **bars** paralelas *fpl*; *adv* en línea paralela a; **your ideas run** ~ **to mine** sus ideas son iguales que las mías; *v* igualar

parallelism paralelismo

parallelogram paralelogramo

paralyse paralizar[7]

paralysis parálisis *f*

paralytic *n+adj* paralítico; (drunk) borracho como una cuba

paramilitary *n* fuerzas paramilitares; *adj* paramilitar

paramount supremo; **of** ~ **importance** de importancia capital

paramour amante *m+f*

paranoia paranoia

paranoiac paranoico

paranoid +*fig* paranoico

parapet parapeto

paraphernalia atavíos *mpl*

paraphrase *n* paráfrasis *f*; *v* parafrasear

paraplegia paraplegia

parapsychology parasicología

parasite parásito

parasitic parasítico

parasitology parasitología

parasol sombrilla

paratrooper paracaidista *m*

paratyphoid paratifoidea

parboil sancochar

parcel *n* paquete *m*; (of land) parcela; ~ **post** servicio de paquetes postales; *v* ~ **out** repartir; ~ **up** empaquetar

parcelling empaque *m*; ~ **out** reparto

parched resecado; **I'm** ~ (**with thirst**) estoy muerto de sed

parching abrasador (-ora)

parchment pergamino

pardon *n* perdón (-ones) *m*; *eccles* indulgencia; *leg* indulto; **beg** ~ pedir (i)[3] perdón; **I beg your** ~ perdone usted; ~? (please repeat) ¿cómo?; **general** ~ amnistía; *v* perdonar; *leg* indultar

pardonable perdonable

pare (peel fruit) mondar; (peel potatoes) pelar; (trim) cortar; **I** ~**d my nails** me corté las uñas; (whittle) adelgazar[7], *fig* reducir[15]; ~ **away/down** ir[19] reduciendo

parent padre *m*, madre *f*; ~**s** padres *mpl*; ~ **company** casa matriz; ~**hood** el tener hijos

parentage linaje *m*

parental paternal

parenthesis: in ~ entre paréntesis *m*

parenthetical(ly) entre paréntesis

par excellence por excelencia

pariah paria *m+f*

parings (fruit) mondaduras *fpl*; (potatoes) peladuras *fpl*; (trimmings) recortes *mpl*

Paris París *m*

parish *n* parroquia; ~ **church** iglesia parroquial; ~ **clerk** sacristán (-anes) *m* (de parroquia); ~ **council** concejo parroquial; ~ **priest** párroco; ~**-pump politics** política local; ~ **register** registro parroquial

parishioner parroquiano, parroquiana

Parisian *n+adj* parisino; parisiense *m+f*

parity paridad *f*; **at ~** a la par

park *n* parque *m*; (flower-gardens) jardines *mpl*; *mot* parking *m*; **~-keeper** guardia del parque; **~way** bulevar *m*; *vt* aparcar⁴; *fam* dejar; *vi* estacionarse

parking aparcamiento; **no ~** prohibido estacionarse; **~-attendant** celador *m*; **~-lights** luces *fpl* de estacionamiento; **~-lot** parking *m*; **~-place** sitio de aparcar; **~-meter** parquímetro; **~-ticket** multa de estacionamiento

parlance lengua; **in common ~** en lenguaje vulgar

parley *n* parlamento; *v* parlamentar (with con)

parliament parlamento; *Sp* las Cortes; **member of ~** diputado; **Houses of Parliament** Cámaras de los Comunes y de los Lores

parliamentarian *n+adj* parlamentario

parliamentary parlamentario; **~ immunity** inmunidad parlamentaria

parlour salón (-ones) *m*; **~-game** juego de salón; **~-maid** camarera

parlous: ~ state estado lamentable

parochial parroquial; (narrow-minded) de miras estrechas

parochialism parroquialismo

parodist parodista *m+f*

parody *n* parodia; *v* parodiar

parole *n* licenciamiento; **on ~** en licenciamiento; *v* licenciar

paroxysm paroxismo

parquet: ~-floor suelo entarimado

parricide (crime) parricidio; (person) parricida *m+f*

parrot loro; **~-fashion** mecánicamente

parry *n* parada; (fencing) quite *m*; *v* parar

parse analizar⁷

Parsee parsí *m*

parsimonious parsimonioso

parsimoniously con parsimonia

parsimony parsimonia

parsing análisis *f*

parsley perejil *m*

parsnip chirivía

parson cura *m*; **~'s nose** rabadilla

parsonage casa del cura

part *n* parte *f*; (of the body) miembro, órgano; *mech* pieza; (place) lugar *m*; **he is from these ~s** él es de esta región;

in foreign **~s** por el extranjero; *cin+theat* papel *m*, **take the ~ of** hacer¹⁹ el papel de; *mus* voz (-ces) *f*, **four-~** para cuatro voces; (duty) deber *m*, **play one's ~** cumplir su deber; **~ of speech** parte *f* de la oración; **three ~s** tres cuartos; **~ and parcel of** parte *f* integrante de; **man of many ~s** hombre *m* de mucho talento; **for my (own) ~**, **on my ~** por mi parte; **for the most ~** por la mayor parte; **in ~** en parte; **look the ~** encajar en el papel; **take ~ in** tomar parte en; **take the ~ of** (act for) hacer¹⁹ de, *theat* hacer¹⁹ el papel de, (support) sacar⁴ la cara a; **he took it in good ~** lo tomó en buena parte; *adj* parcial; **~ author** coautor *m*; **~ owner** condueño; **take in ~ exchange** tomar como cambio parcial; **in ~ payment** como pago parcial; **~-song** canción *f* para varias voces; **~-time work** trabajo por horas; **work ~-time** trabajar por horas; **~-timer** empleado que trabaja media jornada; *adv* en parte; *vt* separar; (open) abrir (*past part* abierto); **~ one's hair** hacerse¹⁹ la raya; *vi* separarse; (open) abrirse (*past part* abierto); (come apart) desmontarse; (break) romperse (*past part* roto); (of roads) dividirse; (leave s.o.) despedirse (i)³ de; **~ with** deshacerse¹⁹ de; (money) pagar⁵

partake: ~ of participar en, (eat) comer

parterre anfiteatro; (garden) parterre

parthenogenesis partenogénesis *f*

partial parcial; **I am ~ to** me gusta

partiality preferencia

participant partícipe *m*; (in fight) combatiente *m*

participate participar (in en)

participation participación *f*

participle participio; **past/present ~** participio pasado/presente

particle partícula; *fam* pizca

particular *n* detalle *m*; **further ~s** más información *f*; **in ~** sobre todo; *adj* (certain) particular; (special) determinado; (fastidious) especial (**about** en cuanto a); **I am very ~ not to offend her** tengo mucho cuidado de no ofenderla

particularity particularidad *f*

particularize *vt* particularizar⁷; *vi* dar¹⁹

todos los detalles
particularly sobre todo
parting *n* separación *f*; (of roads) división *f*; (from s.o.) despedida; (in hair) raya; ~ **of the ways** *fig* momento de separación; *adj* de separación
partisan *n* partidario; *mil* partisano; *adj* partidista; ~ **spirit** partidismo
partition *n* partición *f*; (wall) tabique *m*; *v* repartir; (of country) dividir; ~**ed off** separado con tabique
partly en parte
partner *n* (dance, games, *etc*) pareja; (married) cónyuge *m+f*; *comm* socio; ~ **in crime** codelincuente *m+f*; **junior** ~ socio de menor antigüedad; **senior** ~ socio más antiguo; **sleeping** ~ socio comanditario; *v* acompañar; **be** ~**ed by** ir[19] acompañado de
partnership sociedad *f*; **enter into** ~ (**with**) asociarse (con); **take into** ~ tomar como socio
partridge perdiz (-ces) *f*
party (gathering) fiesta; (youngsters') guateque *m*; **give a** ~ ofrecer[14] un guateque; (informal gathering) tertulia; *pol* partido, **follow the** ~ **line** seguir (i)[3+11] la línea del partido; (hunting *etc*) partida; *comm+leg* interesado; ~ **to the contract** parte *f* contratante; **be** ~ **to** estar[19] interesado en; ~ **line** (telephone) línea de dos o más abonados; ~ **of men** *mil* pelotón (-ones) *m*; ~-**politics** partidismo; ~-**spirit** (festive) juerga, *pol* espíritu del partido; ~-**wall** pared medianera; **two**-~ **system** sistema bipartidista
parvenu advenedizo
paschal pascual
pass *n* (permit) permiso; *mil* salvoconducto; *theat* (free ticket) entrada de favor; *geog* puerto; (narrow) desfiladero; (*sp* + bullfighting) pase *m*, **make a** ~ *sp* efectuar un pase; (examination) nota de aprobado; (crisis) crisis *f*; **make a** ~ **at** (a girl) echar un piropo a; ~-**book** libreta de banco; ~ **key** llave maestra; ~-**out** (**ticket**) billete *m* de reentrada; ~**word** santo y seña; *v* pasar; (hand over) dar[19], ~ **a message to** dar un recado a; *sp* efectuar un pase; (overtake) adelantar, *fam* pasar; (going in opposite direction) cruzarse[7] con, **I** ~**ed her on the**

stairs me crucé con ella en la escalera; (approve) aprobar (ue)[1a]; (law) promulgar[5]; (sentence) pronunciar; (examination) aprobar (ue)[1a]; (test) superar; (at cards) pasar; (forged notes) *sl* colar; ~ **blood** orinar sangre; ~ **the buck** echar la carga a otro; **let it** ~! ¡no haga caso!; **come to** ~ suceder; ~ **the time of day** saludar

~ **away** (of customs) desparecer[14]; (die) fallecer[14]
~ **by** *adv* pasar de largo; *prep* pasar por delante de; (fail to notice) pasar por alto
~ **for** (look like) pasar por
~ **in and out** entrar y salir[19]
~ **off** pasar; (of events) celebrarse; ~ **o.s. off as** hacerse[19] pasar por
~ **on** (hand to s.o.) pasar; (forward) transmitir; (of information) dar[19]; (die) fallecer[14]; (bequeath) dejar como herencia
~ **out** salir[19]; (faint) desmayarse; (graduate) graduarse
~ **over** pasar por; **they** ~ **over the bridge** pasan por el puente; (cross) cruzar[7], **they** ~ **over the river** cruzan el río; *fig* pasar por alto; (for promotion) postergar[5]
~ **round** pasar de uno a otro
~ **through** pasar por
~ **up** rechazar[7]
passable (fair) regular; (of road) transitable
passage (corridor) pasillo; (street) callejón (-ones) *m*; (subterranean) pasadizo; (journey) viaje *m*; (extract) trozo; (of act) promulgación *f*; **bird of** ~ ave *f* de paso
passé pasado de moda
passenger pasajero; ~ **train/boat** tren *m*/barco *m* de pasajeros
passepartout paspartú *m*
passer-by transeúnte *m+f*
passing *n* (death) fallecimiento; **with the** ~ **of time** andando el tiempo; **in** ~ entre paréntesis; *adj* pasajero; ~-**bell** toque *m* de difuntos; ~ **fancy** capricho
passion pasión *f*; *eccles* Pasión *f*; **have a** ~ **for** apasionarse por; ~-**flower** pasionaria; ~-**play** drama *m* de la Pasión
passionate apasionado; ~ **love** amor fogoso

passionately apasionadamente; ~ **in love** locamente enamorado

passionless frío

passive *n*+*adj* pasivo; ~ **resistance** resistencia pasiva

passivity pasividad *f*

Passover pascua de los hebreos

passport pasaporte *m*

past *n* pasado; **in the** ~ en tiempos pasados; *gramm* en tiempo pasado; **she has a** ~ ella tiene una historia; *adj* pasado; **it's all** ~ **and done with** todo eso se acabó; ~ **master** maestro (in en); **for a long time** ~ ya desde hace mucho; *adv* por delante; **go** ~ pasar por delante; *prep* (beyond) más allá de; (in front of) por delante de; (more than) más de; **a quarter** ~ **three** las tres y cuarto; **I wouldn't put it** ~ **her** la creo capaz de; ~ **all doubt** fuera de duda; ~ **bearing** insoportable; **I'm** ~ **caring** ya no me importa nada; ~ **comprehension** incomprensible; ~ **cure** incurable; ~ **hope** sin esperanza

paste *n* (thick liquid) pasta; (for sticking) engrudo; ~**board** cartón *m*; *v* engrudar; *fam* pegar[5], *sl* (hit) pegar[5], *sp* cascar[4]; ~ **up a notice** fijar un anuncio

pastel *n* pastel *m*; (picture) pintura al pastel; ~ **shade** matiz *m* pastel

pasteurize pasterizar[7]

pastiche *lit*+*mus* obra compuesta en el estilo de otro autor

pastille pastilla

pastime pasatiempo

pastor pastor *m*

pastoral *n*+*adj* pastoral *m*; ~ **letter** carta pastoral

pastry (dough) pasta; (art) pastelería; **puff/flaky** ~ hojaldre *m*; ~**-cook** pastelero; ~**-cutter** cortador *m* de pastas; ~**-shop** pastelería

pasturage pastos *mpl*

pasture *n* (field) dehesa; (grass *etc*) pasto; **put out to** ~ llevar a la dehesa; ~**land** dehesa; *vi* pastar

[1] **pasty** *n* (savoury pastry) empanada

[2] **pasty** *adj* pastoso; (pale) pálido, *fam* pocho

pat *n* golpe ligero; (on shoulder) palmadita; (affectionate) caricia; (of butter) porción (-ones) *f*; ~ **on the back** palmad(it)a *m* en la espalda, *fig*

elogio; *adv* (without hesitation) sin vacilar; **know off** ~ saber[19] al dedillo; *v* golpear ligeramente; (on shoulder) dar una palmada, (with affection) acariciar

patch *n* (on garment) remiendo; (on tyre and for eye) parche *m*; (of land) parcela pequeña; (stain + *fig*) mancha; (beat) distrito; (of fog) banco; **good/bad** ~ período próspero/infausto; **not a** ~ **on** muy inferior a; ~ **pocket** bolsillo de parche; ~**work** labor *m* de retazos, (work of uneven quality) chapuza, (mixture) mezcla; ~**work quilt** centón *m*; *v* remendar (ie)[2a]; ~ **up** arreglar (de un modo provisional), *fig* componer[19]

patchiness desigualdad *f*

patchy desigual

pâté paté; ~ **de foie gras** paté de hígado de ganso

patella rótula

patent *n*+*adj* patente *f*; ~ **leather** charol *m*; ~ **medicine** específico; ~ **office** oficina de patentes; **letters** ~ patente *m* de privilegio; *v* patentar

patently evidentemente

pater padre *m*

paterfamilias padre *m* de familia

paternal paternal

paternalism paternalismo

paternity paternidad *f*

paternoster paternoster *m*

path (track) sendero; (way) camino; (pavement) acera; (trajectory) trayectoria; ~ **of a storm** marcha de una tempestad; ~ **to ruin** camino de la ruina; ~**finder** explorador *m*; ~**way** sendero

pathetic patético; **there were a few** ~**-looking dogs** había unos perros de mala muerte

pathological patológico

pathologist patólogo

pathology patología

pathos lo patético

patience paciencia; **have no** ~ **with** no tener[19] simpatía alguna a; (cards) solitario

patient *n*+*adj* paciente *m*+*f*

patio patio

patois dialecto

patriarch patriarca *m*

patrician patricio

patricide (crime) parricidio; (person) parricida *m+f*

Patricia Patricia

Patrick Patricio

patrimony patrimonio

patriot patriota *m+f*

patriotic patriótico

patriotism patriotismo; (extreme) patriotería

patrol *n* patrulla; ~ **car** (*US* ~ **wagon**) coche *m* policía; **on** ~ de patrulla; *US* ~**man** policía *m* municipal; *v* patrullar

patron *n* (customer) cliente; parroquiano; *eccles* patrono; *lit+theat* mecenas *m sing*; ~ **saint** santo patrón

patronage patrocinio; (manner) condescendencia; (patrons of hotel) clientela; *pol* amiguismo

patroness protectora

patronize ser[19] parroquiano de; (adopt superior attitude) condescender (ie)[2b]

patronizing de superioridad; protector

patronymic *n+adj* patronímico

patten zueco

patter *n* (of feet) pasos *mpl* ligeros; (of rain) tamborileo; (speech) parloteo; *v* (of feet) hacer[19] ruido (de pasos); (of rain) tamborilear; ~ **about** andar con pasos ligeros

pattern *n* (+dressmaking) patrón (-ones) *m*; (design) dibujo; (example) modelo; (sample) muestra; ~ **book** revista de figurines; ~**maker** carpintero modelista; *v* ~ **on** modelar sobre

patterning dibujos *mpl*

patty empanada

paucity (**of**) escasez *f* (de)

Paul Pablo

Pauline Paulina

paunch barriga

pauper pobre *m+f*

pauperize empobrecer[14]

pause *n* pausa; **give** ~ **to** dar[19] de pensar a; *v* hacer[19] una pausa

pavane pavana

pave pavimentar; ~ **the way** (**for**) preparar el terreno (a)

pavement acera

pavilion pabellón (-ones) *m*; *sp* vestuario

paving pavimentación *f*; ~**-stone** losa

paw *n* pata; (cat's) garra; (lion's) zarpa; *v* patear; (horse) piafar; *fam* (a person) manosear

[1] **pawn** *n* (chess) peón (-ones) *m*; *fig* instrumento

[2] **pawn:** *n* **in** ~ empeñado; ~**broker** prestamista; ~**shop** casa de empeño; ~ **ticket** papeleta de empeño; *v* empeñar

pay *n* paga, sueldo; (daily) jornal *m*; salario; *mil* paga; **in the** ~ **of** asalariado de; **on half** ~ a medio sueldo; ~ **advance** adelanto; ~**-book** carnet *m* militar; ~**-day** día *m* de paga; ~**load** *mil* carga útil; ~**master** pagador *m*; ~**master's office** pagaduría; ~**-packet** sobre *m* de paga; ~**-roll** nómina; **be on the** ~**-roll of** estar[19] empleado de; *vt* pagar[5]; (debt) liquidar; (subscription) abonarse; (respecto) ofrecer[14]; (visit) hacer[19]; ~ **dearly for** costarle (ue)[1a] a uno caro; ~ **homage to** rendir (i)[3] homenaje a; ~ **for admission** sacar[14] una entrada; ~ **cash** (**down**) pagar[5] al contado; ~ **for a seat** *cin+theat* sacar una entrada; ~ **in full** saldar; ~ **on the nail** pagar[5] en el acto; ~ **the piper** pagar[5] el pato; **it wouldn't** ~ **you to do it** no le compensa(ría) hacerlo; ~ **attention** (**to**) prestar atención (a), (heed) hacer[19] caso (de); **put paid to** acabar con; **it doesn't** ~ **to** más vale no +*infin*; **in two years it will** ~ **for itself** se amortizará en dos años

vi (be profitable) rendir (i)[3] bien

~ **back** devolver (ue)[1b] (*past part* devuelto); *fig* pagar[5] en la misma moneda

~ **for** pagar; **I'll** ~ **for the drinks** yo pago las bebidas

~ **in** ingresar

~**-off** *n* (result) resultado final; ~**-off line** frase chistosa

~ **off** *v* liquidar; (employees) pagar[5] y despedir (i)[3]; ~ **off old scores** ajustar viejas cuentas

~ **out** desembolsar; (of rope) largar[5]

~ **up** pagarlo[5] todo; (unwillingly) pagar[5] de mala gana

payable pagadero; ~ **in advance** pagadero por adelantado; (due for payment) vencido; **cheque** ~ **to** cheque *m* pagadero a; ~ **on delivery** pagadero a la entrega

payee portador *m* (-ora *f*)

payer pagador *m*; *fam* pagano, **I'm always the** ~ siempre soy el pagano

paying *n*: **without** ~ sin pagar; *adj*

(profitable) rentable; ~ **guest** pensionista *m*+*f*

payment +*fig* pago; **in** ~ **for** en pago de; **in full** ~ **for** en saldo de; ~ **in advance** pago adelantado; ~ **in arrears** pago atrasado; ~ **in kind** pago en especie; **part** ~ *comm* pago parcial; **stop** ~ **of a cheque** suspender el pago de un cheque; **on** ~ **of** al pagar; **on** ~ **of the debt** al liquidar la deuda

pea guisante *m*; **they are as like as two** ~**s** se parecen como dos gotas de agua; ~**-green** verde claro; ~**-jacket** chaquetón (-ones) *m* de marinero; ~**nut** cacahuete *m*; ~**nut butter** pasta de cacahuetes tostados; ~**nuts** *fig* cantidad *f* insignificante de dinero; ~**pod** vaina de guisante; ~**-shooter** cerbatana; ~**-soup** sopa de guisantes; ~**-souper** (fog) niebla muy densa

peace paz *f*; (tranquillity) tranquilidad *f*; *leg* orden público; **at** ~ en paz; ~ **of mind** tranquilidad *f*; **keep the** ~ mantener[19] la paz; **make** ~ hacer[1c] las paces; (rest) **in** ~ (descansar) en paz; **hold one's** ~ callarse; ~ **feelers** tentativas *fpl* para la paz; ~ **force** fuerzas *fpl* para mantener la paz; ~**-loving** (people and nations) amante de la paz; ~**maker** pacificador *m*; ~**making** *n* pacificación *f*; ~ **offering** sacrificio propiciatorio; *adj* pacificador (-ora)

peaceable bonachón

peaceful pacífico; ~ **coexistence** coexistencia pacífica

peacefulness quietud *f*

peach melocotón (-ones) *m*; ~ **melba** postre *m* de melocotón, helado y puré de frambuesas; ~ **tree** melocotonero; **dried** ~ *fam* orejón *m*

peacock pavo real

peahen pava real

peak *n* (highest point) cumbre *f*; (top of mountain) pico; (mountain itself) pico; (of cap) visera; (of achievement) cúspide *f*; ~ **hour** hora punta; ~ **load** carga máxima; ~ **period** (of work, traffic) período de afluencia máxima; ~**ed cap** visera

peal *n* (bells) repique *m*; ~ **of laughter** risotada; ~ **of thunder** trueno; *v* (bells) repicar[4]; (thunder) tronar (ue)[1a]

pear pera; ~ **tree** peral *m*; ~**-shaped** de forma de pera

pearl perla; ~ **necklace** collar *m* de perlas; **cast** ~**s before swine** echar margaritas a los puercos; ~**-barley** cebada perlada; ~**-diver** pescador *m* de perlas; ~**-grey** gris perla; **mother-of-**~ nácar *m;* ~ **oyster** ostra perlífera

pearly de perlas; ~ **gates** puertas *fpl* de oro (del cielo); ~ **teeth** dientes *mpl* de perlas

peasant *n*+*adj* campesino, campesina

peasantry campesinos

peat turba; ~ **bog** turbera *m*; ~ **moss** serrín *m* de turba

peaty turboso

pebble guijarro; ~**dash** cubierto de guijarros, *v* cubrir (*past part* cubierto) de guijarros

pebbly guijarroso

pecan (tree + nut) pacana

peccadillo pecadillo

peck *n* picotazo; (light kiss) besito; *v* picotear; (kiss lightly) dar[19] un besito; ~ **at** (eat without appetite) comer melindrosamente; ~ **out** sacar[4] a picotazos

pecker: keep your ~ **up!** ¡ánimo!

peckish: be ~ tener[19] hambre

pectin pectina

pectoral pectoral

peculate pecular

peculation peculado

peculiar (odd) singular; (special) peculiar (**to a**)

peculiarity (oddness) singularidad *f*; (speciality) peculiaridad *f*

pecuniary pecuniario

pedagogic pedagógico

pedagogue pedagogo

pedagogy pedagogía

pedal *n* pedal *m*; **loud/soft** ~ *mus* pedal *m* fuerte/suave; ~**-car** auto de pedales; *v* pedalear; **soft-**~ no subrayar

pedant(ic) pedante *m*

pedantry pedantería

peddle vender de casa en casa; (drugs) traficar[4] en

pederast pederasta *m*

pederasty pederastia

pedestal pedestal *m*; **he puts her on a** ~ él la pone en un pedestal

pedestrian *n* peatón (-ones) *m*; *adj* de/ para peatones; (dull) pedestre; ~

crossing cruce *m* de/para peatones
pedestrianize reservar para peatones
pedigree *n* genealogía; *adj* de buena raza
pediment *archi* frontón (-ones) *m*
pedlar buhonero; (of drugs) traficante *m*, *sl* camello
pedometer pedómetro
pee *n* pis, pipí *m*; *v* hacer[19] pis, pipí; *fam* mear
peek *see* **peep**
peel *n* corteza; (of apple) piel *f*; (of orange, lemon) cáscara; (of potato) mondaduras *fpl*; **candied ~** piel azucarada; *v* pelar; quitar el pellejo; **my arms are starting to ~** empiezan a despellejárseme los brazos
peeler pelador *m*
peelings (*see* **peel**); peladuras *fpl*, mondaduras *fpl*
[1] **peep** *n* (cheep) pío; *v* piar
[2] **peep** *n* mirada furtiva; **at first ~ of day** al despuntar el día; **~-hole** mirilla; **~-show** retablo, *fam* vistas *fpl* sicalípticas; *v* atisbar; **~ out of** asomarse a, (be seen) dejarse ver por primera vez
peeping: ~ Tom mirón (-ones) *m*
peeper (person) atisbador *m*; (eye) ojo
[1] **peer** *n* (lord) par *m*; (equal) igual *m*
[2] **peer** mirar de cerca; **~ at** fisgar[5]; **~ into** mirar adentro
peerage nobleza; (book) catálogo de la nobleza
peeress paresa
peerless sin par
peeved, peevish malhumorado
peevishness mal humor *m*
peewit avefría
peg *n* clavija; (for hanging) gancho; (tent-peg) estaca; (clothes-peg) pinza; **take down a ~ or two** bajarle los humos a uno; **off the ~** de confección **~-board** (for display) tablero, (acoustics) panel acústico; **~-leg** pata de palo; **~-top** peonza; *v* enclavijar; (tent) estacar[4]; (mark out an area) señalar con estacas; (clothes) tender[2b] (con pinzas); (prices) fijar; (salaries) congelar; **~ away** persistir; **~ out** (die) estirar la pata
pegging *comm* sostenimiento de los precios de valores
pejorative peyorativo
pekinese perro pequinés

pelargonium pelargonio
pelican pelícano
pelisse capa larga
pellet pelotilla; (pill) píldora; (shot) perdigón (-ones) *m*; (of airgun) balín (-ines) *m*
pell-mell a troche y moche
pellucid lúcido
pelmet guardamalleta
pelota pelota vasca; *SA* jai alai *m*
[1] **pelt** (skin) pellejo
[2] **pelt** *n*: **at full ~** a toda prisa; *vt* arrojar; **~ s.o. with bad eggs** tirarle a alguien huevos malos; **~ with stones** apedrear; *vi* **~ down with rain** llover (ue)[1b] a cántaros; **he ~ed down the hill** bajó la cuesta corriendo a toda prisa
pelvic pélvico
pelvis pelvis *f*
pemmican pemicán *m*
[1] **pen** *n* pluma; (ballpoint) bolígrafo, *fam* bic (-ques) *m*; (fountain-pen) estilográfica; **~ drawing** dibujo a pluma; **~-friend** persona con la que uno se escribe; **~-holder** portaplumas *m sing+pl*; **~-knife** navaja; **~manship** caligrafía; **~-name** seudónimo; **~-pusher** chupatintas *m sing+pl*; **~-wiper** limpiaplumas *m sing+pl*; *v* escribir (*past part* escrito)
[2] **pen** *n* (enclosure) corral; (pig-~) pocilga; (sheep-~) redil *m*; (play-~) pollera; (penitentiary) *sl* jaula; *v* acorralar
penal penal; **~ code** código penal; **~ servitude** trabajos *mpl* forzados; **~ settlement** colonia penal
penalize penar; (unfairly) perjudicar[4]; *sp* castigar[5]
penalty pena; **on ~ of** so pena de; **pay the ~** sufrir el castigo; **pay the supreme ~** sufrir la pena de muerte; *sp* penalty (-yes) *m*; **award/give away a ~** pitar/incurrir penalty; **penalty area** área (de castigo); **~-kick** golpe *m* de castigo; **~-spot** punto del penalty; **~-clause** *leg* cláusula que establece sanciones para el caso de incumplimiento
penance penitencia; **do ~ (for)** cumplir la penitencia (por)
pence peniques *mpl*
penchant predilección *f* (**for** por)
pencil lápiz (-ces) *m*; **~-box** estuche *m*

para lápices; ~-**sharpener** sacapuntas *m sing*, (machine) afilalápiz *m*; *v* escribir (*past part* escrito) con lápiz

pendant *n*+*adj* pendiente *m*

pending *adj* pendiente; *prep* hasta +*infin*, hasta que +*subj*

pendulous colgante

pendulum péndulo

penetrability penetrabilidad *f*

penetrate penetrar

penetrating penetrante

penetration penetración *f*

penguin pingüino

penicillin penicilina

peninsula península

peninsular peninsular

penis pene *m*; *vet*+*zool*+*sl* verga

penitence arrepentimiento

penitent *n* penitente *m*+*f*; *adj* arrepentido

penitential penitencial

penitentiary (prison) presidio; *eccles* penitenciaría

pennant, pennon gallardete *m*

penniless sin dinero; *fam* a la cuarta pregunta

penny penique *m*; *US* moneda de un céntimo; **cost a pretty** ~ costar (ue)[1a] un dineral; **go and spend a** ~ *euph* ir[19] al servicio; ~-**dreadful** revista juvenil de mala calidad; ~-**in-the-slot machine** tragaperras *m sing*+*pl*; ~-**wise and pound foolish** que escatima en los gastos pequeños y derrocha sumas grandes; ~**worth** valor *m* de un penique, (tiny amount) pizca

pension *n* pensión *f*; **life** ~ pensión vitalicia; *mil* retiro; **old-age** ~ pensión *f* de vejez; *v* pensionar; ~ **off** jubilar

pensioner pensionista *m*+*f*; *mil* inválido; **old-age** ~ viejo jubilado

pensive pensativo

pent: ~ **up** (with emotion) reprimido

pentagon pentágono; **the Pentagon** el Pentágono

pentagonal pentagonal

pentameter pentámetro

Pentateuch Pentateuco

pentathlon pentatlón *m*

Pentecost Pentecostés *f*

penthouse ático

penultimate penúltimo

penumbra penumbra

penurious miserable; (stingy) tacaño

penury miseria

peony peonía

people gente *f*; **many** ~ mucha gente; (nation) pueblo; (lower classes) plebe *f*, *pej* gentuza; **government of the** ~ **by the** ~ **for the** ~ gobierno del pueblo por el pueblo para el pueblo; **Spanish** ~ los españoles; **the Spanish** ~ el pueblo español; **the** ~ **of Manchester** los habitantes de Manchester; **two thousand** ~ dos mil personas; **my** ~ mis padres; **old** ~ los viejos; ~ **say that** se dice que; **some** ~ algunos *mpl*; **little** ~ hadas *fpl*; **some** ~ **sleep in the nude** hay quien duerme desnudo; *v* poblar (ue)[1a] (**with de**)

peopling población *f*

pep *n* vigor *m*; ~-**pill** píldora estimulante; ~-**talk** (encouragement) palabras *fpl* para dar ánimo, (of criticism) rapapolvo; *v* ~ **up** dar[19] ánimo a

pepper *n* (condiment) pimienta; (vegetable) pimiento; ~**corn** grano de pimienta; ~-**pot** pimentero; *v* sazonar con pimienta; *fig* (strew) salpicar[4]; (with shot) acribillar

peppermint (plant) menta; (sweet) pastilla de menta

peppery picante; (of people) de malas pulgas

peptic péptico; ~ **ulcer** úlcera péptica

per por; **twenty miles** ~ **hour** veinte millas por hora; ~ **annum** al año; ~ **cent/head/person** por ciento/barba/persona; ~ **se** por sí mismo; **as** ~ **usual** como siempre

peradventure tal vez

perambulate recorrer

perambulator cochecito de niño

perceivable perceptible

perceive observar; (comprehend) percibir

percentage porcentaje *m*

perceptibility perceptibilidad *f*

perceptible perceptible

perception percepción *f*

perceptive perceptivo

perceptivity perceptividad *f*

[1] **perch** (fish) perca

[2] **perch** *n* (roost) percha; *fig* posición *f* que se cree segura; *v* posar(se); *fig* colocar(se)[4] en una posición elevada; **the village was** ~**ed on the cliff** la aldea colgaba sobre el acantilado

perchance quizá+*subj*
percipient perceptivo
percolate filtrar
percolator cafetera de filtro
percussion percusión *f*; *mus* instrumentos *mpl* de percusión, *fam* batería; ~-**cap** cápsula fulminante
perdition perdición *f*
peregrination peregrinación *f*; ~s vagabundeo
peregrine (falcon) halcón (-ones) peregrino
peremptoriness perentoriedad *f*
peremptory perentorio; (of people) autoritario
perennial *n*+*adj* perenne *m*
perfect *n* (tense) (el) pretérito perfecto; **in the** ~ en pretérito perfecto; **future/conditional** ~ futuro/potencial perfecto; *adj* perfecto; (of knowledge) completo; ~ **silence** silencio absoluto; **you're talking** ~ **nonsense** estás diciendo sandeces de las más grandes; ~ **fifth/fourth** *mus* quinta/cuarta justa; *v* perfeccionar
perfectibility perfectibilidad *f*
perfectible perfectible
perfection perfección *f*; **to** ~ a la perfección
perfectionism perfeccionismo; detallismo
perfectionist perfeccionista *m*+*f*; detallista *m*+*f*
perfectly perfectamente; **you know** ~ **well** usted sabe de sobra
perfidious pérfido
perfidy perfidia
perforate perforar; ~**d** (of stamps) trepado
perforation perforación *f*; (of stamps) trepado
perform *vt* realizar[7]; ~ **the sexual act** realizar[7] el coito; *theat* representar; *mus* ejecutar; *vi mech* funcionar; *theat* actuar; *mus* tocar[4]; *sp* jugar (ue)[1a]
performance *theat* representación *f*, actuación *f*; *mus* ejecución *f*; *mech* funcionamiento; *sp* juego; ~ **rating** rendimiento efectivo
performer *theat* actor *m*, actriz *f*, representante *m*+*f*; *mus* ejecutante *m*+*f*
performing: ~ **animal** animal amaestrado

perfume *n* perfume *m*; *v* perfumar(se)
perfumer perfumista *m*+*f*
perfumery perfumería
perfunctory superficial
pergola pérgola
perhaps tal vez, quizá(s) +*subj*
pericynthion *space* pericintio
perigee *space* perigeo
peril peligro; **at your** ~ por su riesgo; **in** ~ en peligro
perilous peligroso
perilously de modo peligroso
perimeter perímetro
period *n* período; ~ **of grace** plazo de gracia; (epoch) época; (full stop) punto; (school) clase *f*; ~s *med* regla; *adj* de época, ~ **costume** traje *m* de época
periodic periódico
periodical *n*+*adj* periódico; **fortnightly** ~ quincenal *m*; **weekly** ~ semanal *m*
periodicity periodicidad *f*
peripatetic *n*+*adj* ambulante *m*
peripheral periférico
periphery periferia
periphrasis circunlocución *f*
periscope periscopio
perish deteriorarse; (die) perecer[14]; ~ **the thought!** ¡no quiero ni pensarlo!; **she's** ~**ed with cold** ella está aterida
perishable perecedero; (of food) corruptible
perisher: little ~ tunante *m*
perishing: it's ~ **hot** hace un calor insoportable
peritonitis peritonitis *f*
periwinkle *zool* caracol marino; *bot* (vinca) pervinca
perjure: ~ **o.s.** perjurarse
perjury perjurio; **commit** ~ dar[19] falso testimonio
perk: ~ **up** despabilarse
perkiness animación *f*
perks gajes *mpl*
perky despabilado; (in a good mood) de buen humor
perm *n* permanente *f*; *v* hacer[19] la permanente; **have one's hair** ~**ed** hacerse[19] la permanente
permanence, permanency permanencia
permanent permanente; ~ **wave** permanente *f*
permanganate permanganato
permeability permeabilidad *f*

permeable permeable
permeate permear
permissible permisible
permission permiso; **have ~ to** tener[19] autorización para +*infin*; **ask/give ~** pedir (i)[3]/dar[19] permiso; **by ~ of** con permiso de
permissive permisivo; **~ society** sociedad *f* tolerante
permit *n* permiso; **export ~** permiso de exportación; *v* permitir, **weather permitting** si lo permite el tiempo; *fam* dejar, **~ me to help you** déjeme ayudarle; **~ of** permitir
permutable permutable
permutate permutar
permutation permuta(ción) *f*
pernicious pernicioso
pernickety quisquilloso; exigente, *fam* especial
peroration peroración *f*
peroxide peróxido; **~ of hydrogen** agua oxigenada; **~ blonde** rubia teñida
perpendicular perpendicular
perpetrate perpetrar
perpetration perpetración *f*
perpetrator perpetrador *m* (-ora *f*)
perpetual perpetuo; **~ motion** movimiento perpetuo
perpetuate perpetuar
perpetuation perpetuación *f*
perpetuity perpetuidad *f*; **in ~** para siempre
perplex (puzzle) dejar perplejo; (make puzzling) complicar; (distress) dejar preocupado
perplexing confuso
perplexity perplejidad *f*
perquisites gajes *mpl*
persecute perseguir (i)[3+11]
persecution persecución *f*; **~ complex** manía persecutoria
persecutor perseguidor *m* (-ora *f*)
perseverance perseverancia
persevere perseverar (**in/with** en)
persevering perseverante
Persia Persia
Persian *n* +*adj* persa *m*+*f*; **~ cat** gato de angora
persist persistir (**in** en); (endure) perdurar
persistence persistencia
persistent persistente; (enduring) permanente; **~ disease** enfermedad *f* pertinaz

person +*gramm* persona; *fam* cristiano; *pej* individuo; **in ~** en persona; **in the ~ of** en la persona de; **he had it hidden on his ~** lo tenía escondido en su cuerpo; **~-to-~ call** llamada personal; **~ or ~s unknown** desconocido(s)
personable de buen parecer
personage personaje *m*
personal personal; (private) particular; (close) íntimo, **he is a ~ friend of** él es amigo íntimo de; (in person) en persona, **~ interview** entrevista en persona; **make a ~ appearance** aparecer[14] en persona; (of cleanliness) corporal; (rude) ofensivo; **~ remark** alusión *f* ofensiva; **become ~** hacer[19] alusiones personales; **~ column** anuncios *mpl* personales por palabras, *fam* columna de los suspiros; **~ pronoun** pronombre *m* personal; **~ property** bienes *mpl* muebles; **~ stereo** *tr* Walkman *m*
personality personalidad *f*; **~ cult** culto de la persona
personalize personalizar[7]
personate hacerse[19] pasar por otro (*usu* for fraud)
personation el hacerse pasar por otro
personification personificación *f*
personify personificar[4]
personnel personal *m*; (crew) tripulación *f*; **~ management** dirección *f* de personal; **~ manager** jefe *m* de personal
perspective perspectiva; **in ~** en perspectiva; **new ~ on** nuevo punto de vista sobre
Perspex *tr* plexiglás *m*
perspicacious perspicaz (-ces)
perspicacity perspicacia
perspicuity perspicuidad *f*
perspicuous perspicuo
perspiration sudor *m*
perspire sudar
perspiring sudoroso
persuade (s.o. to do something) persuadir; (s.o. of something) convencer[12] de (que)+*subj*; **you can't ~ me that she is not American** a mí no me sacas de la cabeza que ella es americana
persuader persuadidor *m* (-ora *f*)
persuasion persuasión *f*; (faith) creencia
persuasive persuasivo

pert descarado
pertain (refer) referir(se) (ie)[3b] (**to** a); (belong) pertenecer[14] (**to** a)
pertinacious pertinaz (-ces)
pertinacity pertinencia
pertinence, pertinency pertinencia
pertinent pertinente (**to** a)
pertness desparpajo
perturb perturbar
perturbation perturbación *f*
Peru Perú *m*; **she lives in** ~ ella vive en el Perú
perusal lectura (cuidadosa)
peruse leer[17] (con cuidado)
Peruvian n + *adj* peruano; ~ **bark** quina
pervade extenderse (ie)[2b] por; **all-pervading** extenso
pervasion pervasión *f*
pervasive penetrante
perverse perverso
perverseness, perversity perversidad *f*
perversion perversión *f*
pervert *n* pervertido; **sexual** ~ pervertido sexual; *v* pervertir; (talents) emplear mal
perverter pervertidor *m* (-ora *f*)
pervious permeable (**to** a)
pesky *sl* maldito
pessimism pesimismo
pessimist pesimista *m* + *f*
pessimistic pesimista *m* + *f*
pest *ent* insecto nocivo; *zool* animal dañino; *fig* (thing) molestia; (person) pelma, *sl* plasta
pester molestar (con preguntas)
pesticide insecticida
pestiferous pestífero
pestilence pestilencia
pestilent pestilente; (annoying) molesto
pestilential pestilencial
pestle mano de mortero
pet *n* (animal) animal doméstico; (person) favorito; (term of endearment) rico; **be a** ~ **and ...** sé simpático y ...; ~ **name** nombre cariñoso; ~**shop** pajarería; *vt* (stroke) acariciar; (spoil) mimar; *vi* besuquearse
petal pétalo
Peter Pedro
peter: ~ **out** ir[19] disminuyendo; (of plans) resultar en nada
petersham (coat) gabán (-anes) *m*; (ribbon) cinta de seda de cordoncillo
petite pequeña

petition *n* (request) petición *f*; (document) memoria; *v* (beg) suplicar[4]; (present a ~) presentar una memoria a; ~ **for** dirigir[9] una instancia por
petitioner suplicante *m* + *f*
petrel paíño *m*; **stormy** ~ paíño común
petrification petrificación *f*
petrify petrificar(se)[4]; **be petrified** quedarse muerto de susto
petrol gasolina; ~ **can** bidón (-ones) *m* de gasolina; ~ **engine** motor *m* de gasolina; ~ **gauge** medidor *m* de gasolina; ~ **pump** surtidor *m* de gasolina; ~ **station** gasolinera; ~-**station attendant** encargado de gasolinera; ~ **tank** depósito (de gasolina)
petroleum petróleo; ~ **jelly** vaselina
petticoat enagua(s) *fpl*; (slip) combinación (-ones) *f*; (stiff) cancán *m*; ~ **government** gobierno de mujeres
pettifogging insignificante
pettiness insignificancia
pettish enojadizo
petty insignificante; (mean) despreciable; (spiteful) rencoroso; ~ **cash** dinero para gastos *mpl* menores; ~ **intrigue** tiquismiquis *mpl*; ~ **larceny** hurto; ~ **officer** suboficial de marina; ~ **sessions** tribunal presidido por un juez de paz; ~ **thief** ratero, *fam* caco
petulance mal genio
petulant enojadizo
petunia petunia
pew banco (de iglesia); **take a** ~! ¡siéntese!
pewter *n metal* peltre *m*; (vessel) vasija de peltre
Phalange *Sp pol* Falange *f*
Phalangist n + *adj* falangista *m* + *f*
phalanx falange *f*; *anat* falanges *fpl*
phalarope *orni* falaropo
phallic fálico; ~ **symbol** símbolo fálico
phallus falo
phantasm fantasma *m*
phantasmal quimérico
phantasmagoria fantasmagoría
phantom *n* fantasma *m*; *adj* fantasmal
Pharaoh faraón (-ones) *m*
pharisaic farisaico
Pharisee fariseo
pharmaceutical farmacéutico
pharmacist farmacéutico
pharmacology farmacología

pharmacy farmacia
pharyngitis faringitis *f*
pharynx faringe *f*
phase fase *f*; **be in ~** tener[19] una misma fase; **~d** *sl* borracho
pheasant faisán (-anes) *m*; **~ shooting** caza de faisanes
phenomenal fenomenal
phenomenon fenómeno
phew! ¡caramba!
phial frasco pequeño
philander mariposear
philanderer tenorio
philandering galanteo
philanthropic filantrópico
philanthropist filántropo
philanthropy filantropía
philatelic filatélico
philatelist filatelista *m+f*
philately filatelia
philharmonic filarmónico
Philip Felipe
Philippines (Islas) Filipinas *fpl*
philistine filisteo
philistinism incultura
philological filológico
philologist filólogo
philology filología
philosopher filósofo; **~'s stone** piedra filosofal
philosophical filosófico
philosophize filosofar
philosophy filosofía
philtre filtro
philumenist filumenista *m+f*
phlebitis flebitis *f*
phlegm +*fig* flema
phlegmatic flemático
phlox polemonio
phobia fobia
phoenix fénix *m*
phone (*see* **telephone**); **~-in** *n rad+TV* programa *m* en el cual los radioyentes/televidentes toman parte por teléfono
phonetic fonético; **~s** la fonética
phonetician fonetista *m+f*
phoney (insincere) insincero; (sham) falso
phonograph gramófono
phosphate fosfato
phosphoresce fosforescer[12]
phosphorescence fosforescencia
phosphorescent fosforescente

phosphorus fósforo
photo *n* foto *f*; *v* sacar[4] una foto de
photobooth fotomatón (-ones) *m*
photocopy *n* fotocopia; *v* fotocopiar
photoelectric fotoeléctrico
photo-finish fotocontrol *m*
photofit picture foto-robot *m*
photogenic fotogénico
photograph *n* fotografía; **a ~ of me** una fotografía mía; **have one's ~ taken** hacerse[19] retratar; **take a ~** sacar[4] una fotografía; *v* fotografiar
photographer fotógrafo
photographic fotográfico
photography fotografía
photogravure fotograbado
photometer fotómetro
photomontage fotomontaje *m*
photostat *n* fotocopia; *v* fotocopiar
photosynthesis fotosíntesis *f*
phrase *n* frase *f*; *mus* giro; **~-book** libro de frases; *v* frasear; (express) expresar
phraseology fraseología
phrenetic frenético
phrenologist *n+adj* frenólogo
phrenology frenología
physic medicina; **~s** física
physical físico; **~ condition** estado físico; **~ dependence** *med* dependencia somática; **~ exercises** ejercicios físicos; **~ impossibility** imposibilidad física; **~ inventory** inventario material; **~ training** educación *f* física
physician médico
physicist físico
physiognomy fisonomía
physiological fisiológico
physiologist fisiólogo
physiology fisiología
physiotherapist fisioterapista *m+f*
physiotherapy fisioterapia
physique físico; **have a good ~** tener[19] un buen tipo
pianist pianista *m+f*
piano(forte) piano(forte) *m*; **(baby) grand ~** piano de (media) cola; **upright ~** piano vertical; **~-stool** taburete *m* de piano; **~-tuner** afinador *m* de piano
Pianola *tr* pianola
piazza galería; plaza
pica *print* cícero; *med* pica

picaresque picaresco

picayune sin valor

piccalilli mescolanza de mostaza

piccaninny negrito

piccolo flautín (-ines) *m*

pick *n* (~axe) pico; (choice) selección *f*; (right to choose) derecho de escoger; (best) lo más escogido; ~ **of the bunch** el/la mejor de todos; **it's your** ~ a usted le toca escoger; *v* (flowers) coger[8]; (lock) forzar[1a+7]; *mus* (pluck) puntear; (one's nose) hurgarse[5]; (one's teeth) mondarse; (choose) escoger[8]; (team) seleccionar; (fruit) recoger[8]; ~ **a bone** roer un hueso; **have a bone to** ~ **with** habérselas con; ~ **one's way** andar con mucho cuidado; ~ **s.o.'s brains** sacarle[4] a uno el jugo; ~ **s.o.'s pocket** robarle la cartera a alguien; ~ **a quarrel with** meterse con; ~ **and choose** escoger[8] con cuidado; ~**-a-back** a borriquito; **carry** ~**-a-back** llevar a borriquito; ~**pocket** carterista *m*

~ **at** (food) picar[4]

~ **off** quitar; (shooting) matar de un tiro/con tiros sucesivos

~ **on** buscarle[4] la boca a uno

~ **out** (choose) escoger[8]; (mark) señalar; (discern) lograr ver; ~ **out in gold/paint** destacar[4] en oro/pintura

~**-me-up** reconstituyente *m*

~**-up** *n* (gramophone) fonocaptor *m*; (girl) chica facilona; (*US* van) furgoneta; **make a** ~**-up** ligar[6] una chica facilona; ~**-up arm** palanca

~ **up** *vt* recoger[8]; **I'll** ~ **you up at eight** iré a buscarle en mi coche a las ocho; ~ **up a bargain** dar[19] con una ganga; ~ **up a stitch** coger[8] un punto; *rad* sintonizar[7]; (accent) coger[8]; ~ **up a language** aprender un idioma; ~ **up speed** acelerar la marcha; ~ **up strength** recobrar fuerzas; ~ **up the thread of** (argument *etc*) coger[8] el hilo de; *vi* (get better) reponerse[19]

pickaxe pico

picker recogedor *m* (-ora *f*)

picket *n* (stake) estaca; ~**-fence** cerca de estacas; (guard, striker) piquete *m*; *v* (with stakes) cercar[4] con estacas; (with guards) cercar[4] con piquetes

picking (fruit *etc*) recolección *f*; ~**s** ganancia, *fam* trapicheo

pickle *n* (for fish) escabeche *m*; (for meat) adobo; (salt water) salmuera; ~**s** encurtidos, **mixed** ~**s** encurtidos variantes; **I'm in a** ~ estoy en un apuro; *v* (*see n*) escabechar; poner[19] en salmuera; adobar; ~**d** en escabeche/salmuera; ~**d olive** aceituna aliñada; (drunk) achispado, **get** ~**d** agarrar una chufa de bigote

picnic *n* excursión *f* campestre; *fig* cosa fácil; **go on a** ~ ir[19] de excursión; ~ **spot** merendero; *v* merendar (ie)[2a] en el campo

picnicker excursionista *m+f*

picric pícrico

pictorial pictórico; (of magazine) ilustrado

picture *n* cuadro; (in book) lámina; (painting) pintura; (portrait) retrato; *photo* fotografía; (spoken) descripción *f*; **she is a** ~ ella es guapísima; ~ **of health** la salud personificada; ~ **of innocence** imagen *f* de la inocencia; **the other side of the** ~ la otra cara de la moneda; **be in the** ~ (centre of attraction) figurar; **put s.o. in the** ~ **about** poner a uno al corriente de; **go to the** ~**s** ir[19] al cine; ~**-book** libro con láminas/*fam* santos; ~**-frame** marco; ~**-gallery** museo de pintura; ~**-goer** aficionado al cine; ~**-hat** pamela; ~**-palace**, ~**-house** cine *m*; ~**-postcard** tarjeta postal; ~**-writing** pictografía; *v* (describe) pintar; (imagine) imaginar; ~ **to o.s.** imaginarse

picturesque pintoresco

picturesqueness pintoresquismo

piddle hacer[19] pipí/pis

piddling insignificante

pidgin: ~ **English** inglés *m* criollo/macarrónico

pie (sweet) pastel *m*; ~**-crust** pasta de torta; **fruit** ~ pastel de fruta; (savoury) empanada

piebald *n+adj* pío

piece *n* (fragment) pedazo; (coin) moneda; (firearm) arma; *mus+theat+lit* pieza; (chess, draughts *etc*) ficha; *sl* (girl) pizpireta; **all of a** ~ de una sola pieza; **in** ~**s** (broken) hecho pedazos, *mech* desmontado; **take to** ~**s** desmontar; **go to** ~**s** tener[19] un ataque de nervios, *sp* desalentarse (ie)[2a] por completo; ~ **of advice**

consejo; ~ **of furniture** mueble *m*; ~ **of ground** parcela, (building site) solar *m*; ~ **of luck** buena suerte; ~ **of luggage** equipaje *m*; ~ **of news** noticia; ~**meal** a trocitos; ~**work** trabajo a destajo; ~**worker** destajista *m+f*; *v* ~ **together** juntar, *fig* ir¹⁹ comprendiendo

pièce de résistance plato fuerte

pied (animal) pío; (bird) manchado; ~**wagtail** *orni* lavandera blanca

pied-à-terre casa pequeña/piso

pier (jetty) embarcadero; *archi* estribo; (of bridge) pila; (of brickwork) entrepaño (de pared); ~**head** espolón *m*

pierce penetrar

piercing agudo

pierrette pierrette *f*

pierrot pierrot *m*

piety piedad *f*

piffle disparates *mpl*

piffling insignificante

pig *n* +*fig* cerdo, puerco; *metal* lingote *m*; *sl* (policeman) polizonte *m*; **buy a ~ in a poke** cerrar (ie)²ᵃ un trato a ciegas; **make a ~ of o.s.** comer como un cerdo; **make a ~'s ear of** *sl* chafar; ~**headed** tozudo; ~**iron** hierro en lingotes; ~**skin** piel *f* de cerdo; ~**sty**, ~**pen** +*fig* pocilga; ~**tail** coleta; (plait) trenza; *v* ~ **it** vivir como cochino(s)

pigeon paloma; ~ **breeder/fancier** columbicultor *m* (-ora *f*); ~**breeding** columbicultura; ~**hole** *n* casilla, *v* encasillar; ~**loft** palomar *m*; ~**toed** de pies de paloma

piggery pocilga

piggish cochino

piggy-back a borriquito; **carry** ~ llevar a borriquito

piglet cochinillo

pigment pigmento

pigmy *n* +*adj* pigmeo

pike (spear) pica; (fish) lucio; **plain as a** ~**staff** como la luz del día

pilchard sardina arenque

pile *n* (heap) montón (-ones) *m*; (building) mole *m*; (support) estaca; *eng* pilote *m*; (atomic) pila; *fam* (wealth) fortuna; (of carpet) pelusa; ~**s** *med* almorranas *fpl*; ~**driver** martinete *m*; ~**dwelling** palafito; ~**up** (crash) choque *m*; *v* amontonar;

~ **up** amontonar(se); (crash) chocar(se)⁴

pilfer ratear; *fam* birlar

pilferer ratero

pilfering ratería

pilgrim peregrino

pilgrimage peregrinación *f*; **go on a ~** ir¹⁹ en romería

pill píldora; **contraceptive** ~ píldora anticonceptiva, *fam* píldora antibaby; ~**box** cajita de píldoras, *mil* fortín (-ines) *m* armado de ametralladoras

pillage *n* pillaje *m*; *v* saquear

pillar columna; (person) sostén *m*; **he is a ~ of strength** él es una roca; **go/be driven from ~ to post** andar¹⁹ de la Ceca a la Meca; ~**box** buzón (-ones) *m*

pillion asiento de atrás; **ride** ~ ir¹⁹ cn el asiento de atrás

pillock lerdo, *vulg* gilipollas *m sing*

pillory *n* picota; *v* poner¹⁹ en ridículo

pillow *n* almohada; (US cushion) cojín (-ines) *m*; ~**case**, ~**slip** funda de almohada; *v* apoyar (sobre una almohada); ~ **one's head on one's arms** apoyar la cabeza en los brazos

pilot *n* aer piloto *m*; *naut* práctico; ~**boat** buque *m* de práctico; ~**fish** piloto; ~**light** *elect* (luz *f*) piloto, (gas) mechero encendedor; ~ **plant** fábrica experimental; ~ **scheme** proyecto experimental; *v* aer+naut pilotar; (guide) guiar

pilotage *aer* pilotaje *m*; *naut* practicaje *m*

pimento pimiento

pimp *n* alcahuete *m*; *v* alcahuetear

pimpernel pimpinela

pimple grano

pimply con granos

pin *n* (+ brooch) alfiler *m*; (hair) horquilla; (safety-~) imperdible *m*; *carp* clavija; *elect* patilla; *mech* perno; *sp* (skittle) rolo; **like a new ~** como un sol; ~**s and needles** hormigueo; **for two ~s** por menos de nada; ~**cushion** acerico; ~**head** cabeza de alfiler, *fig* tonto; ~**hole** agujero pequeño; ~**money** gastos pequeños; ~**point** indicar⁴ con precisión; ~**prick** alfilerazo, *fig* molestia pequeña; ~**stripe** a rayas; ~**table** billarín (-ines) *m*; *v* sujetar con alfiler(es); ~ **on a**

brooch poner(se)[19] un alfiler; ~ **one's faith on** confiar absolutamente en; ~ **s.o. down** restringir[9]; ~ **s.o.'s arms (to his sides)** sujetarle los brazos a alguien; ~**-up** *n* (foto *f* de una) chica guapa, *fig* mujer *f* ideal; ~ **up** *v* sujetar con alfileres

pinafore delantal *m*

pince-nez quevedos *mpl*

pincer pinza; ~ **movement** movimiento envolvente; ~s tenazas *fpl*

pinch pellizco; *cul* pizca; (of snuff) pulgarada; **feel the** ~ pasar apuros; **at a** ~ si hace falta; *v* pellizcar[4]; (of shoes) apretar (ie)[2a]; ~**ed with cold** acurrucado de frío; ~ **and scrape** escatimar; *sl* (steal) birlar; *sl* (arrest) trincar[4]; ~ **off** (buds) quitar

[1] **pine** *n* pino; ~**apple** piña; ~**-cone** piña; ~**-needle** aguja de pino; ~**-tree** pino; ~**-wood** pinar *m*; ~ **kernel** piñón *m*

[2] **pine** *v*: ~ **away** languidecer[14]; ~ **(away) for** suspirar por

ping *n* sonido metálico; ~**-pong** pinpón *m*; *v* hacer[19] un sonido metálico

pinion *n* piñón (-ones) *m*; *v* (person) sujetar los brazos; (bird) cortar las alas

pink *n bot* clavel *m*; (colour) (color *m* de) rosa; **be in the** ~ **of condition** estar[19] en buena forma; *adj* rosado; *pol* rojillo; *v* (mot+sewing) picar[4]

pinking picadura

pinkish rosáceo

Pinkster Pentecostés *m*

pinnace pinaza

pinnacle *archi* pináculo; (height) cima, *fig* cumbre

pinocle juego de naipes parecido a besique

pinole plato de semillas tostadas con azúcar

pint pinta (0,568 litros)

pioneer *n+adj* explorador *m*; (settler) colonizador *m*; *mil* zapador *m*; (initiator) iniciador *m*; (of a plan) promotor *m*; **be a** ~ **in** ser[19] uno de los primeros en +*infin*; ~ **work** trabajo de introducción; *v* explorar; (settle) colonizar[7]; (initiate) iniciar; (plan) preparar el terreno para

pioneering introducción *f*

pious piadoso; *fam* beato

pip *n bot*+*vet* pepita; (on uniform) estre-

lla; (on playing-card) punto; **it gives me the** ~ me fastidia mucho; ~s (time-signal) señal horaria; ~**-squeak** persona despreciable; *v* (defeat) vencer[12]; (exam) suspender

pipe *n* tubo; **lay** ~s instalar la tubería; (for smoking) pipa, ~ **tobacco** tabaco de pipa; *mus* caramillo; (of organ) cañón (-ones) *m*; (boatswain's) pito; ~s (bagpipes) gaita; **put that into your** ~ **and smoke it!** ¡chúpate eso!; **he is a** ~**-smoker** él fuma en pipa; ~ **of peace** pipa de la paz; ~**clay** *n* albero, *v* blanquear con albero; ~**-cleaner** limpiapipas *m sing* ; ~**-dream** ilusión *f*; ~**-line** cañería, (oil) oleoducto; ~**-organ** órgano de cañones; ~**work** tubería; *v* conducir[15] en cañería; (instal piping) instalar cañerías en; *mus* tocar[4] (la gaita); (sewing) ribetear; ~ **down** callarse; ~ **up** decir[19] con voz aguda

piped: ~ **music** música enlatada

pipeful pipa llena

piper gaitero

pipette pipeta

piping *n* cañería; (sewing) ribete *m*; *mus* música de gaita; *adj* (of voice) agudo; ~ **hot** muy caliente

pipit bisbita

pippin camuesa

piquancy picante *m*

piquant picante

pique *n* pique; **be in a** ~ estar[19] resentido; *v* picar[4]; ~ **o.s. upon** jactarse de; **be** ~**d** estar[19] enojado, *fam* estar[19] amoscado

piquet juego de los cientos

piracy piratería

pirate *n* pirata *m*; ~ **edition** edición pirata; ~ **radio** emisora ilegal; *v* pillar; (publish illegally) hacer una edición piratamente

piratical pirático

pirogue piragua

pirouette *n* pirueta; *v* hacer[19] piruetas

piss *n* meada; *v* mear; ~ **off!** ¡vete a la mierda!; **be** ~**ed** (drunk) *sl* estar[19] pedo; **get** ~**ed** dar[4] tumbos; **take the** ~ **out of** *vulg* coñearse[4] de

pistachio pistacho

pistil pistilo

pistol pistola; *sl* fusca; ~**-shot** pistolazo

piston émbolo; ~**-ring** aro de émbolo;

~-**rod** vástago de émbolo; ~-**stroke** carrera de émbolo

¹ **pit** n (hole) foso; *min* mina (de carbón); (quarry) cantera; *mot* foso de inspección; *theat* patio; (of stomach) boca; *fig* abismo; ~-**a-pat** tictac m, (footsteps) paso ligero; **my heart went** ~-**a-pat** me palpitó el corazón; ~**fall** trampa; ~**head** pozo de mina; ~**head workings** castillete m; ~-**pony** caballito que trabaja en una mina; ~-**prop** puntal; v (mark) cacarañar; ~ **o.s. against** oponer(se)¹⁹ a; **pitted** picoso

² **pit** n (fruit stone) hueso; v deshuesar

¹ **pitch** n pez f, brea; ~-**black** negro como boca de lobo; **in** ~ **darkness** en la mayor oscuridad; v embrear

² **pitch** n (throw) lanzamiento; *naut*+ *space* cabeceo; *sp* terreno; (street vendor's) puesto; (slope) grado de inclinación; (angle of roof) pendiente f; *mus* tono; (extremity) punto, **to such a** ~ **at** a tal punto; **come/go full** ~ **(at)** venir¹⁹/ir¹⁹ con toda fuerza (contra); ~**fork** n horca, v coger⁸ con horca; ~-**pipe** diapasón (-ones) m; v (throw) lanzar⁷; *naut*+*space* cabecear; *mus* graduar el tono; (tent) armar; ~ **camp** asentar (ie)²ᵃ un campamento; ~ **in** empezar (ie)¹ᵇ⁺⁷ a trabajar con furia; ~ **into** atacar⁴; ~**ed battle** batalla campal

¹ **pitcher** cántaro

² **pitcher** (baseball) botador m; ~'s **box** área del botador

pitching *naut*+*space* cabeceo

piteous lastimoso

pith *bot*+*fig* médula

pithy *bot* meduloso; *fig* sucinto

pitiable digno de compasión

pitiful lastimoso; (contemptuous) despreciable

pitiless despiadado

pittance pitanza; **live on a** ~ vivir con poquísimo dinero

pitter-patter n golpeteo m; v golpetear

pitting *metal* picadura; (of fruit) deshuesamiento

pituitary pituitario; ~ **gland** glándula pituitaria

pity n compasión f; **for** ~'s **sake!** ¡por piedad!; **it's a** ~ **that** es lástima que +*subj*; **more's the** ~ desgraciadamente; **take** ~ **(on)** tener¹⁹ lástima

(de); **what a** ~! ¡qué lástima!; v compadecerse¹⁴ de

pivot n pivote m; *fig* punto fundamental; v colocar⁴ sobre un pivote; ~ **on** girar sobre, *fig* depender de

pivotal cardinal

pixie duendecillo; ~-**hood** caperuza

pixilated (crazy) chiflado; (drunk) achispado

pizzicato pizzicato

placable aplacable

placard n letrero; (poster) cartel m; v publicar⁴ por medio de carteles; ~ **the walls** fijar carteles en las paredes

placate aplacar⁴

place n lugar⁵, sitio; **you are in my** ~ usted está en mi sitio; (in book) página, **I've lost my** ~ he perdido la página; (at table) cubierto; (job) empleo; (in competition) puesto; (rank) posición f; ~ **of worship** templo; **my** ~ mi casa (at en); **in his** ~ **I would not do that** en su lugar yo no haría eso; **I'd like to see you in my** ~ quisiera yo verle en mi caso; **I put him in his** ~ le bajé los humos a él; **in the first** ~ en primer lugar; **out of** ~ fuera de (su) lugar, (irrelevant) fuera de propósito; **give** ~ **to** ceder el paso a; **give up one's** ~ **to** ofrecer¹⁴ su asiento a; **know one's** ~ ser¹⁹ respetuoso; **it's not your** ~ **to** a usted no le toca +*infin*; **take** ~ celebrarse, **the ceremony will take** ~ **tomorrow** la ceremonia se celebrará mañana; **to the third (decimal)** ~ en milésimas; ~-**kick** *sp* puntapié m colocado; ~-**man** espía m, *sl* submarino; ~-**name** topónimo; v colocar⁴; (invest) invertir (ie)²ᶜ; (in job) dar¹⁹ empleo a; (remember) recordar (ue)¹ᵃ bien; (identify) identificar⁴; ~ **an order for** encargar⁵; ~ **one's trust in** fiarse de; **be** ~**d** (in competition) quedar clasificado

placebo cúralotodo m

placement empleo; ~ **agency** agencia de colocaciones

placenta placenta

placid plácido

placidity placidez f

placing n colocación f

plagiarism plagio

plagiarist plagiario

plagiarize plagiar

plague *n* peste *f*; *v* infestar; (annoy) molestar
plaice platija
plaid manta escocesa
plain *n* llanura; **~sman** llanero; *adj* sencillo; (unadulterated) natural; (not attractive) sin atractivo, *fam* feíllo; (ugly) feo; (candid) franco; (of cigarette) sin filtro; **it is ~ that** es evidente que, *fam* se ve que; **be very ~ with** hablar claro a; **~chant** canto gregoriano; **~ cooking** cocina casera; **in ~ clothes** de paisano; **~-clothes man** detective *m*; **~ dealing** buena fe; **~ knitting** punto de media; **one ~ and two ~ purl** una del derecho y dos del revés; **~ living** vida sencilla; **~ sailing** cosa fácil, *fam* coser *m* y cantar *m*; **~song** canto llano; **~ speaking** franqueza; **in ~ speech** hablando sin rodeos, *fam* (hablando) en cristiano; **~ truth** pura verdad; **~-spoken** franco; *adv* claro
plainness simplicidad *f*
plaintiff demandante *m+f*
plaintive dolorido
plaintiveness tristeza
plait *n* trenza; **in ~s** en trenzas; *v* trenzar[7]
plan *n* plan *m*, proyecto; (diagram) plano, **~ of the city** plano de la ciudad; *archi* esquema; (technical drawing) proyección *f* horizontal; *v* planificar[4]; **~ for** hacer[19] proyectos para; **~ to** pensar (ie)[2a] +*infin*
[1] **plane** *n* (flat surface) plano, *fig* nivel *m*; *aer* avión *m*; *carp* cepillo de carpintero; **be on a ~ with** estar[19] al mismo nivel que; **~-table** plancheta; *adj* plano; *vt* cepillar; **~ down** desbastar; *vi aer* planear
[2] **plane** *bot* plátano
planet planeta *m*
planetarium planetario
planetary planetario
plangent estrepitoso
planing (a)cepillador (-ora); **~-machine** máquina (a)cepilladora
plank *n* tabla; *pol* artículo de un programa político; **~s** tablaje *m*; **walk the ~** pasear por el tablón; *v* entablar; **~ down** colocar[4] firmemente
planking *bui* entablado; *naut* maderaje *m* de cubierta

plankton plancton *m*
planned: ~ economy economía dirigida
planning planificación *f*
plant *n* planta; (factory) fábrica; *bui* +*mech* maquinaria; *elect* instalación electrógena; *sl* truco para incriminar a una persona; **~-like** como una planta; **~ pot** tiesto; **~ pot stand** jardinera; *v* plantar; (sow) sembrar (ie)[2a]; (put) colocar[4]; **~ something on s.o.** ocultar algo para incriminarle a alguien
plantain llantén *m*
plantation plantación *f*; (tobacco) tabacal *m*, *SA* vega; (of trees) arboleda; (act of planting) plantación *f*, *fig* introducción *f*
planter plantador *m*; (settler) colono, **~pot** tiesto
plaque placa
plasma plasma
plaster *n* yeso; *med* emplasto; (sticking-~) esparadrapo, *fam* tirita; **~ of paris** yeso mate; **~-of-paris bandage** venda escayolada; **layer of ~** enlucido; **~-board** plancha de yeso y cartón; **~ cast** vaciado de yeso, *med* tablilla de yeso, enyesado; *v* enyesar; (fill in cracks *etc*) llenar de yeso; (stick posters *etc*) pegar[5]; (daub) embadurnar; **your shoes are ~ed with mud** sus zapatos están cubiertos de barro; **~ed** (drunk) borracho
plasterer yesero
plastering enyesado; **~-trowel** fratás *m*
plastic *n* plástico; *adj* (de) plástico; **~ arts** artes *fpl* plásticas; (covered with ~) plastificado; **~ raincoat** sira; **~ surgery** cirugía plástica
Plasticine *tr* plasticina
plasticity plasticidad *f*
plate *n* plato; (for collecting money) platillo; (plaque+*phot*) placa; *metal* chapa; (silver) vajilla de plata; (dental) (placa de la) dentadura postiza; (book illustration) lámina; (racing prize) premio; **it was handed to me on a ~** *fig* me lo entregaron en bandeja; **she has a lot on her ~** ella tiene mucho que hacer; **~ armour** cota de escudo; **~glass** vidrio plano; **~layer** (railway) peón (-ones) ferroviario; **~-rack** escurreplatos *m sing*; **~-warmer** calientaplatos *m sing*; *v metal* chapar; (with silver) platear;

(with gold) dorar; (with chromium) cromar; (electro-~) niquelar; (with armour-~) blindar

plateau meseta; *fig* plato *m*

plateful plato

platform plataforma; (at meeting) tribuna; (railway) andén (-enes) *m*; *pol* programa *m* electoral; **~-shoes** zapatos *mpl* de plataforma; **~-ticket** billete *m* de andén

plating enchapado

platinum platino; ~ **blonde** rubia platino

platitude perogrullada

platitudinous lleno de perogrulladas

platonic platónico

platoon pelotón (-ones) *m*

platter fuente *f*

plausibility plausibilidad *f*

plausible plausible; (of people) bien hablado pero de poco fiar

play *n* juego; (play-time) recreo; *mech* (movement) juego; *sp* manera de jugar; *theat* obra dramática; **in** ~ en juego; **out of** ~ *sp* fuera de banda; **fair/foul** ~ juego limpio/sucio; ~ **on words** juego de palabras; **bring into** ~ poner[19] en juego; **come into** ~ entrar en juego; **go to see a** ~ ir[19] al teatro; **make great** ~ **of** insistir en; **~-acting** *fig* fingimiento; **~-bill** cartel *m*; **~-boy** playboy *m*; **~-fellow, ~-mate** compañero de juego; **~-goer** aficionado al teatro; **~-ground** patio (de recreo); **~-house** teatro, (*US* dolls' house) casita de muñecas; **~-pen** corralito (de niño); **~-school** parque *m* infantíl; **~-thing** juguete *m*; **~-time** (hora de) recreo; **~-wright** dramaturgo

v jugar (ue)[1a+5]; (amuse oneself) divertirse (ie)[2c]; *mus* tocar[4]; *theat* representar; (of fountains) correr; (of light) reverberar; ~ **chess** jugar (ue)[1a+5] al ajedrez; ~ **a card** jugar (ue)[1a+5] un naipe; **I'm ~ing Smith** *sp* juego con(tra) Smith; **the captain decided not to ~ Gento** el capitán decidió no incluir a Gento en el equipo; ~ **a part** desempeñar un papel; **he ~s Hamlet** *theat* él hace el papel de Hamlet; ~ **a fish** dejar que se canse un pez; **the firemen ~ the hoses** los bomberos dirigen las mangueras; **~-act** fingir[9]; ~

fair jugar (ic)[1a+5] limpio; ~ **false** engañar; ~ **fast and loose with** portarse irresponsablemente con; ~ **the fool** hacer[19] el tonto; ~ **a joke/trick on s.o.** gastarle una broma a uno; ~ **merry hell with** hacer[19] cisco a; ~ **one's trump card** jugar (uc)[1a+5] la carta más alta; ~ **opposite** *theat* tener[19] de oponente a

~ **at** jugar[1a+5] a; (do half-heartedly) hacer[19] sin entusiasmo

~-back *n* playback *m*

~ **back** *v* repetir lo grabado

~ **for** jugar (ue)[1a+5] por; ~ **for time** tratar de ganar tiempo

~-off *sp* desempate *m*

~ **off** contraponer[19]

~ **on** *vt mus* tocar[4]; **you ~ on my fears** usted explota mi miedo; *vi* seguir (i)[3+11] jugando

~ **out:** ~ **out time** seguir (i)[3+11] jugando (sin entusiasmo) hasta el fin; **be ~ed out** estar[19] agotado

~ **to** tocar[4] para

~ **up** jugar (uc)[1a+5] bien; (mock) burlarse de; ~ **up to** hacer la pelotilla a

player jugador *m* (-ora *f*); *mus* músico; *theat* actor *m*, actriz *f*

playful juguetón; **~ remark** observación *f* hecha en broma

playfulness caracter *m* juguetón

playing juego; **~-card** carta *f*; **~-field** campo de deportes

plea *n* (request) súplica; (excuse) pretexto, **on a ~ of** bajo pretexto de; *leg* (statement) informe *m*; *leg* (defendant's answer) contestación *f* a la demanda

plead (entreat) suplicar[4] (**for** que +*subj*); (claim) pretender, ~ **ignorance/poverty** pretender ignorancia/pobreza; *leg* declarar; *leg* (of counsel) abogar[5] (**for** por); ~ **guilty** confesarse (ie)[2a] culpable; ~ **not guilty** declararse inocente

pleading *n* súplicas *fpl*; *leg* defensa; **~s** *leg* alegatos *mpl*; *adj* implorante

pleasant agradable; (of person) simpático; (entertaining) divertido

pleasantness agrado; (of person) simpatía

pleasantry dicho gracioso

please gustar; ~ **give me** haga el favor de darme, *fam* dame por favor; **as you ~,**

~ **yourself** como quiera; **if you** ~ (if you agree) si le parece bien, (by your permission) con su permiso, *iron* ¡fíjese!; **I'll do as I** ~ haré lo que me parezca bien; **he is easy to** ~ él es fácil de contentar; **say something just to** ~ decir[19] algo por cumplir; **whenever you** ~ cuando quiera; **be** ~**d (to)** estar[19] contento (de); **we are** ~**d to inform you** nos es grato informarle; **I'm** ~**d to meet you** tengo mucho gusto en conocerle; **be** ~**d with** estar[19] satisfecho de; ~**d as Punch** contento como unas pascuas

pleasing, pleasurable agradable

pleasure gusto *m*; (will) voluntad *f*; **it is a** ~ es un placer; **give** ~ **(to)** dar[19] placer (a); **take** ~ **in** deleitarse en +*infin*+*n*; **he does not write for money but for** ~ él no escribe por dinero sino porque le gusta; **with (great)** ~ con (mucho) gusto; ~ **trip** viaje *m* de recreo; ~**boat** barco de recreo; ~**-ground** parque *m* de atracciones; ~**-loving,** ~**-seeking** amigo de los placeres

pleat *n* pliegue *m*; *v* plegar (ie)[2a+5]; plisar; ~**ed skirt** falda plisada

pleating plisado

pleb plebe *f*

plebeian *n+adj* plebeyo

plebiscite plebiscito

plectrum plectro

pledge *n* (security) prenda; (promise) promesa; (toast) brindis *m*; **as a** ~ **of** en prueba de; **sign the** ~ jurar abstenerse del alcohol; *v* (give as security) empeñar; (promise) prometer; (toast) brindar; ~ **o.s.** comprometerse; ~ **support for** prometer apoyo para

plenary plenario; ~ **session** reunión *f* plenaria

plenipotentiary *n+adj* plenipotenciario

plenitude plenitud *f*

plenteous, plentiful abundante

plenty *n* abundancia; **in** ~ en abundancia; **in France** ~ **of people never go to Church** en Francia hay mucha gente que nunca va a la iglesia; **there is** ~ **of food** hay comida de sobra; **she has** ~ **of money** ella tiene dinero de sobra; *adv US* completamente

pleonasm pleonasmo

plethora plétora

pleurisy pleuresía

pliability flexibilidad *f*; *fig* docilidad *f*

pliable, pliant flexible; *fig* dócil

pliers: pair of ~ unos alicates

[1] **plight** *n* apuro

[2] **plight** *v* empeñar; ~ **one's troth** dar[19] palabra de matrimonio

Plimsoll: ~**-line** marca de calado; **plimsoll** (footwear) zapatilla *fpl* de goma

plinth plinto

plod caminar laboriosamente; (work) atrafagar[5] (**away at** en); ~ **on/one's way** avanzar[7] laboriosamente

plodder trafagón *m* (-ona *f*); (student) estudiante *m+f* más aplicado que listo

plodding *n* tráfago; *adj* laborioso

plonk vino peleón

plop *n+interj* paf *m*; **with a** ~ a plomo; *v* caer[19] al agua haciendo paf

[1] **plot** *n* (of land) parcela; (for building) solar *m*; (allotment) cuadro de hortalizas

[2] **plot** (conspiracy) complot *m*, *fam* tejemaneje *m*; (of novel, play *etc*) argumento; *vi* conspirar; *vt* tramar; (route) trazar[7]

plotter conspirador *m* (-ora *f*)

plotting (conspiracy) conspiración *f*; (of route) trazado

plough *n* arado; *astron* Osa Mayor; ~**man** labrador *m*; ~**share** reja del arado; *v* arar; (fail exam) suspender

~ **back** reinvertir (ie)[2c]

~ **through** *fig* abrirse (*past part* abierto) paso por; ~ **through a book** leer[17] con dificultad

~ **under** hundirse

~ **up** arrancar[4] con el arado

ploughing arada

plover *orni* avefría

pluck *n* (tug) tirón (-ones) *m*; (offal) asadura; (courage) valor *m*; *v* (pick) coger[8]; (remove feathers) desplumar; *mus* puntear; ~ **something from s.o.** quitarle algo a alguien

~ **off** quitar

~ **out** arrancar[4]

~ **up courage** armarse de valor

plucky valiente

plug *n* (of sink *etc*) *n* tapón (-ones) *m*; *elect* enchufe *m*, (wall-~) toma; (of switchboard) clavija *f*; *mot* bujía; (chain of w.c.) tirador *m*; (tobacco) rollo; *rad+TV* mención *f* incidental de un disco/una película; ~-**in** *adj* enchufable; ~-**ugly** *US* gamberro; *vt* tapar; (tooth) empastar; *rad*+*TV* dar[19] publicidad *f* incidental a; (shoot) pegar[5] un tiro a; ~ **in** enchufar; *vi* ~ **away** (**at**) seguir (i)[3+11] trabajando con ahinco (en)

plum ciruela; ~ **cake** pastel *m* de fruta; ~ **pudding** pudín *m* inglés de Navidad; ~ **tree** ciruelo

plumage plumaje *m*

plumb plomada; **out of** ~ no vertical; ~-**line** cuerda de plomada; *adj* vertical; *adv* verticalmente; (exactly) *v naut* sondar; (pierce) penetrar

plumber fontanero

plumbing (craft) fontanería; (piping) instalación *f* de cañerías

plume *n* pluma; (on helmet) penacho; ~ **of smoke** penacho de humo; *v orni* limpiarse las plumas; ~**d** emplumado

plummet *n* plomada; *v* caer[19] a plomo

plump *n* caída repentina; *adj* rollizo; (of poultry *etc*) gordo; *v* (drop) dejar(se) caer pesadamente; ~ **for** optar por; ~ **up** engordar

plumpness gordura

plumy plumoso

plunder *n* botín *m*; *v* saquear

plunderer saqueador *m*

plundering saqueo

plunge *n* zambullida; **take the** ~ arriesgarse[5]; *vt* zambullir; (knife) hundir; *vi* zambullirse; (of horse) corcovear; (dress) ser[19] muy escotado; *fig* ~ **o.s. into** arrojarse a

plunger *mech* émbolo; *comm* especulador temerario

pluperfect pluscuamperfecto

plural *n*+*adj* plural *m*; **in the** ~ en el plural; **make** ~ poner[19] en plural

plurality pluralidad *f*

pluralize pluralizar[7]

plus *adj math* positivo; *prep* más; **five** ~ **two are seven** cinco más dos son siete; ~-**fours** pantalones *mpl* bombachos; ~-**sign** signo de más

plush *n* felpa; *adj* felpudo; *sl* lujoso

plushy felpudo; *sl* lujoso

plutocracy plutocracia

plutocrat(ic) plutócrata *m*+*f*

plutonium plutonio

[1] **ply** *n*: **four-**~ (wood) de cuatro capas;

(wool) de cuatro cabos; ~-**wood** madera contrachapada, *fam* panel *m*

[2] **ply** *v* usar; (trade) ejercer[12]; (offer repeatedly) ofrecer[14] repetidas veces; ~ **between** hacer[19] el servicio entre; ~ **with** importunar con

pneumatic neumático; ~ **brake** freno neumático; ~ **drill** perforadora neumática; ~ **tyre** neumático

pneumonia pulmonía; **double** ~ pulmonía doble

[1] **poach** (eggs) escalfar

[2] **poach** (game, fish) cazar[7]/pescar[4] en vedado; *fig* cazar[7] en finca ajena

poacher cazador *m* furtivo

poaching caza furtiva

pock pústula; ~-**mark** hoyo de viruela; ~-**marked** picado de viruela

pocket *n* bolsillo; *aer* bolsa (de aire); *geol* bolsa; (billiards) tronera; ~ **of resistance** *mil* bolsa de resistencia; **be in** ~ salir[19] ganando; **be out of** ~ salir[19] perdiendo; **have s.o. in one's** ~ tener en el bolsillo a alguien; ~-**book** cartera, *SA* billetera; ~-**flap** portezuela; ~-**knife** navaja; cortaplumas *m sing*; ~-**money** dinero para gastos personales (pequeños); **pick s.o.'s** ~ robarle la cartera a alguien; *adj* de bolsillo; ~ **edition** edición *f* de bolsillo; ~ **handkerchief** pañuelo de bolsillo; ~-**size** de bolsillo; *v* (put in one's pocket) meter en el bolsillo; (appropriate) apropiarse de; (take as profit) ganar; (billiards) entronerar

pocketful bolsillo (**of** (lleno) de)

pod vaina

podgy rechoncho

podium podio

poem poema *m*; ~**s of García Lorca** poesías *fpl* de García Lorca

poet poeta *m*; **would-be** ~ poetastro; **Poet Laureate** poeta laureado

poetess poetisa

poetic poético; ~ **licence/justice** licencia/justicia poética

poetry poesía; ~ **book** libro de poesía

pogo(-stick) zanco con resorte (para saltar con él)

pogrom pogrom(o) *m*

poignancy patetismo

poignant patético

point *n* (sharp end) punta; (dot) punto; (decimal point) coma, **six** ~ **four** seis coma cuatro; (of compass) cuarto; *elect* cuerpo; *print* cuerpo, **set up in eight-~** compuesto en cuerpo ocho; *sp* punto, **win on ~s** ganar por puntos; (in rationing) cupón *m*; (item) punto, **the first ~ in his speech** el primer punto de su discurso; **carry one's ~** salirse[19] con la suya; (matter) cuestión *f*, **knotty ~** cuestión *f* difícil; **~ at issue** cuestión *f* bajo consideración; **~ of order** cuestión *f* de procedimiento; **the ~ is that** el hecho es que; **that's beside the ~** eso no viene al caso; **in ~ of fact** en realidad; **off the ~** fuera de propósito; **to the ~** a propósito; **come to the ~** ir[19] al grano; **come to the ~!** ¡déjate de historias!; **when it comes to the ~** cuando llega al caso; **keep to the ~** no apartarse del tema; **speak to the ~** hablar al caso; **make a ~ of** insistir en +*infin*; **make the ~ that** hacer[19] ver que; **stretch a ~** hacer[19] una excepción; (meaning) significado; **see the ~** caer[19] en la cuenta, **I see the ~** ya caigo; **miss the ~** no caer[19] en la cuenta; **get the ~** (take the hint) comprender la indirecta; **get the ~ of something** entender (ie)[2b] lo más importante de algo; (of joke) lo esencial; (purpose) motivo, **what's his ~ in doing that?** ¿qué motivo tiene para hacer eso?; **I don't see the ~** of no creo que sea necesario +*infin*; **is there any ~ in** ¿vale la pena +*infin*?; (moment, place) punto, momento, **~ of departure** punto de partida, **~ of no return** momento decisivo; **~ of view** punto de vista; **at that ~** (then) en aquel momento; **be on the ~ of** estar[19] a punto de +*infin*; **up to a ~** hasta cierto punto; **freezing ~** punto de congelación; **turning ~** *fig* punto decisivo; **~-blank: he refused ~-blank** se negó en rotundo; **to ask ~-blank** preguntar[5] a boca de jarro; **they fired at ~-blank range** dispararon a quemarropa; **~-duty** control *m* de la circulación; **~-to-~** carrera de caballos a través del campo; **~s** (railway) agujas *fpl*, **the train crossed the ~s** el tren entró en agujas; **~sman** (railway) guardagujas *m sing + pl*; **on the ~s** (ballet) de puntillas; **~s of a horse** rasgos *mpl* característicos de un caballo; **he**

has many good ~s él tiene muchas cualidades buenas; *v* (sharpen) afilar; (pencil) sacar[4] punta a; (aim) apuntar (at a); *bui* rejuntar; **the hands of the clock ~ed to six o'clock** las agujas del reloj marcaban las seis; **it ~s north** está orientado hacia el norte

~ at indicar[4]; **~ a finger at** señalar con el dedo

~ out indicar[4]; **he ~ed out that** él advirtió que

~ to indicar[4]

pointed (sharp) puntiagudo; *archi* ojival; (of a remark) lleno de intención; **~ beard** perilla

pointedness mordacidad *f*

pointer (dog) perro de muestra; (on gauge) indicador *m*; (stick) puntero; *fig* índice *m*

pointing *bui* rejuntado; (aim) puntería

pointless inútil

pointlessness inutilidad *f*

poise *n* aplomo; **she has ~** ella tiene confianza en sí misma; *v* balancear(se); **be ~d** estar[19] suspendido; **be ~d to** estar[19] en condiciones de +*infin*

poison *n* veneno; **~ gas** (gas *m*) asfixiante *m*; *v* envenenar

poisoner envenenador *m* (-ora *f*)

poisoning envenenamiento

poisonous venenoso

poke *n* empuje; (with elbow) codazo; **~-bonnet** capelina; *vt* empujar; (with elbow) dar[19] un codazo a; *vulg sl* tirarse a; **~ the fire** atizar[17] el fuego; **~ fun at** burlarse de; **~ a hole** hacer un agujero a empujones; **don't ~ your nose in my business!** ¡no se meta en mis asuntos!; *vi* **~ around** curiosear

[1] **poker** (implement) atizador *m*; **~-work** pirograbado

[2] **poker** (game) póquer *m*; **~-face** cara impasible

poky: ~ room cuartucho

Poland Polonia

polar polar; **~ bear** oso blanco

polarity polaridad *f*

polarization polarización *f*

polarize polarizar[7]

polaroid polaroide

[1] **pole** palo; (athlete's) pértiga; (flag) asta; (telegraph) poste *m*; (tent) poste; *mar* mástil *m*; (measure) medida de lon-

gitud (= 5,029 mctros); **up the ~** chiflado; **~-axe** n hachuela, (butcher's)
mazo, v desnucar[4]; **~-vaulter** saltador
m (-ora f) de pértiga; **~-vault(ing)**
salto de pértiga

[2] **pole** *elect+geog* polo; **~-star** estrella
polar; **from ~ to ~** de polo a polo

Pole polaco

polecat turón m; *SA* mofeta

polemic *adj* polémico; n **~s** polémica

police n policía; *euph* seguridad f; *sl*
bofia; **~ constable, ~man** (agente m
de) policía m; **~ court** tribunal m de
policía; **~ dog** perro policía; **~ force**
(cuerpo de) policía; **~ state** estado
policía (*pl* estados policía); **~ station**
comisaría (de policía); **~ trap** puesto
oculto de la policía; **~ van** furgoneta
de la policía; **~woman** mujer f policía
(*pl* mujeres policía); *v* patrullar

[1] **policy** política; (of newspaper) normas
fpl de conducta

[2] **policy** (insurance) póliza; **~-holder** asegurado

polio(myelitis) polio(mielitis) f

Polish polaco

polish n (wax) cera de lustrar; **metal-~**
sidol m; **shoe-~** betún m, (shine) brillo, **put a ~ on** sacar[4] brillo a; *fig*
finura; *v* (with wax) encerar; (make
shine) sacar[4] brillo a; *fig* (improve
something written) pulir, perfeccionar; **~ off** (finish) acabar con, (kill)
cargarse[5] a

polished *lit* elegante; (of people) fino

polisher (machine + cloth) pulidor m;
(floor-~) enceradora

polishing n pulimento; *adj* de lustrar

polite bien educado; **~ society** gente
guapa

politeness educación f

politic prudente; **body ~** estado

political político; **~ asylum** asilo político

politically: ~ aware politizado

politician político; *pej* politiquero

politicize politiquear

politics política, *pej* politiquería; **he has
no interest in ~** él no tiene política

polka polca; **~-dot** diseño de puntos

[1] **poll** n (election) votación f; (votes cast)
votos *mpl*; (inquiry) encuesta;
public-opinion ~ sondeo de la opinión
pública; **go to the ~s** ir[19] a votar; **take a
~** hacer[19] una encuesta; *v* (votes) re-

cibir, **he will not ~ many votes** él no
recibirá muchos votos

[2] **poll** (cattle) descornar (ue)[1a]; (fighting-
bulls) afeitar

pollard n árbol desmochado; *v* desmochar

pollen polen m; **~-count** cuenta de
pólenes

pollinate fecundar con polen

pollination polinización f; **self-~** auto-
fecundación f

polling votación f; **~-booth** cabina
electoral; **~-card** tarjeta de elector;
~-day día m de elecciones; **~-station**
colegio electoral, *fam* urnas *fpl*

pollster agente m auscultador; encues-
tador m (-ora f)

pollute contaminar; *fig* corromper

pollution contaminación f; *fig* corrupción f

polo polo; **~-necked** de cuello de cisne

polonaise polonesa

poltergeist duende m

polyanthus prímula

polychrome policromo

polygamist polígamo

polygamous polígamo

polygamy poligamia

polyglot n+adj polígloto

polygon polígono

polymath sabio

Polynesia Polinesia

polyp pólipo

polyphonic polifónico

polysyllable, polysyllabic polisílabo

polytechnic n universidad politécnica;
adj politécnico

polytheism politeísmo

polytheist(ic) politeísta m+f

polythene polietileno

pom (dog) perro lulú

pomade pomada

pomegranate granada

pomeranian (dog) perro lulú

pommel n pomo; *v* dar[19] puñetazos a

pomp pompa

Pompeii Pompeya

pompom borla

pomposity pomposidad f; (of language)
ampulosidad f

pompous pomposo; (language) ampuloso

ponce alcahuete m

poncho poncho

pond (natural) charca; (artificial) estanque *m*; (fish-~) vivero

ponder considerar con cuidado; ~ **over** meditar

ponderous pesado

pong *n* tufillo; *v* heder (ie)[2b]

pontiff pontífice *m*

pontifical pontifical

pontificate *n* pontificado; *v eccles* pontificar[4]; *pej* hacer[19] el sabio

Pontius Pilate Poncio Pilato

pontoon pontón (-ones) *m*; (bridge) puente *m* de pontones; (card game) *approx* siete y medio

pony jaca; ~**-tail** (hair style) cola de caballo

poodle perro de lanas

pooh *interj* bah!; *v* ~-~ rechazar[7] con desprecio

[1] **pool** *n* (natural) charca; (artificial) estanque *m*; (fish-~) vivero; (swimming-~) piscina; (of spilt liquid) charco

[2] **pool** (billiards) trucos *mpl*; (cards) banca; *comm* consorcio, fusión de intereses; ~s (gambling) quinielas *fpl*; ~s entry boleto; six-line ~ boleto de seis; ~s forecast acierto; ~s forecaster quinielista *m+f*; ~s promoters Apuestas Mutuas; ~s syndicate peña quinielista; *v* mancomunar intereses

poop popa; ~ **deck** cubierta del alcázar

poor *n* los pobres; *adj* (financially) pobre (*after n*), ~ **country** país *m* pobre; (unfortunate) pobre (*before n*), ~ **girl** pobre chica; (quality) malo; (of character) mezquino; (of land) infértil; (light) *phot* defectuosa; ~ **man/woman** pobre *m+f*; ~ **me!** ¡ay de mí!; ~ **you!** ¡pobre de ti!; **be in** ~ **health** tener[19] mala salud; **have a** ~ **opinion of** tener[19] en poco a; ~**-box** cepillo para los pobres; ~**-house** asilo para los pobres, *fam* misericordia; ~**-law** ley de asistencia pública; ~**-spirited** apocado

poorly *adj* indispuesto; *adv* pobremente

poorness (financial) pobreza; (of quality) mala calidad; (of character) mezquindad *f*; (of land) infertilidad *f*

[1] **pop** *n* (of cork) taponazo; (of gun) detonación *f*; (drink) gaseosa; ~**corn** palomitas *fpl* de maíz; ~**-eyed** de ojos saltones; ~**gun** fusil *m* de juguete; *vt*

(cork) hacer[19] saltar; (firearm) disparar; **she popped the balloon** ella reventó el globo; ~ **the question** declararse; *vi* (of cork) saltar; (of firearm) detonar

~ **along** irse[19]

~ **down(stairs)/up(stairs)** bajar/subir apresuradamente

~ **in** entrar por un momento; (visit) dar[19] un vistazo

~ **off** irse[19] a prisa; (die) *fam* estirar la pata, *sl* diñarla

~ **out** salir[19] por un momento; **I'm going to** ~ **out for some cigarettes** voy a por tabaco; **the cork popped out of the bottle** el corcho saltó de la botella

~ **round** ir[19]/venir[19] a visitar

~ **up** aparecer[14] inesperadamente

[2] **pop** *n* música moderna, *fam* música joven; *adj* moderno, *fam* yeyé *invar*, ~ **art** arte *m+f* pop; ~ **group** conjunto; ~ **music** música (de baile) moderna, *fam* música joven; ~ **singer** cantante *m* yeyé; **this record is top of the** ~**s** este disco es el primero de la lista

[3] **pop** papá *m*

Pope Papa *m*

popery papismo

popish papista *m+f*

poplar (white) álamo; (black) chopo; ~ **grove** alameda

poplin popelina

poppet muñequita

poppy amapola

poppycock *n* + *interj* tonterías *fpl*

populace pueblo; *pej* gentuza

popular popular

popularity popularidad *f*; ~ **chart** *mus* lista del triunfo

popularize popularizar[7]

populate poblar (ue)[1a]

population población *f*; ~ **explosion** explosión demográfica; ~ **growth** crecimiento de la población

populous populoso

porcelain porcelana

porch (of house) portal *m*; (of church) porche *m*

porcupine puerco espín

[1] **pore** *n* poro

[2] **pore**: ~ **over** (be absorbed in) estar[19] absorto en; (examine) estudiar cuidadosamente

pork carne *f* de cerdo; **salt** ~ tocino; ~

butcher chacinero; ~ **chop** chuleta/costilla de cerdo; ~ **pie** pastel *m* de carne de cerdo; ~**-pie hat** sombrero de copa baja y ala estrecha

porker cerdo

porn porno *f*

pornographer pornógrafo

pornographic pornográfico

pornography pornografía

porosity porosidad *f*

porous poroso

porphyry pórfido

porpoise marsopa

porridge: papas *fpl* de avena

porringer plato hondo

¹ **port** *n* puerto; ~ **of call** puerto de escala; ~ **dues** derechos *mpl* portuarios; **put into** ~ tomar puerto; ~**hole** *naut* tronera, *mech* lumbrera

² **port** *n naut* (~ side) babor *m*; *v* ~ **the helm** poner¹⁹ a babor

³ **port** (wine) vino de Oporto

portable portátil; ~ **television set** televisor *m* portátil; (pocket-size) de bolsillo; ~ **transistor** transistor *m* de bolsillo

portage porteo

portal portal *m*

portcullis rastrillo

portend presagiar

portent presagio

portentous portentoso

¹ **porter** (door-keeper) portero; (at university) bedel *m*; ~**'s lodge** portería

² **porter** (railway) mozo, *fam* maletero; (drink) cerveza negra; ~**house steak** mediana

porterage porte *m*

portfolio carpeta; (ministry) ministerio; **minister without** ~ ministro sin cartera

portico portal *m*

portion *n* (part) porción (-ones) *f*; (piece) pedazo; *cul* (helping) porción (-ones) *f*, (in restaurant) ración (-ones) *f*; *v* ~ **out** repartir

portliness corpulencia

portly corpulento; (of manner) grave

portmanteau maleta

portrait retrato; ~ **painter** retratista *m*+*f*; ~ **photographer** fotógrafo de retratos

portraiture arte *m* de retratar

portray retratar; (describe) describir

(*past part* descrito); representar

portrayal representación *f*

Portugal Portugal *m*

Portuguese *n*+*adj* portugués *m* (-esa *f*)

pose *n* postura; *fig* afectación *f*; *vt* ~ **a problem** plantear un problema; ~ **a question** hacer¹⁹ una pregunta; *vi* (model) posar; *fig* darse¹⁹ postín; ~ **as** hacerse¹⁹ pasar por

poser problema *m*/pregunta difícil

posh elegante; *fam* finolis *invar*; (showy) cursi *invar*

posidrive: ~ **screw** tornillo de estrella

position *n* posición *f*; (job) puesto; (opinion) opinión *f*; **be in a** ~ **to** estar¹⁹ en condiciones de +*infin*; **place in** ~ colocar⁴; **take up a** ~ *mil* desplegarse²ᵃ; *v* colocar⁴

positive *elect*+*math*+*phot* positivo; (affirmative) afirmativo; (downright) categórico; (sure) seguro, **I'm** ~ **(that)** estoy seguro (de que)

positively absolutamente

positivism positivismo

positivist positivista *m*+*f*

posse grupo de hombres armados

possess poseer; ~ **o.s. of** tomar posesión de; **be** ~**ed by** (idea, spirit *etc*) estar¹⁹ obsesionado por; **whatever** ~**ed you?** ¿cómo lo ha podido hacer?

possession posesión *f*; ~**s** bienes *mpl*; **in the** ~ **of** en poder de; **take** ~ **of** apoderarse de, (house) ocupar; **he was arrested for being in** ~ **of drugs** le detuvieron por tenencia de drogas; **vacant** ~ posesión *f* libre

possessive posesivo; **she is very** ~ ella es muy dominante; ~ **case** posesivo

possessor poseedor *m* (-ora *f*)

possibility posibilidad *f*; **though he is young he has great possibilities** aunque él es joven tiene condiciones; **there is a (distinct)** ~ **that** es (muy) posible que +*subj*; **within the bounds of** ~ dentro de lo factible

possible posible; **make** ~ posibilitar; **it is** ~ **that** es posible que +*subj*; **it is not** ~ **for me** no me es posible +*infin*; **as much as** ~ lo más posible; **eat as much as** ~ comer todo lo que uno puede; **as often as** ~ lo más frecuentemente posible; **as soon as** ~ lo antes posible

possibly posiblemente; (maybe) tal vez; **if I** ~ **can** de serme posible; **I can't** ~

do it me es absolutamente imposible hacerlo

¹ **post** n (stake) poste m; v (fix) fijar, ~ **no bills** se prohibe fijar carteles

² **post** (job) puesto, cargo; mil puesto; v (appoint) mandar

³ **post** n (mail) correo; (building) casa de correos; (collection) recogida; (delivery) entrega; **by** ~ por correo; **by return of** ~ a vuelta de correo; **I'm going to the** ~ (to the post office) voy a correos, (to the letter-box) voy al buzón; ~ **office** (casa de) correos; ~-**office box number** apartado (de correos); ~-**office savings bank** caja postal de ahorros; ~-**box** buzón (-ones) m; ~**card** (tarjeta) postal f; ~-**code** código postal; ~-**free** porte pagado; ~-**haste** a toda prisa; ~**man** cartero; ~**mark** n matasellos m sing, v poner¹⁹ matasellos a; ~**master** administrador m de correos; ~**mistress** administradora de correos; v/t echar al correo; (enter in ledger) pasar al libro mayor; **keep s.o.** ~**ed** tenerle¹⁹ a uno al corriente

⁴ **post** prep posterior a; ~ **the Industrial Revolution** posterior a la revolución industrial; pref ~-**date** poner¹⁹ fecha posterior a; ~-**dated cheque** cheque m con fecha posterior; ~**graduate** n+adj graduado; ~**graduate studies** curso para graduados; **Post-Impressionism** n+adj postimpresionismo, **Post-Impressionist** postimpresionista m+f; ~-**meridian** postmeridiano; ~**script** posdata m; ~-**war** de la posguerra; ~-**war period** posguerra

postage porte m, franqueo; ~ **due** porte m a pagar; ~ **paid** porte pagado; ~ **stamp** sello postal, SA estampilla

postal de correos; ~ **code** código postal; ~ **order** giro postal

poster cartel m; ~ **artist** cartelista m+f

poste restante lista de correos

posterior n fam asentaderas fpl; adj posterior

posterity posteridad f

posthumous póstumo

postilion postillón m

postmortem autopsia

postpone aplazar⁷

postponement aplazamiento

postulate n postulado; v postular

postulation postulación f

posture n postura; v colocarse⁴ en una postura; (pose for effect) adoptar una actitud afectada

posy ramillete m de flores

¹ **pot** n cul olla, marmita; (jam etc) tarro; (flower-pot) tiesto; (chamber-pot) orinal, fam copa; ~**s of** fam montones mpl de; **go to** ~ echarse a perder; ~-**bellied** tripón; ~-**belly** barriga; ~-**boiler** obra escrita para ganar dinero; ~-**hole** (in road) bache m, geol marmita de gigante; ~-**holer** espeleólogo; ~-**holing** espeleología; **take** ~-**luck** tomar lo que haya; ~-**plant** planta de maceta; ~-**roast** carne asada; ~-**shot** tiro al azar; vt cul conservar (en tarros); hort poner¹⁹ en tiesto; fam matar a tiros; vi ~ **at** disparar contra

² **pot** (marihuana) grifa, sl mierda; ~-**addict** grifómano; ~-**smoker** grifota m+f

potash potasa

potassium potasio; ~ **permanganate** permanganato potásico

potato patata, SA papa; ~ **chips** patatas fpl fritas; ~ **crisps** patatas fpl fritas a la inglesa; ~ **omelette** tortilla de patatas; **jacket** ~**es** patatas fpl sin pelar; ~ **beetle** escarabajo de la patata; ~-**peeler** pelador m de patatas

potency potencia

potent potente

potentate potentado

potential n potencial m; **have** ~ tener¹⁹ posibilidades; adj potencial

potentiality potencialidad f

potion brebaje m

pot-pourri popurrí m

¹ **potter** n alfarero, SA adobero; ~'**s clay** arcilla de alfarería; ~'**s wheel** torno de alfarero

² **potter** v matar el tiempo; ~ **around the house** hacer¹⁹ bagatelas en casa

pottery (craft) alfarería; (pots) cacharros mpl; arch cerámica

potting: ~ **shed/table** caseta/tablero para plantar en macetas

¹ **potty** n orinal pequeño

² **potty** adj chiflado

pouch bolsa; (hunter's) morral m; mil cartuchera; (tobacco-~) petaca; zool bolsa marsupial

pouffe taburete *m* de fantasía; puf; (homosexual) mariquita

poulterer pollero

poultice *n* cataplasma; *v* poner[19] una cataplasma a

poultry aves *fpl* de corral; ~ **dealer** recovero; ~**-farm** granja avícola; ~ **farmer,** ~**man** avicultor *m*; ~ **house** gallinero; ~**-run,** ~**-yard** corral *m*

pounce *n* (attack) ataque repentino; (leap) salto repentino; *v* atacar[4]/saltar repentinamente; ~ **on** +*fig* saltar sobre

[1] **pound** (money) libra (esterlina); (weight) libra (453,6 gramos)

[2] **pound** corral *m* de concejo

[3] **pound** *vt* machacar[4]; (with stick) aporrear; (hit) dar[19] golpes a; (with fists) dar[19] puñetazos a; *mil* bombardear; ~ **at the door** aporrear en la puerta; *vi* (run) correr pesadamente

poundage impuesto de tanto por libra

pour *vt* echar; +*fig* derramar; (of fumes) arrojar; ~ **away/out** vaciar; *vi* (rain) llover (ue)[1b] a cántaros; ~ **in/ out** entrar/salir[19] a montones; ~ **forth** (liquid) correr a chorros, (words) salir[19] rápidamente

pout *n* pucher(it)o; *v* hacer[19] pucher(it)os

poverty pobreza; (extreme) pauperismo; ~**-stricken** paupérrimo

powder *n* polvo; (cosmetic) polvos *mpl*; (gunpowder) pólvora; ~**-compact** polvera; ~**-magazine** polvorín (-ines) *m*; ~**-puff** borla de los polvos; ~**room** *mil* polvorín (-ines) *m*, (in hotel) servicio para señoras; ~**-spray** espolvoreador *m*; *v* espolvorear, pulverizar; ~ **one's face** ponerse polvos en la cara; ~**ed milk** leche *f* en polvo

powdery (like powder) en polvo; (covered with powder) polvoriento; ~ **snow** nieve *f* fina como polvo

power *n* poder *m*; (gift) facultad *f* (of de); (vigour) empuje *m*; *mech* energía, potencia; *elect* fuerza; (influence) influencia; *pol* potencia, **the great** ~**s** las grandes potencias; ~ **politics** política de fuerza; ~**s that be** autoridades *fpl* (actuales); **be in** ~ estar[19] en el poder; **as far as is in my** ~ en cuanto me sea posible; **it is not in my** ~ **to** no está en mi poder +*infin*; **do all in one's**

~ **to** hacer[19] todo lo posible por; ~ **of attorney** poderes *mpl*; **grant** ~ **of attorney to** dar[19] poderes a; ~**-cut** apagón (-ones) *m*; ~**-dive** *n aer* picado a motor en marcha, *v* picar[4] a motor en marcha; ~**-drill** taladradora eléctrica; ~**-driven** mecánico, *elect* eléctrico, (of toys) con motor; ~**-house** central eléctrica, *mech* central eléctrica; ~**-line** línea de fuerza eléctrica; ~**-plant** grupo electrógeno; ~**-point** toma; ~**-station** central eléctrica; ~**steering** *mot* dirección asistida; ~**-tool** herramienta mecánica; *v* alimentar; ~**ed by batteries or from the mains** alimentada con pilas o conectada a la red

powerful poderoso; *anat* fuerte; (of argument) convincente

powerless impotente

pow-wow conferencia

pox sífilis *f*

practicability practicabilidad *f*

practicable practicable

practical práctico; ~ **joke** burla pesada; ~ **subject** (school) asignatura experimental

practicality espíritu práctico; (of plan *etc*) lo práctico

practically (in a practical way) prácticamente; (almost) casi; (in fact) en efecto

practice (not theory) práctica; (custom) costumbre *f*; (repeated exercise) ejercicio; (religious) rito; *med* clientela; **in** ~ (not theory) en la práctica; **be in** ~ (manual skill) tener[19] el tino, *sp* estar[19] entrenado, *leg*+*med* ejercer[12] su profesión; **be out of** ~ haber[19] perdido la costumbre/el tino, *sp* estar[19] desentrenado; **it is not my** ~ **to** no es mi· costumbre +*infin*; **you've had a lot of** ~ **at** usted tiene mucha experiencia de; **make a** ~ **of** acostumbrar a +*infin*; **put into** ~ poner[19] en práctica; ~ **makes perfect** el ejercicio hace maestro; **piano-, gun-**~ ejercicio de piano/cañón

practise practicar[4]; (custom) tener[19] la costumbre de; ejercer[12] (la profesión de); (to train) entrenarse en; ~ **doing s.t.** ensayarse en hacer algo; ~ **medicine** practicar[4] la medicina; ~ **what one preaches** predicar[4] con el ejem-

plo; ~d experto, (manually) mañoso
practitioner médico; **general** ~ médico general, *fam* médico de cabecera
pragmatic pragmático
pragmatism pragmatismo
pragmatist pragmatista *m+f*
Prague Praga
prairie *n* pradera; *SA* pampa; *adj* de la pradera/pampa
praise *n* alabanza(s); ~**worthiness** calidad *f* de loable; ~**worthy** loable; *v* alabar; ~ **to the skies** poner[19] en los cuernos de la luna
pram cochecito de niño
prance *n* cabriola; *v* cabriolar
prank (mischief) travesura; (joke) broma
prate parlotear
prattle *n* parloteo; (childish) balbuceo; *v* parlotear; balbucear
prattler parlanchín (-ines) *m*, parlanchina; (gossip) chismoso
prattling *n* parloteo; (childish) balbuceo; *adj* gárrulo; balbuciente
prawn gamba
pray rezar[7]; ~ **to ... for** orar a ... por
prayer oración *f*, rezo; (entreaty) súplica; **say one's** ~**s** rezar[7]; ~**-book** devocionario; ~**-meeting** reunión *f* para rezar; ~**-rug** alfombra de rezo; ~**-wheel** molino de oraciones
praying rezo; (entreaty) súplica; ~ **mantis** *ent* campanero
preach predicar[4]
preacher predicador *m* (-ora *f*); **turn** ~ meterse a predicar
preaching predicación *f*; *pej* sermoneo
preamble preámbulo
prearrange fijar de antemano
preassembled montado en fábrica
prebendary prebendado
precarious precario
precariousness inseguridad *f*
precaution precaución (-ones) *f*; **take** ~**s** tomar precauciones
precautionary preventivo
precede preceder
precedence precedencia; **take** ~ **over** tener prioridad sobre
precedent *n+adj* precedente *m*; **establish a** ~ establecer[14] un precedente; **without** ~ sin precedente
preceding precedente
precentor chantre *m*

precept precepto
precinct recinto; *US* barrio; **pedestrian** ~ zona para peatones; **shopping** ~ recinto (zona) comercial; ~**s** contornos *mpl*; **within the** ~**s of** dentro de los contornos de
preciosity preciosismo
precious precioso; ~ **stone** piedra preciosa; (affected) afectado; (dearly loved) muy querido; ~ **little** muy poco; ~ **nearly** por poco
preciousness gran valor *m*
precipice precipicio
precipitance precipitación *f*
precipitant precipitado
precipitate *n* precipitado; *v* precipitar
precipitation precipitación *f*
precipitous precipitado
précis resumen (-úmenes) *m*
precise exacto; (of people) escrupuloso; **too** ~ *pej* afectado; **at that** ~ **moment** en ese mismo momento; **to be** ~ por más señas
precisely perfectamente; ~! ¡eso es!; **at ten o'clock** ~ a las diez en punto
precision precisión *f*, exactitud *f*; ~ **tools** herramientas *fpl* de precisión
preclude (exclude) excluir[16]; (make impossible) imposibilitar
preclusion (exclusion) exclusión *f*; (making impossible) imposibilidad *f*
precocious precoz (-ces)
precociousness, precocity precocidad *f*
pre-combustion chamber *mot* antecámara
preconceived preconcebido
preconception preconcepción *f*
precondition condición *f* (hecha de antemano)
precursor precursor *m* (-ora *f*)
pre-date antedatar
predatory rapaz (-ces)
predecease premorir (ue)[1c]
predecessor predecesor *m* (-ora *f*)
predestination predestinación *f*
predestine predestinar
predetermine predeterminar
predicament apuro; **get out of a** ~ salir[19] del paso
predict pronosticar[4]
predictable que se puede pronosticar
prediction pronóstico
predilection predilección *f*
predispose predisponer[19]

predisposition predisposición *f*
predominance predominio
predominant predominante
predominantly (prevailing) por la mayor parte; (dominating) de modo predominante
predominate predominar
pre-eminence preeminencia
pre-eminent preeminente
pre-eminently preeminentemente; (above all) sobre todo; (par excellence) por excelencia
pre-empt anticipar a los sucesos
pre-emptible sometido al derecho de prioridad
pre-emption derecho de prioridad
pre-emptive anticipado
preen: limpiar(se) con el pico; ~ **o.s.** *fig* pavonearse
pre-establish establecer[14] de antemano
pre-exist preexistir
pre-existence preexistencia
pre-existent preexistente
prefab casa prefabricada
prefabricate prefabricar[4]
prefabrication prefabricación *f*
preface *n* prólogo; *v lit* prologar[5]; *fig* introducir[18]; **she ~d her speech by** ella dijo como introducción a su conferencia
prefatory preliminar
prefect prefecto; (school) monitor *m*
prefer preferir (ie)[2c]; **I ~ to stand** prefiero estar de pie; **I ~ fish to meat** prefiero el pescado a la carne; (promote) ascender (ie)[2b]; **~ a charge** hacer[19] una denuncia
preferable preferible
preferably más bien
preference preferencia; **~ shares** acciones *fpl* preferentes
preferential preferente
preferment ascenso
preferred predilecto; **~ stock** *comm* acciones *fpl* preferentes
prefigure imaginar
prefix *n* prefijo; *v* prefijar; (to a word) poner[19] prefijo a
pregnancy embarazo
pregnant embarazada; *euph* en estado; *sl* de compras; *vulg* empollada
pre-heat precalentar (ie)[2a]
prehensile prensil
prehistoric prehistórico

prehistory prehistoria
prejudge prejuzgar[5]
prejudice *n* (preconceived opinion) prejuicio; (harm) perjuicio; *v* (bias) predisponer[19]; (harm) perjudicar[4]; **~d against** lleno de prejuicios contra
prejudicial perjudicial
prelate prelado
prelim examen (-ámenes) *m* preliminar
preliminary *n+adj* preliminar *m*; **preliminaries** preparativos *mpl*
prelude *n* +*mus* preludio; *v* preludiar
pre-marital premarital
premature prematuro
premeditate premeditar
premeditation premeditación *f*
premier *n* primer ministro; *adj* primero, primera; **~ship** cargo de primer ministro
première estreno
premise premisa
premises local *m*; **on the ~** en el local
premium *comm* premio; (insurance) prima; **it is at a ~** está sobre la par, *fig* está en gran demanda; **put a ~ on** dar gran valor a; **~ bond** bono del Estado que mensualmente da al comprador la posibilidad de ganar un premio
premonition presentimiento
pre-natal prenatal
preoccupation preocupación *f*
preoccupied preocupado
preoccupy preocupar
preordain predestinar
prep *n* (single subject) deber *m*; (more than one subject) deberes *mpl*; **~ school** escuela preparatoria
pre-packed, pre-packaged precintado
prepaid porte pagado
preparation preparación *f*; (homework) *see* **prep**; (patent food) preparado; **~s** preparativos *mpl*; **in ~** en preparación (**for** para)
preparatory preparatorio; **~ school** escuela preparatoria; **~ to** como preparación para
prepare preparar(se); (equip) equipar; (train) formar; **be ~d (to)** estar[19] dispuesto a +*infin*; **~ for** hacer[19] preparativos para; *sp* entrenarse para; **~ for an exam** estudiar para un examen; **be ~d for any eventuality** estar[19] dispuesto a aguantarlo todo; **~ to** disponerse[19] a +*infin*

preparedness preparación *f*
prepay pagar[5] por adelantado
prepayment pago adelantado
preponderance preponderancia
preponderant preponderante
preponderantly en su mayoría
preponderate preponderar (**over** sobre)
preposition preposición *f*
prepositional preposicional
prepossessing atractivo
prepossession predisposición *f* favorable
preposterous ridículo, *fam* descabellado
preposterousness ridiculez *f*
Pre-Raphaelite *n*+*adj* prerrafaelista *m*+*f*
prerequisite *n* requisito previo
prerogative prerrogativa
presage *n* presagio; *v* presagiar
Presbyterian *n*+*adj* presbiteriano
Presbyterianism Presbiterianismo
presbytery presbiterio
pre-school: ~ **education** educación *f* preescolar
prescience presciencia
prescribe prescribir (*past part* prescrito); *med* recetar
prescription prescripción *f*; *med* receta
presence presencia; (ghost) aparición *f*; **in the** ~ **of** en presencia de; ~ **of mind** presencia de ánimo
[1] **present** *n* (time) actualidad *f*; *gramm* (tiempo) presente *m*, ~ **indicative** presente *m* de indicativo; **at** ~ actualmente; **for the** ~ por ahora; *adj* presente; (~-day) actual; ~! ¡presente!; **be** ~ **at** asistir a; **those** ~ los presentes; ~ **company excepted** mejorando los presentes; **at the** ~ **time** actualmente; ~ **day** *n* nuestros tiempos *mpl*; ~-**day** *adj* actual
[2] **present** *n* (gift) regalo; **make a** ~ **of** regalar, (sell cheaply) dar[19] medio regalado; **we made Mary a** ~ **of a box of chocolates** a María le regalamos una caja de bombones; *v* regalar; (introduce) presentar; ~ **an argument** exponer[19] un argumento; ~ **arms!** ¡presenten armas!; ~ **s.o. with s.t.** regalarle algo a alguien; **some difficulties** ~**ed themselves** surgieron algunas dificultades; **the occasion** ~**ed itself** se ofreció la ocasión
presentable presentable
presentation *n* presentación *f*; (gift)

obsequio; (display) exposición *f*; ~ **copy** (from author) ejemplar *m* con dedicatoria del autor, (from publisher) ejemplar *m* de obsequio; **on** ~ *comm* a la presentación
presentiment corazonada; **have a** ~ **about** presentir (ie)[2c]; **have a** ~ **that** presentir (ie)[2c] que
presently (at present) actualmente; (soon) dentro de poco
preservation *n* conservación *f*; **in a good state of** ~ bien conservado
preservative *n* +*adj* preservativo
preserve *n* *cul* conserva; (hunting) vedado; *v* conservar; ~ **one's independence** defender (ie)[2b] su independencia; ~**d** *cul* en conserva; **well-~d** bien conservado
preserver (substance) preservante *m*; (person) preservador *m*, (-ora *f*)
preside presidir; **he will** ~ **at/over the function** él presidirá la ceremonia/la función
presidency presidencia
president presidente *m*; (*US comm*) director *m*; (*US* university) rector *m*; **lady-**~ presidenta
presidential presidencial
presiding: ~ **officer** presidente *m* de mesa electoral
press *n* *mech*+*print* prensa; (for extracting juice) exprimidor; (pressure) presión *f*; (weightlifting) presa de los brazos; ~ **advertising** publicidad *f* en la prensa, ~ **conference** rueda de prensa; **go to** ~ entrar en prensa; **have a good/bad** ~ tener[19] buena/mala prensa; ~**-agency** agencia de prensa; ~**-agent** agente *m* de publicidad; ~**-box, -gallery** tribuna de la prensa; ~**-cutting, ~clipping** recorte *m* (de periódico); ~**-gang** *n* patrulla de enganche, *v* enganchar a la fuerza; ~**man** periodista *m*; ~**-release** boletín (-ines) *m* de prensa; ~**-stud** botón (-ones) *m* de presión; *vt* *mech* prensar; (with hand) apretar (ie)[2a]; (electric button) pulsar; (clothes) planchar; ~ **the point** insistir en la cuestión; ~ **home** (an advantage) aprovecharse de; (harass) acosar; *vi* urgir[9]; **time** ~**es** el tiempo apremia
~ **against** pegar(se)[4] con
~ **down** apretar (ie)[2a]

~ **for** pedir (i)[3] con urgencia; **be ~ed for time** tener[19] poco tiempo

~ **forward** seguir (i)[3+11] adelante

~ **into service** utilizar[7]; *mil* enganchar a la fuerza

~ **on** (continue) seguir (i)[3+11]; (go forward) avanzar[7]; (hurry) apretar el paso; ~ **s.t. on s.o.** insistir en que alguien acepte algo

pressing *n* (of clothes) planchado; *adj* urgente

pressure presión *f*; (of the hand) apretón (-ones) *m*; (force) fuerza; *fig* apremio, **do s.t. under** ~ hacer[19] algo bajo apremio; **put** ~ **on** +*fig* apretar (ie)[2a]; ~**-chamber** cámara de presión; ~**-cooker** olla a presión *f*; ~**-gauge** manómetro; ~**-group** camarilla de presión

pressurized: ~ **cabin** cabina a presión

prestige prestigio; ~ **product** producto de reclamo

prestigious prestigioso

presumable presumible

presumably probablemente; ~ **it was Mary** supongo que era María

presume suponer[19]; ~ **to** atreverse a +*infin*; ~ **upon** abusar de

presumption presunción *f*; (effrontery) atrevimiento

presumptive presuntivo; (of heir) presunto

presumptuous presumido; (rude) atrevido

presumptuousness *see* **presumption**

presuppose presuponer[19]

presupposition presuposición *f*

pretence (claim) pretensión *f*; (excuse) pretexto; (show) ostentación *f*; **false** ~**s** fraude *m*

pretend fingir[9]; ~ **to be asleep/dead/ ill** fingirse[9] dormido/muerto/enfermo; (claim) pretender; ~ **to** (make claim to) afirmar tener derecho a

pretender pretendiente *m*

pretension pretensión *f*; **have ~s to** tener[19] pretensiones de +*infin*

pretentious pretencioso; (ostentatious) aparatoso

pretentiousness pretensión *f*

preterite pretérito

preternatural preternatural

pretext pretexto; **under** ~ **of** so pretexto de

prettify adornar (de manera ridícula)

prettily de manera bonita

prettiness lindeza

pretty *adj* bonito, lindo; (of people) guapo, mono; **it cost me a** ~ **penny** me costó un dineral; **I don't like her** ~ **ways** no me gustan sus monerías; *adv* bastante; ~ **easy** bastante fácil; ~ **much the same** poco más o menos lo mismo; ~ **near sold out** casi agotado; ~ **well** medianamente; **be sitting** ~ estar[19] en una posición muy ventajosa; ~**-~** chuchería

pretzel rosquilla

prevail (of condition) reinar; (be victorious) prevalecer[14]; ~ **against/ over** vencer[12] a; ~ **upon s.o.** (**to**) persuadir a alguien (a +*infin*); **be ~ed upon** (**to**) dejarse persuadir (a +*infin*)

prevailing reinante; (of fashion) en boga; ~ **opinion** opinión *f* actual; ~ **prices** precios *mpl* vigentes; ~ **wind** viento predominante

prevalence uso corriente

prevalent corriente; (widespread) común

prevaricate buscar[4] evasivas; *leg* prevaricar[4]

prevarication subterfugio; *leg* prevaricado

prevaricator prevaricador *m* (-ora *f*)

prevent impedir (i)[3]; **they ~ed him from leaving** le impidieron salir; **to** ~ **him from suffering** para evitarle sufrir

preventable evitable

preventative *n* preservativo; (condom) goma (anticoncepcional), condón *m*; *vulg sl* paracaídas *m sing* + *pl*

prevention prevención *f*; **society for the** ~ **of cruelty to animals** sociedad protectora de animales

preventive *adj* preventivo; ~ **medicine** medicina preventiva

preview *cin* pre-estreno; *fig* vista anticipada

previous anterior; *fam* prematuro; ~ **to** antes de

previously antes

pre-war de anteguerra; ~ **era** anteguerra; ~ **prices** precios de anteguerra

prey *n* presa; *fig* víctima; **bird of** ~ ave *f* de rapiña; **be/fall** ~ **to** ser[19] víctima de; *v* ~ (**up**)**on** devorar; (plunder) pillar; **it ~s on my mind** me preocupa mucho; **it ~s on my conscience** me da remordimiento/*fam* calor de conciencia

price *n* precio; **at any ~** a toda costa; **not at any ~** de ninguna manera; **what is the ~ of tomatoes today?** ¿a cómo están los tomates hoy?; **what ~?** (what do you think of?) ¿qué opina usted de?, (what are the chances of?) ¿qué posibilidades hay para?; **~ ceiling** precio máximo; **~ control** control *m* de precios; **~-cutting** reducción *f* de precios; **~-fixing** fijación *f* de precios; **~ increase** escalada de precios; **~-list** lista de precios, (of shares) boletín *m* de cotización; **~ reduction** rebaja; **~-ring** compradores *mpl* que se unen para determinar precios; **~-war** guerra de precios; *v* fijar el precio de; (ask the ~ of) preguntar el precio de

priceless sin precio; (funny) gracioso; (ridiculous) absurdo; **this watch is ~** este reloj no tiene precio

pricey caro

pricing fijación *f* de precios

prick *n* pinchazo; (with pin) alfilerazo; (with spur) espolada; (of conscience) remordimiento, *fam* calor *m*; *vulg* (penis) polla; **~-tease** *vulg* calientapollas *m sing+pl*; **~-eared** amusgado; *v* pinchar; (perforate) agujerear; (of conscience) remorder (ue)[1b]; **~ a balloon/bubble** reventar (ie)[2a] un globo/una burbuja; **~ out** *agri* (tras)plantar, (mark with perforations) marcar[4] con agujerillos; **~ up one's ears** aguzar[7] las orejas, *fig* (listen carefully) aguzar[7] el oído

pricking piquete *m*

prickle espina; (irritation) escozor *m*

prickliness calidad *f* de espinoso; *fig* mal humor *m*

prickly espinoso; *fig* malhumorado; **~ heat** salpullido (causado por el calor); **~ pear** (plant) chumbera, (fruit) higo chumbo

pride *n* orgullo; *pej* arrogancia; **take ~ in** enorgullecerse[14] de; **take ~ of place** ocupar el primer puesto; **~ of lions** manada de leones; *v* **~ o.s. upon** jactarse de

priest sacerdote *m*, cura *m*; **~hood** sacerdocio, (priests collectively) clero;

leave the ~hood secularizarse[7]; **~-ridden** dominado por el clero

priestess sacerdotisa

priestly sacerdotal

prig(gish) pedante *m+f*

prim remilgado; **~ and proper** etiquetero

prima: **~ ballerina** primera bailarina principal; **~ donna** primadonna

primacy primacía

primarily en primer lugar

primary *n* US elección *f* preliminar; *adj* primario; **~ colour** color primario; **~ education** enseñanza primaria; **~ school** escuela de primera enseñanza

primate *eccles* primado; *zool* primate *m*

prime *n*: **~ of life** flor *f* de la vida; *adj* de primera calidad/clase; **Prime Minister** primer ministro; **~ necessity** artículo de primera necesidad; **~ number** número primo; *v* (gun) cebar; (surface) preparar; (with paint) imprimar; (inform) informar de antemano; **~ with drink**[19] beber, (make drunk) emborrachar

primer cartilla; (paint) imprimación *f*

primeval primevo, primitivo

priming preparación *f*; (of gun) cebo; (paint) imprimación *f*; (instruction) instrucción *f*

primitive primitivo; *biol* rudimentario; *fam* sórdido

primitiveness lo primitivo/rudimentario

primly remilgadamente, de manera etiquetera

primness melindre *m*

primogeniture primogenitura

primordial primordial

primrose *n* primavera; *adj* amarillo pálido; **~ path** caminito de rosas, *pej* vida pecaminosa

primula prímula

primus (stove) infiernillo de petróleo

prince príncipe *m*; **~ consort** príncipe consorte; **Prince of Wales** Príncipe de Gales (*Sp equiv* Príncipe *m* de Asturias)

princedom, princehood principado

princely principesco

princess princesa

principal *n* *comm+leg* principal *m*; (college head) director *m* (-ora *f*); *adj* principal; **~ bout** (boxing) combate *m* de fondo; **~ boy:** actriz (-ces) *f* que desempeña el primer papel masculino en una zarzuela navideña; ~ **parts** *gramm* partes *fpl* principales

principality principalidad *f*

principle principio; **in** ~ en principio; **on** ~ por principio

prink adornar(se)

print *n* (mark) impresión *f*; (type) tipo; (fabric) estampado; *phot* copia; (picture) grabado; (writing) letra de imprenta; (finger) huella; **in** ~ impreso, (available) disponible; **in (bold)** ~ en letras de molde; **out of** ~ agotado; **go out of** ~ agotarse; *adj* ~ **blouse** blusa estampada; *v* imprimir; *phot* copiar; (fabrics) estampar; (publish) sacar[4] a luz; (write) escribir (*past part* escrito) en letras de imprenta; (on the memory) grabar

printed impreso; (fabric) estampado; ~**ed matter** impresos *mpl*

printer impresor *m*; ~**'s devil** aprendiz *m* de imprenta; ~**'s ink** tinta de imprenta; ~**'s mark** pie *m* de imprenta

printing impresión *f*; (art of ~) tipografía; (quantity) tirada; (of fabrics) estampación *f*; ~ **frame** *phot* prensa para copiar; ~**-house,** ~**-works** imprenta; ~ **machine** máquina de imprimir; ~ **paper** *phot* papel fotográfico; ~**-press** prensa de imprenta

prior *n* prior *m*; *adj* anterior; ~ **to** antes de

prioress priora

priority prioridad *f*; (road traffic) preferencia

priory priorato

prise: ~ **open** abrir (*past part* abierto) a la fuerza con una palanca; ~ **up** levantar a la fuerza con una palanca

prism prisma

prismatic prismático

prison cárcel *f*, prisión *f*; **put in/send to** ~ encarcelar; ~ **cell** celda; **the** ~ **population of Great Britain** la población reclusa de la Gran Bretaña; ~**-break** huida, evasión (-ones) *f*; ~ **camp** campo para prisioneros; ~ **officer/ warder** guardián (-anes) *m* de prisiones

prisoner prisionero; **take** ~ prender, *mil* hacer[19] prisionero; ~ **of war** prisionero de guerra

prissy remilgado

pristine prístino

privacy soledad *f*; privado; **in the** ~ **of the family** en la intimidad de la familia

private *n* soldado raso; ~**s** *anat* partes pudendas, *fam* bajos *mpl*; **in** ~ en secreto; *adj* privado; (individual) particular; (personal) personal; (of relationships) íntimo; (of reports) confidencial; *leg* (of hearing) a puerta cerrada; ~**!** ¡prohibida la entrada!; **we wish to be** ~ queremos estar a solas; **in** ~ **life** en la intimidad de la familia; ~ **company** sociedad *f* en comandita; ~ **detective/eye** detective privado; ~ **enterprise** iniciativa privada; ~ **house** casa particular; ~ **hotel** pensión *f*; ~ **lessons** clases *fpl* particulares; ~ **matter** asunto privado; ~ **means** rentas *fpl* particulares; ~ **member** *pol* diputado que no es del gobierno; ~ **property** bienes *mpl* particulares, (land) terreno de propiedad particular; ~ **road** camino reservado; ~ **school** colegio de pago; ~ **secretary** secretario particular; ~ **view(ing)** inauguración *f* privada

privatization privatización *f*

privatize privatizar[7]

privateer corsario

privation miseria

privet alheña

privilege *n* privilegio; (immunity) inmunidad *f*; *v* privilegiar; ~**d** privilegiado; **be** ~**d to** tener[19] el privilegio de

privy *n* retrete *m*; *adj* **be** ~ **to** estar[19] enterado de; **Privy Council** consejo privado; ~ **purse** gastos *mpl* personales del monarca

[1] **prize** premio; *naut* presa; ~**-fight** combate *m* de boxeo profesional; ~**-fighter** boxeador *m* profesional; ~**-fighting** boxeo profesional; ~**-giving** reparto de premios; ~**-money** *naut* parte *f* de presa; ~**winner** premiado; *adj* de primera clase; *v* apreciar

[2] **prize** see **prise**

P.R.O. (Public Relations Officer) encargado de relaciones públicas

[1] **pro** en pro de; ~**-forma invoice** factura simulada; ~ **rata** a prorrata; ~**s and cons** el pro y el contra

[2] **pro** profesional *m+f*; (prostitute) prostituta

probability probabilidad *f*; **in all** ~

según toda probabilidad
probable probable
probably probablemente, *fam* a lo
mejor; **he ~ arrived yesterday** habrá
llegado ayer
probate verificación *f* de testamentos
probation probación *f*; *leg* libertad
vigilada; **be on ~** estar[19] a prueba, *leg*
estar[19] en libertad vigilada; **put on ~**
poner[19] en libertad vigilada; **~ officer**
oficial *m* responsable de personas en
libertad vigilada
probationary de prueba; **~ term** *leg*
período de libertad vigilada
probationer (novice) novicio; *med* estudiante *f* de enfermera; *leg* delincuente
m+f en libertad vigilada
probe *n surg* sonda; *mil* exploración *f*;
space cohete *m*; (investigation)
investigación (**into** de); **~ scissors**
tijeras *fpl* de cirujano; *v surg* sondar;
mil explorar; (investigate) investigar[5]
probing (surgical) sondeo; *mil* explo-
raciones *fpl*; (investigation) investi-
gaciones *fpl*
probity probidad *f*
problem problema *m*; **~ child** niño
difícil
problematic(al) problemático
proboscis *ent* trompetilla; *zool* trompa;
fam nariz (-ces) *f*
procedural procesal
procedure procedimiento
proceed seguir (i)[3+11] (adelante); **~ on
one's way** seguir (i)[3+11] el camino;
before we ~ any further antes de ir
más lejos
~ against proceder contra
~ from provenir[19] de
~ to (start) ponerse[19] a +*infin*; **~ to say**
decir[19] a continuación
~ with proseguir (i)[3+11]
proceeding procedimiento; **~s** (trans-
actions) actas *fpl*; *leg* proceso; **take
legal ~s against** poner[19] una demanda
contra
proceeds ganancias *fpl*
[1] **process** *n* procedimiento; **in ~ of** en
curso de; **in ~ of building** en construcción; **in ~ of development** en vía
de desarrollo; **in the ~ of time** con el
tiempo; *v* tratar; *phot* fotografar; **~ed
cheese** queso fundido
[2] **process** *v* ir[19] en procesión

processing tratamiento; (of cheese)
fundición *f*; **data ~** informática
procession desfile *m*; (religious) procesión *f*; (funeral) cortejo; **go in ~** desfilar; *eccles* ir[19] en procesión
proclaim proclamar; **~ o.s. leader** pro-
clamarse caudillo
proclamation proclamación *f*
proclamatory proclamatorio
proclivity propensión *f*
proconsul procónsul *m*
procrastinate tardar en decidirse; (postpone) aplazar[7]
procrastination falta de decisión; (postponement) aplazamiento
procrastinator persona indecisa
procreate procrear
procreation procreación *f*
procreator procreador *m* (-ora *f*)
proctor *leg* procurador *m*; (university)
censor *m* de universidad
procurable asequible
procure *vt* obtener[19]; (achieve) conseguir (i)[3+11]; (for prostitution) solicitar
para prostitución; **~ an abortion** provocar[4] un aborto; *vi* alcahuetear
procurer alcahuete *m*
procuress alcahueta
procurement obtención *f*
prod *n* empuje *m*; (with elbow) codazo;
(with sword *etc*) punzada; *fig* pinchazo; *v* empujar, codear, punzar,
pinchar
prodigal pródigo; **the ~ son** el hijo
pródigo
prodigality prodigalidad *f*
prodigious prodigioso
prodigy prodigio; **infant ~** niño prodigio
produce *n* productos *mpl* (*esp* agrícolas); *v* (yield) producir[15]; (cause)
causar; (in factory) fabricar[4]; *theat*
presentar; *cin* dirigir[9]; *TV* realizar[7];
geom prolongar[5]; (of shares) rendir
(i)[3]; **he ~ed a rabbit from his hat** sacó
un conejo de su sombrero
producer productor *m* (-ora *f*); *theat*
director *m* (-ora *f*) de escena; *cin*
productor *m* (-ora *f*); *TV* realizador *m*
(-ora *f*); **~ nation** nación productora
producible producible
product +*math* producto; (result) resultado
production producción *f*; *cin+theat*

dirección *f*; *TV* realización *f*; (performance) (re)presentación *f*; ~ **costs** costes *mpl* de producción; ~ **line** cadena de fabricación

productive productivo; ~ **of** que produce

productivity productividad *f*; ~ **bonus** prima de producción

prof *sl* profe *m*

profanation profanación *f*

profane *adj* profano; ~ **words** blasfemias; *v* profanar

profanity blasfemia; *fam* taco

profess (declare) afirmar; (faith) profesar; ~ **to be** pretender ser; ~**ed** declarado, (alleged) supuesto

profession profesión *f*; **what is his ~?** ¿qué oficio tiene?; ~ **of faith** profesión *f* de fe

professional *n+adj* profesional *m+f*; **he is a ~ hunter** él es cazador de oficio; ~ **etiquette** etiqueta profesional; ~ **man** hombre *m* de carrera

professionalism profesionalismo

professionalize profesionalizar[7]

professor catedrático; ~**ship** cátedra

professorial de catedrático

proffer ofrecer[14]

proficiency pericia

proficient perito; **be ~ at** ser[19] hábil en

profile perfil *m*; **in ~** de perfil; **keep a low ~** no dejarse ver mucho

profit *n* ganancia; *fig* provecho; ~ **and loss** ganancias *fpl* y pérdidas *fpl*; **clear ~** beneficio neto; ~**-making** con ánimo de lucro; **non-~-making** sin ánimo de lucro; ~**-sharing** (by employees) participación en los beneficios, (by firm) reparto de los beneficios; ~**-sharing system** sistema *m* de cooperación; *vt* servir (i)[3] a; *vi comm* sacar[4] ganancia; ~ **by/from** aprovechar

profitable provechoso; (advantageous) ventajoso; (of investments) rentable

profiteer *n* agiotista *m*; *v* agiotar

profiteering *n* agiotaje *m*; *adj* agiotista

profitless infructuoso

profligacy libertinaje *m*

profligate *n+adj* libertino

profound profundo; ~ **sleep** sueño pesado

profundity profundidad *f*

profuse profuso

profuseness, profusion profusión *f*

progenitor progenitor *m*

progeny progenie *f*; *fam* prole *m*

prognosis pronóstico

prognostic *n+adj* pronóstico

prognosticate pronosticar[4]

prognostication pronóstico

program(me) *n* programa *m*; (of bullfight) cartel *m*; ~ **piece** *mus* pieza descriptiva; ~**-planning** programación *f*; *v* programar

programmer ordenador *m*

programming programación *f*

progress *n* progreso; (improvement) mejora; (of events) marcha; ~ **of work** marcha de la obra; **make ~** hacer[19] progresos, *med* mejorar; *v* progresar; hacer[19] progresos; *med* mejorar

progression progresión *f*

progressive *n pol* progresista *m+f*; *adj* progresivo, *fam* progre

prohibit prohibir; (prevent) impedir (i)[3]

prohibition prohibición *f*

prohibitionist *n+adj* prohibicionista *m+f*

prohibitive prohibitivo

project *n* proyecto; *vt* proyectar; *vi* sobresalir[19]

projectile proyectil *m*

projecting sobresaliente

projection +*cin* proyección *f*; (overhang) saliente *f*; ~ **room** cabina de proyección

projector *cin* proyector *m*

proletarian *n+adj* proletario

proletariat proletariado

proliferate proliferar

proliferation proliferación *f*

prolific prolífico; (**of** en)

prolix prolijo

prologue *n* prólogo; *v* prologar[5]

prolong prolongar[5]

prolongation prolongación *f*

promenade *n* paseo; (at seaside) paseo marítimo; ~ **concert** concierto en el que parte del público está de pie; ~ **deck** cubierta de paseo; *v* pasear(se)

Prometheus Prometeo

prominence prominencia; (importance) eminencia

prominent prominente; (important) eminente; (conspicuous) conspicuo; ~ **eyes** ojos *mpl* saltones; ~ **teeth**

dientes salientes
promiscuity promiscuidad *f*
promiscuous promiscuo
promise *n* promesa; **student of great ~**
estudiante *m+f* que promete mucho;
break/keep one's ~ faltar a/guardar su
promesa; **under ~ of** bajo palabra de;
~ of marriage palabra de matrimonio;
v prometer; **I ~ to write** prometo escribir; (augur) augurar; **I ~ you** yo se
lo aseguro
Promised Land tierra de promisión, *fig*
Jauja
promising que promete (mucho)
promissory: ~ note pagaré *m*
promontory promontorio
promote promover (ue)[1b]; (assist) apoyar; (in rank) ascender (ie)[2b]; **the team
was ~d to the 2nd Division** el equipo
ascendió a la 2ª División; **~ a bill** *pol*
presentar un proyecto de ley; **~ a
campaign** *comm* lanzar[7] una campaña; **~ a company** fundar una compañía; **~ a discussion** estimular una
discusión; **~ a product** promocionar
la venta de un producto; **~ subversion**
instigar[5] a la subversión
promoter promotor *m*; *comm* fundador
m; (boxing) empresario
promotion promoción *f*; (assistance)
apoyo; (in rank) ascenso; (presentation) presentación *f*; (of a campaign)
lanzamiento
prompt *n theat* apunte *m*; *adj* pronto;
(punctual) puntual; *adv* **the concert
starts at eight o'clock ~** el concierto
empieza a las ocho en punto; *v*
(motivate) motivar; (inspire) inspirar
(remind) hacer[19] recordar; (stimulate) estimular; *theat* apuntar; **~-
book** libro del apuntador; **~-box** *theat*
concha
prompter *theat* apuntador *m*
promptitude, promptness prontitud *f*
promptly en punto
promulgate promulgar[5]
promulgation promulgación *f*
prone (lying down) postrado boca
abajo; **~ to** propenso a
proneness propensión *f* (to a)
prong punta; **three-~ed** de tres puntas
pronominal pronominal
pronoun pronombre *m*
pronounce +*leg* pronunciar; (declare)

declarar; **~ on** expresar/*fam* dar[19] su
opinión sobre; **~d** marcado; **he has a
~d accent** él tiene un dejo marcado
pronouncement declaración *f*
pronto pronto
pronunciamento proclama política
pronunciation pronunciación *f*
proof *n* +*phot*+*print* prueba; *math*
comprobación *f*; (of spirits) graduación *f* normal; **in ~ of** en prueba de; **in
~ whereof** en fe de lo cual; **~-read**
corregir[9] pruebas; **~-reader** corrector
m (-ora *f*) (de pruebas); **~-reading**
corrección *f* de pruebas; **~-spirit** licor
m de graduación normal; **~s** *print*
pruebas *fpl*; *adj* (of spirits) de graduación normal; **be ~ against** estar[19]/ser[19]
a prueba de; **bullet-/water-~** a prueba
de balas/de agua; *v* (make water-~)
impermeabilizar[7]
proofing (of cloth) preparación imper-
meabilizadora
[1] **prop** *n bui* puntal *m*; (mining) entibo; *fig*
apoyo; *v* **~ (up)** apuntalar
[2] **props** *theat* accesorio(s)
propaganda propaganda
propagandist *n+adj* propagandista *m+f*
propagandize hacer[19] propaganda
propagate propagar[5]
propagation propagación *f*
propel impulsar
propellant propulsor *m*
propeller hélice *f*
propelling: ~ pencil portaminas *m
sing+pl*
propensity propensión *f* (to a)
proper (correct) propio; (decent) decente; (fully developed) hecho y derecho; (prim and proper) etiquetero;
(suitable) bueno (for para); (true)
verdadero; **he is a ~ rogue** él es un
bribón redomado; **there was a ~ row**
hubo una riña de todos los diablos; **in
the ~ sense of the word** en el sentido
estricto de la palabra; **medicine ~** la
medicina propiamente dicha; **~ fraction** quebrado propio; **~ name/noun**
nombre propio
properly (correctly) correctamente;
(decently) decentemente; **do it ~!**
¡hágalo bien!; **it ~ confused me** me
confundió por completo; **~ speaking**
propiamente dicho
propertied adinerado

properties *theat* accesorios *mpl*
property propiedad *f*; (belongings) posesiones *fpl*; (estate) hacienda; *Sp* finca; (quality) cualidad *f*; **man of ~** hacendado; **~-man** *theat* encargado de los accesorios; **~-tax** impuesto sobre bienes muebles
prophecy profecía
prophesy profetizar⁷
prophet profeta *m*
prophetic(al) profético
prophylactic profiláctico
propinquity propincuidad *f*; (relationship) parentesco
propitiate propiciar
propitiation propiciación *f*
propitiator propiciador *m* (-ora *f*)
propitious propicio
propitiousness lo propicio
proportion *n* proporción *f*; **in ~ as a** medida que; **in ~ to** en proporción con; **out of ~** desproporcionado; **be out of ~ to** no guardar proporción con; **get things out of all ~, lose one's sense of ~** desorbitarse; *v* proporcionar; (share out) repartir; **well-~ed** bien proporcionado
proportional proporcional; **~ representation** representación *f* proporcional
proportionate proporcionado
proposal proposición *f*; (scheme) proyecto; **~ of marriage** oferta de matrimonio; *fam* declaración *f*
propose *vt* proponer¹⁹; (offer) ofrecer¹⁴; **~ a toast to** brindar por; *vi* (marriage) pedir (i)³ la mano, *fam* declararse (**to** a); **~ to pensar** (ie)²ᵃ+*infin*, **I ~ to speak to him** pienso hablarle; **~ that** sugerir (ie)²ᶜ que +*subj*, **I ~ that we write to him** sugiero que le escribamos
proposer proponente *m*+*f*
proposition proposición *f*; (offer) oferta; (suggestion) sugestión *f*; **it's a difficult ~** es un problema difícil
propound proponer¹⁹
proprietary propietario; **~ article** producto patentado; **~ medicine** medicina patentada; **~ name** nombre exclusivo
proprietor dueño
proprietress dueña
propriety decoro; **the proprieties** las convenciones
propulsion propulsión *f*

prorogation prórroga
prorogue prorrogar⁵
prosaic prosaico
proscenium proscenio
proscribe proscribir (*past part* proscrito)
proscription proscripción *f*
prose prosa; **~ works** obras en prosa; **~ writer** prosista *m*+*f*
prosecute (carry on) proseguir (i)³⁺¹¹; *leg* procesar; **~ a claim** entablar una acción judicial
prosecuting: ~ attorney/counsel fiscal *m*
prosecution (carrying out) cumplimiento; *leg* (suit) acusación *f*; (party) parte acusadora
prosecutor acusador *m* (-ora *f*); **public ~** fiscal *m*
proselyte prosélito
proselytism proselitismo
proselytize ganar prosélitos
prosody métrica
prospect *n* (view) vista; (outlook) perspectiva; (expectation) esperanza; (chance) probabilidad; *f*; **he has good ~s** él tiene porvenir; **hold out a ~ of** tener esperanza de; *vt* explorar; *vi* **~ for** buscar⁴
prospecting (for minerals) prospección *f*
prospective anticipado; **~ son-in-law** futuro yerno; **~ visit** próxima visita
prospector prospector *m*
prospectus prospecto
prosper *vt* fomentar; *vi* prosperar
prosperity prosperidad *f*
prosperous próspero
prostate *n* próstata; *adj* prostático
prostitute *n* prostituta; *fam* ramera; *euph* fulana; (male) *sl* chapero; *v* prostituir¹⁶
prostitution prostitución *f*; (male) *sl* chaperismo
prostrate *adj* +*fig* postrado; *v* postrar; **~ o.s.** postrarse
prostration postración *f*
prosy aburrido
protagonist protagonista *m*+*f*
protect proteger⁸ (**from** de, contra)
protection protección *f*; **~ tariff** arancel *m* proteccionista
protectionist *n*+*adj* proteccionista *m*+*f*
protective protector (-ora *f*); **~ coating** película protectora; **in ~ custody** en custodia protectora; **~ wall** pared *f* de protección

protector protector *m* (-ora *f*)

protectorate protectorado

protégé protegido; *fam* criatura, **Quayle was Bush's** ~ Quayle era la criatura de Bush

protein proteína

protest *n* protesta; ~ **song** canción *f* de protesta; **under** ~ haciendo objeciones; *v* (affirm) declarar enérgicamente; ~ **against** protestar de; ~ **that** protestar de que

Protestant *n+adj* protestante *m+f*

Protestantism protestantismo

protestation protestas *fpl*

protester el *m*/la que protesta

protesting *n* protestas *fpl*; *adj* protestador (-ora *f*)

protocol *n* protocolo; *v* protocolizar[7]

proton protón (-ones) *m*

protoplasm protoplasma *m*

prototype prototipo

protract prolongar[5]

protraction prolongación *f*

protractor transportador *m*

protrude *vt* sacar[4] fuera; *vi* sobresalir[19]

protruding: ~ **eyes** ojos *mpl* saltones; ~ **teeth** dientes *mpl* salidos

protrusion proyección *f*; *med* el salir hacia fuera

protuberance protuberancia

protuberant protuberante

proud orgulloso; (arrogant) arrogante; (haughty) altivo; (imposing) imponente; ~ **as a peacock** presumido como un faisán; **be** ~ **of** estar[19] orgulloso de; **do s.o.** ~ tratarle a uno magníficamente; *med* inflamado; (raised) levantado

provable (com)probable

prove *vt* (com)probar (ue)[1a]; ~ **a will** hacer[19] público un testamento; **he** ~**d the experts wrong** él destruyó las previsiones de los expertos; *vi* resultar, **it** ~**d impossible** resultó imposible

proven: non-~ **verdict** veredicto no comprobado

provenance (sitio de) origen *m*

Provençal *n+adj* provenzal *m*

Provence Provenza

provender forraje *m*

proverb refrán (-anes) *m*; **Proverbs** *bibl* Proverbios *mpl*

proverbial proverbial

provide proveer[17]; (stipulate) estipular;

~**d (that)** a condición de que +*subj*

~ **against** precaverse contra

~ **for** (maintain) mantener[19]; (plan) hacer[19] preparativos para; (anticipate) prever[19]

~ **with** abastecer[14] de; ~ **o.s. with** proveerse de

providence providencia; **Divine Providence** Divina Providencia; (thrift) economía

provident providente; (thrifty) previsor; ~ **society** sociedad *f* de ayuda mutua

providential providencial

provider proveedor *m* (-ora *f*)

providing a condición de que +*subj*

province *geog* provincia; (sphere) esfera; **that is not my** ~ eso no es de mi competencia

provincial *n* provinciano; *adj* provincial; *pej* pueblerino

provincialism provincialismo

proving: ~**-ground** campo de prueba

provision *n* estipulación *f*; ~**s** provisiones; **make** ~ **for** (*see* **provide for**), (in future) asegurar el porvenir de; ~ **merchant** vendedor *m* (-ora *f*) de comestibles

provisional interino; (conditional) condicional

provisioning abastecimiento

proviso estipulación (-ones) *f*

provisory provisional

provocation provocación (-ones) *f*

provocative provocativo

provocatively de manera provocativa

provoke provocar[4]; ~ **s.o. to** provocar[4] a uno a que +*subj*; (deliberately) incitar, ~ **s.o. to** incitarle a uno a que +*subj*; ~ **to anger** irritar; **do not** ~ **me!** *fam* ¡no me pinches!

provoker provocador *m* (-ora *f*)

provoking provocativo; (annoying) irritante

provost preboste *m*; (university) rector *m*; (Scots) alcalde *m*

prow proa

prowess (skill) destreza; (valour) valor *m*

prowl *n* (*esp* when searching) ronda; **be on the** ~ rondar; ~**-car** *US* coche *m*/*SA* carro de policía; *v* (*esp* when searching) rondar en busca de; (stroll) vagar[5]; (wander stealthily) merodear

prowler (*esp* when searching) rondador *m* (-ora *f*); (stealthy wanderer) merodeador *m* (-ora *f*)

prowling (*esp* when searching) ronda; (wandering stealthily) merodeo

prox (**proximo**) del mes próximo

proximity proximidad *f*

proxy poder *m*; (person) apoderado; **by ~** por poderes

prude mojigata

prudence prudencia

prudent prudente

prudery mojigatería

prudish mojigato

¹ **prune** *n* (fruit) ciruela pasa

² **prune** *v* (trim) podar

pruner podadera de varilla

pruning poda; **~ hook** podadera; **~ shears** podadera *f*

prurience lascivia

prurient lascivo

Prussia Prusia

Prussian *n* + *adj* prusiano; **~ blue** azul *m* de Prusia

prussic: ~ acid ácido prúsico

pry fisgonear; **~ into** entrometerse en

prying *n* fisgoneo; *adj* fisgón

P.S. (**postscript**) P.D. (posdata)

psalm salmo

psalmist salmista *m*

psalmody salmodia

psalter salterio

pseud *n* (pseudo-intellectual) seudo-intelectual; *adj* seudo, falso

pseudonym seudónimo

pseudonymous seudónimo

pshaw! ¡bah!

psittacosis psitacosis *f*

psyche (p)sique *f*

psychedelic (p)sicodélico

psychiatric (p)siquiátrico

psychiatrist (p)siquiatra *m* + *f*

psychiatry (p)siquiatría

psychic(al) (p)síquico

psychoanalyst (p)sicoanalista *m* + *f*

psychoanalytical (p)sicoanalítico

psychoanalyse (p)sicoanalizar⁷

psychoanalysis (p)sicoanálisis *m*

psychological (p)sicológico

psychologist (p)sicólogo

psychology (p)sicología

psychopath alienado; (p)sicópata *m* + *f*

psychopathic (p)sicopático

psychopathy (p)sicopatía

psychosexual (p)sicosexual

psychosis (p)sicosis *f*

psychosomatic (p)sicosomático

psychotherapist (p)sicoterapeuta *m* + *f*

psychotherapy (p)sicoterapia

psychotic (p)sicótico

P.T. (**physical training**) ejercicios gimnásticos; (school lesson) gimnasia

ptarmigan lagopardo

pterodactyl pterodáctilo

P.T.O. (**please turn over**) v.a.d. (véase al dorso)

pub taberna; pub *m*; *SA* posada; **~-crawl** chateo; **go on a ~-crawl** ir¹⁹ de chateo

puberty pubertad *f*

pubescence pubescencia

pubescent pubescente

pubic púbico

pubis pubis *m*

public *n* + *adj* público; **in ~** en público; **the general ~** el público en general; **make ~** divulgar⁵; **~ address system** sistema de altavoces; **~ assistance** asistencia social; **~ enemy** enemigo público; **~ funds** hacienda pública; **~ house** *see* **pub**; **~ lavatory** servicios públicos; **~ library** biblioteca pública; **commit a ~ nuisance** cometer un atentado contra la decencia pública; **~ official** empleado público; **~ opinion** opinión pública; **~ ownership** nacionalización *f*; **in ~ ownership** nacionalizado; **~ prosecutor** fiscal *m*; **~ relations** (**officer**) (encargado de) relaciones públicas; **~ school** internado privado, *US* escuela pública; **~ spirit** civismo; **~-spirited** lleno de civismo; **~ works** obras públicas

publican tabernero

publication publicación *f*

publicist publicista *m* + *f*

publicity publicidad *f*; **~ agent** agente *m* de publicidad; **~ stunt** montaje *m* publicitario

publicize publicitar

publish publicar⁴; (of book *etc*) editar; **~ abroad** pregonar a los cuatro vientos; **~ the banns of marriage** correr las amonestaciones

publisher editor *m*

publishing publicación *f*, edición *f*; **~ house/firm** casa editorial

puce (de) color purpúreo rojizo

puck duende *m*; (ice-hockey) puck *m*

pucker *n* (facial) arruga; (sewing) frunce *m*; *v* arrugar⁵; fruncir¹³; ∼ **one's brow** fruncir¹³ el ceño

puckering (facial) arrugas *fpl*; (sewing) fruncido

puckish travieso

pudding pudín (-ines) *m*

puddle *n* charco

pudenda partes *fpl* pudendas; *fam* bajos *mpl*

puerile pueril

puerility puerilidad *f*

puerperal: ∼ **fever** fiebre *f* puerperal

Puerto-Rican *n+adj* portorriqueño

puff *n* (of air) soplido; (of tobacco smoke) bocanada; (of locomotive) resoplido; (powder-puff) borla (para polvos); (cake) pastelillo; (advertisement) bombo; (homosexual) marica *m*; ∼ **of wind** ráfaga de aire; ∼ **adder** víbora africana; ∼-**ball** (fungus) bejín (-ines) *m*; ∼-**pastry** hojaldre *m*; *v* soplar; ∼ **at** (pipe) chupar; ∼ **out smoke** (of smoker) lanzar⁷ bocanadas de humo, (of train) echar humo, **the train** ∼**ed out of the station** el tren salió de la estación echando humo; ∼**ed** *med* hinchado; **be** ∼**ed** (out of breath) estar¹⁹ sin aliento; **be** ∼**ed up with pride** engreírse; ∼**ed sleeves** mangas *fpl* de bullón

puffed: ∼ **rice/wheat** arroz/trigo inflado

puffer (train) locomotora

puffin frailecillo

puffiness hinchazón *m*

puffy (of wind) a ráfagas; (swollen) hinchado

pug doguillo; ∼-**nosed** chato

pugilism pugilato

pugilist púgil *m*

pugilistic pugilístico

pugnacious pugnaz (-ces)

pugnacity pugnacidad *f*

puke vomitar

pukka (real) genuino; (posh) elegante

pull *n* tirón (-ones) *m*; **give a** ∼ (at) tirar (de); (at oars) golpe *m* de remos; (at bottle) trago; (at pipe) chupada; *print* primeras pruebas *fpl*; (attraction) atracción *f*; (influence) influencia, **he has plenty of** ∼ él tiene buenas aldabas; **it will be a long hard** ∼ será largo el camino; ∼-**switch** *elect* interruptor

m de tiro; **bell-**∼ cuerda; *v* tirar de; (drag) arrastrar; (gather crop) coger¹⁴; *print* imprimir; (row) remar; ∼ **a face** hacer¹⁹ una mueca; ∼ **a long face** poner¹⁹ cara larga; ∼ **a muscle** torcerse (ue)¹ᵇ⁺¹⁵ un músculo; ∼ **s.o.'s leg** tomar el pelo a alguien; ∼ **a fast one on s.o.** engañar a uno; ∼ **to pieces** despedazar⁷, *fig* ponerle¹⁹ como un trapo a; ∼ **a tooth** sacar⁴ una muela; ∼ **the trigger** apretar el gatillo; ∼ **the wool over s.o.'s eyes** engañarle a uno como a un chino

∼ **about** arrastrar por todas partes; (handle) manosear; (spoil) estropear

∼ **ahead** marchar adelante

∼ **along** arrastrar

∼ **apart** *vt* separar; romper; *vi* separarse

∼ **at** tirar de; ∼ **at a bottle** tomar un trago de una botella; ∼ **at a pipe** fumar la pipa

∼ **back** tirar hacia atrás

∼ **down** (demolish) derribar; (of prices) (re)bajar; (humble) humillar, *fam* tirar

∼-**in** *n* café *esp* para camioneros

∼ **in** *vt* tirar hacia adentro; (rope) cobrar; (arrest) detener¹⁹; *vi mot* pararse al lado de la carretera; (train) llegar⁵ (a la estación)

∼ **off** arrancar⁴ de un tirón; (win) ganar; ∼ **off a deal** cerrar (ie)²ᵃ un negocio; ∼ **it off** llevarlo a cabo

∼ **on** (socks *etc*) ponerse¹⁹; (oars) seguir (i)³⁺¹¹ remando

∼ **open** abrir (*past part* abierto) de un tirón

∼-**out** *n* (section of periodical) coleccionable *m*; *mil* retirada; *adj* extensible; ∼-**out leaf** (of table) hoja extensible

∼ **out** *vt* hacer¹⁹ salir; (teeth, swords, handkerchiefs) sacar⁴; (hair) arrancar⁴; *mil* retirar; *vi mot* conducir¹⁵ más cerca del centro de la carretera; (train) salir¹⁹ (de la estación); *mil* retirarse

∼-**through** *n* cordel *m* de limpiar

∼ **through** *v* reponerse¹⁹

∼ **together** obrar de acuerdo; ∼ **o.s. together** serenarse; ∼ **yourself together!** ¡cálmese!

∼-**up** *n* café *esp* para camioneros

∼ **up** *vt* (by the roots) arrancar⁴; (horse)

sofrenar; *mot* parar; (socks *etc*) subir;
~ **up one's socks** *fig* despabilarse;
(interrupt) interrumpir, (chide) reñir
(i)³; *vi* (halt) pararse; ~ **o.s. up** repri-
mirse
puller (*see* pull); el/la que tira, saca *etc*
pullet poll(it)a
pulley polea; ~ **wheel** roldana
pulling tracción *f*
Pullman: ~ **car** coche *m* Pullman
pullover jersey (-eyes) *m*
pulmonary pulmonar
pulp *n* pulpa; (paper, wood) pasta; **beat
to a** ~ hacer puré; ~ **magazine** revista
sensacionalista; *v* reducir¹⁵ a pulpa/
pasta
pulpiness calidad *f* de pulposo
pulpit púlpito
pulpy pulposo
pulsate latir
pulsation latido
pulse *n* pulso; **feel s.o.'s** ~ tomar el pulso
a alguien; *v* latir
pulverization pulverización *f*
pulverize pulverizar⁷
puma puma
pumice-stone piedra pómez
pummel aporrear
¹ **pump** *n* bomba; *naut* pompa; *v* bombear; (question) sonsacar⁴; ~ **dry**
secar⁴ con bomba; ~ **up** inflar
² **pump** (slipper) zapatilla
pumpernickel pan *m* de centeno
pumpkin calabaza
pun *n* juego de palabras (**on** sobre); *v*
jugar (ue)¹ᵃ del vocablo (**on** a); hacer
juegos de palabras
Punch Don Cristóbal; ~ **and Judy show**
teatro de marionetas
¹ **punch** (blow) puñetazo, golpe *m*;
(energy) vigor *m*; (instrument) punzón (-ones) *m*; **pull one's** ~**es** no emplear toda su fuerza; ~**-bag** saco de
arena; ~**-ball** pelota de boxeo; ~**-
drunk** torta, **he is** ~**-drunk** él está
torta; ~**-line** colofón *m* de un chiste;
~**-up** pelea; *v* dar¹⁹ un puñetazo; **I'll
~ you on the nose!** ¡te romperé las
narices!; (with instrument) agujerear,
~ **a ticket** picar⁴ un billete, ~**ed card**
ficha perforada
² **punch** (drink) ponche *m*; ~**-bowl** ponchera
punching (boxing skill) pegada; ~**-bag**

saco de arena
punctilious etiquetero
punctual puntual
punctuality puntualidad *f*
punctuate +*fig* puntuar
punctuation puntuación *f*; ~**-mark**
signo de puntuación
puncture *n mot* pinchazo; (of skin)
punzada; **have a** ~ tener¹⁹ un pinchazo, *fam* pinchársele a uno la rueda;
mend a ~ reparar un neumático pinchado; *v* pinchar, punzar
pundit experto
pungency picante *m*; *fig* mordacidad *f*
pungent picante; *fig* mordaz
puniness encanijamiento
punish castigar⁵; +*leg* penar, **society
~es traffic in drugs** la sociedad pena
el comercio en drogas; (ill-treat) maltratar
punishable castigable
punishment castigo; (ill-treatment) tratamiento severo; (boxing) encaje *m*;
take ~ encajar, **Urtaín took a lot of
~ in the first round** Urtaín encajó mucho
en el primer asalto; ~**-cell** celda de
castigo, *sl* submarino
punitive punitivo
punk *n* basura; **punky** *m*+*f*; (homosexual) maricón (-ones) *m*; *adj* malo
punnet barqueta
punster persona aficionada a los juegos
de palabras
¹ **punt** *n* batea; ~**-pole** pértiga; *v* impeler
con pértiga; **go** ~**ing** ir¹⁹ en batea
² **punt** (kick) *n* puntapié *m*; *v* dar un
puntapié al balón
³ **punt** *n* apuesta; *v* (gamble) apostar
(ue)¹ᵃ
¹ **punter** *naut* el que impele una batea
² **punter** (kicker) el que da un puntapié al
balón
³ **punter** (gambler) apostador *m*
puny encanijado; ~ **effort** esfuerzo débil
pup *n* cachorro; *v* parir
pupa crisálida
pupil alumno, alumna; *anat* pupila
puppet (glove) títere *m*; (string) marioneta; ~ **government** gobierno de títe-
res; ~**-like** fantochesco; ~**-master**
marionetista *m*; ~**-show** teatro de títe-
res/marionetas
puppy perrito; ~ **fat** gordura juvenil
puppyish parecido a un cachorro

purblind cegato; (short-sighted) +*fig* miope

purchase *n* compra; (hold) agarre seguro; (leverage) apalancamiento; ~ **price** precio de compra; ~ **tax** impuesto sobre compras; **free of** ~ **tax** exento de impuesto; *v* comprar

purchaser comprador *m* (-ora *f*)

purchasing: ~ **power** poder *m* adquisitivo

pure puro; ~-**blooded** de pura sangre; ~-**bred** de raza; ~ **mathematics** matemática pura

purée puré *m*

pureness pureza

purgation purgación *f*

purgative *n* purga; *adj* purgativo

purgatory purgatorio

purge *n* purgación *f*; *med*+*pol* purga; *v* purgar[5]; (kill) liquidar

purification purificación *f*

purificatory purificatorio

purifier purificador *m*; (water-~) depurador *m*

purify purificar[4]; (water) depurar; *metal* acrisolar

purism purismo

purist *n*+*adj* purista *m*+*f*

Puritan *n*+*adj* puritano

puritanical puritano

Puritanism puritanismo

purity pureza

purl *n* punto del revés; **two plain and one** ~ dos del derecho y uno del revés; *v* hacer[19] un punto del revés

purlieu límite *m* (de un bosque); ~**s** alrededores *mpl*, (slums) tugurios *mpl*

purloin robar

purple *n* color morado; *adj* morado; ~ **patch** *lit* trozo florido

purport *n* significado; *v* dar[19] a entender (that que); ~ **to** pretender +*infin*; significar

purpose *n* intención *f*; **for the** ~ **of** con el propósito de; **on** ~ expresamente, *fam* queriendo; **to good** ~ con buenos resultados; **to no** ~ en vano; **it will serve my** ~ servirá para lo que yo quiero; *v* proponerse[19]

purposeful determinado

purposeless sin objeto

purposely queriendo; **she did it** ~ ella lo hizo queriendo

purposive que tiene un objeto

purr *n* *mot*+*zool* ronroneo; *v* ronronear; *fig* decir[19]/hablar melosamente

purse *n* (+boxing) bolsa; monedero; **hold the** ~-**strings** tener[19] las llaves de la casa; *v* ~ **the lips** fruncir[13] los labios

purser contador *m* de navío

pursuance: in ~ **of** cumpliendo

pursuant: ~ **to** de acuerdo con

pursue +*fig* perseguir (i)[3+11]; (seek) buscar[4]; (investigate) proseguir (i)[3+11]; (occupation *etc*) ejercer[14]; ~ **a life of pleasure** dedicarse[4] a una vida de placer

pursuer perseguidor *m* (-ora *f*)

pursuit persecución *f*; (seeking) busca; (investigation) prosecución *f*; (occupation) ejercicio; (dedication) dedicación *f*; (pastime) pasatiempo; **in** ~ **of** en busca de; ~-**plane** (avión *m* de) caza *m*

purulence purulencia

purulent purulento

purvey abastecer[14]

purveyance abastecimiento

purveyor abastecedor *m* (-ora *f*)

purview alcance *m*

pus pus *m*

push *n* empujón (-ones) *m*; (energy) energía; *mil* avance *m*; **at a** ~ en un aprieto; **get the** ~ ser[19] despedido; **give s.o. the** ~ despedir (i)[3] a uno; **make a** ~ hacer[19] un gran esfuerzo; **don't** ~ **your luck** no juegue(s) con la suerte; ~-**bike** bicicleta; ~-**button** botón (-ones) *m* de llamada, *fam* timbre *m*; ~-**button control** mando por botón; ~-**cart** carretilla; ~-**pin** chincheta; ~-**switch** *elect* interruptor *m* de botón; *v* empujar; (claim) proseguir (i)[3+11]; (drugs) traficar[4] en drogas; (incite) incitar; (product) hacer[19] una campaña publicitaria a favor de; (scheme) promover (ue)[1b]; **be** ~**ed for time/money** no tener[19] mucho tiempo/dinero

~ **against** empujar contra

~ **around: no one's going to** ~ **me around** no soy el monigote de nadie

~ **aside/away** apartar con la mano

~ **back** (people) hacer[19] retroceder; (hair) echar atrás

~ **down** empujar hacia abajo; (knock over) derribar a empujones

~ **forward** *vt* empujar hacia delante;

(scheme) llevar adelante; *vi* adelantarse a empujones; *fig* ~ **o.s. forward** darse[19] importancia; (interrupt) entrometerse

~ **in** *vt* introducir[15] a la fuerza; (pin *etc*) clavar; *vi* entrar a la fuerza

~ **off** *vt* rechazar[7] con la mano; *fam* quitar de encima (de); *vi* (go away) marcharse; *naut* desatracar[4]; ~ **off!** ¡quítate de encima!

~ **on** (continue) seguir (i)[3+11] adelante; (advance) avanzar[7]

~ **open** abrir (*past part* abierto) a la fuerza

~ **out** *vt* empujar hacia fuera; (expel) echar; ~ **out one's tongue** sacar[4] la lengua; *vi naut* zarpar

~-**over** *n* cosa muy fácil; (person) persona fácil de (con)vencer; **she's a ~- over** ella es una facilona

~ **over** *v* derribar

~ **through** (task *etc*) despachar rápidamente; ~ **one's way through** abrirse (*past part* abierto) paso empujando

~ **to** cerrar (ie)[2a] empujando

~ **up** empujar hacia arriba; (window) levantar; ~ **up the daisies** estar[19] sepultado

pusher traficante *m+f* de drogas; *sl* camello

pushing *n* empujones *mpl*; **by ~ and shoving** a empujones; *adj* emprendedor (-ora *f*); *pej* agresivo

pusillanimity pusilanimidad *f*

pusillanimous pusilánime

puss minino; ~!~! ¡mis! ¡mis!

pussy minino (-íes) *m*; ~**foot** prohibicionista *m+f*; *v* ~**foot** andar[19] con paso de gato, (not commit oneself) no declararse

pustule pústula

[1] **put** poner[19]; (lay) colocar[4]; (estimate) calcular; ~ **s.o. in the picture** orientarle a uno; ~ **in order** (classify) ordenar, (mend) arreglar, (tidy) recoger[8]; ~ **out of order** desordenar, (machine *etc*) estropear; ~ **in writing** poner[19] por escrito; **I ~ it to you** le digo; **I ~ him on the right lines** le encarrilé; **let me ~ it this way** permítame que lo exprese así; **stay ~** quedarse en su sitio; (for many phrases similar to the following see the relative *n* or *adj*) ~ **a question** hacer[19] una pregunta; ~ **the**

weight lanzar[7] el peso; ~ **wise** poner[19] al tanto

~ **about** *naut* cambiar de rumbo; (spread the news) dar[19] a entender que; (vex) desconcertar (ie)[2a]

~ **across** (communicate) hacer[19] entender; (persuade) hacer[19] aceptar; ~ **it across** (outwit) engañar

~ **ashore** echar en tierra (a)

~ **aside** (~ **to one side**) poner[19] aparte; (hoard) ahorrar[7]

~ **away** (see ~ **aside**); (~ **in its place**) poner[19] en su sitio; *fam* (eat) zampar; (criminal) encarcelar; (lunatic) meter en un manicomio

~ **back** devolver (ue)[1b] (*past part* devuelto) a su sitio; *naut* volver (ue)[1b] (*past part* vuelto) al puerto; (postpone) aplazar[7]; ~ **one's watch back** retrasar el reloj

~ **by** (~ **on one side**) poner[19] aparte; (hoard) ahorrar

~ **down** (burden) poner[19] en el suelo; (umbrella) cerrar (ie)[2a]; (suppress) suprimir; (make a note of) apuntar; (name in a list *etc*) inscribir (*past part* inscrito); *comm* sentar (ie)[2a] (en la cuenta); *vet* matar, **he had the injured dog ~ down** mandó matar al perro herido; **she ~ down the book and turned off the light** ella dejó el libro y apagó la luz; ~ **it down to** atribuirlo[16] a

~ **forth** (sprout) echar

~ **forward** (clock) adelantar[7]; (function) adelantar; (suggest) proponer[19]; ~ **o.s. forward** ofrecerse[14]

~ **in** meter; (claim) presentar; (interpolate) interponer; *naut* hacer[19] escala (**at** en); ~ **in a good word for** hablar a favor de; ~ **in for** (apply for) solicitar; ~ **in a lot of time to** dedicar[4] mucho tiempo a

~ **off** (postpone) aplazar[7]; (discourage) quitar las ganas a; (dissuade) disuadir; (evade) evadir; (mislead) desviar (de); (prevaricate) dar[19] largas (a)

~ **on** (clothes) ponerse[19], (hurriedly) echarse; ~ **on shoes** calzarse[7]; ~ **on a charge** meter un paquete a; ~ **on a good show** *fig* hacer[19] méritos; ~ **on the light** encender (ie)[2b] la luz; ~ **a strain on** poner[19] a prueba; ~ **one's finger on it** *fig* poner[19] el dedo en la llaga; ~ **on weight** engordar; ~ **it on** exagerar, (give o.s. airs) darse[19] tono

~ **out** extender (ie)[2b]; (head) asomar; (hand) alargar[5]; (tongue) sacar[4]; (sprout) echar; *anat* dislocar[4]; *print* publicar[4]; *naut* hacerse[19] a la mar; (expel) poner[19] en la calle; (extinguish) apagar[5]; (bother) molestar; (upset) desconcertar (ie)[2a]

~ **over** (product) hacer[19] aceptar; (meaning) comunicar[4]; ~ **it over on s.o.** engañarle a uno; ~ **o.s. over** impresionar (con su personalidad)

~ **right** (express correctly) expresar correctamente; (correct) corregir[9]; **I ~ my watch right (by the radio)** puse mi reloj (con la radio)

~ **through** *tel* poner[19] con, ~ **me through to …!** ¡póngame con …!; ~ **s.o. through his paces** registrar la capacidad de uno; (proposal) hacer[19] aceptar

~ **to** *naut* dirigir[9] hacia tierra; ~ **to bed** acostar (ue)[1a]; ~ **to death** matar, *leg* ajusticiar; ~ **to the test** poner[19] a prueba; **be hard ~ to** tener[19] dificultad en +*infin*

~ **together** (join) juntar; (assemble) montar; ~ **two and two together** atar cabos

~-**up** *adj* fraudulento; ~-**up job** asunto fraudulento

~ **up** *v* (hand) levantar; (erect) construir[16]; (candidate) nombrar; (guest) hospedar; (prices) aumentar; (tent) montar; (umbrella) abrir (*past part* abierto); **he ~ up a million pesetas** él contribuyó un millón de pesetas; ~ **up for** presentarse como candidato a; ~ **s.o. up to** incitarle a uno; ~ **up with** aguantar

~ **upon** molestar

[2] **put** *see* **putt**

putative putativo

putrefaction putrefacción *f*

putrefy pudrirse

putrescence putrescencia *f*

putrescent putrescente

putrid podrido; pútrido; *fam* malísimo

putsch golpe *m* de estado; alzamiento

putt *n* put(t); *v* hacer[19] un put(t)

puttee polaina

putter (golf) putter *m*

[1] **putting** colocación *f*; ~ **the shot/weight** lanzamiento del peso; ~ **forward of the clocks** adelanto *m* de los relojes; ~-**off** tardanza; ~-**up** (as candidate) candidatura

[2] **putting** put(t)es *mpl*; ~-**green** pista de golf en miniatura

putty *n* masilla; *v* enmasillar

puzzle *n* misterio; problema; (pastime) rompecabezas *m sing+pl*; (jigsaw ~) puzzle *m*; (verbal game) acertijo; *v* (intrigue) intrigar[5]; (perplex) desconcertar (ie)[2a]; dejar perplejo; ~ **out** (decipher) descifrar; (solve) resolver (ue)[1b] (*past part* resuelto); ~ **over** romperse (*past part* roto) la cabeza para descifrar/resolver; **I'm ~d by me** tiene perplejo

puzzler problema *m* difícil

puzzling misterioso

puzzlement enredo; desconcierto

pygmy *n+adj* pigmeo

pyjamas: pair of ~ pijama *m*; ~-**jacket** chaqueta del pijama

pylon pilón *m*; *elect* torre *f*/poste de conducción eléctrica

pyorrhoea piorrea

pyramid pirámide *f*

pyramidal piramidal

pyre pira; *fig* hoguera

Pyrenees Pirineos *mpl*

pyrethrum pietro

pyrotechnic pirotécnico; ~**s** pirotécnica

Pythagoras Pitágoras

python pitón (-ones) *m*

Q

q (letter) ku *f*; Q (question) P (pregunta)

¹ quack *n* graznido; ~-~ cuacuá *m*; *v* graznar

² quack *n* curandero; ~ **remedy** medicina de curandero; *adj* falso

quad (open space) patio; ~s cuatrillizos *mpl*

quadrangle (open space) patio; *geom* cuadrángulo

quadrangular cuadrangular

quadrant cuadrante *m*

quadratic de segundo grado

quadrilateral *n*+*adj* cuadrilátero

quadrille rigodón (-ones) *m*

quadruped cuadrúpedo

quadruple *n*+*adj* cuádruplo; *v* cuadruplicar(se)⁴

quadruplet cuatrillizo

quaff beberse

quagmire tremedal *m*

¹ quail codorniz (-ces) *f*

² quail acobardarse

quaint curioso; (picturesque) pintoresco

quaintness singularidad *f*; (picturesqueness) lo pintoresco

quake *n* terremoto; *v* temblar (ie)²ᵃ

Quaker cuáquero

Quakerism cuaquerismo

qualification (by training) aptitud *f*; (by exam) diploma; (limitation) modificación *f*; *gramm* calificación *f*; **have the necessary** ~s llenar los requisitos; **without** ~ (unreservedly) sin reservas

qualify (by training) habilitar(se); (by exam) diplomar(se); (limit) modificar⁴; *gramm* calificar⁴; **he does not ~ for the post** él no llena los requisitos para el empleo

qualifying eliminatorio; ~ **round** *sp* eliminatoria

qualitative cualitativo

quality (type) calidad *f*; (characteristic) cualidad *f*; (social) categoría, **people of** ~ gente *f* de categoría; **the** ~ la

aristocracia; **of good/poor** ~ de buena/mala calidad

qualm escrúpulo; *med* náusea; ~s **of conscience** remordimiento(s)

quandary dilema *m*; (difficulty) apuro; **be in a** ~ estar¹⁹ en un aprieto

quango ente *m* cuasi autónomo del estado

quantify fijar una cantidad

quantitative cuantitativo

quantity cantidad *f*; (large amount) gran cantidad; **unknown** ~ +*fig* incógnita; ~ **surveyor** aparejador *m*

quantum cantidad *f*; *phys* cuanto; ~ **theory** teoría de los cuantos

quarantine *n* cuarentena; **be in** ~ estar¹⁹ en cuarentena; *v* poner¹⁹ en cuarentena

quarrel *n* riña; *SA* disgusto; **have a** ~ **with** (i)³⁺¹⁸ con; **have no** ~ **(with)** no tener¹⁹ nada en contra (de); **pick a** ~ **(with)** buscar⁴ camorra (con); *v* reñir (i)³⁺¹⁸ **(with** con); (object) oponerse¹⁹ **(with** a)

quarrelsome reñidor (-ora *f*)

¹ quarry *n* cantera; ~**man** cantero; *v* sacar⁴

² quarry (prey) presa

quart cuarto de galón (1,136 litros)

quarter *n* (+ moon) cuarto; (district) barrio, **Latin** ~ barrio latino; (meat) pierna; (direction) parte *f*, **from all** ~s de todas partes; (weight) 28 libras (12,23 kilos); (*US* coin) 25 centavos; *her* cuartel *m*; (three months) trimestre *m*, ~-**day** primer día *m* del trimestre; (mercy) cuartel *m*, **give** ~ **to the enemy** dar¹⁹ cuartel al enemigo; ~s alojamiento, *mil* cuartel *m*; ~ **of an hour** cuarto de hora; **at a** ~ **past eleven** a las once y cuarto; **it's a** ~ **to three** son las tres menos cuarto; **at close** ~s de cerca; **open fire at close** ~s abrir (*past part* abierto) fuego a quemarropa; ~**deck** cubierta de popa; ~-**final** *sp* cuarto de final; ~-**finalist** (team)

940

equipo/(player) jugador *m* en el cuarto de final; ~**master** *mil* furriel *m*, *naut* maestre *m* de víveres; ~**master general** intendente *m* del ejército; ~**master's store** intendencia; ~**sessions** sesión *f* trimestral (del tribunal municipal); ~**-staff** barra; ~**-tone** *mus* cuarto de tono; *v* cuartear; (meat) descuartizar[7]; *her* cuartelar; (in barracks) acuartelar

quarterly *n* publicación *f* trimestral; *adj* trimestral; *adv* cada tres meses

quartet cuarteto; **string** ~ cuarteto de instrumentos de cuerda

quarto *n* (book) libro en cuarto; (paper) papel *m* en cuarto; *adj* en cuarto

quartz cuarzo

quash anular

quasi cuasi

quatrain cuarteta

quaver *n* temblor *m*; *mus* (sound) trémolo; *mus* (note) corchea; *v* temblar, *mus* gorjear; **in a quavering voice** con voz temblorosa

quavery tembloroso, trémolo

quay(side) muelle *m*

queasiness *med* náuseas *fpl*

queasy (sickness) mareado; (on-coming sickness) nauseabundo

queen *n* (+chess) reina; (cards) dama, reina; (*Sp* cards) caballo; (homosexual) mariquita *m*; ~ **bee** abeja reina; ~**-like** regio; ~ **mother** reina madre; *v* (chess) coronar; ~ **it** pavonearse

queenly regio

queer *n* (homosexual) maricón (-ones) *m*; (effeminate male) pisaverde *m*; *adj* (strange) extraño, (mad) chiflado; (unwell) indispuesto; (suspect) sospechoso; (effeminate) afeminado; (homosexual) maricón; *v* ~ **the pitch for** chafar la guitarra a

queerness (strangeness) extrañeza; (madness) chifladura; (illness) indisposición *f*; (suspicion) sospecha; (femininity) afeminación *f*; (homosexuality) homosexualidad *f*

quell calmar; ~ **a riot** sofocar[4] una revuelta

quench (thirst, fire) apagar[5]; (calm) sosegar[5]; ~ **s.o.'s ardour** aplacar[4] el ardor de

quenchless inapagable

querulous quejumbroso

query *n* pregunta; (sign) (signo de) interrogación *f*; (doubt) duda; *v* preguntar; (doubt) expresar dudas acerca de

quest busca; *SA* pesquisa; **in** ~ **of** en busca de

question *n* pregunta; **ask a** ~ hacer[19] una pregunta; (matter) cuestión *f*, **it's a** ~ **of money** es cuestión de dinero; **the** ~ **is** el caso es; **it's a** ~ **of whether** se trata de si; **there can be no** ~ **about** (**what** ...) no cabe la menor duda acerca de (lo que ...); **beg the** ~ ser[19] una petición de principio; **be beyond** ~ estar[19] fuera de duda; **in** ~ de que se trata; **call in** ~ expresar dudas acerca de; **be out of the** ~ ser[19] imposible; **without** ~ indiscutiblemente; ~**-mark** (signo de) interrogación *f*; ~**-master** interrogador *m*; *vt* (ask) preguntar; (interrogate) interrogar[5]; *vi* (doubt) expresar dudas acerca de

questionable dudoso

questioner interrogador *m* (-ora *f*)

questioning *n* interrogatorio *f*; *adj* interrogativo

questionnaire cuestionario

queue *n* cola; **form a** ~ hacer[19] cola; **jump the** ~ calarse (en la cola); ~**-jumper** uno que no espera su turno en la cola; *v* ~ **up (for)** hacer[19] cola (para)

quibble *n* sutileza; *v* sutilizar[7]

quibbler sofista *m*+*f*

quibbling sofistería

quick *n* **the** ~ **and the dead** los vivos y los muertos; **cut to the** ~ herir (ie)[2c] en lo vivo; *adj* rápido; (intelligent) ágil; **be** ~**!** ¡dése prisa!; **be** ~ **about something** hacer[19] algo de prisa; ~ **to become excited** pronto a la emoción; ~ **to take offence** fácilmente ofendido; ~ **march!** ¡de frente, marchen!; ~**-acting** extrarrápido; ~**-change artist** transformista *m*+*f*; ~**-firing** de tiro rápido; ~**lime** cal viva; ~**sand** arena movediza; ~**-set hedge** seto vivo; ~**silver** azogue *m*; ~ **step** paso rápido; ~**step** (dance) *approx* pasodoble *m*; ~**-tempered** de mal genio; ~**-witted** de genio agudo; *adv* pronto; **as** ~ **as I can** tan pronto como yo pueda; **as** ~ **as possible** lo antes posible

quicken acelerar(se); ~ **one's step** apretar el paso; (enliven) vivificar[4]

quicker: be ~ on the draw than ganarle la mano a

quickie pregunta *f* relámpago

quickly rápidamente; (soon) pronto

quickness rapidez *f*; (liveliness) agilidad *f*; (lightness) ligereza; (of mind) penetración *f*, agudeza

quid (tobacco) mascada de tabaco; (£1) libra esterlina; ~ **pro quo** compensación *f*

quiescence quietud *f*

quiescent quieto

quiet *n* (peace) tranquilidad *f*; (silence) silencio; (stillness) quietud *f*; ~, **please!** ¡silencio, por favor!; **all I want is peace and** ~ sólo quiero que me dejen en paz; **on the** ~ a escondidas; *adj* (peaceful) tranquilo; (silent) silencioso; (not talking) callado; (still) quieto; (gentle) apacible; (without fuss) sin ceremonia; ~ **colour** color sufrido; **all** ~ sin novedad; **be/keep** ~ (no noise) no hacer[19] ruido, (no talking) callarse, (still) estarse[19] quieto; **business is** ~ el negocio está encalmado

quieten (calm) calmar; (tranquillize) tranquilizar(se)[7]; (silence) hacer[19] callar

quietly quedamente; *fam* a la chita callando

quietude quietud *f* -

quietus golpe *m* de gracia

quiff copete *m*

quill cañón (-ones) *m* de pluma; (porcupine) púa; (pen) pluma de ave (para escribir); ~ **fishing float** flotador *m*, veleta

quilt *n* colcha; *v* acolchar

quilting acolchado

quin quintillizo

quince membrillo; (tree) membrillero; ~ **jam** carne *f* de membrillo

quincentenary quinto centenario

quinine quinina

quinsy angina

quintessence quintaesencia

quintet quinteto

quintuple *n* quíntuplo; *v* quintuplicar(se)[4]

quintuplet quintillizo

quip agudeza

quire mano *f* de papel

quirk peculiaridad *f*; (flourish) rasgo; (quip) agudeza

quirky peculiar

quisling *n+adj* quisling *m*; *Sp* quinta columnista *m+f*

quit abandonar; **notice to** ~ aviso de desahucio; (leave) despedirse (i)[3]; (cease) dejar de +*infin*; **be** ~ **of** librarse de

quite (completely) absolutamente, **it** ~ **mystified me** me mistificó completamente; (truly) bien, **she is** ~ **happy here** ella está bien contenta aquí; (rather) bastante, **his family is** ~ **rich** su familia es bastante rica; (as an answer) ~ **(so)!** ¡claro!; **she is** ~ **grown-up** ella es toda una mujer; **that is not** ~ **what I'm looking for** éso no es exactamente lo que busco; **it cost me** ~ **a bit** me costó un pico; ~ **a lot** muchito; **he drinks** ~ **a lot** él bebe lo suyo; ~ **the thing** muy de moda

quits en paz; **be** ~ **with** estar[19] en paz con; **cry** ~ hacer[19] las paces

quitter faltón (-ones) *m*; (from fear) cobarde *m+f*

quiver *n* (for arrows) carcaj *m*; (waver) temblor *m*; *v* estremecerse[14]

qui vive: be on the ~ estar[19] en guardia

Quixote: Don ~ Don Quijote

quixotic quijotesco; ~ **deed** quijotada

quiz *n* encuesta; *rad+TV* concurso radiofónico/televisivo; ~-**master** interrogador *m*; *v* interrogar[5]

quizzical burlón

quod *sl* (prison) jaula

quoit tejo; ~s juego de tejos; **play** ~s jugar (ue)[1a] a tejos

quondam antiguo

quorum quórum *m*

quota cuota

quotability calidad *f* de citable

quotable citable; *comm* cotizable

quotation cita; *comm* cotización *f*; (in) ~ **marks** (entre) comillas *fpl*

quote citar; *comm* cotizar[7]

quotient cociente *m*; **intelligence** ~ cociente intelectual

R

r (letter) erre f
rabbi rabino; (title) rabí
rabbit n conejo; mal jugador m; ~-hutch, ~-warren conejera; ~-punch n golpe m en la nuca; Welsh ~ pan m y queso tostados; v (go rabbiting) cazar[7] conejos; ~ on (go on talking/writing) seguir (i)[3+11] hablando/escribiendo
rabble canalla; ~-rouser agitador m (-ora f)
rabid rabioso; fig fanático
rabies rabia
raccoon mapache m
[1] race sp carrera; fig lucha; (current) corriente f; run a ~ competir (i)[3] en una carrera; ~-card programa m de carreras; ~-course hipódromo, SA cancha; ~-goer aficionado a las carreras de caballos/coches/perros; ~-horse caballo de carreras; ~-meeting concurso hípico; ~-track pista, (for dogs) canódromo, (cars) circuito, (cycles) velódromo; v competir (i)[3] (against con); (hurry) correr (de prisa); mech girar/ir[19] a máxima velocidad; ~ a horse/dog hacer[19] competir un caballo/perro
[2] race raza; human ~ género humano; ~-hatred, ~-problem etc see racial
racer bicicleta/caballo etc de carrera
Rachel Raquel
racial racial; ~ hatred odio entre razas; ~ prejudice prejuicio racial; ~ problem problema m racial
racialism racismo
racialist racista m+f
racily con salero
raciness salero
racing n carreras fpl; adj de carreras; ~ car bólido; ~ calendar calendario de reuniones hípicas; ~-driver corredor m automovilista; ~ (motor-)cyclist corredor m (moto)ciclista
racism racismo
racist n+adj racista m+f
rack n estante m; mech cremallera, ~

and pinion cremallera y piñón; (torture) potro; go to ~ and ruin echarse a perder; ~-rent alquiler m exorbitante; hat-~ percha; luggage-~ portaequipajes m sing; parcel-~ rejilla; plate-~ escurreplatos m sing; v atormentar; (with pain) agobiar; ~ one's brains devanarse los sesos, fam romperse (past part roto) la cabeza
[1] racket sp raqueta; ~s especie de tenis jugado en un frontón
[2] racket (noise) estrépito; (swindle) estafa, fam chanchullo
racketeer estafador m (-ora f)
racketeering chantaje m; crimen organizado
racking n tortura; adj torturante; (of cough) persistente
raconteur anecdotista m+f
racy salado
radar radar m; ~ screen pantalla del radar
radial radial; ~ tyre neumático radial
radiance resplandor m
radiant +fig radiante
radiate radiar; (of feelings) difundir
radiation (ir)radiación f
radiator +mot radiador m; ~ grille rejilla del radiador
radical n bot radical m; pol progresista m+f, fam progre m+f; adj radical; progresista
radicalism bot radicalismo; pol izquierdismo
radio n (communication + set) radio f (SA m); on the ~ por la radio; ~ communications radiocomunicaciones fpl; ~-controlled teledirigido; ~-drama comedia radiofónica; ~-fix aer posición determinada por radio; ~-ham, ~-enthusiast radioaficionado; ~-link circuito radiotelefónico; ~-navigation radionavegación f; ~ station/transmitter emisora; ~-telegram radiotelegrama; ~-telescope radiotelescopio; v radiar

radioactive radiactivo
radioactivity radiactividad *f*
radiogram (set) radiogramola, *SA* radiofonógrafo; (message) radiograma *m*
radiograph *n* radiografía; *v* radiografiar
radiographer radiografista *m+f*
radiologist radiólogo
radiology radiología
radiotherapist radioterapeuta *m+f*
radiotherapy radioterapia
radish rábano
radium radio
radius *anat*+*geom* radio; **within a ~ of** en un radio de
raffia rafia
raffish libertino; *naut* que tiene los mástiles inclinados hacia atrás
raffle *n* rifa; *v* rifar
raft balsa
rafter *bui* viga; (raftsman) balsero
[1] **rag** *n* trapo; ~ **doll** muñeca de trapo; (newspaper) periodicucho; ~**s** (worn-out clothes) harapos *mpl*; **in ~s** harapiento; ~**-and-bone-man, ~man** trapero; ~**-bag** bolsa de recortes, (mixture) mezcla; ~**-tag and bobtail** chusma; **wearing one's glad ~s** de gala; ~**time** música sincopada, *fam* jazz *m*
[2] **rag** *n* broma estudiantil; (for charity) función estudiantil benéfica; *vi* bromear; *vt* armar jaleo; (tease) tomar el pelo a
ragamuffin golfillo
rage *n* rabia; **be all the ~** estar[19] muy de moda; *v* rabiar (**against** contra); (of storm) bramar
ragged harapiento; (not smooth) desigual; *mus* poco suave
raggedness estado harapiento; (unevenness) desigualdad *f*; *mus* falta de suavidad
ragging burla
raging rabioso; ~ **toothache** dolor *m* de muelas insoportable
raglan ~ **sleeve** manga raglán
ragout guisado
raid *n* incursión *f*; *aer* ataque *m*; (by thieves) atraco; *v* invadir; *aer* bombardear; (bank, shop) atracar, asaltar; (police) hacer una redada
rail *n* (hand-rail) barandilla; (railway) riel *m*; **by ~** por ferrocarril; **go off the**

~**s** descarrilarse, *fig* perderse (ie)[2b]; ~**bus** ferrobús (-uses) *m*; ~**road** ferrocarril *m*, *v* llevar a cabo muy rápidamente; ~**way** ferrocarril *m*; ~**way guide** guía (oficial) de ferrocarriles; ~**wayman** ferroviario; *v* ~ **off** cercar
[2] **rail** *v* quejarse (**at/against** de)
railing(s) barandilla; (fence) cerca
raillery tomadura de pelo
raiment ropa
rain *n* +*fig* lluvia; (fine ~) llovizna; (sudden downpour) chaparrón (-ones) *m*; ~**bow** arco iris; ~ **cloud** nubarrón (-ones) *m*; ~**coat** impermeable *m*; ~**drop** gota de lluvia; ~**fall** in Spain pluviosidad *f* en España; ~**fall map of Spain** mapa *m* pluviométrico de España; ~**-gauge** pluviómetro; ~**proof** impermeable; ~**storm** temporal *m* (de lluvia); ~**water** agua de lluvia; *v* +*fig* llover (ue)[1b]; ~ **cats and dogs** llover (ue)[1b] a cántaros
rainy lluvioso; ~ **season** época de las lluvias; **save for a ~ day** ahorrar para el día de mañana
raise (lift) levantar; (erect) alzar[7]; (set upright) poner[19] en pie; (hoist) izar[7]; (sunken ship) sacar[4] a flote; (promote) ascender (ie)[2b]; (produce) cultivar; (livestock) criar; *math* elevar (a una potencia); ~ **one's hat** descubrirse (*past part* descubierto); ~ **one's voice** alzar[7] la voz; ~ **an army** reclutar un ejército; ~ **Cain/the devil** armar un lío; ~ **the dead** +*fig* resucitar los muertos; ~ **the eyebrows** enarcar[4] las cejas; ~ **a laugh** provocar[4] la risa; ~ **a loan** reunir fondos; ~ **an objection** poner[19] un reparo, *fam* sacar[4] un pero; ~ **an outcry** armar un alboroto; ~ **a point** hacer[19] una observación; ~ **a problem** plantear un problema; ~ **a siege** levantar un sitio
raised (in relief) en relieve
raisin pasa
raising (lifting) levantamiento; (erecting) alzamiento; (hoisting) iza; (promoting) ascenso; (producing) cultivo; (livestock) crianza; *math* elevación *f*
raison d'être razón *f* de ser
raj: British ~ régimen británico (*esp* en la India)

rajah rajá *m*

[1] **rake** *n* rastrillo; **fire-~** hurgón *m*; *v* rastrillar; (fire) hurgar[5]

~ in acumular

~-off *n sl* tajada

~ off *v* quitar con rastrillo

~ through/over (examine) escudriñar

~ together reunir con rastrillo; *fig* lograr, acumular

~ up sacar[4] del olvido

[2] **rake** (person) calavera *m*

rakish *naut* de palos inclinados; (dissolute) libertino; **he wears his hat at a ~ angle** lleva el sombrero a lo chulo

rally *n pol* reunión (-ones) *f*; (demonstration) manifestación (-ones) *f*; *mot* rallye *m*; (tennis) peloteo; *med* recuperación *f*; *v* reunirse; (demonstrate) hacer[19] una manifestación; *med* recuperarse; *mil* rehacer(se)[19]

ram *n* carnero; *naut* espolón (-ones) *m*; *tech* pilón *m*; *mech* pisón (-ones) *m*; **~-rod** baqueta; *v* dar[19] contra; *naut* atacar[4] con espolón; **~ in(to)** meter por fuerza

Ramadan ramadán *m*

ramble *n* excursión *f* a pie (por el campo); *v* hacer[19] una excursión a pie; (in speech) divagar[5]

rambler excursionista *m+f* a pie: (rose) rosal *m* trepador

rambling *n* excursionismo a pie; *adj* errante; (of building) laberíntico; *bot* trepador (-ora *f*); (of speech) divagador (-ora *f*)

ramification ramificación (-ones) *f*

ramify ramificarse[4]

rammer pisón (-ones) *m*

ramp (slope) rampa; (on roadway) escalón (-ones) *m*; (of metal studs) clavos *mpl*; **beware of ~** ¡atención escalón!; (swindle) estafa

rampage *n*: **be on the ~** destrozarlo todo; *v* alborotar

rampant prevaleciente; *her* rampante; **be ~** cundir

rampart (of earth) terraplén (-enes) *m*; (of stone *etc*) muralla

ramshackle destartalado

ranch hacienda; *SA* rancho

rancher ganadero; *SA* ranchero

rancid rancio

rancidity ranciedad *f*

rancorous rencoroso

rancour rencor *m*

randiness cachondeo

random *n*: **at ~** al azar; *adj* casual; **~ selection** surtido escogido al azar; **~ shot** tiro sin puntería

randy cachondo

range *n* (mountains) cordillera; (open pasture) dehesa; *cul* cocina económica; (selection) surtido; *comm* línea, **the most successful ~** la línea que más éxito tiene; (of colours) gama; (of prices) escala; *elect* (**~ of frequencies**) gama de frecuencias; *mus* extensión *f*; (of ideas) abanico; (distance) alcance *m*, **within/out of ~** al/fuera del alcance; *mil* (butts) campo de tiro; *mil* (distance) alcance *m* de tiro; (limits) radio de acción; *aer+naut* autonomía; **at close ~** de cerca; **at point-blank ~** a quemarropa; **long-~** a largo plazo, *aer* de largo alcance; **take the ~** calcular la distancia; **~-finder** telémetro; **free-~ hens** gallinas *fpl* camperas; *vt* colocar[4]; *vi* extenderse (ie)[2b]; (vary) oscilar, **their ages ~ from forty to fifty** sus edades oscilan entre los cuarenta y los cincuenta años; **~ over** recorrer

ranger (forestry) guardabosques *m sing+pl*; *US* policía *m* (de) a caballo

[1] **rank** *n* +*mil* fila; (position) grado; (quality) categoría; **~ and file** masas *fpl*, *mil* soldados *mpl* rasos; **break ~s** *mil* romper (*past part* roto) filas; **join the ~s** alistarse; **rise from the ~s** ascender (ie)[2b] desde soldado; **close ~s** cerrar (ie)[2a] las filas; **reduce to the ~s** degradar; **taxi-~** estacionamiento de taxis; *v* clasificar(se)[4]

~ above ser[19] superior a

~ among estar[19] al nivel de; **~ high among** ser[19] de los mejores de

~ as equivaler[19] a

~ with figurar entre

[2] **rank** *adj* (of growth) exuberante; (of smell) fétido; **~ hypocrisy** pura hipocresía, hipocresía rematada

ranking: high-~ de alta jerarquía

rankle irritar

rankness (growth) exuberancia; (smell) fetidez *f*

ransack (plunder) saquear; (search) registrar

ransacking (plundering) saqueo;

(searching) registro

ransom *n* rescate *m*; **hold to ~** tener[19] cautivo contra rescate; *v* rescatar

rant declamar a gritos; **~ against** despotricar[4] contra

ranting lenguaje *m* declamatorio

rap *n* golpe ligero y seco; **~ at the door** llamada a la puerta; **take the ~** pagar[5] la multa; **~ over the knuckles** reprensión *f*; **I don't care a ~** (no) me importa un bledo; *v* golpear; **~ s.o. over the knuckles** *fig* reprenderle a alguien; **~ out** espetar

rapacious rapaz (-ces)

rapacity rapacidad *f*

[1] **rape** *n* violación *f*; (of s.o. between the ages of 12 and 23) estupro; *v* violar, estuprar

[2] **rape** *bot* colza; **~seed oil** aceite *m* de colza

rapid *n*: **~s** recial *m*; *adj* rápido

rapidity rapidez *f*

rapier estoque *m*

rapine rapiña

rapist (*see* **rape** *n*) violador *m*; estuprador *m*

rapping golpeo; (of door-knocker) aldabeo

rapport comunicación *f*

rapprochement acercamiento

rapt absorto; (of attention) fijo

rapture éxtasis *m*; **in ~s** extasiado

rapturous extático

rare raro; (first rate) de primera calidad; (of meat) poco hecho

rarefied enrarecido

rareness rareza

rarity rareza; (object) curiosidad *f*

rascal pícaro; *fam* mala pieza; **little ~** pillín *m*

rascally pícaro

[1] **rash** *med* erupción (-ones) *f*

[2] **rash** temerario; (of plans *etc*) precipitado

rasher lonja

rashness temeridad *f*; (of plans *etc*) precipitación *f*

rasp *n* raspador *m*; *v* raspar; (sound) crujir

raspberry frambuesa; **~-cane** frambueso; (noise) pedorreta; **blow a ~** hacer[19] una pedorreta; **get the ~** ser[19] abucheado

rasping *n* raspadura; *adj* áspero

rass *mil sl* obtener[19] ilegalmente

rat *n* rata; (traitor) traidor *m* (-ora *f*); (informer) soplón *m* (-ona *f*); *pol* desertor *m* (-ora *f*); (strike breaker) esquirol *m*; **~s!** ¡narices!, *vulg* ¡mierda!; **smell a ~** sospechar algo; **~-catcher** ratonero; **~-poison** raticida; **~-race** competencia desleal para obtener riqueza/poder; **~-trap** ratonera; *v* cazar[7] ratas; *pol* desertar (ie)[2a]; **~ on** traicionar, *fam* rajar contra; (inform the police) soplar contra

ratchet trinquete *m*; **~ screwdriver** destornillador *m* a presión; **~-wheel** rueda de trinquete

[1] **rate** *n* proporción *f*; (speed) velocidad *f*, **at a ~ of** a una velocidad de; (walking speed) paso, **we'll never get there at this ~** nunca llegaremos a este paso; (price) precio; (at hotel) tarifa; **~(s)** (municipal) contribución *f*; **~s and taxes** contribuciones *fpl* e impuestos *mpl*; **~ for the job** pago adecuado por el trabajo; **~ of depreciation** porcentaje *m*/índice *m* de depreciación; **~ of exchange** cambio; **~ of interest** tipo de interés; **~ of pay** tipo de sueldo; **~ of progress** ritmo de avance; **~ of taxation** nivel *m* de impuestos; **at that/this ~** de ese/este modo; **at a cheap ~** a un precio reducido; **at any ~** de todos modos; **at the ~ of** a razón de; **first, second ~** de primera/segunda categoría; **~payer** contribuyente *m+f*; *v* clasificar[4]; (be judged) ser[19] considerado; **~ highly** estimar mucho

[2] **rate** (chide) reñir (i)[3]

rateable sujeto a contribución

rather mejor; **~ you than I** mejor usted que yo; (somewhat) algo, **she is ~ haughty** ella es algo altiva; (fairly) bastante; *dim suff often used*: **~ difficult** dificilillo; (very) muy; (perhaps) mejor dicho; **~!** ¡ya lo creo!; **I would ~ ...** yo preferiría ...; **~ than** por no +*infin*; **anything ~ than** todo menos; **I ~ imagined that** ya me lo figuraba

ratification ratificación *f*

ratify ratificar[4]

rating categoría; (municipal) contribución *f*; *naut* marinero; **octane ~** octanaje *m*

ratio razón (-ones) *f*; **in the ~ of** a razón de; **in direct ~ to** en razón directa con; **teacher-pupil ~** proporción *f* entre profesores y alumnos

ration *n* ración (-ones) *f*; **~-book** cartilla de racionamiento; *v* racionar

rational racional; (of people) cuerdo

rationale consecuencia lógica

rationalism racionalismo

rationalist *n*+*adj* racionalista *m*+*f*

rationality racionalidad *f*

rationalization racionalización *f*

rationalize racionalizar

rationing racionamiento

ratting caza de ratas; *fam* (squealing) chivetazo

rattle *n* (noise) traqueteo; (instrument) matraca; (baby's) sonajero; **death ~** estertor *m*; **~snake** serpiente *f* de cascabel; *vi* traquetear; (of windows) hacer[19] ruido; *vt* hacer[19] traquetear; (upset) desconcertar (ie)[2a]

~ away (speaking) parlotear

~ off recitar rápidamente

~ on about charlar mucho de

rattler serpiente *f* de cascabel

rattling ruidoso; (wonderful) estupendo

ratty amostazado

raucous ronco

ravage *n* estrago; **~s of time** estragos del tiempo; *v* saquear

rave *n* moda, **be the ~** ser[19] de moda; (praise) elogio entusiasta; *adj* entusiasta; *v* delirar; (with anger) rabiar; **~ about** entusiasmarse por; **~ at** insultar de palabra

ravel enredar(se)

raven cuervo; **~-haired** de pelo negro

ravenous voraz (-ces)

ravine barranco

raving *n*: **~s** delirio; *adj* violento; **~ mad** loco de atar

ravioli ravioles *mpl*

ravish encantar; (rape) violar

ravisher violador *m*

ravishing *n* violación *f*; *adj* encantador (-ora *f*)

raw: **it gets him on the ~** le toca en lo más vivo; *adj* (of food) crudo; (spirits) puro; (unrefined) en bruto; (untrained) inexperto; *meteor* frío y húmedo; **~-hide whip** látigo de cuero verde; **~ deal** mal trato; **~ materials** materias *fpl* primas

rawlplug taco

rawness crudeza; (lack of experience) inexperiencia

[1] **ray** rayo; **~-gun** lanzarrayos *m sing*+*pl*; **~ treatment** *med* tratamiento con rayos

[2] **ray** (fish) raya

Raymond Raimundo

rayon *tr* rayón *m*

raze arrasar

razor (open) navaja; (safety) máquina de afeitar; (electric) afeitadora eléctrica; **~-blade** hoja de afeitar; **~-strop** suavizador *m*

razorbill alca

razzle: **go on the ~** ir[19] de juerga

[1] **re** (concerning) respecto a

[2] **re** *mus* re *m*

reach *n* alcance *m*; (boxing) envergadura; (of river) extensión *f* entre dos recodos; *fig* capacidad *f*; **out of ~** fuera de(l) alcance; **within ~** al alcance; **within easy ~** muy cerca; *v* alcanzar[7]; **I can't ~ it** no lo alcanzo; (go as far as) extenderse (ie)[2b] hasta; (age) cumplir, **the day I ~ed twenty** el día en que cumplí veinte años; **~ (out) one's hand** tender (ie)[2b] la mano; **it won't ~** no llega; **~-me-down** traje *m* hecho

react reaccionar (**to a, against** contra)

reaction reacción *f*

reactionary *n*+*adj pol* reaccionario

reactive reactivo

reactivity reactividad *f*

reactor reactor *m*

[1] **read** *n* lectura; **I had a good long ~** pasé un buen rato leyendo; *v* leer[17]; (study) estudiar; (indicate) indicar[4], **the speedometer ~ 100 k.p.h.** el velocímetro indicó 100 kilómetros por hora; **~ the barometer/thermometer** consultar el barómetro/termómetro; **~ proofs** corregir (i)[3]+[9] pruebas; **~ between the lines** leer[17] entre líneas; **~ the riot act to s.o.** leerle[17] a uno la cartilla; **be able to ~ s.o. like a book** conocerle[14] a uno a fondo; **~ well/badly** (cause good/bad impression) causar buena/mala impresión al leerse; **it ~s well** se lee bien; **that's not how I ~ it** yo no lo interpreto así

~ about leer[17] +*dir obj*

~ aloud leer[17] en voz alta

~ **out** anunciar
~ **through** repasar
~ **up** estudiar
² **read** *adj*: **well-~** instruido
readable legible; (pleasant) ameno
reader lector *m* (-ora *f*); (corrector) co-rrector *m* (-ora *f*); (British university) profesor *m* adjunto; (book) libro de lectura
readdress poner¹⁹ la nueva dirección
readership número de lectores; (British university) puesto de profesor ad-junto
readily de buena gana
readiness (buena) disposición *f*; (of speech) facilidad *f*; (of mind) viveza; **in ~ for** preparado (para)
reading lectura; (of barometer *etc*) indicación *f*; (from text) lección *f*; (interpretation) interpretación *f*; ~ **of a bill** *pol* lectura de un proyecto de ley; **~-desk** atril *m*; **~-glasses** gafas *fpl* de cerca; **~-lamp** lámpara de mesa; **~-room** sala de lectura
readjust reajustar; (reorientate) re-adaptar(se)
readjustment reajuste *m*; reorientación *f*
readmission readmisión *f*
readmit readmitir
ready *n*: **at the ~** *mil* listo para tirar; *adj* listo, preparado (**to/for** para); (in-clined) dispuesto (**to** a); (quick) pronto; (available) disponible; (near at hand) a mano; **get ~** preparar(se), (mentally) disponerse¹⁹; **make ~** pre-parar; ~ **for action** dispuesto para el combate; ~ **to serve** *cul* preparado; ~ **for use** listo para usar; **in ~ cash** en dinero contante; ~ **wit** ingenio agudo; **~-made**, **~-to-wear** confeccionado; **~-reckoner** libro de cálculos; *v* pre-parar
reaffirm reafirmar
reafforestation repoblación *f* forestal
real verdadero; *often expressed by repetition*: **cup of ~ coffee** taza de café café; ~ **estate** bienes *m* raíces
realism realismo
realist *n + adj* realista
realistic realista
reality realidad *f*
realizable realizable
realization comprensión *f*; (of plans)

realización *f*
realize darse¹⁹ cuenta de; (of assets) realizar⁷; (of plans) llevar a cabo
really verdaderamente; **~?** ¿de veras?; **then the fight ~ began** entonces sí que empezó la lucha
realm reino; *fig* campo
realtor *US* corredor *m* de fincas
ream resma; *fam* montón (-ones) *m*
reanimate reanimar
reap segar (ie)²ᵃ; (harvest) +*fig* cose-char; ~ **a profit from** sacar⁴ provecho de
reaper segador *m*; (machine) segadora
reaping siega; **~-hook** hoz (-ces) *f*
reappear reaparecer¹⁴
reappoint nombrar otra vez
reappraisal revaluación *f*
reappraise retasar, revaluar
¹ **rear** *vt* criar; (erect) alzar⁷; *vi* enca-britarse
² **rear** *n* parte trasera; **at the ~ (of)** detrás (de); **bring up the ~** cerrar (ie)¹ᵃ la marcha; **in the ~** *mil* a retaguardia; **view from the ~** vista desde atrás; **~-admiral** contraalmirante *m*; *adj* tra-sero, posterior; **~-engine** *mot* motor trasero; **~-guard** retaguardia; **~-lamp** luz *f* piloto; **~-view mirror** espejo re-trovisor; **~ward(s)** hacia atrás
rearing cría; ~ **of livestock** cría de ganado; ~ **of poultry** avicultura
rearm rearmar
rearrange (arrange again) volver (ue)¹ᵇ (*past part* vuelto) a arreglar; (re-classify) clasificar⁴ otra vez; (place in different order) cambiar el orden de
rearrangement reordenamiento
reason *n* razón (-ones) *f*, motivo; ~ **why** porqué *m*; **by ~ of** a causa de; **within ~** en moderación; **listen to ~** avenirse a razones; **have one's ~s** entenderse (ie)²ᵇ, **I have my ~s** yo me entiendo; **it stands to ~ (that)** es lógico (que); **for the simple ~ (that)** por la sencilla razón de; *v* razonar; (argue) argüir; ~ **with s.o.** intentar convencerle a uno; **~ed** razonado
reasonable razonable; (sensible) sen-sato; (moderate) módico
reasonableness lo razonable, modera-ción *f*
reasoning razonamiento
reassemble (of people) volver (ue)¹ᵇ

(*past part* vuelto) a reunir(se); *mech* montar de nuevo

reassert reafirmar

reassertion reafirmación *f*

reassessment nueva apreciación; (rates) revalorización *f*

reassign asignar de nuevo

reassurance confianza establecida

reassure tranquilizar[7]

reassuring tranquilizador (-ora *f*)

rebate *n* descuento; *v* descontar (ue)[1a]

rebel *n+adj* rebelde *m+f*; *v* sublevarse

rebellion sublevación (-ones) *f*

rebellious rebelde *m+f*

rebirth renacimiento

rebore *n* rectificado; *v* rectificar[4]

reborn: be ~ +*fig* renacer[14]

rebound *n* rebote *m*; **on the ~** de rebote, *fig* de rechazo; *v* rebotar

rebuff *n* repulsa; *v* rechazar

rebuild reedificar[4]

rebuke *n* reprensión (-ones) *f*; *v* reprender

rebut refutar

rebuttal refutación (-ones) *f*

recalcitrant refractario

recall *n* (annulment) revocación *f*; (of diplomat, capital) retirada; *theat* llamada a escena; **beyond ~** irrevocable, (forgotten) olvidado; *v* (annul) revocar; (withdraw) retirar; (remember) recordar (ue)[1a]

recant retractar(se)

recantation retractación (-ones) *f*

recap *n* repaso; (*US* retread) recauchutado; *v* repasar; *US* recauchutar

recapitulate recapitular

recapitulation recapitulación *f*

recapture *n* represa; *v* represar; **~ a memory** hacer[19] revivir un recuerdo

recast refundir

recede retroceder; (of prices) bajar

receding que retrocede; **~ chin** barbilla pequeña

receipt *n* recibo; (recipe) receta; **~s** *comm* ingresos *mpl*; **acknowledge ~ (of)** acusar recibo (de); **~-book** talonario; *v* dar[19] recibo (por)

receive recibir; (guests) acoger[8] a; (money) cobrar; (tennis) estar[19] al resto; (stolen goods) receptar; **~d** recibido; **be well ~d** tener[19] buena acogida

receiver recibidor *m* (-ora *f*); (tele-

phone) auricular *m*; *rad* (radio) receptor *m*; (tennis) restador *m* (-ora *f*); (of stolen goods) encubridor *m* (-ora *f*), *fam* perista *m+f*; **official ~** *approx* síndico

receiving *rad*+*TV* recepción *f*; (of stolen goods) receptación *f* **~ set** *rad* receptor *m*

recent reciente; **in ~ months** en estos últimos meses

recently recientemente; (before *past part*) recién, **~ married** recién casado; **until ~** hasta hace poco

receptacle receptáculo

reception recepción *f*; (welcome) acogida; **~ room** sala de recibo

receptionist, reception clerk recepcionista *m+f*

receptive receptivo

receptiveness, receptivity receptividad *f*

recess *n* (niche) nicho; *mech* rebajo; (vacation) vacaciones *fpl*; (parliamentary) (período de) clausura; (break *esp* between lessons) hora de recreo; **~es** *fig* lo más recóndito

recession retroceso; *comm* recesión *f*

recharge recargar[5]

recherché rebuscado

rechristen rebautizar[7]

recipe receta; **~-book** libro de recetas; *fig* fórmula

recipient recibidor *m* (-ora *f*)

reciprocal *n* inverso; *adj* recíproco

reciprocate (act in return) corresponder (a), (exchange) intercambiar; *mech* alternar

reciprocation reciprocidad *f*

reciprocity reciprocidad *f*

recital (narrative) relación *f*; *mus* recital *m*

recitation recitación *f*

recitative recitado

recite recitar

reciter recitador *m* (-ora *f*)

reckless (person) temerario; (action) precipitado

recklessness temeridad *f*

reckon calcular; (consider) estimar; (suppose) figurarse, **I ~ he will lose** me figuro que él perderá

~ on contar (ue)[1a] con

~ up sumar

~ with tener[19] en cuenta; **he's a man to be ~ed with** él es un hombre a quien hay que tener en cuenta

que tener en cuenta

reckoner calculador *m*

reckoning cuenta; **be wrong in one's ~** equivocarse[4] en el cálculo; **day of ~** día *m* de ajuste de cuentas, (Judgement Day) día *m* del juicio

reclaim reclamar; (land) recuperar; (from sea) ganar; *mech* utilizar[7]

reclaimable reclamable; (recuperable) recuperable

reclamation reclamación *f*; utilización *f*; (of land) aprovechamiento

reclinable: ~ **seat** *mot* asiento abatible

recline recostarse (ue)[1a]

reclining reclinable

recluse recluso

recognition reconocimiento

recognizable reconocible

recognizance +*leg* reconocimiento

recognize reconocer[14]; (admit) admitir; **I ~d your voice** le reconocí por su voz

recoil *n* retroceso; (gun) culatazo; *v* retroceder (de miedo); (gun) dar[19] un culatazo

recoilless: ~ **rifle** fusil *m* sin retroceso

recollect recordar (ue)[1a]; ~ **o.s.** recobrarse

recollection recuerdo

recommence empezar (ie)[2a] de nuevo

recommend recomendar (ie)[2a]; (advise) aconsejar; **~ed for babies and expectant mothers** indicado para niños y futuras madres

recommendable recomendable

recommendation recomendación (-ones) *f*

recommendatory recomendatorio

recompense *n* recompensa; *v* recompensar; (pay) remunerar

recompose recomponer[19]

reconcilable reconciliable

reconcile (re)conciliar; ~ **o.s. (to)** resignarse (a)

reconciliation (re)conciliación *f*

recondite recóndito

recondition reacondicionar

reconnaissance reconocimiento

reconnoitre reconocer[14]

reconquer reconquistar

reconquest reconquista

reconsider reconsiderar

reconsideration reconsideración *f*

reconstitute reconstituir[16]

reconstitution reconstitución *f*

reconstruct reconstruir[16]

reconstruction reconstrucción *f*

reconversion reconversión *f*

reconvert reconvertir (ie)[2c]

record *n* (account) relación (-ones) *f*; *mus* disco; (personal history) antecedentes *mpl*; (soldier's) hoja de servicio; *sp* récord *m*, marca; ~**s** archivos *mpl*, (notes) notas *fpl*, (facts) datos *mpl*, *leg* actas *fpl*; **off the** ~ extraoficial(mente); **be on** ~ estar[19] registrado; **it is on** ~ **that** consta que; **place on** ~ dejar constancia de; **bear** ~ **to** atestar; **break the** ~ batir la marca; **establish a** ~ establecer[14] un récord; ~ **time** tiempo récord; **keeper of the** ~**s** archivero; ~**-breaker** plusmarquista *m+f*; ~**-breaking** que supera la marca; ~ **card** ficha; ~**-fan** discómano; ~ **firm** casa de discos; ~**-holder** plusmarquista *m+f*; ~ **library** discoteca; ~**-player** tocadiscos *m sing+pl*; *v* registrar; tomar nota de; (indicate) indicar; *mus* (on disc/tape) grabar; ~**ed transmission** *rad* emisión difundida

recorder registrador *m*; (magistrate) juez (-ces) *m* municipal; *mus* (instrument) flauta dulce, (tape-~) magnetófono; *mech* indicador *m*

recording grabación (-ones) *f*; (act of ~) registro de la grabación; ~ **apparatus** *cin+rad* máquina de grabar, (scientific) aparato registrador; ~ **level** nivel *m* de registro; ~**-van** coche *m* de grabación

recount referir (ie)[2c]

re-count *n* segundo escrutinio; *v* hacer[19] un segundo escrutinio

recoup recobrar; ~ **one's losses** recobrarse de las pérdidas

recourse: have ~ to recurrir a

recover *vt* recobrar; (money) reembolsarse; *vi med* reponerse[19] (**from** de); (from shock) rehacerse[19]

re-cover volver (ue)[1b] (*past part* vuelto) a cubrir

recoverable recuperable

recovery recuperación *f*; *med* restablecimiento; (of money) recaudación *f*; ~**-room** *med* sala de recuperación

recreant *n+adj* traidor *m* (-ora *f*)

recreate recrear

re-create crear de nuevo

recreation recreación *f*; (play-time) recreo; ~ **ground** patio de recreo, (sports field) campo de deportes

re-creation nueva creación

recreational recreativo

recreative recreativo

recriminate recriminar

recrimination recriminación (-ones) *f*

recriminatory recriminador (-ora *f*)

recrudesce recrudecer(se)[14]

recrudescence recrudescencia

recruit *n* recluta *m*; (newly conscripted) quinto; *fig* novicio; **raw** ~ recluta bisoño; *v* reclutar; *sp + mil* (by lots) quintar; (supplies) restablecer[14]; ~ **one's health** reponerse[19]

recruiting reclutamiento; ~ **officer** oficial *m* reclutador

recruitment reclutamiento

rectangle rectángulo

rectangular rectangular

rectifiable rectificable

rectification rectificación *f*

rectifier rectificador *m*

rectify rectificar[4]

rectitude rectitud *f*

rector cura párroco

rectory casa del párroco

rectum recto

recumbent recostado

recuperate *vt* recuperar; *vi* reponerse[19]; *med* restablecerse[14]

recuperation recuperación *f*; *med* restablecimiento

recuperative recuperativo

recur repetirse (i)[3]; (come to mind again) volver (ue)[1b] (*past part* vuelto) a la mente

recurrence repetición *f*

recurrent repetido; *math* periódico

recurring *math*: **6.3** ~ 6,3 periódica pura

recycle reciclar

recycling reciclado

red rojo; (billiards) mingo; **be in the** ~ tener[19] (la cuenta en) números rojos; **see** ~ encolerizarse[7]; *adj* colorado; +*pol* rojo, *Arg* lacre; (of wine) tinto, (in Catalonia) negro; ~ **as a beetroot** colorado como un pimiento; **paint the town** ~ ir[19] de juerga; ~ **tape** papeleo; ~**breast** petirrojo; ~**-blooded** vigoroso; ~**-brick** (of university) de fundación moderna; ~

cabbage lombarda; ~**cap** policía *m* militar, (*US*) mozo de estación; ~ **clover** trébol morado; ~ **corpuscle** glóbulo rojo; **Red Cross** Cruz Roja; ~**currant** grosella roja; ~ **deer** ciervo común; ~ **flag** bandera roja; ~**-haired** pelirrojo; ~**-handed** con las manos en la masa; ~**head** pelirrojo, *fam* zanahoria; ~ **herring** pista falsa; **draw a** ~ **herring** despistar; ~**-hot** candente, *fig* fanático, (of news) de última hora; ~ **lamp** luz roja; ~**-lead** minio; ~**-letter day** (holiday) día *m* de fiesta, (memorable day) día inolvidable; ~ **mullet** salmonete *m*; ~ **pepper** (vegetable) pimiento, (spice) pimentón *m*; **Red Riding Hood** Caperucita Roja; ~**shank** archibebe *m*; ~**shirt** *pol* camisa roja *m+f*; ~**skin** piel roja *m+f*; ~ **sky** arrebol *m*; ~**start** colirrojo; ~**wing** zorzal alirrojo

redden *vt* enrojecer[14]; (dye) teñir (i)[3] de rojo; *vi* enrojecerse[14]; (with anger) ponerse[19] colorado; (with shame) ruborizarse[7]

reddish rojizo

redecorate renovar

redecoration renovación *f*

redeem redimir; (pledge) rescatar; (promise) cumplir; *comm* amortizar[7]

redeemable redimible; *comm* amortizable

Redeemer Redentor *m*

redeeming: **his one** ~ **characteristic** su única característica compensadora

redemption redención *f*; (of pledge) rescate *m*; *comm* amortización *f*; **beyond** ~ sin remedio

redeploy reorganizar[7]; *mil* desplegar[2a+5] de nuevo

redeployment reorganización *f*; *mil* nuevo despliegue

redirect reexpedir (i)[3]

rediscover descubrir (*past part* descubierto) de nuevo

redistribute volver (ue)[1b] (*past part* vuelto) a distribuir

redistribution nueva distribución

redness rojez *f*

re-do volver (ue)[1b] (*past part* vuelto) a hacer

redolence fragancia

redolent: ~ **of** que huele a; **be** ~ **of** *fig* hacer[19] pensar en

redouble redoblar

redoubtable formidable

redound: ~ **to** redundar en

redraft *n* nuevo borrador; *v* volver (ue)[1b] (*past part* vuelto) a redactar

redress *n* reparación *f*; **have no** ~ no tener[19] remedio; *v* reparar; ~ **the balance** compensarlo

reduce *vt* +*math* reducir[15] (**to** a); (shorten) abreviar; (prices) rebajar; (in rank) degradar; ~ **to the ranks** volver (ue)[1b] (*past part* vuelto) a las filas; ~ **speed sign** señal *f* de limitación de velocidad; **at ~d prices** a precios rebajados; **be in ~d circumstances** estar[19] en la indigencia; *vi* (slim) adelgazar[7]

reducible reducible

reduction reducción *f*; (shortening) acortamiento *f*; (of prices) rebaja; (in rank) degradación *f*

redundancy redundancia

redundant redundante; **be** ~ estar[19] de más

reduplicate reduplicar[14]

reduplication reduplicación *f*

re-echo repercutirse

reed *bot* junco; *mus* (pipe) caramillo; *mus* (vibrator) lengüeta; ~**-warbler** carricero común

reedy (place) juncoso; (sound) silbante

[1] **reef** *geog* arrecife *m*

[2] **reef** *n naut* rizo; ~**-knot** nudo de rizo; *v* arrizar[7]

[3] **reef** *sl* birlar, chorizar

reefer cigarrillo grifado; *sl* porro, petardo; ~**-jacket** chaquetón *m*

reek *n* hedor *m*; *v* heder (ie)[2b] (**of** a)

reel *n* carrete *m*; (fishing) carrete *m*; *cin*+*phot* rollo; *cin* cinta; (dance) baile *m* escocés; **off the** ~ seguido; *v* (wind) devanar; (stagger) tambalear; ~ **off** contar (ue)[1a] rápidamente

re-eligible eligible otra vez

reeling (of ship) cabeceo; (of person) tambaleo

re-emerge salir[19] de nuevo

re-enact decretar otra vez

re-enter volver (ue)[1b] (*past part* vuelto) a entrar

re-entry *space* reentrada

re-establish restablecer[14]

re-examination reexaminación *f*

re-examine reexaminar

re-export reexportar

refashion rehacer

refectory refectorio

refer referir (ie)[2c]; (quote) citar; ~ **to** (concern) referirse (ie)[2c] a; ~ **the matter to** consultar el caso con; ~ **to notes** consultar notas; **surely you're not referring to me!** ¡no lo dirás por mí!

referee *n* árbitro; *fam* soplapitos *m sing*+*pl*; (personal) fiador *m* (-ora *f*); *v* arbitrar

reference referencia; ~ **number** número de referencia; (personal) (carta de) recomendación *f*; (mention) alusión *f* (**to** de); ~**s** *comm* referencias *fpl*; **with** ~ **to** en cuanto a; **make** ~ **to** referirse (ie)[2c] a; **terms of** ~ puntos *mpl* de consulta; mandato; *adj* de consulta; ~ **book/library** libro/biblioteca de consulta

referendum referéndum *m*

refill *n* recambio; (for pen/pencil) mina; *v* rellenar

refine refinar; *metal* acrisolar; (fats) clarificar[4]; *fig* purificar[4]; ~**d** (manners) fino, (affected) afectado

refinement refinamiento; (manners) educación *f*; (subtlety) sutileza; (elegance) elegancia

refinery refinería; (oil) destilería

refit *n* reparación *f*; *v* reparar; (provide supplies) volver (ue)[1b] a equipar

reflation reinflación *f*

reflect (think) reflejar; (consider) reflexionar; (meditate) meditar; ~ **well/ill upon** revelar a uno bajo una luz favorable/poco favorable

reflection (thinking) reflejo; (considering) reflexión *f*; **cast a** ~ **on** (criticize) criticar[4], (dishonour) desprestigiar

reflective meditabundo

reflector reflector *m*; *mot* (rear reflector) captafaros *m sing*+*pl*

reflex *n*+*adj* reflejo; ~ **action** acto reflejo

reflexive reflexivo

refloat sacar[4] a flote

reflux reflujo

reform *n* reforma; *v* reformar(se); ~**-school** reformatorio, *SA* escuela correccional

reformation reforma; (Protestant) Reformation reforma (protestante)

reformatory *n* reformatorio; *SA* escuela correccional, *sl* corre *f*; *adj* reformatorio

reformer reformador *m* (-ora *f*)

refract refractar

refraction refracción *f*

refractive refractivo

refractory refractario

[1] **refrain** *n* estribillo; **the same old ~** *fig* la misma cantilena

[2] **refrain** abstenerse[19] (**from** de); **passengers are requested to ~ from smoking** se ruega a los señores viajeros que no fumen

refresh refrescar[4]

refreshing refrescante

refreshment refresco; **~-room** cantina

refrigerate refrigerar

refrigeration refrigeración *f*

refrigerator frigorífico; **~-lorry** camión (-ones) frigorífico

refuel rellenar (de combustible)

refuelling toma de combustible; **~-plane** avión (-ones) *m* nodriza

refuge refugio; (institution) asilo; (in mountains) albergue *m*; (traffic-island) refugio para peatones; (resort) recurso; **take ~** refugiarse

refugee refugiado; **~ camp** campo de refugiados

refulgence refulgencia

refulgent refulgente

refund *n* reembolso; *v* reembolsar

refurbish restaurar

refurnish amueblar de nuevo

refusal negativa; (option) opción *f*; (rejection) rechazo

[1] **refuse** *n* basura; **~ can** *US* cubo de la basura; **~-lorry**, **~-truck** camión (-ones) *m* de la basura; **~-tip** vertedero

[2] **refuse** *vt* rehusar; (reject) rechazar[7]; **~ o.s. something** privarse de algo; *vi* (of horse) rehusar; **~ to** negarse (ie)[2a] **+***infin*, **she ~d (to do it)** ella se negó a hacerlo

refutable refutable

refutation refutación *f*

refute refutar

regain recobrar; (reconquer) reconquistar; **~ consciousness** volver[1b] (*past part* vuelto) en sí; **~ one's breath** recobrar aliento

regal real

regale regalar

regalia insignias *fpl*; **in full ~** de punta en blanco

regality realeza

regard *n* (gaze) mirada; (consideration) respeto; (esteem) estima; **in/with ~ to** (con) respecto a; **without ~ to** sin hacer caso de; **with due ~ to** considerando; **you have no ~ for my feelings** a usted no le importan mis sentimientos; **~s** recuerdos *mpl*, **kind ~s to your parents** recuerdos a sus padres; *v* (gaze) mirar; (consider) respetar; (esteem) estimar; **as ~s** en cuanto a

regarding en cuanto a

regardless a pesar de todo; **~ of** sin hacer caso de

regatta regata

regency regencia

regenerate *adj* regenerado; *v* regenerar

regeneration regeneración *f*

regent *n+adj* regente *m*

regicide (crime) regicidio; (person) regicida *m+f*

regime régimen (-ímenes) *m*

regiment *n* regimiento; *v* regimentar

regimental del regimiento

regimentation organización muy estricta

region región *f*; **in the ~ of** *fig* alrededor de

regional regional

register *n* (book +*mus*) registro; (of members) registro; (school **~**) lista, **call the ~** pasar lista; **electoral ~** lista de electores; **parish ~** registro parroquial; **cash-~** caja registradora; *mech* indicador *m*; *naut* matrícula; **~ of births, marriages and deaths** registro civil; **~ office** oficina del registro civil; *vt* registrar; **~ed trade mark** marca registrada; (letter) certificar[4]; **~ed parcel** paquete certificado; (luggage) facturar; (of thermometers *etc*) marcar[4]; (emotion) manifestar (ie)[2a]; *mech* indicar[4]; *naut* abanderar; **~ a birth** inscribir (*past part* inscrito) un niño; **~ed office** domicilio social; *vi* (at a hotel) registrarse; **it doesn't ~** (it means nothing to me) no me suena

registrar registrador *m*; **~ of births, marriages and deaths** secretario del registro civil

registration (of emotion) manifestación
f; *mech* indicación *f*; *naut* abande-
ramiento; (of birth *etc*) inscripción *f*;
~ **fee** derechos *mpl* de matrícula; ~
number *mot* matrícula

registry registro *f*; ~ **office** oficina del registro civil

regrade reclasificar[4]

regress *n* retroceso; *v* retroceder

regression retroceso

regret *n* (remorse) remordimiento; **to
my** ~ a mi pesar; **she sends her** ~**s** ella
manda sus excusas; *v* sentir (ie)[2c]; **I**
(very much) ~ **that** siento (mucho)
que +*subj*

regretful pesaroso; arrepentido

regretfully desgraciadamente

regrettable lamentable

regrettably desgraciadamente

regular *n* *mil* soldado de línea; (customer) parroquiano; *adj* regular;
(habitual) asiduo; (methodical) metódico; *mil* de línea; verdadero

regularity regularidad *f*

regularize regularizar[7]

regulate regular; (match) reglamentar;
mech ajustar

regulation *n* regulación (-ones) *f*; (rule)
regla(mento); *adj* reglamentario; (of)
~ **size** de tamaño normal; ~ **football**
balón (-ones) *m* de reglamento

regulator regulador *m*; (clock) registro

regurgitate vomitar

regurgitation regurgitación *f*

rehabilitate rehabilitar

rehabilitation rehabilitación *f*; ~ **centre**
centro de reeducación, (for drug ad-
dicts *etc*) centro de deshabituación

rehash *n* refundición *f*; *v* refundir

rehearsal ensayo; **dress-**~ ensayo general

rehearse *theat*+*mus* ensayar; (repeat)
repetir (i)[3]

rehouse alojar de nuevo

reign *n* reinado; *fig* dominio; *v* reinar; *fig*
prevalecer[14]

reigning reinante

reimburse reembolsar

reimbursement reembolso

reimpose imponer[19] de nuevo

rein *n* rienda; **give** ~ **to** dar[19] rienda
suelta a; **keep a tight** ~ **on** atar corto a;
v gobernar (ie)[2a] (un caballo); ~
back/in refrenar

reincarnate reencarnar

reindeer reno

reinforce reforzar (ue)[1a]; ~**d concrete**
hormigón armado

reinforcement reforzamiento; ~**s** *mil*
refuerzos *mpl*

reinsert reinsertar (ie)[2a]

reinstate reinstalar

reinstatement reinstalación *f*

reintegrate reintegrar

reinvest reinvertir (ie)[2c]

reissue *n* nueva emisión; (of book) reimpresión *f*; (of film) reestreno; (of
record) nueva grabación; (of patent)
reexpedición *f*; *v* hacer[19] una nueva
emisión de; (book) reimprimir; (film)
reestrenar; (patent *etc*) reexpedir (i)[3]

reiterate reiterar

reiteration reiteración *f*

reject *n* (thing) artículo defectuoso;
(person) persona rechazada; *v* rechazar[7]; (request) denegar[5]; (scheme)
desechar; (solution) descartar

rejection rechazamiento; (of request)
denegación *f*; (of scheme) descarte *m*;
surg rechazo

rejoice regocijar(se) (**at** de)

rejoicing *n* regocijo; *adj* regocijado

rejoin reunirse con; (answer) replicar[4]

rejoinder réplica

rejuvenate rejuvenecer[14]

rejuvenation rejuvenecimiento

rekindle volver (ue)[1b] a encender

relapse *n* *med* recaída; (moral) reincidencia; *v* recaer[19], reincidir (**into** en)

relate (tell) narrar; (connect) relacionar; **be** ~**d to** relacionarse con,
(family) tener[19] parentesco con; **I am**
~**d to them** son parientes míos; ~**d
items** similares *mpl*

relation (narration) narración *f*; (connection) relación *f*; (person) pariente
m+*f*; **in** ~ **to** respecto de; **good** ~**s**
buenas relaciones *fpl*; **business** ~**s**
trato comercial; ~**ship** (connection)
relación *f*, (family) parentesco

relative *n* pariente *m*+*f*; *gramm* relativo; *adj* relativo (**to** a)

relatively relativamente; ~ **speaking** a lo
relativo

relativity relatividad *f*

relax *vt* (slacken) aflojar; (make less
rigid) relajar; *vi* descansar; ~! ¡tran-
quilícese!

relaxation (slackening) aflojamiento; (making less rigid) relajación *f*; (rest) descanso; (recreation) recreo; (enjoyment) diversión *f*

relaxing relajante

relay *n* (stage) parada; (of workers) tanda, **work in** ~**s** trabajar en tandas; (of horses) posta; ~-**race** carrera de relevos; **4 × 100 metres** ~ relevos 4 por 100 metros; *rad*+*TV* redifusión *f*; ~ **station** *rad*+*TV* repetidor *m*; *v elect* remitir; *rad*+*TV* retransmitir

re-lay (lay again) colocar[4] de nuevo

release *n* (freeing) liberación *f*; (from gaol) excarcelación *f*; (from undertaking) descargo; (of films, records *etc*) estreno; **listen to his latest** ~ escuchen su última grabación; **press** ~ comunicado de prensa; *v* soltar (ue)[1a], ~ **the brakes!** ¡suelte los frenos!; (emit) emitir; (free) poner[19] en libertad; (lessen pressure) aflojar; (from an undertaking) absolver (ue)[1b]; (bombs *etc*) dejar caer; (news) dar[19] al público; (recording) poner[19] en circulación; *cin* estrenar

relegate relegar[5]; *sp* descender

relegation relegación *f*; *sp* descenso

relent ablandarse

relenting enternecimiento

relentless implacable

relentlessly sin piedad

re-let alquilar de nuevo

relevance, relevancy pertinencia

relevant pertinente

reliability fiabilidad *f*; (of person) formalidad *f*

reliable de confianza; (person) formal; (news) de fuente fidedigna

reliance confianza (**on** en)

reliant confiado (**upon** en)

relic *eccles* reliquia; (trace) vestigio

[1] **relief** alivio; **two aspirins will give you** ~ dos aspirinas le darán alivio; (aid) socorro, ~ **work** trabajos *mpl* de socorro; (guard) relevo; (lifting of siege) descerco; (lightening) aligeramiento; (contrast) contraste *m*; **light** ~ fuerza cómica; **throw into** ~ hacer[19] resaltar; ~ **train** tren suplementario; **what a** ~! ¡menos mal!; **it's a** ~ **that** menos mal que

[2] **relief** (carving) relieve *m*; (painting) realce *m*; ~ **map** mapa *m* en relieve

relieve aliviar; (aid) socorrer; (guard) relevar; (lift siege) descercar[4]; (lighten) aligerar; (reassure) tranquilizar[7]; ~ **s.o. of his post** despedir (i)[3] a uno de su empleo; ~ **a pain** suprimir un dolor; ~ **nature** hacer[19] del cuerpo; ~ **one's feelings** desahogarse[5]

religion religión (-ones) *f*; **get** ~ darle[19] a uno por la religión

religious religioso; ~ **orders** órdenes religiosas

reline poner[19] nuevo forro a

relinquish abandonar

relinquishment abandono

reliquary relicario

relish *n* (appetite) apetito; (pleasure) gusto; (sauce) salsa; *v* (savour) saborear; (enjoy) gustar; **I don't** ~ **the idea (of)** no me apetece mucho la idea (de +*infin*)

relive revivir

reluctance desgana; **with** ~ a desgana

reluctant poco dispuesto (**to** a)

reluctantly de mala gana

rely: ~ **(up)on** fiarse de; (count upon) contar (ue)[1a] con

remain *n*: ~**s** restos *mpl*; **mortal** ~**s** restos mortales; (left-overs) sobras *fpl*; (bits) desperdicios *mpl*; (ruins) ruinas *fpl*; *v* quedar(se); (endure) permanecer[14]; (be left over) sobrar; **it** ~**s the same** sigue como siempre

remainder *n* resto; *math* resto; ~**s** (books) restos *mpl* de edición; *v* (books) saldar

remake rehacer[19]

remand *n* traslado a otro tribunal; *v* enviar a otro tribunal; ~ **in custody** mantener bajo custodia

remark *n* observación *f*; (written) nota; *v* observar; ~ **upon** advertir (ie)[2c]

remarkable notable; (strange) raro

remarriage segundas nupcias *fpl*

remarry casarse en segundas nupcias

remediable remediable

remedial remediador (-ora *f*); *med* terapéutico; ~ **measures** medidas reparadoras

remedy *n* remedio; *v* remediar

remember recordar (ue)[1a]; (bear in mind) tener[19] en cuenta; ~ **me to your parents** salude de mi parte a sus padres

remembrance recuerdo; (commemoration) conmemoración *f*, **service of** ~ acto de conmemoración; **in** ~ **of** en conmemoración de

remind recordar (ue)¹ª, **I** ~**ed Mary of her promise** le recordé su promesa a María; **don't** ~ **me of it!** ¡no me lo recuerde!; ~ **o.s. that** recordarse (ue)¹ª que

reminder recuerdo; (warning) aviso; **gentle** ~ indirecta

reminisce (recall) recordar (ue)¹ª lo pasado; (speak) hablar de lo pasado

reminiscence reminiscencia

reminiscent evocador; **be** ~ **of** recordar (ue)¹ª

remiss negligente

remissible remisible

remission remisión *f*

remit remitir; (send) enviar; (send money) girar

remittance remesa; giro; ~ **charges** gastos *mpl* de transferencia

remitter remitente *m*+*f*

remnant resto; (cloth) retal *m*

remodel reconstruir¹⁶

remonstrance protesta; amonestación *f*

remonstrant protestatario

remonstrate protestar (**against** contra); ~ **with** reconvenir¹⁹ a

remonstrator reprochador *m* (-ora *f*)

remorse remordimiento

remorseful arrepentido

remorseless implacable

remote remoto, ~ **control** mando remoto; (slight) ligero

remoteness lo remoto

remotest: have not the ~ **idea** no tener¹⁹ ni la más mínima idea

remould *mot n* recauchutado; *v* recauchutar

remount *n* remonta; *v* remontar

removable separable; (of collars *etc*) de quita y pon

removal acción *f* de quitar/mover); (of furniture) mudanza; (from office) deposición *f*; *surg* extirpación *f*; (suppression) supresión *f*; (of waste) eliminación *f*; ~ **van** camión (-ones) *m* de mudanzas

remove quitar; (furniture) mudar; (from office) destituir¹⁶; *surg* extirpar; (supress) suprimir; (waste) eliminar

remover agente *m* de mudanzas

remunerate remunerar

remuneration remuneración *f*

remunerative lucrativo

Renaissance *n* Renacimiento; *adj* renacentista

renal renal

rename poner¹⁹ nuevo nombre a

rend rasgar⁵

render (return) devolver (ue)¹ᵇ (*past part* devuelto); (translate) traducir¹⁵; *mus*+*theat* interpretar; (fat) derretir (i)³ y clarificar⁴; ~ **an account** pasar una cuenta; ~ **a service** hacer¹⁹ un favor

rendering, rendition interpretación *f*

rendezvous *n* (date) cita; (place) lugar *m* de una cita; *space* acoplamiento; *v space* acoplar

renegade *n*+*adj* renegado

renegotiation nueva negociación

renew renovar (ue)¹ª; (replace) reemplazar⁷; (start afresh) reanudar; (extend) prorrogar⁵

renewable prorrogable

renewal renovación *f*; (replacement) reemplazamiento; (fresh start) reanudación *f*; (extension) prórroga

rennet cuajo

renounce renunciar; (throne) abdicar⁴

renovate renovar (ue)¹ª

renovation renovación *f*

renovator renovador *m* (-ora *f*)

renown renombre *m*; ~**ed** renombrado

¹ **rent** *n* (tear) rasgón (-ones) *m*; (in cloth) siete *m*; (split) raja; *adj* rasgado

² **rent** *n* alquiler *m*, **pay the** ~ pagar⁵ el alquiler/*fam* la casa; ~**-free** exento de alquiler; ~ **control** control *m* de alquileres; *v* alquilar; **for** ~ a alquilar

rental alquiler *m*

renter inquilino

renumber volver (ue)¹ᵇ (*past part* vuelto) a numerar

renunciation renuncia

reoccupy ocupar de nuevo

reopen reabrir(se) (*past part* reabierto)

reopening reapertura

reorder repetir (i)³ el pedido

reorganization reorganización *f*

reorganize reorganizar⁷

reorientation nueva orientación

rep viajante *m*

repack reenvasar

repaint repintar

repair *n* reparación *f*; (restoration)

restauración *f*; (of shoes) remiendo;
beyond ~ irreparable; **(keep) in good**
~ (conservar) en buen estado; **~-shop**
taller *m* de reparación; **~-truck** furgoneta de auxilio; *v* reparar; restaurar;
remendar (ie)²ᵃ; (put right) remediar
repaper volver (ue)¹ᵇ (*past part* vuelto)
a empapelar
reparable reparable
reparation reparación *f*; *comm* indemnización *f*; *pol* satisfacción *f*; **make**
~ dar¹⁹ satisfacción
repartee respuesta aguda
repast comida
repatriate *n+adj* repatriado; *v* repatriar
repatriation repatriación *f*
repay reembolsar; (compensate) compensar; (revenge oneself) pagar⁵ en la
misma moneda; **it well ~s the effort**
vale la pena
repayable reembolsable
repayment reembolso; (for service)
compensación *f*; *fig* venganza
repeal *n* revocación *f*; *v* revocar⁴
repeat *n* repetición *f*; ~ **broadcast**
reposición *f*; ~ **order** *comm* pedido
reiterado; *v* repetir (i)³; (recite)
recitar; (duplicate) duplicar⁴; ~ **an**
order repetir (i)³ un pedido; ~ **o.s.**
repetirse (i)³
repeatedly repetidas veces
repeater (fusil *m*/reloj *m*) de repetición
repel rechazar⁷; *fig* repugnar
repellent: *n+adj*, anti +*n*, moth-~ anti-
polilla; *adj* repelente
repent arrepentirse (ie)²ᶜ (de)
repentance arrepentimiento
repentant arrepentido
repercussion repercusión *f*; **have ~s** repercutir (on en); **have wide ~s** tener¹⁹
amplias consecuencias
repertoire repertorio
repertory repertorio; ~ **theatre/com-**
pany teatro/compañía de repertorio
repetition repetición *f*
repine desconsolarse (ue)¹ᵃ
replace reemplazar⁷; **his heart was ~d**
by another su corazón fue reempla-
zado por otro; (put back) reponer¹⁹
replacement (thing) repuesto; (person)
sustituto; (action) reposición *f*
replant replantar
replay *sp* repetición *f* de un partido
replenish rellenar; (stock) reapro-

visionar
replenishment rellenado; (of stock) rea-
provisionamiento
replete repleto (**with** de)
repletion hartazgo
replica copia, réplica
replicate *bot* replegado
reply *n* contestación *f*; ~ **paid**
contestación pagada; (**international**)
~ **coupon** cupón (-ones) *m* de
respuesta (internacional); ~ **telegram**
telegrama *m* de porte pagado; **I await**
your ~ espero sus noticias; *v*
contestar; ~ **to a letter** contestar una
carta
repopulate repoblar
report *n* informe *m*; **make a** ~ hacer un
informe; (news item) noticia; (article)
reportaje *m*; (school) nota; (bang)
estampido; **annual** ~ memoria anual;
v informar (**on** acerca de), *SA* reportar; (crime) denunciar; (present
oneself) comparecer¹⁴ (**to** ante); **it is**
~ed that se dice que; ~ **progress** co-
municar⁴ sobre la marcha de un
asunto
reportage relación (-ones) *f*
reportedly según los informes recibidos
reporter reportero
repose *n* descanso; **features in** ~ facciones *fpl* tranquilas; *v* descansar; ~
trust in poner¹⁹ confianza en
repository repositorio; (furniture)
guardamuebles *m sing*
repossess recuperar
reprehend reprender
reprehensible reprensible
represent representar; (mean) signi-
ficar⁴; (symbolize) simbolizar⁷; *leg*
ser¹⁹ apoderado de
representation representación *f*; **make**
~s to … on behalf of hacer¹⁴ gestiones
con … a favor de
representative *n* +*pol* representante
m+f; (delegate) delegado; *comm*
viajante *m*; *leg* apoderado; *adj* representativo; (typical) típico; ~ **sample**
comm muestra representativa
repress reprimir
repression represión *f*
repressive represivo
reprieve *n* aplazamiento; *leg* suspensión
f de la pena de muerte; *v* aplazar⁷; *leg*
suspender la pena de muerte

reprimand n reprensión f; v reprender

reprint n nueva tirada; v reimprimir

reprisal represalia; **take ~s (against)** tomar represalias (contra)

reproach n reproche m; **above ~** sin tacha; v reprochar; fam echar en cara, **they ~ed me for it** me lo echaron en cara

reproachful reprobador(-ora f)

reprobate n + adj réprobo

reprobation reprobación f

reproduce reproducir[15]

reproducible que puede reproducirse[15]

reproduction reproducción (-ones) f; (copy) copia

reproductive reproductor (-ora f); ~ **organs** órganos reproductores

reproof n reprobación f

re-proof v volver (ue)[1b] (past part vuelto) a hacer impermeable

reproval reprobación f

reprove reprobar (ue)[1a]

reptile reptil m

reptilian reptil

republic república

republican n + adj republicano

republicanism republicanismo

republication reedición f

republish reeditar

repudiate (reject) rechazar[7]; (fail to honour) desconocer[14]; (wife) repudiar

repudiation (rejection) rechazamiento; (failure to honour) desconocimiento; (of wife) repudiación f

repugnance, repugnancy repugnancia

repugnant repugnante

repulse n repeler; v repulsar; (refuse) rechazar[7]

repulsion phys repulsión f; (dislike) repugnancia

repulsive repugnante

repurchase (buy back) comprar de nuevo; ~ **agreement** pacto de retroventa

reputable (person) honrado; (firm etc) acreditado

reputation reputación f; fam cartel, **he has the ~ of a Don Juan** él tiene reputación de don Juan

repute reputación f; **by ~** según la opinión pública; **of ~** acreditado; **~d** supuesto; **~d father** padre putativo; **be ~d to be** tener[19] fama de

reputedly según la opinión pública

request n petición f; leg demanda; **at the ~ of** a petición de; **by ~** a petición (of de); ~ **programme** programa a petición (esp de radioyentes); **in ~** en demanda; ~ **stop** parada discrecional; v pedir (i)[3]; **passengers/clients are ~ed to** se ruega a los viajeros/clientes que + subj

requiem: ~ **(mass)** (misa de) réquiem m

require (need) necesitar; (compel) obligar[5] **(to** a); (demand) exigir[9]

requirement requisito; (need) necesidad f; (stipulation) estipulación f

requisite n requisito; adj necesario

requisition n + mil requisición f; v requisar

requital desquite m

requite retornar; ~ **s.o.'s love** corresponder al amor de alguien

reredos retablo

re-release cin reestreno

re-route desviar

re-routing desviación f

re-run cin + TV n reposición f; v reponer[19]

re-saddle ensillar de nuevo

resale reventa

rescind rescindir

rescue n salvamento; (retrieval) rescate m; **go to the ~ of** acudir en socorro de; ~ **party** expedición f de salvamento, mil expedición f de rescate; v salvar; (free) rescatar

rescuer salvador m (-ora f)

research n investigación (into sobre); v investigar[5]; ~ **laboratory** laboratorio de investigación

reseat (provide new seats) proveer[17] de asientos nuevos; (repair a chair etc) poner[19] fondo nuevo; mech reasentar (ie)[2a]

resell revender

resemblance semejanza

resemble parecerse a

resent resentirse (ie)[2c] de

resentful resentido

resentment resentimiento

reservation reserva; (in vehicle) plaza reservada; (wild life) coto; (mental) reserva, **without ~** sin reserva

reserve n reserva; ~ **tank** depósito de/en reserva; (self-control) reticencia; **~s** comm + mil + sp reservas fpl; ~ **price**

precio mínimo fijado; **in** ~ de/en reserva; *v* reservar

reserved reservado; ~ **seat** plaza reservada; (quiet) callado

reservist reservista *m*

reservoir pantano; *fig* fondo

reset *mech* reponer[19]; (watch) poner en hora; ~ **button** botón *m* de reposición

reshape rehacer[19]

reshuffle *n pol* reconstrucción *f*; *v* reconstruir[16]; (cards) barajar de nuevo

reside residir

residence residencia; **in** ~ residente

residency residencia oficial

resident *n+adj* residente *m+f*; *orni* indígena *m+f*

residential residencial; ~ **area** zona de viviendas

residual residual

residuary restante; ~ **legatee** legatario universal

residue resto

residuum residuo

resign dimitir (from de); ~ **o.s. to** conformarse con

resignation resignación *f*; (from a post) dimisión *f*

resignedly con resignación

resilience, resiliency elasticidad *f*; (personal) poder *m* de recuperación

resilient elástico; +*fig* resistente

resin *n* resina; (solidified, for violinists) colofonia

resinous resinoso

resist *vt* oponerse[19] a; ~ **temptation** resistir la tentación; *vi* resistirse; **I just couldn't** ~ **kissing her** no pude por menos de besarla

resistance resistencia; **passive** ~ resistencia pasiva; (opposition) oposición *f*; **resistance (movement)** resistencia

resistant resistente (**to** a)

resister el/la que resiste

resistible resistible

resistless irresistible

resistor resistor *m*

resolute resuelto

resoluteness resolución *f*

resolution resolución *f*; (proposal) acuerdo, **pass a** ~ tomar un acuerdo; **good** ~s buenos propósitos

resolvable resoluble

resolve *n* resolución *f*; *vt* resolver (ue)[1b]

(*past part* resuelto); *vi* resolverse (ue)[1b] (*past part* resuelto) (**to** a)

resonance resonancia

resonant resonante; (of voice) sonoro

resort *n* (place) lugar *m* de veraneo; (recourse) recurso, **as a last** ~ en último caso; *v* ~ **to** recurrir a

resound resonar (ue)[1a]

resounding sonoro; *fig* clamoroso

resource recurso; (of character) inventiva, habilidad; ~**s** (natural) riquezas *fpl*; (money) recursos *mpl*

resourceful inventivo

resourcefulness inventiva; recursos *mpl*

respect *n* respe(c)to, consideración *f*; ~**s** (greetings) recuerdos *mpl*; **in** ~ **of** respecto a; **in every** ~ en todos los aspectos; **in other** ~**s** por lo demás; **in some** ~**s** hasta cierto punto; **in this** ~ respecto a esto; **out of** ~ **for** por consideración a; **with** ~ **to** con respecto a; **pay one's** ~**s to** cumplimentar; *v* respe(c)tar; **as** ~**s** en cuanto a

respectability respetabilidad *f*

respectable respetable; (decent) decente; ~ **sum of money** cantidad *f* considerable de dinero

respectful respetuoso

respectfully: yours ~ le saluda atentamente

respectfulness conducta respetuosa

respecting con respecto a

respective respectivo

respiration respiración *f*

respirator careta antigás (*pl* caretas antigás); *med* respirador *m*

respiratory respiratorio

respire respirar

respite *n* respi(rade)ro; *leg* prórroga; **without** ~ sin tregua; *v* prorrogar (ue)[1a]

resplendence, resplendency resplandor *m*

resplendent resplandeciente

respond (answer) contestar; (react) reaccionar (**to** a)

respondent demandado

response (answer) contestación *f*, respuesta; (reaction) reacción *f*

responsibility responsabilidad *f*

responsible responsable; **be** ~ **for** responder por/de, responsabilizarse[7] de; **hold** ~ hacer[19] responsable

responsive que responde (bien)

[1] **rest** n (support) apoyo; (after activity) descanso; (repose) reposo; (freedom from care) tranquilidad f, paz f; mus silencio; at ~ (dead) en paz; be at ~ estar[19] descansando, (dead) descansar en paz; come to ~ pararse; have a ~ descansar un rato; set one's mind at ~ dejar tranquilo; ~ area parking m; ~-cure cura de reposo; ~-room sala de descanso, US servicio; v (support) apoyar (on en); (cease activity[19]) descansar; ~ assured (that) estar[19] seguro (de que); may (s)he ~ in peace! ¡que en paz descanse!; ~ on one's oars dejar de remar, fig descansar; let the matter ~ que quede ahí el asunto; ~ with depender de; it ~s with you depende de usted

[2] **rest** (remainder) resto; the ~ lo demás, los/las demás; the ~ of the cheese lo que sobra del queso; the ~ of the pupils los demás alumnos; for the ~ por lo demás

restart n sp comienzo del segundo tiempo; v comenzar (ie)[2a+7] de nuevo; mech ponerse[19] de nuevo en marcha

restaurant restorán m, restaurante m; ~-car coche-comedor m

restaurateur dueño de un restaurante

restful descansado

resting: (last) ~-place última morada

restitution restitución f; make ~ indemnizar[7]

restive, restless inquieto; (sleepless) insomne; ~ night noche f en blanco

restlessness inquietud f; (sleeplessness) insomnio

restock (with goods) volver (ue)[1b] (past part vuelto) a surtir; (with animals, trees) repoblar (ue)[1a]

restoration restauración f; (returning) devolución f

restorative n+adj reconstituyente

restore restaurar; (return) devolver (ue)[1b] (past part devuelto); ~ s.o. to health devolver (ue)[1b] (past part devuelto) la salud a una persona

restorer restaurador m (-ora f); hair-~ loción f capilar

restrain contener[19]; fam tener[19] a raya; (lunatic) recluir[16]; ~ s.o. from impedir (i)[3] a alguien que +subj; ~ed refrenado, (of character) cohibido

restraint restricción f; (moderation) moderación f; (of prices etc) contención f

restrict restringir[9]; be ~ed to limitarse a; ~ed (secret) reservado; ~ed area mot zona de velocidad limitada; zona prohibida

restriction restricción f

restrictive restrictivo; ~ practices normas fpl restrictivas

restuff volver (ue)[1b] (past part vuelto) a rellenar

result n resultado; as a ~ en consecuencia; as a ~ of a consecuencia de; v resultar (from de); ~ in terminar en

resultant resultante

resume (take up again) reasumir; (continue after interruption) comenzar (ie)[2a+7] de nuevo; (sum up) resumir; ~ a journey reanudar un viaje; ~ one's seat volver[1b] (past part vuelto) a sentarse

résumé resumen (-úmenes) m

resumption reasunción f; (of journey) reanudación f; sp comienzo del segundo tiempo

resurface vi volver (ue)[1b] (past part vuelto) a la superficie; vt reparar la superficie de

resurgence resurgimiento

resurgent que resurge

resurrect resucitar

resurrection resurrección f

resuscitate resucitar

resuscitation resucitación f

retail n venta al por menor; ~ price precio al por menor; ~ trade comercio minorista; adv al por menor; vt vender al por menor; (gossip) repetir (i)[3]; vi ~ at venderse a

retailer detallista m+f

retain retener[19]; leg ajustar; (player) contratar

retainer (person) criado; (payment) anticipo a cuenta; leg anticipo de honorarios

retake volver (ue)[1b] (past part vuelto) a tomar; phot volver (ue)[1b] a sacar

retaliate tomar represalias

retaliation represalia; in ~ por venganza; como represalia

retaliatory vengativo

retard retrasar; (mentally) ~ed person retrasado mental

retardation retraso; *med* retraso mental

retch (hacer)[19] esfuerzos por) vomitar

retching esfuerzos por vomitar

retell repetir (i)[3]

retention retención *f*

retentive retentivo

rethink *n* reexaminación *f*; *v* volver a pensar (ie)[2a]

reticence reserva

reticent reservado

reticular reticular

reticulate formar a modo de red

retina retina

retinue séquito

retire +*mil* retirarse; (go to bed) recogerse[8]; (from work) jubilarse; ~d jubilado, *mil* retirado

retirement jubilación *f*; *mil* retiro; ~ **pension** pensión *f* de jubilación, *mil* retiro

retiring (shy) reservado; (giving up official position) saliente

[1] **retort** *n chem* retorta; *metal* cámara

[2] **retort** (answer) *n* réplica; *v* replicar[4]

retouch *n phot* retoque *m*; *v* retocar[4]

retrace repasar; ~ **one's steps** volver (ue)[1b] (*past part* vuelto) sobre sus pasos; (recount) narrar

retract retractar(se); *mech* replegar(se) (ie)[2a+5]

retractable retractable; ~ **ball-point pen** bolígrafo retráctil; ~ **undercarriage** tren *m* retráctil

retrac(ta)tion retracción *f*

retranslate traducir[15] de nuevo

retread *n mot* recauchutado; *v* recauchutar

retreat *n* +*mil* retirada; +*eccles* retiro; **beat a** ~ batirse en retirada; *v* retirarse

retrench *vt* reducir; *vi* economizar[7]

retrenchment economías *fpl*

retrial (of person) nuevo proceso; (of case) revisión *f*

retribution retribución *f*

retributive retributivo

retrievable recuperable; (of damage) reparable

retrieve (regain) recobrar; (hunting) cobrar; (an error) remediar; (fortune) reparar; (losses) resarcirse[13] de

retriever perro cobrador

retroactive retroactivo

retrocede retroceder

retrofire *space* maniobra retrógrada

retrograde retrógrado

retrogress retroceder

retrogression retrogresión *f*

retrogressive retrógrado

retro-rocket *space* retrocohete *m*

retrospect retrospección *f*; **in** ~ mirando hacia atrás

retrospection consideración *f* de lo pasado

retrospective retrospectivo; (of legislation) retroactivo

re-try volver a juzgar

return *n* vuelta, regreso; (handingback) devolución *f*; (report) informe *m*; (income-tax) declaración *f*; (reply) respuesta; *pol* elección *f*; (for kindness *etc*) recompensa; (profit) ganancia; ~**s** (figures) estadística, (election) resultados *mpl*; **by** ~ (of post) a vuelta de correo; **in** ~ **for** a cambio de; **many happy** ~**s of the day!** ¡feliz cumpleaños!; ~ **fight** *sp* revancha; ~ **game** partido de vuelta; ~ **journey** viaje *m* de vuelta; ~ **ticket** billete *m* de ida y vuelta; *v* volver (ue)[1b] (*past part* vuelto), regresar; (give back) devolver (ue)[1b] (*past part* devuelto); (elect) elegir (i)[3]; *comm* (produce) rendir (i)[3]; (verdict) dictar; (visit) pagar[5]; ~ **like for like** pagar[5] en la misma moneda; ~ **thanks** dar[19] las gracias (**for** por); '~ **to drawer**' *comm* 'sin fondos'

returnable restituible; ~ **empties** envases *mpl* a devolver

returning: ~ **officer** escudriñador *m*

reunion reunión (-ones) *f*

reunite reunir(se); (reconcile) reconciliar; **become** ~**d** reconciliarse

reusable reutilizable

rev *n mot* revolución *f*; ~**s per second** revoluciones por segundo; ~**-counter** cuentarrevoluciones *m sing*; *v* ~ **up** hacer girar el motor; (while driving) acelerar

revaluation revalorización *f*

revalue revalorizar[7]

reveal revelar; ~ **a secret** revelar un secreto, *fam* soltar (ue)[1a] la consigna

reveille diana; (bugle-call) toque *m* de diana

revel *n* juerga; *v* jaranear; ~ **in** deleitarse en

revelation revelación (-ones) *f*
reveller juerguista *m+f*
revelry jolgorio
revenge *n* venganza; *v* vengar[5]; **be ~d on** vengarse[5] de
revengeful vengativo
revenger vengador *m* (-ora *f*)
revenue renta; (public) rentas *fpl* públicas; **Inland Revenue** Hacienda; **~ authorities** funcionarios *mpl*; **~ cutter** guardacostas *m sing+pl*; **~ officer** aduanero; **~ stamp** sello fiscal
reverberant reverberante
reverberate (sound) retumbar; (light) reverberar
reverberation (sound) retumbar *m*; (light) reverberación *f*
reverberator reverberador *m*
revere venerar
reverence *n* reverencia; **your ~** reverencia; *v* reverenciar
reverend *n* pastor *m*; *adj* reverendo
reverent reverente
reverential reverencial
reverie ensueño
reversal inversión *f*; (of fortune) cambio; (of policy) cambio completo; *leg* revocación *f*
reverse *n* (opposite side) respaldo; (of cloth) revés *m*; (of paper) dorso; (opposite) lo contrario, **quite the ~** al contrario; (setback) contratiempo; *comm* pérdida; *mil* derrota; **in ~** *mot* en marcha atrás; **go in(to) ~** dar[19] marcha atrás; *adj* inverso; **in the ~ direction** en el sentido contrario; **on the ~ side** al dorso; **~ turn** (dancing) vuelta al revés; *v* invertir (ie)[2c]; (movement) ir[19] hacia atrás; *mot* dar[19] marcha atrás, **he ~d into the post** al dar marcha atrás chocó con el poste; (dancing) dar[19] vueltas al revés; *leg* revocar[4]; **~ arms** llevar las armas a la funerala; **~ the charges** (telephone) cobrar al número llamado; **~d charge call** llamada a cobro revertido
reversible (+clothing) reversible
reversing de marcha atrás; **~ lights** faros *mpl* (de) marcha atrás
reversion reversión *f*
revert volver (ue)[1b] (*past part* vuelto) (to a); *biol* saltar atrás; *leg* revertir (ie)[2c]; **~ to type** volver (ue)[1b] (*past part*

vuelto) a las andadas
review *n* (magazine) revista; (critical article) reseña; (revision) repaso; *mil* revista; *leg* revisión *f*; *v* repasar; (write a criticism of) reseñar; *mil* pasar revista a; *leg* revisar[19]
reviewer reseñador *m* (-ora *f*); crítico
revile ultrajar
revise revisar; (a lesson) repasar; (book) corregir (i)[3]
revision revisión *f*; (of lesson) repaso; (of book) corrección *f*
revisionism revisionismo
revisionist *n+adj* revisionista *m+f*
revisit volver (ue)[1b] (*past part* vuelto) a visitar
revitalize revivificar[4]
revival reanimación *f*; *eccles* despertar religioso; *med* resucitación *f*; (of learning *etc*) renacimiento; (of film, play) reestreno
revivalism evangelismo
revivalist predicador *m* evangélico
revive *vt* reanimar; (fire) avivar; *cin+theat* reestrenar; (interest *etc*) despertar (ie)[2a]; (unconscious person) resucitar; *vi* reanimarse; (after unconsciousness) volver (ue)[1b] (*past part* vuelto) en sí
reviver bebida estimulante
revivify revivificar[4]
revocable revocable
revocation revocación *f*
revoke *n* renuncio; *v* revocar[4]; (at cards) renunciar
revolt *n* sublevación (-ones) *f*; *v* sublevarse; (repel) dar[19] asco
revolting (rebellious) sublevado; (disgusting) asqueroso
revolution +*mech*+*pol* revolución (-ones) *f*; (cycle) ciclo
revolutionary *n+adj* revolucionario
revolutionize revolucionar
revolve *vi* (*usu* horizontally) girar; (*usu* vertically) rodar (ue)[19]; *astron* girar; **~ round** depender[2b](ie) de; *vt* hacer[19] girar; (mentally) dar[19] vueltas en la cabeza
revolver revólver *m*
revolving (horizontally) giratorio, **~ stage** *theat* escenario giratorio; (vertically) rotativo
revulsion asco; *med* revulsión *f*
revulsive revulsivo

reward recompensa; (for lost property *etc*) gratificación (-ones) *f*; *v* recompensar (**for** por); gratificar[4]

rewarding remunerador; *fig* satisfaciente

re-wind (on spool) rebobinar, ~ **button** tecla para rebobinar

reword formular en otras palabras

rewrite volver (ue)[1b] a escribir

rhapsodic(al) relativo a la rapsodia

rhapsodize entusiasmarse (**over** por)

rhapsody rapsodia; *fig* transporte *m* (de entusiasmo)

rheostat reostato

rhesus: ~ **factor** factor *m* Rhesus; ~ **monkey** macaco de la India

rhetoric retórica

rhetorical retórico

rhetorician retórico

rheumatic reumático

rheumatism reumatismo

Rhine Rin *m*

rhino(ceros) rinoceronte *m*

Rhodes Rodas *f*

Rhodesia Rodesia

Rhodesian *n+adj* rodesiano

rhododendron rododendro

rhombus rombo

rhubarb ruibarbo

rhyme *n* rima; (poem) poesía; (word) consonante *m*; **without ~ or reason** sin ton ni son; *v* rimar

rhymester rimador *m*

rhythm ritmo; ~ **method** (birth control) método ogino

rhythmic(al) rítmico

rib *n* *anat* costilla; *bot* nervio; *naut* cuaderna; *bui* (beam) viga; *v* tomar el pelo

ribald obsceno

ribaldry obscenidad *f*

riband, ribbon (+ typewriter) cinta; *mil* galón *m*; ~ **development** urbanización *f* al lado de una carretera

ribbed nervudo; *archi* faja

rice arroz *m*; ~-**field** arrozal *m*; ~-**flour** harina de arroz; ~-**paper** papel *m* de arroz; ~-**pudding** arroz *m* con leche

rich *n*: **the** ~ los ricos, *fam* los gordos; ~**es** riqueza(s); *adj* (wealthy) rico; (sumptuous) suntuoso; (of colour) vivo; (of food) rico; *pej* (of food) empalagoso; (of land) fértil; (of style) opulento; (of voice) sonoro; (of wine)

generoso; (amusing) divertido; **be ~ in** abundar de/en; **become ~** enriquecerse[14], *fam* forrarse

Richard Ricardo

richly: ~ **deserved** bien merecido

richness (wealth) riqueza; (sumptuousness) suntuosidad *f*; (of colour) viveza; (of food) lo sabroso, *pej* empalago; (of land) fertilidad *f*; (of style) opulencia; (of voice) sonoridad *f*; (of wine) generosidad *f*

[1] **rick** *n* (hay) henar *m*; (straw) pajar *m*; *v* hacer[19] un henar/pajar

[2] **rick** (in neck) *n* torcedura; *v* torcer (ue)[1b+14]

rickets raquitismo

rickety raquítico; (wobbly) desvencijado

rickshaw carricoche *m* chino

ricochet *n* rebote *m*; *v* rebotar

rid librar; **be ~ of** estar[19] libre de; **get ~ of** deshacerse[19] de

riddance libramiento; **good ~!** ¡vete con viento fresco!

[1] **riddle** *n* (sieve) criba; *v* cribar; (with shot) acribillar, *fam* freír (i)[3] a tiros

[2] **riddle** (puzzle) acertijo; (puzzling fact) enigma *m*

ride *n* (on horseback) cabalgada; (by car/bicycle) paseo en coche/en bicicleta; (bridle-path) camino de herradura; **go for a ~** dar[19] un paseo; **take s.o. for a ~** (deceive) decepcionarle a uno, (take off and kill) dar[19] el paseo a uno; *v* montar (a caballo/en bicicleta); (in car) pasearse (ir) en coche; **he rode ten kilometres** él recorrió (a caballo/en bicicleta) diez kilómetros; ~ **at anchor** estar[19] fondeado; ~ **for a fall** presumir demasiado; ~ **one's high horse** asumir una actitud arrogante; ~ **roughshod over** pisotear los derechos de; ~ **the waves** surcar[4] las olas; ~ **down** atropellar; ~ **out** (storm) capear

rider (on horse) jinete *m*, amazona; (on cycle) ciclista *m+f*; *mech* pilón (-ones) *m*; (additional clause) aditamento

riderless sin jinete

ridge *n* (of hill) cresta; (of hills) sierra; (of roof) caballete *m*; (of furrow) caballón (-ones) *m*; ~-**tent** tienda canadiense; *v* surcar

ridicule *n* burlas *f pl*; *v* poner[19] en solfa

ridiculous ridículo

riding montar *m* a caballo, equitación *f*; ~ **boots/breeches** botas *fpl*/pantalón *m* de montar; ~**-light** *naut* fanal *m* de proa; ~**-school** picadero; ~**-whip** fusta

rife (common) corriente; *fam* a chorros; ~ **with** lleno de; **be** ~ cundir

riff frase repetida en la música moderna

riff-raff gentuza

¹ **rifle** *n* fusil *m*; ~**man** fusilero; ~**-range** campo de tiro; ~**-shot** tiro de fusil; ~**d barrel** cañón *m* rayado

² **rifle** *v* saquear

rifling raya(do)

rift *geol* hendedura; (disagreement) desavenencia

¹ **rig** *n naut* aparejo; (attire) atavío; (oil) torre *f* de perforación; *v* aparejar; ~ **out** ataviar; ~ **up** (assemble) montar, (improvise) improvisar

² **rig:** ~ **an election** amañar⁴ una elección; ~ **the market** manipular la lonja

rigging (ropes) aparejo; (sails) velamen *m*

right *n* (privilege) derecho (**to** a); ~ **of way** derecho de paso; (justice) justicia; (title) título; (not left) derecha, **on/to the** ~ a/hacia la derecha; (boxing) derechazo; *pol* derecha, **politicians of the** ~ políticos de la derecha; ~**s** (copy~) propiedad *f*; **all** ~**s reserved** todos los derechos reservados; **exclusive** ~**s** exclusiva; **by** ~ **of** por razón de; **by** ~**s** según derecho; **in his own** ~ por su propio derecho; **be in the** ~ tener¹⁹ razón; **he doesn't know** ~ **from wrong** él no distingue el bien del mal; *adj* (just) justo; (correct) correcto, **the** ~ **answer** la contestación correcta; (proper) debido, **do what is** ~ hacer¹⁹ lo debido; (sane) cuerdo; (of circumstances) favorable; (not left) derecho; ~ **or wrong, he will do it** con razón o sin ella, él lo hará; ~ **turn!** ¡derecha!; ~ **back** *sp* defensa *m* derecho; ~ **half** *sp* medio derecho; **I'd give my** ~ **hand to** me dejaría sacar los ojos por +*infin*; ~ **wing** *sp* ala derecha; ~ **winger/sweeper** *sp* alero derecho; ~ **you are!** ¡conforme!; **be** ~ tener¹⁹ razón; **you're not thinking on the** ~ **lines** sus pensamientos no van por buen camino; **at the** ~ **moment** al momento (p)sicológico; **all** ~**!**

(agreed) ¡conforme!, (in answer to 'come here!') ¡ya voy!; **be** ~ **to** hacer¹⁹ bien en +*infin*; **be all** ~ estar¹⁹ bien; **be** ~ **as rain** estar¹⁹ de primera; **do the** ~ **thing** saber¹⁹ cómo acertar; **that's** ~ eso es; **put** ~ arreglar; **seem** ~ pegar⁵; **to me it doesn't seem** ~ **to do that** no me gusta hacer eso; **this is the** ~ **machine for the work** ésta es la máquina que hace falta para el trabajo; ~ **about turn!** ¡media vuelta a la derecha!; ~**-angle** ángulo recto; ~**-angled triangle** triángulo rectángulo; ~**-hand drive** *mot* conducción *f* a la derecha; ~**-hand man** hombre *m* de confianza; ~**-handed** (person) que usa la mano derecha, (for a ~-handed person) para la mano derecha; ~**-handed turn** giro hacia la derecha; ~**-minded** (honest) honrado, (sane) cuerdo; ~**-wing, ~-winger** *pol* derechista *m*+*f*; *v* +*naut* enderezar⁷; ~ **a wrong** deshacer¹⁹ un agravio; *adv* bien; **she always does it** ~ ella siempre lo hace bien; **carry on** ~ **ahead** ir¹⁹ todo recto; ~ **at the end of/bottom of** al fin de/al fondo de; ~ **away** en seguida; ~ **here/there** aquí/allí mismo; ~ **now** ahora mismo, *fam* ahorita; ~ **off** en seguida; ~ **on** adelante; **fill** ~ **up** llenar del todo

righteous honrado

righteousness honradez *f*

rightful legítimo

rightist *n*+*adj* derechista *m*+*f*

rightly (correctly) correctamente; (exactly) exactamente; (justly) con razón; ~ **or wrongly** mal que bien

rightness derechura; (justice) justicia

rigid rígido; (harsh) riguroso; (strict) estricto; (of rule) inflexible

rigidity rigidez *f*; (of rule) inflexibilidad *f*

rigmarole galimatías *m sing*; *fam* rollo

rigor: ~ **mortis** rigidez cadavérica

rigorous riguroso; *meteor* severo

rigour rigor *m*; *meteor* severidad *f*

rile irritar

rill riachuelo

rim borde *m*; (of cup) reborde *m*; (of wheel) llanta; *opt* borde (del cristal); (spectacles) montura

rime (frost) escarcha

rimless gafas *fpl* sin montura

rimmed (edged) bordado (**with** de);

gold-~ glasses gafas *fpl* con armadura de oro

rind (of apple+pork) piel *f*; (of cheese) costra; (of orange) cáscara

rindless sin cáscara/costra *etc*

[1] **ring** *n* (plain) anillo; (on drinks can) anilla; (with jewel) sortija; (large) aro; (boxing) cuadrilátero; (bullfight) ruedo; (circus) pista; (of people) corro; (under eyes) ojera; (monopoly) cartel *m*; **~s of Saturn** anillos *mpl* de Saturno; **~ binder** (for documents) carpeta con argollas; **~ finger** dedo anular; **~leader** cabecilla *m*; **~master** director *m* de circo; **~-road** carretera de circunvalación; **~worm** tiña; **wedding-~** alianza; *v* (surround) rodear; (place ring on) poner[19] un anillo a

[2] **ring** *n* (of bell) campanilleo; (of church bells) repique *m*; (of electric bell) toque *m* (de timbre); (of jingle-bells) cascabeleo; (tinkle) tintín *m*; (of phone) telefonazo; (at door) llamada; *vi* sonar; (at the door) llamar; (in one's ears) zumbar; (re-echo) retumbar; *vt* tocar[4] (la campana/el timbre); (large bell) tañer; **~ the doorbell** tocar[4] el timbre; **that ~s a bell** *fig* eso me suena (familiar); **~ the changes on** variar; **~ off** colgar (ue)[1a+5]; **~ up** llamar (por teléfono); **~ up/down the curtain** levantar/bajar el telón

ringer campanero

ringing *see* [2]**ring** *n*; **~ tone** (telephone) tonalidad *f*

ringlet (long) tirabuzón (-ones) *m*; (small) rizo, *fam* caracol *m*

rink pista de patinar

rinse *n* (of mouth) enjuague *m*; (of clothes) aclarado; (hair-dye) tinte *m*; *v* enjuagar[5]; aclarar; teñir (i)[3]; *phot* lavar

rinsing (of mouth) enjuague *m*; (of clothes) aclarado; **~-tank** *phot* tanque *m* de lavado

riot *n* (rebellion) motín (-ines) *m*; (noisy disturbance) alboroto; **run ~** desenfrenarse; **it was a ~!** (great fun) ¡fue una juerga!; **read the ~ act** *see* [1]**read**; *v* amotinarse; alborotarse

rioter (rebel) amotinado; (one who causes noisy disturbance) alborotador *m*

rioting *n* (rebelling) motín (-ines) *m*; (causing noisy disturbance) alboroto

riotous alborotado; (of celebration) ruidoso, bullicioso; **~ assembly** reunión *f* sediciosa; **~ life** vida desenfrenada

riotously: it was ~ funny fue divertidísimo

R.I.P. (Requiescat in Pace) Q.E.P.D. (que en paz descanse)

rip *n* rasgadura; **~cord** *aer* cabo de desgarre; *v* rasgar(se)[5]; **be ripped** estar[19] roto; **~-off** timo; **~ out** arrancar[4]; **~ up** rasgar[5]

ripe maduro; *fig* oportuno; **~ for** en condiciones para; **~ for picking** cogedura

ripen madurar

ripeness madurez *f*

riposte respuesta

ripple *n* onda (pequeña); (sound) murmullo; *v* rizarse[7]; (of sound) murmurar

rip-roaring animadísimo

rise *n* subida, **~ to power** subida al poder; (increase) aumento, **~ in pay** aumento de salario; (in prices) alza; (development) desarrollo; (growth) crecimiento; (in rank) ascenso; (slope) cuesta; (high ground) altura; (of sun *etc*) salida; **give ~ to** motivar; **~ and fall** subida y bajada, (of institutions) grandeza y decadencia, *mus* cadencia, (of voice) ritmo, (of tides) pleamar *m* y bajamar *m*; *v* subir; (get up) levantarse; (to surface) surgir[9]; (rebel) sublevarse; (of buildings + mountains) elevarse; (of meeting) suspenderse; (in rank) ascender (ie)[2b]; (of river) nacer[14]; (of sun *etc*) salir[19]; **~ again** resucitar; **I have ~n in her estimation** he ganado en su estimación; **~ in the world** venir[19] a más; **~ to one's feet** ponerse[19] de pie; **~ to the bait** +*fig* morder (ue)[1b] el anzuelo; **~ to the occasion** estar[19] al nivel de las circunstancias

riser el que se levanta; **early-~** madrugador *m* (-ora *f*)

risibility risibilidad *f*

risible risible

rising *n* subida; (rebellion) sublevación *f*; (of tide) crecida; (overflowing of river) crecimiento; (of sun *etc*) salida; (of bread) levadura; *theat* (of curtain)

subida; (from the dead) resurrección
f; **I like early** ~ me gusta madrugar;
adj naciente, ascendiente; (promising) de porvenir; ~ **generation**
generación *f* nueva; ~ **ground** terreno
en cuesta; ~ **sun** sol *m* naciente; ~
tide marea creciente; **she is** ~ **forty**
ella ronda los cuarenta

risk *n* riesgo; **at the buyer's** ~ *comm* por
cuenta y riesgo del comprador; **at the**
~ **of** con peligro de; **run the** ~ **(of)** correr el peligro (de); *v* arriesgar[5]; ~ **it**
arriesgarse[5]; ~ *+pres part* arriesgarse
a *+infin*; ~ **everything** jugar (ue)[1a] el
todo por el todo; ~ **one's life** jugarse
(ue)[1a] la vida

risky arriesgado

risotto arroz *m* con queso y cebolla

risqué verde

rissole *approx* albóndiga

rite rito; **last** ~**s** exequias *fpl*

ritual *n+adj* ritual *m*

ritualism ritualismo

ritualist ritualista *m+f*

ritualistic ritualista

rival *n+adj* rival *m*; *sp* competidor *m*
(-ora *f*); *v* rivalizar[7] con; competir con

rivalry rivalidad *f*

river río; ~**-bed** lecho; ~ **fish** pez *m* de
río; ~ **mouth** ría; ~ **pilot** práctico de
río; ~**side** orilla; ~**side hotel** hotel ribereño; **down/up** ~ río abajo/arriba;
adj del río; fluvial, ~ **port** puerto fluvial

rivet *n* remache *m*; (for shoe-repairing)
clavito; *v* remachar; (footwear) clavar; ~ **one's attention on** clavar la
atención en

riveter remachador *m*

riveting remachado; ~ **machine** remacha-
chadora

Riviera Costa Azul

rivulet riachuelo

roach (fish) escarcho; (cockroach)
cucaracha

road carretera; (way) *+fig* camino; (in
town) calle *f*; **main** ~ *Sp* carretera
nacional; **secondary** ~ carretera vecinal; **trunk** ~ carretera radial; **the** ~
to Toledo el camino/la carretera de
Toledo; **on the** ~ **to** camino de; **by** ~
por carretera; **get out of the** ~ *fig*
quitarse de en medio; **hold the** ~ agarrarse al camino; ~**s** *naut* rada; ~

accident accidente *m* de carretera; ~-
block barrera (de control); ~ **closed**
paso prohibido; ~ **courtesy** amabilidad *f* en el tráfico; ~**-hog** conductor
desconsiderado; ~**-holding** adherencia; ~**house** parador *m*; ~**-junction**
empalme *m*; ~**man**, ~**mender** peón
m (-ones) caminero; ~**-map** mapa de
carreteras; ~ **network** red *f* arterial de
carreteras; ~**race** carrera sobre carretera; ~**-sense** *mot* instinto de conductor; ~**side** borde *m* de la carretera;
~**side halt** parada al lado de la
carretera; ~**-sign** señal *f* de tráfico; ~
surface firme *m* de la carretera; ~**-
sweeper** (person) barrendero, (mechanical) barrecalles *m* *sing+pl*; ~**-
traffic** tránsito rodado; ~ **up** carretera
en reparación; ~**-user** usuario de las
carreteras; ~ **vehicle** vehículo de carreteras; ~**way** calzada; ~**-works**
obras *fpl*; ~**worthy** en condiciones
para rodar

roadster (bicycle) bicicleta de turismo;
(car) (coche *m* de) turismo

roam *vi* vagar[5]; *vt* vagar[5] por

roamer vagabundo

roaming *n* vagabundeo; *adj* errante

roan caballo ruano

roar *n* rugido; (of bull + angry person)
bramido; (of guns + thunder) estallido; (shout) grito; ~ **of laughter**
carcajada; *vi* rugir[9]; bramar; estallar;
(of fire) crepitar; ~ **with laughter**
reírse (i)[3] a carcajadas; *vt* gritar

roarer bramador *m* (-ora *f*)

roaring rugiente; (of bull) bramante;
(people) vociferante; (of fire) crepitante, *fam* de aúpa; **it was a** ~ **success**
tuvo un éxito formidable

roast *n* asado; *v* asar; (coffee + nuts)
tostar (ue)[1a]; ~**ed almonds** peladillas
fpl

roaster asador *m*; tostador *m*; (poultry)
gallina *etc* para asar

roasting: ~**-spit** asador *m*

rob robar; ~ **s.o. of something** robar
algo a alguién, **they robbed me of my
wallet** me robaron la cartera

robber ladrón (-ones) *m*; (highway)
salteador *m* (de caminos)

robbery robo; ~ **with violence** robo con
atraco; **armed** ~ robo armado; **it's
daylight** ~! ¡es un robo!; **commit** ~

cometer un robo

robe *n* manto; *eccles* sotana; (dressing-gown) bata; ~s **of state** traje *m* de ceremonia; *v* vestir(se) (i)[3]

Robert Roberto

[1] **robin** petirrojo

[2] **robin: round ~** petición *f* firmada colectivamente

robot autómata *m*; *aer* piloto automático

robust robusto

robustness robustez *f*

[1] **rock** roca; *naut* escollo; *sl* diamante *m*; **the Rock** el Peñón (de Gibraltar); **be on the ~s** (ruined) estar[19] a la cuarta pregunta; **whisky on the ~s** whisky *m* con hielo; ~-**bottom** (of prices) bajísimo; **down to ~-bottom** a lo más bajo; ~-**climber** escalador *m* (-ora *f*); ~-**climbing** escalada; ~-**crystal** cuarzo; ~-**fall** deslizamiento (de montaña); ~-**garden** jardín (-ines) rocoso; ~-**painting** pintura rupestre; ~-**plant** planta alpestre; ~-**salt** sal gema

[2] **rock** mecer(se)[14]; (baby) arrullar; (shake violently) sacudir(se); ~ **the boat** *fig* romper (*past part* roto) la baraja

[3] **rock** *mus* rock *m*

rocker balancín (-ines) *m*; (on chair) mecedora; (person) rockero; (*US* rocking-chair) mecedora; **off one's ~** chiflado; ~-**switch** *elect* interruptor *m* con mando basculante

rocket *n* cohete *m*; **space ~** cohete *m* espacial; (reprimand) bronca; ~ **assembly tower** torre *f* de montaje del cohete; ~ **propulsion** propulsión *f* a cohete; ~-**firing plane** caza lanzacohetes *f sing*; ~-**launching** lanzamiento del cohete; *v* subir rápidamente

rocketry ciencia de lanzar cohetes espaciales

rockiness abundancia de rocas

rocking balanceo; (staggering) tambaleo; (of baby) arrullo; ~-**chair** mecedora; ~-**horse** caballito de balancín

[1] **rocky** rocoso; (rugged) peñascoso; (of land) pedregoso; **Rocky Mountains** Montañas *fpl* Rocosas

[2] **rocky** (unstable) inestable

rococo *n+adj* rococó

rod var(ill)a; *mech* barra; (measure) *approx* pértiga; (for punishment) ver-

gajo; (fishing) caña de pescar; (*US* firearm) arma de fuego, *fam* quitapenas *m sing+pl*

rodent *n+adj* roedor *m*

rodeo rodeo

Roderick Rodrigo

rodomontade fanfarronear

roe (fish) hueva; ~-**buck**, ~-**deer** corzo

rogation rogación *f*

Roger Rogelio

rogue pícaro; ~s' **gallery** fichero de delincuentes

roguery *see* **roguishness**

roguish pícaro; (mischievous) travieso

roguishly como un pícaro

roguishness picardía; (mischievousness) travesuras *fpl*

roister bravear

roisterer matasiete *m*

Roland Orlando

role papel *m*; **take the ~ of** hacer[19] el papel de

roll *n* rollo; **he gave me a ~ of tobacco** me dio un rollo de tabaco; (bread) panecillo; (of cloth) pieza; (list) lista, **call the ~** pasar lista; (of thunder) retumbo; (of drum) redoble *m*; (movement + space) balanceo; (gait) bamboleo; ~s (records) archivos *mpl*; ~ **of banknotes** fajo de billetes; ~ **of honour** lista de honor; ~ **of Sellotape** rollo de celo; **have a nautical ~** tener[19] un andar de marinero; ~-**call** acto de pasar lista; ~-**film** rollo de película; ~-**mill** tren *m* de laminación *f*; ~-**top desk** escritorio de cierre enrollable; *vt* hacer[19] rodar; (cigarette) liar; (lawn) allanar; (pastry) aplanar; (drum) redoblar; ~ **one's eyes** poner[19] los ojos en blanco; ~ **one's r's** pronunciar las erres; ~ **the tongue** hacer vibrar la lengua; *vi* rodar; (of thunder) retumbar; (of gait) bambolearse; *naut+space* balancearse; *cin* empezar (ie)[2a] a filmar

~ **about** rodar (ue)[1a]; ~ **about in pain** retorcerse (ue)[1b] de dolor

~ **back** *vi* volver (ue)[1b] (*past part* vuelto); *vt* enrollar

~ **down** bajar rodando

~ **in** llegar[5] en gran cantidad/ (people) en gran número; **he is rolling in money** él está forrado de dinero

~ **off** caer[19] rodando (de)

~-on *n* (girdle) faja elástica

~ **on** *v* seguir (i)[3+11] en marcha; (of time) pasar[7]

~ **out** *metal* laminar; (pastry) aplanar; (unroll) desenrollar

~ **over** *vi* dar[19] la vuelta; (capsize) volcar[4]; *vt* dar[19] la vuelta a; hacer[19] volcar

~ **up** enrollar(se); (of hedgehogs) enroscarse; (arrive) llegar; (sleeves) remangar; ~ **up with laughter** torcerse (ue)[1b] de risa

rolled: ~ **gold** oro laminado; ~ **oats** copos de avena; ~ **steel** hierro laminado

roller (lawn + typewriter) rodillo; (heavy) apisonadora; (for curling hair) rizador *m*; *naut* ola larga; ~-**bearing** cojinete *m* de rodillos; ~-**coaster** montaña rusa; ~-**skate** *n* patín (-ines) *m* de ruedas, *v* patinar sobre ruedas; ~-**skating** patinaje *m* sobre ruedas; ~-**towel** toalla de rodillo

rollicking alegre

rolling *n* rodadura; *naut* balanceo; *adj* (of ground) ondulado; ~-**mill** taller *m* de laminación; ~-**pin** rodillo; ~-**stock** material *m* rodante

roly-poly *n* pudín (-ines) *m* en forma de rollo; *fam* persona gordinflona

Roman *n+adj* romano; **in the** ~ **fashion** a la romana; ~ **Catholic** católico apostólico romano; ~ **Catholicism** catolicismo; ~ **figure/numeral** número romano; ~ **nose** nariz (-ces) aguileña; ~ **road** vía romana

romance *n* (story) romance *m*; (romantic novel) novela romántica; (love-affair) amorío, aventura; **the** ~ **of the Middle Ages** lo romántico de la Edad Media; **Romance** *n+adj* románico; *v* soñar[1a]; (exaggerate) exagerar; (lie) mentir (ie)[2c]

romancing *n* cuento

Romanesque románico

Romania Rumania

Romanian *n+adj* rumano

romantic *n+adj* romántico; (of person) sentimental

romanticism romanticismo

Romany *n+adj* gitano

Rome Roma; **when in** ~ **do as the Romans do** cuando en Roma fueres, haz como vieres

Romish católico (romano)

romp *n* retozo; *v* retozar[7]; ~ **home (an easy winner)** ganar con facilidad

rompers mono (para niño)

Roneo *n* multicopista; *v* multicopiar

rood crucifijo; (measurement) cuarto de acre

roof *n* tejado; (flat) azotea; *mot* capota; (of mouth) paladar *m*; **raise the** ~ hacer[19] mucho ruido; ~-**garden** azotea; ~**top** tejado; **shout from the** ~**tops** *fig* predicar[4] a todo el mundo; *v* (~-over) techar

roofing *n* techumbre *m*; *adj* para techos; ~-**felt** tela asfáltica; ~-**tack** clavo de techar

roofless sin techo

[1] **rook** *n* *orni* corneja; *v* (cheat) engañar; (overcharge) cobrar caro

[2] **rook** (chess) torre *f*

rookery nidada de grajas

rookie bisoño

room *n* cuarto, habitación *f*; (space) sitio; (scope) oportunidad *f*; **they made** ~ **for him at the bar** le hicieron un hueco en la barra del bar; **make** ~ **for me!** ¡déjeme sitio!; **there is no** ~ **for it/them** no cabe/no caben; ~-**mate** compañero de cuarto; **two-**~**ed** de dos habitaciones; *v US* alojar(se)

roomer *US* huésped *m+f*

roomful cuarto lleno

roominess espaciosidad *f*

rooming-house *US* casa de huéspedes

roomy espacioso; (of clothes) holgado

roost *n* (pole) percha; (hen-house) gallinero; **rule the** ~ ser[19] el/la que manda; *v* dormir (ue)[1c] (en una percha)

rooster gallo

[1] **root** *n* raíz (-ces) *f*; *gramm* raíz *f*; (origin) origen (-ígenes) *m*; ~ **vegetable** tubérculo; **take** ~ echar raíces; ~-**stock** rizoma; *v* arraigarse[5]; (of pigs) hocicar[4]; **they** ~**ed through the drawers** revolvieron los cajones; ~ **out** arrancar[4], (destroy) extirpar

[2] **root:** ~ **for** desear el éxito de; (agitate for) hacer[19] propaganda por

rooting arraigo; (of pigs) hozadura

rope *n* cuerda; (+ hangman's) soga; *naut* cabo; (tight-~) cable *m*; (of onions *etc*) ristra; (of pearls) collar *m*; ~**s** (boxing) cuerdas *fpl* del cuadrilátero; **give plenty of** ~ **(to)** dar[19]

rienda suelta (a); **know the ~s** saber[19]
cuántas son cinco; ~ **ladder** escala de
cuerda; ~-**maker** cordelero; ~-
making cordelería; ~ **sandal** alpargata; ~-**trick** truco de la cuerda; ~--
walk cordelería; *v* atar con cuerda/
soga; *naut* amarrar

~ **in** (ask help) pedir (i)[3] ayuda a; (trick)
embaucar[4]

~ **off** acordonar

~ **together** atar con cuerda

ropey de mala calidad; (old-fashioned)
pasado de moda

rosary rosario

rose rosa; (colour) (color *m* de) rosa;
(of watering-can) alcachofa; ~-**bay**
adelfa; ~-**bud** capullo de rosa, *fig*
(girl) chica bonita; ~-**bush**, ~-**tree** rosal *m*; ~-**coloured** (de color de) rosa,
**see things through ~-coloured spec-
tacles** ver[19] las cosas color de rosa; ~-
garden rosaleda; ~-**water** agua de rosas; ~-**window** rosetón (-ones) *m*; ~-
wood palo de rosa

rosé rosado; (wine) *Sp* clarete *m*

roseate rosado

rosemary romero

rosette escarapela

rosin *mus* colofonia

rosiness color *m* de rosa

roster lista (de tandas)

rostrum tribuna

rosy (son)rosado; ~ **cheeks** mejillas
sonrosadas; *fig* prometedor (-ora *f*)

rot *n* putrefacción *f*; (in sheep) comalia,
(in trees) caries seca; (nonsense)
tonterías *fpl*; *v* pudrir(se); (waste)
echarse a perder; **may you ~ in hell!**
¡mal rayo te parta!

rota lista (de tandas)

Rotarian *n* + *adj* rotario

rotary rotativo; ~ **press** (prensa) rotativa; ~-**mower**, ~-**shaver** cortacéspedes *m sing* + *pl* afeitadora de acción
rotativa; **Rotary** rotario; ~ **movement**
rotarismo

rotate *vi* girar; *vt* hacer[19] girar

rotating rotativo

rotation rotación *f*; ~ **of crops** rotación
de cultivos; **in ~** por turno

rotatory rotativo

rote: by ~ de memoria

rotavate roturar

Rotavator motocultor *m*

rotogravure rotograbado

rotor-arm *aer* aspas *fpl*; *elect* + *mot* rotor
m

rotten podrido; (of teeth) cariado; *fig*
corrompido; (of bad quality)
malísimo; **feel ~** encontrarse fatal

rottenness podredumbre *f*

rotter sinvergüenza *m*

rotting *n* pudrición *f*; *adj* que se pudre

rotund rotundo; (of figure) gordinflón

rotunda *archi* rotonda

rotundity rotundidad *f*

rouble rublo

roué libertino

rouge colorete *m*

rough *n* terreno áspero; (golf) obstáculos *mpl*; (person) matón (-ones) *m*;
in (the) ~ en bruto; (roughly drawn)
bosquejado; **take the ~ with the
smooth** estar[19] a las duras y a las
maduras; *adj* (to the touch) áspero,
fam estropajoso; *meteor* tempestuoso; (of sea) agitado; (rude)
grosero; (of manner) bruto; (approximate) aproximado, ~ **idea** idea
aproximada, **at a guess**
aproximadamente; ~ **and ready** tosco
pero bueno; **cut up ~** sulfurarse; ~-
cast mezcla gruesa; ~ **copy** borrador
m; ~ **diamond** + *fig* diamante bruto;
~ **going** camino áspero, *fig* trabajo
arduo; ~-**hew** desbastar; ~-**house** jarana; ~ **life** vida dura; ~**neck** gamberro; ~ **play** juego duro; ~-**rider** domador *m* de caballos; (of people)
nada especial; ~**shod: ride ~shod
over** tratar sin miramientos; ~-**spoken**
malhablado; ~ **treatment** tratamiento
brutal; ~-**and-tumble** camorra; ~
work chapucero; *v* ~ **it** vivir sin
comodidad; ~ **out** bosquejar; ~ **up**
(assault) violentar

roughage forraje *m* (de salvado)

roughen poner(se)[19] áspero; ~ **up**
(assault) violentar

roughly ásperamente; (approximately)
aproximadamente

roughness (to the touch) aspereza; (of
sea) agitación; (rudeness) grosería;
(of manner) brutalidad *f*

roulette (+ ~ **wheel**) ruleta

Roumania Rumania

Roumanian *n* + *adj* rumano

round *n* (circle) círculo; (sphere) esfera; (bullet) cartucho; (shot) tiro, **burst of three** ~s ráfaga de tres tiros; *mus* rondó; (slice) tajada; (of drinks) ronda, **pay for one's** ~ pagar[5] la ronda; (boxing) asalto, **ten-**~ **contest** combate *m* de diez asaltos; (cards) mano *f*; (golf) partido; (lap) circuito, vuelta; (of cup competition) serie *f*; (of negotiation) serie *f*; (patrol) ronda; (tradesman's) recorrido; (doctor's) visitas *fpl*; (of applause *etc*) salva; (daily) rutina; *adj* redondo, ~ **number** número redondo; (spherical) esférico; (categorical) categórico; **at a** ~ **pace** a un buen paso; ~ **dance** baile *m* en ruedo; ~ **table (conference)** mesa redonda; ~ **ticket** billete *m* de ida y vuelta; ~ **trip** viaje *m* de ida y vuelta; **in** ~ **numbers** en cifras globales; ~-**faced** de cara redonda; ~-**game** juego en corro; ~-**hand** letra redonda; ~-**necked** con cuello de caja; ~-**robin** petición firmada colectivamente; ~-**shouldered** cargado de espaldas; ~**sman** repartidor; *v* (make ~) redondear; (go ~) dar[19] (la) vuelta a, *naut* doblar; ~ **a corner** doblar una esquina ~ **off** redondear; (finish) acabar; (perfect) perfeccionar

~ **on** volverse (ue)[1b] (*past part* vuelto) contra

~-**up** *n* rodeo

~ **up** *v* acorralar; rodear

adv alrededor; **all** ~ por todos lados; **all the year** ~ durante todo el año; **bring** ~ traer[19], *med* resucitar; **come** ~ venir[19] (de visita), *med* volver (ue)[1b] (*past part* vuelto) en sí; **come** ~ **to** (point of view) convencerse[14] de; **gather** ~ reunir(se) alrededor; **go** ~ dar[19] la vuelta a; **the planets go** ~ **the sun** los planetas dan la vuelta al sol, (be enough) ser[19] suficiente; **go** ~ **and** ~ dar[19] vueltas; **long way** ~ por el camino más largo; **look** ~ mirar alrededor, (look behind) mirar hacia atrás

prep alrededor de; ~ **about ten o'clock** a eso de las diez; ~ **the bend** despistado; ~ **the city** por la ciudad; **it's** ~ **the corner** está a la vuelta de la esquina; **go** ~ **the world** dar la vuelta al mundo

roundabout *n* (traffic) glorieta; (amusement) tiovivo; *adj* indirecto

rounders (juego de) cuatro esquinas *m sing*

roundhead cabeza pelada

roundly categóricamente

roundness redondez *f*

rouse *vt* despertar (ie)[2a]; (feelings) excitar; (to anger) provocar[4]

rousing conmovedor (-ora *f*); ~ **cheers** aplausos *mpl* calurosos

roustabout chapucero

rout (defeat) derrota completa; (flight) fuga desordenada; *v* (defeat) derrotar completamente; (put to flight) poner[19] en fuga; ~ **out** forzar (ue)[1a+7] a salir

route *n* ruta; (itinerary) itinerario; (tradesman's) recorrido; ~-**march** marcha de entrenamiento; *v* planear la ruta

routine *n* rutina; *adj* rutinario

rove vagar[5]

rover vagabundo

roving errante; (of disposition) andariego

[1] **row** *n* (line) hilera; (string) ristra; *cin* + *theat* fila; **fifteen in a** ~ quince seguidos; **I don't give a** ~ **of beans** (no) me importa un bledo

[2] **row** *n* (in boat) paseo en bote; ~-**boat** bote *m* de remos; ~**lock** escálamera; *v* remar

[3] **row** *n* (noise) alboroto; (quarrel) camorra, disputa; **get into a** ~ ser[19] regañado, (fight) meterse en una pelea; **start a** ~, **kick up a** ~ armar camorra; **there's going to be such a** ~ va a arder Troya; *v* reñir (i)[3] (with con)

rowan serbal *m*

rowdiness (noise) alboroto; (rough behaviour) gamberrismo

rowdy *n* gamberro; *adj* (noisy) alborotador (-ora *f*); (uncouth) grosero

rowdyism gamberrismo

rower remero

rowing *n* (deporte *m* del) remo; *adj* de remos; ~-**boat** bote *m* de remos; ~-**club** club náutico; ~-**stroke** bogada

royal *n* (sail) sobrejuanete *m*; (member of royal family) miembro de la familia real; *adj* real, ~ **family** familia real; ~ **standard** estandarte *m* real; **Royal Academy** Real Academia; **Royal**

Highness Real Alteza
royalism monarquismo
royalist n monarquista m+f; adj monárquico
royally regiamente
royalty realeza; (people) personajes mpl reales; (money) porcentaje m de los ingresos; **royalties** derechos mpl del autor/inventor
rub n (friction) frotamiento; (massage) masaje m; (light touch) roce m; (difficulty) obstáculo; v frotar; (hurt by grazing) raspar; ~ **one's hands** frotarse las manos; ~ **shoulders (with)** codearse (con)
~ **against** rozar[7]; **the pigs ~ against the tree** los cerdos se restriegan contra el árbol
~ **down** (wear down) desgastar; (dry) secar; (groom) almohazar[7]
~ **in** dar[19] fricciones con; (of ideas) machacar[4]
~ **off** vt quitar frotando; vi quitarse; (of bad habits) pegarse[5]
~ **out** borrar, asesinar
~ **up** (polish) pulir, fam sacar[4] brillo a; ~ **up against** restregarse (ie)[2a+5] contra; ~ **up the wrong way** frotar a contrapelo, fig irritar
rub-a-dub rataplán m
[1] **rubber** n caucho; fam (+ eraser) goma; (polisher) paño de pulir; (for blackboard) borrador m; ~s zapatos mpl de goma; ~ **band** gomita; ~ **cheque** cheque m sin fondos; ~ **plant** cauchera; ~ **planter** cauchero; ~ **plantation** cauchal m; ~ **solution** solución f de goma; ~ **stamp** n sello de goma, v aprobar (ue)[1a] automáticamente; ~ **tree** cauchera; ~-**neck** n mirón m (-ona f), v curiosear; adj de goma
[2] **rubber** (bridge etc) juego
rubbery parecido a goma
rubbing (friction) frotación f, fricción f; (of floors) fregado; ~ **alcohol** alcohol quirúrgico
rubbish basura; fig tonterías fpl; **don't talk ~**! ¡no digas disparates!; ~-**bin**, ~-**can** cubo de la basura; ~-**dump** vertedero de basura
rubbishy sin valor; (of goods) de pacotilla
rubble escombros mpl; (hard core) cas-

cotes mpl
rube rústico
rubicund rubicundo
Rubik's cube cubo mágico
rubric rúbrica
ruby n rubí (-íes) m; adj de color rubí; ~ **lips** labios de rubí
ruck n arruga; v arrugar[5]
rucksack mochila
ruction alboroto
rudder timón (-ones) m; ~ **blade** pala del timón
rudderless sin timón
ruddiness rojez f
ruddy rojizo; sl maldito
rude (impolite) descortés m+f; (in speech) grosero; (boorish) grosero; (rough) tosco
rudeness (impoliteness) descortesía; (in speech) grosería; (boorishness) grosería; (roughness) tosquedad f
rudiment biol rudimento; ~s +fig rudimentos
rudimentary biol rudimental; fig rudimentario
Rudolph Rodolfo
[1] **rue** bot ruda
[2] **rue** arrepentirse (ie)[2c] de; (regret) lamentar
rueful triste
ruefulness tristeza
ruff (collar) gorguera; orni collarín (-ines) m de plumas; zool collarín (-ines) m de pelo
ruffian rufián (-anes) m
ruffianly arrufianado
ruffle n (on dress) volante fruncido; v (dressmaking) fruncir[13]; (hair) despeinar; (water) agitar; fig enojar
rug alfombr(ill)a; (travelling-~) manta de viaje
rugby rugby m; **Rugby League** rugby m a trece
rugged (of terrain) áspero; (of facial features) ceñudo; (robust) robusto; (of behaviour) tosco
rugger rugby m
ruin ruina; (downfall) caída; (ruination) perdición f, **it was the ~ of Spain** fue la perdición de España; (financial) quiebra; **in ~s** arruinado; v arruinar; (damage) estropear; (destroy) echar a perder, fam hacer[19] puré de; (a woman) perder (ie)[2b]; ~ **the appetite**

estropear el apetito
ruinate demoler (ue)[16]
ruination ruina; (downfall) caída;
(ruination) perdición *f*
ruinous ruinoso
rule *n* (for measuring) metro, **folding ~**
metro plegable; (ruler) regla; *print* regleta; (authority) dominio; (precept)
norma; (regulation) regla; (reign)
reinado; *leg* fallo; **as a ~** por regla
general; **~ of three** regla de tres; **~ of
thumb** regla empírica; **make it a ~ to**
ser[19] un deber para uno; **work to ~**
huelga de celo; **~s of the road** normas
fpl de la carretera; *v* (with ruler)
trazar[7]; (govern) gobernar (ie)[2a]; (of
monarchs) reinar; (decide) decidir;
(control) dominar; **as ~ that** decretar
que +*subj*; **~d line** raya; **~d paper**
papel reglado; **be ~d by** guiarse por
~ off separar con raya
~ out excluir[16]; *leg* no admitir
~ over gobernar (ie)[2b]
~ through (cross out) borrar
ruler gobernante *m+f*; (for ruling lines)
regla
ruling *n* fallo; (with lines) rayado; *adj*
dominante; **~ class** clase *f* gobernante; **~ price** precio imperante
[1] **rum** ron *m*; **~-runner** contrabandista *m*
de licores; **~-running** contrabando de
licores
[2] **rum** (strange) extraño; (mysterious)
misterioso
Rumania *see* **Roumania**
Rumanian *see* **Roumanian**
rumba rumba
[1] **rumble** *n* ruido sordo; (of thunder)
retumbo; (of stomach) rugido; **~-seat**
asiento trasero; *v* retumbar; (of carts
etc) crujir; (of thunder) tronar (ue)[1a];
his stomach ~d le sonaron las tripas
[2] **rumble** *sl* calar; **he ~d me** él caló mis
intenciones
rumbling ruidos sordos; (of thunder)
retumbos; (of stomach) rugidos
rumbustious ruidoso
ruminant *n+adj* rumiante
ruminate +*fig* rumiar
rumination rumia
ruminative reflexivo
rummage (about in/through) revolverlo
(ue)[1b] (*past part* revuelto) todo +*def
obj*; **~-sale** venta de artículos donados

y generalmente usados (con fines
benéficos)
[1] **rummy** (cards) rummy *m*, juego de
cartas
[2] **rummy** (strange) extraño; (mysterious)
misterioso
rumour *n* rumor *m*; *v* **it is ~ed that** se
rumorea que
rump ancas *fpl*; *cul* cuarto trasero; *fig*
parte *f* inferior; **~ steak** bistec *m*
rumple arrugar[5]
rumpus tumulto; **kick up a ~** armar
jaleo
run *n* +*sp* carrera; *mot* vuelta, **go for a ~**
dar[19] una vuelta (en coche); (distance
by vehicle) trayecto, **it's a good ~
from Madrid to Seville** es buen
trayecto desde Madrid hasta Sevilla;
(distance covered) recorrido, **day's ~**
mot recorrido de un día; *naut* singladura; (in stocking) carrera; (for
poultry) gallinero; (for sheep) terreno
de pasto; (fish) ribazón *m*; (cards)
escaler(ill)a; *mus* glisado; *theat* serie
f de representaciones; (demand) demanda (**on** de); (kind) especie *f*; (of
events) curso; **a ~ of bad luck** *fam* el
cenizo; **~ of good luck** temporada
de buena suerte; **~ of the market**
tendencia del mercado; **~ on a bank**
asedio de un banco; **in the long ~** a la
larga; **on the ~** (of escaped prisoner)
fugado, *mil* (of army) en fuga desordenada, (to avoid conscription)
prófugo; **have the ~ of** tener[19] permiso de usar; **common ~** común *m* de
las gentes; **~way** pista (de aterrizaje)
vi (+ flow) correr; *sp* competir (i)[3] (en
una carrera); (to a spot) acudir, **the
people ran to the entrance** la gente
acudió a la entrada; (rush) precipitarse; (flee) huir[16]; (of traffic) circular, **the buses ~ all night** los autobuses
circulan toda la noche; (ply) hacer[19]
trayecto (**between** entre); (leak) perder (ie)[2b] agua; (of eyes) lloriquear;
med supurar; (of colours) correrse;
(melt) derretirse (i)[3]; (of machines)
funcionar, *fam* andar[19]; (last) durar;
theat representarse consecutiva-
mente; (for office) ser[19] candidato; (of
wording) rezar[7]; **everything was
running smoothly** todo iba sobre ruedas; **~ true to type** obrar como era de

esperarse

vt correr, **he can ~ fifteen kilometres** él puede correr quince kilómetros; **~ a race** competir (i)[3] en una carrera; (water) hacer[19] correr; (drive) conducir[15]; (manage) dirigir[9]; (bus service) hacer[19] el servicio de; (govern) gobernar (ie)[2a]; (nominate) proponer[19], **~ a candidate** proponer[19] un candidato; (smuggle) hacer[19] un recado; **~ a line** trazar[7] una línea; **~ one's eyes/hand over** pasar los ojos/la mano sobre; **~ the gauntlet** pasar por baquetas; **~ a machine** manejar una máquina; **~ a risk** correr un riesgo; **~ a temperature** tener[19] fiebre

~about *n* coche *m* pequeño; **~about ticket** kilométrico

~ about *v* corretear

~ across cruzar[7] corriendo; (meet) tropezar[7] con

~ after +*fig* ir[19] detrás de

~ aground encallar

~ ahead of correr delante de

~ along correr a lo largo de; **~ along!** ¡márchese!

~ amok enloquecer(se)[14]

~away *n* fugitivo; *adj* (of people) fugitivo; (of horses) desbocado; **~away inflation** inflación no controlada; **~away marriage** boda clandestina; **~away victory** victoria fácil

~ away *v* huir[16]; *fam* chaquetear; **~ away with** fugarse[5] con, (win easily) llevarse fácilmente

~ counter to ir[19] en contra de

~down *n* análisis *m*

~ down *v* (catch) cazar[7]; *mot* atropellar; *fam* arrollar; (of clock) acabarse la cuerda; *fig* hablar mal de; **tears ~ down her cheeks** las lágrimas le corren por las mejillas; **be ~ down** *med* estar[19] débil, *elect* (of batteries) estar[19] descargado

~ for (bus) correr para coger; (office) ser[19] candidato para

~ in entrar corriendo; (arrest) detener[19]; *mot* rodar (ue)[1a]

~ into (crash) chocar[4] contra; (knock down) atropellar, *fam* pillar; (meet) tropezar[7] con

~ into debt contraer[19] deudas

~ off huir[16]; *print* tirar; **~ off the rails** descarrilarse; **~ off with** fugarse[5] con

~ out salir[19] corriendo; (end) agotarse; **~ out of** quedarse sin

~ over (overflow) derramarse; *mot* atropellar; (revise) repasar

~ riot enloquecerse[14]

~ short escasear; **I've ~ short of money** me encuentro sin bastante dinero

~-through *n cin* rodaje *m*; (rehearsal) ensayo

~ through *v* correr por; (pierce) traspasar; *cin* rodar; (rehearse) ensayar; (revise) repasar; **~ through a fortune** derrochar una fortuna/*fam* un potosí

~ to (reach) acudir a; **~ to seed** granar

~ up llegar[5] corriendo; (construct) montar; (hoist) izar[7]; **~ up a bill** incurrir en una deuda; **~ up against** (crash) estrellarse contra, (meet) tener[19] que enfrentarse con

~ wild *bot* volver (ue)[1b] (*past part* vuelto) al estado primitivo; (of person) enloquecerse[14]; (of horses) correr a rienda suelta

~ with correr al lado de; **~ with perspiration** estar[19] bañado de sudor

rune runa

rung +*fig* escalón (-ones) *m*

runic rúnico; **~ script** runas *fpl*

runnel arroyuelo

runner +*sp* corredor *m* (-ora *f*); (in horse/dog racing) caballo/perro; (messenger) mensajero; *mil* ordenanza *m*; (on sledge) patín (-ines) *m*; (cloth) tapete *m*; (carpet) alfombra continua; *bot* serpa; **~-bean** judía verde; **~-up** subcampeón *m*

running *n* carrera; *mech* funcionamiento; (management) dirección *f*; (government) gobierno; **be in the ~** tener[19] posibilidades de ganar; **be in the ~ for** tener[19] posibilidades de ser; **be out of the ~** no tener[19] posibilidades; *adj* (*comm* + of water) corriente; (of knots) corredizo; **four times ~** cuatro veces seguidas; **~-board** estribo; **~ commentary** comentario continuo; **~ expenses** gastos *mpl* corrientes; **~ fight** combate *m* en retirada; **~-in** *n mot* rodaje *m*, *adv* en rodaje; **~ out** (expiry) caducidad *f*, (of funds) fuga; **~-shoe** zapatilla de carreras; **~-shorts** pantalón *m* de gimnasia; **~ sore** llaga supurante; **~ start** salida lanzada

runny líquido, derretido
runt redrojo; *pej vulg* mierdica
rupee rupia
Rupert Ruperto
rupture *n* ruptura; *med* hernia; *v* romper (*past part* roto); ~ **o.s.** *med* herniarse
rural rural
ruse ardid *m*
[1] **rush** *bot* junco; ~-**bottomed** con asiento de junco; ~ **light** vela de junco; ~ **mat** estera de junco
[2] **rush** *n* (movement) ímpetu *m*; (charge) acometida; (haste) prisa; (flow) torrente *m*; (demand) demanda extraordinaria (for para); ~ **of work** aumento repentino de trabajo; **with a** ~ de golpe; ~ **hour** hora de máxima circulación, *fam* hora punta (*pl* horas punta); ~ **order** pedido urgente; *v* precipitarse, *fam* darse[19] prisa; (charge) acometer; (send) despachar de prisa
~ **at** arremeter contra
~ **forward** lanzarse con ímpetu
~ **in** entrar precipitadamente; ~ **in upon** sorprender
~ **into** +*fig* entrar precipitadamente en; ~ **into print** publicar[4] sin pensar en las consecuencias
~ **out** salir[19] precipitadamente
~ **through** *vi* pasar de prisa por; *vt* ejecutar de prisa, (parliament) aprobar (ue)[1a] de prisa
rushed: I'm ~ **off my feet** estoy ocupadísimo
rushing *m* abalanzamiento; *adj* precipi-

tante; impetuoso
rushy juncoso
rusk galleta dura
russet *n* manzana asperiega; *adj* rojizo
Russia Rusia
Russian *n*+*adj* ruso
rust *n* orín *m*; oxidación *f*; *bot* roya; ~-**resistant** a prueba de herrumbre; *v* aherrumbrar(se), oxidar(se)
rustic *n*+*adj* rústico; *Cub* guajiro
rusticate *vi* rusticar[4]; *vt* (university) expulsar temporalmente
rustication rusticación *f*
rusticity rusticidad *f*
rustily con orín
[1] **rustle** *n* (of wind) susurro; (of silk, paper) crujido; *v* (hacer[19]) susurrar/crujir; ~ **up** obtener[19] de prisa
[2] **rustle** (steal cattle) robar ganado
rustler cuatrero
rustless inoxidable
rustling *see* [1]**rustle** *n*
rusty oxidado, herrumbroso; I'm ~ soy torpe por falta de práctica
[1] **rut** *zool* celo; *v* estar[19] en celo
[2] **rut** rodera; (in road) bache *m*; *fig* rutina; **get into a** ~ ir[19] encarrilado
rutabaga naba, nabo gallego
ruthless despiadado
ruthlessness implacabilidad *f*
rutted lleno de baches
rutting *zool* en celo; ~ **season** época de celo
rye centeno; (whisky) whisky *m* de centeno; ~ **bread** pan *m* de centeno; ~ **grass** cebadilla

S

s (letter) ese *f*; **S. (Saint)** S (Santo)
Sabbatarian sabatario
sabbath (Christian) domingo; (Jewish) sábado; **keep the ~** guardar el sábado/ (Christian) el domingo
sabbatical sabático
Sabine *n*+*adj* sabino
sable *n* *zool* marta cebellina; (fur) marta; *adj* negro; *her* sable
sabot zueco
sabotage *n* sabotaje *m*; *v* sabotear
saboteur saboteador *m* (-ora *f*)
sabre sable *m*; **~-cut** sablazo; *v* herir (ie)[2c] a sablazos
sac *zool* bolsa
saccharin sacarina
sacerdotal sacerdotal
sachet bolsita
sack *n* saco; *mil* saqueo; (dismissal) despedida; **get the ~** ser[19] despedido; **give the ~** despedir (i)[3], *fam* poner[19] de patitas en la calle; **~cloth** harpillera; **~-race** carrera de sacos; *v* ensacar[4]; *mil* saquear; (dismiss) despedir (i)[3]
sackful saco lleno
sacking (sackcloth) harpillera; *mil* saqueo; (dismissal) despido
sacrament sacramento; **receive the Sacrament** comulgar[5]; **receive the last ~s** recibir los últimos sacramentos; **Blessed Sacrament** Santísimo Sacramento
sacramental sacramental; **~ wine** vino eucarístico
sacred sagrado; **~ music** música sagrada; **you hold nothing ~** usted no respeta nada; **~ to the memory of** consagrado a la memoria de; **Sacred Heart** Sagrado Corazón (de Jesús)
sacredness santidad *f*
sacrifice *n* sacrificio; (victim) víctima; **at a ~** *comm* con pérdida; *v* sacrificar[4]; *comm* malvender
sacrificial de sacrificio
sacrilege sacrilegio
sacrilegious sacrílego

sacristan sacristán (-anes) *m*
sacristy sacristía
sacrosanct sacrosanto
sacrum sacro
sad triste; (of cakes *etc.*) que no ha subido bastante; **~ mistake** error *m* deplorable; **how ~!** ¡qué pena!; **grow ~** entristecerse[14]; **make s.o. ~** entristecer[14] a alguien
sadden entristecer[14]
saddle *n* silla (de montar); (cycle) sillín (-ines) *m*; (of vaulting-horse) silla; (of hill) collado; *anat* espalda; **~ of mutton** lomo de cordero; **in the ~** montado, *fig* en control; **~back** *bui* de caballetes; **~bag** alforja; **~cloth** sudadero; *v* ensillar; (impose) cargar[5] (**with** con)
saddler talabartero
saddlery talabartería
sadism sadismo
sadist sádico
sadistic sádico
sadly tristemente; (very) muy
sadness tristeza
s.a.e. (stamped addressed envelope) sobre *m* con sello y seña
safari safari *f*; **on ~** en safari; **~-park** parque *m* de fieras
safe *n* caja de caudales; **~-blower**, **~-breaker** ladrón (-ones) *m* de cajas de caudales; **~-blowing**, **~-breaking** robo de cajas de caudales (con explosivos); **~-deposit** cámara acorazada; *adj* seguro; (sheltered) al abrigo (**from** de); (trustworthy) digno de confianza; **~ and sound** sano y salvo; **~ load** carga máxima; **to be on the ~ side** para mayor seguridad; **~ conduct** salvoconducto; **~guard** *n* salvaguardia, *v* salvaguardar; **as a ~guard** como precaución; **~ keeping** (place) lugar seguro, (good hands) buenas manos
safely seguramente; **you can ~ tell her** usted puede decírselo con toda seguri-

dad; **he put it away** ~ él lo puso en un lugar seguro; **they arrived** ~ llegaron sin accidente

safety seguridad *f*; **in** ~ en seguro; **I believe in** ~ **first** pongo la seguridad ante todo; **play for** ~ jugar (ue)[1a] seguro; **with complete** ~ con toda seguridad; ~**-belt** cinturón (-ones) *m* de seguridad; ~**-catch** fiador *m*; ~**-chain** cadena/(on jewellery) cadenilla de seguridad; ~ **curtain** *theat* telón (-ones) *m* contra incendios; ~**-device** dispositivo de seguridad; ~**glass** vidrio inastillable; ~ **helmet** *bui* casco protector, (motorcyclist's) casco de motorista; ~**-lamp** lámpara de seguridad; ~**-match** fósforo de seguridad; ~**-net** red *f* paracaídas; ~**-pin** imperdible *m*, *SA* alfiler *m* de gancho; ~**-razor** máquina/maquinilla de afeitar; ~**-valve** válvula de seguridad

saffron azafrán *m*; (colour) de color de azafrán

sag *n* comba; *v* combarse; *fig* aflojarse

saga saga

sagacious sagaz (-ces)

sagacity sagacidad *f*

[1] **sage** *n* + *adj* sabio

[2] **sage** *n bot* salvia

sago sagú *m*

Sahara Sahara *m*; ~ **Desert** Desierto del Sahara

Saharan saharaui

said: the ~ **paragraph** dicho párrafo; **the** ~ **Mr García** el tal señor García; **no sooner** ~ **than done** dicho y hecho; **when all's** ~ **and done** a(l) fin de cuentas

sail *n* vela; (of windmill) aspa; (journey) paseo en barco de vela; **in full** ~ a toda vela; **set** ~ hacerse[19] a la vela (for para); ~**boat** bote *m* de vela; ~**cloth** lona; ~**maker** velero; ~**plane** planeador *m*; *v* navegar[5]; (float) flotar; (bird in sky) cernerse; ~ **close to the wind** ceñir el viento, *fig* correr un peligro; ~ **the Atlantic** cruzar[7] el Atlántico

~ **before:** ~ **before the wind** navegar[5] viento en popa

~ **into** (attack) atacar[4]

~ **round** (headland *etc*) doblar

sailable navegable

sailing navegación *f*; *sp* deporte *m* de la vela; **it's plain** ~ es coser y cantar; ~

date fecha de salida; ~ **orders** últimas instrucciones *fpl*; ~**-boat** bote *m* de vela; ~**-ship** velero

sailor marinero; **be a good** ~ no marearse; **I'm a bad** ~ me mareo fácilmente; ~**-suit** traje *m* de marinero

saint santo, santa; (title) San, Santa, (before *m* names starting with **To-** and **Do-**) Santo; ~**'s day** (día *m* del) santo; **tomorrow is Saint Thomas's Day** mañana es (la fiesta de) Santo Tomás; **he's a** ~ *fig* él es un ángel; **Saint Bernard** (dog) perro de San Bernardo; **Saint Vitus's dance** baile *m* de San Vito

sainted santo; (referring to someone dead) que en la santa gloria esté

saintliness santidad *f*

saintly santo

sake: for the ~ **of** por (motivo de); **do it for my** ~ hazlo por mí; **for brevity's** ~ para mayor brevedad; **for God's/Heaven's** ~ por el amor de Dios; **she talks for talking's** ~ ella habla por hablar; **violence for the** ~ **of violence** violencia por la violencia

sal: ~ **volatile** sal *f* volátil

salaam *n* zalema; *v* hacer[19] zalemas

salacious salaz (-ces)

salaciousness salacidad *f*

salad ensalada; ~ **bowl** ensaladera; ~ **days** juventud *f*; ~ **dressing** mayonesa; ~ **oil** aceite *m* para ensaladas; **fruit-**~ macedonia de frutas

Saladin Saladino

salamander salamandra

salami salchichón *m*

salaried a sueldo; (of post) retribuido; ~ **employee** *approx* oficinista *m* + *f*

salary sueldo

sale venta; (clearance) liquidación *f*; (auction-~) subasta; **be (up) for** ~ estar[19] en venta; **this house is for** ~ se vende esta casa; ~**-price** (retail price) precio de venta, (reduced price) precio de saldo; ~**room** sala de ventas, (auction) sala de subastas; ~**s chart** gráfico de ventas; ~**s forecast** pronóstico de ventas; ~**s organization** red *f* de ventas; ~**s promotion** fomento de ventas; ~**s resistance** oposición *f* a comprar (por parte del público); ~**s tax** impuesto sobre ventas; ~**s-clerk** dependiente *m*, dependienta *f*;

~**sman** dependiente *m*, (traveller) viajante *m*; ~**smanship** arte *m* de vender; ~**swoman** dependienta

salience prominencia *f*

salient *n*+*adj* sobresaliente *m*

saline *n* +*adj* salino

salinity salinidad *f*

saliva saliva

salivary salival

salivate salivar

salivation salivación *f*

¹ **sallow** *n bot* sauce *m*

² **sallow** *adj* cetrino

sallowness amarillez *f*

sally *n mil*+*fig* salida; *v* hacer¹⁹ una salida; ~ **forth** salir¹⁹ atrevidamente

salmon salmón (-ones) *m*; (colour) de color salmón; ~-**trout** trucha asalmonada

salon salón (-ones) *m*

Salonika Salónica

saloon salón (-ones) *m*; (*US* public house) taberna; *mot* sedán *m*; *naut* cámara; **dancing/hairdressing** ~ salón de baile/de peluquería; ~ **bar** barra del bar; ~ **car** (railway) coche-salón *m*

salt *n* sal *f*; ~ **of the earth** sal *f* de la tierra; **old** ~ lobo de mar; **he's not worth his** ~ él no merece el pan que se come; **I'll take it with a pinch of** ~ lo creeré con cierta reserva; ~-**cellar** salero; *adj* salado; ~ **lake** lago salado; ~-**marsh** salina; ~ **meat** carne salada; ~-**mine** mina de sal; ~**petre** salitre *m*; ~-**store** salín *m*; ~ **water** agua salada; ~-**water fish** pez *m* de agua salada; ~-**works** salinas *fpl*; *v* (cure) salar; (season) poner¹⁹ sal en; ~**ed peanuts** cacahuetes salados

saltiness sabor *m* de sal

salty salado

salubrious salubre

salubrity salubridad *f*

salutary de salutación *f*

salutation salutación *f*

salutatory saludable

salute *n* saludo; (of guns) salva; **fire a** ~ hacer¹⁹ salvas; **fire a 21-gun** ~ saludar con 21 salvas; **take the** ~ tomar el saludo; *v* saludar; (with guns) saludar con salvas

saluting: ~ **base** puesto de mando

salvage *n* objetos *mpl* salvados; ~-**tug**, ~-**vessel** barco de salvamento; *v*

salvar

salvation salvación *f*; **Salvation Army** Ejército de Salvación

Salvationist miembro del Ejército de Salvación

¹ **salve** *v* (salvage) salvar

² **salve** *n* (ointment) pomada; *v* curar con pomada, *fig* tranquilizar⁷; ~ **one's conscience** tranquilizar⁷ la conciencia

salver bandeja

salvo salva; ~ **of applause** salva de aplausos; (reservation) reserva

Samaritan *n*+*adj* samaritano

samba samba

same mismo; (similar) igual; **the** ~ **... as** el mismo ... que; **the** ~ **to you** igualmente; **the** ~ **as usual** lo de siempre; **all the** ~ a pesar de todo; **it's all the** ~ **(to me)** (me) es igual; **at the** ~ **time** al mismo tiempo; **at one and the** ~ **time** sobre la marcha; **just the** ~ (nevertheless) sin embargo; **she entered and he did the** ~ ella entró y él hizo lo mismo; **so as not to go to the** ~ **place twice** para no ir otra vez al mismo sitio

sameness igualdad *f*; (monotony) monotonía

Samoan samoano

samovar samovar *m*

sample *n* muestra; ~ **book** muestrario; **random** ~ muestra al azar; *v* probar (ue)¹ᵃ; (wine) catar

sampler probador *m* (-ora *f*); (of wines) catador *m* (-ora *f*); (sewing) dechado

sampling toma de muestra

Samson Sansón

Samuel Samuel

samurai *n*+*adj* samurai *m*

sanatorium sanatorio

sanctification santificación *f*

sanctify santificar⁴

sanctimonious beato

sanction *n* sanción (-ones) *f*; **apply** ~**s against** imponer¹⁹ sanciones contra; *v* sancionar

sanctity santidad *f*; ~ **of human life** inviolabilidad *f* de la vida humana

sanctuary santuario; (refuge) refugio; **seek** ~ acogerse⁸ a

sanctum lugar sagrado; **this is my husband's** ~ éste es el lugar privado de mi esposo

sand *n* arena; ~**s** (beach) playa; ~**bag** *n* saco terrero, *v* proteger[8] con sacos terreros; ~**bank**, ~ **bar** banco de arena; ~-**blast** *n* chorro de arena, *v* deslustrar con un chorro de arena; ~-**castle** castillo de arena, **make** ~-**castles** construir[16] castillos de arena; ~-**dune** duna; ~-**lizard** lagarto común; ~-**martin** avión *m* zapador; ~**paper** *n* papel *m* de lija, *v* lijar; ~-**pit** arenal *m*; ~**stone** piedra arenosa, *fam* piedra pómez; ~**storm** tempestad *f* de arena; *v* arenar; (with sandpaper) lijar

sandal sandalia

sandalwood sándalo

sanding *carp* pulimento con lija; ~-**machine** lijadora

sandwich *n* emparedado; (made with bread roll) bocadillo; (toasted) sandwich *m*; ~ **course** cursillo que comprende estudios teóricos y experiencia práctica en un taller; ~ **loaf** pan *m* de molde; ~-**maker** sandwichera; ~-**man** hombre *m* anuncio; ~-**spread** pasta para sandwich; *v* insertar (entre dos cosas); **be** ~**ed** (crushed) ser[19] aplastado (between entre)

sandy arenoso; (colour) de color de arena; (of hair) rojizo

sane cuerdo; **be** ~ (of a person) estar[19] en su juicio, (of policy) ser[19] prudente

Sanforize sanforizar[7]

sangfroid aplomo

sanguinary sanguinario

sanguine optimista; **be** ~ **about** ser[19] optimista acerca de

sanitary sanitario; ~ **inspector** inspector *m* de sanidad; ~ **towel** paño higiénico, *fam* compresa; ~-**ware** saneamientos

sanitation higiene *f*; (apparatus) instalación sanitaria; (lavatory) servicios *mpl*

sanity cordura; **lose/recover one's** ~ perder (ie)[2b]/recobrar el sano juicio

Sanskrit *n*+*adj* sánscrito

Santa Claus Papá *m* Noel; *Sp equiv* Reyes *mpl* Magos

[1] **sap** *bot* savia; *fam* jugo; (vitality) vitalidad *f*

[2] **sap** *n mil* zapa; *v* zapar; ~ **the strength of** minar las fuerzas de

[3] **sap** (fool) bobo

sapience sapiencia

sapient sabio

sapless sin jugo

sapling árbol *m* joven; +*fig* pimpollo

saponaceous saponáceo

sapper zapador *m*; *mil sl* capador *m*

sapphire zafiro

Sappho Safo

sappy jugoso

saraband zarabanda

Saracen *n*+*adj* sarraceno

Saragossa Zaragoza

sarcasm sarcasmo; **I say it without** ~ lo digo sin sarcasmo

sarcastic sarcástico

sarcophagus sarcófago

sardine sardina; **packed like** ~**s** como sardinas en lata

Sardinia Cerdeña

Sardinian *n*+*adj* sardo

sardonic sardónico

sari sari *m*

sarsaparilla zarzaparrilla

sartorial de sastre

[1] **sash** faja; *mil* fajín (-ines) *m*

[2] **sash** (of window) marco; ~-**window** ventana de guillotina

sassy *US* descarado

Satan Satanás *m*

satanic satánico

satanism satanismo

satchel cartapacio; (school) cartera

sate saciar

sateen satén *m*

satellite *n*+*adj* satélite *m*; ~ **town** ciudad *f* satélite

satiable saciable

satiate saciar

satiety saciedad *f*

satin *n* raso; *adj* de raso

satiny lustroso

satire sátira

satiric(al) satírico

satirist escritor satírico

satirize satirizar[7]

satisfaction satisfacción *f*; (of a debt) pago; (contentment) contento; **give** ~ dar[19] satisfacción

satisfactory satisfactorio

satisfy satisfacer (conjugated as hacer[19]); (convince) convencer[12]; (debt) pagar[5]; ~ **o.s. that** asegurarse de que; ~ **one's thirst** apagar[5] la sed; **I'm not satisfied with her** no estoy satisfecho con ella

satisfying satisfactorio; (nutritious)

nutritivo

satrap sátrapa *m*

satsuma tipo de naranja mandarina

saturate saturar (**with** de)

saturation saturación *f*; ~ **bombing** bombardeo concentrado para destruir las defensas antiaéreas enemigas

Saturday *n* sábado; *adj* sabatino; **his** ~ **bath** su baño de los sábados

Saturn Saturno

saturnine saturnino

satyr sátiro

sauce salsa; (sweet) crema; (impudence) frescura; ~**-boat** salsera; ~**pan** cazo

saucer platillo; **flying** ~ platillo volante

saucy (cheeky) descarado; (cheerful) alegre; (of clothing) coquetón

Saudi (Arabian) (árabe) saudí *m+f*

sauerkraut chucrut *m*

Saul Saúl

sauna(-bath) sauna

saunter *n* paseo lento; *v* pasearse despacio

sausage salchicha, chorizo; **not a** ~! *fig* ¡ni papa!; ~**-machine** choricera; ~**-meat** carne *f* de salchicha; ~**-roll** empanada de salchicha

sauté (ballet) salto; *adj cul* frito ligeramente; *v* freír (i)[3] ligeramente

Sauterne vino de Sauternes

savable conservable

savage *n* salvaje *m+f*; *adj* salvaje; (cruel) cruel; (furious) furioso; *fam* rabioso; ~ **attack** ataque *m* violento; *v* embestir (i)[3]

savagery salvajismo; (cruelty) crueldad *f*; (fury) furia; *fam* rabia

savannah sabana

save *n* (by goalkeeper) parada; *vt* (rescue) salvar (**from** de), **he** ~**d the little girl's life** él le salvó la vida a la niña; (keep) guardar, **will you** ~ **a place for me?** ¿quiere usted guardar un sitio para mí?; (collect) coleccionar, **he** ~**s stamps** él colecciona sellos (postales); (money) ahorrar; (avoid) evitar; *sp* rechazar[7]; ~ **one's neck** conservar el pellejo; ~ **time** ganar tiempo; ~**d by the bell** (boxing) salvado por la campana; *vi* (economize) hacer[19] economías; ~ **for** si no fuera por; *prep* salvo; ~ **that** excepto que

saveloy salchichón (-ones) *m* picante

saver ahorrador *m* (-ora *f*)

saving *n* (rescue) salvamento; *eccles* salvación *f*; (of money) ahorro; (economizing) economía; ~ **grace** único mérito; ~**s** ahorros *mpl*; ~**s bank** caja de ahorros; ~**s bonds** bonos del estado; ~**s fund** montepío; *prep* salvo; *conj* con excepción de que +*subj*

saviour *n+adj* salvador *m* (-ora *f*); **Our Saviour** nuestro Salvador

savoir-faire desparpajo

savory ajedrea

savour *n* sabor *m*; (after-taste) gusto; *vt* saborear; *vi* saber[19] (**of** a)

savoury *n* entremés salado; *adj* sabroso; (not sweet) salado; (of places) respetable; (of character) bueno

Savoy Saboya

savoy col lombarda

savvy *n* entendimiento; *v* entender (ie)[2b]

saw *n* (tool) sierra; ~**bill** pato sierra; ~ **cut** corte *m* de sierra; ~**dust** serrín *m*; ~**fish** pez *m* sierra; ~**mill** aserradero; *vt* (a)serrar (ie)[2a]; *vi* usar la sierra

sawing aserrar *m*; ~**-horse** caballete *m* para aserrar

sawyer (a)serrador *m*

saxifrage saxífraga

Saxon *n+adj* sajón *m* (-ona *f*)

Saxony Sajonia

saxophone saxófono

say *n*: **she has no** ~ **in the matter** ella no tiene ni voz ni voto; **let them have their** ~ **que hablen**; **have your** ~ diga lo que quiera; *v* decir[19]; ~ **goodbye** decir[19] adiós; **I should** ~ **so!** ¡toma no!; **you can** ~ **that again!** ¡eso sí es verdad!; ~**!** *US* ¡oiga!; ~ **one's prayers** rezar[7]; ~ **over and over again** repetir muchas veces; ~ **what you want to** ~ usted dirá; **he didn't** ~ **a word** él no dijo ni palabra/*fam* ni mu; **let us** ~ **that you earn 60,000 pesetas a month** pongamos que usted gana 60.000 pesetas al mes; **that is to** ~ es decir; **that** ~**s a great deal** *fig* es mucho decir; **they** ~ (it is said) se dice; **you don't** ~**!** ¡no me diga!

saying dicho; (proverb) refrán (-anes) *m*; **as the** ~ **goes** como dice el refrán; **it goes without** ~ ni que decir tiene

S-bend curva doble

scab *n med* costra, postilla; (caused by disease) escabro; (blackleg) esquirol *m*; *v* trabajar cuando hay huelga, *fam* esquirollar

scabbard vaina

scabby costroso; (diseased) sarnoso

scabies sarna

scabious escabiosa; sarnosa

scabrous escabroso

scad: ~s of money *US* muchísimo dinero

scaffold cadalso; *bui* andamio; **go to the** ~ acabar en el patíbulo

scaffolding andamiaje *m*

scald *n* escaldadura; *v* escaldar; (milk) hervir (ie)²c; ~ **out** limpiar con agua caliente

scalding: ~ **hot** hirviendo

¹ **scale** *n* (of fish) escama; *v* (fish) escamar; *mech* raspar; ~ **teeth** quitar el sarro a los dientes

² **scale** platillo de balanza; (pair of) ~s balanza; *v* **tip the** ~s pesar, **he tips the** ~s **at 100 kilos** él pesa 100 kilos

³ **scale** *n* +*mus* escala; **to** ~ según escala; **on a big/small** ~ en gran/pequeña escala; ~ **model** maqueta; ~ **of charges** tarifa; ~ **of values** escala de valores; *v* (climb) escalar; ~ **down** reducir¹⁵ a escala; ~ **up** (increase) aumentar a escala

scaliness escamosidad *f*

scaling (of fish) escamadura; *mech* raspadura; (climbing) escalada; ~-**ladder** (fireman's) escalas *fpl* de bombero, *mil* escalas de sitio

scallop *n* concha; (sewing) onda; *v* ondear

scallywag pícaro

scalp *n anat* cuero cabelludo; (trophy) cabellera; ~-**hunter** cazador *m* de cabelleras; *v* escalpar

scalpel escalpelo

scaly escamoso; (of boiler) encrustado

scamp *n* bribón (-ones) *m*; (child) diablillo; *v* (work) frangollar

scamper *n* huida precipitada; *v* ~ **(away/off)** escaparse corriendo

scampi gambas *fpl usu* fritas

scan *vt* (examine) examinar; *TV* explorar; *vi* (of verse) estar¹⁹ bien medido

scandal escándalo; (noise) campanada; (slander) difamación *f*; **what a** ~! ¡qué vergüenza!; **cause a** ~ armar follón; ~-**monger** chismoso, (slanderer) difa-

mador *m* (-ora *f*)

scandalize escandalizar⁷

scandalous escandaloso

Scandinavia Escandinavia

Scandinavian *n* + *adj* escandinavo

scanner antena giratoria; *med* escáner *m*

scansion escansión *f*

scant *see* **scanty**

scantiness escasez *f*

scanty escaso; (of crops) pobre; (of hair) ralo; (of dress) corto

scapegoat cabeza de turco; **be a** ~ **for** ser¹⁹ el chivo expiatorio de

scapula escápula

scapulary escapulario

scar *n* cicatriz (-ces) *f*; *fig* herida; *v* marcar⁴ con una cicatriz; ~ **over** cicatrizarse⁷

scarab escarabajo

scarce escaso; **make o.s.** ~ escabullirse

scarcely apenas; ~ **had I returned when the police came** apenas hube llegado cuando vino la policía; ~ **anyone** casi nadie; ~ **any** casi ningún, casi ninguna; ~ **anything** casi nada; ~ **ever** casi nunca

scarcity escasez *f*

scare *n* susto; **you gave me a** ~ me dio un susto; (panic) pánico; ~-**crow** espantapájaros *m sing*+*pl*; ~-**monger** alarmista *m*+*f*; *v* asustar; ~ **away** ahuyentar; **be** ~**d of** tener¹⁹ miedo de

scarf bufanda; (head ~) pañuelo

scarify escarificar⁴; *fig* criticar⁴ severamente

scarlatina escarlatina

scarlet *n* grana; *adj* de (color) grana; ~ **fever** escarlatina; ~ **hat** capelo (cardenalicio); ~ **pimpernel** pimpinela escarlata; ~ **runner** judía verde; ~ **woman** puta

scarp escarpa

scarper escaparse

scarred señalado de cicatrices

scary asustado

scat! ¡lárguese!

scathing *vt* mordaz (-ces)

scatter *vt* esparcir¹³; *mil* dispersar; *vi* esparcirse,¹³ dispersarse; ~-**brain** cabeza de chorlito; ~-**brained** atolondrado, aturdido; ~-**gun** escopeta; ~**ed showers** chubascos dispersos

scattering esparcimiento; *mil* dispersión *f*; (small number) número pequeño

scatty chiflado

scavenge limpiar las calles; (of animals) alimentarse de carroña

scavenger basurero; *zool* animal *m* que se alimenta de carroña

scenario guión (-ones) *m*

scenarist guionista *m+f*

scene +*theat* escena; (view) vista; (favourite haunt) lugar predilecto; (of events) teatro, **Paris has been the ~ of great events** París ha sido el teatro de grandes acontecimientos; *fam* escándalo; **~ of the crime** escenario del crimen; **behind the ~s** entre bastidores; **the ~ is laid in** la acción pasa en; **come on the ~** entrar en escena; **make a ~** dar¹⁹ un espectáculo, armar un escándalo; **make the ~** lograr hacer algo de moda, (become popular) ponerse¹⁹ de moda; **it turns you on to a whole new ~** revela una nueva perspectiva; **~-painter** escenógrafo; **~-shifter** tramoyista *m + f*

scenery paisaje *m*; *theat* decorado

scenic escénico; **~ railway** montaña rusa

scent *n* (smell) olor *m*; (perfume) perfume *m*; (sense of smell) olfato; (of hunted animal) pista, **follow/lose the ~** seguir (i)³⁺¹¹/perder (ie)²ᵇ la pista; **~-spray** pulverizador *m* de perfume; *v* perfumar; **~ danger** sospechar el peligro; **~ out** olfatear; **~ed** perfumado

scentless sin perfume

sceptic *n + adj* escéptico

sceptical escéptico

scepticism escepticismo

sceptre cetro

schedule lista; +*leg* inventario; (programme) programa *m*; (time-table) horario; (of taxes) clase *f*; **ahead of ~** antes de tiempo; **behind ~** con retraso; **on ~** puntual; **time-~** horario; *v* catalogar⁵; (plan ahead) proyectar; **this house is ~d for modernization** se prevé la modernización de esta casa; **~d flight** vuelo regular; **~d route** itinerario señalado

schematic esquemático

scheme *n* (plan) proyecto; (plot) intriga; (diagram) esquema *m*; **colour ~** combinación *f* de colores; *v* proyectar; (intrigue) intrigar⁵

schemer intrigante *m+f*

scheming *n* (planning) proyectos *mpl*; (plotting) intrigas *fpl*; *adj* astuto

schism cisma *m*

schismatic *n+adj* cismático

schizophrenia esquizofrenia

schizophrenic *n+adj* esquizofrénico

schmaltz exceso de sentimentalismo

schnapps aguardiente *m*

scholar (pupil) alumno, alumna; (holding a ~ship) becario; (learned person) hombre *m*/mujer *f* de letras; **~ship** (learning) erudición *f*, (grant) beca

scholarly erudito

scholastic escolástico; **~ profession** magisterio

¹ **school** *n* (primary) escuela; (secondary) instituto; (fee-paying) colegio; (of university) departamento; (faculty) facultad *f*; **public ~** colegio privado, *US* escuela pública; **~ of motoring** autoescuela; **Sunday ~** escuela dominical; **~ fees** cuota de enseñanza; **in ~** en clase; **~ of thought** escuela de pensamiento; **the Flemish ~** la escuela flamenca; **of the old ~** anticuado; **child of ~ age** niño de edad escolar; **~-bag** cartera; **~boy** colegial *m*; **~days** días *mpl* de escuela/colegio, (time spent in ~) años de colegio, **in my ~days** cuando yo iba a la escuela/al colegio; **~girl** colegiala; **~mate** compañero de clase; **~master** (primary) maestro, (secondary) profesor *m* de instituto; **~mistress** (primary) maestra, (secondary) profesora; **~ report** nota; **~-room** (sala de) clase *f*; **~teacher** *see* **~master, ~mistress**; *v* instruir¹⁶

² **school** (shoal) banco

schooling instrucción *f*; estudios

schooner goleta

sciatica ciática

science ciencia; **on the ~ side** en la parte de ciencias; **~-fiction** ciencia-ficción *f*

scientific científico; (systematic) sistemático

scientist científico

scientology cientología

Scilly Isles Islas *fpl* Sorlingas

scimitar cimitarra

scintillate centellear; (of persons) brillar

scintillating *fig* brillante

scintillation centelleo; (of wit) relámpago

scion +*fig* vástago

scissors (+gymnastics) tijeras *fpl*

sclerosis esclerosis *f*
sclerotic esclerótico
scoff *n* burla; *v* burlarse (**at** de); *sl* engullir[18]
scoffer burlón *m* (-ona *f*)
scoffing *n* burlas *fpl*; *adj* burlón
scold *n* regañina; *v* regañar
scolding regaño
scone bollo
scoop *n* pal(et)a de mano; (water) achicador *m*; (of dredger) cangilón *m*; (of excavating machine) cuchara; *med* espátula; (of newspapers) publicación exclusiva de una noticia; (lucky find) hallazgo; *comm* ganancia; *v* (~ **out**) sacar[4] con pal(et)a; (water) achicar[4]; (excavate) excavar; (of news) publicar[4] exclusivamente; *comm* ganar
scoot escaparse corriendo
scooter (child's) patín (-ines) *m*; *mot* moto *f*, *fam* vespa
scope alcance *m*; (extent) extensión *f*; (opportunity) oportunidad *f*; **have free** ~ tener[19] carta blanca; **there is (plenty of)** ~ **for** hay (mucho) campo para; **within the** ~ **of** dentro del alcance de
scorch chamuscar[4]; (of sun) abrasar, *fam* picar[4]; *mot* ir[19] como un relámpago; ~**ed-earth tactics** táctica de tierra quemada
scorching *n* chamusquina; *adj* abrasador (-ora *f*), *fam* picante
score *n* (cut) muesca; (line) raya; *mus* partitura; *sp* (goals) tanteo, (points) puntuación *f*; (twenty) veintena; **by the** ~ *comm* a granel; **on the** ~ **of** con motivo de; **on that** ~ en ese respecto; **pay off an old** ~ ajustar una cuenta vieja; **what's the** ~? ¿cómo van?; **keep (the)** ~ tantear; ~-**board** tanteador *m*; *vt* (cut) hacer[19] muesca(s) en; (draw a line) rayar; *mus* instrumentar; (total) apuntar; (goal) marcar[4], *fam* puntuar; (point) ganar; *vi sp* marcar[4] un tanto, ganar un punto; (keep the total) tantear; ~ **off s.o.** ganarle un punto a alguien, (win at another's expense) ganar a expensas de otro; ~ **out** (erase) borrar
scorer (one who scores) marcador *m* (-ora *f*); (one who keeps score) tanteador *m* (-ora *f*), *SA* anotador *m* (-ora *f*)

scoria escoria
scoring *sp* puntuación *f*
scorn *n* desprecio, desdén *m*; *v* desdeñar; ~ **to do something** desdeñarse a/*fam* no rebajarse a hacer algo
scornful desdeñoso
scorpion alacrán (-anes) *m*; escorpión *m*
Scot escocés *m* (-esa *f*); ~**land** Escocia; **scot-free** libre de gravámenes; **go scot-free** salir[19] impune
Scotch *n* whisky *m* escocés; (people) escoceses *mpl*; (dialect) dialecto escocés; ~ **pine** pino; ~ **tape** *tr* celo; ~ **terrier** terrier *m* escocés
scotch (thwart) frustrar
Scots *n* (dialect) escocés; *adj* escocés (-esa *f*); ~**man** escocés *m*; ~**woman** escocesa
Scottish escocés (-esa *f*)
scoundrel canalla *m*
scoundrelly canallesco
scour (dishes) fregar (ie)[2a+5]; restregar[4]; *med* purgar[5]; (search) recorrer buscando
scourer (for washing up) estropajo de aluminio/de plástico; (scouring-powder) arena
scourge *n* látigo; *fam* aflicción *f*; *v* azotar
scouse cocido de legumbres y carne de carnero
¹**scout** *n* (+ member of ~ movement) explorador *m*; (exploration) exploración *f*; ~-**car** coche blindado usado para explorar; ~**master** líder *m* de un grupo de exploradores; *v* explorar; ~ **about/around** andar buscando
²**scout** rechazar[7] con desdén
scouting exploración *f*
scowl *n* ceño; *v* mirar con ceño (**at** a)
scowling (theatening) amenazador (-ora *f*)
scrag *n* pescuezo; ~ **end** (meat) aguja y cuello; *v* torcer (ue)[1b+12] el pescuezo; *fam* azotar
scragginess flaqueza
scraggy flaco
scram largarse[5]
scramble *n* (struggle) pelea (**for** por); (climb) subida; *v* (message) *rad* aletear; *aer* despegar[4] rápidamente; ~ **for** pelearse por; ~ **up** subir a gatas a; ~**d eggs** huevos revueltos; ~**d message** mensaje aleatorio

scrambler aparato para hacer incomprensibles los mensajes telefónicos

scrap n (small piece) pedacito; (waste) desechos mpl; (newspaper cutting etc) recorte m; (fight) riña; **have a ~ with** reñir (i)[3] con; **~s** (food) sobras fpl de comida; **~s of news** noticias pequeñas; **not a ~** ni pizca; **~ of paper** pedazo de papel, fig papel mojado; **~ paper** (waste) papel m de desecho; **sheet of ~ paper** hoja de apuntes; **~book** álbum m de recortes; **~-heap** montón (-ones) m de desechos; **throw on the ~-heap** desechar; **~-iron** chatarra; **~-merchant** chatarrero; v (discard as useless) desechar; mot+naut etc reducir[15] a chatarra; (expunge) borrar; (fight) armar camorra

scrape n raspadura; (predicament) aprieto; v raspar; mus pej rascar[4]

~ against rozar[7]

~ along ir[19] tirando

~ away quitar raspando

~ off quitar raspando

~ through (examination) aprobar (ue)[1a] por los pelos

~ together arañar poco a poco

~ up reunir poco a poco; **~ up an acquaintance with** lograr conocer

scraper (for shoes) limpiabarros m sing + pl; mech raspador m

scrappy fragmentario; (incoherent) deshilvanado

scratch n arañazo; (on furniture etc) raya; (of pen) rasgueo; sp línea de salida; **without a ~** ileso; **start from ~** partir de cero; **come up to ~** estar[19] al nivel de las circunstancias; adj (of team etc) improvisado; (player) sin ventaja; **~ team** sp equipo compuesto de novatos; v arañar; (mark furniture) rayar; (rub) rascar[4]; (hen) escarbar; (horse) retirar; **this pen ~es** esta pluma rasguea; **~ one's head** rascarse[4] la cabeza; **~ the surface of** fig tratar superficialmente; **~ out** borrar; **~-pad** bloc m (pl bloques) de apuntes

scratching-ground (for poultry) escarbadero

scratchy (of pen) que rasguea; (tone) áspero

scrawl n garabato(s); v garabatear

scrawny descarnado

scream n chillido; **~ of brakes** chillido de frenos; **she's a perfect ~** ella es para morirse de risa; v chillar; **~ with laughter** reír (i)[3] a carcajadas

screaming n chillidos mpl; adj chillador (-ora f); (piercing) penetrante

screamingly: ~ funny divertidísimo

screech see scream; **~-owl** lechuza común

screed escrito largo y aburrido; fam rollo

screen n (folding) biombo; (rigid) mampara; cin+TV pantalla, **star of the ~** estrella de la pantalla; (of trees) cortina; (sieve and investigation) criba; eccles cancel m; phot retículo; **~ of fire** mil cortina de fuego; **~play** guión (-ones) m; **~ writer** guionista m+f; v proteger[8]; (light) proteger[8] con pantalla; cin+TV proyectar, fam echar; (investigate) cribar, **the police ~ the immigrants** la policía criba a los inmigrantes; (hide) ocultar

screening protección f; cin+TV proyección f; (investigation) criba; (hiding) ocultación f

screw n tornillo; (thread) rosca; aer+naut hélice f; (turn) vuelta de tornillo; sl (wages) paga; sl (gaoler) carcelero; **he has a ~ loose** a él le falta un tornillo; **put the ~s on** apretar los tornillos a; **~-ball** US n+adj excéntrico; **~-on cap** (fountain-pen etc) capuchón m (-ones) de rosca, (lid) tapadera de rosca; **~driver** destornillador m; **~-propeller** hélice f; **~-shot** (billiards) tacada baja; **~-type bulb** bombilla de rosca; v atornillar; (stare at) mirar fijamente; vulg sl (have sexual intercourse with) tirarse a

~ down fijar con tornillos

~ -in adj de rosca

~ in v hacer[19] entrar atornillando

~ -on adj de rosca

~ on v sujetar con tornillos

~ up atornillar; (paper) arrugar[5]; (mess up) fastidiar, vulg joder; **~ up one's courage** cobrar ánimo; **~ up one's eyes** desojarse; **that would ~ me up** eso me dejaría muy preocupado

screwy loco

scribble n garabato; vt escribir (past part escrito) de prisa; vi garabatear

scribbler el/la que tiene letra ilegible; (bad author) autorzuelo

scribbling garabateo; ~-**pad** bloc *m* (*pl* bloques) de notas

scribe *n* copista *m+f*; *bibl* escriba *m*; *v* trazar⁷

scriber punta de trazar

scrimmage *n* escaramuza; (rugby) melé *f*; *v* pelearse

scrimp escatimar

scrimpy escatimoso

script *n* (handwriting) letra cursiva; (manuscript) manuscrito; (examination) examen escrito; *cin+TV* guión (-ones) *m*; ~-**girl** secretaria de dirección; ~-**writer** guionista *m+f*; ~-**writing** composición *f* de guiones; *v* escribir (*past part* escrito) un guión (**for** para)

scriptural bíblico

Scripture Sagrada Escritura; (lesson) Historia Sagrada

scrivener chupatintas *m sing+pl*

scrofula escrófula

scrofulous escrofuloso

scroll (rollo de) pergamino; *archi* (+violin decoration) voluta

scrotum escroto

scrounge *n*: **be on the** ~ ir¹⁹ de gorra; *vi* gorronear; *vt* sacar por medio de gorronería

scrounger gorrón *m* (-ona *f*)

scrounging *n* gorronería; *adj* gorrón

¹ **scrub** matas *fpl*; ~**land** monte bajo

² **scrub** *n* fregado; **it needs a good** ~ hace falta fregarlo bien; *v* fregar (ie)²ᵃ; *fam* (cancel) borrar

³ **scrub** *US* mal jugador; ~ **team** equipo compuesto de novatos

scrubber cepillo para el suelo; (prostitute) ramera

scrubbing fregado; ~-**brush** cepillo para el suelo

scrubby achaparrado

scruff: ~ **of the neck** pescuezo

scruffy piojoso

scrum(mage) *sp* melé *f*; **loose/set** ~ melé espontánea/fija

scrumptious de rechupete

scrunch ronzar⁷

scruple *n* escrúpulo; **have no** ~s no tener¹⁹ escrúpulos; *v* vacilar; **I would not** ~ **to do that** no vacilaría en hacer eso

scrupulous escrupuloso (**about** en cuanto a)

scrupulousness escrupulosidad *f*

scrutineer escudriñador *m*

scrutinize escudriñar; (votes) escrutar

scrutiny escrutinio

scuba: ~-**diver** submarinista *m+f*; ~-**diving** submarinismo

scud ir¹⁹ viento en popa

scuff desgastar la superficie con el uso

scuffle *n* refriega; *v* pelear(se)

scull *n* espadilla; *v* remar con espadilla

scullery recocina

sculptor escultor *m* (-ora *f*)

sculptural escultural

sculpture *n* escultura; *v* esculpir

scum *n* espuma; (on stagnant water) verdín *m*; (dregs) heces *fpl*; ~ **of the earth** heces de la tierra

scummy espumoso

scupper *n* clava; *v* abrir (*past part* abierto) las clavas; *fig* frustrar

scurf caspa

scurfy casposo

scurrility grosería

scurrilous grosero

scurry *n* carrera precipitada; (of rain) chaparrón *m*; (of snow) remolino; *v* echar a correr; ~ **off** escabullirse

scurvy *n* escorbuto; *adj* despreciable; **that was a** ~ **thing to do** eso fue una mala pasada

scut rabito

¹ **scuttle** *n naut* escotilla; *v* barrenar

² **scuttle** (coal-~) cubo

³ **scuttle** *n* (flight) fuga precipitada; *v* escabullirse

scythe *n* guadaña; *v* guadañar

S.E. (south-east) *n+adj* S.E. (sudeste) *m*

sea *n* mar *m+f*; (waves) oleada; *fig* multitud *f*; **by** ~ por mar; **by the** ~(**side**) a orillas del mar; **go to** ~ hacerse¹⁹ marinero; **beyond the** ~s allende el mar; **I'm all at** ~ estoy despistado; **put to** ~ hacerse¹⁹ a la mar; ~-**anemone** anémona de mar; ~**bird** ave *f* marina; ~**board** litoral *m*; ~-**borne** llevado por el mar; ~-**breeze** brisa de mar; ~-**bream** besugo; ~-**captain** capitán (-anes) *m* de mar; ~ **coast** costa marítima; ~-**dog** *zool* foca, *fig* lobo de mar; ~-**eagle** águila pescadora; ~-**farer**, ~-**faring** marinero; ~-**front** (promenade) paseo marítimo, (buildings) edificios *mpl* que dan al mar; ~-**going** navegante; ~-**going vessel** embarcación *f* de alta mar; ~-**green** *n+adj* verdemar *m*; ~**gull** gaviota; ~-**horse** caballo de mar; ~-**legs** pie marino; **get one's** ~-**legs** acostumbrarse a la vida de a bordo; ~-**level** nivel *m* del mar; ~-**lion** león marino; ~-**man** marinero; ~**manship** náutica; ~-**mile** milla náutica; ~-**monster** monstruo marino; ~**plane** hidroavión (-ones) *m*; ~**port** puerto de mar; ~-**power** (naval strength) potencia naval, (country) país *m* con gran potencia naval; ~**quake** maremoto; ~-**serpent** serpiente *f* de mar; ~-**shell** concha; ~-**shore** playa; ~-**sick** mareado; **become** ~-**sick** marearse; ~-**sickness** mareo; ~-**sickness pill** píldora contra el mareo; ~**side** orilla del mar, (beach) playa; ~**side resort** lugar *m* de veraneo a orillas del mar; ~-**trout** trucha asalmonada; ~-**urchin** erizo de mar; ~-**wall** rompeolas *m sing + pl*; dique marítimo; ~-**way** ruta marítima; ~**weed** alga marina; ~**worthy** en condiciones de navegar; ~**worthiness** buen estado marinero

[1] **seal** *zool* foca; ~**skin** piel *f* de foca; *v* cazar[7] focas

[2] **seal** *n* sello; ~-**ring** sortija de sello; *v* (affix a seal) sellar; (letter) cerrar (ie)[2a]; (with wax) lacrar; **my lips are** ~**ed** mis labios están cerrados; **their fate is** ~**ed** su suerte está echada; ~ **off** obturar; ~ **off** (a frontier) impermeabilizar[7]; ~ **up** (letter) cerrar (ie)[2a], *mech* precintar, (with lead) emplomar

[1] **sealing** caza de focas

[2] **sealing:** ~-**wax** lacre *m*

seam (sewing) costura; *geol* veta; *mech* juntura; *surg* sutura; **burst at the** ~**s** descoserse; **it is bursting at the** ~**s** está descosiéndose, *fig* está demasiado lleno

seamless sin costura

seamstress costurera

seamy: ~ **side** revés *m* de la moneda

seance sesión (-ones) *f* de espiritismo

sear (burn) chamuscar[4]; (of wind) abrasar; *med* cauterizar[7]

search *n* busca (**for** de); (exploration+ *surg*) exploración *f*; (examination)

registro; *leg* pesquisa; **in** ~ **of** en busca de; **right of** ~ derecho de visita; ~**light** *n* reflector *m*, *v* enfocar,[4] *fig* escudriñar y aclarar; ~-**warrant** auto de registro; *v* explorar; registrar; pesquisar; (frisk) cachear; ~ **me!** ¡yo qué sé!

~ **for** buscar[4]

~ **into** investigar[5]

~ **out** ir[19] en buscar de

searcher buscador *m* (-ora *f*); (explorer) explorador *m* (-ora *f*); (investigator) investigador *m* (-ora *f*)

searching (question) agudo; (look) penetrante

searing agonizante

seascape marina

season *n* (of year) estación (-ones) *f*; (*sp* ' + **social**) temporada; (opportune time) sazón *f*; **at this** ~ **of the year** en esta época del año; **at the height of the** ~ en plena temporada; **in** ~ en sazón, **strawberries are in** ~ **in June** las fresas están en sazón en junio; **fruit in** ~ (on menu) fruta del tiempo; **in due** ~ a su tiempo; **out of** ~ fuera de temporada; ~ **of goodwill** fiestas *fpl* navideñas; **compliments of the** ~ Felices Navidades; **close** ~ veda; ~-**ticket** billete *m* de abono, *fam* pase *m*; *v* condimentar; (of wood) curar; ~**ed** condimentado, (of wood) maduro, *fig* acostumbrado; **become** ~**ed to** acostumbrarse a; **highly** ~**ed** picante

seasonable propio de la estación; (opportune) oportuno

seasonal estacional; ~ **goods** artículos *mpl* de temporada; ~-**worker** trabajador *m* temporero

seasoning *cul* condimento; (of wood) maduración *f*

seat *n* asiento; (bench) banco; (chair) silla; *cin+theat* localidad *f*; (in bus *etc*) plaza; (buttocks) asentaderas *fpl*; (of trousers) fondillos; (in parliament) escaño; (country residence) casa de campo; ~ **of government** sede *f* del gobierno; ~ **of war** teatro de guerra; **have a good** ~ (horse-riding) montar bien a caballo; **hold a** ~ (in parliament) ser[19] diputado; **take a** ~ tomar asiento; **take a back** ~ dejar de figurar; ~-**back** respaldo; ~-**belt** cinturón (-ones) *m* de seguridad; *v* (a)sentar (ie)²ᵃ; *mech* fijar; (put ~ in a chair) poner¹⁹ asiento a; **this hall ~s 500** esta sala tiene asientos para 500; **be ~ed** estar¹⁹ sentado; **please be ~ed** siéntese por favor

seater: four-~ de cuatro plazas

seating asientos *mpl*; ~ **capacity** número de asientos

S.E.A.T.O. (South-East Asia Treaty Organization) O.T.S.A. (Organización *f* del Tratado del Sudeste Asiático)

seawards hacia el mar

Sebastian Sebastián

secateurs: pair of ~ podadera

secede separarse

secession secesión *f*

secessionist *n*+*adj* secesionista *m*+*f*

secluded apartado

seclusion retiro

¹ **second** *n* +*mus* segundo; (boxing) segundante *m*; (duelling) padrino; **~s** artículos *mpl* de segunda calidad; **just a ~** un moment(it)o; **split ~** santiamén (-enes) *m*; **~-hand** *n* (on watch) segundero; *adj* segundo; **the ~ of May** el dos de mayo; **George the Second** Jorge segundo; **come (in) ~** llegar⁵ el segundo; **be ~ to none** (person) no ser¹⁹ inferior a nadie, (things) no ser¹⁹ inferior a nada; **every ~ day** cada dos días; **he didn't need a ~ invitation** él no se hizo rogar; **on ~ thoughts** pensándolo bien; **without ~ thoughts** sin pensarlo; **I've been having ~ thoughts on the matter** he estado pensando en la cuestión; **in ~ gear** en segunda (velocidad); **play ~ fiddle** desempeñar un papel secundario; **the ~ smallest** el más pequeño menos uno; **~-best** *n* segundo, *adj* el/la mejor después del primero/de la primera; ~ **childhood** chochez *f*, **she's in her ~ childhood** ella está chocheando; ~ **class** segunda clase; **~-class citizen** ciudadano de segunda clase; ~ **cousin** primo segundo, prima segunda; **~-floor flat** apartamento del segundo piso; **~-hand** de segunda mano; (of houses, flats, *etc*) seminuevo; **~-hand bookshop** librería de viejo; **~-hand bookseller** librero de viejo; **~-hand clothes** ropa usada; **~-in-command** subjefe *m*; **~-lieutenant** alférez *m*; ~

mate segundo piloto; ~ **nature** costumbre arraigada; **~-rate** de segunda calidad; ~ **self** alter ego; ~ **sight** intuición *f*, clarividencia; *v* apoyar; *adv* en segundo lugar

² **second** (transfer) trasladar temporalmente

secondary secundario; ~ **school** escuela de segunda enseñanza, *Sp* instituto

seconder el/la que apoya (una proposición)

secondly en segundo lugar

secrecy secreto

secret *n*+*adj* secreto; **in ~** en secreto; **be in the ~** estar¹⁹ en el secreto; **keep ~** tener¹⁹ secreto; **keep a ~** guardar un secreto, *fam* ser¹⁹ una tumba; **open ~** secreto a voces; ~ **policeman** policía *m* secreto, *sl* madaleno; **Secret Service** servicio de espionaje

secretaire secretér *m*

secretarial de secretario, de secretaria; ~ **college** colegio comercial; ~ **course** curso de secretaría

secretariat secretaría

secretary secretario, secretaria; **private ~** secretaria particular; **Secretary of State** (*US*) Ministro de Asuntos Exteriores; **~ship** secretaría

secrete esconder; *med* secretar

secretion secreción (-ones) *f*

secretive callado; **be ~ about** hacer¹⁹ secreto de

sect secta

sectarian *n*+*adj* sectario

section sección (-ones) *f*; (of country) región (-ones) *f*; (of town) barrio; (of road *etc*) tramo; *leg* artículo

sectional seccional; (made in sections) fabricado en secciones; ~ **interests** intereses *mpl* regionales/locales

sector sector *m*

secular secular; (lay) seglar; ~ **music** música profana

secularization secularización *f*

secularize secularizar⁷

secure *adj* seguro; (firm) firme; (confident) confiado (**in** en); ~ **against/from** asegurado contra; *v* asegurar (**against, from** contra); (obtain) obtener¹⁹; (lock) cerrar (ie)²ᵃ con llave

securities valores *mpl*; **government ~** papel *m* del estado

security seguridad *f*; *comm* fianza; (person) fiador *m* (-ora *f*); **stand ~ for** salir[19] fiador de; **~ firm** empresa de seguridad; **~ guard** guardia jurado; **~ risk** peligro para la seguridad nacional; **personal ~** garantía personal; **social ~** seguridad *f* social

sedan *mot* sedán *m*; **~-chair** silla de manos

sedate sosegado

sedateness compostura

sedative *n* + *adj* sedante *m*

sedentary sedentario

sedge juncia

sediment + *geol* sedimento

sedimentary sedimentario

sedition sedición *f*

seditious sedicioso

seduce seducir[15]; *fam* violar

seducer seductor *m*

seduction seducción *f*

seductive seductor (-ora *f*); (attractive) atractivo; (persuasive) persuasivo

sedulous asiduo

[1] **see** *n* sede *f*; **Holy See** Santa Sede

[2] **see** *v* ver[19]; (understand) comprender; (receive) recibir, **I'll ~ her at three** la recibiré a las tres; (visit) visitar, **I'm going to ~ my uncle** voy a visitar a mi tío; **~ page ten** véase la página diez; **let me ~** *fig* vamos a ver; **let's ~** a ver; **go and ~** ir[19] a ver; **~ for o.s.** verlo[19] uno mismo, **~ for yourself!** ¡véalo usted mismo!; **~ you!** ¡hasta la vista!; **~ you later/tomorrow!** ¡hasta luego/mañana!; **I'm not ~ing anyone today** no estoy para nadie hoy; **~ life** ver[19] mundo; **~ red** ponerse[19] furioso; **~ service** servir (i)[3] en las fuerzas armadas; **~ the sights** ver[19] los monumentos

~ about encargarse[5] de

~ home acompañar a casa

~ off despedirse (i)[3] de; **they went to ~ off their friends** fueron a la estación para despedirse de sus amigos

~ out acompañar a la puerta; (film *etc*) quedarse hasta el fin de

~ over inspeccionar

~-through *adj* transparente

~ through *v* ver[19] por; **~ through s.o.** calarle a uno; **~ through a mystery** penetrar un misterio; **~ something through** llevar algo a cabo; **~ s.o.**

through ayudar a alguien hasta el fin

~ to atender (ie)[2b] a; **~ to everything** encargarse[5] de todo; **~ to it that** cuidar de que + *subj*

seed *n* semilla; (of fruit) pepita; *fig* germen (gérmenes) *m*; (offspring) prole *f*; *sp* **~ed** seleccionado; **the two number one ~s** los dos (jugadores) número uno; **go/run to ~** dar[19] grana, *fig* echarse a perder; **~bed** semillero; **~cake** pastel *m* que contiene simientes de alcaravea; **~-pearl** aljófar *m*; **~-potato** patata de siembra; **~sman** vendedor *m* de semillas; **~-time** tiempo de sembrar; *vt* sembrar (ie)[2a]; (tennis) seleccionar; *vi* granar

seedless sin semilla/pepita

seedling planta de semilla

seedy (of appearance) raído; (of place) asqueroso; **I'm feeling ~ today** estoy malucho hoy

seeing *n* vista; **it is worth ~** vale la pena de verse; **~ is believing** ver es creer; **~ eye** (guide-dog) perro guía (*pl* perros guía); *conj* **~ that** visto que

seek *v* (look for) buscar[4]; (search for) recorrer en busca de; (ask for) pedir (i)[3]; **~ after** buscar[4]; **~ to** (do something) tratar de + *infin*; **it is much sought after** es muy solicitado

seeker buscador *m* (-ora *f*)

seem parecer[14], **it ~s to me** me parece; **it ~s (to be) clean** parece limpio; **I ~ to recall** creo recordar; **~ right** parecer[14] correcto, *fam* pegar[5], **it doesn't ~ right for me to do that** no me pega hacer eso; **it ~s that the police came here last night** parece ser que la policía vino aquí anoche; **so it ~s** así parece

seeming *n* apariencia; *adj* aparente

seemingly en apariencia

seemliness decoro

seemly decoroso; (suited to the occasion) indicado

seep filtrar(se)

seepage filtración *f*

seer adivino

see-saw *n* balancín (-ines) *m*; *v* balancear(se)

seethe *v* hervir (ie)[2c]; **he was seething with fury** él estaba muy furioso; **seething with people** concurridísimo

segment segmento

segregate segregar(se)[5]

segregation segregación *f*
Seine Sena *m*
seismic sísmico
seismograph sismógrafo
seismology sismología
seize agarrar; (arrest) prender; *leg* (take possession of) embargar⁵; (by customs officers) decomisar, **customs officers ~d four kilos of marihuana** los aduaneros decomisaron cuatro kilos de marihuana; **~ the opportunity to** aprovechar la oportunidad de +*infin*; **~ up** *mech* agarrotarse, *mot* calarse; **~ upon** *fig* fijarse en; **~ upon an excuse** valerse¹⁹ de un pretexto
seizure (grasping) asimiento; (arrest) prendimiento; *leg* embargo; (goods seized by customs) decomiso; *med* ataque *m*
seldom rara vez
select *adj* escogido; *v* escoger⁸; *sp* seleccionar
selection (act of selecting) selección (-ones) *f*; (things selected) surtido; *mus* selecciones *fpl*; **natural ~** selección *f* natural
selective selectivo
selector *rad* selector *m*; *sp* seleccionador *m*
self *n* uno mismo, una misma; (ego) yo *m*; **my other ~** mi otro yo; **my better ~** mi mejor parte *f*; **dressed as a clown he was his real ~** vestido de payaso era su verdadero yo; **(all) by one~** (unaided) sin ayuda, (unaccompanied) solo; *refl pron* see **myself, himself** *etc*
pref **~-abasement** humillación de sí mismo; **~-abuse** masturbación *f*, *fam* hacer¹⁹ la paja; **~-acting** automático; **~-addressed envelope** sobre dirigido a sí mismo; **~-adhesive** autoadhesivo; **~-adjusting** de ajuste automático; **~-advertisement** autobombo; **~-apparent** evidente; **~-appointed** designado por sí mismo; **~-assertion** presunción *f*; **~-assertive** presumido; **~-assurance** confianza en sí mismo; **~-assured** seguro de sí mismo; **~-centred** egocéntrico; **~-closing** (door) automático; **~-coloured** de su color natural; **~-command** dominio sobre sí mismo; **~-complacent** satisfecho de sí mismo; **~-conceit** arrogancia; **~-confidence** confianza en sí mismo; **~-**

confident seguro de sí mismo; **~-conscious** cohibido; **~-consciousness** cohibición *f*; **~-contained** (of people) poco comunicativo, (of things) completo, (of flats) independiente; **~-contradictory** contradictorio; **~-control** autocontrol *m*; **~-controlled** dueño de sí mismo; **~-convicted** condenado por sus propios hechos; **~-deception** engaño de sí mismo; **~-defence** defensa propia; **~-denial** abnegación *f*; **~-destruction** suicidio, autodestrucción *f*; **~-destructive** auto-destructivo; **~-determination** auto-determinación *f*; **~-discipline** auto-disciplina; **~-drive** sin chófer; **~-drive car hire** alquiler *m* de coches sin chófer; **~-educated** autodidacta; **~-effacement** modestia; **~-effacing** modesto; **~-esteem** amor propio; **~-evident** patente; **~-examination** examen *m* de conciencia; **~-explanatory** que se explica por sí mismo; **~-expression** expresión *f* de la individualidad; **~-fertilization** auto-fecundación *f*; **~-fertilizing** de polinización directa; **~-filling** de relleno automático; **~-governing** autónomo; **~-government** autonomía; **~-help** ayuda propia; **~-importance** presunción *f*; **~-important** presumido; **~-important** darse¹⁹ importancia, *fam* darse¹⁹ postín; **~-indulgence** indulgencia consigo mismo, (of food *etc*) falta de moderación; **~-indulgent** indulgente consigo mismo; **~-inflicted** infligido a sí mismo; **~-interest** egoísmo; **~-justification** autojustificación *f*; **~-knowledge** conocimiento de sí mismo; **~-locking** de cierre automático; **~-love** egolatría; **~-made man** hombre *m* que ha triunfado por su propio esfuerzo; **~-opinionated** terco, *fam* autobombo; **~-pity** auto-compasión *f*; **~-portrait** autorretrato; **~-possessed** dueño/dueña de sí mismo; **~-praise** elogio de sí mismo; **~-preservation** propia conservación; **~-proclaimed** autoproclamado; **~-propelled** autopropulsado; **~-propulsion** autopropulsión *f*; **~-raising flour** harina mezclada con polvos de levadura; **~-reliance** confianza en sí mismo; **~-reliant**

seguro de sí mismo; ~**-respect** dignidad *f*; ~**-righteous** santurrón; ~**-righteousness** santurronería; ~**-sacrifice** abnegación *f*; ~**-same** mismísimo; ~**-satisfied** pagado de sí mismo; ~**-seeker** egoísta *m+f*; ~**-seeking** egoísta; ~**-service** (**shop**) (tienda) de autoservicio; ~**-starter** *mot* arranque automático; ~**-styled** autoproclamado; ~**-sufficiency** independencia; ~**-sufficient** autárquico, independiente; ~**-supporting** que vive de su propio trabajo, independiente; **be** ~**-supporting** autofinanciarse, (of people) vivir de su propio trabajo; ~**-taught** autodidacta; ~**-willed** obstinado; ~**-winding** (clock) de cuerda automática

selfish egoísta

selfishly por egoísmo

selfishness egoísmo

selfless altruista

sell *n* (deception) engaño; (swindle) estafa; *v* vender, **I sold the house for a million pesetas** vendí la casa por un millón de pesetas; ~ **by auction** vender en subasta; **they're trying to** ~ **us the idea** ellos intentan hacernos aceptar la idea; **I'm sold on the idea** estoy cautivado por la idea

~**-by date** fecha de caducidad

~ **off** liquidar

~**-out** *n* traición *f*

~ **out** *v* saldar; *fig* traicionar; **be sold out** (of goods) estar[19] agotado

seller vendedor *m* (-ora *f*); *comm* artículo que se vende bien

selling venta; ~**-off** liquidación *f*; ~**-price** precio de venta al público

Sellotape celo

seltzer (**water**) agua de seltz

selvage, selvedge borde *m*

semantics semántica

semaphore *n* semáforo; *v* comunicar[4] por semáforo

semblance apariencia

semen semen *m*

semester semestre *m*

semi *pref* (semi-detached house) casa semiseparada; ~**-automatic** semiautomático; ~**breve** semibreve *f*; ~**circle** semicírculo; ~**circular** semicircular; ~**colon** punto y coma; ~**-conscious** semiconsciente; ~**-**

detached semiseparado; ~**-final** semifinal *f*; ~**-finalist** *n+adj* semifinalista *m+f*; ~**-invalid** *n+adj* enfermizo; ~**-literate** medio analfabeto; ~**-official** semioficial; ~**-precious** semiprecioso; ~**quaver** semicorchea; ~**-skilled** semicualificado; ~**tone** semitono; ~**vowel** semivocal *f*

seminal seminal

seminar seminario

seminarist *n+adj* seminarista *m+f*

seminary *n* seminario; *joc sl* fábrica de curas; *adj* perteneciente a un seminario

semination propagación *f*

Semite *n* semita *m+f*

Semitic *n* lengua semítica; *adj* semítico

semolina sémola

sempiternal sempiterno

sempstress costurera

senate(-house) senado

senator senador *m*

send enviar, mandar; *comm* remitir; *fig* entusiasmar, **that song** ~**s me** esa canción me entusiasma; ~ **a telegram** poner[19] un telegrama; ~ **word** mandar recado; ~ **packing** mandar a paseo; ~ **mad** enloquecer[14]

~ **away** enviar a otra parte; (scare away) ahuyentar

~ **away for** encargar[5]

~ **back** (persons) volver (ue)[1b] (*past part* vuelto); (things) devolver (ue)[1b] (*past part* devuelto)

~ **down** (persons) hacer[19] bajar; (things) mandar abajo; (expel from university) expulsar; *leg* sentenciar a prisión

~ **for** enviar a buscar; *fam* enviar por

~ **in** (persons) hacer[19] entrar; (things) mandar; (food) servir (i)[3]; (invoice) presentar; (one's name) dar[19]; ~ **in one's resignation** mandar su dimisión; ~ **him in!** ¡que pase!

~**-off** *n* despedida

~ **off** *v see* ~ **away**

~ **on** (letter) hacer[19] seguir; (orders) transmitir

~ **out** (persons) hacer[19] salir; (things) mandar; (emit) emitir; (roots, shoots *etc*) echar

~ **round** (hat, petition *etc*) hacer[19] circular

~ **up** (persons) hacer[19] subir; (things)

enviar arriba; (ball) lanzar[7]

sender remitente *m+f*; *elect* transmisor *m*

sending *n* envío

Seneca Séneca

Senegal Senegal *m*

Senegalese *n+adj* senegalés *m* (-esa *f*)

senile senil

senility senilidad *f*

senior *n* (~ member) decano; ~s **and juniors** (in school) los mayores y los pequeños; **I'm your ~ by two years** tengo dos años más que usted; *adj* (older) mayor (de edad); (of higher rank) más antiguo (to que); **Mr García ~ el Sr García padre; ~ citizen** jubilado (por vejez); ~ **partner** socio más antiguo

seniority antigüedad *f*

senna sena

sensation sensación (-ones) *f*

sensational sensacional

sensationalism sensacionalismo

sensationalist *n+adj* sensacionalista *m+f*

sense *n* sentido; **the five ~s** los cinco sentidos; (sound judgement) juicio; (meaning) opinión *f*; ~ **of balance** equilibrio; ~ **of hearing** oído; ~ **of humour** sentido del humor; ~ **of justice/proportion** sentido de la justicia/la proporción; ~ **of sight** vista; ~ **of smell** olfato; ~ **of taste** paladar *m*; ~ **of touch** tacto; ~ **organ** órgano de los sentidos; **business ~** buena cabeza para los negocios; **colour ~** sentido del color; **common ~** sentido común; **in a ~** en cierto sentido; **in the full ~ of the word** en toda la extensión de la palabra; **be out of one's ~s** haber[19] perdido el juicio; **bring s.o. to his ~s** hacerle[19] a alguien volver en sí; **knock ~ into s.o.** traer[19] a uno a sus sentidos; **it doesn't make ~** no tiene sentido, *fam* no tiene ni pies ni cabeza; **talk ~** hablar con juicio; *v* percibir

senseless (meaningless) sin sentido; (foolish) insensato; (stunned) sin conocimiento; **knock ~** derribar y dejar sin conocimiento

sensibility sensibilidad *f*

sensible sensato; (of clothing *etc*) práctico; (conscious) consciente; (perceptible) sensible; **be ~ of** estar[19]/ser[19] consciente de

sensitive sensible (**to** a); (impressionable) impresionable; (touchy) susceptible, *fam* quisquilloso; *phot* sensibilizado

sensitivity +*phot* sensibilidad *f* (**to** a); (touchy) susceptibilidad *f*, *fam* quisquillosidad *f*

sensitize sensibilizar[7]

sensorial, sensory sensorio

sensual sensual

sensualism sensualismo

sensualist *n+adj* sensualista *m+f*

sensuality sensualidad *f*

sensuous sensual

sentence *n* (punishment) sentencia; *gramm* oración (-ones) *f*; **pass ~** pronunciar sentencia; **serve one's ~** cumplir su condena; **under ~ of** bajo pena de; *v* sentenciar (**to** a)

sententious sentencioso

sententiousness estilo sentencioso

sentient consciente; sensible

sentiment sentimiento; (sentimentality) sentimentalismo; (opinion) opinión *f*

sentimental sentimental; (mawkish) sensiblero; **of ~ value** de valor sentimental

sentimentalist romántico

sentimentality sentimentalismo; (mawkishness) sensiblería

sentimentalize idealizar[7]

sentinel centinela *m+f*

sentry centinela *m+f*; ~-**box** garita de centinela; ~-**duty**, ~-**go** turno de centinela

sepal sépalo

separable separable

separate *adj* separado; (loose) suelto; ~ **development** (apartheid) apartamiento; *v* separar(se) (**from** de); (of races) segregar[5]; *leg* (of husband and wife) separarse

separation separación *f*

separatist *n+adj* separatista *m+f*

separator separador *m*; (in dairy) descremadora

sepia sepia

sepsis sepsis *f*

September se(p)tiembre *m*

septic séptico; ~ **tank** fosa séptica; *fam* pozo negro

septicaemia septicemia

septuagenarian *n+adj* septuagenario

sepulchral sepulcral

sepulchre *n* sepulcro; *v* sepultar

sequel (of story) continuación *f*; (consequence) resultado (**to** de)

sequence (orden *m* de) sucesión *f*; *cin* secuencia; (at cards) serie *f*; ~ **of tenses** concordancia de tiempos

sequester secuestrar; ~**ed spot** sitio aislado

sequestrate secuestrar

sequestration secuestro

sequin lentejuela

seraglio serrallo

seraph serafín (-ines) *m*

seraphic seráfico

Serbia Servia

Serbian *n*+*adj* servio

serenade *n* serenata; *v* dar[19] una serenata

serendipity don *m* de descubrir cosas valorosas

serene sereno; **Your Serene Highness** Su Alteza Serenísima *f*

serenity serenidad *f*

serf siervo

serfdom servidumbre *f*

serge estameña

sergeant sargento; (police) sargento de policía; ~**-at-arms** macero; ~**-major** sargento mayor

serial *n* serial *m*; (novel) novela por entregas; *TV* telenovela; ~ **film, film** ~ película en episodios; *adj* consecutivo; (of numbers) de serie

serialize publicar[4] por entregas; *rad*+ *TV* preparar/presentar en episodios

serially por serie; (of books *etc*) por entregas

series serie *f*; **in** ~ en serie

serifs rajitas *fpl* de adorno

serious (of people) serio; (of news, condition) grave; ~ **inconvenience** grave inconveniente *m*; **be** ~ tomar las cosas en serio; **grow** ~ (of people + events) ponerse[19] grave/serio; **it's not** ~! ¡no es gran cosa!

seriously (of people) seriamente; (of news, conditions) gravemente; **take something** ~ tomar algo en serio, *fam* tomar algo a pecho; **he takes himself very** ~ él se toma muy en serio

seriousness (of people) seriedad *f*; (of news, conditions) gravedad *f*

sermon +*iron* sermón (-ones) *m*

sermonize sermonear

serpent serpiente *f*

serpentine *n min* serpentina; *adj* serpentino

serrated serrado

serration endentadura

serried apretado

serum suero

servant sirviente *m* (-ta *f*); (household) criado, criada, *SA* mucama; ~**s** servidumbre *f*; **your obedient** ~ su seguro servidor; **the** ~ **problem** el problema del servicio; **become a** ~ ir[19] a servir; ~**-girl** criada, *fam* muchacha; ~**s' entrance** entrada de servicio

serve +*mil* servir (i)[3]; (in shop) despachar; (a sentence) cumplir; (on jury) formar parte (**on** de); (tennis) sacar[4]; (of stallion *etc*) cubrir (*past part* cubierto); ~ **an apprenticeship** hacer[19] un aprendizaje; ~ **at table** servir (i)[3] a la mesa; ~ **a writ on** entregar[5] una orden a; **it** ~**s you right** bien se lo merece usted; **it will** ~ **to** (be useful) servirá para +*infin*; ~ **out/up** (food) servir (i)[3]

server (tool) pala; (tennis) saque *m*+*f*; *eccles* monaguillo

service *n* servicio; (of crockery) juego; (of writ *etc*) entrega; (tennis) saque *m*; *eccles* oficio, *fam* misa; **the** ~**s** *mil* las fuerzas armadas; **the three** ~**s** *Sp* los tres ejércitos; ~ **area** (on motorway) área de servicio; ~ **lane** *mot* arcén *m* de servicio; **go into** ~ (of servants) ir[19] a servir; **at your** ~ servidor de usted; **I'm entirely at your** ~ estoy completamente a la disposición de usted; **be of** ~ ayudar, **can I be of** ~ **to you?** ¿puedo ayudarle en algo?; **see** ~ *mil* prestar servicio; **be on active** ~ estar[19] en activo; **it's your** ~ (tennis) le toca a usted sacar; **my car needs a** ~ mi coche necesita atención; ~ **company** empresa de servicio público; **Senior Service** Flota Real; ~**-book** *eccles* misal *m*; ~**-man** militar *m*; ~**-station** estación *f* de servicio; *v* atender (ie)[2b]; *esp mech* mantener; (repair) reparar

serviceable (of things) utilizable; (of people) servicial; (lasting) duradero

serviette servilleta; ~ **ring** servilletero

servile servil

servility servilismo

serving n leg entrega; (tennis) saques mpl; ~-**maid** criada; ~-**hatch** ventanilla de servicio; ~-**table** trinchero

servitude esclavitud f; penal ~ cadena perpetua

servomechanism servomecanismo

sesame sésamo; **open ~!** ¡sésamo ábrete!

session sesión (-ones) f; fam (interview) entrevista; **petty ~s** tribunal presidido por un juez de paz

sessional de una sesión

sestet sexteto

set n (crockery, tools etc) juego, **make the ~** hacer[19] juego; (of stamps etc) serie f, **I need one to make up the ~** necesito uno para completar la serie; (of hair) marcado, **have a shampoo and ~** hacerse[19] lavar y marcar; (of people) clase f; (people with common interest) grupo, **literary ~** grupo literario; cin+theat decorado; rad (aparato de) radio f; TV televisor m; (of gears) tren m; (tennis) set m; agri planta de transplantar, **onion-~** cebolla de transplantar; (of saw teeth) triscamiento; ~ **of false teeth** dentadura postiza; **smart ~** mundo elegante; ~-**designer** escenógrafo; adj (placed) colocado, puesto; (of prices etc) fijo; (of cement) fraguado; (jelly etc) cuajado; (of paint) seco; (of barometer) estable; (inflexible) inflexible, ~ **in one's beliefs** inflexible en sus creencias; (usual) reglamentario, ~ **procedure** trámites mpl reglamentarios; (prescribed) prescrito; **novel ~ in Wales** novela ambientada en Gales; ~ **with** adornado de; **be ~ on** (keen on) empeñarse en +infin; **be dead ~ against** estar[19] completamente opuesto a; **be well ~-up** estar[19] en buen puesto; **he is ~ in his ways** él está establecido en lo suyo; ~ **phrase** frase hecha; ~ **piece** theat grupo; ~ **speech** discurso preparado de antemano para cualquier ocasión; ~**square** cartabón (-ones) m

~ vi (sun) ponerse (past part puesto); (cement) fraguarse; (glue) endurecerse[14]; (jelly) cuajarse

~ **about** (begin to) ponerse[19] (past part puesto) a +infin

~ **forth/off** ponerse[19] (past part puesto)

en camino

~ **in** comenzar[7]; **winter has ~ in** el invierno ha comenzado

~ **out** ponerse[19] (past part puesto) en camino; ~ **out to** ponerse[19] a +infin

~-**to** n lucha

~ **to** v (begin) empezar (ie)[2a] a +infin; **he ~ to work** él empezó a trabajar

~ **up as** constituirse en; (pretend to be) dárselas[19] de

vt colocar[4]; (fashion, problem, table) poner[19] (past part puesto); (bone) reducir[15]; (hair) marcar[4]; (jewel) montar; (prices) fijar; (teeth) apretar (ie)[2a]; (saw) entriscar[4]; (snare) tender (ie)[2b]; (trap) armar; (watch) poner[19] (past part puesto) en hora, fam poner[19] bien; ~ **the alarm-clock** poner[19] (past part puesto) en el despertador (**for** a); ~ **a dog on** azuzar[7] un perro contra; ~ **an example** dar[19] un ejemplo; ~ **free** liberar; ~ **going/in motion** poner[19] (past part puesto) en marcha; ~ **one's heart on** suspirar por; ~ **one's heart against** mostrarse (ue)[1a] contrario a; ~ **eyes on** alcanzar[7] a ver; ~ **fire to** prender fuego a; ~ **foot in** entrar en; ~ **one's teeth on edge** dar[19] dentera; ~ **to music** poner[19] (past part puesto) música a; ~ **sail** (depart) zarpar; ~ **a sail** desplegar (ie)[2a+5] una vela; ~ **a time** fijar una hora; **that ~s me thinking** eso me hace pensar; **it ~ them talking** les dio qué hablar; **it ~ my mind at rest** me tranquilizó; ~ **at ease** hacer[19] cómodo; ~ **at naught** despreciar; ~ **to work** poner[19] (past part puesto) a trabajar; ~ **to rights** poner[19] (past part puesto) en orden; ~ **store by** dar[19] valor a; ~ **the Thames on fire** ser[19] una maravilla

~ **about** (hit) golpear; (start to) emprender

~ **against** indisponer[19] (past part indispuesto) con; ~ **o.s. against** oponerse (past part opuesto) a

~ **apart** separar, segregar

~ **aside** poner[19] (past part puesto) aparte; leg anular; (reject) desatender (ie)[2b]

~**back** n contratiempo

~ **back** v detener[19]; **that car ~ me back 100,000 pesetas** ese coche me costó 100.000 pesetas

~ **before** presentar a

~ **down** depositar; (in writing) poner[19] (*past part* puesto) por escrito; (allow to alight) dejar apearse

~ **forth** exponer[19] (*past part* expuesto)

~-**off** *n* contraste *m*

~ **off** *v* (explode) hacer[19] estallar; (contrast) hacer[19] resaltar (**against** contra)

~ **on** atacar[4]

~ **out** exponer[19] (*past part* expuesto)

~-**up** *n* establecimiento; (arrangement) arreglo

~ **up** *adj*: be well ~ **up for** estar[19] bien provisto de

~ **up** *v* (found) fundar; (erect) erigir[5]; (house, shop) poner[19] (*past part* puesto); (business) establecer[14]; (a shout) dar[19]; *mech* armar; *print* componer[19] (*past part* compuesto); ~ **o.s. up as** darse[19] de

~ **upon** (attack) acometer; be ~ **upon** (determined) estar[19] resuelto a +*infin*

settee sofá *m*

setter sétter *m*

setting *n* (of sun) puesta; (of bones) reducción *f*; (of cement) fraguado; (of jewels) montadura; *mech* ajuste *m*; *mus* arreglo; *theat* escena; (of trap) armadura; (surroundings) alrededores *mpl*; ~-**lotion** fijador *m*; ~-**off** salida; ~-**up** establecimiento; *mech* montaje *m*; *print* composición *f*; *adj* (of sun) poniente

settle *vi* colocar[4]; (pay) ajustar; (an opponent) confundir; (people) establecer[14]; ~ **the land** poblar la tierra; (country) colonizar[7]; (arrange) arreglar; (decide) decidir; (calm) calmar; (arguments *etc*) concertar (ie)[2a]; ~ **money on** dotar; *vi* ~ (**down**) asentarse[2a]; (of liquid, soil) sentarse[2a]; (in new surroundings) establecerse[14]; (of bird) posarse; *naut* hundirse lentamente; *meteor* serenarse, *fig* normalizarse[7]

~ **down to work** ponerse[19] (*past part* puesto) a trabajar

~ **on** (choose) escoger[8]

~ **up** (with) ajustar cuentas (con)

settled permanente; *meteor* sereno

settlement establecimiento; (of people) colonia; (village) caserío; *bui* hundimiento; (arrangement) arreglo; (pact) convenio; *leg* ajuste *m*; (of money) dotación *f*; (of debt) saldo

settler colono

settling *see* **settlement**; ~ **date** fecha de liquidación

seven *n*+*adj* siete *m*; ~ **hundred** setecientos (-as); **it is** ~ **o'clock** son las siete; ~ **deadly sins** siete pecados capitales; ~**fold** *adj* séptuplo; *adv* siete veces

seventeen *n*+*adj* diecisiete *m*; **he is** ~ él tiene diecisiete años

seventeenth *n*+*adj* decimoséptimo *m*, *fam* diecisiete *m*; ~ **of May** el diecisiete de mayo; **Louis the Seventeeth** Luis diecisiete; ~-**century house** casa del siglo diecisiete

seventh *n* séptimo; *fam* séptima parte; *mus* séptima; ~ **of March** el siete de marzo; **Henry the Seventh** Enrique séptimo; *adj* séptimo

seventieth septuagésimo; *fam* setenta; **a** ~ **part** una setentava

seventy *n*+*adj* setenta *m*

sever separar cortando; (relations) romper (*past part* roto)

several varios; **joint and** ~ *leg* solidario

severally respectivamente; (distinctly) separadamente

severance separación *f*; (of relations) ruptura; ~ **pay** indemnización *f*

severe severo; *med* grave; (pain) intenso; (winter, criticism) riguroso; (style) austero

severity severidad *f*; *med* gravedad *f*; (of pain) intensidad *f*; (of style) austeridad *f*; (of weather) inclemencia

Seville Sevilla; ~ **orange** naranja amarga

Sevillian *n*+*adj* sevillano

sew coser; ~ **up** (conclude) concluir[16]

sewage aguas *fpl* residuales; ~ **farm** estación depuradora

sewer alcantarilla

sewerage alcantarillado

sewing *n* costura; *adj* de coser; ~ **cotton** hilo de coser; ~-**machine** máquina de coser

sewn: hand-~ cosido a mano

sex *n* sexo; (physical love) acto sexual; **have** ~ (**with**) realizar[7] el coito (con); **fair** ~ bello sexo; **weaker** ~ sexo débil; ~-**appeal** atracción *f* (sexual), *fam* gancho; ~ **change** transexualismo; ~ **maniac** maniático sexual; ~-**object** objeto sexual; ~-

symbol sexímbolo; *v* (of chicks) sexar; **highly ~ed**, **over ~ed** cachondo
sexagenarian sexagenario
sexennial sexenal
sexily de una manera sexy
sexiness atractivo sexual; cachondez *f*
sexless sin sexo; *fig* frígido
sextant sextante *m*
sextet sexteto
sexton sacristán (-anes) *m*
sextuple séxtuplo
sextuplet sextrillizo
sexual sexual; **~ act** coito; **~ desire** instinto sexual; **~ harassment** agresión *f* sexual; **~ intercourse** trato sexual; **have ~ intercourse** hacer[19] el coito
sexuality sexualidad *f*
sexy cachondo, sexy *invar*
Seychellian seycheliano
sh! ¡chist!
shabbiness (threadbareness) lo raído; (of dress) pobreza de vestido; (dishonesty) poca honradez *f*; (shame) ruindad *f*, mal estado
shabby (threadbare) raído, *fam* zarrapastroso, *Arg* arratonado; (poorly dressed) pobremente vestido; (dishonest) poco honrado; (shameful) ruin; **~ room** habitación *f* en mal estado
shack chabola
shackle *n* traba; **~s** grillos *mpl*; *v* poner[19] trabas a
shade *n* sombra; (*US* curtain) cortina; (of colour, meaning, opinion) matiz (-ces) *m*; (fraction) poquito; (hint) dejo; (eye-shade) visera; (lamp-~) pantalla; (ghost) fantasma *m*; **put in the ~** oscurecer[14], *fig* eclipsar; **thirty-five degrees in the ~** treinta y cinco grados a la sombra; **in the ~ of** a la sombra de; **~-tree** árbol *m* de sombra; *v* dar[19] sombra a; (protect) resguardar; (painting) sombrear; **~ away** cambiar poco a poco; **~ into** transformarse poco a poco en
shadily de una manera sospechosa
shadiness sombra; (of character) falta de honradez
shading *n* sombreado; (painting) degradación *f*; *mus* matiz *m*
shadow *n* sombra; (in picture) toque *m* de oscuro; *fig* compañero inseparable; **cast a ~** proyectar una sombra; **he is**

but a **~ of his former self** él no es ni su sombra; **without a ~ of doubt** sin lugar a dudas; **~ boxing** boxeo con un adversario imaginario; *v* hacer[19] sombra, sombrear; (follow) seguir (i)[3+11]
shadowing (painting) degradación *f*
shadowy umbroso; (vague) vago
shady sombreado; (of people) sospechoso
shaft (of tool) mango; (of spear) asta; (of cart) vara; *mech* árbol *m*; (of mine) pozo; *archi* cañón (-ones) *m* de columna; (ray) rayo; (arrow) flecha; **~ of wit** golpe humorístico
[1] **shag** *n* tabaco de hebra fina; *vulg* comercio sexual; **have a ~** *vulg* echar un polvo; *v vulg* joder, *vulg sl* follar, chingar; **I feel shagged (out)** estoy muerto de cansancio
[2] **shag** *orni* cormorán moñudo
shaggy peludo; **~ dog story** chiste *m* goma
shagreen chagrín *m*
shah cha(h) *m*, sha *m*
shake *n* sacudida; (of the hand) apretón *m* (de manos); (of head) movimiento; **she gave her son a good ~** ella sacudió violentamente a su hijo; **in two ~s** en un santiamén; **it's no great ~s** no es gran cosa; **~-down** cama improvisada, (*US naut*) viaje *m* de pruebas, (*US sl*) exacción *f* de dinero; **~-up** sacudida, *fig* reorganización *f*; *vt* sacudir; (building) hacer[19] temblar; (weaken) debilitar; (surprise) sorprender; (perturb) perturbar; **Legrá was ~n by the fall** Legrá se trastornó por la caída; **~ on it!** ¡chócala!; **~ hands** estrecharse la mano; **~ hands with** dar[19] la mano a; **~ the head** mover (ue)[1b] la cabeza; **~ a leg** menearse; **~ off** sacudir, (of people) librarse de; **~ out** sacudir, (unfold) desplegar (ie)[2a+5]; **~ up** sacudir, (disorder) trastornar, *fam* poner[19] de vuelta y media a; *vi* temblar (ie)[2a]; (of the earth) temblar (ie)[2a+5] (**at, with** de); **~ in one's shoes** temblar (ie)[2a] de miedo; **~ with laughter** desternillarse de risa, *vulg sl* descojonarse de risa
shaker (cocktail-~) coctelera
Shakespearean shakespeariano
shakiness inestabilidad *f*; (of voice) temblor *m*

shaking sacudida

shaky (of voice, hands) tembloroso; (unsafe) movedizo

shale esquisto; ~ **oil** aceite esquistoso

shall: (expressing future) **I ~ do it** lo haré; **they ~ not pass!** ¡no pasarán!; (expressing obligation) **you ~ not do it** usted no debe hacerlo; (expressing intention) ~ **we go out?** ¿quiere usted que salgamos?

shallot chalote *m*

shallow poco profundo; (superficial) superficial; (frivolous) frívolo; ~**s** fondo alto; ~**-brained** torpe

shallowness poca profundidad; (superficiality) superficialidad *f*; (frivolity) frivolidad *f*

sham *n* engaño; (person) impostor *m* (-ora *f*); *adj* fingido; *v* fingir(se)[9]

shamble andar[19] arrastrando los pies

shambles (slaughter) carnicería; (confusion) confusión absoluta; **this room is a ~** esta habitación es una pocilga

shambling: he has a ~ walk él anda arrastrando los pies

shame *n* vergüenza; (dishonour) deshonra; (pity) lástima, **what a ~!** ¡qué lástima!; ~**-faced** avergonzado; *v* avergonzar (ue)[1a+7]; (dishonour) deshonrar; **put to ~** avergonzar (ue)[1a+7]; (beat easily) superar con mucho; ~ **s.o. into** obligar[5] a alguien por vergüenza a +*infin*

shameful vergonzoso

shameless desvergonzado, (cheeky) descarado; (action) vergonzoso

shamelessness desvergüenza

shammy (leather) gamuza

shampoo *n* champú *m*; (act) lavado; *v* (hair, cars) lavar; ~ **and set** lavar y marcar[4]

shamrock trébol *m*

shandy bebida de cerveza y gaseosa, *fam* clara

shanghai embarcar[4] forzosamente (*usu* emborrachando/narcotizando)

shank (leg) pata; *mech* mango; **on Shanks's pony** en el coche de San Fernando, a patita y andando

[1] **shanty** chabola; ~**-town** barrio de chabolas

[2] **shanty** *mus* saloma

S.H.A.P.E. (Supreme Headquarters Allied Powers in Europe) S.S.F.A.E. (Sede Suprema de las Fuerzas Aliadas en Europa)

shape *n* forma; (of clothes) corte *m*; **go out of ~** perder (ie)[2b] la forma; **take ~** tomar forma; ~**-retaining** indeformable; *vt* formar; (of clothes) cortar; (carve) tallar; (of ideas) dar[19] forma a; ~ **one's course (towards)** dirigirse[9] (hacia); *vi* (of events) desarrollarse; ~ **well** prometer bien; ~ **up to** hacer[19] ademán de pelear; ~**d: L-~d** en forma de L

shapeless informe

shapeliness simetría; (of people) buen talle *m*

shapely bien formado; (of people) de buen talle

shards añicos (de porcelana)

[1] **share** *n* (portion) porción (-ones) *f*, parte *f*; (contribution) contribución (-ones) *f*; (part ownership) interés (-eses) *m*; (in a company) acción (-ones) *f*; *Sp* (in lottery ticket) participación (-ones) *f* de lotería; **fall to one's ~** tocar[4] a uno; **have a ~ in** participar en; ~ **and ~ alike** por partes iguales; **go ~s** ir[19] a escote; **take a ~ in a discussion** tomar parte en una discusión; ~**-cropper** aparcero; ~**-cropping** aparcería; ~**holder** accionista *m+f*; ~**-out** repartición *f*; ~**-pusher** vendedor *m* de acciones; *v* (~ out) repartir; ~ **in** participar en

[2] **share** (ploughshare) reja de arado

shark tiburón (-ones) *m*; (swindler) estafador *m* (-ora *f*)

sharp *n mus* sostenido; *adj* (pointed) (punti)agudo; (for cutting) afilado; (steep) empinado; *mus* sostenido; (of outline) definido; *phot* nítido; (of pain) punzante; (clever) listo, *fam* avispado; (unscrupulous) deshonesto; (harsh) acerbo; **have ~ features, be ~-featured** tener[19] las facciones angulosas; ~ **of hearing** fino de oído; ~ **cry of pain** grito agudo de dolor; ~ **bend** curva cerrada; ~ **change** *meteor* cambio repentino; ~**-cut** bien definido; ~**-edged** afilado; ~**-eyed** de buena vista; ~**-nosed** de nariz puntiaguda; ~ **pace** paso rápido; ~ **practice** procedimientos *mpl* poco honrados; ~**-shooter** tirador certero; ~**-shooting** tiro certero; ~**-sighted** de vista penetrante, *fam* de ojos de lince; ~ **smell** olor *m* acre; ~ **sound** ruido seco; ~ **taste** gusto ácido; ~-**tongued** mordaz (-ces); ~-**witted** de inteligencia viva; *adv mus* desafinadamente; **at eight o'clock** ~ a las ocho en punto; **turn** ~ **left** torcer (ue)[1b+14] repentinamente a la izquierda; **look** ~! ¡dése prisa!; **you'll miss the train if you don't look** ~ perderás el tren si no te das prisa

sharpen afilar; +*fig* aguzar; (of appetite) abrir (*past part* abierto); ~ **a pencil** sacar[4] punta a un lápiz

sharpener afilador *m*; (for pencils) sacapuntas *m sing*+*pl*

sharper estafador *m*; (cards) fullero

sharpness (of point) agudeza; (of cutting edge) afiladura; (steepness) lo abrupto; (of outline) definición *f*; *phot* nitidez *f*; (cleverness) listeza; (unscrupulousness) astucia; (harshness) acerbidad *f*

shatter hacer[19] añicos; *fig* destrozar; **my nerves are** ~**ed** mis nervios están destrozados; **you have** ~**ed my hopes** usted ha destruido mis ilusiones; **the news** ~**ed me** la noticia me dejó helado; **the news** ~**ed my health** la noticia me quebrantó la salud

shave *n* afeitado; **have a** ~ afeitarse; **have a close/narrow** ~ escaparse por un pelo; **it was a close** ~ fue una cosa de milagro; *v* afeitarse; *carp* cepillar

shaver afeitadora (eléctrica)

shaving afeitado; (wood ~) viruta; ~-**brush/soap** brocha/jabón *m* de afeitar; ~-**dish** bacía

shawl chal *m*

she *pron* ella, **it is** ~ es ella; ~ **who spoke most** la que habló más; *n* (female) hembra; *zool* (*usu* translated by female ending); ~-**wolf** loba; ~-**devil** diablesa

sheaf gavilla; (of papers) fajo

shear (cut) cortar; (wool) trasquilar; *mech* romper (*past part* roto) por fuerza cortante

shearing trasquileo; ~**s** lana trasquilada

shears: (**pair of**) ~ tijeras grandes; *metal* cizalla

sheath vaina; (contraceptive) goma; ~-**knife** cuchillo de monte

sheathe envainar; *mech* revestir (i)[3]

shebang: the whole ~ todo el asunto

[1] **shed** (hut) cabaña; (lean-to) cobertizo; **assembly-**~ nave *f* de montaje

[2] **shed** *v* (blood) derramar; (leaves, clothes) desprenderse de; (tears) verter (ie)[2b]; **the snake** ~**s its skin** la serpiente muda su camisa; ~ **light on** verter (ie)[2b] luz sobre, *fig* arrojar luz sobre

shedding (of blood) derrame *m*; (of tears) derramamiento; (of skin) muda

sheen lustre *m*

sheep oveja; **they obey like** ~ obedecen como corderitos; **black** ~ **of the family** garbanzo negro de la familia; **look with** ~'**s eyes** (**at**) mirar como un carnero degollado; ~ **breeder**, (*US*) ~**man** ganadero (lanar); ~-**dip** desinfectante *m* para ganado; ~-**dog** perro pastor (perros pastor); ~-**dog trials** concurso de perros pastor; ~-**fold** redil *m*; ~-**like** ovejuno; ~-**run**, ~-**walk** dehesa de ovejas; ~-**shearing** trasquileo; ~-**skin** piel *f* de carnero; ~-**skin jacket** zamarra

sheepish tímido

sheepishness timidez *f*

sheer *adj* completo, puro; (of cloth) diáfano; (of nylons) de cristal; (steep) escarpado; *v* sheer (off) desviarse; *adv* a pico

sheers grúa de tijeras

sheet (bed) sábana; (glass, metal) lámina; (of paper) hoja; (news) periódico; (of fire) cortina; (of water) capa; *naut* escota; ~ **iron** hierro en planchas; ~ **metal** chapa; ~ **steel** chapa de acero; **white as a** ~ blanco como la nieve; ~ **lightning** fucilazos *mpl*; *v* envolver (ue)[1b] (*past part* envuelto) en sábanas

sheeting tela para sábanas

sheik jeque *m*

shekel siclo; ~**s** *fam* pasta

shelduck *orni* tarro blanco

shelf estante *m*; (mountain) saliente *m*; (reef) banco de arena; **be on the** ~ *fig* quedarse para vestir santos; **continental** ~ plataforma continental

shell *n* (of shellfish) concha; (of egg, nut) cáscara; (of pea *etc*) vaina; (of tortoise) caparazón *m*; *mil* obús *m*; *bui* armazón (-ones) *m*; ~-**fire** cañoneo; **be under** ~-**fire** sufrir un bom-

bardeo; ~-**fish** mariscos *mpl*; ~-**proof**
a prueba de obuses; ~-**shock** neurosis
f de guerra; *v* desvainar, descascarar;
mil bombardear; ~ **out** *vt* desembolsar, *vi* aflojar (dinero); ~**ed** (with ~)
dotado de cáscara, (with ~ removed)
sin cáscara

shelling cañoneo

shelter *n* abrigo; (refuge) refugio;
(mountain ~) albergue *m*; (from
wind) +*fig* resguardo[8]; *vt* proteger[8]; *vi*
abrigarse[5]; refugiarse; ~**ed from the
wind** al abrigo del viento; ~**ed life** vida
resguardada

shelve *vt* (postpone) aplazar[7] indefinida-
mente; *vi geol* estar[19] en declive

shelving (in cupboard *etc*) estantería

shemozzle jaleo

shepherd *n* pastor *m*; ~ **boy** pastorcillo;
~ (dog) perro pastor (perros pastor);
~'s **pie** carne *f* con cebolla, cubierta
de puré de patata; ~'s **purse** *bot* bolsa
de pastor; *v* (lead) guiar, cuidar de

shepherdess pastora

shield *n* escudo; *mech*+*mil* blindaje *m*;
her escudo de armas; *fig* defensa; ~-
bearer escudero; **wind-~** resguardo,
mot parabrisas *m sing*+*pl*; *v* proteger[8]

shift *n* (tunic) sayo; (group of workmen)
grupo; (turn) turno; (change) cambio;
(movement) movimiento; ~ **foreman**
encargado de grupo; ~ **key** (typewriter) tecla de las mayúsculas; **make
~ (to)** arreglárselas (para); **make ~
with** arreglárselas con; **make ~ without** pasarse sin; **work in** ~**s** trabajar
por turnos; **day/night** *theat* ~ turno de día/
noche; ~-**stick** (palanca de) cambio
de marchas; *v* (move) mover(se)
(ue)[1b]; (change) cambiar; (of wind)
girar; ~ **the scenes** *theat* cambiar la
decoración; ~ **for o.s.** componér-
selas, valerse[19] por sí mismo

shiftiness falta de honradez

shifting *n see* **shift**; *adj* (of wind) mudable; (of sand) movedizo

shiftless indolente

shiftlessness falta de energía

shifty furtivo; (dishonest) falso; (tricky)
tramposo; ~-**eyed** de mirada furtiva

shilling chelín (-ines) *m*; **cut off with a** ~
desheredar

shilly-shally vacilar

shimmer *n* resplandor *m*; *v* rielar,
relucir

shimmering resplandeciente

shin *n* espinilla; ~-**pad** espinillera; *v* ~
up trepar a

shindy cisco; **kick up a** ~ armar camorra

shine *n* brillo; **in rain or** ~ en buen o mal
tiempo; **give a** ~ **to** sacar[4] brillo a; **take
a** ~ **to** aficionarse a; **take the** ~ **off**
quitar el brillo; **take the** ~ **out of**
eclipsar; *vi*+*fig* brillar; *vt* sacar[4] brillo
a; (shoes) dar[19] lustre a

¹ **shingle** guijarros *mpl*; ~ **beach** playa
guijarrosa/*fam* de piedras

² **shingle** (roof) *n* ripia; *v* cubrir (*past part*
cubierto) con ripias

shingles herpes *m*+*fpl*

shingly guijarroso

shining, **shiny** brillante; (of cloth) con
brillo

ship *n* buque *m*, barco; **merchant** ~
mercante *m*; **steam** ~ vapor *m*; **war**~
buque *m* de guerra; **on board** ~ a
bordo; ~-**breaker** desguazador *m*;
~**builder** constructor *m* naval; ~
building construcción *f* de buques; ~-
canal canal *m* de navegación; ~-**load**
cargamento; ~**mate** compañero de a
bordo; ~-**owner** armador *m*; ~'s **carpenter** carpintero de ribera; ~'s
chandler abastecedor *m* de buques,
fam chiplichandle *m*; ~'s **company**
tripulación *f*; ~-**shape** en buen orden;
~-**to**-~ **missile** proyectil *m* buque-
buque; ~-**to-shore communications**
comunicaciones *fpl* de buque a tierra;
~**wreck** naufragio; ~**wrecked person**
náufrago, náufraga; **be** ~**wrecked**
naufragar[5]; ~**wright** carpintero de
navío; ~**yard** astillero; *v* (take on
board) embarcarse[4]; (send) enviar; ~
oars armar remos; ~ **water** embarcar[4]
agua

shipment envío

shipper exportador *m*

shipping buques *mpl*, flota; ~ **of goods**
embarque *m* de mercancías; ~ **agent**

agente marítimo; ~ **company** compañía naviera; ~ **office(s)** oficinas *fpl* de una compañía naviera

shire condado; ~ **horse** caballo de tiro

shirk *vi* gandulear; *vt* esquivar

shirker gandul *m* (-ula *f*)

shirt camisa; **in** ~-**sleeves** en mangas de camisa; **keep your** ~ **on!** ¡quédate sereno!; **put one's** ~ **on** (betting) apostar (hasta) (ue)¹ᵃ las pestañas a; ~ **collar** cuello de camisa; ~ **front** pechera; ~ **tail** faldón (-ones) *m* de la camisa; ~ **waist** corpiño de mujer

shirting tela para camisas

shirty malhumorado

shit *n+interj* mierda, *fam* caca, *vulg* ful *f*; ~-**house rumour** *mil sl* macutazo; ~**s** *med+fig* cagalera; ~-**scared** *vulg* cagado de miedo; ~**house** *vulg* cagadero; *v* cagar⁵; *euph* hacer¹⁹ de vientre; *vulg* giñar

shiver *n* (cold) escalofrío, tiritona; (excitement) estremecimiento; (fear) temblor *m*; **it gives me the** ~**s to think ...** me da miedo pensar ...; *v* (with cold) tiritar; (with excitement) estremecerse¹⁵; (with fear) temblar (ie)²ᵃ; (shatter) hacer(se)¹⁹ añicos

shivery (cold) friolero; (excitement) estremecido; (fear) tembloroso; **I feel** ~ tengo escalofríos

¹ **shoal** *n* (of fish) banco; *fig* muchedumbre *f*; *v* reunirse en gran número

² **shoal** (reef) bajío; (sandbank) banco de arena

¹ **shock** *n* choque *m*; (earth tremor) temblor *m* de tierra; (fright) sobresalto; (surprise) sorpresa; *elect* sacudida eléctrica, *fam* calambre *m*; **have a** ~ recibir un susto; **you gave me a** ~ usted me dio un susto; **it came as a great** ~ **to me** me impresionó mucho; **suffering from** ~ con conmoción; ~ **troops** tropas *fpl* de asalto; ~-**absorber** +*mot* amortiguador *m*; ~-**proof** a prueba de choques; *v* chocar⁴; (scandalize) escandalizar⁷; (surprise) sorprender; **be** ~**ed** (**at**) asombrarse (de); **I am not easily** ~**ed** no me escandalizo fácilmente

² **shock** (of hair) greña, *fam* escarola; ~-**headed** greñudo

shocker *lit* libro escandaloso; (person) descarado

shocking escandaloso; (of taste) pésimo; (disgusting) horrible; **how** ~! ¡qué horror!

shod calzado; (of horses) herrado

shoddy *adj* de pacotilla

shoe *n* zapato; (horseshoe) herradura; *mech*+*mot* zapata; **put on one's** ~ calzarse⁷; **take off one's** ~**s** descalzarse⁷; **without** ~**s** descalzo; **the horse has cast a** ~ el caballo ha perdido una herradura; **if I were in her** ~**s** si yo estuviera en su pellejo; **if the** ~ **fits, wear it** el que se pica, él mismo se lo aplica; ~**black** limpiabotas *m sing+pl*; ~**horn** calzador *m*; ~-**lace** cordón (-ones) *m*; ~-**leather** cuero para zapatos; **he's heavy on** ~-**leather** él desgasta muchos (pares de) zapatos; ~**maker**, ~-**mender**, ~-**repairer** zapatero; ~-**polish** betún *m*; ~-**shop** zapatería; ~-**string** cordón *m*; **on a** ~-**string** gastando poco dinero; ~-**tree** horma

shoo (**away/off**) oxear; ~! ¡fuera!

shoot *n bot* vástago; (of vine) sarmiento; (chute) tobogán *m*; (hunting) cacería; (at butts) tiro (al blanco); **he has a** ~ **in Scotland** él tiene un coto de caza en Escocia; **the whole** ~ todo

vt (weapon) disparar; (kill by shooting) matar de un tiro, *sl* freír³; (execute) fusilar; (wound by shooting) herir (ie)²ᶜ de un tiro; **he was shot in/through the hand** una bala le hirió en la mano; *cin* filmar; (bolt) correr; ~ **the bridge** pasar debajo del puente; ~ **a line** fanfarronear; ~ **the rapids** salvar el rabión

~ **at** tirar a

~ **down** derribar; *fig* humillar

~-**out** (gun-fight) tiroteo; *sl* ensalada de tiros

~ **out** lanzar⁷

~ **up** destrozar⁷ a tiros

vi bot brotar; (move quickly) moverse (ue)²ᵇ rápidamente; (football) chutar (a la puerta); (of pain) punzar⁷

~ **ahead** adelantarse mucho (**of** a)

~ **off** precipitarse; ~ **off one's mouth** irse¹⁹ de la boca

~ **out** salir¹⁹ disparado

~ **past** pasar rápidamente

~ **up** subir rápidamente; (grow) crecer¹⁴ rápidamente; (of prices) elevarse rápidamente; **prices shot up so much** los precios se han disparado tanto

shooter (football) chutador *m*; *sl* arma de fuego

shooting *n* (of guns) tiroteo, cañoneo; (of arrow + gun) disparo; (of game) caza con escopeta; *cin* rodaje *m*; **go ~** ir[19] a cazar (con escopeta); *adj* (of pain) punzante; **~-brake** *mot* furgoneta; **~-gallery** tiro (al blanco); **~-jacket** sahariana; **~ party** partida de caza; **~ practice** ejercicios *mpl* de tiro; **~-range** campo de tiro; **~-star** estrella fugaz; **~-stick** asiento de caza

shop *n* tienda; (large) almacén *m*; (workshop) taller *m*; **talk ~** hablar de negocios; **all over the ~** por todas partes; **~-assistant** dependiente *m*, dependienta *f*; **~-bell** campanilla automática; **~-floor** *fig* taller *m*; **men on the ~-floor** trabajadores *mpl* de taller; **~-girl** dependienta; **~-keeper** tendero; **~-keeping** trabajo de tendero; **~-lifter** mechero; **~-lifting** mechería; **~-soiled** sobado; **~-steward** representante *m* sindical (en un taller); **~-walker** vigilante *m*; **~-window** escaparate *m*; **~-worn** deteriorado; *v* (purchase) comprar; (go shopping) ir[19] de compras; (inform against) traicionar

shopper comprador *m* (-ora *f*)

shopping compras *fpl*; **go ~** ir[19] de compras; **~-bag/basket** bolsa/cesta de la compra; **~-centre** centro comercial

shore *n* orilla; (beach) playa; **three miles off ~** a tres millas de la costa; **on ~** en tierra; **come on ~** desembarcar[4]

shore (support) puntal *m*; *v* **~ up** apuntalar; *fig* apoyar

shorn: ~ of despojado de

short *n* *cin* corto metraje *m*; *elect* cortocircuito; (drink) bebida pequeña; **~s** pantalones *mpl* cortos; **in ~** en breve; **the long and ~ of it** en resumidas cuentas; *adj* corto, breve; (of height) bajo; (brusque) seco; (in short supply) escaso; (of memory) flaco; **for ~** para abreviar; **cut ~** acortar, (abbreviate) abreviar, (interrupt) interrumpir; **~ for** forma abreviada de; **be ~ (of money)** tener[19] poco dinero; **~ of** (except) salvo, (unless) a

menos de +*infin*; **~ of fighting** excepto luchando; **~ of breath** sin aliento; **go ~** no tener[19] lo suficiente; **go ~ of** pasarse sin; **fall ~** no llegar, **the ball fell ~ of the player** el balón no llegó al jugador; **run ~ of** quedarse sin; **nothing ~ of** nada menos que; **I'm ~ of money** necesito dinero; **I'm 100 pesetas ~** me faltan 100 pesetas; **~ change** no suficiente cambio; **at ~ notice** con poco aviso; **~ pants** (underpants) braslip *m*, (*US* trousers) pantalones *mpl* cortos; **~ story** cuento; **be in ~ supply** escasear; **~ take-off** (de) despegue corto; **by a ~ head** por una cabeza escasa; **a ~ time ago** hace poco; **in a ~ time** (duration) en poco tiempo, (of future) dentro de poco; **be ~ with** tratar con sequedad; **make ~ work of** despachar rápidamente; **stop ~** parar(se) en seco; **stop ~ of** detenerse[19] antes de llegar a; **work ~ time** trabajar en jornadas reducidas; **~-bread, ~-cake** torta seca y quebradiza; **~-change** *v* dar[19] de menos en la vuelta; **~-circuit** *n* cortocircuito, *v* cortocircuitar; **~-coming** defecto; **~ course** cursillo; **~-cut** atajo; **take a ~-cut** atajar el camino; **~-fall** déficit *m*; **~-haired** pelicorto; **~-hand** taquigrafía; **~-hand-typist** taquimecanógrafa, *fam* taquimeca; **be ~-handed** faltar la mano de obra; **~-haul** transporte *m* de corta distancia; **~-horn** tipo de ganado que tiene los cuernos cortos; **~-legged** piernicorto; **~ list** lista restringida; **~-list** seleccionar para una entrevista; **~-lived** de poca duración; **~-necked** cuellicorto; **~-sighted** +*fig* miope; **~-sight(edness)** miopía; **~-sleeved** de manga corta; **~-spoken** brusco; **~-staffed** con personal insuficiente; **~-stop** (baseball) jugador *m* situado entre la segunda base y la tercera; **~-tempered** de mal genio; **~-term** a corto plazo; **~-wave** onda corta; **~ weight** (give ~ weight) engañar en el peso; **~-winded** corto de resuello

shortage escasez *f*

shorten *vi* acortarse; *vt* acortar; (abridge) abreviar; (reduce) reducir[15]

shortening acortamiento; *cul* manteca/

mantequilla para hacer mantecadas

shortly (soon) dentro de poco; (curtly) bruscamente

shortness cortedad *f*; (of a person) poca estatura; (of manner) manera brusca

¹**shot** (shooting) disparo; (pellets) perdigones *mpl*; (marksman) tirador *m* (-ora *f*); (athletics) peso; (football) tiro; (tennis, hockey, billiards) golpe *m*; *cin* fotograma *m*; *phot* fotografía; *med* inyección *f*; (of liquor) trago; (attempt) intento; **dead ~** tirador certero; **exchange ~s** tirotearse; **fire a ~** disparar un tiro; **at one ~** de un tiro, *fig* de un intento; **he left like a ~** él salió disparado; **put the ~** lanzar⁷ el peso; **have a ~** (attempt) probar (ue)¹ᵃ suerte; **have a ~ at** (try) intentar +infin, probar (ue)¹ᵃ +n; **have a ~ at goal** intentar marcar⁴, *sp sl* trallazo; **not by a long ~** ni con mucho; **~ in the dark** golpe a ciegas; **~ in the arm** *fig* estímulo; **big ~** pez gordo; **~gun** escopeta; **~gun wedding** casamiento a la fuerza; **~-put** lanzamiento de peso; **~-tower** torre *f* para hacer perdigones

²**shot** (of silk) tornasolado

should *aux v*: **if I had money I ~** buy it si yo tuviera dinero lo compraría; (ought to) deber, **the train ~ arrive soon** el tren debe llegar pronto; **you ~ have been here yesterday** usted debería haber estado aquí ayer; **I ~ just hope so!** ¡ya lo creo!, *fam* ¡toma no!

shoulder *n* hombro; (of meat) brazo, paletilla; (of hill) lomo; **~s** espaldas *fpl*; **on one's ~s** a espaldas; **~ to ~** hombro a hombro; **he was reading the newspaper over my ~** él estaba leyendo el periódico por encima de mis hombros; **I gave John the cold ~** volví la espalda a Juan; **rub ~s with** codearse con; **put one's ~ to the wheel** arrimar el hombro; **~-blade**, **~-bone** omoplato; **~-pad** hombrera; **~-strap** (on clothing) tirante *m*, (on bag *etc*) bandolera; *v* llevar al hombro; *fig* cargar⁵ con; **~ one's way through** pasar dando codazos; **~ arms!** ¡armas al hombro!; **round-~ed** cargado de hombros

shout *n* grito; **~s of applause** aclama-

ciones *fpl*; **~s of laughter** carcajadas; *v* gritar; **~ from the housetops** pregonar a los cuatro vientos

~ at regañar

~ down silbar hasta hacer callar; *theat* hundir a gritos

~ out gritar

shove *n* empujón (-ones) *m*; *v* empujar; (place) poner¹⁹; **~ off** *naut* alejarse, marcharse

shovel *n* pala; (of excavator) pala de empuje; *v* traspalar

shovelful palada

shoveller *orni* pato cuchara

show *n* exposición (-ones) *f*; *theat* espectáculo; *agri*+*bot* feria; (outward appearance) apariencia; (of feeling) demostración *f*; (vanity) ostentación *f*; **by ~ of hands** a mano alzada; **give the ~ away** tirar de la manta; **run/steal the ~** ser¹⁹ el todo; **motor ~** salón *m* del automóvil; **world of ~ business** mundillo del espectáculo; **~-card** letrero; **~case** vitrina; **~down** momento decisivo; **~-girl** corista; **~ house/flat** casa/piso piloto; **~-jumping** concurso hípico de obstáculos; **~-jumper** caballo de saltos; **~-man** empresario, (at fair) feriante *m*, *fig* exhibicionista *m*+*f*; **~manship** teatralidad *f*; **~piece** obra maestra; **~room** sala de exposiciones; *v* mostrar (ue)¹ᵃ, enseñar; (demonstrate) demostrar (ue)¹ᵃ; (point out) indicar⁴; (prove) probar (ue)¹ᵃ; **~ cause** dar¹⁹ motivo; **~ fight** ofrecer¹⁴ resistencia; **~ one's face** aparecer¹⁴; **~ one's hand** jugar (ue)¹ᵃ a cartas descubiertas; **they ~ed me the door** me pusieron en la calle; **~ the flag** hacer¹⁹ ostensible su presencia

~ in hacer¹⁹ pasar

~-off *n* ostentador *m* (-ora *f*)

~ off *vt* (sacar⁴ a) lucir; *vi* pavonear; (of a child) darse¹⁹ de machote; **don't ~ off!** ¡no hagas teatro!

~ round conducir¹⁵ por

~ through transparentarse

~ up *vi* presentarse; *vt* hacer¹⁹ subir; (unmask) desenmascarar; (shame) dejar mal; **he used powder to ~ up the fingerprints** él empleó polvos para poner en relieve las huellas dactilares

shower *n* chaparrón (-ones) *m*, aguacero; (of spray) chorro; (of missiles) lluvia; (~ bath) ducha; **what a ~!** (of people) ¡vaya pandilla!; (of weather) (ue)[1b], **I think it's going to ~** me parece que va a caer un chaparrón; (take a ~) ducharse; ~ **with** *fig* colmar de

showery lluvioso

showiness ostentación *f*

showing *cin* proyección *f*; (impression) impresión *f*

showy ostentoso

shrapnel metralla

shred *n* tira; (fragment) pizca; **tear to ~s** hacer[19] pedazos; *v* hacer[19] tiras; *cul* desmenuzar[7]

shredder trituradora

shrew *zool* musaraña; *fig* mujer regañona

shrewd astuto; **have a ~ idea of** tener[19] una buena idea de

shrewdly con astucia

shrewdness astucia

shrewish regañón

shriek chillido; ~s **of laughter** carcajadas *fpl*; *v* chillar; ~ **with laughter** reírse (i)[3] a carcajadas

shrieking chillidos *mpl*

shrift: get short ~ ser[19] despachado de prisa

shrill *n* estridente; *v* chillar

shrillness estridencia

shrimp *n* camarón (-ones) *m*, quisquilla; *fig* enano[5]; *v* pescar[4] camarones, quisquillas

shrine santuario; (in church) relicario; (burial place) sepulcro (de santo)

shrink encogerse[8]; *comm* mermar; ~-**proof** (on garment) no encoge

~ **away** retirarse de miedo

~ **back** (show fear) acobardarse; (retire) retroceder **(from de)**

~ **from** no atreverse a +*infin*, retirarse de +*n*

~ **on** *mech* montar en caliente

[2] **shrink** (*US sl*) psiquiatra *m+f*

shrinkage encogimiento; *comm* merma

shrinking tímido

shrivel (up) (of old people) encogerse[8]; (dry up) secarse[4]; (become wrinkled) arrugarse[5]

shroud *n* sudario; *naut* obenque *m*; *v* amortajar; ~ed **in mystery** envuelto en misterio

Shrove: ~ Tuesday martes *m* de carnaval

shrub arbusto

shrubbery (plantío de) arbustos; (growing wild) monte bajo

shrug *n* encogimiento de hombros; *v* encogerse[8] de hombros

shrunken encogido; ~ **head** cabeza reducida

shucks! ¡caramba!

shudder *n* estremecimiento; (of engine) vibración *f*; *v* estremecerse[14], vibrar

shuffle *n* (cards) barajada; (turn to ~) turno de barajar; (of feet) arrastramiento; *vt* (cards) barajar; ~ **off** deshacerse[19] de; *vi* arrastrar los pies; ~ **along** chancletear

shun esquivar

shunt *n* *elect* derivación *f*; (*US* railway) aguja; *v* *elect* poner[19] en derivación; (railway) maniobrar

shunter guardagujas *m sing+pl*

shunting maniobras *fpl*; ~ **engine** locomotora de maniobras; ~-**yard** estación (-ones) *f* de maniobras

shut *v* cerrar(se) (ie)[2a]; ~ **one's eyes to** hacer[19] la vista gorda a; ~ **your mouth!** ¡cállese!

~-**down** *n* paro por los dueños

~ **down** *v* cerrar (ie)[2a]; (machine) parar

~ **in** encerrar (ie)[2a]; (surround) rodear

~ **of: be ~ of** haberse deshecho de; **get ~ of** deshacerse[19] de

~ **off** (supplies) cortar; (isolate) aislar **(from de)**

~ **out** excluir[16]

~ **up** (en)cerrar (ie)[2a]; ~ **up shop** cerrar(se) (ie)[2a] la tienda; (retire) dejar el negocio; (be silent) callarse; (make s.o. be silent) hacer[19] callar

shutter contraventana; *phot* obturador *m*

shuttering *bui* encofrado

shuttle *n* lanzadera; ~ **service** tren *m*/autobús (-uses) *m etc* que hace viajes regulares entre dos puntos; (plane) puente aéreo; *space* transbordador *m* espacial; ~**cock** volante *m*; *v* ir[19] y venir[19]

[1] **shy** *adj* tímido; (of animals) asustadizo; **fight ~ of** preferir (ie)[2c] evitar; **I'm ~ of 100 dollars** me faltan 100 dólares; *v* asustarse **(at al ver)**

[2] **shy** (throw) tiro; **have a ~** intentar; **have a ~ at** hacer[19] una tentativa de +*infin*

shyness timidez *f*

shyster (abogado) trampista *m+f*; *fam* picapleitos *m sing+pl*

Siam Siam *m*

Siamese *n+adj* siamés *m* (-esa *f*); ~ **twins** gemelos siameses

Siberia Siberia

Siberian *n+adj* siberiano

sibilant *n+adj* sibilante *f*

sibling hermano, hermana; (half-brother/-sister) medio/a hermano/hermana

sibyl sibila

sibylline sibilina

Sicilian *n+adj* siciliano

Sicily Sicilia

sick *n* enfermos *mpl*; (vomit) devuelto; *adj* enfermo; (dizzy) mareado; **be ~** estar[19] enfermo; (vomit) devolver (ue)[1b] (*past part* devuelto); **be ~ of** estar[19] harto de; **fall ~** caer[19] enfermo; **feel ~** sentir (ie)[2c] náuseas; **get ~ of** hartarse de; **go ~** ausentarse por enfermedad; **~-bay** enfermería; **~-bed** lecho de enfermo; **~-benefit (fund)** (caja de) subsidio de enfermedad; **~ headache** jaqueca; **~-leave** permiso de convalecencia; **be on the ~-list** estar[19] enfermo; **~-pay** subsidio de enfermedad

sicken *vi* enfermar; **~ at the sight of** sentir (ie)[2c] náuseas ante; **~ for** mostrar (ue)[1a] síntomas de; *vt* dar[19] asco a

sickening nauseabundo; (annoying) fastidioso

sickle hoz (-ces) *f*

sickliness falta de salud; (paleness) palidez *f*

sickly enclenque, enfermizo; (of smell) nauseabundo; (of taste) empalagoso; **~ smile** sonrisa forzada

sickness enfermedad *f*; (dizziness) mareo; (inclination to vomit) náusea; **~-benefit** subsidio de enfermedad

side *n* lado; (of body) costado; (surface) cara; (of hills) falda; (of lake *etc*) orilla; (party) partido; *sp* equipo; *fam* (snobbery) postín *m*; **~ of bacon** loncha de tocino; **~ by ~** lado a lado; **by the ~ of** al lado de; **get s.o. on one's ~** conseguir (i)[3+11] el respaldo de alguien; **she's on my ~** ella está de mi parte; **on all ~s** por todas partes; **make something on the ~** sacar[4] un sobresueldo; **say something on the ~**

decir[19] algo extraoficialmente; **on this ~** en/por este lado; **the other ~ of the picture** la otra cara de la moneda; **on the left-/right-hand ~** a la izquierda/derecha; **take ~s** tomar partido; **~ altar** altar *m* lateral; **~-arms** armas *fpl* de cinto; **~-board** aparador *m*; **~-burns** patillas *fpl*; **~-car** sidecar *m*; **~-dish** entremés (-eses) *m*; **~-door** puerta lateral; **~-drum** tambor *m*; **~-effect** consecuencia indirecta; **~-elevation** alzada; **~-face** (de) perfil *m*; **~-glance** mirada de soslayo; **~ issue** cuestión secundaria; **~-kick** amigo inseparable; **~-light** *mot* luz *f* piloto, *naut* luz *f* de situación, *fig* aspecto incidental; **~-line** *sp* línea de banda, (secondary activity) negocio secundario; **on the ~-lines** *fig* sin tomar parte; **~-long de** soslayo; **~-saddle** silla de señora, **ride ~-saddle** montar a la amazona; **~-shoot** *bot* pimpollo lateral; **~show** espectáculo (menor), barraca de atracciones; **~-splitting** desternillante; **~-step** paso a un lado, (skiing) paso de escalera, *fig* esquivada lateral, *v* tomar un paso a un lado, (skiing) ejecutar el paso de escalera, *fig* esquivar; **~-street** bocacalle *f*; **~-stroke** (swimming) over *m*; **~-track** *n* (railway) apartadero, *fig* distracción *f*, *v* +*fig* desviar; **~-valve** *mot* de válvula lateral; **~-view** vista de lado, **~walk** acera, *Arg* vereda, *Mex* banqueta; **~ward** *adj* oblicuo, *adv* de un lado; **~ways** de lado; *v* **~ with** ponerse de, *fam* estar[19] por

sided: four-~ de cuatro lados

sidereal sidéreo

siding (railway) apartadero, **~s** (yard) estación *f* de clasificación

sidle: ~ away alejarse tímidamente; **~ up (to)** acercarse[4] tímidamente (a)

siege sitio; **lay ~ to** sitiar

sienna tierra de siena

siesta siesta; **have a ~** echar la siesta

sieve *n* tamiz (-ces) *m*; *cul* colador *m*; *v* tamizar[7]; *cul* colar

sift tamizar[7]; *fig* examinar cuidadosamente

sifter tamiz (-ces) *m*

sigh *n* suspiro; *v* suspirar; **~ for** anhelar

sight (sense) vista; (spectacle) espectáculo; (vision) visión *f*; (ridiculous) espantajo; (of gun) mira; **see the ~s** visitar los monumentos; **at (first) ~ a** (primera) vista; **by ~** de vista; **in ~ a** la vista; **(with)in ~ of** a vista de; **come in ~** aparecer[14]; **catch ~ of** lograr ver; **lose ~ of** perder (ie)[2b] de vista; **out of ~** fuera de vista; **go out of ~** desaparecer[14]; **out of ~, out of mind** ojos que no ven, corazón que no siente; **~-reader** persona que lee/canta a primera vista; **~-reading** *mus* ejecución *f* a la primera lectura; **~seeing** turismo; **~seer** turista *m+f*

sightless invidente

sightly vistoso

sign *n* señal *f*; (gesture) seña; (notice) letrero; (shop-sign) rótulo; anuncio; *math* signo; (symptom) síntoma *m*; *mus* (+ of zodiac) signo; (trace) huella; **~s of the times** signo de los tiempos (que vivimos); **as a ~ of** en señal de; **make the ~ of the cross** santiguar(se)[6]; **I didn't see a ~ of her all winter** no le vi el pelo en todo el invierno; **show ~s of** dar[19] señales de; **talk by ~s** hablar por señas; **~-board** letrero; **~-painter** pintor *m* de muestras; **~-post** *n* poste *m* indicador, *fig* hito, *v* señalizar[7], **well ~posted road** carretera bien señalizada; *v* (write one's signature) firmar; **~ a contract** (football) ficharse; **~ on the dotted line/in the space provided** firmar en la línea de puntos/en el lugar indicado; **~ed and sealed** firmado y lacrado

~ away firmar el traspaso de

~ off *rad+TV* cerrar (ie)[2a] la transmisión

~ on/up contratar, *mil* engancharse; **~ on for** (football) fichar por, **he ~ed on for Real Madrid** él fichó por el Real Madrid

signal *n* señal *f*; **~s** *mil* cuerpo de transmisiones; **engaged, US busy ~** *tel* señal *f* de ocupado; **~-box** garita de señales; **~-code** código de señales; **~-man** guardavía; **traffic-~** semáforo, *fam* luces *fpl*; *adj* notable; *v* señalar (to a); **he signalled that the race had started** él comunicó por señales que la carrera había empezado

signalize señalar

signaller *mil* soldado del cuerpo de transmisiones

signatory *n+adj* firmante

signature firma; marca; *mus* signatura; **~ tune** sintonía

signet-ring sortija de sello

significance significación *f*; (meaning) significado

significant significante

signification significación *f*

signify significar[4]; **it doesn't ~** no importa

signing-up (football) fichaje *m*

Sikh *n+adj* sik *m*

silage ensilaje *m*

silence *n* silencio; **observe a two-minute ~** observar un silencio de dos minutos; *v +fig* hacer[19] callar; *mil* apagar[5] el fuego de

silencer silenciador *m*

silent silencioso; (of people) callado; **be ~** callarse; **~ film** película muda; **~ partner** socio comanditario

silhouette silueta; **be ~d against** destacarse[4] sobre/contra

silica sílice *f*

silicon chip *elect* microprocesador *m*, *fam* pulga

silicone silicona; **~ polish** cera de lustrar con siliconas

silk seda; **~ blouse** blusa de seda; **~ hat** sombrero de copa; **~worm** gusano de seda

silken, silky sedoso

silkiness lo sedoso

sill alféizar *m*

silliness tontería

silly tonto; **the blow knocked me ~** el golpe me dejó atontado; **you are a ~ fool** eres un imbécil; **~ bugger** *sl* gilipollas *m sing+pl*; **~ season** época de la serpiente de mar

silo *agri* silo; **~-bin** cámara de silo; *mil* depósito subterráneo de cohetes teledirigidos

silt *n* sedimento; *v* **~ up** obstruirse[16] con sedimentos

silvan selvático

silver *n* plata; (plate) vajilla de plata; (money) monedas *fpl* de plata; **every cloud has a ~ lining** cada semana tiene su día santo; **~ birch** abedul *m*; **~ bullion** plata en barras; **~ chloride** cloruro de plata; **~-fish** lepisma; **~ fox** zorro plateado; **~-haired** de pelo entrecano; **~ jubilee** veinticinco ani-

versario; ~-**paper** papel *m* de estaño;
~**smith** platero; ~**ware** vajilla de
plata; ~ **wedding** bodas *fpl* de plata; *v*
(+ ~-**plate**) platear; (mirror) azogar[5]

silvery argentado; (of voice *etc*) argentino

simian símico

similar semejante; **somewhat** ~ algo
parecido

similarity semejanza

similarly de un modo parecido

simile símil *m*

similitude similitud *f*

simmer *n* hervor *m* a fuego lento; *vi*
hervir (ie)[2b] a fuego lento; *vt* cocer
(ue)[2b] a fuego lento

simper *n* sonrisa tonta y afectada; *v*
sonreír (i)[3] tontamente

simple sencillo; (easy) fácil; (foolish)
bobo; (innocent) ingenuo; (pure) simple; (of style) llano; ~ **equation**
ecuación *f* de primer grado; ~-
hearted candoroso; ~ **interest** interés
m simple; ~-**minded** crédulo, (stupid)
bobo; ~-**mindedness** credulidad *f*,
bobería

simplicity, **simpleness** sencillez *f*;
(foolishness) bobería; (innocence) ingenuidad *f*; (purity) sencillez *m*; (of
style) llanura

simplification simplificación *f*

simplify simplificar[4]

simplistic simplístico

simply sencillamente; (only) solamente;
~ **marvellous** absolutamente maravilloso; **you** ~ **must see that film** de veras
usted debe ver aquella película

simulate simular; ~**d leather** *tr* skay *m*

simulation simulación *f*

simultaneous simultáneo; ~ **equation**
ecuación (-ones) *f* de segundo grado

sin *n* pecado; *v* pecar[4]

since *adv* desde entonces; **long** ~ hace
mucho; **not long** ~ hace poco; *prep*
desde; **I've been waiting** ~ **two o'clock**
estoy esperando desde las dos; *conj*
(because) puesto que; ~ **you have no
money I'll lend you some** puesto que
usted no tiene dinero le prestaré algo

sincere sincero

sincerely sinceramente; **yours** ~ le saluda afectuosamente

sincerity sinceridad *f*

sinecure sinecura; *fam* enchufe *m*, *sl*

chollo

sinew tendón *m*; (in meat) nervio

sinful pecaminoso

sinfulness maldad *f*

sing *n*: **let's have a** ~ vamos a cantar; ~-
song *n* (tone) sonsonete *m*, (gathering) concierto improvisado; *v* cantar;
(of kettle) silbar; (in one's ears) zumbar; ~ **out** gritar; ~ **out of tune** desafinar; ~ **to sleep** arrullar

Singapore Singapur *m*

singe *n* chamusquina; *v* chamuscar[4];
(hair) quemar las puntas de

singeing chamusquina

singer cantor *m* (-ora *f*), cantante *m*+*f*;
~-**composer** cantautor *m* (-ora *f*)

singing canto; (of kettle) silbido; (in
ears) zumbido; **fond of** ~ cantarín
(-ina); ~-**bird** ave cantora

single *n mus* sencillo; ~**s** (tennis) juego
de individuales; *adj* único, solo; (unmarried) soltero; **there was not a** ~
house in sight no había (ni una) casa a
la vista; ~ **bed** cama individual; ~-
breasted sin cruzar; ~-**chamber** *pol*
unicameral; ~ **combat** combate *m*
singular; ~-**cylinder engine** motor de
un cilindro; ~-**decker** (bus) autobús *m*
de un piso; ~-**engined** monomotor;
~-**entry** (bookkeeping) (contabilidad
f) de partida simple; ~ **file** fila india;
~-**handed** sin ayuda; ~-**minded** con
una idea fija; ~-**seater** monoplaza *m*;
~ **ticket** billete *m* de ida; ~-**track** de
una sola vía; *v* ~ **out** distinguir[16]

singlet camiseta

singly uno por uno

singular *n* + *adj* singular *m*

singularity singularidad *f*

singularize singularizar[7]

Sinhalese *n* + *adj* cingalés *m* (-esa *f*)

sinister siniestro

sink *n* fregadero; *mech* sumidero; *vi*
naut hundirse; (of sun) ponerse[19];
med debilitarse; (sit heavily) dejarse
caer; (lessen) menguar; ~ **into oblivion** caer[19] en el olvido; **her heart sank**
se le cayó el alma a los pies; ~ **under
the responsibility** agobiarse bajo la
responsabilidad; ~ **in** penetrar, (of
words) tener[19] efecto; *vt naut* hundir;
(mine-shaft) abrir (*past part* abierto);
(well) perforar; (invest) invertir
(ie)[2c]; (lessen) disminuir[16]; ~ **one's**

teeth into hincar[4] los dientes en; ~ **differences** suprimir la controversia; **be sunk in thought** estar[19] ensimismado

sinkable hundible

sinker plomada; (fishing) plomo

sinking n hundimiento; (of sun) puesta, (of well) cavadura, (with a drill) perforación f; (of mine-shaft) apertura; adj desanimado; ~ **feeling** desánimo; **with ~ heart** con la muerte en el alma; ~-**fund** fondo de amortización

sinless sin pecado

sinner pecador m (-ora f)

Sino-Japanese n +adj chino-japonés m (-esa f)

sinuosity sinuosidad f

sinuous sinuoso

sinus seno

sinusitis sinusitis f

sip n sorbo; v sorber

siphon n sifón (-ones) m; v ~ (**off**) sacar[4] con sifón

sir señor m; (title) sir m; **yes,** ~ **mil** sí, mi capitán/coronel etc; **Dear Sir(s)** Muy señor(es) mío(s)

sire n see **sir**; zool padre m, v ser[19] el padre de

siren sirena; ~-**suit** mono

sirloin solomillo

sirocco siroco

sisal henequén m

siskin lúgano

sissy afeminado; vulg pej marica

sister +eccles hermana; med enfermera jefa; (before nun's Christian name) sor f; ~ **of charity** hermana de la caridad; ~**hood** comunidad f de mujeres; ~-**in-law** cuñada; ~ **ship** buque gemelo

sisterly como hermana

Sistine Chapel Capilla Sixtina

sit vt sentar (ie)[2a]; ~ **an examination** examinarse; ~ **a horse** montar; vi sentarse (ie)[2a]; (be seated) estar[19] sentado; (of an assembly) reunirse; (of clothes) sentar (ie)[2a]; (of birds) posarse; (of hens) empollar; (as model) posar; ~ **for a painter** servir de modelo a un pintor; ~ **pretty** (be safe) estar[19] seguro, (have advantage) tener[19] la ventaja; ~ **still** estarse[19] quieto; ~ **tight** no moverse (ue)[1b]

~-**down:** ~ **strike** huelga de brazos

caídos; pol (as protest) sentada

~ **down** v sentarse (ie)[2a]

~ **for** pol ser[19] diputado por

~-**in** n ocupación f

~ **in** v (baby-sitter) hacer[19] de canguro; ~ **in for s.o.** ocupar el puesto de uno; ~ **in (on)** asistir (a)

~ **on** sentarse (ie)[2a] en/sobre; (committee) ser[19] miembro de; (hatch) empollar; (investigate) investigar[5]; (reprimand) regañar

~ **out** quedarse hasta el fin de; (dance) no bailar

~ **up** incorporarse; ~ **up (at night)** velar; **it made them ~ up** les sorprendió; ~ **up and take notice** despabilarse

site n sitio; (for building) solar m; ~ **office** barraca de la obra; v situar

sitter modelo (de pintor); (hen) gallina clueca; sp gol m que se canta; **baby-~** canguro m+f

sitting n sesión (-ones) f; ~-**room** sala de estar; adj sentado

situate situar; **be ~d** situarse

situation situación (-ones) f; (post) colocación (-ones) f; ~**s vacant** empleos mpl vacantes, (in advertisement) ofertas fpl de trabajo; ~**s wanted** (in advertisement) solicitudes de trabajo

six n+adj seis m; **it is ~ o'clock** son las seis; ~ **hundred** seiscientos (-as); **at** ~**es and sevens** en desorden; ~ **of one and half a dozen of the other** pitos y flautas; **in ~-eight time** mus de seis por ocho; ~-**fold** seis veces; ~-**footer** hombre m que mide seis pies; ~**pence** moneda de seis peniques; ~-**shooter** revólver m de seis tiros

sixteen n+adj dieciséis m; **Mary is ~** María tiene dieciséis años

sixteenth dieciséis; **Louis the Sixteenth** Luis dieciséis

sixth n sexto; fam sexta parte; (date) el seis; mus sexta; **Henry the Sixth** Enrique sexto; adj sexto

sixty n+adj sesenta m; **he's approaching ~** él se acerca a los sesenta; ~-**four dollar question** pregunta clave; ~-**year-old** n+adj sesentón m (-ona f)

[1] **size** n tamaño; (height) altura; (measurement) medida; (of clothes) talla; (shoes) número, **what ~ do you take?** ¿qué número/talla lleva usted?;

v clasificar[4] por tamaños; **large-~d, small-~d** grande, pequeño; **~ up** medir (i)[3]

² **size** *n* (glue) cola; *v* encolar

sizeable bastante grande

sizzle *n* siseo; *v* chisporrotear (al freírse)

sizzling calentísimo

¹ **skate** *m* patín (-ines) *m*; *v* patinar; **~ on thin ice** *fig* correr riesgos; **~ round** *fig* evitar

² **skate** (fish) raya

skating patinaje *m*; **~-rink** pista de patinaje

skedaddle escaparse

skein madeja

skeletal esquelético

skeleton esqueleto; *sl* chasis *m*; *bui* armazón (-ones) *m*; (outline) esquema; (sketch) trazado; **~ in the cupboard** *fig* ropa sucia; **~ crew/staff** equipo/personal mínimo; **~-key** ganzúa

sketch *n* (drawing) croquis *m*; (outline) esquema; *theat* pieza corta; *v* dibujar; **~ out** trazar[7] en esquema

sketching arte *m* de dibujar; **I like ~** me gusta dibujar; **~-block, ~-pad** bloc *m* (*pl* bloques) de dibujos

sketchy incompleto, superficial

skew oblicuo

skewer *n* broqueta; *v* embroquetar; *fig* pinchar

ski *n* esquí *m*; **~-boot** bota de esquí; **~-jacket** plumífero; **~-jump** (action) salto de esquí, (hill) trampolín (-ines) *m* para los saltos (de esquí); **~-jumper** saltador *m* (-ora *f*) de esquí; **~-lift** telesquí *m*; *v* esquiar

skid *n* (of vehicle) patinazo; *aer* patín *m*; *v* patinar; **~-lid** casco protector; **~-pan** pista de deslizamiento

skidoo trineo motorizado

skier esquiador *m* (-ora *f*)

skiff esquife *m*

skiffle música de guitarra con acompañamiento de instrumentos de percusión; **~-group** conjunto de guitarra e instrumentos de percusión

skiing (deporte *m* del) esquí *m*; **go ~** ir[19] a esquiar

skilful hábil; (especially with the hands) mañoso

skill habilidad *f*; (with hands) destreza; (expertise) pericia

skilled hábil; **~ work/worker** trabajo/trabajador especializado

skillet sartén (-enes) *f*

skilly cocido

skim (remove scum) espumar; (milk) desnatar; (graze) rozar[7]; **~ over** pasar rasando; **~ through a book** hojear un libro

skimmed: ~ milk leche desnatada

skimmer espumadera

skimp escatimar; (work) chapucear

skimpy escaso; (of clothes) demasiado corto/estrecho

skin *n* piel *f*; (complexion) cutis *m*; (of animal) pellejo; (hide) cuero; (wineskin) odre *m*; (of fruit) pellejo; (on milk, paint *etc*) nata; **by the ~ of one's teeth** por los pelos; **next to one's ~** sobre la piel; **save one's ~** salvar el pellejo; **be thick-skinned** ser[19] insensible; **be thin-skinned** ser[19] susceptible; **keep one's eyes skinned** estar[19] alerta; **it's no ~ off my nose** no me importa un bledo; **~-deep** superficial; **~-dive** nadar debajo del agua; **~-diver** nadador *m* submarino; **~-diving** natación submarina; **~-flint** *n*+*adj* tacaño; **~-food** (cosmetic) crema de noche; **~-freshener** (cosmetic) loción *f* facial; **~-grafting** injerto de piel; **~-tight** muy ajustado; *v* despellejar; (fruit) pelar; **~ alive** *fam* desollar vivo; **~ over** *med* cicatrizarse[7]

skinful: have a ~ estar[19] achispado

skinner peletero

skinny descarnado, flaco

skint: be ~ estar[19] sin cinco

¹ **skip** *n* salto; *v* saltar; (game) saltar a la comba; (omit) omitir; **~ it!** ¡olvídelo!

² **skip** container *m*

skipper *naut* patrón (-ones) *m*; +*sp* capitán (-anes) *m*

skipping: ~ rope comba

skirl sonido de la gaita escocesa

skirmish *n* escaramuza; *v* escaramuzar[7]

skirmisher escaramuzador *m*

skirt *n* falda; (of coat) faldón (-ones) *m*; (meat) carne *f* de falda; **bit of ~** chica; *v* orillar

skirting: ~-board rodapié *m*

skit pasquín (-ines) *m* (on/against contra); burla; *theat* pieza corta satírica

skittish caprichoso; (nervous, *esp* of horses) asustadizo

skittishness capricho; (nervousness, *esp* of horses) calidad *f* de asustadizo

skittle *n* bolo; (*US* type) bola; ~**s** juego de bolos, (*US* type) juego de (las) bolas; ~**alley** bolera

skive gandulear; ~ **out of a class** fumarse una clase

skiver gandul *m* (-ula *f*)

skivvy fregona

skulduggery embustes *m*

skulk ocultarse

skull calavera; *anat* cráneo; ~ **and cross-bones** calavera y tibias cruzadas; ~**cap** gorro, (priest's) solideo

skunk mofeta; *fig* canalla *m*

sky *n* cielo; **praise to the skies** poner[19] por las nubes; ~**-blue** azul celeste; ~**high** por las nubes; ~**lark** *n* alondra, *v* jaranear; ~**light** claraboya; ~**line** horizonte *m*, (buildings) silueta; ~**rocket** cohete *m*; ~**scraper** rascacielos *m sing+pl*; ~**writing** publicidad aérea; *v* (hacer[19]) subir muy alto

skywards hacia el cielo

slab tabla; (of wood) plancha; (of stone) losa; (of meat) tajada gruesa; (of cake) pedazo; (of chocolate, soap) pastilla

slack *n* lo flojo; **take in the ~** disminuir[16] lo flojo; (small coal) carbón menudo; (~ time) período de inactividad; ~**s** pantalones *mpl* flojos; *adj* flojo; *comm* tranquilo; (lax) negligente; (lazy) perezoso; ~ **season** estación muerta; *v* trabajar poco, *fam* gandulear

slacken (**off**) aflojar; (lessen) disminuir[16]; (of wind) amainar

slackening aflojamiento; (lessening) disminución *f*; (of wind) amaine *m*

slacker gandul *m* (-ula *f*)

slackness flojedad *f*; (carelessness) descuido; (of studies *etc*) pereza

slag escoria; ~**-heap** escorial *m*

slain *mil* caídos *mpl* (en batalla)

slake apagar[5]; ~**d lime** cal muerta

slalom slálom *m*

slam *n* golpe *m*; (of door) portazo; (cards) capote *m*; *v* (hit) golpear; (of door) cerrarse (ie)[2a] de golpe; ~ **down** colocar[4] con violencia; ~ **into** chocar[4] contra

slander *n* calumnia; *v* calumniar

slanderer calumniador *m* (-ora *f*)

slanderous calumnioso

slang *n* argot *m*; (gypsies') caló; (thieves') germanía; *gramm* vulgarismo; *v* poner[19] como un trapo

slanging: ~ match disputa

slangy lleno de vulgarismos

slant *n* inclinación *f*; *fig* punto de vista; **on the ~** inclinado; *v* inclinarse; ~**ed** (biased) partidario

slanting inclinado

slap *n* palmada; (in the face) bofetada; *fig* palmetazo; ~**dash** descuidado, (of work) chapucero; **do s.t. in a ~dash way** chapucear; ~**-happy** alegre, (punch-drunk) torta; ~**jack** hojuela; ~**stick** payasadas *fpl*; ~**-up** de primera; *v* dar[19] una palmada (bofetada); ~ **on the back** golpear en la espalda; *adv* (directly) directamente; (suddenly) de golpe; *interj* ¡zas!

slash *n* cuchillada; (blow) azote *m*; **have a ~** *vulg* mear; *v* acuchillar; (maul) rasgar[5]; (strike) azotar; (prices) rebajar mucho, *fam* machacar[4]; (urinate) *vulg* mear

slashing criticón

slat tablilla

[1] **slate** *n* (+ for writing) pizarra; (for roofing) teja de pizarra; *fig* lista de deudas (en una taberna); *US* lista de candidatos; **put it on the ~** pagaré más tarde; ~**-coloured** apizarrado; ~**pencil** pizarrín (-ines) *m*; ~ **quarry** pizarral *m*; *v* apizarrar

[2] **slate** (reprimand) censurar severamente

slater pizarrero

slating regaño; **give s.o. a ~** regañar a uno

slatted con tablillas

slattern mujer desaseada

slatternly desaseado

slaughter *n* matanza; *fig* carnicería; ~**house** matadero; *v* matar; *SA* carnear

slaughterer matarife *m*

slaughtering matanza; ~**-knife** cuchillo de matarife

Slav *n+adj* eslavo

slave *n* esclavo; **work like a ~** trabajar como un negro; ~**-bangle** esclava; ~**driver** capataz (-ces) *m* de esclavos, *fig* tirano; ~**-labour** (slavery) esclavitud *f*, (people) trabajadores *mpl* forzados; ~**-trade** trata de esclavos; ~**-trader** negrero; *v* trabajar como un negro; ~ **away** sudar tinta

¹ **slaver** *naut* barco negrero; (person) negrero

² **slaver** (dribble) *n* baba(s) *f*; *v* babosear

slavering baboso

slavery esclavitud *f*; *fig* trabajo mal pagado

Slavic eslavo

slavish servil

slavishness servilismo

Slavonic eslavo

slay matar

slayer asesino

sleazy delgado; *fig* de mala fama

¹ **sledge** *n* trineo; (racing) luge *m*; **~-dog** perro esquimal; *vi* ir[19] en trineo; *vt* llevar en trineo

² **sledge**: **~-hammer** acotillo

sledging deslizamiento en luge

sleek *adj* (smooth) liso; (shiny) brillante; (of people) pulcro; *v* alisar; **~ down** suavizar[7]

sleep *n* sueño; **deep ~** sueño pesado; **go to ~** dormirse (ue)[1c]; **my leg has gone to ~** se me ha dormido la pierna; **put to ~** dormir (ue)[1c], (of pets) sacrificar[4]; **send to ~** dormir (ue)[1c]; **talk in one's ~** soñar en voz alta; **~walker** sonámbulo; **~walking** sonambulismo; *v* dormir (ue)[1c], *sl* sobar; **~ like a log** dormir (ue)[1c] como un lirón; **~ on it** *fig* consultarlo con la almohada; **they slept the journey away** pasaron el viaje durmiendo; **this home will ~ six** esta casa tiene camas para seis personas; **~ off** (a hangover) dormir (ue)[1c] la mona; **~ around** llevar una vida promiscua

sleeper durmiente *m+f*; (sleeping-car) cochecama *m*, *SA* carro dormitorio; (track support) traviesa; **be a good ~** dormir (ue)[1c] bien; **she's a heavy/light ~** ella tiene el sueño profundo/ligero

sleepiness somnolencia

sleeping durmiente; **Sleeping Beauty** la Bella Durmiente; **~ partner** socio comanditario; **~ policemen** *mot* clavos *mpl*; **let ~ dogs lie** no meter los perros en danza; **~-bag** saco de dormir; **~-car** *see* **sleeper**; **~-draught** soporífero; **~-out** *pass mil* pase *m* de pernoctar; **~-pill** somnífero; **~-sickness** enfermedad *f* del sueño

sleepless insomne; **~ night** noche *f* en blanco

sleeplessness insomnio

sleepy soñoliento, *fam* medio dormido; **be/feel ~** tener[19] sueño; **~-head** dormilón *m* (-ona *f*)

sleet *n* aguanieve *f*; *US* granizo; *v* caer[19] aguanieve; *US* granizar[7]

sleeve manga; (book/record **~**) funda; *mech* camisa; **have up one's ~** tener[19] de reserva; **laugh up one's ~** reírse con disimulo; **(long-/short-)~d** con mangas (largas/cortas); **~less** sin mangas

sleigh *see* **sledge**; **~ bells** cascabeles *mpl* de trineo

sleight: **~ of hand** escamoteo

slender delgado; (of resources) limitado

slenderize adelgazar[7]

slenderness delgadez *f*; (of resources) escasez *f*

sleuth(-hound) detective *m*; (dog) sabueso

slew: **~ round** torcerse (ue)[2a]

slice *n* tajada; (of bread) rebanada; (of meat) loncha; (of sausage *etc*) raja; (for serving fish *etc*) pala; *v* tajar, rebanar; partir en rodajas; **~ off** cercenar, cortar

slicer rebanador *m*

slick (of people) mañoso; (of movements) hábil; **~ chick** chica bandera

slicker (*US*) embaucador *m*; (raincoat) impermeable *m*; (dandy) petimetre *m*

slide *n* (on ice) resbaladero; *geol* desprendimiento (de tierra); (in playground) tobogán (-anes) *m*; (for hair) pasador *m*; (of trombone) vara corredera; *mech* guía de patín; (microscope) platina; *phot* diapositiva; **~-projector** proyector *m* de diapositivas; **~-rule** regla de cálculo; *v* resbalar; **let ~** no hacer[19] caso de; **let things ~** dejar correr las cosas

sliding *n* deslizamiento; *adj* corredizo; **~ door** puerta corrediza; **~ roof** techo corredizo; **~ scale** escala móvil; **~ seat** asiento movible, (in rowing boat) banca corrediza

slight *n* desaire *m*; *adj* ligero; **~ breeze** brisa ligera; (slender) delgado; (vague) tenue; **he has a ~ fever** él tiene un poco de fiebre; **its influence is ~** su influencia es insignificante; **with a ~ hint of/trace of** con un poco de; *v* desairar

slightest: not in the ~ ni en lo más mínimo

slighting despreciativo

slightly ligeramcnte; (vaguely) tenuemente; **I know her ~** la conozco pero no muy bien

slightness levedad *f*; (slenderness) delgadez *f*; (insignificant) insignificancia

slim delgado; (of resources) escaso; *v* adelgazar[7]

slime légamo; (of snail) baba

slimming *n* adelgazamiento; *adj* para adelgazar[7]; **~-girdle** faja adelgazante

slimness delgadez *f*

slimy fangoso; (of snails) baboso; *fig* servil

sling *n* med cabestrillo; *mil* honda; *naut* eslinga; *v* (throw) tirar; (support) colgar; **~shot** (catapult) tirachinas *m sing+pl*

slink andar[19] furtivamente; **~ away/off** marcharse cabizbajo

slip *n* (slide) resbalón (-ones) *m*; (skid) patinazo; (stumble) traspié *m*; (mistake) falta; (lapse of morals) desliz (-ces) *m*; (petticoat) combinación (-ones) *f*; (cover) funda; *bot* vástago; *geol* dislocación (-ones) *f*; **~s** *naut* gradas *fpl*; **~ of a girl** jovencita; **~** (of paper) tira; **make a ~** (in writing) írsele[19] a uno la mano, **I had made a slip** se me fue la mano, **~ of the pen** lapsus *m* cálami; **~ of the tongue** patinazo; **give s.o. the ~** darle[19] esquinazo a alguien; **there's many a ~ twixt the cup and the lip** del dicho al hecho hay gran trecho; **~-knot** lazo corredizo; **~-road** carretera de acceso; **~shod** (careless) descuidado, (dirty) desaseado; **~stream** viento de la hélice; **~way** gradas *fpl*; *v* deslizarse[7]; (elude) eludir; *med* dislocarse[4]; **~ one's arm around/over** pasar el brazo por/por encima de; **~ one's memory/mind** pasársele a uno, **your name has slipped my mind** se me ha pasado su nombre; **let ~** (drop) dejar caer; **let ~ an exclamation** soltar (ue)[1a] una exclamación; **let ~ a secret** revelar un secreto; **don't let the chance ~** no deje pasar la oportunidad

~ away marcharse desapercibido

~ back regresar desapercibido

~ by pasar inadvertido

~ in entrar inadvertido; (interpolate) deslizar[7]

~ into *vi* introducirse[15] en; *vt* introducir[15]

~ off (clothing) quitarse de prisa; (escape) marcharse desapercibido

~-on *n* faja de goma; (shoe) zapato sin cordones

~ on *v* (clothing) ponerse[19] de prisa

~-over *n* jersey *m* sin mangas

~ round (to) visitar

~ through colarse (ue)[1a]

~-up *n* desliz (-ces) *m*

~ up *v* resbalar; *fig* equivocarse[4]

slipper zapatilla; (heelless) chancleta

slippered en zapatillas

slipperiness lo resbaladizo; *fig* astucia

slippery resbaladizo; *fig* astuto

slit *n* raja; (in screw-head) ranura; *v* rajar

slither deslizarse[7]

slithery resbaladizo

sliver *n* raja; (of wood) astilla; (slice) tajada fina; *v* cortar en rajas

slob patán (-anes) *m*

slobber *n* baba; *v* babear

sloe endrina; (tree) endrino

slog *n* golpe violento; (work) trabajo duro y aburrido; *v* (+cricket) golpear sin arte; **~ (away) at** echar el hígado a

slogan lema

sloop balandro; (naval) corbeta

slop *n* charco; **~s** agua sucia; (food) desperdicios *mpl*; **~-basin/-pail** palangana/cubo para agua sucia; *v* derramar(se); **~ over** desbordar(se)

slope *n* declive *m*; (angle) inclinación *f*; (of mountain) falda; (of roof) vertiente *f*; *vt* inclinar; **~ arms!** ¡armas al hombro!; *vi* inclinarse; **~ off** (depart) largarse[5]

sloping en pendiente; (at angle) inclinado; (of roof) vertedor

sloppy (shapeless) informe; (untidy) desordenado; (over-sentimental) sentimental; (fond of kissing) besucón (-ona *f*); **~-joe** jersey holgado

slosh (hit) cascar[4]; **~ about** chapotear; **~ on** aplicar[4] en gran cantidad

sloshed borracho; **be ~** *sl* estar[19] como una sopa; **get ~** emborracharse

slot *n* ranura; **~-machine** (vending-machine) máquina automática, (for amusement) tragaperras *m sing*+*pl*; *v* hacer[19] una ranura en

sloth *n* (laziness) pereza; *zool* perezoso

slothful perezoso; *fam* gandul (-ula *f*)

slouch *n* postura desgarbada; ~ **hat** sombrero gacho; *v* (sitting) sentarse (ie)[2a] con un aire desgarbado; (walking) andar[19] arrastrando los pies

[1] **slough** *n zool* piel mudada; (snake) camisa; *v* mudar

[2] **slough** (bog) cenegal *m*; *fig* abismo

Slovak(ian) *n*+*adj* eslovaco

sloven persona desaseada

Slovene *n*+*adj* esloveno

slovenliness desaseo, dejadez *f*

slovenly desaseado; (of work) chapucero

slow *adj* lento; (of clock) atrasado, my watch is ~ mi reloj atrasa; (dull) torpe; (boring) aburrido; ~ **heat** *cul* fuego lento; **be ~ to** tardar en; ~**coach** torpe *m*+*f*; ~-**motion** *cin* a cámara lenta; ~**poke** perezoso; ~-**witted** lerdo; ~-**worm** lución (-ones) *m*; *adv* despacio, con pausa; *v* ~ **down/up** retardar; *mech*+*mot* moderar la marcha (de); **the girls ~ed down in order to walk with him** las chicas aminoraron el paso para andar con él; ~-**down** *comm* baja, *mot* embotellamiento

slowing: ~ **down** *comm* reducción *f* en el ritmo de negocios

slowly despacio, con pausa

slowness lentitud *f*; (of intellect) torpeza

sludge (mud) fango; (sediment) sedimento

slug *n zool* babosa; (for gun) perdigón (-ones) *m*; *print* lingote *m*; *v* aporrear

sluggard perezoso, perezosa

sluggish tardo; (river +*comm*) lento

sluice esclusa; (gate) compuerta; (wash) lavado; *v* ~ (**down**) lavar

slum *n* (house) tugurio; ~**s** tugurios *mpl*, barrios *mpl* bajos; *v* (go slumming) visitar los tugurios

slumber *n* sueño; *fig* inactividad *f*; ~-**wear** ropa de dormir; *v* dormir (ue)[1c]; *fig* estar[19] inactivo

slummy escuálido

slump *n* baja repentina; (in morale) bajón (-ones) *m*; *v* bajar repentinamente; **he ~ed into the chair** él se dejó caer en la silla

slur *n* borrón (-ones) *m*; *mus* ligado; *v* ~ **over** pasar por encima, (hide) ocultar; ~ **one's speech** (by omitting letters/ syllables) comerse las letras/las sílabas, (by speaking indistinctly) silbar las eses

slurred (of speech) mal pronunciado

slush (mud) fango; (melting snow) nieve *f* a medio derretir; *fig* sentimentalismo

slushy fangoso; *fig* sentimental

slut marrana; (prostitute) ramera

sluttish marrano

sluttishness marranada

sly socarrón; **on the ~** a hurtadillas

slyness socarronería

[1] **smack** *n* manotazo; (on face) cachete *m*; *fam* torta, (in baby talk) tastás *m*; (noise) chasquido; ~! ¡zas!; ~ **in the eye** *fig* contrariedad *f*; **have a ~ at** intentar; *v* dar[19] un cachete *etc*; dar[19] tastás; ~ **one's lips** relamerse; **run ~ into** chocar[4] contra

[2] **smack** *n*: ~ **of** (taste) sabor *m*, (speech) dejo; *v* saber[19] a

[3] **smack** *naut* barca de pescar

[4] **smack** heroína

small *n*: ~ **of the back** región *f* lumbar; ~**s** ropa interior; *adj* pequeño; (of length) corto; (of stature) bajo (de estatura); (petty) mezquino; **feel ~** sentirse (ie)[2c] humillado; **make s.o. feel/look ~** humillar a alguien; **in a ~ way** modestamente; ~ **ads** anuncios *mpl* por palabras; ~-**arms** armas *fpl* cortas; ~ **beer** cosa insignificante; ~ **change** +*fig* suelto; ~ **craft** embarcación (-ones) *f* pequeña; ~ **fry** pececillos *mpl*, (children) gente menuda; ~-**holding** minifundio; ~ **hours** altas horas *fpl* de la noche; ~ **intestine** intestino delgado; ~ **letter** (letra) minúscula; ~**pox** viruela; ~ **print** letra menuda; ~-**shot** perdigones *mpl*; ~-**size(d)** de reducido tamaño; ~ **sum** pequeña cantidad *f*; ~-**talk** charla frívola; ~-**time** de poca importancia

smallish más bien pequeño

smallness pequeñez *f*

smarmy lisonjero, *sl* cobista *m*+*f*

smart *n* escozor *m*; *adj* (clever) listo, vivo; (cheeky) chulo; (cunning) astuto; (in appearance) elegante; (tidy) aseado; (brisk) rápido; ~ **girl** pizpireta; ~**-alec** sabihondo; *v* escocer (ue)[1b+14]; **it makes my lips** ~ me escuece en los labios; **I'll make him** ~ él me lo pagará; ~ **under/with** resentirse (ie)[2c] de

smarten: ~ **up** hermosear

smartness (cleverness) listeza, vivacidad *f*; (cunning) astucia; (refinement) pulcritud *f*; (tidiness) aseo; (of appearance) elegancia; (briskness) rapidez *f*

smash *n* (crash) choque *m*; (tennis) golpe violento; (bankruptcy) quiebra; **go** ~ (go bankrupt) quebrar (ie)[2a]; ~**-and-grab raid** robo relámpago; ~ **hit** exitazo; ~**-up** *mot* choque *m*; *v* hacer(se)[19] pedazos; (annihilate) destruir[16]; (defeat) derrotar; ~ **into** chocar[4] con

smasher (thing) maravilla; **she is a** ~ ella es una chica bandera

smashing maravilloso

smattering conocimiento superficial

smear *n* mancha; (slander) calumnia; ~ **campaign** campaña de intoxicación/ calumnias; ~**-proof** a prueba de manchas; *v* (spread) untar; (soil) manchar; (slander) calumniar

smell *n* olor *m*; (bad ~) hedor *m*; (sense of ~) olfato; *v* oler (hue)[1a] (**of** a); (sniff) olfatear; **it** ~**s good** huele rico; ~ **a rat** olfatear algo sospechoso; ~ **out** husmear

smelliness olor *m*

smelling: ~**-salts** sales aromáticas

smelly maloliente

smelt fundir

smelter fundidor *m*

smelting fundición *f*; ~**-furnace** horno de fundición de hierro; ~**-works** fundición *f*

smile *n* sonrisa; *v* sonreír(se) (i)[3] (**at** de); ~ **upon** *fig* favorecer[14]

smiling sonriente

smirch *n* mancha; *v* manchar

smirk *n* sonris(ill)a satisfecha; *v* sonreírse(i)[3] satisfecho

smite golpear con fuerza; (punish) castigar[5]

smith herrero

smithy herrería

smitten (in love) enamorado; ~ **with** afligido de, lleno de; **he's** ~ **on her** él

anda perdido por ella

smock *n* blusa; (frock) bata; *v* fruncir[13]

smocking bordado en forma de panal

smog niebla con humo

Smoke *fig* Londres

smoke *n* humo; *fam* (cigarette) pitillo; **have a** ~ echar un pitillo; **cloud of** ~ humareda; **puff of** ~ fumarada; **put that into your pipe and** ~ **it!** ¡chúpate ésa y vuelve por otra!; ~**-bomb** bomba de humo; ~**-dried** ahumado; ~**-screen** cortina de humo; ~**-signal** señal *f* de humo; ~**stack** chimenea; *v* fumar; (emit ~) echar humo; (cure) ahumar; ~ **a pipe** fumar en pipa; ~ **out** ahuyentar con humos; ~**d salmon** salmón ahumado

smokeless sin humo

smoker fumador *m* (-ora *f*); (of drugs) fumadero; (smoking compartment) departamento de fumadores

smokiness fumosidad *f*

smoking fumar *m*; **no** ~ se prohíbe fumar; ~**-compartment** departamento de fumadores; ~**-jacket** chaqueta casera; *adj* humeante

smoky humeante; (filled with smoke) lleno de humo; (of taste, smell) ahumado

smooch besuquear

smoochie romántico

smooching besuqueo

smooth liso, suave; (level) llano; (of water) tranquilo; (without lumps) sin grumos; (of manner) afable; *pej* (of manner) zalamero; (of style) fluido; **take the rough with the** ~ estar[19] a las duras y a las maduras; ~**-faced** barbilampiño, (flattering) lisonjero; ~**-tongued** meloso; *v* ~ (out) alisar, suavizar[7]; ~ **the way for** allanar el camino para; ~ **down** alisar, (a person) tranquilizar[7]; ~ **away/over** *fig* suprimir

smoothing: ~**-iron** plancha; ~**-plane** cepillo de alisar, *Chil* rodó *m*

smoothly (*see* smooth) lisamente, suavemente *etc*; **everything is going** ~ todo marcha sobre ruedas

smoothness lisura, suavidad *f*; (flatness) llanura; (of water) tranquilidad *f*; (of manner) afabilidad *f*; (of style) fluidez *f*

smother sofocar[4]; (extinguish) apagar[5];

~ **a doubt** suprimir una duda; ~ **a yawn** contener[19] un bostezo; ~ **with kisses** abrumar a besos

smoulder *n* rescoldo; *v* arder sin llamas; *fig* estar[19] latente

smouldering que arde lentamente

smudge *n* mancha; *v* manchar

smudgy manchado

smug satisfecho de sí mismo

smuggle *vi* hacer[19] contrabando; *vt* pasar de contrabando; *fam* colar (ue)[1a] contrabando; ~**d goods** contrabando

smuggler contrabandista *m+f*

smuggling contrabando

smugness satisfacción *f* de sí mismo

smut hollín (-ines) *m*; *fig* obscenidad *f*

smutty tiznado; *fig* obsceno; ~ **joke** chiste *m* verde

snack tentempié *m*; (sandwich) bocadillo; ~-**bar** cafetería

snaffle birlar

snag *n* (in wood) nudo; (on fingernail) padrastro; (in stocking) pequeña carrera; (of tooth) raigón (-ones) *m*; (obstacle) tropiezo; (objection) pero

snail caracol *m*; **at a** ~'**s pace** a paso de tortuga

snake *n* culebra, serpiente *f*; ~ **in the grass** enemigo secreto; ~-**charmer** encantador *m* de serpientes; ~**like** serpentino; ~**skin** camisa de serpiente, (material) piel *f* de serpiente; ~**s and ladders** escalera; *v* ~ (**along**) culebrear

snaky serpentino

snap *n* (of fingers) castañeo; (of whip) chasquido; *phot* (foto) instantánea; ~! ¡crac!; **cold** ~ ola de frío; ~**dragon** cabeza de dragón; ~-**fastener** corchete *m* (de presión); ~-**shot** *n* (foto *f*) instantánea; *adj* repentino; ~ **judgement** decisión (-ones) *f* sin deliberación; *v* (break) romperse (*past part* roto); (sound) chasquear; *phot* sacar[4] una foto *f*/instantánea; (speech) decir[19] bruscamente; ~ **in two** romper(se) en dos pedazos; ~ **one's fingers** castañetear; ~ **one's fingers at** *fig* tratar con desprecio

~ **at** mordisquear; *fig* contestar groseramente

~ **into it** despabilarse

~ **off** romper (*past part* roto); **don't** ~

my head off! ¡no me regañes!

~ **out of it** despabilarse; ~ **out of it!** ¡meneáte!

~ **shut** cerrar (ie)[2a] de golpe

~ **up** comprar con avidez

snappish irritable

snappishness irritabilidad *f*

snappy (quick) rápido; (irritable) irritable; (smart) elegante; **look** ~!, **make it** ~! ¡corre!

snare *n* trampa; *fig* engaño; **set a** ~ (**for**) tender (ie)[2b] un lazo (a); *v* coger[8] con trampas; *fig* hacer[19] caer en el lazo

[1] **snarl** *n* gruñido; *v* gruñir[18]

[2] **snarl** *n* enredo; *v* (tangle) enredar; ~ **up** *mot* embotellarse

snatch *n* (action) arrebatamiento; (kidnapping) secuestro; (robbery) robo; *mus* trocito; **by** ~**es** a ratos; *v* arrebatar; (kidnap) secuestrar; (steal) robar; ~ **a glimpse of** vislumbrar; ~ **the opportunity** aprovecharse de la ocasión (to para +*infin*); ~ **at** intentar arrebatar; ~ **up** asir

snatchy inconexo

sneak n soplón *m* (-ona *f*); *fam* chivato; ~-**thief** ratero; *v* hurtar; (move furtively) rondar a hurtadillas

~ **away/off** escabullirse, *sl* pirarse

~ **in/out** entrar/salir[19] a hurtadillas

~ **up (to)** coger[8] desprevenido

sneakers zapatillas de lona, *approx* alpargatas *fpl*

sneaking *adj* secreto

sneer *n* sonrisa de desprecio; *v* sonreír (i)[3] con desprecio; ~ **at** hablar con desprecio de, (mock) burlarse de

sneering despreciativo y burlón

sneeringly despreciativamente

sneeze *n* estornudo; *v* estornudar; **it's not to be** ~**d at** no es moco de pavo

snick *n* corte pequeño; *v* tijeretear

snicker *see* **snigger**

snide criticón (-ona *f*) y malicioso; ~ **remark** observación (-ones) *f* mezquina

sniff *n* (action) husmeo; (breathing in) inspiración (-ones) ruidosa; (smell) olorcillo; (expression of scorn) ademán (-anes) *m* de desdén; *v* oler (hue)[1b]; (breathe in) inspirar con ruido; ~ **at** husmear, *fig* menospreciar

sniffle: have a ~ tener[19] la costumbre de inspirar con ruido; (have a slight cold) estar[19] un poco constipado

snigger n risilla dismulada; v refrse (i)[3] con disimulo

snip n tijeretazo; (bargain) ganga; v tijeretear; ~ **off** recortar

snipe n orni agachadiza; v mil tirar desde un escondite; fig criticar[4]

sniper francotirador m

snippet recorte m; +fig retazo; ~ **of news** noticia suelta

snitch n (tale-bearer) soplón m (-ona f); v soplar

snivel lloriquear

snivelling n lloriqueo; adj llorón

snob (e)snob m+f

snobbery, snobbishness (e)snobismo

snobbily como un (e)snob

snobbish, snobby (e)snob invar

snood redecilla (para el pelo)

snook: cock a ~ at hacer[19] un gesto de desprecio a

snooker cierto juego de billar; ~**ed** tapado, fig fastidiado

snoop fisg(one)ar

snooper fisgón m (-ona f); (inspector) inspector m (esp del gobierno)

snootiness jactancia

snooty jactancioso

snooze n sueñecito; (afternoon nap) siesta; **have a ~** echar la siest(ecit)a; v dormitar

snore n ronquido; v roncar[4]

snoring ronquidos mpl

snorkel tubo snorkel

snort n bufido; vi bufar; vt decir[19] con un bufido

snorter: real ~ cosa difícil/fuera de lo común

snot moco

snotty mocoso; (angry) enojado

snout hocico

snow n nieve f; (cocaine) cocaína; ~**ball** n bola de nieve; ~**ball tree** viburno; ~**ball** v tirar bolas de nieve, (increase) crecer[14] rápidamente; ~**blind** cegado por (el reflejo de) la nieve; ~**blindness** ceguera causada por la nieve; ~**bound** aprisionado por la nieve; ~**capped** coronado de nieve; ~**drift** ventisquero; ~**drop** campanilla de invierno; ~**fall** nevada; ~**flake** copo de nieve; ~**line** límite m de las nieves perpetuas; ~**man** muñeco de nieve; ~**plough** quitanieves m

sing+pl; ~**scape** paisaje m de nieve; ~**shoe** raqueta de nieve; ~**storm** nevasca; ~**-white** blanco como la nieve; **Snow White and the Seven Dwarfs** Blancanieves f y los siete enanitos; v nevar (ie)[2a]; **be ~ed under (with)** estar[19] inundado (de); **be ~ed up** estar[19] aislado por la nieve

snowy nevoso; ~ **owl** buho ártico

[1] **snub** n desaire m; v desairar

[2] **snub** adj corto; ~**-nosed** chato

snuff n rapé m; **take ~** tomar rapé; ~**box** tabaquera; v olfatear; (extinguish) extinguir[16]; (candle) despabilar; ~ **it** sl diñarla, Arg palmar

snuffers despabiladeras fpl

snuffle n gangueo; v ganguear

snug n cuarto cómodo; adj (comfortable) cómodo; (well-fitting) ajustado

snuggle: ~ (up to) arrimarse (a); ~ **down** ponerse[19] cómodo

snugly cómodamente

so tan, **it's ~ pretty** es tan bonito; (thus) así, **do it ~** hágalo así; ~ **as to** para +infin, para que +subj; ~ **be it** así sea; ~ **do I** yo también; ~ **far** hasta ahora; **and ~ forth** y así por el estilo; ~ **long!** ¡hasta luego!; ~ **long as** mientras que; ~ **many** tantos mpl (-as fpl); ~ **much** tanto (that que); ~ **much the better/worse** tanto mejor/peor; ~ **that** (in such a manner that) de modo que, (in order that) para que +subj, (with the result that) así que; ~ **then** conque; ~ **there** ahí lo tiene usted; ~ **to say/speak** por decirlo así; ~ **what?** ¿y qué?; **if ~** en tal caso; **I hope/think ~** espero/creo que sí; **is that ~?** ¿de veras?; **isn't it ~?** ¿no es verdad?; **don't you think ~?** ¿no te parece?; **it can't be ~ bad** no es para tanto; **just ~** ni más ni menos; **or ~** (roughly) más o menos; **very much ~** definitivamente; ~**-and-~** fulano de tal; **I don't like that ~-and-~** no me gusta aquel etcétera; ~**-called** llamado; ~**-~** regular

soak n remojo; (drunkard) borracho; v remojar(se); **leave to ~** dejar en/a remojo; **get ~ed** empaparse, (drunk) emborracharse; ~**ed to the skin** calado hasta los huesos

~ **in** penetrar

~ **through** filtrar

~ **up** empapar

soaking *n* remojo; *adj* mojado hasta los huesos

soap *n* jabón (-ones) *m*; **soft** ~ *n* jabón blando, *fig* coba, *v* dar[19] coba; ~**-box** tribuna (en la calle); ~**-box orator** orador *m* callejero; ~**-bubble** pompa de jabón; ~**-dish** jabonera; ~**-flakes** jabón *m* en escamas; ~**-opera** *rad* serial radiofónico chabacano, *TV* telenovela chabacana; ~**-powder** jabón *m* en polvo; ~**-stone** esteatita; ~**-suds** jabonaduras *fpl*, *fam* espuma; *v* enjabonar

soapy jabonoso; (taste) que sabe a jabón; *fig* (adulatory) lisonjero

soar cerner (ie)[2b]; *fig* encumbrarse

soaring *n* vuelo; *adj* (of prices) en aumento

sob *n* sollozo; **with a** ~ **in one's voice** muy emocionado; ~**-sister** escritora de artículos sentimentales; ~**-stuff** sentimentalismo; *vi* sollozar[7]; *vt* decir[19] entre sollozos; ~ **one's heart out** llorar a lágrima viva

sober *adj* (moderate) sobrio; (sensible) cuerdo; (of colours) apagado; (not drunk) sereno; ~**-minded** serio; *v* ~ **down** calmarse; *v* ~ **up** desintoxicarse[4], *fam* quitarse la sopa

sobriety (moderation) sobriedad *f*; (not drunk) sobriedad *f*; (seriousness) seriedad *f*

sobriquet apodo

soccer fútbol *m*

sociability sociabilidad *f*

sociable sociable

social *n* fiesta social; *adj* social; ~ **climber** arribista *m+f*, *sl* trepa *m*; ~ **insurance** seguros *mpl* sociales; ~ **security** seguridad *f* social; ~ **worker** investigador *m* (-ora *f*) y trabajador *m* (-ora *f*) social; ~**-democrat** socialdemócrata *m+f*

socialism socialismo

socialist *n+adj* socialista *m+f*

socialite persona que alterna en la buena sociedad

socialize socializar[7]

society *n* sociedad *f*; (high ~) buena sociedad; **friendly** ~ mutualidad *f*; **in the** ~ **of** en compañía de; *adj* de la sociedad

socio-economic socioeconómico

sociological sociológico

sociologist sociólogo

sociology sociología

[1] **sock** calcetín (-ines) *m*; (for shoe) plantilla; ~**-suspender** liga

[2] **sock** *n* (blow) torta, **give s.o. a** ~ pegarle[5] a uno una torta; *v* pegar[5]

socket (of eye) cuenca; (of tooth) alveolo; *elect* enchufe *m*; *mech* encaje *m*

Socrates Sócrates

[1] **sod** césped *m*; (cut) tope *m*

[2] **sod** *vulg* cabrón (-ones) *m*

soda sosa; ~**-cracker** cráce(r) *m*; ~**-fountain** puesto donde se venden helados y bebidas no alcohólicas; ~**-water** sifón *m*

sodden saturado

sodium sodio

sodomite *n+adj* sodomita *m+f*

sodomy sodomía

sofa sofá *m*

soft blando; (of skin, sounds) suave; (of colours) delicado; (of metal) dúctil; (of leather) flexible; (of character) débil; (foolish) tonto; ~ **in the head** lerdo; **have a** ~ **spot for** tener[19] una debilidad por; **in a** ~ **voice** en voz baja; ~ **drink** bebida no alcohólica; ~ **job** trabajo fácil; ~ **landing** aterrizaje *m* suave; ~ **line** *pol* blandura; **Russia adopted a** ~ **line towards the Arabs** Rusia mostró blandura hacia los árabes; ~ **palate** paladar blando; ~ **pedal** *mus* ~ *n* pedal *m* suave, *v* disminuir[16] el sonido, *fig* moderar; ~ **soap** *n* jabón líquido, *fig* coba, *v* dar[19] coba; ~ **toy** muñeco de peluche; ~ **water** agua blanda; ~**-boiled egg** huevo pasado por agua; ~**-hearted** tierno de corazón; ~**-heartedness** buen corazón *m*; ~(**ly**)/~**-spoken** de voz baja

soften *vt* ablandar; bajar (la voz) *vi* ablandarse; (of personality) enternecerse[14]

softener +*phot* suavizador *m*

softness blandura; (of skin, sounds) suavidad *f*; (of colours) suavidad; (of leather) flexibilidad *f*; (of character) debilidad *f*; (of textiles) esponjosidad *f*

soggy empapado; (of shoe) lleno de agua

[1] **soil** *n* tierra; **native** ~ tierra patria

[2] **soil** *v* ensuciar; +*fig* manchar; ~ **one's**

hands ensuciarse las manos
soirée velada
sojourn *n* estancia; *v* pasar una temporada
sojourner residente *m+f* temporal
sol *mus* sol *m*
solace *n* consuelo; *v* consolar
solar solar; ~ **eclipse** eclipse *m* de sol; ~
plexus plexo solar; ~ **system** sistema
m solar
solarium solarium *m*
solder soldar
soldier *n* soldado; *sl* chorchi *m*, sorchi
m; *mil sl* guripa *m*; *v* ser[19] soldado; ~
on aguantar y perseverar
soldierly soldadesca
[1] **sole** *n anat* planta; (of shoe) suela; *v*
poner[19] suela a
[2] **sole** (fish) lenguado
[3] **sole** único, exclusivo; ~ **agent** agente
único; ~ **rights** exclusiva
solecism solecismo
solemn solemne; (of person) serio
solemnity solemnidad *f*; (of person)
seriedad *f*
solemnization solemnización *f*
solemnize solemnizar[7]
solenoid solenoide *m*
sol-fa *n* solfa; *v* solfear
solicit solicitar; (importune) importunar; (immorally) intentar seducir[15]
solicitation solicitación (-ones) *f*
solicitor abogado; (for wills, oaths) notario; (US representative) representante *m+f*; **Solicitor General** sub-
fiscal *m* de la corona, US procurador
m general del Estado
solicitous solícito (**about** por)
solicitude solicitud *f*
solid *n* sólido; *adj* sólido; (of gold)
macizo; (of crowds) denso; (of vote)
unánime; ~ **fuel** combustible sólido;
~ **geometry** geometría del espacio; ~
tyre neumático macizo; **I waited a** ~
hour esperé una hora entera
solidarity solidaridad *f*
solidify solidificar(se)[4]
solidity solidez *f*
soliloquize soliloquiar
soliloquy soliloquio
solipsism solipsismo
solitaire (game and gem) solitario
solitary *n* solitario; *adj* solitario; (isolated) apartado; (only) único; **in** ~

confinement incomunicado
solitude soledad *f*
solo *n mus* (+ cards) solo; ~ **machine**
mot máquina sola; ~ **flight** vuelo a
solas; ~ **violin** violín solo; *adv* sólo, a
solas
soloist solista *m+f*
Solomon Salomón *m*
solstice solsticio; **summer/winter** ~ solsticio de verano/de invierno
solubility solubilidad *f*
soluble *n+adj* soluble *m*
solution solución (-ones) *f*
solvable soluble
solve resolver (ue)[1b] (*past part* resuelto);
(riddle) adivinar
solvency solvencia
solvent *n* disolvente *m*: *adj* solvente
Somali *n+adj* somalí
Somalia Somalia
sombre sombrío
some *adj+pron* (number) (alg)unos,
(alg)unas; (quantity) un poco de;
often omitted **do you want** ~ **cheese?**
¿quiere usted queso?; ~ **fifty metres**
unos cincuenta metros; ~ **few** unos
pocos; ~ **people** algunas personas *fpl*;
for ~ **reason** por no sé qué razón;
this is ~ **car!** ¡esto sí que es un coche!;
with ~ **difficulty** con cierta dificultad;
the car was going ~ el coche iba
velozmente; ~**body**, ~**one** alguien;
~**how (or other)** de algún modo (u
otro); ~**how I never liked it** por alguna
que otra razón nunca me gustó; **be**
~**one (of importance)** ser[19] un personaje; ~**one told me** no sé quién me
dijo; ~**one else** otra persona; ~ **place
else** US see ~**where**; ~**thing** algo;
~**thing else** otra cosa; ~**thing else?**
¿algo más?; ~**thing like that** algo por
el estilo; ~**thing or other** alguna cosa;
be ~**thing of a** tener[19] algo de; **have**
~**thing to do** tener[19] qué hacer; **seven
point** ~**thing** siete coma y algo; ~ **time**
algún día *m*; ~ **time last week** durante
la semana pasada; ~ **time soon** un día
de éstos; **the** ~**time president** el antiguo presidente; ~**times** algunas veces;
~**what** algo, un poco; ~**where** en/por
alguna parte; ~**where else** en/por otro
sitio
somersault *n* voltereta; *v* dar[19] una voltereta

somnambulism sonambulismo
somnambulist sonámbulo
somniferous somnífero
somnolence somnolencia
somnolent soñoliento
son hijo; ~ **of the people** hijo del pueblo; ~ **of a bitch** hijo de puta; ~**-in-law** yerno
sonata sonata
song canción (-ones) f; (poem) poema m; ~ **and dance** alharaca; **it's nothing to make a ~ and dance about** no es para tanto; **break into ~** ponerse[19] a cantar; **for a ~** por una bicoca; ~**-bird** pájaro cantor; ~**-book** cancionero; ~**-hit, hit-~** canción (-ones) f de moda; ~**-thrush** tordo; ~**-writer** compositor m (-ora f), autor de canciones; ~**-writer-singer** cantautor m (-ora f)
songster (bird) pájaro cantor; (person) cantante m+f
sonic sónico; ~ **boom** estampido sónico
sonnet soneto
sonneteer escritor m (-ora f) de sonetos
sonny hijito
sonority sonoridad f
sonorous sonoro
soon pronto; ~ **after** poco después (de); **as/so ~ as** tan pronto como; **as ~ as possible** lo antes posible; **see you ~** hasta pronto; **too ~** antes de tiempo; **I would just as ~** igual me daría + infin
sooner más temprano; ~ **or later** tarde o temprano; ~ **than** antes que; **no ~ than** apenas; **no ~ said than done** dicho y hecho; **the ~ the better** cuanto antes, mejor; **I had/would ~** yo preferiría + infin
soot hollín m
sooth: **in ~** de veras; ~**sayer** adivino, adivina
soothe calmar; (pain) aliviar
soothing calmante
sooty holliniento
sop n pan mojado en líquido; fig compensación (-ones) f; sl (fool) tonto; v empapar; ~ **up** absorber
Sophia Sofía
sophism sofismo
sophist sofista m+f
sophisticated sofisticado
sophistication sofisticación f
sophistry sofistería

Sophocles Sófocles
sophomore alumno de segundo curso
soporific n soporífero; adj soporífico
sopping: **be ~ wet** estar[19] mojado hasta los huesos
soprano soprano f
sorcerer hechicero
sorceress hechicera
sorcery hechicería
sordid sórdido, asqueroso; (of motives) vil
sordidness asquerosidad f; (of motives) vileza
sore n llaga; (caused by rubbing harness) matadura; fig herida; **open an old ~** renovar (ue)[1a] la herida; adj dolorido; (angry) enojado; (bad) malo; **she has a ~ throat** ella tiene dolor de garganta
sorely muy
soreness dolor m; (ill-feeling) rencor m; (resentment) resentimiento
soroptimist la que pertenece al club rotario femenino
sorority (US) asociación f de estudiantes
[1] **sorrel** bot acedera
[2] **sorrel** n+adj alazán (-anes) m
sorrow n pesar m; **to my ~** con gran sentimiento mío; ~**-stricken** afligido de pena; v afligirse[9] (at/over de/por)
sorrowful pesaroso
sorrowing n aflicción f; adj afligido
sorry pesaroso; (grieved) triste; (repentant) arrepentido (for de); **you'll be ~ for that** se arrepentirá de eso; (unconvincing) poco convincente; (wretched) ruin, ~ **sight** aspecto ruin; **be ~ for s.o.** compadecerse[14] de uno; **be ~ for o.s.** estar[19] muy alicaído; **I feel ~ for you** lo siento por ti; **be ~ that** sentir (ie)[2c] que +subj; **be ~ to** sentir (ie)[2c] +infin; **I'm ~** lo siento, US ¿qué dice usted?; **I'm very ~** lo siento mucho; (excuse me) perdón
sort n clase f; **he/she is a good ~** él/ella es buena persona; **he has a ~ of scar** él tiene una especie de cicatriz; **she was ~ of angry** ella estuvo algo enfadada; **all ~s of** toda clase de; **it takes all ~s to make a world** hay de todo en este mundo de Dios; **nothing of the ~** nada de eso; **something of the ~** algo por el estilo; **in some ~** hasta cierto punto; **be out of ~s** med estar[19] indispuesto,

(temper) estar[19] malhumorado; *v* ~
(out) (classify) clasificar[4]; (select) escoger[14]; (separate) separar

sorter (at Post Office) distribuidor *m*
(-ora *f*); clasificador *m* (-ora *f*)

sortie salida

sorting (classifying) clasificación *f*; (selecting) selección *f*; (separating) separación *f*; ~**-machine** máquina clasificadora

S.O.S. S.O.S. *m*

sostenuto sostenido

sot borracho

sottish entorpecido por el alcohol

sotto voce en voz baja

soubrette *theat* cómica

soufflé soufflé *m*

sought: ~**-after** solicitado

soul alma; (of the departed) ánima; *mus*
soul *m*; simpatía; **living** ~ ser *m*; **there
was not a living** ~ no había bicho
viviente; **she is the** ~ **of discretion** ella
es la discreción personificada; **Mary is
a simple** ~ María es un alma de Dios;
one must have ~ hay que tener alma;
upon my ~ por mi vida; **All Soul's Day**
día *m* de (los) Difuntos; ~**-stirring**
emocionante

soulful conmovedor (-ora *f*)

soulless desalmado

[1] **sound** (healthy) sano; (of people's
character) digno de confianza; *comm*
solvente; (safe) sólido; (of opinions)
razonable; **on a** ~ **footing** bien fundado; ~ **sleep** sueño profundo; **his** ~
leg is his left one su pierna válida es la
izquierda

[2] **sound** *n* sonido; (noise) ruido, **without a**
~ sin ruido; **she didn't make a** ~ ella
no dijo ni pío; **he didn't like the** ~ **of it**
no le gustó la idea; ~**-barrier** barrera
del sonido; ~**-dubbing** mezcla de sonidos; ~**-effects** efectos *mpl* sonoros;
~**-engineer** ingeniero de sonido; ~**-
film** película sonora; ~**-mixing** *cin,
rad*+*TV* mezcla de sonidos; ~**-proof** a
prueba de ruidos; ~**-proofing** insonorización *f*; ~**-track** *cin* banda sonora; ~**-wave** onda sonora; *vi* sonar
(ue)[1a]; (seem) parecer[14]; *vt* sonar
(ue)[1a]; *mus* tocar[4]; ~ **the charge/retreat** tocar[4] zafarrancho de combate/
retirada

[3] **sound** *naut* sondear; *med* auscultar; *surg*

sondar; ~ **out** sondear

[4] **sound** *geog* estrecho

sounding sondeo; ~**-board** caja armónica

soundless sin ruido

soundness (of health) buena salud;
comm solvencia; (safeness) solidez *f*;
(of people) perspicacia; (of argument) validez *f*

soup (clear) caldo, consomé *m*; (thick)
sopa; **in the** ~ en apuros; ~**-bowl**
plato sopero; ~**-cube** cubito de caldo;
~**-kitchen** cocina de carretilla; ~**-ladle**
cucharón (-ones) *m*; ~**-plate** plato
sopero; ~**-spoon** cuchara sopera; ~**-
tureen** sopera

sour +*fig* agrio; *fam* ácido; ~ **milk** leche
cortada; ~ **soil** tierra maleada; **turn** ~
(milk) cortarse; **it's** ~ **grapes** están
verdes; *v* agriarse

source +*fig* fuente *f*; (of river) nacimiento

sourish agrete

sourness +*fig* agrura; *fam* acidez *f*

souse *n* escabeche *m*; *v* escabechar; (in
water) zambullir; (soak) empapar; ~**d**
cul en escabeche; (drunk) achispado

south *n* sur *m*; ~ **wind** viento del sur;
South Africa África del Sur; **South
African** *n*+*adj* sudafricano; **South
America** América del Sur; **South
American** *n*+*adj* sudamericano; ~**-
east** sudeste *m*; **South East Asia**
Sudeste *m* asiático; ~**-easterly/
eastern** *n*+*adj* sudeste *m*; ~**-paw**
boxeador zurdo; **South Korea** Corea
del Sur; **South Pole** Polo Sur; **South
Seas** mares *m* del Sur; **South Vietnam**
Vietnam del Sur; **South Vietnamese**
n+*adj* sudvietnamita; ~**-west** *n*+*adj*
sudoeste *m*; ~**-westerly**, ~**-western**
n+*adj* sudoeste *m*; *adv* hacia el sur

southern, southerly meridional; **Southern Cross** Cruz *f* del sur

southerner habitante *m*+*f* del Sur

southernmost el más meridional

southwards hacia el sur

souvenir recuerdo

sou'wester *meteor* viento del sudoeste;
(hat) sueste *m*

sovereign *n*+*adj* soberano

sovereignty soberanía

soviet *n* soviet *m*; *adj* soviético; **Soviet
Union** Unión Soviética

sovietize sovietizar[7]
[1] sow v sembrar (ie)[2a]
[2] sow n cerda, marrana; (wild) jabalina
sower sembrador m
sowing siembra; ~**-machine** sembradora; ~**-time** sementera
soya soja; ~ **bean** haba de soja
sozzled trompa; *Arg* curda
Sp. (Spanish) esp. (español, -ola)
spa balneario
space n +*print* espacio; (room) hueco,
there was no ~ in the gallery no había
espacio en la galería; ~ **under the
stairs** hueco de la escalera; ~**-age** era
del espacio; ~**-bar** (on typewriter) barra espaciadora; ~**-capsule** cápsula
espacial; ~**-craft** astronave f; ~ **exploration** exploración f del espacio;
~**-flight** vuelo espacial; ~**-man,
~woman** cosmonauta m+f; ~**-platform** plataforma espacial; ~**-rocket** cohete m espacial; ~**ship** astronave f; ~**-shuttle** transbordador m
espacial; (manned) espacial (tripulada); ~**-station** estación
f espacial (tripulada); ~**-suit** traje m
espacial; ~**-travel** viaje espacial m; v
~ (out) espaciar
spacious espacioso; (of room) amplio;
~ **living** vida holgada
spaciousness espaciosidad f; (of room)
amplitud f
spade n pala; (cards) espada; (negro)
negro; **call a ~ a ~** llamar al pan pan y
al vino vino; ~**-work** trabajo preliminar; v ~ (up) cavar
spadeful palada
spaghetti espaguetis mpl
Spain España
span n (of hand) palmo; *archi* tramo; (of
bridge) luz (-ces) f; *aer* +*orni* envergadura; (US team) pareja (de caballos),
(of oxen) yunta (de bueyes), *fig* (distance) extensión f; (time) duración f;
v tender (ie)[2b] (un puente) sobre; (of
time) abarcar[4]; **the bridge ~s the river**
el puente se extiende sobre el río
spangle n lentejuela; v adornar con
lentejuelas; ~d estrellado (with de)
Spaniard español m (-ola f); *SA sl* gallego
spaniel perro de aguas
Spanish n español, castellano; **speak
good ~** hablar bien/buen castellano,
fam hablar en cristiano; *adj* español

(-ola); **in the ~ fashion** a la española;
~ **chestnut** castaño; ~ **fly** cantárida; ~
Main mar m Caribe; ~ **America**
Hispanoamérica; ~**-American** n+*adj*
hispanoamericano; *sl pej* sudaca m+f
spanish (liquorice) regaliz f
spank zurrar; ~ **along** ir[19] de prisa
spanker *naut* cangreja
spanking n zurra; *adj* excelente; (quick)
rápido
spanner llave f (de tuercas); (adjustable) llave inglesa; **put a ~ in the
works** meter un palo entre los engranajes
[1] spar *naut* verga
[2] spar sp pugilato; v hacer[19] fintas; *fam*
hacer[19] guantes; *fig* disputar amistosamente
spare n recambio; **list of ~s** lista de
recambios; *adj* (thin) enjuto; (left
over) sobrante; (reserve) de reserva;
(replacement) de repuesto; **go ~**
(become frantic) ponerse[19] frenético;
~ **money** *comm* dinero disponible; ~
part (pieza de) recambio; ~**-parts
service** servicio de recambios; ~**-rib**
costilla de cerdo; ~ **room** habitación
(-ones) f para convidados; ~ **time**
ratos libres; ~ **tyre** *fig* (roll of fat)
rosca, *sl* michelín (-ines) m; ~ **wheel**
rueda de recambio; v (pardon) perdonar; **they ~d my life** me perdonaron
la vida; (avoid) evitar; (do without)
pasarse sin; (give) dar[19]; ~ **no expense**
no escatimar, *fig* hacer[19] todo lo posible (to para +*infin*); ~ **me the details**
no me cuente los detalles; **there's no
time to ~** no hay tiempo que perder;
can you ~ me five minutes? ¿puede
usted dedicarme cinco minutos?; **can
you ~ me five hundred pesetas?**
¿quiere usted hacerme el favor de
darme quinientas pesetas?; ~ **o.s.
trouble** ahorrarse trabajo; **to ~** de sobra; **he has money to ~** él dispone de
mucho dinero; **be ~d** (escape) librarse (from de), (escape death) quedar vivo
sparing económico; **be ~ with** escatimar
spark n chispa; (of humour) chispazo;
(electrician) *fam* chispas m sing+pl;
~**s** *naut* telegrafista m; v chispear; ~
off estallar; ~(**ing**)-**plug** bujía
sparkle n destello; *fig* viveza; v destellar;

fig brillar; (of wine) ser[19] espumoso

sparkling destellante; *fig* brillante; (of wine) espumoso

sparring: ~ **match** combate (de boxeo) amistoso; ~ **partner** compañero de entrenamiento, sparring *m*

sparrow gorrión (-ones) *m*; ~**-hawk** gavilán (-anes) *m*

sparse escaso; (of hair) ralo

sparsely aquí y allá

Sparta Esparta

Spartan *n* + *adj* espartano

spasm *med* espasmo; *fig* acceso

spasmodic(al) espasmódico

spastic espástico

spat botín (-ines) *m*

spate torrente *m* (of de); **in** ~ crecido

spatial espacial

spatter salpicar[4] (**with** de)

spattering salpicadura

spatula espátula

spawn *n* freza, hueva; *fig* prole *f*; *vi* frezar[7]; *vt pej* engendrar

spawning freza

spay quitar los ovarios a

speak hablar (**to** a, con); (make a speech) pronunciar un discurso; (say) decir[19]; **so to** ~ por decirlo así; ~ **one's mind** decir[19] lo que se piensa; ~ **the truth** decir[19] la verdad; ~ **well** hablar claro; ~ **well of** hablar bien de; **don't even** ~ **of that!** ¡de eso ni hablar!; ~**easy** taberna clandestina

~ **for** (in favour of) hablar en favor de, (on behalf of) hablar en nombre de; (attest) testimoniar; ~ **for itself** ser[19] evidente; ~ **well for** ser[19] buena recomendación de; **speaking for myself** por mi parte

~ **out** (fearlessly) hablar sin miedo; (loudly) hablar en voz alta

~ **up** hablar alto; ~ **up!** ¡(hable) más fuerte!

speaker el/la que habla; (lecturer) conferenciante *m* + *f*; (orator) orador *m* (-ora *f*); *rad* altavoz (-ces) *f*; **the Speaker** presidente *m* de la Cámara de los Comunes

speaking *n* habla; (on telephone) al habla; **Gómez** ~ soy Gómez; **roughly** ~ más o menos; **without** ~ sin decir nada; ~**-trumpet** bocina; ~**-tube** tubo acústico; *adj* hablante; **we are not on** ~ **terms** no nos hablamos; **within** ~ **dis-**

tance al habla; **English-**~ de habla inglesa

spear *n* lanza; (fishing) arpón (-ones) *m*; ~**head** + *fig* punta de lanza, *sp* **Gento was the** ~**head of the attack** Gento fue el ariete del ataque; ~**mint** menta verde; *v* alancear; (fishing) arponar

spec: on ~ a ver lo que sale; (on approval) a prueba

special *n* (constable) policía *m* auxiliar; (train) tren *m* especial; *adj* especial; ~ **edition** número extraordinario; ~ **commemorative issue** (postage stamps) emisión (-ones) *f* especial conmemorativa; **from our** ~ **correspondent** de nuestro corresponsal extraordinario; **she is my** ~ **friend** ella es la amiga de mi alma; **they're expecting someone** ~ están esperando a alguien de cumplido; **I'll quote you a** ~ **price** le hago un precio de amigos; **what's so** ~ **about it?** ¿qué tiene de particular?; ~ **delivery** entrega especial; ~**-delivery letter** carta urgente; ~**-delivery label** sello de urgencia

specialist *n* + *adj* especialista *m* + *f*

speciality especialidad *f*; **today's** ~ (meal) plato del día

specialize especializarse[7] (**in** en)

specialty contrato sellado

species especie *f*

specific *n* + *adj* específico; ~ **gravity** peso específico

specification especificación (-ones) *f*; *fam* plan *m*

specify especificar[4]

specimen espécimen (especímenes) *m*; ~ **copy** ejemplar *m* de muestra

specious especioso

speciousness lo especioso

speck *n* (mark) manchita; (of dust) partícula; *fam* mota; *v* motear

speckle *n* motita; *v* motear; ~**d** (of cloth) jaspeado

specs gafas *fpl*

spectacle espectáculo; (**pair of**) ~**s** (unas) gafas; ~**-case** estuche *m* de las gafas; ~**-frame** armadura de las gafas; **(be)spectacled** con gafas

spectacular espectacular; ~ **number** *theat* número vistoso

spectator espectador *m* (-ora *f*)

spectral espectral

spectre espectro

spectrum espectro

speculate especular (**on** en); ~ **in** *comm* especular sobre

speculation especulación *f*

speculative especulativo

speculator especulador *m* (-ora *f*)

speech (act) habla; (style) lenguaje *m*; (lecture) conferencia; (oration) discurso; **make a** ~ pronunciar un discurso; **part of** ~ parte *f* de la oración; **~-day** día *m* del reparto *f* de premios; **~-therapist** terapeuta *m+f* de la voz; **~-therapy** terapia de la voz; **~-training** elocución *f*

speechless estupefacto *f*

speechify perorar

speed *n* +*mech*+*mot* velocidad *f*; (rapidity) prisa; **at full** ~ a toda velocidad; **with all** ~ a toda prisa; **~-boat** lancha (motora) de carrera; **~-cop** guardia *m* motorizado; **~-limit** límite *m* de velocidad; **~-limit sign** señal *f* de velocidad limitada; **~-regulator** *mech* regulador *m* de velocidad *f*; **~-way** pista para carreras, (*US*) pista de circulación rápida; *v* (go quickly) ir[19] a gran velocidad; (exceed the ~-limit) exceder la velocidad permitida; **~ s.o. on his way** despedirle (ie)[3] a uno

speeder el/la que va de prisa; *mot* el/la que excede la velocidad permitida

speediness velocidad *f*, rapidez *f*

speeding exceso de velocidad

speedometer velocímetro

speedwell verónica

speedy rápido

speleologist espeleólogo

speleology espeleología

[1] **spell** (period) temporada; (of work) turno; (of disease) ataque *m*; ~ **of good weather** temporada de buen tiempo; **bad** ~ mala racha; **by** ~**s** a ratos

[2] **spell** *n* (magic) hechizo; **cast a** ~ **on/over** hechizar[7], *fig* fascinar; **under the** ~ (**of**) encantado (de), *fig* fascinado (por); **~-binder** (*US*) orador *m* hábil; **~-binding** fascinador (-ora *f*); **~bound** hechizado, (astonished) asombrado, (fascinated) fascinado

[3] **spell** escribir (*past part* escrito), *fig* significar[4]; ~ **a word** deletrear una palabra; **how do you** ~ ...? ¿cómo se deletrea ...?; ~ **out** deletrear, (explain simply) explicar[4] en términos fáciles

speller (book) abecedario; (person) deletreador *m* (-ora *f*); **she's a good** ~ ella sabe deletrear bien

spelling ortografía; ~ **mistake** falta de ortografía; **~-bee** certamen (-ámenes) *m* de ortografía; **~-book** abecedario

spend *v* (money) gastar; (time) pasar; ~ **one's time** (**at/in**) ocuparse (en); ~ **a penny** *fig* ir[19] al servicio, *fam* hacer[19] pis; **~thrift** *n*+*adj* derrochador *m* (-ora *f*)

spender gastador *m* (-ora *f*)

spent gastado; (tired) agotado; (of bullet) frío; **his anger was soon** ~ su ira pronto se calmó

sperm esperma; **~-whale** cachalote *m*

spermatozoon espermatozoo

spew *n* vómito; *fam* devuelto; *v* vomitar; *fam* devolver (ue)[1b] (*past part* devuelto)

sphere +*fig* esfera; *astron* esfera celeste; ~ **of influence** zona de influencia

spherical esférico

spheroid esferoide *m*

sphincter esfínter *m*

sphinx esfinge *m+f*

spice *n* especia; *fig* picante *m*; *v* condimentar; *fig* dar[19] picante a

spiciness picante *m*; *fig* psicalipsis *f*

spick: ~ **and span** (of person) pulcro; (of room *etc*) limpísimo

spicy con especias; *fig* picante, psicalíptico

spider araña; **~'s web** telaraña; **~-man** *bui* constructor *m* de andamiajes

spidery muy delgado; (of writing) de patas de araña

spiel hablar con facilidad

spigot (of cask) espita; *mech* espiga

[1] **spike** *n* pincho; (pointed stud) clavo; (ear of corn) espiga; (hypodermic needle) aguja hipodérmica; *v* clavar, ~ **a gun** clavar un cañón; *fig* ~ **s.o.'s gun** frustrar los planes de alguien; **~d shoes** zapatos con clavos

[2] **spike** asilo de los pobres

spiky erizado

[1] **spill** (fall) *n* caída; **have a** ~ volcarse (ue)[1a]; *v* verter(se) (ie)[2b]; ~ **over** sobresalir[19]; ~ **the beans** revelarlo todo

[2] **spill** (for lighting) pajuela

spin *n* (turn) vuelta; (outing) paseo en

coche/en bicicleta; *aer* barrena; (billiards stroke) tacada de efecto; **be in a flat ~** llenarse de terror; **~-drier** secadora (centrífuga); *vi* (turn) girar; *aer* entrar en barrena; *vt* (turn) hacer¹⁹ girar, (thread) hilar; **~ a ball** hacer¹⁹ girar una pelota; **~ a coin** echar a cara o cruz; **~ a top** hacer¹⁹ bailar una peonza; **~ a yarn** contar (ue)¹ᵃ un cuento; **~ out** alargar⁵; **my head is spinning** estoy mareado; **send spinning** derribar, *mot* atropellar

spinach espinaca

spinal espinal; **~ column** columna vertebral; **~ cord** médula espinal

spindle huso; *mech* eje *m*

spindly largo y delgado

spine *anat* columna vertebral; *fam* espinazo; *bot* espina; *zool* púa; (of book) lomo

spineless invertebrado; *fig* flojo

spinet espineta

spinnaker *naut* balón (-ones) *m*

spinner hilandero

spinney bosquecillo

spinning: ~-jenny máquina de hilar; **~-mill** hilandería; **~-top** peonza; **~-wheel** torno de hilar

spinster soltera; **~hood** soltería

spiny +*fig* espinoso

spiraea espírea

spiral *n* espiral *m*; *adj* de espiral; **~ staircase** escalera en caracol; *v* dar¹⁹ vueltas en espiral; *aer* volar (ue)¹ᵃ en espiral

spire aguja

spirit *n* espíritu *m*; (alcohol) alcohol *m*; (courage) valor *m*; (ghost) fantasma *m*; (real meaning) verdadero significado; (soul) alma; (vivacity) viveza; **in high ~s** animado; **in low ~s** abatido; **keep up one's ~s** no desanimarse; **in a ~ of** movido por un sentimiento de; **evil ~** demonio; **Holy Spirit** Espíritu Santo; **leading ~** primera figura; **public ~** civismo; **surgical ~** alcohol quirúrgico; **~s of salt** sal *f* fumante; **~-lamp** lámpara de alcohol; **~-level** nivel *m* de aire; **motor-~** gasolina; *v* **~ away** hacer¹⁹ desaparecer; **~ed** brioso, (of horses) fogoso; **public-~ed** lleno de civismo

spiritless apocado

spiritual *n* himno religioso de los negros norteamericanos; *adj* espiritual

spiritualism espiritismo

spiritualist *n*+*adj* espiritista *m*+*f*

spirituality espiritualidad *f*

spiritualize espiritualizar⁷

spirituous espirituoso

¹ spit *cul* asador *m* (a rotación); (sandbank) banco de arena; (of land) lengua de tierra; *v cul* espetar

² spit *n* saliva; **he's the very ~ of his father** él es el vivo retrato de su padre; *v* (saliva *etc*) escupir; (rain) lloviznar; (sputter) chisporrotear; **~ on one's hands** escupirse las manos; **~fire** fierabrás *m*

spite *n* rencor *m*; **have a ~ against s.o.** tenerle¹⁹ rencor a alguien; **in ~ of** a pesar de; **in ~ of the fact that** a pesar de que; **in ~ of ourselves** a pesar nuestro; *v* mortificar⁴

spiteful rencoroso

spitefulness rencor *m*

spitting: be the ~ image of ser¹⁹ el vivo retrato de

spittle saliva

spittoon escupidera

spiv (sponger) sablista *m*; (smart-alec) uno que vive del cuento

splash *n* salpicadura; (noise) chapoteo; **~ of colour** mancha de color; **make a ~** hacer¹⁹ gran impresión; **~board** guardabarros *m sing*; *vi* chapotear; *vt* salpicar⁴, (in press) publicar⁴ en lugar prominente

~ about chapotear

~ down *n space* amerizaje *m*

~ down *v* amarar

~ out derrochar dinero

splatter salpicar⁴

splay *n* bisel *m*; **~-footed** zancajoso; *v* biselar

spleen *anat* bazo; (humour) mal humor; **vent one's ~** gastar genio (**on** contra)

splendid espléndido; **~!** ¡magnífico!

splendour esplendor *m*; **add ~ to the party** dar¹⁹ realce a la fiesta

splenetic *anat* esplénico; *med* atrabilioso; *fig* malhumorado

splice *hort*+*naut* empalme *m*; *cin*+*phot* montaje *m*; *mech* junta; **~-grafting** *hort* injerto de empalme; *v* empalmar; montar; juntar; **get ~d (to)** casarse (con)

splicing *cin*+*phot* montaje *m*; **~-kit** estuche *m* de montaje

splint *n* tablilla; **put into** ~s entablillar

splinter *n* astilla; ~ **group** facción *f* de disidentes; *v* astillar(se)

splinterless inastillable

¹ **split** *n* hendidura; (division) división (-ones) *f*; ~ **in the party** división *f* en el partido; **do the** ~s esparrancarse⁴; *adj* hendido; dividido; *v* hender(se); (divide) dividir; (of lips) agrietarse; **Edward and Mary have decided to** ~ **(up)** Eduardo y María han decidido separarse; ~ **hairs** pararse en pelillos; ~ **one's sides** torcerse (ue)¹ᵇ de risa, *vulg sl* descojonarse de risa; ~ **on** *sl* chivarse de; ~ **the atom** desintegrar el átomo; ~ **the difference** partir la diferencia

² **split** (marihuana cigarette) cigarrillo grifado; *sl* petardo

splitting: ~**-up** *n* separación *f*; ~ **head-ache** dolor *m* de cabeza insoportable

splodge, splotch mancha

splurge *n* jactancia; *v* jactarse

splutter *n* balbuceo; (of flame) chisporroteo; *v* balbucear; (of fire) chisporrotear

spoil *n:* ~s despojo; ~s **of power** gajes *mpl* de un cargo público; ~s **of war** trofeos *mpl* de guerra; ~**sman** (*US pol*) miembro de un partido victorioso que acepta un cargo público; *v* estropear(se), *fam* echar(se) a perder; **he spoilt our plans** él chafó nuestros planes; (pamper) mimar; **be** ~**ing for a fight** tener¹⁹ ganas de pelearse; ~ **the fun** aguar⁶ la fiesta, ~**sport** aguafiestas *m sing*

spoilt: ~ **child** niño mimado, niña mimada

spoke rayo; **put a** ~ **in s.o.'s wheel** fastidiar a uno

spokesman portavoz (-ces) *m*

spoliation despojo; *leg* expoliación *f*

spondulicks pasta

¹ **sponge** *n* esponja; (wash) lavado con esponja; **throw up the** ~ darse¹⁹ por vencido; ~**-bag** bolsa de aseo; ~**-cake** bizcocho; ~**-finger** *cul* hueso de santo; *v* lavar(se) con esponja; ~ **up** absorber

² **sponge** (cadge) vivir de gorra; ~ **on** vivir a costa de

sponger sablista *m+f*

sponginess esponjosidad *f*

spongy esponjoso

sponsor *n* patrocinador *m*; *leg* fiador *m*; *rad+TV* costeador *m*; *theat* caballo blanco; *v* patrocinar; ser¹⁹ fiador de; costear; ~ **a project** promover (ue)¹ᵇ un proyecto

sponsorship patrocinio

spontaneity espontaneidad *f*

spontaneous espontáneo; ~ **combustion** combustión espontánea

spoof *n* engaño; broma; *v* engañar con broma(s)

spook fantasma *m*; *fam* coco; *US sl* agente *m* de la C.I.A.

spooky encantado; (frightening) horripilante

spool *n* (textiles + fishing) carrete *m*; (in sewing machine) canilla; (*phot + tape-recorder*) bobina; *phot* rollo; (*US* cotton-reel) bobina; *v* encanillar; enrollar

spoon *n* cuchara; (small) cucharita; *fig* besuqueo; ~**-bait** cucharita; ~**-fed** (of child) que empieza a tomar sólidos, *fig* mimado; *v* ~ **(out)** cucharear; *fig* besuquearse

spoonful cucharada; (small) cucharadita

spoor huella

sporadic esporádico

spore espora

sporran sporran *m*, bolsa escocesa

sport *n* deporte *m*; (game) juego; (pastime) pasatiempo; (fun) broma; (good person) buen chico, buena chica; (good loser) buen perdedor *m*, buena perdedora; **in** ~ en broma; **make** ~ **of** burlarse de; ~s (athletics) juegos *mpl* atléticos; ~s **car** deportivo; ~s **centre** complejo polideportivo; ~s **commentator** comentarista *m+f* de deportes; ~s **cycle** bicicleta de deporte; ~s **day** fiesta de juegos atléticos (de una escuela); ~s **ground** campo de recreo; ~s **jacket** americana; ~**sman** deportista *m*, *fig* persona honrada; ~**smanlike** deportivo, *fig* honrado y leal; ~**smanship** deportividad *f*, *fam* juego limpio; ~s **meeting** juegos *mpl* atléticos; ~s **page** página deportiva; ~s **shirt** camisa de sport; ~s**-wear** trajes *mpl* de deporte; ~**swoman** deportista; *vi* divertirse (ie)²ᶜ; *vt* lucir¹⁵

sporting deportivo; (risky) arriesgado; ~ **chance** posibilidad *f*; ~ **gun** escopeta de caza; ~ **offer** oferta arriesgada; ~ **spirit** espíritu deportivo

sportive juguetón

sporty aficionado a los deportes

spot *n* (place) sitio; (*esp* inhabited place) lugar *m*; (mark) mancha; (pimple) grano; (beauty-~) lunar *m*; (small quantity) poquito; *rad+TV* (advertising space) espacio publicitario; (difficult situation) aprieto; ~ **cash** pago al contado; ~ **on** (well aimed) bien apuntado, (alert) listo; **have a soft ~ for** tener[19] cariño a; **on the ~** (there and then) allí mismo, (immediately) acto continuo, (in danger of death) en peligro de muerte; **blind ~** punto ciego; **tender ~, weak ~** debilidad *f*; **~-ball** (billiards) pinta; **~-remover** quitamanchas *m sing*; **~s before one's eyes** *med* moscas *fpl* volantes; *v* (dirty) manchar; (notice) notar; (pick out) reconocer[14]

spotless limpísimo; +*fig* inmaculado

spotlessness nitidez *f*

spotlight arco; *mot* faro orientable; foco; *fig* luz concentrada; **be in the ~** ser[19] objeto de atención; *v* iluminar; *fig* destacar[4]

spotted (soiled) manchado; ~ **material** tela de/con lunares

spotter observador *m* (*esp* de aviones enemigos); **train-~** aficionado a los trenes

spotting observación *f*

spotty manchado; (pimply) cubierto de granos

spouse esposo, esposa

spout *n* (of vessel) pitorro; (down-~) canalón (-ones) *m*; (jet) chorro; **up the ~** (pawned) empeñado, (pregnant) de compras, (ruined) arruinado; **water-~** tromba de agua; *vi* chorrear; (of whale) soplar; *vt* arrojar a chorros, *fig* declamar

sprain *n* torcedura; *v* torcer (ue)[1b]

sprat arenque pequeño

sprawl (in chair) sentarse (ie)[1a] con las piernas extendidas; (of towns) extenderse (ie)[1b]

[1] **spray** *bot* ramita

[2] **spray** *n* rociada; *naut* espuma; *agri+ hort* pulverizador *m*; (scent ~) atomizador *m*; (aerosol) aerosol *m*; **~-gun** pulverizador *m*; *v* rociar; pulverizar[7]; ~ **the throat** jeringar[5] la garganta

spread *n* extensión *f*; (growth) desarrollo; (of news) difusión *f*; (of branches) ramaje *m*; (wing-span) envergadura; (meal) comilona; **four-column ~** despliegue *m* a cuatro columnas; *v* extender(se)[1b]; (become more popular) popularizarse[7]; (divulge) divulgar(se)[5]; (of seed) sembrar (ie)[2a], *fig* propagar[5]; (of town) ensanchar(se); ~ **one's wings** desplegar[7] las alas; ~ **the butter** untar de/*fam* poner[19] la mantequilla; ~ **o.s.** ponerse[19] a sus anchas, (in speaking) explayarse; ~ **the table** poner[19] la mesa; **~-eagle** (skating) luna, (*US* jingoist) patriotero; **~-eagled** con los miembros extendidos; ~ **about/abroad** divulgar[5]; ~ **out** desplegarse[5], **the six men were ~ out in a semicircle** los hombres estaban desplegados en un semicírculo, (scatter) esparcir(se)[15], (separate) apartarse

spreading extensión *f*; (growing) desarrollo; (of news) difusión *f*; (of knowledge) divulgación *f*

spree parranda; **go on the ~** ir[19] de parranda; **spending-~** derroche *m* de dinero

sprig ramita; *mech* puntilla

sprightliness viveza

sprightly vivo

spring *n* (fountain) manantial *m*; (season) primavera; *mech* muelle *m*; (of watch) resorte *m*; (jump) salto; **with a ~** de un salto; (elasticity) elasticidad *f*; **~-balance** peso de muelle; **~board** trampolín (-ines) *m*; **~-bolt** pestillo de golpe; ~ **chicken** pollo pequeño; **~-clean** hacer limpieza general; **~-cleaning** limpieza general; ~ **fever** fiebre *f* de la primavera; **~-gun** trampa de escopeta y alambre; **~-latch** picaporte *m*; **~-like** primaveral; **~-mattress** colchón *m* de muelles; **~ onion** cebolleta; ~ **tide** aguas *fpl* vivas; **~-time** primavera; **~-washer** arandela de muelle; *v* (jump) saltar; ~ **a criminal** soltar a un presidiario; ~ **a leak** empezar (ie)[2a+7] a hacer agua; ~ **open** abrirse (*past part* abierto) de repente; ~ **a surprise on** dar[19] una sor-

presa a; ~ **a trap** tender (ie)[2b] un lazo
(on a); ~ **to mind** occurrírsele a uno;
~ **to one's feet** ponerse[19] de pie de un
salto

~ **at** precipitarse sobre

~-**back** n libro (de cuentas) con lomo
plegado

~ **back** v saltar hacia atrás

~ **forth** brotar

~ **from** provenir (ie)[19] de; **where did she
~ from?** ¿de dónde ha salido ella?

~ **over** saltar, **he sprang over it** él lo saltó

~ **up** (stand up) ponerse[19] de pie de un
salto; (grow quickly) crecer[14] rápidamente; **bot** brotar; (of wind) levantarse; (of problems) surgir[9]

springbok zool gacela del Cabo; (person) deportista m+f de África del Sur

springiness elasticidad f

springy elástico; (of turf) muelle

sprinkle n rociada; v rociar (**with** de); ~
with holy water asperjar con agua
bendita

sprinkler regadera; aspersor m; eccles
hisopo; ~-**system** instalación f de aspersión automática

sprinkling rociada; +eccles aspersión f;
a ~ of fig unos cuantos

sprint n (e)sprint m; v (e)sprintar

sprinter esprínter m

sprite hada

sprocket rueda dentada; ~-**wheel** rueda
de cadena

sprout n retoño; ~s coles fpl de
Bruselas; vi brotar; bot+zool vt
salirle[19]; **it's ~ing wings** le salen las
alas

[1] **spruce** bot picea

[2] **spruce** adj peripuesto; fam pimpante; v
~ **up** ponerse[19] peripuesto/fam pimpante

spry ágil

spud patata; SA papa

spunk coraje m; vulg huevos mpl

spunky valiente

spur n espuela; (of cock) espolón
(-ones) m;fig estímulo; **on the ~ of the
moment** sin pensarlo; **win one's ~s**
distinguirse[11]; v espolear; ~ **on** animar

spurious espurio; (of writings) apócrifo

spuriousness falsedad f

spurn desdeñar

spurt n (jet) chorro; fig esfuerzo su-

premo; v salir[19] a chorros; fig hacer[19]
un esfuerzo supremo

sputnik sputnik m

spy n espía m+f; ~-**glass** catalejo; ~-
hole mirilla; vi ser[19] espía; vt (notice)
divisar; ~ **on** espiar; ~ **out** explorar;
~ **out the lie of the land** ver[19] como
está el patio

spying espionaje m

squabble n riña; v reñir (i)[3]

squabbler pendenciero (-a f)

squabbling riñas fpl

squad pelotón (-ones) m

squaddie mil soldado raso

squadron escuadrón (-ones) m; aer
escuadrilla; naut escuadra; ~-**leader**
comandante m (de las fuerzas aéreas)

squalid (dirty) escuálido; (despicable)
mezquino

squall n (noise) chillido; (storm) ráfaga,
fig tempestad f; v chillar

squally borrascoso; fig chillón

squalor (dirt) escualidez f; fig mezquindad f

squander despilfarrar (**on** en); ~-**bug** derrochón m (-ona f)

squanderer despilfarrador m (-ora f)

square n geom cuadrado; (in town)
plaza, (small) plazoleta; (scarf) pañuelo; carp+mech escuadra; (on
chess-board) escaque m; (on graph
paper) casilla; mil (defensive formation) cuadro; fam (person) carroza
m+f; ~ **knot** nudo llano; ~ **measure**
medida de superficie; ~-**bashing** instrucción f militar; adj cuadrado; (fair)
equitativo; (old-fashioned) carroza
invar; ~ (**to**) (at a right-angle to) en
ángulo recto (con); **be all ~** estar[19] en
paz; **get ~** (with) desquitarse con; **two
metres ~** dos metros en cuadro; **two ~
metres** dos metros cuadrados; **the
account is ~** la cuenta está justa; ~
bracket corchete m; ~ **dance** baile m
de figuras; ~ **deal** buen trato; ~-**head
pej** teutón m (-ona f); ~ **meal** comida
completa; ~-**necked** de cuello cuadrado; ~ **peg in a round hole** culo mal
asentado; ~-**rigged** de cruz; ~ **root**
raíz (-ces) cuadrada; ~ **sail** vela de
cruz; ~-**shouldered** de hombros
cuadrados; ~-**toed** (of shoes) de
puntera cuadrada; v +math cuadrar;
carp+mech escuadrar; (bribe)

sobornar; ~ **the circle** cuadrar el
círculo; ~ **one's shoulders** cuadrarse;
I'll ~ it up with him lo ajustaré con él;
~ **up accounts** *fig* saldar las cuentas; ~
up to avanzar[7] con amenazas hacia;
~**d paper** papel cuadriculado

squarely en cuadro; (directly) directamente; (honestly) honradamente;
(unambiguously) sin ambigüedades

squareness cuadratura; (honesty) honradez *f*

[1] **squash** *n* (drink) zumo (de. limón *etc*);
(crush) apiñamiento; *vt* aplastar; ~
together *vi* aplastarse

[2] **squash** (gourd) calabaza

[3] **squash** squash *m*; ~-**court** frontón
(-ones) *m*

squat *adj* (desproporcionadamente)
bajo; (of people) rechoncho; *v* ponerse[19] en cuclillas; (on property)
ocupar[14] ilegalmente

squatter ocupante *m+f* ilegal; persona
que ocupa un sitio ilegalmente

squaw india norteamericana

squawk *n* graznido; *fam* protesta; *v*
graznar; *fam* protestar

squeak *n* chirrido; (of mouse *etc*) chillido; **have a narrow ~** escaparse por
un pelo; *v* chirriar; chillar

squeal chillido; *v* chillar; *sl* (inform,
under interrogation) cantar; (inform,
in return for money) soplar

squealer (informer) soplón *m* (-ona *f*)

squealing chillidos *mpl*

squeamish (finicky) remilgado; (nause-
ated) asqueado

squeamishness remilgos *mpl*

squeegee secacristales *m sing+pl*; *phot*
exprimidor *m* de rodillo

squeeze *n* estrujón (-ones) *m*; (of hand)
apretón (-ones) *m*; *comm* restricción *f*
de crédito; **it's a bit of a ~ in here** no
hay mucho sitio aquí adentro; **be in a
tight ~** estar[19] en un aprieto; *v* estrujar; (hard) apretar (ie)[2a]; ~ **a
lemon** exprimir un limón; ~ **money
from** sangrar

~ **in** (hacer[19]) entrar con un esfuerzo;
you can ~ in between us two hay sitio
para usted entre nosotros dos

~ **out** exprimir

~ **through** pasar con un esfuerzo por

squeezer exprimidor *m*

squelch *n* chapoteo; *vi* andar[19] chapo-

teando; *vt* despachurrar

squib buscapiés *m sing+pl*; **damp ~** *fig*
fracaso

squid calamar *m*

squint *n* estrabismo; *fam* mirada bizca;
(quick look) vistazo, **take a ~ at** echar
un vistazo a; *v* bizquear; *fam* torcer
(ue)[1b] la vista; (screw up one's eyes)
mirar con los ojos casi cerrados; ~ **at**
mirar de soslayo

squire escudero; (landowner) terrateniente *m*, hacendado; (*US* magistrate) juez (-ces) *m* de paz

squirearchy caciquismo

squirm *n* retorcimiento; *v* retorcerse
(ue)[1b+14]; ~ **along** arrastrarse

squirrel ardilla

squirt *n* (jet) chorro; (syringe) jeringa;
little ~ *sl* mierdica; *vi* salir[19] a chorros;
vt arrojar a chorros; (with syringe)
inyectar (con jeringa)

S.R.N. (State Registered Nurse) enfermera titulada

S.S. (screw steamer/steamship) v. (vapor *m*)

S.S.E. (south-south-east) S.S.E. (sudsudeste) *m*

S.S.W. (south-south-west) S.S.O. (sudsudoeste) *m*

St (Saint) S (Santo, San), Sta (Santa)

stab *n* puñalada; (of pain) pinchazo;
fam tentativa; **have a ~ at** intentar
+*infin*; ~ **in the back** puñalada por la
espalda; ~-**wound** herida punzante; *v*
apuñalar, *sl* pinchar

stability estabilidad *f*; **economic ~** estabilización económica

stabilization estabilización *f*

stabilize estabilizar[7]

stabilizer estabilizador *m*

[1] **stable** *n* (building) cuadra; (horses)
caballeriza; ~-**boy** mozo de cuadra; *v*
poner[19] en una cuadra

[2] **stable** *adj* estable

staccato *mus* staccato

stack *n* montón (-ones) *m*; (hay-~)
almiar *m*; (chimney-~) cañón (-ones)
m (de la chimenea); (of rifles) pabellón (-ones) *m*; ~**s of** muchos, muchas; *v* amontonar; (hay *etc*) hacinar;
~ **the cards** disponer[19] los naipes para
hacer trampa; **have the cards ~ed
against one** estar[19] en una situación
desventajosa

stadium estadio

¹ **staff** n (stick) bastón (-ones) m; (**flag-~**) asta; *eccles* báculo; *mus* pentagrama m; *fig* apoyo

² **staff** n (plantilla de) personal; (of school *etc*) profesorado; (servants) servidumbre f; *mil* estado mayor; **~-room** (in school) sala de profesores; v proveer[17] de personal; **short-~ed** con personal insuficiente

stag ciervo; *comm* especulador m; **~-beetle** escarabajo cornudo; **~hound** perro de caza; **~-party** tertulia para hombres; despedida de soltero

stage n plataforma; *theat* escena, *fam* las tablas; (of space rocket) cuerpo; (stop) parada; (point in time) estado, **at the present ~** en el estado actual; (phase) etapa, **in ~s** por etapas; **in easy ~s** en cortas etapas; **come/go on ~** salir[19] a la escena; **go on the ~** hacerse[19] actor/actriz, *fam* hacer[19] tablas; **~-box** palco de proscenio; **~ coach** diligencia; **~-craft** arte m teatral; **~ direction** acotación f; **~-door** entrada de artistas; **~-fright** miedo escénico; **~-hand** tramoyista m; **~-manager** director m de escena; **~-whisper** aparte m; v *theat* representar; (recovery *etc*) efectuar; (demonstration) organizar[7]

stager: old ~ veterano, veterana

stagger n tambaleo; v tambalear; (space out) escalonar; (amaze) asombrar; vi tambalearse

staggering tambaleante; (amazing) asombroso

staging (scaffolding) andamio; *theat* producción (-ones) f

stagnant +*fig* estancado; *comm* inactivo

stagnate estancarse[4]; *comm* paralizarse[7]

stagnation estancamiento; *comm* paralización f

stagy teatral

staid serio

stain n +*fig* mancha; (dye) tinte m; **~-remover** quitamanchas m *sing*; v +*fig* manchar(se); (dye) teñir(se) (i)[3+18]

stained: ~ glass vidrio de colores

stainless inmanchable; *fig* inmaculado; **~ steel** acero inoxidable

stair escalón (-ones) m; **~s, ~case, ~way** escalera; **flight of ~s** tramo de escaleras; **~-carpet** alfombra de escalera; **~-rod** varilla para alfombra de escalera

stake n estaca, poste m; (bet) apuesta; *comm* interés (-eses) m; **~s** (prize) premio, (at cards) valor m, (race) carrera; **at ~** en juego; **be burnt at the ~** morir (ue)[1c] en la hoguera; **pull up ~s** mudar de casa; v (mark with ~s) estacar[4]; (bet) apostar (ue)[1a] (on a); *comm* aventurar; **~ a claim** hacer[19] una reclamación (to a); **~ one's all** jugarse (ue)[1a+5] el todo por el todo; **a plant** rodrigar[5] una planta; **~ out** jalonar

stalactite estalactita

stalagmite estalagmita

stale no fresco; (sour) rancio; (of bread) duro; (of tobacco) pasado; (of wine) picado; (of atmosphere) viciado; (of fashion) pasado de moda; (of jokes) trillado; (of news) viejo; **feel ~** estar[19] cansado; **~mate** (chess) mate ahogado, *fig* punto muerto, **reach a ~-mate** *fig* llegar[5] a un punto muerto

staleness (sourness) ranciedad f; (of bread) dureza; (of news) falta de novedad

Stalinism estalinismo

Stalinist n+adj estalinista m+f

¹ **stalk** *bot* tallo; (of cabbage) troncho

² **stalk** vi andar[19] con majestuosidad; vt (game) cazar[7] al acecho; (a person) seguir (i)[3+11] los pasos a

stall n (stable) pesebre m; (in market) puesto; (at fair) barraca; *eccles* sillería; *theat* butaca; **~-fed** cebado en establo; **finger-~** dedal m; vt (horse *etc*) encerrar (ie)[2a] en establo; *mot* parar accidentalmente, (delay) hacer[19] esperar; vi *mot* pararse; *aer* perder (ie)[2b] velocidad; (delay) buscar[4] evasivas; **~ for time** alargar[5] el asunto (para ganar tiempo); **stop/quit stalling!** ¡déjate de rodeos!

stalling *mot* parada accidental; *aer* pérdida de velocidad

stallion caballo semental

stalwart n partidario fiel; *adj* (muscular) fornido; (loyal) fiel

stamen estambre m

stamina resistencia

stammer n tartamudeo; v tartamudear

stammerer tartamudo

stammering n tartamudeo; adj tartamudo

stamp n (postage) sello, SA estampilla;
leg (on document) timbre m; mech
cuño; (rubber-~) estampilla; (with
foot) pisada fuerte; fig (kind) temple
m; fig (sign) sello; ~**-album** álbum
m para sellos/SA estampillas; ~-
collecting filatelia; ~**-collection** colección f de sellos/SA estampillas; ~-
collector filatelista m+f; ~**-duty**
impuesto del timbre; ~**-hinge** fijase-
llos m sing+pl; ~**-machine** expendedor automático de sellos/SA
estampillas; ~**-pad** almohadilla; vt
(put ~s on) poner[19] sello a; (mark)
franquear; (documento) estampar; (a
coin) acuñar; ~ **one's foot** patear; ~
on pisar; ~ **out** (fire) apagar[5] pisando,
fig suprimir; vi patear; (expressing
disapproval) patalear; (horse) piafar;
~**ed envelope** sobre franqueado

stampede n (of animals) estampida; (of
people) fuga precipitada; vi huir[16] en
desorden; vt hacer[19] huir en desorden,
fig hacer[19] perder la cabeza (a)

stance postura

stanchion bui puntal m; naut candelero;
(of cart) telero

stand n (platform) estrado; (stall)
puesto, quiosco; (at exhibition) stand
m; (pedestal) pedestal m; (of table-
lamp, standard-lamp) pie m; (shelf)
estante m; mech sostén (-enes) m; sp
tribuna; (for taxis) parada; (witness-
box) estrado, **take the** ~ subir al estrado; (position) postura, **take a** ~
adoptar una postura; (opinion) opinión f; (resistance) resistencia, **make
a** ~ **(against)** resistir (a); ~ **on** fig basar
sus argumentos sobre; **take a firm** ~
mantenerse[19] firme; ~**-pipe** tubo de la
boca de riego; ~**point** punto de vista;
~**still** parada; **be at a** ~**still** estar[19]
parado; **come to a** ~**still** pararse,
paralizarse[7]

vi (be standing) estar[19] de pie; (of
things) estar[19] (situado); (~ up) ponerse[19] de pie; (remain) quedarse;
(remain in force) mantenerse[19] en
vigor; (endure) (per)durar; (stop)
pararse; (measure) medir (i)[3]; (place
o.s.) colocarse[4], ponerse[19]; pol presentarse como candidato; **in the park**

~**s a statue** en el parque se levanta una
estatua; ~ **aloof** mantenerse[19] apartado; ~ **at/to attention** cuadrarse; ~ **at
ease!** ¡en su lugar descansen!; ~ **fast**
no ceder; ~ **firm** mantenerse[19] firme;
~ **in good stead** ser[19] útil; ~ **on one's
own feet** valerse[19] por sí mismo; ~ **on
tiptoe** estar[19]/ponerse[19] de puntillas;
~ **pat** seguir (i)[3+11] en sus trece; ~ **still**
estarse[19] quieto; ~ **straight** ponerse[19]
derecho; **how do we** ~? ¿cómo estamos?; ~ **in need of** necesitar; ~ **on end**
erizarse[7]; **don't** ~ **on ceremony!** ¡no
gaste cumplidos!; ~ **to lose/win** tener[19]
probabilidad de perder/ganar; **it** ~**s to
reason** es lógico

~ **aside** apartarse

~ **back** retroceder; (be at the rear) estar[19] detrás

~**-by** n recurso; aer lista de espera; adj
de reserva

~ **by** v estar[19] cerca; (be ready) estar[19]
alerta; aer estar en la lista de espera;
(abide by) atenerse[19] a; **I'll** ~ **by you
whatever happens** no te abandonaré
pase lo que pase; ~ **by!** ¡listos!

~ **down** retirarse

~ **for** (represent) representar; (mean)
significar[4]; (put up with) aguantar

~**-in** n sustituto; cin+theat doble m+f

~ **in** v naut acercarse[4] (to a); ~ **in for** suplir a; ~ **in with** declararse por

~**-off** adj: ~**-off half** sp medio de
apertura

~ **off** v apartarse

~**-offish** etiquetero

~**-offishness** altanería

~ **out** (stick out) sobresalir[19]; ~ **out
against** destacarse[4] contra, (oppose)
oponerse[19] a; ~ **out for** no ceder hasta
obtener; ~ **out to sea** hacerse[19] a la
mar

~ **over** quedar aplazado

~ **to** mil estar[19] sobre las armas

~ **together** mantenerse[19] unidos

~**-up** n sl plantón (-ones) m; adj violento, ~**-up fight** pelea violenta

~ **up** v levantarse, ponerse[19] de pie; **she
stood me up** sl ella me dio plantón; ~
up for defender (ie)[2b]; ~ **up to** resistir
a; ~ **up to the test** salir[19] muy bien de la
prueba; ~ **up to wear** ser[19] duradero

vt (place) colocar[4]; (place upright) poner[19] derecho; (bear) soportar, fam

tragar⁵, **I can't stand Raphael's songs**
no trago las canciones de Raphael; **she
can't ~ me** ella no me puede ver; **~ a
chance** tener¹⁹ posibilidades de éxito;
~ one's ground defender su posición
f; **~ investigation** salir bien de la investigación; **~ the test** salir¹⁹ muy bien de
la prueba; **~ the test of time** perdurar;
I'll ~ you a drink te invito a beber
standard *n* (flag) estandarte *m*;
(upright) poste *m*; (for weights *etc*)
norma; (convention) convención
(-ones) *f*; (model) modelo; (type of
tree) árbol *m* en forma natural; **by
today's ~s** a nuestro sentir de hoy; **~
English** inglés correcto; **up to European ~** a nivel europeo; **~ of living**
nivel de vida; **gold ~** patrón *m* (de)
oro; **~-bearer** abanderado, *fig* caudillo; **~-lamp** lámpara vertical; *adj*
normal, corriente; **~ gauge** (railway)
vía normal; **~ make** fabricación *f* corriente; **~ measure** medida tipo; **~
model** modelo standard; **~ packing**
envase normalizado, **~ practice** fórmula habitual; **~ time** hora oficial; **~
type** tipo corriente; **~ wage** salario
base; **~ work** obra clásica
standardization estandarización *f*
standardize estandarizar⁷; **~d production** producción *f* en serie
standing *n* reputación *f*; (quality)
categoría; (of long ago) antigüedad *f*;
of long ~ antiguo; **~-room** sitio para
estar de pie; *adj* en/de pie; **~ army**
ejército permanente; **~ committee**
comité *m* permanente; **~ grievance**
agravio constante; **~ order** orden *f*
vigente, *mil* reglamento; **~ start** *sp*
salida parada
stannic estannífero
stanza estancia
¹ **staple** *m* grapa; *v* sujetar con grapa(s)
² **staple** producto principal; (raw material) materia prima; (textile grade)
fibra textil; *adj* principal; (usual) corriente; **~ commodities** artículos *mpl*
de consumo corriente
stapler grapadora
star *n* astron estrella; *cin+theat* (male)
astro, (female) estrella; *sp* as *m*, estrella; *print* asterisco; **be born under a
lucky ~** tener¹⁹ buena estrella; **see ~s**
ver¹⁹ las estrellas; **five-pointed ~** es-

trella de cinco puntas; **North Star** estrella del norte; **Stars and Stripes** estrellas y barras; **~fish** estrella de mar;
~gazer observador *m* (-ora *f*) de las
estrellas, *fig* distraído; **~gazing** observación *f* de las estrellas, *fig* distracción
f; **~light** luz (-ces) *f* de las estrellas;
~lit iluminado por las estrellas; **~-
spangled** sembrado de estrellas; **Star-
Spangled Banner** bandera de los
Estados Unidos; **~-studded programme** programa *m* estelar; **~ turn**
atracción *f* estelar; *vi cin+theat*
protagonizar⁷; *vt* adornar con estrellas; *cin+theat* presentar como protagonista; *print* señalar con asterisco
starboard *n* estribor *m*; *adj* de estribor
starch *n* almidón *m*; *biol* fécula; **~-
reduced** menos feculento; *v* almidonar
starchiness (of food) feculencia; *fig* (of
people) estiramiento
stardom *cin+theat+TV* estrellato
starchy feculento; (of people) estirado
stare *n* mirada fija; *v* **~ (at)** mirar
fijamente; **it's staring you in the face**
fig está delante de sus narices
staring que mira fijamente; **~ eyes** ojos
mpl saltones
stark (stiff) rígido; (complete) completo; **~ naked** en cueros, *fam* en
pelota; **~ staring mad** loco de atar
starkers en pelota
starless sin estrellas
starlet *cin* estrella joven
starling estornino
starring que presenta como protagonista
starry estrellado; **~-eyed** inocentón
start *n* principio, comienzo; (of race)
salida; (starting-point) *sp* arrancadero; (advantage) ventaja; (when
startled) sobresalto, (of horse) respingo; **by/in fits and ~s** a saltos, (at intervals) a ratos; **for a ~** para empezar;
give a ~ (of surprise) sobresaltarse;
give a five metres' ~ dar¹⁹ una ventaja
de cinco metros; *vt* empezar (ie)²ᵃ⁺⁷,
comenzar (ie)²ᵃ⁺⁷; (cause) causar, **~ a
fire** causar un incendio; (initiate)
iniciar; *mot* arrancar⁴; (game)
levantar; **~ a conversation** entablar
una conversación; **~ a fashion**
inventar una moda; **~ a new line!** (in

dictation) ¡aparte!; ~ **a race** dar[4] la señal de salida; *vi* empezar (ie)[2a+7], comenzar (ie)[2a+7]; (depart) ponerse[19] en camino; (in race) salir[19]; (jump) sobresaltarse

~ **back** emprender el viaje de regreso

~ **off** empezar (ie)[2a+7]; (journey) ponerse[19] en camino; (race) salir[19]

~ **to** ponerse[19] a +*infin*

~ **up** ponerse[19] en marcha

starter *mot* (botón *m* de) arranque *m*; *sp* (judge) juez *m* de salida, *fam* stárter *m*; (competitor) competidor *m*; *cul* entrantes *mpl*

starting *n* (beginning) principio; ~-**handle** manivela de arranque; ~-**judge** juez *m* de salida; ~-**point** punto de partida; ~-**post** poste *m* de salida; ~-**rate** (of pay) sueldo inicial; ~ **signal** señal *f* de partida; ~-**switch** botón (-ones) *m* de arranque

startle asustar

startling alarmante

starvation hambre *f*; *med* inanición *f*; ~ **diet** régimen *m* de hambre; ~ **wage(s)** ración *f* de hambre

starve *vi* morir (ue)[1c] de hambre; *fig* tener[19] mucha hambre; *vt* matar de hambre; *fig* privar de alimento; ~ **out** hacer[19] rendirse por hambre

stash guardar en un escondite

state *n* +*pol* estado; (pomp) pompa, **in** ~ con (gran) pompa; **lie in** ~ estar[19] de cuerpo presente; ~ **of emergency** estado de excepción; ~ **of weightlessness** estado de ingravidez; **be in a** ~ *fam* estar[19] aturrullado; *US* **State Department** Ministerio de Asuntos Exteriores; ~**craft** arte *m* de gobernar; ~**room** camarote *m*, (*US* reception-room) salón *m* de recepción; ~**sman** estadista *m*; ~**smanlike** (propio) de estadista; ~**smanship** arte *m* de gobernar; *adj* del estado; ~ **control** dirigismo estatal; ~ **education/school** educación *f*/escuela pública; ~ **occasion** función *f* de gala; *v* declarar; *leg* formular; (a problem) plantear; **at** ~**d intervals** a intervalos fijos; **on the** ~**d date** en la fecha indicada

stateless desnacionalizado

statelessness desnacionalización *f*

stateliness majestad *f*

stately majestuoso; ~ **home** casa solariega

statement declaración *f*; *leg* deposición *f*; ~ **of account** estado de cuentas

static estático; *fig* estancado

station *n* estación *f*; (railway) estación *f* (de ferrocarril); (police) comisaría; *mil* base *f* militar; *naut* apostadero naval; *rad* emisora; (rank) condición *f*; ~ **in life** posición *f* social; **stations of the Cross** estaciones *fpl* de Vía Crucis; ~-**master** jefe *m* de estación; ~-**wagon** rubia; *v* colocar[4]; *mil* destinar; (park) estacionar

stationary (fixed) estacionario; (not moving) inmóvil; (parked) estacionado; ~ **engine** máquina fija

stationer papelero, papelera; ~'s papelería

stationery papel *m* de escribir

statistical estadístico

statistician estadístico

statistics (science) estadística; (data) datos *mpl* estadísticos

statuary *n* (person) estatuario; (art) estatuaria; (statues) estatuas *fpl*; *adj* estatuario

statue estatua

statuesque escultural

statuette figurina

stature estatura

status (state) estado; (position) posición *f* social; ~ **symbol** símbolo de posición social

statute estatuto; ~ **law** derecho escrito

statutory estatutario

staunch *adj* leal; *v* restañar

stave *n* (of barrel) duela; *mus* pentagrama *m*; *v* ~ **in** (barrel) romper (*past part* roto); ~ **off** evitar

stay *n* (sojourn) estancia; (short) visita; *leg* suspensión (-ones) *f*, aplazamiento; *mech* sostén (-enes) *m*; *naut* estay *m*; ~ **sail** vela de estay; ~**s** corsé *m*; ~-**at-home** *n* persona casera; *vt* detener[19]; *leg* suspender, aplazar[7]; *mech* sostener[19]; ~ **the course** terminar la carrera; ~ **hunger** matar el hambre; ~ **one's hand** contenerse[19]; *vi* (remain) quedar(se); (lodge) hospedarse (at en); **come to** ~ venir[19] a ser permanente, (of visitor) venir[19] a quedarse; ~ **put** quedarse en su sitio

~ **away** ausentarse; (not return) no volver (ue)[1b] (*past part* vuelto)

~ **behind** quedarse

~-**in:** ~-**in strike** huelga en el lugar del trabajo

~ **in** *v* quedarse en casa; ~ **in bed** guardar cama

~ **on** quedarse

~ **out** quedarse fuera; *fig* no tomar parte (of en)

~ **up** no acostarse (ue)[1a]; ~ **up late** acostarse (ue)[1a] tarde; *aer* no bajar

stayer (horse) caballo apto para carreras largas; *fig* persona capaz de un esfuerzo largo

S.T.D. (Subscriber Trunk Dialling) sistema telefónico directo

stead: stand s.o. in good ~ serle[19] útil a alguien; **in his** ~ en su lugar

steadfast constante

steadfastly con constancia

steadfastness constancia

steadily (firmly) firmemente; (stably) establemente; (assiduously) diligentemente; (unwaveringly) constantemente; **I looked** ~ **at him** le miré sin pestañear

steadiness (firmness) firmeza; (stability) estabilidad *f*; (assiduity) regularidad *f*; (constancy) constancia; (of people) seriedad *f*

steady *n* (boy/girl-friend) novio, novia; *adj* (firm) firme; (stable) estable; (uniform) uniforme; (uninterrupted) ininterrumpido; (assiduous) aplicado; (reliable) juicioso; (unwavering) constante; *comm* en calma; ~ **job** empleo seguro; ~ **price** precio estable; ~ **rain** lluvia continua; ~ **rise** subida continua; *v* estabilizar[7]; (nerves) calmar; **she steadied herself against the door** ella se apoyó en la puerta

steak (meat) tajada, filete *m*; bi(f)stec *m*; (fish) tajada

steal *vt* robar (from a); *sl* birlar, *Arg sl* afanar; ~ **a kiss** robar un beso; ~ **a look at** mirar de soslayo; ~ **a march on** obtener[19] una ventaja sobre; ~ **the show** ganar todos los aplausos; *vi* ~ **away/off** escabullirse; (move furtively) andar[19] furtivamente

stealing robo; **that's not** ~ eso no es robar

stealth cautela; **by** ~ **a** hurtadillas

stealthy cauteloso, furtivo

steam *n* vapor *m*; **full** ~ **ahead** a todo

vapor; **get up** ~ hacer[19] subir la presión; **let off** ~ *mech* descargar[5] vapor, *fig* desahogarse; ~-**engine** máquina de vapor; ~-**hammer** martillo pilón; ~-**power** energía de vapor; ~-**radio** radio *f* (comparada con la televisión); ~-**roller** *n* apisonadora; *v fig* aplastar; ~-**ship** (buque *m* de) vapor *m*; ~-**shovel** excavadora; ~-**whistle** silbato de vapor; *vt cul* cocinar al vapor; **he** ~-**ed the letter open** él abrió la carta con vapor; *vi* (emit ~) echar vapor; (function by ~) funcionar a vapor; ~ **along** marchar sin contratiempo

steamer *cul* olla de vapor; *naut* (buque *m* de) vapor

steamy lleno de vapor

steed corcel *m*

steel *n* acero; (sharpener) afilón *m*; **cold** ~ arma blanca; **stainless** ~ acero inoxidable; ~-**clad**, ~-**plated** revestido de acero; ~-**engraving** grabado en acero; ~ **industry** industria siderúrgica; ~-**works** fábrica siderúrgica; ~-**yard** romana; *adj* de acero; ~ **wool** limaduras *fpl* de acero; *v metal* acerar; ~ **o.s.** fortalecerse[14]; **you must** ~ **yourself to tell him** usted tiene que decidirse a decírselo

steely acerado; ~ **look** mirada fría

[1] **steep** *adj* escarpado; (of stairs) empinado; ~ **prices** precios *mpl* exorbitantes

[2] **steep** *n* remojo; **in** ~ en/a remojo; *v* remojar

steeple aguja; ~-**chase** carrera de obstáculos, (horse-race) carrera de vallas; ~-**jack** reparador *m* de chimeneas

steepness lo escarpado; (of stairs) lo empinado

[1] **steer** *n* novillo

[2] **steer** *v mot* conducir[15], *fam* guiar; *naut* gobernar (ie)[2a]; ~ **clear of** evitar; ~ **for** dirigirse a; ~-**sman** timonero

steerage (quarters) entrepuente *m*; (stern) popa; (steering) gobierno; **travel** ~ viajar en tercera clase; ~-**way** empuje *m* (necesario para gobernar un buque)

steering dirección *f*; *naut* gobierno; ~-**column** columna de dirección; ~-**wheel** *mot* volante *m*; *naut* rueda del timón

stellar estelar

¹ **stem** n (of plant) tallo; (of tree) tronco; (of pipe) cañón (-ones) m; (of wine-glass) pie m; gramm tema m; mech vástago; v ~ **from** resultar de

² **stem** n naut tajamar m; **from ~ to stern** de proa a popa

³ **stem** v (stop the flow of) represar; fig contener¹⁹

stemmed: long-~, short-~ de tallo largo/corto

stench hedor m

stencil n estarcido; metal patrón picado; (typing) cliché m; v estarcir¹³

stenographer taquígrafo (-a f)

stenography taquigrafía

stentorian estentóreo

¹ **step** n paso; (stair) escalón m; (rung) peldaño; (of carriage) estribo; fig (measure) medida, paso; ~**s** (ladder) escalera de tijera; (**flight of**) ~**s** escalera; ~ **by** ~ paso a paso; **as a first** ~ como primer paso; **at every** ~ a cada paso; **by such** ~**s** con tales medidas; **in** ~ (**with**) llevando el paso (de), (of music) al compás (de), fig de acuerdo (con); **take** ~**s** (**to**) tomar medidas (para) + infin; **watch one's** ~ ir¹⁹ con cuidado; ~-**ladder** escalera de tijera; v (take a ~) dar¹⁹ un paso; (walk) andar¹⁹; (tread) pisar

~ **aside** hacerse¹⁹ a un lado

~ **back** retroceder

~ **down** bajar, fig ceder su puesto (**in favour of** a)

~ **forward** n adelanto; v adelantarse

~ **in** entrar; (intervene) intervenir¹⁹

~ **inside** entrar; ~ **inside!** ¡pase!

~ **on** pisar; ~ **on it!** (hurry) ¡date prisa!, mot acelerar

~ **out** (walk faster) apretar el paso; (go out) salir¹⁹

~ **outside** salir¹⁹

~-**up** n (promotion) ascenso; (increase) aumento

~ **up** v aumentar

² **step:** ~**brother** hermanastro; ~**child** hijastro (-a f); ~**daughter** hijastra; ~**father** padrastro; ~**mother** madrastra; ~**sister** hermanastra; ~**son** hijastro

Stephen Esteban

steppe estepa

stepping: ~-**stone** pasadera, fig esca-

lón m

stereo(phonic) estereofónico; ~ **film** película estereofónica

stereoscope estereoscopio

stereoscopic estereoscópico; cin tridimensional

stereotype n estereotipo; v estereotipar

sterile estéril; fig improductivo

sterility esterilidad f

sterilization esterilización f

sterilize esterilizar⁷

sterilizer med+surg esterilizador m

sterling esterlina; fig excelente; **one pound** ~ una libra esterlina; ~ **silver** plata de ley

¹ **stern** n popa; ~ **post** barra del cabrestante; ~ **wheel** aer rueda de cola

² **stern** adj severo

sternly con severidad

sternness severidad f

sternum esternón m

stertorous estertor (-ora f)

stethoscope estetoscopio

stevedore estibador m

stew n estofado; cocido; **be in a** ~ sudar la gota gorda; v estofar; (fruit) hacer compota; (tea) posarse; ~ **in one's own juice** fig aguantarse y callar; ~-**pot** cazuela; ~**ed fruit** compota (de fruta)

steward n mayordomo; (manager) administrador m; aer aeromozo; naut camarero; (at race meeting) comisario

stewardess aer azafata, aeromoza; naut camarera

Stewart Estuardo

stewed cocido

¹ **stick** n palo; (stake) estaca; (walking-stick) bastón (-ones) m; (blind man's) tiento; (of office) vara; (baton) batuta; (of toffee, sealing-wax etc) barra; (of chalk) barrita; (of celery) tallo; ~**s** (firewood) leña(s), (hurdles) vallas fpl; (US outskirts) afueras fpl; **in a cleft** ~ entre la espada y la pared; **give s.o. the** ~ darle¹⁹ palos a uno; **have/get hold of the wrong end of the** ~ entender (ie)²ᵇ al revés; **big** ~ **policy** política del gran garrote

² **stick** vt clavar (**into** en); (put) meter (**into** en); (adhere) pegar;⁵ ~ **bills** fijar carteles; **I can't** ~ **her** no la puedo ver; vi clavarse; (adhere) pegarse⁵; (get

stuck) quedarse cogido; (in mud *etc*) atascarse⁴; (stay) quedarse; (at cards) estar¹⁹ servido, **I ~** estoy servido, **~ to the facts** ceñirse (i)³⁺¹⁸ a los hechos; **the words stuck in his throat** las palabras se ahogaron en su garganta; **make something ~** *fig* justificar⁴ algo; **we must ~ together** debemos quedarnos unidos; **the name stuck (to her)** se le quedó (a ella) el apodo; **~ fast** quedarse clavado

~ around esperar por ahí

~ at nothing no tener¹⁹ escrúpulos

~ by (stay near) quedarse cerca de; (be loyal) ser¹⁹ fiel a

~-in-the-mud retrógrado

~-on *adj* engomado; **~-on label** etiqueta engomada, (on luggage) etiqueta con la dirección

~ out *vi* sobresalir¹⁹; **it ~s out a mile** es obvio; *vt* sacar⁴, **~ out one's tongue** sacar⁴ la lengua; **do not ~ your head out of the window!** ¡no se asome a la ventana!; **~ it out!** ¡aguántalo hasta el final!; **~ one's neck out** arriesgarse⁵; **~ out for** no ceder hasta lograr

~ to (persevere) perseverar; (adhere) pegarse⁵ a; (maintain) atenerse¹⁹ a

~-up *n* atraco

~ up *vi* asomarse por encima; (of hair) estar¹⁹ de punta; **~ up for** defender (ie)²ᵇ; *vt* (with gun) atracar⁴; **~ up your hands!** ¡levanta las manos!; **~ up one's nose at** despreciar; **~ it up your jumper!** *vulg* ¡métetelo donde te quepa!

sticker (label) pegote *m*, *usu pol* pegatina; (person) persona perseverante

stickiness pegajosidad *f*

sticking-plaster esparadrapo; *fam* tirita

stickleback espinoso

stickler rigorista *m+f*

sticky pegajoso, *fig* difícil; **~ paper** papel *m* engomado; **bat/be on a ~ wicket** estar¹⁹ en una situación difícil; **come to a ~ end** terminar mal

stiff *n* cadáver *m*; *adj* (rigid) tieso; (starched) almidonado; (of hinge *etc*) duro; (of bone-joints) entumecido; (of paste *etc*) espeso; (with cold) aterido; (formal) reservado; **~ breeze** brisa fuerte; **~ drink** bebida fuerte; **~ price** precio exorbitante; **be bored ~** estar¹⁹ aburrido como una ostra; **be scared ~** estar¹⁹ muerto de miedo;

that's a bit ~! ¡eso pasa de la raya!; **~-necked** terco

stiffen (make rigid) atiesar; (of hinge *etc*) endurecer(se)¹⁴; (of bone-joints) entumecer(se)¹⁴; (of paste *etc*) poner(se)¹⁹ espeso; (of morale) fortalecer(se)¹⁴

stiffener refuerzo; (for shirt-collar) ballena

stiffening *n see* **stiffener**; *adj* de refuerzo; **~ girder** viga rígida; **~ rib** *bui* nervio de refuerzo

stiffness (rigidity) tiesura; (of hinge *etc*) dureza; (of bone-joints) entumecimiento; (of paste *etc*) espesura; (formality) reservación *f*

stifle sofocar(se)⁴; (suppress) suprimir

stifling *n* supresión *f*; *adj* sofocante; *meteor* bochornoso

stigma, stigmata estigma

stigmatize estigmatizar⁷

stile portillo/escalera para pasar una cerca

stiletto estilete *m*: **~ heel** tacón (-ones) *m* de lapicero

¹ **still** *n cin* fotograma *m*; **~s camera** cámara muda; **in the ~ of the evening** en el silencio de la tarde; *adj* inmóvil, quieto; (silent) silencioso; **be ~!** ¡estate quieto!; (non-effervescent) no espumoso; **~-birth** nacimiento de un niño muerto; **~-born** nacido muerto; **~-life** bodegón (-ones) *m*; *v* (calm) calmar; (quieten) hacer¹⁹ callar; (alleviate) aliviar; *adv* (nevertheless) sin embargo

² **still** *adv* (yet) todavía; **I ~ see them from time to time** sigo viéndoles de vez en cuando; **~ more** aún más

³ **still** (for distilling) *n* alambique *m*

stillness inmovilidad *f*, quietud *f*; (silence) silencio

stilt zanco; *orni* zancudo

stilted hinchado

stimulant *n+adj* estimulante *m*

stimulate estimular (**to** a)

stimulation, stimulus estímulo

stimulative estimulador (-ora *f*)

sting *n* (organ) *zool* aguijón (-ones) *m*; *bot* púa; (of scorpion) uña; (of snake) colmillo; (prick with ~) *zool+bot* picadura, (snake's) mordedura; (pain and wound) picadura; (smarting sensation) escozor *m*; *fig* punzada; *adj*

~less sin aguijón/púa; v picar[4]; (smart) escocer (ue)[1b+14]; (of hail) azotar; ~ (s.o.) into action estimular (a uno) para que actúe; ~-ray raya venenosa

stinginess tacañería

stinging picante; (of blows) que duele(n); fig mordaz(-ces); ~-nettle hortiga

stingy tacaño

stink n hedor m; raise a ~ fig armar lío; ~-bomb bomba fétida; v heder (ie)[2b]; cantar; ~ out apestar

stinker persona hedionda; fig (of people) persona poco fiable; (of problem) problema m difícil de resolver

stinking hediondo; he's ~ rich él es un ricachón

stint n (task) tarea; I've done my ~ he hecho mi cuota; vi escatimar; vt restringir[9]

stipend estipendio

stipendiary estipendiario

stipple puntear

stippling punteo; ~-brush brocha de puntear

stipulate estipular

stipulation estipulación f

stir n movimiento; (bustle) bullicio; make a ~ causar una sensación; sl (prison) chirona; vi menearse; John wasn't stirring Juan estaba todavía en cama; vt ~ (up) remover (ue)[1b]; (fire) atizar[7]; (liquid) revolver (ue)[1b] (past part revuelto); fig excitar; ~ up a rebellion fomentar una sublevación

stirring emocionante

stirrup estribo; ~-cup copa de despedida; ~-pump bomba de mano

stitch n puntada; (knitting) punto; (pain) punzada; surg punto de sutura; drop/pick up a ~ perder (ie)[2b]/coger[14] un punto; she was in ~es ella estaba desternillándose de risa; v coser; surg suturar

stitching puntadas; (with sewing-machine) pespunte m; (of book) cosido

stoat armiño

stock n (supply) surtido, stock m; (stump) tronco (cortado); (of vine) cepa; (grafting) patrón (-ones) m; (handle) mango; (of rifle) caja; bot alhelí (-íes) m; (live~) ganado; comm capital m; cul caldo; (lineage) estirpe m; ~s (punishment) cepo (de castigo), comm acciones fpl; naut astillero; on the ~s en vía de construcción, fig en preparación; ~ in hand mercancías fpl en almacén; in ~ en almacén; out of ~ agotado; lay in a ~ (of) hacer[19] provisión (de); take ~ (of) hacer[19] inventario (de), fig asesorarse ~s and shares acciones fpl y obligaciones fpl; chicken ~ caldo de gallina; ~-book libro de almacén; ~-breeder ganadero; ~-broker bolsista m; ~-dove paloma común; Stock Exchange bolsa de valores; ~-holder accionista m+f; ~-in-trade especialidad f; ~-jobber agiotista m; ~-jobbing agiotaje m; ~-man ganadero; ~-market mercado de valores; ~-pile n almacenamiento, v almacenar; ~-pot cazuela de caldo; ~-raiser ganadero; ~-raising ganadería; ~-rider vaquero australiano; ~-room almacén (-enes) m; ~-still absolutamente inmóvil; ~-taking inventario; ~-whip látigo de vaquero; ~-yard corral m; adj acostumbrado; ~ phrase frase hecha; ~ sizes tamaños mpl corrientes; v proveer[17]; comm tener[19] existencias de; do you ~ ...? ¿lleva usted en surtido ...?; ~ up acumular; ~ with (fish, animals etc) poblar (ue)[1a] de

stockade n estacada; v empalizar[7]

stockiness robustez f

stockinet(te) tela de punto

stocking media; (knee-length) calcetín m; ~ stitch punto de media; nylon ~s medias fpl de nilón; in one's ~(ed) feet descalzo

stockist distribuidor m

stocky rechoncho

stodge n comida indigesta

stodginess (of food) carácter indigesto; (of style) pesadez f

stodgy (of food) indigesto; (of style) pesado

stoic n+adj estoico

stoicism estoicismo

stoke echar carbón a; ~-hole cuarto de fogoneros, naut sala de máquinas

stoker fogonero

stole estola

stolid imperturbable

stolidity imperturbabilidad *f*

stomach *n* estómago; (belly) vientre *m*; *fig* (appetite) apetito; (liking) deseo (for de); **have no ~ for** no tener[19] afición a +*infin*; ~**-ache** dolor *m* de estómago/vientre; ~**-pump** bomba gástrica; *v* tragar[5]; **I can't ~ him** no puedo aguantarle

stomp pisar muy fuerte

stone *n* piedra; (pebble) guijarro; (inscribed) lápida; (of fruit) hueso; *med* cálculo; (*UK* weight): *approx* 6,34 kilos; ~ **chippings** gravilla; **leave no ~ unturned** no dejar piedra sin remover; **a ~'s throw from** a poca distancia de; **Stone Age** edad *f* de piedra; **precious ~** piedra preciosa; ~**-axe** hacha para cortar piedra; ~**-blind** ciego por completo; ~**-chat** *orni* tarabilla; ~**-cold** helado; ~**-cold sober** completamente sobrio; ~**-dead** tieso; ~**-deaf** sordo como una tapia; ~**mason** albañil *m*, (quarryman) cantero; ~**-pit**, ~ **quarry** cantera; ~**-wall** *v* ofrecer[14] tenaz resistencia, *sp* jugar (ue)[1a+5] a la defensiva; ~**-walling** táctica de cerrojo; ~**ware** gres *m*; *adj* de piedra; *v bui* revestir (i)[3] de piedra; (throw ~s at) apedrear; (fruit) deshuesar

stoned (of fruit) deshuesado; ~ **raisins** pasas *fpl* sin pepitas; (drunk) borracho como una cuba; (drugged) estupefacto

stoning apedreamiento

stony pedregoso; (made of stone) pétreo; ~ **glance** mirada glacial; **she has a ~ heart** ella tiene el corazón de piedra; ~**-broke** sin una perra

stooge hombre *m* de paja; (yes-man) pelota *m*

stook *n* tresnal *m*; *v* hacer[19] un tresnal de

stool taburete *m*; (faeces) excremento; **fall between two ~s** fracasar por no saber qué hacer; **folding-~** silla de tijera; ~**-pigeon** soplón *m* (-ona *f*)

stoop *n* cargazón *m* de espaldas; *v* agacharse; *fig* humillarse; **I wouldn't ~ to do such a thing** no me rebajaría a hacer semejante cosa

stooping doblado; (of shoulders) cargado (de espaldas)

stop *n* parada, alto; (pause) pausa; (of organ) registro; (full-~) punto; **come to a full-~** pararse de golpe, (cease)

cesar de repente; **put a ~ to** poner[19] fin a; **put a ~ to a rumour** detener[19] un rumor; **bus-~** parada de autobuses; **request-~** parada discrecional; ~**cock** llave *f* de cierre; ~**gap** recurso provisional, (person) sustituto interino; ~**-key** (typewriter) tecla de parada; ~**lights** (traffic-lights) semáforo; ~**press** (as heading) al cerrar la edición, ~**-press news** noticias *fpl* de última hora; ~**-signal** señal *f* de parada, *fam* luz roja; ~**-watch** cronómetro; *vt* parar, detener (ie)[19]; (a hole) tapar; (tooth) empastar; (bleeding) restañar; (forbid) prohibir; (prevent) evitar; **Ali stopped him in the first round** Alí le ganó por K.O. en el primer asalto; **coffee at night ~s me from sleeping** el café por la noche me quita el sueño; ~ **one's ears** taparse los oídos; ~ **payment (of)** suspender pago (de); ~ **the supply** cortar las provisiones; ~ **the traffic** interrumpir la circulación; ~ **s.o. from** +*ger* impedirle (i)[3] +*infin*; **did they ~ anything from your pay?** ¿retuvieron algo de su sueldo?; *vi* parar(se), detenerse[19]; (give up) dejar de +*infin*, **I shall ~ smoking** dejaré de fumar; (stay) quedarse, **why don't you ~ overnight?** ¿por qué no te quedas hasta mañana?; ~ **dead** pararse en seco; ~ **short** detenerse[19] bruscamente; ~ **short of** no llegar[5] a

~ **at** quedarse en; (hotel *etc*) hospedarse en; *naut* hacer[19] escala en; ~ **at nothing** no tener[19] escrúpulo alguno

~ **by** visitar

~ **in** no salir[19]

~ **off (at)** interrumpir el viaje (en)

~ **out** quedarse fuera

~ **over** pasar la noche

~ **up** no acostarse (ue)[1a]

stoppage paro, cese *m*; (of work) suspensión *f*; *mech* obstrucción *f*

stopper *n* tapón (-ones) *m*; *v* cerrar (ie)[2a] con tapón

stopping parada, cese *m*; (of tooth) empaste *m*; **without ~** sin parar; ~**place** parada; ~**-train** tren *m* ómnibus; ~**-up** obturación *f*

storage almacenaje *m*, (furniture) guardamuebles *m sing*; **put into ~** almace-

nar; ~ **battery** acumulador *m*; **cold ~**
almacenaje *m* en frigorífico

store *n* (shop) tienda; (large shop)
almacén (-enes) *m*; (reserve) depósito; **in ~** en almacén; **I was nervous
about what was in ~ for me** yo estaba
nervioso pensando en lo que me
esperaba/*fam* lo que se me venía
encima; **set great/little ~ by** estimar en
mucho/en poco; **~s** provisiones *fpl*,
(food) víveres *mpl*, mil pertrechos
mpl; **~-house** almacén (-enes) *m*, *fig*
mina; **~-keeper** almacenista *m+f*,
(shopkeeper) tendero; **~-room** despensa, *naut* pañolero *m*; *v* almacenar;
~ away guardar, (hold in reserve)
tener[19] en reserva; **~ up** amontonar

storey piso; **top ~** último piso; **two-~,
three-~ house** casa de dos/tres pisos

stork cigüeña

storm *n* +*fig* tempestad *f*; (rain)
aguacero; (snow) nevasca; (thunder)
tormenta; *mil* asalto; **take by ~** tomar
por asalto; **~ in a teacup** tormenta en
un vaso de agua; **~-belt** *meteor* zona
de tempestad; **~-bound** aislado por la
tempestad; **~-centre** centro tempestuoso; **~-cloud** nubarrón *m*; **~-cock**
zorzal *m*; **~-cone** cono/*Sp usu* bola de
tempestad; **~-lantern** linterna contra
el viento; **~-signal** señal *f* de tempestad; **~-tossed** sacudido por la tempestad; **~-troops** tropas *fpl* de asalto; **~-
window** contraventana; *vt* (attack)
asaltar; (capture) tomar por asalto; *vi*
rabiar (**at** contra)

storminess estado tempestuoso

storming asalto; **~-party** pelotón *m* de
asalto

stormy tempestuoso; **~ petrel** petrel *m*

story cuento, historia; (joke) chiste *m*;
(fib) mentira; (plot) argumento;
(news item) reportaje *m*; **as the ~ goes**
según dicen; **that's quite another ~ es**
harina de otro costal; **to cut a long ~
short** para abreviar; **dirty ~** chiste *m*
verde; **short ~** cuento; **that's a tall ~!**
¡eso sí es algo de cuento!; **~-teller**
cuentista *m+f*, (liar) embustero

stoup *eccles* pila para el agua bendita;
(bottle) frasco grande

stout *n approx* cerveza negra; *adj* sólido;
(fat) gordo, *euph* entrado en carnes;
(valiant) valiente; **~-hearted** in-

trépido
stoutly fuertemente, valientemente; **~
made/constructed** resistente

stoutness solidez *f*; (fatness) gordura;
(staunchness) fuerza

stove estufa; *cul* cocina (económica);
gas-~ cocina a/de gas; **electric ~** cocina eléctrica; **~-pipe** tubo de la chimenea; **~-pipe hat** sombrero de copa

stow colocar[4]; (cargo) estibar; **~ it!** ¡cállate!; **~ away** *vi* viajar de polizón;
~-away *n* polizón (-ones) *m*

stowage *naut* arrumaje *m*; (place) bodega

straddle sentarse a horcajadas encima
de; (horse) montar a horcajadas;
(target) cubrir (*past part* cubierto);
US favorecer[14] a ambos lados

Stradivarius (violin) estradivario

strafe bombardear; (with machine-gun)
ametrallar; *fig* castigar[5] severamente

straggle (lag) rezagarse[5]; *bot* lozanear

straggler rezagado; *mil* extraviado

straggling desordenado

straight *n* (racing) recta; *adj* derecho;
(*esp* of road) recto; (of back) erguido;
(of face) serio; (of hair) lacio; (tidy)
ordenado; (fair) justo; (frank) franco;
(honest) honrado; (of drinks) sin
agua; **~ fight** lucha entre dos candidatos; **in a ~ line** en línea recta; *adv*
derecho; (frankly) con franqueza; **~
ahead** todo seguido; **~ away** ahora
mismo; **~ off** de un tirón; **~ out** sin
rodeos; **go ~** formalizarse[7]; **go ~ to
the point** ir[19] al grano; **keep ~ on!**
¡siga todo recto!; **~forward** honrado,
franco; (of task) sencillo; **put things ~**
poner[19] las cosas en orden

straighten enderezar[7]; **~ out** enderezar[7], *fig* arreglar(se); **~ up** enderezarse[7], (tidy) poner[19] en orden, *fam*
recoger[8]

[1] **strain** (lineage) linaje *m*; *mus* tonada;
(style) estilo; **~ of madness** vena de
locura

[2] **strain** *n* tensión *f*, tirantez *f*; *med*
torcedura; (mental) tensión nerviosa;
(effort) esfuerzo; *metal* deformación
f; **put a ~ on** someter a un esfuerzo; *v*
poner[19] tirante; *med* torcer (ue)[1b];
(make an effort) hacer[19] esfuerzos (**to**
por); *metal* deformar; (filter) colar
(ue)[1a]; **~ one's eyes** cansarse los ojos;

~ed atmosphere atmósfera violenta;
~ed relations relaciones *fpl* tirantes;
~ed smile sonrisa forzada

strainer colador *m*

strait *n* estrecho; ~s apuro; in dire ~s en
el mayor apuro; Straits of Gibraltar/
Magellan Estrecho de Gibraltar/Ma-
gallanes; ~jacket camisa de fuerza;
~laced mojigato

straitened: in ~ circumstances apurado
de dinero

¹ strand *n* (beach) playa; *v* encallar; be
~ed hallarse abandonado, (after
missing bus *etc*) quedarse colgado;
leave ~ed dejar abandonado

² strand (filament) brizna; (of hair)
trenza; (fibre) hebra

strange extraño; (foreign) extranjero;
(unknown) desconocido; (unusual)
raro; ~ to relate/say aunque parezca
increíble; he is a ~ man él es un hombre raro; it is ~ that es raro que +*subj*;
I think it's very ~ (that) me extraña
mucho (que +*subj*)

strangeness extrañeza; (uncommon-
ness) rareza

stranger forastero, extraño; (hitherto
unknown) desconocido; he is no ~ to
me él me es conocido

strangle estrangular; *fig* ahogar⁵; ~hold
sp collar *m* de fuerza, *fig* dominio;
have a ~hold on tener¹⁹ asido por la
garganta, *fig* dominar completamente

strangler estrangulador *m*

strangulate estrangular

strangulation estrangulación *f*

strap *n* correa; (in dress) tirante *m*; (in
bus) agarradero; ~-hanger uno/una
que va de pie en un autobús *etc*; *v*
(fasten) atar con correa; (beat) azo-
tar/*fam* pegar⁵ con una correa

strapless sin tirantes

strapping robusto

Strasburg Estrasburgo

stratagem estratagema

strategic estratégico

strategist estratega *m+f*

strategy estrategia

stratification estratificación *f*

stratify estratificar(se)⁴

stratoliner avión estratosférico

stratosphere estratosfera

stratum *geol* estrato; *fig* capa

straw paja; (for drinking) pajita; last ~

golpe *m* de gracia; it's the last ~! ¡no
faltaba más!; man of ~ nulidad *f*;
~board cartón grueso de paja; ~-loft
pajar *m*; *adj* de paja, ~ hat sombrero
de paja; (colour) pajizo; ~ vote votación *f* de tanteo

strawberry fresa; ~ plant fresera; ~
bed/patch fresal *m*; ~ ice helado de
fresa

stray *n* niño/animal perdido o abandonado; *adj* extraviado; (occasional) infrecuente; ~ bullet bala perdida; *v* extraviarse; ~ from apartarse de; ~ into
entrar por equivocación

streak *n* raya; (in marble, wood *etc*)
veta; ~ of lightning rayo; ~ of luck racha de suerte; ~ of cruelty/genius/
madness vena de crueldad/ingenio/
locura; *vi* (go quickly) pasar/correr
como un rayo; (run naked) correr desnudo; *vt* rayar

streaker uno/una que corre desnudo en
un lugar público

streaky rayado; (of bacon) de veta

stream *n* arroyo; (flow) corriente *f*,
against/with the ~ contra/con la corriente; (jet) chorro; he's in the A ~ él
es del grupo A; ~line aerodinamizar⁷,
fig racionalizar⁷; ~lined aerodinámico; *vi* correr; (in breeze) flotar; the
people ~ed into the square la gente entró a raudales en la plaza; my eyes ~ed
lloré a mares; her face was ~ing with
tears ella tenía la cara bañada de lágrimas; ~ forth/out chorrear; *vt* arrojar;
(pupils) clasificar⁴

streamer flámula; (paper) serpentina

street calle *f*; down/up the ~ calle abajo/
arriba; from ~ to ~ de calle en calle;
man in the ~ hombre medio; be on
easy ~ estar¹⁹ con el bolsillo lastrado;
not be in the same ~ (with) no poder
(ue)¹ᵇ compararse (con); it's just up
my ~ es mi especialidad; ~s ahead (of)
mucho mejor (que); on the ~s *fig*
viviendo de prostituta de calle; ~
clothes traje *m* de calle; ~ corner
esquina de la calle; ~ cries gritos *mpl*
de vendedores ambulantes; ~ demonstration manifestación callejera; ~
musician/singer músico/cantante *m*
ambulante; ~-arab, ~urchin golfillo;
~car tranvía, *Mex* trén *m*; ~-door
puerta principal; ~-fighting luchas *fpl*

en las calles; ~-**guide** (plano) callejero; ~-**lamp** farol *m*; ~-**sweeper**
barrendero; ~-**walker** prostituta de
calle, *vulg* puta callejera
strength fuerza; *elect* intensidad *f*; *chem*
concentración *f*; *mil* número; (of
character) firmeza de carácter; ~ **of**
will fuerza de voluntad; **by sheer** ~ a
viva fuerza; **on the** ~ **of** fundándose en
strengthen fortalecerse[14]; (with re-
inforcements) reforzar (ue)[1a+7]; (fortify) fortificar[4]
strenuous enérgico; (arduous) arduo
strenuousness energía; (arduousness)
arduidad *f*
streptococcus estreptococo
streptomycin estreptomicina
stress *n* presión *f*; (emphasis) énfasis *m*;
gramm acento; *med* fatiga nerviosa;
mech+phys tensión *f*; *psych* estrés *m*;
in a state of ~ *psych* estresado; **these**
are times of great ~ éstos son tiempos
turbulentos; **lay** ~ **on** dar[19] importancia a; *v gramm* acentuar; *mech+*
phys cargar[5]; ~ **the importance of** subrayar la importancia de
stretch *n* (stretching) estirón *m*;
(elasticity) elasticidad *f*; (expanse)
extensión *f*; (extent) alcance *m*; (distance) trecho; (of time) período; (gaol
sentence) condena; ~ **of the**
imagination esfuerzo de la imaginación; **at a** ~ de un tirón; **for days at a** ~
durante días enteros; **with two-way** ~
bielástico; *vt* (pull) estirar; (make
bigger) ensanchar; ~ **one's legs** estirar
las piernas; ~ **a point** hacer[19] una concesión; ~ **out** (one's hand *etc*) alargar[5]; *vi* ensancharse; (become longer)
dar[19] de sí; ~ **o.s.** estirarse, (after
sleep) desperezarse[7]; ~ **as far as** extenderse (ie)[2b] hasta; ~ **out on the**
ground tenderse (ie)[2b] en el suelo; **he**
is not sufficiently ~**ed at school** no le
hacen estudiar bastante en la escuela;
my money won't ~ **that far** no me
alcanza el dinero para eso
stretcher *bui* soga; *mech* ensanchador
m; *med* camilla; ~-**bearer** camillero;
~-**party** pareja de camilleros
stretchy elástico
strew esparcir[13]; ~ **the ground with** sembrar (ie)[2a] la tierra de
stricken afligido (**with** por)

strict severo; (exact) riguroso; **too** ~ **a**
judgement un juicio demasiado ta-
jante
strictly severamente, rigurosamente; ~
speaking en rigor
strictness severidad *f*; (exactness) rigor
m
stricture crítica severa; *med* constricción *f*; **pass** ~**s on** criticar[4] severamente
stride zancada; **in one's** ~ sin dificultad
alguna; **get into one's** ~ alcanzar[7] el
ritmo acostumbrado; **make great** ~**s**
progresar mucho; **take it in one's** ~
saber[19] tomarlo bien; *vi* andar[19] a
pasos largos; *vt* cruzar[7] a zancadas;
(straddle) poner[19] una pierna en cada
lado de
stridency estridencia
strident estridente
strife contienda
strike *n* (of workers) huelga; *mil* asalto;
min descubrimiento; (*US* baseball)
golpe *m*; **lucky** ~ hallazgo; **(be) on** ~
(estar[19]) en huelga; **go on** ~ declararse
en huelga; **lightning** ~ huelga relámpago; **sit-down** ~ huelga de brazos
caídos; **stay-in** ~ huelga en el lugar de
trabajo; ~-**breaker** esquirol *m*; ~**fund**
caja de resistencia; ~-**pay** subsidio de
huelga; *v* (hit) pegar[5]; (fishing) tirar
de la caña; (go on ~) declararse en
huelga; *hort* echar raíces; ~ **an atti-**
tude tomar una actitud; ~ **a balance**
arrojar un balance; ~ **a bargain** llegar[5]
a un acuerdo; ~ **a blow** asestar un
golpe; ~ **camp** levantar el campo; ~ **a**
coin acuñar una moneda; ~ **dumb**
dejar sin habla, *fig* pasmar; ~ **home**
dar[19] en el blanco; ~ **a match** encender (ie)[2b] una cerilla; ~ **oil** encontrar
(ue)[1a] petróleo, *fig* hacer[19] los oros y
los moros, tener un golpe de suerte; ~
sail arriar la(s) vela(s); ~ **a snag**
encontrar (ue)[1a] un obstáculo; ~
while the iron's hot aprovechar la
ocasión; **it** ~**s me as very strange** me
parece muy raro; **suddenly it struck**
me de repente se me ocurrió; **the clock**
~**s** el reloj suena; **the clock** ~**s four**
dan las cuatro
~ **against** estrellarse contra
~ **at** asestar un golpe a
~ **down** derribar; **be struck down by ill-**

ness caer[19] enfermo

~ **off** borrar

~ **out** (hit wildly) pegar[5] ciegamente; (erase) borrar

~ **through** (cross out) borrar; (penetrate) penetrar

~ **up** *mus* empezar (ie)[2a+7] a tocar

striker huelguista *m+f*; *mech* percutor *m*; *sp* tanteador *m*, *US* golpeador *m*

striking impresionante; (of colours) llamativo; ~ **girl** chica bandera

strikingly sumamente

string *n* cuerda; (row) hilera; (of onions *etc*) ristra; ~ **of pearls** sarta de perlas; ~ **of curses** retahila de maldiciones; ~ **bag** bolso de malla; ~ **orchestra** orquesta de cuerda; ~ **quartet** (musicians) cuarteto de cuerda; (piece of music) cuarteto para cuerda; ~**s** *mus* instrumentos *mpl* de cuerda, *pol* condiciones *fpl*, **agreement without** ~**s** convenio sin condiciones; **have two** ~**s to one's bow** tener[19] dos cuerdas en su arco; **puppet on a** ~ marioneta en una cuerda; ~-**bean** judía verde; *v* (beads) ensartar; (violin *etc*) encordar (ue)[1a]; ~**ed instrument** instrumento de cuerda

~ **along** (deceive) engañar; ~ **along with** acompañar

~ **out** extender(se) (ie)[2b]

~ **up** *sl* ahorcar[4]

stringency severidad *f*

stringent severo

stringy fibroso

strip *n* (of paper, cloth *etc*) tira; (of wood) listón (-ones) *m*; (of land) franja; (of meat) lonja; (act of undressing) acto de desnudarse; ~-**artist** desnudista; ~-**cartoon** historieta muda; ~-**tease** estriptismo *m*, desnudismo; **comic-**~ tira cómica; *vt* (undress) desnudar; (take off garment) quitar; *mech* desmontar; ~ **the gears** *mot* estropear el engranaje; **they stripped him of his jewellery** le despojaron de sus alhajas; ~ **bark from a tree** descortezar[7] un árbol; *vi* desnudarse; **stripped to the waist** desnudo de la cintura para arriba

stripe *n* raya, banda; *mil* galón (-ones) *m*; (lash) azote *m*; *v* rayar; ~**d** a rayas

stripling mozuelo

stripper *theat* desnudista; **paint-**~ quita-

pinturas *m sing*

stripy rayado

strive afanarse (**after/for** por conseguir); ~ **against** luchar contra; ~ **to** hacer[19] lo posible por

[1] **stroke** *n* (blow) golpe *m*; *sp* jugada; (swimming) brazada; (rowing) remada; (oarsman) primer remero; (of bell) campanada; **at the** ~ **of nine** al acabar de dar las nueve; *mech* carrera; **two-**~ **engine** motor *m* de dos cilindros; *med* ataque *m* fulminante; ~ **of genius** rasgo de ingenio; ~ **of fortune/luck** racha de suerte; **at one** ~ de un golpe; **he has never done a** ~ **(of work)** él jamás ha dado golpe

[2] **stroke** *n* (caress) caricia; (of brush) pincelada; (of pen) rasgo; *v* acariciar; **she** ~**d his hand** ella le acarició la mano

stroll *n* paseo; **take a** ~ dar[19] un paseo

stroller paseante *m+f*

strolling ambulante

strong fuerte; (of coffee, tea) cargado; (of tobacco, cheese) picante; (of colours, emotion) intenso; ~ **accent** acento marcado; ~ **currency** moneda fuerte; ~ **drink** bebida alcohólica; ~ **language** palabras *fpl* indecentes; ~ **man** hombre *m* fuerte, (in circus) hércules *m*; ~ **point** fuerte *m*; **be a** ~ **supporter of** ser[19] partidario acérrimo de; **have** ~ **views on the subject of** tener[19] ideas firmes sobre; **we were fifty** ~ éramos cincuenta; **take** ~ **measures** tomar medidas enérgicas; **in** ~ **terms** enfáticamente; **going** ~ sin perder fuerza; **though he is eighty he's still going** ~ aunque tiene ochenta años él está vivo y coleando; ~-**arm policy** política de mano dura; ~-**box** caja fuerte; ~-**hold** fortaleza; ~-**minded** de espíritu decidido; ~-**room** cámara acorazada; ~-**willed** obstinado

strontium estroncio

strop *n* suavizador *m*; *v* suavizar[7]

struck: I was ~ **by her beauty** me llamó la atención su belleza; **he's** ~ **on her** él está chiflado por ella

structural estructural

structure estructura

struggle *n* lucha; ~ **for existence** lucha por la existencia; **he will not give up**

without a ~ él no se rendirá sin luchar; *v* **~ (for)** luchar (por); **~ to** esforzarse (ue)[1a+7] por; **~ to one's feet** luchar por levantarse

strum *vt* rasguear sin arte; *vi* tocar mal

strumpet ramera

strung: be highly ~ ser[19] muy nervioso

[1] **strut** (walk) contoneo; *v* contonearse; **she strutted out** ella salió de un paso majestuoso

[2] **strut** *n* *bui* puntal *m*; (of chair) varilla guiadora; *v* apuntalar

strychnine estricnina

Stuart Estuardo

stub *n* (of cigarette) colilla; (of cheque) talón (-ones) *m*; (of pencil) cabo; (of tree trunk) tocón (-ones) *m*; *v* **~ one's foot (against)** dar[19] un tropezón (con); **~ out** apagar[5]; **~ up** (trees) desarraigar[5]

stubble *agri* rastrojo; (beard) barba de tres días; **~ field** rastrojera; **~-burning** *agri* quema de rastrojos

stubbly cerdoso

stubborn tenaz; *pej* tozudo

stubbornness tenacidad *f*; *pej* tozudez *f*

stubby pequeño y gordo

stucco *n* estuco; *v* estucar[4]

stuck-up empingorotado

[1] **stud** *n* (nail) tachón (-ones) *m*; (on boots) taco; (collar) botón (-ones) *m* de camisa; *v* tachonar; **studded with** sembrado de; **studded with nails** claveteado

[2] **stud** caballeriza; **~-book** registro genealógico de caballos; **~-farm** potrero; **~-horse** caballo padre

student *n* estudiante *m+f*; *adj* estudiantil

studied premeditado; **~ pose** postura afectada

studio, studio apartment estudio

studious estudioso; (deliberate) intencional; (hard-working) aplicado

studiousness aplicación *f*

study *n* (room) despacho; (music/painting room) estudio; (sketch) bosquejo; (studying) estudio; (investigation) investigación *f*; **he has just finished his studies** acaba de terminar su carrera; *v* estudiar; (investigate) investigar[5]

stuff *n* material *m*; (cloth) tela; (things) cosas *fpl*; (bric-à-brac) cacharros *mpl*; (rubbish) cachivaches *mpl*; **he isn't the**

~ that heroes are made of él no tiene madera de héroe; **~ and nonsense** ¡ni hablar!; *v* (fill) llenar; *cul* rellenar; (with food) llenar, *fam* zampar; (pack untidily) meter sin orden (**into** en); (taxidermy) disecar[4]; *vulg* tirarse a; **~ o.s. with** atiborrarse de; **~ it!** ¡mételo (donde te quepa)!; **get stuffed!** ¡jódete!; **stuffed olive** aceituna rellena; **stuffed shirt** tragavirotes *m sing*

stuffiness mala ventilación; *fam* tufillo; (of character) calidad *f* de relamido

stuffing borra; *cul* relleno; (of furniture) relleno; **he has no ~** él no tiene carácter

stuffy mal ventilado; (narrow-minded) de miras estrechas

stultify anular; (dull the brain of) atontar

stumble *n* tropezón (-ones) *m*; (in speech) desliz *m*; *v* tropezar (ie)[2a+7]; **~ across/upon** tropezar (ie)[2a+7] con; **~ against** tropezar (ie)[2a+7] contra

stumbling-block tropiezo

stump *n* (of limb) muñón (-ones) *m*; (of tree) tocón (-ones) *m*; (of pencil) cabo; (of tooth) raigón (-ones) *m*; (post) poste *m*; (cricket) palo; *vi* (walk with limp) cojear; **~ about** andar[19] cojeando; **~ up** pagar[5]; *vt* (outwit) confundir; **~ the country** *pol* recorrer el país pronunciando discursos; *v* pasearse

stumpy rechoncho

stun aturdir; *fig* despampanar

stunner persona maravillosa; (girl) chica bandera

stunning formidable; (attractive) despampanante

[1] **stunt** impedir (i)[3] el crecimiento de; **~ed** (dwarf) enano, (underdeveloped) subdesarrollado

[2] **stunt** *n* montaje *m* sensacional; *aer* vuelo acrobático; **advertising ~** treta publicitaria; **~-man** *cin* especialista *m*, doble *m*; *v* *aer* hacer[19] maniobras acrobáticas

stupefaction estupefacción *f*

stupefy atolondrar

stupendous estupendo

stupid estúpido; *fam* burro; *sl* berzas *invar*

stupidity estupidez *f*; (stupid act) burrada

stupor estupor *m*
sturdiness robustez *f*
sturdy robusto; *fam* de chapa
sturgeon esturión (-ones) *m*
stutter *n* tartamudeo; *vi* tartamudear; *vt* balbucear
stutterer tartamudo
stuttering *n* tartamudeo; *adj* que tartamudea
[1] **sty** pocilga
[2] **sty(e)** orzuelo
style *n* estilo; (fashion) moda; (elegance) elegancia; (model) modelo; (of address) tratamiento; **do something in** ~ hacer algo lo mejor posible; **live in** ~ darse[19] buena vida; **individual** ~ estilo personal; *v* (name) titular; (hair) moldear; (clothes) hacer[19] a la moda
stylish elegante, a la moda
stylishness elegancia
stylist *n+adj* estilista *m+f*
stylistic estilístico
stylize estilizar[7]
stylus estilete *m* para escribir; (of record-player) aguja
stymie, stymy +*sp* obstaculizar[7]
styptic *n+adj* estíptico; ~ **pencil** estañador *m*
suave afable; (of wine) fino
suavity afabilidad *f*
[1] **sub** *abbr see* **submarine, subordinate, subscription, substitute** *etc*
[2] **sub** *n* (advance of pay) anticipo; *v* pedir (i)[3] un anticipo
[3] **sub:** ~ **judice** bajo juicio
subaltern *n* alférez *m*; *adj* subalterno
subarctic subártico
subcommittee subcomisión *f*
subconscious *n+adj* subconsciente *m*
subconsciousness subconsciencia
subcontinent subcontinente *m*
subcontract *n* subcontrato; *v* subcontratar
subcontractor subcontratista *m*
subculture subcultura
subcutaneous subcutáneo
subdivide subdividir(se)
subdivision subdivisión *f*
subdue subyugar[5]; (one's feelings) dominar; ~**d** (of people) sumiso, (of colours) apagado, (depressed) melancólico; **in a** ~**d voice** en voz baja; ~**d applause** aplausos cerrados

sub-edit redactar
sub-editor redactor subordinado; subeditor
subgroup subgrupo
subheading subtítulo
subhuman infrahumano
subject *n+gramm* sujeto; (citizen) súbdito; (in school) asignatura; (of speech) asunto; (painting + music) tema; **on the** ~ **of** en materia de; **change the** ~ cambiar la conversación; **she is a healthy** ~ *med* ella es un sujeto normal; ~-**matter** tema, (of letter) contenido; *adj* sujeto; (oppressed) subyugado; ~ **to** (liable to) propenso a, (exposed to) expuesto a, (dependent on) supeditado a; ~ **to the approval of** sujeto a la aprobación de; ~ **to change** sujeto a cambio; ~ **to a charge** sujeto a derechos; ~ **to correction** bajo corrección; *v* (conquer) subyugar[5]; (cause to undergo) someter (to a); ~ **o.s. to** someterse a
subjection subyugación *f*
subjective subjetivo
subjectivity subjetividad *f*
subjoin adjuntar
subjugate subyugar[5]
subjugation subyugación *f*
subjunctive *n+adj* subjuntivo
sub-lease, sub-let *n* subarrendamiento; *v* subarrendar
sub-lessee subarrendatario
sub-lieutenant alférez *m* de fragata
sublimate *n* sublimado; *v* sublimar
sublimation sublimación *f*
sublime: the ~ lo sublime
subliminal subconsciente
sublimity sublimidad *f*
sub-machine-gun ametralladora ligera
submarine *n+adj* submarino; ~-**chaser** cazasubmarinos *m sing*
submerge sumergir(se)[9]
submersion sumersión *f*
submission sumisión *f*
submissive sumiso
submissiveness docilidad *f*
submit *vt* someter; (present for consideration) presentar, (in parliament) proponer[19]; **I** ~ **that** me permito decir que; ~ **to arbitration** someter a arbitraje; *vi* someterse; (yield) rendirse (i)[3]
subnormal anormal; subnormal

sub-order subdivisión *f*

subordinate *n+adj* subordinado; (inferior) inferior *m+f*; **be ~ to** depender (ie)²ᵇ de; *v* subordinar

subordination subordinación *f*

suborn sobornar

subornation soborno

sub-plot argumento secundario

subpoena *n* citación *f*; *v* mandar comparecer

sub-post office estafeta (de correos)

subscribe suscribir (*past part* suscrito); (to periodical) abonarse a; *comm* suscribir; **~ to a point of view** estar de acuerdo con un punto de vista

subscriber suscriptor *m* (-ora *f*); (to periodical) abonado

subscription suscripción *f*; (to periodical) abono; (to society) cuota; **~ concert** concierto de abono; **~ rate** tarifa de suscripción

subsection subdivisión *f*

subsequence consecuencia

subsequent subsiguiente; posterior (**to** a)

subsequently después, con posterioridad

subservience subordinación *f*

subservient subordinado

subside (sink) hundirse; (of water) bajar; (of wind) amainar; (of emotions) calmarse; **he ~d into the armchair** él se dejó caer en el sillón

subsidence (of ground) hundimiento; (of water) bajada; (in street) socavón *m*

subsidiary subsidiario; **~ company** empresa filial

subsidize subvencionar

subsidy subvención *f*; subsidio

subsist subsistir

subsistence subsistencia; **~ allowance** dietas *fpl*

subsoil subsuelo

subsonic subsónico

sub-species subespecie *f*

substance sustancia

sub-standard deficiente

substantial (real) sustancial; (strongly made) sólido; (important) importante; **~ part of** parte *f* considerable de

substantiate justificar⁴

substantiation justificación *f*

substantive *n+adj* sustantivo

sub-station subestación *f*

substitute *n* sustituto (**for** por); *v* sustituir¹⁶; *fam* hacer¹⁹ las veces (**for** por)

substitution sustitución *f*

substratum sustrato

substructure subestructura

subtenant subarrendatario

subterfuge subterfugio; *fam* tapujo; **go in for ~s** andar¹⁹ con subterfugios/tapujos

subterranean subterráneo

subtitle subtítulo

subtle (tenuous) sutil; (intelligent) astuto

subtlety (tenuosity) sutileza; (intelligence) astucia

subtract sustraer¹⁹; *fam* restar

subtraction sustracción *f*; *fam* resta

suburb suburbio, barrio; **~s** afueras *fpl*

suburban de barrio; **~ square** plaza de barrio; **~ train** tren *m* de cercanías

suburbia afueras *fpl*

subvention subvención *f*

subversion subversión *f*

subversive subversivo

subvert subvertir (ie)²ᶜ

subway (passage) paso subterráneo; (railway) metro

succeed (be successful) tener¹⁹ éxito; (follow) suceder a; **~ in doing** lograr hacer; **~ to** (position) suceder a

succeeding subsiguiente; (future) futuro; (consecutive) consecutivo

success éxito, **be a (great) ~** tener¹⁹ (mucho) éxito; **it was a ~** salió bien, fue un éxito; **make a ~** tener¹⁹ éxito en

successful que tiene éxito; (prosperous) próspero; **his ~ tour of Canada** su feliz gira del Canadá; **~ negotiations** tratos *mpl* fructíferos

succession sucesión *f*

successive sucesivo

successor sucesor *m* (-ora *f*)

succinct sucinto

succour *n* socorro; *v* socorrer

succulence suculencia

succulent suculento, *fam* riquísimo

succumb sucumbir (**to** a); (die) fallecer¹⁴

such *adj* tal; **~ a girl** tal chica; **~ girls** tales chicas; (so much) tanto, **~ pain** tanto dolor; *adv* tan; **~ a lovely girl** una chica tan guapa; **~ lovely girls** chicas tan guapas; **there's no ~ thing**

no hay tal cosa; ~ **and** ~ tal y cual; ~
as tal como; ~ **as to** de tal manera que;
~ **is life** así es la vida; ~ **men as he**
hombres *mpl* como él; **as** ~ como tal;
there was ~ **fighting!** ¡hubo cada riña!;
~**-like** tales cosas/personas; ~ **as** *pron*
los/las/lo que
suck *n* chupada; (suction) succión *f*; **give**
~ amamantar; *v* chupar; (suckle) ma-
mar; (of vacuum-cleaner) aspirar; ~
one's thumb chuparse el dedo
~ **in** (air) aspirar
~ **down** tragar[5]
~ **up** chupar; (of vacuum-cleaner) aspirar; ~ **up to** *sl* dar[19] coba a
sucker chupador *m* (-ora *f*); (sweet)
chupa; *mech* émbolo; *bot* pimpollo;
(of octopus *etc*) ventosa; *sl* (fool)
crédulo
sucking: ~**-pig** lechón *m*, cochinillo
suckle amamantar
suckling lactante *m*
suction succión *f*; ~**-pump** bomba aspirante
Sudan el Sudán
Sudanese *n + adj* sudanés *m* (-esa *f*)
sudden repentino; **all of a** ~ de repente;
~ **shower** chaparrón imprevisto
suddenly de repente; **did you tell him
like that,** ~? ¿se lo dijo así, de sopetón?
suddenness brusquedad *f*
suds jabonaduras *fpl*
sue *vi* poner[19] pleito; ~ **for peace** pedir
(i)[3] la paz; *vt* ~ **s.o. for** demandarle a
uno por
suede ante *m*; ~ **tie** corbata de ante
suet sebo
suety seboso
Suez: ~ **Canal** canal *m* de Suez
suffer sufrir, padecer[14] (from de); (put
up with) aguantar; (permit) permitir;
he ~**s from an inferiority complex** él
padece de un complejo de inferioridad; **we all** ~ **from our environment**
todos somos víctimas de nuestro ambiente
sufferable soportable
sufferance sufrimiento; **on** ~ por tolerancia
sufferer enfermo, víctima
suffering sufrimiento
suffice bastar
sufficiency suficiencia

sufficient suficiente; **be** ~ bastar
suffix *n* sufijo; *v* añadir como sufijo
suffocate sofocar(se)[4]
suffocating sofocante
suffocation sofocación *f*
suffragan (obispo) sufragáneo
suffrage sufragio
suffragette sufragista
suffuse bañar (**with** de)
suffusion difusión *f*
sugar *n* azúcar *m+f*; ~**-basin,** ~**-bowl**
azucarero; ~**-beet** remolacha; ~**-
candy** azúcar cande; ~**-cane** caña de
azúcar; ~**-coated** azucarado, garapiñado; ~**-coated pill** dragea; ~ **crop**
zafra; ~**-loaf** pan *m* de azúcar; ~**-
lump** terrón *m* de azúcar; ~ **refinery**
fábrica de azúcar; ~**-tongs** pinza para
azúcar; *v* azucarar; ~ **the pill** dorar la
píldora; ~**ed almond** almendra
garapiñada
sugariness lo azucarado
sugary azucarado; *fig* almibarado
suggest sugerir (ie)[2c]; (advise) aconsejar; (hint) insinuar; **I** ~ **that** aconsejo
que +*subj*; **a solution** ~**ed itself to her**
se le ocurrió a ella una solución
suggestibility calidad *f* de sugestionable,
sugestibilidad
suggestible sugestionable
suggestion sugerencia; (trace) sombra;
what a ~! ¡qué idea!
suggestive sugerente; (slightly indecent)
sicalíptico
suggestiveness lo sugestivo *f*
suicidal suicida *invar*
suicide (act) suicidio; (person) suicida
m+f; **commit** ~ suicidarse
suit *n* (clothing) traje *m*; (courtship)
galanteo; *leg* pleito; (request)
petición *f*; (cards) palo; **follow** ~
servir (i)[3] del palo, *fig* hacer[19] lo
mismo; ~ **of armour** armadura; ~**case**
maleta; **live out of a** ~**case** vivir con
una maleta en la mano; *v* (be
convenient) convenir[19] a, **it doesn't** ~
me no me conviene; (of clothes)
sentar (ie)[2a] bien a; ~ **yourself!** ¡como
usted quiera!; **his name** ~**ed him
perfectly** su nombre le sentaba
divinamente; **country life** ~**s me** me
sienta bien la vida campestre; **be** ~**ed
for** ser[19] apropiado para; **they are well**
~**ed** ellos van bien juntos

suitability conveniencia, aptitud *f*; compatibilidad *f*

suitable conveniente, apto; **not ~ for children** no apto para menores; **make something ~ for** adaptar algo a las necesidades de

suite (of retainers) séquito; (of furniture) juego; (of rooms) habitaciones *fpl* particulares; *mus* suite *f*

suiting tela para trajes

suitor pretendiente *m*; *leg* demandante *m+f*

sulk amohinarse

sulkiness, sulks mohína

sulky mohíno

sullen malhumorado; ~ **sky** cielo plomizo

sullenness mal humor *m*

sully manchar

sulphate sulfato

sulphide sulfuro

sulphite sulfito

sulphur *n* azufre *m*

sulphuric sulfúrico

sulphurous sulfuroso

sultan sultán (-anes) *m*

sultana sultana; (fruit) pasa (de Esmirna)

sultriness bochorno

sultry bochornoso; (sexually alluring) provocativo

sum suma, total *m*; *math* suma, cálculo; ~ **total** cifra total; ~**s** aritmética; **do ~s** hacer[19] números; *v* ~ **up** (add) sumar, (give a résumé of) resumir, (assess a situation) justipreciar; **to ~ up** en resumen

summarily sumariamente

summarize resumir

summary *n* resumen (-úmenes) *m*; *adj* sumario; ~ **justice** justicia sumaria

summation *math* suma; (summary) resumen (-úmenes) *m*

summer *n* verano; **I have seen forty ~s** he visto cuarenta abriles; ~ **coat** abrigo de verano; ~ **holiday(s)** veraneo; ~**-house** cenador *m*; casa de verano; ~ **resort** lugar *m* de veraneo; ~**-school** curso de verano; ~ **solstice** solsticio estival; ~**-time** hora de verano; *adj* veraniego; *v* veranear

summery veraniego

summing-up recapitulación *f*

summit +*fig* cumbre *f*; ~ **conference**

conferencia cumbre

summitry negociaciones *fpl* entre (los jefes de) las grandes potencias

summon llamar; (meeting) convocar[4]; *leg* citar; ~ **up** (courage) cobrar, (memory) evocar[4], (devil) invocar[4]

summons *n* llamamiento; *leg* citación *f*; *v* citar

sump *min* sumidero; *mot* cárter *m*

sumptuary suntuario

sumptuous suntuoso

sumptuousness, sumptuosity suntuosidad *f*

sun *n* sol *m*; **the ~ is shining** hace sol; **in the ~** al sol; **bask in the ~** tomar el sol; **place in the ~** *fig* prosperidad *f*; **under the ~** en el mundo; **they talked of everything under the ~** hablaron de todo lo divino y humano; ~**bathe** *n* baño de sol, *v* tomar el sol, *fam* tostarse (ue)[1a] al sol; ~**bathing** baños *mpl* de sol; ~**beam** rayo de sol; ~**-blind** toldo para el sol; ~**-bonnet** papalina; ~**burn** bronceado; ~**burn** bronceado (por el sol); **get ~burnt** broncearse; ~**-deck** cubierta de sol; ~**dial** reloj *m* de sol; ~**down** puesta del sol; **at ~down** al anochecer; ~**downer** vagabundo australiano; ~**flower** girasol *m*; ~**flower seed** pipa; ~**-glasses** gafas *fpl* de sol; ~**-god** dios *m* del sol; ~**-helmet** salacot *m*; ~**-lamp** lámpara de rayos ultravioletas; ~**light** luz *f* solar; **in the ~light** al sol; ~**lit** iluminado por el sol; ~**-lounge** solana; ~**-power** energía solar; ~**-ray lamp** lámpara de rayos ultravioletas; ~**rise** salida del sol; **at ~rise** a la madrugada; ~**-roof** *mot* techo corredizo; ~**set** puesta del sol; **at ~set** a la puesta del sol; ~**shade** sombrilla, (awning) toldo; ~**-shield** *mot* visera; ~**shine** sol *m*; **hours of ~shine** horas de sol; **in the ~shine** al sol; ~**spot** mancha solar; ~**stroke** insolación *f*; **get ~stroke** coger[8] una insolación; ~**tan(ned)** bronceado; ~**-tan lotion** loción *f* solar; ~**-trap** solana; ~**-up** salida del sol; **at ~up** a la salida del sol; ~**-worship** adoración *f* del sol; ~**-worshipper** adorador *m* (-ora *f*) del sol; *v* ~ **o.s.** tomar el sol

sundae helado con frutas, jarabe *etc*

Sunday domingo; **in one's ~ best**

endomingado; **dress in one's ~ best** endomingarse[5]; **~ School** catequesis *f*; **~ driver!** *pej* ¡dominguero!; *adj* dominical

sundry varios; **all and ~** todos y cada uno; **sundries** géneros *mpl* diversos

sunken +*fig* hundido

sunless sin sol

sunny (of places) soleado; (of day) de sol; *fig* risueño; **be ~** hacer[19] sol

sup *n* sorbo; *v* (drink) sorber; (have supper) cenar, **they like to ~ off cold meat** les gusta cenar fiambres

super *n* (superintendent) superintendente *m*; (*US* caretaker) portero; *adj* estupendo, *sl* bárbaro

superabundance superabundancia

superabundant superabundante

superannuate jubilar; **~d** jubilado, (obsolete) anticuado

superannuation jubilación *f*

superb soberbio

supercharge sobrealimentar

supercharger sobrealimentador *m*

supercilious desdeñoso

superciliousness desdén *m*

super-duper fabuloso

supererogatory supererogatorio

superficial superficial

superficiality superficialidad *f*

superfine extrafino; **~ flour** flor *f* de harina

superfluity superfluidad *f*

superfluous superfluo

superhet superheterodino

superhuman sobrehumano

superimpose sobreponer[19]

superintend (direct) dirigir[9]; (supervise) vigilar

superintendence (directing) dirección *f*; (supervising) vigilancia

superintendent superintendente *m*; (police) subjefe *m*; (*US* caretaker) portero

superior *n* superior *m*; *eccles* (mother superior) superiora; *adj* superior; (bad sense) orgulloso; **~ officer** oficial *m* superior; **he is ~ to John** él es superior a Juan/*fam* encima de Juan

superiority superioridad *f*; **~ complex** complejo de superioridad

superlative *n*+*adj* superlativo

superman superhombre *m*

supermarket supermercado

supernatural *n* lo sobrenatural; *adj* sobrenatural

supernaturalism creencia en lo sobrenatural

supernumerary *n*+*adj* supernumerario; *cin*+*theat* extra *m*+*f*

superscribe escribir (*past part* escrito) encima

superscription sobrescrito

supersede reemplazar[7]

supersonic supersónico

superstition superstición (-ones) *f*

superstitious supersticioso

superstructure superestructura

supertanker superpetrolero

supertax sobreimpuesto

supervene sobrevenir[19]

supervise supervisar

supervising: ~ engineer ingeniero inspector

supervision supervisión *f*

supervisor supervisor *m* (-ora *f*)

supervisory fiscalizador (-ora *f*); **act in a ~ capacity** hacer[19] de inspector; **~ staff** personal directivo

supine supino; *fam* boca arriba; (lethargic) letárgico

supper cena; **have ~** cenar; **~-time** hora de cenar

supplant suplantar

supple flexible; (of character) dócil; adaptable

supplement *n* suplemento; *v* suplementar

supplementary suplementario; **~ estimate/tax** presupuesto/impuesto extraordinario

suppleness flexibilidad *f*; (of character) docilidad *f*

suppli(c)ant *n*+*adj* suplicante *m*+*f*

supplicate suplicar[4]

supplication súplica

supplier suministrador *m* (-ora *f*); *comm* proveedor *m* (-ora *f*)

supply *n* suministro; *comm* surtido; **be in short ~** escasear; **law of ~ and demand** ley *f* de la oferta y la demanda; **~ network** red *f* de distribución; **~ teacher** maestro suplente; **supplies** (food) provisiones *fpl*; *mil* material *m*; *v* suministrar; **~ a city** aprovisionar una ciudad; **~ with** abastecer[14] de

support *n*+*fig* apoyo; *bui* soporte *m*;

mech sostén *m*; *moral* ~ adhesión *f*;
thank you for your (moral) ~ gracias
por su apoyo; **in** ~ **of** en apoyo de; ~
costs gastos *mpl* de manutención; *v*
+*fig* apoyar; (campaign) respaldar; ~
a family mantener[19] una familia; ~
o.s. mantenerse[19], *fam* ganarse la
vida
supportable soportable
supporter partidario; *mech* sostén *m*; *sp*
aficionado, *fam* hincha *m*+*f*; ~**s' club**
peña deportiva
supporting justificativo; ~ **programme**
cin películas *fpl* secundarias; **she has a**
~ **role** ella tiene un papel secundario;
~ **statement** *comm* estado demostrativo
suppose suponer[19], imaginarse; (think)
creer[17]; **I** ~ **that she will do it** me
imagino que ella lo hará; **I** ~ **so**
supongo que sí, (with resignation) no
hay más remedio; **I** ~ **not** supongo
que no; **I don't** ~ **that** no creo que
+*subj*; ~ **we go?** ¿y si nos vamos?;
let's ~ **that** pongamos por caso que
+*subj*; **she is** ~**d to be bright** ella tiene
fama de lista; **you're** ~**d to know** usted
debe saberlo; **always supposing** dado
que; ~**d** *adj* supuesto, (feigned) fingido
supposedly según lo que se supone; ~
educated people gente teóricamente
educada
supposition suposición (-ones) *f*
suppository supositorio
suppress suprimir; (dissemble) disimular; (stifle) ahogar[5]; (interrupters) hacer[19] callar
suppressible suprimible
suppression supresión *f*; (dissembling)
disimulación *f*; (stifling) ahogamiento
suppressor *rad* supresor *m*
suppurate supurar
suppuration supuración *f*
supremacy supremacía
supreme supremo; **with** ~ **courage** con
sumo valor; **Supreme Court** tribunal
supremo
surcharge *n* sobrecarga; *v* sobrecargar[5]
sure *adj* seguro, cierto; (accurate)
certero; ~ **enough** efectivamente; **for**
~ sin falta; **to be** ~ estar[19] seguro, **I'm**
~ **that** estoy seguro de que; **be** ~ **to**
(not fail to) no dejar de +*infin*, (be

careful to) tener[19] cuidado de +*infin*;
she is ~ **to see it** ella seguramente lo
verá; **I'm not so** ~ **(of that)** no estoy
convencido por completo de aquello;
make ~ **(that)** asegurarse de que
+*subj*; **make** ~ **of** (facts) cerciorarse
de; **make** ~ **of s.o.'s help** contar (ue)[1a]
con la ayuda de alguien; *US* ~**-fire** de
éxito seguro; ~**-footed** de pie firme;
adv (of course) claro; **she** ~ **is clever**
ella sí (que) es lista
sureness seguridad *f*, certeza
surety (money) fianza; (person) fiador
m (-ora *f*), **go** ~ **(for)** salir[1a] fiador (de)
surf rompientes *mpl*; ~**-board** tabla de
surf; ~**-rider** surfista *m*+*f*; ~**-riding**
surf *m*, surfismo
surface *n* superficie *f*; (of road) firme *m*;
on the ~ *fig* en apariencia; ~ **mail** correo terrestre; ~**-workers** *min* trabajadores *mpl* del exterior; *adj* superficial; *vi* (of submarine *etc*) salir[19] a la
superficie; *vt* (give a smooth surface
to) alisar
surfeit *n* exceso; *v* saciar
surfing surf *m*, surfismo
surge *n* oleada; (of emotions) ola; *v*
agitarse; (of emotions) despertarse
(ie)[2a]; **the blood** ~**d up to her face** la
sangre se le subió a la cara; ~ **forward**
adelantarse en masa
surgeon cirujano; **incompetent** ~ carnicero
surgery (science) cirugía; (place) (sala
de) consulta, *US* sala de operaciones;
~ **hours** horas de consulta
surgical quirúrgico; ~ **clip** laña; ~
cotton algodón hidrófilo; ~ **dressing**
compresa quirúrgica; ~ **instrument**
instrumento quirúrgico; ~ **mask**
mascarilla; ~ **needle** aguja de sutura
surliness displicencia
surly displicente
surmise *n* conjetura; *v* conjeturar
surmount superar; ~**ed by** coronado de
surmountable superable
surname *n* apellido; *v* apellidar
surpass exceder
surpassing superior
surplice sobrepelliz (-ces) *f*
surplus *n* sobrante *m*; *comm* superávit
m; *adj* sobrante; ~ **stock** exceso de
existencias; **sale of** ~ **trousers** saldo de
pantalones sobrantes

surprise *n* sorpresa; ~ **attack** *mil* rebato; **take by** ~ coger[8]/*fam* pillar desprevenido; *v* sorprender; *mil* coger[8] por sorpresa; **be** ~**d** sorprenderse (**at** de), *fam* sobresaltarse

surprising sorprendente; **it's hardly** ~ **that** no es de extrañarse que +*subj*

surrealism surrealismo

surrealist *n*+*adj* surrealista *m*+*f*

surrealistic surrealista

surrender *n* rendición *f*; (handing-over) entrega; (renunciation) renuncia; ~ **value** valor *m* de rescate; *v* rendir(se) (i)[3]; entregar(se); renunciar a

surreptitious subrepticio

surreptitiousness subrepción *f*

surrogate sustituto; *eccles* vicario

surround *n* borde *m*; *v* cercar[4], rodear; *mil* sitiar; ~**ed by** rodeado de

surrounding circundante

surroundings alrededores *mpl*; *fig* ambiente *m*

surtax impuesto adicional (sobre ingresos elevados), sobretaxa

surveillance vigilancia; **under police** ~ bajo vigilancia policial

survey *n* vista panorámica; (study) examen (-ámenes) *m*; (report) informe *m*, **economic** ~ informe económico; *med* medición *f*; ~ **of public opinion** encuesta de la opinión pública; *v* contemplar; (examine) examinar; *med* medir (i)[3]; ~ **the events of the year** pasar revista a los acontecimientos del año

surveying agrimensura; topografía; ~-**rod** piquete *m*

surveyor agrimensor *m*; (of buildings) inspector *m*

survival supervivencia; ~ **of the fittest** supervivencia de los más dotados; ~ **kit** equipo salvavidas

survive sobrevivir (a); (of customs) perdurar

survivor superviviente *m*+*f*

Susan Susana

susceptibility susceptibilidad *f*; **susceptibilities** delicadeza *sing*

susceptible susceptible (**to** a); (easily moved) impresionable

suspect *n* sospechoso; *adj* sospechado, sospechoso; *v* sospechar; (think probable) barruntar; **I** ~ **that** *fam* me huelo que

suspend suspender

suspender liga; (*US* braces) tirantes *mpl*; ~-**belt** portaligas *m sing*, *fam* liguero

suspense incertidumbre *f*; *cin*+*theat* suspenso; **in** ~ en suspenso; **keep in** ~ dejar en la incertidumbre

suspenseful lleno de suspenso

suspension suspensión *f*; ~ **of payments** suspensión *f* de pagos; ~ **of driving licence** privación *f* de permiso de conducir; ~ **bridge** puente *m* colgante

suspicion *n* sospecha; (trace) sombra; **be above** ~ estar[19] por encima de sospecha; **be under** ~ estar[19] bajo sospecha; **I have my** ~**s (that)** sospecho (que)

suspicious sospechoso; (by nature) suspicaz; **make s.o.** ~ hacerle[19] sospechar a alguien; ~ **character** maleante *m*+*f*

suspiciously de un modo sospechoso; **it looks** ~ **like** tiene toda apariencia de

suspiciousness lo sospechoso; (of character) carácter sospechoso

suss *v* (frisk) cachear, (investigate) investigar[5]

sustain sostener[19]; (suffer) sufrir; ~**ed** sostenido; (prolonged) prolongado

sustainment sostener *m*

sustenance sustento

sustentation aguantar *m*

suttee inmolación voluntaria de una viuda hindú

suture *n* sutura; *v* suturar

suzerainty soberanía

svelte esbelto

S.W. (south-west) *n*+*adj* S.O. (sudoeste) *m*

swab *n* estropajo; *naut* lampazo; *surg* tapón *m*; (fool) tonto; *v surg* limpiar con algodón hidrófilo; ~ **(down)** *naut* limpiar con lampazo

swad gran cantidad *f*, montón *m*

swaddle envolver (ue)[1b] (*past part* envuelto); (child) fajar

swaddling-clothes pañales *mpl*

swag botín *m*

swagger *n* fanfarronada; **walk with a** ~ andar[19] de manera fanfarrona; ~-**stick** bastón corto llevado por un militar; *adj* muy elegante; *v* fanfarronear

swain zagal *m*; (lover) amante *m*

[1] **swallow** *n* trago; *v* +*fig* tragar[5]; (in fear) tragar[5] saliva; ~ **an insult** aguantar un

insulto; ~ **one's pride** tragarse el orgullo; ~ **one's words** desdecirse[19]; ~ **up** tragarse[5], (money *etc*) consumir

[2] **swallow** *orni* golondrina; **one ~ does not make a summer** una golondrina no hace verano; ~**-dive** salto de ángel

swamp *n* pantano; (salt-water) marisma; *v* sumergir[9]; (boat) hundir; (inundate) inundar; *fig* abrumar; **I'm ~ed with work** estoy abrumado de trabajo

swampy pantanoso

swan cisne *m*; ~**-dive** salto de ángel; ~**sdown** plumón *m* de cisne; ~**-song** canto del cisne

swank *n* ostentación *f*; *fam* postín *m*; (person) currutaco; *fam* postinero; *v* jactarse (**about** de); *fam* darse[19] postín

swanky ostentoso; *fam* postinero

swannery colonia de cisnes

swap *n* (inter)cambio; *v* cambiar

sward césped *m*

swarm *n* enjambre *m*; *fig* hormigueo; *v* (bees) enjambrar; (people) hormiguear; ~ **up** trepar; ~ **with** estar[19] infestado de

swarthiness tez morena

swarthy atezado

swashbuckler espadachín (-ines) *m*

swastika esvástica

swat aplastar

swath(e) anchura de las hojas de un cortacéspedes

swathe vendar

sway *n* dominio; **hold ~ (over)** tener[19] dominio (sobre); *vt* hacer[19] oscilar; (bear influence on) influir[16] en; ~ **the hips** (when walking) mover las caderas; *vi* oscilar

swaying balanceo; (of train) coletazo

swear +*leg* jurar; (curse) decir[19] palabrotas, *fam* echar pestes; ~ **an oath** prestar un juramento; ~ **blue murder** echar sapos y culebras; ~**-word** palabrota, (blasphemous) blasfemia

~ **at** maldecir[19]

~ **by** jurar por; (have confidence in) tener[19] entera confianza en

~ **in** tomar juramento a

~ **to** declarar bajo juramento +*infin*

swearer jurador *m* (-ora *f*)

swearing palabrotas *fpl*; (blasphemy) blasfemias *fpl*

sweat *n* sudor *m*; *mech* condensación *f*;

by the ~ **of one's brow** con el sudor de la frente; **he's in a ~** él está en un apuro; ~**band** *sp* muñequera; ~**-gland** glándula sudorípara; ~**-shirt** niqui *m*; ~**-shop** taller *m* en que se explota el obrero; *vi* sudar; (work hard) trabajar duro; *vt* (hacer[19]) sudar; (exploit) explotar; *mech* soldar (ue)[1a]; *metal* calentar (ie)[2a] hasta fusión; ~ **blood** *fig* sudar la gota gorda

sweater suéter *m*

sweating *n* transpiración *f*; *fig* (of workers) explotación *f*; *adj* sudoroso

sweaty sudoroso

Swede sueco

swede *agri* nabo sueco

Sweden Suecia

Swedish *n*+*adj* sueco

sweep *n* barrida; (chimney) deshollinador *m*; *mil* redada; (curve) curva; **with a ~ of the hand** con un gesto de la mano; **make a clean ~ of** hacer[19] tabla rasa de; ~**-stake**: lotería en la que el ganador lleva todas las apuestas; *vt* (with brush) barrer; (chimney) deshollinar; *mil* barrer; *naut* (mines) dragar[4]; ~ **the board** llevarse todo; ~ **away** *fig* arrebatar; ~ **out/up** barrer; *vi* barrer; **be swept off one's feet** perder (ie)[2b] el equilibrio, *fig* enamorarse locamente de

~ **by** pasar rápidamente

~ **down** descender (ie)[2b] precipitadamente; (majestically) bajar majestuosamente (**to** hacia)

~ **over** *aer* ir[19] volando por encima (de)

~ **through** pasar majestuosamente por

sweeper (person) barrendero; (carpet) limpialfombras *m* *sing*+*pl*; (footballer) medio, *fam* defensa escoba *m*

sweeping completo; (too general) demasiado general; ~ **changes** cambios *mpl* radicales; ~**-brush** escoba

sweepings barreduras *fpl*

sweet *n* caramelo; (dessert) postre *m*; *adj* dulce; (not stale) fresco; (affectionate) amable; (charming) simpático; (of clothes, ornaments *etc*) mono; ~ **alyssum** *bot* aliso; ~ **face** cara bonita; ~ **smell** olor fragante; **what a ~ smell it has!** ¡qué buen olor tiene!; **be ~ on** sentirse (ie)[2c] atraído por; **have a ~ tooth** ser[19] goloso; ~**bread** lechecillas *fpl*; ~**-corn**

(especie de) maíz *m*; ~**heart** novio, novia; (term of affection) cariño mío; ~**meat** caramelo *m*; ~**-pea** guisante *m* de olor; ~**-potato** batata; ~ **shop** confitería; ~**-smelling** fragante; ~**-tempered** de carácter dulce; ~**-tongued** meloso; ~**-toothed** goloso; ~**-william** minutisa

sweeten +*fig* endulzar[7]

sweetener dulcificante *m*

sweetie (term of endearment) querido/querida

sweetish algo dulce

sweetness +*fig* dulzura

swell *n naut* mar *m* de fondo; (toff) guapo; *sl* (pez) gordo; *mus* crescendo; (increase) aumento; *adj* estupendo; **have a** ~ **time** pasarlo muy bien; *vi* hincharse; (increase) aumentarse; (of river) crecer[14]; ~ **with pride** envanecerse[14]; (of numbers) engrosar; **have a swelled head** estar[19] engreído

swelling hinchazón *m*; *med* chichón *m*

swelter achicharrarse

sweltering sofocante

swept: ~**-back hair** cabello tirado hacia atrás; ~**-back wing** ala en flecha; ~**-back wing plane** avión *m* de ala volante

swerve *n* quite *m*; *v* hacer[19] un quite/viraje; **the other driver made me** ~ el otro conductor me obligó a hacer un viraje; **the centre-forward made the ball** ~ el delantero centro hizo cambiar de trayectoria el balón

swift *n* vencejo común; *adj* veloz; (sudden) repentino

swiftly velozmente; (suddenly) de repente

swiftness velocidad *f*

swig *n* tragantada; (of wine, liqueurs) *fam* latigazo; **have a** ~ echar un trago; *v* pimplar

swill *n* bazofia; *pej* aguachirle *m*; ~**trough** artesa del pienso; *v* (swig) pimplar; ~ **out** enjuagar[5]

swim *n*: **go for a** ~ ir[19] a nadar; **be in the** ~ estar[19] al tanto; ~**suit** bañador *m*; *v* nadar; **go swimming** ir[19] a bañarse; ~ **the Channel** atravesar nadando el canal de la Mancha; **my head is swimming** se me va la cabeza; **everything began to** ~ **before his eyes** todo empezó a bailar ante sus ojos; **be swimming in** *fig* rebosar; **her eyes were**

swimming with tears ella tenía los ojos inundados de lágrimas

swimmer nadador *m* (-ora *f*); **she is a bad/good** ~ ella nada mal/bien

swimming natación *f*; ~**-bath,** ~**-pool** piscina; ~**-costume** bañador *m*

swimmingly: go ~ ir[19] a las mil maravillas

swindle *n* timo; estafa; *sl* guinde *m*; *v* timar; estafar; *sl* guindar

swindler timador *m* (-ora *f*); estafador *m* (-ora *f*)

swine cerdo, puerco; *fig* canalla; **herd of** ~ manada de cerdos; ~**-fever** peste porcina; ~**herd** porquerizo

swing *n* columpio; (movement) balanceo; *fig* oscilación *f*; *mus* ritmo; (type of music) swing *m*; (boxing) golpe *m* lateral; *pol* movimiento, ~ **to the left** movimiento hacia la izquierda; **go with a** ~ ir[19] sobre ruedas; **in full** ~ en plena actividad; ~**-boat** barca voladora; ~**-bridge** puente giratorio; ~**door** puerta giratoria; *vi* columpiarse, oscilar; ~ **round** volver (ue)[1a] (*past part* vuelto) rápidamente; **I'll** ~ **for it** me ahorcarán (por ello); *vt* (wield) blandir; columpiar; balancear; (influence) influir[16] en; ~ **the lead** fingir[9] trabajar

swinging *n* (movement) balanceo; *fig* oscilación *f*; *mus* ritmo; *pol* movimiento; *adj* oscilante; rítmico; **he has a** ~ **stride** él tiene un andar rítmico

swinish cochino

swipe *n* golpe *m* fuerte; ~**s** cerveza floja; *v* golpear fuertemente; *sl* birlar

swingeing formidable

swirl *n* remolino; *v* arremolinarse

swish *n* silbido; (of silk) crujido; ~ **of the tail** meneo del rabo; *adj sl* majo; *v* (cane *etc*) agitar produciendo un silbido; (tail) menear

Swiss *n*+*adj* suizo; ~**-roll** brazo de gitano

switch *n* (stick) varilla; *elect* interruptor *m*, llave *f*; (railway) agujas *fpl*; (change) cambio; ~**back** montaña rusa; ~**board** cuadro de distribución, (telephone) cuadro de conexión manual, (in office) centralita; ~**man** guardagujas *m sing*; *v* (change) cambiar; (to another route) desviar; ~ **on the light** encender (ie)[2b] la luz, *fam* poner[19] la luz; ~ **on the radio** poner[19] la radio; ~ **off** (light) apagar[5], *fam* quitar; (piece of apparatus) desconectar

Switzerland Suiza

swivel *n* eslabón giratorio; ~**-chair** silla giratoria; *vi* girar; *vt* hacer[19] girar

swizzle *n* timo; *v* timar

swizzle-stick varita para mezclar bebidas

swollen hinchado; (of rivers) crecido; ~**-headed** engreído

swoon *n* desmayo; *v* desmayarse

swoop *n* descenso súbito; *orni* calada; *v* ~ **down** precipitarse (**on** sobre); *orni* calar

swop *n* (inter)cambio; *v* cambiar

sword espada; **cross ~s with** cruzar[7] espadas con; ~**-swallower** tragasables *m sing*; **put to the ~** pasar a cuchillo; ~**-arm** brazo derecho; ~**-belt** talabarte *m*; ~**-cut** sablazo; ~**-dance** danza de espadas; ~**fish** pez *m* espada; ~**-play** esgrima; ~**sman** esgrimidor *m*; ~**smanship** esgrima; ~**swoman** esgrimidora; ~**-thrust** golpe *m* de espada, (bull-fighting) estocada

swot *n* empollón (-ones) *m*; *v* empollar

sybarite sibarita *m+f*

sycamore sicomoro

sycophancy adulación *f*

sycophant adulador *m* (-ora *f*)

sycophantic adulatorio

syllabic silábico

syllable sílaba

syllabus programa *m*; (school) programa *m* de estudios

syllogism silogismo

syllogistic silogístico

sylph sílfide *f*

sylvan selvático

Sylvia Silvia

symbiosis simbiosis *f*

symbol símbolo

symbolic(al) simbólico

symbolist simbolista *m+f*

symbolize simbolizar[7]

symmetric(al) simétrico

symmetry simetría

sympathetic compasivo

sympathize compadecer[14]; ~ **with** (ideals) ser[19] partidario de; ~ **with s.o.** acompañarle en sus sentimientos

a alguien

sympathy compasión *f*; ~ **strike** huelga de solidaridad

symphonic sinfónico

symphonist *mus* compositor *m* de sinfonías

symphony sinfonía; ~ **orchestra** orquesta sinfónica

symposium (meeting) simposio, conferencia para estudiar algún tema; (book) colección *f* de artículos

symptom síntoma *m*

symptomatic sintomático

synagogue sinagoga

synchromesh: ~ **gears** velocidades *fpl* sincronizadas

synchronism sincronismo

synchronization sincronización *f*

synchronize *vt* sincronizar[7]; *vi* ser[19] sincrónico (**with** con)

synchronous sincrónico

syncopate sincopar

syncopation síncopa

syndicalism sindicalismo

syndicalist *n+adj* sindicalista *m+f*

syndicate *n* sindicato; *v* sindicar; vender artículos por medio de un sindicato; ~**d article** artículo publicado en varios periódicos

syndrome síndrome *m*; **withdrawal ~** síndrome de abstinencia

synod sínodo

synonym, synonymous sinónimo

synopsis sinopsis *f*

synoptic sinóptico

syntactic(al) sintáctico

syntax sintaxis *f*

synthesis síntesis *f*

synthesize sintetizar[7]

synthetic sintético

syphilis sífilis *f*

syphilitic sifilítico

syphon *n* sifón *m*; *v* ~ **off** sacar[4] con sifón

Syria Siria

Syrian *n+adj* sirio

syringa *bot* jeringuilla

syringe jeringa, *med* jeringuilla; *sl* chuta

syrup jarabe *m*; (sugar) almíbar *m*

syrupy almibarado

system *n* sistema *m*; *med* constitución *f*; *mech* mecanismo; (method) método; ~ **performance** rendimiento de sistema; **decimal ~** sistema *m* decimal;

railway/road ~ red *f* de ferrocarriles/ de carreteras; **tax** ~ sistema tributario; **wiring** ~ *elect* instalación *f*

systematic sistemático
systematization sistematización *f*
systematize sistematizar[7]

T

t (letter) te *f*; **to a** ~ exactamente
ta gracias; ~-~ **(for now)** hasta la vista
tab *n* lengüeta; (cigarette) colilla; (bill)
cuenta; *theat* cortina del escenario;
keep a ~ **on** (person) vigilar, (thing)
tener[19] a la vista
tabard tabardo
tabby (cat with tabby markings) gato
atigrado; (female cat) gata
tabernacle tabernáculo
tabla pequeño tambor indio
table *n* (furniture) mesa; (bedside)
mesilla de noche; (price-list) tarifa;
(of contents) tabla de materias;
(statistical) cuadro; *math* tabla, **multiplication** ~ tabla de multiplicar;
financial ~ cotizaciones *fpl* bancarias;
~ **d'hôte** menú *m*; ~ **lighter**
encendedor *m* de mesa; ~ **salt/wine**
sal *f*/vino de mesa; **at** ~ a la mesa; **sit
down at** ~ sentarse[19] a la mesa; **clear
the** ~ quitar la mesa; **lay the** ~ poner[19]
la mesa; **round** ~ mesa redonda; **turn
the** ~**s on** devolver (ue)[2b] la pelota a;
~**-cloth** mantel *m*; ~**-companion** comensal *m + f*; ~**-football** futbolín *m*;
~**-knife** cuchillo de mesa; ~**land** meseta; ~**-leg** pata de la mesa; ~**-
linen** mantelería; ~**-manners** comportamiento en la mesa; ~**-mat**
salvamanteles *m sing*; ~**-napkin** servilleta; ~**-spoon** cuchara para servir;
~**spoonful** cucharada grande; ~**-talk**
conversación *f* de sobremesa; ~**-
tennis** tenis *m* de mesa; ~**-top** tablero
de la mesa; ~**-turning** (spiritualism)
mesas *fpl* que se mueven; ~**-ware** artículos para la mesa; *v* (motion) presentar; (index) catalogar[5]; (set out)
disponer[19]; ~ **a bill** poner[19] sobre la
mesa un proyecto de ley, *US* dar[19]
carpetazo a un proyecto de ley
tableau cuadro vivo
tablet (soap) pastilla; *med* tableta, comprimido; (stone) lápida; (writing-
paper) bloc (-ques) *m*

tabloid *n* periódico tabloide; *adj* de
forma de tableta
taboo, tabu *n + adj* tabú *m*; *v* tabuizar[7]
tabular tabular
tabulate tabular; ~**d** puesto en forma de
tablas
tabulating *adj* tabulador (-ora *f*)
tabulation tabulación *f*
tabulator (typewriter) tabulador *m*; ~
key tecla del tabulador
tachograph *mot* tacógrafo
tacit tácito
taciturn taciturno
taciturnity taciturnidad *f*
tack *n* (nail) tachuela; (drawing-pin)
chincheta; (sewing) hilván (-anes) *m*;
naut (ship's course) virada; (sail,
rope) amura; *fig* línea de conducta; **be
on the right/wrong** ~ estar[19] en el
buen/mal camino; **hard** ~ rancho
malo; *v* clavar con tachuelas; (sewing)
hilvanar; *naut* virar; ~ **on** *fig* añadir a
tackiness pegajosidad *f*
tacking acción *f* de clavar; (sewing)
acción de hilvanar; *naut* acción de
virar
tackle *n* *mech + naut* aparejo; (pulleys
etc) polea; (football) carga, *fam* corte
m; (rugby) placaje *m*; ~**-block** polea;
v atacar[4]; (try to deal with) abordar;
(undertake) emprender; (football)
cargar[5]; (rugby) placar[4]
tackling *naut* cordaje *m*; (football)
cargas *fpl*; (rugby) placajes *mpl*
tacky pegajoso
tact tacto
tactful diplomático
tactic(s) táctica(s)
tactical táctico
tactician táctico
tactile táctil
tactless indiscreto
tadpole renacuajo
taffeta tafetán *m*
taffrail coronamiento
Taffy habitante *m + f* de Gales

taffy (*US* toffee) caramelo

tag *n* (label) etiqueta; (metal label) herrete *m*; (rag) pingo; (cliché) estribillo; (game) marro; ~ **end** rabito; *v* sujetar una etiqueta/un herrete; ~ **after** pisar los talones a; ~ **along** seguir (i)[3+11]; ~ **along with** acompañar; ~ **on to** unirse a

Tagus Tajo

Tahiti Tahití *m*

Tahitian tahitiano, tahitiana

tail cola, rabo; (of coat, shirt) faldón (-ones) *m*; (hair) trenza; (of music note) rabito; (of comet) cola; (person) seguidor *m* (-ora *f*) de cerca; ~**s** (of coin) cruz (-ces) *f*; ~**s** (evening dress) frac *m*; **put a ~ on** s.o. mandar seguir a alguien; **turn ~** huir[19]; **with his ~ between his legs** con el rabo entre las piernas; ~-**back** *mot* caravana; ~-**board** escalera; ~-**coat** frac *m*; ~-**end** extremo, (remainder) lo que queda; ~-**ender** *sp* colista *m+f*; ~-**feather** pena; ~-**fin** aleta caudal, *aer* timón (-ones) *m* de dirección; ~-**light** (luz (-ces) *f*) piloto; ~-**piece** *print* florón (-ones) *m*, *fig* apéndice; ~-**plane** estabilizador *m* de cola; ~-**skid** *aer* patín (-ines) *m* de cola; ~-**spin** *aer* barrena de cola; ~-**wind** viento de cola; *v* (follow) seguir (i)[3+11] de cerca, **you had me ~ed (by)** usted me hizo seguir (por); (remove ~ from) descolar; ~ **away/off** ir[19] disminuyendo (**into** hasta ser no más que); ~**ed con rabo; **long-~ed** rabilargo; **short-~ed** rabicorto

tailless sin rabo

tailor *n* sastre *m*; ~-**made** *n* traje *m* hecho a (la) medida; *adj* hecho a (la) medida; *fig* sumamente apropiado; ~'**s** (**shop**) sastrería; *v* hacer[19] a la medida

tailoress sastra

tailoring sastrería; (work) corte *m*

taint *n* (blemish) mancha; (tinge) dejo; *v* infeccionar(se); (of meat) corromper(se)

take *n* (money) ingresos *mpl* (de una función); *cin*+*print* toma; *v* tomar, ~ **it or leave it** o lo toma o lo deja; (carry) llevar; (pick up) recoger[8]; (remove) quitar; (choose) escoger[8]; ~ **whatever you fancy!** ¡escoja lo que le apetezca!;

(appropriate) apoderarse de; *phot* sacar[4], ~ **a photo** sacar[4] una fotografía; *cin* filmar; (trick, at cards) hacer[19]; (chess, draughts) comer; (eat, drink) tomar, **will you ~ coffee or tea?** ¿tomará usted café o té?; (capture) hacer[19] prisionero a; (fish) pescar[4]; (trap) atrapar; (grasp) agarrar, **she took my arm** ella me agarró del brazo; (vaccine *etc*) prender; (root) pegar[5], **I don't know if this plant will ~** no sé si pegará esta planta; (be paid) cobrar, **how much will you ~ for that horse?** ¿cuánto cobrará por ese caballo?; (put up with) aguantar, **I can't ~ any more** ya no aguanto más; *med* (catch) contraer[19]; (accompany) acompañar; (guide) conducir[15]; (necessitate) hacer[19] falta, **it will ~ a lot of money** hará falta mucho dinero; (jump over) saltar, **he took the stream in his stride** él saltó el arroyo sin aflojar el paso; **it ~s a little time to get used to it** cuesta un poco acostumbrarse a ello; **it took me two hours to do the journey** tardé dos horas en hacer el viaje; **I ~ it that you will come** supongo que usted vendrá: ~ **things as they come** tomar las cosas como vienen; ~ **by surprise** sorprender; **I took him at his word** me fie de su palabra; **what size do you ~?** ¿qué número gasta usted?

~ **aback** desconcertar (ie)[2a]

~ **after** (follow the example of) seguir (i)[3+11] el ejemplo de; (resemble) parecerse[14] a

~ **amiss** ofenderse

~ **apart** desmontar

~ **away** llevarse; (remove) quitar; (subtract) restar; **it took my breath away** me dejó sin aliento

~ **back** (goods) aceptar la devolución, *fam* descambiar; (return) devolver (ue)[1b]; (statement) retirar lo dicho

~ **down** bajar; (from hook) descolgar (ue)[1a+5]; (write) tomar nota de; (machinery) desmontar; (swallow) tragar[5]; **I took him down a peg or two** le quité los humos

~ **for** tomar por; **did you ~ her for my sister?** ¿la tomó por mi hermana?; ~ **for granted** dar[19] por sentado

~ **from** quitar a; (subtract) restar de

~-**home pay** sueldo líquido

~ **in** hacer[19] entrar; (admit) recibir; (sails) acortar; (comprehend) comprender; (include) abarcar[4]; ~ **it all in** (be deceived) dejarse engañar, (observe closely) mirar con cuidado; **they ~ in washing** lavan la ropa de otros; **I'm going to ~ in this skirt** voy a estrechar esta falda

~ **into:** ~ **into account** tomar en cuenta

~-**off** n aer despegue m; (skit) caricatura (of de)

~ **off** v (remove) quitar, ~ **off your hat!** ¡quítese el sombrero!; (discount) descontar (ue)[1a]; aer despegar[5]; (mimic) parodiar

~ **on** (undertake) tomar; (employ) dar[19] empleo a; (challenge) desafiar; (fight) luchar con; sp jugar (ue)[1a+5] con; **the ship is here to ~ on passengers/supplies** el buque está aquí para embarcar viajeros/cargar[5] provisiones; **don't ~ on so!** ¡no te pongas así!

~ **out** llevar fuera; (extract) sacar[4]; ~ **out a girl** escoltar a una chica, fam salir[19] con una chica; ~ **out a patent** obtener[19] una patente; ~ **out a stain** quitar una mancha; ~ **out for a walk** sacar[4] de paseo; ~ **it out on** (revenge) vengarse[5] en; **it will ~ it out of you** (tire) le cansará

~-**over** n toma de control; ~-**over bid** intento de tomar control

~ **over** v tomar posesión de

~ **to** aficionarse a; (person) coger[8] cariño a; (acquire the habit) coger[8] la costumbre de; ~ **to one's heels** huir[16]

~ **up** (raise) subir; (pick up) recoger[8]; (soak up) absorber; (accept) aceptar; (post) tomar posesión de; ~ **up a carpet** quitar una alfombra; ~ **up the hemline** subir el bajo (de un vestido); ~ **up the matter with** discutir el asunto con; ~ **up residence** establecerse[14]; ~ **up a story** empezar[2a+7] un cuento; ~ **up the study of** dedicarse[4] al estudio de; ~ **up time** ocupar tiempo; **I'll ~ him up on that** (I'll speak to him) le hablaré claro sobre eso, (I can't believe what he says) no puedo aceptar eso; ~ **up with** trabar amistad con

~ **upon o.s.** encargarse[5] de; **she took it upon herself to** ella se encargó de

+*infin*

taken (reserved) ocupado; **be ~ ill** caer[19] enfermo; **be ~ in** (fooled) tragar[5] el anzuelo; **be ~ in by** dejarse engañar por; **be ~ with** (keen on) entusiasmarse por

taker el/la que acepta un desafío/una oferta

taking n toma f; ~**s** ingresos mpl; adj atractivo

talc talco

talcum: ~ **powder** polvos mpl de talco

tale historia; (fable) fábula, +*pej* cuento; **tell ~s** contar (ue)[1a] cuentos, (maliciously) soplar; ~-**bearer** soplón m (-ona f), fam correveidile m+f; ~-**bearing** chivatazos mpl

talent talento; ~**ed** talentoso; ~-**scout** sp cazatalentos m sing+pl

talisman talismán m

talk n conversación f; (formal address) conferencia; (chat) charla; (empty words) palabras vacías; (gossip) rumor m; **give a ~** (on the radio) dar[19] una charla (por la radio/SA el radio); ~ **of the town** comidilla de la ciudad; **there was much ~ of** se hablaba mucho de; **small ~** naderías fpl; v hablar, charlar; ~ **business** hablar de negocios; ~ **English** hablar inglés; ~ **for the sake of talking** hablar por hablar; ~ **the hind leg off a donkey** hablar por los codos; ~ **in one's sleep** hablar en sueños; ~ **nonsense** decir[19] disparates; ~ **shop** hablar de negocios

~ **about** hablar/charlar de

~ **away** seguir (i)[3+11] hablando

~ **down** aer controlar el aterrizaje de; ~ **down to** hablar con desdén a

~ **into** persuadir a; **you've ~ed me into it** me ha convencido usted; ~ **into the microphone** hablar por el micrófono

~ **of** hablar/charlar de; ~ **of the devil!** ¡hablando de Roma, por la puerta asoma!

~ **out of** disuadir de; ~ **out of turn** meterse donde no le llaman

~ **over** discutir; ~ **over a bottle of wine** conversar tomando vino

~ **to** (address) hablar a; (consult) hablar con; (scold) reprender; ~ **to each other/one another** hablarse; ~ **to o.s.** monologar[5]

~ **up** hablar claro

talkative hablador (-ora *f*)

talkativeness locuacidad *f*

talker hablador *m* (-ora *f*); **he's a good ~** él es buen conversador

talkie película sonora

talking parlante; (of birds) parlero; **~-to** (scolding) rapapolvo

tall alto; **be five feet ~** tener[19] cinco pies de altura; **~ order** cosa muy difícil; **~ story** cuento exagerado; **~boy** cómoda alta

tallness altura

tallow sebo; **~ candle** vela de sebo; **~-faced** pálido de cara

tallowy seboso

tally *n* (account) anotación *f*; (stick) tarja; **~-clerk**, **~man** medidor *m*; *v* cuadrar; **~ with** corresponder con

tally-ho! *no equiv* grito del cazador de zorros

Talmud talmud *m*

talon garra

tamable domable

tamarind tamarindo

tamarisk tamarisco

tambour tambor *m*; (for embroidery) bastidor *m* de bordar

tambourine pandereta

tame *adj* manso; (~d) domado; (spiritless) sumiso; (innocuous) inocuo; (unexciting) soso; *v* domar

tameness mansedumbre *f*

tamer domador *m* (-ora *f*)

Tamerlane Tamerlán *m*

taming doma; **'The Taming of the Shrew'** 'La fierecilla domada'

tam-o'-shanter boina escocesa

tamp apisonar

tamper: **~ with** descomponer[19]; (document) falsificar[4]; (witnesses) sobornar

tampon *n* tapón (-ones) *m*; *v* tapar

tan *n* (sunburn) bronceado; (bark) casca; *adj* de color de canela; *v* curtir; broncear; **sun-tanned face** cara curtida/bronceada; *sl* (beat) zurrar

tandem *n* tándem *m*; *adj elect* en tándem

tang (point) espiga; (flavour) sabor *m* picante; *fig* gustillo; (sound) retintín *m*

tangent *n* +*adj* tangente *f*; **go off at a ~** salirse[19] por la tangente

tangential tangencial

tangerine mandarina

tangibility tangibilidad *f*

tangible tangible; *fig* concreto; **~ assets** *comm* valores *mpl* tangibles

Tangier(s) Tánger *m*

tangle *n* +*fig* enredo; *v* enredar(se)

tango *n* tango; *v* bailar el tango

tangy de sabor fuerte

tank +*mil* tanque *m*; **~ engine** locomotora ténder; **~-top** jersey (-eyes) *m* sin mangas; *v* **~ up** beber mucho

tankage cabida de un tanque

tankard pichel *m*

tanker *mot* camión (-ones) *m* cisterna; *naut* petrolero, *SA* tanquero; **~ terminal** puerto petrolero

tanner curtidor *m*; (coin) moneda de seis peniques

tannery curtiduría

tannic: **~ acid** ácido tánico

tannin tanino

tanning curtido; (beating) paliza

Tannoy sistema *m* de comunicación por medio de altavoces

tansy atanasia

tantalize atormentar

tantalizing atormentador (-ora *f*)

tantamount: **~ to** equivalente a

tantrum rabieta

Tanzania Tanzania

Tanzanian tanzanio

Taoiseach primer ministro de la República Irlandesa

[1] **tap** *n* (touch) golpecito; (piece of leather) tapa; **the ~-~-~ of the typewriter** el tecleo de la máquina de escribir; **~-dance** *n* zapateado, *v* zapatear; **~-dancer** zapateador *m* (-ora *f*); *v* golpear ligeramente; **~ s.o. on the shoulder** darle[19] a uno una palmadita en el hombro

[2] **tap** (water) grifo; (of barrel) espita; (gas) llave *f*; *mech* (screw-~) terraja; **~s** *mil* toque *m* de silencio; **on ~** al grifo, (liquor) de barril, *fig* a mano; *tel* (bug) intervención *f*, *sl* pinchazo; **~-room** bodegón (-ones) *m*; **~-root** raíz (-ces) *f* pivotante; **~-water** agua del grifo; *v* (cask) espitar; (resources) explotar; (tree) sangrar; *elect* derivar; **~ a telephone** intervenir[19] una comunicación telefónica, *sl* pinchar

tape *n* +*sp* cinta; (ceremonial) cinta simbólica; (recording ~) cinta magnetofónica; (ticker-~) cinta de teletipo; **have on** ~ tener[19] grabado en cinta; **~-measure** cinta métrica, *fam* metro; **~-recording** grabación (-ones) *f* en cinta; **~-recorder** magnetófono; **~-worm** solitaria; *v* (tie) atar con cinta; (record) hacer[19] una grabación (sonora) de; **I've got it ~d** *fig* lo comprendo perfectamente

taper *n* vela; *eccles* cirio; *v* afilar(se); ~ **away/off** *vt* afilar, *vi* ir[19] disminuyendo; **~ed trousers** pantalón ajustado

tapering ahusado

tapestried entapizado

tapestry tapiz (-ces) *m*; **~-work** tapicería

tapioca tapioca

tapir tapir *m*

tapper *elect* manipulador *m*

tappet *mech* excéntrica; *mot* alzaválvula

tapping golpecitos; *med* paracentesis *f*

tar *n* alquitrán *m*; (sailor) marinero; *v* alquitranar; ~ **and feather** emplumar; **touch of the ~ brush** algo de sangre negra; **be tarred with the same brush** estar[19] cortados por el mismo patrón

tarantula tarántula

tardiness tardanza

tardy tardío

¹ **tare** *bot* arveja

² **tare** *bibl* cizaña; *comm* tara; ~ **weight** tara

target blanco; (aim) meta; **hit the ~** dar[19] en el blanco; **~-practice** tiro al blanco

tariff tarifa; (duty) arancel *m*; **put a ~ on** arancelar; ~ **wall** barrera aduanera

tarmac *n*+*adj* alquitranado; **on the ~** *aer* en la pista de aterrizaje

tarn lago pequeño

tarnish *n* deslustre *m*; *v* deslustrar

tarpaulin lona alquitranada

tarragon estragón *m*

¹ **tarry** *v* detenerse[19]; quedarse atrás

² **tarry** *adj* alquitranado

tarsus tarso

tart *n* pastel *m* (de fruta); (prostitute) ramera; *adj* ácido, *fig* aspero; *v* ~ **up** embellecer[14]; ~ **o.s. up** ponerse[19] las mejores galas

tartan *n* tartán *m*; *adj* de cuadros escoceses

Tartar tártaro; *fig* arpía

tartar *chem* tártaro

tartaric tartárico

Tartary Tartaria

tartlet pastelillo de fruta

tartness acidez *f*; *fig* aspereza

tartuffe tartufa *m*+*f*

tarty como una ramera

task tarea; **take to ~ (for)** reprender; ~ **force** *mil* fuerzas reunidas para una misión especial, (police) equipo de policía con una misión especial; **~-master** capataz (-ces) *m*

Tasmania Tasmania

Tasmanian (habitante *m*+*f*) de Tasmania

tassel *n* borla; *v* adornar con borlas

taste *n* (flavour) sabor *m*, ~ **of honey** sabor a miel; (appreciation) gusto; (sample) muestra; (sip) sorbo; **just a ~, please** una pizca, por favor; **in good/bad ~** de buen/mal gusto; **add salt to ~** añadir sal a gusto; **acquire a ~ for** tomar gusto a; **have a ~ for** tener[19] afición a; **it is just to my ~** me gusta; *vt* (savour) saborear; (try) probar (ue)[1a]; (professionally) catar; *vi* saber[19] a; **it ~s of cheese** sabe a queso; **it ~s good** está riquísimo

tasteful de buen gusto

tasteless soso; (in bad taste) de mal gusto; (lacking charm) *sl invar* soseras

taster catador *m* (-ora *f*)

tasting degustación *f*

tasty sabroso

tattered, in tatters andrajoso

tatting encaje *m* de hilo *m*

tattle *n* charlas *fpl*; (gossip) chismes *mpl*; *v* parlotear; (gossip) chismear

tattler charlatán *m* (-ana *f*); (gossip) chismoso

¹ **tattoo** *mil* (call) toque *m* de retreta; (display) espectáculo militar

² **tattoo** *n* tatuaje *m*; *v* tatuar

tatty desaseado

taunt *n* mofa; *v* mofarse de

taut +*fig* tirante

tauten tensar (ie)[2a]

tautological tautológico

tautology tautología

tavern taberna

tawdriness lo cursi

tawdry cursi

tawny leonado; ~ **owl** cárabo

tax *n* contribución (-ones) *f*, impuesto;

(strain) cargo; ~ **on excess profits** impuesto sobre ganancias excesivas; ~ **allowance** desgravación *f*; ~ **collector** recaudador *m* de contribuciones; ~ **cut** reducción *f* de impuestos/contribuciones; ~ **evasion** evasión *f* fiscal; ~ **exemption** exención *f* de impuestos; ~ **gatherer** recaudador *m* de contribuciones; ~**free** exento de contribución; ~**-haven** país *m* donde se pagan pocos impuestos; ~**payer** contribuyente *m+f*; *v* imponer[19] contribuciones a; *comm* (costs) tasar; **it ~es my patience** me agota la paciencia; **it ~es her intelligence** es demasiado para su inteligencia; ~ **s.o. with** acusarle a uno de

taxable sujeto a contribución; ~ **income** renta imponible; ~ **value** valor *m* impositivo

taxation (payment) contribuciones *fpl*, impuestos *mpl*; (system) sistema *m* tributario; **rate of** ~ tarifa de impuestos

taxi *n* taxi *m*; ~**cab** taxi *m*; ~**-driver** taxista *m+f* ; ~**meter** taxímetro; ~**rank** parada de taxis; *v* ir[19] en taxi, *aer* rodar (ue)[1a] de suelo

taxidermist taxidermista *m+f*

taxidermy taxidermia

tea té *m*; (green) mate *m*; **make** ~ hacer[19] té, *Arg* cebar té/mate; (meal) merienda; *sl* infusión *f* de marihuana; **have** ~ (drink) tomar té, (meal) merendar (ie)[2a]; **high** ~ merienda-cena; **not for all the** ~ **in China** por nada del mundo; ~**bag** bolsita de té; ~**-break** intervalo para tomar té; ~**caddy** bote *m* del té; ~**-chest** caja de té; ~**-cloth** mantelito, (for dishes) paño de secar (la vajilla); ~**-cosy** cubretetera; ~**cup** taza de té; **storm in a** ~**cup** tormenta en un vaso de agua; ~**cupful** taza llena; ~**-dance** té-baile *m*; ~**-garden** plantación *f* de té, (restaurant) restaurante *m* al aire libre; ~**-leaf** hoja de té; ~**-party** té *m*, **she is always out at** ~**-parties** ella siempre está en sus tés; ~**-plant** arbusto de té; ~**-pot** tetera; ~**-room** salón (-ones) *m* de té; ~**-rose** rosa de té; ~**-set**, ~**-service** juego de té; ~**shop** salón (-ones) *m* de té; ~**spoon** cucharita; ~**spoonful** cucharadita; ~

strainer colador *m* de té; ~**-table** mesita para té; ~**-things** tazas, platos *etc* de té; ~**-time** hora del/para el té; ~**-towel** paño de secar (la vajilla); ~**urn** samovar *m*

teach enseñar; (lecture on) ser[19] profesor de; (give a lesson) dar[19] clase, **he** ~**es French this morning** él da clase de francés esta mañana; ~ **how to** enseñar a +*infin*; ~ **s.o. a lesson** *fig* escarmentar (ie)[2a] a uno; ~**-in** seminario

teachable educable

teacher profesor *m* (-ora *f*); **Spanish/ mathematics** ~ profesor *m* (-ora *f*) de español/matemáticas; ~**-training** formación pedagógica; ~ **training college** escuela normal; ~**'s pet** (pupil) diuca *m+f*

teaching *n* enseñanza; *adj* docente; ~ **profession** magisterio

teak (tree) teca; (wood) madera de teca

teal cerceta

team equipo; (*esp* football) selección *f*, **goalkeeper of the Spanish** ~ portero de la selección española; (horses) tiro; (oxen) yunta; (of adjudicators) tribunal *m*; ~**-mate** compañero de juego; ~**-spirit** compañerismo; ~**sports** deportes *mpl* en equipo; ~**work** cooperación *f*; *v* ~ **up** formar un equipo; ~ **up against** aliarse contra; ~ **up with** asociarse con

teamster cochero; (*US* lorry-driver) camionero

[1] **tear** *n* lágrima; **in** ~**s** llorando; **wipe away one's** ~**s** secarse[4] las lágrimas; **with** ~**s in one's eyes** con los ojos llenos de lágrimas; ~**-drop** lágrima; ~**-duct** conducto lacrimal; ~**-gas** gas lacrimógeno; ~**-gas bomb** bomba lacrimógena

[2] **tear** *n* desgarrón (-ones) *m*; *v* rasgar[5]; (flesh) lacerar; (snatch) arrancar[4]

~ **apart** despedazar[7]

~**away** *n* gamberro

~ **away** *vi* huir[16] precipitadamente; *vt* arrancar[4] violentamente

~ **down** (building) derribar; (curtains *etc*) quitar arrancando

~ **off** *vt* arrancar[4]; *vi* salir[19] como un rayo

~ **to pieces** despedazar[7]

~ **up** (paper) romper (*past part* roto); (uproot) desarraigar[5]

tearful lloroso

tease *n* bromista *m+f*; *v* tomar el pelo a; ~ **wool** cardar lana

teasel *bot* cardencha; (textile) carda

teaser (person) bromista *m+f*; (problem) rompecabezas *m sing+pl*

teat teta; (man's) tetilla; (on feeding bottle) tetina

tech *see* **technical college**

technical técnico; ~ **adviser** asesor técnico; ~ **college** *approx* escuela de formación profesional; ~ **drawing** dibujo técnico; ~ **offence** cuasidelito

technicality tecnicidad *f*; (technical term) tecnicismo

technician técnico

technicolo(u)r: in ~ en tecnicolor

technique técnica

technocracy tecnocracia

technocrat tecnócrata *m+f*

technological tecnológico

technologist tecnólogo

technology tecnología; **college of** ~ *approx* universidad *f* laboral

techy quisquilloso

teddy: ~**-bear** osito de trapo; **Teddy boy** petimetre *m* inglés de los años cincuenta

Te Deum tedeum *m*

tedious aburrido

tedium tedio

tee *n* tee *m*; *v* colocar⁴ en el tee; ~ **off** golpear la pelota desde el tee

teem hormiguear; ~ **with** estar¹⁹ lleno de; ~ **with rain** llover (ue)¹ᵇ a cántaros

teeming abundante; ~ **with** lleno de

teenage: ~ **problems** problemas *mpl* de la adolescencia

teenager adolescente *m+f*

teens (numbers) números desde trece hasta diecinueve; (age) edad *f* de trece a diecinueve años; **be in one's** ~ tener¹⁹ de trece a diecinueve años

teeny-weeny *n* chiquito; ~ **bit** trocito; *adv* un poco

teeter balancearse; *fig* vacilar; ~**-totter** balancín (-ines) *m* de sube y baja

teethe echar los (primeros) dientes

teething dentición *f*; ~**-ring** masticador *m*; ~**-troubles** *fig* dificultades *fpl* iniciales de dentición

teetotal abstemio

teetotalism abstinencia completa de bebidas alcohólicas

teetotaller abstemio

telecast *n* programa televisado; *v* televisar

telecommunications telecomunicaciones *fpl*

telegram telegrama *m*

telegraph *n* telégrafo; ~ **pole/wire** poste *m*/hilo telegráfico; *v* telegrafiar

telegraphic telegráfico

telegraphist telegrafista *m+f*

telegraphy telegrafía

telematic telemático

telemetering *space* telemedida

telepathic telepático

telepathist telépata *m+f*

telepathy telepatía

telephone *n* teléfono; *sl* tubo; ~ **box/kiosk** cabina telefónica; ~ **call** llamada telefónica, *fam* telefonazo, *sl* canutazo; ~ **directory** guía telefónica; ~ **exchange** central *f* telefónica, (private exchange) centralilla; ~ **operator** telefonista *m+f*; **she's on the** ~ (has a ~) ella tiene teléfono, (is talking) ella está hablando por teléfono; *v* telefonear

telephonic telefónico

telephonist telefonista *m+f*

telephony telefonía

telephoto telefoto; ~ **lens** teleobjetivo

teleprinter teletipo

telerecord grabar (un programa televisado)

telerecording grabación (-ones) *f* de un programa de televisión

telescope *n* telescopio; *vi* enchufarse; *vt* reducir

telescopic telescópico; ~ **sight** mira telescópica

teletype teletipo; ~**writer** máquina teletipo

televiewer telespectador *m* (-ora *f*)

televise televisar

television televisión *f*; (~ set) televisor *m*; ~ **film** telefilme *m*; ~ **personality** telepersonaje *m*; ~ **screen** telepantalla

telex télex *m*

tell decir¹⁹; **he will** ~ **you the time** él le dirá la hora; (relate) contar (ue)¹ᵃ; (distinguish) distinguir, **he can't** ~ **a waltz from a tango** él no sabe distinguir un vals de un tango; (influence) producir[15] efecto (**on** a); (notice) notar, **I can ~ if he has been drinking** yo noto si ha estado bebiendo; (recognize) (re)conocer[14], **you'll ~ her by her hair** la conocerá por su pelo; **~ s.o. to** decirle[19] a uno que +*subj*; **I'm told that** me han dicho que; **~ me** (say what's on your mind) usted me dirá; **you can never ~** no se puede saber; **who can ~?** ¿quién sabe?; **~ that to the marines!** ¡a otro perro con ese hueso!; **you're telling me!** ¡a quién se lo cuenta!; **~ tales** soplar; **~-tale** soplón *m* (-ona *f*); **~ against/on** contar (ue)[1a] contra, *fam* soplar contra; **~ off** (count) contar (ue)[1a], *mil* designar; (rebuke) regañar

tellable que se puede contar

teller (of stories) narrador *m* (-ora *f*); (bank official) cajero; (parliament) escrutador *m*

telling eficaz (-ces)

telly tele *f*

temerarious atrevido

temerity temeridad *f*

temper *n metal* temple *m*; (humour) humor *m*; (bad temper) mal genio; **keep one's ~** contenerse[19]; **lose one's ~** enfadarse, *SA* entromparse; **get into a ~** ponerse[19] furioso; **in a ~** enfadado; **be in a bad/good ~** estar[19] de mal/buen humor; *v metal* templar; (calm) moderar; (adjust) ajustar; **~ed** *metal* templado; **bad-~ed** de mal humor, *fam* con malas pulgas; **good-~ed** de buen humor

tempera temple *m*; **in ~** al temple

temperament temperamento

temperamental excitable; **be ~** tener[19] genio

temperance moderación *f*; (teetotalism) abstinencia

temperate moderado; (teetotal) abstemio; *meteor* templado

temperature temperatura; **have/run a ~** tener[19] fiebre; **~ chart** gráfico de temperatura

tempest tempestad *f*

tempestuous tempestuoso

Templar templario

template molde *m*

temple templo; *anat* sien *f*

tempo tiempo, ritmo

temporal +*anat* temporal

temporarily temporalmente

temporary temporal, provisional; (employee) eventual; (official) interino; **~ teacher** profesor contratado, profesora contratada

temporize contemporizar[7]

tempt tentar (ie)[2a] (**to** a); (attract) atraer[19]

temptation tentación *f*

tempter tentador *m*

tempting tentador (-ora *f*); (of food) apetitoso

temptress tentadora

ten *n+adj* diez *m*; **~fold** *adj* décuplo, *adv* diez veces; **~-pin bowling** boleras *fpl* americanas; **~-yard circle** (football) círculo central; **~-yard line** (rugby) línea de diez metros

tenable sostenible

tenacious tenaz (-ces)

tenacity tenacidad *f*; **~ of purpose** tesón *m*

tenancy tenencia

tenant *n* inquilino; *fig* habitante *m+f*; **~s' association** comunidad *f* de vecinos; *v* alquilar; *fig* ocupar

tenantry inquilinos *mpl*

tench tenca

¹**tend** *vt* cuidar; (machine) manejar; **he ~s the sheep** él guarda las ovejas

²**tend: ~ to/towards** tender (ie)[2a] a

tendency tendencia

tendentious tendencioso

¹**tender** *n comm* oferta; *naut* gabarra auxiliar; (railway) ténder *m*; **legal ~** moneda de curso legal

²**tender** *adj* tierno; (of wound) dolorido; **~foot** novato; **~-hearted** compasivo; **~loin** *US* filete *m*, *US fam* barrio de mala vida

³**tender** *v* (offer) ofrecer[14]; **~ one's resignation** presentar su dimisión; **~ apologies** presentar excusas; **~ for** presentar una oferta para

tenderness ternura

tendon tendón (-ones) *m*

tendril zarcillo; (of vine) tijereta

tenebrous tenebroso

tenement vivienda; (house) casa de vecindad

tenet dogma *m*

tennis tenis *m*; **play ~** jugar (ue)[1a] al tenis; **~ ball/court** pelota/pista de tenis; **~-elbow** inflamación *f* del codo; **~**

player tenista *m+f*; ~ **racket** raqueta de tenis

tenon *carp* espiga; ~-**saw** sierra de espigas

tenor *n* +*mus* tenor *m*; *adj* de tenor; ~ **part** voz (-ces) *f* de tenor; ~ **horn** corno en fa; ~ **trombone** trombón *m* tenor

tense *n gramm* tiempo, **in the future** ~ en tiempo futuro

tense *adj* tenso; (exciting) lleno de emoción; (foreboding) tirante

tenseness tensión *f*; (foreboding) tirantez *f*

tensile extensible

tension *see* **tenseness**; *elect* voltaje *m*

tent tienda (de campaña); *med* lechino; ~ **peg** estaca; ~ **pole** mastil *m* de la tienda

tentacle tentáculo

tentative tentativo

tenterhook escarpia; **on** ~**s** sobre ascuas

tenth *n* décimo; *fam* décima parte; (of month) el diez; *adj* décimo

tenthly en décimo lugar

tenuity tenuidad *f*

tenuous tenue

tenure tenencia; (of office) ejercicio

tepee tipi *m*

tepid tibio

tepidity tibieza

tercentenary *n* tricentenario; *adj* de trescientos años

Terence Terencio

term *n gramm* + *math* término; (period) plazo; (in prison) condena; (of office) mandato; (school) trimestre *m*, ~ **paper** deber *m* para el fin de trimestre; ~**s** (conditions) condiciones *fpl*, (prices) precios, (relationship) relaciones *fpl*; ~**s of reference** puntos *mpl* de consulta; ~**s of sale** condiciones *fpl* de venta; **in** ~**s of** en términos de; ~**s available** *comm* se puede comprar a plazos; **on easy** ~**s** *comm* a plazos; **I'm on good** ~**s with** estoy en buenas relaciones con; **come to** ~**s** llegar[5] a un acuerdo; **come to** ~**s with** conformarse con; *v* nombrar

termagant fiera

terminable terminable

terminal *n elect* polo; (port) terminal *m*, *SA* estación *f* de cabeza; *adj* (final) terminal; (of school term) trimestral;

~ **velocity** velocidad máxima de caer una cosa

terminate terminar(se)

termination terminación *f*

terminator *space* límite *m* de iluminación

terminology terminología

terminus término; (railway *etc*) estación *f* terminal/*SA* de cabeza

termite termita

tern charrán (-anes) *m*

terra: ~ **firma** tierra firme

terrace *n* terraza; (bank) terraplén (-enes) *m*; (of houses) hilera; *v* terraplenar

terracotta terracota

terrain terreno

terrestrial terrestre

terrible terrible; *fam* malísimo

terribly terriblemente; *fam* de mala manera; *sl* endiabladamente

terrier perro de busca, terrier *m*

terrific tremendo; *fam* estupendo

terrified aterrorizado, *sl* cagado de miedo, *sl* acojonado

terrify aterrorizar[7]

terrifying espantoso

territorial *n* reservista *m*; *adj* territorial; ~ **waters** aguas *fpl* jurisdiccionales

territory territorio

terror terror *m*; **reign of** ~ reinado del terror; ~-**stricken** muerto de miedo

terrorism terrorismo

terrorist *n* + *adj* terrorista *m+f*

terrorize aterrorizar[7]

terry felpa; albornoz *m*

terse sucinto

terseness concisión *f*

tertiary terciario

Terylene *tr* tergal *m*

test *n* prueba, ensayo; *chem* análisis *m*; *psych etc* test *m*; (school) examen (-ámenes) *m*; (standard) piedra de toque; **acid** ~ prueba decisiva; **put to the** ~ poner[19] a prueba; **stand the** ~ soportar la prueba; ~-**ban** acuerdo que prohibe las pruebas de armas nucleares; ~ **card** *TV* carta de ajuste; ~ **case** acción *f* de ensayo para determinar la interpretación de una ley; ~-**flight** vuelo de prueba; ~ **match** partido internacional; ~-**paper** papel *m* de examen, *chem* papel reactivo; ~-**pilot** piloto de pruebas; ~

print *phot* (copia de) prueba; ∼-**tube** tubo de ensayo; ∼-**tube baby** niño probeta; *v* probar (ue)[1a], ensayar; (school) examinar; ∼ **blood-pressure** tomar la tensión; ∼ **eyesight** graduar la vista

testable que puede probarse

testament testamento

testamentary testamentario

testator testador *m*

testatrix testadora

tester ensayador *m* (-ora *f*)

testicle testículo; *vulg* huevo

testification testificación *f*

testify testificar[4] (**that** que); ∼ **to** +*fig* atestar

testimonial recomendación *f*; (appreciation) homenaje *m*; *leg* testimonio; *adj* testimonial

testimony testimonio

testy enojadizo

tetanus tétano

tetchy quisquilloso

tête-à-tête conversación íntima

tether *n* atadura; **be at the end of one's** ∼ estar[19] para volverse (ue)[1b] (*past part* vuelto) loco; *v* atar

tetrahedron tetraedro

tetter herpe *m*+*f*

Teuton teutón *m* (-ona *f*)

Teutonic teutónico

text texto; (topic) tema *m*; (motto) lema; *mus* letra; ∼-**book** libro de texto

textile *n* tejidos *mpl*; ∼ **mill** fábrica de tejidos; *adj* textil

textual textual

texture textura

Thai tailandés *m* (-esa *f*)

Thailand Tailandia

thalidomide talidomida; ∼ **baby** niño talidomídico

Thames Támesis *m*

than que; (before numeral) de, **she has more** ∼ **you/twenty** ella tiene más que usted/más de veinte; **he has more friends** ∼ **you think** él tiene más amigos de los que usted cree

thank: ∼s gracias *fpl*; ∼s **to** gracias a; **many** ∼s muchas gracias; **give/return** ∼s dar[19] las gracias; **vote of** ∼s voto de gracias; ∼**sgiving** acción *f* de gracias; *US* **Thanksgiving Day** día *m* de acción de gracias; *v* dar[19] las gracias a (**for** por); (**no**) ∼ **you** (no) gracias, *iron* ¡a

usted!; **you have only yourself to** ∼ **for it** usted solo tiene la culpa de ello; **I'll** ∼ **you to be more careful** le agradecería que tuviese más cuidado; ∼ **goodness!** ¡gracias a Dios!

thankful agradecido; **I'm** ∼ **to find you** me alegro de encontrarle a usted

thankfulness agradecimiento

thankless (person) ingrato; (task) sin recompensa; *fam* en balde

thanklessness ingratitud *f*

that *dem adj* ese *m*, esa; (more remote) aquel *m*, aquella; ∼ **way** por allí, (less precise) por ahí; *adv* tan, ∼ **far** tan lejos; ∼ **many** tantos *mpl*, tantas *fpl*; ∼ **much** tanto, **I didn't like it all** ∼ **much** no me gustó tanto; *dem pron* ése *m*, ésa, eso *neut*; (more remote) aquél *m*, aquélla, aquello *neut*; (**so**) ∼'s ∼! ¡se acabó!; ∼ **was** ∼ allí fue el acabose; ∼ **is** (**to say**) es decir; ∼'s **the way to do it** así se hace; ∼'s **what I'm going to do** eso es lo que pienso hacer; **for all** ∼ a pesar de eso; **what did he mean by** ∼? ¿qué quería decir con eso?; **I hope it won't come to** ∼ espero que no llegue a ese punto; **her face is** ∼ **of a film-star** su cara es la de una estrella de cine; **at** ∼ acto seguido; **like** ∼ así; **with** ∼ con eso; *rel pron* que, el/la cual; (∼ **which**) el que, la que, lo que; **all** ∼ **he said** todo lo que dijo él; *conj* (para) que; **so** ∼ (purpose) para que +*subj*, (result) de modo que; ∼'s **life!** ¡así es la vida!

thatch *n* techo de paja; *v* bardar

thatcher bardador *m*

thaw *n* deshielo; *v* deshelar(se) (ie)[2a]; *fig* hacerse[19] más tratable

the el *m*, la, lo *neut*, los, las; (omitted before number of king *etc*) **Philip** ∼ **Second** Felipe segundo; ∼ **more ...** ∼ **more** cuanto más ... (tanto) más, ∼ **more he eats** ∼ **fatter he gets** cuanto más come más engorda; ∼ **more** ∼ **merrier** cuanto(s) más, mejor; ∼ **sooner** ∼ **better** cuanto antes, mejor

theatre teatro; (for lectures) aula; *surg* quirófano, *fam* sala de operaciones; ∼ **agency** despacho de localidades para teatro; ∼ **attendant** acomodador *m* (-ora *f*); ∼**goer** aficionado/aficionada al teatro; ∼ **in-the-round** teatro redondo con el escenario en el centro;

~ **workshop** taller *m* de teatro

theatrical teatral; ~**s** *n* funciones *fpl* teatrales

thee te; (*after prep*) ti; **with** ~ contigo

theft robo; ~-**proof** a prueba de ladrones

their su(s); ~**s** el suyo, la suya, los suyos, las suyas

theism teísmo

theist *n+adj* teísta *m+f*

theistic teísta

them (things) los, las; (persons) *Sp* les *m*, *SA* los, las; *dat* les, **I've sent ~ a letter** les he mandado una carta; (*after prep*) ellos/ellas, **he arrived with ~** él llegó con ellos/ellas; *reflex* sí; **they brought it with ~** lo trajeron consigo

thematic temático

theme tema; ~ **song** música sintónica, tema musical

themselves ellos mismos, ellas mismas; *reflex* se, **they dressed ~** se vistieron

then *adj* (de) entonces, **the ~ ruler** el gobernante de entonces; *adv* entonces; (later) luego; ~ **and there** acto seguido; **before ~** antes de ese momento; **by ~** para entonces; **now ~** ahora bien; **now and ~** de vez en cuando; **since ~** desde entonces; **what ~?** ¿y qué más?; *conj* (well ~) pues

thence de allí; (therefore) por eso; ~-**forth**, ~**forward** de allí en adelante, (time) desde entonces

theocentric teocéntrico

theocracy teocracia

theocratic teocrático

theodolite teodolito

Theodore Teodoro

theologian teólogo

theological teológico; ~ **college** seminario, *joc* fábrica de curas

theologize hacerse[19] el teólogo

theology teología

theorem teorema *m*

theoretic(al) teórico

theorist teórico

theorize teorizar[7]

theory teoría

theosophical teosófico

theosophist teósofo

theosophy teosofía

therapeutic terapéutico; ~**s** **therapy** terapéutica

therapist terapeuta *m+f*

therapy terapéutica, terapia

there allí; (less precise) allá; (omitted before verb followed by its subject) ~ **came a time when** vino una época en que; ~ **you are!** (demonstration) ¡allí lo tiene usted!, (that's all) ¡eso es todo!; ~, ~! ¡vaya, vaya!; **she's all ~** ella es despierta; **he's not all ~** él está chiflado; ~ **is/are** hay; ~ **isn't any/aren't any** no hay; ~ **has/had been** ha/había habido; ~ **may be** puede haber; ~ **must be** tiene que haber; ~ **was/were** había; ~ **will be** habrá; ~ **would be** habría; **down/up** ~ allí abajo/arriba; **over** ~ (in another country) allá; **in/out** ~ allí dentro/fuera; **go** ~ **and back** ir[19] y volver (ue)[1b] (*past part* vuelto); ~**abouts** por allí, (of time) por entonces; ~**after** desde entonces; ~**by** por lo cual; ~**in** a ese respecto; ~**upon** por lo tanto; ~**with** con eso

therefore por eso

Theresa Teresa

therm unidad térmica

thermal térmico; ~ **springs** termas *fpl*; ~ **water** aguas *fpl* termales

thermic térmico

thermionic: ~ **valve** *rad* lámpara termiónica

thermodynamics termodinámica

thermoelectric termoeléctrico

thermometer termómetro

thermometric(al) termométrico

thermonuclear termonuclear

thermoplastic termoplástico

Thermopylae Termópilas

Thermos(-flask) *tr* termo(s) *m*

thermostat termostato

thermostatic termostático

thesaurus tesauro

these *adj* estos, estas; *pron* éstos, éstas

Theseus Teseo

thesis tesis *f*; (short) tesina

Thessalonian *n+adj* tesalónico

Thessaly Tesalia

they ellos, ellas; ~ **who** los que

thick *n* parte gruesa; ~ **of the fight** lo más reñido de la lucha; **in the ~ of** en medio de; **through ~ and thin** a toda prueba; *adj* (big) grueso; (of smoke *etc*) denso; (muddy) turbio; (of voice) ronco; (abundant) abundante; (stupid) estúpido; (intimate) íntimo; **one metre ~** de un metro de espesor; **the**

room was ~ **with** el cuarto estaba atestado de; **the air was ~ with** el aire estaba lleno de; **be ~ with** (friendly) tener[19] intimidad con, *fam* tener[19] buenas migas con; **be as ~ as thieves** ser[19] uña y carne; **lay it on ~** exagerar mucho; **that's a bit ~**! ¡no hay derecho a eso!; **I'll give you a ~ ear** te daré una bofetada; **~ stroke** (of letter) grueso; **~-headed** torpe; **~-lipped** de labios gruesos; **~-set** grueso; **~-skinned** *fig* insensible

thicken espesar(se); (of mystery) complicarse[4]

thickening hinchamiento; (*cul* +paints) espesante *m*

thicket matorral *m*

thickish algo espeso

thickness espesor *m*; (consistency) consistencia; (denseness) densidad *f*

thief ladrón *m* (-ona *f*), *fam* caco, *sl* chorizo

thieve robar; *sl* chorizar[7]

thievery, thieving robo, latrocinio

thievish ladrón

thigh muslo; **~-bone** fémur *m*

thimble dedal *m*

thimbleful *fig* gota

thin *adj* delgado; (of air, sounds) tenue; (lightweight) ligero, **~ material** tela ligera; (sparse) escaso; (watery) aguado; (of wine) aguado, *fam* bautizado; (transparent) transparente; (of argument) flojo; **~ on the ground** escaso; **~ on top** algo calvo; **grow ~** adelgazar[7]; **make ~** hacer[19] adelgazar; **rather ~** (of people) algo flaco; **~-clad** ligero de ropa; **~-faced** de cara delgada; **~-lipped** de labios finos; **~-skinned** *fig* sensible; *v* (slim) adelgazar[7]; (disperse) reducir(se)[15]; (add water) aguar[6], *fam* bautizar[7]; **~ out** (hair) *vt* entresacar[4], *vi* caer[19]

thine (el) tuyo, (la) tuya, (los) tuyos, (las) tuyas

thing cosa; **~s** (belongings) efectos *mpl*, (clothing) efectos personales, (life) vida, **~s are easier nowadays** la vida es más fácil hoy día; **the best ~** lo mejor; **the worst ~** lo peor; **the only ~** lo único; **poor ~**! ¡pobre!; **above all ~s** sobre todo; **as ~s are/stand** tal como están las cosas; **for one ~** en primer lugar; **just the ~, the very ~** exacta-

mente lo que hace falta; **of all ~s**! (pleasant surprise) ¡qué sorpresa!, (disgust) ¡qué asco!; **no such ~**! ¡nada de eso!; **the ~ is that** el caso es que; **the ~ is to** lo más importante es +*infin*; **I don't know the first ~ about** no sé nada en absoluto de; **she knows a ~ or two** ella sabe cuántas son cinco; **how are ~s?** *fam* ¿qué tal?; **have a ~ about** *fam* tener[19] manía de; **it's the ~** *fam* está de moda; **it's not the done ~** no se hace eso; **do one's ~** hacer[19] lo que uno quiere

thingummy(bob) chisme *m*

think *n*: **have a good, long ~** pensar (ie)[2a] mucho; **~-tank** comisión *f* de expertos; *v* pensar (ie)[2a]; (believe) creer[17], **I ~ so/not** creo que sí/no; (meditate) meditar; **I should ~ so!** ¡ya lo creo!, **I don't ~!** (expressing disbelief) ¡no lo creo!, *fam* ¡y un jamón!; **I don't know what to ~** no sé qué pensar; **if you ~ fit** si usted quiere; **you're not thinking on the right lines** sus pensamientos no van por buen camino; **~ nothing of it!** ¡no faltaba más!

~ about pensar (ie)[2a] en; **what do you ~ about the monarchy?** ¿qué opina usted de la monarquía?; **what on earth am I thinking about today?** ¿dónde demonios tengo hoy la cabeza?; **if you ~ about it, it's sad having no children** bien mirado, es triste no tener hijos

~ of pensar (ie)[2a] en; (opinion) pensar (ie)[2a] de; **~ better of it** mudar de parecer; **~ highly of s.o.** tener[19] en gran estima a alguien; **~ little of** tener[19] en poco; **~ nothing of** tener[19] en poco, (ignore) no hacer caso de; **~ well of** tener[19] buena opinión de

~ out resolver (ue)[1a] (*past part* resuelto)

~ over meditar

~ up idear; *US* resolver (ue)[1a] (*past part* resuelto)

thinkable concebible

thinker pensador *m* (-ora *f*)

thinking *n* pensamiento; **way of ~** modo de pensar; **to my way of ~** a mi parecer; *adj* pensante

thinner(s) aguarrás *m*

thinness delgadez *f*; (of air, sounds) tenuidad *f*; (sparseness) escasez *f*; (of argument) flojedad *f*

third n tercero; fam tercera parte; mus tercera; ~ **of May** (el) tres de mayo; **Henry the Third** Enrique tercero; adj tercero; **he came in** ~ él llegó en tercer lugar; ~-**class** de tercera clase; ~-**class road** carretera de tercer orden; ~-**degree** interrogación violenta/severa; ~ **party** tercero; ~-**party insurance** seguro contra terceros; ~ **person** gramm tercera persona; ~ **quarter** (of moon) luna menguante; ~-**rate** de tercera clase; ~ **time lucky!** ¡a la tercera va la vencida!; **Third World** n tercer mundo; adj tercermundista m+f

thirdly en tercer lugar

thirst n sed f; v +fig tener[19] sed (**after**, **for** de)

thirsty sediento; **be** ~ tener[19] sed; **go** ~ pasar sed; ~ **work** trabajo que hace sudar

thirteen n+adj trece m

thirteenth n+adj decimotercero; **Alphonso the Thirteenth** Alfonso trece; ~ **of June** (el) trece de junio

thirtieth n treintavo; adj trigésimo; (date) (el) treinta

thirty n+adj treinta m; **the thirties** los años treinta; ~-**first**, ~-**second** treinta y uno/y dos

this adj este m, esta; ~ **afternoon** esta tarde; **by** ~ **time** ya; ~ **way** (in this direction) por aquí, (like this) de este modo; pron éste m, ésta, esto neut; ~ **and that** esto y lo otro; ~ **is my birthday** hoy es mi cumpleaños; **what's** ~? ¿qué es esto?

thistle cardo; ~**down** vilano de cardo

thistly lleno de cardos

thither (hacia) allá

Thomas Tomás

thong correa

thorax tórax m

thorn espina; **be a** ~ **in the flesh of** ser[19] una espina clavada en; ~-**brake** espinal m; ~-**bush** espino

thornless sin espinas

thorny espinoso

thorough (complete) completo; (careful) cuidadoso; (conscientious) concienzudo; ~**bred** n caballo/perro de pura sangre, adj de pura sangre; ~**fare** vía pública; **no** ~**fare** se prohibe el paso; ~-**going** (uncompromising)

intransigente, (complete) completo

thoroughly de fondo; **you are a** ~ **selfish person** eres un egoísta de marca

thoroughness perfección f

those adj esos mpl, esas fpl; (more remote) aquellos mpl, aquellas fpl; pron ésos mpl, ésas fpl; (more remote) aquéllos mpl, aquéllas fpl; ~ **who** los que

thou tú

though aunque +subj (if doubt is implied); (nevertheless) sin embargo; **as** ~ como si +subj; **even** ~ aunque +subj

thought pensamiento; (care) cuidado; (intention) idea; **the** ~ **struck me** se me ocurrió la idea; **it's the** ~ **that counts** la intención es lo que vale; **give** (**much**) ~ **to** considerar (bien); **on second** ~s después de pensarlo bien; ~-**reader** adivinador m (-ora f) de pensamientos; ~-**reading** adivinación f de pensamientos; ~-**transference** telepatía

thoughtful pensativo; (careful) cuidadoso; (pensive) meditabundo; (kind) considerado

thoughtfulness seriedad f; (kindness) consideración f; (forethought) previsión f

thoughtless (careless) descuidado; (inconsiderate) desconsiderado

thoughtlessness (carelessness) descuido; (unkindness) desconsideración f

thousand n+adj mil m; **two** ~ **soldiers** dos mil soldados; ~s **of demonstrators** miles mpl de manifestantes

thousandth n+adj milésimo

thraldom esclavitud f

thrall esclavitud f; **hold in** ~ fig fascinar

thrash (beat) zurrar; agri trillar; (defeat) derrotar rotundamente; ~ **about** agitarse; ~ **out** (resolve) resolver (ue)[1a] (past part resuelto) después de una larga discusión

thrashing (beating) zurra; agri trillo; (defeat) derrota; ~-**floor** era; ~-**machine** trilladora

thread (sewing) hilo; (of silkworm/spider) hebra; (of screw) rosca; fig hilo, **take up the** ~ coger el hilo; v (sewing) enhebrar; (beads) ensartar; ~ **one's way through** abrirse (past part abierto) paso por; **~bare** raído

threat amenaza

threaten amenazar[7]

threatening n amenazas fpl; adj amenazador (-ora f)

three n+adj tres m; **~-colour(ed)** de tres colores; **~-cornered** triangular; **~-cornered hat** tricornio; **~-decker** naut navío de tres puentes; **~-dimensional** tridimensional; **~-eight time, ~-four time** mus tres m por ocho/por cuatro; **~-engined plane** (avión m) trimotor m; **~-figure** (of sums) de tres cifras; **~fold** adj triple, adv tres veces; **~-foot rule** metro; **~ hundred** trescientos (-as); **~-legged** de tres patas; **~-masted** de tres palos; **~-master** velero de tres palos; **~pence** tres peniques mpl; **~penny** de tres peniques; **~-phase** trifásico; **~-piece suite** tresillo; **~-pin plug/socket** elect enchufe m/ toma trifásica; **~-ply** (wood) de tres capas, (wool) triple; **~-point turn** mot vuelta completa de tres movimientos; **~-quarter** (size of bed) de entrecama; **~-quarter sheet** sábana de entrecama; **~some** grupo de tres, sp partida jugada entre tres personas; **~ thousand** tres mil; **~-wheeled** de tres ruedas; **~-wheeler** mot coche m de tres ruedas, (cycle) triciclo

thresh trillar

threshing n trilla; adj de trilla; **~ floor** era; **~ machine** trilladora

threshold umbral m; **on the ~ of** fig en los umbrales de; **~ agreement** acuerdo condicional colectivo

thrice tres veces

thrift frugalidad f

thriftiness frugalidad f

thriftless malgastador (-ora f)

thriftlessness falta de frugalidad

thrifty frugal

thrill n emoción f; (tingle) estremecimiento; **what a ~!** ¡qué emoción!; **the big ~ comes at the end** el momento emocionante viene al final; v emocionar(se); estremecer(se)[12]; **be ~ed by** estar[19] cautivado por

thriller novela de suspense; cin película de suspense

thrilling emocionante

thrive prosperar; (grow) crecer[12]; (grow strong) desarrollarse; bot acertar

(ie)[2a]

thriving próspero

throat garganta; **clear one's ~** carraspear; **cut one's ~** cortarse el cuello; **~-pastille** pastilla para la tos

throaty ronco

throb n latido; v latir; mot (vibrate) vibrar; (noise) runrunear

throbbing latidos mpl; mot vibración f; (noise) runruneo

throes agonía; **be in the ~ of** estar[19] luchando con; **be in the ~ of childbirth** sufrir los dolores de parto; **death-~** agonía de la muerte

thrombosis trombosis f

throne n trono; (regal powers) corona; v elevar al trono

throng n muchedumbre f; vt atestar; vi apiñarse, afluir

throstle tordo

throttle n mech reguladora; mot acelerador m; fam (throat) pescuezo; v estrangular; fig ahogar[5]

through adj sin obstrucción; (train) directo; **~ ticket** billete m directo; **~ traffic** vehículos mpl interurbanos; prep por, a través de; **~ the window** por la ventana; (by means of) por medio de; (due to) debido a; adv (time) desde el principio hasta el fin; (place) por todas partes; **~ and ~** enteramente; **be ~ (with)** haber[19] terminado (con); **I'm ~ (I quit)** para mí se acabó; **I'll be ~ in a moment** en seguida termino; **you're ~** tel está usted al habla; **~out** durante todo, hasta el final; **~out the world** mundialmente

throw n tirada, tiro; (wrestling) derribo; **it's your ~** a usted le toca tirar; **within a stone's ~ (of)** a tiro de piedra (de); v tirar, arrojar; cer hacer[19]; (twist) torcer (ue)[1b]; (wrestling) derribar; **he threw himself to the ground** él se tumbó; **she threw herself from the train** ella se arrojó del tren; **~ a glance** echar una mirada; **this horse will not ~ you** este caballo no le tirará de la silla; **I knew the boxer was going to ~ the fight** ya sabía yo que el boxeador iba a perder con premeditación; **snakes ~ their skins** las serpientes mudan la piel; **~ open** abrir (past part abierto) de par en par; **~ open the discussion**

dar[19] la palabra al público; ~ **overboard** echar al mar, *fig* abandonar; ~ **the book at s.o.** *fig* echarle a alguien el paquete

~ **about** esparcir[15]; (money) derrochar

~ **aside** echar a un lado; *fig* abandonar

~**away** *adj*: ~ **container/bottle** envase *m*/botella sin devolución

~ **away** *v* tirar; *sl* chindar; *fig* (money) malgastar; (opportunity) desperdiciar; ~ **away one's life** sacrificar[4] la vida

~ **back** *n* reversión *f*

~ **back** *v* (ball) devolver (ue)[1b]; (foe) arrollar; (offer) rechazar

~ **down** echar a tierra; (demolish) derribar; ~ **down the gauntlet** arrojar el guante; ~ **down one's arms** rendirse (i)[3]

~**in** *n sp* saque *m* (de banda)

~ **in** *v* (give extra) dar[19] de más; (interpolate) meter; (football) sacar[4]; ~ **in the towel** darse[19] por vencido

~ **off** (clothing) quitarse; (get rid of) deshacerse[19] de; (write quickly) hacer[19] de prisa

~ **on** echar sobre; (clothing) ponerse[19]; ~ **light on** +*fig* esclarecer[14]

~**out** *n* artículo sin valor

~ **out** *v see* ~ **away**; (person) poner[19] en la calle; (one's chest) sacar[4] pecho; ~ **out of gear** *fig* trastornar

~ **over** (bridge) tender (ie)[2b] sobre; (desert) abandonar

~ **up** lanzar[7] por el aire; (erect) levantar; (vomit) vomitar; (renounce) renunciar; ~ **up the sponge** darse[19] por vencido

~ **o.s. upon** lanzarse[7] sobre

thrower tirador *m* (-ora *f*)

throwing *n* lanzamiento; ~ **the discus/ hammer** lanzamiento del disco/martillo; *adj* arrojadizo; ~ **knife** cuchillo arrojadizo

thru *see* **through**

thrum *n* (string instrument) rasgueo; (keyed instrument) tecleo; *v* rasguear; teclear

[1] **thrush** tordo

[2] **thrush** *med* afta

thrust *n* empujón (-ones) *m*; *mech* empuje *m*; *mil* ataque *m*; (with lance) lanzazo; (with sword) estocada; *fig* determinación *f*; *v* (push) empujar;

(put) meter

~ **aside** empujar a un lado; (reject) rechazar[7]

~ **in** introducir[15]; **with his hands ~ in his pockets** con las manos metidas en los bolsillos

~ **upon** imponer[19]; ~ **o.s. upon** entrometerse con

thud *n* ruido sordo; *v* golpear con ruido sordo

thug (murderer) asesino; (hooligan) gamberro

thuggery asesinatos *mpl*; (hooliganism) gamberrismo

thumb *n* pulgar *m*; **under the ~ of** bajo el dominio de; **rule of ~** métodos empíricos; ~**-index** uñeras; ~**-nail** *n* uña del pulgar, *adj* en miniatura; ~**-nut** tuerca de orejas; ~**-print** impresión *f* del pulgar; ~**screw** empulgueras *fpl*; ~**-tack** chincheta; *v* manosear; ~ **a lift** hacer[19] autostop; ~ **through** hojear

thump *n* golpe *m*; *vt* golpear; *vi* (of heart) palpitar

thumping *adj* enorme

thunder *n* trueno; *fig* estruendo; (of hooves) estampido; ~**bolt** +*fig* rayo; ~**clap** trueno; ~**cloud** nube *f* de tormenta; ~**flash** petardo; ~**storm** tormenta de truenos; ~**struck** *fig* pasmado; **I was ~struck by the news** me dejaron atónito las noticias; *v* tronar (ue)[1a]; *fig* retumbar; (in speech) fulminar (**against** contra)

thunderer fulminador *m* (-ora *f*)

thundering *fam* enorme

thunderous atronador (-ora *f*)

thundery tronador (-ora *f*)

thurible incensario

Thursday jueves *m*; **on ~** el jueves; **on ~s** los jueves; **Maundy ~** Jueves Santo

thus así; (in this way) de esta manera; ~ **far** hasta aquí

thwack *n* golpe *m*; *v* golpear

thwart *n* bancada; *v* frustrar

thy tu(s); ~**self** (subject) tú mismo/ misma, (object) te, (after *prep*) ti mismo/misma

thyme tomillo

thyroid tiroideo; ~ **gland** tiroides *m*

tiara tiara

Tiberius Tiberio

Tibet Tibet *m*

Tibetan *n+adj* tibetano

tibia tibia

tic tic *m*

[1] **tick** *ent* garrapata

[2] **tick** (bedding) funda

[3] **tick** *fam* crédito; **on** ~ de fiado

[4] **tick** (sound) tictac *m*; (mark) contraseña; *fam* (moment) momento; *v* hacer[19] tictac; ~ **over** *mot* marchar en punto muerto; (put a ~ against) poner[19] una señal contra; ~ **off** *fam* echar un rapapolvo a

ticker (heart) corazón (-ones) *m*; (watch) reloj *m* de bolsillo; ~**-tape** cinta de cotizaciones

ticket *n* (for travel) billete *m*; (for entertainment) entrada; (counterfoil) talón *m*; (label) etiqueta; *mot* (fine) multa; *US pol* candidatura; **buy a** ~ sacar[4] un billete/una entrada; **that's the** ~ *fam* eso es lo que hacía falta; ~ **agency** (travel) agencia de viajes, (entertainments) agencia de venta de localidades; ~ **collector/inspector/taker** revisor *m*; ~ **holder** abonado; ~ **office/window** taquilla, (railway) despacho de billetes; ~**-of-leave** libertad *f* condicional; ~**-punch** sacabocados *m sing* de billetes; ~ **seller** taquillero, taquillera; ~**-tout** revendedor *m* de billetes; ~**-touting** reventa de billetes; *v* poner[19] etiqueta(s) a

ticking funda; ~**-off** rapapolvo

tickle *n* cosquilla; **give s.o. a** ~ hacer[19] cosquillas a; **slap and** ~ jugueteo amoroso; *vi* tener[19] cosquillas; **my leg** ~**s** tengo cosquillas en la pierna; *vt* hacer[19] cosquillas a; (amuse) divertir (ie)[2c]

tickler *rad* bobina de regeneración

tickling cosquillas *fpl*

ticklish cosquilloso; (difficult) peliagudo

tick-tack-toe tres en raye

tidal de marea; ~ **wave** ola de marea

tiddler pececillo; (stickleback) espinoso

tiddly achispado; ~**-winks** juego de la pulga; **play** ~**-winks** jugar (ue)[1a] a la pulga

tide *n* marea; *fig* corriente *f*; **against the** ~ contra la corriente; **high** ~ pleamar *f*, *fig* apogeo; **low** ~ bajamar *f*, *fig* punto más bajo; **at the turn of the** ~ al cambio de la marea, *fig* al momento

de cambio decisivo; ~ **table** tabla de mareas; ~ **mark** línea de la marea alta, *fig* costra; *v* ~ **over** superar

tidiness aseo

tidings noticias *fpl*

tidy aseado; (of tidy habits) ordenado, *fig* considerable; *v* (+ ~up) asear, poner[19] en orden; ~ **o.s.** (up) arreglarse

tie *n* (neck-~) corbata; *bui* tirante *m*; *mus* ligado; (railway) traviesa; *fig* (bond) vínculo; (hindrance) estorbo; *sp* (drawn game) empate *m*; *sp* (match) partido, **cup**~ partido de copa; ~**-breaker** *sp* partido de desempate; ~**-clip**, ~**-pin** alfiler *m* de corbata; ~**-tack** sujetador *m* de corbata; *vi sp* empatar; *vt* atar; *mus* ligar[4]; (neck-~) hacer[19] el nudo de; ~ **a knot** hacer[19] un nudo

~ **down** *fig* limitar; (hinder) estorbar

~ **in with** concordar (ue)[1a] con

~ **together** unir

~**-up** *n* conexión (-ones) *f*

~ **up** *v* atar; *naut* amarrar; (parcel) hacer[19]; (traffic) obstruir[16]; ~ **up a matter** arreglar un asunto; ~ **up money** invertir (ie)[2c] dinero; ~ **up with** concordar (ue)[1a] con; **be tied up (with)** *fig* estar[19] ocupado (en)

tied: ~ **cottage** casa que pertenece al empleador del inquilino; ~ **house** taberna que pertenece a una fábrica de cerveza

tier (of seats) grada; (of wedding cake) piso

tiff riña ligera

tiffin almuerzo ligero

tig marro

tiger tigre *m*; *US* jaguar norteamericano; ~**-cat** ocelote *m*; ~**-lily** tigridia; ~**-moth** arctia caja

tigerish feroz (-ces)

tight (~-fitting) apretado; (of clothing, shoes *etc*) estrecho; (shut) bien cerrado; (leak-proof) hermético; (taut) tieso; (of supplies) escaso; (drunk) bebido; (dangerous) peligroso; **be in a** ~ **corner/spot** estar[19] en una encrucijada; (mean) tacaño; **be** ~**-fisted** ser[19] roñoso; **hold** ~ agarrarse fuerte (**on to** a); ~ **trousers are in fashion** los pantalones ajustados están de moda; ~**-lipped** callado; ~**rope** cuerda floja;

~**rope artist** equilibrista *m*+*f*, *Cub* caballitero; ~ **wad** tacaño; ~**s** *n* panty *m*, *theat* leotardo

tighten *vt* apretar (ie)²ᵃ; (make narrower) estrechar; (stretch) estirar; ~ **one's belt** hacer¹⁹ economías; ~ **a screw** apretar (ie)²ᵃ un tornillo; *vi* apretarse (ie)²ᵃ; estrecharse; estirarse

tightness (narrowness) estrechez *f*; (tautness) tirantez *f*; (intoxication) emborrachamiento; (meanness) tacañería

tigress tigresa

tike (boor) gamberro; (*US* mischievous child) diablillo; (mongrel) perro callejero

tilde tilde *f*

tile *n* teja; (for floor) baldosa; (glazed) azulejo; *v* tejar; embaldosar; poner¹⁹ azulejos; ~**d floor** embaldosado; ~**maker** fabricante *m* de baldosas/azulejos/tejas

tiler (of roof tiles) tejero; (of floor tiles) solador *m*

¹ **till** *n* (drawer) cajón (-ones) *m*; (cashregister) (caja) registradora

² **till** *v agri* cultivar

³ **till** *prep* hasta; *conj* hasta que +*subj* (if future is referred to)

tillable cultivable

tillage cultivo

tiller *agri* labrador *m*; *naut* caña del timón

tilt *n* inclinación *f*; (joust) torneo; (at) **full** ~ a toda velocidad; *v* inclinar(se); (joust) tornear; ~ **at** atacar⁴

tilting *see* tilt

timber *bui* madera de construcción; (trees) árboles *mpl* del monte; ~! ¡bolva!; ~**s** *bui* vigas *fpl*; *naut* cuaderna; ~**-merchant** maderero; ~**wolf** lobo gris; ~**-work** maderaje *m*; ~**-yard** maderería; *v* enmaderar, ~**ed** enmaderado; (with trees) arbolado

timbre timbre *m*

timbrel tamboril *m*

time *n* tiempo; **a long** ~ mucho tiempo; (era) época; (of the clock) hora, **what** ~ **is it?** ¿qué hora es?; (of the year) estación (-ones) *f*; (occasion) ocasión (-ones) *f*; *mus* compás *m*, **mark** ~ marcar⁴ el compás; (respite) plazo; (numerical) vez *f*; ~ **and** (~) **again** una y otra vez; **have the** ~ **of one's life**

pasarlo bomba; ~ **out of mind** tiempo inmemorial; ~ **to come** tiempos *mpl* venideros; ~ **to get up/go to bed** hora de levantarse/acostarse¹⁴; ~ **was when** en otro tiempo; ~ **will tell** el tiempo dirá; **it's not the** ~ **for** no es el momento propicio para; **the** ~ **was not ripe** no estaba el horno para bollos; ~ **flies** el tiempo vuela; **it's about** ~! ¡ya es hora!; **two/three at a** ~ dos/tres a la vez; ~**-and-motion study** estudio de tiempos y movimientos; **at no** ~ nunca; **at the** ~ entonces; **at the present** ~ actualmente, (at this moment) en este momento; **at the proper** ~ a la hora debida; **at the same** ~ a la vez, (however) sin embargo; **at that** ~ en aquella época, (at that moment) en aquel instante; **at** ~**s** a veces; **any** ~ (hour) a cualquier hora, (occasion) en cualquier momento; **behind the** ~**s** atrasado, (unfashionable) pasado de moda; **between** ~**s** entre medias; **by the** ~ **that** para cuando +*subj*; **by that** ~ para entonces; **each/every** ~ cada vez; **for some** ~ durante algún tiempo; **for the** ~ **being** de momento; **for all** ~ para siempre; **from this** ~ **forth** desde ahora en adelante; **from** ~ **to** ~ de vez en cuando; **in** ~ (punctual) a tiempo, *mus* al compás; **in** ~ **you will understand** con el tiempo comprenderá usted; **in a short** ~ en breve; **in an hour's** ~ dentro de una hora; **(in) a long** ~ (en) mucho tiempo; **a long** ~ **ago** hace mucho tiempo; **in no** ~ en un santiamén; **in** ~**(s) gone by** antiguamente; **in these** ~**s** hoy día; **in my** ~ en mis tiempos, (in my youth) en mi juventud; **when my** ~ **comes** cuando me llegue la hora; **on** ~ a tiempo; **be on** ~ ser¹⁹ puntual; **be out of one's** ~ haber¹⁹ servido su aprendizaje; **once upon a** ~ (there was) érase una vez; **some** ~ **or other** algún día; **do** ~ cumplir una condena; **have a bad/good** ~ pasarlo mal/bien; **have no** ~ **to** no tener tiempo para; **kill** ~ matar el tiempo, *sl* matar la araña; **take one's** ~ tardar lo suyo; **take your** ~! ¡tómeselo con calma!; **waste** ~ perder (ie)²ᵇ el tiempo, (deliberately) pasar el rato; **spare** ~ ratos *mpl* libres; ~**-bomb** bomba de relojería; ~**-clock** (in factory) reloj *m* registrador; ~-**exposure** exposición (-ones) *f*; ~-**fuse** espoleta de tiempo; ~-**honoured** consagrado; ~**keeper** cronometrador *m*; ~**keeping** cronometraje *m*, (punctuality) puntualidad *f*; ~-**lag** retraso; ~-**payment** compra a plazos; ~**piece** reloj *m*; ~-**saving** que ahorra tiempo; ~-**server**, ~-**serving** contemporizador *m* (-ora *f*); ~-**sheet** tarjeta registradora (de horas trabajadas); ~-**signal** señales *fpl* horarias, *fam* hora; ~-**switch** interruptor automático; ~**table** (programme) programa *m*, (railway) horario, (published) guía de ferrocarriles; ~-**trial** prueba contra reloj; ~**worn** gastado; *v* calcular el tiempo necesario para; (regulate) regular; (choose the best moment) hacer[19] en el momento oportuno; ~ **a blow** calcular un golpe; ~**d** calculado; **ill-~d** inoportuno; **well-~d** oportuno

timeless eterno

timeliness oportunidad *f*

timely oportuno

timer marcador *m* de tiempo

timid tímido; (shy) vergonzoso

timidity timidez *f*; (shyness) vergüenza

timing cronometraje *m*; (synchronization) sincronización *f*; *mech* regulación *f*; ~ **of the trains** horario de los trenes

timorous asustadizo

timorousness timidez *f*

Timothy Timoteo

timpano timbal *m* (de orquesta)

tin *n* metal estaño; (can) lata; *cul* molde *m*; (drum) bidón (-ones) *m*; (~plate) hojalata; *sl* (money) pasta; (loaf) pan *m* de molde; ~ **hat/lid** *sl* cacerola; ~ **soldier** soldado de plomo; ~-**can** lata; ~**foil** papel *m* de estaño; ~-**opener** abrelatas *m sing*; ~**pot** de mala muerte; ~**smith** hojalatero; ~**smith's** hojalatería; ~**tack** tachuela; ~**ware** hojalatería; *v* estañar; (put in ~s) enlatar, envasar en latas

tincture *n* +*med* tintura; (veneer) capa; *v* tinturar

tinder yesca; ~-**box** caja de yesca

ting *n* retintín (-ines) *m*; ~-**a-ling!** tilín *m*; *v* tintinar

tinge *n* tinte *m*; (shade) sombra; (hint)

dejo; *v* teñir (i)[3]; *fig* tocar[4]

tingle *n* hormigueo; (thrill) estremecimiento; *v* producir[15] hormigueo; (vibrate) vibrar; (thrill) estremecerse[14]

tingling hormigueo; (thrill) estremecimiento; (vibration) vibración (-ones) *f*

tinker *n* hojalatero; (tramp) agitanado; *v* remendar (ie)[2a]; ~ **with** jugar (ue)[1a] con

tinkle *n* retintín (-ines) *m*; (of cow/sheep bells) cencerreo; ~~~! ¡tilín-tilín!; *v* tintinar

tinkling tintineo

tinned enlatado; ~ **food** comida en lata

tinny *mus* que suena a lata; *mot* hecho de chapa demasiado delgada

tinsel *n* oropel *m*; *v* oropelar

tint *n* tinte *m*; (shade) sombra; **hair-~** tinte *m*; ~ **of gold in her hair** reflejo de oro en su pelo; *v* teñir (i)[3]

tinting (hair) *n* teñido

tintinnabulation campanilleo

tiny pequeñito, menudito

[1] **tip** *n* (end) punta; (of shoe) puntera; (of finger) yema; (of stick) regatón (-ones) *m*; (of cigarette) boquilla; (of mountain) cima; **from ~ to toe** de pies a cabeza; **have at one's finger-~s** saber[19] al dedillo; **it's on the ~ of my tongue** lo tengo en la punta de la lengua; ~**staff** alguacil *m* de vara; **(go) on ~-toes** (andar[19]) de puntillas; ~**top** excelente; *v* (put a ~ on) poner[19] regatón a

[2] **tip** *n* (for rubbish) vertedero; *v* depositar; (lean) ladear; ~ **back** abatir; ~-**back seat** *mot* asiento abatible; ~ **up/over** volcar(se) (ue)[1a+4]; ~-**up cart/lorry** volquete *m*; ~-**up seat** (in taxi *etc*) traspontín (-ines) *m*

[3] **tip** *n* (gratuity) propina; (advice) consejo; (news) informe oportuno; *v* (money) dar[19] propina a; (winner) recomendar (ie)[2a]; ~ **the wink** advertir (ie)[2c] clandestinamente; ~ **off** avisar; ~-**off** aviso

tipple *n* pimple *m*; *v* pimplar

tippler borracho

tipsiness borrachera

tipster pronosticador *m* de las carreras de caballos

tipsy achispado; **be ~** estar[19] achispado/piripi

tirade arenga

¹ **tire** (*US mot etc*) *see* **tyre**

² **tire** *vt* cansar; (bore) aburrir; *vi* cansarse (of de), aburrirse (of con); ~ **out** agotar; ~**some** molesto; (boring) aburrido, *sl* pesado; **be** ~**d of** estar¹⁹ harto de; **grow** ~**d** empezar (ie)²ᵃ⁺⁷ a cansarse

tiredness cansancio, aburrimiento

tireless incansable

tiresome, tiring tedioso

tiro novicio

tissue +*med* tejido; (paper handkerchief) tisú *m*, *fam* Kleenex *m*; ~ **of lies** sarta de mentiras; ~-**paper** papel *m* de seda

¹ **tit:** ~ **for tat** donde las dan las toman; ~**bit** +*fig* golosina

² **tit** (~**mouse**) *orni* paro

³ **tit** *see* **teat**

Titan titán *m*

titanic titánico

tithe diezmo

Titian Ticiano

titillate estimular

titillation excitación *f*

titivate ataviar(se)

title *n* título; *sp* campeonato; ~ **to** derecho a; **give a** ~ **to** titular, (raise to nobility) ennoblecer¹⁴; ~-**deeds** escritura de propiedad; ~-**fight** combate *m* para el título; ~-**holder** *leg* tenedor *m* (-ora *f*) de la escritura de propiedad, *sp* campeón (-ones) *m*; ~-**page** portada; ~-**role** papel *m* principal; *v* (in)titular, ennoblecer¹⁴; ~**d** (of person) que tiene título

titrate valorar

titter risa sofocada; *v* reírse (i)³ entre dientes

tittle pizca; ~-**tattle** *n* chismes *mpl*, *v* chismear

titular titular

Titus Tito

T-junction intersección *f* en T

TNT trinitrotolueno

to (direction) a, **he's going** ~ **Gijón** él va a Gijón; (purpose) para, **expedition** ~ **discover unknown lands** expedición *f* para descubrir tierras desconocidas; (often not translated before *infin*) ~ **eat** comer; ~ **and fro** de un lado a otro; ~ **my way of thinking** a mi parecer; ~ **this day** hasta hoy; **road** ~

Palencia carretera de Palencia; **she is secretary** ~ **the minister** ella es secretaria del ministro; **ten** ~ **three** las tres menos diez; **here's** ~ **you!** ¡por usted!; **from tree** ~ **tree** de árbol en árbol; **I have a lot of work** ~ **do** tengo mucho trabajo que hacer; **the letters are** ~ **be typed** las cartas deben ser escritas a máquina; **I laugh** ~ **think of him** me río con sólo pensar en él; **be kind** ~ ser¹⁹ simpático con; **what a** ~-**do!** ¡qué lío!

toad sapo; ~-**in-the-hole** salchichas rebozadas; ~**stool** hongo venenoso

toady *n* pelotillero; *v* adular servilmente (**to** a)

toadying adulación *f* servil

toast *n* tostada; (drink) brindis *m* (**to** por); ~-**rack** portatostadas *m sing*; *v* tostar (ue)¹ᵃ; (drink) brindar por

toaster tostadora

toasting tostadura; ~-**fork** tostadera

tobacco tabaco; ~ **addiction/dependence** tabaquismo; ~ **plantation** plantación *f* de tabaco; ~-**pouch** petaca

tobacconist estanquero; ~'**s** estanco

toboggan *n* tobogán (-anes) *m*; ~ **slope** deslizamiento; *v* deslizarse⁷ en tobogán

toby-jug jarra grande en forma de hombre

toccata tocata

tocsin campanadas de alarma

today hoy; ~ **week** de hoy en ocho días

toddle (of a baby) hacer¹⁹ pin(it)os; (stroll) pasearse; ~ **off** marcharse

toddler niño que aprende a andar

toddy ponche *m*

toe *n* *anat* dedo del pie; (of shoe) puntera; (of sock) punta; **be on one's** ~**s** *fig* estar¹⁹ atento; ~-**cap** puntera; ~-**dance**, ~-**dancing** baile *m* de puntillas; ~-**dancer** bailarín *m* (-ina *f*); ~**hold** asidero pequeño para el pie; ~**nail** uña del dedo del pie; ~-**strap** piel *f* de foca; *v* tocar⁴ con la punta del pie; ~ **the line** ponerse¹⁹ en la raya/ *Mex* catrín *m*, obedecer¹⁴ órdenes, *fig* seguir (i)³⁺¹¹ la línea del partido

toff petimetre *m*

toffee caramelo; ~ **apple** manzana recubierta de caramelo

toga toga

together juntos/as; junto (**with** con):

(simultaneously) a la vez (**with que**); (without interruption) sin interrupción; **all** ~ todos juntos; **all** ~! (pulling) ¡ahora!

togetherness compañerismo, solidaridad *f*

toggle *n* cazonete *m*; *v* asegurar con cazonete

togs ropa

toil *n* afán *m*; **in the** ~**s of** enredado en; *v* afanarse; **they** ~**ed up the hill** subieron penosamente la colina

toiler trabajador *m* (**-ora** *f*)

toilet aseo; (wash-room) cuarto de aseo; (w.c.) servicio, retrete *m*; ~ **articles** artículos *mpl* de aseo personal; ~**-case** neceser *m*; ~**-paper** papel *m* higiénico; ~**-paper holder** soporte *m* del papel higiénico; ~**-powder** polvos *mpl* de talco; ~**-roll** rollo de papel higiénico; ~**-set** juego de tocador; ~**-soap** jabón *m* de tocador; ~**-table** tocador *m*; ~**-water** colonia

toiletries artículos de aseo

token *n* muestra; (disc) ficha; (proof) prueba; *adj* simbólico; ~ **payment** depósito en señal; **as a** ~ **of** en señal de; ~ **stoppage/strike** huelga simbólica

Tokyo Tokio

told: all ~ en total

tolerability tolerabilidad *f*

tolerable tolerable; (fair) regular

tolerance tolerancia; *fam* tragaderas *fpl*; *mech* espacio (para permitir movimiento)

tolerant tolerante

tolerate tolerar

toleration tolerancia

[1] **toll** peaje *m*; *fig* número de víctimas; **there was a heavy** ~ hubo gran mortalidad *f*; **take** ~ **of** *fig* costar (ue)[1a] caro a; ~ **barrier/bridge/road** barrera/puente *m*/carretera de peaje; ~**-call** *tel* conferencia interurbana; ~**-gate** barrera de peaje

[2] **toll** doblar; ~ **the hour** dar[19] la hora

tolling tañido

Tom: every ~, **Dick and Harry** fulano, zutano y mengano; ~ **Thumb** Pulgarcito; **peeping** ~ mirón *m*

tomahawk tomahawk *m*

tomato tomate *m*; ~ **plant** tomatero; ~ **sauce/soup** salsa/sopa de tomate

tomb tumba; ~**stone** lápida

tombola tómbola

tomboy marimacho *m*

tomcat gato (macho)

tome librote *m*

tomfool *adj* necio; *v* hacer[19] necedades

tomfoolery payasadas *fpl*

tommy soldado inglés; ~**-gun** pistola ametralladora; ~**-rot** sandeces *fpl*

tomorrow *n+adv* mañana *f*; ~ **afternoon/morning/night** mañana por la tarde/mañana/noche, *SA* mañana en la tarde *etc*; **day after** ~ pasado mañana; **a week/fortnight** ~ mañana en ocho días/quince días

tomtom tantán (**-anes**) *m*

ton tonelada; ~**s of** montones *mpl* de; **do a** ~**-up** *mot* pasar la velocidad de cien millas por hora; ~**-up boy** joven motociclista aficionado a grandes velocidades

tonal tonal

tonality tonalidad *f*

tone *n* tono; ~ **control** regulador *m* del tono; ~ **poem** poema sinfónico; ~**-deaf: he is** ~ él tiene mal oído musical; *v mus* tonar; *phot* virar; ~ **down** suavizar[7] el tono de, *fig* moderarse; ~ **up** tonificar[4]; ~ **in with** armonizar[7] con

toneless monótono

Tongan tongano

tongs tenazas *fpl*; (small) tenacillas *fpl*; (pair of) pinzas

tongue (*anat* +language) lengua; *mech* (+shoe-~) lengüeta; *sl* húmeda, *sl* sinhueso; **give** ~ empezar (ie)[2a+7] a ladrar; **hold one's** ~ callarse; **hold your** ~! ¡cállate!; **with** ~ **in cheek** irónicamente; **my** ~ **ran away with me** se me escapó la lengua; ~ **of fire** lengua de fuego; ~**-tied** con impedimento en el habla, *fig* tímido; ~**-twister** trabalenguas *m sing+pl*; **sharp-**~**d** de lengua viperina

tonic *n+adj* tónico; ~ **water** (agua) tónica; ~ **wine** vino tonificante

tonight esta noche

tonnage tonelaje *m*; (charge) derechos *mpl* de tonelaje

tonner: thousand ~ (barco) de mil toneladas

tonsil amígdala

tonsillitis amigdalitis *f*, *fam* anginas

tonsure *n* tonsura; *v* tonsurar

tontine tontina

tony *US* aristocrático

too demasiado; (also) también; ~ **bad** *US* lo siento; **all** ~ demasiado; ~ **many** demasiados; ~ **much** demasiado, *sl* demasié; **this is really** ~ **much!** ¡esto pasa de la raya!; **if it isn't** ~ **much trouble** si no es mucha molestia; **she's** ~ **much for her parents** sus padres no pueden con ella; **none** ~ **much** no muy; **only** ~ **well** de sobra

tool *n* herramienta; *fig* instrumento; *vulg* (penis) pito; **set of** ~**s** utillaje *m*; ~**-allowance** compensación *f* por desgaste de herramientas; ~ **bag/box** bolsa/caja de herramientas; ~**-shed** cobertizo de herramientas; *v* (bookbinding) estampar

tooling estampación *f*

toot *n* (on horn) bocinazo; (on whistle) silbido; *v* tocar⁴ la bocina/el silbato

tooth diente *m*; (back tooth) muela; (eye-tooth) colmillo; (of comb) púa; ~ **and nail** encarnizadamente; **have a sweet** ~ ser¹⁹ muy goloso; **have a** ~ **pulled (out)** sacarse⁴ una muela; **false teeth** dentadura postiza; **armed to the teeth** armado hasta los dientes; ~**ache** dolor *m* de muelas; ~**brush** cepillo de dientes; ~**paste** pasta de dientes; ~**pick** palillo; ~**some** sabroso

toothed (serrated) aserrado; ~ **wheel** rueda dentada

toothless sin dientes; ~ **smile** sonrisa desdentada

tootle *see* **toot**

¹**top** *n* (peak) cima; (upper part) parte *f* superior; (surface) superficie *f*; (lid) tapa; (of bus) imperial *f*; (of car) capota; (of fountain-pen) capuchón (-ones) *m*; (of head) coronilla; (of page) encabezamiento (de página); (of roof) remate *m*; (of tree) copa; **at the** ~ **of** a la cabeza de; **he's (at the)** ~ **of his class** él es el primero de su clase; **at the** ~ **of one's voice** a voz en grito; **from** ~ **to bottom** de arriba abajo; **from** ~ **to toe** de pies a cabeza; **on** ~ encima (de), (victorious) victorioso, (winning) ganando; **come out on** ~ salir¹⁹ ganando; **one on** ~ **of the other** uno encima de otro; **wait until he's right on** ~ **of us** espere hasta que le tengamos encima; **and on** ~ **of all**

that y además; **go over the** ~ entrar en batalla; ~**-boot** bota-polaina; ~**-coat** sobretodo, abrigo; **be** ~**-dog** ser¹⁹ el gallito; ~**-dressing** abono aplicado a la superficie; ~**-flight** sobresaliente; ~**gallant mast** mastelerillo; ~**gallant sail** juanete *m*; ~ **gear** *mot* directa; ~**hat** sombrero de copa; ~**-heavy** más pesado por arriba que por abajo; ~**-hole** de primera; ~**knot** moño; ~**mast** mastelero; ~**most** (el) más alto; ~**notch** sobresaliente; ~**-ranking** de primera categoría; ~**sail** gavia; **lower/upper** ~**sail** gavia baja/alta; ~**sail schooner** goleta a velacho; *adj* (el) más alto; ~ **floor** último piso; ~ **people** gente *f* de bien; ~ **priority** de alta prioridad; ~ **scorer** (football) plusmarquista *m*; ~ **secret** extremadamente confidencial; ~**-security** (de) alta seguridad; ~ **sergeant** sargento primero; ~ **speed** velocidad máxima; **they went at** ~ **speed** fueron a toda velocidad; *v* (rise above) coronar; (be better than) aventajar; *agri* (cut the ~ off) descabezar⁷; ~ **off** rematar; ~ **off with** terminar con; ~ **up** (drink) llenar

²**top** (toy) peonza; **sleep like a** ~ dormir (ue)¹ᶜ como un lirón

³**top** (execute) ajusticiar, (kill) cargarse⁵

topaz topacio

topee casco colonial

toper borrachín *m*

topiary arte *m* de recortar setos artísticamente

topic tema *m*

topical tópico

topless con el pecho al descubierto

topographer topógrafo

topographic(al) topográfico

topography topografía

topper sombrero de copa

topping *n cul* crema artificial (que se sirve con fruta *etc*); *adj* estupendo

topple: ~ **down/over** volcar(se)⁴

topsy-turvy (in disorder) en desorden; (upside down) al revés

tor colina rocosa

torch antorcha; *elect* linterna (eléctrica); **carry the** ~ **for** estar¹⁹ enamorado de; ~**-bearer** portahachón (-ones) *m*; ~**light** luz *f* de antorcha; ~**light procession** desfile *m* de portahachones; **by** ~**light** a la luz de antorchas; ~-**song** US canción f de amor

toreador torero

torment n tormento; **souls in** ~ almas fpl en pena; v atormentar

tormentor atormentador m (-ora f)

tornado huracán (-anes) m

torpedo n torpedo; ~-**boat** torpedero; ~-**boat destroyer** cazatorpederos m sing+pl; ~-**net(ting)** red f contra torpedos; ~-**tube** lanzatorpedos m sing+pl; v torpedear

torpid (clumsy) torpe; (lethargic) aletargado

torpidity torpor, letargo

torque par m de torsión

torrent +fig torrente m

torrential torrencial

torrid tórrido

torso torso

tort agravio

tortoise tortuga; ~**shell** carey m; ~**shell comb** peine m de carey

tortuosity tortuosidad f

tortuous +fig tortuoso; (person) torcido

torture n tortura; v torturar

torturer verdugo

Tory n+adj conservador m (-ora f)

Toryism conservadurismo

tosh disparates mpl

toss n (sudden shake) sacudida; (of bull) cogida; (fall) caída; (of coin) echada a cara o cruz; **argue the** ~ insistir con vehemencia; **win the** ~ ganar el sorteo; **take a** ~ caer[19]; vt (throw) tirar al aire; (shake) sacudir; (bull) coger[8]; (coin) echar a cara o cruz; ~ **the head** levantar airosamente la cabeza; ~ **in a blanket** mantear; vi agitarse; ~ **and turn** revolverse (ue)[1b] (past part revuelto)

~ **aside** abandonar

~ **off** (drink) beber de un trago; vulg sl meneársela

~-**up** n (of coin) echada a cara o cruz; **it's a** ~-**up** es cuestión de suerte

~ **up** v echar a cara o cruz; sp (at start of game) sortear

tot n (child) nene m, nena; (drink) trag(uit)o; (glass) copita; (sum) cuenta; v ~ **up** sumar

total n+adj total m; ~ **war** guerra total; vt sumar; vi ascender a, **the volunteers totalled six hundred** los voluntarios ascendieron a seiscientos

totalitarian totalitario

totalitarianism totalitarismo

totality totalidad f

totalizator totalizador m (para registrar apuestas)

totalize totalizar[7]

tote n totalizador m (para registrar apuestas); v (carry) llevar

totem tótem m; ~-**pole** poste totémico

totter tambalearse

tottering tambaleante; fig ruinoso

tottery a punto de caer

toucan tucán (-anes) m

touch n (sense) tacto; (contact) toque m; mus pulsación f; (paint) pincelada; med pequeño ataque; (small quantity) poquito; **by** ~ a tiento; **finishing** ~ último toque; **be in** ~ **with** (s.o.) estar[19] en comunicación con, (s.t.) estar[19] al tanto de; **get in** ~ **with** ponerse[19] en contacto con; **keep in** ~ **with** mantener[19] relaciones con, mantenerse al corriente de; **lose** ~ perder (ie)[2b] la costumbre; **lose** ~ **with** perder (ie)[2b] contacto con; ~ **of the sun** una leve insolación; **the ball is in** ~ sp el balón está fuera de banda; **kick into** ~ (rugby) lanzar[7] a la lateral; **in that picture can be seen the master's** ~ en ese cuadro se puede ver la mano del maestro; **blue with a** ~ **of green** azul tirando a verde; ~-**and-go** dudoso; **it's** ~-**and-go** (whether) está en un hilo (si); ~-**judge** sp juez m de línea; ~-**line** sp línea lateral, fam banda; ~-**me-not** bot cohombrillo; ~-**stone** +fig piedra de toque; ~-**type** mecanografiar al tacto; ~-**typing** mecanografía al tacto; ~-**typist** mecanógrafa al tacto; v tocar[4]; (brush against) rozar[7]; (adjoin) estar[19] contiguo a; (reach) alcanzar[7]; (eat) tomar; (feelings) conmover (ue)[1b]; sl (borrow money) dar[19] un sablazo a (**for para sacar**); **I've not** ~**ed food all day** en todo el día no he probado bocado

~ **at** naut hacer[19] escala en

~-**down** n aer aterrizaje m; (rugby) (by defender) anulado, (by attacker) apoyo (del balón)

~ **down** v aer aterrizar[7]; (rugby) (by defender) anular, (by attacker) apoyar (el balón)

~ **off** +fig hacer[19] estallar

~ **on** aludir a

~**-up** n retoque m; ~**-up paint** pintura para retocar

~ **up** v +*phot* retocar[4]

touched (crazy) chiflado; (greatly moved) emocionado

touchiness susceptibilidad f

touching adj conmovedor (-ora f); prep tocante a

touchy quisquilloso; (wary) escamón

tough n matón (-ones) m; adj (hard) duro; (strong) fuerte; (leathery) correoso; (bullying) testarudo; **he's as ~ as nails** a él no le entran balas; ~ **job** faena difícil; ~ **journey** viaje arduo; ~ **luck!** ¡mala suerte!

toughen endurecer[14]; ~**ed glass** vidrio templado

toughness (hardness) dureza; (strength) resistencia; (tenacity) tenacidad f

Toulon Tolón m

Toulouse Tolosa

toupee tupé m

tour viaje m (largo); (round trip) recorrido; (organized) circuito; (of duty) turno; sp+*theat* gira, **on ~** de gira; vt viajar por; vi viajar (de turista)

tour-de-force proeza

tourer *mot* coche m descapotable

touring n turismo; adj turístico; adj ~ **car** coche m descapotable; ~ **circus** circo ambulante

tourism turismo

tourist turista m+f; ~ **agency** agencia de viajes; ~ **class** clase turística; ~**-class tickets** billetes mpl de clase turística

tourmaline turmalina

tournament, tourney torneo; sp concurso

tourniquet torniquete m

tousle: ~**-headed person** *fam* escarola

tout n (agent) gancho; (racing) pronosticador m; **ticket-~** revendedor m (de billetes); v intentar (re)vender; ~ **for** solicitar

¹ **tow** n remolque m; **on ~** a remolque; **take in ~** remolcar a, *fig* encargarse[5] de; ~**line** sirga; ~**path** camino de sirga; ~**-rope** sirga; v remolcar[4]

² **tow** estopa

towage (derechos mpl de) remolque m

towards hacia; (of time) cerca de; (concerning) respecto a; **go ~** *fig* contribuir[16] a

towel n toalla; ~**-rack,** ~**-rail** toallero; **roller-~** toalla continua; v secar[4] con toalla

towelling género para toallas

tower n torre f; (of church) campanario; (fortress) fortaleza; v elevarse; ~ **over** dominar, *fig* descollar entre

towering dominante; (violent) violento

town n ciudad f; (small) pueblo; **he has a ~ house and a country house** él tiene una casa en la ciudad y una casa de campo; ~ **meeting** reunión f de ciudadanos; **new ~** (for overspill population) poblado de absorción; ~ **clerk** secretario del ayuntamiento; ~ **council** ayuntamiento; ~ **councillor** concejal m; ~**-crier** pregonero; ~ **hall** ayuntamiento; ~**-planner** urbanista m+f; ~**-planning** n urbanismo, adj urbanista; ~**sfolk,** ~**speople** ciudadanos mpl; ~**ship** término municipal; ~**sman** ciudadano

toxaemia toxemia

toxic tóxico

toxicologist toxicólogo

toxicology toxicología

toxin toxina

toy n juguete m; ~**-maker** fabricante m de juguetes; ~**shop** juguetería; adj (not real) de jugar; (tiny) muy pequeño; ~ **dog** perro miniatura; v ~ **with** jugar (ue)[1a] con, (food) comer sin ganas, (ideas) acariciar; **do not ~ with her affections!** ¡no te diviertas con ella!

trace n (track) huella; (sign) vestigio; (tiny amount) pizca; (fishing) hijuela; v (follow) seguir (i)[3+11] la pista de; (discover whereabouts of) averiguar[6] el paradero de; ~ **a curve** trazar[7] una curva; ~ **back to** averiguar[6] el origen, (of ancestry) remontarse a; ~ **to** rastrear hasta llegar a; ~ **a drawing** calcar[4] un dibujo

traceability calidad f de averiguable/trazable

traceable (of whereabouts) averiguable; (of drawing) trazable

tracer trazador m (-ora f); ~**-bullet** bala trazadora

tracery tracería

trachea tráquea

trachoma tracoma

tracing calco (**of** sobre); ~ **paper** papel

m de calco

track *n* rastro; (footprint *etc*) huella; (footpath) senda; (course) ruta; *aer* trayectoria; (railway) vía (férrea); (runners) carriles *mpl*; (of tank *etc*) oruga; *sp* pista, **grass ~** pista de hierba; (of tape-recorder) pista *m*, **four-~ recorder** magnetófono de cuatro pistas; **off the ~** (railway) descarrilado, *fig* despistado; **go off the ~** descarrilarse; **put off the ~** despistar; **on the ~ of** en la pista de; **be on s.o.'s ~** andar[19] tras la pista de uno; **keep ~ of** *fig* estar[19] al tanto de; **~ event** atletismo en pista; **~-suit** mono de deporte; *v* rastrear; **~ down** lograr descubrir; **~ed vehicle** vehículo de oruga

tracker rastreador *m*; **~ dog** perro rastreador

tracking-station; *space* estación (-ones) *f* de seguimiento

trackless sin caminos

tract +*anat* región (-ones) *f*; (plot of land) terreno; (writing) folleto; **digestive ~** canal digestivo; **respiratory ~** vías *fpl* respiratorias

tractability tratabilidad *f*

tractable tratable

traction tracción *f*; **~ engine** locomóvil *m*

tractive de tracción

tractor tractor *m*

trade *n* comercio; (industry) industria; (job) oficio, **he's a carpenter by ~** él es carpintero de oficio; **~ agreement** convenio comercial; **~ journal** revista profesional; **~ price** precio al por mayor; **~ school** escuela de artes y oficios; **~ secret** secreto industrial; **~-fair** feria de muestras; **~-mark** marca registrada; **~-name** nombre *m* comercial; **~sman** tendero, (industrial) artesano; **~smen's entrance** puerta de servicio; **~speople** tenderos *mpl*; **~ union** sindicato; **~-unionism** sindicalismo; **~-unionist** sindicalista *m+f*; **~-winds** vientos alisios; *vi* comerciar (**in** en) (**with** con); (*US* do the shopping) hacer[19] las compras; **~ on** (exploit) aprovecharse de; *vt* cambiar (**for** por); **~ in** (part exchange) dar[19] como parte del pago; **~-in** cambio; **~ value** valor *m* en cambio

trader comerciante *m+f*

trading comercial; **~ post** factoría; **~ stamp** cupón (-ones) *m*; **~ unit** unidad *f* negociable

tradition tradición (-ones) *f*

traditional tradicional

traditionalism tradicionalismo

traditionalist *n+adj* tradicionalista *m+f*

traduce calumniar

traffic *n* *mot etc* circulación *f*; (trade) comercio; *pej* trata (**in** de); **cause a block in the ~** interrumpir la circulación; **~ accident** accidente *m* de circulación; **~ indicator** indicador *m* de dirección; **~ island** refugio de peatones, *fam* burladero; **~ jam** embotellamiento; **~-lights** semáforo; **~ offence** infracción *f* de circulación; **~ patrol** patrulla de la policía de tráfico; **~ policeman/cop** guardia *m* de circulación; **~ roundabout** redondel *m*; **~ sign** señal *f* de circulación; *v* traficar[4], *pej* tratar (**in** en)

trafficator indicador *m* de dirección

trafficker traficante *m*

tragacanth tragacanto

tragedian (actor) trágico; (author) autor *m* de tragedias

tragedy tragedia

tragic trágico

tragi-comedian tragicómico

tragi-comedy tragicomedia

trail rastro; (footprint *etc*) huella; (footpath) senda; (tail) cola; **on the ~ (of)** en la pista (de); *vt* seguir (i)[3+11] la pista de; (drag) arrastrar; **~ arms** *mil* bajar armas; *vi* arrastrarse; *bot* trepar; **~ along** arrastrarse; **~ away/off** ir[19] desapareciendo; **~ behind** rezagarse[5]

trailer *mot* remolque *m*; (*US* caravan) coche-vivienda *m*; *bot* planta trepadora; *cin* trailer *m*; **~ park** parking *m* para coches-vivienda, (camp-site) camping *m* para coches-vivienda; **~-truck** camión (-ones) *m* con remolque

[1] **train** *n* tren *m*; *min* vagonera; (company) séquito; (of dress) cola; (of gunpowder) reguero; (series) sucesión *f* (**of** de); **~ of thought** hilo del pensamiento; **go by ~** ir[19] en tren; **~ service** servicio de trenes; **~-bearer** paje *m* que lleva la cola; **~-ferry** barco portatrén (-enes); **~load** carga completa de un tren; **~-sick** mareado; **~**

sickness mareo; *v* ir[19] en tren

[2] **train** *vt* (animal) amaestrar; (child) educar; (teach) enseñar; (plant) guiar; (gun) apuntar (**on** a); *sp* entrenar; *vi* entrenarse

trainee aprendiz *m* (-za *f*) profesional; ~ **teacher** normalista *m+f*

trainer *aer* avión (-ones) *m* de escuela; (of animals) domador *m* (-ora *f*); *sp* entrenador *m*, míster *m*, (boxing + horse-racing) preparador *m*

training educación *f*; *sp* entrenamiento, (boxing) preparación *f*; (of animals) doma; ~**-college** centro de formación del profesorado; ~**-ship** buque-escuela *m*; **physical** ~ gimnasia; **professional** ~ formación *f* profesional

traipse trajinar

trait rasgo

traitor traidor *m*; **be a** ~ **to** traicionar

traitorous traidor (-ora *f*)

traitress traidora

trajectory trayectoria

tram tranvía *m*; ~**car** tranvía *m*; ~ **depot** cochera de tranvías; ~**-line** vía de tranvía

trammel: ~**s** impedimentos *mpl*; *v* impedir (i)[3]

tramp *n* (wanderer) vagabundo; (prostitute) furcia; (steamer) vapor *m* volandero; (walk) paseo largo; (of feet) marcha pesada; *vi* viajar a pie; marchar pesadamente; *vt* pisar con fuerza

trample (on/underfoot) pisotear

trampoline cama elástica

trance (dream) éxtasis *m*; (spiritualism) estado hipnótico; **be in a** ~ estar[19] hipnotizado; **put into a** ~ hipnotizar[7]

tranquil tranquilo; *sl* huevón

tranquillity tranquilidad *f*

tranquillize tranquilizar[7]

tranquillizer calmante *m*

tranquillizing tranquilizante

transact despachar

transaction negocio; ~**s** actas *fpl*

transatlantic transatlántico

transcend superar

transcendence superioridad *f*

transcendent sobresaliente

transcendental trascendental

transcendentalism trascendentalismo

transcontinental transcontinental

transcribe transcribir (*past part* transcrito)

transcript copia

transcription transcripción *f*

transept cruccro

transfer *n* transferencia; *leg+sp* traspaso; (to another job) traslado; (picture) calcomanía; *vt* transferir (ie)[2c]; *leg +sp* traspasar; (to another job) trasladar; *vi* trasladarse

transferability cesibilidad *f*

transferable transferible; **not** ~ intransferible

transferee cesionario

transference transferencia

transferor cesionista *m+f*

transfiguration transfiguración *f*

transfigure transfigurar

transfix traspasar; *fig* pasmar, ~**ed with** pasmado de

transform transformar

transformation transformación *f*

transformer transformador *m*

transfuse transfundir; (blood) hacer[19] una transfusión de; *fig* ~ **with** impregnar de

transfusion transfusión (-ones) *f*

transgress *vi* pecar[4]; *vt* violar

transgression infracción (-ones) *f*

transgressor transgresor *m* (-ora *f*)

tranship transbordar

transhipment transbordo

transience, transiency lo pasajero

transient pasajero

transistor: ~ **radio** transistor *m*

transistorize transistorizar[7]

transit tránsito; **in** ~ en tránsito

transition transición *f*; ~ **period** período de transición

transitional transicional

transitive transitivo

transitory transitorio

translatable traducible

translate traducir[15]; ~ **into English** traducir[15] al inglés/en inglés

translation traducción (-ones) *f*

translator traductor *m* (-ora *f*)

transliterate transcribir (*past part* transcrito)

translucence translucidez *f*

translucent translúcido

translunar: ~ **coast** *space* viaje *m* a la luna

transmigrate transmigrar

transmigration transmigración f
transmissible transmisible
transmission transmisión f
transmit transmitir
transmitter transmisor m; *rad* emisora
transmitting-station estación f transmisora
transmogrify transformar como por magia
transmutable transmutable
transmutation transmutación f; *biol* transformismo
transmute transmutar
transom travesaño
transparency transparencia; (colourslide) diapositiva; ~ **frame** marco de la diapositiva; ~ **projector** proyector m de diapositivas
transparent transparente; (of underwear) vaporoso
transpiration transpiración f
transpire transpirar; *fig* suceder; **it ~d that** se supo que
transplant n trasplante m; adj de trasplante; ~ **operation** operación f de trasplante; v trasplantar
transplantation trasplante m
transplanter *agri* máquina para trasplantar árboles; *med* trasplantador m (-ora f)
transport n transporte m; (fit) paroxismo; (ecstasy) éxtasis m; ~ **plane** avión (-ones) m de transporte; **Ministry of Transport** Ministerio de Transportes; v +*fig* transportar
transportable transportable
transportation transportación f; (exile) deportación f
transporter transportador m
transpose transponer[19]; *mus* transportar
transposition +*mus* transposición (-ones) f
transubstantiate transubstanciar
transubstantiation transubstanciación f
transversal n línea transversal; adj transversal
transverse transversal
transvest(it)ism travestismo
transvestite travestido, *sl* travesti m
trap n trampa; *mech* bombillo; (vehicle) coche m ligero de dos ruedas; (mouth) boca; (on dog-racing track) cajón m; ~**s** equipaje m; **be caught in a** ~ caer[19] en la trampa; **set a** ~ poner[19] una

trampa (**for** a); ~-**door** escotilla; *theat* escotillón (-ones) m; v atrapar; (football) parar con los pies
trapes trajinar
trapeze trapecio; ~ **artist** trapecista m+f
trapezist n+adj trapecista m+f
trapper trampero
trapping caza; (of football) control m del balón; ~**s** arreos *mpl*, *fig* adornos *mpl*
Trappist n trapense m; adj trapense, trapensa
trash (rubbish) basura; (bad writing) escritos *mpl* sin valor; (*US* people) gentuza; ~-**can** cubo de la basura
trashy de mala calidad
trauma trauma(tismo)
traumatic traumático
travail dolores *mpl* del parto; **be in** ~ estar[19] de parto
travel n viajar m; ~**s** viajes *mpl*; ~-**agent**, ~-**agency** agente m/agencia de viajes; ~-**bureau** oficina de viajes; v viajar; *mech* (move) correr; ~ **at full speed** ir[19] a toda velocidad; **this fruit does not** ~ **well** esta fruta no se puede transportar; **much-travelled** que ha viajado mucho; ~ **along/over** viajar por
traveller viajero; (salesman) viajante m, *SA* agente viajero; ~'**s cheque** cheque m de viajero
travelling n viajes *mpl*; adj viajero; (itinerant) ambulante; ~-**clock** reloj m de petaca; ~ **crane** grúa corrediza; ~ **expenses** gastos *mpl* de viaje; ~-**rug** manta de viaje; ~ **salesman** (pedlar) vendedor m ambulante, (commercial traveller) viajante m; ~ **show** circo ambulante
travelogue *cin* película sobre viajes; (talk) conferencia sobre viajes
traverse n *mech* travesaño; *mil* través m; v atravesar; *mil* mover (ue)[1a] lateralmente
traversable atravesable
travesty n parodia; v parodiar
trawl n red f rastrera; v pescar[4] al arrastre
trawler barco rastreador; ~-**man** pescador m de arrastre
tray bandeja; *phot* cubeta
treacherous traidor (-ora f); (unsafe) in-

seguro
treachery traición f
treacle melaza
treacly melado
tread n pisada; (of stair) huella; mot dibujo; ~**mill** molino de rueda de escalones, fig rueda; v pisar; ~ **water** pedalear en el agua; ~ **underfoot** pisotear; ~ **down** aplastar con los pies; ~ **on** pisar; ~ **on air** estar[19] sin preocupaciones; ~ **on the heels of** pisar los talones a; ~ **on s.o.'s toes** fig ofenderle a uno
treadle pedal m
treason traición f
treasonable traidor (-ora f)
treasure n tesoro; ~ **trove** tesoro hallado; v atesorar; (be fond of) apreciar mucho; (hoard) guardar como tesoro
treasurer tesorero
treasury tesorería; pol Ministerio de Hacienda; ~ **note** billete m de curso legal
treat n placer m; (reward) recompensa; **it's my** ~ yo pago; v +med tratar; (invite) convidar (**to** a); ~ **of** tratar de; ~ **with** negociar con
treatise tratado
treatment +med tratamiento, **I'm under** ~ estoy en tratamiento; lit manera de tratar
treaty tratado
treble n mus triple m+f; ~ **clef** clave f de sol; ~ **control** regulador m de notas agudas; adj triple; mus de tiple; ~ **chance** apuesta triple; v triplicar(se)[4]
tree n árbol m; **family** ~ árbol genealógico; ~**-frog** rana de San Antonio; ~**-sparrow** gorrión molinero; ~**-stump** tocón (-ones) m; ~**-top** copa (de árbol)
treeless despoblado de árboles
trefoil +archi trébol m
trek n marcha; (migration) migración f; (day's) jornada; v hacer[19] una marcha
trellis espaldera; ~**-work** enrejado
tremble n temblor m; (of emotion) estremecimiento; v temblar (ie)[2a], estremecerse[14] (**with** de); ~ **like a leaf/jelly** temblar (ie)[2a] como un flan
trembler temblador m (-ora f)
trembly trémolo
tremendous tremendo
tremolo trémolo

tremor temblor m; (vibration) vibración f; **without a** ~ sin conmoverse
tremulous trémulo
trench n zanja; mil trinchera; ~**-coat** trinchera; ~ **warfare** guerra de trincheras; v zanjar; cavar una trinchera
trenchancy mordacidad f
trenchant mordaz (-ces)
trencher tajadero
trend n tendencia; **follow the** ~ seguir (i)[3+11] la moda; ~**-setter** persona que saca la moda; v tender (ie)[2a]
trendy de moda
trepan n trépano; v trepanar
trepidation trepidación f
trespass n transgresión (-ones) f; (illegal intrusion) entrada sin permiso; eccles pecado; v entrar sin permiso (**on** en); ~ **against** pecar[4] contra; ~ **upon** violar, fig abusar de
trespasser intruso; ~**s will be prosecuted** se procederá contra los intrusos
trespassing: no ~ prohibida la entrada
tress trenza
trestle caballete m; ~**-bridge** puente m; ~**-table** mesa de tijera
triad tríada
trial n (test) prueba; (adversity) adversidad f; (affliction) aflicción f; leg proceso, juicio; ~**s** sp concurso, **sheepdog** ~**s** concurso de perros pastor; ~ **and error** tanteo; ~ **lawyer** US abogado; ~ **by jury** juicio por jurado; ~ **of strength** prueba de fuerza; **on** ~ a prueba, leg procesado; **bring to** ~ procesar; **I'll give it a** ~ lo ensayaré; adj experimental; ~ **run/trip** viaje m de ensayo; ~ **balance** balance m de comprobación; ~ **marriage** matrimonio de prueba
triangle +mus triángulo
triangular, triangulate triangular
triangulation triangulación f
tribal tribal
tribalism sociedad f tribal
tribe tribu f; pej tropel m; ~**sman** miembro de una tribu
tribulation tribulación (-ones) f
tribunal +fig tribunal m
tribune tribuna
tributary n+adj tributario
tribute tributo; fig homenaje m; **pay** ~ **to** rendir (i)[3] homenaje a
trice: in a ~ en un santiamén

trick *n* (ruse) truco; (swindle) estafa; (joke) burla; (mischief) travesura; (knack) maña; (illusion) ilusión *f*; (conjuring) juego de manos; (of style) peculiaridad *f*; (cards) baza; **play a ~ on** gastar una broma a; **my eyesight plays me ~s** mis ojos me engañan; **it was a dirty/rotten ~** fue una mala pasada; **~ riding/cycling** acrobacia ecuestre/en bicicleta; **~ photography** trucaje *m*; **~ question** pregunta de pega; *v* engañar; **~ s.o. into** lograr con engaños que uno +*subj*; **be ~ed into** dejarse persuadir por engaños +*infin*; **~ out** ataviar; **~ out of** estafar

trickery astucia; (swindle) fraude *m*

trickiness trampería

trickle *n* chorrito; *v* gotear

trickster estafador *m* (-ora *f*)

tricky (of people) tramposo; (of problem *etc*) difícil; (of situation) delicado

tricolour (bandera) tricolor

tricycle triciclo

trident tridente *m*

tried probado; (of people) leal

triennial trienal

trier persona que se esfuerza

trifle *n* bagatela; (small sum) poquito; *cul approx equiv* bizcocho borracho; **argue over a ~** discutir por tan poca cosa; *adv* un poco; **a ~ drunk** un poco borracho; *v* chancear; **~ away** malgastar; **~ with** jugar (ue)[1a+5] con

trifler persona frívola; (with affections) seductor *m*, *fam* tenorio

trifling insignificante

trigger *n* gatillo; *mech* disparador *m*; **~-happy** deseoso de disparar; *v* **~ off** +*fig* hacer[19] estallar; (person) provocar[4]

trigonometry trigonometría

trilateral trilátero

trilby sombrero flexible

trilingual trilingüe

trill *n* +*mus* trino; *phon* vibración (-ones) *f*; *v* trinar; hacer[19] vibrar

trillion trillón (-ones) *m*; *US* billón (-ones) *m*

trilogy trilogía

trim *n* (condition) buena condición; (of hair) recorte *m*; *naut* (of vessel) asiento; (of sails) orientación *f*; *adj* bien arreglado, (of people) aseado; *v* *agri* podar; (cut) cortar; (hair *etc*) recortar; (lamp) despabilar; (sails) orientar; (wallpaper) orillar; (sewing) guarnecer[14] (**with** de); (tidy) arreglar (vessel) equilibrar

trimaran velero de tres cascos

trimester trimestre *m*

trimly en regla

trimmer guarnecedor *m* (-ora *f*)

trimming guarnición *f*; **~s** accesorios *mpl*, (off-cuts) recortes *mpl*

trimness elegancia

Trinidad Isla de la Trinidad; **citizen of ~** trinitario

Trinitarian trinitario

trinity trinidad *f*; **Holy Trinity** Santísima Trinidad

trinket chuchería

trio trío

trip *n* excursión *f*; (+ drug bout) viaje *m*; (slip) tropiezo; (wrestling) zancadilla; *mech* trinquete *m*; **~-wire** alambre *m* que hace funcionar una trampa cuando un animal/enemigo lo toca; *vt* **~ up** hacer[19] tropezar (ie)[2a], (wrestling) poner[19] la zancadilla, *fig* coger[8] en una falta; *vi* (run) correr a paso ligero; **~ on/over** tropezar (ie)[2a] en/con; **~ up** (err) equivocarse[4]

tripartite tripartito

tripe *cul* callos *mpl*; (nonsense) tonterías *fpl*; (bad writing) bodrios *mpl*

triple *adj* triple; **~-play** (recording tape) de triple duración; *v* triplicar(se)[4]

triplet (person) trillizo; *mus* tresillo; (trio) terceto

triplicate *n* tercera copia; *adj* triplicado; **in ~** por triplicado; *v* triplicar[4]

triplication triplicación *f*

tripod trípode *m*

tripper excursionista *m*+*f*

tripping ágil

triptych tríptico

trireme trirreme *m*

trisect trisecar[4]

trisection trisección *f*

Tristram Tristán

trisyllabic trisilábico

trisyllable trisílabo

trite trivial

triteness vulgaridad *f*

triturate triturar

triumph *n* triunfo; *v* **~ (over)** triunfar (sobre)

triumphal triunfal; ~ **arch** arco de triunfo

triumphant triunfante

triumvirate triunvirato

trivet trípode *m*

trivia naderías *fpl*

trivial trivial

triviality nadería; (state) trivialidad *f*

trochee troqueo

troglodyte troglodita *m+f*

troika troica

Trojan *n+adj* troyano; **work like a** ~ trabajar como un negro

troll (fishing) arrastrar; ~**-hook** curricán (-anes) *m*

trolley carretilla; (tea) carrito, mesita de ruedas; (trolley-car) tranvía; *elect* trole *f*; ~**-bus** trolebús *m*

trollop ramera

trombone trombón (-ones) *m*

troop *n* tropa; (cavalry) escuadrón (-ones) *m*; *theat* compañía; ~**s** tropas *fpl*; ~**-carrier** camión (-ones) blindado; ~**-ship** buque *m* de transporte militar; *v* reunirse; ~ **away/off** marcharse en tropel

trooper soldado de caballería

trophy trofeo

tropic trópico; ~**s** trópicos *mpl*

tropical tropical

trot *n* trote *m*; **at a** ~ al trote; (consecutively) seguidos; **she's always on the** ~ *fig* ella siempre está activa; *v* ir[19] al trote; ~ **out** sacar[4] a relucir

troth promesa; **plight one's** ~ dar[19] palabra de matrimonio

trotter (horse) caballo trotón; *cul* mano *f* de cerdo

trotting *n* trote *m*; *adj* trotón

troubadour trovador *m*

trouble *n* molestia; *med* enfermedad *f*; *mech+mot* avería; (misfortune) desgracia; (unpleasantness) disgusto; **the** ~ **is** lo malo es; **be in** ~ hallarse en un apuro, (be pregnant) estar[19] embarazada; **be worth the** ~ valer[19] la pena; **cause** ~ (of people) armar un lío, *fam* gibar, (of things) traer[19] cola; **get s.o. into** ~ meter a uno en un lío; **he got her into** ~ (pregnant) *sl* él la metió en un berenjenal; **give s.o. a lot of** ~ darle[19] a uno mucho sinsabor; **go to the** ~ **of/take** ~ **to** tomarse la molestia de +*infin*; **go to great** ~ **to** hacer[19] un gran esfuerzo para +*infin*; **look for** ~ buscarle[4] tres pies al gato; **tell me your** ~**s** cuénteme sus penas; ~**-free** sin preocupaciones, *mot* sin averías; ~**maker** alborotador *m* (-ora *f*); (agitator) agitador *m* (-ora *f*); ~**shooter** mediador *m* en una disputa; ~**some** molesto, (awkward) dificultoso; *v* (annoy) molestar; (badger) importunar; (cause to worry) inquietar; (disturb) (per)turbar; (necessitate an effort) costar (ue)[1a] trabajo, **learning to drive did not** ~ **him** no le costó trabajo aprender a conducir; **may I** ~ **you for a light?** ¿me dará fuego, por favor?; **don't** ~ **yourself!** ¡no se moleste!; ~**d** inquieto; **these are** ~**d times** estos tiempos son turbulentos; ~**d waters** aguas revueltas

trough (baker's) artesa; (drinking-~) abrevadero; *meteor* área de baja presión; (of waves) seno

trounce zumbar; (triumph over) vencer[12]

troupe compañía

trouper actor veterano, actriz (-ces) veterana

trousered que lleva pantalones

trousers pantalón (-ones) *m*; *sl* alares

trousseau ajuar *m*

trout trucha

trowel *agri* desplantador *m*; *bui* paleta

Troy Troya; **troy weight** peso troy

truancy faltar *m* a clase sin permiso

truant *n* gandul *m*; persona que hace novillos; **play** ~ hacer[19] novillos; *adj* haragán (ana); *v* faltar a clase sin permiso

truce tregua

¹ **truck** *mot* camión (-ones) *m*; (railway) vagón (-ones) *m* de mercancías; (hand-propelled) carretilla; ~**-driver** camionero; ~**-farm** huerto, (large) huerta; ~**-farmer** hortelano; ~**load** carga completa de un camión

² **truck** trueque *m*; ~ **system** pago del salario en especie; **have no** ~ **with** no tener[19] trato con

trucker camionero

trucking ~ **company** empresa de transporte por camiones

truckle ~ **to s.o.** someterse servilmente a alguien; ~**-bed** carriola

truculence truculencia

truculent truculento

trudge *n* caminata; *v* caminar trabajosamente

true verdadero; (exact) exacto; (genuine) auténtico; (level) uniforme; (loyal) leal; (vertical) a plomo; ~ **copy** copia fiel; ~ **to life** conforme a la realidad; ~ **to type** conforme con su carácter; **be** ~ ser[19] verdad; **be** ~ **to** ser[19] fiel a; **come** ~ realizarse[7]; **how (very)** ~! ¡cuánta razón tiene usted!; **out of** ~ descentrado; ~-**blue** sumamente leal, *pol* n+*adj* conservador *m* (-ora *f*); ~-**born** bien nacido; ~-**bred** bien criado; ~-**hearted** fiel; ~ **love** amor verdadero; ~-**love** amante *m*+*f*

truffle trufa

truism perogrullada; **it's a** ~ **to say that** es un tópico decir que

truly verdaderamente; (exactly) exactamente; (faithfully) fielmente; **yours** ~ su seguro servidor; (in letters) le saluda atentamente

trump *n* (cards) triunfo; **last** ~ juicio final; ~-**card** (naipe *m* de) triunfo, *fig* pieza reina; *v* jugar un triunfo, *fam* ganar una baza con la pinta; ~ **up** falsificar[4]

trumpery sin importancia

trumpet *n* trompeta; *mil* clarín (-ines) *m*; ~-**blast**, ~-**call** trompetazo; ~ **daffodil** narciso trompón; ~-**shaped** atrompetado; **ear**-~ trompetilla (acústica); *v* trompetear; (of elephant) barritar; ~ **(forth)** pregonar (a son de trompeta)

trumpeter trompeta *m*; *mil* clarín *m*

truncate truncar[4]

truncation truncamiento

truncheon porra; **hit with a** ~ aporrear

trundle *vi* rodar (ue)[1a]; *vt* hacer[19] rodar

trunk (case) baúl *m*; (body and tree) tronco; (elephant's) trompa; *mot* (boot) maletero; ~s taparrabos *m sing*+*pl*; ~-**call** conferencia interurbana; ~ **line** línea principal; ~ **road** carretera de primera clase, *Sp* carretera nacional

trunnion muñón (-ones) *m*

truss *n* (bundle) lío; (of grapes) racimo; *bui* entramado; *surg* braguero; *v* liar; (poultry) espetar; *bui* apoyar con entramado

trust *n* confianza; (hope) esperanza; *leg* fideicomiso; *comm* crédito; *comm* (organization) monopolio; **have** ~ **in** tener[19] confianza en; **in** ~ en confianza, *leg* en depósito; **on** ~ a fiado, *fam* a ojos cerrados; ~ **company** grupo financiero; ~ **funds** fondos *mpl* fiduciarios; ~-**worthiness** confiabilidad *f*, (of people) honradez *f*; ~**worthy** fidedigno; ~**worthy young man** chico de confianza; *vt* confiar en; ~ **s.o. with s.t.** confiar algo a alguien; ~ **s.o. to** confiar en que uno +*subj*; ~ **her to say that!** ¡no me extraña que ella haya dicho eso!; **I wouldn't** ~ **her with your fountain-pen** no la dejaría usar tu estilográfica; *vi* confiar (**to** en, **that** que); **I** ~ **I shall see you again** espero verle a usted otra vez

trustee síndico; *leg* fideicomisario; ~-**ship** cargo de fideicomisario

trustful, trusting confiado

trustiness confianza

trusty leal

truth verdad *f*; **in** ~ en verdad; **it's Gospel** ~ es la pura verdad; **tell the** ~ decir[19] la verdad; ~-**drug** suero de la verdad

truthful verídico

truthfulness veracidad *f*

[1] **try** *n* tentativa; (rugby) ensayo; **have a** ~ intentar; *v* (test) probar (ue)[1a]; *leg* (person) procesar (**for** por), (case) ver[19]; *sl* empalmar; ~ **and ...** tratar de +*infin*; ~ **another tack** tratar sobre otra base; ~ **one's hand at** hacer[19] la prueba de; ~ **one's luck** probar (ue)[1a] fortuna; ~ **the key in the lock** manipular la llave en el cerrojo; ~-**your-strength machine** máquina de probar la fuerza

~ **for** intentar obtener

~-**on** *n* trampa

~ **on** *v* probarse (ue)[1a]

~-**out** *n* prueba

~ **out** *v* someter a prueba; (clothes) probarse (ue)[1a]

~ **to** intentar; **she punished him to** ~ **to correct him** ella le castigó para intentar corregirle

[2] **try:** ~**sail** vela cangreja; ~-**square** gramil *m*

trying molesto

tryst (lugar *m* de una) cita

tsar zar *m*

tsarina zarina

tsetse tsetsé *m*; ~ **fly** mosca tsetsé

T-shaped en forma de T

T-shirt camiseta, *sl* nicki *m*, niqui *m*

T-square regla T

tub tina; (bath) baño; *naut* carcamán *m*; **take a** ~ bañarse; **~-thumper** *pol* agitador *m*, *eccles* predicador *m*; **~-thumping** *pol* agitación *f*, *eccles* sermoneo

tuba tuba

tubby gordinflón

tube +*TV* tubo; (underground railway) metro; (*US* valve) lámpara; **inner** ~ cámara

tubeless: ~ **tyre** neumático sin cámara

tuber tubérculo

tubercular tubercular

tuberculosis tuberculosis *f*

tuberculous tuberculoso

tubing tubería

tubular tubular; ~ **furniture** muebles *mpl* de tubo de acero

tuck *n* recogido; *fam* comestibles dulces *mpl*; **~-box** caja de comestibles; **~-shop** confitería en/cerca de una escuela; *v* (sewing) plegar (ie)[2a]

~ **away** (hide) ocultar; *sl* (eat) zampar

~-in *n* banquete *m*

~ **in (to)** *sl* (eat) *v* zampar

~ **up** (skirt, sleeves *etc*) remangar[5]; ~ **up in bed** arreglar el embozo a

[1] **tucker** *n* camisolín (-ines) *m*; **in one's best bib and** ~ en sus mejores galas; *Aust* comestibles *mpl*; **~-bag** *Aust* bolsa de comida

[2] **tucker** *v US* cansar

Tuesday martes *m*

tuft copete *m*; (hair) mechón *m*; (feathers) penacho; (of grass) manojo; **~ed carpet** alfombra de nudos

tug *n* tirón (-ones) *m*; *naut* remolcador *m*; **~-of-war** lucha de la cuerda, *fig* lucha decisiva; *vt* ~ **at** tirar de; *naut* remolcar; *vi* tirar con fuerza; ~ **at one's beard** arrancarse[4] la barba

tuition enseñanza

tulip tulipán (-anes) *m*; **~-tree** tulipanero

tumble *n* caída; **take a** ~ caerse[19]; *v* caer[19]

~-down *adj* destartalado

~ **down** *v* venirse[19] abajo

~ **out** *vi* salir[19] en desorden; *vt* echar en desorden

~ **over** tropezar (ie)[2a+7] en

~ **to it** (realize) caer[19] en la cuenta

tumbler (glass) vaso; (of lock) seguro; (acrobat) volteador *m* (-ora *f*); *orni* pichón (-ones) *m* volteador

tumbrel, tumbril chirrión (-ones) *m*; *mil* carro de artillería

tummy estómago; (belly) barriga

tumour tumor *m*

tumult tumulto

tumultuous tumultuoso

tumulus túmulo

tun tonel *m*

tuna atún *m*

tundra tundra

tune *n* melodía; **in** ~ afinado; **be in** ~ **with** armonizar[7] con, *fig* concordar con; **out of** ~ desafinado; **be out of** ~ **with** no armonizar[7] con, *fig* desentonar con; **change one's** ~ mudar de tono; **to the** ~ **of** por la suma de; *v* (+ ~ **up**) *mus* afinar; *mot* poner[19] a punto; (+ ~ **in**) *rad* sintonizar[7]; **I can't** ~ **in to Madrid** no puedo sintonizar con Madrid

tuneful melodioso

tuneless disonante

tuner afinador *m*; *rad* sintonizador *m*

tungsten tungsteno

tunic túnica

tuning *m* afinación *f*; *rad* sintonización *f*; **~-coil** sintonizadora; **~-fork** diapasón *m*

Tunis, Tunisia Túnez *m*

Tunisian *n*+*adj* tunecino

tunnel *n* túnel *m*; *min* galería; *v* construir[16] un túnel (**under** bajo)

tunny atún *m*

tuppence dos peniques

turban turbante *m*

turbid turbio

turbine turbina

turbo-jet *n*+*adj* turborreactor *m*

turbo-prop *n* turbohélice *m*; ~ **plane** avión (-ones) *m* de turbohélices

turbot rodaballo

turbulence turbulencia

turbulent turbulento

turd *vulg* caca

tureen sopera

turf *n* césped *m*; (piece of) tepe *m*; (peat) turba; *sp* turf *m*; **~-accountant** apostador *m* de profesión; *v* encespe-

dar; ~ **out** expulsar
turfing césped *m*
turgid turgente; *fig* hinchado
turgidity turgencia
Turk turco; *fig* pícaro
Turkey Turquía
turkey pavo; **talk** ~ *US* no tener[19] pelos en la lengua
Turkish *n+adj* turco; ~ **bath** baño turco; ~ **Cypriot** *n+adj* turcochipriota *m+f*; ~ **delight** miel *f* turca; ~ **towel** toalla de felpa
turmeric cúrcuma
turmoil desorden *m*
turn *n* vuelta; (in road) curva; (sharp bend) recodo; (on axis) giro; (of events) marcha; (change) cambio; (spell) turno; *med* vahído; *theat* número; (move) jugada; ~ **of mind** disposición *f*; ~ **of phrase** giro; **bad** ~ mala jugada; **good** ~ favor *m*; **take a** ~ (walk) dar[19] una vuelta; **take a** ~ **at** contribuir[16] con su trabajo a; **take** ~**s at washing up** fregar (ie)[2a+5] los platos en turno; **take one's** ~ esperar su turno; **take** ~**s** turnarse; **whose** ~ **is it?** ¿a quién le toca?; **it's my** ~ me toca a mí; **by** ~**s** por turnos; **in** ~ por turno; **in her/his** ~ a su vez; **out of** ~ fuera de orden; **take a** ~ **for the better** mejorar(se); **take a** ~ **for the worse** empeorar(se); **the situation has taken a new** ~ la situación ha cambiado de aspecto; **done to a** ~ en su punto; **at every** ~ a cada paso; ~**coat** renegado; *fam* chaquetero; ~**cock** llave *f* de paso (de agua); ~**key** llavero; ~**pike** barrera de portazgo, *US* autopista de peaje; ~**stile** torniquete *m*; ~**table** (gramophone) placa giratoria, (railway) plataforma giratoria; *vt* volver (ue)[1b] (*past part* vuelto); *mech* tornear; (on axis) hacer[19] girar; ~ **one's ankle** torcerse (ue)[1b+12] el tobillo; ~ **one's back (on)** volver (ue)[1b] (*past part* vuelto) la espalda (a); ~ **colour** cambiar de color; **the leaves** ~ **yellow** las hojas se tornan/vuelven amarillas; ~ **a corner** doblar una esquina; ~ **a deaf ear to** hacerse[19] el sordo a; ~ **the handle** dar[19] vueltas al manubrio; ~ **an honest penny** ganarse la vida honradamente; ~ **the key** echar la llave; ~ **s.o.'s head** traerle[19] a

uno de coronilla; ~ **the stomach** revolver (ue)[1b] (*past part* revuelto) el estómago, (with disgust/anger) reventar (ie)[2a] las tripas; ~ **the scales** (be a decisive factor) ser[19] decisivo; ~ **the scales at** pesar; ~ **the tables on** cambiar la suerte; ~ **tail** darse[19] a la fuga; **he didn't even** ~ **a hair** él ni pestañeó; **hot weather will** ~ **the milk** el tiempo caluroso agriará la leche; **she's** ~**ed forty** ella tiene a lo menos cuarenta años; *vi* girar, ~ **to the right** girar a la derecha; *mot* torcer (ue)[1b]; (become) hacerse[19] +*n*, ponerse[19] +*adj*; (of milk) cortarse; (of wine) avinagrarse; (of tide) cambiar de marea; (of weather) cambiar; ~ **turtle** zozobrar
~ **about** dar una vuelta completa
~ **s.o. against** predisponerle[19] a uno en contra
~ **aside** desviar(se)
~ **away** *vt* despedir (i)[3]; *vi* volver (ue)[1b] (*past part* vuelto) la espalda (**from** a)
~ **back** *vt* (fold) doblar; (person) hacer[19] retroceder; *vi* volver (ue)[1b] (*past part* vuelto) atrás
~-**down** *n* doblado hacia abajo
~ **down** *vt* (fold) doblar; (reject) rehusar; (person) no aceptar; (gas *etc*) bajar; *vi* torcer (ue)[1b] por
~ **from** apartarse de
~ **in** *vt* doblar hacia adentro; (hand over) entregar[5]; (denounce) denunciar; *vi* doblarse hacia adentro; *fig* acostarse (ue)[1a]
~ **inside out** volver (ue)[1b] (*past part* vuelto) al revés
~ **into** convertir(se) (ie)[2c] en; (translate) traducir[15] en
~ **off** *vt* elect apagar[5], *fam* quitar; (tap) cerrar (ie)[2a]; (gas) cortar; *vi* (stray) desviarse
~ **on** *vt* rad+TV *etc* poner[19]; (light, heating) encender (ie)[2b]; (tap) abrir (*past part* abierto); (inspire) inspirar; (attack) volverse (ue)[1b] (*past part* vuelto) contra; *vi* depender de
~-**out** *n* (crowd) concurrencia; (production) producción *f*; (pomp) atuendo; (appearance) asco; **my wife has a general** ~-**out every spring** mi esposa hace una limpieza general cada primavera

~ **out** *vt* (extinguish) apagar⁵; (cake) sacar⁴; (expel) echar; (produce) fabricar⁴; (empty) vaciar; *vi* salir¹⁹ a la calle; (result) resultar; (get up) levantarse (de la cama); ~ **out to be** resultar; ~ **out well/badly** salir¹⁹ bien/mal; **she is well ~ed out** ella va bien vestida

~**-over** *n comm* volumen *m* de transacciones; (of personnel) cambio; *cul* pastel *m* con repulgo

~ **over** *vt* dar¹⁹ la vuelta a; ~ **over and over** dar¹⁹ vueltas a; ~ **over and over again** dar¹⁹ vueltas y vueltas; (upset) volcar⁴; (hand over) entregar⁵ (to a); *leg* rendir (i)³; ~ **over the engine** *mot* hacer¹⁹ girar el motor; ~ **over in one's mind** pensar (ie)²ᵃ bien; ~ **over a new leaf** dar¹⁹ la vuelta a la tortilla; ~ **over the page** pasar la hoja; **the police wanted to** ~ **over the room** la policia quería registrar la habitación; *vi* revolverse (ue)¹ᵇ (*past part* revuelto); *aer+mot* volcar⁴

~ **round** girar

~ **to** (for aid) recurrir; (change into) convertirse (ie)²ᶜ en; ~ **to account** sacar⁴ partido de

~**-up** *n* conmoción *f*; (of trousers) vuelta; ~**-up for the book** racha de buena suerte, (racing) buen resultado (para los apostadores profesionales)

~ **up** *vt* doblar hacia arriba; (soil) levantar; (gas) abrir (*past part* abierto) más; (reference) consultar; *rad+TV* poner¹⁹ más alto; (sleeves *etc*) remangar⁵; ~ **up one's nose at** mirar con desprecio; ~ **it up!** (be quiet!) ¡cállate!; *vi* doblarse hacia arriba; (appear) aparecer¹⁴; (arrive) llegar⁵; ~**ed-up:** ~ **nose** nariz (-ces) *f* respingona

~ **upside down** dar¹⁹ la vuelta a; *fig* trastornar

turner tornero

turning (action) vuelta; (angle) ángulo; (side-street) bocacalle *f*; *mech* torneado; ~**-circle** *mot* radio de dirección cerrada; ~**-lathe** torno (de tornero); ~**-point** momento decisivo

turnip nabo; ~ **field** nabar *m*

turpentine trementina

turpitude infamia

turquoise turquesa

turret *bui* torreón (-ones) *m*; *mil* torre *f*; *naut* torreta acorazada; (*US* capstan)

cabrestante *m*; ~**-lathe** torno revolvedor

turreted (with turrets) con torres; (turret-shaped) en forma de torre

turtle tortuga marina; (*US* tortoise) tortuga; **turn** ~ zozobrar; ~**-dove** tórtola

Tuscan *n+adj* toscano

Tuscany Toscana

tusk colmillo

tusked colmilludo

tussle *n* pelea; *v* ~ **over** reñir (i)³ a causa de; ~ **with** pelear con

tussock montecillo de hierba

tut! ¡bah!

tutelage tutela

tutelary tutelar

tutor *n* preceptor *m*; (private teacher) profesor *m* particular; *leg* tutor *m*; ~**ship** preceptorado, *leg* tutela; *v* ~ **in** enseñar

tutorial *n* clase *f* particular; *adj* preceptoral; *leg* tutelar

tutu tutú *m*

tuxedo smoking *m*

T.V. (television) T.V. (televisión *f*); **Spanish** ~ T.V.E. (Televisión Española)

twaddle tonterías *fpl*

twain dos

twang (of stringed instrument) punteado; (spoken) gangueo; *v mus* puntear

tweak *n* pellizco *m*; *v* pellizcar⁴ retorciendo

twee (small) pequeñito; (attractive) mono

tweed cheviot; **in** ~**s** llevando un traje de cheviot

tweet pío

tweezers pinzas *fpl*; **pair of** ~ unas pinzas

twelfth *n+adj* duodécimo; (fraction) dozavo; **Charles the Twelfth** Carlos doce; **the** ~ **of July** (el) doce de julio; **Twelfth Night** Día *m* de Reyes

twelve *n+adj* doce *m*

twentieth *n+adj* vigésimo; (of month) (el) veinte; (fraction) veintavo

twenty *n+adj* veinte *m*; ~**-five-yard line** (rugby) línea de veintidós metros; ~**fold** veinte veces; ~**-odd** veintitantos; ~**-year-old** *n+adj* veinteañero

twerp idiota *m+f*

twice dos veces; ~ **as many** otros tantos; ~ **as much** el doble (de); ~ **two are four** dos por dos son cuatro

twiddle jugar (ue)[1a] distraídamente (**with** con)

[1] **twig** ramita

[2] **twig** *fam* caer[19] en la cuenta; **now I ~ it** ahora caigo

twiggy con muchas ramitas; (thin) muy delgado como una ramita

twilight *n* crepúsculo; *adj* crepuscular; ~ **sleep** sueño crepuscular

twill tela cruzada

twin *n+adj* (identical) gemelo, (non-identical) mellizo; ~-**engined** bi-motor; ~-**jet** birreactor *m*; ~-**pram** cochecito para mellizos; ~-**screw** de dos hélices; ~-**set** juego de jersey y rebeca; **twinned towns** ciudades *fpl* hermanadas; *v* (be twinned with) hermanarse con

twine *n* bramante *m*; *vt* torcer (ue)[1b]; *vi* enroscarse[4]

twinge punzada; ~ **of conscience** remordimiento de conciencia

twining *bot* sarmentoso

twinkle *n* centelleo; (of eye) parpadeo; *v* centellear; (of eye) parpadear

twinkling *see* **twinkle**; **in the ~ of an eye** en un dos por tres

twirl *n* vuelta rápida; *vt* hacer[19] girar; *vi* girar

twist *n* torcedura; (of tobacco) rollo; (bend) recodo; (of screw) enrosca-dura; (dance) twist *m*; ~ **of the mind** peculiaridad *f* de la mente; **round the ~** chiflado; ~-**grip** *mot* puño giratorio; *v* torcerse (ue)[1b]; (screw) enroscar[4]; (swindle) estafar; (dance) bailar el twist; **you ~ my words** usted desfigura mis palabras

twister estafador *m* (-ora *f*)

twit *n* tonto; *v* tomar el pelo

twitch *n* sacudida repentina; *med* con-tracción *f* nerviosa; **facial** ~ tic *m*; *vt* tirar ligeramente a; *vi* temblar (ie)[2a]

twitter *orni* gorjeo; (excitement) agita-ción *f*; **be all of a ~** estar[19] agitado; *v* *orni* gorjear; *fig* algazar

two *n+adj* dos *m*; ~ **against** ~ dos a dos; ~ **hundred** doscientos *mpl* (-as *fpl*); ~ **of a kind** tal para cual; ~ **weeks** quince días *mpl*; **in** ~ en dos; **in/by** ~s de dos en dos; **one or** ~ algunos; **put** ~ **and** ~

together atar cabos; ~-**berth cabin** camarote *m* de dos camas; ~-**edged** de dos filos; ~-**faced** falso; ~**fold** *adj* dos veces; **in** ~-**four**, ~-~ **time** *mus* en dos por cuatro/dos por dos; ~-**handed** de/para dos manos, (ambidextrous) ambidextro; ~-**handed saw** tronzador *m*; ~-**horsed carriage** carruaje *m* de dos caballos; ~-**hundredth** ducentésima parte; ~-**legged** bípedo; ~-**masted** de dos palos; ~-**party system** sistema *m* bipartidista; ~-**pence** dos peniques; ~**penny** de dos peniques; ~-**ply** (wood) de dos capas, (wool) de dos cabos; ~-**seater** *aer+mot* de dos plazas; ~-**seater car/plane** biplaza *m*; ~**some** *sp* partido de dos; ~-**stage rocket** cohete *m* de dos etapas; ~**step** paso doble; ~-**storey** de dos pisos; ~-**stroke** *mot* de dos tiempos; ~-**time** (betray) traicionar, (be unfaithful) ser[19] infiel; ~-**tone** bicolor; ~-**way** de dos direcciones; ~-**way switch** conmutador de dos direcciones; ~-**way stretch** bielástico

tycoon magnate *m*

tying atadura

tyke perro callejero

tympanum tímpano

type *n* +*print* tipo; **goods of this** ~ artí-culos del ramo; ~**cast** *v* escoger un actor porque tiene experiencia en papeles parecidos; ~-**face** tipo; ~-**script** original mecanografiado; ~-**setter** (person) cajista *m*, (machine) máquina de componer; ~**setting** com-posición *f*; ~-**writer** (person) mecanó-grafo, (machine) máquina de escribir; ~**writer ribbon** cinta tintadora; ~-**written** mecanografiado; *v* escribir (*past part* escrito) a máquina; (clas-sify) clasificar[4]; ~ **with two fingers** es-cribir (*past part* escrito) a máquina con dos dedos

typhoid fiebre *f* tifoidea

typhoon tifón (-ones) *m*

typhus tifus *m*

typical típico

typify simbolizar[7]

typing mecanografía; ~-**paper** papel *m* de escribir a máquina

typist mecanógrafo, mecanógrafa

typographer tipógrafo

typographical tipográfico

typography tipografía
typological tipológico
typology typología
tyrannic(al) tiránico
tyrannize (over) tiranizar[7]
tyrannous tiránico
tyranny tiranía
tyrant tirano
tyre neumático; *SA* llanta; (outer cover)
cubierta; (inner tube) cámara; (of
cart) calce *m*; ~ **lever** desmontable *m*
de cubiertas
Tyre Tiro
tyro novicio
Tyrol Tirol *m*
Tyrolean *n* + *adj* tirolés *m* (-esa *f*)
tzar zar *m*
tzarina zarina

U

u (letter) u *f*

U *cin*: ~ **film** *approx* película tolerada para menores

U.A.R. (United Arab Republic) R.A.U. (República Árabe Unida)

U-bend curva en U

ubiquitous omnipresente

ubiquity ubicuidad *f*

U-boat submarino alemán

udder ubre *f*

U.F.O. (unidentified flying object) O.V.N.I. (objecto volante no identificado)

Uganda Uganda

Ugandan ugandés *m* (-esa *f*)

ugh! ¡uf!

ugliness fealdad *f*

ugly feo; **be in an ~ mood** estar[19] de muy mal humor; **the crowd was in an ~ mood** la muchedumbre amenazaba violencia; ~ **customer** tipo antipático; ~ **situation** situación peligrosa; **the situation is getting ~** la situación se pone peligrosa; ~ **sky** cielo amenazador

U.H.F. (ultra high frequency) F.M. frecuencia modulada

U.K. (United Kingdom) Reino Unido

ukelele ukelele *m*

Ukraine Ucrania

Ukrainian *n* + *adj* ucranio

ulcer úlcera

ulcerate ulcerar(se)

ulceration ulceración *f*

ulcerous ulceroso

ullage + *space* pérdida por evaporación

Ulster Úlster *m*

Ulsterman ciudadano del Úlster

ult. (ultimo) del mes pasado

ulterior ulterior; ~ **motive** intención oculta

ultimate último; (basic) fundamental

ultimately finalmente; (basically) en esencia

ultimatum ultimátum *m*

ultra: ~-**fashionable** muy de moda;

~**marine** ultramarino, (colour) color *m* de ultramar; ~-**modern** ultramoderno; ~-**montane** ultramontano; ~-**short-wave (de)** onda ultracorta; ~**violet** ultravioleta

ululate ulular

ululation ululato

Ulysses Ulises *m*

umbel umbela

umber lugar *m* de sombra

umbilical umbilical; ~ **cord** + *fig* cordón *m* umbilical

umbilicus ombligo

umbrage resentimiento; **take ~ (at)** ofenderse (por)

umbrella paraguas *m sing* + *pl*; *aer* protección *f* de aviones de caza; ~-**barrage** cortina de fuego antiaéreo; ~-**stand** paragüero

umpire *n* árbitro; *v* arbitrar

umpteen muchísimos

umpteenth enésimo

unabashed descarado

unabated sin disminución

unabbreviated íntegro

unable incapaz (-ces); **be ~ to** no poder[19] + *infin*

unabridged íntegro

unaccented sin acento

unacceptable inaceptable

unaccommodating poco amable

unaccompanied sin acompañamiento

unaccomplished no acabado

unaccountable inexplicable

unaccountably inexplicablemente

unaccounted sin noticias; **three of them were ~ for** no había noticias de tres de ellos

unaccustomed no acostumbrado

unacknowledged sin reconocer; (of letter) por contestar

unacquainted desconocido; **be ~ with** no conocer

unadaptable inadaptable

unaddressed sin dirección

unadjusted no ajustado

unadorned sin adorno

unadulterated sin mezcla

unadventurous poco aventurero

unadvisable poco aconsejable

unadvisably imprudentemente

unaesthetic antiestético

unaffected sin afectación: **he was ~ by the news** las noticias no le hicieron ningún efecto

unaffectedly sin afectación

unafraid sin temor

unaided sin ayuda

unalleviated sin aliviar

unalloyed sin mezcla

unalterable inalterable

unalterably de modo inalterable

unaltered inalterado

unambiguous inequívoco

unambiguously de modo inequívoco

unambitious poco ambicioso

un-American antiamericano

unamiable poco simpático

unanimity unanimidad *f*

unanimous unánime

unanswerable incontestable

unanswered sin contestar

unappealable inapelable

unappetizing poco apetitoso

unappreciative desagradecido

unapproachable inaccesible

unappropriated no asignado

unarm desarmar; **~ed combat** lucha sin armas

unartistic poco artístico

unashamed desvergonzado

unasked sin pedir permiso; (at function) sin ser invitado

unassailable inexpugnable

unassisted sin ayuda

unassuming modesto

unattached suelto; (person) no prometido; *mil* de reemplazo; *pol* independiente

unattainable inasequible

unattended desatendido

unattractive poco atractivo

unauthorized sin autorización

unavailable, unavailing inaprovechable

unavoidable inevitable

unaware inconsciente (**of** de); **be ~ ignorar**; **be ~ that** ignorar que; **~s** de improviso; **take ~s** coger[14] desprevenido

unbalance desequilibrio; **~d** (mentally) desequilibrado

unbandage quitar la venda

unbaptized sin bautizar

unbar desatrancar[4]

unbearable insoportable

unbeatable imbatible; (of prices) inmejorable

unbeaten (of team) imbatido; (of record) no superado

unbecoming impropio (**for** de); (of dress) que sienta mal

unbefriended sin amigos

unbeknown: ~ to him sin saberlo él

unbelief descreimiento

unbelievable increíble

unbeliever no creyente *m+f*

unbelieving incrédulo

unbend enderezar(se)[7]

unbending inflexible

unbiased imparcial

unbidden sin ser invitado

unbind (free) soltar (ue)[1a]; (of bandages) quitar las vendas

unbleached sin blanquear; **~ linen** hilo crudo

unblemished sin tacha

unblushing desvergonzado

unbolt desatrancar[4]

unborn no nacido aún

unbosom desahogarse[5]

unbound sin encuadernar

unbounded ilimitado

unbowed erguido

unbreakable irrompible; (of glass) inastillable

unbreeched sin calzones

unbridled +*fig* desenfrenado

unbroken (intact) intacto; (of time) no interrumpido; (of animals) no domado; *sp* (of record) no superado

unbuckle deshebillar

unburden: ~ o.s. of aliviarse de; (confess) confesar; **~ one's heart** desahogarse[5]

unbusinesslike anticomercial; (impractical) poco práctico

unbutton desabrochar

uncalled-for innecesario; **that insinuation is ~** esa insinuación es impropia

uncanny misterioso

uncap *vt* destapar; *vi* descubrirse (*past part* descubierto) para saludar

uncared-for abandonado

unceasing incesante

uncensored sin censurar

unceremonious poco ceremonioso

unceremoniously sin ceremonia; (rudely) bruscamente

uncertain incierto; (undecided) indeciso; **I am ~ of** no estoy seguro de

uncertainty incertidumbre f; (football pools) variante f, **this week there are many uncertainties** esta semana hay muchas variantes

unchain desencadenar

unchallengeable incontestable

unchallenged incontestado

unchangeable, unchanging incambiable

unchanged inalterado

unchanging inalterable

uncharitable poco caritativo

uncharted inexplorado

unchaste impúdico

unchastised impune, sin castigo

unchecked adj desenfrenado; (not verified) no comprobado; adv sin restricción

unchristian anticristiano; fig poco caritativo

uncircumcised n los gentiles; adj incircunciso

uncivil descortés m+f

uncivilized incivilizado

unclaimed sin reclamar

unclasp desabrochar; (let go) soltar (ue)[1a]

unclassed sin clasificar

unclassifiable inclasificable

unclassified sin clasificar

uncle tío; (pawn-broker) prestamista m; theat agente m; theat caballo blanco; **talk like a Dutch ~** reprender severamente; **Bob's your ~!** ¡todo está de primera!

unclean sucio; fig impuro

uncleanliness suciedad f; fig impureza

uncleanly de modales sucios

unclench desagarrar

uncloak quitar la capa

unclothe desnudar

unclouded despejado

unclubbable insociable

uncoil desenrollar

uncomfortable incómodo

uncommercial no comercial

uncommitted no comprometido; (impartial) imparcial

uncommon poco común (-unes)

uncommonly excepcionalmente

uncommunicative poco comunicativo

uncompanionable poco sociable

uncomplaining resignado

uncomplicated poco complicado

uncomplimentary poco lisonjero

uncompromising intransigente

unconcern indiferencia; **~ed** indiferente

unconditional incondicional; **~ surrender** rendición f sin condiciones

unconfessed sin confesar

unconfined ilimitado

unconfirmed sin confirmar

unconformity desconformidad f

uncongenial antipático

unconnected inconexo

unconquerable inconquistable

unconquered sin conquistar

unconscionable exorbitante

unconscious n inconsciente; adj inconsciente (**of** de); med sin conocimiento

unconsciously sin saber

unconsciousness inconsciencia; med insensibilidad f

unconsecrated sin consagrar

unconsidered inconsiderado

unconstitutional inconstitucional

unconstrained no cohibido

uncontaminated sin contaminar

uncontrollable incontrolable

uncontrolled libre

uncontroversial poco contencioso

unconventional poco convencional; (contrary to custom) fuera de lo común

unconverted no convertido

unconvinced no convencido

uncooked sin cocer[14]

uncooperative poco cooperativo

uncoordinated sin coordinar

uncork descorchar

uncorrected sin corregir[9]

uncorroborated no confirmado

uncorrupted incorrupto

uncouple desacoplar

uncouth grosero

uncouthness grosería

uncover descubrir (past part descubierto)

uncreditworthy poco digno de crédito

uncritical con poco sentido crítico

uncropped no cortado

uncross descruzar[7]

uncrowned sin corona; ~ **king** *fig* el que más influencia tiene

uncrushable inarrugable

unction *eccles* unción *f*; (manner) zalamería

unctuous zalamero, *sl* cobista

unctuousness zalamería, *sl* coba

uncultivated +*fig* inculto

uncultured inculto

uncut (book) sin cortar; (stone) sin tallar

undamaged ileso

undamped *fig* no disminuido

undated sin fecha

undaunted intrépido

undeceive desengañar

undecided indeciso

undecipherable indescifrable

undeclared no declarado

undefeated imbatido

undefended indefenso; *leg* perdido por incomparecimiento

undefiled puro

undefinable indefinible

undefined indefinido

undemonstrative reservado

undeniable innegable

undenominational no sectario

undependable no de fiar

under *adj* inferior; ~**side of** parte *f* inferior de; *adv* debajo, abajo, ~ **there** allí abajo; *prep* debajo de; (less precise) bajo; (fewer than) menos de, **she is** ~ **forty** ella tiene menos de cuarenta años; ~ **age** menor de edad; **you are** ~ **arrest** queda usted detenido; ~ **consideration** en consideración; ~ **fire** en combate; ~ **one's nose** delante de sus narices; ~ **pain of** bajo pena de; ~ **separate cover** aparte; ~ **the circumstances** dadas las circunstancias; ~ **the microscope** +*fig* bajo el microscopio; ~ **water** inundado; ~ **way** en marcha; ~-**five**, ~-**fourteen** *n* menor *m*+*f* de cinco/catorce años; ~-**belly** vientre *m*, *fig* parte *f* más vulnerable; ~**bid** *n* oferta más baja, *v* ofrecer[14] menos que; ~-**blanket** manta bajera; ~**bred** vulgar; ~**brush** maleza; ~**carriage** tren *m* de aterrizaje; ~-**charge** cobrar menos de lo debido; ~**clothing**, ~**clothes** ropa interior; ~**coat** *n* primera mano (de pintura), *v* dar[19] la primera mano (de pin-

tura); ~-**cover** secreto; ~-**cover agent** espía; ~**current** resaca, (of opinion) tendencia oculta a creer; ~**cut** *n* (meat) solomillo, *v* (prices) rebajar, (competitor) vender a menos precio que; ~**develop** *phot* no revelar bastante; ~**developed country** país subdesarrollado; ~**dog** marginado; ~**done** (deliberately ~-cooked) poco hecho, (accidentally ~-cooked) no bastante hecho; ~**employment** infraempleo; ~**estimate** menospreciar, (miscalculate) calcular mal; ~**expose** exponer[19] insuficientemente; ~**exposure** exposición *f* insuficiente; ~**fed** subalimentado; ~**feeding** subalimentación *f*; ~**felt** felpa que se pone debajo de una alfombra; ~**foot** debajo de los pies; **trample** ~**foot** pisotear; ~**garment** pieza de ropa interior; ~**go** (experience) experimentar, (suffer) sufrir; ~**graduate** *n* estudiante *m*+*f* universitario, *adj* estudiantil; ~**ground** *n* metro, *mil* resistencia, *mus* underground *m*, *adj* subterráneo, (secret) clandestino, *adv* bajo tierra, (secretly) clandestinamente; ~**growth** maleza; ~**hand** (deceitful) poco limpio, (secret) clandestino; ~**hand service** *sp* hecho con la mano debajo del hombro; ~**handed** disimulado; ~**lay** *n* refuerzo, *print* calzo, *v* reforzar (ue)[1a+7], *print* calzar[7]; ~**lie** ser[19] la razón fundamental de; ~**line** +*fig* subrayar; ~**linen** ropa interior; ~**ling** subordinado, *pej* lacayo; ~**lying** fundamental; ~**manned** sin bastantes obreros/*naut* tripulantes; ~**mentioned** abajo citado; ~**mine** socavar, *fig* debilitar; ~**most** (el) más bajo, la más baja; ~**neath** *adv* debajo, *prep* debajo de; ~**nourished** desnutrido; ~**nourishment** desnutrición *f*; ~**paid** mal pagado; ~**pants** calzoncillos *mpl*; ~**pass** paso inferior; ~**pay** pagar[5] insuficientemente; ~**pin** apuntalar; ~**pinning** apuntalamiento; ~**privilege** marginación *f*, *v* marginar; ~**production** producción *f* insuficiente; ~**quote** ofrecer precio más bajo que; ~**rate** menospreciar; ~**score** subrayar; ~-**secretary** subsecretario; ~**sell** vender más barato que; ~**shirt** camiseta; ~**side** superficie *f* inferior, (of paper) revés *m*; ~**sign** suscribir (*past part* suscrito); ~**signed** *n* suscrito(s); ~**sized** más pequeño que lo normal, (baby) sietemesino; ~**skirt** enaguas *fpl*; ~**slung** *mot* debajo del eje; ~**staffed** sin suficiente personal; ~**stand** entender (ie)[2b], (sympathize) comprender, (realize) darse[19] cuenta de, (have heard) haber[19] oído decir, **I ~stand she is Russian** he oído decir que ella es rusa, **give to ~stand** dar[19] a entender; **make o.s. understood** hacerse[19] entender, (in foreign language) defenderse (ie)[2b]; **it is understood that** se entiende que; ~**standable** comprensible; ~**standing** *n* entendimiento, (agreement) acuerdo, (interpretation) interpretación *f*, (sympathy) sensibilidad *f*; **on the ~standing that** bien entendido que, *adj* sensible; ~**state** exponer[19] incompletamente; ~**statement** declaración incompleta; ~**study** *n* suplente *m*+*f*, *v* aprender el papel para poder suplir; ~**take** (embark upon) emprender, (promise) comprometerse a, (take on responsibility for) encargarse[5] de; ~**taker** director *m* de pompas fúnebres; ~**taker's** funeraria; ~**taking** (enterprise) empresa, (promise) promesa, (funeral business) funeraria; ~**-the-counter** *fig* por la trastienda; ~**tone** voz baja (**in an en**), (implication) trasfondo; ~**tow** resaca; ~**value** menospreciar; ~**water** submarino; ~**wear** ropa interior; ~**weight** de peso insuficiente; ~**work** no dar[19] suficiente trabajo a, **I am ~worked** no tengo suficiente trabajo; ~**world** (hell) infierno, (criminal) hampa; ~**write** asegurar; ~**writer** asegurador *m*; *sp* ~**-21 team** equipo sub-21

undeserved inmerecido
undeserving indigno
undesigned impremeditado
undesirable *n* persona *f* indeseable; *adj* indeseable
undetected sin descubrir
undetermined incierto
undeterred que no se deja intimidar
undeveloped sin desarrollar; (of land) sin explotar; *phot* sin revelar
undies prendas *fpl* íntimas

undifferentiated sin diferenciar
undigested indigesto
undignified sin dignidad
undiluted puro
undiminished no disminuido
undiplomatic poco diplomático
undiscerning sin discernimiento
undischarged (unpaid) no pagado; (gun) no disparado
undisciplined indisciplinado
undisclosed secreto
undiscovered desconocido
undiscriminating sin discriminación
undisguised sin disfraz
undismayed impávido
undisputed incontestable
undistinguished mediocre
undisturbed (of people) imperturbado; (of things) sin tocar
undivided entero
undo deshacer[19]; (untie) desatar; (unwrap) abrir (*past part* abierto); (unclasp, unbutton) desabrochar; (ruin) arruinar, *fig* deshonrar
undoing perdición *f*
undone deshecho; (untied) desatado; (unwrapped) abierto; (unclasped, unbuttoned) desabrochado; (ruined) arruinado, *fig* deshonrado; **come ~** deshacerse[19]; desatarse; abrirse; desabrocharse; arruinarse; **leave ~** dejar por hacer; **leave nothing ~** no dejar nada por hacer; **she is ~** ella está perdida
undoubted indudable
undoubting que no tiene dudas
undramatic poco dramático
undreamed-of no soñado
undress *n* bata; **in a state of ~** en bata; ~ **uniform** uniforme *m* de fatigas; *v* desnudar; ~ **o.s., get ~ed** desnudarse; ~ **a wound** quitar el vendaje a una herida; ~**ed** (naked) desnudo, (unbandaged) sin vendar, *cul* sin preparar, (leather) sin curtir
undrinkable no potable
undue excesivo
undulate ondular
undulating ondulante
undulation ondulación *f*
undulatory ondulatorio
unduly con exceso
undying imperecedero
unearned no ganado; ~ **income** renta

diferida; ~ **interest** interés (-eses) *m* no devengado

unearth desenterrar (ie)[2a]

unearthly sobrenatural; *fig* espantoso; **at an ~ hour** a una hora intempestiva

uneasiness inquietud *f*

uneasy inquieto

uneatable incomible

uneconomic(al) antieconómico

unedifying indecoroso

unedited inédito

uneducated inculto; (bad-mannered) sin educación

unemotional impasible

unemployable inapto para ser empleado

unemployed *n* parados *mpl*; *adj* en paro

unemployment desempleo; ~ **benefit** subsidio de desempleo; ~ **insurance** seguro contra el paro

unending interminable

unendurable inaguantable

unengaged libre

un-English (untypical) nada típico de un inglés; (anti-English) contrario a los intereses ingleses

unenlightened poco instruido; (of behaviour) ignorante

unenterprising poco emprendedor (-ora *f*)

unenthusiastic sin entusiasmo

unenviable poco envidiable

unequal desigual; **he was ~ to the work** no estaba a la altura del trabajo

unequalled sin par

unequivocal inequívoco

unerring infalible

unessential no esencial

unethical inmoral

uneven desigual; (of roads) accidentado; (of numbers) impar

unevenness desigualdad *f*; (of roads) desnivelación *f*

uneventful tranquilo

unexampled sin paralelo

unexceptionable intachable

unexceptional normal

unexpected inesperado

unexpectedly inesperadamente; *fam* de manos a boca

unexpired sin caducar[4]; (ticket *etc*) no caducado; (bill) no vencido

unexplained inexplicado

unexplored inexplorado

unexposed (sheltered) abrigado; *phot* inexpuesto

unexpressed no expresado

unexpurgated sin expurgar

unfading inmarcesible

unfailing infalible

unfair injusto; ~ **competition** competencia desleal; **that's ~!** ¡no hay derecho!

unfairness injusticia

unfaithful infiel; (disloyal) desleal

unfaithfulness infidelidad *f*; (disloyalty) deslealtad *f*

unfamiliar desconocido; **be ~ with** desconocer[14]

unfamiliarity desconocimiento

unfashionable pasado de moda

unfashioned informe

unfasten soltar (ue)[1a]; (untie) desatar

unfathomable insondable

unfavourable desfavorable

unfeathered desplumado

unfeeling insensible

unfeigned verdadero

unfetter destrabar; ~**ed** sin trabas

unfilled: ~ **orders** pedidos *mpl* sin despachar

unfinished inacabado; ~ **symphony** sinfonía incompleta

unfit (out of condition) desentrenado; (injured) **he is ~** él está lesionado; ~ **for** no apto para; ~ **for human consumption** impropio para el consumo humano; **it is ~ for human habitation** no reúne las condiciones (mínimas) de habitabilidad

unfitness incapacidad *f*

unfitted for incapacitado para

unfitting indecoroso

unfix soltar (ue)[1a]; ~**ed** suelto

unflagging incansable

unflattering poco lisonjero

unflinching impávido

unfold desplegar (ie)[2a+5]; (reveal) revelar; (story) desarrollarse

unforced espontáneo

unforeseeable imprevisible

unforeseen imprevisto

unforgettable inolvidable

unforgivable imperdonable

unforgiving implacable

unforgotten no olvidado, sin olvidar

unformed sin formar aún

unfortified sin fortificar; ~ **town** ciudad abierta

unfortunate *n+adj* desgraciado; ~ **occurrence** acontecimiento funesto; ~ **remark** observación *f* desacertada

unfounded infundado; *leg* improcedente

unfreeze +*fig* descongelar

unfrequented poco frecuentado

unfriended sin amigos

unfriendliness insociabilidad *f*; (hostility) hostilidad *f*

unfriendly insociable; (hostile) hostil

unfrock (of priests) degradar; (of monks) exclaustrar

unfrozen sin congelar; (thawed) descongelado

unfruitful infructuoso

unfulfilled incumplido

unfurl desplegar (ie)²ᵃ⁺⁵; (sail) desaferrar

unfurnished desamueblado; ~ **house** casa sin muebles

ungainliness torpeza

ungainly torpe

ungallant descortés *invar*

ungenerous poco generoso

ungentlemanly indigno de un caballero

unget-at-able inaccesible

ungifted sin talento

unglazed no vidriado

ungodliness impiedad *f*

ungodly impío

ungovernable ingobernable

ungracious descortés *invar*

ungrammatical incorrecto

ungrateful ingrato

ungratefulness ingratitud *f*

ungrounded sin fundamento

ungrudgingly de buena gana

unguarded sin guarda; (careless) imprudente

unguent ungüento

unguided sin guía

ungulate ungulado

ungullible astuto

unhallowed profano

unhampered sin estorbos

unhand soltar (ue)¹ᵃ

unhandled sin manosear

unhandy desmañado

unhappily desgraciadamente

unhappiness infelicidad *f*

unhappy infeliz (-ces)

unharmed ileso

unharnessed desguarnecido

unhealthy (person) enfermizo; (place *etc*) insalubre

unheard que no se ha oído; ~ **of** inaudito

unheeded desatendido; **go** ~ ser¹⁹ desatendido

unhelpful poco servicial

unheralded inesperado

unhesitating resuelto

unhesitatingly sin vacilar

unhinge +*fig* desquiciar

unhistorical legendario

unhitch desenganchar; (animal) desuncir¹³

unholy impío; **what an** ~ **row!** ¡qué ruido tan atroz!

unhook desenganchar

unhoped-for inesperado

unhopeful poco prometedor

unhorse: be ~**d** caerse¹⁹ del caballo

unhurt ileso

unhygienic antihigiénico

unicellular unicelular

unicorn unicornio

unicycle monocicleta

unidentified no identificado; ~ **flying object** objeto volante no identificado

unification unificación *f*

uniform *n* uniforme *m*; **full** ~ uniforme *m* de gala; *adj* uniforme; **make** ~ uniformar

uniformity uniformidad *f*

unify unificar⁴

unilateral unilateral; ~ **disarmament** desarme *m* unilateral

unimaginable inimaginable

unimaginative sin imaginación

unimpaired intacto

unimpassioned sin pasión

unimpeachable intachable

unimpeded sin estorbo

unimportance insignificancia

unimportant insignificante

unimposing poco imponente

unimpressive poco impresionante; ~ **man** hombre insignificante

unimproved no mejorado; (of land) sin urbanizar

uninfluenced no afectado (**by** por)

uninformed poco instruido

uninhabitable inhabitable

uninhabited (house) deshabitado; (land) despoblado

uninhibited; desinhibido

uninitiated novicio
uninjured ileso
uninspired sin inspiración; (of writings *etc*) mediocre
uninstructed ignorante
uninstructive nada instructivo
uninsured no asegurado
unintelligent ininteligente
unintelligible ininteligible
unintended, unintentional involuntario
unintentionally sin querer
uninterested sin interés
uninteresting faltando interés; (of food) soso; (of people) aburrido
uninterrupted ininterrumpido
uninvited (person) no invitado; (comment) gratuito; (unlooked for) no buscado
uninviting poco atractivo; (of food) poco apetitoso
union *n* +*mech* unión *f*; (trade union) sindicato; (marriage) enlace *m*; (university) asociación *f* estudiantil; (workhouse) asilo; **Union Jack** bandera del Reino Unido; **state of the Union** estado de los Estados Unidos de América; ~ **suit** ropa interior de una sola pieza; *adj* sindical
unionism unionismo; (trade-unionism) sindicalismo
unionist *n*+*adj* unionista *m*+*f*; (trade-unionist) sindicalista *m*+*f*
unique único
uniqueness lo singular
unisex: ~ **clothes** ropa unisex
unisexual unisexual
unison unisonancia; **in** ~ al unísono, *fam* todos juntos
unit unidad *f*; ~ **furniture** muebles *mpl* por elementos; ~ **trust** cooperativa de inversiones; ~-**built house** vivienda por elementos
Unitarian *n*+*adj* unitario
Unitarianism unitarismo
unitary unitario
unite unir(se); (marry) casar; ~**d** unido; **United Kingdom** Reino Unido; **United Nations** Naciones *fpl* Unidas; **United States of America** Estados *mpl* Unidos de América
unity unidad *f*; (harmony) concordia
universal universal; ~ **joint** junta universal; **Universal Postal Union** Unión *f* Postal Universal

universality universalidad *f*
universalize universalizar[7]
universe universo
university *n* universidad *f*; *adj* universitario
unjust injusto
unjustifiable injustificable
unkempt despeinado; *fig* desaseado
unkind poco simpático; (words) malintencionado
unkindness dureza; (single act) acción (-ones) *f* cruel
unknown *n* lo desconocido; *adj* desconocido; ~ **to me** *adv* sin saberlo yo; ~ **quantity** incógnita
unlace desenlazar[7]
unladylike impropio de una señora
unlamented no lamentado
unlatch abrir (*past part* abierto) levantando el picaporte
unlawful ilegal; ~ **possession** tenencia ilícita
unlearn desaprender; ~**ed** ignorante
unleash soltar (ue)[1a]; *fig* desencadenar
unleavened sin levadura; ~ **bread** pan ácimo
unled sin líder
unless a menos que +*subj*
unlettered iletrado
unlicensed sin licencia
unlike *adj* diferente; *elect* de signo contrario; *prep* a diferencia de
unlikelihood improbabilidad *f*
unlikely improbable
unlimited (boundless) ilimitado; (unrestricted) sin restricción
unlined (clothing) sin forro; (paper) sin rayas; (skin) sin arrugas
unlisted *tel* privado
unlit sin luz
unload descargar[5]; *comm* deshacerse[19] de
unlock abrir (*past part* abierto); *fig* resolver (ue)[1b]
unlooked-for inesperado
unloose(n) soltar (ue)[1a]
unlovable poco apetecible; (person) antipático
unloved no querido
unlovely desgarbado
unloving nada cariñoso
unlucky desgraciado; (ill-fated) nefasto; **is it** ~ **to?** ¿trae mala suerte +*infin*?; **it was an** ~ **break** fue mala pata

unmaidenly indigno de una señorita
unmake deshacer[19]
unman acobardar
unmanageable inmanejable; (person) incontrolable
unmanly (cowardly) cobarde; (effeminate) afeminado
unmanned; *aer+space* sin tripulación
unmannered mal educado
unmarked sin marcar[4]; (unnoticed) inadvertido; *sp* desmarcado
unmarketable invendible
unmarriageable incasable
unmarried soltero
unmask desenmascarar
unmatched sin par; sin pareja
unmeasurable infinito
unmentionable *adj* indecible; ~s *n* ropa interior
unmerciful despiadado
unmerited inmerecido
unmethodical poco metódico
unmindful: be ~ of no pensar (ie)[2a] en
unmistakable inconfundible
unmitigated absoluto; profundo; (inhuman) inhumano
unmixed sin mezcla
unmolested tranquilo
unmortgaged sin hipoteca
unmounted desmontado; *phot* sin encuadrar
unmoved (unemotional) impasible; (unshaken) inflexible
unmusical sin afición a la música; (tone deaf) sin oído (para la música)
unmuzzle quitar el bozal; *fig* relevar de la obligación de guardar silencio
unnameable que no se puede nombrar
unnamed sin nombre; ~ sources fuentes *fpl* no divulgadas
unnatural (against nature) antinatural; ~ act acto contra la naturaleza
unnavigable no navegable
unnecessarily sin necesidad *f*
unnecessary innecesario; (useless) superfluo
unneighbourly poco amistoso
unnerve acobardar
unnerving desalentador (-ora *f*)
unnoticed inadvertido
unnumbered sin numerar
U.N.O. (United Nations Organization) O.N.U. (Organización *f* de las Naciones Unidas)

unobjectionable intachable
unobservant distraído
unobserved inadvertido
unobtainable inasequible
unobtrusive discreto
unoccupied (house) deshabitado; (land) sin colonizar; (post) vacante; (person) desocupado; (seat, lavatory *etc*) libre
unoffending inofensivo
unofficial extraoficial; (news) sin confirmar; (of strikes) ilegal
unopened sin abrir
unopposed sin oposición
unorganized sin organización
unoriginal poco original
unorthodox no ortodoxo; *eccles* heterodoxo
unostentatious sin ostentación
unpack desempaquetar; (suitcase) deshacer[19]
unpacking desembalaje *m*
unpaid no pagado; (bill) por pagar
unpalatable +*fig* intragable
unparalleled sin igual
unpardonable imperdonable
unparliamentary antiparlamentario; ~ language palabras *fpl* obscenas/feas
unpatented sin patentar
unpatriotic antipatriótico
unpaved sin asfaltar
unpeg (prices) descongelar
unpen soltar (ue)[1a] del redil
unperceived desapercibido
unperturbed impertérrito
unpick (sewing) descoser; *fam* soltar (ue)[1a]
unpin desprender
unplaced *sp* no colocado
unplanned casual
unpleasant, unpleasing desagradable; (person) antipático
unpleasantness antipatía; (ill-feeling) desavenencia; (quarrel) disgusto
unplug *elect* desenchufar; (drain) destapar
unplumbed no sondado
unpolished sin pulir; *fig* inculto; ~ diamond diamante *m* en bruto
unpolluted impoluto
unpopular impopular
unpopularity impopularidad *f*
unposted (packet, letter *etc*) no echado al buzón; (not informed) no al corriente

unpotable no potable
unpractical poco práctico
unpractised inexperto
unprecedented inaudito
unpredictable imprevisible; (person) de acciones imprevisibles
unprejudiced imparcial
unpremeditated impremeditado
unprepared no preparado; (improvised) improvisado; (unready) desprevenido
unprepossessing poco atractivo
unpresentable no presentable
unpretending, unpretentious sin pretensiones
unpriced sin precio
unprincipled poco escrupuloso
unprintable impublicable
unprocurable inasequible
unproductive improductivo
unprofessional antiprofesional
unprofitable nada lucrativo
unprofitably sin lucro
unpromising poco prometedor (-ora f)
unprompted sin apuntar
unpronounceable inpronunciable
unpropitious impropicio
unprotected indefenso; (against weather) a la intemperie; ~ **level-crossing** paso a nivel sin guarda
unproved, unproven no probado
unprovided desprovisto (with de); ~ **for** imprevisto
unprovoked no provocado
unpublished inédito
unpunctual impuntual
unpunctuality impuntualidad f
unpunished impune; go ~ escaparse sin castigo
unqualified incompetente; (teacher *etc*) sin título; (success) incondicional; he's an ~ liar él es un mentiroso redomado
unquenchable inextinguible
unquestionable incuestionable
unquestionably indudablemente
unquestioned incontestable
unquestioning incurioso
unquiet inquieto
unquote terminar una cita; (in dictation) fin *m* de la cita
unravel desenmarañar
unreachable inalcanzable
unread (book) no leído; (person) inculto

unreadable ilegible
unreadiness falta de preparación
unready desprevenido
unreal irreal
unrealistic fantástico; (person) poco realista
unreality irrealidad f
unrealizable irrealizable
unreason insensatez f
unreasonable irrazonable; (of request) excesivo
unreclaimed sin reclamar
unrecognizable irreconocible
unrecognized no reconocido
unrecorded sin registrar
unredeemed (pledge) no desempeñado; (promise) sin cumplir
unreel desenrollar
unrefined sin refinar; (vulgar) inculto
unreflecting irreflexivo
unreformed sin reformar
unregarded desatendido
unregistered (letter) sin certificar; (birth) sin registrar
unregretted sin lamentar
unrehearsed espontáneo
unrelated inconexo
unrelenting implacable
unreliability incertidumbre f; (person) informalidad f
unreliable incierto; (news) nada fidedigno; (person) informal
unrelieved continuo
unremarkable nada especial
unremarked inadvertido
unremitting infatigable
unremunerative nada lucrativo
unrepentant impenitente
unrepresentative poco representativo
unrequited no correspondido
unreserved (vacant) sin reservar; (outspoken) comunicativo
unreservedly sin reserva
unresisting sumiso
unresolved sin resolver
unresponsive insensible
unrest (disquiet) zozobra; *pol* desorden *m*; **labour** ~ agitación *mpl* entre los obreros
unrestful desasosegado
unrestrained desenfrenado
unrestricted sin restricciones; (*US*) sin barrera de color/raza

unrevealed sin divulgar[5]
unrewarded sin recompensa; **go** ~ no tener[19] recompensa
unrewarding infructuoso
unriddle resolver (ue)[1b] (*past part* resuelto); (code) descifrar
unrighteous injusto
unrighteousness injusticia
unrip abrir (*past part* abierto) rompiendo
unripe inmaduro; *fam* verde
unrivalled sin par
unrobe desnudar(se)
unroll desenrollar
unromantic nada romántico
unruffled imperturbable
unruliness indisciplina
unruly ingobernable
unsaddle (horse) desensillar; (rider) desmontar
unsafe inseguro
unsaid sin decir
unsalaried sin salario
unsal(e)able invendible
unsalted sin sal
unsanctified sin sanctificar
unsanctioned sin autorización
unsanitary insalubre
unsatisfactory insatisfactorio
unsatisfied insatisfecho
unsatisfying insuficiente
unsavoury desagradable; (food) insípido; (person) indeseable
unsay retractar
unscathed ileso
unscented sin perfume
unscheduled no incluido; (unexpected) imprevisto
unscholarly poco erudito
unscientific anticientífico
unscrambled descifrado
unscratched ileso
unscreened *fig* sin investigar
unscrew desatornillar
unscripted sin guión
unscrupulous sin escrúpulos
unseal abrir (*past part* abierto)
unseasonable fuera de tiempo
unseasoned sin sazonar; (timber) verde
unseat (horse) desensillar; (rider) desmontar; **be** ~**ed** *fig* ser[19] expulsado
unseaworthy innavegable
unseeing (blind) ciego; (unsuspecting) sin sospechar

unseemliness falta de decoro
unseemly indecoroso
unseen *n* traducción (-ones) hecha a primera vista; *adj* invisible; (hidden) oculto; (unnoticed) inadvertido
unsegregated sin barreras de color
unselfish desinteresado
unselfishness generosidad *f*
unsentimental no sentimental
unserviceable inservible
unsettle desarreglar; (person) trastornar; ~**d** (not populated) sin colonizar, (of mind) trastornado, (of no fixed abode) sin residencia fija, (pending) pendiente, (unsolved) sin resolver; ~**d account** cuenta por pagar; ~**d market** mercado inestable; ~**d weather** tiempo variable
unsettling inquietante
unsex quitar las cualidades propias del sexo
unshackle desencadenar
unshaded sin sombra; (drawing *etc*) no sombreado
unshakeable inquebrantable
unshaken impertérrito
unshapely desproporcionado
unshaven sin afeitar
unsheathe desenvainar
unsheltered desabrigado
unship desembarcar[4]
unshod (barefoot) descalzo; (of horse) sin herraduras
unshrinkable inencogible
unshrinking impávido
unsighted que tiene impedida la vista
unsightly feo
unsigned sin firmar; ~ **note** besamanos *m sing + pl*
unsinkable que no se puede hundir
unskilful inexperto
unskilled inexperto; ~ **worker** obrero no cualificado
unsleeping sin dormir
unsociability insociabilidad *f*
unsociable insociable
unsocial antisocial
unsocialized (lacking social feeling) sin sentido social; (not nationalized) sin nacionalizar
unsoldierly indigno de un militar
unsolicited no solicitado
unsolvable irresoluble
unsolved sin resolver

unsophisticated sencillo
unsought no solicitado
unsound defectuoso; (argument) falso; (of fruit) podrido; **of ~ mind** insano
unsparing generoso; (cruel) despiadado
unspeakable (bad) incalificable; (indescribable) indecible
unspecialized sin especializar
unspecified sin especificar
unspent no gastado
unspoilt sin estropear; (of child) no mimado
unspoken tácito
unsporting, unsportsmanlike antideportivo; **~ play** juego desleal
unspotted sin observar
unsprung sin muelles
unstable inestable
unstamped sin franquear
unstatesmanlike indigno de un estadista
unsteady inestable; (irresolute) irresoluto
unstick despegar[5]
unstinting sin escatimar
unstitch descoser
unstop destapar
unstoppered destapado
unstrap aflojar una correa
unstring (beads) desensartar; *mus* desencordar (ue)[1a]; (of nerves) trastornar
unstuck despegado; **come ~** *fig* fracasar
unstudied no afectado
unsubdued sin subyugar
unsubsidized sin subvención
unsubstantial insustancial
unsubstantiated no verificado
unsuccessful (effort) ineficaz (-ces); (person) fracasado; **be ~** no tener[19] éxito
unsuccessfully sin éxito
unsuitability inconveniencia
unsuitable inconveniente; (incongruous) incongruo; **~ man for the job** hombre incompetente para el trabajo
unsuited inapto (**for** para); (inappropriate) impropio
unsullied inmaculado
unsupported sin apoyo
unsure poco seguro
unsurpassed insuperado
unsuspected insospechado
unsuspecting, unsuspicious confiado
unswerving firme

unsympathetic antipático
unsystematic no metódico
untack deshilvanar
untainted inmaculado
untam(e)able indomable
untamed indomado
untangle desenredar
untarnished sin tacha
untasted sin probar
untaught no enseñado
untaxed libre de impuestos
unteachable ineducable
untenable insostenible
untenanted desalquilado
untether soltar (ue)[1a]
unthankful ingrato
unthinkable increíble
unthinking irreflexivo
unthought of inconcebible; (unexpected) inesperado
unthread (needle) desenhebrar; (beads) desensartar
unthrone destronar (ue)[1a]
untidiness desaseo; (of room) desorden *m*
untidy desaseado; **~ room** habitación *f* en desorden
untie desatar
until *prep* hasta, **~ next Friday** hasta el viernes próximo; *conj* hasta que (+*subj* if future is referred to), **I'll wait ~ they come** esperaré hasta que vengan, (+*indic* if past is referred to), **I waited ~ they came** esperé hasta que vinieron; **~ further notice** por tiempo indefinido; **~ Heaven knows when** Dios sabe hasta cuándo
untilled sin cultivar
untimely inoportuno; **~ end** muerte *f* prematura; **come to an ~ end** malograrse
untold nunca contado; (incalculable) incalculable
untouchable *n* intocable; *adj* intangible; (caste) intocable
untouched sin tocar; (unhurt) ileso; (unmoved) insensible
untoward (unfavourable) desfavorable; (unfortunate) adverso
untraceable que no se puede encontrar
untrained (of animals) no amaestrado; *sp* sin entrenamiento
untrammelled libre
untransferable intransferible

untranslatable intraducible

untravelled (road) no frecuentado; (person) provinciano

untried no probado; *leg* (case) no visto, (defendant) no procesado

untrodden no pisado; (snow) virgen

untroubled tranquilo; (water) tranquila

untrue falso; (disloyal) desleal; (unfaithful) infiel

untrustworthy indigno de confianza; (treacherous) pérfido

untruth mentira

untruthful mentiroso

untruthfulness falsedad *f*

untutored indocto

untwine destorcer (ue)[1b]

untwist destorcer (ue)[1b]

unused inusitado; (stamp) sin usar; ~ **to** desacostumbrado a

unusual inusitado; (not customary) insólito

unutterable indecible

unvalued desestimado

unvaried sin variación

unvarnished sin barnizar; ~ **truth** pura verdad

unvarying invariable

unveil quitar(se) el velo; (uncover) descubrir (*past part* descubierto); (monument) inaugurar

unverifiable que no se puede verificar

unverified sin verificar

unversed in poco ducho en

unvoiced *gramm* sordo

unvouched-for no garantizado

unwanted no deseado; (superfluous) superfluo

unwarily imprudentemente

unwariness falta de precaución

unwarlike nada belicoso

unwarrantable injustificable

unwarranted injustificado

unwary incauto

unwashed sin lavar; (person) sucio; **the great** ~ los carasucias

unwavering resuelto

unweaned sin destetar

unwearable que no se puede llevar

unwearying incansable

unwelcome inoportuno; (unpleasant) desagradable; **make** ~ acoger[14] mal

unwell indispuesto

unwholesome insalubre; (person) indeseable

unwieldy difícil de manejar; (bulky) abultado

unwilling desinclinado; **be** ~ **to** no estar[19] dispuesto a

unwillingly de mala gana

unwillingness desgana *f*; **his** ~ **to come** el que no quiera venir

unwind (paper) desenrollar; (thread) devanar; *fig* recobrar la tranquilidad

unwinking con los ojos abiertos

unwinnable inganable

unwisdom imprudencia

unwise imprudente; (ill-advised) poco aconsejable

unwished-for no deseado

unwittingly sin saber

unwomanly poco femenino

unwonted insólito

unworkable impracticable

unworkmanlike impropio de un trabajador

unworldly poco mundano

unworn sin llevar

unworthy indigno

unwounded ileso

unwrap desenvolver (ue)[1b] (*past part* desenvuelto)

unwritten no escrito; ~ **law** derecho tradicional

unwrought sin labrar

unyielding +*fig* inflexible

unyoke desuncir[13]

unzip desabrochar la cremallera

unzoned no dividido en zonas

up *n*: be on the ~ **and** ~ ir[19] cada vez mejor; ~**s and downs** altibajos *mpl*; *adj*: ~ **train** tren *m* ascendente; ~-**and-coming** joven y prometedor (-ora *f*)

v he ~**s and hits me** sin más, me pega; ~ **with it!** ¡levántelo!

adv (hacia) arriba; (out of bed) levantado; (on horseback) montado; (standing ~) de pie; **the sun is** ~ el sol ha salido; **time is** ~ es la hora; **what's** ~ **(with you)?** ¿qué (le) pasa?; **it's all** ~ **(with them)** se acabó todo (para ellos); ~ **above** allí arriba, (in Heaven) en el paraíso; **be** ~ **against** enfrentarse; **be** ~ **against it** estar[19] en apuros; ~ **and down** (everywhere) acá y allá; **go** ~ **and down** (vertically) subir y bajar, (horizontally) ir[19] de un lado para otro; **look** ~ **and down** mirar de arriba abajo; **walk ~ and down** pasearse (por); ~ **before the magistrate** ante el juez de paz; ~ **in arms** sublevado, *fig* alborotado; **be well ~ in** scr[19] experto en, (well informed) estar[19] al corriente de; **be ~ to** (fit) estar[19] en condiciones para, (willing) estar[19] dispuesto a; ~ **to the eyes** *fig* hasta la coronilla; **what is she ~ to?** ¿qué pretende ella?; **it's not ~ to much** no vale gran cosa; ~ **to date** hasta la fecha; ~ **to standard** de acuerdo con las normas; **it's ~ to you** depende de usted

prep en (lo alto de); ~ **a tree** en un árbol; ~ **a gum-tree** confuso; **have ~ one's sleeve** guardar en secreto, (in reserve) tener[19] en reserva; **laugh ~ one's sleeve** reírse (i)[3] interiormente; *interj* ¡arriba!; ~ **the reds!** ¡arriba los rojos!

pref ~**beat** *mus* tiempo débil; ~**bringing** crianza; ~**braid** reprender; ~**country** *adj* del interior, *adv* tierra adentro; ~**date** poner[19] al día, (modernize) modernizar[7]; ~**end** poner(se)[19] en posición vertical; ~**grade** *n* cuesta arriba; **be on the ~grade** *fig* ir[19] mejorando, ascender (ie)[2b], ~**heaval** trastorno; ~**hill** cuesta arriba; ~**hill work** trabajo penoso; ~**hold** apoyar, (protect) defender (ie)[2b], (confirm) confirmar; ~**holder** defensor *m* (-ora *f*); ~**keep** conservación *f*, (cost) mantenimiento; ~**land** tierra alta; ~**lift** *n* (enthusiasm) fervor *m*, *iron* elevación *f*, *v* elevar; ~**link data** *space* datos *mpl* de enlace; ~**market** vendible a la gente adinerada; ~**most** supremo; ~**on** en, sobre; ~**on my word/soul** bajo mi palabra, *interj* ¿habráse visto (semejante cosa)?; ~**on oath** bajo juramento; ~**right** *n* montante *m*, *adj* derecho, *fig* honrado; ~**right piano** piano vertical; ~**rightness** honradez *f*; ~**rising** sublevación *f*; ~**roar** alboroto; ~**roarious** estrepitoso; **laugh ~roariously** reírse (i)[3] a carcajadas; ~**root** desarraigar[5]; ~**rush** oleada repentina; ~**set** *n* trastorno, *med* indisposición *f*, *adj* trastornado, *med* indispuesto; **I have an ~set stomach** tengo trastornos gástricos; **become ~set** ponerse[19] malo;

~**set** *v* (overthrow) volcar[4], (boat) zozobrar, *med* trastornar, (disturb) desbarajustar, (untidy) desarreglar, (worry) inquietar; **fried things ~set me las cosas fritas me sientan mal; ~**setting** inquietante; ~**shot** resultado; ~**side** lado superior; ~**sidedown** al revés, (untidy) en desorden; **turn ~side-down** poner[19] al revés, (disorder) revolver (ue)[1b] (*past part* revuelto); ~**stage** en el fondo del escenario; **go ~stage** ir[19] hacia el fondo del escenario; ~**stairs** arriba; **go ~stairs** subir (al piso de arriba); ~**stairs room** habitación *f* de arriba; ~**standing** honrado; **an ~standing young fellow** buen mozo; ~**standing young woman** buena moza; ~**start** advenedizo; ~**stream** aguas *fpl* arriba, *fig* contra corriente; ~**swing** *comm* mejora (de los negocios); ~**take: be quick/slow on the ~take** tener[19] los reflejos rápidos/lentos; ~**tight** ansioso; ~**-to-date** al día; ~**-to-the-minute** de gran actualidad; ~**town** *adj* de moda, *adv* hacia/en la parte alta (de una ciudad); ~**turn** mejora; ~**wards** hacia arriba; ~**wards of** más de

upholster tapizar[7]

upholsterer tapicero; ~**'s** tapicería

upholstery tapicería; *mot* almohadillado

upper *n* (of shoe) pala; **be down on one's ~s** estar[19] en aprietos; *adj* superior; **be in the ~ (income) bracket** ser[19] de los que más ganan; ~ **case** mayúsculas *fpl*; ~ **circle** *theat* anfiteatro; ~ **class** (de la) clase alta; ~ **crust** *fam* aristocracia; ~**-cut** *sp* upper *m*; ~ **deck** cubierta alta; **have the ~ hand** llevar la ventaja; ~ **house** *pol* cámara alta, (*UK*) Cámara de los Lores; ~ **jaw/lip** mandíbula/labio superior; ~ **lights** *theat* diabla; ~ **topsail** gavia alta; ~**most** *adj* supremo; **be ~most** predominar; **thought ~most in one's mind** lo primero que piensa uno; ~**most** *adv* encima, (first) en primer lugar

uppish arrogante

uppity pidiendo sus derechos arrogantemente

upsy-daisy! ¡aúpa!

uralite uralita

Urals Urales *mpl*

uranium uranio; ~ **isotope** isótopo de uranio

Uranus Urano

urban urbano

urbane cortés *invar*

urbanity cortesía

urbanization urbanización *f*

urbanize urbanizar[7]

urchin golfillo; ~-**cut** corte *m* a lo garsón

urge *n* impulso; (desire) ganas *fpl*; **have a sudden** ~ **to** tener[19] ganas repentinas de; *v* sentir (ie)[2c] impulsos de; (entreat) instar con ahínco; (incite) incitar; (recommend) recomendar

urgency urgencia

urgent urgente

uric úrico

urinal urinario; (vessel) orinal *m*

urinary urinario

urinate orinar

urination micción *f*

urine orina (-ines)

urn urna; (coffee) cafetera; (tea) tetera; **burial** ~ tumba sepulcral, sepulcro

Uruguay El Uruguay

Uruguayan *n + adj* uruguayo

us (direct + indirect *obj*) nos; (after *prep*) nosotros, nosotras

U.S.A. (**United States of America**) EE.UU. (Estados Unidos)

usable utilizable

usage tratamiento; (custom) uso; (meaning) acepción *f*

usance costumbre *f*

use *n* uso; (custom) costumbre *f*; *eccles* liturgia; (handling) manejo; **in** ~ en uso, (being used) usándose; **of** ~ útil; **of no** ~ inútil; **it's no** ~ ... es inútil +*infin*; **have the** ~ **of** (right to use) tener[19] a la disposición *f*; **have no** ~ **for** no necesitar, (of people) tener[19] en poco; **make** ~ **of** servirse (i)[3] de; **every two minutes he made** ~ **of the word 'complex'** cada dos minutos él echaba mano de la palabra 'complejo'; **make good** ~ **of, put to good** ~ sacar[4] partido de; **out of** ~ pasado de moda; **what's the** ~? ¿para qué?; **what's the** ~ **of working?** ¿de qué sirve trabajar?; **room with** ~ **of kitchen** habitación *f* con derecho a cocina; **directions for** ~ modo de empleo; *v* usar; (consume) consumir, *fam* gastar; (handle) mane-

jar; (treat) tratar; (take advantage of) aprovecharse de; **do you** ~ **a belt or braces?** ¿lleva usted cinturón o tirantes?; ~ **up** consumir, *fam* gastar

used usado; (second-hand) de segunda mano; (worn out) gastado; **be** ~ **to** estar[19] acostumbrado a; **get** ~ **to** acostumbrarse a; **I** ~ **to live in Spain** yo solía vivir en España

useful útil; (helpful) servicial; *sl* apto; ~ **life/load** vida/carga útil

usefully con provecho

usefulness utilidad *f*

useless inútil; (people) inepto

uselessness inutilidad *f*

user usuario, el que usa

usher ujier *m*; (doorman) portero; *theat* acomodador *m*

usherette *theat* acomodadora

U.S.S.R. (**Union of Soviet Socialist Republics**) U.R.S.S. (Unión *f* de las Repúblicas Socialistas Soviéticas)

usual normal; **the** ~ (drink *etc*) lo de siempre; **as** ~ como de costumbre

usually por lo general

usurer usurero

usurious usurario

usurp usurpar

usurpation usurpación *f*

usurpatory usurpador (-ora *f*)

usurper usurpador *m* (-ora *f*)

usurping *adj* usurpador (-ora *f*)

usury usura

utensil utensilio

uterine uterino

uterus útero

utilitarian *n* utilitarista *m+f*; *adj* utilitario

utility utilidad *f*; (public) ~ empresa de servicio público; ~ **furniture** muebles *mpl* utilitarios

utilization utilización *f*

utilize utilizar[7]

utmost *n* lo más; **do one's** ~ hacer[19] todo lo posible; **to the** ~ al máximo; *adj* (size) máximo; (distance) más lejano

Utopia utopía

Utopian utópico

utter *adj* absoluto; **he's an** ~ **fool** él es un tonto de remate; ~**most** *see* **utmost**; *v* pronunciar; ~ **a cry** dar[19] un grito; ~ **a dud cheque** pasar un cheque falso; ~ **false money** poner[19] en circulación dinero falso; ~ **a sigh** suspirar; ~ **a**

  groan gemir (i)[3]
utterance palabras *fpl*; **give ~ to** expresar
utterly del todo
U-turn *n mot* viraje *m* en uve; *v* dar[19]

  una vuelta en uve
uvula úvula
uvular uvular
uxorious gurrumino
uxoriously con gurrumina

V

v (letter) uve *f*

vacancy (post) vacante *f*; (in boarding-house) habitación *f* libre; (abstracted-ness) vacuidad *f*

vacant vacante; (seat, toilet) libre; (look) distraído; (stupid) estúpido; with ~ possession con entrega

vacate dejar libre; (post) dejar vacante

vacation *n* vacaciones *fpl*; *v* US pasar las vacaciones

vacationist veraneante *m+f*

vaccinate vacunar; she's going to have her baby ~d ella va a vacunar a su niño

vaccination vacunación *f*; ~ certificate certificado de vacunación

vaccinator vacunador *m* (-ora *f*)

vaccine vacuna

vacillate vacilar

vacillating vacilante

vacillation vacilación *f*

vacuity vacuidad *f*

vacuous vacuo

vacuum *n* vacío; ~-brake freno de vacío; ~-cleaner aspiradora; ~-container, ~-flask termo; ~-packed envasado al vacío; ~-pump bomba de vacío; ~-tube tubo de vacío; *v* limpiar con aspiradora

vade-mecum vademécum *m*

vagabond *n+adj* vagabundo, *sl* carrilano

vagabondage vagabundeo

vagary capricho

vagina vagina

vaginal vaginal

vagrancy vagabundeo

vagrant *n+adj* vagabundo

vague vago; (of people) distraído

vagueness vaguedad *f*; (of people) distracción *f*

vain (conceited) vanidoso; (useless) vano; in ~ en vano; ~glorious vanaglorioso; ~glory vanagloria

valance cenefa

vale valle *m*

valediction despedida

valedictory de despedida

Valencian *n+adj* valenciano

valency valencia

Valentine Valentín; St ~'s Day Día *m* de los Enamorados

valentine (card) tarjeta del Día de los Enamorados; (person) novio, novia

valerian valeriana

valet ayuda *m* de cámara

valiant valiente

valid válido; *comm* vigente; it is not ~ no vale

validate validar

validity validez *f*

valise portamantas *m sing+pl*

Valkyrie Valquiria

valley valle *m*

valorous valeroso

valour valor *m*

valuable *n*: ~s objetos *mpl* de valor; *adj* valioso

valuation valuación (-ones) *f*

value *n* valor *m*; (price) precio; *v* tasar (at en); (esteem) estimar

valueless sin valor

valuer tasador *m* (-ora *f*)

valve válvula; *SA rad* bulbo; *bot* valva; ~ cap *mot* capuchón (-ones) *m* protector (de la válvula)

vamoose largarse[5]

vamp *n* vampiresa; *v* coquetear con; *mus* improvisar

vampire vampiro; *fig* vampiresa

van *mot* camioneta; (railway) furgón (-ones) *m*; (vanguard) +*fig* vanguardia; ~-driver conductor *m* de camioneta

vandal vándalo

vandalism vandalismo

Vandyke cuadro de Vandyke; ~ beard perilla; ~ collar cuello de encaje

vane (of mill-wheel) aspa; (of propeller) paleta; (of rocket) timón (-ones) *m*; weather-~ veleta

vanilla vainilla

1102

vanish desaparecer[14]; (fade away) desvanecerse[14]
vanishing desaparición *f*; (fading away)
desvanecimiento; **~-cream** crema de
belleza; **~-point** punto de fuga
vanity vanidad *f*; *fam* ventolera; **~-bag,
~-case** neceser *m* (de belleza); **~-
table** tocador *m*
vanquish vencer[12]
vantage-point lugar estratégico; (for
views) punto panorámico
vapid insípido
vapidity insipidez *f*
vaporization vaporización *f*
vaporize vaporizar[7]
vaporizer vaporizador *m*
vaporous vaporoso
vapour vapor *m*; (condensed, on windows) vaho; **~-bath** baño de vapor; **~
trail** (of rocket) estela de condensación
vapourings palabras *fpl* sin sentido
variability variabilidad *f*
variable *n+adj* variable; **~ condenser**
rad bobina del circuito oscilatorio
variance variación *f*; *leg* discrepancia; **be
at ~ (with)** estar[19] reñido (con)
variant variante *m*
variation variación *f*
varicoloured abigarrado
varicose varicoso; **~ veins** varices *fpl*
varied *see* vary
variegated abigarrado
variegation abigarramiento
variety variedad *f*; (class) especie *f*; *theat*
variedades *fpl*; **for a ~ of reasons** por
varias razones; **~ artist/theatre** artista
m+f/teatro de variedades
variola viruela
various varios, varias
varnish *n* barniz *m*; **~-remover** quitaesmaltes *m sing*; *v* barnizar[7]
varsity universidad *f*
vary variar; (modify) modificar[4]
vascular vascular
vase jarrón (-ones) *m*; **flower-~** florero
vasectomy vasectomía
Vaseline *tr* vaselina
vassal vasallo
vassalage vasallaje *m*
vast inmenso
vastly enormemente
vastness inmensidad *f*
V.A.T. (Value Added Tax) I.V.A. (im-

puesto de valor añadido/sobre el valor
añadido)
vat *n* tina; *v* poner[19] en tina
Vatican Vaticano
vaudeville variedades *fpl*, vodevil *m*; **~
theatre** teatro de variedades
¹ **vault** *n archi* bóveda; (cellar) bodega;
(in bank) cámara acorazada; (tomb)
tumba; *v archi* abovedar
² **vault** *n* salto; *v* (+ ~ over) saltar
¹ **vaulting** *archi* abovedado
² **vaulting** salto; **~-horse** potro de madera; **~-pole** pértiga
vaunt *vi* jactarse; *vt* jactarse de
vaunted alardeado
V-belt *mech* correa en uve
veal (carne *f* de) ternera
vedette centinela de avanzada
veer *naut* virar; (of wind) cambiar
vegan uno que no consume nada de
origen animal
veganism abstinencia total de productos
de origen animal
vegetable *n* legumbre *f*; (greenstuff)
verduras *fpl*; **~-garden** huerta (de legumbres); **~-man, ~-seller** verdulero; **~-marrow** calabacín *m*; *adj*
vegetal; **~ oil** aceite *m* vegetal
vegetal vegetal
vegetarian *n+adj* vegetariano
vegetarianism vegetarianismo
vegetation vegetación *f*
vegetative vegetativo
vehemence vehemencia
vehement vehemente
vehemently con vehemencia
vehicle vehículo
vehicular de vehículos; **~ traffic** circulación rodada
veil *n +fig* velo; **take the ~** profesar de
religioso/religiosa; *v* velar; (conceal)
correr un velo sobre; **~ed question**
pregunta indirecta
veiling material *m* para velos; *phot* velo
vein *n* vena; (in marble) veta; (mood)
humor *m*; **in a serious ~** en plan más
serio
veined venoso; (of marble) veteado
veldt llanura (de África del Sur)
vellum vitela
velocity velocidad *f*
velour felpa de pelo de liebre
velvet *n* terciopelo; (hunting) piel ve-
lluda; **on ~** *fig* en situación muy ven-

tajosa; *adj* aterciopelado
velveteen pana lisa
velvety aterciopelado
venal venal
venality venalidad *f*
vend vender
vendetta vendeta
vending-machine distribuidor automático
vendor vendedor *m*; (street-~) buhonero
veneer *n* chapeado; (appearance) aspecto exterior; *v* chapear; *fig* disfrazar[7]
veneering chapeado
venerability venerabilidad *f*
venerable venerable
venerate venerar
veneration veneración *f*
venereal venéreo; ~ **disease** enfermedad venérea
Venetian veneciano
Venezuela Venezuela
Venezuelan *n* + *adj* venezolano
vengeance venganza; **with a** ~ con creces
vengeful vengativo
venial venial
veniality venialidad *f*
Venice Venecia
venison (carne *f* de) venado
venom veneno
venomous venenoso; *fig* maligno
venous venoso
vent respiradero; (hole) orificio de escape; (slit on jacket) apertura; **give** ~ **to** desahogarse[5]
ventilate +*fig* ventilar
ventilation ventilación *f*; ~ **shaft** *min* pozo de ventilación
ventilator ventilador *m*
ventral ventral
ventricle ventrículo
ventricular ventricular
ventriloquism ventriloquia
ventriloquist ventrílocuo
venture *n* empresa arriesgada; **at a** ~ a la ventura; *v* osar (**to** *infin*), arriesgarse (**on** en); ~ **an opinion** atreverse a decir; **he** ~**d near the precipice** se acercó aventuradamente al precipicio; ~**some** atrevido
venue lugar *m* de reunión
Venus Venus *f*; ~ **fly-trap** *bot* atrapa-

moscas *m sing* + *pl*
Venusian venusiano
veracious veraz (-ces)
veracity veracidad *f*
verandah balcón (-ones) *m* largo; (porch) pórtico
verb verbo
verbal verbal; ~ **contract** contrato de palabra; ~ **noun** substantivo verbal
verbalize *vt* expresar con palabras; *vi* ser prolijo
verbally de palabra
verbatim palabra por palabra
verbiage palabrería
verbose verboso
verbosity verbosidad *f*
verdancy verdor *m*
verdant verde
verdict *leg* veredicto; *fig* opinión *f* (**on** sobre); **bring in a** ~ dictar un veredicto
verdigris cardenillo
verdure verdura
verdurous verdoso
verge *n* borde *m*; (of lake) orilla; **grass** ~ margen *m* de hierba; **be on the** ~ **of** estar[19] al borde de + *n*, estar[19] al punto de + *infin*; *v* ~ **upon** rayar en
verger *approx* sacristán (-anes) *m*
Vergil Virgilio
verifiable verificable
verification verificación *f*
verify verificar[4]
verisimilitude verosimilitud *f*
veritable verdadero
verity verdad *f*
vermicelli fideos *mpl*
vermilion *n* bermellón *m*; *adj* de color rojo vivo
vermin (insects) bichos *mpl*; (animals) sabandijas *fpl*
verminous verminoso; *fam* piojoso
vermouth vermut *m*
vernacular *n* lengua vernácula; *adj* vernáculo
vernal primaveral
veronal veronal *m*
veronica verónica
verruca verruga
versatile versátil; (adaptable) adaptable
versatility versatilidad *f*; (adaptability) adaptabilidad *f*
verse *n* (poetry + line of poetry) verso; (stanza) estrofa; *bibl* versículo; *v*

versificar

versed: be well ~ in estar[19] versado en

versification versificación *f*

versify versificar[4]

version versión (-ones) *f*

versus contra

vertebrae vértebras *fpl*

vertebral vertebral

vertebrate *n+adj* vertebrado

vertex vértice *m*

vertical *n+adj* vertical *f*; ~ **take-off (plane)** (avión (-ones) *m* de) despegue *m* vertical; ~ **trade union** sindicato vertical

verticality verticalidad *f*

vertiginous vertiginoso

vertigo vértigo

verve brío

very *adj* mis(mísi)mo; **the ~ idea!** ¡ni hablar!; **the ~ thing** exactamente lo que necesitaba/necesitábamos; *adv* muy

vespers vísperas *fpl*

vessel vasija; (match) cerilla; *naut* barco

vest *n* camiseta; (waistcoat) chaleco; ~**-pocket** *adj* en miniatura; *v* ~ **with** investir (i)[3] de; ~ **with authority** armar de autoridad; ~**ed interests** intereses creados

vesta (match) cerilla

vestal *n+adj* vestal *f*

vestibule vestíbulo; (*US* railway) coche *m* de vestíbulo

vestige vestigio

vestigial vestigial

vestment vestidura

vestry sacristía; (body) junta parroquial; ~**man** miembro de la junta parroquial

Vesuvius Vesubio

[1] **vet (veterinary surgeon)** vetcrinario

[2] **vet** *v* repasar y corregir[9]

vetch arveja

veteran *n+adj* veterano; (ex-soldier) excombatiente *m*; **Veterans' Day** *US* día del excombatiente; ~ **car** coche *m* de época

veterinarian, veterinary surgeon veterinario

veterinary veterinario; ~ **studies** veterinaria

veto *n* veto; **put a ~ on** vedar; *v* vetar

vex fastidiar; ~**ed question** cuestión *f* muy reñida

vexation irritación *f*

vexatious fastidioso

vexing fastidioso

V.H.F. (very high frequency) F.M. frecuencia modulada; ~ **aerial** antena bipolar

via por

viability viabilidad *f*

viable viable

viaduct viaducto

vial frasquito

viands manjares *mpl*

viaticum viático

vibrancy calidad *f* de vibrante

vibrant vibrante

vibraphone vibráfono

vibrate vibrar

vibration vibración (-ones) *f*

vibrato vibrato

vibrator vibrador *m* consolador

vibratory vibratorio

viburnum viburno

vicar vicario; (Anglican) párroco

vicarage casa del párroco

vicarious experimentado por otro

[1] **vice** *n* (evil) vicio; ~ **squad** *approx* Brigada de Investigación Criminal

[2] **vice** *n mech* torno de banco

[3] **vice** (in place of) en lugar de; ~**-admiral** vicealmirante *m*; ~**-chairman** vicepresidente *m* (-ta *f*); ~**-chancellor** vicecanciller *m*; (of university) rector *m*; ~**-consul** vicecónsul *m*; ~**-president** vicepresidente *m* (-ta *f*); ~**-regal** de virrey; ~**-reine** virreina; ~**-roy** virrey *m*

vice versa viceversa

vicinity vecindad *f*; **in the ~ (of)** cerca (de); (approximately) alrededor de

vicious vicioso; (remark) virulento; (of dogs) malo; (of horses) arisco; ~ **circle** círculo vicioso

vicissitude vicisitud *f*

victim víctima

victimize tomar represalias contra

victimization represalias *fpl*

victor vencedor *m*

victoria (coach) victoria

Victorian victoriano

victorious victorioso

victory victoria

victual *n*: ~**s** víveres *mpl*; *v* abastecer[14]

victualler abastecedor *m*; **licensed ~** vendedor *m* de bebidas alcohólicas

vide véase

videlicet a saber

video vídeo; ~ **mixer** mezclador *m* de imágenes; ~ **nasty** vídeo repugnante; ~ **piracy** piratería del vídeo; ~**-pirate** pirata del vídeo; ~**-recording** grabación en vídeo; *v* grabar en vídeo

vie competir (**with** con)

Vienna Viena; ~ **roll** pan de Viena

Viennese *n+adj* vienés *m* (-esa *f*)

Vietnam Vietnam *m*

Vietnamese vietnamita *m+f*

view *n* vista; *phot* panorama; (opinion) opinión *f*; **in** ~ a la vista; **in** ~ **of** en vista de; **in my** ~ a mi parecer; **keep in** ~ no perder (ie)²ᵇ de vista; **point of** ~ punto de vista; **with a** ~ **to** con el propósito de; **she has strong** ~**s on** ella tiene ideas muy firmes sobre; ~**finder** visor *m* de imagen; ~**point** mirador *m*, *fig* punto de vista; *v* (see) mirar; (inspect) inspeccionar; (consider) considerar

viewer espectador *m* (-ora *f*); *TV* telespectador *m* (-ora *f*)

viewing inspección *f*

viewless invisible; (having no opinion) sin opiniones

vigil vigilia

vigilance vigilancia

vigilant *adj* vigilante

vignette viñeta

vigorous vigoroso

vigour vigor *m*

Viking *n+adj* vikingo

vile vil; (very bad) malísimo, (smell) asqueroso; (of weather) malísimo

vileness vileza; (extreme badness) maldad, (smell) asquerosidad *f*

vilification vilipendio

vilify vilipendiar

villa (at seaside) chalé *m*, chalet *m*; (in country) casa de campo; **Roman** ~ villa romana

village *n* aldea; *adj* aldeano

villager aldeano

villain desalmado; *theat* malo

villainous desalmado

villainy villanía

villein villano

vim energía

Vincent Vicente

vindicate vindicar⁴

vindication vindicación *f*

vindicator vindicador *m* (-ora *f*)

vindictive vengativo

vindictiveness deseo de venganza

vine vid *f*; (climbing) parra; ~**-dresser** viñador *m* (-ora *f*); ~**-grower** viticultor *m*; ~**-growing** viticultura; ~**yard** viña

vinegar *n* vinagre *m*; *v* avinagrar

vinegary avinagrado

vingt-et-un (card game) *equiv* siete y media

viniculture viticultura

vin ordinaire vino de mesa

vinous vinoso

vintage *n* vendimia; *adj* añejo; ~ **wine** vino añejo; ~ **car** coche de la época 1914–30

vintner vinatero

vinyl vinilo *m*

viola *bot+mus* viola

violable violable

violate violar

violation violación *f*; ~ **of rules** infracción *f* de las reglas

violator violador *m*

violence violencia; **do** ~ **to** agredir, *fig* violentar; **robbery with** ~ robo a mano armada

violent violento

violet *n* violeta; (colour) violado; *adj* violado

violin violín (-ines) *m*

violinist violinista *m+f*

violoncellist violoncelista *m+f*

violoncello violoncelo

V.I.P. persona famosa; ~ **lounge** sala de autoridades

viper víbora

viperish, viperous viperino

virago sargentona

virgin *n+adj* virgen (vírgenes) *f*

virginal *n mus* espineta; *adj* virginal

Virginia *adj* (of tobacco) rubio; ~ **creeper** viña virgen

virginity virginidad *f*

viridescence verdura

viridescent verdoso

virile viril

virility virilidad *f*

virology virología

virtual virtual

virtue virtud *f*

virtuosity virtuosismo

virtuoso virtuoso

virtuous virtuoso

virulence virulencia; (feeling) acrimonia

virulent virulento; (feeling) cáustico

virus virus; ~ **disease** enfermedad *f* por virus

visa *n* visado; *v* visar

visage semblante *m*

vis-à-vis *prep* respecto a; *adv* cara a cara

viscera vísceras *fpl*

viscid viscoso

viscose *n* + *adj* viscoso

viscosity viscosidad *f*

viscount vizconde *m*

viscountess vizcondesa

viscous viscoso

vise *see* **vice**

visé visado

visibility visibilidad *f*

visible visible

Visigoth visigodo

Visigothic visigótico

vision (sight) vista; (dream) visión *f*; **field of** ~ campo visual

visionary *n* + *adj* visionario; (idealist) soñador *m* (-ora *f*)

visit *n* visita; **pay a** ~ hacer[19] una visita; *v* visitar; ~ **s.t. on s.o.** castigar[5] a uno con algo; *US* ~ **with** visitar, (chat to) charlar con

visitant visitante *m*

visitation *eccles* visitación *f*; *fam* visita larguísima

visiting visitante; **go** ~ ir[19] de visita; ~-**card** tarjeta de visita

visitor visita(nte) *m* + *f*; (tourist) turista *m* + *f*; (summer holidaymaker) veraneante *m* + *f*; ~**s' book** libro de honor; ~**s' gallery** tribuna de visitantes

visor visera

vista panorama

visual visual; ~ **aid** enseñanza visual; ~ **control/tuner** *TV* sintonizador *m* óptico

visualization evocación *f*

visualize imaginar(se); (foresee) prever[19]

vital vital; (important) esencial (**to** para); ~ **parts** partes *fpl* vitales; ~ **statistics** estadística vital

vitality vitalidad *f*

vitalize vitalizar[7]

vitals partes *fpl* vitales

vitamin vitamina; ~ **deficiency** deficiencia vitamínica

vitaminized reforzado con vitaminas

vitiate + *leg* viciar

vitiation viciamiento

viticulture viticultura

vitreous vítreo; ~-**enamelled** esmaltado vidriado

vitrification vitrificación *f*

vitrify vitrificar[4]

vitriol vitriolo

vitriolic vitriólico; *fig* cáustico

vituperate vituperar

vituperation vituperación *f*

vituperative injurioso

Vitus: St ~**' dance** baile *m* de San Vito

viva (voce) examen *m* oral

vivacious animado

vivacity animación *f*

vivarium vivero

Vivian Bibiano

Vivienne Bibiana

vivid vivo; (of colour, light) intenso; (of description) gráfico

vividness vivacidad *f*; (of light *etc*) intensidad *f*

viviparous vivíparo

vivisect hacer la vivisección a

vivisection vivisección *f*

vixen raposa; *fig* arpía

viz o sea

vizier visir *m*

vizor visera

V-neck escote *m* en pico

V-shaped cn uvc

vocabulary vocabulario

vocal + *mus* vocal; *gramm* vocálico; *fig* ruidoso; ~ **chords** cuerdas *fpl* vocales; ~ **music** música vocal

vocalist cantante *m* + *f*; (in cabaret) vocalista *m* + *f*

vocalization vocalización *f*

vocalize vocalizar[7]

vocation vocación *f*

vocational vocacional; ~ **guidance** guía *f* vocacional

vocative vocativo

vociferate vociferar

vociferation vociferación *f*

vociferous vocinglero

vodka vodka *m*

vogue moda; **in** ~ en boga

voice *n* voz *f*; (opinion) opinión *f*; (right to express opinion) voto; **give** ~ **to** expresar; **have no** ~ *fig* no tener[19] ni voz ni voto; **be in good** ~ cantar bien; **lose one's** ~ perder (ie)[2b] la voz; *v* expresar; ~d hablado

voiceless sin voz

void *n*+*adj* vacío; (invalid) nulo; ~ **of** falto de; *v* (excrete) excretar; (vomit) vomitar; (invalidate) anular

voidable anulable

volatile volátil

volatility volatilidad *f*

volatilize volatilizarse[7]

vol-au-vent pastel *m* de hojaldre

volcanic volcánico; ~ **glass** obsidiana

volcano volcán (-anes) *m*

vole campañol *m*

volition voluntad *f*; **of one's own** ~ por su propia voluntad

volley *n* *mil* descarga; *sp* voleo; (of abuse) retahíla; ~ **of applause** salva de aplausos; ~ **of stones** lluvia de piedras; **fire a** ~ lanzar[7] una descarga; **on the** ~ de voleo; ~**ball** balonvolea *m*; ~**-kick** (rugby) puntapié *m* de volea; *v* *mil* lanzar[7] una descarga; (tennis) volear

volt voltio; ~**meter** voltímetro

voltage voltaje *m*

volte-face cambio total de opinión

volubility locuacidad *f*

voluble locuaz (-ces)

volume *n* volumen (-úmenes) *m*; ~ **control** *rad etc* control *m* de volumen; ~ **control knob** regulador *m* del volumen

voluminosity lo voluminoso

voluminous voluminoso; (of writings) prolífico

voluntary *n* *mus* solo de órgano; *adj* voluntario

volunteer *n* voluntario; *v* ofrecerse[14] de voluntario

voluptuous voluptuoso

voluptuousness voluptuosidad *f*

volute voluta; ~**d** en forma de volutas

vomit *n* vómito; *v* vomitar; *fam* devolver (ue)[1b] (*past part* devuelto)

voodoo vudú *m*

voracious voraz (-ces)

voracity voracidad *f*

vortex vórtice *m*

votaress devota

votary devoto; (supporter) partidario

vote *n* voto; (right to ~) derecho de voto; (budget) presupuesto; (voting) votación *f*; ~ **of confidence** voto de confianza; **by a majority** ~ por mayoría de los votos; **cast a** ~ dar[19] un voto; **put to the** ~, **take a** ~ **on** someter a votación; *v* votar; (suggest) sugerir (ie)[2c], **I** ~ **that** sugiero que +*subj*; ~ **down** rechazar[7] por votación; ~ **for** votar por; ~ **in** elegir (i)[3+9]

voter votante *m*

voting votación *f*; ~**-machine** máquina electoral; ~**-paper** papeleta (de votación)

votive votivo; ~ **offering** exvoto

vouch: ~ **for** s.t. responder de algo; ~ **for** s.o. responder por uno; ~**safe** conceder

voucher vale *m*

vow *n* promesa (solemne); *eccles* voto; **make a** ~ **to** prometer solemnemente; **take a** ~ **of chastity** hacer[19] voto de castidad; ~**-taking** *eccles* profesión *f*; *v* ~ **(to)** prometer solemnemente +*infin*

vowel vocal *f*

voyage *n* viaje *m* (por mar); *v* viajar (por mar)

voyeur mirón m (-ona *f*)

Vulcan Vulcano

vulcanite vulcanita

vulcanize vulcanizar[7]

vulcasbestos amianto vulcanizado

vulgar (of the people) populachero; (in speech) vulgar; (indecent) indecente; **given to** ~ **talk** grosero; ~ **fraction** quebrado común; ~ **joke** chiste *m* verde; ~ **tongue** lengua vulgar

vulgarism vulgarismo

vulgarity indecencia

vulgarization vulgarización *f*

vulgarize vulgarizar[7]

Vulgate Vulgata

vulnerability vulnerabilidad *f*

vulnerable vulnerable

vulpine vulpino

vulture +*fig* buitre *m*

vulva vulva

vying rivalizando (**with** con)

X

x (letter) equis *f sing+pl*; **let's say that the murderer waited for** ~ **hours** digamos que el asesino esperó durante equis horas; ~ **marks the spot** la equis indica el lugar

Xavier Javier

xenophobe xenófobo

xenophobia xenofobia

xenophobic xenofóbico

xerox *n* fotocopia; *v* fotocopiar

Xerxes Jerjes

Xmas *see* **Christmas**

X-ray *n* (picture) radiografía; ~ **film** película radiográfica; ~ **photograph** radiografía; ~s rayos *mpl* X; *adj* radiográfico; *v* radiografiar

xylograph grabado en madera

xylographer xilógrafo

xylography xilografía

xylophone xilófono

xylophonist xilofonista *m+f*

Y

y (letter) i griega

yacht n yate m; (small) balandro; ~-club club náutico; ~-race regata de yates/balandros; ~sman deportista m náutico, balandrista m; v pasear en yate/balandro

yachting n deporte m de vela; go ~ pasear en yate/balandro; adj de balandrista; ~-cap gorra de balandrista

yahoo patán (-anes) m; fam burro

yak yak m

yale: ~ key/lock llave f/cerradura yale

yam batata; SA ñame m

yank n (tug) tirón (-ones) m; (jerk) sacudida; v dar[19] un tirón; ~ out sacar[4] de un tirón

Yank(ee) n+adj yanqui m+f

yap n ladrido agudo; v ladrar agudamente; fam hablar necedades; (nag) regañar continuamente

yapping n ladridos mpl; adj que ladra

[1] yard corral m; (paved) patio

[2] yard (measure) yarda (91,44 cm), approx vara; how much a ~ is ...? ¿a cómo está la yarda de ...?; five-~-line sp equiv línea de cinco metros; twenty-five-~-line sp equiv línea de veintidós metros; ~stick yarda de medir, fig norma

[3] yard naut verga; ~arm penol m de verga

[1] yarn (thread) hilo; (wool) estambre m

[2] yarn (story) cuento; (traveller's) cuento chino; spin a ~ contar (ue)[1a] una historia

yarrow milenrama

yashmak velo que llevan las musulmanas

yaw n aer serpenteo; naut+space guiñar; v serpentear; guiñar

yawl yola

yawn n bostezo; stifle a ~ ahogar[5] un bostezo; v bostezar[7]

yawning n bostezos mpl; adj abierto

yawp (yawn) bostezar[7]; (chatter) cotorrear

~ea: ~ or nay sí o no

yeah sí

year n año; ~ after ~, ~ in ~ out año tras año; ~ before last el año antepasado; ~ of grace año de gracia; a ~ (per annum) al año; all the ~ round todo el año; by the ~ por año; ~s (age) edad f; ~s ago hace años; be ... ~s old tener[19] ... años; he is getting on in ~s él va para viejo; New Year's Day/Eve día m de Año Nuevo/Noche f Vieja; Happy New Year! ¡Feliz Año Nuevo!; ~-book anuario; ~-long que dura un año

yearling n+adj primal m+f; (cattle) añojo; (horses) añal

yearly adj anual; ~ income renta anual; adv (every year) todos los años; (once a year) una vez al año

yearn anhelar; ~ after añorar; ~ for suspirar por; ~ to do s.t. tener[19] muchas ganas de hacer algo

yearning n anhelo; (after s.t.) añoranza; (to do s.t.) ganas fpl; adj anhelante; (tender) tierno

yeast levadura

yeasty (yeast-like) semejante a la levadura; (frivolous) frívolo

yell n grito; let out a ~ dar[19] un grito; v gritar; ~ for s.o. llamar a alguien a gritos; ~ for help pedir (i)[3] ayuda a gritos; don't ~ at me like that! ¡no me des voces!, sl ¡no me vengas con coñas!

yelling n gritos mpl

yellow n+adj amarillo; (of complexion) amarillento; (of hair) rubio; (cowardly) blanco; vulg cagado; have a ~ streak ser[19] gallina; turn ~ (of complexion) ponerse[19] amarillento; (of leaves) volverse (ue)[1b] (past part vuelto) amarillo; ~-back (book) novelucha sensacionalista; ~ fever/jack fiebre amarilla; ~ flag/jack bandera de cuarentena; ~hammer emberizo, US picamaderos m sing+pl; ~ peril peligro amarillo; ~ press prensa sen-

1130

sacionalista; *v see* turn ~; ~ **with age**
amarillear por el tiempo
yellowish, yellowy amarillento
yellowness amarillez *f*
yelp *n* aullido; *v* aullar
yelping aullidos *mpl*
Yemen el Yemen
Yemeni *n+adj* yemení *m+f*
¹ **yen** (coin) yen *m*
² **yen**: have a ~ **for** tener¹⁹ un deseo vivo
de +*infin*
yeoman hacendado; **do ~ service** servir
(i)³ lealmente; ~ **of the guard** alabardero de palacio
yeomanry regimiento de soldados de
caballería
yes sí; ~? (on phone) dígame; **say ~**
decir¹⁹ que sí, (accept marriage offer)
dar¹⁹ el sí; ~ **indeed** ya lo creo; ~ **man**
pelotillero
yesterday (día de) ayer *m*; ~ **morning/**
evening ayer por la mañana/tarde; **day**
before ~ anteayer
yesteryear antaño
yet *adv* todavía; ~ **again** otra vez; **as** ~
hasta ahora; **it is** ~ **to be done** está por
hacer; **nor** ~ ni aún; **not** ~ todavía no;
conj sin embargo
yeti yeti *m*
yew tejo; (wood) madera de tejo
Yid(dish) *n + adj* judío
yield *n agri* cosecha; *comm* renta; (production) producción *f*; *v* ceder; (consent) consentir (ie)²ᶜ; *comm* dar¹⁹ rédito; (produce) producir¹⁵; (surrender) rendirse (i)³; ~ **to** ceder a; ~ **up**
entregar⁵
yielding flexible; (soft) blando; (weak)
flojo; *fig* dócil
yippy! ¡hurra!
yob gamberro
yobbish como un gamberro
yobbishness gamberrismo
yodel cantar en falsete
yodeller cantador *m* (-ora *f*) a la tirolesa
yoga yoga *m*
yoghurt yogur *m*; ~; ~**-maker** (appliance) yogurtera
yogi yogui *m*
yoke *n* yugo; (of clothes) canesú *m*; (for
buckets) balancín (-ines) *m*; ~ **of oxen**
yunta de bueyes; *v* uncir; ~ **to** acoplar
a
yokel palurdo, paleto

yolk yema; **double-~** **egg** huevo de dos
yemas
yon *adj* aquel, aquella, aquellos, aquellas
yonder allá
yonks hace mucho tiempo
yore: **of** ~ de antaño; **in days of** ~ en
otro tiempo
you (subject *pron*) tú, vosotros; (formal) usted, ustedes; (object *pron*) te,
os, (formal) le, les; (after *prep*) tí,
vosotros, (formal) usted, ustedes;
(indefinite *pron*) uno, ~ **never can tell**
uno no sabe nunca; **are** ~ **there?** (on
phone) oiga; **between** ~ **and me** entre
tú y yo; **if I were** ~ *fam* yo que tú/usted
young (of animal) cría; (human) jóvenes
mpl; **with** ~ embarazada; *adj* joven,
SA nuevo; **grow** ~ **again** rejuvene-
cerse¹⁴; **the night is** ~ la noche es joven; ~ **fellow** chico; ~ **girl** chica; ~
people jóvenes *mpl*
youngish bastante joven
youngster (child) niño; (youth) jo-
ven(cito)
your (familiar) tu (*pl* vuestro); (formal)
su; ~ **books** sus libros (de usted/
ustedes); ~**self** tú/usted mismo, (after
prep) tí, *reflex* sí; ~**selves** vosotros/
ustedes mismos, (after *prep*) vosotros, *reflex* sí
yours *pron* (familiar) el tuyo, la tuya, el
vuestro, la vuestra; (formal) el suyo,
la suya; ~ **faithfully** le(s) saluda
atentamente; ~ **sincerely** un abrazo
de; ~ **truly** (in letter) su seguro
servidor; ~ **truly** (in speech) su
servidor
youth juventud *f*; (young man) jo-
ven(cito); **the** ~ **of Great Britain** los
jóvenes de la Gran Bretaña; ~ **club**
club *m* juvenil; **Youth Hostel** albergue
m de la juventud
youthful juvenil; **she has a** ~ **appearance**
ella parece muy juvenil; ~ **exploits**
mocedades *fpl*
yowl *n* aullido; *v* aullar
yo-yo yoyo
Yucatan *n* Yucatán *m*; *adj* yucateco
yucca yuca
Yugoslav *n+adj* yugoeslavo
Yugoslavia Yugoeslavia
Yukon Yucón *m*
yule: ~**-log** leña de Navidad; ~**-tide**

Navidades *fpl*

yum-yum! ¡ñam-ñam!

yuppify hacer[19] subir de categoria un barrio (por la presencia de **yuppies**)

yuppy joven y adinerado hombre *m* de
negocios

Z

z (letter) zeta; ~-car coche zeta
Zambia Zambia
Zambian zambiano
zany n payaso; adj chiflado
Zanzibar Zanzibar m
zeal entusiasmo
zealot fanático
zealotry fanatismo
zealous entusiasta m+f (for de)
zealously con entusiasmo
zebra cebra; ~ stripes rayas fpl de la cebra, (on zebra-crossing) rayas fpl indi-
   cadoras; ~-crossing paso de peatones
zebu cebú m
zeitgeist espíritu de la época
Zen: ~ Buddhism budismo zen; ~ Buddhist budista m+f zen
zenith cenit m; fig apogeo
zephyr céfiro
zeppelin dirigible m
zero cero; above/below ~ sobre/bajo
   cero; ~ hour hora H
zest (pleasure) gusto; (energy) entusiasmo (for por)
zestful lleno de entusiasmo
zigzag n zigzag m; adj zigzagueante; v
   zigzaguear; (while walking) andar[19]
   haciendo eses; mot ir[19]/conducir[15]
   haciendo eses
zinc n cinc; ~ bucket cubo galvanizado;
   ~ ointment pomada de cinc; ~ oxide

óxido de cinc; v cubrir (past part
   cubierto) de cinc
zinnia rascamoño
Zion Sión m; fig paraíso
zionism sionismo
zionist n+adj sionista m+f
zip n (noise) silbido; (zip-fastener
   zipper) cremallera, SA riqui m; US
   Zip code código postal; v ~ by pasar
   silbando; ~ up cerrar (ie)[2a] con cremallera, sl (shut up) echarse la cremallera
zipper see zip
zippy enérgico
zircon circón m
zither cítara
zodiac zodíaco
zodiacal zodiacal
zonal zonal
zone n zona; v dividir en zonas
zoning zonificación f
zoo parque zoológico
zoological zoológico
zoologist zoólogo
zoology zoología
zoom (noise) zumbido; aer empinadura;
   ~-lens cin+phot objectivo zoom; v
   zumbar; aer empinarse
Zoroaster Zoroastro
Zulu n+adj zulú m; ~land Zululandia
Zwingli Zuinglio

READ MORE IN PENGUIN

In every corner of the world, on every subject under the sun, Penguin represents quality and variety – the very best in publishing today.

For complete information about books available from Penguin – including Puffins, Penguin Classics and Arkana – and how to order them, write to us at the appropriate address below. Please note that for copyright reasons the selection of books varies from country to country.

In the United Kingdom: Please write to *Dept. JC, Penguin Books Ltd, FREEPOST, West Drayton, Middlesex UB7 0BR*

If you have any difficulty in obtaining a title, please send your order with the correct money, plus ten per cent for postage and packaging, to *PO Box No. 11, West Drayton, Middlesex UB7 0BR*

In the United States: Please write to *Penguin USA Inc., 375 Hudson Street, New York, NY 10014*

In Canada: Please write to *Penguin Books Canada Ltd, 10 Alcorn Avenue, Suite 300, Toronto, Ontario M4V 3B2*

In Australia: Please write to *Penguin Books Australia Ltd, 487 Maroondah Highway, Ringwood, Victoria 3134*

In New Zealand: Please write to *Penguin Books (NZ) Ltd, 182–190 Wairau Road, Private Bag, Takapuna, Auckland 9*

In India: Please write to *Penguin Books India Pvt Ltd, 706 Eros Apartments, 56 Nehru Place, New Delhi 110 019*

In the Netherlands: Please write to *Penguin Books Netherlands B.V., Keizersgracht 231 NL–1016 DV Amsterdam*

In Germany: Please write to *Penguin Books Deutschland GmbH, Friedrichstrasse 10–12, W–6000 Frankfurt/Main 1*

In Spain: Please write to *Penguin Books S. A., C. San Bernardo 117–6° E–28015 Madrid*

In Italy: Please write to *Penguin Italia s.r.l., Via Felice Casati 20, I–20124 Milano*

In France: Please write to *Penguin France S. A., 17 rue Lejeune, F–31000 Toulouse*

In Japan: Please write to *Penguin Books Japan, Ishikiribashi Building, 2–5–4, Suido, Tokyo 112*

In Greece: Please write to *Penguin Hellas Ltd, Dimocritou 3, GR–106 71 Athens*

In South Africa: Please write to *Longman Penguin Southern Africa (Pty) Ltd, Private Bag X08, Bertsham 2013*